Schäfer
Wirtschaftswörterbuch

Wirtschaftswörterbuch

Band II: Deutsch – Englisch

von

Dr. Wilhelm Schäfer
o. Professor
an der Universität Erlangen-Nürnberg

Verlag Franz Vahlen München

CIP-Kurztitelaufnahme der Deutschen Bibliothek

Schäfer, Wilhelm:
Wirtschaftswörterbuch / von Wilhelm Schäfer. – München: Vahlen
NE: HST
Bd. 2. Deutsch–Englisch. – 1983.
ISBN 3-8006-0794-8

ISBN 3 8006 0794 8

© 1983 Verlag Franz Vahlen GmbH, München
Satz und Druck der C. H. Beck'schen Buchdruckerei, Nördlingen

Vorwort

Mit diesem Band wird der ungleich schwierigere, wenngleich in mancher Hinsicht reizvollere Teil des Gesamtwerkes der Öffentlichkeit vorgelegt.

Um einem größeren Benutzerkreis hilfreich zu sein, wurde die Zahl der Stichwörter aus der allgemeinen Sprache der Wirtschaft erheblich vergrößert. Auch die Terminologie des wirtschaftlich relevanten Rechts wurde stärker berücksichtigt. Dies geschah im großen und ganzen in dem von großen deutschen Wirtschaftslexika abgesteckten Rahmen. Schließlich wurde auf vielseitigen Wunsch das Grundvokabular der Datenverarbeitung mit einigen Tausend Einheiten aufgenommen. Neu ist ein Anhang mit einer Reihe zweisprachiger Tabellen und Schemata, die das Kontextverständnis oft vorkommender Schlüsseltermini fördern.

Gelegentlich wird von Rezensenten und Lexikologen bemängelt, Wörterbuchverfasser unterließen es, Rechenschaft zu geben über die ,,theoretischen" Grundlagen ihrer Arbeit. Diese Unterlassungssünde scheint indes verzeihlich. Denn Hand aufs Herz: Wer (außer Rezensenten) nimmt sich schon die Zeit, das Vorwort eines Wörterbuches zu lesen? Benutzer suchen verläßliche Auskunft, um einen Text verstehen und/oder übersetzen zu können. Und schnell muß es gehen. Ist nach längerem Gebrauch die Trefferquote erfreulich hoch, gilt dies als Beweis für die Leistungsfähigkeit des Bauprinzips, dessen langatmige Erklärung sich erübrigt.

Dennoch fühlt sich der Verfasser gedrängt, einige wenige Anmerkungen zur Systematik zu machen. Sie können in Abschnitt 5 nachgelesen werden.

Wieder waren viele Hände hilfreich. Dank gebührt in- und ausländischen Kollegen und Institutionen für Rat und Kritik. Hervorzuheben ist die Hilfsbereitschaft amerikanischer Universitätsbibliotheken, vor allem Columbia, Yale und Princeton. Für viel mühevolle Routinearbeit gebührt Dank Fräulein *Pia Wirtgen*, Frau *Bärbel Seibold-Bauer*, Herrn *Bernd Schmidt-Liermann* und Fräulein *Elke Künzel*. Frau *Heidi Thiesen*, Lehrstuhl-Sekretärin, danke ich herzlich für ermutigende, stets rasche Hilfe.

Auch für diesen Band gilt, daß ich ohne die finanzielle Förderung durch das Kuratorium der Hans-Frisch-Stiftung, Nürnberg, und das Verständnis seines Vorsitzenden, Herrn Prof. em. Dr. *Ernst Weigt*, an Weiterführung und Abschluß des Projekts nicht hätte denken können.

Schließlich gilt mein Dank der verlegerischen Betreuung und dem geduldigen Zuwarten von Herrn Dipl.-Volkswirt *Dieter Sobotka*, München.

Nürnberg, August 1983 *Wilhelm Schäfer**

* *Wirtschafts- und Sozialwissenschaftliche Fakultät, Lange Gasse 20, D 8500 Nürnberg*

Preface

It was more than a quarter century ago that I began the project with great confidence. It is with humility that I finish it. And it is with the hope that it will help make the handling of economic and business texts more rewarding that I now submit volume II to its potential users.

This time around, the number of keywords taken form general business terminology has been substantially expanded in order to appeal to a wider range of users. Greater account has also been taken of legal parlance as it relates to business. By and large, this was done on the lines established by major German business encyclopedias. Finally, in response to a widely expressed need, a few thousand terms making up the basic vocabulary of automatic data processing have been included. A new feature is an Appendix containing a number of bilingual tables and layouts which should help the user to understand certain often encountered key terms in context.

A criticism occasionally leveled by reviewers and lexicologists is that people constructing a specialized dictionary of this sort omit to explain the ,,theoretical" foundation of their work. The omission is quite understandable, isn't it, for if we are honest with ourselves, who bothers to read a foreword to a dictionary? Users want reliable information in trying to understand and/or translate a text. And they want it quickly. If use over a long period shows that the dictionary is right in a satisfying large number of cases, this is in itself enough to show that the underlying principle works and there is no need for it to be explained at length.

Nevertheless, the author feels that at least some remarks should be made on the general system but these can be read in section 6.

Many people again lent a helping hand. I would like to extend my thanks to German and foreign colleagues and institutions for constructive comments and suggestions. Special mention must be made of the great helpfulness of American university libraries, especially those at Columbia, Yale, and Princeton. *Pia Wirtgen, Bärbel Seibold-Bauer, Bernd Schmidt-Liermann,* and *Elke Künzel* patiently toiled over the uninspiring routine work that still defies the wonders of automatic data processing. Particular thanks are due to *Heidi Thiesen,* Department Secretary, for her encouraging and unfailingly prompt assistance.

With this volume, too, I could not have thought of continuing and completing the project without the financial sponsorship of the Board of Trustees of the Hans Frisch Foundation in Nuremberg and the understanding cooperation of its Chairman, Dr. *Ernst Weigt,* emeritus professor in this faculty.

I am grateful to *Dieter Sobotka,* Munich, for his patience and persistence in taking care of the publishing side.

Finally, my wife has been almost wholly without enthusiasm since I announced the project to her. And yet she has listened to whatever problems I brought to her during the long time the book has been in the making. It is therefore right that it should again be dedicated to her.

Nuremberg, August 1983   *Wilhelm Schäfer*

Inhalt

1. Vorwort V
2. Preface VI
3. Benutzerhinweise VIII
4. Guide to the Dictionary IX
5. Bemerkungen zur Lexikographie X
6. A Note on Lexicography XVI
7. Abkürzungen – Abbreviations XXII
8. Wörterbuch – Dictionary 1
9. Anhang 695
   9.1 Rentabilitätsbegriffe 696
   9.2 DuPont-(RoI-)Kennzahlensystem 696
   9.3 Kapitalflußrechnung 698
   9.4 Jahresabschluß nach §§ 151 und 157 AktG 700
   9.5 Jahresabschluß nach der 4. EG-Richtlinie 706
   9.6 VGR: Produktionskonto eines Unternehmens 710
   9.7 VGR: Sozialprodukt und Volkseinkommen 712
   9.8 Schema der Zahlungsbilanz 714
   9.9 Währungsbezeichnungen 716

Benutzerhinweise

1. Schneller Zugriff soll unter anderem erreicht werden durch Verzicht auf Wortfeldartikel. Jeder Ausdruck erscheint unter seinem Anfangsbuchstaben, ohne Rücksicht darauf, ob es sich um Basiswort oder Kollokation handelt. Längere und meist umständliche Grundartikel, wie sie unter ,,Abschreibung" oder ,,machen" möglich wären, erübrigen sich so. Es ist also zum Beispiel nachzuschlagen unter ,,lineare Abschreibung", ,,digitale Abschreibung", ,,Gewinne machen".
2. Entsprechend den Grundsätzen, die in den ,,Bemerkungen zur Lexikographie" skizziert sind, werden den Übersetzungen zahlreicher deutscher Ausdrücke englische Kurzdefinitionen beigefügt, wenn englische Begriffe fehlen oder diese nicht deckungsgleich mit deutschen Begriffen sind. Diese Definitionen sind erfahrungsgemäß eine willkommene Hilfe bei der Anfertigung von Texten oder Übersetzungen. Wiederholt sei an dieser Stelle: *Wörter und Ausdrücke sind etwas anderes als Begriffe!*
3. Von ausschließlich britischen Ausdrücken abgesehen, wird wie im 1. Band die amerikanische Schreibweise angewendet. Dem Benutzer eines Fachwörterbuches sollte zugemutet werden dürfen, sich über die geringen Unterschiede (z. B. Verdoppelung von Endkonsonanten) anhand eines einsprachigen Wörterbuches selbst Klarheit zu verschaffen.
4. Die Kodierung (US) und (GB) wurde dort gesetzt, wo es unumgänglich schien. Sie schließt nicht aus, daß ein Ausdruck auch im jeweils anderen Sprachgebiet bekannt ist und dort verwendet wird.
5. Werden zu einem Basiswort mehrere Kollokatoren angegeben, so erscheint das Basiswort nach folgendem Muster nur einmal:

    Bestellung ausführen   – *to carry out*
                                    – *to fill*
                                    – *to complete*
                                    – *to execute . . . an order*

    Komplementär   – *general*
                             – *unlimited*
                             – *full . . . partner*

    scharfer Wettbewerb   – *bitter*
                                   – *fierce*
                                   – *intense*
                                   – *keen*
                                   – *severe*
                                   – *stiff . . . competition.*

6. Reflexivverben sind unter ihrem Grundwort eingeordnet. Beispiel: *bewerben, sich*.
7. Unter Mißachtung der Regeln der Lexikographie wurde nicht davor zurückgeschreckt, eine begrenzte Anzahl synkategorematischer Ausdrücke zu alphabetisieren, wie *nach geltendem Recht, mit Wirkung vom.*
8. Alles weitere – Auslassungen und Mängel eingeschlossen – ergibt sich bei häufiger Benutzung von selbst.

Guide to the dictionary

1. The whole project started with the notion of user friendliness. One way to achieve fast reference is by dispensing with main entries. Every expression appears under its initial letter, no matter whether it is a root word or a collocating item. Thus, lengthy and often awkward main entries, as would be possible under ,,*Abschreibung*" or ,,*machen*" are unnecessary. The idea is therefore to look up under ,,*lineare Abschreibung*", ,,*digitale Abschreibung*", ,,*Gewinne machen*", etc.
2. Following the principles briefly set out in ,,A Note on Lexicography", many of the translations of German terms and expressions are explained by short definitions in English if the concept does not exist in English or if the concept is not quite the same as the German one. From experience, these definitions are often an aid in preparing translations or other written material. Readers should, for instance, be aware that European concepts such as ,,*earnings*", ,,*cash flow*", and ,,*shareholders' equity*" in many cases bear little direct relation to their U.S. counterparts.
3. Barring exclusively British expressions, American spelling is used throughout as in volume I. It should be reasonable to expect the user of a specialist dictionary to look up minor differences, such as the doubling of terminal consonants, in a general monolingual dictionary.
4. The abbreviations (US) and (GB) have been used where it appeared appropriate. This is not to imply that a coded expression is not known and used in the other English-speaking area as well.
5. If a set of collates is added to a root word, the latter appears only once as is illustrated below:

Bestellung ausführen	– to carry out
	– to fill
	– to complete
	– to execute ... an order
Komplementär	– general
	– unlimited
	– full ... partner
scharfer Wettbewerb	– bitter
	– fierce
	– intense
	– keen
	– severe
	– stiff ... competition.

6. Reflexive German verbs are entered under their root components, for example: *bewerben, sich*.
7. In a limited number of cases, an established rule of lexicography was deliberately disregarded by alphabetically sorting even syncategorematical terms which are part of meaningful expressions but have no meaning by themselves, such as *nach geltendem Recht, mit Wirkung vom*.
8. The rest (including omissions and shortcomings) will become clear on its own through constant use.

> Für viele Widersprüche findet man meistens leicht eine Lösung, wenn man zeigen kann, daß verschiedene Verfasser die gleichen Worte in verschiedener Bedeutung verwendeten.
>
> *Abaelard,* Sic et Non

Bemerkungen zur Lexikographie

Fachwörterbücher lassen sich einteilen nach dem Prinzip der Äquivalenz, der Definition, der Kollokation.

1. Äquivalenzwörterbücher

Äquivalenz bedeutet Gleichwertigkeit. Diese Beziehung wird von alters her genutzt für das Lernen von Vokabeln im elementaren und gehobenen Sprachunterricht. Der Lernende kennt zum Beispiel den Terminus „x" im Deutschen und sucht im Wörterbuch die englische Entsprechung „y", gläubig vertrauend, die beiden Ausdrücke seien gleichwertig, äquivalent.

Wir fragen uns indessen oft, warum wir von den nach dieser einfachen Methode gelernten Wörtern viele rasch vergessen, wie wir überhaupt ständig das Gefühl haben, zu wenig „Vokabeln" zu kennen. Gelänge es uns – so die Meinung –, weitere 10 000 oder gar 100 000 Vokabeln im Langzeitgedächtnis zu behalten, müßten die Schwierigkeiten des Hörens und Lesens, des Sprechens und Schreibens mit einem Schlage verschwinden. Offenbar funktioniert dies aber nicht, wie unermüdliche Vokabel-Lerner verdrießlich registrieren. Zweifler wird man leicht überzeugen: Man lege ihnen einen Text vor, der nicht eine unbekannte „Vokabel" enthält und den sie gleichwohl nicht entschlüsseln oder übersetzen können.

Daß endloses Vokabellernen das Hineinwachsen in eine fremde Sprache eher behindert, hat – neben anderen Faktoren – eine einfache Ursache: wir ordnen den Gegenständen, Vorgängen und Vorstellungen mehr oder weniger willkürlich Wörter zu. Der springende Punkt hierbei ist, daß die Zahl der Gegenstände samt ihrer Kombinationen praktisch *unbegrenzt* ist, während die Zahl der Wörter trotz täglicher Neubildungen zwar sehr groß, aber *begrenzt* ist.

Daraus folgt, daß die Wörter einer Sprache nicht mit nur je einem Gegenstand oder je einer Vorstellung besetzt werden können. Anders gesagt: Wörter sind zwangsläufig mehr- oder vieldeutig. Sollen aber Sprachen für alle Zwecke funktionieren, und sie tun es offensichtlich, müssen sie ihre Mehrdeutigkeit bewahren. Dies ist notwendige Bedingung jeder höheren Form von Sprachverwendung, bis hin zu den Meisterwerken der Weltliteratur.

Nun meinen viele Sprachbenutzer zu wissen, daß es Mehrdeutigkeit von Wörtern, Ausdrücken, Sätzen nur in der meist (Gott sei Dank) nicht genau definierten Alltagssprache gebe. Fachsprachen dagegen bemühten sich um strenge Logik, seien grammatisch einfach bis simpel, und die Bedeutung von Fachausdrücken sei eindeutig. Als klassisches Beispiel terminologischer Präzision könne etwa die Pariser Nomenklatur der Anatomie von 1955 gelten, die sich auf 1:1-Entsprechungen beschränke. Auch sonst werde in Fachsprachen auf stilistische Effekte, Anspielungen, gefühlsmäßig mitschwingende Nebenbedeutungen verzichtet, so daß Mehr- und Vieldeutigkeit ausgeschlossen sei.

Äquivalenzwörterbücher wären dann so etwas wie eine ,,Rosinen"-Sammlung. Die rasch gefundenen englischen Entsprechungen von ,,*Gleitzeit*", ,,*Umsatzgewinnrate*", ,,*Wirtschaftsordnung*" würden dann ausreichen, die Leerstellen im einfach gebauten Satz der Fachsprache zu füllen. Diese Meinung wird explizit oder implizit selbst von Fachleuten in Praxis und Wissenschaft vertreten. Sie ist falsch, wie im zweiten Abschnitt gezeigt wird. Hier wäre noch anzumerken, daß die wichtigsten Wörter nicht immer auch die häufigsten sind.

2. Definitionswörterbücher

Wir gehen von der banalen Feststellung der Sprachlogik aus, daß Wörter gesprochen und geschrieben werden, also der *sprachlichen Ebene* zugehören. Scharf von ihnen zu trennen sind Begriffe, die man (philosophisch umstritten) als Denkinhalte bezeichnen kann. Das Verhältnis zwischen beiden wird durch den wichtigen Satz ausgedrückt: *Das Wort benennt den Begriff*. Die zwei Ebenen stehen in einem bestimmten Verhältnis zu einer dritten Ebene, auf der wir Gegenstände, Tatsachen, Sachverhalte vorfinden.

Aus Wörtern bilden wir zusammengesetzte Ausdrücke, Sätze und ganze Sprachen. Die zunehmende Kompliziertheit ändert nichts an dieser Grundstruktur.

Definitionswörterbücher werden in der Regel in *einer* Sprache geschrieben. Der Bearbeiter macht zu einem Ausdruck in zuverlässigen Primärquellen eine bereits vorhandene Definition ausfindig. Er *stellt sie fest*. Hätte ein Wissenschaftler einen neu aufgedeckten Sachverhalt zu definieren, würde er (als erster) die Definition formulieren, sie *festlegen*.

Eigentlich dürfte es keinen Zweifel geben, welcher der beiden Ebenen die Definition zugehört. Es kann nur die sprachliche sein: durch die Aufzählung definierender Hauptmerkmale wird der Begriff abgesteckt, fixiert, seine Vagheitszone eingeengt. Mit Hilfe der Definition wird aus der Menge der denkbaren Vorstellungen eine bestimmte Vorstellung abgegrenzt.

Einer der häufigsten sprachlogischen Fehler – mit einem hohen Grad an Resistenz – ist die angebliche Austauschbarkeit von ,Wort' und ,,Begriff".[1] Der Satz ,Der Begriff soziale Sicherheit wird in mehreren Bedeutungen gebraucht' ist logisch nicht statthaft. Was der Schreiber zum Ausdruck bringen wollte, ist folgendes: Der Terminus ,soziale Sicherheit' muß wegen der (relativen) Wortarmut unserer Sprache mehrere Begriffe bezeichnen, die als abgrenzbare Merkmalebündel durchaus unterscheidbar definiert werden können (oder sollten). Das Wort, der Ausdruck, der Terminus ist mehrfach besetzt.

So hat es ja auch wenig Sinn, sich auf eine Debatte über ,Eigentum' einzulassen, wenn nicht allen Diskutanten klar ist, über welchen der mehreren Begriffe geredet werden soll: den liberalen Eigentumsbegriff im Sinne der §§ 903ff. BGB, den Eigentumsbegriff des Art. 14 GG mit der dort verankerten Sozialbindung oder gar den Eigentumsbegriff des Pierre-Joseph Proudhon (,la proprieté c'est le vol'). Wer mit marxistisch-dialektischen Techniken vertraut ist, weiß, daß dort nichts so sehr gefürchtet wird wie begriffliche Eindeutigkeit und Klarheit.

Zur Verdeutlichung möge ein weiteres Beispiel aus der Sprache der Wirtschaft dienen. Der Ausdruck ,*Zwangsanleihe*' benennt zwei Begriffe ,,*Zwangsanleihe*". Der ältere und häufigere wird definiert durch die Aufzählung folgender Merkmale:

,,*Zwangsanleihe* = $_{df}$ *Öffentliche Schuldaufnahme durch zwangsweisen Verkauf von Staatspapieren, deren Rückzahlungs- und Zinsbedingungen meist unvorteilhafter für die Gläubiger sind als eine Kreditvergabe auf dem freien Markt.*"[2]

---

[1] Die Zugehörigkeit zur sprachlichen Ebene wird durch einfache Anführungszeichen (,), die zur begrifflichen Ebene durch doppelte Anführungszeichen (,,) kenntlich gemacht.
[2] Zimmermann/Henke: Einführung in die Finanzwissenschaft. 3. Auflage. München 1982. S. 386.

Der zweite Begriff stammt aus der jüngsten Diskussion über das Haushaltsdefizit der Bundesrepublik. Hier bezeichnet der Ausdruck ‚Zwangsanleihe' einen rückzahlbaren (?) unverzinslichen Zuschlag zur Einkommensteuer Besserverdienender.

Definitionswörterbücher sind Sammlungen solcher Begriffsbeschreibungen. Diese werden häufig ergänzt durch mehr oder weniger lange Begriffsexplikationen, das heißt weiterführende Erläuterungen. Definitionen sind in der Regel für den Fachmann als Gedächtnisstütze oder Formulierungshilfe oder für Lernende mit Grundwissen gedacht. Mit der oben zitierten Definition kann ja nur arbeiten, wer die definierenden Ausdrücke schon kennt, wer also über *„Staatspapiere", „öffentliche Schuldaufnahme", „Kreditvergabe auf dem freien Markt"* mittels entsprechender Definitionen Auskunft geben kann. Oft ungern gehört, aber sicher richtig ist die Forderung, die systematische Erörterung von Definitionen gehöre nicht in methodologische Erörterungen über Begriffe, sondern sei in den entsprechenden Fachgebieten zu behandeln.

Im vorliegenden Wörterbuch wurde diesen Sachverhalten dadurch Rechnung zu tragen versucht, daß die englischen Entsprechungen deutscher Termini wie im ersten Band durch Kodierung einem oder mehreren Fachgebieten zugeordnet wurden. Der Fachmann weiß, daß diese Zuordnung nicht immer befriedigen kann. So wird etwa der Komplex der Abschreibung sowohl im Rechnungswesen als auch in der Finanzwirtschaft der Unternehmung behandelt.

Was zur allgemeinen Sprache der Wirtschaft gehört, darüber wird von Linguisten und sonstigen *cognoscenti* der allgemeinen und angewandten Sprachwissenschaft mit großem metasprachlichem Arsenal mehr oder weniger trefflich gestritten. Dieser Streit dürfte ausgehen wie das Hornberger Schießen: Letztlich entscheidend sind im Einzelfall Wissensstand und Erfahrung des Sprachbenutzers.

Über die Kodierung hinaus wurden einer größeren Zahl von englischen Einträgen Kurzdefinitionen, Beispiele, Synonymverweise, Angabe von Gesetzes-Fundstellen und sonstige Hinweise beigegeben, die es leichter machen, die Eignung eines bestimmten Stichwortes für einen vorgegebenen Kontext zu prüfen. Die Zahl der Definitionen und Beispiele mußte sich aus Raumgründen in Grenzen halten. Der Zufall spielte hierbei keine geringe Rolle. Das Ideal eines vollständigen zweisprachigen Definitionswörterbuches für alle Fälle begrifflicher Nicht-Äquivalenz ist technisch zwar möglich, aber über den Markt kaum zu finanzieren.

Das folgende Schema veranschaulicht die besprochenen drei Ebenen:[3]

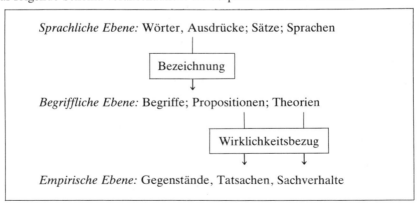

Der bisher unerwähnte Ausdruck ‚Proposition', für den es im Deutschen keine Entsprechung gibt, ist das begriffliche Gegenstück zum ‚Satz' – gewissermaßen ein „Satz an sich" (Bolzano).

---

[3] M. Bunge: Scientific Research I. Berlin-Heidelberg-New York 1967. S. 58.

Die Gepflogenheit, dem Benutzer inhaltliche Gleichheit zu suggerieren, wenn Wörter und Ausdrücke in Ausgangs- und Zielsprache sich oberflächlich entsprechen, läßt sich einfach veranschaulichen:

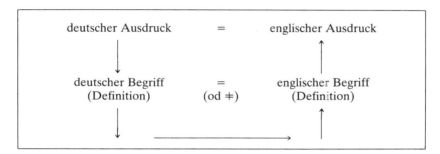

Auf dieser „nur" sprachlichen Ebene lautet die einzige Frage zu Recht: gibt es für einen deutschen Ausdruck eine englische Entsprechung und umgekehrt? In Wirklichkeit gibt es eine logisch zwingende Stufenfolge, auch wenn diese häufig verdeckt wird durch Interferenzen anderer Informationskanäle (Expertenbefragung usw.):

```
    deutscher Ausdruck      =        englischer Ausdruck
            │                                 ▲
            ▼                                 │
    deutscher Begriff        =        englischer Begriff
      (Definition)         (od ǂ)       (Definition)
            │                                 ▲
            ▼                                 │
            └─────────────────────────────────┘
```

Der Suchpfeil läuft vom deutschen Wort oder Ausdruck zunächst zum deutschen Begriff, der durch Aufzählung von Merkmalen definiert ist. Die nächste Station: Gibt es einen Begriff, der nach Inhalt und/oder Umfang dem deutschen Begriff entspricht? Wenn ja, wird der Pfeil zum englischen Begriff und von dort zum englischen Wort oder Ausdruck gezogen, und es darf Bedeutungsgleichheit zwischen D und E als sicher angenommen werden. Sind Begriffe nach Inhalt und Umfang (d. h. intensional und extensional) nicht deckungsgleich, kann es Äquivalenz auch nicht auf der sprachlichen Ebene geben.

Ein Beispiel aus der Rechtssprache möge dies erläutern. Der Jurist erhält eine gewisse Vorstellung, wenn ihm ‚geldwerte Gegenleistung' als Übersetzung von ‚valuable consideration' angeboten wird. Die bloß wörtliche Übersetzung ist indes kein Schlüssel zur englischen Consideration-Lehre. Benötigt er eine Definition und eine daran anschließende ausführlichere Begriffserläuterung, wird er wie in zahllosen anderen Fällen begrifflicher Nichtäquivalenz zur Fachliteratur greifen, in der Begriffe im systematischen Zusammenhang behandelt werden.

Zitiert sei aus Arthur Curtis in vielen Punkten überholter, in Anlage und Durchführung aber nach wie vor lesenswerter rechtsvergleichender Darstellung:

„Die Consideration ist eine der bedeutsamsten Eigentümlichkeiten des englischen Rechts ... Es ist nicht möglich, den Begriff dieses technischen Ausdrucks ... in einem einzigen Worte in einer anderen Sprache wiederzugeben ... Aus dem Vertrag soll klar hervorgehen, daß das Versprechen zu einer Leistung gemacht wurde gegen einen Vorteil oder Schaden, ein Unterlassen, eine Übernahme einer Verantwortung, mögen diese ‚Gegenleistungen' auch ohne greifbaren Wert sein ... *Es ist nicht nötig, daß der Versprechende durch die Gegenleistung einen in Geld oder sonst objektiv wertbaren Vorteil erlangt* ... (Hervorhebung vom Vf.) ... Die Consideration kann sogar in der Verwandtschaft (z. B. in der bevorstehenden Ehe) oder in der Freundschaft bestehen. Ob die Considera-

Bemerkungen zur Lexikographie

tion vorhanden ist, darüber steht dem Richter freies Ermessen zu. Genau fassen läßt sich der Begriff nicht, oft mögen Gefühlsmomente den Ausschlag geben."[2]

Auf schwachem Fuß steht also der Versuch, vom deutschen rechtstechnischen Begriffspaar Leistung–Gegenleistung her, das als Kernmerkmal stets die Vermögensmehrung enthält, eine Äquivalenzbeziehung zu ,,consideration" herzustellen. Unschädlich ist die Gleichsetzung nur, wenn eine bestimmte Teilmenge des englischen Begriffs dem deutschen Begriff gleichgesetzt werden kann. Dies ist im Einzelfall festzustellen, setzt jedenfalls die über Wort und Begriff hinausgehende Kenntnis beider Rechtssysteme voraus.

Auf die Spitze getrieben wird der begriffslogische Unverstand, wenn durch Umkehrung einer Karteikarte zum Beispiel die Übersetzung ‚geldwerte Gegenleistung' als deutscher Original-Terminus ausgegeben wird. Im Pfeilschema geschieht dabei folgendes:

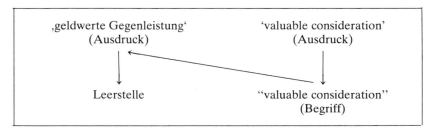

Begriffliche Äquivalenz wird vorgetäuscht, obgleich der Suchpfeil auf eine Leerstelle trifft.

Der Leser, der bis hierher gefolgt ist, mag die Qualität von Fachwörterbüchern anhand des Gesagten selbst prüfen. So ist ‚Vorstand' nicht gleich ‚board of directors', die Übersetzung ‚deed of purchase' = ‚Kaufbrief' ist kein deutscher Terminus; die deutsche Umsatzsteuer läßt sich nicht mit ‚purchase tax' bezeichnen, die in England am 1. April 1973 durch die MWSt abgelöst wurde; ‚Königsfriede' = ‚the queen's peace' wird auch ein Laie nicht für ein Wort der deutschen Rechtssprache halten wollen; und so weiter, und so fort.

3. Kollokationswörterbücher

Diese Wörterbücher tragen dem Sachverhalt Rechnung, daß wir als ursprüngliche sinnvolle Einheiten der Sprache *Sätze* und nicht *Wörter* auffassen. Denn es sind Sätze und nicht Wörter, die wir im alltäglichen und wissenschaftlichen Sprachgebrauch behaupten und bestreiten (W. Stegmüller). Dies heißt, daß Kollokationswörterbücher über die Wort-Äquivalenz hinausgehen. Sie bieten zu Grundwörtern (= Basiseintragungen) sachlich und stilistisch passende Beiwörter (= Kollokatoren) an. Beispiel:

Kapitaldecke = *Basis*
dünne = *Kollokator.*

Bei konsequenter Anwendung der Kollokationsmethode ergeben sich für den Wörterbuch-Hersteller gewisse Schwierigkeiten. Bevorzugt er die Wortfeldmethode, wird er in der Tat den Ausdruck auflösen und ‚Kapitaldecke' unter ‚K' einordnen und dort den oder die Kollokatoren angeben. In extremen Fällen wird ein Basis-Eintrag allerdings so aufgeschwemmt, daß der – stets eilige – Benutzer die Suche oft vorzeitig aufgibt.

[2] A. Curtis: Englands Privat- und Handelsrecht. Band 2. Berlin 1927. S. 10–12.

Im vorliegenden Band mußte wegen des einmal gewählten Prinzips der durchgehenden Alphabetisierung ein anderer Weg beschritten werden, der nach Ansicht des Vf. den zeitlichen Zugriff verkürzt. So wird der Benutzer die Wendung „dünne Kapitaldecke" unter ‚d' finden, weil es sich um einen fixierten, dem Finanzfachmann bekannten Ausdruck handelt, der nicht zerlegt werden sollte:

      dünne Kapitaldecke   = *slender*
                                             thin
                                             inadequate . . . capital base.

An die alphabetische Einordnung der nicht allzu zahlreichen Kollokatoren wird sich der Benutzer rasch gewöhnen.

A Note on Lexicography

> In Turkey, it is said, the color of the fez on the outside of the head was once changed to provoke novel ideas inside the head.
>
> *Sydney Weintraub*

A Note on Lexicography

The main organizing principles in compiling technical or specialized dictionaries are equivalence, definition, and collocation. We shall take up each one of them in turn.

1. Equivalence dictionaries

This is the common and garden type of dictionary. Its main thrust has always been to carry the idea of equivalence into elementary and advanced language learning. For instance, a learner knows what „x" stands for in German and flies to his two-language dictionary to look for the English term „y", relying on the naive faith that the two terms have identical meanings in both languages, in short, that they are equivalent.

However, we often ask ourselves why we forget so quickly so many of the words learned by this hard-and-fast rule and why we constantly worry over the low level of our word inventory. If we had yet another 10,000 or even 100,000 words and phrases at our fingers' tips – the common opinion –, we should no doubt be able to converse with native speakers almost on a par. Many people, though, stuffing their heads with simple word equations wholesale, soon find to their dismay that what little progress they make is out of step with the vast amount of time and effort they put into the undertaking. This is easy to show: take any group of learners and assign a text to them of which they know every word; yet the message the text seeks to convey may be out of their reach.

There is a simple reason – among other factors – why the drudgery of learning long lists of words does not automatically ensure a better command of a foreign language: It is more or less arbitrarily that names are given to things, processes, and ideas. Think of today's computerese where computer fanatics – called „hackers" at M.I.T. and elsewhere – like to invent new terms that are as mystifying to an outsider as the secret password of an esoteric cult. Anyone who objects to such jargon is, to the computer literate, not merely uninformed but „bletcherous".

The general point is that the number of things and their combinations is practically *infinite,* while the number of words is very large indeed but still *finite.*

This is to say that no word in a language is normally set aside to designate one single object or abstraction only. Put differently: Words rarely have less than two or more meanings. If languages are to serve the full gamut of purposes in all walks of life, as in fact they do, they must not be robbed of this superb feature of ambiguity. Even the mathematical logician, who works on perfecting artificial sign languages, would readily admit that this is a necessary condition of every advanced language usage culminating in the world's masterpieces of poetry and prose.

Now many language users are certain that the ambiguity of words, phrases, and sentences has its proper place in ordinary, everyday language which – thank God – defies clear-cut definition. Technical languages, the argument goes, strive for impeccable logic, are grammatically easy if not simple, and the meaning of terms is straightforward. As a classical example of terminological precision they would perhaps – rightly or wrongly – hold up the 1955 Paris Nomenclature of Anatomy with its sure-fire principle of one-to-one correspondence. Technical languages, we hear them say, stay unadorned with metaphorical allusions, things half said, and emotionally resonant secondary meanings, which, again, helps to eliminate ambiguity.

For the practicing speaker and writer, equivalence dictionaries would then be something like an unassorted mass of brickbats to be tossed around more or less at random. For example, the English terms corresponding to ,,*Wirtschaftsordnung*", ,,*Gleitzeit*", ,,*Umsatzgewinnrate*" would duly fill the blanks in an otherwise bare-bone sentence of a technical language. This view put about in academic quarters and by seasoned practical men is wrong. It has its roots in a time-honored logical mistake to be discussed below. Suffice it to say in passing that the most important words are not always those that occur most frequently.

2. Definition dictionaries

To start again with the most obvious: one of the basics in the logic of language is that a *word* is spoken and written and therefore belongs to the *linguistic level*. Strictly separated from it is the *concept* which may be called a ,,thought content" although philosophers have differed on this throughout the centuries. Concepts are on the second, the *conceptual level*. The two levels are related in a way that should be hammered home to all language users: *The word names the concept.* A third level is the *physical* where we find things, facts, properties.

Definition dictionaries are usually of the one-language type. The compiler works (or should work) through primary-source material written by experts in the field in order to find a definition or set of definitions that goes with a given term. In other words, his job is one of ,,*constating*". If a scientist or scholar were to describe or to define a newly discovered combination of facts, he would be the first to formulate or establish a definition. His would be a *creative* task.

A learner may now ask: to which of the first two levels does a definition belong? No doubt the linguistic. In listing the defining earmarks, we delimit a concept and reduce its vagueness zone. Definitions are used to separate a specific idea from the set of all other ideas, real or potential.

One of the commonest logical mistakes – certainly never to be eradicated – is the alleged interchangeability of ,*Wort*' and ,,*Begriff*', of ,*term*' and ,*concept*".[1] A sentence like ,*Der Begriff soziale Sicherheit wird in mehreren Bedeutungen gebraucht*' (ie, the concept of social security has more than one meaning) is logically unacceptable. What the writer had in mind is that the term ,soziale Sicherheit' (due to the paucity of our vocabulary) need be used to designate several concepts each of which can (or should) be clearly defined.

Let's take another example. The term ,*Zwangsanleihe*' is a label attached to two concepts of ,,*Zwangsanleihe*". The first, older and of wider currency, is defined as follows:

,,*Zwangsanleihe* = $_{df}$ *Öffentliche Schuldaufnahme durch zwangsweisen Verkauf von Staatspapieren, deren Rückzahlungs- und Zinsbedingungen meist unvorteilhafter für die Gläubiger sind als eine Kreditvergabe auf dem freien Markt.*"[2]

In English this is something like:

,,*Forced loan* = $_{df}$ *Public sector borrowing through compulsory sale of government bonds, with repayment and interest terms usually being less profitable to a creditor than lending in the free market.*"

---

[1] Linguistic objects, such as terms and sentences, are enclosed in simple quotes (,), while conceptual objects, such as the propositions expressed by sentences, are enclosed in double quotes (,,).

The second concept recently introduced when West Germany's budget plight was discussed is differently defined, it has a different meaning, but the same word-tag ‚Zwangsanleihe': what budget experts refer to is a repayable (or non-repayable) income tax surcharge imposed on the higher income brackets. British journalists call it a ‚*mandatory loan*'.

Conceptual confusion would no doubt be greatly reduced – with savings in time and money –, if this basic distinction between ‚*Wort*' and ,,*Begriff*", between ‚*term*' and ,,*concept*" were being kept in mind.

Definition dictionaries are written for the expert – to freshen his memory – or for the learner with a basic knowledge of the subject. The above definition does in fact make sense only for someone familiar with the defining terms, that is, for someone who can work with ease in any given situation with the terms ‚Staatspapiere', ‚öffentliche Schuldaufnahme', ‚Kreditvergabe auf dem freien Markt'.

An unpopular but surely valid claim is that the proper place for a formal discussion of concepts and definitions is not in the methodological chapter but should rather be discussed in the relevant subject area.

Passing to bilingualism, we should now see at once that mere comparison of terms or literal word-by-word translations will not take us far. Whether correspondence of *words* implies equivalence of *concepts* is a matter to be decided by inquiring into definitions or even theories. This inquiry is sometimes unproblematic but more often than not assumes a well-grounded knowledge of the subjects in which the terms and concepts occur.

Learners and other people should be told time and again that *there is no automatic, perfect transfer of meaning at the linguistic level:* Words, or fine oratory for that matter, can be no substitute for a systematic body of knowledge. Ignorance or sloppy disregard of this basic fact explains the deplorable quality of a great deal of technical translations fabricated by native and non-native speakers alike. This is in part due to an ingrained overdependence on *the* dictionary once dubbed by a wisecrack as Mr Shortcut to Proficiency.

The dictionary before you tries to account for this state of affairs by coding the English equivalents of German terms into one or more subject areas. The knowledgeable user is aware that this cannot be fully satisfactory. For instance, the subject of depreciation is given systematic treatment in accounting as well as in business finance. And where to draw a dividing line between the everyday jargon of business and economics and the higher reaches of this kind of specialized language is an issue that will remain unresolved for some time to come.

It may not be unfair to say that this line of demarcation is determined by an individual's level of knowledge and experience.

Above and beyond the coding system, a large number of entries supply short definitions, examples, synonyms, indications of statutory sources, and other references which should help to test a word's suitability in a specific context.

Space has often been an unwelcome constraint on the total volume of definitions and examples, and the role of random choice here is none too small. The ideal complete bilingual definition dictionary offering comments for all cases of conceptual non-equivalence, though technically possible, could not be sold for a reasonable price.

To set ideas, the three levels might be pictured schematically as below:[3]

---

[3] M. Bunge: Scientific Research I. Berlin-Heidelberg-New York 1967. p. 58.

A Note on Lexicography

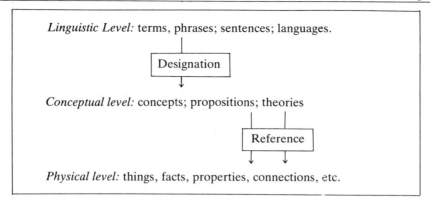

The term ‚proposition', so far unmentioned and without equivalent in German, is the conceptual counterpart of ‚sentence'.

The insidious habit of suggesting conceptual equivalence to the user of a dictionary whenever terms and phrases in both source and target language look superficially alike, is simple to illustrate:

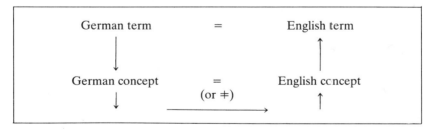

If we decide not to go beyond the linguistic level, the only question and one that is legitimately asked is: What is the English equivalent of a German term and vice versa? This and nothing else.

In actual fact, however, the logic of languages forces us to cast our net wider even if the logical sequence inherent in all languages is blurred by interference from other information channels, such as queries answered by experts, etc.:

```
German term         =        English term
    │                              ↑
    ↓                              │
German concept      =        English concept
    │            (or ≠)            ↑
    ↓            ─────────→        │
```

The ‚search arrow' starting from the German term first moves to the German concept which is defined by listing a number of properties or earmarks. The next step is to find an English concept that – intensionally and/or extensionally – is equivalent to the German concept. If we do, the arrow is allowed to proceed to the English term, and we may be certain that G and E are also equivalent. Be sure to note that, if there is no equivalence on the conceptual level, there can be none on the linguistic either.

This simple flowchart may be brought to life by an example taken from legal language. A German lawyer would get a first idea if the English term ‚valuable consideration' were translated for him as ‚geldwerte Gegenleistung'. But this naturally does not provide a clue to the English doctrine of consideration. In this and countless other cases, the toing and froing between German and English technical languages demands the study of concepts in their systematic setting.

I may quote from Arthur Curtis who as far back as 1927 published a comparative study that is outdated on many points but still eminently readable:

,,Consideration is one of the outstanding peculiarities of English law ... It is impossible to make the concept intelligible through a single expression in another language ... A contract is to establish beyond doubt that the promise to perform was made in return for a benefit or detriment, a forbearance, the assuming of a responsibility, even though such ‚Gegenleistungen' may have no tangible value ... *It is not of the essence that the promisor, in receiving consideration, obtains a benefit that can be expressed in money's worth or by any other yardstick of value* ... [Italics are mine]. Consideration may even consist in kinship (eg, in a forthcoming marriage) or in friendship. It is in the court's discretion to determine whether consideration does in fact exist. The concept is an elusive one, and elements of emotion often have the upper hand."[2]

Since an increase of property (= Vermögensmehrung) is at the heart of the German pair ‚Leistung' and ‚Gegenleistung', the attempt to construe a relation of equivalence with the concept of consideration is bound to fail. Such relation does not exist unless a specified subset of the English concept is co-extensive with the narrower German concept. Words and concepts do not suffice to find out whether this is so in the individual case, and therefore the investigator needs to make up his mind in the context of both legal systems: Outside their proper context terms and definitions may become pointless.

The failure to apply elementary logic is carried to nonsensical extremes when a dictionary card index is mechanically reversed and, for example, the translated term ‚geldwerte Gegenleistung' is sold to the public as an original item of German legal parlance. Please see what happens in the flowchart below:

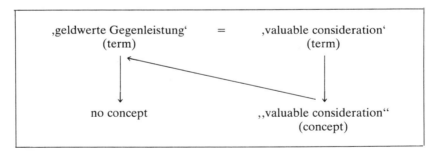

There is a pretense of conceptual equivalence although the search arrow sent out by the German term does not arrive at a conceptual referent.

The reader who has patiently followed may now check the quality of specialist dictionaries in terms of the foregoing.

To give him a lead: ‚Vorstand' is not the same as ‚board of directors'; the translation of ‚deed of purchase' = ‚Kaufbrief' is no original German term; the German turnover tax cannot be labeled as ‚purchase tax' which, by the way, has been an obsolete British term since the introduction of VAT on 1 April 1973; ‚Königsfriede' = ‚the queen's peace' is certainly not of German origin; and so on, and so forth.

---

[2] A. Curtis: Englands Privat- und Handelsrecht. Vol. 2. Berlin 1927. pp. 10–12. (Quote translated by author.)

3. Collocation dictionaries

This type of dictionary also goes beyond the pure equivalence principle. It offers qualifiers fitting the basic terms factually and stylistically. Example:

Kapitaldecke   = *basis term*
dünne   = *collating item.*

Trying to construct a dictionary along these lines, a compiler soon faces problems. If he sticks to the word-field method and looks upon a dictionary as a substitute for knowing a field of study, he will cut the phrase in two and place ‚Kapitaldecke' under ‚K' and list all collating items there. In extreme cases, a basis entry will be swelled to unmanageable proportions, so that the unfortunate user – always hard pressed for time – throws up the sponge before he hits upon the item he is after.

As only a minority of users can be expected to have a keen sense for sifting page after page of sometimes questionable evidence, the present volume again follows the strict alphabetical order which the author feels makes access faster. So you will find ‚dünne Kapitaldecke' under ‚d', because it is a fixed phrase that is known as such to financial experts and to professional translators and should therefore not be torn asunder:

dünne Kapitaldecke   = *slender*
                                   thin
                                   inadequate . . . capital base.

Abkürzungsverzeichnis   List of Abbreviations

a. B.	außergewöhnliche Belastungen	Extraordinary Financial Burdens
AB	Ausführungsbestimmungen	Implementing Regulations
AbfG	Gesetz über die Beseitigung von Abfällen	Waste Disposal Law
AblEG	Amtsblatt der Europäischen Gemeinschaften	Official Journal of the European Communities
AbwAG	Abwasserabgabengesetz	Law Relating to a Water Pollution Control Levy
AbzG	Gesetz betreffend die Abzahlungsgeschäfte	Law Relating to Deferred Payments Sales
ADB	Allgemeine Deutsche Binnentransportbedingungen	General Domestic Transport Conditions
ADS	Allgemeine Deutsche Seeversicherungsbedingungen	General German Ocean Marine Insurance Conditions
ADSp	Allgemeine Deutsche Spediteurbedingungen	General German Forwarders' Conditions
ADV	Automatische Datenverarbeitung	Automatic Data Processing
AE	Ausfuhrerklärung	Export Declaration
AfA	Absetzung für Abnutzung	Depreciation for Income-Tax Purposes
AfaA	Absetzung für außergewöhnliche Abnutzung	Tax Depreciation Due to Extraordinary Wear and Tear
AFG	Arbeitsförderungsgesetz	Labor Promotion Law
AFIZ	Ausschuß für Internationale Zusammenarbeit	Committee for International Cooperation
AfS	Absetzung für Substanzverringerung	Depletion Allowance for Income-Tax Purposes
AG	1. Aktiengesellschaft	German Stock Corporation
	2. Amtsgericht	Local First-Instance Court
	3. Ausführungsgesetz	German State Law Implementing a Federal Law
AGB	Allgemeine Geschäftsbedingungen	Standard Terms and Conditions
AGBG	Gesetz zur Regelung des Rechts der Allgemeinen Geschäftsbedingungen (AGB-Gesetz)	Law Relating to Standard Terms and Conditions
AHB	Außenhandelsbank	Foreign Trade Bank
AKA	Ausfuhrkredit-Gesellschaft	German Export Credit Company
AkB	Allgemeine Bedingungen für die Kraftverkehrsversicherung	General Conditions Relating to Motor Vehicle Insurance
AktG	Aktiengesetz	German Stock Corporation Law
AKV	Allgemeine Kreditvereinbarungen	General Arrangements to Borrow
ALALC	Lateinamerikanische Freihandelszone	Latin American Free Trade Zone
ALB	Allgemeine Lagerbedingungen des deutschen Möbeltransports	General Storage Conditions of German Furniture Removers
AnfG	Gesetz betreffend die Anfechtung von Rechtshandlungen eines Schuldners außerhalb des Konkurses (Anfechtungsgesetz)	Law Relating to the Avoidance of Debtor's Legal Transactions
AO	Abgabenordnung	Federal Fiscal Code
appr	etwa	approximately
AR	Aufsichtsrat	Supervisory Board
ARB	Allgemeine Rollfuhrbedingungen	General Cartage Conditions
ArbGG	Arbeitsgerichtsgesetz	Law Relating to Labor Courts
ArbPlSchG	Gesetz über den Schutz des Arbeitsplatzes bei Einberufung zum Wehrdienst (Arbeitsplatzschutzgesetz)	Job Protection Law
AStG	Gesetz über die Besteuerung bei Auslandsbeziehungen (Außensteuergesetz)	Law on External Tax Relations
AStO	Ausgleichsteuerordnung	Ordinance Regulating the Turnover Equalization Tax
AStR	Außensteuerrecht	Legislation on External Tax Relations

Abkürzungsverzeichnis List of Abbreviations

Abk.	Deutsch	Englisch
ASU	Arbeitsgemeinschaft selbständiger Unternehmer	Association of Independent Businessmen
AuslInvG	Gesetz über steuerliche Maßnahmen bei Auslandsinvestitionen der deutschen Wirtschaft (Auslandsinvestitionsgesetz)	Foreign Investment Law
AuW	Außenwirtschaft	International Trade
AVB	Allgemeine Versicherungsbedingungen	General Insurance Conditions
AWG	Außenwirtschaftsgesetz	Foreign Trade Law
AWV	Außenwirtschaftsverordnung	Foreign Trade Ordinance
AZO	1. Allgemeine Zollordnung	General Customs Ordinance
	2. Arbeitszeitordnung	Code Regulating Working Hours
BA	1. Bundesaufsichtsamt für das Kreditwesen	Federal Banking Supervisory Office
	2. Berichtigungsaktie	Bonus Share
BAB	Betriebsabrechnungsbogen	Expense Distribution Sheet
BAföG	Bundesgesetz über individuelle Förderung der Ausbildung (Bundesausbildungsförderungsgesetz)	Federal Law on Education and Training Promotion
BAG	Bundesarbeitsgericht	Federal Labor Court
BAK	Bundesaufsichtsamt für das Kreditwesen	Federal Banking Supervisory Office
BAM	Bundesarbeitsminister	Federal Minister of Labor and Social Affairs
BAnz	Bundesanzeiger	Federal Official Gazette
BaSta	Bankenstatistik	Banking Statistics
BAT	Bundes-Angestellten-Tarifvertrag	Federal Collective Agreement for Public Employees
BAV	Bundesaufsichtsamt für das Versicherungs- und Bausparwesen	Federal Supervisory Office for Insurance Companies and for Building and Loan Associations
BAW	Bundesamt für gewerbliche Wirtschaft	Federal Trade and Industry Office
BBankG	Bundesbankgesetz	Federal Bank Law
BBiG	Berufsbildungsgesetz	Occupational Training Law
BBk	Deutsche Bundesbank	German Federal Bank
BDA	Bundesvereinigung der Deutschen Arbeitgeberverbände	Federation of Employers' Associations
BFH	Bundesfinanzhof	Federal Fiscal Court
BFM	Bundesminister der Finanzen	Federal Minister of Finance
BdI	Bundesminister des Innern	Federal Minister of the Interior
BDI	Bundesverband der Deutschen Industrie	Federation of German Industry
BDSG	Bundesdatenschutzgesetz	Federal Data Protection Law
BefStG	Beförderungsteuergesetz	Transportation Tax Law
BerlinFG	Gesetz zur Förderung der Berlin-Wirtschaft (Berlinförderungsgesetz)	Law for the Promotion of the Economy of West Berlin
BetrVG	Betriebsverfassungsgesetz	Industrial Constitution Law
BewDV	Durchführungsverordnung zum Bewertungsgesetz	Ordinance Regulating the Valuation Law
BewG	Bewertungsgesetz	Valuation Law
Bf	Buchführung	Accounting
BfA	1. Bundesanstalt für Arbeit	Federal Labor Office
	2. Bundesversicherungsanstalt für Angestellte	Federal Social Insurance Office for Salaried Employees
	3. Bundesstelle für Außenhandelsinformationen	Federal Foreign Trade Information Office
BFA	Bankenfachausschuß	Banking Expert Committee
BfF	Bundesamt für Finanzen	Federal Tax Office
bfn	brutto für netto	gross for net
BGB	Bürgerliches Gesetzbuch	German Civil Code
BGBl	Bundesgesetzblatt	Federal Official Gazette
BGH	Bundesgerichtshof	Federal Supreme Court
BHO	Bundeshaushaltsordnung	Federal Budget Code
BICC	Internationales Büro der Handelskammern	International Bureau of Chambers of Commerce
BIZ	Bank für Internationalen Zahlungsausgleich	Bank for International Settlements

XXIII

Abkürzungsverzeichnis List of Abbreviations

BLZ	Bankleitzahl	Bank Routing Number
BMA	Bundesministerium für Arbeit und Sozialordnung	Federal Ministry of Labor and Social Affairs
BMBau	Bundesministerium für Raumordnung, Bauwesen und Städtebau	Federal Ministry of Urban Planning and Housing
BMBW	Bundesministerium für Bildung und Wissenschaft	Federal Ministry of Education
BMF	Bundesministerium für Finanzen	Federal Ministry of Finance
BMFT	Bundesministerium für Forschung und Technologie	Federal Ministry for Research and Technology
BMI	Bundesministerium des Innern	Federal Ministry of the Interior
BMJ	Bundesministerium der Justiz	Federal Ministry of Justice
BMJFG	Bundesministerium für Jugend, Familie und Gesundheit	Federal Ministry for Youth, Family Affairs and Health
BML	Bundesministerium für Ernährung, Landwirtschaft und Forsten	Federal Ministry of Food, Agriculture and Forestry
BMP	Bundesministerium für Post und Fernmeldewesen	Federal Ministry of Post and Telecommunications
BMV	Bundesministerium für Verkehr	Federal Ministry of Transportation
BMVg	Bundesministerium der Verteidigung	Federal Minstry of Defense
BMWi	Bundesministerium für Wirtschaft	Federal Ministry of Economics
BMZ	Bundesministerium für wirtschaftliche Zusammenarbeit	Federal Ministry of Economic Cooperation
BP	Deutsche Bundespost	Federal Post Office
BPflV	Verordnung zur Regelung der Krankenhauspflegesätze	Ordinance Regulating Hospital Operating Cost Rates
BPG	Buchprüfungsgesellschaft	Firm of Lincensed Public Accountants
BPV	Betriebspachtvertrag	Plant Leasing Agreement
BRD	Bundesrepublik Deutschland	Federal Republic of Germany
BRVS	Bahnrollfuhr-Versicherungsschein	Cartage Contractor's Insurance Policy
BSG	1. Bausparkassengesetz 2. Bundessozialgericht	Law on Building and Loan Associations Federal Court for Social Security and Social Matters
BSP	Bruttosozialprodukt	Gross National Product
BSpKG	Gesetz über Bausparkassen (Bausparkassengesetz)	Law on Building and Loan Associations
BStBl	Bundessteuerblatt	Official Gazette of the Federal Ministry of Finance
BUSt	Börsenumsatzsteuer	Exchange Turnover Tax
BÜV	Betriebsüberlassungsvertrag	Plant Transfer Agreement
BVerfG	Bundesverfassungsgericht	Federal Constitutional Court
BVerwG	Bundesverwaltungsgericht	Federal Administrative Court
BVG	Betriebsverfassungsgesetz	Industrial Constitution Law
BWM	Bundeswirtschaftsminister	Federal Minister of Economics
CGB	Christlicher Gewerkschaftsbund	Christian Trade Union Federation
com	Allgemeine Sprache der Wirtschaft	General Commercial English
CpD	Konto pro Diverse	Collective Suspense Account
CST	Internationales Warenverzeichnis für den Außenhandel	Statistical and Tariff Classification for International Trade
DAG	Deutsche Angestelltengewerkschaft	German Salaried Employee Union
DB	Deutsche Bundesbahn	Federal Railways
DBA	Doppelbesteuerungsabkommen	Double Taxation Agreement
DBB	Deutscher Beamtenbund	German Public Service Federation
DBP	Deutsches Bundespatentamt	German Federal Patent Office
DBPa	für Deutsches Bundespatent angemeldet	Application Pending for German Federal Patent
DE	Datenerfassung	Data Acquisition
DEMV	Deutscher Einheitsmietvertrag	German Standard Tenancy Agreement
DepG	Depotgesetz	Law on the Deposit and Acquisition of Securities
DES	Datenerfassungssystem	Data Acquisition System
DGB	Deutscher Gewerkschaftsbund	German Labor Federation

Abkürzungsverzeichnis List of Abbreviations

DGBa	Deutsche Genossenschaftsbank	Central Bank of German Cooperatives
DGFB	Deutsche Gesellschaft für Betriebswirtschaft	West German Management Association
DIW	Deutsches Institut für Wirtschaftsforschung	German Institute for Economic Research
DTV	Deutscher Transportversicherungsverband	German Transport Insurance Association
DV	Datenverarbeitung	Data Processing
DVO	Durchführungsverordnung	Regulating Ordinance
EAB	Europäische Ausfuhrbank	European Export Bank
EAGFL	Europäischer Ausrichtungs- und Garantiefonds Landwirtschaft	European Agricultural Guidance and Guarantee Fund, AEGGF
EAN	Europäische Artikelnumerierung	European Product Code
EDV	Elektronische Datenverarbeitung	Electronic Data Processing, EDP
EE	Einfuhrerklärung	Import Declaration
EEF	Europäischer Entwicklungsfonds	European Development Fund
EFTA	Europäische Freihandelsassoziation	European Free Trade Association
EFWS	Europäisches Forschungsinstitut für Wirtschafts- und Sozialpolitik	European Economic and Social Policy Research Institute
EFWZ	Europäischer Fonds für währungspolitische Zusammenarbeit	European Monetary Cooperation Fund
eg	zum Beispiel	for instance
EG	Europäische Gemeinschaften	European Communities
EGAktG	Einführungsgesetz zum Aktiengesetz	Introductory Law to the German Stock Corporation Law
EGKS	Europäische Gemeinschaft für Kohle und Stahl (Montanunion)	European Coal and Steel Community
eGmbH	eingetragene Genossenschaft mit beschränkter Haftpflicht	Registered Limited-Liability Cooperative
eGmuH	eingetragene Genossenschaft mit unbeschränkter Haftpflicht	Registered Cooperative with Unlimited Liability
EIB	Europäische Investitionsbank	European Investment Bank
EK	Eigenkapital	Equity Capital
EL	Entwicklungsländer	Developing Countries
ERA	Einheitliche Richtlinien und Gebräuche für Dokumenten-Akkreditive	Uniform Customs and Practice for Commercial Documentary Credits
ErbSt	Erbschaftsteuer	Inheritance Tax
ErbStDV	Erbschaftsteuer-Durchführungsverordnung	Ordinance Regulating the Inheritance Tax Law
ErbStG	Erbschaftsteuergesetz	Inheritance Tax Law
ERI	Einheitliche Richtlinien für das Inkasso von Handelspapieren	Uniform Rules for the Collection of Commercial Paper
ERV	Einheitliche Richtlinien für Vertragsgarantien	Uniform Rules for Contract Guarantees
esp	insbesondere	especially
ESt	Einkommensteuer	Income Tax
EStDV	Einkommensteuer-Durchführungsverordnung	Ordinance Regulating the Income Tax Law
EStG	Einkommensteuergesetz	Income Tax Law
EStR	Einkommensteuer-Richtlinien	Income Tax Regulations
EUA	Europäische Rechnungseinheit	European Unit of Account, EUA
EuGH	Europäischer Gerichtshof	European Court of Justice
euphem	Euphemismus	euphemism
EUSt	Einfuhrumsatzsteuer	Import Turnover Tax
e. V.	eingetragener Verein	Registered Association
E. v.	Eingang vorbehalten	Subject to Collection
EVO	Eisenbahnverkehrsordnung	Rail Freight Traffic Ordinance
EVSt	Einfuhr- und Vorratsstelle	Intervention Board for Agricultural Products
EWA	Europäisches Währungsabkommen	European Monetary Agreement, AME
EWF	Europäischer Währungsfonds	European Monetary Fund
EWS	Europäisches Währungssystem	European Monetary System
EZU	Europäische Zahlungsunion	European Payments Union, EPU

XXV

Abkürzungsverzeichnis List of Abbreviations

f	femininum	feminine
FA	Finanzamt	Local Tax Office
fab	frei an Bord	free on board, fob
FG	Finanzgericht	Fiscal Court
FGO	Finanzgerichtsordnung	Code of Fiscal Procedure
Fin	Finanzwirtschaft der Unternehmen, einschl. Banken	Business Finance, incl. Banking
FiW	Öffentliche Finanzwirtschaft	Public Finance
FK	Fremdkapital	Borrowed Capital
FLR	freie Liquiditätsreserven	Free Liquid Reserves
FVG	Gesetz über die Finanzverwaltung	Law on Fiscal Administration
GAB	Allgemeine Kreditvereinbarungen	General Arrangements to Borrow
GAZ	Gemeinsamer Außenzolltarif	Common External Tariff
GB	Großbritannien	Great Britain
GbR	Gesellschaft des bürgerlichen Rechts (BGB-Gesellschaft)	Civil Law Association
GenG	Gesetz betreffend die Erwerbs- und Wirtschaftsgenossenschaften (Genossenschaftsgesetz)	Law on Cooperatives
GesSt	Gesellschaftsteuer	Company Tax
GewStDV	Gewerbesteuer-Durchführungsverordnung	Ordinance Regulating the Trade Tax Law
GewStG	Gewerbesteuergesetz	Trade Tax Law
GewStR	Gewerbesteuer-Richtlinien	Trade Tax Regulations
GG	Grundgesetz	Basic Law of the Federal Republic
GKR	Gemeinschaftskontenrahmen industrieller Verbände	Joint Standard Accounting System of Industrial Associations
GKV	Gesetzliche Krankenversicherung	Statutory Health Insurance
GmbH	Gesellschaft mit beschränkter Haftung	Limited Liability Company
GmbH-Ges	Gesetz betreffend die Gesellschaften mit beschränkter Haftung	Law on Limited Liability Companies
GoA	1. Grundsätze ordnungsmäßiger Durchführung von Abschlußprüfungen	Principles of Orderly Auditing
	2. Geschäftsführung ohne Auftrag	Management of Affairs without Mandate
GoB	Grundsätze ordnungsmäßiger Buchführung	Principles of Orderly Accounting
GoD	Grundsätze ordnungsmäßiger Datenverarbeitung	Principles of Orderly Data Processing
GrdstVG	Gesetz über Maßnahmen zur Verbesserung der Agrarstruktur und zur Sicherung land- und forstwirtschaftlicher Betriebe (Grundstücksverkehrsgesetz)	Law on Real Estate Transactions
GrEStDV	Durchführungsverordnung zum Grunderwerbsteuer-Gesetz	Ordinance Regulating the Real Property Transfer Tax Law
GrEStG	Grunderwerbsteuergesetz	Real Property Transfer Tax Law
GrStDV	Verordnung zur Durchführung des Grundsteuergesetzes	Ordinance Regulating the Real Property Tax Law
GrStG	Grundsteuergesetz	Real Property Tax Law
GrStR	Grundsteuer-Richtlinien	Real Property Tax Regulations
GüKG	Güterkraftverkehrsgesetz	Law on Road Haulage
GuV	Gewinn- und Verlustrechnung	Income Statement
Gvf	Geschäftsvorfall	Accounting Transaction
GVG	Gerichtsverfassungsgesetz	Law on the Constitution of Courts
GWB	Gesetz gegen Wettbewerbsbeschränkungen	Law Against Restraints of Competition
GZT	Gemeinsamer Zolltarif	Common Customs Tariff
HandwO	Handwerksordnung	Artisans' Code
HAÜ	Hauptabschlußübersicht	Condensed Statement of Annual Accounts Figures
HGB	Handelsgesetzbuch	German Commercial Code
HR	Handelsregister	Commercial Register
HV	Hauptversammlung	General Shareholders' Meeting

i. A.	1. im Auftrag	by order of
	2. in Abwicklung	in liquidation
IAA	Internationales Arbeitsamt	International Labor Office
IBRD	Internationale Bank für Wiederaufbau und wirtschaftliche Entwicklung (Weltbank)	International Bank for Reconstruction and Development (World Bank)
IdW	Institut der Wirtschaftsprüfer	Institute of German Certified Public Accountants
ie	das heißt	that is
IEA	Internationale Energie-Agentur	International Energy Agency
i. e. S.	im engeren Sinne	in its narrower sense
IHK	1. Industrie- und Handelskammer	Chamber of Industry and Commerce
	2. Internationale Handelskammer	International Chamber of Commerce
IKR	Industriekontenrahmen	Uniform Classification of Accounts for Industrial Enterprises
i. L.	in Liquidation	in liquidation
ILO	Internationale Arbeitsorganisation	International Labor Organization
IndE	Industriebetriebslehre	Industrial Engineering
infml	informell	informal
IR	Investitionsrechnung	Preinvestment Analysis
IStR	Internationales Steuerrecht	International Law of Taxation
ITVV	Internationaler Transportversicherungsverband	International Union of Marine Insurance
IWF	Internationaler Währungsfonds	International Monetary Fund
i. w. S.	im weiteren Sinne	in its wider sense
joc	jocular	scherzhaft
KAGG	Gesetz über die Kapitalanlagegesellschaften	Law on Investment Companies
KAP	Konsolidierungsausgleichsposten	Consolidation Excess
KapErtrSt	Kapitalertragsteuer	Tax on Income from Capital
KapStDV	Kapitalertragsteuer-Durchführungsverordnung	Ordinance Regulating the Withholding of Tax from Income from Capital
Kart	Kartellrecht	Antitrust Law
KfW	Kreditanstalt für Wiederaufbau	Reconstruction Loan Corporation
KG	Kommanditgesellschaft	Limited Commercial Partnership
KGaA	Kommanditgesellschaft auf Aktien	Commercial Partnership Limited by Shares
KGV	Kurs-Gewinn-Verhältnis	Price-Earnings Ratio
KO	Konkursordnung	Bankruptcy Law
KoR	Kostenrechnung	Cost Accounting
KSchG	Kündigungsschutzgesetz	Dismissals Protection Law
KSt	Körperschaftsteuer	Corporation Income Tax
KStDV	Verordnung zur Durchführung des Körperschaftsteuergesetzes	Ordinance Regulating the Corporation Income Tax Law
KStG	Körperschaftsteuergesetz	Corporation Income Tax Law
KStR	Körperschaftsteuer-Richtlinien	Corporation Income Tax Regulations
KVSt	Kapitalverkehrsteuer	Capital Transfer Tax
KVStDV	Kapitalverkehrsteuer-Durchführungsverordnung	Ordinance Regulating the Capital Transfer Tax Law
KVStG	Kapitalverkehrsteuergesetz	Capital Transfer Tax Law
KWG	Gesetz über das Kreditwesen (Kreditwesengesetz)	German Banking Law
LP	Lineare Programmierung	Linear Programming
LStDV	Lohnsteuer-Durchführungsverordnung	Ordinance Regulating the Wage Tax
LStR	Lohnsteuer-Richtlinien	Wage Tax Regulations
LZB	Landeszentralbank	Central Bank of a Land
m	masculinum	masculine
Math	Mathematik	Mathematics
MaW	Materialwirtschaft	Materials Management and Control

Abkürzungsverzeichnis List of Abbreviations

Mk	Marketing	Marketing
MNU	Multinationale Unternehmungen	Multinational Enterprises
MWSt	Mehrwertsteuer	Value Added Tax
n	neutrum	neuter
NRZZ	Brüsseler Zolltarifschema	Brussel's Tariff Nomenclature
od	oder	or
OFD	Oberfinanzdirektion	Regional Finance Office
OFH	Oberster Finanzgerichtshof	Federal Fiscal Court
OHG	Offene Handelsgesellschaft	General Commercial Partnership
OLG	Oberlandesgericht	Intermediate Court of Appeals
opp	Gegensatz	opposed to
OR	Operations Research	Operations Research
ÖTV	Gewerkschaft Öffentliche Dienste, Transport und Verkehr	Public Services and Transport Workers' Union
Pat	Gewerbliche Schutzrechte	Industrial Property Rights
PatG	Patentgesetz	German Patent Law
PKK	persönlicher Kleinkredit	Loan for Personal Use
pl	Plural	plural
PR	Pensionsrückstellungen	Pension Reserves
PrüfO	Prüfungsordnung für Wirtschaftsprüfer	CAP Examination Code
PublG	Gesetz über die Rechnungslegung von bestimmten Unternehmen und Konzernen (Publizitätsgesetz)	Disclosure Law
PVÜ	Pariser Verbands-Übereinkunft	Paris Convention
Pw	Personalwirtschaft	Personnel Management
qv	siehe	which see
RAP	Rechnungsabgrenzungsposten	Accruals and Deferrals
RechbkVVO	Rechnungslegungsvorschriften für Versicherungsunternehmen	Accounting Standards for Insurance Companies
RE	Rechnungseinheit	Unit of Account
REFA	REFA-Verband für Arbeitsstudien und Betriebsorganisation	REFA – Work Study Organization
RFH	Reichsfinanzhof	Fiscal Court of the former Reich
RRVU	Richtlinien für die Aufstellung des zu veröffentlichenden Rechnungsabschlusses von Versicherungsunternehmen	Rules for Preparing Financial Statements of Insurance Companies
RVO	Reichsversicherungsordnung	West German Social Insurance Code
SAEG	Statistisches Amt der Europäischen Gemeinschaften	Statistical Office of the European Communities
ScheckG	Scheckgesetz	German Law Relating to Checks
SeeV	Seeversicherung	Ocean Marine Insurance
SGB	Sozialgesetzbuch	Social Security Code
SKE	Steinkohleeinheit	Coal Equivalent
sl	Slang	slang
SozV	Soziale Sicherheit	Social Security
SparPG	Sparprämiengesetz	Law on Premiums Paid by the Government on Savings and Investments of Resident Individuals
StabG	Stabilitätsgesetz	Stabilization Law
StAnpG	Steueranpassungsgesetz	Law on the Adaptation of Taxes
Stat	Statistik	Statistics
StBA	Statistisches Bundesamt	Federal Statistical Office
StBerG	Steuerberatungsgesetz	Law on Tax Counseling
StGB	Strafgesetzbuch	German Penal Code
StR	Steuerrecht	Tax Law

Abkürzungsverzeichnis List of Abbreviations

StVZO	Straßenverkehrszulassungsordnung	Ordinance for Road Vehicle Licensing
SVR	Sachverständigenrat	Council of Economic Advisers
SVS	Speditionsversicherungsschein	Forwarder's Risk Insurance Policy
SvZ	System vorbestimmter Zeiten	System of Predetermined Times
syn	synonym	synonymous
SZR	Sonderziehungsrechte	Special Drawings Rights
TVG	Tarifvertragsgesetz	German Collective Agreements Law
TWA	Technologiewirkungsanalyse	Technology Assessment
UmwG	Umwandlungsgesetz	Reorganization Law
UmwStG	Gesetz über steuerliche Maßnahmen bei Änderung der Unternehmensform (Umwandlungs-Steuergesetz)	Reorganization Tax Law
US	Vereinigte Staaten	United States
USt	Umsatzsteuer	Turnover Tax
UStDV	Umsatzsteuer-Durchführungsverordnung	Ordinance Regulating the Turnover Tax
UStG	Umsatzsteuergesetz	Turnover Tax Law
UWG	Gesetz gegen Unlauteren Wettbewerb	Law Against Unfair Competition
VAG	Versicherungsaufsichtsgesetz	Law on the Supervision of Insurance Companies
VAT	Mehrwertsteuer	Value Added Tax
VDA	Verband der Automobilindustrie	German Motor Industry Federation
VDMA	Verein Deutscher Maschinenbauanstalten	Association of German Machinery Manufacturers
Vers	Versicherungswirtschaft	Insurance Industry
VerSt	Versicherungsteuer	Insurance Tax
VerStG	Versicherungsteuergesetz	Insurance Tax Law
VGH	Verwaltungsgerichtshof	Appellate Administrative Court
VGR	Volkswirtschaftliche Gesamtrechnung	National Accounting
VSt	Vermögensteuer	Net Worth Tax
VStDV	Vermögensteuer-Durchführungsverordnung	Ordinance Regulating the Net Worth Tax Law
VStG	Vermögensteuergesetz	Net Worth Tax Law
VStR	Vermögensteuer-Richtlinien	Net Worth Tax Regulations
VVaaG	Versicherungsverein auf Gegenseitigkeit	Mutual Insurance Association
Vw	Volkswirtschaftslehre	Economics
VwGO	Verwaltungsgerichtsordnung	Administrative Tribunals Code
VwVfg	Verwaltungsverfahrensgesetz	Law on Administrative Procedures
VZ	Veranlagungszeitraum	Tax Assessment Period
VVG	Gesetz über den Versicherungsvertrag (Versicherungsvertragsgesetz)	Law on Insurance Contracts
WährG	Währungsgesetz	Reorganization of Currency Law
WeR	Wertpapierrecht	Negotiable Instruments
WG	Wechselgesetz	German Law on Bills of Exchange
WP	Wirtschaftsprüfer	Certified Public Accountant, CPA
WPO	Wirtschaftsprüferordnung	Law Regulating the CPA Profession
WPK	Wirtschaftsprüferkammer	CPA Professional Organization
WStG	Wechselsteuergesetz	Law Regulating the Taxes on Bills of Exchange, Drafts, and Acceptances
WWU	Wirtschafts- und Währungsunion	Economic and Monetary Union
ZDH	Zentralverband des Deutschen Handwerks	Central Association of German Handicrafts
ZE	Zentraleinheit	Central Processing Unit
ZG	Zollgesetz	Tariff Law
ZKMA	Zentraler Kapitalmarktausschuß	Central Capital Market Committee
Zo	Zollwesen	Customs
ZPO	Zivilprozeßordnung	Code of Civil Procedure

Abkürzungsverzeichnis List of Abbreviations

ZVEI	Zentralverband der Elektrotechnischen Industrie	Central Association of the Electrical Industry
ZVG	Gesetz über die Zwangsversteigerung und Zwangsverwaltung	Law on Forced Sale and Administration

A

Abandon *m*
(com) relinquishment of a right in order to be discharged from a duty
(Re) abandonment *(ie, of a share to a company if shareholder objects to change of AG into GmbH or vice versa, §§ 375, 383 AktG)*
(SeeV) abandonment *(ie, surrender of insured property to the underwriter in return for full payment of sum insured, § 861 HGB)*
(Vers) abandonment *(ie, right of transport insurer to pay or deposit the full amount of sum insured in order to disclaim any further liability)*
Abandonerklärung *f* (SeeV) notice of abandonment
Abandonist *m* (SeeV) abandoner
Abandonklausel *f* (Vers) abandonment clause
abandonnieren (Re, Vers) to abandon
Abandonrecht *n* (Re) right of abandonment
Abandonrevers *m*
(Vers) declaration of abandonment *(ie, in transportation insurance)*
(SeeV) abandonment acknowledgment *(ie, authenticated document of acknowledgment concerning the subrogation of rights occurring by reason of the notice of abandonment, § 871 HGB)*
Abänderungsantrag *m* **einbringen** (Re) to introduce an amendment
Abänderungsantrag *m* **zustimmen** (Re) to agree to an amendment
Abänderungsklage *f* (Re) civil action seeking to modify enforceable judgment for recurrent payments, § 323 ZPO
Abänderungskündigung *f* (Pw) notice of dismissal + offer for re-employment at less favorable terms, §§ 2, 8 KSchG
Abänderungsvertrag *m* (Re) agreement concluded to change an existing contract
abarbeiten (com) to work off *(eg, debts)*
Abbaubetrieb *m* (com) extractive enterprise *(or company)*
Abbau *m* **der Belegschaft** (Pw) cutting down *(or reduction) of workforce (or personnel)*
 – job pruning
 – slimming *(eg, upwards of 20,000)* jobs
 – slashing of manning level
abbauen
(com) to reduce *(eg, prices, wages)*
(com) to abolish gradually *(eg, tariffs, tax advantages)*
(com) to work off *(eg, backlog of orders on hand)*
(com) to run down *(eg, stocks)*
(Fin) to repay *(eg, debt)*
(Pw) to cut down *(eg, labor force)*
 – to slim
 – to reduce
abbaufähige Betriebsfläche *f* (Bw) wasting asset
Abbaugerechtigkeit *f* (Re) mineral *(or mining)* right *(ie, right equivalent to ownership of real property and existing under a servitude or easement = Grunddienstbarkeit)*
Abbaukonzession *f* (Re) operating license *(or lease)*
Abbauland *n* (StR) wasting assets *(eg, mining land, quarries, gravel pits; ie, assets diminishing in value commensurately with the removal of a natural product, § 43 BewG)*
Abbau *m* **nichttarifärer Handelshemmnisse** (AuW) nontariff reductions
Abbaurecht *n* (Re) mineral *(or mining)* right
Abbau *m* **von Devisenreserven** (AuW) rundown of foreign exchange reserves
Abbau *m* **von Handelsschranken** (AuW) lowering *(or dismantling)* of trade barriers
Abbau *m* **von Lagerbeständen**
(Vw) disinvestment in stocks
(Bw) inventory liquidation *(or runoff)*
Abbau *m* **von Staatsverschuldung** (FiW) reduction in government *(or public)* debt
Abbau *m* **von Zöllen**
(AuW) abolition of tariffs
(AuW) reduction of customs duties
Abbau *m* **von Zollschranken** (AuW) removal of customs barriers
abberufen
(Re) to recall *(ie, from office)*
 – to withdraw
 – to dismiss *(eg, supervisory board member)*
Abberufung *f*
(com) dismissal
 – recall
 – withdrawal
abbestellen
(com) to cancel an order (for)
(com) to cancel a subscription (for)
abbezahlen
(Fin) to pay off
 – to pay by installments
abbilden auf *(od* **in)** (Math) to map *(or transform)* into
Abbildtheorie *f* (Math) theory of mapping
Abbildung *f*
(Math) function
 – mapping
 – transformation
abbrechen
(com) to break off *(eg, negotiations)*
(EDV) to abort a job or system *(ie, mostly due to malfunction)*
(EDV) to truncate *(ie, to suppress insignificant digits of a number)*
Abbrechen *n*
(Stat) cutoff *(eg, cf survey)*
(EDV) abortion
(EDV) truncation
Abbrechfehler *m* (EDV) truncation error
abbröckeln

(Bö) to ease off
- to edge down
- to drift down *(eg, bond and equity prices)*

abbröckelnd
(Bö) slackening
- easing
- crumbling

Abbruch *m*
(com) break off *(eg, of negotiations)*
(Bw) demolition *(eg, buildings)*
- dismantlement *(eg, plant and equipment)*

Abbruchbetrieb *m*
(com) demolition contractor
- salvage company

Abbrucherlöse *mpl*
(ReW) revenue from disposal of dismantled buildings, plant and equipment
- revenue from scrap disposal

Abbruchkosten *pl*
(ReW) cost of demolition
- cost of dismantling
- removal expenses *(ie, capitalized and written off as incidental acquisition cost)*

Abbruchmaterial *n* (com) demolition rubbish *(or* waste*)*

Abbruchunternehmen *n*
(com) demolition contractor
- salvage company

Abbruchwert *m* (ReW) break-up value

abbuchen
(com) to debit *(eg, bank debited my account with $50)*
- to enter a debit against
- to take out of the books
(ReW) to charge off *(ie, as an expense or loss)*
(ReW) to write off *(eg, bad debt as uncollectible)*
(ReW) to close out *(eg, cost of plant removed)*

Abbuchen *n* **e-r uneinbringlichen Forderung**
(ReW) bad debt writeoff

Abbuchungsauftrag *m* (Fin) credit transfer instruction

Abbuchungsverfahren *n*
(Fin) direct debiting service
- preauthorized payment method

ABC-Analyse *f* **der Lagerhaltung**
(MaW) ABC inventory control system
- selective inventory control
- usage value analysis

abdecken
(Fin) to repay *(eg, a credit or debt)*
(Bö) to conclude covering transaction *(ie, in forward operations)*

Abdeckung *f* **des Marktes** (Mk) market coverage

abdingbar
(Re) *(provisions of contract are)* modifiable
- may be modified *(or* altered*)*

abdisponieren
(Fin) to transfer
(Fin) to withdraw

Abdisposition *f*
(Fin) transfer
(Fin) withdrawal

abelsche Gruppe *f* (Math) abelian group
abelsches Integral *n* (Math) abelian integral
Abendschule *f* (Pw) evening *(or* night*)* school

Abendverkauf *m*
(Mk) nighttime sales
- late opening

Aberdepot *n* (Fin) deposit of fungible securities *(ie, bank need only return paper of same description and quantity)*

ab Fabrik
(com) ex works
- ex factory

Abfahrtsdatum *n* (com) date of sailing *(ie, in ocean shipping)*

Abfall *m*
(MaW) spoilage *(ie, junked and sold for disposal value)*
- scrap *(ie, of measurable but relatively minor recovery value; eg, shavings, filings, turnings; may be sold or reused)*
- waste *(ie, no measurable recovery value or lost in the process; eg, dust, smoke)*

Abfallanalyse *f* (MaW) volume analysis of scrap, waste, and spoilage

Abfallaufkommen *n*
(MaW) solid waste production
- quantity discarded

Abfallbeseitigung *f* (IndE) waste disposal

Abfallbeseitigungsanlage *f* (IndE) solid waste plant *(ie, set up for processing and disposal)*

Abfallbeseitigungsgesetz *n* (Re) Waste Disposal Law, as amended 5 Jan 1977

Abfallbörse *f* (com) exchange set up by German Chambers of Commerce for the purchase and sale of residues, waste, and rejects, such as paper, plastics, etc.

Abfallerzeugnis *n*
(Bw) byproduct
- product made from scrap, waste, or spoilage

Abfallmaterial *n*
(IndE) spoilage *(ie, products not meeting quality standards, sold for disposal value)*
- waste *(ie, lost in manufacturing, no recovery value)*
- scrap *(ie, residue from manufacturing, sold or reused)*

Abfallmengenplanung *f* (KoR) volume planning of waste, scrap, and spoilage *(ie, carried out by OR methods as part of direct materials planning in standard cost accounting)*

Abfallpapier *n* (com) waste paper
Abfallprodukt *n* (Bw) = *Abfallerzeugnis*
Abfallstoffe *mpl* (IndE) waste material
Abfallstück *n*
(IndE) reject
- (infml) waster

Abfallverminderungsprämie *f* (Pw) scrap-cutting bonus *(ie, an additional component of premium wage systems)*

Abfallverwertung *f* (com) disposition *(ie, sale or reuse)* of spoilage or scrap

Abfallwirtschaft *f* (IndE) waste management *(or* control*)*

Abfassung *f* **von Werbetexten** (Mk) copy writing

abfertigen
(com) to attend
- to serve
- to wait on customers

Abfertigung

(com) to deal with
– to process *(esp. in public offices)*
(com) to dispatch
– to forward
– to expedite *(eg, consignment)*
(Zo) to clear under customs procedure *(or* through the customs)
Abfertigung *f*
(com) dispatch *(ie, preparing, concluding, and implementing railroad transportation contract)*
(Zo) customs clearance of goods
(OR) service unit *(or* station)
Abfertigung *f* **im Reiseverkehr** (Zo) control of tourist traffic
Abfertigungsbeamter *m* (Zo) customs clearance officer
Abfertigungsbescheinigung *f* (Zo) certificate of acceptance
Abfertigungsgebühr *f* (com) incidental railroad charges *(ie, other than actual freightage; eg, for loading and unloading)*
Abfertigungshafen *m* (Zo) port of clearance
Abfertigungsprozeß *m* (OR) service process
Abfertigungsrate *f* (OR) service rate
Abfertigungsreihenfolge *f* (OR) service order
Abfertigungsschalter *m* (Zo) passport control point
Abfertigungsspediteur *m* (com) truck haulage carrier *(ie, appointed by a higher-level transportation authority under § 34 GüKG)*
Abfertigungsstelle *f*
(com) freight office
– (GB) goods office
(OR) channel
– service point
– service station
– service unit
Abfertigungszeit *f* (OR) service time *(syn, Bedienungszeit, Servicezeit)*
Abfertigungsvorschriften *fpl*
(com) forwarding regulations
(Zo) clearance regulations
Abfertigungszollstelle *f* (Zo) office of clearance
Abfertigung *f* **von Waren** (Zo) customs clearance of goods
Abfertigung *f* **zum Dauerverbleib** (Zo) clearance for home use
Abfertigung *f* **zum freien Verkehr beantragen** (Zo) to enter (goods) for consumption
Abfertigung *f* **zum zollrechtlich freien Verkehr** (Zo) release for free circulation
Abfertigung *f* **zum zoll- und steuerrechtlich freien Verkehr** (Zo) release for home use
Abfertigung *f* **zur Anweisung** (Zo) clearance for transit
Abfertigung *f* **zur Wiedereinfuhr** (Zo) clearance on re-importation *(or* re-entry)
Abfinanzierung *f* (Fin) repayment of debt and/or equity
abfinden
(com, Re) to compensate
– to indemnify
(Re) to settle with
(Fin) to pay off
– to satisfy *(eg, creditor)*

(Fin) to buy out *(ie, an established company, a partner)*
Abfindung *f*
(Re) indemnity *(ie, one-time money compensation to settle a legal claim)*
(Pw) dismissal pay
– severance pay
– terminal bonus *(or* wage)
– termination pay
– ex gratia payment
– lump-sum settlement *(ie, fixed by a labor court, § 10 KSchG)*
– (infml) golden handshake
Abfindungsangebot *n*
(com) offer of lump-sum compensation *(ie, in settlement of a claim)*
(Fin) takeover bid
(Pw) retirement offer
– early retirement scheme
Abfindungsbefugnis *f* (Re) right to perform an obligation other than that originally stipulated, § 241 I BGB
Abfindungserklärung *f*
(Re) release
– declaration accepting indemnity in full settlement of claim
(Vers) release *(ie, document signed by insured stating that any further claims, present and future, are waived)*
Abfindungsguthaben *n* (Re) compensation *(ie, due to a partner at the time of his withdrawal from the partnership or company)*
Abfindungsvertrag *m* (Pw) termination agreement
Abfindungszahlung *f*
(Pw) redundancy payment
– severance pay
– termination pay
abflachen (com) to level off
Abfluß *m* (Fin) outflow *(ie, of funds)*
Abfluß *m* **liquider Mittel** (Fin) cash drain
Abfrage *f* (EDV) inquiry *(ie, request for information from storage)*
– query
abfragebereit (EDV) ready for inquiry
Abfrageblattschreiber *m* (EDV) interrogating typewriter
Abfrageeinheit *f* (EDV) inquiry unit
Abfrageimpuls *m* (EDV) read(ing) pulse
abfragen
(EDV) to inquire
– to interrogate
(EDV) to scan
Abfrageplatz *m* (EDV) inquiry station
Abfrageprogramm *n* (EDV) inquiry program
Abfrageregister *n* (EDV) inquiry register
Abfragesequenz *f* (EDV) calling sequence
Abfragesprache *f* (EDV) inquiry *(or* query) language
Abfragestation *f* (EDV) inquiry station *(or* unit)
Abfragesystem *n* (EDV) inquiry system
Abfragetaste *f* (EDV) „who are you" key
Abfühlbürste *f* (EDV) reading *(or* sensing) brush
Abfühleinrichtung *f* (EDV) reading *(or* sensing) mechanism
abfühlen

(EDV) to sense *(syn, abtasten)*
– to read
Abfühlfehler *m* (EDV) read(ing) error
Abfühlstation *f* (EDV) sensing (*or* reading) station
Abfühlstift *m*
(EDV) sensing pin
– pecker
abführen (Fin) to pay over *(ie, to make formal payment; eg, to revenue authorities)*
Abgabe *f* **der Steuererklärung** (StR) filing a tax return, § 149 AO
Abgabe *f* **der Zollanmeldung** (Zo) lodgment of the goods declaration
Abgabedruck *m* (Bö) sales (*or* selling) pressure
Abgabefrist *f*
(com) due date
– filing date
– final date for acceptance
Abgabehoheit *f* (FiW) = *Steuerhoheit*
Abgabekurs *m* (Bö) issue price
Abgaben *fpl*
(StR) fiscal (*or* public) charges *(ie, general term denoting all compulsory payments to public or quasi-public authorities; eg, taxes, duties, levies, dues)*
(KoR) taxes and fiscal charges *(ie, treated as administrative overhead)*
(Bö) sales (of securities)
Abgabenautonomie *f* (FiW) right of municipalities to levy taxes and duties
Abgabeneigung *f* (Bö) selling tendency
Abgabenerhebung *f*
(StR) collection of taxes (and other fiscal charges)
(Zo) collection of duties and taxes
abgabenfrei (StR) free of tax
abgabenfreie Einfuhr *f*
(Zo) duty and tax-free importation
– free admission
Abgabenfreiheit *f* (StR) exemption from taxes (and other fiscal charges)
Abgabenordnung *f* (StR) German Fiscal Code *(ie, basic tax law, as amended in 1976, incorporating substantive and procedural provisions common to all special tax legislation)*
Abgabenorientierung *f* (Bw) tax-orientation of plant location *(ie, choice of location determined by general level of fiscal charges)*
abgabenpflichtig
(StR) liable to pay taxes (*or* other fiscal charges)
– subject to payment of taxes
abgabenpflichtige Waren *fpl* (Zo) chargeable (*or* dutiable) goods
Abgabenschuldner *m* (StR) person liable to duties or taxes
Abgabenstruktur *f* (StR) tax structure
Abgabensystem *n* (StR) system of levies
Abgabenvergünstigung *f* (AuW) preferential tariff treatment
Abgaben *fpl* **zollgleicher Wirkung** (Zo) charges equivalent to customs duties
Abgabepreis *m* (Mk) selling price *(ie, in retailing)*
Abgabesatz *m*
(com) amount of fiscal charges *(ie, in % of income)*

(Fin) selling rate *(ie, charged by German Bundesbank for money market paper; opp, Rücknahmesatz)*
Abgabetermin *m*
(com) due date
– filing date (for acceptance)
– time for filing *(eg, report, tax return)*
Abgabe *f* **von Angeboten**
(com) submission of bids
– bidding
Abgabe *f* **von Spielbanken** (StR) tax on gambling casinos
Abgabe *f* **von Zollanmeldungen für bestimmte Zeiträume** (Zo) periodic lodgment of declarations
Abgang *m*
(com) loss of weight *(ie, due to storage)*
(MaW) quantity issued *(ie, from stock)*
(Bw) asset disposal (*or* retirement)
(Pw) separation
– leave *(ie, termination of employment contract)*
(Vers) termination *(ie, of policy)*
Abgänge *mpl*
(ReW) disposals
– retirements *(eg, fixed assets, inventory items)*
(Pw) leavers
(Vers) actual deaths
Abgänger *m* (OR) branch emanating from node
Abgangsalter *n* (Vers) age at expiry
Abgangsdatum *n* (com) date of dispatch (*or* forwarding)
Abgangsflughafen *m* (Zo) airport of departure
Abgangshafen *m* (Zo) port of clearance (*or* departure)
Abgangskurve *f* (Bw, Vers) mortality curve
– survivor-life curve
Abgangsland *n* (Zo) country of departure
Abgangsmitgliedstaat *m* (Zo) Member State of departure
Abgangsordnung *f*
(Bw) mortality sequence *(ie, of technical products, such as automobiles, railroad sleepers)*
(Bw) mortality table *(ie, showing retirement sequence of fixed assets)*
Abgangsort *m* (Zo) place of departure
Abgangsrate *f* (Pw) separation (*or* layoff) rate
Abgangsrechnung *f* (ReW) asset retirement accounting
Abgangstabelle *f* (Stat) mortality (*or* retirement) table
Abgangswahrscheinlichkeit *f*
(Bw) mortality probability
(Vers) probability of exit
Abgangszeugnis *n* (Pw) school leaving certificate
Abgangszollstelle *f* (Zo) office of departure
Abgang *m* **von Gegenständen des Anlagevermögens** (ReW) disposal of fixed assets
abgebende Buchhaltung *f* (ReW) transferring accounting unit
abgebender Sektor *m* (Vw) supplying sector *(ie, in input-output analysis)*
abgebrochene Prüfung *f* (Stat) curtailed inspection
abgebrochene Rente *f* (Math) curtate annuity
abgebrochene Stichprobenprüfung *f* (Stat) curtailed (*or* truncated) sampling

abgekürzte Außenprüfung f (StR) summary examination, § 203 AO *(ie, of small businesses not subject to periodic review)*
abgekürzte Division f (Math) short division
abgekürzte Lebenserwartung f (Vers) reduced life expectancy
abgekürztes Zollverfahren n (Zo, US) summary judgment
abgekürzte Versicherung f (Vers) endowment life insurance *(ie, payable to the insured at the end of the contract or covered period or to beneficiary if insured dies prior to maturity date)*
abgekürzte Todesfallversicherung f (Vers) term insurance *(syn, Risikoversicherung: life insurance for a stipulated term only, beneficiary receiving the face value of the policy upon death, but nothing upon survival at completion of term)*
abgelagerte Ware f (com) seasoned goods
abgelaufene Frist f (com) expired term
abgelaufene Police f (Vers) expired policy
abgelaufenes Patent n (Pat) expired patent
abgelaufene Zeit f (EDV) elapsed time
Abgeld n (Fin) discount *(syn, Disagio)*
abgeleitete Bilanz f (ReW) derived balance sheet *(ie, prepared from the commercial balance sheet but based on different valuation rules)*
abgeleitete Firma f (Re) derived firm, §§ 21, 22 HGB
abgeleitete Informationsquelle f (Bw) source of processed information
abgeleitete Kostenarten fpl (KoR) derived
– composite
– mixed
– secondary . . . cost types
abgeleitete Maßzahl f (Stat) derived statistic
abgeleitete Menge f (Math) (weak) derived set
abgeleitete Nachfrage f (Vw) derived (*or* indirect) demand
abgeleiteter Anspruch m (Re) derivative claim
abgeleiteter Besitz m (Re) derivative possession
abgeleiteter Erwerb m (Re) derivative acquisition
abgeleiteter Produktionsfaktor m (Vw) derived factor of production
abgeleitetes Einkommen n (Vw) derived income *(ie, other than primary income)*
abgeleitetes Ereignis n (OR) derived event
abgeleitete Steuerhoheit f (FiW) derived taxing power *(ie, delegated to subordinate governmental units, such as ‚Gemeinde', ‚Kreis')*
abgelten (com) to pay in settlement of claim
abgepackte Ware f (com) packaged goods *(opp, bulk goods)*
abgerechnete Leistungen fpl (ReW) invoiced sales
abgeschlossene Hülle f **e-r Punktmenge** (Math) closure of a set of points
abgeschlossene Menge f (Math) closed set
abgeschlossenes Börsengeschäft n (Bö) round transaction
abgeschlossenes Studium n (Pw) full course of study *(eg, completed a . . . at a university)*
abgeschlossene Struktur f (Math) closed structure
abgeschlossenes Unterprogramm n (EDV) closed subroutine
abgeschwächte Nachfrage f (Vw) weaker demand

abgesonderte Befriedigung f (Re) preferential settlement of claim, §§ 47–52 KO
abgesonderter Gläubiger m (Re) creditor entitled to preferential settlement, § 4 KO
abgestimmte Betriebsgröße f (IndE) balanced plant size
abgestimmtes Verhalten n (Kart) concerted action
– concerted practice
– parallel behavior
abgetretene Forderung f (ReW) account receivable discounted *(ie, in factoring: contingent liability of seller up to time of payment by debtor)*
– (Re) assigned claim
abgewanderter Bevölkerungsüberschuß m (Vw) population overspill
ABG-Gesetz n (Re) Law Regulating Standard Terms and Conditions (1976)
abgleichen
(EDV) to collate
– to merge
abgrenzen (ReW) to charge to subsequent accounting years
Abgrenzung f
(ReW) accruals and deferrals *(ie, to reflect the lack of coincidence of the accounting period and the benefit period)*
(KoR) assignment of cost or expense not relating to accounting period or operating purpose
Abgrenzung f **des Küstenmeeres** (Re) delimitation of the territorial sea
Abgrenzung f **regionaler Teilmärkte** (Mk) market zoning
Abgrenzungsbogen m (ReW) reconciliation sheet *(ie, statistical statement showing allocation of expenses to financial and plant accounts)*
Abgrenzungsergebnis n (ReW) result of expense allocation statement *(ie, showing accruals and deferrals)*
Abgrenzungskonten npl (ReW) accounts receiving accruals and deferrals
Abgrenzungsposten mpl (ReW) items of accrual and deferral
Abgrenzungsrechnung f (ReW) statement of expense allocation
Abgrenzungssammelkonto n (ReW) account collecting accruals and deferrals
Abgruppierung f (Pw) downgrading *(ie, of a job)*
abhaken (com) to tick off *(eg, items on a list)*
Abhakungszeichen n
(com) check
– tick
abhanden gekommene Sache f (Re) movable thing either lost or stolen *(ie, ownership cannot be acquired from any person other than the true owner, § 935 BGB)*
abhängig Beschäftigte mpl (Pw) = *Abhängige*
Abhängige mpl
(Pw) wage and salary earners (*or* workers)
– wage earners and salaried employees
– persons in dependent employment
– employees
abhängige Beschäftigung f (Pw) dependent employment
abhängige Erwerbspersonen fpl (Stat) dependent labor force

abhängige Erwerbstätige *pl* (Pw) dependent workers
abhängige Gesellschaft *f* (Bw) dependent (*or* controlled) company
abhängiger Wartezustand *m* (EDV) normal disconnected mode, NDM
abhängiges Patent *n* (Pat) dependent patent
abhängiges Unternehmen *n* (Bw) controlled (*or* dependent) enterprise, § 17 AktG
abhängige Variable *f* (Math) dependent variable
Abhängigkeitsanalyse *f* (KoR) analysis determining relation between costs and changes of plant parameters
Abhängigkeitsbericht *m* (ReW) dependence report *(ie, report disclosing relations to affiliated companies, § 312 AktG)*
Abhängigkeitsprüfung *f* (ReW) dependence audit, § 313 AktG
Abhängigkeitsverhältnis *n* (Bw) relationship of dependence
abheben
(Fin) to draw
– to withdraw *(ie, money from a bank account)*
Abhebung *f* (Fin) withdrawal
Abhilfemaßnahmen *f pl* **in Gang setzen** (com) to instigate corrective action
abholen
(com) to collect
– to pick up *(eg, parcels, consignment)*
Abholgrossist *m* (Mk) cash and carry wholesaler
Abitur *n* (Pw) secondary school final *(ie, the equivalent of two years of college in US, and of ‚A' level in GB; entitles successful candidate forthwith to matriculation at any German university)*
Abiturient *m* (Pw) ‚gymnasium' graduate
Abiturzeugnis *n* (Pw) final secondary school leaving certificate
ab Kai (com) ex quay
ab Kai (unverzollt) (com) ex quay (duty on buyer's account)
ab Kai verzollt (com, *Incoterms*) ex quay duty paid (... named port of destination)
Abkommen *n*
(Re, *bilateral*) agreement *(ie, on economic, financial, technical matters, see ‚treaty')*
(Re, *multilateral*) convention
(Note: the two terms are sometimes used interchangeably)
Abkommen *n* **mit den Gläubigern** (Re) arrangement (*or* settlement) with creditors
Abkommen *n* **über das Zolltarifschema für die Einreihung der Waren in die Zolltarife** (AuW) Convention on nomenclature for the classification of goods in customs tariffs
Abkommen *n* **über den Schutz des gewerblichen Eigentums** (Re) Convention for the Protection of Industrial Property
Abkommen *n* **über den Zollwert der Waren** (AuW) Convention on the valuation of goods for customs purposes
Abkommen *n* **zur Stabilisierung der Rohstoffpreise** (Vw) commodity stabilization agreement
Abkommen *n* **zur Vermeidung von Doppelbesteuerung** (StR) double taxation treaty

abkoppeln (AuW) to de-couple *(ie, Europe from U.S. interest rates)*
Abladegeschäft *n* (com) import transaction where shipping port is deemed to be the place of performance *(ie, echtes Abladegeschäft; see also: unechtes Abladegeschäft)*
Abladegewicht *n* (com) unloading weight *(ie, determined by the carrier upon arrival at point of destination)*
Abladehafen *m* (com) port of discharge
Abladeklauseln *f pl* (com) trade terms relating to transportation cost, place and time of fulfillment *(eg, cif, fob, freight prepaid etc.)*
Abladekosten *pl* (com) unloading charges
Ablader *m*
(com) shipper
– forwarder
(ie, neither exporter nor carrier, § 442 HGB)
Abladung *f*
(com) unloading
– discharge
Abladungshafen *m* (com) port of discharge
Ablage *f*
(com) filing
(com) file system *(ie, systematic arrangements for storing office papers)*
Ablagefach *n* (EDV) card stacker
Ablagekorb *m* (com) letter tray
Ablagemappe *f* (com) letter folder *(ie, folded cardboard used for holding loose papers)*
ab Lager
(com) ex store
– ex warehouse
(com, infml) off the shelf
ab Lager liefern (com) to deliver from stock
Ablagerutsche *f* (EDV) stacker chute
Ablageschacht *m* (EDV) = *Ablagefach*
Ablagesteuerung *f* (EDV) stacker control
Ablagesystem *n* (com) filing system
Ablagevermerk *m* (com) filing stamp
Ablauf *m*
(Bw) operation
– operational sequence
– execution
– procedure
(Re) expiration
– lapse
– termination
(WeR) maturity
(Pat) lapse
– expiration
(Vers) expiry *(eg, of life insurance policy)*
Ablaufabschnitt *m* (IndE) phase of work flow *(eg, project stage, activity)*
Ablaufanalyse *f* (IndE) analysis of work flow
Ablaufanforderung *f* (EDV) sequence request
Ablaufauswahl *f* (EDV) sequence selection
ablaufbedingte Brachzeit *f* (IndE) machine idle time
ablaufbedingte Wartezeit *f* (IndE) unoccupied time
Ablaufbeschreibung *f* (EDV) operational sequence description
Ablaufdauer *f* (IndE) time of operations flow
Ablauf *m* **der Gültigkeitsdauer der Einfuhrlizenz**

(Zo) expiry of the period of validity of the import licence
Ablauf *m* **der Gültigkeitsdauer des Carnet** (Zo) expiry of the validity of the carnet
Ablaufdiagramm *n*
(EDV) flowchart
– flow diagram
– process chart *(sub-terms: Befehlsdiagramm, Datenflußplan, Programmablaufplan)*
(Stat) flow *(or* route) diagram
(IndE) straight-line scheduling
ablaufen
(EDV) to execute
– to run
Ablauf *m* **e-s Patents**
(Pat) lapse of a patent
Ablauf *m* **e–s Programms** (EDV) program run
Ablauffrist *f*
(com) time limit
Ablaufgraph *m*
(Stat) flow *(or* route) diagram
(IndE) straight-line scheduling
Ablaufhemmung *f* (Re) suspension of the statute of limitations, § 205 BGB *(ie, period of limitations is extended for the duration of the suspending event)*
ablaufinvariant
(EDV) re-entrant
– re-enterable
– sharable
Ablaufkontrolle *f* (IndE) flow control *(ie, in continuous manufacture)*
Ablauflinie *f* (EDV) flow line
Ablauforganisation *f* (Bw, *roughly*) structuring of operations *(ie, in simple German defined as: ‚raumzeitliche Gestaltung der in allen Bereichen e-s organisatorischen Gebildes zur Aufgabenerfüllung erforderlichen Prozesse'; opp, Aufbauorganisation)*
Ablaufplan *m* (EDV) = *Ablaufdiagramm*
Ablaufplanung *f*
(Bw) operations planning
– scheduling and sequencing
– ordonnancement
(IndE) job shop scheduling *(ie, determining when and where each operation in the production process will be done; syn, Durchführungsplanung, Produktionsvollzugsplanung)*
Ablaufplanung *f* **mit überlappenden Phasen**
(IndE) lap phasing
– overlapped scheduling
– telescoping
Ablaufplanungsdilemma *n* (IndE) operations-planning dilemma
Ablaufprinzipien *npl* (IndE) classification by type of manufacturing processes *(eg, job shop, flow line, automated production)*
Ablaufprogramm *n* (IndE) operating cycle
Ablaufschaubild *n* (EDV) = *Ablaufdiagramm*
Ablaufschema *n* (EDV) = *Ablaufdiagramm*
Ablaufsteuerkarte *f* (EDV) job control card
Ablaufsteuerung *f*
(EDV) scheduler *(subterms: job scheduler + task scheduler)*
(EDV) sequential control

Ablaufteil *m* (EDV) executive (program)
Ablauftermin *m*
(Re) date of expiry
(Fin) due date
– date of maturity
Ablaufüberwacher *m*
(EDV) tracer
– tracing program
Ablaufverfolger *m* (EDV) = *Ablaufüberwacher*
ablegen (com) to file
ablehnen
(com, Re) to refuse *(ie, general word)*
– to reject *(ie, stronger implication)*
– to decline *(ie, more formal and courteous)*
Ablehngrenze *f*
(Stat) lot tolerance limit
– lot tolerance percent defective
– rejectable quality level
– rejection line
Ablehnung *f*
(com, Re) refusal
– rejection
– decline
Ablehnung *f* **durch Gegenangebot** (Re) rejection by counter-offer
Ablehnung *f* **e-s Risikos** (Vers) rejection of risk
Ablehnungsbereich *m* (Stat) rejection region
Ablehnungsbescheid *m* (Re) notice of denial
Ablehnung *f* **von Prämienerhöhungen** (Vers) turndown on rate requests *(ie, by supervisory authority)*
ableichtern (com) to tranship *(or* transship) *(ie, to reload cargo, in whole or in part, from one ship to another)*
ableitbar (Log) deducible *(syn, erzeugbar)*
Ableitbarkeit *f*
(Log, Math) deducibility
(Math) derivability
Ableitung *f*
(Log) inference *(ie, derivation of a proposition, the conclusion, from a set of other propositions, the premises)*
(Math) derivation
(Math) derivative
– differential quotient
Ableitungen *fpl* (Math) derivations
Ableitung *f* **höherer Ordnung** (Math) derivative of higher order
Ableitung *f* **nach der Zeit** (Math) time derivative
Ableitungsbeziehung *f* (Log) consequence
Ableitungsregel *f* (Log) rule of inference
Ablenkungsmanöver *n* (com) diversionary tactics *(or* exercise)
abliefern (com) to deliver *(eg, goods)*
Ablieferung *f* (com) delivery
Ablieferungsbescheid *m* (com) notice *(or* notification) of delivery
Ablieferungsbescheinigung *f* (com) receipt of delivery
Ablieferungsfrist *f*
(com) time of delivery
– delivery period
Ablieferungsgewicht *n* (com) weight delivered
Ablieferungshindernis *n* (com) obstacle to delivery,

7

§ 437 HGB *(ie, if such obstacle arises, carrier shall notify the sender of the goods)*
Ablieferungskontingent *n* (com) delivery quota
Ablieferungsort *m* (com) place of delivery *(or destination)* *(ie, frequently identical with „Erfüllungsort' = place of performance)*
Ablieferungspflicht *f* (com) obligation to deliver *(ie, mostly farm products)*
Ablieferungspreis *m*
  (com) price of delivery
  – delivery price
Ablieferungssoll *n* (com) delivery quota
Ablieferungstermin *m* (com) date appointed *(or* fixed *or* settled) for delivery
Ablochbeleg *m* (EDV) punch form
ablochen
  (EDV) to punch
  – to perforate
Ablochen *n*
  (EDV) punching
  – perforating
Ablochfehler *m* (EDV) punch error
Ablochvordruck *m* (EDV) = *Ablochbeleg*
ablösbar
  (Fin) redeemable
  – repayable
ablösen
  (Fin) to redeem
  – to repay
Ablösung *f*
  (Fin) discharge
  – redemption
  – repayment *(ie, in a single sum)*
Ablösung *f* **e-r Anleihe** (Fin) anticipatory redemption of a loan
Ablösungsanleihe *f* (FiW) commutation loan *(or* bonds) *(ie, short-term bonds issued to creditors and equivalent to the depreciated debt of public borrowers)*
Ablösungsbetrag *m*
  (Fin) amount required for redemption
  – redemption sum
Ablösungsfinanzierung *f* (Fin) consolidation financing *(ie, provision of equity capital to repay borrowed funds)*
Ablösungsfonds *m* (Fin) sinking fund
Ablösungsrecht *n*
  (Re) right to avert seizure by satisfying the judgment debt on debtor's behalf, § 268 BGB
  (Re) right of redemption
Ablösungsschuld *f* (FiW) commutation debt
Ablösungssumme *f* (Re) redemption sum *(ie, paid to extinguish encumbrance, § 1199ff BGB)*
abmachen
  (com) to arrange
  – to make arrangements
Abmachung *f* (com) arrangement
Abmachungen *fpl* **einhalten** (com) to honor arrangements
Abmachung *f* **treffen** (com) to make an arrangement *(or* agreement)
Abmahnung *f* (Kart) urgent request *(ie, by German Cartel Office to discontinue anti-competitive behavior)*
Abmattung *f* (com) dunnage *(eg, material laid beneath objects carried by rail or ship to prevent damage)*
abmelden (com) to deregister *(eg, automobile)*
Abnahme *f*
  (com) purchase *(ie, of goods)*
  – order
  (com) acceptance *(ie, of goods by customer)*
  (com) taking delivery
  (IndE) final inspection *(ie, of products ready for delivery)*
Abnahmeabschnitt *m* (Zo) voucher for customs control
Abnahmebeamter *m* (IndE) quality inspector
Abnahmebedingungen *fpl*
  (IndE) acceptability standards
  – conditions laid down for acceptance
Abnahmebericht *m* (IndE) acceptance *(or* inspection) report
Abnahmebescheinigung *f* (IndE) inspection certificate
Abnahme *f* **des Nutzungspotentials** (Bw) diminution of service yield *(ie, of depreciable assets)*
Abnahme *f* **größerer Mengen**
  (com) ordering *(or* purchasing) of large quantities
  – bulk buying
  (syn, Großeinkauf)
Abnahmekontrolle *f* **durch Stichproben**
  (Stat) sampling inspection
Abnahmepflicht *f* (com) obligation to take delivery *(ie, of merchandise tendered)*
Abnahmeprotokoll *n*
  (IndE) acceptance certificate
  – test report
Abnahmeprüfung *f*
  (IndE) inspection test *(ie, made by manufacturer)*
  (IndE) acceptance *(or* specification) test *(ie, made by customer)*
Abnahmeprüfung *f* **nach qualitativen Merkmalen** (Stat) inspection by attributes
Abnahmeprüfung *f* **nach quantitativen Merkmalen** (Stat) inspection by variables
Abnahmetest *m* (EDV) acceptance test
Abnahmeverpflichtung *f*
  (com) purchase commitment
  (Re) obligation to take delivery
Abnahmevorschriften *fpl*
  (IndE) quality specifications
  – acceptance standards
Abnahmezeugnis *n*
  (IndE) test certificate
  (com) acceptance certificate
abnehmen
  (com) to order
  – to purchase *(eg, goods, merchandise, products)*
  (com) to accept
  – to take delivery *(ie, of goods)*
  (Fin, infml) to soak
  – (GB) to rush *(eg, how much did they rush you for that car?)*
abnehmende Funktion *f* **e-r Variablen**
  (Math) decreasing function of a variable

abnehmende Grenzleistungsfähigkeit f **des Kapitals**
(Vw) declining marginal efficiency of capital
abnehmende Grenzproduktivität f (Vw) diminishing marginal productivity
abnehmende Grenzrate f **der technischen Substitution** (Vw) diminishing marginal rate of substitution
abnehmende Niveaugrenzerträge *mpl* (Vw) diminishing returns to scale
abnehmender Grenznutzen m (Vw) diminishing marginal utility
abnehmende Skalenerträge *mpl* (Vw) diminishing returns to scale
Abnehmer m
(com) buyer
– purchaser
– customer
– client
(Bö) taker
(StR, VAT) recipient of a delivery *(ie, Empfänger e-r Lieferung)*
Abnehmer *mpl* **finden** (com) to find a market
Abnehmerkreis m (com) customers
Abnehmerland n (AuW) customer *(or* importing) country
abnormale Krümmung f (Stat) allokurtosis
abnutzbare Betriebsmittel *npl* (Bw) depreciable plant assets
abnutzbares Anlagevermögen n (ReW) depreciable fixed assets
abnutzbare Wirtschaftsgüter *npl* **des Anlagevermögens** (ReW) depreciable fixed assets
Abnutzung f
(IndE) wear and tear
(ReW) depreciation *(ie, in the sense of diminution of service yield)*
(StR) depreciation for tax purposes
(Vers) new for old *(ie, applying discount based upon depreciation of a new part that is installed in settlement of a claim)*
Abnutzung f **durch Gebrauch** (IndE) wear and tear
Abnutzungswert m (ReW) carrying rate of asset
Abonnement n (com) subscription
Abonnent (com) subscriber (to)
Abonnentenversicherung f (Vers) subscribers' insurance *(ie, publisher of periodicals taking out policies on account of his subscribers)*
abonnieren
(com) to subscribe (to)
– to take out a subscription
Abordnung f (Pw) transfer *(ie, of employee to another location)*
Abordnungsgeld n (Pw) living allowance *(ie, paid to an employee transferred to another duty station)*
Abraumbeseitigung f (IndE) removal of overburden
abrechnen
(com) to account for
– to give an accounting
– to settle the accounts
(com) to invoice *(ie, goods and services)*
(ReW) to charge an account
(Fin) to clear *(eg, checks)*
(Bö) to liquidate
– to settle

Abrechnung f
(com) accounting
– settlement of accounts
(com) statement of accounts
(com) invoicing
– billing
(Fin) clearing
(Bö) liquidation
– settlement
(Bö) contract note
Abrechnung f **des Einkaufskommissionärs** (com) account purchases (A/P)
Abrechnung f **des Verkaufskommissionärs** (com) account sales (A/S)
Abrechnungsbeleg m (ReW) voucher
Abrechnungsbuch n (Re) job ledger
Abrechnungscomputer m (EDV) accounting computer
Abrechnungsdaten *pl* (com) account information
Abrechnungseinheit f (ReW) reporting subunit
Abrechnungskurs m
(Bö) making-up price
(Bö) settlement rate
Abrechnungsmaschine f (EDV) accounting machine *(eg, Fakturiermaschine, Buchungsmaschine)*
Abrechnungsperiode f (Bö) account period
abrechnungsreife Leistungen *fpl* (ReW) accountable cost of unbilled contracts
Abrechnungsroutine f (EDV) accounting routine
Abrechnungssaldo m (Fin) clearing balance
Abrechnungsspitzen *fpl* (Bö) settlement fractions
Abrechnungsstellen *fpl* (Fin) clearing offices *(ie, run by the Landeszentralbanken – central banks of the Laender*
Abrechnungsstufen *fpl* (KoR) levels of costing
Abrechnungssystem n (EDV) job accounting system
Abrechnungstag m (Bö) pay *(or* settlement) day
Abrechnungstermin m (Fin) due *(or* settlement) date
Abrechnungsvaluta f (Bö) settlement currency
Abrechnungsverkehr m
(Fin) clearing system
– system of clearing transactions *(ie, set up to settle mutual accounts of banks, which arise from transfers, checks, bills, etc.)*
Abrechnungszeitraum m (ReW) accounting period
Abrechnung f **von Zollverkehren** (Zo) settling of accounts in connection with special customs procedures
abreißen
(com) to tear down
– (GB) to pull down
Abreißkalender m (com) sheet calendar
Abrollkosten *pl*
(com) cartage
– (US) drayage
Abruf m (com) call-forward notice *(ie, instruction to send off consignment)*
Abrufauftrag m (com) call order
Abrufbetrieb m (EDV) polling mode
abrufen
(com) to call off *(ie, goods ordered and ready for shipment)*

(Fin) to call *(ie, funds made available by a bank)*
(EDV) to call in
− to fetch from storage
Abrufmenge *f* (MaW) call-off amount of materials *(ie, requested by production centers)*
(com) part shipment called off under a continuing purchase contract
Abrufphase *f* (EDV) fetch cycle
Abruftaste *f* (EDV) attention key *(syn, Unterbrechungstaste)*
Abrufvertrag *m* (com) call-off purchase agreement
Abrufzeichen *n* (EDV) polling character
abrunden (Math) to round off
Abrüstzeit *f* (IndE) dismantling time
abrutschen (com) to nose downward *(eg, economy into recession)*
Absatz *m*
  (com) sales volume
  (Mk) marketing
  − selling
  − distribution
  (ReW) sales
  − (GB) turnover *(ie, in terms of volume and money)*
Absatzaktivität *f* (Mk) marketing *(or* sales) activity
Absatzanalyse *f* (Mk) sales analysis *(ie, part of market analysis)*
Absatzausschuß *m* (Mk) marketing *(or* distribution) committee
Absatzbarometer *n* (Vw) sales barometer
Absatzbedingungen *fpl* (Mk) marketing *(or* sales) conditions
Absatzbelebung *f* (com) sales resurgence
− revival of sales
Absatzbemühungen *fpl* (Mk) marketing
− sales
− selling ... efforts *(or* endeavors)
Absatzbereich *m* (Mk) market coverage
Absatzbeschränkung *f* (Mk) sales restriction
Absatzbezirk *m*
  (Mk) marketing area *(or* territory)
  − distribution area *(or* territory)
Absatzbudget *n* (Mk) sales *(or* volume) budget
Absatzchancen *fpl*
  (Mk) marketing *(or* sales) opportunities
  − sales prospects
  − potential market
Absatzdirektor *m* (Mk) general sales manager
Absatz *m* **durch ein Kartell** (Kart) pool selling
Absatzeinbruch *m* (Mk) slump in sales
Absatzelastizität *f* (Vw) sales elasticity *(ie, ratio of relative change of sales volume to relative change of commodity price)*
Absatzergebnis *n* (KoR) sales result *(ie, in standard costing = Plankostenrechnung: difference between standard mill cost and net revenue = Unterschied zw Standardselbstkosten und Reinerlös)*
Absatzertrag *m* (ReW) sales revenue *(opp, unrealisierter Ertrag: auf Lager genommene Güter = unrealized revenue from inventory additions)*
Absatzerwartungen *fpl* (Mk) sales anticipations *(or* expectations)

Absatzfachmann *m* (Mk) marketing man *(or* specialist)
absatzfähig
  (Mk) marketable
  − salable
Absatz *m* **festverzinslicher Wertpapiere** (Fin) bond sales
Absatzfinanzierung *f* (Fin) sales *(or* customer) financing *(ie, German term now obsolete)*
Absatz *m* **finden** (com) to find a market
Absatzflaute *f*
  (com) dull
  − flagging
  − slack ... sales
  − low level of sales
Absatzfonds *m* **der deutschen Land-, Forst- und Ernährungswirtschaft** (com) Sales Promotion Fund of the German Farming, Forestry, and Food Industries *(ie, established in 1969)*
Absatzförderung *f* (Mk) sales promotion
Absatzforschung *f* (Mk) marketing research
Absatzfunktion *f* (Mk) marketing *(or* selling) activity
Absatzgebiet *n*
  (Mk) distribution area
  − market(ing) area
  − sales area *(or* territory)
  − marketing outlet
  − trading area
Absatzgebietsstaffel *f* (Mk) graduated prices *(ie, for identical products, fixed for each sales area)*
Absatzgenossenschaft *f*
  (Mk) cooperative marketing association
  − marketing cooperative
Absatzgeschwindigkeit *f* (Mk) rate of selling *(ie, number of units sold in a given period; eg, per week, month, etc.)*
Absatzkanal *m*
  (Mk) channel of distribution
  − distributive
  − marketing
  − trade ... channel
Absatzkapazität *f*
  (Mk) selling capacity
  − sales potential
Absatzkartell *n*
  (Kart) sales
  − distribution
  − marketing ... cartel
Absatzkette *f* (Mk) sales chain
Absatzkontingent *n* (Mk) market *(or* sales) quota
Absatzkontrolle *f* (Mk) sales control
Absatzkosten *pl*
  (Mk) marketing costs *(or* expenses)
  − sales costs
  − distribution costs *(or* expenses)
  − cost of disposition
Absatzkrise *f* (Vw) slump in sales
Absatzlage *f*
  (Mk) market situation
  − sales position
Absatzleiter *m* (Pw) marketing manager *(or* executive)
Absatzmangel *m* (Mk) lack of sales

Absatzmarkt m
(Vw) output market
(Mk) sales market
Absatzmarkt m für industrielle Erzeugnisse
(Mk) industrial market
Absatzmenge f
(Mk) sales volume
- quantity sold
- amount of sales
Absatzmengenplan m
(Mk) volume budget
- budget of sales volume *(ie, part of overall sales planning)*
Absatzmethoden fpl
(Mk) marketing
- distribution
- sales ... methods
- marketing *(or* selling) techniques
Absatzmittler m
(Mk) sales *(or* distribution) middleman
- marketing institution
Absatzmöglichkeiten fpl
(Mk) sales potential
- potential market
Absatznetz n (Mk) sales network
Absatzorganisation f (Mk) sales *(or* marketing) organization
absatzorientiert (Mk) marketing-oriented
Absatzperiode f (Mk) selling period
Absatzphase f nach Neuemission (Bö) period of digestion
Absatzplan m
(Mk) distribution
- marketing
- sales ... plan
- sales budget
Absatzplanung f (Mk) marketing *(or* sales) planning
Absatzpolitik f (Mk) distribution *(or* marketing) policy
Absatzpotential n (Mk) marketing *(or* sales) potential
Absatzpreis m (Mk) selling price
Absatzproduktion f (Mk) production of goods for an anonymous market
Absatzprognose f
(Mk) forward sales projection
- sales forecast
Absatzprozeß m (Mk) distribution *(or* marketing) process
Absatzquote f (Mk) sales quota
Absatzregion f
(Mk) market area
- marketing territory
Absatzrisiko n (Mk) marketing *(or* merchandising) risk
Absatzrückgang m
(com) decrease
- decline
- drop
- slump ... in sales
Absatzschwierigkeiten fpl (Mk) marketing difficulties *(or* problems)
Absatzsegment n (Mk) marketing segment
Absatzsoll n (Mk) target sales *(ie, fixed for the various sales areas)*

Absatzstatistik f (Mk) sales *(or* distribution) statistics
Absatzsteigerung f (com) sales increase *(or* jump) *(eg, to DM 1.8bn)*
Absatzstellen fpl (Mk) marketing institutions *(or* agencies)
Absatzstrategie f
(Mk) market
- marketing
- sales ... strategy
Absatzstudie f (Mk) market study
Absatzsystem n (Mk) distribution *(or* marketing) system
Absatzvereinigung f (Mk) marketing association
Absatzverhältnisse npl (Mk) market situation *(or* conditions)
Absatzvolumen n
(Mk) sales volume
- volume of goods sold
Absatz m von Massenerzeugnissen (Mk) mass marketing
Absatzweg m = *Absatzkanal*
Absatzwirtschaft f
(Mk) marketing
- distributive trade
absatzwirtschaftliche Kennzahlen fpl (Mk) marketing ratios
Absatzzahlen fpl
(Mk) sales figures
- market data
Absatzzeitenstaffel f (Mk) graduated prices *(ie, for identical seasonal goods)*
Absatzzentrum n (Mk) distribution center
Absatzziel n (Mk) sales goal
Absatzzielgruppe f (Mk) market target
Absatzzusammenschluß m (Mk) marketing association
Abschaffung f der Zölle
(AuW) abolition of tariffs
- elimination of customs duties
abschalten (Pw, infml) to turn off *(ie, to become less involved in one's work)*
Abschichtungsbilanz f (ReW) balance sheet of a partnership prepared when a partner retires
abschicken
(com) to send off
- to forward
- to dispatch
- (US) to ship *(eg, a letter)*
ab Schiff (com) ex ship
Abschlag m
(com) price reduction
- reduction in price
(com) payment on account
- installment
(Fin) discount *(eg, on forward dollars)*
(Fin) payment of interim dividend
(Bö) markdown *(ie, of share prices)*
(Pw) advance pay *(or* wage)
(StR) deduction
Abschlagsdividende f (Fin) interim dividend
Abschlagsverteilung f (Re) intermediate distribution of cash to creditors, § 149 KO
Abschlagszahlung f
(com) part payment

11

Abschlagszahlung auf den Bilanzgewinn

(com) payment on account
(com) progress payment
(Re) installment, § 266 BGB
Abschlagszahlung f **auf den Bilanzgewinn**
(Fin) interim dividend
abschlägige Antwort f (com) refusal
abschlägiger Bescheid m (com) negative reply
Abschleppwagen m
(com) tow truck
– (GB) breakdown van (or lorry)
abschließen
(com) to close a deal
– to strike a bargain
(ReW) to close (out) an account
(Re) to conclude a contract
(Pw) to complete
– to finish (eg, education or training course)
abschließende Abnahmeprüfung f (Stat) final checkout (or inspection)
abschließen über (ReW) to close into (eg, nominal accounts into income statement)
Abschließungseffekt m (AuW) trade diverting effect
Abschluß m
(com) sales contract (eg, § 94 HGB)
(Re) conclusion (or making) of a contract
(ReW) closing the accounts
(ReW) financial statements
– (GB) annual accounts
(Bö) bargain (eg, finalized by contract note)
(Pw) wage settlement
Abschlußagent m (Vers) policy writing agent (opp, Vermittlungsagent)
Abschlußanalyse f (ReW) financial statement analysis
Abschlußanlage f (ReW) supplement to financial statement
Abschlußanweisung f (EDV, Cobol) close statement
Abschluß m **auf Abladung** (Bö) transaction for delivery within a specified period (ie, made on commodity exchanges)
Abschlußbericht m (com) final report
Abschlußbesprechung f (com) final discussion
(ReW) discussion of financial statement
Abschlußblatt n (ReW) = Abschlußtabelle
Abschlußbogen m (ReW) = Abschlußtabelle
Abschlußbuchung f (ReW) closing (or final) entry
Abschlußdividende f (Fin) final (or year-end) dividend
Abschlüsse mpl **am Sekundärmarkt** (Fin) secondary dealings
Abschlüsse mpl **machen** (ReW) to prepare financial statements
Abschlußergebnis n (ReW) annual result
Abschlußerläuterungen fpl (ReW) notes to financial statements
Abschluß m **e-s Geschäfts** (com) conclusion of a transaction
Abschluß m **e-s Kaufvertrages** (com) conclusion of a purchase order contract
Abschlußgebühr f
(com) sales charge
(Vers) acquisition fee

Abschlußvertreter

Abschlußgliederungsprinzip n (ReW) principle of classifying accounts
Abschluß m **in rollender od schwimmender Ware** (Bö) transaction for delivery of goods in transit (ie, made on commodity exchanges)
Abschlußkonsolidierung f (ReW) consolidation of financial statements
Abschlußkonto n (ReW) closing account
Abschlußkosten pl
(Vers) acquisition cost
– initial expenses
Abschlußkurs m (Bö) contract price
Abschluß m **machen**
(ReW) to draw up
– to make up
– to prepare ... a financial statement
– (GB) to make up the accounts
Abschluß m **mit Bestätigungsvermerk** (ReW) certified financial statement
Abschlußnormen fpl (Pw) rules written into collective agreements and dealing with the conclusion of new employment contracts
Abschlußprämie f (com) „signature bonus" (ie, lump sums paid up for the privilege of getting any oil at all)
Abschlußpreis m (Bö) strike (or striking) price
Abschlußprovision f
(com) commission for business transactions concluded by commercial agent, § 87 HGB
(Vers) acquisition commission
– initial commission
Abschlußprüfer m
(ReW) balance sheet auditor, § 162 AktG
– independent auditor
– (often simply) auditor
Abschlußprüfung f
(ReW) statutory balance sheet audit, §§ 162–169 AktG
– (GB) audit of annual accounts
(Pw) final examination
– final
Abschlußrechnung f
(ReW) final accounts
(Bö) settlement note
Abschlußstichtag m
(ReW) balance sheet
– closing
– cutoff ... date
Abschlußtabelle f
Abschlußtag m (Bö) settlement day
Abschlußtest m (EDV) final program test
(ReW) condensed tabular statement of balance sheet figures
– (GB) balance sheet in schedule form
– work sheet
Abschlußübersicht f
(ReW) = Abschlußtabelle
Abschlußunterlagen pl
(ReW) balance sheet and income statement
– balance sheet and profit and loss accounts
– financial statements
Abschlußvertreter m (com) commercial agent authorized to sign sales contracts (opp, Vermittlungsvertreter)

12

Abschlußvollmacht *f* (Re) authority to transact business for a third party, § 164 I BGB
Abschlußvorschriften *fpl* (ReW) legal rules governing the closing of accounts, §§ 151–159 AktG
Abschlußzahlung *f*
(com) final payment
(Re, *also*) complete payment
(Fin) final installment (*or* payment)
(StR) final tax payment, § 36 IV EStG
Abschlußzeugnis *n* (Pw) school leaving certificate
Abschlußzwang *m* (Re) obligation to accept contracts, § 453 HGB
Abschlußzyklus *m* (EDV) termination cycle
Abschneiden *n* (EDV, Cobol) truncation
Abschnitt *m*
(com) stub *(ie, counterfoil in a check book)*
(WeR) bill of exchange
(Math) subset of ordered set where each element includes all smaller elements
(EDV) segment (of a program)
Abschnitt *m* **der x-Achse** (Math) x-intercept
Abschnitt *m* **der y-Achse** (Math) y-intercept
Abschnitte *mpl*
(Fin) bills (of exchange)
(Fin) denominations *(eg, securities)*
Abschnittsetikett *n* (EDV) tape mark label
Abschnittsmarke *f* (EDV) tape mark, TM
Abschnittsnummer *f* (EDV) segment number
abschöpfen
(Vw) to absorb
– to skim off
– to siphon off *(ie, purchasing power)*
Abschöpfung *f*
(EG) variable import levy
– agricultural levy
Abschöpfungserhebungsgesetz *n* (EG) Levy Imposition Law
abschöpfungsfrei (EG) exempt from agricultural levies
abschöpfungsfreie Einfuhr *f* (EG) free-of-levy import
Abschöpfungspreispolitik *f* (Mk) skimming-the-market policy
Abschöpfungstarif *m* (EG) price-adjustment levy rate
abschreibbare Kosten *pl* (ReW) depreciable cost
abschreiben
(ReW) to depreciate
– to write off
– to write down
– to charge off
– to charge depreciation *(eg, on properties)*
(ReW) to deplete
(ReW) to amortize
(Vers) to write off *(ie, a policy)*
(Vers) to declare off
Abschreibepolice *f* (Vers) floater policy *(ie, special type of ‚laufende Versicherung', mostly in transportation)*
Abschreibung *f*
(ReW) depreciation
– writedown
– writeoff *(ie, all general terms)*
(ReW) depreciation *(usu. of fixed assets)*
(ReW) depletion *(ie, implies removal of natural resource)*
(ReW) amortization *(ie, of intangible assets)*
(ReW) depreciation accounting *(ie, systematic, periodic writedown of cost = Anschaffungs- od Herstellungskosten of limited life assets = Anlagegüter mit begrenzter Nutzungsdauer)*
Abschreibung *f* **auf Anlagevermögen** (ReW) depreciation of fixed assets and long-term investments
Abschreibung *f* **auf Basis der Produktion**
(ReW) production-basis method of depreciation
– production-unit-basis method
– service-output method
– unit-of-product method
Abschreibung *f* **auf Basis der Wiederbeschaffungskosten** (ReW) replacement method (of depreciation)
Abschreibung *f* **auf Beteiligungen**
(ReW) writedown of investments in shares of affiliated companies
– writeoff on trade investments
Abschreibung *f* **auf Betriebsanlagen** (ReW) depreciation of plant and equipment
Abschreibung *f* **auf Finanzanlagen**
(ReW) depreciation on financial assets
– writedown of investments
Abschreibung *f* **auf Forderungen**
(ReW) allowance for bad or doubtful accounts
(ReW) writedown of uncollectible receivables
(ReW) valuation account *(ie, = Wertberichtigung, set up to account for estimated losses from receivables)*
Abschreibung *f* **auf Gebäude** (ReW) building depreciation
Abschreibung *f* **auf Geschäftswert** (ReW) amortization of goodwill
Abschreibung *f* **auf Lagerräume** (ReW) depreciation of storerooms
Abschreibung *f* **auf Rentenbestand** (Fin) writeoff on fixed-income securities
Abschreibung *f* **auf Sachanlagen**
(ReW) fixed-asset depreciation
– depreciation of property, plant, and equipment
Abschreibung *f* **auf Warenbestände**
(ReW) depreciation of inventories
– inventory depreciation
Abschreibung *f* **auf Wertpapiere**
(Fin) write-off on securities portfolio
– writedowns of securities
Abschreibung *f* **auf Zugänge des Geschäftsjahres** (ReW) depreciation on additions during the year
Abschreibung *f* **aus bilanz- od finanzpolitischen Gründen**
(ReW) policy depreciation
– in-lieu depreciation
Abschreibungen *fpl*
(VGR) capital (asset) consumption
– provision for the consumption of fixed capital *(syn, Kapitalverschleiß)*
Abschreibungen *fpl* **auf Zugänge des Geschäftsjahres** (ReW) depreciation on additions made during the fiscal year
Abschreibungen *fpl* **und Wertberichtigungen** *fpl*

auf Forderungen und Wertpapiere (ReW) write-offs and value adjustments

Abschreibung *f* **geringwertiger Wirtschaftsgüter** (StR) write-off of low-cost assets

Abschreibung *f* **mit konstanten Quoten** (ReW) straight-line depreciation

Abschreibung *f* **nach Maßgabe der Beanspruchung** (ReW) production-basis method of depreciation
- production-unit-basis method
- service-output method
- unit-of-product method

Abschreibungsarten *fpl* (ReW) methods of depreciation
(eg, balance sheet/imputed
- *unit/group*
- *direct/indirect)*

Abschreibungsaufwand *m* (ReW) depreciation expense *(or* expenditures) *(ie, depreciation base × depreciation rate)*

Abschreibungs-Ausgangsbetrag *m* (ReW) depreciation base
- cost to be depreciated
- depreciable cost
- service cost
(ie, total depreciation during useful life, excluding resale or salvage value)

Abschreibungsbasis *f* (ReW) = Abschreibungs-Ausgangsbetrag

Abschreibungsbedarf *m* (ReW) depreciation requirements

Abschreibungsbetrag *m*

Abschreibungsdauer *f* (ReW) period of depreciation
(ReW) amount of depreciation
- depreciation allowance

Abschreibungsergebnis *n* (ReW) depreciation result *(ie, difference between commercial and cost-accounting depreciation allowances, zwischen handelsrechtlicher und kalkulatorischer Abschreibung)*

Abschreibungserleichterungen *fpl* (StR) writcoff facilities

abschreibungsfähig (ReW) depreciable and amortizable *(ie, depreciable used in connection with tangible fixed assets, while amortizable refers to intangible assets)*

abschreibungsfähige Güter *npl* (ReW) depreciable assets

Abschreibungsfinanzierung *f* (Fin) ‚depreciation financing' *(ie, recovery of fixed-asset costs through depreciation charges)*

Abschreibungsfonds *m* (ReW) depreciation fund

Abschreibungsfunktion *f* (Bw) depreciation function

Abschreibungsgegenstand *m* (ReW) depreciation unit

Abschreibungsgesellschaft *f*
(Fin) depreciation company
- project write-off company
- company selling depreciation allowances
- tax loss company
(ie, scheme offering tax savings by producing artificial accounting losses)

Abschreibungsgrundlage *f* (ReW) depreciation base

Abschreibungskonto *n* (ReW) depreciation account

Abschreibungskorrektur *f* (ReW) adjustment for depreciation

Abschreibungskriterium *n* (ReW) depreciation criterion

Abschreibungsmethode *f* (ReW) depreciation method *(or* procedure)

Abschreibungsmöglichkeiten *fpl* (StR) write-off facilities

Abschreibungsplan *m* (ReW) depreciation program *(or* schedule)

Abschreibungspolitik *f* (ReW) depreciation policy

Abschreibungspräferenz *f* (ReW) special depreciation allowance

Abschreibungsprojekt *n* (StR) tax-saving write-off project *(ie, high losses offered in the initial phases can be set against the individual's taxable income from other sources)*

Abschreibungsprozentsatz *m* (ReW) depreciation rate

Abschreibungsquote *f* (od -rate *f*)
(ReW) annual depreciation charge *(or* expense)
- depreciation per period
- periodical depreciation charge *(or* expense)

Abschreibungsrechnung *f* (ReW) depreciation accounting

Abschreibungsrichtsätze *mpl*
(Bw) statistically observed useful lives of certain fixed assets
(StR) standard depreciation rates *(ie, recommended depreciation tables published by the Federal Ministry of Finance and classified by branches of commerce and industry)*

Abschreibungssatz *m* (ReW) rate of depreciation

Abschreibungssumme *f*
(ReW) depreciation charge
(ReW) depreciation base
- depreciable cost
- cost to be depreciated
- service cost *(ie, total depreciation during useful life, excluding resale or salvage value)*

Abschreibungstabellen *fpl*
(StR) depreciation-rate tables
- (US) guideline lives

Abschreibungsursachen *fpl*
(ReW) causes of expiration of fixed-asset cost *(ie, technical, economic, legal)*
- factors of depreciation

Abschreibungsvergünstigungen *fpl* (StR) tax privileges in the form of special or accelerated depreciation

Abschreibungswagnis *n* (ReW) depreciation risk *(ie, risk of premature retirement or loss of fixed assets, due to obsolescence and other factors; eg, fire)*

Abschreibungswagniskonto *n* (ReW) depreciation risk account

Abschreibungszeitraum *m*
(ReW) depreciation period
- period of depreciation

Abschreibung *f* **unter Berücksichtigung von Zinseszinsen**
(ReW) annuity depreciation method

- equal-annual-payment method of depreciation
- compound-interest method of depreciation

Abschreibung *f* **vom Wiederbeschaffungspreis** (ReW) replacement method of depreciation *(ie, based on the cost of replacing assets actually in use)*

Abschrift *f* (com, Re) copy *(eg, business letter, entries of commercial register; § 38 II HGB, § 140 AO)*

Abschwächung *f*
(com) decline
- fall
(eg, in business activity or in the trend of capital investment)
(Bö) easing
- sagging *(ie, of prices)*

Abschwächung *f* **des Wachstums** (Vw) slowdown in economic growth

Abschwächungsmöglichkeiten *fpl* (Bö) downside potential

Abschwung *m*
(Vw) downturn
- downswing *(eg, of economic or business activity)*

Abschwungphase *f* (Vw) contraction phase *(ie, of business cycle)*

absehbare Zeit *f* (Re) foreseeable future *(eg, in tax matters interpreted by the courts to mean ,,approximately six years")*

absenden
(com) to send off
- to forward
- to dispatch
- (US) to ship *(eg, a letter)*
(syn, abschicken)

Absender *m*
(com) sender *(eg, of letters, parcels)*
- consignor *(ie, concluding freight contract with carrier in his own name)*

Absenderfreistempler *m*
(com) postage meter
- (GB) franking machine

Absendung *f* (com) dispatch

Absentismus *m* (Pw) absenteeism

absetzbar
(Mk) marketable
- salable
(StR) tax deductible

Absetzbarkeit *f*
(Mk) marketability
- salability
(StR) tax deductibility

absetzen
(Mk) to sell
- to market
(StR) to deduct *(ie, for tax purposes)*
(EDV) to relocate

Absetzung *f* **für Abnutzung (AfA)**
(StR) tax depreciation
- tax writeoff *(ie, ordinary depreciation of income producing assets, § 7 EStG; syn, steuerliche Abschreibung)*

Absetzung *f* **für außergewöhnliche technische od wirtschaftliche Abnutzung** (StR) extraordinary depreciation *(ie, due to unexpected wear and tear, incorrect estimate of useful life, § 7 EStG)*

Absetzung *f* **für Substanzverringerung** (StR) depletion allowance *(ie, expenses allowed for removal of natural resource; eg, coal, ore, peat, petroleum, § 7 VI EStG)*

absichern (Fin) to hedge

Absicht *f* **der Einnahmeerzielung** (StR) intent to realize receipts, § 2 I UStG

Absicht *f* **der Gewinnerzielung**
(Re) intent to realize profits
- gainful intent

Absichtsanfechtung *f* (Re) avoidance of transactions which a bankrupt concludes prior to the proceedings with the intent to damage his creditors, § 31 KO

Absichtserklärung *f* (com) letter of intent

absolut (com) in absolute terms

absolute Abweichung *f* (Stat) absolute deviation

absolute Adresse *f*
(EDV) absolute
- actual
- direct
- explicit
- machine
- specific ... address
(opp, symbolische, relative, virtuelle Adresse)

absolute Adressierung *f* (EDV) absolute addressing

absolute Codierung *f* (EDV) = absolute Programmierung

absolute Einkommenshypothese *f* (Vw) absolute-income theory

absolute Häufigkeit *f* (Stat) absolute frequency

absolute Konstante *f* (Math) absolute constant

absolute Konvergenz *f* (Math) absolute (*or* unconditional) convergence

absolute Meistbegünstigung *f* (AuW) unconditional most-favored-nation treatment

absolute Minimalität *f* (OR) crash time

absolute Priorität *f* (OR) preemptive priority *(ie, in waiting-line theory; opp, relative Priorität)*

absolute Programmierung *f* (EDV) absolute programming (*or* coding) *(opp, symbolische Programmierung)*

absoluter Ausdruck *m* (EDV) absolute expression

absoluter Betrag *m* (Math) absolute value

absoluter Code *m* (EDV) absolute code

absoluter Fehler *m* (EDV) absolute error

absoluter Höchststand *m* (com) all-time high

absoluter Kostenvorteil *m* (AuW) absolute advantage

absoluter Tiefstand *m* (com) all-time low

absoluter Vorrang *m* (OR) = absolute Priorität

absolutes Glied *n* (Math) constant term

absolutes Maximum *n* (Math) absolute maximum

absolutes Minimum *n* (Math) absolute minimum

absolute Speicheradresse *f* (EDV) absolute storage address

absolutes Programm *n* (EDV) absolute program *(opp, symbolic program)*

absolutes Recht *n* (Re) absolute right *(ie, available against the whole world, equivalent to the English ‚jus ad rem')*

15

absolutes Streuungsmaß *n* (Stat) absolute measure of dispersion
absolute Supposition *f* (Log) simple supposition
absolute Unmöglichkeit *f* (Re) absolute impossibility
absolute Verschlüsselung *f* (EDV) absolute programming
absolute Zahl *f* (Math) absolute (*or* abstract) number
Absolutglied *n* (Math) constant term
Absolutlader *m* (EDV) absolute program loader
Absolutwert *m* (EDV) absolute value
Absolutwert *m* **e–r Abweichung** (Math) absolute deviation
Absolutwert *m* **e–r komplexen Zahl** (Math) modulus
Absolutzeitgeber *m* (EDV) real time clock
Absolvent *m*
 (Pw) graduate *(ie, of any educational institution; in GB: restricted to university degree)*
 – diploma holder
Absonderung *f* (Re) right to preferential settlement of claim, §§ 47–52 KO
Absonderungsrecht *n* (Re) preferential right of creditor
absorbierender Rand (od **Zustand**) *m* (Math) absorbing barrier
Absorption *f* (VGR) absorption *(ie, total spending of residents on domestic and foreign goods and services)*
Absorptionsschirm *m* (Math) absorbing barrier
Absorptionstheorie *f* (AuW) absorption approach
abspecken (com, infml) to slim down *(eg, a business, an industry)*
Absperrklausel *f* (Pw) provision in a collective agreement stating that employers will only hire unionized workers *(ie, violates the Federal Basic Law)*
Absprache *f*
 (com) arrangement
 (Re) agreement
 (Kart) gentlemen's agreement
 – coordinated business practice
abspringen
 (EDV) to branch
 – to jump
 (ie, to depart from normal sequence of instructions)
Abstand *m* (Re) indemnity payment
Abstandssumme *f*
 (Re) compensation
 – indemnity
absteigende Arbeitspartizipation *f* (Pw) descending worker participation *(eg, managerial functions carried out at workers' own level)*
absteigender Sortierbegriff *m* (EDV, Cobol) descending key
abstellen
 (Pw) to transfer temporarily
 – to second *(ie, employee to another position)*
Abstellgleis *n*
 (com) siding
 – sidetrack *(ie, opening onto main track at both ends)*

Abstellung *f* (Pw) temporary transfer *(ie, of employee to another position)*
Abstempelung *f* (Fin) official stamping of shares *(eg, on capital reduction, change of firm, reduction of bond interest)*
Absterbeordnung *f*
 (Stat) mortality table
 (Vers) observed life table
Abstiegsmobilität *f* (Pw) downward mobility
abstimmen
 (com) to vote
 (ReW) to reconcile
Abstimmkarte *f* (EDV) summation check card
Abstimmung *f*
 (ReW) matching
 – reconciliation
 (ie, bringing the balances of accounts into agreement)
Abstimmung *f* **des Produktionsprogramms** (IndE) matching of production program
Abstimmung *f* **laufender Einnahmen und Ausgaben** (Fin) cash management
Abstimmungsbogen *m* (ReW) reconciliation sheet *(ie, statistical statement showing allocation of expenses to financial and plant accounts)*
Abstimmungsmechanismus *m* (Bw) coordinating mechanism
Abstimmungsparadoxon *n* (Vw) voting paradox
Abstimmungsverfahren *n* (com) procedure on voting
Abstimmung *f* **zwischen Produktion und Lager** (IndE) production smoothing
Abstinenztheorie *f* (Vw) abstinence theory of interest
abstoßen
 (com) to sell off *(eg, merchandise)*
 (Fin) to divest
 – to sell off
 – to shed
 – to unload
 (eg, security holdings, foreign assets, subsidiaries)
 (Pw) to shed *(eg, labor)*
abstrahieren
 (Log, Math) to abstract
 – to generalize
Abstrakt *n*
 (EDV) abstract
 – summary, *(syn, Kurzfassung, Referat, Abstract)*
abstrakter Raum *m* (Math) abstract space
abstrakter Term *m* (Log) abstract term
abstrakter Vertrag *m* (Re) abstract agreement *(ie, by which one of the parties incurs a liability without reference to the reason or motive inducing him to incur such liability; eg, Anweisung, Wechsel, Scheck, Inhaberschuldverschreibung)*
abstraktes Rechtsgeschäft *n* (Re) abstract (legal) transaction *(ie, one standardized by law to such an extent that the circumstances of the individual case can only to a very slight extent be taken into consideration in appreciating their legal consequences)*
abstraktes Schuldversprechen *n*
 (Re) abstract contractual performance
 – abstract promise to perform

(ie, unilateral contract not tied to the underlying transaction)
abstrakte Zahl *f* (Math) abstract number
Abstraktion *f*
(Log, Math) abstraction
– generalization
Abstraktionsniveau *n* (Log) level of abstraction *(or* generalization *or* generality)
Abstraktionsstufe *f*
(Log) = *Abstraktionsniveau*
(EDV) refinement step *(ie, in program design)*
Abszisse *f* (Math) abscissa
Abszissendifferenz *f* zweier Punkte (Math) run
Abtastbefehl *m* (EDV) scan command
Abtastbürste *f* (EDV) reading *(or* sensing) brush
Abtasteinheit *f* (EDV) scanning unit
abtasten (EDV) to scan
Abtaster *m* (EDV) scanner
Abtastfehler *m* (EDV) read(ing) error
Abtastimpuls *m* (EDV) sample pulse
Abtastkopf *m* (EDV) sensing head
Abtastmatrix *f* (EDV) scan matrix
Abtastprogramm *n* (EDV) scan program
Abtastregler *m* (EDV) sampled data feedback controller *(syn,* digitaler Regler)
Abtastverfahren *n* (EDV) scanning method
Abtastvorrichtung *f* (EDV) scanner
Abteilung *f* (com) department *(ie, any division of a business enterprise)*
Abteilung *f* **Einkauf** (com) purchasing department
Abteilungen *fpl* **außerhalb der Linienhierarchie** (Bw) collateral units *(eg, staff management units)*
Abteilung *f* **Forderungsinkasso** (Fin) collection department
Abteilungsbildung *f* (Bw) departmentation
Abteilung *f* **Schaden** (Vers) claim *(or* loss) department
Abteilungserfolgsrechnung *f*
(KoR) profit center accounting
– activity accounting
Abteilungsgemeinkosten *pl* (KoR) departmental overhead *(or* expenses *or* burden)
Abteilungsgewinn *m* (KoR) departmental profit
Abteilungsgliederung *f* (Bw) departmental structure *(ie, of an organization)*
Abteilungs-Handbuch *n* (Bw) department manual *(ie, loose-leaf presentation of department work processes through texts and graphs)*
Abteilungshierarchie *f* (Bw) departmental hierarchy *(ie, of an organization)*
abteilungsintern (Bw) intra-departmental
Abteilungskalkulation *f* (KoR) departmental costing *(or* cost estimation)
Abteilungskostenrechnung *f* (KoR) departmental costing
Abteilungsleiter *m*
(Pw) department(al) head
– head of department
– department manager *(or* chief)
– head of division
– superintendent
Abteilungsorganisation *f* (Bw) departmental organization
Abteilungsrechnung *f* (KoR) departmental costing

Abteilungsspanne *f* (KoR) departmental profit margin
abteilungsübergreifend (Bw) *(eg, problems)* cutting across departmental boundaries
Abteilungsumlage *f* (KoR) departmental charge
Abteilungsverrechnungssatz *m* (KoR) departmental rate
Abteilungszeichen *n* (com) departmental code *(ie, used in correspondence to ensure speedy routing of incoming mail)*
Abteilungszuschlag *m* (KoR) departmental rate
Abteilung *f* **Verkauf** (com) sales department
Abteilung *f* **Verkaufsförderung** (Mk) promotion services department
abtragen
(Math) to lay off *(or* up)
(Fin) to pay off (debt)
abtransportieren (com) to truck away
abtrennbarer Optionsschein *m* (Fin) detachable purchase warrant
Abtrennungsregel *f* (Log) law of detachment
abtretbar
(Re) assignable
– transferable
Abtretbarkeit *f*
(Re) assignability
– transferability
abtreten
(Re) to assign *(eg, rights, claims)*
– to make an assignment
– to transfer
– to make over
– to set over
(Re) to convey *(ie, real estate)*
Abtretender *m*
(Re) assignor
– transferor
(syn, Zedent, Altgläubiger; opp, Abtretungsempfänger, Zessionar)
Abtretung *f*
(Re) assignment *(ie, transfer of a right by agreement only;* §§ 398ff BGB)
Abtretung *f* **kraft Gesetzes** (Re) assignment by operation of law
– (GB) assignment by act of law
Abtretungsanzeige *f* (Re) notice of assignment
Abtretungsempfänger *m*
(Re) assignee
– assign
– transferee
– *(Scot)* cessionary
(syn, Zessionar, Neugläubiger; opp, Abtretender, Zedent)
Abtretungserklärung *f* (Re) declaration of assignment
Abtretung *f* **und Übergabe** *f* (WeR) assignment and delivery
Abtretungsurkunde *f* (Re) deed *(or* instrument) of assignment
Abtretungsverbotsklausel *f* (Re) non-assignment clause
Abtretungsvertrag *m* (Re) contract of assignment
Abtretung *f* **von Bezugsrechten** (Fin) letter of renunciation

Abtretung f von Forderungen (Fin) assignment of accounts receivable
abundante Zahl f (Math) abundant (*or* redundant) number
abwählen (com) to vote out of office *(eg, chairman)*
abwälzen
  (com) to pass on to *(eg, cost, taxes)*
  – to shift
Abwälzung f (FiW) = *Steuerüberwälzung*
abwandern (Pw) to float off *(eg, workers)*
abwarten (Bö, infml) to stay on the sidelines
Abwärtsbewegung f
  (com) downward movement (*or* slide) *(eg, of prices)*
  (Vw) downtrend
  – downward trend
Abwärtsstrukturierung f (EDV) top down design
Abwärtstrend m
  (Stat) downtrend
  (Fin) downside trend
  – down market *(ie, in charting)*
Abwasserabgabe f (FiW) sewage levy *(ie, imposed by the Länder)*
Abwasserabgabengesetz n (Re) Water Pollution Control Levy Law
Abwehranspruch m (Re) claim to protection against abridgment of legal rights, § 1004 BGB
Abwehrklage f
  (Re) action brought to repel unlawful interference
  – *(civil law)* actio negatoria (*or* negativa) *(ie, to safeguard an absolute right, such as property, property rights, etc.; umbrella term covering ‚Beseitigungsklage' and ‚Unterlassungsklage')*
Abwehrkonditionen fpl (com) defensive conditions *(ie, resulting from full capacity operations)*
Abwehrwerbung f (Mk) counter-offensive advertising
Abwehrzölle mpl (FiW) protective tariffs
abweichend (com) out-of-line
abweichendes Votum n (Re) dissenting opinion
Abweichung f
  (Math) azimuth
  – polar angle *(ie, in polar coordinate system)*
  (Stat) deviation
  (KoR) variance
Abweichungsanalyse f
  (Stat) variance analysis
  (KoR) cost variance analysis
  – analysis of cost variances
Abweichungsindikator m
  (EG) indicator of divergence
  – divergence indicator *(ie, in EMS, European Monetary System)*
Abweichungsklausel f (SeeV) deviation clause
Abweichungskoeffizient m (Stat) coefficient of variation
Abweichungsschwelle f (AuW) divergence threshold *(ie, level at which central banks are expected to take corrective action; syn, Divergenzschwelle)*
Abweichungsspanne f (AuW) divergence margin
Abweichungsverteilung f (KoR) allocation of variances

Abweichung f **zweiten Grades** (KoR) composite (*or* incidental) variation
Abweisung f **e-r Klage beantragen** (Re) to seek to have a case dismissed
Abwendung f **des Konkurses** (Re) avoidance of bankruptcy
abwerben
  (Mk) to alienate
  – to contract away customers
  (Pw) to bid away
  – to entice away
  – to hire away
  – (infml) to poach
Abwerber m (Pw) head hunter
Abwerbung f
  (Mk) alienation
  – contracting away *(ie, customers)*
  (Pw) bidding away
  – enticing away
  – hiring away
  – (infml) poaching
  – labor piracy
abwerfen (Fin) to yield (*or* return) a profit
ab Werk
  (com) ex works *(Incoterm)*
  – ex factory
  – ex mill
  – (US) ex *(point of origin)*
  – free at point of dispatch
ab-Werk-Preis m (com) price ex works (*or* at factory)
abwerten
  (AuW) to depreciate
  – to devalue
Abwertung f (AuW) currency devaluation
Abwertung f **auf Fertigerzeugnisse** (ReW) inventory adjustments – finished goods
Abwertung f **auf Roh-, Hilfs- und Betriebsstoffe, Waren** (ReW) inventory adjustments – raw materials and supplies
Abwertung f **auf unfertige Erzeugnisse** (ReW) inventory adjustments – work in process
Abwertungskonkurrenz f (AuW) = *Abwertungswettlauf*
Abwertungssatz m (AuW) rate of currency devaluation
Abwertungsspirale f (AuW) depreciation spiral
Abwertungsstrategie f (AuW) depreciation strategy
abwertungsverdächtige Währung f (Vw) depreciation-prone currency
Abwertungswettlauf m (AuW) competitive currency devaluation
Abwertungszyklus m (AuW) devaluation cycle
Abwertung f **wegen Leihwarenrisiko** (ReW) adjustment for risk relating to equipment loaned to customers
Abwertung f **wegen Mengenrisiko** (ReW) adjustment for quantitative risk
Abwertung f **wegen Preisrisiko** (ReW) adjustment for price risk
Abwertung f **wegen Skonti und Niederstwert** (ReW) adjustment for cash discounts and lowest value

Abwertung*f* **wegen Sonderlager** (ReW) adjustment for special inventory risks
Abwertung*f* **wegen technischen Risikos** (ReW) adjustment for technical risks
Abwesenheitsprotest *m* (WeR) protest for absence (of drawer) *(syn, Platzprotest)*
Abwesenheitsquote *f* (Pw) rate of absenteeism
Abwesenheitsrate *f* (Pw) = *Abwesenheitsquote*
Abwesenheitszeit *f* (IndE) absence time
abwickeln
 (com) to handle *(eg, order, business)*
 – to process
 – to carry out
 – to deal with
 (Re) to liquidate *(ie, a company)*
 – to wind up
 (Fin) to settle *(eg, transaction)*
 – to complete arrangements *(eg, for a loan)*
Abwickler *m* (Re) liquidator
Abwickler *m* **bestellen** (Re) to appoint a liquidator
Abwicklung *f*
 (com) handling
 – processing
 (Re) liquidation
 – winding-up
 (Bö) settlement
Abwicklung *f* **des Versicherungsgeschäfts** (Vers) conduct of insurance business
Abwicklungs-Anfangsvermögen *n* (Fin) net worth at beginning of winding-up
Abwicklungsbank *f* (Fin) liquidating bank
Abwicklungsbilanz *f*
 (ReW) liquidating balance-sheet
 – (GB) winding-up accounts
Abwicklungs-Endvermögen *n* (Fin) net worth at end of winding-up
Abwicklungseröffnungsbilanz *f* (ReW) opening balance sheet of a business in liquidation
Abwicklungsfirma *f* (Re) company in liquidation *(ie, with the statutory abbreviation ,,i. L." annexed to its name, § 153 HGB, § 269 AktG)*
Abwicklungsschlußbilanz *f* (ReW) closing balance sheet of a business in liquidation
Abwicklungstermin *m* (Bö) settlement date
Abwicklungsverfahren *n* (Re) liquidation *(or winding-up) procedure*
Abwicklungszeit *f* (com) handling *(or processing)* time *(eg, of order, of work on hand)*
Abwicklungszeitraum *m* (Re) liquidation *(or winding-up)* period
Abwicklung *f* **von Havarieschäden** (SeeV) adjustment of average losses
abzählbare Menge *f*
 (Math) denumerable
 – enumerable
 – countable . . . set
Abzählbarkeitsaxiom *n* (Math) axiom of countability
abzählbar unendlich
 (Math) denumerably
 – enumerably
 – countably . . . infinite
abzahlen
 (Fin) to pay off
 – to pay by installments

Abzahlung *f* (com) payment of installments
Abzahlungsgeschäft *n*
 (com) installment contract *(or sale)*
 – (GB) hire purchase
 – (GB, infml) the never never
 (ie, sale of movable goods (a) which seller delivers to buyer and for which buyer pays in periodic payments; (b) which may be delivered in separate lots against payment by installment; (c) which may be the object of a continuing contract.
 Syn, Teilzahlungskauf, Ratenkauf, Abzahlungskauf.
 Note: German legal and commercial practice is different and should not be pressed into the conceptual framework, for instance, of the British Hire Purchase Act of 1965 or of comparable American arrangements.)
Abzahlungshypothek *f* (Re) installment mortgage *(ie, equal redemptions and falling interest payments)*
Abzahlungskauf *m* (com) = *Abzahlungsgeschäft*
Abzahlungskredit *m* (Fin) installment credit
Abzahlungsperiode *f* (Fin) repayment period
Abzahlungspreis *m* (com) installment price
Abzahlungswechsel *mpl* (Fin) installment bills of exchange *(ie, drawn for each separate installment under an installment sale; do not confuse with ,Ratenwechsel' which is a multimaturity bill)*
abzeichnen (com) to initial *(eg, letter, memo)*
abziehbar (com) deductible
abziehbare Aufwendungen *mpl* (StR) deductible expenditure
abziehbare Reisekosten *pl* (StR) deductible traveling expenses, § 119 III EStR
abziehbare Vorsteuerbeträge *mpl* (StR) deductible portion of the prior turnover tax, § 15 III UStG
Abziehbild *n*
 (com) decal
 – decalcomania
 – transfer picture
 – transfer design
abziehen
 (com) to deduct
 – (infml) to knock off
 (com) to divert
 – to turn off
 – to siphon off *(eg, traffic from common carriers)*
 (ReW) to net *(eg, loss against profit)*
abzinsen (Math) to discount
Abzinsung *f*
 (Math) discounting
 – discounting process
Abzinsungsfaktor *m*
 (Math) discount factor $(1 + i)^{-n}$
 – conversion factor in compound discounting
Abzinsungspapiere *npl* (Fin) securities sold at a discount
Abzinsungssatz *m* (StR) discount rate allowed on advance payment of taxes
Abzinsungstabelle *f* (Math) discount table
Abzug *m*
 (com) deduction
 (com) allowance

– discount *(ie, in the sense of ‚Nachlaß')*
(Stat) penalty *(ie, in quality control)*
Abzug *m* **alt für neu** (Vers) discount new for old, § 86 VVG *(ie, based upon depreciation of a new part that is installed in settlement of a claim; discount approaches the wearing out of the item indemnified)*
Abzüge *mpl* (Pw) deductions from wage or salary
abzüglich
(com) less
– net of *(eg, agreed price net of turnover tax)*
Abzugsbeträge *mpl* (StR) statutory deductions
abzugsfähig
(StR) allowable
– deductable *(eg, income-related expenses)*
abzugsfähige Ausgaben *fpl* (StR) tax-deductible expenses *(ie, collective term covering ‚Betriebsausgaben, Werbungskosten, Sonderausgaben und außergewöhnliche Belastungen')*
abzugsfähiger Betrag *m* (StR) allowable deduction
Abzugsfähigkeit *f* (StR) deductibility
Abzugsformat *n* (EDV) dump format
Abzugsfranchise *f* (Vers) deductible *(ie, paid by the insured)*
Abzugskapital *n* (Fin) capital items deducted from total *(ie, in determining the amount of operating capital needed = bei Ermittlung des betriebsnotwendigen Kapitals)*
Abzugsmethode *f* (StR) exclusion method *(ie, exclusion of income from tax base to mitigate double taxation; used in all tax treaties signed by the Federal Republic of Germany)*
Abzugsroutine *f* (EDV) dump routine
Abzugssteuern *fpl*
(StR) withholding taxes
– taxes stopped at source
(ie, taxes withheld from wages and salary and paid direct to the government; eg, wages tax, supervisory board tax, capital yield tax; opp, veranlagte Steuern)
abzweigen (com) to detour *(eg, taxes to other uses)*
Account-Manager *m* (Mk) account manager, AM
Achsenabschnitt *m* (Math) intercept of an axis
Acht-Bit-Byte *n* (EDV) octet
Achteralphabet *n* (EDV) eight-level code
Achtstundentag *m* (Pw) eight-hour working day
à condition (com) sale under the suspensive condition of resale; if condition is not satisfied, goods are returned to producer
A-conto-Zahlung *f* (com) payment on account
ad acta legen
(com) to close off *(eg, plan, program)*
– to lay to rest
adaptive Regelung *f* (EDV) adaptive control (system) *(subterms: gesteuerte a.R. + a.R. mit Rückführung = open loop adaptation + closed loop adaptation)*
adaptive Regelung *f* **mit Rückführung** (EDV) closed loop adaptation
a dato (WeR) from the day of making out *(eg, a bill of exchange)*
Addend *m* (EDV) addend *(ie, added to the augend to form the sum)*
Addendenregister *n* (EDV) addend register *(syn, Summandenregister)*

Addierbefehl *m* (EDV) add instruction
addieren
(com) to add up
– to cast up
– to foot up
– (infml) to tot up
Addierer *m* **mit Übertragungsweiterleitung für Dualzahlen**
(EDV) carry-ripple adder
(syn, Carry-Ripple Addierer)
Addierglied *n* (EDV) = *Addierwerk*
Addierlocher *m* (EDV) add-punch machine
Addiermaschine *f* (EDV) adding machine
Addierschaltkreis *m* (EDV) adding circuit
Addierwerk *n* (EDV) (digital) adder
Addierzähler *m* (EDV) adding counter
Addition *f*
(com) addition
– summation
– footing
Additionsanweisung *f* (EDV, Cobol) add statement
Additionsaxiom *n* (Math) addition axiom
Additionsbefehl *m* (EDV) add instruction
Additionsmaschine *f* (EDV) = *Addiermaschine*
Additionssätze *mpl* **der Wahrscheinlichkeit** (Stat) addition theorems of probability
Additionsschaltung *f* (EDV) = *Addierschaltkreis*
Additionsstreifen *m* (EDV) addition slip
Additionstheorem *n* (Math) addition theorem
Additions-Subtraktionszeit *f* (EDV) add-subtract time *(ie, exclusive of fetch time)*
Additionstabelle *f* (EDV) addition table
Additionsübertrag *m* (EDV) add carry
Additionszeit *f* (EDV) add time
Addition *f* **von Matrizen** (Math) matrix addition
Addition *f* **von Zufallsvariablen** (Stat) addition of variates
additive Grenzkosten *pl* (Vw) additive marginal cost *(Pigou)*
additive Gruppe *f* (Math) additive group
additive Präferenzen *fpl* (Vw) additive preferences *(or utilities)*
additiver Fehler *m* (EDV) accumulated error
additiver Feldrechner *m* (EDV) distributed array processor
additiver Zufallsprozeß *m* (Stat) additive random walk process
Additivität *f* (Stat) additive property
Adhäsionsverschluß *m* (com) adhesion flap *(ie, used for printed matter consignments)*
Adhäsionsvertrag *m* (Re) adhesion contract
ad hoc-Ausschuß *m* (com) ad hoc committee
ad-hoc-Verband *m* (Re) single-purpose association
Adjazenzmatrix *f* (Math) adjacency matrix
Adjungierte *f* **e–r Matrix** (Math) adjoint *(or adjugate)* of a matrix
Adjunktion *f* (Log) inclusive disjunction
Adjustierung *f* (SeeV) adjustment of average
administrative Handelshemmnisse *npl* (AuW) administrative barriers to trade
administrativer Protektionismus *m* (AuW) administrative protectionism *(eg, non-tariff trade barriers)*
administrierte Preisfestsetzung *f* (Vw) business-controlled pricing

administrierte Preisinflation f (Vw) administered price inflation
administrierter Preis m (Vw) administered price
administrierter Zinssatz m (Vw) administered rate of interest
Adressat m (com) addressee
Adreßbereich m (EDV) address range
Adreßbuch n (EDV) index register
Adreßbus m (EDV) address bus
Adresse f (EDV) address
Adressenänderung f (EDV) address modification
Adressenarithmetik f (EDV) = *Adreßrechnung*
Adressenauswahl f (EDV) address selection
Adressenauswahleinrichtung f (EDV) address selection unit
Adressenbüro n (com) agency selling specified sets of addresses
Adressendatei f (EDV) address file
Adressenerzeugung f (EDV) address generation *(syn, randomization)*
Adressenfeld n (EDV) address field
Adressenkapazität f (EDV) address capacity
Adressenliste f
 (com) list of addresses
 – mailing list
adressenloser Befehl m (EDV) addressless (*or* zero address) instruction
Adressenmodifikation f (EDV) address modification
Adressenrechnung f (EDV) address computation
Adressenregister n (EDV) = *Adreßregister*
Addressensammlung f (com) set of addresses
Adressensubstitution f (EDV) address substitution
Adressensystem n (EDV) address system
Adressenteil m (EDV) = *Adreßteil*
Adressenübersetzung f (EDV) address translation
Adressenumwandlung f (EDV) address conversion
Adressenverkettung f (EDV) address chaining
Adressenverzeichnis n (com) list of addresses
Adressenzuweisung f (EDV) address assignment
adressieren (com, EDV) to address
Adressierkarte f (com) address card
Adressiermaschine f
 (com) addressing machine
 – addressor
 – addressograph
Adressiermethode f (EDV) addressing
Adressiersystem n (EDV) addressing system
Adressierverfahren n (EDV) addressing
Adreßindex m (EDV) address index
Adreßkarte f (EDV) address card
Adreßkonstante f (EDV) address constant *(syn, ADCON)*
Adreßmarke f (EDV) address marker
Adreßmodifikation f (EDV) address modification
Adreßpegel m (EDV) location counter
Adreßspediteur m (com) receiving forwarding agent
Adreßpfad m (EDV) address highway (*or* bus *or* trunk)
Adreßraum m (EDV) address space
Adreßrechnen n (EDV) address arithmetic (*or* computation)
Adreßregister n (EDV) address register
Adreßschlüssel m (EDV, Cobol) actual key

Adreßspur f (EDV) address track
Adreßteil m (EDV) address part (*or* portion) *(syn, Operandenteil)*
Adreßwiederholung f (EDV) repetitive addressing
Adreßzuordnung f (EDV) address assignment
AD-Umsetzer m (EDV) = *Analog-Digital-Umsetzer*
ad valorem-Zoll m (Zo) ad valorem customs duty (*or* tariff)
Aerogramm n (com) aerogram
Afa-Nutzungsdauer f (StR) writeoff period *(ie, for income tax purposes)*
Afa-Tabellen fpl (StR) tax depreciation tables *(ie, tables listing statutory economic lives of assets for the purpose of computing tax depreciation)*
Affektionswert m (com) fancy value *(ie, subjective value of a good higher than its objective value)*
Affiche f (Mk) bill
Affiliation f
 (Bw) affiliation
 (Fin) subsidiary bank *(ie, controlled by another large bank)*
affine Funktion f (Math) affine function
affine Gruppe f (Math) affine group
affines Koordinatensystem n (Math) affine coordinate system
affine Transformation f (Math) affine transformation
à fonds perdu (com) (money) paid without prospect of getting it back
à forfait (WeR) without recourse
Agent m
 (com) commercial agent
 – sales agent (*or* representative)
 – selling agent
Agentenprovision f (com) agent's commission
Agentur f
 (com) representation *(ie, of a firm by an agent)*
 (com) branch office
 (com) news agency
Agenturgeschäft n (com) agency business
Agentur-Vergütung f (com) agency commission
Agenturvertrag m (Re) agency agreement *(ie, signed between commercial agent and principal = Unternehmer, § 84 HGB)*
Agenturvertreter m (com) agency representative
Agenturwaren fpl (Zo) agency goods
A-Geschäft n (Fin) installment credit granted to consumer directly
Agglomeration f (Vw) agglomeration *(ie, in location theory, A. Weber)*
Agglomerationsziffer f (Stat) agglomeration index
Aggregat n
 (Stat, Vw) aggregate
 (IndE) set of machines *(eg, turbo-generator set)*
Aggregation f
 (Stat) aggregation
 – summation
Aggregations-Methode f (Log) bottom-up method
aggregierte Größe f (Stat, Vw) aggregate (quantity)
aggregierter Index m (Stat) aggregative index number
aggregiertes Modell n (Vw) aggregative model
aggressiv
 (Mk) aggressive

– thrusting
(Bw) fast expanding
– competing head-on
aggressiv expandiern (com) be set on an aggressively expansionary conrse
aggressive Absatzmethode *f* (Mk) hard-sell technique
aggressives Marketing *n*
(Mk) aggressive marketing
– (infml) hell-for-leather marketing
aggressives Verkaufsgespräch *n*
(Mk) high-pressure sales talk
Agio *n*
(Fin) premium *(syn, Aufgeld)*
(ReW, EG) share premium account
Agio *n* **aus Aktienemission**
(Fin) premium on capital stock
– share premium
Agioerträge *mpl* (Fin) premiums received
Agiopapier *n* (Fin) premium bond
Agiorücklage *f* (ReW) share premium reserve *(ie, not available for distribution)*
Agiotage *f*
(Fin) agiotage *(ie, business of dealing in foreign exchange)*
(Fin, *rare*) agiotage *(ie, speculative dealing in securities)*
Agioteur *m*
(Fin) agioteur
– foreign-exchange dealer
Agiotheorie *f* (Vw) agio theory of interest *(E. v. Böhm-Bawerk)*
agiotieren
(Fin) to deal in foreign exchange
(Fin, *rare*) to deal speculatively in securities
Agrarabschöpfung *f* (EG) agricultural levy
Agrarbevölkerung *f* (Vw) rural population
Agrareinkommen *n* (EG) farm income
Agrarerzeugnisse *npl*
(EG) agricultural products
– farm goods
– farm products
Agrarexporte *mpl*
(EG) agricultural exports
– farm exports
– agri-exports
Agrarfonds *m* (AuW) European Agricultural Guidance and Guarantee Fund, AEGGF
Agrargenossenschaft *f* (com) farm cooperative
Agrargeographie *f* (Vw) rural geography
Agrarimporte *mpl*
(EG) agricultural imports
– farm imports
– agri-imports
agrarische Rohstoffe *mpl* (com) agricultural commodities
Agrarkonjunktur *f* (Vw) cyclical movements in agricultural markets
Agrarkredit *m*
(Vw) agricultural credit *(or* loan)
– farm credit
– farming credit
Agrarkrise *f* (Vw) farm crisis
Agrarland *n* (Vw) agrarian country *(opp, industrial country)*

Agrarmarkt *m* (Vw) agricultural commodities market
Agrarmarktordnung *f* (EG) agricultural market organization *(or* regulation)
Agrarministerrat *m* (EG) Council of Agricultural Ministers
Agrarpolitik *f* (EG) agricultural *(or* farm) policy
agrarpolitisch (EG) relating to farm policy
Agrarpreise *mpl* (EG) agricultural *(or* farm) prices
Agrarpreisregelung *f* (EG) farm price settlement
Agrarpreisstützung *f* (EG) support of agricultural prices *(ie, by ‚Preis- und Abnahmegarantien, Exportsubventionen, Zölle, Abschöpfungen, Einfuhrkontingentierung, Interventionskäufe‘, which see)*
Agrarpreissystem *n*
(EG) CAP system of prices
– farm price system
Agrarprodukte *npl* (EG) agricultural *(or* farm) products
Agrarproduktion *f* (EG) agricultural *(or* farm) production
Agrarquote *f* (Stat) ratio of farming population to total labor force
Agrarsektor *m* (Vw) agricultural sector
Agrarstatistik *f* (Stat) agricultural statistics
Agrarstruktur *f* (Vw) farm structure
Agrarsubventionen *fpl*
(EG) agricultural aids
– aids to farmers
– farm aids
Agrarüberschüsse *mpl* (EG) farm product surpluses
Agrarvermarktung *f* (EG) marketing of farm products
Agrarverordnung *f* (EG) agricultural regulation
Agrarwirtschaft *f* (Vw) farming
Agrarwissenschaft *f* (Vw) agricultural economics
Agrarzölle *mpl*
(AuW) customs duties levied on exported and imported products
– agricultural duties
AG und Co. (Bw) combination of ‚Offene Handelsgesellschaft‘ and ‚Kommanditgesellschaft‘, qv.
ähnlich geordnete Menge *f* (Math) similarly ordered set
Ähnlichkeitsverhältnis *n* (Math) ratio of similitude
à jour (com) updated
Akademiker *m* (Pw) person of university education *(ie, not an academic which in English is a person holding a teaching job at a college or university)*
akademischer Grad *m* (Pw) university degree
Akkommodation *f* (Stat) accommodation
Akkord *m*
(com) amicable *(or* friendly) settlement of disputes
(Re) composition proceedings
(IndE) piece work
Akkordabrechnung *f* (IndE) piece-work payroll accounting
Akkordarbeit *f* (IndE) piecework
Akkordarbeiter *m* (IndE) piece worker
Akkordausgleich *m* (IndE) timeworkers' bonus
Akkordbrecher *m*
(IndE) job spoiler

– rate buster
– (inful) high flier
– (sl) rat
Akkordkarte *f* (IndE) job ticket
Akkordköpfen *n* (IndE) rate cutting *(ie, in piece work; syn, Akkordschere)*
Akkordlohn *m*
(IndE) piecework rate *(or* wage)
– piece rate
– payment by piece rates
Akkordlohnsatz *m* (IndE) piece *(or* job) rate
Akkordrichtarbeiter *m* (IndE) pace setter
Akkordrichtsatz *m* (IndE) basic piece rate *(ie, amount earned at a normal pace per time unit)*
Akkordschere *f* (IndE) rate cutting *(ie, in piece work)*
Akkordstundenanteil *m* (IndE) hours on incentive
Akkordsystem *n* (IndE) piecework system
Akkordzeit *f* (IndE) allowed *(or* incentive) time
Akkordzettel *m* (IndE) piecework slip *(syn, Lohnzettel, Lohnschein)*
Akkordzuschlag *m* (IndE) bonus increment
Akkreditierung *f* (Fin) opening of a letter of credit *(or* L/C)
Akkreditiv *n* (Fin) commercial letter of credit *(or* L/C)
Akkreditivabrechnungskonto *n* (Fin) credit settlement account
Akkreditivanzeige *f* (Fin) notification of credit
Akkreditiv *n* **anzeigen** (Fin) to advise *(or* notify) a letter of credit
Akkreditivbank *f*
(Fin) credit-issuing bank
– opening bank
Akkreditivbedingungen *fpl* (Fin) terms of a credit
Akkreditiv *n* **bestätigen** (Fin) to confirm a credit
Akkreditivbestätigung *f* (Fin) credit confirmation
Akkreditivbevorschußung *f* (Fin) anticipatory credit
Akkreditiv *n* **brieflich eröffnen** (Fin) to open a credit by letter
Akkreditivdeckung *f* (Fin) credit cover
Akkreditivermächtigung *f* (Fin) letter of authority
Akkreditiv *n* **eröffnen**
(Fin) to open
– to issue
– to establish . . . a credit
Akkreditiveröffnung *f*
(Fin) issue
– issuance
– opening . . . of a letter of credit
Akkreditivgeschäft *n* (Fin) documentary credit business
Akkreditiv *n* **hinauslegen** (Fin) = *Akkreditiv eröffnen*
Akkreditiv *n* **in Anspruch nehmen** (Fin) to draw on a letter of credit
Akkreditivklausel *f* (Fin) letter of credit clause
Akkreditiv *n* **mit aufgeschobener Zahlung** (Fin) deferred-payments credit
Akkreditivpartei *f* (Fin) party to a letter of credit
Akkreditivstellung *f* (Fin) opening a letter of credit
Akkreditiv *n* **telegraphisch eröffnen** (Fin) to open a credit by cable

Akkreditivverpflichtung *f* (Fin) liability under a letter of credit
Akkreditivwährung *f* (Fin) currency of the credit
Akkreditivwährungsdeckungskonto *n* (Fin) foreign currency credit cover account
Akkumulation *f* (Vw) accumulation *(ie, Marxist term for investment)*
Akkumulationsquote *f* (Vw) rate of accumulation *(ie, obsolete for ‚investment ratio')*
Akkumulator *m*
(EDV) accumulator
– accumulator register
(ie, register in which arithmetic results are kept)
Akkumulatorregister *n* (EDV) = *Akkumulator*
akkumulierte Abschreibung *f* (ReW) accumulated depreciation
Akontozahlung *f* (com) payment on account
AKP-Länder *npl* (AuW) ACP countries *(ie, African, Caribbean, and Pacific States)*
Akquisiteur *m*
(Mk) canvasser
– solicitor
Akquisition *f*
(Mk) sales canvassing
– acquisition
Akquisitionskosten *pl*
(Mk) canvassing costs
– sales development costs
(Vers) acquisition cost
Akte *f* (com) file *(ie, collection of papers on one subject)*
Aktendeckel *m* (com) folder
Akteneinsicht *f* (Re) inspection of records
aktenkundig (Re) on the record
aktenkundig machen (com) to place on record
Aktennotiz *f* (com) memo(randum)
Aktenordner *m* (com) standing file
Aktenplan *m* (com) filing plan *(ie, based on decimal classification)*
Aktenvermerk *m* (com) memo
Aktenzeichen *n*
(com) reference code *(ie, on letters)*
(com) file number
Aktie *f*
(com) stock
– (GB) share
(ie, stocks, in British financial circles, are ‚government bonds')
(WeR) share *(or* stock) certificate *(ie, evidence of ownership = Mitgliedsschaftsurkunde)*
(Fin) share of stock
– corporate share
(ie, one of the equal fractional parts into which the capital stock of a corporation is divided)
Aktie *f* **mittlerer Güte** (Fin) medium grade stock
Aktienabstempelung *f* (Fin) official stamping of shares *(eg, on capital reduction, change of firm, reduction of bond interest)*
Aktienagio *n* (Fin) stock *(or* share) premium
Aktienaufschlag *m* (Fin) = *Aktienagio*
Aktienausgabe *f* (Fin) issue of shares *(or* stock)
Aktien *fpl* **ausgeben** (Fin) to issue shares *(or* stock)
Aktienaustausch *m* (Fin) exchange of shares *(or* stock)

Aktienbestand *m* (Fin) shareholding
- stockholding
- stock portfolio

Aktienbeteiligung *f* (Fin) equity interest (*or* stake)

Aktienbewertung *f* (Fin) stock valuation

Aktienbezugsrecht *n*
(Fin) stock purchase warrant
- (GB) stock right

Aktienbezugsschein *m* (Fin) stock allotment warrant

Aktienbörse *f* (Fin) stock exchange (*or* market)

Aktienbuch *n* (Re) share (*or* stock) register, § 67 AktG

Aktiendisagio *n* (Fin) stock (*or* share) discount

Aktien *fpl* **einreichen** (Fin) to surrender share certificates

Aktien *fpl* **einziehen** (Fin) to call in shares

Aktieneinziehung *f* (Fin) redemption of shares (*or* stock), § 237 AktG

Aktienemission *f* (Fin) issue of shares (*or* stock)

Aktienemissions-Agio *n* (Fin) stock-issue premium

Aktienemissions-Disagio *n* (Fin) stock-issue discount

Aktienemissions-Kosten *pl* (Fin) stock-issue cost

Aktienemissions-Kurs *m* (Fin) share (*or* stock) offering price

Aktien *fpl* **emittieren** (Fin) to issue shares (*or* stock)

Aktienfinanzierung *f* (Fin) financing through common stock *(Note: ‚equity financing' may include funds generated in the business = Selbstfinanzierung')*

Aktienfonds *m*
(Fin) stock fund
- share-based investment fund

Aktienführer *m* (Bö) stock guide

Aktiengattung *f* (Fin) class of shares (*or* stock)

Aktiengattungen *fpl* (Fin) types of stock

Aktiengesellschaft *f*
(Bw) stock corporation
- (GB) company limited by shares
- (GB) full public company
(ie, with limited liability and quoted shares)

Aktiengesetz *n* (Re) German Stock Corporation Law, of 6 Sep 1965

Aktienhandel *m* (Bö) equity (*or* stock) trading

Aktien *fpl* **im Sammeldepot** (Fin) shares in collective deposit *(ie, bank serving as central depository for securities)*

Aktienindex *m*
(Bö) stock index
- share price index

Aktieninhaber *m*
(Fin) shareholder
- stockholder
- equity holder
- equity shareholder

Aktienkaduzierung *f* (Fin) forfeiture of shares, § 64 AktG

Aktienkapital *n* (Fin) share capital of a corporation *(ie, no difference between authorized and unissued because entire capital must be subscribed for upon organization)*

Aktienkauf *m*
(Fin) buying of shares (*or* stock)
- purchase of shares (*or* stock)

Aktienkaufplan *m* (Pw) stock purchase plan

Aktien *fpl* **konjunkturempfindlicher Unternehmen** (Fin) cyclical stocks

Aktienkurs *m*
(Fin) share (*or* stock) price
- market price of share

Aktienkursindex *m* (Bö) share (*or* stock) price index

Aktienmarkt *m*
(Bö) equity
- stock
- share ... market

Aktienmehrheit *f*
(Fin) controlling portion of common stock
- majority of stock

Aktien *fpl* **mit Konsortialbindung** (Fin) shares under syndicate agreements

Aktiennotierung *f* (Bö) stock quotation

Aktienoption *f* (Fin) right to convert bonds into shares

Aktienpaket *n* (Fin) block (*or* parcel) of shares

Aktienportefeuille *n* (Fin) stock portfolio

Aktienrecht *n* (Re) stock corporation law

aktienrechtliche Gliederungsvorschriften *fpl* (Re) rules of classification as established in the German Stock Corporation Law

aktienrechtliche Vorschriften *fpl* (Re) rules as established under the German Stock Corporation Law

Aktienrechtsreform *f* (Re) reform of German stock corporation law

Aktienrendite *f*
(Fin) stock yield
- yield on shares

Aktienrückgabe *f* (Fin) surrender of shares

Aktiensparen *n* (Fin) equity saving

Aktienspekulation *f* (Bö) speculation in shares (*or* stock)

Aktiensplit *m* (Fin) stock splitup

Aktien *fpl* **splitten** (Fin) to split shares (*or* stock)

Aktienstreubesitz *m* (Fin) widely scattered shareholdings

Aktientausch *m*
(Fin) exchange of shares
- stock swap
(ie, in acquisition or merger operation)

Aktienübernahme *f* (Fin) stock takeover

Aktienübertragung *f* (WeR) transfer of shares (*or* stocks)

Aktienumtausch *m* (Fin) exchange of share certificates

Aktienurkunde *f* (WeR) stock (*or* share) certificate

Aktien *fpl* **zeichnen** (Fin) to subscribe to shares

Aktienzeichner *m*
(Fin) applicant for shares
- share applicant

Aktienzeichnung *f* (Fin) application for shares

Aktienzertifikat *n* (WeR) = *Aktienurkunde*

Aktien *fpl* **zur Zeichnung auflegen** (Fin) to invite subscription to shares

Aktienzusammenlegung *f*
(Fin) share consolidation
- reverse stock split

Aktienzuteilung *f* (Fin) stock (*or* share) allotment

Aktionär *m*
(Fin) shareholder
– stockholder
– equity holder
– equity shareholder
Aktionäre *mpl* **abfinden** (Fin) to indemnify shareholders
Aktionäre *mpl* **einberufen** (Bw) to convene shareholders *(eg, to general meeting)*
Aktionärsbanken *fpl* (Fin) shareholding banks
Aktionärsbrief *m* (com) shareholders' letter *(eg, company stated in a . . .)*
Aktionärsgruppe *f* (Fin) shareholder group
Aktionärspflege *f* (Fin) shareholder *(or* stockholder*)* relations
Aktionärsrechte *npl* (Fin) shareholders' *(or* stockholders' rights
Aktionärsschutzvereinigung *f* (Fin) shareholders' protective association
Aktionärsvereinigung *f* (Fin) association of shareholders
Aktionärsvertreter *mpl* (Pw) stockholder representatives *(ie, in co-determination matters)*
Aktionen *fpl* **zur Stützung von Währungen** (AuW) monetary support operations
Aktionseinheit *f*
(Bw) organization unit
– administrative unit
– job
Aktionsparameter *m*
(Vw) action parameter
– parameter of action
Aktiva *npl* (ReW) assets
Aktiva *npl* **monetisieren** (Fin) to monetize assets
Aktiv-Antizipation *f*
(ReW) accrued assets
– accrued expense
– accrued income
– accrued liabilities
aktive Datenstation *f* (EDV) active station
aktive Handelsbilanz *f*
(AuW) favorable trade balance
– active trade balance
aktive Jahresabgrenzung *f* (ReW) accrued income
aktive Leistungsbilanz *f* (AuW) surplus on current account
aktive Leitung *f* (EDV) active line *(ie, available for data transmission)*
aktive Lohnveredelung *f* (AuW) processing of goods for foreign account
aktive Rechnungsabgrenzung *f* (ReW) accruals *(ie, accrued assets/income/revenue)*
aktiver Speicher *m* (EDV) active storage
aktiver Teilhaber *m* (Re) active partner
aktiver Transithandel *m* (AuW) active transit trade
aktiver Veredelungsverkehr *m* (Zo) inward processing arrangements
aktiver Verrechnungssaldo *m* (Fin) credit balance on inter-branch account, § 53 II 2 KWG
aktives Element *n* (EDV) active element *(syn, aktives Glied)*
aktive Veredelung *f* (Zo) inward processing
aktive Vertretung *f* (Re) active agency *(ie, agent makes a declaration of intent on his principal's behalf)*
aktive Zahlungsbilanz *f* (AuW) active *(or* favorable*)* balance of payments
Aktiv-Finanzierung *f* (Fin) lending of funds to third parties *(ie, by banks or business enterprises)*
Aktivforderung *f* (com) claim outstanding *(ie, no technical term in accounting)*
Aktivgeschäft *n* (Fin) lending business
Aktivhandel *m* (AuW) foreign trade carried on by domestic firms *(opp, Passivhandel)*
Aktivhypotheken *fpl* (Fin) mortgage lendings
aktivieren
(ReW) to capitalize
– to recognize *(or* carry*)* as an asset
– to charge to capital
aktivierte Eigenleistungen *fpl*
(ReW) internally produced and capitalized assets
– company-produced additions to plant and equipment
– material, wages and overhead capitalized as additions to plant and equipment
(ReW, EG) work performed by the undertaking for its own purposes and capitalized
aktivierte Kosten *pl* (ReW) capitalized cost
Aktivierung *f* (ReW) capitalization
– carrying as assets
(AuW) moving *(or* heading*)* into surplus *(ie, said of balance of payments; opp, Passivierung)*
aktivierungsfähig (ReW) ... which may be capitalized
Aktivierungspflicht *f* (ReW) legal obligation to capitalize *(or* to itemize assets in the balance sheet*)*, § 40 HGB
aktivierungspflichtige Gemeinkosten *pl* (ReW) capitalized overhead *(or* indirect cost*)*
aktivierungspflichtiger Aufwand *m* (ReW) expenditure to be capitalized
Aktivierungsrecht *n* (ReW) right to capitalize *(ie, certain assets; eg, discount, startup cost, acquired goodwill)*
Aktivierungsverbot *n* (ReW) legal prohibition to capitalize *(ie, certain asset items)*
aktiv Innovierender *m* (Bw) change agent
aktivisch abgegrenzt (ReW) deferred
Aktivitätsanalyse *f* (OR) activity analysis
Aktivitäts-Kennzahl *f* (Fin) activity ratio
Aktivitätsordnung *f* (Vers) active life table *(ie, actuarial table showing number of persons of a specific age group that are still alive or gainfully employed)*
Aktivitätssektor *m* (Math) activity vector
Aktivitätsstrahl *m* (Math) activity ray
Aktivitätsvektor *m* (Math) activity vector
Aktivkonto *n* (ReW) asset account
Aktivkredit *m* (Fin) business lending to outside parties
Aktivlegitimation *f* (Re) capacity to sue, § 50 ZPO *(ie, term is now extended to include the wider concept of ‚Sachbefugnis' = accrual of substantive claim to plaintiff)*
aktiv legitimiert
(Re) capable of suing
– having capacity to sue

25

Aktivposten *m*
 (VGR) credit item *(ie, of balance of payments)*
 (ReW) asset item *(or* unit)
Aktivsaldo *m* (ReW) credit balance
Aktivsaldo *m* **der Zahlungsbilanz** (AuW) balance of payments surplus
Aktivseite *f* (ReW) asset side *(ie, of balance sheet)*
Aktivspeicher *m* (EDV) programmable read only memory, PROM
Aktivtausch *m* (ReW) accounting exchange on the assets side *(ie, of financial statements)*
Aktivum *n* (ReW) asset
Aktivvermögen *n* (Fin) actual net worth *(or* assets)
Aktivwechsel *mpl* (ReW) bills outstanding
Aktivwert *m* (ReW) asset value
Aktivzins *m* (Fin) interest charged
aktualisieren (com) to update *(eg, operating figures)*
Aktualisierungsprogramm *n* (EDV) updating program
Aktualitätsverlust *m* (com) loss of up-to-dateness
aktuelle Ertragslage *f* (Fin) current profitability
aktueller Adreßschlüssel *m* (EDV, Cobol) actual key
aktuelles Programm *n* (EDV) active *(or* current) program
akustische Anzeige *f* (EDV) audible alarm
akustischer Koppler *m* (EDV) acoustic coupler
akustischer Speicher *m* (EDV) acoustic memory *(or* storage *or* store)
 (ie, using the properties of an acoustic delay line)
akustische Verzögerung *f* (EDV) acoustic delay
akustische Verzögerungsstrecke *f* (EDV) acoustic delay line
Akzelerationskoeffizient *m* (Vw) acceleration coefficient
Akzelerationsprinzip *n* (Vw) acceleration principle
Akzelerator *m* (Vw) accelerator
Akzelerator-Multiplikator-Modell *n* (Vw) accelerator-multiplier model
Akzelerator-Multiplikator-Wirkung *f* (Vw) accelerator-multiplier interaction
Akzelerator-Rückkopplung *f* (Vw) accelerator loop
Akzept *n* (WeR) acceptance
Akzeptant *m* (WeR) acceptor *(syn, Bezogener, Trassat = drawee)*
Akzeptanz *f* (Mk) market acceptance
Akzeptanzproblem *n*
 (EDV) problem of acceptance
 (syn, mangelnde Nutzung)
Akzeptaustausch *m* (Fin) exchange of acceptances
 (ie, among banks)
 (Fin) exchange of accommodation bills
Akzeptbuch *n* (ReW) register of bills payable
Akzepte *npl* **im Umlauf** (Fin) acceptances outstanding
Akzeptgebühr *f* (Fin) acceptance charge
akzeptieren
 (com) to accept
 – to approve of *(eg, plan, proposal, scheme)*
Akzeptkredit *m* (Fin) acceptance credit
Akzeptleistung *f* (WeR) acceptance
Akzeptlinie *f* (Fin) acceptance line *(ie, limit or ceiling of acceptance credit which a foreign bank allows a domestic bank for drafts of its customers)*
Akzeptmeldung *f* (Fin) notification of acceptance
Akzeptobligo *n* (ReW) bills payable
Akzeptprovision *f* (Fin) acceptance commission
Akzeptumlauf *m*
 (Fin) acceptances outstanding
 – acceptance commitments
Akzeptverbindlichkeiten *fpl* (Fin) acceptance liabilities *(or* commitments)
Akzeptverweigerung *f* (WeR) dishonor by nonacceptance
Akzeptvorlage *f* (WeR) presentation for acceptance
Akzession *f*
 (com) accession
 – acquisition *(eg, of books in library)*
 (Re) accession
 – adherence
 (ie, act of becoming joined to; eg, Greece to EEC)
akzessorisch (Re) accessory
akzessorische Sicherheit *f*
 (Re) collateral security
 – (GB) asset cover
Akzisen *fpl*
 (FiW) excise taxes
 – indirect taxes *(eg, consumption taxes, customs duties)*
à la baisse spekulieren
 (Bö) to speculate for a decline in prices
 – to bear
à la hausse spekulieren
 (Bö) to speculate for a rise in prices
 – to bull
Alarmeinrichtung *f* (EDV) alarm equipment
aleatorischer Vertrag *m* (Re) aleatory *(or* hazardous) contract
 (ie, where the performance depends on an uncertain event; eg, insurance, engagement to pay annuity)
Algebra *f* (Math) algebra
Algebra *f* **der Logik** (EDV) Boolean algebra *(or* logic)
algebraische Funktion *f* (Math) algebraic function
algebraische Gleichung *f* (Math) algebraic equation
algebraische Körpererweiterung *f* (Math) algebraic *(or* separable) extension of a field *(syn, separable Körpererweiterung, Körpererweiterung 1. Art)*
algebraischer Addierer *m* (EDV) algebraic adder
algebraisches Komplement *n*
 (Math) algebraic complement
 – cofactor
algebraische Struktur *f* (Math) algebraic structure
algebraische Topologie *f* (Math) algebraic topology
algebraische Zahl *f* (Math) algebraic number *(ie, root of an algebraic equation with integral coefficients = ganzzahlige Koeffizienten)*
algebraisch irrationale Zahl *f* (Math) algebraic irrational number
algorithmisch (EDV) algorithmic
algorithmische Linguistik *f* (EDV) computational linguistics
algorithmisieren (EDV) to algorithmize
Algorithmisierung *f* (EDV) algorithmization

Algorithmus m (Math) algorithm *(ie, problem-solving procedure; effektives Berechnungsverfahren)*
Alimente pl (Re) alimony *(ie, an allowance payable for maintenance of illegitimate children)*
Aliud-Lieferung f (Re) delivery of goods other than those ordered *(ie, does not constitute performance of contract)*
Alleinbetrieb m
  (Re) one-man business
  – sole proprietor
  – (GB) sole trader
Allbranchen-Versicherung f
  (Vers) all-lines insurance
  (Vers) all-lines insurance company
Alleinbesitz m (Re) exclusive possession
Alleineigentum n (Re) sole ownership
Alleineigentümer m (Re) sole owner
Alleinerbe m (Re) sole heir
Alleinfinanzierung f (Fin) sole financing *(opp, joint financing)*
alleiniger Abnehmer m (com) sole buyer *(ie, franchise dealer for a specified sales district)*
alleiniger Eigentümer m (Re) sole owner
alleiniger Erfinder m (Pat) sole inventor
alleiniger Patentinhaber m (Pat) sole patent holder
alleiniges Eigentumsrecht n (Re) sole ownership *(or proprietorship)*
alleiniges Vertriebsrecht n (Re) sole selling right
Alleininhaber m (Re) sole holder *(or owner)*
Alleinkonzessionär m (com) sole concessionaire
Alleinrecht n (Pat) exclusive right
Alleinstellung f (Pat) unique position *(ie, special protection of a well-known trade mark on account of its unequaled nature)*
Alleinsteuer f (FiW) single tax *(= impôt unique)*
Alleinverkaufsrechte npl
  (com) sole and exclusive selling rights
  – exclusive franchise
Alleinverkaufsvertrag m (Re) exclusive sales contract
Alleinvertreter m
  (com) sole agent
  – sole distributor
  (ie, buys and sells in his own name and for his own account, seeking to make middleman's profit)
  (Re) sole (and exclusive) agent *(opp, Gesamtvertreter)*
  (Mk) exclusive distributor
Alleinvertretung f (com) sole and exclusive agency *(or representation)*
Alleinvertrieb m (Mk) exclusive marketing *(ie, by a sole agent, a sole proprietor, or a company-owned trading operation)*
Alleinvertriebsabkommen n (Re) exclusive sales contract
Alleinvertriebsberechtigter m (com) exclusive distributor
Alleinwerbung f (Mk) individual advertising *(opp, Gemeinschaftswerbung)*
„Alle Rechte vorbehalten" (Re) all rights reserved
Alles-oder-Nichts-Klausel f (Fin) all-or-nothing clause

allgemein (com) across-the-board *(eg, pay rises, price and wage controls)*
Allgemeinbegriff m
  (com) general term
  (Log) universal (concept)
allgemein-bejahendes Urteil n
  (Log) universal affirmative
  – A-proposition
allgemeine Arbeitslosigkeit f (Vw) general unemployment
allgemeine Bankgeschäfte npl (Fin) general banking operations
allgemeine Bedingungen fpl (Re) standard terms and conditions
Allgemeine Bedingungen fpl **für die Kraftverkehrsversicherung** (Vers) General Conditions Relating to Motor Vehicle Insurance
Allgemeine Bemessungsgrundlage f (SozV) general basis of assessment
allgemeine Betriebskosten pl (KoR) general (operating) costs
Allgemeine Betriebswirtschaftslehre f (Bw, roughly) general business economics
allgemeine Bewertungsvorschriften fpl (StR) general valuation rules, §§ 1–16 BewG
Allgemeine Deutsche Seeversicherungsbedingungen fpl (Re) General German Ocean Marine Insurance Conditions
Allgemeine Deutsche Spediteurbedingungen fpl (com) General German Forwarders' Conditions
allgemeine Erhöhung f (com) across-the-board increase *(eg, prices, wages)*
allgemeine Erklärungsfrist f
  (StR) general due date for filing annual tax return, § 149 I AO
  – filing period
  (ie, within 5 months after the period or date unless otherwise specified)
Allgemeine-Erlang-Verteilung f
  (EDV) Cox distribution
  – general Erlang distribution
  – phase-type distribution
  (syn, Cox-Verteilung, gemischte-Erlangverteilung, allgemeine Phasenverteilung)
allgemeine Geburtenziffer f (Stat) crude birth rate
Allgemeine Geschäftsbedingungen fpl (Re) Standard Terms and Conditions
allgemeine Geschäftskosten pl (com) general business expense *(ie, nontechnical term for ‚administrative overhead')*
allgemeine Havarie f (SeeV) general average
allgemeine Hilfsabteilung f (KoR) general service department
allgemeine Hilfskostenstelle f
  (KoR) general indirect-cost center
  – general service department
  (eg, buildings, heating, welfare facilities)
allgemeine Kapitalgesellschaft f
  (Bw) public(ly held) company
  – publicly held corporation
allgemeine Kostenstelle f
  (KoR) general cost center
  – service department
  (eg, accounting, legal, personnel; opp, production department)

Allgemeine Kreditvereinbarungen *fpl* (IWF) General Agreements to Borrow
Allgemeine Lieferbedingungen *fpl* (com) General Terms and Conditions of Delivery
allgemeine Lohnerhöhung *f* (Pw) across-the-board wage increase
allgemeine Preiserhöhung *f*
  (Vw) general price increase
  (Mk) across-the-board price increase *(ie, affecting all company products)*
Allgemeine Rollfuhrbedingungen *fpl* (com) General Cartage Conditions
allgemeiner Satz *m*
  (Log) strictly universal statement
  – all-statement
  (opp, singulärer Satz)
allgemeiner Term *m* (Math) general term
allgemeiner Überblick *m* (com) broad (*or* general) overview (of)
allgemeines Glied *n* (Math) general term *(ie, of a series)*
allgemeine Sicherheitsrücklage *f* (Vers) contingency reserve
allgemeines Kindergeld *n* (SozV) general children's benefits
allgemeines Lohnniveau *n* (Vw) general wage level
allgemeine Sorgfaltspflicht *f* (Re) common duty of care
allgemeines Preisniveau *n* (Vw) general price level
allgemeines Rechnungswesen *n* (ReW) general accounting
Allgemeines Schuldrecht *n* (Re) general part of the law of obligations, §§ 241–432 BGB
allgemeines Tauschmittel *n* (Vw) general means of exchange
allgemeine Sterbeziffer *f* (Stat) crude death (*or* mortality) rate
allgemeine Steuermeßzahl *f* (StR) general basic rate, § 15 GrStG
allgemeine Steuermittel *pl*
  (FiW) general revenue
  – (infml) public purse (*or* till)
allgemeine Steuern *fpl* (FiW) general (*or* broad-based) taxes
allgemeine Steuersenkung *f* (FiW) general cut in taxes
allgemeines Urteil *n* (Log) universal (proposition)
allgemeines Veräußerungsverbot *n* (Re) general prohibition to sell or otherwise dispose of individual assets, § 106 KO, § 59 VerglO
Allgemeines Wirtschaftsrecht *n* (Re) General Law of the Economy *(ie, juristic basis of economic activities)*
Allgemeines Zoll- und Handelsabkommen *n* (AuW) General Agreement on Tariffs and Trade, GATT
allgemeine Tarifierungs-Vorschriften *fpl* **zum Schema des gemeinsamen Zolltarifs** (EG) Rules for the Interpretation of the Nomenclature of the Common Customs Tariff
allgemeine Unkosten *pl* (com) general expense *(ie, obsolete term for ‚overhead')*
allgemeine Verbrauchsteuer *f* (StR) general consumption tax

Allgemeine Verkaufsbedingungen *fpl* (Re) General (*or* Standard) Conditions of Sale
Allgemeine Versicherungsbedingungen *fpl* (Vers) General Insurance Conditions
allgemeine Volkswirtschaftslehre *f* (Vw) general economics
Allgemeine Vorschriften *fpl* **über die Zollsätze** (Zo) General Rules concerning duties
allgemeine Wirtschaftsdaten *pl* (com) general business statistics
allgemeine Wirtschaftslage *f* (Vw) general business conditions
  – general economic activity
  – state of the economy
allgemeine Zinstendenz *f* (Vw) general interest tendency
Allgemeine Zollordnung *f* (Zo) General Customs Regulations
Allgemeinheit *f*
  (Re) general public
  – public at large
Allgemeinheitsstufe *f* (Log) level of generality (*or* universality)
allgemeinstes Entscheidungsnetzwerk *n* (OR) generalized activity network
allgemein-verneinendes Urteil *n*
  (Log) universal negative
  – E-proposition
Allklasse *f* (Log) universal class
Allokation *f* **der Ressourcen**
  (Vw) resource allocation
  – allocation of resources
Allokationsabteilung *f* (FiW) allocation branch *(Musgrave)*
Allokationseffekt *m* (Vw) allocative effect
Allokationseffizienz *f* (Vw) allocative efficiency
Allokationsfunktion *f* (Vw) allocative function
Allokationsmechanismus *m* (Vw) allocative mechanism
Allonge *f*
  (WeR) allonge
  – rider
  (ie, strip of paper annexed to a bill of exchange, on which to write indorsements for which there is no room left on the instrument itself)
Alloperator *m* (Log) universal quantifier
  (ie, name given to the notation (x) prefixed to a logical formula A (containing the free variable x to express that A holds for all values of x – usu. for all values of x within a certain range)
Allphasen-Brutto-Umsatzsteuer *f* (StR) all-stage gross turnover tax *(ie, abolished on 31 Dec 1967)*
Allphasen-Netto-Umsatzsteuer *f* (StR) all-stage net turnover tax *(ie, value-added tax, or VAT, introduced on 1 Jan 1968)*
Allphasen-Netto-Umsatzsteuer *f* **mit Vorsteuerabzug** (StR) all-stage net turnover tax entitling ‚entrepreneur' to deduct prior turnover tax
Allphasensteuer *f* (FiW) all-stage (turnover) tax
Allsatz *m*
  (Log) strictly universal statement
  – all-statement
Allzweckrechner *m* (EDV) general-purpose computer

al pari

al pari (Fin) at par *(ie, market price of security is equal to its face value)*
alphabetischer Code *m* (EDV) alphabetic code *(syn, Alphacode)*
alphabetischer Locher *m* (EDV) alphabetic punch
alphabetische Sortierung *f* (EDV) = *Alphabetsortierung*
Alphabetprüflocher *m* (EDV) alphabetic verifier
Alphabetsortierung *f* (EDV) alphabetic sort
Alphacode *m* (EDV) alphabetic code
Alphacodierung *f* (EDV) alphabetic coding
alphanumerisch
 (EDV) alphameric
 – (Cobol) alphanumeric
alphanumerische Adresse *f* (EDV) alphameric *(or* alphanumeric) address
alphanumerische Codierung *f* (EDV) alphameric *(or* alphanumeric) coding
alphanumerische Daten *pl* (EDV) alphameric *(or* alphanumeric) data
alphanumerischer Code *m* (EDV) alphameric *(or* alphanumeric) code
alphanumerischer Leser *m* (EDV) alphameric *(or* alphanumeric) reader
alphanumerisches Codesystem *n* (EDV) alphameric *(or* alphanumeric) coding system
alphanumerische Tastatur *f* (EDV) alphanumeric keyboard
als Aufwand verrechnen
 (ReW) to expense
 – to charge against the operations of an accounting period
 – to charge as present operating cost
als Gegenleistung (Re) in return for
als Vertreter (Re) in representative capacity
als Zollwert der Waren anerkennen (Zo) to accept the price as the value of goods for customs purposes
Altbausanierung *f*
 (com) modernizing and refitting older buildings
 (com) area rehabilitation *(ie, als Flächensanierung)*
Altbauwohnungen *fpl* (StR) older homes
alte Aktie *f* (Fin) old share
alteingesessenes Unternehmen *n* (com) old-established business
Altenteil *n* (StR) residential building (or part thereof) used by retired owner of an agricultural enterprise, § 34 III BewG
Altenteiler *m* (StR) retired owner (of an agricultural establishment), § 34 III BewG
älterer Arbeitnehmer *m*
 (Pw) older employee *(or* worker)
 – elderly employee
ältere Erfindung *f* (Pat) prior invention
älteres Patent *n* (Pat) prior patent
Alternative *f*
 (Log) alternative
 – inclusive disjunction
 (EDV) inclusive OR
 (com) alternative *(ie, one or the other of two conditions or courses of action)*
alternative Kosten *pl* (Vw) alternative *(or* opportunity) costs

Alterssicherung

alternative Produktion *f* (IndE) alternative production *(ie, in a multi-product plant where an increase in output of one product reduces the output potential of others)*
alternative Substitution *f* (Bw) alternative substitution
Alternativ-Frage *f*
 (Mk) closed
 – dichotomous
 – alternative ... question
Alternativhypothese *f* (Log) alternative hypothesis *(opp, null hypothesis)*
Alternativklausel *f* (Fin) *(obsolete for:)* Fakultativklausel, qv
Alternativkosten *pl* (Vw) opportunity *(or* alternative) cost *(syn, Opportunitätskosten)*
Alternativlösung *f* (Bw) alternative solution
Alternativplan *m* (Bw) contingency *(or* alternative) plan
Alternativplanung *f* (Bw) contingency *(or* alternative) planning
Alternativprognose *f* (Bw) alternative forecast
Alternativprogramm *n* (Bw) alternative program
Alternativsanierung *f* (Fin) alternative reorganization *(ie, where members of a company may choose between voluntary prorata payments or reduction of par value of their shares)*
Alternativsubstitution *f* (Vw) alternative substitution
Alternativvorschlag *m* (com) alternative suggestion *(or* proposal)
Alternativweg *m* (EDV) alternative route *(ie, secondary route if primary route is unavailable)*
alternierende Gruppe *f* (Math) alternating group
alternierende Reihe *f* (Math) alternating series
Altersaufbau *m*
 (Bw) age ranking of fixed assets *(ie, based on year of acquisition)*
 (Stat) age distribution
 – age pattern
 – age structure
Alterseinkommen *n* (Pw) retirement income
Altersentlastungsbetrag *m* (StR) old age percentage reduction, § 24a EStG *(ie, maximum 40 percent, not exceeding DM 3,000)*
Altersfreibetrag *m* (StR) old-age tax free allowance, § 32 II EStG
Altersgliederung *f* (Stat) age distribution *(or* structure)
Altersgrenze *f*
 (Pw) age limit
 (Pw) retirement age
Altersgruppe *f*
 (com) age group
 (Stat) age cohort
Altershilfe *f* **für Landwirte** (SozV) farmers' old-age pension scheme
Altersprofil *n* (Mk) age profile *(ie, of a product)*
Alterspyramide *f* (Stat) age pyramid
Altersruhegeld *n*
 (Pw) old-age pension
 – retirement pension
 – retired pay
Alterssicherung *f* (SozV) old-age protection

29

altersspezifisch
(Pw) age-specific *(eg, death rate)*
– by age
altersspezifische Sterbeintensität *f* (Vers) force of mortality
altersspezifische Sterbeziffer *f* (Stat) refined death rate
Altersstruktur *f* (Pw) = *Altersaufbau*
Alters- und Hinterbliebenenversorgung *f* (SozV) old age, disabled, and survivors' social security system
Altersverteilung *f* (Bw) age distribution *(ie, of fixed assets)*
altes Ziel *n* (Vw, Bw) long-standing goal
Altgläubiger *m* (Re) assignor *(syn, Abtretender, Zedent)*
Altlastzahlungen *fpl* (FiW) payments to meet restructuring costs run up before the 1969 reorganization of the West German coal industry
Altmaterial *n* (com) scrap
Altmaterialhändler *m* (com) scrap dealer
Altmaterialwert *m* (ReW) scrap *(or* salvage) value
Altpapier *n*
(com) waste paper
(com) paper stock *(ie, raw material or merchandise)*
Altwarenhandel *m* (com) second-hand trade
Aluminiumindustrie *f*
(com) aluminum industry
– (GB) aluminium industry
(ie, this is what is generally called „Leichtmetallindustrie')
Ambivalenzkonflikt *m* (Bw) plus-minus conflict
ambulante Behandlung *f* (SozV) out-patient treatment
ambulanter Handel *m* (com) itinerant selling
ambulantes Gewerbe *n* (com) itinerant trade
amerikanische Buchführung *f* (ReW) columnar *(or* tabular) bookkeeping
Amoroso-Robinson-Relation *f* (Vw) Amoroso-Robinson relation *(ie, between marginal outlay and direct price elasticity)*
Amortisation *f*
(Fin) amortization
– repayment *(ie, gradual extinction of long-term debt according to an agreed plan)*
(Fin) payback
– payoff
– payout *(ie, of investment projects)*
Amortisationsanleihe *f* (Fin) redemption *(or* refunding) loan *(syn, Tilgungsanleihe)*
Amortisationsdauer *f* (Fin) = *Amortisationszeitraum*
Amortisationsfonds *m*
(Fin) amortization
– redemption
– sinking ... fund *(syn, Tilgungsfonds)*
Amortisationshypothek *f* (Fin) redemption mortgage *(ie, debtor repays in equal annual installments; syn, Annuitätenhypothek, Tilgungshypothek)*
Amortisationsmethode *f* (Fin) payback *(or* payoff) analysis *(ie, used in evaluating investment projects)*

Amortisationsplan *m* (Fin) amortization *(or* redemption) schedule
Amortisationsrechnung *f* (Fin) payback (time) method *(ie, in preinvestment analysis)*
Amortisationszeitraum *m*
(Fin) period of amortization *(or* redemption *or* repayment)
(Fin) payback
– payoff
– payout ... period *(ie, in preinvestment analysis)*
amortisierbar
(Fin) amortizable
– repayable
– redeemable
amortisieren
(com) to pay off *(eg, purchase has long paid off)*
(Fin) to amortize *(ie, to retire debt gradually and as planned)*
(Fin) to pay back *(or* off *or* out) *(ie, said of investment projects)*
Amortisierung *f* (Fin) = *Amortisation*
amtlich beglaubigt
(Re) legalized
– officially attested *(or* authenticated)
amtlich bestellter Sachverständiger *m* (com) officially appointed expert
amtlich beurkundet (Re) officially recorded
amtliche Bekanntmachung *f* (Re) official announcement
amtliche Börsennotiz *f* (Bö) official quotation
amtliche Finanzstatistik *f* (FiW) official financial statistics
amtliche Genehmigung *f* (Re) official approval
amtliche Güteprüfung *f* (Stat) government inspection
amtliche Hinterlegungsstelle *f* (Re) official depository
amtlich eingeführte Aktie *f*
(Bö) listed share
– officially quoted share
– share admitted to official stock exchange dealings
amtliche Notierung *f* (Bö) official quotation
amtliche Preisüberwachung *f* (Vw) official price surveillance
amtliche Prognose *f* (Vw) official forecast *(or* prognosis)
amtlicher Börsenmakler *m* (Bö) official stock exchange broker
amtlicher Börsenpreis *m* (Bö) official exchange quotation
amtlicher Devisenkurs *m* (AuW) official foreign exchange quotation
amtlicher Handel *m* (Bö) official dealings *(or* trading)
amtlicher Kurs *m*
(Bö) official rate of exchange
(Bö) official price *(or* quotation)
amtlicher Kursmakler *m* (Bö) official broker
amtlicher Markt *m* (Bö) official market *(ie, for trading in securities)*
amtlicher Sachverständiger *m* (com) officially appointed expert
amtlicher Vordruck *m* (com) official form

amtlicher Wechselkurs *m* (AuW) official exchange rate
amtliches Kursblatt *n* (Bö) official price list
– (GB) Official List
amtliche Statistik *f* (Stat) official statistics
amtliche Vorprüfung *f* (Pat) preliminary search
amtliche Währungsreserven *fpl* (AuW) official reserves
amtliche Wertpapierbörse *f* (Bö) official (*or* recognized) stock exchange
amtlich nicht notierte Werte *mpl* (Bö) unlisted securities
amtlich notiert (Bö) officially listed (*or* quoted)
amtlich notierte Wertpapiere *npl* (Bö) listed (*or* on-board) securities
amtlich vorgeschriebenes Muster *n* (com) officially designated (*or* required) form
amtlich zugelassen (Bö) officially listed (*or* quoted)
amtlich zugelassener Makler *m* (Bö) official broker
Amtsblatt *n* **der Europäischen Gemeinschaften** (EG) Official Journal of the European Community
Amtsbonus *m* (com) advantage of incumbency
Amtsgericht *n* (Re) local first-instance court *(ie, hears cases involving minor offenses or smaller claims)*
Amtshaftungsklage *f* (Re) suit to establish liability of public authorities
Amtshandlung *f* **der Zollbehörden** (Zo) customs operation
Amtshilfe *f* (Re) administrative cooperation
Amtspfleger *m* (Re) official guardian
Amtspflichtsverletzung *f* (Re) breach of official duties by civil (*or* public) servants, § 839 BGB
Amtsplatz *m* (Zo) place where the business of customs offices is usually conducted
Amtsstunden *fpl* (com) authorized (*or* official) hours
Analogdarstellung *f* (EDV) analog representation
Analog-Digital-Umsetzer *m* (EDV) analog-digital converter, ADC
– AD converter
(syn, Analog-Digital-Wandler, AD-Umsetzer, AD-Wandler)
analoge Daten *pl* (EDV) analog data *(opp, digitale Daten)*
analoges Signal *n* (EDV) analog signal
Analogkanal *m* (EDV) analog channel
Analognetz *n* (EDV) analog network
Analogrechner *m* (EDV) analog computer
Analogsichtgerät *n* (EDV) analog display unit
Analyse *f* **der strategischen Lücke des Unternehmens** (Bw) gap analysis
Analyse *f* **der strategischen Mission des Unternehmens** (Bw) mission analysis
Analyse *f* **der strategischen Möglichkeiten des Unternehmens** (Bw) opportunity analysis
Analysenprobe *f* (Stat) test sample
Analysenzertifikat *n* (com) certificate of analysis
analysierende Entscheidungstheorie *f* (Bw) decision analysis
analytische Arbeitsbewertung *f* (IndE) analytic job evaluation (*or* rating)
analytische Definition *f* (Log) lexical definition

analytische Fortsetzung *f* (Math) analytic continuation
analytische Funktion *f* (Math) analytic (*or* regular) function
analytische Geometrie *f* (Math) analytic geometry
analytische Methode *f* **der Arbeitsbewertung** (IndE) analytic job evaluation
analytischer Beweis *m* (Math) analytic proof
analytischer Satz *m* (Log) analytic proposition (*or* statement) *(ie, one in which the predicate concept is included within the subject concept; requires no verification by experience; its sole criterion is the law of contradiction; opp, synthetischer Satz)*
analytische Statistik *f* (Stat) inferential statistics *(syn, induktive, schließende Statistik)*
Anbauten *mpl*
(com) additions to buildings
– attachments to buildings
(opp, detached buildings)
Anbauverfahren *n* (KoR) expense distribution transfer sheet
Anbieter *m*
(com) supplier
(com) bidder
– tenderer *(ie, connoting a formal buying approach)*
(Mk) marketer
Anbieterabsprache *f* (com) collusive bidding (*or* tendering)
anbieter-determinierte Preise *mpl* (Vw) inflexible prices
Anbieter-Einheit *f* (Mk) selling center
Anbieter-Inflation *f* (Vw) supply inflation
Anden-Gruppe *f* (AuW) Andean Group *(ie, members are Bolivia, Colombia, Ecuador, Peru, and Venezuela)*
Andenpakt *m* (AuW) Andean Pact *(ie, successor organization of the Latin American Free Trade Zone)*
an der Börse gehandelt (Bö) traded on the stock exchange
Anderdepot *n* (Fin) third-party security deposit *(ie, securities left to banks for safekeeping by lawyers, public accountants, and trust companies on behalf of their clients)*
andere aktivierte Eigenleistungen *fpl* (ReW) other company-produced additions to plant and equipment
andere Verbindlichkeiten *fpl* (ReW) other undetermined liabilities
Anderkonto *n* (Fin) third-party (*or* trust) account *(ie, held in a bank by trustees on behalf of third-party assets; syn, Treuhandkonto)*
Anderkonten *npl* (Fin) client accounts
Änderung *f* **der Sätze des gemeinsamen Zolltarifs** (EG) modification of duties of the common customs tariff
Änderung *f* **der Unternehmensform** (Re) transformation of legal form of business organization
Änderung *f* **der Vergleichsbasis** (StR) re-basing
Änderung *f* **der Zollsätze** (Zo) alteration of customs duties
Änderung *f* **des Beschäftigungsgrades** (Vw) change in the level of activity

Änderung *f* **des Steuerbescheides** (StR) alteration of tax assessment notice, § 172 AO
Änderungen *fpl* **der Bedarfsstruktur** (Vw) changes in tastes
Änderungen *fpl* **vorbehalten** (com) subject to change without notice
Änderungsgesetz *n* (Re) amending statute
Änderungsband *n*
  (EDV) amendment
  – change
  – updating ... tape
Änderungsdatei *f*
  (EDV) amendment
  – activity
  – change
  – detail
  – transaction ... file
  (syn, Bewegungsdatei, Fortschreibungsdatei)
Änderungsdaten *pl* (EDV) change data
Änderungsdienst *m* (EDV) updating service
Änderungskarte *f* (EDV) patch card *(syn, Korrekturkarte, Patch-Karte)*
Änderungskündigung *f* (Pw) notice of dismissal + offer for re-employment at less favorable terms, §§ 2, 8 KSchG
Änderungsprogramm *n* (EDV) updating program
Änderungsrate *f* (com) rate of change
Änderungsroutine *f* (EDV) = *Änderungsprogramm*
Änderungssatz *m*
  (EDV) amendment
  – change
  – transaction ... record
Änderungsvorschlag *m* (com) proposal for modification *(or* to modify)
andienen
  (com) to tender *(ie, goods)*
  (Fin) to tender *(ie, documents)*
  (SeeV) to advance a claim
aneignen, sich
  (com) to acquire
  (Re) to appropriate
Aneignung *f* (Re) acquisition of ownership by occupancy, § 958 BGB
an ein Zollamt anweisen (Zo) to clear for transit to a customs office
an Erfüllungs Statt (Re) in lieu of performance *(ie, creditor accepts a substituted obligation in lieu of the promised act, § 364 I BGB)*
anerkannter Ausbildungsberuf *m* (Pw) officially recognized training occupation
anerkannter Beleg *m* (ReW) approved voucher
Anerkenntnis *n* (Re) acknowledgment of debt *(ie, takes it out of the Statute of Limitations, § 208 BGB)*
Anerkennungsbedürfnis *n* (Pw) need of recognition
Anerkennungsstreik *m* (Pw) recognition strike
anfallen
  (Fin) to accumulate *(eg, interest)*
  – to accrue
Anfallsberechtigter *m*
  (Re) person having a future interest in income
  – remainderman

Anfängerkurs *m* (Pw) beginning course *(eg, in math)*
anfängliche Unmöglichkeit *f*
  (Re) initial *(or* original) impossibility
  – impossibility ab initio
  – impossibility at the time of making
Anfangsadresse *f* (EDV) starting address
Anfangsauszahlung *f* (Fin) initial investment
Anfangsbelastung *f* (Fin) initial debt service *(ie, including interest and repayment of principal)*
Anfangsbestand *m*
  (ReW) beginning *(or* opening) inventory
  (MaW) level of initial inventory
Anfangsbilanz *f* (ReW) opening balance sheet
Anfangsdividende *f* (Fin) initial dividend
Anfangsereignis *n* (OR) initial event
Anfangsetikett *n* (EDV) header label
Anfangsfehler *m* (EDV) inherited error
Anfangsgehalt *n*
  (Pw) commencing
  – initial
  – starting ... salary
Anfangsgewinne *mpl* (Bö) early gains
Anfangsglied *n* (Math) first term *(ie, of a series or progression = Reihe od Folge)*
Anfangskapital *n*
  (Fin) initial *(or* starting) capital
  – start-up funding
  (Math) initial investment
  – original principal, K_O
Anfangskennsatz *m* (EDV, Cobol) file *(or* header) label
Anfangsknoten *m*
  (Math) initial vertex
  – starting node
Anfangskurs *m*
  (Bö) first quotation
  – opening price
  (ie, for a security quoted in the variable market)
Anfangslohn *m*
  (Pw) starting *(or* entrance) wage
  – hiring *(or* entrance) rate
Anfangsmarke *f*
  (EDV) beginning of information marker
  – load point
Anfangsnotierung *f* (Bö) = *Anfangskurs*
Anfangsrendite *f* (Fin) initial rate of return
Anfangsstadium *n* (com) initial stage
Anfangsverteilung *f* (Math) boundary *(or* initial) distribution
Anfangsverzinsung *f* (Fin) initial coupon
Anfangszeichen *n* (EDV) starting character
anfechtbar
  (Re) contestable
  (Re) avoidable
  (Log) refutable
anfechtbare Behauptung *f* (Log) refutable assertion
anfechtbare Rechtshandlung *f* (Re) voidable transaction *(ie, favoring or discriminating one or more creditors)*
anfechtbarer Vertrag *m* (Re) voidable contract
anfechtbares Rechtsgeschäft *n* (Re) voidable transaction *(or* act-in-the-law)
Anfechtbarkeit *f* (Re) right of avoidance

Anfechtbarkeit f **wegen falscher Übermittlung** (Re) voidability due to incorrect transmission, § 120 BGB
Anfechtbarkeit f **wegen Irrtum** (Re) voidability due to error, § 119 BGB
Anfechtbarkeit f **wegen Täuschung od Drohung** (Re) voidability due to fraud or threat, § 123 BGB
anfechten
  (Re) to challenge
  – to contest *(eg, administrative act)*
  (Re) to avoid
  – to rescind
  – to dispute *(eg, a contract)*
  (Re) to oppose *(eg, a will)*
  (Re) to appeal against *(eg, a judgment)*
Anfechtung f
  (Re) challenge
  – contestation
  (Re) avoidance
  – rescission
  (Re) opposition
  (Re) appeal
Anfechtung f **außerhalb des Konkurses** (Re) avoidance outside of bankruptcy proceedings
Anfechtungsfrist f (Re) period during which right of avoidance can be exercised, § 124 BGB
Anfechtungsgegner m (Re) party subject to avoidance
  – opposing party, § 143 BGB
Anfechtungsklage f
  (Re, *general*) action for annulment
  (Re) action for the invalidation of a contract *(= im Schuldrecht)*
  (Re) action to set aside a conveyance *(= im Grundstücksrecht)*
  (Pat) interference proceedings
  (StR) action to contest an administrative decision, § 40 I FGO
  – complaint directed at the extinction or modification of an administrative act
Anfechtungsklausel f (Re) avoidance clause
Anforderung f
  (EDV) intervention required
  – request
Anforderungsbetrieb m (EDV) contention mode
Anforderungsdefinition f
  (EDV) requirements definition
  (syn, Aufgabendefinition, Bedarfsbeschreibung)
Anforderungsprofil n (Pw) job specification
Angaben fpl
  (com) details
  – particulars
  – statement
Angaben fpl **über den Zollwert** (Zo) particulars relating to the value of goods for customs purposes
Angabe f **von Ankaufs- und Verkaufskurs** (Bö) double-barrelled quotation
Angebot n
  (com) offer
  – quotation
  – quote
  – proposal *(ie, general terms)*
  (com) bid

– tender *(ie, terms in contract awarding)*
(Re) offer *(syn, Offerte)*
(Vw) supply *(opp, Nachfrage = demand)*
Angebot n **einholen**
(com) to obtain an offer
– to send out requests for quotations
Angebot n **einreichen** (com) to put out *(or* submit) a proposal
Angebot n **geht ein** (com) bid is received
Angebot n **ohne Festpreis** (com) subject bid
Angebotsabgabe f (com) tendering
Angebotsanalyse f (com) comparative evaluation sheet *(ie, in bid analysis)*
Angebotsänderung f
  (com) change in supply
  (Vw) shift in supply
Angebotsbearbeiter m (com) proposal writer
Angebotsbedingungen fpl (com) terms of a bid
Angebotsdruck m (Bö) selling pressure
Angebotseinholung f (com) request to submit offer
angebotselastisch (Bw) supply elastic *(eg, plant)*
Angebotselastizität f
  (Vw) elasticity of supply
  – supply elasticity
Angebotseröffnung f
  (com) bid opening
  – opening of tenders
Angebotsformular n (com) bid form
Angebotsfunktion f (Vw) supply function
Angebotsgarantie f (com) tender guaranty *(or* bond)
Angebotsgesetz n (Vw) law of supply
angebotsinduzierte Rezession f (Vw) supply induced recession
Angebotsinflation f (Vw) sellers' *(or* supply push) inflation
Angebotskalkulation f (com) cost estimating *(ie, on which supply offer is based)*
Angebotskurve f (Vw) supply curve
Angebotslücke f (com) supply gap
Angebotsmenge f (Vw) quantity supplied
angebotsorientierte Wirtschaftspolitik f
  (Vw) supply-oriented economic policy
  – (US) supply side economics
Angebotspalette f (com) range of goods *(and/or* services) offered
Angebotspreis m
  (com) offer price
  – bid price
  – quoted price
  – quotation
  – price stated in bid *(or* tender)
  – supply price
angebotsstarr (Bw) supply inelastic *(eg, plant)*
Angebotstabelle f (Vw) supply schedule
Angebotsüberhang m (Vw) = *Angebotsüberschuß*
  (Bö) sellers over
  – surplus of selling orders
Angebotsüberschuß m
  (Vw) excess (in) supply
  – excess of supply over demand
  – surplus offers
Angebotsunterlagen fpl (com) tender documents
Angebotsverschiebung f (Vw) shift in supply
Angebotszeichnungen fpl (com) proposal drawings

Angebot n und Annahme f (Re) offer and acceptance *(ie, in contract law)*
Angebot n **und Nachfrage** f (Vw) supply and demand
Angebot n **verwerfen** (com) to reject an offer *(or bid)*
Angebot n **vorlegen** (com) to submit an offer *(or bid)*
Angebot n **zurückziehen** (com) to withdraw a bid
angefochtener Verwaltungsakt m (StR) contested administrative action, § 40 FGO
angegliedertes Unternehmen n (Bw) affiliated *(or associated)* enterprise
angekündigter Bezugspreis m (Mk) advertised price
Angeld n (Re) earnest money *(syn, Draufgabe)*
angelernte Arbeitskräfte fpl (Pw) semi-skilled labor
angemessene Entschädigung f
(com) fair and reasonable compensation
(Re) just compensation *(eg, payable under condemnation proceedings = Enteignungsverfahren)*
angemessene Frist f (Re) reasonable time
angemessene Frist f **setzen** (com) to set a reasonable period of time
angemessene Gegenleistung f (Re) fair and reasonable consideration
angemessene Kündigungsfrist f (Re) reasonable notice
angemessener Marktpreis m (com) fair market value
angemessener Preis m (com) reasonable *(or bona fide)* price
angemessener Schadenersatz m (Re) fair damages
angemessener Wert m (ReW) fair value
angemessene Sorgfalt f (Re) reasonable care and skill
angemessenes Wachstum n (Vw) adequate rate of growth
angemessene Vergütung f (com) reasonable compensation
angemessene Verzinsung f (Fin) fair rate of return
angemessen reagieren (com) to respond adequately
angenommene Lieferung f (Stat) accepted lot (of goods)
angenommener Totalverlust m (SeeV) constructive total loss
angepaßte Stichprobe f (Stat) balanced sample
angepeiltes Wachstumsziel n (Vw) targeted growth rate
angeschlossene Bank f (Fin) affiliated bank
angeschlossenes Unternehmen n (Bw) = *angegliedertes Unternehmen*
angeschmutzte Ware f (com) shop-soiled goods
angespannte Finanzlage f (Fin) situation of strained resources
angespannte Haushaltslage f
(FiW) tight budget situation
– strained budget
angespannte Liquiditätslage f (Fin) tight liquidity position
angespannter Arbeitsmarkt m (Vw) tight labor market

angesparte Eigenmittel pl (Fin) personal resources saved
Angestelltenversicherung f (SozV) salary earners' pension insurance
Angestellter m
(Pw) nonmanual employee
– salaried employee
– salary *(or office)* worker
– (infml) white-collar worker
angestrebte Kapitalverzinsung f (Fin) target rate of return
angestrebte Mindestverzinsung f (Fin) required rate of return *(ie, in investment analysis)*
angestrebter Preis m (Mk) target price
angestrebtes Zielausmaß n (Bw) targeted goal accomplishment
angewandte Forschung f (com) applied research
angewandte Mathematik f (Math) applied mathematics
angewandte Statistik f (Stat) applied statistics
angewandte Wirtschaftsforschung f (Vw) applied economic research
Angleichung f **von Zollsätzen** (Zo) adjustment *(or alignment)* of tariff rates
angliedern (Bw) to affiliate (to)
Angliederungsfinanzierung f (Fin) procurement of funds to finance a holding in, or the acquisition of, another company
angrenzende Küstenstaaten mpl (Re) adjoining coastal States
Angstkäufe mpl
(com) panic buying *(or purchasing)*
– scare buying
Angstklausel f (WeR) no-recourse clause
Angstverkäufe mpl (Bö) panic selling
anhaltend
(com) persistent
– sustained
anhaltende Kurserholung f (Bö) sustained rally
anhaltende Nachfrage f (com) persistent demand
anhaltende Nachfrageschwäche f (com) persistent weakness of demand
anhaltender Umschwung m (com) sustained reversal *(eg, in current transactions)*
Anhalten n **der Ware auf dem Transport** (Re) stoppage in transit *(see: Verfolgungsrecht)*
anhaltendes Exportwachstum n (Vw) sustained growth of exports
Anhaltepunkt m
(EDV) checkpoint
– conditional breakpoint *(syn, Fixpunkt)*
Anhang m
(com) appendix
(ReW, EG) notes to the accounts
(WeR) alonge
– rider
(Re) codicil *(ie, supplement to a will)*
Anhang m **zum Konzernabschluß** (ReW) notes to the consolidated accounts
Anhängekalkulation f (KoR) cost estimate in which bases are not corrected if direct costs have changed
anhängiges Verfahren n
(Re) proceeding pending before a court
– lis pendens

anheben
(com) to raise *(eg, prices)*
– to increase
– to lift
(Bö) to mark up
anheuern (Pw) to sign up *(ie, as a sailor)*
Anhörung *f* (com) hearing
an Inhaber (WeR) payable to bearer
Ankauf *m* (com) acquisition (*or* purchase) of goods in bulk, or of objects of value *(ie, securities, precious metals, real estate)*
ankaufen
(com) to buy goods in bulk or objects of value *(eg, shares, grain)*
(Fin) to negotiate *(eg, a draft)*
Ankäufer *m*
(com) buyer
– purchaser
Ankaufermächtigung *f*
(com) authority to buy *(on behalf of a third party)*
(AuW) authority to pay (*or* to purchase)
(Fin) order to negotiate *(ie, Form des Negoziierungskredits)*
Ankaufskurs *m* (Bö) buying rate *(ie, of foreign exchange)*
Ankaufspreis *m*
(com) buying-in price
(EG) intervention price *(ie, minimum price in EC farm policy)*
Ankaufsrecht *n*
(Re) right to acquire *(ie, nonlegal ambiguous term:)*
– unilateral offer for contract of sale held open for limited period of time
– preliminary agreement giving right to specific contract offer
– contract of sale subject to condition precedent that party entitled will use its rights
Ankaufssatz *m* (Bö) check price
(Bö) = *Ankaufskurs*
Ankergebühr *f* (com) anchorage
ankommen bei (com, infml) to go down well with *(eg, product)*
ankreuzen
(com) „please check in appropriate space"
– to mark
Ankündigungseffekt *m* (Vw, FiW) announcement effect
Ankündigungsschreiben *n* (com) announcement letter
Ankunftsrate *f* (OR) arrival rate
Ankunftszeit *f* (OR) arrival time
ankurbeln
(Vw) to boost *(ie, the economy)*
– to stimulate *(ie, economic activity)*
(Vw, infml) to pep up
– to give a shot in the arm
Ankurbelung *f* (Vw) pump priming *(ie, of the economy by public sector spending)*
Ankurbelungsmaßnahmen *fpl* (Vw) pump priming measures *(ie, to boost or pep up the economy)*
Ankurbelungspolitik *f* (Vw) reflationary policy

Anlage *f*
(IndE) plant
(Fin) investment
Anlageberater *m*
(Fin) investment adviser
– investment consultant
– investment counsel
– investment counselor
Anlageberatung *f* (Fin) investment counseling
anlagebereite Mittel *pl*
(Fin) idle balances (*or* funds) seeking investment
Anlagebereitschaft *f*
(Fin) readiness
– willingness
– propensity . . . to invest
Anlagebetrag *m* (Fin) amount invested
Anlagebewertung *f*
(ReW) fixed asset valuation
(Fin) evaluation of securities
(Fin) investment appraisal (*or* rating)
Anlagebuchhaltung *f* (ReW) plant records
– fixed-asset accounting
Anlagechance *f* (Fin) investment outlet (*or* opportunity)
Anlagedeckungsgrad *m* (Bw) fixed-assets-to-net-worth ratio
Anlagedispositionen *fpl* (Fin) investment decisions
Anlageerträge *mpl* (Fin) investment income
Anlagefinanzierung *f* (Fin) investment financing
Anlageformen *fpl* (Fin) investment vehicles
Anlagegegenstand *m*
(ReW) fixed asset
(Bw) capital asset
Anlagegruppen-Ersatzpolitik *f* (Bw) group replacement policy
Anlagegüter *npl*
(Bw) capital assets
– (fixed) capital goods
Anlagegut *n* **mit begrenzter Nutzungsdauer** (Bw) limited-life asset
Anlageinstrument *n* (Fin) investment asset
Anlageinvestitionen *fpl*
(VGR) gross fixed capital formation
(VGR) business capital spending
– fixed asset investment
– business outlay for plant and equipment
– private investment in plant and equipment
(Bw) capital equipment spending
– capital investment
– expenditures for plant and equipment
– outlays for fixed asset investment
Anlageinvestitionen *fpl* **des Unternehmensbereichs**
(VGR) business fixed investment
Anlageinvestitionsgüter *npl*
(Bw) capital
– investment
– industrial
– equipment . . . goods
Anlage *f* **in Wertpapieren** (Fin) paper investment *(opp, gold)*
Anlagekapital *n* (Bw) fixed (*or* capital) assets *(ie, nontechnical term for ‚Anlagevermögen')*
Anlagekäufe *mpl* (Fin) portfolio buying
Anlagekäufe *mpl* **des Publikums** (Fin) public investment buying

35

Anlagekonten *npl* (ReW) fixed-asset and investment accounts
Anlagekonto *n* (ReW) fixed-asset account
Anlagekonto *n* **im Investmentgeschäft** (Fin) open account
Anlagekredit *m* (Fin) investment credit *(ie, long-term borrowed capital used for financing production plant)*
Anlagemöglichkeiten *fpl*
  (Fin) investment outlet (*or* opportunities)
  – outlet for funds
Anlagen *fpl*
  (IndE) plants
  (ReW) fixed assets
  (Fin) investments
Anlagenabgänge *mpl*
  (Bw) fixed assets retirements
  – deductions during period
  – disposals during period
Anlagenausmusterung *f* (Bw) retirement of fixed assets (*or* plant and equipment) *(ie, removal from service)*
Anlagenbau *m* (IndE) plant engineering and construction
Anlagenbauer *m* (IndE) plant and equipment maker
Anlagenbeurteilung *f* (EDV) system evaluation
Anlagenbewertung *f* (ReW) fixed asset appraisal (*or* valuation)
Anlagenbuchhaltung *f*
  (ReW) fixed-asset accounting
  (ReW) fixed-asset accounting department *(= für Sachanlagen)*
  (ReW) investment accounting department *(= für Finanzanlagen)*
Anlagendeckung *f*
  (Fin) equity-to-fixed assets ratio
  – ratio of equity capital to fixed assets
Anlagenerneuerung *f*
  (Bw) renewal of plant and equipment
  – replacement investment
Anlagenfinanzierung *f*
  (Fin) plant and equipment financing
  – investment financing
  – provision of finance for renewed or expanded plant facilities
Anlagengeschäft *n* (com) systems business *(eg, ‚Großanlagenbau‘ covered by major contracts)*
Anlagen *fpl* **im Bau**
  (ReW) plant under construction
  (ReW, EG) tangible assets in course of construction
Anlagenintensität *f* (Bw) capitalization ratio *(ie, fixed assets to total assets)*
anlagenintensiv (Bw) capital intensive *(ie, production in which substantial use is made of fixed assets)*
anlageninterne Codierung *f* (EDV) absolute (*or* specific) coding *(syn, Maschinencodierung, maschineninterne Codierung)*
anlageninterner Code *m* (EDV) absolute (*or* specific) code *(syn, Maschinencode)*
Anlagenkartei *f*
  (ReW) fixed-asset card file

  – plant ledger
  – unit asset records
Anlagenkonfiguration *f* (EDV) system (*or* hardware) configuration
Anlagenkonto *n*
  (ReW) fixed asset account *(Sachanlagen)*
  (ReW) investment account *(Finanzanlagen)*
Anlagen *fpl* **Kraft, Licht, Heizung** (ReW) installations for power, light and heating
Anlagen-Marketing *n* (Mk) industrial marketing
Anlagennachweis *m* (ReW) fixed asset inventory
Anlagenorganisation *f* (Bw) product-group-oriented structure (of a company)
Anlagenplanung *f* (Bw) planning for industrial installations
Anlagenrechnung *f* (ReW) fixed-asset accounting
Anlagenstatistik *f* (Bw) fixed-assets statistics
Anlagenüberträge *mpl* (ReW) fixed-asset transfers
Anlagen *fpl* **umbuchen** (ReW) to reclassify fixed assets
Anlagenumbuchungen *fpl* (ReW) reclassification of fixed assets
Anlagen *fpl* **umschichten** (Fin) to regroup investments
Anlagen-Umschichtung *f* (Fin) regrouping of investments
Anlagenvergleich *m* (EDV) system comparison
Anlagenwirtschaft *f* (Bw) fixed-asset management
Anlagenzugänge *mpl*
  (ReW) asset additions *(ie, Sachanlagen)*
  – addition of fixed asset units
  – additions to plant and equipment
  – additions to capital account
  (ReW) additions to capital investments *(ie, Finanzanlagen)*
Anlagenpalette *f* (Fin) range of investment vehicles
Anlagepapiere *npl* (Fin) investment securities
Anlageplanung *f* (IndE) plant layout and design
Anlagepolitik *f* (Fin) investment management policy
Anlagepublikum *n*
  (Fin) investing public
  (Bö) buying public
Anlagerisiko *n* (Fin) investment risk
Anlagespezialist *m* (Fin) investment specialist
Anlagespiegel *m*
  (ReW) fixed-asset transactions statement
  – six-column statement
  (ie, itemizing additions and disposals, appreciations, annual depreciation, and reposting of fixed and financial assets, § 152 I 2 AktG; syn, Sechsspaltenausweis)
Anlagestreuung *f* (Fin) investment diversification
anlagesuchendes Publikum *n* (Fin) investing public
Anlage *f* **umrüsten** (IndE) to refit plant
Anlage- und Ausrüstungsinvestitionen *fpl* (VGR) business investment in plant and equipment
Anlagevermögen *n* (ReW) fixed assets *(ie, intended for use on a continuing basis for the purpose of an undertaking's activities)*
Anlagevermögen *n* **zum Anschaffungswert** (ReW) fixed assets at cost
Anlagevermögen *n* **zum Nettobuchwert** (ReW) fixed assets valued at net book value
Anlagevolumen *n* (Fin) volume of assets invested

Anlagewagnis *n*
(ReW) depreciation risk *(ie, risk of premature retirement or loss of fixed assets, due to obsolescence and other factors; eg, fire)*
(Fin) investment risk
Anlagewagniskonto *n* (ReW) depreciation risk account
Anlagewährung *f* (AuW) investment currency
Anlageziel *n* (Fin) investment goal
Anlanden *n* (com) landing
Anlandevertreter *m* (com) landing agent *(ie, of a shipping company)*
Anlaufen *n*
(com) phase-in *(eg, programs, projects)*
(IndE) starting
– startup
– launching
– breaking-in *(eg, of machine)*
Anlaufhafen *m* (com) port of call
Anlaufkosten *pl*
(ReW) starting cost
– starting-load cost
– start-up cost *(or expense)*
– launching cost
– pre-operating expense
(KoR) breaking-in cost *(eg, of machine)*
Anlaufperiode *f* **der Entwicklung** (Vw) takeoff period
Anlaufphase *f* (com) start-up phase
Anlaufschritt *m* (EDV) start element
Anlaufverluste *mpl* (ReW) startup losses
Anlaufzeit *f*
(com) phase-in period
(IndE) break-in period
– start-up period
– launching period
anlegen
(com, infml) to spend
(Fin) to invest
Anleger *m* (Fin) investor
Anlegerinteresse *n* (Fin) buying interest
Anlegerpublikum *n* (Fin) = *Anlagepublikum*
Anlegerrisiko *n* (Bö) investor's risk
Anlehnungsmodell *n* (Fin) rescue model
Anleihe *f*
(Fin) loan *(ie, large-scale long-term borrowing on the capital market against the issue of fixed-interest bearer bonds = Inhaberschuldverschreibungen)*
(Fin) bond issue
– bonds
Anleiheablösung *f* (Fin) redemption of a loan
Anleiheagio *n*
(Fin) bond *(or* loan) premium
– premium on bonds
Anleihe *f* **auflegen**
(Fin) to launch a bond offering
– to float a bond issue
– to float a loan
– to offer bonds for subscription
Anleihe *f* **aufnehmen** (Fin) to contract *(or* raise) a loan
Anleiheausstattung *f*
(Fin) terms of a loan
– bond features

Anleihe *f* **bedienen** (Fin) to service a loan
Anleihebedingungen *fpl* (Fin) loan terms
Anleihe *f* **begeben** (Fin) = *Anleihe auflegen*
Anleihedienst *m* (Fin) loan debt service
Anleihedisagio *n*
(Fin) discount on bonds
– (GB) debenture discount
Anleiheemission *f* (Fin) bond issue
Anleihe-Emissionsagio *n* (Fin) bond *(or* loan) premium
Anleihe *f* **emittieren** (Fin) to float a bond issue
Anleiheerlös *m*
(Fin) bond yield
– loan proceeds
– avail
– (GB) debenture capital
Anleihefinanzierung *f* (Fin) bond financing
Anleihegeschäft *n* (Fin) bond issue operations
Anleihegläubiger *m* (Fin) bond creditor *(or* holder)
Anleiheinhaber *m* (Fin) bondholder
Anleihekapital *n* (Fin) bond *(or* loan) capital
Anleihekonsortium *n* (Fin) bond *(or* loan) syndicate
Anleihekonversion *f* (Fin) bond conversion
Anleihekosten *pl* (Fin) bond issue costs
Anleihekündigung *f* (Fin) call-in of a loan
Anleihekupon *m* (Fin) bond coupon
Anleihekurs *m* (Fin) loan quotation
Anleihelaufzeit *f* (Fin) term of a loan
Anleihemantel *m* (Fin) bond certificate
Anleihemarkt *m* (Fin) bond market
Anleihe *f* **mit Endfälligkeit** (Fin) bullet maturity issue
Anleihe *f* **mit Optionsscheinen** (Fin) bond with warrants
Anleihe *f* **mit Umtauschrecht** (Fin) convertible bond
Anleihe *f* **mit variabler Verzinsung** *f*
(Fin) floater
– floating rate note
(eg, minimum rate 7 per cent + ¼ pct over 6-months Libor)
Anleihe *f* **mit Zinseinschluß im Kurs** (Fin) flat bond
Anleihemodalitäten *fpl* (Fin) = *Anleiheausstattung*
Anleihen *fpl,* **davon konvertibel** (ReW, EG) debenture loans, showing convertible loans separately
Anleihen *fpl* **der öffentlichen Hand** (Fin) public bonds
Anleihen *fpl* **ohne Zinssatz** (Fin) zero bonds *(ie, mostly much below par, medium term)*
Anleihepolitik *f* (Fin) loan issue policy
Anleiheportefeuille *n* (Fin) bond portfolio
Anleiherechnung *f* (Math) bond mathematics
Anleiherendite *f* (Fin) loan *(or* bond) yield
Anleiherückzahlung *f* (Fin) bond redemption
Anleiheschuld *f* (Fin) loan *(or* bonded) debt
Anleiheschuldner *m* (Fin) loan debtor
Anleiheschuldverschreibung *f* (WeR) bond made out to order
Anleihestückelung *f* (Fin) bond denomination
Anleihe *f* **tilgen** (Fin) to redeem *(or* repay) a loan
Anleihetilgung *f* (Fin) loan redemption
Anleihetilgungsfonds *m* (Fin) sinking fund

Anleiheübernahmekonsortium *n* (Fin) underwriting syndicate
Anleiheumlauf *m* (Fin) bonds outstanding
Anleiheumschuldung *f* (Fin) rescheduling of a loan
Anleihe *f* **unterbringen** (Fin) to place a loan
Anleiheunterbringung *f* (Fin) placing of a loan
Anleiheverbindlichkeiten *fpl* (Fin) bonded debt (*or* indebtedness)
Anleihevertrag *m* (Fin) loan agreement
Anleiheverzinsung *f* (Fin) loan interest
Anleihezeichner *m* (Fin) loan subscriber
Anleihezeichnungskurs *m* (Fin) loan subscription price
Anleihezinssatz *m* (Fin) loan interest rate
Anleihezuteilung *f* (Fin) loan allotment
Anlernling *m* (Pw) trainee *(ie, in a semi-apprenticeship)*
anliefern (com) to deliver
Anlieferung *f* (com) delivery
Anlieferungszeit *f* (EDV) response time
Anlieger *m* (Re) abutting owner
Anliegerbeitrag *m* (FiW) = *Erschließungsbeitrag*
Anliegerstaat *m* (Re) bordering state
Anlocken *n* **von Kunden** (Kart) baiting of customers *(eg, by unsolicited consignments, leading articles, bait and switch advertising)*
Anmeldedatum *n*
 (com) date of application
 (Pat) filing date of application
Anmeldeformular *n*
 (com) application form (*or* blank)
 – registration form
Anmeldefrist *f*
 (com) time limited for application (*or* registration)
 (Pat) filing period
Anmeldegebühr *f*
 (com) application (*or* registration) fee
 (Pat) application (*or* filing) fee
Anmeldekartell *n* (Kart) application cartel *(ie, effective upon application submitted to the Federal Cartel Office, § 5 I GWB)*
anmelden
 (com) to apply for
 (Zo) to declare *(ie, goods for duty)*
 (Re) to file for registration
 – to register
 (Re) to advance *(ie, a claim)*
 – to lodge
 – to put forward
 – to submit
 (Pat) to file *(ie, a patent application)*
 (EDV) to sign on
 – to log in
Anmeldepflicht *f* (Re) legal obligation to register *(ie, with a public authority)*
anmeldepflichtig
 (Kart) notifiable
 – subject to notification
 – subject to filing requirement
anmeldepflichtige Waren *fpl* (Zo) goods to declare
anmeldepflichtiges Gewerbe *n* (Re) business (*or* trade) subject to registration
Anmelder *m*
 (com) applicant

(Re) declarant *(ie, person making a declaration or statement)*
(Pat) applicant
Anmeldeschluß *m*
 (com) closing date
 – deadline
 – final deadline
 – time limit for application
Anmeldestelle *f* (com) filing (*or* registration) office
Anmeldesystem *n* (Pat) registration system, § 3 PatG *(opp, Prüfsystem = pre-examination system as used in the U.S.)*
Anmeldetermin *m*
 (com) time fixed for application (*or* registration)
 (Pat) latest filing date
Anmeldeunterlagen *fpl*
 (com) application (*or* registration) documents
 (Pat) application documents (*or* papers)
Anmeldeverfahren *n*
 (com) application procedure
 (Pat) patent application proceedings
Anmeldevordruck *m*
 (com) registration form
 (SeeV) declaration form
Anmeldevorschriften *fpl* (Pat) application requirements
Anmeldung *f*
 (com) application
 (Re) (filing for) registration
 (Re) registry *(ie, place where register is kept)*
 (Re) advancement *(ie, of a claim)*
 – lodgment
 – putting forward
 – submission
 (Pat) patent application
 (Kart) notification of cartel, § 9 II GWB
Anmeldung *f* **bei der Ankunft des Schiffes** (Zo) ship's arrival declaration
Anmeldung *f* **der Gesellschaft** (Re) application to record the company, § 36 AktG
Anmeldung *f* **der Ladung** (Zo) freight declaration
Anmeldung *f* **der Waren(ausfuhr)** (Zo) goods declaration (outwards)
Anmeldung *f* **der Waren(einfuhr)**
 (Zo) goods declaration (inwards)
 – (GB) entry of goods (on importation)
Anmeldung *f* **des Schiffes (Einfuhr)** (Zo) declaration of ship's particulars (inwards)
Anmeldung *f* **e–s ausgeschiedenen Teiles e–r Anmeldung** (Pat) divisional application
Anmeldung *f* **in e–m Verbandsland** (Pat) Convention application
Anmeldung *f* **nach Zusammenschluß** (Kart) post-merger notification, § 23 I GWB
Anmeldung *f* **offenlegen** (Pat) to disclose a patent application
Anmeldungsstau *m* (Pat) backlog of pending applications
Anmeldung *f* **von Kartellen** (Kart) notification of cartels
Anmeldung *f* **von Transporten** (Vers) declaration of consignments
Anmeldung *f* **vor Zusammenschluß** (Kart) pre-merger notification, § 24a I GWB

Anmeldung f zum gemeinschaftlichen Versandverfahren (EG) declaration for Community transit
Anmeldung f zurückweisen (Pat) to refuse a patent application
Annäherung f (Math) approximation
Annäherungskurs m (Bö) approximate price
Annahme f
 (com) acceptance *(eg, goods, orders)*
 – receipt
 (Log) assumption
 – supposition
 (Stat) acceptance *(ie, of submitted lots of goods in quality control)*
 (Re) acceptance *(ie, following offer by contracting party)*
 (Re) passage *(ie, enactment of bill into law)*
 (WeR) acceptance *(ie, promise to pay by the drawee of a bill of exchange)*
Annahme f an Erfüllungs Statt (Re) acceptance in lieu of performance
Annahmebereich m (Stat) accept(ance) region
Annahmebestätigung f (com) acknowledgment of receipt
Annahme f erfüllungshalber (Re) acceptance on account of performance
Annahmeerklärung f (Re) declaration of acceptance
Annahme f e–r nicht geschuldeten Leistung (Re) substituted mode of performance *(ie, in lieu of + on account of performance)*
Annahmefrist f
 (com) time stated for acceptance
 (Re) time within which offer must be accepted, § 147 BGB
Annahmefrist f setzen (com) to limit the time for acceptance
Abnahmegrenze f
 (Stat) acceptance boundary
 – acceptable quality level, AQL
Annahmekennlinie f (Stat) operating characteristic
Annahmekontrolle f durch Stichproben (Stat) lot acceptance sampling
Annahmelinie f (Stat) acceptance line
Annahmelos n (Stat) acceptance lot
Annahmepflicht f
 (com) duty to accept *(or to take delivery) (ie, of merchandise tendered)*
 (Vers) obligation to accept application for insurance cover
Annahmeprüfung f (Stat) acceptance inspection
Annahmerichtzahl f (Stat) acceptance number
Annahme-Stichprobenplan m (Stat) acceptance sampling plan
Annahmevermerk m (com) note of acceptance
Annahme f verweigern
 (com) to refuse to accept
 – to refuse to take delivery
 (Re) to refuse acceptance
Annahmeverweigerung f
 (com, Re) refusal to accept
 – refusal of acceptance
 – nonacceptance
Annahmeverzug m
 (Re) default in acceptance, § 373 HGB

– default in accepting the delivery of goods
– *(civil law)* mora accipiendi
Annahmewahrscheinlichkeit f (Stat) probability of acceptance
Annahmezahl f (Stat) acceptance number
annehmbare Qualitätslage f (Stat) acceptable quality level, AQL
annehmbarer Preis m (com) reasonable (*or* acceptable) price
annehmen
 (com) to accept *(eg, goods, orders)*
 – to receive
 (Re) to accept *(ie, an offer for contract)*
 (Re) to pass *(ie, a bill)*
 (WeR) to accept *(ie, a bill of exchange)*
 (Stat) to accept
 (Log) to assume
 – to suppose
 – to proceed on the assumption
 (Math) to take on *(eg, variables . . . integer values or whole numbers)*
Annehmer m (WeR) acceptor *(syn, Akzeptant; same as drawee = Bezogener od Trassat)*
Annonce f (Mk) advertisement *(syn, Anzeige)*
Annoncenexpedition f
 (Mk) advertising agency (*or* office)
 – space buyer
Annotation f (EDV) annotation *(ie, explanatory notes in flowcharting)*
Annuität f
 (Fin) annuity *(ie, income payable at stated intervals; syn, Zeitrente)*
 (Fin) regular annual payment *(ie, covering interest and repayment of principal)*
Annuitätenanleihe f (Fin) perpetual bond
Annuitätendarlehen n (Fin) annuity loan *(ie, repayable by annuities made up of interest plus repayment)*
Annuitätenhypothek f (Fin) redemption mortgage *(ie, debtor repays in equal annual installments; syn, Tilgungshypothek, Amortisationshypothek)*
Annuitätsmethode f (Fin) annuity method *(ie, of preinvestment analysis)*
annullieren
 (com) to cancel *(eg, an order)*
 (Re) to avoid
 – to declare null and void
 – to rescind
 (Re) to set aside *(eg, a judgment)*
Annullierung f
 (com) cancellation
 (Re) avoidance
 – annulment
 – rescission
 (Re) setting aside
anomale Angebotskurve f (Vw) backward bending supply curve
anomale Nachfragekurve f (Vw) backward bending demand curve
Anomalie f
 (Math) azimuth
 – polar angle *(ie, in the polar coordinate system)*
anonymer Aktienbesitz m (Fin) nominal holdings *(ie, through straw men, often in preparation of a takeover)*

anonymes Sparen *n* (Fin) anonymous saving *(ie, by holder of passbook unknown to bank, not allowed in West Germany, § 154 I AO)*
an Order (WeR) to order
an Order ausstellen (WeR) to make out to order
Anordnung *f* (Math, Stat) array *(ie, generic term = Sammelbegriff covering rows and columns)*
Anordnungsmaßzahl *f* (Stat) order statistic
Anordnungspatent *n* (Pat) arrangement patent
Anordnungstest *m* (Stat) order test
anormale Häufigkeitskurve *f* (Stat) abnormal frequency curve
anpassen
   (com) to adjust *(eg, figures in the light of changing circumstances)*
   (Bw) to shape *(eg, business to prevailing economic conditions)*
Anpassung *f* (com) adjustment *(eg, of plant to cyclical conditions)*
Anpassung *f* **der Trendlinie an den Kurvenverlauf** (Stat) fitting the trendline
Anpassungsbeihilfe *f* (FiW) adjustment assistance *(or* aid*)*
Anpassungsbereitschaft *f* (Pw) willingness to adapt *(eg, to changing conditions)*
Anpassungsdarlehen *n* (Fin) adjustment loan
Anpassungsfähigkeit *f* (Pw) action flexibility
Anpassungshilfe *f* (Vw) financial assistance to enterprises or industries to facilitate their adaptation to new economic conditions
Anpassungsinflation *f* (Vw) adjustment inflation
Anpassungsinvestition *f* (Fin) rationalization investment *(ie, to bring plant in line with changed conditions)*
Anpassungsmaßnahme *f* (com) adjustment measure
Anpassungsperiode *f* (Vw) period of adjustment
Anpassungsprozeß *m* (Vw) adjustment process
Anpassungstransaktionen *fpl* (AuW) settling transactions
Anrainerstaat *m* (Re) littoral state *(ie, in Sea Law)*
anrechenbar (com, StR) creditable
anrechenbarer Betrag *m* (StR) creditable amount
anrechenbare Steuer *f* (StR) creditable tax
anrechnen
   (com) to credit against
   – to offset
   (com) to count against *(eg, a quota)*
Anrechnung *f*
   (Re) mode of appropriation, § 367 BGB
   (StR) imputation
Anrechnung *f* **auf mehrere Schulden** (Re) appropriation of performance where several obligations are outstanding
Anrechnung *f* **ausländischer Steuern** (StR) foreign tax credit
Anrechnung *f* **gezahlter Steuern** (StR) tax credit
anrechnungsberechtigt (StR) entitled to imputation credit
anrechnungsberechtigter Anteilseigner *m* (StR) shareholder entitled to an imputation credit
anrechnungsfähiges Jahr *n* (SozV) year of coverage
anrechnungsfähige Versicherungsjahre *npl* (SozV) eligible insured years

Anrechnungsverfahren *n*
   (StR) imputation system *(ie, in corporate income tax law; opp, split rate system)*
   (StR) tax credit system *(ie, applicable to foreign taxes)*
Anrechnungswert *m* (com) accepted value
Anrechnungszeitraum *m* (StR) tax credit period
Anrechtsschein *m* (WeR) intermediate share certificate
Anrede *f* (com) salutation *(ie, in business letters)*
Anregungsphase *f* (Bw) orientation phase *(ie, in decision theory: pointing up problems, perceiving problems requiring solutions)*
Anreiz *m*
   (Vw, Bw) incentive
   – inducement
Anreizartikel *m* (Mk) leader *(or* inducement*)* article
Anreizsystem *n*
   (Pw) incentive system
   (IndE) productivity incentive system
Anreiz *m* **zur Integration** (Bw) incentive to integrate
Anruf *m* **an Organisationsprogramm** (EDV) supervisor call
Anrufbeantworter *m* (com) automatic answering set
Anrufer *m*
   (EDV) calling party
   – (GB) caller
Anruftaste *f* (EDV) request button
Ansager *m*
   (com) newscaster
   – (GB) newsreader
Ansatz *m*
   (Log) approach
   (ReW) amount reported
   (ReW) valuation
Ansatzfehler *m* (Math) error in equation
anschaffen
   (com) to buy
   – to purchase
   (Fin) to provide cover
   (Fin) to remit
Anschaffung *f*
   (com) acquisition
   (Re) acquisition
   (ie, legal transaction involving transfer of movable things and negotiable instruments for a consideration)
   (Fin) remittance
   (Fin) provision of cover
Anschaffungsausgabe *f* (Fin) investment outlay *(ie, in preinvestment analysis)*
Anschaffungsdarlehen *n* (Fin) personal loan *(ie, medium-term installment credit of 2,000 to 25,000 DM extended to individuals and small businesses)*
Anschaffungsgeschäfte *npl*
   (StR) acquisition deals
   – acquisition of securities
   (ie, contractual transfer for a consideration through which the transferee acquires title to stocks and bonds, § 18 KVStG)

Anschaffungskosten *pl*
(com) purchase (*or* acquisition) cost
(ReW) cost
- historical cost
(ie, other terms: first, initial, original, asset, (infml) up-front ... cost)
Anschaffungskostenprinzip *n* (ReW) historical cost concept
Anschaffungskosten *pl* **von Investitionsobjekten**
(Fin) initial investment
- original cash outlay
- original investment
Anschaffungskredit *m* (Fin) medium-sized personal loan
anschaffungsnaher Aufwand *m* (ReW) expense following closely upon acquisition of asset
Anschaffungsnebenkosten *pl* (ReW) incidental acquisition cost
Anschaffungs- od Herstellungskosten *pl* (ReW) costs of acquisition or production
Anschaffungs- od Herstellungspreis *m* (ReW) cost price *(ie, component of acquisition cost)*
Anschaffungswert *m*
(ReW) = *Anschaffungspreis*
(Fin) net cash outflow *(ie, in preinvestment analysis)*
Anschaffungswert-Methode *f*
(Fin) cost value method
- legal basis method
(ie, method of evaluating permanent investments)
Anschaffungszeitpunkt *m* (ReW) date of acquisition
Anschauungen *fpl* **des Verkehrs** (StR) custom and usage, § 2 BewG
Anschauungsmaterial *n* (Mk) visual demonstration material
Anscheinsbeweis *m* (Re) prima facie evidence
Anscheinsbeweis *m* **erbringen** (Re) to establish a prima facie case
Anschlag *m* (Pw) bulletin board notice
Anschlagdrucker *m* (EDV) impact printer *(syn, mechanischer Drucker)*
Anschlagflächen *fpl*
(MK) billboards
- (GB) hoardings *(syn, Reklameflächen)*
anschlagloser Drucker *m* (EDV) non-impact printer *(syn, nichtmechanischer Drucker)*
Anschlag *m* **machen** (Pw) to post a notice on the bulletin board
Anschlagtafel *f*
(Mk) billboard
- (GB) hoarding
Anschlagwerbung *f* (Mk) billboard advertising
Anschlußabsatz *m* (Mk) joint use of sales organization
Anschluß-Arbeitslosenhilfe *f* (SozV) follow-up unemployment assistance
Anschlußauftrag *m*
(com) follow-up
- renewal
- sequence ... order
(com, infml) add-on sale
(ie, made to a customer satisfied on earlier occasions)

Anschlußaufträge *mpl* (Bö) follow-through support
Anschlußfinanzierung *f* (Fin) follow-up financing
Anschlußflug *m* (com) connecting flight
Anschlußgerät *n* (EDV) peripheral unit *(syn, periphere Einheit)*
Anschlußgeschäft *n* (com) follow-up contract
Anschlußgleis *n*
(com) siding
- sidetrack
(ie, opening onto main track at both ends)
(com) spur (*or* stub) track *(ie, connected to main track at one end only)*
Anschlußkonkurs *m* (Re) bankruptcy proceedings following failure of composition proceedings
Anschlußkunde *m* (Fin) client *(ie, in factoring)*
Anschlußleitung *f* (EDV) access line
Anschlußnorm *f* (IndE) follow-up standard specification *(ie, one that allows replacement of machine parts of different origin; eg, standard fit systems, screw thread standardization)*
Anschlußpfändung *f* (Re) renewed attachment of ‚thing' previously attached, §§ 826, 827 ZPO
Anschlußplanung *f* (Bw) follow-up planning
Anschlußstelle *f* (EDV) exit point
Anschlußzone *f* (Re) contiguous zone *(ie, in Sea Law)*
Anschlußzone *f* **für Fischereirechte** (Re) contiguous fishing zone
Anschlußzone *f* **für die Zollkontrolle** (Zo) customs supervision zone
Anschreibekonto *n*
(com) charge account
- (GB) account
anschreiben
(com) to charge to account
- (infml) to chalk up
Anschreibung *f* **über die Waren führen** (Zo) to keep a stock-account of goods
Anschrift *f* (com) address
anschwärzende Werbung *f* (Kart) denigration *(ie, of competitive products in advertising)*
Anschwärzung *f*
(Kart) disparagement (*or* slander) of goods *(ie, making a false statement about a competitor's product)*
- injurious (*or* malicious) falsehood
ansetzen
(com) to estimate
- (infml) to put at
(ReW) to state
- to report
- to show
Ansichtsexemplar *n* (com) inspection specimen
Ansichtssendung *f*
(com) consignment on approval
- (GB, infml) ... on áppro
(ie, merchandise taken but returnable at customer's option)
Anspannungsgrad *m* (KoR) tightness
Anspannungsindex *m* (Vw) employment index *(ie, ratio of number of jobless and number of vacancies)*
Anspannungskoeffizient *m* (Fin) debt to total capital *(ie, balance sheet ratio)*

41

ansparen (com) to save up *(ie, by putting aside money regularly and for a specific purpose)*
Anspruch *m*
  (com) claim
  (Re) claim
  (ie, legal capability to require a positive or negative act – Tun od Unterlassen – of another person, § 194 BGB)
  (SozV) entitlement
Anspruch *m* **abweisen** (Re) to dismiss (*or* reject) a claim
Anspruch *m* **anerkennen** (Re) to admit (*or* recognize) a claim
Anspruch *m* **aufgeben**
  (Re) to abandon
  – to renounce
  – to waive ... a claim
  – to disclaim
Anspruch *m* **auf Versicherungsleistung** (Vers) insurance claim
Anspruch *m* **aus Sachschaden** (Re) property claim
Anspruch *m* **aus unerlaubter Handlung**
  (Re) tort claim
  – claim arising out of an unlawful act
Anspruch *m* **aus Vertrag** (Re) contractual claim
Anspruch *m* **durchsetzen** (Re) to enforce a claim
Ansprüche *mpl* **aus dem Steuerschuldverhältnis** (StR) claims arising out of the government-taxpayer relationship, § 38 AO
Ansprüche *mpl* **Dritter** (Re) third-party claims
Ansprüche *mpl* **erlöschen** (Re) rights of claim are invalidated *(eg, by non-observance of ...)*
Anspruch *m* **einklagen** (Re) to litigate a claim
Ansprüche *mpl* **erlassen** (StR) to grant administrative relief
Anspruch *m* **entsteht** (Re) claim arises
Anspruch *m* **erlischt** (Re) claim expires *(eg, non-observance of ... invalidates any rights of claim)*
Anspruch *m* **geltend machen**
  (Re) to advance
  – to assert
  – to bring forward
  – to prefer
  – to put forth ... a claim
Anspruch *m* **haben auf**
  (Re) to have a claim to
  – to be entitled to
anspruchminderndes Mitverschulden *n* (Re) comparative negligence
Anspruchsanpassung *f* (Mk) adjustment of aspiration level
Anspruchsberechtigter *m*
  (Re) claimant
  – beneficiary
Anspruchsgesellschaft *f* (Vw) ‚entitlement' society
Anspruchsgrundlage *f* (Re) subject-matter of a claim
Anspruchshäufung *f* (Re) multiplicity (*or* plurality) of claims *(ie, against the same defendant, § 260 ZPO)*
Anspruchsniveau *n* (Vw) level of aspirations
Anspruchsteller *m* (Re) claimant *(ie, one who may assert a right, demand, or claim)*
Anspruchsverwirkung *f* (Vers) forfeiture of insurance claim

Anspruch *m* **verjährt** (Re) claim is barred
Anspruch *m* **zurückweisen** (Re) to reject (*or* repudiate) a claim
Anstalt *f*
  (Re) incorporated public-law institution
  – institution unter public law, § 196 BGB
anstellen (Pw) = *einstellen*
Anstellung *f* **auf Lebenszeit** (Pw) life (*or* permanent) tenure
Anstellung *f* **auf Probe** (Pw) hiring on probation
Anstellungsvertrag *m*
  (Pw) contract of employment
  – employment contract
  – hiring contract
  – service agreement
Ansteuerungsprüfung *f* (EDV) selection check
Anstieg *m*
  (com) increase
  – rise
  – (infml) uphill climb *(eg, in interest rates is still in gear)*
Anstoß *m* (com) initiative
Anstoßmultiplikator *m* (Vw) impact multiplier
Anstoßwirkung *f*
  (Bw) knock-on impact *(eg, of a decision)*
  (FiW) impact effect
anstreben (com, fml) to aspire to *(eg, the job of vice president marketing)*
an Subunternehmer vergeben (com) to subcontract
  – to farm out a contract
antagonistische Kooperation *f* (Bw) antagonistic cooperation
Anteil *m* (Fin) share
  (Fin) = *Beteiligung*
Anteil *m* **am Investmentfonds**
  (Fin) share
  – (GB) unit
Anteil *m* **der geprüften Stücke** (Stat) average fraction inspected
Anteil *m* **der Kontingentsmenge** (Zo) quota share
Anteil *m* **des Warenhandels am Außenhandel** (AuW) commodity concentration
Anteile *mpl* (Re) shares *(ie, term covers shares, interests, or participations in: AG, OHG, KG, BGB-Gesellschaft and other forms of associations as well as all foreign corporations, partnerships or associations)*
Anteile *mpl* **an verbundenen Unternehmen** (ReW, EG) shares in affiliated undertakings
Anteile *mpl* **in Fremdbesitz** (Fin) minority interests
Anteil *m* **fehlerhafter Einheiten** (Stat) fraction defective
Anteile *m* **fehlerhafter Stücke in der Stichprobe** (Stat) sample fraction defective
anteilig belasten (KoR) to charge pro rate
anteilige Befriedigung *f* (Re) prorata payment (*or* settlement)
anteilige Finanzierung *f* (Fin) prorata financing
anteilige Gemeinkosten *pl* (KoR) prorated overhead
anteilige Kosten *pl* (KoR) prorated cost
anteilige Personalkosten *pl* (KoR) prorated employment cost
anteiliger Beitragswert *m* (SeeV) rateable contribution

anteiliger Betrag m (com) proportionate (or prorated) amount
anteiliger Bilanzverlust m (ReW) proportionate share in loss
anteilige Zahlung f (Fin) prorata payment
anteilig geschichtete Stichprobe f (Stat) proportional stratified sampling
anteilig verrechnete Gemeinkosten pl (KoR) prorated overhead
anteilig verteilen (ReW) to prorate *(eg, cost over productive life of an asset)*
anteilig zu verrechnende Kosten pl (KoR) prorateable cost
anteilmäßige Kostenumlage f (KoR) prorata apportionment of cost
anteilmäßige Zahlungen fpl (Fin) prorata payments
anteilmäßig verrechnen
 (KoR) to absorb
 – to prorate
Anteilpapier n (Fin) equity security
Anteilsbesitz m (Fin) share ownership
Anteilschein m
 (Fin) interim certificate *(ie, issued to shareholders prior to issuance of share certificates, § 8 IV AktG)*
 (Fin) investment fund share
Anteilscheine mpl **an Kapitalgesellschaften** (Fin) certificates issued by German investment funds, § 19 I 3 KVStG
Anteilseigner m
 (Fin) shareholder
 – stockholder
 – equity holder
 (Fin) quotaholder of a GmbH
 (Fin) shareholder *(ie, of investment fund)*
 – (GB) unitholder
Anteilseignervertreter mpl
 (Pw) stockholder side
 – capital side
 (ie, supervisory board members representing stockholders)
Anteilsinhaber m (Fin) = Anteilseigner
Anteilskurs m (Fin) unit price
Anteilsmengen fpl **eines Kontingents** (Zo) volume of quota share
Anteilsrechte npl (Fin) equity interests
Anteilsumlauf m
 (Fin) shares outstanding
 – (GB) units outstanding
Anteilszertifikat n
 (Fin) share certificate
 – (GB) unit certificate
Anteilszoll m (Zo) compensatory levy
Antezedens n
 (Log) antecedent
 – protasis
 (ie, clause expressing the condition in a conditional statement; opp, Konsequens = apodosis)
Anthropotechnik f (Bw) human engineering
Antidumping-Verfahren n (AuW) anti-dumping procedure
Antidumpingzoll m (AuW) anti-dumping duty
Anti-Inflationspolitik f
 (Vw) anti-inflation policy
 – inflation-fighting policy

Antilogarithmus m (Math) antilogarithm
Anti-Marginalist m (Vw) anti-piecemeal approacher
Anti-Marketing n (Mk) demarketing
Antiquariat n
 (com) second-hand book selling
 (com) second-hand book store
 – (GB) second-hand book shop
 (com) second-hand department *(ie, in a book store)*
Antiselektion f
 (Vers) adverse selection
 – anti-selection
Antisubventionsverfahren n (EG) anti-subsidy procedure
Antitrust-Bewegung f (Vw) antitrust movement
Antitrust-Gesetzgebung f (Kart) antitrust legislation
Antitrustrecht n (Kart) antitrust law
Antivalenz f
 (EDV) exclusive-OR
 – non-equivalence
 – anti-coincidence ... operation
 (syn, Kontravalenz, ausschließendes ODER)
Antivalenzglied n
 (EDV) exclusive-OR element
 – except gate
 – non-equivalence element
 (syn, ODER-Glied)
Antizipationsaufwand m (ReW) anticipated cost
Antizipationsläger npl (Bw) anticipation inventories
antizipative Aktiva npl
 (ReW) accrued assets
 – accrued expense
 – accrued income
 – accrued liabilities
antizipative Zinsabgrenzung f (ReW) deferred interest
antizipierter Vertragsbruch m (Re) anticipatory breach of contract
antizyklische Fiskalpolitik f
 (FiW) countercyclical fiscal policy
 – compensatory finance
antizyklische Haushaltspolitik f (FiW) anticyclical budgeting
antizyklische Politik f (Vw) anticyclical (or countercyclical) policy
antizyklische Wirtschaftspolitik f (Vw) countercyclical (or anti-cyclical) economic policy *(ie, measures to mitigate the effects of cyclical booms and recessions)*
Antrag m (com) application
Antrag m **auf Aktienzuteilung** (Fin) application for shares
Antrag m **auf Börseneinführung** (Bö) application for listing
Antrag m **auf Entlassungen** (Pw) request for dismissal of redundant personnel *(ie, made to the local labor office)*
Antrag m **auf Eröffnung des Konkursverfahrens stellen**
 (Re) to apply for bankruptcy proceedings
 – to file a petition in bankruptcy

43

Antrag *m* **auf Fristverlängerung** (com) request for an extension of time
Antrag *m* **auf Konkurseröffnung** (Re) petition in bankruptcy
Antrag *m* **auf Konkurseröffnung stellen** (Re) to file a petition in bankruptcy
Antrag *m* **auf Lohnsteuerjahresausgleich** (StR) application for annual computation of wage tax
Antrag *m* **auf Schluß der Debatte** (com) closure motion
Antrag *m* **auf Steuerrückerstattung stellen** (StR) to file a refund claim
Antrag *m* **auf Zollabfertigung für den freien Warenverkehr** (Zo) consumption entry
antragsberechtigt (Re) entitled to make an application
Antragsberechtigter *m* (com) party entitled to make an application
Antragsempfänger *m* (Re) offeree *(ie, in formation of contract)*
Antragsformular *n*
  (com) application form
  – application blank
  – form of application
  – proposal form
Antragsgrund *m* (com) reason for application
Antrag *m* **stellen**
  (com) to make an application
  – to apply for
  (Re) to file a petition
  (StR) to file a claim *(eg, for a tax credit)*
Antragsteller *m* (com) applicant
Antragsverfahren *n* (Re) filing procedure
Antriebsermüdung *f* (Pw) psychically-induced fatigue
Antriebskräfte *fpl* (Vw) expansionary *(or* stimulating) forces
Antrittsbesuch *m* (com) „get-acquainted" visit
Antrittsvorlesung *f* (Pw) inaugural lecture
Antwort bezahlt (com) answer prepaid
Antwortkarte *f* (com) business reply card
Antwortschein *m* (com) reply coupon
Antwortzeit *f* (EDV) response time
anwählen (EDV) to dial
Anwachsung *f* (Re) accrual *(ie, of company share to the other members, § 738 BGB)*
Anwalt *m*
  (Re) = *Rechtsanwalt*
Anwaltsgebühren *fpl* (Re) attorney fees
Anwaltskammer *f*
  (Re, appr.) Bar Association
  – (GB) Law Society *(ie, of solicitors)*
  – (GB) General Council of the Bar *(ie, confined to barristers)*
Anwaltssozietät *f* (Re) law firm
Anwaltszwang *m* (Re) mandatory legal counsel *(ie, in court proceedings; syn, Vertretungszwang)*
Anwärterkreis *m* (Pw) recruiting sources *(ie, which may be external or internal)*
Anwartschaft *f*
  (Re) right in course of acquisition
  (Pw) legal right to future pension payments
  – expectancy of future benefits
Anwartschaft *f* **auf Pension** (SozV) vested right to future pension payments

Anwartschaftsrecht *n* **auf Altersversorgung** (SozV) right to an old-age pension
anweisen
  (com) to instruct
  (Fin) to remit *(eg, amount of money)*
Anweisender *m* (WeR) drawer *(ie, person issuing an order to pay or to deliver a thing)*
Anweisung *f*
  (com) instruction
  (WeR) order to pay a sum of money or to deliver a thing
  (Zo) transit
  (EDV) statement
Anweisungen *fpl* **entgegennehmen** (Pw) to take orders (from)
Anweisung *f* **in der Auftragssprache** (EDV) job control statement
Anweisungsblatt *n* (Zo) transit sheet *(ie, comprises counterfoil and voucher = Stammabschnitt und Trennabschnitt)*
Anweisungsempfänger *m* (WeR) payee *(ie, person to whom or to whose order payment or delivery is to be made)*
Anweisung *f* **zur Arbeitsunterbrechung** *f* (IndE) stop work order
Anwender *m* (com) user
Anwenderprogramm *n*
  (EDV) applications *(or* user) program
Anwendersoftware *f*
  (EDV) applications software
  (EDV) user software
Anwendung *f* **der Zollsätze aussetzen** (Zo) to suspend collection of the duties applicable
Anwendungsbereich *m*
  (com) scope of application
  (Re) scope *(eg, of a law)*
anwendungsbezogene Forschung *f* (com) action *(or* applied) research
Anwendungsentwicklung *f* (Bw) application management
Anwendungsgenerator *m* (EDV) applications generator
anwendungsorientierte Informatik *f* (EDV) application-oriented computer science
Anwendungsprogrammierer *m*
  (EDV) application programmer
  (syn, Organisationsprogrammierer)
Anwendungssystem *n* (EDV) applications system
Anwendungstechnik *f* (IndE) applications engineering
Anwendungstechniker *m* (IndE) applications engineer
Anwerbegebühr *f* (Pw) recruitment fee
Anwerbeland *n* (Pw) recruitment country
anwerben (Pw) to recruit (labor)
Anwerbestopp *m* (Pw) recruitment ban *(or* stop)
Anwerbevereinbarung *f* (Vw) recruitment agreement *(ie, between two countries)*
Anwerbung *f* (Pw) recruitment
Anwesenheitskarte *f* (Pw) attendance card
Anwesenheitsliste *f* (com) attendance sheet *(or* register)
Anwesenheitsprämie *f* (Pw) attendance bonus
Anwesenheitszeit *f*
  (Pw) attendance time

anzahlen (OR) attendance time *(ie, waiting time + processing time)*
anzahlen
(com) to pay down
– to make a down payment
(Re) to pay as a deposit
Anzahl *f* **in e–r Klasse** (Stat) absolute frequency
Anzahlung *f*
(com) down payment
– advance payment
(Re) deposit (payment)
(ReW) customer prepayment
(Fin) cash deposit
Anzahlungen *fpl* **auf Anlagen** (ReW) installment payments for facilities
Anzahlungen *fpl* **finanzieren** (Fin) to fund downpayments
Anzahlungsgarantie *f*
(Fin) advance payment bond
– advance guaranty
– security bond for down payment
an Zahlungs Statt
(Re) in payment
– in lieu of payment
– *(civil law)* datio in solutum
Anzeige *f*
(Mk) advertisement
– (infml) ad
– (infml, GB) ádvert
(EDV) indicator
(EDV) display
Anzeige *f* **aufgeben** (Mk) to advertise
Anzeigedatei *f* (EDV) display file
anzeigefreies Bauvorhaben *n* (Re) building project exempt from notification of authorities
Anzeigegerät *n* (EDV) indicating instrument
Anzeigehintergrund *m*
(EDV) background display *(or* image)
– static image
Anzeigenabteilung *f* (Mk) advertising department
Anzeigenagentur *f* (Mk) advertising agency
Anzeigenakquisiteur *m* (Mk) advertisement canvasser
Anzeigenannahme *f* (Mk) advertising office
Anzeigenauftrag *m* (Mk) advertising *(or* space) order
Anzeigenbeilage *f* (Mk) advertising insert *(or* supplement)
Anzeigenblatt *n* (Mk) advertising journal
Anzeigenexpedition *f* (Mk) advertising agency
Anzeigenfachmann *m*
(Mk) advertising specialist
– adman
Anzeigengrundpreis *m*
(Mk) advertising base price
– open rate
Anzeigenkosten *pl*
(Mk) advertising charges *(or* costs)
– advertising rates
– space costs
Anzeigenmittler *m* (Mk) advertising agency *(or* office)
Anzeigenplazierung *f* (Mk) advertisement positioning
Anzeigenpreisliste *f* (Mk) advertising rate list

Anzeigenraum *m* (Mk) (advertising) space
Anzeigenraum *m* **buchen** (Mk) to book advertising space
Anzeigenraumvermittler *m*
(Mk) advertising space salesman
– space buyer
Anzeigenspalte *f* (Mk) advertisement column
Anzeigen-Split *m* (Mk) split run advertising
Anzeigentarife *mpl* (Mk) advertising rates
Anzeigentermin *m* (Mk) copy deadline
Anzeigentext *m* (Mk) advertising copy
Anzeigentexter *m* (Mk) copy writer
Anzeigenvertrag *m* (Mk) advertising contract
Anzeigenvertreter *m*
(Mk) ad agent
– advertising representative
– advertising sales agency
Anzeigepflicht *f*
(Re) duty to notify
– duty of notification
– duty to give notice
– duty of disclosure
Anzeigepflicht *f* **bei Fusionen** (Kart) premerger notification duty
Anzeigepflichten *fpl* (Re) reporting requirements
anzeigepflichtiges Bauvorhaben *n* (Re) building project requiring notification of authorities
Anzeigeregister *n* (EDV) condition code register
Anzeigeröhre *f* (EDV) display tube
Anzeigetafel *f* (Bö) quotations board
Anzeigevordergrund *m*
(EDV) foreground display *(or* image)
– dynamic image
anziehen
(Bö) to advance *(ie, prices)*
– to firm
– to move up
Anziehen *n*
(com, Bö) firming up
– upturn *(eg, prices, interest rates)*
anzuwendende Berichtigung *f* (EG) corrective amount *(ie, applicable to the refund of . . .)*
aperiodische Aufwendungen *mpl* (ReW) expenses not identified with a specified period
A-Phase *f* (EDV) execution phase *(syn, Ausführungsphase)*
apodiktische Aussage *f* (Log) apodictic statement *(ie, asserting that something must be the case; opp, assertorische und problematische Aussage)*
apodiktisches Urteil *n* (Log) apodictic proposition
a posteriori-Wahrscheinlichkeit *f* (Stat) posterior *(or* a posteriori) probability *(opp, a priori-Wahrscheinlichkeit)*
Apotheke *f*
(com) drugstore
– pharmacy
– (GB) chemist's (shop)
Apotheker *m*
(com) pharmacist
– (GB) dispenser
Apparatur *f* (EDV) hardware
A-priori-Schätzung *f* (Stat) extraneous estimate
a priori-Wahrscheinlichkeit *f* (Stat) prior *(or* a priori) probability *(opp, a posteriori-Wahrscheinlichkeit)*

Äquipollenz f (Log) equipollence
äquivalente Binärstellen fpl (EDV) equivalent binary digits
äquivalente Mengen fpl
  (Math) equivalent
  – equinumerable
  – equipotent ... sets
äquivalente Struktur f
  (Math) equivalent structure
  – indistinguishable structure
äquivalente Waren fpl
  (Zo) equivalent goods
  – equivalents
Äquivalenz f
  (Log) equivalence
  – biconditional
Äquivalenzbeziehung f (Log) equivalence relation
Äquivalenzglied n (EDV) equivalence (or coincidence) element
Äquivalenzklasse f (Math) equivalence class
Äquivalenzkonflikt m (Bw) plus-plus conflict
Äquivalenzoperator m (Log) iff
Äquivalenzprinzip n
  (FiW) benefit received principle
  – benefits received principle
  – compensatory principle of taxation
  – cost-of-service principle
  (Vers) principle of equivalence
Äquivalenzverkehr m (Zo) setting-off with equivalent goods
Äquivalenzverknüpfung f
  (EDV) equivalence operation
  – if and only if-operation
  – matching
Äquivalenzziffer f (KoR) weighting figure *(ie, applied in process cost accounting [= Divisionskalkulation] and in handling joint production [= Kuppelproduktion] in standard costing [= Plankostenrechnung] to find a common base for cost allocation)*
Äquivokation f (Log) equivocation *(ie, an argument in which an equivocal expression is used in one sense in one premise and in a different sense in another premise or in the conclusion)*
arabische Zahlen fpl (Math) Arabic numerals
Arbeit f
  (Vw) labor *(ie, as one of the factors of production)*
  (Bw) work *(ie, labor × working time)*
Arbeit f **annehmen** (Pw) to take employment
Arbeit f **aufnehmen** (Pw) to take up work (or employment)
Arbeiten fpl **außerhalb des Arbeitstaktes** (IndE) out-of-cycle work
Arbeiten n **mit mehrfacher Wortlänge** (EDV) multiple-length working
Arbeiten fpl **mit Zeitrichtwerten** (IndE) controlled work
Arbeiten fpl **vergeben** (com) to contract out work
Arbeiter m (Pw) worker *(ie, general term denoting varying degrees of qualification; eg, manual worker, research worker)*
  – laborer *(mostly heavy work)*
  – hourly paid employee
  – manual worker
  – blue-collar worker
Arbeiter mpl
  (Pw) labor
  – labor force
  – workers
  – wage-earning community
Arbeiteraktie f (Pw) employee share
Arbeiterin f (Pw) female worker
Arbeiterrentenversicherung f (SozV) invalidism and old-age insurance for wage earners
Arbeiterschutzgesetzgebung f (Re) protective labor legislation
Arbeiterselbstverwaltung f (Bw) autogestion
Arbeiterstunde f
  (Pw) manhour
  – manpower hour
Arbeitgeber m (Pw) employer
Arbeigeberanteil m (SozV) employer's contribution
Arbeitgeber-Arbeitnehmer-Beziehungen fpl (Pw) employer-employee relations
Arbeitgeberbeitrag m (SozV) employer's contribution
Arbeitgeberdarlehen n (Pw) loan by employer to employee
Arbeitgeber-Übergewicht n (Pw) employer supremacy *(ie, in matters of co-determination)*
Arbeitgebervereinigung f (com) Employers' Federation
Arbeitnehmer m (Pw) employee
Arbeitnehmeraktie f (Pw) employee share
Arbeitnehmeranteil m (SozV) employee's contribution
Arbeitnehmereinkommen n (Pw) employee compensation (or earnings)
Arbeitnehmererfindung f (Pw) employee invention *(ie, made by one or several employees in the course of their employment, either on or off duty)*
Arbeitnehmer-Erfindervergütung f (StR) compensation received by an employee as an inventor
Arbeitnehmerflügel m (Pw) worker wing *(ie, of a political party)*
Arbeitnehmerhandbuch n (Pw) company information manual
Arbeitnehmerseite f (Pw) = *Arbeitnehmervertreter*
Arbeitnehmer-Sparzulage f (Pw) employee's savings premium
Arbeitnehmervertreter mpl
  (Pw) board employee representatives
  – employee representatives on the supervisory board
  – employee members
  – members representing employees
  – worker board members
  – worker representatives
  – labor side
Arbeitsablauf m
  (Bw) operational sequence
  – flow of work
Arbeitsablaufabweichung f (KoR) nonstandard operation variance
arbeitsablaufbedingte Brachzeit f **bei Mehrstellenarbeit** (IndE) interference time
Arbeitsablaufbogen m (IndE) flow process chart

Arbeitsablaufdiagramm n
(IndE) flowchart
– labor explosion chart *(syn, Arbeitsablaufplan)*
Arbeitsablaufgestaltung f (IndE) work flow structuring
Arbeitsablauf-Handbuch n (Bw) procedures manual
Arbeitsablaufkarte f (IndE) route sheet
Arbeitsablauforganisation f (IndE) work flow organization *(ie, term used in industrial plant organization to denote planning of job scheduling; opp, Strukturorganisation)*
Arbeitsablaufplan m
(IndE) sequence of operations schedule
(IndE) flowchart
(syn, Arbeitsablaufdiagramm)
Arbeitsablaufplanung f (IndE) work flow planning
Arbeitsablaufschaubild n (IndE) outline process chart
Arbeitsablaufskizze f (IndE) outline process chart
Arbeitsablaufstudie f (IndE) analysis of work flow
– work flow study
Arbeitsamt n (Pw) local Labor Office *(ie, a government-run employment agency)*
Arbeitsanalyse f
(IndE) job analysis
– breakdown of job operations
Arbeitsangebot n (Vw) labor supply
Arbeitsangebotskurve f (Vw) labor supply curve
Arbeitsanreiz m (Vw) incentive to work
Arbeitsanweisungen fpl
(Pw) job instructions
– work assignments
– orders directing employees on their jobs
Arbeitsaufbau m (IndE) job analysis
Arbeitsaufgabe f
(IndE) job
– task
Arbeitsauftrag m
(IndE) job *(or* shop*)* order
– labor voucher
– operation ticket
– work order *(or* ticket*)*
Arbeitsauftragnummer f (IndE) job number
Arbeitsband n (EDV) work *(or* scratch*)* tape
Arbeitsbedingungen fpl (Pw) conditions of employment
– working conditions
Arbeitsbegleitpapiere npl (IndE) job routing documents
Arbeitsbelastung f (Pw) workload
Arbeitsbereich m
(Log) study area *(or* field*)*
– field of attention *(or* concentration*)*
(IndE) working area
(Pw) area of operations
Arbeitsbereichsbewertung f (Pw) job evaluation *(or* rating*)*
Arbeitsbeschaffungsmaßnahmen fpl
(Vw) employment *(or* job*)* creating measures *(or* scheme*)*
(Vw) make-work policies
Arbeitsbeschaffungsprogramm n
(Vw) job creation *(or* creating*)* programm
– job fostering scheme

Arbeitsbeschaffungsprojekt n (Vw) make-work project
Arbeitsbeschreibung f (IndE) work specification
Arbeitsbestgestaltung f (Bw) measures taken to ensure optimum efficiency in combining labor, equipment, and materials
Arbeitsbewertung f (IndE) job evaluation
Arbeitsblatt n (ReW) work sheet
Arbeitsdatei f (EDV) work file
Arbeitsdefinition f (Log) working definition
Arbeitsdiagramm n (EDV) flow diagram *(syn, Datenflußplan)*
Arbeitsdirektor m
(Pw) personnel director *(ie, union approved and appointed to the managing board)*
– director of industrial relations
– *(for U.S. readers:)* vice president personnel
(Note that ‚worker director' is a convenient but incorrect translation
Arbeitsdurchlaufkarte f (IndE) operations routing sheet
Arbeitseignung f (Pw) aptitude for work
Arbeitseinheit f
(IndE) activity
– service unit
Arbeitseinkommen n
(Vw) earned
– employment
– service ... income *(opp, Besitzeinkommen = property income, unearned income)*
Arbeitseinsatz m (Pw) amount of work
– (Pw, infml) habit of getting stuck into work
Arbeitseinsatzplanung f (IndE) manload planning
Arbeitseinteilung f (Pw) work management
Arbeitselement n (IndE) work element
Arbeitsentfremdung f (Vw) alienation from work
Arbeitsentgelt n
(Pw) employee compensation
– employee pay
Arbeitsergiebigkeit f (Bw) labor productivity
Arbeitserlaubnis f (Pw) employment *(or* work*)* permit *(ie, issued to foreign workers)*
Arbeitsermüdung f
(Pw) work fatigue
– fatigue due to work
Arbeitserprobung f (Pw) aptitude test *(ie, for a period of up to 4 weeks, cost paid by Federal Labor Office)*
Arbeitsertrag m (Vw) return to labor
Arbeitsessen n (com) working lunch *(or* dinner*)*
arbeitsfähig
(Pw) able *(or* capable*)* to work
– employable
– fit for work
arbeitsfähige Mehrheit f (Re) working majority
arbeitsfähiges Alter n (Pw) working *(or* employable*)* age
Arbeitsfähigkeit f
(Pw) capacity to work
– fitness for work
Arbeitsfluß m (IndE) work flow
Arbeitsflußdarstellung f (IndE) route diagram
Arbeitsflußdiagramm n (IndE) operation flow chart

Arbeitsfolge f
(IndE) operating sequence
– sequence of work
Arbeitsfolge f **der Werkstattfertigung** (IndE) job shop sequencing
Arbeitsfolgen fpl (IndE) routings
Arbeitsförderung f (Vw) employment (or work) promotion
Arbeitsförderungsgesetz n (Re) Labor Promotion Law, of 1 July 1969
Arbeitsfortschritt m (IndE) status of progress (or project)
Arbeitsfortschritts-Ausweis m (com) work progress certificate
Arbeitsfortschritts-Diagramm n (IndE) progress chart
Arbeitsfortschrittsplanung f (IndE) progress planning
arbeitsfreie Zeit f (Pw) time off duty
Arbeitsfreude f (Pw) delight in work
Arbeitsfrieden m
(Pw) industrial peace
– labor-management peace
– peaceful labor relations
Arbeitsgang m
(IndE) work cycle
– pass
– run
Arbeitsgebiet n
(Log) study area (or field)
– field of attention (or concentration)
Arbeitsgemeinschaft f
(Re) special partnership
(Bw) joint venture (group)
– (ad hoc) consortium
(ie, adopted for specific schemes, mostly in the legal form of ‚joint venture')
(Pw) team
(Pw) study group
Arbeitsgemeinschaft f **selbständiger Unternehmer**
(com) Association of Independent Businessmen
Arbeitsgericht n (Re) (first-instance) labor court
Arbeitsgerichtsbarkeit f (Re) labor jurisdiction
Arbeitsgesetzgebung f (Re) labor legislation
Arbeitsgestaltung f
(Bw) optimum combination of labor, equipment, and materials
(Bw) job design
– work structuring
Arbeitsgruppe f
(Pw) task force (or group)
– team
– working group (or party)
(Pw) gang
Arbeitsgruppe f **leiten** (Pw) to head a task force
Arbeitshypothese f (Log) working hypothesis
Arbeitsinhalt m (Pw) job content
arbeitsintensiv (Bw) labor intensive
Arbeitskampf m
(Pw) industrial conflict (or dispute)
– labor dispute
– industrial action (or strife)
(syn, Arbeitsstreitigkeiten)
Arbeitskampfmaßnahmen fpl **ergreifen** (Pw) to take industrial action

Arbeitskampfrecht n (Re) labor dispute law
Arbeitskleidung f (Pw) working clothes
Arbeitskoeffizient m (Vw) labor-output ratio (ie, reciprocal of labor productivity)
Arbeitskolonne f (Pw) gang
Arbeitskosten pl
(Pw) labor cost
– employment cost
– bill for wages, salaries, and social cost
– sum total of wages and salaries + fringe benefits
(KoR) variable cost (ie, fully determined by output or ‚labor')
Arbeitskostentheorien fpl (Vw) labor cost theories (opp, production cost theories)
Arbeitskraft f
(Bw) labor (ie, as productive factor)
(Pw) capacity to work
(Pw) employee
– worker
Arbeitskräfte fpl
(Pw) manpower
– workers
– labor
– labor force
Arbeitskräfteabgang m
(Pw) labor wastage
– attrition
Arbeitskräfteangebot n (Vw) labor supply
Arbeitskräfteangebotskurve f (Vw) labor supply curve
Arbeitskräfte-Auslastungskurve f (Bw) workload curve (or graph)
Arbeitskräftebedarf m (Pw) manpower requirements
Arbeitskräftebedarfs-Bericht m (Bw) manpower loading report
Arbeitskräftedefizit n (Vw) labor shortage
Arbeitskräfte fpl **einstellen**
(Pw) to hire
– to engage
– to add ... workers (or employees)
– to take on labor
Arbeitskräfteengpaß m (Vw) labor (or manpower) bottleneck
Arbeitskräfte fpl **horten** (Pw) to hoard labor
Arbeitskräfteknappheit f (Vw) = Arbeitskräftemangel
Arbeitskräftemangel m
(Vw) scarcity of labor
– shortage of labor
– manpower shortage
– tight labor market
Arbeitskräftenachfrage f (Vw) labor demand
Arbeitskräfteplanung f (Pw) manpower planning
Arbeitskräftepotential n
(Vw) manpower potential
– labor force potential
(ie, pool of workers potentially available for work)
Arbeitskräftereserve f (Vw) manpower (or labor) reserve
arbeitskräftesparende Fertigung f (IndE) labor-saving production

Arbeitskräftestatistik *f*
(Stat) manpower statistics
– labor force statistics
Arbeitskräftestunde *f*
(Pw) manhour
– manpower-hour
Arbeitskräfteüberangebot *n* (Vw) excess supply of labor (*or* manpower)
Arbeitskräfteüberschuß *m* (Vw) labor (*or* manpower) surplus
Arbeitskräfteverknappung *f* (Pw) labor (*or* manpower) shortage
Arbeitskräftewanderung *f* (Vw) labor (*or* manpower) migration
Arbeitskreis *m* (com) working group (*or* party)
Arbeitsleben *n*
(Pw) working
– occupational
– professional ... life
Arbeitsleistung *f*
(IndE) output
(Pw) job performance
– performance level
Arbeitsleistungsabweichung *f*
(KoR) labor efficiency variance
– labor time variance
– labor usage variance
Arbeitsliste *f*
(IndE) operating list
Arbeitslohn *m*
(Vw) wage(s)
(Vw) wage rate
(IndE) employment compensation
(StR) employment income *(ie, including wages, salaries, commissions, bonuses, etc.)*
arbeitslos
(Pw) unemployed
– jobless
– out of work
– off the payroll
– (infml) sitting on the sidelines of business
Arbeitslose *pl*
(Vw) unemployed
– jobless
– persons out of work
Arbeitslosengeld *n* (SozV) unemployment benefit (*or* pay) *(ie, has replaced the earlier term ‚Arbeitslosenunterstützung‘: currently 68% of the erstwhile earnings for the first year out of work)*
Arbeitslosenhilfe *f* (SozV) unemployment aid (*or* assistance) *(ie, earlier term ‚Arbeitslosenfürsorge‘)*
Arbeitslosenpflichtversicherung *f* (SozV) compulsory unemployment insurance
Arbeitslosenquote *f* (Vw) unemployment (*or* jobless) rate *(ie, ratio of jobless to total labor force)*
Arbeitslosenschlangen *fpl* (Vw) lines of jobless workers
Arbeitslosenstatistik *f*
(Stat) unemployment statistics
– jobless tally
Arbeitslosenunterstützung *f* (SozV) unemployment payment
Arbeitslosenversicherung *f* (Pw) unemployment insurance

Arbeitslosenversicherungsbeitrag *m* (SozV) unemployment insurance contribution
Arbeitslosenzahl *f*
(Vw) jobless total
– unemployment figure
– number of people out of work (*or* unemployed)
Arbeitsloser *m*
(Pw) jobless (*or* unemployed) person
– person out of work
arbeitsloses Einkommen *n* (Vw) unearned (*or* property) income *(syn, Besitzeinkommen; opp, Arbeitseinkommen)*
Arbeitslosigkeit *f*
(Pw) unemployment
– joblessness
(Pw) level of unemployment
– number of people out of work
Arbeitslosigkeit *f* **bekämpfen** (Vw) to fight (*or* combat) unemployment
Arbeitsmarkt *m*
(Vw) job
– labor
– unemployment ... market
Arbeitsmarktabgabe *f* (Vw) labor market levy
Arbeitsmarktanpassung *f* (Vw) labor (*or* job) market adjustment *(ie, by removing bottlenecks or surpluses)*
Arbeitsmarktaussichten *fpl*
(Vw) employment outlook (*or* perspectives)
– job outlook (*or* perspectives)
Arbeitsmarktbehörde *f*
(Vw) manpower administration
– labor administration
– labor market authorities
Arbeitsmarktdaten *pl* (Stat) labor market data
Arbeitsmarktentwicklung *f* (Vw) labor market development (*or* trend)
Arbeitsmarkterhebung *f* (Stat) labor force survey
Arbeitsmarktforschung *f* (Vw) labor market research
Arbeitsmarktgleichgewicht *n* (Vw) labor market equilibrium (*or* balance)
Arbeitsmarktmonopol *n* (Vw) labor monopoly
Arbeitsmarktpolitik *f*
(Vw) labor market policy
– manpower policy
Arbeitsmarktsituation *f*
(Vw) labor market
– employment
– manpower ... situation
Arbeitsmarktstatistik *f*
(Vw) labor (market) statistics
– labor force statistics
Arbeitsmarkttheorie *f*
(Vw) labor market theory
– labor economics
Arbeitsmarktungleichgewicht *n* (Vw) labor market disequilibrium (*or* imbalance)
Arbeitsmarktverhalten *n*
(Vw) labor market behavior
– labor force behavior
Arbeitsmedizin *f* (Pw) industrial medicine
Arbeitsmethode *f* (IndE) working method

Arbeitsmobilität f
(Vw) labor mobility
– mobility of labor
Arbeitsmöglichkeiten fpl (Pw) employment (or job) opportunities
Arbeitsmoral f
(Pw) work attitude
– on-the-job morale
– staff morale
Arbeitsnachweis m (Pw) daily performance record
Arbeitsniederlegung f
(Pw) stoppage of work
– industrial stoppage
– walkout
Arbeitsnorm f (Pw) labor standard
Arbeitsorientierung f (Bw) labor orientation *(ie, in location theory = Standorttheorie)*
Arbeitspapier n
(com) working paper
– exposure draft
Arbeitspapiere npl (Pw) employee (or working) papers *(ie, wage tax card, social insurance card, employment permit for foreign workers)*
arbeitsparende Technologie f (IndE) labor-saving technology
Arbeitspartizipation f (Pw) worker participation
Arbeitsplan m (IndE) schedule of job operations *(ie, based on drawings and design data)*
Arbeitsplaner m (IndE) work scheduler
Arbeitsplanung f (IndE) work scheduling
Arbeitsplanungsbogen m (IndE) multiple activity chart
Arbeitsplatz m
(Pw) job
– position
– post
(Pw) job
– job site
– workplace
– work station
– duty station *(ie, im Sinne von Einsatzort)*
Arbeitsplatzanalyse f (IndE) job description
Arbeitsplatzangebot n
(Vw) availability (or supply) of jobs
(Pw) job offer
Arbeitsplatzbeschaffung f (Pw) job creation
Arbeitsplatzbeschreibung f (Pw) job description
Arbeitsplatz m **besetzen** (Pw) to fill a job (or vacancy)
Arbeitsplatzbesetzung f (Pw) filling vacant jobs
Arbeitsplatzbewertung f (Pw) job evaluation (or rating)
Arbeitsplatzbezogenheit f (Pw) job relatedness
Arbeitsplatz-Computer m (EDV) desk-top personal computer
Arbeitsplätze mpl **einsparen** (Pw) to shed jobs
Arbeitsplätze mpl **erhalten** (Pw) to preserve jobs
Arbeitsplätze mpl **gefährden** (Vw) to endanger jobs
Arbeitsplatzerhaltung f (Pw) preservation of jobs
Arbeitsplätze mpl **schaffen** (Vw) to create (or generate) jobs
Arbeitsplatzexport m (AuW) job export
Arbeitsplatzförderung f
(Vw) job promotion
– promotion of jobs

Arbeitsplatzgestaltung f
(Pw) job engineering
– workplace layout
Arbeitsplatz m **haben** (Pw) to have (or hold) a job
Arbeitsplatzmangel m
(Vw) job scarcity (or shortage)
– lack of jobs
Arbeitsplatzmerkmal n (Pw) job characteristic
Arbeitsplatz m **ohne Aufstiegsmöglichkeiten** (Pw) dead-end job
Arbeitsplatzprofil n (Pw) job profile
Arbeitsplatzrisiko n (Pw) occupational hazard
Arbeitsplatzsicherheit f
(Pw) job security (or safety)
– employment security
Arbeitsplatzsicherung f (Pw) safeguarding of jobs
Arbeitsplatzumsetzung f (Pw) job relocation
Arbeitsplatz m **verlieren** (Pw) to lose a job
Arbeitsplatzverluste mpl (Pw) job losses
Arbeitsplatzvernichtung f (Pw) job shedding (or destruction)
Arbeitsplatzwahl f (Vw) job choice
Arbeitsplatzwechsel m (Pw) job change (or shift)
Arbeitsproduktivität f
(Vw) labor productivity (or efficiency) *(ie, ratio of output to labor input)*
Arbeitsproduktivitäts-Abweichung f (KoR) labor productivity variance
Arbeitsprogramm n (EDV) working program
Arbeitsrechner m (EDV) host (computer) *(syn, Dienstleistungsrechner, Hostrechner, Verarbeitungsrechner, Wirtsrechner)*
Arbeitsrecht n
(Re) labor law
– (GB) industrial law
arbeitsrechtliche Gesetzgebung f (Re) labor legislation
arbeitsrechtliche Streitigkeit f (Pw) = *Arbeitsstreitigkeiten*
arbeitsrechtliche Vorschriften fpl (Re) labor legislation rules
Arbeitsregister n (EDV) general register
Arbeitsrückstand m (com) backlog of work
Arbeitsschein m (IndE) work slip
Arbeitsschluß m
(Pw) end of working day
(Pw, infml) knocking-off time
Arbeitsschutz m (Pw) labor (or job) protection
Arbeitsschutzgesetz n (Re) labor (or job) protection law
Arbeitssicherheit f (Pw) on-the-job safety
Arbeitssitzung f (com) working session
arbeitssparende Technologie f (IndE) labor-saving technology
Arbeitsspeicher m
(EDV) main memory
– working storage
(syn, Hauptspeicher, Zentralspeicher, Primärspeicher, Speicherwerk)
Arbeitsspeicherabzug m (EDV) working storage dump
Arbeitsspeicheradresse f (EDV) main memory address
Arbeitsspeicherbereich m (EDV) (main) memory area

Arbeitsspeicherblock *m*
(EDV) main memory block
- storage block
Arbeitsspeichergröße *f* (EDV) main memory size
Arbeitsspeicherplatz *m* (EDV) (main) memory location
Arbeitsstatistik *f*
(Vw) labor (market) statistics
- labor force statistics
Arbeitsstätte *f* (Pw) place of work
Arbeitsstelle *f* (Pw) = *Arbeitsplatz*
Arbeitsstreitigkeiten *fpl*
(Pw) industrial
- labor
- trade ... dispute
- industrial conflict (*or* strife)
(*syn, Arbeitskampf*)
Arbeitsstrukturierung *f*
(Pw) job redesign (*or* structuring)
- work restructuring
(*ie, umbrella term covering job enrichment, job rotation, employee participation etc. in varying degrees*)
Arbeitsstückliste *f* (IndE) schedule of job operations (*ie, based on drawings and design data*)
Arbeitsstudie *f* (IndE) time and motion study
Arbeitsstudium *n* (IndE) work study
Arbeitsstunde *f* (com) manhour (*ie, work done by one man in one hour*)
Arbeitssuche *f*
(Pw) job seeking
- job search
- job hunting
Arbeitssystem *n* (IndE) work system (*ie, interpreted as a socio-technical system or as a man-machine control loop*)
Arbeitstag *m*
(Pw) workday
- (GB) working day
(Bw) stream day (*ie, day of real productive work*)
Arbeitstagung *f* (com) workshop
Arbeitstakt *m* (IndE) work cycle
Arbeitsteilung *f* (Vw) division of labor
Arbeitsüberwachung *f* (IndE) job control
Arbeit *f* **suchen**
(Pw) to look for a job (*or* for work)
- to seek a job (*or* work)
Arbeitsuchender *m* (Pw) job seeker
Arbeitsumgebung *f* (Pw) job environment (*or* context)
arbeitsunfähig (Pw) unfit for work (*ie, for the time being*)
(Pw) incapacitated
- unable to work
Arbeitsunfähiger *m* (Pw) disabled person
Arbeitsunfähigkeit *f*
(Pw) unfitness for work
(Pw) inability to work
- disability
Arbeitsunfall *m* (Pw) industrial (*or* occupational *or* work) accident
Arbeitsunterbrechung *f*
(IndE) interruption of work
- work stoppage
- delay
Arbeitsunterbrechungsanweisung *f* (IndE) hold order
Arbeitsunterlagen *fpl* (com) working papers
Arbeitsunterteilung *f* (IndE) job breakdown
Arbeitsunzufriedenheit *f* (Pw) job dissatisfaction
Arbeitsurlaub *m* (Pw) working vacation (*ie, managers and politicians sometimes claim to be in that frame of mind*)
Arbeitsvereinfachung *f* (IndE) work simplification
Arbeitsverfahren *n* (com) working method
Arbeitsverhältnis *n* (Pw) employer-employee relationship
arbeitsvermittlungsfähig (Pw) employable
Arbeitsvermittlungsfähigkeit *f* (Pw) employability
Arbeitsvermögen *n* (Vw) human capital (*or* wealth) (*ie, part of the productive assets of the economy; syn, Humankapital*)
arbeitsvernichtende Technologien *fpl* (IndE) job-displacing technologies
Arbeitsverrichtung *f* (IndE) task
Arbeitsverteilung *f* (Pw) assignment of activities
Arbeitsvertrag *m*
(Pw) employment
- labor
- service ... contract
- contract of employment
Arbeitsverwaltung *f*
(Vw) labor (*or* manpower) administration
- labor market authorities
Arbeitsvolumen *n* (Vw) total number of man-hours worked
Arbeitsvorbereiter *m* (IndE) process planning engineer
Arbeitsvorbereitung *f*
(IndE) production (*or* operations) scheduling
- process planning
- operation and process planning
- planning of process layout
(EDV) job preparation
Arbeitsvorgang *m* (IndE) job
Arbeitswertlehre *f* (Vw) labor theory of value
Arbeitswertlohn *m* (IndE) evaluated rate
Arbeitswilligkeit *f* (Pw) willingness to be employed (*ie, preferred term now: employability*)
Arbeitszeichnung *f* (IndE) working drawing
Arbeitszeit *f*
(Pw) hours of work
- working hours
- working time
Arbeitszeitabweichung *f*
(KoR) labor efficiency variance
- labor time variance
- labor usage variance
Arbeitszeitkategorie *f* (Pw) working-time category (*eg, normal time, overtime*)
Arbeitszeitnachweis *m* (IndE) time sheet (*or* slip)
Arbeitszeitordnung *f* (Re) working-time ordinance (as of 30 April 1938)
Arbeitszeitplan *m* (IndE) (schematic) job time plan
Arbeitszeitstudie *f* (IndE) work time study
Arbeitszeitverkürzung *f*
(Pw) cut in working time

- reduction of (working) hours
- shorter working hours

Arbeitszeitvorgabe *f*
(KoR) labor efficiency standard
- labor performance standard
- labor quantity standard
- labor time standard
(IndE) operation time standard

Arbeitszerlegung *f*
(IndE) job analysis
- breakdown of job operations

Arbeitszerlegung *f* **in Teilvorgänge** (IndE) element breakdown

Arbeitszerlegungsdiagramm *n* (IndE) breakdown structure

Arbeitszeugnis *n* (Pw) employment certificate

Arbeitszufriedenheit *f* (Pw) job satisfaction

Arbeitszuordnung *f* (Pw) assignment of activities

Arbeitszyklus *m*
(EDV) operation cycle
(EDV) cycle time

Arbitrage *f* (AuW) arbitrage

Arbitrage *f* **bei unternormalen Preis- od Kursdifferenzen** (Fin) backspread

Arbitragehändler *m* (AuW) arbitrage dealer

Arbitrage-Interventionspunkte *mpl* (AuW) arbitrage support points

Arbitrage-Klausel *f*
(Re) clause of arbitration
(AuW) arbitrage clause

Arbitrage-Rechnung *f* (Fin) arbitrage calculation

Arbitrage-Transaktionen *fpl* (AuW) arbitrage dealings (*or* operations *or* transactions)

Arbitrageur *m*
(AuW) arbitrager
- arbitrageur
- (GB) shunter

Arbitragewerte *mpl* (Bö) arbitrage stocks

Arbitrage *f* **zwischen zwei Parallelmärkten** (AuW, GB) shunting

Arbitriumwert *m* (Bw) value of an enterprise as a whole *(ie, as determined by an arbitrating expert; syn, Schiedsspruchwert)*

Architekt *m* (com) architect

Architektengruppe *f* (com) architectural firm

Argand-Diagramm *n* (Math) Argand diagram

Arglist *f* (Re) intention to deceive
(ie, term denoting acts made in violation of good faith; eg, any act done willfully by means of which damage is done to another in a manner contra bonos mores, § 826 BGB)

arglistig (Re) fraudulent

arglistiges Verschweigen *n* **e–s Fehlers** (Re) malicious silence with regard to a defect, § 463 BGB

arglistige Täuschung *f*
(Re) fraud
- misrepresentation intended to deceive
(ie, a legal transaction so induced is voidable at the option of the party deceived, § 123 BGB)

Argument *n* (Math, Log) argument

argumentationszugänglich
(Log) open to analytical argument (*or* to logical reasoning)

arithmetisch-degressive Abschreibung *f*
(ReW) sum-of-the-years-digit method of depreciation
- life period method
(syn, digitale Abschreibung)

arithmetische Anweisung *f* (EDV) arithmetic statement

arithmetische Einheit *f* (EDV) arithmetic unit (*or* element *or* section *or* organ) *(syn, Rechenwerk)*

arithemtische Folge *f* (Math) arithmetic progression (*or* sequence)

arithmetische Operation *f* (EDV) arithmetic operation

arithmetische Prüfung *f* (EDV) arithmetic (*or* mathematical) check

arithmetischer Ausdruck *m* (EDV, Cobol) arithmetic expression

arithmetischer Befehl *m* (EDV) arithmetic instruction

arithmetischer Durchschnitt *m* (Stat) arithmetic mean (*or* average)

arithmetische Reihe *f* (Math) arithmetic series

arithmetischer Lag *m* (Vw) arithmetic lag

arithmetischer Mittelwert *m* (Stat) = *arithmetischer Durchschnitt*

arithmetischer Operator *m* (EDV) arithmetic operator

arithmetisches Element *n* (EDV) = *arithmetische Einheit*

arithmetisches Mittel *n* (Stat) = *arithmetischer Durchschnitt*

arithmetisches Register *n* (EDV) arithmetic register *(syn, Operandenregister, Rechenregister)*

arithmetisches Unterprogramm *n* (EDV) arithmetic subroutine

arithmetisches Verschieben *n* (EDV) arithmetic shift

Armenrecht *n* (Re) right to cost exemption *(ie, in civil proceedings)*

Arrest *m*
(Re) attachment
- (GB) distraint

Arrestbeschluß *m*
(Re) attachment order
- (GB) distraint order
(ie, secured or sued out to seize property, §§ 916ff ZPO)

Arrestverfahren *n* (Re) attachment procedure

Arrondierungskauf *m* (com) rounding-off buying *(eg, real property, stock exchange securities)*

Artikel *m*
(com) article (*or* item) of goods
- product
(Re) section *(ie, in laws or contracts)*
- article

Artikelanalyse *f* (Mk) item analysis

Artikelaufschlag *m* (Mk) item markup

artikelbezogene Prüfung *f* (Stat) commodity test

Artikeleinstandswert *m* (Mk) item cost

Artikel *m* **im Sonderangebot** (Mk) flash item

Artikelkarte *f* (EDV) commodity card

Artikelnummerndatei *f*
(Mk, US) master universal product (UPC) order file

Artikelspanne *f* (Mk) item-related profit margin

(ie, difference between purchase and sales prices of a single article)
Artikelstatistik *f* (Mk) item analysis
Ärztekammer *f*
  (com, US) State Medical Board of Registration
  – (GB) General Medical Council
Ärztemuster *n* (Mk) free drug sample *(ie, said to be lavishly distributed to medical practitioners as a sales boosting measure)*
Asiatische Entwicklungsbank *f* (Vw) Asian Development Bank
Assekurant *m*
  (Vers) insurer
  – insurance company
  (ie, German term now obsolete)
Assekuranz *f* (Vers) insurance industry
Assembler *m*
  (EDV) assembler
  – assembly program *(syn, Assemblierer)*
Assemblerprotokoll *n* (EDV) assembly list
Assemblersprache *f* (EDV) assembly language *(syn, Assemblierersprache)*
assemblieren (EDV) to assemble *(ie, to translate a source program into an object program; syn, übersetzen)*
Assemblierer *m* (EDV) = *Assembler*
Assemblierinstruktion *f* (EDV) assembly instruction
Assemblierprotokoll *n* (EDV) assembler listing
Assemblierersprache *f* (EDV) = *Assemblersprache*
assertorische Aussage *f* (Log) assertoric statement *(ie, asserting that something is the case; opp, apodiktische und problematische Aussage)*
assertorischer Eid *m* (Re) assertory oath
assertorisches Urteil *n* (Log) assertoric proposition
Assistenzarzt *m* (Pw) assistant physician *(ie, employed by a hospital)*
  – (US) intern
  – (GB) houseman
assortieren (Mk) to assort *(ie, goods or commodities)*
Assoziationskoeffizient *m* (Stat) coefficient of association
Assoziationsrat *m* (EG) Association Council
assoziatives Gesetz *n* (Math) associative law
Assoziativspeicher *m*
  (EDV) associative storage
  – content addressed memory, CAM
  – data addressed memory
  – parallel search storage
  (syn, inhaltsadressierbarer Speicher)
assoziiert (EG) to have *(or* to hold) associate status (with)
assoziiertes Gebiet *n* (EG) associated territory
assoziiertes Land *n* (EG) associated country
assoziiertes Mitglied *n* (EG) associate member
assoziiertes Unternehmen *n* (Re) associated undertaking *(ie, one over which another undertaking exercises a significant influence)*
Assoziierungsabkommen *n* (EG) agreement of association
Ast *m* (OR) tree arc
astronomische Höhe *f* (com) sky-scraping levels *(eg, prices remain at . . .)*

Asylant *m* (Re) person seeking asylum
Asylrecht *n* (Re) right to seek asylum
asymmetrische Verteilung *f* (Stat) asymmetric distribution
Asymptote *f* (Math) asymptote
asymptotisch (Math) asymptotic
asymptotisch beste Schätzung *f* (Stat) asymptotically efficient estimate
asymptotische Eigenschaft *f* (Math) asymptotic property
asymptotische Entwicklung *f* (Stat) asymptotic expansion
asymptotische Methoden *fpl* (Math) asymptotic methods
asymptotische Normalität *f* (od **Normalverteilung** *f*) (Stat) asymptotic normality
asymptotisch erwartungstreue Schätzfunktion *f* (Stat) asymptotically unbiased estimator
asymptotische Streuungs-Kovarianz-Matrix *f* (Math) matrix of asymptotic variances and covariances
asymptotisches Verhalten *n* (Math) asymptotic behavior
asymptotische Verzerrung *f* (Stat) asymptotic bias
asynchrone Arbeitsweise *f* (EDV) asynchronous mode
Asynchronrechenanlage *f* (EDV) = *Asynchronrechner*
Asynchronrechner *m* (EDV) asynchronous computer
Asynchronübertragung *f* (EDV) asynchronous data transmission
Asynchronverfahren *n* (EDV) asynchronous method
ATA-Vorgang *m* (Zo) ATA-operation
Atempause *f* (com) breathing space
atomare Wirtschaft *f* (Vw) nuclear-based industry
Atomgesetz *n* (Re) Atomic Energy Law, as amended 31 Oct 1976
atomistische Konkurrenz *f* (Vw) atomistic competition
Atomkraftwerk *n* (IndE) nuclear power station
Atomprogramm *n* (Vw) nuclear energy program *(ie, to promote research and technological development)*
Atomrisiko-Versicherung *f* (Re) nuclear risk insurance
Atomsatz *m* (Log) atomistic proposition
Attentismus *m* (Bö) wait-and-see attitude
Attest *n*
  (Pw) doctor's certificate
  – (GB) medical certificate
  (ie, evidencing a person's temporary unfitness for work)
Attest *n* **ausstellen** (Pw) to write out a certificate
attraktive Ausstattung *f* (Fin) attractive terms *(eg, of bond)*
attraktives Risiko *n* (Vers) target risk
Attribut *n*
  (Stat) attribute
  – qualitative characteristic
Attributenkontrolle *f*
  (Stat) go-and-not-go gage
  – sampling by attributes
Attributenmerkmal *n* (Stat) attribute

Attributenprüfung f
(Stat) attribute gage (*or* test *or* testing)
– inspection by attributes
Attributenvariable f (Log, Math) attribute variable
atypischer stiller Gesellschafter m (Bw) nontypical silent partner *(ie, one who participates in the assets and capital of a business in addition to its profits and losses)*
atypische stille Gesellschaft f (Bw) nontypical silent partnership
auf Abzahlung kaufen
(com) to buy on the installment plan
– (GB) to buy on hire purchase
aufaddieren
(com) to add up
– to sum up
– to foot up
– (infml) to tot up
auf Antrag
(com) upon application
– upon request
aufarbeiten
(com) to work off *(eg, arrears of correspondence)*
(IndE) to recondition
– to rework
auf Baisse spekulieren (Bö) to sell a bear
Aufbaudarlehen n (Fin) reconstruction loan
Aufbauorganisation f (Bw) company organization structure
Aufbau m **von Lagerbeständen**
(MaW) inventory buildup
– stockbuilding
aufbereiten (EDV) to edit
Aufbereitung f
(Stat) organization of data
(EDV) editing
Aufbereitungsfehler m (Stat) processing error
aufbessern (Pw) to raise *(ie, salary of a staff member)*
Aufbewahrungsfristen fpl (Re) retention periods *(ie, during which books of account and business records must be preserved, 10 and 7 years, respectively; § 44 HGB)*
Aufbewahrungsgebühr f (Fin) safe deposit fee
Aufbewahrungspflicht f (ReW) duty (*or* obligation) to preserve books of account and other records for a specified period, § 44 HGB
aufbrauchen
(com) to use up
– to finish completely
aufbringen
(Fin) to raise (*or* put up) money
– (infml) to cough up
– (infml) to stump up *(eg, an extra $50bn in finance)*
auf dem Dienstweg (Bw) through formal channels
auf dem Submissionswege (com) by tender
auf den Markt bringen (com) to put on the market
auf den neuesten Stand bringen (com) to bring up to date
auf die Tagesordnung setzen (com) to put down on the agenda
aufdrängen (com) to pressure (customers) to take *(eg, a certain product)*

auf eigene Gefahr (com) at one's own risk (*or* peril)
auf eigene Rechnung (com) on one's own account
aufeinander bezogene Ereignisse npl (Bw) related events
auf Eis legen (com, infml) to put *(a matter)* on ice
Aufenthaltsbeschränkung f (Re) limitation of residence
Aufenthaltserlaubnis f (Re) = **Aufenthaltsgenehmigung**
Aufenthaltsgenehmigung f (Re) residence permit *(ie, issued to a foreigner)*
Aufenthaltsort m (Re) (place of) residence *(ie, permanent address)*
Aufenthaltsverlängerung f (Re) extension of stay *(ie, issued to foreigners)*
auf erstes Anfordern (com) upon first demand
auffangen (com) to cushion the impact *(eg, of cost increases)*
Auffanggesellschaft f (Bw) rescue company
Auffangkonsortium n (Fin) support group
auffordern (com) to request *(eg, to pay)*
Auffordern n (EDV) prompting
Aufforderungsbetrieb m (EDV) normal response mode, NRM
Aufforderungsschreiben n (com) letter of invitation
Aufforderung f **zur Einzahlung auf Aktien** (Fin) call on shares
auffrischende Ausbildung f
(Pw) booster
– refresher
– updating
– upgraded ... training
Auffrischungskurs m (Pw) refresher course
auffüllen
(MaW) to accumulate
– to build up
– to replenish ... inventories (*or* stocks)
Auffüllen n (EDV, Cobol) padding
Auffüllung f **von Lagerbeständen**
(MaW) inventory buildup
– accumulation of inventories (*or* stocks)
– stockbuilding
– replenishment of inventories (*or* stocks)
Auffüllzeichen n (EDV) pad character
Aufgabe f
(com) mailing *(eg, a letter)*
– (GB) posting
(com) placing *(eg, an order)*
(Re) discontinuance *(eg, of a business)*
(Pw) task
– job
– (work) assignment
(Math) problem
(Mk) inserting *(ie, an advertisement)*
(EDV) task
(EDV) problem
Aufgabebescheinigung f (com) postal receipt
Aufgabe f **e–r Anwartschaft** (StR) renunciation of an expectancy § 24 Ib EStG
Aufgabe f **e–r Gewinnbeteiligung** (StR) renunciation of a right to a profit participation, § 24 Ib EStG
Aufgabe f **e–r Tätigkeit** (StR) discontinuance of a taxable activity, § 24 Ib EStG

Aufgabe *f* **e–s Gewerbebetriebes** (Re) discontinuance of a commercial business
Aufgabemakler *m* (Bö) broker concluding a deal for his own account
Aufgabenanalyse *f* (Bw) functional analysis
Aufgabenbereich *m* (Bw) area (*or* scope) of responsibilities
– task area
(Pw) scope of position
(Pw) field (*or* scope) of duties
Aufgabengebiet *n* (Pw) = *Aufgabenbereich*
Aufgabenbereicherung *f* (Pw) job enrichment
Aufgabendefinition *f* (EDV) requirements definition
Aufgabenerweiterung *f* (Pw) job enlargement
Aufgabengliederung *f* (Bw) task structuring *(syn, Objektgliederung)*
Aufgabenkatalog *m* **der Wirtschaftspolitik** (Vw) set of economic policy objectives (*or* targets)
aufgabenorientierter Führungsstil *m* (Bw) task-oriented style of leadership *(R. Likert)*
aufgabenorientiertes Terminal *n* (EDV) job oriented terminal
aufgabenorientierte Variable *f* (Mk) task variable
Aufgabensammlung *f* (Math) collection of problems
Aufgabenstellung *f* (com) terms of reference
Aufgabenstrukturierung *f* (Pw) job structuring
Aufgabenteilung *f*
(Bw) division of responsibilities
(EDV) task sharing
Aufgabenträger *m* (Bw) ultimate unit of responsibility
Aufgaben *fpl* **übernehmen** (Pw) to take on responsibilities (*or* tasks)
Aufgabenveränderungs-Programm *n* (Pw) job readjustment program
Aufgabenverteilung *f*
(Pw) task (*or* job) assignment
(EDV) task assignment
Aufgabenverwaltung *f* (EDV) task management
Aufgabenziele *npl* (Bw) task goals
Aufgabenzuteiler *m* (EDV) task dispatcher
Aufgaben *fpl* **zuweisen** (Pw) to assign problems
Aufgabenzuweisung *f* (Pw) assignment of tasks
Aufgabeort *m*
(com) place of mailing
– (GB) place of posting
Aufgabeschein *m* (com) postal receipt
Aufgabestempel *m*
(com) date stamp
– postmark
Aufgabe *f* **übertragen** (Pw) to assign a task (*or* job) (to)
Aufgabe *f* **von Rechten**
(Re) parting with rights
– surrender of rights
Aufgabezeit *f* (com) time of dispatch
Aufgabe *f* **zuweisen** (Pw) to assign a task (to)
aufgeben
(com) to mail *(eg, letter, parcel)*
– (GB) to post
(com) to place *(eg, order, advertisement)*
(Re) to abandon *(eg, right, claim)*
– to give up

– to part with
– to renounce
– to waive
(com) to close down
– to discontinue
– to give up ... a business
aufgeblähte Bilanz *f* (ReW) blown-up balance sheet
Aufgebot *n* (Pat) public invitation to advance claims *(ie, following preliminary examination by Patent Office)*
Aufgebotssystem *n* (Pat) examination-plus-opposition system *(ie, grounds of opposition are ‚prior use' and ‚prior patent grant')*
Aufgebotsverfahren *n*
(Re) cancellation proceeding, § 72 I AktG
(Re) process of public notice, § 946 ZPO
auf Gefahr des Empfängers (com) at receiver's risk
auf Gefahr des Käufers (com) at buyer's risk
aufgegebenes Unternehmen *n* (Re) discontinued business
aufgeklärte Unternehmensführung *f* (Bw) enlightened form of management
aufgelaufene Abschreibungen *fpl* (ReW) accrued (*or* accumulated) depreciation
aufgelaufene Dividende *f* (Fin) accumulated dividend
aufgelaufene Gemeinkosten *pl* (KoR) accumulated overhead
aufgelaufene Zinsen *mpl* (Fin) accrued interest
Aufgeld *n* (com) extra charge
– surcharge
(Fin) premium *(syn, Agio)*
aufgelegt (Fin) open (*or* issued) for subscription
aufgenommene Gelder *npl*
(Fin) creditors' account *(ie, in bank balance sheet)*
(Fin) borrowing by banks *(ie, to strengthen liquidity position)*
aufgenommene langfristige Darlehen *npl* (Fin) long-term borrowing *(ie, item on bank balance sheet)*
aufgenommene Mittel *pl* (Fin) borrowed funds
auf Geschäftskonto (com) on expense account
auf Geschäftskosten reisen (com) to travel at company's expense
aufgeschobene Dividende *f* (Fin) deferred dividend
aufgeschobene Nachfrage *f* (Vw) deferred demand
aufgeschobene Prüfung *f* (Pat) deferred patent examination
aufgeschobene Rente *f* (Math) deferred (*or* intercepted) annuity
aufgeschobene Steuerverbindlichkeiten *fpl* (ReW) deferred tax liabilities
aufgeschobene Versicherung *f* (Vers) deferred insurance
aufgeschobene Zahlung *f* (Fin) deferred payment
aufgliedern
(com) to break down
– to classify
– to itemize
Aufgliederung *f*
(com) breakdown
– classification
– itemization

55

Aufgliederung *f* **in Matrizenform** (ReW) spread sheet
aufhängen
  (com) to put back the receiver
  – to hang up
Aufhänger *m*
  (com, infml) peg
  (Mk, infml) sales anchor
  (ie, to overcome buying resistance)
auf Hausse spekulieren
  (Bö) to bull
  – to go a bull
aufheben
  (com) to close *(eg, meeting, debate)*
  – to end
  – to terminate
  (Vw) to lift *(eg, price controls)*
  (Zo) to abolish *(ie, customs duties)*
  (Pw) to call off *(ie, a strike)*
  (Re) to annul
  – to avoid
  – to cancel
  – to rescind
  – to nullify
  – to terminate ... a contract
  (Re) to disaffirm *(eg, a legal transaction)*
  (Re) to set aside *(eg, a will)*
  (Re) to disaffirm *(eg, a decision)*
  – to reverse
  (Re) to rescind *(ie, a judgment)*
  – to quash
  – to set aside
  (StR) to abolish *(ie, a tax)*
  – to lift
aufheben, sich (Math) to cancel (each other) out
Aufhebung *f* **der öffentlichen Bindung** (Vw) deregulation *(ie, returning ,regulated industries' to the private sector of the economy)*
Aufhebung *f* **von Zöllen**
  (AuW) abolition of tariffs
  – elimination of customs duties
Aufhebung *f* **des Steuerbescheides** (StR) revocation of tax assessment notice, § 172 AO
Aufhebung *f* **des Wohnsitzes** (Re) discontinuance of residence, § 7 BGB
Aufhebung *f* **e-r Sitzung** (com) termination of a meeting
Aufhebungserklärung *f* (Re) declaration of avoidance *(eg, of a contract)*
Aufhebungsklage *f* (Re) action for rescission *(ie, taking proceedings to have a contract judicially set aside)*
Aufhebungsvertrag *m* (Re) agreement to annul an obligatory relation
Aufhebung *f* **von Kreditkontrollen** (Fin) removal of credit controls
aufholen (com) to pick up *(eg, prices)*
  (Bö) to rally
Aufholhypothese *f* (Vw) catching-up hypothesis
Aufholprozeß *m* (Vw) catching-up process
auf Inhaber ausstellen (WeR) to make out to bearer
auf Inhaber lauten (WeR) made out to bearer
auf Jahresbasis umgerechnet
  (Stat) at an annual rate
  – annualized

auf Jahresbasis umrechnen (Stat) to annualize
Aufkauf *m*
  (com) buying up
  (Re) acquisition
  – buying out *(or up)*
  – takeover
aufkaufen
  (com) to buy up *(ie, all the supplies of a commodity)*
  (Re) to buy out *(or up)* *(ie, a business to gain complete control)*
  – to acquire
  – to take over
Aufkäufer *m*
  (com) buyer
  – purchaser
  (com) speculative buyer
Aufkaufhandel *m* (com) buying-up trade
Aufklärungspflicht *f* (Re) duty to warn *(ie, imposed on producer)*
Aufklebeadresse *f* (com) gummed address label
Aufkleber *m* (com) sticker
Aufklebezettel *m* (com) adhesive label
Aufkommen *n* **an Finanzierungsmitteln** (Fin) inflow of financial resources
Aufkommen *n* **an Steuern** (FiW) revenue from taxes
aufkommen für
  (com) to make good *(eg, damage)*
  (com) to pay expenses
  – to pay for
Aufkommenselastizität *f* (FiW) elasticity of tax revenue *(syn, Steuerflexibilität)*
auf Kredit
  (com) on credit
  – (infml) on the cuff
  – (GB, infml) on tick
  – (GB, infml) on the slate *(eg, put it on the slate)*
auf Kredit bestellen
  (com) to order on account *(or* credit)
  – (GB, infml) to order on tick
auf Kredit kaufen (com) to buy on credit
auf Kredit verkaufen (com) to sell on credit terms
aufkündigen (Re) to give notice to terminate *(eg, contract, lease)*
  (Fin) to call in *(eg, a loan)*
Auflage *f*
  (com) edition *(ie, of a book)*
  (com) circulation *(ie, of a newspaper)*
  (Bw) lot
  – lot size
  – batch
  (syn, Los, Partie, Serie)
  (Re) condition *(eg, imposed by a contract; eg, on condition that ...)*
  (Re) requirement
  (ie, by a public authority: to do or omit an act)
  (Re, *civil law*) modus
  (ie, qualification of restriction annexed to the conveyance of land)
  (Re) burden *(ie, imposed by a testator)*
Auflagendegression *f* (KoR) reduction of fixed setup cost per output unit *(ie, resulting from increased lot size)*
Auflagen *fpl* **erfüllen** (Re) to satisfy requirements

Auflagenhöhe f (com) circulation *(ie, number of copies of each issue)*
auf Lager
(com) in stock (*or* store)
– on hand
auf Lager haben (com) to have in stock
auf Lager produzieren (Bw) to manufacture for warehouse
auflassen (Re) to convey real property
Auflassung f
(Re) conveyance by agreement
– formal *in rem* transfer agreement
(ie, agreement on transfer of property between vendor and vendee, sale and transfer being distinct transactions, § 925 BGB)
auflaufen (com) to accrue *(eg, interest on bank account)*
aufleben lassen (Re) to revitalize *(eg, a company)*
auflegen
(com) to put back the receiver
– to hang up
(Fin) to issue *(ie, a bond issue)*
– to float
– to launch
(Fin) to invite subscriptions
– to offer for subscription
(IndE) to run *(eg, a production lot)*
Auflegung f
(Fin) issue
– floating
– launching
Auflegung f **zur öffentlichen Zeichnung** (Fin) invitation (*or* offer) for public subscription
Auflieferer m (com) sender
aufliefern
(com) to send
– to dispatch
– to consign
auflisten (com) to list
Auflisten n
(EDV) listing
– printout
Auflockerung f **der Geldpolitik** (Vw) relaxation of monetary policy
auflösen (Re) to dissolve *(eg, a company)*
(Re) to cancel *(eg, a contract)*
(Kart) to break up *(ie, a cartel)*
(Math) to solve *(eg, an equation)*
(Fin) to close *(ie, one's account with a bank)*
(ReW) to retransfer *(ie, reserves, provisions)*
– to return to source
– to release
– to appropriate
– to withdraw
– to write back
(Pw) to terminate *(ie, an employment contract; eg, by notice to quit)*
auflösend bedingt (Re) subject to a condition subsequent
auflösende Bedingung f (Re) condition subsequent, § 158 II BGB
Auflösung f (Re) dissolution *(eg, of a company)*
(Kart) breaking up *(ie, of a cartel)*
(Re) cancellation *(of a contract)*
(Math) solution *(eg, of an equation)*

(Fin) closing *(ie, an account)*
(ReW) retransfer *(ie, of reserves, provisions)*
– return to source
– release
– appropriation
– withdrawal
– writing back
(Pw) termination *(ie, of employment contract)*
Auflösungsbeschluß m (Re) resolution to liquidate a business
Auflösungsfehler m (EDV) quantization error *(syn, Diskretisierungsfehler, Quantisierungsfehler)*
Auflösungsgraph m (Stat) explosion graph
Auflösungsgründe mpl (Re) statutory grounds for dissolution, § 131 HGB
Auflösung f **von Rechnungsabgrenzungsposten** (ReW) amortization of accruals and deferrals
aufmachen (SeeV) to draw up *(ie, Dispache)*
Aufmachung f
(Mk) presentation
– getup
(Mk) layout *(ie, of printed material)*
Aufmaßliste f (com) list of measurements
auf meine Rechnung, bitte!
(com, GB) Put it down, please
– Please book it to me
– Book it to my account
Aufmerksamkeitserreger m (Mk) attention getter
Aufnahme f
(Re) admission
(Fin) raising *(ie, funds, a loan)*
Aufnahmeantrag m (Re) application for admission
Aufnahmeantrag m **stellen**
(com) to apply for admission
(EG) to apply to join the Community
Aufnahmebedingungen fpl (Re) conditions for admission
aufnahmebereiter Markt m (com) receptive market
Aufnahme f **der Geschäftstätigkeit** (com) commencement of business operations
Aufnahme f **der Steuererklärung an Amtsstelle** (StR) oral declaration by taxpayer before the local tax office, § 151 AO
Aufnahme f **e-s Protokolls** (com) taking of minutes
aufnahmefähiger Markt m (Bö) ready market
(Mk) market capable to absorb (*or* to take up)
Aufnahmefähigkeit f (Mk) absorptive capacity *(ie, of a market)*
(Bö) absorbing capacity
– market receptiveness
Aufnahmegebühr f (com) admission fee *(ie, general term)*
(com) initiation fee
– (GB) entrance fee
(ie, paid on joining a club)
Aufnahmegesuch n (com) application for admission
Aufnahme f **in die Kursnotiz** (Bö) listing
Aufnahmeinterview n (Mk) initial (*or* intake) interview
Aufnahmeland n (Vw) receiving country *(ie, for migrant workers)*
Aufnahme f **langfristigen Fremdkapitals** (Fin) long-term borrowing

57

Aufnahmeprüfung *f* (Pw) entrance examination
Aufnahme *f* **von Fremdkapital** (Fin) borrowing
Aufnahme *f* **von Fremdmitteln** (Fin) borrowing (*or* raising) external funds
Aufnahme *f* **von Gütern** (com) inland collection (*ie, from exporter*)
aufnehmen
 (Re) to introduce (*eg, provisions into a contract*)
 – to include
 (Fin) to borrow
 – to raise
 – to take up (*ie, money, funds, loan*)
 (Fin) to accept
 – to take up (*ie, documents*)
 (Mk) to absorb
 – to accept
 – to take up (*eg, products, merchandise*)
aufnehmende Gesellschaft *f* (Bw) absorbing company
Auf- *od* **Abschlag** *m* **bei Aufträgen auf Bruchschluß** (Bö) trading difference
Aufpreis *m*
 (com) extra charge
 – additional price
auf Probe
 (com) on approval
 (Pw) on probation
auf Pump (com, infml) on tick
aufrechnen
 (Re) to offset
 (StR) to offset
 (ReW) to balance against
 – to counterbalance
 – to offset (*eg, debits against credits*)
Aufrechnung *f*
 (Re) offset
 – setoff
 (*ie, element not of procedural but of substantive law; results in discharge of obligation, §§ 387ff BGB*)
 (StR) offset
 – setoff
 (*ie, of a tax against other tax liabilities, § 226 AO*)
 (ReW) offset
 – setoff
 – balancing against
 – counterbalancing
Aufrißzeichnung *f* (IndE) front view (*or* elevation)
Aufruf *m*
 (EDV) call
 – cue
 (*ie, transference of control to a closed subroutine*)
Aufrufbefehl *m* (EDV) call instruction
Aufrufbetrieb *m* (EDV) polling (*or* selecting) mode
aufrufen
 (Vw) to call in (*ie, to remove banknotes from circulation*)
 (Fin) to call up (*or* in) (*ie, for redemption*)
Aufrufliste *f* (EDV) polling list
aufrunden (EDV) to round off
Aufrunden *n* (EDV) rounding off
auf Schadenersatz klagen (Re) to sue for damages

aufschieben
 (com) to put off (*or* back) (*till/until*) (*eg, decision, appointment, talks until year-end*)
 – to postpone (*until/to*)
 – to delay (*doing sth*)
 – to defer
Aufschieben *n*
 (com) putting off
 – postponement
 – delay
 – deferment
aufschiebend bedingt (Re) subject to a condition precedent
aufschiebend bedingte Lasten *fpl* (StR) conditional liabilities and burdens (on property), § 6 BewG
aufschiebende Bedingung *f*
 (Re) condition precedent
 – suspensive condition, § 158 BGB
 (*eg, it shall be a condition precedent to this contract that . . .*)
aufschiebende Einrede *f* (Re) dilatory defense (*or* exception) (*syn, dilatorische od rechtshemmende Einrede*)
aufschiebende Wirkung *f* (Re) suspensive effect
Aufschlag *m*
 (com) extra charge
 (com) premium
 (com) recargo
 (Mk) markup
 (Bö) markup
aufschlagen (com) to mark up (*ie, prices*)
Aufschlag *m* **für Bearbeitung** (com) service charge
Aufschlag *m* **für vorzeitige Tilgung**
 (Fin) prepayment penalty
 – (GB) redemption fee
 (*ie, fee charged for paying off a mortgage before maturity*)
aufschließen (IndE) to develop (*eg, land or natural resources*)
Aufschließung *f* (IndE) development work in mining (*ie, removal of overburden in strip mining, and shaft sinking in underground mining*)
Aufschließungseffekt *m* (AuW) trade creating effect
Aufschließungskosten *pl* (com) development cost
 (KoR) mine development cost (*or* expense) (*ie, capitalized and written off by the unit-of-product method*)
Aufschließungsmaßnahmen *fpl* (com) land improvements
aufschlüsseln
 (com) to break down
 – to apportion
 – to subdivide
 – to classify
 – to subclassify
Aufschlüsselung *f*
 (com) breaking down
 – apportionment
 – allocation
 – subdivision
 – classification
 – subclassification
aufschreiben (com) to write (*or* put) down

Aufschrift *f*
(com) name (*or* sign) of business
(com) address
– label *(ie, in postal service)*
(com) inscription
Aufschub *m*
(com) delay
– deferment
– extension
Aufschubanmeldung *f* (Zo) deferment notification
Aufschubfrist *f* (Fin) time limit for payment
Aufschub *m* **gewähren** (com) to grant a delay (*or* respite)
Aufschubkonto *n* (Zo) deferment account
aufschwänzen (Bö) to corner *(syn, schwänzen)*
aufschwatzen (Mk) to talk *(a customer)* into taking sth
Aufschwung *m*
(Vw) (cyclical) upswing
– upturn
– turn-up
– burst of expansion
– business cycle expansion
aufsetzen
(com) to draw up *(eg, letter, minutes, contract, advertisement)*
(Re) to draft *(eg, a contract)*
Aufsetzpunkt *m* (EDV, Cobol) rerun point
auf Sicht
(WeR) at sight
– on demand *(ie, subject to payment upon presentation and demand)*
Aufsichtsamt *n* (Re) supervisory office
Aufsichtsführung *f* (Pw) supervision
Aufsichtsrat *m* (Bw) supervisory board
(ie, determines the overall policy of the company. Note: This is the Central European version of the ‚board of directors'. It is not a component of a two-tier management system, but is playing essentially the same advisory role as its American counterpart. Top managers cannot sit on the board.)
Aufsichtsratsbericht *m* (ReW) supervisory board's annual report *(ie, prepared on the basis of management and audit reports, § 171 AktG)*
Aufsichtsratsmandat *n* (Bw) supervisory board seat
Aufsichtsratsmitglied *n*
(Bw) supervisory board member
– member of supervisory board *(ie, may be equated with the non-executive directors on an English board of directors)*
Aufsichtsratssitz *m* (Bw) supervisory board seat
Aufsichtsratsteuer *f* (StR) directors' tax *(ie, deducted at source – Quellensteuer – from directors' fees receivable by nonresident members of supervisory board)*
Aufsichtsratsvergütung *f* (Re) supervisory board fee, § 113 AktG
Aufspaltung *f*
(Stat) disaggregation
(EDV) switching point
aufspannen
(Math) to occupy
– to span

aufspannender Baum *m* (OR) spanning tree
aufsummieren
(com) to add up
– to sump up
– (infml) to tot up
aufsummieren über (Math) to sum over
aufsummierte Abweichung *f* (Stat) accumulated deviation
Aufsummierung *f*
(com) adding up
– summing up
(Math) summation
Aufstaulager *n* (IndE) bottled-up store *(ie, in serial production where output per time unit is larger than that of subsequent operations)*
aufsteigen
(Pw) to rise
– to be promoted
aufsteigende Arbeitspartizipation *f* (Pw) ascending worker participation *(ie, influence at levels above one's own)*
aufstellen
(com) to draw up
– to prepare *(eg, statement, balance sheet)*
(IndE) to install *(eg, machinery)*
Aufstellen *n* **e-r Präferenzordnung** (Vw) ordering (*or* ranking) of preferences
Aufstellung *f*
(com) list
– breakdown
– schedule
(ReW) drawing up
– preparation *(eg, statement, balance sheet)*
(IndE) installation *(eg, machinery)*
(EDV) tabulation *(ie, a printed report)*
Aufstellung *f* **des Jahresabschlusses**
(ReW) preparation of year-end financial statement
– (GB) drawing up of the annual accounts
Aufstellung *f* **e-s Inventars** (ReW) preparation (*or* taking) of an inventory, § 39 II HGB
Aufstellungszeichnung *f* (com) installation drawing
Aufstieg *m*
(Pw) advancement
– career development
– (fml) ascendancy
Aufstiegschancen *fpl*
(Pw) career development prospects
– scope for advancement
Aufstiegsmobilität *f* (Pw) upward mobility
Aufstiegsmöglichkeiten *fpl*
(Pw) career prospects
– career development prospects
– career growth opportunities
– scope for advancement
aufstocken
(com) to increase *(eg, credit by DM 10bn, reserves, liquid funds)*
– to top up *(eg, pension)*
(Bw) to build up *(eg, inventory)*
Aufstockung *f* **des Grundkapitals** (Fin) increase of capital stock
Aufstockung *f* **e-s Zollkontingents** (Zo) quota increase
Aufstockungsaktie *f* (Fin) bonus share

Aufstockungs-Koeffizient *m* (ReW) revaluation coefficient
aufsuchen (Mk) to call on *(eg, a customer)*
auftabellierbar (com) tabulable
auftabellieren
 (com) to tabulate
 – to put in tabular form
 – to tabularize
 – to formulate tabularly
Auftabellierung *f* (com) tabulation
aufteilen
 (com) to break up
 – to split up
 – to apportion
 – to allocate
 (ReW) to divide *(eg, profits)*
 (Stat) to allocate *(ie, a sample)*
 (FiW) to apportion *(ie, tax revenues)*
 (Mk) to divide *(ie, a market)*
 – to partition
 – (infml) to carve up
Aufteilung *f*
 (com) allocation
 – apportionment
 – breakup
 (ReW) division *(eg, of profits)*
 (Stat) allocation *(eg, of a sample)*
 (FiW) apportionment *(ie, of tax revenues)*
 (Mk) division *(ie, of a market)*
 – partition
 – (infml) carving up
Aufteilung *f* **e-s Kontingents** (Zo) allocation of a tariff quota
Aufteilungsmaßstab *m* (StR) procedural rule governing the apportionment of taxes, §§ 268–280 AO
auf Termin kaufen (Bö) to purchase forward
Auftrag *m*
 (com) order
 – purchase order
 – sales order (for)
 (Re) mandate *(ie, gratuitous contract by which one party undertakes to do something on behalf of the other without receiving any compensation = Gegenleistung; § 662 BGB)*
 (EDV) job *(syn, Abschnitt, Aufgabe, Bearbeitung)*
Auftrag *m* **ausführen**
 (com) to carry out
 – to complete
 – to execute
 – to fill ... an order
Auftrag *m* **bearbeiten** (com) to process an order
Aufträge *mpl* **ablehnen** (com) to turn away business
Aufträge *mpl* **abwickeln**
 (com) to transact business
 (com) to fill
 – to handle
 – to process ... orders
Aufträge *mpl* **beschaffen**
 (com) to attract *(or* solicit) new business
 – to canvass
 – to obtain
 – to secure ... new orders

Aufträge *mpl* **hereinholen** (com) = *Aufträge beschaffen*
Aufträge *mpl* **hereinnehmen** (com) to take on business
Auftrag *m* **erhalten**
 (com) to obtain
 – to secure ... an order
 (com) to win a contract *(ie, esp. in construction and systems engineering)*
Auftrag *m* **erteilen**
 (com) to place an order (for)
 – to award a contract
Aufträge *mpl* **zu regulärem Festpreis** (com, US) straight-fixed-price contracts
Aufträge *mpl* **zurückhalten** (com) to cut back on orders
Auftraggeber *m*
 (com) customer
 – client
 (Fin) principal
 (Re) mandant *(ie, person at whose request unremunerated services are performed, § 662 BGB)*
 (StR, VAT) recipient of another performance *(= Empfänger e-r sonstigen Leistung)*
 (EDV) user
Auftraggebereffekt *m* (Log) sponsorship bias
Auftrag *m* **hereinholen** (com) to secure an order
Auftrag *m* **mit interessewahrender Ausführung** (Bö) not-held order
auftragsabhängige Kosten *pl* (KoR) cost traceable to a specific job order
Auftragsabrechnung *f*
 (KoR) job order cost accounting
 – accounting for job order costs
 (EDV) job accounting
Auftragsabrechnungsdatei *f* (EDV) job account file
Auftragsabrechnungssystem *n* (EDV) job accounting system
Auftragsabwicklung *f*
 (com) order filling
 – order handling
 – order processing
 (EDV) job handling
auftragsähnliches Rechtsverhältnis *n* (Re) mandate, employment or other contractual relationship
Auftragsänderung *f* (com) change order
Auftragsaufgaben *fpl* **der Zollverwaltung** (Zo) functions of the customs administration carried out on behalf of other government bodies
Auftragsaufruf *m* (EDV) job macro call
Auftragsausführung *f* (com) job execution
Auftragsbearbeitung *f* (com) sales order processing
Auftragsbeschaffung *f* (com) order getting
Auftragsbestand *m*
 (com) backlog *(or* level *or* volume) of orders
 – backlog order books *(eg, look relatively healthy)*
 – state of order book
 – orders on hand
 – unfilled orders
 – orders on the book
 – order book

Auftragsbestandskartei *f* (MaW) open purchase-order file
Auftragsbestätigung *f*
(com) acknowledgment of order *(ie, sent by seller to customer)*
(com) confirmation of order *(ie, sent by buyer to vendor)*
Auftragsbewegung *f* (com) statement of changes in order backlog
auftragsbezogen (EDV) job oriented
auftragsbezogen produzieren (com) to make *(or* produce*)* to order
Auftragsbuch *n* (com) order book
Auftragsbuchführung *f* (com) order filing department
Auftragseingabe *f* (EDV) job input
Auftragseingabeband *n* (EDV) job input tape
Auftragseingang *m*
(com) booking of new orders
– incoming business *(or* orders*)*
– inflow of orders
– intake of new orders
– new orders
– order bookings *(or* flow*)*
– orders received *(or* taken*)*
– rate of new orders *(eg, started to show slight improvement)*
Auftragseingang *m* **aus dem Ausland** (com) foreign bookings
Auftragseingangs-Statistik *f* (Stat) statistics on orders received
Auftragsende *n* (EDV) end of job *(or* run*)*
Auftragserteilung *f*
(com) placing an order
– placing of order
Auftragsferneingabe *f* (EDV) remote job entry, RJE
Auftragsfertigung *f* (IndE) make-to-order production
Auftragsforschung *f* (com) committed *(or* contract *or* outside*)* research
auftragsgebundenes Material *n*
(MaW) allotted
– allocated
– apportioned
– applicable
– assigned
– obligated
– reserved ... materials
auftragsgemäß (com) as per order
Auftragsgeschäft *n* (Fin) commission business
Auftragsgröße *f* (Bw) lot size
Auftragsgruppen-Überwachung *f* (Bw) block control
Auftragskalkulation *f* (KoR) estimate of job order costs
Auftragskarte *f*
(com) order card
(EDV) job macro card
Auftragskartei *f* (com) order file *(ie, comprising customer and production orders)*
Auftragskennzeichen *n* (com) job order code
Auftragskosten *pl* (KoR) job costs
Auftragskostenrechnung *f* (KoR) job *(or* order*)* costing

Auftragskostensammelblatt *n* (KoR) job cost sheet
Auftragskostenverfahren *n* (KoR) job order cost system
Auftragslage *f* (com) orders position
Auftragsmakro *n* (EDV) job macro
Auftragsmangel *m* (com) lack *(or* dearth*)* of orders
Auftragsmaterial *n* (MaW) materials purchased to fill a particular order
Auftragsmeldung *f* (com) order note
Auftragsname *m* (EDV) job name
Auftragspapiere *npl* (Fin) documents accepted for collection
Auftragsplanung *f* (IndE) job order planning *(ie, part of production planning: made to smooth out fluctuations in plant utilization)*
Auftragspolster *n*
(com) cushion of existing orders
– comfortable backlog of orders
– full order books
Auftragspriorität *f* (EDV) job priority
Auftragsprioritätssteuergerät *n* (EDV) job scheduler
Auftragsproduktion *f* (IndE) make-to-order production
Auftragsreserven *fpl* (com) order backlog
Auftragsrückgang *m*
(com) drop in orders
– drop-off in orders
– falling-off of orders
– order decline *(eg, in capital goods)*
Auftragsrückstand *m* (com) unfilled orders
Auftragsschritt *m* (EDV) job step
Auftragsschwemme *f* (com) boom in orders
Auftragssprache *f* (EDV) = *Auftragssteuersprache*
Auftragssteuersprache *f* (EDV) job control language
Auftragssteuerung *f* (EDV) job control
Auftragssteuerungsstelle *f* (Kart) central order distribution agency
Auftrag *m* **stornieren** (com) to cancel an order
Auftragsstornierung *f* (com) cancellation of order
Auftragsüberwachung *f* (com) order control
Auftragsumlaufzeit *f* (EDV) elapsed *(or* job around*)* time *(syn, Verweilzeit)*
Auftragsvergabe *f* (com) contract award process
(com) placing of orders
Auftragsverteilung *f* **auf mehrere Lieferanten** (MaW) order splitting
Auftragsverwaltung *f*
(Re) administration by the states *(= Länder)* acting as agents for the Federal Government
(EDV) job management
auftragsweise Kostenerfassung *f* (KoR) determination of costs by job order
Auftragswert *m* (com) contract value
Auftragszeit *f* (IndE) total process time *(ie, setup time + actual process time)*
Auftragszusammensetzung *f* (KoR) job order setup
Auftrag *m* **vergeben**
(com) to give *(or* place*)* an order (for)
(com) to award *(or* let out*)* a contract
– to accept a bid *(or* tender*)*
Auftrag *m* **zu Festpreisen** (com) fixed-price contract *(ie, no escalator clause)*

Auftrag *m* zur Bestandsauffüllung (MaW) replacement order
Auftrag *m* zu regulärem Festpreis (com) straight fixed-price contract
Auftrag *m* zur Nachbesserung (IndE) spoiled-work order
– rework order
Auftriebskräfte *fpl* (Vw, Bö) buoyant (*or* propellant) forces
auf unbestimmte Zeit vertagen (com) to adjourn indefinitely
auf veränderte Bedingungen reagieren (Bw) to respond to changing circumstances
auf Veranlassung von (com) at the instance of
auf Vermögensausgleich gerichtetes Schuldrecht *n* (Re) remedial obligatory right
Aufwand *m*
(com) cost
– expense
– expenditure
– outlay
(ReW) expense *(opp, Ertrag = revenue)*
Aufwand *m* für ungenutzte Anlagen (ReW) carrying charges
Aufwandsart *f* (ReW) type of expense
Aufwandsausgleichskonto *n* (ReW) expense matching account
Aufwandsentschädigung *f* (Pw) expense allowance
– representation allowance
aufwandsgleiche Ausgaben *fpl* (ReW) revenue expenditure
(KoR) current-outlay costs
Aufwandskonto *n* (ReW) expense account
Aufwandskosten *pl* (KoR) current-outlay costs
Aufwandsposten *m* (ReW) expense item
Aufwandsrückstellung *f* (ReW) provision for operating expense
Aufwandsteuer *f* (StR) expenditure tax
Aufwands- und Ertragskonten *npl*
(ReW) revenue and expense accounts
– nominal accounts
– (US) income accounts
Aufwands- und Ertragsrechnung *f* (ReW) = *Gewinn- und Verlustrechnung*
Aufwandszinsen *mpl* (Fin) interest charges (*or* expenses)
Aufwand *m* und Ertrag *m*
(ReW) revenue and expense
– (US) income and expense
Aufwärtsentwicklung *f*
(com) rising (*or* upward) trend
– rising tendency
– uphill trend
Aufwärtsstrukturierung *f* (EDV) bottom-up design
Aufwärtstrend *m* (com) = *Aufwärtsentwicklung*
aufwenden
(com) to spend
– to expend *(eg, money on)*
aufwendig
(com) expensive
– entailing great expense
– costly
Aufwendungen *mpl*
(Re, ReW) expenses
(ReW, EG) charges

Aufwendungen *mpl* aus Verlustübernahme (ReW) charge resulting from agreements to assume losses
Aufwendungen *mpl* für Arbeitsmittel (StR) expenses for tools and other professional necessities *(eg, work clothes, professional literature, § 9 I 6 EStG)*
Aufwendungen *mpl* für die Berufsfortbildung (StR) educational expenses *(ie, expenses incurred for maintaining or improving existing skills needed in the taxpayer's profession or employment, § 10 I 7 EStG)*
Aufwendungen *mpl* für die Bewirtung (StR) expenditures incurred in connection with the entertainment of persons other than employees, § 4 V No. 2 EStG
Aufwendungen *mpl* für die Eigenkapitalbeschaffung (Fin) commissions and expense on capital
Aufwendungen *mpl* für die Errichtung und Erweiterung des Unternehmens (ReW, EG) formation expenses
Aufwendungen *mpl* für Fahrten zwischen Wohnung und Arbeitsstätte (StR) commuting expenses *(ie, for daily travel between home and place of work, § 9 I 4 EStG)*
Aufwendungen *mpl* für Forschung und Entwicklung (Bw) spending on research and development
Aufwendungen *mpl* für Geschäftsfreundebewirtung (StR) entertaining expenses
Aufwendungen *mpl* und Erträge *mpl*
(ReW) revenue and expense
– (US) income and expense
Aufwendungen *mpl* zur Erwerbung, Sicherung und Erhaltung der Einnahmen (StR) expenditures made to create, protect, or preserve the income
Aufwendungsersatz *m* (com) repayment of expenses, § 87d HGB
aufwerten
(com) to upgrade
(AuW) to appreciate (*or* upvalue) a currency
Aufwertung *f*
(AuW) appreciation
– upvaluation
– upward revaluation *(ie, of a currency)*
Aufwertungsdruck *m* (AuW) upward pressure *(eg, on the $, £)*
Aufwertungsland *n* (AuW) upvaluing country
Aufwertungssatz *m* (AuW) revaluation rate
Aufwertungstendenz *f* (AuW) tendency towards depreciation
aufwertungsverdächtig (AuW) revaluation prone
Aufwuchs- und Fanggründe *pl* (com) maturing and fishing grounds
aufzehren
(com) to use up
– to clean out *(eg, savings)*
aufzeichnen
(com) to note
– to put down
– to record
(EDV) to record *(syn, speichern)*
Aufzeichnung *f* (EDV) recording
Aufzeichnung *f* des Warenausgangs (StR) records of merchandise sales, § 144 AO

Aufzeichnung f des Wareneingangs (StR) records of merchandise purchases, § 143 AO
Aufzeichnungen fpl
(com) notes
(ReW) books and records
Aufzeichnungsband n (EDV) log tape
Aufzeichnungsdichte f (EDV) recording density
Aufzeichnungsfehler m (EDV) recording error
Aufzeichnungsformat n (EDV) record format
Aufzeichnungsmedium n (EDV) recording medium
Aufzeichnungspflicht f (StR) legal obligation to keep books and records, §§ 140ff AO
auf Ziel kaufen (com) to buy on credit
aufzinsen
(Math) to accumulate
– to compound
(Fin) to add unaccrued interest
Aufzinsung f (Math) accumulation
Aufzinsungsfaktor m
(Math) accumulation factor $(1 + i)^n$
– compound amount of 1
(ie, amount of 1 at compound interest)
Aufzinsungspapiere npl (Fin) securities sold at a premium
Auf-Zu-Regler m (EDV) on-off controller
Augenblicksänderung f (Math) instantaneous rate of change
Augenblicksverband m (Re) single-purpose association
Augenblicksverzinsung f (Fin) continuous convertible interest
Auktion f
(com) sale at auction
– (GB) sale by auction
Auktionator m (com) auctioneer
Auktionssystem n (com) system of establishing prices by auction
A-Urteil n
(Log) universal affirmation
– A-proposition
– material implication
(ie, equivalent of ‚subalternation' of traditional logic)
ausarbeiten
(com) to prepare
– to work out
Ausarbeitung f
(com) draft
– preparation
(com) paper
– memorandum
– memo
ausbaden
(com, infml) be left holding the bag (or baby)
Ausbau m (Bw) plant extension
Ausbau m **der Fertigungskapazität** (Bw) upstepping of productive capacity
ausbauen
(Bw) to extend *(eg, plant facilities)*
– to expand
ausbaufähig (Bw) extensible
Ausbaugebiet n (Vw) structural-improvement region

Ausbaugewerbe n (com) fitting-out trade *(eg, plumbing, painting, etc.)*
Ausbaupatent n (Pat) improvement patent
ausbedingen (Re) to stipulate
Ausbesserungen fpl (com) maintenance and repair work
Ausbeute f
(Bw) output
– yield
(Bw) yield coefficient *(ie, relation between usable output and processed output)*
(Fin) distributable profit *(ie, of a mining company)*
(Re) yield, § 99 BGB
Ausbeuteabweichung f (KoR) yield variation
Ausbeutesatz m (Bw) rate of yield *(ie, in processing)*
Ausbeutung f **auf Wettbewerbsbasis** (Vw) competitive exploitation *(ie, of the oceans)*
Ausbeutungsrate f (IndE) yield rate
ausbieten (com) to put up for sale (by auction)
Ausbietung f (com) putting up for sale by auction
Ausbietungsgarantie f (Re) contractual obligation of a party in a forced sale to bid up to the amount of the mortgage so that the other party suffers no loss through a delinquent claim
Ausbildender m
(Pw) instructor
(Pw) enterprise or company in which apprentice is trained
Ausbildung f
(Pw) schooling
– education
– training
– instruction
Ausbildung f **abschließen**
(Pw) to complete (or finish) education (or training)
Ausbildung f **am Arbeitsplatz**
(Pw) on-the-job training
– on-the-site training
– desk training
Ausbildung f **außerhalb des Arbeitsplatzes** (Pw) off-the-job training
Ausbildungsabgabe f (Pw) apprenticeship levy
Ausbildungsabgabe f **einführen** (Pw) to introduce (or impose) a training levy
Ausbildungsabschlußprüfung f (Pw) final trainee examination
Ausbildungsbeihilfe f (Pw) training allowance *(ie, paid to apprentice)*
Ausbildungsdauer f
(Pw) length (or duration) of education (or training)
Ausbildungsförderung f (Pw) promotion of vocational (or professional) training
Ausbildungsförderungsgesetz n (Pw) Federal Law on Education and Training Promotion
Ausbildungsfreibetrag m
(StR) education allowance
– deduction for educational expenses
Ausbildungsgang m (Pw) course of training
Ausbildungskosten pl (Pw) training costs
Ausbildungslehrgang m (Pw) training course
Ausbildungsleiter m (Pw) training officer

63

Ausbildungsort *m* (StR) town where training takes place
Ausbildungspersonal *n* (Pw) training personnel
Ausbildungsplatz *m* (Pw) (apprentice) training place
Ausbildungsplatz-Abzugsbetrag *m* (StR) deduction for creating training opening, § 24 b EStG
Ausbildungsplätze *mpl* (Pw) openings for apprentices
Ausbildungsplatzförderungsgesetz *n* (Re) Apprentice Hiring Law
Ausbildungsprogramm *n* (Pw) training scheme (*or* program)
Ausbildungsstand *m* (Pw) level of training
Ausbildungsstätte *f*
  (Pw) training shop (*or* facilities)
  – training center
Ausbildungsvergütung *f* (Pw) trainee compensation
Ausbildungsversicherung *f* (Vers) educational endowment insurance
Ausbildungsvertrag *m* (Pw) articles of apprenticeship
Ausbildungswerkstatt *f* (Pw) training shop
Ausbildungszeit *f* (Pw) length (*or* duration) of training or education
Ausbildungszeiten *fpl* (Pw) periods of professional (*or* vocational) training
Ausblendbefehl *m* (EDV) mask (*or* extract) instruction
ausblenden (EDV) to mask out
Ausblenden *n*
  (EDV) masking out
  (EDV) reverse clipping
  – shielding
Ausbreitungseffekt *m* (Vw) spread effec (*G. Myrdal*)
Ausbringung *f*
  (Bw) output
  – production
  – yield
Ausbringung *f* **bei Vollbeschäftigung** (Vw) full employment output
ausbuchen
  (com) to debit
  – to take out of the books
  – to enter a debit against (*eg, bank debited my account with $50*)
  (ReW) to charge off (*eg, as expense or loss*)
  (ReW) to write off (*eg, bad debt as uncollectible*)
  (ReW) to close out (*eg, cost of plant removed*)
  (Fin) to balance (*ie, an account*)
Ausbuchung *f*
  (com) debit
  (ReW) charge off
  (ReW) write off
  (ReW) closing out
  (Fin) balancing
aus dem Erwerbsleben ausscheiden
  (Pw) to leave the labor force
  – to withdraw from working life
  – to drop out of the labor force
aus dem Markt nehmen (Fin) to soak up
aus der Notierung nehmen (Bö) to suspend a quotation

Ausdruck *m*
  (Log) term
  (EDV, Cobol) arithmetic expression
  (EDV) printout
  (EDV) memory dump
Ausdruck *m* **des Systems** (Log) well-formed formula, wff
ausdrucken (EDV) to print out
ausdrückliche Bedingung *f* (Re) express condition
ausdrückliche Garantie *f* (Re) express guaranty
ausdrückliche od stillschweigende Gewährleistung *f* (Re) express or implied warranty
ausdrückliche Vereinbarung *f*
  (Re) special arrangement
  – express agreement
ausdrückliche Zusicherung *f* (Re) express warranty
ausdrücklich od stillschweigend
  (Re) expressly or impliedly
  – expressly or by implication
ausdrücklich vereinbaren (Re) to stipulate expressly
Auseinandersetzung *f*
  (Re) division
  – apportionment
  (*ie, of property – surplus or deficiency – among partners pro rata of their shares, §§ 730–735 BGB*)
  (Re) partition of an estate, § 2042 BGB
Auseinandersetzung *f* **e-r Gemeinschaft** (Re) partition of a community of interest
Auseinandersetzungsbilanz *f* (ReW) balance sheet for settlement purposes (*ie, division of property among members of partnership*)
Auseinandersetzungsguthaben *n* (Re) credit balance of a retiring partner's capital account (*usu, plus his share of secret reserves resulting from an undervaluation of the business' fixed assets*)
Auseisung *f* (SeeV) de-icing
aus e-m Vertrag klagen (Re) to sue on a contract
Ausfall *m*
  (Fin) financial loss
  – loss
  – deficiency
  (*eg, from default in payment, of receivables, sales revenue*)
  (Stat) failure
  (Mk) non-response rate
  (IndE) failure (*ie, of machinery*)
  – breakdown
  (EDV) cutage
  – failure
Ausfallbürge *m*
  (Re) guarantor of collection
  – (GB) deficiency guarantor
Ausfallbürgschaft *f*
  (Re) guaranty of collection
  – (GB) deficiency (*or* deficit) guarantee
  – (GB) indemnity bond
  (*ie, surety assumes only subsidiary liability: creditor must first exhaust his legal remedies against the principal*)
Ausfalldichte *f* (Stat) failure density
Ausfälle *mpl* (Fin) loan losses

Ausfallforderung *f* (Re) claim of preferential creditor *(ie, in bankruptcy proceedings)*
Ausfallhaftung *f* (Re) liability for non-collection
Ausfallhäufigkeit *f* (Stat) failure frequency
Ausfallhäufigkeitsverteilung *f* (Stat) failure frequency distribution
Ausfallklasse *f* (Stat) risk allowance group
Ausfallkriterien *npl* (Stat) failure criteria
Ausfallmuster *n* (com) reference pattern
Ausfallquote *f*
 (Stat) failure quota
 (Fin) loan chargeoff ratio
Ausfallrate *f*
 (Stat) non-achievement rate *(ie, in surveys)*
 – failure *(or* non-response) rate
 (Stat) proportion of defectives
 – refusal rate
 (IndE) failure rate
Ausfallrisiko *n*
 (Fin) risk of default *(or* nonpayment)
 – non-payment risk *(ie, relating to receivables)*
 (Fin) loan loss risk
ausfallsichere Betriebsweise *f* (EDV) fail safe mode
Ausfallursache *f* (Stat) failure cause
Ausfallwahrscheinlichkeit *f* (Stat) probability of failure
Ausfallwahrscheinlichkeitsdichte *f* (Stat) failure probability density
Ausfallwahrscheinlichkeitsverteilung *f* (Stat) failure probability distribution
Ausfallwahrscheinlichkeit *f* **von Leitungen** (EDV) network reliability
Ausfallzeit *f*
 (IndE) downtime
 (EDV) down *(or* fault) time
ausfertigen (Re) to write out *(eg, document, agreement, contract)*
Ausfertigung *f*
 (com) copy *(ie, of official document)*
 (com) counterpart *(eg, of bill of lading)*
Ausfertigungsgebühr *f*
 (com) issue fee
 (com) charge for making out *(eg, duplicate, copy)*
 (Vers) policy issue fee
Ausfertigungstag *m* (com) day of issue
Ausfischung *f* (com) devastation of fishery resources
Ausflaggen *n* (com) sailing under a foreign flag
Ausfolgungsprotest *m* (WeR) protest for non-delivery *(ie, of bill of exchange)*
Ausfuhr *f* (AuW) export *(ie, act of exporting)*
 – exportation
 (AuW) export *(ie, article exported)*
 (AuW) exports *(ie, volume of goods exported)*
Ausfuhrabfertigung *f* (Zo) clearance on exportation
Ausfuhrabgaben *fpl* (EG) export levies
 – duties at exportation
 (ie, payable if world-market price levels are higher than Community prices)
Ausfuhrabschöpfung *f*
 (EG) price adjustment levy
 – export farm levy
 (ie, imposed in order to keep prices at high EEC levels)
Ausfuhragent *m* (AuW) export agent
Ausfuhranmeldung *f*
 (Zo) clearance on exportation
 – (GB) entry outwards
Ausfuhrartikel *m*
 (com) article exported
 – article of exportation
Ausfuhrbescheinigung *f* (Zo) certificate of exportation
Ausfuhrbeschränkung *f* (AuW) export restriction
Ausfuhrbestimmungen *fpl* (AuW) export regulations
Ausfuhrbewilligung *f* (AuW) export license
Ausfuhrblatt *n* (Zo) exportation sheet *(ie, Stammabschnitt und Trennabschnitt: counterfoil and voucher)*
Ausfuhrbürgschaft *f* (AuW) export guaranty *(ie, covers risks inherent in transactions with foreign governments; see also „Hermesdeckung')*
Ausfuhrdokument *n* (AuW) export document
ausführen
 (com) to carry out *(eg, an order)*
 – to execute
 – to fill
 (AuW) to export *(syn, exportieren)*
ausführende Arbeit *f* (Bw) operative performance
ausführende Arbeitskraft *f* (Pw) operative
Ausführer *m* (AuW) exporter *(syn, Exporteur)*
Ausfuhrerklärung *f* (Zo) export declaration
Ausfuhrerlaubnis *f* (AuW) export permit *(or* license)
Ausfuhrerlösschwankungen *fpl* (AuW) export revenue fluctuations
Ausfuhrerstattung *f* (EG) export refund *(ie, rebate of domestic tax to exporter)*
Ausfuhrfinanzierung *f* (AuW) export financing
Ausfuhrforderung *f* (AuW) export claim
Ausfuhrförderung *f* (AuW) export promotion *(ie, sum total of measures designed to increase volume of exports of a particular country)*
Ausfuhrförderungskredit *m* (AuW) export promotion credit
Ausfuhrförmlichkeiten *fpl* **erfüllen** (AuW) to carry out export formalities
Ausfuhrgarantie *f* (AuW) export credit guaranty *(ie, covers risks inherent in transactions with private foreign firms; see also „Hermesdeckung')*
Ausfuhrgenehmigung *f* (EG) export authorization
Ausfuhr-Grundquote *f* (Zo) basic export quota
Ausfuhrgüter *npl*
 (AuW) export commodities *(or* goods)
 – exports
Ausfuhrhafen *m* (Zo) port of exit
Ausfuhrhandel *m* (AuW) export trade
Ausfuhrhändler *m* (AuW) export trader
Ausfuhrhändlervergütung *f* (AuW) refund of VAT to exporter
Ausfuhrkartell *n* (Kart) export-promoting cartel *(syn, Exportkartell)*
Ausfuhrkommissionär *m* (com) export commission agent
Ausfuhrkontingent *n* (AuW) export quota

Ausfuhrkontrolle f (AuW) export control *(ie, pursuant to German foreign trade legislation)*
Ausfuhrkontrollmeldung f (Zo) export notification for purposes of record
Ausfuhrkredit m (Fin) export credit
Ausfuhr-Kreditgesellschaft f (AuW) Export Credit Company *(ie, set up in 1952 by a group of West-German credit institutions for medium and long-term export financing; abbr. AKA)*
Ausfuhrkreditversicherung f (AuW) export credit insurance
Ausfuhrland n
 (AuW) country of export
 – exporting country
ausführlich beschreiben (com) to describe in detail
 – to detail
ausführliche Bewerbung f (Pw) detailed application
ausführlicher Lebenslauf m
 (Pw) detailed curriculum vitae
 – career monograph
 – detailed *(or* full) career history
ausführlicher Prüfungsbericht m (ReW) accountant's detailed report
Ausfuhrlieferungen fpl (StR) export deliveries *(ie, exempt from turnover tax, § 4 No. 1, § 6 UStG)*
Ausfuhrlizenz f (EG) export license *(ie, needed for farm products supplied to non-member countries)*
Ausfuhrlizenz f **beantragen** (AuW) to file an application for an export license
Ausfuhrmarkt m (AuW) export market
Ausfuhrmeldung f (AuW) export notification *(ie, submitted together with the export declaration, in the form of one copying set)*
Ausfuhrmitgliedsstaat m (EG) Member State of export
Ausfuhr f **nach aktiver Veredelung** (Zo) exportation after inward processing
Ausfuhrnachweis m (StR) evidence of export shipment *(ie, requirement for exemption from turnover tax, § 6 No. 3 UStG)*
Ausfuhrort m
 (AuW) place of dispatch
 (Zo) exit point
Ausfuhrpapier n (Zo) export document
Ausfuhrprämie f (AuW) export bounty
Ausfuhrpreisbestimmung f (AuW) export price regulation, § 9 AWG
Ausfuhrpreisindex m (AuW) export price index
Ausfuhrquote f (AuW) export quota
Ausfuhrrisiko n (AuW) export risk
Ausfuhrschein m (AuW) export declaration as per § 8 AWV
Ausfuhrsendung f (AuW) export consigment
Ausfuhrsperre f (AuW) embargo on exports
Ausfuhrsubvention f (AuW) export subsidy
Ausfuhrtag m (com) day of exportation
Ausfuhrüberschuß m (AuW) export surplus
Ausfuhrüberwachung f (AuW) export control *(ie, pursuant to German foreign trade legislation)*
Ausführung f (com) carrying out *(eg, of orders)*
 – execution
 (com) model
 (com) quality
Ausführungsanzeige f (Bö) contract note

Ausführungsbeispiel n (Pat) embodiment *(eg, of an invention)*
Ausführungsbestimmungen fpl (Re) implementing regulations
Ausführungsform f (Pat) = *Ausführungsbeispiel*
Ausführungsgeschäft n (Re) business transaction made by commission agent with a third party, of which he is to render an account to the principal, § 384 II HGB
Ausführungsgrenzen fpl (com) scope of tender
Ausführungsphase f
 (EDV) execution phase *(syn, A-Phase)*
 (OR) contract-in-process phase
Ausführungsverordnung f (Re) implementing ordinance
Ausführungszeichnung f (IndE) workshop drawing
Ausführungszeit f
 (EDV) execution *(or* object) time
 (IndE) setup time + portion of job time
Ausführungszyklus m (EDV) execute cycle *(or* phase)
Ausfuhrverbot n
 (AuW) ban on exports
 – export prohibition
 – prohibition on exportation
Ausfuhrverbot n **wirtschaftlicher Art** (AuW) export prohibition imposed in the interest of the national economy
Ausfuhrverfahren n (Zo) export procedure
Ausfuhrvergütung f (StR) export rebate *(ie, applicable until 1967 when VAT was introduced)*
Ausfuhrvertrag m (AuW) export contract *(ie, legal transaction by which a resident agrees to supply goods to a customer in a foreign country)*
Ausfuhrvolumen n (AuW) volume of exports *(ie, total value of goods and services sent out of the country)*
Ausfuhr f **von Arbeitslosigkeit** (Vw) transfer of unemployment to other countries *(ie, through beggar-my-neighbor policy)*
Ausfuhr f **von Waren** (AuW) export of commodities
Ausfuhr-Vorfinanzierungsversicherung f (Vers) insurance of export advance-financing *(ie, taken out to protect credit institute against the risk of exporter's insolvency)*
Ausfuhrwaren fpl (AuW) goods to be exported
Ausfuhrzahlen fpl (AuW) export figures *(ie, foreign trade statistics about cross-frontier movement of goods, broken down by types of commodities)*
Ausfuhrzoll m (Zo) customs duty on exportation
Ausfuhr-Zolldeklaration f (Zo) export declaration
Ausfuhrzollförmlichkeiten fpl (Zo) customs export formalities
Ausfuhrzollstelle f (Zo) customs office of exports
ausfüllen
 (com) to fill in
 – to fill out *(ie, a form)*
 – (GB) to fill in
 – (GB, *nonstandard*) to fill up
Ausgabe f
 (com) outlay
 – expense
 – expenditure

(Fin) issue (*or* issuance) *(eg, shares)*
(EDV) data output
Ausgabeabgeld *n* (Fin) offering discount
Ausgabeanforderung *f* (EDV) output request
Ausgabeaufgeld *n* (Fin) offering premium *(ie, excess of issue price over par value)*
Ausgabebank *f*
(Vw) bank of issue
– issue bank
Ausgabebedingungen *fpl* (Fin) terms of issue
Ausgabebefehl *m* (EDV) output instruction
Ausgabebereich *m* (EDV) output area
Ausgabebetrag *m* (Fin) amount for which shares are issued
Ausgabeblock *m* (EDV) output block
Ausgabebuch *n* (ReW) cash (*or* expense) book
Ausgabecode *m* (EDV) output code
Ausgabedaten *pl* (EDV) output data
Ausgabeeinheit *f* (EDV) = *Ausgabegerät*
Ausgabeermächtigung *f*
(FiW) total obligational authority, TOA
– (US) Budget Authority
Ausgabefunktion *f* (Vw) expenditure function
Ausgabegerät *n* (EDV) output device (*or* unit)
Ausgabegewohnheiten *fpl* (Mk) spending habits
Ausgabekanal *m* (EDV) output channel
Ausgabekurs *m*
(Fin) issue price
– initial offering price *(syn, Emissionskurs)*
Ausgabekurve *f* (Vw) outlay curve
Ausgabeliste *f* (OR) analysis sheet
Ausgabemagazin *n* (EDV) output magazine
Ausgaben *fpl*
(com) expenditure
– expenses
– outlay
(Fin) outflows *(ie, in preinvestment analysis)*
Ausgabenansätze *mpl* (FiW) expenditure estimates
Ausgabenbegrenzung *f* (FiW) spending limitation
Ausgabenbeleg *m* (ReW) disbursement voucher
Ausgabenbewilligung *f* (FiW, Fin) budget appropriation
Ausgaben *fpl* **decken** (com) to cover expenses
Ausgabeneigung *f* (Vw) propensity to spend
Ausgaben/Einnahmen *fpl* (ReW) outlays/receipts
Ausgaben *fpl* **einschränken**
(com) to curtail
– to cut
– to limit ... expenditures
Ausgaben-Entscheidung *f* (Mk) spending decision
Ausgaben *fpl* **erhöhen** (Fin) to step up spending
Ausgabe *f* **neuer Aktien** (Fin) issue of new shares
Ausgabenfunktion *f* (Vw) expenditure function
Ausgaben *fpl* **für Auslandsreisen**
(VGR) tourist outlays abroad
– spending of tourists abroad
Ausgaben *fpl* **für Hausverwaltung** (StR) expenses for housekeeping
ausgabengleiche Kosten *pl* (KoR) cash-outlay costs *(ie, costs set equal to expenses; eg, taxes paid)*
Ausgabengleichung *f* (Vw) spending equation
Ausgabengrenze *f*
(FiW) budget ceiling
– spending target
(eg, set forth in fiscal blueprint)

Ausgabenkompetenz *f* (FiW) spending power
Ausgaben-Konsum-Kurve *f* (Vw) expenditure-consumption curve
Ausgabenkurve *f* (Vw) outlay curve
Ausgabenkurve *f* **der Nachfrager** (Vw) demand-outlay curve
Ausgaben *fpl* **kürzen**
(Fin) to cut spending
– to make cuts in spending
– (infml) to put a lid on spending
– (infml) to clamp down on spending
Ausgabenkürzung *f* (FiW) spending cut
Ausgabenmultiplikator *m* (Vw) expenditure multiplier
Ausgabenplan *m* (Fin) outgoing payments budget *(ie, part of overall financial budget)*
Ausgabenpolitik *f* (FiW) spending policy
Ausgabenquote *f* (FiW) quota of expenditure
Ausgabenquote *f* **für Auslandsreisen** (VGR) travel ratio
Ausgaben *fpl* **reduzieren**
(com) to cut spending
– (infml) to tighten purse strings
Ausgabenreste *mpl* (FiW) unspent budget balances
Ausgabenschub *m* (FiW) sharp rise of expenditure
Ausgabensteuer *f* (FiW) expenditure tax *(ie, imposed on use of income, described by N. Kaldor)*
Ausgabenstruktur *f* (Vw) pattern of expenditure
Ausgabenwährung *f* (Vw) expenditure currency
Ausgabepreis *m* (Fin) issue price *(ie, of investment fund share)*
Ausgabeprogramm *n* (EDV) output program (*or* routine)
Ausgabepufferspeicher *m* (EDV) output buffer
Ausgabesatz *m* (EDV) output record
Ausgabeschalter *m* (com) delivery counter
Ausgabeschreiber *m* (EDV) output writer
Ausgabeschreibmaschine *f* (EDV) output typewriter
Ausgabespeicher *m* (EDV) output storage
Ausgabewelle *f* (Vw) wave of expenditures
Ausgabewerk *n* (EDV) output control
Ausgabewert *m* (Fin) issue price
ausgabewirksame (Perioden)kosten *pl* (KoR) out-of-pocket cost (*or* expense)
ausgabenwirksames Gesetz *n* (FiW) spending bill
Ausgabenzuweisung *f* (ReW) allocation of expenditure
Ausgang *m* (EDV) output
Ausgang *m* **aus der Gemeinschaft** *f* (Zo) exit from the Community
Ausgänge *mpl* (Fin) outgoings
Ausgangsabfertigung *f* (Zo, GB) clearance outwards
Ausgangsabgaben *fpl* (StR) export duties and taxes
ausgangsabgabenpflichtig (StR) liable to export duties and taxes
Ausgangsdaten *pl* (Stat) raw (*or* source) data
Ausgangs-Durchgangszollstelle *f* (Zo) office of exit en route
Ausgangsfinanzierung *f* (Fin) initial finance
Ausgangsfracht *f*
(com) freight out
– (GB) carriage outward

Ausgangsfunktion f
 (OR) distributive function
 – emitting function
 – output function
Ausgangsgesamtheit f (Stat) parent population
Ausgangsgewicht n (Stat) base weight
Ausgangshypothese f (Log) starting assumption
Ausgangskapital n (Fin) initial capital
Ausgangsknoten m (OR) output (or starting) node
Ausgangsland n (AuW) country of departure
Ausgangsmatrix f (OR) original matrix
Ausgangspunkt m **der Trendlinie** (Stat) pivot of linear trend
Ausgangsraum m (Stat) sample space
Ausgangssignal n (EDV) zero output
Ausgangssprache f (Log) source language *(opp, Zielsprache = target language)*
Ausgangsstelle f (EDV) outconnector
Ausgangsversand m (Zo) outward transit
Ausgangswert m
 (Stat) basic dimension
 (StR) basic value *(ie, of real estate or plot of land, comprising value of land, buildings, and external improvements)*
Ausgangszahl f (Stat) benchmark figure
Ausgangszollsatz m (Zo) basic duty
Ausgangszollstelle f
 (Zo) customs office outward
 – customs office at point of exit
 – office of exit
Ausgangszustand m
 (EDV) initial state
 (OR) starting state
ausgeben
 (com) to spend
 – to disburse
 – to expend
 – to lay out
 – to pay out
 (Fin) to issue *(eg, shares, banknotes)*
ausgebucht
 (com) booked up *(eg, for eight weeks ahead)*
 (ReW) expensed
 (ReW) charged off
 – written off
ausgedient
 (com) worn out
 (com, infml, GB) clapped out *(eg, equipment, vehicle)*
 (Pw) retired
ausgegebene Aktien fpl (Fin) issued shares
ausgegebenes Aktienkapital n (Fin) capital stock issued
ausgeglichener Haushalt m (FiW) balanced (or in-balance) budget
ausgeglichenes Budget n (FiW) = *ausgeglichener Haushalt*
ausgeglichenes Ergebnis n (ReW) break-even result
ausgeglichenes Konto n (ReW) closed account
ausgehen (com) to eat out in restaurants
ausgehende Post f (com) outgoing mail
ausgelastete Knoten mpl (OR) rejected nodes
ausgelegte Kredite mpl (Fin) loans extended (or granted)

ausgeschiedenes Wirtschaftsgut n (StR) replaced (or retired) asset, Abschn. 35 II EStR
ausgeschlossener Aktionär m (Re) expelled shareholder
ausgeschüttete Dividende f (Fin) declared dividend
ausgeschüttete Gewinnanteile mpl (StR) distributive share of profits
ausgeschütteter Gewinn m (Fin) distributed profit
ausgesetzte Steuerfestsetzung f (StR) suspended tax assessment, § 165 II AO
ausgesperrt (Pw) locked-out
ausgewiesene eigene Mittel pl (ReW) equity *(ie, as reported in the balance sheet)*
ausgewiesener Gewinn m (ReW) reported earnings (or income)
ausgewiesenes Eigenkapital n (ReW) reported net worth
ausgewiesenes Grundkapital n (ReW) capital stock disclosed in balance sheet
ausgewogene Stichprobe f (Stat) balanced sample
ausgezahlte Einkommen npl (VGR) income receipts
ausgezahlter Betrag m (Fin) amount paid out *(ie, to borrower)*
ausgezahlter Gewinnanteil m (Vers) bonus in cash
Ausgleich m
 (com) balance
 – compensation
 – adjustment
 – equalization
 – settlement
 – squaring
Ausgleich m **der Produktlebenszyklen** (Bw) life cycle balance
Ausgleich m **der Zahlungsbilanz**
 (VGR) adjusting the balance of payments
 (VGR) balance of payments equilibrium
Ausgleich m **der Zolltarife** (Zo) tariff harmonization
Ausgleich m **des Kapazitätsbedarfs** (OR) leveling of capacity requirements
Ausgleich m **durch Kauf od Verkauf** (Bö) evening up
ausgleichen
 (com) to make up the difference
 (com) to balance *(eg, an account)*
 – to compensate *(eg, for a loss)*
 – to equalize *(eg, incomes)*
 – to settle *(eg, an account, claim)*
 – to square *(eg, a debt)*
 – to offset (or smooth out) *(eg, cyclical fluctuations)*
ausgleichender Fehler m (ReW) offsetting error
Ausgleichsabgabe f
 (FiW) equalization levy
 (EG) compensatory tariff
 – contingent duty
 – countervailing duty (or tariff)
 (Pw) equalizing levy
 (ie, payable by private and public employers in the amount of DM 100 a month for each severely handicapped person not employed as provided for in § 8 of the ‚Schwerbehindertengesetz')
Ausgleichsabgaben fpl (StR) contributions under the equalization of burdens law

Ausgleichsamt *n* (FiW) Equalization of Burdens Office *(ie, handling equalization cases on a lower administrative level, such as Land- and Stadtkreise)*
Ausgleichsanspruch *m* (Re) claim for adjustment *(made by a commercial agent, § 89b HGB)*
Ausgleichsarbitrage *f* (AuW) foreign-exchange arbitrage seeking the lowest rates to pay off a claim
Ausgleichsbetrag *m* **Beitritt** (EG) accession compensatory amount
Ausgleichsbuchung *f*
 (ReW) offsetting entry
 (ReW) charge back
Ausgleichsdividende *f* (Fin) equalizing dividend
Ausgleichsfonds *m* (FiW) Equalization Fund *(ie, special-purpose fund, part of Equalization of Burdens system, receives levies and funds from public-sector budgets)*
 (AuW) Exchange Stabilization Fund *(or* GB: Exchange Equalisation Account)
 (ReW) equalizing fund *(ie, set up by groups of companies or other business combinations to spread profits and losses evenly)*
Ausgleichsforderungen *fpl* (FiW) equalization claims *(ie, claims by banks and insurance companies against Federation and Laender, created by the West German Currency Reform)*
Ausgleichsgesetz *n* **der Planung** (Bw) law of balancing organizational plans *(ie, implies continuous appraisal of interrelated operating plans or financial programs and removal of discrepancies among them; the overall planning or master budgeting is subject to the constraints of the ‚minimum (bottleneck) sector')*
Ausgleichskredite *mpl* (FiW) borrowing to smooth budgetary irregularities
Ausgleichskürzungen *fpl* (FiW) compensatory cuts *(eg, made elsewhere in the budget)*
Ausgleichslager *n* (AuW) buffer stock
Ausgleichsleistung *f*
 (FiW) equalization of burdens payment
 (Fin) compensating payment
Ausgleichsmeßzahl *f* (StR) equalization figure *(ie, per capita collection figure multiplied by the number of inhabitants of each state)*
Ausgleichsposten *m*
 (ReW) balancing item
 – compensating item
 – offsetting item
 – per contra item
 (ReW) adjustment item *(eg, aus der Erstkonsolidierung = from initial consolidation)*
Ausgleichsposten *m* **aus der Konsolidierung** (ReW) adjustment resulting from consolidation
Ausgleichsposten *m* **zur Auslandsposition** (VGR) balance on official settlements
Ausgleichsprämie *f*
 (Pw) catch-up allowance
 (IndE) compensating bonus
Ausgleichsrücklage *f* (ReW) equalization reserve
Ausgleichsschleife *f* (EDV) tape loop
Ausgleichsteuer *f*
 (FiW) regulatory tax
 (StR) turnover equalization tax *(ie, under the former law imposed on imported goods in order to equalize the tax burden of imported goods and of domestic goods; now ‚Einfuhrumsatzsteuer')*
Ausgleichsteuerordnung *f* (StR) Ordinance Regulating the Turnover Equalization Tax
Ausgleichstransaktionen *fpl*
 (AuW) accommodating movements
 – accommodating transactions
 – settling transactions
Ausgleichszahlung *f*
 (com) adjusting payment *(ie, made to commercial agent, § 89b HGB)*
 (FiW) deficiency *(or* equalization) payment
 (Fin) recurrent payments to minority stockholders based on § 304 AktG
 (Bw) side payment
Ausgleichszoll *m*
 – countervailing duty
 (AuW) compensating tariff
 – compensatory duty *(or* tariff)
 – contingent duty
 – matching duty *(ie, a special type of antidumping duty)*
Ausgleichszugeständnisse *npl* (AuW) compensatory concessions
Ausgleichszuweisungen *fpl* (FiW) equalization payments
Ausgleichungspflicht *f* (Re) hodgepodge (GB: hotchpotch) liability *(ie, liability to account for certain kinds of gift received from the deceased during his life, §§ 2050ff, 2316 BGB)*
ausgliedern (Bw) to spin off *(ie, part of a company)*
ausgründen (Re, GB) to hive off *(ie, to separate parts of a company and start a new firm)*
aushandeln (com) to negotiate
aushändigen
 (com) to hand over
 (com) to deliver
Aushilfe *f* (Pw) temporary worker *(ie, employed for a limited period)*
Aushilfskraft *f* (Pw) casual worker
Aushilfspersonal *n* (Pw) temporary personnel
Aushöhlung *f* (EDV) bucket *(ie, in direct access storage)*
Aushöhlung *f* **der Steuerbasis** (FiW) tax erosion
Aushöhlung *f* **e-s Gesetzes** (Re) dismantling of a law
Aushöhlungseffekt *m* (Vw) backwash effect *(ie, in developing countries)*
auskalkulieren (com) to make a complete estimate
auskehren (Fin) to pay out
Auskehrung *f* (FiW) rundown of public authorities' bank balances
ausklammern (Math) to factor out a term
Auskunftei *f*
 (com) commercial agency
 – *(rare)* mercantile agency
 – (GB) credit inquiry agency
Auskunftsersuchen *n* (Re) request for information
Auskunftspflicht *f* (com) duty to disclose information *(ie, in various contexts; eg, by employers, by taxpayers as laid down in §§ 93ff AO, for statistical purposes, in competition law, in foreign trade law)*
Auskunftsrecht *n* (Re) right to demand informa-

tion *(ie, from the managing board during a general meeting of a stock corporation, § 131 AktG)*
Auskunftsschein m (com) information slip *(eg, supplied by commercial agencies)*
Auskunftsstellen fpl **für den Außenhandel** (AuW) foreign-trade information agencies *(ie, chambers of commerce or other trade associations)*
Auskunftssystem n
  (EDV) information system
  (EDV) inquiry system
Auskunftsverlangen n (Kart) request for information
Ausladebahnhof m (com) unloading railroad station
ausladen
  (com) to unload
  – to discharge
Auslage f
  (Mk) window display
  – goods displayed
Auslagefenster n (Mk) shop window
Auslagematerial n (Mk) display materials *(ie, for shop window)*
Auslagen fpl
  (com) expenses
  – outlays
Auslagenersatz m (com) reimbursement of expenses *(ie, under civil and commercial law, under civil procedure provisions, and under wages tax law)*
Auslagenklausel f (SeeV) disbursement clause
auslagern
  (com) to take out of stock and transfer to another place
  (Mk) to sell from stock
Auslagerung f (EDV) roll in/roll out
Auslagetisch m (com) display counter
Ausland n
  (Re) foreign country *(eg, in turnover tax law and foreign trade law)*
  (VGR) rest of the world
Ausländer m (Re) non-resident
Ausländerdepot n (Fin) non-resident securities account
Ausländerguthaben npl (Fin) external assets
Ausländerkonten npl (Fin) non-resident accounts *(ie, with German banks, held by natural or legal persons domiciled abroad)*
Ausländerkonvertibilität f (AuW) external *(or* non-resident) convertibility
Ausländerrecht n (Re) law relating to non-residents
Ausländerreiseverkehr m (AuW) foreign tourist trade
Ausländersicherheit f (Re) foreigner's security *(ie, at request of defendant deposited in German court by foreign plaintiff to cover estimated cost of litigation)*
Ausländersonderkonto n (AuW) special non-resident account
ausländische Anleihe f
  (Fin) foreign bond
  – external loan
  (ie, loan raised by a foreigner in Germany; see also: Auslandsanleihe)

ausländische Arbeitnehmer mpl (Pw) foreign employees *(or* workers)
ausländische Arbeitskräfte fpl (Pw) = *ausländische Arbeitnehmer*
ausländische Betriebsstätte f (StR) permanent establishment abroad
ausländische Direktinvestitionen fpl (AuW) direct foreign *(or* outward) investment
ausländische DM-Anleihe f (Fin) international DM bond
ausländische Einkünfte pl
  (StR) foreign-source income
  – income received from abroad
  (ie, by natural or legal persons subject to unlimited tax liability)
ausländische Emittenten mpl (Bö) foreign issuers
ausländische Investitionen fpl (AuW) non-residents' investments *(ie, in West Germany)*
ausländische Konkurrenz f (com) foreign rivals *(or* competitors)
ausländische Körperschaften fpl (Re, StR) foreign corporations
ausländische Märkte mpl (com) foreign markets
ausländische Märkte mpl **erobern** (com) to conquer *(or* penetrate) foreign markets
ausländische Mitarbeiter mpl
  (Pw) non-German personnel
  – foreign employees
ausländische Quellensteuer f (StR) foreign tax withheld at source
ausländischer Abnehmer m (StR) foreign customer *(ie, term used in turnover tax law, § 6 I 1 UStG)*
ausländischer Anteilseigner m (Fin) non-resident shareholder
ausländischer Arbeitnehmer m (Pw) foreign employee *(or* worker)
ausländische Rentenwerte mpl (Fin) foreign bonds
ausländischer Schiedsspruch m (Re) foreign arbitral *(or* arbitration) award
ausländischer Versicherer m (Vers) foreign insurer
ausländisches Fabrikat n (com) foreign product
ausländisches Vermögen n (StR) assets held abroad *(ie, part of total taxable assets, except if tax liability is limited; valuation as per § 31 BewG)*
ausländische Tochtergesellschaft f (Re) foreign subsidiary *(ie, a corporation abroad in which a domestic company holds at least a material interest)*
ausländische Unternehmungen fpl **im Inland** (Re) domestic enterprises in which non-residents hold an equity stake
ausländische Währung f (AuW) foreign currency
ausländische Werte mpl (StR) invoice amounts in foreign currency, § 53 UStDV
Auslandsabsatz m (com) export *(or* external) sales
Auslandsabteilung f
  (com) foreign operations department
  (Fin) international department *(of a bank)*
Auslandsakkreditiv n (Fin) credit opened in a foreign country
Auslandsaktiva npl (AuW) external *(or* foreign) assets
Auslandsakzept n (Fin) foreign acceptance *(ie, draft accepted by foreign buyer)*

Auslandsanlage f (Fin) foreign investment
Auslandsanleihe f (Fin) external loan
– foreign bond
(ie, issued abroad by a domestic debtor in foreign or domestic currency or loan issued by a foreigner in Germany, the latter also being termed ‚ausländische Anleihe')
Auslandsarbitrage f (AuW) outward arbitrage
Auslandsauftrag m
(AuW) order from abroad
– foreign order
Auslandsbank f (Fin) foreign bank *(ie, one mainly operating abroad)*
Auslandsbelegschaft f
(Pw) employees operating abroad
– employees outside Germany
Auslandsbesitz m (AuW) non-resident's holding
Auslandsbestellung f (AuW) = *Auslandsauftrag*
Auslandsbeteiligung f
(Fin) foreign participations *(or* shareholdings)
(Fin) associated company abroad
Auslandsbezug m (com) purchase from foreign suppliers
Auslandsbilanz f (VGR) foreign balance sheet
Auslandsbonds pl (AuW) external bonds *(ie, German fixed-interest bonds in foreign currency)*
Auslandsbrief m (com) letter sent abroad
Auslandsdebitoren pl (Fin) foreign receivables *(or* debtors)
Auslandseinlage f (Fin) non-resident deposit
Auslandsemission f (Fin) foreign issue
Auslandsfiliale f
(com) foreign branch
– branch abroad
– overseas branch
Auslandsfiliale f **eröffnen** (com) to establish a foreign branch *(or* a branch abroad)
Auslandsflug m (com) nondomestic flight
Auslandsforderungen fpl
(AuW) external claims
(ReW) foreign receivables
Auslandsfracht f (com) cargo *(or* freight) sent abroad
Auslandsgelder npl (Fin) foreign funds
Auslandsgeschäft n
(com) international business
(Fin) provision of international banking services
(Fin) external transactions *(ie, in securities, made either abroad or between resident and non-resident, § 24 KVStG)*
Auslandsgespräch n (com) foreign telephone call
Auslandsguthaben npl
(AuW) foreign assets *(or* claims)
(Fin) funds *(or* balances) abroad
(Fin) non-resident deposits
Auslandshandelskammer (AuW) foreign-trade chamber of commerce
Auslandshilfe f (Vw) external economic aid
Auslandsinvestition f
(Bw) foreign investment
– investment abroad
(ie, may be either direct or portfolio investment)
Auslandsinvestitionsgesetz n (Re) Law on Foreign Investments, of 18 Aug 1969, as amended

Auslands-Investmentgesetz n (Re) Foreign Investment Law, of 28 July 1969, as amended
Auslandskapital n (AuW) foreign capital *(ie, capital supplied from other countries, as direct or portfolio investment or as loans)*
Auslandskäufe mpl (Bö) foreign buying
Auslandskonkurrenz f
(AuW) foreign competitors *(or* rivals)
– competition from abroad
Auslandskontakte mpl (com) contacts abroad *(or* in foreign countries)
Auslandskonto n
(VGR) rest-of-the-world account
(Fin) foreign account *(ie, account held at a bank abroad)*
Auslandskorrespondent m
(com) clerk handling foreign correspondence
(Fin) foreign correspondent (bank)
Auslandskorrespondenz f (com) foreign correspondence
Auslandskredit m
(Fin) foreign lending
– loan extended to foreigner
(Fin) foreign borrowing
– loan obtained abroad
Auslandskreditgeschäft n (Fin) international lending business
Auslandskunde m
(AuW) foreign customer
– overseas buyer
Auslandsmarkt m (AuW) foreign market
Auslandsmesse f (com) foreign fair
Auslandsnachfrage f (AuW) external *(or* foreign) demand
Auslandsnetz n (Mk) foreign network
Auslandsniederlassung f (com) foreign branch *(ie, set up by residents in foreign countries to establish permanent business relations)*
Auslandsobligo n (Fin) total lendings to foreigners
Auslandspassiva npl (AuW) external liabilities
Auslandspatent n (Pat) foreign patent *(ie, obtained abroad or granted to foreigners)*
Auslandsposition f (AuW) external position
Auslandspostanweisung f (Fin) international money order
Auslandsreiseverkehr m (AuW) foreign travel
Auslandsreise-Versicherung f (Vers) foreign travel insurance
Auslandsrente f (Pw) pension payable to non-residents
Auslandsrepräsentanz f (Fin) representative office abroad
Auslandssaldo m (AuW) net foreign position
Auslandsscheck m (Fin) foreign check
Auslandsschulden fpl
(AuW) external *(or* foreign) debt
(Fin) foreign liabilities
Auslandssendung f (com) postal consignment sent abroad or received from abroad
Auslandsstatus m (Fin) foreign assets and liabilities *(or* position)
Auslandstochter f (Re) foreign *(or* overseas) subsidiary
Auslandstourismus m (VGR) international tourism

Auslandsumsatz *m*
(Stat) sales abroad *(ie, all direct supplies of goods and services to a consignee abroad, plus deliveries to German exporters)*
(com) international sales
– export turnover

Auslandsverbindlichkeit *f*
(AuW) external indebtedness
– liability to non-resident
– foreign liability

Auslandsverkäufe *mpl* (Bö) foreign selling

Auslandsvermögen *n*
(VGR) foreign
– external
– international ... assets *(ie, German assets abroad)*

Auslandsverpflichtung *f* (AuW) international capital links

Auslandsverschuldung *f* (AuW) foreign indebtedness *(ie, volume of claims due to foreigners)*

Auslandsvertreter *m*
(AuW) foreign representative
– agent abroad

Auslandswährung *f* (Vw) foreign currency

Auslandswechsel *m* (Fin) external (*or* foreign) bill *(ie, drawn by a bank on a foreign correspondent bank)*

Auslandswerte *mpl*
(AuW) foreign assets
(ie, fixed assets abroad, DM claims against non-residents, foreign means of payment, receivables and securities, § 4 II AWG)
(Bö) foreigners

Auslandszahlung *f*
(Fin) foreign payment
(Fin) payment from abroad

Auslandszahlungsverkehr *m* (AuW) foreign (*or* international) payments transactions

Auslandszulage *f*
(Pw) foreign service allowance
– expatriation allowance

auslasten
(IndE) to utilize *(eg, capacity of plant)*
– to work a plant at ... pct

Auslastung *f* (com) load factor *(ie, of commercial airplanes)*
(IndE) = *Auslastungsgrad*

Auslastungsgrad *m*
(IndE) rate of capacity utilization
– plant utilization rate
– operating rate
– operating performance *(eg, was only 90% of normal)*
(EDV) relative throughput
– utilization *(syn, relativer Durchsatz)*

Auslastungsgrad *m* **von Arbeitskräften** (Pw) overall performance

Auslastungskontrollkarte *f* (IndE) load chart

Auslastungsplan *m* (IndE) loading schedule

auslastungssensible Bereiche *mpl* (Bw) areas sensitive to capacity utilization

auslaufen
(com) to run out
– to discontinue
– to phase out

Auslaufen *n* (com) phase-out *(eg, programs, projects)*

auslaufender Brief *m* (com) outgoing letter

auslaufender Vertrag *m* (Re) expiring contract

auslaufen lassen (com) to taper off *(eg, subsidies)*

Auslaufen *n* **von Häufigkeitsverteilungen** (Stat) tail off

auslegen
(Re) to interpret
– to construe
(Pat) to open applications to public inspection
(IndE) to design
– to lay out

Auslegeschrift *f* (Pat) patent specification open to public inspection *(ie, comprises description and drawings)*

Auslegung *f*
(Re) construction
– interpretation
(eg, to put a broad or strict construction upon; see §§ 133, 157 BGB, § 1 StAnpG)

Auslegungsregeln *fpl* (com, Re) rules of interpretation (*or* construction)

Auslegung *f* **von Betriebsanlagen** (IndE) plant layout

ausleihen (Fin) to lend

Ausleiher *m* (Fin) lender

Ausleihquote *f* (Fin) lendings ratio

Ausleihungen *fpl*
(Fin) total lendings
– total amount loaned

Ausleihungen *fpl* **mit e-r Laufzeit von mindestens 4 Jahren** (Fin) loans for a term of at least 4 years

auslesen (EDV) to read out

Auslesen *n* (EDV) readout

ausliefern (com) to deliver

Auslieferung *f* (com) delivery *(eg, of goods, securities)*

Auslieferungsanspruch *m* (com) right (*or* claim) to delivery

Auslieferungsauftrag *m* (com) delivery order

Auslieferungslager *n*
(com) consignment stock *(ie, inventory of consigned goods committed to the consignee at consignor's expense)*
(com) distributing warehouse
– field store
(ie, from which customers are supplied direct)

Auslieferungsprovision *f* (Re) delivery commission *(ie, payable to commission agent when transaction, that is, receipt, storage, and delivery, has been carried out, § 396 HGB)*

Auslieferungsversprechen *n* (com) promise to deliver

Auslobung *f* (Re) public offer (*or* promise) of reward, § 657 BGB *(ie, example of an obligation arising from a unilateral declaration, not from contract)*

Auslobungstarife *mpl* (com) exceptional rates in railroad transport for delivery of minimum quantities

auslosbar
(Fin) redeemable by drawings
– drawable

Auslöseimpuls *m* (EDV) trigger pulse

auslosen (Fin) to draw by lot
auslösen
   (com) to set off
   – to spark off
   – to trigger off
auslösender Faktor *m* (com) initiating source *(eg, of excess demand and a soaring price level)*
Auslosung *f*
   (Fin) bond drawing *(ie, form of repayment of bonds during their life)*
   (Mk) prize competition *(eg, in advertising)*
Auslösung *f*
   (Pw) field allowance *(ie, paid during employment abroad)*
   (Pw) termination (or severance) payment *(ie, for early retirement)*
Auslosungsanleihe *f*
   (Fin) lottery loan (*or* bonds)
   – bonds issued by public authorities and redeemable by drawings
Auslosungsanzeige *f* (Fin) notice of drawing
Auslosungskurs *m* (Fin) drawing price
Auslösungspreis *m* (EG) activating price *(ie, on EEC farm markets)*
Auslosungstermin *m* (Fin) drawing date
ausmachender Betrag *m* (Fin) actual amount *(ie, market price + interest for fixed-interest securities; market price for variable-interest securities)*
ausmultiplizieren (Math) to multiply out
ausmustern
   (com) to sort out and discard *(eg, models, vehicles)*
   (com) to produce new designs or patterns
Ausmusterung *f* (com) sorting out and discarding
   (com) production of new designs or patterns
Ausnahmen *fpl* **von der Besteuerung** (StR) nontaxable transactions, § 22 KVStG
Ausnahmetarife *mpl* (com) low freight rates in railroad or commercial long-distance transport, granted for economic or social reasons
ausnutzen (Pat) to work a patent
Ausnutzungsgrad *m* (IndE) = *Auslastungsgrad*
Ausnutzungsmodus *m* **eines Kontingents** (Zo) system of utilization of quota
Ausnutzung *f* **vorhandener Anlagen** (Bw) utilization of existing plant
auspacken
   (com) to unpack
   (Pw, infml) to speak out (*or* up)
Auspendler *m* (com) commuter
ausprägen
   (Vw) to coin
   – to mint
Ausprägung *f*
   (Stat) attribute
   – characteristic
   (Vw) coining
   – minting
auspreisen (com) to price *(ie, to put price tags on articles)*
ausrechnen
   (com) to calculate
   – to work out *(eg, a sum)*
   – (US) to figure out

Ausrechnung *f*
   (com) worked-out figures
   (com) calculation
ausreichen (Fin) to extend *(eg, a loan)*
ausreichendes Kapital *n*
   (Fin) sufficient capital
   – capital adequacy
ausreichende Sorgfalt *f* (Re) adequate care
Ausreißer *m*
   (Stat) outlier
   – maverick
   (Stat) ,,runaway" product
ausrüsten
   (com) to equip
   – to outfit
Ausrüster *m*
   (com) outfitter
   (com) managing owner *(of a ship)*
Ausrüstung *f*
   (com) equipment
   – plant
Ausrüstungsgegenstand *m* (com) piece of equipment
Ausrüstungsgüter *npl* (com) machinery and equipment
Ausrüstungsinvestitionen *fpl*
   (Bw) plant and equipment expenditure
   – plant and equipment outlay
   – plant and equipment spending
   – equipment investment
   – equipment spending
   – investments in machinery and equipment
Ausrüstungsvermietung *f* (Fin) equipment leasing
Aussage *f* (Log) statement
(ie, in a declarative sentence; note that ‚proposition' is usually reserved to denote the content of meaning of a declarative sentence)
Aussageform *f*
   (Log) propositional formula
   – sentential formula
   (Log) well-formed formula, wff
Aussagefunktion *f* (Log) propositional (*or* statement) function
Aussagefunktor *m*
   (Log) propositional connective
   – sentential operator
Aussagekraft *f* (Log) informative value
Aussagenkalkül *n* (Log) propositional (*or* sentential) calculus *(ie, system containing ‚Aussagenvariable' and ‚aussagenlogische Verknüpfungen' = propositional variables and logical connectives)*
Aussagenkomplex *m*
   (Log) molecular statement
   (Log) set of interrelated propositions
Aussagenlogik *f* (Log) propositional (*or* sentential) logic *(ie, theory of truth-functions)*
aussagenlogische Ableitbarkeit *f* (Log) propositional deducibility
aussagenlogische Deduktion *f* (Log) sentential inference
aussagenlogische Konstante *f* (Log) propositional constant
aussagenlogisches Argument *n* (Log) sentential logic argument

aussagenlogische Verknüpfung *f* (Log) propositional (*or* sentential) connective
Aussagenvariable *f* (Log) propositional variable
Aussagenwahrscheinlichkeit *f* (Log) probability of statement
Aussagenzusammenhang *m* (Log) set of interrelated propositions
Aussagewahrscheinlichkeit *f* (Stat) confidence coefficient *(syn, Vertrauenskoeffizient)*
ausschalten
 (com, infml) to cut out *(eg, go-between, financial institutions)*
 (EDV) to deactivate
 – to disable
Ausschalten *n* **von Saisonbewegungen** (Stat) seasonal adjustment
Ausschaltung *f* **der Konkurrenz** (Bw) elimination of competitors (*or* rivals)
ausscheiden
 (com) to retire
 – to withdraw
Ausscheiden *n*
 (Re) retirement *(eg, of a partner)*
 – withdrawal
 (Pw) retirement
 (Vw) exit *(ie, of supplier or demander)*
Ausscheiden *n* **aus dem Erwerbsleben** (Pw) withdrawal from employment (*or* working life *or* labor force)
Ausscheiden *n* **aus dem EWS** (AuW) withdrawal from the European Monetary System, EMS
ausscheidend (com) outgoing *(eg, chairman)*
ausscheidender Gesellschafter *m* (Re) retiring (*or* withdrawing) partner
Ausscheiden *n* **e–s Wirtschaftsgutes** (Bw) retirement of an asset
Ausscheidetafel *f* (Vers) table of decrements
Ausscheidungsrate *f* (Fin) cut-off point (*or* rate) *(ie, in preinvestment analysis)*
ausscheren (com) to pull out *(ie, of business, sector, industry)*
ausschiffen
 (com) to land
 – to discharge
 – to unload
ausschlachten
 (com) to cannibalize
 – to disassemble
 (ie, to use a broken or retired machine or plant for the repair of another)
ausschlaggebende Interessen *npl* (Re) overriding interests
ausschlaggebende Stimme *f*
 (Pw) casting
 – decisive
 – tie-breaking ... vote *(eg, on supervisory board)*
Ausschlagung *f* **e–r Erbschaft**
 (StR) disclaimer of an inheritance (GB: of an estate), § 3 II 4 ErbStG
Ausschlagung *f* **e–s Vermächtnisses** (Re) disclaimer of a testamentary gift (*or* specific legacy)
Ausschlagungsfrist *f* (Re) period of disclaimer, § 1956 BGB
Ausschließen *n* (EDV) justified setting *(ie, in text processing)*

ausschließende Disjunktion *f* (Log) exclusive disjunction
ausschließende Einrede *f* (Re) peremptory defense (*or* exception) *(syn, dauernde od zerstörliche od peremptorische Einrede)*
ausschließendes ODER *n*
 (EDV) exclusive OR
 – non-equivalence
 – anti-coincidence ... operation
 – diversity
 – except
 – exjunction
 – symmetric difference
 (syn, Antivalenz, Kontravalenz)
„ausschließendes-Oder"-Knoten *m* (OR) exclusive-or node
ausschließlich (com) exclusive of
ausschließliche Benutzung *f* (Pat) exclusive use
ausschließliche Lizenz *f* (Pat) exclusive license
ausschließliche Zuständigkeit *f* (Re) exclusive jurisdiction *(ie, proceedings can be brought in only one court; opp, konkurrierende Z.)*
Ausschließlichkeitsbindung *f* (Kart) exclusive dealing
Ausschließlichkeitserklärung *f* (Re) agreement to deal exclusively with one business partner in certain types of transactions *(eg, in cartel or broker agreements, also often requested in banking)*
Ausschließlichkeitsklausel *f* (Kart) tying clause
Ausschließlichkeitspatent *n* (Pat) exclusive patent
Ausschließlichkeitsvertrag *m*
 (Mk) exclusive dealer arrangement
 (Pat) exclusive licensing agreement
Ausschließung *f* **e–s Gesellschafters** (Re) exclusion (*or* expulsion) of a partner *(eg, by virtue of § 140 HGB)*
Ausschließungsgrund *m* (Re) personal circumstance with respect to a partner, which would entitle the other members of a partnership to demand its dissolution under § 140 HGB
Ausschließungsklage *f* (Re) litigation seeking exclusion of one or several members of a OHG or KG
Ausschließungsurteil *n* (Re) court order to exclude partner from OHG or KG
Ausschluß *m* **der Haftung** (Re) exclusion of liability
Ausschluß *m* **der Steuerbefreiung für Ausfuhrlieferungen** (StR) exemption of export deliveries
Ausschlußfrist *f* (Re) preclusive (*or* bar) period *(ie, compulsory period prescribed for the exercise of certain rights, such as the right to avoid a legal transaction on the ground of error or fraud)*
Ausschlußprinzip *n* **des Preises** (FiW) exclusion principle *(ie, applied to distinguish between private and public goods)*
Ausschlußrecht *n* (Re) exclusive (*or* exclusionary) right
ausschöpfen
 (com) to exhaust
 – to utilize *(eg, a loan)*
Ausschöpfung *f* **e–s Kontingents** (AuW) exhausting a quota

ausschreiben
(com) to invite tenders
– to put out (*or* up) for tender
– to advertise for bids
Ausschreibung *f* (com) invitation to bid (*or* tender)
– request for bids
(ie, published notice that competitive bids are requested; syn, Submission)
Ausschreibung *f* **der Ausfuhrabschöpfung** (EG) tendering for export levies
Ausschreibung *f* **e–r Emission** (Fin) offer for sale by competitive bidding
Ausschreibung *f* **im Tenderverfahren** (Bö) offer for sale by tender *(ie, relating to new issues of equities)*
Ausschreibungsbedingungen *fpl*
(com) terms (*or* conditions) of tender
– bidding requirements
Ausschreibungsfrist *f* (com) bidding period
Ausschreibungsgarantie *f* (com) bid bond
Ausschreibungskonsortium *n* (com) bidding syndicate
Ausschreibungsunterlagen *fpl* (com) tender documents (*or* specifications)
Ausschreibungsverfahren *n* (com) bid process (*or* procedure)
Ausschreibungswettbewerb *m* (com) competitive bidding on a tender basis
Ausschuß *m*
(com) committee
(IndE) lost units
– rejects
– spoilage *(ie, not reprocessed or sold)*
(IndE) defective (*or* subquality) units *(ie, reworked and sold)*
Ausschußabweichung *f* (KoR) spoilage rate variance *(ie, difference between budgeted and actual rates)*
Ausschußanteil *m*
(IndE) rate of lost units
(IndE) fraction defective
– rate of defectives
Ausschuß *m* **der Präsidenten der Zentralbanken der Mitgliedstaaten der EG** (EG) Committee of the Governors of the Central Banks of the EC Member States
Ausschuß *m* **für allgemeine Zollregelungen** (EG) General Customs Procedures Committee
Ausschuß *m* **für das gemeinschaftliche Versandverfahren** (EG) Committee on Community transit operations
Ausschuß *m* **für das harmonisierte System** (EG) Harmonized System Committee
Ausschuß *m* **für das Schema des Gemeinsamen Zolltarifs** (EG) Committee on Common Customs Tariff Nomenclature
Ausschuß *m* **für das Zolltarifschema** (EG) Nomenclature Committee
Ausschuß *m* **für den aktiven Veredelungsverkehr** (EG) Inward Processing Committee
Ausschuß *m* **für den Zollwert** (EG) Valuation Committee
Ausschuß *m* **für die Reform des internationalen Währungssystems und damit verbundene Fragen** (AuW) Committee on the Reform of the International Monetary System and Related Issues *(ie, Committee of 20)*
Ausschuß *m* **für Umweltfragen** (com) environmental committee
Ausschuß *m* **für Wirtschaft** (com) committee on economic affairs
Ausschuß *m* **für wirtschaftliche Zusammenarbeit** (com) committee on economic cooperation
Ausschuß *m* **für Wirtschaftspolitik** (EG) Economic Policy Committee
Ausschuß *m* **für Zollbefreiungen** (EG) Committee on duty-free arrangements
Ausschuß *m* **für Zollveredelungsverkehr** (EG) Customs Processing Arrangement Committee
Ausschuß *m* **für Zusammenarbeit im Zollwesen** (EG) Customs Cooperation Committee
Ausschußgrenze *f*
(Stat) limiting quality
– lot tolerance percent defective, LTPD
Ausschußkostenverrechnung *f* (KoR) accounting (*or* costing) for spoiled goods (*or* units)
Ausschußmitglied *n* (com) committee member
Ausschußplanung *f* (IndE) planned spoilage
Ausschußprozentsatz *m*
(IndE) percentage defective
– percentage of defective items
(Stat) attribute
Ausschußprüfung *f* (Stat) attribute gage (*or* test)
Ausschußquote *f* (IndE) reject frequency
Ausschußsenkung *f* (IndE) lowering rates of spoilage
Ausschußsitzung *f* (com) committee meeting
Ausschußstücke *npl* (IndE) rejects
Ausschußverhütung *f* (IndE) elimination of spoilage (to a minimum)
Ausschußverwertung *f* (IndE) utilization of unavoidable defectives *(ie, through sale as seconds, reprocessing, recycling as raw material, scrapping and sale)*
Ausschußvorsitzender *m* (com) committee chairman
Ausschußwagnis *n* (ReW) risk of spoilage
Ausschußware *f* (com) defective (*or* substandard) goods
ausschüttbarer Gewinn *m* (Fin) distributable profit
ausschütten (Fin) to distribute *(ie, dividends)*
ausschüttende Körperschaft *f* (StR) distributing corporate body
Ausschüttung *f*
(Fin) distribution of dividends
– dividend outpayment (*or* payout)
Ausschüttung *f* **erhöhen** (Fin) to raise (dividend) distribution
Ausschüttungsbelastung *f*
(StR) burden on distributions
– distribution rate
(ie, corporate tax rate that applies to distributed profits; set at a uniform 36%)
ausschüttungsfähiger Gewinn *m*
(Fin) net earnings available for distribution (*or* payout)
– distributable profit
Ausschüttungspolitik *f* (Fin) dividend policy
Ausschüttungssatz *m* (Fin) (dividend) payout rate

Ausschüttungstermin *m* (Fin) profit distribution date
Außenanlagen *fpl* (StR) external improvements of a property other than buildings, § 89 BewG *(eg, fencing, paving)*
Außenbeitrag *m*
 (VGR) net export (of goods and services) *(ie, including net factor income accruing to residents from abroad)*
 (Vw) net foreign demand *(ie, difference between planned foreign demand and planned imports of goods and services)*
Außenbilanz *f* (AuW) external balance
Außendienst *m*
 (com) field service
 – customer engineering
 (Vers) field organization
 – (US) agency plant
 (ie, total force of agents representing an insurer)
Außendienstberichtssystem *n* (Bw) field-service reporting system
Außendienstkosten *pl* (KoR) field expense
Außendienstleiter *m* (Vers) agency manager
Außendienstmitarbeiter *mpl*
 (com) outdoor staff
 (Mk) field workes
Außendiensttechniker *m*
 (com) customer engineer
 – field service technician
Außenfinanzbedarf *m* (Fin) external finance requirements
Außenfinanzierung *f* (Fin) debt financing
 – external financing
 – financing out of outside funds
 – outside financing
 (eg, there is a limit to the amount of money that can be raised from outside sources)
Außengeld *n* (Vw) outside money
Außengrenze *f* (EG) external frontier
Außengroßhandel *m* (AuW) foreign trade wholesaling
Außenhandel *m* (AuW) foreign (*or* external) trade *(ie, commerce with other nations)*
Außenhandelsabteilung *f* (com) foreign trade department *(eg, in banks)*
Außenhandelsakzelerator *m* (Vw) foreign trade accelerator
Außenhandelsbeziehungen *fpl* (AuW) foreign trade relations
Außenhandelsbilanz *f* (AuW) (foreign) trade balance
Außenhandelsdefizit *n*
 (AuW) trade deficit
 – (US) deficit on merchandise trade
Außenhandelsfinanzierung *f* (Fin) foreign trade financing
Außenhandelsförderung *f* (AuW) foreign trade promotion
Außenhandelsgeschäft *n*
 (AuW) external transaction
 – export/import transaction
Außenhandelsgewinn *m* (AuW) gains from trade
Außenhandelskaufmann *m* (AuW) export and import merchant

Außenhandelsmonopol *n* (AuW) foreign trade monopoly
Außenhandelsmultiplikator *m* (AuW) foreign trade multiplier
Außenhandelspolitik *f*
 (AuW) foreign trade policy
 – foreign trading policy
 – trade policy
Außenhandelsquote *f* (AuW) ratio of total trade turnover – *exports and imports* – to national income *(ie, national income: as a rule gnp at market prices)*
Außenhandelsstatistik *f* (AuW) foreign (*or* external) trade statistics
Außenhandelstätigkeit *f* (AuW) foreign trade activity
Außenhandelstheoretiker *m* (Vw) foreign trade theorist
Außenhandelsüberschuß *m*
 (AuW) trade surplus
 – (US) surplus on merchandise trade
Außenhandelsunternehmen *n*
 (AuW) foreign trade firm
 – foreign trader
 – international trader
 – (GB) import/export merchant
 – (US) export management company, EMC
Außenhandelsvolumen *n* (AuW) volume of foreign trade
Außenhändler *m* (AuW) foreign trader
Außenkonsolidierung *f* (ReW) external consolidation *(ie, carried out to prepare global or worldwide financial statements of company groups)*
Außenmarkt *m* (Vw) external market *(ie, total of all external national economies which are potential trading partners)*
Außenmontage *f* (com) field assembly
Außenmontagegehälter *npl* (Pw) field assembly salaries
Außenmontagelöhne *mpl* (Pw) field assembly wages
Außenprüfer *m*
 (ReW) field auditor
 (StR) qualified government auditor
Außenprüfung *f*
 (ReW) field audit
 (StR) periodic tax examination (*or* government audit) *(ie, of large business, agricultural and professional establishments by government auditors, §§ 193–207ff AO)*
Außenseiter *m*
 (Kart) outsider *(ie, firm or company not affiliated with a cartel or pressure group)*
 (Vers) independent (insurer), pl. independents
Außensicherung *f* (Vw) hot-money defense policy
Außenstände *pl*
 (ReW) accounts receivable
 – debts outstanding (*or* receivable)
 – receivables outstanding
 – outstanding accounts
 – uncollected receivables
Außenstation *f*
 (EDV) remote terminal
 – outstation
Außenstehender *m* (Re) bystander

außenstehende Anteilseigner mpl (Fin) outside shareholders
Außensteuererlaß m (StR) Introductory Decree to the ,,Außensteuergesetz", of 11 July 1974
Außensteuergesetz n (StR) Law on External Tax Relations, of 8 Sept 1972, as amended
Außensteuerrecht n (StR) tax legislation relating to non-residents
Außentarif m (EG) external (or extra-bloc) tariff
Außenumsatzerlöse mpl (ReW) external sales
 – customer sales proceeds
 (ie, of a group of companies)
Außenverhältnis n (Re) (rights and duties) as to third parties
Außenverpackung f (com) packing (opp, packaging als Grundverpackung)
Außenversicherung f (Vers) external insurance (ie, covering temporary removal of property from its usual site)
Außenvertreter m (com) field representative
Außenwährungspolitik f (Vw) monetary policy toward the outside world
Außenwanderung f (Vw) external migration (ie, persons moving from one country to another)
Außenwanderungsstatistik f (Vw) external-migration statistics
Außenwerbung f (Mk) outdoor advertising
Außenwert m e–r Währung
 (AuW) external value of a currency
 (Fin) trade-weighted exchange rate
 – trade weighting (eg, improved from 90 to 90.2)
Außenwinkel m (Math) exterior angle
Außenwirtschaft f
 (AuW) external economic relations
 – external sector of the economy
außenwirtschaftliche Lage f (AuW) external position (or situation)
außenwirtschaftliche Komponente f (VGR) external component (ie, balance of goods and service transactions with the rest of the world)
außenwirtschaftliche Probleme npl (AuW) external problems
außenwirtschaftlicher Geldwert m (Vw) external value of money
außenwirtschaftliches Gleichgewicht n (AuW) equilibrium in a country's international balance of payments
 – external equilibrium
außenwirtschaftliche Stabilität f (AuW) external stability
außenwirtschaftliches Ungleichgewicht n (AuW) external imbalance
Außenwirtschaftsbestimmungen fpl (Re) foreign trade and payments provisions
Außenwirtschaftsgesetz n (Re) Foreign Trade Law, of 28 Apr 1961
Außenwirtschaftspolitik f (AuW) foreign economic policy
Außenwirtschaftsrecht n (Re) foreign trade and payments legislation
Außenwirtschaftstheorie f (Vw) international economics

Außenwirtschaftsverkehr m (AuW) foreign trade and payments transactions
Außenwirtschaftsverordnung f (Re) Foreign Trade and Payments Ordinance (ie, newly amended as of 31 Dec 1973)
Außenzoll m (AuW) external tariff
Außenzollsatz m (EG) external rate of duty
außer Betrieb
 (com) inoperative
 – out of action
 – out of operation
 – out of work
außerbetrieblicher Vergleich m (Bw) inter-plant comparison
außerbetriebliche Weiterbildung f (Pw) off-the-job training
außer Betrieb nehmen
 (com) to take out of operation
 (ReW) to abandon (ie, fixed assets)
 – to retire
außerbörslicher Handel m (Bö) off board (or off the floor) trading (ie, refers to transactions over-the-counter)
außerbörslicher Kurs m (Bö) off-the-board price
außerbörslich handeln (Bö) to trade off the floor
äußere Konvertibilität f (AuW) external convertibility
äußerer Speicher m
 (EDV) storage
 (EDV) backing storage
äußere Umstände mpl (com) external facts (eg, are controlling)
äußere Verschuldung f (FiW) borrowing abroad
außergerichtliche Einigung f (Re) out-of-court settlement
außergerichtlicher Rechtsbehelf m (StR) administrative appeal (or remedy), § 44 FGO, §§ 348, 349 AO
außergerichtlicher Vergleich m
 (Re) out-of-court
 – amicable
 – voluntary ... settlement
 – (GB) arrangement before receiving order
außergerichtlich vertreten (Re) to represent out of court
außergewöhnliche Aufwendungen mpl (ReW) extraordinary (or nonrecurrent) expenditure (ie, part of nonoperating expense)
außergewöhnliche Belastungen fpl (StR) extraordinary financial burdens, §§ 33, 33a EStG
außergewöhnlicher Preisnachlaß m (com) abnormal discount
außergewöhnlicher Verschleiß m (ReW) extraordinary loss of service life (or utility) (ie, due to unexpected occurrences; eg, accidents, explosion, fire)
außer Kraft setzen
 (Re) to cancel
 – to set aside
 – to rescind
Außerkrafttreten n von Rechtssätzen (Re) inoperativeness of legal rules
 (ie, by lapse of time – by formal cancellation – by collision with another legal rule of the same or a higher standing)

Außerkurssetzung *f* (Bö) suspension of a quotation
außerökonomisch bedingte Arbeitslosigkeit *f* (Vw) incidental unemployment *(eg, due to act of God, fire, inundation)*
außerordentliche Abschreibungen *fpl* (ReW) extraordinary depreciation
außerordentliche Aufwendungen *mpl* (ReW) extraordinary *(or* nonrecurrent) expenditure *(ie, part of nonoperating expense)*
außerordentliche Bilanz *f* (ReW) special balance sheet
außerordentliche Einkünfte *pl* (StR) extraordinary income, § 34 I EStG
außerordentliche Erträge *mpl* (ReW) extraordinary income
– extraordinary gains
– nonrecurrent income
außerordentliche Gewinne *mpl* **und Verluste** *mpl* (ReW) extraordinary profit and loss
außerordentliche Hauptversammlung *f* (Bw) special meeting of shareholders *(or* stockholders)
– (GB) extraordinary general meeting
außerordentliche Kündigung *f* (Pw) notice to quit for cause *(= aus wichtigem Grund)*
außerordentlicher Aufwand *m* (ReW) extraordinary expenses
– nonrecurrent charges
außerordentlicher Haushalt *m* (FiW) extraordinary budget
außerordentlicher Reparaturaufwand *m* (ReW) extraordinary repairs
außerordentliche Rücklagenzuführung *f* (ReW) extraordinary charge to reserves
außerordentliches Ergebnis *n* (ReW, EG) extraordinary profit or loss
außerordentliche Zuwendungen *fpl* (ReW) extraordinary benefits *(ie, accruing to an enterprise through gift, inheritance, remission of debt, etc.)*
außerplanmäßige Abschreibung *f* (ReW) unplanned *(or* non-scheduled) depreciation, § 154 II AktG *(ie, due to sudden and unexpected loss of usefulness)*
außerplanmäßige Ausgaben *fpl* (Fin) unbudgeted expenditure
außerplanmäßige Tilgung *f* (Fin) off-schedule redemption
außerpreislicher Wettbewerb *m* (Vw) nonprice competition
außerschulische Ausbildung *f* (Pw) out-of-school education *(or* training)
außertarifliches Personal *n* (Pw) staff members to whom the regular pay scale does not apply
außertarifliche Zollvergünstigung *f* (Zo) non-tariff customs relief
außervertragliche Haftung *f*
(Re) noncontract liability
– noncontractual liability
– liability based on violation of non-contract right
äußerlich gute Beschaffenheit *f* (SeeV) apparent good order and condition
äußerster Kurs *m* (Bö) ceiling price

äußerster Preis *m*
(com) lowest
– bottom
– knock-down
– rock-bottom ... price
aussetzen
(Re) to stay
– to suspend *(eg, execution of judgment)*
(StR) to suspend *(eg, assessment or payment of taxes)*
(Bö) to suspend *(eg, quotation of shares)*
Aussetzung *f* **der degressiven Afa** (StR) suspension of declining-balance depreciation
Aussetzung *f* **der Eingangsabgaben** (Zo) conditional relief from import duties and taxes
Aussetzung *f* **der Sätze des Gemeinsamen Zolltarifs** (EG) suspension of duties of the common customs tariff
Aussetzung *f* **der Steuerfestsetzung** (StR) suspension of tax assessment, § 165 AO
Aussetzung *f* **der Vollziehung** (StR) suspension of execution
Aussetzung *f* **e–r Gerichtsentscheidung** (Re) suspension of judgment
Aussetzung *f* **von Kursnotizen** (Bö) suspension of price quotations
aussondern (Re) to segregate
Aussonderung *f*
(Re) stoppage in transit, § 44 KO
(Re) segregation *(ie, of an asset from bankrupt's estate)*
Aussonderungsaxiom *n* (Log) axiom *(or* schema) of separation
Aussonderungsrecht *n* (Re) right of segregation, §§ 43–46 KO
aussortieren (com) to sort out
Aussortierung *f* (com) sorting out
Ausspannen *n* **von Kunden** (Kart) enticing away of customers
ausspeichern (EDV) to roll out
aussperren (Pw) to lock out
Aussperrung *f* (Pw) lockout
Ausstand *m* (Pw) strike
ausstatten
(Fin) to lay down the terms *(eg, of a loan issue)*
(Fin) to provide funds
– to fund
Ausstattung *f*
(Fin) terms of issue
(Fin) provision of funds
– funding
(Fin) structure *(ie, of a bond issue; eg, 25-year domestic sterling bond, including amount, price, coupon, maturity, register or bearer, placement and underwriting group)*
(Mk) design of packing
Ausstattungsmerkmale *npl* (Fin) structure *(or* terms) *(ie, of a bond issue)*
aussteigen
(com, infml) to pull out
(EDV) to abort a job or system *(syn, abbrechen)*
aussteuern
(EDV) to select
– to outsort
Aussteuerungsbefehl *m* (EDV) select instruction

Aussteuerungsfach n
  (EDV) reject stacker
  (EDV) reject pocket
austauschbare Dateien fpl (EDV) interchangeable files
Austauschpufferung f (EDV) exchange buffering
Austauschvertrag m
  (Re) reciprocal
  – bilateral
  – synallagmatic ... contract
  (ie, agreement intending to create obligations on both sides)
ausstehende Aktien fpl (ReW) outstanding capital stock *(ie, issued minus treasury shares)*
ausstehende Einlagen fpl
  (ReW) outstanding contributions
  – unpaid subscriptions
  – (GB) outstanding calls on shares
  – (GB) unpaid call on capital
ausstehende Einlagen fpl **auf das gezeichnete Kapital** (ReW, EG) subscribed capital unpaid
ausstehende Forderung f
  (ReW) account receivable
  (Fin) debt outstanding
ausstehender Betrag m (com) amount outstanding
ausstehende Rechnungen fpl (ReW) invoices not yet received
ausstehendes Aktienkapital n
  (ReW) capital outstanding
  – outstanding capital stock
aussteigen
  (com) to back out
  – to drop out
  – to pull out
  – to opt out *(eg, of a contract, deal, project)*
ausstellen
  (com) to draw up *(eg, contract, document)*
  – to make out *(eg, bill, invoice)*
  – to write out *(eg, check, receipt)*
  (Mk) to exhibit *(eg, at a fair)*
  (Vers) to close out *(ie, a policy)*
ausstellende Behörde f (com) issuing body
ausstellende Dienststelle f (com) issuing office
Aussteller m (WeR) drawer
  – *(Solawechsel:)* maker
  (Mk) exhibitor
Aussteller m **e–s Gefälligkeitsakzepts** (WeR) accommodation maker (*or* party)
Ausstellung f
  (com) fair
  – exhibition
  – show
  – exposition
Ausstellungsdatum n (com) date of issue
Ausstellungsfläche f (com) exhibition space
Ausstellungsgegenstände mpl (com) equipment for shows and exhibits
Ausstellungsgelände n (com) exhibition (*or* fair) grounds
Ausstellungsgut n (com) exhibits *(ie, exported or imported for use at trade fairs)*
Ausstellungsjahr n (com) year of issue
Ausstellungskosten pl (com) expenses arising in connection with exhibition at, and visits to, trade fairs

Ausstellungsmodell n (com) display model
Ausstellungsort m (WeR) place of issue
Ausstellungsraum m (com) show room
Ausstellungsstand m (com) exhibition stand
Ausstellungsstück n
  (com) exhibit
  – display article
  – showpiece
Ausstellungstag m (com) issuing date *(eg, of a policy)*
Ausstellungs-Versicherung f (Vers) trade fair insurance
Ausstellungswerbung f (Mk) exhibition advertising
aussteuern (Vers) to discontinue insurance benefits
Aussteuerversicherung f (Vers) daughters' endowment insurance
Ausstiegskurs m (Bö) take-out price
Ausstoß m (Bw) output *(syn, Ausbringung, Produktionsmenge)*
Ausstoßmaximierung f **unter Nebenbedingungen** (Vw) constrained-output maximization
Ausstoßrate f (Bw) rate of output
Ausstrahlungseffekt m (Mk) spillover effect
ausstreichen
  (com) to strike out
  – to delete
Ausstreichungen fpl (com) deletions
Austakten n (IndE) assembly line balancing
Austaktverfahren n (IndE) line-of-balance system
Austauschbeziehung f
  (com) trade relationship
  (Vw) tradeoff
Austauschrelation f (Vw) exchange ratio
Austauschvolumen n
  (AuW) volume of exports and imports
  (AuW) total value of exports and imports
Austausch m **von Informationen** (Bw) information exchange
austesten (EDV) to debug
Austestzeit f (EDV) program development time *(syn, Programmprüfzeit)*
austretende Variable f (OR) departing variable
Austritt m (Re) voluntary retirement (*or* withdrawal) of partner *(ie, in partnerships, associations, cooperatives, stock corporations)*
Austrittsort m (Zo) place (*or* point) of exit
Ausübung f **der Steuerhoheit** f (FiW) exercise of taxing power
Ausübung f **des Stimmrechts** (Re) exercise of the right to vote
Ausübung f **e–s freien Berufes** (com) practice of a profession
Ausverkauf m
  (com) clean-up sale
  – close-out sale
  – closeout
  – sellout
  – clearance sale
  – cleanout of inventories of unsold goods
ausverkaufen (com) to sell out
ausverkauft
  (com) out of stock
  – sold out
aus von uns nicht zu vertretenden Gründen (Re) for reasons beyond our control

Auswahl *f*
 (com) range of goods (*or* products)
 − assortment
 (Stat) sample
Auswahlantwort *f* (EDV) multiple choice
Auswahlantwort *f* (EDV) multiple choice
Auswahl *f* **aus e–m Herstellersortiment** (Mk) short line
Auswahlaxiom *n*
 (Math) axiom of choice
 − multiplicative axiom
 − Zermelo's axiom
Auswahlbetrieb *m* (EDV) selective calling
Auswahl *f* **der Lieferquelle** (MaW) selection of sources of supply
Auswahleinheit *f*
 (Stat) unit of sampling
 − sampling unit
Auswahleinheit *f* **erster Stufe** (Stat) first-stage unit
Auswahleinheit *f* **zweiter Stufe** (Stat) second-stage unit
Auswahlfrage *f*
 (Mk) cafeteria question
 − multiple choice question
Auswahlgrundlage *f* (Stat) frame
Auswahlkriterium *n* (Stat) eligibility (*or* selection) criterion
Auswahlphase *f*
 (Bw) choice activity *(ie, in decision theory)*
 − phase of selecting the best alternative
 − phase of selecting the plan to follow
Auswahlplan *m*
 (Stat) sample design
 − sample plan
 − sampling plan
Auswahlsatz *m* (Stat) sampling fraction (*or* ratio)
Auswahlsendung *f* (com) ,,on approval" consignment
Auswahlverfahren *n* (Stat) sampling (procedure)
auswärtige Unterbringung *f* (StR) room and board away from home
Auswärtsvergabe *f* (com) farming out *(ie, of contracts)*
auswechselbare Platten *fpl* (EDV) interchangeable disks
auswechselbare Typenstange *f* (EDV) interchangeable type bar
Ausweichklausel *f* (AuW) escape clause
Ausweichkurs *m* (Bö) fictitious security price *(syn, Scheinkurs)*
Ausweis *m*
 (com) identity card
 (ReW) statement *(eg, balance sheet)*
 (Fin) bank return
ausweisen
 (com) to prove one's identity
 (ReW) to report
 − to show *(eg, on the books)*
 − to recognize *(eg, in an account)*
 − to list
Ausweiskontrolle *f* (Zo) identity control
Ausweisleser *m* (EDV) badge reader
Ausweismethode *f* (Fin) recording method
Ausweispapier *n* (WeR) identification document *(ie, simple instrument evidencing title to ownership; eg, credit card, cloakroom ticket)*
Ausweispflicht *f* (com) duty (*or* obligation) to publish (*or* disclose) certain information
auswerten
 (com) to appraise
 − to evaluate
 (Stat) to evaluate
 − to interpret
 (Pat) to exploit
Auswertung *f*
 (com) evaluation
 − appraisal *(ie, to determine the value of sth)*
 (Stat) evaluation
 − interpretation
 (Pat) exploitation *(eg, of an invention)*
auszahlen
 (com) to disburse
 − to pay out
 (Fin) to pay off *(eg, a partner)*
Auszahlung *f*
 (com) disbursement
 − outpayment
 − outgo
 (Fin) payoff
 (Fin) amount paid out *(eg, mortgage)*
 (Fin) payout
 − net proceeds
 − avail
 (ie, of loan; eg, 5% interest, 100% payout, minus 1% bank handling fee)
Auszählung *f* (Stat) tabulating (*or* tallying) of data
Auszahlungsanweisung *f* (Fin) payment order
Auszahlungsbetrag *m* (Fin) net loan proceeds
Auszahlungsbewilligung *f* (Fin) payment authorization
Auszahlungsdisagio *n* (Fin) loan discount
Auszahlungsermächtigung *f* (Fin) authority to pay
Auszahlungskurs *m* (Fin) payout ratio *(ie, loan amount less discount)*
Auszahlungsmatrix *f* (Bw) payoff matrix
Auszahlungsreihe *f* (Fin) (stream of) cash outflows *(ie, in preinvestment analysis)*
Auszahlungsstelle *f* (Fin) paying agency
Auszahlungstabelle *f* (Bw) payoff table
Auszahlungsüberschuß *m* (Fin) net outpayments
Auszahlungsvolumen *n* (Fin) volume of loans granted
Auszahlungswert *m* (Fin) net loan proceeds
auszeichnen
 (com) to price
 − to mark with prices
 (ie, to put price tags on articles)
Auszeichnen *n* (EDV) typographic styling *(ie, in text processing)*
Auszeichnung *f*
 (com) price marking
 − marking with price tags
 (com) price mark (*or* tag)
Auszeichnungspflicht *f* (com) legal duty to price goods displayed
Auszubildender *m*
 (Pw) apprentice
 − trainee

Auszug *m*
(Re) extract *(eg, from official register)*
(com) statement of account
autark
(Vw) autarchic *(eg, energy policy)*
– self-reliant
– self-sufficient
Autarkie *f*
(Vw) economic self-sufficiency
– autarchy
authentische Interpretation *f* (Re) authentic interpretation
Autobranche *f* (com) motor industry (*or* sector)
Autocode *m*
(EDV) autocode
– low-level language *(syn, maschinenorientierte Programmiersprache)*
Autodidakt *m*
(Pw) self-trained (*or* self-educated) person
autodidaktisches Lernen *n* (Pw) self-education *(ie, without outside help)*
Autohändler *m*
(com) motor dealer
– auto dealer
Autohersteller *m*
(com) car manufacturer
– auto maker
Autoindustrie *f*
(com) motor car industry
– auto industry
Autokonsolidierung *f* **von Staatsdefiziten** (FiW) automatic consolidation of public-sector deficits
Autokorrelation *f* (Stat) autocorrelation
Autokorrelations-Koeffizient *m* (Stat) autocorrelation coefficient
Autokovarianz-Funktion *f* (Stat) autocovariance function
autokratische Führung *f* (Bw) autocratic (*or* Caesar) management
autokratischer Führungsstil *m* (Bw) autocratic managerial style
Automat *m*
(com) vending machine
– (GB) slot machine
(IndE) automatic machine
Automatentheorie *f*
(EDV) theory of automation
– automatics
Automatenverkauf *m* (com) sale by automatic vendors
Automatik *f* (IndE) (programmed) automatic cycle
Automation *f* (IndE) automation *(ie, fully mechanized production with the aid of automated equipment)*
Automationsgrad *m* (IndE) degree of automation
automatische Ausschaltung *f* (EDV) automatic cutout
automatische Codierung *f* (EDV) automatic coding (*or* programming) *(syn, automatische od maschinenunterstützte Programmierung)*
automatische Datenverarbeitung *f* (EDV) automatic data processing, ADP
automatische Fehlerkorrektur *f* (EDV) automatic error correction

automatische Fristverlängerung *f* (StR) automatic extension *(ie, of time for the filing of returns)*
automatische Geräteprüfung *f*
(EDV) automatic
– built-in
– hardware . . . check *(syn, Selbstprüfung)*
automatische Lohnbindung *f* (Vw) automatic wage-indexation *(eg, ‚scala mobile' in Italy)*
automatische Produktionssteuerung *f* (IndE) automated production control
automatische Programmierung *f* (EDV) automatic programming (*or* coding) *(syn, maschinenunterstützte Programmierung, automatische Codierung)*
automatische Prüfung *f* (EDV) built-in (*or* hardware) check *(syn, Selbstprüfung)*
automatische Quoten *fpl* (EG) automatic quotas
automatischer Abrufbetrieb *m*
(EDV) automatic polling
– autopoll
automatischer Konjunkturstabilisator *m*
(Vw) automatic fiscal stabilizer
– built-in flexibility
– built-in stabilizer
automatischer Stanzer *m*
(EDV) automatic (feed) punch
– card punch *(syn, (Loch-)Kartenstanzer)*
automatischer Stopp *m* (EDV) automatic stop
automatische Rückstellung *f* (EDV) self-resetting
automatischer Vorschub *m* (EDV) automatic feed
automatische Saldenaufnahme *f* (ReW) automatic balance pickup
automatische Scheckbearbeitung *f* (Fin) automatic check handling
automatische Schreibmaschine *f* (com) automatic typewriter
automatische Speichervermittlung *f*
(EDV) automatic (message) switching center
– switching center
(ie, transferring traffic between circuits)
automatische Stabilisatoren *mpl* (Vw) automatic stabilizers
automatisches Wörterbuch *n* (EDV) automatic dictionary *(ie, providing a word for word substitution between languages)*
automatische Unterbrechung *f* (EDV) automatic interrupt
automatische Vorrangsteuerung *f* (EDV) automatic priority control
automatische Weiterversicherung *f* (Vers) automatic loss reinstatement *(ie, of full value of the policy after payment of a loss)*
automatische Zeichengenerierung *f* (EDV) automatic character generation
automatisch in Kraft tretend (Re) self-operative
automatisieren (IndE) to automate
automatisierte Produktion *f* (IndE) automated production
automatisierter Arbeitsprozeß *m* (IndE) automated operating procedure
Automatisierung *f* (IndE) automation *(ie, operating in an advanced stage of mechanization by highly automatic means)*
Auto *n* **mieten** (com) to rent (*or* hire) a car

Automobilindustrie f
(com) automotive industry
– motor car industry
Automobilwerte mpl (Bö) automative stock
autonome Arbeitsgruppe f (Pw) autonomous work group
autonome Ausgaben fpl (Vw) autonomous expenditure
autonome Funktion f (Math) autonomous function
autonome Größen fpl (Vw) autonomous variables
autonome Investition f (Vw) autonomous investment
autonome Nachfrage f
(Vw) autonomous demand
(OR) final bill of goods
autonomer Konsum m (Vw) autonomous consumption
autonomer technischer Fortschritt m (Vw) autonomous technical progress
autonomer Zoll m (AuW) autonomous tariff
autonomes Verhalten n (Vw) autonomous behavior
autonome Transaktion f (Vw) autonomous (or regular) transaction
autonome Variable f (Math) autonomous variable
Autonomiegrad m (Bw) scope of authority
Autonomieprinzip n (Re, Bw) principle of autonomy
Autorenexemplar n (com) author's copy
Autorenhonorar n (com) (author's) royalty *(ie, percentage of retail price of each copy sold)*
Autorenrechte npl (Re) author's rights
autorisieren (Re) to authorize
autorisierte Übersetzung f (com) authorized translation
Autorisierung f (com) authorization
Autorität f
(com) authority *(ie, authoritative power)*
(com) authority
– expert *(ie, in a special field)*
autoritärer Führungsstil m (Bw) authoritative (or directive) style of leadership
Autoritätsprinzip n (Pw) principle of authority
Autoritätsstruktur f (Bw) authority structure
Autoschalter m (Fin) drive-in window
Autoverleih m (com) car rental service
Autovermietung f (com) car rental service
Autoversicherung f (Vers) motor insurance
Aval m od n
(Fin) guaranty
– (GB) guarantee
(ie, irrevocable bank guaranty for a bill of exchange)
Avalakzept n (Fin) collateral (or guaranteed) acceptance by bank
Avalbegünstigter m (Re) beneficiary under a guaranty
Avale mpl (Fin) guaranteed bills outstanding
avalieren (Fin) to guarantee *(ie, a bill of exchange)*

avalierter Wechsel m (Fin) backed (or guaranteed) bill of exchange
Avalist m (Fin) guarantor of bill of exchange
Avalkredit m (Fin) credit by way of bank guaranty
Avalobligo n (Fin) guaranty commitments
Avalprovision f (Fin) commission on guaranty
Avis m od n
(com) advice
– notice
– notification
avisieren
(com) to inform *(eg, that consignment is under way)*
– to advise
– to notify
– to give notice of
avisierende Bank f (Fin) advising bank *(ie, under a letter of credit)*
Avisierung f
(com) advice
– notification
a vista (WeR) (payable) at sight
à vue (WeR) (payable) at sight
Axiologie f (Re, Vw) axiology *(ie, branch of science dealing with values)*
axiologisch (Re, Vw) axiological
Axiom n (Log, Math) axiom
Axiomatik f (Log) axiomatics *(ie, the total of logical operations proceeding from axioms)*
axiomatische Definition f (Log) axiomatic definition
axiomatische Mengenlehre f (Math) axiomatic set theory
axiomatische Methode f (Log) axiomatic method
– model theory *(ie, sometimes in empirical sciences)*
axiomatischer Begriff m (Log) axiomatic concept (or term)
axiomatischer Satz m (Log) axiomatic proposition (or statement)
axiomatische Theorie f
(Math) axiometric theory
– *(also often called:)* deductive system
axiomatisieren (Log, Math) to axiomatize
Axiom n der Fundierung (Math) axiom of foundation (or regularity) *(ie, an axiom in set theory stating that every non-empty set a) contains a member b) which has no member in common with a))*
Axiom n der vollständigen Ordnung (Math) complete-ordering axiom
Axiomensystem n (Math) system of axioms
Axonometrie f (Math) axonometrics
axonometrische Zeichnung f (Math) axonometric drawing
Azubi m
(Pw) apprentice
– trainee *(ie, acronym for ‚Auszubildender')*
azyklisches Netzwerk n (OR) acyclic network

B

baden gehen (com, infml) to take a bath
Bagatellausgaben *fpl* (com) minor disbursements
Bagatellbetrag *m*
  (com) trifle
  – trifling amount
Bagatellfehler *m* (ReW) negligible mistake *(ie, in preparing the annual financial statement)*
bagatellisieren (com) to play down *(opp, to play up = hochspielen)*
Bagatellkartell *n* (Kart) minor cartel *(ie, not deemed to be in violation of the public interest)*
Bagatellklausel *f*
  (Kart) minor-merger clause *(ie, taking such mergers outside the scope of statutory merger control, if a market for goods and commercial services produces less than DM 10 million in sales revenue, § 24 VIII GWB)*
  (Vers) franchise clause *(ie, claims below a stated limit not payable by insurer)*
Bagatellsache *f* (Re) petty case *(or* cause*) (ie, civil litigation where the amount in controversy is negligible; the concept is foreign to the German legal system)*
Bagatellschaden *m*
  (com) trivial *(or* petty*)* damage
  (Vers) small loss *(ie, costing more to process than the actual settlement amount)*
Bagatellsteuer *f* (FiW) nuisance tax *(ie, small rate, excessive red tape)*
Bagatellstrafsache *f* (Re) petty *(or* summary*)* offense
Bagatellzölle *mpl* (FiW) nuisance rates *(ie, below 5 percent)*
Bahn *f*
  (com) railroad
  – (GB) railway
Bahnaktien *fpl*
  (Fin) railroad shares *(or* stocks*)*
  – railroads
  – rails
bahnamtlich (com) in accordance with railroad rules and regulations
bahnamtliche Bestimmungen *fpl* (com) rules and regulations issued by railroad authorities
bahnamtlicher Rollfuhrdienst *m* (com) contract carrier *(ie, authorized by and acting on behalf of the Federal Railways)*
Bahnanschluß *m*
  (com) rail connection
  – (GB *also:* connexion)
Bahnanschlußgleis *n*
  (com) railroad siding
  – private siding
Bahnbeamter *m* (com) railroad official
Bahnbeförderung *f* (com) carriage *(or* transport*)* by rail
Bahnbehörde *f* (com) railroad authorities
bahnbrechend
  (com) pioneering
  – epoch-making
  – (infml) trail-blazing
  (eg, discoveries, inventions, innovations)
Bahnfracht *f*
  (com) railroad freight
  – rail freight
  (com) rail charges
  (com) rail carriage
Bahnfrachtbrief *m*
  (com) railroad bill of lading
  – (GB) railway consignment note
Bahnfrachtgeschäft *n* (com) rail transport *(or* carriage*)*
Bahnfrachtsätze *mpl* (com) railroad rates
Bahnfrachtverkehr *m* (com) railroad freight traffic
bahnfrei
  (com) free on board *(railroad station)*
  – (GB) free on rail, FOR, f. o. r.
  (com, GB) carriage paid
  (ie, charges for delivery prepaid)
bahngesteuerter Betrieb *m* (IndE) continuous-path operation
Bahnhofstarif *m* (com) tariff rates for railroad transport between loading station and unloading station
Bahnhofswerbung *f* (Mk) commercial advertising in railroad stations
bahnlagernde Sendung *f* (com) consignment to be called for at railroad station
Bahnlieferung *f*
  (com) transport by rail
  – (GB) carriage by rail
bahnmäßig verpackt
  (com) packed for rail shipment
  – (GB) packed for carriage by rail
Bahnpost *f* (com) railroad mail service
Bahnpostamt *n* (com) station post office
bahnpostlagernd (com) to be called for at station office
Bahnrechner *m* (EDV) path computer
Bahnrollfuhr-Versicherungsschein *m* (Vers) cartage contractor's insurance policy
Bahnspediteur *m*
  (com) railroad agent
  – (GB) railway carrier
  – cartage contractor
Bahnsteuerung *f* (IndE) continuous-path control
Bahntransport *m*
  (com) rail(road) transport
  – transportation by rail
  – (GB) railway transport
Bahnverkehr *m* (com) railroad traffic
Bahnversand *m* (com) forwarding by rail
Bahnzustellung *f* (com) railroad delivery
Baisse *f*
  (Fin) downturn phase
  (Bö) slump at the stock market
  – falling prices
  – sharp drop

Baisseangebot *n* (Bö) short offer
Baissebewegung *f* (Bö) bearish (*or* downward) movement
Baisse-Engagement *n*
(Bö) engagement to sell short
– short account
– short interest
– short position
Baissegeschäft *n*
(Bö) bear transaction
– short selling
Baissemanöver *n* (Bö) bear raid
Baissemarkt *m* (Bö) bear (*or* short) market
Baissepartei *f* (Bö) short side
Baisseposition *f*
(Bö) bear account
– short position
Baissespekulant *m*
(Bö) bear
– speculator for a fall in prices
– (infml) banger
Baissespekulation *f*
(Bö) bear operation (*or* speculation *or* transaction)
– speculation for a fall in prices
– going short
Baissestimmung *f*
(Bö) bearish tone of the market
– bearishness
– bearish tendency
Baissetendenz *f* = *Baissestimmung*
Baissetermingeschäft *n* (Bö) trading on the short side
Baisseverkauf *m* (Bö) bear sale
Baisseverkäufer *m* (Bö) short seller
Baissier *m*
(Bö) bear
– speculator for a fall in prices
– short seller
Balkencode *m* (EDV) bar code *(syn, Strichcode)*
Balkencodeleser *m* (EDV) bar code scanner *(syn, Strichcodeleser)*
Balkendiagramm *n* (Stat) bar chart (*or* graph)
Ballungsgebiet *n*
(com) congested urban area
(Vw) area of industrial concentration
– agglomeration area
Ballungsraum *m* = *Ballungsgebiet*
Band *n*
(EDV) tape
(IndE) assembly line
Bandabgleich *m* (IndE) assembly line balancing
Bandabschnittsmarke *f* (EDV) tape mark
Bandanfang *m* (EDV) leading end
Bandanfangkennsatz *m* (EDV, Cobol) beginning reel label
Bandanfangs-Etikett *n* (EDV) tape header label
Bandanfangsmarke *f* (EDV) beginning of tape marker, BOT
Bandarchiv *n* (EDV) magnetic tape library
Bandaufbereitung *f* (EDV) tape editing
Bandauszug *m* (EDV) selective tape dump
Bandbetriebssystem *n* (EDV) Tape Operating System, TOS *(ie, for IBM computers)*
Bandbibliothek *f* (EDV) tape library

Bandblock *m* (EDV) magnetic tape block (*or* cluster *or* group)
Bandbreite *f*
(AuW) currency band
– exchange margins
– support points
– margin (*or* range) of fluctuations
– official spread
(eg, margin of 2¼% on either side of nominal rates)
Bandbreiten-Flexibilität *f* (Vw) flexible target range *(eg, of monetary growth)*
Banddatei *f* (EDV) magnetic tape file
Banddiagramm *n* (Stat) band chart
Banddichte *f* (EDV) tape packing density
Banddruckroutine *f* (EDV) tape edit routine
Bandeingabe *f* (EDV) tape input
Bandende *n*
(EDV) end of tape
(EDV, Cobol) end of reel
(EDV) trailing end
Bandendemarke *f* (EDV) end of tape marker, EOT
Bandenschmuggel *m* (StR) joint contraband smuggling, § 373 AO
Banderole *f* (StR) revenue stamp *(ie, printed on pasted label)*
Banderolensteuer *f* (StR) revenue stamp tax (*or* duty)
Bänderschaubild *n* (Stat) band chart
Bandetikett *n* (EDV) tape label
Bandfehler *m* (EDV) tape error *(syn, Magnetbandfehler)*
Bandfertigung *f* (IndE) synchronous assembly-line production
Bandgerät *n* (EDV) magnetic tape unit (*or* deck *or* station) *(syn, Laufwerk)*
Bandgeschwindigkeit *f* (EDV) tape speed
bandgesteuert (EDV) tape controlled
Band-Karte-Umsetzer *m* (EDV) tape-to-card converter
Bandlader *m* (EDV) tape loading routine
Bandlänge *f* (EDV) tape length
Bandlaufwerk *n* (EDV) magnetic tape drive
Bandlesebereich *m* (EDV) tape read area
Band-Lochstreifen-Umsetzer *m* (EDV) tape-to-punched-tape converter
Bandmarke *f* (EDV) tape mark
Bandmontage *f* (IndE) progressive assembly
Bandnummer *f* (EDV) tape number
Bandprüfung *f* (EDV) tape test
Bandrücksetzen *n* (EDV) backspace
Bandrückspulen *n* (EDV) rewind
Bandsatz *m* (EDV) tape record
Bandschreibmarke *f* (EDV) tape mark
Bandsicherung *f* (EDV) file protection
Bandspeicher *m* (EDV) magnetic tape storage
Bandsprosse *f* (EDV) frame
Bandspule *f* (EDV) reel
Bandspur *f* (EDV) tape track
Bandsteuerung *f* (EDV) tape control
Bandvergleich *m* (EDV) tape compare
Bandvorschub *m* (EDV) tape feed
Bandwagon-Effekt *m*
(Vw) bandwagon effect
– demonstration effect

Bank *f*
(Fin) bank
- banker
- banking establishment (*or* house)

Bankabrufverfahren *n* (Fin) automatic debit transfer system *(eg, taxpayer authorizes his bank by standing order = ‚Dauerauftrag' to make payment to the revenue receiving office = ‚Finanzkasse' when this calls for it)*

Bankadresse *f*
(com) bank address
(Fin) bank name *(eg, on a bill of exchange)*

Bankagent *m* (Fin) bank representative

Bankagio *n* (Fin) share (*or* bond) premium charged by banks

Bankakkreditiv *n*
(Fin) clean credit *(ie, based on the terms ‚‚documents against payment")*
(Fin) instruction by a bank to another bank to pay out a specified amount in cash to a third party

Bankaktien *fpl* (Fin) bank shares (*or* stock) *(ie, issued by joint-stock banks)*

Bankaktiengesellschaft *f*
(Fin) joint-stock bank
- banking corporation

Bankakzept *n*
(Fin) banker's acceptance
- (GB) bank bill
(ie, bill accepted by a bank, more easily resold)

Bank-an-Bank-Kredit *m* (Fin) interbank lending (*or* loan)

Bankangestellter *m*
(com) bank clerk
- bank employee
- bank officer (*or* official)

Bankanleihen *fpl* (Fin) bank bonds *(ie, issued by banks for refinance purposes, esp. by real estate credit institutions, rarely by credit banks)*

Bank *f* **anweisen** (Fin) to instruct a bank

Bankanweisung *f* (Fin) order to a bank to transfer title to a fungible thing, mostly money, to a third party *(eg, check, letter of credit)*

Bankarchiv *n* (Fin) bank's archives *(ie, today replaced by the ‚economics department' of a bank)*

Bankauftrag *m*
(Fin) instruction to a bank
- bank order
(Re) contract concluded with a bank for transaction of business, Ziff. 6ff AGB

Bankauskunft *f*
(Fin) information supplied by bank
- bank reference

Bankausweis *m* (Fin) bank return

Bankauszug *m* (Fin) bank statement

Bankautomat *m*
(Fin) automated teller machine, ATM *(syn, Bankomat)*

Bankautomation *f* (Fin) automation of banking services

Bankaval *n* (Fin) bank guaranty

Bankavis *n*
(com) bank advice *(ie, confirming letter of credit to exporter)*

(Fin) LZB credit advice *(ie, sent to the receiving LZB)*

Bankbeamter *m* (com) bank official *(ie, term obsolescent)*

Bank-bei-Bank-Einlage *f* (Fin) interbank deposit

Bankbestände *mpl* (Fin) banks' holdings

Bankbeteiligung *f*
(Fin) banking interest
- interest (*or* holding *or* stake) in a bank
(Fin) affiliated bank

Bankbetrieb *m*
(Fin) bank *(ie, handling all bank operations from inception to completion; includes savings banks)*
(Fin) bank(ing) operations

Bankbetriebslehre *f* (Fin) bank management science *(ie, dealing with money and credit in terms of banking operations)*

Bankbevollmächtigter *m* (Fin) bank's authorized agent

Bankbilanz *f* (ReW) bank balance sheet

Bankbote *m* (Fin) bank messenger

Bankbuchhaltung *f*
(ReW) bank accounting system
(ReW) bank's accounting department

Bankbürgschaft *f* (Fin) bank guaranty

Bankdarlehen *n* (Fin) bank loan

Bankdeckung *f*
(Vw) bank cover *(ie, of notes issued; comprising bankable instruments, such as bills of exchange, checks, Lombard claims, stocks and bonds)*
(Fin) cover provided by bank

Bankdepositen *pl* (Fin) bank deposits

Bankdepot *n* (Fin) safe custody (at a bank)

Bank *f* **der Banken** (Vw) bankers' bank

Bankdienstleistung *f* (Fin) banking service

Bankdirektor *m* (Fin) bank manager *(ie, esp. board members of joint-stock banks = ‚Aktienbanken'; title is not protected and need not be entered in the commercial register)*

Bankdiskont *m*
(Fin) bank discount rate
(Fin) discount rate *(ie, charged by central bank)*

Bankeigenschaft *f* (Fin) bank status

Bankeinbruchversicherung *f* (Vers) bank burglary insurance

Bankeneinlage *f* (Fin) bank deposit

Bankeinlagenversicherung *f* (Vers) bank deposit insurance

Bank *f* **einschalten** (Fin) to interpose a bank *(eg, between seller and buyer)*

Bankeinzug *m* (Fin) payment by automatic debit transfer

Bankeinzugsverfahren *n* (Fin) automatic debit transfer system

Bankenabrechnungsstelle *f* (Fin) bankers' clearing house

Bankenapparat *m* (Vw) banking system

Bankenaufsicht *f* (Fin) bank supervision *(ie, organized under public and private law)*

Bankenaufsichtsbehörde *f* (Fin) banking supervisory authority

Bankenbonifikation *f* (Fin) agency commission *(ie, between banks)*

85

Banken-Clearing n
(Fin) clearing
- settling inter-bank transactions

Bankendebitoren pl (ReW) due from banks

Bankendekonzentration f (Fin) deconcentration of banks

Bankenerlaß m (StR) „banking decree" *(ie, administrative decree issued in 1949 imposing restraint on the fiscal authorities in tracing taxable transactions)*

Bankenfilialsystem n (Fin) multiple branch *(or* office) banking

Bankengeldmarkt m (Fin) interbank money market

Bankengesetzgebung f (Re) banking legislation *(ie, all statutory provisions relating to the money and credit system of a country)*

Bankengruppe f
(Fin) group of banks
- banking group

Bankenkonsortium n
(Fin) banking consortium
- consortium of banks
- banking syndicate
- syndicate
- bank group *(or* group of banks)
- underwriting group

Bankenkonzentration f (Fin) concentration of banks

Bankenkreditoren pl (ReW) due to banks

Bankenkrise f (Vw) bank crisis

Bankenliquidität f (Fin) bank liquidity

Bankenmarkt m (Fin) interbank market

Bankenmoratorium n (Fin) moratorium by banks

Bankennumerierung f (Fin) system of bank routing numbers

Bankenpublikum n (Bö) bank traders

Bankensektor m (Vw) banking sector

Bankenstatistik f (Fin) banking statistics

Bankenstimmrecht n
(Fin) right of banks to vote proxies
- bank's right to vote deposited shares at a general meeting

Bankensystem n (Fin) banking system

Banken-Überweisungsverkehr m (Fin) bank transfer system

Bankerträge mpl (Fin) bank's earnings

Bankfach n
(Fin) banking business
(Fin) bank safe

Bankfachmann m (Fin) banking specialist *(or* professional)

bankfähiger Wechsel m (Fin) bankable bill (of exchange)

bankfähiges Papier n (Fin) paper eligible for discount

Bankfazilitäten fpl
(Fin) bank facilities
- credit facilities (at a bank)

Bankfeiertage mpl (Fin) bank holidays *(ie, in Germany all Saturdays)*

Bankfiliale f (Fin) branch bank

bankenfinanziert (Fin) bank-financed

Bankfinanzierung f (Fin) financing through a bank

Bank f **für Internationalen Zahlungsausgleich** (AuW) Bank for International Settlements, BIS

Bankfusion f (Fin) bank merger *(or* consolidation)

Bankgarantie f (Fin) bank guaranty

Bankgarantiefonds m (Fin) bank guaranty fund

Bankgebühren fpl (Fin) bank charges

Bankgeheimnis n (Fin) banking secrecy

Bankgeld n (Vw) bank *(or* book) money

Bankgelder npl
(Fin) bank moneys
- deposits of banks

Bankgeldschöpfung f (Vw) creation of bank money

Bankgeschäft n
(Fin) banking
- banking activity
- banking business
- banking operations
- banking transactions

bankgeschäftlicher Betrieb m (Fin) banking operation

Bankgesetz n (Re) Law on the Federal Central Bank, of 27 July 1957

Bankgesetzgebung f (Re) bank legislation *(ie, all statutory provisions relating to the money and credit system of a country)*

Bankgewerbe n (Fin) banking industry, § 1 HGB

bankgiriert (Fin) bank indorsed

bankgirierter Warenwechsel m (Fin) banker's trade acceptance *(ie, bill resulting from a trade transaction, discounted by the bank and bearing bank's indorsement; rediscountable)*

Bankgiro n
(Fin) noncash clearing under Giro system
- Bank Giro
(Fin) bank indorsement

Bankgläubiger m (Fin) bank creditor

Bankguthaben n
(ReW) cash in bank
(Fin) bank balance *(or* deposit)
- balance in bank

Bankhaus n (Fin) banking firm *(or* house)

Bank-Holding f (Fin) bank holding (company)

Bankier m
(Fin) banker *(ie, the KWG amendment of 1976 prohibits the legal form of sole proprietorship in licensing new credit institutions, § 2a KWG)*
(Fin) *(loosely also:)* any top executive in the banking business

Bankierbonifikation f (Fin) banker's commission *(ie, for taking over part of a securities issue from an underwriting group)*

Bankindossament n (Fin) bank stamp *(ie, on bill of exchange)*

Bankinstitut n
(Fin) bank
- banking establishment *(or* institution)

Bankkalkulation f (Fin) bank's cost and revenue accounting

Bankkapital n (Fin) bank capital *(ie, own funds + outside capital)*

Bankkassierer m (Fin) bank teller

Bankkaufmann m (Fin) bank employee *(with a 3-year training period)*

Bankkonditionen fpl (Fin) credit conditions of a bank

Bankkonsortium *n*
(Fin) banking consortium
- consortium of banks
- banking syndicate
- syndicate
- bank group (*or* group of banks)
- underwriting group

Bankkonto *n* (Fin) bank account

Bankkonto *n* **eröffnen**
(com) to open a bank account
- to open an account with a bank

Bankkonto *n* **haben**
(com) to carry (*or* have) an account (with)
- to bank with (*eg, Where do you bank?*)

Bankkontokorrent *m* (Fin) current account with a bank

Bankkonto *n* **sperren** (Fin) to block a bank account

Bankkonto *n* **überziehen** (Fin) to overdraw a bank account

Bankkontrolle *f* (Fin) bank audit

Bankkonzern *m*
(Fin) group of banks
- banking group

Bankkonzerngeschäfte *npl* (Fin) group banking

Bankkostenrechnung *f* (KoR) bank cost accounting (*ie, mostly based on departmental costing, aimed at efficiency analysis and control*)

Bankkrach *m* (Fin) bank crash

Bankkredit *m*
(Fin) bank loan
- (GB) overdraft (*ie, universal British term for a bank loan*)

Bankkredite *mpl* (Fin) bank lending

Bankkreise *mpl*
(Fin) banking quarters (*or* circles)
- the banking community

Bankkrise *f* (Vw) bank crisis

Bankkunde *m* (Fin) bank customer

Bankkundschaft *f*
(Fin) bank's customers
- bank's clientele

Banklehre *f* (Pw) bank apprenticeship

Bankleistungen *fpl* (Fin) banking services

Bankleitzahl *f*
(Fin) transit number
- routing symbol
- (GB) bank code

Banklombardgeschäft *n* (Fin) collateral loan business

bankmäßige Zahlung *f* (Fin) bank payment (*ie, by means of check, remittance, or debit transfer; opp, cash payment*)

Bank *f* **mit mehreren Zweigstellen** (Fin) multiple-office bank

Banknebenstelle *f* (Fin) secondary bank place

Banknote *f*
(Vw) banknote
(com, infml) bill
- (esp GB) note

Banknoten *fpl* **aufrufen** (Vw) to call in notes

Banknoten *fpl* **aus dem Verkehr ziehen** (Vw) to withdraw notes from circulation

Banknotenausgabe *f* (Vw) note issue

Banknoten *fpl* **ausgeben** (Vw) to issue bank notes

Banknotenbündel *n*
(Fin) bankroll
- wad of notes
- (GB) sheaf of notes

Banknoten *fpl* **einziehen** (Vw) to withdraw notes from circulation

Banknotenemission *f* (Vw) note issue

Banknotenfälschung *f* (Vw) counterfeiting (*or* forgery) of bank notes

Banknoten *fpl* **in Umlauf setzen** (Vw) to issue bank notes

Banknotenmonopol *n* (Vw) note-issuing monopoly

Banknotenpapier *n* (Vw) bank note paper

Banknotensteuer *f* (FiW) tax on note issue

Banknotenumlauf *m*
(Vw) bank notes in circulation
- active circulation of bank notes

Bankobligationen *fpl* (Fin) bank bonds (*ie, issued by banks for refinance purposes, esp. by real estate credit institutions, but rarely by credit banks*)

Bankomat *m*
(Fin) automated teller machine, ATM
- (GB) cash dispenser

Bankorganisation *f* (BwL) bank's organization system

Bankpapiere *npl* (Fin) securities issued by a bank

Bankplatz *m* (Fin) bank place (*ie, where a LZB establishment is domiciled*)

Bankpolitik *f* (Vw) banking policy (*ie, pursued by the central bank or by government agencies*)

Bankpraxis *f* (Fin) banking practice

Bankprovision *f* (Fin) banking commission

Bankprüfung *f* (ReW) complete audit of bank balance sheet

Bankpublizität *f* (Fin) banks' disclosure requirements

Bankquittungen *fpl*
(Fin) bank receipts (*ie, mainly used in borrowed-funds trading*)
(Fin) receipts made out by branded-article dealers and sent to banks for collection

Bankrate *f* (Vw) official discount rate

Bankrechnen *n* (Fin) mathematics of banking

Bankrecht *n* (Fin) banking law

Bankreferenz *f* (Fin) banker's reference

Bankregel *f* (Fin) Golden Bank Rule (*ie, liquidity rule of credit institutions, requires sufficient availability of funds at any time*)

Bankrembours *m* (Fin) bank documentary credit

Bankreserve *f* (Vw) bank reserve

Bankrevision *f* (Fin) banking audit

bankrott
(com) bankrupt
- (infml) bust
- (sl) broke/flat broke

Bankrott *m* (com) bankruptcy

bankrott machen
(com) to go bankrupt (*or* into bankruptcy)
- (infml) to go broke
- (infml) to go bust
- (sl) to take a bath
- (sl) to lose one's shirt
- (GB, sl) to put up the shutters

Banksafe *m* od *n* (Fin) bank safe

Banksaldenbestätigung *f* (Fin) confirmation of bank balance
Banksaldo *m*
  (Fin) balance of a bank account
  – bank balance
Banksatz *m* (Fin) discount rate
Bankschalter *m* (Fin) bank counter
Bankscheck *m*
  (Fin) bank check *(ie, drawn on a bank)*
  (Fin) bank draft *(ie, bill or check drawn by a bank on another bank)*
Bankschließfach *n* (Fin) bank safe deposit box
Bankschulden *fpl*
  (ReW) due to banks
  – indebtedness to banks
Bankschuldner *m* (Fin) bank's debtor
Bankschuldschein *m* (Fin) borrower's note issued by bank
Bankschuldverschreibung *f* (Fin) bank bond
Banksicherheit *f* (Fin) security provided by bank
Banksparbrief *m* (Fin) bank savings bond
Banksparen *n* (Fin) bank savings scheme
Bankspesen *pl* (Fin) bank(ing) charges
Bankstatistik *f* (Fin) banking statistics
bankstatistische Gesamtrechnung *f* (Fin) overall monetary survey
Bankstatus *m* (Fin) bank statement
Bankstellen *fpl* (Fin) banks including their branch establishments and offices
Banksysteme *npl* (Vw) bank systems
banktechnische Abläufe *mpl* (Fin) banking procedures *(or* operations)
Banktransaktion *f* (Fin) banking operation *(or* transaction)
Banktresor *m* (Fin) bank vault
Banküberweisung *f*
  (Fin) bank transfer
  – bank credit transfer
  – banker's order
  – bank remittance
Banküberziehungskredit *m* (Fin) bank overdraft facilities
banküblich (Fin) customary in banking
Bankumsätze *mpl* (Fin) bank turnovers
Bank- und Börsenverkehr *m* (Fin) bank and stock exchange operations *(or* transactions)
Bankusancen *pl*
  (Fin) banking customs
  – bank usages
Bankverbindlichkeiten *fpl*
  (ReW) due to banks
  – indebtedness to banks
Bankverbindung *f* (Fin) banking connection
Bankverkehr *m*
  (Fin) banking business
  (Fin) interbank operations
  – interbank dealings
Bankvollmacht *f* (Re) power of attorney granted to a bank
Bankwechsel *m*
  (Fin) bank acceptance
  – bank bill
  – bank draft
Bankwerte *mpl*
  (Bö) bank stock
  – bank shares
  – banks
Bankwesen *n* (Fin) banking
Bankwirtschaft *f* (Fin) banking industry
Bankziehungen *fpl* (Fin) bank's own drafts on customers or on other banks
Bankzinsen *mpl* (Fin) bank interest
Bank-zu-Bank-Ausleihungen *fpl* (Fin) interbank lendings
Bank-zu-Bank-Einlagen *fpl* (Fin) interbank deposits
Bank-zu-Bank-Fazilitäten *fpl* (Fin) interbank credit lines
Bank-zu-Bank-Geschäfte *npl* (Fin) interbank transactions
Bank-zu-Bank-Kredit *m* (Fin) interbank credit
Bankzusammenbruch *m* (Fin) bank failure *(or* collapse)
Bannbruch *m* (StR) illegal export, import, or transit of goods without due customs clearance, § 369 AO
Banngut *n* (com, Re) contraband goods
Bannware *f* (com, Re) = *Banngut*
bar
  (com) in cash
  – cash down *(ie, by money payment or by check)*
Barabfindung *f* (Fin) money compensation, § 320 V AktG
Barabhebung *f* (Fin) cash withdrawal
Barablösung *f*
  (Fin) cash repayment
  – cash settlement
Barablösungswert *m* (Vers) cash surrender value
Barabstimmung *f* (com) register cash balance *(ie, in retailing)*
Barabzug *m* (com) cash deduction
Barakkreditiv *n* (Fin) cash letter of credit
Baraufwendungen *mpl* (ReW) out-of-pocket cost *(or* expense)
Barausgaben *fpl* (Fin) cash expenditure *(or* outlay)
Barausgänge *mpl* (com) cash outgoings
Barauslagen *fpl*
  (com) cash outlays
  – out-of-pocket costs *(or* expense)
Barausschüttung *f*
  (Fin) cash distribution
  – cash dividend
Barauszahlung *f* (Fin) cash payment
Barbestand *m* (ReW) cash on hand
Barbetrag *m* (com) cash amount
bar bezahlen
  (com) to pay cash down
  – (sl) to pay spot cash
  – (us, sl) to pay on the barrel head
  – (GB, sl) to pay on the nail
Barbezüge *pl* (Pw) compensation in cash
Bardepot *n* (Vw) cash deposit, § 23 AWG
Bardepotpflicht *f* (Vw) cash deposit requirement
Bardepotsatz *m* (Vw) cash deposit ratio
Bardividende *f*
  (Fin) cash dividend
  (Vers) cash bonus
  – bonus in cash
Bareingänge *mpl* (com) cash receipts
Bareinkauf *m* (com) cash buying *(or* purchase)

Bareinlage *f*
(Fin) contribution in cash
- cash contribution *(opp, Sacheinlage = contribution in kind or noncash contribution)*
Bareinnahmen *fpl*
(com) cash receipts
- takings *(esp. in retailing)*
Bareinschuß *m* (Bö) cash margin *(ie, cash put up by a client in part payment of the purchase of a stock under a forward contract = Termingeschäft)*
Bareinschußpflicht *f* (Bö) cash margin requirement
Bareinzahlung *f*
(com) inpayment
(Fin) cash deposit
Bareinzahlungen *fpl* (IWF) subscription payments in cash
Barentnahme *f* (com) cash withdrawal
Barerlös *m*
(com) net proceeds
- proceeds in cash
Barerstattung *f* (com) cash refund
Barforderung *f* (com) money claim
Barfreimachung *f* (com) bulk franking (of mail)
Bargebot *n* (Re) minimum cash bid *(ie, in forced sales: difference between lowest and highest bid + cost of auction, §§ 10, 12 ZVG)*
Bargeld *n*
(com) cash *(ie, money in notes and coin)*
(com, infml) hard cash
- (GB) ready cash *(ie, coll: ready)*
- (esp US) cash on the barrelhead
Bargeldausgaben *fpl* (Fin) outgoing cash payments
Bargeldautomat *m*
(Fin) automated teller machine, ATM
- (GB) cash dispenser
(syn, Bankomat, Bankautomat)
Bargeldbestand *m*
(Fin) cash in hand
- cash holding
Bargeldeinnahmen *fpl* (Fin) incoming cash receipts
Bargeldknappheit *f*
(Fin) cash shortage
- cash squeeze
bargeldlos
(Fin) cashless
- noncash
(ie, payment by check or bank transfer)
bargeldlose Lohnzahlung *f* (Pw) cashless pay
bargeldloser Einkauf *m* (com) cashless shopping
bargeldloser Zahlungsverkehr *m* (Fin) cashless money transfer
bargeldlose Zahlung *f* (Fin) cashless *(or* noncash*)* payment
bargeldloser Zahlungsverkehr *m* (Fin) bank giro credit system
Bargeldrückfluß *m* (Vw) reflux of notes and coin
Bargeldumlauf *m*
(Vw) currency in circulation
- (GB) notes and coin in circulation
- currency circuit
- cash circuit
(ie, component of money supply M_1)
Bargeldvolumen *n* (Vw) volume of notes and coin in circulation
Bargeldzahlung *f* (Fin) cash payment

Bargeschäft *n* (com) cash sale *(or* transaction*)*
Bargründung *f* (Bw) formation of stock corporation by cash subscriptions
Barguthaben *n* (ReW) cash in hand
Barkauf *m* (com) cash sale *(ie, payment being made in full on receipt of goods; opp, Kreditkauf = sale on credit)*
Barkaution *f* (Vers) cash bond
Barkredit *m* (Fin) cash advance *(or* credit*)*
Barleistungen *fpl* (SozV) cash benefits
Barliquidität *f*
(Fin) liquid cash resources
- cash position
Barliquidität *f* **der Kreditinstitute** (Fin) available cash *(ie, ratio of cash in hand and central bank balances to total liabilities less savings deposits)*
Barlohn *m* (Pw) money wages *(or* compensation*)*
Barlohnumwandlung *f* (Pw) conversion of cash wages into insurance premium, § 40b EStG *(ie, direct insurance through cuts in cash wages)*
Barmittel *pl*
(Fin) cash
- liquid funds
Barpreis *m* (com) cash price
Barrabatt *m* (com) cash discount
Barrengold *n* (Fin) gold bullion
Barrensilber *n* (Fin) silver bullion
Barrentabilität *f* (Fin) cash return
Barreserve *f*
(Fin) bank's cash reserve
- legal reserve
- vault cash *(or* money*)*
(ie, bank notes + deposits with central bank)
Barsaldo *m* (Fin) cash balance
Barscheck *m*
(Fin) cashable check
- open check
Barsicherheit *f* (Fin) cash deposit
Bartergeschäft *n* (com) barter transaction
Barüberschuß *m* (Fin) cash surplus
Barüberweisung *f* (Fin) cash remittance *(or* transfer*)*
Barumsatz *m* (com) net cash
Barumsätze *mpl* (com) cash transactions
Barvergütung *f* (com) compensation in cash
Barverkauf *m* (com) cash sale
Barverkehr *m* (com) trading on cash terms
Barvermögen *n* (Fin) liquid funds *(ie, cash in hand, bank and postal check balances, checks, discountable bills)*
Barvorschuß *m* (Fin) cash advance
Barwert *m*
(Fin) present value *(or* worth*)* *(syn, Gegenwartswert)*
(Fin) cash value *(eg, of lease that has seven years to run)*
Barwertanwartschaft *f* (Vers) present value of an expectancy
Barwert *m* **der nachschüssigen Rente** (Math) present value of ordinary annuity
Barwert *m* **der Rückflüsse** (Fin) present value of net cash inflows *(ie, in preinvestment analysis)*
Barwertfaktor *m* (Fin) present-value factor
bar zahlen (com) to pay in cash

Barzahlung f
(com) cash payment
– (infml) cash down
– (infml) hard cash
Barzahlung f **bei Lieferung** (com) cash on delivery, COD
Barzahlungsgeschäft n (com) cash transaction
Barzahlungsnachlaß m (com) cash discount *(syn, Skonto)*
Barzahlungspreis m (com) cash price *(opp, Teilzahlungspreis)*
Barzahlungsrabatt m (com) cash discount *(or* rebate*)*
Barzahlungsverkehr m (Fin) cash payments *(or* transactions*)*
Barzahlung f **vor Lieferung** (com) cash before delivery
Barzufluß m (Fin) cash inflow
Basis f
(Pw) rank and file *(ie, of a union)*
(Math) base *(ie, of a power = Potenz)*
(Math) radix *(ie, of a logarithm)*
(OR) basics
(Bö) basis
(ie, difference between spot and forward prices in commodity futures trading = Warenterminhandel)
(EDV) base
– radix
(eg, the radix of each place in the decimal notation is ten)
Basisadresse f (EDV) base *(or* reference*)* address *(syn, Bezugsadresse, Grundadresse)*
Basisadreßregister n (EDV) base address register
Basisausgleichsbeträge mpl **für den innergemeinschaftlichen Warenverkehr** (EG) basic compensatory amounts for intra-Community exchanges
Basisbeschäftigung f (KoR) basic volume of activity
Basis-Betriebssystem n (EDV) basic operating system
Basis-Datensystem n (EDV) small business computer
Basiseinkommen n **des Haushalts** (Vw) breakeven level of income
Basiseinstandspreis m (com) base cost
Basis f **e-r Topologie** (Math) base of topology
Basis f **e-s Logarithmussystems** (Math) radix
Basisgesellschaft f (StR) foreign base company *(ie, domiciled in a low-tax country to accumulate profits or to take advantage of double-taxation agreements)*
Basisgewicht n (Stat) base weight
Basisjahr n (Stat) base year *(syn, Basisperiode)*
Basiskalkulation f (KoR) standardized cost estimate *(ie, covering all fixed and variable cost)*
Basiskomplement n (EDV) radix *(or* true*)* complement
Basiskurs m (Bö) initial price
Basislaufzeit f
(com) effective base period
(KoR) period used in standard cost calculation *(ie, during which basic prices remain unchanged)*
Basislinie f (Stat) base line
Basislösung f (OR) basic solution

Basismatrix f **des geschlossenen Kantenzuges** (Math) circuit-basis matrix
Basispatent n (Pat) basic patent
Basisperiode f (Stat) base period *(syn, Basisjahr)*
Basispreis m
(com) basic price
(Bö) basis *(ie, in options trading = ‚Optionshandel' on German stock exchanges)*
Basispunktsystem n (com) basing point system *(ie, for computation of freight charges)*
Basisregister n (EDV) base register
Basissatz m (Log) basic statement
Basisstichtag m (com) base reference date
Basissystem n (EDV) small computer
Basistrend m (Stat) basic trend
Basisvariable f (OR) basic variable
Basiswährung f (AuW) reference currency
Basiswert m (Stat) basic dimension
Basiswinkel m (Math) base angle
Basiszeitraum m (Stat) base *(or* origin*)* period *(ie, of a time series)*
Basiszins m (Fin) base interest rate
Basiszugriffsmethode f (EDV) basic access method *(syn, einfache Zugriffsmethode)*
Basiszyklus m (Stat) reference cycle
Basler Abkommen n
(AuW) Basle Agreement
– Reciprocal Currency Agreement
(syn, Stillhalteabkommen; ie, beetwenn 1931 and 1962)
Bauabnahme f
(Re) final inspection of completed building by appropriate authority
(com) acceptance of building work by owner
Bauabrechnung f (com) work measurement and billing
Bauabschnitt m
(com) phase of construction
(com) section of construction
Bauaktien fpl (Bö) building shares
Bauamt n (Re) building authority
Bauantrag m (com) application for building license
Bauarbeit f (com) construction work
Bauarbeiter m (Pw) construction worker
Bauarbeitsgemeinschaft f (com) construction consortium
Bauartgenehmigung f (com) type approval
Bauauflage f (Re) specific condition imposed on the performance of construction work *(ie, by building authority)*
Bauaufsicht f (com) supervision of construction work
Bauaufsichtsbehörde f (Re) building supervisory authority
Bauaufwand m
(com) cost of construction
– building cost
Bau m **ausführen** (com) to carry out *(or* complete*)* a building *(or* construction*)* project
Bauausschreibung f (com) invitation to tender for construction work
Baubeginn m (com) start of building *(or* construction*)* work
Baubehörde f (Re) building authority
Baubeschränkungen fpl (Re) building restrictions

Baubeteiligte *mpl* (com) parties to a construction project
Baubewilligung *f* (Re) = *Baugenehmigung*
Bauboom *m* (Vw) construction boom
Bauchlandung *f* (Fin, sl) belly flop
Baudarlehen *n* (Fin) building loan
Baueinheit *f* (EDV) physical unit
Bauelement *n*
 (EDV) component
 (IndE) guzzinta
Bauerlaubnis *f* (Re) = *Baugenehmigung*
bäuerlicher Familienbetrieb *m* (com) family farm
Bauernverband *m* (com) farmers' association
Bauerwartungsland *n*
 (com) prospective building land
 – land earmarked for development
Baufinanzierung *f*
 (Fin) financing of building projects
 – construction financing
Baufinanzierungsmittel *pl* (Fin) construction finance
Baufirma *f*
 (com) firm of builders (*or* constructors)
 – construction company
Bauführer *m* (com) construction site supervisor
Baugebiet *n* (com) building area
Baugelände *n* (com) building site
Baugeld *n* (Fin) building loans
Baugeldhypothek *f* (Fin) building mortgage
Baugeldkredit *m* (Fin) intermediate building credit
Baugenehmigung *f* (Re) building license (*or* permit)
Baugenossenschaft *f* (Bw) building cooperative
Baugewerbe *n*
 (com) construction industry
 – (GB) building trade
 (ie, excluding building materials industry and trade)
Baugrundstück *n*
 (com) building lot (*or* plot)
 – home site
Baugruppe *f* (IndE) assembly
Baugruppennummer *f* (IndE) indent number
Bauhaftpflichtversicherung *f* (Vers) builder's risk insurance
Bauhandwerk *n* (com) building trade
Bauhandwerker *m* (com) construction worker
Bauhauptgewerbe *n* (com) construction industry
Bauherr *m* (com) owner of a building *(ie, in the planning stage, under construction, and upon completion)*
Bauherrenhaftung *f* (Re) liability of builder-owner
Bauherrenmodell *n* (StR) model for tax-favored construction of residential properties *(ie, purchasers, mostly of condominiums in a large building system, are deemed to be the original owners, and may deduct substantial portion of costs as income-related expenses – Werbungskosten – during the construction period; allocation of losses – Verlustzuweisungen – result from commissions, cost of finance, and depreciation on construction cost)*
Bauhilfsgewerbe *n* (com) construction-related trade
Bauhypothek *f* (Fin) building mortgage

Bauindex *m* (Stat) construction price index
Bauindustrie *f* (com) building (*or* construction) industry
Bauinvestitionen *fpl*
 (Vw) building investments
 – capital spending on new construction
Baukastenprinzip *n*
 (IndE) building block concept
 – concept of modular assembly
 – modular concept
 – modularity
Baukonjunktur *f* (Vw) overall construction activity
Baukonsortium *n* (com) group of building contractors
Baukosten *pl* (com) building (*or* construction) cost
Baukostenindex *m* (Stat) construction cost index
Baukostenvoranschlag *m* (com) building estimate
 – estimate of construction cost
Baukostenzuschuß *m* (com) tenant's contribution to building cost
Baukostenzuschüsse *mpl* (com) building subsidies
Bauland *n*
 (com) building (*or* developed) land
 (StR) land suitable for residential construction, § 69 I BewG
Baulandbeschaffung *f* (Re) provision of land for building sites
Baulanderschließung *f*
 (com) development of real estate
 – property development
Baulandsteuer *f* (StR) site value tax *(ie, conceived as ‚land hoarding charge' = graduated tax on land ready for building but not yet improved; introduced on 23 June 1960 and repealed as of 1 Jan 1963)*
Bauleistungen *fpl* (com) construction work performed
Bauleitplan *m* (com) general plan for the development of local real estate
bauliche Mängel *mpl* (StR) structural defects, § 85 BewG
Baumalgorithmus *m* (OR) tree search type algorithm
Baumaschinen-Hersteller *m* (com) construction machinery producer
Baumaßnahmen *fpl* (com) construction work
Baumaterial *n* (com) building (*or* construction) materials
Baumateriallieferant *m* (com) building supply firm
 – (GB) builder's merchant
Baumdiagramm *n* (Stat) tree diagram
Baumwollbörse *f* (Bö) cotton exchange
Baumwollterminbörse *f*
 (Bö) forward cotton exchange
 – cotton futures market
 – trading in cotton futures
Baunebengewerbe *n* (com) construction-related trade
Bauobjekt *n* (com) construction project
Bauplanung *f* (com) planning of construction work
Bauplatz *m* (com) building lot (*or* plot)
 (com) building (*or* construction) site *(ie, after starting work; syn, Baustelle)*
Baupreise *mpl* (com) building prices

Baupreisverhältnisse *npl* (StR) building cost index, § 85 BewG
Bauprogramm *n* (com) construction schedule (*or* program)
Bauprojekt *n* (com) construction project
Baureederei *f* (com) joint ship building
baureife Grundstücke *npl* (com) land ready for building (StR) land considered likely to be improved in the near future and included in a building plan, § 73 II BewG
Baureihe *f* (IndE) production series
Baurezession *f* (Vw) construction slump
Baurisikoversicherung *f* (Vers) builder's risk insurance *(ie, insurance of a building under construction)*
Bausachverständiger *m* (com) building expert
– quantity surveyor
Bauschäden *mpl* (com) structural damage
Bauschädenversicherung *f* (Vers) building liability insurance
Bausektor *m* (Vw) building sector
Bausparbeitrag *m* (Fin) saver's payment to savings and loan association (*or* GB: to building society)
Bauspardarlehen *n* (Fin) loan from savings and loan association *(ie, paid out when savings quota (= Mindestsparguthaben) is reached)*
Bausparen *n* (Fin) saving through a savings and loan association
Bausparer *m* (Fin) member of a savings and loan association
– (GB) person saving through a building society
Bausparguthaben *n* (Fin) balance on savings account with a savings and loan association (*or* GB: a building society)
Bausparkasse *f* (Fin) home loan association
(Fin, US) savings and loan association
– (GB) building society
Bausparkassengesetz *n* (Re) Law on Savings and Loan Associations, of 16 Nov 1972
Bausparprämie *f* (Fin) government premium allowed to savers in savings and loan association
Bausparsumme *f* (Fin) target amount of savings *(ie, which qualifies for a building loan under a ‚Bausparvertrag')*
Bausparvertrag *m* (Fin) agreement under which a loan is granted by a savings and loan association *(ie, for the purchase, construction, or improvement of residential properties)*
Baustein *m* (Bw) building block *(ie, of systems)*
(EDV) module
Bausteinsystem *n* (EDV) modular system
Baustelle *f* (com) building site
– construction site
– job site
Baustellenfertigung *f* (IndE) job-site production
– fixed-site production *(eg, large-scale equipment and machinery, construction industry)*
Baustoffe *mpl* (com) building (*or* construction) materials

Baustoffhandlung *f* (com) building supply firm
– (GB) builder's merchant
Baustoffindustrie *f* (com) building (*or* construction) materials industry
Bausumme *f* (com) total construction cost
Bautätigkeit *f* (Vw) building activity
Bauteil *n* (IndE) structural component
– guzzinta
Bauträger *m* (com) property developer
– company building and selling completed residential properties
Bauträger-Gesellschaft *f* (com) real estate developing company *(ie, one that subdivides land into sites, builds houses and sells them)*
Bauüberhang *m* (com) volume of unfinished building projects
Bauüberwachung *f* (Re) building inspection
Bau- und Prüfvorschriften *fpl* (com) specifications for construction and testing
Bauunternehmer *m* (com) building contractor
– construction firm
Bauvergabe *f* (com) award of construction contract
Bau *m* **vergeben** (com) to award (*or* let) a building contract
Bauverwaltung *f* (Re) building authorities
Bauvolumen *n* (Vw) volume of construction output
Bauvorhaben *n* (com) construction project
Bauvorschriften *fpl* (Re) building code (*or* regulations)
Bauwert *m* (com) construction cost of a building *(ie, taken as a basis for determining the lending value = ‚Beleihungswert' of a plot of land)*
Bauwerte *mpl* (Bö) buildings
Bauwesenversicherung *f* (Vers) builder's risk insurance *(ie, insurance on a building during construction)*
Bauwirtschaft *f* (com) construction industry
– (GB) building trade
Bauzeit *f* (com) construction period
Bauzinsen *mpl* (com) interest for building finance
(Fin) fixed interest paid during the build-up period of a new company, § 57 III AktG
Bauzuschuß *m* (FiW) building subsidy
Bauzwischenkredit *m* (Fin) intermediate building credit *(ie, replaced by a mortgage credit upon completion of the building)*
Bayessche Schätzung *f* (Stat) Bayes' estimation
Bayessches Theorem *n* (Stat) Bayes' theorem
BCD-Darstellung *f* (EDV) binary coded decimal representation
beabsichtigte Geschäftspolitik *f* (Bw) prospective business policy
beabsichtigte Nettoinvestition *f* (Vw) intended (*or* planned) net investment
beachtlicher Irrtum *m* (Re) substantial (*or* operative) mistake
Beamter *m* (Pw) public official *(ie, for life)*
– (GB) civil servant

(ie, not only administrative personnel in direct government service, but also school teachers, university staff, police, part of armed forces, clergy, judiciary, senior employees in the Post Office and railways)
beanspruchen
(Re) to claim
– to lay claim to
Beanspruchung *f* **der Priorität** (Pat) claim to priority
beanstanden
(com) to complain about
– to reject *(eg, defective goods)*
Beanstandung *f*
(com) complaint (about)
– objection (to)
(ReW) exception (to) *(ie, in balance sheet audit)*
beantragen
(com) to apply for
– to make an application for
– to make a request
(Re) to file *(or* lodge) an application
Beantwortung *f*
(com) answer
– reply
Beantwortungsfrist *f* (Re) time limit set for filing a reply
Beantwortungszeit *f* (EDV) response time
bearbeiten
(com) to deal with
– handle
– to process *(eg, incoming mail)*
(IndE) to process
– to treat
bearbeitende Industrie *f* (com) manufacturing *(or* processing) industry
Bearbeiter *m* (com) person in charge of (sth)
Bearbeitung *f*
(com) handling
– processing *(eg, incoming mail)*
(Zo) working of goods *(= Veredelung)*
(IndE) processing
– treatment
Bearbeitungsaufschlag *m* (com) service charge
Bearbeitungsbetrieb *m* (IndE) processing plant
Bearbeitungsfehler *m* (com) processing error
Bearbeitungsgebühr *f*
(com) service charge
– handling *(or* processing) fee
(Fin) management charge *(or* fee)
– bank service charge
Bearbeitungskosten *pl*
(com) handling cost
(Vers) cost of writing insurance
(Vers) claim expenses
(IndE) manufacturing *(or* processing) cost
Bearbeitungsmethode *f* (IndE) manufacturing method *(or* technique)
Bearbeitungsprogramm *n* **für die Großproduktion** (IndE) retooling program
Bearbeitungsprovision *f* (Fin) handling fee *(ie, charged by credit granting bank)*
Bearbeitungsschädenklausel *f* (Re) clause relating to processing risks
Bearbeitungsschritt *m* (EDV) job step

Bearbeitungsstempel *m* (com) date *(or* receipt) stamp
Bearbeitungsverfahren *n* (IndE) manufacturing method *(or* technique)
Bearbeitungsvorgang *m*
(com) processing operation
(Zo) manufacturing operation *(ie, im Veredelungsverkehr)*
Bearbeitungszeit *f*
(IndE) process(ing) time
(OR) holding time
(EDV) process time *(eg, in teleprocessing)*
beaufsichtigen (Pw) to supervise
Beaufsichtigung *f* (Pw) supervision
beauftragen
(com) to charge with
– to put in charge with
– to instruct
(Re) to authorize
– to empower
beauftragte Bank *f* (Fin) paying bank
Beauftragter *m*
(com) agent
– representative
(Re) attorney-in-fact
– private attorney
(Re) mandatary *(ie, person agreeing to perform unremunerated services involving the transaction of business for another, § 662 BGB)*
Beauftragter *m* **für den Datenschutz** (EDV) data protection officer *(syn, Datenschutzbeauftragter)*
bebauen
(com) to build upon
– to develop *(ie, to build on land)*
bebaute Fläche *f* (com) improved *(or* built-up) area
bebaute Grundstücke *npl*
(com) developed real estate
(ReW) land and buildings
– land built-upon
(StR) improved real property *(ie, carrying buildings and other structures, §§ 74–90 BewG)*
bebautes Gelände *n* (com) built-up area
Bebauungsgebiet *n* (com) building *(or* development) area
Bebauungskosten *pl*
(com) building costs
– cost of buildings
Bebauungsplan *m* (com) building *(or* development) plan *(ie, for the area in which land is located, § 69 III BewG)*
BCD-Code *m* (EDV) BCD (binary coded decimal) code
Bedarf *m*
(com, Vw) demand *(an: for)*
– need (for)
– requirements (of)
Bedarf *m* **an Arbeitskräften** (Pw) manpower requirements
Bedarf *m* **an liquiden Mitteln** (Fin) cash requirements
Bedarf *m* **decken**
(com) to meet
– to satisfy
– to supply ... demand *(or* needs *or* requirements)

Bedarf *m* **neu ausschreiben** (com) to rebid a requirement
Bedarfsanalyse *f* (Mk) demand analysis
Bedarfsartikel *mpl* (Mk) necessaries
Bedarfsbefriedigung *f* (Vw) satisfaction of demand
Bedarfsbeschreibung *f* (EDV) requirements definition *(syn, Anforderungsdefinition, Aufgabendefinition)*
Bedarfsdeckung *f*
  (com) satisfaction of requirements
  – supply of needs
Bedarfsdeckungswirtschaft *f* (Vw) subsistence economy *(ie, supplying only survival needs: the minimum of food, clothing, and shelter)*
Bedarfselastizität *f* (Mk) demand elasticity
Bedarfserkennung *f* (Mk) demand recognition
Bedarfsfaktoren *mpl* (Mk) factors of demand *(ie, determined in market analyses)*
Bedarfsforschung *f* (Mk) demand research *(ie, aimed at potential sales volume)*
bedarfsgerecht (Mk) tailored to suit the needs of the market
Bedarfsgüter *npl*
  (Vw) necessaries
  (com) consumer goods
Bedarfslenkung *f* (Vw) re-directing consumer demand
Bedarfslücke *f*
  (Vw) demand gap
  – unsatisfied demand
Bedarfsmaterial *n* (MaW) materials purchased to fill a particular order
Bedarfsmeldung *f* (MaW) purchase requisition
Bedarfsmengenplanung *f* (MaW) materials requirements planning, MRP
Bedarfsmeßzahl *f* (FiW) figure indicating the average expenditure burden of a municipality
bedarfsorientiert (Mk) demand oriented
bedarfsorientierte Fertigung *f* (IndE) demand-oriented production
Bedarfsplanung *f* (MaW) requirement planning *(ie, by plant divisions for materials and operating supplies)*
Bedarfsprämie *f* (Vers) net premium *(or* rate) *ie, the net charge for insurance cost only, minus expenses or contingencies)*
Bedarfsprüfung *f* (Re) public need test *(ie, prior to licensing a business establishment)*
Bedarfsquote *f* (Pw) vacancy ratio *(ie, job openings to number of unemployed)*
Bedarfsrate *f* (OR) demand rate
Bedarfsspanne *f*
  (Fin) net expense ratio *(ie, of banks)*
  – cover-requiring margin
  – required margin
Bedarfsspannenrechnung *f* (Fin) calculation of net expense ratio
Bedarfsspitze *f* (Mk) peak demand
Bedarfsstruktur *f*
  (Vw) order of preference
  – preference system
Bedarfsstruktur *f* **des Haushalts** (Vw) tastes of household
Bedarfsverlagerung *f* (Mk) shift in demand

Bedarfsverlust *m* (com) loss of demand *(ie, if stockouts cannot be supplied)*
Bedarfswandel *m* (Mk) change in demand
Bedarfsweckung *f* (Mk) creation of demand
Bedarfswirtschaft *f* (Vw) needs-economy *(opp, wants-or-aspirations economy)*
Bedenkfrist *f* (WeR) time allowed for re-presentation *(of a bill of exchange, Art. 24 WG)*
bedeutsame Ziffer *f* (EDV) significant digit
bedienen
  (com) to attend to *(eg, customers, clients)*
  (Fin) to service *(eg, a loan)*
Bediener *m* (IndE) operator
Bedieneranweisung *f* (EDV) run chart *(or* diagram)
Bedienerführung *f* (EDV) operator prompting
Bedienerstation *f* (EDV) control station
Bedienperson *f* (EDV) operator
Bedienplatz *m* (EDV) operator console
bedienter Betrieb *m* (EDV) attended operation
Bedienung *f* **e–s Kredits** (Fin) debt service
Bedienung *f* **mit Vorrang** (OR) preemptive service
Bedienung *f* **ohne Vorrang** (OR) nonpreemptive service
Bedienungsanforderung *f* (EDV) service call *(or* request)
Bedienungsanleitung *f*
  (com) instructions for use
  (IndE) operating instructions
Bedienungsanweisung *f* (EDV) operating instructions
Bedienungsaufruf *m* (EDV) operator request
Bedienungsaufschlag *m* (com) service charge
Bedienungsblattschreiber *m* (EDV) console typewriter, CTW
Bedienungseinrichtungen *fpl* (EDV) operating facilities
Bedienungselement *n* (EDV) control element
Bedienungsfeld *n* (EDV) operator control panel
bedienungsfreier Betrieb *m* (EDV) unattended operation
Bedienungshandbuch *n* (IndE) service manual
Bedienungskonsole *f* (EDV) = *Bedienungsplatz*
Bedienungsperson *f* (EDV) operator
Bedienungspersonal *n* (IndE) operating personnel
Bedienungsplatz *m*
  (EDV) operator console
  – operator control station
Bedienungspult *n* (EDV) control console
Bedienungsrate *f* (OR) service rate
Bedienungsrelation *f* (IndE) relation between operator's process time and machine time
Bedienungsstation *f*
  (OR) server
  – channel
  – service facility *(or* point *or* station *or* unit) *(ie, in waiting-line models)*
Bedienungsstelle *f* (OR) service facility *(or* point)
Bedienungssteuerung *f* (EDV) master scheduler
Bedienungsstrategie *f* (OR) service strategy
Bedienungssystem *n* (OR) system of service points *(ie, in waiting-line theory)*
Bedienungstisch *m* (EDV) control desk
Bedienungszeit *f* (OR) service time *(syn, Abfertigungszeit, Servicezeit)*

bedingt (Re) conditional
bedingt arbeitsfähig (Pw) fit for limited employment (*or* service)
bedingte Abfertigung *f* **zum Dauerverbleib** (Zo) conditional clearance for home use
bedingte Annahme *f* (Re) conditional acceptance
bedingte Anweisung *f* (EDV, Cobol) conditional statement
bedingte Ausfallwahrscheinlichkeit *f* (IndE) conditional probability of failure
bedingte Befreiung *f* **von Eingangsabgaben** (Zo) conditional relief from import duties and taxes
bedingte Definition *f* (Log) conditional definition
bedingte Einfuhr *f* (AuW) conditional imports
bedingte Fälligkeit *f* (Fin) contingent payment
bedingte Kapitalerhöhung *f* (Fin) conditional increase of capital stock, §§ 192 ff AktG
bedingte Klausel *f* (com) conditional clause
bedingte Meistbegünstigungsklausel *f* (AuW) conditional most-favored nation clause
bedingte Option *f* (com) qualified option
bedingter Anspruch *m* (Re) contingent claim
bedingter Ausdruck *m* (EDV, Cobol) condition(al) expression
bedingter Befehl *m* (EDV) conditional instruction
bedingte Regression *f* (Stat) conditional regression
bedingter Erwartungswert *m* (Stat) conditional expectation
– conditional expected value
bedingt erhöhen (Fin) to increase subject to a contingency
bedingter paralleler Fortschritt *m* (OR) conditional parallel progress
bedingter Sprung *m* (EDV) conditional branch (*or* jump) *(syn, bedingte Verzweigung)*
bedingter Sprungbefehl *m* (EDV) conditional branch (*or* jump) instruction
– discrimination instruction
(syn, bedingter Verzweigungsbefehl)
bedingter Test *m* (Stat) conditional test
bedingter Vertrag *m* (Re) conditional contract
bedingter Verzweigungsbefehl *m* (EDV) = *bedingter Sprungbefehl*
bedingt erwartungstreue Schätzfunktion *f* (Stat) conditionally unbiased estimator
bedingtes Anschaffungsgeschäft *n* (StR) acquisition of securities subject to a condition, § 18 II 3 KVStG
bedingtes Fremdkapital *n* (Fin) contingent assets
bedingtes Indossament *n* (WeR) conditional indorsement
bedingtes Kapital *n* (Fin) authorized but unissued capital
bedingtes Maximum *n* (Math) conditioned maximum
bedingtes Recht *n* (Re) conditional right
bedingtes Rechtsgeschäft *n*
(Re) conditional transaction
– (GB) act of the parties subject to a condition
bedingte Störungsrate *f*
(IndE) conditional rate of failure
– hazard rate of failure
bedingtes Urteil *n* (Log) conditional proposition
bedingtes Ziel *n* (Log) conditional target

bedingte Trennschärfefunktion *f* (Stat) conditional power function
bedingte Überlebenswahrscheinlichkeit *f* (OR) conditional probability of survival
bedingte Verbindlichkeiten *fpl* (Re) contingent liabilities
bedingte Versicherung *f* (Vers) contingent insurance
bedingte Verteilung *f* (Stat) conditional distribution
bedingte Verzweigung *f* (EDV) conditional branch (*or* jump) *(syn, bedingter Sprung)*
bedingte Wahrscheinlichkeit *f* (Stat) conditional probability
bedingte Wahrscheinlichkeit *f* **der Ausfallzeit** (IndE) conditional rate of failure
Bedingtgeschäft *n* (Re) conditional transaction
Bedingtlieferung *f* (com) sale qualified by right of return *(ie, esp. in book selling)*
bedingt verfügbare Liquidität *f* (AuW) conditional liquidity
bedingt verfügbare Pufferzeit *f* (OR) interfering (*or* dependent) float
Bedingung *f*
(Re) condition *(general term)*, §§ 158 ff BGB
– stipulation *(eg, of a contract)*
(Log, Math) condition
Bedingung *f* **der Zug-um-Zug-Erfüllung** (Re) concurrent condition
Bedingungen *fpl* (com) terms and conditions
Bedingungen *fpl* **auferlegen** (Re) to impose conditions
Bedingungen *fpl* **festsetzen** (Re) to stipulate terms (*or* conditions)
Bedingungen *fpl* **vereinbaren**
(Re) to agree on conditions
– to settle terms
Bedingung *f* **erfüllen**
(Re) to comply with
– to fulfill
– to perform
– to satisfy ... a condition
Bedingung *f* **erster Ordnung** (Math) first-order condition
bedingungsfeindliche Geschäfte *npl*
(Re) absolute (*or* unconditional) transactions
– *(civil law)* actus legitimi
(ie, conditional acceptance is inoperative = rechtsunwirksam)
Bedingungsgleichung *f* (Math) conditional equation
Bedingungskonstellation *f* (Bw, Vw) combination of circumstances
bedingungslos
(Re) unconditional
– without qualification
– without stipulations
bedingungslose Abfertigung *f* **zum Dauerverbleib** (Zo) unconditional clearance for home use
bedingungslose Zuwendung *f* (Re) outright gift
bedingungslos verfügbare Liquidität *f* (IWF) unconditional liquidity
Bedingungsname *m* (EDV, Cobol) condition name
Bedingungsvariable *f* (Math) conditional variable

Bedingung *f* **tritt ein**
(Re) condition happens (*or* is performed)
- contingency comes to pass

Bedingung *f* **zweiter Ordnung** (Math) second-order condition

bedungene Einlage *f* (Fin) stipulated capital contribution

Bedürfnis *n* (Vw) want

Bedürfnis *n* **befriedigen** (Vw) to meet (*or* satisfy) a want

Bedürfnisbefriedigung *f* (Vw) satisfaction (*or* satiation) of wants

Bedürfnis *n* **der Selbstverwirklichung** (Pw) self-actualization need

Bedürfnishierarchie *f* (Bw) hierarchy of needs (*Maslow*)

Bedürfniskoinzidenz *f* (Vw) (double) coincidence of wants

Bedürfnislohn *m*
(Vw) living wage
- cultural wage

Bedürfnisprüfung *f* (Re) public need test (*ie, prior to licensing a business establishment*)

Bedürfnispyramide *f* (Bw) = *Bedürfnishierarchie*

Bedürfnisse *npl*
(Vw) wants
- wants and needs
- tastes and preferences

Bedürfnisskala *f* (Vw) scale of preferences

Bedürfnisstruktur *f* (Vw) want pattern (*or* structure)

bedürftige Angehörige *mpl* (Re) dependents in need

Bedürftigkeitsprüfung *f*
(SozV) means test
- no-means test
- test of need

beeidigter Dolmetscher *m* (com) sworn interpreter

beeidigter Sachverständiger *m* (Re) sworn expert (*or* appraiser)

Beeidigung *f* (Re) administration of oath

beeinflußbare Kosten *pl* (KoR) controllable cost (*ie, term used in ‚responsibility accounting'*)

beeinflußbare Maschinenzeit *f* (IndE) controlled machine time

beeinflußbare Variable *f* (Math) controlled variable

Beeinflusser *m* (Mk) influencer

beeinträchtigen
(Re) to abridge
- to encroach upon
- to impair
- to interfere (upon *or* on)
- to interfere with (*eg, a right*)

Beeinträchtigung *f*
(Re) encroachment (on)
- infringement (of)
- interference (with)

beenden (Re) to terminate (*eg, a contract*)

Beendigung *f* (Re) termination

Beendigung *f* **e–s Vertragsverhältnisses**
(Re) discharge of a contract (*ie, by performance or otherwise*)
- termination of a contractual relationship

Beendigung *f* **von Schuldverhältnissen** (Re) discharge of obligations (*eg, termination of contract by performance*)

beerben
(Re) to inherit from
- to succeed to (*eg, the family estate*)

Beerdigungskosten *pl* (StR) funeral expenses (*ie, extraordinary burden = ‚außergewöhnliche Belastung' for income-tax purposes*)

befähigt
(Pw) capable of
- qualified for

Befähigung *f*
(Pw) ability
- aptitude
- capacity
- qualification

Befähigung *f* **nachweisen**
(Pw) to prove qualifications
- to furnish proof of qualifications
- to submit evidence as to qualifications

Befähigungsnachweis *m*
(com) proof of ability (*or* competence)
- evidence of formal qualifications
- (Re) certificate of qualification

Befähigung *f* **zum Richteramt** (Re) qualification for judicial office

Befehl *m*
(EDV) instruction
- command
(EDV) command (*ie, as part of an instruction*)

Befehlsablauf *m* (EDV) instruction cycle

Befehlsabrufphase *f* (EDV) instruction fetch phase

Befehlsadresse *f* (EDV) instruction address (*syn, Instruktionsadresse*)

Befehlsadreßregister *n*
(EDV) instruction address register
- program address counter
- program register
- sequence control register

Befehlsänderung *f* (EDV) instruction modification

Befehlsaufbau *m* (EDV) instruction format

Befehlsausführung *f* (EDV) instruction execution

Befehlsausführungszeit *f* (EDV) instruction time

Befehlsbereich *m* (EDV) instruction area

Befehlscode *m* (EDV) instruction code

Befehlsdecoder *m* (EDV) instruction decoder

Befehlsdiagramm *n* (EDV) instruction flowchart

Befehlsergänzung *f* (EDV) instruction modification

Befehlsfolge *f* (EDV) instruction sequence

Befehlsfolgeregister *n* (EDV) instruction counter

Befehlsformat *n* (EDV) instruction format

Befehlsindex *m* (EDV) instruction index

Befehlsinterpretation *f* (EDV) instruction decomposition (*ie, step in pipelining*)

Befehlskette *f*
(Bw) chain of command
- internal lines of command
(EDV) instruction chain

Befehlskettung *f* (EDV) command chaining

Befehlslänge *f* (EDV) instruction length

Befehlsleitwerk *n* (EDV) instruction control unit

Befehlsliste *f* (EDV) instruction list

Befehlsregister *n* (EDV) instruction register

Befehlsschleife *f* (EDV) instruction loop

Befehlsschlüssel *m* (EDV) instruction code
Befehlsstruktur *f* (EDV) command structure
Befehlsteil *m* (EDV) operation part
Befehlstyp *m* (EDV) instruction type
Befehlsübertragung *f* (EDV) instruction fetch *(ie, from main memory to control unit)*
Befehlsverschlüsselung *f* (EDV) instruction coding
Befehlsvorrat *m* (EDV) instruction repertoire *(or set)*
Befehlsweg *m* (Bw) = *Befehlskette*
Befehlswort *n* (EDV) instruction word
Befehlszähler *m* (EDV) instruction *(or* program) counter
– control register
Befehlszählerregister *n* (EDV) = *Befehlszähler*
befördern
(com) to transport
– to carry
– to forward
– to convey
– to ship *(eg, goods)*
(Pw) to advance
– to promote
Beförderer *m* (Zo) carrier
Beförderung *f*
(com) transport(ation)
– carriage
– conveyance
– freighting
– shipment
– haulage
(Pw) advancement
– promotion
Beförderung *f* **ablehnen** (Pw) to turn down a promotion
Beförderung *f* **auf dem Landwege** (com) land transport
Beförderung *f* **auf dem Luftwege** (com) air transport
Beförderung *f* **im Straßenverkehr** (com) road haulage
Beförderung *f* **im Transitverkehr** (com) transport in transit
Beförderung *f* **im Zollgutversand** (Zo) transport (of goods) under customs transit
Beförderung *f* **per Bahn** (com) rail transport
Beförderung *f* **per Schiff** (com) waterborne transport
Beförderung *f* **von Stückgut** (com) transport of general cargo
Beförderungsangebot *n* (com) offer of transportation
Beförderungsanspruch *m*
(Pw) seniority right
– right to be advanced *(or* promoted)
Beförderungsart *f* (com) mode of transport
Beförderungsaussichten *fpl*
(Pw) career prospects
– prospects of promotion
Beförderungsbedingungen *fpl* (com) conditions of transport
Beförderungseinheit *f* (com) transport unit
Beförderungsentgelte *npl* (com) transport charges *(or* rates)

Beförderungsgeschäfte *npl* (Re) transport activities *(or* operations) *(ie, comprising passenger and goods traffic)*
Beförderungsgut *n* (com) cargo
Beförderungskosten *pl*
(com, Zo) cost of transport
– freight
– transport expenses
(com) railroad charges
(com) haulage *(ie, in road transport)*
Beförderungsleistung *f*
(com) volume of traffic
(StR) transport operations *(ie, within the meaning of the turnover tax law)*
Beförderungsleiter *f* (Pw) promotion ladder
Beförderungsmittel *npl*
(com) means of transportation
– transport facilities
Beförderungspapier *n* (Zo) transit *(or* transport) document
Beförderungspflicht *f* (Re) statutory duty of public carriers to undertake transportation
Beförderungsrisiko *n* (com) risk of transport
Beförderungssteuer *f* (StR) transportation tax *(ie, superseded by the value-added tax, as of 1 Jan 1968)*
Beförderungssteuergesetz *n* (StR) Law Regulating the Transportation Tax Law, of 13 June 1955, as amended
Beförderungstarif *m* (com) scale of transport charges
Beförderungsunternehmen *n*
(com) transport company
– private carrier
Beförderungsvertrag *m*
(Re) shipping contract
– (GB) contract of carriage
– forwarding contract
Beförderungsvorschriften *fpl* (com) forwarding instructions
Beförderungswege *mpl*
(com) transport routes
(Zo) transit routes
Beförderungszulage *f* (Pw) seniority pay
Beförderung *f* **unter Zollverschluß** (Zo) transport under customs seal
befrachten
(com) to load *(ie, on board a ship)*
– to freight *(eg, ship is freighted with . . .)*
(com) to forward freight *(ie, up to ship's berth, putting it at disposal of ocean carrier)*
Befrachter *m*
(com) inland waterway forwarding agent
(com) freighter
– shipper *(ie, for whom freight is transported, contracts with ocean carrier)*
Befrachtung *f* (com) freighting
Befrachtungsmakler *m* (com) chartering broker
Befrachtungsvertrag *m* (Re) contract of affreightment
Befragter *m* (Mk) respondent
Befragung *f*
(Stat) public-opinion survey
– opinion poll
Befragung *f* **e-r Grundgesamtheit** (Mk) canvass

befreien
(com) to discharge
- to dispense
- to exempt
- to exonerate
- to free
- to relieve
(Re) to excuse *(eg, performance)*
(Re) to insulate from *(or* against) *(eg, risk of liability, imposition of liability)*
(Re) to relieve *(eg, of liability)*
(Fin) to discharge *(eg, of debt)*
befreiende Lebensversicherung *f* (SozV) exempt life insurance
befreiender Dienst *m* (StR) alternate service *(ie, instead of military service)*
befreiende Schuldübernahme *f* (Re) assumption of debt *(or* liability) in discharge of the old debtor
befreiende Wirkung *f* (Re) discharging effect
befreit (Re) immune from
- relieved of *(eg, liability to)*
(StR) exempt
Befreiung *f*
(StR) tax exemption
- exemption from tax liability
Befreiungen *fpl* (StR) exemptions
Befreiungsklausel *f* (AuW, GATT) escape clause
Befreiung *f* **von den Eingangsabgaben** (Zo) exemption from *(or* waiver of) import duties and taxes
Befreiung *f* **von der geschuldeten Leistung** (Re) discharge of obligation
Befreiung *f* **von e-r Schuld** (StR) forgiveness of a debt *(or* indebtedness), § 13 I 5 ErbStG
Befreiung *f* **von e-r Verbindlichkeit**
(Re) discharge
- release from an obligation
Befreiungsversicherung *f* (SozV) insurance taken out to exempt beneficiary from compulsory social insurance
befreundete Zahlen *fpl* (Math) amicable numbers
befriedigen
(Vw) to meet
- to satisfy *(eg, want, need)*
(Re) to satisfy *(eg, claim)*
(Re) to pay off
- to satisfy *(eg, creditor)*
Befriedigung *f*
(Re) satisfaction *(eg, claim, creditor)*
(Vw) satisfaction
- satiation *(eg, want)*
Befriedigung *f* **des Bedarfs** (Vw) satisfaction of demand
Befriedigung *f* **e-s Gläubigers vereiteln** (Re) to frustrate the satisfaction of a creditor
Befriedigungsrecht *n* (Re) right to obtain satisfaction, § 371 HGB
Befriedigungsvorrecht *n* (Re) right to preferential payment
Befriedigung *f* **von Gläubigern** (Re) paying off creditors
befristen
(com) to place
- to set
- to fix ... a deadline (on)
- to put a time limit on

befristet
(com) limited in time
- having a time limit *(or* cutoff date)
- with a limited time *(eg, for acceptance of an offer)*
befristete Einlagen *fpl* (Fin) time deposits *(eg, at no less than 30 days' notice)*
befristete Exportförderung *f* (AuW) export promotion limited in time
befristete Guthaben *npl* (Fin) time balances
befristete Police *f* (Vers) time policy
befristeter Kredit *m* (Fin) time loan
befristeter Vertrag *m* (Re) contract of limited duration
befristetes Angebot *n* (com) offer open for a specified time
befristetes Anschaffungsgeschäft *n* (StR) acquisition of securities subject to a time limitation, § 18 II 3 KVStG
befristetes Arbeitsverhältnis *n* (Pw) limited employment contract
befristetes Darlehen *n* (Fin) loan with fixed date for repayment
befristete Verbindlichkeiten *fpl* (Fin) term liabilities
Befristung *f* (com) setting a time limit *(or* deadline)
Befugnis *f*
(com) authority *(or* powers)
- competence
- power
Befugnisse *fpl* **überschreiten** (com) to exceed authority *(or* powers)
Befugnisse *fpl* **übertragen** (com) to delegate authority *(or* powers)
befugt
(com) authorized
- competent
- empowered
begebbar
(WeR) negotiable *(ie, referring to ‚Inhaber- und Orderpapiere' = bearer and order instruments; transfer by indorsement and delivery)*
(WeR) transferable
- assignable
(ie, referring to ‚Rekta-/Namenspapiere' = registered or nonnegotiable instruments; transfer by assignment)
begebbare Schuldverschreibung *f* (WeR) negotiable bond
begebbare Wertpapiere *npl*
(WeR) negotiable instruments
(WeR) transferable *(or* assignable) instruments
Begebbarkeit *f* (WeR) negotiability *(ie, restricted to order and bearer papers)*
begeben
(WeR) to negotiate *(ie, to hand over 1. Inhaberpapiere, by indorsement and delivery, Indossament und Übergabe; 2. Orderpapiere, by mere delivery, bloße Übergabe; see also ‚Einwendungsausschluß')*
(Fin) to issue *(eg, bond issue)*
- to float
- to launch
(Fin) to sell *(eg, a loan)*
(Fin) to negotiate *(eg, at the stock exchange)*

Begebung *f*
(WeR) negotiation
(Fin) issue *(ie, of shares and other securities)*
Begebung *f* **e-s Wechsels** (WeR) negotiation of a bill of exchange
Begebungsfähigkeit *f* (Fin) negotiability
Begebungskonsortium *n*
(Fin) issuing group (*or* syndicate)
– selling group
Begebungskosten *pl* (Fin) issue costs
Begebungskurs *m*
(Fin) issue
– subscription
– coming-out ... price
Begebung *f* **von Aktien** (Fin) issue of shares (*or* stock)
Begebung *f* **von Anleihen**
(Fin) issue
– flotation
– launching ... of a loan (*or* bonds)
Begebung *f* **von Auslandsanleihen** (Fin) issue of foreign bonds
Begehen *n* **e-r unerlaubten Handlung** (Re) commission of an unlawful act (*or* tort)
Begeher *m* **e-r unerlaubten Handlung**
(Re) tortfeasor
– person committing an unlawful act
Beginn *m* **der Rechtsfähigkeit** (Re) beginning of legal capacity, § 1 BGB
beglaubigen
(Re) to authenticate
– to legalize *(eg, a signature)*
– to certify *(eg, certified to be a true and correct copy of the original)*
beglaubigte Kopie *f* (com) certified copy
beglaubigte Übersetzung *f* (com) certified translation
beglaubigte Urkunde *f* (Re) authenticated document
beglaubigte Vollmacht *f* (Re) certified power of attorney
Beglaubigung *f*
(Re) authentication
– certification
– verification
(ie, stating that a document is in due legal form)
Beglaubigungsgebühr *f* (Re) certification fee
Beglaubigungsvermerk *m*
(Re) attestation clause
– certificate of acknowledgment
begleichen
(com) to pay *(eg, a debt)*
– to defray *(eg, cost, expenses)*
– to discharge *(eg, a debt)*
– to settle *(eg, bill or money claimed)*
– to square *(eg, an account)*
Begleichung *f*
(com) payment
– discharge
– settlement
Begleitblatt *n* (com) advice note
Begleitdokumente *npl* (com) accompanying documents
Begleitpapier *n* (com) accompanying document
Begleitschreiben *n*
(com) accompanying letter
– covering letter
– letter of transmittal
Begleitumstände *mpl* (Re) attendant (*or* surrounding) circumstances
Begleitungsdienst *m* **im Zoll- und Verbrauchsteuerverkehr** (Zo) escort duties with respect to customs and excise matters
begrenzen
(com) to limit
– to restrict
– (infml) to put a cap on *(eg, railroad rates)*
(EDV) to delimit
begrenzende Wortmarke *f* (EDV) defining word mark
Begrenzer *m* (EDV) delimiter
begrenzter Markt *m*
(com, Bö) narrow
– thin
– tight ... market
begrenzter Markttest *m* (Mk) consumer acceptance test
Begrenzungszeichen *n* (EDV) data delimiter
Begriff *m*
(Log) concept
– notion
(Note: „term', strictly speaking, is not the equivalent of „Begriff'; it is simply a word or expression = Bezeichnung, Benennung; unfortunately, however, „term' and „concept', like their German counterparts, are used interchangeably by scholars and non-scholars alike)
Begriff *m* **des Obersatzes** (Log) major term *(ie, the predicate of the conclusion in a categorical syllogism)*
Begriff *m* **des Untersatzes** (Log) minor term *(ie, the term that is the subject of the conclusion in a categorical syllogism)*
begrifflich (Log) conceptual
begrifflicher Bezugsrahmen *m* (Log) conceptual frame of reference (*or* framework)
begriffliche Supposition *f* (Log) logical supposition
Begriff *m* **präzisieren** (Log) to respecify a concept
Begriffsbestimmung *f* (Log) definition of a concept
Begriffsbestimmung *f* **des Warenursprungs** (Zo) definition of the concept of originating products
Begriffsbestimmung *f* **des Zollwerts** (Zo) definition of value for customs purposes
Begriffsbildung *f* (Log) concept formation
Begriffsinhalt *m*
(Log) intension *(ie, of a concept)*
– connotation
Begriffslogik *f* (Log) logic of concepts
Begriffsumfang *m*
(Log) extension *(ie, of a concept)*
– denotation
begründen
(Re) to create (*or* establish) *(ie, at right)*
(Re) to justify
– to substantiate *(eg, a claim in a law court)*
begründet (Re) supported by a reasoned opinion
begründete Einrede *f* (Re) good defense
begründete Entlassung *f* (Pw) dismissal for cause
begründete Weigerung *f* (Re) reasonable refusal

Begründung f
(com) statement of reasons
(com) explanatory notes (*or* memorandum)
Begründung f **e-s Gerichtsstandes** (Re) establishment of a forum
Begründung f **e-s Gesellschaftsverhältnisses** (Re) establishment of a partnership
Begründung f **e-s Rechts** (Re) creation of a right
Begründung f **e-s Wohnsitzes** (Re) establishment of a residence, § 7 BGB
Begründungsfrist f (StR) time limit set for stating reasons of an administrative appeal
Begründungszusammenhang m (Log) context of justification
Begründungszwang m (Re) duty to submit supporting arguments
begünstigen
(com) to favor
– to foster
– to support
– to promote
(Re) to benefit
begünstigte Aufwendungen mpl (StR) expenses subject to preferential treatment
begünstigte Einfuhr f
(Zo) preferential import
– importation on preferential terms
Begünstigter m (Re) beneficiary
begünstigter Warenverkehr m (Zo) preferential trade
begünstigtes Ausfuhrland n (AuW) exporting beneficiary country
begünstigtes Land n (Zo) beneficiary country
Begünstigung f
(com) support
– preferential treatment
Begünstigungsklausel f (Re) beneficiary clause
begutachten (com, Re) to give an expert opinion
(com) to appraise
– to assess
– to evaluate
Begutachtung f
(com, Re) appraisal
– valuation
– expert valuation
behaftet (com) surrounded (*eg, forecasts are surrounded by a number of uncertainties*)
Behälterabkommen n (Zo) Customs Convention on Containers, of 1956
Behälterverkehr m (com) container traffic
behandeln
(com) to address oneself to (*eg, task, problem, business in hand*)
– to deal with
– to approach
– to tackle
– to treat
Behandlung f **e-r Großspeicherdatei** (EDV) random processing (*ie, treatment of data without respect to their location in external storage*)
Beharrungstendenz f (Bö) tendency to inertia
behaupten
(Log, Re) to allege (*ie, facts, without proof*)
– to assert (*ie, forcefully; eg, a right*)
– to claim (*ie, in the face of opposition*)

– to contend (*ie, say with strength*)
– to maintain (*ie, to argue for an opinion*)
behauptende Aussage f (Log) assertion
behauptendes Urteil n (Log) assertoric proposition
behauptet (Bö) steady
Behauptung f
(Log, Re) allegation
– assertion
– claim
– contention
Behauptung f **aufstellen** (Log, Re) = *behaupten*
Behauptung f **beweisen** (Log) to prove an assertion (*or* contention)
Behauptung f **ohne Grundlage**
(Log) unfounded assertion
– assertion without substance
Behauptungszeichen n (Log) assertion (*Frege*)
Behauptung f **zurückweisen** (Log) to reject an allegation
Beheizungskosten pl (KoR) heating cost
beherrschende Gesellschaft f (Bw) controlling company
beherrschender Einfluß m
(Bw) control
– dominating influence
beherrschendes Unternehmen n (Bw) controlling (*or* dominant) enterprise
beherrschte Fertigung f
(Stat) controlled process
– process under control
beherrschte Gesellschaft f (Bw) controlled company
beherrschter Fertigungsprozeß m (IndE) controlled process
beherrschtes Unternehmen n (Bw) controlled enterprise
Beherrschungsvertrag m (Re) control (*or* subordination) agreement (*ie, agreement under which a corporation subordinates its management to that of another enterprise, § 291 I AktG*)
Behinderte mpl (SozV) disabled people (*ie, physically handicapped, deaf, hard of hearing, blind, partially sighted, speech impaired, mentally handicapped or ill*)
Behinderungswettbewerb m (Kart) restraint of competition
Behörde f
(Re) public authority (*or* agency)
– administrative agency
Behördeneinkauf m
(FiW) public purchasing
– purchasing by governmental agencies
(*syn, öffentliche Auftragsvergabe, Staatseinkauf*)
Behördenhandel m (com) purchasing and distribution of merchandise within a government agency
Behördenleiter m
(Bw) administrator
– head of a government agency
Behördensprache f (com) officialese
Behördenvertrag m (Re) government contract
behördlich anerkannte Wirtschaftsprüferstelle f (ReW) officially recognized accounting agency
behördliche Genehmigung f (Re) official license (*or* permit)
behördliche Zulassung f (Re) concession

Beiakten *fpl* (Re) related files
bei Auftragserteilung (com) with order
beiderseitiges Einverständnis *n* (Re) mutual consent
beiderseitiges Verschulden *n* (Re) mutual fault
Beidhanddiagramm *n*
  (IndE) simultaneous motion cycle chart
  – simo chart
Beidhand-Analysebogen *m* (IndE) two-handed process chart
bei Fälligkeit
  (Fin) at maturity
  – when due
Beihilfe *f* (Pw) allowance paid by the government to public employees *(ie, as contribution to costs of removal, illness, death, etc.)*
Beihilfe *f* **zu Patentverletzung** (Pat) aiding and abetting infringement
Beiladung *f*
  (com) additional *(or* extra) cargo
  (Re) summoning a person who is not a party to an administrative legal procedure, § 65 VwGO
Beilage *f* (com) enclosure (same as *„Anlage')*
Beilegung *f* **von Streitigkeiten** (Re) settlement of disputes
Beinahe-Geld *n*
  (Vw) quasi-money
  – near-money
„bei Nichtgefallen Geld zurück"
  (com) satisfaction or money back
  – money back guarantee
Beipacksendung *f* (com) collective *(or* pooled) consignment
Beipackzettel *m*
  (com) drug guide
  – package leaflet
Beirat *m* (com) advisory council
bei Sicht
  (WeR) at sight
  – on demand
  (ie, subject to payment upon presentation and demand)
Beistand *m*
  (com) aid
  – assistance
  – support
  (Re) legal advisor, § 1685 BGB, § 14 VwVfg
Beistandsfazilität *f* (AuW) support facility
Beistandskredit *m* (Fin) standby credit
Beistandspflicht *f* (StR) duty to assist *(ie, the local finance office in taxation procedures, examinations and supervisions)*
Beistandssystem *n* (AuW) support system
Beistellung *f* (com) provision of materials
Beitrag *m*
  (com) contribution
  (Fin) financial contribution
  – subscription
Beiträge *mpl*
  (StR) special public charges *(ie, recurrent or onetime; eg, improvement costs payable by real property owner)*
  (SozV) social insurance contributions
Beiträge *mpl* **an Bausparkassen**
  (Fin) periodic savings deposits with a savings or loan association

  – payments made to a savings and loan association
Beiträge *mpl* **zu Berufsverbänden** (com) membership dues paid to trade or professional organizations
Beiträge *mpl* **zur gesetzlichen Rentenversicherung** (Pw) mandatory social insurance contributions
Beitragsabführung *f* (SozV) remittance of social insurance contributions
Beitragsabzug *m* (Pw) deduction of social insurance contributions *(ie, from wages or salaries)*
Beitragsaufkommen *n* (SozV) yield from contributions
Beitragsbefreiung *f*
  (SozV) exemption from contributions
  (Vers) waiver of premium
Beitragsbemessungsgrenze *f*
  (SozV) income threshold
  (ie, income limit up to which contributions are payable)
Beitragsberechnung *f* (SozV) computation of contributions
Beitragseinnahmen *fpl* (com) contribution receipts
Beitragseinzugsverfahren *n* (SozV) contributions checkoff system
Beitragserstattung *f* (SozV) refunding *(or* reimbursement) of contributions
beitragsfrei (SozV) non-contributory
beitragsfreie Police *f* (Vers) free policy
beitragsfreie Versicherung *f* (Vers) = *beitragsfreie Police*
beitragsfreie Zeiten *fpl* (SozV) no-contribution periods
Beitragsfreiheit *f* (SozV) exemption from contributions
Beitragsjahre *npl* (SozV) contribution years
Beitragsklasse *f* (SozV) scale of contributions
Beitragsleistung *f* (SozV) payment of contributions
Beitragspflicht *f* (SozV) liability to pay contributions
beitragspflichtig (SozV) liable to contribute
Beitragspflichtiger *m*
  (com) person liable to contribute *(or* to pay contributions)
beitragspflichtige Vermögenswerte *mpl* (SeeV) contributing values
Beitragsrückerstattung *f* (Vers) refund of premium
Beitragsrückstände *mpl*
  (SozV) arrears of contributions
  (Vers) arrears of premiums
Beitragssatz *m*
  (SozV) rate of contribution
  (com) membership fee
Beitragsstaffelung *f* (Vers) grading of premiums
Beitragsüberwachung *f* (SozV) control of contributions checkoff *(or* collection)
Beitragswert *m* (SeeV) contributory value
beitreiben
  (Fin) to collect
  (Re) to enforce payment
Beitreibung *f*
  (com) collection of money due
  (StR) enforced collection of amounts due to public authorities *(eg, taxes, fees, fines, penalties, etc.)*

101

Beitreibung f der Steuerschuld (StR) enforced collection of taxes due
Beitreibungskosten pl (Fin) collection expenses
Beitreibungsverfahren n
  (Fin) recovery proceedings
  (Fin) collection procedure
Beitreibung f von Außenständen (Fin) recovery of accounts receivable
Beitreibung f von Zöllen (Zo) recovery of duties
beitreten
  (Re) to enter
  – to accede to
Beitritt m
  (EG) accession to the EEC
  – EEC accession
  – entry into the EEC
Beitrittsakte f (EG) Act of Accession
Beitrittsantrag m (Re) application for entry (or membership)
Beitrittsausgleichsbetrag m (EG) accession compensatory amount
Beitrittserklärung f (Re) declaration of accession (or adhesion) (eg, to EEC)
Beitrittsgegner m (EG) anti-marketeer
Beitrittsklausel f (Re) accession clause
Beitrittsländer npl (EG) acceding countries
Beitrittsurkunde f (Re) document (or instrument) of accession
Beitrittsverhandlungen fpl
  (EG) entry negotiations
  – membership negotiations
  – accession talks
Beitrittsvertrag m (EG) treaty of accession
bei Versand (com) on shipment
bei Vorlage
  (WeR) on presentation
  (WeR) at sight
  – on demand
bejahendes Urteil n (Log) affirmative (proposition)
Bekanntmachung f
  (com) announcement (eg, in newspapers, circular letters, etc.)
  (Re) public notice (or announcement)
Bekanntmachung f der Börsenorgane (Bö) notification by stock exchange authorities
Bekanntmachung f der Firmenänderung (com) notification of change of corporate (or firm) name
Bekanntmachungspflicht f (ReW) diclosure requirement (ie, relating to annual financial statement)
Beklagter m (Re) defendant
  (ie, party against whom recovery is sought in a civil action or suit)
Bekleidungsindustrie f (com) apparel (or garment) industry
bekräftigen
  (com, Re) to affirm
  – to confirm
  (Log, Re) to corroborate
  – to substantiate
Bekräftigung f
  (Re) affirmation (ie, of the truth of a statement)
  – corroboration
  – substantiation

bekundete Präferenzen fpl (Vw) revealed preferences (syn, offenbarte Präferenzen)
Beladung f
  (com) loading
  (com) load
  – cargo
Beladungsgrenze f
  (com) load limit
  – maximum load
belasten
  (ReW) to charge (eg, an account)
  – to debit
  (Re) to burden (eg, property)
  – to encumber
belastetes Eigentum n (Re) encumbered property
belastete Ware f (AuW) taxed product
Belastung f (com) burden (eg, interest, taxes)
  – load
  (ReW) charge
  – debit
  (Re) charge
  – burden
  – encumbrance (eg, of property by lien or mortgage)
  (AuW) pressure (eg, on the balance of payments)
Belastungsanzeige f (ReW) debit note
Belastungsausgleich m (OR) leveling
Belastungsfaktoren mpl (OR) load factors (ie, coefficients assigned to the variables in capacity restraints of mathematical programming)
Belastungsgrenze f (Re) limit for land encumbrances
Belastungsprinzip n (FiW) burden principle (ie, loan repayments and grants are deducted from total expenditures; the result is the net expenditure)
Belastungsquote f des BSP (FiW) public-sector share of gnp
belaufen auf, sich
  (com) to amount to
  – to add up to
  – (infml) to tot up to (eg, total debt)
beleben
  (com) to revive
  – to stimulate
  – to reinvigorate
  – to revitalize
Belebung f der Investitionstätigkeit (Vw) investment upturn
Belebung f der Konjunktur (Vw) economic upturn (or recovery)
Belebung f der Nachfrage
  (com) recovery of demand
  – upturn in demand
Belebung f des Auftragseingangs (com) picking up of orders
Belebungseffekt m (Vw) reinvigorating (or revitalizing) effect
Beleg m
  (ReW) voucher
  – slip
  – record
  (ie, written evidence of a business or accounting transaction)
Belegabriß m (com) stub (ie, in garment retailing)

Belegabschnitt *m*
(com) check voucher
- stub
- (GB) counterfoil
Belegaufbereitung *f* (Fin) voucher processing
Belegbearbeitung *f* (com) document handling
Belegblock *m* (com) pad of forms
Belegbuchhaltung *f*
(ReW) bookless accounting
- file posting
- ledgerless accounting
- slip system of accounting
Belegdoppel *n* (ReW) voucher copy
Belege *mpl* (ReW) supporting data (*or* records)
belegen
(com) to prove
(Re) situate *(eg, a parcel of land ... in)*
(EDV) to occupy
- to use
(EDV) to allocate
- to assign
belegene Sache *f* (Re) property situated at
Belegenheit *f* (Re) situs *(eg, property that has a situs in Germany)*
Belegenheitsfinanzamt *n* (StR) local finance office where taxable property is situated, § 72 AO *(ie, now ‚Lagefinanzamt', § 18 AO 1977)*
Belegenheitsgemeinde *f* (StR) municipality where taxable property is situated
Belegenheitsstaat *m*
(StR) country where property is situated
- state of situs
Belegerstellung *f* (ReW) voucher (*or* document) preparation
Belegexemplar *n* (com) author's (*or* courtesy) copy
Belegfeld *n* (EDV) document field
beleggebundener Einzugsverkehr *m* (Fin) paper-based collections
beleggebundene Zahlung *f* (Fin) paper-based transfer
Belegkopie *f* (ReW) voucher (*or* document) copy
Beleglauf *m* (ReW) voucher routing
Belegleser *m* (EDV) document (*or* mark) reader
belegloses Scheckinkasso *n* (Fin) check truncation procedure
belegloser Überweisungsverkehr *m* (Fin) electronic funds transfer
beleglose Zahlung *f* (Fin) paperless transfer
belegmäßige Bestandsaufnahme *f* (ReW) voucher-based materials inventory
belegmäßiger Nachweis *m* (ReW) audit trail
Belegnumerierung *f* (ReW) item numbering (*or* indorsing)
Belegnummer *f* (ReW) voucher number
Belegprinzip *n* (ReW) „no posting without voucher" principle
Belegprüfung *f*
(ReW) voucher audit
(Zo) documentary check
- scrutiny of documents
Belegregister *n*
(ReW) voucher register
- voucher journal
- voucher record
Belegsatz *m* (com) form set

Belegschaft *f*
(Pw) employees
- staff
- personnel
- workforce
Belegschaft *f* **reduzieren**
(Pw) to reduce the workforce
- to trim staff
- (infml) to winnow staff
- to slash jobs
Belegschaftsaktien *fpl*
(Pw) employee shares (*or* stocks)
- shares offered and sold to employees
- (infml) buckshee shares *(eg, employees get further ... on a 1:1 basis)*
Belegschaftsaktienplan *m* (Pw) share purchase plan for employees
Belegschaftsaktionär *m* (Fw) shareholder (*or* stockholder) employee
Belegschaftsangehöriger *m* (Pw) company employee
Belegschaftsversammlung *f* (Pw) employee meeting
Belegschaftsversicherung *f* (Vers) employee insurance
(ie, taken out, and often fully paid, by the employer as an additional safeguard against the risks of disability, old age, and death)
Belegsortierer *m* (EDV) document sorter
Belegstelle *f* (Log) supporting authority
Belegstreifen *m* (ReW) detail strip
Belegsystem *n* (ReW) voucher system
Belegungsdauer *f* (EDV) holding time *(ie, message time + operating time)*
Belegverarbeitung *f* (EDV) document handling
Belegverweis *m* (ReW) audit trail
Belegzuführung *f* (EDV) document feeding
Belegzwang *m* (StR) legal duty of taxpayer to keep records *(ie, on business, income-related, and special expenses, § 205 AO in connection with §§ 170–182 AO)*
beleihbar (Fin) eligible (*or* suitable) as collateral
beleihbare Effekten *pl* (Fin) securities eligible as collateral
beleihen (Fin) to lend against collateral security
Beleihung *f* (Fin) lending against collateral security
Beleihung *f* **e-r Police od Versicherung** (Vers) policy loan
beleihungsfähig (Fin) eligible (*or* suitable) to serve as collateral
beleihungsfähiges Objekt *n* (Fin) property eligible as security
Beleihungsgrenze *f* (Fin) lending ceiling (*or* limit) *(ie, in respect of collateral security)*
Beleihungsgrundsätze *mpl* (Fin) lending principles
Beleihungskredit *m* (Fin) advance on collateral
Beleihungsobjekt *n* (Fin) real estate used as collateral
Beleihungsquote *f* (Fin) loan-to-value ratio
beleihungsreifes Bauobjekt *n* (Fin) construction project qualifying for mortgage loans
Beleihungssatz *m* (Fin) = *Beleihungsquote*
Beleihungswert *m*
(Fin) value of collateral

(Vers) loan value *(ie, of an insurance policy, based on its cash value)*
Beleihung *f* **von Versicherungspolicen** (Fin) loans and advances on insurance policies
Beleuchtungskosten *pl* (KoR) lighting cost
beliehenes Unternehmen *n* (Re) independent private enterprise charged with specific functions in the national interest
beliehene Wertpapiere *npl* (Fin) collateral securities
Belieferung *f* (com) supply *(ie, transport between producer and customer)*
Bemerkungseintrag *m* (EDV) comments entry
Bemerkungsfeld *n* (EDV) comments field
bemessen
    (com) to assess
    – to determine
    (Re) to award *(eg, damages)*
Bemessung *f*
    (com) assessment
    – determination
    (Re) awarding
Bemessung *f* **der Eingangsabgaben** (Zo) assessment of import duties
Bemessung *f* **e-r Steuer** (StR) computing a tax
Bemessungsgrundlage *f*
    (com) basis of proration
    (Re) measure *(eg, of damages)*
    (StR) tax *(or* taxable) base
    – basis of assessment
Bemessungsgrundlage *f* **für den Gewinn** (Vers) rate base
Bemessungsgrundlage *f* **für die Zollerhebung** (Zo) basis upon which customs charges are determined
Bemessungsmaßstab *m* (com) standard of assessment
Bemessungszeitraum *m* (StR) income year *(ie, the calendar year, § 2 VII EStG; co-extensive with the period of assessment)*
bemustern
    (com) to attach samples to an offer
    (com) to sample *(ie, drawing samples to determine the average quality of staple goods)*
benachbarte Kanten *fpl* (OR) adjacent edges *(or* vertices)
benachbarte Küstenstaaten *mpl* (Re) adjoining coastal States
benachbarter Kanal *m* (EDV) adjacent channel
benachbarte Staaten *mpl* (Re) adjoining States
benachrichtigen (com) to advise
    – to inform
    – to give notice
    (Re) to notify
Benachrichtigung *f*
    (com) advice
    – information
    – notice
    (Re) notification
Benachrichtigungsadresse *f* (com) notify party
Benachrichtigungspflicht *f*
    (Re) duty of commercial agent to notify principal, § 86 II HGB
    (WeR) duty (of holder) to notify certain obligors, Art. 45 WG

Benachrichtigungsschreiben *n* (com) letter of advice
benachteiligen
    (Re) to discriminate
    – to place at a disadvantage
Benachteiligter *m* (Re) injured party
Benachteiligung *f*
    (Re) discrimination
    – unfavorable treatment
Benachteiligung *f* **am Arbeitsplatz** (Pw) job discrimination
benannte Zahl *f* (Math) concrete *(or* denominate) number
beneficium discussionis *n* (Re) = Einrede der Vorausklage *(ie, privilege by which a surety is bound to sue the principal debtor first, and can only sue the sureties for that which he himself cannot recover from the principal, § 771 BGB)*
Benennung *f* (Log) term *(ie, see: Begriff)*
Benennungssystem *n* (Log) nomenclature
Benutzer *m* (EDV) user
Benutzerakzeptanz *f* (EDV) user acceptance
Benutzer *m* **e-s Warenzeichens** (Pat) rightful user of a trade mark
Benutzeretikett *n* (EDV) user label
benutzerfreundlich (EDV) user friendly
Benutzerfreundlichkeit *f* (EDV) user friendliness
Benutzerhandbuch *n* (com) user's guide *(or* manual)
Benutzerprogramm *n* (EDV) application *(or* user) program
Benutzerroutine *f* (EDV) own module
Benutzerstation *f* (EDV) user terminal
Benutzungsanleitung *f* (EDV) handling specification *(syn, Hantierungsvorschrift)*
Benutzungsgebühr *f*
    (FiW) charge *(or* fee) for the use of ...
    – user fee
Benutzungskosten *pl* (com) user cost
Benutzungslizenz *f* (Pat) license to use
Benutzungsrecht *n* (Re) right to use
Benutzungszwang *m* (Re) compulsory use *(ie, of public utility services; eg, postal services, water, light, etc.)*
beobachtbare Variable *f* (Stat) observable variable
beobachteter Leistungsgrad *m* (IndE) observed rating
beobachteter Wert *m* (Stat) observation
beobachtete Verfügbarkeit *f* (Stat) observed availability
Beobachtungsdaten *pl* (Stat) observational data
Beobachtungsfehler *m* (Stat) error of observation
Beobachtungswert *m* (Stat) observed value
Beobachtungszeit *f*
    (IndE) elapsed time *(ie, of machine operator)*
    (IndE) effective time *(ie, of operator, incl. setup and inspection time)*
bequeme Finanzierung *f* (Fin) easy financing facilities
bequemer Zinsfuß *m* (Math) convenient base
beraten
    (com) to advise
    (com) to consult *(eg, with fellow workers)*
    – to confer (with)
    (Re) to deliberate

beratende Abteilung f (Bw) advisory department
beratende Funktion f (com) advisory function (or capacity)
beratender Ausschuß m (com) consultative committee
Beratender Ausschuß m **für Zollfragen** (EG) Advisory Committee on Customs Matters
beratendes Gremium n (com) advisory body
Berater m
  (com) consultant
  – adviser
  – counselor
Beratung f
  (com) advice
  (com) consulting
  – consultation
  – counseling
  (com) consultancy
  (Re) deliberation
Beratungsfirma f
  (com) consulting firm
  – consultancy
Beratungsgegenstand m
  (com) item on the agenda
  – subject of discussion
Beratungsgesellschaft f (com) consulting company
Beratungsingenieur m (com) consulting engineer
Beratungskosten pl (com) consultation fee
Beratungspflicht f (StR) duty to furnish tax counsel (ie, imposed upon local tax offices under § 89 AO)
Beratungsservice m (com) consulting service
Beratungsstelle f (com) consulting agency
Beratungstätigkeit f (com) consulting (or advisory) activity
Beraubung f (SeeV) pilferage
Beraubungsversicherung f (Vers) robbery insurance policy (ie, coverage protecting against loss from the unlawful taking of property by violence, force, or intimidation)
Berechenbarkeit f (com) computability
Berechnung f
  (com) calculation
  (com) estimate
  (com) billing
  – invoicing
  (EDV) computation
Berechnung f **der Fristen** (Re) computation of time limits
Berechnung f **der Zinstage** (Math) computing elapsed time in days
Berechnung f **der Zölle und sonstigen Abgaben** (Zo) assessment of duties and taxes
Berechnungsart f (com) method of calculation
Berechnungsformel f (com) computational formula
Berechnungsgrundlage f (com) basis of computation (or calculation)
Berechnungsmethode f (com) method of calculation
Berechnungsschema n (com) = **Berechnungsformel**
Berechnungsschlüssel m (com) = **Berechnungsformel**
Berechnungszeitraum m (com) period of computation

berechnen
  (com) to calculate
  – to work out (eg, prices, costs)
  (com) to bill
  – to charge
  – to invoice
  (com) to estimate (eg, in cost calculation)
  (EDV) to compute
berechtigen
  (Re) to entitle
  – to qualify
Berechtigter m
  (Re) beneficiary
  – obligee
  – promisee
  – party entitled to ...
berechtigtes Interesse n (Re) vital interest (ie, of a factual or legal kind; eg, access to inspect official files)
Bereich m
  (com) area
  – domain
  – range
  – scope
  – sector
  – sphere
  (Bw) group (ie, of a company)
  – division
  – operations
  (Bw) segment (eg, the metals ... reported heavy losses)
  (EDV) area
Bereicherung f (Re) enrichment (ie, obtaining a thing without consideration = ohne rechtlichen Grund, § 812 BGB)
Bereicherungsabsicht f (Re) intent to enrich oneself
Bereicherungsanspruch m (Re) claim on account of unjust enrichment
Bereicherungsklage f (Re) action on grounds on unjust enrichment
  – (civil law) condictio sine causa
Bereich m **e-r Variablen** (Math) range of a variable
Bereich m **für ein Warteschlangenelement** (OR) queue element area
Bereich m **mit selbständiger Ergebnisrechnung** (Bw) profit center
Bereich m **realisierbarer Verbrauchspläne** (Vw) budget space
Bereichsadresse f (EDV) area address
Bereichsangabe f (EDV) area specification
Bereichsausgangspreis m (KoR) internal price agreed upon between groups (or divisions)
Bereichsausnahmen fpl (Kart) industry-wide exemptions (ie, agriculture, banks, insurance companies, public utilities)
Bereichs-Controller m (Bw) area controller
Bereichsdefinition f (Log) area definition
Bereichsgrenze f (EDV) area limit (or boundary)
bereichsintern (Bw) internal
Bereichskapital n (Fin) equity capital allocated to a group (or division)
Bereichsleiter m (Bw) division manager
  – (US, also) vice president ... (eg, marketing)
  – (GB) divisional director

Bereichsmatrix f (EDV) area matrix
Bereichsschutz m (EDV) memory protect feature
bereichsspezifisch (Bw) area specific
Bereichsüberschreitung f (EDV) limit error
Bereichsunterschreitung f (EDV) underflow
Bereichsvariable f (Stat) array variable
Bereichsvorstand m
  (Bw) divisional board of management
  (Bw) top executive in command of a functional area
bereinigen
  (com) to adjust
  – to correct
  – to settle
  – to straighten out
bereinigter Betriebserfolg m (ReW) net operating profit *(ie, total profit minus nonoperating profit)*
bereinigter Index m (Stat) adjusted index
bereinigtes Kassenbudget n (FiW) consolidated cash budget
Bereinigung f
  (com) adjustment
  – correction
  – settlement
  (IndE) streamlining *(eg, of operations sequence)*
Bereinigung f **des Sortiments** (Mk) streamlining of product range
bereitgestellte Investitionsmittel pl
  (Fin) capital appropriation
  – funds available for capital spending
bereitschaftsabhängige Kosten pl (KoR) standby costs
Bereitschaftsdienst m (Pw) standby duty (or services)
Bereitschaftskosten pl (KoR) standby costs
Bereitschaftskredit m (IWF) standby credit (or facility) *(ie, additional device to assist IMF members in temporary difficulties; under these Arrangements members may negotiate lines of credit in anticipation of their actual needs)*
Bereitschaftskredit-Abkommen n (IWF) standby agreement
Bereitschaftsprämie f (Pw) on-call premium
Bereitschaftsrechner m (EDV) standby computer
Bereitschaftssystem n (IndE, EDV) standby system
Bereitschaftswahrscheinlichkeit f (IndE) operational readiness *(ie, of machines)*
Bereitschaftszeit f (IndE) waiting time
Bereitschaftszusage f (Fin) credit commitment
bereitstellen
  (com) to furnish
  – to make available
  – to make ready for use
  – to provide
  – to supply
  (Fin) to allocate
  – to appropriate
  – to earmark
Bereitstellung f
  (com) provision
  – supply
  (Fin) allocation
  – appropriation
  – earmarking
  (EDV) load

Bereitstellungsadresse f (EDV) load area address
Bereitstellungsprogramm n (EDV) job control program
Bereitstellungsteil m (EDV) load field
Bereitstellung f **von Ressourcen** (Bw) resourcing
Bereitstellungsfonds m (Fin) earmarked fund
Bereitstellungsgebühr f (Fin) standby fee
Bereitstellungskonto n
  (ReW) appropriation account
  (Fin) credit account open to drawings
Bereitstellungskosten pl
  (MaW) expenses for maintaining reserve inventory costs
  (ie, incidental to material procurement cost and allocable as material overhead)
  (KoR) standby cost
Bereitstellungskredit m (Fin) commitment credit
Bereitstellungsplanung f (IndE) procurement budgeting *(ie, part of manufacturing planning and scheduling)*
Bereitstellungsmenge f (MaW) service level
Bereitstellungsplafonds m (Fin) commitment ceiling
Bereitstellungsprinzipien npl (MaW) principles of procurement
Bereitstellungsprovision f (Fin) loan commitment fee *(ie, now ‚Kreditprovision')*
Bereitstellungszins m (Fin) commitment interest
Bergbau m
  (com) mining
  (com) mining industry
Bergbauberufsgenossenschaft f (SozV) compulsory miners' accident insurance
Bergbaufreiheit f (Re) equal opportunity of mining *(ie, accruing to the first finder of mineral deposits, except gypsum, platinum, tungsten, bod iron ore = Raseneisenerz, and hard coal; the latter falling under the right of eminent domain)*
bergbautreibende Vereinigung f (com) mining association
Bergbehörde f (Re) mining authorities *(ie, Bergamt, Oberbergamt, and the appropriate Laenderminister)*
Bergegeld n (com) salvage money
Bergelohn m (com) = *Bergegeld*
Bergelohnforderung f (com) salvage claim
Bergewert m
  (com) salvage value
  – residual value
Berggrundbuch n (Re) public land register for mining assets
Bergmannsprämie f (StR) (tax-free) miner's bonus *(ie, not subject to social insurance)*
Bergmannsrente f (SozV) miners' old-age pension
Bergrecht n (Re) mining law
bergrechtliche Gesellschaft f (Re) mining company
bergrechtliche Gewerkschaft f (Re) mining company
  (ie, share capital divided into ‚Kuxe' evidencing a prorata share; partners are called ‚Gewerken'; many companies are now converted into stock corporations)
Bergschäden mpl (Re) mining damage *(ie, due to subsidence; see: §§ 82, 87ff BewG)*
Bergung f (SeeV) salvage

Bergungsgesellschaft f (com) salvage company
Bergungskosten pl (com, SeeV) salvage charges
Bergungsrecht n (Re) right of salvage
Bergungsschaden m (SeeV) salvage loss
Bergungsvertrag m (Re) salvage agreement (or contract)
Bergwerksaktie f (Fin) mining share
Bergwerksanteil m (WeR) registered mining share (= Kux) (ie, = Rektapapier, no par value, subject to contributions by members)
Bergwerkseigentum n (Re) right to economic exploitation of a certain mining district (ie, this is a right equivalent to real property)
Bergwerksgesellschaft f (com) mining company
Bergwerkskonzession f (Re) mining license
Bergwerksrecht n (Re) mining right
Bericht m (com) report
Bericht m **e-r Auskunftei**
 (com) mercantile report
 – status report
Bericht m **ausarbeiten** (com) to draw up (or prepare) a report
berichtende Abrechnungseinheit f (ReW) reporting subunit
berichtende Gesellschaft f (ReW) reporting company
Berichterstattung f
 (com) reporting
 (ReW) disclosure
Berichterstattungs-Grundsatz m (ReW) basic standard of reporting
Berichterstellung f (com) report preparation
Bericht m **frisieren** (com) to doctor a report
berichtigen
 (com) to correct
 – to put right
 – to rectify
 – to straighten out (eg, mistakes in a bill)
 (ReW) to adjust
berichtigende Werbung f (Mk) corrective advertising
berichtigte Bilanz f (ReW) adjusted balance sheet
berichtigter Bruttoauftragseingang m (com) adjusted gross sales
berichtigter Bruttoumsatz m (com) adjusted gross income
Berichtigung f
 (com) adjustment
 – correction
 – rectification
Berichtigung f **der Steuerfestsetzung** (StR) change of tax assessment
Berichtigung f **der Währungsausgleichsbeträge** (EG) correction of the monetary compensating amounts
Berichtigung f **des Aktienkapitals** (Fin) adjustment of capital stock
Berichtigungsaktien fpl (Fin) bonus (or scrip) shares (ie, equivalent to a capital increase out of retained earnings = zu Lasten der offenen Rücklagen, §§ 207ff AktG; syn, Gratisaktien)
Berichtigungsbetrag m
 (StR) correcting amount
 (EG) corrective amount

Berichtigungsbuchung f (ReW) adjusting (or correcting) entry
Berichtigungsbuchung f **am Jahresende** (ReW) year-end adjustment
Berichtigungsbuchung f **nach Abschlußprüfung** (ReW) audit adjustment
Berichtigungsfeststellung f (StR) adjusting assessment (ie, setting aside or changing a notice of assessment)
Berichtigungsfortschreibung f (StR) adjustment of assessed value to correct a mistake (ie, made in the last-preceding assessment, § 22 IV 2 BewG)
Berichtigungshaushalt m (FiW) amended budget
Berichtigungskonto n (ReW) adjustment (or reconciliation) account
Berichtigungsposten m
 (ReW) adjusting entry (ie, in general bookkeeping)
 (ReW) valuation account (ie, as a means of providing for indirect depreciation)
Berichtigungsposten mpl **zum Eigenkapital** (ReW) adjustments to capital account
Berichtigungssatz m (Zo) rate of adjustment (ie, relating to customs value)
Berichtigungsveranlagung f (StR) adjusting assessment (ie, setting aside or changing a notice of assessment)
Berichtsdaten pl (com) reporting data
Berichtsformular n (com) report form
Berichtsgrundlage f (com) terms of reference
Berichtsjahr n (com) year under review
Berichtsnormen fpl (ReW) reporting standards
Berichtsperiode f (com) period under review
Berichtsvorlage f (com) presentation of a report
Berichtswesen n (com) reporting
Berichtszeit f
 (com) reporting period
 – period under review
Berichtszeitpunkt m (com) key (or reporting) date
Berichtszeitraum m
 (com) reporting period
 – period under review
Bericht m **über die wichtigsten Ereignisse** (com) highlight report
Bericht m **über Umsatzverlust** (com) lost revenue report
Bericht m **vorlegen** (com) to present (or submit) a report
Berlin-Darlehen n (Fin) Berlin loan (ie, extended under § 17 BerlinFG)
Berliner Kammergericht n (Kart) West Berlin Appeal Court
Berlinförderungsgesetz n (Re) Berlin Promotion Law, as amended 22 Dec 1978
Berlinhilfe f (Vw) Berlin aid
Berlinhilfegesetz n (Re) = (now) Berlinförderungsgesetz
Berlin-Vergünstigung f (StR) tax preferences for West Berlin (ie, consisting of reductions of the turnover tax, laid down in BerlinFG)
Berlin-Zulage f (StR) Berlin premium (ie, cash premium added to employment income from sources in West Berlin, § 28 BerlinFG)
Berner Verband m (Pat) Berne Union

Berner Verbands-Übereinkunft *f* (Pat) Berne Convention
Bernoulli-Experiment *n* (Stat) Bernoulli trial
Bernoulli-Prinzip *n* (Bw) Bernoulli principle *(ie, decision rule under risk)*
Bernoulli-Verteilung *f*
 (Stat) Bernoulli distribution
 (Math) binomial distribution
Bertrand-Modell *n* (Vw) Edgeworth-Bertrand model *(ie, of oligopolistic dyopoly)*
berücksichtigungsfähig (StR) tax deductible
berücksichtigungsfähige Ausschüttungen *fpl* (StR, KSt) dividend payments subject to reduced tax rates *(ie, superseded by the corporate tax imputation procedure = körperschaftsteuerliches Anrechnungsverfahren)*
Beruf *m*
 (Pw) occupation *(ie, most inclusive term: work or employment habitually pursued and requiring a certain training; eg, architect, teacher, bookbinder)*
 (Pw) profession *(ie, requires – often university – training in some special branch of knowledge; eg, law, medicine)*
 (Pw) career *(ie, job or profession for which one is trained and which is often pursued for a whole lifetime)*
 (Pw) vocation *(ie, requires a special fitness for a special call)*
 (Pw) trade *(ie, job needing manual skills; eg, a carpenter by trade)*
Beruf *m* **ausüben** (Pw) to practice an occupation or profession
berufen (com) to appoint *(eg, to an office)*
berufen auf, sich (Re) to invoke *(eg, a special legal provision)*
Beruf *m* **ergreifen** (Pw) to take up career *(eg, in a particular trade or industry)*
berufliche Bildung *f* (Pw) vocational (*or* occupational) training
berufliche Eignung *f* (Pw) occupational competence
berufliche Eignungsprüfung *f* (Pw) examination of professional competence *(ie, at graduate level)*
berufliche Fortbildung *f*
 (Pw) further occupational (*or* professional) training
 (Pw) measures to maintain or improve existing skills in a profession or occupation, § 1 III BBiG
berufliche Gliederung *f* (Stat) occupational classification
berufliche Mobilität *f* (Vw) occupational mobility
berufliche Rehabilitation *f* (Pw) vocational rehabilitation
beruflicher Ehrenkodex *m*
 (Bw) professional code of ethics
 – deontology
beruflicher Werdegang *m*
 (Pw) career path (*or* history)
 – work history
berufliche Umschulung *f* (Pw) vocational retraining, § 1 IV BBiG
Berufsanfänger *m* (Pw) entry-level employee (*or* job seeker)
Berufsauffassung *f* (com) professional standard

Berufsausbildung *f*
 (Pw) professional or vocational training
 – pre-employment training
Berufsausbildungsabgabe *f* (Pw) levy for the creation of apprentice training places *(ie, imposed by virtue of the Federal Law of 23 Dec 1977)*
Berufsausbildungsbeihilfe *f* (Pw) grant or loan paid by the Federal Labor Office to youths or adults to finance occupational training
Berufsausbildungsförderung *f* (Pw) promotion of training for an occupation or profession
Berufsausbildungskosten *pl* (Pw) cost of occupational or professional training *(ie, may be deducted as extraordinary tax burden, § 33 a EStG)*
Berufsausbildungsverhältnis *n* (Pw) employer/apprentice relationship, §§ 3 ff BBiG
Berufsausbildungsvertrag *m*
 (Pw) contract creating an employer/apprentice relationship
 – employer/apprentice agreement
Berufsausrüstung *f* (Zo) occupational outfit *(ie, duty-free in the Federal Republic)*
Berufsaussichten *fpl* (Pw) employment outlook (*or* prospects)
Berufsausübung *f* (Pw) exercise of a trade, occupation or profession
Berufsberater *m* (Pw) vocational (*or* job) counselor
Berufsberatung *f*
 (Pw) career
 – vocational
 – occupational ... guidance
 – job counselling
 (ie, a monopoly of the Nuremberg-based Federal Labor Office)
Berufsbezeichnung *f* (Pw) job title
berufsbezogene Ausbildung *f* (Pw) career-oriented training
Berufsbild *n*
 (Pw) detailed description of a specific occupation, § 40 a HandwO
 (Pw) professional activity description
Berufsbildung *f* (Pw) generic term of the ‚*Berufsbildungsgesetz*' covering 1) occupational or professional training, and 2) all retraining measures
Berufsbildungsgesetz *n* (Pw) Occupational Training Law, of 14 Aug 1969 and variously amended
Berufserfahrung *f*
 (Pw) vocational
 – professional
 – proven ... experience *(eg, several years of ...)*
Berufsfeld *n* (Pw) group of ‚training' occupations
Berufsfreiheit *f* (Re) right to freely choose one's occupation, place of work and place of training, Art. 12 GG
Berufsfortbildung *f* (Pw) training to improve existing skills in the taxpayer's profession or employment, § 10 EStG
Berufsfürsorge *f* (SozV) = (*now*) Berufshilfe
Berufsgefahren *fpl* (Pw) occupational hazards
Berufsgeheimnis *n* (com) professional secrecy (*or* discretion)
Berufsgenossenschaft *f* (SozV) social insurance against occupational accidents
Berufsgliederung *f* (Stat) occupational classifica-

tion *(ie, criteria: a) sex, b) economic sectors, c) social status, d) occupation)*
Berufsgruppe *f*
(Pw) occupational
– professional
– trade ... group
Berufsgruppen-Einteilung *f* (Stat) occupational classification
Berufshaftpflichtversicherung *f* (Vers) professional liability insurance
Berufshandel *m*
(Bö) professional (securities) dealing
– professional trading
Berufshilfe *f* (SozV) training promotion provided by the statutory accident insurance fund
Berufskammer *f* (com) professional organization *(ie, semi-autonomous corporations under public law)*
Berufskodex *m* (com) code of professional guidelines
Berufskrankheit *f* (Pw) industrial *(or* occupational*)* disease
Berufsleben *n* (Pw) working life
berufsmäßige Spekulation *f*
(Bö) professional speculation
– professional stock exchange operations
Berufsorganisation *f* (com) professional *(or* trade*)* association
Berufspflicht *f* (Pw) professional duty
Berufspflichtverletzung *f* (Pw) professional misconduct
Berufspsychologie *f* (Pw) occupational psychology
Berufsrichter *m* (Re) permanent judge
Berufsrisiko *n* (Pw) occupational hazard
Berufsschule *f* (Pw) vocational school *(ie, attended part-time in conjunction with practical apprenticeship)*
berufsständische Vertretung *f* (com) professional representation
Berufsstatistik *f* (Stat) occupational statistics
Berufsstellung *f* (Pw) occupational *(or* professional*)* status
Berufssystematik *f*
(Pw) occupational classification
– structure of occupational groups
Berufsstruktur *f* (Stat) occupational structure *(or* pattern *or* distribution*)*
berufstätig
(Pw) working
– (fml) gainfully employed
Berufstätige *mpl* (Stat) gainfully employed persons
berufstätige Bevölkerung *f* (Stat) gainfully employed population
Berufstätigkeit *f*
(Pw) work
– employment
– occupation
– professional activity
– (fml) gainful employment
Berufsumschulung *f* (Pw) vocational retraining
Berufsunfähigkeit *f* (SozV) occupational disability *(ie, below 50% of capacity, § 1246 RVO)*
Berufsunfähigkeitsrente *f* (SozV) pension for occupational invalidity *(ie, due to decline in earning capacity)*

Berufsunfall *m* (SozV) occupational accident
Berufsunfallversicherung *f* (SozV) occupational accident insurance
Berufsverband *m* (com) professional association
Berufsverbot *n*
(Re) non-admission to a profession
(Re) revocation of the license to practise
Berufsvereinigung *f*
(com) trade association
– professional body
Berufsvertretung *f* (com) representation of professional group
Berufswahl *f* (Pw) choice of occupation
Berufswechsel *m* (Pw) job change
Berufszählung *f* (Stat) occupational census
Berufszuschlag *m* (Vers) added premium for occupational risks
Berufszweig *m* (Pw) line of occupation
Berufung *f*
(Pw) appointment
(Re) appeal *(ie, against judgment, on questions of fact or law)*
Berufung *f* **einlegen**
(Re) to appeal a decision
– to take an appeal *(ie, to a higher or superior court)*
– to appeal against *(ie, a decision)*
Berufungsbeklagter *m*
(Re) appellee
– respondent
(ie, in civil proceedings)
Berufungsfrist *f* (Re) period set aside for appeal
Berufungsgegner *m* (Re) appellee
Berufungsgericht *n* (Re) appellate court
Berufungsinstanz *f* (Re) appellate instance
Berufungskläger *m* (Re) appellant *(ie, in civil proceedings)*
Berufungsmöglichkeit *f* (Re) resort to an appellate court
Berufung *f* **stattgeben** (Re) to allow an appeal
Berufung *f* **verwerfen** (Re) to dismiss *(or* negative*)* an appeal
Berufung *f* **zurückweisen** (Re) to dismiss an appeal
Beruhigungsfrist *f* (Pw) cooling-off period
Berührungspunkt *m* (Math) point of tangency
Beschädigtenrente *f* (SozV) disablement pension *(ie, paid to war veterans if earning capacity is reduced to at least 30%)*
Beschädigter *m* (SozV) disabled person
beschädigte Waren *fpl*
(com) damaged goods
(Zo) goods deteriorated or spoiled *(eg, by accident or force majeure)*
beschaffen
(com) to procure
– to furnish
– to supply
Beschaffenheit *f* (com) quality
Beschaffenheit *f* **der Waren** (Zo) nature of goods
Beschaffenheitsangabe *f* (com) quality description
Beschaffenheitsschaden *m* (SeeV) inherent defect *(or* vice*)*
Beschaffenheitssicherung *f* (com) quality protection *(ie, of merchandise)*

Beschaffenheitszeugnis *n* (com) certificate of inspection
Beschaffung *f*
(MaW, *i. w. S.*) procurement
– resource acquisition
– resourcing *(ie, covers labor, materials, equipment, services, rights, capital)*
(MaW, *i. e. S.*) purchasing
Beschaffung *f* **für die lagerlose Fertigung** (MaW) hand-to-mouth buying
Beschaffung *f* **neuen Fremdkapitals** (Fin) provision of fresh outside finance
Beschaffungsamt *n* (FiW) government purchasing authority *(ie, set up to buy specific requirements)*
Beschaffungsaufgabe *f* (Mk) buying task
Beschaffungsbegleitkarte *f* (MaW) purchase traveler
Beschaffungsbudget *n* (MaW) procurement budget
Beschaffungseinrichtung *f*
(Kart) purchasing organization, § 5 III GWB
– procurement facilities
Beschaffungsermächtigung *f* (MaW) procurement authorization
Beschaffungsforschung *f* (MaW) procurement research *(ie, market study and market survey)*
Beschaffungsfunktion *f* (MaW) procurement function
Beschaffungsgruppe *f* (Mk) buying center
Beschaffungskartell *n* (Kart) buying cartel
Beschaffungskosten *pl*
(MaW) procurement cost
– ordering cost
– cost of acquisition
(MaW, KoR) incidental procurement expense *(eg, freight, cartage, insurance)*
Beschaffungskredit *m* (Fin) buyer credit
Beschaffungsmarkt *m* (Bw) input market
beschaffungsmäßige Verflechtung *f* (Vw) backward linkage
Beschaffungsnebenkosten *pl* (Maw, KoR) incidental procurement cost *(eg, freight, cartage, insurance)*
Beschaffungsplan *m* (MaW) procurement budget
Beschaffungsplanung *f* (MaW) procurement planning *(or budgeting)*
Beschaffungspolitik *f* (MaW) purchasing policy
Beschaffungspreis *m* (MaW) purchase price *(ie, invoice price of goods + expenses incidental thereto; eg, transportation, insurance, packing, customs duties)*
Beschaffungsproblem *n* (OR) procurement problem
Beschaffungsprogramm *n* (MaW) buying *(or* purchasing*)* program
Beschaffungsstatistik *f* (MaW) procurement statistics *(ie, comprises a) external market statistics, b) order statistics, c) purchase statistics)*
Beschaffungsvertrag *m* (FiW) procurement contract
Beschaffungsvollzugsplanung *f* (MaW) detailed procurement planning *(ie, broken down on a quarterly and monthly basis)*
Beschaffungsweg *m* (MaW) procurement channel *(ie, either direct or indirect purchasing: Bezug beim Hersteller od Einkauf beim Handel)*

Beschaffungswert *m* (ReW) acquisition value
Beschaffungswesen *n*
(MaW) purchasing and materials management
– procurement system
(FiW) government procurement
Beschaffungszeit *f*
(MaW) purchasing
– procurement
– inventory
– vendor
– replenishment . . . lead time
– procurement cycle
beschäftigen
(Pw) to employ
– to occupy
Beschäftigte *mpl*
(Pw) employed persons
– employees
– wage and salary earners
Beschäftigte *mpl* **in der Stablinienorganisation** (Pw) staff operatives
Beschäftigtenstand *m*
(Pw) level *(or* volume*)* of employment
(Pw) number of persons employed
Beschäftigung *f*
(Vw, Bw) output
– production volume *(or* level*)*
(KoR) activity
– volume
(Pw) employment
– occupation
(Pw) total number of employees
Beschäftigung *f* **an der Kapazitätsgrenze** (Vw) capacity output *(or* production*)*
Beschäftigung *f* **annehmen** (Pw) to take employment
Beschäftigung *f* **aufnehmen** (Pw) to take up work *(or* employment*)*
Beschäftigungsabweichung *f*
(KoR) activity
– capacity
– idle capacity
– noncontrollable
– volume . . . variance
Beschäftigungsart *f* (Stat) employment category
Beschäftigungsaussichten *fpl*
(Pw) employment prospects *(or* outlook*)*
– job prospects *(or* outlook *or* perspectives*)*
Beschäftigungsbedingungen *fpl*
(Vw) conditions of employment
– employment conditions
Beschäftigungsbereich *m* (KoR) range of activity
Beschäftigungsbescheinigung *f* (Pw) certificate of employment
Beschäftigungschancen *fpl*
(Vw) employment opportunities *(or* prospects*)*
– job opportunities *(or* prospects*)*
Beschäftigungsdauer *f*
(Pw) duration of employment *(or* service*)*
– length of employment *(or* service*)*
Beschäftigungseffekt *m* (Vw) employment effect
Beschäftigungseinbruch *m*
(Vw) drop in economic activity
(Pw) sudden slump in employment

Beschäftigungsengpaß m (Vw) employment bottleneck
Beschäftigungsentwicklung f (Vw) trend in economic activity
(Vw) employment trend
Beschäftigungsförderung f (Vw) promotion of employment (or work)
Beschäftigungsgrad m
(Bw) capacity utilization rate
– degree of capacity utilization
– operating rate
Also:
– activity level
– level (or volume) of activity (or operations or output or production)
– volume point (eg, to run a mill at a high . . .)
Beschäftigungsindex m
(Vw) employment index
(KoR) index of volume
Beschäftigungsindikator m (Vw) employment indicator
Beschäftigungslage f
(Vw) level of employment
– current employment figures
– employment situation
Beschäftigungsland n (StR) country of employment
Beschäftigungsmöglichkeiten fpl (Pw) employment (or job) opportunities
Beschäftigungsniveau n (Vw) level of employment (ie, jobless rate or number of unemployed)
Beschäftigungsort m (Pw) place of employment
Beschäftigungsplanung f (KoR) planning of activity level
Beschäftigungspolitik f
(Vw) manpower policy
(Vw) = Vollbeschäftigungspolitik
Beschäftigungspotential n (Vw) potential labor force
Beschäftigungsprogramm n
(Vw) job creation program
– make-work scheme
– (infml) jobs plan
(ie, spending program to create jobs or to promote employment and increase investment)
Beschäftigungsreserve f (Vw) reserve of potential labor
Beschäftigungsschwankungen fpl (KoR) fluctuations in activity
beschäftigungssichernde Finanzpolitik f (FiW) fiscal policy safeguarding a targeted level of employment
Beschäftigungssituation f
(Vw) employment
– job
– manpower
– labor market . . . situation
Beschäftigungsstand m (Pw) employment level
Beschäftigungsstatistik f (Stat) statistics of employment
Beschäftigungsstruktur f (Vw) pattern of employment (ie, distribution of gainfully employed persons among various sectors or regions of a national economy, either in absolute or percentage terms)

Beschäftigungstheorie f (Vw) theory of income and employment
Beschäftigung f **suchen** (Pw) to look for (or seek) employment
beschäftigungsunabhängige Kosten pl (KoR) standby (or noncontrollable) cost
Beschäftigungsverhältnis n (Pw) employment (relationship)
Beschäftigungsvolumen n (Pw) employment volume (ie, total hours worked)
beschäftigungswirksam (Vw) having a positive impact on employment
Beschau f **der Waren** (Zo) physical inspection of the goods
Bescheid m (Re) administrative decision
Bescheid m **erteilen** (Re) to render an administrative decision
bescheinigen (com) to certify (eg, This is to certify that . . . = Hiermit wird bescheinigt, daß . . .)
bescheinigende Stelle f (com) certifying body
Bescheinigung f
(com) certificate
– ,,to whom(soever) it may concern"
Bescheinigung f **ausstellen** (com) to make out a certificate
Bescheinigung f **beibringen** (com) to submit (or furnish) a certificate
Bescheinigung f **der Ursprungsbezeichnung** (Zo) certificate of designation of origin
Bescheinigung f **der Zollstelle** (Zo) customs certificate
Bescheinigungs- und Zulassungsvorschriften fpl (AuW) certification and approval requirements
Bescheinigung f **über abgabenfreie Verbringung ins Zollgebiet** (Zo) duty-free entry certificate
Bescheinigung f **über die Einfuhr aus einem Nicht-Mitgliedsland** (EG) certificate of import from a nonmember country
Bescheinigung f **über die Wiederausfuhr** (Zo) certificate of re-exportation
Bescheinigung f **über die Wiedereinfuhr** (Zo) certificate of re-importation
Bescheinigung f **über zusätzliche Nämlichkeitszeichen** (Zo) certificate concerning additional identification marks
Bescheinigung f **über zuviel gezahlte Zollgebühren** (Zo) over-entry certificate
Beschläge mpl
(com) hardware
– (GB) fixings
Beschlagnahme f
(Re) attachment (ie, to satisfy the judgment debt)
(Re) arrest (ie, of ship or cargo)
Beschlagnahme f **aufheben** (Re) to set aside an attachment
Beschlagnahmebeschluß m (Re) order of attachment
beschlagnahmefähig (Re) attachable
Beschlagnahmerisiko n (AuW) risk of capture and seizure
Beschlagnahmeverfügung f (Re) warrant of attachment
Beschlagnahmeversicherung f (Vers) capture-risk insurance

beschlagnahmte Forderung *f* (Re) claim attached by a judgment creditor, § 392 BGB
beschleunigte Abschreibung *f* (ReW) accelerated depreciation
beschleunigtes wirtschaftliches Wachstum *n* (Vw) accelerated growth
– forced-draught expansion
beschließen
(com) to adopt (*or* pass) a resolution
(Fin) to declare *(eg, a dividend)*
beschließendes Organ *n* (Re) decision-making body
Beschluß *m*
(Re) decision
– resolution
(eg, passed in a meeting)
Beschlußabteilungen *fpl* (Kart) Deciding Divisions *(ie, of the Federal Cartel Office)*
Beschluß *m* **beantragen** (Re) to sue out a writ
beschlußfähig (com) constituting a quorum
beschlußfähige Anzahl *f* (com) quorum *(ie, taken from the phrase: ‚numerus membrorum quorum praesentia necesse est')*
beschlußfähige Versammlung *f* (com) quorate meeting
Beschlußfähigkeit *f* (com) presence of a quorum
beschlußfähig sein (com) to form a quorum
Beschluß *m* **fassen** (com) to adopt (*or* pass) a resolution
beschlußfassendes Organ *n* (Re) decision-making body
Beschlußfassung *f* (com) adoption (*or* passing) of a resolution
Beschluß *m* **mit einfacher Mehrheit** (com) resolution by simple majority
beschlußreif (com) ready to be voted on
Beschluß *m* **über die Eröffnung des Konkursverfahrens** (Re) order of adjudication in bankruptcy
Beschluß *m* **über Dividendenausschüttung** (Fin) declaration of dividend
Beschlußunfähigkeit *f* (com) absence of quorum
beschneiden
(com) to cut back on
– to pare (down)
– to trim
– to clamp a lid on *(eg, spending)*
beschränkte Deliktsfähigkeit *f* (Re) limited capacity to commit unlawful acts, § 828 BGB
beschränkte Einkommensteuerpflicht *f* (StR) non-residents' income tax liability
beschränkte Geschäftsfähigkeit *f*
(Re) limited capacity to contract
– restricted capacity to transact business
beschränkte Haftung *f* (Re) limited liability
beschränkt einkommensteuerpflichtig (StR) subject to limited taxation of income
beschränkte Konvertibilität *f*
(AuW) limited
– partial
– restricted ... convertibility
beschränkte Meistbegünstigung *f* (AuW) conditional most-favored-nation treatment
beschränkte Nachschußpflicht *f* (Re) limited liability of members to make additional contributions

beschränkte persönliche Dienstbarkeit *f* (Re) limited personal servitude, § 1090 BGB
beschränkter Handel *m* (Bö) restricted trading
beschränkter Markt *m* (com) restricted market
beschränktes Eigentum *n* (Re) qualified ownership
beschränktes Giro *n* (WeR) qualified indorsement
beschränktes Recht *n* (Re) limited right
beschränkte Steuerpflicht *f* (StR) limited tax liability
beschränkte Variable *f* (Math) bounded variable
beschränkte Vollmacht *f* (Re) limited authority
beschränkte Zuständigkeit *f* (Re) limited jurisdiction *(opp, unbeschränkte Zuständigkeit)*
beschränkte Zuteilung *f* (Fin) limited allotment
beschränkt geschäftsfähig
(Re) of limited contractual capacity
– limited in competence to enter into legal transactions, § 8 BGB
beschränkt Geschäftsfähiger *m* (Re) person with limited capacity *(ie, to transact legal business)*
beschränkt haftender Gesellschafter *m* (Bw) limited partner
beschränkt konvertierbar (AuW) limitedly convertible
beschränkt persönliche Dienstbarkeit *f* (Re) easement restricted to the benefit of an individual
beschränkt steuerpflichtig (StR) subject to limited tax liability *(ie, applies to nonresident individuals, § 1 EStG)*
beschränkt Steuerpflichtiger *m*
(StR) non-resident
– person subject to limited taxation
Beschränkung *f*
(com) restriction
(Math) constraint
– restriction
– limiting condition
Beschränkung *f* **ausländischer Investitionen** (AuW) controls over foreign investment
Beschränkung *f* **des Kapitalverkehrs** (AuW) restrictions on capital movements
Beschränkungen *fpl* **auferlegen** (com) to impose restrictions
Beschränkungen *fpl* **aufheben** (com) to lift (*or* remove) restrictions
Beschränkungen *fpl* **verschärfen** (com) to intensify restrictions
Beschränkungsvektor *m* (OR) restriction vector
beschreiben
(com) to describe
– to specify
(EDV) to record
Beschreiben *n* **e-r Spur** (EDV) recording of a track
Beschreibung *f*
(com) description
– account
– report
– specification
(Pat) patent specification
(EDV, Cobol) description
beschriften (com) to inscribe
Beschriftung *f*
(com) inscription
– marking

Beschriftungsschild *n*
(com) placard
– placard strip
– name plate *(ie, of a machine)*
(EDV) marking label
Beschwerde *f*
(Re) appeal
(StR) administrative appeal *(ie, against a decision which rejects the application for administrative relief, § 349 AO)*
Beschwerdeausschuß *m* (Pw) grievance committee
Beschwerdebrief *m* (com) letter of complaint
Beschwerde *f* **einlegen**
(Re) to appeal a decision *(ie, to court)*
– to take an appeal (to)
Beschwerdefrist *f*
(Re) time for bringing an appeal
– time limit for appealing a decision
Beschwerde *f* **führen**
(Re) to appeal a decision
– to lodge an appeal
– to take an appeal *(ie, to a court)*
Beschwerdeführer *m*
(Re) appellant
– complainant
– person filing an appeal
Beschwerdegegner *m*
(Re) appellee
– respondent
Beschwerdegericht *n* (Re) appellate court
Beschwerdegrund *m* (Re) grounds of appeal
Beschwerdeinstanz *f* (Re) appellate instance
Beschwerden *fpl* **nachgehen** (com) to monitor complaints
Beschwerdequote *f* (Pw) rate of grievances
Beschwerderecht *n*
(Re) right of complaint
– right to appeal
Beschwerdeverfahren *n* (Re) complaint proceedings
Beschwerde *f* **verwerfen** (Re) to refuse an appeal
Beschwerde *f* **zurückziehen** (Re) to withdraw an appeal
Beseitigung *f* **der Zölle**
(AuW) abolition of tariffs
– elimination of customs duties
Beseitigung *f* **e-s Rechtsmangels** (Re) removing a deficiency in title
besetzt
(com) busy *(ie, telephone line)*
– (GB) engaged
Besetztzeichen *n*
(com) busy signal
– (GB) engaged tone
Besetzung *f* **e-s Tabellenfeldes** (Stat) cell frequency
Besetzungsproblem *n* (Stat) occupancy problem
Besetzungszahl *f* (Stat) (absolute) frequency
besichern
(Fin) to collateralize
– to supply security for a loan
besichertes Darlehen *n*
(Fin) collateralized loan
– loan against collateral

Besicherung *f*
(Fin) provision of collateral
– collateralization
besichtigen
(com) to examine
– to inspect
(SeeV) to hold survey
Besichtigung *f*
(com) tour of a plant *(=Betriebsbesichtigung)*
(com) drawing samples *(ie, to determine the average quality of goods)*
(Zo) physical inspection of goods
Besichtigungsbericht *m* (SeeV) survey report
Besitz *m*
(com) property *(= im wirtschaftlichen Sinne)*
(Re) possession *(= im rechtlichen Sinne, § 854 BGB)*
(Fin) holding *(ie, of shares and stock = Wertpapierbesitz)*
Besitzanspruch *m* (Re) possessory claim
Besitz *m* **aufgeben** (Re) to surrender possession
Besitzdiener *m* (Re) possessory servant, § 855 BGB *(ie, exercising actual power over a thing for another, but not having possession)*
Besitzeinkommen *n*
(Vw) unearned income
– unearned revenue
– income from property
– property income
besitzen
(com) to own
(Re) to possess
– to hold in possession)
– *(als Vertragsformel)* to have and to hold
Besitz *m* **entziehen** (Re) to dispossess
Besitzentziehung *f*
(Re) dispossession
– divestment
Besitzer *m*
(com) owner
– proprietor
(Re) possessor
– holder
– occupier
Besitzer *m* **auf Lebenszeit** (Re) holder for life
Besitz *m* **ergreifen** (Re) to take possession
Besitzerwerb *m* (Re) obtaining possession
Besitz *m* **erwerben**
(Re) to acquire possession
– to acquire property
Besitzgesellschaft *f*
(Bw) company leasing its fixed assets to a ‚Kapitalgesellschaft' *(ie, frequently in the form of OHG, KG or BGB-Gesellschaft)*
(Bw) holding company (*or* unit)
Besitzkonstitut *n*
(Re, *civil law*) constitutum possessorium *(ie, agreement replacing delivery of movables by indirect possession; eg, in the form of tenancy)*
– constructive possession, §§ 930ff BGB
Besitzloser *m* (Re) nonproperty owner
Besitznachfolger *m* (Re) subsequent holder
Besitzstand *m*
(Re) vested (*or* acquired) rights
– status of possession, § 920 BGB

Besitzstand *m* **wahren** (Pw) to stay even *(eg, union leaders hope . . .)*
Besitzstandswahrung *f* (Re) non-impairment (*or* protection) of vested rights
Besitzsteuern *fpl* (FiW) taxes from income and property
Besitzstörung *f* (Re) unlawful interference with possession, § 862 BGB
Besitzteile *mpl* (com) assets = *Aktiva*
Besitztitel *m* (Re) right to possession
Besitzübertragung *f* (Re) transfer of possession
Besitz- und Verkehrsteuern *fpl* (FiW) taxes on property and transactions
Besitzwechsel *m*
  (ReW) bills (*or* notes) receivables
  – (GB) trade notes receivable
besoldet (Pw) salaried
Besoldung *f* (Pw) salary
Besoldungsgruppe *f* (Pw) pay grade
besondere Ausfuhrabgabe *f* (Zo) special charge on exports
besondere Ausfuhrabschöpfung *f* (Zo) special export levy
besondere Bewertungsvorschriften *fpl* (StR) special valuation rules, §§ 17–124 BewG
besondere Havarie *f*
  (SeeV) particular
  – common
  – petty
  – simple . . . average, § 701 HGB
besonderer Satz *m* (Log) particular statement *(opp, Allsatz, allgemeiner Satz = universal statement)*
besonderes Ausgleichskonto *n* (IWF) Special Settlement Account
Besonderes Schuldrecht *n* (Re) law relating to individual types of obligations *(eg, sale, donation, unjust enrichment, torts, §§ 433–853 BGB)*
Besonderes Wirtschaftsrecht *n* (Re) Particular Law of the Economy *(ie, concerned with the powers of public authorities and their exercise)*
Besorgnis *f* **der Befangenheit**
  (Re) doubt as to impartiality
  – fear of prejudice
  (eg, to challenge a jugde for . . .)
besprechen
  (com) to discuss
  (com) to review *(eg, a book)*
Besprechung *f*
  (com) discussion
  – meeting
  (com) book review
Besprechungsexemplar *n* (com) review copy
Bessel-Verteilung *f* (Stat) Bessel function distribution
Bestand *m*
  (MaW) inventory
  – stock
  (Fin) bank's asset portfolio
  (Vers) portfolio of insurance
  – policies in force
  – in-force business
Bestand *m* **an Aufträgen mit Rückgaberecht** (com) backlog of orders subject to cancellation
Bestand *m* **an fertigen Erzeugnissen** (ReW) inventory of finishd goods

Bestand *m* **an festen Aufträgen** (com) backlog of final orders
Bestand *m* **an unfertigen Erzeugnissen** (ReW) work-in-process inventory
  – work-in-progress inventory
  – in-process inventory
  – inventory of intermediate goods
Bestände *mpl*
  (MaW) inventory
  – inventories
  – stock(s)
  – merchandise on hand
  – stock on hand
  – (GB) stock-in-trade
Bestände *mpl* **an Handelswaren** (com) merchandise inventory
Bestände *mpl* **an Waren** (com) stocks of goods on hand
Bestände *mpl* **auffüllen** (MaW) to replenish inventory
Bestände *mpl* **aufnehmen**
  (ReW) to take inventory (*or* stock)
  – to inventory
Beständeeinheitswert *m* (ReW) inventory unit value
beständelose Beschaffungswirtschaft *f* (MaW) job lot control
Beständerechnung *f*
  (ReW) inventory
  – stocktaking
Beständeschwund *m* (MaW) inventory shrinkage
Bestände-Stückwert *m* (ReW) inventory unit value
Bestände *mpl* **verringern**
  (MaW) to destock
  – to trim inventories
Beständewagnis *n* (ReW) inventory risk
Bestandsabbau *m*
  (MaW) decrease
  – reduction
  – liquidation . . . of inventories
Bestandsänderungen *fpl* (com) change of inventories
Bestandsänderungen *fpl* **an eigenen Erzeugnissen** (VGR) change in inventories
Bestandsänderungsgröße *f* (VGR) change in stocks
Bestandsänderungsrechnung *f* (VGR) statement showing changes in stocks
Bestandsaufbau *m*
  (MaW) increase in inventories
  – replenishment of inventories
Bestandsaufnahme *f*
  (Bw) situation audit
  – position audit
  – corporate appraisal
  – assessment of current position
  (ReW) inventory taking
  – stocktaking
Bestandsband *n* (EDV) master tape
Bestandsbedingungen *fpl* (Vw) stock conditions
Bestandsberichtigungen *fpl* (ReW) inventory adjustments
Bestandsbericht *m* **über Lagervorräte** (MaW) balance-of-stores record
Bestandsbewegung *f* (Vers) changes of business in force

Bestandsbewertung f (ReW) inventory valuation
Bestandsbewertung f **zu Anschaffungs- od Herstellungskosten** (ReW) inventory pricing (*or* valuation) at acquisition or production costs
Bestandsdatei f (EDV) master file
Bestandsdaten pl (ReW) inventory data
Bestandsdifferenz f (ReW) inventory discrepancy *(ie, posted as extraordinary expense)*
Bestandserfolgskonten npl (ReW) mixed accounts *(ie, representing both balance sheet items and revenue or expense items)*
Bestandserhöhung f **der Erzeugnisse** (ReW) increase in product inventories
Bestandsermittlung f (ReW) inventory taking
– stocktaking
Bestandsfortschreibung f (MaW) inventory updating
Bestandsführung f (MaW) inventory management
Bestandsgewinn m (ReW) inventory profit *(ie, excess of one valuation base over another; eg, fifo vs lifo; unavailable for reinvestment or dividend payout)*
Bestandsgröße f (Vw) stock (variable)
Bestandshöhe f
(MaW) amount of inventory carried
– service level
Bestandskarte f
(ReW) balance card
– inventory record card
(EDV) master card
Bestandskartei f (ReW) inventory file
Bestandskonto n (ReW) asset (*or* real) account
Bestandskontrolle f (MaW) inventory control
Bestandsliste f
(ReW) inventory
– stock list
Bestandsmasse f (Stat) point-in-time population *(opp, Bewegungsmasse)*
Bestandsminderung f (MaW) drop in inventories
Bestandsobergrenze f (MaW) maximum inventory level
Bestandspflege f
(Vers) policy service
– conservation of issued insurance
Bestandsprüfer m (MaW) inventory checker
Bestandsprüfung f (MaW) inventory audit
Bestandsrechnung f (VGR) statement of stocks
Bestandsrente f (SozV) existing pension
Bestandsrisiko n (ReW) inventory risk
Bestandssteuerung f (MaW) inventory control
Bestandsüberschuß m (MaW) overage
Bestandsübertragung f (MaW) transfer of stock
Bestandsveränderungen fpl (MaW) inventory changes
Bestandsvergleich m (StR) „simplified" method of net worth comparison *(ie, also called ‚Vermögensvergleich', § 4 I EStG)*
Bestandsverlust m (MaW) inventory shrinkage
Bestandsverwaltung f (MaW) inventory management
Bestandsverzeichnis n
(ReW) inventory (*or* stock) list
(StR) list of fixed assets, Abschn. 31 I EStR *(=*

Verzeichnis der Gegenstände des beweglichen Anlagevermögens)
Bestandswagnis n (ReW) inventory risk
Bestandswesen n (MaW) inventory management
Bestandszuwachs m (MaW) increase in inventories
Bestandteile mpl (Re) components *(ie, objects other than buildings, firmly attached to the realty and including rights attaching to the ownership, such as easements or servitudes, §§ 93, 94, 96 BGB)*
bestätigen
(com) to acknowledge *(eg, receipt of a letter)*
(com) to confirm *(eg, what I told you over the phone)*
(Re) to indorse
– to ratify
– to certify *(eg, this is to certify that... = hiermit wird bestätigt, daß ...)*
bestätigende Bank f (Fin) confirming bank
bestätigter Scheck m (Fin) certified check *(ie, see § 23 BBankG)*
bestätigtes Akkreditiv n (Fin) confirmed letter of credit
bestätigtes unwiderrufliches Akkreditiv n (Fin) confirmed irrevocable letter of credit
Bestätigung f
(com) acknowledgment
– confirmation
(Re) indorsement
– ratification
– validation
– verification
Bestätigung f **des Jahresabschlusses** (ReW) certification of annual financial statements, § 167 AktG
Bestätigungskarte f (Vers) cover note
Bestätigungsmeldung f (EVD) acknowledgment, ACK *(ie, confirming receipt of a message; syn, Rückmeldung)*
Bestätigungsprovision f (Fin) confirming commission
Bestätigungsschreiben n
(com) letter of acknowledgment
– letter of confirmation *(ie, see distinction made under ‚bestätigen')*
Bestätigungsvermerk m
(ReW) auditors' examination certificate, § 167 AktG
– audit certificate (*or* report)
– (US) short-form audit report *(syn, Testat)*
Bestätigungsvermerk m **einschränken** (ReW) to qualify the auditor's certificate
Bestätigungsvermerk m **versagen** (ReW) to refuse the auditor's certificate
Bestattungskosten pl (StR) funeral expenses *(ie, extraordinary burden = außergewöhnliche Belastung for income-tax purposes)*
Bestbeschäftigung f (KoR) optimum level of activity *(syn, Optimalbeschäftigung)*
Bestbietender m (com) highest bidder
beste Anpassung f (Stat) best fit
bestechen
(com) to bribe
– to buy off

- GB, *also*) to buy over
- (infml) to grease

bestechen lassen, sich (com) to take bribes
Bestechung *f* (com) bribery
Bestechungsaffäre *f* (com) bribery affair
Bestechungsgeld *n*
   (com) bribe money
- (corporate) payoff
- improper payments
- (sl) boodle

Besteckindustrie *f* (com) cutlery industry
beste lineare Schätzung *f* (Stat) best linear estimate
Bestellabstand *m* (MaW) ordering interval
Bestellbestand *m*
   (MaW) reorder point
- reordering quantity

Bestellbuch *n* (com) order book
Bestelleingang *m*
   (com) booking of new orders
- incoming business (*or* orders)
- inflow of orders
- intake of new orders
- new orders
- order bookings
- orders received
- rate of new orders *(eg, started to show slight improvement)*

bestellen
   (com) to order
- to place (*or* give) an order for
   (Re) to appoint *(eg, annual auditor)*
   (Re) to create *(eg, a mortgage)*

Besteller *m*
   (com) customer
- buyer
- purchaser

Bestellerkredit *m* (Fin) buyer's credit
Bestellerrisiko *n* (Stat) consumer's risk
bestellfixe Kosten *pl* (MaW) fixed order cost
Bestellformular *n* (MaW) purchase order form
Bestellhäufigkeit *f* (MaW) frequency of ordering (*or* acquisition)
Bestellintervall *n* (MaW) replenishment cycle
Bestellkarte *f* (com) return order card *(ie, in mail order business)*
Bestellkosten *pl* (MaW) ordering costs
Bestelliste *f* (com) list of orders
Bestellmenge *f*
   (MaW) order(ing) quantity
- order size

Bestellmuster *n* (com) sample of goods which are made after receipt of orders *(eg, textiles, wallpaper)*
Bestellnummer *f* (com) purchase order number
Bestellpolitik *f* (MaW) ordering policy
Bestellpraxis *f* (com) system of appointment *(eg, physicians, hair-dressers)*
Bestellproduktion *f* (IndE) make-to-order production
Bestellpunkt *m* (MaW) order point
Bestellpunktsystem *n*
   (MaW) max-min system
- order point system
- fixed-order variable-cycle system *(ie, of inventory control)*

Bestellrhythmussystem *n*
   (MaW) periodic review system
- order cycling system
- fixed-cycle (variable-order) system
- fixed reorder-cycle system *(ie, of inventory control)*

Bestellschein *m* (com) order note *(ie, either contract offer binding customer for some time, or acceptance of contract)*
Bestellsystem *n* (MaW) reorder system
Bestellsystem *n* **mit Fixgrößen**
   (MaW) fixed-order system
- maximum-minimum inventory control

Bestellsystem *n* **mit Intervallüberprüfung** (MaW) periodic inventory review system
bestellt
   (com) on order
- ordered
- booked
   (com) having an appointment *(eg, to see . . .*
   (Re) appointed

Bestelltätigkeit *f* (com) booking (*or* placing) orders
bestellter Vertreter *m* (Re) appointed representative
bestelltes Material *n* (MaW) material on order
Bestellung *f*
   (com) *(auf/über)* order (for)
- purchase order
- customer order
- sales order
   (Re) appointment *(eg, as/to be chairman of the managing board)*

Bestellung *f* **annehmen** (com) to accept an order
Bestellung *f* **aufgeben**
   (com) to order
- to place (*or* give) an order for

Bestellung *f* **ausführen**
   (com) to carry out
- to complete
- to execute
- to fill . . . an order

Bestellungen *fpl* **einschränken** (com) to slash orders
Bestellung *f* **e-r Sicherheit**
   (Fin) collateralization
- provision of security *(ie, for a loan)*

Bestellungsannahme *f*
   (com) acceptance of an order
   (com) acknowledgment of an order

Bestellung *f* **stornieren** (com) to cancel an order
Bestellungsstatistik *f* (com) order statistics
Bestellwert *m* (com) order (*or* contract) value
Bestellwesen *n* (MaW) purchase order processing
bestens
   (Bö) at best
- at market

„bestens" absetzen (Fin) to sell on „best efforts basis" *(ie, securities through banks)*
bestens-Auftrag *m*
   (Bö) discretionary order
- market order
- order at the market
- order to buy at best

„bestens" kaufen (Bö) to buy irrespective of price

bester kritischer Bereich *m* (Stat) best critical region
bester Test *m* (Stat) optimum test
beste Schätzfunktion *f* (Stat) best estimator
beste statistische Maßzahl *f* (Stat) optimum statistic
beste Übereinstimmung *f* (Stat) best fit
besteuerbar
(StR) subject to taxation
– taxable
besteuern
(StR) to tax
– to levy taxes
– to impose taxes
– (GB) to charge (sth) to tax
besteuert (StR) taxed
Besteuerung *f* (StR) taxation
Besteuerung *f* **nach Durchschnittssätzen** (StR) taxation at flat rates, § 23 UStG
Besteuerungseinheit *f* (StR) tax unit
Besteuerungsgegenstand *m* (StR) taxable event
Besteuerungsgrundlagen *fpl*
(StR) basic principles of taxation
(StR) basis of taxation *(ie, all factual and legal elements from which tax liability is derived, § 157 AO)*
Besteuerungsgrundsätze *mpl* (FiW) canons of taxation
Besteuerungshoheit *f*
(StR) power to tax
– taxing power
Besteuerungsunterschiede *mpl* (StR) discrepancies in taxation
Besteuerungsverfahren *n* (StR) tax proceedings
Besteuerungszeitraum *m* (StR) taxable period
Besteuerung *f* **von Wohlfahrtstransfers** (Vw) clawback
bestimmender Teilvorgang *m* (IndE) governing element
bestimmte Geldsumme *f* (WeR) sum certain in money
bestimmter Wert *m* (Math) assigned value
bestimmtes Integral *n* (Math) definite integral
Bestimmtheitsmaß *n* (Stat) coefficient of determination
Bestimmung *f*
(com) use for which an article is intended
(Re) provision
– stipulation
– term
(ie, of a contract)
(Re) regulation
– rule
Bestimmungen *fpl* **für den Aktienhandel** (Bö) trading rules
Bestimmungen *fpl* **über den Zahlungsverkehr** (AuW) exchange arrangements
Bestimmungsbahnhof *m* (com) station of destination
Bestimmungsfaktor *m*
(com) determining factor
(Log) determinant
Bestimmungsflughafen *m* (com) airport of destination
bestimmungsgemäß
(com) in accordance with the intended (*or* appointed) use
(Re) as set down in the contract
– according to the terms of the contract
bestimmungsgemäßer Gebrauch *m* (com) intended (*or* contractual) use
Bestimmungshafen *m* (com) port of destination
Bestimmungskauf *m* (Re) sale subject to buyer's specifications, § 375 I HGB
(ie, usually in the iron and steel, wood, and paper industries)
Bestimmungsland *n* (com) country of destination
Bestimmungsmitgliedsstaat *m* (Zo) Member State of destination
Bestimmungsort *m*
(com) place of destination
– final destination
Bestimmungszollstelle *f* (Zo) office of destination
Bestimmungszone *f* (Zo) destination zone
Bestkauf *m* (com) purchase at lowest price
Bestleistung *f* (KoR) optimum performance *(ie, term used in standard costing)*
bestmöglich absetzen (Fin) to sell on ,,best efforts basis'' *(ie, securities through banks)*
Bestpreis *m* (com) best (*or* highest) price
bestreiken
(Pw) to strike *(eg, a plant)*
– to go on strike *(eg, against a plant)*
Bestreiken *n* **von Drittbetrieben** (Pw) secondary picketing
bestreikter Betrieb *m* (Pw) strike-bound firm (*or* plant)
bestreiten
(com) to pay *(eg, expenses)*
– to defray
(Re) to challenge
– to dispute
Bestreiten *n*
(com) defrayal *(ie, of expenses)*
(Re) contestation
– denial
betagte Forderungen *fpl* (Re) claim maturing at a certain future date, § 54 KO
Betakoeffizient *m* (Stat) beta coefficient
Betaverteilung *f* (Stat) beta distribution
beteiligen (Fin) to give an interest (*or* share) (in)
beteiligen, sich
(com) to participate
– to take part *(eg, in a project)*
(Fin) to acquire an interest (in)
– to take an equity stake
Beteiligung *f*
(Fin) interest
– holding
– stake
– participation
– participating interest (*or* share)
(Fin) equity holding (*or* stake)
– industrial holding
– share of equity capital
(Fin) investment
Beteiligung *f* **abstoßen**
(Fin) to spin off
– to hive off
– to unload ... a stake

Beteiligung f am Gewinn
(Fin) profit share
– share in the profit
Beteiligung f an börsennotierten Unternehmen
(Fin) quoted (*or* listed) investment
Beteiligung f an der Patentverwertung (Pat) interest in patent exploitation
Beteiligungen fpl
(ReW) investments
– equity interests
– (GB) trade investments
(ReW, EG) participating interests
(Fin) investments in subsidiaries and affiliated companies
– shareholdings in outside companies
Beteiligungen fpl an nicht konsolidierten Tochtergesellschaften (Fin) unconsolidated investments
Beteiligungen fpl zum Buchwert (Fin) investments at amortized cost
Beteiligung f erwerben
(Fin) to acquire an interest
– to acquire an equity investment *(eg, in a foreign corporation)*
Beteiligungsbesitz m (Fin) shareholding
Beteiligungscharakter m (Fin) equity feature *(eg, of a loan)*
Beteiligungsdarlehen n (Fin) loan taken up to finance a participation
Beteiligungserträge mpl
(Fin) direct investment income
(ReW) income from investments in affiliates
Beteiligungserwerb m (Fin) acquisition of participations
Beteiligungsfähigkeit f (Re) capacity to participate in proceedings
Beteiligungsfinanzierung f (Fin) equity financing *(ie, supply of share capital by all existing or new members of a company; takes the form of contributions, shares, mining shares, drilling interests, etc.)*
Beteiligungsfonds m (Fin) equity fund
Beteiligungsgeschäft n (Fin) participation transaction *(ie, carried out to secure control or major influence)*
Beteiligungsgesellschaft f
(Bw) associated company *(ie, often restricted to an interest of not more than 50%)*
(Re) holding company
(Fin) investment company
Beteiligungsgewinn m (Fin) investment earnings
Beteiligungs-Investition f
(Fin) direct investment
(Fin) portfolio investment
Beteiligungskapital n
(Fin) outside (*or* equity) capital
(Fin) direct-investment capital
Beteiligungskäufe mpl (Fin) acquisition of shareholdings
Beteiligungspapier n (WeR) equity security
Beteiligungsquote f
(Fin) participation quota
– amount of holding
Beteiligungsrechte npl (Fin) equities
Beteiligungstitel mpl (Fin) equity securities

Beteiligungsveräußerung f (Fin) sale of participation
Beteiligungsverhältnis n (FiW) Federal and Länder portions *(ie, of total tax revenues)*
Beteiligungsvertrag m (Re) contract of participation
Beteiligungswert m (Fin) book value of investment *(ie, in subsidiaries and associated companies)*
Betrag m abbuchen
(com) to debit an amount
– to charge (amount) to an account
Betrag m abheben (com) to withdraw an amount (from)
Betrag m abzweigen (com) to set aside (*or* earmark) an amount
Betrag m anrechnen (com) to credit an amount
Betrag m auszahlen (com) to pay out an amount
betragen
(com) to amount to
– to add up to
– to come to
– to run at
Betragsfeld n (EDV) amount field
Betragsspanne f (Mk) gross margin *(ie, absolute difference between cost price and sales price of an article)*
Betrag m überweisen (Fin) to remit an amount *(ie, through a bank)*
betrauen mit (com) to put in charge of
Betreiben n (IndE) operation
Betreiber m (Bw) operator *(eg, of a plant)*
Betreuungsgebühr f (com) attendance fee
Betrieb m
(Bw) business enterprise
– enterprise
– firm
– undertaking
– company *(see: Unternehmen)*
– (IndE) plant
– operation
(IndE) operation
– running
– working
– duty
(EDV) mode
Betrieb m aufgeben
(Bw) to close
– to discontinue
– to terminate ... a business
– (infml) to shut up shop
Betrieb m aufnehmen
(Bw) to start business
(IndE) to start operations
– to commission
– to take into operation
– to put on stream
Betrieb m der Urproduktion (com) extractive (*or* natural resource) enterprise
Betriebe mpl der Land- und Forstwirtschaft (StR) agricultural establishments, § 34 BewG
Betrieb m einstellen
(com) to shut down shop
– (infml) to put up the shutters
(IndE) to close down a plant

Betrieb *m* **eröffnen**
(com) to open a business
- (infml) to put up shop

Betrieb *m* **für die Eigenfertigung** (Bw) captive shop

Betrieb *m* **gewerblicher Art** (StR) business enterprise of a public corporation *(eg, public utility)*

betriebliche Altersversorgung *f* (Pw) employee pension scheme *(ie, covering old age, disability, and survivors' pensions)*

betriebliche Aufwendungen *mpl*
(ReW) operating cost (*or* expense)
(ReW, EG) operating charges

betriebliche Ausbildung *f*
(Pw) in-plant
- in-service
- industrial
- in-house ... training

betriebliche Bruttoerträge *mpl* (ReW) gross operating revenue

betriebliche Finanzwirtschaft *f* (Fin) business (*or* corporate) finance

betriebliche Fortbildung *f* (Pw) in-plant training

betriebliche Gesamtplanung *f* (Bw) overall corporate planning

betriebliche Instanzen *fpl* (Bw) organizational lines

betriebliche Leistungserstellung *f* (Bw) production process *(ie, turnout of goods and services)*

betriebliche Leistungsfähigkeit *f* (IndE) operating efficiency

betriebliche Lohnsumme *f* (Pw) establishment payroll

betriebliche Mitbestimmung *f* (Pw) codetermination at plant level

betriebliche Pensionskasse *f* (Pw) employer's pension scheme

betriebliche Planung *f* (Bw) company (*or* corporate) planning

betriebliche Prozesse *mpl* (Bw) operations

betrieblicher Ertrag *m* (ReW) operating revenue

betrieblicher Standort *m* (Bw) plant location

betrieblicher Teilbereich *m*
(Bw) department
- division
- group

betriebliche Ruhegeldverpflichtung *f* (Pw) employer's pension commitment

betriebliches Förderwesen *n* (IndE) internal (*or* inplant) transportation

betriebliches Gesamtbudget *n* (Bw) business budget

betriebliches Kommunikationssystem *n* (Bw) organizational communications system

betriebliche Sonderzahlung *f* (Pw) bonus payment

betriebliches Potential *n* (Bw) operational capabilities

betriebliche Steuerlehre *f* (Bw) company tax law

betriebliches Umfeld *n* (Bw) external (*or* business) environment

betriebliches Umsystem *n* (Bw) organizational environment

betriebliches Verantwortungszentrum *n* (Bw) responsibility center

betriebliches Vorschlagswesen *n* (Pw) suggestion system *(ie, through which employees submit ideas for increasing productivity)*

betriebliche Umwelt *f* (Bw) external (*or* business) environment

betriebliche Wohlfahrtseinrichtungen *fpl* (Pw) plant welfare facilities

Betrieb *m* **mit Kundenauftragsfertigung**
(IndE) job shop
- job order plant
- make-to-order plant

Betrieb *m* **mit Lagerfertigung** (IndE) make-to-stock plant

Betriebsablauf *m*
(com) sequence of operations
(IndE) inplant flow of operations

Betriebsabrechnung *f*
(KoR) industrial cost accounting
- operational accounting
- internal accounting

Betriebsabrechnungsbogen *m*
(KoR) expense distribution sheet
- assignment sheet for non-manufacturing cost
- overhead allocation sheet

Betriebsabteilung *f*
(Bw) division
- operating division
- plant division

Betriebsanalyse *f* (Bw) operational analysis

Betriebsänderung *f* (Re) change in plant operation *(ie, closure, restriction, locational shift, object of company, etc.)*

Betriebsangehörige *mpl*
(Pw) employees
- personnel
- staff of a firm

Betriebsanlage *f*
(IndE) (operating) equipment
- facility
- plant

Betriebsanleitung *f* (IndE) operating instructions

Betriebsanweisung *f* (EDV) job control statement

Betriebsart *f* (EDV) operating mode

Betriebsart *f* „**Eingriff**" (EDV) interrupt (*or* hold) mode

Betriebsarten *fpl* (Bw) classification of business enterprises

Betriebsart *f* „**Halten**" (EDV) hold mode

Betriebsart *f* „**Lesen**" (EDV) read mode

Betriebsart *f* „**Pause**" (EDV) reset mode

Betriebsart *f* „**Rechnen**" (EDV) compute (*or* operate) mode

Betriebsart *f* „**Rücksetzen**" (EDV) reset mode

Betriebsart *f* „**Schreiben**" (EDV) write mode

Betriebsarzt *m* (Pw) company physician

Betriebsassistent *m* (IndE) assistant to works manager

Betriebsaufgabe *f* (Bw) termination of a business

Betriebsaufnahme *f*
(Bw) starting business
(IndE) commissioning
- putting on stream
- taking into operation *(eg, a plant)*

Betriebsaufspaltung *f* (StR) split of a unitary enterprise *(ie, into a Besitzunternehmen = property holding unit, usu. in the form of a sole proprietorship or partnership, and a Betriebsunternehmen = operating unit, usu. in the form of a GmbH)*

119

Betriebsaufwand *m* (ReW) operating expense
Betriebsaufwendungen *mpl* (ReW) operating expense
Betriebsausflug *m* (Pw) annual works outing
Betriebsausgaben *fpl* (StR) business expenses, § 4 IV EStG
Betriebsausstattung *f*
(IndE) plant and equipment
– machinery and equipment
betriebsbedingter Aufwand *m* (ReW) operating expense
betriebsbedingter Ertrag *m* (ReW) operating revenue
betriebsbedingtes Kapital *n* (ReW) necessary operating capital *(ie, term used in ‚Grundsätze für das Rechnungswesen' = principles of accountancy)*
Betriebsbedingungen *fpl* (com) operating conditions
Betriebsbegehung *f*
(com) plant inspection
– touring the plant
Betriebsberater *m* (com) management consultant
Betriebsberatung *f* (com) management consulting
betriebsbereit
(IndE) ready to operate
– ready for operation
– ready to go into operation
– in operating (*or* working) order
– operational
Betriebsbereitschaft *f* (IndE) readiness to operate
Betriebsbesichtigung *f*
(com) plant visit
– touring the plant
Betriebsbit *n* (EDV) operation bit
betriebsblind
(com) blunted by habit
– blind to organizational deficiencies
Betriebsblindheit *f* (com) habitual blindness to organizational deficiencies
Betriebsbuchführung *f* (ReW) = *Betriebsbuchhaltung*
Betriebsbuchhalter *m* (KoR) plant accountant
Betriebsbuchhaltung *f*
(ReW) internal cost accounting
– industrial accounting
– factory accounting
Betrieb *m* **schließen**
(com) to go out of business
(IndE) to close down a plant
Betriebscode *m* (EDV) operation code
Betriebsdaten *pl*
(com) operational information
(EDV) production data
Betriebsdatenerfassung *f*
(IndE) production data acquisition
(EDV) industrial data capture
Betriebsdatenrückmeldung *f* (Bw) feedback of operational data
Betriebsdichte *f* (Stat) ratio of number and size of business enterprises to territory or number of population
Betriebseinheit *f* (Bw) operating center (*or* unit)

Betriebseinnahmen *fpl*
(ReW) operating receipts
(StR) business receipts
Betriebseinnahmen *fpl* **aus freiberuflicher Tätigkeit** (StR) business income from independent professional services
Betriebseinrichtungen *fpl*
(IndE) operating (*or* production) equipment
– plant facilities
Betriebseinrichtungskosten *pl* (ReW) expenses for the startup of operations *(ie, may be included under fixed assets, § 153 IV AktG)*
Betriebseinschränkung *f* (com) cutting back of operations
Betriebserfahrung *f* (com) operational experience
Betriebserfindung *f* (Pat) employee invention *(ie, automatically attributed to the owner of an enterprise; now replaced by ‚Diensterfindung')*
Betriebserfolg *m* (ReW) = *Betriebsergebnis*
Betriebserfordernisse *npl* (com) operational requirements
Betriebsergebnis *n*
(ReW) operating result *(ie, either net profit or loss)*
– earnings from operations
– operating income (*or* profit)
– results from operations
– (GB) trading result
Betriebsergebnisquote *f* (Fin) profit ratio
Betriebsergebnisrechnung *f*
(ReW) operating income statement
– operating statement
Betriebserlaubnis *f* (Re) operating license (*or* permit)
Betriebseröffnung *f* (com, StR) opening of a business, § 137 AO
Betriebsertrag *m* (ReW) operating income (*or* revenue)
Betriebserweiterung *f*
(Bw) plant extension
– expansion of plant facilities
betriebsfähig (IndE) in working order
Betriebsfähigkeit *f*
(IndE) operating condition
– working order
Betriebsferien *pl*
(Bw) plant (closure for) holidays
– vacation close-down *(syn, Werksferien)*
betriebsfertig = *betriebsbereit*
Betriebsfinanzamt *n* (StR) tax office in whose district the management of an enterprise or a permanent establishment = *Betriebsstätte* is domiciled, § 18 AO
Betriebsfläche *f* (com) plant area
Betriebsfonds *m* (Bw) operating fund *(ie, capital needed to keep fixed assets employed at a reasonable level; part of necessary current assets = betriebsnotwendiges Umlaufvermögen)*
Betriebsformen *fpl* **des Einzelhandels** (Bw) organizational forms of retail trade
betriebsfremd (ReW) nonoperating
betriebsfremde Aufwendungen *mpl*
(ReW) nonoperating expense
– other expense

betriebsfremde Erträge *mpl*
(ReW) nonoperating revenue
– other revenue (*or* income)
betriebsfremder Aufwand *m*
(ReW) nonoperating expense
– other expense
Betriebsführung *f* (IndE) plant management
Betriebsführungsrechner *m* (EDV) operation control computer
Betriebsführungsvertrag *m* (Re) business management agreement *(syn, Verwaltungsvertrag)*
Betriebsgebäude *n*
(com) factory building
(com) company buildings
Betriebsgefahr *f* (com) operational hazard (*or* risk)
Betriebsgefährdung *f* (Kart) disparagement of competitor, § 14 UWG *(ie, making a false statement about a competitor's business, its management and products)*
Betriebsgeheimnis *n*
(com) business
– trade
– industrial ... secret
Betriebsgemeinde *f* (StR) municipality of employer
Betriebsgemeinkosten *pl*
(KoR) factory overhead
– operating overhead
– factory indirect expense
Betriebsgenehmigung *f* (Re) operating license (*or* permit)
Betriebsgesellschaft *f* (Bw) operating company (*or* unit)
Betriebsgewerkschaft *f* (Pw) company union
Betriebsgewinn *m*
(ReW) earnings from operations
– operating incom (*or* profit)
– earned surplus
– (GB) trading profit
(ie, operating revenue minus operating cost of a period)
betriebsgewöhnliche Nutzungsdauer *f*
(StR) useful life expectancy, § 7 I EStG
– average (*or* useful) life
– asset depreciation range
Betriebsgröße *f*
(Bw) plant size
– scale of plant
Betriebsgrößenvariation *f* (Bw) variation of plant scale *(ie, through quantitative adjustment)*
Betriebsgrundstücke *npl*
(Bw) company premises
– factory-site land
– plant-site land
– land in use as a plant site
(StR) business real property, § 99 BewG
Betriebshaftpflichtversicherung *f* (Vers) business liability insurance *(ie, taken by owner or operator)*
Betriebshandbuch *n* (Pw) company information manual
Betriebshandelsspanne *f*
(com) gross (merchandise) margin
– operating margin
Betriebshierarchie *f* Bw) management structure
Betriebshygiene *f* (Bw) plant hygiene

Betriebsingenieur *m* (IndE) plant engineer
Betriebsinhaber *m* (com) owner (*or* proprietor) of a business
betriebsinterne Abfälle *mpl* (IndE) home scrap *(syn, Rücklaufschrott)*
betriebsinterne Größennachteile *mpl* (Bw) internal diseconomies of scale
betriebsinterne Größenvorteile *mpl* (Bw) internal economies of scale
Betriebsjahr *n*
(com) operating year
– working year
Betriebskapazität *f* (IndE) plant (*or* operating) capacity
Betriebskapital *n*
(com) working capital
(Fin) current operating capital
(ie, in commercial language equal to ‚Umlaufvermögen' = current assets) (Note: Do not confound with ‚working capital' or ‚net working capital' which, being a liquidity ratio, is defined as ‚current assets minus current liabilities'. The term ‚working capital' is either used as a loan word or translated as ‚Liquiditätskoeffizient'.)
Betriebsklima *n* (Pw) organization climate
Betriebskoeffizient *m* (Bw) input-output ratio
Betriebskonfiguration *f* (EDV) operating environment
Betriebskonto *n* (ReW) contra account of internal accounting *(ie, maintained in financial accounting)*
Betriebskosten *pl*
(KoR) operating cost (*or* expense)
– operational cost
– cost of operation
– operationals
– running cost *(eg, wages, rent, taxes)*
Betriebskosten *pl* **bei Unterbeschäftigung** (KoR) partial-capacity operating cost
Betriebskostenkalkulation *f* (Bw, appr) cost effectiveness analysis *(ie, esp. by means of cost center accounting = Kostenstellenrechnung)*
Betriebskostenzuschlag *m* (Vers) loading for expenses
Betriebskrankenkasse *f* (Pw) company (*or* plant) health insurance fund
Betriebskredit *m* (Fin) short-term operating credit *(ie, may take the form of any short-term bank credit)*
Betriebsleistung *f*
(Vw) share of a business enterprise in the overall performance of the economy
(Bw) operating performance *(ie, measured by comparing actual output with maximum output)*
Betriebsleiter *m*
(IndE) plant
– works
– operating ... manager
– (GB) plant superintendent
Betriebsleitung *f* (IndE) plant (*or* factory) management
Betriebsmaterial *n* (IndE) factory supplies
Betriebsmaximum *n* (Bw) maximum capacity
Betriebsminimum *n* (KoR) minimum of variable average costs

121

Betriebsmittel *npl*
(Bw) operating resources *(ie, conceptual counterpart of the term ‚Produktionsmittel' as used in economics)*
(IndE) production facilities
(IndE) operating media
– expendables *(eg, power, water)*
(Fin) operating (*or* working) funds
Betriebsmittelbedarf *m*
(Bw) resource requirements
(Fin) working fund requirements
Betriebsmittelgrundzeit *f* (IndE) equipment base time
Betriebsmittelkredit *m* (Fin) short-term operating credit *(ie, to cover temporary finance requirements; opp, long-term investment credit)*
Betriebsmittelplanung *f* (EDV) resource scheduling
Betriebsmittelrücklage *f* (Fin) operating cash reserve
Betriebsmittelrüstzeit *f* (IndE) machine setup time
Betriebsmittelverbund *m* (EDV) resource sharing
Betriebsmittelverwaltung *f* (EDV) resource management
Betriebsmittelzeit *f*
(IndE) available machine time
– available process time
Betriebsmittelzuschüsse *mpl* (FiW) operating subsidies
Betriebsmittelzuweisung *f*
(FiW) appropriation of operating funds
(EDV) resource allocation
betriebsnotwendiges Kapital *n* (Bw) necessary operating capital
betriebsnotwendiges Vermögen *n* (KoR) necessary business assets
Betriebsobmann *m* (Pw) plant steward *(ie, takes the place of ‚Betriebsrat' in small enterprises, § 9 BetrVerfG)*
betriebsoptimale Ausbringung *f* (Bw) optimum output
Betriebsoptimum *n*
(Bw) ideal (*or* practical) capacity
– optimum scale of operations
(ie, minimum of total average costs)
Betriebsorganisation *f* (Bw) plant organization
Betriebspachtvertrag *m* (Re) company lease agreement, § 292 I No. 3 AktG *(ie, leasing an entire enterprise to another)*
„Betriebspapst" *m* (Pw, sl) „works pope" *(ie, often used by the shop floor to refer to a powerful chairman of a works council at divisional or corporate level)*
Betriebsperiode *f* (OR) busy period
Betriebspersonal *n*
(Pw) personnel
– staff
Betriebspflicht *f* (Re) statutory obligation to operate *(eg, public carriers, utilities)*
Betriebsplanung *f* (Bw) business (*or* corporate) planning
Betriebspolitik *f* (Bw) business (*or* company) policy
Betriebspreis *m* (KoR) product price (*or* value)

used in intra-plant cost allocation *(eg, pricing of semi-finished goods between departments)*
Betriebsprogramm *n* (EDV) operating program
Betriebsprüfer *m*
(StR) government tax auditor
– tax investigator
(ie, term now replaced by ‚Außenprüfer')
Betriebsprüferbilanz *f* (StR) tax auditors' balance sheet *(syn, Prüferbilanz, Prüfungsbilanz)*
Betriebsprüfung *f*
(Zo) external audits
(StR) government tax audit
– tax investigation
(ie, periodic examination by tax auditors, term now replaced by ‚Außenprüfung', § 193 AO)
(EDV) operating test
– dynamic test (*or* check)
Betriebsprüfungsbilanz *f* = *Betriebsprüferbilanz*
Betriebsprüfungsordnung *f* (StR) Regulations on Procedural Rules to be Observed in Tax Examinations, of 27 Apr 1978
Betriebsrat *m*
(Pw) works
– plant
– company
– employee ... council
Betriebsratsvorsitzender *m* (Pw) chairman of works council
Betriebsratswahl *f* (Pw) election of works council members
Betriebsrechner *m* (EDV) plant computer
Betriebsrentabilität *f* (Fin) operating return *(ie, pretax ‚,as if'– kalkulatorisch – operating income to necessary operating capital)*
Betriebsrente *f*
(Pw) business (*or* company) pension
– occupational pension
Betriebsrentengesetz *n* (Pw) Law Relating to Company Pension Plans, of 19 Dec 1974
Betriebsrisiko *n*
(com) business risk
(IndE) operational hazard (*or* risk)
Betriebsschließung *f*
(Bw) factory closure
– plant shutdown
Betriebsschluß *m* (com) closing hours
Betriebsschulden *fpl* (StR) business debt (*or* indebtedness, § 103 BewG) *(opp, Privatschulden)*
Betriebsschwund *m* (com) shrinking number of enterprises
Betriebsselbstkosten *pl* (KoR) net production cost
Betriebsspaltung *f* (StR) = *Betriebsaufspaltung*
Betriebssprache *f*
(EDV) job control language, JCL
– job description language, JDL
(EDV) operating language
Betriebsstätte *f*
(IndE) plant
– operational facility
(StR) permanent establishment, § 12 AO
Betriebsstillegung *f* (Bw) plant closing (*or* closure)
Betriebsstoffe *mpl*
(ReW) supplies
(IndE) factory supplies
– operating supplies

(KoR) expendables
- expendable supplies
- expense material
- single-use items
Betriebsstörung *f*
(IndE) equipment failure
- breakdown
- plant interruption
- stoppage
Betriebsstruktur *f* (Bw) corporate structure
Betriebssystem *n*
(IndE) production system
(EDV) operating system, OS
- executive system
Betriebssystem-Residenz *f* (EDV) operating system residence
Betriebssystem-Stammband *n* (EDV) operating system master tape
Betriebsteil *m* (Bw) operating unit
Betriebsteile *mpl* **ausgliedern** (Bw) to split off (*or* hive off) operations
Betriebsteuer *f* (FiW) operating tax *(ie, discussed under tax reform plans as a means of uniformly taxing all commercial operating profits)*
Betriebstreuhandversicherung *f* (Vers) plant fidelity insurance *(ie, lump-sum insurance protecting employer against losses through employee action)*
Betriebsübergabe *f* (Bw) transfer of an enterprise
Betriebsüberlassungsvertrag *m* (Bw) company surrender agreement, § 292 I No. 3 AktG *(ie, handing over the operation of an entire enterprise to another)*
Betriebsübernahme *f* (Bw) takeover of a business (*or* plant)
Betriebsüberschuß *m*
(ReW) operating surplus
(VGR) operating surplus *(ie, Einkommen aus Unternehmertätigkeit und Vermögen = income from property and entrepreneurship)*
Betriebsübersicht *f* (ReW) condensed tabular statement of balance sheet figures
Betriebs- und Geschäftsausstattung *f* (ReW) office and plant equipment
- furnitures and fixtures
Betriebs- und Geschäftsgeheimnis *n* (Re) business secrecy *(ie, term used in labor law)*
Betriebsunfall *m*
(SozV) industrial
- occupational
- work... accident
Betriebsunkosten *pl* (KoR) overhead cost *(ie, obsolete term for ‚Gemeinkosten')*
Betriebsunterbrechung *f*
(Bw) plant interruption
- (infml) tie-up
Betriebsunterbrechungsversicherung *f* (Vers) business interruption insurance
Betriebsunterlagen *fpl* (com) operational data
Betriebsuntersuchung *f* (Bw) operational analysis *(syn, Betriebsanalyse)*
Betriebsveräußerung *f* (Bw) sale of a business
Betriebsvereinbarung *f* (Pw) plant agreement *(ie, between employer and works council, not permissible to supersede collective agreements)*

Betriebsverfassungsgesetz *n* (Pw) Industrial Constitution Law, of 15 Jan 1972
Betriebsvergleich *m*
(Bw) interfirm comparison
- interplant comparison
- comparative analysis
- external analysis
Betriebsverlegung *f*
(Bw) relocation of a plant
- movement of operations *(eg, into another country)*
Betriebsverlust *m* (ReW) operating loss *(ie, net of nonoperating result)*
Betriebsvermögen *n*
(StR) business capital
- business property
- business assets and liabilities, §§ 95–109 a BewG and § 5 EStG
Betriebsvermögensvergleich *m* (Fin) balance-sheet comparison
Betriebsversammlung *f* (Pw) employee meeting
Betriebsversicherung *f* (Vers) group insurance *(ie, for the benefit of employees)*
Betriebsvertrauensleute *pl* (Pw) shop representatives
Betriebsverwaltungsgemeinkosten *pl* (KoR) administrative overhead
Betriebsvorrichtungen *fpl* (StR) plant facilities, § 68 BewG
Betriebswagnis *n* (Bw) operating risk
Betriebswert *m* (KoR) product price (*or* value) used in intra-plant cost allocation *(eg, pricing of semi-finished goods between departments)*
Betriebswirt *m* (Pw, *roughly*) graduate in business economics
Betriebswirtschaft *f* (Bw) = *Betriebswirtschaftslehre*
betriebswirtschaftlich
(Bw) economic *(eg, merger is absolutely necessary for economic reasons)*
- operational *(eg, aspects)*
- managerial
betriebswirtschaftliche Kennziffern *fpl*
(Bw) ratios
- management ratios
betriebswirtschaftliche Logistik *f* (Bw) industrial logistics
betriebswirtschaftliche Planungsabteilung *f*
(OR) operations research unit
- (GB) operational research unit
betriebswirtschaftlicher Verlust *m* (ReW) operating loss
betriebswirtschaftliches Instrument *n* (Bw) administrative vehicle
betriebswirtschaftliches Risiko *n* (Bw) commercial risk *(opp, economic, political, currency risks)*
betriebswirtschaftliche Statistik *f* (Stat) business statistics
betriebswirtschaftliche Steuerlehre *f* (Bw) business taxation *(ie, as a field of study)*
Betriebswirtschaftslehre *f*
(Bw) ,,business economics" *(ie, business meaning any undertaker of economic activity)*
- science of business management

(Note: There is no exact equivalent in American or British usage)
Betriebswirtschaftspolitik f (Bw) business (*or* company) policy
Betriebswirtschaftsstelle f (IndE) fuel power department
Betriebswissenschaft f
  (Bw) management science
  (Bw) scientific management *(ie, today often referred to as ‚Arbeitswissenschaft' in its wider sense)*
Betriebszeit f (IndE) attended time
Betriebszuschuß m (FiW) operating subsidy (*or* grant)
Betriebszweig m (com) branch of business
Betrieb m **verlegen**
  (Bw) to relocate a plant
  – to move operations
Betrug m (Re) fraud, § 263 StGB
betrügerischer Konkurs m (Re) fraudulent bankruptcy
beurkunden
  (Re) to record
  – to place on record
  – to register
  – to authenticate
beurkundet
  (Re) authenticated
  – evidenced
  – recorded
  – registered
  – certified
Beurkundung f
  (Re) authentication
  – (judicial or notarial) recording
Beurlaubung f
  (Pw) furlough *(eg, part of a company's workforce)*
  (Pw) suspension from office
Beurteilender m (Pw) rater
Beurteilter m (Pw) ratee
Beurteilung f **durch Gleichgestellte** (Pw) peer rating
Beurteilung f **durch Untergebene** (Pw) rating by subordinates
Beurteilungsgespräch n (Pw) appraisal interview
Beurteilungskriterien npl (Pw) appraisal factors
Beurteilungszeitraum m (Pw) period of appraisal
Bevölkerungsaufbau m (Stat) population structure
Bevölkerungsdichte f (Stat) density of population
Bevölkerungsdruck m (Vw) population pressure
Bevölkerungsexplosion f (Vw) population explosion
Bevölkerungsfalle f (Vw) population trap *(ie, in developing countries)*
Bevölkerungsgruppe f (Stat) segment of the population
Bevölkerungsmodell n (Stat) demographic model
Bevölkerungspolitik f (Vw) population policy *(ie, seeking to affect the birth rate)*
Bevölkerungspyramide f (Stat) age pyramid
Bevölkerungsschicht f
  (Stat) social stratum
  – demographic stratum
Bevölkerungsstatistik f (Stat) demographic (*or* vital) statistics *(ie, concerning the maintenance of population)*
Bevölkerungsstruktur f (Stat) population structure
Bevölkerungsüberschuß m (Stat) surplus population
bevollmächtigen
  (com) to authorize
  – to empower
  (Re) to appoint (someone) attorney-in-fact
  – to grant power of attorney
bevollmächtigt
  (com) authorized
  – empowered
  (Re) invested with (*or* having) power of attorney
Bevollmächtigter m
  (com) authorized person
  – proxy *(ie, authorized to act at a meeting of stockholders)*
  (Re) attorney-in-fact
  – duly authorized agent (*or* representative)
bevollmächtigter Vertreter m (Re) authorized representative
Bevollmächtigung f
  (Re) authorization *(ie, delegation of power enabling another to act as agent or attorney)*
  (Re) power of attorney *(ie, instrument authorizing such agent or attorney-in-fact)*
bevorraten
  (Vw) to stockpile
  – to stock up
Bevorratung f
  (Vw) stockpiling
  – building up of stocks
bevorrechtigen (Re) to grant privileges (*or* preferences)
bevorrechtigte Forderung f
  (Re) preferred claim (*or* debt)
  – preferential claim
  – prior charge
bevorrechtigter Gläubiger m
  (Re) preferred
  – preferential
  – privilege
  – secured
  – senior ... creditor
Bevorrechtigung f
  (Re) preference
  – privilege
  – priority
bevorschussen (Fin) to advance money
Bevorschussung f (Fin) advancement of funds
bevorstehend
  (com) forthcoming
  – upcoming *(eg, negotiations)*
  (Vw) oncoming *(eg, recession)*
bevorzugte Annahmegrenze f (Stat) preferred average quality level
bevorzugte Befriedigung f (Re) preferential payment
bevorzugte Behandlung f (com) preferential treatment
Bevorzugung f (com) preferential treatment
bewährte Technologie f (IndE) proven technology
Bewährungsaufstieg m (Pw) automatic progression

Bewältigung f strategischer Probleme (Bw) strategic issue management
Bewässerungsprojekt n (com) irrigation scheme
bewegliche Gegenstände mpl (Re) movable objects
bewegliche Güter npl (Re) movable goods
bewegliche Kosten pl (KoR) variable cost
bewegliche Sachanlagen fpl (Bw) non-real-estate fixed assets
bewegliche Sache f
  (Re) movable (or personal) property
  – personal estate (or chattel)
  – personalty
bewegliche Sachen fpl (Re) movables
bewegliches Anlagevermögen n (Bw) non-real-estate fixed assets
bewegliches Vermögen n (Re) movable property
bewegliche Wirtschaftsgüter npl (Bw) movable assets
bewegte Konten npl (ReW) active accounts
Bewegungsbilanz f
  (Fin) flow statement
  – flow of funds analysis
  – statement of application of funds
  – statement of sources and application of funds
  – statement of changes in financial position
  – sources-and-uses statement
Bewegungsdatei f
  (EDV) amendment
  – change
  – activity
  – transaction ... file
  (syn, Änderungsdatei, Fortschreibungsdatei)
Bewegungsdaten pl (EDV) transaction data (ie, used to update a file)
Bewegungsgrundelement n (IndE) elemental movement
Bewegungshäufigkeit f (EDV) activity ratio
Bewegungskomponenten fpl (Stat) movements (ie, in time series)
Bewegungsmasse f (Stat) period-based population (syn, Ereignismasse; opp, Bestandsmasse)
Bewegungsökonomie f
  (IndE) motion economy
  – economy in human movements
Bewegungsstudie f
  (IndE) motion study
  – motion analysis
Bewegungs-Zeit-Studie f (IndE) time and motion study
Beweis m
  (Log, Math) proof
  – demonstration
  (Re) proof
  – evidence
Beweisantrag m
  (StR) submission of evidence
  – evidence submitted by the parties, § 76 I FGO, § 88 AO
Beweis m **antreten**
  (Re) to furnish evidence
  – to offer proof
Beweis m **des ersten Anscheins** (Re) prima facie evidence
Beweis m **des ersten Anscheins erbringen** (Re) to establish a prima facie case

Beweise mpl **erheben** (Re) to take evidence
Beweiskette f (Log) chain of evidence
Beweiskraft f (StR) probative force, § 158 AO (eg, of an inventory)
Beweiskraft f **e-r Urkunde** (Re) inherent (or internal) evidence of a legal instrument
beweiskräftige Unterlage f (Re) substantiating document
Beweislast f (Re) burden (or onus) of proof
Beweismittel n (Re) evidence
Beweisregel f (Log) rule of inference
Beweisurkunde f (WeR) instrument of evidence
Beweisvermutung f (Re) evidentiary presumption
Beweiswert m (Re) evidentiary value
bewerben, sich (Pw) to apply for (ie, job, position, vacancy; to a company)
Bewerber m
  (Pw) (job) applicant
  (Pw) job candidate
Bewerbung f (Pw) job application (syn, Stellengesuch)
Bewerbungsschluß m (Pw) closing date of/for an application
Bewerbungsschreiben n (Pw) letter of application
bewerten
  (com) to appraise
  – to assess
  – to evaluate
  – to value
Bewertung f
  (com) appraisal
  – evaluation
  – valuation
  (ReW) valuation
Bewertung f **aufgrund des gezahlten Preises** (Zo) valuation on the basis of the price paid
Bewertung f **des Materialverbrauchs** (KoR) costing of material usage
Bewertung f **des Vertriebsplanes** (Mk) marketing plan evaluation
Bewertung f **des Vorratsvermögens** (ReW) inventory valuation
Bewertung f **e-r Unternehmung als Ganzes** (Bw) valuation of an enterprise as a whole
Bewertung f **für Zollzwecke** (Zo) customs valuation
Bewertung f **nicht notierter Aktien** (Fin) valuation of unlisted (or unquoted) shares
Bewertungsabschlag m (StR) downward valuation adjustment, § 80 EStDV (ie, relating to certain current assets supplied from abroad)
Bewertungsabschreibung f (ReW) valuation of an asset below the last-preceding balance-sheet valuation (ie, as a rule, down to the lower going-concern value)
Bewertungsänderung f (ReW) valuation adjustment
Bewertungsaufgabe f (EDV) benchmark problem
Bewertungsbasis f (ReW) basis of valuation
Bewertungsbeirat m (StR) advisory council set up to determine the values of agricultural model enterprises (ie, attached to the Federal Ministry of Finance, §§ 39 I, 63–66 BewG)
Bewertungsdifferenzen fpl (ReW) valuation variances (ie, important correcting items in operating statements)

Bewertungseinheit f (StR) separate valuation unit, § 2 BewG
Bewertung f **selbsterstellter Erzeugnisse** (ReW) product costing
Bewertungsfachmann m (Bw) appraiser
Bewertungsfreiheit f
(StR) freedom of choice in the valuation of assets
– discretionary valuation
Bewertungsgebühr f (com) appraisal fee
Bewertungsgesetz n (StR) Valuation Law, of 10 Dec 1965
Bewertungsgrößen fpl (Bw) factors of evaluation
Bewertungsgrundlage f
(com) basis of value
(ReW) basis of valuation
– valuation basis
Bewertungsgrundsatz m
(ReW) standard of valuation
(StR) standard of value, § 9 BewG
Bewertungskonglomerat n (ReW) valuation mix *(ie, consolidation balance sheet based on different valuation standards; eg, commercial code, stock corporation law)*
Bewertungskontinuität f (ReW) continuity of valuation
Bewertungsmaßstab m (ReW) standard of valuation *(eg, fair market value, going concern value, etc.)*
Bewertungsmatrix f (OR) value matrix
Bewertungsmethoden fpl **für Zollzwecke** (Zo) customs valuation techniques
Bewertungsrecht n (StR) law regulating the valuation of property
Bewertungsskala f (Log) rating scale
Bewertungsstichtag m (StR) effective valuation date, § 106 BewG
Bewertungsstützpunkte mpl (StR) index figures determined to assure equality of valuation, § 39 I BewG *(ie, based on operating conditions and results of representative agricultural enterprises)*
Bewertungsüberschuß m (ReW) appraisal (*or* appreciation) surplus
Bewertungs- und Gliederungsvorschriften fpl (ReW) rules of valuation and classification
Bewertungsunterlagen fpl (com) valuation data
Bewertungsunterschied m (ReW) valuation variance
Bewertungsverfahren n (ReW) valuation method (*or* procedure)
Bewertungsverstoß m (ReW) infringement of valuation rule
Bewertungsvorschrift f (ReW) valuation rule
Bewertungswahlrecht n
(ReW) option to choose cost or market valuation
(StR) freedom of choice in the valuation of assets
– discretionary valuation
Bewertung f **und Erfolgsermittlung** f
(ReW) principles of evaluating balance sheet items and of determining results *(ie, als theoretisches Sachgebiet)*

Bewertung f **von Büroarbeiten** (Pw) clerical work evaluation
Bewertung f **zu Durchschnittspreisen** (ReW) average cost method
Bewertung f **zu festen Verrechnungspreisen** (ReW) standard cost method
Bewertung f **zum Niederstwertprinzip** (ReW) valuation at the lower of cost or market
Bewertung f **zum Wiederbeschaffungspreis** (ReW) valuation at replacement cost
bewilligen (FiW) to appropriate
bewilligte Mittel pl
(FiW) appropriations
– appropriated funds
Bewilligung f (FiW) appropriation
Bewilligung f **des aktiven Veredelungsverkehrs** (Zo) authorization granting the benefit of the inward processing arrangements
Bewilligungsausschuß m (FiW) appropriations committee
Bewilligungsinhaber m (Zo) holder of the authorization
Bewilligungszeitraum m (FiW) appropriation period
bewirtschaften (Vw) to control
bewirtschaftete Währung f (AuW) controlled currency
Bewirtschaftung f (Vw) control
Bewirtungskosten pl (StR) entertainment expenses
beworbener Artikel m (Mk) advertised article
bewußte Auswahl f (Stat) purposive sample *(ie, today often used as a quota sample)*
bewußte Fahrlässigkeit f
(Re) intentional negligence
– *(civil law)* luxuria
bewußt gewählte Stichprobe f (Stat) purposive sample
bezahlen (com) to pay
bezahlte Freizeit f (Pw) time off with pay
bezahlter Jahresurlaub m (Pw) annual vacation with pay
bezahlter Urlaub m
(Pw) paid holidays (*or* leave)
– vacation with pay
Bezahlt-Kurs m (Bö) price agreed upon
bezahlt machen, sich (com, infml) to pay for itself
bezahlt und Geld
(Bö) buyers ahead
– dealt and bid
Bezahlung f (com) payment
bezeichnen
(Log) to denote
– to name
– to designate
(com) to mark
Bezeichner m (EDV Cobol) identifier
Bezeichnung f (Log) term *(see also: ‚Begriff')*
Bezeichnung f **e-r Erfindung** (Pat) title (*or* designation) of an invention
Bezeichnungsweise f (Log) terminology
beziehen
(com) to buy
– to purchase
(Pw) to draw *(ie, wages or salary)*

Bezieher *mpl* **fester Einkommen** (Vw) persons on fixed income
Beziehungskauf *m* (com) direct purchase *(ie, bypassing the retailing trade)*
Bezirksdirektion *f* (Vers) district management
Bezirksdirektor *m* (Vers) district manager
Bezirksfiliale *f* (Vers) regional main office
Bezirksfinanzdirektion *f* (StR) regional tax office
Bezirksleiter *m* (Pw) district leader *(ie, second-tier union functionary)*
Bezirksvertreter *m* (com) agent to whom a certain district or group of customers is assigned, § 87 II HGB
bezogene Bank *f*
 (Fin) bank drawn upon (*or* as drawee)
 – drawee bank
Bezogener *m* (WeR) drawee *(syn, Trassat)*
bezogene Teile *npl* (MaW) purchased components
Bezug *m*
 (MaW) buying
 – purchase
 – procurement *(ie, goods, merchandise)*
 (com) subscription *(ie, of regular publications, such as newspapers, periodicals)*
Bezüge *pl*
 (Pw) pay *(ie, the most general word)*
 – earnings
 – salary
 – (fml) remuneration
 – (fml) emoluments *(ie, may include fringe benefits)*
Bezugnahme *f* (com) reference
Bezug *m* **neuer Aktien** (Fin) allocation of new shares
Bezugsadresse *f* (EDV) base (*or* reference) address *(syn, Basisadresse, Grundadresse)*
Bezugsaktien *fpl* (Fin) preemptive shares *(ie, resulting from a conditional capital increase, §§ 192ff AktG)*
Bezugsangebot *n*
 (Fin) rights offer
 – offer of new shares
Bezugsaufforderung *f* (Fin) request to exercise option right
Bezugsband *n* (EDV) standard tape
Bezugsbasis *f* (Stat) benchmark (*or* reference) figures
Bezugsbedingungen *fpl*
 (com) terms and conditions of sale
 (Fin) terms of subscription
bezugsberechtigt (Fin) entitled to subscribe
Bezugsberechtigter *m*
 (Re) beneficiary *(ie, of a foundation)*
 (Fin) allottee *(ie, person entitled to new shares)*
 (Vers) beneficiary *(ie, of an insurance policy)*
Bezugsberechtigung *f* (Vers) appointment of beneficiary
Bezugsbescheinigung *f* (Fin) allotment certificate
bezugsfertiges Gebäude *n* (com) building ready for use
Bezugsfrist *f* (Fin) time limit for subscription
Bezugsgenossenschaft *f* (com) agricultural purchasing cooperative
Bezugsgröße *f* (KoR) reference figure
 (SozV) basic amount, § 18 SGB IV *(ie, average compensation of all workers and salaried employees in the penultimate calendar year, rounded up to the next higher amount which is divisible through 600)*
Bezugsgröße *f* **des Währungssystems** (AuW) numéraire
Bezugsgrößenkalkulation *f* (KoR) costing on the basis of reference figures, independent of the production method used
Bezugskalkulation *f* (Mk) cost price estimate *(ie, in retail trading)*
Bezugskante *f* (EDV) document reference edge
Bezugsklasse *f* (Stat) reference class
Bezugskosten *pl* (KoR) delivery costs
Bezugskurs *m* (Fin) stock subscription price *(ie, mostly in percent of par value)*
Bezugsland *n*
 (AuW) supplying country
 (AuW) customer country
Bezugsmarke *f* (EDV) benchmark
Bezugsmaß *n* (Stat) basic size *(ie, in quality control)*
Bezugsobligationen *fpl* (Fin) bonds with stock subscription rights
Bezugsoption *f*
 (Bö) call
 – call option
 – option to buy new shares (*or* stock)
Bezugsperiode *f* (Stat) reference period
Bezugspflicht *f* (com) obligation to buy
Bezugspreis *m*
 (com) price of delivery
 (Fin) subscription price
Bezugspunkt *m* (EDV) benchmark *(ie, reference point from which measurements can be made)*
Bezugsquelle *f* (com) supply source
Bezugsquellenverzeichnis *n* (com) trade directory (*or* register)
Bezugsrahmen *m* (Log) frame of reference
Bezugsrecht *n*
 (Fin) subscription right
 – stock right
 Also:
 – right
 – preemptive (*or* preemption) right
 – stock purchase warrant
 (Vers) right to life insurance benefits
Bezugsrecht *n* **auf neue Aktien**
 (Fin) option on new stock
 – stock option
 – stock subscription right
Bezugsrecht *n* **ausgeübt** (Fin) ex rights
Bezugsrecht *n* **ausüben** (Fin) to exercise (*or* take up) an option
Bezugsrechte *npl* **auf Dividendenwerte** (Fin) subscription rights to dividend-bearing securities, § 19 III KVStG
Bezugsrechtsabschlag *m* (Fin) subscription ex rights
Bezugsrechtsangebot *n* (Fin) rights offering
Bezugsrechtsankündigung *f* (Fin) announcement of rights issue
Bezugsrechtsausgabe *f* (Fin) rights issue
Bezugsrechtsausübung *f* (Fin) exercise of subscription rights

Bezugsrechtsemission *f*
(Fin) rights issue
− capitalization issue
Bezugsrechtshandel *m* (Bö) trading in subscription rights
Bezugsrechtskurs *m* (Fin) subscription price
Bezugsrechtsobligation *f* (Fin) option bond
Bezugsrechtsschein *m* (Fin) subscription warrant
Bezugsrechtsstichtag *m* (Fin) record date
Bezugssperre *f* (Kart) refusal to buy, § 26 GWB
Bezugsstelle *f* (Fin) subscription agent
Bezugstermin *m*
(com) date fixed for moving into a building
(Fin) date of delivery *(ie, of shares)*
Bezugsverhältnis *n* (Fin) exchange (*or* subscription) ratio
Bezugsvertrag *m*
(Re) continuous purchase contract
− open-end contract
(ie, extends over a longer period of time)
Bezugswert *m*
(Stat) base
(com) reference value
(Fin) security carrying subscription rights
Bezugszeitpunkt *m* (Fin) initial date *(eg, in preinvestment analysis)*
Bezugszeitraum *m* (Stat) base period
BGB-Gesellschaft *f*
(Re) civil-law association
− company constituted under civil law
− civil-code company
− (US, *roughly*) non-trading partnership
(ie, company constituted under German civil law, §§ 705–740 BGB; syn, Gesellschaft des bürgerlichen Rechts)
Bibliothek *f* (EDV, Cobol) library
Bibliothek *f* **ladbarer Programme** (EDV) core image library
Bibliotheksband *n* (EDV) library tape
Bibliotheksplatte *f* (EDV) library disk
Bibliotheksprogramm *n* (EDV) library program (*or* routine)
Bibliotheksunterprogramm *n* (EDV) library subroutine
Bibliotheksverwaltungsprogramm *n*
(EDV) librarian (program)
− library maintenance program
bichromatischer Graph *m* (Math) bipartite graph
Biersteuer *f* (StR) beer tax
bieten
(com) to bid
− to make (*or* submit) a bid
− to offer
Bieten *n* (com) bidding *(ie, at an auction)*
Bieter *m* (com) bidder
Bietproblem *n* (OR) bidding problem
Bietungsgarantie *f*
(com) bid bond
− earnest money
− proposal bond
− provisional deposit
(ie, furnished by a bank, esp. in public invitations to bid)
Bietungskonsortium *n* (com) bidding syndicate

Bikonditional *n*
(Log) biconditional
− equivalence
(ie, binary propositional connective = 2-stelliger Funktor der Aussagenlogik, ,,if and only if", ,,iff")
Bilanz *f*
(ReW) balance sheet
− annual financial stament
− year-end financial statement
− (GB) annual accounts
(ie, comprehensive term: includes balance sheet, profit and loss statement, and other related documents)
Bilanzanalyse *f*
(ReW) balance sheet
− financial statement
− statement ... analysis
Bilanzänderung *f* (StR) alteration of a balance sheet, Abschn. 4 II EStR *(ie, one permissible entry in the financial statements is replaced by another permissible entry)*
Bilanzanlage *f* (ReW) balance sheet supplement
Bilanzansatz *m*
(ReW) balance sheet item (*or* figure)
(ReW) recording of a balance sheet item
(ReW) valuation of a balance sheet item
Bilanzaufbereitung *f* (ReW) reshuffling of balance-sheet items for the purpose of detailed analysis
Bilanz *f* **auf Nettoliquiditätsbasis** (AuW) net liquidity balance
Bilanz *f* **aufstellen** (ReW) to prepare a balance sheet
Bilanzaufstellung *f* (ReW) preparation of a balance sheet
Bilanzausgleichsposten *m* (ReW) balance sheet adjustment item
Bilanzausschuß *m* (Bw) financial audit committee *(ie, on managing boards)*
Bilanzauswertung *f*
(ReW) evaluation of a balance sheet
− balance sheet evaluation
Bilanzauszug *m*
(ReW) condensed balance sheet
− summarized balance sheet
Bilanzbereinigung *f* (ReW) balance sheet adjustment
Bilanzbericht *m* (ReW) notes added to the balance sheet
Bilanzberichtigung *f* (StR) correction of a balance sheet, Abschn. 4 I EStR *(ie, either by taxpayer or by the local tax office)*
Bilanzbewertung *f* (StR) balance sheet valuation *(ie, valuation of business assets for purposes of income determination, § 6 EStG)*
Bilanzbuch *n* (ReW) balance sheet book
Bilanzbuchhalter *m* (ReW) accountant qualified to prepare balance sheets
Bilanzdelikt *n* (Re) balance sheet offense, § 400 AktG
Bilanz *f* **der laufenden Posten**
(AuW) balance on current account
− current account
− balance of payments on current account

– balance on goods, services, and remittances
(See note under ‚Leistungsbilanz')
Bilanz f der offiziellen Reservetransaktionen (VGR) balance on official reserve transactions *(ie, foreign exchange balance + official liabilities to foreign currency authorities)*
Bilanz f der unentgeltlichen Leistungen (AuW) balance on unilateral transfers
Bilanz f der unsichtbaren Leistungen (VGR) invisible balance
– balance on services account
Bilanz f des kurzfristigen Kapitalverkehrs (VGR) balance on short-term capital account
Bilanz f des langfristigen Kapitalverkehrs (VGR) balance on long-term capital account
Bilanz f des Warenhandels (VGR) visible balance
– balance on merchandise account
Bilanzebene f (Vw) budget surface
Bilanzentwurf m (ReW) draft balance sheet
Bilanz f e-r AG (ReW) corporate statement
Bilanzergebnis n
(ReW) net result (for the year)
– balance sheet profit or loss
Bilanzergebnisvortrag m (ReW) undistributed net result of prior year
Bilanzerläuterungen fpl (ReW) balance sheet notes
Bilanz f e-r Muttergesellschaft (ReW) parent company balance sheet *(ie, consolidating the subsidiaries into ‚investment in subsidiaries')*
Bilanz f erstellen (ReW) to prepare a balance sheet
Bilanzfälschung f (ReW) falsification of a balance sheet, § 400 AktG
Bilanz f frisieren (ReW, infml) to cook *(or* doctor) a balance sheet
Bilanzfrisur f (ReW, infml) window dressing
Bilanzgerade f
(Vw) budget (constraint) line
– opportunity curve
– price line
Bilanzgewinn m
(ReW) net profit for the year, § 157 AktG
Also:
– unappropriated retained earnings
– net income shown in the balance sheet
Bilanzgleichung f
(Vw) budget equation *(ie, for the household)*
(ReW) accounting equation
– accounting identity
– balance sheet equation
– fundamental accounting equation
Bilanzgliederung f (ReW) layout of balance sheet
Bilanzhochrechnung f (ReW) balance sheet extrapolation
Bilanzidentität f (ReW) identity between closing balance sheet of the current year and opening balance sheet of the following year
bilanzielle Abschreibung f
(ReW) depreciation for reporting purposes
– balance sheet depreciation expense
– bookkeeping allowance for depreciation
– accounting provision for depreciation *(opp, steuerliche Abschreibung)*
bilanzieren
(ReW) to balance *(ie, an account)*

(ReW) to prepare a balance sheet
(ReW) to report *(ie, in the balance sheet)*
Bilanzierung f
(ReW) balancing of an account
(ReW) preparation of a balance sheet
Bilanzierungsgesetzgebung f (ReW) accounting legislation
Bilanzierungsgrundsatz m der kaufmännischen Vorsicht (ReW) principle of prudence
Bilanzierungsgrundsätze rnpl (ReW) accounting principles *(or* rules)
Bilanzierungshandbuch n (ReW) manual of accounting
Bilanzierungspolitik f
(ReW) practice of balance sheet make-up
– financial presentation practice
Bilanzierungsrichtlinien fpl (ReW) rules for the preparation of balance sheets
Bilanzierungsvorschriften fpl (ReW) statutory provisions relating to the make-up of balance sheets
Bilanz f in Matrizenform (ReW) matrix balance sheet
Bilanzjahr n (ReW) financial *(or* fiscal) year
Bilanzkennzahl f (ReW) balance sheet ratio
Bilanzklarheit f (ReW) principle of unambiguous presentation of balance sheet items
Bilanzkontinuität f (ReW) continuity of balance sheet presentation
Bilanzkonto n (ReW) balance sheet account
Bilanzkritik f (ReW) critical appraisal *(or* evaluation) of balance sheet
Bilanzkurs m
(ReW) book value *(ie, of assets)*
(Bö) value of a corporate share *(ie, ratio of reported equity to stated capital = ausgewiesenes Eigenkapital zu Grundkapital)*
bilanzmäßige Abschreibung f (ReW) = *bilanzielle Abschreibung*
Bilanzmaterial n (ReW) balance sheet material
bilanzoptisch (ReW) for window-dressing purposes
Bilanzpolitik f (ReW) accounting policy
Bilanzposition f (ReW) balance-sheet item *(or* title)
Bilanzposten m (ReW) balance sheet item
Bilanzprüfer m
(ReW) balance sheet auditor, § 162 AktG
– independent auditor
– *(often simply)* auditor
Bilanzprüfung f (ReW) statutory balance sheet audit, §§ 162–169 AktG
bilanzrechtliche Vorschriften fpl (ReW) accounting regulations
Bilanzreform f
(ReW) balance sheet reform *(ie, attempts to combine the tax and commercial balance sheets into a single balance sheet = ‚Einheitsbilanz')*
(ReW) rearrangement of the corporate balance sheet classification
Bilanzrelationen fpl (ReW) balance sheet ratios
Bilanzrevision f (ReW) internal balance sheet audit *(ie, detailed voluntary audit of balance sheet and profit and loss statement)*
Bilanzsanierung f (ReW) balance sheet restructuring

Bilanzschema *n* (ReW) balance sheet classification, § 151 AktG
Bilanzstatistik *f* (ReW) balance sheet statistics
Bilanzsteuerrecht *n* (StR) statutory provisions relating to the preparation of tax balance sheets
Bilanzstichtag *m* (ReW) balance sheet date
Bilanzstruktur *f* (ReW) balance sheet structure
Bilanzsumme *f* (ReW) balance sheet total
Bilanzsumme *f* **verlängert sich** (ReW) balance sheet totals increase
Bilanz *f* „**über Kreuz**" (ReW) matrix balance sheet
bilanz- und finanzpolitische Abschreibung *f* (ReW) policy depreciation
– in-lieu depreciation
Bilanzvergleich *m* (ReW) comparison of balance sheets
Bilanzverkürzung *f* (ReW) balance sheet contraction *(ie, reduction on both sides of a balance sheet)*
Bilanzverlängerung *f* (ReW) balance sheet extension *(ie, rise on both sides of a balance sheet)*
Bilanzverlust *m* (ReW) net loss for the year
Bilanzvermerk *m* (ReW) balance sheet note
Bilanz *f* **verschleiern** (ReW) to cook *(or* doctor*)* a balance sheet
Bilanzverschleierung *f* (ReW) doctoring a balance sheet
Bilanzvolumen *n* (ReW) balance sheet total
Bilanzvorlage *f* (ReW) presentation of a balance sheet
Bilanzwahrheit *f* (ReW) true and correct presentation of balance sheet items
Bilanzwert *m* (ReW) value of a balance sheet item *(ie, determined on the basis of all applicable commercial and tax valuation rules)*
Bilanz *f* **ziehen** (com) to strike a balance
Bilanzzusammenhang *m* (ReW) continuity of balance sheet presentation
bilateral (Vw) bilateral *(opp, multilateral)*
bilaterale Interventionspunkte *mpl* (AuW) bilateral exchange limits
bilateraler Beistand *m* (EG) bilateral assistance
bilateraler Handel *m* (AuW) bilaterial *(or* two-way*)* trade
bilateraler Strukturdialog *m* (Vw) bilateral discussions on structural policy measures
bilateraler Zahlungsverkehr *m* (AuW) bilateral settlements
bilaterales Clearing *n* (AuW) bilateral clearing
bilaterales Handelsabkommen *n* (AuW) bilateral trade agreement
bilaterales Länderkontingent *n* (AuW) negotiated bilateral quota
bilaterales Monopol *n* (Vw) bilateral monopoly
bilaterales Oligopol *n* (Vw) bilateral oligopoly
bilaterales Verrechnungsabkommen *n* (AuW) bilateral clearing agreement
bilaterale Verträge *mpl* (Re) bilateral agreements *(ie, mostly based on the reciprocity principle)*
Bilateralismus *m* (AuW) bilateralism
Bildfernsprechverkehr *m* (EDV) video telephone service
bildliche Darstellung *f* (Stat) visual portrayal
Bildmenge *f* (Math) image set
Bildplatte *f* (EDV) videodisc

Bildschirm *m* (EDV) display screen
Bildschirmarbeitsplatz *m* (EDV) video workstation
Bildschirmcomputer *m* (EDV) video computer
Bildschirmgerät *n* (EDV) visual display unit *(syn, Sichtgerät)*
Bildschirmtelefon *n* (EDV) video telephone
Bildschirmterminal *n* (EDV) visual display terminal
Bildschirmtext *m* (EDV) videotext
Bildschirmtext-Dienst *m* (EDV) videotext service
Bildungschancen *fpl* (Pw) educational opportunities
Bildungsgang *m* (Pw) educational background
Bildungsinvestition *f* (Vw) investment in the educational system
Bildungsökonomie *f* (Vw) economics of education
Bildungsregel *f* (Log) rule of formation
Bildung *f* **steuerfreier Rücklagen** (ReW) accruals – non taxable
Bildungsurlaub *m* (Pw) educational leave
Bildungswesen *n* (Pw) training and education system
Bildung *f* **von Rücklagen** (ReW) formation *(or* setting-up*)* of reserves
Bildwerbung *f* (Mk) pictorial advertising
billige Flaggen *fpl* (Re) flags of convenience *(ie, Panama, Honduras, Liberia; benefits: tax preferences and subsidies)*
Billigeinfuhren *fpl* (AuW) cut-price imports
billige Produkte *npl* (com) low-priced products
billiges Geld *n* (Vw) cheap money
Billigflugpreise *mpl* (com) cut-price fares *(ie, of airlines)*
Billigimporte *mpl* (com) cut-price imports
Billigkeit *f* (Re) equity
Billigkeitsentscheidung *f* (Re) decision ex aequo et bono
– equitable decision
Billigkeitserlaß *m* (StR) equitable tax relief, § 227 AO
Billigkredit *m* (Fin) cheap loan
Billigpreisgeschäft *n* (Mk) cut-price store
Billigpreisländer *npl* (AuW) low-price countries
billigst
(Bö) at best
– at market
billigst-Auftrag *m* (Bö) buy order at market
billigstens kaufen (Bö) to buy at the lowest price
billigster Anbieter *m* (com) lowest bidder
Billigst-Gebot *n* (com) lowest bid *(ie, bid with no indication of price = „Gebot ohne Angabe e–s Bietungskurses')*
Billigst-Order *f* (Bö) order to buy at the lowest possible price
Billigtarif *m*
(com) cheap fare
– cut-price fare *(eg, of airlines)*
Billigung *f* (Re) approval
Bimetallismus *m* (Vw) bimetalism *(ie, currency system where the monetary unit – Währungseinheit – is defined in two metals; eg, gold and silver)*
bimodale Verteilung *f* (Stat) bimodal distribution
Binärcode *m* (EDV) binary code

Binärcode m für Dezimalziffern (EDV) binary coded decimal, BCD
binär codierte Dezimaldarstellung f (EDV) binary coded decimal representation *(syn, BCD-Darstellung)*
binär codierte Dezimalziffer f (EDV) binary coded decimal, BCD
binär codiertes Zeichen n (EDV) binary coded character
Binärdaten pl (EDV) binary-coded data
Binär-Dezimal-Umwandlung f (EDV) binary-to-decimal conversion
binäre Arithmetik f (EDV) binary arithmetic *(ie, in which the operands are binary numbers)*
binäre Ausgabe f (EDV) binary output
binäre Datencodierung f (EDV) binary data coding
binäre Prüfziffer f (EDV) check bit
binärer Dezimalcode m (EDV) binary-coded decimal code
binärer Fehlererkennungscode m (EDV) binary error detecting code
binärer Funktor m (Log) binary connective
binärer Halbaddierer m (EDV) binary half adder
binärer Speicherabzug m (EDV) binary dump
binäres Addierwerk n (EDV) binary adder
binäre Schreibweise f (EDV) binary notation *(or representation)*
binäres Komplement n (EDV) complement on two
binäres Programm n (EDV) binary program
binäres Suchen n
(EDV) binary search *(or chop)*
– dichotomizing
(syn, dichotomische Suche)
binäres Zeichensystem n (EDV) binary character system
binäre Variable f (EDV) binary variable *(ie, can have one of two values, 0 or 1; can contain a binary number)*
Binärkomma n (EDV) binary point
Binärlochkarte f (EDV) row binary card
Binärmuster n (EDV) bit configuration (or pattern)
Binäroperation f (EDV) binary arithmetic operation *(syn, dyadische Verknüpfung)*
Binäroperator m (EDV) binary operator
Binärsignal n (EDV) binary signal
Binärspalte f (EDV) binary column
Binärstelle f (EDV) binary digit
Binärsuche f (EDV) binary search
Binärzahl f (EDV) binary number
Binärzähler m (EDV) binary counter *(syn, Dualzähler)*
Binärzeichen n (EDV) binary character
Binärzeichenfolge f (EDV) bit string *(or stream) (syn, Bitkette)*
Binärzelle f (EDV) binary cell *(ie, storage element able to represent one binary digit)*
Binärziffer f (EDV) binary digit *(or numeral) (usu. abbreviated to ‚bit')*
Bindeglied n (EDV) link
Bindeglieder npl (OR) linking pins *(ie, between systems of groups)*
bindende Abmachung f
(Re) binding agreement
– agreement binding upon the parties

bindendes Angebot n (com) binding *(or firm)* offer
bindendes Schiedsgerichtsverfahren n (Re) binding adjudication
bindende Wirkung f (Re) binding effect
bindende Zusage f (Re) binding promise
Binder m
(EDV) linkage editor
– composer
Binderlauf m (EDV) linkage run
Bindungsermächtigung f (FiW) commitment authorization
Bindungsvektor m (Math) constraint vector
Bindung f **von Entwicklungshilfe an Auflagen** (Vw) aid tying
Bindung f **von Geldmitteln** (Fin) appropriation *(or earmarking)* of funds
Bindung f **von Währungen** (Vw) linking of currencies *(eg, to the US-$)*
Binnenfischerei f (com) freshwater fishery
Binnengewässer npl (Re) inland *(or internal)* waters
Binnengrenze f (Zo) internal frontier
Binnengroßhandel m (com) domestic wholesaling
Binnenhafen m (com) inland port
Binnenhandel m (Vw) domestic *(or internal)* trade
Binnenkaufkraft f (Vw) domestic purchasing power
Binnenklassen-Korrelation f (Stat) intra-class correlation
Binnenklassen-Streuung f (Stat) intra-class variance
Binnenkonjunktur f
(Vw) domestic economic situation *(or trend)*
– domestic activity
Binnenkonnossement n (com) inland waterway bill of lading
Binnenmarkt m
(com) domestic market
– home market
(EG) internal market
Binnenmarktpreis m (Zo) domestic price
Binnenmarktpreise mpl **des Ausfuhrlandes** (Zo) internal prices in a country of exportation
Binnennachfrage f (Vw) domestic demand
Binnenschiffahrt f (com) inland waterway transportation
Binnenschiffahrtunternehmen n (com) inland waterway carrier
Binnenschiffahrtverkehr m (com) inland waterway traffic *(or transportation)*
Binnenschiffahrtversicherung f (Vers) inland waterway insurance
Binnenschiffer m (com) inland waterway operator
Binnentarif m
(com) inland rate
(com) domestic tariff
(EG) intra-bloc tariff
Binnentransportversicherung f (Vers) inland marine insurance
Binnenumsätze mpl (StR) internal turnovers *(ie, between divisions of the same enterprise or several enterprises owned by the same person)*
Binnenverkehr m (com) internal traffic
Binnenversand m (Zo) interior transit
Binnenwährung f (Vw) domestic currency

Binnenwanderung f (Stat) internal migration
Binnenwasserstraßen fpl (com) inland waterways
Binnenwert m **e-r Währung** (Vw) internal value of a currency
Binnenwirtschaft f (Vw) domestic economy
binnenwirtschaftliche Lage f (Vw) domestic situation
binnenwirtschaftliche Notwendigkeiten fpl (Vw) domestic requirements
binnenwirtschaftlicher Einkommensmultiplikator m (Vw) national income multiplier
binnenwirtschaftlicher Geldwert m (Vw) domestic (or internal) value of money
binnenwirtschaftliches Gleichgewicht n
  (EG) internal economic equilibrium
  – (GB) domestic economic equilibrium
binnenwirtschaftliche Stabilität f (Vw) internal economic stability
Binnenzoll m
  (Zo) internal tariff
  – (GB) internal customs duty
Binnenzollamt n (Zo) inland customs office
Binnenzollsatz m (EG) internal rate of duty
Binnenzollstelle f (Zo) inland customs office
binomiale Grundgesamtheit f (Stat) binomial population
Binomialkoeffizient m (Math) binomial coefficient
Binomialverteilung f (Math) binomial distribution
  – point binomial
  – Bernoulli distribution
Binomialwahrscheinlichkeit f (Stat) binomial probability
binomische Reihe f (Math) binomial series
binomischer Lehrsatz m (Math) binomial theorem
BIP n **zu Marktpreisen** (VGR) GDP *(gross domestic product)* at market prices
biquadratische Gleichung f
  (Math) biquadratic equation
  – quartic equation
Biquinärcode m (EDV) biquinary code *(ie, used to represent each decimal digit)*
bis auf weiteres (com) until further notice
bistabile Kippschaltung f (EDV) bistable multivibrator
  – flipflop circuit
  – Eccles-Jordan circuit
bistabile Kippstufe f (EDV) bistable circuit
  – binary pair
  – flip-flop circuit
bistabile Multivibratorschaltung f
  (EDV) bistable multivibrator
  – Eccles-Jordan circuit (*or* mulivibrator)
  – flip-flop circuit
  – trigger circuit
Bisubjunktion f
  (Log) biconditional
  – equivalence
  (ie, binary propositional connective = ,2-stelliger Funktor der Aussagenlogik', ,,if and only if", ,,iff")
Bisubtraktion f (Math) symmetric difference of sets
Bit n
  (EDV) bit
  – binary digit
Bitdichte f (EDV) bit density

Bitebene f (EDV) digit plane
Bitfehlerwahrscheinlichkeit f (EDV) bit error probability
Bitgeschwindigkeit f (EDV) bit rate *(syn, Übertragungsgeschwindigkeit)*
Bitkette f (EDV) bit string (*or* stream) *(syn, Binärzeichenfolge)*
Bitmuster n (EDV) = *Binärmuster*
Bitposition f (EDV) bit location (*or* position) *(syn, Bitstelle, Bitadresse)*
bitseriell (EDV) bit serial
bitte wenden
  (com) over
  – (GB) p.t.o. *(= please turn over)*
Bitversatz m (EDV) skew
Bitzahlprüfung f (EDV) bit check
b-Komplement n (Math) complement on b
Blankett n
  (com) document signed in blank
  (WeR) blank form
Blankoabtretung f (Re) assignment in blank
Blankoakzept n
  (WeR) acceptance in blank
  – blank acceptance
blanko akzeptieren (WeR) to accept in blank
Blankoannahme f
  (WeR) acceptance in blank
  – blank acceptance
Blankoauftrag m (com) blank order
blanko ausstellen (com) to make out in blank
Blankoformular n (com) blank form
Blankogeschäft n (Bö) uncovered transaction
blanko girieren (WeR) to indorse in blank
Blankoindossament n
  (WeR) blank (*or* general) indorsement
  – indorsement in blank *(opp, Vollindossament)*
blanko indossiert (WeR) blank indorsed
Blankokarte f (EDV) blank (*or* dummy) card *(syn, Leerkarte)*
Blankokredit m
  (Fin) blank credit
  – clean credit
  – open (book) account
  (ie, not secured by documents or credit commitment)
Blankoofferte f (com) offer in blank
Blankopapiere npl (WeR) blank instruments *(ie, not yet bearing the name of the beneficiary or other essential details)*
Blankopolice f (Vers) blank policy
Blankoquittung f (com) blank receipt
Blankoscheck m (Fin) blank check
blanko übertragen (Re) to assign in blank
Blankoübertragung f (WeR) transfer in blank
Blankounterschrift f (com) blank signature
Blankoverkauf m (Bö) short sale
blanko verkaufen (Bö) to sell short
Blankoverkäufer m (Bö) short seller
Blankovollmacht f (Re) blank (*or* unlimited) power of attorney
Blankowechsel m (WeR) blank bill
Blankozession f
  (Re) assignment in blank
  – blank assignment
Blankstahl m (com) bright steel

blaß (Pw) unassertive
Blasenchip *m* (EDV) bubble chip
Blasenspeicher *m* (EDV) bubble memory
Blattleser *m* (EDV) document reader *(syn, Belegleser)*
Blattschreiber *m* (EDV) page printer
Blaupausen-Export *m* (com) export of patents, licenses, engineering documentations, etc.
blendfreie Tastatur *f* (EDV) nonglare keyboard
blendfreie Tasten *fpl* (EDV) glare-free keys *(ie, of typewriter)*
Blickfang *m* (Mk) attention getter
Blindanweisung *f* (EDV) null statement
blind buchen (com) to book blind *(eg, from single advertisement)*
Blitzprogramm *n* (com) crash programm
„Blitzprüfung" *f* (StR) lightning check
blitzschnelle Entscheidung *f* (com) split second decision
Blitzstreik *m* (Pw) lightning strike
Blitzumfrage *f* (Mk) snap poll
Block *m*
  (EDV) block *(syn, group of records treated as an individual unit)*
  (EDV) physical record
  – tape block
Blockadresse *f* (EDV) block address
Blockanfangsadresse *f* (EDV) block start address
Blockdiagramm *n* (Stat) block diagram
Blockdiagrammsymbol *n* ‚Entscheidung' (EDV) decision box
blocken (EDV) to block
Blocken *n* (EDV) blocking *(ie, combination into blocks)*
Blockende *n* (EDV) end of block
Blockendesicherungszeichen *n* (EDV) cyclical redundancy check character
Blockendezeichen *n* (EDV) end-of-block signal
Blockfaktor *m* (EDV) blocking factor
Blockfehlerrate *f* (EDV) block error rate
Blockfloaten *n*
  (AuW) block floating
  – common float
  – joint float
Blockformat *n* (EDV) block format
Blockierpatent *n* (Pat) blocking-off patent
Blockierung *f* **von Vermögenswerten** (Vw) freezing of assets
Blocklänge *f* (EDV) block length
Blocklücke *f* (EDV) = *Blockzwischenraum*
Blockmarke *f* (EDV) block mark
Blockmultiplexkanal *m* (EDV) block multiplex channel
Blockpolice *f* (Vers) ticket policy
Blockposten *m* (Fin) block *(eg, of shares or bonds)*
Blockprüfung *f*
  (ReW) block check
  (EDV) longitudinal (redundancy) check *(syn, Längssummenprüfung, Längsprüfung)*
Blockprüfzeichen *n* (EDV) longitudinal (redundancy) check character, LRC
Blocksicherung *f* (EDV) cross checking *(syn, Kreuzsicherung)*
Blocksortierung *f* (EDV) block sort
Blocksuche *f* (EDV) block search

Blocktransfer *m* (EDV) block transfer
Blockübertragung *f* (EDV) = *Blocktransfer*
Blockungsfaktor *m* (EDV) blocking factor *(ie, number of records in a block)*
Blockungültigkeitszeichen *n*
  (EDV) block cancel character
  – block ignore character
blockweiser Datentransfer *m* (EDV) burst mode
blockweise Übertragung *f* (EDV) = *Blocktransfer*
Blockzwischenraum *m* (EDV) block
  – interblock
  – interrecord
  – recording ... gap
  – interblock space
  (syn, Blocklücke, Kluft)
B-minus-1-Komplement *n* (EDV) radix-minus-one complement
Bocksprungtest *m* (EDV) leapfrog test
Bodenbeschaffungsplan *m* (Vw) land-acquisition program
Bodenbonitierung *f* (com) appraisal of farm land
Bodenertrag *m* (Vw) return to land
Bodenertragsgesetz *n* (Vw) law of diminishing *(or* non-proportional) returns to land
Bodenkredit *m* (Fin) mortgage *(or* land-secured) credit
Bodenkreditinstitut *n*
  (Fin) real estate credit institution
  – land mortgage bank
Bodenpreis *m* (com) land price
Bodenrente *f* (Vw) ground rent
Bodensatz *m*
  (Fin) deposit base
  – permanent average balances
Bodensatzarbeitslosigkeit *f* (Vw) hard-core unemployment *(syn, Restarbeitslosigkeit)*
Bodensatz *m* **eigener Akzepte** (Fin) working inventory
Bodenschätze *mpl* (Vw) natural resources
Bodenschätzung *f* (com) appraisal of farm land
Bodenschätzungsgesetz *n* (Re) Law on the Appraisal of Farm Land, of 16 Oct 1934
Bodenspekulation *f* (com) speculation in real estate
Bodentransport *m* (com) surface transport *(opp, air transport)*
Bodenwertzuwachssteuer *f* (FiW) land-value tax
Bodmerei *f*
  (SeeV) bottomry
  – gross adventure *(ie, repealed on 21 June 1972)*
Bodmereibrief *m*
  (Re) bill of adventure
  – bottomry bond
  – maritime loan
Bodmereigelder *npl* (com) loans on bottomry
Bogen *m*
  (com) sheet of paper
  (Fin) coupon sheet *(ie, sheet made up of dividend coupons)*
Bogenanschlag *m* (Mk) bill advertising *(opp, Daueranschlag)*
Bogenelastizität *f* (Vw) arc elasticity
Bogenerneuerung *f* (Fin) renewal of coupon sheets
Bon *m* (com) cash register slip
Bona-Fide-Klausel *f* (Fin) bona fide clause *(ie, part of a commercial letter of credit)*

Bonifikation f
(com) bonus
– premium
(ie, paid to agents in wholesaling or in the insurance industry)
(Fin) agency commission *(ie, between banks)*
Bonität f
(com) credit standing
– credit worthiness
– financial standing
(Vw) quality of farm land
Bonitätsprüfung f (Fin) credit investigation *(or review) (ie, relating to capacity, capital, conditions)*
(ReW) examination of debtors' financial standing *(ie, part of annual audit)*
bonitieren (com) to classify and appraise soil
Bonitierung f (com) classification and appraisal of soil
Bonus m
(com) bonus
– premium
(Vers) extra *(or* special) dividend
Boole-Operator m
(EDV) Boolean *(or* logical) connective
– logical operator
(syn, boolescher Operator)
boolesche Algebra f
(Log, Math) algebra of logic
– Boolean algebra
boolesche Komplementierung f
(EDV) Boolean complementation
– negation
– NOT operation *(syn, Negation)*
boolesche Menge f (Math) symmetric difference
boolesche Operation f (EDV) Boolean operation *(syn, boolesche Verknüpfung)*
boolescher Befehl m (EDV) logical instruction
boolescher Elementarausdruck m
(EDV) logical element
– gate
boolescher Operator m
(EDV) Boolean connective *(or* operator)
– logical connective *(or* operator)
boolescher Primärausdruck m (Math) logical primary
boolescher Term m (Math) logical term
boolescher Verband m (Math) Boolean lattice
boolescher Wert m (EDV, Cobol) logical value
boolesche Variable f (Math) Boolean variable
boolesche Verknüpfung f (EDV) Boolean operation *(syn, boolesche Operation)*
Bordbescheinigung f (com) mate's receipt
Bordcomputer m (EDV) vehicle-borne computer
Bordkonnossement n
(com) on board bill of lading
– on board B/L
– ocean bill of lading
– shipped bill of lading
Borel-Menge f (Stat) Borel set
Borel-meßbare Funktion f (Stat) Borel measurable function
Börse f
(Bö) exchange
(Bö) stock exchange = *Effektenbörse*

(Bö) commodity exchange = *Warenbörse*
(Note that stock exchanges on the Continent are often called ,Bourses' by the British; eg, Paris Bourse)
Börsenabrechnung f (Bö) stock exchange settlement
Börsenabschluß m
(Bö) stock market transaction
– (GB) bargain
Börsenabschlußeinheit f (Bö) full *(or* regular) lot
Börsenagent m (Bö) bank's stock exchange agent *(or* representative)
Börsenaufsicht f (Bö) stock exchange supervision
Börsenaufsichtsbehörde f
(Bö) stock market supervisory authority
– (US) Securities and Exchange Commission, SEC
Börsenauftrag m (Bö) stock exchange order
Börsenausschuß m (Bö) stock exchange committee
Börsenbedingungen fpl (Bö) stock exchange rules
Börsenbericht m
(Bö) stock exchange report
– market report
Börsenbesucher mpl (Bö) groups of persons having access to the stock or commodity exchanges
Börsenbewertung f
(Bö) market assessment *(eg, of equities)*
– stock market rating
Börsenblatt n
(com) German book trade gazette *(ie, ,Börsenblatt des deutschen Buchhandels')*
(Bö) stock exchange gazette
Börseneffekten pl (Bö) securities traded on the stock exchange
Börseneinführung f (Bö) admission to official listing *(or* quotation)
Börseneinführungsgebühr f (Bö) stock exchange admission fee
Börseneinführungsprospekt m (Bö) prospectus
Börseneinführungsprovision f
(Fin) commission charged for stock exchange admission
– listing commission
Börsenengagement n (Bö) stock exchange commitment
Börsenerholung f (Bö) stock market rally
Börseneröffnung f (Bö) opening of the stock exchange
Börsenfachmann m (Bö) stock exchange *(or* trading) specialist
börsenfähige Aktie f (Bö) marketable share
börsenfähige Wertpapiere npl (Bö) stock exchange securities
Börsenfähigkeit f
(Bö) marketableness
– qualification for trading on the stock exchange
Börsenflaute f (Bö) dullness of the market
börsengängig
(Bö) marketable
– listed *(or* traded) on the stock exchange
börsengängige Papiere npl (Bö) marketable *(or* stock exchange) securities
Börsengeschäft n
(Bö) stock market transaction
– (GB) bargain

Börsengesetz n (Re) German Stock Exchange Law (ie, as amended in 1975)
Börsenhandel m (Bö) stock exchange trading
Börsenhändler m (Bö) stock exchange trader (ie, Angestellte von Unternehmen mit Händlerbefugnis)
Börsenhausse f (Bö) bull market
Börsenindex m (Bö) stock exchange index
Börsenklima n (Bö) market climate (or sentiment)
Börsenkommissionsfirma f (Bö) commission brokers
Börsenkonsortium n (Bö) stock exchange syndicate
Börsenkrach m (Bö) stock exchange collapse (or crash)
Börsenkredit m (Fin) bank loan for financing stock exchange dealings
Börsenkurs m
(Bö) stock exchange price (or quotation)
– market price
– list price (of a security)
– officially quoted price
Börsenmakler m (Bö) stock (exchange) broker
börsenmäßiger Handel m (Bö) stock exchange trading
börsenmäßig gehandelte Waren fpl (Bö) commodities (or goods) dealt in on an exchange
Börsenmitglied n (Bö) member of a stock exchange
börsennotiert (Bö) listed (or quoted) on the stock exchange
börsennotiertes Unternehmen n (Bö) quoted company
börsennotierte Wertpapiere npl
(Bö) listed securities
– quoted investments
– on-board securities
Börsennotierung f (Bö) exchange quotation (or listing)
Börsennotiz f (Bö) quotation
Börsen- od Marktpreis m
(ReW) current market price
– exchange or market value
Börsenordnung f (Bö) stock exchange rules
Börsenorgane npl (Bö) stock exchange authorities
Börsenpapiere npl (Bö) quoted (or listed) securities
Börsenparkett n (Bö) floor
Börsenpflichtblatt n (Bö) authorized journal for the publication of mandatory stock exchange announcements
Börsenplatz m (Bö) stock exchange
Börsenpreis m
(Bö) exchange price (or quotation)
– market price
Börsenprospekt m (Bö) prospectus
Börsenrecht n (Re) law governing stock exchange transactions
Börsenrendite f (Bö) stock market yield
Börsenschiedsgericht n (Bö) exchange arbitration tribunal
Börsenschluß m
(Bö) close of stock exchange
– market close
(Bö) lot
– trading unit
Börsensitz m (Bö) exchange seat

Börsensitzung f (Bö) trading session
Börsenspekulant m
(Bö) stock exchange speculator
– stag
Börsenspekulation f (Bö) stock exchange speculation
Börsensprache f (Bö) stock exchange jargon
Börsenstimmung f (Bö) tone (or mood or sentiment) of the market
Börsenstunden fpl (Bö) official (or trading) hours
Börsentag m (Bö) trading day
Börsentendenz f (Bö) stock market trend
Börsentermingeschäft n
(Bö) forward exchange transactions
– trading in futures
Börsenterminhandel m
(Bö) forward trading
– trading in futures
Börsenticker m (Bö) tape
Börsentransaktion f
(Bö) stock exchange transaction
– (GB) bargain
Börsenumsätze mpl
(Bö) stock exchange turnover
– value of trading
– sales figures
Börsenumsatzsteuer f
(StR) exchange turnover tax
– stock exchange transfer tax
– (GB) stamp duty on stock exchange transactions
(ie, imposed on the acquisition – other than the original issuance – of certain securities for a consideration, § 17 KVStG)
börsenumsatzsteuerfrei (StR) exempt from exchange turnover tax
Börsenusancen fpl (Bö) stock exchange usages
Börsenverkehr m (Bö) stock exchange dealings (or transactions)
Börsenvertreter m (Fin) bank's representative at a stock exchange
Börsenvolumen n (Bö) volume of securities traded
Börsenvorstand m (Bö) managing committee of the stock exchange
Börsenwert m
(ReW) market value
(Fin) market capitalization (ie, Kurswert e-r Kapitalgesellschaft)
Börsenwerte mpl (Bö) quoted securities
Börsenzeiten fpl (Bö) trading hours
Börsenzeitung f (Bö) stock exchange journal
Börsenzettel m
(Bö) list of quotations
– stock list
Börsenzulassung f (Bö) admission (of securities) to the stock exchange
Börsenzulassung f **beantragen** (Bö) to apply for official quotation
Börsenzulassungsausschuß m (Bö) listing committee
Börsenzulassungsprospekt m (Bö) prospectus
Börsenzulassungsverfahren n (Bö) listing procedure
Börsenzwang m (Bö) stock exchange monopoly (ie,

bars securities trading outside official stock exchanges)
Börse f schließen (Bö) to suspend trading
Börsianer m
  (Bö) stock exchange
  – market
  – bourse ... operator
böser Glaube m
  (Re) bad faith
  – mala fides
bösgläubig (Re) in bad faith, §§ 932 ff BGB
bösgläubiger Besitzer m (Re) possessor in bad faith *(or mala fide)*
böswillige Beschädigung f (SeeV) malicious damage
Bote m (Re) messenger *(ie, person transmitting declaration of intent = Willenserklärung, § 120 BGB)*
Box-Pierce-Test m (Mk) portmanteau lack of fit test
Boykott m (com, Pw) boycott
Boykott-Streik m (Pw) boycott strike
brachliegendes Geld n
  (Fin) idle money
  – unemployed funds
Brachzeit f
  (IndE) dead *(or lost)* time
  (IndE) machine down time *(störungsbedingt)*
  (IndE) machine idle time *(ablaufbedingt)*
  (IndE) machine interference time *(überlappend)*
Branch-and-Bound-Verfahren n (OR) branch-and-bound-process
Branche f
  (com) branch of business *(or industry)*
  – line of business
  – industry
  – sector of industry
Branchenanalyse f (Fin) sector analysis
Branchenbeobachtung f (Vw) industry survey and appraisal
Branchenerlöse mpl (Fin) industry revenue
branchenfremde Fusion f (Kart) merger in (totally) different lines
branchenfremder Zusammenschluß m (Bw) inter-industry business combination
Branchenführer m
  (Mk) industry leader
  – (infml) bellwether of an industry
Branchenkennziffer f (Bw) industry ratio
Branchenkonjunktur f
  (Vw) economic activity in a specific industry
  – sector trends
Branchenposition f (com) industry position
Branchenquotenziele npl (com) industry quota objectives
Branchenspanne f (Mk) average industry margin
Branchenstatistik f (Stat) industry statistics
branchenüblicher Gewinn m (Fin) conventional profit
Branchenuntersuchung f
  (Bw) industry study
  – study of a particular branch of business
Branchenverzeichnis n
  (com) classified (telephone) directory
  – (infml) the yellow pages

Branchenvorausschau f (com) industry forecast
brandeiliger Auftrag m (com) hot job
Brandschaden m (Vers) loss by fire, lightning, explosion
Brandversicherung f (Vers) fire insurance
Branntweinmonopol n (FiW) alcohol *(or spirits)* monopoly
Branntweinmonopolstelle f (Zo) spirits monopoly agency
Branntweinsteuer f
  (StR) spirits duty
  – tax on distilled spirits
Brauch m (com) commercial *(or trade)* usage
brauchbares Kriterium n (Log) acceptable criterion
Brauchbarkeit f **der Erfindung** (Pat) usefulness of an invention
Brauchbarkeitsminderung f
  (Bw) lost usefulness (of fixed assets)
  – loss of serviceability
  – decline in economic usefulness
  – diminution of service yield
  – expired utility
Brauchbarkeitsdauer f (IndE) service life
braune Ware f (com) brown goods *(eg, radio, TV set, recorder; opp, weiße Ware = white goods)*
Braunkohlekraftwerk n (IndE) lignite-based power station
Break-Even-Analyse f (KoR) break-even analysis
Brauereiaktien fpl (Fin) brewery stock
Bravais-Pearsonscher-Korrelationskoeffizient m (Stat) Bravais correlation coefficient
Briefe mpl **diktieren** (com) to dictate letters
Breitbandleitung f (EDV) wideband line
breite Nachfrageschichten fpl (Mk) large groups of consumers *(or demanders)*
breite Produktpalette f (Mk) diversified product range
breites Sortiment n
  (Mk) wide range of goods
  – wide assortment of products
breit gestreut (Bö) broadly diversified
breit gestreuter Aktienbesitz m (Fin) widespread shareholdings
Brief m
  (com) letter
  (Bö) ask
  – offer
  – offer price
Briefablage f (com) letter filing
Briefentwurf m (com) draft letter
Briefgeheimnis n (com) secrecy of mails
Briefgrundschuld f (Re) certificated land charge *(ie, registered charge for which a transferable instrument is issued, §§ 1191–1196 BGB)*
Briefhypothek f (Re) certificated mortgage, § 1116 I BGB
Briefkasten m
  (com) mailbox
  – (GB) letter-box
  – post(ing) box
  – pillar box
Briefkastenfirma f (com) letter box company *(ie, empty cover without economic functions of its own)*

Briefkopf m
(com) heading
- letterhead
Briefkurs m
(Fin) selling rate *(ie, of foreign exchange)*
(Bö) asked price
- offered
- offer price
- price offered
- rate asked
- sellers' rate
Briefkursnotiz f (Bö) offer quotation
briefliche Auszahlung f (Fin) mail transfer
briefliche Befragung f
(Mk) mail interview *(or* survey)
- postal inquiry
Briefmarke f
(com) postage stamp
- postal stamp
- stamp
Briefnotiz f (Bö) offer quotation
Brieföffner m (com) letter opener
Briefsendung f (com) consignment by mail
Brieftelegramm n
(com) lettergram
- letter telegram
Briefträger m
(com) mailman
- (GB) postman
Briefumschlag m (com) envelope
Briefumschlagklappe f (com) envelope flap
Brief und Geld
(Bö) asked and bid
- sellers and buyers
Briefwahl f
(com) voting by mail *(or* post)
- absentee ballot
- (GB) postal ballot *(or* vote)
Briefwechsel m (com) correspondence
Briefzustellung f (com) delivery of letters
Briggscher Logarithmus m
(Math) Briggs' *(or* Briggsian) logarithm
- common logarithm
Bringschuld f (Re) obligation to be performed at creditor's habitual residence *(ie, mostly by agreement or by virtue of trade usages)*
Bringsystem n (MaW) delivery system *(ie, materials are supplied to work stations; opp, Holsystem)*
Broschüre f
(com) broschure
- booklet
- folder
Bruch m
(Re) violation *(eg, of contracts)*
(SeeV) breakage
Bruch m **kürzen** (Math) to cancel factors
Bruchrechnen n (com) fractions *(eg, using fractions in business)*
Bruchrisiko n (com) risk of breakage
Bruchschaden m (com) damage by breakage
Bruchschadenversicherung f (Vers) insurance against breakage
Bruchstrich m (Math) (fraction) bar
bruchteilige Gewinne mpl (Bö) fractional gains
Bruchteilsaktie f (Fin) fractional share certificate

Bruchteilseigentum n
(Re) fractional share of property
- tenancy in common
Bruchteilseigentümer m (Re) owner of a fractional share of property
Bruchteilsgemeinschaft f
(Re) community of part owners
- tenancy in common
(ie, each owner holds an undivided interest in property, §§ 741 ff BGB)
Bruchteilversicherung f (Vers) fractional value insurance *(ie, taken out to cover warehouse against the risks of burglary and water damage; fraction usually between 5% and 25% of total value)*
Bruchzins m (Fin) broken interest
Brüsseler Begriffsbestimmung f (Zo) Brussels definition *(ie, of value for customs purposes)*
Brüsseler Bewertungsgrundsätze mpl (Zo) Brussels principles of valuation
Brüsseler Zollrat m (EC) Customs Cooperation Council, CCC *(ie, now ‚Rat für die Zusammenarbeit auf dem Gebiet des Zollwesens')*
Brüsseler Zolltarifschema n (EC) Brussels tariff nomenclature, CCCN
brutto (com) gross
Brutto-Allphasen-Umsatzsteuer f
(StR) cumulative all-stage turnover tax
- cascade tax
(ie, replaced by the value-added tax as of 1 Jan 1968)
Bruttoanlageinvestitionen fpl (VGR) gross fixed capital formation
Bruttoarbeitseinkommen n (Pw) earned income before deductions
Bruttoarbeitslohn m
(Pw) gross amount of wages or salaries
- gross pay
Bruttoaufschlag m (com) gross (merchandise) margin
Bruttoauftragseingang m (com) gross sales
Bruttoaustauschverhältnis n (AuW) gross barter terms of trade
Bruttoausweis m (ReW) gross statement *(ie, of fixed assets before deducting accumulated depreciation)*
Bruttobetrag m (com) gross amount
Brutto-Betriebsvermögen n
(Bw) operating investment
- gross operating assets
Bruttobilanz f (ReW) statement of account transactions *(syn, Summenbilanz, Umsatzbilanz)*
Bruttobuchwert m (ReW) book value before adjustment
Bruttodividende f (Fin) gross dividend
Brutto-Eigenkapitalrendite f (Fin) gross return on net assets
Bruttoeinkaufspreis m (com) gross *(or* invoiced) purchase price *(ie, acquisition cost less invoice deductions = Nettoeinkaufspreis)*
Bruttoeinkommen n
(Pw) gross earnings
- gross income
- gross pay

Bruttoeinkommen n **aus unselbständiger Arbeit** (VGR) gross wage and salary income
Bruttoeinkommen n **aus Vermögen** (VGR) gross property income
Bruttoeinkünfte pl (StR) total gross income
Bruttoeinnahmen fpl (com) gross receipts (or takings)
Bruttoentgelt n (Pw) gross pay
Bruttoerfolgsrechnung f (ReW) grossed income statement *(ie, listing all expense and revenue items on an income statement without balancing, § 157 AktG; opp, Nettoerfolgsrechnung)*
Bruttoergebnis n
(ReW) gross operating result
– earnings before taxes
Bruttoerlös m (ReW) gross revenue (or sales)
Bruttoersparnis f (com) gross savings
Bruttoertrag m
(com) gross proceeds
(Fin) gross yield from investment
Bruttoetat m (FiW) gross budget *(ie, showing receipts and expenditures separately for each budget item; opp, Nettoetat)*
Bruttofracht f (com) gross freight
brutto für netto (com) gross for net *(ie, price is quoted for the weight of the goods inclusive of packing, § 380 HGB)*
Bruttogehalt n (Pw) gross salary
Bruttogewicht n (com) gross weight
Bruttogewinn m
(com) gross profit on sales *(ie, in retailing and wholesaling: difference between purchase and sales prices)*
(KoR) contribution margin
– marginal income
– profit contribution
– variable gross margin
(ie, difference between price and variable unit costs = Deckungsbeitrag)
Bruttogewinnanalyse f (KoR) gross profit analysis *(ie, method of short-term results accounting, based on standard costing)*
Bruttogewinnmarge f (com) gross profit margin
Bruttogewinn m **pro Einheit der Engpaßbelastung** (KoR) marginal income per scarce factor
Bruttogewinnspanne f (com) gross (merchandise) margin
Bruttogewinnzuschlag m (com) gross markon
Bruttoinlandsinvestitionen fpl (VGR) gross domestic fixed capital formation
Bruttoinlandsprodukt n (VGR) gross domestic product, GDP, gdp
Bruttoinlandsprodukt n **zu Faktorkosten** (VGR) gross domestic product at factor cost
Bruttoinlandsprodukt n **zu konstanten Preisen** (VGR) gross domestic product at constant cost
Bruttoinlandsprodukt n **zu Marktpreisen** (VGR) gross domestic product at market prices
Bruttoinvestitionen fpl
(VGR) gross capital expenditure (or formation)
– gross investment
Bruttoinvestitionsquote f (VGR) gross investment ratio
Bruttojahresarbeitsentgelt n (Pw) annual gross wages or salaries

Brutto-Kapitalproduktivität f (Vw) gross capital productivity
Bruttoladefähigkeit f (com) deadweight cargo
Bruttolohn m (Pw) gross earnings (or pay)
Bruttolohnberechnung f (Pw) determination of gross earnings per period *(ie, including taxes and social insurance)*
bruttolohnbezogene Rentenformel f (SozV) pension formula based on gross, wages and salaries
Bruttolohnsumme f
(Stat) total of wages and salaries
– total payroll
(ie, plus all extras and premiums directly related to the work performed, excluding employer's contributions and fringe benefits)
Bruttolohnzusammenstellungsliste f (KoR) tabular list of gross earnings *(ie, prepared for certain cost centers and the overall plant)*
Bruttomehrwertsteuer f (FiW) output tax
Bruttomietwert m (StR) gross annual rental
Bruttoprämie f (Vers) gross premium
Bruttopreis m (com) gross price *(ie, prior to discounts or rebates)*
Bruttopreisliste f (com) gross-price list
Bruttoprinzip n (FiW) principle of recording all planned receipts and expenditures in the budget
Bruttoproduktion f
(VGR) gross output (or product)
– total volume of output
Bruttoproduktionswert m (VGR) gross output
Bruttorechnung f (ReW) = *Bruttoerfolgsrechnung*
Bruttorendite f (Fin) gross return
Brutto-Selbstfinanzierung f
(Fin) gross self-financing
– (GB) gross plough-back
Bruttosozialprodukt n (VGR) gross national product, GNP, gnp
Bruttosozialprodukt n **bei Vollbeschäftigung** (Vw) full employment GNP
Bruttosozialprodukt n **zu Faktorkosten** (VGR) gross national product at factor cost
Bruttosozialprodukt n **zu Marktpreisen** (VGR) gross national product at market prices
Bruttospanne f **ohne Skontoabzug** (Mk) gross merchandising margin
Bruttosteuerbelastung f (FiW) gross tax load ratio
Bruttostundenlohn m **im Fertigungsbereich** (Pw) gross hourly wages in manufacturing
Bruttoumsatz m
(ReW) gross sales
– (GB) gross turnover
Bruttoumsatzerlös m
(ReW) gross sales revenue
– sales including VAT
Bruttoverbuchung f (ReW) gross accounting procedure
Bruttoverdienst m (Pw) gross earnings
Bruttoverdienstspanne f (com) gross margin
Bruttoverkaufspreis m (com) gross selling price
Bruttoverkaufswert m (ReW) gross sales
Bruttoverlust m (ReW) gross loss
Bruttovermögen n (VGR) gross wealth
Bruttoverzinsung f (Fin) gross interest return
Bruttovolkseinkommen n (VGR) gross national income

Bruttowarengewinn *m* (ReW) gross trading profit
Bruttowarenumsatz *m* (ReW) gross sales
Bruttowertschöpfung *f* (VGR) gross value added *(ie, net value added + indirect taxes (− subsidies) + depreciation)*
Bruttoziehungen *fpl* (IWF) gross drawings
Bruttozins *m* (Fin) gross interest
Bruttozinsdifferenz *f* (AuW) uncovered interest-rate differential
Bruttozinsspanne *f* (Fin) gross interest margin
BSP-Deflator *m* (Vw) gross national product deflator
BSP-Lücke *f* (Vw) gross national product gap
Buchauszug *m* (com) statement of account, § 87 c HGB
Bucheinsicht *f* (ReW) inspection of books of account
buchen
 (com) to reserve *(eg, hotel rooms, rental cars)*
 − (GB *also*) to book
 − (ReW) to post
 − to enter in the books
 − to make an entry in the accounts
Bücher *npl*
 (ReW) (account) books
 − books of account
 − books and records
Bücher *npl* **abschließen** (ReW) to close the books
Bücher *npl* **einsehen** (ReW) to inspect books and records
Bücher *npl* **fälschen** (ReW) to doctor (*or* falsify) books and records
Bücher *npl* **führen** (ReW) to keep commercial books
Bücher *npl* **und sonstige Aufzeichnungen** (ReW) books and records
Buchforderungen *fpl*
 (ReW) accounts receivables
 − book receivables
 − outstanding accounts
Buchführung *f*
 (ReW) bookkeeping
 − accounting
 − accountancy
Buchführungspflicht *f*
 (ReW) duty to keep books of account, § 38 HGB
 (StR) legal obligation to keep commercial books of account and to prepare financial statements at regular intervals, §§ 140ff AO
Buchführungsrichtlinien *fpl* (ReW) accounting rules *(ie, originally issued in 1937, but still regarded as properly spelling out the basic elements of ‚orderly accounting' = ordnungsgemäße Buchführung')*
Buchführungssystem *n* (ReW) accounting system
Buchführungstechnik *f* (ReW) accounting methods
Buchgeld *n*
 (Vw) deposit money
 Also:
 − bank deposit money
 − book money
 − deposit currency
 − primary deposits
 (syn, Giralgeld)

Buchgewinn *m* (Fin) book (*or* accounting) profit
Buchgrundschuld *f* (Re) registered land charge
Buchhalter *m* (ReW) accounting clerk
buchhalterische Abschreibung *f* (ReW) accounting depreciation
buchhalterische Behandlung *f* (ReW) accounting treatment
Buchhalternase *f* (ReW) ruling off *(syn, Buchhalterknie, Buchhalterriegel)*
Buchhaltung *f*
 (ReW) = *Buchführung*
 (ReW) accounting department
 − bookkeeping department
 − (GB) accounts department
Buchhaltungsrichtlinien *fpl* (ReW) = *Buchführungsrichtlinien*
Buchhaltungstheorie *f* (ReW) accountancy theory
Buchhonorar *n* (com) book royalty
Buchhypothek *f*
 (Re) mortgage entered in the land register, § 1116 II BGB
 − registered mortgage
Buchinventur *f* (ReW) book (*or* perpetual) inventory
Buchkredit *m*
 (Fin) book credit
 − current account credit
 − open (book) credit
 − open account credit
buchmäßig angefallene Wagnisse *npl* (ReW) risks recorded in the books of account
buchmäßige Abschreibung *f* (ReW) book (*or* recorded) depreciation
buchmäßige Erfassung *f* (ReW) entry in the accounts
buchmäßige Gewinnverteilung *f* (ReW) appropriation of earnings
buchmäßige Informationen *fpl* (ReW) accounting information
buchmäßiger Gewinn *m* (ReW) accounting profit
buchmäßiger Nachweis *m* (ReW) evidence of a transaction (in the books of account)
buchmäßiger Restwert *m* (ReW) residual value recorded in the books
buchmäßiger Überschuß *m* (Fin) book surplus
buchmäßiger Verlust *m* (ReW) accounting loss
buchmäßiges Ergebnis *n* (ReW) result as shown in the books
Buchmesse *f* (com) book fair
Buchprüfung *f* (ReW) audit
Buchprüfungsgesellschaft *f* (ReW) firm of licensed public accountants
Buchprüfungsgesellschaft *f* (ReW) auditing firm
 − company of licensed public accountants
Buchrestwert *m* (ReW) salvage value shown in the books
Buchsachverständiger *m* (ReW) accounting expert *(ie, comprehensive term covering certified public accountants = Wirtschaftsprüfer, sworn auditors = vereidigte Buchprüfer, and other experts)*
Buchstabendrucker *m*
 (EDV) character printer
 − charakter-at-a-time printer *(syn, Zeichendrucker)*
Buchstabenkette *f* (EDV) alphabetic string

139

Buchstabenschlüssel m (EDV) alphabetic code
Buchstabenwechsel m (EDV) letters shift, LET
Buchstaben-Ziffern-Umschaltung f (EDV) case shift
Buchstabierwörter npl (com) identification words
Buchstelle f (ReW) accounting agency
Buch- und Betriebsprüfung f (StR) periodic examination by tax auditors *(ie, term now replaced by ‚Außenprüfung')*
Buchung f
  (com) reservation
  – (GB *also*) booking
  (ReW) entry
Buchung f **berichtigen** (ReW) to correct a bookkeeping entry
Buchungen fpl **erzeugen** (ReW) to generate entries
Buchung f **ohne Gegenbuchung** (ReW) unbalanced entry
Buchungsautomat m (EDV) automatic accounting machine
Buchungsbeleg m (ReW) bookkeeping voucher
  – voucher supporting book entry
Buchungsdatum n (ReW) date of entry
Buchungsfehler m (ReW) false entry
Buchungsformel f (ReW) entry formula
Buchungsgebühr f (Fin) account management fee *(eg, DM 0.50 for each credit and/or debit)*
Buchungskarte f (ReW) posting card
Buchungskontrolle f (ReW) audit trail
Buchungsmaschine f (EDV) accounting machine *(ie, used to prepare accounting records)*
buchungspflichtig (ReW) accountable
Buchungsplatz m (EDV) booking (*or* reservation) terminal
Buchungssatz m (ReW) entry formula
Buchungsschluß m (ReW) closing date of entries
Buchungstext m
  (ReW) entry description
  – memo
Buchung f **stornieren** (ReW) to reverse an entry
Buchungsunterlage f
  (ReW) accounting document (*or* record)
  – posting medium
  – records and vouchers
Buchungsvermerk m (ReW) posting reference *(eg, voucher number, account identification)*
Buchungsvorfall m
  (ReW) accounting event
  – internal transaction
Buchungsvorgang m (ReW) bookkeeping operation
Buchungszeitpunkt m (ReW) date of entry
Buchung f **von Eliminierungen** (Re) eliminating entry *(ie, in preparing group accounts = Konzernabschlüsse)*
Buchverleger m (com) book publisher
Buchverlust m (ReW) book loss
Buchwert m
  (ReW) book value
  – amortized cost
  – carrying value
  – depreciated book value (*or* cost) *(ie, original cost less applicable portions of accounting depreciation)*
  (Fin) book value *(ie, nominal amount of liability less unamortized discount = nicht abgeschriebenes Disagio od Damnum)*
Buchwertabschreibung f
  (ReW) declining-balance method *(of depreciation)*
  – diminishing-provision method
  (syn, geometrisch-degressive Abschreibung, Restwertabschreibung)
Buchwert m **des Anlagevermögens** (ReW) net investment in property, plant, and equipment
Buckel-Effekt m (Stat) bulge effect *(eg, in the cost-of-living index, due to an increase in VAT)*
Budget n
  (FiW) budget *(ie, annual estimates of public receipts and expenditures)*
  (Bw) budget
Budgetabweichung f (KoR) budget variance
Budgetanforderung f (Fin) budget request
Budget n **aufstellen** (FiW, Bw) to prepare a budget
Budgetaufstellung f
  (FiW, Bw) budgeting
  – preparing the budget
Budgetausgleich m (FiW) balancing the budget
Budget n **ausgleichen** (FiW) to balance a budget
Budgetausgleichsfonds m (Fin) budget equalization fund
Budgetausschuß m (FiW) budget committee
Budgetbeschränkung f (Vw) budget balance
Budget n **der Wartungskosten** (Bw) maintenance budget
Budget n **des Fertigungsbereichs** (Bw) production budget
Budget n **des Materialbereichs** (MaW) inventory and purchases budget
Budgeteinsparungen fpl (FiW) budget cuts
Budgetentwurf m (FiW) = *Haushaltsentwurf*
Budget-Genehmigigungsblatt n (Bw, Fin) budget authorization form
Budgetgerade f
  (Vw) budget line
  – iso-expenditure line
  – opportunity curve
  – price line
  – budget constraint line
  – consumption possibility line
Budgetgleichung f (Vw) budget equation
Budgetierung f
  (Bw) budgeting *(ie, operational planning)*
  (Fin) budgeting *(ie, in the sense of financial planning)*
Budgetierungszeitraum m (Bw) budget period
Budgetimpuls m (FiW) budget impulse
Budgetinflation f (Vw) public demand-pull inflation
Budgetinzidenz f (FiW) budget incidence
Budgetkontrolle f (KoR) budgetary control
Budgetkosten pl
  (KoR) budgeted
  – target
  – attainable standard
  – current standard
  – ideal standard ... cost
  (syn, Soll- od Vorgabekosten)
Budgetkreislauf m (FiW) budget cycle
Budgetkürzung f (FiW, Bw) budget cut

Budgetperiode f (FiW) budget period
Budgetposten m (FiW) budget item
Budgetprinzipien npl (FiW) budget principles
Budgetprojektion f (Bw) budget forecast
Budgetrestriktion f (Vw) budget constraint
Budgetsoll n (Bw) budgeted figure
Budgetüberschreitung f (FiW, Bw) budget overrun
– over budget
Budgetüberschuß m (FiW) budget surplus
Budgetüberschuß m **bei Vollbeschäftigung** (Vw) high employment budget surplus
Budgetübertragungen fpl (FiW) carryover funds (ie, from one fiscal year to the next)
Budgetunterschreitung f (FiW, Bw) budget underrun
– under budget
Budgetziel n (Bw) budget target (ie, in the shape of a numberized goal)
Budgetzyklus m (FiW) budget cycle
Bumerang-Methode f (Mk) boomerang method (ie, of sales talk)
Bummelstreik m (Pw) slowdown strike
– labor slowdown
– go-slow
Bund m **der Steuerzahler** m (com) Tax Payers' Association
Bündelpatent n (Pat) batch patent
Bundesamt n **für Finanzen** (StR) Federal Tax Agency (ie, domiciled in Bonn-Bad Godesberg)
Bundesamt n **für gewerbliche Wirtschaft** (com) Federal Office for Trade and Industry (ie, domiciled in Frankfurt)
Bundes-Angestellten-Tarifvertrag m (Pw) Federal Collective Agreement for Public Employees, BAT
Bundesanleihe f (FiW) federal loan (or bond)
Bundesanleihekonsortium n (Fin) federal loan syndicate
Bundesanstalt f **für Arbeit** (Pw) Federal Labor Office (ie, central labor administration, Nuremberg-based, holds a strict labor exchange monopoly)
Bundesanzeiger m (com) Federal Official Gazette
Bundesarbeitsgericht n (Re) Federal Labor Court (at Kassel)
Bundesarbeitsminister m (com) Federal Minister of Labor
Bundesaufsichtsamt n (com) Federal Supervisory Office
Bundesaufsichtsamt n **für das Kreditwesen** (Fin) Federal Banking Supervisory Office (ie, domiciled in Berlin)
Bundesaufsichtsamt n **für das Versicherungs- und Bausparwesen** (Vers) Federal Supervisoy Office for Insurance and for Building and Loan Associations (ie, domiciled in Berlin)
Bundesausbildungsförderungsgesetz n (Pw) Federal Law on Education and Training Promotion, of 26 Aug 1971, as amended
Bundesausgaben fpl (FiW) federal expenditure
Bundesbahn f (com) Federal Railways
Bundesbank f (Fin) West German Central Bank
– Deutsche Bundesbank
– Bundesbank
Bundesbankausschüttung f (FiW) payout of Bundesbank surplus (ie, to improve the deficit position of the Federal budget)
bundesbankfähig (Fin) eligible for rediscount (or rediscountable) at the Bundesbank
bundesbankfähige Abschnitte mpl (Fin) bills rediscountable at the Bundesbank
bundesbankfähige Wechsel mpl (Fin) = bundesbankfähige Abschnitte
Bundesbankfähigkeit f (Fin) eligibility for rediscount at the Bundesbank (ie, refers to bills of exchange and other negotiable instruments)
Bundesbankgiro n (Fin) Bundesbank transfer
Bundesbankguthaben npl (Fin) Bundesbank balances
Bundesbankrat m (Fin) Federal Bank Council
Bundesbank- und Postscheckguthaben npl (ReW) deposits at Bundesbank and in postal checking accounts
Bundesbeauftragter m **für den Datenschutz** (EDV) Federal Data Protection Commissioner
Bundesbedienstete pl (Pw) employees of the Federal Government
Bundesbehörde f (com) federal authority
Bundesbeihilfe f (FiW) federal grant
Bundesberggesetz n (Re) Federal Mining Law
Bundesbetriebsprüfungsstelle f (StR) Federal Tax Examination Office (ie, superseded by the Federal Tax Office = Bundesamt für Finanzen)
Bundesbürgschaft f
(Fin) federal guaranty
– state-backed guaranty
– state backing
(ie, for credits that are in the public interest and cannot otherwise be secured)
Bundesdatenschutzgesetz n (Re) West German Data Protection Law
bundeseigene Unternehmen npl (FiW) federal commercial enterprises under public and private law
Bundeseinkommen n (FiW) federal income
Bundesemittent m (Fin) issuer of federal bonds
Bundesetat m (FiW) Federal Government budget
Bundesfinanzbehörden fpl (FiW) federal revenue authorities
Bundesfinanzhof m (StR) Federal Fiscal Court (ie, supreme court in tax controversies, domiciled in Munich)
Bundesfinanzminister m (com) Federal Minister of Finance
Bundesfinanzministerium n (com) Federal Ministry of Finance
Bundesfinanzverwaltung f (FiW) Federal Revenue Administration
Bundesgarantie f (Fin) federal guaranty
Bundesgebührenordnung f (Re) federal fee scale regulation
Bundesgerichtshof m (Re) Federal Supreme Court (ie, in civil and criminal proceedings, domiciled in Karlsruhe)
Bundesgesetzblatt n (Re) Official Federal Gazette
Bundeshauptkasse f (FiW) Federal Chief Cash Office

Bundeshaushalt *m* (FiW) federal budget
Bundeskartellamt *n* (Re) Federal Cartel Office *(domiciled in Berlin)*
Bundeskasse *f* (FiW) Federal Cash Office
Bundeskindergeldgesetz *n* (Re) Law on Support Payments for Children, of 31 Jan 1975, as amended
Bundeskompetenzen *fpl* **verlagern** (FiW) to shift federal responsibilities *(eg, to states and local authorities)*
Bundesminister *m* **der Finanzen** (com) Federal Minister of Finance
Bundesminister *m* **der Justiz** (com) Federal Minister of Justice
Bundesminister *m* **der Verteidigung** (com) Federal Minister of Defense
Bundesminister *m* **des Auswärtigen** (com) Federal Minister for Foreign Affairs
Bundesminister *m* **des Innern** (com) Federal Minister of the Interior
Bundesminister *m* **für Arbeit und Sozialordnung** (com) Federal Minister of Labor and Social Affairs
Bundesminister *m* **für Bildung und Wissenschaft** (com) Federal Minister of Education and Science
Bundesminister *m* **für Ernährung, Landwirtschaft und Forsten** (com) Federal Minister of Food, Agriculture and Forestry
Bundesminister *m* **für Forschung und Technologie** (com) Federal Minister for Research and Technology
Bundesminister *m* **für innerdeutsche Beziehungen** (com) Federal Minister for Intra-German Relations
Bundesminister *m* **für Jugend, Familie und Gesundheit** (com) Federal Minister for Youth, Family Affairs and Health
Bundesminister *m* **für Post- und Fernmeldewesen** (com) Federal Minister of Posts and Telecommunications
Bundesminister *m* **für Raumordnung, Bauwesen und Städtebau** (com) Federal Minister for Regional Planing, Building and Urban Planning
Bundesminister *m* **für Verkehr** (com) Federal Minister of Transport
Bundesminister *m* **für Wirtschaft** (com) Federal Minister of Economics
Bundesminister *m* **für wirtschaftliche Zusammenarbeit** (com) Federal Minister for Economic Co-operation
Bundesministerium *m* (com) federal ministry
Bundesministerium *n* **der Finanzen** (com) Federal Ministry of Finance
Bundesministerium *n* **der Justiz** (com) Federal Ministry of Justice
Bundesministerium *n* **der Verteidigung** (com) Federal Ministry of Defense
Bundesministerium *n* **des Auswärtigen** (com) Federal Ministry for Foreign Affairs
Bundesministerium *n* **des Innern** (com) Federal Ministry of the Interior
Bundesministerium *n* **für Arbeit und Sozialordnung** (com) Federal Ministry of Labor and Social Affairs *(or Matters)*

Bundesministerium *n* **für Bildung und Wissenschaft** (com) Federal Ministry for Education and Science
Bundesministerium *n* **für das Post- und Fernmeldewesen** (com) Federal Ministry of Posts and Telecommunications
Bundesministerium *n* **für Ernährung, Landwirtschaft und Forsten** (com) Federal Ministry for Food, Agriculture and Forestry
Bundesministerium *n* **für Forschung und Technologie** (com) Federal Ministry for Research and Technology
Bundesministerium *n* **für innerdeutsche Beziehungen** (com) Federal Ministry for Intra-German Relations
Bundesministerium *n* **für Jugend, Familie und Gesundheit** (com) Federal Ministry for Youth, Family Affairs and Health
Bundesministerium *n* **für Raumordnung, Bauwesen und Städtebau** (com) Federal Ministry for Regional Planning, Building and Urban Development
Bundesministerium *n* **für Verkehr** (com) Federal Ministry of Transport
Bundesministerium *n* **für wirtschaftliche Zusammenarbeit** (com) Federal Ministry for Economic Cooperation
Bundesmonopolverwaltung *f* **für Branntwein** (FiW) Federal Spirits Monopoly Administration
Bundesoberseeamt *n* (Re) Federal Admiralty Court *(at Hamburg)*
Bundesobligation *f* (FiW) federal bond
Bundespatentgericht *n* (Re) Federal Patent Tribunal
Bundespost *f*
(com) Federal Post Administration
– (GB) Federal Post Office
Bundesrat *m*
(com) Federal Council
– Federal Upper House
– Council of States
(ie, representing the German Laender)
Bundesrechnungshof *m* (FiW) Federal Audit Office *(ie, charged with the accounting and budgetary control of all government functions)*
Bundesschatzanweisung *f* (Fin) federal treasury note
Bundesschatzbrief *m* (Fin) federal treasury bill
Bundesschuld *f* (FiW) federal debt
Bundesschuldbuch *n* (FiW) Federal Debt Register
Bundesschuldenverwaltung *f* (FiW) Federal Debt Administration *(ie, reporting to the Federal Ministry of Finance; domiciled at Bad Homburg v. d. Höhe)*
Bundesschuldverschreibung *f* (Fin) federal bond
Bundessozialgericht *n* (Re) Federal Court for Social Security and Related Matters *(domiciled at Kassel)*
Bundesstatistik *f* (Stat) federal statistics
Bundesstelle *f* **für Außenhandelsinformation** (com) Federal Foreign Trade Information Office
Bundessteuer *f* (FiW) federal tax
Bundessteuerblatt *n* (StR) Official Gazette of the Federal Ministry of Finance

bundesunmittelbare juristische Person *f* **des öffentlichen Rechts** (Re) federal public law body
bundesunmittelbare Körperschaft *f* (Re) federal corporation
bundesunmittelbares Unternehmen *n* (FiW) directly operated federal government enterprise
Bundesverband *m* **der deutschen Arbeitgeberverbände** (com) Confederation of German Employers' Federations
Bundesverband *m* **der Deutschen Industrie** (com) Federal Association of German Industry
Bundesverband *m* **der Deutschen Volksbanken und Raiffeisenbanken** (Fin) Federal Association of German Commercial and Rural Credit Association
Bundesverband *m* **Deutscher Banken** (Fin) Federal Association of German Banks
Bundesvereinigung *f* **der deutschen Arbeitgeberverbände** (com) Federal Confederation of German Employers' Association
Bundesverfassungsgericht *n* (Re) Federal Constitutional Court *(at Karlsruhe)*
Bundesvermögen *n* (FiW) federal government property
Bundesvermögensstelle *f* (FiW) Federal Property Agency
Bundesvermögensverwaltung *f* (FiW) Federal Property Administration
Bundesversicherungsamt *n* (SozV) Federal Insurance Office *(at Berlin)*
Bundesversicherungsanstalt *f* **für Angestellte** (SozV) Federal Social Insurance Office for Salaried Employees *(at Berlin)*
Bundesverwaltungsgericht *n* (Re) Federal Administrative Court *(at Berlin)*
bundesweiter Streik *m* (Pw) all-out national strike
Bundeszollbehörde *f* (FiW) federal customs authority
Bundeszollblatt *n* (StR) Federal Customs Gazette
Bundeszollverwaltung *f* (FiW) Federal Customs Administration
Bundeszuschuß *m* (FiW) federal grant
Bürge *m*
(Re) guarantor
– surety
bürgender Verband *m* (com) guaranteeing association
Bürgerinitiative *f* (com) civic action group
bürgerliche Rechtsstreitigkeiten *fpl* (Re) civil litigation
bürgerliches Recht *n*
(Re) private law
(ie, governing the legal relations between private persons, including legal entities; opp, public law)
(Re) civil law
(eg, as laid down in the German Civil Code = BGB)
bürgerlich-rechtliche Gesellschaft *f* (Re) = *BGB-Gesellschaft*
Bürgschaft *f*
(Re) suretyship, §§ 765 ff BGB
– (US) guaranty
– (GB) guarantee

Bürgschaft *f* **leisten**
(Re) to accept a guaranty
– to stand surety (for)
Bürgschaftserklärung *f* (Re) statement of guaranty
Bürgschaftskredit *m* (Fin) guaranty credit
Bürgschaftsnehmer *m*
(Re) guaranteed creditor
– guarantee
Bürgschaftsplafond *m* (Fin) guaranty line *(or ceiling)*
Bürgschaftsprovision *f* (Fin) guaranty commission
Bürgschaftsrahmen *m* (Fin) = *Bürgschaftsplafond*
Bürgschaftsrisiko *n* (ReW) guaranty risk
Bürgschaftsschuld *f*
(Re) guaranty indebtedness
– principal debt
Bürgschaftsverhältnis *n* (Re) principal-surety relationship
Bürgschaftsverpflichtungen *fpl* (ReW) guaranties
Bürgschaftsversicherung *f* (Vers) guaranty insurance
Bürgschaftsvertrag *m* (Re) contract of guaranty *(or suretyship)*
Bürgschaft *f* **übernehmen**
(Re) to accept a guaranty
– to stand surety
Büro *n* (com) office
Büroangestellte *pl*
(Pw) office workers
– clerical personnel
– white-collar *(or* black-coated) workers
Büroangestellter *m* (Pw) office worker
Büroarbeiten *fpl*
(com) office work
– clerical operations
Bürobedarf *m* (com) office supplies *(ie, stationery, etc.)*
Büroberufe *mpl* (Pw) white-collar occupations
Bürobote *m* (com) interoffice messenger
– office boy
– (sl) office goofer
– (sl) prat boy
Büro *n* **der Zukunft** (EDV) office of the future
Bürofachkraft *f* (com) trained clerical help
Bürofernschreiben *n* (EDV) hard copy communication
Bürogebäude *n* (com) office building
Bürogemeinschaft *f* (com) sharing office facilities *(ie, used by free professionals)*
Bürogeräte *npl* (EDV) electronic office equipment
Bürohandel *m* (Bö) unofficial trading
Büroklammer *f*
(com) paper clip
– (US) bulldog clip
Bürokommunikation *f* (EDV) office automation
bürokratische Autorität *f* (Bw) bureaucratic type of administrative organization *(ie, translation of M. Weber's German term)*
bürokratische Schwerfälligkeit *f* (Bw) bureaucratic inflexibility
Bürolandschaft *f*
(com) landscaped office
– open office area
– panoramic office

Büromaschinenhändler m (com) office equipment dealer
Büromaschinenhersteller m (com) office equipment manufacturer
Büromaterial n (com) stationery and office supplies
Bürorechner m (EDV) office computer
Büro- und Geschäftseinrichtung f (com) office equipment
Bürozeit f (com) office hours
Bürozubehörmarkt m (com) office supplies market
Bus m
  (EDV) bus
  – highway
  – trunk *(syn, Pfad, Sammelweg)*
Büschelkarte f (Stat) bunch graph (*or* map)
Büschelkartenanalyse f (Stat) bunch map analysis
Bußgeld n
  (Re) monetary fine
  – penalty
Bußgeldbescheid m (Re) penalty notice
Bußgeldbestimmungen fpl (Re) monetary fine regulations
Bußgeldverfahren n (Kart) administrative fine proceedings
Bußgeld n **verhängen**
  (Kart) to impose a fine *(eg, on a company)*
  – (infml) to slap a fine (on)
Bußgeld n **zahlen**
  (Kart) to pay a fine
  – to pay in fines ...
BU-Versicherung f (Vers) business interruption insurance
Bu-Zi-Umschaltung f (EDV) = *Buchstaben-Ziffern-Umschaltung*
Byte n (EDV) byte *(ie, 8 information bits + 1 control bit)*
Bytemultiplexkanal m (EDV) byte multiplex channel
byteweise Serienübertragung f (EDV) byte-serial transmission

C

Cache-Speicher m (EDV) cache memory
Cantor-Paradoxon n (Math) Cantor paradox
Cantorsche Menge f (Math) Cantor set
Cantorsche Reihe f (Math) Cantor series
Cantorsches Diskontinuum n (Math) Cantor set
Carnet n für die vorübergehende Einfuhr (AuW) carnet for temporary admission
Carter Bonds pl
  (Fin) DM-denominated bearer treasury bonds
  – Carter bonds
  (ie, issued by the U.S. Treasury in the German capital market)
Cauchy-Riemannsche Differentialgleichung f (Math) Cauchy-Riemann equation
Cauchyscher Integralsatz m (Math) Cauchy integral law
Cauchysches Konvergenzkriterium n (Math) Cauchy principle of convergence
Cauchysches Restglied n (Math) Cauchy's form of remainder
Cauchy-Standardverteilung f (Stat) standard Cauchy distribution
Cauchy-Verteilung f (Math) Cauchy distribution
CES-Funktion f (Vw) CES *(constant elasticity of substitution)* function
ceteris paribus (Vw) other things being equal
C-Geschäft n (Fin) installment credit based on bills of exchange
charakteristische Determinante f (Math) characteristic determinant
charakteristische Funktion f (Math) characteristic function
charakteristische Gleichung f (Math) characteristic equation
charakteristische Matrix f (Math) characteristic matrix
charakteristischer Wert m e–r Grundgesamtheit (Stat) summary measure
charakteristische Wurzel f
  (Math) characteristic (*or* latent) root
  – proper value
  – eigenwert
charakterliche Zuverlässigkeit f (Pw) character firmness
Charge f (IndE) batch
Chargenfertigung f (IndE) batch production *(ie, no continuous or standardized production)*
Chargenkalkulation f (KoR) batch-type costing *(ie, special type of 'Divisionskalkulation')*
Chargenproduktion f (IndE) = *Chargenfertigung*
Chargenstreuung f (IndE) batch variation
Chart-Analyst m (Fin) chartist
Charterer m (com) charterer
Charterflug m (com) charter flight
Chartergeschäft n (com) charter business
Chartermaschine f (com) charter plane
chartern
  (com) to charter
  – to hire
Chartern n (com) chartering *(ie, of ocean-going vessel or airplane)*
Charterpartie f (com) charter party, § 557 HGB
Chartervertrag m
  (com) contract of affreightment
  – charter party
Checkliste f (com) check list
Check-List-Methode f (Stat) check list method
Chef m
  (com) head *(ie, of a firm)*
  – (infml) boss
Chefetage f (com) executive floor
Chefredakteur m (com) editor-in-chief
Chefsekretärin f
  (Pw) personal secretary
  – personal assistant, PA
Chemieindustrie f (com) chemicals industry
Chemiekonzern m (com) chemicals group
Chemiemärkte mpl (com) chemicals markets
Chemieriese m (com) chemical giant *(eg, BASF, Hoechst, Bayer)*

Chemieunternehmen *n* (com) chemicals company
Chemiewerte *mpl* (Bö) chemicals
chemische Industrie *f* (com) = *Chemieindustrie*
Chiffreanzeige *f* (Pw) blind ad *(ie, one that does not identify the employer, a box number being provided for responses)*
(Mk) box number advertisement
– keyed advertisement
Chiffrenummer *f* (Pw) box (*or* reference) number
Chip *m* (EDV) chip
Chi-Quadrat-Kriterium *n* (Stat) test of goodness of fit
Chi-Quadrat-Test *m* (Stat) chi square test
chiquadratverteilt (Stat) chi square distributed
Chi-Quadrat-Verteilung *f* (Stat) chi square distribution
cif-Agent *m* (com) CIF agent
cif-Geschäft *n* (com) CIF contract (*or* transaction)
Clausula *f* **rebus sic stantibus** (Re) clausula rebus sic stantibus *(ie, tacit condition attaching to all contracts which cease to be binding when underlying facts have changed)*
Clearing *n* (Fin) clearing
Clearing-Forderungen *fpl* (Fin) clearing receivables
Clearing-Guthaben *n* (Fin) clearing assets
Clearingstelle *f* (Fin) clearing house
Clearingverkehr *m* (Fin) clearing transactions
Cobb-Douglas-Funktion *f* (Vw) Cobb Douglas function *(ie, macroeconomic production function)*
COBOL-Programm *n* (EDV) COBOL source program
COBOL-Übersetzer *m* (EDV) COBOL compiler
COBOL-Zielprogramm *n* (EDV) COBOL object program
Codeelement *n* (EDV) code element
Codeklausel *f* (EDV, Cobol) code clause
Codeloch *n* (EDV) code hole
Codeprüfung *f* (EDV) code check
Codetabelle *f* (EDV) code table
Code-Umsetzer *m* (EDV) code converter
Codierblatt *n* (EDV) coding sheet
codieren
(EDV) to code
– to encode
Codierer *m*
(EDV) coder *(ie, person writing computer instructions)*
(EDV) coding device
– encoder
Codiermatrix *f* (EDV) coding matrix
codiert dezimal (EDV) coded decimal
codierter Befehl *m* (EDV) coded instruction
codiertes Programm *n* (EDV) coded program
Codierung *f* (EDV) coding
Codierungsformular *n* (EDV) = *Codierblatt*
Codierzeile *f* (EDV) code line
Cod-Sendung *f* (com) consignment „cash on delivery"

Compact-Rechner *m* (EDV) compact computer
compilierendes Programm *n* (EDV) compiling routine
Computerbrief *m* (com) personalized computer letter
computer-geführte Fertigung *f* (IndE) computer-aided manufacturing, CAM
Computergeld *n* (Fin) electronic (*or* disk) money
computergestützt (EDV) computer-aided (*or* -based)
– computerized
computergestützte Informationserschließung *f* (EDV) information retrieval
computergestützte Produktionsplanung *f* (Bw) computer-based production planning
computergestütztes Arbeitsvermittlungssystem *n* (Pw) computerized job bank network
computergestütztes Konstruieren *n* (EDV) computer-aided design, CAD
computergestütztes Telefoninterview-Verfahren *n* (Mk) computer-aided telephone interviewing
– CATY system
Computerlauf *m* (EDV) computer run
computerlesbar (EDV) machine readable
Computerprogramm *n* (EDV) computer program
Computersteuerung *f* (EDV) computer control
Computerverbund *m* (EDV) computer network
Computer-Wörterbuch *n* (EDV) electronic dictionary
Container *m* (com) container
Containerfracht *f* (com) containerized freight
– capsule cargo
Container-Frachtbrief *m* (com) container bill of lading
Container-Linie *f* (com) container line
Containerschiff *n* (com) container ship
Containerstapel *m* (com) unit load
Containerstapler *m* (com) container carrier truck
Containerterminal *m od n* (com) container terminal
Container-Verkehr *m* (com) container traffic
contradictio *f* **in adiecto** (Log) contradiction in terms *(ie, a phrase of which the parts are expressly inconsistent)*
Contremineur *m*
(Bö) bear
– speculator for a fall of prices
Courtage *f* (Fin) brokerage
Courtagerechnung *f* (Bö) brokerage statement
Courtagesatz *m* (Fin) brokerage rate
CpD-Konto *n* (Fin) account held for uncleared settlements, undisclosed customers, etc.
CPFF-Vertrag *m* (com) cost plus fixed fee contract
CPIF-Vertrag *m* (com) cost plus incentive fee contract
CPM-Methode *f* (OR) critical path analysis
Cramèr-Raosche Ungleichung *f* (Math) Cramèr Rao inequality
CRC-Prüfzeichen *n* (EDV) cyclic redundancy check character

D

Dachfonds *m*
(Fin) pyramiding fund
– fund of funds
(ie, assets consist of shares of other investment funds, legally prohibited in 1969)
Dachgesellschaft *f* (Fin) holding company *(ie, either an AG or a GmbH, set up to control and dominate affiliated companies)*
Dachorganisation *f* (com) umbrella organization
Dachprogramm *n* (EDV) = *Organisationsprogramm*
Dachschädenversicherung *f* (Vers) roof damage insurance *(ie, introduction several times attempted but not permitted by insurance supervisory authorities)*
Dachverband *m* (com) umbrella organization
Damnum *n*
(Fin) debt discount *(ie, difference between amount of repayment of a loan and payout amount, § 156 III AktG)*
(Fin) loss *(eg, on exchange rates, securities)*
dämpfen
(com) to check
– to curb
– to damp down
– to retard
– to slow down
Dämpfung *f*
(Vw) curb
– slackening
– slowdown
Dämpfungsfunktion *f* (Math) loss function
Dankschreiben *n*
(com) letter of thanks
(infml) bread-and-butter letter
– (GB) Collins
– (GB) roofer
Darbietung *f* (Mk) presentation
Dargebot *n* (IndE) supply *(eg, water, energy)*
Darlegung *f* (Zo) presentation of goods to be cleared, ready for inspection
Darlehen *n*
(Fin) loan
– advance
(Re) loan *(ie, of money and other fungible things, § 607 I BGB)*
Darlehen *npl* **an Tochtergesellschaften** (ReW) advances to subsidiary companies
Darlehen *n* **aufnehmen**
(Fin) to raise
– to obtain
– to secure
– to take on
– to take up ... a loan
Darlehen *n* **aushandeln**
(Fin) to negotiate *(or* arrange*)* a loan
– to negotiate the terms of a loan
Darlehen *n* **gegen Pfandbestellung**
(Fin) loan secured by chattel mortgage

– collateralized loan
Darlehen *n* **gewähren**
(Fin) to extend
– to grant
– to make ... a loan
Darlehen *n* **kündigen** (Fin) to call *(or* recall*)* a loan
Darlehen *n* **mit täglicher Kündigung** (Fin) loan at call
Darlehensabgeld *n* (Fin) loan discount
Darlehensagio *n* (Fin) loan premium
Darlehensantrag *m* (Fin) application for a loan
Darlehensbedingungen *fpl* (Fin) terms of a loan
Darlehensbestand *m* (Fin) loan portfolio
Darlehensbetrag *m* (Fin) loan amount
Darlehensempfänger *m* (Fin) borrower
Darlehensfinanzierung *f* (Fin) loan financing *(ie, general term to denote financing through outside lenders)*
Darlehensforderung *f*
(Fin) claim under a loan
– loan receivable
Darlehensforderungen *fpl* **abzüglich Wertberichtigungen** (Fin) loans less provisions
Darlehensforderungen *fpl* **gegenüber Betriebsangehörigen** (ReW) due from officers and employees
Darlehensgeber *m* (Fin) lender
Darlehensgeschäft *n* (Fin) lending *(or* loan*)* business
Darlehensgewährung *f* (Fin) loan grant
Darlehenshypothek *f* (Re) mortage securing a loan
Darlehenskasse *f* (Fin) loan bank
Darlehenskonten *npl* **der Töchter** (ReW) loan accounts – subsidiaries of ...
Darlehenskonten *npl* **eigene Tochtergesellschaften** (ReW) loan accounts – own subsidiaries
Darlehenskonto *n* (ReW) loan account
Darlehenskosten *pl* (Fin) loan charges
Darlehensnehmer *m* (Fin) borrower
Darlehenspolitik *f* (Fin) lending policy
Darlehensrückzahlung *f* (Fin) amortization *(or* repayment*)* of a loan
Darlehensschuld *f* (Fin) loan debt
Darlehensschulden *fpl* (Fin) loan debts
Darlehensschuldner *m* (Fin) borrower
Darlehenssumme *f* (Fin) amount of loan
Darlehensvaluta *f* (Fin) loan proceeds
Darlehensverbindlichkeiten *fpl* (Fin) loan liabilities
Darlehensvermittler *m* (Fin) loan broker
Darlehensversprechen *n* (Fin) promise to extend a loan, § 610 BGB
Darlehensvertrag *m* (Fin) loan agreement *(or* contract*)*
Darlehensvertrag *m* **abschließen** (Fin) to conclude a loan agreement
Darlehensvorvertrag *m* (Fin) preliminary loan agreement
Darlehenszinsen *mpl* (Fin) interest on loans, § 608 BGB and §§ 354 II, 352 HGB

Darlehenszinssatz *m*
(Fin) loan interest
– lending rate
Darlehenszusage *f*
(Fin) loan commitment
– promise to grant a loan
Darlehen *n* **tilgen** (Fin) to repay a loan
Darlehen *npl* **von Kreditinstituten** (ReW) bank loans
Darlehen *n* **zurückzahlen** (Fin) to pay off (*or* repay) a loan
darstellende Geometrie *f* (Math) projective geometry
Darstellung *f* (EDV) representation
Darstellungsbasis *f* (EDV) radix factor
Datei *f*
(EDV) (computer) file
– data file
Dateiabschlußanweisung *f* (EDV, Cobol) close statement
Dateiabschnitt *m* (EDV) file section
Dateianfangsetikett *n* (EDV) file header label
Dateianfangskennsatz *m* (EDV, Cobol) beginning file label
Dateiaufbau *m* (EDV) file (*or* record) layout
Dateiaufbereiter *m* (EDV) file editor
Dateiaufbereitungsprogramm *n* (EDV) file edit routine
Dateibereich *m* (EDV) file area
Dateibezeichnung *f* (EDV) file name
Dateidefinition *f* (EDV) file definition
Dateidefinitionsanweisung *f* (EDV) data definition statement
Dateidefinitionsname *m* (EDV) dd name
Dateiende *n* (EDV, Cobol) end of file
Datei-Endekennsatz *m* (EDV, Cobol) end of file label
Dateiendetikett *n*
(EDV) trailer label
– end of file label
Dateiendmarke *f* (EDV) end of file marker (*or* indicator)
Dateikatalog *m* (EDV) data set catalog
Dateikennsatz *m* (EDV, Cobol) file identifier (*or* label)
Dateilücke *f* (EDV) file gap
Dateiname *m* (EDV) file name
Dateischutz *m* (EDV) file protection
Dateisteuerblock *m* (EDV) data control block, DCB
Dateisteuerung *f* (EDV) data file control
Dateiverarbeitung *f* (EDV) file processing
Dateiverbundsystem *n* (EDV) linked file system
Dateiverwaltung *f* (EDV) file management
Dateiwartung *f* (EDV) file maintenance
Dateldienste *mpl* (EDV) datel services
Daten *pl*
(com) data
– facts and figures
– particulars
– conditions
datenabhängiger Fehler *m* (EDV) pattern sensitive fault
Daten *pl* **abrufen** (EDV) to recall data
Datenabruftechnik *f* (EDV) polling method

Datenanzeigeeinrichtung *f* (EDV) data display
Datenaufbereitung *f* (EDV) data preparation
Datenausgabe *f* (EDV) data output
Datenaustausch *m* (EDV) data communication exchange
Datenaustauscheinheit *f* (EDV) data exchange unit
Datenaustauschsteuerung *f* (EDV) data exchange control, DXC
Datenauswahlsteuerung *f* (EDV) data select control
Datenauswertung *f* (Stat) data evaluation
Datenbank *f* (EDV) data bank (*or* base)
Datenbankabfragesystem *n* (EDV) data base inquiry system
Datenbank-Management-System *n* (EDV) data base management system, DBMS
Datenbanksprachen *fpl* (EDV) data base languages (*ie, generic term covering ‚Datenbeschreibungssprachen' and ‚Datenmanipulationssprachen'*)
Datenbanksystem *n* (EDV) data base system
Datenbankverwaltung *f* (EDV) data base management (facilities)
Datenbasis *f* (EDV) data base
Datenbearbeitung *f* (EDV) data manipulation
Datenbehandlungssprache *f* (EDV) data manipulation language
Datenbeschreibung *f* (EDV) data definition
Datenbeschreibungssprache *f* (EDV) data definition language, DDL
Datenbestand *m* (EDV) data stock
Datenbestandsschutz *m* (EDV) data file protection
Datenbit *n* (EDV) information bit (*opp, Kontrollbit = control bit*)
Datenblatt *n* (EDV) spec sheet
Datenblock *m* (EDV) data block
Datenblockadresse *f* (EDV) data block address
Datenbus *m* (EDV) data bus
Datendarstellung *f* (EDV) data representation
Datendirektübertragung *f* (EDV) on-line data transmission
Datendurchsatz *m* (EDV) data throughput
Datenebene *f* (EDV, Cobol) data level
Dateneingabe *f* (EDV) data input
Dateneingabegerät *n* (EDV) data entry unit
Dateneinheit *f* (EDV) data unit
Datenelement *n*
(EDV, Cobol) data element
– elementary item
Datenendeinrichtung *f* (EDV) data processing terminal equipment
Datenendgerät *n*
(EDV) data terminal
– terminal (unit)
Datenendplatz *m*
(EDV) data terminal
– terminal
Datenendstation *f* (EDV) communication terminal
Datenerfassung *f*
(EDV) data acquisition
– data capture
– data collection
– data gathering
Datenerfassungskasse *f* (EDV) point-of-sale (POS) system

Datenfehler *m* (EDV) data error
Datenfeld *n*
 (EDV, Cobol) data item
 – item of date
 – item
 (EDV) data field
Datenfernübertragung *f* (EDV) remote data transmission
Datenfernübertragungssystem *n* **der Kreditinstitute** (Fin) direct fund transfer system
Datenfernverarbeitung *f*
 (EDV) remote data processing
 – telecomputing
 – teleprocessing
Datenfluß *m* (EDV) data flow
Datenflußplan *m* (EDV) data flowchart
Datenflußsteuerung *f* (EDV) data flow control
Datenformat *n* (EDV) data format
Datengewinnung *f* (EDV) data acquisition *(syn, Datenerfassung)*
Datengruppe *f*
 (EDV) array
 (EDV, Cobol) group item
Datenkanal *m* (EDV) data channel
Datenkanalmultiplexor *m* (EDV) data channel multiplexor
Datenkarte *f* (EDV) data card
Datenkasse *f*
 (EDV) POS terminal
 (Mk) stand-alone terminal
Datenkennsatz *m*
 (EDV) dataset label, DSL
 – header label
Datenkettung *f* (EDV) data chaining
Daten-Kompatibilität *f* (EDV) data compatibility
Datenkonstellation *f*
 (com) facts
 – situation
Datenkonvertierung *f* (EDV, Cobol) conversion of data
Datenkonzentrator *m* (EDV) data concentrator
Datenkranz *m*
 (Vw) set of non-economic factors
 – non-economic environment
Datenleitung *f* (EDV) data line *(or circuit)*
Datenlogger *m* (EDV) data logger
Datenmanagement *n* (EDV) data management
Datenmanipulationssprache *f* (EDV) data manipulation language, DML
Datenmißbrauch *m* (EDV) data abuse
Datenname *m* (EDV, Cobol) data name
Datenorganisation *f* (EDV) data organization
Datenpaket *n* (EDV) data packet
Datenpaketübertragung *f* (EDV) packet switching
Datenpfad *m* (EDV) data highway *(or* bus *or* trunk)
Datenprozeßsteuerung *f* (EDV) data processing system
Datenquelle *f* (EDV) data source *(opp, Datensenke)*
Datenreduktion *f* (Stat) reduction of data
Datenretrieval *n* (EDV) data retrieval
Datensammeleinrichtung *f* (EDV) data pooling equipment
Datensatz *m* (EDV, Cobol) data record

Datenschutz *m* (EDV) data privacy protection
Datenschutzbeauftragter *m*
 (EDV) Federal Data Protection Commissioner
 (EDV) data protection officer
Datenschutzgesetz *n* (Re) Federal Data Protection Law
Datensenke *f* (EDV) data sink *(opp, Datenquelle)*
Datensicherung *f* (EDV) data protection
Datensicherung *f* **mit Rückübertragung** (EDV) information feedback system
Datensichtgerät *n*
 (EDV) visual display unit, VDU
 – video terminal
Datensichtplatz *m* (EDV) data display console
Datenspeicher *m* (EDV) data memory *(or* storage)
Datenspeicherorganisation *f* (EDV) data memory organization
Datenstation *f* (EDV) data station *(or* terminal) *(subterms: Dialogstation and Stapelstation; syn, Endstation, Terminal)*
Datenstationsrechner *m* (EDV) terminal computer
Datensteuerung *f* (EDV) data control
Datenstruktur *f* (EDV) data format
Datensucheinrichtung *f* (EDV) file scan unit
Datentechnik *f* (EDV) data systems technology
Datenteil *m* (EDV, Cobol) data division
Datenträger *m* (EDV) data medium *(or* carrier)
Datenträger-Buchführung *f* (ReW) books and recordings in the form of storage media, § 43 IV HGB *(eg, tapes, microfilms, discs)*
Datenträgeretikett *n* (EDV) volume label
Datenträger-Inhaltsverzeichnis *n* (EDV) volume table of contents, VTOC
Datenträgerkatalog *m* (EDV) volume catalog
Datenträgerspeicher *m* (EDV) data carrier storage
Datentransfer *m* (EDV) data transfer
Datenübermittlung *f* (EDV) data communication
Datenübermittlungsabschnitt *m* (EDV) communication *(or* data) link
Datenübermittlungsgerät *n* (EDV) data transmission unit
Daten *pl* **übertragen** (EDV) to transfer data
Datenübertragung *f*
 (EDV) data transfer
 (EDV) data communication
 (EDV) data transmission
Datenübertragungsblock *m* (EDV) frame
Datenübertragungs-Einrichtungen *fpl* (EDV) data transmission facilities
Datenübertragungsgeschwindigkeit *f* (EDV) transmission speed
Datenübertragungskanal *m* (EDV) data channel
Datenübertragungsleitung *f* (EDV) data transmission line
Datenübertragungsprogramm *n* (EDV) communication control program, CCP
Datenübertragungssteuerung *f* (EDV) communication control
Datenübertragungssteuerzeichen *n* (EDV) transmission control character
Datenübertragungsvorrechner *m* (EDV) front-end processor
Datenübertragungsweg *m* (EDV) data bus
Datenumsetzung *f* (EDV) data conversion

Datenverarbeitung *f* (EDV) data (*or* information) processing
Datenverarbeitungsanlage *f* (EDV) computer
– data processing (*or* dp) equipment
(syn, Rechenanlage)
Datenverarbeitungssystem *n* (EDV) data processing system *(syn, Rechensystem)*
Datenverbund *m* (EDV) data combination
Datenverdichtung *f* (EDV) data reduction
Datenvermittlungstechnik *f* (EDV) data switching
Datenverwaltung *f* (EDV) data management
Datenwort *n* (EDV) data word
datieren (com) to date
Datierung *f* (com) dating *(eg, of a document)*
dato (com, *obsolete*) date
Datowechsel *m*
(Fin) after-date bill of exchange
– bill (payable) after date
(opp, Tageswechsel, Datumswechsel)
Datum *n* **des Angebots** (com) date of quotation
Datum *n* **des Inkrafttretens** (Re) effective date
Datum *n* **des Poststempels** (com) date as postmark
Datumsangabe *f*
(com) date *(eg, undated letter)*
(Mk) code date *(eg, printed on perishable goods)*
Datumsstempel *m*
(com) dater
– date stamp
Datumswechsel *m*
(Fin) bill payable at a fixed date
– day bill
(syn, Tagwechsel; opp, Datowechsel)
Dauer *f*
(com) duration
(Re) term
(OR) elapsed time
Dauerabfluß *m*
(Vw) permanent drain
Daueranlage *f*
(Fin) permanent holding
– long-term investment
Daueranleger *m* (Fin) long-term investor
Daueranschlag *m* (Mk) permanent advertising *(ie, mostly for several years; opp, Bogenanschlag)*
Dauerarbeitslosigkeit *f* (Vw) chronic unemployment
Dauerauftrag *m*
(com) standing order
(Fin) money transfer order *(ie, the practice is rare in America)*
– (GB) banker's order
– mandate
Dauerausschreibung *f* (com) standing invitation to tender
Dauerbelastung *f* (com) permanent burden
Dauerbeschäftigung *f* (Pw) permanent employment
Dauerbetrieb *m* (IndE) continuous operation
Dauer *f* **der Beschäftigung** (Pw) length of employment (*or* service)
Daueremission *f*
(Fin) constant issue
– issue offered continuously
– tap issue

(ie, by mortgage banks and certain banks making communal loans)
Daueremittent *m*
(Fin) constant issuer
(Bö) tap issuer
Dauerfinanzierung *f* (Fin) continuous funding
dauerhafte Güter *npl*
(Vw) durable goods
– durables
dauerhafte Konsumgüter *npl*
(Vw) durable consumer goods
– consumer durables
dauerhafte Nutzung *f* (Bw) permanent use (*or* flow of services)
dauerhafte Produktionsmittel *npl* (Vw) producer durables
Dauerinflation *f* (Vw) persistent inflation
Dauerinserent *m* (Mk) rate holder
Dauerkonsortium *n* (Fin) standing loan syndicate
Dauerkredit *m* (Fin) long-term credit
Dauerkrise *f* (Vw) permanent crisis
Dauerkunde *m*
(com) regular customer
– repeat buyer
Dauerkundschaft *f* (com) established clientele
dauernde Einrede *f* (Re) peremptory defense (*or* exception) *(syn, ausschließende od zerstörliche od peremptorische Einrede)*
dauernde Erwerbsunfähigkeit *f* (SozV) permanent incapacity for self-support
dauernde Invalidität *f* (SozV) permanent disablement
dauernde Lasten *fpl* (StR) permanent burden (*or* charges) *(ie, obligation imposed on a person, or, more often, an encumbrance of real property, § 9 I No. 1 EStG)*
dauernd getrennt lebend (StR) permanently separated, § 10 I No. 1 EStG
dauernd pflegebedürftig (SozV) permanently in need of care
Dauernutzungsrecht *n* (Re) proprietary lease
Dauerposten *m* (Pw) permanent job (*or* position)
Dauerprüfung *f*
(ReW) continuing audit
(Stat) endurance test
Dauerregelung *f* (com) permanent arrangement
Dauerrente *f* (SozV) permanent pension *(ie, paid to injured persons by the statutory accident insurance fund)*
Dauerschaden *m* (SozV) permanent injury
Dauerschulden *fpl* (StR) permanent debts *(ie, serving to strengthen the capital structure of a business for a substantial length of time, § 8 No. 1 GewStG)*
Dauerschuldverhältnis *n* (Re) continuous obligation *(ie, contracts under which debtor's performance extends over a longer period of time, esp. if performance takes place in installments)*
Dauerschuldzinsen *mpl* (StR) interest on permanent debt, § 8 No. 1 GewStG
Dauersparauftrag *m* (Fin) automatic deduction plan *(ie, under which a bank transfers to a savings account a specified sum at fixed intervals)*
Dauersparen *n* (Fin) long-term saving
Dauerspeicher *m* (EDV) non-erasable (*or* perma-

149

nent) storage *(syn, Permanentspeicher, Strukturspeicher)*
Dauerstellung *f* (Pw) permanent position
Dauerverpflichtungen *fpl* (FiW) permanent obligations
Dauerversuch *m* (Stat) endurance test
Dauervollmacht *f* (Re) permanent power of attorney
Dauerwerkzeuge *npl* (KoR) permanent tools
Dauerwohnrecht *n* (Re) permanent residential *(or* occupancy) right *(ie, recorded on the land register = Grundbuch, may be sold and inherited)*
Dauerwohnrechtsvertrag *m* (Re) contract relating to permanent residential right
Dauerwohnsitz *m* (Re) permanent residence
D/A-Umsetzer *m*
 (EDV) digital-analog converter
 – digitizer
davonlaufende Preise *mpl* (com) skyrocketing prices
DCF-Analyse *f*
 (Fin) discounted cash flow analysis
 – DCF *(or* dcf) analysis
DD-Anweisung *f* (EDV) data definition statement *(syn, Dateidefinitionsanweisung)*
Debet *n* (ReW) debit side *(ie, of an account)*
Debetbuchung *f* (ReW) debit entry
Debetsaldo *m*
 (ReW) balance due
 – debit balance
Debetseite *f* (ReW) debit side *(ie, of an account)*
Debetspalte *f* (ReW) debit column
Debetzins *m* (Fin) interest on debit balance
Debitoren *pl*
 (ReW) accounts receivable
 – customer's accounts
 – receivables
 (Fin) lendings
Debitorenausfälle *mpl* (Fin) loan writeoffs
Debitorenbewegungsdatei *f* (ReW) accounts receivable *(or* A/R) journal entry file
Debitorenbuch *n* (ReW) accounts receivable transactions register
Debitorenbuchhaltung *f* (ReW) accounts receivable department
Debitorenbuchung *f* (ReW) accounts receivable entry
Debitorengeschäft *n* (Fin) lending business
Debitorenjournal *n* (ReW) accounts receivable transactions register
Debitorenkonto *n* (ReW) accounts receivable account
Debitorenkontoauszug *m* (ReW) A/R statement
Debitorenkredit *m* (Fin) accounts receivable loan
Debitorensaldo *m* (ReW) balance due
Debitorensätze *mpl* (Fin) lending rates
Debitorenverkauf *m* (Fin) sale of accounts receivable
Debitorenversicherung *f* (Vers) accounts receivable insurance
Debitorenwagnis *n* (ReW) accounts receivable risk *(syn, Vertriebswagnis)*
Debitorenziehung *f* (Fin) bill drawn by a bank on a debtor *(ie, may also be a promissory note made out by a debtor and presented to his bank)*

Deckladung *f* (com) deck cargo
Deckladungsversicherung *f* (Vers) deck cargo insurance
Deckung *f*
 (Vw) backing *(ie, of a currency)*
 (Bö) covering purchase
 – short covering
 (Vers) insurance coverage
 – (GB) insurance cover
 (ie, indicating the aggregate risks covered by a particular policy)
Deckung *f* **anschaffen** (Fin) to provide cover
Deckung *f* **der Anleihezinsen durch die Gewinne des Unternehmens** (Fin) interest times earned
Deckung *f* **im Leergeschäft** (Bö) short covering
Deckungsanschaffung *f* (Fin) provision of cover
Deckungsauflage *f* (com) break-even number of printed copies *(ie, of a book that must be sold to cover direct cost and prorated overhead)*
Deckungsauftrag *m* (Bö) covering order
Deckungsbedürfnisse *npl* (FiW) budgetary requirements
Deckungsbeitrag *m*
 (KoR) contribution margin
 – profit contribution
 – variable gross margin *(or* profit)
 – marginal balance
 – marginal income
 (ie, net sales – all variable expenses)
Deckungsbeitrag *m* **in %** (KoR) contribution margin percentage
Deckungsbeitrag *m* **je Engpaßeinheit** (KoR) contribution per unit of limiting factor
Deckungsbeitrag *m* **pro Ausbringungseinheit** (KoR) unit contribution margin
Deckungsbeitragsplan *m* (KoR) contribution budget
Deckungsbeitragsrechnung *f* (KoR) contribution costing *(or* analysis)
 – contribution margin technique
 – (US) = *direct costing*
 – (GB) = *marginal costing*
 (ie, today mostly synonymous with ‚Grenzplankostenrechnung')
Deckungsbeschränkung *f* (Fin) cover restriction
Deckungsbestätigung *f*
 (Fin) confirmation of cover
 – cover note
Deckungsbetrag *m* (com) amount of coverage
Deckungsdarlehen *n* (Fin) covering loan
deckungsfähiges Risiko *n* (Fin) coverable risk
deckungsfähige Wertpapiere *npl* (Fin) fixed-interest securities which the central bank may use as cover in its open market operations
Deckungsfonds *m* (Fin) cover fund
Deckungsforderungen *fpl* (Fin) covering claims
Deckungsfrist *f* (Vers) duration of cover
Deckungsgeschäft *n* (com, Bö) covering transaction
Deckungsgrad *m* (Fin) cover *(or* liquidity) ratio *(eg, balance sheet ratios, such as: fixed assets to equity + long-term debt; cash and short-term receivables to current liablities; debt-equity ratio)*
Deckungsgrenze *f* (Fin) cover limit
Deckungsguthaben *n*
 (Fin) coverage deposit

Deckungsguthaben
— covering balance
(Fin) bond-covered mortgage *(ie, zur Deckung von Hypothekenpfandbriefen)*
(Vers) mortgage investment based upon premium reserve stock
Deckungskapital *n*
(Fin) guaranty fund
(Vers) premium reserve
— unearned premium reserve
— mathematical reserve
— reimbursement fund
— (GB) cover of assurance
Deckungskauf *m*
(com) covering purchase
(Bö) covering
— short covering
— hedge transaction
Deckungsklausel *f* (FiW) cover clause *(ie, exceptional authorization to appropriate funds for purposes other than those specified in the budget)*
Deckungskonto *n* (Fin) cover account
Deckungslücke *f*
(FiW) budgetary deficit
— shortfall
(SozV) deficit
Deckungslücke *f* **schließen** (FiW) to close the gap *(ie, between receipts and expenditures)*
Deckungsmittel *pl* (FiW) cover funds
Deckungsorder *f* (Bö) covering order
Deckungspapiere *npl* (Fin) securities pledged as collateral
Deckungspunktanalyse *f* (KoR) breakeven analysis
Deckungspunkt *m* (KoR) breakeven point
Deckungsquote *f* (Fin) cover ratio
Deckungsrücklage *f* (Vers) = *Deckungskapital*
Deckungsrückstellung *f*
(Vers) pro rata unearned premium reserve
— (GB) cover of assurance
(ie, the terms ‚Deckungsrücklage' and ‚Prämienreservefonds', though often used, are inappropriate; the reserve is set up as an interest-bearing pool of premiums)
Deckungssatz *m* (Vers) cover (*or* reserve) ratio
Deckungsschutz *m* (Vers) insurance protection
Deckungsstock *m*
(Vers) premium reserve stock
— cover fund
(ie, total assets available as cover for the sum total of premium reserves, separately administered and supervised by a trustee)
deckungsstockfähig (Vers) eligible for investment in premium reserve stock
Deckungsstockfähigkeit *f* (Vers) eligibility for investment in premium reserve stock
Deckungsstockgrundsatz *m* (Vers) cover fund principle
Deckungssumme *f* (Vers) amount insured
Deckungssysteme *npl* (Vers, SozV) cover systems
Deckungsumsatz *m* (KoR) breakeven sales *(ie, sales volume absorbing all costs)*
Deckungsverhältnis *n* (Vw) cover ratio *(ie, currency to gold or foreign exchange)*
Deckungsverkauf *m*
(Re) resale of goods by unpaid seller

(Bö) covering sale
— hedging sale
Deckungszeitpunkt *m* (KoR) breakeven time *(ie, term used in cumulative profit analysis: point of time in a planning period where the cumulative profit contributions are higher than the cumulative fixed costs)*
Deckungszusage *f*
(Vers) cover note *(ie, prepared by an agent)*
— binder *(ie, prepared by the insurance company)*
— slip *(ie, used in property and transportation insurance)*
decodieren (EDV) to decode
Decodierer *m* (EDV) decoder
Decodiermatrix *f* (EDV) decoder matrix
Découvert *n* (Bö) = *Leerverkauf*
Dedikationsexemplar *n*
(com) complimentary (*or* courtesy) copy *(syn, Widmungsexemplar)*
Deduktion *f*
(Log) deduction
— inference
Deduktionsgesetz *n* (Log) theorem of deduction
Deduktionsregel *f* (Log) rule of inference
Deduktionsschluß *m* (Log) inference
Deduktionstheorem *n* (Log) theorem of deduction
deduktive Methode *f* (Log, Math) deductive (*or* axiomatic) method
deduktiver Beweis *m* (Log) deductive proof
deduzieren
(Log) to deduce
— to infer
Defekt *m* **der Matrix** (Math) nullity of a matrix
defensive Investitionspolitik *f* (Bw) defensive investment policy
Defensivstrategie *f* (Bw) defensive strategy
Defensivzeichen *n* (Pat) defensive trademark, § 2 I WZG
Deficit Spending *n*
(FiW) deficit spending
— budgetary reflation
(ie, stimulating demand by widening the public sector's debt)
definieren (Log) to define
Definition *f* (Log) definition
Definition *f* **durch Induktion** (Log) recursive definition
Definitionsbereich *m* (Math) universal set of reference
Definitionsbereich *m* **e–r Funktion** (Math) domain of a function
Definitionsgleichung *f* (Vw) definitional equation
Definitionsintervall *n* (Math) defining range
definitorische Beziehung *f* (Log) definitional relationship
definitorische Identität *f* (Log) definitional identity
defiziente Zahl *f* (Math) defective (*or* deficient) number
Defizit *n*
(com, FiW) deficit
— shortfall
defizitär
(Fin) in deficit

– (infml) deficit-ridden
(AuW) in a deficit position
Defizit *n* **der Leistungsbilanz**
(AuW) deficit on current account
– current account deficit
Defizit *n* **der Zahlungsbilanz**
(AuW) balance of payments deficit
– external deficit
Defizit-Finanzierung *f* (FiW) deficit financing (*or* spending)
Defizit *n* **in laufender Rechnung** (AuW) deficit on current account
Defizitland *n* (AuW) deficit country
Defizitmultiplikator *m* (FiW) deficit multiplier
Deflation *f* (Vw) deflation
deflationäre Tendenzen *fpl* (Vw) deflationary tendencies
deflationieren
(Stat) to deflate
(Vw) to revalue
Deflationierungsfaktor *m* (Vw) deflator
deflationistisch (Vw) deflationary
Deflationsspirale *f* (Vw) deflationary spiral
Deflator *m* (Vw) deflator *(ie, GNP ‚implicit price deflator': compensating subtraction to determine the effect of rising prices)*
deflatorische Impulse *mpl* (Vw) deflationary impulses
deflatorische Lücke *f* (Vw) deflationary gap
deflatorisches Gleichgewicht *n* (Vw) equilibrium under deflationary conditions
Deformation *f* (SeeV) deformation
Degeneration *f* (OR) degenerate solution
Degenerationsphase *f* (Mk) decline stage *(ie, of product life cycle)*
degenerierte Lösung *f* (OR) degenerate solution
Degression *f* (FiW, KoR) degression
Degressionsgewinne *mpl*
(Vw) economies of scale
– scale economies
Degressionsschwelle *f* (KoR) level of activity where the unit costs are at a minimum and equal to marginal costs
degressive Abschreibung *f*
(ReW) declining balance method *(of depreciation)*
– diminishing provision method
– reducing balance method
(syn, geometrisch-degressive Abschreibung; opp, arithmetisch-degressive Abschreibung)
degressive Afa *f* (StR) declining-balance tax depreciation *(ie, includes sum-of-the-years-digit method = digitale Abschreibung, § 7 II 2 EStG*
degressive Akkorde *mpl* (IndE) degressive premiums *(eg, Rowan-Lohn)*
degressive Doppelraten-Abschreibung *f* (ReW) double-rate declining balance method (of depreciation)
degressive Kosten *pl* (KoR) degressive costs *(ie, falling average, unit or total costs in relation to a level of activity)*
degressiver Tarif *m* (com) tapering rate
degressive Steuer *f* (FiW) degressive tax
dehnbarer Begriff *m* (Log) elastic concept

dekadischer Logarithmus *m*
(Math) common logarithm
– Briggs' (*or* Briggsian) logarithm
Dekartellisierung *f*
(Kart) decartelization *(ie, general term)*
– deconcentration *(ie, term used in banking)*
Deklaration *f*
(com) declaration *(ie, of contents and value in postal consignments)*
(StR) tax return
(Zo) customs declaration
Deklaration *f* **für zollfreie Waren** (Zo) entry for duty-free goods
Deklarationsprinzip *n* (StR) declaration principle *(ie, duty of taxpayer to cooperate in determining tax liability; eg, by filing tax returns; opp, Quellenprinzip, retained in wages tax)*
Deklarationsprotest *m* (WeR) declaratory protest
Deklarationsschein *m* (Zo) declaration certificate
Deklarationswert *m* (Zo) declared value
Deklaration *f* **zur Einlagerung unter Zollverschluß** (Zo) warehousing entry
deklaratorischer Charakter *m* (Re) declaratory effect
deklaratorische Urkunde *f* (Re) declaratory instrument
(eg, receipt, declaratory judgment = Feststellungsurteil; it declares a right, but does not establish it: it is not a ‚constating instrument')
deklarieren (Zo) to declare goods
Dekomposition *f* (OR) decomposition *(ie, of a program)*
Dekompositions-Algorithmus *m* (OR) decomposition algorithm
Dekompositionsprinzip *n* (OR) principle of decomposition
Dekonzentration *f* (Kart) deconcentration *(ie, in banking)*
Dekoration *f* (Mk) window dressing (*or* display)
Dekort *m*
(com) deduction for substandard quality
(com) cash discount in wholesaling
(com) rebate in export business
Delegation *f* (Bw) delegation *(ie, of authority and activity to subordinate units = untergeordnete Stellen)*
Delegation *f* **funktionaler Kompetenz** (Bw) function authority delegation
Delegationsbefugnis *f* (Bw) power of delegation
Delegationsbereich *m* (Bw) delegated decision area
Delegation *f* **von Kompetenzen** (Bw) delegation of authority
Delikt *n* (Re) unlawful (*or* wrongful) act
– tort
– tortious act
(ie, does not include breach of contract; syn, ‚unerlaubte Handlung')
deliktische Haftung *f* (Re) tortious (*or* delictual) liability
deliktsfähig (Re) capable of unlawful acts
Deliktsfähigkeit *f* (Re) capacity to commit unlawful acts
Deliktshaftung *f* (Re) liability in tort

Delkredere *n*
(Re) del credere *(ie, direct personal liability of assignor or commission agent to make good a loss arising from failure of purchaser to pay)*
(ReW) provision for contingent losses
– writeoff of uncollectible receivables *(or* uncollectible accounts)
Delkredereagent *m* (com) del credere agent
Delkrederegeschäft *n* (com) del credere business
Delkrederehaftung *f* (Re) del credere liability
Delkredereklausel *f* (com) del credere clause
Delkrederekonto *n*
(ReW) reserve set up to cover losses of receivables *(ie, expected for the end of the business year)*
– provision for doubtful debts
Delkredereprovision *f* (com) del credere commission *(ie, paid for undertaking to guarantee the fulfillment of obligations arising from a deal, § 86 b HGB)*
Delkrederereserven *fpl* (Fin) additional loan loss allowances
Delkredererisiko *n* (com) collection risk *(ie, particularly high in export trade)*
Delkredererückstellung *f* (ReW) provision for doubtful debts *(ie, set up to meet a del credere liability)*
Delkredere *n* **übernehmen** (com) to assume del credere liability
Delkredere-Versicherung *f* (Vers) del credere insurance
Delkredere-Vertrag *m* (com) del credere agreement
Delkredere-Vertreter *m* (com) del credere agent
Delkredere-Wertberichtigung *f* (ReW) (indirect) writedown of uncollectible receivables
Delphi-Methode *f* (Bw) delphi method *(ie, using structured group interviews, developed by RAND Corporation)*
Delphi-Prognose *f* (Bw) jury-of-executive opinion
Demigrossist *m* (com) semi-wholesaler *(ie, wholesaler who also engages in retailing)*
demnächst
(com) coming
– fortcoming
Demographie *f* (Stat) demography
demokratischer Führungsstil *m* (Bw) democratic style of leadership *(or* management)
Demometrie *f* (Stat) demometry
demonetisieren
(Vw) to demonetize *(ie, to divest a monetary standard – Münzeinheit – of value)*
(Vw) to withdraw *(ie, money from use)*
Demonetisierung *f*
(Vw) demonetization
(Vw) withdrawal
Demonstrationsanlage *f* (IndE) demonstration *(or* pilot) plant
Demontage *f* (com) dismantlement
Demoskopie *f* (Stat) public opinion research *(ie, by means of surveys or polls)*
Denkgesetze *npl* (Log) laws of thought
Denkmodell *n* (Log) conceptual model
Denomination *f* (Fin) form of capital reduction of a German stock corporation

Denotation *f*
(Log) denotation *(ie, of a concept)*
– extension
(opp, Konnotation, Intension)
denotative Definition *f* (Log) denotative definition
deontische Logik *f* (Log) deontic logic
Deponent *m*
(Fin) depositor *(eg, of money)*
(Fin) bailor *(ie, in safekeeping)*
Deponentenaktien *fpl* (Fin) deposited shares *(ie, for which banks may vote proxies in their own name)*
deponieren
(Fin) to deposit
(Fin) to hand over for safe-keeping
Deport *m*
(Bö) delayed delivery penalty
– (GB) backwardation *(ie, London Stock Exchange term: percentage of the selling price payable by the seller of shares for the privilege of delaying their delivery; opp, Report)*
Deportgeschäft *n* (Bö) backwardation business *(opp, Reportgeschäft)*
Deportsatz *m* (Bö) backwardation rate
Depositalschein *m* (Fin) = *Depotschein*
Depositen *pl* (Fin) deposits *(ie, demand and time deposits)*
Depositenbank *f* (Fin) deposit bank
Depositeneinlage *f* (Fin) deposit
Depositengelder *npl*
(Fin) deposit money
– deposits
Depositengeschäft *n* (Fin) deposit banking *(or* business)
Depositenkonto *n* (Fin) deposit account
Depositenkonto *n* **mit festgesetzter Fälligkeit** (Fin) deposit account with fixed maturity
Depositenkonto *n* **mit vereinbarter Kündigungsfrist** (Fin) deposit account at notice
Depositenmultiplikator *m* (Vw) deposit multiplier
Depositenschein *m* (com) deposit receipt
Depositenversicherung *f* (Vers) bank deposit insurance *(ie, not used in Germany; see U. S. Banking Act, 1935)*
Depositenzertifikat *n* (Fin) Certificate of Deposit
Depositenzinsen *mpl* (Fin) deposit rate
Depot *n*
(com) storehouse
– warehouse *(ie, where freight is deposited)*
(Fin) securities account
Depot A *n* (Fin) own security deposit, § 13 DepG *(syn, Eigendepot)*
Depot B *n* (Fin) third-party securities account *(syn, Anderdepot)*
Depot C *n* (Fin) pledged securities deposit *(syn, Pfanddepot)*
Depot D *n* (Fin) special pledged-securities deposit *(syn, Sonderpfanddepot)*
Depotabstimmung *f* (Fin) securities account reconciliation
Depotabteilung *f* (Fin) securities deposit department
Depotaktien *fpl* (Fin) deposited shares *(ie, for which banks may vote proxies in their own name)*
Depotaufstellung *f* (Fin) list of securities deposited

Depotauszug m (Fin) statement of securities
Depotbank f (Fin) depositary bank
Depotberechtigter m (Fin) depositor
Depotbescheinigung f (Fin) deposit certificate
Depotbesitz m (Fin) holding of deposited securities
Depotbuch n (Fin) deposit ledger *(ie, maintained by bailee of deposited securities, § 14 DepG)*
Depotbuchhaltung f (Fin) securities accounts department
Depotgebühr f (Fin) safe custody charge (*or* fee)
Depotgeschäft n
  (Fin) custody business
  − security deposit business
  − portfolio management
  (ie, custody and administration of securities for the account of others)
Depotgesetz n (Re) Law on the Deposit and Acquisition of Securities, of 4 Feb 1937
Depotinhaber m (Fin) securities account holder
Depotkonto n
  (Fin) security deposit account
  − securities account
Depotprüfer m (Fin) securities deposit auditor
Depotprüfung f (Fin) audit of security deposit holdings *(ie, annually by auditors appointed by the Federal Supervisory Office or by the Bundesbank, § 30 KWG)*
Depotschein m
  (Fin) safe custody receipt
  − deposit receipt
Depotstimmrecht n
  (Fin) proxy voting power
  − right of banks to vote proxies
  − bank's right to vote deposited shares at a general meeting
  (ie, under German law, a bank automatically votes all proxies according to the decisions of its management, unless shareholders have given instructions to the contrary)
Depotstück n (Fin) security deposited at a bank
Depotumbuchung f (Fin) transfer of securities
Depotverpfändung f (Fin) pledging of security holding
Depotversicherung f (Vers) deposit insurance
Depotvertrag m (Fin) safe custody agreement *(ie, relating to the custody and management of securities, §§ 688ff BGB and relevant provisions of ‚Depotgesetz')*
Depotverwaltung f
  (Fin) management of deposited securities
  − portfolio management
Depotwechsel m (Fin) collateral bill *(ie, deposited with a bank)*
Depression f
  (Vw) depression
  − (US) business panic
Deputat n (Pw) payment in kind *(eg, free coal for miners)*
Dereliktion f (Pw) voluntary abandonment of a movable thing, § 959 BGB
derivativer Firmenwert m (ReW) acquired goodwill, § 153 V AktG and § 6 I No. 2 EStG
Derivierte f (Math) derivative
derzeitiger Wohnort m (Re) current residence

Desaggregation f
  (Stat) disaggregation
  − breakdown
desaggregierte Größe f (Vw) subaggregate
Designat n (Log) designatum
Designierungsverfahren n (IWF) designation procedure
Desinflation f (Vw) disinflation *(ie, reduction of price level to the plateau of long-term marginal costs)*
Desinvestition f
  (Vw) disinvestment
  − negative investment
Desinvestitionsperiode f (Fin) recovery period *(ie, period in which the tied-up capital flows back with interest)*
Desinvestitionsprogramm n (Bw) disinvestment program *(ie, to shed unnecessary assets)*
Desinvestitionsvorgang m (Fin) disinvestment process
deskriptive Anweisung f (EDV) non-executable statement
deskriptiver Satz m (Log) descriptive (*or* positive) statement
deskriptive Statistik f (Stat) descriptive statistics
Deskriptorenverknüpfung f (EDV) interfixing of descriptors
Desorganisation f (Bw) disorganization
Destinatar m
  (com) consignee *(ie, recipient of goods named in a waybill*
  (Re) beneficiary *(ie, of a foundation)*
destruktives Lesen n (EDV) destructive reading
Detailflußdiagramm n (EDV) detail flowchart
Detailhandel m (com) *(obsolescent term for:)* retail trade
Detailkollektion f (com) primary collection *(eg, of scrap, eggs)*
detaillierte Aufstellung f
  (com) detailed list
  − breakdown
detaillierte Berichterstattung f (ReW) detailed (*or* segmental) reporting
detaillierte Übersicht f
  (com) detailed report
  − detailed statement
  − rundown
Detaillist m (com) *(obsolescent term for:)* retailer
Detailplanung f (Bw) detailed planning
Detailreisehandel m (com) traveling salesman's trade *(ie, door-to-door canvassing of mail orders)*
Determinante f (Math) determinant
Determinantengleichung f (Math) determinantal equation
Determinantenschreibweise f (Math) determinant form (*or* notation)
deterministische Entscheidung f (Stat) deterministic decision
Deutsche Angestelltengewerkschaft f (Pw) German Salaried Employee Union
Deutsche Bundesbahn f (com) German Federal Railways
Deutsche Bundesbank f
  (Fin) West German Central Bank

- Deutsche Bundesbank
- the Bundesbank

Deutsche Bundespost *f* (com) German Federal Post Office

Deutsche Genossenschaftsbank *f* (com) Central Bank of German Cooperatives

Deutscher Beamtenbund *m* (Pw) German Public Service Federation

Deutscher Einheitsmietvertrag *m* (Re) German Standard Tenancy Agreement, DEMV

Deutscher Gewerkschaftsbund *m* (Pw) German Trade Union Federation

Deutscher Industrie- und Handelstag *m* (com) German Industrial and Trade Association *(ie, umbrella organization covering the 69 German chambers of commerce)*

Deutscher Sparkassen- und Giroverband *m* (Fin) German Savings Banks' and Giro Association

Deutscher Städtetag *m* (com) Federation of German Towns
- German City Diet

Deutsches Bundespatentamt *n* (Pat) German Federal Patent Office
- West German Patent Office

Deutsches Institut *n* **für Wirtschaftsforschung** (Vw) *(Berlin-based)* German Institute for Economic Research

Devalvation *f* (Vw) currency depreciation

Deviation *f* (com) deviation from scheduled route

Devisen *pl* (Fin) foreign exchange
- exchange
- foreign currency

Devisenabfluß *m* (AuW) outflow of foreign exchange

Devisenabkommen *n* (AuW) foreign exchange agreement

Devisenabrechnung *f* (Fin) foreign exchange note

Devisenankaufskurs *m* (Fin) buying rate

Devisenarbitrage *f*
(Fin) arbitration of exchange
- currency arbitrage
- exchange arbitrage

Devisenaufgeld *n* (Fin) premium on exchange

Devisenausgleichsabkommen *n* (AuW) foreign exchange offset agreement

Devisenausländer *m* (AuW) non-resident *(ie, term replaced by ‚Gebietsfremder')*

Devisenbeschränkungen *fpl* (AuW) foreign exchange restrictions

Devisenbestände *mpl*
(Fin) currency holdings *(or* reserves*)*
- foreign exchange holdings *(or* reserves*)*
- exchange holdings
- holdings of exchange
(Vw) reserve balances

Devisenbestimmungen *fpl* (AuW) exchange *(or* currency*)* regulations

Devisenbewirtschaftung *f*
(AuW) control of foreign exchange
- currency control
- exchange control
- foreign exchange control
- (US *also*) monetary controls

Devisenbewirtschaftungsmaßnahmen *fpl* (AuW) exchange controls

Devisenbilanz *f*
(AuW) foreign exchange account
- net exchange movements

Devisenbörse *f* (Bö) foreign exchange market

Devisenbringer *mpl* (AuW) foreign exchange earners *(eg, machinery exports, oil, tin, rubber)*

Devisendefizitland *n* (AuW) exchange deficit country

Deviseneigenhandel *m* (Fin) foreign exchange dealings for own account *(of a bank)*

Deviseneinnahmen *fpl*
(Fin) currency receipts
- exchange proceeds

Devisenengagements *npl* (Fin) foreign exchange commitments

Devisenerlöse *mpl* (AuW) foreign exchange earnings

Devisengeschäft *n*
(Fin) foreign exchange transaction
(Fin) foreign exchange trading

Devisenguthaben *n* (Fin) foreign exchange holdings

Devisenhandel *m*
(Fin) foreign exchange trade *(or* trading*)*
- dealings in foreign exchange
- foreign exchange dealings

Devisenhändler *m*
(Fin) exchange dealer *(or* trader*)*
- foreign exchange dealer *(or* trader*)*

Deviseninländer *m* (AuW) resident *(ie, term replaced by ‚Gebietsansässiger')*

Devisenkassageschäft *n* (Bö) spot exchange transaction

Devisenkassahandel *m* (Bö) spot exchange trading

Devisenkassakurs *m* (Bö) spot exchange rate

Devisenkassamarkt *m* (Bö) spot exchange market

Devisenknappheit *f* (AuW) shortage of foreign exchange

Devisenkontingent *n* (AuW) foreign exchange quota

Devisenkontingentierung *f* (AuW) foreign exchange allocation

Devisenkonto *n* (Fin) foreign exchange account *(syn, Währungskonto, Fremdwährungskonto)*

Devisenkontrolle *f* (AuW) exchange control

Devisenkontrolle *f* **an der Grenze** (AuW) currency check at the border

Devisenkontrollerklärung *f* (AuW) exchange control declaration

Devisenkredit *m* (Fin) foreign exchange loan

Devisenkurs *m*
(Fin) foreign exchange rate
- exchange rate
- rate of exchange

Devisenkursarbitrage *f* (Fin) foreign exchange arbitrage

Devisenkursfeststellung *f* (Bö) exchange rate fixing

Devisenkursnotierung *f* (Bö) exchange rate quotation

Devisenkurssicherung *f* (Fin) exchange rate hedging

Devisenkurszettel *m* (Bö) list of foreign exchange

155

Devisenmakler *m*
   (Bö) foreign exchange broker
   – exchange broker
   – cambist
Devisenmangel *m* (AuW) scarcity of foreign exchange
Devisenmarkt *m*
   (Bö) foreign exchange market
   – exchange market
   – currency market
Devisenmarktintervention *f* (Fin) exchange market intervention
Devisenmarktkurs *m* (Fin) market exchange rate
Devisenmittelkurs *m* (Fin) middle rate
Devisen-Pensionsgeschäft *n*
   (Fin) purchase of foreign exchange for later resale
   – foreign exchange transaction under repurchase agreement
Devisenplafond *m* (AuW) foreign exchange ceiling
Devisenpolitik *f* (AuW) foreign exchange policy
Devisenpolster *n* (AuW) foreign exchange cushion (*or* reserve)
Devisenportefeuille *n* (Fin) foreign exchange holdings
Devisenposition *f* (AuW) foreign exchange position
Devisenquoten *fpl* (AuW) foreign exchange quotas (*ie, allocated to importers, instrument of bilateralism*)
Devisenreserven *fpl*
   (AuW) foreign currency reserves
   – foreign exchange reserves
   – currency reserves
Devisenrestriktionen *fpl* (AuW) exchange restrictions
Devisenschmuggel *m*
   (com) smuggling of foreign exchange
   – currency smuggling
Devisenspekulation *f* (Fin) foreign exchange speculation
Devisenspekulationsgewinn *m* (Fin) gain on foreign exchange speculation
Devisen-Swapgeschäft *n* (Fin) foreign exchange swap
Devisenterminbörse *f* (Bö) forward market in currency
Devisentermingeschäft *n*
   (Bö) forward exchange dealing
   – forward exchange
   – exchange futures
   – future exchange transaction
Devisenterminhandel *m* (Bö) forward exchange trading
Devisenterminkurs *m* (Bö) forward exchange rate
Devisenterminmarkt *m* (Bö) forward exchange market
Devisenterminpolitik *f* (AuW) forward exchange policy
Devisentransfer *m* (Fin) currency transfer
Devisenüberschuß *m* (AuW) foreign exchange surplus
Devisenverfügbarkeit *f* (AuW) availability of foreign exchange
Devisenvergehen *n* (AuW) violation of foreign exchange regulations

Devisenverkaufskurs *m* (Fin) selling rate
Devisenverkehr *m* (Fin) foreign exchange transactions
Devisenverkehrsbeschränkungen *fpl* (AuW) exchange restrictions
Devisen-Verrechnungsabkommen *n* (AuW) exchange clearing agreement
Devisenvorschriften *fpl* (AuW) foreign exchange regulations
Devisenwährung *f* (AuW) currency exchange standard
Devisenwechsel *m*
   (Fin) foreign exchange bill *(ie, payable abroad)*
   – bill in foreign currency
Devisenwerte *mpl* (Fin) foreign exchange assets
Devisenzufluß *m* (AuW) inflow of foreign exchange
Devisenzuteilung *f*
   (AuW) allocation of foreign exchange *(ie, to travelers)*
   – exchange allowance
Devisenzwangswirtschaft *f* (AuW) foreign exchange control
dezentrale Datenverarbeitung *f* (EDV) distributed data processing *(ie, terminals located at remote sites)*
dezentralisierte Datenerfassung *f* (EDV) decentralized data acquisition
dezentrale Planung *f* (Bw) decentralized planning
dezentrales Führungssystem *n* (Bw) decentralized management system
dezentrales Lager *n* (MaW) decentralized inventory
Dezentralisation *f* (Bw) decentralization
dezentralisieren (Bw) to decentralize
dezentralisierte Arbeitszuweisung *f* (IndE) decentralized dispatching
dezentralisierte Willensbildung *f* (Bw) decentralized decision-making
Dezentralisierung *f* (Bw) decentralization
Dezil *n* (Stat) decile
Dezimal-Binär-Code *m*
   (EDV) binary-coded decimal code
   – BCD code
Dezimal-Binär-Konvertierung *f* (EDV) = *Dezimal-Binär-Umwandlung*
Dezimal-Binär-Umwandlung *f* (EDV) decimal-to-binary conversion
Dezimalbruch *m*
   (Math) decimal fraction
   – decimal
Dezimalkomma *n* (EDV) decimal point
Dezimalpunkt *m* (EDV) decimal point
Dezimalschreibweise *f* (Math) decimal notation
Dezimalstelle *f* (Math) decimal digit (*or* place)
Dezimalsystem *n* (EDV) decimal system
Dezimalwert *m* (Math) decimal value
Dezimalzahl *f* (Math) decimal number
Dezimalziffer *f* (Math) decimal digit
DGB-Vorstand *m* (Pw) DGB executive board
d'Hondtsches Wahlverfahren *n* (Pw) d'Hondt proportional-election procedure
Diagnoseprogramm *n* (EDV) diagnostic program (*or* routine)
Diagnosetest *m* (EDV) diagnostic check (*or* test)

diagonales Wachstum n (Bw) diagonal expansion
Diagonalmatrix f (Math) diagonal matrix
Diagonal-Produkt-Regel f (Math) diagonal product rule
Diagonal-Regression f (Stat) diagonal regression
Diagramm n
  (Stat) diagram
  – chart
  – graph
Dialogbetrieb m (EDV) conversational mode
Dialogbetriebsteilnehmer m (EDV) conversational user
Dialogdatenverarbeitung f (EDV) dialog (or interactive) processing
Dialogfernverarbeitung f (EDV) remote dialog processing
Dialog-Kompilierer m (EDV) conversational compiler
Dialogprogrammierung f (EDV) conversational mode programming
Dialogrechner m (EDV) interactive computer
Dialogstation f (EDV) conversational terminal
Dialogsystem n (EDV) conversational system
Dialogverkehr m (EDV) interactive mode
Dibit n (EDV) dibit *(ie, a group of two bits)*
dichotomische Suche f
  (EDV) binary search (or chop)
  – dichotomizing search *(syn, binäres Suchen)*
Dichte f (Stat) density
Dichte f **des Seeverkehrs** (com) density of marine traffic
Dichte f **e-r Menge** (Math) density of a set
Dichtefunktion f (Stat) density function
dichte Menge f (Math) dense set
dichtester Wert m (Stat) mode
Dienstalter n (Pw) (job) seniority
Dienst m **antreten** (Pw) to take up duties
Dienstantritt m (Pw) commencement of duties
Dienstanweisung f (Bw) service (or standing) instructions *(ie, for handling routine activities)*
Dienstaufsichtsbehörde f (Re) supervisory authority
Dienstaufsichtsbeschwerde f (Re) informal remonstration about an official *(ie, because of an allegedly arbitrary decision)*
Dienstauftrag m (Ber) service order
Dienstaufwandsentschädigung f (StR) expense allowance *(ie, paid to private employees, treated as part of employment compensation = Teil des Arbeitslohnes)*
Dienstbarkeit f
  (Re) easement
  – servitude
  (ie, portion of a right of ownership enjoyed by a person other than the owner of the thing itself; eg, ‚Nießbrauch' and ‚Grunddienstbarkeiten')
Dienstbezüge pl (Pw) remuneration *(ie, paid to public employees)*
Diensterfindung f (Pat) employee invention *(ie, made in the course of employment)*
Dienstfahrzeug n (com) service vehicle
Dienstgang m (StR) temporary employment in a location less than 15 km from the regular duty station

Dienstgeheimnis n
  (Bw) business
  – trade
  – industrial ... secret
Dienstgeschäfte npl (Pw) official business
Dienstgespräch n
  (com) business call
  (com) official call
Dienstleistung f (com) business service
Dienstleistungen fpl (Vw) services *(eg, encompassing transportation, public utilities, wholesale and retail trade, finance, health, education, business services, entertainment)*
Dienstleistungen fpl **erbringen** (com) to provide (or render) services
Dienstleistungsauftrag m (Bw) service order
Dienstleistungsbereich m (Vw) = Dienstleistungssektor
Dienstleistungsbetrieb m
  (com) service company (or enterprise)
  (com) service center (or establishment)
Dienstleistungsbilanz f
  (VGR) balance on services
  – services account
  – (GB) invisible balance
Dienstleistungsentgelt n (com) service charge (or fee)
Dienstleistungsgeschäft n
  (com) service transaction
  – sale of services
Dienstleistungsgesellschaft f
  (Re) nontrading partnership
  (Bw) service company *(eg, in a group of companies = Konzern)*
Dienstleistungsgewerbe n (Vw) service industry
Dienstleistungskosten pl (com) cost of services
Dienstleistungsmarke f (Pat) service mark *(ie, allowed under German patent law as from 1 Apr 1979)*
Dienstleistungspalette f
  (com) range
  – array
  – palette ... of services
Dienstleistungspflicht f (Re) duty (or obligation) to render services
Dienstleistungsrechenzentrum n (EDV) service computing center
Dienstleistungsrechner m (EDV) host (computer) *(syn, Arbeitsrechner, Verarbeitungsrechner, Wirtsrechner)*
Dienstleistungssektor m
  (Vw) service (producing) sector
  – tertiary sector
Dienstleistungsunternehmen n
  (com) service business
  – service-producing company
Dienstleistungsverkehr m (AuW) service transactions
Dienst m **nach Vorschrift**
  (Pw) work by the book
  – (GB) work to rule
Dienstort m (Pw) duty station
Dienstprogramm n (EDV) service (or utility) program
Dienstreise f (StR) business travel *(ie, temporary*

employment in a location at least 15 km from the regular duty station)
Dienstsitz *m* (Pw) duty station
Dienststelle *f*
  (com) office
  – administrative office (*or* agency)
  – official agency
  (Bw) activity
Dienststellengliederung *f* (Bw) departmental structure
Dienststellung *f* (Pw) position
Dienststunden *fpl*
  (com) business (*or* office) hours
  (com) hours of service (*or* attendance)
  – official hours
  – (*or simply*) hours
Dienstverhältnis *n* (Pw) employment
Dienstvertrag *m*
  (Re) contract of service (*or* employment) §§ 661 ff BGB
  – service agreement (*or* contract)
Dienstweg *m* (Bw) official channels
Dienstwohnung *f* (Pw) official residence
Dienstzeit *f*
  (com) business (*or office) hours*
  (com) hours of service (*or* attendance)
  – official hours
  (Pw) length (*or* period) of service
  – term of office
Differential *n* (Math) differential *(ie, of a function)*
Differentialeinkommen *n* (Vw) differential income
Differentialfracht *f* (com) differential freight rate
Differentialgleichung *f* (Math) differential equation
Differentialgleichung *f* **erster Ordnung** (Math) first-order differential equation
Differentialkosten *pl* (Vw) differential cost
Differentiallohnsystem *n* (IndE) differential piecerate system *(developed by Taylor)*
Differentialoperatior *m* **zweiter Ordnung** (Math) Laplacian operator
Differentialprozeß *m* (Stat) additive random walk process
Differentialquotient *m* (Math) differential quotient
Differentialrechnung *f* (Math) differential calculus
Differentialrente *f* (Vw) differential rent *(developed by Anderson and Ricardo)*
Differentialstücklohn *m* (Pw) differential piece rate
Differentialzoll *m*
  (AuW) differential duty (*or* tariff)
  – discriminating duty
Differentiation *f* (Math) differentiation
Differentiationsregel *f* (Math) differentiation formula
Differentiationszeichen *n* (Math) differentiation sign
differentieller Parameter *m* (Math) differential parameter
Differenzbetrag *m* (com) residual balance
Differenzbeträge *mpl* (EG) differential amounts
Differenz *f* **der Zahlenfolge** (Math) common difference *(ie, of an arithmetic progression or series)*
Differenzengleichung *f* **erster Ordnung** (Math) difference equation of the first order

Differenzenquotient *m* (Math) difference quotient
Differenzenrechnung *f* (Math) calculus of differences
Differenzgeber *m* (EDV) bias transmitter
Differenzgeschäft *n*
  (Bö) gambling in futures
  – margin business (*or* trading)
  (ie, not allowed in Germany, treated as gambling under § 764 BGB)
Differenzhandel *m* (Bö) margin business (*or* trading)
differenzierbar (Math) differentiable
differenzierbare Funktion *f* (Math) differentiable function
differenzierte Produktanforderungen *fpl* (Mk) demand for sophisticated products
differenzierter Akkordsatz *m* (IndE) differential piece rate
Differenzinvestition *f* (Fin) fictitious investment made in preinvestment analysis *(ie, to compare various spending alternatives)*
Differenzkosten *pl*
  (Vw, Bw) differential cost
  (KoR) marginal
  – incremental
  – relevant
  – avoidable
  – alternative ... cost
Differenzmenge *f*
  (Math) difference set
  – difference of sets
Differenzmethode *f* (Stat) variate difference method *(developed by O. Anderson)*
Differenzposten *m* **bei der Abstimmung** (ReW) reconciling item
Differenzzahlung *f* (com) marginal payment
Diffusionsindex *m* (Stat) diffusion index
Diffusionstheorie *f* (FiW) diffusion theory of taxation *(ie, tax on a particular kind of commodity, exchange, or occupation is shifted on to other classes of taxpayers, so that the tax is spread, ,,diffused", over a large area)*
Diffusion *f* **von Innovationen** (Vw) diffusion of innovations
Digitalabschreibung *f*
  (ReW) sum-of-the-years-digit method of depreciation
  – life-period method of depreciation
  (syn, arithmetisch-degressive Abschreibung)
Digital-Analog-Umsetzer *m* (EDV) digital-analog converter
Digitalanzeige *f* (EDV) digital display
Digitalausgabe *f* (EDV) digital output
Digitalbaustein *m* (EDV) logical unit
Digitalbildröhre *f* (EDV) display tube
digital darstellen (EDV) to digitize
Digitaldrucker *m* (EDV) digital printer
digitale Abschreibung *f* (ReW) = *Digitalabschreibung*
digitale Darstellung *f* (EDV) digital representation
digitale Daten *pl* (EDV) digital (*or* discrete) data *(opp, analoge Daten)*
digitale Datenverarbeitung *f* (EDV) digital data processing
Digitaleingabe *f* (EDV) digital input

digitale Rechenanlage *f* (EDV) digital computer
digitaler Regler *m* (EDV) sampled data feedback controller *(syn, Abtastregler)*
digitales Integriergerät *n* (EDV) digital differential analyzer
– incremental computer
digitale Verarbeitungsanlage *f* (EDV) digital computer
Digitalisiergerät *n* (EDV) digitizer *(syn, D/A-Umsetzer, Digital-Analog-Umsetzer)*
Digitalplotter *m* (EDV) data *(or* graphic) plotter
– plotter
Digitalrechner *m* (EDV) digital computer
Digitaluhr *f* (EDV) digital clock
Digraph *m* (Math) digraph
Diktat *n* (com) shorthand dictation
Diktat *n* **aufnehmen** (com) to take dictation
Diktat *n* **übertragen** (com) to transcribe notes
Diktatzeichen *n* (com) identification initials
– (GB) reference initials
diktierter Vertrag *m* (Re) adhesion contract
dilatorische Einrede *f* (Re) dilatory defense *(or* exception) *(syn, aufschiebende od rechtshemmende Einrede)*
Dilemma *n* **der Planung** (Bw) planning dilemma
Dilemma *n* **des Untersuchungsgefangenen** (OR) prisoner's dilemma
Dilemmasituation *f* (Log) double-bind situation
diligentia quam in suis (rebus adhibere solet) (Re) ordinary diligence *(see: konkrete Fahrlässigkeit)*
Dimensionsanalyse *f* (Stat) factor analysis
dimensionslose Maßzahl *f* (Math) absolute measure
dinglich besichern (Re) to secure by real property
dingliche Belastung *f* (Re) encumbrance
dinglicher Anspruch *m* (Re) claim ad rem
dinglicher Arrest *m* (Re) attachment
(Re) attachment order *(ie, blocking debtor's assets)*
dingliche Rechte *npl* **an Grundstücken** (Re) real right in land
dinglicher Vertrag *m* (Re) real agreement
– deed of conveyance
dingliche Sicherheit *f* (Re) real security *(ie, property pledged for the satisfaction of a debt)*
dingliches Recht *n* (Re) right in rem
dingliches Vorkaufsrecht *n* (Re) real right of preemption
dingliches Wohnrecht *n* (Re) limited personal servitude *(ie, in residential property)*
dinglich gesicherte Verbindlichkeiten *fpl* (Fin) debt secured by real property
diophantische Gleichung *f* (Math) diophantine equation
Direktabsatz *m* (com) = *Direktverkauf*
Direktanspruch *m* (Vers) direct claim *(ie, of injured third party against motor insurance company)*
Direktausgabe *f* (EDV) direct output
Direktbedarfsmatrix *f* (OR) matrix of direct requirements *(ie, of assemblies, components, raw materials which are incorporated into a unit of next higher complexity)*
Direktbefehl *m* (EDV) direct instruction
Direktbezug *m* (com) direct buying *(or* purchasing)
Direktbuchungssystem *n* (EDV) direct accounting system
Direktcode *m* (EDV) direct code *(syn, Maschinencode, Rechnercode)*
Direktcodierung *f* (EDV) direct coding
Direktdiskont *m* (Fin) direct rediscounting *(ie, without intermediation of banks, not provided for in the law on the Deutsche Bundesbank)*
direkte Abschreibung *f* (ReW) direct method of depreciation *(ie, debiting to fixed-asset account)*
direkte Adresse *f* (EDV) direct *(or* one-level) address
direkte Adressierung *f* (EDV) direct *(or* first-level) addressing
direkte Arbitrage *f* (Fin) two-point arbitrage
direkte Ausfuhr *f* (com) direct export
direkte Auswahl *f* (Stat) direct sampling
direkte Beschaffung *f* (MaW) direct purchasing *(ie, bypassing all trade intermediaries)*
direkte Buchung *f* (ReW) straightforward entry
direkte Devisenarbitrage *f* (Fin) simple arbitrage
direkte Einkommensverbesserungen *fpl* (EC) cash-in-hand income supplements *(ie, paid to farmers)*
Direkteingabe *f* (EDV) direct input
Direkteinkauf *m* (com) direct buying *(or* purchasing)
direkte Investitionen *fpl* (AuW) direct investment
direkte Kosten *pl* (KoR) direct cost *(or* expense)
Direktemission *f* (Fin) direct offering
direkte Programmierung *f* (EDV) direct programming
direkter Export *m* (AuW) direct export selling
direkter Import *m* (AuW) direct importing
direkter Speicherzugriff *m* (EDV) direct memory access, DMA
direkter Vertrieb *m* (com) direct selling *(ie, from manufacturer to final user)*
direkter Zugriff *m* (EDV) direct *(or* immediate) access
direkte Speicherplatzzuweisung *f* (EDV) direct storage allocation *(opp, dynamische Speicherplatzzuweisung)*
direkte Steuern *fpl* (FiW) direct taxes
direkte Stichprobennahme *f* (Stat) direct sampling
Direktexport *m* (AuW) direct export(ing)
Direktexporte *mpl* AuW) direct exports
Direktfinanzierung *f* (Fin) direct financing *(ie, bypassing the capital market and banking syndicates)*
Direktgeschäfte *npl* (com) direct business *(ie, done by principal with third parties without using the services of the commercial agent)*
Direkthändler *m* (com) dealer
Direktimport *m* (AuW) direct importing
Direktimporte *mpl* (AuW) direct imports
Direktimporteur *m* (AuW) direct importer
Direktinvestition *f* (AuW) direct investment
Direktion *f* (Bw) management

(com) headquarters
- (GB) head (*or* main) office
Direktionsassistent *m* (Pw) assistant to top management
Direktionsrecht *n* (Bw) right to issue instructions to employees
Direktkorrektur *f* (EDV) patch
Direktkostenrechnung *f* (KoR) direct costing
Direktkredit *m* (Fin) direct loan
Direktkredite *mpl*
(Fin) borrowings
(Fin) lendings
Direktlieferung *f* (com) direct (*or* drop) shipment
direkt meßbare Größe *f* (Math) quantity
Direktor *m*
(com) manager
- head of ...
Direktplazierung *f* (Fin) direct placement *(ie, of an issue)*
Direktrufanschluß *m* (EDV) quick line service
Direktschuldner *m* (Re) direct debtor
Direktsteuerung *f* (EDV) direct control
Direktsubventionen *fpl* (EG) direct aid (*or* subsidies) *(eg, to farmers)*
Direktübertragung *f* (EDV) direct transmission
Direktverkauf *m*
(com) direct selling *(im weiteren Sinne: no intermediaries of trade)*
(com) direct selling *(im engeren Sinne: sale of consumer goods to ultimate consumers through retail outlets, door-to-door selling, mail ordering, etc.)*
(com) direct selling *(ie, also called ‚anonymer Warenweg' = ‚anonymous distribution channels', or ‚grauer Markt' = ‚gray market'; its various forms: (1) Belegschaftshandel = sale to outsiders through employees; (3) Beziehungshandel = direct sale to ultimate consumer by manufacturer or wholesaler.)*
Direktverkauf *m* **über Haushaltsreisende**
(com) door-to-door selling
- personal selling
Direktversicherer *m*
(Vers) original isurer
- ceding company
- reinsured (*or* reassured)
(ie, in reinsurance; syn, Zedent, Erstversicherer)
Direktversicherung *f* (Vers) direct insurance *(ie, insurance premiums paid direct by employers on behalf of employees)*
Direktvertrieb *m* (com) = *Direktverkauf*
Direktweg *m* (EDV) primary route *(syn, normaler Weg; opp, Alternativweg)*
Direktwerbung *f* (Mk) direct advertising
Direktzugriff *m* (EDV) direct (*or* random) access
Direktzugriffsspeicher *m* (EDV) direct (*or* random) access storage *(syn, Randomspeicher)*
Direktzugriffsverfahren *n* (EDV) random-access (*or* direct-access) method
direkt zurechenbare Kosten *pl*
(KoR) directly allocable (*or* apportionable *or* assignable *or* traceable) cost
- specific cost
Direktzusage *f* (Pw) employer's pension commitment

Disagio *n*
(Fin) discount
- below par
- disagio
Disagio-Anleihe *f* (Fin) noninterest-bearing discount bond *(ie, interest paid at maturity)*
Disagio-Darlehen *n* (Fin) loan granted at a discount
Disagioerträge *mpl* (Fin) discounts earned
Disagiokonto *n* (Fin) account stating difference between repayment amount and payout amount
- *Auszahlungsbetrag* - arising in connection with the issue of loans and other liabilities, § 156 III AktG
Discounter *m*
(Mk) discounter
- discount house
disjunkte Mengen *fpl* (Math) disjoint sets
Disjunktion *f* (Log) disjunction
Disjunktionsglied *n* (EDV) = *inklusives ODER-Glied*
disjunktive Normalform *f* (Log) disjunctive normal form
disjunktive Supposition *f* (Log) discrete supposition
disjunktives Urteil *n* (Log) disjunctive proposition
Diskette *f*
(EDV) diskette
Disketten-Betriebssystem *n* (EDV) diskette operating system
Diskettenlaufwerk *n* floppy disk drive
Diskettenspeicher *m* (EDV) diskette storage
Diskont *m* (Fin) discount
Diskontabrechnung *f* (Fin) discount note
Diskontaufwendungen *mpl* (ReW) discounts allowed
Diskontbank *f* (Fin) discounting bank
Diskontbedingungen *fpl* (Fin) discount terms
Diskonteinreichung *f* (Fin) presentation for discount
Diskonten *pl* (Fin) domestic bills of exchange *(opp, foreign exchange bills)*
Diskont *m* **erhöhen** (Fin) to increase (*or* raise) the discount rate
Diskonterhöhung *f* (Fin) raising the discount rate
Diskonterholung *f* (Fin) discount rate rise
Diskonterlöse *mpl* (ReW) discounts earned
Diskonterträge *mpl* (ReW) discounts received
diskontfähig
(Fin) discountable
- bankable
- eligible for discount
diskontfähiger Wechsel *m* (Fin) discountable bill
diskontfähiges Papier *n* (Fin) paper eligible for discount
Diskonfähigkeit *f* (Fin) eligibility for discount
Diskontgefälle *n* (Fin) discount rate differential
Diskontgeschäft *n* (Fin) discount business *(ie, purchase of bills of exchange, promissory notes, and checks)*
Diskonthäuser *npl* (com) discount houses *(ie, retailing outlets selling far below usual or suggested prices, mostly self-service)*
diskontierbar
(Fin) discountable

– bankable
– eligible for discount
diskontieren (Fin) to discount *(ie, to purchase or sell a bill at a reduction based on the interest for the time it has still to run)*
diskontierende Bank *f* (Fin) discounting bank
diskontierter Einnahmeüberschuß *m* (Fin) discounted cash flow
– DCF, dcf
diskontierter Rückfluß *m* **von Barmitteln** (Fin) discounted cash flowback
diskontierte Wechsel *mpl* (Fin) discounts
– discounted bills
Diskontierung *f* (Math) discounting
– discounting process
Diskontierungsfaktor *m* (Math) discount factor $(1 + i)^{-n}$
– conversion factor in compound discounting *(syn, Abzinsungsfaktor)*
Diskontierungszeitraum *m* (Fin) discount period
diskontinuierliche Hypothese *f* (Stat) discontinuous hypothesis
diskontinuierliches Produktionsverfahren *n* (IndE) discrete production process
diskontinuierliche Verteilung *f* (Stat) discrete distribution
Diskontkredit *m* (Fin) discount credit
Diskontmakler *m* (Fin) discount broker
Diskontmarkt *m* (Fin) discount market
Diskontnota *f* (Fin) list of bills or checks presented for discount *(usu. a bank's multipart form = Vordrucksatz)*
Diskontpolitik *f* (Vw) discount-rate policy *(ie, one of the traditional instruments of central-bank monetary policy)*
Diskontprovision *f* (Fin) discount commission *(ie, charged by the bill-buying bank as a service fee)*
Diskontrechnung *f*
(Math) computation of simple discount
(Fin) discount note
Diskontsatz *m*
(Fin) discount rate *(ie, charged for buying bills of exchange in advance of maturity)*
(Vw) central-bank discount rate
– official rate of discount
– (US) rediscount rate
Diskontsatz *m* **erhöhen** (Fin) to raise the discount rate
Diskontsatz *m* **senken** (Fin) to lower the discount rate
Diskontsenkung *f* (Fin) reduction of discount rate
Diskontspesen *pl* (Fin discount charges
Diskonttage *mpl* (Fin) discount days
Diskont-Warenhaus *n*
(Mk) discounter
– discount house
Diskontwechsel *m* (Fin) discount(ed) bill
Diskontzusage *f* (Fin) discount commitment
diskreditierende Werbung *f* (Kart) denigration *(ie, of competitive products in advertising)*
diskret
(Math) discountinuous
– discrete

diskrete Punktmenge *f* (Math) discrete set of points
diskreter stochastischer Prozeß *m* (Stat) discrete process
diskrete Spesenzahlungen *fpl* (StR) discreet expense payments
diskrete Variable *f* (Math) discontinuous variable
diskrete Zeitvariable *f* (Math) discontinucus time variable
diskrete Zufallsvariable *f* (Math) discontinuous variate
diskretionäre Entscheidungsspielräume *mpl* (Vw) discretionary power
diskretionäre Fiskalpolitik *f* (FiW) discretionary fiscal policy
Diskriminanzanalyse *f* (Stat) discriminatory analysis *(ie, goes back to R. A. Fisher)*
diskriminieren (Kart, Vw) to discriminate (against)
diskriminierende Behandlung *f* (AuW) discriminatory treatment
diskriminierende Besteuerung *f* (FiW) discriminatory taxation
diskriminierende Preisgestaltung *f* (Mk) differential pricing
diskriminierender Frachtausgleich *m* (Kart) freight equalization
diskriminierende Wechselkurse *mpl* (AuW) discriminatory exchange rates
diskriminierende Zollpolitik *f* (AuW) tariff discrimination
Diskriminierung *f* (AuW) discrimination *(eg, the various nontariff barriers to trade)*
Diskriminierung *f* **am Arbeitsplatz** (PwW) job discrimination
Diskriminierungsverbot *n* (Kart) prohibition of discrimination
Diskussionsbereich *m* (Log) universe of discourse
Diskussionspapier *n*
(com) discussion paper *(or document)*
– exposure draft
Dispache *f*
(SeeV) adjustment of average, §§ 727 ff HGB
(SeeV) general average statement
– statement of average
Dispache *f* **aufmachen** (SeeV) to make up the average
Dispachekosten *pl* (SeeV) adjustment charges
Dispacheur *m*
(SeeV) average adjuster *(or stater)*
– general average adjuster
dispachieren (SeeV) to adjust averages
Dispachierung *f* (SeeV) adjustment of average
Disparität *f* (Vw) disparity
Dispersion *f* (Stat) dispersion
Dispersionsindex *m* (Stat) index of dispersion
Dispersions-Parameter *m* (Stat) measure of dispersion
Disponent *m*
(com) expediter
(com) managing clerk
(Fin) fund *(or* money) manager
Disponibilität *f* (AuW) availability (of monetary reserves)
disponibles Einkommen *n* (VGR) disposable income

disponible Ware *f*
(Bö) cash commodity *(ie, in spot transactions)*
– spots
disponieren
(com) to make arrangements
(com) to place orders
Dispositionen *fpl*
(com) arrangements
– operations
– planning
(IndE) scheduling
(Fin) drawings *(ie, on a bank account)*
Dispositionen *fpl* **der öffentlichen Haushalte** (FiW) public authorities' operations
Dispositionen *fpl* **des Handels** (com) ordering by the trade
Dispositionsausdruck *m* (Log) dispositional term
Dispositionsbegriff *m*
(Log) dispositional
– dispositional concept
Dispositionsfonds *m* (FiW) fund at free disposal of executive or administrative head *(eg, Federal Chancellor, ministers, mayors)*
Dispositionsguthaben *n* (Fin) balance available
Dispositionskartei *f* (MaW) materials planning file
Dispositionskredit *m* (Fin) drawing credit
Dispositionspapiere *npl* (WeR) documents of title *(syn, Traditionspapiere)*
Dispositionsrechner *m* (EDV) scheduling computer
Dispositionsreserve *f* (Fin) general operating reserve
Dispositionsschein *m* (WeR) certificate of obligation, § 363 I HGB *(ie, made out by a bank which promises to pay a sum certain in money to a third party)*
Dispositionsterminus *m* (Log) intervening variable
Dispositionszeichnung *f*
(com) general arrangement drawing
– layout plan
– outline drawing
dispositive Arbeit *f* (Bw) directing activity *(ie, of an entrepreneur or manager; term coined by E. Gutenberg)*
Disproportionalitätstheorien *fpl* (Vw) generic term covering a group of business cycle theories which assume that economic activities are set in motion by ‚disproportionalities' in the overall economic structure
Dissens *m* (Re) lack of agreement
Dissertation *f* **einreichen** (Pw) to submit a doctoral dissertation
Dissertation *f* **schreiben** (Pw) to write a doctoral dissertation
Distanzadresse *f* (EDV) symbolic *(or* floating*)* address *(syn, symbolische Adresse)*
(EDV) displacement address
Distanzfracht *f*
(com) distance freightage
– freight by distance
(ie, shipper pays freightage in the same proportion as the part of the voyage covered stands to the whole, § 630 HGB)
– freight pro rate
– prorata freight

Distanzgeschäft *n* (com) contract of sale where seller agrees to ship the goods to buyer's destination at the latter's risk *(ie, basis of transaction may be sample, catalog or indication of standard quality)*
Distanzhandel *m* (com) mail-order business *(ie, based on catalog-type advertising)*
Distanzkauf *m* (com) = *Distanzgeschäft*
Distanzscheck *m* (Fin) out-of-town check
Distanzwechsel *m* (Fin) out-of-town bill *(opp, Platzwechsel)*
Distribution *f*
(Vw) income distribution
(Mk) distribution
Distributionsfunktion *f* **des Preises** (Vw) distributive function of prices
Distributions-Index *m* (Mk) distribution index
Distributionskette *f* (Mk) distribution chain
Distributions-Mix *m* (Mk) distribution mix
Distributions-Planung *f* (Mk) distribution planning
Distributionspolitik *f* (Mk) distribution mix
Distributionsproblem *n* (OR) transport problem
Distributionstheorie *f* (Vw) theory of distribution
Distributionsweg *m* (Mk) channel of distribution
distributive Supposition *f* (Log) distributive supposition
Disziplinarverfahren *n* (Re) disciplinary proceedings
Disziplinierungseffekt *m* (Pw) labor disciplining mechanism *(ie, of unemployment)*
divergente Reihe *f* (Math) divergent series
Divergenzschwelle *f* (AuW) threshold of divergence *(ie, level at which central banks are expected to take corrective action; syn, Abweichungsschwelle)*
Diversifikation *f*
(Mk) diversification
– branching out
diversifizierte Intervention *f*
(AuW) diversified intervention *(ie, in the EMS: European Monetary System)*
Diversifizierung *f* (Mk) = *Diversifikation*
Diversifizierungsinvestition *f* (Bw) investment made to produce a qualitative change in the marketing program and/or organization
Dividende *f*
(Fin) (shareholder) dividend
(Vers) dividend
Dividende *f* **ankündigen** (Fin) to announce a dividend payout
Dividende *f* **auf Stammaktien** (Fin) ordinary dividend
Dividende *f* **ausfallen lassen** (Fin) to pass dividends *(eg, because of plunging profits)*
Dividende *f* **ausschütten** (Fin) to distribute *(or* pay*)* a dividend
Dividende *f* **kürzen** (Fin) to reduce a dividend
dividendenabhängig (Fin) linked to dividend payout
Dividendenabrechnung *f* (Fin) dividend note
Dividendenabschlag *m*
(Fin) interim dividend
(Bö) quotation ex dividend
Dividendenabschnitt *m* (Fin) dividend coupon
Dividendenanspruch *m* (Fin) right to a dividend

Dividendenausfall *m* (Fin) passing of a dividend
Dividenden-Ausgleichskonto *n* (ReW) dividend equalization account (*or* reserve)
Dividendenausschüttung *f*
(Fin) dividend distribution
– dividend payment (*or* payout)
dividendenberechtigt
(Fin) entitled to dividend
(Fin) bearing dividend
Dividendenberechtigungsschein *m* (Fin) dividend warrant
Dividendenbogen *m* (Fin) dividend coupon sheet
Dividendendeckung *f*
(Fin) earnings cover *(ie, ratio of earnings to dividend)*
(Fin) payout ratio *(ie, earnings percentage paid out in dividends)*
Dividendeneinkommen *n* (Fin) dividend income
Dividendeneinnahmen *fpl* (Fin) = *Dividendeneinkommen*
Dividendenerhöhung *f* (Fin) dividend increase
Dividendenerklärung *f* (Fin) declaration of a dividend
Dividendenerträge *mpl* (ReW) dividend earnings (*or* income)
Dividendenforderungen *fpl* (ReW) dividends receivable
Dividendengarantie *f* (Fin) dividend guaranty *(ie, promise to pay a minimum dividend by third parties; eg, by government or municipality; such promise cannot be extended to company's own shareholders, § 57 II AktG)*
Dividendeninkasso *n*
(Fin) dividend collection
– collection of dividend
Dividendenkontinuität *f* (Fin) payment of unchanged dividend over a period of years
Dividendenkonto *n* (ReW) dividend payout account
Dividendenkürzung *f* (Fin) dividend cut
Dividendenpapier *n*
(Fin) equity security
– dividend-bearing share
– dividend paper
Dividendenpapiere *npl*
(Fin) shares
– equities
Dividendenpolitik *f* (Fin) dividend payout policy
Dividendenrendite *f* (Fin) dividend yield *(ie, gross cash dividend per share in % of the market price)*
Dividendenrücklage *f* (ReW) dividend reserve fund
Dividendenrückstände *mpl* (Fin) arrears of dividends
Dividendensatz *m* (Fin) dividend rate
Dividendenschein *m* (Fin) dividend coupon (*or* warrant)
Dividendenschnitt *m* (Fin) dividend cut
Dividendensenkung *f* (Fin) dividend cut
Dividendensteuer *f* (StR) dividend tax
Dividendenstopp *m* (Fin) dividend stop
Dividendentermin *m* (Fin) dividend due date
Dividendenvorschlag *m* (Fin) dividend proposal (*or* recommendation)

Dividendenwerte *mpl*
(WeR) dividend-bearing securities *(ie, corporate shares, parts of limited liability companies, quotas of mining companies, and other securities evidencing an equity investment in a domestic or foreign ‚Kapitalgesellschaft', § 19 II KVStG)*
(Bö) shares
– equities
Dividendenzahlstelle *f* (Fin) dividend disbursing agent
Dividendenzahlung *f* (Fin) dividend payment (*or* payout)
Dividende *f* **pro Aktie** (Fin) dividend per share
Dividende *f* **vorschlagen** (Fin) to recommend (*or* propose) a dividend
Dividierwerk *n* (EDV) digital divider *(syn, Divisionsschaltung)*
Division *f* (Bw) division
divisionale Organisation *f* (Bw) divisional organization
divisionale Struktur *f* (Bw) divisional structure *(syn, Spartenstruktur)*
Divisionalisierung *f* (Bw) divisionalization
Divisionsanweisung *f* (EDV, Cobol) divide statement
Divisionskalkulation *f*
(KoR) process costing
– process system of accounting
Divisionsmanagement *n* (Bw) divisional management
Divisionsmanager *m* (Bw) divisional manager
Divisionsschaltung *f* (EDV) digital divider *(syn, Dividierwerk)*
DM-Auslandsanleihe *f* (Fin) foreign (*or* international) DM bond
DM-Schuldscheine *mpl* (Fin) D-Mark denominated promissory notes
Dock *n*
(com) dock
– wharf
Dockempfangsschein *m* (com) dock warrant
Dockgebühren *fpl* (com) dock charges (*or* dues)
Dogmengeschichte *f* (Vw) history of economic thought
Doktorand *m* (Pw) candidate for a doctor's degree (*or* doctorate)
Dokument *n*
(Re) document
– instrument
Dokument *n* **ausstellen** (com) to prepare a document
Dokumente *npl* (com) documents
Dokumente *npl* **aufnehmen** (Fin) to take up (*or* accept) documents
Dokumente *npl* **gegen Akzept** (com) documents against acceptance, D/A
Dokumente *npl* **gegen Zahlung** (com) documents against payment, D/P
Dokumentenakkreditiv *n*
(Fin) documentary letter of credit
– documentary credit
– commercial letter of credit
Dokumentenaufnahme *f* (Fin) taking up of documents

Dokumenteneinreichung *f* (Fin) presentation of documents
Dokumentengegenwert *m* (Fin) currency equivalent of documents
Dokumentengeschäft *n* (Fin) documentary business
Dokumenteninkasso *n* (Fin) documentary collection *(ie, documents are handed over by the bank to the importer against payment of invoice amount)*
Dokumentenkredit *m* (Fin) documentary credit
Dokumententratte *f*
(Fin) documentary draft *(or* bill)
– acceptance bill
– draft with documents attached
Dokumentenwechsel *m* (Fin) documentary bill
Dokument *n* **vorlegen**
(WeR) to present an instrument (to)
– to produce a document (to)
Dollaranleihen *fpl* (Fin) dollar bonds
Dollaranstieg *m* **bremsen** (AuW) to slow advance of dollar
Dollarguthaben *n* (Fin) dollar balance
Dollarklausel *f*
(Fin) dollar clause *(ie, stipulating that invoicing and payment must be made in dollars)*
Dollarknappheit *f* (AuW) dollar gap *(or* shortage)
Dollarlücke *f* (AuW) dollar gap
Dollarparität *f* (AuW) dollar parity
Dollarrembours *m* (Fin) dollar documentary *(or* acceptance) credit
Dollarschwäche *f* (AuW) weakness of the dollar
Dollarsteigerung *f*
(AuW) advance
– climb
– ascent ... of the dollar
– surge in the dollar
Dollarüberfluß *m* (AuW) dollar glut
Dollarzinssätze *mpl* **am Eurogeld- und Euroanleihemarkt** (Fin) Eurodollar deposit rates and bond yields
Domänentransportspeicher *m* (EDV) bubble memory *(syn, Magnetblasenspeicher, Magnetdomänenspeicher)*
dominanter Baum *m* (OR) dominant requirement tree
dominante Strategie *f* (OR) dominant strategy
dominante Werbung *f* (Mk) dominant advertising
Domizil *n*
(Re) residence
– domicile
(WeR) domicile
Domizilgesellschaft *f* (StR) foreign base company *(ie, domiciled in a low-tax country to accumulate profits or to take advantage of double-taxation agreements)*
Domiziliant *m* (WeR) payer of a domiciled bill
domizilierter Wechsel *m* (WeR) domiciled bill
Domizilort *m* (WeR) place of payment of a domiciled bill
Domizilprovision *f* (Fin) domicile commission
Domizilstelle *f* (Fin) place for presentment
Domizilvermerk *m* (WeR) domicile clause

Domizilwechsel *m* (WeR) domiciled *(or* addressed) bill
Doppel *n* (com) duplicate
Doppelbelastung *f* (StR) double economic burden
Doppelbeschäftigung *f* (Pw) double employment
Doppelbesteuerung *f* (StR) double taxation of corporate profits *(ie, first to the corporation and, upon distribution, to the shareholders; removed by superseding legislation)*
Doppelbesteuerungsabkommen *n* (StR) double taxation convention *(or* treaty)
Doppelbesteuerung *f* **von Kapitalerträgen** (StR) double taxation of portfolio income
Doppelbrief *m* (com) overweight letter
Doppelbruch *m* (Math) complex *(or* compound) fraction
Doppelgesellschaft *f* (StR) split company *(ie, operating unit + holding unit)*
Doppelgesellschafter *m*
(Re) simultaneous partner *(ie, in two partnerships)*
(Re) simultaneous member *(ie, in two companies)*
Doppelimpuls *m* (EDV) double pulse
Doppelimpulsschreibverfahren *n* (EDV) double pulse recording
Doppelintegral *n* (Math) double integral
Doppellochkontrolle *f* (EDV) double punch detection
Doppellochung *f* (EDV) double punching
doppeln (EDV) to duplicate
Doppelpatentierung *f* (Pat) double patenting
Doppelprüfung *f* (EDV) duplication *(or* twin) check
Doppelquittung *f* (com) double receipt *(ie, made out by a third party for another)*
doppelseitige Anzeige *f* (Mk) double-page spread
Doppelsitz *m* (Re) double seat *(ie, of a commercial company)*
Doppelstichprobennahme *f* (Stat) double sampling
Doppelstichprobenplan *m* (Stat) double sampling plan
Doppelstichprobenprüfung *f* (Stat) double sampling inspection
doppelstöckige GmbH & Co. KG *f* (Re) two-tier GmbH & Co. KG *(ie, a ‚Kommanditgesellschaft' = partnership limited by shares where the limited partner is a ‚GmbH & Co. KG')*
Doppelstrategie *f* (Bw) double-barrelled strategy
doppelstufige Sanierung *f* (Fin) capital writedown + immediate increase of capital
Doppelsystem *n* (EDV) twin system
Doppeltarif *m* (Zo) double tariff *(ie, two rates for each customs item)*
doppelte Buchführung *f* (ReW) double-entry bookkeeping
doppelte Dichotomie *f* (Stat) double dichotomy
doppelte Genauigkeit *f* (EDV) double precision
doppelte Haushaltsführung *f*
(StR) double housekeeping
– maintenance of two households, §9 I No. 5 EStG
doppelte Preisauszeichnung *f* (Mk) double pricing
doppelte Pufferung *f* (EDV) double buffering

doppelter Boden m (EDV) false (or raised) floor (ie, in computer centers)
doppelt erhobene Stichprobe f (Stat) duplicate sample
doppelter Shefferstrich m (Log) joint denial
doppelter Vorschub m (EDV) double feed
doppelter Zeilenabstand m (EDV) double space
doppeltes Integral n (Math) double integral sign
doppelt faktorales Austauschverhältnis n (AuW) double factoral terms of trade
doppelt lange Zahl f (EDV) double-length (or double-precision) number
doppelt-logarithmisches Netz n (Math) double-logarithmic chart
doppelt-logarithmisches Papier n (Math) log-log paper
doppelt-logarithmische Transformation f (Stat) log-log transformation
Doppelverdiener m (Pw) dual jobholder
Doppelverdienerehe f (StR) two-earner married couple
Doppelverrechnung f (ReW) double counting
Doppelversicherung f (Vers) double insurance
Doppelversicherungsklausel f (Vers) double indemnity clause
Doppelwährung f
 (Vw) double currency
 – double monetary standard
 – double standard
 – bimetallism
Doppelwohnsitz m (Re) second domicile (or residence)
Doppelwort n (EDV) doubleword
Doppelzählung f (com) double counting
Doppik f (ReW) double-entry bookkeeping
Doppler m (EDV) card reproducer
Dotationen fpl (FiW) unappropriated payments made by a higher government unit – within the system of revenue sharing – to subordinate units, such as municipal associations, churches, etc.
Dotationskapital n (Fin) dotation capital (ie, equity capital of credit institutions organized under public law, § 10 II No. 5 KWG)
dotieren
 (Fin) to allocate funds
 – to endow (eg, a foundation)
 (ReW) to allocate to reserves (= Rücklagen)
dotiert mit (Pw) remuneration is . . .
Dotierung f
 (Fin) allocation (or provision) of funds
 – endowment
 – dotation
Dotierung f **der Rücklagen** (ReW) transfer (or allocation) to reserves
Doxologie f (Mk) public opinion research
Drahtdrucker m (EDV) wire (or stylus) printer
Drahtspeicher m (EDV) plated-wire memory
drastischer Anstieg m (com) dramatic rise (eg, of oil prices)
drastischer Rückgang m (com) sharp fall
drastisch kürzen (com) to curtail drastically
Draufgabe f
 (Re) earnest money, § 336 BGB (ie, as evidence of a completed bargain)
 – bargain money
 – token payment
Draufgeld n (Re) = Draufgabe
Draufgeld n **leisten** (Re) give in earnest (ie, to bind the contract)
Draufsicht f (IndE) top view
Drehbleistift m
 (com) mechanical pencil
 – (GB) propelling pencil
Drehen n **an der Diskontschraube** (Fin) turning the discount screw
Drehungsachse f (Math) axis of revolution
Drei-Abweichungsmethode f (KoR) three-way overhead analysis
Dreiadreßbefehl m (EDV) three-address instruction
Dreiadreßcode m (EDV) three-address code
Dreiadreßmaschine f (EDV) three-address machine
Dreiadreßsystem n (EDV) three-address system
dreidimensionaler Raum m (Math) ordinary (or three-dimensional) space
dreidimensionales Gitter n (Math) three-dimensional lattice
dreieckiger Graph m (Math) triangulated graph
Dreiecksarbitrage f (AuW) triangular arbitrage
Dreiecksgeschäft n
 (AuW) triangular (or trilateral) barter
 (com) three-cornered deal
 – three-way switch deal
Dreieckshandel m (AuW) triangular trade
Dreiecksmatrix f (OR) triangular matrix
Dreiecksverhältnis n (Re three-cornered relationship
dreiecksverteilte Dichte f (Stat) triangular density
Dreieck-Verkehr m (AuW) triangular system
Dreieckverkehr m **bewilligen** (AuW) to authorize recourse to the triangular system
Dreierprodukt n (Math) triple product
Drei-Exzeß-Code m (EDV) excess three code (syn, Stibitz-Code)
Dreifachadresse f (EDV) three address
Dreifachintegral n (Math) triple integral
Dreimeilengrenze f (com) three-mile limit
Dreimonatsakzept n (Fin) three months' acceptance
Dreimonatsgeld n (Fin) three-month funds
Dreimonatsinterbanksatz m (Fin) interbank rate for three-month funds
Dreimonatspapiere npl (Fin) three-month maturities
Dreimonatswechsel m (Fin) three months' bill of exchange
Dreiprodukttest m (Mk) triadic product test
Dreischichtler m (IndE) three-shift worker (ie, working early, late, and night shifts; opp, Einschichtler, Zweischichtler, Kontiarbeiter)
dreiseitige Gespräche npl (com) tripartite talks
Drei-Sektoren-Wirtschaft f (VGR) three-sector economy
Dreispaltentarif m (Zo) triple-column tariff
dreistelliger Junktor m
 (Log) three-place
 – ternary
 – triadic . . . connective

165

dreistufiges Leitungssystem *n* (Bw) three-tier system of control *(ie, shareholders' meeting, board of management, supervisory board)*
3-Tupel *n* (Math, Log) ordered triple
Dreiviertelmehrheit *f* (Bw) three-quarter majority
dreiwertige Logik *f* (Log) three-valued logic
dreiwertiger Graph *m* (Math) trivalent graph
Driftausfall *m* (EDV, Cobol) degradation failure
Driftfehler *m* (EDV) drift error
driftkorrigierter Verstärker *m* (EDV) drift-corrected amplifier
Dringlichkeitsstufe *f* (Bw) precedence rating
Drittanspruch *m* (Re) third-party claim
Drittausfertigung *f*
 (com) third copy
 (WeR) third of exchange
Drittbegünstigter *m* (Re) tertiary (*or* third-party) beneficiary
Dritteigentümer *m* (Re) third-party owner
dritter Markt *m*
 (Bö) third market
 – over-the-counter market
 (ie, operating outside the stock exchange among traders and the investing public; syn, vor- und nachbörslicher Handel, Telefonhandel; opp, Primärmarkt, Sekundärmarkt)
dritter Produktionsfaktor *m* (Vw) residual factor
Dritterwerber *m* (Re) third-party purchaser
3. UN-Seerechtskonferenz *f* (Re) UNCLOS III, Third United Nations Conference on the Law of the Sea
dritte Wahl *f*
 (com) third-class quality
 – (infml) thirds
Drittgläubiger *m* (Re) third-party creditor
Drittkontrahent *m* (Re) third contracting party
Drittland *n*
 (EG) third country
 – non-EEC state
Drittlandswaren *fpl* (EG) third country products
Drittlandszoll *m* (EG) rate of duty applicable to third countries
Drittmarkt *m* (AuW) export (*or* outside) market
Drittschaden *m* (Re) third-party damage (*or* injury)
Drittschadenversicherung *f* (Vers) third-party damage insurance
Drittschuldner *m* (Re) third-party debtor, §§ 829, 835 ZPO
Drittvergleich *m* (StR) dealing-at-arm's-length rule *(syn, Fremdvergleich, which see)*
Drittvermögen *n* (Re) third-party assets
Drittverwahrung *f* (Fin) custody (of securities) by third party
Drittwiderspruch *m* (Re) third-party opposition *(ie, against execution = Zwangsvollstreckung)*
Drittwiderspruchsklage *f* (StR) third-party action against execution, § 262 AO
drohende Enteignung *f* (Re) imminence (*or* threat) of condemnation
drohender Verderb *m* (com) imminent deterioration
drohende Verluste *mpl* (ReW) impending losses
Drohung *f* (Re) duress, §§ 123, 124 BGB

drosseln
 (com) to curb
 – to reduce
 – to restrict
Drosselung *f*
 (com) curb
 – cutdown
 – reduction
Drosselungsbetrag *m* (ReW) amount of revaluation
Druckaggregat *n* (EDV) printing unit
Druckaufbereitung *f* (EDV, Cobol) editing
Druck *m* **auf die Gewinnspanne** (com) price-cost squeeze
Druck *m* **auf die Zinsspanne** (Fin) pressure on interest margins
Druckausgabebereich *m* (EDV) printout area
Druckausgabespeicher *m* (EDV) printout storage
Druckband *n* (EDV) printer tape
druckbares Zeichen *n* (EDV) printable character
Druckbefehl *m* (EDV) print instruction
Druckdezimalpunkt *m* (EDV, Cobol) actual decimal point
drucken (EDV) to print
Drucker *m* (EDV) printer
Drucker *m* **mit fliegendem Abdruck**
 (EDV) hit-on-the-fly
 – on-the-fly printer
Druckfehler *m*
 (com) misprint
 – literal error
 – (GB) typo (*= typographical error*)
 – literal
Druckformat *n* (EDV) print format
Druckformular *n* (EDV) printer form
Druckkette *f* (EDV) print chain
Druckleiste *f* (EDV, Cobol) print group
Druckkontrastsignal *n* (EDV) print contrast signal, PCS
Druckprogramm *n* (EDV) print program
Drucksachen *fpl*
 (com) printed matter
 – (GB) printed papers
Drucksachenwerbung *f* (Mk) direct-mail advertising
Druckstab *m* (EDV) = *Typenstange*
Druckstange *f* (EDV) = *Typenstange*
Druckstelle *f* (EDV) print position
Drucksteuerzeichen *n* (EDV) print control character
Drucktastentelefon *n* (EDV) pushbutton phone
Drucktrommel *f*
 (EDV) print barrel
 – type drum
Druck *m* **verstärken** (com) to step up pressure (on)
Druckvorlage *f* (EDV) print layout
Druckzeichen *n* (EDV) print character
Druckzusatz *m* **beim Schreiblocher** (EDV) punched card interpreter
Dualbasis *f* (OR) dual base
Dualcode *m* (EDV) binary code
dualer Algorithmus *m* (OR) dual algorithm
dualer Graph *m* (Math) dual graph
dualer Vektorraum *m* (Math) dual vector space

duales Problem n
(OR) dual
- dual problem
duale Wirtschaft f (Vw) dual economy
dualistisches System n
(ReW) dual system of bookkeeping
- dual accounting system *(ie, financial + internal accounting; syn, Zweikreissystem)*
Dualitätsprinzip n (Log) principle of duality
Dualitätstheorem n (OR) duality theorem
Dualitätsrestriktionen fpl (OR) dual constraints
Dualsystem n (EDV) binary system
Dualzahl f (EDV) binary number
Dualzähler m (EDV) binary counter
Dualziffer f (EDV) binary digit
dual zulässiger Vektor m (OR) dual feasible vector
dubiose Forderungen fpl (ReW) = *Dubiosen*
Dubiosen pl (ReW) doubtful accounts
Dumping n (AuW) dumping
Dumpingbekämpfungszoll m (AuW) anti-dumping tariff
Dumpingeinfuhr f (AuW) dumped import
Dumping-Praktiken pl (Kart) dumping practices *(or activities)*
Dumpingpreis m (AuW) dumping price
Dumpingraten fpl (com) uncommercial rates *(ie, in shipping)*
Dumpingspanne f (AuW) dumping margin
Dumpingverbot n (AuW) ban on dumping
Dumpingverbotsgesetz n (Re) anti-dumping law
Düngemittel pl (com) fertilizer
Düngemittelstatistik f (com) fertilizer statistics
Dunkelziffer f (com) number of undisclosed cases
dunkle Geschäfte npl (com) shady dealings *(ie, of doubtful honesty)*
dünne Kapitaldecke f
(Fin) thin
- slender
- inadequate ... capital *(or* equity) base
Dünnschichtspeicher m (EDV) thin film memory *(ie, less than one micrometer)*
Duopol n (Vw) duopoly
Duopson n (Vw) duopsony
Duplexbetrieb m (EDV) duplex operation *(opp, Simplexbetrieb)*
Duplexkanal m (EDV) duplex channel
Duplexsystem n (EDV) duplex system
Duplikat n (com) duplicate
Duplikatfrachtbrief m (com) duplicate of railroad bill of lading
duplizieren (EDV) to duplicate
Duplizierprogramm n (EDV) duplicating program
durchboxen (com, infml) to ram through *(eg, plan, project)*
durchbringen (com) to carry through *(eg, a plan through a committee meeting)*
durchdringende Stichprobe f (Stat) interpenetrating sample
durcheinanderbringen (com, infml) to throw *(eg, a spending plan)* off balance
Durchfinanzierung f (Fin) complete financing (package)
Durchflußwirtschaft f (Vw) throughput economy
Durchfracht f (com) through freight

Durchfrachtkonnossement n (com) through bill of lading *(or* B/L)
Durchfrachtverladung f (com) through-freight shipment
Durchfuhr f (AuW) transit
Durchfuhrabgaben fpl (Zo) transit duties
durchführbar
(com) workable
- feasible
Durchführbarkeit f
- workability
(com) feasibility
Durchführbarkeitsstudie f (Bw) feasibility study
Durchfuhrberechtigungsschein m (AuW) transit permit
Durchfuhrbeschränkung f (Zo) restriction on transit
durchführen
(com) carry out *(or* through)
- to perform
- to implement
Durchfuhrfreiheit f (Zo) freedom of transit
Durchfuhrhandel m (AuW) transit trade
Durchfuhrland n (AuW) country of transit
Durchführung f
(com) implementation
- performance
Durchführung f **der Geldpolitik** (Vw) execution of monetary policy
Durchführung f **e-s Gesetzes** (Re) administration of a law *(or* statute)
Durchführung f **e-s Vertrages** (Re) implementation of an agreement *(or* contract)
Durchführungsbestimmungen fpl (Re) implementing regulations
Durchführungsbestimmungen fpl **zum Umsatzsteuergesetz** (StR) Ordinance Regulating the Turnover Tax
Durchführungsphase f
(Bw, *Entscheidungsphase*) phase of actual decision making
- phase of putting solution to work
Durchführungsplanung f (Bw) operational planning *(syn. Ablaufplanung)*
Durchführungsverordnung f (Re) implementing *(or* regulatory) ordinance *(eg, supporting a tax statute)*
Durchfuhrverbot n (Zo) prohibition on transit
Durchfuhrverkehr m (Zo) traffic in transit
Durchfuhrzoll m (Zo) transit duty
Durchgangsfracht f (com) through freight
Durchgangsgüter npl (com) transit goods
Durchgangskonnossement n (com) through bill of lading *(or* B/L)
Durchgangskonto n
(ReW) internal transfer account
- transit account
Durchgangsladung f (com) through shipment
Durchgangsland n (AuW) transit country
Durchgangsposten m (ReW) transitory item *(ie, accruals and deferrals)*
Durchgangstarif m (com) through rate
Durchgangstransport m (com) transit transport
Durchgangsverkehr m (com) transit traffic
Durchgangswaren fpl (com) goods in transit
Durchgangszoll m (Zo) transit duty
Durchgangszollstelle f (Zo) customs office en route

167

Durchgangszollstelle f beim Ausgang (Zo) customs office of exit en route
Durchgangszollstelle f beim Eingang (Zo) customs office of entry en route
durchgehendes Frachtpapier n (com) through bill of lading
durchgehende Versicherung f (Vers) = *durchstehende Versicherung*
Durchgriffshaftung f (Re) ,,piercing the corporate veil" *(ie, direct liability of partners and shareholders beyond corporate assets, if legal person is abused to restrict liability or is used in violation of the principle of good faith)*
Durchkonnossement n (com) through bill of lading *(or B/L)*
Durchlauf m
(OR) transmittance
(IndE) pass
– run
(EDV) run
Durchlaufanweisung f (EDV, Cobol) perform statement
durchlaufende Gelder npl (Fin) transitory funds
durchlaufende Kredite mpl
(Fin) loans on a trust basis
– loans in transit
– conduit credits
(ie, bank acting in its own name but for the account of another; syn, Treuhandkredite)
durchlaufende Mittel pl (Fin) transmitted funds *(or money)*
durchlaufender Posten m
(ReW) item in transit
– transitory item *(or account)*
– self-balancing item
Durchlauf m e–r Schleife (OR) traversal
Durchlaufkonto n (ReW) interim account
Durchlaufposten m (ReW) = *durchlaufender Posten*
Durchlaufrichtung f **e–r Randkurve** (Math) contour traversal
Durchlaufwahrscheinlichkeit f (OR) reliability
Durchlaufwirtschaft f (Vw) throughput economy
Durchlaufzeit f
(com) time from receipt of order till dispatch
(Bw) processing time
(IndE) door-to-door time
– throughput time
durchleiten
(com) to channel through
– to transmit
Durchleitgelder npl (Fin) transmitted funds
Durchleitkredit m (Fin) transmitted credit
Durchleitmarge f (Fin) bank's margin on transmitted credit
Durchleitung f
(com) channeling through
– transmission
Durchleitungsrecht n (Re) right-of-way
durch Organe handeln (Re) to act through its primary agents
durchrechnen
(com) to make a detailed estimate
(com) to go over *(eg, set of figures, Projekt, Kalkulation)*

Durchsatz m
(IndE) throughput
(EDV) throughput *(syn, Durchsatzrate, Datenrate)*
Durchsatzkapazität f (IndE) throughput capacity
Durchschalt-Vermittlung f (EDV) circuit switching *(syn, Leitungs-Vermittlung)*
Durchschlag m
(com) copy
– carbon copy
– carbon
(eg, mit drei Durchschlägen = with three copies)
durchschlagen (com) to feed through *(eg, auf die Preise = into the prices)*
Durchschlagpapier n
(com) manifold
– flimsy
(ie, thin inexpensive paper for making carbon copies on a typewriter)
(com) carbon paper *(= Kohlepapier)*
Durchschlupf m (Stat) average outgoing quality, AOQ
Durchschnitt m
(Math) intersection *(von Mengen: of sets)*
– meet
(Stat) average
– mean
– mean value
Durchschnitt m ermitteln (com) to average out *(eg, profit, cost, revenue, for a period of . . .)*
durchschnittlich anfallende Zinskosten pl (Fin) average interest expenses
durchschnittlich betragen (com) to average out *(eg, output, takings, salary)*
durchschnittliche Abweichung f (Stat) mean deviation
durchschnittliche Auslastung f (OR) average utilization *(ie, of server in waiting-line models)*
durchschnittliche Exportquote f (Vw) average propensity to export
durchschnittliche Fertigungsqualität f (Stat) process average
durchschnittliche fixe Kosten pl (Vw) average fixed cost
durchschnittliche Gesamtkosten pl (Vw) average total cost
durchschnittliche Importquote f (Vw) average propensity to import *(ie, ratio of imports to net national product at market prices)*
durchschnittliche Kapitalproduktivität f (Vw) average investment productivity
durchschnittliche Konsumquote f (Vw) average propensity to consume
durchschnittliche Lebenserwartung f (Vers) average life expectancy
durchschnittliche Nutzungsdauer f (Bw) average useful life
durchschnittlicher Fehler m (Stat) mean absolute error
durchschnittlicher Fehleranteil m (Stat) process average defective
durchschnittlicher Normalverdienst m
(Pw) normal average earnings
– average straight-time earnings
– standard average earnings

durchschnittlicher Preisaufschlag *m* (com) average markon
durchschnittlicher Prüfaufwand *m* (Stat) average fraction inspected
durchschnittlicher Stichprobenumfang *m* (Stat) average sample number
durchschnittliche Schadenhöhe *f* (Vers) loss ratio *(ie, percentage of losses in relation to premiums)*
durchschnittliche Schadensgröße *f* (Vers) average size of loss
durchschnittliche Sparquote *f* (Vw) average propensity to save, S/Y
Durchschnittsbeitragssatz *m* (SozV) average rate of social insurance contribution
Durchschnittsbestand *m* (MaW) standard inventory
Durchschnittsbetrag *m* (com) average amount
Durchschnittsbewertung *f* (ReW) inventory valuation at average prices, Abschn. 36 II EStR
Durchschnittseinkommen *n* (Pw) average income
Durchschnittseinstandspreis *m* (ReW) average cost price
Durchschnittsentgelt *n* (Pw) average pay (*or* compensation)
Durchschnittserlös *m*
(Vw) average revenue
(Bw) average sales revenue
Durchschnittsertrag *m*
(Vw) average product
(Fin) average yield
Durchschnittsfachmann *m*
(Pat) average mechanic skilled in the art
– average person familiar with the art
Durchschnitts-Gemeinkostensatz *m* (KoR) average overhead (*or* burden) rate
Durchschnittsgewinn *m* (Fin) average profit
Durchschnittskosten *pl* (Vw, KoR) average cost
Durchschnittskostendeckung *f* (Bw) principle of long-term pricing policy: product prices should cover average unit costs
Durchschnittskostenmethode *f* (ReW) average cost method *(ie, of inventory valuation)*
Durchschnittskostenrechnung *f* (KoR) absorption costing
Durchschnittskurs *m* (Bö) average market price
Durchschnittsleistung *f*
(com) average performance
(IndE) average output (per worker)
Durchschnittslohn *m* (Pw) average wage
Durchschnittsmenge *f*
(Math) intersection of sets
– logical product of sets
– meet of sets
Durchschnittsprämie *f* (Vers) flat rate
Durchschnittspreis *m* (ReW, KoR) average price
Durchschnittspreisermittlung *f* (KoR) determining average prices
Durchschnittsprodukt *n* (Vw) average product
Durchschnitts-Produktivität *f* (Bw) average productivity
Durchschnittsqualität *f* (com) fair average quality, faq
Durchschnittsrendite *f* (Fin) average yield
Durchschnittssatz *m* (com) average rate
Durchschnittssatzbesteuerung *f* (StR) average rates method of computing taxes, §§ 13a, 29 EStG, § 24 UStG
Durchschnittssätze *mpl* (StR) average rates of return, § 29 EStG *(repealed in 1980)*
Durchschnittssatz-Verordnung *f* (StR) 8. UStDV = Regulatory Ordinance of 3 Jan 1968 specifying the average rates at which prior turnover tax (= *Vorsteuer*) can be deducted by certain businesses
Durchschnittsspanne *f* (com) average profit margin
Durchschnitts-Stückkosten *pl*
(KoR) average cost per unit
– average unit cost
Durchschnitts-Stundenverdienst *m* (Pw) average hourly earnings
Durchschnittsverdienste *mpl*
(Pw) average wages and salaries
– average earnings
Durchschnittsverzinsung *f*
(Fin) average interest rates
– yield mix
Durchschnittsware *f* (com) merchandise of average quality
Durchschnittswerte *mpl*
(Bö) market averages
(Zo) customs averages
Durchschreibeblock *m* (com) carbon-copy pad
Durchschreibebuchführung *f*
(ReW) mechanical bookkeeping
– one-write system of bookkeeping
(ie, duplicate recording system using carbon copies)
Durchschreibsatz *m* (com) multi-part form set
Durchschrift *f* (com) carbon copy
Durchschrift *f* **Kassenzettel** (com) tissue form of sales check
durchsehen (com) to skim through *(eg, notes)*
Durchsetzungsvermögen *n* (Pw) ability to get things done
durchstehende Versicherung *f* (Vers) uniform application of marine transportation conditions to all other forms of transportation *(eg, by rail, truck, plane)*
durch Steuerabzug erhobene Einkommensteuer *f* (StR) income tax withheld at the source, § 36 EStG
durchstreichen
(com) to cancel
– to strike out
– to cross out
– to delete
Durchsuchungsbefehl *m* (Re) search warrant
Durchwahl *f* (com) direct dialing
Durchwahlnummer *f* (com) direct dial number
durchwurschteln
– to muddle through
(com, infml) to fumble along from day to day
durch Zession übertragbar (WeR) transferable by assignment
düstere Prognose *f* (Vw) gloomy forecast
dyadische Relation *f* (Log) dyadic relation
dyadischer Funktor *m* (Log) binary connective
dyadischer Wahrheitswertfunktor *m* (Log) binary connective

dyadische Verknüpfung *f*
(EDV) binary arithmetic operation
– dyadic operation
(syn, Binäroperation)
Dynamik *f* (Vw) = *dynamische Analyse*
dynamische Adreßumsetzung *f* (EDV) dynamic address translation
dynamische Adreßverschiebung *f* (EDV) dynamic memory relocation
dynamische Analyse *f*
(Vw) dynamic analysis
– dynamics
dynamische Arbeitsspeicherzuweisung *f* (EDV) dynamic storage allocation
dynamische Außenhandelsgewinne *mpl*
(AuW) dynamic gains from trade
– nonallocative gains from trade
Dynamische Bilanz *f* (ReW) Dynamic Accounting *(E. Schmalenbach)*
dynamische Marktlagengewinne *mpl* (Vw) windfall profits
dynamische Methoden *fpl*
(Fin) time adjusted (*or* time-weighted) methods (of investment analyis)
– *(sometimes also:)* dcf methods
– (GB) discounted cash flow methods
dynamische Partialanalyse *f* (Vw) partial dynamics
dynamische Programmierung *f* (OR) dynamic programming
dynamische Programmverschiebung *f* (EDV) dynamic program relocation
dynamische Prüfung *f* (EDV) dynamic test (*or* check)
dynamischer Anpassungsprozeß *m* (Vw) dynamic adjustment process
dynamische Rente *f*
(SozV) wage-related pension
– earnings-linked pension
(ie, pension linked with current changes in the general level of money incomes)
dynamischer Fehler *m* (EDV) dynamic error
dynamischer Multiplikator *m* (Vw) dynamic (*or* long-run) multiplier
dynamischer Schräglauf *m* (EDV) dynamic skew
dynamischer Speicherabzug *m* (EDV) dynamic dump
dynamische Speicherplatzzuweisung *f* (EDV) dynamic storage allocation *(opp, direkte Speicherplatzzuweisung)*
dynamischer Stopp *m* (EDV) dynamic stop *(syn, Fehlerstopp: raising an error condition by the invocation of a closed loop)*
dynamischer Wachstumsfonds *m* (Fin) growth fund
dynamisches Modell *n* (Vw) dynamic model
dynamisches Ungleichgewichtsmodell *n* (Vw) model of disequilibrium dynamics
dynamisches Unternehmen *n*
(Bw) dynamic enterprise
– go-ahead company
dynamisches Unterprogramm *n* (EDV) dynamic subroutine
dynamische Verfahren *npl* **der Investitionsrechnung**
(Fin) time-adjusted (*or* time-weighted) methods of investment analysis
– *(sometimes also:)* dcf methods
– (GB) discounted cash flow methods
dynamische Wirtschaftstheorie *f*
(Vw) dynamic economic analysis
– dynamics
dynamische Zinstheorie *f* (Vw) dynamic interest theory
Dynamisierung *f* (Pw) dynamization *(eg, of company pensions)*

E

EAN-Codierung *f* (Mk) EAN bar coding
Ebene f
(Bw) level
– echelon *(ie, of a business organization)*
ebene Geometrie *f* (Math) plane (*or* two-dimensional) geometry
ebene Koordinaten *fpl* (Math) plane coordinates
ebene Kurve *f* (Math) plane curve
ebener Schnitt *m* (Math) plane cross-section
ebener Umlauf *m* (Math) plane contour
ebenes Polarkoordinatensystem *n* (Math) polar coordinates in the plane
ebene Trigonometrie *f* (Math) plane trigonometry
Eccles-Jordan-Schaltung *f*
(EDV) Eccles-Jordan circuit
– bistable multivibrator
– trigger circuit
Echokontrolle *f* (EDV) echo (*or* read-back) check
echte Addition *f* (EDV) true add
echte Adresse *f*
(EDV) actual
– absolute
– specific . . . address

echte Entscheidung *f* (Bw) genuine (*or* non-programmable) decision
echte Gemeinkosten *pl* (KoR) true overhead (costs)
echte Monatsprämie *f* (Vers) genuine monthly premium *(opp, unechte Monatsprämie)*
echter Bruch *m* (Math) proper fraction
echtes Abladegeschäft *n* (AuW) import transaction where shipping port is deemed to be the place of performance
echtes Angebotsmonopol *n* (Vw) pure monopoly
echte Schnittmengen *fpl* (Math) proper cut sets
echtes Dokument *n* (Re) authentic document
echtes Factoring *n* (Fin) old-line factoring
echte Teilmenge *f* (Math) proper (*or* true) subset
Echtheitszeugnis *n* (Zo) certificate of authenticity
Echtheit *f* **von Urkunden bestätigen** (Re) to authenticate documents
Echtzeitausgabe *f* (EDV) real time output
Echtzeitbetrieb *m* (EDV) real time operation
Echtzeiteingabe *f* (EDV) real time input
Echtzeitprogrammiersprache *f* (EDV) real time programming language

Echtzeitsimulation *f* (EDV) real time simulation
Echtzeitsystem *n* (EDV) real time system
Echtzeituhr *f* (EDV) real time clock
Echtzeitverarbeitung *f* (EDV) real time processing
Eckdaten *pl*
(com) key data
– benchmark figures
Ecke *f*
(OR) node
– vertex
Eckenabschnitt *m* (EDV) corner cut
Eckenlösung *f* (Vw) corner solution
eckige Klammer *f* (Math) bracket
Ecklohn *m*
(Pw) basic (*or* benchmark) rate
– standard wage
(ie, collectively agreed hourly earnings for a normal skilled-worker group over 21 years of age)
Eckpunkt *m* (OR) = *Ecke*
Eckpunkt *m* **e–r Matrix** (Math) corner
Eckpunkt *m* **zweier Tangenten** (Math) cusp
Ecktermin *m* (Bw) basic time limit
Eckwert *m* (com) benchmark figure
Eckzins *m* (Fin) basic rate of interest *(ie, fixed for savings account at statutory notice = bei gesetzlicher Kündigungsfrist)*
ECU-Leitkurs *m* (Fin) ECU central rate
Edelmetall *n* (com) precious metal
Edelmetallbörse *f* (Bö) precious-metals market
Edelmetallgeschäft *n* (com) precious-metals business
Edelmetallgewicht *n* (com) troy weight
Edelmetallhandel *m*
(Fin) precious-metals dealing
– bullion trade
Edelmetallhausse *f* (Fin) upswing in bullion prices
Edelmetallombardgeschäft *n* (Fin) lending on precious metals
Edelmetallmarkt *m* (Fin) precious-metals market
Edelmetallrechnung *f* (Fin) computing the gross weight and the standard of purity of gold and silver bullion and of coins
Edelsteinbörse *f* (com) precious-stone market
Edgeworth-Bertrand-Modell *n* (Vw) Edgeworth-Bertrand model *(ie, of oligopolistic duopoly)*
Edgeworthsches Kastendiagramm *n* (Vw) Edgeworth box diagram
Edinburgh-Regel *f* (FiW) leave them as you find them-rule
EDV-Abteilung *f* (EDV) data processing department
EDV-Analphabet *m* (EDV, infml) computer illiterate
EDV-Großanlage *f* (EDV) mainframe computer
EDV-Personal *n*
(EDV) data processing personnel
– liveware
EDV-Überweisungsverkehr *m* (Fin) electronic funds transfer, EFT
EEV-Steuern *fpl* (StR) taxes on corporate income, business profits, and net worth
Effekten *pl*
(Fin) stocks and bonds
– stock exchange securities
Effektenabrechnung *f* (Fin) contract note

Effektenabteilung *f* (Fin) investment (*or* securities) department *(ie, mostly organizationally related to security deposit department)*
Effektenanlage *f* (Fin) investment in securities
Effektenanlageberater *m* (Fin) investment consultant
Effektenarbitrage *f*
(Bö) securities arbitrage
– arbitrage in securities (*or* stock)
– stock arbitrage
Effektenauftrag *m* (Fin) buying or selling order
Effektenaustausch *m* (Fin) portfolio switch (of investment fund)
Effektenbank *f* (Fin) investment bank *(ie, outside West Germany: special bank dealing with provision of finance, setting up new businesses, securities issues)*
Effektenbankgeschäft *n* (Fin) investment banking
Effekten *pl* **beleihen** (Fin) to make a loan on securities
Effektenbeleihung *f* (Fin) advance on securities
Effektenberatung *f* (Fin) investment counseling
Effektenbestand *m* (Fin) security holding
Effektenbörse *f*
(Bö) stock exchange
– stock market
– market
(ie, exchanges on the European Continent are often called ‚Bourses')
Effektendepot *n*
(Fin) deposit of securities
– securities deposit
– stock deposit
Effektendifferenzgeschäft *n* (Fin) margin business (*or* trading)
Effektendiskont *m*
(Fin) securities discounting
(Fin) securities discount *(ie, slightly above central-bank discount rate, deducted on buying securities drawn by lot prior to the redemption date)*
Effekteneigenhandelsgeschäfte *npl* (Fin) security trading for own account
Effekteneinführung *f* (Fin) marketing of securities
Effektenemission *f* (Fin) issue of securities
Effektenemissionsgeschäft *n* (Fin) underwriting business
Effektenengagement *n* (Bö) stock market commitment
Effektenferngiroverkehr *m* (Fin) securities clearing system between different stock exchange locations
Effektenfinanzierung *f* (Fin) financing through securities
Effektengeschäft *n* (Fin) securities business *(ie, purchase and sale of securities for the account of others)*
Effektengirobank *f* (Fin) giro-type security deposit bank *(ie, financial institution operating collective security systems and giro transfer systems; syn, Wertpapiersammelbank, Kassenverein)*
Effektengiroverkehr *m* (Fin) clearing system for settling securities operations
Effektenhandel *m*
(Bö) dealing (*or* trading) in stock

- stock trading
- securities trading

Effektenhändler m (Bö) stock dealer (or trader)
- dealer in securities
(ie, bank employee dealing in certain types of securities)

Effektenhaus n (Fin) securities trading house *(eg, Merrill Lynch, Salomon, Shearson Loeb Rhoades, E. F. Hutton)*

Effektenkauf m (Fin) security purchase

Effektenkaufabrechnung f (Bö) bought note

Effektenkauf m **mit Einschuß** (Bö) buying on margin

Effektenkommissionär m (Fin) securities commission agent *(ie, banks act as such in their own name and on behalf of another)*

Effektenkommissionsgeschäft n (Fin) securities transactions on commission *(ie, by banks, for officially listed securities)*

Effektenkonto n (Fin) stock account

Effektenkredit m
(Fin) loan on securities
- security loan
- stock loan

Effektenkundschaft f (Fin) customers investing in stocks and bonds

Effektenkurs m
(Bö) stock exchange quotation
- stock market price

Effektenlombard m
(Fin) loan collateralized by securities
- collateral advance
- advance on securities

Effekten pl **lombardieren** (Fin) to borrow on stocks and bonds (or securities)

Effektenmakler m (Fin) stock broker

Effektenmarkt m (Bö) stock market

Effektennotierung f
(Bö) stock exchange quotation
- stock market price

Effektenorder f (Bö) stock order *(ie, order to buy or sell shares)*

Effektenpaket n (Fin) block (or parcel) of shares

Effektenplazierung f (Fin) placing of new securities issue *(ie, by public sale or subscription)*

Effektenportfolio n (Fin) investment portfolio

Effektenrechnung f (Fin) computation of effective interest rate *(syn, Wertpapierrechnung)*

Effektensammeldepot n
(Fin) collective securities deposit

Effektenschalter m (Fin) security department counter

Effektenscheck m (Fin) security transfer check *(syn, grüner Scheck)*

Effektenskontro n (Fin) securities ledger

Effektensparen n (Fin) saving through investment in securities

Effektenspekulation f (Fin) speculation in securities

Effektensubstitution f (Fin) substitution of security by another *(ie, financed through the issue of own shares, bonds, etc.)*

Effektentermingeschäft n (Fin) forward operation (or transaction) in securities

Effektenübertragung f (Fin) transfer of securities

Effektenverkauf m (Fin) sale of securities

Effektenverkaufsabrechnung f (Fin) sold note

Effektenverwahrung f
(Fin) security deposit business
(Fin) security custody

Effektenverwaltung f
(Fin) portfolio management
(Fin) security deposit department (of banks)

effektive Adresse f (EDV) effective address

effektive gearbeitete Zeit f (Pw) working time

effektive Inventur f (ReW) physical inventory

effektive Kosten pl (Vw) explicit cost

effektive Lieferzeit f (com) actual delivery time

effektive Nachfrage f (Vw) effective (or monetary) demand

effektiver Befehl m (EDV) effective instruction

effektiver Übergangspfad m (Vw) effective transition path

effektiver Zins m
(Fin) effective interest rate
- market (or real or negotiated) rate of interest
- yield rate *(ie, in bond valuations)*

effektiver Zinsfuß m (Math) effective rate

effektive Steuerbelastung f (StR) actual tax load

effektive Stücke npl (Bö) actual securities

effektive Übertragungsgeschwindigkeit f (EDV) effective bit rate *(syn, Transfergeschwindigkeit: not the same as Übertragungsgeschwindigkeit)*

Effektivgarantieklausel f (Pw) clause safeguarding effective pay *(ie, when negotiated pay is increased)*

Effektivgeschäft n (Bö) spot market transactions *(ie, on commodity exchanges, include ‚Lokogeschäfte‘, ‚Abschlüsse auf Abladung‘, ‚Abschlüsse in rollender od schwimmender Ware‘)*

Effektivhandel m (com) transactions directed at actual delivery *(opp, speculative trade)*

Effektivklausel f
(WeR) currency clause *(ie, ,,effektiv" on bills of exchange)*
(Pw) stipulation in a collective agreement that a percentage pay rise is granted to all employees across the board

Effektivkosten pl (KoR) actual cost

Effektivlohn m (Vw) actual earnings (or wages)

Effektivrendite f (Fin) dividend yield

Effektivverdienst m (Pw) actual earnings

Effektivverzinsung f
(Fin) effective rate (of a bond)
- effective (interest) yield
- effective annual yield
- market rate
- redemption yield
- true yield (or rate of return)
- yield rate

Effektivwert m
(Bö) actual price *(ie, esp. of stocks and bonds, generally market price less expenses)*
(Stat) root mean square (or rms) value

Effektivzins m (Fin) bond (or market) rate

Effektivzoll m (Zo) effective tariff

effiziente Schätzfunktion f (Stat) efficient estimate

effiziente Schätzung f (Stat) efficient estimate

Effizienz f (com) efficiency

Effizienzeinbußen fpl (Vw) efficiency losses

Effizienzkriterium *n* (Vw, Bw) performance criterion
Effizienzmangel *m* (Bw) organizational slack *(ie, in organizations)*
Effizienztheorem *n* (OR) efficiency theorem
EG-Agrarminister *m* (EG) Community agricultural minister
EG-Haushalt *m* (EG) EEC budget
EG-Länder *npl*
 (EG) EEC countries
 – members of the European Community
EG-Marktpreis *m* (EG) Community market price
EG-Präferenz *f* (EG) EEC preference
EG-Richtlinie *f* (EG) EEC directive
EGKS-Waren *fpl* (EC) ECSC treaty products
Eheberater *m* (StR) marriage guidance counselor
Ehegattenbesteuerung *f* (StR) taxation of husband and wife (*or* spouses)
Ehekonflikt *m* (OR) battle of sexes
eheliches Güterrecht *n* (Re) matrimonial regime, §§ 1363 ff BGB
ehernes Lohngesetz *n* (Vw) iron (*or* brazen) law of wages *(D. Ricardo)*
Eheschließungsrate *f* (Stat) marriage rate *(ie, per 1,000 inhabitants)*
Ehrenakzept *n*
 (WeR) acceptance for honor
 – acceptance supra protest
 – acceptance by intervention
Ehrenakzeptant *m*
 (WeR) acceptor for honor
 – acceptor by intervention
ehrenamtlicher Richter *m* (StR) lay judge, § 5 III FGO
ehrenamtlich tätig (com) acting on an honorary basis
Ehrenannahme *f* (WeR) = *Ehrenakzept*
Ehreneintritt *m*
 (WeR) act of honor
 – intervention supra protest
Ehrenkodex *m* (com) code of ethical practice
Ehrenzahlung *f*
 (WeR) payment for honor
 – payment supra protest
 – payment by intervention
Ehrenzahlung *f* **nach Protest** (WeR) payment for honor supra protest
ehrgeiziges Projekt *n* (com) ambitious project (*or* scheme)
eichen (com) to calibrate
Eichung *f* (com) calibration
Eid *m* **abnehmen**
 (Re) to administer an oath
 – to swear in
eidesstattliche Versicherung *f*
 (Re) statement in lieu of an oath *(ie, affirmed and signed)*
 – affirmation (*or* declaration) in lieu of an oath
 – affidavit *(ie, the use of this term in English law is confined to civil proceedings)*
Eid *m* **leisten** (Re) to take an oath
eidliche Vernehmung *f* (StR) examination (*or* statement) under oath, § 94 AO
eidliche Versicherung *f* (Re) assertory oath

Eigenanzeige *f* (StR) self-accusation of tax evasion reported to the local tax office, § 371 AO
Eigenbedarf *m*
 (com) personal requirements
 (Bw) in – house needs
 (AuW) domestic requirements
Eigenbehalt *m* (Vers) retention *(ie, amount of liability assumed by the writing company and not reinsured)*
Eigenbelastung *f* (StR) amount of extraordinary expenditure (= *außergewöhnliche Belastungen*) which the taxpayer can reasonably be expected to bear himself, § 33 EStG
Eigenbeleg *m*
 (ReW) internal voucher
 – self-prepared document (*or* voucher)
Eigenbesitz *m*
 (Re, StR) possession under claim of right, § 872 BGB, § 39 II 1 AO
 (Fin) own holdings of securities
Eigenbesitzer *m* (Re) proprietary possessor
Eigenbestand *m* (Fin) own holdings
Eigenbestand *m* **von Emittenten** (Fin) issuers' holdings of their own bonds
Eigenbetrieb *m*
 (FiW) owner-operated municipal enterprise
 – municipal public utility undertaking
 (ie, gas, power, water, transportation; set up as a special fund = Sondervermögen; no independent legal entity)
Eigendepot *n* (Fin) own security deposit, §§ 13, 15 DepG (syn, Depot A)
Eigendiagnose *f* (EDV) self diagnosis *(eg, with self-diagnostic features)*
eigene Aktien *fpl*
 (Fin) own shares, § 71 AktG
 – (US) treasury shares
 – shares held in treasury
 – reacquired (*or* repurchased) shares
eigene Akzepte *npl* (Fin) (bank's) acceptances outstanding
eigene Leistungen *fpl*
 (ReW) non-market output of goods and services
 – goods and services for own account
 (ie, usu. rechanneled into input flow)
Eigenelement *n* (Math) eigenfunction
eigene Mittel *pl*
 (Fin) own (*or* capital) resources *(ie, capital and reserves; may include depreciation allowances and unappropriated earnings)*
 (Fin) self-generated funds
eigener Hausstand *m* (StR) own household
eigener Wechsel *m* (WeR) promissory note
eigenerwirtschaftete Mittel *pl* (Fin) internally generated funds
Eigenerzeugnis *n* (KoR) company-manufactured product
eigene Währungsreserven *fpl* (AuW) earned reserves
eigene Ziehungen *fpl* (Fin) bills drawn by a bank
Eigenfertigung *f*
 (IndE) internal production
 (IndE) internally-produced goods
Eigenfinanzierung *f* (Fin) financing from own resources

(ie, the two components of this type of financing are a) eigene Mittel: equity financing, and b) Selbstfinanzierung: funds generated in the business; opp, Fremdfinanzierung)
Eigenfinanzierungsmittel *pl* (Fin) internal resources *(ie, capital consumption, investment grants, retained income)*
Eigenfinanzierungsquote *f* (Fin) self-financing ratio
Eigenfunktion *f*
 (Math) eigenfunction
 – proper function
eigengenutzte Grundstücke *npl* (com) owner-occupied land
eigengenutztes Haus *n* (StR) owner-occupied home
Eigengeschäft *n*
 (com) independent operation *(or* transaction) *(ie, for one's own account)*
 (Fin) trade for one's own account
Eigengewässer *npl* (Re) inland *(or* internal) waters
Eigengewicht *n* (Zo) net weight
Eigenhandel *m* (Fin) trade for one's own account
Eigenhandelsgewinne *mpl* (Fin) profits from dealing for bank's own account
eigenhändig
 (com) ,,hand to addressee only"
 (Re) holographic *(ie, written with one's own hand)*
eigenhändiges Testament *n*
 (Re) holograph
 – holographic will *(ie, not witnessed or attested)*
eigenhändige Unterschrift *f* (Re) autograph *(or* personal) signature
eigenhändig geschriebener Brief *m* (com) autograph letter
eigenhändig geschriebene Urkunde *f* (Re) holograph
eigenhändig unterschrieben (Re) signed personally *(or* in one's own hand)
Eigenhändler *m* (com) dealer *(ie, other than agent)*
Eigenhändlergeschäft *n* (Fin) trading for (bank's) own account *(ie, not on commission)*
Eigenhändlervertrag *m* (com) exclusive dealer agreement
Eigenheim *n* (com) owner-occupied home
Eigenheim *n* **mit Einliegerwohnung** (com) owner-occupied home with separate apartment
Eigeninvestition *f* (Bw) internal investment *(opp, Fremdinvestition)*
Eigenkapital *n*
 (Fin) equity (share) capital
 – stockholders' equity
 – net worth *(or* assets)
 – capital employed *(or* invested)
 – owners' capital *(or* equity)
 – corporate net worth
 – (GB) total equity
 (Vers) net total assets
 – capital at risk
Eigenkapitalanteil *m* (Fin) proprietary interest
Eigenkapitalausstattung *f* (Fin) equity capitalization
Eigenkapitalbasis *f* (Fin) equity capital base *(ie,*

about 22% in West Germany, which is less than half of that in U. S. and U. K.)
Eigenkapitalbedarf *m* (Fin) equity requirements *(or* needs)
Eigenkapital-Bewegungsbilanz *f* (Fin) statement of shareholders' equity *(or* net worth)
Eigenkapitalbildung *f* (Fin) equity capital formation
Eigenkapitaldecke *f* (Fin) equity position *(eg, thin)*
Eigenkapitalfinanzierung *f* (Fin) equity financing
Eigenkapitalgliederung *f* (ReW) breakdown of net worth
Eigenkapital *n* **je Aktie** (Fin) net assets per share
Eigenkapitalkonsolidierung *f* (Fin) equity funding
Eigenkapitalkonto *n*
 (ReW) equity account
 – (GB) proprietary *(or* proprietorship) account
Eigenkapitalkosten *pl* (Fin) cost of equity
Eigenkapitalminderung *f* (Fin) decrease in equity
Eigenkapitalquote *f* (Fin) equity ratio *(eg, 14% of total assets)*
Eigenkapitalrendite *f* (Fin) = *Eigenkapitalrentabilität*
Eigenkapitalrentabilität *f*
 (Fin) equity return
 – income-to-equity ratio
 – percentage return on equity
 – return on (shareholders') equity
Eigenkapitalverzinsung *f*
 (Fin) equity yield rate
 – rate of return on equity
Eigenleistung *f* (Fin) borrower's own funding
Eigenleistungen *fpl* (Bw) services rendered for own account
 (ReW) = *eigene Leistungen*
Eigenmacht *f* (Re) unlawful interference with possession, § 858 BGB
Eigenmarke *f* (Mk) house brand
Eigenmittel *pl*
 (Fin) own funds
 – capital resources
Eigennachfrage *f* (Vw) reverse demand
Eigennutzung *f* (com) internal use
Eigenschaft *f*
 (Log, Math) attribute
 – property
 – characteristic
 – feature
 – earmark
eigentliches Dumping *n* (AuW) dumping proper
Eigentest *m*
 (EDV) open-shop testing
 (EDV) open-shop test run *(opp, Ferntest)*
eigentrassierter Wechsel *m* (WeR) bill drawn by the maker
Eigentum *n*
 (Re) ownership, §§ 903 ff BGB
 – perfect ownership
 – complete ownership
 – property
 (Note: Be careful in using the term ,title'. It does not indicate whether a person holds property for his own benefit or as trustee.)
Eigentümer *m*
 (Re) owner

(ie, in English the term is a ‚nomen generalissimum', its meaning to be gathered from the connection in which it is used)
– proprietor
(ie, having exclusive title to anything; in many instances synonymous with ‚owner')
Eigentümergrundschuld f (Re) owner's land charge, § 1196 BGB
Eigentümerhypothek f (Re) owner's mortgage, § 1163 BGB
Eigentümerin f (Re) proprietoress
Eigentümer-Unternehmer m (Bw) owner-manager
Eigentum n **erwerben** (Re) to acquire ownership (of)
Eigentum n **geht über** (Re) property (*or* title) passes (to)
Eigentum n **nach Bruchteilen** (Re) tenancy in common *(ie, each owner holds an undivided interest in property, §§ 741 ff BGB)*
Eigentum n **retten** (SeeV) to preserve property
Eigentumsanspruch m (Re) right of ownership
Eigentumsaufgabe f
 (Re) voluntary abandonment of ownership, § 959 BGB
 – *(civil law)* dereliction
Eigentumsbildung f (Pw) formation of property (*or* wealth)
Eigentumserwerb m (Re) acquisition of ownership
Eigentumsformen fpl (Re) types of ownership
Eigentumsrecht n
 – right of ownership
 – legal right of property
 – legal title
 – proprietary right
 – property right
Eigentumsschutz m (Re) protection of ownership
Eigentumsübergang m
 (Re) passage (*or* transfer) of title to property
 – passage of ownership
 – passing of title
Eigentumsübertragung f (Re) transfer of ownership
Eigentumsurkunde f (Re) document of ownership
Eigentumsverhältnisse npl (Re) ownership structure
Eigentumsverlust m (Re) loss of ownership *(ie, through destruction, abandonment, and transfer of property)*
Eigentumsvermutung f (Re) presumption of ownership, § 1006 BGB
Eigentumsverzicht m (Re) = *Eigentumsaufgabe*
Eigentumsvorbehalt m
 (Re) reservation of ownership
 – reservation of right of disposal
 – retention of (title to) ownership
 (ie, ownership should not pass before payment of purchase price, § 455 BGB; civil law: pactum reservati dominii)
Eigentumsvorbehaltsklausel f (Re) retention-of-title clause
Eigentumswohnung f
 (Re) condominium
 – cooperative apartment
 (ie, system of separate ownership of individual units in multiple-unit building)

Eigentum n **übertragen**
 (Re) to convey
 – to transfer
 – to transmit . . . ownership *(to others)*
 – to pass title
Eigentum n **verschaffen** (Re) to transfer property
Eigentum n **vorbehalten** (Re) to reserve title to ownership
Eigentum n **zur gesamten Hand** (Re) joint property
Eigenumsatz m (com) internal turnover *(ie, use of own finished products, own repairs, own buildings, etc.)*
Eigen- und Fremdkapital n (Fin) equity and debt capital
Eigenvektor m
 (Math) characteristic vector
 – eigenfunction
 – latent vector
Eigenverbrauch m
 (com) personal consumption
 (VGR) consumption by owner
 (Bw) in-house consumption
 – in-feeding (of goods and services)
 (StR, VAT) appropriation (*or* withdrawal) of business property for non-business purposes of the owner, § 1 I 2 UStG
 – personal use by taxpayer
Eigenveredelung f (com) processing for own account
Eigenverkehr m (Bw) plant-operated traffic *(ie, delivering goods to private and public households)*
Eigenversicherung f (Vers) self-insurance *(eg, business places aside sufficient sums to cover liability losses that may be sustained)*
Eigenwechsel m (WeR) promissory note *(syn, Solawechsel)*
Eigenwerbung f
 (Mk) individual advertising
 – self-advertising
 (opp, ‚Gemeinschaftswerbung' and ‚Sammelwerbung')
Eigenwert m
 (Math) characteristic root
 – eigenfunction
 – eigenwert
 – eigenvector
 – latent root
 – proper value
Eigenwirtschaftlichkeit f (FiW) profitability (*or* efficiency) of public enterprises *(ie, pursued to ensure continued existence or viability)*
Eignung f
 (Pw) aptitude
 – qualification
 – suitability
Eignungsbeurteilung f (Pw) appraisal of aptitude *(ie, through aptitude tests or testing)*
Eignungsprüfung f
 (Pw) aptitude test
 – qualifying examination
Eilauftrag m
 (com) rush order
 (Fin) „urgent order" *(ie, instruction in postal check handling)*

Eilbestellung f (com) = *Eilauftrag*
Eilbote m
(com) special delivery messenger
– (GB) express messenger
Eilbotensendung f (com) express delivery consignment
Eilfracht f
(com) fast freight
– (GB) express freight
Eilfrachtbrief m (com) fast-freight waybill
Eilgebühr f (com) express delivery charge
Eilgeld n **in Höhe des halben Liegegeldes** (com) dispatch half demurrage
Eilgeld n **nur im Ladehafen** (com) dispatch loading only
Eilgut n (com) fast freight
Eilpaket n (com) express parcel
Eilpost f (com) express postal service
Eilüberweisung f (Fin) rapid money transfer *(ie, straight through to the final account-holding bank; settlement still passing through Giro center)*
Eilzuschlag m (com) extra charge for urgent work
Eilzustellung f (com) rush delivery
Einadreßbefehl m (EDV) single *(or* one-address) instruction
Einadreßmaschine f (EDV) single address computer
Einadreßsystem n (EDV) single address system
Einarbeitung f
(Pw) orientation
– familiarization
– settling-in *(ie, of new employees)*
Einarbeitungskosten pl (Pw) cost of employee orientation
Einarbeitungsprogramm n (Pw) orientation program
Einarbeitungszeit f
(Pw) lead-in period
– orientation period
– period of familiarization
– settling-in period
Einarbeitungszuschlag m (IndE) learner allowance
Einarbeitungszuschuß m (Pw) job familiarization allowance
Ein-Ausgabe-Bereich m (EDV) input output area
Ein-Ausgabe-Kanal m (EDV) input output channel
Ein-Ausgabe-Operation f (EDV) input output operation
Ein-Ausgabe-Prozessor m (EDV) input output processor
Ein-Ausgabe-System n (EDV) input output system, IOS
Ein-Ausgabe-Werk n (EDV) input output control
Einbauten pl **in gemietete Räume** (ReW) leasehold improvements
Einbauten pl **in Mietobjekte** (ReW) = *Einbauten in gemietete Räume*
einbehalten
(Fin) to retain *(eg, earnings)*
(StR) to withhold *(ie, taxes)*
einbehaltene Gewinne mpl
(Fin) earnings *(or* net income *or* profits) retained in the business

– profit retentions
– reinvested earnings
– retained earnings *(or* income *or* profit)
– undistributed profits
– (GB) ploughed-back profits
einbehaltene Lohnsteuer f (StR) wages tax withheld
einbehaltener Gewinn m (ReW) earnings retained for use in the business
einbehaltene Steuern fpl
(ReW) tax withholdings
– withheld taxes
Einbehaltung f **der Lohnsteuer** (Pw) withholding of wages tax *(ie, by employer)*
Einbehaltung f **von Gewinnen**
(Fin) earnings *(or* profit) retention
– (GB) ploughing-back of profits
Einbehaltung f **von Steuern** (StR) withholding of taxes
einberufen (com) to call *(or* convene) *(eg, a meeting)*
Einberufung f **der Hauptversammlung** (Bw) calling of shareholders' meeting, §§ 121ff AktG
Einberufungsbefehl m
(Pw) draft card
– (GB) call-up card
Einberufungsbekanntmachung f (Bw) notice of meeting
Einberufungsfrist f (Re) period of notice of meeting, § 123 AktG
einbezahlen (com) to pay in
einbezahlt
(com) paid-in
– paid-up
Ein-Bit-Verzögerungsglied n (EDV) digit delay element
einbringen
(com) to earn
– to yield
(Fin) to contribute
– to bring contributions to
– to put in contributions
Einbringung f (Fin) transfer of property to a company in exchange for stock
Einbringung f **e-s Unternehmens** (Bw) contribution of an enterprise, § 31 III AktG
Einbringungsvertrag m (Fin) agreement relating to contribution of capital
Einbringung f **von Sachwerten** (Fin) contribution of physical assets
Einbruch m
(com) setback
(com) slump
– sharp tumble *(eg, in prices)*
Einbruchdiebstahl-Versicherung f (Vers) burglary insurance
Einbruch m **in den Markt** (Mk) inroads into a market
Einbuße f
(com) damage
– loss
Einbußen fpl **des Realeinkommens** (Vw) real income losses
eindämmen
(com) to check

- to curb
- to damp

eindecken, sich
(com) to buy ahead
- to cover requirements
- to stock up

Eindeckung *f*
(com) stocking up
(com) precautionary buying
(MaW) least-cost replenishment of inventories

eindeutig
(Log) unequivocally
(com) fairly and squarely

eindeutig abhängig (Math, Log) uniquely related
eindeutig definiert (Log) uniquely defined
eindeutige Abbildung *f* (Math) single-valued function
eindeutige Aufgabe *f* (Bw) specified task
eindeutige Definition *f*
(Log) clear-cut
- hard-and-fast
- unique ... definition

eindeutige Funktion *f* (Math) one-valued (*or* single-valued) function
eindeutige Lösung *f* (Math) determinate (*or* unique) solution
eindeutiges Ergebnis *n* (Math) unique solution
eindeutiges Optimum *n* (OR) unique optimum
Eindeutigkeitssatz *m* (Math) identity (*or* uniqueness) theorem
eindimensionale Verteilung *f* (Stat) univariate distribution
eindringen (com) to penetrate (*eg, a market*)
eineindeutige Abbildung *f*
(Math) bijection
- biunique mapping
- one-to-one mapping (*or* function *or* transformation)

Einerkomplement *n* (EDV) ones complement
Einerstelle *f* (EDV) low-order position
Einfachadresse *f* (EDV) one (*or* single) address
Einfachbeleg *m* (com) single-part form
einfache Buchführung *f* (ReW) single-entry bookkeeping
einfache Codierung *f* (EDV) absolute (*or* basic) coding (*syn, Grundcodierung*)
einfache Devisenarbitrage *f* (Fin) direct arbitrage
einfache Fahrkarte *f*
(com) one-way ticket
- (GB) single ticket

einfache Gesellschaft *f* (Re) civil partnership (*syn, Gesellschaft des bürgerlichen Rechts, BGB-Gesellschaft*)
einfache Havarie *f* (SeeV) simple (*or* ordinary) average
einfache Lizenz *f* (Pat) nonexclusive license (*ie, essentially an agreement that patent owner will not sue the licensee*)
einfache Mehrheit *f* (com) simple majority
einfache mittlere Abweichung *f* (Stat) average deviation
einfacher Ausdruck *m*
(Log) primitive (*or* simple) expression
- simple term

einfacher durchschnittlicher Abstand *m* (Stat) = *einfache mittlere Abweichung*
einfacher exponentieller Lag *m* (Math) simple exponential lag
einfacher Gitterplan *m* (Stat) simple lattice design
einfacher Mittelwert *m* (Stat) simple average
einfacher Name *m* (EDV) simple name
einfacher Summenzuwachs *m* (Vers) simple reversionary bonus
einfacher Zeitlohn *m* (Pw) plain time rate
einfaches Akkreditiv *n* (Fin) clean (*or* open) credit
einfaches Inkasso *n* (Fin) clean collection
einfaches Termingeschäft *n* (Bö) outright forward transaction
einfache Stichprobe *f* (Stat) simple sample
einfache Stichprobenahme *f* (Stat) single sampling
einfache Unstetigkeit *f* (Math) ordinary discontinuity
einfache Vermutung *f*
(Re) rebuttable
- disputable
- inconclusive ... presumption
- (*civil law*) praesumptio juris tantum (*ie, counter-evidence permitted* = Widerlegungsmöglichkeiten zugelassen; opp, unwiderlegliche Vermutung)

einfache Zinsen *mpl* (Fin) simple interest
einfache Zufallsauswahl *f* (Stat) simple (*or* unrestricted) random sampling
einfache Zufallsstichprobe *f* (Stat) simple sample
einfache Zugriffsmethode *f* (EDV) basic access method (*syn, Basiszugriffsmethode*)
einfach faktorales Austauschverhältnis *n* (AuW) single factoral terms of trade
Einfachfertigung *f* (IndE) single-process production
Einfachklassifikation *f* (Stat) one-way classification
Einfachkorrelation *f* (Stat) simple correlation
einfach-logarithmischer Maßstab *m* (Math) ratio scale
einfach-logarithmisches Netz *n* (Math) semilogarithmic chart
einfach-logarithmisches Papier *n* (Math) semi-log paper
Einfachstichprobenahme *f* (Stat) single sampling
Einfachstichprobenprüfplan *m* (Stat) single sampling plan
Einfachstichprobenprüfung *f* (Stat) single sampling inspection
einfach zusammenhängender Bereich *m* (Math) simply connected region
einfahren
(com, infml) to break in (*ie, a new car*)
- (GB) to run in

Einfaktortheorie *f* (Stat) single-factor theory
Einfamilienhaus *n* (StR) single-family home (*or* unit) (*ie, may be used in part for business or professional purposes, § 75 V BewG*)
einfarbiges Farbband *n* (com) monochrome (typewriter) ribbon
Einfirmenvertreter *m* (Re) commercial agent contractually barred from working for other principals, § 92a HGB
einfordern (Fin) to call in (*or* call up) capital

Einfordern *n* **nicht eingezahlter Zeichnungen** (Fin) call on unpaid subscriptions
Einfordern *n* **von Kapitaleinlagen** (Fin) call-in of unpaid capital contributions
einfrieren (Fin) to freeze *(eg, external assets)*
Einfuhr *f* (AuW) importation
Einfuhrabfertigung *f*
  (Zo) clearance on importation
  – clearance inwards
Einfuhrabgaben *fpl* (Zo) import charges
Einfuhrabgabenbefreiung *f* (Zo) exemption from import duties
Einfuhrabschöpfung *f* (EG) variable import farm levy *(ie, difference between a lower world market price and a high domestic price)*
Einfuhranmeldung *f* (Zo) import notification *(ie, submitted to the Federal Office of Statistics)*
Einfuhr *f* **auf dem Seeweg** (Zo) importation by sea
Einfuhrausgleichsabgabe *f* (Zo) import equalization levy
Einfuhrbelastung *f* (Zo) import charges
Einfuhrbescheinigung *f* (Zo) entry certificate
  – certificate of clearance inwards
Einfuhrbeschränkungen *fpl*
  (AuW) import restrictions *(or* curbs)
  – restrictions on imports
  – restrictions on the entry of goods
  – bar on imports
Einfuhrbeschränkungen *fpl* **verschärfen** (AuW) to intensify import restrictions
Einfuhrbesteuerung *f* (FiW) imposition of taxes on importation
Einfuhrbestimmungen *fpl* (AuW) import regulations
Einfuhrbewilligung *f* (AuW) import permit
Einfuhrbewilligungsverfahren *n* (AuW) import licensing system
Einfuhrdeklaration *f* (Zo) import entry *(or* declaration)
Einfuhrdokument *n* (Zo) import document
einführen
  (AuW) to import (into)
  (Mk) to launch *(eg, product on a market)*
Einfuhren *fpl*
  (AuW) imports
  – imported goods
Einfuhren *fpl* **auf die Gemeinschaftsplafonds anrechnen** (EG) to charge imports against the Community ceilings
Einfuhren *fpl* **aus Staatshandelsländern** (AuW) imports from state trading countries
einführender Mitgliedstaat *m* (EG) importing Member State
Einfuhren *fpl* **durch Agenturen** (Zo) agency importations
Einführer *m* (AuW) importer
Einfuhrerklärung *f* (Zo) import entry *(or* declaration)
Einfuhrerleichterung *f* (AuW) import facility
Einfuhrerleichterungen *fpl* **gewähren** (AuW) to ease the importation procedure
Einfuhrfinanzierung *f* (AuW) import financing *(ie, raising debt money for handling import transactions)*
Einfuhrfreigabe *f* (AuW) import release

Einfuhrfreiliste *f* (AuW) import calendar
Einfuhrgebiet *n* (AuW) importing territory
Einfuhrgenehmigung *f* (AuW) import authorization
Einfuhrgeschäft *n* (AuW) import transaction
Einfuhrhafen *m* (Zo) port of import
Einfuhrhandel *m* (AuW) import trade
Einfuhrhändler *m* (AuW) importer
Einfuhrkartell *n* (Kart) import cartel
Einfuhrkommissionär *m* (AuW) import commission agent
Einfuhrkontingent *n* (AuW) import quota
Einfuhrkontingentierung *f*
  (AuW) quota allocation for imports
  – imposing import quotas
  – limitation on imports
Einfuhrkontrollmeldung *f* (Zo) import control declaration *(or* notification)
Einfuhrkredit *m* (Fin) import credit
Einfuhrland *n*
  (AuW) country of importation
  – importing country
Einfuhrliberalisierung *f* (AuW) liberalization of imports
Einfuhrliste *f* (AuW) import calendar
Einfuhrlizenz *f* **beantragen** (EG) to apply for an import licence
Einfuhrlizenz *f* **erteilen** (EG) to grant an import licence
Einfuhrmakler *m* (AuW) import broker
Einfuhrmengen *fpl* (AuW) volume of imports
Einfuhrmonopol *n* (AuW) import monopoly
Einfuhr *f* **nach passiver Veredelung** (Zo) importation after outward processing
Einfuhrort *m* (Zo) place of entry *(or* importation)
Einfuhrpapier *n* (AuW) import document
Einfuhrpapiere *npl* (AuW) import documentation
Einfuhrplafond *m* (AuW) import ceiling
Einfuhrprämie *f* (AuW) import bonus
Einfuhrpreis *m* (AuW) entry *(or* import) price
Einfuhrpreisindex *m* (AuW) import price index
einfuhrrechtlich abfertigen (Zo) to carry out *(or* effect) import procedure
Einfuhrregelung *f*
  (AuW) import rules
  – rules for imports
Einfuhrrestriktionen *fpl* (AuW) = **Einfuhrbeschränkungen**
Einfuhrsaison *f* (AuW) importing season
Einfuhrschleuse *f* (AuW) import sluice
Einfuhrschranken *fpl* (AuW) import barriers
Einfuhrsendung *f* (AuW) import consignment
Einfuhrsog *m* (AuW) import pull
Einfuhrsteuer *f* (FiW) import levy *(ie, imposed to protect domestic industries or to better the balance of payments situation)*
Einfuhrstopp *m* (AuW) import ban
Einfuhrstrom *m* (AuW) flow of imports
Einfuhrsubvention *f* (AuW) import subsidy
Einfuhrtag *m* (AuW) day of importation
Einfuhrüberschuß *m* (AuW) import surplus
Einfuhrüberwachung *f* (EG) surveillance over imports
Einfuhrumsatzsteuer *f* (StR) turnover tax on imports, § 21 UStG *(ie, levied on imported goods*

at the rates applicable to domestic deliveries of equivalent merchandise)
Einfuhrumsatzsteuer-Wert *m* (StR) basis for calculation of import turnover tax
Einfuhrunbedenklichkeitsbescheinigung *f* (AuW) certificate of non-objection to import
Einfuhr- und Vorratsstelle *f* **für landwirtschaftliche Erzeugnisse** (AuW) intervention board for agricultural products
Einführung *f* **in die Rechtswissenschaft** (Re) elements of jurisprudence
Einführung *f* **neuer Produkte** (Mk) launching of new products
– product pioneering
Einführungsangebot *n* (Bö) opening offer
Einführungsgesetz *n* (Re) introductory act (*or* law)
Einführungskonsortium *n* (Bö) introduction syndicate
Einführungskurs *m* (Bö) introduction (*or* issue) price
Einführungsphase *f* (Mk) introduction (*or* pioneering) stage *(ie, of product life cycle)*
Einführungspreis *m* (Mk) introductory (*or* advertising) price
Einführungsprospekt *m* (Bö) listing prospectus
Einführungsprovision *f* (Bö) listing commission
Einführungsrabatt *m* (Mk) get-acquainted discount
Einführungstag *m* (Bö) first day of listing
Einführungstest *m* (Mk) product placement test
Einführungswerbung *f*
(Mk) announcement advertising (campaign)
– launch advertising
– (GB) initial advertising
Einführung *f* **von Kreditkontrollen** (Fin) imposition of credit controls
Einfuhr *f* **unter Zollverschluß** (Zo) importation in bond
Einfuhrverbot *n*
(AuW) import embargo
– ban on imports
Einfuhrverfahren *n* (Zo) import procedure
Einfuhrvertrag *m* (AuW) contract for importation, § 22 AWV
Einfuhrvolumen *n*
(AuW) volume of imports
(Stat) value of imports for one period, measured in prices of a specified base year
Einfuhrvorgang *m* (AuW) import operation (*or* transaction)
Einfuhrwaren *fpl* (AuW) import goods
Einfuhrzoll *m*
(Zo) customs duty on importation
– import duty
– duty on entry (*or* imports)
– customs inward
Einfuhrzollanmeldung *f* (Zo) import declaration
Einfuhrzollerklärung *f* (Zo) duty paid entry
Einfuhrzollförmlichkeiten *fpl*
(Zo) customs formalities for putting into free circulation
– customs import formalities
Einfuhrzollkontingent *n* (Zo) import tariff quota
Einfuhrzuschuß *m* (AuW) import subsidy
Eingabe *f* (EDV) (data) input

Eingabe-Ausgabe-Einheit *f* (EDV, Cobol) input output unit
Eingabe-Ausgabe-Gerät *n* (EDV) input output device
Eingabe-Ausgabe-Puffer *m* (EDV) input output buffer
Eingabe-Ausgabe-Steuerung *f* (EDV) input output (traffic) control
Eingabe-Ausgabe-System *n*
(EDV) input output control system, IOCS
– file control processor, FCP
Eingabe-Ausgabe-Unterbrechung *f* (EDV) input output interrupt
Eingabebefehl *m* (EDV) read instruction *(syn, Lesebefehl)*
Eingabebereich *m* (EDV) input area (*or* block)
Eingabecode *m* (EDV) input code
Eingabedaten *pl* (EDV) input data
Eingabeeinheit *f* (EDV) input unit
Eingabefach *n* (EDV) input hopper
Eingabegerät *n* (EDV) input device (*or* unit)
Eingabekanal *m* (EDV) input channel
Eingabemedium *n* (EDV) input medium
Eingabemittel *n* (EDV) = *Eingabemedium*
Eingabeprogramm *n* (EDV) input program (*or* routine)
Eingabepuffer *m* (EDV) input buffer
Eingaberegister *n* (EDV) input register
Eingabesatz *m* (EDV) input record
Eingabespeicher *m* (EDV) input storage (*or* area)
Eingabestation *f* (EDV) input station
Eingabetastatur *f* (EDV) keyboard
Eingabevorgang *m* (EDV) input process
Eingabewarteschlange *f*
(EDV) input job queue
– input work queue
Eingabewerk *n* (EDV) input control
Eingabezustand *m* (EDV) input state
Eingang *m*
(com) arrival
(com) incoming mail
(Fin) receipts
(EDV) input
Eingänge *mpl* (Fin) receipts
Eingang *m* **e–r Zahlung** (Fin) receipt of payment
Eingang *m* **in die Gemeinschaft** (EC) entry into the Community
Eingangsabfertigung *f* (Zo) inward clearance formalities (on arrival)
Eingangsabgaben *fpl*
(StR) import duties and taxes, § 1 III ZG
– import charges
eingangsabgabenpflichtig (StR) liable to import duties and taxes
Eingangsabteilung *f* (com) receiving department
Eingangsanzeige *f* (com) acknowledgment of receipt
Eingangsbefehl *m* (EDV) entry instruction
Eingangsbescheinigung *f* (EG) receipt *(ie, common shipping procedure)*
Eingangsbestätigung *f*
(com) acknowledgment of receipt
(Zo) confirmation of procedure as declared
Eingangsbuch *n* (MaW) register of merchandise received

Eingangsbuchung *f* (ReW) original entry
Eingangsdatum *n* (com) date of receipt
Eingangsdurchgangszollstelle *f* (Zo) office of entry en route
Eingangsdurchschnittspreis *m* (KoR) average price of raw materials and supplies, restricted to current additions *(ie, disregarding the beginning inventory of an accounting period)*
Eingangsfehler *m* (EDV) inherited error
Eingangsfracht *f*
 (com) carriage inward
 – freight in
 – freight inward
Eingangsfunktion *f*
 (OR) contributive function
 – input function
 – receiving function
Eingangs-Informationsträger *m* (EDV) input medium
Eingangslager *n* (MaW) incoming stores
Eingangsmeldung *f* (com) receiving report
Eingangsmitgliedstaat *m* (EG) Member State of entry
Eingangsort *m* (Zo) port of entry
Eingangsprüfung *f* (MaW) receiving inspection *(ie, of incoming goods)*
Eingangsprüfung *f* **ablegen**
 (Pw) to sit for
 – to take
 – to sustain ... a qualifying examination *(eg, at university level)*
Eingangsrechnung *f* (ReW) purchase invoice
Eingangsstelle *f* (EDV) inconnector
Eingangsstempel *m* (com) date *(or* receipt) stamp
Eingangsstufe *f* (Pw) entry level
Eingangsstufe *f* **des Steuertarifs** (StR) first-bracket rate of tax
Eingangstag *m* (com) date of receipt
Eingangsvermerk *m* (com) file mark
Eingangsversand *m* (Zo) inward transit
Eingangszoll *m* (Zo) inward duty
Eingangszollamt *n* (Zo) import customs office
Eingangszollstelle *f* (Zo) customs office of entry
Eingang *m* **vorbehalten** (Fin) ,,subject to collection" *(ie, clause on credit note for bills of exchange and checks turned in to a bank for collection)*
eingebaute Funktion *f*
 (IndE) preparatory function
 (EDV) built-in function
eingeben (EDV) to input
eingebrachtes Kapital *n*
 (Fin) contributed capital
 – capital brought into the company
eingeforderter Betrag *m* (Fin) amount called in, § 63 II AktG
eingefordertes Kapital *n* (Fin) called-up capital
eingefrorene Forderung *f* (Fin) blocked *(or* frozen) claim
eingefrorenes Guthaben *n* (Fin) frozen *(or* blocked) assets
eingegliederte Gesellschaft *f* (Bw) integrated company, §§ 319–327 AktG
eingegliedertes Unternehmen *n* (StR) integrated entity, § 2 II No. 2 GewStG *(ie, subordinated to another resident business enterprise to the extent that it has no freedom of decision)*
eingehen
 (Re) to assume *(eg, obligation)*
 (Fin) to incur *(eg, debt, liabilities)*
eingehende Beschau *f* **der Waren** (Zo) detailed *(or* full) examination of the goods
eingehende Post *f* (com) incoming mail
eingehender Bericht *m* (com) detailed *(or* full) report
eingelöster Scheck *m* (Fin) paid check
eingerichteter Geschäftsbetrieb *m* (com) organized enterprise
eingeschaltete Bank *f* (Fin) intermediary bank
eingeschränkte Ermessensfreiheit *f* (Bw) bounded discretion
eingeschränkte Randomisierung *f* (Stat) restricted randomization
eingeschränkte Rationalität *f* (Bw) bounded rationality *(ie, permitting no optimum solutions)*
eingeschränkter Bestätigungsvermerk *m* (ReW) qualified certificate *(or* opinion)
 – with-the-exception-of opinion
eingeschränktes Akzept *n* (WeR) qualified *(or* special) acceptance
eingeschränktes Eigentum *n* (Re) qualified title (to property)
eingeschränktes Indossament *n* (WeR) qualified indorsement
eingeschränkte Zufallsauswahl *f* (Stat) restricted random sampling
eingeschriebener Brief *m* (com) registered letter
eingeschriebenes Mitglied *n* (Pw) card-carrying member *(eg, of a union)*
eingesetztes Kapital *n* (Fin) capital employed
eingetragene Genossenschaft *f* (Re) registered cooperative society
eingetragene Genossenschaft *f* **mit beschränkter Haftpflicht, eGmbH** (Re) registered cooperative society with limited liability
eingetragener Inhaber *m* (Re) registered holder
eingetragener Verein *m* (Re) registered association *(or* society), §§ 55–79 BGB
eingetragenes Warenzeichen *n* (Pat) registered trademark
eingetretene Anlagenwagnisse *npl* (ReW) encountered risks on fixed assets and investments
eingetretene sonstige Wagnisse *npl* (ReW) miscellaneous encountered risks
eingetretene Todesfälle *mpl* (Vers) actual deaths
eingezahlte Aktie *f* (Fin) fully paid-in share
eingezahlter Betrag *m* (com) amount paid in *(or* tendered)
eingezahltes Aktienkapital *n* (Fin) paid-up share capital
eingezahltes Kapital *n* (Fin) paid-in capital *(ie, including contributions in kind)*
eingezogene Aktie *f* (Fin) redeemed *(or* called-in) share
eingipfelige Verteilung *f* (Stat) unimodal distribution
eingliedern (Bw) to integrate *(a company etc.)*
Eingliederung *f*
 (Bw, StR) integration
 – subordination of a dependent entity

(ie, temporary affiliation of a company with/to another – main – company, §§ 319–327 AktG, § 2 II No. 2 GewStG)
Eingliederung f in den Arbeitsprozeß (Pw) integration into the labor force
Eingliederungsbeihilfe f (SozV) settling-in allowance *(ie, paid by the Federal Labor Office to employers offering a permanent job to a jobseeker, usu. for one year)*
Eingliederungsdarlehen n (Vw) integration loan
Eingliederungshilfe f (Vw) integration aid
Eingriff m (Re) impairment *(ie, of existing right)*
Eingriff m im Ausnahmefall (Bw) management by exception
Eingriffsintensität f (Kart) intensity of interference
Eingriffsrechte npl (Re) powers to intervene *(eg, in the running of the economy)*
Eingriffsschwelle f (Kart) threshold of interference *(ie, threshold at which cartel authorities start investigations; eg, volume of sales, number of employees, market shares)*
Eingriffssignal n (EDV) interrupt signal
Einhaltung f e–r Frist
(com) keeping a time limit
– meeting a deadline
Einhaltung f e–s Vertrages (Re) compliance with the terms of a contract
Einhaltung f staatlicher Vorschriften (Re) compliance with government regulations
einheimische Arbeitskräfte fpl (Pw) indigenous workers
einheimisches Unternehmen n
(com) domestic enterprise
(AuW) indigenous enterprise
Einheit f der Auftragserteilung (Bw) unity of command *(ie, in business organizations)*
Einheit f der ersten Auswahlstufe (Stat) first-stage (*or* primary) unit
Einheit f der zweiten Auswahlstufe (Stat) second-stage (*or* secondary) unit
einheitlich abschreiben (ReW) to subject to uniform depreciation rules, Abschn. 31 II EStR
einheitliche Bedingungen fpl (com) standard terms
einheitliche Geschäftsbedingungen fpl (Re) standard business conditions
einheitliche Gewinnfeststellung f (StR) uniform determination of profits, §§ 179, 180 I 2a AO
einheitliche Grundsätze mpl der Kostenrechnung (KoR) uniform cost accounting rules
einheitliche Lebensverhältnisse npl (Re) identical social and economic conditions (*or* relations)
einheitliche Leitung f
(Bw) central
– centralized
– unified ... management
– common control
einheitliche Preise mpl (com) uniform prices
einheitlicher Auswahlsatz m (Stat) uniform sampling fraction
einheitlicher Bezugspunkt m (Fin) uniform base period *(ie, in investment analysis)*
einheitlicher Gewerbesteuermeßbetrag m (StR) uniform tentative tax *(ie, obtained by combining the tentative taxes on business profits and on business capital)*

Einheitliche Richtlinien fpl für Dokumentenakkreditive (com) Uniform Customs and Practice for Commercial Documentary Credits
Einheitliche Richtlinien fpl für Inkassi (Fin) Uniform Rules for Collections
einheitlicher Markt m (Bö) uniform market
einheitlicher Satz m (com) uniform rate
einheitlicher Steuermeßbetrag m (StR) uniform tentative tax *(ie, established by the local tax office which combines the tentative taxes [= Steuermeßbeträge] on business profits and business capital)*
einheitliches Bewertungssystem n (Bw) uniform valuation system
einheitliches Kaufvertragsrecht n (Re) uniform law on sale of goods
einheitliches Preisgefüge n (Mk) unified price structure
einheitliche Unternehmenspolitik f (Bw) uniformity of corporate policy
einheitliche Währung f (EG) sole (*or* single) currency
Einheitlichkeit f der Lebensverhältnisse (Re) economic unity of the country *(see: einheitliche Lebensverhältnisse)*
Einheitlichkeit f der Zollsysteme (Zo) uniformity in the customs systems
Einheitsbewertung f (StR) assessed valuation, §§ 19–109a BewG *(ie, designed to establish uniform and separate values for the greatest possible variety of taxes)*
Einheitsbilanz f (ReW) unified balance sheet *(ie, term suggesting the goal of making the commercial and tax balance sheets co-extensive. Current statutory obstacle are different valuation rules)*
Einheitsbudget n (FiW) unified budget *(ie, developed in U. S. in 1967)*
Einheitsformular n (com) standard form
Einheitsfrachttarif m (com) all-commodity freight rate
Einheitsgewerkschaft f (Pw) nonpartisan industry-based union *(ie, open to all skills, grades and specialists in the branch of employment covered by the union; there are 17 of them under the umbrella of the union federation – DGB – at Düsseldorf)*
Einheitsgraph m (Math) unitary graph
Einheitsgründung f (Re) single-step formation (of a stock corporation = AG) *(ie, corporation and capital issue at one go; syn, Simultangründung; opp, Stufengründung)*
Einheitskosten pl
(KoR) unit cost
– cost per unit of output *(opp, ‚Gesamtkosten')*
Einheitskurs m
(Bö) daily
– single
– standard ... quotation
– middle price
Einheitsmarkt m (Bö) single-price (*or* single-quotation) market *(opp, variabler Markt)*
Einheitsmatrix f
(Math) identical
– identity

- unit
- universal... matrix
Einheitsmietvertrag *m* (Re) standard tenancy agreement
Einheitsnotiz *f* (Bö) single quotation
Einheitsprämie *f* (Vers) flat premium (*or* rate)
Einheitspreis *m*
(com) standard price
- unit price
(Vw) uniform price *(ie, set for government price control purposes)*
Einheitspreisgeschäft *n* (Mk) variety store *(ie, retail outlet carrying 2,000–3,000 low-priced articles in fixed price classes)*
Einheitssatz *m* (KoR) standard rate
Einheitsscheck *m* (Fin) standard check form
Einheitssprung *m* (Math) unit step
Einheits-Sprungfunktion *f* (Math) unit-step function
Einheitssteuer *f* (FiW) flat rate tax
Einheitsstücklohn *m* (IndE) standard piece wage
Einheitstarif *m*
(com) flat rate
(Zo) general tariff
- single-schedule tariff
- unilinear tariff
Einheitstheorie *f* (ReW) theory of economic unity of a company group
Einheitsvektor *m* (Math) unit vector
Einheitsverpackung *f* (com) standard packing, § 62 I EVO
Einheitsversicherung *f* (Vers) combined-risk insurance *(ie, restricted to a number of industries, such as textiles, leather clothing, tobacco, furs, dying, laundries, chemical cleaning)*
Einheitsvertrag *m* (Re) standard agreement (*or* contract)
Einheitsvordruck *m* (com) standard form
Einheitswechsel *m* (Fin) standard form of bill of exchange
Einheitswert *m* (com) standard value
(StR) assessed value *(ie, computed for agricultural, real, and business property, §§ 19–109a BewG)*
Einheitswertbescheid *m* (StR) assessment notice
Einheitswertsteuern *fpl* (StR) taxes based on assessed values *(eg, net worth tax, real property tax, trade tax, inheritance tax)*
Einheitswertzuschlag *m* (StR) assessed value adjustment, § 121a BewG *(ie, raises the 1964 assessed values of real property by 40%)*
Einheitswurzel *f* (Math) root of unity
Einheitszoll *m* (Zo) uniform duty
Einheitszolltarif *m* (Zo) single-schedule tariff
Einigung *f*
(com) agreement
(Re) mutual consent
- meeting (*or* union) of minds *(ie, in contract law)*
(Re) agreement that property should pass, § 929 BGB
Einigung *f* **mit den Gläubigern** (Re) arrangement (*or* composition) with creditors
- composition in bankruptcy
(ie, discharge is by operation of law)

Einigungsmangel *m* (Re) lack of agreement
Einigungsstelle *f* (Pw) conciliation board, § 76 BetrVerfG
Einigungsstellen *fpl* **für Wettbewerbsstreitigkeiten** (Kart) conciliation boards for the settlement of disputes on restrictive trade practices *(ie, working under the jurisdiction of the Chambers of Industry and Commerce)*
Einigung *f* **und Übergabe** *f* (Re) agreement and delivery, § 929 BGB
Einkanalmodell *n* (OR) single channel (*or* station) model
Ein-Kanten-Netzwerk *n* (OR) one-branch network
Einkauf *m*
(com) buying
- purchase
(MaW) purchasing *(ie, terms like purchasing, procurement, supply, materials management, and logistics are used almost interchangeably)*
einkaufen
(com, infml) to go shopping
(com) to buy
- to purchase
Einkaufen *n*
(com, infml) shopping
- (US) marketing
(com) to do shopping
- to go marketing
Einkäufer *m*
(com) shopper
(Mk) buyer
- buying agent
Einkauf *m* **nach Katalog** (Mk) catalog buying *(opp, buying through retail outlets)*
Einkaufsabteilung *f* (Bw) purchasing department
Einkaufsabweichung *f* (KoR) purchasing variance *(ie, difference between planned price and actual cost price)*
Einkaufsagent *m* (AuW) purchasing agent *(ie, employed by American and European department stores)*
Einkaufsakkreditiv *n* (Fin) buying letter of credit
Einkaufsauftrag *m* (com) purchase order
Einkaufsbedingungen *fpl* (com) conditions of purchase *(ie, in commercial practice: conditions of delivery and payment)*
Einkaufsbruttopreis *m* (KoR) gross purchase price *(ie, includes all acquisition costs)*
Einkaufsbuch *n* (MaW) purchase journal
Einkaufsbudget *n* (Bw) purchase budget
Einkaufsgemeinschaft *f*
(Mk) purchasing association
- buying group
(ie, comprising retail traders, artisans, wholesalers, and department stores)
Einkaufsgenossenschaft *f* (Bw) purchasing (*or* wholesale) cooperative
Einkaufsgewohnheiten *fpl* (Mk) buying habits
Einkaufshandbuch *n* (MaW) purchasing manual
Einkaufshäufigkeit *f* (Mk) purchasing frequency
Einkaufskartell *n* (Kart) buying (*or* purchasing) cartel
Einkaufskommission *f* (Re) commission to purchase goods, § 391 HGB

Einkaufskommissionär *m*
(com) commission buyer
- purchasing commission agent
- buying agent

Einkaufskommittent *m* (Fin) securities account holder

Einkaufskontingent *n* (com) buying quota

Einkaufskonto *n* (ReW) purchasing account

Einkaufsland *n* (Zo) country of purchase

Einkaufsleiter *m*
(MaW) head of purchasing
- purchasing director (*or* officer)

Einkaufsniederlassung *f* (Bw) purchasing branch office

Einkaufsplanung *f* (Bw) purchasing planning

Einkaufspolitik *f* (MaW) procurement policy

Einkaufspreis *m* (com) purchase price *(ie, invoiced by seller)*

Einkaufsprogramm *n* (MaW) purchasing program

Einkaufsprovision *f* (com) buying commission

Einkaufsrechnungspreis *m* (com) invoiced purchase price *(ie, charged by supplier)*

Einkaufsstatistik *f* (MaW) procurement statistics

Einkaufssyndikat *n* (Bw) buying syndicate

Einkaufsverband *m* (Mk) purchasing association

Einkaufsvereinigung *f* (Mk) buying group

Einkaufsverhalten *n* (Mk) buying behavior (*or* pattern)

Einkaufsvertreter *m* (com) buying agent

Einkaufszentrale *f* (Bw) buying office

Einkaufszentrum *n* (Mk) shopping center

einklagbare Forderung *f* (Re) enforceable claim

einklagen (Re) to sue for

Einklarierung *f* (Zo) clearance inwards

Einkommen *n* (com, Pw) income *(ie, usu. money income)*
- earnings
(StR) net income *(ie, taxable base of income tax)*

Einkommen *n* **angestellter Unternehmer** (VGR) contractual entrepreneurial income

Einkommen-Ausgaben-Modell *n* (Vw) income-expenditure approach

Einkommen *n* **aus selbständiger Arbeit** (VGR) self-employment income

Einkommen *n* **aus unselbständiger Arbeit** (VGR) income from employment

Einkommen *n* **aus Unternehmertätigkeit und Vermögen** (VGR) income from property and entrepreneurship

Einkommen *n* **der unselbständigen Beschäftigten** (VGR) employee compensation (*or* earnings)

Einkommen-Konsum-Funktion *f* (Vw) income-consumption function
- Engels curve

Einkommen-Konsumkurve *f* (Vw) income-consumption curve

Einkommen *n* **pro Kopf der Bevölkerung** (VGR) per capita income

Einkommensaktien *fpl* (Fin) income equities *(ie, shares with a high price-dividend ratio)*

Einkommensaustauschverhältnis *n* (AuW) income terms of trade

einkommensbedingte Inflation *f* (Vw) inflation due to disproportionate claims to income rises

Einkommensbesteuerung *f* (FiW) income taxation

Einkommensbezieher *m* (com) income recipient

Einkommensdisparität *f* (Pw) pay inequalities
(Vw) income disparity *(ie, income differential between employed persons of various sectors or various societal groups)*

Einkommenseffekt *m* (Vw) income effect *(ie, in the theory of the household)*
(Vw) income generating effect *(ie, in macroeconomics)*

Einkommenselastizität *f* (Vw) income elasticity

Einkommenselastizität *f* **der Importnachfrage** (Vw) income elasticity of demand for imports

Einkommenselastizität *f* **der Nachfrage** (Vw) income elasticity of demand

Einkommensempfänger *m* (com) income recipient

Einkommensermittlung *f* (StR) determination (*or* computation) of taxable income:

Summe der Einkünfte aus den 7 Einkunftsarten (§§ 13–24 EStG)	Adjusted gross income from all applicable sources
– Altersentlastungsbetrag	– Old age percentage reduction
= Gesamtbetrag der Einkünfte	= Adjusted gross income
– Sonderausgaben (§§ 10–10d EStG)	– Special expenses
– außergewöhnliche Belastungen (§§ 33–33b EStG)	– Extraordinary financial burdens
= Einkommen	= Income
– Altersfreibetrag (§ 32 II EStG)	– Old age allowance
– Haushaltsfreibetrag (§ 32 III EStG)	– Household allowance
– sonstige vom Einkommen abzuziehende Beträge	– Other deductions
= Zu versteuerndes Einkommen	= Taxable Income

Einkommensfonds *m* (Fin) income fund *(opp, Wachstumsfonds, Thesaurierungsfonds)*

Einkommensgefälle *n* (Pw) earnings gap

Einkommensgleichung *f* (Vw) cash balance equation

Einkommensgruppe *f*
(Vw) income group
(StR) income bracket

Einkommenshöhe *f* (com) income level

Einkommens-Konsumkurve *f* (Vw) income consumption curve

Einkommenskonto *n* (VGR) income account

Einkommenskreislauf *m*
(Vw) circular flow of income
- flow of income

Einkommenskreislaufgeschwindigkeit *f* **des Geldes** (Vw) income velocity of circulation

Einkommensmechanismus *m* (AuW) income mechanism

Einkommens-Nachfrage-Funktion *f* (Vw) income demand function
Einkommensnivellierung *f* (Vw) leveling of incomes
Einkommenspolitik *f* (Vw) incomes policy *(ie, strategy aimed at directly holding down wages and prices)*
Einkommensprobleme *npl* **der Landwirtschaft** (Vw) farm income problems
Einkommenspyramide *f* (Vw) income pyramid
Einkommensredistribution *f* (Vw) income redistribution
Einkommensschere *f* (Vw) income gap *(eg, between the farming and industrial sectors)*
Einkommensschmälerung *f* (Pw) reduction of earnings
Einkommenssicherung *f* (SozV) income maintenance *(or* protection)
Einkommenssituation *f* (Vw) income situation *(ie, of market participants)*
Einkommensstatistik *f* (Stat) income statistics
Einkommensstufe *f* (StR) income bracket
Einkommensteuer *f* (StR) income tax *(ie, including ‚Lohnsteuer' = wages tax and ‚Körperschaftsteuer' = corporation income tax)*
Einkommensteuerbilanz *f* (StR) income-tax balance sheet
Einkommensteuer-Durchführungsverordnung *f* (StR) Ordinance Regulating the Income Tax Law
Einkommensteuererklärung *f* (StR) individual income tax return
Einkommensteuergesetz *n* (StR) Income Tax Law
Einkommensteuer-Grundtabelle *f* (StR) basic income-tax scale
Einkommensteuerpflicht *f* (StR) income tax liability
einkommensteuerpflichtig
  (StR) taxable to income tax
  – liable in/to income tax
Einkommensteuerpflichtiger *m* (StR) person liable in income tax
  – income tax payer
Einkommensteuerreformgesetz *n* (StR) Income Tax Reform Law
Einkommensteuer-Richtlinien *fpl* (StR) Income Tax Regulations
Einkommensteuer-Rückvergütung *f* (StR) refund of income tax
Einkommensteuerschätzung *f* (StR) arbitrary assessment of income tax
Einkommensteuer-Splittingtabelle *f* (StR) joint marital income-tax scale
Einkommensteuer-Tarif *m* (StR) income tax scale
Einkommensteuer-Vorauszahlung *f* (StR) prepayment of estimated income tax, § 37 EStG
Einkommenstheorie *f* (Vw) theory of income determination
  (VGR) national income theory
Einkommensstufe *f* (StR) income bracket
Einkommensträger *m* (Stat) income-receiving person
Einkommensübertragungen *fpl* (VGR) transfer payments
Einkommensumverteilung *f* (Vw) income redistribution *(ie, through labor-union wage policy + government (secondary) redistribution, such as taxes, transfer payments, public goods)*
Einkommens- und Beschäftigungstheorie *f* (Vw) income and employment analysis
Einkommensverlust *m*
  (Pw) income loss
  – loss of income
Einkommen *n* **verringern**
  (com) to cut down
  – to diminish
  – to pare down
  – to reduce
  – to whittle down ... income/earnings
Einkommensverteilung *f* (Vw) income *(or* earnings) distribution
Einkommensverteilungs-Inflation *f* (Vw) income-share inflation
Einkommensverwendung *f* (StR) application of income
Einkreisungspatent *n* (Pat) fencing-in patent
Einkünfte *pl*
  (com) earnings
  – income
  – emoluments
  – revenue
  (StR) adjusted gross income *(ie, gross income from one or several of the seven sources listed in § 2 EStG)*
Einkünfte *pl* **aus bebauten Grundstücken** (StR) income from improved properties
Einkünfte *pl* **aus Gewerbebetrieb** (StR) income from trade or business, § 2 I No. 2 EStG
Einkünfte *pl* **aus Kapitalvermögen** (StR) income from investment of capital, § 2 I No. 5 EStG
Einkünfte *pl* **aus Land- und Forstwirtschaft** (StR) income from agriculture and forestry, § 2 I No. 1 EStG
Einkünfte *pl* **aus nichtselbständiger Arbeit** (StR) employment income *(ie, on which income tax is withheld at the source, § 2 I No. 4 EStG)*
Einkünfte *pl* **aus öffentlichen Erwerbsunternehmungen**
  (FiW) revenue from government-owned enterprises
  – proprietary receipts
Einkünfte *pl* **aus Schwarzarbeit** (Pw) black earnings
Einkünfte *pl* **aus selbständiger Arbeit** (StR) income from independent personal services, § 2 I No. 3 EStG
Einkünfte *pl* **aus unbebauten Grundstücken** (StR) income from lease of unimproved properties
Einkünfte *pl* **aus Vermietung und Verpachtung** (StR) income from rentals and royalties, § 2 I No. 6 EStG
Einkünfte *pl* **aus wissenschaftlicher, künstlerischer, schriftstellerischer, unterrichtender od erzieherischer Tätigkeit** (StR) income from scientific, artistic, literary, or teaching activity
Einkunftsarten *fpl*
  (StR) sources of taxable income, § 2 I EStG
  – categories of income
Einladung *f* **zur Zeichnung** (Bö) subscription offer
Einlagekonto *n* (Fin) account of ‚dormant' partner

showing the current position of his participation *(ie, see §§ 335ff HGB!)*
Einlagen *fpl*
(Fin) bank deposits
(Re) contribution *(ie, cash or property, made to any type of commercial undertaking, such as AG, OHG, KG, stille Gesellschaft)*
(StR) contributions to capital during the business year, § 4 I 3 EStG
(Mk) inserts
Einlagen *fpl* **abbauen** (Fin) to run down *(eg, central bank deposits)*
Einlagenabgänge *mpl* (Fin) outflow of deposits
Einlagenbestand *m* (Fin) volume of deposits
Einlagenentwicklung *f* (Fin) movement of deposits
Einlagengeschäft *n* (Fin) deposit-taking business *(ie, of a bank)*
Einlagen *fpl* **mit Kündigungsfrist** (Fin) deposits at notice
Einlagen *fpl* **mit kurzer Kündigungsfrist** (Fin) short-term deposits
Einlagenpolitik *f* (FiW) government deposit policy
Einlagenschutz *m* (Fin) deposit security arrangements *(ie, multi-stage system set up by the German savings banks)*
Einlagensicherung *f* (Fin) safeguarding depositors' accounts *(ie, general term; accomplished through private arrangements of the banking industry, such as guaranty funds, joint liability agreements, ect.)*
Einlagensicherungs-Fonds *m* (Fin) deposit guaranty fund
– fire-fighting fund *(ie, set up by the ‚Bundesverband der deutschen Banken' = Federation of the German Banking Industry)*
Einlagenüberschuß *m* (Fin) surplus of deposits
Einlagenumschichtung *f* (Fin) shift in deposits
Einlagenversicherung *f* (Vers) deposit insurance
Einlagenvolumen *n* (Fin) volume of deposits
Einlagen *fpl* **von Anteilseignern** (Fin) capital contribution by shareholders
Einlagenzins *m* (Fin) deposit rate
Einlagenzuflüsse *mpl* (Fin) inflow of deposits
Einlagerer *m* (com, Zo) depositor
einlagern
(com) to store
– to stock
– to warehouse
Einlagerung *f*
(com) storage, §§ 416ff HGB
– warehousing
(Zo) admission into warehouse
Einlagerungsgewicht *n* (com) storage weight of goods receipted by the warehouse keeper
Einlagerungskredit *m* (Fin) stockpiling loan
Einlagerungsland *n* (Zo) country of warehousing
Einlagerungsschein *m* (com) warehouse receipt
Einlagerungswechsel *m* (com) storage *(or* warehouse*)* bill
Einlauf *m* (com) incoming mail
Einlaufkurve *f* (Bw) regular pattern of startup cost curve *(ie, established in the motor industry and other large-series production)*
Einleger *m* (com, Fin) depositor

einlesen
(EDV) to read in
– to input
Einleseroutine *f* (EDV) read-in routine
Einlesespeicher *m* (EDV) input storage
Einlieferung *f*
(com) mailing
– (GB) posting
(com) delivery
– surrender
Einlieferungsbescheinigung *f* (com) postal receipt *(eg, for registered letters, inpayments)*
(Fin) paying-in slip
(Fin) safe custody receipt
Einliniensystem *n*
(Bw) single-line system
– straight-line organization
– unity of command
einlösbar
(Fin) redeemable
– repayable
(Fin) payable *(eg, check, bill of exchange)*
einlösen
(Fin) to cash *(eg, check, coupon)*
(WeR) to honor *(eg, draft)*
(Fin) to redeem
– to repay *(eg, loan, mortgage)*
einlösende Bank *f* (Fin) negotiating bank *(ie, in letter of credit transaction)*
Einlösung *f*
(WeR) discharging
– honoring
– payment *(ie, of a bill)*
(Fin) encashment *(eg, check, coupon)*
(Fin) redemption
– repayment *(eg, loan, mortgage)*
Einlösung *f* **e–s Wechsels** (WeR) payment of a bill
Einlösungsaufforderung *f* (Fin) call *(ie, to bondholders for payment, esp. by formal notice)*
Einlösungsbedingungen *fpl* (Fin) terms of redemption
Einlösungsfonds *m* (Fin) sinking fund
Einlösungsfrist *f*
(Fin) maturity deadline
– redemption period
Einlösungsgewinn *m* (Fin) gain on redemption
Einlösungskurs *m* (Fin) redemption price
Einlösungsprovision *f* (Fin) payment commission
Einlösungsstelle *f* (Fin) paying agent
Einlösung *f* **von Zinsscheinen** (Fin) coupon collection
Einmalbeitrag *m* (Vers) one-time *(or* single*)* premium
Einmalemission *f* (Bö) one-off issue *(opp, Daueremission: tap issue)*
einmalige Aufwendungen *fpl* (ReW) non-recurrent expenditure
einmalige Ausgabe *f* (Fin) non-recurring *(or* one-off*)* expenditure
einmalige Berechnung *f* (com) one-time charge
einmalige Bezüge *pl* (Pw) non-recurring income
einmalige Einnahmen *fpl* (Fin) non-recurrent *(or* one-time*)* receipts
einmalige Entscheidung *f* (OR) one-shot decision
einmalige Erhöhung *f* (com) one-shot increase *(eg,*

in special energy allowances to persons receiving supplemental government payments)
einmalige Erträge *mpl* (ReW) noncurrent income *(or* revenue)
einmalige Gebühr *f*
(com) non-recurrent charge
(com) single-use charge
einmalige Produktionskosten *pl* (KoR) sunk costs
einmaliger Versicherungsvertrag *m* (Vers) one-time insurance contract
einmaliges Stück *n*
(com) one of a kind
– (GB, infml) one-off *(eg, a one-off model)*
einmalige Vermögensabgabe *f* (StR) one-time capital levy
einmalige Vermögensanfälle *mpl* (StR) one-time wealth accruals *(eg, gift, inheritance, lottery gains)*
einmalige Zahlung *f*
(Fin) commutation payment
(Fin) one-off *(or* one-time) payment
Einmal-Käufer *m* (Mk) one-time buyer
Einmal-Kohlepapier *n* (com) one-time carbon paper
Einmalkosten *pl* (com) non-recurring *(or* one-time) costs
Einmalprämie *f* (Vers) one-time *(or* single) premium *(opp, current premiums)*
Einmalprämien-Lebensversicherung *f* (Vers) single-premium life insurance
Einmal-Rückstellung *f* (ReW) non-recurrent transfer to reserve
Einmaltarif *m* (Mk) one-time rate *(ie, of advertising)*
Einmann-AG *f* (Re) one-man stock corporation
Einmannbetrieb *m*
(Bw) one-man business
– (sl) one-man band
Einmanngesellschaft *f*
(Re) one-man company *(ie, most frequently as limited liability company = GmbH)*
(Re) one-man corporation *(ie, may come into existence by the acquisition of all shares)*
Ein-Mann-GmbH *f* (Re) one-man GmbH
Einmonatsbilanz *f* (ReW) monthly balance sheet
Einmünder *m* (OR) branch leading into node
Einnahmeausfall *m* (FiW) revenue shortfall
Einnahmeerzielung *f* (StR) income-producing activity
Einnahmen *fpl*
(com) receipts *(ie, do not confuse with ‚Einzahlung')*
(com) (retail) takings
(Fin) inflows *(ie, term used in preinvestment analysis)*
(StR) gross income, § 4 III EStG
Einnahmen *fpl* **aus der Veräußerung von Dividendenscheinen** (StR) income from disposition of dividend certificate
Einnahmen-Ausgaben-Plan *m* (Fin) cash budget
Einnahmen-Ausgaben-Planung *f* (Fin) cash budgeting
Einnahmen *fpl* **aus Umlagen** (StR) income from encumbrances *(eg, fees for water, central heating etc.)*

Einnahmen *fpl* **aus unsichtbaren Leistungen** (VGR) invisible earnings
Einnahmen *fpl* **beschaffen** (FiW) to raise revenues
Einnahmenbuch *n* (ReW) cash receipts journal
Einnahmen *fpl* **in laufender Rechnung** (VGR) current account receipts
Einnahmenplan *m* (Fin) incoming receipts budget
Einnahmenpolitik *f* (FiW) revenue policy
Einnahmenreihe *f* (Fin) stream of earnings *(ie, term used in preinvestment analysis = Investitionsrechnung)*
Einnahmenstruktur *f* (FiW) pattern of revenue
Einnahmenüberschuß *m* (FiW) revenue surplus
Einnahmen *fpl* **und Ausgaben** *fpl*
(ReW) receipts and disbursements
(com) *(a store's)* income and outgo
Einnahmen- und Ausgabenrechnung *f* (ReW) cash-based accounting (StR) = *Einnahmeüberschußrechnung*
Einnahmequelle *f*
(com) income source
(FiW) source of revenue
– income source
Einnahmeschätzungen *fpl* (FiW) receipts projections
Einnahme-Überschüsse *mpl*
(Fin) cumulative annual net cash savings *(ie, term used in preinvestment analysis)*
(Fin) cash flows
Einnahmeüberschußrechnung *f*
(StR) cash receipts and disbursement method, § 4 III EStG
– net income method
Einnahmeunterdeckung *f* (Fin) negative cash flow
Einnahmewirkungen *fpl* (FiW) revenue effects
einordnen (com) to pigeonhole *(ie, to put into proper class or group)*
einpendeln (com) to settle down *(eg, prices settle down at a lower level)*
Einpendler *m* (com) commuter
Einpersonen-Gesellschaft *f* (Re) one-man corporation *(ie, corporation with a single shareholder)*
Ein-Personen-Haushalt *m* (Stat) single person household
Ein-Pfeil-Schleife *f* (OR) self loop
Einphasensteuer *f* (FiW) single-stage tax
Einphasen-Umsatzsteuer *f* (FiW) single-stage turnover tax *(eg, production tax, wholesale tax, retail tax)*
einplanen
(Bw) to plan
(IndE) to schedule
Einplanwirtschaft *f* (Vw) single-plan economy *(E. Preiser) (syn, Planwirtschaft, zentralgeleitete Wirtschaft, Befehlswirtschaft)*
Einproduktbetrieb *m* (IndE) single-product firm
Einprodukt-Unternehmen *n* (Vw) single-product firm
einräumen
(com) to admit
– to allow
(Fin) to grant *(eg, credit, loan)*
– to extend

Einrede *f*
(Re) defense
— plea
Einrede *f* **begründen mit** (Re) to establish a defense on the ground of *(eg, necessity = Notstand)*
einredebehaftete Forderung *f* (Re) claim which can be met by a plea of confession and avoidance, § 390 BGB
Einrede *f* **der Arglist**
(Re) exception of fraud
— *(civil law)* exceptio doli mali
Einrede *f* **der Aufrechnung** (Re) defense of setoff
Einrede *f* **der Erfüllung** (Re) defense of discharge *(ie, of contract)*
Einrede *f* **der Verjährung**
(Re) plea of the statute of limitations
— *(civil law)* exceptio temporis
(ie, defense that a claim is statute-barred or that time prescribed for bringing suit has expired)
Einrede *f* **der Verjährung geltend machen**
(Re) to plead the statute of limitations
— to plead lapse of time *(ie, as a defense to an action)*
— to set up the statute of limitations *(ie, against a claim)*
— to assert the bar of the statute of limitations
Einrede *f* **der Vorausklage**
(Re) defense of preliminary proceedings against principal debtor
— benefit of discussion
— *(civil law)* beneficium discussionis
(ie, surety — Bürge — may refuse to satisfy creditor unless the latter has unsuccessfully attempted to levy compulsory execution against principal debtor, § 771 BGB)
Einrede *f* **des nicht erfüllten Vertrages**
(Re) defense of nonperformance of contract
— defense that plaintiff has not performed
— *(civil law)* exceptio non adimpleti contractus
(ie, exception in an action that plaintiff is not entitled to sue because he has not performed his own part of the agreement)
Einrede *f* **des Notstandes** (Re) defense of necessity
Einrede *f* **geltend machen**
(Re) to put forward
— to set up
— to interpose
— to establish
— to urge ... a defense
— to allege an objection
(eg, to urge fraud or rescission as a defense)
einreichen
(com) to file
— to hand (to)
— to lodge
— to submit
(Fin) to bring *(or* present) *(eg, a bill for discount)*
(Fin) to deposit *(eg, for collection or safe custody)*
Einreicher *m* (com) presenting party
Einreichung *f*
(com) filing
— lodgment
— submission
(Fin) presentment
— presentation
— deposit
Einreichung *f* **e–r Patentanmeldung** (Pat) filing of patent application
Einreichung *f* **e–s Antrags** (com) filing of an application
Einreichungsdatum *n* (com) filing date
Einreichungsfrist *f*
(com) closing date *(eg, invitation to tender)*
(com) deadline for application
(Fin) period for presentment
Einreichungsschluß *m*
(com) cut-off date for applications
— closing date
(com) bid closing
Einreichungstermin *m*
(com) closing date *(eg, for receipt of applications)*
— last day *(eg, on which we are to receive ...)*
Einreichungsverzeichnis *n* (Fin) list of bills or checks submitted for discount *(usu. a bank's multipart form = Vordrucksatz)*
Einreichung *f* **von Schriftstücken** (com) filing of documents
einreihen (Zo) to classify *(ie, under a tariff heading = ‚unter eine Tarifnummer')*
Einrichtelöhne *mpl* (KoR) setup wages *(ie, traced to costing units or included in overhead rate)*
einrichten
(com) to arrange
— to organize
— to set up
Einrichtezeit *f* (IndE) setup time
Einrichtkosten *pl* (KoR) setup cost *(ie, incurred in retooling machinery for new operations)*
Einrichtung *f*
(com) office equipment and furnishings
(ReW) furnitures and fixtures *(= Betriebsausstattung)*
(IndE) machine setup *(ie, to change to another type of production)*
Einrichtungskosten *pl*
(ReW) cost *(or* expense) of setting up, organizing, and extending a plant *(ie, capitalized and written off, but see § 6 EStG)*
Einrichtung *f* **und Betrieb** *m* **industrieller Anlagen**
(Bw) plant engineering
Einsatz *m*
(com) use
— utilization
(Pw) employment
einsatzbereiter Zustand *m* (IndE) operating condition
Einsatzbereitschaft *f* (Pw) willingness to engage in purposeful action
Einsatzergebnis *n* (KoR) difference between purchase price and predetermined price *(ie, term used in standard costing: may be a shadow price or a standard price)*
Einsatzfaktor *m* (Bw) input factor
Einsatzgewicht *n*
(IndE) input weight
— charge weight

Einsatzgüter *npl*
(Bw) input *(ie, sum total of all productive factors)*
(IndE) start materials
– charge materials
– feedstocks
Einsatzhäufigkeit *f* (Bw) incidence of usage
Einsatzmaterial *n*
(IndE) charge materials
– feed materials
– feedstocks
– input materials
– start (*or* starting) materials
Einsatzmenge *f* **des variablen Faktors** (Bw) input of variable factor
Einsatzniveau *n* (Vw) input level
Einsatzplanung *f* (Bw) applications planning
Einsatzpreis *m* (com) starting price *(ie, at auction)*
Einsatzstoffe *mpl* (KoR) input materials
einsatzsynchrone Anlieferung *f*
(MaW) stockless buying
– systems contracting
einschalten (com) to use the services of
Einschaltquote *f* (Mk) share of audience *(ie, in television)*
Einschaltung *f* **e–r Bank** (Fin) interposition of a bank
Einschichtler *m* (IndE) one-shift worker *(ie, either early or late shift; opp, Zwei- und Dreischichtler, Kontiarbeiter)*
einschießen
(Fin) to contribute money (*or* capital)
– to put money into a business
einschlägige Bestimmung *f* (Re) relevant provision
einschleusen (Mk) to channel *(ie, goods into a market)*
Einschleusung *f* (Mk) channeling
Einschleusungspreis *m* (EG) sluice gate price
einschließendes ODER *n*
(EDV) inclusive-OR operation
– disjunction
– logical sum
einschließlich aller Rechte (Bö) cum all
einschließlich Bezugsrechte (Bö) cum rights
einschließlich Dividende (Bö) cum dividend
Einschlußklausel *f* (Vers) omnibus clause
einschränken (com, infml) to cut down on *(eg, smoking, capital spending)*
einschränkende Bedingung *f*
(Re) limiting condition
(Re) proviso *(ie, a condition or limitation inserted in a contract; usu. beginning with the words ‚provided that . . .')*
einschränkendes Konnossement *n* (com) claused bill of lading
Einschreibebrief *m* (com) registered letter
Einschreibegebühr *f* (com) registration fee
einschreiben (EDV) to write in
Einschreiben *n*
(com) registered mail
– (GB) registered post
Einschreiben *n* **mit Rückschein** (com) registered letter with acknowledgment of receipt
Einschreibesendung *f*
(com) registered mail
– (US) certified mail

Einschub *m* (EDV) slide-in module
Einschuß *m*
(Bö) contribution (*or* trading) margin
– margin requirement
– initial deposit
(ie, usu. 10% of contract value)
(SeeV) contribution
– general average deposit
Einschußquittung *f* (SeeV) contribution receipt
einseitig
(Re) unilateral
– one-sided
– ex parte *(eg, notice to determine a lease)*
einseitige Ableitung *f* (Math) one-sided derivative
einseitige empfangsbedürftige Erklärung *f* (Re) unilateral declaration requiring communication *(eg, on the part of a debtor)*
einseitige Handelsgeschäfte *npl* (Re) one-sided (*or* unilateral) commercial transactions
einseitige Rechtsetzung *f* (Re) unilateral legislative action
einseitiger Irrtum *m* (Re) unilateral mistake
einseitiger Schuldvertrag *m* (Re) unilateral contract
einseitiger Test *m*
(Stat) one-sided test
– single-tail test
einseitiger Transfer *m* (VGR) unilateral transfer
einseitiger Vertrag *m*
(Re) unilateral
– one-sided
– ex-parte . . . contract
einseitiges Rechtsgeschäft *n* (Re) unilateral act (*or* transaction) *(eg, declaration containing a notice to terminate a lease)*
einseitige Überlebensrente *f*
(Fin) reversionary annuity
– survivorship annuity
einseitige Übertragung *f* (VGR) unilateral transfer
einseitige Verpflichtung *f* (Re) unilateral obligation
einseitige Willenserklärung *f* (Re) unilateral manifestation of intent
einseitig festgesetztes Importkontingent *n* (AuW) unilateral quota
einseitig offene Klasse *f* (Stat) open-ended class
Einsendeabschnitt *m* (com) return coupon
einsenden
(com) to send in
– to submit
Einsender *m*
(com) sender
– submitter
Einsendeschluß *m*
(com) deadline
– closing date
Einserkomplement *n* (EDV) ones complement
Einsetzen *n* (Vw) onset *(eg, of an economic upturn)*
Einsetzungsregel *f* (Log) rule of substitution
Einsicht *f* **in die Bücher** (ReW) inspection of books and records
Einsichtsrecht *n* (Re) right to inspect books and records
Einsmenge *f* (Math) unitary set
Einsoperator *m* (Math) unit operator
Einspaltenlochung *f* (EDV) single-column punch

Einspaltentarif m (Zo) unilinear tariff
einsparen
  (com) to save
  – to cut expenses
  – to economize (on)
  – (infml) to shave (costs)
Einsparung f
  (com) reduction of costs
  – cutting expenses
  – economizing
Einsparungsmöglichkeit f (com) savings possibility
einspeichern
  (EDV) to store
  (EDV) to roll in
einspiegeln (ReW) to reflect *(eg, fixed assets in a consolidated financial statement)*
Einspruch m
  (Re) objection
  – exception
  (StR) protest against tax assessment, § 348 AO
  (Pat) opposition
Einspruch m **einlegen** (Re) to file (*or* lodge) an objection
Einspruch m **einleiten** (Pat) to give notice of an opposition
Einspruch m **erheben**
  (Re) to make (*or* raise) an objection
  – to object (to)
Einspruch m **gegen Erteilung e–s Patents erheben** (Pat) to oppose the grant of a patent
Einspruch m **gegen Patentanmeldung erheben** (Pat) to oppose an application
Einspruchsabteilung f (Pat) Opposition Division *(ie, of the Patent Office)*
Einspruchsbegründung f (Pat) grounds for opposition
Einspruchseinlegung f (Pat) notice of opposition
Einspruchsentscheid m (Pat) decision relating to an opposition
Einspruchserwiderung f (Pat) rejoinder to an opposition
Einspruchsfrist f (Pat) time limit for entering opposition
Einspruchsgebühr f (Pat) opposition fee
Einspruchspartei f
  (Pat) party in opposition
  – opponent
Einspruchsrecht n (Re) right to object (to)
Einspruchsschriftsatz m (Pat) memorandum supporting opposition
Einspruchsverfahren n (Pat) opposition proceedings
Einspruch m **wegen mangelnder Neuheit** (Pat) opposition for lack of novelty
Einspruch m **wurde nicht erhoben** (Pat) application was left unopposed
Einspruch m **verwerfen** (Pat) to reject (*or* dismiss) an opposition
Einspruch m **zurücknehmen** (Pat) to withdraw an opposition
Einspruch m **zurückweisen** (Pat) to reject an opposition
Einsprungbedingungen fpl (EDV) initial (*or* entry) conditions
Einsprungstelle f (EDV) entry (point)

Einspulen n (EDV) spooling
Einstandskosten pl (Fin) cost of funds *(ie, in banking)*
Einstandspreis m (KoR) = *Einstandswert*
Einstandspreis m **verkaufter Handelsware** (ReW) cost of merchandise sold
Einstandswert m
  (KoR, *in retailing*) acquisition cost
  – cost price
  (ie, price delivered free stock)
einstellen
  (Re) to discontinue
  – to stop
  – to suspend *(eg, payment of debts)*
  (Bw) to close (*or* shut) down *(eg, a plant)*
  (ReW) to allocate *(eg, to open reserves)*
  (Pw) to engage
  – to hire
Einstellenarbeit f (IndE) single-place job *(ie, one assignment, one worker)*
einstellig
  (Log) one-place
  – monadic
einstelliger Junktor m (Log) singular connective
einstelliges Addierwerk n (EDV) half (*or* one-digit) adder
Einstellkosten pl (Pw) hiring cost (*or* expenses)
Einstellquote f
  (Pw) hiring rate *(ie, of labor)*
  – (GB) accessions rate
Einstellung f
  (Re) discontinuance
  – stoppage
  – suspension
  (Bw) closure
  (ReW) allocation *(eg, to special reserves)*
  (Pw) hiring
  (IndE) setup
  – adjustment
Einstellungen fpl **aus dem Jahresüberschuß** (ReW) transfer from net income for the business year
Einstellungen fpl **in offene Rücklagen** (ReW) transfer to general reserves
Einstellungen fpl **in Sonderposten mit Rücklageanteil** (ReW) allocations to special accounts which in part constitute reserves
Einstellung f **in Rücklage** (ReW) transfer to reserve
Einstellung f **in Sonderposten** (ReW) transfer to special allowances
Einstellungsgespräch n
  (Pw) job
  – employment
  – hiring ... interview
Einstellungskosten pl (Pw) recruiting expenses
Einstellungsquote (Pw) hiring rate
  – (GB) accession(s) rate
Einstellungssperre f (Pw) employment (*or* job *or* hiring) freeze
Einstellungsstopp m (Pw) = *Einstellungssperre*
Einstellungstermin m (Pw) first date of service
Einstellungsverfahren n (Pw) hiring procedure
Einsteuer f (FiW) single tax *(= impôt unique)*
Einstiegspreis m (Bö) strike (*or* striking) price

einstimmige Entscheidung *f* (Bw) unanimous decision *(eg, was taken)*
einstimmiger Beschluß *m* (Bw) unanimous resolution *(eg, was adopted)*
einstufen
  (com) to categorize
  – to classify
  – to grade
  – to scale
einstufige Kostenplanung *f* (KoR) formula method (of cost budgeting)
einstufiger Betrieb *m* (IndE) single-stage plant system
einstufiger Stichprobenplan *m* (Stat) unitary sampling plan
einstufiges Leitungssystem *n* (Bw) single-tier *(or* unitary*)* board structure *(eg, in the Anglo-Saxon and French company law systems)*
einstufiges Mischgeldsystem *n* (Vw) single-tier mixed-money system
einstufiges Reihenfolgeproblem *n* (IndE) one-machine *(or* single-machine*)* sequencing problem
einstufiges Unternehmen *n* (Bw) single-stage business
Einstufung *f* **der Tätigkeit** (IndE) job ranking
Einstufungstest *m* (Pw) placement test
einstweiliges Fischereiabkommen *n* (Re) temporary fishing agreement
einstweilige Verfügung *f*
  (Re) preliminary
  – interim
  – interlocutory ... injunction
  – temporary restraining order
  (eg, is issued or granted)
einstweilige Verfügung *f* **erwirken** (Re) to sue out a preliminary injunction
Einsystem *n* (ReW) interlinked system of financial and cost accounting *(ie, all postings are made in journal and general ledger)*
Einszustand *m*
  (EDV) one state
  – one condition
einteilen
  (com) to classify
  – to grade
  – to scale
Einteilung *f*
  (com) classification
  – gradation
  – division
  – subdivision
Einteilung *f* **nach einem Merkmal** (Stat) one-way classification
Einteilungsmethode *f* (Log) classification approach
Einteilung *f* **zollpflichtiger Güter nach Eigenschaften** (AuW) attribute method of tariff classification
eintragen
  (com) to enter
  – to register
  – to make an entry
  – to post
Eintragung *f*
  (com) entry
  – registration
  – posting
Eintragungsbewilligung *f* (Re) consent to entry in land register *(ie, requires official authentication)*
Eintragung *f* **löschen** (com) to cancel an entry
eintreibbare Forderung *f* (Fin) recoverable debt
eintreiben (Fin) to collect *(ie, debts outstanding)*
Eintreibung *f*
  (Fin) collection
  – recovery
eintretende Variable *f* (OR) entering variable
Eintritt *m* **der Geschäftsunfähigkeit** (Re) supervening incapacity, § 791 BGB
Eintritt *m* **der Rechtshängigkeit** (Re) date at which a claim is brought forward, § 291 BGB
Eintritt *m* **des Schadensfalles** (Vers) occurrence of risk
Eintritt *m* **des Versicherungsfalles** (Vers) insurance contingency
Eintritt *m* **e–r Bedingung** (Re) fulfillment of a condition
Eintritt *m* **in Rechte** (Re) subrogation *(ie, substitution of a third party in place of a party having a claim against another person, eg; insurance companies or guarantors generally have such right)*
Eintritt *m* **ins Erwerbsleben** (Pw) entry into the labor force
Eintrittsalter *n* (Vers) age at entry
Eintrittsbilanz *f* (ReW) special balance sheet prepared when a new member joins a partnership
Eintrittsgrenzzollamt *n* (Zo) customs office at place of entry
Eintrittshafen *m* (Zo) port of entry
Eintrittshäufigkeit *f* (Stat) frequency of occurrence
Eintrittspreis *m* (com) admission fee
Eintrittssperre *f*
  (Vw) restriction of entry
  – barrier to entry
Eintrittssperrenpreis *m* (Vw) limit price
Einverfahren-Maschine *f* (IndE) single-process machine
Einverständnis *n*
  (com) approval
  (Re) assent
  – consent
Einwand *m* **der unzulässigen Rechtsausübung**
  (Re) defense *(or* exception*)* of fraud
  – *(civil law)* exceptio doli generalis
  (ie, made irrelevant by the general principle of fair dealing, §§ 157, 242, 226 BGB)
Einwand *m* **der Verwirkung** (Re) defense available in cases of belated assertion of rights
Einwand *m* **des Rechtsmißbrauchs** (Re) = **Einwand der unzulässigen Rechtsausübung**
Einwände *mpl* **geltend machen**
  (Re) to set up
  – to raise
  – to urge
  – to interpose
  – to establish
  – to put forward ... defenses
einwandfreier äußerer Zustand *m* (Re) apparent good order and condition
einwandfrei funktionieren (com) to work properly

Einwegbehälter *m* (com) disposable (*or* one-way) container
Einwegflasche *f*
(com) non-returnable bottle
– non-refillable
– one-way bottle
Einwegverpackung *f* (com) disposable (*or* non-returnable) package (*or* packaging)
einweisen (Pw) to familiarize
Einwendungsausschluß *m* (WeR) holder in due course (= *rechtmäßiger od legitimierter Inhaber*) is free of equitable defenses available to prior parties
einwertige Funktion *f* (Math) single-value function
Einwilligung *f* (Re) prior approval (*ie, authorization of an act-in-the law, § 183 BGB*)
Ein-Wort-Karte *f* (EDV) one-word card
einzahlen
(Fin) to pay in
(Fin, fml) to pay over
Einzahler *m*
(com) payer
(Fin) depositor
Einzahlung *f*
(Fin) inpayment
(Fin) deposit
Einzahlungsaufforderung *f*
(com) request for payment
(Fin) call letter
– notice of call
Einzahlungsformular *n* (Fin) in-payment form
Einzahlungspflicht *f* (Re) obligation to pay up shares, § 54 AktG
Einzahlungsquittung *f* (Fin) deposit receipt
Einzahlungsreihe *f*
(Fin) stream of cash inflows
– cash inflows
(*ie, term used in evaluating alternative investment projects*)
Einzahlungsschein *m*
(Fin) deposit slip
– (GB) paying-in slip
– credit slip
Einzahlungsströme *mpl* (Fin) cash inflows (*ie, in preinvestment analysis*)
einzeiliger Beleg *m* (ReW) single-line document
Ein-Zeit-Verfahren *n* (OR) single-phase planning method (*eg, critical path method [CPM], metra potential method [MPM]*)
Einzelabnehmer *m* (com) individual customer
Einzelabschluß *m* (ReW) individual accounts (*ie, in group accounting*)
Einzelabschreibung *f*
(ReW) single-asset depreciation
– unit depreciation
(*syn, individuelle Abschreibung; opp, Pauschal- od Summenabschreibung*)
Einzelakkord *m*
(IndE) individual piece-work
(IndE) individual piece-work rate
Einzelanfertigung *f*
(IndE) manufacture to specification
– single-unit production
Einzelanleger *m* (Fin) individual investor

Einzelarbeitsvertrag *m* (Pw) individual employment contract
Einzelaufgliederung *f* (com) detailed breakdown
Einzelaufstellung *f*
(com) detailed statement
– itemized list
Einzelauftrag *m* (com) individual order
Einzelaufzeichnungen *fpl* (ReW) detail records
Einzelausgebot *n* (Re) invitation of bids (*ie, for each individual parcel of real estate, in judicial sales, § 63 ZVG; opp, Gesamtausgebot*)
Einzelausnahmen *fpl* (Kart) individual exemptions, §§ 2–8 GWB
Einzelaussteller *m* (Mk) individual exhibitor
Einzelbegriff *m* (Log) individual concept
Einzelbeleg *m* (ReW) single voucher (*or* form)
Einzelbelegprüfung *f* (ReW) detailed checking
Einzelbeschaffung *f* im Bedarfsfall (MaW) individual buying
Einzelbesteuerung *f* (StR) individual taxation
Einzelbewertung *f*
(ReW) individual
– single-asset
– single ... valuation
– unit account method of valuation (*opp, Gruppenbewertung*)
Einzelbilanz *f* (ReW) individual balance sheet (*ie, part of consolidated balance sheet*)
Einzelbürgschaft *f* (Re) individual guaranty
Einzeldokument *n* (com) single document
Einzelerfinder *m* (Pat) individual (*or* sole) inventor
Einzelertragswertverfahren *n* (StR) individual appraisal of potential yield, § 37 II BewG
Einzelfertigung *f*
(IndE) individual
– job
– one-off
– single-unit
– unique-product
– unit
– single-item ... production
(IndE) tailor-made (*or* unique) products
Einzelfirma *f*
(com) one-man business
(Bw) sole (*or* individual) proprietorship
– individual business
– (GB) sole trader
(*syn, Einzelkaufmann, Einzelunternehmung*)
Einzelgang *m* (EDV) detail printing (*opp, Sammelgang*)
Einzelgeschäftsführung *f* (Re) capacity to transact business of each individual partner of OHG and KG, §§ 114ff HGB
Einzelgesellschaften *fpl* (Bw) individual companies
Einzelgewerbetreibender *m* (StR) individual proprietor (*or* trader) (*ie, carries on business independently, permanently, and for profit, excluding agriculture and independent personal services*)
Einzelgewerkschaft *f* (Pw) single-industry union
Einzelhandel *m* (Mk) retail industry (*or* trade)
Einzelhandelberatung *f* (Mk) retail advisory services
Einzelhandel-Einkaufsgenossenschaft *f* (com) retail cooperative

Einzelhandelsbetrieb *m*
(com) retail business (*or* establishment)
– retail store
Einzelhandels-Factoring *n* (Mk) retail factoring
Einzelhandelsgeschäft *n* (com) retail store (*or* outlet)
Einzelhandelskette *f* (Mk) retailing chain
Einzelhandelskontenrahmen *m* (ReW) (simplified) classification-of-account system tailored to retailing needs
Einzelhandelskunde *m* (com) retail customer
Einzelhandelsorganisation *f* (com) retail sales organization
Einzelhandelspolitik *f* (Vw) retail trade policy
Einzelhandelspreis *m* (com) retail price
Einzelhandelspreisindex *m* (Stat) retail price index
Einzelhandelsrabatt *m* (com) retail rebate
Einzelhandelsrichtpreis *m* (com) recommended retail price
Einzelhandelsspanne *f* (com) retail margin
Einzelhandelsumsätze *mpl*
(com) retail sales
– (GB) retail turnover
– shop sales
– sales of retail stores
Einzelhandelsunternehmen *n* (com) retail establishment
Einzelhandelsvertrieb *m* (com) retail marketing (*or* sales)
Einzelhändler *m*
(com) retailer
– retail trader
Einzelhonorar *n*
(com) individual fee
– fee for service (*opp, flat fee*)
Einzelkalkulation *f* (KoR) job-order (*or* single-item) calculation
Einzelkartenverdichtung *f* (EDV) accumulated-totals punching
Einzelkaufmann *m* (Bw) = *Einzelfirma*
Einzelkontingent *n* (AuW) selectively administered quota
Einzelkosten *pl*
(KoR) direct cost
– direct expense
– direct charge
Einzelkostenabweichung *f* (KoR) direct-cost variance
Einzelkostenlohn *m* (KoR) direct labor
Einzelkostenmaterial *n* (KoR) direct material
Einzelkostenplanung *f* (KoR) direct cost planning
Einzelkredit *m* (Fin) individual credit (*ie, funds loaned to a single borrower*)
Einzelkreditversicherung *f* (Vers) individual credit insurance
Einzelleistung *f* (Re) individual performance
Einzellizenz *f* (Pat) individual license
Einzellöhne *mpl* (KoR) direct labor
Einzellohnkosten *pl* (KoR) productive labor (*or* wages)
Einzellohnsatzabweichung *f* (KoR) labor rate variance
Einzellohnzeitabweichung *f*
(KoR) labor efficiency

– labor time
– labor usage ... variance
Einzelmaterial *n* (KoR) direct material
Einzelmaterialkosten *pl* (KoR) cost of direct material
Einzelmaterialmischungsabweichung *f* (KoR) mixture subvariance
Einzelmaterialpreisabweichung *f* (KoR) material price variance
Einzelmaterialverbrauchsabweichung *f* (KoR) materials quantity variance
– material usage variance
Einzelmieter *m* (Re) sole tenant
Einzelnachfolge *f* (Re) singular succession (*ie, not to the entire estate of another, but only to individual legal relations*)
Einzelnachweis *m* **führen** (StR) to itemize expenses (*ie, instead of claiming blanket allowance*)
einzeln aufführen (com) to itemize
Einzelobjekt *n* (Bw) individual item
Einzelplan *m* (Bw) individual plan
Einzelplanung *f* (Bw) detail planning
Einzelpolice *f* (Vers) individual (*or* voyage) policy
Einzelpreis *m* (com) unit price
Einzelpreiserrechnung *f* (com) unit price calculation
Einzelprodukt *n* (KoR) specific product
Einzel-Produkttest *m* (Mk) monadic product test
Einzelprogramm *n* (EDV) individual routine
Einzelprokura *f* (Re) individual ,,Prokura" (*ie, general power of commercial representation*)
Einzelprüfer *m* (ReW) independent auditor (*opp, auditing partnership*)
Einzelpunktsteuerung *f* (IndE) point-to-point system
Einzelrechtsnachfolge *f* (Re) = *Einzelnachfolge*
Einzelstoffkosten *pl* (KoR) direct material
Einzelschuldner *m* (Re) sole debtor
Einzelspanne *f* (Mk) item-related profit margin (*ie, difference between purchase and sales price of a single article*)
einzelstaatliche Rechtsvorschriften *fpl* (EG) national legislation
einzelstaatlicher Markt *m* (EG) national market
einzelstaatliches Durchfuhrpapier *n* (Zo) national transit document
Einzelstrategie *f* (Bw) individual strategy
Einzelteile *npl* (com) (component) parts
Einzelübertragung *f* (Re) = *Einzelnachfolge*
Einzelunternehmen *n* (Bw) = *Einzelfirma*
Einzelveräußerungspreis *m* (com) unit sales price
Einzelverpackung *f* (com) individual (*or* unit) packing
Einzelversicherer *m* (Vers) individual insurer
Einzelversicherung *f* (Vers) individual (*or* private) insurance
Einzelvertretung *f* (Re) sole representation (*opp, Gesamtvertretung*)
Einzelverwahrung *f* (Fin) individual safekeeping
Einzelvollmacht *f* (Re) individual power of representation (*ie, to undertake certain transactions or certain kinds of transaction, § 125 II HGB; opp, Generalvollmacht*)
Einzelwerbung *f* (Mk) individual advertising (*opp, Gemeinschaftswerbung*)

Einzelwertberichtigung *f*
(ReW) individual value adjustment
(Fin) provision for losses on individual loan accounts
Einzelwertberichtigung *f* **zu Kundenforderungen**
(ReW) reserve for doubtful accounts – direct
einzelwirtschaftlich (Vw) applying to individual economic units
einzelwirtschaftliche Nachfragefunktion *f* (Vw) individual demand function
Einzelzeit *f* (IndE) element time
Einzelzeitverfahren *n* (IndE) flyback timing
Einzelziele *npl* (Bw) individual (*or* personal) goals
Einzelzuweisung *f* (FiW) segregated appropriation
einziehen
(Vw) to call in *(eg, old notes from circulation)*
(Fin) to call in
– to redeem *(ie, securities)*
(Fin) to collect *(eg, debt outstanding, checks)*
(Fin) to debit
Einziehung *f*
(Re) forfeiture
(Vw) calling in
(Fin) redemption
– call in
(Fin) collection
(Fin) debiting
(StR) collection of a tax, § 227 AO
Einziehungsgebühr *f* (Fin) collection charge
Einziehungsgeschäft *n* (Fin) collection business
Einziehungsverfahren *n* (Fin) collection procedure
Einzug *m* = *Einziehung*
Einzugsauftrag *m* (Fin) collection order
Einzugsbank *f* (Fin) collecting bank
Einzugsermächtigung *f* (Fin) direct debit authorization
Einzugsgebiet *n*
(Mk, Pw) catchment area
– area of supply
– trading area
Einzugskosten *pl* (Fin) collecting charges
Einzugsstelle *f* (Fin) collecting agency
Einzugsverfahren *n*
(Fin) direct debiting service
– automatic debit transfer
Einzugswechsel *m* (Fin) bill for collection
Einzweck-Maschine *f* (IndE) single-purpose machine
Eisenbahner-Gewerkschaft *f* (Pw) railwaymens' union
Eisenbahnerstreik *m* (Pw) rail strike
Eisenbahnfrachtbrief *m*
(com) railroad bill of lading (*or* waybill) *(ie, this is a document of title* = *Dispositions- od Traditionspapier)*
– (GB) consignment note
Eisenbahnfrachtgeschäft *n* (com) carriage of goods by public railroads, §§ 453ff HGB
Eisenbahngütertarif *m*
(com) railroad freight tariff
– railroad rates
Eisenbahngüterverkehr *m* (com) rail freight traffic
Eisenbahntarif *m*
(com) railroad rates
– (GB) railway rates

Eisenbahnwerte *mpl*
(Bö) railroad stocks
– rails
– (GB) railway shares
Eisenerzbergbau *m* (com) iron ore mining
Eisengalluspause *f* (com) black-and-white print
eisenschaffende Industrie *f* (com) iron and steel industry
Eiserne-Bestands-Methode *f* (ReW) base (*or* reserve) stock method of valuation *(ie, assets always needed in the business are carried on the books at cost)*
eiserner Bestand *m*
(MaW) base stock
– base stock inventory
– minimum inventory level
– reserve stock
– safety level (*or* stock)
(Fin) reserve fund
eiserne Reserve *f* (com) iron reserve *(ie, against unpleasant surprises such as escalation of prices)*
elastische Geldmenge *f* (Vw) elastic money supply
elastische Nachfrage *f* (Vw) elastic demand
elastischer Bereich *m* **der Nachfragekurve** (Vw) elastic range of demand
elastisches Angebot *n* (Vw) elastic supply
Elastizität *f* (Vw) elasticity
Elastizität *f* **der Nachfrage** (Vw) elasticity of demand
Elastizität *f* **des Angebots** (Vw) elasticity of supply
Elastizitätsansatz *m* (AuW) elasticity approach
Elastizitätskoeffizient *m*
(Vw) elasticity coefficient
– coefficient of elasticity
„Elefanten"-Hochzeit *f*
(Kart) giant (*or* jumbo) merger
– (infml) juggernaut marriage
– (US) megadollar merger
elektrische Abtastung *f*
(EDV) electrical (*or* brush) sensing
– brush reading
(opp, magnetische und optische Abtastung)
elektrische Buchungsmaschine *f* (EDV) electric accounting machine, EAM
Elektrizitätsversorgung *f* (com) electricity (*or* power) supply
Elektrizitätswirtschaft *f* (com) electricity (supply) industry
Elektrobranche *f* (com) = *elektrotechnische Industrie*
Elektroindustrie *f* (com) = *elektrotechnische Industrie*
Elektrokonzern *m*
(com) electrical group
Elektronikindustrie *f* (com) electronics industry
elektronisch bestellen (com) to teleorder
elektronische Ablage *f*
(EDV) electronic filing system
– electronic file cabinets
elektronische Datenverarbeitung *f* (EDV) electronic data processing, EDP
elektronische Datenverarbeitungsanlage *f* (EDV) electronic data processing machine, EDPM
elektronischer Drucker *m* (EDV) electrostatic printer

elektronische Rechenmaschine f (EDV) electronic calculator
elektronischer Rechenlocher m (EDV) electronic calculating punch
elektronische Schreibmaschine f (EDV) electronic typewriter
elektronisches Datenverarbeitungssystem n (EDV) electronic data processing system *(opp, electromechanical equipment)*
elektronisches Datenverarbeitungszentrum n (EDV) electronic data processing center
– EDP center
– computer center
elektrostatischer Speicher m (EDV) electrostatic storage *(or* memory)
elektrotechnische Gebrauchsgüter npl (com) electrical applicances
elektrotechnische Industrie f (com) electrical engineering industry
Elektrowerte mpl (Bö) electricals
Element n
(Stat) element
– unit
(OR) input unit
– customer *(ie, in waiting-line models)*
Elementaraufgabe f (Pw) elementary task
Elementarbewegung f
(IndE) basic motion
– elemental movement
elementare Algebra f (Math) basic algebra
elementare Mengenlehre f (Math) intuitive set theory
elementare Stichprobentheorie f (Stat) basic sampling theory
Elementarfaktoren mpl (Bw) basic factors of production *(ie, umbrella term used by E. Gutenberg; opp, ‚dispositive Faktoren')*
Elementarkombination f
(Bw) combination of basic factors of production
– basic-factor combination
Elementarmarkt m
(com) individual market
(Vw) elemental market
– single-market model
Elementarsatz m
(Log) atomistic proposition
– elementary statement
Elementarschadenversicherung f (Vers) insurance against damage by natural forces
Elementbeziehung f (Math) membership relation
Elemente npl **der Menge** (Math) elements of a set
Element n **e–r Menge** (Math) element of a set
elementfremde Mengen fpl (Math) disjoint sets
Elferausschuß m (Fin) Central Capital Market Committee *(ie, represents the large issuing banks)*
Elfer-Lochung f (EDV) eleven *(or* X) punch *(syn, X-Lochung)*
Eliminierung f **des Trends** (Stat) trend elimination
Emballage f (com) packaging *(ie, all-inclusive term)*
Embargo n (AuW) embargo
Embargo n **aufheben** (AuW) to lift an embargo
Embargo n **durchsetzen** (AuW) to enforce an embargo
Embargo n **nicht beachten** (AuW) to defy an embargo

Embargorisiko n (Fin) risk of embargo *(ie, in export credit insurance)*
Embargo n **verhängen** (AuW) to impose *(or* put) an embargo (on)
Emission f (Fin) issue
Emission f **auf dem Submissionswege** (Fin) issue by tender
Emission f **begeben** (Fin) to launch an issue
Emission f **fest übernehmen** (Fin) to underwrite an issue
Emission f **mit variablem Zinssatz** (Fin) floating rate notes
Emission f **placieren** (Fin) = Emission unterbringen
Emissionsabteilung f (Fin) issue department *(ie, of banks)*
Emissionsagio n
(Fin) issue premium
– underwriting premium
(Fin, GB) share premium
(Fin) bond premium
Emissionsbank f
(Vw) bank of issue
(Fin) issuing bank
– underwriter
Emissionsbedingungen fpl
(Fin) offering terms
– terms of an issue
Emissionsdisagio n
(Fin) issuing discount *(ie, discount to subscribers of a share or bond issue)*
(Fin) bond *(or* debt) discount
Emissionserlös m (Fin) proceeds of an issue
Emissionsfahrplan m (Fin) calendar for new issues
Emissionsfenster n (Fin) new issue window *(eg, for fixed-interest public bonds)*
Emissionsgenehmigung f (Fin) authorization to issue securities *(ie, granted by economics minister for bearer and order bonds, §§ 795 and 808a BGB)*
Emissionsgeschäft n (Fin) issuing *(or* underwriting) business
Emissionsgesellschaft f (Fin) issuing company
Emissionsgewinn m (Fin) underwriting profit *(ie, issue premium less cost of issue)*
Emissionsgläubiger m (Fin) issuing creditor
Emissionshaus n (Fin, GB) issuing house
Emissionsinstitut n (Fin) issuing institution
Emissionsjahr n (Fin) year of issue
Emissionskalender m (Fin) new issue calendar
Emissionsklima n (Fin) climate for new issues
Emissionskonditionen fpl (Fin) terms of issue
Emissionskonsortialvertrag m
(Fin) agreement among underwriters
– underwriting agreement
Emissionskonsortium n
(Fin) underwriting group *(or* syndicate)
– buying syndicate
Emissionskontrolle f (Fin) control of security issues *(ie, as an instrument of capital market policy)*
Emissionskosten pl (Fin) cost of issue *(ie, expenses of issuing shares or bonds)*
Emissionskredit m
(Fin) readiness of market to take certain securities

(Fin) credit granted to security issuer by issuing bank
Emissionskurs *m* (Fin) initial offering (*or* issue) price
Emissions-Kursniveau *n* (Fin) issue-price level
Emissions-Limit *n* (Fin) ceiling of new issues
Emissionsmakler *m* (Fin) issue broker
Emissionsmarkt *m* (Fin) primary issue market *(ie, for the initial issue of securities, opp, ‚Umlaufmarkt')*
Emissionsmodalitäten *fpl* (Fin) terms of an issue
Emissionsnebenkosten *pl* (Fin) ancillary issuance (*or* issue) costs
Emissionsnotenbank *f* (Vw) issuing central bank
Emissionspause *f* (Fin) pause preceding a new issue
Emissionspolitik *f*
(Fin) issue policy
– policy of issuing securities
Emissionsprospekt *m*
(Fin) prospectus
– issuing (*or* underwriting) prospectus
Emissionsrecht *n* (Fin) right to issue
Emissionsrendite *f*
(Fin) yield on newly issued bonds
– yield on new issue
– new issue rate
Emissionsrisiko *n* (Fin) underwriting risk
Emissionssatz *m* (Fin) tender rate
Emissionsschuldner *m* (Fin) issue debtor
Emissionsschwemme *f* (Fin) wave (*or* deluge) of new issues
Emissionssperre *f* (Fin) blocking of new issues *(ie, instrument of capital market policy)*
Emissionsspitze *f* (Fin) portion of an unsold issue
Emissionsstatistik *f* (Fin) security issue statistics
Emissionsstoß *m* (Fin) flurry of new issue activity
Emissionstag *m* (Fin) date of issue
Emissionstätigkeit *f* (Fin) issuing activity
Emissionsteuer *f* (StR) security issue tax
Emissionsübernahmevertrag *m* (Fin) underwriting contract
Emissionsvergütung *f* (Fin) issuing commission
Emissionsvertrag *m* (Fin) underwriting agreement
Emissionsvolumen *n* (Fin) total volume of issues
Emissionswährung *f* (Fin) issuing currency
Emission *f* **unterbringen** (Fin) to place an issue
Emission *f* **von Wertpapieren** (Fin) issue of securities
Emittent *m* (Fin) issuer
emittieren
(Fin) to issue *(eg, shares)*
– to float *(eg, an issue)*
emittierende Bank *f* (Fin) issuing bank
emittierende Gesellschaft *f* (Fin) issuing company
emittierte Aktien *fpl* (Fin) shares issued and outstanding
empfangender Sektor *m* (Vw) receiving sector *(ie, in input-output analysis)*
Empfänger *m*
(com) addressee *(eg, letters, parcels)*
– receiver
– recipient
(com) consignee *(ie, of merchandise)*
(Fin) payee *(ie, of money)*
– remittee

(Fin) borrower *(ie, of loan)*
(Re) warrantee *(ie, of guaranty)*
Empfängerland *n*
(AuW) host
– recipient
– donee ... country
Empfängerteil *m* e–s Knotens (OR) receiver of a node
empfangsbedürftig (Re) requiring communication
Empfangsberechtigter *m*
(com) authorized recipient
(Re) beneficiary
Empfangsbescheinigung *f*
(com) receipt
– acknowledgment of receipt
Empfangsbestätigung *f*
(com) = *Empfangsbescheinigung*
(com) receipt for goods shipped
Empfangsbevollmächtigter *m* (Re) person authorized to take delivery
Empfangsdaten *pl* (EDV) received data
Empfangsknoten *m* (OR) receiver node
Empfangskonnossement *n* (com) received-for-shipment bill of lading (*or* B/L)
Empfangslocher *m*
(EDV) paper tape reproducer
– reperforator
Empfangsschein *m* (com) counterfoil *(ie, of a delivery note = ‚Lieferschein')*
Empfangsspediteur *m* (com) receiving forwarding agent *(ie, routing individual consignments of a collective shipment to final destinations)*
Empfangsspediteurvergütung *f* (com) fee paid to receiving forwarding agent *(ie, covering unloading, distribution, and office expenses)*
Empfehlungsschreiben *n*
(com) letter of recommendation (*or* introduction)
(Pw) letter of appraisal
Empfehlungsvereinbarungen *fpl* (com) recommended arrangements
Empfindlichkeitsanalyse *f* (Bw) sensitivity analysis
empfohlener Abgabepreis *m* (Mk) suggested retail price
empfohlener Richtpreis *m* (com) recommended (*or* suggested) retail price
empirische Kurvenbestimmung *f* (Stat) curve fitting
empirische Varianz *f* (Stat) sample variance
empirische Wahrheit *f* (Log) empirical truth
empirische Wirtschaftsforschung *f* (Vw) empirical economic research
empirische Wissenschaft *f* (Log) empirical (*or* factual) science
emporschnellen
(com) to soar *(eg, prices)*
– to zoom
Endabnahme *f* (IndE) final inspection
Endabnehmer *m*
(com) ultimate buyer (*or* consumer)
– end user
– intended user
Endabrechnung *f* (ReW) final account
Endadresse *f* (EDV) end address
Endalter *n* (Vers) age at expiry

Endauswertung f (com) final evaluation
Endbestand m
　(com) final balance
　(ReW) net balance end of period
　(MaW) closing inventory
　– ending balance
Ende n **der Laufzeit** (Fin) maturity date *(ie, of bonds)*
Ende n **der Versicherung** (Vers) termination (*or* expiry) of insurance contract
Ende n **des Beschäftigungsverhältnisses** (Pw) termination (*or* cessation) of employment
Endereignis n (OR) terminal event
Endergebnis n (com) final (*or* net) result
Enderzeugnis n (com) end (*or* final) product
Endezeichen n
　(EDV) end character
　(EDV) end marker
Endfälligkeit f (Fin) final maturity
Endfläche f **e–r Verteilung** (Stat) tail area of a distribution
Endgehalt n (Pw) final salary
Endgerät n (EDV) terminal
Endglied n **e–r Reihe** (Math) last term (*or* extreme) of a series
endgültig (Re) final and binding
endgültige Einfuhr f (Zo) outright (*or* permanent) importation
endgültig entscheiden (Re) to settle finally
endgültige Patentbeschreibung f (Pat) = *endgültige Patentschrift*
endgültige Patentschrift f (Pat) complete patent specification
endgültiger Bescheid m
　(com) final information
　(com) final notice
　(Re) final decision
endgültiger Bestimmungsort m (com) final destination
endgültiger Steuerbescheid m (StR) final notice of assessment
endgültiges Patent n (Pat) complete patent *(opp, provisional patent = vorläufiges Patent)*
endgültige Steuerfestsetzung f (StR) final tax assessment, § 165 II AO
endgültiges Urteil n (Re) final (*or* valid and binding) judgment
Endkapital n (**K**ₙ)
　(Math) compound amount at end of n years
　– end value
　– new principal
Endknoten m (OR) terminal node (*or* vertex)
Endkostenstelle f (KoR) final cost center
Endkreditnehmer m (Fin) final (*or* ultimate) borrower
Endlaufzeit f (Fin) period to maturity
endliche Anzahl f (Math) finite number
endliche Folge f (Math) finite sequence
endliche Folge f **von Gliedern** (Math) finite set of terms
endliche Grundgesamtheit f (Stat) finite population
endliche Körpererweiterung f (Math) finite extension of a field *(syn, Körpergrad)*
endlicher Dezimalbruch m (Math) finite (*or* terminating) decimal

endliche Reihe f (Math) finite series
endlicher Graph m (OR) finite graph
endlicher Warteraum m (OR) finite queue
endliches Kundenreservoir n (OR) finite source population
endliches Spiel n (OR) finite game
endliche Streuung f (Stat) finite variance
endliche Zahl f (Math) finite number (*or* integer)
Endlichkeitsbeweis m (OR) finiteness proof
Endlosformular n (EDV) continuous form
Endloslochstreifen m (EDV) continuous tape
Endlospapier n (EDV) continuous stationery
Endlospapier n **in Faltstapeln** (EDV) continuous fanfold stock *(syn, Leporello-Endlospapier)*
Endlosvordruck m (EDV) = *Endlosformular*
Endmarke f (EDV) end mark
Endmontage f (IndE) final assembly
Endnachfrage f
　(Vw) final demand (for goods and services)
　(OR) final bill of goods
endogene Bestimmungsgröße f (Vw) endogenous determinant
endogene Finanzierung f (Fin) internal financing *(ie, profit retentions, reserves, depreciation, restructuring of assets)*
endogene Konjunkturtheorie f (Vw) endogenous business-cycle theory
endogenes Geld n (Vw) inside money
endogene Variable f (Vw) endogenous variable
Endpreis m
　(com) price charged to ultimate customer
　– final price
　(com) retail price
Endprodukt n
　(com) final product
　(Vw) output *(ie, measured by social indicators)*
Endprüfung f (Stat) final inspection
Endpunkt m **der Beförderung** (Zo) terminal point of transportation
Endpunkt m **e–r Kante** (OR) end point
Endrente f (SozV) maximum payable pension
Endsaldo m (ReW) closing (*or* ending) balance
Endschuldner m (Fin) final debtor *(eg, in the international credit system)*
Endspalte f (ReW) end column
Endsumme f
　(com) total
　(com) grand (*or* final) total
Endtermin m
　(com) target date
　– deadline
　– finish date
Endübertrag m (EDV) end around carry *(syn, Ringübertrag)*
Endverbrauch m (VGR) final consumption
Endverbraucher m
　(com) end user
　(com) retail customer
　(Vw) final (*or* ultimate) consumer
Endverbrauchernachfrage f (Mk) demand from ultimate consumers
Endverbraucherpreis m
　(com) retail price
　(com) consumer price

Endverbraucherwerbung f (Mk) consumer (or retail) advertising
Endverkaufspreis m (com) final sales (or selling) price
Endvermögen n (Bw) final net worth *(ie, at end of winding-up procedure)*
Endvermögensmaximierung f (Fin) maximization of assets at end of total planning period *(ie, targeted goal in evaluating investment projects)*
Endwert m
 (Math) end (or terminal) value
 (Fin) total accumulation of annuity
Endwertmodell n (Fin) final-value model *(ie, used in planning optimum capital budget, related to date of discontinuance of an enterprise or to cutoff date of planning horizon)*
Endzinssatz m
 (Fin) all-in interest rate
 (Fin) interest rate charged to borrower
Endzuführung f (EDV) endwise feed
energieabhängiger Speicher m (EDV) volatile storage
Energieanlagen fpl (IndE) utilities *(ie, power, steam, water, air, fuels)*
Energieaufwand m (IndE) energy input
Energieausfall m (IndE) power failure
Energiebedarf m (IndE) energy requirements
Energieberater m (com) advisor on energy
Energiebereich m (com) energy industry
Energiebilanz f (IndE) energy balance statement *(ie, recording aggregate supply and utilization of power)*
Energieeinsatz m (IndE) energy input
Energieeinsatz m **pro Produktionseinheit** (IndE) energy input per unit of production
Energieeinsparung f (com) energy saving
Energieerzeugung f (IndE) power generation
Energiefluß m (IndE) energy flow
Energiegewinnung f (Vw) production of energy
Energiehaushalt m (Vw) ratio of power generation to energy requirements
energieintensiv (IndE) energy intensive
Energiekonzept n (Vw) energy concept
Energiekosten pl (KoR) cost of energy *(ie, power, steam, gas)*
Energiekrise f (Vw) energy crisis (or crunch)
Energielage f (Vw) energy supply situation
Energielücke f (Vw) energy gap
Energielücke f **füllen** (Vw) to plug the energy gap
Energiemarkt m
 (Vw) energy market
 (com) power-supply market
Energiepolitik f (Vw) energy policy
Energiepreis m (IndE) energy price
Energieproblem n (Vw) energy supply problem
Energieprogramm n
 (Vw) energy-generating program
 (Vw) power-plant program
Energiequelle f (Vw) source of energy
Energiereserve f (Vw) energy reserve
Energiesektor m
 (Vw) energy sector
 (com) power-supply sector
Energiesicherung f (Vw) energy conservation

Energiesparprogramm n (Bw) energy thrift campaign
Energiesystem n (IndE) power distribution system
Energietechnik f (IndE) power engineering
Energieträger m
 (IndE) fuel
 (IndE) source of energy
energieunabhängiger Speicher m (EDV) non-erasable (or non-volatile) storage
Energieunternehmen n
 (com) utility company
 – power-supply company
Energieverbrauch m (IndE) energy consumption
Energieverlust m (IndE) energy loss
Energieversorgung f (Vw) energy supply
Energieversorgungsunternehmen n (com) public utility
Energieverteilungsplan m (IndE) power distribution plan
Energieverwendung f (IndE) utilization of energy
Energiewerte mpl (Bö) utilities
Energiewirtschaft f
 (com) energy industry
 – power-supply industry
energiewirtschaftliche Probleme npl (Vw) energy problems
Energiewirtschaftsgesetz n (Re) Energy Industry Law
Energiezufuhr-Funktion f (Bw) energy supply function
Engagement n
 (Bö) commitment
 (Pw) personal involvement
eng auslegen (Re) to put a narrow (or restricted) construction upon
enge Auslegung f (Re) narrow (or restricted) construction
Engel-Kurve f (Vw) Engel curve
enger Markt m (Bö) tight (or narrow) market
enge Verflechtung f (com) tight interlocking *(eg, of the banking and industrial sectors)*
Engpaß m (Bw) bottleneck
Engpaßbereich m (Bw) bottleneck area
Engpaßfaktor m
 (KoR) limiting factor
 (IndE) constraining (or critical) factor
Engpaßinvestition f (Bw) bottleneck investment
Engpaßmonopol n (Kart) bottleneck monopoly *(ie, operating a key physical facility)*
Engpaßplanung f (Bw) overall planning paying particular attention to the bottleneck area of an enterprise
en gros (com) wholesale
Engrosabnehmer m (com) wholesale buyer (or customer)
Engrosbezug m (com) wholesale buying
Enkelgesellschaft f (StR) second-tier subsidiary *(ie, enterprise controlled by another subsidiary, § 120 BewG)*
Enquete-Kommission f
 (com) study committee
 – commission of inquiry
entartete Lösung f (OR) degenerate solution
entarteter Graph m (OR) degenerate graph
Entartung f (OR) degeneracy

Entartungsfall m (OR) degenerate case
Entbindungskosten-Pauschbetrag m (StR) flat-rate birth benefit *(ie, paid by the statutory health insurance fund, at present DM 100, § 198 RVO)*
entblocken (EDV) to deblock
Entbündelung f (EDV) unbundling *(ie, separate supply and pricing of hardware and software)*
Entdeckungszusammenhang m (Log) context of discovery
enteignen (Re) to condemn property *(ie, for public purposes)*
  (AuW) to expropriate
Enteignung f
  (AuW) expropriation
  (Re, US) condemnation
  – *(almost synonymous)* expropriation
  – (GB) compulsory purchase
  (ie, taking private property under the power of eminent domain)
Enteignungsbeschluß m (Re) condemnation order
Enteignungsentschädigung f (Re) condemnation award
enteignungsgleich (Re) confiscatory
Enteignungsrecht n **des Staates** (Re) right (*or* power) of eminent domain
Enteignungsverfahren n
  (Re) formal eminent domain proceedings
  – condemnation proceedings
entfallende Ausschüttungsbelastung f (StR) applicable distribution burden
entferntes Endgerät n (EDV) remote terminal
Entfernungsmatrix f (Math) distance matrix
Entfernungsstaffel f (com) graded distance schedule
entflechten
  (Re) to deglomerate
  (Kart) to divest
  (Kart) to decartelize
  – to deconcentrate
Entflechtung f
  (Re) deglomeration
  (Kart) divestiture
  (Kart) decartelization
  – deconcentration
Entflechtungsanordnung f (Kart) divesting (*or* dismemberment) order
Entfremdung f **am Arbeitsplatz** (Pw) shop-floor alienation
entfusionieren (Kart) to demerge *(ie, to break up into independent smaller units)*
entgangener Gewinn m
  (com) lost profits
  (Re) loss of prospective profits, § 252 BGB
  – *(civil law)* lucrum cessans
  – *(Scotland)* ceasing gain
  (ReW) profit loss *(ie, from potential sale)*
  – loss of expected return
entgegengehaltenes Patent n (Pat) reference (*or* cited) patent
entgegengesetztes Ereignis n (Stat) complementary event
entgegenhandeln (Re) to act in contravention (*or* violation) *(ie, of legal provisions)*
Entgegennahme f **von Einlagen** (Fin) acceptance of deposits

entgegenstehende Anmeldung f (Pat) interfering application
entgegenstehender Anspruch m (Pat) conflicting claim
Entgelt n
  (com) payment
  (Re) consideration *(ie, see ‚Note on Terminology')*
  (StR) consideration *(ie, for deliveries and services, § 13 UStG)*
  (Pw) compensation
  – remuneration
  (SozV) benefit *(ie, cash or in kind)*
Entgelt n **für die Unternehmensführung** (VGR) remuneration of management
entgeltlich
  (Re) for (valuable) consideration
  (com) against payment
entgeltliche Einfuhr f (AuW) imports against payment
entgeltlich erwerben
  (Re) to aquire for a consideration
  (WeR) to take for value
entgeltlich od unentgeltlich (Re) gratuitously or for a consideration
Entgeltpolitik f (Pw) pay policy
Entgeltüberträge mpl (Vers) premiums unearned on balance sheet date, § 14 VAG
enthorten (Vw) to dishoard
Enthorten n (Vw) dishoarding
entkartellisieren (Kart) to decartelize
Entkartellisierung f (Kart) decartelization
Entladehafen m (com) port of discharge (*or* unloading)
Entladekosten pl (Zo) unloading charges
entladen
  (com) to discharge
  – to unload
Entladeort m (com) place of unloading
Entladerampe f (com) unloading platform
Entladung f
  (com) discharge
  – unloading
Entladung f **auf Zollboden** (Zo) unloading to temporary store
entlassen
  (Re) to discharge
  – to release
  – to remove from office
  (Pw) to dismiss
  – (infml) to fire
  – (GB, infml) to sack (*or* give the sack)
Entlassung f
  (Re) discharge
  – release
  – removal from (office)
  (Pw) dismissal
  – permanent layoff
Entlassungen fpl (Pw) terminations
Entlassungsabfindung f
  (Pw) severance pay
  – dismissal pay
  – (GB) redundancy pay
Entlassungsentschädigung f (Pw) = *Entlassungsabfindung*

Entlassungsgeld n (Pw) = *Entlassungsabfindung*
Entlassungsgrund m (Pw) grounds for dismissal (*or* discharge)
Entlassungspapiere npl
(Pw) dismissal papers
– (infml) walking papers (*or* ticket)
Entlassungsschreiben n
(Pw) letter (*or* notice) of dismissal
– layoff notice
entlasten
(com) to ease the strain (on)
(ReW) to credit (*ie, someone's account*)
(Re) to discharge (*ie, from debt or obligation*)
(Bw) to give discharge (to) (*eg, managing board, auditor, § 120 AktG*)
– to ratify (*eg, acts of management for a business year*)
entlasteter Gemeinschuldner m (Re) discharged bankrupt
Entlastung f
(ReW) credit entry
(Re) formal approval
– vote of formal approval
– (grant of) discharge
– release
– ratification
Entlastung f **beschließen** (Bw) to ratify the acts of management, § 30 III AktG
Entlastung f **der Wirtschaft** (Vw) easing the pressure on the economy
Entlastung f **der Zahlungsbilanz** (VGR) easing the strain on the balance of payments
Entlastung f **des Abschlußprüfers** (ReW) discharge of the statutory auditor
Entlastung f **des Gemeinschuldners** (Re) discharge of bankrupt
Entlastung f **des Vorstandes** (Bw) release of managing board from responsibility for management
– discharge of managing board
Entlastung f **erteilen**
(Re) to release members of a board from responsibility for management during the preceding year, § 120 AktG
– to approve (*or* vote for) a general release at an annual shareholders' meeting
Entlastungsanzeige f (ReW) credit note
Entlastungsauftrag m (IndE) relief order
Entlastungsbeweis m (Re) exculpatory evidence
Entlastungserteilung f
(Re) vote of formal approval
– grant of release
Entlastungsfertigung f (IndE) production in connection with relief orders
entlohnen
(Pw) to pay
– to compensate
Entlohnung f (Pw) compensation (*ie, of employees*)
Entlohnungsverfahren npl (Pw) payments system (*syn, Lohnformen*)
entmischte Tätigkeit f (Pw) work mix comprising only video station work (*ie, to the exclusion of ordinary office work; see: Mischtätigkeit*)
entmonetisieren (Vw) to demonetize
Entmonetisierung f (Vw) demonetization

entmündigen
(Re) to interdict (*wegen* · on the ground of)
– to place under guardianship
entmündigt (Re) officially placed under guardianship
Entmündigung f
(Re) interdiction
– placing under guardianship, § 6 BGB
Entmündigungsbeschluß m (Re) judicial decree of interdiction (*ie, by which a person is deprived of the exercise of his civil rights*)
Entnahme f
(MaW) withdrawal
(Fin) distribution
(Fin) withdrawal (*eg, cash, capital*)
– drawings (*eg, to take . . .*)
(IndE) sampling
– taking samples
Entnahme f **aus der Gemeinschaftsreserve** (EG) drawing on the Community reserve
Entnahmemaximierung f (Fin) maximization of annual withdrawals (*ie, target requirement in evaluating investment projects*)
Entnahme f **von Kapital** (Fin) withdrawal from capital
Entnahme f **von Proben**
(IndE) sampling of test specimens
– taking of samples
entnehmen
(com) to withdraw
– to take drawings
entpacken (EDV) to unpack
entrichten (Fin) to pay (*eg, taxes and duties*)
Entrichtung f (Fin) payment
Entrichtung f **der Eingangsabgaben** (Zo) payment of import duties and taxes
Entropie f
(EDV) entropy
– average information content
Entsalzungsanlage f (IndE) desalination plant
entschädigen
(com) to reimburse
(Re) to compensate
– to indemnify
Entschädigung f
(com) reimbursement
(Re) compensation
– indemnification
(*ie, give reimbursement of loss incurred*)
(Re) indemnity
– compensation
(*eg, given by government for private property turned to public use*)
Entschädigungen fpl **für entgangene Einnahmen** (StR) indemnities received for loss of income, § 24 I a EStG
Entschädigung f **in Geld** (Re) pecuniary compensation
Entschädigungsanspruch m (Re) claim for compensation
Entschädigungsfonds m (Vers) Indemnity Fund (*ie, set up to adjust injuries suffered from motor accidents*)
Entschädigungsforderungen fpl (com) indemnity claims (*ie, arising under freight contracts signed with the Deutsche Bundesbahn*)

Entschädigungsleistung *f*
  (Re) compensatory payment
  – compensation
  (Vers) adjustment
Entschädigungspflicht *f* (Re) liability to pay compensation
entschädigungspflichtig (Re) liable to pay compensation
Entschädigungspflichtiger *m* (Re) person (*or* party) liable to pay compensation
Entschädigungssumme *f*
  (Re) amount of compensation
  – indemnity
Entschädigungszahlung *f* (Re) (payment of) compensation
entschärfen (com) to defuse (*eg, shopfloor unrest*)
Entscheidbarkeit *f* (Log) decidability
Entscheider *m*
  (Vw, Bw) decider
  – decision maker
Entscheidung *f*
  (com) decision
  (Re) decision
  – ruling
  – judgment
Entscheidung *f* **anfechten** (Re) to contest a decision
Entscheidung *f* **aufheben** (Re) to disaffirm (*or* reverse) a decision
Entscheidung *f* **aufschieben** (com) to shelve a decision
Entscheidung *f* **bei Unsicherheit und Risiko** (Bw) decision under risk and uncertainty
Entscheidung *f* **fällen** (com) to make a decision
Entscheidung *f* **in mündlicher Verhandlung** (StR) hearing a case in open court, § 90 I FGO
Entscheidung *f* **ohne mündliche Verhandlung** (StR) decision of a controversy on the basis of the record, § 90 II FGO
Entscheidung *f* **realisieren** (Bw) to implement a decision
Entscheidungsanalyse *f* (Bw) decision analysis
Entscheidungsautonomie *f* (Bw) autonomy of decision making
Entscheidungsbaum *m* (Bw) decision (*or* logical) tree
Entscheidungsbefehl *m* (EDV) decision instruction
Entscheidungsbefugnis *f*
  (Bw) authority (*or* competence) to decide
  – power to take decisions
  – decision-making power
Entscheidungsbereitschaft *f*
  (Bw) willingness to take decision
  – decisiveness
Entscheidungsdaten *pl* (Bw) decision data (*or* parameter)
Entscheidungsdelegation *f* (Bw) delegation of decision-making
Entscheidungsdezentralisation *f*
  (Bw) decentralization of decisions
  – delegation of authority
Entscheidungseinheit *f*
  (Vw, Bw) decision unit
  – decision-taking unit
Entscheidungselement *n* (EDV) decision element

Entscheidungsfehler *m* (Stat) error of decision (*ie, first and second kind*)
Entscheidungsfeld *n* (Bw) decision area
Entscheidungsfindung *f* (Bw) decision making
Entscheidungsfunktion *f* (Stat) decision function
Entscheidungsgehalt *m* (Bw) decision content
Entscheidungsgrund *m* (Re) ratio decidendi (*ie, the ground of decision*)
Entscheidungshierarchie *f*
  (Bw) hierarchy of authority
  – decision-making hierarchy
Entscheidungsinstanz *f*
  (Bw) authority
  – decision center
  – decision-making unit
Entscheidungsknoten *m* (OR) decision box
Entscheidungskriterien *npl* (Bw) criteria of decision
Entscheidungslogik *f* (Bw) decision logic
Entscheidungsmatrix *f* (Bw) decision matrix
Entscheidungsmodell *n* (Bw) decision model
Entscheidungsmodell *n* **mit mehreren Zielfunktionen** (Bw) multi-objective decision model
entscheidungsorientierte Kostenrechnung *f* (KoR) functional accounting
Entscheidungspaket *n* (Bw) decision package
Entscheidungsparameter *m* (Bw) decision parameter
Entscheidungsphasen *fpl* (Bw) phases of the decision-making process
Entscheidungsproblem *n* (Bw) decision problem
Entscheidungsprogramm *n* (Bw) decision program (*ie, written to solve routine decisions*)
Entscheidungsprozeß *m* (Bw) decision making process
Entscheidungsprozeß *m* **an der Front** (Bw) process of operational decision-making
Entscheidungsraum *m* (Bw) decision space
Entscheidungsregeln *fpl* (Bw) decision rules
entscheidungsrelevante Größen *fpl* (Bw) decision variables
entscheidungsrelevante Kosten *pl* (KoR) relevant costs
entscheidungsrelevante Kriterien *npl* (Bw) choice criteria
Entscheidungssequenzen *fpl* (Bw) interlocked sequence of decision steps
Entscheidungsspeicher *m* (EDV) decision storage
Entscheidungsspielraum *m* (Bw) scope of decision-making
Entscheidungsstufe *f* (Bw) level of decision-making
Entscheidungssubjekt *n* (Bw) decision maker (*or* unit)
Entscheidungstabelle *f* (EDV) decision table
Entscheidungstechnologie *f* (Bw) decision technology
Entscheidungstheorie *f* (Bw) decision (making) theory
Entscheidungsträger *m*
  (Vw, Bw) decider
  – decision-taking unit
  – decision unit
Entscheidungsunterstützungssystem *n* (Bw) decision support system
Entscheidungsvariable *f* (Bw) decision variable

Entscheidungsverfahren n
(Bw) decision making process
(Log) decision rule
Entscheidungsverhalten n (Bw) decision making behavior
Entscheidungsverzögerung f (FiW) decision lag
Entscheidungsverzögerung f **konjunkturpolitischer Maßnahmen** (Vw) action lag
Entscheidungswege mpl (Bw) lines of decision
entscheidungswirksame Kosten pl (KoR) decision making cost
Entscheidungszentrum n
(Bw) decision center
– locus of decision making
Entscheidung f **unter Unsicherheit** (Bw) decision under uncertainty
entschlüsseln (EDV) to decode
Entschlüsselungsmatrix f (EDV) decoder matrix
entschulden
(Re) to disencumber
– to free of debts
(Fin) to reduce indebtedness
entschuldigtes Fernbleiben n (Pw) authorized absence
Entschuldung f
(Re) disencumberment
(Fin) reduction of indebtedness
Entsendeland n (Pw) sending country
Entspannung f (Fin) easing (eg, of financial position)
Entsparen n
(Vw) dissaving
– negative saving
Entstaatlichung f (Vw) privatization (ie, of nationalized industries)
entstehendes Recht n (Re) inchoate right (opp, vested right)
Entstehung f **der Zollschuld** (Zo) creation of the customs debt
Entstehung f **des Bruttoinlandsprodukts** (VGR) industrial origin of gross domestic product
Entstehungsrechnung f
(VGR) commodity-service method
– (GB) output method
Entstehungsseite f (VGR) output side
Entweder-Oder-Regel f (Log) rule of alternatives
entwerfen
(com) to draft
– to make a draft
entwerten
(com) to cancel
– to invalidate
Entwertung f
(com) cancellation
– invalidation
(Bw) decline in economic usefulness
Entwertung f **durch technischen Fortschritt** (Bw) obsolescence
Entwertungsfaktoren mpl
(ReW) factors of depreciation
– causes of expiration of fixed-asset cost (ie, technical, economic, legal)
Entwertungsstempel m (com) cancellation stamp
entwickeln
(com) to develop

(Math) to expand
entwickelte Volkswirtschaft f (Vw) developed (or commercial) economy (opp, subsistence economy)
entwickelt von Rechtsprechung und Lehre (Re) developed in and out of court
Entwicklung f
(com) development
– movement
– trend
– tendency
Entwicklung f **des Führungskräftepotentials** (Pw) management development
Entwicklung f **e–r Funktion** (Math) expansion of a function
Entwicklungsabteilung f (IndE) development department (ie, closely cooperating with research and dealing with improvement, rationalization, new salable products)
Entwicklungsanleihe f (Fin) development loan
Entwicklungsaufwand m (ReW) development expense
Entwicklungsausschuß m (AuW) Development Committee (ie, Joint Ministerial Committee of the Governors of the World Bank and the IMF on the transfer of Real Resources to Developing Countries)
Entwicklungsbank f (Vw) development bank (eg, European Investment Bank)
Entwicklungsfonds m (Vw) development fund
Entwicklungsforschung f (Bw) development engineering
Entwicklungsgebiet n (Vw) development area
Entwicklungsgefahren fpl (Bw) risks of product development
Entwicklungsgesellschaft f
(Vw) development corporation
(Bw) research and development company
– R & D company
Entwicklungshilfe f (Vw) aid (or assistance) to developing nations
Entwicklungshilfeanleihe f (Fin) development aid loan
Entwicklungshilfekredit m
(Vw) development loan
– aid loan
Entwicklungshilfepolitik f (Vw) development aid policy
Entwicklungshilfe-Steuergesetz n (StR) Development Aid Tax Law
Entwicklungskapazität f (Bw) product development potential
Entwicklungskosten pl (ReW) development cost (or expense)
Entwicklungsland n
(Vw) developing country
– less developed country
– LDC, ldc
Entwicklungsländer-Steuergesetz n (StR) Law on Tax Incentives for Investments in Developing Countries
Entwicklungsmöglichkeiten fpl (com) open-ended capabilities
Entwicklungsprojekt n (AuW) development project

Entwicklungsstadium n (Bw) stage of development
Entwicklungsvorhaben n (Vw) development project
Entwicklungswagnis n (ReW) R & D (research and development) risk
Entwicklung f **von Erzeugnissen** (Bw) product engineering
Entwurf m
 (com) draft *(eg, of letter, document)*
 – outline
 (IndE) design
Entwurfsphase f **des Entscheidungsprozesses** (Bw) design activity
entzerren (com) to correct the distorted pattern *(eg, of interest rates, prices)*
Entzerrung f **(der Zinsstruktur)** (Vw) correcting the distortion (in the pattern of interest rates)
entziehbare Betriebsmittel pl (EDV) preemptive resources
Entzugseffekte mpl (Vw) withdrawals
Enumeration f (OR) enumeration
Erbanfall m (StR) acquisition of property by will or intestacy, § 1942 BGB, § 3 I ErbStG
Erbanfallsteuer f
 (StR) inheritance tax
 – (GB) estate duty *(ie, in 1975 replaced by the Capital Transfer Tax)*
Erbauseinandersetzung f (Re) apportionment and division of a decedent's estate
Erbbaurechte npl (Re) inheritable building rights
Erbe m (Re) heir
Erbe n (Re) inheritance
Erbengemeinschaft f (Re) community of heirs, §§ 2032 ff BGB
Erbfolge f (StR) succession of the testamentary or intestate heir to the property and debts of the testator or decedent
Erblasser m (Re) testator *(ie, one who makes a will or testament)*
Erbportion f (Re) portion of the estate received by a beneficiary
Erbrecht n (Re) Law of Succession *(ie, laid down in the fifth book of the German Civil Code, BGB; treats both testate and intestate succession)*
erbringen
 (com) to perform
 – to render
 – to furnish
 (Fin) to yield
Erbringung f **von Dienstleistungen** (com) performance of services
Erbschaft f **ausschlagen** (StR) to disclaim an inheritance, § 3 II 4 ErbStG
Erbschaftsgut n (Zo) inherited goods, § 24 I ZG
Erbschaftsteuer f
 (StR) inheritance tax
 (FiW) estate or inheritance tax *(ie, the estate tax is a ‚Nachlaßsteuer' levied on the undivided decedent's estate, while the inheritance tax is an ‚Erbanfallsteuer' levied – as in West Germany – on the heir receiving a portion of the estate. Note that the British ‚estate duty' was replaced in 1975 by a ‚capital transfer tax')*
Erbschaftsteuer-Durchführungsverordnung f (StR) Ordinance Regulating the Inheritance Tax Law, of 19 Jan 1962
Erbschaftsteuer- und Schenkungsteuergesetz n (StR) Inheritance Tax Law, of 17 Apr 1974 *(ie, amended by Introductory Decree on the Fiscal Code of 14 Dec 1976)*
Erbschein m (Re) certificate of inheritance
Erbteil n (Re) portion of estate received by a beneficiary
Erdbebenversicherung f (Vers) earthquake insurance
erdölexportierende Länder npl (Vw) oil exporting countries
Erdölindustrie f (com) oil industry
Erdölwerte mpl (Bö) oils
Ereignis n (OR) event
Ereignisbit n (EDV) event bit
Ereigniseintritt m (com) occurrence of an event
Ereignisfolgen fpl (Stat) runs
Ereignismasse f (Stat) period-based population *(syn, Bewegungsmasse; opp, Bestandsmasse)*
Ereignispuffer m (OR) slack
Ereignisraum m (Stat) sample space *(syn, Stichprobenraum)*
Ereignissteuerblock m (EDV) event control block, ECB
Ereigniswahrscheinlichkeit f (Stat) probability of occurrence (*or* events)
erfahren (Pw) widely experienced
Erfahrungsaustausch m (com) interchange of know-how
Erfahrungsbericht m (com) progress report
Erfahrungssatz m (Log) statement based on experience
Erfahrungswerte mpl (com) experience figures
Erfahrungswissenschaft f (Log) empirical science
erfassen
 (KoR) to accumulate
 – to acquire
 – to collect ... data
erfaßt (com) covered
Erfassung f **an der Quelle** (StR) stoppage at source
Erfassungsbereich m (com) scope *(eg, of survey, estimate, assessment)*
Erfassungsbreite f (com) scope of coverage
Erfassungsstation f (EDV) point of acquisition
Erfassungszeitraum m (Stat) period under review
Erfassung f **von Daten** (EDV) data acquisition
Erfassung f **von Geschäftsvorfällen** (ReW) recording of business transactions
Erfinder m (Pat) (first and true) inventor
Erfinder m **der Haupterfindung** (Pat) original inventor
Erfindergeist m (Pw) inventive talent
erfinderrechtliche Vindikation f (Pat) claim to transfer of property *(ie, patterned after § 985 BGB)*
Erfinderschutz m (Pat) safeguarding of inventor's rights
Erfindervergütung f (Pw) inventor's compensation
Erfindung f (Pat) invention
Erfindung f **anmelden** (Pat) to apply for a patent of an invention
Erfindung f **nutzen** (Pat) exploit an invention
Erfindungsaufgabe f (Pat) object of an invention

Erfindungeigenschaft f (Pat) sufficiency of an invention
Erfindungsgedanke m (Pat) inventive idea
Erfindungsgegenstand m (Pat) object (*or* subject matter) of an invention
– claimed subject matter
Erfindungshöhe f
(Pat) inventive level (*or* height *or* step)
– level of invention
– degree of novelty
– amount of invention
Erfindungshöhe f **verneinen** (Pat) to deny an inventive step
Erfindungsmaßstab m (Pat) standard of invention
Erfindungspatent n (Pat) patent for an invention
Erfindungspriorität f (Pat) priority of invention
Erfindungsschutz m (Pat) protection of an invention
Erfindungsvorteil m (Pat) benefit of an invention
Erfolg m
(com) result of economic activity
– performance
(ReW) profit
– result
erfolgloses Übernahmeangebot n (Fin) abortive takeover bid
erfolgreicher Anbieter m (com) successful bidder
erfolgreiches Unternehmen n
(com) successful venture
– going business
Erfolgsanalyse f (ReW) profit analysis *(eg, break even analysis, profit-maximizing production program)*
Erfolgsbeitrag m (KoR) profit contribution
Erfolgsbeteiligung f (Pw) profit-sharing plan for employees
Erfolgsbilanz f
(ReW) = *Gewinn- und Verlustrechnung*
(ReW) results accounting *(ie, based on Schmalenbach's concept of ‚Dynamische Bilanz')*
Erfolgsermittlung f
(Bw) performance evaluation
(ReW) income determination
– determination of earnings
Erfolgsfaktoren mpl (Bw) factors of performance
Erfolgsgrößen fpl (Bw) performance data
Erfolgshaftung f
(Re) strict (*or* absolute) liability
– liability without fault
Erfolgshonorar n (com) contingent fee
Erfolgskennziffer f (Bw) operating ratio *(ie, measuring the effectiveness of operations)*
Erfolgskonsolidierung f
(ReW) consolidation of earnings
– intercompany elimination, §§ 331 ff AktG
Erfolgskonto n
(ReW) nominal account
– revenue and expense account
– operating account
– income statement account
Erfolgskontrolle f
(Bw) efficiency review
(KoR) cost-revenue control
(ie, analysis of period income for 1. an enterprise

as a whole; 2. a plant unit; 3. individual departments; and 4. individual profit units)
Erfolgslohn m
(Pw) incentive pay
– payment by results
Erfolgsmaßstab m
(Bw) yardstick of performance
– performance criterion
– indicator of performance
Erfolgsplan m (Bw) profit plan
Erfolgsplanung f (Bw) profit planning
Erfolgsposten m (ReW) item of income statement (*or* GB: of profit and loss account)
Erfolgsquote f (Stat) success rate
Erfolgsrate f (Bw) yield
Erfolgsrechnung f
(ReW) income statement
– profit and loss statement
Erfolgsrelationen fpl (Bw) performance ratios *(eg, productivity, economic efficiency, rates of return)*
Erfolgsspaltung f (ReW) breakdown of total profit into operating income and nonoperating income
Erfolgsvergleichsrechnung f (Fin) comparative earnings analysis *(ie, carried out to evaluate investment projects)*
Erfolgswert m (Fin) = *Ertragswert*
erfolgswirksam (ReW) affecting current-period result (*or* operating result)
erfolgswirksame Kosten pl (ReW) expired cost (*or* expense)
erfolgswirksamer Aufwand m (ReW) revenue expenditure *(ie, non-capitalized expense affecting operating result)*
Erfolgsziele npl (Bw) goals of performance
Erfolgszurechnung f (Fin) allocation of earnings *(ie, to various organizational units)*
erfolgversprechender Markt m (Mk) promising market
Erfordernis n **der Schriftform** (Re) writing requirement
Erforschung f **des Meeresbodens** (com) sea-bed exploration
Erfüllbarkeit f (Log) satisfiability
erfüllen
(com) to satisfy *(eg, conditions)*
(Re) to perform a contract
– to carry out the terms of a contract
– to discharge obligations under a contract
– to render performance
Erfüllung f
(Re) performance, § 362 I BGB
– discharge
– fulfillment
– extinction
Erfüllung f **der Einfuhrförmlichkeiten** (Zo) carrying out the import formalities
Erfüllung f **durchsetzen** (Re) to force performance
Erfüllung f **e-r Bedingung** (Re) satisfaction (*or* performance) of a condition *(eg, a condition precedent is one which must be performed . . .)*
Erfüllung f **e-r Forderung** (Re) satisfaction of a claim
Erfüllung f **e-r Verbindlichkeit** (Re) discharge of a debt

Erfüllung *f* **e-s Anspruchs** (Re) satisfaction of a claim
Erfüllung *f* **e-s Vertrages** (Re) performance of a contract
Erfüllung *f* **e-s Wertpapiergeschäfts** (Bö) execution of a bargain
Erfüllungsangebot *n* (Re) tender of performance
Erfüllungsannahme *f* (Re) acceptance as performance
Erfüllungsfrist *f* (Re) time fixed for performance
Erfüllungsgarantie *f*
 (Re) performance guaranty
 – guaranty against defective materials and workmanship
 – completion (*or* contract) bond
Erfüllungsgehilfe *m* (Re) person employed in performing an obligation, § 278 BGB
Erfüllungsgeschäft *n* (Re) legal transaction in fulfillment of an obligation
erfüllungshalber (Re) on account of performance *(ie, where the undertaking of a new obligation by the debtor does not operate as a discharge of the former obligation, such new obligation is said to be undertaken ‚erfüllungshalber')*
Erfüllungshindernis *n* (Re) obstacle to performance
Erfüllungsinteresse *n* (Re) positive interest *(ie, claim to indemnity for breach at an amount equal to the full performance of the contract; syn, positives Interesse; opp, Vertrauensinteresse, negatives Interesse)*
Erfüllungsmenge *f* (Math) solution set
Erfüllungsort *m*
 (Re) place of performance (*or* fulfillment), § 269 BGB
 – *(civil law)* domicilium executandi
Erfüllungsort *m* **und Gerichtsstand** *m*
 (Re) place of fulfillment and jurisdiction
 – *(civil law)* domicilium citandi et executandi *(eg, place of fulfillment for either party shall be Munich; any disputes arising out of the contract shall be referred to the court having jurisdiction in Munich)*
Erfüllungspflicht *f* (Re) obligation to perform
Erfüllungstag *m* (com) due date
Erfüllungstermin *m* (Bö) settlement day
Erfüllungsübernahme *f* (Re) assumption of an obligation to perform, § 329 BGB
Erfüllungsverweigerung *f* (Re) repudiation of a contract
Erfüllungszeitpunkt *m* (Re) time (*or* date) of performance
Erfüllung *f* **Zug um Zug** (Re) mutual concurrent performance
Ergänzungsabgabe *f* (StR) supplemental income tax *(ie, on upper-bracket individuals)*
Ergänzungsabgabegesetz *n* (StR) Law on Surcharge of Income Tax and Corporation Income Tax
Ergänzungsfrage *f* (Stat) probe question
Ergänzungsgesetz *n* (Re) supplementary law
Ergänzungshaushalt *m* (FiW) supplementary budget *(ie, changing a budget not yet approved by parliament)*
Ergänzungsklasse *f* (Log) difference class

Ergänzungslieferungen *fpl* (com) supplements *(ie, to loose leaf volumes)*
Ergänzungspatent *n* (Pat) supplementary patent
Ergänzungsprodukt *n* (com) add-on product
Ergänzungsspeicher *m*
 (EDV) auxiliary
 – backing
 – secondary . . . storage
 (syn, Hilfsspeicher, Zubringerspeicher)
Ergänzungswerbung *f* (Mk) accessory advertising
Ergänzungswinkel *m* (Math) conjugate angle
Ergänzungszone *f* (Re) contiguous zone *(ie, in Sea Law)*
Ergänzungszuweisungen *fpl* (FiW) supplementary appropriations (*or* payments) *(ie, out of federal funds to indigent Länder, Art. 107 II GG)*
Ergebnis *n*
 (com) result
 – showing *(eg, the best . . . since 1980)*
 – performance
 (Bw) (positive or negative) payoff
 (ReW) profit
 – net earnings
 – operating result
Ergebnisabführungsvertrag *m* (Bw) profit and loss transfer agreement *(ie, corporation undertakes to transfer its entire profits to another enterprise, §§ 291 ff AktG; syn, Gewinnabführungsvertrag)*
Ergebnisanalyse *f* (Vw) performance analysis *(ie, ratio analysis)*
Ergebnisausschlußvereinbarung *f* (ReW) profit and loss exclusion agreement
Ergebnisberichtigung *f* **früherer Jahre** (ReW) prior-period adjustment
Ergebnisbeteiligung *f* (Pw) profit sharing
ergebnisbezogene Leistungsbewertung *f* (Pw) appraisal of (*or* by) results
Ergebnis *n* **der normalen Geschäftstätigkeit** (ReW, EG) profit or loss on ordinary activities
Ergebnis *n* **des Geschäftsjahres** (ReW, EG) profit or loss for the financial year
Ergebniseinheit *f* (Bw) profit center
Ergebnis *n* **je Aktie** (Fin) net earnings per share
Ergebnislohn *m* (Pw) payment by results
Ergebnismatrize *f* (Bw) payoff matrix
Ergebnis *n* **nach Steuern** (ReW) result after taxes
ergebnisneutral (ReW) not affecting net income (*or* operating result)
Ergebnisprotokoll *n* (com) minutes of a meeting
Ergebnisrechnung *f*
 (ReW) statement of operating results
 (ReW) = *Erfolgsrechnung*
Ergebnisübernahmevertrag *m* (Re) = *Ergebnisabführungsvertrag*
Ergebnisübersicht *f* (ReW) statement of results
Ergebnisverantwortung *f* (Bw) profit responsibility
Ergebnisverbesserung *f* (Bw) improvement in performance
Ergebnisverwendung *f* (ReW) appropriation of net income
Ergebnisvortrag *m*
 (ReW) result brought forward
 – unappropriated net income
 (ReW, EG) profit or loss brought forward
ergebniswirksam (ReW) affecting net income

ergebniswirksame Konsolidierung f (ReW) consolidation affecting net income
Ergibt-Anweisung f (EDV) assignment statement
ergiebige Steuer f (StR) tax yielding a large amount of revenue
Ergiebigkeit f (Bw) productivity
Ergiebigkeit f **des technischen Fortschritts** (Vw) yield of technical progress
Ergonomie f
  (IndE) ergonomics
  – human-factors engineering
ergonomischer Arbeitsplatz m
  (IndE) ergonomically designed workplace
  – workplace designed to fit man's physiological makeup
erhaltene Anzahlungen fpl
  (ReW) advance payments from customers
  – customer prepayments
  – advances received from customers
erhaltene Anzahlungen fpl **auf Bestellungen** (ReW, EG) payments received on account of orders
Erhaltungsaufwand m (StR) maintenance expenditure *(ie, fully tax allowable for the year in which payment was made, up to DM 4,000 – exclusive of VAT – for each building)*
Erhaltungsinvestition f (Bw) replacement investment
Erhaltungssubvention f (Vw) maintenance subsidy
Erhaltungswerbung f (Mk) maintenance advertising
Erhaltungszustand m (com) state of repair
Erhaltung f **von Arbeitsplätzen** (Pw) job preservation
erheben
  (StR) to charge
  – to levy
  – to impose
erheblicher Marktanteil m (Mk) substantial market share
erheblicher Umstand m (Re) material circumstance
erhebliche Schädigung f (AuW) material injury
erhebliche Vorteile mpl (com) substantial benefits
Erheblichkeitsschwelle f (Kart) relevance threshold
Erhebung f
  (Stat) survey
  – census
  (StR) collection
  – levying
  – charging
  – imposition
Erhebung f **durchführen** (Stat) to carry out a survey
Erhebung f **im Groß- und Einzelhandel** (Stat) census of distribution
Erhebung f **im produzierenden Gewerbe** (Stat) census of production
Erhebungsanalyse f (Stat) survey analysis
Erhebungsbogen m (Stat) questionnaire
Erhebungseinheit f (Stat) survey unit *(syn, statistische Einheit)*
Erhebungsfehler m
  (Stat) ascertainment error
  – error in survey
Erhebungsforschung f (Stat) observational (*or* survey) research
Erhebungsgebiet n (Stat) collection area
Erhebungsgesamtheit f (Stat) coverage
Erhebungskosten pl
  (Stat) cost of collection
  (StR) collection expenses
  – cost of collecting a tax
Erhebungsobjekt n (Stat) element of survey population
Erhebungsstichtag m (Stat) statistical reference date
Erhebungsverfahren n (Stat) collection method (*or* procedure)
Erhebungszeitraum m
  (Stat) survey period
  (Stat) check period
  – period of collection
  (StR) levying period, § 14 II GewStG
erhöhen
  (com) to increase *(eg, prices, wages)*
  – to raise
  – to advance
  – to lift
  – to put up
  (com, infml) to boost
  – to beef up
  – to bump up
  – to hike up
  – to step up
erhöhte Abschreibung f (ReW) increased depreciation
erhöhte Absetzungen fpl (StR) accelerated depreciation, § 7 b EStG
erhöhtes Risiko n
  (Vers) aggravated risk
  – classified risk
Erhöhung f
  (com) increase
  – rise
  – (US) raise
Erhöhung f **der Bestände** (MaW) inventory increase (*or* buildup)
Erhöhung f **des Bestandes** (ReW), EG) increase in stocks *(eg, of finished goods and work in progress)*
Erhöhung f **liquider Mittel** (Fin) increase in net funds
erholen, sich
  (com) to recover
  – to revive
  – (infml) to pick up
  (Bö) to rally
Erholung f
  (Vw) economic recovery
  – pickup *(ie, in economic activity)*
Erholung f **am Aktienmarkt** m (Bö) stock market rally
Erholung f **am Rentenmarkt** (Bö) bond market rally
Erholungszeit f (IndE) compensating rest
Erholungszeitzuschlag m (IndE) relaxation allowance
Erholungszuschlag m (IndE) fatigue allowance

Erinnerungsposten *m* (ReW) memorandum (*or* pro memoria) item
Erinnerungsschreiben *n* (com) follow-up letter
Erinnerungswerbung *f* (Mk) follow-up (*or* reminder) advertising
Erinnerungswert *m* (ReW) pro mem(oria) figure *(eg, to write down to the . . .)*
erkennbare Umstände *mpl* (com) recognizable facts
erkennen (ReW) to credit
 – to enter on the credit side
Erkenntnislogik *f* (Log) logic of knowledge
Erkennungsteil *m* (EDV, Cobol) identification division
Erkennungsverzögerung *f* (Vw) recognition lag
erklärende Definition *f* (Log) lexical definition
Erklärender *m* (Re) declaring person
 – person making a declaration
 – declarant
erklärende Variable *f* (Stat) explanatory variable
erklärter Zollwert *m* (Zo) declared value
Erklärung *f* (com) declaration
 – statement
Erklärung *f* **des Ausführers** (Zo) declaration by the exporter
Erklärung *f* **für die vorübergehende Ausfuhr** (Zo) temporary export declaration
Erklärung *f* **für die vorübergehende Einfuhr** (Zo) temporary importation declaration
Erklärung *f* **für die Wiedereinfuhr** (Zo) re-importation declaration
Erklärungsansatz *m* (Log) explanatory approach
Erklärungsbote *m* (Re) messenger transmitting a declaration
Erklärungsempfänger *m* (Re) addressee of declaration
Erklärungsfrist *f* (Re) time fixed for making a declaration
Erklärungsirrtum *m* (Re) mistake as to the expression of intention, § 119 I BGB
Erklärungsmittler *m* (Re) person transmitting declaration of intent
Erklärungstheorie *f* (Re) doctrine of declared intention *(eg, in formation of contract)*
Erklärungsvariable *f* (Log) explaining variable
Erklärungsversuch *m* (Log) approach
Erklärungswert *m* (Log) explanatory power (*or* usefulness)
Erklärungswille *m* (Re) will or intention to state something having legal consequences *(ie, creation, transfer, or extinction of a right)*
Erklärung *f* **zur Anweisung** (Zo) declaration of despatch in transit
Erklärung *f* **zur Feststellung des Einheitswerts** (StR) report disclosing the factual data on which the determination of the assessed value of property is based *(ie, to be filed as of each principal assessment date, § 28 I BewG)*
Erklärung *f* **zur gesonderten und einheitlichen Feststellung** (StR) statement of a separate and uniform determination

Erlaß *m* (Re) waiver of right to performance of contract, § 397 BGB
 (Re) decree
 – ordinance
 (StR) abatement *(eg, of assessed taxes)*
Erlaß *m* **der Eingangsabgaben** (Zo) remission of import duties and taxes
Erlaß *m* **e-r einstweiligen Verfügung** (Re) issue of a temporary injunction
Erlaß *m* **e-r Schuld** (Re) release (*or* remission) of a debt *(ie, by act of party = durch Rechtsgeschäft)*
erlassen (Re) to release
 – to remit *(ie, debt, liability)*
Erlaßvertrag *m* (Re) release agreement *(ie, informal agreement between creditor and debtor by which an obligation is gratuitously – ohne Gegenleistung – discharged, § 397 I BGB)*
Erlaubnis *f* **erlöscht** (Re) license expires
Erlaubnis *f* **erteilen** (Re) to issue a license
Erlaubniskartell *n* (Kart) authorized cartel
Erlaubnis *f* **versagen** (Re) to refuse a license
Erläuterungen *fpl* **zum Brüsseler Zolltarifschema** (Zo) Explanatory Notes to the Brussels Nomenclature
Erläuterungen *fpl* **zum Jahresabschluß** (ReW) notes to the annual (*or* year-end) financial statements
Erläuterungen *fpl* **zur Bilanz und zur G+V** (Re) notes to the financial statements
Erlebens-Rentenversicherung *f* (Vers) retirement income policy
Erlebensversicherung *f* (Vers) pure endowment insurance
Erlebenswahrscheinlichkeit *f* (Vers) average life expectancy
erledigen (com) to arrange for
 – to dispatch
 – to discharge
 – to see to it
 – to settle
Erledigung *f* (com) dispatch
 – discharge
 – settlement
Erledigung *f* **e-s Rechtsstreits** (Re) settlement of litigation
Erledigung *f* **des Versandvorganges** (Zo) termination of the customs transit operation
Erledigungsbescheinigung *f* (Zo) certificate of discharge
Erleichterung *f* **bewilligen** (StR) to grant relief *(eg, from statutory requirements)*
Erlös *m* (com) revenue
 – proceeds
 (ReW) revenue
Erlöschen *n* (Re) extinguishment (of a debt) *(ie, by operation of law)*
erloschene Firma *f* (Re) defunct firm
erloschene Forderung *f* (Re) extinct (*or* extinguished) claim
erloschene Gesellschaft *f* (Re) defunct company

erloschenes Patent *n* (Pat) extinct (*or* expired *or* lapsed) patent
Erlöschen *n* **e-r Hypothek** (Re) cancellation of a mortgage
Erlöschen *n* **e-r Steuerbefreiung** (StR) termination (*or* extinction) of tax exemption
Erlöschen *n* **e-r Versicherung** (Vers) expiration of an insurance policy
Erlöschen *n* **e-s Patents** (Pat) lapse (*or* expiry) of a patent
Erlöschen *n* **e-s Rechts** (Re) extinction of a right
Erlöse *mpl* **aus dem Verkauf von Fertigprodukten an andere Unternehmen** (VGR) finished goods sold to other enterprises
Erlöseinbuße *f* (Fin) fall (*or* drop) in sales revenue
Erlösfunktion *f* (Vw) revenue function
Erlöskonten *npl* (ReW) revenue accounts
Erlös *m* **maximieren** (Bw) to maximize revenue
Erlösmaximierung *f* (Bw) revenue maximization
Erlösmaximierung *f* **unter Nebenbedingungen** (Vw) constrained-revenue maximization
erlösmindernd (ReW) revenue-reducing
Erlösrechnung *f* (ReW) revenue accounting
Erlösschmälerungen *fpl*
  (ReW) sales deductions
  – reduction of proceeds
Erlössituation *f* (com) revenue picture *(eg, is improving)*
ermächtigen
  (Re) to authorize
  – to empower
Ermächtigter *m* (Re) authorized person
ermächtigter Ausführer *m* (Zo) approved exporter
ermächtigter Vertreter *m*
  (Re) authorized agent
  – agent acting on behalf of . . .
Ermächtigung *f*
  (Re) authorization
  (Re) authority
  – power
Ermächtigungsindossament *n* (WeR) indorsement for collection only
Ermächtigungsschreiben *n* (com) letter of authority
Ermächtigungsvorschriften *fpl* (Re) authorization provisions
ermäßigen
  (com) to reduce
  – to lower
  – to mark down
ermäßigte Gebühr *f* (com) reduced rate
ermäßigter Satz *m* (com) reduced rate
ermäßigter Steuersatz *m* (StR) reduced tax rate, § 12 II UStG
Ermäßigung *f*
  (com) allowance
  – reduction
  – markdown
Ermessensauswahl *f*
  (Stat) judgmental
  – convenience
  – nonprobability . . . sampling
Ermessensbereich *m* (Re) scope of discretion
Ermessensentscheidung *f* (StR) discretionary decision, § 102 FGO
Ermessensfrage *f* (Re) matter of discretion

Ermessensfreiheit *f*
  (Re) discretionary power
  – power of discretion
Ermessensmißbrauch *m* (Re) abuse of discretion
Ermessensreserven *fpl* (ReW) discretionary reserves
Ermessensspielraum *m* (Re) scope of discretion
Ermittlung *f* **der Erwartungen von Unternehmen und Haushalten** (Stat) anticipations survey
Ermittlung *f* **des Einkommens** (StR) determination of income
Ermittlung *f* **des Preises** (com) determination of price
Ermittlung *f* **des Zollwertes** (Zo) determination of the value for customs purposes
Ermittlung *f* **des zu versteuernden Einkommens** (StR) computation of taxable income
Ermittlungen *fpl* **führen** (Kart) to conduct investigations
Ermittlungszeitraum *m* (StR) period for which income is determined
Ermittlung *f* **von Amts wegen** (StR) examination (by the tax office) of the facts of a case on its own initiative (*or* motion), § 88 AO
Ermüdung *f* (Pw) fatigue
Ernannter *m* (com) appointee
ernennen (com) to appoint (as/to be) *(eg, to a post or vacancy, as/to be chairman of a board)*
Ernennung *f* (com) appointment
Ernennung *f* **auf Lebenszeit** (Pw) appointment for life
Ernennungsproblem *n* (OR) assignment problem
Ernennung *f* **widerrufen** (Re) to revoke an appointment
Erneuerung *f* (com) renewal *(eg, contract, loan)*
Erneuerungsbedarf *m* (Bw) replacement demand
Erneuerungsfonds *m* (ReW) = *Erneuerungsrücklage*
Erneuerungskonto *n* (ReW) renewal fund account
Erneuerungspolice *f* (Vers) renewal policy
Erneuerungsprämie *f* (Vers) renewal bonus
Erneuerungsrücklage *f* (ReW) renewal (*or* replacement) fund *(ie, a free reserve, § 58 AktG, set up to provide for increased prices of plant and equipment at the time of replacement)*
Erneuerungsschein *m*
  (Fin) renewal coupon
  – coupon sheet
  (syn, Talon, Leiste, Leistenschein)
Erneuerungswert *m* (ReW) replacement value
erneut zusammentreten
  (com) to meet again
  – to reconvene
Ernteüberschüsse *mpl* (EG) crop surpluses
Ernteversicherung *f* (Vers) crop insurance
Eroberungsdumping *n* (AuW) predatory dumping
eröffnen
  (com) to open
  – to set up *(eg, business)*
  (Fin) to open *(eg, account)*
  (Re) to open *(eg, legal proceedings)*
  (Pw) to offer *(eg, opportunities)*
eröffnende Bank *f* (Fin) opening (*or* issuing) bank *(ie, in the case of a letter of credit)*
Eröffnungsanweisung *f* (EDV) open statement

Eröffnungsbeschluß *m*
(Re) order for the commencement of proceedings
(Re) bankruptcy order, § 108 I KO *(ie, issued by the court in charge)*
– (US) adjudication of bankruptcy
Eröffnungsbestand *m* (ReW) opening balance
Eröffnungsbilanz *f* (ReW) opening balance sheet
Eröffnungsbuchung *f* (ReW) opening entry
Eröffnungskurs *m* (Bö) opening quotation
Eröffnungsnotierung *f* (Bö) = *Eröffnungskurs*
Eröffnungssatz *m* (Fin) daily opening rate
Eröffnungsschreiben *n* (Fin) advice of credit
Eröffnung *f* **von Zollpräferenzen** (Zo) opening of tariff preferences
Erpressung *f* (Re) extortion *(ie, demanding money with menaces, § 253 StGB)*
Erprobungsphase *f* (com) trial phase
Errechnung *f* **der Grundzeit** (IndE) extension
erreichbare Fertigungsgenauigkeit *f* (Stat) process capability
erreichbarer Nettoproduktivitätsvektor *m* (Vw) attainable point in commodity space
Erreichbarkeitsmatrix *f* (OR) reachability matrix
errichten
(com) to set up
– to establish
Errichtung *f* **e–r Gesellschaft** (Re) formation of a company
Errichtung *f* **e–r Zollunion** (AuW) establishment of a customs union
Ersatzaktie *f* (Fin) substitute share certificate, § 74 AktG
Ersatzanspruch *m*
(Re) damage claim
– claim for compensation
Ersatz *m* **barer Auslagen** (com) reimbursement of cash outlay
Ersatzbedarf *m* (Bw) replacement demand
Ersatzbeschaffung *f* (Bw) replacement
Ersatzbeschaffung *f* **aus Abschreibungen** (ReW) replacements funded from depreciation allowances
Ersatzbeschaffungsrücklage *f* (ReW) replacement reserve
Ersatzbescheinigung *f* (com) substitute certificate
Ersatz *m* **des tatsächlichen Schadens** (Re) compensatory damages
Ersatz *m* **erhalten** (Re) to recover for a loss
Ersatzgeschäft *n* (Re) substituted purchase
Ersatzgut *n* (Zo) compensating good
Ersatzindikator *m* (Vw, Bw) proxy indicator
Ersatzinvestition *f*
(VGR) reinvestment
(Bw) replacement investment
(Fin) capital spending on replacement
Ersatzkennzahl *f* (Vw, Bw) = *Ersatzindikator*
Ersatzkonto *n* (IWF) Substitution Account
Ersatzleistung *f*
(Re) indemnification
(Re) indemnity
– compensation
Ersatzlieferung *f* (com) substitute delivery
Ersatzmitglied *n* (Pw) substitute member *(ie, of works council)*

Ersatzpflicht *f* (Re) obligation to pay damages *(or* compensation)
Ersatzpflicht *f* **ausschließen** (Re) to preclude liability for damages
Ersatzpflichtiger *m* (Re) party liable
Ersatzproblem *n* (Bw) replacement problem
Ersatz-Reservewährung *f* (AuW) substitute reserve currency
Ersatzscheck *m* (Fin) replacement check
Ersatzstück *n* (Fin) replacement certificate
Ersatzteil *n*
(com) spare
– renewal
– replacement ... part
Ersatzteildienst *m* (MaW) spare parts service
Ersatzteile *npl* **einbauen** (IndE) to fit replacement parts
Ersatzteillager *n* (MaW) stock of spare *(or* replacement) parts
Ersatztheorie *f* (OR) replacement *(or* renewal) theory
Ersatzvariable *f* (Vw) proxy variable
Ersatz *m* **von Aufwendungen** (Re) reimbursement of outlay
Ersatz *m* **von Barauslagen** (com) reimbursement of cash expenses
Ersatz *m* **von Reisekosten** (Pw) reimbursement of travel cost
Ersatzwirtschaftsgut *n* (StR) replacement asset, Abschn. 35 II EStR
Ersatzzeiten *fpl* (SozV) fictitious qualifying periods, § 1251 RVO
Ersatzzeitpunkt *m* (Bw) reinvestment *(or* replacement) time
erschließen
(com) to develop *(eg, land)*
– to improve
(Mk) to open up *(ie, markets)*
Erschließung *f* (com) land development
Erschließungsabgabe *f* (FiW) development charge
Erschließungsanlagen *fpl* (com) land *(or* public) improvements
Erschließungsaufwendungen *fpl* (com) development and improvement costs
Erschließungsbedarf *m* (Mk) latent demand
Erschließungsbeitrag *m* (FiW) assessment *(ie, earlier term: Anliegerbeitrag)*
Erschließungsgebiet *n* (com) improvement area
Erschließungsgelände *n* (com) land ready for building
Erschließungskosten *pl*
(com) development costs
– cost of developing real estate
erschlossene Grundstücke *npl* (com) improved real property
erschlossenes Gelände *n* (com) developed *(or* improved) site
erschöpfende Aufzählung *f* (com) exhaustive enumeration
Erschöpfung *f* **des Rechtsweges** (Re) exhaustion of rights *(ie, a doctrine which is foreign to English law)*
Erschwerniszulage *f* (Pw) bonus for hazardous or unpleasant work

Ersetzungsbefugnis *f*
(Re) right to offer alternative performance
– *(civil law)* facultas alternativa
ersitzen (Re) to acquire by adverse possession
Ersitzung *f* (Re) adverse possession, §§ 937 ff BGB
– acquisitive prescription
(ie, acquisition of ownership by long possession)
Ersparnis *f* (Fin) savings
Ersparnisbildung *f* (Fin) formation of savings
Ersparnisse *fpl* **angreifen** (com) to dip into savings
Erstabsatz *m* **neu aufgelegter Wertpapiere** (Fin) initial sales of newly issued securities
Erstanmeldedatum *n* (Pat) first filing date
Erstanmeldung *f*
(Pat) original filing *(ie, of a patent application)*
(Pat) original application
erstatten
(com) to pay back
– to refund
– to reimburse
– to repay
– to return
Erstattung *f*
(com) refund
– repayment
– reimbursement *(eg, of cost or expenses)*
(Re) restitution *(ie, as a measure of damages)*
(StR) tax refund, § 37 II AO
Erstattung *f* **beantragen** (StR) to claim credit, § 36 II EStG *(eg, for corporate income tax)*
Erstattungsanspruch *m*
(Re) claim to reimbursement
(Re) claim to restitution
(StR) claim for refund, § 37 AO
Erstattungsantrag *m* (com) claim for repayment
Erstattungsbetrag *m* (com) amount of refund
erstattungsfähig
(com) recoverable
– refundable
– repayable
Erstattungsrückstände *mpl* (Fin) repayment arrears
Erstattungssatz *m* (com) rate of refund
Erstattung *f* **zuviel erhobener Beträge** (com) repayment of amounts overpaid
Erstauftrag *m* (com) first (*or* initial) order
Erstausfertigung *f* (com) original
Erstausgabepreis *m* (Bö) issuing price
Erstausstattung *f*
(com) initial supply
(WeR) first of exchange
(IndE) initial equipment
Erstbegünstigter *m* (Re) primary beneficiary
Erstbestellung *f* (com) first (*or* initial) order
erste Ableitung *f* (Math) first-order derivative
erste Adresse *f*
(Fin) top-quality (*or* top-rated) borrower
– quality borrower
– prime borrower (*or* firm)
– prime industrial firm
– firm with impeccable credit standing
erste Gefahr *f* (Vers) first (*or* initial) risk
erstehen
(com) to buy
– to purchase

ersteigern (com) to buy at an auction
erstellen
(com) to prepare
– to draw up
– to make up
Erstellung *f*
(com) preparation *(eg, report, balance-sheet)*
(EDV) creation *(ie, in file processing)*
Erstellung *f* **e–s konsolidierten Abschlusses** (ReW) consolidation
Erstellungskosten *pl* (com) cost of construction
erste Mahnung *f* (com) first reminder
erste partielle Ableitung *f* (Math) first-order partial derivative
erster Entwurf *m* (com) rough (*or* preliminary) draft
Ersterfassung *f*
(Stat) source data
– initial data
– original data
– primary data ... collection
Ersterfassungsbeleg *m* (ReW) source document
Ersterfinder *m* (Pat) original inventor
erster Grenzwertsatz *m* (Stat) first limit theorem
erster Kapitalaufwand *m* (Fin) initial capital outlay
erster Kurs *m* (Bö) initial quotation
Ersterwerb *m*
(Re) first acquisition *(eg, of membership rights)*
(Fin) purchase of newly issued securites
Ersterwerber *m*
(com) first buyer (*or* purchaser)
(Bö) original subscriber
Ersterwerb *m* **von Wertpapieren** (StR) initial acquisition of securities, § 22 KVStG
erstes Bestimmungsland *n* (com) first country of destination
erstes Gebot *n* (com) opening bid *(ie, at an auction)*
erste Wahl *f*
(com) prime quality
– (infml) firsts
erste Zahlungsaufforderung *f*
(com) first request to pay an amount due
(Fin) first call *(ie, going out to shareholders after allotment)*
Erstfinanzierung *f* (Fin) initial financing
Erstgebot *n* (com) first bid
Erstgüteprüfung *f* (Stat) original inspection
Ersthand-Leasing *n* (Fin) first-hand leasing
Ersthypothek *f*
(Re) first
– principal
– prior
– priority
– senior ... mortgage
erstinstanzliche Entscheidung *f* (Re) first-instance decision
Erstinvestition *f* (Fin) start-up investment
Erstkartenbahn *f* (EDV) primary feed
erstklassig
(com) first class
– first tier
– top flight
erstklassige Anlage *f* (Fin) prime investment
erstklassige Bank *f* (Fin, infml) blue-blooded bank

14 Schäfer, Wirtschaftsw. II

erstklassige Geldmarktpapiere *npl* (Fin) prime paper
erstklassiger Wechsel *m*
  (Fin) approved bill of exchange
  – fine bill
  – prime bill
erstklassige Schuldverschreibung *f*
  (Fin) top-line bond
  – high-grade bond
erstklassiges Material *n* (Fin) first-category paper
erstklassige Wertpapiere *npl* (Fin) top-grade securities
Erstkonsolidierung *f* (ReW) initial consolidation
erstmalig Arbeitsuchender *m*
  (Pw) first-time job seeker
  – entry-level job seeker
Erstplazierung *f* (Fin) initial placing of securities
Erstprämie *f* (Vers) first premium
erstrangiges Grundpfandrecht *n* (Re) first mortgage
erstrebte Mindestverzinsung *f* (Fin) minimum acceptable rate (of return)
Erstrisikoversicherung *f* (Vers) first loss insurance
Erstschrift *f* (com) original
Erstschuldner *m* (Re) primary debtor
erststellige Grundschuld *f* (Re) senior land charge
erststellige Hypothek *f* (Re) = *Ersthypothek*
erststellige Schuldverschreibung *f* (Fin) senior bond
erststellige Sicherheit *f* (Fin) first-charge security
Erstverkauf *m* (com) initial sale
Erstverpflichteter *m* (WeR) principal *(eg, guarantor, indorser)*
Erstversicherer *m*
  (Vers) original insurer
  – reinsured
  – reassured
  – ceding company
  (ie, in reinsurance; syn, Zedent, Direktversicherer)
Erstversicherung *f*
  (Vers) direct insurance
  – original insurance
  – primary insurance
Erstversicherungsgeschäft *n* (Vers) prime insurance business
Erstverwahrer *m* (Fin) original custodian
Erstzeichner *m* (Fin) original subscriber
Erstzeichnung *f* (Fin) initial subscription
Ersuchen *n* (Re) request
ersuchende Verwaltung *f* (Re) requesting administration
Erteilungsgebühr *f*
  (Pat) fee for the grant of a patent
  – patent fec
Ertrag *m*
  (Vw, Bw) output
  – yield
  (ReW) revenue *(opp, expenditure)*
  – earnings
  – proceeds
  – yield
  – income
Ertrag *m* **aus der Nominalverzinsung** (Fin) nominal yield

ertragbringend
  (com) earning
  – income-producing
  – profitable
ertragbringende Aktiva *npl* (Fin) earning assets *(eg, stocks and bonds; opp, cash or capital equipment)*
Ertrag *m* **des investierten Kapitals**
  (Fin) return on investment
  – return on capital employed
Erträge *mpl* (ReW, EG) income
Erträge *mpl* **aus Beteiligungen**
  (Fin) income from investments
  – investment income
  (ReW, EG) income from participating interests
Erträge *mpl* **aus Beteiligungen an Tochtergesellschaften** (Fin) income from subsidiaries
Erträge *mpl* **aus der Auflösung von Rückstellungen** (ReW) income from writing back provisions
Erträge *mpl* **aus festverzinslichen Wertpapieren** (Fin) receipts from bonds
Erträge *mpl* **aus Investmentanteilen** (Fin) income from investment shares
ertragloses Kapital *n* (Fin) dead assets
ertragreiche Anbausorten *fpl* (com) high-yield crops
ertragsabhängige Steuern *fpl* (StR) earnings-linked taxes
Ertragsabweichung *f* (KoR) yield variance *(ie, in standard costing)*
Ertragsanteil *m* (StR) interest portion of an annuity payment, § 9 I No. 1, § 22 No. 1a EStG
Ertragsaufteilung *f* (ReW) earnings apportionment
Ertragsausfall *m* (Fin) loss of earnings
Ertragsausschüttung *f* (Fin) distribution of earnings
Ertragsaussichten *fpl*
  (StR) earnings capacity *(eg, based on the average profits for a number of preceding years)*
  – prospective earnings
Ertragsbeteiligung *f* (Pw) profit sharing
Ertragsbewertung *f* (Fin) valuation of prospective earnings *(or* of earning power*)*
Ertragsbilanz *f* (ReW) = *Gewinn- und Verlustrechnung*
Ertragscontrolling *n* (ReW) revenue controlling *(ie, increase of revenues while keeping cost constant)*
Ertragsdifferenz *f* (Fin) yield differential
Ertragseinbruch *m* (Fin) sharp drop in earnings
Ertragseinbußen *fpl* (Fin) reductions in profit
Ertragsentwicklung *f*
  (Fin) trend of earnings *(or* profits*)*
  – trend of profitability
Ertragserwartungen *fpl* (com) earnings *(or* profit*)* expectations
Ertragsfähigkeit *f*
  (com) income productivity *(eg, of land)*
  (Fin) earning power
  – earning capacity value *(syn, Ertragskraft)*
Ertragsfunktion *f* (Vw, Bw) production function
Ertragsfunktion *f* **bei Niveauvariation** (Vw) returns-to-scale function
Ertragsgebirge *n* (Vw) (physical) production surface
Ertragsgesetz *n*
  (Vw) law of diminishing returns

- law of non-proportional returns
- law of variable proportions

Ertragsisoquanten *fpl* (Vw) revenue isoquants

Ertragskonsolidierung *f* (ReW) consolidation of earnings

Ertragskonto *n*
(ReW) revenue
- income
- nominal ... account

Ertragskraft *f*
(Fin) earning power
- earning capacity value
- profitability

Ertragskurve *f*
(Vw) total product curve
(Fin) yield curve *(ie, spread betwen long-term and short-term interest rates)*

Ertragslage *f*
(Fin) earnings *(or* operating) position *(eg, of a group of companies, § 329 II AktG)*
- income *(or* profit) situation
- profitability *(eg, remains under pressure)*

Ertragslage *f* **verbessern** (Fin) to improve profitability

Ertragsmarge *f* (com) profit margin

Ertragsminderung *f* (com) reduction of earnings *(or* profit)

ertragsorientiertes Budget *n* (FiW) performance budget

Ertragsrechnung *f*
(ReW) income statement
- statement of income

Ertragsrückgang *m* (Fin) drop in earnings

Ertragsschwelle *f* (Fin) break-even point

Ertragssituation *f*
(com) revenue picture *(eg, is worsening)*
(Fin) earnings situation

Ertragsspanne *f* (Fin) earnings margin *(ie, ratio of operating cost to average volume of business)*

Ertragssteigerung *f* (Fin) earnings growth

Ertragsströme *mpl* (Vw) flow of yields

Ertragsteuerbilanz *f* (ReW) earnings-tax balance sheet

Ertragsteuern *fpl* (StR) taxes on income *(or* earnings) *(ie, Einkommen-, Körperschaft- und Gewerbeertragsteuern)*

ertragsunabhängige Steuern *fpl* (StR) taxes independent of income

Ertrags- und Aufwandposten *mpl* (ReW) revenue and expense items

Ertragsverbesserung *f* (Fin) improvement of profitability

Ertragsvorschau *f* (Fin) profit and loss forecast

Ertragswert *m*
(Fin) capitalized value of potential earnings
- earning power
- earning capacity value

Ertragswertverfahren *n* (StR) gross rental method *(ie, value of property is determined by applying statutory multipliers to the annual rental, §§ 78ff BewG)*

Ertragszahlen *fpl* (Fin) operational figures *(ie, revenue and expense as reported in the statement of profit and loss)*

Ertragszentrum *n* (Fin) profit center

Ertragszinsen *mpl* (Fin) interest earned or received

erwartete Abweichung *f* (KoR) budgeted variance

erwartete Leistung *f* (Pw, IndE) expected attainment *(or* performance)

erwartete Mindestrendite *f*
(Fin) hurdle rate of return
- expected minimum rate of return

erwartete mittlere Nutzungsdauer *f* (Bw) anticipated average life *(ie, of a fixed asset item)*

erwartete Nutzungsdauer *f*
(Bw) expected useful life
- life expectancy

erwarteter Aufschwung *m* (Vw) anticipated economic upswing

Erwartungen *fpl* **zurücknehmen** (com) to scale back expectations

Erwartungen *fpl* **zurückschrauben** (SozV) to cool off popular expectations

Erwartungsgrad *m* (Stat) degree of rational belief

Erwartungshypothese *f* (Stat) expectation hypothesis

Erwartungsparameter *m* (Vw) expectation parameter

Erwartungstreue *f* (Stat) unbiasedness

Erwartungstreue *f* **e–r Schätzfunktion** (Stat) accuracy

erwartungstreue Schätzfunktion *f* (Stat) unbiased estimator

Erwartungswert *m*
(Stat) expected value
(Vw) anticipation term

erweiterte Aussagenlogik *f* (Log) extended propositional calculus *(ie, quantifiers whose operator variables are propositional variables are added)*

erweiterte Bandbreiten *fpl* (AuW) widened parity bands

erweiterte Fondsfazilität *f* (IWF) extended Fund facility

erweiterte Gemeinschaft *f* (EG) enlarged Community

erweiterte Hoheitszone *f* (Re) contiguous zone *(ie, in Sea Law)*

erweiterte Matrix *f* (Math) augmented matrix

erweiterte Mitbestimmung *f* (Pw) extended codetermination

erweiterter Arbeitscode *m* (EDV) augmented operation code

erweiterter Befehlsvorrat *m* (EDV) extended instruction set

erweiterter Binärcode *m* **für Dezimalziffern** (EDV) extended binary-code decimal interchange code

erweiterter Eigentumsvorbehalt *m* (Re) extended reservation of ownership

erweiterter Prädikatenkalkül *m* (Log) extended predicate *(or* functional) calculus

erweiterter Rohertrag *m* (ReW) amplified gross earnings

erweiterter Versicherungsschutz *m* (Vers) extended insurance coverage

erweiterte Steuerpflicht *f* (StR) extended tax liability

erweiterte Zugriffsmethode *f* (EDV) queued access method

Erweiterung *f* **der Arbeitsaufgaben** (Pw) job enlargement
Erweiterung *f* **der Haftung** (Re) extension of liability
Erweiterungsbedarf *m* (Mk) expansion demand
Erweiterungsinvestition *f*
 (Vw) capital widening
 (Bw) investment in new plant capacity
 – investment in the extension of productive capacity
 – expansion investment
 – capital expansion
 – capital expenditure expansion
Erweiterungskörper *m* (Math) extension of a field *(syn, Körpererweiterung, Oberkörper)*
Erwerb *m* (com) acquisition
Erwerb *m* **aus Konkursmasse** (Re) acquisition from the estate of a bankrupt
Erwerb *m* **eigener Aktien** (Re) acquisition of own shares, §§ 71, 305, 320 AktG
Erwerb *m* **e–r Kaufoption** (Bö) giving for the call
erwerben
 (com) to acquire
 – to buy
 – to earn
Erwerber *m*
 (com) buyer
 – purchaser
 (Re) transferee
 – vendee
 (Re) alienee *(ie, in real property law)*
 (StR) beneficiary, § 2 I ErbStG
 – donee
Erwerber *m* **e–r Sachgesamtheit** (Re) bulk transferee
Erwerbsberechtigter *m* (Re) authorized transferee
Erwerbsbeteiligung *f* (Vw) labor force participation
Erwerbsbevölkerung *f*
 (Stat) working population *(ie, employed and unemployed)*
 – economically (*or* gainfully) active population
erwerbsfähig
 (Pw) capable of work
 – employable
erwerbsfähiges Alter *n* (Pw) working (*or* employable) age
Erwerbsfähigkeit *f* (Pw) ability (*or* capacity) to work
Erwerbsgartenbau *m*
 (com) truck farming (*or* gardening)
 – (GB) market gardening
Erwerbsgenossenschaft *f* (Re) commercial cooperative
Erwerbskurs *m*
 (Fin) basis price
 (Bö) flat price *(ie, including accrued interest)*
Erwerbsleben *n* (Pw) working life
erwerbslos
 (Pw) unemployed
 – jobless
 – out of work
Erwerbslose *pl*
 (Pw) persons out of work
 – unemployed persons

Erwerbsminderung *f* (SozV) reduction in earning capacity, expressed in percent
Erwerbspersonen *fpl* (Stat) economically active population
Erwerbspersonenstatistik *f* (Stat) manpower statistics
Erwerbsquote *f*
 (Vw) activity rate
 – employee activity rate
 – labor force participation rate
 – employment rate
 – labor force activity
erwerbstätig (Stat) gainfully active (*or* employed)
Erwerbstätige *mpl* (Stat) wage and salary earners (*or* workers)
 – wage earners and salaried employees
 – persons in dependent employment
Erwerbstätigkeit *f*
 (Stat) gainful employment
 – remunerative occupation
erwerbsunfähig (SozV) incapable of self-support
 – incapacitated
Erwerbsunfähigkeit *f* (SozV) general disability *(ie, not ‚Berufsunfähigkeit' which is inability to work in one's occupation or profession)*
Erwerbsunfähigkeitsklausel *f*
 (Vers) disability clause
Erwerbsunfähigkeitsrente *f*
 (SozV) invalidism pension
 – pension for general disability *(ie, loss of earning capacity)*
Erwerb *m* **unter aufschiebender Bedingung** (StR) conditional transfer of property, § 9 I ErbStG
Erwerb *m* **unter Lebenden** (Re) acquisition inter vivos
Erwerb *m* **von Todes wegen** (Re) acquisition mortis causa
 (StR) transfer of property by reason of death, § 1 ErbStG
Erwerb *m* **von Wertpapieren durch Gebietsfremde** (Fin) nonresident purchase of securities
erwirken
 (Re) to secure
 – to sue out *(eg, order from court)*
erzeugen
 (com) to produce
 (EDV) to generate
Erzeugende *f* (Math) generatrix
erzeugendes Modell *n* (Stat) generating model
erzeugende Zeile *f* (OR) generating (*or* source) row
Erzeugerhandel *m*
 (com) direct acquisition and selling *(ie, by manufacturers)*
 (com) direct selling *(ie, with no intermediaries to the ultimate consumer)*
Erzeugerkosten *pl* (com) cost of production
Erzeugermitgliedstaat *m* (EG) producer Member State
Erzeugerpreis *m* (com) producer price
Erzeugerpreisindex *m* (Stat) producer price index
Erzeugerrichtpreis *m* (EG) producer target price
Erzeugersachkapital *n* (Vw) stock of capital
Erzeugnis *n* (com) product

Erzeugnisbestände mpl (ReW) inventories of finished and unfinished products
Erzeugnisfixkosten pl (KoR) product-traceable fixed cost
Erzeugnisgliederung f (Bw) product classification
Erzeugnisgruppe f (com) product group
Erzeugnisgruppenfixkosten pl (KoR) fixed cost traceable to product groups
Erzeugniskapazität f (Bw) product capacity *(opp, plant capacity = ‚Betriebskapazität' relating to the entire production program)*
Erzeugnispatent n (Pat) product patent
Erzeugnisplanung f (Bw) product planning
Erzeugnisspektrum n (com) product range
Erzeugung f (com) production
Erzeugungsgebiet n (com) production area
Erziehungszoll m (AuW) educational tariff
Erziehungszoll-Argument n (FiW) infant-industry argument
Es-gibt-nicht Satz m (Log) nonexistence statement
Es-gibt Satz m (Log) existential statement
Essensmarken fpl
 (Pw) lunch coupons
 – (GB) luncheon vouchers, L. V.
etablierte Konkurrenz f (com) established competitors
etablierte Wettbewerber mpl (com) competitors *(or rivals)* firmly established in the market
Etat m (FiW, Fin) budget
Etatansatz m
 (FiW) budget estimate
 (Fin) planned budget figure
etatisieren (FiW) to budget
Etatkunde m (Mk) (advertising) account
etatmäßig (FiW, Fin) budgetary
Etatmittel pl (FiW) budget funds
Etatrecht n (FiW) budget law
Etat-Spielraum m (FiW) budgetary scope
Etatüberschreitung f (FiW) spending in excess of appropriated funds
Etatzuweisung f (FiW) budget appropriation
Etikett n
 (com) ticket
 – tag
 (EDV) label
Etikettangaben fpl (EDV) label information
Etikettanweisung f (EDV) label statement
Etikettbehandlung f (EDV) label processing
Etiketterzeugung f (EDV) label generation
Etikettfehler m (EDV) label error
Etikettfeld n (EDV) label field
Etikettfolge f (EDV) label sequence
Etikettformat n (EDV) label format
Etikettgruppe f (EDV) label set
Etikettprüfprogramm n (EDV) label checking routine
Eulersches Theorem n (Math) adding-up theorem *(ie, in linear-homogeneous production functions)*
Euro-Anleihe f (Fin) Eurocurrency loan
Euro-Anleihemarkt m (Fin) Eurocurrency loan market
Eurobondmarkt m (Fin) Eurobond market
Eurobonds pl (Fin) Eurobonds
Euro-Devisen pl (Fin) Euro currencies
Euro-Dollar m (Fin) Eurodollar

Euro-Dollareinlagen fpl (Fin) Eurodollar deposits
Euro-Dollarkredit m (Fin) Eurodollar borrowing
Euro-Dollarmarkt m (Fin) Eurodollar market
Euro-Emission f (Fin) Euro issue (of bonds)
Euro-Geldmarkt m (Fin) Eurocurrency market
Euro-Geldmarktgeschäfte npl (Fin) Eurocurrency business (*or* transactions)
Euro-Kapitalmarkt m (Fin) Eurocapital market
Euro-Konsortialkredit m (Fin) syndicated Euroloan
Eurokraten mpl (EG) Eurocrats
Euro-Kreditaufnahme f (Fin) borrowing in the Eurocredit market
Eurokreditgeschäft n (Fin) Euromarket lending business
Euro-Kreditmarkt m (Fin) Eurocredit market
Europäische Artikelnumerierung f (Mk) European product coding, EAN
Europäische Ausfuhrbank f (EG) European Export Bank, EEB
Europäische Freihandelsassoziation f (AuW) European Free Trade Association, EFTA
Europäische Gemeinschaft f (EG) European Community
Europäische Gemeinschaft f für Kohle und Stahl (EG) European Coal and Steel Community, ECSC
Europäische Handelsgesellschaft f (EG) European trading company
Europäische Investitionsbank f (EG) European Investment Bank, EIB *(ie, set up by the EEC countries to encourage regional and economic integration, Luxembourg-based)*
europäische Parallelwährung f (EG) European parallel currency
Europäische Patentorganisation f (Pat) European Patent Organization
europäische Patentschrift f (Pat) specification of the European patent
Europäischer Ausrichtungs- und Garantiefonds m Landwirtschaft (EG) European Agricultural Guidance and Guarantee Fund
Europäische Rechnungseinheit f (AuW) European unit of account, EUA
Europäischer Entwicklungsfonds m (EG) European Development Fund, EDF
Europäischer Fonds m für währungspolitische Zusammenarbeit (EG) European Monetary Cooperation Fund, EMCF
Europäischer Sozialfonds m (EG) European Social Fund, ESF
Europäischer Währungsfonds m (EG) European Monetary Fund, EMF
Europäischer Wechselkursverbund m (Fin) Currency Snake
Europäischer Wirtschaftsrat m (EG) European Economic Council
Europäisches Forschungsinstitut n für Wirtschafts- und Sozialpolitik (EG) European Economic and Social Policy Research Institute
Europäisches Patent n (Pat) = *Europa-Patent*
Europäisches Patentamt n (Pat) European Patent Office
Europäisches Patentregister n (Pat) Register of European Patents

213

Europäisches Patentübereinkommen n (Pat) European Patent Convention, EPC
Europäisches Währungsabkommen n (AuW) European Monetary Agreement, EMA
Europäisches Währungssystem n (EG) European monetary system, EMS
Europäische Union f (EG) European union
Europäische Währungseinheit f (EG) European Currency Unit, ECU, ecu
Europäische Wirtschaftsgemeinschaft f (EG) European Economic Community, EEC
Europäische Zahlungsunion f (AuW) European Payments Union, EPU
Europäische Zollunion f (AuW) European Customs Union, ECU
Europa-Patent n (Pat) Europatent *(ie, granted for a term of 20 years)*
Euro-Pfund n (Fin) Euro sterling
Euroschlange f (AuW) European snake *(ie, snake in the tunnel + blockfloating)*
Euro-Währung f (AuW) Eurocurrency
Euro-Währungskredit m (Fin) Eurocurrency loan
Euro-Währungsmarkt m (Fin) Eurocurrency market
Euro-Zinsen mpl (Fin) Euromarket interest rates
E-Urteil n
 (Log) E-proposition
 – alternative denial
 – universal negative
Evaluierung f
 (AuW) project evaluation
 – control of implementation of industrial projects *(ie, in developing countries)*
Eventualbudget n (FiW) = *Eventualhaushalt*
Eventualfonds m (Fin) contingent fund
Eventualforderung f (Re) contingent claim
Eventualhaftung f (Re) contingent liability
Eventualhaushalt m (FiW) contingency budget *(ie, prepared for fiscal policy purposes)*
Eventualplan m (Bw, FiW) contingency plan
Eventualplanung f (FiW, Bw) contingency *(or alternative)* planning
Eventualverbindlichkeit f (ReW) contingent liability
Evidenzzentrale f (Fin) Central Risk Office, § 14 KWG
EWG-Vertrag m
 (EG) EEC Treaty
 – Treaty of Rome
EWG-Waren fpl (EC) EEC products
ewige Rente f (Fin) perpetuity *(ie, an annuity that continues forever)*
exakt identifiziert (Log) uniquely identified
Examensarbeit f (Pw) examination paper *(or GB: script)*
ex ante-Analyse f (Vw) ex ante analysis
ex ante-Beziehungen fpl (Vw) ex ante constructions
ex ante-Ersparnis f (Vw) planned savings
ex ante-Größe f (Vw) anticipation term
ex Berichtigungsaktien (Bö) ex capitalization issue
ex Bezugsaktien (Bö) ex cap(italization)
ex Bezugsrecht (Bö) ex allotment *(or rights)*
ex Dividende
 (Bö) dividend off
 – coupon detached
 – ex dividend *(or ex-d)*
Exemplar n **Abgang** (EG) departure copy
Exemplar n **Bestimmung** (EG) destination copy
Exemplar n **für statistische Zwecke** (EG) copy for statistical purposes *(ie, in Community transit operations)*
Exim-Regelung f (com) exim arrangements
Existenzgrundlage f (StR) essential basis for gaining a livelihood, § 69 II BewG
Existenzminimum n
 (Vw) subsistence level
 – minimum survival needs
Existenzminimumtheorie f **des Lohnes** (Vw) subsistence theory
Existenzoperator m (Log) existential *(or particular)* quantifier
Existenzsatz m **für Fixpunkte** (OR) fixed-point theorem
Exklusion f (Log) alternative *(or joint)* denial
Exklusivbetrieb m (Mk) exclusive dealing
exklusive Disjunktion f (Log) nonequivalence
exklusives ODER-Glied n (EDV) = *ODER-Glied*
exklusives Segment n (EDV) exclusive segment
Exklusivrecht n (com) exclusive dealing right
Exklusivvertrag m
 (com) exclusive rights contract
 (Kart) exclusive purchasing agreement
Exkulpationsbeweis m (Re) exculpatory proof
exkulpieren
 (Re) to exculpate
 – to exonerate
ex Kupon (Bö) ex coupon
Exnotierung f (Bö) quotation ex ... *(eg, rights)*
exogene Bestimmungsgröße f (Vw) exogenous determinant
exogene Finanzierung f (Fin) external financing *(ie, equity + debt)*
exogene Konjunkturtheorie f (Vw) exogenous *(or external)* business cycle theory
exogenes Geld n
 (Vw) monetary base
 – primary money
 (ie, central bank money + demand deposits with central bank; syn, Geldbasis, monetäre Basis, Primärgeld)
exogene Variable f (Vw) exogenous variable
exogene Zufallsvariable f (Stat) exogenous variate
Exoten pl
 (Bö) securities offered by issuers from exotic countries
 (Bö) speculative papers *(ie, unlisted and outside over-the-counter business)*
expandierender Markt m (com) growing *(or expanding)* market
Expansion f (Vw, Bw) expansion
Expansionsgrenze f (Vw) ceiling
Expansionskurve f (Vw) expansion curve *(ie, locus of all least cost combinations resulting from constant factors prices and successive output variations)*
Expansionsmultiplikator m (Vw) expansion multiplier
Expansionspfad m (Vw) expansion path

Expansionsrate *f* (Vw) rate of growth (*or* expansion)
expansive Einflüsse *mpl* (Vw) expansionary forces
expansive Fiskalpolitik *f* (FiW) expansive fiscal policy
expansive Geldpolitik *f* (Vw) expansionary monetary policy
expansive Haushaltspolitik *f* (FiW) expansionary budget policy
expansive Impulse *mpl* (Vw) expansionary impact
expansive Lohnpolitik *f* (Vw) expansionary wages policy *(ie, suggested by labor unions)*
expansive Offenmarktpolitik *f* (Fin) expansionary open market policy
expansiver Prozeß *m* (Vw) expansionary movement (*or* process)
– business cycle expansion
Expedient *m* (com) dispatcher
Expedition *f*
(com) forwarding
– shipping
Expeditionsabteilung *f* (com) forwarding (*or* shipping) department
Experiment *n* **durch Versuch und Irrtum** (Log) trial and error
Experte *m*
(com) expert
– specialist
Expertengruppe *f* (com) panel of experts
Expertise *f* (com) expert opinion
explizite Adresse *f* (EDV) explicit address
explizite Definition *f* (Log) explicit definition
explizite Funktion *f* (Math) explicit function
explosive Oszillation *f* (Vw) explosive oscillation
explosive Schwingung *f* (Vw) = *explosive Oszillation*
explosives Cobweb *n* (Vw) explosive cobweb
Exponent *m* (Math) exponent
Exponentialgleichung *f* (Math) exponential equation
Exponentialkurve *f* (Math) exponential curve
Exponentiallag *m* (Vw) exponential lag
Exponentialtrend *m* (Vw) exponential trend *(syn, logarithmischer Trend)*
exponentialverteilte Abfertigungszeit *f* (OR) exponential holding time
exponentialverteilte Zwischenankunftszeiten *fpl* (OR) exponential interarrival times
Exponentialverteilung *f* (Math) exponential distribution
exponentielle Beziehung *f* (Math) exponential (*or* curvilinear) relationship
exponentielle Dichte *f* (Stat) exponential density
exponentielle Glättung *f* (Stat) exponential smoothing
exponentielle Glättung *f* **erster Ordnung** (Stat) first-order exponential smoothing
exponentielle Glättung *f* **zweiter Ordnung** (Stat) second-order exponential smoothing
exponentieller Bedienungskanal *m* (OR) exponential service channel
exponentielles Wachstum *n* (Vw) exponential growth
Export *m*
(AuW) exportation

(AuW) exports
exportabgabepflichtig (AuW) liable to export duty
exportabhängige Beschäftigung *f* (Vw) base employment *(ie, of a region)*
Exportabhängigkeit *f* (AuW) export dependency
Exportabteilung *f* (AuW) export department
Exportagent *m* (AuW) export agent
Exportakkreditiv *n* (Fin) export letter of credit (*or* L/C)
Exportangebot *n* (AuW) export offer
Exportanteil *m* (AuW) export content
Exportartikel *m* (AuW) export article (*or* item)
Exportauftrag *m* (AuW) export order
Exportbasis *f* (AuW) export base
Exportbasis-Analyse *f* (Vw) base analysis
Exportbasisanteil *m* (Vw) base component
Exportbasiseinkommen *n* (Vw) basic income
Exportbasisindustrie *f* (Vw) basic industry
Exportbasis-Multiplikator *m* (Vw) base multiplier
Exportbasis-Sektor *m* (Vw) basic sector
Exportbasis-Theorie *f*
(Vw) base theory
– economic base concept
Exportbedingungen *fpl* (AuW) export terms
Exportbeschränkungen *fpl* (AuW) export restraints (*or* restrictions)
Exportbestimmungen *fpl* (AuW) export regulations
Exportbonus *m* (AuW) export bonus *(ie, subsidy or special benefit or credit)*
Exportbürgschaft *f* (AuW) export guaranty
Exportdeklaration *f* (Zo) entry outwards
Exportdevisen *pl* (AuW) foreign exchange resulting from export transactions
Exportdokumente *npl* (AuW) export documents
Exporte *mpl* **behindern** (AuW) to hamstring exports *(eg, with countervailing duties)*
Export *m* **entwickelter Länder an Entwicklungsländer** (AuW) downstream trade
Exporterlös *m*
(AuW) export earnings (*or* proceeds)
– proceeds from exports
Exporteur *m*
(AuW) exporter
– export firm
Exportfinanzierung *f* (Fin) export financing
Exportfinanzierungsinstrumente *npl* (Fin) export financing instruments
Exportfirma *f* (AuW) export trader
Exportförderung *f* (AuW) export promotion
Exportförderungskredit *m* (Fin) export promotion credit
Exportgemeinschaft *f* (AuW) export association
Exportgeschäft *n* (AuW) export business
(AuW) export transactions
Exportgeschäft *n* **abwickeln** (AuW) to process an export transaction
Exportgeschäft *n* **finanzieren** (Fin) to finance an export transaction
Exportgüterstruktur *f* (Vw) commodity pattern
Exporthandel *m* (AuW) export trade
Exporthändler *m* (AuW) export merchant
exportieren (AuW) to export
exportierte Arbeitslosigkeit *f* (Vw) exported unemployment

Exportindustrie f (AuW) export industry
exportinduziert (Vw) export-led
exportinduzierter Aufschwung m (Vw) export-led recovery
exportinduziertes Wachstum n (Vw) export-led expansion (or growth)
Exportinformationen fpl (AuW) export intelligence
Exportintensität f (AuW) export intensity *(ie, ratio of exports to total production, see ‚Exportquote')*
exportintensive Branche f (AuW) export intensive industry
exportintensive Industrie f (AuW) export-intensive industry
Exportkalkulation f (AuW) export cost accounting
Exportkartell n (Kart) export-promoting cartel
Exportkatalog m (AuW) export catalog
Exportkommissionär m (AuW) export commission agent
Exportkonnossement n (AuW) outward bill of lading
Exportkontingent n (AuW) export quota
Exportkredit m (Fin) export (trade) credit
Exportkredit-Vereinbarungen fpl (AuW) export credit arrangements
Exportkreditversicherung f (Fin) export credit insurance *(eg, Hermes in Germany, ECGD in Great Britain)*
Exportkunde m (AuW) export customer
Exportland n (AuW) exporting country
Exportleiter m
 (AuW) head of export department
 – export sales manager
Exportlizenz f (AuW) export license
Exportmakler m (AuW) export agent *(syn, Ausfuhragent)*
Exportmarkt m (AuW) export market
Exportmesse f (AuW) export exhibition (or fair)
Exportmöglichkeiten fpl (AuW) export opportunities
Exportmultiplikator m (AuW) export multiplier
Exportneigung f (Vw) propensity to export
Export m **ohne Gegenleistung** (AuW) unrequited exports
exportorientierte Wirtschaft f
 (AuW) export-oriented economy
 (AuW) export trade
Exportpolitik f (AuW) export policy
Exportpotential n (AuW) export potential
Exportprämie f (AuW) export bounty *(ie, paid by government or private associations to promote the exportation of specific goods)*
Exportpraxis f (AuW) export practice
Exportpreis m (AuW) export price
Exportquote f (AuW) export-income ratio *(ie, assets side of trade balance to gnp at market prices)*
 (VGR) net exports of goods and services *(syn, Außenbeitrag)*
 (Vw) propensity to export
 (AuW) export quota per period
 (Bw) export share *(ie, of sales abroad to total sales)*
Exportrestriktionen fpl (AuW) export restrictions
Exportrisiko n (AuW) export-related risk

Exportrisikohaftung f (AuW) export risk liability
Export-Schutzversicherung f (Vers) (additional) insurance of exports
Exportselbstbehalt m (AuW, Fin) exporter's retention *(ie, share of financing)*
Exportselbstbeschränkung f (AuW) voluntary export restraint
Exportsperre f (AuW) export embargo
Exportsteuer f (StR) export levy *(ie, on products destined for export, 4%; syn, Sonderumsatzsteuer; inapplicable as of 11 Oct 1969)*
Exportstruktur f (AuW) structure of the export industry
Exportsubvention f (AuW) export subsidy
Exporttratte f (Fin) export draft
Exportüberschuß m (AuW) export surplus
Exportverbot n (AuW) export ban
Exportverpackung f (AuW) export packing
Exportversicherung f
 (Vers) export insurance
 – insurance of exports
Exportvertreter m (AuW) export agent
Export m **von Arbeitslosigkeit** (Vw) beggar-my-neighbor policy *(ie, attempts to switch a certain amount of unemployment to other countries)*
Exportware f (AuW) exported articles
Exportwelle f
 (AuW) export wave
 – surge of export orders
Exportwerbung f (AuW) export advertising
Exportwirtschaft f
 (AuW) export sector
 – export business
 – export trade
Exportzoll m (Zo) export duty
ex post-Analyse f (Vw) ex post-analysis *(eg, national accounting)*
ex post-Analyse f **des Volkseinkommens** (Vw) ex-post analysis of national income
Expreßgut n (com) express consignment
Expreßgutschein m (com) express parcels consignment note
Extension f
 (Log) extension *(ie, of a concept)*
 – domain of applicability
extensionale Definition f (Log) extensional (or denotative) definition
extensionale Logik f (Log) extensional logic *(ie, one in which truth-values may be substituted for sentences)*
extensionaler Junktor m (Log) extensional connective
extensionale Semantik f (Log) theory of reference
Extensionalitätsaxiom n (Log) axiom of extensionality
extensive Auswahl f (Stat) extensive sampling
Externalitäten fpl
 (Vw) external effects
 – externalities
 – neighborhood effects
 – spillovers
externe Adresse f (EDV) external address
externe Aufwendungen pl (ReW, EG) external charges
externe Effekte mpl (Vw) = *Externalitäten*

externe Informationsquelle *f* (Bw) external source of information *(eg, competitors, markets)*
externe Kosten *pl*
(Vw) social costs
– discommodities
externe Leistungen *fpl* (ReW) external performance
externe Nachteile *mpl* (Vw) external diseconomies
externer Arbeitsmarkt *m* (Pw) external labor market
externer Bilanzvergleich *m* (ReW) external balance sheet comparison *(ie, covering several firms in the same industry, of about the same size, and for the same period)*
externe Referenz *f* (EDV) external reference
externe Revision *f* (ReW) external *(or* independent*)* audit
externer gemeinschaftlicher Versandschein *m* (EG) external Community transit document
externer Konsumeffekt *m* (Vw) external effects of consumption *(ie, bandwagon effect = ‚Mitläufereffekt', snob effect, and Veblen effect)*
externer Speicher *m* (EDV) external *(or* peripheral*)* storage
externe Sortierung *f* (EDV) offline sorting
externe Steuerung *f* (EDV) external control
externes Wachstum *n* (Bw) external growth

externe Umwelt *f* (Bw) external environment
externe Unterbrechung *f* (EDV) external interrupt
externe Verschuldung *f* (FiW) borrowing abroad
externe Verzögerung *f* (EDV) external delay
externe Vorteile *mpl* (Vw) external benefits *(or* economies*)*
Extrapolation *f* (Math) extrapolation
Extrarisiko *n* (Vers) special risk
Extratara *f* (com) additional packing required for prolonged transportation
extraterritoriale Anwendung *f* (Kart) extraterritorial application *(eg, of competition rules)*
Extremalpunkt *m* (Math) extreme point
Extremkostenversicherung *f* (Vers) catastrophic coverage
Extremwert *m* **e-r Funktion** (Math) extreme *(or* extremum*)* of a function *(ie, maxiumum or minimum value)*
Exzedent *m* (Vers) excess of line *(or* loss*)*
Exzedentenfranchise *f* (Vers) free from average in excess of ... pct
Exzedentenrückversicherung *f*
(Vers) excess loss insurance
– surplus treaty reinsurance
ex Ziehung (Bö) ex drawing
ex Zinsen (Fin) without interest

F

Fabrik *f*
(IndE) factory
– manufacturing plant
– plant
(IndE) factory building(s)
(Pw) labor force of a factory
Fabrikabgabepreis *m* (com) price ex works
Fabrikanlage *f* (IndE) factory *(ie, including site, buildings, and all other facilities)*
Fabrikant *m*
(com) manufacturer
(com) factory owner
Fabrikarbeit *f*
(com) factory work
(Pw) activity of a factory worker
Fabrikarbeiter *m*
(Pw) factory worker
– *(euphem)* operative
Fabrikarbeiterin *f*
(Pw) female factory worker *(or* operative*)*
Fabrikat *n*
(com) product
– make
– brand
(IndE) manufactured product
Fabrikategemeinkosten *pl*
(KoR) product overhead
– indirect cost of work in progress and finished products
Fabrikategruppe *f* (IndE) product group
Fabrikategruppenleiter *m* (IndE) product group manager

Fabrikatekonto *n* (ReW) finished products account *(ie, in the ‚Gemeinschaftskontenrahmen' = joint account classification, placed between the manufacturing and sales accounts)*
Fabrikation *f*
(IndE) *(older term for ‚Produktion':)* production
– manufacturing
Fabrikationsanforderungen *fpl* (IndE) manufacturing requirements
Fabrikationsanlagen *fpl* (IndE) manufacturing facilities
Fabrikationsauftrag *m* (IndE) production order
Fabrikationsbetrieb *m* (IndE) small-sized manufacturing establishment *(ie, often affiliated to a larger enterprise and specialized in making a single product)*
Fabrikationsdampf *m* (IndE) process steam
Fabrikationseinrichtungen *fpl*
(IndE) production facilities
– plant equipment
Fabrikationsgeheimnis *n* (IndE) industrial secret
Fabrikationsgemeinkosten *pl* (KoR) manufacturing overhead *(or* expense*)*
Fabrikationsgrundstück *n* (IndE) manufacturing premises
Fabrikationskonto *n*
(ReW) work-in-process account
– goods-in-progress account
(ReW) process account
Fabrikationskosten *pl* (KoR) production *(or* manufacturing*)* cost
Fabrikationsleiter *m* (IndE) production manager

Fabrikationsnummer *f* (com) serial number
Fabrikationsprogramm *n*
(IndE) manufacturing program *(ie, together with the sales program it makes up the overall production program)*
(com) total number of orders scheduled for a certain plant planning period
Fabrikationsstätte *f*
(IndE) production plant
– factory
Fabrikationssteuer *f* (FiW) production tax *(ie, special mode of levying a consumption tax, based on features such as raw materials, equipment, semi-finished products; syn, Produktionsteuer)*
Fabrikationsverfahren *n* (IndE) manufacturing process
Fabrikationszweig *m* (IndE) branch (*or* line) of production
Fabrikatsteuer *f* (FiW) product tax *(ie, another type of consumption tax levied on the product as it leaves the production facilities; eg, mineral oil, tobacco, playing cards)*
Fabrikbauten *pl*
(IndE) factory buildings
– plant facilities
Fabrikbesitzer *m* (com) factory owner
Fabrikbuchhaltung *f*
(ReW) factory accounting *(ie, accounting system based on a special account classification plan)*
(ReW) *(obsolete term replaced by ‚Betriebsbuchhaltung' =)* cost accounting
Fabrikdirektor *m* (Pw) factory manager
Fabrikeinrichtung *f* (IndE) factory equipment
Fabrikenplanung *f*
(IndE) planning and design of factories
(IndE) *(= Raumplanung)* intra-plant layout
Fabrikgebäude *n*
(ReW) factory (*or* plant) building
– factory premises
– industrial building
Fabrikgelände *n* (com) factory site
Fabrikgleis *n*
(com) siding (*or* sidetrack) *(ie, opening onto main track at both ends)*
(com) spur (*or* stub) track *(ie, connected to main track at one end only)*
Fabrikgrundstück *n* (com) factory (*or* plant) site
Fabrikhalle *f* (IndE) factory (*or* plant) building
Fabrikhandel *m*
(com) direct purchasing from producer
(com) direkt selling to final user
Fabrikklausel *f* (com) ex factory clause
Fabrikleitung *f* (IndE) factory management
Fabrikleitungsgemeinkosten *pl* (KoR) plant management overhead
Fabrikmarke *f* (Mk) manufacturer's brand *(opp, Handelsmarke)*
fabrikmäßig (com) industrial *(eg, production)*
fabrikmäßig herstellen (IndE) to manufacture
Fabrikmusterlager *n* (com) permanent display of sample *(ie, by producer or in main marketing centers, representing entire production program)*
fabrikneu
(com) brand-new
– straight from the factory

– virgin
Fabrikpreis *m*
(com) price ex works
(Mk) factory price *(ie, based on cost price plus profit markup)*
Fabrik *f* **stillegen** (com) to close down a factory
Fabrik *f* **unter Zollverschluß**
(com) bonded factory
– bonded manufacturing warehouse
Fach *n*
(Log) subject matter
(com) special area (*or* field)
Fachabteilung *f* (Bw) operating department *(eg, accounting, organization, marketing)*
Fachanwalt *m* (Re) specialized lawyer
Fachanwalt *m* **für Steuerrecht** (StR) tax lawyer
Facharbeiter *m* (Pw) skilled worker *(ie, has served formal apprenticeship in a particular occupation or trade and passed a qualifying examination)*
Facharbeiter *mpl*
(Pw) skilled workers
– skilled labor
– skilled manpower
Facharbeiterbrief *m* (Pw) skilled worker's certificate *(ie, obtained by passing an examination at the end of the apprenticeship)*
Facharbeiterlohn *m* (Pw) wage of skilled worker
Fachaufsicht *f* (Re) government supervision of certain economic branches *(opp, Dienstaufsicht)*
Fachausbildung *f* (Pw) special (*or* technical) training
Fachausdrücke *mpl*
(Log) technical terms
– words of art
Fachausschuß *m*
(com) technical committee
– committee of experts
– professional committee
Fachausstellung *f* (Mk) trade show
Fachberater *m* (com) technical consultant
Fachbereich *m* (com) special field (*or* line *or* domain)
Fachbericht *m* (com) technical report
Fachblatt *n*
(com) technical journal
(com) trade journal
(com) professional journal
Facheinzelhandel *m* (com) specialized retail trade
Facheinzelhändler *m* (com) specialized retail dealer
Fachgebiet *n* (com) special field (*or* line *or* domain)
Fachgeschäft *n*
(com) specialty store
– single-line retail store
– (GB) specialist shop
Fachgespräch *n* (com) expert (*or* technical) discussion
Fachgremium *n* (com) expert body (*or* group)
Fachgroßhandel *m* (com) specialist wholesaling trade
Fachgroßhändler *m* (com) specialist wholesaler
Fachgruppe *f*
(com) special group
– working party
Fachgutachten *n* (com) expert opinion

Fachgütermesse *f* (Mk) specialized trade fair
Fachhandel *m* (com) specialized trade
Fachhändler *m* (com) specialized dealer
Fachhochschule *f* (Pw, appr) senior technical college
Fachingenieur *m* (Pw) specialist engineer
Fachjargon *m* (Log) technical jargon
Fachkaufmann *m* (Pw) operational specialist at middle-management level *(eg, in balance-sheet and cost accounting, personnel, materials control)*
Fachkenntnisse *fpl* (Pw) specialized (*or* technical) knowledge *(ie, resulting from job training + job experience)*
Fachkompetenz *f* (Pw) technical competence
Fachkraft *f*
 (Pw) skilled worker
 – specialist
Fachkräfte *fpl*
 (Pw) skilled labor (*or* personnel)
 – specialized labor
 – qualified operators (*or* personnel)
 (Pw) specialist staff
Fachleute *pl*
 (Pw) experts
 – specialists
 – persons knowledgeable in a specialized field
fachliche Eignung *f* (Pw) professional qualification
fachliche Mobilität *f* (Pw) occupational mobility
fachliche Qualifikation *f* (Pw) professional qualification
fachliches Können *n* (Pw) technical competence (*or* expertise)
fachliche Vorbildung *f* (Pw) professional background
fachliche Zwecke *mpl* (com) specialist purposes
fachlich geeignet (Pw) professionally (*or* technically) qualified
Fachliteratur *f* (com) specialized (*or* technical) literature
Fachmann *m*
 (Pw) expert
 – specialist
 – authority *(eg, in the field)*
 (Pat) average person familiar with the art
Fachmarkt *m* (Mk) specialized discount store
Fachmesse *f* (Mk) trade fair (*or* show)
Fachnorm *f* (IndE) special standard *(ie, for a special segment of production; eg, ribbon cartridges for typewriters)*
Fachpersonal *n* (Pw) skilled personnel (*or* staff)
Fachpresse *f* (com) trade press
Fachsprache *f*
 (Log) technical (*or* professional) language
 – technical terminology
Fachtagung *f* (com) special (*or* trade) conference
Fachtechnik *f* (IndE) special engineering
Fachübersetzer *m* (com) technical (*or* specialized) translator
Fachübersetzung *f* (com) technical translation
Fachunternehmer *m* (com) specialized enterprise
Fachverband *m*
 (com) trade association
 (com) professional association
Fachverkäufer *m*
 (com) trained salesclerk
 – (GB) trained salesman
Fachvorgesetzter *m* (Pw) operating supervisor
Fachwelt *f*
 (com) profession
 – experts
 – trade
Fachwort *n* (Log) technical term
Fachwörterbuch *n* (Log) specialized dictionary
Fachzeitschrift *f*
 (com) professional
 – technical
 – trade ... journal
Façonwert *m* (Bw) goodwill
Factoring *n* (Fin) factoring *(ie, buying of accounts receivable)*
Factoring-Gebühr *f* (Fin) factor's commission
Factoring-Institut *n*
 (Fin) factor
 – factoring company
Factoring *n* **mit Kreditrisiko und Forderungsverwaltung** (Fin) maturity factoring
Factoringvertrag *m* (Re) factoring agreement *(ie, sale of accounts receivable of a firm to a factor = ‚Finanzierungsinstitut' at a discounted price)*
facultas alternativa *f* (Re) right to offer alternative performance, § 251 II BGB *(syn, Ersetzungsbefugnis)*
Fadendiagramm *n* (Stat) string diagram
Fähigkeit *f* (Pw) skill
Fähigkeiten *fpl* (Pw) skills and abilities
Fahndungsdienste *mpl* (Zo) investigation services
Fahnenabzug *m* (com) galley proof
fahren
 (IndE) to run
 – to operate
 – to use
fahrende Ladung *f* (com) revenue freight
Fahrgelderstattung *f* (com) reimbursement of travel expenses
Fahrgemeinschaft *f* (com) ride-sharing group *(ie, as a measure to conserve energy)*
Fahrkarte *f* **einfach**
 (com) one-way ticket
 – (GB) single
fahrlässig (Re) negligent
fahrlässige Handlung *f* (Re) negligent act
fahrlässige Steuerumgehung *f* (StR) negligent tax avoidance
fahrlässig handeln (Re) to act negligently
Fahrlässigkeit *f*
 (com) want of proper care
 (Re) negligence *(ie, failure to use such care as a reasonable and prudent person would use under similar circumstances, § 276 BGB)*
Fahrnis *f*
 (Re) movable (*or* personal) property
 – personal estate (*or* chattel)
 – personalty
Fahrnishypothek *f* (Re) chattel mortgage
Fahrnisversicherung *f* (Vers) insurance of movable property
Fahrnisvollstreckung *f* (Re) seizure and sale of movable property

Fahrradversicherung f (Vers) bicycle insurance
Fahrstrahl m (Math) radius vector
Fahrtauslagen fpl (com) travel expenses
Fahrtenbuch n (com) log book, § 31a StVZO
Fahrtenschreiber m
(com) tachograph
– vehicle performance recorder
(ie, meter recording driving speeds and length of journeys)
Fahrtkosten pl
(com) travel expenses
(StR) commuting expenses
Fahrtkostenentschädigung f (com) compensation for travel expenses
Fahrtkostenzuschuß m (Pw) commuting allowance
Fahrtschreiber m (com) = *Fahrtenschreiber*
Fahrzeugbau m (com) vehicle construction
Fahrzeugdichte f (Stat) motor vehicle density *(ie, number of motor vehicles per square kilometer, per road km or per head of population)*
Fahrzeugpark m (com) vehicle *(or* automobile) fleet
Fahrzeugversicherung f (Vers) vehicle insurance
Fahrzeugvollversicherung f (Vers) fully comprehensive car insurance
Fahrzeugwerte mpl (Bö) motor shares
Faksimile n (com) facsimile
Faksimilestempel m (com) signature stamp
Faksimileunterschrift f (com) facsimile signature
faktische Beherrschung f (Bw) factual control
faktische Gesellschaft f
(Re) de facto company *(ie, one without legal basis, perhaps due to nullity of constituting agreement, but accepted for all practical purposes)*
– company frappe; du nullite;
faktische Präferenz f (Vw) revealed preference *(syn, offenbarte Präferenz)*
faktischer Vertrag m (Re) de facto agreement *(or* contract) *(ie, held to be valid against the outside world but defective in some element)*
faktisches Arbeitsverhältnis n (Pw) de facto employer/employee relationship *(ie, existing if employee works for employer without legally valid contract)*
faktisches Beschäftigungsverhältnis n (Pw) = *faktisches Arbeitsverhältnis*
faktisches Vertragsverhältnis n (Re) de facto contractual relationship
Faktor m
(Math) factor *(ie, multiplicand and multiplier)*
(Vw) factor of production
(com) department head in printing trade
(com) foreman in outdoor industry *(ie, handing out raw materials and receiving finished products)*
faktorales Austauschverhältnis n (AuW) factoral terms of trade
Faktoranalyse f (Stat) = *Faktorenanalyse*
Faktorangebot n (Vw) factor supply
Faktoranpassungskurve f (Vw) expansion path
Faktorausstattung f (Vw) factor endowment
Faktordifferential n
(Vw) factor differential
– differential of factor function

Faktoreinkommen n
(Vw) factor earnings
– factor income
– factor payments
Faktoreinkommen n **an das Ausland** (VGR) factor incomes paid to foreigners
Faktoreinkommen n **aus dem Ausland** (VGR) factor incomes received from abroad
Faktoreinsatz m (Vw) factor input
Faktoreinsatzfunktion f (Vw) factor input function
Faktoreinsatzmengen fpl
(Vw, Bw) input of resources
– volume input
Faktorenanalyse f (Stat) factor analysis
Faktorengewichtung f (IndE) factor weighting *(ie, in job evaluation)*
Faktorenspeicher m (EDV) factor storage
Faktorentlohnung f (Vw) factor payments
Faktorenzerlegung f
(Math) factorizing
– factorization
Faktorerträge mpl
(Vw) earnings of factors of production
– factor returns
Faktorexpansionspfad m (Vw) input expansion path
Faktorfehlleitung f (Vw) misallocation of resources
Faktorfunktion f (Bw) input function *(syn, Produktorfunktion)*
Faktorgrenzkosten pl
(Vw) marginal cost of acquisition
– marginal factor cost
Faktorgruppe f (Math) quotient *(or* factor) group
Faktorielle f (Math) factorial
faktorielles Experiment n (Stat) factorial experiment
Faktorintensität f (Vw) input ratio of the factors of production *(ie, at a given output volume)*
faktorisierbar (Math) factorable
faktorisieren
(Math) to factor
– to factorize
Faktorisierung f
(Math) factorizing
– factorization
Faktorisoquante f
(Vw) factor isoquant
– transformation curve
Faktorkoeffizient m (Vw) production *(or* technical) coefficient *(syn, Produktions- od Inputkoeffizient)*
Faktorkombination f
(Vw) combination of inputs
– factor mix
Faktorkosten pl (Vw) factor cost
Faktorkurve f
(Vw) factor curve
– graph of factor function
Faktorleistungen fpl (Vw) productive services
Faktorlücke f
(Vw) factor gap
– inflationary gap in the factor market
Faktormarkt m
(Vw) factor market
– input market

Faktormatrize

- resource market
Faktormatrize *f* (Math) component matrix
Faktormengen *fpl* (Vw) fixed inputs
Faktorminimierung *f* unter Nebenbedingungen (Vw) constrained-input minimization
Faktormobilität *f* (Vw) (spatial, inter-state, and sectoral) mobility of production factors
Faktornachfrage *f* (Vw) factor demand
Faktorpreis *m* (Vw, VGR) input (*or* resource) price
- factor price
Faktorpreisausgleich *m* (AuW) equalization of factor prices
Faktorpreisausgleichstheorem *n* (AuW) factor price equalization theorem
Faktorpreisgleichgewicht *n* (Vw) factor price equilibrium
Faktorpreistheorem *n* (Vw) factor price theorem
Faktorproduktivität *f* (Vw) factor productivity *(ie, total output to input quantity of one factor)*
Faktorproportionen *fpl* (Vw) factor proportions
Faktorproportionen-Theorem *n* (AuW) factor proportions (endowment) theorem
- Heckscher-Ohlin theorem
Faktorqualität *f* (Vw) factor quality *(ie, may be expressed through productivity measures)*
Faktorstrom *m* (Vw) factor flow
Faktorsubstitution *f* (Vw) substitution of factor (of production)
- factor substitution
Faktorumkehrprobe *f* (Stat) factor reversal test
faktorunabhängige Kosten *pl* (Vw) nonfactor cost
Faktorvariation *f* (Vw) factor variation *(ie, may be total or partial)*
Faktorverlagerung *f* (Vw) shift of resources
faktorvervielfachend (Vw) factor-augmenting *(ie, technical progress)*
Faktorwanderungen *fpl* (Vw) factor movements
Faktorwert *m* (Vw) input level
Faktura *f* (com) invoice
- bill
Fakturawährung *f* (com) invoicing currency
Fakturenabteilung *f* (com) billing (*or* invoicing) department
Fakturenwert *m* (com) invoice value
Fakturierautomat *m* (EDV) automatic billing machine
Fakturiercomputer *m* (EDV) invoicing computer
fakturieren (com) to invoice
- to bill
Fakturiermaschine *f* (EDV) automatic billing machine
Fakturierung *f* (com) billing
- invoicing
Fakturist *m* (com) invoice clerk
Fakultät *f* (Math) factorial
fakultative Normen *fpl* (com) voluntary standards
fakultative Rückversicherung *f* (Vers) facultative reinsurance *(ie, reinsurer has the option of accepting the tendered part of the original insurer's risk)*
fakultatives Geld *n* (Vw) facultative money *(ie, money which is not legal tender)*

Fälligkeitsgrundschuld

Fakultativklausel *f* (Fin) optional clause *(ie „oder anderes Konto des Empfängers" = „or creditable to another account of beneficiary")*
Fakultätschreibweise *f* (Math) factorial notation
Fall *m*
(com) matter
(Re) case
Fall *m* **bearbeiten** (com) to handle a case
fallen
(com) to fall *(eg, prices, interest rates)*
- to decline
- to decrease
- to dip
- to drop
- to go down
- to sag
- to lower
fallende Abschreibung *f* (ReW) accelerated method of depreciation *(ie, declining balance and sum-of-the-years-digit = degressive und digitale Abschreibung)*
fallende Annuität *f* (Fin) decreasing annuity
fallende Funktion *f* (Math) decreasing function
fallende Nachfragekurve *f* (Vw) downward sloping demand curve
fallende Preise *mpl* (com) dropping (*or* falling) prices
fallende Reihe *f* (Math) descending series
fallende Tendenz *f* (com) downward tendency
Fällen *n* **von Entscheidungen** (Bw) decision making
Fall *m* **erledigen** (com) to settle a case
Fallibilismus *m* (Log) fallibilism *(ie, posits the principle that no statement can be accepted as true beyond possible doubt)*
fallieren
(Re) to go bankrupt
- (infml) to go bust
- (infml) to go to the wall
fällig
(Fin) due
- payable
- due and payable
- matured
fällige Forderung *f* (Fin) debt due
fälliger Anspruch *m* (Re) matured claim
fälliger Betrag *m* (Fin) amount due
fälliger Wechsel *m* (WeR) payable bill of exchange
fällige Verbindlichkeit *f*
(Fin) matured liability
(ReW) liability due
fällige Zahlungen *fpl* **leisten** (Fin) to meet payments when due
Fälligkeit *f*
(com) maturity
- due date
(ie, the date at which an obligation becomes due)
Fälligkeit *f* **der Prämie** (Vers) premium due date
Fälligkeiten *fpl* (Fin) maturities
Fälligkeitsdatum *n* (Fin) = *Fälligkeitstag*
Fälligkeitsgliederung *f* (Fin) spacing of maturities
Fälligkeitsgrundlage *f* (Fin) maturity basis *(ie, difference between future and spot prices)*
Fälligkeitsgrundschuld *f* (Re) fixed-term land charge, § 1193 BGB

221

Fälligkeitshypothek *f* (Re) fixed-term mortgage
Fälligkeitsjahr *n* (Fin) year of maturity
Fälligkeitsklausel *f* (Fin) accelerating clause
Fälligkeitssteuern *fpl* (StR) taxes payable by operation of law *(ie, assessment not normally required)*
Fälligkeitsstruktur *f* (Fin) maturity structure
Fälligkeitstabelle *f* (Fin) aging schedule
Fälligkeitstag *m*
  (Fin) accrual date *(ie, for recurrent payments, such as interest, annuities)*
  (Fin) date of maturity
  – maturity date
  – due date
  – date of payment
  – date of expiration *(or* expiry*)*
Fälligkeitstermin *m* (Fin) = *Fälligkeitstag*
Fälligkeitswert *m* (Fin) maturity value *(eg, of a bond)*
Fälligkeitszeitpunkt *m* (Fin) = *Fälligkeitstag*
Fälligkeitszinsen *mpl* (Fin) interest after due date, § 353 HGB
Fälligkeit *f* **vorverlegen** (Fin) to accelerate the due date *(or* maturity*)*
fällig werden
  (Fin) to become due
  – to fall due
  – to mature
Falliment *n* (od **Fallissement** *n*) (Re) bankruptcy
Fallit *m* (Re) bankrupt
Fallmethode *f*
  (Bw) case-by-case approach
  – case method
Fallrecht *n* (Re) case law *(ie, aggregate of reported cases as forming a body of jurisprudence; opp, statutes and other sources of law)*
Fallstudie *f* (Bw) case study
falls unzustellbar, zurück an (com) if undelivered return to
fallweise Beschaffung *f*
  (MaW) individual buying
  – procurement on a case-to-case basis
Fall *m* **wieder aufrollen** (Re) to reopen a case
Fall *m* **wird verhandelt** (Re) case comes before a court
falsa demonstratio non nocet (Re) false description does not injure or vitiate *(eg, a contract or manifestation of intent = Willenserklärung)*
Falschanmeldung *f* (Zo) false declaration
Falschbuchung *f* (ReW) false entry
fälschen
  (com) to counterfeit
  – to fake
  – to falsify
  – (GB) to forge
  (eg, bank notes, documents, receipts)
Fälschen *n* **von Buchungsunterlagen** (ReW, infml) padding of accounting records
Falschgeld *n*
  (Fin) counterfeit
  – fake
  – (GB) forged ... money
Falschlieferung *f* (Re) delivery of merchandise other than that stipulated, § 378 HGB
Falschlochung *f* (EDV) mispunch

Falschmünzen *fpl* (Fin) base *(or* counterfeit*)* coin
Falschmünzer *m* (Fin) counterfeiter
Falschmünzerei *f* (Fin) forging of false currency
Fälschung *f*
  (com) falsification
  (Re) forgery and counterfeiting *(ie, of notes and coin, documents, securities)*
  (com, Re) counterfeit
  – fake
Fälschungen *fpl*
  (Mk) counterfeit products
  – bogus merchandise
  – fakes
  (ie, a well-known label of a manufacturer's brand name is illegally fixed to inferior merchandise which is sold at an inflated markup = zu überhöhten Preisen)
Falschwerbung *f* (Mk) misleading advertising
Falsifikat *n*
  (com) counterfeit
  – fake
Falsifikation *f*
  (Log) falsification
  (Re) = *Fälschung*
falsifizieren (Log) to falsify
Falsifizierung *f* (Log) falsification
falsus procurator *m* (Re) attorney-in-fact without proper authority, §§ 177 ff BGB
Faltabstand *m* (EDV) fold spacing
Faltprospekt *m*
  (com) folder
  – leaflet
Faltschachtel *f* (com) folding box
Faltungsintegral *n* (Math) convolution integral
Familienaktiengesellschaft *f* (Bw) family-owned corporation, § 157 IV 2 AktG
Familien-Aktionär *m* (Bw) family shareholder
Familienarbeitskräfte *fpl* (com) unpaid familiy workers *(ie, of a farm)*
Familienbesteuerung *f* (StR) familiy taxation
Familienbetrieb *m*
  (com) family farm
  (Re) family-owned business *(or* concern*)*
Familieneinkommen *n* (Stat) family income
Familiengeld *n* (SozV) benefit paid to the family of a disabled person *(ie, through legal accident insurance)*
Familiengesellschaft *f*
  (Bw) family partnership
  (Bw) family-owned corporation, § 157 IV 2 AktG
Familienheimfahrt *f* (StR) trip home
Familienhilfe *f* (SozV) family assistance *(ie, benefits paid under statutory health insurance scheme to dependents of insured)*
Familienlohn *m*
  (Pw) socially subsidized wage *(syn, Soziallohn)*
  (StR) family-based income *(opp, income by results)*
Familienmarke *f* (com) family brand
Familienpackung *f* (com) family size package
Familienrecht *n*
  (Re) family law
  – law of domestic relations
Familienstand *m* (StR) marital status

Familienstiftung f (StR) family foundation, § 1 I 4 ErbStG
Familienunternehmen n
(Bw) family-owned business (or concern)
(Bw) family partnership
(Bw) family-owned corporation
Familienunterstützung f (SozV) = Familiengeld
Familienversicherung f
(Vers) family income insurance
(ie, type of life insurance: part of policy amount is paid if the insured dies and installments are paid to the family until the expiration date)
(Vers) family health insurance
Familienzulage f (SozV) family allowance *(ie, being paid as ‚Kindergeld' = childrens' allowance since 1955)*
Familienzusammenführung f (Pw) family reunion
Familienzuschlag m (SozV) additionel family allowance *(ie, paid in addition to the basic amount of unemployment benefit or aid)*
Familie f **unterhalten** (Pw) to carry the family
Fangabkommen n (Re) fishery-limiting agreement
Fangbeschränkung f (Re) fishing limitation
Fangergebnis n (com) catch *(ie, in fishery)*
Fanggebiete npl (com) fishing grounds
Fanggründe mpl (com) = Fanggebiete
Fangplätze mpl (com) = Fanggebiete
Fangquote f (com) catch (or fishing) quota
Fangquotenaufteilung f (com) allocation of fishing quota
Fangquotenfestlegung f (com) allocation of fishing
Fangrechte npl (Re) fishery (or fishing) rights
Fangverbot n
(com) fishing ban
– ban on fishing *(eg, of Norway pout)*
Farbband n
(com) (typewriter) ribbon
– ink ribbon
Farbbanddrucker m (EDV) ribbon printer
Farbbandwechsel m (com) changing the ribbon
Farbenindustrie f (com) paint (or dye-stuffs) industry
Farbkissen n (com) inking pad
Farbstoffindustrie f (com) dyestuffs industry
Faser-Importrestriktionen fpl (Kart) trade barriers against cheap man-made fibers
Fassongründung f (Re) formation of a shell company *(ie, either AG or GmbH, with no intention of carrying on business, regarded as violating § 134 BGB)*
Fassonwert m (Bw) goodwill
fastperiodische Funktion f (Math) almost periodic function
Faustpfand n (Re) pledge *(ie, security interest in a chattel, usually in direct possession of the creditor)*
Faustpfandkredit m (Fin) loan secured by pledge (or movable property) *(eg, merchandise, securities)*
Faustregel f (Log) rule-of-thumb
Fautfracht f (com) dead freight, § 580 HGB *(ie, payable by a charterer for such part of the carrying capacity of a ship as he does not in fact use; it is damages for loss of freight)*
Favoriten mpl (Bö) favorites

Fazilität f (Fin) credit facility
– facility
Fazilität f **zur Finanzierung von Rohstofflagern** (IWF) buffer stock financing facility
federführend
com) acting as general coordinator
– handling a contract
(Fin) leading
– taking the lead *(eg, in arrangements made for a credit)*
federführende Börse f (Bö) leading stock exchange *(ie, on the occasion of a stock or loan issue)*
federführende Firma f (com) leading member *(eg, of a group)*
federführende Konsortialbank f
(Fin) leading bank
– lead manager
federführender Ausschuß m (com) responsible committee
federführendes Konsortialmitglied n
(Fin) leader
– manager
(Vers) leader
– leading company
federführend sein (com) to lead manage
Federführung f
(com) central handling
– lead management
Fehlallokation f **von Ressourcen** (Vw) misallocation of resources
Fehlanzeige f (com) nil return
Fehlarbeit f (com) = Ausschuß
Fehlbedarf m (com) uncovered demand
Fehlbestand m
(com) deficiency
(MaW) stockout
Fehlbestands-Wahrscheinlichkeitsdiagramm n
(Bw) stockout probability chart
Fehlbetrag m
(com) deficit
– deficiency
– short
– shortfall
– wantage
Fehlbuchung f (ReW) incorrect entry
fehlende Erfindungseigenschaft f (Pat) lack of invention
Fehlen n **der Erfindungshöhe** (Pat) obviousness of an invention (or inventive idea)
Fehlen n **der Gegenleistung** (Re) absence of consideration
Fehlen n **der Geschäftsgrundlage** (Re) absence of valid subject-matter
Fehlen n **e-r zugesicherten Eigenschaft** (Re) lack of quality which has been promised, § 463 BGB
Fehlen n **gesetzlicher Grundlage** (Re) lack of legal (or statutory) basis
Fehler m
(com) error
(Stat, EDV) error
(IndE) defect
– fault
fehleranfällig
(IndE) fault prone
(EDV) error prone

Fehler-Anpassungsmechanismus *m* (Vw) error adjustment mechanism
Fehleranzeige *f* (EDV) error display
Fehleranzeiger *m* (EDV) error indicator
Fehlerband *n* (EDV) error tape
Fehlerbaum-Analyse *f* (Bw) fault tree analysis *(ie, in accident prevention, DIN 25 424)*
Fehlerbehandlung *f* (EDV) error control processing
Fehlerbereich *m*
  (Stat) band of error
  (EDV) range of error
Fehlerberichtigung *f* (EDV) error correction
Fehlerbündel *n* (EDV) error burst
Fehlerbyte *n* (EDV) error byte
Fehlercode *m* (EDV) error code
Fehler *m* **dritter Art** (Stat) error of third kind
Fehlererkennung *f* (EDV) error detection
Fehlererkennungscode *m*
  (EDV) error detecting code
  – self-checking code
  (syn, selbstprüfender Code)
Fehlererkennungsprogramm *n* (EDV) error detection routine
Fehler *m* **erster Art**
  (Stat) error of first kind
  – alpha error
Fehlerfach *n* (EDV) reject stacker
Fehlerfortpflanzung *f* (Stat) propagation of error
fehlerfreie Regression *f* (Stat) true regression
fehlerfreies Stück *n* (Stat) effective unit
Fehlerfunktion *f* (Math) error function
Fehlergrenze *f*
  (Stat) error limit
  – margin of error
  (Pw) performance tolerance
fehlerhafte Arbeit *f* (IndE) faulty *(or* defective) work
fehlerhafte Lieferung *f* (com) defective delivery
fehlerhafter Anspruch *m* (Re) defective claim
fehlerhafter Besitz *m* (Re) faulty possession
fehlerhaftes Eigentumsrecht *n* (Re) bad title
fehlerhaftes Produkt *n*
  (com) defective product
  – product in defective condition
fehlerhafte Stücke *npl* (Stat) defective items *(or* units)
fehlerhafte Teile *npl* (com) defective parts
Fehlerhaftigkeit *f* (Re) defective condition
Fehlerhäufigkeit *f* (EDV) error rate
Fehlerhäufigkeit *f* **beim Tasten** (EDV) keying error rate
Fehler *m* **in der Gleichung** (Math) error in equation
Fehlerkennbit *n* (EDV) error indication bit
Fehlerklassifizierung *f* (Stat) classification of defects
Fehlerkontrolle *f* **mit Rückwärtsübertragung** (EDV) busback
  – loop checking
  – information *(or* message) feedback
Fehlerkorrektur *f* (EDV) error correction
Fehlerkorrekturcode *m* (EDV) error correcting code
Fehlerkorrekturprogramm *n* (EDV) error correction routine

Fehlerliste *f* (EDV) error list
Fehlermeldung *f* (EDV) error message
Fehlernachricht *f* (EDV) error message
Fehlerprotokoll *n* (EDV) error list *(or* report)
Fehlerprüfcode *m* (EDV) error detecting code
Fehlerprüfprogramm *n* (EDV) error checking program
Fehlerprüfung *f* (EDV) error check
Fehlerrate *f* (EDV) error rate
Fehlerrechnung *f* (Math) calculus of error
Fehlerregister *n* (EDV) error register
Fehlerrisiko *n* (Stat) risk of error
Fehlersicherung *f* (EDV) error protection
Fehlerstopp *m* (EDV) dynamic stop *(syn, dynamischer Stopp)*
Fehlersuche *f*
  (IndE) troubleshooting
  – troubleshoot
  (EDV) error debugging
Fehler *mpl* **suchen**
  (IndE) to troubleshoot
  (EDV) to debug
Fehlersuchprogramm *n* (EDV) debugging *(or* checkout) routine
Fehlertheorie *f* (Stat) theory of error
Fehlerunterbrechung *f* (EDV) error interrupt
Fehlervariable *f* (Stat) error term
Fehlervarianz *f* (Stat) error variance
Fehlerverwaltung *f* (EDV) recovery management
Fehlerwahrscheinlichkeit *f* (Stat) error probability
Fehlerzähler *m* (EDV) error counter
Fehler *m* **zweiter Art** (Stat) error of second kind
  – beta error
Fehlfracht *f* (com) = *Fautfracht*
Fehlinvestition *f*
  (com) bad investment
  (Fin) unprofitable investment
  (Fin) misdirected capital spending
Fehlkonstruktion *f* (IndE) faulty design
Fehlleitung *f* **volkswirtschaftlicher Produktivkräfte** (Vw) misallocation of productive resources
Fehlmenge *f* (com) shortage
  – shortfall
Fehlmengenkosten *pl*
  (MaW) cost of not carrying
  – out-of-stock cost
  – stockout cost
  (OR) penalty cost
Fehlmengensituation *f* (MaW) stocking-out situation
Fehlschluß *m*
  (Log) fallacy
  – paralogism
  (ie, any fallacious reasoning: an argument which seems to be valid but really is not)
Fehlschluß *m* **der Desaggregation** (Log) fallacy of division *(ie, an argument in which one assumes that various parts have a property solely because the whole has that property)*
Fehlschluß *m* **der Verallgemeinerung** (Log) fallacy of composition *(ie, an argument in which one assumes that a whole has a property solely)*
Fehlzeit *f* (Pw) time off
Fehlzeitenquote *f*
  (Pw) rate of absenteeism

- absence rate
Feierschicht *f*
(IndE) off-shift time *(eg, in one-shift operation, 16 hours are off shift)*
(Pw) day off in lieu
Feiertagsarbeit *f*
(Pw) rest-day working
- work on a public holiday
Feiertagslohn *m* (Pw) holiday pay
Feiertagszuschlag *m* (Pw) holiday premium
feilschen (com) to haggle *(eg, over EEC farm prices)*
Feingehalt *m*
(Fin) fineness
- percentage of purity
(eg, designating the purity of gold or silber in carat or lot)
Feinplanung *f* (Bw) detailed *(or* fine-tuned) planning
Feinsteuerung *f* (Vw) fine tuning *(eg, of economic policy)*
Feld *n*
(Math) field
(EDV) array
(EDV, Cobol) data item
Feldbild *n* (Math) flow map
Feldelement *n* (EDV) array element
Feldforschung *f* (Mk) field research *(syn, Primärforschung)*
Feldgruppe *f* (EDV) array
Feldlinien *fpl* (Math) flow lines
Feldrechner *m* (EDV) array processor
Fensterumschlag *m* (com) window envelope
Ferienvertretung *f*
(Pw) deputy during vacations
(Pw) deputizing during vacations
Ferienwetterversicherung *f* (Vers) holiday weather insurance
Fernanfrage *f* (EDV) remote inquiry
Fernanzeige *f* (EDV) remote indication
Fernbuchführung *f*
(ReW) accounting center bookkeeping *(ie, servicing small businesses, farmers, professions)*
(EDV) remote accounting
Ferndatenstation *f* (EDV) remote station
Ferneingabe *f* (EDV) remote input
Ferneingabestation *f* (EDV) remote input station
fernere mittlere Lebensdauer *f* (Stat) average life expectancy *(syn, mittlere Lebenserwartung)*
ferne Sichten *pl* (Bö) distant deliveries
Fernfischerei *f*
(com) distant
- distant-water
- long-range ... fishing
Fernfrachtverkehr *m* (com) long-haul freight traffic
Ferngespräch *n*
(com) long distance call
- (GB) trunk call
Ferngiroverkehr *m* (Fin) distant giro transfers
Fernkauf *m* (com) contract of sale where seller agrees to ship the goods to buyer's destination at the latter's risk, § 447 BGB
Fernkopierer *m*
(EDV) remote copier

(EDV) facsimile terminal
- telecopier
Fernlastverkehr *m*
(com) long-distance trucking
- (GB) long-distance haulage
Fernmeldegebühren *fpl* (com) telephone charges
Fernmeldesatellit *m* (EDV) telecommunication satellite
Fernmeldetechnik *f* (EDV) telecommunication engineering
Fernmeldewesen *n* (EDV) telecommunication
fernmündliche Befragung *f* (Mk) telephone survey
Fernscheck *m* (Fin) out-of-town check
fernschreiben (EDV) to teletype
Fernschreiben *n* (EDV) telex
Fernschreiber *m*
(EDV) teletypewriter
- (GB) teleprinter
Fernschreibverkehr *m* (EDV) telex traffic
fernschriftlich (com) by telex
Fernsehen *n*
(Mk) television, TV
- (GB, infml) telly
- (infml) goggle box
Fernsehinterview *n*
(Mk) television
- televised
- TV ... interview
Fernsehwerbung *f* (Mk) TV advertising
Fernsprechanschluß *m* (com) telephone connection
Fernsprechauftragsdienst *m* (com) answering service
Fernsprechbuch *n*
(com) telephone directory
- (infml) phone book
Fernsprechgebühren *fpl* (com) telephone charges
Fernsprechleitung *f* (com) telephone line
Fernsprechteilnehmer *m* (com) telephone subscriber
Fernsprechverkehr *m* (com) telephone communications
Fernstapelverarbeitung *f* (EDV) remote batch processing
Fernsteuereinrichtung *f* (IndE) remote control equipment
Fernsteuerung *f* (IndE) remote control
Ferntest *m* (EDV) remote *(or* closed-shop) testing *(opp, Eigentest)*
Fernüberweisung *f* (Fin) out-of-town credit transfer
Fernüberweisungsverfahren *n* (Fin) intercity transfer procedure
Fernverkehr *m* (com) long-distance transport
Fernwartung *f* (EDV) remote maintenance
Fernwirksystem *n* (EDV) remote control system
Fernzahlungsverkehr *m* (Fin) intercity payments
Ferritkern *m* (EDV) ferrite *(or* magnetic) core
Ferritkernspeicher *m* (EDV) ferrite core memory
fertigen
(com) to produce
- to manufacture
- to make
Fertigerzeugnis *n* (com) finished product
Fertigerzeugniskonto *n* (ReW) finished products account

Fertigfabrikat *n* (com) = *Fertigerzeugnis n*
Fertiggewicht *n*
(IndE) finished weight
– weight of finished product
Fertiggüterbranche *f* (com) finished goods industry
Fertigladenbau *m* (com) preassembly shop fitting
Fertiglager *n* (MaW) finished goods (*or* products) inventory
Fertigmeldung *f* (IndE) order completion report
Fertigmontage *f* (IndE) final assembly
Fertigprodukt *n* (com) finished product
Fertigstellung *f* (com) completion
Fertigstellungsbescheinigung *f* (com) certificate of manufacture
Fertigstellungstermin *m* (com) finish date
Fertigteile *npl*
(IndE) finished parts
(KoR) purchased parts
– bought-out parts (*or* components)
Fertigteilelager *n* (MaW) finished parts store
Fertigung *f*
(IndE) production
– manufacture
– manufacturing operation(s)
Fertigung *f* **nach Flußprinzip**
(IndE) flow-line (*or* process) production *(ie, Fließfertigung = continuous production; eg, assembly-line production + Reihenfertigung = continuous production without cycle times)*
Fertigungsablauf *m* (IndE) production sequence
Fertigungsablaufplan *m*
(IndE) master operation list
– master route chart
– manufacturing data sheet
– process chart
Fertigungsablaufplanung *f* (IndE) production sequencing
Fertigungsablaufstudie *f* (IndE) production study
Fertigungsabteilung *f*
(IndE) production department (*or* division)
– manufacturing department
Fertigungsanteil *m* (AuW, *im Abnehmerland*) local content
Fertigungsauftrag *m* (IndE) production (*or* manufacturing) order
Fertigungsbeobachtung *f* (Stat) production surveillance
Fertigungsbereich *m* (IndE) manufacturing sector
Fertigungsbereich *m* **reorganisieren** (IndE) to restructure manufacturing operations
Fertigungsbetrieb *m* (IndE) manufacturing enterprise
fertigungsbezogener Lohn *m* (Pw) production-related wages
Fertigungseinheit *f* (IndE) unit of product
Fertigungseinrichtungen *fpl* (IndE) manufacturing (*or* production) facilities
Fertigungseinzelkosten *pl* (KoR) prime cost *(ie, include all direct manufacturing expense)*
Fertigungsendstellen *fpl* (KoR) final production cost centers
Fertigungsergebnis *n* (Bw) production result
Fertigungsgehälter *npl* (KoR) direct salaries
Fertigungsgemeinkosten *pl*
(KoR) factory overhead (*or* expense)

– applied manufacturing cost
– indirect manufacturing overhead
– production overhead
Fertigungsgemeinkostenlohn *m* (KoR) indirect labor
Fertigungsgemeinkostenmaterial *n* (KoR) indirect material
Fertigungsgemeinkosten-Überdeckung *f* (KoR) overapplied factory expense
Fertigungsgemeinkosten-Unterdeckung *f* (KoR) underabsorbed production overhead
Fertigungsgemeinkostenzuschlag *m* (KoR) allocated production overhead
Fertigungshauptkostenstelle *f* (KoR) production cost center (*or* department)
Fertigungshauptstelle *f* (KoR) = *Fertigungshauptkostenstelle*
Fertigungshilfskostenstelle *f*
(KoR) indirect production cost center
– indirect department
Fertigungshilfsstelle *f* (KoR) = *Fertigungshilfskostenstelle*
Fertigungskapazität *f* (IndE) production capacity
Fertigungskontrolle *f*
(Stat) process control
(IndE) control engineering
– production control
Fertigungskosten *pl*
(KoR) manufacturing
– production
– factory
– conversion ... cost
Fertigungskostenstelle *f* (KoR) production cost center
Fertigungslenkung *f* (IndE) production control
Fertigungslohn *m*
(KoR) direct labor
– manufacturing labor
– productive labor (*or* wages)
Fertigungslohnzettel *m* (IndE) direct labor slip (*or* ticket)
Fertigungslos *n*
(IndE) manufacturing lot
– production batch
Fertigungsmaterial *n*
(KoR) direct and indirect material
(IndE) charge material
Fertigungsmaterialkosten *pl* (KoR) direct material
Fertigungsmethode *f* (IndE) production method
Fertigungsperiode *f* (KoR) operating period
Fertigungsplan *m* (IndE) production schedule (*or* plan)
Fertigungsplanung *f*
(IndE) production planning (*or* scheduling)
– process planning
Fertigungsprogramm *n* (Bw) production program *(syn, Produktionsprogramm)*
Fertigungssonderkosten *pl* (KoR) special production costs *(eg, of patents, special tools, patterns)*
Fertigungssortiment *n* (IndE) product mix
Fertigungsspannweite *f* (Stat) process range
Fertigungsstätten *fpl* (IndE) production facilities
Fertigungsstelle *f* (KoR) = *Fertigungskostenstelle*
Fertigungsstellengemeinkosten *pl* (KoR) plant departmental overhead

Fertigungssteuerung *f*
(IndE) manufacturing
— process
— production ... control
(IndE) production planning
Fertigungssteuerungssystem *n* (IndE) production control system
Fertigungsstückliste *f* (MaW) manufacturing bill of materials
Fertigungstechnik *f*
(IndE) production (*or* manufacturing) technology
— product engineering
Fertigungsterminübersicht *f* (IndE) master schedule
Fertigungstoleranz *f* (Stat) process tolerance
Fertigungsüberwachung *f*
(IndE) production control
(Stat) process inspection
Fertigungsunternehmen *n* (Bw) manufacturing enterprise (*or* organization)
Fertigungsvereinfachung *f* (IndE) product simplification
Fertigungsverfahren *n* (IndE) method (*or* system) of production
Fertigungsvertriebsrechnung *f* (KoR) production/ sales cost accounting
Fertigungsvollzugsplanung *f* (IndE) planning of overall production process
Fertigungsvorbereitung *f* (IndE) production scheduling
Fertigungswagnis *n* (KoR) manufacturing (*or* production) risk
Fertigungszeit *f*
(IndE) production (*or* manufacturing) cycle
— production lead time
Fertigungszuschlag *m* (KoR) combined rate for direct labor and overhead
Fertigwaren *fpl* (com) finished goods (*or* products)
Fertigwarenimporte *mpl* (AuW) imported finished products
Fertigwarenlager *n* (MaW) inventory of finished products
Fertilität *f* (Stat) fertility
Fertilitätsmaße *npl* (Stat) fertility ratios
Fertilitätsökonomie *f* (Vw) economics of familiy
Festangestellte *pl* (Pw) permanently employed salaried personnel
Festanlage *f* (Fin) funds deposited for a fixed period
Festauftrag *m* (com) firm order
Festbewertung *f* (ReW) valuation of assets based on standard values
feste Abfälle *mpl* (com) solid waste
feste Annuität *f* (Fin) fixed-amount annuity
feste Anstellung *f* (Pw) fixed (*or* permanent) appointment
feste Ausgangsstichprobe *f* (Stat) master sample
feste Belastung *f* (Fin) fixed charge
feste Bestellung *f* (com) firm order
feste Blocklänge *f* (EDV) fixed block length
feste Börse *f* (Bö) up market
feste Gelder *npl*
(Fin) fixed bank deposits
(*ie, for at least one month*)

(Fin) longer-term funds traded in the money market for fixed periods *(eg, three months)*
feste Grundstimmung *f* (Bö) firm undertone
feste Kosten *pl* (KoR) fixed costs
feste Kurse *mpl* (Bö) firm prices
feste Laufzeit *f* (Fin) fixed period to maturity
feste Laufzeiten *fpl* (Fin) fixed maturities
fester Gemeinkostenzuschlag *m* (KoR) standard costing rate
fester Kostenvoranschlag *m* (com) firm estimate
fester Kundenkreis *m* (com) established clientele
fester Kurs *m* (Bö) firm price
fester Markt *m* (Bö) firm (*or* steady) market
fester Schluß *m* (Bö) firm closing
fester Verrechnungspreis *m* (KoR) standard price
fester Wechselkurs *m* (AuW) fixed (*or* pegged) exchange rate
festes Angebot *n* (com) firm (*or* binding) offer
feste Satzlänge *f* (EDV) fixed record length
festes Einkommen *n*
(com) regular income
(com) fixed income
festes Format *n* (EDV) fixed format
festes Gebot *n* (com) firm (*or* fixed) offer
feste Stichprobe *f* (Stat) fixed sample
festes Zeitelement *n* (IndE) constant element *(ie, in time studies)*
feste Tendenz *f* (Bö) firm tendency
feste Übernahme *f* (Fin) firm commitment underwriting *(ie, of a bond issue by an issuing bank)*
feste Wechselkursparität *f* (AuW) fixed parity
feste Wortlänge *f* (EDV) fixed word length
Festgebot *n* (com) firm offer
Festgehalt *n* (Pw) fixed salary
Festgehaltsklausel *f* (Pw) fixed-salary clause
(ie, relates the amount of a regular payment to a specified salary bracket)
Festgeld *n* (Fin) fixed-term deposits *(opp, Tagesgeld)*
Festgeldanlage *f* (Fin) fixed-term deposit investment
Festgeldkonto *n* (Fin) fixed-term deposit account
Festgeldzinsen *mpl* (Fin) interest on fixed-term deposits
festgelegte Bestellmenge *f* (MaW) fixed-order quantity
festgelegter Beschaffungsrhythmus *m* (MaW) fixed cycle
Festgeschäft *n* (com) firm bargain (*or* deal)
festgestellter Jahresabschluß *m* (ReW) certified financial statement, § 177 AktG
Festgrundschuld *f* (Re) fixed-date land charge
Festhypothek *f* (Re) fixed-date mortgage loan *(opp, Tilgungshypothek)*
Festjahre *npl* (Fin) call-free years
Festkauf *m* (com) firm purchase
fest kaufen (com) to buy firm
Festkomma *n* (EDV) fixed decimal point
Festkonditionen *fpl* (Fin) fixed lending rates
Festkonto *n* (Fin) fixed-date time account
Festkörperbauelement *n* (EDV) solid state component
(ie, a component utilizing the electric or magnetic phenomena of solids; eg, a transistor, a ferrite core)

Festkörperelement n (EDV) solid state element
Festkörperschaltkreis m (EDV) solid state circuit
Festkosten pl (KoR) fixed cost
Festkredit m (Fin) fixed-rate loan
Festkurs m (Bö) fixed quotation
Festkurs-System n (AuW) fixed-exchange-rate system
Festlandsockel m (Re) continental shelf
Festlandsockelgrenzen fpl (Re) continental shelf boundaries
Festlandsproduzent m (com) land-based mineral producer
Festlaufzeit f (Fin) fixed term *(ie, of a loan)*
festlegen
 (Fin) to lock up *(eg, capital)*
 (Pw) to lock away *(eg, shares for two years in a share ownership scheme)*
Festlegen n **von Akkordsätzen** (Pw) rate fixing
Festlegung f **der Arbeitsfolge** (IndE) routing *(ie, defining the product's path through the production process)*
Festlegungsfrist f (Fin) fixed period of investment
Festlegung f **von Kapital** (Fin) locking-up of capital
Festlegung f **von Prioritäten** (Bw) priority assignment
Festlohn m (Pw) fixed wage
Festnotierung f (Bö) fixed quotation
Festplattenspeicher m (EDV) fixed disk storage
Festpreis m
 (com) firm price
 (Vw) fixed price *(or rate)*
 (ReW) standard intercompany price *(ie, in cartels and groups of affiliated companies)*
 (ReW) fixed price *(ie, in valuation)*
Festpreisauftrag m (com) fixed price order
Festpreisaufträge mpl **mit Neufestsetzung des Preises** (com, US) fixed-price contracts with provision for redetermination of price
Festpreisverfahren n (KoR) fixed-price method *(ie, of valuating intra-plant service output)*
Festpreiszuschlag m (com) fixed-price charge
Festpunktaddition f (EDV) fixed point addition
Festpunktarithmetik f (EDV) fixed point arithmetic
Festpunktoperation f (EDV) fixed point operation
Festpunktrechnung f (EDV) fixed point arithmetic *(or computation)*
Festpunktschreibweise f (EDV) fixed point representation
festsetzen
 (com) to determine
 – to fix
 (Re) to lay down
 – to stipulate
Festsetzen n **von Zielen** (Bw) goal setting
Festsetzung f **der Lohnsätze** (IndE) rate setting *(ie, based on time and motion studies)*
Festsetzung f **der Prämie nach Schadenshäufigkeit** (Vers) retrospective rating
Festsetzung f **des Goldpreises** (Bö) gold fixing
Festsetzung f **e-s Exportpreises** (AuW) costing an export price
Festsetzungen fpl (Log) conventions
Festsetzungsfrist f (StR) assessment period, § 169 AO

Festsetzung f **von Abgabepreisen** (com) rate making *(or setting)*
Festspeicher m
 (EDV) read only memory, ROM
 – fixed *(or non-erasable or permanent)* storage *(syn, Festwertspeicher, Dauerspeicher, Permanentspeicher)*
feststellen
 (com) *sagen* = to state
 – *herausfinden* = to find out
 – *bemerken* = to notice
 – *festsetzen* = to determine
 (ReW) to approve *(ie, annual accounts)*
Feststellen n **der Kreditwürdigkeit** (Fin) credit investigation
Feststellung f **der Satzung** (Re) execution of articles of incorporation, § 23 AktG
Feststellung f **des amtlichen Kurses** (Bö) fixing of official quotation
Feststellung f **des Jahresabschlusses** (ReW) approval of year-end financial statements *(ie, by supervisory board or general meeting)*
Feststellung f **des Schadens** (Re) ascertainment of loss *(or damage)*
Feststellungsbescheid m (StR) notice of determination, §§ 157, 179 AO *(ie, establishes the factual and legal data from which tax liability follows but does not compute a tax or demand its payment)*
Feststellungsklage f
 (StR) action for a declaratory judgment
 – (GB) friendly action
 (ie, to establish the existence of a fiscal obligation between taxpayer and government or the invalidity of an administrative act, § 41 FGO)
Feststellungsurteil n (Re) declaratory judgment, § 256 ZPO
Festübernahme f (Fin) firm underwriting *(ie, of a loan issue)*
festverdrahtetes Programm n (EDV) hard-wired program
festverdrahtete Steuerung f (EDV) hard-wired controller
Festverkauf m (com) fixed sale
festverzinslich (Fin) fixed-interest bearing
festverzinsliche pl (Fin) fixed-interest bearing securities
festverzinsliche Anlagepapiere npl (Fin) investment bonds
festverzinsliche Anleihe f (Fin) fixed-interest loan
festverzinsliche Kapitalanlage f (Fin) fixed-interest investment
festverzinsliche Schuldverschreibung f (Fin) fixed-interest bearing bond
festverzinsliches Wertpapier n (Fin) fixed-interest (bearing) security
festverzinsliche Werte mpl (Fin) fixed-interest-bearing securities
Festwert m (ReW) fixed valuation *(ie, over a period of several years)*
Festwertregelung f (EDV) constant value control
Festwertspeicher m (EDV) = *Festspeicher*
Festwort n (EDV) fixed-length word
Festzinsdarlehen n (Fin) fixed-rate term loan
Festzinshypothek f (Fin) fixed-rate mortgage
Festzinskredit m (Fin) fixed-interest loan

Festzinssatz *m* (Fin) fixed interest rate
Feuergefahr *f* (Vers) fire hazard
Feuerrisiko *n* (Vers) = *Feuergefahr*
Feuerschaden *m* (Vers) fire damage
Feuerschadenabteilung *f* (Vers) fire department
Feuerschutzsteuer *f* (StR) fire protection tax *(ie, collected from public or commercial fire insurance companies)*
Feuerschutzsteuergesetz *n* (StR) Law Regulating the Fire Protection Tax, of 21 Dec 1979
Feuerversicherer *m* (Vers) fire insurer
Feuerversicherung *f* (Vers) fire insurance
Feuerversicherungsgesellschaft *f* (Vers) fire insurance company
Feuerversicherungsprämie *f* (Vers) fire insurance premium
Feuerversicherungsteuer *f* (StR) fire insurance tax
Feuerwehrfonds *m* (Fin) fire-fighting fund *(ie, as a measure of safety to bank customers' accounts; today ‚Einlagensicherungsfonds')*
Feuerwehrkosten *pl* (KoR) fire protection expense
Feuerwehr-Unfallversicherung *f* (SozV) fire brigade accident insurance *(ie, mostly incorporated into the social accident insurance schemes)*
FFP-Vertrag *m* (com) firm fixed price contract
Fibonacci-Folge *f* (EDV) Fibonacci series
Fiduzialgrenze *f* (Stat) probability limit
Fiduzialschluß *m* (Stat) fiducial inference
Fiduzialverteilung *f* (Stat) fiducial distribution
fiduziarische Abtretung *f* (Re) fiduciary assignment *(eg, for the purpose of giving security to a creditor)*
fiduziarisches Rechtsgeschäft *n* (Re) fiduciary transaction
Fifo-Methode *f* (ReW) first-in, first-out method *(ie, of inventory valuation)*
figurative Konstante *f* (EDV) figurative constant
fiktive Buchung *f*
 (VGR) imputation
 (ReW) imputed (*or* fictitious) entry
fiktive Dividende *f* (Fin) sham dividend
fiktive Prämie *f* (Vers) fictitious premium *(ie, used in computing pension reserves qualifying for tax exemption)*
fiktiver Besitz *m* (Re) constructive possession
fiktiver Wert *m* (com) fictitious value
fiktiver Wohnsitz *m* (Re) sham domicile
fiktives Einkommen *n*
 (StR) imputed income *(eg, from owner-occupied residence)*
 – (GB) notional income
Filialbank *f*
 (Fin) branch bank
 (Fin) multiple-branch bank
Filialbanksystem *n*
 (Fin) branch-banking system
 – multiple-branch banking
Filialbetrieb *m*
 (com) company (*or* firm) having branches
 (com) branch operation *(ie, under central management)*
 (Mk) branch (*or* chain) store
Filialbetriebsorganisation *f* (Mk) branch (*or* chain) store organization

Filialbuchführung *f* (ReW) retail branch accounting
Filiale *f*
 (com) branch
 (com) branch (*or* field) office
 (com) branch operation *(ie, may be an independent retail outlet, a field store from which customers are supplied = Auslieferungslager, etc.)*
 (Mk) branch (*or* chain) store
 (Re) branch establishment
Filialgeschäft *n* (Mk) retail (*or* chain) store
Filialgesellschaft *f* (Mk) chain store company
Filialkalkulation *f* (ReW) branch office accounting
Filialkette *f*
 (Mk) chain store
 – (GB) multiple shops
Filialleiter *m*
 (com) branch manager
 (Mk) branch (*or* chain) store manager
Filialnetz *n* (com) network of branches
Filialunternehmen *n* (com) = *Filialbetrieb*
Filialwechsel *m* (Fin) house bill
Filmausgabeeinheit *f* (EDV) film recorder
Filmlochkarte *f* (EDV) aperture card
Filmspeicher *m* (EDV) photographic storage
Filmverleih *m* (com) film rental
Filterbasis *f* (Math) filter *(ie, family of nonempty subsets of a set; syn, Raster)*
Filterfrage *f* (Mk) filter (*or* strip) question
Filtern *n* (Stat) filtering
Finanz *f*
 (Fin) (management of) finance
 (Fin, infml) financial community
Finanzabgaben *fpl* (FiW) fiscal charges *(ie, general term denoting all compulsory payments to public authorities; eg, taxes, duties, levies)*
Finanzabkommen *n* (FiW) financial agreement
Finanzabteilung *f* (Fin) financial department
Finanzakzept *n* (Fin) accepted finance bill *(ie, with no underlying sale of goods)*
Finanzamt *n*
 (StR) local tax office
 – (infml) tax collector
 – (infml) taxman
Finanzamtsvorsteher *m* (StR) head of local tax office
Finanzanalyse *f* (Fin) financial analysis
Finanzanalyst *m* (Fin) financial analyst
Finanzanlageinvestition *f*
 (Fin) investment in financial assets
 – (GB) trade investment
Finanzanlagen *fpl*
 (ReW) financial investments
 (ReW, EG) financial assets
 (Fin) long-term investments
Finanzanlagevermögen *n* (Fin) = *Finanzanlagen*
Finanzanteil *m* e-s Zolls (FiW) fiscal element of a duty
Finanzaufkommen *n* (FiW) budgetary revenue (*or* receipts)
Finanzausgleich *m*
 (FiW) fiscal (*or* intergovernmental) equalization
 (EG) financial compensation
Finanzausgleichsgesetz *n* (FiW) Tax Equalization Law, of 28 Aug 1968

Finanzausgleichsmittel *pl*
(FiW) revenue sharing funds
– shared revenues
Finanzausgleichssystem *n* (FiW) financial equalization system
Finanzausgleichs-Zahlungen *fpl*
(FiW) intergovernmental transfers
(EG) compensatory payments
Finanzausgleich *m* **zwischen Händlern** (com) pass-over system
Finanzausschuß *m*
(Fin) committee on finance
– finance committee
– financial policy committee
Finanzausweis *m*
(ReW) financial statement
– statement of financial position
Finanzautonomie *f* (FiW) = *Finanzhoheit*
Finanzbeamter *m* (FiW) tax official
Finanzbedarf *m* (Fin) financial requirements (*or* needs)
Finanzbedarf *m* **der öffentlichen Hand** (FiW) public sector borrowing requirements, PSBR
Finanzbedarfsplanung *f* (Fin) planning of financial requirements
Finanzbedarfsrechnung *f* (Fin) financial requirements analysis
Finanzbefehl *m* (FiW) fiscal order *(ie, administrative act imposing upon a taxpayer the duty to do or to refrain from doing something)*
Finanzbehörde *f*
(StR) revenue
– fiscal
– tax ... authority
Finanzbeitrag *m* (EG) financial contribution
Finanzberater *m* (Fin) financial consultant (*or* adviser)
Finanzberatung *f* (Fin) financial counseling
Finanzbericht *m* (Fin) financial report
Finanzbeteiligung *f* (Fin) financial participation
Finanzbrief *m* (Fin) financial letter
Finanzbuchhalter *m* (ReW) financial accountant
Finanzbuchhaltung *f*
(ReW) financial
– general
– administrative ... accounting
(ReW) general accounting department
Finanzbudget *n* (Fin) capital (*or* financial) budget
Finanzdecke *f* (Fin) available operating funds
Finanzdirektor *m* (Fin) = *Finanzleiter*
Finanzdisposition *f*
(Fin, FiW) management of financial investments *(ie, seeking to optimize the asset mix)*
(Fin) implementation of a company's financial policy
Finanzen *pl*
(Fin) matters of finance
– finances
(FiW) public revenue and other pecuniary resources *(ie, of governmental units)*
Finanzentscheidung *f* (Fin) financial decision
Finanzexperte *m* (Fin) expert in financial management
Finanzfachleute *pl* (Fin) finance specialists (*or* men)

Finanzflußelemente *npl* (Fin) cash flow elements
Finanzflußrechnung *f*
(Fin) funds statement
– financial flow statement
– cash flow statement
Finanzgebaren *n*
(Fin, FiW) practice of financial management
– management (*or* practice) of finances
Finanzgebarung *f* (FiW) = *Finanzgebaren*
Finanzgenie *n* (Fin, infml) financial wizard
Finanzgericht *n*
(StR) first-instance fiscal court, § 2 FGO
– tax court
finanzgerichtliche Entscheidung *f* (StR) tax court ruling
Finanzgerichtsbarkeit *f* (StR) fiscal jurisdiction, § 1 FGO
Finanzgerichtsordnung *f* (StR) Code of Fiscal Procedure, of 6 Oct 1965
Finanzgeschäft *n* (Fin) financial (*or* money) transaction
Finanzgeschäfte *npl* (Fin) financial operations
Finanzgesellschaft *f* (Fin) finance company
Finanzgesetzgebung *f* (FiW) fiscal legislation
Finanzgewaltiger *m* (Fin, infml) financial tycoon
Finanzgruppe *f* (Fin) financial services group
– financial (*or* financiers') group
Finanzhedging *n* (Fin) financial hedging
Finanzhilfe *f*
(Fin) financial aid (*or* assistance *or* support)
(FiW) fiscal aid, § 12 StabG
Finanzhoheit *f* (FiW) = *Steuerhoheit*
Finanzholding *f* (Fin) financial holding (company)
finanziell (Fin) financial
finanziell angeschlagen (Fin) financially-stricken *(eg, electrical group)*
finanzielle Aktiva *npl* (Fin) financial assets *(eg, money, receivables, property rights)*
finanzielle Angelegenheiten *fpl* (Fin) financial affairs (*or* matters)
finanzielle Anreize *mpl* (Vw) financial inducements *(ie, offered by the state)*
finanzielle Ausstattung *f* (Fin) funding
finanzielle Belastung *f* (Fin) financial burden
finanzielle Beteiligung *f* (Fin) financial interest (*or* participation)
finanzielle Eingliederung *f* (Fin) financial integration
finanzielle Entschädigung *f* (Fin) pecuniary compensation
finanzielle Führung *f* (Fin) financial management
finanzielle Hilfe *f* (FiW) financial aid (*or* assistance)
finanzielle Konsolidierung *f* (Fin) financial restructuring
finanzielle Lage *f* (Fin) financial position (*or* condition)
finanzielle Leistungsfähigkeit *f* (Fin) financial strength (*or* power)
finanzielle Mittel *pl*
(Fin) funds
– financial resources
finanzielle Mittler *mpl* (Fin) financial intermediaries
finanzielle Notlage *f* (Fin) financial emergency

finanziellen Verpflichtungen *fpl* **nachkommen** (Fin) to fulfill (one's) financial obligations
finanzieller Beitrag *m* (Fin) financial contribution
finanzieller Engpaß *m* (Fin) financial straits (*or* plight *or* squeze)
finanzielle Rettungsaktion *f* (Fin) financial rescue deal (*or* package)
finanzieller Status *m* (Fin) financial condition (*or* position)
finanzieller Vorteil *m* (Fin) financial advantage (*or* benefit)
finanzieller Zusammenbruch *m* (Fin) financial collapse (*or* failure)
finanzielle Schwierigkeiten *fpl*
  (Fin) financial difficulties (*or* trouble)
  – (infml) troubled waters
finanzielles Ergebnis *n* (Fin) financial result
finanzielles Gleichgewicht *n* (Fin) financial equilibrium
finanzielle Sphäre *f* (Fin) area of finance
finanzielles Polster *n* (Fin) financial cushion
finanzielle Unterstützung *f* (Fin) financial aid (*or* assistance *or* backing *or* support)
finanzielle Verflechtung *f* (Fin) financial interpenetration
finanzielle Vermögenswerte *mpl* (Fin) financial assets
finanzielle Verpflichtung *f* (Fin) financial commitment (*or* obligation)
finanziell solide (FiW) financially sound *(eg, government budget!)*
finanziell unterstützen (Fin) to back financially
finanziell verpflichtet (Fin) financially obligated (to)
finanzieren
  (com) to finance *(ie, to buy or sell on credit; eg, automobile)*
  (Fin) to finance
  – to fund
  – to provide (*or* raise) funds (*or* capital *or* money)
Finanzierung *f*
  (Fin) financing *(ie, act, process, instance of raising or providing funds)*
  – provision of finance
  – funding
  (Fin) finance *(ie, capital, funds)*
  (Fin) lending *(ie, extension of credits)*
Finanzierung *f* **durch Aktienfinanzierung** (Fin) stock financing
Finanzierung *f* **durch Fremdmittel** (Fin) financing with outside funds
Finanzierung *f* **durch Verkauf offener Buchforderungen** (Fin) accounts receivable financing
Finanzierung *f* **e-s Projektes** (Fin) funding of a project
Finanzierungsabschnitt *m* (Fin) phase of financing
Finanzierungsarten *fpl* (Fin) types of financing
Finanzierungsaufwand *m* (Fin) finance charges (*or* expenditure)
Finanzierungsbasis *f* (Fin) = *Finanzierungsgrundlage*
Finanzierungsbedarf *m*
  (Fin) financing requirements
  (Fin) borrowing requirements

Finanzierungsdarlehen *n* (Fin) loan for financing purposes
Finanzierungsdefizit *n* (FiW) financing deficit
Finanzierungsdienst *m* (Fin) financing service
Finanzierungsentscheidung *f* (Fin) financial decision
finanzierungsfähig (Fin) eligible for financing
Finanzierungs-Fazilität *f* (Vw) financing facility *(ie, of the Bank for International Settlements, BIS)*
Finanzierungsform *f* (Fin) method of financing
Finanzierungsfunktion *f* (Fin) finance function
Finanzierungsgebühren *fpl* (Fin) financing charges
Finanzierungsgeschäft *n*
  (Fin) financing transaction
  (Fin) financing business *(eg, selling securities issues)*
Finanzierungsgesellschaft *f*
  (Fin) finance (*or* financing) company
  – loan company
Finanzierungs-Gleichgewicht *n* (Fin) balance of financing
Finanzierungsgrundlage *f*
  (Fin) financial base
  – basis for granting credit (*or* loans)
Finanzierungsgrundsätze *mpl* (Fin) rules of financing
Finanzierungshandbuch *n* (Fin) financing manual
Finanzierungshilfe *f* (Fin) financing aid
Finanzierung *f* **sichern** (Fin) to procure adequate financing
Finanzierungsinstitut *n* (Fin) financial institution
Finanzierungsinstrument *n* (Fin) financing instrument (*or* vehicle)
Finanzierungskonsortium *n* (Fin) financial (*or* financing) syndicate
Finanzierungskontrolle *f*
  (Fin) internal financial control
  – cash control
Finanzierungskosten *pl*
  (Fin) cost of finance
  – finance charges
  – financial charges (*or* expense)
  – funding cost
Finanzierungskredit *m* (Fin) credit for financing purposes
Finanzierungslast *f* (Fin) financing burden
Finanzierungs-Leasing *n* (Fin) financial leasing *(ie, medium- and long-term; opp, operating leasing)*
Finanzierungslücke *f*
  (Fin) financing gap
  (FiW) budgetary gap
Finanzierungsmakler *m* (Fin) credit broker
Finanzierungsmethode *f* (Fin) method of financing
Finanzierungsmittel *pl*
  (Fin) funds
  – finance
Finanzierungsmittelmarkt *m*
  (Fin) finance market
  – fund raising market
  (eg, money and capital markets, stock exchange)
Finanzierungsmodalitäten *fpl* (Fin) financing terms
Finanzierungsmöglichkeit *f* (Fin) source of finance
Finanzierungspaket *n* (Fin) financial package
Finanzierungspapiere *npl* (FiW) finance paper *(ie,*

treasury bills and notes issued by public authorities)
Finanzierungsplan *m* (Fin) financing plan (*or* scheme)
Finanzierungspolitik *f* (Fin) financial policy
Finanzierungspotential *n* (Fin) available capital and credit sources
Finanzierungspraxis *f* (Fin) practise of finance
Finanzierungsquelle *f*
(Fin) financing source
– source of finance
Finanzierungsrechnung *f* (ReW) statement of changes in financial position
Finanzierungsregeln *fpl* (Fin) rules for structuring debt capital
Finanzierungsreserve *f* (Fin) financial reserve *(ie, lump-sum amount added to cash requirements as a safety margin)*
Finanzierungssalden *mpl* (AuW) debit and credit balances
Finanzierungssaldo *m* (VGR) net financial investment
Finanzierungsschätze *pl* (FiW) financing Treasury bonds
Finanzierungsspielraum *m* (Fin) financial margin
Finanzierungsströme *mpl* (VGR) financial flows
Finanzierungstätigkeit *f* (Fin) financing activity
Finanzierungstheorie *f* (Fin) theory of managerial finance
Finanzierungsträger *m* (Fin) financing institution
Finanzierungsüberschuß *m* (Fin) surplus cash
Finanzierungsüberschüsse *mpl* **anlegen** (Fin) to invest cash temporarily *(eg, in interest-bearing securities)*
Finanzierungsunterlagen *fpl* (Fin) documents to be submitted for financing
Finanzierungsvertrag *m* (Fin) financing agreement
Finanzierungswechsel *mpl* (Fin) finance acceptances and notes
Finanzierungsziele *npl* (Fin) objectives of financial decisions
Finanzierungszusage *f*
(Fin) promise to finance
– financial commitment
– commitment to provide finance
Finanzierungszusageprovision *f* (Fin) finance commitment commission
Finanzimperium *n* (Fin) financial empire
Finanzinstitut *n* (Fin) financial institution
Finanzinvestition *f* (Fin) financial investment *(ie, loans, securities, participations)*
Finanzjahr *n* (Fin) financial (*or* fiscal) year
Finanzklemme *f* (Fin) financial squeeze
Finanzkonten *npl* (ReW) financial accounts
Finanzkontrolle *f* (FiW) (continuous) budgetary control *(ie, comprises: Kassenkontrolle, Rechnungskontrolle, Verwaltungskontrolle)*
Finanzkonzern *m* (Fin) financial group (of companies)
Finanzkraft *f* (Fin) financial strength (*or* power) (Fin, infml) financial clout
finanzkräftig (Fin) financially strong *(eg, company)*
Finanzkredit *m*
(Fin) finance loan
– financing credit

Finanzkrise *f* (Fin) financial crisis
Finanzlage *f* (Fin) financial position (*or* condition)
Finanzleiter *m*
(Fin) financial manager
– treasurer
– (US *usu.*) vice president finance *(ie, placed at the second level of the management structure)*
Finanzmagnat *m* (Fin) financial tycoon
Finanzmakler *m* (Fin) finance broker *(ie, making available medium- and long-term credits, participations, and enterprises as a whole)*
Finanzmanagement *n* (Fin) financial management *(ie, institutional and functional)*
Finanzmann *m* (Fin) financier
Finanzmarkt *m* (Fin) financial market
Finanzmathematik *f* (Math) mathematics of finance (*or* investment)
finanzmathematische Methoden *fpl* **der Investitionsrechnung**
(Fin) discounted cash flow methods
– time-adjusted methods
(ie, of preinvestment analysis; syn, dynamische Methoden)
Finanzminister *m*
(FiW) Minister of Finance
– Finance Minister
– (US) Secretary of the Treasury
– (GB) Chancellor of the Exchequer
Finanzministerium *n*
(FiW) Ministry of Finance
– (US) Treasury Department
– (GB) Treasury
Finanzmisere *f* (FiW) financial trouble (*or* straits)
Finanzmittel *pl*
(Fin) financial resources
– funds
Finanzmittelbindung *f* (Fin) absorption of funds
Finanzmonopol *n* (FiW) fiscal monopoly *(ie, exclusive right to appropriate the proceeds from the sale of certain goods for the compensation for certain services rendered)*
Finanznot *f* (FiW) financial straits *(eg, of municipalities)*
Finanzorganisation *f*
(Fin) administrative organization for financial decisions
– administrative arrangement for financial matters
Finanzperiode *f* (Fin) budgetary period
Finanzplan *m* (Fin) financial plan (*or* budget)
Finanzplanung *f*
(FiW) fiscal planning
(Fin) budgetary planning
– financial forecasting (*or* planning)
Finanzplanungsrat *m* (FiW) Financial Planning Council *(ie, composed of representatives of local government)*
Finanzplatz *m* (Fin) financial center
Finanzpolitik *f* (FiW, Fin) financial policy
finanzpolitisch
(FiW, Fin) financial
– fiscal
finanzpolitische Instrumente *npl* (FiW) fiscal policy mix

finanzpolitischer Hebel *m* (FiW) fiscal leverage *(Musgrave)*
finanzpolitischer Spielraum *m* (FiW) budgetary room for maneuver
- fiscal leverage
- scope for action within the fiscal system

Finanzrecht *n* (FiW) financial *(or* fiscal) law *(ie, comprises: Recht der Finanzverwaltung, Haushaltsrecht, Steuerrecht)*
Finanzreform *f* (FiW) fiscal reform
Finanzreformgesetz *n* (StR) Fiscal Reform Law, of 12 May 1969
Finanzregelung *f* (FiW) financial arrangements
Finanzriese *m* (Fin, infml) financial juggernaut
Finanzsachverständiger *m* (Fin) financial expert
finanzschwach (Fin) financially weak
Finanzschwierigkeiten *fpl* (Fin) = *finanzielle Schwierigkeiten*
Finanzsenator *m* (FiW) senator for finance *(ie, in the city states of Hamburg and Bremen, and in West Berlin)*
Finanzspritze *f*
 (Fin) cash infusion *(or* injection)
- injection of fresh funds
- (infml) fiscal hypo
- (infml) fiscal shot in the arm
finanzstark (Fin) financially strong
Finanzstatistik *f* (Fin) financial statistics
Finanzstatus *m* (Fin) statement of financial position
Finanzsteuer *f*
 (FiW) revenue tax *(ie, tax as a revenue-raising instrument or a source of general revenue)*
- tax levied for revenue
- (infml) revenue raiser
Finanzsteuerung *f* (Fin) financial engineering
Finanzstruktur *f*
 (Fin) financial structure
- pattern of finance
Finanzsystem *n* (FiW) fiscal system (of a country)
finanztechnisch
 (FiW) financial
- fiscal
 (ie, relating to the technical arrangements of public finance)
Finanzterminbörse *f* (Bö) financial futures market *(eg, in Chicago and London)*
Finanztermingeschäfte *npl* (Fin) financial futures *(ie, comprising futures contracts in interest rates and exchange rates; eg, dealing facilities exist notably in Chicago, and, since Sept 1982 in London: LIFFE: London International Financial Futures Exchange)*
Finanztheorie *f* (FiW) theory of public finance
Finanztransaktion *f* (Fin) financial operation *(or* transaction)
Finanzüberschuß *m* (Fin) cash flow
Finanzüberschußanalyse *f* (Fin) cash flow analysis
Finanzumlaufvermögen *n* (ReW) current financial assets
Finanzunternehmen *n* (Vw) business undertaking engaged in the provision of finance
Finanzverfassung *f*
 (FiW) constitutional provisions governing public finance *(eg, Art 105 ff GG)*

 (FiW) system of public finance
Finanzverfassungsrecht *n* (FiW) fiscal constitutional law
Finanzverhältnisse *npl* (Fin) financial conditions
Finanzvermögen *n*
 (Fin) financial assets
 (FiW) revenue-producing assets in public ownership *(eg, forestry, government farms)*
Finanzverwaltung *f* (FiW) fiscal administration *(ie, general term denoting all tax offices and revenue authorities)*
Finanzverwaltungsgesetz *n* (StR) Law on Fiscal Administration, as republished on 30 Aug 1971
Finanzverwaltungsrecht *n* (FiW) fiscal administration law
Finanzvorschau *f* (Fin) financial forecast
Finanzvorstand *m*
 (Fin) (corporate) financial manager
- financial executive
- (US) vice president finance
Finanzwechsel *m* (Fin) finance *(or* financial) bill
Finanzwelt *f* (Fin) financial community
Finanzwesen *n* (FiW) system of public finance
Finanzwirtschaft *f*
 (FiW) public finance *(ie, management of public revenues and expenditures)*
 (Fin) business *(or* managerial *or* corporate) finance
finanzwirtschaftlich
 (Fin) financial
 (FiW) relating to public finance
finanzwirtschaftliche Bewegungsbilanz *f*
 (Fin) source and application of funds statement
- funds statement
finanzwirtschaftliche Entscheidung *f* (Fin) financial decision
finanzwirtschaftliche Kennzahlen *fpl* (ReW) accounting *(or* financial) ratios
finanzwirtschaftliche Modellbildung *f* (Fin) financial modeling
Finanzwissenschaft *f*
 (FiW) public finance
- theory of public finance
- fiscal *(or* public sector) economics
Finanzzeitung *f* (Fin) financial paper
Finanzzentrum *n* (Fin) financial center
Finanzzoll *m*
 (FiW) financial *(or* revenue) duty
- revenue-raising duty
- revenue tariff
- customs duty of a fiscal nature
Finanzzuweisung *f* (FiW) revenue appropriation *(ie, by the Federal government to the Laender, Art. 106 IV GG)*
Finderlohn *m* (Re) finder's reward, § 971 BGB
fingierte Order *f* (com) fictitious order *(ie, submitted by commercial agent to his principal; cause for dismissal without notice)*
fingierter Besitz *m* (Re) constructive *(or* indirect) possession
fingierter Totalverlust *m* (SeeV) constructive total loss
fingierte Veräußerungsgewinne *mpl* (StR) fictitious disposal gains

233

Firma *f*
(Bw) firm
- business enterprise (*or* undertaking) *(ie, any economic unit of whatever type and size)*
(Re) firm (*or* business) name *(ie, the name under which a single trader carries on business and signs documents, § 17 HGB)*
Firma *f* **gründen**
(Re) to set up
- to organize
- to create
- to found ... a business
Firmenbezeichnung *f* (Bw) firm name
firmeneigene Vermittlungsgesellschaft *f* (Vers) captive agent
firmeneigene Versicherung *f* (Vers) self-insurance
firmeneigene Versicherungsgesellschaft *f* (Vers) captive insurance company
Firmenfortführung *f* (Bw) continued existence of a firm
Firmengeschichte *f* (Bw) business history
Firmengründung *f* (Bw) establishment of a business undertaking
Firmengruppe *f*
(Bw) group of firms (*or* companies)
- company group
Firmen-Gruppenversicherung *f* (Vers) group contract
Firmeninhaber *m* (com) proprietor of a firm (*or* business)
Firmenjargon *m* (com) in-house jargon
Firmenkauf *m* (Bw) acquisition of a firm
Firmenkern *m* (Bw) essential elements of a firm name *(eg, family name and first name of owner)*
Firmenkunde *m* (Fin) corporate customer
Firmenkundschaft *f* (Bw) business (*or* commercial) customers *(opp, Privatkundschaft)*
Firmenleitungskosten *pl* (KoR) general management cost
Firmenmantel *m*
(Bw) corporate shell
- shell company (*or* firm)
- nonoperating company
Firmenmarke *f* (Pat) trade name *(ie, covers all products of a company)*
Firmenname *m*
(Bw) business
- commercial
- corporate
- firm
- trade ... name
Firmenpleiten *fpl* (Bw) business failures
Firmenregister *n* (Re) = *Handelsregister*
Firmenschutz *m* (Re) protection of firm name
Firmensitz *m* (Bw) registered office
- domicile of a firm (*or* company)
- headquarters
Firmensprecher *m* (com) company spokesman
Firmentarif *m* (Pw) pay scale negotiated by single employer
Firmenverband *m* (Bw) group of companies
Firmenvertreter *m* (Bw) firm's representative
Firmenwagen *m* (Pw) company-supplied car
Firmenwerbung *f* (Mk) institutional advertising
Firmenwert *m* (Fin) goodwill *(syn, Geschäftswert)*

Firmenwertabschreibung *f* (Fin) goodwill amortization *(ie, method of determining the value of an enterprise as a whole)*
Firmenzeichen *n* (Bw) firm's distinctive symbol
firmieren
(Bw) to carry on business under the firm of ...
- to trade under the firm of ...
Fischbestände *mpl*
(com) fish stocks
- fishery resources
Fischereiabkommen *n*
(Re) fisheries agreement
- fishing pact
Fischereianschlußzone *f* (Re) contiguous fishing zone
Fischereiflotte *f* (com) fishing fleet
Fischereigrenzen *fpl* (com) fishery limits *(eg, 200 miles)*
Fischerei-Industrie *f* (com) fishing industry
Fischereipolitik *f* (EG) EEC fisheries policy
Fischereirechte *npl* (Re) fishery rights
Fischereischutzzone *f*
(Re) fishery conservation zone
- fisheries protection zone
Fischereistreit *m* (Re) fisheries dispute
Fischereiwirtschaft *f* (com) fisheries
Fischindustrie *f* (com) fish processing industry
Fischverarbeitung *f* (com) fish processing
fiskalische Besteuerung *f* (FiW) revenue taxation
fiskalische Bremse *f* (FiW) fiscal drag
fiskalischer Anreiz *m* (FiW) fiscal stimulus (*or* incentive)
fiskalisch strafbare Handlungen *fpl* (FiW) fiscal offenses
Fiskalzoll *m* (FiW) = *Finanzzoll*
Fiskus *m*
(FiW) revenue (*or* tax) authorities
- government as a tax collector
(Re) public fisc *(ie, government as a public body)*
fixe Fertigungsgemeinkosten *pl* (KoR) fixed factory overhead
fixe Gemeinkosten *pl* (KoR) fixed overhead
fixe Koeffizienten *mpl* (Vw) fixed coefficients
fixe Kosten *pl*
(com) inflexible expenses
(KoR, Vw) fixed
- constant
- nonvariable
- standby
- standing
- volume
- capacity ... cost (*or* expense)
fixe Kurse *mpl* (AuW) pegged rates
fixen
(Bö) to bear the market
- to sell a bear
- to sell short
Fixer *m* (Bö) bear (*or* short) seller
fixer Kapitalkoeffizient *m* (Vw) constant (*or* fixed) capital-output ratio
fixer Wechselkurs *m* (AuW) fixed exchange rate
fixe Stückkosten *pl* (KoR) fixed cost per unit
fixe Werksgemeinkosten *pl* (KoR) fixed factory overhead

Fixgeschäft n
(com) firm deal (or bargain)
(com) fixed-date purchase
(Re) contract where time is of the essence *(ie, performance at an exact point of time, or within a strictly defined period, § 361 BGB, § 376 HGB)*
(Bö) short sale
(Bö) time bargain
fixierte Wechselkurse mpl (AuW) fixed exchange rates
– pegged rates
Fixkauf m (com) = *Fixgeschäft*
Fixklausel f (com) fixed-date clause
Fixkosten pl (Vw, KoR) = *fixe Kosten*
Fixkosten-Aggregat n (KoR) block of fixed costs
Fixkostenbestandteil m (KoR) fixed-cost component
Fixkostenblock m (KoR) pool (or total) of fixed costs
Fixkostendeckung f (KoR) covering of fixed costs *(ie, by aggregate profit contribution = gesamte Deckungsbeiträge)*
Fixkostendeckungsrechnung f (KoR) analysis of fixed-cost allocation
Fixkostendegression f (KoR) decline of fixed unit costs when output rises
– fixed cost degression
Fixkostenkoeffizient m (KoR) fixed-cost coefficient *(ie, indicating the percentage share of fixed costs in total plant costs)*
fixkostenrelevante Beschäftigung f (KoR) relevant range
Fixkostenschichten fpl (KoR) blocks of fixed costs
Fixpunkt m
(EDV) checkpoint
– dump point
– conditional breakpoint *(syn, Anhaltepunkt)*
Fixpunktetikett n
(EDV) checkpoint label
Fixsummenspiel n (OR) constant sum game
Fixum n
(Pw) fixed salary (or compensation or remuneration)
(com) fixed allowance *(ie, guaranteed minimum income, as paid to commercial traveler)*
Fixverkauf m (com) fixed-date sale
Flachbaugruppe f
(EDV) printed circuit board
– board *(syn, gedruckte Schaltung)*
Fläche f **in dreidimensionaler Darstellung** (Math) surface in space
Flächendiagramm n (Stat) area diagram
Flächenintegral n (Math) surface integral
Flächennutzungsplan m (Re) municipal development plan
Flächenstaat m (Re) territorial state
Flächenstichprobe f (Stat) area sample
Flächenstichprobenverfahren n (Stat) area sampling
Flächenvergleichsfaktor m (Stat) area comparability factor
Flächenverteilung f (Math) surface distribution
flacher Trend m (Stat) flat trend
Fläche f **zweiten Grades** (Math) quadratic surface
Flachglasmarkt m (com) flat-glass market

flankierende Maßnahmen fpl (Vw) supporting measures
flankierende Werbung f (Mk) accessory advertising *(syn, unterstützende od Randwerbung)*
Flaschenhals m (com) = *Engpaß*
Flaschenpfand n (com) returnable-bottle deposit
Flaute f
(com) dullness
(Bö) slackness
– sluggishness
Fleischabteilung f
(com) meat department
– (GB) butchery
Flexibilität f **der Wechselkursparitäten** (AuW) flexibility in exchange rate parities
flexible Altersgrenze f
(Pw) flexible age limit
– flexible retirement (or retiring) age
– flexible pensionable age
flexible Arbeitszeit f (Pw) = *gleitende Arbeitszeit*
flexible Investmentgesellschaft f (Fin) management company
flexible Magnetplatte f
(EDV) floppy disk
flexible Normalkosten pl (KoR) normal standard cost
flexible Plankosten pl (KoR) flexible standard cost
flexible Plankostenrechnung f (KoR) flexible budgeting
flexible Planung f (Bw) contingency planning *(syn, Alternativplanung, Schubladenplanung)*
(OR) flexible planning *(ie, multi-phase decision process under conditions of uncertainty)*
flexible Preise mpl (Vw) flexible prices
flexibler Akzelerator m (Vw) flexible accelerator
flexibler Wechselkurs m
(AuW) flexible
– floating
– fluctuating ... exchange rate
flexibles Budget n
(Bw) flexible
– variable
– sliding-scale ... budget
(KoR) expense control (or formula) budget
– performance budget
flexible Vollkostenrechnung f (KoR) modified absorption costing
fliegender Streikposten m (Pw) roving picket
Fließarbeit f (IndE) continuous sequence of operations *(eg, Fließfertigung, Fließbandfertigung)*
Fließband n (IndE) assembly line
Fließbandabgleich m (IndE) assembly line balancing
Fließbandarbeiter m (Pw) assembly line worker
Fließbandfertigung f (IndE) assembly line (or belt) production
Fließbandprinzip n (IndE) conveyor belt system
Fließbandstation f (IndE) assembly station
Fließfertigung f
(IndE) continuous process production
– flow line (or shop) production
Fließprinzip n (IndE) principle of continuous production
Fließstraße f (IndE) production line
Fließverfahren n (IndE) flow process

Flipflop n (EDV) flipflop *(syn, bistabile Kippschaltung od Multivibratorschaltung, Eccles-Jordan-Schaltung)*
Floaten n (AuW) = *Floating*
Floatgewinn m (Fin) profit from different value dates
Floating n
  (AuW) floating
  – float *(ie, of foreign exchange rates)*
Floprate f (Mk) flop rate
flottant (Fin) non-permanent *(ie, security holdings)*
Flotte f
  (com) vehicle pool
  – fleet of trucks
Flottenrabatt m (Vers) vehicle pool rebate *(ie, granted for at least thirty insured automobiles)*
Flucht f **aus dem Dollar** (Fin) flight from the dollar
Flucht f **aus der DM** (Fin) flight of funds out of the Deutschemark
Fluchtgelder npl (Fin) = *Fluchtkapital*
flüchtiger Schuldner m
  (Re) absconding debtor
  – (sl) fly-by-night
flüchtiger Speicher m (EDV) volatile storage
Flucht f **in Gold od Edelmetalle** (Fin) flight *(eg, from a paper currency)* to gold and precious metals
Fluchtkapital n (Fin) flight (*or* runaway) capital
Fluchtlinientafel f (Math) alignment chart
Fluchtsteuer f (FiW) tax on capital flight
Flugblatt n
  (Mk) handbill
  – leaflet
  – throwaway leaflet
  – (US) flier, flyer
Flugpreise mpl (com) air fares
Flugunfallentschädigung f (Vers) air accident compensation
Fluktuation f
  (Pw) employee
  – labor
  – manpower
  – personnel
  – staff ... turnover
  (Fin) flow of funds *(ie, between markets)*
Fluktuationsarbeitslosigkeit f (Vw) frictional unemployment *(syn, friktionelle Arbeitslosigkeit)*
Fluktuationskennzahl f (Pw) net turnover rate
fluktuieren
  (Fin) to float
  – to flow
fluktuierende Gelder npl (AuW) hot money *(ie, transferred from one country to another to escape devaluation)*
fluktuierende Wechselkurse mpl (AuW) = *flexible Wechselkurse*
Flußbild n
  (Stat) flow chart (*or* diagram)
  – route diagram
Flußdiagramm n
  (Bw) flowchart
  – flow diagram
  (IndE) flow process chart
  (EDV) flowchart *(syn, Ablaufdiagramm)*

Flüsse mpl **in kontinuierlichen Medien** (OR) flows in continua
Flußfrachtgeschäft n (com) inland waterway transportation business
Flußfrachtsendung f (com) consignment carried by inland waterway
Flußgraph m (OR) flowgraph
Flußgraphtheorie f (OR) flowgraph theory
flüssige Mittel pl
  (Fin) cash resources
  – current funds
  – liquid funds *(ie, cash and bank balances, notes, and marketable securities)*
flüssiger Arbeitsablauf m
  (IndE) speedy dispatch of work
  – uninterrupted performance of work
Flüssigkeit f **des Geldmarktes** (Fin) ease in the money market
Flüssigkeitsverlust m (com) ullage
Flüssigkristallanzeige f (EDV) liquid crystal display
flüssigmachen (Fin) to mobilize *(eg, several million DM)*
Flußkonnossement n
  (WeR) shipping note, §§ 444–450 HGB
  – inland waterway bill of lading
Flußladeschein m (com) inland waterway bill of lading
Flußrichtung f (EDV) flow direction
fob-Geschäft n (AuW) f.o.b. sale
fob-Kalkulation f (AuW) f.o.b. calculation *(ie, of export prices)*
fob-Lieferung f (AuW) f.o.b. delivery
fob-Preis m (AuW) f.o.b. price
fob Schiff (AuW) free on board vessel
Folgeadresse f (EDV) link address
Folgeausgaben fpl (Fin) follow-up (*or* subsequent) expenditure
Folgebetrieb m (EDV) serial operation
Folge f **der arithmetischen Mittel** (Stat) arithmetic mean sequence
Folge f **der Länge Eins** (EDV) unit string
Folgeentscheidung f (Bw) follow-up (*or* sequential) decision
Folgeerzeugnis n (IndE) derived product
Folgefehler m (EDV) sequence error
Folgeinvestitionen fpl (Bw) follow-up investments
Folgekarte f (EDV) continuation card
Folgekartenbeschriftung f (EDV) repetitive printing
Folgekosten pl
  (com) follow-up costs
  (Vers) ongoing maintenance charges
Folgeleistungs-Sektor m (Vw) nonbasic sector
Folgen fpl **tragen** (com) to answer for the consequences
Folgeprämie f (Vers) subsequent premium *(ie, every premium which is not an ,,Erstprämie' = initial premium)*
Folgeprovision f (Vers) installment commission
Folgeprüfung f
  (Stat) sequential analysis (*or* sampling)
  (EDV) sequence check
Folgeregelung f (EDV) sequence control

Folgeregelungssystem n (EDV) adaptive control constraint, ACC
folgerichtig (Log) consistent
Folgerichtigkeit f (Log) consistency *(ie, a set of propositions has consistency or is consistent when no contradiction can be derived from the joint assertion of the propositions in the set)*
folgern
(Log) to conclude
– to infer from
Folgerückversicherung f (Vers) retrocession *(ie, cession of reinsurance by one reinsurer to another reinsurer; syn, Retrozession)*
Folgerung f
(Log) conclusion
– inference
Folgerungsbeziehung f (Log) entailment relation
Folgeschaden m
(Re) consequential
– constructive
– indirect ... damage *(or loss)*
Folgeschadenversicherung f (Vers) consequential loss insurance
Folgespalte f (ReW) continue column
Folgestanzen n (EDV) gang punching
Folgestanzer m (EDV) gang punch
Folgesteuern fpl (FiW) follow-up taxes *(ie, levied to stop loopholes in the tax system; eg, inheritance tax followed by gift tax)*
Folgesteuerung f (EDV) sequential control
Folgetestverfahren n (Stat) sequential analysis *(or sampling)*
Folgeverarbeitung f (EDV) sequential scheduling
Folge f **von Ereignissen** (Stat) sequence of occurrences
Folgezeitverfahren n (IndE) differential timing
Fonds m
(com) fund
(Fin) earmarked reserve fund
(FiW) bonds of public authorities *(ie, often restricted to funded loans, exclusive of short-term treasury notes)*
(Fin) = investment fund
(Fin) = real property fund
Fondsanlage f (Fin) fund investment
Fondsanteil m
(Fin) share
– (GB) unit
Fondsanteilseigner m
(Fin) shareholder
– (GB) unitholder
Fondsbeitrag m (Fin) contribution to fund
Fondsbörse f
(Bö) stock exchange *(opp, commodity exchange)*
(Bö) fixed-interest security exchange
Fonds m **der flüssigen Mittel** (Fin) cash fund *(ie, in Kapitalflußrechnung = funds statement)*
Fonds m **des Nettoumlaufvermögens** (Fin) working-capital fund
fondsgebundene Lebensversicherung f
(Vers) variable life insurance
– (US) share-linked life insurance
– (GB) unit-linked life assurance
Fondsgesellschaft f (Fin) investment company
Fonds m **liquider Mittel** (Fin) cash fund

Fondsprinzip n (FiW) principle permitting earmarking of public funds for specific purposes *(opp, Non-Affektationsprinzip)*
Fondsrechnung f (ReW) funds statement
Fondsvermögen n (Fin) fund's assets
Fondsverwaltung f (Fin) fund management
forcieren
(com) to force up
– to speed up
– to step up
Förderabgabe f (FiW) mining royalty
Förderland n (Vw) producing country
Fördermittel npl (IndE) materials handling equipment
Förderprämie f (com) output bonus
Förderung f
(IndE) production
(IndE) output
förderungswürdig (StR) worthy of support
– meritorius
(eg, officially recognized as ..., § 10b I EStG)
Förderziele npl (IndE) production targets
Förderziffern fpl (IndE) production *(or output)* figures
fordern
(Re) to claim
– to assert a claim *(or right)*
Forderung f
(com) demand *(ie, for money or property)*
(com) claim
(Re) claim *(ie, contract claim + tort = Forderung aus Vertrag + unerlaubter Handlung)*
(ReW) receivable
Forderung f **abtreten** (Re) to assign a claim *(or debt)*
Forderung f **anerkennen** (Re) to allow a claim
Forderung f **anmelden** (Re) to prove a debt *(ie, in bankruptcy proceedings)*
Forderung f **aufgeben**
(Re) to abandon
– to resign
– to waive ... a claim
Forderung f **befriedigen** (Re) to satisfy a claim
Förderung f **der Allgemeinheit** (StR) furtherance *(or promotion)* of public welfare
Förderung f **des Warenhandels** (AuW) promotion of commodity trade
Forderung f **einklagen** (Re) to sue for the recovery of a debt
Forderungen fpl
(ReW) accounts receivables
Also:
– customers' accounts
– debt outstanding
– debts receivable
– outstanding accounts
– receivables
– trade debtors
Forderungen fpl **abschreiben** (ReW) to write off delinquent accounts
Forderungen fpl **an Konzernunternehmen**
(ReW) due from affiliated companies *(or affiliates)*
– indebtedness of affiliates

237

Forderungen *fpl* **an Kreditinstitute** (ReW) due from banks
Forderungen *fpl* **an Kunden** (ReW, Fin) due from non-bank customers
Forderungen *fpl* **an verbundene Unternehmen** (ReW) due from subsidiaries and affiliated companies
– accounts receivable from related enterprises
Forderungen *fpl* **aus Aktienzeichnungen** (Fin) stock subscriptions receivable
Forderungen *fpl* **aus Inkassogeschäften** (Fin) collections receivable
Forderungen *fpl* **aus Kreditgeschäften** (Fin) receivables from lending operations
Forderungen *fpl* **aus Lieferungen und Leistungen** (ReW, EG) trade debtors
Forderungen *fpl* **aus Warenlieferungen und Leistungen (a. W. u. L.)** (ReW) accounts receivable from sales and services
– trade accounts receivable
– customers' accounts
– outstanding trade debts
– trade debtors (*or* receivables)
Forderungen *fpl* **a.W.u.L. an eigene Tochtergesellschaften** (ReW) accounts receivable from sales and services – subsidiaries
Forderungen *fpl* **a.W.u.L. – Ausland** (ReW) accounts receivable from sales and services – foreign
Forderungen *fpl* **a.W.u.L. – Inland** (ReW) accounts receivable from sales and services – domestic
Forderungen *fpl* **einziehen** (Fin) to collect accounts (*or* receivables)
Forderungen *fpl* **gegenüber leitenden Angestellten und Aktionären** (ReW) accounts receivable from officers, directors, and stockholders
Forderungen *fpl* **gegen verbundene Unternehmen** (ReW, EG) loans to affiliated undertakings
Forderung *f* **erfüllen**
(com) to satisfy (*or* answer) a claim
– to fulfill (*or* meet) a demand
– to agree to (*or* respond to) a demand
Forderung *f* **erlassen** (Re) to forgo (*or* release from) a debt
Forderung *f* **geltend machen**
(Re) to assert
– to make
– to prefer
– to put in
– to raise
– to set up ... a claim
Förderung *f* **gewerblicher Interessen** (com) furtherance of commercial interests
Forderungsabschreibung *f* (ReW) writedown of uncollectible receivables, § 40 III HGB
Forderungsabtretung *f* (Re) assignment of claim (*or* debt), §§ 398 ff BGB
Forderungsanmeldung *f* (Re) filing a debt *(ie, in bankruptcy proceedings)*
Forderungsausfall *m* (ReW) loss of receivables outstanding
Forderungsausfallquote *f* (Fin) loss chargeoff ratio *(ie, in banking)*

Forderungsberechtigter *m* (Re) rightful claimant *(ie, one who may assert a right, demand, or claim)*
Forderungseinzug *m* (Fin) collection of accounts receivable
Forderungsgarantie *f* (Re) guaranty of receivables outstanding
Förderungsgebiet *n* (Vw) development area
Forderung *f* **sichern** (Fin) to secure an existing debt
Forderungs-Inkasso *n* (Fin) collection of accounts receivable
Forderungskauf *m* (Fin) purchase of accounts receivable, § 437 BGB
Förderungsmaßnahmen *fpl*
(Vw) (state *or* government) promotion measures
(Pw) employee development measures
Forderungspapiere *npl* (WeR) securities representing money claims *(opp, Mitgliedschaftspapiere und sachenrechtliche Papiere)*
Forderungspfändung *f* (Re) attachment of debt
Forderungspodest *n* (Pw) intitial pay settlement claim *(ie, made by a union during the first bargaining round)*
Förderungsprogramm *n* (Vw) development plan
Forderungsrecht *n* (Re) *(personal)* right to recover a debt *(ie, sustainable against a specific person, not the world at large; eg, money claims, claims under contracts, unjust enrichment, tort)*
Forderungsrisiko *n* (ReW) risk on receivables
Forderungsstrom *m* (VGR) flow of monetary claims
Forderungsstundung *f* (Re) respite for payment of debt *(ie, time or delay obtained for the payment of sums owed)*
Forderungstilgung *f* (Fin) repayment of debt
Forderungstransfer *m* (Vw) transfer of claims (*or* accounts outstanding)
Forderungsübergang *m* (Re) transmission of claim
Forderungsübernahme *f* (Re) assumption of indebtedness *(ie, one person binds himself to pay debt incurred by another)*
Forderungsumschlag *m* (Fin) receivables turnover (ratio)
Forderungsverletzung *f* (Re) breach of an obligation
Forderungsvermögen *n* (Fin) financial assets
Forderungsverzicht *m*
(Re) remission (*or* release) of a debt
– waiver of claims outstanding
förderungswürdig
(FiW) eligible for favorable tax treatment
(com) eligible for promotion
Förderungswürdigkeit *f* (com) eligbility for aid (*or* promotion)
Forderung *f* **zurückweisen**
(Re) to reject a claim
– to refuse to recognize a claim
Forfaitierung *f* (AuW) nonrecourse export financing
Forfaitierungsgeschäft *n* (Fin) forfaiting transaction
formale Äquivalenz *f* (Log) formal equivalence
formale Entscheidungslogik *f* (Bw) formal decision logic
formale Inzidenz *f* (FiW) formal incidence

formale Logik *f* (Log) formal logic
formaler Einwand *m* (Re) technical objection
formaler Kommunikationsweg *m* (Bw) formal communication channel *(ie, based on a chain of command from the top of the organization down)*
formale Supposition *f* (Log) formal supposition
– use of a term
formale Unternehmensplanung *f* (Bw) formal corporate planning
Formalitäten *fpl* **klären** (Re) to handle formalities
Formalprüfung *f* (Pat) examination as to formal requirements
Formalstruktur *f* **der Organisation** (Bw) formal organizational structure
Formalwissenschaft *f* (Log) formal science
Format *n* (EDV) format
formatieren (EDV) to format
formatierter Datenbestand *m* (EDV) formatted data set
Formatsteuerzeichen *n*
(EDV) layout character
– format effector
formbedürftiger Vertrag *m* (Re) formal contract
Formblatt *n*
(com) form
– blank
(ReW) financial statement form
Formbrief *m* (com) form letter *(ie, business or advertising letter composed of carefully phrased but repetitive elements; opp, Schemabrief)*
Formelflexibilität *f* (FiW) formula flexibility *(ie, instrument designed to flatten out cyclical fluctuations)*
formelle Kreditwürdigkeitsprüfung *f* (Fin) formal test of credit standing
formeller Führungsstil *m* (Bw) formal management style
formelles Recht *n*
(Re) procedural
– remedial
– adjective . . . law
– law of procedure
Formalsprache *f* (EDV) formula language
Formerfordernis *n* (Re) requirement (*or* requisite) of form
Formfehler *m*
(Re) defect (*or* insufficiency) of form
(EDV) syntax error
formfreier Vertrag *m* (Re) informal contract
Formfreiheit *f*
(Re) freedom of form *(ie, contracts under German law as a rule do not require any form)*
– absence of formal requirements
Formgebung *f* (com) industrial design
Formgestalter *m* (com) industrial designer
Formkaufmann *m* (Re) association on which the law confers the attributes of a merchant, regardless of the object of its business, § 6 II HGB
förmlich (Re) in due form
förmliche Beschwerde *f* (StR) administrative appeal *(ie, against a decision rejecting the application for administrative relief, § 349 AO)*
förmlicher Vertrag *m* (Re) formal contract (*or* agreement)

förmlich in Ordnung (StR) formally in order, Abschn. 29 I EStR
formlos (com) informal
formlose Befragung *f* (Mk) informal interview
formloser Antrag *m* (com) simple application
formloser Vertrag *m* (Re) informal agreement
formlose Vereinbarung *f* (com) informal arrangement
formlos übertragbar (Re, WeR) freely transferable
formlos übertragen (WeR) to negotiate by delivery only
Formmangel *m*
(Re) deficiency in form
– defect in form
– insufficiency of form
– noncompliance with required form
Formregel *f* (Log) rule of formation
Formsache *f*
(com) formality
– matter of form
Formular *n*
(com) blank
– form
– blank form
– printed form
(EDV) form
Formularbrief *m* (com) = *Formbrief*
Formularformatspeicher *m* (EDV) (vertical) format buffer
Formularkopf *m* (EDV) form title field
Formulartransport *m* (EDV) form feed
Formularvertrag *m* (Re) standard form contract
Formularvorschubzeichen *n* (EDV) form feed character
form- und fristgerecht (Re) in due form and time
Formvorschrift *f*
(Re) form requirement
– requisite of form
Formvorschriften *fpl* **für die Anmeldung** (Pat) formal filing requirements
formwechselnde Umwandlung *f* (Re) transformation of a company
formwidrig (Re) contrary to formal requirements
Formzwang *m*
(Re) requisites of form
– required formalities *(eg, it is not essential that any particular formalities be complied with)*
Forschungsabteilung *f* (Bw) research department
Forschungsansatz *m* (Log) approach
Forschungsanstalt *f* (com) research institute
Forschungsauftrag *m* (Bw) research assignment (*or* contract)
Forschungseinrichtungen *fpl* (Bw) research facilities
Forschungsetat *m* (Bw) research budget
Forschungsgelder *npl* (Bw) research funds
Forschungshaushalt *m* (Bw) research budget
Forschungsinstitut *n* (com) research institute
Forschungskosten *pl* (ReW) research costs
Forschungsökonomik *f* (Vw) research economics
Forschungsprogramm *n* (Bw) research program
Forschungsprojekt *n* (Bw) research project
Forschungs- und Entwicklungskosten *pl* (Rew, EG) cost of research and development
Forschungsvorhaben *n* (Bw) research project

Forschungszuschuß *m* (FiW) research grant
Forschung *f* **und Entwicklung** *f* (Bw) research and development, R & D
Forstwirtschaft *f* (Vw) forestry
forstwirtschaftlicher Betrieb *m* (Bw) forestry operation
Fortbestand *m* **e-s Unternehmens** (Bw) ongoing (*or* continued) existence of a company
Fortbestehen *n*
 (Bw) continuity of existence
 – continued existence
Fortbildung *f*
 (Pw) further training (*or* education)
 – advanced training
Fortbildungsbedarf *m* (Pw) training needs (*or* requirements)
Fortbildungskosten *pl* (StR) cost of further training
Fortbildungs-Maßnahmen *fpl* (Pw) training measures
Fortbildungs-Methoden *fpl* (Pw) training techniques
Fortbildungsprogramm *n*
 (Pw) training program
 – employee development program
Fortbildungsziel *n* (Pw) training objective
Fortführung *f* **der Firma**
 (com) continuation of business
 (Re) continuation of firm name
fortgeführte Anlagekosten *pl* (ReW) carrying rate of asset
fortgeführte Kosten *pl* (ReW) depreciated book value (*or* cost)
fortgeführter Anschaffungswert *m* (ReW) net book value
fortgeschrittene Informationsverarbeitung *f* (EDV) advanced information processing, AIP
fortlaufende Kreditbürgschaft *f* (Fin) continuing guaranty
fortlaufende Notierung *f*
 (Bö) consecutive (*or* continuous) quotation
 – variable-price quotation (*opp, Einheitskurs*)
fortlaufender Handel *m* (Bö) continuous market
fortlaufende Verzinsung *f* (Fin) continuous interest (*or* compounding)
fortlaufend numeriert (com) consecutively numbered
fortschreiben (ReW, EDV) to update
Fortschreiben *n* (com) file maintenance
Fortschreibung *f* (ReW, EDV) updating
 (StR) adjustment of assessed value, § 22 BewG
Fortschreibungsdatei *f*
 (EDV) amendment
 – change
 – activity
 – transaction
 – up date . . . file
 (*syn, Änderungsdatei, Bewegungsdatei*)
Fortschreibungsdifferenz *f* (ReW) updating difference
Fortschreibungsverfahren *n* (ReW) application of estimation or grossing-up procedure
fortschreitender Mittelwert *m* (Stat) progressive average
fortschreitendes Gleichgewicht *n* (Vw) progressive equilibrium

Fortschrittsbericht *m* (com) progress report *(ie, submitted in multi-phase project realization)*
Fortschrittsmöglichkeitsfunktion *f* (Bw) innovation possibility function
Fortschrittszeitverfahren *n* (IndE) cumulative timing
Fortsetzungszeile *f* (EDV, Cobol) continuation line
Fortwälzung *f* (FiW) forward shifting
Fotokopie *f*
 (com) photocopy
 – photostat (copy)
fotokopieren (com) to photocopy
Fotokopiergerät *n* (com) photocopier
Fototermin *m* (com) photograph session
F. P. A.-Deckung *f* (SeeV) f.p.a. cover
FPI-Vertrag *m* (com) fixed-price incentive contract
Fracht *f*
 (com) cargo
 – freight
 – load
 (com) = *Frachtgebühr*
Frachtabnahme *f* (com) acceptance of consignment (*or* shipment)
Frachtabschluß *m* (com) freight fixing
Frachtangebot *n* (com freight offered
Frachtannahme *f* (com) = *Frachtabnahme*
Frachtanspruch *m* (com) freight claim
Frachtaufkommen *n* (com) freight volume
Frachtaufschlag *m* (com freight surcharge
Frachtaufseher *m* (com) cargo superintendent
Frachtausgleich *m* (com freight equalization
Frachtausschuß *m* (com) freight bureau
Frachtaval *n* (Fin) guaranty of freight payment
Frachtbasis *f*
 (com) freight basis
 – basing point
 – equalization point
Frachtbasissystem *n*
 (com) basing point system
Frachtbedingungen *fpl* (com) terms of freight
Frachtbeförderung *f* (com) freightage
Fracht *f* **berechnen** (com) to charge freight
Frachtberechnung *f*
 (com) calculation of freight
 (com) freight charges
Fracht bezahlt
 (com) freight prepaid
 – (GB) carriage paid, C/P
Fracht bezahlt Empfänger (com) freight forward
Frachtbilanz *f* (VGR) net freights
Frachtbörse *f* (com) = *Frachtenbörse*
Frachtbrief *m*
 (com) railroad bill of lading
 – railroad waybill
 – freight bill
 – (GB) consignment note
 – (GB) letter of consignment
 (ie, unlike the German document which is a mere instrument of evidence = Beweisurkunde, the English counterparts are transferable or negotiable)
Frachtbriefabrechnung *f* (com) waybill accounting
Frachtbriefdoppel *n*
 (com) duplicate freight bill

- counterfoil waybill
- (GB) duplicate consignment note

Frachtbuchung f (com) freight booking
Frachtbüro n (com) freight office
Frachtenausgleich m (com) equalization of freight rates
Frachtenausschuß m (com) = *Frachtausschuß*
Frachtenaval n (Fin) bank guaranty for deferred freight payment
Frachtenbörse f (com) shipping exchange
Frachtermäßigung f (com) freight reduction
Frachtertrag m (com) freight receipts (*or* revenue)
frachtfrei
 (com) freight prepaid
- (GB) carriage paid, C. P.
 (com, *Incoterms 1953*) freight or carriage paid to ... *(named port of destination)*
frachtfreie Beförderung f (com) transport at no charge to customer
frachtfrei Grenze (com) carriage paid to frontier
Frachtführer m
 (com) carrier
- haulage contractor
 (ie, individual or organization engaged in transporting goods by land, river or other inland waterway for hire = gewerbsmäßig; called ‚Verfrachter' = ‚ocean carrier' in sea transport)
Frachtführer-Klausel f (Vers) carrier clause *(ie, insurance protection does not extend to carriers, shipowners and warehousemen who are employed or in the service of the insured)*
Frachtgebühr f
 (com) freight
- freight charge
- (GB) carriage charge
Fracht f **gegen Nachnahme**
 (com) freight collect
- (GB) freight forward, frt fwd
 (opp, frachtfrei = freight prepaid)
Frachtgeschäft n (com) freight business
frachtgünstig (com) low freight
Frachtgut n
 (com) freight *(ie, in all types of transportation)*
- (GB) freight *(ie, in sea and air transport)*
- cargo
Fracht f **im voraus bezahlt**
 (com) freight prepaid
- (GB) carriage paid, C. P.
Fracht f **in Bausch und Bogen** (com) flat rate (*or* lump sum) freight *(syn, Pauschalfracht)*
Frachtinkasso n (com) collection of freight charges
Frachtkosten pl
 (com) freight
- freightage
- freight charges
- carrying charges
Frachtmakler m (com) freight broker
Frachtmaklergebühr f (com) freight brokerage
Frachtmaklergeschäft n (com) freight broking
Frachtmanifest n **des Luftfahrzeugs** (com) aircraft cargo manifest
Frachtnachlaß m (com) freight rebate
Frachtnotierung f (Bö) freight quotation
Frachtpapier n (com) transport document
Frachtparität f (com) basing point

Fracht f **per Nachnahme**
 (com) freight collect (*or* forward)
- (GB) carriage forward
Frachtrate f (com) shipping rate
Frachtraum m (com) freight capacity
Frachtraum m **belegen** (com) to book freight
Frachtrechnung f (com) freight note (*or* account)
Frachtsatz m (com) freight rate
Frachtstundung f (com) deferred freight payment *(ie, method used by ‚Deutsche Verkehrskreditbank' for cashless settlement of freightage, fees and other Bundesbahn claims)*
Frachttarif m
 (com) freight rates (*or* tariff)
- prices for rail freight
Fracht– und Liegegeld n (com) freight and demurrage
fracht- und spesenfrei (com) freight and charges prepaid
Fracht f **und Versicherung** f (com) freight and insurance
frachtungünstig (com) high freight
Frachtunterbietung f (com) rate cutting *(ie, in ocean shipping)*
Frachtverkehr m (com) freight traffic
Frachtverlag m (com) = *Frachtvorlage*
Frachtvermerk m (com) freight clause
Frachtversicherer m (Vers) cargo underwriter
Frachtversicherung f (Vers) cargo (*or* freight) insurance
Frachtversicherungspolice f (Vers) cargo policy
Frachtvertrag m
 (com) freight contract
- (GB) contract of carriage
Fracht f **vorausbezahlt**
 (com) freight prepaid
- (GB) carriage paid, C. P.
Frachtvorlage f (com) advance payment of freight charges by forwarder
Frachtvorschuß m (com) advance on freight
Frachtweg m (com) freight route
Fracht f **zahlt der Empfänger**
 (com) freight collect (*or* forward)
- (GB) carriage forward, C/F
Frachtzahlung f **im Bestimmungshafen** (com) freight payable at destination
Fracht-Zone f (com) freight zone
Frachtzuschlag m
 (com) extra freight
- (GB) additional carriage
Frachtzustellung f (com) freight delivery
Frachtzuteilung f (com) space allocation
Frage f **anschneiden**
 (com) to address
- to broach
- to take up ... a question
Fragebogen m (Mk) questionnaire
Fragebogen m **ausfüllen** (Mk) to fill out (*or* make out) a questionnaire
Fragebogen m **mit Strichmarkierung** (EDV) bar markable request form
Fraktil n (Stat) fractile *(ie, of a distribution)*
Fraktionssitzung f (Pw) caucus session
Franchise f
 (com) weight variation allowance

(Mk) franchise
- franchising
(Vers) deductible
- excess insurance
- percentage exempion
(SeeV) free average
Franchisegeber *m* (Mk) franchisor *(ie, Hersteller/ Großhändler)*
Franchise-Klausel *f* (Vers) franchise clause *(ie, claims below a stated limit are not payable by insurer)*
Franchisenehmer *m* (Mk) franchisee *(ie, Einzelhändler)*
Franchisesystem *n* (Mk) franchising system
Franchiseunternehmen *n* (Mk) franchise company
Franchisevertrag *m* (Mk) franchise agreement
Frankatur *f* (com) prepayment of freight
Frankaturvermerk *m* (com) freight prepayment mark
Frankaturzwang *m* (com) compulsory prepayment of freight
frankieren
(com) to stamp *(ie, a letter)*
(com) to frank *(ie, using a metering machine)*
Frankiermaschine *f*
(com) postage meter
- (GB) franking machine
frankiert
(com) stamped
- post paid
- postage paid
frankierter Brief *m* (com) free-paid letter
franko (com) charges prepaid by sender
franko Fracht und Zoll (com) carriage and duty prepaid
franko Kurtage (Bö) no brokerage
Frankoposten *mpl* (Fin) free-of-charge items in current account statements
franko Provision (Bö) free of commission *(ie, in stock exchange orders for over-the-counter securities)*
Frauenbeschäftigung *f*
(Pw) female employment
- women in the labor force
- female labor force activity
Frauenerwerbsarbeit *f* (Pw) gainful occupation of women
frei (Pw) time off work *(eg, a day, two weeks, a morning off)*
Freiaktie *f*
(Fin) gratuitous share *(ie, illegal under German stock corporation law)*
(Fin) bonus share *(ie, backed by retained earnings or reserves)*
frei an Bord (com, *Incoterms*) free on board, F.O.B., fob
Freiantwort *f* (com) prepaid answer
frei Bahnstation (com) free on board *(ie, railroad station)*
frei Bau (com) free construction site
frei beantwortbare Frage *f* (Stat) open-ended question
frei benannter Abflughafen (com, *Incoterms*) F.O.B. *(or* fob) airport

freieruflich (com) free lance *(eg, journalist, interpreter)*
Freiberuflicher *m*
(com) (free) professional
- professional worker
freiberuflicher Mitarbeiter *m* (com) free lance contributor
freiberuflicher Werbeberater *m* (Mk) advertising consultant *(or* counselor)
freiberufliche Tätigkeit *f*
(Pw) self-employment
- free-lance work
frei Bestimmungsort
(com) free domicile
- free delivered
Freibetrag *m*
(Zo) amount of exemption
(StR) allowable deduction
- exemption
- tax-free amount
Freibetrag *m* **für außergewöhnliche Belastung** (StR) allowance for extraordinary financial burden
Freibezirk *m* (Zo) free port area
freibleibend
(com) subject to change without notice
- without engagement
(Fin) subject to prior sale
freibleibend anbieten (com) to offer subject to confirmation
freibleibende Offerte *f* (com) = *freibleibendes Angebot*
freibleibendes Angebot *n* (com) offer without engagement
Freibordabkommen *n* (Re) Load-Line Convention
Freibordzeugnis *n* (com) freeboard certificate
freie Berufe *mpl* (com) liberal professions
freie Berufswahl *f* (Re) freedom of choise of occupation or profession
freie Beweiswürdigung *f* (StR) free evaluation of facts and evidence, § 96 I FGO
freie Forschung *f* (com) uncommitted research
frei Eisenbahnwaggon (com, *Incoterms*) free on rail, F.O.R., for
freie Kapazität *f*
(Bw) idle
- spare
- unused ... capacity
freie Konkurrenz *f* (Vw) free competition
freie Konsumwahl *f*
(Vw) freedom of choice by consumers
- free consumers' choice
freie Lieferung *f* (com) delivery free of charge
freie Liquiditätsreserven *fpl* (Vw) free liquid reserves
freie Marktwirtschaft *f* (Vw) free *(or* liberal) market economy
freie Pufferzeit *f* (OR) (early) free float
freier Aktionär *m* (Fin) outside shareholder
freier Beruf *m* (com) (liberal) profession
freier Devisenverkehr *m* (AuW) freedom of exchange operations
freier Erfinder *m* (Pat) independent inventor
freie Reserven *fpl* (Vw) free reserves
freier Goldmarkt *m* (Fin) free-tier gold market

freier Handel *m* (Bö) unofficial trading
freier Importeur *m* (com) outside importer
freier Kapitalverkehr *m* (AuW) freedom of capital movements
freier Lombardspielraum *m* (Vw) scope for raising lombard loans
freier Makler *m*
 (com) outside broker
 (Bö) unofficial (*or* private) broker *(syn, Privatmakler; opp, amtlicher Kursmakler)*
freier Markt *m*
 (com) free (*or* open) market
 (Bö) unofficial market
 – off-board trading
freier Marktpreis *m* (com) competitive (*or* free market) price
freier Marktzutritt *m*
 (Vw) freedom of entry
 – free entry into a market
freier Mitarbeiter *m* (com) free-lance collaborator
freier Parameter *m* (Math) arbitrary parameter
freie Rücklagen *fpl*
 (ReW) free
 – voluntary
 – uncommitted ... reserves
 – retained earnings – voluntary portion
freier Verkehr *m* (Zo) = *freier Warenverkehr*
freier Vorgangspuffer *m* (OR) = *freie Pufferzeit*
freier Warenverkehr *m* (Zo) free movement of goods
freier Wechselkurs *m* (AuW) = *frei schwankender Wechselkurs*
freier Wettbewerbspreis *m* (Vw) open market price
freier Wohnungsbau *m* (com) privately (*or* market) financed housing
freier Zugang *m* (Pw) unrestricted entry *(eg, to institutions of higher learning)*
freies Band *n* (EDV) clear band *(ie, in OCR)*
freies Einkommen *n*
 (Pw) net income
 – take-home pay
freies Ermessen *n* (Re) absolute discretion
freies Gut *n*
 (Vw) free good (*or* resource)
 – common property resource
freies Guthaben *n* (Vw) free balance
freies Interview *n* (Stat) nonstructured interview
freie Spanne *f* (Mk) free mark-up
freies Rediskontkontingent *n* (Vw) unused rediscount quota
freies Spiel *n* **der Marktkräfte** (Vw) free play of market forces
freies Spiel *n* **des Wettbewerbs** (Vw) unrestrained interaction of competitive forces
freie Stelle *f*
 (Pw) vacant job
 – vacancy
 – job opening
 – job on offer
freie Stücke *npl* (Fin) freely disposable securities *(opp, Sperrstücke)*
freies Vermögen *n* (Vers) free assets
freie Tankstelle *f*
 (com) independent filling station
 – (US) private-brand gas station (*or* retailer)

freie Übertragbarkeit *f*
 (WeR) free transferability
 – negotiability
freie Wahl *f* **des Arbeitsplatzes** (Pw) free choice of employment
freie Wirtschaft *f*
 (Vw) free (*or* liberal) market economy
 – private enterprise
freie Wohnung *f* (StR) free living quarters
Freiexemplar *n* (com) free (*or* complimentary) copy
frei finanziert (Fin) privately financed
frei finanzierter Wohnungsbau *m* (com) = *freier Wohnungsbau*
frei Flughafen (com) free airport
Freigabe *f* (Fin) unfreezing *(eg, of blocked assets)*
Freigabedatum *n* (EDV) purge date
Freigabe *f* **der Waren**
 (Zo) release of the goods
Freigabesignal *n* (EDV) enabling signal
Freigabe *f* **von Mitteln** (Fin) unblocking (*or* unfreezing) of funds
Freigabe *f* **von Wechselkursen**
 (AuW) unpegging of foreign exchange rates
 – floating
Freigelände *n* (com) open-air space (*or* site) *(ie, at fairs and exhibitions)*
freigemacht
 (com) prepaid
 – postage paid
freigemachter Umschlag *m* (com) postage-free envelope
frei-gemeinnützige Betriebe *mpl* (Re) private non-profit enterprises *(ie, seeking to satisfy public welfare goals)*
freigesetzte Arbeitskräfte *fpl*
 (Pw) redundant workers (*or* labor)
 – displaced workers
freigestellt (Pw) freed for full-time works council activity
 (Pw) laid off
frei Grenze (com) free frontier
Freigrenze *f*
 (StR) tax-free amount
 (Zo) duty-free allowance
Freigut *n* (Zo) goods in free circulation
Freigutumwandlung *f* (Zo) conversion of duty-free goods
Freigutveredelung *f* (Zo) processing of duty-free goods
Freihafen *m*
 (Zo) free port (area)
 – free trade zone
Freihafengebiet *n* (Zo) free port area
Freihafengrenze *f* (Zo) free port frontier
Freihafenlager *n* (com) free port store (*or* warehouse)
Freihafen-Veredelungsverkehr *m* (Zo) free port processing
Freihandel *m*
 (Vw) free (*or* liberal) trade
 (Bö) over-the-counter trade
Freihandelsabkommen *n* (AuW) free-trade agreement
Freihandelsgebiet *n*
 (AuW) free trade area

- (US) foreign trade zone
Freihandels-Gleichgewicht *n* (AuW) free trade equilibrium
Freihandelspolitik *f* (Vw) liberal trade policy
Freihandelsprinzip *n* (AuW) principle of free trade
Freihandelszone *f*
(AuW) free trade area
- (US) foreign trade zone
freihändig (com) by private contract
freihändige Auftragsvergabe *f* (com) discretionary award of contract
freihändiger Ankauf *m* (Fin) purchase at market rates
freihändiger Rückkauf *m* (Fin) repurchase *(eg, of mortgage bonds)* in the open market
freihändiger Verkauf *m* (Fin) direct offering *(or sale) (eg, of a loan issue)*
freihändig verkaufen
(com) to sell privately
- to sell by private contract
freihändig verwerten (com) to sell in the open market
Freihandverfahren *n* (Stat) freehand method
frei Haus
(com) free of charge to address of buyer
- franco domicile
- free house (*or* domicile)
frei Haus unverzollt (com) free at domicile not cleared through customs
frei Haus verzollt (com) free at domicile after customs clearance
Freiheit *f* **des Dienstleistungsverkehrs** (Vw) freedom to provide services
Freiheitsgrad *m* (Math) degree of freedom
Freiheitsstrafe *f* (Re) confinement in a penitentiary
Freijahr *n* (Vers) year for which premium payment is suspended
Freijahre *npl*
(Fin) grace period
- years of grace
- repayment holiday
(eg, three grace = principal repayment beginning in the fourth year; or: life of 10 years, with 8 grace)
Freikarte *f* (com) free ticket
frei konvertierbare Währungen *fpl* (AuW) freely convertible currencies
Freiladegleis *n* (com) loading track provided free of charge
frei Lager (com) free warehouse
Freilager *n* (Zo) bonded (*or* customs) warehouse
Freilandeier *npl*
(com) eggs from uncooped hens
- (GB) free-range eggs *(opp, battery eggs)*
frei längsseit Kai (com) free alongside quay, faq
frei Längsseite Schiff (com, *Incoterms*) free alongside ship, F. A. S., fas
Freiliste *f*
(Zo) free list
- list of tax-free goods
frei Lkw (com, *Incoterms*) free on truck, F. O. T., fot
freimachen
(com) to stamp
- to prepay postage

Freimakler *m* (Bö) = *freier Makler*
Freiperiode *f* (Fin) = *Freijahre*
- (OR) idle period
Freischicht *f*
(Pw) nonworking shift
- paid nonwork shift *(ie, in mining and steelmaking)*
frei Schiff (com) free on board
Freischreibungserklärung *f* (WeR) officially recorded declaration by which the holder of a ‚Rektapapier' = *non-negotiable instrument* hands a title of execution to a pledgee; allows satisfaction of claim without assignment of instrument
frei schwankender (schwebender) Wechselkurs *m*
(AuW) freely flexible
- floating
- fluctuating ... exchange rate
freisetzen
(Pw) to lay off
- to make redundant
Freisetzung *f* **von Arbeitskräften**
(Pw) displacement of labor
(Pw) redundancy *(ie, which may be due to structural changes)*
freistehende Bauten *mpl* (com) detached buildings
freistellen
(Fin) to indemnify *(eg, for losses)*
(Pw) to release
(Pw) = *freisetzen*
Freistellungen *fpl* (Pw) job layoffs
Freistellungsanspruch *m* (Re) right of indemnity
Freistellungsantrag *m* (SozV) application for exemption from compulsory old-age insurance coverage
Freistellungsbescheid *m* (StR) notice of nonliability for tax, § 155 I AO
Freistellungsgarantie *f* (Re) indemnification guaranty
Freistellungsklausel *f* (Re) exemption clause
Freistellungsvertrag *m* (SeeV) indemnification agreement
Freistellung *f* **von Haftung** (Re) indemnity against liability
freistempeln (com) to frank
Freistempler *m*
(com) postage meter
- (GB) franking machine
Freiteil-Klausel *f* (Vers) franchise clause *(ie, claims below a stated limit are not payable by insurer)*
frei übertragen (WeR) to transfer freely
Freiumschlag *m*
(com) postage-paid
- reply-paid
- stamped ... envelope
frei verfügbares Einkommen *n*
(Vw) discretionary income
(Pw) available income
Freiverkauf *m* (com) voluntary sale
Freiverkehr *m*
(Bö, *geregelter*) over-the-counter market
(Bö, *ungeregelter*) unofficial dealing (*or* market)
- outside market
- unlisted trading
- off-floor trading

Freiverkehrsbescheinigung f (Zo) free circulation certificate
Freiverkehrsbörse f (Bö) unofficial market
Freiverkehrshändler m (Bö) dealer in unlisted securities
Freiverkehrskurs m (Bö) unofficial quotation
– free market price
Freiverkehrsmakler m (Bö) outside (or unoffical) broker
– broker for unofficial dealings
Freiverkehrsmarkt m (Bö) unofficial market
Freiverkehrsumsätze mpl (Bö) outside transactions
Freiverkehrswerte mpl (Bö) unlisted securities
frei verwerten (com) to sell in the open market
frei von Beschädigung (SeeV) free from damage (ie, now obsolete)
frei von Beschädigung außer im Strandungsfalle (SeeV) (essentially co-extensive with) free from particular average, F.P.A.
frei von Beschlagnahme und Aufbringung (SeeV) free of capture and seizure
frei von Bruch (com) free from breakage
frei von gewissen ersten Prozenten (Vers) free from certain first percentage points (ie, the agreed percentage is deducted from a damage claim)
frei von gewissen Prozenten (Vers) free from certain percentage points (ie, insurer is not liable to indemnify unless the claim exceeds the agreed percentage rate)
frei von Havarie (com) free from average
frei von Schäden in besonderer Havarie (SeeV) free of particular average
frei Waggon (com) free on rail, FOR, f.o.r.
freiwillige Abfindungsaktion f (Pw) voluntary termination program
freiwillige Altersversorgung f (SozV) voluntary old-age provision
freiwillige Arbeitslosigkeit f (Vw) voluntary unemployment
freiwillige Beschränkung f (Kart) voluntary restraint
freiwillige Entschädigung f (Re) ex gratia payment
freiwillige Ersparnis f **der privaten Haushalte** (Vw) voluntary savings of private households
freiwillige Exportbeschränkungen fpl (AuW) „voluntary" export restraint (or reductions)
freiwillige Gerichtsbarkeit f (Re) voluntary (or noncontentious) jurisdiction
freiwillige Großhandelskette f (Mk) voluntary chain of wholesalers
freiwillige Kapitalbildung f (Vw) voluntary capital formation
freiwillige Kette f (Mk) voluntary retail buying chain
freiwillige Leistungen fpl (SozV) noncompulsory contributions
freiwillige Produktionsbeschränkung f (EG) voluntary system of limiting production (eg, Eurofer II)
– voluntary output curbs
freiwillige Quotenvereinbarung f (EG) voluntary quota agreement

freiwilliger Preisstopp m (Bw) voluntary price freeze
freiwillige Rücklagen fpl (ReW) = freie Rücklagen
freiwilliger Zusammenschluß m (Re) voluntary association (eg, of two or more persons to carry on as co-owners a business for profit)
freiwilliges Ausscheiden n (Pw) voluntary redundancy
– voluntary retirement
freiwillige Sozialleistungen fpl (SozV) voluntary welfare payments
freiwillige Versicherung f (Vers) voluntary insurance
(SozV) voluntary social insurance
freiwillige Weiterversicherung f (SozV) continued voluntary insurance
freiwillige Zusammenarbeit f (Bw) voluntary cooperation
freiwillige Zuwendungen fpl (StR) voluntary payments to others, § 12 No. 2 EStG
freiwillig versichert (SozV) insured on a voluntary basis
Freizeichen n (Pat) unprotected mark
– trade mark not in general use
– non-registrable trademark
freizeichnen (Re) to contract out of (eg, liability, agreement)
– to disclaim
Freizeichnung f (Re) contracting out of (total or partial) statutory liability
Freizeichnungsgrenze f (Vers) percentage exemption
(SeeV) free average
Freizeichnungsklausel f (com) without-engagement clause
(Re) contracting-out clause
– disclaimer (clause)
– exemption clause
– exculpatory contract clause
– exoneration clause
– hold-harmless clause
– non-warranty clause
(ie, disclaiming defects liability)
(Vers) accepted perils clause
Freizeit f (Pw) leisure (or vacation) time
freizeitbezogene Dienstleistungen fpl (Vw) leisure-time-related services
Freizeitgestaltung f (com) organization of leisure activities
Freizeitindustrie f (com) leisure time industry
Freizeitökonomik f (Vw) leisure time economics
Freizone f (Zo) free zone
freizügig (AuW) liberal
Freizügigkeit f
(Fin) freedom of capital movements
(Pw) labor mobility
– free movement of labor
Fremdanteile mpl (Fin) minority interests
Fremdanzeige f (Fin) third-party deposit notice
Fremdarbeiter m (Pw) foreign worker
Fremdauftrag m (com) outside contract
Fremdbeleg m (ReW) external voucher
Fremdbeteiligung f (Fin) minority interest (or stake)

fremdbezogene Stoffe *mpl* (MaW) bought-out materials
fremdbezogene Teile *npl*
(MaW) bought-in (*or* bought-out) parts
– bought-in supplies
– purchased components
Fremdbezug *m*
(MaW) outside purchasing
– external procurement
Fremddepot *n* (Fin) third-party security deposit
fremde Gelder *npl*
(Fin) outside funds
– borrowings
(Fin) customers' deposits (*or* balances)
Fremdemission *f* (Fin) securities issue for account of another
fremde Mittel *pl*
(Fin) borrowed funds
– funds from outside sources
Fremdenförderung *f* (com) promotion of tourism
Fremdenverkehr *m* (com) tourism
Fremdenverkehrsabgabe *f* (com) tourist tax
Fremdenverkehrsgewerbe *n* (com) tourist industry
Fremdenverkehrswerbung *f* (Mk) tourist advertising
fremdes Bankakzept *n* (Fin) acceptance by another bank
fremdes Eigentum *n* (Re) third-party property
fremde Währung *f* (AuW) foreign currency
fremdfinanzieren
(Fin) to borrow
– to finance through borrowing
Fremdfinanzierung *f*
(Fin) debt
– external
– loan
– outside ... financing
– borrowing
Fremdfinanzierungsmittel *pl* (Fin) borrowed (*or* outside) funds
Fremdfinanzierungsquote *f* (Fin) borrowing ratio
Fremdgeld *n* (Fin) trust fund (*or* money)
Fremdgelder *npl* (Fin) third-party funds
Fremdgrundschuld *f* (Re) third-party beneficiary land charge
Fremdinvestition *f*
(Fin) external investment
– investment in other enterprises
Fremdkapital *n*
(Fin) outside
– debt
– borrowed
– loan ... capital
– capital from outside sources
– creditors' equity
– debt (*eg, in debt/equity ratio*)
(ReW) current liabilities + long-term debt – stockholders' equity – valuation accounts
Fremdkapitalbeschaffung *f* (Fin) procurement of outside capital
Fremdkapitalgeber *m* (Fin) lender
Fremdkapitalkosten *pl* (Fin) cost of debt
Fremdkapitalzins *m* (Fin) interest rate on borrowings
Fremdkosten *pl* (KoR) = *Fremdleistungskosten*

Fremdleistungen *fpl* (Bw) external (*or* outside) services
Fremdleistungskosten *pl* (KoR) cost of outside services *(eg, rent, brought-in energy supplies, patents)*
Fremdmittel *pl*
(Fin) borrowed
– external
– outside ... funds
Fremdmittelbedarf *m* (Fin) borrowing requirements
Fremdnutzung *f* (com) utilization by third parties
Fremdspeicher *m* (EDV) external memory (*or* storage)
Fremdsprachenkorrespondent *m* (com) foreign language correspondent
Fremdumsatz *m* (com) external sales (*or* GB: turnover)
Fremdvergleich *m* (StR) dealing-at-arm's-length rule *(ie, standard methods under this rule are: (1) Preisvergleichsmethode = comparable uncontrolled price method, (2) Wiederverkaufspreismethode = resale price method, and (3) Selbstkostenpreismethode = cost-plus method)*
Fremdvergleichspreis *m* (Fin) external reference price *(ie, to charge such prices between branches of the same bank is not permissible)*
Fremdvermutung *f* (Fin) non-property presumption *(ie, that securities which a bank placed with third-party depository are not its property: protects customer by restricting rights of retention and attachment)*
Fremdversicherung *f* (Vers) third-party insurance
Fremdwährung *f*
(Fin) foreign currency
– xenocurrency
(ie, currency on deposit in a bank owned by someone outside the issuing country)
Fremdwährungsanleihe *f* (Fin) foreign currency loan issue
Fremdwährungseinlagen *fpl* (Fin) foreign currency deposits
Fremdwährungsguthaben *npl* (Fin) foreign exchange balances *(syn, Währungsguthaben)*
Fremdwährungsklausel *f* (Fin) foreign currency clause
Fremdwährungskonto *n* (Fin) foreign exchange account *(syn, Währungskonto, Devisenkonto)*
Fremdwährungskredit *m* (Fin) foreign currency loan
Fremdwährungskreditaufnahme *f* (Fin) foreign currency borrowing
Fremdwährungsposition *f* (AuW) foreign currency position
Fremdwährungsrisiko *n* (Fin) foreign currency exposure (*or* risk)
Fremdwährungsscheck *m* (Fin) foreign currency check
Fremdwährungsschuld *f* (Fin) debt expressed in a foreign currency
Fremdwährungsschuldverschreibung *f* (Fin) foreign currency bond
Fremdwährungsumrechnung *f* (Fin) translation of foreign currencies

Fremdwährungsverbindlichkeiten *fpl*
(Fin) foreign currency liabilities
– foreign currency debt
– foreign currency indebtedness
Fremdwährungsversicherung *f* (Vers) foreign currency insurance
Fremdwährungswechsel *m*
(Fin) foreign currency bill
– foreign bill
– foreign exchange draft
Frequenz *f* (Stat) frequency
Frequenzreihen *fpl* (Stat) frequency series
Frequenzverwerfung *f* (EDV) drift
freundliche Börse *f* (Bö) cheerful market
Friedenspflicht *f*
(Pw) peacekeeping duty
– obligation to keep the peace
(ie, during the continuance of a wage agreement; it is the very essence of the West German collective bargaining process)
friktionelle Arbeitslosigkeit *f* (Vw) frictional unemployment *(syn, Fluktuationsarbeitslosigkeit)*
frisch gebacken (Pw, infml) freshly minted *(eg, lawyer)*
frisieren (com) to doctor *(eg, report, balance sheet)*
Frisieren *n* **der Bilanz** (ReW) doctoring a balance sheet
Frist *f*
(com) time limit *(eg, within the ... provided in the contract)*
– time allowed *(eg, for cancellation)*
– period of time
– time span
– extension of time *(eg, a 10-day ... in which to consummate a deal)*
Fristablauf *m*
(com) expiration of time *(or* period)
– lapse of time
Frist *f* **bewilligen** (com) to grant a deadline
Frist *f* **einhalten**
(com) to keep a time limit
– to meet a deadline
Frist *f* **einräumen** (com) to grant a period of time
Fristen *fpl* **berechnen** (com) to compute time limits
Fristen *fpl* **einhalten** (com) to observe time limits
Fristeninkongruenz *f* (Fin) mis-match in maturity
Fristenkategorie *f* (Fin) maturity category
fristenkongruente Finanzierung *f* (Fin) financing based on matched maturities *(ie, of outflows and inflows)*
fristenkongruent finanzieren (Fin) to finance by funds with matching maturities
Fristenkongruenz *f* (Fin) identity *(or* matching) of maturities
Fristenraum *m* (Fin) maturity range
Fristenrisiko *n* (Fin) risk of maturity gaps (of ‚Schuldscheindarlehen') *(ie, risk that no follow-up loan is available when amounts are due with terms shorter than those of the overall loan)*
Fristenstruktur *f* (Fin) maturity structure *(or* pattern)
Fristentransformation *f*
(com) rephasing of time periods

(Fin) maturity transformation *(ie, borrowing short-term deposits to make longer-term loans)*
Fristen *fpl* **verlängern** (StR) to grant extensions of time for the filing of returns, § 109 AO
Frist *f* **festsetzen** (com) to fix a time limit
fristgemäß
(Re) within the time stipulated
– within the agreed time limit
– at due date
– when due
– as promised
– on schedule
fristgemäße Rückzahlung *f* (Fin) repayment at due date
fristgerecht (Re) = *fristgemäß*
Frist *f* **gewähren** (com) to grant a time limit
Fristhemmung *f* (Re) suspension of prescription
Fristigkeit *f*
(Fin) time to maturity
– *(or* simply) maturity
Fristigkeiten *fpl* (Fin) maturities
Fristigkeitsstruktur *f* (Fin) = *Fristenstruktur*
Frist *f* **in Lauf setzen** (Re) to appoint time to run against a party
Frist *f* **läuft ab** (Re) period set aside for ... runs out
fristlos (Pw) without notice
fristlose Entlassung *f*
(Pw) instant dismissal
– dismissal without notice
fristlose Kündigung *f* (Pw) termination without notice
fristlos entlassen (Pw) to dismiss without notice
fristlos kündigen (Pw) to terminate without notice
Frist *f* **setzen**
(com) to set a deadline
– to fix a time limit
Frist *f* **überschreiten**
(com) to disregard a time limit
– to pass a deadline
– to fail to meet a time target
Fristüberschreitung *f*
(com) failure to keep within the time limit
– passing a deadline
frist- und formgerecht (Re) in due form and time
Frist *f* **verlängern** (com) to extend a time limit *(or* deadline)
Fristverlängerung *f*
(com) extension of deadline *(or* time limit)
(StR) extension of time for the filing of returns, § 109 AO
Frist *f* **versäumen** (com) to fail to meet a deadline
Frist *f* **wahren** (com) to observe a time limit
Fristwahrung *f* (com) observance of deadline
Frist *f* **zur Äußerung** (Re) final date for reply
Frostschadenversicherung *f* (Vers) frost insurance *(ie, widely used in US, unknown in Germany)*
Früchte *fpl* **und Nutzungen** *fpl* (Re) fruits and profits, §§ 99, 100 BGB
Frühbezugsrabatt *m* (com) dead-season rebate *(ie, granted for buying in advance of actual season sales)*
früherer Erfinder *m* (Pat) preceding inventor
frühester Anfangszeitpunkt *m* (OR) earliest starting time

247

frühester Endzeitpunkt *m* (OR) earliest completion time
frühest möglicher Zeitpunkt *m* (OR) earliest expected time
Frühindikator *m*
 (Vw) leading indicator
 – leader
 (eg, new orders, money supply, stock prices)
Frühinvalidität *f* (SozV) pre-retirement disablement
Frühjahrsmesse *f* (com) spring fair
Frühkapitalismus *m* (Vw) early capitalism
Frühpensionierung *f* (Pw) early retirement
Frührentner *m* (Pw) early retirer
Frühschicht *f* (Pw) morning shift
Frühstückskartell *n* (Kart) gentlemen's agreement
Frühverrentung *f* (SozV) early retirement
Frühwarnsignal *n* (Bw) early warning signal
Frühwarnsystem *n* (Bw) early warning system
Fühler *mpl* **ausstrecken** (com, infml) to put out *(or* send out) one's feelers
Fühlungnahme *f* (com) exploratory contacts
führen
 (Bw) to manage
 – to direct
 – to lead
 – to run *(eg, the show day by day)*
 (com) to carry *(eg, in stock a wide variety of products)*
 (Fin) to lead manage *(eg, an underwriting syndicate)*
führende Aktienwerte *mpl* (Bö) equity leaders
führende Null *f* (EDV, Cobol) leading zero
führender Hersteller *m* (com) leading *(or* premier) producer
führende Stellung *f* (Pw) leading position
führende Werte *mpl* (Bö) leading shares
Führerpersönlichkeit *f* (Pw) born leader
Führerschein *m*
 (com) driver's license
 – (GB) driving licence
Fuhrpark *m*
 (com) vehicles park
 – vehicle fleet
 – motor pool
Führung *f*
 (com) guided tour *(eg, of a plant)*
 (Bw) directing
 – direction
 – management
 – leadership
Führung *f* **der Bücher** (ReW) keeping books of account
Führung *f* **der Geschäfte** (com) conduct of a business
Führungsabstand *m* (EDV) guide margin
Führungsaufgaben *fpl* (Bw) = *Führungsfunktionen*
Führungsausschuß *m* (com) management committee
Führungsbefähigung *f* (Pw) managerial qualities
Führungscrew *f* (Bw, infml) management team
Führungsebene *f*
 (Bw) level *(or* layer) of management
 – managerial level
Führungseigenschaften *fpl* (Pw) executive talent

Führungselite *f* (Bw) managerial elite
Führungsentscheidung *f* (Bw) executive decision
Führungsfunktionen *fpl* (Bw) management *(or* mangerial) functions
Führungsgremium *n* (Bw) management group *(or* committee)
Führungsgröße *f* (EDV) controlling variable
Führungsgrundsätze *mpl* (Bw) principles of management
Führungsgruppe *f*
 (com) management team
 (Fin) lead management group
Führungshierarchie *f* (Bw) managerial hierarchy
Führungsinformation *f* (Bw) management information
Führungsinstrument *n*
 (Bw) directional device
 – instrument of management
Führungskante *f* (EDV) guide *(or* guided) edge
Führungsklausel *f* (Vers) lead management clause
Führungskonzeption *f* (Bw) management concept
Führungskraft *f*
 (Bw) manager
 – executive
Führungskräfte *fpl*
 (Pw) executive personnel
 – senior staff
Führungskräfte *fpl* **aller Ebenen** (Bw) managers at all levels
Führungsloch *n* (EDV) feed *(or* sprocket) hole *(syn, Vorschubloch)*
Führungslochung *f* (EDV) sprocket holes
Führungsmannschaft *f* (Bw) management team
Führungsmittel *npl* (Bw) managerial instruments
Führungsmodell *n* (Bw) management model
Führungsnachwuchs *m* (Pw) young executives
Führungsposition *f*
 (Bw) management
 – executive
 – supervisory ... position
Führungsprovision *f* (Fin) management fee
Führungssituation *f* (Bw) directional *(or* managerial) situation
Führungsspanne *f* (Bw) span of control
Führungsspitze *f*
 (Bw) corporate summit
 – top management *(or* echelon)
Führungsstil *m*
 (Bw) pattern *(or* style) of leadership
 – management style
Führungsstruktur *f*
 (Bw) management structure
 – management and control structure
Führungstheorie *f* (Bw) theory of management
Führungsverhalten *n*
 (Bw) pattern of management
 – leadership attitude
Führungswechsel *m* (Bw) change in leadership
Führungszeugnis *n* (Pw) certificate of conduct
Führungsziele *npl* (Bw) managerial objectives
Fuhrunternehmen *n* (com) haulage contractor
Füllauftrag *m*
 (com) stop gap order
 – fill-in order
Füllbefehl *m* (EDV) dummy instruction

Füllfeld *n* (EDV, Cobol) filler
Füllsteuerkarte *f* (EDV) dummy control card
Füllzeichen *n*
  (EDV) fill character
  – filler *(syn, Leerzeichen)*
Füllziffer *f* (EDV) gap digit
Fundamentalanalyse *f* (Bö) fundamental analysis
Fundamentalsatz *m* **der Algebra** (Math) fundamental theorem of algebra
Fundbüro *n*
  (com) lost and found
  – (GB) Lost Property Office
  – baggage service
fundieren (Fin) to fund (*or* consolidate) *(eg, a debt or loan)*
fundierte Schätzung *f* (Stat) informed estimate
fundierte Schulden *fpl* (Fin) funded (*or* long-term) debt
fundiertes Einkommen *n* (StR) unearned income
fundierte Staatsschuld *f*
  (FiW) funded
  – consolidated
  – long-term . . . public debt
Fundierung *f*
  (Fin) funding
  – consolidation
Fundierungsanleihe *f* (Fin) funding loan
Fundierungsmethode *f* (ReW) sinking fund method (of depreciation)
Fundierungsschuldverschreibung *f* (Fin) funding bond
Fünfercode *m* (EDV) five-level code
Fünftagewoche *f* (Pw) five-day work week
fungibel
  (com) fungible
  – marketable
  – merchantable
Fungibilien *pl* (Re) fungible goods, § 91 BGB
Fungibilität *f* (com) fungibility
fungible Waren *fpl*
  (com) fungible (*or* merchantable) goods
  – fungibles
fungieren (com) to act as
Funktion *f*
  (Math) function
  – transformation
  – mapping
  – map
  – graph
Funktional-Determinante *f* (Math) Jacobian determinant
funktionale Autorität *f* (Bw) functional authority *(ie, based on power, status, or job)*
funktionale Organisation *f* (Bw) functional organization
funktionale Organisationsstruktur *f* (Bw) functional organization structure
funktionaler Entscheidungsträger *m* (Bw) decision-making unit
  – decider
funktionaler Leiter *m* (Bw) functional manager
funktionales Weisungsrecht *n* (Bw) functional authority
funktionale Verteilungsquoten *fpl* (Vw) factor shares

Funktionalgliederung *f* (FiW) functional breakdown *(ie, of expenditures)*
Funktionallehre *f* (Bw) functional specialty
Funktionär *m* (Pw) functionary
Funktion *f* **des mittleren Stichprobenumfangs** (Stat) average sample number function
funktionelle Einkommensverteilung *f* (Vw) functional income distribution *(ie, income accruing to the factors of production, such as land, labor, capital)*
funktionelle Lohnquote *f* (Vw) functional share
funktionelle Planung *f* (EDV) functional design
funktionelle Untergliederung *f* (Bw) functional grouping
Funktionen *fpl* **ausgliedern** (Bw) to split off enterprise functions
Funktionenbudget *n* (FiW) functional budget
Funktionendiagramm *n* (Bw) function chart
Funktion *f* **mit absoluten Werten** (Math) levels function
Funktionsbereich *m*
  (Bw) area of activities
  – functional area
Funktionscode *m* (EDV) function code
Funktionsdarstellung *f* (Bw) function chart
Funktionseinheit *f* (EDV) functional unit
funktionsfähig
  (com) workable
  (IndE) operative
funktionsfähiger Wettbewerb *m* (Vw) workable competition
Funktionsgenerator *m* (EDV) function generator
Funktionsgliederung *f* (Bw) functional departmentation
Funktionsmanager *m* (Bw) functional manager
Funktionsmeister *m* (Bw) functional foreman
Funktionsorganisation *f* (Bw) function-oriented structure
Funktionsplan *m* (FiW) functional budget plan
Funktionsprüfung *f* (EDV) acceptance test
Funktionsrabatt *m* (Mk) functional discount
Funktionsschwäche *f* (Bw) functional weakness
funktionsspezifische Leistung *f* (Bw) function-related service
Funktionsstörung *f* (EDV) malfunction
Funktionsüberschneidungen *fpl* (Bw) instances of multiple functions
Funktionsübersicht *f*
  (Bw) function chart
  (EDV) functional diagramm
Funktionsunfähigkeit *f* (IndE) failure to function properly
Funktionsvariable *f* (Log) functional variable
Funktionszeichen *n* (EDV) functional character
Funktionszustandsregister *n* (EDV) interrupt status register
Funktor *m* (Log) logical connective (*or* operator)
Funkwerbung *f* (Mk) broadcast advertising
für die Richtigkeit der Abschrift (com) certified to be a true and correct copy of the original
für ehelich erklärte Kinder *npl* (StR) legitimated children, § 6 II VStG
für fremde Rechnung
  (com) for third party account
  – on/in behalf of another person

für nichtig erklären
(Re) to avoid
– to nullify
für Rechnung wen es angeht (com) for the account of whom it may concern
Fürsorge f (SozV) = *(now) Sozialhilfe*
Fürsorgepflicht f
(Re) principal's duty to ensure welfare (to commercial clerks, § 62 HGB)
Fürsorgepflicht f **des Arbeitgebers** (Pw) employer's duty of care
Fürstensuite f (Pw, joc) top executives' office suite
Fusion f (Re) merger
Fusion f **durch Aufnahme** od **Neubildung** (Bw) merger or consolidation
fusionieren (Fin) to merge
Fusionsangebot n (Fin) merger offer
Fusionsbilanz f (ReW) merger balance sheet
Fusionsfieber n (Bw) merger fever
Fusionsgewinn m (Fin) consolidation profit

Fusionskontrolle f (Kart) merger control, §§ 23, 24 GWB
Fusionsstrategie f (Bw) merger strategy
Fusionsvertrag m (Kart) merger agreement
Fusionswelle f
(Bw) spate (*or* wave) of mergers
– takeover wave
Fuß fassen
(Mk) to get a toehold in a market
– to breach a market
– to carve out a market niche
Fußgängerüberweg m
(com) pedestrian crossing
– (GB) pelican crossing *(ie, short for: pedestrian light controlled crossing)*
– (GB) zebra crossing
Fußgängerzone f
(Mk) pedestrian mall
– (GB) pedestrian precinct

G

Gabelungspunkt m (KoR) splitoff point *(ie, in joint-product production the point of separation of the different products)*
Gage f (Pw) artist's pay or fee
galoppierende Inflation f
(Vw) galloping
– runaway
– cantering . . . inflation
Gammadichte-Funktion f (Stat) gamma density function
Gang m (EDV) cycle
gängig
(com) marketable
– (readily) salable (*or* saleable)
– readily sold
– easily sold
gängige Größe f (com) stock size
gängige Münzen fpl
(Vw) current coins
– coins in circulation
gängiger Artikel m
(com) fast-selling article
– high-volume product
gängiger Lohnsatz m (Pw) going rate
gängige Waren fpl (com) readily salable goods
Gängigkeit f
(com) marketability
– salability (*or* saleability)
Gangzähler m (EDV) cycle counter
Gangzählung f (EDV) cycle count
Gannt-Chart f
(IndE) Gannt chart
– daily balance chart
Gannt-Karte f (IndE) = *Gannt Chart*
Gannt-Prämienlohnsystem n (IndE) Gannt premium plan
Ganzcharter f (com) chartering a whole ship
ganze Dualzahl f (EDV) binary integer
ganze rationale Funktion f (Math) rational integral function

ganze Zahl f
(Math) integer
– whole number
ganzjährig geöffnet (com) open all the year round
ganz leichte Fahrlässigkeit f (Re) culpa levissima *(ie, very slight negligence; the term is foreign to the BGB, but is used in labor-court decisions when risk-prone work is involved)*
ganz od **teilweise** (com) wholly or in part
ganzseitige Anzeige f (Mk) full-page advertisement
Ganzstelle f (Mk) entire billboard *(ie, reserved for a single advertiser)*
ganztägig arbeiten (Pw) to work full time
Ganztagsarbeit f (Pw) full-time job
Ganztagsbeschäftigung f (Pw) full-time employment (*or* job *or* work)
ganzwertige Funktion f (Math) integer-valued function
ganzzahlig (Math) integer-valued
ganzzahlige Potenz f (Math) integer power
ganzzahlige Programmierung f (OR) integer (*or* diophantine *or* discrete) programming
ganzzahliges Vielfaches n (Math) integer multiple
ganzzahlige Variable f (Math) integer-valued variable
ganzzahlige Verteilung f (Stat) integer-valued distribution
Ganzzahligkeitsbedingung f (OR) discreteness stipulation
Garant m
(Re) guarantor
– warrantor
(Fin) underwriter
Garanten mpl (Vers) guarantors *(ie, people who have put up the funds for the formation and initial operation of a mutual insurance association)*
Garantie f
(Re) guaranty
– (GB) guarantee
(ie, making guarantor secondarily liable for debt

or default of another person, but see „selbstschuldnerische Bürgschaft')
(com) guarantee
– warranty
(ie, written promise by maker of a product to repair or replace it if it is found defective within a period of time)
(Fin) underwriting
Garantieabteilung *f*
(Fin) guaranty department *(ie, of a bank)*
(Fin) underwriting department
Garantieanspruch *m*
(Re) claim under a warranty
– warranty claim
Garantiearbeiten *fpl* (com) repair work under a guaranty
Garantiedeckungsbetrag *m* (Fin) guaranty cover amount
Garantiedeckungskonto *n* (ReW) guaranty cover account
Garantiedividende *f* (Fin) guaranteed dividend *(ie, adequate annual compensation payable to minority shareholders, § 304 AktG)*
Garantieeffekt *m* (WeR) guaranty effect *(ie, resulting from payment guaranty given by indorser of bill of exchange or check)*
Garantieerklärung *f*
(Re) guaranty bond
– warranty
Garantiefall *m* (Fin) event making a guaranty operative
Garantiefonds *m* (Vers) guaranty fund
Garantiefrist *f*
(com) guarantee period
– period of warranty
Garantiegeber *m* (Re) guarantor
Garantiegemeinschaft *f* (Re) guaranty association
Garantiegeschäft *n* (Fin) guaranty business *(ie, of banks)*
Garantiegruppe *f* (Fin) underwriting group
Garantie *f* **haben** (com) guaranteed *(eg, for 3 years)*
Garantiehaftung *f* (Re) liability under a guaranty
Garantie *f* **in Anspruch nehmen** (Re) to implement a guaranty
– to call a guaranty
– to make a claim under a guaranty
Garantiekapital *n* (ReW) equity capital *(ie, insofar as it serves as security for loans or other liabilities)*
(Fin) equity capital of real estate credit institutions
Garantieklausel *f* (Re) warranty clause
Garantiekonsortium *n*
(Re) guaranty syndicate
(Fin) underwriting syndicate
– (GB) underwriters
(ie, rare in Germany: syndicate guarantees to take up any unsold portion of a security issue for its own account)
Garantiekosten *pl*
(KoR) cost of a company's guarantee commitments
(Fin) cost of government or bank guaranties
Garantie *f* **läuft ab** (com) guarantee expires

Garantie *f* **leisten**
(Re) to guarantee
– to give (*or* furnish) guaranty
Garantieleistung *f* (Re) giving (*or* furnishing) a guaranty
Garantieleistungen *fpl* (ReW) warranties
Garantielohn *m* (IndE) = *garantierter Mindestlohn*
Garantiemittel *pl*
(Fin) guaranty funds
(Vers) equity capital (*or* net worth) of an insurance company + technical reserves
Garantienehmer *m* (Re) warrantee
Garantien *fpl* **für Kapitalanlagen im Ausland** (AuW) guaranties for capital investments abroad *(ie, provided by the Federal Government to cover political risks of direct investments in developing countries)*
Garantiepreis *m* (com, EG) guaranteed price
Garantieprovision *f*
(Fin) guaranty commission
(Fin) underwriting commission
Garantierahmen *m* (Fin) guaranty ceiling (*or* limit)
garantieren
(Re) to guarantee (*or* guaranty)
(com) to guarantee *(eg, a machine for 5 years)*
– to warrant
garantierter Erzeugermindestpreis *m* (EG) guaranteed minimum producer price
garantierter Jahreslohn *m* (Pw) guaranteed annual wage *(ie, paid by some U. S. companies)*
garantierter Mindestlohn *m* (Pw) guaranteed minimum wage
– minimum entitlement (*or* wage)
(ie, supplements the straight piece-rate system)
garantierter Mindestpreis *m* (EG) intervention price
garantiertes jährliches Mindesteinkommen *n* (FiW) guaranteed annual income
Garantierückstellungen *fpl* (ReW) provisions for guarantees
Garantiesatz *m* (AuW) guaranteed proportion (of export credit)
Garantieschein *m* (com) certificate of guarantee (*or* warranty)
Garantieschreiben *n* (com) letter of guarantee
Garantiestempel *m* (com) warranty stamp
Garantieübernahme *f* (com) acceptance of a guarantee
Garantie *f* **übernehmen**
(Re) to guarantee
– to give (*or* furnish) guaranty
Garantieverbund *m* (Fin) joint security scheme *(ie, operated by banks as a means to protect customers' accounts)*
Garantieverletzung *f* (Re) breach of warranty
Garantieverpflichtung *f*
(Re) guaranty obligation
– obligation under a guaranty
Garantieversicherung *f* (Vers) guaranty insurance *(ie, nontechnical term – untechnischer Ausdruck – covering „Kautionsversicherung', Veruntreuungsversicherung' and a special type of „Maschinenversicherung')*
Garantievertrag *m* (Re) contract of guaranty

Garantiezeit *f* (com) guarantee (*or* warranty) period
Gartenbaubetrieb *m*
(com) truck farm (*or* garden)
– (GB) market garden
Gasgigant *m* (com, infml) gas supply juggernaut
Gastarbeiter *m*
(Pw) foreign worker
– guest worker
– temporary immigrant worker
Gastarbeiterrimessen *fpl* (VGR) = *Gastarbeiterüberweisungen*
Gastarbeiterüberweisungen *fpl* (VGR) remittances of foreign workers
Gastgeberland *n* (AuW) host country
Gasthörer *m* (Pw) extramural student
Gastland *n* (AuW) host (*or* receiving) country
Gaststättengewerbe *n*
(com) restaurant business
– (GB) catering trade
Gaststätteninhaber *m*
(com) restaurateur
– (GB) caterer
Gaststätten- und Beherbungsgewerbe *n* (VGR) hotels and restaurants
Gastwirtversicherung *f* (Vers) innkeeper's insurance
Gate Arrays *pl*
(EDV) gate arrays
(*ie, halbkundenspezifische integrierte Schaltungen = semi-custom ICs; syn, Logik-Arrays*)
Gatter *n* (EDV) gate
Gattung *f*
(Re) genus
– a general class or division
(Fin) class (*eg, of shares*)
Gattungsanspruch *m* (Re) generic claim
Gattungsbegriff *m* (Log) generic term
Gattungsbezeichnung *f* (Kart, Pat) generic (*or* established) name (*ie, of a product, not protected by industrial property law*)
Gattungskauf *m*
(Re) sale by description
– sale of unascertained goods
Gattungsname *m*
(Log) generic name
– general term
Gattungssachen *fpl*
(Re) generic (*or* unascertained) goods (*opp, konkrete Sachen: specific or ascertained goods*)
– generics
Gattungsschuld *f*
(Re) obligation in kind
– generic obligation
(Re) obligation to supply unascertained goods
– obligation to deliver a generically defined thing
(*ie, merchantable goods of average kind and quality, § 243 BGB*)
Gattungsware *f* (Re) = *Gattungssachen*
Gauß-Markoffscher Satz *m* (Stat) Gauss-Markov theorem
Gaußsche Einheitsvariable *f* (Stat) unit normal variate

Gaußsche Normalverteilung *f* (Stat) Gaussian distribution
Gaußsche Zahlenebene *f*
(Math) Argand diagram
– Gaussian plane
geätzte Schaltung *f* (EDV) etched circuit *(syn, gedruckte Schaltung)*
Gebaren *n*
(com) behavior
– practices
– mode of handling
Gebarung *f* (com) = *Gebaren*
Gebäude *npl* (ReW, *balance sheet item*) buildings
Gebäudeabschreibungen *fpl* (ReW, KoR) building depreciation
Gebäudebesteuerung *f* (StR) taxation of buildings *(ie, may comprise elements of real property tax, net worth tax, income tax, and real property transfer tax)*
Gebäudekosten *pl* (KoR) building occupancy expenses *(ie, depreciation, interest, repairs, heating, lighting, etc.)*
Gebäudereparaturen *fpl* (KoR) building repairs
Gebäudeschaden *m* (Vers) damage to a building
Gebäudeunterhaltung *f* (KoR) building maintenance and upkeep
Gebäudeversicherung *f* (Vers) building insurance
Gebäudewert *m* (StR) value of building *(ie, construction cost + income)*
Geber *m*
(StR) payor, § 10 I No. 1 EStG
(EDV) generator
Geber *m* **für analytische Funktionen** (EDV) analytical (*or* natural) function generator
Geber *m* **für empirische Funktionen** (EDV) empiric-function generator
Geber *m* **für variable Funktionen** (EDV) variable-function generator
Geberland *n*
(Vw) donor country
(IWF) selling country
Gebiet *n*
(Log) subject area
gebietsansässig (AuW) resident
Gebietsansässiger *m* (AuW) resident
Gebietsaufteilung *f* (Vw) zoning
gebietsfremde Einlagen *fpl* (Fin) non-resident deposits
Gebietsfremden-Kontingent *n* (AuW) nonresident quota
Gebietsfremder *m* (AuW) nonresident
Gebietshoheit *f* (Re) territorial jurisdiction
Gebietskartell *n* (Kart) market sharing cartel *(ie, limited agreement allocating markets with a view to saving transport and advertising costs)*
Gebietskörperschaft *f*
(Re) government unit
– governmental unit
– unit of government
– political subdivision
– territorial division
Gebietskörperschaften *fpl* (Re) central, regional, and local authorities
Gebietsleiter *m*
(com) regional manager

– division area supervisor
Gebietsprovision *f* (com) overriding commission *(ie, of a commercial agent)*
Gebietsvertreter *m* (com) regional commercial representative
Gebinde *n*
(com) barrel
– cask
(ie, used for storing alcoholic beverages)
geborene Orderpapiere *npl* (WeR) original order papers *(opp, gekorene Orderpapiere)*
Gebot *n*
(com) bid *(eg, at auction)*
(Bö) buyers
Gebot *n* **abgeben** (com) to make a bid
gebotener Preis *m* (com) bid price
Gebrauchsabnahme *f* (com) final acceptance of completed building
Gebrauchsabweichung *f* (KoR) use variance
Gebrauchsanweisung *f* (com) instructions for use
Gebrauchsartikel *m* (com) article of daily use
Gebrauchsdefinition *f*
(Log) contextual definition
– definition in use
– postulational definition
Gebrauchsgraphik *f* (Mk) advertising *(or* commercial*)* art
Gebrauchsgraphiker *m* od **-in** *f* (Mk) commercial *(or* industrial*)* artist
Gebrauchsgüter *npl*
(Vw) durable consumer goods
– consumer durables
– durables
Gebrauchsgüterpanel *n* (Mk) consumer durables panel
Gebrauchslizenz *f* (Pat) license for use
Gebrauchsmuster *n* (Pat) utility-model patent *(ie, second-class patent for ‚petty‘ inventions of useful articles)*
– utility patent
– petty patent
– design patent
Gebrauchsmusterberühmung *f* (Pat) holding out as a utility-patented article
Gebrauchsmusterhilfsanmeldung *f* (Pat) auxiliary utility model registration
Gebrauchsmusterschutz *m* (Pat) legal protection of utility patents
Gebrauchsstarif *m* (AuW) autonomous tariff
Gebrauchsüberlassung *f* (Re) transfer for use
Gebrauchsüberlassungsvertrag *m* (Re) contract for the transfer of use
Gebrauchsvermögen *n* (VGR) national wealth earmarked for consumption
Gebrauchsverschleiß *m* (ReW) depreciation based on use *(eg, through ordinary or normal wear and tear)*
Gebrauchswert *m*
(com) practical value
(Vw) value in use
Gebrauchszolltarif *m* (Zo) working tariff
Gebrauchtmaschinen *fpl* (com) used equipment
Gebrauchtwagen *m* (com) second-hand *(or* used*)* car
Gebrauchtwagenmarkt *m* (com) used-car market

Gebrauchtwagenpreisliste *f* (com, GB) Glass's guide *(ie, equivalent, for instance, to ‚Schwacke‘)*
Gebrauchtwaren *fpl* (com) second-hand articles
Gebrauchtwarenhändler *m* (com) second-hand dealer
Gebrauchtwarenmarkt *m* (com) second-hand market
gebrochene Abschreibung *f* (KoR) broken-down depreciation *(ie, into fixed and proportional elements; used in standard direct costing = Grenzplankostenrechnung)*
gebrochener Exponent *m* (Math) fractional exponent
gebrochener Schluß *m* (Bö) odd lot
gebrochener Verkehr *m* (com) combined transportation *(eg, rail/road, rail/truck)*
gebrochene Währung *f* (Fin) more than one currency
gebrochen rationale Funktion *f* (Math) fractional equation
Gebühren *fpl*
(com) charges
– fees
(ReW) professional fees *(or* charges*)*
(FiW) public charges
– direct-user charges
– benefit taxes
(Fin, *sometimes*) commission
Gebührenanzeiger *m*
(com) tollcharge meter
– (GB) call-charge indicator
Gebührenaufstellung *f* (com) account of charges
Gebühren *fpl* **berechnen** (com) to charge fees
Gebühreneinheit *f* (com) (telephone) call charge unit
Gebühren *fpl* **entrichten** (com) to pay fees
Gebühren *fpl* **erheben** (FiW) to levy fees
Gebührenerhöhung *f* (com) increase of charges or fees
Gebührenerlaß *m* (com) remission of charge *(or* fee*)*
Gebührenerstattung *f* (com) refund of charges
Gebühren *fpl* **festsetzen** (com) to fix fees
gebührenfrei
(com) at no charge
– free of charge
– without charge
gebührenfreies Konto *n* (Fin) account on a non-charge basis
Gebühren *fpl* **für Müllabfuhr** (com) fees for garbage disposal
Gebührenmarke *f* (com) fee stamp
Gebührenordnung *f*
(com) fee scale
– schedule of fees
Gebührenordnung *f* **für Kursmakler** (Bö) brokers' pricing schedule
Gebührenrechnung *f* (com) bill of charges *(or* costs*)*
Gebührensatz *m*
(com) billing rate *(eg, per accountant hour)*
(Re) rate of charges
Gebührentabelle *f*
(com) scale of charges
(Re) schedule of fees

253

(Fin) scale of interest rates and charges *(ie, in banking)*
Gebühren-Tableau *n* (Fin) list of banking charges
Gebührentarif *m* (Re) fee schedule
Gebühr *f* **für ungenutzte Liegetage** (com) dispatch money
gebunden
(Re) bound *(eg, by contract)*
– committed
gebundene Entwicklungshilfe *f*
(AuW) tied aid
– procurement tying
gebundene Erfindung *f* (Pat) employee's invention made available to the employer
gebundene Finanzmittel *pl*
(MaW) funds tied up in inventories
– cash (*or* capital) lockup in raw materials and supplies
gebundene Mindestreserven *fpl* (Vw) nonavailable (*or* immobilized) liquidity
gebundene Namensaktie *f* (Fin) registered share of restricted transferability
gebundener Preis *m*
(Vw) controlled price *(opp, free market price)*
(Kart) maintained (*or* fixed) price *(see: resale price maintenance)*
gebundener Zahlungsverkehr *m* (Vw) payments by means of currencies agreed upon between two countries
gebundenes Kapital *n*
(ReW) fixed capital
(Fin) tied-up (*or* locked-up) capital
gebundene Spanne *f* (Mk) restricted margin
gebundenes Vermögen *n* (Vers) restricted assets
gebundene Variable *f* (Log, Math) bound(ed) variable *(syn, scheinbare Variable)*
gebundene Vermögenswerte *mpl* (Bw) blocked (*or* frozen) assets
Geburtenhäufigkeit *f* (Stat) fertility
Geburtenstatistik *f* (Stat) birth statistics
Geburtenziffer *f* (Stat) birth rate
Geburtsbeihilfe *f* (StR) birth benefit, § 3 No. 15 EStG
Geburtshilfe *f* (SozV) childbirth care
Gedächtnisprotokoll *n* (com) minutes from memory
Gedächtnistest *m* (Mk) (aided) recall test
gedämpfte Schwingung *f* (Vw) damped oscillation
Gedankenaustausch *m*
(com) exchange of ideas (on)
– (infml) swapping ideas (on)
Gedankengang *m* (com) line of thought
gedeckter Kredit *m* (Fin) secured loan (*or* credit)
gedeckter Wagen *m*
(com) boxcar
– (GB) covered goods waggon *(syn, G-Wagen)*
gedecktes Risiko *n* (Vers) risk covered
Gedingelohn *m* (Pw) job (*or* piece) wage *(ie, in the mining industry)*
gedrückter Markt *m* (Bö) depressed market
gedruckter Schaltkreis *m* (EDV) printed circuit
gedruckte Schaltung *f* (EDV) printed circuit board *(syn, geätzte Schaltung, Flachbaugruppe)*
geeignete Schritte *mpl* (com) appropriate action *(eg, to take ...)*

Gefahr *f*
(Vers) risk
– hazard
– peril
gefährdeter Beruf *m* (Pw) hazardous occupation
Gefährdungshaftung *f*
(Re) strict (*or* absolute) liability
– liability based on causation irrespective of fault
(ie, responsibility for hazardous activities where damage was caused neither intentionally nor negligently)
Gefahrengemeinschaft *f*
(Vers) community of risks
(SeeV) contributing interests
Gefahrenklasse *f*
(Vers) class (*or* category) of risks
– experience rating
Gefahrenklausel *f* (Vers) emergency (*or* perils) clause
Gefahrenmerkmale *npl* (Vers) particulars of risk
Gefahrenprämie *f* (Vers) extraordinary perils bonus
Gefahrenquelle *f* (Vers) safety hazard
Gefahrenrückstellung *f* (Vers) reserve for special risks
Gefahren *fpl* **tragen** (com) to bear risks
Gefahrenübergang *m* (Re) = *Gefahrübergang*
Gefahrenübernahme *f* (Re) assumption (*or* acceptance) of risk
Gefahrenzulage *f*
(Pw) danger pay
– danger zone bonus
– hazard bonus
Gefahrerhöhung *f* (Vers) extended risk (*or* hazard)
Gefahr *f* **geht über** (Re) risk passes
gefahrgeneigte Arbeit *f*
(Pw) accident prone work
– hazardous occupation
Gefahrgüter *npl* (com) dangerous goods
Gefahrminderung *f* (Vers) risk-reducing measure (*or* arrangement)
Gefahrübergang *m* (Re) passage of risk
(ie, in German law the maxim ‚cujus periculum ejus est commodum' applies: the burdens and advantages of the object which has been sold pass to the purchaser at the time the risk passes, § 446 BGB)
Gefälligkeitsadresse *f* (WeR) accommodation address
Gefälligkeitsakzept *n* (Fin) accommodation acceptance
Gefälligkeitsakzeptant *m* (Fin) accommodation acceptor
Gefälligkeitsdeckung *f* (Vers) accommodation line
Gefälligkeitsgiro *n* (WeR) = *Gefälligkeitsindossament*
Gefälligkeitsindossament *n* (WeR) accommodation indorsement
Gefälligkeitskonnossement *n* (com) accomodation bill of lading (*or* B/L)
Gefälligkeitswechsel *m* (Fin) accommodation bill (*or* note *or* paper)
Gefälligkeitszeichner *m* (WeR) accommodation party

gefälschte Banknote f
(Fin) counterfeit bill
- (GB) forged note
Gefangenendilemma n (OR) prisoner's dilemma
gefragt (com) in demand
Gefriergut n
(com) frozen food
- (GB) frosted foods
Gefriertrocknung f (Mk) freeze-drying *(eg, of vegetables)*
gegabelte Befragung f (Mk) split ballot
Gegenakkreditiv n
(Fin) back-to-back
- countervailing
- secondary ... credit
gegen alle Gefahren (Vers) against all risks
Gegenangebot n
(com) counterbid
- counter-offer
Gegenanspruch m (Re) counterclaim
Gegenauslese f
(Vers) anti-selection
- adverse selection
gegen bar verkaufen (com) to sell for cash
gegen Barzahlung (com) cash down
Gegenbestätigung f (com) counterconfirmation
Gegenbetrieb m (EDV) duplex transmission
Gegenbewegung f
(Stat) countermovement
- scissor movement
(eg, of time series in a business cycle diagram)
Gegenbeweis m (Re) rebutting (*or* counter) evidence
Gegenbieter m (com) competitive bidder
Gegenbuchung f
(ReW) contra
- cross
- offsetting
- reversing ... entry
Gegenbürge m (Re) counter surety
Gegendarstellung f
(com) counterstatement
(Mk) (voluntary) counter advertising
Gegendienst m
(com) reciprocal service
- service in return
gegen Entgelt
(Re) for a consideration
- against ‚quid pro quo'
Gegenerklärung f (com) counterstatement
Gegenforderung f (com) counterclaim
Gegengarantie f (Re) counter indemnity
Gegengeschäft n
(com) back-to-back transaction
(AuW) counter-purchasing
(Bö) offsetting transaction
(Vers) reciprocity business *(ie, in reinsurance)*
gegengewichtige Marktmacht f (Vw) countervailing power *(K. Galbraith)*
Gegengutachten n (com) opposing expert opinion
Gegenhypothese f (Stat) non-null hypothesis
Gegenkaperbrief m (SeeV) letter of countermart
Gegenkonto n (ReW) contra account
gegenläufige Güter- und Geldströme mpl (Vw) bilateral flows

gegenläufiger Zyklus m
(Vw) counter-cyclical pattern
- anticyclical pattern
- reciprocal cycle
(eg, of prices, unemployment)
Gegenleistung f (Re) quid pro quo *(ie, strictly speaking, the doctrine of ‚consideration' has no counterpart in German law! See ‚Note on Terminology')*
(Re) counter-performance, §§ 323–325 BGB
gegenlesen (com) to compare
Gegenmacht f (Vw) countervailing power *(K. Galbraith)*
Gegenmaßnahme f
(AuW) countermeasure
- retaliation
- retaliatory action
gegen Null konvergieren (Math) to approach toward zero
Gegenofferte f (com) counter-offer
Gegenposten m
(VGR) contra entry *(ie, changes in the external position)*
(ReW) per contra item
Gegenrechnung f
(com) bill in return
- invoice for setoff purposes
Gegensaldo m (ReW) counter balance
gegenseitig ausschließende Ereignisse npl (OR) mutually exclusive events
gegenseitige Bankforderungen fpl (Fin) interbank balances
gegenseitige Bedingungen fpl (Re) concurrent (*or* mutual) conditions
gegenseitige Kostenstellenverrechnungen fpl (KoR) mutual cost center charge transfers
gegenseitige Kreditlinie f (AuW) swing
gegenseitige Lizenzgewährung f (Pat) cross-licensing
gegenseitiger Vertrag m
(Re) reciprocal
- bilateral
- synallagmatic ... contract
(ie, agreement intending to create obligations on both sides)
gegenseitige Vereinbarung f (Re) mutual agreement
gegenseitige Verpflichtung f (Re) mutual (*or* reciprocal) obligation
Gegenseitigkeit f
(Re) reciprocity
- mutuality
Gegenseitigkeitsabkommen n (AuW) reciprocal trade agreement
Gegenseitigkeitsgeschäft n (AuW) reciprocal deal (*or* transaction)
Gegenseitigkeitsgesellschaft f (Re) noncommercial civil-law partnership *(ie, most frequently used in the insurance industry: mutual insurance company)*
Gegenseitigkeitsklausel f (AuW) reciprocity clause
Gegenstand m **des Anlagevermögens** (ReW) fixed asset
Gegenstand m **des Geschäftsverkehrs** (StR) activity of economic significance

255

Gegenstände *mpl* **des täglichen Bedarfs**
(com) necessaries
– convenience goods
Gegenstand *m* **e–r Gesellschaft** (Re) object (*or* purpose) of a company
Gegenstand *m* **e–r Patentanmeldung** (Pat) subject matter of a patent application
Gegenstand *m* **e–s Patents** (Pat) subject matter of a patent
Gegenstand *m* **e–s Vertrages** (Re) subject matter of a contract
Gegenstandsbereich *m*
(Log) universe of discourse
– domain of individuals
– field of attention (*or* concentration *or* study) (Math) reference set
Gegenstromverfahren *n* (Bw) mixed top-down/bottom-up planning system
Gegenverkauf *m*
(com) sale in return
– counter-sale
Gegenverpflichtung *f* (Re) mutual promise
Gegenversicherung *f* (Vers) mutual (*or* reciprocal) insurance
Gegenwahrscheinlichkeit *f* (Stat) inverse probability
gegenwärtiger Preis *m* (com) current (*or* prevailing) price
Gegenwartswert *m*
(ReW) current purchase price
(Fin) present value (*or* worth)
Gegenwechsel *m* (WeR) cross bill
Gegenwert *m*
(Fin) equivalent amount
(Fin) countervalue *(eg, bills and checks)*
(Fin) proceeds *(ie, in the sense of ‚Erlös')*
Gegenwert *m* **e–r Anwartschaft** (Vers) present value of an expectancy
Gegenwertfonds *m* (Vw) = *Gegenwertmittel*
Gegenwertmittel *pl* (Vw) counterpart funds
Gegenwert *m* **überweisen** (Fin) to transfer counter-value
gegenzeichnen (com) to countersign
Gegenzeichnung *f* (com) counter-signature
Gehalt *n* (Pw) salary
Gehalt *n* **beziehen** (Pw) to draw (*or* receive) a salary
Gehalt *n* **erhöhen** (Pw) to increase the salary
Gehaltsabrechnung *f* (EDV) salary printout
Gehaltsabzug *m*
(Pw) deduction from salary
– paycheck deductions
Gehaltsansprüche *mpl* (Pw) desired pay (*or* salary)
Gehaltsaufbesserung *f* (Pw) = *Gehaltserhöhung*
Gehaltseinzelkosten *pl* (KoR) direct salary costs
Gehaltsempfänger *mpl*
(Pw) salaried employees
– salaried personnel
– salaried workers
– salary earners
Gehaltserhöhung *f*
(Pw) salary increase
– pay rise (*or* US: raise)
Gehaltsfortzahlung *f* (SozV) continued payment of salary *(ie, im Krankheitsfalle: in case of illness)*

Gehaltsklasse *f* (Pw) salary bracket
Gehaltskonto *n*
(ReW) salary account
(Pw) employee's salary account
Gehaltskurve *f* (Pw) wage curve
Gehaltskürzung *f*
(Pw) salary cut
– reduction in salary
Gehaltsliste *f*
(Pw) payroll
– salary roll
Gehaltsniveau *n* (Pw) salary level
Gehaltspfändung *f* (Re) attachment (*or* garnishment) of salary
Gehaltspolitik *f* (Pw) compensation policy
Gehaltsstreifen *m* (Pw) pay slip
Gehaltsstruktur *f* (Pw) salary structure
Gehaltssummenstatistik *f* (Pw) payroll statistics
Gehaltsunterschiede *mpl* (Pw) salary differential
Gehaltsverrechnungskonto *n* (ReW) payroll account
Gehaltsvorschuß *m* (Pw) salary advance
Gehaltszettel *m* (Pw) pay slip
Gehaltszulage *f* (Pw) additional salary
gehandelt
(Bö) quoted
– listed
– traded *(ie, on the stock exchange)*
gehandelt und Brief (Bö) dealt and offered
Geheimbuchführung *f* (ReW) undisclosed accounting *(ie, employees have no access to key portions of books and records; this is not against principles of orderly accounting)*
geheimer Mangel *m*
(Re) latent
– hidden
– concealed ... defect
(ie, not apparent on the face of product, document, etc.)
geheimer Vorbehalt *m*
(Re) mental reservation
– hidden intention
(ie, denotes a dishonest excuse for evading a contractual promise, § 116 BGB)
geheimes Einverständnis *n* (Re) collusion
geheimes Wettbewerbsverbot *n* (Kart) blacklisting, § 75 HGB
geheime Wahl *f* (Pw) election by secret ballot
Geheimhaltungspflicht *f* (Pw) obligation to maintain secrecy
Geheimnisverrat *m* (Kart) disclosure of business secrets, §§ 17ff UWG
Geheimpatent *n* (Pat) secret patent
Geheimsache *f*
(com) secret matter
– classified item
gehemmtes Exportwachstum *n* (Vw) constrained export growth
gehobener Bedarf *m* (Mk) non-essential demand
Gehorsamspflicht *f* (Re) duty (*or* obligation) to comply with instructions
gehortetes Geld *n* (Vw) inactive money
geht gegen unendlich (Math) tends to infinity
geh- und stehbehindert (SozV) unable to walk and stand properly

Geisteskranker *m*
(Re) person of unsound mind
– person non compos mentis
Geisteskrankheit *f*
(Re) mental illness, § 104 BGB
– unsoundness of mind
– insanity
Geistesschwäche *f*
(Re) mental infirmity (*or* weakness)
– feebleness of mind
geistiges Eigentum *n* (Pat) intellectual property
gekettete Adressierung *f* (EDV) chained addressing
gekettete Liste *f* (EDV) chained list
geknickte Nachfragekurve *f*
(Vw) kinked (*or* kinky) demand curve
– cornered demand curve
gekoppelte Börsengeschäfte *npl* (Bö) matched sales
gekoppelte Stichproben *fpl* (Stat) linked samples
gekorene Orderpapiere *npl* (WeR) order papers by transaction (*or* GB: act) of party (*opp, geborene Orderpapiere*)
gekreuzter Scheck *m* (WeR) crossed check, §§ 37ff ScheckG
gekrümmte Nachfragekurve *f* (Vw) curvilinear demand curve
gekündigt (Pw) under notice
Geländeerschließungskosten *pl* (com) site development (*or* preparation) cost
Geld *n*
(Vw) money (*ie, notes and coins*)
(com) money
– (infml) cash (*ie, money in any form*)
(Bö) bid
– buyers
Geldabfluß *m* (Fin) outflow of funds
Geld *n* **abheben** (Fin) to draw (*or* withdraw) money (*ie, from bank account*)
Geld *n* **abschöpfen** (FiW) to skim money from the economy (*ie, through higher taxes*)
Geldabundanz *f* (Fin) abundance of money (*ie, in the banking system and in the money market*)
Geldakkord *m* (Pw) money piece rate
Geldangebot *n*
(Vw) money supply
(Fin) money supply (*eg, in the money market*)
Geldangebotsmultiplikator *m* (Vw) money supply multiplier
Geldanlage *f*
(Fin) (financial) investment
– employment of funds
Geldanlagen *fpl* **der privaten Haushalte** (VGR) private savings
Geldanlagen *fpl* **entgegennehmen** (Fin) to accept deposits
Geldanlagen *fpl* **im Ausland** (Fin) funds employed abroad
Geldanlagen *fpl* **von Gebietsfremden** (Fin) nonresident investments
Geld *n* **anlegen**
(Fin) to invest
– to put money (into)
– to sink money (into)
Geldanleger *m* (Fin) investor

Geldanspruch *m* (Re) monetary claim
Geld *n* **aufbringen** (Fin) to raise (*or* borrow) money
Geld *n* **aufnehmen** (Fin) to borrow (*or* take up) money
Geldausgabeautomat *m*
(Fin) automated teller machine, ATM
– (GB) cash dispenser
(*syn, Bankomat*)
Geldausgang *m* (Fin) cash disbursement
Geld *n* **ausleihen**
(Fin) to lend
– to give out money (to)
Geldautomat *m* (Fin) = *Geldausgabeautomat*
Geldautomatensystem *n*
(Fin) ATM (automatic teller machine) system
– (GB) cash dispenser system
Geldbasis *f* (Vw) monetary base (*ie, central bank money + demand deposits with central bank; syn, monetäre Basis, Primärgeld, exogenes Geld*)
Geldbedarf *m* (Fin) cash requirements
Geld *n* **bei e–r Bank haben** (Fin) to have/keep money in/with a bank
Geld *n* **bereitstellen** (Fin) to put up money (*ie, for a project*)
Geld *n* **beschaffen**
(Fin) to find
– to procure
– to raise ... money
– (infml) to dig up money somewhere
Geldbeschaffung *f* (Fin) provision of funds (*ie, converting nonliquid assets into cash*)
Geldbeschaffungskosten *pl*
(Fin) cost of finance
– cost of raising (*or* procuring) money
(Fin) financing costs for the bank itself
Geldbestand *m* (Fin) monetary holdings
Geld-Brief-Schlußkurs *m* (Bö) bid-ask close
Geld-Brief-Spanne *f* (Bö) price spread
Geldbuße *f*
(Re) administrative fine
(StR) fine
(Kart) monetary fine
Gelddeckung *f*
(Vw) gold or foreign exchange cover (*ie, of money in circulation*)
(Fin) sum total of liquid funds (*ie, raised through realizing physical assets or procuring money*)
Gelddisponent *m* (Fin) money manager
Gelddisponibilitäten *fpl* (Fin) available liquid funds
Gelddisposition *f* (Fin) cash management
Gelddispositions-Stelle *f* (Fin) money-management department
Geldeingang *m*
(Fin) cash receipt
(Fin) inflow of liquid funds (*ie, from sales of goods, services, or receivables*)
Geldeinheit *f* (Vw) monetary unit
Geldeingänge *mpl* (Fin) monies received
Geldeinkommen *n* (Vw) money income
Geldeinkommen *n* **des Haushalts** (Vw) consumer's money income
Geldeinlage *f*
(Re) contribution in cash

- cash contribution
  (opp, Sacheinlage = contribution in kind od noncash contribution)
Geldeinstandskosten *pl* (Fin) cost of money *(ie, bank's own financing cost)*
Geld *n* **einzahlen**
  (Fin) to pay in money
  (Fin) to deposit money at/with a bank
Geldeinzug *m* (Fin) collection of receivables
Geldentschädigung *f* (Re) money *(or* pecuniary) compensation
Geldentwertung *f*
  (Vw) inflation
  – fall in the value of money
Geldentwertungsindex *m* (Stat) inflation index
Geldentwertungsrate *f* (Vw) rate of inflation
Gelder *npl* **abziehen** (Fin) to withdraw funds
Gelder *npl* **anlegen** (Fin) to invest funds
Gelder *pl* **der öffentlichen Hand** (FiW) public funds
Geldersatzmittel *n* (Fin) substitute money
Gelderwerb *m* (Fin) money-making
Geld *n* **fest anlegen** (Fin) to tie up money
Geldflüssigkeit *f* (Fin) = *Geldmarktverflüssigung*
Geldflußrechnung *f* (Fin) cash flow statement *(Note: ‚Finanzflußrechnung' is the preferred term in German managerial finance)*
Geldforderung *f*
  (Fin) money *(or* monetary) claim
  – outstanding debt
Geldfunktionen *fpl* (Vw) functions of money
Geldgeber *m*
  (Fin) (money) lender
  (com) financial backer
  – sponsor
Geldgeschäft *n*
  (Fin) money-market business
  (Fin) money *(or* financial) transaction
  (Fin) procurement and disposal of funds
Geldhahn *m* (Fin, infml) money faucet *(eg, opens up)*
Geldhandel *m* (Fin) money-market dealings *(ie, in central bank money between banks)*
Geld *n* **hinauswerfen** (com, infml) to throw money down the sink
Geld *n* **hineinstecken** (Fin) to invest money (into)
  – to sink money into
Geld *n* **horten** (Vw) to hoard money
Geldhortung *f* (Vw) hoarding of money
Geldillusion *f*
  (Vw) money illusion *(I. Fisher)*
  – veil of money
Geldinstitut *n* (Fin) financial institution
Geld *n* **investieren** (Fin) to invest money (into)
Geldkapital *n* (Vw) monetary capital *(opp, Real- od Sachkapital)*
Geldkapitalbildung *f* (Vw) formation of monetary capital
Geldkapitalerhaltung *f* (ReW) maintenance of money capital
Geld *n* **knapp halten** (Vw) to keep credit tight
Geldknappheit *f*
  (Vw) money squeeze *(or* stringency)
  (Fin) scarcity *(or* shortage) of money
  – (infml) money crunch

Geldkosten *pl* (KoR) money cost *(ie, equivalent of materials used)*
Geldkredit *m* (Fin) monetary credit
Geldkreislauf *m*
  (Vw) circular flow of money
  – money circuit
Geld *n* **kündigen** (Fin) to call in money
Geldkurs *m*
  (AuW) buying rate *(ie, of foreign currency)*
  (Bö) bid
  – bid price
  – buyers' rate
  – demand price
  – money rate
Geldleihe *f* (Fin) lending business *(ie, comprises loans, advances on current account, and credits by way of bills discounted)*
Geld *n* **leihen** (Fin) to borrow money
Geldleihverkehr *m* (Fin) money loan business between banks
Geldleistung *f* (com) payment
Geldleistungen *fpl* (SozV) cash benefits
Geld *n* **locker machen** (com, infml) to stump up money
Geldlohn *m* (Pw) money wage *(opp, Naturallohn)*
Geldmangel *m*
  (Fin) lack of money
  – want of finance
Geldmarkt *m*
  (Fin) money market
  – (GB, infml) Lombard Street
  – (US, infml) Wall Street
Geldmarktanlage *f*
  (Fin) employment of funds in the money market
  – money market investments
geldmarktfähige Aktiva *pl* (Fin) assets eligible for the money market
  (ie, those which are also eligible for discount with the central bank)
geldmarktfähige Papiere *npl* (Fin) paper eligible for the money market
Geldmarktgeschäfte *npl* (Fin) money market dealings
Geldmarktkredite *mpl* (Fin) money market loans
Geldmarktpapiere *npl* (Fin) money market paper
Geldmarktsätze *mpl* (Vw) money (market) rates
Geldmarktsätze *mpl* **unter Banken** (Fin) interbank money market rates
Geldmarktsteuerung *f* (Fin) money market control
Geldmarkttitel *mpl* (Fin) = *Geldmarktpapiere*
Geldmarktverflüssigung *f* (Fin) easing of money market *(ie, supply of loan funds satisfies demand)*
Geldmarktverschuldung *f* (Fin) money market indebtedness
Geldmarktwechsel *m* (Fin) money market bill
Geldmarktzinsen *mpl* (Fin) money market (interest) rates
Geldmenge *f* (Vw) money supply *(or* stock)
Geldmenge *f* **in der Abgrenzung M_1** (Vw) money supply M_1 *(ie, currency and sight deposits)*
Geldmenge *f* **in der Abgrenzung M_2** (Vw) money supply M_2 *(ie, M_1 + time deposits and funds borrowed for less than 4 years)*
Geldmenge *f* **in der Abgrenzung M_3** (Vw) money

supply M_3 *(ie, M_2 + savings deposits at statutory notice)*
Geldmenge *f* **in der engen Abgrenzung** (Vw) narrowly defined money supply
Geldmenge *f* **in der engsten Definition** (Vw) money supply in the narrowest definition (M21) *(ie, Bargeld und Sichteinlagen: currency and sight deposits)*
Geldmenge *f* **in der weiten Abgrenzung** (Vw) broadly defined money supply (M_3) *(ie, Bargeld, Sichteinlagen, Termingelder unter 4 Jahren, Spareinlagen mit gesetzlicher Kündigungsfrist: currency, sight deposits, time deposits and funds borrowed for less than 4 years, savings deposits at statutory notice)*
Geldmenge *f* **knapp halten** (Vw) to keep a tight grip on the money supply
Geldmengenausweitung *f*
(Vw) money supply expansion
– monetary expansion
Geldmengen-Einkommensmechanismus *m* (AuW) money supply/income mechanism
Geldmengenexpansion *f* (Vw) growth of money supply (*or* stock)
Geldmengen-Preismechanismus *m* (AuW) money supply/price-mechanism
Geldmengenregulierung *f* (Vw) management of money supply
Geldmengensteuerung *f* (Vw) monetary targeting
Geldmengen- und Kreditzunahme *f* **beschränken** (Vw) to restrain the growth of money and credit
Geldmengenwachstum *n* (Vw) monetary growth (*or* expansion)
Geldmengenziel *n*
(Vw) monetary growth target
– monetary target
– money supply target
Geldmenge *f* **regeln** (Vw) to regulate the money supply
Geldmittel *pl* (Fin) cash resources
Geldmittelbestand *m* (Fin) cash position
Geldmittelbewegung *f* (Fin) flow of funds *(ie, updated statement of liquid funds extending over a period up to three months)*
Geld *n* **mit niedrigem Kreditschöpfungsmultiplikator** (Vw) low-powered money
Geldnachfrage *f* (Vw) demand for cash
Geldnähe *f* (Fin) degree of liquidity
Geldnutzen *m* (Vw) utility of liquid funds (*or* cash)
Geld *n* **ohne Edelmetalldeckung** (Vw) credit money
Geldplan *m* (Fin) cash plan
Geldplanung (Fin) cash planning
Geldpolitik *f* (Vw) monetary policy
geldpolitisch (Vw) monetary
geldpolitische Bremsen *fpl* (Vw) monetary brakes
geldpolitische Maßnahmen *fpl* (Vw) measures of monetary policy
geldpolitischer Indikator *m* (Vw) monetary policy indicator
geldpolitisches Instrumentarium *n* (Vw) tools of monetary policy
geldpolitische Ziele *npl* (Vw) monetary targets
Geldquelle *f* (Fin) money source
Geldrente *f* (Re) annuity *(ie, right to receive periodic payments in compensation for loss of occupational ability or death, § 843 BGB)*
Geldrepartierung *f* (Bö) scale-down of purchase orders
Geldreserve *f* (Vw) money reserve
Geldrückgabe *f* (com) money back
Geldsatz *m* (Fin) buying rate
Geldschaffung *f* (Vw) = *Geldschöpfung*
Geldschleier *m* (Vw) veil of money *(syn, Geldillusion)*
Geld *n* **schöpfen** (Vw) to create money
Geldschöpfung *f*
(Vw) creation of money
– process of creating money
Geldschöpfungs-Gewinn *m* (Vw) seigniorage
Geldschöpfungskoeffizient *m* (Vw) money creation coefficient
Geldschöpfungsmultiplikator *m*
(Vw) bank money creation multiplier
– money creation multipler
– money supply expansion multiplier
– deposit multiplier
Geldschuld *f* (Re) money debt (*or* owed), § 244 BGB
Geldsendung *f* (VGR) remittance
Geldsorten *fpl* (Fin) foreign notes and coin
Geld *n* **spielt keine Rolle** (com, infml) money no consideration
Geldspritze *f*
(Fin) injection of money
– (infml) fiscal shot in the arm
Geldsteuerung *f* (Vw) money supply control
Geld *n* **stillegen**
(Vw) to immobilize
– to neutralize
– to sterilize ... money
Geldstillegung *f*
(Fin) locking up
– tying up
– sterilization ... of money
Geldstrafe *f* (Re) penalty
– fine
Geldstromanalyse *f*
(Vw) analysis of moneyflows
– flow-of-funds analysis
– money flow analysis
Geldsubstitut *n* (Fin) near money
Geldsumme *f* (Fin) sum of money
Geldsurrogat *n* (Fin) substitute money
Geldtheorie *f*
(Vw) theory of money
– monetary economics
Geldtransfer *m* (FiW) cash grants
Geldüberhang *m* (Vw) excess money supply
Geld *n* **überweisen** (Fin) to remit money *(ie, by mail or post)*
Geldüberweisung *f*
(Fin) money transfer
– remittance
(Fin) remittance
– amount of money remitted
Geldumlauf *m*
(Vw) circulation of money
(Vw) money in circulation
– money supply (*or* stock)

Geldumlaufgeschwindigkeit f (Vw) velocity of circulation
Geldumsatz m (Fin) money turnover
Geld und Brief (Bö) bid and asked
Geld- und Kapitalvermittler mpl (Fin) financial intermediaries
Geld- und Kreditpolitik f (Vw) monetary policy
Geld- und Kredittheorie f (Vw) monetary theory
geld- und kreditwirtschaftliches Unternehmen n (Fin) financial enterprise
Geld- und Währungsordnung f (Vw) monetary order (or system)
Geld n **unterschlagen**
 (Re) to embezzle
 – to convert another's money to one's own use
 – to take another's money
Geldunterschlagung f (Re) embezzlement
Geld n **verdienen**
 (Fin) to make money
 (Pw) to earn money *(ie, by working)*
Geldverfassung f (Vw) monetary structure
Geldverkehr m (Fin) monetary movements (or transactions)
Geldverknappung f
 (Fin) contraction of money supply
 – monetary tightness
 – money squeeze
Geldverleiher m (Fin) moneylender
Geldvermögen n (VGR) financial assets
Geldvermögensbildung f
 (VGR) acquisition of financial assets
 (Vw) monetary wealth formation
Geldvermögensneubildung f (Vw) new capital formation
Geldvermögenswerte mpl (Fin) cash assets
Geldvernichtung f
 (Vw) reduction of money supply
 – destruction of money *(opp, Geldschöpfung)*
Geldverschlechterung f (Vw) currency depreciation
Geld n **verschwenden**
 (Fin) to squander money
 – (infml) to throw one's money about/around
Geldversorgung f **der Wirtschaft** (Vw) money supply
Geldversorgungsgeschäfte npl (Fin) money creation and payments transactions *(ie, by banks)*
Geldvolumen n
 (Vw) money supply (or stock)
 – volume of money
Geldvolumen n **der Wirtschaft** (Fin) volume of money in the economy
Geldvolumen n **M$_1$** (Vw) money supply M$_1$ *(ie, currency in circulation, excluding cash holdings of banks + sight deposits of domestic nonbanks)*
Geldvolumen n **M$_2$** (Vw) money supply M$_2$ *(ie, money supply M$_1$ + time deposits and funds borrowed for less than 4 years)*
Geldvolumen n **M$_3$** (Vw) money supply M$_3$ *(ie, money supply M$_2$ + savings deposits at statutory notice)*
Geldwechselgeschäft n (Fin) currency exchange transactions
Geld n **wechseln** (Fin) to change money
Geldwechsler m (Fin) moneychanger
Geldwert m (Vw) value of money

Geldwerte mpl (Vw) money assets
geldwertes Recht n (Vw) financial claim
geldwerte Vorteile mpl (Pw) benefits in money's worth
Geldwertschwankungen fpl (Vw) fluctuations in the value of money
Geldwertschwund m (Vw) monetary erosion
Geldwertstabilität f (Vw) monetary stability
Geldwertverschlechterung f (Vw) currency depreciation
Geldwesen n
 (Vw) currency system
 – monetary system (or order)
Geldwirtschaft f (Vw) money economy *(opp, Naturalwirtschaft = barter economy)*
Geldzins m (Vw) money interest *(opp, Naturalzins)*
Geldzuflüsse mpl (Fin) inflow (or influx) of funds
Geld n **zurückerstatten** (Fin) to refund (or pay back) money
Gelegenheitsagent m (com) occasional agent *(ie, he is not a commercial representative)*
Gelegenheitsarbeit f
 (Pw) temporary employment (or work)
 – casual work (or labor)
Gelegenheitsarbeiter m
 (Pw) occasional (or transient) worker
 – (GB) casual labourer
 (ie, not confined to heavy labor)
Gelegenheitsbeschäftigung f (Pw) = *Gelegenheitsarbeit*
Gelegenheitsemittent m (Fin) occasional issuer
Gelegenheitsfrachtführer m (com) occasional carrier
Gelegenheitsgeschäfte npl
 (com) occasional deals (or transactions)
 (com) transactions of single-venture partnerships
Gelegenheitsgesellschaft f
 (com) temporary (special) venture
 – ad hoc consortium
 (ie, ‚Arbeitsgemeinschaft' in construction, ‚Konsortium' in the credit industry)
 (Re) ad hoc association
 – single-venture partnership
 – occasional partnership *(ie, association of persons combining funds for a single joint transaction with a view to profit, such as a syndicate, joint management of property)*
Gelegenheitskauf m
 (com) chance bargain
 (Kart) bargain *(ie, offering goods for sale below the current market price)*
Gelegenheitskunde m (com) casual customer
Gelegenheitspreis m (com) bargain price
Gelegenheitsspediteur m (com) occasional forwarder
Gelegenheitsstichprobe f (Stat) chunk sample
geleistete Anzahlungen fpl
 (ReW) advance payments to suppliers
 – payments in advance
 – advances to supply
 – deposits with suppliers
 (ReW, EG) payments on account
geleistete Anzahlungen fpl **auf Anlagevermögen**
 (ReW) down-payments for fixed assets

geleistete Arbeitsstunden *fpl* (Pw) hours worked
gelenkter Außenhandel *m* (AuW) controlled international trade
gelenkte Wirtschaft *f* (Vw) controlled (*or* directed) economy
gelieferte Menge *f* (com) quantity shipped
geliefert Grenze benannter Lieferort (com, *Incoterms*) delivered at frontier named place of delivery
geliefert verzollt benannter Ort im Einfuhrland (com, *Incoterms*) delivered named place of destination in country of importation duty paid
geliehene Währungsreserven *fpl* (AuW) borrowed reserves
geltender Lohnsatz *m* (Pw) prevailing wage rate
geltender Preis *m* (com) current (*or* ruling) price
geltender Satz *m* (com) current rate
geltendes Recht *n* (Re) established (*or* applicable) law
geltende Ziffer *f* (Math) significant number
geltend machen
 (Re) to assert *(eg, a right)*
 – to put forward *(eg, a claim)*
 (StR) to claim *(eg, expenses as tax exempt)*
 (Pat) to interfere
Geltendmachen *n* **von Rechten** (Re) assertion of rights
Geltendmachung *f* **von Ersatzansprüchen** (Re) assertion of claims for damages
Geltungsbereich *m* (Re) scope *(eg, of law or statute)*
Geltungsdauer *f*
 (Re) duration
 – period of validity (*or* operation)
Geltungsdauer *f* **e–s Patents** (Pat) life of a patent
Geltungsfrage *f* (Log) question of justification (*or* validity)
Geltungskonsum *m* (Vw) conspicuous (*or* ostentatious) consumption
Gemeinbedarf *m* (FiW) public requirements
Gemeinbedürfnisse *npl* (FiW) collective (*or* public) wants
Gemeinde *f* (FiW) municipality
 (ie, lowest level of government in the German three-tier system)
Gemeindeabgaben *fpl* (FiW) municipal taxes and charges
Gemeindeabgabengesetz *n* (FiW) municipal-revenue law
Gemeindeanleihe *f* (FiW) municipal loan
Gemeindeanteil *m* (FiW) municipal share in income tax revenue
Gemeindefinanzen *pl* (FiW) municipal (*or* local) finance
Gemeindefinanzreformgesetz *n* (FiW) Municipal Finance Reform Law, of 8 Sept 1969
Gemeindehaushalt *m* (FiW) municipal budget
Gemeindehaushaltsrecht *n* (FiW) municipal budget law
Gemeindelasten *fpl* (StR) municipal burdens *(ie, which result from the existence of a business establishment, § 30 GewStG)*
Gemeindesteuer *f* (StR) municipal tax
Gemeindesteuersystem *n* (FiW) municipal tax structure

Gemeindeverband *m* (Re) communal association
 – association of municipalities
 (ie, autonomous governmental unit discharging supra-regional functions, such as road construction, water and electricity supply)
Gemeineigentum *n* (Re) public ownership
gemeiner Handelswert *m* (com) common market value, § 659 HGB
gemeiner Logarithmus *m* (Math) common logarithm
gemeiner Wert *m* (StR) fair market value, § 9 BewG
 (ie, the price which can be realized for an asset under normal market conditions; applicable unless a different measure of value is specifically prescribed)
Gemeinhaftung *f* (Re) joint liability *(of GmbH shareholders, § 31 III GmbHG)*
Gemeinkosten *pl*
 (KoR) overhead
 – overhead cost
 – indirect cost (*or* expense)
 – burden
 – (GB) oncost
Gemeinkostenabweichung *f* (KoR) overhead variance
Gemeinkostenausgleichsrücklage *f* (ReW) reserve for overhead
Gemeinkostenbereich *m* (KoR) overhead (*or* burden) department
Gemeinkostenbudget *n* (KoR) overhead budget
Gemeinkostenergebnis *n* (KoR) balance between estimated and absorbed overhead
gemeinkostenintensiv (KoR) costly on overheads
Gemeinkostenkarten *fpl* (KoR) expense cards
Gemeinkostenleistungen *fpl* (KoR) overhead-type services *(ie, not sold, but immediately used for plant purposes; traceable as secondary expense)*
Gemeinkostenlohn *m* (KoR) indirect labor
Gemeinkostenmaterial *n* (KoR) indirect material
Gemeinkostenplan *m* (KoR) overhead budget
Gemeinkostenplanung *f* (KoR) overhead budgeting (*or* planning)
Gemeinkostensatz *m* (KoR) overhead rate
Gemeinkostenschlüssel *m* (KoR) overhead allocation base
Gemeinkostenschlüsselung *f* (KoR) establishing standards for allocating overhead cost to costing units or cost centers
Gemeinkostenstelle *f* (KoR) overhead department
Gemeinkostenstoffe *mpl* (KoR) = *Gemeinkostenmaterial*
Gemeinkostenüberdeckung *f*
 (KoR) overabsorption of overhead
 (KoR) overabsorbed (*or* overapplied) overhead
Gemeinkostenumlage *f*
 (KoR) allocation of overhead
 – overhead cost allocation
 – overhead distribution
Gemeinkostenunterdeckung *f* (KoR) underabsorption of overhead
 (KoR) underabsorbed (*or* underapplied) overhead
Gemeinkosten-Verrechnungsbasis *f* (KoR) overhead distribution base

Gemeinkosten-Verrechnungssatz *m* (KoR) percentage overhead rate
– burden rate
Gemeinkosten-Verrechnungssatzbasis *f* (KoR) overhead (*or* burden) base
Gemeinkostenzuschlag *m* (KoR) overhead rate
gemeinnützig (Bw) nonprofit
– nonprofit making
– on a public benefit and cooperative basis
(see ‚gemeinwirtschaftlich' for conceptual explanation)
(StR) of public benefit, § 10b I EStG *(ie, excludes religious and scientific purposes)*
gemeinnützige Gesellschaft *f* (Bw) company not for profit (*or* gain)
gemeinnützige Körperschaft *f* (Re) nonprofit corporation
gemeinnützige Organisation *f* (Re) nonprofit organization
gemeinnütziger Verein *m* (Re) nonprofit association
gemeinnütziger Zweck *m* (StR) public-benefit purpose
gemeinnützige Stiftung *f* (Re) nonprofit foundation
gemeinnütziges Unternehmen *n* (Bw) nonprofit enterprise
Gemeinnützigkeit *f* (Bw) nonprofit-making character
gemeinsam abhängige Variable *f* (Math) jointly dependent variable
gemeinsam benutzte Datei *f* (EDV) shared files
gemeinsame Abgaben *fpl* (EG) co-responsibility levies *(eg, on farm overproduction)*
gemeinsame Agrarmarktorganisation *f* (EG) common organization of the agricultural markets
gemeinsame Agrarpolitik *f* (EG) Common Agricultural Policy, CAP
gemeinsame Anmelder *pl* (Pat) joint applicants
gemeinsame Bewirtschaftung *f* (Bw) joint management
gemeinsame Bildung *f* **von Reserven** (EG) pooling of reserves
gemeinsame Dichtefunktion *f* (Math) joint density function
gemeinsame Einfuhrregelung *f* (EG) common rule for import
gemeinsame Erfinder *pl* (Pat) joint inventors
gemeinsame Erklärung *f* (StR) joint statement *(ie, of special expenses and extraordinary financial burdens, § 57 EStDV)*
gemeinsame Federführung *f* (com) co-general contracting
(eg, for Western participants in gas pipeline project)
gemeinsame Fischereipolitik *f* (EG) common fisheries (*or* fishing) policy
gemeinsame Gefahr *f* (SeeV) common peril
gemeinsame Gesamtleistung *f* (Bw) joint overall performance
gemeinsame Gewinnmaximierung *f* (Vw) joint profit maximization
gemeinsame Handelspolitik *f* (EG) common commercial policy
gemeinsame Marktforschung *f* (Mk) syndicated market research

gemeinsame Marktorganisation *f* (EG) common market organization *(ie, for products such as grain, rice, vegetables, hop, tobacco, etc.)*
gemeinsame Patentanmeldung *f* (Pat) common patent application
Gemeinsamer Agrarmarkt *m* (EG) Common Agricultural Market
gemeinsame Rangzahlen *fpl* (Stat) tied ranks
gemeinsamer Ausschluß *m* (com) joint committee
gemeinsamer Außenzolltarif *m* (EG) common external tariff
gemeinsamer Fonds *m* (EG) common fund
– (infml) common kitty
(eg, to which all members contribute)
gemeinsamer Haushalt *m* (StR) common household
gemeinsamer Konsum *m* (Vw) non-rivalry in consumption
gemeinsamer Markt *m* (EG) Common Market
gemeinsamer Nenner *m* (Math) common denominator
gemeinsamer Rechtsgeschäftswille *m* (Re) meeting (*or* union) of minds
– concurrence of intention
gemeinsamer Teiler *m* (Math) common divisor
Gemeinsame Rundverfügung *f* (StR) Joint Decree *(ie, of Regional Tax Offices = Oberfinanzdirektionen)*
Gemeinsamer Zolltarif *m* (EG) Common Customs Tariff, CCT
gemeinsames Patent *n* (Pat) joint patent
gemeinsame Steuererklärung *f* (StR) joint (tax) return
gemeinsames Umsatzsteuersystem *n* (EG) Common Turnover Tax System
gemeinsames Vielfaches *n* (Math) common multiple
gemeinsames Zollgebiet *n* (EG) common customs territory
gemeinsame Währung *f* (EG) common currency
gemeinsame Wirtschaftspolitik *f* (EG) common economic policy
gemeinsam haften (Re) be jointly liable (for)
gemeinschädliche Sachbeschädigung *f* (Re) malicious damage to public property, § 304 StGB
Gemeinschaft *f* (EG) Community
gemeinschaftliche Absatzorgane *npl* (Mk) joint sales organization
(ie, sales office, distributing warehouse, traveling salesmen, etc.)
gemeinschaftliche Einfuhrüberwachung *f* (EG) Community surveillance over imports
gemeinschaftliche Gefahrenübernahme *f* (Re) pooling of risk
gemeinschaftliche Havarie *f* (com) general average, § 700 HGB
gemeinschaftlicher Besitz *m* (Re) joint possession
gemeinschaftlicher Versandschein *m* (EG) Community transit document
gemeinschaftliches Bankkonto *n* (Fin) joint bank account
gemeinschaftliches Eigentum *n* (Re) joint ownership
gemeinschaftliches Risiko *n* (Vers) joint risk

gemeinschaftliches Tarifkontingent *n* (EG) Community tariff quota
gemeinschaftliches Versandverfahren *n* (EG) Community transit operation (*or* procedure)
gemeinschaftliches Wirtschaftsrecht *n* (EG) economic Community law
gemeinschaftliches Zollrecht *n* (EG) Community provisions on customs matters
gemeinschaftliche Überwachung *f* (EG) Community surveillance (over)
Gemeinschaft *f* **nach Bruchteilen** (Re) tenancy in common *(ie, each owner holds an undivided interest in property, §§ 741 ff BGB)*
Gemeinschaftsabgabe *f* (EG) Community levy
Gemeinschaftsangebot *n* (Fin) syndicated bid
Gemeinschaftsanleihe *f* (EG) Community loan
Gemeinschaftsaufgabe *f* (FiW) community task
Gemeinschaftsausschuß *m* **der Deutschen Gewerblichen Wirtschaft** (com) Joint Association of German Trade and Industry *(ie, headquartered in Cologne)*
Gemeinschaftsbehandlung *f*
(EG) Community treatment
– intra-Community treatment
Gemeinschaftsbeschaffung *f* (Mk) group buying (*or* purchasing) *(ie, by retail traders, artisans, wholesalers, and department stores)*
Gemeinschaftsbeteiligung *f* (Re) jointly owned company
Gemeinschaftsbudget *n* (EG) Community budget
Gemeinschaftscharakter *m* **von Waren** (EG) Community nature of goods
Gemeinschaftsdepot *n* (Fin) joint security deposit *(ie, for the account of one or several depositors)*
Gemeinschaftseinfuhr *f* **von Waren** (EG) Community import of goods
Gemeinschaftseinkauf *m* (Mk) joint buying (*or* purchasing)
Gemeinschaftsemission *f* (Fin) joint loan issue
Gemeinschaftserfindung *f* (Pat) joint invention
Gemeinschaftserzeuger *m* (EG) Community producer
Gemeinschaftserzeugnis *n* (EG) Community product
Gemeinschaftsetat *m* (EG) Community budget
Gemeinschaftsfinanzierung *f*
(Fin) joint (*or* group) financing
(Fin) co-financing deal
Gemeinschaftsforschung *f* (Bw) joint research *(ie, undertaken by several firms)*
Gemeinschaftsgenehmigung *f* (EG) Community authorization
Gemeinschaftsgeschäft *n* (Fin) joint business
Gemeinschaftsgründung *f* (Re) joint venture
Gemeinschaftsinstrumente *npl* (EG) Community instruments
Gemeinschaftskontenrahmen *m* **industrieller Verbände** (ReW) Joint Standard Accounting System of Industrial Associations *(superseded in 1971 by IKR)*
Gemeinschaftskonto *n* (Fin) joint account *(ie, which may be ‚Oder-Konto' or ‚Und-Konto', which see)*
Gemeinschaftskredit *m*
(Fin) joint loan

– syndicated credit
Gemeinschaftsland *n* (EG) Community country
Gemeinschaftsmarkt *m* (EG) Community market
Gemeinschaftsmittel *pl* (EG) Community funds (*or* cash)
Gemeinschaftsorgane *npl* (EG) Community institutions
Gemeinschaftspatent *n* (Pat) jointly owned patent
Gemeinschaftsplafond *m* (EG) Community ceiling
Gemeinschaftspräferenz *f* (EG) Community preference
Gemeinschaftsproduktion *f* (EG) Community production
Gemeinschaftsprojekt *n* (com) community (*or* consortium) project
Gemeinschaftsrechner *m* (EDV) multi-user computer
Gemeinschaftsrecht *n* (EG) Community law
Gemeinschaftsregelung *f* (EG) Community rules
Gemeinschaftsreserve *f* (EG) Community reserve
Gemeinschaftsschlange *f* (EG) Community snake
Gemeinschaftssinn *m* (Pw) sense of communality
Gemeinschaftssparen *n* (Fin) collective saving *(opp, Individualsparen/Einzelsparen)*
Gemeinschaftssteuern *fpl*
(FiW) shared taxes *(ie, apportioned between Federation and Länder)*
(EG) Community taxes
Gemeinschaftsunternehmung *f*
(com) joint undertaking
(Re) joint venture *(ie, entered into for a limited time or for the completion of a particular project; may be established as corporation, partnership, civil law association = BGB-Gesellschaft, or any other legal form)*
Gemeinschaftsursprung *m* (EG) Community origin
Gemeinschaftsverfahren *n* (EG) Community procedure
Gemeinschaftsversicherung *f* (Vers) group insurance
Gemeinschaftsvertrag *m* (Re) joint contract
Gemeinschaftsvertrieb *m* (Mk) joint selling (*or* marketing)
Gemeinschaftswährung *f* (EG) common (*or* Community) currency
Gemeinschaftswaren *fpl* (EG) Community goods
Gemeinschafts-Warenhaus *n* (Mk) shop-in-the-shop system
Gemeinschafts-Wechselkurssystem *n* (EG) Community exchange rate system
Gemeinschaftswerbung *f*
(Mk) cooperative
– joint
– collective
– association ... advertising
Gemeinschaftszoll *m* (EG) Community tariff
Gemeinschaftszollkontingent *n* (EG) Community tariff quota
Gemeinschaft *f* **zur gesamten Hand** (Re) community of „united hands" *(ie, similar concept found in English law is the institution of joint ownership, see §§ 718ff BGB)*
Gemeinschuldner *m*
(Re) bankrupt
– common debtor

– adjucated bankrupt
Gemeinwirtschaft *f* (Bw) public-benefit and cooperative sector of the economy
*(ie, profit objective is subordinated to certain economic and sociopolitical goals; the difficulty of translating the term is illustrated by the following subclassification of ‚Gemeinwirtschaft':
(1) öffentliche Unternehmen = public enterprises
(2) frei-gemeinwirtschaftliche Unternehmen = based on ‚free', private initiative:*
  (a) Selbsthilfebetriebe, such as Genossenschaften, cooperatives
  (b) widmungswirtschaftliche Betriebe, such as hospitals, Red Cross
(3) öffentlich gebundene Unternehmen, such as ‚Versorgungsbetriebe' = public utilities
gemeinwirtschaftlich
(Bw) nonprofit
– nonprofit making
– on a public benefit and cooperative basis
(The German term and its common translation ‚nonprofit' do not imply that such organizations disown the profit motive; they profess as their overriding goal the promotion of public-welfare tasks which, by definition, lie outside the direct operational range of private enterprise committed to both the profitability and the payout principle; note, however, that the German term has moral and, sometimes, self-righteous undertones)
Gemeinwirtschaftlichkeitsprinzip *n* (Bw) principle (*or* concept) of ,,commonweal" *(ie, chief objective of business ought to be to improve social and economic conditions and not to maximize profits)*
gemeldete offene Stellen *fpl* (Pw) vacancies notified
gemietete Grundstücke *npl* **und Gebäude** *npl* (ReW) leasehold land and buildings
Gemischtbasis-Schreibweise *f* (EDV) mixed radix notation
gemischte Basis *f* (EDV) mixed base
gemischte Entscheidungsfunktion *f* (Stat) randomized decision function
gemischte Hypothekenbank *f* (Fin) mixed mortgage bank
gemischte Kommission *f* (Re) joint commission
gemischte Konten *npl* (ReW) mixed accounts *(syn, Bestands-Erfolgs-Konten)*
gemischte Kostenarten *fpl*
(KoR) mixed
– composite
– derived
– secondary ... cost types
gemischte Lebensversicherung *f* (Vers) endowment life insurance
(ie, payable to the insured at the end of contract or covered period or to beneficiary if insured dies prior to maturity date)
gemischte Nachfrage-Kosten-Inflation *f* (Vw) mixed demand-cost inflation
gemischte Produktausdrücke *mpl* (Math) cross-product terms
gemischter Fonds *m* (Fin) mixed fund
gemischter Vertrag *m* (Re) mixed contract
gemischtes Konto *n* (ReW) mixed account

gemischtes Modell *n* (Stat) mixed model
gemischte Strategie *f* (OR) mixed strategy
gemischtes Stichprobenverfahren *n* (Stat) mixed sampling
gemischte Versicherung *f*
(Vers) combined insurance
(Vers) combined endowment and whole-life insurance *(ie, nontechnical term in German insurance language)*
gemischte Wirtschaft *f* (Vw) mixed economy *(ie, combining elements of capitalist and socialist systems)*
gemischte Zahl *f* (Math) mixed number
Gemischtfertigung *f* (IndE) mixed production (*or* manufacturing) *(ie, halfway between Werkstattfertigung = job shop production and Fließfertigung = flow line production; syn, Gruppenfertigung)*
gemischt-ganzzahlige Programmierung *f* (OR) mixed-integer programming
gemischtgenutzte Grundstücke *npl* (StR) mixed property, § 75 IV BewG *(ie, serving residential as well as business or public purposes)*
Gemischtwarengeschäft *n* (Mk) general store
gemischtwirtschaftliche Gesellschaft *f* (Re) quasi-public company
gemischtwirtschaftliches System *n* (Vw) mixed economy
gemischtwirtschaftliches Unternehmen *n* (Re) mixed (*or* semi-public) enterprise
genannter Verschiffungshafen *m* (com) named port of shipment
genaue Beschreibung *f* **der Waren** (com) detailed description of goods
Genauigkeit *f* (Math, EDV) accuracy
genehmigte Bilanz *f* (ReW) approved balance sheet
genehmigte Investition *f* (Fin) authorized investment
genehmigtes Kapital *n* (Re) approved capital, §§ 202ff AktG *(ie, not identical with the English term ‚authorized capital' which is often translated as ‚autorisiertes Kapital')*
Genehmigung *f*
(com) authorization
– approval
– permit
(Re) subsequent approval *(ie, ratification of an act-in-the-law, § 184 BGB)*
Genehmigung *f* **der Bilanz** (ReW) adoption of the balance sheet
Genehmigung *f* **des Jahresberichts** (ReW) adoption of the annual report
Genehmigungsantrag *m* (Re) application for a permit
Genehmigungsbehörde *f* (Re) approving authority
Genehmigungsbescheid *m* (Re) notice of approval
genehmigungspflichtig
(Re) requiring official approval
(Kart) to be registered
– must be filed for approval *(ie, with the Berlin-based Federal Cartel Office)*
Genehmigungsverfahren *n* (com) licensing procedure
Genehmigungsvermerk *m* (Re) note of approval

Genehmigung f von Investitionsprojekten
(Fin) capital spending authorization
– capital appropriation
geneigte Ebene f (Math) oblique plane
Generalagent m (Vers) general agent *(ie, of an insurance company)*
Generalagentur f (com) general agency
Generalbevollmächtigter m
(Re) manager holding a general power of attorney
– universal agent *(see: Generalvollmacht)*
(Fin) executive manager
Generalbilanzen fpl (ReW) overall balance sheets *(ie, comprising ‚Sammelbilanzen' and ‚konsolidierte Bilanzen')*
Generaldirektor m
(Bw) chief executive
– general manager
(ie, rarely used additional title)
(EG) Director General
Generalhandel m (AuW) general commodity trade
Generalisator m (Log) universal quantifier
Generalklausel f
(com) all-purpose clause
– blanket clause
(Re) general rule of law
– legal principle of general application
(ie, one sanctioned by the recognition of authorities and expressed in the form of a maxim or logical proposition)
Generalkonto n (IWF) General Account
Generallizenznehmer m (Pat) general licensee
Generalpolice f
(Vers) floating (*or* floater) policy
(SeeV) open cargo policy
– open cover
Generalstreik m (Pw) general strike
Generaltarif m
(Zo) general
– single-schedule
– unilinear ... tariff
Generalüberholung f (IndE) general overhaul
Generalunternehmer m
(com) general
– main
– primary
– prime ... contractor
Generalversammlung f
(Re) general meeting of shareholders
– (GB) company in general meeting
Generalvertrag m (Re) blanket contract
Generalvertreter m (com) general agent (*or* representative)
Generalvertretung f (com) general agency
Generalvollmacht f (Re) universal agency
– general power of representation
– blanket (*or* unlimited) power of attorney
(opp, Sondervollmacht/Einzelvollmacht)
Generator m
(EDV) generator
– generator program
– generating program (*or* routine)
Generatorprogramm n (EDV) = *Generator*
generelle Abgaben fpl (FiW) general fiscal charges
(ie, taxes, duties, levies)

generelle Exportförderung f (AuW) across-the-board export promotion
generieren (EDV) to generate
generierte Adresse f (EDV) generated address
genormte Größe f (com) standardized size
Genosse m (Re) member of a cooperative
Genossenschaft f
(com) cooperative
– co-op
Genossenschaft f **des Einzelhandels**
(com) retail co-op
– retailer cooperative
genossenschaftlicher Prüfungsverband m (ReW) cooperative auditing association
genossenschaftliche Zentralbanken fpl (Fin) central institutions of credit cooperatives
Genossenschaftsanteil m (Fin) share in a cooperative
Genossenschaftsbank f
(Fin) cooperative bank
– credit cooperative
Genossenschaftsgesetz n (Re) Cooperative Association Law, as amended in 1973
Genossenschaftskasse f (Fin) cooperative bank
Genossenschaftsprüfung f (ReW) auditing of cooperatives
Genossenschaftsregister n (Re) public register of cooperatives
Genossenschaftstheorie f (Vw) theory of cooperative societies
Genossenschaftsverband m (Bw) cooperative union
Genossenschaftswesen n (Bw) cooperative movement (*or* system)
Genossenschaftswissenschaft f (Bw) cooperative science
Genuskauf m
(Re) sale of unascertained goods
– sale by description
(ie, contract of sale in which the goods have been designated by their kind only)
Genus-Sachen fpl (Re) unascertained goods
Genußaktie f (Fin) bonus share *(ie, unknown in Germany)*
Genußberechtigter m (Re) beneficiary
Genußschuld f
(Re) generic (*or* generically defined) obligation
– obligation in kind
– unascertained debt
Genußrechte npl (Fin) profit participation rights
Genußschein m
(Fin) partipating (*or* participation) certificate
– qualified dividend instrument
– certificate of beneficial interest
genutzte Kapazität f (Bw) utilized (*or* used) capacity
geographische Mobilität f (Vw) geographical (*or* regional) mobility
geometrisch-degressive Abschreibung f
(ReW) declining-balance method *(of depreciation)*
– diminishing-provision method
(syn, Buchwertabschreibung, Restwertabschreibung)
geometrische Folge f (Math) geometric progression (*or* sequence)

265

geometrische Kante f (OR) geometric edge
geometrische Programmierung f (OR) geometric programming
geometrische Reihe f (Math) geometric series
geometrischer Knoten m (OR) geometric vertex
geometrischer Lag m (Vw) geometric lag
geometrischer Ort m (pl Örter) (Math) locus (pl loci)
geometrisches Mittel n (Stat) geometric mean
geometrische Spannweite f (Stat) geometric range
geometrische Verteilung f (Stat) geometric distribution
geordnete Marktverhältnisse npl (Vw) orderly market conditions
geordnete Menge f (Math) (partially) ordered set
geordnete Mengen fpl (Math) nested sets
geordnete Menge f **von Mengen** (Math) chain
– nest
– tower
geordneter Markt m (Bö) regular market
geordnetes Paar n (Math) ordered pair
Gepäcknetz n
(com) luggage rack
– (GB) roof rack
Gepäckschein m (WeR) baggage (or luggage) check
Gepäckversicherung f (Vers) baggage (or luggage) insurance
geplante Desinvestition f (Vw) intended (or planned) disinvestment
geplante Emissionen fpl (Fin) slated issues
geplante Ersparnis f (Vw) planned savings
geplante Investition f
(Vw) intended (or planned) investment
(Fin) proposed investment expenditure
geplante Konsumsumme f (Vw) planned consumption expenditure
geplante Kosten pl (KoR) predetermined cost
geplanter Verrechnungspreis m (ReW) budgeted transfer price
geplantes Entsparen n (Vw) intended dissaving
geplantes Sparen n (Vw) planned saving
geplantes Veralten n (Bw) built-in obsolescence
geplatzter Scheck m (Fin, sl) bounced check
geprüfte Bilanz f (ReW) audited balance sheet
gepufferte Ein-Ausgabe f (EDV) buffered input/output
Geradenabschnitt m (Math) line segment
Geradenschar f (Math) family (or system) of straight lines
gerade Parität f (EDV) even parity
gerade Zahl f (Math) even number
geradliniger Graph m (Math) straight graph
geradliniges Segment n (Math) straight-line segment
geränderte Determinante f (Math) bordered determinante
Gerätebyte n (EDV) standard device byte
Gerätefehler m (EDV) equipment failure
Gerätefehlerkorrektur f (EDV) device error recovery
Gerätekompatibilität f (EDV) equipment compatibility
Gerätemiete f (com) equipment rental

Gerätesteuerung f (EDV) device controller
Gerätesteuerzeichen n (EDV) device control character
Geräteverwaltungsprogramm n (EDV) device management program
Gerätezuordnung f (EDV) device allocation
Gerätezustandsbyte n (EDV) = *Gerätebyte*
Gerätezuweisung f (EDV) = *Gerätezuordnung*
gerechte Beurteilung f (Pw) fair appraisal
geregelter Devisenmarkt m (AuW) regulated foreign exchange market
geregelter Freiverkehr m
(Bö) regulated over-the-counter market
– regulated inofficial dealing
– semi-official trading
(ie, securities permitted on the trading floor, but not on the official list)
geregelter Wertpapiermarkt m (Bö) organized stock market
Gericht n (Re) court of law
gerichtete Gerade f (Math) directed line
gerichtete Inzidenzabbildung f (Math) directed incidence mapping
gerichtete Kante f
(OR) arc
– directed arc (or edge)
– oriented branch
gerichtete Kantenprogression f **der Länge** (OR) arc progression of length
gerichtete Kette f (OR) directed chain
gerichtete Pfeile mpl (OR) directed branches
gerichteter Graph m
(Math) directed graph
– digraph
gerichteter Zyklus m (OR) directed cycle
gerichtetes Abtasten n (EDV) directed scan
gerichtliche Beurkundung f (Re) judicial record
gerichtliche od notarielle Beurkundung f (Re) authentication by public act
gerichtlicher Vergleich m (Re) court settlement
gerichtliche Schritte mpl (Re) legal action
gerichtliche Schritte mpl **unternehmen**
(Re) to take legal action
– (infml) to go to court
gerichtliches Vergleichsverfahren n (Re) judicial composition proceedings *(see: Vergleich)*
gerichtliche Versteigerung f (Re) judicial sale
gerichtlich vertreten (Re) to represent in court
Gerichtsbarkeit f (Re) jurisdiction
Gerichtsbeschluß m **beantragen** (Re) to sue out a writ
Gerichtsdiener m (Re) court attendant
Gerichtsgebühren fpl (Re) court fees
Gerichtshof m
(Re) court of law
– court of justice
– tribunal
Gerichtshof m **erster Instanz** (Re) first-instance court
Gerichtshof m **zweiter Instanz** (Re) court of second instance
Gerichtskosten pl (Re) legal fees (or charges)
Gerichtsstand m
(Re) place of jurisdiction
– venue

– *(civil law)* domicilium disputandi
Gerichtsstand *m* **des Erfüllungsortes** (Re) jurisdiction at the place of performance
Gerichtsstand *m* **des Wohnsitzes** (Re) forum domicilii *(ie, forum or court of the domicile, considered as a place of jurisdiction)*
Gerichtsverfahren *n* (Re) legal proceedings
Gerichtsvollzieher *m* (Re, appr) bailiff
geringe Besteuerung *f* (StR) light taxation
geringe Lagerbestände *mpl* (MaW) lean inventories
geringe Nachfrage *f* (com) slack *(or* sluggish) demand
geringer Zuwachs *m* (com) marginal gain *(eg, in sales)*
geringe Umsätze *mpl*
 (Bö) calm
 – quiet
 – thin ... trading
geringfügige Beschäftigung *f*
 (SozV) low-paid *(or* side-line) employment *(eg, 15 hours per week or DM390 per month or one sixth of total income)*
 (StR) part-time employment *(ie, for wage tax purposes)*
geringfügiger Rückgang *m* (com) slight dip *(or* decline) *(eg, in value of mergers)*
geringfügig fester (Bö) slightly firmer
geringfügig schwächer (Bö) a fraction easier
geringstes Gebot *n* (Re) minimum bid *(ie, in judicial sales of real estate, § 44 ZVG)*
geringste Stückkosten *pl* (KoR) minimum unit cost
Geringverdiener *m* (SozV) low-income earner *(ie, whose monthly income is not more than one tenth of the monthly social insurance income limit = ¹⁄₁₀ der monatlichen Beitragsbemessungsgrenze)*
geringwertig
 (com) low-valued
 – of minor value
geringwertige Geschäftsausstattung *f* (ReW) low-value office equipment
geringwertiges Wirtschaftsgut *n*
 (ReW) low-value item
 – minor asset
 (StR) depreciable movable fixed asset of low value
 (ie, capable of separate use, deductible as current expense – Betriebsausgaben – in the year of acquisition or production, if cost does not exceed DM800, less VAT paid in connection with its acquisition)
Gerücht *n* **ausstreuen**
 (com, infml) to plant a rumor
 – (GB) to put it about*(that...)*
Gerüchteküche *f* (Bw, infml) grapevine *(ie, oral, one-to-one channel through which rumors can spread throughout the organization extremely rapidly)*
gerufener Teilnehmer *m* (EDV) called party
Gesamtabsatz *m* (com) total sales
Gesamtabschreibung *f* (ReW) lump-sum depreciation
Gesamtabweichung *f* (KoR) gross *(or* overall) variation
Gesamtaktie *f* (Fin) multiple share certificate *(ie,*

evidencing a large share holding, not widely used in Germany; syn, Gesamttitel od Globalaktie)
Gesamtangebot *n* (Vw) aggregate *(or* overall *or* total) supply
Gesamtannuität *f* (Fin) total annuity
Gesamtarbeitslosigkeit *f* (Vw) overall *(or* total) unemployment
Gesamtarbeitswert *m* (IndE) total work value
Gesamtaufkommen *n*
 (FiW) total tax collections
 – total revenue
Gesamtauftragswert *m*
 (com) total contract value
 (com) value of total orders received
Gesamtaufwand *m* (ReW) total expenditure
Gesamtausgaben *fpl* **der Inländer für Güter und Dienste**
 (VGR) domestic expenditure
 – absorption
Gesamtausgebot *n* (Re) invitation of combined bid *(ie, for several parcels of real estate, in judicial sales, § 63 ZVG; opp, Einzelausgebot)*
Gesamtausleihungen *fpl* (Fin) total lendings
Gesamtbedarf *m* (com) total requirements
Gesamtbelastung *f* (StR. VAT) total tax burden *(ie, on the final sales price of a product)*
Gesamtbelegschaft *f* (Pw) total labor force
Gesamtbeschäftigung *f* (Bw) total activity
Gesamtbetrag *m*
 (com) total
 – total amount
 – sum total
 – grand total
Gesamtbetrag *m* **der Einkünfte** (StR) adjusted gross income
Gesamtbetriebskalkulation *f* (Mk) overall costing system *(ie, covering the entire flow of goods and services from purchasing to sales)*
Gesamtbetriebsrat *m* (Pw) central works council
Gesamtbewertung *f* (StR) valuation of an enterprise as a whole
Gesamtbilanz *f*
 (ReW) overall balance sheet *(eg, consolidated balance sheet)*
 (AuW) overall balance *(ie, all balance-of-payments items, except changes in currency reserves)*
Gesamtbuchhaltung *f* (ReW) unified accounting *(ie, no separation of general and cost accounting, etc.)*
Gesamtbudget *n* (Bw) master budget
Gesamtbürgschaft *f* (Re) comprehensive guaranty
Gesamtdefizit *n* (FiW) overall budget deficit
Gesamtdividende *f* (Fin) total dividend
Gesamtdurchlaufzeit *f*
 (IndE) total door-to-door time
 – total processing time
gesamte außenwirtschaftliche Transaktionen *fpl* (VGR) total external transactions
gesamte Erwerbspersonen *fpl* (Stat) total labor force
Gesamteigenhandel *m* (AuW) total cross-frontier traffic of goods *(ie, including direct transit trade)*
Gesamteigentum *n* (Re) joint ownership
Gesamteinkommen *n* (SozV) total income *(ie, includes ‚Arbeitsentgelt' and ‚Arbeitseinkommen'*

= *employment income and earned income*, § 16 SGB IV)
Gesamtentwicklung *f* (com) overall trend (*or* development)
gesamte Pufferzeit *f* (OR) total float
gesamter Auftragsbestand *m* (com) total backlog
Gesamterbe *m* (Re) universal heir
Gesamterfolg *m* (ReW) overall result(*or* performance)
Gesamtergebnis *n* (Bw) overall result
Gesamtergebnisplan *m* (Bw) overall earnings budget *(ie, listing a number of annual pretax earnings figures)*
Gesamtergebnisrechnung *f* (ReW) statement of income and accumulated earnings
Gesamterhebung *f* (Stat) universal census
Gesamterlös *m*
(Vw) total revenue
(com) total proceeds
Gesamtertrag *m*
(Vw) total revenue
(Bw) total output *(ie, used in mapping the production function)*
(com) total yield *(ie, in farming)*
Gesamterwartungsschaden *m* (Vers) total expected loss
Gesamtfahrleistung *f* (StR) total distance driven in fiscal year
gesamtfällige Anleihen *fpl* (Fin) issues falling due en bloc
Gesamtfinanzierung *f* (Fin) total financing *(opp, Grenzfinanzierung)*
Gesamtforderung *f* (Re) claim of several joint creditors, §§ 428 to 430 BGB *(ie, each being entitled to request full performance; opp, Teilforderung)*
Gesamtgeschäft *n* (com) package deal
Gesamtgeschäftsführung *f*
(Re) joint management
– management by more than one partner *(ie, requires consent by all managing partners, § 115 HGB)*
Gesamtgläubiger *mpl*
(Re) joint creditors, § 428 BGB
– plurality of creditors
Gesamtgleichgewicht *n* (Bw) overall equilibrium *(ie, of receipts and expenditures)*
Gesamtgrundschuld *f* (Re) comprehensive land charge
Gesamthaftung *f*
(Re) joint and several liability
(Re) aggregate liability
Gesamthand *f* (Re) = *Gemeinschaft zur gesamten Hand*
Gesamthandeigentum *n* (Re) joint ownership of property
Gesamthandeigentümer *m* (Re) joint owner (of undivided interest)
Gesamthandforderung *f* (Re) joint claim (of several creditors)
Gesamthandgläubiger *m* (Re) joint and several creditor
Gesamthandsbesitz *m* (Re) common possession of a thing *(ie, physical control by several persons)*
Gesamthandschuld *f* (Re) joint debt (*or* liability)

Gesamthandschuldner *m* (Re) joint and several debtor
Gesamthandsgemeinschaft *f* (Re) community of joint owners
Gesamthandvermögen *n* (Re) joint property
Gesamthaushalt *m* (FiW) overall budget
Gesamthaushaltseinkommen *n* (Vw) aggregate consumer income
Gesamthypothek *f* (Re) blanket mortgage *(ie, one creating a lien on several parcels of land to secure payment of the same claim, § 1132 BGB)*
Gesamtindex *m* (Stat) overall index
Gesamtinvestitionen *fpl* (Fin) total capital spending
Gesamtkapazität *f* (Bw) overall capacity
Gesamtkapital *n* (Fin) total capital
Gesamtkapitalausstattung *f* (Fin) total capitalization
Gesamtkapitalrentabilität *f*
(Fin) return on total investment
– return on total assets
– percentage return on total capital employed *(ie, profit + interest on borrowed capital × 100, divided by total capital)*
Gesamtkassendefizit *n* (FiW) overall cash deficit
Gesamtkaufpreis *m* (com) total purchase value
Gesamtkonjunktur *f*
(Vw) level of general economic activity
(Vw) overall health of the economy
Gesamtkonsum *m* (Vw) aggregate consumption expenditure
Gesamtkonzern *m* (Re) combined group
Gesamtkosten *pl* (KoR) total cost
(ie, sum of (a) fixed and variable cost = fixe und variable Kosten; (b) direct cost and overhead = Einzel- und Gemeinkosten; opp, Einheitskosten)
Gesamtkosten *pl* **der Materialbeschaffung** (MaW) total cost of acquisition
Gesamtkostenfunktion *f* (Bw) total cost function
Gesamtkostenkurve *f* (Bw) total cost curve
Gesamtkostenverfahren *n* (KoR) „total cost"-type of short-term results accounting *(ie, gross sales revenue − sales deductions = net sales revenue ± inventory change − cost of sales [Herstellkosten der gefertigten Erzeugnisse] = operating result = Betriebsergebnis; opp. Umsatzkostenverfahren)*
Gesamtlaufzeit *f* (Fin) total life *(eg, of a bond issue)*
Gesamtleistung *f* (Bw) total operating performance (ReW) gross performance
(ie, Umsatzerlöse + Bestandsänderungen + aktivierte Eigenleistungen = sales revenue + inventory changes + internally produced and capitalized assets)
(Bw) total operating performance
Gesamtmarktanalyse *f* (Mk) census survey *(opp, sample survey)*
Gesamtnachfolge *f* (Re) = *Gesamtrechtsnachfolge*
Gesamtnachfolger *m* (Re) = *Gesamtrechtsnachfolger*
Gesamtnachfrage *f*
(Vw) aggregate
– overall
– total . . . demand

Gesamtnachfragefunktion *f* (Vw) aggregate demand function
Gesamtnachfragekurve *f* (Vw) aggregate demand curve
Gesamtnennbetrag *m* (Fin) total par value
Gesamtnutzen *m* (Vw) total utility
Gesamtnutzungsdauer *f* (Bw) total life
Gesamtpersonalrat *m* (Pw) central works council
Gesamtplan *m* (com) master (*or* overall) plan
Gesamtplanung *f*
 (com) general layout
 (Bw) master (*or* overall) planning
Gesamtprämienaufkommen *n* (Vers) total premium earned
Gesamtpreis *m*
 (com) overall (*or* total) price
 (Zo) inclusive price
Gesamtproduktion *f* (com) total production (*or* output)
Gesamtproduktivität *f*
 (Vw) aggregate
 – overall
 – total ... productivity
 (Bw) corporate productivity
Gesamtprokura *f*
 (com, appr) joint proxy
 (Re) ‚Prokura' granted to several persons who must act jointly, § 48 II HGB
Gesamtqualifikation *f* (Pw) overall qualification
Gesamtrechtsnachfolge *f* (Re) universal succession *(ie, to predecessor's entire property which includes all his active and passive legal relations)*
Gesamtrechtsnachfolger *m* (Re) universal successor
Gesamtrendite *f* (Fin) total yield (of a loan) *(opp, Einzelrendite)*
Gesamtrentabilität *f*
 (Fin) overall profitability
 – operating efficiency
 (ie, as measured by return on total assets)
Gesamtrisiko *n* (Bw) total risk
Gesamtsaldo *m* **der Zahlungsbilanz** (VGR) overall net total
Gesamtschaden *m* (Re, Vers) total loss
Gesamtschaden-Exzedenten-Rückversicherung *f* (Vers) aggregate excess of loss reinsurance
Gesamtschätzung *f* (Stat) overall estimate
Gesamtschuld *f* (Re) joint and several obligation
Gesamtschuldner *mpl*
 (Re) co-debtors, § 421 BGB
 – debtors jointly and severally liable
 – joint and several debtors
 – plurality of debtors
gesamtschuldnerisch (Re) jointly and severally
gesamtschuldnerische Bürgschaft *f* (Re) joint and several guaranty
gesamtschuldnerische Haftung *f* (Re) joint and several liability
gesamtschuldnerisch haftbar (Re) jointly and severally liable
Gesamtschuldnerschaft *f* (StR) joint tax liability, § 44 AO
Gesamtsparverhalten *n* (Vw) aggregate savings behavior
Gesamtstatus *m* (ReW) consolidated statement

Gesamtsteueraufkommen *n* (FiW) total tax collections *(ie, at all levels of government: federal, Laender, municipal)*
Gesamtstillegung *f* (Bw) final discontinuance of an enterprise as a whole
Gesamtstückzeit *f* (IndE) cycle time
Gesamtsumme *f*
 (com) total amount
 – total
 – sum total
 – grand total
Gesamttextil *f* (com) West German Textile Federation
Gesamtüberschuß *m* (FiW) overall budget surplus
Gesamtumlaufvermögen *n* (ReW) total current assets
Gesamtumsatz *m*
 (ReW) total sales
 – (GB) total turnover
 (StR) total of taxable sales, net of imports
Gesamtumsatzvolumen *n* **aller Waren** (Mk, *retailing*) all-commodity volume
Gesamtumschuldung *f* (Fin) total debt rescheduling
Gesamtunternehmer *m*
 (com) general
 – main
 – primary
 – prime ... contractor
Gesamtverband *m*
 (com) central
 – general
 – umbrella ... association
Gesamtverband *m* **der deutschen Versicherungswirtschaft** (Vers) Central Association of the German Insurance Industry
Gesamtverband *m* **der Textilindustrie** (com) Central Association of the Textile Industry
Gesamtverband *m* **des Groß- und Außenhandels** (com) General Association of Wholesale and Foreign Trade
Gesamtverbindlichkeiten *fpl*
 (ReW) overall debt burden
 – overall debt exposure
 – overall indebtedness
Gesamtverbrauch *m* (Vw) total (*or* overall) consumption
Gesamtverbuchung *f* **e–s Geschäftsfalles** (ReW) covering entry
Gesamtvergütung *f* (Pw) total compensation package *(ie, salary + fringe benefits)*
Gesamtvermögen *n*
 (com) total (*or* entire) assets
 – entire property
 (Fin) total capital employed (*or* invested) *(ie, fixed assets + current assets)*
 – total investment
 (StR) total property, §§ 114–120 BewG
Gesamtversicherung *f*
 (Vers) all-risk comprehensive insurance
 – (GB) all-in insurance
Gesamtversicherungssumme *f* (Vers) total sum insured
Gesamtvertrag *m* (SozV) overall agreement
Gesamtvertretung *f* (Re) collective representation, § 125 II HGB

Gesamtvollmacht *f* (Re) collective power of attorney
Gesamtvolumen *n* (FiW) total volume *(eg, of farm budget)*
Gesamtwartezeit *f* (OR) total waiting time
Gesamtwert *m*
  (com) aggregate
  – total
  – overall ... value
  (StR) total value of a commercial enterprise, § 103 BewG *(ie, total assets minus liabilities and reserves)*
Gesamtwert *m* **der Einfuhr** (Zo) aggregate value of importation
Gesamtwert *m* **e–r Unternehmung** (Bw) value of an enterprise as a whole
Gesamtwirtschaft *f*
  (Vw) economy as a whole
  – overall economy
  – entire economy
gesamtwirtschaftliche Abgabenquote *f* (FiW) overall ratio of levies
gesamtwirtschaftliche Aktivität *f* (Vw) general business activity
gesamtwirtschaftliche Angebotsfunktion *f* (Vw) aggregate supply function
gesamtwirtschaftliche Arbeitsproduktivität *f* (Vw) overall labor productivity
gesamtwirtschaftliche Eckdaten *pl* (Vw) key economic data
gesamtwirtschaftliche Endnachfrage *f* (Vw) total final demand
gesamtwirtschaftliche Entwicklung *f*
  (Vw) aggregate
  – overall
  – macroeconomic ... development
gesamtwirtschaftliche Finanzierungsrechnung *f*
  (VGR) capital finance account
  – money flow analysis
gesamtwirtschaftliche Größen *fpl* (Vw) economic aggregates (*or* quantities)
gesamtwirtschaftliche Kosten *pl* (Vw) social costs
gesamtwirtschaftliche Nachfrage *f* (Vw) total (*or* aggregate *or* overall) demand
gesamtwirtschaftliche Nutzen *mpl* (Vw) social benefits
gesamtwirtschaftliche Sparquote *f* (Vw) aggregate savings ratio
gesamtwirtschaftliche Steuerquote *f* (FiW) overall tax receipts *(ie, total tax receipts to gnp)*
gesamtwirtschaftliche Tätigkeit *f* (Vw) aggregate (*or* overall) economic activity
gesamtwirtschaftliche Theorie *f* (Vw) aggregative theory
gesamtwirtschaftliche Zielvariable *f* (Vw) economic policy goal
Gesamtzahl *f* **der offenen Stellen** (Vw) number of job vacancies in the economy as a whole
Gesamtzahlungsbilanz *f* (AuW) overall balance of payments
Gesamtzollbelastung *f* (Zo) total customs charges
gesamtwirtschaftliche Nachfrage *f* (Vw) overall (*or* aggregate) level of demand
gesamtwirtschaftliche Produktion *f* (Vw) aggregate output

gesamtwirtschaftliche Produktionsfunktion *f* (Vw) aggregate production function
gesamtwirtschaftlicher Konsum *m* (Vw) aggregate consumption
gesamtwirtschaftliche Produktivität *f* (Vw) overall productivity
gesamtwirtschaftliches Gleichgewicht *n* (Vw) overall economic equilibrium
gesamtwirtschaftliches Interesse *n* (Vw) interest of the whole economy
gesamtwirtschaftliche Sparquote *f* (Vw) aggregate savings ratio
gesamtwirtschaftliches Produktionspotential *n* (Vw) overall production potential
gesamtwirtschaftliche Tätigkeit *f* (Vw) overall business activity
gesamtwirtschaftliche Ziele *npl* (Vw) overall economic goals
Gesamtziel *n* (Vw, Bw) overall objective
Gesamtzinsspannenrechnung *f* (Fin) calculation of total interest margin *(ie, to determine gross and net margins)*
Gesamtzuladungsgewicht *n* (com) deadweight tonnage *(ie, capacity of vessel in tons of cargo, passengers, fuel, etc.)*
gesättigter Markt *m* (Mk) saturated (*or* mature) market
geschachtelt (EDV, Cobol) nested
geschädigte Partei *f* (Re) aggrieved (*or* injured) party *(ie, entitled to legal remedy)*
Geschädigter *m*
  (Re) injured party
  – person injured
  (Vers) claimant
Geschäft *n*
  (com) business *(ie, general term)*
  (com) store
  – (GB) shop
  (com) bargain
  – deal
  – transaction
Geschäft *n* **abschließen**
  (com) to make a bargain (*or* deal)
  – to strike a deal
  – to enter into a transaction
  – to sign a contract (with)
  – to consummate a transaction
Geschäft *n* **abwickeln**
  (com) to carry out a transaction
  (Re) to wind up (*or* liquidate) a business
Geschäft *n* **aufgeben**
  (com) to discontinue (*or* give up) a business
  – to go out of business
  (com) to close down a shop
  – (infml) to shut shop
Geschäft *n* **betreiben**
  (com) to carry on business
  (com) to run (*or* operate) a business
Geschäfte *npl* **der Kreditinstitute** (Fin) banking operations (*or* transactions)
Geschäftemacherei *f* (com) profiteering
Geschäft *n* **eröffnen**
  (com) to put up shop
  – (infml) to hang out one's shingle

– (infml, GB) to put up one's brass plate
Geschäfte *npl* **tätigen** (com) to do business
Geschäfte *npl* **vermitteln** (com) to negotiate business *(ie, said of an agent)*
Geschäft *n* **für wen es angeht** (Re) legal transaction for whom it may concern
(ie, an instance of indirect agency in which the disclosure principle (= Offenkundigkeitsprinzip) is waived)
geschäftlich (com) on business
geschäftliche Transaktion *f* (com) business *(or* commercial) transaction
geschäftliche Verabredung *f* (com) business appointment
Geschäft *n* **ohne Rechnung** (com) non-invoiced transaction
Geschäft *n* **rückgängig machen** (com) to cancel an order
Geschäftsablauf *m* (com) course of business
Geschäftsabschluß *m* (com) conclusion of a deal *(or* transaction)
Geschäftsabwicklungspflichten *fpl* (Re) responsibilities of the parties to perform the contract
Geschäftsanteil *m*
  (Re) share
  – interest
  – participation
  (ie, in GmbH and Genossenschaft)
Geschäftsarten *fpl* (StR) types of transactions, § 20 KVStG
Geschäftsaufgabe *f* (com) discontinuance *(or* termination) of a business
Geschäftsauflösung *f* (com) dissolution of a business
Geschäftsausstattung *f* (ReW) furnitures and fixtures
Geschäftsausweitung *f* (com) business expansion
Geschäftsbank *f* (Fin) commercial bank
Geschäftsbauten *mpl*
  (com) commercial buildings
  (ReW) office buildings
Geschäftsbedingungen *fpl* (Re) general terms and conditions
Geschäftsbeginn *m*
  (com) commencement of business
  (com) opening hours
Geschäftsbereich *m*
  (Bw) division
  (Bw) functional *(or* operating) area
  – operation
  – area of responsibility
Geschäftsbereichsgruppe *f* (Bw) operational group
Geschäftsbericht *m*
  (Bw) annual report
  – year-end report
  – report of managing board
  (ie, comprising (a) report on operations, (b) company welfare report, (c) report on board composition, (d) audit report)
Geschäftsbesorgungsvertrag *m* (Re) non-gratuitous contract for services or work, § 675 BGB *(ie, services of attorney or bank)*
Geschäftsbetrieb *m*
  (com) business establishment
  (com) sum total of business activities

Geschäftsbewegungen *fpl* (com) sales activities
Geschäftsbezeichnung *f*
  (Re) trade name, § 16 UWG
  (Re) firm name
Geschäftsbeziehungen *fpl* (com) business relations *(or* contacts)
Geschäftsbrief *m* (com) business *(or* commercial) letter
Geschäftsbücher *npl* (ReW) (commercial) books of account
Geschäftsbuchhaltung *f* (ReW) financial *(or* general) accounting
Geschäftsergebnis *n* (ReW) operating result
Geschäftseröffnung *f* (com) opening of a business
Geschäftserweiterung *f* (com) expansion of business
geschäftsfähig (Re) competent to contract
geschäftsfähige Partei *f* (Re) competent party
Geschäftsfähigkeit *f*
  (Re) legal capacity to contract
  – contractual capacity
  – capacity to transact legal business
  – capacity to enter into legal transactions
  – capacity to perform legal acts
  – capacity for acts-in-the law
Geschäftsfrau *f* (com) business woman
Geschäftsfreund *m*
  (com) business associate
  – customer
  – business friend
  (com) correspondent *(ie, one who has regular business relations with another, esp. at a distance)*
Geschäftsfreundebewirtung *f* (StR) entertainment of visitors
geschäftsführend
  (com) directing the affairs
  – managing
geschäftsführender Bereich *m* (Bw) management sector
geschäftsführender Direktor *m*
  (com) managing director
  – head manager
geschäftsführender Gesellschafter *m* (com) managing partner
geschäftsführender Partner *m*
  (com) acting
  – active
  – managing ... partner
geschäftsführendes Mitglied *n* (com) managing member
Geschäftsführer *m*
  (com) manager
  (Re) single chief executive of GmbH and KG
  (Mk) store manager
Geschäftsführer *m* **ohne Auftrag** (Re) agent without mandate
Geschäftsführer *m* **Technik** (Bw) technical director
Geschäftsführung *f*
  (com) conduct of business
  (Bw) management
Geschäftsführung *f* **ohne Auftrag**
  (Re) management of affairs without mandate
  – *(civil law)* negotiorum gestio
  (ie, creates a semi-contractual relation; performs a number of functions which in English law are

271

allotted to the law of trust; eg, duty to act with due care)
Geschäftsführungsbefugnis *f*
(com) managing authority
– power of management
– power to direct a business
(Re) authority granted by principal to agent *(opp, Vertretungsmacht: power to represent principal towards third parties)*
Geschäftsgebaren *n* (com) business methods *(or* practices)
Geschäftsgebäude *n* (com) office building
Geschäftsgebiet *n* (Bw) operational sector *(or* segment)
Geschäftsgebrauch *m* (com) official use
Geschäftsgegend *f* (Mk) shopping area
(or district)
Geschäftsgeheimnis *n* (com) trade *(or* business) secret
Geschäftsgrundlage *f* (Re) basis of a transaction
Geschäftsgrundlage *f* **zerstören** (Re) to upset the economy of a contract
Geschäftsgrundstücke *npl* (StR) business property, § 75 III BewG
(ie, more than 80% of it used for commercial or industrial purposes; opp, Betriebsgrundstücke)
Geschäftsgründung *f* (Re) formation of a business enterprise
Geschäftsguthaben *n*
(Fin) capital share *(ie, held by member of cooperative: includes cash contributions and prorata profit credited to contribution account = Barzahlung und Zuschreibung von Gewinnanteilen)*
– paid-up cooperative share
Geschäftsguthabendividende *f* (Fin) capital dividend distributed by cooperative
Geschäftshaus *n*
(com) trading firm
– business firm
– business establishment
(com) commercial building
Geschäftsherr *m* (Re) principal
Geschäftsinhaber *m*
(Re) owner *(or* proprietor) of a business
(com) storekeeper
– (GB) shopkeeper
Geschäftsinhaberin *f* (com) proprieteress of a business
Geschäftsjahr *n*
(com) business
– financial
– fiscal ... year
– (infml) fiscal *(eg, in fiscal 1983)*
Geschäftskarte *f* (com) business card *(ie, card with businessman's name, firm, business address, and phone number)*
Geschäftskette *f*
(com) retailing chain
– chain of retail stores
Geschäftskonto *n* (ReW) contra account linking financial accounting and cost accounting
Geschäftskorrespondenz *f* (com) business *(or* commercial) correspondence
Geschäftskredit *m* (Fin) business loan

Geschäftskunde *m*
(com) customer
– client
Geschäftslage *f*
(Vw) business conditions
(Mk) store location
Geschäftsleben *n* (com) business *(eg, to retire from business)*
Geschäftsleiter *m* (com, Fin) manager
Geschäftsleitung *f*
(com) management
(com) place of management
Geschäftsleute *pl* (com) business men
Geschäftslokal *n*
(com) business premises
(Mk) retail store
Geschäftsmann *m* (com) business man *(Americans now prefer ‚business person' if the term is understood to include both male and female)*
geschäftsmäßig
(com) businesslike
geschäftsmäßige Hilfe *f* **in Steuersachen** (StR) tax advice on a professional basis
Geschäftsordnung *f*
(Re) internal rules of procedure *(ie, of managing or supervisory board)*
(Bw) set of procedural rules implementing the organization chart
– code of procedure
Geschäftsordnung *f* **erlassen** (Re) to establish rules of procedure
Geschäftspapiere *npl*
(com) business papers
(Re) business records *(eg, books of account, business letters)*
Geschäftspartner *m*
(com) business partner
– associate
(Re) partner
(Re) party to a transaction
Geschäftspolitik *f*
(Bw) business
– company
– corporate ... policy
geschäftspolitische Entscheidung *f* (Bw) business decision
Geschäftsräume *mpl* (com) business premises
Geschäftsreise *f* (com) business tour *(or* trip)
Geschäftsrückgang *m* (com) shrinkage in volume of business *(or* trade)
geschäftsschädigend (com) damaging *(or* injuring) the interests and reputation of a firm
Geschäftsschädigung *f* (com) act by which a firm's standing is affected
Geschäftsschluß *m* (com) closing time
Geschäftssitz *m*
(Re) place of business
– registered office
Geschäftssparte *f* (com) line of business
Geschäftsspartenkalkulation *f* (Fin) cost accounting by lines of business *(ie, a type of departmental cost accounting practiced by banks)*
Geschäftssprache *f* (Re) official language
Geschäftsstelle *f*
(com) office(s)

(com) branch (*or* field) office
Geschäftsstellenleiter *m* (com) branch manager
Geschäftsstellennetz *n* (com) branch network
Geschäftsstunden *fpl* (com) business hours
Geschäftstagebuch *n* (ReW) daily transactions journal *(ie, posting all receipts and expenditures and all cashless transactions)*
Geschäftstätigkeit *f*
  (com) business activity
  (Vw) economic activity
Geschäftstätigkeit *f* **aufnehmen** (com) to commence business operations
Geschäftsübernahme *f* (com) takeover of a business
Geschäfts- und Fabrikgebäude *npl*
  (ReW) buildings
  – administrative and plant buildings
geschäftsunfähig
  (Re) incapacitated
  – incompetent
  – incapable (*or* wholly unable) to enter into legal transactions
Geschäftsunfähiger *m* (Re) incapacitated person
Geschäftsunfähigkeit *f*
  (Re) contractual incapacity
  – incapacity to contract
  – legal disability
  – contractual incompetence
  (ie, total absence of capacity for legal transactions; opp, beschränkte Geschäftsfähigkeit)
Geschäftsunterbrechung *f* (Bw) interruption of business
Geschäftsveräußerung *f* **im ganzen** (Bw) sale of an enterprise as a whole
Geschäftsverbindung *f* (com) business relations (*or* contacts)
Geschäftsverkehr *m* (com) business
  (ie, the total of all reciprocal business or commercial relations)
Geschäftsvermögen *n* (ReW) business assets *(opp, Privatvermögen = private assets)*
Geschäftsverteilung *f*
  (Bw) assignment of business
  – division of responsibilities
Geschäftsverteilungsplan *m*
  (Bw) distribution-of-business plan
  – plan of task division
Geschäftsvolumen *n*
  (com) business volume
  – volume of business
  (Bö) trading volume
Geschäftsvorfall *m*
  (ReW) accountable event (*or* condition)
  – business transaction
  – external transaction
  – transaction with an outsider
Geschäftsvorgang *m* (com) business transaction
Geschäftswagen *m* (com) business car
Geschäftswelt *f* (com) business community
Geschäftswert *m*
  (ReW) goodwill (*syn*, Firmenwert)
  (Re) value of subject matter in issue, § 153 V AktG
Geschäftszeichen *n* (com) reference (*or* file) number

Geschäftszeit *f*
  (com) business hours
  (Mk) shopping hours
Geschäftszentrum *n* (Mk) business center
Geschäftszimmer *n* (com) office
Geschäftszweig *m* (com) = Wirtschaftszweig, Branche
Geschäft *n* **tätigen** (com) to transact business
Geschäft *n* **zustandebringen**
  (com) to negotiate a deal (*or* transaction)
  – to conclude a contract
  – to strike a deal
  – (infml) to engineer a deal
geschätzte Ankunftszeit *f* (OR) estimated time of arrival
geschätzte Kosten *pl* (KoR) estimated cost
geschätzte Nutzungsdauer *f*
  (ReW) estimated useful life *(ie, of a fixed asset)*
  – expected life
  – estimated service life
  – life expectancy
  (StR) guideline service life
geschätzter mittlerer Fehleranteil *m* (Stat) estimated process average
geschätzter Wert *m* (com) estimated value (*or* price)
geschätzter Wertminderungsverlauf *m*
  (ReW) estimated loss of service life (*or* utility)
  – estimated diminution of service life
Geschenk *n* (com) gift
Geschenkabonnement *n* (com) gift subscription
Geschenke *npl* (StR) gratuities and presents, § 4 V EStG
Geschenke *npl* **verteilen** (SozV, infml) to hand out largesse
Geschenksendungen *fpl* (Zo) gift parcels
Geschichte *f* **der ökonomischen Theorie** (Vw) history of economic thought
geschichteter Stichprobenplan *m* (Stat) stratified sampling plan
geschichtete Stichprobe *f* (Stat) stratified sample
geschichtete Zufallsstichprobe *f* (Stat) stratified random sample
Geschicklichkeit *f* (IndE) skill
geschlossene Anlage *f* (StR) integrated unit, Abschn. 31 III EStR
geschlossene Erfassungsgruppe *f* (Stat) cluster
geschlossene Kantenzugprogression *f* (OR) circuit progression
geschlossene Kurve *f* (Math) loop
geschlossene Randkurve *f* (Math) closed contour
geschlossener Fonds *m* (Fin) closed-end fund
geschlossener Halbraum *m* (Math) closed half-space
geschlossener Immobilienfonds *m* (Fin) closed-end real estate fund
geschlossener Investmentfonds *m* (Fin) closed-end investment fund
geschlossener Kantenzug *m* (OR) circuit
geschlossener Markt *m* (Vw) closed market *(ie, one barred to new entrants)*
geschlossener Regelkreis *m* (EDV) closed loop (circuit)
geschlossenes Entscheidungsmodell *n* (Bw) closed decision model *(ie, based on fully formulated*

decision matrix and given decision rule; eg, linear programming model)
geschlossenes Netzwerk *n* (OR) closed network
geschlossenes Unterprogramm *n* (EDV) linked (*or* closed) subroutine
geschlossene Volkswirtschaft *f* (Vw) closed economy *(ie, one for which no external transactions are assumed)*
geschlossene Wirtschaft *f* **ohne staatliche Aktivität** (Vw) closed economy, with no government budget
geschlossen prozeßgekoppelter Betrieb *m* (EDV) closed loop operation
Geschmacksmuster *n*
  (Pat) design patent
  – ornamental design
geschuldeter Betrag *m* (com) sum due (*or* owing)
geschützte Bezeichnung *f* (Pat) proprietary designation
geschützter Speicher *m* (EDV) protected memory
geschützter Speicherplatz *m* (EDV) isolated location
geschweifte Klammern *fpl* (Math) braces
Geschwindigkeitsumsetzer *m* (EDV) remote multiplexer
Geselle *m* (Pw) journeyman *(ie, skilled worker with formal apprenticeship qualification)*
Gesellschaft *f*
  (Re) partnership *(ie, as the basic type of ‚Personengesellschaft')*
  (Re) corporation
  – company
  (ie, as the basic type of ‚Kapitalgesellschaft')
Gesellschaft *f* **auflösen** (Re) to dissolve a partnership (*or* company)
Gesellschaft *f* **ausgliedern** (Re) to remove a subsidiary from an affiliated group of companies
Gesellschaft *f* **beherrschen** (Re) to control another company
Gesellschaft *f* **des bürgerlichen Rechts** (Re) = *BGB-Gesellschaft*
Gesellschafter *m*
  (Re) *(Personengesellschaft:)* partner
  – member of partnership
  (Re) *(Kapitalgesellschaft:)* shareholder
  – stockholder
  – company member
Gesellschafterbeschluß *m*
  (Re) resolution adopted by the partners
  – shareholders' decision (*or* resolution)
Gesellschafterdarlehen *n*
  (com) member's loan
  (Fin) partner's loan (to a partnership) *(ie, a genuine loan in the case of limited partners = Kommanditisten, if capital is fully paid, but a contribution only if paid in by unlimited partners = Komplementäre, Vollhafter)*
  (Fin) shareholder loan
  (ie, one granted to ‚Kapitalgesellschaften'; genuine loan and as such subject to trade tax = Gewerbesteuer)
Gesellschaftereinlage *f* (Fin) partner's contribution
Gesellschafter-Geschäftsführer *m* (com) managing partner
Gesellschafterkapital *n* (Fin) partner's capital

Gesellschafterliste *f*
  (Bw) shareholder list
  (ie, containing names and residence of all shareholders of a stock corporation present at a general meeting)
  (Re) list of shareholders *(ie, submitted annually to the Commercial Register, § 40 GmbHG)*
Gesellschaft *f* **errichten**
  (Re) to constitute
  – to establish
  – to found
  – to set up ... a partnership *or* company
Gesellschafterversammlung *f*
  (Re) shareholders' meeting
  – general meeting of members
  (ie, organ of a GmbH, § 48 GmbHG)
Gesellschaft *f* **gründen**
  (Re) to form
  – to create
  – to organize ... a partnership
  (Re) to create
  – to establish
  – to form ... a corporation
gesellschaftliche Indifferenzkurve *f* (Vw) community indifference curve
gesellschaftliche Indikatoren *mpl* (Vw) social indicators
gesellschaftliche Kosten *pl* (Vw) social cost
gesellschaftliche Nutzen *mpl* (Vw) social benefits
gesellschaftliche Präferenzfunktion *f* (Vw) social preference function
gesellschaftliche Rechtfertigung *f* (Bw) societal justification *(eg, for the existence of a business firm)*
gesellschaftlicher Konsens *m* (Vw) social consensus *(eg, in Germany and Austria)*
gesellschaftlicher Nutzen *m* (Vw) social utility
gesellschaftliche Wohlfahrt *f* (Vw) social welfare
gesellschaftliche Wohlfahrtsfunktion *f* (Vw) social welfare function
Gesellschaft *f* **mit beschränktem Aktionärskreis**
  (Re) closely held corporation
  – (GB) closely held company
  (ie, most of the shares and voting control are held by a small group)
Gesellschaft *f* **mit beschränkter Haftung**
  (Re) limited liability company, GmbH *(ie, private legal entity, unquoted)*
  – (US, *roughly*) close corporation
  – (GB, *roughly*) private company
Gesellschaft *f* **ohne Geschäftsbetrieb** (Bw) inactive company
Gesellschaftsanteil *m* **der OHG** (Re) share or other membership right in a commercial partnership, §§ 105 II HGB, 719 BGB
Gesellschaftsbeiträge *mpl* (Re) monetary and non-monetary contributions of partners, § 706 BGB
Gesellschaftsbeschluß *m* (Re) corporate resolution
gesellschaftsbezogene Rechnungslegung *f* (ReW) corporate socio-economic accounting *(syn, Sozialbilanz)*
Gesellschaftsbilanz *f*
  (ReW) partnership balance sheet
  (ReW) company (*or* corporate) balance sheet
Gesellschaftsblätter *npl* (Re) publications named

in the company's articles of incorporation, § 20 VI AktG
Gesellschaftsbücher *npl*
(ReW) partnership books
– company books
Gesellschaftseinlage *f* (Fin) contribution to partnership capital
Gesellschaftsformen *fpl* (Re) legal forms of commercial entities *(ie, OHG, KG, atypische stille Gesellschaft, AG, KGaA, GmbH, Genossenschaft, Versicherungsverein auf Gegenseitigkeit)*
Gesellschaftsjustitiar *m* (Re) legal adviser *(or officer)* of a company
Gesellschaftskapital *n*
(Fin) partnership capital
(Fin) corporate capital
– share capital
Gesellschaftskonkurs *m* (Re) bankruptcy of legal entities and partnerships *(ie, juristische Personen and Personengesellschaften, §§ 207–213 KO)*
Gesellschaftsmantel *m* (Re) corporate shell
Gesellschaftsmittel *pl* (Fin) corporate funds
Gesellschaftsrecht *n*
(Re) law of partnerships and corporations *(ie, including also part of the law relating to ‚Vereine' = private-law associations)*
– (GB) company law
Gesellschaftsrechte *npl*
(StR) membership rights in corporations and other companies *(ie, corporate shares, GmbH participations, quotas of mining companies = Kuxe, participations in the profits of a company = Genußrechte, etc.)*
gesellschaftsrechtliche Einlagen *fpl* (StR) deposits under company law
Gesellschaftsschulden *fpl*
(Re) partnership liabilities
(Re) company liabilities
– corporate debts
Gesellschaftssitz *m*
(Re) corporate domicile
– (GB) registered office
Gesellschaftsstatuten *pl* (Re) bylaws
Gesellschaftsstruktur *f* (Vw) societal structure
Gesellschaftsteuer *f*
(StR) company tax
– capital investment tax
(ie, levied on contributions made by stockholders; see: ‚Kapitalverkehrsteuer')
Gesellschaftsvergleich *m* (Re) composition proceedings relating to legal persons *(ie, Vergleichsverfahren von nicht natürlichen Personen)*
Gesellschaftsvermögen *n*
(Fin) partnership assets *(ie, of ‚Personengesellschaften')*
(Fin) company *(or* corporate*)* assets *(ie, of ‚Kapitalgesellschaften')*
Gesellschaftsvertrag *m*
(Re) partnership agreement
– articles of partnership
– articles of copartnership
(ie, relating to Gesellschaft des bürgerlichen Rechts, OHG, KG, stille Gesellschaft)
(Re) company agreement *(or* contract*) (ie, equivalent to the articles of AG and KGaG; US:*

articles of incorporation + bylaws; GB: memorandum of association + articles of association)
(Re) articles of a GmbH
Gesellschaftszweck *m*
(Re) purposes of a partnership
(Re) corporate purpose
– object of company
Gesetz *n*
(Log) universal law
(Re) statute
– (US) Law
(ie, after legislation ‚law' and ‚act' may be used interchangeably)
– (GB) Act
Gesetzblatt *n* (Re) legal gazette
Gesetz *n* **der abnehmenden Grenzrate der Substitution** (Vw) law of diminishing marginal rate of substitution
Gesetz *n* **der doppelten Negation** (Log) law of double negation
Gesetz *n* **der großen Zahlen** (Stat) law of large numbers
Gesetz *n* **der komparativen Kosten** (AuW) law of comparative costs
Gesetz *n* **der Kontraposition** (Log) law of contraposition
Gesetz *n* **der Massenproduktion** (Bw) law of mass production *(ie, formulated by K. Bücher in 1910)*
Gesetz *n* **der Unterschiedslosigkeit der Preise** (Vw) law of indifference *(Jevons)*
Gesetz *n* **der wachsenden Staatsausgaben** (FiW) law of rising public expenditure *(A. Wagner, 1861)*
Gesetz *n* **des abnehmenden Bodenertrages** (Vw) law of diminishing marginal productivity
Gesetz *n* **des komparativen Vorteils** (AuW) law of comparative advantage
Gesetzesauslegung *f* (Re) interpretation *(or* construction*)* of a law
Gesetzesbegriff *m*
(Re) legal term
– statutory concept
Gesetzesentwurf *m* (Re) draft statute
Gesetzeskraft *f* (Re) force of law
Gesetzeslücke *f* (Re) loophole
Gesetzesvollzug *m* (Re) law enforcement
Gesetzgebungsverfahren *n*
(Re) legislative procedure
– bill-to-law process
Gesetz *n* **gegen den Unlauteren Wettbewerb** (Kart) Law Against Unfair Competition *(ie, as of 7 June 1906, variously amended)*
Gesetz *n* **gegen Wettbewerbsbeschränkungen** (Kart) Law Against Restraints of Competition *(1957, last amended 1974)*
– German Antitrust Act
gesetzlich
(Re) lawful
– legal
(ie, the principal distinction between the two terms is that the former contemplates the substance of law, the latter the form of law)
– statutory *(ie, conforming to a statute)*
– by operation of law

gesetzliche Beschränkung f (Re) statutory restriction
gesetzliche Bestandteile mpl (WeR) statutory features *(eg, of checks or bills of exchange)*
gesetzliche Bestimmung f (Re) legal *(or* statutory) provision
gesetzliche Dauerverpflichtungen fpl (FiW) permanent statutory obligations
gesetzliche Einlagen fpl (Fin) legal minimum deposits
gesetzliche Erbfolge f (Re) intestate succession
gesetzliche Exportbeschränkungen fpl (AuW) legally enforced export controls
gesetzliche Forderung f (Re) legal claim
gesetzliche Forderungsabtretung f (Re) assignment by operation of law
gesetzliche Formvorschriften fpl (Re) formal legal requirements
gesetzliche Frist f (Re) statutory time limit (Re) statutory period
gesetzliche Gebühr f (Re) legal fee
gesetzliche Gewährleistung f
 (Re) statutory warranty
 – warranty implied in law
gesetzliche Grundlage f (Re) statutory basis
gesetzliche Haftpflicht f (Re) legal *(or* statutory) liability
gesetzliche Haftung f (Re) legal *(or* statutory) liability
gesetzliche Krankenversicherung f
 (SozV) statutory *(or* compulsory) health insurance
 (SozV) statutory health insurance fund
gesetzliche Kündigungsfrist f (Re) statutory period of notice
gesetzliche Lizenz f (Pat) legal *(or* statutory) license
gesetzliche Orderpapiere npl (WeR) original order paper *(syn, geborene Orderpapiere; opp, gekorene Orderpapiere = order paper by act of the party)*
gesetzlicher Arbeitgeberzuschuß m (SozV) employer's statutory social security contribution
gesetzliche Rentenversicherung f (SozV) statutory pension insurance fund
gesetzlicher Feiertag m (Pw) public holiday
gesetzlicher Güterstand m (Re) statutory regime of matrimonial property *(ie, considered as adopted by the spouses whenever they have not expressly agreed on choosing another regime)*
gesetzlicher Hinderungsgrund m (Re) statutory bar
gesetzliche Rücklagen fpl
 (ReW) legal *(or* statutory) reserves
 – retained earnings – compulsory portion, § 150 AktG
gesetzlicher Vertreter m (Re) legal *(or* statutory) representative *(eg, parents for their minor children, guardian, managing board of stock corporation, trustee in bankruptcy)*
gesetzlicher Zinsfuß m (Re) legal *(or* statutory) rate of interest
gesetzlicher Zinssatz m (Re) legal rate of interest
gesetzliche Schriftform f (Re) writing prescribed by law

gesetzliche soziale Abgaben fpl (SozV) statutory social security contributions
gesetzliches Pfandrecht n
 (Re) lien by operation of law
 – statutory lien
 (ie, where either law or statute itself raises a lien, § 1257 BGB)
gesetzliches Rentenalter n (SozV) statutory retirement age
gesetzliches Schuldverhältnis n (Re) obligation created by operation of law *(ie, otherwise than by act of the parties)*
gesetzliches Veräußerungsverbot n (Re) statutory prohibition of alienation, § 135 BGB)
gesetzliches Zahlungsmittel n
 (Vw) legal tender
 – lawful money
 (ie, for all debts, public and private, public charges, taxes, duties, and dues)
gesetzliche Unfallversicherung f (SozV) statutory accident insurance
gesetzliche Unterhaltspflicht f (StR) statutory obligation to support *(eg, devolving upon the taxpayer)*
gesetzliche Verjährungsfrist f (Re) statutory period of limitation
gesetzliche Verpflichtung f (Re) legal *(or* statutory) obligation
gesetzliche Vertretung f (Re) legal representation
gesetzliche Vertretungsmacht f (Re) agency by operation of law
 (opp, gewillkürte Vertretungsmacht = agency by act of the parties)
gesetzliche Vollmachten fpl (Re) statutory powers
gesetzliche Vorschrift f (Re) statutory provision *(or* requirement)
gesetzliche Zinsen mpl (Re) legal *(or* statutory) rate of interest
gesetzlich geschützt
 (Pat) legally protected
 – patented *(ie, inventions)*
 – registered *(ie, trade marks)*
gesetzlich geschütztes Verfahren n (Pat) proprietory process
gesetzlich vorgeschriebenes Deckungsverhältnis n (Vers) legal reserve requirements
Gesetzmäßigkeit f (Log) universal tendency
Gesetz n **novellieren** (Re) to amend a law
Gesetz n **über Abgaben für das Einleiten von Abwässer in Gewässer** (Re) Law Providing for a Levy for Discharging Effluents Into Running and Standing Waters = *Abwasserabgabengesetz*
Gesetz n **über die Deutsche Bundesbank** (Re) Federal Bank Law
Gesetz n **über die Ermittlung des Gewinns aus Land- und Forstwirtschaft nach Durchschnittssätzen** (StR) Law Regulating the Establishment of Average Rates of Return for Computing Profits from Agriculture and Forestry
Gesetz n **über die Finanzverwaltung** (Re) Law on Fiscal Administration *(as of 30 Auf 1971 and amended thereafter)*
Gesetz n **über die Mitbestimmung** (Pw) Codetermination Law
Gesetz n **über die Rechtsverhältnisse der Steuerbe-**

rater und Steuerbevollmächtigten (Re) Law on Tax Advisers
Gesetz *n* **über Kapitalanlagegesellschaften** (Fin) Law Relating to Investment Companies, as amended 14 Jan 1970
Gesetz *n* **vom abnehmenden Ertragszuwachs** (Vw) law of diminishing returns
– law of non-proportional returns
– law of variable proportions
Gesetz *n* **vom abnehmenden Grenznutzen** (Vw) law of diminishing marginal utility
– law of satiation
Gesetz *n* **vom ausgeschlossenen Dritten** (Log) law of excluded middle
– law of bivalence
– law of tertium non datur
Gesetz *n* **vom Ausgleich der Grenznutzen** (Vw) equimarginal principle
– law of equi-marginal returns
Gesetz *n* **vom Rangabfall** (Math) Sylvester's law of degeneracy (*or* nullity)
Gesetz *n* **von Angebot und Nachfrage** (Vw) law of supply and demand
Gesetz *n* **von der Steigerung der fixen Kosten** (KoR) law of increasing fixed cost *(K. Mellerowicz)*
gesetzwidriges Verhalten *n* (Re) illegal conduct
Gesetz *n* **zur Entlastung des Bundesfinanzhofs** (StR) Law for the Relief of the Federal Fiscal Court, of 7 Aug 1975, amending the FGO
Gesetz *n* **zur Förderung der Berliner Wirtschaft** (Re) Law for the Promotion of the Economy of West Berlin, of 29 Oct 1970 (and numerous amendments)
Gesetz *n* **zur Förderung der Stabilität und des Wachstums der Wirtschaft** (Vw) Law Promoting Stability and Growth of the Economy, as of 8 June 1967 (*= Stabilitätsgesetz*)
Gesetz *n* **zur Verbesserung der betrieblichen Altersversorgung** (Re) Business Pension Law, 19 Sep 1974
Gesetz *n* **zur Vermögensbildung der Arbeitnehmer** (Pw) Law to Promote Capital Formation by Employees
gesicherte Forderung *f* (Fin) secured debt
gesicherte Gläubiger *m* (Re) secured creditor
gesicherter Kredit *m* (Fin) secured credit
gesichertes Darlehen *n* (Fin) secured loan
gesondert anmelden (Zo) to declare separately
gesondert ausweisen (ReW) to present (*or* show) separately
gesonderte Feststellung *f* (StR) separate determination, § 180 AO
gesonderte Gewinnfeststellung *f* (StR) separate determination of profits, § 180 AO
gespaltener Devisenmarkt *m* (AuW) split
– two-tier
– dual ... foreign exchange market
gespaltener Goldmarkt *m* (Fin) two-tier gold market
gespaltener Goldpreis *m* (Fin) two-tier gold price
gespaltener KSt-Satz *m* (StR) split corporation income tax rate
gespaltener Preis *m* (Mk) split price

gespaltener Steuersatz *m* (StR) split tax rate
gespaltener Wechselkurs *m* (AuW) multiple (*or* split) exchange rate *(syn, multipler od differenzierter Wechselkurs)*
gespaltenes Wechselkurssystem *n* (AuW) two-tier foreign exchange system
gespannter Kurs *m* (Bö) close quotation of foreign exchange
gespeichertes Programm *n* (EDV) stored program
gesperrte Guthaben *npl* (Fin) blocked assets
gesperrter Scheck *m* (Fin) stopped check
gesperrtes Depot *n* (Fin) blocked deposit *(ie, of securities)*
gesperrte Stücke *npl* (Fin) blocked securities
Gespräch *n* **anmelden** (com) to book a (telephone) call
Gespräch *n* **durchstellen** (com) to put a call through
Gesprächsbetrieb *m* (EDV) dialog processing *(opp, Stapelbetrieb)*
Gesprächsgebühren *fpl* (com) call charges
Gesprächssystem *n* (EDV) time sharing
Gesprächsnotiz *f*
(com) memo of a discussion
– notes on a discussion
gestaffelt (com) graduated
gestaffelte Rückzahlung *f* (Fin) repayment by installments
gestaffelter Zinssatz *m* (Fin) staggered rate of interest
gestaltungsfähige Kapitalertragsteuer *f* (StR) flexible capital yields tax
Gestaltungsfreiheit *f*
(com) freedom of scope
(Re) liberty of the parties (to a contract) to make their own arrangements
(StR) freedom to shape one's transactions so as to accomplish the most favorable tax result
Gestaltungsklage *f* (Re) action for a modification of rights
Gestaltungsrecht *n* (Re) right to establish, alter or terminate a legal relationship
Gestehungskosten *pl* (KoR) cost price
Gestehungswert *m* (com) cost of production or acquisition
Gestellung *f* **der Waren** (Zo) presentation of goods
Gestellung *f* **e-s Akkreditivs** (Fin) opening a letter of credit
Gestellungsverzeichnis *n* (Zo) customs declaration list, § 6 ZG
gesteuerte Ablage *f* (EDV) controlled stacker
gesteuerter Preis *m* (Vw, Kart) controlled price *(opp, Marktpreis)*
gesteuertes Floating *n* (AuW) controlled floating
gesteuerte Variable *f* (EDV) controlled variable
gestörtes Gleichgewicht *n*
(Vw) disequilibrium
– imbalance
gestreckte Programmierung *f* (EDV) straight line coding
gestreute Anlagen *fpl* (Fin) diversified investments
gestreute Datenorganisation *f* (EDV) scattered data organization
gestreutes Laden *n* (EDV) scatter loading (*or* reading)

277

gestreutes Lesen *n* (EDV) = *gestreutes Laden*
gestreute Speicherung *f* (EDV) random organization
gestreutes Schreiben *n* (EDV) gather write
gestrichelte Linie *f* (Math) dashed (*or* broken) line
gestrichen (Bö) quotation canceled *(ie, no price, no dealings)*
gestützter Preis *m* (com) pegged (*or* supported) price
gestützter Wechselkurs *m* (Fin) pegged rate of exchange
gestutzte Verteilung *f* (Stat) truncated distribution
Gesuch *n*
 (com) application
 – request
Gesuch *n* **ablehnen** (com) to refuse a request
Gesuch *n* **bearbeiten** (com) to handle an application (*or* request)
Gesuch *n* **bewilligen** (com) to grant an application
Gesuch *n* **einreichen**
 (com) to file an application
 – to submit a request
gesunde finanzielle Lage *f* (Fin) sound financial position
Gesundheitsattest *n*
 (com) bill of health
 – health (*or* sanitary) certificate
Gesundheitseinrichtungen *fpl* (SozV) health care facilities
Gesundheitsindikatoren *mpl* (Bw) health indicators *(eg, length of patient stay, etc.)*
Gesundheitsinformationssystem *n* (EDV) health information system
Gesundheitsmarkt *m* (Vw) health care market
Gesundheitsökonomik *f* (Vw) health economics *(ie, instruments are theory of public goods, theory of externalities, cost-benefit analysis, etc.)*
gesundheitspolitische Bestimmungen *fpl* (AuW) sanitary regulations (*or* standards)
gesundheitspolitische Überwachung *f* (AuW) sanitation
Gesundheitsrisiko *n* (SozV) health hazard
gesundheitsschädigende Wirkungen *fpl* (SozV) adverse health effects
Gesundheitsschutz *m* (Pw) health protection
Gesundheitswesen *n* (SozV) health care system
Gesundheitszertifikat *n* (AuW) = *Gesundheitsattest*
Gesundheitszeugnis *n* (com) = *Gesundheitsattest*
gesundschrumpfen
 (com, infml) to pare down
 – to whittle down
 (ie, a company to a more profitable or leaner and more viable core)
Gesundwert *m* (SeeV) sound value
getaktete Arbeitsweise *f* (EDV) clocked operation
Getränkebesteuerung *f* (StR) taxation of beverages
Getränkeindustrie *f* (com) beverage industry
Getränkesteuer *f* (StR) beverage tax
Getreideausfuhrland *n* (AuW) grain exporting country
Getreidebörse *f*
 (Bö) grain exchange
 – (GB) (London) Corn Exchange
 (ie, mostly part of produce exchange = Produktenbörse)

Getreideeinfuhr- und Vorratsstelle *f* (AuW) grain import and storage agency
Getreideembargo *n* (AuW) grain embargo *(eg, on the Soviet Union)*
Getreidehandel *m* (com) grain trade
Getreidehändler *m* (com) grain merchant (*or* dealer)
Getreidemarktregelung *f* (Vw) grain market regulation
Getreidepreis *m* (com) grain price
Getreide-Schweine-Zyklus *m* (Vw) corn-hog cycle
Getreidetermingeschäfte *npl* (Bö) grain futures
Getreidezoll *m* (Zo) duty on imported grain
getrennte Schleife *f* (OR) disjoint (*or* nontouching) loop
getrennte Veranlagung *f* (StR) separate assessment *(ie, independent taxation of wife's and husband's income, § 26a EStG)*
gewähren
 (com) to allow
 – to grant
Gewährfrist *f* (Re) period of guarantee, § 482 BGB
gewährleisten (com) to warrant
Gewährleistung *f* (com) warranty *(ie, agreement by seller that article sold has certain qualities)*
Gewährleistungen *fpl* **aus Einzelrisiko** (ReW) warranties – direct
Gewährleistungen *fpl* **pauschal** (ReW) warranties – indirect
Gewährleistung *f* **für Rechtsmängel** (Re) warranty of title
Gewährleistung *f* **für Sachmängel** (Re) warranty of merchantable quality
Gewährleistungsansprüche *mpl* (ReW) warranty claims
Gewährleistungsfrist *f* (Re) warranty period
Gewährleistungsgarantie *f*
 (Re) performance bond (*or* guaranty)
 – defects liability guaranty
 – guaranty against defective material and workmanship
 – guaranty deposit
 – maintenance guaranty
Gewährleistungskosten *pl* (ReW) cost of guaranty commitments
Gewährleistungsverpflichtungen *fpl* (ReW) warranties
Gewährleistungsvertrag *m* (Re) indemnity agreement
Gewährleistungswagnis *n* (ReW) warranty risk *(ie, amounts to self-insurance of noninsurable risks)*
Gewährleistung *f* **übernehmen** (Re) to give warranty
Gewährträger *m* (Fin) guaranty authority *(ie, city or municipality which covers liability of savings banks operating within its jurisdiction)*
Gewährträgerhaftung *f* (Re) liability of guaranty authority
Gewährung *f* **e-s Kredits** (Fin) granting of a credit
Gewährung *f* **von Ansprüchen** (Re) acceptance of claims
Gewährverband *m* (Re) = *Gewährträger*
Gewährvertrag *m* (Re) contract of guaranty *(syn, Garantievertrag)*

Gewerbe *n*
No English equivalent exists of the German term that in its most general sense is taken to mean any permanent, gainful economic activity. The English terms *'business'*, *'trade'*, and *'industry'*, together with the adjectives *'commercial'* and *'industrial'* may be used to approximate a specific German context.
The general idea of ‚**Gewerbe**' *is variously described as follows:*
(1) any gainful activity, as opposed to leisure time pursuits;
(2) the total of all nonfarm activities carried on by economically inpendent units = **gewerbliche Wirtschaft:** *mining, industry, crafts, trade and commerce, transportation, catering trade, banks and insurance companies, service industries;*
(3) a specific segment of the economy as described under (2) and defined in the German **Gewerbeordnung** *= Trade Regulation Act, which exludes the mining industry;*
(4) a still more restricted extension of the term, used esp. in economics, covers the entire nonfarm production of goods and services (industry, crafts, and homework on contract);
(5) **Kleingewerbe:** *small and medium-sized business engaged in the production of goods;*
(6) **mittelständisches Gewerbe:** *the entire group of small and medium-sized business, industrial and commercial, that is, exclusive of large enterprises in industry, trade, etc.*

Gewerbe *n* **anmelden** (Re) to apply for a trading license
Gewerbeanmeldung *f* (Re) registration of a trade or business, § 14 GewO
Gewerbeaufsicht *f* (Re) trade supervision
Gewerbeaufsichtsamt *n* (Re) trade supervisory authority
Gewerbe *n* **ausüben** (com) to carry on a trade
Gewerbebescheinigung *f* (com) trade certificate
Gewerbebesteuerung *f* (StR) trade taxation
Gewerbe *n* **betreiben** (com) to carry on a trade
Gewerbebetrieb *m* (StR) business establishment, § 1 GewStDV
(ie, includes every activity which is carried on independently, continuously, for profit, and which constitutes a participation in the general commerce of the country = Selbständigkeit, Nachhaltigkeit der Betätigung, Gewinnerzielungsabsicht, Beteiligung am allgemeinen wirtschaftlichen Verkehr)
Gewerbeerlaubnis *f* (Re) business license, §§ 30 ff GewO
Gewerbeertrag *m* (StR) trade earnings
Gewerbeertragsteuer *f*
(StR) trade tax on earnings
– trade earnings tax *(ie, geared to annual profits)*
Gewerbeförderung *f* (Vw) promotion of small and medium-size enterprises *(ie, designed to increase efficiency and rationalization)*
Gewerbefreiheit *f* (Re) right freely to choose one's occupation, Art 12 II GG
Gewerbegenehmigung *f* (Re) = *Gewerbeerlaubnis*
Gewerbegesetzgebung *f* (Re) legal rules relating to trade regulation
Gewerbekapital *n* (StR) trading capital, § 12 GewStG
Gewerbekapitalsteuer *f* (StR) trading capital tax *(ie, levied on capital employed!)*
Gewerbelegitimationskarte *f* (com) commercial card, § 55b GewO *(= carte de commercant, valid for trading abroad)*
Gewerbeordnung *f* (Re) Trade Regulation Act, 21 June 1869, as amended 1 Jan 1978 *(ie, postulates the desirability of freely chosen trade or occupation as a matter of principle)*
Gewerbepolitik *f* (Vw) trade policy *(ie, umbrella term covering industrial policy, policy relating to the crafts, and policy directed at all other activities which are neither industry nor craft)*

Gewerbeschein *m* (com) trading license
Gewerbesteuer *f* (StR) trade tax *(ie, levied by local authorities, including tax on earnings and capital = Gewerbeertrag- und Gewerbekapitalsteuer)*
Gewerbesteuerausgleich *m* (FiW) equalization of revenue from trade tax
Gewerbesteuerbefreiung *f* (StR) exemption from trade tax
Gewerbesteuerbescheid *m* (StR) trade tax assessment notice
Gewerbesteuer-Durchführungsverordnung *f* (StR) Ordinance Regulating the Trade Tax Law, republished on 26 Jan 1978
Gewerbesteuererklärung *f* (StR) trade tax return, § 25 GewStDV
Gewerbesteuergesetz *n* (StR) Trade Tax Law, republished on 22 Sept 1978
Gewerbesteuerhebesatz *m* (StR) factor by which the uniform tentative tax = *einheitlicher Steuermeßbetrag* is multiplied *(ie, established for one or several calender years, § 16 II GewStG)*
Gewerbesteuermeßbescheid *m* (StR) formal notice of applicable basic rate, § 184 AO
Gewerbesteuermeßbetrag *m* (StR) tentative tax *(ie, product of applicable tax rate and taxable business profits)*
Gewerbesteuer-Richtlinien *fpl* (StR) Trade Tax Regulations, republished on 21 June 1979
Gewerbesteuerrückstellung *f* (StR) reserve for trade taxes, Abschn. 22 II EStR
Gewerbesteuerumlage *f* (FiW) participation of federal and state governments in the municipal trade tax, Art 106 VI GG
Gewerbetreibender *m*
(com) businessman *(ie, anyone carrying on a trade or business in his own name and for his own account)*
(StR) nonfarm self-employed *(ie, excluding liberal professions)*
Gewerbeunfallversicherung *f* (Vers) industrial accident insurance
Gewerbeverlust *m* (StR) trading loss, § 10a GewStG
Gewerbezentralregister *n* (Re) Central Trade Register, §§ 149 ff GewO
Gewerbezulassung *f* (Re) trading license
Gewerbezweig *m* (com) branch of industry *(or trade)*

gewerbliche Ausfuhr *f* (AuW) industrial exports
gewerbliche Ausrüstungsinvestitionen *fpl* (VGR) business investment of plant and equipment
gewerbliche Bauten *pl*
(com) non-residential buildings
– commercial and industrial buildings
gewerbliche Berufe *mpl* (Pw) industrial occupations
gewerbliche Betriebsgebäude *npl* (Bw) plant buildings
gewerbliche Bodenbewirtschaftung *f* (StR) commercial extraction of minerals and other deposits *(ie, mining, extraction of peat, stones, earths, etc., § 15 I No. 1 EStG)*
gewerbliche Einfuhr *f* (AuW) commercial and industrial imports
gewerbliche Erfahrung *f* (com) industrial experience
gewerbliche Erzeugnisse *npl* (com) industrial products
gewerbliche Fahrzeuge *npl* (com) commercial vehicles
gewerbliche Gebäude *npl* (Bw) commercial (*or* non-residential) buildings
gewerbliche Hypothek *f* (Fin) industrial mortgage
gewerbliche Investition *f* (Bw) business investment
gewerbliche Investitionen *fpl* (VGR) business investment in plant and equipment
gewerbliche Kreditaufnahme *f* (Fin) industrial and business borrowing
gewerbliche Kreditgenossenschaft *f* (Fin) industrial credit cooperative *(ie, mainly ‚Volksbanken')*
gewerbliche Kreditnachfrage *f* (Fin) business-sector credit demand
gewerbliche Leistungen *fpl* (Kart) commercial services
gewerbliche Niederlassung *f* (Bw) business establishment
gewerbliche Produkte *npl* (Bw) industrial products
gewerbliche Produktion *f* (Stat) industrial production
gewerblicher Abnehmer *m* (Bw) industrial buyer (*or* user)
gewerblicher Arbeiter *m* (Pw) industrial worker
gewerbliche Räume *mpl* (Bw) business premises
gewerblicher Betrieb *m* (StR) business enterprise, § 95 BewG
gewerblicher Gewinn *m* (StR) business income
gewerblicher Güterfernverkehr *m* (com) commercial long haul trucking
gewerblicher Hochbau *m* (com) industrial construction
gewerblicher Kredit *m* (Fin) industrial loan
gewerblicher Kreditnehmer *m* (Fin) industrial borrower
gewerblicher Rechtsschutz *m* (Pat) protection of industrial property rights
gewerbliche Schutzrechte *npl* (Pat) industrial property rights
gewerbliches Eigentum *n* (Pat) industrial property
gewerbliches Fahrzeug *n* (com) commercial vehicle
gewerbliches Unternehmen *n* (Bw) business (*or* commercial) enterprise
gewerbliches Verfahren *n* (IndE) industrial production method

gewerbliche Tätigkeit *f* (com) business (*or* commercial) activity
gewerbliche Tätigkeit *f* **ausüben** (com) to carry on a business
gewerbliche Verbrauchsgüter *npl* (Mk) industrially produced consumer goods
gewerbliche Verwertbarkeit *f* (Pat) commercial utilization
gewerbliche Wirtschaft *f* (com) trade and industry
gewerbliche Zwecke *mpl* (com) industrial or commercial purposes
gewerblich genutzte Grundstücke *npl* (com) industrial real estate
gewerblich-industrielle Bauten *mpl* (com) industrial and commercial buildings
gewerbsmäßig
(com) professionally
– by way of business or trade
gewerbsmäßiger Frachtführer *m* (com) common carrier
Gewerke *m* (Re) member of mining company
Gewerkenbuch *n* (Re) register of mining-share holders
Gewerkschaft *f*
(Pw) labor union
– (GB) trade union
(Bw) mining company
Gewerkschaft *f* **Druck und Papier** (Pw) Print and Paper Workers' Union
Gewerkschaftler *m*
(Pw) union member
(Pw) union official
gewerkschaftliche Kampfmaßnahmen *fpl*
(Pw) industrial action
– strike action unleashed by unions
gewerkschaftlich genehmigter Streik *m* (Pw) authorized strike
gewerkschaftlich organisieren (Pw) to unionize
gewerkschaftlich organisiert (Pw) unionized
gewerkschaftlich organisierte Arbeitnehmer *mpl* (Pw) union-member employees
Gewerkschaft *f* **Öffentliche Dienste, Transport und Verkehr** (Pw) Public Services and Transport Workers' Union
Gewerkschaftsbeiträge *mpl* (Pw) union dues
Gewerkschaftsbewegung *f*
(Pw) unionism
– union movement
Gewerkschaftsführer *m* (Pw) union (*or* labor) leader
Gewerkschaftsfunktionär *m* (Pw) union official (*or* functionary)
Gewerkschaftskartell *n* (Pw) combination of unions
Gewerkschaftsmitglied *n* (Pw) union member
Gewerkschaftspolitik *f* (Pw) union policy
Gewerkschaftsvertreter *m*
(Pw) union representative
(Pw, pl) the union side
Gewichte *npl* (com) weights
gewichten (Stat) to weight
gewichtetes Mittel *n* (Stat) weighted average
gewichtete Stichprobe *f* (Stat) differential sample
Gewichtsangabe *f* (com) declaration of weight
Gewichtsbescheinigung *f* (com) weight certificate

Gewichtsermittlung f (com) determination of weights
Gewichtsgrenze f (com) weight limit
Gewichtskoeffizient m (Stat) weighting coefficient
Gewichtsliste f (com) weight list
Gewichtstarif m (com) weight-based transport rate *(opp, Stück- und Raumtarife)*
Gewichtsverlust m (com) loss in weight
Gewichtsverzollung f (Zo) duty based on weight
Gewichtszoll m (Zo) specific duty *(ie, based on weight)*
Gewichtszollsatz m (Zo) tariff rate based on weight
Gewichtung f (Stat) weighting
Gewichtungsfehler m (Stat) weighting bias
Gewichtungsziffer f (KoR) weighting figure *(cp, Äquivalenzziffer)*
gewillkürte Orderpapiere npl (WeR) order paper by act of party
gewillkürtes Betriebsvermögen n (StR) voluntary business property *(ie, assets which may be private or business, depending on their appropriation)*
gewillkürte Vertretungsmacht f (Re) agency by act of the parties *(opp, gesetzliche Vertretungsmacht = by operation of law)*
Gewinn m
(com) profit
(ReW) profit
– income
– earnings
– gain
(ie, subordinate concepts: Betriebsgewinn and Unternehmungsgewinn, which see)
Gewinnabführung f (Fin) transfer of profits
Gewinnabführungsvertrag m (Bw) profit transfer agreement *(ie, corporation undertakes to transfer its entire profits to another enterprise, § 291 I AktG; syn, Ergebnisabführungsvertrag)*
gewinnabhängige Steuern fpl (StR) taxes on profits
gewinnabhängige Zulage f (Pw) profit-linked bonus
Gewinnabrechnungsgemeinschaft f (Fin) profit pool
Gewinnabschöpfung f (Fin) siphoning-off *(or skimming-off)* profits
Gewinnabsicht f (com) gainful intent
Gewinnanalyse f **nach Marktsegmenten** (ReW) segment profit analysis
Gewinnanspruch m (Fin) claim on pro rata share in annual net profits *(ie, divident and interest coupons)*
Gewinnanteil m
(Fin) profit share
(Vers) policy dividend
– bonus
– profit commission
Gewinnanteilschein m (WeR) profit sharing certificate, § 234 BGB
(Fin) dividend coupon *(or warrant)*
Gewinnanteilscheinbogen m (Fin) coupon sheet
Gewinnanteil-Staffel f (Vers) graded scale of profit commission
Gewinnaufschlag m (com) mark-up
Gewinn m **aus Anlagenverkauf** (Fin) profit on asset disposal

Gewinn m **aus der Auflösung stiller Rücklagen** (StR) gain from the dissolution of secret reserves, Abschn. 35 EStR
– gain from involuntary conversion
Gewinn m **aus der Veräußerung von Wertpapieren** (ReW) profit *(or* gain) on securities
Gewinnausfallversicherung f (Vers) loss of profit insurance
Gewinnausgleichssystem n (Kart) profit pass-over *(ie, protected traders receive part of the sales profit)*
Gewinn m **aus konzerninternen Geschäften** (ReW) intercompany profit
Gewinn m **aus Neubewertung** (ReW) surplus arising from revaluation
Gewinnausschließungsvertrag m (Fin) non-profit agreement
– profit-exclusion agreement
Gewinnausschluß- und Verlustübernahmevertrag m (Fin) = *Gewinnabführungsvertrag*
Gewinnausschüttung f
(Fin) distribution of profits
– profit distribution
– dividend payout
Gewinnaussichten fpl (Fin) profit prospects
Gewinn m **ausweisen** (ReW) to post a profit
Gewinn m **aus Wertpapieranlagen** (Fin) income from security holdings
gewinnberechtigt (Fin) entitled to profit share
gewinnberechtigte Aktien fpl (Fin) shares entitled to dividend
Gewinnbesteuerung f (StR) tax on earnings
Gewinnbeteiligung f (Pw) profit sharing
Gewinnbeteiligung f **der Arbeitnehmer** (Pw) employee profit sharing
Gewinnbeteiligungsplan m (Pw) profit-sharing plan *(or* scheme)
Gewinnbeteiligungsrechte npl (Fin) participating rights
gewinnbringend (com) profitable
Gewinn m **der Minderheitsaktionäre** (Fin) profit accruing to minority shareholders
Gewinn m **des Geschäftsjahres** (ReW, EG) profit for the financial year
Gewinndruck m (Bw) profit squeeze
Gewinndruck-Inflation f (Vw) profit-push inflation
Gewinne mpl **abschöpfen** (Fin) to siphon off *(or* skim off) profits
Gewinn m **einbringen** (com) to turn in profits
Gewinneinbruch m (Fin) profit collapse
Gewinneinbußen fpl (Fin) squeeze on margins
Gewinneinkommen n (Vw) profit income
Gewinneinkommensbezieher mpl (Vw) profit income recipients
Gewinnentgang m (com) loss of profits
Gewinnentwicklung f (Fin) earnings performance
Gewinne mpl **realisieren**
(Fin) to realize profits
(Bö) to take profits
Gewinnerhaltung f (Fin) maintenance of profit levels
Gewinnermittlung f (StR) determination of income *(or* profit *or* earnings)
Gewinnermittlungsarten fpl (StR) methods of determining taxable income

Gewinnermittlungsbilanz *f*
(ReW) income statement
– profit and loss account
Gewinnermittlungsweg *m* (StR) method of computing taxable income
Gewinne *mpl* **erwirtschaften** (com) to generate income (*or* profits)
Gewinn *m* **erzielen** (com) to make a profit
Gewinnerzielung *f* (Fin) making (*or* realization) of profits
Gewinnerzielungsabsicht *f* (StR) intent to realize a profit
Gewinne *mpl* **subventionieren** (Bw) to subsidize profits
Gewinne *mpl* **überweisen** (Fin) to forward profits *(eg, to parent company)*
Gewinne *mpl* **und Verluste** *mpl*
(Bö) gains and losses
– (GB) rises and falls
Gewinne *mpl* **von Kapitalgesellschaften** (ReW) corporate profits (*or* income)
Gewinnfeststellung *f* (StR) income determination *(ie, by tax authorities)*
Gewinnfunktion *f* (Bw) profit function *(ie, revenue minus cost)*
Gewinngemeinschaft *f*
(Bw) profit and loss pooling
– profit-pooling agreement, § 292 I No. 1 AktG
Gewinnherausgabeanspruch *m* (Pat) right to claim infringement profits
Gewinninflation *f*
(Vw) markup pricing inflation
– profit-push inflation
Gewinn *m* **in % des investierten Kapitals** (Fin) rate of return on investment (*or* capital employed)
Gewinn *m* **in % des Umsatzes** (Fin) percentage return on sales
(syn, Umsatzrentabilität, Umsatzrendite, Umsatzgewinnrate)
Gewinn *m* **je Aktie** (Fin) earnings per share
Gewinnkennziffern *fpl* (Fin) earnings ratios
Gewinnlinse *f*
(KoR) profits wedge
– net income area *(ie, in breakeven diagram; syn, Gewinnzone)*
gewinnlose Konkurrenz *f* (Vw) no-profit competition *(ie, where market price is equal to minimum of total average cost)*
Gewinn *m* **machen**
(com) to make a profit
(com, infml) to make a turn
(com, infml) to turn in a profit
Gewinnmarge *f* (com) profit margin
Gewinnmatrix *f* (Fin) payoff (*or* gain) matrix
gewinnmaximale Ausbringung *f* (Bw) profit maximization output
Gewinnmaximierung *f* (Bw) profit maximization
Gewinnmitnahme *f* (Bö) profit taking
Gewinnmitnahme *f* **durch den Berufshandel** (Bö) professional profit taking
Gewinn *m* **mitnehmen** (Bö) to take profits
Gewinn *m* **nach Steuern**
(ReW) after-tax profit
– post-tax income
– earnings after taxes

Gewinnobligation *f* (Fin) income (*or* participating) bond
gewinnorientiert (Bw) profit-minded (*eg, managers*)
Gewinnorientierung *f* (Bw) profit orientation
Gewinnplan *m*
(Bw) profit plan
(Vers) bonus scheme
Gewinnplanung *f* (Bw) profit planning and budgeting
Gewinnpolster *n* (Fin) earnings cushion
Gewinnpoolung *f* (Re) profit-pooling agreement, § 291 I 1 AktG
Gewinnprinzip *n* (Bw) profitability principle
Gewinn *m* **pro Aktie** (Fin) earnings per share
Gewinnprognose *f* (Fin) profit (*or* earnings) forecast
Gewinnpunkt *m* (Fin) breakeven point *(ie, point of activity or sales volume where total revenues and total expenses are equal, that is, there is neither profit nor loss)*
Gewinnpunktrechnung *f* (Fin) breakeven analysis
Gewinnquote *f* (Vw) profit share *(ie, in national income)*
Gewinnrate *f* (Fin) rate of profit
Gewinnrealisierung *f*
(ReW) realization of profits *(ie, by disclosing secret reserves)*
(Bö) profit taking
– realization of profits
Gewinnrückgang *m* (com) drop in profits
Gewinnschuldverschreibung *f*
(Fin) income (*or* participating) bond
– profit-related bond
– (GB) profit-sharing loan stock
gewinnschwache Tochtergesellschaft *f* (Bw) marginal subsidiary
Gewinnschwelle *f* (KoR) breakeven point *(syn, Nutzschwelle, Kostendeckungspunkt, toter Punkt)*
Gewinnschwelle *f* **erreichen** (KoR) to break even
Gewinnschwellenanalyse *f* (KoR) breakeven analysis
Gewinnschwellendiagramm *n*
(KoR) breakeven chart
– profitgraph
Gewinnschwellenrechnung *f* (KoR) breakeven analysis
Gewinnspanne *f*
(com) profit margin
– margin of profit
– gross profit
– operating margin
Gewinnspanne *f* **e–r Emissionsbank** (Fin) gross spread
Gewinnspanne *f* **komprimieren** (com) to squeeze the profit margin
Gewinnsteuern *fpl* (StR) taxes on income (*or* earnings)
Gewinnsteuerung *f* (Fin) profit management
Gewinnsubventionierung *f* (Bw) subsidization of profits
Gewinnthesaurierung *f*
(ReW) income retention
– (GB) ploughing back of profits

gewinnträchtig (Bw) high-profit-margin *(eg, speciality chemicals)*
Gewinntreiber *m* (com) profiteer
Gewinn-Umsatz-Kennziffer *f* (KoR) profit-volume ratio
Gewinn-Umsatz-Schaubild *n* (Fin) profit-volume graph
Gewinn- und Kapitalverlagerung *f* (StR) (arbitrary) shifting of profits and capital *(ie, among affiliated businesses)*
Gewinn- und Sicherheitszuschlag *m* (Vers) profit and contingencies
Gewinn- und Verlustbeteiligung *f* (Re) participation in profits and losses *(ie, in the absence of provisions written into partnerships agreements, statutory rules apply, such as §§ 121, 168, 336 HGB)*
Gewinn- und Verlustkonto *n* (ReW) profit and loss account
Gewinn- und Verlustrechnung *f* (ReW) income statement
– (GB) profit and loss account
– statement of earnings
– statement of loss and gain
(syn, Erfolgsbilanz, Ertragsbilanz, Ergebnisrechnung, Umsatzrechnung, Aufwands- und Ertragsrechnung)
Gewinn- und Verlustübernahmevertrag *m* (Fin) profit and loss assumption *(or* absorption*)* agreement
Gewinnungsbetriebe *mpl* (Bw) extractive industries
Gewinnungskosten *pl* (com) resource cost *(ie, of obtaining primary energies)*
Gewinnung *f* **von Steinen und Erden** (VGR) quarrying
Gewinnvergleichsrechnung *f* (Fin) profit comparison method
(ie, in preinvestment analysis)
Gewinnverlagerung *f*
(Fin) shift *(or* transfer*)* of profits
– profit shifting
Gewinnverlagerungspolitik *f* (Fin) profit shifting policy
gewinnversprechend (com) profitable
Gewinnverteilung *f*
(Fin) profit distribution
(Vers) bonus distribution
Gewinnverteilungsbeschluß *m* (Bw) resolution ordering the distribution of profits
Gewinnverteilungskartell *n* (Kart) profit-distribution cartel
Gewinnverteilungsplan *m* (Vers) contribution plan
Gewinnverwendung *f*
(ReW) application *(or* appropriation*)* of profits
– disposal of corporate profits
– disposition of retained earnings
Gewinnverwendungsbilanz *f* (ReW) profit appropriation statement
Gewinnverwendungsrücklage *f* (ReW) profit utilization reserve
Gewinnverwendungsvorschlag *m* (Fin) proposed appropriation of earnings
Gewinnverwirklichung *f* (ReW) profit realization
Gewinnvorschau *f* (Fin) profit forecast

Gewinn *m* **vor Steuern**
(ReW) profit *(or* income *or* earnings*)* before taxes
– pretax profit
– taxable profit
Gewinnvortrag *m*
(ReW) portion of profit carried forward as unappropriated surplus, § 174 II 4 AktG
– net earnings brought forward
– profit carried forward
– prior year's earnings
Gewinnzielkalkulation *f* (Bw) target return pricing
Gewinnzone *f*
(KoR) profits wedge
– net income area *(ie, in breakeven diagram; syn, Gewinnlinse)*
Gewinnzuschlag *m* (Mk) profit markup *(ie, in retail trading)*
gewogener arithmetischer Mittelwertindex *m* (Stat) weighted arithmetic mean of relatives
gewogener Außenwert *m* (AuW) weighted external value
gewogener Außenwert *m* **e–r Währung** (AuW) trade-weighted exchange rate
gewogener Mittelwert *m* (Stat) weighted average
gewogener Summenindex *m*
(Stat) index of weighted aggregatives
– weighted aggregative relative
gewogenes Mittel *n* (Stat) weighted average
gewöhnliche Erhaltungskosten *pl* (StR) regular maintenance cost
gewöhnliche Fahrlässigkeit *f*
(Re) ordinary negligence, § 276 BGB
– *(civil law)* culpa levis
gewöhnliche Nutzungsdauer *f* (Bw) expected life
gewöhnliche Post *f*
(com) ordinary mail
– (com, US) surface mail
gewöhnlicher Aufenthalt *m*
(StR) habitual residence, § 90 AO
– customary *(or* usual*)* place of abode
(ie, implies mere physical presence for a somewhat extended period of time)
gewöhnlicher Bruch *m*
(com) ordinary breakage
(Math) common fraction
gewöhnlicher Logarithmus *m* (Math) common logarithm
gewöhnlicher Verschleiß *m* (ReW) ordinary loss of utility *(ie, through wear and tear, action of the elements, depletion)*
gewöhnliche Zinsen *mpl* (Math) simple *(or* ordinary*)* interest *(ie, based on 360 days)*
geworfene Güter *npl* (SeeV) jettisoned goods, § 720 HGB
gezeichnete Aktien *fpl* (Fin) subscribed shares
gezeichnetes Kapital *n* (ReW, EG) subscribed capital
gezielte Anzeigenwerbung *f* (Mk) targeted advertising
gezielte Aufklärung *f* (Mk) pinpointed information campaign
gezielte Förderung *f* (com) selective incentives
gezielte Programme *npl* (FiW) selectively targeted programs

gezielte Stichprobe *f* (Stat) precision sample
gezogener Wechsel *m* (WeR) draft
Gibson-Paradoxon *n* (Vw) Gibson paradox *(ie, empirical evidence that rising prices also pull up rates of interest)*
Gießkannenprinzip *n* (Vw, SozV) ,,watering can" principle *(eg, of investment subsidies, social benefits)*
Giffen-Effekt *m* (Vw) Giffen effect
Giffenscher Fall *m* (Vw) Giffen case
Gipfelgespräche *npl* (Vw) summit talks
Gipfelkonferenz *f* (Vw) summit conference
Gipfelteilnehmer *m* (Vw) summiteer
Gipfelwert *m* (Stat) peak
Giralgeld *n*
  (Vw) bank deposit money
  – bank account money
  – book money
  – deposit currency (*or* money)
  – primary deposits
  – (US) checkbook money
Giralgeld *n* **der Kreditbanken** (Fin) commercial bank book money
Giralgeld *n* **der Zentralbank** (Fin) central bank book money
Giralgeldkontraktion *f* (Vw) deposit contraction
Giralgeldschöpfung *f* (Vw) deposit money creation (*or* expansion)
Giralgeldvernichtung *f* (Vw) destruction of commercial bank deposits
Girant *m*
  (WeR) indorser
  – backer
  – (GB) endorser
Girat(ar) *m*
  (WeR) indorsee
  – (GB) endorsee
girierbar (WeR) indorsable
girieren
  (WeR) to indorse
  – (GB) to endorse *(syn, indossieren)*
girierter Wechsel *m* (WeR) indorsed bill of exchange
Girierung *f* (WeR) transfer by indorsement
Giro *n*
  (WeR) indorsement
  (Fin) giro
Giroabteilung *f* (Fin) giro department *(syn, Überweisungsabteilung)*
Giroauftrag *m* (Fin) credit transfer order
Giroeinlage *f* (Fin) deposit on current account
Girogelder *npl* (Fin) funds available for credit transfer
Girogeschäft *n* (Fin) giro business, § 1 I 9 KWG *(ie, cashless payments and clearings)*
Girogläubiger *m* (WeR) creditor by indorsement
Giroguthaben *n*
  (Fin) credit balance on current account
Girokonto *n*
  (Fin) current account *(ie, in a bank)*
  – Giro account
Girokunden *mpl* (Fin) current account customers
Gironetz *n* (Fin) giro system *(ie, branch system of a group of banks through which payments are cleared)*

Giro *n* **ohne Gewähr** (WeR) indorsement without recourse
Giroprovision *f* (Fin) credit transfer commission
Girosammelanteil *m* (Fin) share in a collective securities account
Girosammeldepot *n* (Fin) = Girosammelverwahrung
Girosammelverwahrung *f* (Fin) collective safe deposit of negotiable securities
Giroschuldner *m* (WeR) debtor by indorsement
Girostelle *f* (Fin) giro center *(ie, credit transfer clearing house)*
Giroüberweisung *f* (Fin) credit (*or* bank) transfer
Giroüberzugslombard *m* (Fin) Bundesbank advance
Giroverbände *mpl* (Fin) giro center associations *(ie, set up by savings banks and credit cooperatives)*
Giroverkehr *m*
  (Fin) giro credit transfers
  – giro transactions
  (ie, payment by cashless bank transfers; syn, Überweisungsverkehr)
Girozentrale *f* (Fin) central giro institution
Girozentralen *fpl* (Fin) giro centers *(ie, central credit institutions of public savings banks)*
Gitterauswahlverfahren *n* (Stat) lattice sampling
Gitter *n* **bilateraler Leitkurse**
  (AuW) grid of bilateral central rates
  – parity grid
Gitter-Stichprobenverfahren *n* (Stat) configurational (*or* grid) sampling
Glasindustrie *f* (com) glass industry
Glasversicherung *f*
  (Vers) glass insurance
  – *(sometimes called)* plate glass insurance
glatte Komponente *f* (Stat) systematic component *(ie, in time series)*
glattstellen
  (Bö) to balance
  – to even up
  – to liquidate
  – to realize
  – to sell off
  – to settle
  – to square
Glattstellung *f* (Bö) realization sale
Glattstellungsauftrag *m* (Bö) realization order
Glattstellungsgeschäft *n* (Bö) evening-up transaction
Glattstellungsverkauf *m*
  (Bö) realization sale
  – sell off
Glättung *f* (Stat) smoothing
Glättung *f* **der Trendkurve** (Stat) fitting the trendline
Glättungsfaktor *m* (Stat) smoothing factor
Glättungskoeffizient *m* (Stat) smoothing coefficient
Glättungskonstante *f* (Stat) smoothing constant
Gläubiger *m*
  (com) creditor *(ie, one to whom money is due)*
  (Re) creditor, § 241 BGB
  – *(fml)* obligee

(ie, one having the right to require the performance of any legal obligation)
Gläubigeranfechtung *f* (Re) avoidance of debtor's transactions by creditor
Gläubigeranfechtungsgesetz *n* (Re) Creditor's Avoidance of Transfers Act, 1898
Gläubigerarbitrage *f* (AuW) creditor arbitrage
Gläubigerausschuß *m* (Re) committee of creditors, § 87 KO
Gläubiger *m* **befriedigen** (Re) to satisfy (*or* pay off) a creditor
Gläubigerbefriedigung *f* (Re) satisfaction of creditors
Gläubiger *m* **begünstigen** (Re) to prefer a creditor
Gläubigerbegünstigung *f* (Re) preference of a creditor
Gläubigerbeirat *m* (Re) creditors' committee *(ie, appointed by the court, § 44 VerglO)*
Gläubigerbenachteiligung *f* (Re) delay of creditors
Gläubigerland *n* (AuW) creditor country
Gläubigerliste *f* (Re) = *Gläubigerverzeichnis*
Gläubigerpapiere *npl* (WeR) fixed-interest securities
Gläubigerquote *f* (EG) creditor quota
Gläubigerrallonge *f* (EG) creditor rallonge
Gläubigerrechte *npl* (Re) creditor claims
Gläubigerschädigung *f* (Re) prejudicial treatment of creditors
Gläubiger-Schuldner-Hypothese *f* (Vw) debtor-creditor hypothesis *(ie, claims a positive correlation between inflation and growth)*
Gläubigerschutz *m*
 (Re) creditor protection
 – proctecting the rights of creditors
Gläubigerversammlung *f*
 (Re) creditors' meeting, § 93 KO
 – meeting of creditors
Gläubigerverzeichnis *n* (Re) schedule (*or* list) of creditors
Gläubigerverzicht *m* (Re) forgiveness of indebtedness
Gläubigerverzug *m*
 (Re) creditor's delay *(ie, in accepting performance)*, § 293 BGB
 – *(civil law)* mora accipiendi
Gläubigerwechsel *m* (Re) subrogation of creditors
Gläubigerzentralbank *f* (AuW) creditor central bank
gleichartige Geschäfte *npl* (com) similar transactions
gleichartige Ware *f* (AuW) like product
gleich behandeln (StR) to treat equivalently
Gleichbehandlung *f*
 (AuW) nondiscrimination
 (Pw) equal treatment *(ie, of all employees)*
Gleichbehandlungspflicht *f* (Pw) rule of equal treatment
gleichbleibende Prämie *f* (Vers) level premium
gleiche Mengen *fpl* (Math) equal sets
gleichförmiges Verhalten *n* (Kart) parallel behavior
gleichgerichtete Kursbildung *f* (Bö) parallel pricing
gleichgerichtete Preisgestaltung *f* (Kart) parallel pricing
gleichgestellter Mitarbeiter *m* (Pw) peer
gleichgestreut (Stat) homoscedastic
Gleichgewicht *n* (Vw, Bw) equilibrium
Gleichgewicht *n* **am Gütermarkt** (Vw) goods market equilibrium
Gleichgewicht *n* **bei Maximalgewinn** (Vw) best profit equilibrium
Gleichgewicht *n* **bei Unterbeschäftigung** (Vw) underemployment equilibrium
Gleichgewicht *n* **bei Vollbeschäftigung** (Vw) full employment equilibrium
gleichgewichtige Expansion *f* (Vw) moving equilibrium
gleichgewichtiger Code *m*
 (EDV) constant ratio
 – fixed count
 – fixed ratio ... code
gleichgewichtiges Wachstum *n* (Vw) steady growth
Gleichgewichtsbedingung *f* (Vw) equilibrium condition (*or* position)
Gleichgewichtseinkommen *n* (Vw) equilibrium level of income
Gleichgewichtslohnsatz *m* (Vw) adjustment rate of wages
Gleichgewichtsmenge *f* (Vw) equilibrium quantity
Gleichgewichtsmodell *n* (Vw) equilibrium model
Gleichgewichtspfad *m* (Vw) equilibrium path
Gleichgewichtspreis *m* (Vw) equilibrium price
Gleichgewichtsproduktion *f* (Bw) production by which the goal function of an enterprise is maximized
Gleichgewichtstheorie *f* (Vw) equilibrium theory
Gleichgewichtswachstum *n* (Vw) balanced growth
Gleichgewichts-Wachstumsrate *f* (Vw) warranted rate of growth *(Harrod)*
Gleichgewichts-Wechselkurs *m* (AuW) equilibrium exchange rate
Gleichgewichtszins *m* (Vw) equilibrium interest rate
Gleichheitsglied *n* (EDV) equality circuit (*or* unit)
Gleichheitszeichen *n* (Math) equals sign
gleichlaufende Reihe *f* (Stat) coincident series
Gleichlaufsteuerung *f* (EDV) clocking
gleichmächtig (Math) equipollent *(ie, used of sets between which there exists a one-to-one correspondence)*
gleichmächtige Mengen *fpl*
 (Math) equipotent
 – equinumerable
 – equivalent ... sets
Gleichmächtigkeit *f* (Math) equipollence
gleichmäßig beste Schätzfunktion *f* (Stat) uniformly best constant risk estimator
gleichmäßige Besteuerung *f* (FiW) equal and uniform taxation
gleichmäßiges Wachstum *n* (Vw) steady (*or* sustained) growth
gleichmäßige Toleranz *f* (Stat) uniform tolerance
Gleichmäßigkeit *f* **der Besteuerung** (FiW) uniformity and equality of taxation
gleichmäßig schärfster Test *m* (Stat) uniformly most powerful test
gleichmäßig verzerrungsfreie Schätzfunktion *f* (Stat) uniformly unbiased estimator
Gleichmöglichkeit *f* (Stat) equal probability *(ie, basic term of Laplacean probability theory)*

(Stat) equal chance sampling
gleich Null setzen (Math) to set to zero
Gleichordnungskonzern *m* (Bw) horizontal group *(of affiliated companies)*
gleichrangig
  (Re) of equal rank (*or* status)
  – pari passu
gleichrangiger Gläubiger *m* (Re) creditor ranking pari passu
gleichrangige Schuldverschreibung *f* (Fin) pari passu bond
gleichrangige Verbindlichkeiten *fpl* (Re) liabilities of equal priority
Gleichrangrahmen *m* (Fin) scope for equally ranking charges
gleichschenkeliges Dreieck *n* (Math) isosceles triangle
gleichseitige Hyperbel *f* (Math) equilateral (*or* rectangular) hyperbola
gleichseitiges Polygon *n* (Math) equilateral polygon
gleichsetzen
  (Math) to equate
  – to set equal to
gleichsinnige Abweichung *f* (Stat) concurrent deviation
Gleichung *f* (Math) equation
Gleichung *f* **dritten Grades**
  (Math) cubic equation
  – equation of third degree
Gleichungssystem *n* (Math) set (*or* system) of equations
Gleichung *f* **vierten Grades**
  (Math) biquadratic (*or* quartic) equation
  – equation of fourth degree
Gleichung *f* **zweiten Grades**
  (Math) linear (*or* quadratic equation
  – equation of second degree
Gleichverteilung *f* (Stat) uniform distribution
Gleichverteilungshypothese *f*
  (Stat) equal-chance hypothesis
  – equi-probability hypothesis
Gleichwahrscheinlichkeit *f* (Stat) = *Gleichmöglichkeit*
gleichwertige Beschäftigung *f* (Pw) equivalent occupation
gleichwertige Zugeständnisse *npl* (AuW) equivalent concessions
Gleichwertigkeit *f* (Math) equipollence
gleichwinkeliges Polygon *n* (Math) equiangular polygon
gleichzeitig schwebende Anmeldung *f* (Pat) co-pending application
Gleisanschluß *m*
  (com) railroad siding
  – private siding
gleitende Arbeitswoche *f* (Pw) fluctuating workweek
gleitende Arbeitszeit *f*
  (Pw) flexible working hours
  – flextime
gleitende Bandbreiten *fpl*
  (AuW) crawling peg
  – sliding parity (*or* peg)
gleitende Budgetprognose *f* (Bw) moving projection

gleitende Lohnskala *f* (Pw) escalator scale
gleitender Durchschnitt *m* (Stat) moving average
gleitender Lohn *m* (Pw) indexed wage
gleitender Mittelwert *m* (Stat) moving average
gleitender Zoll *m* (Zo) escalator (*or* sliding scale) tariff
gleitende Saisonschwankung *f* (Stat) moving seasonal variation
gleitende Summenanpassung *f* (Vers) automatic cover
Gleitkomma *n* (EDV) floating point decimal
Gleitkommabefehl *m* (EDV) floating point instruction
Gleitkommarechnung *f* (EDV) floating point arithmetic
Gleitparität *f* (AuW) crawling peg
Gleitpreisklausel *f* (com) escalator (*or* escalation) clause
Gleitpunkt *m* (EDV) floating point
Gleitpunktarithmetik *f* (EDV) floating point arithmetic
Gleichpunktcharakteristik *f* (EDV) floating point characteristic
Gleitpunktoperation *f* (EDV) floating point operation
Gleitpunktrechnung *f* (EDV) floating point computation
Gleitpunktschreibweise *f* (EDV) floating point representation
Gleitpunktwort *n* (EDV) floating point word
Gleitpunktzahl *f* (EDV) floating point number
Gleitzeit *f*
  (Pw) flextime
  – flexible (working) hours
Gleitziffer *f* (Stat) link relative
Gleitzoll *m* (Zo) = *gleitender Zoll*
Glied *n* (Math) term
Glied *n* **e–r Datei** (EDV) member of a file
Gliederdrucker *m* (EDV) train printer
gliedern
  (com) to arrange
  – to classify
  – to subdivide
Gliedertaxe *f* (SozV) rate of dismemberment benefit
Gliederung *f*
  (Log) breakdown
  – classification
  – subdivision
  (ReW) layout (*or* format) (*eg, of financial statements, § 151 AktG*)
Gliederung *f* **der Jahresbilanz** (ReW) classification of annual balance sheet
Gliederungsvordruck *m* (StR) form for the breakdown of distributable equity capital, §§ 27–43 KStG
Gliederungsvorschriften *fpl* (Rew) legal requirements for the classification of financial statements
Glieder *npl* **zusammenfassen** (Math) to collect terms
gliedweise Ableitung *f* (Math) term-by-term derivation
Gliedziffern *fpl* (Stat) linked relatives
global (com) in aggregate terms

Globalabtretung f (Re) blank (or blanket) assignment
Globalaktie f
(Fin) multiple share certificate
– stock certificate
(ie, evidencing a large share holding, not widely used in West Germany; syn, Sammelaktie)
Globalangebot n (com) comprehensive offer
Globalanleihe f (Fin) blanket loan
Globalbewilligung f (FiW) block appropriation
Globaldarlehen n (Fin) blanket (or lump sum) loan
globale Ausgabeneigung f (Vw) global propensity to spend
globale Vorgabe f (Bw) overall standard
Globalfinanzierung f (Fin) block financing
Globalkontingent n (AuW) overall quota
Globalkürzung f (com) across-the-board cut
Globalplanung f (Bw) master planning
Globalpolice f (Vers) blanket policy
Globalsteuerung f (Vw) demand management (ie, by monetary or fiscal policies or both)
Globalurkunde f (Fin) global bond certificate
Globalversicherung f (Vers) blanket insurance
Globalwertberichtigung f (ReW) lump-sum value adjustment
global zurechenbare Kosten pl (OR) indirect cost (or expense)
Glockenkurve f (Stat) bell-shaped (or gaussian) curve
Glücksspiel n (Stat, Re) game of chance, § 284 StGB
GmbH-Gesetz n (Re) Law on Limited Liability Companies
GmbH-Novelle f (Re) statute amending the GmbH Law (effective 1 Jan 1981)
GmbH & Co f
(Bw) limited partnership
(ie, whose general partner – nominally liable without limit for the partnership's debts – is a private company and whose limited partners are the same persons as the shareholders of the company)
GmbH & Co. KG f (Bw) limited commercial partnership (= KG) formed with a limited liability company (= GmbH) as general partner and the members of the GmbH, their families, or outsiders, as limited partners
Goldabfluß m (Vw) gold outflow
Goldagio n (Vw) gold premium
Goldaktien fpl (Bö) gold mines
Goldankaufspreis m (Fin) gold buying price
Goldarbitrage f
(AuW) arbitrage in bullion
– gold arbitrage
Goldaufgeld n (Fin) gold premium
Goldauktion f (IWF) gold auction
Goldausfuhrpunkt m (AuW) export gold point
Goldautomatismus m (AuW) specie-flow adjustment mechanism (ie, correcting an adverse balance of payment, or restoring equilibrium; reference is had to a ‚self-regulating' or ‚automatic' gold standard)
Goldbarren m (Fin) gold bullion
Goldbarrenmarkt m (Fin) bullion market
Goldbarrenwährung f (Vw) gold bullion standard

Goldbestand m (Fin) gold inventory
Goldbestände mpl
(AuW) gold holdings (or reserves)
– gold stock
Goldbewegungen fpl (AuW) gold flow (or movements)
Goldbindung f (Vw) linkage to gold
Goldbörse f (Bö) gold exchange
Golddeckung f (Vw) gold cover (or backing)
Golddevisenwährung f (Vw) gold exchange standard
Goldeinfuhrpunkt m (AuW) gold import point
Goldeinlagen fpl **der Zentralbanken** (IWF) gold contributions of Central Banks
Goldene Bankregel f (Fin) Golden Bank Rule (ie, liquidity rule of credit institutions, requires sufficient availability of funds at any time)
Goldene Bilanzregel f (ReW) golden balance-sheet rule (ie, requires that fixed assets be backed by long-term capital, and current assets by short-term funds)
Goldene Finanzregel f (Fin) golden rule of financing (ie, requires that long-term investments be not financed with short-term funds)
goldener Wachstumspfad m
(Vw) complete (or total) equilibrium
– golden age path
– unique steady-state equilibrium
Goldexportpunkt m (AuW) gold export point
Goldhandel m (AuW) gold trading
Goldhorte pl (Vw) gold hoardings
Goldimportpunkt m (AuW) gold import point
Goldkernwährung f (Vw) gold bullion standard
Goldmarkt m (Fin) gold market
Goldmünzen fpl (Fin) gold coins
Goldmünzwährung f (Vw) gold coin standard
Goldnotierung f (Fin) gold quote
Goldoptionen fpl (Fin) gold options
Goldparität f (Vw) gold parity
Goldpreis m (Fin) gold price
Goldproduktion f (Vw) gold production (or output)
Goldpunkte mpl
(Vw) gold points
– gold specie points
– bullion points
Goldreserven fpl (AuW) gold holdings (or reserves)
Goldstandard m (Vw) gold standard
Goldtranche f (IWF) gold tranche (ie, term preceding that of the ‚reserve tranche')
Goldtransaktionen fpl (AuW) gold transactions
Goldumlaufwährung f (Vw) gold specie currency (or standard)
Gold- und Devisenbilanz f (AuW) gold and foreign exchange balance
(ie, shows the changes in foreign exchange reserves; equal to a positive or negative change in ‚net external assets' = Nettoauslandsaktiva der Bundesbank)
Gold- und Devisenwährung f (AuW) gold and foreign currency reserves
Goldverkäufe mpl **am freien Markt** (Fin) gold sales in the open market
Goldwährung f (Vw) gold currency (or standard)

Goldwährung f **aufgeben** (Vw) to go off the gold standard
Goldwährungsmechanismus m (AuW) = *Goldautomatismus*
Goldwährungssystem n (Vw) gold-based monetary system
Goldwertklausel f (Fin) gold clause
Goldzufluß m (Vw) gold influx
Gomory-Schnitt m (OR) generating (*or* source) row
Gomory-Zeile f (OR) = *Gomory-Schnitt*
Goodwill m (ReW) = *Firmenwert*
Gossensche Gesetze *npl* (Vw) Gossen's Laws *(ie, First Law: postulates the principle of diminishing utility, and Second Law: this is in fact a theorem stating that, to maximize utility, a given quantity of a good must be divided among different uses in such a manner that the marginal utilities are equal in all uses)*
Grad m **der Anforderung** (IndE) degree of factor
Grad m **der Entartung** (OR) degree of degeneracy
Grad m **der erreichten Marktdurchdringung** (Mk) achieved market penetration
Grad m **der Neuheit** (Pat) degree of novelty
Grad m **des Folgeschadens** (Re) remoteness of damage
Grad m **des Verschuldens** (Re) degree of fault
Grad m **e–r algebraischen Bestimmungsgleichung** (Math) degree of an algebraic equation
Grade *mpl* **von Fahrlässigkeit** (Re) degrees of negligence *(ie, in English law the prevailing view is that there are no degrees of care in negligence, but only different amounts of care as a matter of fact)*
Gradient m (Mat) gradient
Gradientenmethode f
  (Math) gradient method
  – method of successive approximation
Gradientenvektor m (OR) gradient vector
gradzahlige Paritätskontrolle f (EDV) even parity check
Grafik f
  (Stat) chart
  – graph
Graph m (OR) graph
Graphenreduktion f (OR) graph reduction
graphentheoretisch (OR) graph theoretic
Graphentheorie f
  (OR) graph theory
  – theory of graphs
graphisch darstellen
  (Stat) to graph
  – to represent graphically
graphische Anzeige f
  (EDV) graphic display
  – graphics *(syn, graphische Datendarstellung)*
graphische Darstellung f
  (Stat) graph
  – graphic(al) representation
  – arithmetic chart (*or* graph)
graphische Datenverarbeitung f
  (EDV) graphic data processing
  – computer graphics
graphische Papiere *npl* (com) graphic papers
graphischer Arbeitsplatz m
  (EDV) graphics workstation
  (EDV) display console
graphisches Gewerbe n (com) printing industry *(ie, German term obsolete, but still used in places)*
graphisches Kernsystem n (EDV) graphical kernel system, GKS
Graphitstift m (com) conductive pencil
Gratifikation f (Pw) bonus *(eg, Christmas, vacation, loyalty)*
gratis
  (com) at no charge
  – free
  – free of charge
Gratisaktie f (Fin) bonus share (*or* stock) *(ie, a special type of self-financing: a formal dividend payout is subsequently treated as a new capital contribution, §§ 207ff AktG; syn, Berichtigungsaktie)*
Gratisangebot n (com) free offer
Gratismuster n (com) free sample
Gratiszuteilung f (Fin) bonus allotment
grauer Markt m (com) gray market
Graupappe f (com) chipboard
Gray-Code m (EDV) Gray (*or* cyclic) code
Grenzanalyse f (Vw) marginal analysis
Grenzanbieter m (Vw) marginal seller
Grenzanbieter m **von Kapital** (Vw) marginal lender
Grenzausgabe f (Vw) marginal outlay
Grenzausgleich m
  (EG) border adjustment for internal taxes
Grenzausgleichsabgabe f (FiW) border tax on imports
Grenzausgleichsteuer f (AuW) border tax adjustment
Grenzausgleichszahlungen *fpl* (EG) Monetary Compensatory Amounts *(ie, subsidizing exports from a country with higher prices to one with lower prices, and correspondingly taxing trade in the opposite direction)*
Grenzbereich m (Log) interface
Grenzbesteuerungsquote f (FiW) marginal propensity to tax
Grenzbetrieb m
  (Bw) marginal firm (*or* producer)
  – marginal unit of production
Grenzböden *mpl* (Vw) marginal land
Grenzen *fpl* **der Besteuerung** (FiW) limits of taxation
Grenzen *fpl* **des Wachstums** (Vw) growth limits
Grenzerlös m (Vw) marginal revenue
Grenzerlösfunktion f (Vw) marginal revenue function
Grenzerlösproduktion f (Vw) marginal revenue product
Grenzertrag m
  (Vw) marginal yield
  (Vw) marginal return (*or* income)
Grenzertrag m **des Kapitals** (Vw) marginal yield on capital
Grenzerzeugnis n (Vw) marginal product
Grenzfall m (Log) borderline case
Grenzfinanzierung f (Fin) marginal financing *(opp, Gesamtfinanzierung)*
Grenzform f **e–r Funktion** (Math) limiting form of a function

Grenzgänger *m*
(StR) frontier worker
– cross-frontier commuter
Grenzgebiet *n* (Log) borderline subject
Grenzkapazität *f* (Vw) marginal capacity
Grenzkäufer *m* (Vw) marginal buyer
Grenzkonsum *m* (Vw) marginal consumption
Grenzkosten *pl*
(Vw, Bw) marginal
– incremental
– differential ... cost
(KoR) alternative cost
Grenzkostenergebnis *n*
(KoR) profit contribution
– variable gross margin (*or* profit)
– marginal balance
– marginal income *(syn, Deckungsbeitrag)*
Grenzkostenkalkulation *f* (KoR) marginal costing
Grenzkostenrechnung *f*
(KoR) direct costing
– (GB) marginal costing
Grenzkreditnehmer *m* (Fin) marginal borrower
Grenzkurs *m* (Fin) marginal rate
Grenzleerkosten *pl* (KoR) marginal idle-capacity cost
Grenzleid *n* **der Arbeit** (Vw) marginal disutility of labor
Grenzleistungsfähigkeit *f* **des Kapitals**
(Vw) marginal efficiency of capital
– marginal rate of return
Grenzliquidität *f* (Fin) marginal liquidity
Grenzmultiplikator *m* (Vw) marginal multiplier
Grenznachfrager *m* (Vw) marginal buyer
Grenznachfrager *m* **nach Kapital** (Vw) marginal borrower
Grenznutzen *m*
(Vw) marginal utility
– final degree of utility *(St. Jevons)*
Grenznutzenanalyse *f* (Vw) marginal utility analysis
Grenznutzen *m* **des Geldes** (Vw) marginal utility of money
Grenznutzenschule *f*
(Vw) marginalist school
– marginal utility school
Grenznutzentheorie *f* (Vw) marginal utility theory (of value)
Grenzplankostenrechnung *f*
(KoR) standard direct costing
– direct costing
– differential costing
– variable cost accounting
– (GB) marginal costing
– activity accounting
– functional accounting
(syn, Teilkostenrechnung, Deckungsbeitragsrechnung)
Grenzprinzip *n* (Vw) principle of marginality
Grenzprodukt *n* (Vw) marginal product
Grenzprodukt *n* **der Arbeit** (Vw) marginal product of labor
Grenzproduktivität *f* (Vw) marginal productivity
Grenzproduktivität *f* **der Arbeit** (Vw) marginal productivity of labor
Grenzproduktivität *f* **des Geldes** (Vw) marginal productivity of money *(ie, reciprocal of marginal cost)*
Grenzproduktivitätstheorie *f* (Vw) marginal productivity theory *(ie, developed by J. B. Clark)*
Grenzproduzent *m*
(Vw) marginal firm (*or* producer)
– least efficient producer
– marginal unit of production
Grenzpunkt *m* **e-r Menge** (Math) boundary point of a set
Grenzrate *f* **der Substitution** (Vw) marginal rate of substitution
Grenzrate *f* **der technischen Substitution** (Vw) marginal rate of technical substitution
Grenzrate *f* **der Transformation** (Vw) marginal rate of transformation *(ie, equal to the negative reciprocal ratio of marginal productivities)*
Grenzrate *f* **der Zeitpräferenz** (Vw) intertemporal marginal rate of substitution
Grenzsituation *f* (Log) sensitive situation
Grenzsparen *n* (Vw) marginal saving
Grenzsteuersatz *m*
(FiW) marginal tax rate
– marginal rate of taxation
– marginal propensity to tax, MPT
Grenzstückkosten *pl* (KoR) marginal unit cost
Grenzübergang *m*
(com) border crossing
(Zo) point of entry
grenzüberschreitend
(com) international
– cross-frontier
grenzüberschreitende Beförderung *f* (Zo) international transport
grenzüberschreitender Kapitalverkehr *m* (AuW) international (*or* cross-frontier) capital movements
grenzüberschreitender Warenverkehr *m*
(AuW) cross-frontier movements of goods (*or* traffic *or* trade)
– cross-border commerce (*or* trade)
grenzüberschreitendes Leasing *n* (Fin) cross-border leasing
grenzüberschreitendes Projekt *n* (com) cross-frontier project
grenzüberschreitende Transportmittel *npl* (AuW) international means of transport
Grenzumsatz *m* (Vw) marginal revenue
Grenzumsatzprodukt *n* (Vw) marginal revenue (*or* value) product
Grenzverbraucher *m* (Vw) marginal consumer
Grenzverkäufer *m* (Vw) marginal seller
Grenzverkehr *m* (Zo) border traffic
Grenzwert *m*
(Math) limiting value
– limit
Grenzwertanalyse *f* (Vw) marginal analysis
Grenzwertaxiom *n*
(Stat) axiom of convergence
– limit axiom
Grenzwertbegriff *m* (Math) limit concept
Grenzwertproblem *n* (Math) boundary value problem
Grenzwertprüfung *f* (EDV) marginal check (*or* test)

Greshamsches Gesetz n (Vw) Gresham's law
Griffbereich m (IndE) working area
grobe Fahrlässigkeit f
  (Re) gross negligence
  – (civil law) culpa lata
  (ie, intentional failure to perform a duty in disregard of the consequences as affecting the life or property of another, § 277 BGB)
grobe Pflichtverletzung f (Pw) gross breach of duty
grobe Schätung f (com) rough estimate
grob fahrlässig (Re) grossly negligent
grob gerechnet
  (com) as a rough estimate
  – roughly calculated
Grobplanung f (Bw) overall planning
Großabnehmer m
  (com) bulk buyer (or purchaser)
  – big industrial user
  – heavy consumer
  – large buyer
  – quantity buyer
Großabschluß m
  (com) large contract (or deal)
  – big-ticket transaction
Großaktionär m (Fin) major shareholder
Großanlage f (EDV) mainframe computer
Großanlagenbau m
  (IndE) large-scale plant engineering and construction
  – systems engineering
Großanleger m (Fin) big (or large-scale) investor
Großauftrag m
  (com) large-scale order
  – big ticket item
Großbank f (Fin) big bank
Großbestellung f (com) bulk order
Großbetrieb m
  (Bw) large-scale enterprise (ie, defining categories are: size of labor force, capital, or sales volume)
  (Bw) large farm
Großbrand m (Vers) conflagration
Größe f
  (com) size
  – dimensions
  – measurements
  (Math) magnitude
  – variable
große Alternative f
  (Log) exclusive disjunction
  – alternation
große Havarie f (SeeV) general (or gross) average, § 700 HGB
Großeinkauf m
  (Mk) bulk buying
  – volume purchasing
Großeinkäufer m
  (Mk) bulk purchaser
  – wholesale buyer
Großeinlagengeschäft n (Fin) big-ticket deposit-taking (ie, by banks)
große Kontrollspanne f (Bw) shallow (or broad) span of control
große Leitungsspanne f (Bw) = große Kontrollspanne

Großemission f (Fin) jumbo loan issue
Großemittent m (Fin) major debt issuer
Größendegression f (Bw) economies of scale
Größennachteile mpl
  (Bw) diseconomies of scale
  – inefficiencies of scale
größenordnungsmäßig (com) in order of magnitude
größenproportionale Auswahl f (Stat) proportionale sampling
Größenverteilung f (Stat) size distribution
Größenvorteile mpl (Bw) economies of scale
großer Spielraum m (com) plenty of room to operate
großer Steuertermin m (StR) major tax payment date
großes Sortiment n (com) large variety of goods
große Steuerreform f (FiW) top-to-bottom (or root and branch) reform of the tax system
Große Tarifkommission f (Pw) Central Union Bargaining Committee
Großfusion f (Bw) large-scale (or jumbo) merger
Großgeschäft n (Fin) wholesale banking
Großhandel m
  (com) wholesale business (or trade)
  – wholesaling
Großhandelsbetrieb m (com) wholesale establishment
Großhandelsfunktion f (Mk) wholesaling function
Großhandelsindex m (Stat) index of wholesale prices
Großhandelslager n (com) wholesale stock
Großhandelspreis m (com) wholesale price
Großhandels-Preisindex m (Stat) index of wholesale prices
Großhandelsrabatt m (com) wholesale discount
Großhandelsspanne f (com) wholesale margin
Großhandelsunternehmen n (com) wholesale firm
Großhandelsvereinigung f (com) wholesaling association
Großhandelsvertreter m (com) wholesale representative
Großhandelswerte mpl (Bö) big volume stock
Großhandelszentrum n (com) wholesale center
Großhändler m
  (com) wholesale dealer
  – wholesaler
  – distributor
Grossist m (com) wholesaler
Großkredit m
  (Fin) big
  – large-scale
  – massive
  – (infml) jumbo ... loan
  (ie, extended in excess of 15% of a bank's equity capital, § 13 KWG)
Großkreditgeschäft n (Fin) large-scale lending business
Großkreditnehmer m
  (Fin) major
  – massive
  – big ... borrower
Großkunde m
  (com) big customer
  – large-lot (or bulk) buyer
  – major account

- leading edge account
- (infml) big-ticket customer
- (Mk) key account *(ie, in industrial marketing)*

Großkundensteuerung *f* (Mk) account management

Großleben *n* (Vers) ordinary branch business

Großlebenbranche *f* (Vers) ordinary life insurance

Großlebensversicherung *f* (Vers) ordinary *(or* straight) life insurance

Großlieferant *m* (com) major supplier

Großmarkt *m* (com) wholesale market

Groß-M-Methode *f* (OR) big M method

Großpackung *f*
 (com) large
 - bulk
 - giant
 - jumbo
 - familiy size ... package

Großproduktion *f* (IndE) large-scale production

Großprojekt *n*
 (com) large-scale project
 - big-ticket project *(or* item)
 - jumbo scheme

Großraumbüro *n* (com) open plan office

Großraumkernspeicher *m* (EDV) bulk core storage

Großraumspeicher *m* (EDV) bulk storage

Großreparatur *f* (ReW) general overhaul

Großrisiko *n* (Vers) jumbo risk

Großschaden *m* (Vers) major damage

Großserie *f* (IndE) large-scale production

Großspeicher *m* (EDV) mass storage

Großspeichersteuerung *f* (EDV) random access controller, RAC

großtechnische Anlage *f* (IndE) commercial *(or* full-scale) plant

großtechnische Demonstrationsanlage *f* (IndE) commercial demonstration *(or* pilot) plant

großtechnische Fertigung *f* (IndE) commercial production *(opp, Pilotfertigung = pilot plant scale production)*

größter Durchschlupf *m* (Stat) average outgoing quality limit, AOQL

größter gemeinsamer Teiler *m*
 (Math) greatest common divisor
 - highest common factor

größte Schranke *f* (Math) infimum

größte untere Schranke *f* (Math) greatest lower bound

Größtrechner *m* (EDV) ultra-large computer

Großvater *m* (EDV) grandfather *(ie, data set that is two generations earlier than the data set under consideration)*

Großvaterzyklus *m* (EDV) grandfather cycle

Großverbraucher *m* (com) bulk consumer

Großverbundnetz *n* (com) large-scale integrated system

Großverdiener *m* (com) big income earner

Großwetterlage *f*
 (Vw, infml) general business conditions
 - shape of the economy

Großwirtschaftsraum *m* (Vw) large economic region

Großzahlforschung *f* (Stat) large-number research

Großzählung *m* (Stat) census

großzügige Kreditbedingungen *fpl* (Fin) (very) easy credit terms

Grubenvorstand *m* (com) managing board of mining company

Grundadresse *f* (EDV) base *(or* reference) address *(syn, Basisadresse, Bezugsadresse)*

Grundaktivität *f* (Bw) basic activity

Grundaufbaubefehl *m* (EDV) basic instruction

Grundausbildung *f* (Pw) basic training

Grundbedürfnisse *npl* (Vw) basic wants

Grundbefehl *m* (EDV) basic instruction

Grundbegriff *m* (Log) basic concept

Grundbesitz *m* (StR) real property *(ie, comprises property in agriculture and forestry, and plant sites, § 19 BewG)*

Grundbestand *m*
 (MaW) lead time
 - working
 - cycle
 - turnover ... inventory
 (com) basic stock

Grundbetrag *m*
 (com) basic amount
 (StR) gross rental
 (ie, 1.4% of assessed value = Einheitswert)

Grundbetriebssystem *n* (EDV) Basic Operation System, BOS

Grundbilanz *f* (AuW) basic balance *(ie, balance on current account and long-term capital = Leistungsbilanz + Bilanz des langfristigen Kapitalverkehrs)*

Grundbilanz *f* **und kurzfristiger Kapitalverkehr** (AuW, US) official settlement balance

Grundbuch *n*
 (ReW) book of original entry
 - journal
 - daybook
 (syn, Tagebuch, Memorial, Journal, Primanota)
 (Re) official real estate register

Grundbuchamt *n*
 (Re) real estate registry
 - (US) Land Records Office
 - (GB) Land Registry

Grundbuchauszug *m*
 (Re) abstract of land register
 - (GB) office copy of land register

Grundbucheinsicht *f* (Re) inspection of real estate register

Grundbucheintragung *f*
 (Re) entry in the land register
 - (GB) registration of title to land

Grundbuchlöschung *f* (Re) cancellation of an entry in the land register

Grundbuchung *f* (ReW) original entry

Grundcodierung *f* (EDV) absolute *(or* basic) coding *(syn, einfache Codierung)*

Grunddaten *pl* (Stat) source data

Grunddefiniton *f* (Log) core definition

Grunddienstbarkeit *f* (Re) real servitude, § 1018 BGB

Grundeigentum *n* (Re) property in land

Grundeigentümer *m* (Re) land owner

gründen
 (Bw) to form
 - to create

- to establish
- to launch
- to organize
- to set up ... a business *(ie, of any kind)*
(Bw) to incorporate *(ie, Kapitalgesellschaft)*
- (GB) to promote (a company)

Gründer *m*
(Bw) founder *(ie, of any type of business)*
(Bw) incorporator *(ie, of a Kapitalgesellschaft, usu. of an AG)*
- (GB) promoter

Gründer *m* **e-r AG**
(Bw) incorporator of a stock corporation, § 2 AktG
- (GB) promoter of a company

Gründerlohn *m* (Fin) founders' fee
Grunderwerb *m* (Re) acquisition of land
Grunderwerbsteuer *f* (StR) land transfer tax
Grunderwerbsteuer-Durchführungsverordnung *f* (StR) Ordinance Regulating the Real Property Transfer Tax Law, of 30 March 1940
Grunderwerbsteuergesetz *n* (StR) Real Property Transfer Tax Law, of 29 March 1940
Grundformen *fpl* **der Betriebsorganisation** (Bw) basic patterns of departmentation
Grundfreibetrag *m* (StR) basic tax-free amount
Grundgebühr *f* (com) basic fee *(or* charge)
Grundgehalt *n* (Pw) basic salary
Grundgesamtheit *f*
(Stat) parent population
- population
- universe *(obsolescent term)*

Grundgeschäft *n*
(Re) basic transaction
- underlying deal *(or* transaction)
(Mk) bottom lines
- (infml) bread-and-butter lines
- (infml) meat and potatoes

Grundgesetz *n* (Re) Bonn Basic Law
Grundhandelsgeschäft *n* (com) general commercial transaction, § 1 II HGB
Grundhandelsgewerbe *n* (com) general commercial business, § 1 II HGB
Grundkapital *n*
(Fin, appr) stated
- nominal
- legal
- share ... capital
- capital stock
(ie, of a corporation, identical with the total par value of all its shares, minimum amount DM 100,000, § 7 AktG)

Grundkapital-Dividende *f* (Fin) dividend out of capital
Grundkonjunktor *m* (Log) primitive connective
Grundkosten *pl* (KoR) basic cost *(ie, expenditure spread by costing over the period under review, opp, Zusatzkosten)*
Grundkredit *m* (Fin) real estate credit
Grundkreditanstalt *f* (Fin) mortgage bank
Grundkurve *f* (Math) master curve
Grundlagenbescheid *m* (StR) basic assessment
Grundlagenforschung *f* (com) basic research
Grundlageninvestition *f* (Vw) investment in infrastructure

Grundleistungssektor *m* (Vw) basic sector
gründliche Analyse *f*
(com) in-depth analysis
- (infml) seat-of-the-pants analysis

Grundlinie *f*
(Vw) underlying tendency
(Stat) base line

Grundlohn *m* (Pw) base pay
Grundlohnsatz *m* (Pw) base pay rate
grundlose Entlassung *f*
(Pw) unfair dismissal
- dismissal without cause

Grundmenge *f* (Log, Math) universal set of reference
(Stat) universe

Grundmetall *n* (com) base metal
Grundnahrungsmittel *npl* (Vw) basic foodstuffs
Grundpatent *n* (Pat) basic *(or* master) patent
Grundpfand *n* (Re) real estate mortgage
Grundpfandbrief *m* (Re) official mortgage certificate
Grundpfanddarlehen *n* (Fin) mortgage loan
Grundpfandgläubiger *m* (Re) mortgagee
Grundpfandrechte *npl*
(Re) encumbrances on real property
- rights in rem
- real rights
(ie, securing a claim attaching to a real estate; general term covering Hypothek, Grundschuld, Rentenschuld, qv)

grundpfandrechtlich gesichert (Re) secured by mortgage
Grundpfandschuld *f* (Re) mortgage debt
Grundpfandschuldner *m* (Re) mortgagor
Grundprämie *f* (Vers) basic premium *(or* rate)
Grundpreis *m*
(com) basic price
(EG) basic price *(ie, laid down for pigmeat under CAP)*

Grundrechnungsarten *fpl* (Math) first rules of arithmetic
Grundrechtsgarantie *f* (Re) constitutional safeguard of basic rights
Grundrendite *f* (Fin) basic yield
Grundrente *f* (Vw) ground rent
Grundrichtpreis *m* (EG) basic target price
Grundsatzabkommen *n* (Re) basic agreement
Grundsatz *m* **der Ausfuhrfreiheit** (AuW) principle of freedom of export
Grundsatz *m* **der Einzelbewertung** (ReW) rule of individual *(or* unit) valuation
Grundsatz *m* **der Gesamtbewertung** (StR) principle of appraising each economic unit by itself, § 2 I BewG
Grundsatz *m* **der Maßgeblichkeit der Handelsbilanz** (StR) principle of dependency of the tax balance sheet on the commercial balance sheet
Grundsatz *m* **der materiellen Bilanzkontinuität** (ReW) consistency principle
Grundsatz *m* **der mittleren Prädikation** (Log) fundamental principle of mediate predication *(syn, nota-notae-Prinzip)*
Grundsatz *m* **der Nichtdiskriminierung** (AuW) principle of nondiscrimination
Grundsatz *m* **der steuerlichen Gleichbehandlung**

(StR) principle of the equal treatment of taxpayers
Grundsatz m **der steuerlichen Leistungsfähigkeit** (FiW) ability-to-pay principle
- faculty principle of taxation
Grundsatz m **der Unmerklichkeit** (FiW) principle of imperceptibly imposing tax burdens
Grundsatz m **der Wesentlichkeit** (ReW) principle of materiality
Grundsatzdiskussion f (com) discussion in principle
Grundsätze mpl **der Rechnungslegung** (ReW) reporting policies
Grundsätze mpl **der Unternehmensführung**
(Bw) business
- company
- corporate ... policies
Grundsätze mpl **des Verfahrens** (Re) procedural principles
Grundsatzentscheidung f
(Re) leading (or landmark) decision
(com) pivotal decision
Grundsätze mpl **für das Rechnungswesen** (ReW) principles of accountancy
Grundsätze mpl **ordnungsmäßiger Buchführung** (ReW) principles of proper (or orderly) accounting
- financial accounting standards
- principles of orderly bookkeeping and balance-sheet makeup
- (US) Generally Accepted Accounting Principles
(ie, GAAP do not have the same significance, because even detailed valuation principles and financial reporting requirements are prescribed by German law)
Grundsätze mpl **ordnungsmäßiger Prüfung** (ReW) generally accepted auditing standards
Grundsatzfragen fpl
(com) basic
- key
- pivotal ... issues
grundsätzlich
(Re) basically
- in broad principle
grundsätzliche Einigung f (Re) agreement in principle
Grundsatzreferat n (com) key note speech
Grundsatzvertrag m (Re) agreement in principle
Grundsatz m **von Treu und Glauben** (Re) principle of equity and fair dealing *(ie, each party shall act ex aequo et bono = nach pflichtgemäßem Ermessen, § 242 BGB)*
Grundschaltung f (EDV) basic circuit arrangement
Grundschuld f
(Re) land charge
- encumbrance of real property
(ie, abstract charge for a money payment, § 1191 BGB)
Grundschuldbrief m (Re) land charge certificate
Grundschuldforderung f (Re) claim secured by a land charge
Grundschuldgläubiger m (Re) holder of a land charge
Grundschuldlöschung f (Re) cancellation of land charge

Grundschule f
(Pw) grade school
- (GB) elementary school
Grundsicherung f
(SozV) basic minimum floor of income
- basic level of protection
Grundsprache-Programm n (EDV) basic (or low-level) language program
Grundsteuer f (StR) real property tax *(ie, levied by municipalities on land and buildings situated within their jurisdiction)*
Grundsteuer-Durchführungsverordnung f (StR) Ordinance Regulating the Real Property Tax Law
Grundsteuergesetz n (StR) Real Property Tax Law, of 7 Aug 1973, as amended
Grundsteuer-Richtlinien fpl (StR) Real Property Tax Regulations, of 9 Dec 1978
Grundstichprobe f (Stat) master sample
Grundstoffe mpl
(com) basic goods (or commodities)
- basic materials
- primary products
Grundstoffgewerbe n (com) basic goods sector
Grundstoffindustrie f
(com) primary
- basic
- extractive ... industry
Grundstoffsektor m (com) basic goods sector
Grundstoffunternehmen n (Bw) natural-resource company
Grundstoffwirtschaft f (Vw) basic industry
Grundstück n
(com) plot of land
- parcel of real estate (or real property)
- real estate tract
- real estate
(ie, may include buildings)
Grundstück n **belasten** (Re) to encumber real property
Grundstücke npl (ReW) land
- real estate (or property)
Grundstücke npl **für den Gemeinbedarf** (StR) land set aside for public purposes
Grundstücke npl **ohne Bauten** (ReW) unimproved real property
Grundstücke und Bauten pl (ReW) land and buildings
Grundstücke npl **und grundstücksgleiche Rechte** npl (Re) real estate and equivalent titles
Grundstücksarten fpl (StR) types of real estate, § 75 BewG
Grundstücksauflassung f (Re) notarized transfer of ownership, § 925 BGB
Grundstücksbelastung f (Re) encumbrance
Grundstücksbestandteile mpl
(Re) fixtures, § 94 BGB
- things affixed to the soil
- appurtenances
Grundstücksbewertung f
(Fin, StR) valuation of real property
- site value appraisal
Grundstückseigentümer m (com) real estate owner
Grundstückseinrichtungen fpl (com) land improvements

Grundstückserschließung f (com) real estate (or property) development
Grundstückserschließungsplan m (com) land development plan
Grundstücksfonds m (Fin) real estate fund
Grundstücksgeschäfte npl (com) real estate transactions
Grundstücksgesellschaft f (com) real estate company *(ie, engaged in buying and selling)*
grundstücksgleiche Rechte npl (Re) rights equivalent to real property
Grundstückskauf m (com) purchase of real estate
Grundstückskäufer m (com) purchaser of land
Grundstückskaufvertrag m (Re) contract for sale of land
Grundstückskosten pl (com) land cost
Grundstücksmakler m
  (com) real estate broker (or agent)
  – (GB) estate agent
  – (GB) land agent
  (syn, Immobilienmakler)
Grundstücksmarkt m
  (com) real estate market
  – property market
Grundstücksmiteigentümer m (Re) co-owner of real estate
Grundstückspreise mpl (com) real estate prices
Grundstücksübertragung f
  (Re) conveyance
  – transfer of land
Grundstücksveräußerung f (Re) real estate transfer
Grundstücksveräußerungsrecht n (Re) right to convey real estate
Grundstücksverkäufer m
  (com) real estate operator
  – (GB) property dealer
Grundstücksverkehr m (Re) real estate transactions
Grundstücksverkehrsgesetz n (Re) Law Regulating Real Estate Transactions, as of 28 July 1961
Grundstücksvermittler m (com) = *Grundstücksmakler*
Grundstücksversicherung f (Vers) real property insurance
Grundstücksverwalter m (com) real estate manager
Grundstücksverwaltung f (com) real estate management
Grundstücksverzeichnis n (com) list of real estate holdings
Grundstückswert m (com) real estate value
Grundstückszubehör n (Re) accessory to realty fixtures and fittings of the premises
Grundtabelle f (StR) Basic Tax Table, § 32a EStG
Grundtarif m (Zo) autonomous tariff
Grundtendenz f (com) underlying trend
Grund m **und Boden** m (com) real estate (or property)
Grund- und Hilfsstoffhandel m (com) wholesale trading in basic and auxiliary materials *(ie, branch of domestic wholesaling)*
Gründung f
  (Bw) formation *(ie, of any type of business)*
  – foundation
  – organization

(Bw) incorporation *(ie, of a Kapitalgesellschaft)*
  – (GB) promotion *(ie, of a company)*
Gründungsaufwand m
  (Fin) formation expense, § 26 AktG
  – organization expense
Gründungsbericht m (Bw) formation report, § 32 AktG
Gründungsbilanz f (ReW) commencement balance sheet, § 39 HGB
Gründungseinlage f (Fin) original investment
Gründungsfinanzierung f (Fin) funding at commencement of a business enterprise
Gründungsfonds m (Vers) foundation fund *(ie, serving as a guaranty fund for the benefit of the insured and for the provision of the working expenses)*
Gründungsformalitäten fpl
  (Re) formalities of formation
  – technical incorporation requirements
  (ie, to be met in the case of stock corporations)
Gründungsjahr n (Bw) year of formation (or foundation)
Gründungskapital n (Fin) original capital
  – initial capital stock
Gründungskonsortium n (Fin) foundation (or underlying) syndicate
Gründungskosten pl
  (ReW) organization expense (or cost)
  – development expense
  – formation expense
  – setup (or setting-up) expense
  – (GB) preliminary expense
Gründungskosten pl **abschreiben** (ReW) to write off formation expenses
Gründungsmitglied n
  (com) charter member
  – (GB) foundation member
Gründungsprüfer m (ReW) auditor of the formation, § 33 II AktG *(ie, appointed by a court to report on the formation process)*
Gründungsprüfung f (ReW) examination of company formation, § 33 AktG
Gründungsstock m (Vers) = *Gründungsfonds*
Gründungsurkunde f
  (Re) organization certificate
  – corporate charter
Gründungsversammlung f (Re) organization meeting
Grundverkehr m (Re) = *Grundstücksverkehr*
Grundvermögen n
  (com) property in land
  (StR) real property
  – real estate, §§ 68–94 BewG
Grundverpackung f (com) packaging *(opp, packing = Außenverpackung)*
Grundwehrdienst m (StR) basic military service
Grundwert m
  (com) basic amount *(ie, in commercial calculations)*
  (StR) real estate value
Grundwertsteigerung f (Fin) real estate appreciation
Grundzahl f (Math) base
Grundzeichen n (Log) primitive symbol
Grundzeit f (IndE) basic time

grüner Ausgang m (Zo) green exit
grüner Dollar m (EG) green dollar *(ie, unit of account in the EC farm system)*
grüner Durchgang m (Zo) green channel
grüne RE f (EG) agricultural unit of account, AUA
Grüner Plan m (Vw) Green Plan *(ie, annual farming plan published by the Federal Government)*
grüner Scheck m (Fin) security transfer check *(syn, Effektenscheck)*
Grünes Heft n (Vw) Green Booklet *(ie, setting forth Standard Business Conditions of Deutsche Bundesbank)*
grünes Licht n **geben** (com) to give the go-ahead *(eg, for final agreement, for an investment project)*
grüne Umrechnungskurse mpl (EG) green rates
grüne Wiese f (com) greenfield site *(ie, building plot without infrastructure; eg, to build a plant on a greenfield site)*
Gruppe f der Einzelfloater (AuW) group with individually floating currencies
Gruppe f der Vierundzwanzig (AuW) Group of Twenty-Four *(ie, Intergovernmental Group of 24 on International Monetary Affairs)*
Gruppenabschluß m
 (ReW) group financial statements
 – (GB) group accounts
Gruppenabschreibung f
 (ReW) composite depreciation
 – composite-life method of depreciation
Gruppenadresse f (EDV) group address
Gruppenadressierung f (EDV) group addressing
Gruppenakkord m
 (Pw) group piecework
 – group scheme
Gruppenakkordkarte f (Pw) gang job card
Gruppenakkordlohn m (IndE) group piecework rate
Gruppenakkordsatz m (Pw) group piece rate
Gruppenanzeige f
 (EDV) group indication
 – first item list
Gruppenarbeit f (Pw) group *(or* team) work
Gruppenbegriff m (EDV, Cobol) control break item
Gruppenbeurteilung f (Pw) group appraisal
Gruppenbewertung f
 (ReW) composite method of valuation
 – group valuation
 – group-of-asset valuation
 (ie, of items similar in kind and at average prices)
gruppenbezogene Hierarchie f (Bw) group-oriented hierarchy
Gruppencode m (EDV) group code
gruppencodierte Aufzeichnung f (EDV) group coded recording
Gruppenfertigung f (IndE) mixed-type production *(ie, where optimum of continuous production is not yet reached)*
Gruppenfloating n (AuW) block *(or* joint) floating
Gruppenfrachtrate f (com) blanket *(or* class) rate
Gruppengemeinkosten pl (KoR) indirect product group cost
Gruppenkapazität f (Bw) group capacity *(ie, total capacity of a number of comparable plants of the same type, mostly of a branch of industry)*
Gruppenkosten pl (KoR) product group overhead
Gruppenlebensversicherung f (Vers) group life insurance
Gruppenleiter m
 (Bw) head of organizational group
 – group manager
Gruppenlöhne mpl (Pw) gang rates
Gruppenmarke f (EDV) group mark(er)
Gruppenname m (EDV) group name
Gruppenprämiensystem n (Pw) group bonus system
Gruppenpreisverfahren n (Bw) product group pricing
Gruppenrendite f (Fin) group yield
gruppenspezifische Steuerlastquote f (FiW) group-based tax ratio
Gruppen-Stabdiagramm n (Stat) multiple bar chart
Gruppentarif m (com) blanket rate
Gruppentrennzeichen n (EDV) group separator
Gruppenvergleich m (EDV) card-to-card comparing
Gruppenversicherung f (Vers) group *(or* collective) insurance
Gruppenversicherung f auf den Todes- und Erlebensfall (Vers) group endowment policy
Gruppenverteiler m (com) group distributer
Gruppenwechsel m
 (EDV) group control change
 (EDV, Cobol) control break
Gruppenwechselplan m (Stat) changeover design *(or* trial)
Gruppenwechselstufe f (EDV) control break level
Gruppenziel n (Bw) unit objective
 – group goal
Gruppe f von Anbietern (Vw) industry
gültig bis auf Widerruf (com) valid until canceled
gültiger Rechtsanspruch m (Re) good title
gültiger Verkaufspreis m (com) actual selling price
gültiges Patent n (Pat) patent in force
gültige Ziffer f (Math) significant number
Gültigkeit f (Log, Re) validity
Gültigkeitsdauer f
 (Re) currency *(eg, of a contract)*
 – life
 – duration
 – period of validity
Gültigkeitserklärung f (Re) validation certificate
Gültigkeitsprüfung f (EDV) validity check
G+V-Rechnung f (ReW) = *Gewinn- und Verlustrechnung*
günstige Bedingungen fpl (com) easy *(or* reasonable) terms
günstiges Angebot n (com) attractive *(or* favorable) offer
günstige Zahlungsbedingungen fpl (Fin) easy terms of payment
Gunstvertrag m (Re) third-party beneficiary contract
Gürtel m enger schnallen
 (com, infml) to tighten belt
 – to notch belt tighter
Gut n
 (Vw) commodity *(ie, in economic theory)*

– *(sometimes even)* a good
gut abschneiden (Fin) to perform well
Gutachten *n*
(com) expert opinion
– report
– experts report
– appraisal report *(ie, of valuer)*
– (esp GB) expertise
Gutachten *n* **einholen** (com) to ask for an expert opinion
Gutachten *n* **erstatten** (com) to submit an expert opinion
Gutachter *m* (com) expert
Gutachterausschuß *m* (com) committee of experts
gutachterliche Stellungnahme *f* (com) advisory opinion
Gutachtertätigkeit *f* (com) expert's advisory services
Gutbereich *m* (Stat) accept(ance) region
gutbezahlte Stelle *f*
(Pw) well-paid job
– (GB, infml) plum job
Güte *f* (com) quality
Güteantrag *m* (Re) petition for concilition
Güteaufpreis *m* (com) quality extra
gute Auftragslage *f* (com) strong orders position
Güte *f* **der Anpassung** (Stat) goodness of fit
gute Durchschnittsqualität *f*
(com) fair average quality, faq
(com) good middling
Güte *f* **e-r Schätzung** (Stat) closeness in estimation
Gütefunktion *f* (Stat) power function *(ie, of a test)*
Güteklassen *fpl*
(com) quality categories
(com) grades
Güteklassenbezeichnung *f* (com) grade label
Güteklassen *fpl* **einteilen, in** (com) to grade
Güteklasseneinteilung *f* (com) grading
Gütemarke *f* (Pat) certification mark
Gütemerkmal *n* (Stat) quality (*or* qualitative characteristic)
Gütenorm *f* (com) quality standard
Güteprämie *f* (Pw) quality bonus
Güteprüfung *f* (Stat) inspection test
Güteprüfung *f* **durch den Lieferanten** (Stat) vendor inspection
Güter *npl*
(Vw) goods
– commodities
– resources
(com) commodities
– merchandise
– goods
– freight
Güterabfertigung *f*
(com) dispatching of goods
(com) freight office
Güterannahme *f* (com) freight receiving office
Güterausgabe *f* (com) freight delivery office
Güterbahnhof *m*
(com) freight station (*or* depot)
– (GB) goods station
Güterbeförderung *f* (com) transportation of goods
Güterbeförderung *f* **zur See**
(com) maritime transportation of goods

– (GB) carriage of goods by sea
Güterbündel *n*
(Vw) batch of commodities
(OR) bill of goods
Güter *npl* **des Anlagevermögens**
(Bw) fixed assets
– fixed capital goods
Güter *npl* **des gehobenen Bedarfs** (com) luxuries and semi-luxuries
Güter *npl* **des täglichen Bedarfs**
(Vw) essential goods
– essentials
– necessaries
(Mk) convenience goods
Güterexpedition *f* (com) forwarding agency
Güterfernverkehr *m*
(com) long-distance freight transportation
– long-distance transport
– long-haul trucking
– (GB) long-distance haulage
Güterfernverkehrs-Unternehmer *m*
(com) long-haul trucker
– (GB) long-distance road haulier
Gütergemeinschaft *f* (Re) community of property
guter Glaube *m* (Re) good faith *(ie, implies reasonable commercial standards of fair dealing in trade)*
Güter *npl* **in enger Substitutionskonkurrenz** (Vw) close substitutes
Güterkombination *f* (Vw) commodity combination
Güter *n* **konkretisieren** (Re) to appropriate goods
Güterkraftverkehr *m*
(com) trucking
– (GB) road (*or* freight) haulage
Güterkreislauf *m* (Vw) circular flow of goods and services
Güterlücke *f*
(Vw) goods gap
– inflationary gap in the goods market
Gütermarkt *m* (Vw) commodity (*or* product) market
Gütermengenkombination *f* (Vw) quantity combination
Güternahverkehr *m* (com) short haul transportation
güterorientierter Ansatz *m* (Mk) commodity approach
Güterpreise *mpl* (Vw) output prices
Güterschuppen *m* (com) freight shed
Güterspediteur *m* (com) freight forwarder
Güterstand *m* (StR) property regime
Güterstrom *m* (VRG) flow of goods and services
Gütertarif *m* (com) freight rates
Gütertausch *m* (Vw) barter
(ie, exchange of goods and services without the use of money)
Gütertransport *m*
(com) freight transportation
– transit of goods
Gütertransportmarkt *m* (com) freight market
Gütertransportversicherung *f*
(Vers) freight insurance
– goods in transit insurance
Güter *npl* **und Dienste** *mpl* (com) goods and services

Güter- und Kapitalverkehr *m* (Vw) goods and capital movement
Güterverkehr *m*
(com) freight (*or* goods) traffic
– freight business
– freight movement
– transportation of freight
Güterverladung *f* (com) freight handling
Güterverladungsanlagen *fpl* (com) freight handling facilities
Güterversicherung *f* (Vers) cargo (*or* freight) insurance *(ie, 'cargo' being the marine term in U. S.; syn, Kargoversicherung)*
Güterwagen *m*
(com) freight car
– (GB) goods waggon
güterwirtschaftliche Komponente *f* (Vw) component in real terms
güterwirtschaftliches Gleichgewicht *n*
(Vw) overall equilibrium in real terms
– commodity equilibrium
güterwirtschaftliche Theorie *f* **des internationalen Handels** (AuW) pure theory of international trade
güterwirtschaftliche Überinvestitionstheorie *f* (Vw) nonmonetary overinvestment theory
Güterzug *m*
(com) freight train
– (GB) goods train
Gütesicherung *f* (Stat) quality assurance
gute Sitten *pl* (Re) boni mores *(eg, verstößt gegen die guten Sitten = is contra bonos mores)*
Gütestempel *m* (Stat) compliance stamp
Gütesteuerung *f* (Stat) process control
Gütevorschrift *f* (com) quality standard (*or* classification)
Gütezeichen *n*
(Mk) quality label
– quality mark
– brand name
– collective brand name *(eg, RAL is the brand name of Gütegemeinschaft Deutsche Möbel)*
(Pat) mark of quality
– quality mark
Gütezeichengemeinschaft *f* (Kart) association for marks of quality
Gütezeichenliste *f* (com) register of quality labels *(ie, kept by RAL = Ausschuß für Lieferbedingungen und Gütesicherung)*
gut gehende Produkte *npl* (Mk) well-running lines
Gutglaubenserwerb *m* (Re) bona fide acquisition
Gutglaubensschutz *m* (Re) protection of bona fide purchaser
gutgläubiger Benutzer *m*
(Re) user in good faith
– bona fide user
gutgläubiger Besitz *m* (Re) bona fide possession
gutgläubiger Besitzer *m*
(Re) bona fide possessor
– possessor in good faith
(ie, ignorant that his title is contested)
(WeR) holder in good faith
gutgläubiger Dritter *m*
(Re) innocent third party
– third party acting in good faith

gutgläubiger Eigentümer *m* (Re) bona fide owner, § 932 BGB
gutgläubiger Erwerb *m*
(Re) bona fide purchase
– acquisition in good faith
gutgläubiger Erwerber *m*
(Re) bona fide purchaser
(ie, one purchasing without notice of any defects in the title of seller)
(WeR) bona fide purchaser *(ie, without notice of any defense or claim to document or property)*
gutgläubiger Inhaber *m*
(WeR) bona fide holder
– holder in good faith
gutgläubig erwerben (Re) to acquire in good faith (*or* bona fide)
Gutgrenze *f* (Stat) acceptable quality level, AQL
Guthaben *n*
(Fin) balance
– credit balance
(Fin) deposits
– funds
Guthaben *n* **ausweisen** (Fin) to show a balance
Guthabenbewegungen *fpl* (Fin) changes in credit balances
Guthaben *n* **freigeben** (Fin) to unfreeze funds
Guthaben *npl* **Gebietsfremder** (Fin) nonresident holdings
Guthabenklausel *f* (Fin) sufficient-funds proviso
Guthaben *n* **pfänden** (Re) to attach an account
Guthabensaldo *m* (Fin) credit balance
Guthaben *n* **sperren** (Re) to block (*or* to freeze) an account
gut halten, sich
(Bö) *(prices)* hold steady
– hold up well
gütliche Einigung *f* (Re) amicable (*or* out-of-court) settlement
gütlich einigen (Re) to settle amicably (*or* out of court)
gütliche Regelung *f* (Re) amicable settlement
Gut-Schlecht-Prüfung *f*
(Stat) go-and-not-go gage
– good-defective inspection test
– sampling by attributes
gutschreiben (ReW) to credit *(eg, an account with an amount)*
Gutschrift *f*
(com) credit note
(ReW) credit entry
(Mk) refund credit slip *(ie, in retail trade)*
Gutschriftsanzeige *f*
(Fin) credit memo(randum)
– credit slip
– (GB) credit note
Gutschriftsbeleg *m* (ReW) credit voucher
Gutschriftskondition *f* **verschlechtern** (Fin) to tighten terms for crediting items
gut strukturierte Aufgabe *f* (Bw) well-structured task
gut verkaufen lassen, sich
(com) to sell readily
– to find a ready market
Gutzahl *f* (Stat) acceptance number
G-Wagen *m* (com) = *gedeckter Wagen*

297

H

Haager Übereinkommen *n* (Re) Hague Convention
haarsträubender Fehler *m* (com, infml) glaring flaw
Haavelmo-Theorem *n*
(FiW) balanced-budget multiplier theorem
– Haavelmo's proposition
Haben *n* (ReW) credit (side) *(ie, of an account)*
Habenbuchung *f* (ReW) credit entry
Habenposten *m* (ReW) credit item
Habensaldo *m* (ReW) credit balance
Habenseite *f*
(ReW) credit side *(ie, of an account)*
– creditor
Habenzinsen *mpl*
(Fin) interest earned
– interest earnings
– credit interest
Habenzinssatz *m* (Fin) creditor (interest) rate
Habilitand *m* (Pw) habilitation candidate
Habilitation *f* (Pw) formel promotion to professorial status
Habilitationsschrift *f* (Pw) professorial thesis
Hack- und Freßordnung *f* (Pw, infml) pecking order
Hafen *m*
(com) port *(ie, artificial)*
– harbor *(ie, natural or artificial)*
Hafenabgaben und -gebühren *fpl* (com) port dues and charges
Hafenanlagen *fpl* (com) port facilities
Hafen *m* **anlaufen** (com) to call at a port
Hafenarbeiter *m*
(com) dock worker
– docker
– (US) longshoreman
Hafengebühren *fpl* (com) port dues *(or* charges)
Hafenkonnossement *n*
(com) port bill of lading
– port B/L
Hafenordnung *f* (com) part *(or* habor) regulations
haftbar
(Re) (legally) liable (to) (for)
– subject to liability *(eg, for all partnership obligations)*
– responsible (to) (for)
– answerable (to) (for)
– accountable (to) (for)
haftbar machen
(Re) to hold *(or* make) liable in damages
– to hold responsible for
– to hold accountable for
– to saddle with liability
haften
(Re) to be liable (to) (for)
– to be responsible (to) (for)
– to be liable in *(eg, damages)*
Haftender *m*
(Re) party liable
– obligor

haftendes Eigenkapital *n* (Fin) liable equity capital *(ie, of banks)*, § 10 KWG
Haftetikett *n*
(com) self-adhering label
– sticker
Haftpflicht *f* (Re) legal *(or* third party) liability
Haftpflicht *f* **des Versicherten** (Vers) insured's legal liability (towards)
Haftpflichtgeschäft *n* (Vers) liability field *(or* business)
Haftpflichtsumme *f* (Re) uncalled liability *(ie, of a cooperative's member)*
Haftpflichtverband *m* (Vers) liability association
Haftpflichtversicherer *m* (Vers) third party risk insurer
Haftpflichtversicherung *f*
(Vers) liability insurance
– (GB) third-party insurance
Haftpflichtversicherung *f* **freier Berufe**
(Vers) malpractice insurance
– professional liability insurance
Haftpflichtversicherung *f* **mit Kaskoversicherung** (Vers) automobile personal liability and property damage insurance
Haftpflichtversicherung *f* **mit Vollkaskoversicherung** (Vers) fully comprehensive insurance
Haftsummenverpflichtung *f* (Fin) uncalled liabilities of members *(ie, of a cooperative society)*
Haftung *f* (Re) (legal) liability
Haftung *f* **ablehnen**
(Re) to disclaim
– to refuse
– to refuse to accept ... liability
Haftung *f* **aus der Bestellung von Sicherheiten für fremde Verbindlichkeiten** (ReW) liabilities arising out of collateral put up to secure third parties
Haftung *f* **ausschließen** (Re) to rule out *(or* negative) liability
Haftung *f* **aus unerlaubter Handlung**
(Re) liability for unlawful acts, § 823 BGB
– tort liability
– liability in tort
– delictual *(or* tortious) liability
(ie, in civil-law countries predicated upon proof of fault = Verschuldensprinzip)
Haftung *f* **aus Vertrag** (Re) contract *(or* contractual) liability
Haftung *f* **bestreiten** (Re) to deny liability
Haftung *f* **des Wiederverkäufers** (Re) liability of reseller
Haftung *f* **erweitern**
(Re) to extend scope of liability
– to increase responsibility
Haftung *f* **für fremdes Verschulden** (Re) vicarious liability *(ie, debtor is answerable for any default on the part of his assistants as though it had been his own*, § 278 BGB)
Haftung *f* **für vertragsgemäßen Gebrauch** (Re) warranty of fitness for contractual use

Haftung *f* **nach dem Verursacherprinzip** (Re) source responsibility
Haftung *f* **ohne Verschulden** (Re) strict liability
– liability based on causation
– liability without (*or* irrespective of) fault
Haftungsansprüche *mpl* **Dritter** (Re) third party liability claims
Haftungsausschluß *m* (Re) disclaimer (*or* exclusion) of liability
Haftungsausschlußklausel *f* (Re) disclaimer (*or* non-liability) clause
Haftungsbefreiung *f* (Re) exemption from liability
Haftungsbescheid *m* (StR) notice of liability, §§ 191, 218 AO
Haftungsbeschränkung *f* (Re) limitation of liability (*ie, usu.* in strict liability = *Gefährdungshaftung*)
Haftungsbeschränkung *f* **des Transportunternehmens** (com) risk note
Haftungsbeschränkungsklausel *f* (Re) liability exemption clause
Haftungsdauer *f* (Re) indemnity period
Haftungsfonds *m* (Re) liability fund, § 487 HGB
Haftungsfreistellung *f* (Re) release from liability
Haftungsfreistellungsvertrag *m* (Re) contract of indemnity
Haftungsgrenze *f* (Vers) limit of liability (*ie, maximum amount for which insurer is liable*)
Haftungsgrundsätze *mpl* (Re) principles (*or* rules) governing liability
Haftungskapital *n* (Fin) liable equity capital
Haftungsschuldner *m* (StR) person held liable for the payment of the tax of another, § 191 AO (*eg, withholding liability of the employer for wage tax*)
Haftungssumme *f*
(Re) maximum amount of liability
(Vers) liability coverage
Haftungsträger *m* (Re) party liable
Haftungsübernahme *f* (Re) assumption of liability
Haftungsübernahmevertrag *m* (Re) assumption of liability agreement
Haftungsumfang *m* (Re) extent of liability
Haftungsverbund *m* (Fin) joint liability scheme (*ie, operated by the savings banks' guaranty fund and the desposit security reserve of the ‚Landesbanken' and ‚Girozentralen'*)
Haftungsverzicht *m* (Re) waiver of liability
Haftungsverzichtsklausel *f* (Re) liability waiver clause
Haftungszusage *f* (Fin) guaranty commitment
Haftung *f* **übernehmen**
(Re) to assume liability
– to make oneself responsible (for)
Hagelversicherung *f* (Vers) hail insurance
Halbaddierer *m*
(EDV) half
– one-digit
– two-input . . . adder
Halbaddierglied *n* (EDV) half adder
halbamtlicher Verkehr *m* (Bö) over-the-counter market
Halbbelegung *f* (SozV) half-cover (*syn, Halbdeckung*)
Halbduplex *m* (EDV) half duplex

Halbduplexbetrieb *m* (EDV) half duplex operation (*syn, Wechselbetrieb*)
Halbduplexkanal *m* (EDV) half duplex channel
Halbebene *f* (Math) half plane
halber Quartilsabstand *m*
(Stat) quartile deviation
– semi-interquartile range
Halberzeugnisse *npl* (com) semi-finished goods (*or* products)
Halbfabrikate *npl* (com) = *Halberzeugnisse*
halbfertige Erzeugnisse *npl* (ReW) goods in process
– work in process (*or* progress)
– material in process
(*syn, unfertige Erzeugnisse*)
Halbgerade *f* (Math) half line
Halbgrossist *m* (com) semi-wholesaler (*ie, wholesaler who also engages in retailing*)
Halbierungsmethode *f* (Stat) split-half method (*or* technique)
Halbjahresabschluß *m*
(ReW) first-half report
– interim accounts and report
– semi-annual accounts
– half-yearly accounts
Halbjahresbericht *m*
(ReW) interim report (*ie, for the first or second half of . . .*)
– six-months figures
– semi-annual report
Halbjahres-Betriebsergebnis *n*
(ReW) first-half operating profit
– operating profit in the first six months
Halbjahresbilanz *f* (Fin) semi-annual balance sheet
Halbjahresdividende *f* (Fin) semi-annual dividend
Halbjahresprämie *f* (Vers) semi-annual (*or* half-yearly) premium
Halbjahreszahlung *f* (Fin) semi-annual payment
halbjährlich
(com) semi-annual
– (GB) half-yearly
halbkundenspezifisch
(com, EDV) semi-custom
Halbleiter *m* (EDV) semiconductor
Halbleiterfestwertspeicher *m* (EDV) semiconductor read only memory
Halbleiterspeicher *m* (EDV) semiconductor memory
Halbleitertechnik *f* (EDV) semiconductor technology
halblogarithmische Schreibweise *f* (EDV) variable-point representation (*syn, Gleitpunktschreibweise: floating point representation*)
Halbraum *m* (Math) half space
halbstetige Funktion *f* (Math) semi-continuous function
Halbsubtrahierer *m* (EDV) half subtractor
Halbtagsbeschäftigung *f* (Pw) half time work
Halbteilungsgrundsatz *m* (StR) rule of splitting
Halbwaren *fpl* (com) semi-finished goods
Halbwort *n* (EDV) half word
Halbzeug *n* (com) semi-finished products
Haltbefehl *m* (EDV) halt (*or* checkpoint) instruction (*syn, Stoppbefehl*)
Halteklammer *f* (com) retaining clip

Haltepršmie f (AuW) maintenance bonus (or premium)
Hamiltonscher Weg m (OR) Hamilton path
Handapparat m (EDV) telephone handset
Handbetrieb m (IndE) manual operation
Handbuch n (com) manual
Handeingabe f (EDV) keyboard input (or entry)
Handel m
  (com) trade (ie, process of buying, selling, or exchanging commodities)
  – commerce (esp. on a large scale)
  (AuW) trade and commercial dealings (ie, with a particular country)
  (com) deal
  – bargain
  – commercial transaction
  (Mk) distributive trade
  (Bö) trading
  – dealing
  (Bö) professional traders (syn, Berufshandel)
Handel m **abschließen** (com) to strike a bargain
Handel m **aussetzen** (Bö) to suspend trading
handelbare Option f (Bö) traded option
Handel m **in Festverzinslichen** (Bö) bond trading
Handel m **in Freiverkehrswerten** (Bö) over-the-counter trading in unlisted securities
Handel m **in Wertpapieren** (Bö) trading (or dealing) in securities
Handel m **mit aufgeschobener Erfüllung** (Bö) trading per account
Handel m **mit Bezugsrechten** (Fin) rights dealings
Handel m **mit eigenen Aktien** (Fin) traffic in (a company's) own shares
Handel m **mit Waren zweiter Hand** (com) trade with second-hand goods (ie, usually revamped prior to resale)
handeln
  (com) to buy and sell
  – to trade
  – to carry on trade
  (Bö) to trade (ie, on the stock exchange)
Handel m **nach festgelegten Eigenschaften** (com) dealing by graded description
Handeln n **auf eigene Gefahr** (Re) acting at own risk
handeln für den es angeht
  (com) to act for whom it may concern
  – to act ad personam incertam
handeln, im Freiverkehr (Bö) to trade over the counter
handeln, im Telefonverkehr (Bö) to trade in the unofficial market
handeln mit
  (com) to deal in (eg, certain commodities)
  – to trade in
Handel m **per Erscheinen** (Bö) trading in securities not yet issued
Handel m **per Termin** (Bö) trading for future delivery
Handelsabkommen n (AuW) trade agreement
handelsablenkende Wirkungen fpl (AuW) trade diversion (ie, of a customs union)
Handelsagent m
  (com) commercial agent
  – trade representative

Handelsakzept n (Fin) trade acceptance
Handelsattaché m (AuW) commercial attaché (ie, of an embassy)
Handelsbeschränkungen fpl (AuW) trade restrictions
Handelsbetrieb m (Mk) business engaged in the distributive trade (ie, general term covering wholesale and retail establishments)
Handelsbevollmächtigter m (Re) = Handlungsbevollmächtigter
Handelsbezeichnung f (Pat) trade name
Handelsbeziehungen fpl
  (com) trade relations
  – trading links
Handelsbeziehungen fpl **aufnehmen** (com) to enter into trade relations
Handelsbilanz f
  (ReW) commercial balance sheet (opp, Steuerbilanz = tax balance sheet)
  (AuW) balance to trade
  – trade balance
  – balance on merchandise trade
  – merchandise account (or balance)
Handelsbilanzüberschuß m
  (AuW) trade surplus
  – surplus on visible trade
Handelsblöcke mpl (AuW) trade (or trading) blocs
Handelsbrauch m
  (com) trade
  – business
  – commercial
  – mercantile ... usage
  – custom of the trade
  – mercantile custom
  – usage of the market (or trade)
Handelsbrief m (com) commercial (or business) letter
Handelsbücher npl (ReW) commercial books of account
Handelsbürgschaft f (Re) guaranty in the nature of a commercial transaction, §§ 349, 350 HGB
handelschaffende Wirkungen fpl (AuW) trade creation (ie, of a customs union)
Handelsdefizit n (AuW) trade deficit
Handelseinheit f
  (Bö) unit of trading
  – marketable parcel
  – regular lot
Handelsembargo n
  (AuW) trade embargo
  – embargo on trade
Handelserleichterungen fpl (AuW) trade concessions
Handelsfachzeitschrift f (com) trade journal
handelsfähig
  (com) marketable
  – merchantable
  (WeR) negotiable
Handelsfaktura f (com) commercial invoice
Handelsfixkauf m (Re) executory commercial contract (ie, performance of one party taking place at a fixed time or within a fixed period, § 376 HGB)
Handelsflagge f (com) trading flag
Handelsflotte f (com) merchant fleet

Handelsfrau *f* (com) female merchant
Handelsfreiheit *f* (AuW) freedom of trade
Handelsfunktionen *fpl* (Vw) functions of the distributive trade
Handelsgericht *n* (Re) commercial court *(ie, now reduced to ‚Kammer für Handelssachen der Landgerichte')*
Handelsgeschäft *n*
(com) trading establishment
(Re) commercial business, §§ 22–28 HGB
(Re) commercial act *(ie, act of a merchant which pertains to the carrying on of his trade or business, § 343 HGB)*
Handelsgesellschaft *f*
(com) trading partnership
– trading company
(Re) ‚commercial company' *(ie, the referent of the German term is in fact untranslatable; it covers: OHG, KG, AG, KGaA, GmbH; not included are: stille Gesellschaft, Erwerbs- und Wirtschaftsgenossenschaften)*
Handelsgesetzbuch *n* (Re) German Commercial Code, 10 May 1897
Handelsgewerbe *n* (Re) commercial enterprise *(ie, comprises the legal forms of: Mußkaufmann, Sollkaufmann, Kannkaufmann, Formkaufmann, as defined in §§ 1–6 HGB)*
Handelsgut *n*
(com) merchandise
– merchantable good
(ie, of average description and quality, § 360 HGB)
Handelsgut *n* **mittlerer Art und Güte** (com) fair average quality, faq
Handelshemmnisse *npl*
(AuW) barriers to trade
– trade barriers (*or* restrictions)
Handelsindifferenzkurve *f* (AuW) trade indifference curve
Handelskammer *f* (com) Chamber of Commerce
Handelskauf *m* (Re) commercial sale, §§ 373–382 HGB
Handelskette *f* (Mk) sales (*or* marketing) chain
Handelsklassen *fpl* (com) grades *(ie, quality standards for farm and fishery products)*
Handelsklauseln *fpl* (com) trade terms *(eg, ex works, CIF, FOB)*
Handelskorrespondenz *f* (com) business (*or* commercial) correspondence
Handelskosten *pl* (Bö) trading costs
Handelskredit *m* (Fin) trade credit
Handelskreditbrief *m* (Fin) commercial letter of credit
Handelskrieg *m*
(AuW) economic warfare
– trade war
Handelsliberalisierung *f* (AuW) trade liberalization
Handelsmakler *m*
(com) commercial
– mercantile
- merchandise ... broker
– mercantile agent, § 93 HGB
Handelsmarine *f* (com) merchant marine
Handelsmarke *f* (Mk) dealer's brand *(ie, used by wholesalers and retailers; syn, Handelszeichen; opp, Fabrikmarke)*
Handelsmarke *f* **e-s Großhändlers** (Mk) dealer brand
handelsmäßige Bewertung *f* (Zo) commercial valuation
handelsmäßige Tatsachen *fpl* (Zo) commercial facts
Handelsmesse *f* (com) trade fair
Handelsmißbrauch *m* (Kart) trade custom violating ‚bonos mores'
Handelsmittler *m*
(com) trade intermediary
– middleman
Handelsname *m* (Re) name of a firm *(ie, designating a natural or legal person, or the members of a partnership)*
Handelsniederlassung *f* (com) trading establishment
Handelsoptimum *n* (Vw) exchange optimum *(syn, Tauschoptimum)*
Handelspapiere *npl*
(com) commercial documents
(WeR) commercial paper *(ie, mainly comprising instruments made out to bearer and to order)*
Handelspartner *m* (com) trading partner
Handelspolitik *f* (AuW) foreign trade policy
handelspolitisch
(AuW) in terms of
– relating to
– affecting ... foreign trade policy
Handelspräferenzen *fpl* (AuW) trade preferences
Handelsprivileg *n, mostly* pl. (Vw, *historical*) trade privilege
Handelsrabatt *m* (com) trade rebate *(ie, final retail price minus ‚Handelsrabatt')*
Handelsrechnung *f*
(com) commercial invoice
– (GB) trading invoice
Handelsrecht *n* (Re) commercial (*or* business) law
handelsrechtlich
(Re) in terms of
– relating to
– affecting ... commercial law
handelsrechtliche Bewertung *f* (StR) commercial valuation *(opp, steuerrechtliche Bewertung = tax-based valuation)*
handelsrechtliche Buchführungsvorschriften *fpl* (ReW) commercial accounting standards *(see: §§ 38–47 HGB, §§ 148 and 151ff AktG, and §§ 41ff GmbHG, and ministerial ordinance of 11 Nov 1937)*
Handelsregister *n*
(Re) Commercial Register
– *(British equivalent)* Register of Business Names
Handelsregisterauszug *m* (Re) certificate of registration
Handelsregistereinsicht *f* (Re) inspection of Commercial Register *(ie, includes all documents submitted to it, § 9 HGB)*
Handelsreisender *m* (com) commercial traveler
Handelsrestriktionen *fpl*
(AuW) trade restrictions
– barriers to trade

Handelsrichter *m* (Re) honorary commercial judge *(ie, appointed at the suggestion of a chamber of industry and commerce for a term of three years, §§ 107–113 GVG)*
Handelssachen *fpl* (Re) commercial matters in controvery (*or* dispute)
Handelsschiffahrt *f* (com) commercial shipping
Handelsschranke *f*
 (AuW) barrier to trade
 – trade barrier (*or* restriction)
Handelsschranken *fpl* **abbauen** (Vw) to dismantle (*or* reduce) trade barriers
Handelsschranken *fpl* **errichten** (Vw) to put up (*or* erect) trade barriers
Handelssitten *fpl* (com) = *Handelsbrauch*
Handelsspanne *f*
 (com) margin
 – operating margin
 – price margin
 – trade margin
 (ie, equal to difference between selling and purchase price)
Handelssperre *f* (AuW) trade embargo
Handelssprache *f* (com) commercial jargon
Handelsstatistik *f* (Stat) trade statistics *(ie, covering domestic trade and foreign trade)*
Handelsstrom *m* (AuW) flow of trade
Handelsüberschuß *m* (AuW) trade surplus
handelsüblich
 (com) customary in trade or commerce
 (com) commercially available
handelsübliche Bezeichnung *f*
 (com) commercial description
 – customary description (*or* designation)
handelsübliche Brauchbarkeit *f* (com) merchantableness
handelsübliche Dokumente *npl* (com) commercial documents *(eg, warehouse receipt, bill of lading)*
handelsübliche Güte *f* **und Beschaffenheit** *f* (com) good merchantable quality and condition
handelsübliche Mengen *fpl* (com) commercial quantities
handelsübliche Qualität *f* (com) merchantable quality
handelsübliches Risiko *n* (com) customary risk
handelsübliche Vertragsklauseln *fpl* (com) trade terms
handelsüblich verpackt (com) packed to commercial standards
Handels- und Entwicklungskonferenz *f* **der Vereinten Nationen** (Vw) UNCTAD: United Nations Conference on Trade and Development
Handels- und Zahlungsabkommen *n* (AuW) trade and payments agreement
Handelsunternehmen *n* (com) trading firm
Handelsusancen *fpl* (com) = *Handelsbrauch*
Handelsverbindungen *fpl* (com) trade connections
Handelsvereinbarungen *fpl* (AuW) trade agreements
Handelsverkehr *m* (com) trade and commerce
Handelsvertrag *m* (AuW) trade agreement
Handelsvertreter *m*
 (Re) commercial agent (*or* representative), § 84 HGB
 (com) traveling salesman

 – (GB) commercial traveller
Handelsvertreter *m* **mit delcredere** (com) delcredere agent
Handelsvertretung *f* (com) commercial (*or* sales) agency
handelsverzerrende Maßnahmen *fpl* (AuW) trade distorting policies
Handelsvolumen *n* (AuW) foreign trade volume
Handelswaren *fpl*
 (com) merchandise
 (Bw) merchandise held for resale
Handelswechsel *m*
 (Fin) trade
 – commercial
 – commodity ... bill *(syn, Warenwechsel)*
Handelsweg *m*
 (com) distributive channel
 – channel of distribution
Handelswert *m*
 (com) commercial (*or* market) value *(ie, subcategory of ‚gemeiner Wert')*
 (SeeV) common market value
Handelszeichen *n* (Mk) = *Handelsmarke*
Handelszensus *m* (Stat) trade census
Handelszentrum *n* (com) trade center
Handelszoll *m* (Zo) trading tariff
handhabbar (com) manageable
Handhabungsgeräte *npl* (IndE) handling equipment
Handhabungskosten *pl* (KoR) handling cost
Handkauf *m* (com) cash sale *(ie, payment being made in full on receipt of goods; syn, Realkauf)*
Handlager *n* (MaW) stock of small parts *(ie, held available at job stations)*
Händler *m* (com) trader *(ie, general term describing wholesaler, retail saler, itinerant trader, etc.)*
 (Bö) dealer or trader in securities
 (ie, includes domestic and foreign banks and other credit institutions, domestic and foreign exchange brokers, the Bundesbank, etc., § 21 KVStG)
Händlerarbitrage *f* (AuW) dealer (*or* trader) arbitrage
Händlergeschäfte *npl* (Bö) dealer transactions, § 22 KVStG *(ie, transactions among dealers or traders in securities, § 20 KVStG)*
Händlergewinn *m* (Bö) turn
Händlerinterview *n* (Mk) dealer interview
Händlerkette *f* (Mk) dealer chain
Händlermarke *f* (Mk) private (*or* dealer's) brand
Händlernetz *n* (Mk) dealer network
Händlerorganisation *f*
 (Mk) dealership network
 – dealer organization
Händlerprovision *f* (Bö) dealer commission
Händlerrabatt *m*
 (com) dealer rebate
 – distributor discount
Händlerspanne *f* (com) dealer's margin
Händlerzusammenschluß *m* (com) dealer organization
Handleser *m*
 (EDV) hand-held reader
 – code (*or* data) pen
 (syn, Lesestift, Lesepistole)

Handlocher *m* (EDV) keypunch
Handlochkarte *f* (EDV) hand-operated punched card *(syn, Nadellochkarte)*
Handlungen *fpl* **und Unterlassungen** *fpl* (Re) acts and forbearances
Handlung *f* **od Unterlassung** *f* (Re) act or failure to act
Handlungsagent *m* (com) = *Handelsvertreter*
Handlungsalternative *f*
 (Vw, Bw) alternative course of action
 – action alternative
Handlungs-Autoritäts-Struktur *f* (Bw) activity-authority structure
Handlungsbevollmächtigter *m* (Re) *(no counterpart in English)* holder of commercial authority, § 54 HGB *(ie, ranking below ‚Prokurist')*
Handlungseinheit *f*
 (Bw) operating unit
 – actor *(eg, household, company)*
Handlungsfähigkeit *f* (Re, *generic term*) capacity for acts in the law and for unlawful acts *(ie, Geschäftsfähigkeit + Deliktsfähigkeit)*
Handlungsgehilfe *m*
 (Re) commercial clerk, § 59 HGB
 – dependent commercial employee
 (ie, term now obsolete)
Handlungslehrling *m* (com) commercial apprentice *(ie, §§ 66ff HGB repealed; current term: Auszubildender, Azubi)*
Handlungsprogramm *n* (Bw) action program
Handlungsrahmen *m* (Bw) universe of actions
Handlungsreisender *m* (com) traveling salesman
Handlungsspielraum *m* (com) room for maneuver
Handlungstheorie *f* (Vw) theory of action
Handlungsunkosten *pl* (KoR, *obsolete term*) overhead expenses
Handlungsvollmacht *f* (Re) „commercial authority" *(ie, limited authority to represent a firm or company, defined in § 54 HGB, narrower than ‚Prokura' and not entered in the Commercial Register)*
Handlungsvollzug *m* (Bw) action
Hand-Mund-Kauf *m* (Mk) hand-to-mouth buying
Handsteuerung *f* (EDV) manual control
Handverkauf *m*
 (com) open sale
 (Bö) over-the-counter sale
Handwerk *n*
 (com) craft
 – trade
 (ie, trade or occupation requiring prolonged training and special skill; eg, the craft of a mason, the trade of a carpenter)
 (com) craft *(ie, members of trade collectively)*
Handwerker *mpl* (com) artisans and tradesmen
Handwerkerinnung *f* (com) trade *(or* craft*)* guild
handwerkliche Ausbildung *f* (Pw) training for a trade
handwerkliche Erzeugnisse *npl* (com) craft products
Handwerksbetrieb *m* (com) craft business *(or* establishment*) (ie, formal criterion is the entry into a special register, the ‚Handwerksrolle')*
Handwerkskammer *f* (com) Chamber of Handicrafts
Handwerkslehre *f* (Pw) craft apprenticeship
Handwerksmeister *m* (com) master craftsman
Handwerksrolle *f* (com) Register of Craftsmen
Handzeichen *n* (com) initials
Handzettel *m*
 (Mk) handbill
 – throwaway
Handzuführungslocher *m* (EDV) hand feed punch
Hängeablage *f* (com) suspension file
Hanseatische Wertpapierbörse *f* (Bö) Hamburg Stock Exchange
Hantierungsvorschrift *f* (EDV) handling specification
harmonische Analyse *f* (Math) harmonic analysis
harmonische Folge *f* (Math) harmonic progression
harmonische Funktion *f* (Math) harmonic function
harmonische Reihe *f* (Stat) harmonic series
harmonischer Mittelwert *m* (Stat) harmonic average *(or* mean*)*
Harmonisierung *f* (Bw, Vw, EG) harmonization
Harrod-neutraler Fortschritt *m* (Vw) Harrod-neutral technical progress
Harrod-Paradoxon *n* (Vw) Harrod paradox
Härtefall *m* (Re) case of hardship
harte Währung *f* (AuW) hard currency *(ie, freely convertible and steadily priced at foreign exchange markets)*
Hartgeld *n* (Vw) coins
Hartkopie *f* (EDV) hard copy
Hartwährungsland *n* (AuW) hard currency country
Hardware *f* (EDV) hardware
Hardware-Wartung *f* (EDV) hardware maintenance
Hartweizen *m* (com) hard *(or* durum*)* wheat
hauchdünne Minderheit *f*
 (Pw) tiny
 – thin
 – (infml) skinny ... majority
häufiger Stellenwechsel *m* (Pw) job hopping
Häufigkeit *f* (Stat) frequency
Häufigkeitsdichte *f* (Stat) frequency density
Häufigkeitsfunktion *f* (Stat) frequency function
Häufigkeitskurve *f* (Stat) frequency curve
Häufigkeitsmaß *n* (Stat) measure of frequency
Häufigkeitsmoment *n* (Stat) frequency moment
Häufigkeitspolygon *n* (Stat) frequency polygon *(syn, Treppen-Polygon)*
Häufigkeitssummenkurve *f* (Stat) Galton ogive
Häufigkeitstabelle *f* (Stat) frequency table
Häufigkeitstheorie *f* **der Wahrscheinlichkeit** (Stat) frequency theory of probability
Häufigkeitsverteilung *f* (Stat) frequency distribution
häufigster Wert *m* (Stat) mode
Häufigkeitspunkt *m* **e-r Menge**
 (Math) accumulation
 – cluster
 – limit ... point
 – point of condensation
Hauptablage *f* (com) central filing department
Hauptabsatzgebiet *n* (Mk) principal market area
Hauptabsatzmarkt *m* (Mk) main *(or* prime*)* market
Hauptabschlußübersicht *f*
 (ReW) condensed tabular statement of balance sheet figures, § 60 II EStDV

– general ledger trial balance
Hauptabschnittsdeterminante *f* (Math) principal minor
Hauptabteilung *f* (Bw) main (*or* principal) department
Hauptaktionär *m*
(Fin) principal shareholder (*or* stockholder)
– principal member
hauptamtlicher Richter *m* (Re) full-time (*or* permanent) judge
Hauptanbieter *m* (com) main (*or* principal) bidder
Hauptanmeldung *f* (Pat) basic application
Hauptanspruch *m*
(Re) principal claim
(Pat) first (*or* main) claim
Hauptaufgabenbereich *m*
(Pw) major job segment
– main operational task
Hauptauftragnehmer *m* (Bw) prime contractor
Hauptausfall *m* (Stat) major failure
Hauptband *n* (EDV) master tape
Hauptbedienungsplatz *m* (EDV) main console
Hauptbereich *m* (com) key area
Hauptberuf *m* (Stat) main occupation
hauptberuflicher Vertreter *m* (Vers) full-time agent
Hauptbetrieb *m* (IndE) principal plant
Hauptbieter *m* (com) base bidder *(ie, in contract awarding)*
Hauptbuch *n*
(ReW) general ledger
– book of secondary (*or* final) entry
Hauptbuchhaltung *f* (ReW) general bookkeeping department
Hauptbuchkonto *n* (ReW) general ledger account *(syn, Sachkonto)*
Hauptbuchprobe *f* (ReW) general ledger test *(ie, adding the debit and credit sides of all accounts must produce identical totals)*
Hauptbuchunterlagen *fpl* (ReW) general records
Hauptbürge *m* (Re) chief guarantor *(eg, for most of the borrowings of the principal leasing company)*
Hauptbüro *n* (Bw) head office
Hauptdatei *f* (EDV) master file
Hauptdiagonale *f* (Math) main (*or* principal) diagonal of a matrix
Hauptdimension *f* (com) key dimension
Hauptergebnisbereich *m* (Bw) key result area
Haupterfindung *f* (Pat) main invention
Haupterwerbsstelle *f* (com) full-time farm *(opp, Nebenerwerbsstelle = part-time farm)*
Haupterzeugnis *n*
(Bw) main
– major
– chief . . . product
(ie, in joint production; opp, Nebenerzeugnis, Nebenprodukt = byproduct)
Hauptfach *n*
(Pw) major
– (GB) main subject
(ie, read by university students; opp, Nebenfach)
Hauptfehler *m* (Stat) major defect
Hauptfeststellung *f* (StR) principal assessment *(ie, regularly occurring determination of assessed values, § 21 BewG)*

Hauptfeststellungszeitpunkt *m* (StR) principal assessment date, § 21 II BewG
Hauptfeststellungszeitraum *m* (StR) principal assessment period, § 21 I BewG
Hauptforderung *f* (Re) principal claim
Hauptfrachtvertrag *m* (com) head charter
Hauptgemeinschaft *f* **des deutschen Einzelhandels** (com) Central Association of German Retail Traders
Hauptgenossenschaft *f* (com) central cooperative *(ie, supplying the ‚Raiffeisengenossenschaften' with fertilizer, farm machinery, etc.)*
Hauptgeschäftsführer *m* (com) chief manager
Hauptgeschäftsgegend *f* (com) main business area
Hauptgeschäftssitz *m* (Re) main (*or* principal) place of business
Hauptgeschäftsstelle *f* (com) principal office
Hauptgeschäftszeit *f* (com) peak business hours
Hauptgesellschaft *f* (Bw) principal company, § 319 AktG
Hauptgläubiger *m*
(Re) main
– primary
– principal . . . creditor
– principal obligor
Hauptgruppenkontrolle *f* (EDV) intermediate control
Hauptgruppentrennung *f* (EDV) intermediate control change
Hauptgruppentrennzeichen *n* (EDV) file separator
Hauptgruppenwechsel *m* (EDV) intermediate control change
Haupthandelspartner *m* (AuW) major trading partner
Hauptindex *m* (EDV) master index
Hauptindustrieländer *npl* (Vw) key industrial countries
Hauptkapazität *f* (IndE) main capacity *(eg, crude steel and rolled products in iron and steel plants)*
Hauptkarte *f* (EDV) master card
Hauptkasse *f* (Fin) main cashier's office
Hauptkassierer *m* (Fin) chief cashier
Hauptkonto *n* (ReW) ledger account
Hauptkontrakt *m* (Bw) prime (*or* system) contract
Hauptkostenstelle *f*
(KoR) production cost center
– direct cost center
– direct department
Hauptkunde *m* (com) main (*or* principal) customer
Hauptlager *n* (MaW) central store (*or* stockroom)
Hauptlieferant *m* (com) main supplier
Hauptmangel *m* (Re) principal defect
Hauptmarkt *m* (com) primary (*or* principal) market
Hauptmerkmal *n* (com) key (*or* leading) feature
Hauptmerkmal *n* **e-s Begriffs** (Log) earmark of a concept
Hauptminor *m* (Math) principal minor
Hauptniederlassung *f* (com) principal establishment
Hauptorganisationseinheit *f* (Bw) main organizational unit
Hauptpatent *n*
(Pat) independent
– main
– original . . . patent

Hauptpflichten *fpl* (Re) principal obligations
Hauptplan *m* (Bw) master (*or* major) plan
Hauptplatz *m* (Fin) main center *(ie, in foreign exchange trading this is the place where currency must be delivered; eg, Copenhagen, Frankfurt, New York, Montreal; often shown in foreign exchange list of quotations)*
Hauptpolice *f* (Vers) master policy
Hauptprodukt *n* (com) main (*or* leading) product
Hauptprogramm *n* (EDV) main program (*or* routine)
Hauptprozeß *m* (EDV) major task
Hauptprüfer *m*
 (ReW) principal *(ie, in a CPA firm)*
 (Pat) examiner-in-chief
 – chief examiner
Hauptreservewährungsland *n* (AuW) principal reserve currency country
Hauptsache *f* (Re) principal thing, § 97 BGB
Hauptsaison *f* (com) peak season
Hauptsatz *m*
 (Math) central theorem
 (EDV) master record
Hauptsatz *m* **der Algebra** (Math) fundamental law (*or* theorem) of algebra
Hauptsatz *m* **der Differential- und Integralrechnung** (Math) fundamental theorem of calculus
Hauptschiffahrtsweg *m* (com) major shipping lane
Hauptschuldner *m*
 (Re) principal debtor, § 767 BGB
 – principal
 – primary debtor (*or* obligor)
Hauptschule *f* (Pw) non-selective secondary modern school
Hauptsendezeit *f*
 (Mk) prime time *(ie, in television)*
 – (GB) peak viewing time
Hauptsicherheit *f* (Re) primary security
Hauptsitz *m*
 (com) head office
 – headquarters
 (Re) principal (*or* main) place of business
Hauptsparte *f*
 (com) main line
 – bottom line
 (ie, of a business, trade, or industry)
Hauptspediteur *m* (com) principal forwarding agent
Hauptspeicher *m* (EDV) main (*or* primary) storage
Hauptsteuertermin *m* (StR) big tax date
Haupttätigkeit *f* (IndE) core activity
Haupttheorem *n* (Log) major theorem
Hauptunterbrechungsregister *n* (EDV) main interrupt register
Hauptunternehmer *m* (com) general (*or* prime) contractor
Haupturkunde *f* (WeR) principal instrument
Hauptveranlagung *f* (StR) principal assessment, § 15 VStG, § 16 GrStG
Hauptveranlagungszeitpunkt *m* (StR) date of basic assessment, § 24 VStG
Hauptveranlagungszeitraum *m* (StR) basic assessment period
Hauptverantwortungsbereich *m* (Bw) key responsibility center

Hauptverband *m* **der Deutschen Bauindustrie** (com) German Building Industry Association
Hauptverbindlichkeit *f*
 (Re) principal obligation, § 767 BGB
 (WR) primary liability
Hauptversammlung *f*
 (Re) general meeting of shareholders
 – (GB, *also*) the company in general meeting *(ie, legal organ of ‚Aktiengesellschaft' and ‚Kommanditgesellschaft auf Aktien', §§ 118–128, 285 AktG)*
Hauptversammlungsbeschluß *m* (Re) shareholders' (*or* stockholders') resolution
Hauptversicherer *m* (Vers) primary insurer
Hauptversicherung *f* (Vers) direct insurance
Hauptverteiler *m* (EDV) main distribution frame
Hauptvertrag *m* (Re) main (*or* original) contract
Hauptverwaltung *f*
 (com) headquarters
 – central headquarters
 – corporate (*or* company) headquarters
 – head office
 – main office
Hauptvorstand *m* (com) executive (*or* governing) board
Hauptzahlstelle *f* (Fin) principal paying agent
Hauptziel *n* (Vw, Bw) key goal
Hauptzinstermin *m* (Fin) principal coupon date
Hauptzollamt *n* (Zo) principal custom house, § 13 FVG
Hauptzweigstelle *f* (Fin) principal branch office *(ie, of savings banks, handling inpayments, outpayments, and customers' accounts)*
Hausadresse *f* (EDV) home (*or* track) address
Hausadressesatz *m* (EDV) home record
Hausangestellte *f* (Pw) household employee
Hausbank *f*
 (Fin) house bank *(ie, affiliated to a company and acting as principal banker in its behalf)*
 (FiW) house bank
 – principal banker
 (ie, affiliated to a governmental unit; eg, Federal Bank operating on behalf of Bund and Länder, savings banks on behalf of municipalities)
Hausbestand *m* (Vw) housing stock
hauseigener Rechner *m* (EDV) in-house computer
Hausgehilfin *f* (StR) domestic help
hausgemachte Inflation *f* (Vw) home-made (*or* internal) inflation
hausgemachter Preisauftrieb *m* (Vw) home-made price increase
Hausgeräteindustrie *f* (com) domestic (*or* home) appliance industry
Haushalt *m*
 (Vw, Stat) household
 (FiW) budget
Haushalts ...
 (FiW) budget
 – budgetary
Haushaltsansatz *m* (FiW) budget estimate
Haushaltsausgaben *fpl* (FiW) budget expenditure
Haushaltsausgleich *m* (FiW) balancing of budget, Art 110 GG
Haushaltsausschuß *m* (FiW) budget committee

− committee on the budget
− appropriations committee
Haushaltsbelastung f (FiW) burden on the budget
Haushaltsbesteuerung f (StR) taxation of households *(ie, of spouses and children liable in taxes)*
Haushaltsbewilligung f (FiW) appropriation
haushaltsbezogene Dienstleistungen fpl (VGR) household-related services
Haushaltsdebatte f (FiW) budget debate
Haushaltsdefizit n (FiW) budget deficit (*or* shortfall)
Haushaltsdefizit n **abbauen** (FiW) to reduce (*or* pare down) a budget deficit
Haushaltseinkommen n (VGR) income of individual household
Haushaltseinnahmen fpl (FiW) budget receipts (*or* revenue)
Haushaltsentwurf m
(FiW) draft budget
− budget draft
− proposed budget
− fiscal blueprint
Haushaltsfehlbetrag m (FiW) = *Haushaltsdefizit*
Haushaltsforschung f (Mk) household research
Haushaltsfragen fpl (FiW) budget matters
Haushaltsfreibetrag m (StR) household allowance, EStG 32 III
Haushaltsgebaren n (FiW) budgetary behavior *(ie, of public sector)*
Haushaltsgelder npl (FiW) public money
Haushaltsgerätehersteller m (com) household appliances manufacturer
Haushaltsgesetz n (FiW) budget law
Haushaltsgrundsätze mpl (FiW) basic rules governing budget law *(ie, of Bund and Länder, laid down in law of 19 Aug 1969)*
Haushaltshilfe f
(StR) household allowance
(StR) part-time domestic help
Haushaltsjahr n (FiW) financial (*or* fiscal) year
Haushaltskonsolidierung f (FiW) budget consolidation
Haushaltskontrolle f (FiW) budget control
Haushaltskürzung f (FiW) budget cut (*or* slash)
Haushaltslage f (FiW) budgetary position
Haushaltsliste f (Stat) household census form
Haushaltslücke f (FiW) budget gap
Haushaltsmittel pl (FiW) budget (*or* public) funds
Haushaltsmittel pl **beantragen** (FiW) to apply for the appropriation of budget funds
Haushaltsmittel pl **bewilligen** (FiW) to approve (*or* grant) the appropriation of budget funds
Haushaltsmittel pl **kürzen**
(FiW) to cut
− to pare down
− to trim ... budget funds
Haushaltsmittel pl **übertragen** (FiW) to transfer budget funds
Haushaltsmittel pl **zuteilen** (FiW) to allocate budget funds
Haushaltsnachfrage f (Vw) consumer demand
Haushaltsoptimum n (Vw) optimum commodity combination of household
Haushaltspackung f (Mk) family size package
Haushaltspanel n (Mk) household panel

Haushaltsperiode f (FiW) budget period
Haushaltsplan m (FiW) budget
Haushaltsplan m **aufstellen**
(FiW) to draw up
− to draft
− to prepare ... a budget
Haushaltsplanung f (FiW) budgetary planning
Haushaltsplan m **verabschieden** (FiW) to pass a budget
Haushaltspolitik f (FiW) budgetary policies
Haushaltsprüfung f (FiW) budget (*or* public) audit
Haushaltsrechnung f (FiW) receipt-expenditure accounting *(ie, of government units = Gebietskörperschaften)*
Haushalts-Rechnungseinheit f (EG) budgetary unit of account
Haushaltsrecht n (FiW) budget law
haushaltsrechtliche Beschränkungen fpl (FiW) budgetary restrictions
haushaltsrechtliche Bestimmungen fpl (FiW) budgetary regulations
Haushaltsreform f (FiW) budget reform
Haushaltsrest m (FiW) unexpended balance of budgetary appropriation
Haushaltsstichprobe f (Stat) household sample
Haushaltsstrukturgesetz n (FiW) Budget Structure Law
haushaltstechnisch (FiW) pertaining to budget procedure
Haushaltstheorie f (Vw) consumer theory
Haushaltstitel m (FiW) budgetary item
Haushaltsüberschreitung f (FiW) budget runover
Haushaltsüberschuß m (FiW) budget surplus
Haushalt m **umschichten** (FiW) to revamp a budget
Haushaltsvoranschlag m (FiW) budget estimate (*or* proposal)
Haushaltswaren fpl (com) (durable and nondurable) consumer goods
Haushaltungsvorstand m (StR) head of household
Haus-Haus-Verkehr m (com) door-to-door delivery service
Hausierer m (com) door-to-door peddler
Hausindustrie f (com) domestic industry *(syn, Heimindustrie)*
Hausjurist m
(Re) in-house counsel
− company lawyer
− corporate attorney (*or* counsel)
„Hausmann" m (com) househusband
Hausmarke f (com) private (*or* house) brand
Hausratversicherung f (Vers) household and personal effects insurance
Haussatz m (EDV) home record *(syn, Mitlesesatz)*
Hausse f
(Bö) boom
(Bö) bull market
Hausse-Engagement n (Bö) long position
Haussekauf m (Bö) bull buying
Haussemarkt m (Bö) bullish market
Hausseposition f
(Bö) bull account
− long position
Haussespekulant m (Bö) bull
Haussespekulation f
(Bö) buying long

- bull operation (or speculation or transaction)
Haussetendenz f (Bö) bullish tendency
Haussier m
(Bö) bull
- bull operator
haussieren (Bö) to rise sharply
Haustürverkauf m (Mk) door-to-door selling
Hausvertreter m (Vers) home-service insurance man
Hauswirtschaftslehre f
(Pw) home economics
- (GB) domestic science
Hauszeitschrift f (com) house journal (or magazine)
Haus-zu-Haus-Container m (com) door-to-door container
Hauszustellung f
(com) door (or home) delivery
- delivery-by-hand service
Havarie f (SeeV) average
Havarieagent m (SeeV) average agent
Havarieaufmachung f (SeeV) settlement of average
Havarieberechnung f (SeeV) average assessment
Havariebericht m (SeeV) damage report
Havariebeteiligte mpl (SeeV) shipowner and the other cargo owners
Havariebond m (SeeV) general average bond
Havarie-Dispacheur m (SeeV) average adjuster
Havarieeinschuß m (SeeV) average contribution
Havarieerklärung f
(SeeV) average statement
- ship's protest
Havarieexperte m (SeeV) average surveyor
havariefrei (SeeV) free from average
Havariegeld n (SeeV) average disbursement
Havariegelder npl (SeeV) general average contributions
Havariegenossen mpl (SeeV) contributing interests
Havarie f **große** (SeeV) general average
Havarie-große-Beitrag m (SeeV) general average contribution
Havarie-große-Einschuß m (SeeV) general average deposit
Havarie-große-Ereignis n (SeeV) general average act
Havarie-große-Klausel f (SeeV) general average clause
Havarie-große-Verpflichtungsschein m (SeeV) general average bond
Havariegutachten n (SeeV) damage survey
Havarie-Kommissar m
(SeeV) claims agent
- average adjuster
Havarie f **nach Seebrauch** (SeeV) average accustomed
Havarieregelung f (SeeV) average adjustment
Havarie-Sachverständiger m (SeeV) (general) average adjuster
Havarieschaden m (SeeV) loss or damage to a vessel or to its cargo during a voyage
Havarieschäden mpl **abwickeln** (SeeV) to adjust average losses
Havarieschein m (SeeV) average certificate (or bond)

Havarieverteilung f (SeeV) average distribution
Havarievertrag m (SeeV) average agreement
Havariezertifikat n (SeeV) certificate of average
HDLC-Prozedur f (EDV) high level data link control
Hebegebühr f (Vers) premium collection fee
Hebelwirkung f **der Finanzstruktur** (Fin) leverage effect
Hebesatz m (StR) municipal factor (or percentage) *(ie, percentage of the basic rate = Steuermeßzahl, established annually by each municipality, § 16 GewStG and §§ 25, 26, 27 II GrStG; applied in determining trade and real property taxes)*
Heckscher-Ohlin-Theorem n
(AuW) Heckscher-Ohlin theorem (or law)
- factor proportions (endowment) theorem
Hedgegeschäft n (Bö) hedge transaction *(ie, in forward commodity business)*
Heftapparat m (com) stapler
heftige Kursausschläge mpl (Bö) erratic price movements
Heftklammer f
(com) staple *(ie, thin wire driven into sheets of paper)*
(com) paper clip (syn, Büroklammer)
Heftzwecke f
(com) thumbtack
- (GB) drawing pin
- (GB) push pin
Heimarbeit f (com) homework on contract
Heimathafen m (com) port of registry
Heimfahrten fpl (StR) trips home
Heimindustrie f (com) domestic industry
heimische Industrie f (Vw) domestic industry
heimischer Markt m (Vw) domestic market
heimisches Gericht n (Re) domestic court
heimische Waren fpl (Zo) home produced goods
heimische Wirtschaft f (Vw) domestic economy (or industry)
Heimrechner m (EDV) home computer
heißes Geld n (AuW) hot money *(ie, flowing between countries to benefit from interest-rate differentials)*
heiß umkämpfter Markt m
(com) fiercely competitive market
- hotly (or keenly) contested market
Heizkostenbeihilfe f (FiW) heating expenses subsidy
Heizölsteuer f
(StR) excise tax on heating oil
- heating oil tax
Heizungskosten pl (KoR) heating cost
hemmende Einrede f (Re) dilatory exception *(ie, not tending to defeat the action, but only to retard its progress)*
Hemmung f **der Verjährung**
(Re) stay of the period of limitation
- suspension of prescriptive period, § 202 BGB
herabgesetzter Preis m (com) reduced (or cut-rate) price
herabsetzen
(com) to reduce
- to lower
- to cut
(Fin) to reduce *(eg, capital)*

(Bö) to mark down *(ie, prices)*
herabsetzende Feststellung *f* (Re) injurious falsehood
herabsetzende Hinweise *mpl* (Kart) disparaging references *(ie, to a competitor's product)*
herabsetzende Werbung *f* (Mk) disparaging advertising
Herabsetzung *f* (Kart) denigration *(ie, of competitive products in advertising)*
Herabsetzung *f* **der Altersgrenze** (Pw) lowering *(or* reduction) of retirement age
Herabsetzung *f* **des Grundkapitals** (Re) reduction of capital
Herabsetzung *f* **des Kaufpreises** (com) reduction *(or* abatement) of purchase price
Herabsetzung *f* **des Rentenalters** (SozV) reduction of pensionable age
Herabstufung *f* **von Arbeitsplätzen** (Pw) downgrading (*or* de-skilling) of jobs
heraufsetzen
(com) to increase *(eg, prices)*
(Bö) to mark up *(ie, security prices)*
Herausgabeanspruch *m* (Re) right to recover possession
Herausgabeklage *f* (Re) action to recover possession
Herausgabepflicht *f* (Re) obligation to surrender possession
herauslegen
(com) to open
– to establish *(eg, a letter of credit)*
(Fin) to put out
– to lend out *(ie, money, funds)*
– to grant *(ie, a credit)*
herauszuholen suchen (com, infml) to hold out (*or* stick out) for *(eg, a higher profit during negotiations)*
Hereinnahme *f* **von Wechseln** (Fin) discounting of bills
hereinnehmen
(Fin) to take on deposit *(ie, funds)*
(Fin) to discount *(ie, a bill)*
Herkunftsbezeichnung *f*
(AuW) mark of origin
(Mk) informative labeling
– origin marking *(eg, of consumer goods)*
Herkunftsland *n* (com) country of origin
Herkunfts- und Verwendungsrechnung *f* (ReW) statement of changes in financial position
Herkunftszeichen *n* (com) mark of origin
Hermesdeckung *f* (AuW) Hermes export credit guaranty
(ie, covers transactions with private firms = Ausfuhrgarantie, and with foreign governments = Ausfuhrbürgschaft)
Hermes-Kreditversicherungs-AG *f* (AuW) West German Government-backed Hermes export credit insurance institution
hermitesche Form *f* (Math) Hermitian form
hermitesche Matrix *f* (Math) Hermitian matrix
Herrenausstatter *m* (com) men's outfitter
herrenlose Sachen *fpl* (Re) unpossessed property
herrschender Lohnsatz *m* (Vw) going (*or* prevailing) wage rate
herrschender Preis *m* (com) ruling price

herrschendes Unternehmen *n* (Bw) controlling (*or* dominant) enterprise, § 17 AktG
herstellen
(IndE) to make
– to manufacture *(esp. in large volume)*
– to produce *(ie, to make from sth)*
– to fabricate *(ie, by putting parts together)*
Hersteller *m*
(IndE) maker
– manufacturer
– producer
herstellereigener Bedarf *m* (com) in-house requirements
Herstellerfinanzierung *f* (Fin) financing of production *(ie, credit line offered by AKA)*
Herstellermarke *f* (Pat) manufacturer's brand *(eg, IBM, Coca-Cola)*
Herstellerwerbung *f* (Mk) producer advertising
Herstellkonto *n*
(ReW) manufacturing account
– work-in-process account
Herstellkosten *pl*
(com) cost of production
(KoR) product cost *(ie, Summe der Einzelkosten; opp, Periodenkosten)*
Herstellung *f*
(IndE) production
– manufacturing
Herstellungsaufwand *m*
(KoR) = *Herstellungskosten*
(StR) construction expenditure, Abschn. 157 EStR
Herstellungsgemeinkosten *pl* (KoR) productive fixed overhead *(ie, Materialgemeinkosten + Fertigungsgemeinkosten + Verwaltungsgemeinkosten, traceable to the materials and manufacturing sector)*
Herstellungskosten *pl*
(ReW) cost of production, § 153 AktG, § 6 EStG
– final manufacturing cost
– mill cost of sales
Herstellungsland *n* (AuW) producer country
Herstellungslizenz *f*
(Pat) license to manufacture
– manufacturing license
Herstellungsort *m* (com) place of manufacture
Herstellungswert *m* (ReW) cost of production
herunterhandeln
(com) to bargain down *(eg, your car dealer)*
– to beat down *(ie, prices)*
heruntersetzen
(com) to reduce
– to scale down
herunterspielen (com) to down-play *(eg, consequences)*
Herunterstufen *n* (Pw) downgrading
Hessesche Determinante *f* (Math) bordered Hessian determinant
heterogene Güter *npl* (Vw) heterogeneous goods
heterogene Konkurrenz *f* (Vw) heterogeneous competition *(see: Surrogatkonkurrenz)*
heterogenes Oligopol *n* (Vw) imperfect oligopoly
Heuer *f* (com) sailor's pay
heuristische Methode *f* (Bw) heuristic method

heuristische Programmierung *f* (OR) heuristic programming
heuristisches Modell *n* (Bw) heuristic model
heuristische Verfahren *npl* (Bw) heuristics
Hicks-arbeitsparender Fortschritt *m* (Vw) Hicks labor saving progress
Hicksches Diagramm *n* (Vw) Hick (IS-LM) diagram
Hierarchie *f* (Bw) hierarchy
Hierarchiestufen *fpl* (Bw) levels (*or* echelons) of authority
hierarchische Planung *f* (Bw) hierarchical planning
hierarchische Verdichtung *f* (EDV) hierarchical collation
Hifo (ReW) highest in-first out *(ie, method of valuing inventory, not permitted under German tax law)*
Hilfe *f* **bei der Wohnungsbeschaffung** (Pw) assisted housing
Hilfsabteilung *f* (Bw) general service department
Hilfsarbeit *f* (Pw) lowest-grade work
Hilfsarbeiter *m* (Pw) unskilled worker (*or* labor)
Hilfsarbeiterlöhne *mpl* (Pw) wages going to unskilled and semi-skilled employees *(ie, not to be confused with ‚indirect labor' = Hilfslöhne in cost accounting)*
Hilfsbetrieb *m* (IndE) auxiliary plant *(ie, such as power generation, maintenance, materials handling)*
Hilfsbogen *m* (ReW) work sheet
Hilfsbücher *npl* (ReW) subsidiary books of account *(eg, Kontokorrentbuch, Effektenbücher, Wareneingangs- und -ausgangsbuch)*
Hilfsfiskus *m* (FiW) auxiliary fiscal agent *(eg, churches, religious organizations, social insurance carriers, professional organizations, EC, World Bank)*
Hilfsgeschäfte *npl* (com) auxiliary (*or* subsidiary) transactions
Hilfsgewerbe *n* (Vers) auxiliary sector
Hilfskanal *m* (EDV) backward channel
Hilfskonto *n* (ReW) subsidiary account
Hilfskostenstelle *f* (KoR) indirect (*or* service) cost center
(syn, sekundäre Kostenstelle)
Hilfskräfte *fpl*
(Pw) auxiliary personnel
(Pw) supporting staff
Hilfslager *n* (MaW) standby inventory *(opp, Hauptlager = central store)*
Hilfsleistung *f* (SeeV) marine assistance, §§ 740–753 HGB
Hilfslohn *m* (SeeV) assistance money, § 740 HGB
Hilfslöhne *mpl* (KoR) indirect (*or* auxiliary) labor
Hilfsmaßzahl *f* (Stat) ancillary statistic
Hilfsmaterial *n* (KoR) indirect material
Hilfsmatrix *f* (Math) auxiliary matrix
Hilfspersonal *n* (Pw) supporting staff
Hilfsprüfer *m* (Pat) assistant examiner
Hilfsregister *n* (EDV) auxiliary register
Hilfssatz *m*
(Log) corollary
– helping theorem
– lemma
– subsidiary proposition

Hilfsspeicher *m* (EDV) auxiliary (*or* backing) store
(syn, Ergänzungsspeicher, Zubringerspeicher)
Hilfsstoffe *mpl*
(KoR) supplies
– factory supplies
– manufacturing supplies
– auxiliary material
Hilfstheorem *n* (Log) helping theorem *(syn, Hilfssatz)*
Hilfs- und Betriebsstoffe *mpl*
(ReW) supplies
– manufacturing supplies
Hilfs- und Nebengeschäfte *npl* (Fin) ancillary credit business *(ie, in the banking industry)*
Hilfsursprung *m* (Stat) arbitrary origin
Hilfsvariable *f* (OR) slack variable
hinaufsetzen
(com) to raise
– to mark up
hinausgeworfenes Geld *n* (com, infml) money thrown down the sink
hinauslegen
(com) to open *(ie, a letter of credit)*
(Fin) to put out *(ie, money)*
(Fin) to grant
– to extend *(ie, a loan or credit)*
Hinausschieben *n* **der Fälligkeiten** (Fin) postponement of maturity dates
Hinfracht *f*
(com) freight outward
– outward cargo (*or* freight)
Hingabe *f* **an Erfüllungs Statt**
(Re) delivery in full discharge
– transfer in lieu of performance
Hingabe *f* **an Zahlungs Statt** (Re) transfer in lieu of payment
Hingabe *f* **von Darlehen** (an) (Fin) lending of credit (to)
hinkende Goldwährung *f* (Vw) limping gold standard
hinkendes Inhaberpapier *n* (WeR) restricted bearer instrument
hinreichende Bedingung *f* (Log) sufficient condition
Hinreise *f* **e-s Schiffes** (com) outward-bound voyage
Hinterbliebene *pl*
(SozV) surviving dependents
– survivors
Hinterbliebenenbezüge *pl*
(SozV) surviving dependents' benefits
– survivors' benefits
Hinterbliebenenrente *f* (SozV) survivors' pension
Hinterbliebenenversicherung *f* (Vers) survivors' insurance
Hinterbliebenenversorgung *f* (SozV) survivors' pension
hintereinander geschaltete Kanäle *mpl* (OR) servers in series (*or* in tandem)
Hintergrunddaten *pl* (Bö) fundamentals
Hintergrundprogramm *n* (EDV) background program
Hintergrundspeicher *m* (EDV) backing storage
Hintergrundverarbeitung *f* (EDV) background processing

309

hinterherhinken (com) to lag behind
Hinterkante f (EDV) card trailing edge
hinterlassen (com) to leave *(ie, as an estate)*
 – (GB, sl) to cut up for *(eg, how much did he cut up for?)*
Hinterleger m (Re) bailor
hinterlegte Sache f (Re) deposited object, § 373 BGB
Hinterlegung f
 (Re) deposit *(or* lodgment) with a public authority, §§ 372ff BGB
 – safekeeping
 – warehousing
Hinterlegungsbescheinigung f
 (com) deposit receipt
 – certificate of deposit
Hinterlegungsgebühr f (com) deposit fee
Hinterlegungsort m (Re) place of lodgment, § 374 BGB
Hinterlegungsschein m (com) deposit certificate
Hinterlegungsstelle f (Re) depositing agent
Hinterlegungsvertrag m
 (Re) contract of deposit
 – deposit agreement
Hintermann m (com) straw man
Hintersatz m
 (Log) consequent
 – apodosis
hinterziehen (StR) to evade *(ie, taxes, customs duties)*
Hinterziehung f **von Steuern** (StR) tax evasion
Hin- und Rückflug m (com) outward and inward flight
Hin- und Rückfracht f (com) freight out and home
Hin- und Rückreise f (com) round trip
Hinweisdefinition f (Log) ostensive definition
Hinzurechnungen fpl (StR) additions, §§ 8, 12 II GewStG
Hinzuziehung f **von Sachverständigen** (com) employment of outside experts
Histogramm n
 (Stat) histogram
 – bar graph *(or* chart)
 – column diagram
 – frequency bar chart
historische Anschaffungskurse mpl (ReW) historical rates of exchange
historische Kosten pl
 (ReW) historical cost
 – (GB *also*) historic cost
historische Kosten pl**, auf Tageswert umgerechnet** (KoR) adjusted historical cost
 – historical cost translated to current market values
historische Kurse mpl (Fin) historical exchange rates
historische Schule f (Vw) historical school of economists
 (opp, classical school)
hocharbeiten (Pw) to work one's way through the ranks
Hochbau m (com) building construction
hochentwickelt (com) sophisticated
Hochfinanz f (Fin) high finance *(ie, dealing with large sums of money)*

hochgerechnete Erfolgsrechnung f (ReW) extrapolated income statement
hochgestellter Index m
 (Math) superscript
 – upper index
Hochhaus n
 (com) high rise building
 – (GB) multi-storey building
hochkarätiges Management n (com) high-caliber *(or* top-flight) management
Hochkonjunktur f
 (Vw) high-level economic activity
 – boom
 – prosperity
Hochleistungsrechner m (EDV) high performance computer
hochliquide Anlagen fpl (Fin) near cash
hochliquide Forderung f (Fin) highly liquid claim
Hochprozenter mpl (Fin) high-interest-rate bonds
hochqualifizierte Arbeitskräfte fpl (Pw) highly qualified manpower
hochrechnen
 (Stat) to extrapolate
 – to blow up *(ie, a sample)*
Hochrechnung f
 Stat) extrapolation
 – trend extrapolation
Hochrechnungsergebnis n (Stat) result of extrapolation
Hochrechnungsfaktor m (Stat) inflation *(or* raising) factor
Hochregallagersteuerung f (EDV) racking control system
hochrentierende Papiere npl
 (Fin) high yielding securities
 – high yielders
Hochsaison f (com) peak season
hochschleusen (EG) to push up *(ie, prices)*
Hochschreiben n **von Devisenbeständen** (AuW) write-up of currency holdings
Hochschulabschluß m (Pw) university degree
Hochschulausbildung f (Pw) university-type higher education
Hochschule f
 (Pw) university
 (Pw) establishment of higher education
Hochschulreife f
 (Pw) (attainment of) university entrance level
Hochschutzzollpolitik f (AuW) high protectionism
Hochseefischerei f (com) deap-sea *(or* deep-water) fishing
Hochseeschiffahrt f (com) ocean shipping
Hochspannungsmast m
 (IndE) high tension tower
 – pylon
Höchstabschreibung f (ReW) writeoff ceiling
Höchstangebot n (com) highest offer *(or* tender)
Höchstbeitrag m (SozV) maximum contribution
Höchstbelastungssatz m (FiW) psychological breaking point
 (eg, of a progressive income tax)
Höchstbetrag m (Fin) maximum *(or* threshold) amount
Höchstbetrag m **der Rallonge** (EG) maximum rallonge

Höchstbetragshypothek *f* (Fin) maximum-sum mortgage, § 1190 BGB
Höchstbietender *m* (com) highest bidder
Höchstdauer *f* (com) maximum duration
höchsteffiziente Schätzfunktion *f* (Stat) most efficient estimator
hochstehend (Bö) high priced
höchster Gruppenbegriff *m* (EDV, Cobol) final
Hochsteuerland *n* (AuW) high-tax country
Höchstgebot *n*
  (com) highest (*or* best) bid
  – highest tender
  – closing bid
Höchstgebühren *fpl* (com) fee ceilings
Höchstgehalt *n* (Pw) maximum salary
Höchsthaftungssumme *f* (Vers) maximum liability cover
Höchstkapazität *f* (Bw) maximum capacity
Höchstkurs *m*
  (Bö) highest price
  – all-time high
  – peak price
Höchstkurs *m* **im EWS** (AuW) upper exchange limit in the EMS
Höchstleistung *f* (Vers) maximum on claims payments
Höchstlohn *m*
  (Pw) top (*or* maximum) wage rate
  – wage ceiling
Höchstmiete *f* (Re) rent ceiling
höchstpersönliche Rechte *npl* (Re) rights which cannot be transferred
Höchstpreis *m*
  (com) maximum price
  – ceiling price
  – price ceiling
  – premium price
  – top price
  (Mk) price plateau *(ie, as accepted by buyers)*
Höchstqualität *f* (com) top quality
höchstrichterliche Entscheidung *f*
  (Re) decision of the highest court
  – supreme-court decision
Höchstschaden *m* (Vers) maximum possible loss *(ie, largest probable loss expected for a given risk assuming the most unfortuitous circumstances)*
Höchststand *m* (com) high
Höchststeuerland *n* (FiW) high tax country
Höchstsumme *f*
  (Vers) maximum limit
  – fixed insurance cover
höchstverzinsliche Wertpapiere *npl* (Bö) high yielders
Höchstwert *m* (ReW) highest value *(eg, under commercial valuation rules: original cost less depreciation for depreciable fixed assets, and the lower of cost or market for current assets)*
höchstwertiges Zeichen *n* (EDV) most significant character
Hochtechnologie *f*
  (IndE) high
  – advanced
  – state-of-the-art ... technology
  – (infml) high tech
  (syn, Spitzentechnologie)

hochtreiben (com) to drive up *(eg, prices)*
Hoch- und Tiefbau *m* (com) structural and civil engineering
hochverzinslich (Fin) high interest yielding
hochverzinsliche Anleihe *f* (Fin) high coupon loan
hochverzinsliche Langläufer *mpl* (Fin) high-coupon longs
hochverzinsliche Wertpapiere *npl*
  (Fin) high-yield instruments
  – high yielders
hochwertige Anlagen *fpl* (IndE) sophisticated equipment
hochwertige Erzeugnisse *npl* (com) high-quality products
hochwertiges Produkt *n* (Mk) high-technology product
Hochzahl *f* (Math) exponent
Hochzinsphase *f* (Fin) period of high interest rates
Hochzinspolitik *f* (Vw) high interest policy
Hochzollpolitik *f* (AuW) protectionist policy
hohe Aufwendungen *fpl* (com) heavy spending
Hohe Behörde *f* (EG) High Authority *(ie, of the European Coal and Steel Community = Montanunion; in 1967 merged with the Commissions of the other two Communities)*
hohe Bußgelder *npl* (Kart) stiff penalties
Höhe *f* **der Beschäftigung** (Vw) level of employment
Höhe *f* **der Einlage** (Re) amount of (capital) investment
Höhe *f* **des Schadenersatzes** (Re) measure of damages
Hoheitsbetrieb *m* (StR) enterprise vested with public authority
Hoheitsgebiet *n* (Re) territorial area
Hoheitsgewässer *npl* (Re) territorial waters
Hoheitsträger *m* (Re) holder of sovereignty
hohe kurzfristige Verschuldung *f* (Fin) mountain of short-term debt
hoher Auftragsbestand *m*
  (com) high level of order backlog
  – strong order book
hoher Beschäftigungsstand *m* (Vw) high employment level
Höherbewertung *f* (ReW) upward revaluation
höhere Einkommensgruppen *fpl* (Stat) higher-income brackets
höhere Gewalt *f*
  (Re) act of God
  – *(civil law)* vis major
  (ie, assumed to exist where the nonperformance of an obligation could not have been avoided, even by the exercise of the highest degree of diligence)
  – force majeure *(ie, wider meaning than act of God, includes strike, war, etc.)*
höher einstufen
  (Pw) to upgrade
  – to put into a higher group
höhere Preise *mpl* **verlangen** (com) to charge higher prices
höhere Programmiersprache *f* (EDV) high-level language
höherer Verwaltungsdienst *m* (Re) higher administrative service

höhere Steuerbelastung f
(StR) increased taxation
– heavier tax load (or burden)
hoher Gewinn m (Fin) high (or sizeable) profit
Höhergruppierung f (Pw) upgrading (ie, of a job)
höher notieren
(Bö) to mark up
– to trade higher
hoher Preis m (com) high price (tag)
höherstufen (com, Pw) to upgrade
höherverzinslich (Fin) higher-yielding
höherverzinsliche Anlagen fpl (Fin) higher-yield investments
höherwertiges Bit n (EDV) high order bit
hohe Steuern fpl **erheben** (FiW) to levy stiff taxes
hohe Stückzahlen fpl (IndE) large product numbers
hohe Verschuldung f (Fin) heavy debt load
hohe Zinsen mpl (Fin) steep interest rates
Holding (-Gesellschaft) f (Re) holding company
holographischer Speicher m (EDV) holographic memory
holographisches Testament n (Re) holograph testament
holomorphe Funktion f (Math) analytic (or regular) function
Holschuld f (Re) obligation where place of performance is debtor's residence or business seat (ie, creditor must fetch goods or money from debtor)
Holsystem n (MaW) pick-up system (ie, operator fetches materials from storeroom; opp, Bringsystem)
Holzbearbeitungsindustrie f (com) wood working industry
Holzhandel m (com) timber trade
Holzhändler m (com) timber merchant
Holzindustrie f (com) timber industry
holzverarbeitende Industrie f (com) wood processing industry
Holzwolle f
(com) excelsior
– (GB) wood wool (or shavings)
homogene Differentialgleichung f (Math) homogeneous differential equation
homogene Funktion f **vom Grade 1** (Math) homogeneous function of the first degree
homogene Funktion f **vom Grade Null** (Math) homogeneous function of zero degree
homogene Güter npl
(Vw) homogeneous goods (or products)
– identical products
homogene kartesische Koordinaten fpl (Math) homogeneous coordinates
homogene Markoffsche Kette f (Stat) homogeneous Markov chain
homogener Markt m (Vw) homogeneous market
homogenes algebraisches Polynom n (Math) homogeneous algebraic polynomial
homogenes Gleichungssystem n (Math) homogeneous set of equations
homogenes Oligopol n (Vw) pure oligopoly
homogenes Polynom n (Math) homogeneous algebraic polynomial
– quantic

Homogenität f **e-r Funktion** (Math) homogeneity of a function
Homogenitätsgrad m (Math) degree of homogeneity
homograde Größe f (Stat) intensive magnitude
homogrades Merkmal n (Stat) attribute
homograde Statistik f (Stat) attribute-based statistics
homo oeconomicus m (Vw) economic man
Honorant m (WeR) acceptor for honor (or supra protest)
Honorar n
(com) fee
– professional fee
– fee for professional services
– remuneration
– honorarium
Honorarfestsetzung f (com) fee setting
Honorarrechnung f
(com) bill for professional services
– bill of costs
– bill of fees
Honorarumsatz m (com) volume of professional fees
Honorarvertrag m (com) fee contract
Honorarvorschuß m (com) fees (or charges) paid in advance
honorieren
(Fin) to honor
– to pay
Hörer m **abheben** (com) to lift the receiver (ie, off its hook)
Hörer m **auflegen**
(com) to put back the receiver
– (infml) to hang up (ie, as an unfriendly act)
horizontale Arbeitsmobilität f (Pw) horizontal labor mobility
horizontale Diversifikation f (Bw) horizontal diversification
horizontale Integration f
(Bw) horizontal integration (or merger)
– horizontal expansion
– lateral integration
horizontale Konzentration f (Bw) horizontal integration
horizontale Kooperation f (Bw) horizontal cooperation
horizontale Mobilität f (Vw) horizontal mobility
horizontale Preisbindung f (Kart) collective resale price maintenance
horizontaler Finanzausgleich m
(FiW) horizontal system of tax revenue
– tax equalization
horizontaler Kommunikationsweg m (Bw) horizontal communication channel
horizontaler Zusammenschluß m (Re) horizontal combination
horizontale Steuergerechtigkeit f (FiW) horizontal tax equity
horizontale Wettbewerbsbeschränkungen fpl (Kart) horizontal restraints of competition (ie, comprising cartel agreements and cartel resolutions, §§ 1–14 GWB)
Horizontalkonzern m (Bw) horizontal group (ie, of affiliated companies)

Horten n (Vw) hoarding of money *(ie, by households and businesses)*
Horten n von Arbeitskräften (Pw) labor hoarding
Hortung f
(Vw) hoarding *(ie, of money)*
(Bw) stockpiling *(ie, of goods and commodities)*
Hortungskäufe mpl (Vw) hoarding purchases
Hotelgewerbe n (com) hotel industry
Hotelkette f (com) hotel chain
Hotelschlüssel m (com) hotel booking code
Hotel- und Gaststättengewerbe n
(com) hotels and restaurants
– (GB) catering trade
Huckepack-System n (com) piggyback export scheme
Huckepackverkehr m
(com) piggyback traffic
– roll on/roll off-service
Hüllkurve f (Math) envelope
Humanisierung f der Arbeit
(Pw) humanizing of work
– work humanization
Humankapital n (Vw) human capital (*or* wealth) *(syn, Arbeitsvermögen)*
Humankapitalrechnung f (ReW) human asset (*or* resource) accounting
Humanökologie f (Vw) human ecology
Humanvermögen n (ReW) human assets (*or* resources)
Humanvermögensrechnung f (ReW) = *Humankapitalrechnung*
hundertprozentige Tochtergesellschaft f (Re) wholly-owned subsidiary
Hundesteuer f (StR) dog tax
Hüttenwerk n (IndE) iron and steel works
Hybridrechner m
(EDV) hybrid computer
– analog-digital computer
Hygiene-Faktoren mpl
(Pw) job context factors
– hygiene factors *(ie, in Herzberg's theory)*
Hyperbel f (Math) hyperbola
Hyperbelfunktion f (Math) hyperbolic function
hyperbolisch (Math) hyperbolic
Hyperebene f
(Math) hyperplane
– hypersurface
hypergeometrisch (Math) hypergeometric
hypergeometrische Reihe f (Math) Gaussian series
hypergeometrische Verteilung f (Stat) hypergeometric distribution
Hyperinflation f
(Vw) hyperinflation
– runaway inflation
Hypotenuse f (Math) hypotenuse
Hypothek f (Re) mortgage *(ie, long-term loan based on the security of the property itself)*
Hypothek f ablösen (Re) to redeem a mortgage
hypothekarische Belastung f (Re) mortgage charge
hypothekarisches Darlehen n (Fin) mortgage loan
hypothekarische Sicherheit f (Fin) security by real-estate mortgage
hypothekarisch gesicherte Forderung f (Fin) mortgage debt

hypothekarisch gesicherte Schuldverschreibung f (Fin) mortgage bond
Hypothekarkredit m (Fin) mortgage loan *(ie, mainly for financing residential construction)*
Hypothek f aufnehmen (Fin) to take up a mortgage
Hypothek f bestellen (Re) to create a mortgage
Hypothekenablösung f (Fin) redemption of mortgage
Hypothekenbank f (Fin) mortgage bank *(ie, there are 39 of them, chiefly engaged in long-term lending against security or public guaranty)*
Hypothekenbankgeschäft n (Fin) mortgage banking business
Hypothekenbestellung f (Re) creation of a mortgage
Hypothekenbrief m (Re) mortgage certificate, § 1116 BGB
Hypothekendamnum n (Fin) mortgage discount
Hypothekendarlehen n (Fin) mortgage loan
Hypothekeneintragung f (Re) registration of a mortgage
hypothekenfrei (Fin) clear of mortgages
Hypothekengewinnabgabe f (StR) levy on profits from the redemption of mortgage loans *(ie, imposed under the Equalization of Burdens Law and ended 10 Nov 1979)*
Hypothekengläubiger m
(Re) mortgage creditor
– mortgagee
Hyothekenkredit m (Fin) mortgage loan
Hypothekenkreditgeschäft n (Fin) mortgage lending business
Hypothekenkredit m mit 100% Auszahlung (Fin) real-estate mortgage paid out in full
Hypothekenkredit m mit 90% Auszahlung (Fin) real-estate mortgage, paid out at a discount of 10%
Hypothekenlaufzeit f (Fin) term (*or* currency) of a real-estate mortgage
Hypothekenmarkt m (Fin) mortgage market *(ie, long-term loans for house purchases; no such market exists in GB)*
Hypothekenpfandbrief m (Fin) mortgage bond
Hypothekenpfandrecht n (Re) mortgage lien
Hypothekenregister n (Re) register of real-estate mortgages
Hypothekenschuld f (Re) mortgage debt
Hypothekenschuldner m
(Re) mortgage debtor
– mortgagor
Hypothekenschuldverschreibung f (Fin) collateral mortgage bond
Hypothekentilgung f (Re) mortgage redemption
Hypothekentilgungsversicherung f (Vers) mortgage redemption life insurance *(syn, Hypothekenversicherung, Tilgungslebensversicherung)*
Hypothekenurkunde f (Re) mortgage deed (*or* instrument)
Hypothekenvaluta f (Fin) mortgage loan money (*or* proceeds)
Hypothekenvermittlungsgebühr f (Re) mortgage broker's fee
Hypothekenversicherung f (Vers) = *Hypothekentilgungsversicherung*
Hypothekenzinsen mpl (Fin) mortgage interest

Hypothekenzusage f (Fin) mortgage loan commitment
Hypothek f **löschen** (Re) to cancel a mortgage
Hypothek f **tilgen** (Fin) to pay off a mortgage
Hypothese f (Log) hypothesis, pl. hypotheses
Hypothese f **aufstellen**
  (Log) to put forward a hypothesis
  – to hypothesize
Hypothese f **der Fristensynchronisierung** (Fin) hedging pressure hypothesis
Hypothese f **kontinuierlicher Konsumgewohnheiten** (Mk) habit persistence hypothesis
Hypothesenprüfung f (Stat) test of hypothesis (or significance)
Hypothesenwahrscheinlichkeit f (Stat) probability of hypotheses
Hypothese f **von der Kapitalmarkteffizienz** (Fin) efficient market hypothesis
hypothetische Grundgesamtheit f (Stat) hypothetical population
hypothetisches Urteil n
  (Log) conditional proposition
  – logical conditional

I

IATA-Sammelladungsagent m (com) consolidator
Idealstandardkosten pl (KoR) ideal (or perfect) standard cost
Idealverein m (Re) incorporated society established for non-economic purposes, §§ 21, 55 ff BGB
ideeller Schaden m
  (Re) immaterial damage
  – intangible damage
  – damage not resulting in pecuniary loss
Identifikationsproblem n (Vw) identification problem (Leontief and Frisch)
Identifikationstest m (Mk) identification test (ie, in advertising)
identische Gleichung f (Math) identical equation
identische Größen fpl (Math) identical quantities
identischer Operator m (Math) unit operator
identische Transformation f (Math) identity transformation
identisch falsch
  (Log) identically false
identisch wahr
  (Log) identically true
identisch wiederholen
  (Math) to duplicate
Identität f
  (Math) identity
  (Zo) identity (ie, of goods)
Identitätsgleichung f (Vw) identity (equation)
Identitätsprinzip n (ReW, Zo) principle of identity
IFO-Institut n **für Wirtschaftsforschung**
  (Vw) (Munich-based) IFO Economic Research Institute
IFO-Konjunkturtest m (Vw) IFO barometer for the business climate
IG Metall f (Pw) West German engineering workers' union
Ikosaeder m (Math) icosahedron
illegaler Streik m
  (Pw) illegal strike
  – (infml) snap strike
illiquide
  (Fin) insolvent
illiquide werden
  (Fin, infml) to run out of money (ie, to pay bills)
Illiquidität f
  (Fin) inability to pay
  – illiquidity
  – insolvency
  – shortage of liquid funds
Imagepflege f (Bw) image building
imaginärer Gewinn m
  (Re) paper profit
  (com, Vers) anticipated (or imaginary) profit (eg, profit expected upon arrival of the goods at place of destination)
imaginäre Zahl f (Math) imaginary number
Imaginärteil m (Math) imaginary part (ie, of a complex number)
im Amt bleiben
  (Pw) to stay in office
im Angebot
  (com) on sale
  – (GB) on offer (eg, article is on offer this week)
im Aufsichtsrat sitzen
  (Pw) to sit on the supervisory board
im Auftrag
  (com) by order of
im Bau
  (com) under construction
im Bau befindliche Anlagen fpl (ReW) construction in process
im Freiverkehr handeln
  (Bö) to trade over the counter
im internationalen Vergleich m (com) by international standards
Immaterialgüter npl (Re) intangible assets
Immaterialgüterrechte npl (Re) rights over immaterial property (eg, patent rights, trademarks, commercial goodwill)
immaterielle Aktiva npl
  (ReW) intangible assets
  – intangibles
immaterielle Anlagewerte mpl (ReW) intangible fixed assets (ie, patents, licenses, trademarks, goodwill)
immaterielle Bedürfnisse npl (Vw) nonmaterial wants
immaterielle Gegenstände mpl (Re) incorporeal things
immaterielle Güter npl (Vw) intangible (or noneconomic) goods
immaterielle Güter npl **des Anlagevermögens**
  (Bw) = immaterielles Anlagevermögen

immaterielle Investitionen *fpl* (Bw) intangible investments
(eg, in advertising, personnel development, organization)
immaterieller Schaden *m*
(Re) immaterial (*or* intangible) damage
– damage not resulting in pecuniary loss
immaterielles Anlagevermögen *n* (ReW) intangible fixed assets
immaterielles Recht *n* (Re) intangible right
immaterielle Vermögenswerte *mpl* (Re) intangible assets
immaterielle Ware *f* (EDV) software
immaterielle Werte *mpl* (StR) = *immaterielle Wirtschaftsgüter*
immaterielle Wirtschaftsgüter *npl* (StR) intangible assets
immerwährende Nutzungen *fpl* **od Leistungen** *fpl* (StR) perpetual payments or other benefits, § 13 II BewG
Immobiliarkredit *m* (Fin) real estate credit
Immobiliarpfandrechte *npl* (Re) = *Grundpfandrechte*
Immobiliarvermögen *n* (Re) real property
Immobiliarversicherung *f*
(Vers) real estate (*or* real property) insurance
– building insurance
Immobiliarvollstreckung *f* (Re) levy of execution on real property
Immobilien *pl*
(com) real estate
– real property
– property (*also:* properties)
Immobilienabteilung *f* (Fin) real estate department *(ie, of a bank)*
Immobilienanlage *f* (Fin) real estate investment
Immobilienanlagegesellschaft *f* (Fin) real estate investment fund
Immobilienbranche *f* (com) real estate industry
Immobilienfirma *f* (com) real estate firm (*or* venture)
Immobilienfonds *m*
(Fin) real estate investment trust, REIT
– (GB) property fund
Immobilienfondsanteil *m*
(Fin) REIT share
– (GB) property fund unit
Immobiliengesellschaft *f*
(com) real estate company
– property company
Immobilienhandel *m* (com) real estate business (*or* trading)
Immobilien-Investition *f* (Fin) real estate investment
Immobilienkredit *m* (Fin) real estate loan
Immobilienmakler *m*
(com) real estate broker
– (GB) estate (*or* land) agent
(syn, Grundstücksmakler)
Immobilienmarkt *m*
(com) property market
– real estate market
Immobilien-Mischfonds *m* (Fin) commingled property fund
Immobilienpreise *mpl* (com) real estate prices

Immobilienunternehmen *n* (com) real estate developer (*or* operator)
Immobilienverkauf *m* (com) sale of real estate (*or* property)
Immobilienversicherung *f* (Vers) = *Immobiliarversicherung*
im Original (com) in the original
Imparitätsprinzip *n* (ReW) principle of unequal treatment of losses and income *(ie, valuation rule requiring disclosure of unrealized losses which are in the course of materializing, while unrealized income or profit must not be shown)*
imperative Anweisung *f* (EDV) executable statement
Implementierung *f* (EDV) implementation
Implementierungssprache *f* (EDV) implementation (*or* system programming) language
Implikans *n* (Log) antecedent *(ie, in 'if A then B', A is the antecedent)*
Implikat *n* (Log) consequent *(ie, in 'if A then B', B is the consequent)*
Implikation *f*
(Log) implication
– logical conditional
– implicative proposition
(ie, a binary propositional connective, usually read 'if – then')
(EDV) conditional implication operation
– if-then operation
– inclusion operation
implizieren
(Log) to imply
– to entail
implizite Definition *f* (Log) implicit definition
implizite Differentiation *f* (Math) implicit differentiation
implizite Funktion *f* (Math) implicit function
Import *m*
(AuW) import
– importation
Importabgabe *f* (AuW) import levy
Importabteilung *f* (AuW) import department
Importakkreditiv *n* (Fin) import letter of credit
Importausgleich *m* (EG) import price adjustment levy
Importbedarf *m* (AuW) import requirements
Importbeschränkungen *fpl* (AuW) = *Einfuhrbeschränkungen*
Importe *mpl* (AuW) imports
Importerstfinanzierung *f* (Fin) initial import financing
Importeur *m* (AuW) importer
Importfinanzierung *f* (Fin) import financing
Importfirma *f*
(AuW) importer
– importing firm
Importgüter *npl* (AuW) imported goods (*or* materials)
Importhandel *m* (AuW) import (*or* passive) trade
importieren (AuW) to import
importierte Deflation *f* (Vw) imported deflation
importierte Inflation *f* (Vw) imported inflation
importierte Vorleistungen *fpl* (VGR) imported input
Importkartell *n* (Kart) import cartel

Importkonnossement n (com) inward bill of lading
Importkontingent n (AuW) import quota
Importkontingentierung f (AuW) imposition of import quotas
Importkredit m (Fin) import credit
Importlager n (AuW) stock of imported goods
Importland n (AuW) importing country
Importlizenz f (EG) import license
Importneigung f (Vw) propensity to import
Import-Niederlassung f
 (AuW) import branch
 – import branch office (or operation)
Importquote f
 (AuW) import quota
 (Vw) propensity to import (ie, ratio of imports to net national product at market prices; equal to ‚durchschnittliche Importquote' = average propensity to import; see: marginale Importquote)
Importrechnung f (AuW) import bill
Importrestriktionen fpl (AuW) = Importbeschränkungen, Einfuhrbeschränkungen
Importüberschuß m (AuW) import surplus
Importverbot n (AuW) ban on imports
Importvolumen n
 (AuW) volume of imports
 (AuW) import bill
Importware f (AuW) imported merchandise (or goods)
Importwarenabschlag m (AuW) reduction of price paid on imported goods
Importwirtschaft f (AuW) import trade (or business)
Import-Zertifikat n (AuW) certificate of import
improvisierende Planung f (Bw) intuitive-anticipatory planning
Impulsabfallzeit f (EDV) decay time
Impulskauf m (Mk) impulse purchase
im Rahmen der Vertretungsmacht (Re) within the scope of one's authority
im Rahmen des Unternehmens (com) within the scope of the enterprise
im Sinne des Vertrages (Re) as contemplated by the contract
im Telefonverkehr handeln (Bö) to trade in the unofficial market
im voraus zahlen (Fin) to pay in advance
im Wert fallen
 (com) to fall in value
 – to depreciate
 – to lose (or fall) (eg, against another currency)
im Wert steigen
 (com) to increase in value
 – to appreciate
 – to gain (or rise) (eg, against another currency)
in Abwicklung
 (Re) in liquidation
 – in process of winding up
inaktive Datenstation f (EDV) inactive station
inaktives Geld n (Fin) idle money
Inanspruchnahme f **der Zentralbank** (Fin) recourse to central bank
Inanspruchnahme f **des Geldmarktes** (Fin) borrowing in the money market
Inanspruchnahme f **des Kapitalmarktes** (Fin) tapping the capital market

Inanspruchnahme f **e-r Garantie** (Re) implementation of a guaranty
Inanspruchnahme f **e-s Akkreditivs** (Fin) drawing on a letter of credit
Inanspruchnahme f **von Leistungen** (SozV) claiming (or utilization) of benefits
in Arbeit = in Bearbeitung
in Arbeit befindliche Aufträge mpl (com) active backlog of orders
in Ausbildung (Pw) being educated for a profession or employment
in bar (com) cash down
 – (in) cash
in Bausch und Bogen (com) by the bulk
in Bearbeitung
 (com) in process
 – being handled (or processed)
 – under way
 (com, infml) in the works
 – (GB) on the stocks (ie, already started)
in Betrieb
 (IndE) in operation
 – on stream (eg, plant, machinery)
in Betrieb gehen
 (IndE) to go into operation
 – to come on stream
 – to be commissioned
Inbetriebnahme f
 (IndE) coming on stream
 – going into operation
 – commissioning
in Betrieb nehmen
 (IndE) to commission
 – to put into operation (or service or action)
 – to take into operation
 – to put (or bring) on stream
 – to start up (eg, continuous caster)
 – to fire up (eg, coke-oven battery)
in das Privatvermögen pfänden (Re) to attach private assets
in das Vermögen übergehen (Fin) to pass into the assets (of)
Indemnitätsbriefe mpl (com) letters of indemnity
in den Aufwand buchen (Rew) to expense
in den Aufwand gebucht (Rew) expensed
in den roten Zahlen stecken
 (com) to operate (or stay) in the red
 – to write red figures
in den Ruhestand versetzen
 (Pw) to pension off
Indentgeschäft n (AuW) indent
Indentkunde m (Mk, US) resident buyer
in der Fassung vom
 (Re) as amended
Index m (Stat) index
Indexanleihe f (Fin) index-linked loan
Indexautomatik f (Pw) automatic cost-of-living increases
Indexbindung f
 (Vw) indexation
 – index-linking
 – indexing
Indexdatenfeld n (EDV, Cobol) index data item
Index m **der Aktienkurse** (Bö) index of stocks and shares

Index m der Arbeitsproduktivität (Stat) index of labor productivity
Index m der Einzelhandelspreise (Stat) retail price index
Index m der Erzeugerpreise industrieller Produkte (Stat) index of industrial producer prices
Index m der Großhandelspreise (Stat) wholesale price index
Index m der industriellen Nettoproduktion (Stat) index of industrial net output
Index m der industriellen Produktion (Stat) industrial production index
Index m der Lebenshaltungskosten (Stat) index of retail prices
Index m der Rentenwerte (Fin) fixed-securities index
Index m der Verbraucherpreise (Stat) consumer price index
Index m des gesamten Handelsgewinns (AuW) index of total gain from trade
Index m des Verbraucherverhaltens (Stat) index of consumer sentiment
Indexfamilie f (Stat) standardized family household
indexiert (Stat) index-linked
Indexierung f (Vw) indexation
– index-linking
– indexing
Indexierung f **des Außenwertes** (AuW) trade weighting *(ie, of a country's exchange rate; weighting applied to arrive at the indexes is based on foreign trade figures [exports + imports])*
Indexierungs-Vereinbarung f (Vw) indexation arrangements
Indexklausel f (Stat) index clause
Indexliste f (EDV) index register *(syn, Adreßbuch)*
Indexlohn m (Pw) index-linked wage
Indexmethode f (EDV) index method
Indexposition f (EDV) index *(or punch)* position
Indexpreis m (Vw) index-linked price
Indexpunkt m (EDV) index point
Indexregister n (EDV) index *(or modifier)* register
Indexrente f (SozV) index-linked pension *(syn, dynamische Rente)*
Indexsatz m (EDV) index record
indexsequentielle Datei f (EDV) indexed sequential file
Indexstabilität f (Vw) index stability
Indextheorie f (Stat) index theory
Indexverfahren n (EDV) indexed sequential access method, ISAM
index-verkettete Speicherung f (EDV) chaining
Indexverknüpfung f (Stat) index linking
Indexversicherung f (Vers) index-linked insurance
Indexwährung f (Vw) index-based currency
Indexwort n (EDV) index word
Indexzahl f
 (Stat) index number
 (Bw) ratio
Indexziffer f (Stat) = *Indexzahl*
in die Höhe treiben (com) to force up *(eg, prices)*
in die roten Zahlen geraten (com) to go *(or* plunge) into the red
in die Tagesordnung eintreten (com) to get down to business

Indifferenzbereich m (Vw) zone of indifference
Indifferenzebene f (Vw) indifference surface
Indifferenzfunktion f (Vw) indifference function
Indifferenz-Hyperbene f (Vw) indifference hypersurface
Indifferenzkurve f
 (Vw) indifference curve
 – iso-utility curve
Indifferenzkurvenanalyse f (Vw) indifference analysis
Indifferenzkurvensystem n (Vw) indifference map
Indifferenzort m (Vw) locus of indifference
Indifferenzpunkt m
 (Stat) indifference quality
 – point of control
indikative Planung f (Vw) indicative planning
Indikator m (Vw) indicator
Indikatorenanalyse f (Stat) item analysis
Indikatorenstabilität f (Vw) formula flexibility
indirekte Abschreibung f (ReW) indirect method of depreciation *(ie, debit through valuation account, which is treated as ‚Erneuerungskonto')*
indirekte Adresse f
 (EDV) indirect
 – second-level
 – multi-level ... address
indirekte Adressierung f (EDV) indirect *(or* multi-level) addressing
indirekte Arbitrage f (AuW) multiple point *(or* triangular) arbitrage
indirekte Ausfuhr f (AuW) indirect export
indirekte Auswahl f (Stat) indirect sampling
indirekte Datenfernverarbeitung f (EDV) offline teleprocessing
indirekte Devisenarbitrage f (AuW) indirect arbitrage
indirekte Erhebung f (Mk) desk research
indirekte Investition f (Fin) portfolio investment
indirekte Kosten pl (KoR) indirect cost *(or* expense) *(ie, in network planning those costs that can be traced to a specific project only on a lump-sum basis)*
indirekte Parität f (AuW) cross rate
indirekter Betrieb m (EDV) offline operation
indirekter Boykott m (Pw) secondary boycott
indirekter Import m (AuW) indirect import
indirekter Nutzen m (Vw) indirect benefit
indirekter Vertrieb m (Mk) indirect selling of industrial products
indirekter Wechselkurs m (AuW) cross-rate of exchange
indirekte Stellenkosten pl
 (KoR) cost center overhead
 – departmental overhead
 – departmental burden
indirekte Steuer f (FiW) indirect tax
indirekte Steueranrechnung f (StR) indirect tax credit
indirekte Stichprobennahme f (Stat) indirect sampling
Individualbegriff m (Log) individual concept
Individualeinkommen n (Vw) individual income
Individualentscheidung f (Bw) decision of an individual transactor
Individualgüter npl (Vw) private goods

Individualhaftung *f* (Re) individual liability
individualisierter Vertragsgegenstand *m* (Re) specified (*or* ascertained) good
Individualpanel *n* (Mk) individual panel
Individualsparen *n* (Fin) individual saving *(opp, Kollektivsparen)*
Individualverkehr *m* (com) private transportation (GB) transport system
Individualversicherung *f* (Vers) individual (*or* private) insurance *(opp, Sozialversicherung = social insurance)*
Individualvertrag *m* (Re) contract between individuals
individuelle Abschreibung *f*
  (ReW) single-unit depreciation
  – unit depreciation
  (syn, Einzelabschreibung; opp, Pauschal- od Summenabschreibung)
individuelle Absetzungen *fpl* (ReW) individual adjustments
individuelle Bedürfnisse *npl* (Vw) private wants
individuelle Fahrlässigkeit *f* (Re) negligence disregarding the care which a person ordinarily gives to his own affairs
  – *(civil law)* culpa in concreto
  – violation of diligentia quam in suis *(rebus adhibere solet)*
individuelle Nachfragefunktion *f* (Vw) individual demand function
individuelle Nachfragekurve *f* (Vw) individual demand curve
individueller Nutzen *m* (Vw) subjective utility (*or* satisfaction)
individuelles Delkredere *n* (ReW) individual contingency reserve
individuelle Steuerquote *f* (Pw) individual tax ratio *(ie, taxes paid to taxpayer's gross earnings)*
individuelle Wertberichtigung *f*
  (ReW) individual value adjustment
  – individual allowance
Individuenkonstante *f* (Log) individual constant
Indizienbeweis *m* (Re) circumstantial evidence
indizieren (Stat) to index
indizierte Adresse *f* (EDV) indexed (*or* variable) address
indizierte Adressierung *f* (EDV) indexed addressing
indizierte Jahresabschlußrechnung *f* (ReW) price-level-adjusted accounting
indizierte Variable *f* (Math) subscripted variable
indiziert sequentielle Datei *f* (EDV) indexed sequential data set
indiziert sequentielle Zugriffsmethode *f* (EDV) index sequential access (*or* file) method
Indizierung *f* (EDV, Cobol) indexing
in Dollar fakturieren (com) to invoice in dollars
indossabel
  (WeR) indorsable
  – (GB) endorsable
indossable Wertpapiere *npl* (WeR) indorsable securities
Indossament *n*
  (WeR) indorsement
  – (GB) endorsement
  – backing

Indossamentschuldner *m* (WeR) debtor by indorsement
Indossamentshaftung *f* (WeR) indorser's liability
Indossamentskette *f* (WeR) chain of indorsements
Indossamentsverbindlichkeiten *fpl*
  (ReW) commitments arising from indorsements
  – indorsement liabilities
Indossamentsverbindlichkeiten *fpl* **aus weitergegebenen Wechseln** (Fin) bills sold with the indorsement of the ... bank
Indossamentsvollmacht *f* (WeR) power to indorse
Indossant *m*
  (WeR) indorser
  – (GB) endorser
  – backer *(syn, Girant)*
Indossatar *m*
  (WeR) indorsee
  – (GB) endorsee
indossierbar
  (WeR) indorsable
  – (GB) endorsable
indossieren
  (WeR) to indorse
  – (GB) to endorse
  – to back
indossierter Fremdwechsel *m* (Fin) bill discounted
Induktionslogik *f* (Log) inductive logic
Induktionsschluß *m* (Log) inductive inference
induktive Definition *f* (Log) inductive definition
induktive Logik *f* (Log) inductive logic
induktiver Schluß *m* (Log) inductive inference
induktive Statistik *f* (Stat) inferential statistics *(syn, Inferenz-Statistik, analytische, beurteilende, schließende Statistik)*
Industrial Engineering *n* (IndE) industrial (*or* management) engineering
industrialisieren (Vw) to industrialize
Industrialisierung *f* (Vw) industrialization
Industrie *f* (com) industry
Industrieabgabepreis *m* (com) industrial selling price
Industrieaktien *fpl* (Fin) industrial shares (*or* equities) *(opp, Bank-, Versicherungs-, Verkehrsaktien)*
Industrieanlage *f* (IndE) industrial plant
Industrieanlagen *fpl*
  (IndE) industrial plant and equipment
  – industrial facilities
Industrieanleihe *f* (Fin) industrial (*or* corporate) loan
Industrieansiedlung *f* (Vw) settlement (*or* establishment) of industries
Industriearbeiter *m* (Pw) industrial worker
Industriebauten *mpl* (com) industrial buildings
Industriebeteiligung *f*
  (Fin) industrial (equity) holding
  – industrial equities
  – equity stakes banks hold in industry
Industriebetrieb *m* (Bw) industrial undertaking
Industriebetriebslehre *f* (Bw, appr) science of managing industrial undertakings *(eg, as opposed to service sector enterprises)*
Industriebörse *f* (Bö) industrial exchange *(ie, on which fungible products, esp. textiles, are traded; eg, Stuttgart, Manchester, Tourcoing)*

Industrieerzeugnis n (com) industrial product
Industriefahrzeuge npl (com) industrial vehicles
Industrieförderung f (Vw) promotion of industry
Industriegebiet n (Vw) industrial area (or region)
Industriegelände n (com) industrial site (or area)
Industriegesellschaft f (Vw) industrial society
Industriegewerkschaft f (Pw) industry-wide union
Industriegruppen fpl (Stat) groups of industry
Industriegüter npl (com) industrial goods
Industriegüter-Ausrüster m (com) heavy equipment maker
Industriegütermarketing n (Mk) industrial marketing
Industriegüterwerbung f (Mk) industrial (goods) advertising
Industriehypothek f (Fin) mortgage on industrial sites
Industriekartell n (Kart) industrial cartel
Industriekaufmann m (Pw, appr) industrial clerk (ie, ex-apprentice in areas like Finance, Sales, Personnel, etc.)
Industriekontenrahmen m (ReW) uniform classification of accounts for industrial enterprises
Industriekredit m (Fin) corporate loan
Industriekreditbank f (Fin) industrial credit bank
Industriekreditgeschäft n (Fin) corporate loan business
Industrieland n
  (Vw) industrial country
  (StR) land suitable for industrial construction, § 69 I BewG
industrielle Beteiligung f (Fin) industrial participation (or holding)
industrielle Datenverarbeitung f (EDV) industrial data processing
industrielle Entwicklung f (Vw) industrial development
industrielle Formgebung f
  (IndE) industrial design
  – styling
industrielle Konzentration f (Kart) industrial concentration
industrielle Kostenstruktur f (KoR) cost structure in industrial enterprises
industrielle Produktion f (Stat) industrial output (or production)
industrielle Produzentenrente f (Vw) quasi rent (A. Marshall)
industrielle Revolution f (Vw) industrial revolution
industrielles Rechnungswesen n (ReW) industry accounting (ie, financial and cost accounting, statistics, planning)
Industriemesse f (com) industrial fair
Industriemüll m (IndE) manufacturing and processing waste
Industrienorm f (IndE) industry standard
Industrieobligation f (Fin) corporate (or industrial) bond
Industriepark m
  (com) industrial park (or estate)
  – (GB) trading estate
Industriepolitik f (Vw) industrial policy
Industrieproduktion f (Stat) industrial production (or output)

Industrieroboter m
  (IndE) industrial robot
  – universal transfer device, UTD
  (ie, programmable micro-processor controlled machine tool)
Industrieroboter m **der zweiten Generation** (IndE) intelligent industrial robot (ie, equipped with sensing and feeling functions and controllable by optical signals)
Industrieschuldverschreibung f (Fin) corporate (or industrial) bond
Industriespion m (Bw) industrial spy
Industriespionage f (Bw) industrial espionage
Industriestaat m (Vw) industrial nation
Industriestandort m (Bw) industry location
Industriestatistik f (Stat) industrial statistics
Industrie- und Handelskammer f (com) (German) Chamber of Industry and Commerce
Industrieunternehmen n (com) industrial undertaking
Industrieverlagerung f (Vw) relocation of industries
Industriewaren fpl (com) manufactured goods
Industriewerbung f (Mk) industrial advertising
Industriewerte mpl (Bö) industrials
Industriezensus m (Stat) industry census
Industriezweig m (com) branch (or segment) of industry
induzierte Größe f (Vw) induced variable
induzierte Investitionen fpl (Vw) induced investment
induzierter technischer Fortschritt m (Vw) induced technical progress
induzierte Transaktionen fpl
  (AuW) accommodating movements (or transactions)
  – settling transactions
induzierte Variable f (Vw) induced variable
ineffiziente Maßzahl f (Stat) inefficient statistic
in eigenem Namen (com) in one's own name
in eigenem Namen abschließen (com) to contract in one's own name
ineinandergeschachtelte Intervalle npl (Math) nested intervals
ineinandergreifende Stichprobe f
  (Stat) interpenetrating sample
  – network of samples
in ein Zollager bringen (Zo) to place in a bonded warehouse
Inferenzstatistik f (Stat) inferential statistics (ie, deals with inferences from samples to populations)
inferiore Güter npl (Vw) inferior goods
Infimum n (Math) infimum
Infinitesimalrechnung f
  (Math) calculus
  – infinitesimal calculus (or analysis)
Infixschreibweise f (EDV) infix notation
Inflation f (Vw) inflation
Inflation f **anheizen** (Vw) to stoke up inflation
Inflation f **bekämpfen**
  (Vw) to fight
  – to combat
  – to counter
  – to battle ... inflation

Inflation *f* **durch fahrlässiges Finanzgebaren des Staates** (FiW) government inflation
Inflationsausgleich *m*
(StR) inflation relief
− compensating for inflation
Inflationsauslöser *m* (Vw) inflation trigger
inflationsbedingte Lohnerhöhung *f* (Pw) inflation-triggered pay rise
Inflationsbekämpfung *f*
(Vw) containment of inflation
− fighting inflation
− fight against inflation
inflationsbereinigt
(ReW) inflation-adjusted
− adjusted for inflation
inflationsbewußt (Fin) inflation-conscious
Inflationsdruck *m* (Vw) inflationary pressure
Inflationserwartungen *fpl* (Vw) inflationary expectations
inflationsfreies Wachstum *n* (Vw) non-inflationary growth
Inlationsgefahr *f* (Vw) risk of inflation
Inflationsgefälle *n*
(Vw) inflation differential
− inflation rate differential
− differences in countries' inflation rates
Inflationsgeleitzug *m* (Vw) inflation league
Inflationsgewinn *m* (Vw) inflation gain
Inflationsindex *m* (Stat) inflation index
Inflationsklima *n* (Vw) inflationary climate *(ie, unduly depresses personal savings)*
Inflationslücke *f* (Vw) inflationary gap
Inflationsmentalität *f* (Vw) inflation mentality
inflationsneutrale (od **inflationsbereinigte**) **Rechnungslegung** *f* (ReW) inflation accounting
Inflationsrate *f* (Vw) rate of inflation
Inflationsschub *m* (Vw) inflationary push
Inflationsschutz *m* (Pw) inflation protection
Inflationssicherung *f* (Fin) hedge against inflation
Inflationsspirale *f*
(Vw) inflationary spiral
− spiralling inflation
Inflationsstoß *m* (Vw) upsurge in inflation
Inflationstheorie *f* (Vw) theory of inflation
Inflationsursachen *fpl* (Vw) roots of inflation
Inflations-Verlangsamung *f* (Vw) deceleration of inflation
Inflationszuschlag *m* (ReW) inflation charge
inflatorische Lücke *f* (Vw) inflationary gap
inflatorischer Gewinnstoß *m* (Vw) inflationary profit push
informaler Kommunikationsweg *m* (Bw) informal communication channel
Informand *m* (Pw) trainee
Informatik *f*
(EDV) information science
− informatics
− computer science
− information processing science
Informatiker *m* (EDV) information scientist
Informationsabsprache *f* (Kart) price-reporting agreement *(ie, related to prices and other conditions)*
informationsaktiver Verbraucher *m* (Mk) information seeker, IS

Informationsanordnung *f* (EDV) information format
Informationsaustausch *m* (EDV) information exchange
Informationsbank *f* (EDV) data bank
Informationsbeschaffungsphase *f* (Bw) phase of information search
Informationsbit *n* (EDV) information bit
Informationsbrief *m* (com) news letter
Informationsdarstellung *f* (EDV) data representation
Informationseingabe *f* (EDV) information input
Informationseinheit *f* (EDV) information unit
Informationsfluß *m* (EDV) information flow
Informationsflußanalyse *f* (EDV) information flow analysis
Informationsgehalt *m* (EDV) information content
Informationskartell *n* (Kart) price-reporting cartel
Informationskette *f* (EDV) information-transmitting chain
Informationskosten *pl* (Bw) cost of collecting information
Informationsloch *n* (EDV) code hole
Informationspflicht *f* (Bw) duty to inform
Informationsprozeß *m* (Bw) information process
Informationsquelle *f* (Bw) source of information
Informationsrecht *n* (Bw) right to be given information
Informationsregulator *m* (EDV) gatekeeper
Informationsrückfluß *m* (EDV) feedback
Informationsspeicherung *f* (EDV) information storage
Informationsspur *f* (EDV) information track
Informationssteuer *f* (FiW) information tax *(ie, levied on imported information to protect domestic information industries)*
Informationssystem *n* (EDV) information system
Informationstheorie *f*
(EDV) information theory
− theory of communication
(syn, Kommunikationstheorie)
Informationsträger *m* (EDV) information carrier
Informationstransformation *f* (EDV) storage, transmission, and processing of information
Informationstrennzeichen *n* (EDV) information separator
Informationsübermittlung *f* (EDV) transmission of information
Informationsüberschuß *m* (EDV) information overload
informationsverarbeitende Maschine *f* (EDV) information processing machine
Informationsverarbeitung *f* (EDV) information *(or* data*)* processing
Informationsweg *m* (Bw) channel of information
Informationswiedergewinnung *f* (EDV) information *(or* data*)* retrieval
Information *f* **von oben nach unten** (Bw) top-down information
Information *f* **von unten nach oben** (Bw) bottom-up information
informative Werbung *f* (Mk) information-based advertising *(opp, Suggestivwerbung)*
informelles Kommunikationssystem *n* (Bw) informal communications system *(ie, mostly oral;*

information transmitted is often called ,,scuttlebutt")
informelle Untersuchung *f* (Mk) informal survey
Infrakosten *pl* (Vw) social costs
Infrastruktur *f*
(Vw) infrastructure
– social overhead capital
Infrastrukturinvestition *f* (FiW) government investment in infrastructure
Infrastrukturkredit *m* (Fin) infrastructure loan
Ingangsetzung *f* (Bw) start-up *(eg, of a plant)*
Ingangsetzungskosten *pl* (ReW) startup costs, § 153 IV AktG *(syn, Anlaufkosten)*
Ingenieurbüro *n* (com) firm of consulting engineers
Ingenieurhonorar *n* (com) engineering fee
in Güteklassen einteilen
(com) to grade
– to gate into quality categories
Inhaber *m*
(Re) proprietor *(eg, of a business)*
(WeR) bearer
– holder *(ie, of a negotiable instrument)*
Inhaberaktie *f* (WeR) bearer share *(or* stock)
Inhabergrundschuld *f* (Re) bearer land charge, § 1195 BGB
Inhaberhypothek *f* (Re) bearer-type mortgage *(ie, mortgage securing a claim under a bearer security, such as bond, bill of exchange, §§ 1187–1189 BGB)*
Inhaberindossament *n* (WeR) indorsement to bearer *(ie, treated as a blank indorsement, Art. 12 WG)*
Inhaberklausel *f* (WeR) bearer clause *(ie, entitling the holder of a security to require payment)*
Inhaberkonnossement *n*
(WeR) bill of lading made out to bearer
– bearer bill of lading *(or* B/L)
Inhaberkreditbrief *m* (Fin) open letter of credit
Inhaberlagerschein *m* (WeR) negotiable warehouse receipt made out to bearer
Inhaber- od Orderkonnossement *n* (com) negotiable bill of lading
Inhaberpapier *n*
(WeR) bearer paper *(or* instrument)
– instrument made out to bearer
(ie, negotiated by delivery alone)
Inhaberpolice *f*
(Vers) (insurance) policy made out to bearer
– bearer policy
Inhaberscheck *m*
(WeR) bearer check
– check to bearer
Inhaberschuldverschreibung *f* (WeR) bearer bond, §§ 793–806 BGB
Inhaberwechsel *m* (WeR) bill payable to bearer
Inhalt *m* **des Geschäftsberichts** (ReW) contents of the annual report, § 160 AktG
inhaltsadressierbarer Speicher *m*
(EDV) content addressable memory, CAM
– associative memory *(syn, Assoziativspeicher)*
inhaltsadressierter Speicher *m* (EDV) content-addressed *(or* associative) memory
Inhaltsanalyse *f* (Mk) content analysis
Inhaltsverzeichnis *n*
(com) table of contents

(com) directory
Initialwerbung *f* (Mk) pioneering advertising
Initialzündung *f* (Vw) pump priming
in jeweiligen Preisen (Stat) at current prices
Inkasso *n*
(Fin) collection *(ie, by commercial agents or banks)*
– encashment
(Fin) collection procedure
(AuW) cash against documents
Inkassoabtretung *f* (Re) assignment of receivables for collection
Inkassoakzept *n* (Fin) acceptance for collection
Inkassoanweisungen *fpl* (Fin) collection instructions
Inkassoanzeige *f* (Fin) advice of collection
Inkassoauftrag *m* (Fin) collection order
Inkassobank *f* (Fin) collecting bank
inkassobevollmächtigt (Fin) authorized to collect
Inkassobüro *n*
(Fin) collection agency
– debt collecting agency
– debt collector
Inkassoerlös *m* (Fin) collection proceeds
Inkassoermächtigung *f* (Fin) collection authority
inkassofähig (Fin) collectible
Inkassoforderungen *fpl* (ReW) uncollected cash items
Inkassogebühr *f* (Fin) collection charge *(or* fee)
Inkassogegenwert *m* (Fin) collection proceeds
Inkassogeschäft *n*
(Fin) collection business *(ie, of banks)*
– debt recovery service
Inkassoindossament *n* (WeR) indorsement ,for collection'
(ie, instructing a bank to collect amount of bill or draft)
Inkassokommission *f* (Fin) collection commission
Inkassopapiere *npl* (Fin) paper for collection
Inkassoprovision *f* (Fin, Vers) collection commission
Inkassorisiko *n* (Fin) collection risk
Inkassospesen *pl*
(Fin) collecting charges
– collection charges
– collection commission
– encashment charges
Inkassostelle *f* (Fin) collecting *(or* collection) agency
Inkassovereinbarungen *fpl* (Fin) collection arrangements
Inkassovertreter *m* (Fin, Vers) collecting agent
Inkassovollmacht *f*
(Fin) authority to collect *(ie, third-party or assigned receivables, § 55 HGB)*
– collection authority
Inkassowechsel *m*
(Fin) bill for collection
– collection draft
Inkassozession *f* (Re) assignment of receivables for collection
Inklusion *f* (Math, Log) inclusion
Inklusionsbeziehung *f* (Math) inclusive relation *(ie, of sets)*
inklusives ODER-Glied *n* (EDV) inclusive-OR

element (*or* circuit) *(syn, Disjunktionsglied, Mischgatter, Odergatter, Oderglied)*
inkommensurable Zahlen *fpl* (Math) incommensurable numbers
in Kommission (com) on consignment
in Kommission geben (com) to consign
Inkompatibilität *f* (Vw) incompatibility *(eg, of economic policy targets)*
Inkompatibilitätsprinzip *n* (Re) principle of incompatible offices
inkongruente Darlehen *npl* (Fin) mismatched loans *(ie, fixed-term loans financed with more expensive floating-rate funds)*
in Konkurs geraten (Re) to become (*or* go) bankrupt
in Konsignation (com) on consignment
in Konsignation geben (com) to consign
in Kost geben
  (Bö) to carry over
  – to defer payment
in Kost nehmen (Fin) to take in *(ie, securities)*
in Kraft
  (Re) legally effective
  – in force
in Kraft setzen (Re) to put into force
in Kraft treten
  (Re) to come (*or* enter) into force
  – to take effect
Inkreis *m* (Math) incircle
Inkreismittelpunkt *m* (Math) incenter
inkrementale Ausfallwahrscheinlichkeit *f* (OR) incremental probability of failure
inkrementale Darstellung *f* (EDV) incremental representation
inkrementaler Digitalplotter *m* (EDV) digital incremental plotter
Inkrementalrechner *m* (EDV) incremental computer *(opp, absolute value computer)*
Inkrement *n* **e–r Funktion** (Math) increment of a function
inkulant
  (com) unaccommodating
  – petty
  – picayune
Inländer *m* (AuW) resident
Inländer-Konvertibilität *f*
  (AuW) internal convertibility
  – convertibility for national residents
  – resident convertibility
Inländerkonzept *n* (VGR) method of determining ‚value added' – *Wertschöpfung* – on the basis of resident status, irrespective of place of performance *(opp, Inlandskonzept)*
inländische Abgaben *fpl* (FiW) internal duties and taxes
inländische Beförderungskosten *pl* (com) inland carriage
inländische Betriebsstätte *f* (StR) domestic permanent establishment
inländische DM-Anleihe *f* (Fin) German domestic bond
inländische Einkünfte *pl* (StR) domestic income
inländische Emittenten *mpl* (Bö) domestic issuers
inländische Güterverwendung *f* (Vw) domestic consumption of goods

inländische Konkurrenz *f* (com) domestic rivals (*or* competitors)
inländische Kreditausweitung *f* (Vw) domestic credit expansion
inländische Nichtbanken *fpl* (Fin) domestic non-banks
inländischer Arbeitnehmer *m* (Pw) domestic (*or* indigenous) worker
inländischer Arbeitsmarkt *m* (Vw) domestic labor market
inländischer Emittent *m* (Fin) domestic issuer
inländische Rentenwerte *mpl* (Fin) domestic bonds
inländischer Erzeuger *m* (com) domestic producer
inländischer Marktanteil *m* (com) domestic market share
inländischer Produzent *m* (Vw) domestic producer
inländischer Schiedsspruch *m* (Re) domestic arbitral award
inländischer Steuerpflichtiger *m* (StR) resident taxpayer
inländischer Verkaufspreis *m* (com) domestic selling price
inländischer Wirtschaftszweig *m* (com) domestic industry
inländisches Fabrikat *n* (com) domestic product
inländisches Kreditinstitut *n* (Fin) domestic bank (*or* banking institution)
inländisches land- und forstwirtschaftliches Vermögen *n* (StR) property appropriated to the use of a domestic agricultural establishment, § 121 II 1 BewG
inländisches Vermögen *n* (StR) = *Inlandsvermögen*
inländische Währung *f* (AuW) local (*or* domestic) currency
inländische Wertpapiere *npl* (Fin) domestic securites *(ie, made out by a national resident)*
Inlandsabsatz *m* (com) domestic sales
Inlandsanleihe *f* (Fin) domestic loan
Inlandsanmeldung *f* (Pat) application in home country
Inlandsauftrag *m* (com) domestic (*or* home) order
Inlandsbestellung *f* (com) = *Inlandsauftrag*
Inlandsbeteiligung *f*
  (Fin) domestic participation
  – (GB) domestic trade investment
Inlandsemission *f* (Fin) domestic issue
Inlandsflug *m*
  (com) domestic flight
  – (GB) internal flight
Inlandsgeschäft *n*
  (com) inland (*or* domestic) sale
  – inland transaction
  (com) domestic business
Inlandshafen *m* (com) domestic port
Inlandsinvestitionen *fpl* (Vw) domestic investment
Inlandskapital *n* (Fin) domestic capital
Inlandskonjunktur *f* (Vw) domestic economic activity
Inlandskonzept *n* (VGR) domestic concept *(ie, method of determining value added – Wertschöpfung – of an economic area, irrespective of whether the goods and services were produced by residents or not; opp, Inländerkonzept)*

Inlandsmarkt *m*
(com) domestic (*or* home) market (*syn, Binnenmarkt*)
(EG) internal market
Inlandsmonopol *n*
(Vw) domestic monopoly
– (GB) sheltered trade
(ie, business getting no competition from abroad)
Inlandsnachfrage *f* (Vw) domestic (*or* internal) demand
Inlandspatent *n* (Pat) domestic patent
Inlandsprodukt *n* (VGR) domestic product
Inlandsumsatz *m* (ReW) domestic sales
Inlandsverbrauch *m* (Vw) domestic consumption
Inlandsvermögen *n* (StR) domestic property *(ie, of nonresident taxpayers = beschränkt Steuerpflichtige, § 121 BewG; certain property has a situs in the territory of the Federal Republic or West Berlin)*
Inlandsvertreter *m* (com) resident agent
Inlandswährung *f* (Vw) domestic (*or* local) currency
Inlandswechsel *m* (Fin) domestic bill of exchange
Inlandswerte *mpl* (Bö) domestic securities
in Liquidation
(Re) in liquidation
– in process of winding up
Innenauftrag *m*
(Bw) internal order *(ie, issued by a plant division, not by a customer:*
1. Vorratsauftrag zur Lagerergänzung = make-to-stock order to replenish inventory; 2. Auftrag zur Erstellung innerbetrieblicher Leistungen = intraplant order for products or services)
Innenauftragsabrechnung *f* (ReW) internal-order accounting
Innenfinanzierung *f* (Fin) internal finance (*or* financing)
Innenfinanzierungsmittel *pl* (Fin) internal financing resources
Innenfinanzierungsquote *f* (Fin) internal financing ratio
Innengeld *n* (Vw) inside money
Innengemeinschaft *f* (Bw) association not dealing as such with the outside world
Innengesellschaft *f* (Re) internal partnership *(ie, civil-law partnership doing no business with the outside world)*
Innenkonsolidierung *f* (ReW) consolidation within a group
Innenrevision *f*
(ReW) internal
– administrative
– operational... audit
Innenrevisor *m* (ReW) internal auditor
Innentransport *m* (Bw) internal handling
Innenumsätze *mpl*
(ReW) intercompany sales
– internal deliveries (*or* turnover)
– intra-group sales
Innenumsatzerlöse *mpl*
(ReW) internal sales (revenues) *(ie, of an affiliated group of companies)*
– proceeds from intercompany sales
Innenverhältnis *n* (Re) internal relationship

innerbetrieblich
(com) internal
– in-company (*or* intra-company)
– in-plant (*or* intra-plant)
– interoffice
innerbetriebliche Ausbildung *f*
(Pw) in-company
– in-plant
– in-service
– shop... training
innerbetriebliche Kommunikationswege *mpl* (Bw) internal lines of communication
innerbetriebliche Leistungen *fpl*
(Bw) internal services
(KoR) intra-plant service output
– auxiliary plant services
– non-market plant output
(ie, usu. re-channeled into input flow)
innerbetriebliche Leistungsverrechnung *f* (KoR) intra-plant cost allocation *(ie, the problem is one of tracing costs from service cost centers to production cost centers)*
innerbetriebliche Lieferung *f* (KoR) internal delivery
innerbetriebliche Mitteilung *f* (com) inter-office memo
innerbetriebliche Mobilität *f* (Pw) intra-plant mobility
innerbetriebliche Preisverrechnung *f* (KoR) cross-charging of prices
innerbetrieblicher Arbeitsmarkt *m* (Pw) intra-company job market
innerbetrieblicher Aufstieg *m* (Pw) advancement within the organization pyramid
innerbetrieblicher Materialtransport *m* (MaW) in-plant materials movement
innerbetrieblicher Prüfer *m* (ReW) internal (*or* staff) auditor
innerbetrieblicher Transportauftrag *m*
(IndE) move card
– move order
– move ticket
innerbetrieblicher Vergleich *m* (Bw) intrafirm comparison
innerbetrieblicher Verrechnungspreis *m*
(ReW) shadow price
– internal (*or* intracompany) transfer price
innerbetriebliches System *n* (EDV) in-plant system
innerbetriebliches Transportwesen *n* (IndE) intra-plant materials handling
innerbetriebliche Transportplanung *f* (IndE) planning of intra-plant handling
innerbetriebliche Umsetzungen *fpl* (Pw) intra-company transfers
innerbetriebliche Weiterbildung *f* (Pw) in-service training
innerbetriebliche Werbung *f* (Pw) in-plant advertising *(opp, Verkaufswerbung als außerbetriebliche Werbung)*
innere Konvertibilität *f* (AuW) internal convertibility
innerer Fehler *m* (Re) inherent defect (*or* vice)
innerer Punkt *m* **e–r Menge** (Math) point interior to a set
innerer Verderb *m* (com) intrinsic decay

innerer Wert *m* (Fin) intrinsic value *(ie, of a share of stock, determined by dividing the net worth of the issuing company by the number of shares)*
inneres Produkt *n*
  (Math) inner
  – dot
  – scalar ... product
innere Staatsverschuldung *f* (FiW) domestic borrowing
innere Unruhen *fpl* (com) civil commotion
innergemeinschaftlich (EG) intra-Community
innergemeinschaftlicher Saldenausgleich *m* (EG) intra-Community settlements
innergemeinschaftlicher Warenverkehr *m* (EG) intra-Community trade
innerstaatliche Beförderung *f* (Zo) domestic transport operation
Innovation *f* (Bw) innovation *(eg, realization of new products, and new methods in production, management, and organization)*
innovationsbewußt (Bw) receptive to innovation
Innovationsförderung *f* (Vw) promotion of original innovation
Innovationsforschung *f* (Bw) innovation research
Innovationspotential *n* (Bw) innovation capabilities *(or* potential*)*
Innovationsstruktur *f* (Bw) innovative structure
in Pension geben (Fin) to park *(eg, shares with a bank for sale later to the public)*
in Pension gehen (Pw, infml) to retire
Inputkoeffizient *m* (Vw) production *(or* technical*)* coefficient *(syn, Produktions- od Faktorkoeffizient)*
inputorientierte Budgetaufstellung *f* (FiW) input-oriented budgeting
Input-Output-Analyse *f* (Vw) input-output *(or* interindustry*)* analysis
Input-Output-Koeffizient *m* (Vw) input-output coefficient
Input-Output-Tabelle *f* (Vw) input-output table
in Raten (Fin) in *(or* by*)* installments
in Rente gehen (Pw, infml) to retire
Insasse *m* (Vers) passenger
Insassen-Unfallversicherung *f* (Vers) passenger accident insurance
Insassenversicherung *f* (Vers) motor car passenger insurance
inseparables Polynom *n* (Math) inseparable polynomial *(syn, Polynom 2. Art)*
Inserat *n* (Mk) advertisement
  – ad
Inserat *n* **aufgeben** (Mk) to advertise
Inserent *m* (Mk) advertiser
in Serie geschaltete Kanten *fpl* (OR) branches in series
inserieren (Mk) to insert an advertisement
Insertion *f* (Mk) insertion of an advertisement
ins Haus stehen
  (com) forthcoming
  – upcoming
Insichgeschäft *n*
  (Re) self-contracting
  – self-dealing
  (ie, an agent cannot as such conclude a transaction between the principal and himself or another party represented by himself, except if he has been granted express authority to do so, § 181 BGB)
insolvent
  (Fin) insolvent
  – unable to pay one's debts
Insolvenz *f*
  (Fin) inability to pay
  – insolvency
  (syn, Zahlungsunfähigkeit; opp, Zahlungsfähigkeit, Solvenz)
Insolvenzen *fpl* (Re) business failures
Insolvenzniveau *n* (Fin) volume of insolvencies
Insolvenzquote *f* (Bw) insolvency rate
Insolvenzsicherung *f* (Pw) insolvency insurance, § 3 No. 65 EStG *(ie, taken out by an employer to protect his employees in the event of a business failure; carrier is the ‚Pensions-Sicherungs-Verein a. G.')*
Inspektionszertifikat *n* (com) certificate of inspection
instabiler Wachstumspfad *m* (Vw) knife-edge equilibrium
Installation *f* (com) installation *(eg, of plant and machinery)*
Installationskosten *pl* (ReW) cost of installation
installieren
  (com) to install
  – to set up
Instandhaltung *f*
  (IndE) maintenance
  – maintenance and repair
  – upkeep
Instandhaltungsintervall *n* (IndE) maintenance interval
Instandhaltungskosten *pl*
  (KoR) maintenance charges *(or* expense*)*
  – cost of upkeep
Instandhaltungsrückstellung *f* (ReW) provision for deferred repairs
Instandhaltungs- und Reparaturplanung *f* (IndE) planning of maintenance and repair
Instandsetzung *f*
  (com) repair
  (IndE) complete overhaul
  (ie, of fixed assets in order to restore them to full operating condition)
Instandsetzungsauftrag *m* (IndE) repair order
Instandsetzungsdauer *f* (IndE) active repair time
Instandsetzungskosten *pl* (KoR) cost of repair
Instandsetzungszeit *f* (EDV) repair time
Instanz *f*
  (Bw) management *(or* managerial*)* unit
  – organizational unit
  – unit of supervision
  – level of authority
  (ie, vested with rights of decision, directing, and control)
Instanzen *fpl* (Bw) organizational lines
Instanzenaufbau *m* (Bw) pyramid of authority
Instanzenzug *m* (Bw) hierarchy of organizational units
institutionell bedingte Arbeitslosigkeit *f* (Vw) institutional unemployment
institutionelle Bedingungen *fpl* (Vw) institutional constraints

institutionelle Gleichung f (Vw) institutional equation
institutioneller Aktionär m (Fin) institutional shareholder
institutioneller Anleger m (Fin) institutional investor (or buyer) (syn, Kapitalsammelstelle)
Institutionenlehre f (Bw) theory of business structures
Institutsgruppen fpl (Fin) banking groups
Instruktionsadresse f (EDV) instruction address
Instruktionsaufbau m (EDV) instruction format
Instruktionslänge f (EDV) instruction length
instrumentale Wissenschaft f (Log) formal science
Instrumentalvariable f (Bw) = Instrumentvariable
Instrumentarium n (Log) tool kit
Instrumentarium n **der Wirtschaftspolitik** (Vw) economic policy instruments
Instrumentvariable f
  (Vw) instrument variable
  – policy instrument (or variable)
  (Bw) decision variable
in Stücken von (Fin) in denominations of
Insular-Philosophie f (EDV) insular philosophy (ie, expensive side-by-side operation of data and text processing systems)
Integral n (Math) integral
Integralfranchise f (Vers) free from average under ... pct.
Integralgleichung f (Math) integral equation
Integralrechnung f (Math) integral calculus
Integraltafel f (Math) integrable table
Integralzeichen n (Math) integral sign
Integrand m (Math) integrand
Integration f
  (Math) integration
  (Bw, Vw) integration
Integrationsbereich m (Math) integral domain
Integrationsgebäude n (Vw) integrating economic structure
Integrationskonstante f
  (Math) constant of integration
  – integration constant
Integrationsmuster n (Vw) pattern of economic integration
Integrationsweg m (Math) path of integration
integrative Prozeßstrukturierung f (Bw) structuring of operations (syn, Ablauforganisation)
Integrator m (EDV) integrator
integrierbare Funktion f (Math) integrable function
integrieren (Math, Vw, Bw) to integrate
Integrierer m **mit Begrenzer** (EDV) limited integrator (ie, functions only while its output signal falls within specified limits)
Integrierglied n (EDV) = Integrierwerk
integrierte Datenverarbeitung f (EDV) integrated data processing, IDP
integrierte Finanzplanung f (Fin) integrated financial planning
integrierte Großschaltung f (EDV) large-scale integration, LSI
integrierte Halbleiterschaltung f (EDV) integrated semiconductor circuit
integrierte Hybridschaltung f (EDV) hybrid integrated circuit

integrierte Planung f (Bw) integrated planning
integrierter Halbleiterschaltkreis m (EDV) integrated semiconductor circuit
integrierter Schaltkreis m (EDV) integrated circuit
integrierte Schaltung f (EDV) integrated circuit, IC
integriertes Hüttenwerk n (IndE) integrated iron and steel works
integriertes Planungssystem n (Bw) integrated planning system
integriertes Rechnungswesen n (ReW) integrated accounting system (ie, interconnected through an information system)
integrierte Unternehmensplanung f (Bw) integrated corporate planning
Integrierwerk n (EDV) digital integrator (syn, Integrierglied)
Integritätsbereich m (Math) integral domain
intelligente Datenstation f (EDV) intelligent data terminal
intelligentes Terminal n (EDV) intelligent (or programmable) terminal
Intelligenz- und Begabungstest m (Pw) intelligence test
Intension f
  (Log) intension (ie, of a concept)
  – connotation
  – comprehension
  (ie, in contemporary logical works this has come to be synonymous with ‚sense')
intensionale Logik f (Log) intensional logic
intensionaler Junktor m (Log) intensional connective
intensionale Semantik f (Log) theory of meaning (ie, studies the sense or connotation of symbols; opp, extensionale Semantik)
Intensität f
  (IndE) efficiency
  – effectiveness
  (ie, measure of technical performance of a machine, defined as: number of output units divided by unit of time; eg, 4 units/hr)
Intensitätsabweichung f
  (KoR) efficiency variance
  – machine effectiveness variation
Intensitätsgrad m (IndE) degree of utilization (ie, ratio of actual output per time unit to planned output per time unit)
intensitätsmäßige Anpassung f (IndE) variation of efficiency (ie, in order to increase or reduce output while keeping operating time constant)
Intensitätsnachteil m (Fin) operating inferiority (Terborgh)
Intensivberatung f (com) intensive counseling (or consulting)
intensive Ausbildung f (Pw, infml) hands-on training (eg, on computers)
intensive Auswahl f (Stat) intensive sampling
Intensivinterview n (Mk) depth (or qualitative) interview
Intensivwerbung f
  (Mk) intensive coverage (ie, frequent, large-scale advertising in a market)
  – (infml) heavy drumbeating (eg, in print and on TV)
intentionale Supposition f (Log) logical supposition

Interaktionshäufigkeit *f* (Bw) frequency of interaction *(ie, in organizations)*
Interaktionsmatrix *f* (Bw) interaction matrix
Interaktionstheorie *f* (Bw) theory of interaction *(ie, branch of organizational theory)*
interaktive Anzeige *f* (EDV) interactive display *(syn, interaktive Datendarstellung)*
interaktive Arbeitsweise *f* (EDV) interactive mode
interaktives Programmieren *n* (EDV) conversational-mode programming
Interamerikanische Entwicklungsbank *f* (Vw) Inter-American-Development Bank, IDB
Interbankaktiva *npl* (Fin) interbank assets
Interbanken-Einlagen *fpl* (Fin) interbank deposits
Interbanken-Geldmarkt *m* (Fin) interbank money market
Interbanken-Markt *m* (Fin) interbank market
Interbankgeschäft *n*
  (Fin) interbank business
  (Fin) interbank operation (*or* transaction)
Interbankrate *f* (Fin) interbank rate
Inter-Branchen-Konkurrenz *f* (Vw) interindustry competition
interdisziplinäre Arbeitsgruppe *f* (Pw) cross-skilled team
interdisziplinärer Ansatz *m* (Log) interdisciplinary (*or* cross-skilled) approach
Interessenabwägung *f* (Re) weighing of interests
Interessengemeinschaft *f*
  (Re) community of interests *(ie, any civil-law partnership, § 705 BGB)*
  (Bw) community of interests *(ie, 1. contractual pooling of interests, with contributors remaining legally independent; 2. pooling of profits and losses) (Note: in German literature ‚IG' and ‚pool' are not identical)*
Interessenkäufe *mpl* (Bö) special-purpose buying *(eg, to acquire a majority stake or a blocking minority)*
Interessenkollision *f* (Re) conflict of interests
Interessent *m*
  (com) prospective buyer (*or* customer)
  – potential buyer
  – prospect
  (Re) interested party
  (Fin) potential acquiree *(ie, in merger or acquisition)*
Interessen- und Neigungstest *m* (Pw) interest inventory
Interessenverband *m* (Re) pressure group
Interessenvereinigung *f* (Bw) pooling of interests *(syn, Interessengemeinschaft)*
Interessen *npl* **wahrnehmen**
  (Re) to promote (*or* safeguard) interests
  – to attend to interests
Interessenwahrnehmung *f*
  (Re) promotion
  – protection
  – safeguarding ... of interests
Interessenwahrung *f* (Re) = *Interessenwahrnehmung*
Interimsausschuß *m* (com) interim committee
Interimsbilanz *f* (ReW) interim balance sheet *(syn, Zwischenbilanz)*
Interimsdividende *f* (Fin) interim dividend

Interimskonto *n* (ReW) transitory account
Interimsschein *m* (WeR) interim certificate, § 10 AktG *(ie, obsolete term replaced by ‚Zwischenschein')*
interindustrielle Neuverschuldung *f* (Fin) interindustrial incurrence of liabilities
intermediäre Finanzgewalt *f* (FiW) auxiliary fiscal agent *(F. K. Mann)*
(syn, Hilfsfiskus, Parafiskus, Nebenfiskus)
intermediäres Finanzinstitut *n*
  (Fin) financial intermediary
  – nonbank financial institution
Internalisierung *f* **sozialer Kosten** (Vw) allocation of social costs
international ausschreiben (com) to put up to international tender
Internationale Arbeitgeberorganisation *f* (com) International Organization of Employers, IOE
Internationale Arbeitsorganisation *f* (Pw) International Labour Organization, ILO
internationale Arbeitsteilung *f* (AuW) international division of labor
internationale Arbitrage *f* (AuW) international arbitrage activity
Internationale Bank *f* **für Wiederaufbau und Entwicklung** (AuW) International Bank for Reconstruction and Development
  – World Bank
internationale Bürgschaftskette *f* (Zo) international guaranty chain
internationale Devisenspekulation *f* (AuW) international currency speculation
Internationale Energieagentur *f* (AuW) International Energy Agency, IEA
Internationale Entwicklungsorganisation *f* (AuW) International Development Association, IDA
Internationale Finanzierungsgesellschaft *f* (AuW) International Finance Corporation, IFC
internationale Garantiekette *f* (Zo) international chain of customs guarantees
Internationale Handelskammer *f* (com) International Chamber of Commerce, ICC
internationale Handelspolitik *f* (AuW) international trade policy
internationale Kapitalbewegungen *fpl* (AuW) international capital movements
Internationale Klassifikation *f* (Pat) International Patent Classification
internationale Kreditmärkte *mpl* (Fin) international credit markets
internationale Liquidität *f* (AuW) international liquidity
internationale Messe *f* (com) international fair
Internationale Organisation *f* **für Normung** (com) International Standards Organization, ISO
internationaler Anleihemarkt *m* (Fin) international bond market
Internationaler Antwortschein *m* (com) international reply coupon
internationaler Behälterverkehr *m* (com) international container transport
internationale Recheneinheit *f* (AuW) international unit of account
internationale Reservewährung *f* (AuW) international reserve currency

internationaler Expressgutschein *m* (com) international express parcels consignment note
internationaler Frachtbrief *m* (com) international consignment note
internationaler Geldhandel *m* (Fin) international money trade
internationaler Handel *m* (AuW) international trade
internationaler Kapitalverkehr *m* (AuW) international capital movements
internationaler Kreditverkehr *m* (Fin) international lending
Internationaler Normen-Ausschuß *m* (com) International Organization for Standardization
internationaler Preiszusammenhang *m* (AuW) international price system
Internationaler Transportversicherungs-Verband *m* (Vers) International Union of Marine Insurance
Internationaler Verband *m* **für die Veröffentlichung der Zolltarife** (Zo) International Union for the Publication of Customs Tariffs
Internationaler Verband *m* **zum Schutz des gewerblichen Eigentums** (Pat) International Union for the Protection of Industrial Property
Internationaler Währungsfonds *m* (AuW) International Monetary Fund, IMF *(ie, headquartered in Washington, D. C.)*
internationale Währungsordnung *f* (AuW) international monetary system
Internationaler Weizenrat *m* (AuW) International Wheat Council
internationaler Zahlungsauftrag *m* (Fin) international payment order *(ie, im Auftrag und zugunsten Dritter = by order and for the account of a third party)*
internationaler Zahlungsverkehr *m* (AuW) international payments
Internationaler Zinnrat *m* (AuW) International Tin Council
Internationaler Zuckerrat *m* (AuW) International Sugar Council
internationales Abkommen *n* (Re) *(zweiseitig:)* international agreement; *(mehrseitig:)* international convention
Internationales Abkommen *n* **zur Erleichterung der Einfuhr von Warenmustern und Werbematerial** (Re) International Convention to facilitate the importation of commercial samples and advertising material
internationales Anlagepublikum *n* (Fin) international investing public
Internationales Arbeitsamt *n* (Pw) (Geneva-based) International Labor Office, ILO
internationales Bankgeschäft *n* (Fin) international banking
internationale Schiedsklauseln *fpl* (Re) international clauses of arbitration
Internationales Freibord-Abkommen *n* (Re) load-line convention
internationales Freibordzeugnis *n* (com) international loadline certificate
internationales Gewohnheitsrecht *n* (Re) customary international law
Internationales Institut *n* **der Sparkassen** (Fin) *(Geneva-based)* International Savings Banks Institute
internationales Patent *n* (Pat) international patent
internationale Spedition *f* (com) international forwarders *(or* transport company*)*
internationales Privatrecht *n* (Re) Conflict of laws – *(less commonly called)* private international law
internationales Rohstoffabkommen *n* (AuW) international commodity agreement
internationales Spediteur(durch)konnossement *n* (com) Forwarding Agent's Certificate of Receipt
internationales Steuerabkommen *n* (StR) international tax treaty
internationales Steuerrecht *n* (StR) international law of taxation
Internationale Standardklassifikation *f* **der Berufe** (Vw) International Standard Classification of Occupation, ISCO
internationales Vertragsrecht *n* (Re) conventional international law
internationales Währungssystem *n* (AuW) international monetary system
Internationales Warenverzeichnis *n* **für den Außenhandel** (com) Standard International Trade Classification
internationale Übereinkunft *f* (Re) international agreement
internationale Unternehmung *f* (Bw) multinational
– transnational
– international
– supranational . . . enterprise *(or* corporation*)*
Internationale Vereinigung *f* **der Seeversicherer** (Vers) International Union of Marine Insurance
Internationale Vereinigung *f* **zur Erforschung des Volkseinkommens** (Vw) International Association for Research in Income and Wealth, ARIW
internationale Verflechtungen *fpl* (StR) international interrelations
internationale Vertriebskosten *pl* (Mk) international marketing cost *(or* expenses*)*
internationale Währungsbeziehungen *fpl* (AuW) international monetary relations
internationale Währungskrise *f* (AuW) international monetary crisis
internationale Währungsordnung *f* (AuW) international monetary system
internationale Währungsreserven *fpl* (Vw) international currency reserves
internationale Waren- und Güterverzeichnisse *npl* (AuW) international classifications of goods and services
internationale Warenverzeichnisse *npl* (AuW) standard international trade classification
internationale Wettbewerbsfähigkeit *f* (AuW) international competitiveness
internationale Wirtschaftspolitik *f* (Vw) international economic policy
internationale Wirtschaftsprüfungsgesellschaft (ReW) international accounting group *(eg, Arthur Anderson, Touche Ross, Price Waterhouse)*
internationale Zahlungen *fpl* (AuW) international payments *(or* settlements*)*

internationales Zahlungsabkommen n (AuW) international payments agreement
international gebräuchlich (com) internationally recognized
intern beschaffen (Bw) to get *(eg, raw materials)* in-house
interne Annullierung f **von Aufträgen** (com) internal cancellation of orders
interne Auseinandersetzungen fpl (Pw) internal feuding
interne Beteiligung f (Fin) intercompany participation
interne Buchungsfälle mpl (ReW) accounting transactions *(ie, depreciation, cost allocations, valuation accounts = Wertberichtigungen)*
interne Fernsehanlage f (EDV) closed circuit TV
interne Informationsquelle f (Bw) internal source of information
interne Konten npl (ReW) inter-company accounts
interne Kontrolle f (EDV) internal check
interne Kostendegression f (Bw) internal economies of scale
interne Leistungen fpl (Bw) internal services *(or performance)*
interne Nachfrage f (Vw) domestic demand
interner Bilanzvergleich m (ReW) internal balance-sheet comparison *(ie, covering several successive fiscal years)*
interne Revision f
   (ReW) internal
   – administrative
   – operational ... audit
interner gemeinschaftlicher Versandschein m (EG) internal Community transit document
interner Kostenausgleich m (Bw) internal cost-equalizing process
interner Speicher m (EDV) internal memory *(or storage)*
   (ie, in the sense of 'Arbeitsspeicher')
interner Umsatz m
   (ReW) intercompany sales
   – internal deliveries *(or turnover)*
   – intra-group sales
interner Verrechnungspreis m (ReW) intercompany billing price
interner Zinsfuß m
   (Fin) internal rate of return
   – dcf rate of return
   – time-adjusted rate of return
   (Fin) yield to maturity
   (Vw) marginal efficiency of capital *(or investment)*
   – marginal rate of return (over cost)
   – marginal productivity of investment
internes Berichtswesen n (com) internal reporting
internes gemeinschaftliches Versandpapier n (EG) internal Community transit document
internes gemeinschaftliches Versandverfahren n (EG) Community transit operation
internes Kontrollsystem n
   (ReW) system of internal audits
   – internal audits
interne Sortierung f (EDV) online sorting
internes Rechnungswesen n (ReW) internal *(or cost)* accounting

interne Staatsverschuldung f (FiW) domestic borrowing
interne Stellenausschreibung f (Pw) in-house job posting *(ie, publication of openings within a company)*
interne Steuerung f (EDV) internal control
interne Ströme mpl (VGR) internal flows
interne Umwelt f (Bw) internal environment
interne Verarbeitung f (EDV) internal processing
interne Vereinbarung f (Bw) intercompany agreement
interne Zinsen mpl (Fin) internal interest
Interne-Zinsfußmethode f
   (Fin) internal rate of return method
   – IRR method of analysis
   – discounted cash flow method
   – (GB) yield method
   (ie, of preinvestment analysis)
interne Zinsrechnung f (Fin) internal-interest accounting
interne Zulieferungen fpl (Bw) internal supplies
interpersoneller Nutzenvergleich m (Vw) interpersonal comparison of utility
Interpolation f (Math) interpolation
interpretierendes Programm n (EDV) interpretive program
   – interpreter
interpretierendes Protokollprogramm n (EDV) interpretive trace program
Interpretierer m (EDV) = *Interpretierprogramm*
Interpretierprogramm n (EDV) interpretive program
intersektorale Kreditströme mpl (Fin) intra-sectoral credit flows
intertemporale Grenzrate f **der Substitution** (Vw) intertemporal marginal rate of substitution *(syn, Grenzrate der Zeitpräferenz)*
intertemporale Nutzenfunktion f (Vw) intertemporal utility function
Intervall n (Stat) class interval
intervallfixe Kosten pl
   (KoR) step variable cost
   – fixed cost rising in steps
   (syn, Sprungkosten, sprungfixe Kosten)
Intervallschachtelung f (Math) nested intervals
Intervallschachtelungs-Axiom n (Math) nested interval theorem
Intervallschätzung f (Stat) interval estimation
Intervallzeitgeber m (EDV) interval time clocker
intervalutarischer Devisenhandel m (Bö) cross-exchange dealings
intervenieren (Bö) to intervene *(ie, if prices fluctuate erratically)*
intervenierende Variable f (Log) intervening variable
Intervention f (Bö) intervention
Intervention f **am freien Markt** (AuW) intervention in the open market
Intervention f **an den Devisenmärkten** (AuW) intervention in foreign exchange markets
Intervention f **der Zentralbank** (Vw) central-bank intervention
Interventionismus m (Vw) interventionism
interventionistische Finanzpolitik f (FiW) monetary-fiscal policy

interventionistische Marktwirtschaft *f* (Vw) economics of control
interventionistische Wirtschaftspolitik *f* (Vw) interventionist (or infml: hands-on) economic policy
interventionsfreie Wirtschaftspolitik *f* (Vw) non-interventionist (or infml: hands-off) economic policy
Interventionskäufe *mpl* (Vw) support purchases (or buying)
Interventionsklage *f* (Re) action of third party opposition
Interventionskurs *m* (AuW) support price
Interventionskurs *m* **im EWS** (AuW) intervention rate
Interventionsmechanismus *m* (EG) intervention mechanism
Interventionspolitik *f* (Vw) intervention policy *(ie, of a central bank)*
Interventionspreis *m* (EG) intervention price *(ie, minimum prices in EEC farm policy)*
Interventionspunkte *mpl*
 (AuW) dealing limits
 – bank's upper and lower limits
 – peg points
 – support points
 (ie, in foreign exchange trading)
Interventionsregeln *fpl* (EG) intervention rules
Interventionswährung *f* (AuW) intervention currency
Interventionszahlung *f* (WeR) payment for honor
intramarginale Intervention *f* (AuW) intramarginal intervention
intuitionistische Aussagenlogik *f* (Log) intuitionistic propositional calculus
in Übereinstimmung mit
 (com) in accordance with
 – in agreement (or conformity) with
 – in keeping with
 – conformably to
Invalidenrente *f* (SozV) disability pension *(now: Rente wegen Berufsunfähigkeit od Erwerbsunfähigkeit)*
Invalidenversicherung *f* (SozV) workers' disability insurance *(now: Arbeiterrentenversicherung)*
Invalidität *f* (SozV) disablement *(ie, permanent total or partial disability to work)*
Inventar *n*
 (ReW) inventory
 – list of assets and liabilities *(syn, Inventarliste)*
Inventar *n* **aufstellen** (ReW) to prepare (or take) an inventory, § 39 II HGB
inventarisierbar (ReW) inventoriable
inventarisieren
 (ReW) to take inventory (or stock)
 – to inventory
Inventarnummer *f* (MaW) inventory number
Inventarwert *m* **e–s Fondsanteils** (Fin) net asset value per share
 (ie, total assets minus total liabilities divided by total shares outstanding)
Inventur *f*
 (ReW) inventory
 – physical inventory
 – stocktaking

Inventurabstimmliste *f* (ReW) inventory reconciliation list
Inventuraufnahmeliste *f* (ReW) inventory sheet
Inventurausverkauf *m* (com) pre-inventory sale
Inventurbewertung *f* (MaW) inventory valuation
Inventurbuch *n* (ReW) inventory register
Inventurdifferenzen *fpl* (ReW) inventory discrepancies
Inventur *f* **machen** (ReW) to take inventory (or stock)
Inventurprüfung *f* (ReW) inventory audit *(ie, part of annual balance-sheet audit)*
Inventurrichtlinien *fpl*
 (ReW) inventory rules
 – (GB) stocktaking rules
Inventurstichtag *m* (ReW) inventory date
Inventurverkauf *m* (com) inventory sale *(ie, permitted only as seasonal sale)*
Inventurvorbereitungsliste *f* (ReW) physical inventory list
Inventurzählkarten *fpl* (ReW) physical inventory cards
Inverse *f* (Math) inverse
inverse Angebotskurve *f* (Vw) regressive supply curve
inverse Auswahl *f* (Stat) inverse sampling
Inverse *f* **der Matrix** (Math) resolvent of a matrix
inverse Funktion *f* (Math) inverse function
inverse Matrix *f* (Math) inverse (or reciprocal) matrix
inverse Tangente *f* (Math) arc (or inverse) tangent
inverse Zinsstruktur *f* (Vw) inverse interest rate structure
Inversschaltung *f* (EDV) inverse integrator
invertierte Datei *f* (EDV) inverted file
in Vertretung (com) *(to sign)* for and on behalf of
in Verzug
 (Re) defaulting
 (Fin) in arrears
in Verzug geraten (Re) to default on payment (or performance)
investieren
 (Fin) to invest (into)
 – (infml) to sink *(eg, $50m into an enterprise)*
investiertes Kapital *n* (Fin) invested capital *(ie, current assets and fixed assets)*
 – capital employed
Investition *f*
 (Vw) investment
 (Bw) investment
 – capital spending (or expenditure)
 – capital outlay
Investition *f* **auf nachgelagerter Wirtschaftsstufe** (Vw) downstream investment
Investition *f* **auf vorgelagerter Wirtschaftsstufe** (Vw) upstream investment
Investitionen *fpl* **der gewerblichen Wirtschaft** (VGR) business investment spending
Investitionen *fpl* **genehmigen** (Fin) to authorize investments
Investitionen *fpl* **im Dienstleistungssektor** (com) service investment
Investitionen *fpl* **kürzen** (Bw) to cut (or slash) spending for capital investment
Investitionsabgabe *f* (FiW) investment tax

Investitionsanreiz *m*
(Bw) investment incentive
– incentive to invest
Investitionsantrag *m* (Fin) capital spending requisition *(ie, by division, department, subsidiary, etc.)*
Investitionsaufwand *m*
(Fin) capital expenditure
– capital outlay
– capital spending
– investment expenditure
Investitionsaufwendungen *pl* (Fin) = *Investitionsaufwand*
Investitionsausgaben *fpl* (Fin) = *Investitionsaufwand*
Investitionsbedarf *m*
(Vw) capital investment needs *(eg, of the economy)*
(Bw) capital expenditure requirements
Investitionsbelebung *f* (Vw) pickup in capital spending
Investitionsbereitschaft *f*
(Vw) propensity to invest *(standard term in economics: Investitionsquote, I/Y)*
(Bw) willingness to invest
– investment confidence *(eg, has been remarkably strong)*
Investitionsbewilligung *f* (Fin) capital appropriation
Investitionsbilanz *f* (ReW) capital-flow balance sheet
Investitionsboom *m* (Vw) boom in capital investment
Investitionsbudget *n*
(FiW) capital budget
(Fin) capital expenditure budget
Investitionsdarlehen *n* (Fin) loan to fund investment project
Investitionseinnahmen *fpl* (Fin) investment receipts
Investitionsentscheidung *f* (Fin) capital spending decision
Investitionsfinanzierung *f*
(Fin) (capital) investment financing
– financing of capital projects
Investitionsförderung *f*
(Vw) investment assistance
– promotion of capital spending activity
Investitionsfreudigkeit *f* (Bw) inclination to invest
Investitionsfunktion *f* (Vw) investment function
investitionsgebundener technischer Fortschritt *m* (Vw) embodied technical progress
Investitionsgenehmigung *f* (Fin) capital spending authorization
Investitionsgüter *npl*
(Bw) capital
– investment
– industrial
– equipment ... goods
(ie, more precise: Anlageinvestitionsgüter)
Investitionsgüter-Gewerbe *n* (com) capital goods sector
Investitionsgüter-Gruppe *f* (Bw) group of capital goods producers
Investitionsgüter-Hersteller *m* (com) capital goods manufacturer

Investitionsgüterindex *m* (Stat) capital goods index *(ie, a special production index used in official statistics: determines the salable output of the capital goods industry)*
Investitionsgüterindustrie *f* (com) capital goods industry
Investitionsgüter-Leasing *n* (Fin) equipment leasing
Investitionsgütermarketing *n* (Mk) industrial marketing *(ie, industrial goods comprising physical products, services, rights, nominal goods; opp, Konsumgütermarketing)*
Investitionsgütermarkt *m* (Bw) capital goods market
Investitionsgütermesse *f* (Mk) exhibition of capital goods
Investitionsgüterproduktion *f* (Bw) production of capital goods
Investitionsprogramm *n* (Fin) capital program
Investitionshaushalt *m* (FiW) capital budget
Investitionshemmnisse *npl* (Vw) barriers to investment
Investitionshilfe *f* (Vw) investment aid *(ie, one-off contribution of DM 1bn by the ‚gewerbliche Wirtschaft' designed to pump-prime investments in industrial bottleneck sectors; statutory basis was the ‚Investitionshilfegesetz' of 7 Jan 1952)*
Investitionshilfeabgabe *f*
(FiW) investment aid deduction
– (infml) mandatory loan
(ie, interest-free, refundable loan by high-income earners to the government, equal to 5% of income tax burden, to help encourage a general economic upswing; syn, Zwangsanleihe)
investitionsinduziertes Wachstum *n* (Vw) investmend-led expansion
Investitionskalkül *n* (Fin) investment analysis
Investitionskapital *n* (Fin) investment capital
Investitionskette *f* (Fin) stream of investment
Investitionsklima *n*
(Vw) investment climate
– climate for investment
Investitionskonjunktur *f* (Vw) investment activity
Investitionskontrolle *f*
(Vw) investment control *(or steering)*
(Bw) capital spending control *(ie, comparison of budgeted and actual figures to determine budget variances)*
Investitionskosten *pl*
(Fin) capital outlay cost
– investment cost
– up-front costs
Investitionskredit *m* (Fin) investment credit *(ie, long-term borrowed capital used for financing production plant)*
Investitionskreditversicherung *f* (Vers) investment credit insurance
Investitionskürzungen *fpl* (Fin) cuts in capital spending
Investitionsleistung *f* (Bw) capital spending volume
Investitionslenkung *f* (Vw) = *Investitionskontrolle*
Investitionslücke *f* (Vw) investment deficit (or gap)
Investitionsmaßnahme *f* (Fin) investment
Investitionsmöglichkeiten *fpl* (Fin) investment opportunities *(or outlets)*

Investitionsmöglichkeitskurve *f* (Vw) investment opportunity line
Investitionsmultiplikator *m* (Vw) investment multiplier *(ie, reciprocal of marginal propensity to save)*
Investitionsnachfrage *f* (Vw) demand for capital goods
Investitions-Nachtragshaushalt *m* (FiW) additional investment budget
Investitionsneigung *f*
(Vw) propensity to invest
(Bw) = *Investitionsbereitschaft*
Investitionsobjekt *n*
(Fin) capital expenditure (or spending) project
– capital investment project
– investment project (*or* object *or* proposal)
Investitionsperiode *f* (Fin) investment period *(ie, during which the sum of outpayments is greater than the sum of receipts)*
Investitionsplan *m*
(Bw) capital spending plan
– capital budget
– investment plan
Investitionsplanung *f*
(Fin) capital budgeting
– capital expenditure planning
– capital investment planning
Investitionspolitik *f* **des Unternehmens** (Bw) capital spending policy *(ie, based on preinvestment analysis = Investitionsrechnung, and on planning procedures)*
Investitionsprogramm *n*
(Fin) capital expenditure program
– capital (investment) spending program
– capital spending budget
Investitionsprojekt *n* (Fin) = *Investitionsobjekt*
Investitionsquote *f* (Vw) propensity to invest, I/Y *(ie, durchschnittliche I. = average propensity to invest I/C; marginale I. = marginal propensity to invest dI/dY)*
Investitionsrate *f*
(VGR) ratio of gross investment to gnp at market prices
– investment-income ratio
Investitionsrechnung *f*
(Fin) capital budgeting
– preinvestment analysis
– investment appraisal
– estimate of investment profitability
(ie, method of comparing the profitability of alternative investment projects; or: technique of capital expenditure evaluation)
Investitionsrisiko *n*
(Fin) investment risk
– risk of capital spending
Investitionsrückgang *m* (Vw) decline in capital spending
Investitionsschub *m* (Bw) investment surge
Investitions-Spar-Kurve *f*
(Vw) investment-spending curve
– IS (investment-saving) curve
Investitionsstau *m*
(Vw) pile-up (*or* backlog) of investment projects
– piles of investment projects waiting to be started

Investitionssteuer *f*
(FiW) capital investment tax
Investitionsstoß *m*
(Vw) investment shock
– single injection of capital spending
Investitionsstrom *m* (Vw) investment flow
Investitionssumme *f* (Fin) amount to be invested
Investitionstätigkeit *f*
(Vw) capital spending
– investment activity
Investitionstätigkeit *f* **der Unternehmer** (Vw) business purchases of capital goods
investitionsunabhängiger technischer Fortschritt *m* (Vw) disembodied technical progress
Investitionsverbot *n* (Vw) investment ban
Investitionsverhalten *n* (Vw) investment behavior
Investitionsvorgang *m* (Fin) investment process
Investitionsvorhaben *n*
(Fin) capital spending plan
– (capital) investment project
Investitionsvorhaben *n* **zurückstellen** (Fin) to shelve spending plan (*or* investment project)
Investitionszulage *f*
(FiW) capital investment bonus
– government premium to aid investment
– investmend subsidy (*or* grant)
(ie, to stimulate lagging expenditure on plant and equipment)
Investitionszulagengesetz *n* (Re) Investment Subsidy Law, 2 Jan 1979, as amended
Investitionszuweisung *f* (FiW) investment grant, *(ie, made to local authorities)*
investive Ausgaben *fpl* (FiW) investment spending (*or* expenditure)
investive Verflechtung *f* (Vw) cross investment
Investmentanteil *m*
(Fin) share
– (GB) unit
Investmentfonds *m*
(Fin) investment fund
– (US) mutual fund
– (GB) unit trust
Investmentfonds *m* **mit auswechselbarem Portefeuille** (Fin) flexible (*or* managed) fund
Investmentfonds *m* **mit begrenzter Emissionshöhe** (Fin) closed end fund
Investmentfonds *m* **mit Sitz in e-r Steueroase** (Fin) offshore fund
Investmentfonds *m* **mit unbeschränkter Anteilsemission** (Fin) open end fund
Investmentgeschäft *n* (Fin) investment business
Investmentgeschäfte *npl* (Fin) operations of investment companies
Investmentgesellschaft *f* (Fin) investment company
Investmentgesellschaft *f* **mit gesetzlicher Risikoverteilung** (Fin) diversified company
Investmentgesellschaft *f* **mit konstantem Anlagekapital** (Fin) closed end investment trust
Investmentgesellschaft *f* **ohne gesetzliche Anlagestreuung** (Fin) non-diversified company
Investmentsparen *n* (Fin) saving through investment companies
Investmentzertifikat *n* (Fin) investment fund certificate
Investor *m* (Fin) investor

in voller Höhe abzugsfähig (StR) fully tax deductible
in Vorlage treten (Fin) to advance funds
in Zahlung geben
  (com) to trade in
  – to turn in
  – (GB) to give in part exchange *(eg, old car, TV set)*
in Zahlung nehmen (com) to receive *(or* take) in payment
Inzidenz *f* (FiW) incidence *(ie, of taxes)*
Inzidenzabbildung *f* (Math) incidence mapping
Inzidenz *f* **des Steueranstoßes** (FiW) impact incidence
Inzidenzmatrix *f* (Math) incidence matrix
irrationale Zahl *f* (Math) irrational number
irrealer Bedingungssatz *m*
  (Log) contrary-to-fact *(or* counterfactual) conditional
  – counterfactual
irreduzibles Polynom *n* (Math) irreducible *(or* prime) polynomial
irreduzible Wurzel *f* (Math) irreducible radical
irreführende Angaben *fpl* (Kart) misleading *(or* deceptive) representations
irreführende Kennzeichen *npl* (Kart) deceptive marks
irreführende Praktiken *pl* (Kart) deceptive practises
irreführende Reklame *f* (Mk) = *irreführende Werbung*
irreführende Warenzeichen *npl* (Pat) deceptive marks
irreführende Werbung *f* (Mk) deceptive advertising
irrelevante Information *f*
  (Log) prevarication
  (com) irrelevant information
Irrelevanz *f*
  (Log) irrelevance
  – prevarication
Irrtum *m* (Re) mistake
Irrtum *m* **im Beweggrund** (Re) mistake as to formation of intention, § 119 II BGB
Irrtumsanfechtung *f* (Re) avoidance on account of mistake
Irrtum *m* **über den Vertragsgegenstand** (Re) mistake as to subject matter of contract
Irrtumswahrscheinlichkeit *f* (Stat) level of significance
Irrtum *m* **vorbehalten** (Re) errors and omissions excepted, E&OE
Irrungszeichen *n* (EDV) error character
IS-Kurve *f* (Vw) IS (investment-saving) curve
isoelastische Funktionen *fpl* (Vw) isoelastic functions
isoelastische Nachfragekurve *f* (Vw) isoelastic demand curve
Isogewinngerade *f* (Vw) isorevenue line
Isogewinnkurve *f* (Vw) isorevenue curve
Isokosten *pl* (Vw) isocost
Isokostengerade *f* (Vw) isocost line
Isokostenkurve *f* (Vw) iso-outlay curve
Isokostenlinie *f* (Vw) outlay contour
isolierte Menge *f* (Math) isolated set

Isolinie *f* (Math) contour line
isometrisches Schaubild *n* (Stat) isometric chart *(or* plot)
Isophoren *fpl* (Vw) isophores *(syn, Isoquanten, Indifferenzkurven)*
Isoproduktkurve *f* (Vw) product contour
Isoquante *f*
  (Vw) isoquant
  – product indifference curve
  – equal products curve
  – iso-product curve
Isoquant-Ebene *f* (Vw) isoquant plane
Isoquantenanalyse *f* (Vw) isoquant analysis
Ist-Ausbringung *f* (Bw) actual output
Istausgaben *fpl* (Fin) actual outlay *(or* expenditure)
Istbestand *m*
  (com) actual stock
  (ReW) actual balance
  (MaW) stock on hand
Istbetrag *m* (Fin) actual amount *(ie, of outlay or expenditure)*
Isteindeckungszeit *f* (MaW) ratio of existing inventory to daily requirements
Isteinnahmen *fpl* (com) actual receipts
Ist-Ist-Vergleich *m* (Bw) comparison of actual performances
Istkosten *pl* (KoR) actual cost
  – outlay cost
  (opp, kalkulatorische Kosten = implicit cost und Opportunitätskosten = opportunity cost)
Istkosten *pl* **der Gegenwart** (KoR) current-outlay cost
Istkosten *pl* **der Vergangenheit** (KoR) historical cost
Istkostenrechnung *f*
  (ReW) historical cost accounting
  (KoR) actual cost system
Istleistung *f*
  (Bw) actual output
  – out-turn *(opp, estimate)*
  (Pw) actual attainment
Ist-Prämie *f* (Vers) actual premium
Ist-Reserve *f* (Vw) actual reserve *(ie, average monthly balance of a bank with the Deutsche Bundesbank)*
Ist-Satz *m* (Log) Is Statement *(opp, Sollsatz = Ought Statement)*
Ist-Spanne *f* (ReW) ratio of gross margin to sales
Ist-Stunden *fpl* (Pw) actual manhours
Ist-System *n* **der Rechnungslegung** (ReW) cash accounting
Istversteuerung *f* (StR) actual payment of turnover taxes
Ist-Wert *m*
  (com) actual value
  (IndE) instantaneous value *(ie, in process control)*
Ist-Zeit *f* (IndE) actual *(or* clock) time
Iteration *f* (Math) iteration
Iterationstest *m* (Stat) iteration test
Iterationsverfahren *n* (EDV) iterative procedure
iterative Operation *f* (EDV) iterative process
iterieren (Math) to iterate
I-Urteil *n*
  (Log) I-proposition

- particular affirmative categorical proposition *(eg, some companies have a high RoI)*

IWF-Quote *f* (AuW) IMF quota
- quota in the IMF

J

Jacobische Determinante *f* (Math) Jacobian determinant
Jagdsteuer *f* (StR) hunting tax
Jahresabgrenzung *f* (ReW) year-end deferrals
Jahresabonnement *n* (com) annual subscription
Jahresabrechnung *f*
(com) annual (*or* yearly) settlement
(ReW) annual statement of accounts
Jahresabschluß *m*
(ReW) annual (*or* year-end) financial statements
- (GB) annual accounts
(ie, comprising balance sheet, income statement, annual report, and audit report)
Jahresabschlußanalyse *f* (ReW) financial statement analysis
Jahresabschluß *m* **aufstellen**
(ReW) to prepare annual financial statements
- (GB) to draw up the annual accounts
Jahresabschlußbuchungen *fpl*
(ReW) entries made at annual closing of accounts
- year-end closing entries
Jahresabschluß *m* **feststellen** (ReW) to establish the annual financial statements
Jahresabschlußprüfung *f* (ReW) annual audit
Jahresabschlußzahlungen *fpl* (Fin) end-of-year payments
Jahresabschreibung *f*
(ReW) annual depreciation charge (*or* expense)
- depreciation per period
- periodical depreciation charge (*or* expense)
Jahresarbeitslohn *m* (Pw) annual wage
Jahresarbeitsverdienst *m* (SoZV) annual earnings
Jahresarbeitsverdienstgrenze *f* (SozV) taxable wage base *(ie, monthly earnings ceiling for the assessment of social insurance contributions; syn, Versicherungspflichtgrenze)*
Jahresausgleich *m* (StR) = *Lohnsteuerjahresausgleich*
Jahresbedarf *m* (com) annual requirements
Jahresbeitrag *m* (com) annual membership fee
Jahresbericht *m* (ReW, StR) annual report
Jahresbilanz *f* (ReW) annual balance sheet
Jahresbonus *m* (com) annual quantity discount
Jahresbruttolohn *m* (StR) gross annual earnings
Jahreseinkommen *n* (Pw) annual income (*or* earnings)
Jahreserfolg *m* (ReW) profit (*or* results) for the year
Jahresergebnis *n* (ReW) = *Jahreserfolg*
Jahresfehlbetrag *m*
(ReW) loss for the year, § 157 I No. 28 AktG
(Fin) annual deficit (*or* shortfall)
Jahresfreibetrag *m* (StR) annual allowance
Jahresfrist *f* (com) one-year-period
Jahresgebühr *f* (com) annual fee

Jahresgehalt *n* (Pw) annual (*or* yearly) salary
Jahresgewinn *m*
(ReW) net profit for the year
(Fin) annual net cash inflow *(ie, determined in preinvestment analysis)*
Jahreshauptversammlung *f*
(Bw) annual meeting of shareholders (*or* stockholders)
- (GB) annual general meeting, AGM
Jahreshöchstkurs *m* (Bö) yearly high
Jahresinventur *f* (ReW) annual (*or* year-end) inventory
Jahreslohn *m* (Pw) annual wage
Jahreslohnrunde *f* (Pw) annual round of wage bargaining
Jahresprämie *f* (Vers) annual premium
Jahresprojektion *f* (Vw) annual projection of economic activity
Jahresrate *f* (com) annual rate *(eg, construction costs rise at an ... of 13%)*
(Fin) annual installment
Jahresreingewinn *m* (ReW) net profit for the year
Jahresrohmiete *f* (StR) gross annual rental *(ie, total annual consideration payable for the use of property; based on net rentals which, for the purpose of administrative simplification, are converted into gross rentals, § 79 BewG)*
Jahressteuer *f* (StR) tax computed on a fiscal year basis, § 2 VII EStG
Jahrestiefstkurs *m* (Bö) yearly low
Jahresüberschadenrückversicherung *f* (Vers) aggregate excess of loss reinsurance
Jahresüberschuß *m* (ReW) profit for the year, § 157 I No. 28 AktG
Jahresüberschuß *m* **vor Steuern** (ReW) pre-tax profit for the year
Jahresübersicht *f* (com) annual review
Jahresultimo *m* (com) end of year
Jahresumsatz *m*
(ReW) annual sales
- (GB) annual turnover
Jahresurlaub *m* (Pw) annual vacation
Jahresverdienst *m* (Pw) annual earnings
Jahresversammlung *f* (com) annual general meeting
Jahresvertrag *m* (Re) one-year contract (*or* agreement)
Jahreswert *m* **von Nutzungen** (StR) annual value of benefits, §§ 15, 16 BewG *(ie, fruits or proceeds of property)*
Jahreswirtschaftsbericht *m* (Vw) Annual Economic Report *(ie, submitted by the Federal Government)*
jahreszeitliche Schwankungen *fpl* (Stat) seasonal variations
Jahreszinsen *mpl* (Fin) annual interest

Jahreszins *m* **Festverzinslicher** (Fin) coupon yield
jährliche Abschreibung *f* (ReW) = *Jahresabschreibung*
jährliche Änderungsrate *f* (Vw) annualized rate of change
jährliche Einkommensteuererklärung *f* (StR) annual income tax return
jährliche Gesamtbelastung *f* (Fin) annual percentage rate
jährlicher Abschreibungsaufwand *m* (ReW) annual depreciation expense
jährlicher Einnahmeüberschuß *m* (Fin) annual cash flow
jährliche Rendite *f* (Fin) annual return
jährlicher Lagerabgang *m* (MaW) annual usage
jederzeit (Re) at all reasonable times
jederzeit kündbar (Fin) terminable at call
jedes Kollo eine Taxe (com) each package separately insured
je Stück (com) apiece *(eg, price is ... apiece)*
jeweilig
 (com) currrent
 – obtaining
 – prevailing
 – in effect
jeweiliger (Re) ... for the time being *(eg, holder, owner, president for the time being)*
Jobdisponent *m* (EDV) job scheduler
Jobeingabefluß *m* (EDV) input job stream
Jobmanagement *n* (EDV) job management *(ie, general term that describes the functions of job scheduler and high-level scheduler)*
Jobverarbeitung *f* (EDV) job shop system
Journal *n*
 (ReW) journal
 – daybook
 – book of original entry
 (syn, Tagebuch, Memorial, Grundbuch, Primanota)
Journalbeleg *m* (ReW) journal voucher
Journalbuchung *f* (ReW) journal entry
Jugendarbeitslosigkeit *f* (Vw) youth unemployment
Jumbo-Ehe *f* (Fin) giant merger
Jumbo-Rat *m* (EG) jumbo council
junge Aktie *f* (Fin) new share *(syn, neue Aktie)*
jüngere Anmeldung *f* (Pat) subsequent application
jüngeres Patent *n* (Pat) subsequent patent
junger Wirtschaftszweig *m* (Vw) infant industry

Junktimklausel *f* (Re) package-deal clause
Junktor *m* (Log) propositional (*or* sentential) connective
Junktor *m* **der Aussagenlogik** (Log) connective of propositional logic
Junktorenlogik *f* (Log) propositional (*or* sentential) logic
Jurastudent *m* (Re) law student
Jura studieren
 (Re) to study for the bar
 – (GB) to read law
 – (GB, infml) to eat one's dinners
Jurist *m* (Re) lawyer *(ie, any person learned in the law; not ‚jurist': a term that is preferably used to describe a ‚Rechtsgelehrter')*
juristische Fakultät *f*
 (Re) law school
 – (GB) law faculty
juristische Fiktion *f*
 (Re) legal fiction
 – (GB *also*) legal figment
juristische Handlung *f* (Re) legal (*or* juristic) act *(ie, act of a private individual directed to the origin, termination, or alteration of a right)*
juristische Person *f*
 (Re) legal person
 Also:
 – legal entity
 – artificial (*or* juristic) person
 – juridical personality
 – body corporate
 – corporate body
juristische Person *f* **des öffentlichen Rechts**
 (Re) legal person under public law
 – public law body
juristische Person *f* **des privaten Rechts** (Re) legal person under private law
juristischer Berater *m* (Re) legal adviser
juristischer Fachausdruck *m*
 (Re) legal term
 – term of legal parlance
juristisches Kleid *n* (Re) legal shell
Jurist *m* **werden wollen** (Pw) to seek a career as a lawyer
justitiabel (Re) justiciable *(ie, capable of being settled by law or in court)*
Justitiar *m*
 (Re) corporate attorney (*or* counsel)
 – in-house counsel

K

Kabelauszahlungen *fpl* (Fin) cable transfers, C. T. *(ie, no longer quoted in German foreign exchange markets)*
Kabelbuch *n* (Re) Ocean Cable Register *(ie, kept by the ‚Kabelbuchamt' at the Amtsgericht Berlin-Schöneberg)*
Kabelfernsehen *n* (Mk) cable television
Kabeljaukrieg *m* (EG) Cod War
Kabotage *f* (com) cabotage *(ie, coasting trade)*
 (com) cabotage *(ie, right of a country to license air transport within its borders; of little relevance in Europe)*
kaduzierte Aktie *f* (Fin) forfeited share
Kaduzierung *f* (Re) exclusion of defaulting shareholder *(ie, through cancellation or forfeiture of shares, § 64 AktG, § 21 GmbHG)*
Kaffeepause *f* (Pw) coffee break
Kaffeesteuer *f* (StR) coffee tax
Kaffeeterminbörse *f*
 (Bö) forward coffee exchange

- trading in coffee futures
Kahlpfändung f (Re) attachment and sale of all assets of a debtor, § 811 ZPO
Kaiablieferungsschein m (com) wharf's receipt
Kaianschlußgleis n (com) dock siding
Kaiempfangsschein m
(com) dock receipt
- wharfinger's note
Kaigebühren fpl
(com) dockage
- dock charges (or dues)
- wharfage charges
- quayage (or quay dues)
Kaigeld n (com) pierage
Kai-Receipt n (com) quay receipt
Kaldor-Hicks-Kriterium n (Vw) Kaldor-Hicks criterion
Kalenderabweichung f (Stat) calendar variation
kalenderbereinigt (Stat) after adjustment for working-day variations
Kalendereinflüsse mpl (Stat) working-day variations
Kalenderjahr n (com) calendar year
Kalendervierteljahr n (com) calendar quarter
Kalenderzeitanalyse f (Bw) clock time analysis (ie, developed by McDongall and Neal)
Kalkül n
(com) estimate
- consideration
(Vw, Bw) analysis
(Log, Math) calculus (ie, the two most important types of logical calculi are ‚propositional‘ or ‚sentential‘ and ‚predicate‘ or ‚functional‘, respectively = Aussagen- und Prädikatenkalkül)
Kalkulation f
(KoR) cost estimating
- costing (ie, activity)
(KoR) cost estimate (ie, result)
(KoR) cost estimate system (ie, part of cost accounting system)
Kalkulationsabschlag m (Mk) markdown
Kalkulationsabteilung f
(KoR) cost estimating department
- costing department
Kalkulationsaufschlag m (Mk) markup
Kalkulationsdaten pl
(KoR) cost estimate data
- costing data
Kalkulationsfaktor m (com) markup factor
Kalkulationskarte f (KoR) product cost card
Kalkulationskartell n (Kart) cost estimating cartel (ie, prices are fixed on the basis of a unified cost calculating system)
Kalkulationsleitfaden m (KoR) cost accounting guide
Kalkulationsschema n (KoR) cost estimate sheet
Kalkulationsspanne f (Mk) pricing margin
Kalkulationsstichtag m (KoR) costing reference date
Kalkulationsunterlagen fpl
(KoR) costing data
- cost estimate data
Kalkulationsverfahren n (KoR) costing technique
Kalkulationszinsfuß m
(Fin) internal rate of discount

- proper discount rate
- required rate of return (ie, applied in preinvestment analysis = Investitionsrechnung)
Also:
- adequate target rate
- minimum acceptable rate
- conventional (or prevailing or stipulated) interest rate
Kalkulationszuschlag m (KoR) costing rate
Kalkulator m
(Kor) cost estimator
- costing clerk
kalkulatorisch
(ReW) implicit
- imputed
- as if
- fictitious
kalkulatorische Abschreibung f
(ReW) imputed (or implicit) depreciation allowance
- cost-accounting depreciation allowance
kalkulatorische Bewertung f (KoR) pricing of input factors (ie, for cost accounting purposes)
kalkulatorische Kosten pl (ReW) implicit (or imputed) costs
kalkulatorische Kostenarten fpl (ReW) implicit (or imputed) cost categories
kalkulatorischer Faktorertrag m (Vw) implicit factor return
kalkulatorischer Gewinn m (ReW) imputed profit (ie, based on the ‚Leitsätze für die Preisermittlung auf Grund von Selbstkosten', LSP; covering a general entrepreneurial risk)
kalkulatorische Risiken npl (KoR) = kalkulatorische Wagnisse
kalkulatorischer Restwert m (KoR) calculated residual value
kalkulatorischer Unternehmerlohn m
(ReW) fictitious compensation (for owner's services)
- implicit entrepreneurial wages
- imputed wages of management
kalkulatorische Wagnisse npl
(KoR) imputed risks
- imputed risk premium
kalkulatorische Zinsen mpl
(ReW) imputed
- implicit
- fictitious ... interest charge
(ie, on owner's investment)
kalkulierbare Risiken npl (Bw) insurable and imputed risks (ie, special risks are fire, theft, mining subsidence damage = Bergschäden; opp, Unternehmerrisiko)
kalkulieren
(KoR) to estimate costs
- to cost
kalkulierte Auftragskosten pl (KoR) estimated job order costs
kalkulierter Wert m (com) estimated value
Kaltlagerung f (com) cold storage
Kaltstart m (EDV) cold start
Kameralismus m (Vw) cameralism (ie, variety of mercantilism in Germany and Austria in the 17th and 18th centuries)

Kameralistik f (FiW) cameralistics *(ie, science of public finance, esp. its peculiar style of accountancy)*
kameralistische Buchführung f (FiW) governmental accounting *(ie, cash receipts-expenditure accounting, not accrual accounting)*
Kameralwissenschaft f (Vw) = *Kameralismus*
Kammer f
  (com) chamber
  (ie, statutory association organized to promote the interests of a particular trade or commerce; eg, Industrie- und Handelskammer, Handwerkskammer)
  (Re) court division *(eg, dealing with commercial matters = Kammer für Handelssachen)*
Kammerbörsen fpl (Bö) securities exchanges *set up and maintained by local chambers of commerce and industry, which act as institutional carriers: Berlin, Hamburg, Frankfurt; opp, Vereinsbörsen*
Kammer f **für Handelssachen** (Re) court division handling commercial matters
Kammergericht n (Kart) Court of Appeals *(ie, in Berlin, competent to decide appeals taken against decisions of the Federal Cartel Office = Bundeskartellamt)*
Kammlinie f (Vw) ridge line
Kampagnebetrieb m (com) crop season enterprise *(eg, based on sugar beet harvesting)*
Kampfabstimmung f
  (Pw) divisive voting *(eg, on the supervisory board)*
  – vote on a controversial issue
Kampfbereitschaft f (Pw) willingness *(ie, of labor unions)* to embark upon industrial action
Kampfmaßnahmen fpl (Pw) industrial action
Kampfparität f (Pw) parity of weapons in industrial disputes *(ie, strike v. lockout)*
Kampfpreis m (com) cut-rate price
Kampfstrategie f (Vw) strategy of economic warfare *(ie, boycott, strike, lockout, cutthroat undercutting, economic duress)*
Kampfzoll m (AuW) retaliatory duty *(or tariff)*
Kanal m
  (EDV) channel
  – trunk
Kanaladreßwort n
  (EDV) channel address word
Kanalbefehlswort n (EDV) channel command word
Kanalkapazität f (EDV) channel capacity
Kanalprogramm n (EDV) channel program
Kanalsprungbefehl m (EDV) transfer-in-channel command
Kanalzustandsbyte n (EDV) channel status byte, CSB
Kanalzustandsregister n (EDV) channel status register
Kandidat m (Pw) candidate
Kandidatur f
  (Pw) candidacy
  – (GB) candidature
Kandidatur f **zurückziehen** (com) to withdraw one's candidacy
kandidieren (com) to stand as a candidate
Kannkaufmann m (Re) undertaking entitled, but not obliged, to be entered on the Commercial Register, § 3 HGB
Kann-Knoten m (OR) may-follow node
Kannleistungen fpl (SozV) discretionary benefits *(ie, not based on legal claims)*
Kannvorschrift f (Re) facultative provision *(ie, one operating at the will of the party or parties concerned)*
kanonische Analyse f (Stat) canonical analysis *(ie, establishing a simultaneous prognosis of several dependent variables)*
kanonische Form f **der Matrix** (Math) canonical *(or* normal) form of matrix
kanonische Koeffizienten mpl (Stat) canonical coefficients *(ie, the end result of canonical analysis)*
kanonische Korrelation f (Stat) canonical correlation
kanonische Studentverteilung f (Stat) canonical Student distribution
kanonische Zufallsvariable f (Stat) canonical variate
Kante f
  (OR) branch
  – edge
Kantenfluß m (OR) arc flow
Kantenprogression f (OR) chain *(or* edge) progression
Kanzleideutsch n (com) offialese
Kapazität f (Bw) capacity *(ie, potential output of a plant per period)*
Kapazität f **ausfahren**
  (IndE) to produce to maximum potential
  – to operate
  – to run
  – to work ... to capacity
Kapazitäten fpl **abbauen** (Bw) to close manufacturing facilities
Kapazitäten fpl **einmotten** (Bw, infml) to mothball capacities
Kapazitäten fpl **stillegen** (Bw) to close down plant facilities
Kapazität f **erweitern**
  (Bw) to expand plant capacity
  – to extend operations
Kapazität f **e-s Betriebes** (Bw) plant capacity
Kapazität f **e-s Marktes**
  (Mk) absorptive capacity of a market
  – market potential
Kapazität f **e-s Schnittes** (Math) capacity of a cut
Kapazität f **reduzieren** (Bw) to cut (back) capacity
Kapazitätsabbau m
  (Bw) cut in production capacity
  – cutback in capacity
  – reduction in capacity
  – shutting capacity
Kapazitätsabweichung f (KoR) capacity variance
Kapazitätsanpassung f (Bw) capacity adjustment
Kapazitätsauslastung f (Bw) = *Kapazitätsausnutzung*
Kapazitätsausnutzung f
  (Bw) capacity utilization *(eg, is down to 75%, or: is at a healthy 90%)*
  Also:
  – plant utilization

Kapazitätsausnutzungsgrad
– capacity working
Kapazitätsausnutzungsgrad *m*
(Bw) degree (*or* level) of capacity utilization
– (capacity) utilization rate
– operating rate
– plant utilization rate
(ie, ratio of actual utilization to attainable capacity working)
Kapazitätsausweitung *f* (Bw) = *Kapazitätserweiterung*
Kapazitätsbedarf *m* (OR) amount of work (RAMPS)
Kapazitätsbedarf *m* **ausgleichen** (Bw) to level capacity requirements
Kapazitätsbedarfsermittlung *f* (OR) resource allocation
Kapazitätsbelastungsplanung *f* (IndE) planning of machine operating rates
Kapazitätsbeschränkungen *fpl* (IndE) capacity constraints (*or* limitations)
Kapazitätseffekt *m* (Vw) capacity-increasing effect of investments *(ie, measured with the aid of the capital-output ratio = Kapazitätskoeffizient)*
Kapazitätsengpaß *m* (IndE) production bottleneck
Kapazitätserweiterung *f*
(Vw) expansion of capital stock
(Bw) addition to capacity
– increase in capacity
– expansion of plant facilities
(ie, expansion, purchase, and construction of plants)
Kapazitätserweiterungseffekt *m* (Bw) capacity increasing effect *(syn, Lohmann-Ruchti-Effekt: depreciation through use as a potential source of new investments)*
Kapazitätsfaktor *m* (Bw) capacity (*or* load) factor
Kapazitätsgrenze *f*
(Bw) capacity barrier (*or* limit)
– limit of plant capacity
Kapazitätskosten *pl*
(KoR) capacity cost *(ie, when operating at full capacity)*
(KoR) fixed cost *(ie, to the extent that it is a function of capacity, fixed cost often varies with the size of a plant)*
Kapazitätslinie *f*
(Vw) capacity frontier (*or* line)
– transformation curve
Kapazitätslücke *f* (Bw) capacity gap
Kapazitätsmatrix *f* (OR) capacity matrix
Kapazitätsoptimum *n* (Bw) ideal capacity
Kapazitätsplanung *f* (Bw) capacity planning
Kapazitätspolitik *f* (Bw) capacity policy
Kapazitätsquerschnitt *m* (IndE) capacity cross-section
Kapazitätsreserve *f* (Bw) idle (*or* unused) capacity
Kapazitätsüberhang *m* (Bw) excess (*or* unused) capacity
Kapazitätsverminderung *f* (Bw) capacity decrease
Kaperbrief *m* (SeeV) letter of mart
Kapital *n* (Math) principal *(ie, basic amount without interest)*
(Vw) capital *(ie, one of the factors of production)*
– capital *(ie, funds for capital spending purposes)*

Kapitalbedarfsplan
(Bw) capital of a business undertaking *(ie, total assets of a firm)*
(Fin) capital *(ie, funds employed in a business firm)*
Kapitalabfindung *f* (Re, SozV) lump-sump compensation (*or* payment)
Kapitalabfluß *m*
(Vw) capital drain
(AuW) capital outflow
Kapitalablösung *f* (Fin) redemption (*or* substitution) of capital
Kapitalabwanderung *f* (Vw) capital drain
Kapitalakkumulation *f* (Vw) capital accumulation
Kapitalanlage *f*
(Fin) investment
– capital investment
– financial investment
– employment of capital (*or* funds)
Kapitalanlagegesellschaft *f* (Fin) capital investment company
Kapitalanlagen *fpl* **von Gebietsfremden** (VGR) nonresident capital investments
Kapitalanleger *m* (Fin) investor
Kapitalanlegerschutzverband *m* (Fin) investors' protection society
Kapitalanpassungs-Intervall *n* (Vw) capital adjustment period
Kapitalanteil *m* (Fin) capital share *(ie, in a partnership)*
Kapitalaufbau *m* (Fin) capital structure
Kapital *n* **aufbringen** (Fin) to put up (*or* to raise) capital
Kapitalaufbringung *f* (Fin) putting up (*or* raising) capital
Kapitalaufnahme *f*
(Fin) long-term borrowing
– raising of capital
(Fin) procurement of equity
Kapital *n* **aufnehmen** (Fin) to take up capital
Kapital *n* **aufstocken** (Fin) to inject fresh capital *(eg, into a company)*
Kapitalaufstockung *f*
(Fin) stocking-up of funds
– capital increase
(Fin) cash injection *(eg, an extra DM30m are pumped into the company)*
Kapitalaufwand *m* (Fin) capital expenditure (*or* spending)
Kapitalausfallrisiko *n* (Fin) loan loss risk
Kapitalausfuhr *f* (AuW) export of capital
Kapitalausfuhrland *n* (AuW) capital exporting country
Kapitalausstattung *f*
(Fin) capitalization
– capital resources
Kapitalausweitung *f* (Vw) capital widening
Kapitalbasis *f*
(Fin) capital base
– equity base
Kapitalbedarf *m*
(Fin) capital requirements
– funding needs
Kapitalbedarfsplan *m* (Fin) incoming and outgoing payments plan *(ie, part of long-term financial planning)*

Kapitalbedarfsrechnung *f*
(Fin) capital budget
(Fin) capital budgeting
Kapitalbereitstellung *f* (Fin) provision of funds
Kapitalbereitstellungskosten *pl* (Fin) loan commitment charges
Kapitalberichtigung *f* (Fin) capital adjustment
Kapitalberichtigungsaktie *f* (Fin) bonus share *(ie, issued for the adjustment of capital)*
Kapital *n* **beschaffen**
(Fin) to procure capital
– to raise funds
Kapitalbeschaffung *f*
(Fin) procurement of capital
– capital procurement
– raising of funds
Kapitalbeschaffungskosten *pl*
(Fin) capital procurement cost
– cost of funds
Kapitalbestand *m* (Vw) total capital
Kapitalbeteiligung *f* (Fin) (equity) participation
Kapitalbeteiligung *f* **des Arbeiters** (Pw) worker participation in the capital of a company
Kapitalbeteiligungsdividende *f* (Fin) = *Kapitaldividende*
Kapitalbeteiligungsgesellschaften *fpl* (Fin) capital investment companies *(ie, investing their funds in enterprises unable to issue securities)*
Kapitalbewegungen *fpl* (AuW) capital movements *(or* flow*)*
Kapitalbilanz *f*
(AuW) capital account
– balance on capital account
– balance of capital movements *(or* transactions*)*
(ie, subclassification of balance of payments; syn, Kapitalverkehrsbilanz)
Kapitalbildung *f*
(Vw) formation *(or* accumulation*)* of capital
– capital formation
Kapital *n* **binden** (Fin) to tie up *(or* lock up*)* capital *(eg, in raw materials and supplies)*
Kapitalbindung *f* (Fin) capital lockup *(or* tie-up*)*
Kapitalbindungsdauer *f* (Fin) duration of capital tie-up
Kapitalbindungsfrist *f* (Fin) period of capital tie-up
Kapitalbudget *n* (FiW, Fin) capital budget
Kapitaldecke *f*
(Fin) capital resources
– equity basis
Kapitaldeckungsplan *m*
(Fin) capital coverage plan *(ie, part of long-term financial planning)*
Kapitaldeckungsstock *m* (Vers) capital cover fund
Kapitaldeckungsverfahren *n* (SozV) funding principle
(ie, social insurance on a fully funded or invested basis; opp, Umlageververfahren = pay-as-you-go basis)
Kapitaldienst *m* (Fin) debt service *(ie, payment of matured interest and principal on borrowed funds)*
Kapitaldienstfaktor *m* (Fin) capital recovery factor *(syn, Wiedergewinnungsfaktor, applied in preinvestment analysis = Investitionsrechnung)*

Kapitaldividende *f* (Fin) capital dividend *(ie, paid by cooperatives)*
Kapitaleigner *m*
(Fin) proprietor
(Fin) shareholder *(eg, of a corporation)*
– stockholder
Kapital *n* **einbringen** (Fin) to contribute capital
– to bring capital into *(eg, a company)*
Kapitaleinbringung *f* (Fin) contribution of capital
Kapitaleinfuhr *f* (AuW) import of capital
Kapitaleinfuhrland *n* (AuW) capital importing country
Kapitaleinlage *f* (Fin) capital contribution
Kapitaleinsatz *m* (Fin) (amount of) capital employed *(or* invested*)*
Kapitaleinsatz *m* **pro Beschäftigtem** (Vw) capital labor ratio
Kapital-Embargo *n*
(AuW) capital embargo
– ban on capital exports
Kapitalentnahme *f* (Fin) withdrawal of capital
Kapital *n* **entnehmen** (Fin) to withdraw capital
Kapitalerhaltung *f*
(Bw) capital maintenance
– maintenance of capital
– preservation of corporate assets
Kapital *n* **erhöhen** (Fin) to increase capital
Kapitalerhöhung *f*
(Fin) capital increase *(or* raising*)*
– increase of share capital *(or* capital stock*)*
(ie, through self-financing or additional capital contributions by old or new members; eg, injection of DM200m of new funds)
Kapitalerhöhung *f* **aus Gesellschaftsmitteln** (Fin) capital increase out of retained earnings, §§ 207 ff AktG *(ie, by converting disclosed reserves into stated capital = Nennkapital)*
Kapitalertrag *m*
(Vw) return to capital
(ReW) income from investments
(Fin) capital yield
– income on investment
(StR) investment income
(Vers) investment earnings on funds
Kapitalertragsbilanz *f* (AuW) balance of investment income
Kapitalertragsteuer *f*
(StR) investment income tax
– tax on income from capital
– withholding tax on capital
(ie, capital yields tax on dividends and other distributions of company profits)
Kapitalertragsteuer-Durchführungsverordnung *f*
(StR) Ordinance Regulating the Withholding Tax on Income from Capital
Kapital *n* **e-s Fonds** (Fin) corpus
Kapitalexporte *mpl*
(AuW) capital exports
– export of capital
Kapitalfehlleitung *f* (Vw) misallocation of capital *(ie, channeling financial resources into suboptimum uses, often resulting in excess capacities)*
Kapital *n* **festlegen** (Fin) to tie up *(or* lock up*)* capital
Kapitalfestlegung *f* (Fin) tying up capital

Kapitalflucht *f*
(AuW) capital flight
– flight of capital
Kapitalfluß *m* (Fin) flow of funds
Kapitalflußrechnung *f*
(Fin) flow statement
– flow of funds analysis
– statement of application of funds
– statement of sources and application of funds
– statement of changes in financial position
– sources-and-uses statement
Kapitalfonds *m* (Fin) capital fund *(ie, sum of long-term borrowing and capital repayments; E. Gutenberg)*
Kapitalforderung *f* (Fin) money claim *(opp, Forderung auf andere Leistungen, such as goods, services, securities)*
Kapital *n* **freisetzen** (Fin) to free up capital
Kapitalfreisetzungseffekt *m* (Bw) = *Lohmann-Ruchti-Effekt*
Kapitalgeber *m*
(Fin) lender
(Fin) investor
Kapitalgesellschaft *f*
(Re) *(roughly)* corporation
– incorporated firm
– entity of the commercial law
(ie, general category comprising AG, GmbH, KGaA, bergrechtliche Gewerkschaft; opp, Personengesellschaft)
Kapitalgüter *npl*
(Vw) capital
– investment
– instrumental ... goods
Kapital *n* **herabsetzen** (Fin) to reduce capital
Kapitalherabsetzung *f*
(Fin) capital reduction, §§ 222 ff AktG, § 58 GmbHG
– reduction of share capital
– writedown of corporate capital *(eg, in the ratio of 6:1)*
(see: ordentliche K. and vereinfachte K.)
Kapitalherabsetzung *f* **durch Einziehung von Aktien** (Fin) reduction of capital by redemption of shares
Kapitalherkunft *f* (Fin) sources of finance
Kapitalhilfe *f* (AuW) financial assistance
Kapitalhilfe *f* **ohne politische Auflagen** (AuW) capital aid with no strings attached
Kapitalimporte *mpl* (AuW) capital imports
Kapitalintensität *f*
(Vw) capital-labor ratio *(ie, of production)*
– capital intensity
(ie, ratio of capital stock C to labor input L = main determinant of labor productivity)
kapitalintensiv (Bw) capital intensive
kapitalintensive Betriebe *mpl* (Vw) capital intensive companies (*or* enterprises)
kapitalintensive Produktion *f* (Bw) capital-intensive production
kapitalintensive Wirtschaftszweige *mpl* (Vw) capital intensive industries
kapitalisierbar (Fin) capitalizable
kapitalisieren
(ReW) to capitalize *(ie, to carry as asset; opp, to expense = als Aufwand – der Periode – verbuchen)*
(Fin) to capitalize *(ie, to discount the present value of future earnings)*
kapitalisierte Aufwendungen *pl* (ReW) capitalized expense
kapitalisierte Zinsen *mpl* (Fin) capitalized interest
Kapitalisierung *f* (ReW, Fin) capitalization
Kapitalisierungsfaktor *m* (Fin) capitalization factor
Kapitalisierungsformel *f*
(Bw) earning capacity standard *(ie, used in the valuation of enterprises as a whole = Unternehmensbewertung)*
(Fin) capitalized value standard
Kapitalismus *m* (Vw) capitalism
Kapitalist *m* (Vw) capitalist
kapitalistisch
(Vw) capitalist
– capitalistic
kapitalistische Wirtschaft *f* (Vw) capitalist economy
Kapitalknappheit *f* (Fin) shortage of capital
Kapitalkoeffizient *m* (Vw) capital-output ratio
Kapitalkonsolidierung *f* (Fin) consolidation of investment
Kapitalkonto *n*
(ReW) proprietary account
(ie, in the case of sole proprietorships and partnerships)
(ReW) capital account
(ie, showing the fixed amount of capital stock of incorporated entities)
Kapitalkontrolle *f* (AuW) capital control
Kapital-Konvertibilität *f* (AuW) capital-account convertibility *(ie, allowing unrestricted convertibility in capital transactions)*
Kapitalkonzentration *f* (Bw) capital concentration
Kapitalkosten *pl*
(Fin) cost of capital
– cost of borrowed funds
(Fin) capital charges *(ie, interest, depreciation, repayment)*
Kapitalkosten *pl* **je Leistungseinheit** (Fin) capital cost compound
Kapitalkosten *pl* **je Produkteinheit** (Vw) capital cost per unit of output
Kapitalkraft *f*
(Fin) strength of capital resources
– financial strength
kapitalkräftig
(Fin) well-funded
– financially powerful
Kapitallebensversicherung *f*
(Vers) capital sum life insurance
– endowment insurance
Kapitallenkung *f* (Vw) capital (*or* investment) control
Kapitallücke *f* (Fin) capital gap
Kapitalmangel *m* (Fin) lack of capital
Kapitalmarkt *m* (Fin) capital market
Kapitalmarkt *m* **anzapfen** (Fin) to tap the capital market
Kapitalmarktausschuß *m* (Fin) German Capital Market Subcommittee
Kapitalmarkteffizienz *f* (Fin) capital market effi-

ciency *(ie, hypothesis trying to explain stock price movements)*
Kapitalmarktforschung *f* (Bw) capital market research
Kapitalmarkt-Gesellschaft *f* (Fin) publicly quoted company (*or* corporation)
Kapitalmarkt *m* **in Anspruch nehmen** (Fin) to go to (*or* draw on) the capital market
Kapitalmarktinstitute *npl* (Fin) banking institutions operating in the capital market *(ie, commercial banks, savings banks, credit cooperatives, but not 'Bausparkassen')*
Kapitalmarktintervention *f* (Fin) intervention in the capital market
Kapitalmarktklima *n* (Fin) capital market conditions
Kapitalmarktpapiere *npl* (Fin) capital market paper
Kapitalmarktpflege *f* (Fin) supporting the capital market
Kapitalmarktstatistik *f* (Fin) capital market statistics *(ie, prepared by the Deutsche Bundesbank)*
Kapitalmarktsteuerung *f* (Fin) capital market control
Kapitalmarktzins *m* (Fin) capital-market interest rate
kapitalmäßige Bindung *f* (Fin) capital linkage (*or* tie-in)
kapitalmäßige Verflechtung *f* (Fin) capital tie-up
Kapitalmehrheit *f*
(Fin) equity majority
– majority shareholding
Kapitalnachfrage *f* (Fin) demand for capital
Kapitalnutzung *f* (Fin) capital utilization
Kapitalnutzungsentschädigung *f* (Fin) service charge for the use of money
Kapitalnutzungskosten *pl* (Fin) capital user cost
Kapitalpolster *n* (Fin) equity cushion
Kapitalproduktivität *f* (Vw) output-capital ratio *(ie, reciprocal of 'Kapitalkoeffizient')*
Kapitalquellen *fpl* (Fin) sources of capital
Kapitalrendite *f* (Fin) (rate of) return on investment, RoI
Kapitalrentabilität *f*
(Fin) return on capital employed
– return on investment
(Fin) earning power of capital employed
Kapitalrente *f*
(Vw) capital rent
(Fin) annuity
– pension from capital yield
Kapital-Restriktionen *fpl* (Fin) capital constraints
Kapitalrückfluß *m* (Fin) capital recovery
Kapitalrückflußdauer *f* (Fin) payback period
Kapitalrückflußmethode *f* (Fin) payback (*or* payoff) analysis *(ie, in evaluating investment projects)*
Kapitalrückflußrate *f* (Fin) capital recapture rate
Kapitalrückführung *f* (Fin) repatriation of capital
Kapitalrückgewinnung *f* (Fin) capital recovery
Kapitalrückzahlung *f* (Fin) repayment of capital
Kapitalsammelstelle *f* (Fin) institutional investor (*or* buyer)
Kapitalschnitt *m*
(Fin) capital writedown

– (sharp) writedown of capital
Kapitalspritze *f*
(Fin) injection of capital
– cash injection
Kapitalstau *m* (Fin) piling up of investment capital
Kapitalstock *m*
(Vw) capital stock
– stock of capital
Kapitalstockanpassungsprinzip *n* (Vw) principle of capital-stock adjustment *(ie, modifies the accelerator principle)*
Kapitalstrom *m* (AuW) capital flow
Kapitalstruktur *f*
(Fin) capital (*or* financial) structure
– financing mix
Kapitalstrukturpolitik *f* (Bw) capital structure policy
Kapitalsubstanz *f* (Fin) real capital
Kapitalsumme *f* (Fin) principal *(ie, basic amount without interest)*
Kapitaltransfer *m* (Fin) transfer of capital
Kapitalüberweisungen *fpl* (Fin) capital transfers
Kapitalumschichtung *f* (Fin) switching of capital
Kapitalumschlag *m*
(Fin) capital (*or* asset) turnover
– (GB) turnover to average total assets
(ie, one of the components of the RoI ratio system; opp, Umsatzrentabilität, qv)
Kapitalumschlaghäufigkeit *f* (Fin) = *Kapitalumschlag*
Kapitalumstellung *f* (Fin) capital reorganization
Kapital *n* **und Rücklagen** *fpl* (ReW) capital and retained earnings
Kapital *n* **und Zinsen** *mpl* (Fin) principal and interest
Kapitalverflechtung *f*
(AuW) capital links
(Fin) financial interlocking (*or* interrelation)
– interlocking capital arrangements
Kapitalverkehr *m*
(AuW) movements of capital
– capital movements
– capital transactions
Kapitalverkehrsbilanz *f* (AuW) = *Kapitalbilanz*
Kapitalverkehrskontrolle *f*
(AuW) control on the movement of capital
– capital controls
(ie, restricting international currency transactions)
Kapitalverkehrsteuer *f* (StR) capital transfer tax *(ie, includes Gesellschaftsteuer = company tax, and Börsenumsatzsteuer = exchange turnover tax)*
Kapitalverkehrsteuer-Durchführungsverordnung *f* (StR) Ordinance Regulating the Capital Transfer Tax Law
Kapitalverkehrsteuergesetz *n* (StR) Capital Transfer Tax Law, of 17 Nov 1972
Kapitalvernichtung *f* (Vw) destruction of capital
Kapitalverschleiß *m*
(VGR) capital (asset) consumption
– capital consumption allowance
Kapitalversicherung *f* (Vers) endowment insurance
Kapitalvertiefung *f* (Vw) capital deepening
Kapitalvertreter *pl* (Fin) stockholders' side

Kapitalverwaltungsgesellschaft (Fin) investment company (*or* fund)
Kapitalverwässerung *f*
(Fin) capital dilution
– dilution of equity
– stock watering
Kapitalverwendung *f* (Fin) employment of capital (*or* funds)
Kapitalverzinsung *f*
(Fin) interest on principal
(Fin) = *Kapitalrendite*
Kapitalwert *m*
(Fin) net present
– capital
– capitalized . . . value
(eg, of an annuity or right of use)
(Vers) cash value *(ie, of policy)*
Kapitalwertmethode *f* (Fin) net present value (*or* NPV) method *(ie, used in investment analysis)*
Kapitalzins *m*
(Fin) long-term interest rate
(Fin) = *Kapitalverzinsung*
(Fin) rate of return on investment (*or* on capital employed)
Kapitalzufluß *m*
(AuW) capital inflow
– influx of capital
(Fin) inflow of funds
Kapital *n* **zuführen** (Fin) to inject fresh capital *(ie, into a company or plant)*
Kapitalzuführung *f*
(Fin) new capital injection
– injection of fresh funds (*or* new capital)
Kapitalzusammenlegung *f* (Fin) capital reduction (*or* merger)
Kapitalzuwachs *m* (Fin) capital accretion
Kapitalzuwachs *m* **aus Höherbewertung von Vermögensteilen** (ReW) revaluation reserve (*or* excess *or* surplus)
Kapitel *n* (EDV, Cobol) section
Kapitellisten *fpl* (EDV, Cobol) report sections
Kapitelname *m* (EDV) section name
Kapitelüberschrift *f* (EDV, Cobol) section header
kardinale Nutzentheorie *f* (Vw) theory of cardinal utility
kardinaler Nutzen *m* (Vw) cardinal utility *(opp, ordinaler Nutzen = ordinal utility)*
kardinales Meßkonzept *n* (Vw) cardinal utility approach
kardinales Nutzenmaß *n* (Vw) cardinal utility measure
Kardinalzahl *f* (Math) cardinal number
Karenzentschädigung *f* (Re) compensation paid for the period of prohibition of competition, § 74 II HGB
Karenzklausel *f* (Kart) restraint of competition clause
Karenzzeit *f* (Pw) cooling period
(Vers) qualifying (*or* waiting) period
Kargo *m* (com) cargo, *pl.* cargoes, cargos *(ie, freight carried by ship, plane, or vehicle)*
Kargoversicherung *f* (Vers) cargo insurance *(ie, insurance against loss to cargo carried in ships or by other means of transportation, such as trucks,* planes; *opp, Kaskoversicherung = hull coverage)*
Karriere *f* (Pw) career
Karrierefrau *f* (Pw) career woman (*or* girl)
Karriere *f* **machen** (Pw) to make a fast career
Karrieremacher *m* (Pw) careerist *(ie, perhaps willing to act unfairly to advance up the organization pyramid)*
Karriere *f* **planen** (Pw) to plan one's own career
Karriereplanung *f* (Pw) career planning
Karriereplanungs-Seminar *n* (Pw) career planning workshop
Karrierismus *m* (Pw) careerism
Karrierist *m* (Pw) = *Karrieremacher*
Karte *f* (EDV) (punched) card
– magnetic card
Karte-Band-Umsetzer *m* (EDV) card-to-tape converter
Kartei *f* (com) card file
Karteiauswahl *f* (Stat) file sampling
Karteibuchführung *f* (ReW) card accounting
Karteikarte *f*
(com) index card
– (GB) record card
karteimäßige Bestandsaufnahme *f* (ReW) card-file monitored inventory
Karte-Karte-Programm *n* (EDV) card-to-card program
Kartell *n* (Bw) cartel *(ie, in the United States, cartels are better known under the term ‚loose combinations')*
Kartellabsprache *f* (Kart) cartel agreement
Kartellamt *n* (Kart) *(Berlin-based)* Federal Cartel Office
Kartellanmeldung *f* (Kart) filing a cartel agreement
Kartell *n* **auflösen** (Kart) to break up a cartel
Kartellbehörde *f*
(Kart) cartel authority
– (US) antitrust enforcement agency *(ie, Department of Justice and Federal Trade Commission)*
Kartellbeschluß *m* (Kart) cartel decision
Kartellbeteiligung *f* (Kart) cartel participation
Kartelle *npl* **bekämpfen** (Kart) to combat cartels
Kartellgesetz *n* (kart) West German Antitrust Law *(syn, Gesetz gegen Wettbewerbsbeschränkungen, GWB = Law Against Restraint of Competition)*
Kartellhürde *f* **nehmen** (Kart) to clear the antitrust hurdle
Kartellhüter *mpl* (Kart, infml) cartel watchdogs
kartellieren (Kart) to cartelize
Kartellierung *f* (Kart) cartelization
Kartelljurist *m* (Kart) antitrust lawyer
Kartellnovelle *f* (Kart) amendment of the cartel law
Kartellpolitik *f* (Kart) cartel policy
Kartellquote *f* (Kart) pool quota
Kartellrecht *n* (Kart) antitrust law
kartellrechtliche Hürden *fpl*
(Kart) antitrust hurdles
– obstacles on antitrust grounds
kartellrechtlicher Grundsatz *m* (Kart) antitrust principle (*or* standard)
Kartellregister *n* (Kart) Federal Cartel Register *(ie, kept at the Federal Cartel Office, § 9 I GWB)*

Kartellverbot n (Kart) general ban on cartels
Kartellvereinbarung f (Kart) cartel agreement
Kartellvertrag m (Kart) cartel agreement
Kartellvertreter m (Kart) cartel representative
Kartenabfühler m (EDV) card reader
Kartenablage f (EDV) card ejection
Kartenablagefach n (EDV) card stacker
Kartenabtaster m (EDV) = *Kartenabfühler*
Kartenanstoß m (EDV) card jam (*or* wreck) *(syn, Lochkartenstau, Kartensalat)*
Kartenbahn f (EDV) card bed (*or* track)
Kartencode m (EDV) card code
Kartendatei f (EDV) card file
Kartendoppler m (EDV) card reproducer
Kartendurchlauf m (EDV) pass
Karteneingabe f (EDV) card input
Karteneingabefach n (EDV) card hopper (*or* magazine)
Kartenfeld n (EDV) card field
Kartenformat n (EDV) card format
Kartenführung f (EDV) card bed (*or* track)
Kartengang m (EDV) card cycle
kartengesteuerter Streifenlocher m (EDV) card-to-tape converter
Kartenhinterkante f (EDV) (card) trailing edge
Kartenlader m (EDV) card loader
Kartenleser m (EDV) card reader
Kartenlochen n (EDV) card punching
Kartenlocher m (EDV) card (*or* keyboard) punch
Kartenmagazin n (EDV) card magazine (*or* hopper)
Kartenmischer m
  (EDV) collator
  – interpolator
kartenprogrammiert (EDV) card-programmed
Kartenprüfer m (EDV) card verifier
Kartenprüfung f (EDV) card verifying
Kartenrückseite f (EDV) card back
Kartensalat m (EDV) card jam (*or* wreck) *(syn, Lochkartenstau, Kartenausstoß)*
Kartenspalte f (EDV) card column
Kartenstanzen n (EDV) card punching
Kartenstanzer m
  (EDV) automatic (feed) punch
  – card punch
  (syn, automatischer od Lochkartenstanzer)
Kartenstapel m
  (EDV) deck of cards
  – pack of punched cards
Kartensteuer f (StR) tax on playing cards
Kartenvorderkante f (EDV) (card) leading edge
Kartenvorderseite f (EDV) card face
Kartenvorschub m (EDV) card feed
Kartenzeile f (EDV) card row (*or* track)
Kartenzuführung f (EDV) card feed
Kartenzyklus m (EDV) card cycle
kartesisches Koordinatensystem n (Math) rectangular Cartesian coordinates
kartesisches Produkt n **von Mengen** (Math) Cartesian (*or* direct) product of sets
Kartogramm n (Stat) cartogram
Kaskadenbesteuerung f (FiW) cascade (*or* pyramiding) type of taxation *(ie, imposed at every stage of the economic process)*
Kaskaden-Netzwerk n (OR) cascaded network

Kaskadensteuerung f (EDV) cascade control
Kasko m (com) means of transportation = *Transportmittel*
  (Vers) = *Kaskoversicherung*
Kaskoversicherung f (Vers) collision damage insurance
  – insurance against damage to one's own automobile
  (Vers) hull insurance (*or* coverage)
  (ie, ocean marine or aviation insurance covering the ship or plane itself)
Kassabuch n (ReW) cash book
Kassadevisen pl (Bö) spot exchange
Kassadollar mpl (Fin) spot dollars
Kassageschäft n
  (Bö) cash sale (*or* operation *or* transaction)
  – spot sale (*or* deal *or* transaction)
  (opp, Termingeschäft = forward transaction)
Kassageschäfte npl
  (Bö) dealings for cash
  – cash dealings (*or* trade)
  – spot trading
Kassahandel m
  (Bö) spot dealings
  – trading for cash
Kassakauf m
  (Bö) cash purchase
  – buying outright
Kassakonto n (ReW) cash account
Kassakurs m
  (Bö) spot rate (*or* price) *(ie, of foreign exchange)*
  (Bö) daily quotation
Kassalieferung f (Bö) spot delivery
Kassamarkt m
  (Bö) cash
  – physical
  – spot ... market
Kassanotierung f (Bö) spot quotation
Kassapapiere npl (Fin) securities traded for cash
Kassaverkauf m (com) cash sale
Kassaware f (Bö) cash commodity
Kasse f
  (ReW, Fin) cash on hand
  (com) cash register
  – POS (point of sale) terminal
  (Fin) cash (*or* cahier's) office
  (Fin) cash payments handling department *(of a bank)*
Kasse f **gegen Dokumente** (com) cash against documents, c. a. d.
Kassekonto n (ReW) cash account
Kasse machen (Fin) to cash up
Kassenabstimmung f (ReW) reconciliation of cash
Kassenanweisung f (Fin) disbursement instruction
Kassenarzt m (SozV) panel doctor
Kassenärztliche Bundesvereinigung f (SozV) Federal Association of Panel Doctors
Kassenausgaben fpl (FiW) cash expenditure
Kassenausgänge mpl (Fin) cash disbursements
Kassenausgangsbuch n (ReW) cash disbursement journal
Kassenbeleg m (Rew) cash voucher
Kassenbericht m (ReW) cash report (*or* statement)
Kassenbestand m
  (ReW) cash

- cash in hand
- cash balance
- cash holding

Kassenbestandsdifferenz *f* (ReW) over and short account

Kassenbestandsnachweis *m* (Fin) records of cash totals

Kassenbestand *m* **und Guthaben** *npl* **bei Kreditinstituten** (ReW) cash and due from banks

Kassenbon *m*
(com) sales slip
- cash receipt

Kassenbuch *n*
(ReW) cashbook
- cash journal

Kassenbuchkonto *n* (ReW) cashbook account

Kassenbuchung *f* (ReW) cash entry

Kassenbudget *n* (FiW) cash budget

Kassendefizit *n*
(Fin) cash deficit (*or* shortfall)
- shorts

Kassendifferenz *f* (Fin) cash over or short

Kassendisposition *f* (Fin) cash management plan

Kassendispositionen *fpl* (Fin, FiW) cash arrangements (*or* transactions)

Kasseneingänge *mpl* (ReW) = *Kasseneinnahmen*

Kasseneinnahmen *fpl*
(ReW) cash receipts
- takings

Kassenfehlbetrag *m*
(Fin) cash deficit (*or* shortfall)
- shorts

Kassenführung *f* (Fin) cash management

Kassenguthaben *n*
(ReW) cash in hand
- cash balance

Kassenhaltung *f*
(Vw) money holding
(Fin) cash management
(Fin) cash balances
(Fin) till money (*ie, of a bank*)

Kassenhaltungseffekt *m* (Vw) cash balance effect (*M. Friedman*)

Kassenhaltungsgleichung *f* (Vw) cash balance equation ($M = k.Y$)

Kassenhaltungskoeffizient *m* (Vw) Cambridge k

Kassenhaltungsplan *m* (Fin) estimate of cash requirements

Kassenhaltungspolitik *f* (Fin) policy of optimum cash holdings

Kassenhaltungstheorie *f* (Vw) cash balance theory

Kassenkredit *m*
(FiW) cash advance
- central bank advance (*ie, to government agencies*)
- (GB) ways and means advance

Kassenkredite *mpl* (FiW) short-term lending (*ie, to governmental units*)

Kassenkreditzusage *f* (Fin) cash advance facility

Kassenlage *f* (Fin) cash position

Kassenmanko *n* (Fin) cash shortfall (*ie, determined through cash audit*)

kassenmäßige Abgrenzung *f* (FiW) in cash terms

kassenmäßige Entwicklung *f* (FiW) movement in cash position

Kassenmittel *pl*
(Fin) cash
- cash resources

Kassenobligationen *fpl*
(FiW) medium-term fixed-rate notes (*ie, issued by Federal Government, Bundesbahn, Bundespost, and a number of banks*)
- (US) DM-nominated bearer treasury notes
- (*Austria*) cash bonds

Kassenprüfung *f*
(ReW) cash audit
- spot check

Kassenquittung *f* (Fin) receipt evidencing payment for securities not yet issued

Kassenrevision *f* (ReW) cash audit

Kassensaldo *m* (ReW) cash balance

Kassenscheck *m* (Fin) open check

Kassenschlager *m* (com, infml) money-spinner

Kassenskonto *m od n* (Fin) cash discount

Kassensturz *m* (Fin) making the cash

Kassensturz *m* **machen** (Fin) to make the cash

Kassensystem *n* (Mk) checkout facility

Kassensystem *n* **auf Festbestand** (ReW) cash fund on imprest basis

Kassenterminal *n*
(EDV) point-of-sale (POS) terminal
- POS system
(*ie, microprocessor-controlled DP system used to register cash and credit sales*)

Kassentransaktion *f* (Fin) cash transaction

Kassenverein *m* (Fin) securities deposit association (*ie, financial institution operating collective security deposits and giro transfer systems; syn, Wertpapiersammelbank, Effektengirobank*)

Kassenzettel *m*
(com) sales check
- (GB) sales slip

kassieren
(com) to cash
- to collect

Kassierer *m*
(Fin) teller
- (GB) cashier

Kastendiagramm *n* (Stat) box diagram

Katallaktik *f* (Vw) catallactics (*ie, artificial term that has never won wide acceptance: political economy as the science of exchanges = politische Ökonomie als Tauschwirtschaft*)

katalogisiertes Verfahren *n* (EDV) cataloged procedure

Katalogpreis *m* (com) catalog price

Kataster *m od n* (Re) cadastre (*ie, official inventory of real property, kept by the ‚Vermessungsamt' = land surveying office*)

Katastrophenrisiko *n* (Vers) catastrophe hazard (*or* risk)

Katastrophen-Rückversicherung *f* (Vers) catastrophe reinsurance

Katastrophenverlust *m* (Vers) catastrophe loss

Katastrophenverschleiß *m* (ReW) depreciation (*or* loss of utility) through catastrophic events (*eg, fire, explosion, inundation*)

Katastrophenversicherung *f* (Vers) catastrophal hazard insurance

Katastrophenwagnis *n* (Bw) catastrophal hazard

343

(ie, included in the general entrepreneurial risk)
kategorematisches Zeichen *n* (Log) categorematic symbol *(ie, one having independent meaning; opp, synkategorematisches Zeichen)*
kategorischer Syllogismus *m* (Log) categorical syllogism
kategorisches Urteil *n* (Log) categorical *(or* subject-predicate) proposition *(ie, affirming or denying that something has a property or is a member of a class)*
kategorisieren (Log) to categorize
Kathedersozialisten *mpl* (Vw) ,,socialists of the professorial chair"
(ie, group of political economists and law professors belonging to what in the history of economics is known as the ‚historical school'; dominated German universities during the last third of the 19th century and set the stage for Bismarck's social legislation)
Kauf *m*
  (com) purchase
  (Re) sale
Kaufabrechnung *f* (Bö) bought note
Kauf *m* **abschließen**
  (com) to conclude a sale
  – to conclude a contract of sale
  – (infml) to make a deal *(or* bargain)
Kaufabsicht *f* (Mk) buying intention
Kaufangebot *n*
  (com) offer to buy
  – bid
Kaufanreiz *m* (Mk) buying incentive
Kauf *m* **auf Abruf** (com) call purchase
Kauf *m* **auf Hausse**
  (Bö) buying for a rise
  – bull buying
Kauf *m* **auf Probe** (com) sale on approval *(ie, goods may be returned though they conform to the contract)*
Kauf *m* **auf Raten**
  (com) installment purchase
  – (infml) buying on time
Kaufauftrag *m* (com) buying *(or* purchase) order
  (Bö) buy order
  – securities trading order
Kaufauftrag *m* **billigst** (Bö) buy order at market
Kauf *m* **auf Umtausch** (com) sale or exchange *(eg, a store allows purchasers to exchange goods)*
Kauf *m* **auf Ziel** (com) credit sale
Kaufbereitschaft *f* (Mk) willingness to buy
Kaufempfehlung *f* (Bö) buy recommendation
Kaufentscheidung *f* (Mk) purchase decision
Kaufschlußanalyse *f* (Mk) activation research
Käufer *m*
  (com) buyer
  – purchaser
  – (fml) vendee
Käuferabruf *m* (Bö) buyer's call
Käuferandrang *m* (Mk) run *(or* rush) of customers
Käufer *m* **e-r Rückprämie** (Bö) taker for a put
Käufer *m* **e-r Stellage** (Bö) taker for a put and call
Käufer *m* **e-r Vorprämie** (Bö) giver for a call
Käufer *m* **e-s Nochgeschäfts** (Bö) giver for a call of more
Käuferforschung *f* (Mk) psychological buyer research *(ie, emphasis on buying motives, impulse buying, brand change and loyalty, etc.)*
Käufergewohnheiten *fpl* (Mk) buying habits *(or* pattern)
Käufergruppe *f* (com) group of buyers
Käuferinteresse *n* (Bö) buying interest
Käuferkredit *m* (Fin) buyer credit *(eg, granted by a consortium led by Deutsche Bank)*
Käuferkreis *m* (com) category of buyers
Käuferland *n* (AuW) buyer country
Käufermangel *m* (Bö) lack of buying orders
Käufermarkt *m* (Vw) buyer's market *(opp, Verkäufermarkt = seller's market)*
Käuferpflichten *fpl* (Re) buyer's duties
Käuferschicht *f* (Mk) category *(or* stratum) of buyers
Käufersouveränität *f* (Mk) consumer sovereignty *(preferred syn: Konsumentensouveränität)*
Käuferstrukturanalyse *f* (Mk) category analysis
Käufer *mpl* **suchen** (com) to seek purchasers
Kauffahrteischiff *n* (com) trading vessel
Kauffahrteischiffahrt *f* (com) commercial navigation
Kauffrau *f* (com) female merchant
Kaufgegenstand *m* (com) object sold
Kaufgeldforderung *f* (com) claim for purchase price
Kaufgewohnheiten *fpl* (Mk) buying habits
Kaufhaus *n* (Mk) *(inexpensive)* department store
  – (GB) departmental store
Kaufhausgruppe *f* (Mk) department stores group
Kaufhauskonzern *m* (com) retail stores group
Kaufhauswerte *pl* (Bö) stores
Kauf *m* **in Bausch und Bogen**
  (com) bulk sale
  – purchase in bulk
  (Re, *civil law*) sale per aversionem *(ie, where goods are taken in bulk, not by weight or measure, and for a single price, usu. limited to sale of immovable property)*
Kaufinteressent *m* (com) prospective *(or* potential) buyer *(syn, Interessent)*
Kaufkosten *pl* (MaW) cost of acquisition *(eg, telephone, telex, postage, commissions, brokerage)*
Kaufkraft *f* (Vw) purchasing *(or* spending) power
Kaufkraft *f* **abschöpfen** (FiW) to skim off *(or* siphon off) purchasing power
Kaufkraftabschöpfung *f* (FiW) absorption of excess purchasing power
Kaufkraft *f* **entziehen** (FiW) to drain off purchasing power
Kaufkraftentzug *m* (FiW) drain on purchasing power
Kaufkrafterhöhung *f* (Vw) increase of purchasing power
Kaufkraftforschung *f* (Mk) purchasing power research *(ie, part of consumer analysis)*
kaufkräftige Nachfrage *f* (Vw) effective demand
Kaufkraft *f* **in die Wirtschaft pumpen** (Vw) to pump purchasing power into the economy
kaufkraftindizierte Rechnungslegung *f* (ReW) current purchasing power accounting
Kaufkraftkennzahlen *fpl* (Mk) purchasing power indices *(or* indexes)

Kaufkraftminderung *f* (Vw) loss of purchasing power
Kaufkraftparität *f* (AuW) purchasing-power parity
Kaufkraftparitätentheorie *f* (Vw) purchasing-power parity theory
Kaufkraftschöpfung *f* (Vw) creation of purchasing power
Kaufkraftstabilität *f* (Vw) stability of purchasing power
Kaufkraftüberhang *m*
(Vw) excess money supply
– excess of purchasing power
Kaufkraftvergleich *m* (Stat) comparison of purchasing power *(ie, made by OECD)*
Kaufkraftverteilung *f* (Mk) spatial pattern of purchasing power
Kaufkraftwährung *f* (Vw) index-linked currency
Kaufkredit *m* (Fin) loan to finance purchases *(ie, mostly of durable goods)*
Kaufkurs *m* (Bö) buying rate
käuflich erwerben
(com) to acquire by purchase
– to buy
– to purchase
Kaufmann *m*
(com) businessman
Also:
– trader
– dealer
– merchant
kaufmännisch buchen (ReW) to keep commercial accounts
kaufmännische Anweisung *f* (WeR) bill of exchange drawn on a merchant
kaufmännische Buchhaltung *f* (ReW) financial *(or* general) accounting
kaufmännische Datenverarbeitung *f* (EDV) business data processing
kaufmännisch eingerichteter Betrieb *m* (com) commercial enterprise
kaufmännische Lehre *f* (Pw) commercial apprenticeship
kaufmännische Orderpapiere *npl* (WeR) commercial negotiable instruments, § 363 HGB
kaufmännischer Geschäftsbetrieb *m* (com) commercially organized business operation
kaufmännischer Verpflichtungsschein *m* (WeR) certificate of obligation drawn up by a merchant
kaufmännisches Rechnen *n* (Math) business *(or* commercial) arithmetic
kaufmännisches Zurückbehaltungsrecht *n* (Re) mercantile lien *(ie, right to retain possession until claim is satisfied, but including the right of sale,* § 369 HGB)
kaufmännische Urkunde *f* (WeR) commercial document *(eg, warehouse receipt, bill of lading,* § 363 HGB)
Kauf *m* **mit Rückgaberecht** (com) sale or return
Kaufmotiv *n* (Mk) buying motive
Kauf *m* **nach Muster** (com) = *Kauf nach Probe*
Kauf *m* **nach Probe**
(Re) sale by sample, § 494 BGB
– purchase on sample
Kauf *m* **nach Warenbeschreibung** (com) sale by description

Kaufneigung *f* (Mk) inclination to buy
Kaufoption *f*
(com) buyer's option
– purchase option
(Bö) call
– call option
Kauforder *f* (Bö) buying order
Kaufortinterview *n* (Mk) point-of-purchase interview
Kaufpreis *m* (com) purchase *(or* contract) price, § 433 II BGB
Kaufpreis *m* **erstatten** (com) to refund the purchase price
Kaufpreisforderung *f* (com) purchase money claim
Kaufpreishypothek *f* (Re) purchase money mortgage
Kaufpreisminderung *f* (com) reduction in price
Kaufpreis *m* **überweisen** (com) to remit the purchase price
Kauf *m* **rückgängig machen**
(Re) to cancel
– to rescind
– to set aside ... a sale
Kauf *m* **unter Eigentumsvorbehalt** (Re) conditional sales contract *(ie, where seller reserves title until buyer pays for the goods)*
Kaufverhalten *n* (Mk) buying *(or* purchasing) pattern
Kaufverhandlungen *fpl* (com) sales negotiations
Kaufvertrag *m*
(Re) contract for sale
– purchase contract
(Note that transfer of ownership requires transfer of possession, whereas in English law mere sale as a rule transfers title to the goods, § 433 BGB)
Kaufvertrag *m* **abschließen** (com) to conclude a purchase order contract
Kaufvertragsrecht *n* (Re) law of sales
Kauf *m* **von Wertpapieren zur sofortigen Lieferung** (Bö) cash buying
Kaufwelle *f* (Bö) buying surge
Kaufwert *m*
(com) contract price
– purchase price *(or* value)
Kaufwiderstand *m* (Mk) buyer's *(or* buying) resistance
Kauf *m* **zur späteren Auslieferung** (com) forward purchase
Kaufzwang *m* (Mk) obligation to buy
Kausalanalyse *f* (Bw) causal analysis
kausaler Schluß *m* (Log) causal inference
Kausalgesetz *n* (Log) law of causation
Kausalhaftung *f* (Re) liability based on causation *(ie, irrespective of fault)*
Kausalitätsprinzip *n*
(Log) principle of causation *(or* causality)
– cause-effect principle
Kausalkette *f* (Log) chain of causation
Kausalkette *f* **der Beziehungen** (Stat) causal ordering
Kausalzusammenhang *m*
(Log) chain of causation
– causal chain
– causal connection
– causal nexus

345

– causal concatenation
Kaution f (Fin) security deposit
Kaution f **leisten** (Re) to put up bail (for)
Kautionseffekten pl (Fin) deposited securities *(ie, of a bank)*
Kautionskredit m (Fin) credit as security for a contingent liability *(opp, Avalkreditgeschäft)*
Kautionsversicherung f
(Vers) guaranty *(or* surety) insurance
– fidelity bond
Kautionsversicherungs-Gesellschaft f (Vers) guaranty association
Kautionswechsel m (Fin) bill of exchange deposited as a guaranty
Kegelschnitt m (Math) conic section
Kegelstumpf m (Math) frustrum of a cone
Kehrmatrix f (Math) inverse *(or* reciprocal) matrix
Kehrtwendung f (Vw) reversal *(eg, in central bank policy)*
kein Anschluß unter dieser Nummer (com) „no subscriber at this number"
Kellerspeicher m
(EDV) cellar
– push-down store *(syn, Stapelspeicher)*
Kellerwechsel m
(WeR) fictitious bill
– kite
– windmill
Kelley-Algorithmus m (OR) Kelley algorithm
Kennbegriff m (EDV) key
Kennbegriffsfeld n (EDV) key field
Kennbit n (EDV) marker *(or* flag) bit
Kennblock m (EDV) control block *(syn, Steuerblock)*
Kennbuchstabe m (com) identification letter
Kennedy-Runde f (AuW) Kennedy Round *(ie, of negotiations in 1967 seeking to reduce tariff levels on industrial products by about one-third)*
Kennlinie f (Math) characteristic
Kennlochung f (EDV) identifying punching
Kenn-Nummer f
(com) identification number
(ReW) account number
Kennquote f (Stat) statistical ratio
Kennsatz m (EDV, Cobol) label (record)
Kennung f
(EDV) answerback code
– station identification *(syn, Stationskennung)*
Kennungsgeber m (EDV) answerback unit
Kennungsgeberwalze f (EDV) answerback drum
Kennwort n (EDV) password
Kennzahl f
(com) code number
– reference number
(Bw) ratio
Kennzahlenanalyse f (Bw) ratio analysis
Kennzahlenhierarchie f (Fin) ratio pyramid *(eg, RoI system of E. I. du Pont de Nemours, ZVEI-Kennzahlensystem)*
Kennzeichen n (EDV) flag
Kennzeichner m (EDV, Cobol) qualifier
Kennzeichnungsbestimmungen fpl (Mk) labeling provisions
Kennzeichnungsoperator m (Log) description *(or* iota) operator

Kennzeichnungsvorschriften fpl (AuW) labeling *(or* marking) requirements
Kennziffer f
(ReW) code number *(ie, used to identify accounting items)*
(Bw) ratio
Kennziffer-Anzeige f (Pw) blind ad *(ie, one that does not identify the employer; a box number is provided for responses)*
Kennziffernanalyse f (Bw) ratio analysis
Kerblochkarte f
(EDV) edge-notched
– margin-notched
– margin punched ... card *(syn, Randlochkarte)*
Kernarbeitszeit f (Pw) core time *(ie, periods during the day when all employees are required to be present at work; the rest is flexible time = Gleitzeit)*
Kernbegriff m (Log) core concept
Kernbereiche mpl (Bw) core businesses *(or* operations)
Kern m **e-r Erfindung** (Pat) pith and marrow of an invention
Kernfamilie f (Stat) core family *(opp, Vollfamilie)*
Kernfunktion f (Bw) key *(or* basic) function
Kerngeschäft n
(Bw) bottom line
– (infml) staple diet
Kerngesellschaft f (Bw) central company
Kerninhalt m **e-s Begriffs** (Log) core intension
Kernproblem n (com) focal *(or* key) problem
Kernspeicher m (EDV) (magnetic) core memory
Kernspeicherabzug m (EDV) core (memory) dump
Kernspeicheradresse f (EDV) core memory address
Kernspeicherbelegung f (EDV) assignment of core memory space
Kernspeicherblock m (EDV) core memory stack
Kernspeicherfehler m (EDV) core memory error
Kernspeichermatrix f (EDV) core matrix
Kernspeicherplatz m (EDV) core memory location
kernspeicherresident (EDV) core memory resident
Kernspeicherwort n (EDV) core memory word
Kessel- und Maschinenversicherung f
(Vers) boiler and machinery insurance
– use and occupancy insurance
Kette f
(Mk) chain store
(EDV) chain
– catena
Kette f **e-s Graphen** (Math) chain of a graph
ketten
(EDV) to chain
– to concatenate
Kettenabschluß m (Bö) chain transaction *(ie, in forward commodity trading)*
Kettenarbeitsvertrag m (Pw) = *Kettenvertrag*
Kettenbanksystem n (Fin) chain banking
Kettenbruch m (Math) continued fraction
Kettencode m (EDV) chain code
Kettendrucker m (EDV) chain printer
Kettenhandel m (Mk) chain trade
Kettenindex m (Stat) chain relative
Kettenläden mpl (Mk) chain stores

Kettenregel f
  (Math) chain rule
  – composite-function rule
  – function-of-a-function rule
Kettenziffern fpl (Stat) chain relatives
Keynessche Theorie f (Vw) Keynesian theory
Kfz-Finanzierung f
  (com) auto financing
  – financing auto purchase
Kfz-Haftpflichtversicherung f
  (Vers) third-party motor insurance
  – motor vehicle liability insurance
Kfz-Kennzeichen n (com) automobile identification number
Kfz-Versicherung f (Vers) automobile insurance
Kilometergeld n (com) mileage allowance
Kilometerpauschale f (StR) blanket amount per km
Kinderfreibetrag m (StR) allowance for dependent children
Kindergeld n (SozV) support payment for dependent children (ie, under the ‚Bundeskindergeldgesetz')
  (StR) children's (or family) allowance
Kinderkrankheiten fpl (IndE, infml) teething troubles
Kinderkrippe f
  (Pw) crib
  – (GB) crèche
  – day nursery
Kinderzuschuß m (SozV) children's grant
kinetische Gewinne mpl (Vw) windfall profits
Kippschalter m (EDV) toggle switch
Kippschaltung f (EDV) trigger circuit
Kirchensteuer f (StR) church tax
  (ie, an addition to the income tax which the Federal states collect on behalf of the established religious bodies)
Kirchtumspolitik f (com) parish-pump (or parochial) politics (ie, putting narrow sectoral interests ahead of the common good or any other overarching goal)
Kladde f
  (ReW) daybook
  – (GB waste book
  (ie, in which the transactions of the day are entered in the order of their occurrency; syn, Vorbuch, Strazze)
Klage f
  (Re) action (ie, in a civil court)
  – lawsuit (ie, vernacular term)
  – legal proceedings (ie, in a civil court)
  – suit (ie, at law or in equity)
  – process in law (ie, instituted by one party to compel the other to do him justice)
  (StR) complaint, §§ 40ff FGO
Klage f **abweisen** (Re) to dismiss a case
Klageabweisung f (Re) dismissal of action
Klageänderung f (Re) amendment of action, §§ 263ff ZPO
Klage f **anhängig machen**
  (Re) to bring action (or suit)
  – to file (or lodge) a suit
  – to bring (or institute) legal proceedings
  – to proceed against

Klage f **auf Aufhebung e-s Vertrages** (Re) action for cancellation of contract
Klage f **auf Herausgabe** (Re) action for restitution
Klage f **auf Schadenersatz** (Re) action for damages
Klage f **auf Wandlung**
  (Re) action for cancellation of sales contract
  – (civil law) redhibitory action
  (ie, action to avoid a sale on account of some defect in the thing sold)
Klage f **aus Geschäftsführung ohne Auftrag** (Re) action on the grounds of ‚negotiorum gestio'
Klage f **aus schuldrechtlichem Vertrag** (Re) action ‚ex contractu' (ie, arising out of a contract)
Klage f **aus unerlaubter Handlung** (Re) action ‚ex delictu' (or in tort)
Klage f **aus ungerechtfertigter Bereicherung** (Re) action to remedy unjustified unrichment
Klage f **aus Vertrag** (Re) action ‚ex contractu' (or based on contract)
Klagebegehren n **entsprechen** (Re) to permit relief
Klage f **einreichen** (Re) = Klage anhängig machen
Klage f **erheben** (Re) = Klage anhängig machen
Klageerhebung f
  (Re) bringing action (or suit)
  (Kart, GB) notice of reference
Klagegrund m (Re) cause of action
Klagehäufung f (Re) consolidation of actions
Klage f **ist nicht gegeben** (Re) no action will lie
klagen
  (Re) to bring action (or suit)
  – to sue (for)
  – to go to court
  – to take legal action
Klagenschema n (StR) types of action, §§ 40, 41 FGO
Kläger m (Re) plaintiff (ie, party bringing an action or suing in a civil action)
Klagerecht n
  (Re) right of action
  – right to bring suit
Klagerücknahme f (Re) voluntary discontinuance of proceedings, § 269 ZPO
Klageschrift f (Re) statement of claim, § 253 ZPO
Klage f **stattgeben**
  (Re) to entertain an action
  – to allow an action to be brought against
Klageverjährung f (Re) limitation of action
Klammer auf (com) left parenthesis
Klammerausdruck m (Math) parenthesized expression
klammerfreie Schreibweise f
  (EDV) parenthesis-free
  – Polish
  – prefix ... notation
  (syn, polnische od Präfixschreibweise)
Klammer f **zu** (com) right parenthesis
Klarschriftleser m (EDV) optical character reader, OCR (syn, optischer Beleglesser)
Klarsichtpackung f (com) see-through pack
Klartextbelegleser m (EDV) optical character reader (syn, Klarschriftbelegleser)
Klasse f
  (Log, Math) class
  – category
  – classification

(Stat) class
— cell
Klassenanzahl *f* (Stat) number of classes (*or* cells)
Klassenbesetzung *f* (Stat) number of variates of a class
Klassenbildung *f* (Stat) grouping into classes
Klassenbreite *f* (Stat) class interval
Klasseneinteilung *f* (Math) partition of a set
Klassengrenze *f* (Stat) class boundary (*or* limit)
Klassenhäufigkeit *f* (Stat) class (*or* cell) frequency
Klassenintervall *n* (Stab) rlass interval
Klassenkalkül *n* (Log) calculus of classes
Klassenkampf *m* (Vw) class warfare
Klassenlogik *f* (Log) logic of classes
klassenlose Gesellschaft *f* (Vw) classless society
Klassenmitte *f*
(Stat) class midpoint
— class mark
— mid-value of class interval
Klassenpunkt *m* (Math) class mark
Klassensumme *f* (Math) class sum
Klassensymbol *n* (Stat) class symbol
Klassifikation *f* (Stat, Log) classification
(*ie, process of grouping individuals into classes*)
(com) classification
(*ie, of ships, by classification societies, such as Germanischer Lloyd, Norske Veritas*)
Klassifikationsattest *n* (com) certificate of classification (*ie, issued by a classification society, such as Germanischer Lloyd*)
Klassifikations-Institut *n* (com) classification society (*eg, Lloyd's Register of Shipping, Germanischer Lloyd*)
Klassifikationsschema *n* (Log) classification scheme (*or* approach)
klassifizieren
(Stat) to classify
— to categorize
— to grade
Klassifizierung *f* (com) = *Klassifikation*
Klassifizierungsgesellschaft *f* (com) classification society (*eg, Germanischer Lloyd*)
Klassifizierungsmaßzahl *f* (Stat) classification statistic
Klassiker *mpl* (Vw) classical economists (*eg, D. Hume, A. Smith, D. Ricardo, J. St. Mill*)
klassische Junktorenlogik *f* (Log) traditional (two-valued) propositional logic
Klausel *f* (Re) clause
Klausel *f* ,,**beiderseitiges Verschulden**'' (com) ,,both to blame'' collision clause
Klausel *f* ,,**frei von Bruch außer im Strandungsfall**'' (com) ,,free from wreck except in case of stranding'' clause, § 852 HGB
Klausel *f* ,,**für behaltene Ankunft**'' (com) ,,safe arrival'' clause, § 850 HGB
Klausel *f* ,,**ohne Franchise**'' (Vers) irrespective of percentage clause
Klausel *f* **über Schadenabwendung und Schadenminderung** (SeeV) sue and labor clause
Klebeeinrichtung *f* (EDV) splicer
Klebezettel *m* (com) self-adhering label
Klebstreifen *m* (com) glue strip
,,**Kleckerkonten**'' *npl* (Fin) mini-volume customer accounts

Kleinaktie *f*
(Fin) small
— micro
— midget ... stock
(*ie, stock with a minimum par value of DM50, § 8 AktG*)
Kleinaktionär *m* (Fin) small shareholder
Kleinanzeige *f*
(Mk) classified advertisement
— classified ad
— want ad
(*ie, dealing with offers or requests for jobs, used cars, apartments, etc.*)
Kleinanzeigenwerbung *f* (MK) classified (or small space) advertising
Kleinbetrieb *m* (com) small business
Kleincomputer *m* (EDV) small computer
kleine Freihandelszone *f* (AuW) European Free Trade Area, EFTA
kleine Havarie *f* (SeeV) petty average, § 621 HGB
kleine Kasse *f*
(Fin) petty cash fund
— (GB) float
(com, infml) kitty
kleine Kontroll- od Leitungsspanne *f* (Bw) narrow span of control
kleine Stückelung *f* (Fin) small denomination (*ie, of securities*)
kleine und mittlere Betriebe *mpl* (com) small and medium-sized businesses
Kleingedrucktes *n* (com) small print
Kleingeld *n* (com) small change
Kleingeschäft *n* **der Banken** (Fin) retail banking
Kleingruppenforschung *f* (Mk) small-group research
Kleinkredit *m* (Fin) loan for personal (non-business) use
Kleinleben
(Vers) industrial branch business
— industrial life insurance
— (GB) industrial assurance
kleinlich (com) narrow-minded
Kleinmaterial *n* (MaW) sundry supplies (*ie, nails, screws, etc.*)
Kleinpreisgeschäft *n* (Mk) low-price store
Kleinrechner *m* (EDV) small computer
Kleinserie *f* (IndE) small batch (*or* lot)
Kleinserienfertigung *f* (IndE) small batch production
Kleinserienprogramm *n* (IndE) (automated) small batch program
Kleinstbewegung *f* (IndE) elemental movement
kleinste obere Schranke *f*
(Math) least upper bound
— supremum
kleinster gemeinsamer Nenner *m* (Math, com) lowest common denominator
kleinstes Glied *n* (Math) least term
kleinste Untersuchungseinheit *f* (Stat) elementary unit
Kleinstrechner *m* (EDV) minicomputer
Klein- und Mittelunternehmen *npl* (com) small and medium-sized businesses
Kleinunternehmer *m*
(com, infml) small fry operator

348

(StR) small trader (*or* entrepreneur), § 19 UStG
Kleinverkaufspreis *m* (com) retail price
Kleinverkehr *m* (com) trading of goods in retail, § 104 HGB
Klient *m* (com) client
Klimaanlage *f* (com) air conditioning equipment
Klinken *fpl* **putzen**
  (com, sl) to work from door to door
  – (GB) to work on the knocker
Kluft *f* (EDV) = *Blockzwischenraum*
Klumpen *m* (Stat) cluster
Klumpenauswahl *f* (Stat) cluster sampling
Klumpenauswahlverfahren *n* (Stat) nested sampling
Klumpeneffekt *m* (Stat) cluster effect
Klumpenstichprobe *f* (Stat) cluster sample
knapp (Vw) scarce
knapp behauptet (Bö) barely steady
knapp bei Kasse (com, infml) short of funds
knappe Akkord-Vorgabezeit *f* (IndE) tight rate
knappe Liquiditätsausstattung *f* (Vw) shortage of liquid funds
knappe Mehrheit *f* (Re) narrow (*or* bare) majority
knappe Mittel *pl* (Vw) scarce resources
knapper Termin *m* (com) tight deadline
knappes Geld *n* (Vw) tight money
knappe Verfassung *f* **des Marktes** (Vw) tightness of the market
Knappheit *f*
  (Vw) scarcity
  (com) scarcity
  – (infml) crunch
Kanppheitsgewinne *mpl* (Vw) scarcity-induced profits
Knappschaft *f* (SozV) social miners' and mine-employees' insurance
knappschaftliche Rentenversicherung *f* (SozV) miners' pension insurance *(ie, branch of ‚Knappschaftsversicherung')*
Knappschaftsrente *f* (SozV) miner's pension
Knappschaftsruhegeld *n* (SozV) miner's pension on early retirement
Knappschaftsversicherung *f* (SozV) miners' social insurance system
Knapsack-Problem *n* (OR) knapsack problem
Knebelungsvertrag *m*
  (Re) adhesion contract
  – oppressive contract
  (ie, weaker party has no realistic choice as to its terms and usu. loses its economic independence in favor of another person)
Knoten *m*
  (OR) node
  – vertex *(ie, of a graph)*
knoten-beschränktes Netzwerk *n* (OR) node-constraint network
knotendisjunkt (OR) node disjoint
Knotenereignis *n* (OR) node event
Knotenpunkt *m* (EDV) nodal point
Knotenpunkt *m* **einer Kurve** (Math) node of a curve
Knowhow *n*
  (com) know-how
  – (infml) savvy *(eg, marketing ...)*
Know-how-Vertrag *m* (Re) know-how agreement

Koalition *f* (Bw) coalition *(ie, expansion of a core group by one or several satellite groups)*
Koalitionsfreiheit *f* (Pw) freedom of association
Koalitionsrecht *n* (Pw) right of association
Kodierung *f* (EDV) coding
Kodifikation *f* (Re) codification *(ie, arranging a variety of legal provisions or laws into a single code*
Koeffizient *m* (Math, Stat) coefficient
Koeffizient *m* **der Asymmetrie** (Stat) skewness
Koeffizient *m* **der Kreuzelastizität** (Vw) coefficient of cross-elasticity
Koeffizienten-Matrix *f* (Math) matrix of coefficients
Kofaktor *m* (Math) cofactor
Kofaktor *m* **der Elemente e-r anderen Matrizenzeile** (Math) alien factor
Kohleausfuhr *f* (com) coal exports
Kohlebergbau *m*
  (IndE) coal mining
  (com) coal mining industry
Kohlefarbband *n* (com) carbon ribbon
Kohlehalden *fpl* (com) mountains of unsold coal
Kohlekraftwerk *n* (com) coal-fired power station
Kohlenwertstoffindustrie *f* (com) coal chemicals industry
  – coal derivative industry
  (ie, industry related to the recovery of coal chemicals)
Kohlepapier *n* (com) carbon paper
Kohlepfennig *m* (FiW) additional amount charged on every unit of gas and electricity *(ie, a hidden tax used to subsidize building of coal-fueled power stations and cheapen German coal to power industry)*
Kohleveredelung *f* (IndE) coal conversion *(or* transformation) *(ie, includes gasification and liquefaction)*
Kohleveredelungsanlage *f* (IndE) coal conversion plant
Kohleveredelungsprogramm *n* (Vw) coal transformation program
Kohorte *f* (Stat) age cohort
Kohortenanalyse *f* (Stat) age cohort analysis *(ie, in population statistics)*
Koinzidenz *f* (Stat) coincidence
Kokskohlebeihilfe *f* (FiW) coaking coal equalization grant *(ie, supposed to make up the difference between imported and domestic coal prices)*
kollationieren
  (com) to compare
  – to collate
  – to reconcile
Kollegialsystem *n* (Bw) collegial system of top management
Kollektion *f* (Mk) collection
  – set of samples
Kollektiv *n* (Stat) parent population
  – *(obsolete)* universe
Kollektivabschreibung *f* (ReW) lump-sum depreciation *(ie, a form of valuation adjustment of fixed assets in small and medium-sized businesses)*
Kollektivanzeige *f* (Mk) composite advertisment
Kollektivbedürfnisse *npl*
  (Vw) collective needs

349

– public wants
– social wants
Kollektiventscheidung *f* (Bw) collective decision
kollektive Preispolitik *f* (Bw) collective pricing policy
kollektive Supposition *f* (Log) collective supposition
Kollektivgüter *npl*
(Vw) public goods
– collective goods
Kollektivismus *m* (Vw) collectivism *(ie, catch-all label for all socialist economic orientations)*
Kollektivmarke *f* (Mk, Pat) collective mark
Kollektivmonopol *n* (Vw) collective monopoly *(ie, special type of cartel set up to avoid oligopolistic pricing and cut-throat competition)*
Kollektivsparen *n* (Fin) collective saving *(opp, Individualsparen/Einzelsparen)*
Kollektivversicherung *f* (Vers) group *(or* blanket*)* insurance
Kollektivvertretung *f* (Re) collective representation *(syn, Gesamtvertretung)*
Kollektivwerbung *f* (Mk) collective advertising *(ie, of a group of firms to promote joint objectives)*
Kollektivzeichen *n* (Pat) collective trade mark
Kollektor *m* (EDV) collector
kollidieren
(Re) to conflict *(eg, interests)*
– to clash
(Pat) to interfere
kollidierende Erfindung *f* (Pat) interfering invention
kollidierende Interessen *npl* (Re) conflicting *(or* clashing*)* interests
kollidierender Anspruch *m* (Pat) interfering claim
kollidierendes Patent *n* (Pat) interfering patent
Kollinearität *f* (Stat) collinearity
Kollision *f*
(Re) conflict *(eg, of interests)*
(Pat) interference *(ie, of one claim with another)*
(Vers) collision
Kollisionsklausel *f*
(SeeV) collision clause
– running-down clause
Kollisionsklausel *f* **bei beiderseitigem Verschulden** (SeeV) both-to-blame-collision clause
Kollisionspatent *n* (Pat) interfering patent
Kollisionsversicherung *f* (SeeV) collision insurance
Kollisionsschaden *m* (SeeV) damage due to collision
Kollo *n, pl.* **Kolli**
(com) unit of freight
– package
Kollusion *f* (Vw) collusion
Kolonnenaddition *f* (Pw) footing of gross to net pay *(ie, in processing payrolls)*
Kombination *f* (Math) combination *(ie, in combinatorial mathematics)*
Kombinationspatent *n* (Pat) combination patent
Kombinationswerbung *f* (Mk) tie-in advertising
Kombinatorik *f* (Math) combinatorial analysis *(or* mathematics*)*
kombinatorische Topologie *f* (Math) combinatorial topology
kombinierte Police *f* (Vers) mixed policy

kombinierter Anzeigentarif *m* (Mk) combination rate
kombinierter Diffusionsindex *m* (Stat) cumulative diffusion index
kombinierter Index *m* (Stat) aggregative index number
kombinierter Sprung *m* (EDV) combined branch
kombinierte Schaltungsplatte *f* (EDV) combination board
kombiniertes Transportkonnossement *n* (com) combined transport bill of lading, CT-BL
kombinierte Versicherung *f* (Vers) multiple risk insurance
kombinierte Währungsklausel *f* (Vw) combined currency clause
Kommanditaktionär *m* (Bw) shareholder in a KGaG
Kommanditanteil *m* (Bw) limited partner's share
Kommanditbeteiligung *f* (Bw) participation in a limited partnership
Kommanditeinlage *f* (Fin) limited partner's contribution *(or* holding*)*
Kommanditgesellschaft *f* (Bw) limited commercial partnership
Kommanditgesellschaft *f* **auf Aktien** (Bw) commercial partnership limited by shares *(ie, no equivalent in US and GB)*
Kommanditist *m* (Bw) limited *(or* special*)* partner *(ie, contributing in cash payments a specific sum as capital to the common stock and not liable beyond the fund so contributed; syn, Teilhafter; opp, Komplementär, Vollhafter = general partner)*
Kommanditkapital *n* (Fin) limited liability capital
Kommanditvertrag *m* (Re) agreement setting up a limited commercial partnership
Kommandowerk *n* (EDV) control unit
kommerzialisieren (com) to commercialize
Kommerzialisierung *f* (com) commercialization
kommerziell (com) commercial
kommerzielle Datenverarbeitung *f* (EDV) business data processing
kommerzielle Einfuhren *fpl* (AuW) commercial importations
kommerzielle Konvertibilität *f* (AuW) current-account convertibility
kommerzieller Außenhandel *m* (AuW) commercial trade
kommerzielle Warensendung *f* (com) commercial consignment
Kommission *f*
(com) consignment
– production order
(Bw) committee
(EG) Commission
Kommissionär *m*
(Re) commission agent
– commission merchant
– mercantile agent
(ie, person professionally undertaking to buy or sell goods or securities in his own name for the account of another, § 383 HGB)
Kommission *f* **der Europäischen Gemeinschaften** (EG) Commission of the European Communities

Kommission f einsetzen (Re) to appoint (*or* set up) a commission
kommissionieren (com) to make out a production order *(ie, based on specifications of customer purchase order)*
Kommissionsagent *m* (com) commission agent *(syn, Kommissionsvertreter)*
Kommissionsbuch *n* (com) order book
Kommissionsgeschäft *n*
(Re) commission agency, §§ 383–406 HGB *(ie, based on a reciprocal contract, § 675 BGB)*
(com) commission business *(ie, dealing in commodities and securities)*
Kommissionsgut *n* (com) goods consigned (*or* on consignment)
Kommissionshandel *m* (com) commission trade *(opp, Agenturhandel und Eigenhandel)*
Kommissionskonto *n* (ReW) consignment account
Kommissionslager *n*
(com) consignment stock
– stock on commission
Kommissionsprovision *f* (com) consignment commission
Kommissionsrechnung *f* (com) consignment invoice
Kommissionstratte *f* (com) bill of exchange drawn for account of a third party, Art. 3 WG
Kommissionsverkauf *m* (com) sale on commission
Kommissionsverkauf *m* **mit Selbsteintrittsrecht** (com) sale with self-contracting right
Kommissionsvertrag *m* (com) consignment agreement
Kommissionsvertreter *m* (com) = *Kommissionsagent*
Kommissionsware *f*
(com) goods in consignment
– consignment goods
– consigned goods
– goods on commission
Kommissionswechsel *m* (com) = *Kommissionstratte*
kommissionsweise (com) on commission
Kommittent *m*
(Re) principal, § 383 HGB
(com) consignor
Kommunalabgaben *fpl* (FiW) municipal charges
Kommunalanleihe *f* (FiW) municipal loan
Kommunalbetrieb *m* (FiW) municipal enterprise
Kommunaldarlehen *n* (FiW) municipal loan
kommunaler Eigenbetrieb *m* (FiW) municipal enterprise
kommunaler Zweckverband *m* (FiW) municipal special-purpose association
Kommunalkredit *m* (FiW) municipal loan
Kommunalobligationen *fpl* (FiW) municipal bonds
Kommunalsteuern *fpl* (FiW) municipal taxes *(syn, Gemeindesteuern)*
Kommunalverband *m* (FiW) municipal organization
Kommune *f* (FiW) municipality *(syn, Gemeinde)*
Kommunikation *f* (Bw) communication
Kommunikationsbefehl *m* (EDV) access instruction
Kommunikationsnetz *n* (Bw) communications network

Kommunikationsprozeß *m* (Bw) communications process
Kommunikationsrechner *m* (EDV) front-end processor
Kommunikationsstörung *f*
(Bw) communications breakdown *(ie, a distorted version of the message is received)*
– distortion in communications
Kommunikationsstruktur *f* (Bw) lines of information
Kommunikationssystem *n* (Bw) communications system
Kommunikationstechnik *f* (Bw) communications techniques (*or* methods)
Kommunikationstheorie *f*
(EDV) information theory
– theory of communication
(syn, Informationstheorie)
Kommunikationsweg *m* (Bw) communication channel *(ie, oral or written, formal or informal, one-to-one, one-to-many)*
kommutative Gruppe *f* (Math) abelian group
kommutativer Körper *m* (Math) commutative field
kommutatives Gesetz *n* (Math) commutative law
Kompaktbauweise *f* (EDV) compact design
kompakte Menge *f* (Math) compact set
komparative Dynamik *f* (Vw) comparative dynamics
komparative Kosten *pl* (AuW) comparative cost *(D. Ricardo)*
komparativer Vorteil *m* (AuW) comparative advantage
komparative Statik *f* (Vw) comparative statics
Komparativreklame *f* (Kart) comparative advertising
komparativ-statische Analyse *f* (Vw) comparative-static analysis
Kompatibilität *f*
(Vw) compatibility *(eg, of goals)*
(EDV) compatibility *(syn, Verträglichkeit)*
Kompensation *f*
(Re) compensation
– set off
Kompensationsabkommen *n* (AuW) offsetting agreement
Kompensationsbetrieb *m* (com) compensatory type enterprise *(ie, single-product firm trying to bridge seasonal or cyclical downtimes by extending production program)*
Kompensationsgeschäft *n*
(AuW) barter transaction
– compensation trading deal
(Bö) interbank transaction bypassing the stock exchange
Kompensationskriterien *npl* (Vw) tradeoff criteria *(ie, in welfare economics; developed by Kaldor, Hicks, Scitovsky, and Little)*
Kompensationskurs *m* (Bö) settlement price in forward operations *(syn, Liquidationskurs)*
Kompensationsmarkt *m* (Fin) compensation market
kompensatorische Fiskalpolitik *f* (FiW) compensatory fiscal policy
kompensatorische Kosten *pl* (KoR) offsetting costs
kompensatorisches Budget *n* (FiW) compensatory budgeting

kompensatorische Transaktionen *fpl* (AuW) settling transactions
kompensieren
(com) to compensate
– to counterbalance
– to offset
Kompetenz *f* (Bw) authority
Kompetenzabgrenzung *f* (Bw) delineation of powers
Kompetenzbereich *m* (Bw) area of authority (*or* discretion)
Kompetenzdelegation *f* (Bw) delegation of authority (*or* responsibility)
Kompetenz *f* **delegieren** (Bw) to delegate authority (*or* responsibility)
Kompetenzspielraum *m* (Bw) room for competence (to decide)
Kompetenzstreitigkeiten *fpl*
(Re) jurisdictional disputes
(Bw) conflicting lines of authority
– conflicts over competence to decide
– jurisdictional disputes
– (GB) demarcation disputes
(*ie, between different departments in any organization*)
Kompetenzsysteme *npl* (Bw) forms of organization structure
Kompetenzüberschneidungen *fpl*
(Bw) confusion of lines of authority
– instances of plural executives
– multiple command
(*ie, leading to multiple subordination*)
kompilieren (EDV) to compile
Kompilieren *n* (EDV) compilation
Kompilierer *m*
(EDV) compiler
– compiling program (*or* routine)
Kompilierungsanlage *f* (EDV) source computer (*opp, object computer*)
Kompilierzeit *f* (EDV) compiling (*or* compilation) time
Komplement *n*
(Math) absolute complement
(EDV) complement (*syn, Zahlenkomplement*)
Komplementär *m*
(Re) general
– unlimited
– full ... partner
(*ie, personally liable for all debts of a partnership; syn, Vollhafter; opp, Kommanditist, Teilhafter = limited partner*)
komplementäre Addition *f* (EDV) complement add
komplementäre Diversifikation *f* (Bw) complementary diversification
komplementäre Güter *npl*
(Vw) complementary goods
– complements
– joint goods
komplementäre Nachfrage *f* (Vw) joint demand
Komplementärgüter *npl* (Vw) = *komplementäre Güter*
Komplementärinvestition *f* (Fin) complementary investment (*ie, in preinvestment analysis; syn, Differenzinvestition, Supplementinvestition*)

Komplementarität *f* (Vw) complementarity (*ie, of two goods*)
Komplementärmenge *f* **e-r Punktmenge** (Math) complementary set
Komplement *n* **e-r Menge** (Math) complement of a set
Komplementmenge *f* (Math) complement
komplexe Kosten *pl* (KoR) compound (*or* composite) costs
komplexe Zahl *f* (Math) complex number
komplexwertige Funktion *f* (Math) complex-valued function
Komponentenschreibweise *f* (Math) component form
Kompositversicherer *m*
(Vers) composite insurance company
– (infml) pup company
(*ie, operating several types of insurance business*)
Kompromißvorschlag *m* (com) compromise proposal
Kondiktion *f* (Re, *civil law*) claim to regaining unlawful enrichment
Konditional *n*
(Log) conditional
– material implication
– ‚if-then' proposition
konditionale Aussage *f* (Log) hypothetical
Konditionalsatz *m* (Log) conditional statement
Konditionen *fpl*
(com) terms and conditions
(Fin) terms (*eg, of a loan or credit*)
Konditionenanpassung *f* (Fin) adjustment of terms
Konditionenbindung *f* (Fin) commitment to fixed terms
Konditionengestaltung *f* (Fin) arrangement of terms
Konditionenkartell *n* (Kart) condition cartel, § 2 GWB (*ie, involving uniform application of trade terms, terms of delivery or payment, including cash discounts*)
Konditionenpolitik *f* (Fin) terms policy
Konditionen *fpl* **ziehen an** (Fin) interest rates go up
Konditionskartell *n* (Kart) = *Konditionenkartell*
Kondratieff-Zyklus *m*
(Vw) Kondratieff cycle
– long-wave business cycle (*ie, 54 to 60 years*)
Konfektion *f* (com) off the rack
– ready-to-wear
– (GB) off the peg ... clothes
Konferenz *f* **der Vereinten Nationen für Handel und Entwicklung** (AuW) United Nations Conference on Trade and Development, UNCTAD
Konferenzfrachten *fpl* (com) conference (freight) rates (*ie, in ocean shipping*)
Konferenzraten *fpl* (com) = *Konferenzfrachten*
Konferenzteilnehmer *m* (com) conference participant
Konfidenz *f*
(Stat) confidence
– significance
Konfidenzbereich *m* (Stat) confidence belt (*or* interval *or* range *or* region) (*syn, Vertrauensbereich*)
Konfidenzgrenze *f* (Stat) confidence limit
Konfidenzintervall *n* (Stat) = *Konfidenzbereich*

Konfidenzkoeffizient *m* (Stat) confidence coefficient
Konfidenzmodell *n* (Stat) confidence model
Konfidenzniveau *n* (Stat) confidence (*or* significance) level *(syn, Vertrauensniveau)*
Konfidenzstreifen *m* (Stat) = *Konfidenzbereich*
Konfiguration *f* (EDV) configuration
konfiskatorische Steuer *f* (FiW) confiscatory tax
konfliktinduzierte Inflation *f* (Vw) struggle-for-income inflation
Konfliktkurve *f* (Vw) contract curve
konforme Abbildung *f* (Math) conformal mapping
Konfusion *f* (Re) confusion of rights *(ie, union of the qualities of debtor and creditor in the same person)*
Konglomerat *n*
(Bw) conglomerate company (*or* group)
– conglomerate
(ie, heterogeneous group of affiliated companies; syn, Mischkonzern)
kongruente Abbildung *f* (Math) congruent transformation
konjekturale Anpassung *f* (Vw) conjectural adjustment *(ie, of sales quantity to ‚expected' price, or of prices to expected sales quantity)*
konjekturale Preis-Absatz-Funktion *f* (Vw) expected price-sales function
Konjugate *f* (Math) conjugate
Konjunktion *f*
(Log) conjunction
(ie, a binary propositional connective, usu. read ‚and')
(EDV) AND operation *(syn, UND-Funktion, UND-Verknüpfung)*
konjunktive Normalform *f* (Log) conjunction normal form
Konjunktur *f*
(Vw) level of business activity
– level of economic activity
– business (*or* economic) activity
– economic situation
konjunkturabhängige Erzeugnisse *npl* (Bw) cyclical products
konjunkturabhängiger Wirtschaftszweig *m* (Vw) cyclical industry
Konjunkturabhängigkeit *f* (Vw) cyclicality
Konjunkturabkühlung *f* (Vw) economic decline
Konjunkturabschwächung *f*
(Vw) slowing down in/of the economy
– weakening in the economy
– slackening (*or* weakening) of economic activity
– tail-off in the pace of economic activity
Konjunkturabschwung *m*
(Vw) cyclical downturn
– cyclical downswing
– contraction
– decline in economic activity
– slump
Konjunkturanalyse *f* (Vw) analysis of economic trends
konjunkturanfällig (Vw) sensitive to cyclical influences
Konjunkturaufschwung *m*
(Vw) business expansion (*or* upturn)
– business upswing
– cyclical expansion (*or* recovery *or* upswing *or* upturn *or* uptick)
– economic upswing (*or* upturn)
– revival of economic activity
Konjunkturauftrieb *m*
(Vw) economic upswing
– further expansion of economic activity
Konjunkturausgleichsrücklage *f*
(FiW) anticyclical reserve
– business cycle reserve
– business cycle equalization reserve
– counter-cyclical funds
Konjunkturaussichten *fpl* (Vw) economic outlook
Konjunkturbarometer *n* (Vw) business barometer
konjunkturbedingt (Vw) cyclical
konjunkturbedingter Vor- und Nachlauf *m* (Vw) cyclical leads and lags
Konjunkturbelebung *f*
(Vw) pickup in economic activity
– business revival
– rise of economic activity
Konjunkturbelebungsprogramm *n* (Vw) economic stimulation program
Konjunkturberuhigung *f* (Vw) easing of cyclical strains
Konjunkturbewegung *f* (Vw) cyclical movement
Konjunkturbild *n* (Vw) economic situation
Konjunkturdebatte *f* (Vw) economic policy debate
Konjunktureinbruch *m*
(Vw) setback in economic activity
– steep downturn
konjunkturell bedingte Zunahme *f* (Vw) cyclical increase
konjunkturelle Abkühlung *f* (Vw) economic slowdown
konjunkturelle Arbeitslosigkeit *f*
(Vw) cyclical unemployment
– *(frequently also)* deficiency-of-demand unemployment
konjunkturelle Entwicklung *f*
(Vw) development of business activity
– cyclical movement (*or* trend)
konjunkturelle Flaute *f* (Vw) economic slowdown
konjunkturelle Gegensteuerung *f* (Vw) counter-cyclical response
konjunkturelle Instabilität *f* (Vw) cyclical instability
konjunkturelle Preisschwankungen *fpl* (Vw) cyclical price swings
konjunktureller Abschwung *m*
(Vw) slide (*or* decline) in economic activity
– cyclical downturn
konjunktureller Aufschwung *m*
(Vw) improvement in general economic situation
– cyclical upturn
– economic recovery
konjunktureller Wendepunkt *m* (Vw) turning point in economic activity
konjunkturelle Schwankungen *fpl* (Vw) cyclical fluctuations
konjunkturelle Talsohle *f*
(Vw) bottom *(ie, of economic activity)*
– economic tailspin

konjunkturelle Talsohle *f* **verlassen** (Vw) to bottom out
konjunkturempfindlich (Vw) cyclically sensitive
Konjunkturempfindlichkeit *f* (Vw) cyclical sensitivity
Konjunkturentwicklung *f* (Vw) economic trend
Konjunkturerwartungen *fpl* (Vw) expected future business conditions
Konjunkturfaktor *m* (Vw) cyclical factor
Konjunkturförderung *f*
(Vw) cyclical stimulation
– promotion of economic activity
Konjunkturförderungsprogramm *n* (Vw) government spending program to boost economic activity
Konkunkturforscher *m* (Vw) business cycle analyst
Konjunkturforschung *f* (Vw) business cycle research
Konjunkturforschungsinstitut *n*
(Vw) economic research institute
– institute for economic research
– (US) business research institute
– *(rarely used)* conjuncture institute
Konjunkturgeschichte *f* (Vw) history of business cycles
Konjunkturgewinne *mpl* (Vw) cyclical (*or* boom) profits
Konjunkturhilfeprogramm *n* (Vw) counter-cycle aid program
Konjunkturindikator *m*
(Vw) business cycle indicator
– business indicator
– cyclical indicator
– economic indicator
Konjunkturinstitut *n* (Vw) economic research institute
Konjunkturkartell *n* (Kart) business cycle cartel
Konjunkturklima *n* (Vw) business (*or* economic) climate
Konjunkturlage *f*
(Vw) economic condition
– business cycle situation
Konjunkturmodell *n* (Vw) business cycle model
konjunkturneutral (Vw) cyclically neutral
konjunkturneutraler Haushalt *m* (FiW) cyclically balanced budget
Konjunkturphase *f*
(Vw) phase of a business cycle
– business cycle
– (GB) trade cycle
Konjunkturpolitik *f*
(Vw) business cycle policy
– (GB) trade cycle policy
– countercyclical policy
– economic stabilization policy
konjunkturpolitisch (Vw) relating to cyclical policy
– business cycle ...
konjunkturpolitisches Instrumentarium *n* (Vw) economic policy tools
konjunkturpolitisch motivierte Steuern *fpl* (FiW) special anticyclical taxes
Konjunkturprognose *f*
(Vw) business forecast
– business scenario
– (GB) economic forecast

Konjunkturprogramm *n*
(Vw) anticyclical program
– economic policy program
– stimulus program *(eg, West Germany should not adopt a ...)*
Konjunkturrat *m* (Vw) Business Cycle Council, § 18 StabG
konjunkturreagibel (Vw) responsive to cyclical trends
konjunkturreagible Steuer *f* (FiW) tax sensitive to economic trends
Konjunkturrückgang *m*
(Vw) decline in economic activity
– falling economic activity
– economic slowdown
– slowdown in the economy
– tail-off in the pace of economic activity
Konjunkturschwäche *f* (Vw) weakness of economic activity
Konjunkturschwankungen *fpl*
(Vw) business (or cyclical) fluctuations
– cyclical swings in economic activity
– economic fluctuations
– swings in the economic cycle
konjunktursicherer Bereich *m* (Vw) recession-proof industry
Konjunkturspritze *f*
(Vw) injection of public funds to support economic activity
– (US, infml) hypo
Konjunkturstabilisator *m* (Vw) economic stabilizer
Konjunkturstabilisierung *f* (Vw) stabilization of the economy
Konjunkturtest *m* (Stat) business opinion poll
Konjunkturtheoretiker *m* (Vw) business cycle theorist
Konjunkturtheorie *f*
(Vw) business cycle theory
– (GB) trade cycle theory
Konjunkturtief *n*
(Vw) economic low
– bottom (of economic activity)
– trough
Konjunkturüberhitzung *f*
(Vw) cyclical overstrain
– overheating of the economy
Konjunkturumschwung *m* (Vw) turnaround in economic activity
Konjunkturverlauf *m*
(Vw) cyclical course (*or* trend)
– economic course (*or* trend)
– course (*or* trend *or* thrust) of economic activity
– run of business
– path of the economy
– economic development
Konjunkturwellen *fpl* (Vw) cyclical fluctuations
Konjunkturwende *f* (Vw) turnaround of the economy
Konjunkturzuschlag *m* (FiW) anticyclical surcharge *(ie, on income taxes)*
Konjunkturzyklus *m*
(Vw) business (*or* economic) cycle
– (GB) trade cycle

konkave Kostenfunktion *f* (Bw) concave cost function
konkave Programmierung *f* (OR) concave programming
konkludente Handlung *f* (Re) intention declared by conduct
– action implying legal intent
– passive manifestation of will
(eg, contract may be implied from the conduct of the parties, such as silence, deliberate acquiescence)
Konklusion *f* (Log) conclusion *(ie, statement inferred from the premises of a given argument)*
konkordante Stichprobe *f* (Stat) concordant sample
Konkordanzkoeffizient *m* (Stat) coefficient of agreement
konkrete Fahrlässigkeit *f*
(Re) ordinary negligence
– *(civil law)* culpa in concreto
(ie, failure to use such care as a man of common prudence takes of his own concerns, responsibility being confined to ‚Sorgfalt in eigenen Angelegenheiten' = diligentia quam in suis (rebus adhibere solet), § 277 BGB)
konkrete Güter *npl* (Re) specific goods
konkreter Fall *m* (com) case in point
konkretisieren (Re) to appropriate *(or* identify) goods to a contract
konkretisierte Gattungsschuld *f* (Re) particular goods identified
konkretisierter Vertragsgegenstand *m* (Re) specified *(or* ascertained) goods
Konkretisierung *f*
(Re) appropriation (of goods) to a contract
– ascertainment of goods
Konkurrent *m*
(com) competitor
– rival
– contender *(eg, top contenders in a faltering market)*
Konkurrenz *f*
(com) the competition
– (GB, infml) the opposition *(ie, competing firms in one's business or profession)*
Konkurrenz *f* **abhängen** (com, infml) to outdistance competitors
Konkurrenzangebot *n*
(com) rival offer *(or* bid)
(Mk) rival supply
Konkurrenz-Aufwertung *f* (Vw) competitive appreciation
Konkurrenz *f* **aus dem Felde schlagen** (com) to outdistance rivals
Konkurrenz *f* **ausschalten** (com) to outbid *(or* defeat) one's competitors
Konkurrenz *f* **besänftigen** (com) to mollify competitors
(eg, by orderly marketing agreements)
Konkurrenzbetrieb *m*
(com) rival firm
– competitor
(EDV) contention mode
Konkurrenzdruck *m* (com) competitive pressure
Konkurrenzerzeugnis *n* (com) competing product

Konkurrenzfähigkeit *f*
(com) competitiveness
– competitive edge *(or* position)
Konkurrenzkampf *m* (com) competitive struggle
Konkurrenzklausel *f*
(Re) stipulation *(or* covenant) in restraint of trade
– ancillary covenant against competition
– restraining clause
– restrictive covenant
(Pw) restraint of competition clause *(syn, Wettbewerbsklausel)*
konkurrenzlose Preise *mpl* (com) unmatched prices, §§ 3, 4 UWG
Konkurrenzmodell *n* (Vw) competitive model
Konkurrenzpreis *m* (com) competitive price
Konkurrenzprodukt *n* (com) rival product
Konkurrenzreaktion *f* (Vw) response of rival firms
Konkurrenzspiel *n* (OR) competitive game
Konkurrenzunternehmen *n*
(com) rival firm
– competitor
Konkurrenzverbot *n* (Re) prohibition to compete *(ie, applies to commercial clerks, voluntary apprentices, personally liable partners of OHG and KG, and managing board members, §§ 60, 82a, 112 HGB, § 88 AktG; syn, Wettbewerbsverbot)*
Konkurrenz *f* **verdrängen** (Kart) to cut out *(or* wipe out) rivals *(or* competitors)
konkurrieren (com) to compete (with) *(eg, in a foreign market)*
konkurrierende Einzelwerbung *f* (Mk) competitive advertising
konkurrierende Ziele *npl* (Bw) conflicting goals
konkurrierende Zuständigkeit *f* (Re) concurrent jurisdiction *(ie, proceeding can be brought in any one of several courts; opp, ausschließliche Z.)*
Konkurs *m*
(Re) bankruptcy
– (GB) compulsory winding-up *(according to the Companies Act)*
Konkurs *m* **abwenden**
(Re) to avoid
– to avert
– to stave off ... bankruptcy
Konkurs *m* **abwickeln** (Re) to administer the bankrupt's estate *(ie, reduce to money the property of the estate)*
Konkursabwicklung *f* (Re) administration of the property of the bankrupt
Konkursanfechtung *f* (Re) avoidance *(or* contestation) of bankruptcy, §§ 29–42 KO
Konkurs *m* **anmelden** (Re) to file a petition in bankruptcy
Konkursantrag *m*
(Re) petition in bankrupty
– application for bankruptcy, § 103 KO
Konkursantrag *m* **stellen**
(Re) to file a petition in bankruptcy
– to file for bankruptcy
Konkursausfallgeld *n* (Pw) payment of net earnings over three months before bankruptcy proceedings are opened *(ie, financed through employers' contributions levied by ‚Berufsgenossenschaften')*

Konkurs *m* **beantragen** (Re) to apply for commencement of bankruptcy proceedings
Konkursbilanz *f* (Re) statement of bankrupt's assets and liabilities, § 124 KO *(syn, Konkursstatus)*
Konkursdelikte *npl* (Re) = Konkursstraftaten
Konkursdividende *f* (Re) dividend in bankruptcy
– percentage of recovery
(ie, in bankruptcy proceedings)
Konkurs *m* **einstellen** (Re) to suspend bankruptcy proceedings
Konkurseinstellung *f* (Re) suspension of bankruptcy proceedings
Konkurs *m* **eröffnen** (Re) to open *(or* institute) bankruptcy proceedings (against)
Konkurseröffnung *f* (Re) commencement of bankruptcy proceedings
Konkurseröffnung *f* **beantragen** (Re) to file a petition in bankruptcy
Konkursforderung *f* (Re) claim against a bankrupt estate
(opp, Anspruch auf Aussonderung, Absonderung und Masseanspruch)
konkursgefährdet (com, infml) cliffhanging *(eg, company)*
Konkursgericht *n* (Re) bankruptcy court
Konkursgläubiger *m*
(Re) bankrupt's creditor
– creditor in bankruptcy
– creditor to a bankrupt
Konkursgrund *m* (Re) act of bankruptcy
Konkurs *m* **machen**
(Re) to go bankrupt
(com, infml) to go bust
– to go to the wall
Konkursmasse *f*
(Re) bankrupt estate
– bankruptcy estate
– debtor's assets
– estate in bankruptcy
– insolvent assets
Konkursordnung *f* (Re) Bankruptcy Law, as of 1 Jan 1900, variously amended
Konkursquote *f* (Re) dividend in bankruptcy
Konkursrecht *n* (Re) bankruptcy law
Konkursrichter *m*
(Re) judge in bankruptcy
– judge in charge of bankruptcy proceedings
Konkursschuldner *m*
(Re) bankrupt
– debtor in bankruptcy *(syn, Gemeinschuldner)*
Konkursschuldnerverzeichnis *n* (Re) list of adjudicated bankrupts
Konkursstatus *m* (Re) = *Konkursbilanz*
Konkursstraftaten *fpl* (Re) bankruptcy offenses, §§ 283–283 d StGB
Konkurstabelle *f* (Re) bankruptcy schedule *(ie, listing bankrupt's assets, liabilities, and all unsecured creditors, § 145 KO)*
Konkursverfahren *n* (Re) bankruptcy proceedings
Konkursverfahren *n* **eröffnen** (Re) to open bankruptcy proceedings
Konkursverfahren *n* **mangels Masse einstellen** (Re) to dismiss petition in bankruptcy for insufficiency of assets

Konkursvergleich *m* (Re) composition in bankruptcy
Konkursverlust *m* (Re) loss due to bankruptcy
Konkursverwalter *m* (Re) bankruptcy trustee *(ie, appointed by court to take charge of bankrupt estate)*
Konkursverwaltung *f* (Re) administration of bankrupt estate
Konkursvorrecht *n* (Re) priority rights in bankruptcy proceedings *(see: bevorrechtiger Gläubiger)*
Konkurswelle *f* (Re) wave of bankruptcies
Konnossement *n* (com) bill of lading *(ie, document evidencing receipt of goods for shipment, issued by person engaged in business of transporting or forwarding goods, §§ 642 ff HGB)*
Konnossement *n* **ausstellen** (com) to make out a bill of lading
Konnossement *n* **gegen Kasse** (Fin) cash against bill of lading
Konnossement *n* **mit einschränkendem Vermerk** (com) unclean bill of lading *(or* B/L)
Konnossementsanteilsschein *m* (com) delivery order, D/O
Konnossementsgarantie *f* (com) letter of indemnity
Konnossementsklauseln *fpl* (com) bill of lading clauses
Konnossements-Teilschein *m* (com) delivery note
Konnotation *f* (Log) connotation *(ie, of a concept)*
– intension
– comprehension
(opp, Denotation)
Konsens-orientiertes Planungssystem *n* (Bw) consensus system of planning
Konsequens *n*
(Log) consequent
– apodosis
(ie, clause expressing the consequence in a conditional sentence; opp. Antezedens = antecedent, protasis)
Konsignant *m* (AuW) consignor *(ie, shipper of consigned goods)*
Konsignatar *m* (AuW) consignee *(ie, party receiving goods on consignment; usu. commission merchant acting as selling agent for a commission fee or factorage)*
Konsignationsgeschäft *n* (AuW) consignation transaction *(or* sale)
Konsignationshandel *m* (AuW) consignation selling *(ie, type of export selling in which consignee does not take title to the goods which passes upon sale to final buyer)*
Konsignationskonto *n* (com) consignment account
Konsignationslager *n*
(AuW) consignment stock *(ie, carried by commission merchant)*
(MaW) consignment stock *(syn, Auslieferungslager)*
Konsignationsverkauf *m* (AuW) consignment sale
Konsignationsvertrag *m* (AuW, MaW) consignment contract
Konsignationsware *f*
(AuW, MaW) consigned goods
– consignment merchandise
– goods out on consignment

konsignieren (AuW) to ship goods on consignment
konsistente Schätzfunktion f (Stat) consistent estimator
Konsistenz f (Stat) consistence
Konsistenzkoeffizient m (Stat) coefficient of consistence
Konsistenzmodell n (Vw) fixed-target policy model
Konsoldrucker m (EDV) console printer
Konsole f (EDV) = *Bedienungsplatz*
Konsolidation f
 (Fin) consolidation
 – funding
konsolidieren
 (Fin) to consolidate
 – to fund a debt
konsolidierte Anleihe f
 (Fin) consolidated (*or* consolidation) bond
 – unified bond
 – unifying bond
konsolidierte Bilanz f
 (ReW) consolidated balance sheet
 – (GB) consolidated accounts
 – (GB) group balance sheet
konsolidierte Gewinn- und Verlustrechnung f
 (ReW) consolidated income statement
 – (GB) consolidated profit and loss account
 – group income statement
konsolidierte Konzernbilanz f (ReW) group consolidated balance sheet
konsolidierte Konzerngewinn- und Verlustrechnung f (ReW) group consolidated profit and loss account
konsolidierte Kredite mpl (FiW) funded debt
konsolidierter Abschluß m
 (ReW) consolidated financial statement (*or* set of accounts)
 – group financial statement
 – (GB) group assounts
konsolidierter Sonderabschluß m (ReW) special consolidated accounts
konsolidierter Teilkonzernabschluß m (ReW) consolidated subgroup accounts
konsolidierte Schuld f (FiW) consolidated (*or* permanent) debt
konsolidierte Sektorenkonten npl (VGR) consolidated sector accounts
konsolidierte Staatsschuld f (FiW) consolidated (*or* long-term) public debt
konsolidierte Tochtergesellschaft f (Re) consolidated subsidiary
konsolidierte Unternehmensgruppe f
 (Bw) consolidated group of enterprises
 – consolidation
 (ie, combination of two or more enterprises, with transfer of net assets to a new corporation organized for the purpose)
Konsolidierung f
 (ReW) consolidation
 (Fin) consolidation
 – funding
Konsolidierungsanleihe f
 (Fin) debt-consolidating loan
 – funding loan
Konsolidierungsausgleichsposten m (ReW) consolidation excess

Konsolidierungsbuchung f (ReW) consolidating entry
Konsolidierung schwebender Schulden (Fin) funding of floating debts
Konsolidierungskreis m (ReW) consolidated group
Konsolidierungsstufe f (ReW) level of consolidation
Konsolidierungsvorschriften fpl (ReW) consolidation rules
Konsorte m
 (Fin) syndicate member
 – underwriter
Konsortialanteil m (Fin) share in a syndicate
Konsortialbank f (Fin) consortium bank
Konsortialbeteiligung f (Fin) participation in a syndicate
konsortialführende Bank f (Fin) = *Konsortialführerin*
Konsortialführerin f
 (Fin) leader manager
 – manager
 – managing bank
 – managing underwriter
 – prime underwriter
 – principal manager
 – syndicate leader (*or* manager)
 – consortium leader
Konsortialführung f (Fin) lead management
Konsortialgebühr f (Fin) management charge (*or* fee)
Konsortialgeschäft n
 (Fin) syndicate (*or* underwriting) transaction
 (Fin) underwriting business
Konsortialkredit m (Fin) syndicated loan
Konsortialmarge f (Fin) issuing banks' commission
Konsortialmitglied n (Fin) syndicate member
Konsortialprovision f
 (Fin) underwriter's commission
 – spread
Konsortialquote f (Fin) underwriting share
Konsortialrechnung f (Fin) syndicate accounting
Konsortialspanne f
 (Fin) overriding commission
 – spread
Konsortialsystem n (Vers) syndicate system
Konsortialverbindlichkeiten fpl (Fin) syndicated loans
Konsortialvertrag m (Fin) consortium (*or* underwriting) agreement
Konsortium n
 (Bw) consortium (*pl.* consortia)
 (Fin) management group
 – financial syndicate
 – syndicate of security underwriters
 (ie, civil-law partnership formed by banks to carry on underwriting business)
Konstante f (Math) absolute (*or* constant) term
konstante Absatzgeschwindigkeit f (Mk) constant rate of selling
konstante Differenz f (Math) common difference
 (ie, of an arithmetic progression or series)
konstante Kosten pl
 (KoR) fixed total cost *(ie, constant over a period)*
 (KoR) fixed average production cost *(ie, constant per unit of output)*

konstante Lohnquote f (Vw) constant wage share
Konstantenbereich m (EDV) constant area
konstante Preise mpl (Vw) constant prices base-period prices
konstanter Abschreibungssatz m (ReW) constant (or fixed) rate of depreciation
konstanter Produktionskoeffizient m (Vw) fixed coefficient of production
konstanter Prozentsatz m (com) fixed percentage
konstanter Skalenertrag m (Vw) constant returns to scale
konstantes Kapitalkonto n (ReW) constant capital account
konstante Substitutionselastizität f (Vw) constant elasticity of substitution
konstante Zusatz- od Grenzkosten pl (Vw) constant relative costs
Konstanz f **der Lohnquote** (Vw) constancy of labor's share
Konstellation f (com) combination of circumstances
Konstrukteur m (IndE) design engineer
Konstruktion f (IndE) design
Konstruktionsfehler m (IndE) faulty design
Konstruktionsgemeinkosten pl (KoR) indirect design costs
Konstruktionskosten pl (KoR) design costs
Konstruktionsprinzipien npl (IndE) design philosophy
Konstruktionsstand m (IndE) engineering level
Konstruktionsstellen fpl (KoR) design departments
Konstruktions-Stückliste f (MaW) engineering bill of materials
Konstruktionstechnik f (IndE) design engineering
Konstruktionsunterlagen fpl (IndE) design data
Konstruktionszeichnung f (IndE) working drawing
Konsularfaktura f (com) = Konsulatsfaktura
Konsulargebühren fpl (com) consular fees (or charges)
Konsulargut n (Zo) consular goods, § 68 AZO
konsularische Amtshandlung f (Re) consular transaction
Konsulat n (com) consulate
Konsulatsfaktura f (pl.-fakturen) (com) consular invoice
Konsulatsgebühren fpl (com) consular fees
Konsum m (com) consumption
Konsumaufwand m (Vw) = Konsumausgaben
Konsumausgaben fpl (Vw) consumption expenditure
Konsumebene f (Vw) consumption surface
Konsumeinheit f (Mk) spending unit
Konsumelektronik f (com) consumer electronics
Konsument m (com) consumer
Konsumentenanalyse f (Mk) consumer analysis
Konsumentengesellschaft f (Vw) consumer society
Konsumentengeschäft n (Fin) consumer lending
Konsumentengewohnheiten fpl (Mk) consumer habits
Konsumentenhandel m (com) consumer buying (com) special forms of retail trading, such as consumer cooperatives
Konsumentenkäufe mpl (com) consumer sales

Konsumentenkredit m (Fin) = Konsumkredit
Konsumentennachfrage f (Vw) consumer demand
Konsumentenrente f (Vw) consumer's (or buyer's) surplus
Konsumentenrisiko n (Stat) consumer's risk
Konsumentensouveränität f (Vw) consumer sovereignty
Konsumerismus m (Vw) consumerism
Konsumfinanzierung f (Fin) consumer credit
 – financing of installment sales
Konsumforschung f (Mk) consumer research
Konsumfreiheit f (Vw) consumer's freedom to dispose
 – freedom of choice by consumers
Konsumfunktion f (Vw) consumption function
Konsumgenossenschaft f (Bw) consumers' co-operative
Konsumgewohnheiten fpl (Vw) habits of consumption
 – consumption patterns
Konsumgüter npl (Vw) consumer (or consumption) goods (ie, identical with ‚Verbrauchsgüter')
Konsumgüterhersteller m (com) consumer goods maker
Konsumgüterindustrie f (com) consumer goods industry
Konsumgütermärkte mpl (Mk) consumer goods markets
Konsumgütermesse f (Mk) trade fair for consumer goods
Konsumgüternachfrage f (Mk) consumption demand
Konsumklima n (Mk) consumer sentiment
 – buyer confidence
Konsumgüter-Marketing n (Mk) consumer goods marketing (opp. Investitionsgüter-Marketing)
Konsumkredit m (Fin) consumer credit (ie, usu. granted as Teilzahlungskredit, Kleinkredit, Anschaffungsdarlehen)
Konsumkreditgenossenschaft f (Bw) consumer credit co-operative
Konsumlinie f (Vw) consumption line
Konsumneigung f (Vw) propensity to consume
Konsumplan m (Vw) consumption plan
Konsumquote f (Vw) propensity to consume, C/Y (ie, durchschnittliche K. = average propensity to consume C/Y; marginale K. = marginal propensity to consume dC/dY)
Konsumtabelle f (Vw) consumption schedule
Konsumtheorie f (Vw) theory of consumption
Konsumtion f (Vw) = Konsum
konsumtive Ausgaben fpl (Vw) consumption expenditure
Konsumtivkredit m (Fin) = Konsumkredit
Konsumvereine mpl (Bw) = Konsumgenossenschaften
Konsumverhalten n (Vw) consumption pattern
Konsumwaren fpl (com) (durable and nondurable) consumer goods
Konsumwerbung f (Mk) consumer product advertising
Konsumzeit f (Vw) time needed for consumption
Kontaktbürste f (EDV) reading brush

Kontakter *m* (Mk) account executive
Kontaktmann *m* (Mk) = *Kontakter*
Kontaktpflege *f* (Bw) human relations
Kontaktstelle *f* (com) contact point
Konten *npl (sg.* **Konto)** (ReW) accounts
Kontenabbuchung *f* (Fin) automatic debit transfer
Kontenabgleichung *f* (ReW) balancing of accounts
Konten *npl* **abstimmen** (ReW) to reconcile accounts
Kontenabstimmung *f* (ReW) reconciliation of accounts
Kontenanruf *m* (ReW) entry formula
Kontenauflösung *f* (ReW) fanout (into several other accounts)
Kontenaufteilung *f* (ReW) accounts specification *(eg, according to cost center, product group)*
Konten *npl* **ausgleichen** (ReW) to square accounts
Kontenbezeichnung *f* (ReW) account title
Kontenblatt *n* (ReW) account form
Kontenführer *m* (ReW) person in charge of an account
Kontenführung *f* (ReW) account keeping
Kontenglattstellung *f* (ReW) squaring *(or* adjustment) of accounts
Kontengliederung *f* (ReW) account classification
Kontengruppe *f* (ReW) group of accounts
Kontengruppenbezeichnung *f* (ReW) account group title
Kontenkarte *f* (ReW) account card
Kontenklasse *f* (ReW) account class
Kontenkontrolle *f* (ReW) account control *(ie, by collating)*
kontenlose Buchführung *f*
(ReW) ledgerless accounting
– open item system
(syn, Offene-Posten-Buchführung)
kontenmäßige Darstellung *f* (ReW) account-type presentation
Kontenplan *m*
(ReW) chart of accounts
– classification of accounts
Kontenrahmen *m* (ReW) uniform system of accounts
Kontenspalte *f* (ReW) account column
Kontensparen *n*
(Fin) deposit account saving
– savings through accounts
Kontenstand *m*
(ReW) balance of an account
– state of an account
Kontenüberziehung *f* (Fin) bank overdraft
Kontenumschreibung *f* (ReW) transfer from one account to another
Kontenzusammenlegung *f* (ReW) pooling of accounts
Konterbande *f* (Zo) contra band goods
Kontereffekte *mpl* (Vw) backwash effects *(G. Myrdal)*
Kontermine *mpl* (Bö) group of bull operators
Kontextdefinition *f* (Log) contextual definition
kontextuale Definition *f* (Log) = *Kontextdefinition*
Kontiarbeiter *m* (IndE) all-shift worker *(ie, working early, late, and night shifts: on workdays, Sundays and holidays; opp, Ein-, Zwei- und Dreischichtler)*

kontieren (ReW) to allocate *(or* assign) to an account
Kontierung *f* (ReW) allocation to an account
Kontinentalsockel *m* (Re) continental shelf
Kontingent *n* (com) quota
Kontingentbeschränkungen *fpl* (com) quota limitations
Kontingent *n* **erschöpfen** (AuW) to exhaust a quota
kontingentieren (AuW) to fix a quota
Kontingentierung *f*
(Vw) rationing
(AuW) quota setting
(Kart) output limitation *(ie, in a ‚Quotenkartell')*
Kontingentierungskartell *n* (Bw) quota-allocation cartel *(ie, restriction of production by allocating quotas to the individual members)*
Kontingent *n* **überziehen** (com) to exceed a quota
Kontingenz *f* (Stat) contingency
Kontingenzkoeffizient *m* (Stat) coefficient of contingency
Kontingenztafel *f* (Stat) contingency table
Kontinuante *f* (Math) continuant
kontinuierliche Arbeitszeit *f* (Pw) fluctuating workweek
(ie, the day off must no longer be a Sunday; practiced in steelworks and other continuous flow-process plants; syn, gleitende Arbeitswoche)
kontinuierliches Verfahren *n* (IndE) flow process
kontinuierliche Verzinsung *f* (Fin) continuous convertible interest
Kontinuumshypothese *f* (Math) continuum hypothesis
Konto *n (pl.* **Konten)** (ReW) account
Konto *n* **abgeschlossen** (Fin) account closed
Konto *n* **abschließen**
(ReW) to balance
– to close
– to make up
– (infml) to tot up ... an account
(ReW) to rule off an account
Kontoabschluß *m* (ReW) balancing of an account
Kontoabstimmung *f* (Fin) account reconciliation
Konto *n* **anlegen** (ReW) to open an account
Konto *n* **ausgleichen** (ReW) to balance an account
Kontoauszug *m*
(Fin) statement of account
– bank statement
Konto *n* **belasten** (ReW) to charge *(or* debit) an account
Kontobewegungen *fpl* (Fin) account movements
Konto *n* **der Sonderziehungsrechte** (AuW) Special Drawing Account
Konto *n* **einrichten** (ReW) to set up an account
Kontoeinrichtung *f* (ReW) setting up an account
Kontoeinzahlung *f* (Fin) payment into an account
Konto *n* **erkennen** (ReW) to credit an account (with)
Konto *n* **eröffnen** (Fin) to open *(or* set up) an account (with/at a bank)
Kontoeröffnung *f* (Fin) opening of an account
Kontoform *f* **der Bilanz** (ReW) account form of a balance sheet

Konto n führen (ReW) to keep an account
kontoführende Bank f (Fin) bank in charge of an account
Kontoführung f (Fin) account management
Kontoführungsgebühr f
  (Fin) service charge
  – account management charge
Konto n glattstellen (Fin) to square an account
Kontoinhaber m (Fin) account holder
Kontokarte f (ReW) account card
Kontokorrent n
  (Fin) account current
  – current account
  – open account
Kontokorrentauszug m
  (Fin) statement of account
  – account current
Kontokorrentbuch n (ReW) accounts receivable (or accounts payable) ledger
Kontokorrenteinlagen fpl (Fin) current deposits
Kontokorrentgeschäft n (Fin) overdraft business
Kontokorrentguthaben n (Fin) balance on current account
Kontokorrentkonto n
  (Fin) current account
  – cash account
  – operating account
  – (US) checking account
Kontokorrentkredit m
  (Fin) credit in current account
  – advance in current account
  – (GB) overdraft facility
Kontokorrentverbindlichkeiten fpl (ReW) liabilities on current account
Kontokorrentvertrag m (Fin) open account agreement
Kontokorrentvorbehalt m (Fin) current account reservation
Kontokorrentzinsen mpl
  (Fin) interest on current account
  – current account rates
Konto n mit laufenden Umsätzen (ReW) active account
Kontonummer f (ReW) account number
Konto n ohne Bewegung (ReW) inactive account
Konto n pro Diverse (Fin) collective suspense account
  (ie, receiving sundry transfers awaiting final clarification)
Konto n prüfen (Fin) to verify an account
Konto n sperren (Fin) to block an account
Kontospesen pl (Fin) account carrying charges
Kontostand m
  (ReW) balance of an account
  – state of an account
Konto n stillegen (ReW) to flag an account (ie, temporarily)
Kontoüberziehung f (Fin) overdrawing of an account
Kontoumsatz m (Fin) account turnover
Konto n unterhalten (Fin) to have an account (with/at a bank)
Kontounterlagen fpl (Fin) account files
Kontovollmacht f (Fin) power to draw on an account

kontradiktorischer Gegensatz m (Log) contradictory opposition
Kontrahent m (Re) contracting party
kontrahieren
  (Re) to agree
  – to conclude an agreement (or contract)
Kontrahierungsmix m (Mk) contract mix
Kontrahierungszwang m (Re) legal obligation to accept contracts, § 453 HGB
Kontrakt m (com) contract
kontraktbestimmtes Einkommen n
  (Vw) contractual income
  – income paid under contract
Kontrakteinkommen n (Vw) = *kontraktbestimmtes Einkommen*
Kontraktforschung f (Bw) contract research *(ie, awarded to research institutes, universities, or other firms)*
Kontraktfrachten fpl (com) contract (freight) rates *(ie, in ocean shipping)*
kontraktgebundene Sparformen fpl (Pw) contractual forms of saving
Kontraktgerade f (Vw) contract line
kontraktive Geldpolitik f (Fin) tight money policy
kontraktive Maßnahmen fpl (Vw) restrictive measures
kontraktive Offenmarktpolitik f (Vw) restrictive open market policy
kontraktiver Prozeß m
  (Vw) contractionary process
  – business cycle contraction
Kontraktkurve f (Vw) contract curve *(syn, Konfliktkurve)*
Kontraposition f (Log) contraposition
kontrárer Gegensatz m (Log) contrary opposition
Kontrastverhältnis n (EDV) print-contrast ratio
Kontravalenz f
  (Log) exclusive disjunction
  – alternation
  (EDV) exclusive-OR operation
  – non-equivalence operation
  – anti-coincidence operation
  (syn, Antivalenz, ausschließendes ODER)
Kontrollabschnitt m
  (Fin) stub
  – (GB) counterfoil
Kontrollbit n (EDV) control bit *(opp, Datenbit = information bit)*
Kontrollbudget n (FiW) accounting-control budget
Kontrolle f **von Einnahmen und Ausgaben** (ReW) monitoring of receipts and outlays
Kontrollfeld n (EDV) control field *(syn, Steuerfeld)*
Kontrollgrenze f (Stat) control limit
Kontrollinformation f (EDV) check(ing) information
Kontrollinterview n
  (Stat) check interview
  (Mk) callback
Kontrollkarte f
  (Stat) control chart
  (IndE) schedule chart
Kontrollkonto n (ReW) check account
Kontrolliste f (com) check list
Kontrollmitteilung f (StR) tax-audit tracer note *(ie,*

sent by tax auditors to local tax office of income recipient)
Kontrollmuster *n* (com) countersample
Kontrollprogramm *n* (EDV) executive routine
Kontrollpunkt *m*
(Stat) indifference quality
− point of control
(EDV) checkpoint
Kontrollspanne *f*
(Bw) span of control
− span of command
− span of management
− span of supervision
− span of responsibility
(syn, Leitungsspanne, Subordinationsquote)
Kontrollsteuer *f* (FiW) controlling tax *(eg, turnover tax v. income tax, inheritance tax v. net worth tax)*
Kontrollsumme *f*
(EDV) check
− control
− proof
− hash
− gibberish ... total
− check sum
Kontrolluhr *f* (com) time clock
Kontrollwort *n* (EDV) check word
Kontrollzeitstudie *f* (IndE) check study
Kontrollziffer *f* (EDV) check digit
Konventionalstrafe *f*
(Re) contract penalty
− time penalty under contract
− penalty for breach of contract
− (GB) liquidated damages
(ie, payable if work is not carried out within stipulated time, §§ 339ff BGB; syn, Vertragsstrafe)
Konventional-Zolltarif *m* (Zo) contractual (*or* conventional) tariff
konventioneller Linienfrachter *m* (com) general cargo ship (*or* liner)
konventionelles Budget *n* (Fin) administrative budget
konvergente Reihe *f* (Math) convergent series
Konvergenz *f* (Math) convergence
Konvergenzaxiom *n* (Math) axiom of convergence
Konvergenzhypothese *f* (Vw) theory of convergence *(ie, positing gradual assimilation of economic systems in West and East)*
Konvergenzsatz *m* (Stat) convergence theorem
konverser Begriff *m* (Log) converse concept
Konversion *f*
(Re) conversion of legal transaction, § 140 BGB *(ie, if transaction is void but requirements for the validity of another transaction which has the same effect are complied with, such other transaction will be allowed to take the place of the intended transaction)*
Konversion *f* **e-r Anleihe** (Fin) bond conversion
Konversionsanleihe *f* (Fin) conversion loan
Konversionsguthaben *n* (Fin) conversion balance
Konversionskurs *m* (Fin) conversion price
konvertibel (Vw) convertible
Konvertibilität *f* (AuW) = *Konvertierbarkeit*
Konvertibilität *f* **in laufender Rechnung** (AuW) current-account convertibility

Konvertibilität *f* **in primäre Reserve-Aktiva** (AuW) reserve-asset convertibility
Konvertibilität *f* **zwischen den Gemeinschaftswährungen** (EG) convertibility of Community currencies against each other
konvertierbar (Vw) convertible
konvertierbare Währung *f* (Vw) convertible currency
Konvertierbarkeit *f* (AuW) (market) convertibility *(ie, to ensure freedom of international payments and capital transactions)*
Konvertierbarkeit *f* **im Rahmen der Leistungsbilanz** (AuW) current account convertibility
konvertieren (Vw) to convert
Konvertierung *f* (Fin) conversion
Konvertierungsangebot *n* (Fin) conversion offer
Konvertierungsanleihe *f* (FiW) conversion issue
Konvertierungsrisiko *n* (AuW) exchange transfer risk
konvexe Kostenfunktion *f* (Bw) convex cost function
konvexe Linearkombination *f* (Math) convex linear combination
konvexe Menge *f* (Math) convex set
konvexe Programmierung *f* (OR) convex programming
Konzentration *f* (Bw) concentration
Konzentrationsanalyse *f* (Stat) concentration analysis
Konzentrationsbewegung *f* (Kart) concentration movement
Konzentrationsindex *m* (Vw) index of concentration
Konzentrationsmaß *n* (Stat) measure of concentration
Konzentration *f* **wirtschaftlicher Macht** (Vw) concentration of economic power
Konzentrator *m* (EDV) concentrator *(ie, device having several input channels and a smaller number of output channels)*
konzentrierte Modellfunktion *f* (Stat) concentrated likelihood function
Konzept *n* **der einheitlichen Leitung** (Bw) unity of direction
konzeptualisieren (Log) to conceptualize
konzeptueller Bezugsrahmen *m* (Log) conceptual frame of reference (*or* framework)
Konzern *m*
(Bw) group of affiliated companies
− *(usu. shortened to)* group
(ie, under common centralized management of the controlling enterprise)
(Note that English law has not developed a distinct body of law governing the relationship between holding companies and subsidiaries, and between companies which have substantial shareholdings in other companies not conferring legal powers of control and those of other companies. In this respect English law is less advanced than the German legislation governing public companies, §§ 15–21 and §§ 291–338 AktG)
Konzernabschluß *m*
(ReW) consolidated financial statement, § 329 AktG
− consolidated accounts

361

- (GB) group accounts
- group financial statement

Konzern-Auftragseingang *m* (com) group order intake

Konzernausgleich *m* (ReW) inter-company squaring

Konzernaußenumsatz *m*
(ReW) group external sales
- (GB) group external turnover

Konzernbereich *m* (Bw) group division

Konzernberichtswesen *n* (ReW) group reporting

Konzernbeteiligungen *fpl* (ReW) securities of affiliates

Konzernbetriebsrat *m* (Pw) corporate works council

Konzernbilanz *f* (ReW) consolidated balance sheet, § 331 AktG

Konzernbilanzgewinn *m* (ReW) consolidated net earnings *(ie, after reserve transfers)*

Konzernbilanz-Summe *f* (ReW) group balance-sheet total

Konzernbuchgewinn *m* (ReW) inter-company (*or* consolidated) profit

Konzernchef *m*
(Bw) chairman of the group
- group's chief executive

konzerneigene Anteile *mpl* (Fin) group's own shares

konzerneigene Handelsgesellschaft *f* (com) trading subsidiary

Konzern-Erfolgsrechnung *f* (ReW) consolidated income statement

konzernfremde Interessen *npl* (Fin) interests held by parties outside a group (of companies)

Konzernfremder *m* (Fin) outsider to a group

Konzerngeschäfte *npl* (com) intra-group transactions

Konzerngeschäftsbericht *m* (ReW) consolidated annual report, § 334 AktG

Konzerngesellschaft *f*
(Bw) group company
- group-related company
- company belonging to a group
- constituent company

Konzerngewinn *m*
(ReW) consolidated (*or* group) profits
- consolidated net income

Konzern-Gewinn und Verlustrechnung *f* (ReW) consolidated statement of income

Konzerngewinn *m* **vor Steuern** (ReW) group pre-tax profits

konzernintern
(Bw) intergroup
- within the group

konzerninterne Forderungen *fpl* (ReW) intercompany receivables

konzerninterne Kapitalströme *mpl* (Fin) intra-group capital flows

konzerninterner Lieferungs- und Leistungsverkehr *m* (Bw) intergroup shipments (*or* supplies)

konzerninterne Umsätze *mpl* (ReW) intercompany sales

konzerninterne Vereinbarung *f* (Re) intercompany agreement

konzerninterne Zwischengewinne *mpl* (ReW) intra-group intermediate profits

Konzerninvestitionen *fpl* (Fin) group capital investment

Konzern-Kapitalflußrechnung *f* (Fin) group cash flow statement

Konzernlagebericht *m* (ReW) group annual report

Konzernleitung *f* (Bw) central management of a group

Konzern-Probebilanz *f* (ReW) consolidating financial statement

Konzernprüfung *f* (StR) group tax audit *(ie, made if external group sales are DM50m annually and over)*

Konzernrechnungslegung *f* (ReW) consolidated accounting

Konzernrecht *n* (Re) law relating to groups of affiliated companies *(ie, §§ 291–338 AktG, esp. provisions on group accounting)*

Konzern-Rentabilität *f* (ReW) group profitability

Konzernrücklagen *fpl* (ReW) consolidated reserves

Konzernspitze *f*
(Bw) principal company of a group
(Bw) = *Konzernleitung*

Konzern *m* **steuern** (Bw) to steer (*or* direct) a group

Konzernsyndikus *m* (Re) corporate lawyer

Konzerntöchter *fpl* (Re) consolidated subsidiaries

Konzernüberschuß *m* (ReW) consolidated surplus

Konzernumsatz *m*
(ReW) consolidated sales
- group deliveries
- group sales
- group's business volume
- intercompany sales
- internal deliveries

Konzernunternehmen *n*
(Bw) member of an affiliated group of companies, § 18 I AktG
- affiliate
- allied company
- associate company

Konzernverbindlichkeiten *fpl*
(ReW) group indebtedness
- intra-group liabilities

Konzernverflechtung *f* (Bw) group integration

Konzernverrechnung *f* (ReW) intercompany pricing

Konzernverrechnungspreise *mpl* (ReW) intercompany prices

Konzernverwaltung *f* (Bw) group headquarters

Konzernvorbehalt *m* (Re) extended reservation of ownership *(ie, title is reserved until all claims of group affiliates are satisfied)*

Konzernvorstand *m* (Bw) group executive board

Konzernweltbilanz *f* (ReW) global consolidated accounts

Konzernzwischengewinn *m* (ReW) intergroup profit

konzertierte Aktion *f* (Vw) ,,concerted action" *(ie, procedure by which the economics minister meets at regular intervals with employer and union representatives to discuss the state of the economy –*

ended in 1977 after a row about the employers' attitude about codetermination)
konzertierte Reservenpolitik *f* (EG) concerted policy on reserves
Konzertzeichner *m* (Bö) stag
Konzertzeichnung *f* (Bö) stagging
Konzession *f*
(Re) franchise
– license
– concession
Konzession *f* **beantragen** (Re) to apply for a license
Konzession *f* **entziehen** (Re) to disfranchise
Konzession *f* **erteilen** (Re) to grant a license
konzessionieren
(Re) to license
– to grant a license
– to franchise
– (US) to grant a concession
konzessioniert (com) certified
Konzessionsentzug *m* (Re) withdrawing of a license
Konzessionserteiler *m*
(Re) licensor
– franchiser
Konzessionserteilung *f* (Re) issue of a license
Konzessionsgebühr *f*
(Re) license *(or* concession) fee
– royalty
Konzessionsinhaber *m*
(Re) holder of a license
– franchisee
– concessionaire
Konzessionsvertrag *m* (com) franchise agreement
Kooperation *f* (Bw, Kart) cooperation
Kooperationsfibel *f* (Kart) Cooperation Guide *(ie, put out by the Federal Economics Ministry, indicating areas of cooperation between enterprises which should not normally be regarded as coming within the terms of § 1 GWB)*
Kooperationskartell *n* (Kart) cooperation cartel
Kooperationsvertrag *m* (Re) cooperation agreement
kooperativer Führungsstil *m*
(Bw) cooperative style of leadership
– supportive pattern of leadership
kooperatives Oligopol *n* (Vw) cooperative oligopoly
kooperatives Spiel *n* (OR) cooperative game
Koordinate *f* (Math) coordinate
Koordinatenanfang *m* (Math) origin of Cartesian coordinates
Koordinatenebene *f* (Math) coordinate plane
Koordinatenspeicher *m* (EDV) coordinate *(or* matrix) store *(syn, Matrixspeicher, Matrizenspeicher)*
Koordinatentransformation *f*
(Math) coordinate transformation
– transformation of coordinates
Koordination *f* (Bw) coordination *(eg, of corporate activities)*
Koordinationskonzern *m* (Bw) coordinated group of affiliated companies *(opp, Subordinationskonzern)*
Koordinator *m* **der Produktionsplanung** (IndE) production scheduler

Kopfbogen *m* (com) letter head
Kopfetikett *n* (EDV) header (label)
„Kopfjäger" *m*
(Pw) executive search consultant
– (infml) headhunter
Kopfkarte *f* (EDV) header card
Kopfsteuer *f*
(FiW) capitation
– head
– poll . . . tax
Kopie *f*
(com) copy
– duplicate
– carbon copy
Kopiendrucker *m* (EDV) hard copy terminal
Kopieranweisung *f* (EDV, Cobol) copy statement
Kopiergerät *n* (com) copier
Kopiergerätemarkt *m* (com) copier market
Kopplungsgeschäft *n*
(com) package deal
– linked transaction
(Kart) tie-in sale *(ie, one product cannot be bought without another)*
Kopplungsklausel *f* (Re) tie-in clause
kopulative Supposition *f* (Log) common supposition
Korbflasche *f* (com) demijohn *(ie, large bottle encased in wickerwork, frequently used in export trade for transporting chemicals)*
Korbwährung *f* (AuW) basket currency
Körper *m*
(Math) number field *(or* domain)
– domain of rationality
– commutative field *(syn, Rationalitätsbereich)*
körperbehindert (Pw) physically handicapped
Körperbehindertenpauschale *f* (StR) lump sum tax benefit for handicapped persons
Körperbehinderter *m* (SozV) handicapped person
Körperdiagramm *n* (Stat) three-dimensional diagram
Körpererweiterung *f* (Math) extension of a field *(syn, Erweiterungskörper, Oberkörper)*
Körpererweiterung *f* **1. Art** (Math) separable *(or* algebraic) extension of a field *(syn, separable od algebraische Körpererweiterung)*
Körpergrad *m* (Math) finite extension of a field *(syn, endliche Körpererweiterung)*
körperliche Bestandsaufnahme *f*
(MaW) phyiscal inventory
– physical stocktaking
– physical count
körperliche Eigenschaften *fpl* **der Waren** (com) physical characteristics of the goods
körperliche Gegenstände *mpl* (Re) corporeal objects
körperliche Inventur *f* (ReW) = *körperliche Bestandsaufnahme*
Körperschaden *m* (Re) bodily *(or* physical) injury
Körperschaft *f*
(Re) statutory corporation
– corporate body
– body corporate
(ie, legal persons organized under public and private law, represented by their own statutory agents)

Körperschaftbesteuerung *f* (StR) taxation of corporations
Körperschaft *f* **des öffentlichen Rechts**
(Re) corporation under public law
– public body
– public corporation
– public-law corporation
– entity of the public law
Körperschaft *f* **des privaten Rechts** (Re) corporation under private law
Körperschaftsteuer *f* (StR) corporation (*or* corporate) income tax
Körperschaftsteuer-Befreiung *f* (StR) exemption from corporation tax
Körperschaftsteuer-Durchführungsverordnung *f* (StR) Ordinance Regulating the Corporation Income Tax Law
Körperschaftsteuererklärung *f* (StR) corporation income tax return
Körperschaftsteuergesetz *n* (StR) Corporation Income Tax Law, of 31 Aug 1976
körperschaftsteuerliches Anrechnungsverfahren *n* (StR) corporate tax imputation procedure
körperschaftsteuerpflichtig (StR) liable in corporate income taxes
Körperschaftsteuer-Reform *f* (StR) corporate tax reform
Körperschaftsteuerreformgesetz *n* (StR) corporation tax reform law
Körperschaftsteuer-Richtlinien *fpl* (StR) Corporation Income Tax Regulations
Körperschaftsteuer-Vorauszahlung *f* (StR) prepayment of estimated corporation income tax, § 48 KStG
– advance corporation tax, ACT
Körperverletzung *f*
(Re) bodily injury
– (US *also*) personal injury
Korrektionsfaktor *m* (Stat) correction factor
Korrektivposten *m* (ReW) = *Korrekturposten*
Korrektur *f* **endlicher Grundgesamtheiten** (Stat) finite sampling correction
Korrekturkarte *f* (EDV) patch card (*syn, Änderungskarte, Patch-Karte*)
Korrektur *f* **nach oben**
(com) upward revision
– scaling up
Korrektur *f* **nach unten**
(com) downward revision
– scaling down
Korrekturposten *m*
(ReW) correcting entry
– offsetting item
Korrekturroutine *f* (EDV) patch
Korrektur *f* **überhöhter Preise** (Mk) disappreciation
Korrelation *f* (Stat) correlation
Korrelationsanalyse *f* (Stat) correlational analysis
Korrelationsdiagramm *n* (Stat) correlation diagram
Korrelationsindex *m* (Stat) correlation index
Korrelationskoeffizient *m*
(Stat) correlation coefficient
– coefficient of correlation
Korrelationsmaße *npl* (Stat) measures of correlation

Korrelationsmatrix *f* (Stat) correlation matrix
Korrelationsparameter *m* (Stat) correlation parameter
Korrelationsquotient *m* (Stat) correlation ratio
Korrelationstabelle *f*
(Stat) correlation table
– bivariate table
Korrespondent *m*
(com) correspondent (*ie, person handling commercial correspondence*)
(Fin) correspondent bank
Korrespondentreeder *m* (com) managing owner (*ie, of a ship*)
Korrespondenzabteilung *f* (com) correspondence department
Korrespondenzbank *f*
(Fin) correspondent bank
– foreign correspondent
(*ie, foreign bank with which a domestic bank is doing business on a continuous basis*)
Korrespondenzspediteur *m* (com) correspondent forwarder
Korrespondenzversicherung *f* (Vers) home-foreign insurance
korrespondierende Buchhaltung *f* (ReW) corresponding accounting unit
korrespondierende Reihe *f* (Math) coincident series
korrigierbarer Code *m* (EDV) error correcting code
korrigieren
(com) to correct
– to rectify
– to remedy
– to set to rights
– to straighten out
Kosinusfunktion *f* (Math) cosine function
Kosinussatz *m* (Math) law of cosine
Kosten *pl*
(com) cost(s)
– charges
– expense(s)
– expenditure
– outlay
Kostenabweichung *f* (KoR) cost variance (*ie, between actual and standard cost*)
Kostenanalyse *f* (KoR) cost analysis
Kostenanschlag *m*
(com) cost estimate
(com) bid
– quotation
Kostenanstieg *m* (com) increase (*or* rise) in costs
Kostenarten *fpl* (KoR) categories (*or* types) of costs
Kostenartenkonto *n* (KoR) cost account
Kostenartenrechnung *f* (KoR) cost type accounting
Kostenartenverteilung *f* (KoR) allocation of cost types
(*ie, to cost centers and costing units = Kostenstellen and Kostenträger*)
Kostenaufbau *m* (KoR) cost structure (*ie, of a unit of output, may be wage intensive, materials intensive, etc.*)
Kosten *pl* **auffangen** (com) to absorb costs
Kosten *pl* **aufgliedern** (com) to itemize costs

Kostenaufgliederung f (KoR) cost breakdown (or splitup)
Kostenauflösung f (KoR) breakdown of total costs (ie, into fixed and proportional elements)
Kosten pl **aufschlüsseln** (com) to break down expenses
Kostenaufteilung f (KoR) allocation of costs
Kostenbelastung f (KoR) cost burden
Kostenbeschränkung f (Vw) cost constraint
Kostenbestandteile mpl (KoR) cost components (or elements)
Kostenbestimmungsfaktoren mpl (KoR) cost determinants
Kosten pl **bestreiten** (com) to defray costs
Kostenbeteiligung f
  (com) cost sharing
  – assuming a share of costs
  (com) shared cost
Kosten pl **bewerten** (KoR) to cost
Kostenbewertung f (KoR) costing
Kostenbewertung f **von Vorräten** (ReW) inventory costing
kostenbewußt (Bw) cost conscious
Kosten pl **bis dahin** (KoR) final manufacturing cost
Kostenblock m (KoR) pool of costs (eg, total pool of manufacturing cost)
Kostendämmung f
  (com) cost cutting
  – curbing costs
  – cost containment
Kostendämpfungsgesetz n (SozV) Law to Curb the Cost Expansion (of Health Insurance)
Kosten pl **decken** (com) to cover (or recover) costs
kostendeckende Prämie f (Vers) net premium
kostendeckender Betrieb m (Bw) self-supporting enterprise
kostendeckender Preis m (com) cost covering price
Kostendeckung f (com) cost coverage (or recovery) (eg, was not achieved)
Kostendeckungsbeitrag m
  (KoR) contribution margin
  – marginal income
  (ie, sales minus variable expenses)
Kostendeckungspunkt m (KoR) breakeven point (syn, Gewinnschwelle, Nutzschwelle, toter Punkt)
Kostendegression f (Bw) decline of marginal unit cost (ie, one phase of the cost behavior pattern)
Kostendenken n (KoR) cost conciousness
Kosten pl **der Aktienausgabe**
  (Fin) expense of issuing shares
  – expense incurred in connection with the issuance of shares
Kosten pl **der allgemeinen Geschäftsführung** (KoR) general management cost
Kosten pl **der Auftragsabwicklung** (com) order filling costs
Kosten pl **der Auftragsbeschaffung** (com) order getting costs
Kosten pl **der Betriebsbereitschaft**
  (KoR) cost (of keeping plant in) readiness
  – ready-to-serve cost
  – standby cost
  – capacity cost
Kosten pl **der fehlenden Lieferbereitschaft** (KoR) out-of-stock costs

Kosten pl **der Kapitalbeschaffung** (Fin) capital procurement cost
Kosten pl **der Kuppelprodukte** (KoR) joint-product cost (ie, total costs incurred up to the point of separation of the different products = Gabelungspunkt)
Kosten pl **der Kuppelproduktion** (KoR) joint
  – common
  – related ... cost
Kosten pl **der Lagerhaltung**
  (KoR) carrying cost (or charges)
  – cost of carrying
  – holding cost
Kosten pl **der Nacharbeit** (com, KoR) cost of rework
Kosten pl **der Nichtverfügbarkeit** (KoR) outage cost
Kosten pl **der Rechtsverfolgung**
  (Re) cost of litigation
  – cost of seeking judicial remedy
Kosten pl **der Umrüstung** (KoR) change-over cost
Kosten pl **der verkauften Erzeugnisse**
  (ReW) cost of goods sold
  – cost of sales
Kosten pl **der Werbemaßnahmen** (KoR) media advertising and public relations cost
Kostendruck m
  (com) upward pressure on costs
  – cost pressure
Kostendruck-Inflation f (Vw) cost-push inflation
Kosteneffizienz f (Vw, FiW) engineering efficiency (ie, relation between volume output and costed input)
Kosteneinflußgrößen fpl (KoR) cost determinants
Kosteneinsparung f
  (com) cost cutting
  – cost saving
  – (infml) rampage on expenses
Kostenelement n (KoR) cost component (or element)
Kostenerfassung f
  (KoR) cost finding
  – cost accumulation
  – cost recording
Kosten pl **ermitteln** (com) to determine costs
Kostenermittlung f (KoR) cost finding
Kosten pl **ersetzen** (com) to refund (or reimburse) costs
Kostenersparnis f (com) cost saving
Kosten pl **erstatten** (com) to reimburse (or refund) expenses
Kostenerstattung f (com) reimbursement (or refund) of costs
Kostenexplosion f
  (com) cost explosion
  – runaway costs
Kostenfluß m (KoR) cost flow
Kostenfluß-Nachweis m (KoR) cost flow statement
Kostenfunktion f (Bw) cost function
Kosten pl **für Leichterung und Handhabung** (com) lightering and handling charges
kosteninduzierte Inflation f (Vw) cost-push inflation

Kostenkategorien *fpl*
 (KoR) types of cost *(E. Schmalenbach)*
 – cost categories
Kostenkennzahlen *fpl* (KoR) cost ratios
Kostenkoeffizient *m* (IndE) cost coefficient
Kostenkonten *npl* (KoR) cost accounts
Kostenkontrolle *f* (KoR) cost (*or* expense) control
Kostenkurve *f* (Vw, Bw) cost curve
Kosten-Leistungs-Verhältnis *n* (IndE) cost-to-performance ratio
kostenlos
 (com) at no charge
 – free of charge
 – without charge
kostenlose Ersatzlieferung *f* (com) replacement free of charge
Kostenmatrix *f* (OR) cost matrix
kostenminimaler Fluß *m* (OR) minimal cost flow
Kosten *pl* **minimieren** (Bw) to minimize cost
Kostenminimierung *f* (Bw) cost minimization
Kostenminimum *n* (Bw) cost minimum *(ie, level of activity at which unit costs are minimized)*
Kostenmodell *n* (Bw) cost model *(eg, of a multiproduct firm)*
Kosten *pl* **niedrig halten** (com) to hold down cost
Kosten-Nutzen-Analyse *f* (Vw, Bw) cost-benefit analysis
Kosten-Nutzen-Verhältnis *n* (Vw, Bw) cost-benefit ratio
Kostenoptimum *n* (Bw) cost optimum *(ie, at which the ratio of total cost to number of units of output is lowest; average cost and marginal cost are equal at this intersection)*
Kostenpaket *n* (OR) cost package
kostenpflichtig abweisen (Re) to dismiss (a case) with cost
Kostenplan *m* (KoR) cost plan (*or* budget)
Kostenplanung *f*
 (KoR) cost planning
 – expense budgeting
Kostenplatz *m* (KoR) workplace
Kostenpreis *m* (Bw) cost price *(ie, based on cost + percentage of cost as profit and risk element)*
Kosten-Preis-Schere *f* (Vw) cost-and-price scissors
Kostenprinzip *n* (Bw) full-recovery principle of costing *(ie, cost price + profit markup)*
Kostenrechner *m* (KoR) cost accountant
Kostenrechnung *f* (KoR) cost accounting
Kostenrechnung *f* **nach Verantwortungsbereichen** (KoR) responsibility accounting
Kostenrechnungssystem *n* (KoR) cost (*or* costing) system
Kostenremanenz *f* (KoR) cost lag
Kostensammelblatt *n*
 (KoR) job cost sheet
 – job order cost sheet
Kostensammelkarte *f* (KoR) cost card
Kostensammelkonten *npl* (KoR) collective cost accounts
Kostensatz *m* (KoR) cost unit rate
Kostenschlüssel *m* (KoR) cost allocation base
Kosten *pl* **senken**
 (com) to cut
 – to reduce
 – to trim . . . costs

Kostensenkung *f* (com) cost cutting (*or* reduction)
Kostensenkungsprogramm *n* (com) cost-cutting program
Kosten *pl* **sparen** (com) to save costs (*or* charges)
kostensparende Maßnahmen *fpl* (com) cost-reducing improvements
Kostenspielraum *m* (KoR) cost latitude
Kostenspirale *f* (Bw) cost spiral
Kostenstatistik *f* (KoR) cost statistics
Kosten *pl* **steigen** (com) costs increase (*or* rise *or* go up)
Kostenstelle *f*
 (KoR) cost center
 – cost (*or* costing) unit
 – department
 – expense center
 – unit of activity
Kostenstellenausgleichsverfahren *n* (KoR) cost center squaring
Kostenstellenblatt *n* (KoR) cost center summary sheet
Kostenstellengemeinkosten *pl*
 (KoR) cost center overhead
 – departmental overhead
 – departmental burden
Kostenstellen-Gemeinkostenzuschlag *m* (KoR) cost center overhead rate
Kostenstellengliederung *f*
 (KoR) functional expense classification
 – departmentalization
 (KoR) cost center structure
Kostenstellengruppe *f* (KoR) cost center group
Kostenstellenkonten *npl* (ReW) cost center accounts
Kostenstellenkosten *pl* (KoR) cost center cost
Kostenstellen-Lagebericht *m* (Bw) operating unit status report
Kostenstellenplan *m* (ReW) chart of functional accounts
Kostenstellenrechnung *f*
 (KoR) cost center accounting
 – departmental costing
Kostenstellenüberdeckung *f* (KoR) cost center surplus
Kostenstellenumlage *f* (KoR) cost center charge transfer
Kostenstellenumlageverfahren *n* (KoR) step ladder method
Kostenstellenunterdeckung *f* (KoR) cost center deficit
Kostenstellenvergleich *m* (KoR) cost center comparison
Kostenstellenverrechnung *f* (KoR) cost center charge transfer
Kostensteuern *fpl* (StR) taxes chargeable as expenses
Kostenstoß-Inflation *f* (Vw) cost-push inflation
Kosten *pl* **tragen** (com) to bear costs
Kostenträger *m*
 (KoR) cost (*or* costing) unit
 – cost objective
 – unit of output
Kostenträger-Erfolgsrechnung *f* (KoR) cost-unit statement of income
Kostenträgergruppe *f* (KoR) cost unit group

Kostenträgerrechnung *f*
(KoR) unit-of-output costing
– job order cost system
Kostenträger-Stückrechnung *f* (KoR) cost unit accounting
Kostenträgerzeitrechnung *f* (KoR) cost unit period accounting
Kostenüberdeckung *f* (KoR) cost surplus
Kosten *pl* **übernehmen** (com) to bear (*or* take over) costs
Kostenüberschreitung *f* (com) cost overrun
Kostenübertragung *f* (KoR) cost transfers
Kostenüberwachung *f* (KoR) expense control
Kostenumlage *f*
(KoR) cost allocation
– cost distribution
– cost apportionment
Kosten- und Ertragslage *f* (Bw) cost-earnings situation
Kosten- und Leistungsrechnung *f* (KoR) cost accounting and results accounts
Kosten- und Produktionsmittel-Revision *f* (OR) cost and resources updating worksheet
Kosten- und Terminbilanz *f* (OR) cost of work report
Kosten *pl* **ungenutzter Kapazität** (KoR) idle capacity cost
Kosten *pl* **verbundener Produktion** (KoR) common cost
Kostenvergleich *m* (KoR) cost comparison
Kostenvergleichsrechnung *f* (Fin) cost comparison method *(ie, in preinvestment analysis)*
Kostenverhalten *n* (KoR) cost behavior
Kostenverlauf *m*
(KoR) pattern of cost behavior
– cost behavior pattern
Kostenverrechnung *f*
(KoR) cost allocation
– cost apportionment
– cost distribution
– expense distribution
Kosten *pl* **verteilen** (ReW) to spread cost *(eg, over some years)*
Kostenverteilung *f* (KoR) = *Kostenverrechnung*
Kostenverteilungsbogen *m* (KoR) cost allocation sheet
Kostenverursachungsprinzip *n* (KoR) principle of allocation by which variable costs must be traced to cost centers and costing units where such costs originated
Kostenvoranschlag *m*
(com) cost estimate
– preliminary estimate
– (GB) bill of quantity *(ie, in the building contracting business)*
(com) bid
– quotation
Kostenvorgabe *f* (KoR) cost objective
Kostenvorlauf *m* (KoR) cost anticipation
Kostenvorschau *f* (KoR) cost-outlook report
Kostenvorschuß *m* (Re) advance on the costs
Kostenwirksamkeitsanalyse *f* (FiW) cost effectiveness analysis
Kostenziel *n* (KoR) cost objective
Kostenzurechnung *f* (KoR) = *Kostenverrechnung*

Kostenzusammenstellung *f* (KoR) cost sheet
Kostgeschäft *n* (Fin) take-in transaction
Kotangente *f* (Math) cotangent
Kotieren *n* (Bö) official listing of a security
kovariante Komponente *f* (Math) covariant component
Kovarianz *f* (Stat) covariance
Kovarianzanalyse *f* (Stat) analysis of covariance
Kovarianz *f* **der Grundgesamtheit** (Stat) parent covariance
Kovarianzmatrix *f* (Stat) covariance matrix
Kraftfahrzeug *n* (com) motor vehicle
Kraftfahrzeugbrief *m* (com, GB) registration (*or* log) book
Kraftfahrzeughaftpflichtversicherung *f*
(Vers) third-party automobile insurance
– (GB) motor insurance
Kraftfahrzeugindustrie *f*
(com) automobile (*or* automotive) industry
– (GB) motor (vehicle) industry
Kraftfahrzeugsteuer *f* (StR) tax on motor vehicles
Kraftfahrzeugversicherer *m* (Vers, GB) motor insurer
Kraftfahrzeugversicherung *f*
(Vers) automobile insurance
– (GB) motor insurance
kraft Gesetzes (Re) by operation of the law
– by act of law
kräftig anziehen (Bö) to advance strongly
Kraftloserklärung *f*
(Re) invalidation
– forfeiture
– cancellation
Kraftpapier *n* (com) kraft paper *(ie, strong, usu. brown paper made from pulp and used for wrapping)*
Kraftverkehrspedition *f*
(com) trucking company
– (GB) haulage contractor
Kraftverkehrsversicherung *f* (Vers) = *Kraftfahrzeugversicherung*
Kraftwagenkosten *pl* (StR) automobile expenses
Krankengeld *n* (SozV) sickness benefit (*or* pay)
Krankengeldversicherung *f* (Vers) temporary disability insurance
Krankenhauskosten *pl* (Vers) hospital charges
Krankenhauskostenversicherung *f* (Vers) hospital cost insurance
Krankenhauspflegesatz *m* (SozV) hospital perdiem charge
Krankenkasse *f* (SozV) health insurance fund (*or* scheme)
Krankenkassenbeiträge *mpl* **des Arbeitgebers** (SozV) employer's contribution to health insurance fund
Krankentagegeldversicherung *f* (Vers) daily benefits insurance
Krankenversicherung *f*
(SozV) compulsory health insurance
(Vers) health insurance
Krankenversicherungsbeitrag *m*
(SozV) health insurance contribution
(Vers) health insurance premium
Krankenversicherungsträger *m* (SozV) health insurance carrier

krankfeiern (Pw) to go sick *(ie, often for trivial reasons)*
— (infml) to take a holiday pretending sickness
krankhafte Störung *f* **der Geistestätigkeit** (Re) morbid disturbance of mind, § 104 BGB
krankheitsbedingtes Fehlen *n*
(Pw) absence due to illness
— sickness absenteeism
Krankheitshäufigkeitsziffer *f* (Pw) illness frequency rate
krankschreiben lassen (Pw) to get oneself certified unfit for work
Krankwert *m* (SeeV) damaged value
Kredit *m*
(Fin) credit
— loan
— advance
(ie, types of credit: Kontokorrentkredit, Diskontkredit, Lombardkredit, Akzeptkredit, Akkreditiv)
Kreditabbau *m* (Fin) loan repayment
Kreditabschnitte *mpl* (Fin) loans
Kreditabsicherung *f* (Fin) credit security arrangements
Kreditabteilung *f* (Fin) loan department
Kredit *m* **abwickeln** (Fin) to process a loan
Kreditabwicklung *f* (Fin) loan processing
Kreditakte *f* (Fin) borrower's file *(ie, kept by bank)*
Kreditakzept *n* (Fin) financial acceptance *(ie, accepted finance bill)*
Kreditangebotsfunktion *f* (Vw) credit supply function
Kreditanspannung *f* (Fin) tight credit situation
Kreditanstalt *f* **des öffentlichen Rechts** (Fin) credit institution of the public law
Kreditanstalt *f* **für Wiederaufbau** (Fin) Reconstruction Loan Corporation, KfW, KW *(ie, Frankfurt-based, channel for public aid to developing countries)*
Kreditantrag *m*
(Fin) loan application
— request for a loan
Kreditantragsteller *m* (Fin) loan applicant
Kreditapparat *m* (Fin) banking system
Kreditaufnahme *f*
(Fin, FiW) credit intake
— borrowing
— raising credits *(or* loans)
— taking up *(or* on) credits
Kreditaufnahme *f* **der öffentlichen Hand** (FiW) government *(or* public sector) borrowing
Kreditaufnahme *f* **im Ausland** (Fin) borrowing abroad
Kreditaufnahme-Vollmacht *f* (Fin) borrowing authority
Kreditaufnahme *f* **von Unternehmen** (Fin) corporate borrowing
Kredit *m* **aufnehmen**
(Fin) to borrow
— to raise a loan
— to take on/up a credit
Kreditauftrag *m* (Re) credit-extending instruction, § 778 BGB
Kreditausfall *m* (Fin) loan loss
Kreditausfallquote *f* (Fin) loan loss ratio

Kredit *m* **aushandeln**
(Fin) to arrange a loan
— to negotiate the terms of a credit
Kreditauskunft *f*
(Fin) credit information *(or* report)
— (GB) banker's reference
Kreditauskunftei *f*
(Fin) credit reporting agency
— (GB) credit reference agency
Kreditauslese *f* (Fin) credit selection
Kreditausschuß *m* (Fin) credit *(or* loan) committee
Kreditausweitung *f* (Vw) expansion of credit volume
Kreditauszahlung *f* (Fin) loan payout
Kreditbank *f* (Fin) bank
Kredit *m* **bearbeiten**
(Fin) to process a credit application
— to handle *(or* manage) a credit
Kreditbearbeitung *f*
(Fin) processing of credit applications
— loan processing
— credit management
Kreditbearbeitungsprovision *f* (Fin) loan processing charge
Kreditbedarf *m* (Fin) borrowing needs *(or* requirements)
Kreditbedarf *m* **der öffentlichen Hand** (FiW) public sector borrowing requirements, PSBR
Kreditbedarfsplan *m* (Fin) credit requirements plan
Kreditbedingungen *fpl*
(Fin) terms of credit
(Fin) lending terms *(ie, of a bank)*
Kreditbereitschaft *f* (Fin) readiness to grant a credit
Kreditbereitstellung *f*
(Fin) allocation of loan funds
(Fin) extension of a loan *(ie, by a bank)*
Kreditbeschaffung *f* (Fin) borrowing
Kreditbeschaffungsprovision *f* (Fin) credit procurement fee
Kreditbeschränkungen *fpl* (Fin) lending restrictions
Kredit *m* **besichern** (Fin) to collateralize a loan
Kredit *m* **bewilligen** (Fin) to approve a loan
Kreditbeziehung *f* (Fin) relationship involving credit
Kreditbilanz *f* (Fin) = *Kreditstatus*
Kreditbremse *f*
(Fin) credit *(or* monetary) brake
— restraint on credit
Kreditbremse *f* **ziehen**
(Vw, infml) to clamp down on credits
— (sl) to jam on the credit brake
Kreditbrief *m* (Fin) letter of credit
Kreditbürgschaft *f* (Fin) credit guaranty
Kreditbüro *n* (Fin) credit sales agency
Kredite *mpl* **aufnehmen** (Fin) to borrow funds (from)
Kredite *mpl* **der Kreditinstitute** (Vw) lending by banks
Kredit-Einlagen-Relation *f* (Fin) loan-deposit ratio
Kredit *m* **einräumen** (Fin) to grant a credit
Krediteinschränkung *f* (Fin) credit restriction

Krediterleichterungen *fpl* (Vw) easing of credit policy
Kredit *m* **erneuern**
(Fin) to renew a loan
– to refresh an expiring loan
Kredit *m* **eröffnen** (Fin) to open a credit
krediteröffnende Bank *f* (Fin) issuing (*or* opening) bank
Krediteröffnung *f* (Fin) opening of a credit
Krediteröffnungsvertrag *m* (Fin) credit agreement
Kreditexpansion *f*
(Vw) credit expansion
(Fin) growth of lending
Kreditfachmann *m* (Fin) credit expert
Kreditfähigkeit *f*
(Fin) borrowing power
– financial standing
Kreditfazilität *f* (Fin) borrowing (*or* credit) facility
kreditfinanzierte Ausgaben *fpl* (FiW) credit-financed public expenditure
Kreditfinanzierung *f*
(Fin) loan financing
– borrowing
Kreditgarantie *f* (Fin) loan guaranty
Kreditgarantiegemeinschaften *fpl* (com) credit guaranty associations (*ie, set up in the legal form of GmbH*)
kreditgebende Bank *f* (Fin) lending bank
Kreditgeber *m* (Fin) lender
Kreditgebühren *fpl* (Fin) loan charges
Kreditgefährdung *f* (Re) disparagement of another's credit standing, § 824 BGB
Kreditgeld *n* (Vw) credit money
Kreditgenossenschaft *f* (Fin) credit cooperative
Kreditgeschäft *n*
(Fin) credit (*or* loan) transaction (*ie, extension of money loans and acceptance credits*)
(Fin) lending business
Kredit *m* **gewähren**
(Fin) to extend a credit
– to make a loan
Kreditgewährung *f*
(Fin) credit extension
– extension of credits and loans
– lending
Kreditgewährung *f* **der Banken** (Fin) bank lending
Kreditgewerbe *n* (Fin) banking industry
Kreditgewinnabgabe *f* (StR) levy on gains from the conversion of Reichsmark liabilities under § 211 I LAG
Kreditgrenze *f* (Fin) credit ceiling
Kredithahn *m* **zudrehen** (Fin, infml) to cut off credit (to)
Kredithai *m* (Fin, infml) loan shark
kreditieren (Fin) to credit
Kreditierung *f* (Fin) crediting
Kredit *m* **in Anspruch nehmen**
(Fin) to draw upon
– to make use of
– to utilize . . . a credit
Kreditinflation *f* (Vw) inflation induced by disproportionate expansion of credit volume
Kredit *m* **in laufender Rechnung**
(Fin) credit on current account
– open account credit

Kreditinstitut *n* (Fin) bank
Kreditinstitut *n* **mit Sonderaufgaben**
(Fin) specialized credit institution
– credit institution with special functions
(*eg, Kreditanstalt für Wiederaufbau, Lastenausgleichsbank, etc.*)
Kreditinstitut *n* **mit Warengeschäft** (Fin) banking institution trading in goods
Kreditinstrument *n* (Fin) credit instrument
Kredit *m* **in unbeschränkter Höhe** (Fin) unlimited credit line
Kreditkapazität *f* (Fin) lending capacity
Kreditkarte *f* (Fin) credit card
Kreditkartengeschäft *n* (Fin) credit card business
Kreditkauf *m*
(com) credit sale (*ie, as ‚Zielkauf' if agreed upon between merchants under stipulated terms of payment and delivery*)
(com) consumer credit sale (*ie, identical to Teilzahlungs- od Abzahlungsgeschäft*)
Kreditkauf *m* **von Effekten od Waren** (Bö) trading on margin
Kreditkette *f* (Fin) credit chain
Kreditklemme *f* (Fin) credit squeeze
Kreditknappheit *f*
(Fin) credit crunch
– credit stringency
– tight credit
Kreditkonsortium *n* (Fin) loan syndicate
Kreditkonto *n* (Fin) credit (*or* loan) account
Kreditkontrolle *f* (Fin) credit control
Kreditkosten *pl*
(Fin) borrowing cost (*or* fees)
– cost of borrowing
Kreditkostenfinanzierung *f* (Fin) financing of borrowing costs
Kreditkunde *m* (Fin) borrowing (*or* credit) customer
Kreditkundschaft *f* (Fin) borrower customers (*ie, of a bank*)
Kreditlaufzeit *f*
(Fin) credit period
– period of credit extension
– time span for which credit is granted
Kreditlaufzeiten *fpl* (Fin) loan maturities
Kreditleihe *f* (Fin) credit commitment (*ie, bank does not grant a money credit, but its credit standing in the form of guaranty, acceptance credit*)
Kreditlimit *n* (Fin) borrowing limit
Kreditlinie *f*
(Fin) credit line
– line of credit
– lending line (*or* ceiling)
(*ie, the nearest British equivalent is the ‚overdraft'*)
(AuW) credit line (*ie, in bilateral and multilateral clearing agreements*)
Kreditlinie *f* **vereinbaren** (Fin) to arrange a line of credit
Kreditliste *f* (Fin) black list of borrowers with low credit standing
Kreditlücke *f* (Fin) credit gap
Kreditmakler *m* (Fin) money broker
Kreditmarkt *m* (Fin) credit market (*ie, includes money market and capital market*)

Kreditmärkte *mpl* (Fin) financial markets
Kreditmarktschulden *fpl* (FiW) credit market debt (*or* indebtedness)
Kreditmarktverschuldung *f* (Fin) market indebtedness
Kreditmechanismus *m* (Fin) credit mechanism
Kredit *m* **mit Ablöseautomatik** (Fin) droplock credit agreement
Kredit *m* **mit fester Laufzeit**
(Fin) time loan
– fixed term loan
Kredit *m* **mit gleichbleibendem Zinssatz** (Fin) straight loan
Kredit *m* **mit häufiger Neufestsetzung des Zinssatzes während der Laufzeit od mit Kopplung an die Interbanksätze** (Fin) rollover credit
Kreditmittel *pl* (Fin) borrowed funds
Kredit *m* **mit variabler Verzinsung** (Fin) variable interest loan
– floating rate loan
Kredit *m* **mit Warenbindung** (AuW) tied loan
Kreditnachfrage *f*
(Fin) credit demand
(Fin) volume of credit demand
Kreditnachfrage *f* **der gewerblichen Wirtschaft** (Fin) business loan demand
Kreditnachfragefunktion *f* (Vw) credit demand function
Kreditnehmer *m* (Fin) borrower
Kreditobergrenze *f* (Fin) credit limit
Kreditobligo *n* (Fin) loan commitments
Kreditoren *mpl*
(ReW) accounts payable
– payables
– creditors
Kreditorenbuch *n* (ReW) creditor's ledger
Kreditorenbuchhaltung *f* (ReW) accounts payable department
Kreditorenbuchung *f* (ReW) accounts payable entry
Kreditoren-Journal *n* (ReW) invoice journal
Kreditplafond *m* (FiW) loan ceiling *(ie, extended to a public debtor, usu. on a statutory basis)*
Kreditplan *m* (Fin) credit budget
Kreditpolitik *f* (Fin) lending (*or* credit) policy
kreditpolitische Maßnahmen *fpl* (Vw) credit policies
kreditpolitischer Kurs *m* (Vw) monetary policy
kreditpolitische Schocktherapie *f* (Vw) monetary shock therapy
kreditpolitisches Instrumentarium *n* (Vw) instruments of credit control
Kreditportefeuille *n* (Fin) total lendings
Kreditpotential *n* (Fin) lending capacity
Kreditprolongation *f* (Fin) renewal of a loan
Kreditprovision *f* (Fin) credit fee *(ie, equal to credit risk premium)*
Kreditprüfung *f*
(ReW) audit for credit purposes
(Fin) credit investigation (*or* evaluation)
Kreditpyramide *f* **bei der Geldschöpfung** (Vw) pyramid of credit
Kreditrahmen *f* (Fin) framework of credit
Kreditrahmenkontingent *n* (Fin) general credit line
Kreditreserve *f* (Fin) credit reserve

Kreditrestriktion *f* (Vw) credit restriction (*or* squeeze)
Kreditrisiko *n*
(Fin) credit risk
– risk exposure
Kreditrisiko *n* **übernehmen**
(Fin) to take a credit risk upon oneself
– to assume a credit risk
Kreditrisikoversicherung *f* (Vers) credit risk insurance
Kreditrückflüsse *mpl* (Fin) loan repayments
Kreditrückzahlung *f* (Fin) repayment of a loan
Kreditsachbearbeiter *m* (Fin) bank clerk handling loan applications
Kreditsaldo *m* (Fin) credit balance
Kreditschöpfung *f*
(Vw) credit creation
– credit expansion
– credit formation
Kreditschöpfungsmultiplikator *m*
(Vw) credit (*or* deposit) multiplier
– credit expansion multiplier
Kreditschraube *f* (Fin) credit screw
Kreditschutz *m* (Fin) credit protection
Kreditseite *f*
(ReW) credit side (of an account)
– creditor
Kreditselektion *f* (Fin) credit selection
Kreditsicherheit *f* (Fin) collateral for secured loan
Kreditsicherung *f*
(Fin) securing a loan
– collateralization of loan
Kreditsonderkonto *n* (Fin) special loan account
Kreditsperre *f*
(Fin) stoppage of credit
– credit freeze
Kredit *m* **sperren** (Fin) to block (*or* freeze) a credit
Kreditspielraum *m* (Fin) lending potential *(of a bank)*
Kreditstatistik *f* (Fin) bank lending statistics
Kreditstatus *m* (Fin) statement of credit position *(ie, prepared to determine net worth and liquidity of borrower)*
Kreditstreuung *f* (Fin) loan diversification
Kreditsumme *f* (Fin) loan amount
Kredittranche *f* (IWF) credit tranche
Kreditüberwachung *f* (Fin) credit surveillance
Kredit *m* **überziehen** (Fin) to overdraw one's account
Kreditüberziehung *f* (Fin) overdraft
Kreditumschuldung *f* (Fin) rescheduling of a loan
Kreditunterlagen *fpl* (Fin) information required for credits
Kreditunternehmen *n* (Fin) credit institution
Kreditvaluta *f* (Fin) loan moneys
Kreditverbilligung *f* (Fin) easier credit terms
Kreditvereinbarung *f* (Fin) credit agreement (*or* arrangement)
Kreditverflechtung *f* (Fin) credit links (*or* ties) *(eg, among business enterprises)*
Kreditvergabepolitik *f* (Fin) lending policy
Kreditvergünstigungen *fpl* (AuW) credit concessions
Kreditverkauf *m*
(com) credit sale

− sale on credit
Kreditverkehr *m* (Fin) credit transactions
Kredit *m* **verlängern** (Fin) to renew a credit
Kreditverlängerung *f* (Fin) credit renewal
Kreditvermittler *m* (Fin) credit broker
Kreditversicherer *m* (Vers) credit insurer
Kreditversicherung *f* (Vers) credit insurance
Kreditversicherungspolice *f* (Vers) credit insurance policy
Kreditvertrag *m* (Fin) credit agreement (*or* contract) *(ie, made between lender and borrower)*
Kreditvertrag *m* **abschließen** (Fin) to conclude a loan agreement
Kreditverträge *mpl* (Fin) borrowing and lending agreements
Kreditverwaltung *f* (Fin) credit management
Kreditverwendung *f* (Fin) utilization of loan funds
Kreditvolumen *n*
(Fin) lending volume *(ie, of a bank)*
− volume of credits
− outstanding credits
Kreditvolumen *n* **steuern** (Vw) to control (*or* regulate) the volume of credit
Kreditwesengesetz *n* (Fin) German Banking Law, KWG
Kreditwirtschaft *f* (Fin) banking industry
Kreditwucher *m* (Re) lending at usurious interest rates, § 302a StGB
kreditwürdig (Fin) creditworthy
Kreditwürdigkeit *f*
(Fin) credit worthiness
− credit rating
− credit standing
Kreditwürdigkeit *f* **bestätigen** (Fin) to approve credit
Kreditwürdigkeit *f* **prüfen** (Fin) to test the credit standing
Kreditwürdigkeitsprüfung *f* (Fin) credit investigation (*or* review)
Kreditzins *m* (Fin) lending (*or* loan) rate
Kreditzinsen *mpl*
(Fin) interest on borrowings
(Fin) loan interest
(Fin) lending margin
Kredit *m* **zu günstigen Bedingungen** (Fin) soft loan
Kredit *m* **zurückzahlen**
(Fin) to pay back
− to repay
− to retire ... a loan
Kreditzusage *f*
(IWF) standby arrangement
(Fin) loan commitment
Kreisdiagramm *n*
(Stat) circular chart (*or* diagram)
− circle chart
− pie chart
− wheel diagram
Kreislauf *m* (Vw) circular flow
Kreislaufmaterial *n* (IndE) recycled auxiliary material
Kreislaufschema *n* (Vw) circular-flow scheme
Kreislauftheorie *f* (Vw) circular-flow theory
Kreisverkehr *m*
(com) traffic circle
− (GB) roundabout

Kreisverkehrsbeleg *m* (EDV) turnaround document
Kreuzelastizität *f* (Vw) cross elasticity
Kreuzelastizität *f* **der Nachfrage** (Vw) cross-elasticity of demand
Kreuzelastizität *f* **des Angebots** (Vw) cross-elasticity of supply
Kreuzmenge *f* (Math) cross set
Kreuzparität *f* (Fin) cross rate
Kreuzpreiselastizität *f* (Vw) cross price elasticity
Kreuzprodukt *n* (Math) cross (*or* vector) product
Kreuzsicherung *f* (EDV) cross checking *(syn, Blocksicherung)*
Kreuzungspunkt *m*
(Math) saddle point
− point of stagnation
Kreuzwechselkurs *m* (AuW) cross-rate of exchange
Kriegsdienstverweigerer *m*
(Pw) conscientious objector
− (GB, sl) conchy
Kriegsdienst *m* **verweigern** (Pw) to sign up as a conscientious objector
Kriegsopferversorgung *f* (SozV) war victim's support
Kriegsrisikoklausel *f* (Vers) war risk clause
Krisenfrachtzuschlag *m* (com) emergency freight surcharge
krisengeschüttelte Branchen *fpl* (Vw) crisis-ridden sectors *(eg, steel, shipbuilding, automobiles)*
Krisenkartell *n* (Kart) anti-crisis cartel
Krisenmanagement *n* (Bw) crisis management
Krisenvorräte *mpl* (Vw) emergency stockpiles
Kriterium *n*
(Log) criterion
− test
− yardstick
Kriterium *n* **der Effizienz** (Stat) efficiency criterion
Kriterium *n* **der Minimalstreuung** (Stat) efficiency criterion
Kriterium *n* **der Nichtausschließbarkeit** (FiW) principle of non-exclusion
kritische Aktivität *f* (OR) critical activity
kritische Menge *f* (Bw) critical output *(ie, intersection of total cost curves of production methods I and II)*
kritischer Ausfall *m* (Stat) critical failure
kritischer Bereich *m* (Stat) critical (*or* rejection) region
kritischer Fehler *m* (Stat) critical defect
kritischer Lagerbestand *m*
(MaW) order point
− reorder point
− reordering quantity
kritischer Quotient *m* (Stat) critical ratio
kritischer Vorgang *m* (OR) critical activity
kritischer Weg *m* (OR) critical path
kritischer Wert *m* (Fin) critical variable
Kryotronspeicher *m* (EDV) cryotron memory *(syn, Supraleitungsspeicher)*
KSt-Tarif *m* (StR) corporate income tax rate scale
KT-Risiko *n* (Fin) conversion and transfer risk
Kubikwurzel *f* (Math) cube root
kubische Gleichung *f* (Math) cubic equation
Kugelkoordinaten *fpl* (Math) spherical coordinates

Kugelkopf *m* (EDV) print element
Kugellagerindustrie *f* (com) ball-bearing industry
Kugelschreiber *m*
  (com) ball point pen
  – (GB) biro *(ie, generic use of trademark)*
Kühlanlage *f* (com) cold storage plant
Kühlgüterversicherung *f* (Vers) cold storage insurance *(ie, designed to protect operators from risks during on-and-off transport and actual storage)*
Kühlhaus *n* (com) cold store
Kühlladung *f* (com) refrigerated cargo
Kühlschiff *n* (com) refrigerator ship
Kühlwagen *m*
  (com) refrigerator car
  (com) refrigerated truck
Kuhnsche Methode *f* (OR) Hungarian method
kulant (com) accommodating
Kulanz *f* (com) good will
Kulanzregelung *f* (com) broad-minded, liberal settlement of customer's complaint
Kulisse *f* (Bö) unofficial market *(ie, non-official stock market + group of professional traders doing business on their own account; opp, Parkett: offizieller Börsenverkehr in amtlich notierten Werten durch Kursmakler)*
Kumulationswirkung *f* (StR) cumulative effect
kumulative Allphasensteuer *f* (FiW) cumulative all-stage turnover tax
kumulative Dividende *f* (Fin) cumulative dividend
kumulative Effekte *mpl* (Vw) aggregative effects
kumulative Häufigkeitskurve *f* (Stat) cumulative frequency curve
kumulative Häufigkeitsverteilung *f* (Stat) cumulative frequency distribution
kumulative Kausalreihe *f* (Log) cumulative causation
kumulative Mehrphasensteuer *f* (StR) cumulative multi-stage tax
kumulativer Multiplikator *m* (Vw) truncated multiplier
kumulativer Summenzuwachs *m* (Vers) compound reversionary bonus system
kumulativer Ursprung *m* (Zo) cumulative origin
kumulatives Banddiagramm *n*
  (Stat) band curve chart
  – cumulative band chart
  – surface chart
kumulative Schuldübernahme *f* (Re) cumulative assumption of debt *(ie, no equivalent in English = person acquiring all the assets of another thereby automatically becomes liable to this persons's creditors for all his debts, the old debtor remaining liable in addition to the new debtor, § 305 BGB)*
kumulative Umsatzsteuer *f* (StR) cumulative turnover tax
kumulative Verteilung *f* (Stat) cumulative distribution
kumulierte Abweichung *f* (Stat) accumulated deviation
kumulierter Jahresgewinn *m* (Fin) cumulative annual net cash savings *(ie, determined in preinvestment analysis)*
kündbar
  (Fin) callable

  – redeemable
kündbare Einlagen *fpl* (Fin) deposits at notice
kündbare Obligationen *fpl* (Fin) redeemable bonds
kündbare Rente *f* (Fin) redeemable *(or* terminable*)* annuity
kündbare Schuldverschreibungen *fpl* (Fin) redeemable bonds
kündbares Darlehen *n* (Fin) callable loan
Kündbarkeit *f* (Fin) terminability
Kunde *m*
  (com) customer
  – client
  – (GB) custom
  (com) accounts
Kunden *mpl* **abfertigen** (OR) to process customers
Kundenabrechnung *f* (ReW) customer accounting
Kunden *mpl* **abwerben** (com) to divert custom
Kundenabwerbung *f* (Kart) enticing away *(or* poaching*)* customers
Kundenanzahlung *f*
  (com) advance *(or* down*)* payment
  – customer's deposit
Kundenauftrag *m*
  (com) customer order
  (IndE) production order *(ie, based on a customer order)*
Kundenauftragsfertigung *f*
  (IndE) custom manufacturing
  – make-to-order production
  – job order production
  – production to order
  (opp, Lagerfertigung = make-to-stock production)
Kunden *mpl* **ausspannen** (Kart) to alienate *(or* entice away*)* customers
Kundenbankkunde *m* (Fin) nonbank customer
Kundenberater *m* (com) advisor to customers
Kundenbuchführung *f* (ReW) customer accounting
Kundenbuchhalter *m* (ReW) accounts receivable accountant
Kundenbuchhaltung *f* (ReW) accounts receivable department
Kundendepot *n* (Fin) third-party securities account
Kundendienst *m*
  (com) customer
  – client
  – after-sales
  – post-sales
  – sales ... service
Kundendienstabteilung *f* (com) service department
Kundendienstorganisation *f* (com) customer service organization
Kundeneinlagen *fpl* (Fin) customer deposits
Kundenentnahmen *fpl* (Fin) customers' drawings
Kundenetat *m* (Mk) (advertising) account
Kundenfinanzierung *f*
  (Fin) customer financing
  – financing of customers
Kundengeschäft *n*
  (Fin) customer business *(ie, of banks; opp, Geschäft für eigene Rechnung)*
  (StR) transaction in which one of the parties is a resident dealer or trader in securities, § 20 KVStG
Kundengruppe *f* (com) group of customers

Kundenkartei f (com) customer file
Kundenkredit m
(Fin) credit extended to customer
(Fin) credit extended by customer to supplier
(ie, as advance financing of high-value projects)
Kundenkreditbank f (Fin) sales finance company
Kundenkreditvolumen n (Fin) lendings to customers
Kundenkreis m
(com) customers
– clientele
Kundenpreis m (com) customer price
Kundenproduktion f
(Vw) custom manufacturing *(opp, Marktproduktion)*
(IndE) make-to-order production *(syn, Kundenauftragsfertigung, qv)*
Kundenrabatt m (com) patronage refund
Kundenreservoir n (OR) source population *(ie, in waiting-line models)*
Kundenschutz m (com) protection of patronage *(ie, if a certain district or a certain group of customers is assigned to the commercial agent, he is entitled to receive a commission also for business concluded without his participation, § 87 II HGB)*
Kunden-Segmentierung f (Mk) customer segmentation
Kundenskonto m od n
(com) discount allowance
– cash discount paid
kundenspezifisch
(com) customized
– custom
– tailored
– made-to-order *(eg, circuits)*
kundenspezifische Logik-Arrays pl (EDV) uncommitted logic arrays, ULAs *(ie, chips tailored to a customer's specification; syn, gate arrays)*
Kundenstamm m
(com) regular customers
– established clientele
Kundensuche f
(Mk) search for customers
– soliciting *(or locating)* customers
Kundentreue f (Mk) consumer loyalty
Kundenverkehr m (com) business with customers
Kundenverlust m (com) loss of custom
Kundenwechsel m
(Fin) customer's acceptance
– bill receivable
Kundenwerbung f (Mk) canvassing *(or soliciting)* customers
kündigen
(Re) to give notice to terminate *(eg, contract, lease)*
(Pw, *by employee*) to give notice to quit
(Pw, *by employer*) to give notice to terminate
(Pw, *collective agreement*) to abrogate
(Fin) to call in *(eg, a loan)*
Kündigung f
(Re) notice
(Pw, *general term*) separation
(Pw, *by employee*) notice to quit
(Pw, *by employer*) notice to terminate
– notice of dismissal

(Pw, *collective agreement*) abrogation
(Fin) calling in
Kündigung f **e-r Anleihe** (Fin) redemption of loan
Kündigung f **e-s Guthabens** (Fin) notice of withdrawal
Kündigung f **e-s Vertrages** (Re) notice to terminate a contract
Kündigung f **einreichen** (Fw) to submit (*or* hand in) notice to quit
Kündigungsfrist f
(Re) period of notice
– notice term
– period to terminate
(Pw) dismissal notice period
(Fin) withdrawal notice
Kündigungsgeld n (Fin) deposits at notice
Kündigungsgrund m (Re) reason for termination
Kündigungsgrundschuld f (Fin) mortgage with a call-in provision
Kündigungsklausel f
(Re) notice clause
– contractual clause on unilateral termination
– (Fin) call(-in) provision
Kündigungsrecht n
(Re) right of notice (*or* termination)
– right of cancellation
(Fin) right to call for repayment
(Pw) right to terminate an employment contract
Kündigungsschreiben n
(Re) notice of termination
(Pw) dismissal notice
– letter of dismissal
– notice to terminate
– termination notice
Kündigungsschutz m
(Pw) dismissal protection
– security against dismissal
(ie, protection from unjustified termination)
Kündigungsschutzgesetz n (Pw) dismissals protection law
Kündigungsschutzklage f (Re) dismissals protection suit
Kündigungsschutzvorschriften fpl (Pw) dismissal protection regulations
Kündigungssperrfrist f
(Fin) period during which redemptions is barred
– non-calling period
Kündigungstermin m
(Fin) call-in date
(Fin) withdrawal date
Kündigung f **von Einlagen** (Fin) notice of withdrawal of funds
Kündigung f **von Wertpapieren** (Fin) notice of redemption
Kündigung f **zum Quartalsende** (Re) quarter notice
Kundschaft f
(com) customers
– clients
– clientele
– patronage
– (GB) custom
Kundschaft f **aufbauen** (com) to develop a clientele
Kunstgewerbetreibender m (com) commercial (*or* industrial) artist
künstliche Basis f (OR) artificial basis

künstlicher Nullpunkt *m* (Stat) arbitrary origin
künstliche Variable *f* (OR) artificial variable
Kunststoffindustrie *f* (com) plastics industry
kunststoffverarbeitende Industrie *f* (com) plastics processing industry
Kupon *m*
  (Fin) coupon
  – dividend coupon
  – interest coupon
Kuponbogen *m*
  (Fin) coupon sheet
Kuponeinlösung *f* (Fin) collection of coupons
Kuponinhaber *m* (Fin) coupon holder
Kuponkurs *m* (Fin) price of matured coupons of foreign securities
Kuponsteuer *f* (StR) coupon tax *(ie, imposed on fixed-interest bearing industrial or government bonds; collected through withholding at the source)*
Kupontermin *m* (Fin) coupon date *(ie, frequent dates are 2 Jan and 1 July – J/J – and 1 Apr and 1 Oct – A/O)*
Kuppelkalkulation *f* (KoR) joint-product costing
Kuppelprodukte *npl* (IndE) joint *(or* complementary*)* products
Kuppelproduktion *f* (IndE) joint-product production
Kurantgeld *n* (Vw) current money *(ie, treated as legal tender in unlimited amounts; previously gold coins, now bank notes; opp. Scheidemünzen = low-value coin)*
Kurantmünze *f* (Vw) full-bodied coin
Kurs *m*
  (com) rate
  (Vw) policy
  – direction *(or* thrust*)* of policy
  (Fin) exchange rate
  (Bö) price
  – market price *(or* rate*)*
  – quotation
Kursabbröckelung *f* (Bö) slight drop in market prices
Kursabschlag *m* (Bö) markdown
Kursabschwächung *f* (Bö) easing of market prices
Kurs *m* **alte Aktien** (Fin) market price
Kursangleichung *f* (Bö) adjustment of rates
Kursanstieg *m* (Bö) rise in market prices
Kursanstieg *m* **auf breiter Front** (Bö) price rises across the board
Kursanzeigetafel *f* (Bö) marking *(or* quotations*)* board
Kursaufschlag *m* (Bö) markup
Kursaufschwung *m* (Bö) upturn in prices
Kursausschläge *mpl*
  (AuW) movements *(eg, of $, £, DM)*
  – exchange rate movements
  (Bö) price fluctuations
Kurs *m* **aussetzen** (Bö) to suspend a quotation
Kursaussetzung *f* (Bö) suspension of a quotation
Kursbefestigung *f* (Bö) firming up of prices
Kursbericht *m* (Bö) = *Kurszettel*
Kursbewegung *f* (Bö) movement in prices
Kursbildung *f* (Bö) formation of rates
Kursbindung *f* (AuW) pegging of exchange rates
Kursblatt *n* (Bö) = *Kurszettel*

Kursdiagramm *n* (Fin) chart
Kursdifferenz *f* (AuW) exchange difference
Kursdruck *m* (Bö) downward pressure on prices
Kurs *m* **drücken** (Bö) to pull down prices
Kurse *mpl* **auf breiter Front zurücknehmen** (Bö) to reduce prices across the board
Kurseinbruch *m* (Bö) sudden price fall
Kurseinbußen *fpl*
  (Fin) losses on exchange
  (Bö) price losses
Kursentwicklung *f*
  (Bö) price movement
  – trends in quotations
Kurserholung *f* (Bö) rally *(or* recovery*)* in prices
Kurse *mpl* **stützen** (Bö) to peg quotations
Kurse *mpl* **zurücknehmen** (Bö) to mark down prices
Kursfeststellung *f*
  (Fin) fixing of official exchange rate
  (Bö) determination of prices
Kurs *m* **Festverzinslicher** (Fin) bond price
Kursfixierung *f* (AuW) official pegging *(ie, by central banks)*
Kursgefälle *n*
  (AuW) exchange-rate differential
  (Bö) price differential
Kursgefüge *n*
  (Bö) price structure
  – structure of market rates
kursgesicherte Devisen *pl* (Fin) rate-hedged foreign exchange
Kurs gestrichen (Bö) no dealings
Kursgewinn *m*
  (Fin) exchange gain *(or* profit*)*
  (Bö) stock price gain
Kursgewinn-Chancen *fpl* (Bö) upside price potential
Kursgewinne *mpl* **auf breiter Front** (Bö) price gains across the board
Kurs-Gewinn-Verhältnis *n*
  (Fin) price-earnings ratio
  – p/e ratio
  – price-earnings multiple
  – times earnings
kursglättende Interventionen *fpl* (AuW) interventions to smooth out exchange rate fluctuations
Kursgraphik *f* (Fin) stock chart
Kurshöhe *f* (Bö) price level
Kurs *m* **im Freiverkehr** (Fin) dealer *(or* inside*)* price
Kursindex *m*
  (Bö) stock price index
  – (GB) share price index
Kursintervention *f*
  (Fin) exchange intervention
  (Fin) price intervention
Kursklausel *f* (Fin) exchange clause *(ie, now obsolete)*
Kurskorrektur *f* (Bö) corrective price adjustment
Kurskorrektur *f* **nach oben** (Bö) upward price adjustment
Kurskorrektur *f* **nach unten** (Bö) downward price adjustment
Kurslimit *n* (Bö) price limit
Kursmakler *m* (Bö) official exchange broker

Kursmanipulation *f*
(Bö) market rigging
– rigging the market
Kursmaterial *n* (Pw) course (*or* back-up) material *(eg, text-books, records)*
Kursniveau *n* (Bö) price level
Kursnotierung *f*
(Bö) market (*or* price) quotation
– quoted price
– stock quotation
– (GB) share quotation
Kursnotierung *f* **aussetzen** (Bö) to stop (*or* suspend) a quotation
Kursnotierung *f* **ohne Zinsen** (Bö) flat quotation
Kursnotiz *f* (Bö) market quotation
Kursnotizen *fpl* **aussetzen** (Bö) to suspend price quotations
Kursparität *f* (AuW) parity of foreign exchange rates
Kurspflege *f*
(Bö) price management (*or* support)
(FiW) pegging of public debt
Kurspflegeverkäufe *mpl* (Fin) market regulation sales
Kurspflege-Operationen *fpl* (Fin) price support operations
Kursrechnung *f* (Fin) bond valuation
Kursregulierung *f*
(Fin) regulation of the market
– price support
Kursregulierungs-Konsortium *n* (Bö) price support syndicate
Kursrelationen *fpl* (AuW) exchange rate relations
Kursrisiko *n*
(AuW) exchange risk
(Bö) price risk
Kursrückgang *m* (Bö) decline in prices
Kursrückgänge *mpl* **auf breiter Front** (Bö) fall in prices across the board
Kursrücklage *f* (Vers) investment reserve
Kursrücknahme *f* (Bö) price markdown
Kursschnitt *m* (Bö) price fraud *(ie, by a commission agent*
Kursschwäche *f* (AuW) weakness *(eg, of $, £, DM)*
Kursschwankungen *fpl*
(Bö) price fluctuations (*or* variations)
– fluctuations of the market
– ups and downs of the market
kurssichernde Interventionen *fpl* (AuW) rate supporting interventions
Kurssicherung *f* (AuW) rate support (*or* hedging)
Kurssicherung *f* **am Devisenmarkt** (AuW) forward exchange cover
Kurssicherungsabschlüsse *mpl* (AuW) commercial covering
Kurssicherungsgeschäft *n* (Fin) hedging transaction
Kurssicherungsklausel *f* (AuW) exchange-rate-fluctuation clause
Kurssicherungskosten *pl*
(Fin) cost of exchange cover
(Fin) cost of forward exchange cover
Kursspanne *f*
(Bö) difference in quotations
– spread
Kurssprünge *mpl* (Bö) jumps in prices

Kursstabilisierungsmaßnahmen *fpl* (AuW) official support
Kurssteigerung *f* (Bö) price advance
Kurssturz *m*
(Bö) sharp tumble in stock/bond prices
– plunge of prices
kursstützende Intervention *f* (AuW) intervention in support of exchange rate
Kursstützung *f*
(AuW) pegging of exchange rates
(Bö) price maintenance
– price stabilization
– price support
Kursstützungskäufe *mpl* (Fin) price supporting purchases
Kurstabelle *f*
(Bö) quotation record
– stock market table
Kurstafel *f* (Bö) marking (*or* quotations) board
Kurstreiberei *f*
(Bö) rigging the market
– share pushing
Kurs *m* **unter Nennwert** (Bö) price below par
Kursverbesserung *f* (Bö) improvement in market rates
Kursverfall *m*
(Bö) substantial decline in prices
– price collapse
Kursverlust *m*
(Fin) exchange loss
– loss on fluctuations of the rate of exchange
(Fin) price loss
Kursverwässerung *f* (Bö) watering of stock exchange prices
Kurswert *m*
(Bö) market value
– list price
(StR) official price *(ie, of securities traded on a domestic stock exchange, § 11 I BewG)*
Kurswertberichtigung *f* **von Wertpapierbeständen** (Bö) writedown of securities portfolio
Kurswert *m* **ohne Dividende** (Bö) ex dividend (*or* ex-d)
Kurswertreserven *fpl* (Fin) gains arising from the increase in security prices
Kurszettel *m*
(Bö) list of quotations
– daily official list
– stock market report
Kursziel *n* (Bö) upside target
Kurszuschlag *m*
(Bö) continuation rate
– carrying-over rate
Kurtage *f* (Fin) courtage
Kurtaxe *f* (FiW) health resort tax
Kurve *f* (Math) graph
Kurve *f* **ausziehen** (Math) to trace out a curve
Kurve *f* **der monetären Nachfrage** (Vw) outlay curve
Kurve *f* **der Verteilungsfunktion** (Stat) distribution curve
Kurve *f* **des mittleren Stichprobenumfangs** (Stat) average sample number curve
Kurve *f* **gleicher Produktion** (Vw) product indifference curve

Kurve *f* **gleicher Trennschärfe** (Stat) curve of equidetectability
Kurve *f* **gleicher Wahrscheinlichkeit** (Stat) equiprobability curve
Kurvenabschnitt *m* (Math) reach of a curve
Kurvenanpassung *f* (Math) curve fitting
Kurvenanpassung *f* **an den Trend** (Stat) trend fitting
Kurvenblatt *n* (Stat) graph
Kurvenintegral *n* (Math) line integral
Kurvenknick *m* (Math) kink of a curve
Kurvenschar *f*
   (Math) family of curves
   – set of curves
   – array of curves
Kurvenschreiber *m*
   (EDV) graph plotter
   – plotter
Kurvenstück *n* (Math) branch of a curve
Kurvenverlauf *m* (Math) curve shape
Kurzarbeit *f* (Pw) short-time working
kurzarbeiten
   (Bw) to operate short-time working
   (Pw) to work short time
Kurzarbeiter *m*
   (Pw) short-time worker
   – worker (put) on short time
   – *(pl)* people on short-time working
Kurzarbeitergeld *n* (Pw) short-time allowance (*or* money)
Kurzarbeitsunterstützung *f* (SozV) short-time working benefits
Kurzbericht *m*
   (com) brief
   – summary (*or* condensed) report
kurze Arbeitsniederlegung *f*
   (Pw, infml) downer
   – quickie strike
kürzen
   (com) to cut
   – to cut back
   – to pare down
   – to reduce
   – to trim
kurzer Bereich *m* (Fin) short end of the market
kurzer Warnstreik *m* (Pw) hit-and-run strike
kürzestes Konfidenz-Intervall *n* (Stat) shortest confidence interval
Kurzfassung *f* **e–s Patents** (Pat) title of a patent
kurzfristig (com) over the short term
kurzfristig ausleihen (Fin) to lend short term
kurzfristig beschäftigte Arbeitnehmer *mpl* (Pw) part-time employees
kurzfristige Analyse *f* (Vw) short-run analysis
kurzfristige Ausleihungen *fpl* (Fin) short-term lendings
kurzfristige Einlagen *fpl*
   (Fin) short-term deposits
   – (GB) deposits at short notice
kurzfristige Erfolgsrechnung *f* (ReW) operating statement of income (*ie, covering period of less than 12 months)*
kurzfristige Finanzanlage *f* (Fin) cash fund
kurzfristige Finanzierung *f* (Fin) short-term financing

kurzfristige Finanzplanung *f* (Fin) short-term financial planning
kurzfristige Geldmarktpapiere *npl* (Fin) short-term paper
kurzfristige Kapitalanlage *f* (Fin) short-dated (*or* temporary) investment of funds
kurzfristige Kapitalbewegungen *fpl* (AuW) short-term capital movements
kurzfristige Kapitalbilanz *f* (VGR) short-term capital account
kurzfristige Kapitaleinfuhr *f* (AuW) short-term capital imports
kurzfristige Konjunkturprognose *f* (Vw) short-term forecast
kurzfristige Konsumfunktion *f* (Vw) short-period consumption function
kurzfristige Kreditaufnahme *f* (Fin) short-term borrowing
kurzfristige Kreditnachfrage *f* (Fin) short-term loan demand
kurzfristige Kredite *mpl* (Fin) short-term lending (*ie, by banks)*
kurzfristige Lieferung *f* (com) delivery at short notice
kurzfristige Mittel *pl* (Fin) short-term funds (*or* money)
kurzfristige Nettoverbindlichkeiten *fpl* (ReW) net current liabilities
kurzfristige Obligationen *fpl* (Fin) short-term bonds
kurzfristige Passivgelder *npl* (Fin) short-term liabilities
kurzfristige Planung *f* (Bw) short-term planning
kurzfristiger Erfolgszwang *m* (Bw) pressure to make short-term profits
kurzfristiger Kapitalverkehr *m* (VGR) short-term capital movements (*or* transactions)
kurzfristiger Kredit *m* (Fin) short-term credit (*or* loan)
kurzfristiger Kreditbedarf *m* (FiW, Fin) short-term borrowing requirements
kurzfristiger Planabschnitt *m* (Fin) short-range budget period
kurzfristiger Schuldschein *m* (Fin) short note
kurzfristiger Verlust *m* (Bw) short-term loss
kurzfristiger Währungsbeistand *m* (EG) short-term monetary support
kurzfristiger Warenkredit *m* (Fin) commercial credit
kurzfristiger Wechsel *m* (WeR) short-dated bill
kurzfristige Schuldverschreibungen *fpl* (Fin) short-dated bonds
kurzfristiges Darlehen *n* (Fin) short-term loan
kurzfristiges Dumping *n* (AuW) short-run dumping
kurzfristiges Gleichgewicht *n* (Vw) short-run (*or* shifting) equilibrium
kurzfristiges Ziel *n* (Bw) short-run (*or* tactical) goal (*ie, lying ahead typically one year or less)*
kurzfristige Todesfallversicherung *f* (Vers) term insurance (*syn, Risikoversicherung)*
kurzfristige Verbindlichkeiten *fpl*
   (ReW) current liabilities
   – short-term liabilities
   – current debt

kurzfristig lieferbar (com) available for prompt delivery (*or* at short notice)
Kurzfristplan *m* (Bw) short-term plan
kurzlaufende Bankschuldverschreibungen *fpl* (Fin) short-dated bank bonds
Kurzläufer *mpl*
(Fin) short-dated bonds
 – shorts
Kurzläufer-Rendite *f* (Fin) yield on shorts
kurzlebige Konsumgüter *npl* (Vw) consumer disposables
Kurzlochkarte *f* (EDV) stub (*or* scored) card
Kurzperiodenanalyse *f* (Vw) short-period analysis (A. Marshall)
Kurzprospekt *m* (Bö) offering circular
Kurzschrift *f* (com) shorthand
Kurzspeicher *m* (EDV) short-time storage
Kurzstreckenflugzeug *n* (com) short-haul airliner
Kurzstreckenfracht *f* (com) shorthaul
Kürzung *f*
(com) cut
 – cutback
 – reduction
 – deduction
 – curtailment
Kürzung *f* **von Sozialleistungen** (SozV) cuts in social benefits
Kurzwaren *pl*
(com) notions
 – (GB) haberdashery
Kurzzeitversuch *m* (Stat) accelerated test
Küstenfischerei *f*
(com) coastal fisheries
 – inshore fishing
Küstengewässer *npl* (Re) coastal waters
Küstenhandel *m* (com) inter-coastal trade
Küstenmeer *n* (Re) territorial sea
Küstenschiffahrt *f* (com) coastal shipping
Küstenstaat *m* (Re, Sea Law) littoral state
Kux *m* (*pl. Kuxe*)
(WeR) quota of a mining company
 – registered mining share
(ie, Rektapapier, no par value, subject to contributions by members; syn, Bergwerksanteil)
Kybernetik *f* (EDV) cybernetics

L

Ladeadresse *f* (EDV) load address (*or* point)
Ladeanweisung *f* (EDV) load instruction
Ladebaum *m* (com) derrick
Ladebefehl *m* (EDV) = *Ladeanweisung*
ladefähiges Programm *n* (EDV) loadable (*or* executable) program
Ladefähigkeit *f*
(com) carrying (*or* load) capacity
(com) *(gewichtsmäßige L. =)* deadweight capacity *(ie, of ocean-going ships)*
 – *(räumliche L. =)* bulk capacity
(com) payload capacity *(ie, of planes)*
Ladefläche *f* (com) loading (*or* cargo) area
Ladefristen *fpl* (com) loading days
Ladegebühr *f* (com) (railroad) loading charges
Ladegeld *n* (com) = *Ladegebühr*
Ladegeschäft *n* (com) loading and unloading business
Ladegeschirr *n* (com) ship's loading gear (*or* tackle)
Ladegewicht *n* (com) shipping weight
Ladegut *n*
(com) cargo
 – freight
 – (US) cargo *(ie, as a marine term)*
Ladehilfsmittel *npl* (IndE) loading equipment
Ladeinstruktion *f* (EDV) = *Ladeanweisung*
Ladekai *m* (com) cargo dock
Ladekapazität *f* (com) loading (*or* carrying) capacity
Ladekosten *pl*
(com) loading (*or* handling) charges
 – *(ships also)* lading charges
Ladelinie *f* (com) = *Lademarke*
Ladeliste *f*
(com) freight list
(com) manifest *(ie, list of cargo carried by vessel or plane)*
Ladeluke *f* (com) cargo hatch
Lademakler *m* (com) loading broker
Lademarke *f*
(com) loadline
 – loadline mark
 – Plimsoll line (*or* mark)
Lademodul *n* (EDV) load module
Lademodus *m* (EDV) load mode *(ie, delimiters being moved with the data; opp, Übertragungsmodus)*
laden
(com) to load
 – to put (cargo) on/in
(EDV) to load
Laden *m*
(com) store
 – (GB) shop
(Mk) retail store
Laden *n* (EDV) loading
Ladenaufsicht *f*
(com) floorwalker
 – shopwalker
Ladenausrüstung *f*
(com) store fixtures
 – (GB) shop fittings
Ladenbau *m* (com) shop fitting (*or* design)
Ladendieb *m* (Re) shoplifter
Ladendiebstahl *m* (Re) shoplifting
Ladeneinrichtung *f*
(com) store fixtures
 – (GB) shop fittings
Ladeneinzelhandel *m* (Mk) retail selling
Ladengeschäft *n*
(com) retail store

377

- (GB) retail shop
Ladenhüter *m*
(com) non-moving item
- unsalable article
- (infml) cats and dogs
- (infml) drug on the market
- (infml) shelf warmer
- (infml) slicker
Ladeninhaber *m*
(com) store owner
- (GB) shopkeeper
Ladenkasse *f*
(com) cash box
- (GB) till
Ladenkette *f*
(com) retailing chain
- chain of retail stores
Laden *m* **mit Fremdbedienung** (com) over-the-counter store (*or* shop)
Ladenöffnungszeiten *fpl* (com) shop hours
Ladenpreis *m* (com) retail price
Ladenregal *n* (com) shelf
Ladenschluß *m* (com) closing time
Ladenschlußgesetz *n* (ReW) Shop Closing Law, of 28 Nov 1956
Ladenschlußzeiten *fpl* (com) shop closing hours
LADEN-Taste *f* (EDV) load key
Ladentisch *m*
(com) counter
- display (*or* sales) counter
Ladenverkauf *m* (com) retail selling
Ladenwerbung *f* (Mk) in-store advertising *(ie, by mass display of goods)*
Ladepapiere *npl* (com) shipping documents (*or* papers)
Ladeparameter *m* (EDV) load parameter
Ladeplatz *m*
(com) loading berth (*or* wharf)
- place of shipment
Ladeprogramm *n* (EDV) = *Lader*
Ladepunkt *m* (EDV) load point
Lader *m*
(EDV) loader
- load program (*or* module)
- loading program (*or* routine) *(syn, Ladeprogramm, Programmlader)*
Laderampe *f* (com) loading (*or* shipping) ramp
Laderaum *m*
(com) loading space
(com, *ships*) cargo hold
Laderost *m* (com) pallet
Laderoutine *f* (EDV) routine used to load programs into memory
Ladeschein *m*
(WeR) shipping note, §§ 444–450 HGB
- inland waterway bill of lading, § 72 BinnSchG = *Flußkonnossement*
Ladestelle *f* (com) loading berth
Ladetätigkeit *f*
(com) handling
- loading and unloading
Ladetonnage *f* (com) load displacement
Ladeverzeichnis *n* (com) = *Ladeliste*
Ladevorrichtungen *fpl* (com) ship's loading gear (*or* tackle)

Ladezeit *f* (com) loading time
Ladung *f*
(com) loading
(com) cargo
- freight
- consignment
- load
- shipment
Ladung *f* **löschen** (com) to unload (*or* discharge) cargo
Ladungsaufseher *m* (com) supercargo
Ladungsbeteiligte *mpl*
(com) parties interested in the cargo, § 485 HGB
- cargo owners
Ladungsbuchung *f* (com) booking of cargo
Ladungsempfänger *m* (com) consignee
ladungsgekoppelte Schaltung *f* (EDV) charge coupled device, CCD
Ladungskontrolleur *m* (com) tallyman
Ladungsmanifest *n* (com) manifest of cargo
Ladungsschäden *mpl* **durch Seewurf** (SeeV) damage to cargo by jettison
Ladungstüchtigkeit *f* (com) fitness for storage
Ladung *f* **über Bord werfen** (SeeV) to jettison a cargo
Ladung *f* **übernehmen** (com) to take up cargo
Ladung *f* **zustellen** (Re) to serve a citation (*or* summon) (upon)
Lagebericht *m*
(com) status report
(ReW) annual report
Lagebesprechung *f* (com) discussion of current situation
Lagemaßzahl *f*
(Stat) measure of central tendency
- measure of central location
- measure of central position
- parameter of location
Lageparameter *m* (Stat) = *Lagemeßzahl*
Lageplan *m* (com) layout plan
(com) site plan
Lager *n*
(com) stock of goods (*or* merchandise)
(MaW) inventory held in storage
(MaW) store
- storeroom
- stockroom
- storage area
- warehouse
Lagerabbau *m*
(MaW) inventory cutting (*or* decline *or* workoff)
- destocking
- liquidation of inventories
- reduction of inventories
- stock reduction
Lager *npl* **abbauen**
(MaW) to cut
- to run down
- to trim
- to work off
- to reduce
- to liquidate . . . inventories (*or* stock)
- to destock
- to pare down inventory levels *(eg, to the bone)*

Lagerabgangsrate f
(MaW) rate of usage
− usage rate
Lageranordnung f (MaW) layout of storage area
Lager-Anteil m (MaW) ratio of inventory level to total assets of firm
Lagerarbeiter m (MaW) stockroom worker
Lager npl **auffüllen**
(MaW) to rebuild
− to fill up
− to refill
− to replenish ... inventories
− to restock
− (infml) to load the pipelines
Lagerauffüllung f
(MaW) inventory buildup (or rebuilding)
− inventory accumulation
− inventory replenishment
− refilling of inventories
− replenishment of stocks
Lageraufnahme f
(MaW) physical inventory
− stocktaking
Lageraufseher m (MaW) stockroom supervisor
Lager npl **aufstocken** (MaW) = Lager auffüllen
Lageraufstockung f (MaW) = Lagerauffüllung
Lagerauftrag m (Bw) stock order
Lagerauslastung f (MaW) utilization of storage capacity
Lagerbehälter m (MaW) storage bin
Lagerbehandlung f (MaW) handling of goods in storage (eg, refilling, drying, etc.)
Lagerbestand m
(MaW) goods on hand (or in stock)
− inventory level
− stock
− stock on hand
− stores
Lagerbestände mpl **aufnehmen** (MaW) to compile inventory
Lagerbestände mpl **des Einzelhandels** (com) retail inventories
Lagerbestandsaufnahme f (ReW) stock taking
Lagerbestandsaufstellung f (MaW) inventory status report
Lagerbestandsbericht m (MaW) stock status report
Lagerbestandsbewertung f (ReW) inventory valuation
Lagerbestandsfortschreibung f (MaW) updating of inventory
Lagerbestandsführung f
(MaW) inventory (or stock) accounting
− inventory control
Lagerbestandskarte f (ReW) stock record card
Lagerbestandsliste f (MaW) = Lagerbestandsverzeichnis
Lagerbestandsvergleich m (MaW) comparison of inventory movements
(ie, by preparing statistics over a number of periods)
Lagerbestandsverzeichnis n
(MaW) inventory
− inventory status report
Lagerbetrieb m (com) warehousing business, §§ 416–424 HGB

Lagerbewegungen fpl (MaW) inventory (or stock) movements
Lagerbewertung f (ReW) inventory valuation (or costing)
Lagerbuch n (MaW) stock (or stores) ledger
Lagerbuchführung f
(MaW) inventory accounting
(MaW) inventory records file
− stockroom record system
− stockroom records
(ie, keeping track of all items on inventory and on order)
Lagerbuchhaltung f (ReW) inventory accounting department (Note: In commercial jargon, the terms ‚Lagerbuchführung‘ and ‚Lagerbuchhaltung‘ are often used interchangeably)
Lagerdaten pl (MaW) inventory data (or figures)
Lagerdauer f
(MaW) period of storage
− days of inventories
Lagerdisposition f
(MaW) stockbuilding (activity)
− stock ordering
Lagerdispositionen fpl (MaW) storage dispositions
Lagerempfangsschein m (WeR) warehouse receipt
Lagerente f (Bw) rent due to favorable location
Lagerentnahme f (MaW) withdrawal from stock
Lagerergänzung f (MaW) = Lagerauffüllung
Lagerfach n (MaW) storage bin (or slot)
Lagerfachkarte f (MaW) bin card
lagerfähig (com) fit for storage
Lagerfähigkeit f (MaW) storage (or shelf) life
Lagerfertigung f
(IndE) make-to-stock production
− production to stock
Lagefinanzamt n (StR) local finance office where taxable property is situated, § 18 AO
Lagerfinanzierung f (Fin) inventory financing
Lagerfrist f (MaW) = Lagerdauer
Lagerfunktion f (MaW) inventory (carrying) function
Lagergebäude n
(MaW) storehouse
− storage building
Lagergebühren fpl (com) = Lagergeld
Lagergeld n (com) warehouse (or storage) charges
Lagergeschäft n
(com) warehousing business, §§ 416–424 HGB (Mk) procurement to stock up inventory (opp, Streckengeschäft)
Lagergewinne mpl (ReW) inventory profits
Lagergröße f
(MaW) inventory level
− size of inventory
Lagergut n
(com) goods fit for storage
(Zo) = Zollagergut
Lagerhalle f (MaW) storage building
Lagerhallenkonnossement n (com) custody bill of lading
Lagerhalter m
(com) warehouse keeper
− warehouseman
(ie, person undertaking the storage and custody of goods, § 416 HGB)

379

Lagerhaltung f
(MaW) = *Lagerwirtschaft*
(MaW) stockkeeping
- warehousing
Lagerhaltung f **mit konstanten Beständen** (MaW) constant-cycle system of inventory control
Lagerhaltung f **mit konstanten Bestellintervallen** (MaW) periodic ordering
Lagerhaltung f **nach ABC-Klassifikation** (MaW) ABC inventory control
- split inventory method
Lagerhaltungsanalyse f (OR) inventory analysis
Lagerhaltungskosten pl
(KoR) inventory carrying (or holding) costs
- expenses of carrying inventories
Lagerhaltungsmodell n (OR) inventory model
Lagerhaltungsplanung f (MaW) inventory scheduling
Lagerhaltungspolitik f (MaW) inventory policy
Lagerhaltungs-Rezession f (Vw) inventory recession
Lagerhaltungsschwankungen fpl (MaW) inventory fluctuations
Lagerhaltungssystem n (MaW) inventory control system
Lagerhaltungszyklus m (Vw) inventory cycle
Lagerhaus n (MaW) warehouse
Lagerhüter m (MaW) inactive inventory item
Lagerinvestitionen fpl
(VGR) net changes in business inventory
- inventory changes (or investment)
- investment in inventories of goods
(MaW) inventory investment
Lagerist m
(MaW) stock clerk
- stockkeeper
- stockroom clerk
- storekeeper
Lagerjournal n (MaW) inventory journal
Lagerkapazität f (MaW) storage capacity
Lagerkarte f
(MaW) inventory card
- stock record card
Lagerkartei f
(MaW) inventory records
- stock file
Lagerkennzahlen fpl (MaW) inventory turnover ratios
Lager n **klein halten** (MaW) to keep stocks trim
Lagerkonto n (Rew) inventory (asset) account
Lagerkontrolle f (MaW) inventory audit
Lagerkosten pl
(ReW) inventory cost
- inventory carrying cost
- holding cast
- storage cost (or expenses)
(com) warehouse charges
Lagerkostenabgabe f (EG) levy on storage
Lagerleistungen fpl (Bw) make-to-stock output *(ie, to replenish inventory)*
lagerlose Fertigung f (IndE) stockless production *(ie, based on hand-to-mouth buying of input materials)*
Lagermaterial n (MaW) regular stock on hand *(opp, Auftragsmaterial)*

Lagermiete f (KoR) storage rental fee
Lagermodell n (MaW) procurement inventory model
lagern
(MaW) to stock
- to store
Lagerort m (MaW) stock location
Lagerortkarte f (MaW) bin tag
Lagerpersonal n (MaW) inventory clerks
Lagerplan m (Bw) inventory budget
Lagerplanung f
(MaW) materials requirements planning
- inventory planning
Lagerpolitik f (MaW) inventory policy
Lagerraum m
(MaW) storage area
- stockroom
Lagerraum m **bereitstellen** (MaW) to provide storage space
Lager n **räumen**
(com) to clear stocks
- (infml) to offload stocks
Lagerräumung f
(com) clearance of stocks
- clearnout of inventories of unsold goods
Lagerrisiko n (com) storage risk
Lagerschein m (WeR) warehouse receipt (or certificate)
Lagerspesen pl (MaW) storage charges
Lagerstatistik f (MaW) inventory statistics
Lagerüberwachung f
(MaW) stockchasing
- monitoring the status of inventory
Lagerumsatz m (MaW) = *Lagerumschlag*
Lagerumschlag m
(MaW) inventory-sales ratio
- rate of inventory turnover
- turnover of inventories
- merchandise (or stock) turnover
Lagerung f
(MaW) storage
- keeping in stock
Lagerungskosten pl (MaW) storage costs
Lagerverkehr m (Zo) warehouse transactions
Lagerverluste mpl (MaW) inventory losses
Lagerversicherung f (Vers) storage insurance
Lagervertrag m (com) warehousing contract
Lagerverwalter m
(com) warehouse keeper (or manager)
(MaW) stock clerk
- stockkeeper
- stockroom clerk
- storekeeper
Lagervorrat m
(MaW) stock
- supply
Lagerwirtschaft f
(MaW) inventory management (or control)
- administration of inventory
- stock control
Lagerzeit f (MaW) period of storage
Lagerzins m
(MaW) implicit interest charges for average inventory period

(ie, equal to opportunity cost of capital tied in inventories)
Lagerzugang m (MaW) addition to stocks
Lagerzugänge mpl (MaW) inventory receipts
Lagerzugangsliste f (MaW) stock receipts register
Lagerzyklus m
 (Vw) inventory cycle
 – inventory investment cycle
 – (GB) stock cycle
Lagrangescher Multiplikator m (Math) Lagrange (*or* Lagrangian) multiplier
Lagrangesches Restglied n (Math) Lagrange's form of remainder
Land n
 (FiW) (West German) Land, *pl.* Länder (*or* Laender)
 – federal state
 – provincial state
Landarbeiter m
 (Pw) farmhand
 – (GB) agricultural labourer
Land n **des steuerlichen Wohnsitzes** (StR) country of fiscal domicile
Landegebühr f (com) landing charge
Landeier npl
 (com) free-range eggs
 – (US) eggs from uncooped hens *(opp, battery eggs)*
Länder npl **der Andengruppe** (AuW) Andean Group countries
Länderfinanzausgleichsgesetz n (FiW) Law on Fiscal Equalization among the States, of 28 Aug 1969, as amended
Länderfinanzverwaltungen fpl (FiW) Länder taxation authorities
Ländergruppe f (AuW) group of countries
Länderhaushalte mpl (FiW) Länder budgets
Länderkontingent n (AuW) quota accorded to an individual country
 – negotiated quota
Länderquoten fpl (AuW) country-by-country quotas
Länderrisiko n (AuW) country risk
Landesarbeitsgericht n (Re) appellate labor court
Landesbank f (Fin) regional bank *(ie, central giro institution of a Federal state)*
Landesbodenkreditanstalt f (Fin) Land mortgage bank
Landesfinanzamt n (StR) Land tax office
Landesfinanzminister m (StR) state minister of finance
Landesfinanzministerium n (StR) state ministry of finance
Landesjustizverwaltung f (Re) state justice administration
Landeskartellbehörde f (Kart) State Cartel Office
Landeskreditanstalt f (Fin) semi-public bank in a German state
Landesplanung f (Vw) regional planning
Landesplanungsgesetz n (Re) Land Planning Law
Landesrentenbank f (Fin) Land mortgage bank
Landessozialgericht n (Re) Appellate Court for Social Security and Related Matters
Landessteuern fpl
 (FiW) taxes levied by the West German Länder
 (*or* provincial states)
 – state taxes
landesüblicher Zinssatz m (Fin) current (*or* prevailing) rate of interest
Landesversicherungsanstalt f (SozV) Land social insurance office *(ie, for workers)*
Landesverwaltungsgericht n (Re) Land administrative tribunal
Landeswährung f (Vw) domestic (*or* local) currency
Landeszentralbank f (Fin) State Central Bank *(ie, regional central bank branch)*
Landfracht f (com) land-borne freight
Landfrachtgeschäfte npl
 (com) land-borne freight
 – (GB) land carriage
Land n **für Verkehrszwecke** (StR) land suitable for the building of highways or airports, § 69 I BewG
Landgericht n
 (Re) regional court
 – first-instance district court
 (ie, normal superior court having both first instance jurisdiction in civil and commercial matters and appellate jurisdiction from ,Amtsgericht')
ländliche Kreditgenossenschaft f
 (Fin) agricultural credit cooperative
 – rural credit association
 (ie, Spar- und Darlehnskassen od Raiffeisenkassen)
Landmaschinen fpl (com) agricultural (*or* farm) machinery
Landmaschinenbranche f (com) farm equipment industry
land- od forstwirtschaftliches Vermögen n (StR) agricultural property
Landtransport m
 (com) carriage by land
 – land carriage
Landtransportrisiko n (Vers) land risk
Landtransportversicherung f (Vers) insurance of goods in transit by land
Land- und Forstwirtschaft f (Vw) agriculture and forestry
land- und forstwirtschaftlicher Nebenbetrieb m
 (StR) business
 – enterprise
 – establishment ... incident to agriculture and forestry, § 15 I 1 EStG
land- und forstwirtschaftliches Einkommen n (StR) agricultural and forestry income
land- und forstwirtschaftliches Vermögen n (StR) property used in agriculture or forestry, §§ 33–67 BewG
Landwirtschaft f
 (com) agriculture
 – farming
 (com) agricultural industry
 – agri-business
landwirtschaftliche Ausstellung f
 (com) state *or* county fair
 – (GB) agricultural show
landwirtschaftliche Buchführung f (ReW) accounting of farm and forestry establishments

landwirtschaftliche Erzeugnisse *npl*
  (com) farm products
  – agricultural products
  – produce
  (ie, farm products collectively)
landwirtschaftliche Genossenschaft *f* (com) agricultural cooperative
landwirtschaftliche Marktordnung *f* (EG) farming market regime
landwirtschaftliche Messe *f* (com) agricultural fair
landwirtschaftliche Produkte *npl* (com) = *landwirtschaftliche Erzeugnisse*
landwirtschaftliche Produktivität *f* (Vw) agricultural productivity *(ie, input yield of labor and capital for a given unit of land)*
landwirtschaftlicher Betrieb *m* (com) agricultural undertaking
landwirtschaftlicher Hypothekarkredit *m* (Fin) agricultural real estate loan
landwirtschaftlicher Marktordnungswechsel *m* (FiW) agricultural market organization bill
landwirtschaftlicher Nebenerwerb *m* (com) part-time farm
landwirtschaftliches Einkommen *n* (EC) farmer's *(or* farm*)* income
landwirtschaftliche Überschußproduktion *f*
  (EG) farm overproduction
  (EG) farm surplus
Landwirtschaftskammer *f* (com) agricultural chamber
Landwirtschaftsschau *f*
  (com) state *(or* country*)* fair
  – (GB) agricultural show
längerfristige Finanzierung *f*
  (Fin) longer-term financing
  – provision of longer-period finance
langes Ende *n* **des Kapitalmarktes** (Fin) long end of the capital market
langfristig ausleihen (Fin) to lend long term
langfristig disponieren (Fin) to invest long term
langfristige Anlage *f* (Fin) long-dated *(or* permanent*)* investment
langfristige Anleihe *f* (Fin) long-term bond
langfristige Ausleihungen *fpl*
  (Fin) money loaned long-term
  – long-term lendings
langfristige Bankkredite *mpl* (Fin) long-term bank credits
langfristige Durchschnittskosten *pl* (Vw) long-run average cost
langfristige Emission *f* (Fin) long-dated issue
langfristige Erfolgsplanung *f* (Bw) long-term profit planning
langfristige Finanzanlagen *fpl* (ReW) long-term investments
langfristige Finanzierung *f* (Fin) long-term financing
langfristige Finanzierungsmittel *pl* (Fin) long-term financial resources *(or* funds*)*
langfristige Forderung *f* (Rew) long-term receivable
langfristige Grundsatzplanung *f* (Bw) long-range corporate planning
langfristige Kapitalanlage *f*
  (Fin) long-term
  – fixed

  – permanent ... investment
langfristige Kapitalbewegungen *fpl* (VGR) long-term capital movements
langfristige Kapitalbilanz *f* (VGR) long-term capital account
langfristige Konsumfunktion *f* (Vw) long-period consumption function
langfristige Kredite *mpl* (Fin) long-term indebtedness
langfristige Kreditgeschäfte *npl* (Fin) long-term lending
langfristige Kreditlücke *f* (Fin) long-term credit gap
langfristige Planung *f* (Bw) long-range *(or* long-term*)* planning
langfristiger Abschluß *m* (com) long-term contract
langfristige Rentabilität *f* (Fin) long-term profitability
langfristiger Kapitalverkehr *m* (AuW) long-term capital transactions *(or* movements*)*
langfristiger Kredit *m*
  (Fin) long-term credit *(or* loan*)*
  (FiW) funded debt
langfristiger Liefervertrag *m* (com) long-term supply agreement *(or* contract*)*
langfristiger Plan *m* (Bw) long-range plan
langfristiger Planabschnitt *m* (Fin) long-range budget period
langfristiger Vertrag *m* (Re) long-term contract *(eg, in the production of heavy equipment)*
langfristiger Wechsel *m*
  (WeR) long-dated bill
  – long bill
langfristiges Anlagevermögen *n* (Bw) long-term fixed assets
langfristiges Darlehen *n* (Fin) long-term *(or* fixed*)* loan
langfristiges Gleichgewicht *n* (Vw) long-period equilibrium
langfristiges Kapital *n* (ReW) capital and long-term liabilities
langfristiges Kreditgeschäft *n* (Fin) long-term loan business
langfristige Staatsschuld *f* (FiW) long-term public debt
langfristiges Ziel *n* (Bw) long-run *(or* strategic*)* goal *(ie, typically over 3 years)*
langfristige Unternehmenspolitik *f*
  (Bw) long-term company *(or* corporate*)* policy
  – long-term lines of approach
langfristige Unternehmenstrategie *f* (Bw) long-term corporate strategy
langfristige Verbindlichkeiten *fpl*
  (ReW) long-term liabilities
  – long-term debt *(or* indebtedness*)*
  – noncurrent liabilities
langfristige Verlaufsrichtung *f* (Stat) secular trend
langfristig investieren (Bw) to invest (for the) long term
Langfristplanung *f* (Bw) long-term *(or* long-range*)* planning
langlaufende Terminkonten *npl* (Fin) long-term time accounts
Langläufer *mpl*
  (Fin) long-dated securities

– long maturities
– longs
Langläufer-Rendite *f*
(Fin) long-term yield on bonds
– yield on longs
langlebige Konsumgüter *npl* (Mk) durable consumer goods
langlebige Wirtschaftsgüter *npl* (Bw) long-lived assets
langsamer Speicher *m* (EDV) slow access storage
Längsparitätskontrolle *f* (EDV) = *Längssummenprüfung*
Längsprüfzeichen *n* (EDV) horizontal parity bit
Längsseit-Konnossement *n* (com) alongside bill of lading
Längsseitlieferung *f* (com) delivery alongside ship
längsseit Schiff (com) alongside ship
Längssummenprüfung *f* (EDV) longitudinal (redundancy) check *(syn, Blockprüfung)*
Langzeitarbeitsloser *m* (Pw) long-term unemployed
Langzeitlagerung *f* (MaW) long-term storage
Langzeitplan *m* (Bw) long-range plan
Langzeitplanung *f* (Bw) long-range (*or* long-term) planning
Langzeitprognose *f* (Bw) long-term (*or* long-range) forecast
Laplacescher Grenzwertsatz *m* (Stat) Laplace's theorem
Laplacescher Operator *m* (Math) Laplacian operator
Laplace-Transformation *f* (Stat) Laplace transform
Lärmbelastung *f* (IndE) exposure to noise
Lärmschutz *m* (IndE) noise protection
Laser-Drucker *m* (EDV) laser printer
Lash-Verfahren *n* (com) lighter-aboard-ship method
Last *f* **der öffentlichen Schuld** (FiW) burden of the public debt
Lastenausgleich *m* (FiW) equalization of burdens
lastenfrei
(Re) free from encumbrances
– unencumbered
lastenfreies Eigentum *n* (Re) unencumbered property
Lastenheft *n*
(com) tender specifications
– specification
– cahier des charges
lästige Bedingung *f* (Re) onerous clause
lästiger Parameter *m* (Stat) nuisance parameter
Lastkraftwagen *m*
(com) truck
– (GB) lorry
Lastschrift *f*
(ReW) debit entry
(Fin) direct debit *(ie, im Lastschriftverfahren)*
Lastschriftanzeige *f*
(ReW) charge slip
– debit advice (*or* memo *or* note)
– advice of debit
Lastschriftbeleg *m* (ReW) debit voucher
Lastschriftverfahren *n* (Fin) direct debiting
Lastschriftverkehr *m* (Fin) direct debiting transactions

Lastschriftzettel *m* (Fin) direct debit slip
Lastspiel *n* (IndE) operating cycle
Last- und Gutschriften *fpl* (ReW) debit and credit entries
Lastverbund *m* (EDV) load link
Lastverteilung *f* (FiW) distribution of tax burden *(ie, structural criteria are: functional, personal, sociological, sectoral, regional, temporal)*
Last-Zeit-Funktion *f*
(IndE) history of loading
– service-loading history
lateinisches Quadrat *n* (Stat) Latin square
lateinisches Rechteck *n* (Stat) Latin rectangle
lateinisches Standardquadrat *n* (Stat) standard Latin square
latent-deterministischer Prozeß *m* (Stat) crypto-deterministic process
latente Konkurrenz *f* (Vw) latent competition *(ie, by potential suppliers)*
latenter Bedarf *m* (Mk) latent demand
latente Steuern *fpl* (ReW) deferred taxes *(ie, in Germany still regarded as violating the principle of realization)*
latente Variable *f* (Stat) latent variable
Latenzinformation *f* (Mk) latent information
Lattenkiste *f* (com) crate
Lauf *m* (IndE, EDV) run
Laufbahn *f* (Pw) career (path)
Laufbahnplanung *f*
(Pw) career planning
(Pw) in-house career path planning
laufende Aufwendungen *fpl* (ReW) current expenditure
laufende Auswertung *f* (Bw) periodic evaluation and reporting
laufende Bestandsaufnahme *f* (MaW) perpetual inventory
laufende Bestandskartei *f* (MaW) perpetual inventory file (*or* records)
laufende Buchungsnummer *f* (ReW) journal number
laufende Dividende *f* (Fin) regular dividend
laufende Emission *f* (Fin) tap issue
laufende Erträge *mpl* (Fin) current income *(eg, from bonds)*
laufende Instandhaltung *f* (com) current maintenance
laufende Inventur *f* (MaW) perpetual inventory
laufende Kontenabrechnung *f* (Fin) demand deposit accounting
laufende Leistungen *fpl* (SozV) current benefits
laufende Lohnrunde *f* (Pw) on-going wage round
laufende Numerierung *f* (com) consecutive numbering
laufende Pensionszahlungen *fpl* (Pw) current pension payments
laufende Planung *f* (Bw) current planning
laufende Police *f*
(Vers) floating policy
– open cover (*or* slip)
laufende Prämie *f* (Vers) regular premium
laufender Betrieb *m* (com) day-to-day business
laufende Rechnung *f*
(com) account current
– current account

laufende Rendite f (Fin) flat yield
laufender Faktoreinsatz m (Vw) current input
laufender Geschäftsbetrieb m
 (com) day-to-day business
 – running operations
laufender Kurvenzug m (Math) smooth curve
laufender Zins m (Fin) interest accrued
laufendes Budget n (FiW) current budget
laufendes Geschäftsjahr n (com) current financial year
laufendes Konto n
 (Fin) checking account
 – (GB) current account
laufendes Patent n (Pat) pending patent
laufendes Programm n (EDV) active program
laufendes Steuerjahr n (StR) current taxable year
laufende Summe f (EDV) running total
laufendes Unternehmen n (Bw) going concern
laufende Verbindlichkeiten fpl (ReW) current liabilities
laufende Versicherung f
 (Vers) floater policy
 – open policy
 (ie, esp. in transport insurance; more properly called ,open certificate')
laufende Wartung f (EDV) maintenance routine
laufende Wirtschaftsperiode f (Vw) market *(or instantaneous)* period
laufend numerieren (com) to number consecutively
laufend senken (com) to lower progressively
laufend veranlagte Steuern fpl (StR) currently assessed taxes
Laufkarte f
 (IndE) job *(or* move) ticket
 – travel card
 – batch card
Laufkunde m
 (com) casual customer
 – (infml) off-the-street customer
Laufkundschaft f (com) occasional customers
Laufwerk n (EDV) magnetic tape unit *(or* station or deck) *(syn, Magnetbandgerät)*
Laufzahl f (Math) number of terms *(ie, in a progression)*
Laufzeit f
 (Re) term
 – continuance
 – currency *(eg, during the . . . of the contract)*
 (Fin) life
 – life span
 – maturity period
 – time to maturity *(eg, of bond issue)*
 – length of time to maturity *(eg, 5 years to maturity)*
 (EDV) run
 – running
 – object . . . time
Laufzeit f **der Verzinsung** (Math) number of terms
Laufzeitenstruktur f (Fin) maturity pattern
Laufzeit f **e–r Anleihe**
 (Fin) duration
 – length
 – period . . . of a loan
 – repayment period
 (IndE) operating *(or* running) time

Laufzeit f **e–r Police** (Vers) life of a policy
Laufzeit f **e–s Patents** (Pat) term of a patent
Laufzeit f **e–s Wechsels** (WeR) term of a bill
Laufzeitglied n (EDV) transport delay unit *(ie, in analog computers)*
laufzeitkongruent (Fin) of/with identical maturity
Laufzeitkongruenz f (Fin) identity *(or* matching) of maturities
Laufzeitregister n (EDV) delay line register
Laufzeitspeicher m (EDV) delay-line memory *(or* storage)
Laufzettel m (com) routing slip
lauten auf (Fin) denominated *(or* issued) in *(eg, DM, £, $)*
lauterer Wettbewerb m (Kart) fair competition
Layouter m (Mk) layout man
Leasinggeber m (Fin) lessor
Leasingnehmer m (Fin) lessee
Leasing n **von Wagenparks** (Fin) fleet leasing
lebendes Inventar n
 (com) livestock
 (opp, totes Inventar; eg, farm machinery and implements)
Lebensarbeitszeit f (Pw) total working of life
Lebensdauer f
 (SozV) life expectancy
 (Bw) physical life
 – life (span)
 (eg, fixed asset, investment project)
Lebensdauer f **e–s Investitionsobjektes** (Bw) project life
Lebensdauer f **nach der Pensionierung** (Vw) retirement span
Lebenseinkommen n (Vw) lifetime income
Lebenserhaltung f (SozV) life conservation
Lebenserwartung f (Bw) life
 (Vers) life expectancy *(ie, number of years remaining for a person)*
Lebensfall-Versicherung f (Vers) endowment insurance *(ie, more frequent term: Erlebensfall-Versicherung)*
Lebenshaltungsindex m (Stat) = *Lebenshaltungs-Preisindex*
Lebenshaltungskosten pl
 (Stat) cost of living
 – living cost
Lebenshaltungs-Preisindex m (Stat) cost-of-living index
lebenslängliche Nutzungen fpl **und Leistungen** fpl (StR) payments and other benefits limited by the life of a person, § 14 BewG
lebenslängliche Rente f (Fin) life annuity
lebenslänglich laufende Leistungen fpl (Vers) current benefits for the lifetime of the beneficiaries
Lebenslauf m
 (Pw) curriculum vitae
 – personal history *(or* record)
 (IndE) history of a machine
Lebensmittelbranche f (com) food trade *(or* business)
Lebensmitteleinzelhandel m
 (Mk) grocery retailing
 (Mk) grocery retailing industry
Lebensmittelgeschäft n (com) food *(or* grocery) store

Lebensmittelgroßhandel m (Mk) food trade
Lebensmittelhandel m (Mk) grocery trade
Lebensmittelindustrie f (com) food processing industry
Lebensmittelkennzeichnung f (Mk) food labeling
Lebensmittelkette f
 (Mk) food store chain
 – multiple food retailers
Lebensmittelrecht n (Re) law relating to food processing and distribution
Lebensqualität f (Vw) quality of life
Lebensstandard m (Vw) standard of living
Lebensstellung f (Pw) tenured post (or position)
Lebensversicherer m (Vers) life insurer
Lebensversicherung f
 (Vers) life insurance
 – (GB) life assurance
Lebensversicherung f **abschließen**
 (Vers) to take out a life insurance policy
 – to buy life insurance
Lebensversicherung f **auf den Erlebensfall**
 (Vers) endowment insurance
 – (GB) endowment assurance
Lebensversicherung f **auf den Todesfall**
 (Vers) ordinary life insurance
 – whole life assurance
Lebensversicherung f **gegen Einmalprämie** (Vers) single premium insurance
Lebensversicherung f **mit abgekürzter Prämienzahlung** (Vers) limited payment life policy
Lebensversicherung f **mit gestaffelten Prämienzahlungen** (Vers) graded premium policy
Lebensversicherung f **mit Gewinnbeteiligung**
 (Vers) life insurance with profits
 – participating life policy
Lebensversicherung f **ohne Gewinnbeteiligung**
 (Vers) non-participating insurance
 – without-profits insurance
Lebensversicherung f **ohne Rückkaufswert** (Vers) term policy (preferred term: Risikoversicherung)
Lebensversicherungsabschlüsse mpl **machen** (Vers) to write life insurance
Lebensversicherungsgesellschaft f
 (Vers) life insurance company
 – (GB) life assurance company
Lebensversicherungspolice f (Vers) life insurance policy
Lebensversicherungsprämie f (Vers) life insurance premium
Lebensversicherungsunternehmen n (Vers) life insurance company
Lebensversicherungsverein m **auf Gegenseitigkeit** (Vers) mutual life insurance company
Lebensversicherungsvertrag m (Vers) life insurance contract
lebenswichtiger Bedarf m
 (Vw) essential supplies
 – necessities of life
Lebenszeitanstellung f (Pw) life-time employment
Lebenszeit-Beamter m (Pw) public servant (or GB: civil servant) appointed for life
Lebenszeit-Hypothese f (Vw) life cycle hypothesis (ie, planning of consumption expenditure over a whole life span)
Lebenszeitplanung f (Vw) lifetime planning

Lebenszyklus m (IndE) life cycle (ie, of an industrial product)
lebhafte Börse f (Bö) brisk market
lebhafte Käufer mpl (Bö) active buyers
lebhafte Nachfrage f (com) brisk demand
lebhafter Handel m (Bö) active trading (or dealings)
lebhafter Markt m (Bö) brisk market
lebhafte Umsätze mpl
 (Bö) active market (or trading)
 – brisk trading
 – broad market
 – heavy market
lebhaft gehandelte Werte mpl
 (Bö) active
 – actively traded
 – high-volume ... shares or stocks
lebhaft handeln (Bö) to trade briskly
Leckage f (com) leakage
Leckage-Klausel f (com) leakage clause
Lec-Verfahren n EDV liquid encapsulated czochralski process (ie, applied to produce galliumarsenide chips that switch optical as well as digital electronic signals)
Lederindustrie f (com) leather industry
Lederwarenmesse f (com) leather goods fair
Leerabgabe f (Bö) short selling
Leeraktie f (Fin) corporate share not fully paid up, § 60 AktG
Leeranweisung f (EDV, Cobol) exit statement
Leeraussage f (Log) empty statement (or proposition)
Leerbefehl m (EDV) dummy instruction
Leerbeleg m (EDV) blank document
Leerbit n (EDV) dummy bit
Leerdruck m (EDV) = Leergang
leere Menge f
 (Math) empty
 – null
 – void ... set
leerer Begriff m (Log) empty (or insignificant) term
leererfüllt (Log) vacuously satisfied
leeres Wartesystem n (Or) empty waiting-line system
Leerformel f
 (Log) empty phrase
 – vacuous expression (or phrase)
 – insignificant term
Leerfracht f (com) dead freight (ie, payable by charterer for such part of the carrying capacity of a ship he does not in fact use: it is damages for loss of freight)
Leergang m (EDV) idling cycle (syn, Leerdruck, Leerzeile)
Leergut n (com) empties
Leerkarte f (EDV) blank (or dummy) card (syn, Blankokarte)
Leerkauf m (Bö) uncovered sale
Leerkosten pl (Bw) idle capacity cost (O. Bredt)
Leerkostenanalyse f (Bw) idle-capacity-cost analysis
Leerkostenfunktion f (Bw) idle-capacity-cost function (ie, [maximum output – actual output] × [fixed cost/maximum output])

Leerkostenprozentsätze *mpl* (Bw) idle-capacity-cost percentages
Leerlauf *m*
   (Bw) organizational slack
   (EDV) floating
   – drifting
Leerlaufvariable *f* (OR) slack variable
Leerlaufzeit *f* (Bw) idle time
Leerpackung *f* (com) empty package
Leerposten *m* (ReW) empty heading
Leerstelle *f*
   (Log) argument place
   (EDV) blank character
Leertabelle *f* (Stat) dummy table
Leerübertragung *f* **der Firma** (Re) transfer of firm name *(ie, independently of the commercial business for which it is employed, § 23 HGB; in the case of stock corporations this is achieved through sale of the corporate shell = Mantel)*
Leerverkauf *m*
   (Bö) bear sale
   – short sale
   – short
Leerverkäufe *mpl* **abschließen** (Bö) to sell short
Leerverkäufe *mpl* **als Baissemanöver** (Bö) bear raiding
leer verkaufen (Bö) to sell short
Leerverkäufer *m*
   (Bö) bear (*or* short) seller
   – short
Leerverkaufsposition *f* (Bö) short position
leerverkaufte Aktien *fpl* (Bö) shorts
Leerzeichen *n*
   (EDV) blank
   (EDV, Cobol) space
Leerzeile *f* (EDV) = *Leergang*
Leerzeit *f* (IndE) idle time *(ie, unproductive time caused by machine breakdowns, material shortages, sloppy production scheduling)*
Legaldefinition *f* (Re) statutory definition
legalisieren (com) to legalize *(eg, a consular invoice)*
Legalzession *f* (Re) assignment by operation of law
legitim (com, Re) legitimate
Legitimationsaktionär *m* (Re) proxy shareholder
Legitimationsübertragung *f* (Re) transfer of right to vote
legitimieren
   (Re) to authorize
   – to legitimate
   – to legitimatise
   – to legitimise
legitimiert (Re) authorized
legitimierter Inhaber *m* (WeR) holder in due course
Lehre *f* **machen** (Pw) be apprenticed to a trade
Lehrenprüfung *f* (Stat) go-and-not-go gage
Lehrgang *m* (Pw) course
Lehrkräfte *fpl* (Pw) teaching staff
Lehrling *m*
   (Pw) apprentice *(ie, this term was officially changed to ‚Auszubildender' – Azubi –)*
   – trainee
Lehrlingsausbildung *f* (Pw) apprenticeship training
Lehrpersonal *n* (Pw) = *Lehrkräfte*

Lehrsatz *m* (Log, Math) theorem
Lehrstelle *f* (Pw) apprenticeship (*or* trainee) place
Lehrstelle *f* **besetzen** (Pw) to fill an apprenticeship
Lehrstuhlinhaber *m*
   (Pw) occupant of a professorship
   – holder of a chair
Lehrverhältnis *n* (Pw) apprenticeship
Lehrvertrag *m* (Pw) apprenticeship contract
Lehrwerkstätte *f*
   (Pw) apprentice
   – training
   – trainee ... workshop
Leibrente *f*
   (Fin) annuity for life
   – life annuity
   – contingent annuity
Leibrentenempfänger *m* (Fin) annuitant
leicht abgeschwächt (Bö) slightly lower
leichte Beschaffung *f* **von Fremdkapital** (Fin) ease of borrowing money
leichte Erholung *f* (Bö) slight rally (*or* recovery)
leichte Fahrlässigkeit *f*
   (Re) ordinary negligence, § 276 BGB
   – slight (*or* culpable) negligence
   (ie, omission to use ordinary care, or failure to exercise such care as is reasonably necessary, usu. referred to as ‚culpa levis')
leichte Finanzierung *f* (Fin) ease of raising capital
leichte Inflation *f* (Vw) moderate inflation
leichte Papiere *npl* (Bö) low-priced securities
Leichter *m*
   (com) barge
   – lighter
leichter eröffnen (Bö) to open lower *(ie, at the start of trading)*
Leichtergebühr *f* (com) lighterage *(ie, fee paid for loading and unloading a ship)*
Leichtergefahr *f* (com) ligther risk
leicht erholen (Bö) to manage a slim gain
leicht erholt (Bö) slightly higher
Leichterklausel *f* (SeeV) craft etc. clause
Leichtern *n*
   (com) lightering
   – lighterage
leichter nach anfänglichen Kursgewinnen (Bö) easier after early gains
leichter nach Glattstellungen durch den Berufshandel (Bö) lower on professional liquidation
leichter schließen (Bö) to close lower
leichter tendieren (Bö) to turn lower
Leichtindustrie *f* (com) lighter manufacturing
Leichtmetallindustrie *f* (com) light metals industry *(ie, also called ‚Aluminiumindustrie')*
leicht nachgeben (Bö) to turn a shade easier
leicht nachgebend (Bö) slightly easier
leicht verderbliche Güter *npl* (com) perishable goods
Leiharbeit *f* (Pw) loan employment
Leiharbeiter *m* (Pw) loan worker
Leiharbeitsfirma *f* (Pw) loan-employment agency
Leiharbeitskräfte *fpl* (Pw) loaned employees
Leiharbeitsverhältnis *n* (Pw) loan employment
Leihbibliothek *f*
   (com) lending library
   – (GB) subscription library

Leihdevisen *pl* (Fin) short-term currency borrowings
Leihe *f* (Re) gratuitous loan of a chattel, §§ 598–606 BGB
Leihemballagen *fpl* (com) loan containers
leihen (Re) to lend
Leihkapital *n* (Fin) loan capital *(ie, obsolete term for ‚Fremdkapital')*
Leihwagengeschäft *n* (com) rented car business
Leihwaren *fpl* (com) equipment loaned to customers
leihweise (com) on loan
Leichtlohn *m* (Pw) bottom wage
Leichtlohngruppe *f* (Pw) bottom wage group
Leiste *f* (Fin) renewal coupon *(syn, Erneuerungsschein)*
leisten
(Re) to perform
– to tender performance
Leistung *f*
(Bw) output
– performance
– result
(Re) performance *(ie, act or forbearance, § 241 BGB)*
(Pw) performance
– achievement
(StR) performance
(ie, umbrella term of German turnover tax law denoting every activity or nonperformance of an activity which can be the object of an agreement or which is otherwise legally relevant: sales, withdrawals and other ‚performances')
(SozV) benefits
– payments
(Vers) benefits
– *(also)* liability *(see: Leistungspflicht)*
– indemnity
(ie, not recommended; the term is constantly misused even in the U. S. insurance industry)
Leistung *f* **anbieten** (Re) to tender performance, § 298 BGB
Leistung *f* **an Erfüllungs Statt** (Re) performance in full discharge of an obligation, § 364 I BGB
Leistung *f* **an Zahlungs Statt**
(Re) performance in lieu of payment
– *(civil law)* dation in payment
Leistung *f* **des Geschuldeten** (Re) specific performance
Leistung *f* **durch Dritte** (Re) performance by a third party, § 267 BGB
Leistungen *fpl* (Vers) claims payments
Leistung *f* **e–r Nichtschuld**
(Re) payment of a non-existent debt, § 813 BGB
– *(civil law)* condictio indebiti
Leistungen *fpl* **abrechnen** (com) to invoice sales (and/or services)
Leistungen *fpl* **aus der Sozialversicherung** (SozV) social insurance benefits
Leistungen *fpl* **aus der Sterbeversicherung** (Vers) death benefits *(ie, amounts paid under insurance policy on death of insured)*
Leistungen *fpl* **erbringen**
(com) to perform

– to render services
– (infml) to deliver the goods
(Vers) to pay benefits
Leistungen *fpl* **für ausländischen Auftraggeber** (StR) services rendered to a foreign customer, § 4 No. 3 UStG
Leistungen *fpl* **kürzen** (SozV) to cut back benefits
Leistungen *fpl* **umsetzen** (StR) to sell goods and services
Leistungen *fpl* **zur beruflichen Förderung** (Pw) vocational assistance measures
Leistung *f* **erbringen** (Re) to perform an obligation
Leistung *f* **erfüllungshalber** (Re) = *Leistung an Erfüllungs Statt*
Leistungsabfall *m* (com) drop in performance
Leistungsabgabe *f* (IndE) output
leistungsabhängige Abschreibung *f* (ReW) = *leistungsbezogene Abschreibung*
leistungsabhängige Kosten *pl* (KoR) output-related costs
leistungsabhängiges Honorar *n* (com) fee per unit of services rendered
Leistungsabstimmung *f* (IndE) work balancing *(ie, at the assembly line)*
Leistungsabweichung *f*
(KoR) efficiency variance
– machine effectiveness variance
– physical variance
Leistungs-Afa *f* (StR) unit-of-product method of tax depreciation, § 7 I 3 EStG
Leistungsangabe *f* (Bw) performance specification
Leistungsangaben *fpl* (com) performance figures
Leistungsangebot *n*
(Re) offer to perform
(Vers) benefits offered
Leistungsanreiz *m*
(Pw) incentive
– inducement
Leistungsanspruch *m* (SozV) right (*or* entitlement) to benefits
Leistungsanwärter *m* (Vers, Pw) potential (*or* qualifying) beneficiary
Leistungsaustausch *m* (StR, VAT) exchange of performance, § 1 No. 1 UStG
leistungsbedingte Abschreibung *f* (ReW) = *leistungsbezogene Abschreibung*
Leistungsberechtigter *m* (SozV) person entitled to (*or* eligible for) benefits
Leistungsberechtigung *f* (SozV) = *Leistungsanspruch*
Leistungsbereitschaft *f*
(IndE) readiness to operate
(Pw) willingness to achieve
Leistungsbeschreibung *f* (Pw) performance description
Leistungsbeurteilung *f*
(Pw) performance appraisal
Also:
– performance evaluation (*or* review)
– employee evaluation (*or* rating)
– personnel rating
– efficiency rating
– merit rating
– service rating
– results appraisal

Leistungsbeurteilungssystem n (Pw) performance appraisal plan
Leistungsbewertung f **nach Einzelfaktoren** (Pw) factor rating
leistungsbezogene Abschreibung f
(ReW) production-method of depreciation
– unit-of-production method
– production-unit-basis method
– service output (or yield) method
(ie, original price minus scrap value divided by total volume output; syn, verbrauchsbedingte od technische od Mengenabschreibung)
leistungsbezogene Gehaltssteigerung f (Pw) merit increase
Leistungsbilanz f
(VGR) balance on acurrent account
– balance of payments on current account
– balance on goods, services, and unilateral transfers
(Note: ‚unilateral transfers' = unentgeltliche Leistungen are included in the Bundesbank's definition of Leistungsbilanz, while the Federal Statistical Office and part of the technical literature on the subject limit their definition to the exchange of goods and services)
Leistungsbilanzdefizit n
(AuW) current account deficit
– deficit on current account
– deficit on external account
– shortfall in the balance of payments on current account
Leistungsbilanzmultiplikator m (AuW) balance of payments multiplier *(ie, the usual term is ‚Zahlungsbilanzmultiplikator')*
Leistungsbilanzsaldo m
(AuW) balance on current account
– current account balance
Leistungsbilanzüberschuß m
(AuW) current account surplus
– surplus on current account
– balance-of-payments surplus on current account
– external deficit on current account
Leistungsbudget n (FiW) performance budget
Leistungsdaten pl (IndE) performance figures
Leistungsdauer f (Vers) benefit period
Leistungsdefizit n (Pw) performance deficit
Leistungs-Dschungel m (SozV, infml) benefits maze
Leistungseinheit f
(IndE) unit of output
– output unit
– service unit
Leistungseinkomen n (Vw) factor income
Leistungsempfänger m
(Re) beneficiary
(StR, VAT) recipient of performance
(Vers, SozV) beneficiary
– recipient of benefits
Leistungsentgelt n
(Re) consideration
– compensation
– quid pro quo
(Kart) compensation for services rendered, § 3 I GWB

(StR, VAT) consideration for a performance
Leistungsentgelte npl **der öffentlichen Hand** (FiW) nontransfer expenditures
Leistungsentlohnung f (Pw) incentive wage
Leistungserfüllung f (Re) performance of engagement
Leistungsergebnis n
(Bw) operating result
(Pw) work results
Leistungsergebnisgrad m (IndE) operator performance
Leistungsergebnisgrad m **e-r Abteilung** (IndE) departmental performance
Leistungserstellung f (Bw) production (or creation or output) of goods and services
Leistungserwartungen fpl (Pw) specific performance expectations
leistungsfähig (Pw) capable of achievement
Leistungsfähigkeit f
(Bw) operative capability
– efficiency
– productive capacity
(Pw) achievement potential
Leistungsfähigkeitsprinzip n (FiW) ability-to-pay principle *(ie, of taxation)*
Leistungsfaktoren mpl
(Bw) factors of production
– productive factors
– productive resources
– inputs
Leistungsfall m (SozV) benefit case
Leistungsfrist f (Re) time for performance
Leistungsgarantie f
(Re) performance bond (or guaranty)
– bank bond
– cash bond
– contract bond
– guaranty deposit
– guaranty against defective material and workmanship
– maintenance guaranty
leistungsgerechter Wettbewerb m (Kart) competition based on efficiency
Leistungsgesellschaft f (Vw) achievement-oriented society
Leistungsgewinn m (Bw) = *Leistungsergebnis*
Leistungsgrad m
(Bw) performance level
– performance index
– performance efficiency
(IndE) rate of working
Leistungsgradabweichung f (IndE) off-standard performance
Leistungsgradschätzen n (IndE) performance rating
Leistungsgradstandard m (Bw) standard performance
Leistungsgradüberschreitung f (IndE) = *Leistungsgradabweichung*
Leistungsgrenze f
(Bw) limit of performance
– output maximum
leistungshemmender Einfluß m (Pw) disincentive
Leistungsindex m (IndE) level-of-performance index

Leistungsklage *f* (StR) action for the performance *(ie, of an act other than the issuance of an administrative decision, § 40 I FGO; eg, refund of an overpaid tax)*
Leistungskonten *npl* (ReW) sales accounts
Leistungskontrolle *f* (Bw) performance control
Leistungskontroll-Schaubild *n* (IndE) Gantt chart
– daily balance chart
Leistungskurve *f* (IndE) performance (*or* work) curve
Leistungslohn *m* (Pw) payment by results
– performance-linked pay
– incentive wage
Leistungslohnausgleich *m* (IndE) lieu bonus
Leistungslohnsystem *n* (Pw) wage incentive system
Leistungsmaßstab *m* (Pw) standard of performance
– performance objective
Leistungsmessung *f* (Bw) performance measurement
(EDV) tuning
Leistungsmotivation *f* (Pw) achievement motivation
Leistungsniveau *n* (Bw) performance (level)
leistungsorientiert (Pw) achievement (*or* performance) oriented
leistungsorientiertes Budget *n* (Bw, FiW) output-oriented budget
Leistungsort *m* (Re) place of performance, § 269 BGB
Leistungspflicht *f* (Re) obligation
– obligation (*or* duty) to perform
– duty of performance
(Vers) liability
(ie, to pay for a loss coming under the terms of an insurance contract)
(Note: In common insurance usage the term 'liability' also specifies the amount for which the insurer is obligated by law)
Leistungspflichtiger *m* (Re) person liable to perform
Leistungspotential *n* (Bw) capability *(eg, of an company)*
(Pw) performance (*or* achievement) potential
Leistungsprämie *f* (Pw) incentive (*or* production) bonus
– efficiency premium
Leistungsprämiensystem *n* (Pw) efficiency bonus plan
Leistungsprinzip *n* (Vw) achievement principle
leistungsproportionale Abschreibung *f* (ReW) = *leistungsbezogene Abschreibung*
Leistungsrechnung *f* (ReW) results accounting
Leistungsreihe *f* (ReW) sales-purchases accounts
Leistungsrestriktion *f* (Bw) restricted performance *(eg, work to rule)*
Leistungsschau *f* (Mk) trade exhibition
Leistungssoll *n* (IndE) production target
Leistungsstand *m* (com) level of performance
Leistungsstandards *mpl* (Pw) performance standards
– standards of performance

Leistungssteigerung *f* (Bw) increase in efficiency (*or* performance)
(Bw) improved performance
Leistungsstörung *f* (Re) default in performance
– defective performance
(eg, delayed acceptance, default, impossibility)
Leistungsstrom *m* (AuW) flow of goods and services
Leistungsstruktur *f* (SozV) benefit structure
Leistungsstudien *fpl* (Pw) achievement studies *(ie, in work psychology)*
Leistungstest *m* (Pw) achievement (*or* performance) test
Leistungstoleranz *f* (Pw) performance tolerance
Leistungsträger *m* (Pw) high (*or* top) performer
– high contributor
– (infml) topnotcher
– *(pl, infml)* the tops
Leistungsübersicht *f* (Bw) statement of performance (*or* operations)
– operational statement
Leistungs- und Erlöskonten *npl* (ReW) sales and income accounts
Leistungsverbesserung *f* (com) improved performance
(Vers) improvement of benefits
Leistungsverhalten *n* (Pw) job
– performance
– work ... behavior
Leistungsverkehr *m* (AuW) current transactions *(ie, with other countries)*
Leistungsvermögen *n* (Bw, Pw) = *Leistungsfähigkeit*
Leistungsverrechnungen *fpl* (ReW) charges resulting from services
Leistungsversprechen *n* (Re) promise to perform
Leistungsverweigerung *f* (Re) refusal of performance
Leistungsverweigerungsrecht *n* (Re) right to refuse performance
Leistungsverzeichnis *n* (com) specification and schedule of prices
(com) bill of quantities
Leistungsverzögerung *f* (Re) delay in performance
Leistungsverzug *m* (Re) statutory delay in performance, §§ 284–286 BGB *(syn, Schuldnerverzug)*
Leistungsvolumen *n* (Bw) volume of output
(SozV) volume of benefits
Leistungsvoraussetzungen *fpl* (SozV) requirements for entitlement to benefits
Leistungsvorgabe *f* (Pw) standard of performance
Leistungswettbewerb *m* (Bw) competition in efficiency *(opp, Behinderungswettbewerb)*
Leistungswille *m* (Pw) will to achieve
Leistungswucher *m* (Re) transaction where financial advantages are strikingly out of proportion to performance rendered, § 302a I 3 StGB
Leistungszeit *f* (Re) time of performance, § 271 BGB
Leistungsziel *n* (Pw) performance objective

Leistungszulage *f* (Pw) efficiency (*or* incentive) bonus
Leistung *f* **und Gegenleistung** *f* (Re) performance and counter performance
Leistung *f* **verweigern** (Re) to refuse performance
Leistung *f* **Zug um Zug** (Re) contemporaneous performance
Leitbegriff *m* (Log) key concept
Leitbörse *f* (Bö) central stock exchange *(ie, Frankfurt Bourse)*
Leitemission *f* (Fin) signpost issue
leitender Angestellter *m*
 (Pw, *no single statutory definition*)
 – executive employee *(ie, discharging a number of employer functions)*
 Also:
 – management (*or* managerial) employee
 – manager below managing board level
 – senior executive
 – *(pl)* senior staff
Leitentscheidung *f* (Re) landmark decision
Leiterbahn *f* (EDV) conducting path
Leiter *m* **der Einkaufsabteilung** (Bw) head of purchasing department
Leiter *m* der Exportabteilung (com) export manager
Leiter *m* **der Finanzabteilung** (Fin) finance director
Leiter *m* **der Verkaufsabteilung** (com) sales manager
Leiter *m* **des Beschaffungswesens** (MaW) procurement manager
Leiter *m* **e–r Kontaktgruppe** (Mk) group head
Leiter *m* **Finanzen**
 (Fin) head of finance
 – finance director
Leiter *m* **Vermögensverwaltung** (Vers) chief investment manager
Leitkarte *f* (com) master card
Leitkurs *m* (AuW) central rate
Leitkursraster *m* (AuW) grid of central rates
Leitlinien *fpl*
 (Vw) quidelines
 – guideposts
Leitlochungen *fpl*
 (EDV) control (*or* function) holes
 – control punchings
 (syn, Steuerlochungen)
Leitprodukt *n* (IndE) main product *(opp, Koprodukt)*
Leitstation *f* (EDV) control station (*or* terminal)
Leitstrahl *m* (Math) radius vector *(ie, in the polar coordinate system)*
Leitstudie *f*
 (com) pilot
 – exploratory
 – preliminary ... study
Leitung *f*
 (Bw) *(als Führungsfunktion:)* directing
 – leading
 (Bw) management
Leitung *f* **der Geschäftsbereiche** (Bw) operational management
Leitungsanschlußschaltung *f* (EDV) line termination circuit
Leitungsbeauftragter *m* (Bw) executive

Leitungsbefugnis *f*
 (Bw) power of direction
 – decision-making powers
Leitungsbündel *n* (EDV) line group *(ie, catering for terminals with similar characteristics)*
Leitungsebene *f* (Bw) level of management
Leitungsfunktion *f* (Bw) executive function *(ie, of running a business)*
Leitungskosten *pl* (KoR) managerial costs *(ie, needing separate treatment as services; are not quantifiable)*
Leitungskostenstelle *f* (KoR) managerial cost center
Leitungsmacht *f* **ausüben** (Pw) to exercise the power of direction
Leitungsorgane *npl* **e–r AG** (Bw) administrative organs of a corporation
Leitungspuffer *m* (EDV) line buffer
Leitungsspanne *f*
 (Bw) span of control
 – span of command
 – span of management
 – span of supervision
 – span of responsibility
 (syn, Kontrollspanne, Subordinationsquote)
Leitungsstruktur *f*
 (Bw) management (*or* managerial) structure
 – management and control structure
 – lines of authority
 – lines of command
Leitungssystem *n*
 (Bw) directional system
 – form of organization structure
 – regular management chain of command
 – system of command
Leitungs-Vermittlung *f* (EDV) line (*or* circuit) switching *(syn, Durchschalte-Vermittlung)*
Leitungswasserversicherung *f* (Vers) pipe water damage insurance
Leitvariable *f* (Bw) leading variable
Leitwährung *f*
 (AuW) key currency
 (AuW) reserve currency *(ie, wider term covering gold and key reserve currencies)*
Leitwährungsland *n* (AuW) key currency country
Leitwerk *n* (EDV) control unit *(syn, Steuerwerk, Kommandowerk)*
Leitzins *m*
 (Vw) central bank discount rate
 – key rate
 – key interest rate
 (Fin) basic interest rate for savings at statutory notice *(syn, Spareckzins)*
Lemma *n*
 (Log) lemma
 – helping theorem
 – subsidiary proposition
Lenkungsausschuß *m* (Bw) steering committee (*or* group)
Leontief-Funktionen *fpl* (Vw) Leontief functions
Leontief-Paradoxon *n* (Vw) Leontief paradox
Leporello-Endlospapier *n* (EDV) fanfold stationery
Lernberufe *mpl* (Pw) occupations for which an officially recognized apprenticeship exists

Lerner-Effekt *m* (FiW) Lerner effect
Lernfunktion *f* (Bw) learning function
Lernkurve *f* (Bw) learning curve
Lernprozeß *m* (com) learning process *(ie, taking place between a system and its environment)*
Lernziel *n* (Pw) objective
Leseranalyse *f*
  (Mk) audience analysis
  – reader survey
Leseanweisung *f* (EDV, Cobol) read statement
Lesebefehl *m* (EDV) read instruction
Lesefehler *m* (EDV) read error
Lesegerät *n* (EDV) reader
Lesegeschwindigkeit *f* (EDV) read rate
Leseimpuls *m* (EDV) read pulse
Lesekopf *m* (EDV) read head
Lesepistole *f*
  (EDV) code (*or* data) pen *(syn, Handleser, Lesestift)*
  – wand reader
Leseprogramm *n* (EDV) input program
Leserforschung *f* (Mk) reader research
Leserschaft *f*
  (Mk) readership
  – print media audience
Leserschaftanalyse *f* (Mk) readership survey
Leseschreibkopf *m*
  (EDV) combined head
  – read/write head
Lese-Stanz-Einheit *f* (EDV) card punch reader
Lesestation *f* (EDV) reading station
Lesestift *f* (EDV) = *Lesepistole*
Letztangebot *n* (com) last offer
Letztbegünstigter *m* (Re) ultimate beneficiary
Letztbietender *m* (com) last and highest bidder
letzte Auswahleinheit *f* (Stat) ultimate sampling unit
letzte Bestimmungszollstelle *f* (Zo) office of final destination
letzte Börsennotiz *m* (Bö) last price (*or* quotation)
letzte Mahnung *f* (com) final reminder
letzte Ratenzahlung *f* (Fin) terminal payment
letzter Kurs *m* (Bö) closing price
letzter Verbrauch *m* (Vw) final (*or* ultimate) consumption
letztes Gebot *n* (com) last bid
letztes Zahlungsdatum *n* (Fin) final date of payment
Letztkäufer *m*
  (Mk) final purchaser
  – ultimate buyer
Letztverbrauch *m*
  (com) end use
  – ultimate consumption
Letztverbraucher *m*
  (com) ultimate (*or* final) consumer
  (Bw) end user
  (Mk) retail consumer
Letztverwender *m* (com) ultimate user
letztwillige Verfügung *f* (Re) testamentary disposition
Leuchtmittelsteuer *f* (StR) tax on electric bulbs and fluorescent fittings
Leuchtröhren-Versicherung *f* (Vers) insurance of fluorescent fittings *(ie, part of glass insurance)*

Leuchtwerbung *f* (Mk) illuminated advertising
liberale Schule *f* (Vw) liberal school of economic thought
liberalisieren (AuW) to liberalize foreign trade
liberalisierte Einfuhr *f* (AuW) liberalized imports *(ie, unrestricted in terms of volume and money)*
Liberalisierung *f* (AuW) liberalization of foreign trade
Liberalisierung *f* **der Zollpolitik** (AuW) tariff liberalization
Liberalisierungsliste *f* (AuW) free list
Liberalismus *m* (Vw) liberalism
liberalistischer Führungsstil *m* (Bw) liberal style of leadership
libertäre Schule *f* (Vw) libertarian economics *(ie, main proponents are v. Hayek and L. v. Mises; syn, New Austrian School)*
LIBOR-Zuschlag *m* (Fin) spread
Lichtgriffel *m* (EDV) light pen
Lichtpunktabtaster *m* (EDV) flying spot scanner
Lichtpunktabtastung *f* (EDV) flying spot scan
Lichtstift *m* (EDV) light pen
Liebhaberpreis *m* (com) fancy price
Lieferangebot *n*
  (com) tender of delivery
  – offer to supply goods
Lieferant *m*
  (com) supplier
  – seller
  – vendor
Lieferantenauswahl *f*
  (MaW) selection of suppliers
  – supplier selection
Lieferantenbeurteilung *f* (MaW) supplier evaluation
Lieferantenbuch *n* (ReW) accounts payable ledger
Lieferantenbuchhaltung *f* (ReW) accounts payable accounting
Lieferantenkartei *f* (ReW) vendor card file
Lieferantenkonto *n* (ReW) supplier account
Lieferantenkontokorrent *n* (ReW) supplier current account
Lieferantenkredit *m* (Fin) trade (*or* supplier) credit
Lieferantennummer *f* (com) vendor number
Lieferantenrechnung *f* (com) supplier's invoice
Lieferantenrisiko *n* (Stat) producer's risk
Lieferantenskonti *pl* (Fin) cash discount received
Lieferantenwechsel *m* (Fin) supplier's bill (*or* note)
Lieferanweisung *f* (com) instructions for delivery
Lieferanzeige *f*
  (com) advice note
  – delivery note
  – letter of advice
Lieferauftrag *m* (com) purchase order
lieferbar
  (com) available
  – in stock
  (com) ready for delivery
lieferbare Mengen *fpl*
  (com) quantities to be supplied
  (com) quantities available
lieferbares Stück *n* (Bö) good-delivery security *(ie, one without external defects)*
Lieferbarkeitsbescheinigung *f* (Bö) validation certificate

Lieferbedingungen *fpl*
(com) terms and conditions of sale
– terms of delivery
Lieferbereitschaft *f* (com) readiness to deliver
Lieferbereitschaftsgrad *m* (MaW) service degree (*or* level) *(ie, ratio indicating supply capability of a stock in inventory;* syn, *Servicegrad; see: optimaler L.)*
Lieferdatum *n*
(com) date shipped
– delivery date
Lieferengpaß *m* (com) supply shortage
Lieferer *m*
(com) supplier
– seller
– vendor
Lieferfirma *f*
(com) supplying firm
– supplier
Lieferfrist *f*
(com) time of delivery
– delivery deadline
– period of delivery
Lieferfristüberschreitung *f* (com) failure to keep the delivery date
Liefergarantie *f* (Re) trade guaranty *(ie, that products supplied are suitable for the intended purpose)*
Liefergegenstand *m* (com) delivery item
Liefergeschäft *n*
(com) delivery transaction
(com) series-produced products business *(opp, Anlagengeschäft)*
Lieferklauseln *fpl*
(AuW) international commercial terms,
– Inco-Terms
Lieferkosten *pl* (com) delivery charges
Lieferland *n* (AuW) supplier country
Lieferort *m*
(Re) place of delivery (*or* performance)
(StR) place of delivery
Lieferposten *m*
(com) lot
– supply item
Lieferpreis *m*
(com) contract price
– price of delivery
– supply price
Lieferprogramm *n*
(com) program of delivery
(Mk) line
Lieferquelle *f* (com) source of supply
Lieferrückstand *m*
(com) back order *(ie, portion of undelivered order)*
– order backlog
Lieferschein *m*
(com) delivery note
– delivery ticket
– bill of sale
– receiving slip (*or* ticket)
Liefersperre *f* (Kart) refusal to sell
Liefertag *m* (Bö) delivery day
Liefertermin *m*
(com) date of delivery

– delivery date
– time of delivery
– target date
Liefertermin *m* **einhalten**
(com) to meet a delivery date *(eg, set by a buyer)*
Lieferung *f*
(com) supply
(com) delivery
Lieferung *f* **auf Abruf** (com) delivery on call
Lieferung *f* **durchführen** (com) to effect (*or* execute) delivery
Lieferung *f* **effektiver Stücke** (Bö) delivery of actual securities
Lieferungen *fpl* (StR) deliveries, § 3 I UStG *(ie, essentially sales: performance by which an entrepreneur puts the recipient in a position to dispose of property in his own name)*
Lieferungen *fpl* **ins Ausland** (StR) export deliveries
Lieferungen *fpl* **kürzen** (com) to cut (*or* slash) supplies
Lieferungen *fpl* **und sonstige Leistungen** *fpl* (StR, VAT) deliveries and other ‚performances'
Lieferung *f* **frei Bestimmungsort** (com) free delivery
Lieferung *f* **frei Haus** (com) delivery free domicile
Lieferung *f* **gegen Barzahlung** (com) cash on delivery
Lieferung *f* **gegen Nachnahme** (com) cash basis delivery
Lieferung *f* **nach Eingang der Bestellung** (com) ready delivery
Lieferungsbedingungen *fpl* (com) = *Lieferbedingungen*
Lieferungsgarantie *f* (Re) = *Liefergarantie*
Lieferungsort *m* (Re, StR) = *Lieferort*
Lieferungssperre *f* (Bö) blocking period *(ie, subscriber to securities undertakes not to sell the paper before expiry of such blocking period)*
Lieferungs- und Zahlungsbedingungen *fpl* (com) terms of payment and delivery
Lieferungsvertrag *m* (com) supply agreement (*or* contract)
Lieferungsverzug *m* (Re) delayed delivery
Lieferung *f* **und Zahlung** *f* **am Abschlußtag** (Bö) cash delivery
Lieferung *f* **von Haus zu Haus** (com) door-to-door delivery
Lieferverpflichtung *f* (com) supply commitment
Liefervertrag *m* (com) supply agreement (*or* contract)
Liefervertrag *m* **mit Ausschließlichkeitsbindung** (Re) requirements contract
Lieferverzögerung *f* (com) delay in delivery
Lieferverzug *m* (Re) default of delivery
Liefervorschriften *fpl* (com) delivery instructions
Lieferzeit *f*
(com) period of delivery
(MaW) purchasing lead time
Lieferzeit *f* **einhalten**
(com) to meet the delivery deadline
– to deliver on time
Lieferzeitpunkt *m* (com) delivery date
Lieferzusage *f* (com) delivery promise
Liegegebühren *fpl* (com) anchorage dues *(ie, charge for anchoring a vessel)*

Liegegeld *n* (com) demurrage (charge) *(ie, charterer's contractual obligation under a charterparty to pay a certain sum to the shipowner if he fails to discharge the chartered vessel within the lay-time stipulated)*
Liegenschaften *pl* (Re) real property
Liegenschaftsrecht *n* (Re) law of real property
Liegeplatz *m* (com) berth *(ie, of a ship at port)*
Liegezeit *f* (com) lay-days *(ie, needed for unloading and loading of cargo)*
Lifo-Methode *f* (ReW) last in, first out (method of inventory valuation)
Likelihoodfunktion *f* (Stat) likelihood function
Likelihood-Quotient *m* (Stat) likelihood ratio
Limes *m* (Math) limiting value
Limit *n*
  (com) price limit
  – margin
limitationale Faktoreinsatzmengen *fpl* (Vw) fixed factor inputs
limitationale Produktionsfaktoren *mpl* (Vw) fixed (*or* limitational) factors of production
limitationale Produktionsfunktion *f* (Vw) fixed (*or* limitational) production function
Limitationalität *f* (Vw) fixed technological relationship *(ie, of input resources)*
Limitauftrag *m*
  (Bö) limited (*or* stop) order
  – limited (price) order
  – order at limit
Limit *n* **einhalten** (com) to remain within a limit
limitieren (com) to limit
limitierte Order *f* (Bö) = *Limitauftrag*
limitierter Auftrag *m* (Bö) = *Limitauftrag*
limitierter Auftrag *m* **bis auf Widerruf** (Bö) open order
limitierter Kaufauftrag *m* (Bö) stop loss order
limitierter Kurs *m* (Bö) limited price
limitierter Verkaufsauftrag *m* (Bö) selling order at limit
limitierte Stufenflexibilität *f* (Vw) adjustable peg system
Limitpreis *m*
  (Vw) limit price
  (com) price set for commission agent, § 386 HGB
  (Bö) limit price
Limit *n* **überschreiten** (com) to overshoot a limit *(eg, of external finance)*
lineare Abbildung *f* (Math) linear mapping
lineare Abhängigkeit *f* (Math) linear dependence
lineare Abschreibung *f* (ReW) straight-line method of depreciation
lineare Afa *f* (StR) straight-line tax depreciation, § 7 EStG
lineare Algebra *f* (Math) linear algebra
lineare algebraische Gleichung *f* (Math) linear algebraic equation
lineare Anhebung *f* (com) across-the-board rise
lineare Approximation *f* (Math) linear approximation
lineare Einheit *f* (EDV) linear unit
lineare Homogenität *f* (Math) linear homogeneity *(ie, of a function)*
lineare Hypothese *f* (Stat) linear hypothesis

lineare Interpolation *f* (Math) linear (*or* straight-line) interpolation
lineare Kausalität *f*
  (Log) multiple causation
  – one-to-one causation
lineare Lohnerhöhung *f* (Pw) across-the-board pay rise
lineare Nachfragekurve *f* (Vw) straight-line demand curve
lineare Nebenbedingung *f* (Math) linear constraint
lineare Optimierung *f* (OR) = *lineare Programmierung*
lineare Planungsrechnung *f* (OR) = *lineare Programmierung*
lineare Programmierung *f* (OR) linear programming
linearer Akkord *m* (Pw) straight piecework
lineare Regression *f* (Stat) linear regression
linearer Filter *m* (Stat) linear filtering
linearer Trend *m* (Stat) linear trend
lineare Schätzfunktion *f* (Stat) linear estimator
lineare Schätzung *f* (Stat) linear estimate
lineares Modell *n* (Stat) linear model
lineare Steuersenkung *f* (FiW) across-the-board tax increase *(opp, targeted tax breaks benefiting specific groups or strata)*
lineare Transformation *f* (Math) collineation
lineare Trennfunktion *f* (Math) linear discriminant function
lineare Überlagerung *f* (Math) linear superposition
lineare Zollsenkung *f* (AuW) linear tariff cut
linear gebrochene Form *f* (Math) linear fractional form
linear geordnete Menge *f*
  (Math) linearly ordered set
  – serially ordered set
  – chain
linear homogene Produktionsfunktion *f* (Vw) linearly homogeneous production function
Linearitätsannahme *f* (Math) linear assumption
Linearkombination *f* (Math) linear combination
linear limitationale Produktionsfunktion *f* (Vw) linearly limitational production function
Linie *f* (Bw) line *(opp, Stab)*
Linienagent *m* (com) shipping line agent
Liniendiagramm *n* (Stat) line diagram
Linienfertigung *f* (IndE) line production
linienförmige Quellenverteilung *f* (Math) filamental source distribution
Linienfrachtraten *fpl* (com) liner rates
Linienfunktion *f* (Bw) line function *(eg, purchasing, production, marketing)*
Liniengraph *m* (Math) line graph
Linienintegral *n* (Math) line integral
Linien-Konnossementsbedingungen *fpl* (com) shipping-line bill-of-lading terms
Linienkräfte *fpl* (Pw) the line
Linienmanager *m* (Bw) line manager
Linienorganisation *f* (Bw) line organization
Linienschiff *n* (com) liner
Linienschiffahrt *f* (com) shipping line service *(opp, Trampschiffahrt)*
Linienstelle *f* (Bw) line position
Linienstichprobenverfahren *n* (Stat) line sampling
Linientätigkeit *f* (Bw) line activity

393

Linienverkehr m (EDV) party line technique
Linienverteilung f (Math) filamental distribution
Linksasymmetrie f (Stat) positive skewness
linksbündig (EDV) left justified
linksbündig machen (EDV) to left-justify
Linksmultiplikation f (Math) premultiplication
Linksschrauben-Regel f (Math) left-hand screw rule
Linksverschiebung f
 (Vw) leftward shifting *(ie, of demand and supply curves)*
 (EDV) left shift
Lippenbekenntnis n
 (com) lip service *(ie, to pay . . .)*
 – pious pledge *(eg, to make . . .)*
liquid
 (Fin) liquid
 – solvent
Liquidation f
 (com) note (*or* bill) of fees
 (Re) realization
 (Re) liquidation *(ie, of a company; not ‚dissolution'!)*
 – (GB) winding up
 (Bö) settlement
 (Bö) clearance
Liquidationsbeschluß m (Re) winding-up resolution
Liquidationsbilanz f
 (ReW) liquidation balance sheet
 – (GB) winding-up balance sheet
 (ie, statement of assets and liabilities of a company in liquidation)
Liquidationserlös m (Fin) liquidation proceeds
Liquidationsgesellschaft f (Re) company in liquidation
Liquidationsgewinn m (Fin) winding-up profit
Liquidationsguthaben n (Fin) clearing balance
Liquidationskosten pl (Fin) liquidation costs
Liquidationskurs m
 (Bö) making-up price
 (Bö) settlement price in forward transactions *(syn, Kompensationskurs)*
Liquidationsquote f (Re) liquidating dividend
Liquidationsrate f (ReW) installment of liquidation proceeds
Liquidationstermin m (Bö) pay day
Liquidationsvergleich m (Re) „liquidation-type" composition
 (ie, debtor hands over to creditors part or all of his property for sale, § 7 IV VerglO)
Liquidationsverkauf m
 (Re) liquidation sale
 – (GB) winding-up sale
Liquidationswert m (ReW) liquidation (*or* realization) value
 (Re) sum total of liquidation (*or* winding-up) proceeds
 (Fin) net assets value *(ie, determined by investment trusts)*
Liquidationszeitraum m (Re) liquidation period
Liquidator m (Re) liquidator
liquide
 (Fin) liquid
 – (infml) flush with cash

liquide bleiben (Fin) to stay solvent
liquide Mittel pl
 (Fin) liquid funds *(ie, cash, short-term claims, and marketable securities)*
 – cash and cash items
 – cash assets
liquide Mittel pl **ersten Grades** (Fin) unrestricted cash
liquide Mittel pl **zweiten und dritten Grades** (Fin) assets held for conversion within a relatively short time
liquide Titel mpl **höchster Ordnung** (Fin) liquidity of last resort
liquidieren
 (com) to charge *(ie, for services rendered)*
 (Re) to realize
 (Re) to liquidate *(ie, a company)*
 – (GB) to wind up
 (Bö) to sell off
 (Bö) to settle
Liquidität f
 (Fin) liquidity
 – ability to pay
 – financial solvency
 (Fin) availability of financial resources
 (Fin) liquid funds (*or* resources)
Liquidität f **dritten Grades** (Fin) current ratio *(ie, total current assets to current liabilities)*
Liquidität f **ersten Grades**
 (Fin) cash ratio
 – (absolute) liquid ratio
 (ie, cash + short-term receivables to current liabilities)
 – (US) acid-test ratio
 (ie, total cash + trade receivables + marketable securities to current liabilities)
Liquiditätsabfluß m (Vw) outflow of liquidity
liquiditätsabschöpfende Maßnahmen fpl (Vw) measures designed to skim off liquidity
Liquiditätsanspannung f (Fin) strain on liquidity
Liquiditätsausstattung f (Fin) availability of liquid funds
Liquiditätsausweitung f (Fin) expansion of liquidity
Liquiditätsbedarf m (Fin) liquidity requirements
Liquiditätsbereitstellung f (Fin) supply of liquidity
Liquiditätsbeschaffung f (Fin) procurement of liquidity
Liquiditätsbilanz f
 (AuW) net liquidity balance
 (ReW) financial statement *(ie, submitted by borrowers to banks, with items arranged in decreasing order of liquidity, § 16 KWG)*
Liquiditätsbudget n (Fin) cash budget *(ie, itemizing receipts and disbursements)*
Liquiditätsdecke f (Fin) extent of liquidity
Liquiditätsdefizit n (Fin) shortfall of liquidity
Liquiditätseffekt m (Vw) availability effect
Liquiditätsengpaß m (Fin) liquidity squeeze
Liquiditätsentzug m (Fin) liquidity drain
Liquiditätserhaltung f (Fin) maintenance of liquidity
Liquiditätsfalle f (Vw) liquidity trap
Liquiditätsgarantie f (Fin) debt service guaranty
liquiditätsgebende Aktiva pl (Vw) assets conferring liquidity

Liquiditätsgefälle *n* (Fin) different levels of liquidity
Liquiditätsgrad *m* (Fin) liquidity ratio *(syn, Deckungsgrad; see: Liquidität ersten, zweiten und dritten Grades)*
Liquiditätsgrundsätze *mpl* (Fin) liquidity directives *(ie, issued by the 'Bundesaufsichtsamt für das Kreditgewerbe = Banking Supervisory Authority')*
Liquiditätshilfe *f*
(Vw) temporary release of extra reserves to the banks
– temporary injection of new liquidity into the money market by the central bank
Liquiditätskennzahlen *fpl* (Fin) liquid asset rations
Liquiditätsklemme *f*
(Fin) liquidity squeeze
– cash bind
– cash crunch
– cash squeeze
Liquiditätsknappheit *f* (Fin) lack of cash
Liquiditäts-Koeffizient *m* (ReW) (net) working capital ratio *(ie, current assets minus current liabilities)*
Liquiditäts-Konsortialbank *f* (Fin) liquidity bank
Liquiditätskosten *pl* (Fin) cost of liquidity *(ie, opportunity cost of cash holdings + interest payable on borrowed capital)*
Liquiditätskredit *m* (Fin) loan to maintain liquidity
Liquiditätskrise *f* (Fin) liquidity crisis
Liquiditätslage *f* (Fin) cash *(or* liquidity) position
Liquiditätsmarge *f* (Vers) solvency margin
Liquiditätsmechanismus *m* (Vw) liquidity mechanism *(ie, concept of liquidity theory of money)*
Liquiditätsneigung *f* (Vw) = *Liquiditätspräferenz*
Liquiditätspapier *n* (FiW) liquidity paper *(ie, unverzinsliche Schatzanweisungen + Schatzwechsel*
Liquiditätsplanung *f* (Fin) liquidity planning
Liquiditätspolitik *f* (Fin) liquidity policy
Liquiditätspräferenz *f* (Vw) liquidity preference
Liquiditätspräferenztheorie *f* (Vw) liquidity preference theory *(J. M. Keynes)*
Liquiditätsprämie *f* (Fin) liquidity premium
Liquiditätsprüfung *f* (Fin) liquidity audit
Liquiditätsquote *f* (Fin) liquidity ratio *(ie, ratio of free liquidity reserves of commercial banks to deposit volume held by nonbanks and foreign banks)*
Liquiditätsrahmen *m* (Vw) ceiling for new injections of liquidity *(ie, by the Bundesbank)*
Liquiditätsreservehaltung *f* (Fin) liquidity reserve management
Liquiditätsreserven *fpl* (Fin) liquid reserves
Liquiditätssaldo *m* (Vw) liquidity balance *(ie, indicator of monetary policy: sum of minimum reserves and free liquidity reserves of banks)*
Liquiditätsschraube *f* (Fin) liquidity screw
Liquiditätsschwierigkeiten *fpl*
(Fin) cash pressures *(or* problems)
– (infml) financial hot water
Liquiditätssicherung *f* (Fin) measures safeguarding liquidity
Liquiditätsspritze *f* (Fin) cash injection

Liquiditätstheorie *f* (Vw) liquidity preference theory
Liquiditätsüberhang *m* (Fin) excess liquidity
Liquiditätsüberschuß *m*
(Fin) cash surplus
– surplus cash resources
– surplus funds
Liquiditätsumschichtung *f* (Fin) transfer *(or* switch) of liquidity
Liquiditätsverknappung *f* (Vw) shortage of liquidity
Liquidität *f* **zweiten Grades** (Fin) ratio of financial current assets to current liabilities
Liste *f*
(com) list
(EDV, Cobal) report
Liste *f* **aufstellen**
(com) to draw up *(or* compile) a list
Liste *f* **der gelöschten Ladungsmengen** (com) statement of outturn
Listenbild *n* (EDV) printer layout
Listengenerator *m* (EDV) list generator
Listengrundpreis *m* (com) basic list price
Listenpreis *m*
(com) list price
(com) sticker price *(eg, of cars)*
(AuW) posted price *(ie, of crude oil)*
Listenpreis *m* **zahlen**
(com) to pay the list price
– (infml) to pay list
Listenprogramm *n* (EDV) report program
Listenprogrammgenerator *m* (EDV) report program generator
Listenschreiben *n*
(EDV) listing
– printout
Listenverarbeitung *f* (EDV) list processing
Literal *n* (EDV, Cobol) literal
Litfaßsäule *f* (Mk) advertising pillar *(or* post)
lizensieren (Pat) to license
Lizensierung *f* (Pat) licensing
Lizenz *f*
(Re) permit
(Pat) license
Lizenzabgabe *f*
(Pat) license fee
– royalty
Lizenzabkommen *n* (Pat) license agreement
Lizenzabkommen *n* **auf Gegenseitigkeit** (Pat) cross-license agreement
Lizenzabrechnung *f* (Pat) royalty statement
Lizenzaustausch *m* (Pat) cross-licensing
Lizenzaustauschvertrag *m* (Pat) cross-license agreement
Lizenzbau *m* (com) licensed construction
Lizenzdauer *f* (Pat) term of a license
Lizenzeinnahmen *fpl*
(ReW) income under license agreements
– income from royalties
Lizenzeinräumung *f* (Pat) licensing
Lizenz *f* **erteilen** (Pat) to grant a license
Lizenzerteilung *f* (Pat) issue of a license
Lizenzfertigung *f*
(com) licensed production
– production under license

Lizenzgeber *m*
  (Pat) licensor
  – grantor of a license
Lizenzgebühren *fpl*
  (Pat) license fees
  – royalties
Lizenzgewährung *f* (Pat) licensing
Lizenzinhaber *m*
  (Pat) license holder
  – licensee
Lizenzkosten *pl* (ReW) cost of license agreements
Lizenznehmer *m*
  (Pat) license holder
  – licensee
Lizenzrechte *npl* (Pat) rights of licensee under a patent
Lizenzsucher *m*
  (Pat) licensee
  – party seeking license
Lizenzträger *m* (Pat) licensee
Lizenzverbund *m* (Pat) network of licenses
Lizenzvereinbarung *f* (Pat) license agreement
Lizenzvergabegesellschaft *f* (Pat) franchise company
Lizenzverlängerung *f* (Pat) renewal of a license
Lizenzvertrag *m* (Pat) license agreement
Lizenzverwertung *f* (Pat) exploitation of a license
Lizenzzahlung *f* (Pat) payment of royalties
Lkw *m*
  (com) truck
  – (GB) lorry
Lkw-Anhänger *m* (com) truck trailer
Lkw-Fahrer *m*
  (com) truck driver
  – (infml) teamster
  – (GB) lorry driver
Lkw-Fracht *f* (com) truck freight
Lkw-Ladung *f* (com) truck load
Lkw-Produktion *f* (com) truck production
Lkw-Transportunternehmen *n*
  (com) trucking company
  – (GB) haulage contractor
LM-Kurve *f* (Vw) LM *(liquidity-money)* curve
LMS-System *n* (IndE) leveling system *(ie, of performance rating = Leistungsgradschätzen; syn, Nivellierungsmethode, Westinghouse-System)*
Lochaggregat *n* (EDV) punching unit
Lochband *n* (EDV) = *Lochbandschleife*
Lochbandabtaster *m* (EDV) paper tape reader
Lochbandlocher *m* (EDV) carriage tape punch
Lochbandschleife *f*
  (EDV) control loop *(or* tape*)*
  – paper tape loop
  – printer carriage tape
  (ie, closed loop of tape to control the operation of printing devices; syn, Lochband, Vorschubband)
Lochbandvorschub *m* (EDV) tape controlled carriage
Lochbeleg *m* (EDV) punch form *(syn, Ablochvordruck)*
lochen
  (EDV) to punch
  – to perforate
Locher *m*
  (EDV) punch
  – perforator
Lochfehler *m* (EDV) punch error
Lochfeld *n* (EDV) field
Lochkarte *f*
  (EDV) card
  – punch(ed) card
  (syn, Maschinenlochkarte; opp, Handlochkarte)
Lochkartenabtaster *m* (EDV) card reader unit
Lochkartenbeschrifter *m* (EDV) printing punch
Lochkartencode *m* (EDV) card code
Lochkartendoppler *m* (EDV) duplicator
Lochkarteneingabe *f* (EDV) card input
Lochkarteneingabebereich *m* (EDV) card input area
Lochkartenfeld *n* (EDV) card field
Lochkartenformat *n* (EDV) card format
Lochkartengeräte *npl* (EDV) card equipment
Lochkartengewinnung *f* (EDV) card punching
Lochkartenleser *m* (EDV) card reader
Lochkartenlocher *m* (EDV) card punch
Lochkartenmagazin *n* (EDV) card magazine *(or* hopper*)*
Lochkartenmaschine *f* (EDV) punched card machine
Lochkartenmischer *m*
  (EDV) collator
  – interpolator
Lochkartenprüfer *m* (EDV) punched card verifier
Lochkartenprüfung *f* (EDV) card verifying
Lochkartenschlüssel *m* (EDV) card code
Lochkartenselektor *m* (EDV) selector
Lochkartenspalte *f* (EDV) card column
Lochkartenstanzer *m*
  (EDV) automatic (feed) punch
  – card punch
  (syn, automatischer od Kartenstanzer)
Lochkartenstapel *m*
  (EDV) deck of cards
  – pack of punched cards
Lochkartenstau *m* (EDV) card jam *(or* wreck*)* *(syn, Kartenanstoß, Kartensalat)*
Lochkartenstelle *f* (EDV) code *(or* punch*)* position
Lochkartenverdichtung *f* (EDV) data reduction
Lochkartenvorderseite *f* (EDV) card face
Lochkartenvorschub *m* (EDV) card feed
Lochkartenzeile *f* (EDV) card row *(or* track*)*
Lochkartenziehkartei *f* (EDV) tub file
Lochkartenzuführung *f* (EDV) card feed (mechanism)
Lochkombination *f* (EDV) code hole combination
Lochprogramm *n* (EDV) punching programm
Lochprüfer *m*
  (EDV) verifier
  – verifying unit
Lochprüfung *f* (EDV) punch verifying
Lochschrift *f* (EDV) punch code
Lochschriftübersetzer *m* (EDV) card interpreter
Lochspalte *f* (EDV) card column
Lochstation *f* (EDV) punching station
Lochstelle *f* (EDV) hole site
Lochstreifen *m*
  (EDV) paper
  – punched
  – punched paper ... tape
Lochstreifenabtaster *m* (EDV) paper tape reader

Lochstreifencode *m* (EDV) paper tape code
Lochstreifendoppler *m*
 (EDV) paper tape reproducer
 – reperforator
Lochstreifenempfänger *m* (EDV) reperforator
Lochstreifengerät *n* (EDV) paper tape unit
Lochstreifenkarte *f* (EDV) edge-punched (*or* tape) card
Lochstreifenkartenlocher *m* (EDV) tape card punch
Lochstreifenleser *m* (EDV) paper tape reader
Lochstreifenlocher *m*
 (EDV) paper tape punch
 – tape punch
 (EDV) automatic paper tape punch
 – automatic tape punch
Lochstreifensender *m* (EDV) tape transmitter
Lochstreifenspule *f*
 (EDV) spool
 – reel
 – roll
Lochstreifenstanzer *m* (EDV) = *Lochstreifenlocher*
Lochstreifenvorschub *m* (EDV) tape feed (*or* transport)
Lochung *f*
 (EDV) perforation
 (EDV) punching
Lochungszone *f* (EDV) curtate (*ie, group of adjacent punched rows on a card*)
Lochzange *f*
 (EDV) spot punch
 – unipunch
Lochzeile *f* (EDV) card row
Lockangebot *n* (Mk) = *Lockvogelangebot*
Lockartikel *m*
 (Mk) bait
 – leader
 – leading article
 – loss leader
 – (infml) lure
Locke *f* (OR) self loop
Lockerung *f*
 (com) easing
 – loosening
 – relaxation
 – relieving
Lockerung *f* **am Geldmarkt** (Vw) relieving tightness in the money market
Lockerung *f* **der Geldpolitik** (Vw) easing (*or* relaxation) of monetary policy
 – loosening the monetary reins
Lockerung *f* **der Hochzinspolitik** (Vw) slackening of current high interest rates
Lockerung *f* **der restriktiven Geldpolitik** (Vw) let-up in monetary restraint
Lockerung *f* **von Preiskontrollen** (Vw) relaxation of price controls
Lockvogel *m* (Mk) = *Lockartikel*
Lockvogelangebot *n* (Mk) advertising unavailable goods at reduced prices, § 3 UWG
Lockvogelwerbung *f*
 (Mk) loss-leader sales promotion
 – loss-leader selling
 – advertising by enticement
 – bait-type advertising
Logarithmand *m* (Math) inverse logarithm
Logarithmentafel *f* (Math) log table
logarithmieren (Math) to logarithm
logarithmische Darstellung *f* (Math) logarithmic chart
logarithmische Gleichung *f* (Math) logarithmic equation
logarithmische Normalverteilung *f* (Stat) lognormal distribution
logarithmisches Papier *n* (Math) log paper
Logarithmus *m* (Math) logarithm
Logik-Arrays *pl.* (EDV) gate arrays (*ie, halbkundenspezifische integrierte Schaltungen = semi-custom ICs*)
Logikbaustein *m* (EDV) logical unit
Logik *f* **der Widerspruchslosigkeit** (Log) consistency logic
logische Adresse *f* (EDV) logical address
logische Datei *f* (EDV) logical file
logische Ebene *f* (EDV) logical level
logische Elemente *npl* (EDV) logical components (*or* elements)
logische Entscheidung *f* (EDV) logical decision
logische Konzeption *f* (EDV) logic(al) design
logische Matrix *f* (Log) truth table
logische Nähe *f* (Log) logical proximity
logische Operation *f* (EDV) logical operation
logische Partikel *mpl* (Log) connectives
logischer Befehl *m* (EDV) logical instruction
logischer Funktor *m* (Log) logical functor (*or* operator)
logischer Identitätsvergleich *m* (EDV) logical comparison (*ie, between two operands*)
logischer Knoten *m* (Log) logical node
logischer Operator *m* (Log) logical operator (*or* functor)
logischer Plan *m* (EDV) logical diagram
logischer Satz *m* (EDV) logical record
logischer Vergleich *m* (EDV) logical comparison
logische Schaltung *f* (EDV) logical circuit
logisches Diagramm *n*
 (EDV) logic chart (*or* flowchart)
 – logical diagram
logisches Prinzip *n* **vom Widerspruch** (Log) law of contradiction
logisches Produkt *n* (Log) conjunction
logisches Quadrat *n* (Log) square of opposition
logisches Schaltelement *n*
 (EDV) logic element
 – gate
logische Summe *f* (Log) inclusive disjunction
logische Supposition *f* (Log) logical supposition
logisches Verschieben *n*
 (EDV) logical (*or* end around) shift
 – non-arithmetic shift
logische Verknüpfung *f* (EDV) logical operation
logistische Kurve *f* (Stat) logistic curve
logistischer Trend *m* (Stat) logistic trend
logistische Systeme *npl* (Bw) industrial logistics
logistisches System *n* **von Betriebswirtschaften**
 (Bw) business logistics
 – logistics of the firm
Log-Normalverteilung *f*
 (Stat) lognormal

397

- logarithmic-normal
- Gibrat ... Verteilung
Lohmann-Ruchti-Effekt *m* (Bw) capacity increasing effect *(syn, Kapazitätserweiterungseffekt: depreciation through use as a source of new investments)*
Lohn *m*
(Pw) wage
- pay
lohnabhängige Gemeinkosten *pl* (KoR) wage-related overhead
Lohnabrechnung *f*
(ReW) payroll *(or* wage) accounting
(ReW) payroll accounts department
(Pw) pay slip
Lohnabschlagszahlung *f* (Pw) wage advance payment *(ie, at short intervals; eg, one week, 10 days)*
Lohnabschluß *m*
(Pw) pay *(or* wage *or* labor) settlement
- wage agreement
Lohnabtretung *f* (Re) assignment of wages
Lohnabzüge *mpl* (Pw) pay deductions
Lohnabzugsverfahren *n* (ReW) withholding of taxes and social security contributions from wages and salaries
Lohn-Angebots-Kurve *f* (Vw) wage supply curve
Lohnarbeitsrechenzentrum *n* (EDV) job shop computer center
Lohnauftrag *m*
(com) farming-out contract
- commission order
Lohnaufträge *mpl* **vergeben** (com) to farm out work to sub-contractors
Lohnausfall *m* (Pw) loss of pay
Lohnausgleich *m* (Pw) pay compensation *(ie, reduction of weekly working hours to 40 or less without pay cuts)*
Lohnbeihilfe *f* (AuW) employment subsidy
Lohnbeleg *m* (Re) pay slip, § 134 II GewO
Lohnbezieher *m* (Pw) = *Lohnempfänger*
Lohnbuchführung *f* (ReW) payroll *(or* wage) accounting
Lohnbuchhalter *m* (Pw) payroll clerk
Lohnbuchhaltung *f* (ReW) payroll department
Lohnbüro *n*
(ReW) pay *(or* payroll) office
- payroll bureau
Lohndrift *f* (Vw) earnings *(or* wage) drift
Lohndruckinflation *f* (Vw) wage-push inflation
Löhne *mpl* **für Ausfallstunden und Ausbildung** (Pw) wages paid for hours not worked and for training
Lohneinzelkosten *pl* (KoR) direct labor (cost)
Löhne *mpl* **künstlich niedrig halten** (Vw) to keep wages artificially low
Lohnempfänger *m* (Pw) wage earner *(or* recipient)
Lohnerhöhung *f*
(Pw) wage increase
- pay rise
- (US) pay raise
- (US) wage hike
Lohnerhöhungsspielraum *m* (Vw) margin available for wage increases

Löhne *mpl* **und Gehälter** *npl* (Pw) wages and salaries
Löhne *mpl* **während der Abwesenheit** (ReW) wages paid during absence from work
Lohnexplosion *f* (Vw) wage explosion
Lohnfonds *m* (Vw) wage(s) fund
Lohnfondstheorie *f* (Vw) wage(s) fund theory
Lohnforderungen *fpl*
(Pw) wage demands
- demands for higher wages
Lohnformen *fpl*
(Pw) payments system *(syn, Entlohnungsverfahren)*
Lohnfortzahlung *f* (Pw) continued pay *(ie, in case of sickness, generally for six weeks)*
Lohnfortzahlungsgesetz *n* (Re) Continuation of Wage Payments Law, of 27 July 1969, as amended
Lohngefälle *n*
(Pw) earnings gap
- pay differential
Lohngefüge *n* (Pw) wage structure
Lohngemeinkosten *pl* (KoR) payroll overhead
Lohngruppe *f* (Pw) wage bracket
Lohngruppenkatalog *m* (Pw) wage bracket catalog
Lohngruppenverfahren *n* (IndE) job classification method
Lohnhöhe *f* (Pw) wage level
Lohnindexbindung *f* (Vw) wage indexation
lohninduzierte Arbeitslosigkeit *f* (Vw) wage-induced unemployment *(syn, stabilisierte Arbeitslosigkeit)*
lohninduzierte Inflation *f* (Vw) wage-induced inflation
Lohninflation *f* (Pw) wage cost inflation
Lohnintensität *f* (Pw) payload ratio *(ie, proportion of wages to costs)*
lohnintensiv (Bw) wage *(or* manpower) intensive
Lohnjournal *n* (ReW) = *Lohnliste*
Lohnkarte *f* (ReW) payroll card
Lohnklasse *f* (Pw) wage group
Lohnkonto *n* (ReW) payroll account *(ie, to be kept for every employee, § 41 I EStG, § 7 LStDV)*
Lohnkosten *pl*
(KoR) labor costs
- payload
- costs incurred in wages
lohnkosteninduzierte Inflation *f* (Vw) cost-induced inflation
Lohnkosten *pl* **je Ausbringungseinheit** (Vw) labor cost per unit of output
Lohnkosten *pl* **je Produkteinheit** (KoR) unit labor cost
Lohnkurve *f* (Pw) wage curve
Lohnkürzungen *fpl* **hinnehmen** (Pw) to take pay cuts
Lohnleitlinien *fpl* (Vw) wage guidelines
Lohnliste *f*
(ReW) payroll register
- (GB) wages sheet
Lohnnachschlag *m* (Pw) supplementary wage rise *(eg, to compensate for effects of oil price increases)*
Lohnnachzahlung *f* (Pw) back pay

Lohnnebenkosten *pl*
(KoR) incidental wage costs
– associated employer outlay
– nonwage labor costs
Lohnnebenleistungen *fpl* (Pw) ancillary pay
Lohnniveau *n* (Vw) wage level
Lohnpause *f*
(Pw) pay pause
– temporary wage freeze
Lohn *m* **pfänden** (Re) to attach (wages) by garnishment
Lohnpfändung *f* (Re) attachment (*or* garnishment) of wages, §§ 850-850k ZPO
Lohnpfändungstabelle *f* (Re) permissible wage garnishment scale
Lohnpolitik *f* (Vw) pay (*or* wages) policy
Lohnprämie *f* (Pw) earmarked wage bonus *(ie, on quality, economizing, accident prevention, etc.)*
Lohn-Preis-Spirale *f* (Vw) wage-price spiral
Lohn-Preis-Struktur *f* (Vw) wage-price structure
Lohnquote *f* (Vw) labor's share in national income *(ie, ratio of total wage bill to national income or of average real wage rate to labor productivity)*
Lohnrückstände *mpl* (Pw) wage arrears
Lohnrunde *f*
(Pw) pay round
– wage(s) round
– round of pay bargaining
Lohnrunde *f* **einläuten** (Pw, infml) to kick off a wage round
Lohnsatz *m*
(Vw) wage rate
(Pw) rate of pay
Lohnsatzabweichung *f* (KoR) rate variance
Lohnsatzmischungsabweichung *f* (KoR) labor mix variance
Lohnsatzvorgabe *f* (KoR) labor rate standard
Lohnschein *m* (IndE) piecework slip *(syn, Lohnzettel, Akkordzettel)*
Lohnskala *f* (Pw) wage scale
Lohnspanne *f* (Vw) wage spread
Lohnstatistik *f* (Stat) wage statistics
Lohnsteuer *f*
(StR) wage(s) tax
– income tax on wages and salaries
Lohnsteuerabzug *m* (ReW) wage tax withholding
Lohnsteueranmeldung *f* (StR) wage debt return, § 41a EStG
Lohnsteueraußenprüfung *f* (StR) external wage tax audit
Lohnsteuerbescheinigung *f* (StR) certificate of wage-tax deduction
Lohnsteuer-Durchführungsverordnung *f* (StR) Wage Tax Ordinance
Lohnsteuer-Ermäßigungsverfahren *n* (StR) wage tax reduction method *(ie, tax-free amount is entered on wage tax card)*
Lohnsteuerfreibetrag *m* (StR) wage earners' tax allowance
Lohnsteuerjahresausgleich *m* (StR) annual wage tax recomputation
(ie, if not employed on a regular basis, taxpayers get back most or all of their income tax withheld by their employers if they file an application to their local tax office, §§ 42–42b EStG)

Lohnsteuerjahresausgleich-Bescheid *m* (StR) annual recomputation of wage tax decision
Lohnsteuerkarte *f* (StR) wage tax card
Lohnsteuerpflicht *f* (StR) wage tax liability
lohnsteuerpflichtig
(StR) subject to wage tax
– liable in wage tax
lohnsteuerpflichtige Beschäftigung *f* (StR) employment subject to wage tax
lohnsteuerpflichtige Einkünfte *pl* (StR) earnings subject to wage tax
Lohnsteuerprüfung *f* (StR) = *Lohnsteueraußenprüfung*
Lohnsteuerquote *f* (StR) wage tax ratio *(ie, wage tax revenue to gross wage/salary income)*
Lohnsteuer-Richtlinien *fpl* (StR) Wage Tax Regulations
Lohnsteuerrückvergütung *f* (StR) wage tax refund
Lohnsteuertabellen *fpl* (StR) wage tax withholding tables
Lohnstopp *m*
(Pw) wage control (*or* freeze)
– (GB) wage restraint
Lohnstreifen *m* (Pw) pay slip
Lohnstruktur *f*
(Pw) pay (*or* wage) structure
– pay pattern
Lohnstückkosten *pl* (KoR) unit (*or* unitized) labor cost
Lohnstundensatz *m*
(Pw) hourly wage rate
(KoR) direct labor hour rate
Lohnsumme *f*
(Pw) payroll
– total payroll
– wage bill
(ie, sum total of wages and salaries paid)
Lohnsummensteuer *f*
(StR) municipal tax on total wages paid
– municipal payroll tax *(ie, abolished in 1979)*
Lohnsystem *n*
(Pw) payments system
– worker's compensation system
Lohntheorie *f* (Vw) wage theory
Lohntüte *f*
(Pw) pay envelope
– (GB) pay packet
Lohn- und Gehaltsabrechnung *f* (ReW) payroll accounting
Lohn- und Gehaltseinzelkosten *pl* (KoR) direct wages and salaries
Lohn- und Gehaltskonten *npl* (Fin) wage and salary accounts
(ie, kept by banks and receiving cashless payments by employers)
Lohn- und Gehaltskürzungen *fpl* (Pw) pay cuts
Lohn- und Gehaltspolitik *f* (Pw) compensation policy
Lohn- und Gehaltsverbindlichkeiten *fpl* (ReW) wages and salaries accrued
Lohn- und Gehaltsvorschüsse *mpl* (ReW) wage and salary advances
Lohn- und Preisleitlinien *fpl* (Vw) wage and price guidelines
Lohnunterschiede *mpl* (Pw) pay differentials

Lohnveredelung f
(AuW) commission processing
– contract processing
– job processing
(StR) conversion, processing, or improvement of property, § 7 UStG
Lohnveredelungsverkehr m (com) commission processing transactions
Lohnvereinbarung f (Pw) = Lohnabschluß
Lohnverhandlungen fpl
(Pw) pay negotiations
– wage bargaining (or negotiations)
Lohnverrechnungskonto n (ReW) payroll transitory account
Lohnvorschuß m
(Pw) advance wage
– advance against (or on) wages
– pay advance
Lohnzugeständnisse npl (Pw) wage concessions
Lohnzulage f
(Pw) premium pay
– bonus
Lohnzuschlag m (Pw) premium pay (or payment) (ie, for overtime, etc.)
lokale Werte mpl (Bö) securities traded on regional stock exchanges
Lokalisationsparameter m
(Stat) measure of central tendency
– parameter of location
Lokalmarkt m (Bö) local stocks
Lokalpapier n (Bö) security traded on local exchange only
Lokalverarbeitung f (EDV) home loop operation
Lokogeschäft n (Bö) spot transaction (or bargain) (ie, made on commodity exchanges)
Lokohandel m (Bö) spot trading
Loko-Kauf m (Bö) spot purchase
Loko-Kurs m (Bö) spot price
Loko-Markt m (Bö) spot market
Loko-Preis m (Bö) spot price
loko verkaufen (com) to sell for spot delivery
Loko-Ware f (Bö) spot commodity
Lokowaren fpl (Bö) spots
Lombardbestand m (Fin) collateral holdings
Lombarddarlehen n (Fin) collateralized loan
Lombardeffekten pl (Fin) pledged securities (syn, Pfandeffekten)
lombardfähige Wertpapiere npl (Fin) securities eligible as collateral for borrowings from Deutsche Bundesbank
Lombardfenster n (Fin) Lombard facility (or window)
Lombardforderungen fpl (Fin) Lombard loans
Lombardgeschäfte npl (Fin) advances on securities
lombardieren (Fin) to accept collateral for a loan
lombardierte Wertpapiere npl
(Fin) collateral securities
– securities pledged as security for a loan
Lombardierung f (Fin) borrowing from the central bank against securities
Lombardkredit m
(Vw) Lombard loan
– central-bank advance against security
(Fin) collateral loan
– advance against security

Lombardlinien fpl (Fin) ceilings on lombard credit
Lombardsatz m (Fin) Lombard rate (ie, the rate at which the Bundesbank provides overnight liquidity to the banking system)
Lombardverzeichnis n (Fin) Lombard list (ie, list of securities eligible as collateral against central-bank advances, kept by the Deutsche Bundesbank)
Lombardwechsel m (Fin) collateralized bill (or note)
Lombardzinssatz m (Vw) lombard lending rate
Londoner Finanzwechsel m (Fin) international trade bill
Londoner Interbanken-Angebotssatz m (Fin) LIBOR rate
Londoner Metallbörse f (Bö) London Metal Exchange
Londoner Parität f (AuW) London equivalent (ie, in foreign exchange quotations)
Lorenzkurven fpl (Stat) Lorenz curves
Loroeffekten pl (Fin) securities held by one bank for the account of another bank
Loroguthaben n (Fin) credit balance on loro account
Lorokonto n (Fin) loro account (ie, current account of another bank)
Los n
(MaW) lot
(IndE) lot
– batch
(syn, Auflage, Partie, Serie)
Losanleihe f (Fin) lottery loan
löschbarer Speicher m (EDV) erasable storage
löschbares PROM n (EDV) erasable-programmable-read-only memory
Löschbescheinigung f (com) landing certificate
Löschdatum n (EDV) purge date
löschen
(com) to discharge goods (or cargo)
– to unload
(Re) to cancel
– to delete
(EDV) to erase
– to destroy
löschendes Lesen n
(EDV) destructive read(ing)
– destructive readout
Löschhafen m (com) port of discharge (or delivery)
Löschkopf m (EDV) erase head
Löschkosten pl (com) unloading charges
Löschplatz m
(com) place of discharge
– unloading berth
Löschung f e–r **Eintragung** (Re) cancellation of an entry
Löschung f e–r **Hypothek** (Re) extinction of a mortgage in the land register
Löschung f e–r **Ladung**
(com) discharge of cargo
– unloading
Löschung f e–s **Warenzeichens** (Pat) cancellation of a trademark
Löschungskosten pl (com) landing charges
Löschzeichen n
(EDV) delete

- erase
- ignore
- rub-out . . . character

Loseblattausgabe *f* (com) loose-leaf edition
Loseblattbuchführung *f* (ReW) loose-leaf system of bookkeeping
Loseblattsystem *n* (com, ReW) loose-leaf system
lose Zusammenschlüsse *mpl* (Kart) loose combinations
Losgröße *f*
  (Stat) lot size
  (IndE) batch size *(syn, Seriengröße)*
Losgrößenbestimmung *f* (Bw) lot-size calculation
Losung *f* (com, *obsolete*) daily cash receipts *(ie, in retailing)*
Lösungsansatz *m* (com) approach to problem-solving
Lösungsmenge *f*
  (Math) set of solutions
  - solution set
Lösungsraum *m* (Math) solution space
losweise Prüfung *f* (Stat) lot-by-lot inspection
Lotsengeld *n* (com) pilotage fee
Lotterieanleihe *f* (Fin) = *Losanleihe*
Lotterieauswahl *f* (Stat) lottery sampling
Lotterieeinnehmer *m* (com) lottery collector
Lotteriemethode *f* (OR) wagering technique *(Neumann-Morgenstern)*
Lotteriesteuer *f* (StR) tax on lotteries
Lotteriestichprobe *f* (Stat) lottery sample
LRC-Prüfzeichen *n* (EDV) longitudinal redundancy check character
Lücke *f* **in der Gesamtnachfrage** (Vw) aggregate deficiency in demand
Lückenbüßer *m* (com) stopgap *(eg, act as a stopgap, stopgap arrangement)*
Lückenbüßertheorem *n* (Vw) stop-gap theorem *(ie, discussed in connection with problems of ‚Gemeinwirtschaft')*
lückenlose Prüfung *f* (ReW) detail test
lückenlose Prüfung *f* **e–r Beleggruppe** (ReW) block vouching test
Lücke *f* **schließen** (com) to plug a gap
„Luft" *f* (com) water *(eg, some water in the mill order books)*
Luftpreßfracht *f* (com) air express
Luftpreßtarif *m* (com) air express tariff
Luftfahrtindustrie *f* (com) airline industry
Luftfahrtversicherung *f* (Vers) aviation insurance *(ie, general term covering accident, cargo, liability risks)*
Luftfahrtwerte *mpl* (Bö) aircrafts
Luftfracht *f* (com) air cargo (*or* freight)
Luftfrachtbrief *m*
  (com) air waybill
  - airbill
  - (GB) air consignment note
Luftfrachtbüro *n* (com) cargo office
Luftfrachtführer *m* (com) air carrier

- air freight forwarder

Luftfrachtgeschäft *n* (com) airfreight forwarding
Luftfrachtkosten *pl* (com) air freight charges
Luftfrachtraum *m* (com) air freight space
Luftfrachtsendung *f* (com) air cargo shipment
Luftfrachtspedition *f* (com) air freight forwarding
Luftfrachttarif *m* (com) air cargo rate
Luftfrachtverkehr *m* (com) air freight service
Luftgüterversicherung *f* (Vers) air cargo insurance
Lufthansa *f* (com) LH German Airways
Luft *f* **herauslassen** (com, infml) to knock the stuffing out of *(eg, assets traded, such as stocks, bonds, commodities)*
Luftkaskoversicherung *f* (Vers) hull coverage - aviation insurance policy *(ie, coverage against loss to an aircraft or its machinery or equipment)*
Luftpost *f* (com) airmail
Luftpostbeförderung *f* (com) carriage of airmail
Luftpostbrief *m* (com) airmail(ed) letter
Luftpostdienst *m* (com) airmail service
Luftpostleichtbrief *m*
  (com) air letter
  - aerogramme
Luftpostpaket *n* (com) air parcel
Luftposttarif *m* (com) airmail rate
Luftpostzuschlag *m* (com) air surcharge
Lufttaxi *n* (com) air taxi
Lufttransportspediteur *m* (com) air carrier
Luftunfallversicherung *f* (Vers) air travel insurance
Luftverkehr *m* (com) air transport
Luftverkehrsgesellschaft *f* (com) airline
Luftversicherung *f* (Vers) air-risk insurance
Luftverunreinigung *f* (com) air pollution
lukratives Geschäft *n* (com) high-margin business
Lumpensammler *m*
  (com, infml) junkman
  - (GB) rag-and-bone man
lustlos
  (Bö) dull
  - flat
  - inactive
  - listless
  - sluggish
  - stale
lustlose Börse *f* = *lustloser Markt*
lustloser Markt *m*
  (Bö) dull
  - flat
  - inactive . . . market
Luxusartikel *m*
  (Mk) fancy (*or* luxury) article
Luxusgüter *npl*
  (Vw) luxury goods
  - luxuries
  - prestige goods
Luxussteuer *f* (FiW) luxury tax
  - sumptuary excise
  (ie, imposed on items which are not necessaries; eg, liquor, tobacco products)
Luxusware *f* (com) highest (*or* quality) goods

M

Macht *f* **durch Legitimation** (Bw) legitimate power *(ie, in leadership behavior)*
Macht *f* **durch Persönlichkeitswirkung** (Bw) referent power *(ie, in leadership behavior)*
Macht *f* **durch Wissen und Fähigkeiten** (Bw) expert power *(ie, in leadership behavior)*
Macht *f* **durch Zwang** (Bw) coercive power *(ie, in leadership behavior)*
Mächtigkeit *f* **der Mengen der natürlichen Zahlen** (Math) aleph-null (*or* aleph-zero)
Mächtigkeit *f* **e–r Menge** (Math) cardinality
– power (*or* potency)
– manyness
– cardinal number ... of a given set
Mächtigkeitszahl *f* **e–r Menge** (Math) cardinal number of a set
mächtigster biasfreier Test *m* (Stat) most powerful unbiased test
Machtmißbrauch *m* (Re) abuse of discretionary power
Machtpolitik *f* **der Gewerkschaften** (Pw) union power politics
Machttheorie *f* (Vw) theory of economic power
Machtverteilung *f* (Vw) distribution of power
Mafo-Daten *pl* (Mk) = *Marktforschungsdaten*
Magazin *n*
(MaW, *obsolete*) = *Lager*
(EDV) magazine
Magazinbuchhaltung *f* (MaW) = *Lagerbuchhaltung*
magisches Dreieck *n* (Vw) uneasy triangle (of economic policy)
(ie, refers to three policy objectives which cannot be achieved simultaneously: (1) full employment, (2) stable prices, and (3) external balance; the original British concept stresses free collective collective bargaining instead of external equilibrium)
magisches Sechseck *n* (Vw) uneasy hexagon (*or* polygon of six sides)
(ie, reference to the six-cornered incompatibility between economic policy objectives: (1) full employment, (2) stable price level, (3) external equilibrium, (4) sustained growth, (5) reasonably balanced sizes of private and public sectors of the economy, and (6) equitable distribution of incomes and wealth; neither theoretically nor in practice is it possible to have all six at the same time)
magisches Vieleck *n* (Vw) uneasy polygon (of economic policy)
(ie, reference to a set of policy objectives which are in part mutually exclusive; eg, full employment at the expense of a higher rate of inflation)
magisches Viereck *n* (Vw) uneasy quadrangle (of economic policy)
(ie, set of four incompatible policy objectives: (1) full employment, (2) stable prices, (3) steady growth, and (4) external equilibrium; see ‚German Stabilization Law', StabG, § 1)
Magnetband *n* (EDV) magnetic tape
Magnetbandabzug *m*
(EDV) magnetic tape dump
– tape edit
Magnetbandarchiv *n* (EDV) magnetic tape library
Magnetbandarchivnummer *f* (EDV) tape serial number, TSN
Magnetbandaufzeichnung *f* (EDV) tape recording
Magnetbandauszug *m* (EDV) selective tape dump
Magnetbandbefehle *mpl* (EDV) magnetic tape instructions (*or* commands)
Magnetbandbibliothek *f* (EDV) magnetic tape library
Magnetbandbibliothekssystem *n*
(EDV) online tape library, OLTL
– tape library system
Magnetbandblock *m* (EDV) magnetic tape block
Magnetbandcode *m* (EDV) magnetic tape code
Magnetbanddatei *f* (EDV) magnetic tape file
Magnetbandeinheit *f* (EDV) magnetic tape unit (*or* deck)
Magnetbandetikett *n* (EDV) tape label
Magnetbandfehler *m* (EDV) magnetic tape error *(ie, may be Signalausfall = drop out, or Störsignal = drop in)*
Magnetbandgerät *n* (EDV) magnetic tape unit (*or* deck *or* station)
Magnetbandkassette *f* (EDV) tape cassette
Magnetbandlaufwerk *n*
(EDV) magnetic tape drive
– tape transport
Magnetbandprüfung *f* (EDV) magnetic tape check
Magnetbandsicherungssystem *n* (EDV) tape protection system
Magnetband-Sortierprogramm *n* (EDV) tape sort
Magnetbandspeicher *m* (EDV) magnetic tape storage
Magnetbandsteuerung *f* (EDV) magnetic tape controller
Magnetblasen *fpl* (EDV) bubbles *(syn, Magnetdomänen, Bubbles)*
Magnetblasenspeicher *m* (EDV) bubble memory *(syn, Magnetdomänenspeicher, Domänentransportspeicher)*
Magnetdomänen *fpl* (EDV) bubbles *(syn, Magnetblasen, Bubbles)*
Magnetdomänenspeicher *m* (EDV) bubble memory *(syn, Magnetblasenspeicher, Domänentransportspeicher)*
Magnetdrahtspeicher *m* (EDV) plated-wire memory
Magnetfilmspeicher *m* (EDV) thin-film memory
magnetische Abtastung *f* (EDV) magnetic reading *(opp, elektrische und optische Abtastung)*
magnetische Aufzeichnung *f* (EDV) magnetic recording
magnetischer Speicher *m* (EDV) magnetic storage

402

magnetisches Speicherelement n (EDV) magnetic cell
magnetisierbare Tinte f (EDV) magnetized (or magnetic) ink
Magnetkarte f (EDV) magnetic card
Magnetkartenmagazin n (EDV) magnetic card magazine
Magnetkartenspeicher m (EDV) magnetic card storage
Magnetkartenspeicherdatei f (EDV) magnetic card file
Magnetkern m (EDV) magnetic core
Magnetkernspeicher m (EDV) magnetic core memory
Magnetkonten-Automat m (EDV) magnetic ledger card computer
Magnetkontokarte f (EDV) magnetic account card
Magnetkopf m
(EDV) magnetic head
– read/write head
Magnetplatte f (EDV) magnetic disk
Magnetplattendatei f (EDV) disk file
Magnetplattenkassette f (EDV) magnetic disk cartridge (or pack)
– disk cartridge
Magnetplattenspeicher m (EDV) magnetic disk storage
(subterms: Festplattenspeicher + Wechselplattenspeicher)
Magnetplattenstapel m (EDV) magnetic disk pack (syn, Plattenturm, Plattensatz)
Magnetscheibe f (EDV) magnetic disk
Magnetscheibenspeicher m (EDV) magnetic disk storage
Magnetschichtdatenträger m (EDV) (data) volume
Magnetschichtspeicher m (EDV) magnetic layer storage
Magnetschrift f (EDV) magnetic ink font
Magnetschriftbeleg m (EDV) magnetic ink document
Magnetschriftleser m (EDV) magnetic ink character reader, MICR
Magnetschriftzeichenerkennung f (EDV) magnetic ink character recognition, MICR
Magnetspeicher m (EDV) magnetic storage (or memory or store)
Magnetspur f (EDV) magnetic track
Magnetstreifen m (EDV) data cell
Magnetstreifenspeicher m (EDV) magnetic strip
Magnettinte f (EDV) magnetic ink
Magnettrommel f (EDV) magnetic drum
Magnettrommelspeicher m (EDV) magnetic drum storage
Mahnbescheid m (Re) summory court notice to pay a debt, §§ 688–703 d ZPO
mahnen (com) to dun (ie, demand payment of a debt)
Mahngebühr f (com) dunning charge
Mahnschreiben n
(com) letter of reminder
– dunning letter
(ie, pressing for payment of a debt)
Mahnung f (com) dunning notice
Mahnung f **vor Fälligkeit der neuen Prämie** (Vers) renewal notice

Majorante f
(Math) dominant
– majorant
majorisieren (Math) to dominate
Majoritätsbeteiligung f (Fin) = Mehrheitsbeteiligung
Majoritätskäufe mpl (Bö) stock purchases designed to acquire a majority stake
Makler m (com) broker, § 652 BGB and §§ 93–104 HGB
Maklerbuch n (Bö) broker's journal (ie, registering all buy and sell orders and security prices)
Maklercourtage f
(com) broker's commission
– brokerage
Maklerfirma f
(com) brokerage firm
– (GB) broking firm
Maklergebühr f
(com) brokerage
– brokerage commission
– broker's commission
Maklergeschäft n
(com) brokerage business
(com) brokerage
– brokerage operation
Maklerkammer f (Bö) brokers' association (ie, now ‚Kursmaklerkammer')
Maklerordnung f (Bö) brokers' code of conduct
Maklerprovision f (com) broker's commission
Maklervertrag m (com) brokerage contract
Makro-Assembler m (EDV) macro assembler
Makroaufruf m (EDV) macro call
Makrobefehl m
(EDV) macro
– macro instruction (or code)
Makrobibliothek f (EDV) macro library
Makrocodierung f (EDV) macro coding
makrodynamische Analyse f
(Vw) macrodynamics
– microdynamic analysis
Makroerklärung f (EDV) macro definition
Makroinstruktion f (EDV) macro instruction
Makroökonomie f (od **Makroökonomik** f)
(Vw) macroeconomics
– macroeconomic analysis
– economics of aggregates
makroökonomisch (Vw) macroeconomic
makroökonomische Größen fpl (Vw) economic aggregates
makroökonomischer Kapitalkoeffizient m (Vw) gross incremental capital-output ratio
makroökonomisches Modell n (Vw) macroeconomic (or aggregative) model
makroökonomische Theorie f
(Vw) macroeconomic theory
– macroeconomics
– aggregative theory
Makroprogrammierung f
(EDV) macro programming
– programming-in-the-large
Makrosprache f (EDV) macro language
Makrotheorie f (Vw) macroeconomic (or aggregative) theory
Makroumwandlung f (EDV) macro expansion

Malrabatt *m* (Mk) rebate granted for repeat advertising *(syn, Wiederholungsrabatt)*
Malus *m* (Vers) extra premium *(ie, extra amount added to the basic premium on account of bad risk experience)*
Mammutfusion *f*
 (Fin) giant merger
 – (US) megabuck merger
Mammutgesellschaft *f* (Bw) mammoth *(or* giant*)* company
Management-Ausbildung *f* (Bw) management education
Managementberatung *f* (Bw) management consulting
Management-Informationsystem *n* (Bw) management information system
 (syn, computergestütztes Informationssystem, integriertes Management-Informations- und Kontrollsystem)
Management-Karussell *n*
 (com, infml) management turntable
 – management carousel
 – (GB) management roundabout
Managementprozeß *m* (Bw) management process
Management-Schwelle *f* (Pw) management threshold *(ie, phase marking transition on career ladder from specialist to generalist function)*
Management-Unternehmen *n* (Bw) management company
Manager-Krankheit *f* (Bw) manager sickness *(ie, physical wear and tear of high achievers; chief symptoms are heart trouble and circulatory failure)*
Mandant *m* (Re) client
Manganknollen *pl* (com) manganese *(or* deep-sea*)* nodules
Mangel *m*
 (Re) physical defect
 (Re) deficiency in title
Mängelanzeige *f* (com) notice of defects, § 478 BGB
Mangel *m* **beheben**
 (com) to remedy *(or* rectify*)* a defect
 (Re) to remedy a deficiency
Mängelbeseitigung *f* (Re) correction of faults
Mängeleinrede *f* (Re) defense based on warranty for defects
Mangel *m* **feststellen** (com) to discover a defect
Mängelgewähr *f* (Re) warranty for defects
mangelhafte Erfüllung *f* (Re) defective performance
mangelhafte Lieferung *f* (com) defective delivery
mangelhaftes Patent *n* (Pat) defective patent
mangelhafte Verpackung *f* (com) defective packing
Mängelhaftung *f*
 (com) warranty
 (Re) liability for defects, § 478 BGB
Mangel *m* **im Recht** (Re) defect in title
mangelnde Erfindungshöhe *f* (Pat) lack of inventiveness
mangelnde Neuheit *f* (Pat) want of novelty
mangelnde Patentfähigkeit *f* (Pat) lack of patentability
mangelnde Vertragserfüllung *f* (Re) defective performance

Mängelrüge *f*
 (com) customer's complaint, § 377 HGB
 – notice of defects
 – letter of complaint
Mängelrüge *f* **geltend machen** (com) to make *(or* lodge*)* a complaint
mangels
 (Re) in the absence of
 – unless otherwise ...
 (Examples:
 – *in the absence of specific provision to the contrary*
 – *in the absence of express agreement*
 – *unless the agreement specifically provides otherwise*
 – *in default of a contrary provision in the agreement)*
mangels Annahme (WeR) for lack of acceptance
mangels ausdrücklicher Vereinbarung
 (Re) in the absence of any express agreement
 – if the parties fail to make express arrangements
mangels gegenteiliger Vereinbarungen
 (Re) in the absence of stipulations to the contrary
 – unless otherwise agreed upon
mangels Masse (Re) for insufficiency of assets
mangels Zahlung (WeR) in default of payment
Mangelware *f*
 (com) goods in short supply
 – scarce articles
Manipulation *f* (Mk) handling of merchandise to suit it to consumer tastes and preferences *(ie, sorting, cleaning, mixing, repacking, or processing)*
manipulieren
 (com) to manage
 (Bö) to rig the market
manipulierte Währung *f* (Vw) managed currency
Manko *n* (Fin) cash shorts
Mankogeld *n* (com) cashier's allowance for shortages
Mannmonate *mpl* (com) man months
Mantel *m*
 (Fin) share certificate *(opp, coupons)*
 (Re) corporate shell *(ie, without significant assets or active business operations of its own)*
Mantelabtretungsvertrag *m* (Re) blanket assignment
Mantelform *f* **e–r Funktion** (Math) portmanteau formula
Mantelgründung *f* (Re) formation of a shell company *(ie, either as AG or GmbH, with no intention of carrying on business, regarded as violating § 134 BGB)*
Mantelkauf *m*
 (Re) purchase of a corporate shell *(or* shell company*)*
Mantelpolice *f* (Vers) global policy
Manteltarif *m* (Pw) industry-wide collective agreement
 (ie, union agreement regulating work week, vacation, and time off)
Mantelvertrag *m* (Re) framework *(or* skeleton*)* agreement

Mantelzession *f* (Re) blanket assignment of receivables *(ie, used esp. to secure bank credits)*
Mantisse *f*
(Math) mantissa *(ie, of logarithm)*
(EDV) coefficient
– fixed point part
– mantissa
manuelle Buchung *f* (ReW) manual posting
manuelle Dateneingabe *f* (EDV) manual input
manuelle Eingabe *f* (EDV) keyboard entry
manuelle Fertigung *f* (IndE) manual (*or* hand) assembly
manueller Betrieb *m* (EDV) manual operation
Marathonläufer *mpl* (Fin) securities running to extremely long maturities
Marathon-Sitzung *f* (com) ,,jumbo" meeting
Marge *f*
(Mk) gross margin
(com) spread
(ie, between buying and selling price, debtor and creditor interest rates, etc.)
(Bö) margin
(ie, cash put up by a client in part payment of stock buying under a forward contract = Termingeschäft; syn, Einschuß)
Marginalanalyse *f* (Vw) marginal analysis (*or* theory)
marginale Ausgabeneigung *f* (Vw) marginal propensity to spend
marginale Böden *mpl* (Vw) marginal soils
marginale Gewinnerzielung *f* (Bö) margin convenience yield *(ie, in the futures market, at spot availability of a commodity)*
marginale Importquote *f* (Vw) marginal propensity to import *(ie, change of imports to infinitesimal change of NNP at market prices)*
marginale interne Ertragsquote *f* (Fin) marginal internal rate of return
marginale Investitionsquote *f* (Vw) marginal propensity to invest
marginale Konsumquote *f* (Vw) marginal propensity to consume, dC/dY
marginale Produktivität *f* **der Investition** (Vw) marginal productivity of investment
marginaler Anbieter *m* (Vw) marginal supplier
marginale Refinanzierungskosten *pl* (Fin) marginal cost of funds
marginaler Kapitalkoeffizient *m* (Vw) marginal capital-output ratio
marginale Sickerquote *f* (Vw) marginal leakage
marginale Sparquote *f* (Vw) marginal propensity to save, dS/dY
Marke *f*
(com) brand
(Pat) trademark
(Pat) proprietary name
Markenabkommen *n* (Pat) trademark convention
Markenakzeptanz *f* (Mk) brand acceptance
Markenanmeldung *f* (Pat) filing a trademark registration
Markenartikel *m*
(com) brand *(eg, the best brand of coffee)*
– branded article (*or* product *or* good)
– (Mk) proprietary article
– trademarked article

Markenartikelwerbung *f* (Mk) brand advertising
Markenbetreuer *m* (Mk) brand manager
Markenbevorzugung *f* (Mk) brand preference
Markenbewußtsein *n* (Mk) brand recognition
Markenbild *n* (Mk) brand image
Markenerzeugnis *n* (Mk) branded article
Markenetikett *n* (Mk) brand label
Markenfamilie *f* (Mk) brand family
markenfreie Produkte *npl* (Mk) no-name products *(ie, unbranded lower-cost items found in supermarkets)*
Markenführer *m* (Mk) brand leader
Markenidentität *f* (Mk) brand identification
Markenimage *n* (Mk) brand image
Markenindex *m* (Mk) brand trend survey
Markenname *m*
(Re) proprietary name (*or*, label)
(Mk) brand name
Markenpolitik *f* (Mk) brand policy
Markenpräferenz *f* (Mk) brand preference
Markenprofil *n* (Mk) brand image
Markenrecht *n*
(Pat) trademark law
(Pat) right in a trademark
– trademark right
(Pat) proprietary right
Markenschutz *m* (Pat) protection of proprietary rights
Markenschutzrecht *n* (Pat) proprietary right
markenspezifischer Wettbewerb *m* (Mk) intra-brand competition
Markentreue *f* (Mk) brand name loyalty
Markenvergleich *m* (Mk) brand comparison
Markenwahl *f* (Mk) brand selection
Markenware *f* (Mk) = *Markenartikel*
Markenwerbung *f* (Mk) brand advertising
Markenwettbewerb *m* (Mk) brand competition
Markenwiedererkennung *f* (Mk) brand recognition
Markenzeichen *n* (Mk) brand figure
Marketing-Abteilung *f* (Mk) marketing department (*or* division)
Marketing-Berater *m* (Mk) marketing consultant
Marketing-Fachmann *m* (Mk) marketing man (*or* specialist)
Marketing-Konzept *n* (Mk) marketing concept
Marketing-Kosten *pl* (ReW) marketing costs
Marketing-Logistik *f* (Mk) marketing logistics
Marketing-Manager *m* (Mk) marketing director (*or* manager)
Marketing-Methoden *fpl* (Mk) marketing techniques
Marketing-Mix *n* (Mk) marketing mix
Marketing-Modell *n* (Mk) marketing model
Marketing-Philosophie *f* (Mk) marketing philosophy
Marketing-Plan *m* (Mk) marketing plan
Marketing-Spezialist *m* (Mk) marketing specialist
Marketing-Strategie *f* (Mk) marketing strategy
Marketing-Ziel *n* (Mk) marketing goal (*or* objective)
Marketing-Zyklus *m* (Mk) marketing cycle *(ie, comprising planning, performance, and control)*
Markierung *f*
(com) marking
– labeling

(EDV) mark
Markierungsbeleg *m* (EDV) mark sheet
Markierungsbelegleser *m* (EDV) mark sheet reader
Markierungslesen *n*
(EDV) optical bar-code reading
— mark reading (*or* sensing *or* scanning)
Markierungsleser *m*
(EDV) optical bar mark reader (*or* scanner)
— mark reader
Markierungslochkarte *f* (EDV) mark sense card
Markierungsverfahren *n* (OR) labeling method *(ie, for getting maximum flow)*
Markierungsvorschriften *fpl* (com) marking (*or* labeling) instructions
Markierungszeichen *npl* (com) shipping marks
Markov-Algorithmus *m* (Stat) Markoff algorithm
Markov-Kette *f* (Stat) Markoff chain
Markov-Prozeß *m* (Stat) Markoff process
Markov-Schätzwert *m* (Stat) Markoff estimate
Markov-Theorem *n* (Stat) Markoff theorem
Markov-Ungleichung *f* (Stat) Markoff inequality
Markt *m*
(com) market
— marketplace
Marktabgrenzungsabkommen *n* (Mk) interpenetration agreement *(eg, French and German companies limit volume of steel exported into one another's home markets)*
Marktabschwächung *f*
(com) sagging market
— weakening of the market
Marktabsprache *f* (Mk) informal marketing agreement
Markt *m* **abtasten** (com) to explore (*or* sound out) a market
Marktanalyse *f* (Mk) market analysis
Marktangebot *n* (com) market offering (*or* supply)
Marktangebotskurve *f* (Vw) market supply curve
Marktanpassung *f* (Vw) market adjustment *(ie, over time)*
Marktanspannung *f* (Mk) tightness of a market
Marktanteil *m*
(Mk) market share
— share of the market
— market coverage
Marktanteil *m* **erobern**
(com) to conquer a share of the market
— (infml) to grab a chunk of the market
Marktanteil *m* **halten** (com) to maintain a share of the market
Marktanteil *m* **zurückerobern** (com) to win back a market share
Markt *m* **aufteilen**
(Kart) to divide up
— to fragment
— to partition ... a market
Marktaufteilung *f*
(Kart) market sharing
— allocation of sales territories *(eg, by a pricing cartel)*
Marktaufteilungsabkommen *n* (Kart) market sharing agreement (*or* pact)
Marktausgleichslager *n* (Vw) buffer stock
Marktaussichten *fpl* (Mk) market outlook

Marktaustrittsschranken *fpl* (Vw) barriers to exit
Marktautomatik *f* (Vw) automatic market adjustment *(ie, matching of supply and demand in the open market)*
Marktbedingungen *fpl*
(Mk) market conditions
— circumstances of the market
Marktbefestigung *f* (Mk) consolidation of a market
Markt *m* **beherrschen**
(com) to lead a market
(Kart) to dominate a market
marktbeherrschende Stellung *f*
(Kart) dominant market position
— market dominant role
marktbeherrschendes Unternehmen *n*
(Kart) dominant firm
— market dominating company (*or* enterprise), § 22 I GWB
Marktbeherrschung *f* (Kart) domination of a market
Marktbeherrschungs-Vermutung *f* (Kart) presumption of market domination
Markt *m* **beobachten** (Mk) to watch (*or* investigate) a market
Marktbeobachter *m* (Fin) market observer
Marktbeobachtung *f*
(Mk) market investigation
— watching the market
Marktberichte *mpl* (Mk) market reports
Marktbeteiligte *mpl* (Kart) participants in the market, § 3 III GWB
Marktbewegungen *fpl* (Mk) movements of a market *(eg, seasonal, cyclical)*
Marktchancen *fpl* (com) marketing (*or* sales) opportunities
Marktdaten *pl* (Mk) market data (*or* information)
marktdeterminierte Preise *mpl* (Vw) flexible prices
Markt-Diversifizierung *f* (Mk) market diversification
Marktdurchdringung *f* (Mk) market penetration
Markt *m* **eindringen, in e–n** (com) to penetrate a market
Markteinfluß *m* (com) influence on the market
Markteinschätzung *f* (Mk) market assessment
Markteintrittsschranken *fpl* (Vw) barriers to entry
Marktelastizität *f* (com) market flexibility
Marktenge *f* (Bö) tightness of a market
Marktentwicklung *f*
(Mk) development of a market
— market trend
Marktergebnis *n* (Vw) market performance
Markterholung *f* (Bö) market recovery
Markt *m* **erkunden** (Mk) to study a market
Markterkundung *f*
(Mk) (occasional) probing of a market
— market reconnaissance
(opp, marketing research)
Markt *m* **erobern** (Mk) to capture a market
Markteroberungsstrategie *f* (Mk) strategy for conquering markets
Markt *m* **erschließen** (com) to tap (*or* open up) a market
Markterschließung *f* (com) opening up (*or* tapping) new markets
Markterwartungen *fpl* (Mk) market anticipations

Markterweiterungs-Zusammenschluß m (Kart) market extension merger
marktfähig
(com) marketable
– salable
marktfähige Papiere npl (Fin) = *marktfähige Wertpapiere*
marktfähiges Erzeugnis n (com) salable product
marktfähige Wertpapiere npl (Fin) marketable securities
Marktfinanzierung f
(Fin) external financing
– outside financing
Marktform f (Vw) market form
Marktformenlehre f (Vw) theory of market forms (ie, as developed by W. Eucken)
Marktforscher m (Mk) market researcher
Marktforschung f (Mk) marketing (or market) research
Marktforschung f **für Investitionsgüter** (Mk) industrial market research
Marktforschungsdaten pl (Mk) market research data
Marktforschungsgesellschaft f (Mk) marketing research company
Marktforschungsinstitut n (Mk) marketing research institute
Marktführer m
(Bw) market leader
(Bö) leading security
Markt m **für Festverzinsliche** (Fin) bond market
Markt m **für Kurzläufer** (Bö) short end of the market
Markt m **für Langläufer** (Bö) long end of the market
Markt m **für Neuemissionen** (Fin) primary market
Markt m **für öffentliche Güter** (Vw) political market
Markt m **für unnotierte Werte** (Bö) unlisted securities market
marktgängig
(com) marketable
– merchantable
marktgängige Größe f (com) commercial size
marktgängige Währung f (AuW) negotiable currency
Marktgebiet n (Mk) marketing area
Marktgefüge n (com) pattern (or structure) of a market
marktgemäße Verzinsung f (Fin) interest in line with market conditions
marktgerechter Preis m (com) fair market price
marktgerechtes Verhalten n (Kart) action in conformity with market trends
marktgerechte Zinsen mpl (Fin) interest rates in line with market conditions
Marktgleichgewicht n (Vw) market equilibrium
Marktgröße f **der eigenen Branche** (Mk) branch potential
Marktklima n (com) market conditions
Marktkonfiguration f (Mk) current condition of a market
marktkonforme Mittel pl (Vw) market-conforming policies
(ie, economic policies that do not unduly interfere with the price mechanism and self-regulating forces of the market; concept developed by German neoliberals)
Marktkonstellation f (Mk) = *Marktkonfiguration*
Marktkonzentration f (Kart) concentration of the market
Marktkräfte fpl
(Vw) forces of the market
– market forces
Marktkurs m (AuW) market exchange rate
Marktlage f (com) market situation (or status)
Marktlagengewinne mpl (Vw) windfall gains (syn, Quasimonopolgewinne, Q-Gewinne)
Marktlohn m (Vw) wage determined by market forces
Marktlücke f
(com) gap in the market
– untapped market
Marktlücken-Analyse f (Mk) gap analysis
Marktlücke f **schließen** (com) to bridge a gap in the market
Marktmacht f (Vw) market power
Marktmechanismus m (Vw) price mechanism
Markt m **mit amtlicher Notierung** (Bö) official market
Markt m **mit stabiler Preisentwicklung** (com) firm market
Markt m **mit starken Schwankungen** (com) jumpy market
Marktnachfrage f (Vw) market demand
Marktnachfragekurve f (Vw) market demand curve
marktnahe (Mk) close to the market
Marktnähe f (Mk) market proximity
Marktnische f (Mk) market niche
Marktnische f **erobern** (Mk) to carve out a market niche
Marktordnung f
(Vw) market regime
– market regulations
Marktordnungsabkommen n (AuW) orderly market agreement
Marktordnungspreise mpl (EG) Common support prices
Marktordnungsstelle f (EG) market regulating agency
Marktorientierung f (Mk) market orientation
Marktpflege f
(Mk) cultivation of a market
(Fin) market support
Marktpflegekäufe mpl (Fin) market regulation purchases
Markt m **pflegen** (Mk) to cultivate a market
Marktphase f (Mk) market phase
Marktpolitik f (Vw) market policy
Marktportefeuille n (Fin) market portfolio
Marktpotential n (Mk) market potential
Marktpreis m
(com) going price
(Vw) market price
(ReW) current price
Marktpreisbildung f (Vw) formation of market prices
Marktpreise mpl (VGR) market prices (ie, factor cost + indirect taxes – subsidies)

Marktpreis-Mechanismus *m* (Vw) price mechanism
Marktproduktion *f* (com) production for the market *(opp, Kundenproduktion, Vorratsproduktion)*
Marktprofil *n* (Mk) market profile
Marktprognose *f* (Mk) market forecast
marktreagibel (com) sensitive to the market
Marktregulierung *f* (com) market regulating arrangements
marktreif
(com) ready for the market
– fully developed
– market ripe
Marktreife *f* (Mk) market maturity *(ie, of a product)*
Marktrichtsatz *m* (Fin) key interest rate *(syn, Leitzins)*
Marktsättigung *f* (Mk) market saturation
Marktschwankungen *fpl* (Mk) market fluctuations *(ie, seasonal and cylical)*
Marktsegment *n* (Mk) market segment
Markt *m* **segmentieren** (Mk) to segment a market
Marktsegmentierung *f* (Mk) market segmentation
Marktsituation *f* (com) market situation
Marktspaltung *f* (Bw) division of a market into several submarkets *(ie, through price differentials, dumping, most-favored-nation clause, etc.)*
Marktstellung *f* (com) market position
Marktstörungen *fpl* (Fin) disturbances of a market
Marktstrategie *f* (Mk) market strategy
Marktstruktur *f* (Mk) market structure
Marktstrukturanalyse *f* (Mk) market structure analysis
Marktstudie *f* (Mk) market study
Marktstützung *f* (com) market support
markttechnische Erholung *f* (Bö) technical rally
markttechnischer Kursrückgang *m* (Bö) technical decline
Marktteilnehmer *m*
(Mk) market participant
(Bö) market operator
Markttendenzen *fpl*
(Mk) market trends
– tendencies of a market
Markttest *m*
(Mk) acceptance test
– market testing
– pretest
– product placement test
Markttransparenz *f* (Vw) transparency of the market *(ie, perfect knowledge of all conditions surrounding the market)*
Marktübersättigung *f* (Mk) market saturation
Markt *m* **überschwemmen** (com) to flood a market *(eg, with high-quality equipment)*
Marktübersicht *f* (Mk) market survey *(or study)*
Marktüberwachung *f* (Fin) market scrutiny *(eg, supported by German banks)*
marktüblicher Zins *m* (Fin) market interest rate *(ie, for first-class capital investments; often equal to the interest rate charged for senior mortgages)*
Marktumfang *m* (Mk) market volume *(or size)*
Marktumschwung *m* (Bö) turnabout of the market

Markt- und Meinungsforschung *f* (Mk) market and opinion research
Markt- und Preisstützung *f* (com) supporting the market
Marktuntersuchung *f* (Mk) market analysis *(or audit)*
Marktverfassung *f* (com) state of the market
Marktverflechtung *f* (Bw) integration *(or interpenetration)* of markets
Marktverhalten *n*
(Vw) market behavior
– market conduct
– market performance
Marktverhältnisse *npl* (com) market conditions
Marktversteifung *f* (com) stiffening of the market
Marktverzerrung *f* (Vw) distortion of a market
Marktvolumen *n*
(Mk) size of the market
– market volume
Marktwende *f* (Bö) = *Marktumschwung*
Marktwert *m*
(com) commercial value
(ReW) current value
– current market value
– market price *(or value) (syn, Tageswert, qv)*
Marktwiderstand *m* (Mk) market resistance
Marktwirtschaft *f* (Vw) market (directed) economy
marktwirtschaftliche Ordnung *f* (Vw) free market system
marktwirtschaftlicher Koordinationsmechanismus *m* (Vw) free-market coordinating mechanism
marktwirtschaftliches Gleichgewicht *n* (Vw) free market equilibrium
Marktzerrüttung *f*
(AuW) market disruption
(Mk) dislocation of markets
Marktzersplitterung *f* (Bö) market fragmentation
Marktzins *m*
(Vw) average market rate of interest
– current interest rate
(ie, prevailing on the money and capital markets of an economy during a given period)
Markt *m* **zurückerobern** (Mk) to reconquer a market
Marktzutritt *m* (Vw) entry into a market
Marktzwänge *mpl* (Mk) market compulsions
marodes Unternehmen *n* (com) moribund company *(or undertaking)*
Maschennetz *n* (EDV) intermeshed network
maschinelle Anlagen *fpl* (ReW) plant and equipment
maschinelle Lagerbuchhaltung *f* (ReW) mechanical storage records
maschinelle Prüfanlagen *fpl* (IndE) mechanical testing facilities
maschinell lesbar (EDV) machine readable
Maschinenadresse *f* (EDV) = *absolute Adresse*
Maschinenaufstellung *f* (IndE) installation of machinery
Maschinenausfall *m* (IndE) machine breakdown *(or failure)*
Maschinenausfallzeit *f* (IndE) machine idle time
Maschinenauslastung *f* (IndE) machine utilization
Maschinenbau *m* (com) mechanical engineering

Maschinenbaugruppe *f* (com) mechanical engineering group
Maschinenbauindustrie *f* (com) mechanical engineering industry
Maschinenbauunternehmen *n* (com) mechanical engineering company
Maschinenbauwerte *mpl* (Bö) engineerings
Maschinenbediener *m*
(IndE) operator
– machine operator
– operative
maschinenbedingte Ausfallzeit *f* (EDV) machine-spoilt processing time
Maschinenbefehl *m* (EDV) computer (*or* machine) instruction
Maschinenbefehlscode *m*
(EDV) machine (*or* computer) instruction code
– machine code
Maschinenbelastung *f* (EDV) machine load
Maschinenbelegung *f* (IndE) machine loading and scheduling
– job shop sequencing
Maschinenbelegungsplan *m* (IndE) job shop schedule
Maschinenbelegungsübersicht *f* (IndE) loading board
Maschinenbesetzungsplan *m* (IndE) = *Maschinenbelegungsplan*
Maschinenbetriebsversicherung *f* (Vers) machinery breakdown insurance
Maschinenbuchführung *f* (ReW) machine accounting
Maschinenbuchhaltung *f* (ReW) = *Maschinenbuchführung*
Maschinencode *m*
(EDV) absolute
– actual
– specific ... code *(syn, Rechnercode)*
Maschinencodierung *f* (EDV) absolute (*or* specific) coding
(syn, maschinen- od anlageninterne Codierung)
Maschinenerneuerungskonto *n* (ReW) machine renewal account
(ie, receives depreciation in excess of the original cost of a machine and is therefore part of taxable income)
Maschinenfehler *m* (EDV) machine error
Maschinengang *m* (EDV) machine cycle
Maschinen-Garantieversicherung *f* (Vers) machine guaranty insurance
maschinengeschriebenes Schriftstück *n*
(com) typewritten document
– typescript
maschineninterne Codierung *f* (EDV) = *Maschinencodierung*
Maschinenkosten *pl* (ReW) cost of plant and machinery
Maschinenkostensatz *m* (KoR) machine overhead rate
Maschinenlauf *m*
(IndE) run
(EDV) machine run
Maschinenlaufzeit *f*
(IndE) machine time
– running time

maschinenlesbar (EDV) machine readable
maschinenlesbarer Datenträger *m* (EDV) machine readable medium
Maschinenlieferant *m* (com) supplier of machinery
Maschinenlochkarte *f* (EDV) machine-operated punched card
maschinennahe Programmiersprache *f* (EDV) machine oriented (*or* low-level) language
Maschinennummer *f* (IndE) machine serial number
Maschinenoperation *f* (EDV) computer (*or* machine) operation
maschinenorientierte Programmiersprache *f* (EDV) computer-oriented (*or* low-level) language
– autocode
maschinenorientierte Sprache *f* (EDV) machine-oriented language
Maschinenprogramm *n* (EDV) machine program
Maschinenprogrammcode *m* (EDV) object code
Maschinenring *m*
(com) „ring" system for sharing machinery
– farm machinery cooperative
(ie, organization for the joint use of farm equipment)
Maschinensprache *f* (EDV) computer (*or* machine) language
Maschinenstillstandszeit *f* (IndE) machine down time
Maschinenstörung *f*
(IndE) machine failure (*or* malfunctioning)
(EDV) machine fault
– hardware failure
Maschinenstundenrechnung *f* (KoR) machine hour accounting
Maschinenstundensatz *m* (KoR) machine hour rate
Maschinenteil *m* (EDV, Cobol) environment division
Maschinenüberwachungszeit *f* (IndE) attention time
maschinenunabhängig (EDV) machine independent
Maschinen und maschinelle Anlagen *pl* (ReW) plant and machinery
maschinenunterstützte Programmierung *f*
(EDV) automatic (*or* machine-aided) programming
– automatic coding
(syn, automatische Programmierung, automatische Codierung)
Maschinenversicherung *f* (Vers) machinery insurance
Maschinenwerte *mpl*
(Bö) mechanical engineering shares
– engineerings
Maschinenwort *n* (EDV) machine (*or* computer) word
Maschinenzeit *f* (EDV) machine (*or* computer) time
Maschinenzyklus *m* (EDV) machine cycle
maschineschreiben (com) to type
Maske *f*
(EDV) mask
– extractor
– filter

(EDV, Cobol) picture
Maskenprogrammierung *f* (EDV) mask programming
Maskenregister *n* (EDV) mask register
maskieren (EDV) to mask
Maskierung *f* (EDV) masking
Maslow'sche Bedürfnishierarchie *f* (Bw) Maslow's hierarchy of needs
Masse *f*
(Re) bankrupt estate
– insolvent assets
Masseansprüche *mpl* (Re) preferred claims, §§ 57–60 KO *(ie, Massekosten + Masseschulden; to be satisfied direct from the bankrupt estate)*
Massebestand *m* (Re) = *Masse*
Masseforderung *f* (Re) claim to bankrupt estate
Massegläubiger *m*
(Re) creditor of bankrupt's estate
– nonprivileged creditor
– ordinary creditor
Massekosten *pl* (Re) cost of bankruptcy
Massenarbeitslosigkeit *f*
(Vw) mass (*or* large-scale) unemployment
– (infml) wholesale unemployment
Massenartikel *m* (com) mass-produced articles
Masseneinkommen *n* (Vw) mass income
Massenentlassungen *fpl* (Pw) mass dismissals
Massenfertigung *f* (IndE) = *Massenproduktion*
Massenfilialbetrieb *m* (Mk) large-scale chain operation
Massenfrachtgut *n* (com) bulk cargo
Massengeschäft *n*
(Mk) bottom lines
– bulk business
(Fin) retail banking
– bulk business
(ie, banking services for everyone)
Massengut *n* (com) bulk commodity
Massengütertransport *m* (com) bulk goods transport
Massengüterverkehr *m* (com) = *Massengütertransport*
Massengutladung *f* (com) bulk cargo
Massengutschiff *n* (com) bulk freighter
Massenherstellung *f* (IndE) mass production
Massenkaufkraft *f* (Vw) mass (*or* households') purchasing power
Massenkommunikationsmittel *npl* (Mk) mass communication media
Massenkonsum *m* (Mk) mass consumption
Massenlieferung *f* (com) bulk consignment
Massenmarkt *m* (Mk) mass market
Massenprodukt *n* (com) mass product
Massenproduktion *f*
(IndE) large-scale production
– mass production
– production in bulk
Massenproduktionsvorteile *mpl* (Bw) economies of scale
Massenspeicher *m* (EDV) mass storage
Massensteuer *f* (FiW) mass tax
Massenstahl *m* (IndE) tonnage steel
Massentourismus *m* (com) mass tourism
Massenverkauf *m* (Mk) mass selling

Massenverkauf *m* **von Wertpapieren** (Fin) large-scale selling (*or* unloading) of equities
Massenverkehrsmittel *npl* (com) mass transportation facilities
Massenverteilung *f* (Re) liquidating distribution
Massenvertrieb *m* (Mk) mass selling
Massenverzeichnis *n* (com) schedule of quantities *(ie, in a tender or building contract)*
Massenwahrscheinlichkeit *f* (Stat) a posteriori probability
Massenwerbung *f* (Mk) mass (*or* large-scale) advertising
Masseschulden *fpl* (Re) debt of the estate
Maße *npl* **und Gewichte** *npl* (com) weights and measures
Masseverwalter *m* (Re) administrator of a bankrupt's estate
Masseverwaltung *f* (Re) administration of bankrupt's estate
Masseverzeichnis *n* (Re) list of assets
Maß *n* **der Glättungsfähigkeit** (Stat) error reducing power
Maß *n* **der Zentraltendenz** (Stat) central tendency *(eg, arithmetic mean, mode, median)*
Maßfracht *f* (com) freighting on measurement
maßgebender Marktanteil *m* (Kart) qualifying market share
maßgebliche Beteiligung *f* (Fin) controlling (*or* substantial) interest
maßgeblicher Hersteller *m* (com) leading producer
maßgeblicher Indikator *m* (Stat) key indicator
Maßgeblichkeit *f* **der Handelsbilanz** (ReW) principle that the commercial accounts should be identical with the tax accounts
maßgeschneidert
(com, EDV) tailor-made
– custom(ized)
maßgeschneidertes Bauteil *n* (EDV) tailor-made component (*or* element)
maßgeschneidertes System *n* (com) tailored system
Maßgröße *f* (Math) quantity
Maßgröße *f* **der Produktion** (KoR) measure of production
Maßhalteappelle *mpl* (Vw) moral suasion
mäßige Umsätze *mpl* (Bö) moderate trading
massive Abgaben *fpl* (Bö) heavy selling
massiver Auftragsrückgang *m* (com) massive (*or* marked) fall in orders
Maßkleidung *f* (com) customized clothes
Maßkosten *pl* (KoR) basic standard cost
Maßnahmebündel *n* (com) package
Maßnahmebündel *n* **der Geld- und Fiskalpolitik** (Vw) fiscal monetary mix
Maßnahmen *fpl* **der Ausgabendämpfung** (FiW) expenditure dampening policies
Maßnahmen *fpl* **der Ausgabenumschichtung** (FiW) expenditure switching policies
Maßnahmen *fpl* **treffen** (com) to take measures
Maßnahmen *fpl* **zur Änderung der relativen Preise** (AuW) switching policy
(ie, measures designed to change the ratio of import prices to domestic prices, and thus improve the balance-of-payments situation)
Maßnahmen *fpl* **zur beruflichen Förderung** (Pw) vocational assistance measures

(ie, vocational training, vocational rehabilitation, and job-creating schemes)
maßvolle Politik *f*
(Vw) moderate policy
– (infml) middle-of-the-road policy
maßvoller Lohnabschluß *m* (Pw) moderate pay settlement
Maßzahl *f* (Stat) statistical parameter
Master-Scheduler *m* (EDV) master (*or* high-level) scheduler
Material *n*
(IndE) materials *(ie, raw materials and supplies, small parts, bought-out standard parts, etc.)*
(Bö) securities
Materialabfall *m*
(IndE) spoilage *(ie, junked and sold for disposal value)*
(IndE) scrap *(ie, measurable but of relatively minor recovery value; eg, shavings, filings, turnings; may be sold or reused)*
(IndE) waste *(ie, no measurable recovery value or lost in the process; eg, dust, smoke)*
Materialabgaben *fpl* (Bö) selling of securities
Materialabgang *m* (MaW) material withdrawal
Materialabrechnung *f* (KoR) materials accounting
Materialanforderung *f*
(IndE) materials requisition
– stores issue order
– stores materials requisition
Materialannahme *f* (MaW) materials receiving
Materialannahmeschein *m* (MaW) receiving slip
Materialannahmestelle *f* (MaW) point of receipt
Materialaufwand *m*
(ReW, EG) raw materials and consumables
(IndE) material input
(KoR) cost of materials
Materialausbeute *f* (IndE) material yield
Materialausgabe *f*
(MaW) issue
– issuance
– issuing . . . of materials
(MaW) materials issue counter
Materialausgang *m* (MaW) materials issue
Materialbedarf *m* (MaW) material requirements
Materialbedarfsermittlung *f* (MaW) = *Materialbedarfsplanung*
Materialbedarfsplanung *f*
(MaW) materials requirements planning, MRP
– requirements planning
(ie, computerized method of production scheduling)
Materialbedarfsrechnung *f* (MaW) assessment of materials requirements
Materialbedarfsvorhersagen *fpl* (MaW) (statistical) forecasting of materials requirements
Materialbegleitkarte *f*
(IndE) shop traveler
– traveler
Material *n* **beistellen** (MaW) to supply (*or* provide) materials
Materialbeistellung *f* (MaW) supply (*or* provision) of materials
Materialbelege *f* (MaW) materials records
Materialbereich *m* (MaW) materials management function (*or* area)

Materialbereitstellungsplan *m* (MaW) supply-of-materials plan
Materialbeschaffenheit *f* (MaW) quality of materials
Materialbeschaffung *f*
(MaW) materials purchasing
– procurement of materials
Materialbeschaffungsplan *m* (MaW) materials purchase budget
Materialbeschaffungspolitik *f* (MaW) materials purchasing policy
Materialbestand *m* (MaW) stock of materials
Materialbestandskarte *f* (MaW) bin card *(syn, Lagerfachkarte)*
Materialbestandskonten *npl* (ReW) material accounts
Materialbestandsrechnung *f* (MaW) materials status evaluation
Materialbestimmungskarte *f* (IndE) order bill of materials
Materialbezüge *mpl* (ReW) intercompany material purchases
Materialbilanz *f* (IndE) materials input-output statement
Materialbuchführung *f* (MaW) = *Lagerbuchführung*
Materialbudget *n* (MaW) materials budget
materiale Implikation *f* (Log) material implication
(ie, ,,If A then B" is true in all cases except when A is true and B is false; opp, strict implication = strikte od strenge Implikation)
Materialeingang *m*
(MaW) receiving materials
– inventory additions
Materialeinkauf *m* (MaW) materials purchasing
Materialeinsatz *m*
(KoR) spending on materials
– materials usage
Materialeinsparung *f*
(MaW) materials saving
– economizing on materials
Materialeinzelkosten *pl*
(KoR) cost of direct material
– direct material
Materialempfangsbescheinigung *f* (MaW) materials receiving report
Materialentnahme *f*
(MaW) materials requisition
– withdrawal of material
Materialentnahmeschein *m* (MaW) materials order
Materialersparnis *f* (IndE) saving of material
materiale Supposition *f*
(Log) material supposition
– mention of a term
(ie, possessed of a term that stands for an expression; opp, formale Supposition)
Materialfehler *m* (MaW) defect in material
Materialfluß *m* (IndE) material flow *(ie, through the various stages of manufacturing)*
Materialflußgestaltung *f* (MaW) materials flow layout
Materialflußkontrolle *f* (MaW) materials flow control
Materialflußkosten *pl* (MaW) cost of materials flow

Materialflußmatrix f (MaW) materials flow matrix
Materialflußoptimierung f
   (MaW) materials flow optimization
   – optimization of materials flow system
Materialflußsystem n (MaW) materials flow system
Materialflußtechnik f (MaW) materials flow methods
Materialgemeinkosten pl
   (KoR) materials handling overhead
   – indirect material
Materialgemeinkostenzuschlag m (KoR) materials overhead rate
Material(hilfs)stellen fpl (KoR) indirect materials center
materialintensive Industrien fpl (Bw) materials intensive industries
Materialkäufe mpl (MaW) materials purchasing
Materialknappheit f (MaW) material shortage
Materialkontrolle f (MaW) testing of materials
Materialkosten pl (KoR) cost of materials *(ie, Summe Einzelkosten für Einzelmaterial + Materialgemeinkosten = direct and indirect materials)*
Materialkostenermittlung f (KoR) materials costing
Materialkostenplan m (KoR) materials used budget
Materialkostenstelle f (KoR) materials cost center
Materiallager n (MaW) store of materials and supplies
Materiallagerung f (MaW) storage of materials and supplies
Materialliste f
   (MaW) materials list
   – takeoff
   (ie, list used primarily for purchasing and costing purposes: the most simple type of bill of materials = Stückliste)
Materialmangel m
   (com) shortage of materials
   (Bö) shortage of securities on offer
   (or of offerings)
Materialmengenabweichung f (KoR) materials quantity variance
Materialmischung f (MaW) materials mix
Materialplanung f (MaW) materials planning
Materialpreis m (KoR) materials price
Materialpreisabweichung f (KoR) materials price variance
Materialprüfung f
   (MaW) inspection of incoming materials
   (Stat) testing of materials
Materialprüfungskosten pl (KoR) expense of materials inspection
Materialqualität f (MaW) quality of materials
Materialrechnung f (MaW) materials accounting
Materialrückgabeschein m (MaW) materials return record
Materialstelle f (KoR) materials cost center
Materialsteuerung f (MaW) materials control
Materialtransport m (MaW) material handling
Materialumarbeitung f (IndE) reprocessing of materials
Material- und Herstellungsfehler mpl (com) defective material and workmanship

Materialverarbeitung f (IndE) processing of materials
Materialverbrauch m (KoR) materials usage
Materialverbrauchsabweichung f (KoR) materials quantity *(or* usage*)* variance
Materialveredelung f (IndE) improvement of materials
Materialverfügbarkeit f (MaW) availability of materials
Materialverkauf m (com) sale of materials
Materialverlust m (com) loss of materials
Materialversorgung f (MaW) supply of materials
Materialverteuerung f (MaW) increased cost of materials
Materialverwaltung f (MaW) inventory *(or* materials*)* management
Materialverwertung f (MaW) utilization of materials
Materialverzeichnis n (MaW) list of materials
Materialwert m (KoR) value of raw materials and supplies
   (ie, based on average purchase price)
Materialwirtschaft f (MaW) materials and logistics management
Materialzugang m (MaW) inventory additions
Materialzuschlag m (KoR) materials overhead rate
materielle abnutzbare Anlagegüter npl (ReW) depreciable fixed *(or* tangible*)* assets *(ie, any capital asset other than intangible)*
materielle Bedürfnisse npl (Vw) material needs
materielle Besserstellung f (Vw) material advancement
materielle Buchführungsmängel mpl (ReW) substantive accounting deficiencies
materielle Güter npl
   (com) physical assets
   – tangible goods
materielle Implikation f (Log) = materiale Implikation
materielle Lebenslage f
   (Vw) economic well-being
   – material condition of life
materielle Prüfung f (Pat) substantive examination, § 28b PatG
materielle Rechtsvorschrift f (Re) substantive rule of law *(eg, this rule is one of substance)*
materieller Mangel m (StR) substantive defect *(or* mistake*)*, Abschn. 29 II No. 6 EStR
materielles Anlagevermögen n (ReW) tangible fixed assets
materielles Patentrecht n (Pat) substantive patent law
materielles Recht n (Re) substantive law
materielles Schadenersatzrecht n (Re) substantive tort law
materielle Vermögenswerte mpl (Bw) tangible assets
materielle Ware f (EDV) hardware
materielle Wirtschaftsgüter npl (Bw) physical assets
materiell-rechtlich (Re) substantive
materiell-rechtliche Bedeutung f (Re) import in substantive law
materiell-rechtliche Vorschriften fpl (Re) substantive provisions

Mathematiker *m* **für Anlagenrechnung** (Bw) actuary
mathematische Erwartung *f* (Stat) mathematical expectation
mathematische Kostenauflösung *f* (KoR) high-low points method
mathematische Programmierung *f* (OR) mathematical programming
mathematischer Erwartungswert *m* (Stat) expectation value
mathematisches Modell *n* (Vw) mathematical model
mathematisches Stichprobenverfahren *n* (Stat) statistical sampling
Matrikularbeiträge *mpl* (FiW) contributions of the states to the German Reich *(ie, discontinued in 1918)*
Matrix *f* (*pl*, **Matrizen**) (Math, EDV) matrix (*pl*, matrices)
  – array
Matrixaddierer *m* (EDV) matrix adder
Matrixbilanz *f* (KoR) articulation statement
Matrixdaten *pl* (Math) matrix data
Matrix *f* **der Schnittmenge** (Math) cut-set matrix
Matrix *f* **der Übergangswahrscheinlichkeit** (OR) transition probability matrix
Matrix *f* **des geschlossenen Kantenzuges** (Math) circuit matrix
Matrixdrucker *m* (EDV) matrix (*or* dot) printer *(syn, Rasterdrucker)*
Matrix-Inversion *f* (Math) matrix inversion
Matrix-Korrelation *f* (Stat) matrix correlation
Matrixmanagement *n* (Bw) = *Matrixorganisation*
Matrixorganisation *f* (Bw) matrix organization
Matrixprinzip *n* (Bw) matrix principle
Matrixspeicher *m* (EDV) coordinate (*or* matrix) store *(syn, Koordinatenspeicher)*
Matrixspiel *n* (OR) rectangular game
Matrixspiele *npl* (Math) matrix games
Matrixstruktur *f* (Bw) matrix structure
Matrixtabelle *f* (Math) matrix table
Matrixvariable *f* (Math) array variable
Matrizenalgebra *f* (Math) algebra of matrices
Matrizengleichung *f* (Math) matrix equation
Matrizeninversion *f* (Math) matrix inversion
Matrizenkarte *f* (EDV) master card
Matrizen-Multiplikator *m* (Vw) matrix multiplier
Matrizenrechnung *f* (Math) matrix calculus
Matrizenschreibweise *f* (Math) matrix notation
Matrizenspalte *f* (Math) matrix column
Matrizenspeicher *m* (EDV) = *Matrixspeicher*
Matrizenzeile *f* (Math) matrix row
maximale Abweichungsspanne *f* (EG) maximum spread of divergence
Maximaleindeckung *f* (MaW) maximum inventory level
maximale Kapazität *f* (Bw) ideal capacity *(ie, of plant and equipment)*
maximale Kapazitätsauslastung *f* (Bw) peak operating rate
maximale Maschinen-Nutzungszeit *f* (IndE) machine maximum time
maximale Pufferzeit *f* (OR) total float
maximaler aufspannender Baum *m* (OR) maximum spanning tree

maximaler Bestand *m* (MaW) maximum inventory
maximaler Griffbereich *m* (IndE) maximum working area
Maximalerlös-Kombination *f* (Bw) maximum-revenue product mix
maximale Schadenersatzleistung *f* (Vers) aggregate indemnity
Maximalkapazität *f* (Bw) theoretical capacity
Maximalzoll *m* (Zo) maximum revenue tariff
Maximax-Regel *f* (Bw) maximax rule
maximieren (Math) to maximize
Maximierung *f* **ohne Nebenbedingung** (Math) unconstrained maximization
Maximierung *f* **unter Nebenbedingungen** (Math) constrained maximization
Maximin-Kriterium *n* (OR) maximin criterion
Maximum-Likelihood-Methode *f* (Stat) maximum likelihood method
Maximum *n* **unter Nebenbedingungen** (Math) constrained maximum
mechanische Abtastung *f* (EDV) mechanical sensing
mechanischer Drucker *m* (EDV) impact printer
Mechanisierung *f* (Bw) mechanization
Mechanismus *m* **der relativen Preise** (Fin) mechanism of relative prices *(ie, in portfolio selection)*
Mechanismus *m* **für den mittelfristigen finanziellen Beistand** (EG) mechanism for medium-term financial assistance
Mechatronik *f* (IndE) mechatronics *(ie, linking mechanics with electronics: application of advanced technologies, computers, microprocessors, and integrated circuits to achieve greater efficiency in the design, production, and operation of machinery)*
Media *npl* (Mk) advertising media
Media-Abteilung *f* (Mk) media department
Media-Auswahl *f* (Mk) advertising media selection
Media-Fachmann *m* (Mk) media specialist
Media-Feldzug *m* (Mk) media campaign
Media-Forschung *f* (Mk) media research
Media-Planer *m* (Mk) media mix planner
Media-Mix-Planung *f* (Mk) media mix planning
Median *m* (Stat) median *(syn, Zentralwert)*
Mediaselektion *f* (Mk) media selection
Media-Zielgruppe *f* (Mk) media target group
Medien *npl* **der Außenwerbung** (Mk) outdoor media
Medienrabatt *m* (Mk) media discount
Medienreichweite *f* (Mk) media reach
Medio-Abrechnung *f* (Fin) mid-month settlement
Medio-Ausweis *m* (Fin) mid-monthly statement
Mediogelder *npl* (Bö) funds or bills repayable at mid-month
Mediogeschäft *n* (Fin) transaction for mid-month settlement
Medioliquidation *f* (Bö) mid-month settlement
Medio-Wechsel *m* (Fin) fortnightly bill
Medium *n* (Mk) medium, *pl.* media
Meeresbergbau *m* (com) deep-sea mining
Meeresboden-Grundsatzerklärung *f* (Re) Declaration of Principles Governing the Sea-Bed and Ocean Floor
Meeresbodenschätze *mpl* (com) marine mineral resources

– mineral resources of the sea bed
Meeresnutzung f (Re) use of the seas
Meeresnutzung f **auf Wettbewerbsbasis** (Vw) competing use of the oceans
Meeresschätze mpl **im Eigentum der Völkergemeinschaft** (Re) common property resources
Meeresuntergrund m (com) subsoil of sea-bed
Mehrabschreibung f (ReW) additional depreciation allowance *(ie, amounts beyond budgeted depreciation allowances)*
Mehradreßbefehl m (EDV) multi-address (*or* multiple) instruction
Mehradreßmaschine f (EDV) multiple address computer
Mehradreßsystem n (EDV) multiple address system
Mehrarbeit f (Pw) additional (*or* extra) work
Mehrarbeitsvergütung f (Pw) extra-work pay
Mehrarbeitszuschlag m (Pw) bonus paid for extra work
Mehraufwand m (com) additional expenditure (*or* outlay)
Mehraufwendungen mpl **für doppelte Haushaltsführung** (StR) additional expenses of maintaining two households
Mehraufwendungen mpl **für Verpflegung** (StR) additional expenses for board
Mehrausgabe f (com) extra expense
Mehrbankensystem n (Vw) system of several banks
Mehrbenutzersystem n (EDV) multi-user system *(ie, mostly time sharing operation)*
Mehrbedarf m (com) additional requirements
Mehrbelastung f (com) additional charge
Mehrbetrag m (com) additional amount
Mehrbietender m (com) outbidder
mehrdeutig
(Log) ambiguous
– equivocal
mehrdeutig determiniertes Gleichgewicht n (Vw) multiple equilibrium
mehrdeutige Bezugnahme f (Log) ambiguous reference
mehrdeutige Funktion f (Math) relation
Mehrdeutigkeit f (Log) ambiguity
(ie, capability of being understood in two or more ways)
mehrdimensionale Analyse f (Stat) multi-variate analysis
mehrdimensionale Inhaltsanalyse f (Mk) multidimensional content analysis
mehrdimensionale polynomische Verteilung f (Stat) multi-variate multi-nominal distribution
mehreindeutige Relation f (Log) many-one correspondence
Mehreinnahmen fpl (com) additional receipts
Mehrerlös m
(com) additional proceeds
(ReW) excess sales revenue *(ie, difference between the admissible and the actual price)*
Mehrerlösabschöpfung f (Kart) elimination of additional revenues
Mehrertrag m (com) extra proceeds
Mehrfachadresse f
(EDV) multi-address
– multiple address

Mehrfachadressierung f (EDV) multi-addressing
Mehrfachadreßnachricht f (EDV) multiple-address message
Mehrfacharbitrage f (AuW) compound (*or* indirect) arbitrage
Mehrfachbandgerät n (EDV) multiple tape unit
Mehrfachbeleg m (ReW) multipart form
Mehrfachbelegung f **des haftenden Eigenkapitals** (Fin) multiple use of liable capital
Mehrfachbeschäftigte mpl (Pw) = *Teilbeschäftigte*
Mehrfachbeschäftigung f (Pw) multiple employment
Mehrfachbesteuerung f
(StR) multiple (*or* recurrent) taxation
– tax overlapping
Mehrfachbetrieb m (EDV) multi-job operation
Mehrfach-Beurteilung f (Pw) multiple rating
Mehrfachbezieher m (SozV) recipient of several types of benefits
Mehrfachbuchung f (ReW) multiple posting
Mehrfach-Bus-System n (EDV) multiple common-data-bus system
mehrfache Eigenwerte mpl (Math) repeated latent roots
mehrfache Integration f (Math) multiple integration
Mehrfacheinteilung f (Stat) manifold classification
mehrfache Versicherung f (Vers) multiple identical-risk coverage by several insurers
mehrfache Wechselkurse mpl (Vw) multiple exchange rates
mehrfache Wortlänge f (EDV) multiple precision
Mehrfachfertigung f (IndE) multiple-process production
mehrfach gegliederte Tafel f (Stat) complex table
Mehrfachintegral n (Math) multiple (*or* iterated) integral
Mehrfachklassifikation f (Stat) multiple classification
Mehrfachkonten npl (ReW) multiple accounts
Mehrfachkopie f (com) multiple copy
Mehrfachlochung f (EDV) multiple punching
Mehrfachlösung f (OR) multiple solution
Mehrfachregelungskreis m (EDV) multiple control circuit
Mehrfachregelungssystem n (EDV) multiple control system
Mehrfachregression f (Stat) multiple regression
Mehrfachsatz m (com) multipart form
Mehrfachschichtung f (Stat) multiple stratification
Mehrfachstichprobenprüfplan m (Stat) multiple sampling plan
Mehrfachstichprobenprüfung f (Stat) multiple sampling inspection
Mehrfachunterstellung f (Bw) multiple command (*or* subordination)
Mehrfachversicherung f (Vers) multiple-line insurance
Mehrfachzoll m (Zo) multiple tariff
mehrfach zusammenhängender Bereich m (Math) multiply connected region
mehrfaktorieller Versuchsplan m (Stat) multi-factorial design
Mehrfamilienhaus n
(StR) multiple dwelling unit

– multi-family unit
Mehrfunktionskarteneinheit *f* (EDV) multi-function card machine
Mehrgangkartenzuführung *f* (EDV) multicycle card feeding
Mehrgebot *n* (com) higher bid
mehrgemeindliche Betriebsstätte *f* (StR) establishment extending over more than one municipality, § 30 GewStG
mehrgipfelige Verteilung *f* (Stat) multi-modal distribution
Mehrgipfeligkeit *f* (Stat) multimodality
Mehrheit *f*
  (com) plurality *(ie, a voting term)*
  – (GB) majority *(ie, more than 50% = clear majority)*
  (Fin) majority *(or* controlling) interest
Mehrheit *f* **erwerben** (Fin) to win control (of)
Mehrheitsaktionär *m*
  (Fin) majority shareholder *(or* stockholder)
  – controlling shareholder
Mehrheitsbeschluß *m*
  (Re) majority vote
  – resolution adopted by a majority of votes
Mehrheitsbeteiligung *f*
  (Fin) majority interest *(or* holding *or* stake), § 16 AktG
  – controlling interest
  (Bw) majority-owned subsidiary
Mehrheitsglied *n* (EDV) majority element
Mehrheit *f* **von Forderungen** (Re) several co-existing obligations, § 396 BGB
Mehrheit *f* **von Schuldner und Gläubigern** (Re) plurality of debtor and creditors, § 420 BGB
Mehrkanal-Datenübertragung *f* (EDV) multi-channel communication
Mehrkanal-Kabelfernsehen *n* (com) multi-channel cable television
Mehrkanalmodell *n*
  (OR) multi-channel model
  – multi-station model
Mehrkanalschalter *m* (EDV) multi-channel switch
Mehrkosten *pl*
  (com) extra cost
  (Bw) cost overrun
  (KoR) additional expense *(or* charges)
Mehrkostenwagnis *n* (KoR) risk of unanticipated extra cost
mehrlagiges Papier *n* (EDV) multi-part paper
Mehrleistung *f*
  (Bw) extra output
  (Bw) productivity gain
  (com) additional payment
  (SozV) additional benefit
Mehrleistungszulage *f* (Pw) production bonus
Mehrliniensystem *n* (Bw) multiple-line system
Mehrlochkern *m* (EDV) multiple aperture core
Mehrmaschinenbedienung *f* (IndE) = **Mehrstellenarbeit**
mehrmehrdeutige Relation *f* (Log) many-many correspondence
Mehrperioden-Analyse *f* (Vw) multi-period analysis
mehrperiodiges Totalmodell *n* (Bw) multi-period comprehensive model

Mehr-Personen-Nullsummenspiel *n* (OR) n-person zero sum game
Mehrphasenauswahl *f* (Stat) multiphase sampling
Mehrphasen-Lagerhaltungsproblem *n* (MaW) multi-echelon inventory problem
Mehrphasensteuer *f* (StR) multi-stage tax
Mehrphasen-Stichprobenverfahren *n* (Stat) multiphase sampling
Mehrphasen-Umsatzsteuer *f* (FiW) multi-stage turnover tax
Mehrproduktbetrieb *m* (Bw) multi-product firm
Mehrprogrammbetrieb *m* (EDV) multiprogramming (operation)
Mehrprogrammverarbeitung *f* (EDV) multi-programming
Mehrprozessorbetrieb *m* (EDV) multiprocessing
Mehrpunktnetz *n* (EDV) party line *(syn, Liniennetz, Mehrpunktverbindung, Multipointverbindung, Kettennetz, Gruppenverbindung)*
Mehrpunktschaltung *f* (EDV) multi-drop circuit
Mehrrechnersystem *n* (EDV) multiprocessor *(or* multiprocessing) system
Mehrschichtbetrieb *m* (Bw) multiple shift operation
mehrschichtiges Lagerhaltungsproblem *n* (MaW) multi-level inventory problem
Mehrschichtkosten *pl* (KoR) multiple shift cost
mehrseitiger Vertrag *m* (Re) multilateral contract
Mehrspaltenjournal *n* (ReW) multi-column journal
Mehrsparten-Geschäft (Vers) multiple-line insurance
mehrspartige Unternehmensgruppe *f* (Bw) multi-division group
Mehrspulendatei *f* (EDV) multi-reel file
Mehrspurkopf *m* (EDV) head stack
Mehrstellenarbeit *f* (IndE) multiple-machine work
mehrstellig (Log) many-place
mehrstellige Zahl *f* (Math) multi-digit number
Mehrstimmrechte *npl* (Re) multiple voting rights, § 12 II AktG
Mehrstimmrechtsaktien *fpl*
  (Fin) multiple-voting shares *(or* stock)
Mehrstückpackung *f* (com) multipack
Mehrstufenbefragung *f* (Mk) multistage interview
Mehrstufen-Stichproben-Verfahren *n* (Stat) multi-stage sampling
mehrstufige Auswahl *f* (Stat) nested sampling
mehrstufige Divisionskalkulation *f* (KoR) process costing *(ie, costs are traced to products resulting from continuous operations)*
mehrstufige Entscheidung *f* (Bw) multi-phase decision *(ie, breaking down a decision into a temporal sequence of subdecisions)*
mehrstufige Flächenschichtung *f* (Stat) area substratification
mehrstufige Probenahme *f* (Stat) multi-stage sampling
mehrstufiger Betrieb *m* (IndE) multi-stage plant *(ie, in which a sequence of operational stages with salable intermediate products is combined)*
mehrstufiger Konzern *m* (Bw) multi-level group of companies
mehrstufiges Lagerhaltungsmodell *n* (OR) multi-echelon inventory model

mehrstufiges Stichprobensystem *n* (Stat) multiple sampling
mehrstufige Stichprobe *f*
  (Stat) multiple sample
  – multi-stage sample
  – nested sample
  – network of samples
mehrstufiges Unternehmen *n* (Bw) multi-stage business
mehrteiliges Etikett *n* (com) multiple label (*or* tag)
Mehrthemen-Befragung *f*
  (Mk) multi-purpose survey
  – omnibus survey
Mehrverbrauch *m* (com) additional consumption
Mehrwegpackung *f* (Mk) two-way package
Mehrwert *m* (Vw) surplus value
mehrwertige Entscheidung *f* (Stat) multi-valued decision
mehrwertige Funktion *f* (Math) multi-valued function
mehrwertige Logik *f* (Log) many-valued logic (*or* calculus)
Mehrwertigkeit *f* (Log) polyvalence
Mehrwertsteuer *f* (StR) value-added tax, VAT
Mehrwertsteuer *f* **ausweisen** (StR) to indicate VAT on an invoice
Mehrwertsteuerbefreiung *f*
  (StR) exemption from VAT
  – (GB) zero rating
Mehrwertsteuer *f* **erhöhen** (FiW) to put up value-added tax
Mehrwertsteuer-Gesamtbelastung *f* (StR) total amount of VAT
Mehrwertsteuer-Überschuß *m* (StR) unabsorbed balance of VAT, § 18 II UStG
Mehrwertsteuer-Vorbelastung *f* (StR) prior VAT charges
Mehrwertversicherung *f* (Vers) increased-value insurance *(ie, taken out by importers)*
Mehrzweckfunktionsgeber *m* (EDV) general-purpose function generator
Mehrzweckrechner *m* (EDV) multi-purpose computer
Mehrzweckstichprobe *f* (Stat) all-purpose sample
Mehrzweckzeiten *fpl* (IndE) multi-purpose times
Meilensteinbericht *m* (OR) milestone report
Meilenstein-Druckausgaben *fpl* (EDV) milestone printouts
Meinungsaustausch *m* (com) exchange of views
Meinungsbefragung *f* (Mk) opinion survey (*or* poll)
Meinungsforschung *f* (Mk) public opinion research
Meinungsfreiheit *f*
  (Re) free expression of opinion
  – freedom of discussion
Meinungsführermodell *n* (Mk) opinion leader model
Meinungskauf *m* (Bö) speculative buying
Meinungstest *m* (Mk) opinion test
Meinungsumfrage *f* (Mk) public opinion poll (*or* survey)
Meinungsumfrage *f* **durchführen** (Mk) to conduct a public opinion survey
Meinungsumfrage *f* **in Auftrag geben** (Mk) to commission a public opinion survey
Meinungsverkauf *m* (Bö) speculative selling

Meinungsverschiedenheit *f*
  (Re) difference
  – disagreement
Meistbegünstigung *f* (AuW) most-favored-nation treatment
Meistbegünstigungsklausel *f* (AuW) most-favored-nation clause
Meistbegünstigungsprinzip *n* (AuW) most-favored-nation principle
Meistbegünstigungssatz *m* (AuW) most-favored-nation rate
meistbietend (com) highest bidding
Meistbietender *m* (com) highest (*or* best) bidder
meistbietend verkaufen (com) to sell to the highest bidder
meistbietend versteigern (com) to auction off to the highest bidder
Meister *m* (Pw) foreman
Meisterbrief *m* (Pw) foreman's certificate *(ie, of qualificational ability to become a foreman)*
Meisterprüfung *f* (Pw) foreman's qualifying examination
Meistgebot *n* (com) last and highest bid
meist gehandelte Aktie *f* (Bö) volume leader
meist gehandelte Werte *mpl* (Bö) most active issues
Meldebestand *m*
  (MaW) reordering quantity
  – reorder point
  – protective inventory
Meldemenge *f* (MaW) = *Meldebestand*
melden
  (com) to notify
  – to report
Meldepflicht *f* (com) duty to report
meldepflichtig (com) subject to reporting requirements
Meldeschluß *m* (com) deadline set for receiving applications
Meldetermin *m* (com) reporting deadline
Meldewesen *n* (com) reporting
Menge *f*
  (Math) set
  – aggregate
  – assemblage
  – complex *(ie, of elements)*
Menge *f* **aller äußeren Punkte e-r Punktmenge** (Math) exterior
Menge *f* **der Basisvariablen** (OR) basics
Menge *f* **mit genau zwei Elementen** (Math) pair set
Mengenabnahme *f* (com) bulk purchasing
Mengenabsatz *m* (com) quantity (*or* volume) sale
Mengenabschreibung *f*
  (ReW) production-method of depreciation
  – unit-of-production method
  – production-unit-basis method
  – service output (*or* yield) method
  (ie, original price minus scrap value divided by total volume output; syn, leistungsbezogene od verbrauchsbedingte od technische Abschreibung)
Mengenabweichung *f* (KoR) quantity (*or* usage) variance
Mengenalgebra *f* (Math) algebra of sets
Mengenanpasser *m*
  (Vw) quantity adjuster

– price taker
Mengenanpassermarkt *m* (Vw) price taker market *(ie, sellers have no say in the matter of selling price)*
Mengenanpassung *f* (Mk) quantity adjustment
Mengenbeschränkung *f* (AuW) quota restriction
Mengenbudget *n* (KoR) physical budget
Mengeneffekt *m* (Vw) quantity effect *(eg, of open-market operations)*
Mengeneinkauf *m* (MaW) bulk buying
Mengenfixierung *f* (Vw) quantity *(or* volume) fixing
Mengengerüst *n* **der Kosten** (KoR) quantity structure of costs
Mengengeschäft *n* (Fin) = *Massengeschäft*
Mengenindex *m* (Stat) quantity index
Mengenindex *m* **mit fester Basis** (Stat) fixed base index
Mengenkombination *f*
(Vw) combination of goods *(or* commodities)
– commodity combination
– bundle of goods
Mengenkonjuktur *f* (Vw) effective-demand boom *(ie, with prices falling, and revenues rising)*
Mengenkurs *m* (AuW) = *Mengennotierung*
Mengenlehre *f* (Math) theory of sets
Mengenleistungsprämie *f* (IndE) quantity bonus *(ie, mixed system of time and piece-rate wages)*
mengenmäßig
(com) by volume *(eg, imports dropped 2% by volume)*
– in terms of volume *(or* quantity)
mengenmäßige Ausfuhrbeschränkung *f* (AuW) quantitative restriction on exportation
mengenmäßige Beschränkung *f* (com) quantitative restriction
mengenmäßige Einfuhrbeschränkung *f* (AuW) quantitative restriction on importation
mengenmäßige Lageraufzeichnungen *fpl* (MaW) stockroom quantity records
mengenmäßige Nachfrage *f*
(Vw) quantity demanded
– demand in physical terms
– physical demand
mengenmäßiger Zuwachs *m* (com) rise in volume terms
mengenmäßiges Ausfuhrkontingent *n* (AuW) quantitative export quota
mengenmäßige Veränderungen *fpl* (Vw) quantum changes
Mengenmeßziffer *f* (Stat) quantity relative
Mengennachlaß *m* (com) = *Mengenrabatt*
Mengennotierung *f*
(AuW) indirect quotation
– indirect method of quoting foreign exchange *(eg, price of $ in DM; ie, number of units of foreign currency that will buy a unit of domestic currency; opp, Preisnotierung)*
Mengenoperationen *fpl*
(Math) operations on sets
– set operations
Mengenpreis *m* (com) bulk price
Mengenproduktion *f* (Bw) quantity production
Mengenrabatt *m*
(com) large-quantity discount

– quantity rebate
– bulk discount
– volume discount
Mengenrechnung *f* (MaW) volume accounting
Mengenrelationen *fpl* (IndE) output ratio *(ie, in joint production = Kuppelproduktion)*
Mengenrisiko *n* (Bw) quantitative *(or* volume) risk
Mengenschreibweise *f* (Math) set notation
Mengenspesen *pl* (com) volume-related expenses
Mengenstaffel *f* (com) volume-based scale of prices
Mengenstandard *m* (KoR) volume standard
Mengensteuern *fpl* (FiW) quantitative taxes
Mengensystem *n*
(Math) system of sets
– family of sets
– collection of sets
Mengentarif *m* (com) bulk supply tariff
mengentheoretisch (Math) set theoretic
mengentheoretische Topologie *f* (Math) set-theoretic topology
Mengenumsatz *m*
(com) volume sales
– sales in terms of volume
Mengenverluste *mpl* (KoR) volume losses *(ie, difference between input and output volumes; eg, in steelmaking and chemicals processing)*
Menge *f* **von Handlungsalternativen** (Bw) set of action alternatives
Mengenvorgabe *f* (KoR) quantity standard
Mengenwachstum *n* (Mk) volume growth
menschbezogen (Pw) people oriented
menschliche Arbeitsleistung *f* (Vw) human labor
menschliches Kapital *n* (Vw) human capital
Mensch-Maschine-Dialog *m* (EDV) man-machine dialog
meritorische Bedürfnisse *npl* (FiW) merit wants
meritorische Güter *npl* (FiW) merit goods
merkantiler Minderwert *m*
(com) reduced market value
– loss in value upon resale
(ie, of damaged automobile, due to hidden defects supposed to remain after repair)
Merkantilismus *m* (Vw) mercantilism
Merkmal *n*
(Log) property
(Stat) attribute
Merkmale *npl* **der Leistungsbeurteilung** (Pw) merit factors
Merkmalsfolge *f* (Stat) sequence of properties
Merkmalsklasse *f* (Stat) property class
Merkmalsraum *m* (Stat) variable space
Merkmalsträger *m* (Stat) statistical unit *(syn, statistische Einheit)*
Merkmalsvergleich *m* (IndE) factor comparison *(ie, made in job evaluation)*
Merkmalswahrscheinlichkeit *f* (Stat) a priori probability
Merkposten *m* (ReW) pro memoria item
Merkzeichen *n*
(Mk) distinctive marking, § 445 HGB
– identification mark
meßbares Leistungsergebnis *n* (Pw) measurable performance
Messe *f*
(Mk) fair

– trade fair
– show
– exhibition
Messeamt *n* (com) fair office
Messeausweis *m* (com) fair pass
Messe *f* beschicken (com) to participate in a fair
Messe *f* besuchen (com) to visit a fair
Messebesucher *m* (com) visitor of a fair
Messebeteiligung *f* (com) number of exhibitors
Messe *f* eröffnen (com) to open a fair
Messegelände *n* (com) exhibition site (*or* grounds)
Messekatalog *m* (com) fair catalog
Messeleitung *f* (com) trade fair management
Messestand *m* (Mk) exhibition stand
Messeteilnehmer *m* (com) participant in a fair
Messe- und Ausstellungsversicherung *f* (Vers) exhibitions insurance
Messe *f* veranstalten (com) to organize a fair
Messeveranstalter *m* (com) organizer of a fair
Messewerbung *f* (Mk) exhibition advertising
Meßfehler *m* (Stat) error of measurement
Meßfühler *m* (EDV) primary element
Meßglied *n* (EDV) measuring means
Meßleitung *f* (EDV) control line (*or* tubing)
Meßort *m* (EDV) measuring point
Meßschleife *f* (EDV) loop
Meßstelle *f* (EDV) measuring point
Messungskosten *pl* (KoR) basic standard cost
Meßverstärker *m* (EDV) booster unit
Meßwert *m* (EDV) process variable
Meßwertwandler *m* (EDV) transmitter
– transducer
Meßzahl *f* (Stat) index number
Meßzahl *f* mit fester Basis (Stat) fixed base relative
Meßzahl *f* mit wechselnder Basis (Stat) chain relative
Meßziffer *f* (Stat) relative
Metaentscheidung *f* (Bw) metadecision
Metageschäft *n* (com) transaction on joint account
Metakonto *n* (Fin) joint account
Metakredit *m* (Fin) loan on joint account *(ie, extended on equal terms with another bank)*
Metallbearbeitungsmaschinen *fpl* (IndE) metalworking machinery
Metallbörse *f* (Bö) metal exchange *(ie, on which nonferrous metals are traded; the leading exchanges are New York and London)*
Metallhandel *m* (com) metal trading
Metallindustrie *f*
(com) metal industry
– non-ferrous metals industry
Metallismus *m* (Vw) metalism
Metallnotierungen *fpl* (Bö) metal prices
metallverarbeitende Industrie *f* (com) metal-working industry
metallverarbeitendes Gewerbe *n* (com) = **metallverarbeitende Industrie**
Metallwährung *f* (Vw) metallic standard (*or* currency)
Metasprache *f* (Log) metalanguage
Meterware *f* (com) yard goods
Methode *f*
(Log) method
– approach

– technique
Methode *f* der gleitenden Mittelwerte (Stat) moving-average method
Methode *f* der größten Dichte (Stat) maximum likelihood method
Methode *f* der kleinsten Quadrate
(Stat) method of least squares
– least squares method
Methode *f* der Zahlungsbereitschaft (Vw) willingness-to-pay method *(ie, used in dealing with shadow prices)*
Methodenbank *f* (EDV) methods storage bank
Methodenstreit *m* (Vw) clash over economic methods *(ie, between Menger's Austrian School and Schmoller's German Historical School)*
Methode *f* zur Bestimmung der Saisonbereinigung (Stat) ratio-to-moving average method of seasonal adjustment
Metist *m* (com) party to a joint transaction
metrische Packung *f* (com) metric pack
metrisches System *n* (com) metric system *(ie, of weights and measures)*
Middleware *f* (EDV) middleware *(ie, software tailored to the needs of a particular installation)*
Mietablösung *f* (com) compensation to outgoing tenant
Mietanlagen *fpl* (ReW) rental equipment
Mietanlagengeschäft *n* (Bw) leasing activities
Mietaufwand *m* (ReW) rental expense
Mietausfallversicherung *f* (Vers) insurance against loss of rent
Mitbeihilfe *f* (Re) rent subsidy
Mietdauer *f* (Re) term of tenancy
Miete *f*
(com) rent
(com) hire charge *(eg, for renting a car)*
Miete *f* erhöhen
(com) to raise rent
– (GB) to put up rent
Miete *f* mit Kaufoption (Re) lease with purchase option
mieten (Re) to rent *(eg, house, building)*
– to lease
– to hire
Mieter *m*
(Re) tenant
– lessee
– hirer
Mieterschutz *m* (Re) legal protection of tenants
Mieterschutzgesetz *n* (Re) Tenants' Protection Law
Mietertrag *m* (ReW) rental income
Mietervereinigung *f* (Re) tenants' association
Miete *f* und Pacht *f* (Re) tenancy *(ie, of movables and immovables; note that nothing in German law is comparable to the estate of leasehold under English law, §§ 535ff BGB)*
Mietfläche *f* (com) rented floor space
Mietgebühr *f* (com) rental fee
Mietgesetz *n* (Re) rental law
Mietgrundstück *n* (com) tenancy property
Miethaus *n* (com) tenant-occupied house (*or* dwelling)
Mietkauf *m* (com) lease-purchase agreement *(ie, a*

special type of leasing in which the lessee may negotiate a purchase at the end of the basic lease term, may renew the lease for stated periods, or may return the leased asset to the lessor.

Note that ‚Mietkauf' has little in common with the British practice of ‚hire-purchase agreements' for which there is no equivalent in German.)

Mietkosten *pl* (KoR) rental cost
– rentals
Mietnebenkosten *pl* (KoR) incidental rental expenses
Mietobjekt *n* (com) rented property
Mietpreisbindung *f* (Re) rent control
Mietpreisfreigabe *f* (Re) decontrolling of rents
Mietrecht *n* (Re) law of tenancy
Mietrückstände *mpl* (com) rent arrears *(eg, due to increasing unemployment)*
Mietspiegel *m* (com) representative list of rents
Miet- und Pachteinnahmen *fpl* (ReW) rentals
Miet- und Pachtrechte *npl* (Re) leaseholds
Mietvereinbarung *f* (Re) tenancy agreement
Mietverhältnis *n* (Re) tenancy
Mietverlängerung *f* (Re) extension (*or* renewal) of tenancy
Mietverlust-Versicherung *f* (Vers) rental value insurance
Mietvertrag *m* (Re) tenancy agreement
Mietvorauszahlung *f*
(com) prepayment of rent
(com) rent paid in advance
Mietwert *m* **der selbstgenutzten Wohnung** (StR) rental value of appartment used by taxpayer
Mietwohnungsgrundstücke *npl* (StR) rental (residential) property, § 75 I BewG
Mietwucher *m* (Re, GB) rackrenting *(see: Wuchermiete)*
Mietzuschuß *m* (Re) rent allowance (*or* supplement)
mifrifi (FiW) medium-term fiscal planning *(acronym: mittelfristige Finanzplanung)*
Mikrobaustein *m* (EDV) chip
Mikrobefehl *m* (EDV) micro instruction
Mikrobefehlscode *m* (EDV) micro code (*or* instruction)
Mikrobewegungsanalyse *f* (IndE) micromotion analysis
Mikrocode *m* (EDV) micro code
Mikrocomputer *m* (EDV) microcomputer
Mikroelektronik *f* (EDV) microelectronics
Mikrofilmausgabe *f* (EDV) computer output to microfilm, COM
Mikrofilmeingabe *f* (EDV) computer input from microfilm, CIM
Mikrofilmlesegerät *n* (EDV) microfilm reader
Mikrogröße *f* (Vw) microeconomic magnitude (*or* quantity)
Mikromodul *m* (EDV) micromodule
Mikroökonomie *f* **(od Mikroökonomik** *f*)
(Vw) microeconomics
(ie, concerned with data in individual form as opposed to aggregate form)
mikroökonomisch (Vw) microeconomic
mikroökonomische Theorie *f*
(Vw) microeconomic theory

– microeconomics
Mikroplättchen *n* (EDV) (silicon) wafer
Mikroprogramm *n* (EDV) microprogram
Mikroprogramm-Speicher *m* (EDV) control memory
Mikroprozessor *m* (EDV) microprocessor
Mikroschaltung *f*
(EDV) chip
– microcircuit
Mikrotheorie *f*
(Vw) microeconomics
– microeconomic theory
Mikroverfilmung *f* (EDV) micofilming
Mikrozensus *m* (Stat) micro (*or* sample) census *(ie, 1 percent annually)*
Milchmädchenrechnung *f* (com, infml) 'milkmaid's calculation *(ie, speculation based on false reasoning)*
Milchwirtschaft *f* (com) dairy farming (*or* industry)
mildtätige Einrichtung *f* (com) charitable institution
mildtätiger Zweck *m* (StR) charitable purpose
militante Gewerkschaft *f* (Pw) militant union
Millimeterpapier *n*
(com) cross-section
– plotting
– ruled
– squared . . . paper
Millionenkredit *m* (Fin) credit of DM 1 million or more, § 14 I KWG
Minderausgabe *f* (com) reduction of expenditure
Mindereinnahmen *fpl* (com) shortfall in receipts
Mindererlös *m* (com) deficiency in proceeds
Mindererlös *m* **aus Anlageverkäufen** (ReW) loss on disposal of fixed assets
Mindererlös *m* **aus Finanzanlagen** (ReW) loss on disposal of financial assets
Mindergewicht *n*
(com) short weight
– underweight
– reduced weight
Minderheitsaktionär *m* (Re) minority shareholder (*or* stockholder)
Minderheitsbeteiligung *f* (Fin) minority interest (*or* holding *or* stake *or* participation)
Minderheitspaket *n* (Fin) minority holding
Minderheitsrechte *npl* (Re) minority rights, §§ 147, 163 II, 122 I, 254 AktG
Minderheitsvotum *n* (Re) dissenting opinion
Minderjähriger *m*
(Re) minor
– person of non-age
Minderjährigkeit *f*
(Re) non-age (*or* nonage)
– under age *(ie, lack of requisite legal age)*
Minderkaufmann (Re) small merchant, § 4 HGB *(ie, artisan or person engaged in a smaller trade; provisions relating to firm name, commercial books and records, and ‚Prokura' do not apply)*
Minderkonditionen *fpl* (Fin) highly favorable loan terms
Minderleistung *f*
(com) short-fall in output
– loss of efficiency
Minderlieferung *f* (com) short shipment

mindern (Re) to demand a reduction of purchase price

Minderung *f*
(Re) reduction (*or* abatement) of purchase price, § 472 BGB *(ie, by an amount equal to the deficiency in value)*
(SeeV) deterioration

Minderung *f* **der Erwerbsfähigkeit** (SozV) impairment of earning capacity

Minderung *f* **liquider Mittel** (Fin) decrease in net funds

Minderungsklage *f* (Re) action for reduction of purchase price

Minderwertigkeitskomplex *m* (Pw) inferiority complex

Mindestabnahme *f* (com) minimum purchasing quantity

Mindestabschlußbetrag *m* (Bö) minimum dealing quota

Mindestakkordsatz *m* (Pw) minimum piece rate

Mindestangebot *n* (com) lowest bid

Mindestanlage *f* (Fin) minimum investment

Mindestarbeitsbedingungen *fpl* (Pw) minimum employment standards

Mindestauflage *f* (com) minimum circulation

Mindestbargebot *n* (Re) minimum cash bid, § 49 ZVG *(ie, in forced sales: difference between lowest and highest bid + cost of auction)*

Mindestbestand *m*
(MaW) inventory reserve
– inventory safety stock
– minimum inventory level
– reserve stock
– protective inventory
– safety level

Mindestbesteuerung *f* (StR) minimum taxation

Mindestbewertung *f* (StR) minimum valuation *(eg, of fixed and current assets)*

Mindestbietkurs *m* (Bö) minimum bidding price

Mindesteindeckung *f* (MaW) = *Mindestbestand*

Mindesteinkommen *n* (Vw) minimum income

Mindesteinlage *f*
(Fin) minimum contribution, § 7 I GenG
(Fin) minimum deposit *(ie, 1DM on savings accounts, 5DM on postal check accounts)*

Mindesteinschuß *m* (Bö) minimum margin requirements

Mindesterfordernisse *npl* (Re) minimum requirements

Mindesterzeugerpreis *m* (EG) minimum producer price

Mindestfracht *f* (com) minimum freight rate

Mindestfreibetrag *m* (StR) minimum standard deduction

Mindestgebot *n*
(com) lowest bid
(com, infml) knocked-down bid

Mindestgewinnspanne *f*
(com) minimum margin
(Bö) bottom-line profit margin

Mindestgrundkapital *n* (Fin) = *Mindestkapital*

Mindestguthaben *n* (Fin) minimum balance

Mindestkapazität *f* (IndE) minimum operating rate *(eg, blast furnace, brick kiln, engine)*

Mindestkapital *n* (Fin) minimum capital *(ie, AG =* *DM 100,000; GmbH = DM 20,000; no minimum for sole proprietorship, general and limited commercial partnerships, mining company)*

Mindestkurs *m* (Bö) floor price

Mindestlohn *m* (Pw) minimum wage

Mindestlohnarbeitslosigkeit *f* (Vw) unemployment due to minimum wage arrangements

Mindestmenge *f*
(Bö) contract unit
– unit of trading

Mindestmengenaufpreis *m* (com) low-quantity extra

Mindestnennbetrag *m* (Fin) minimum par value of shares, § 8 AktG *(ie, DM 50, higher amounts must be DM 100 or a multiple thereof)*

Mindestprämie *f* **für bestimmte Gruppen von Risiken** (Vers) class rate

Mindestpreis *m*
(com) knocked-down (*or* minimum) price
– price floor
(EG) floor (*or* reference) price
(Mk) fall-back price
– reserve price
– upset price

Mindestpreismechanismus *m* (AuW) trigger price mechanism *(ie, to reduce U.S. steel imports)*

Mindestprüfstoff *m* (Pat) minimum documentation

Mindestqualität *f* (com) minimum acceptable quality

Mindestrendite *f* (Fin) minimum yield

Mindestreservedispositionen *fpl* (Fin) arrangements to maintain minimum reserves

Mindestreserveeinlagen *fpl* (Fin) minimum reserve deposits

Mindestreserveerhöhung *f* (Fin) increase in minimum reserves

Mindestreserveguthaben *npl* (Fin) minimum reserve balances

Mindestreserven *fpl*
(Vw) minimum reserve requirements
– minimum reserves
(ie, minimum amounts which legally have to be kept on deposit with central bank)

mindestreservepflichtige Einlagen *fpl* (Fin) deposits subject to minimum reserve requirements

mindestreservepflichtige Verbindlichkeiten *fpl* (Fin) reserve-carrying liabilities

Mindestreservepolitik *f* (Vw) minimum reserve policy

Mindestreserveprüfung *f* (Fin) minimum reserve audit

Mindestreservesatz *m*
(Fin) minimum reserve ratio
– (GB) reserve assets ratio

Mindestreservesenkung *f* (Fin) lowering of minimum reserve ratios

Mindestreservesoll *n* (Fin) minimum reserve requirements

Mindestschluß *m* (Bö) minimum lot

Mindeststundenlohn *m* (Pw) minimum time rate

Mindestumsatz *m*
(com) minimum sales
– (GB) minimum turnover

Mindestverkaufspreis *m* (Mk) fixed resale price

Mindestversicherungszeit f (SozV) minimum period of coverage
Mindestverzinsung f
(Fin) minimum rate of return
- cutoff rate (or point)
(ie, minimum acceptable rate of return expected of investment projects)
Mineralgewinnungsrechte npl (StR) mining rights, §§ 19, 100 BewG
Mineralölindustrie f (com) mineral oil industry
Mineralölstatistik f (Stat) mineral oil statistics
Mineralölsteuer f (StR) mineral oil tax
Mineralölsteuergesetz n (StR) Law on Excise Tax on Oil and Oil Products
Mineralölverarbeitung f (IndE) mineral oil processing
Miniaturmodell n (IndE) lilliputian model
Minimal-Bodenbearbeitung f (com, US) minimum tillage
Minimaldauer f (OR) crash duration
minimale Losgröße f (Bw) minimum manufacturing quantity
minimaler aufspannender Baum m (OR) minimum spanning tree
minimale Schnittmenge f (OR) minimum cut
Minimalfracht f (com) minimum freight rate *(ie, in ocean and inland waterway transport: charged to cover carriage between loading and unloading port)*
Minimalkosten pl (Bw) minimum cost *(ie, lowest average or total cost for optimum capacity working)*
Minimalkostenkombination f
(Bw) least cost combination
- minimum cost combination
Minimalschätzung f (Stat) minimum variance estimate
Minimalzoll m (Zo) minimum tariff
Minimax-Entscheidungsfunktion f (Stat) minimax decision function
Minimax-Kriterium n (OR) minimax criterion
Minimax-Regel f (Bw) minimax rule *(syn, Wald-Regel)*
Minimax-Schätzung f (Stat) minimax estimation
Minimax-Theorem n (OR) minimax theorem
Minimierung f **unter Nebenbedingungen** (Math) constrained minimization
Minimumsektor m (Bw) bottleneck segment *(ie, in operative planning)*
Minirezession f (Vw) mini (or near) recession
Ministerrat m (EG) Council of Ministers
Ministerratssitzung f (EG) EC council meeting
Min-Max-System n (MaW) min-max system of inventory control
Minor m
(pl. Minoren)
(Math) minor
Minorante f
(Math) minorant
- lower bound
Minor m **erster Ordnung** (Math) first minor
Minoritätsbeteiligung f (Fin) = *Minderheitsbeteiligung*
Minoritätsrechte npl (Re) = *Minderheitsrechte*
Minor m **zweiter Ordnung** (Math) second minor

Minusankündigung f (Bö) sharp markdown
Minusbetriebsvermögen n (StR) negative value of business assets
(ie, form of tax valuation of businesses with a debt overload, § 12 GewStG)
Minuskorrektur f
(Bö) markdown
- downward adjustment
Minusposition f (Bö) shortage of cover
Minuszeichen n
(Math) negative sign
(Bö) markdown
Mischarbeitsplatz m (EDV) work station handling data and text processing
Mischbauart f (EDV) hybrid design
Mischbetrieb m (EDV) asynchronous balanced mode, ABM
Mischdurchlauf m (EDV) merge run
mischen
(EDV) to merge
- to collate
Mischer m
(EDV) collator
- interpolator
Mischfinanzierung f
(Fin) mixed financing *(ie, combination of several funding sources)*
(FiW) joint financing *(eg, put up by Federal and state governments)*
Mischfolge f (EDV) collating (or collation) sequence *(syn, Sortierfolge)*
Mischgatter n (EDV) inclusive-OR element (or circuit) *(syn, inklusives ODER-Glied, Odergatter, Oderglied)*
Mischgeldsystem n (Vw) mixed money system
Mischgüter npl (Vw) mixed goods
Mischkonzern m
(Bw) conglomerate company (or group)
- conglomerate
(ie, multi-industry or multi-market company: heterogeneous group of affiliated companies; syn, Konglomerat)
Mischkosten pl (KoR) mixed cost *(ie, composed of fixed and variable elements)*
Mischkredit m (Fin) mixed credit
Mischpreis m (com) composite (or mixed) price
Mischproblem n (OR) product mix problem
Mischprogramm n (EDV) merge program
Mischsortieren n (EDV) merge (or classical) sorting
Mischtätigkeit f (Pw) work mix comprising ordinary office work + video station work *(see: entmischte Tätigkeit)*
Mischungsabweichung f (KoR) mix variance
Mischungsproblem n (OR) blending problem
Mischungsrechnung f
(Math) alligation
- alligation alternate
- alligation medial
Mischzinssatz m (Fin) composite interest rate
Mischzoll m
(Zo) compound duty (or tariff)
- mixed tariff
Mißbrauch m **abstellen** (Kart) to desist from an abuse *(of market power)*

Mißbrauch m des Ermessens (Re) abuse of discretion
Mißbrauch m eindämmen (StR) to curb an abuse *(eg, of tax relief provisions)*
mißbräuchliche Patentbenutzung f (Pat) abuse of patent
Mißbrauchsaufsicht f (Kart) control of abusive practices *(ie, by market-dominant firms)*
Mißbrauchsprinzip n (Kart) principle of abuse
Mißbrauchsverfahren n (Kart) abuse proceedings
Mißbrauch m von Marktmacht (Kart) abuse of market power
Mißtrauensantrag m stellen (Pw) to propose a vote of no confidence
Mißtrauensvotum n (Pw) no-confidence vote
Mitaktionär m (Fin) joint shareholder (*or* stockholder)
mit allen Einreden (Re) subject to equities
Mitanmelder m
 (Pat) coapplicant
 – joint applicant
Mitanmelder mpl e-s Patents (Pat) joint applicants for a patent
Mitarbeiter m
 (Pw) employee
 – subordinate
 (com) collaborator
 – co-worker
Mitarbeiter mpl
 – personnel
 – staff
 – manpower
Mitarbeiter-Analyse f (Pw) manpower analysis
Mitarbeiter mpl einstellen
 (Pw) to hire employees
 – to take on (new) workers
Mitarbeiter-Förderung f (Pw) personnel development
Mitarbeiter mpl im Außendienst (com) field staff
Mitarbeiter mpl im Innendienst
 (com) indoor staff
 – in-house staff
Mitarbeiter m in der Linie (Bw) line subordinate
Mitarbeiter-Interview n (Pw) interviewing of personnel
Mitarbeiterorientierung f (Bw) employee-oriented style of leadership
Mitarbeiterstab m
 (com) staff
 – team of subordinates
Mitbegünstigter m (Re) co-beneficiary
Mitbenutzungsrecht n (Re) right of joint use
mit besonderer Havarie (com) with particular average, wpa
mitbestimmtes Unternehmen n (Bw) co-determined business enterprise
Mitbestimmung f (Pw) codetermination *(ie, employee participation in the management of German enterprises)*
Mitbestimmungsergänzungsgesetz n (Pw) Amendment to Codetermination Law, of 27 Apr 1967
Mitbestimmungsgesetz n (Pw) Law on Codetermination, of 4 May 1976
Mitbestimmungsrecht n (Pw) codetermination right *(ie, right of Works Council to give its consent on certain matters)*
Mitbeteiligung f
 (Fin) co-partnership
 – joint interest
 – participation
Mitbewerber m
 (com) competitor
 – rival
mit Bezugsrecht (Fin) cum rights
Mitbürge m (Re) joint guarantor
Mitbürgschaft f (Re) joint guaranty
mit dem Außenhandelsvolumen gewichtet (AuW) trade-weighted
mit Dividende (Fin) cum dividend
Miteigentum n
 (Re) joint ownership, §§ 1008–1011 BGB
 (Pw) joint employee ownership
Miteigentum n an Grundstücken (Re) co-ownership in land
Miteigentümer m
 (Re) co-owner
 – joint owner
Miteigentümer m nach Bruchteilen (Re) fractional co-owner
Miteigentum n nach Bruchteilen (Re) co-ownership by fractional shares
mit einem Durchschlag (com) *(letter)* in duplicate
Miterbe m
 (Re) co-heir
 – joint heir
Miterbengemeinschaft f (Re) community subsisting between co-heirs
Miterfinder m (Pat) co-inventor
mitfinanzieren (Fin) to join in the financing of ...
Mitführung f
 (Fin) co-management
 – joint lead management *(ie, of loan issue)*
Mitgesellschafter m (Re) co-partner
mit Gewähr (Re) with recourse
mit Gewinn arbeiten
 (com) to operate in the black
Mitgläubiger m
 (Re) co-creditor
 – joint creditor
mit gleicher Post (com) under separate cover
Mitglied n der Geschäftsleitung
 (Bw) member of the top management team
 – top executive
Mitglieder npl abjagen (com) to siphon off membership
Mitgliederversammlung f (com) meeting of members
Mitgliedsbeiträge mpl (com) membership dues
Mitgliedschaftspapiere npl (WeR) securities evidencing membership *(eg, corporates shares = Aktien)*
Mitgliedsland n (EG) member state (*or* country)
Mitgliedsunternehmen n (Kart) member
Mithaftung f (Re) secondary liability
mithelfende Familienangehörige mpl (StR) assisting family members
mit 100%-iger Auszahlung (Fin) paid out in full
mit 90%-iger Auszahlung (Fin) paid out at a discount of 10%

Mitinhaber m **e-r Lizenz** (Pat) joint licensee
Mitinhaber m **e-s Patents** (Pat) joint patentee
mit Kupon (Fin) cum coupon
mit (laufenden) Zinsen (Bö) cum interest
mitlaufende Verarbeitung f
   (EDV) demand processing
   – *(sometimes)* in-line processing
   (syn, unmittelbare Verarbeitung)
Mitläufereffekt m (Vw) bandwagon effect *(syn, Nachahmereffekt)*
Mitnahme f (Bö) profit taking
mitnehmen
   (Bö) to take profits
   – to cash in on profits
Mitreeder m
   (com) co-owner of a ship, § 490 HGB
   – joint shipowner
mitschneiden (EDV) to tape *(eg, a telephone conversation)*
Mitschuldner m (Re) co-debtor
mit sofortiger Wirkung (Re) immediately effective
mit Sonderdividende (Bö) cum bonus
mit späteren Änderungen (Re) as amended
Mittagsschicht f (Pw) late shift
mitteilen
   (com) to inform
   (com, fml) to notify
mitteilende Partei f (Re) notifying party
Mitteilung f (com) notification
Mitteilungsfeld n (EDV) communication region
Mitteilungspatent n (Pat, GB) communicated patent
Mitteilungspflicht f (com) duty to notify
Mitteilungspflichten fpl (Re) disclosure requirements, § 20 AktG
mitteilungspflichtig (Re) subject to disclosure requirements
Mittel pl
   (Fin) funds
   – resources
Mittelabfluß m (Fin) outflow of funds
Mittel pl **aufbringen** (com) to raise money (*or* funds)
Mittelaufbringung f
   (Fin) raising of funds (*or* money)
   – fund raising
Mittelaufkommen n
   (Fin) funds raised
   – inflow of funds
   (FiW) yield of revenue
Mittelaufkommen n **und Mittelverwendung** f (ReW) sources and uses of funds
Mittelaufnahme f (Fin) borrowing
Mittelaufnahme f **am Geldmarkt** (Fin) borrowing in the money market
Mittelaufnahme f **am Kapitalmarkt** (Fin) borrowing in the capital market
Mittel pl **aus Innenfinanzierung** (Fin) internally generated funds
Mittelausstattung f (Fin) financial resources
mittelbare Arbeiten fpl (IndE) auxiliary work
mittelbare Ausfuhr f (AuW) indirect export
mittelbare Beteiligung f (StR) indirect holdings of securities *(eg, through a domestic or foreign holding company)*

mittelbare Patentverletzung f (Pat) contributory infringement of patent
mittelbarer Besitz m
   (Re) constructive possession, § 868 BGB
   – indirect possession
mittelbarer Besitzer m (Re) indirect possessor
mittelbarer Boykott-Streik m (Pw) secondary boycott strike
mittelbarer Schaden m
   (Re) consequential damage (*or* loss)
   – indirect damage
mittelbares Arbeitsverhältnis n (Pw) indirect employment
mittelbares Interesse n (Log) indirect (*or* proximate) interest *(opp, ultimate interest)*
mittelbares Verhalten n (Re) passive manifestation of will
mittelbare Ursache f (Re) remote cause
Mittelbegriff m (Log) middle term *(ie, occurring in both premises but not in the conclusion of a categorical syllogism)*
Mittel pl **beschaffen** (Fin) to raise cash (*or* funds)
Mittelbeschaffung f
   (Fin) borrowing
   – procurement of capital
   – raising of funds
Mittelbetrieb m (Bw) medium-sized business
Mittel pl **binden** (Fin) to tie up (*or* lock up) funds *(eg, in receivables or inventories)*
Mittelbindung f
   (Fin) commitment of
   – tying up
   – locking up ... funds
Mittel npl **der Einflußnahme** (Bw) control devices
Mittel n **der Flügelwerte** (Stat) class midpoint
Mittel n **der Grundgesamtheit** (Stat) parent mean
Mittelentzug m (Fin) withdrawal of funds
Mittel pl **freigeben** (FiW) to release funds
mittelfristige Anleihen fpl
   (Fin) medium-term bonds
   – mediums
mittelfristige Finanzplanung f
   (Fin) intermediate financing
   (FiW) medium-term fiscal planning
mittelfristige Optionsanleihe f (Fin) convertible notes
mittelfristige Papiere npl (Fin) medium-term securities
mittelfristige Prognose f (Vw) medium-term (*or* intermediate-range) forecast
mittelfristiger Beistand m (EG) medium-term assistance
mittelfristiger finanzieller Beistand m (EG) medium-term financial assistance
mittelfristiger Kredit m
   (Fin) medium-term loan
   – intermediate credit
mittelfristiger Zinssatz m (Fin) medium-term rate
mittelfristige Schatzanweisungen fpl (Fin) medium-term Treasury bonds
mittelfristiges Ziel n
   (Bw) medium-range target
   – midrange goal
   – intermediate goal
   (ie, typically two or three years)

mittelfristig garantierter Paritätsanstieg *m* (AuW) crawling peg
Mittelfristplan *m* (Bw) medium-term plan
Mittelherkunft *f* (Fin) sources of funds
Mittelherkunft *f* **und -verwendung** *f* (Fin) sources and application of funds
Mittelkurs *m*
  (Fin) mean (*or* middle) rate *(ie, arithmetic mean of buying and selling price of foreign exchange)*
  (Bö) middle market price
Mittel *pl* **kürzen** (Fin) to slash funds
Mittel *pl* **mobilisieren** (FiW) to mobilize funds
Mittelpreis *m* **des Verbrauchsorts** (StR) average retail price at the place where non-monetary benefits are appraised, § 15 II BewG
Mittelpunktswinkel *m* (Math) central angle
Mittelrückfluß *m* (Fin) return flow of funds
Mittelsmann *m*
  (com) go-between
  – (GB) link
Mittelsorte *f*
  (com) medium quality
  – middling
Mittelstand *m* (com) small and medium-sized businesses
mittelständischer Kredit *m* (Fin) loan to small and medium-sized enterprises
mittelständische Unternehmen *npl* (com) small to medium-sized businesses
mittelständische Wirtschaft *f* (com) small and medium-scale sector of the economy
Mittelständler *mpl* (com) small and medium-sized businessmen
Mittelstandskartell *n* (Kart) cartel relating to co-operation (other than rationalization) between small and medium-sized businesses to increase their productivity
Mittelstandskredit *m* (Fin) loan to small or medium-sized business
Mittelstreckenflugzeug *n* (com) medium-haul airliner
mittel- und langfristige Bilanzposten *mpl* (ReW) noncurrent items
mittel- und langfristiges Leasing *n* (Fin) financial leasing
Mittelvaluta *f* (Fin) mean value date
Mittelverwendung *f*
  (Vw) allocation of resources
  (Fin) application (*or* uses) of funds
Mittel *pl* **weitergeben** (Fin) to relend funds (to)
Mittelwert *m*
  (Stat) average
  – mean
Mittelwert *m* **bilden aus** (Stat) to average over
Mittelwert *m* **der Abweichungsquadrate** (Stat) mean square
Mittelzuführung *f* (Fin) injection of new funds
Mittelzuweisung *f* (FiW) apportionment of funds *(eg, to government agency, project, period of time)*
Mittler *m*
  (Re) go-between
  – middleman
  – intermediary
mittlere Abfertigungsrate *f* (OR) mean service rate

mittlere Abweichung *f* (Stat) average (*or* mean) deviation
mittlere Ankunftsrate *f* (OR) mean arrival rate
mittlere Bedienungszeit *f* (OR) mean service time
mittlere Beschleunigungskosten *pl* (OR) average variable cost
mittlere Datentechnik *f* (EDV) office computers
mittlere Fertigungsgüte *f* (Stat) process average quality
mittlere Führungsspitze *f* (Pw) middle management
mittlere Lebenserwartung *f* (Stat) average life expectancy
  (syn, fernere mittlere Lebensdauer)
mittlere Leitungsebene *f* (Bw) middle management
mittlere quadratische Abweichung *f* (Stat) standard deviation σ *(ie, positive square root of the variance; syn, Standardabweichung)*
mittlere quadratische Kontingenz *f* (Stat) mean-square contingency
mittlere Qualität *f* (com) medium quality
mittlere Qualitätslage *f* **der Fertigung** (Stat) process average
mittlerer Anteil *m* **voll geprüfter Lose** (Stat) average total inspection
mittlerer Ausschußanteil *m* **in der Fertigung** (Stat) process average fraction defective
mittlerer Betrieb *m*
  (Bw) medium-sized business
  (Mk) medium account
mittlerer Börsenpreis *m* (Bö) average list price
mittlerer Durchschlupf *m* (Stat) average outgoing quality
mittlere Reife *f* (Pw) examination taken at 16 and approximating to ‚0‘ level in England
mittlerer Fälligkeitstermin *m* (Fin) average due date
mittlerer Fehler *m* (Stat) mean deviation
mittlerer Informationsgehalt *m*
  (EDV) average information content
  – entropy
mittlerer Kapitalkoeffizient *m* (Vw) average capital-output ratio
mittlerer Lagerbestand *m* (MaW) average inventory on hand
mittlerer Prüfumfang *m* (Stat) average amount of inspection
mittlerer quadratischer Fehler *m*
  (Stat) root-mean-square error
  – standard error (of the mean)
mittlerer Stichprobenumfang *m* (Stat) average sample number function
mittlerer Verfalltag *m* (Fin) mean due date *(ie, of bills of exchange)*
mittleres Abweichungsquadrat *n* (Stat) mean square
mittleres Fehlerquadrat *n*
  (Stat) error mean square
  – mean-square error
mittleres Management *n* (Bw) middle management
mittlere Spannweite *f* (Stat) mean range
mittlere Unternehmen *n* (Bw) medium-sized business
mittlere Transportentfernung *f* (com) average haul distance
mittlere Verfallzeit *f* (Fin) = *mittlerer Verfalltag*

Mitunternehmer *m*
(Re) co-partner
– joint contractor
(StR) co-entrepreneur
Mitunternehmeranteil *m* (Re) partnership share
Mitunterzeichner *m*
(com) co-signer
(WeR) co-maker
Mitverantwortungsabgabe *f* (EG) co-responsibility levy *(ie, la taxe de la coresponsabilité)*
mit Verlust abschließen
(ReW) to report a loss
– to close at a loss
Mitverschulden *n* (Re) contributory default *(or* negligence), § 254 BGB
Mitversicherer *m*
(Vers) co-insurer
(Vers) additional insured
Mitversicherung *f* (Vers) co-insurance
mitwirkendes Verschulden *n* (Re) = *Mitverschulden*
Mitwirkungspflicht *f* (StR) duty (of taxpayer) to cooperate
Mitwirkungsrecht *n*
(Pw) participatory right
– right of participation *(eg, of the works council)*
mit Wirkung vom
(Re) as of *(ie, such-and-such a date)*
– (GB) as from
mnemotechnischer Code *m* (EDV) mnemonic code
mnemonisches Symbol *n* (EDV) mnemonic (symbol)
Möbelwagen *m*
(com) moving van
– (GB) pantechnicon *(ie, becoming rare)*
– (GB) removal van
mobile Einsatzgruppe *f* (Bw) flying crew *(or* squad) *(ie, to handle urgent situations)*
Mobiliarkredit *m* (Fin) credit secured by personal property or securities *(ie, term no longer in current usage)*
Mobiliarvollstreckung *f* (Re) seizure and sale of movable property
Mobilien *pl* (Re) movable property
Mobilisierungspapiere *npl* (Fin) mobilisation paper *(or* instruments) *(ie, sold by Deutsche Bundesbank to the banking industry)*
Mobilität *f* **der Arbeitnehmer** (Pw) labor mobility
Mobilitätshilfe *f* (Vw) mobility allowance *(or* assistance)
Mobilitätsziffer *f* (Stat) mobility ratio *(ie, total number of migrations, related to 1,000s of resident population)*
Modalitäten fpl
(com, Fin) arrangements
– details
– features
– terms
Modalwert *m* (Stat) mode
Modeartikel *m*
(com) style item
– fashionable article
Modegag *m* (com) the latest rag *(or* thing)
Modell *n* (Math) model

Modellbildung *f* (Log) model building
Modellbildung *f* **industrieller Prozesse** (IndE) modeling of industrial processes
Modell *m* **entwickeln** (Vw, Bw) to develop *(or* build) a model
Modellhaus *n*
(com) model home
– (GB) show house
Modell *n* **mit Lagerhaltung** (Vw) model with stocks
Modell *n* **mit Zufallsstörungen** (Stat) shock model
Modellrechnung *f* (com) model calculation
Modellreihe *f* (com) model range *(eg, of motor cars)*
Modenschau *f*
(com) fashion show
– (GB) dress show
moderne Anlagen *fpl* (IndE) up-to-date equipment
moderne Technologie *f* (come) state-of-the-art technology
modernisieren (com) to modernize
Modernisierung *f* (com) modernization
Modernisierungsbeihilfe *f* (StR) modernization aid
Modernisierungsdarlehen *n* (Fin) home improvement loan
Modernisierungs- und Energieeinsparungsgesetz *n* (Re) Modernization and Energy Conservation Law
Modifizierfaktor *m* (EDV) modifier
modifizierte Adjazenz-Matrix *f* (OR) modified adjacency matrix
modifizierte Ausfallbürgschaft *f* (Re) modified guaranty of collection
modifizierter Mittelwert *m* (Stat) modified mean
Modul *m*
(Math) module
– absolute value
(EDV) module
modulares Programmieren *n* (EDV) modular programming
Modularsystem *n* (EDV) modular system
Modulbauweise *f*
(IndE) modular construction *(or* design)
Modulbibliothek *f* (EDV) relocatable library
Modulbinder *m* (EDV) linkage editor *(syn, Binder)*
Modulo-N-Prüfung *f*
(EDV) modulo n check
– residue check
Modul-Werbung *f* (Mk) modular advertising
Modus *m* (Log) mode
Modus-Ponens-Regel *f* (Log) law of detachment
Mogelpackung *f*
(Mk) deceptive packing *(or* packaging)
– deception packaging
– dummy package
Möglichkeit *f* **ausschließen** (com) to rule out a possibility *(eg, of a cut in interest rates)*
Möglichkeiten *fpl* **erkunden** (com) to explore possibilities
Möglichkeiten *fpl* **nutzen** (com) to exploit (business) opportunities *(eg, presented by ...)*
Molekularsatz *m* (Log) molecular statement
Molkereigenossenschaft *f* (com) cooperative processing and distributing dairy products

425

Moment *n* (Stat) moment (about)
Momentanverzinsung *f* (Math) continuous convertible interest
Moment *n* **e-r Stichprobenverteilung** (Stat) sampling moment
momentenerzeugende Funktion *f* (Stat) moment generating function
Momentenmatrix *f* (Math) moment matrix
Momentenmethode *f* (Stat) method of moments
Moment *n* **erster Ordnung** (Stat) first order moment
Moment *n* **zweiter Ordnung** (Stat) second order moment
monadischer Wahrheitswertfunktor *m* (Log) singular connective
monatliche Erfolgsrechnung *f* (ReW) monthly income statement
monatliches Abrechnungssystem *n* (ReW) monthly accounting (*or* reporting) system
monatliche Zahlung *f* (Fin) monthly payment (*or* installment)
Monatsabgrenzung *f* (ReW) budgetary equalization – month end
Monatsabschluß *m* (ReW) monthly balance (*or* settlement)
Monatsausweis *m* (ReW) monthly return
Monatsbeitrag *m* (com) monthly contribution
Monatsbericht *m* (com) monthly report
Monatsbilanz *f* (ReW) monthly balance sheet
Monatsergebnis *n* (ReW) monthly result
Monatsgehalt *n* (Pw) monthly salary
Monatsgeld *n* (Fin) one-month money (*or* loans)
Monatszahlung *f* (Fin) monthly payment (*or* installment)
monetäre Aggregate *npl* (Vw) monetary aggregates
monetäre Basis *f* (Vw) monetary base *(ie, central bank money + demand deposits with central bank; syn, Geldbasis, Primärgeld, exogenes Geld)*
monetäre Bremsen *fpl* **lockern** (Vw) to ease (*or* relax) monetary restrictions
monetäre Expansion *f* (Vw) expansion of money supply
monetäre Gesamtgrößen *fpl* (Vw) monetary aggregates
monetäre Gesamtnachfrage *f* (Vw) total monetary demand
monetäre Grenzproduktivität *f* (Vw) marginal revenue productivity
monetäre Größen *fpl* (Vw) monetary aggregates
monetäre Instabilität *f* (Vw) monetary instability
monetäre Integration *f* (AuW) monetary integration
monetäre Komponente *f* (Vw) monetary component
montäre Konjunkturpolitik *f* (Vw) monetary business cycle policy
monetäre Konjunkturtheorie *f* (Vw) monetary business cycle theory
monetäre Koordinierung *f* (AuW) monetary coordination
monetäre Kosten *pl* (Bw) money cost of factor input
monetäre Kostenkurve *f* (Bw) monetary cost curve
monetäre Märkte *mpl* (Fin) financial markets

monetäre Nachfrage *f* (Vw) monetary (*or* effective) demand
monetäre Nachfragefunktion *f* (Vw) monetary demand function
monetärer externer Effekt *m* (Vw) pecuniary spillover
monetärer Gegenwert *m* (ReW) money equivalent – money's worth
monetärer Konsum *m* (Vw) money consumption – consumption in monetary terms
monetäres Gleichgewicht *n* (Vw) monetary equilibrium
monetäres Umlaufvermögen *n* (ReW) current financial assets
monetäre Überinvestitionstheorie *f* (Vw) monetary overinvestment theory
monetäre Zusammenarbeit *f* (AuW) monetary cooperation
Monetarismus *m* (Vw) monetarism
Monetarist *m* (Vw) monetarist
Monetärkredit *m* (Fin) monetary credit
monetisieren (Vw) to monetize *(ie, to give character of money; eg, to bonds)*
Monetisierung *f* **der Staatsschuld** (FiW) monetization of public debt
monistisches System *n* **der Kostenrechnung** (KoR) tied-in cost system
Monitorprogramm *n* (EDV) monitor (routine)
monoindustrielle Agglomeration *f* (Vw) single-industry agglomeration
Monokausalität *f* (Log) one-to-one causation
Monokultur *f*
  (com) monoculture
  (Vw) one-product economy
monolithischer Speicher *m* (EDV) monolithic storage *(syn, Halbleiterspeicher)*
monolithisch integrierte Schaltung *f* (EDV) monolithic integrated circuit
Monolith-Technik *f* (EDV) solid-state circuitry
Monemetallismus *m*
  (Vw) monometallism
  – single standard
Monopol *n* (Vw) monopoly
Monopolgesetzgebung *f* (Kart) monopoly legislation
Monopolgewinne *mpl* (Vw) monopoly profits
Monopolgrad *m* (Vw) Lerner's degree of monopoly
Monopolist *m* (Vw) monopolist
monopolistische Angebotsbeschränkung *f* (Vw) monopolistic supply restriction
monopolistische Konkurrenz *f* (Vw) monopolistic competition *(E. Chamberlain)*
monopolistische Preisdifferenzierung *f* (Vw) price discrimination
monopolistischer Markt *m* (Vw) monopolistic market
Monopolkommission *f* (Vw) monopolies commission, § 24b GWB *(ie, an independent five-man body set up in 1973 to evaluate competition policy)*
Monopolpreis *m* (Vw) monopoly price
Monopolunternehmen *n* (Vw) monopolistic firm

Monopolverwaltung f des Bundes (FiW) federal monopoly administration
Monopson n (Vw) monopsony
monoton abnehmende Funktion f (Math) monotone decreasing function
monotone Funktion f (Math) monotonic function
monotone Transformation f (Math) monotonous (or monotonic) transformation
monoton fallend (Math) monotonically decreasing
Monotonie f (Math) monotonicity
monoton wachsend (Vw) monotonically increasing
Montage f
  (com) assembly
  – fitting
  – installation
  (IndE) assembly work (or operations)
Montageabteilung f (IndE) assembly department
Montagearbeit f (IndE) field-assembly work (or operations)
Montagearbeiter m (Pw) assemblyman
Montageband n (IndE) assembly line
Montagebetrieb m (IndE) assembly plant
Montageboden m (EDV) false floor (ie, of computer center)
Montagefirma f (com) assembler
Montagegehälter npl (Pw) installation salaries
Montagekosten pl (com) installation charges
Montagelöhne mpl (Pw) installation wages
Montageplan m (IndE) assembly schedule
Montageroboter m (IndE) assembly robot
Montageversicherung f (Vers) installation insurance
Montagewerkstatt f (IndE) assembly shop
Montagezeichnung f (IndE) assembly drawing
Montanaktien fpl (Fin) shares of the coal, iron, and steel industries
Montanbereich m (com) coal, iron, and steel sector
Montangesellschaften fpl (com) coal, iron, and steel companies
Montanindustrie f (com) coal, iron, and steel industry
Montanmitbestimmung f (Pw) codetermination in the coal, iron and steel industry
Montan-Mitbestimmungsgesetz n (Pw) Iron and Steel Codetermination Law, of 21 May 1951
Montanumlage f (EG) ECSC levy
Montanunion f
  (EG) European Coal and Steel Community, ECSC
Montanwerte mpl (Bö) mining and steel shares
Monte-Carlo-Methode f (OR) random walk process
Monteur m
  (Pw) assemblyman
  – assembly operator
  – assembler
  – fitter
Moratorium n
  (Re) standstill agreement
  (Fin) debt deferral
  – deferral (or suspension) of debt repayment
  – moratorium
Morgenschicht f (Pw) morning shift
morphologische Forschung f (Mk) morphological research (ie, in product design)

Mosaikdrucker m (EDV) dot matrix printer (syn, Matrixdrucker, Rasterdrucker)
MOS-FET-Technologie f (EDV) mosfet technology (ie, field effect transistor utilizing metal oxide semiconductor, MOS)
Motivatoren mpl
  (Pw) motivators
  – job content factors
Motivforschung f (Mk) motivation(al) research
Motivirrtum m (Re) mistake as to formation of intention, § 119 II BGB
Motivstudie f (Mk) motivation study
Motorenwerte mpl (Bö) motors
Motorlocher m (EDV) motor drive punch
MTM-Verfahren n (IndE) methods time measurement
MTS-Verfahren n (IndE) methods time sharing
Müllabfuhr f
  (com garbage collection
  – (GB) refuse collection
Müllkunde f (Mk) garbology
Mülldeponie f
  (com) garbage dump
  – (GB) refuse tip
Müllfahrzeug n (com) refuse collection vehicle
Mülltonne f
  (com) garbage can
  – (GB) dustbin
Müllwagen m
  (com) garbage truck
  – (GB) dustcart
Müllwerker m
  (com) garbage collector
  – (GB) dustbinman
  (earlier Briticism: dustman)
Multidevisenstandard m (AuW) multiple foreign exchange currency
multifunktionale Geräte npl (EDV) multifunctionals
Multikausalität f (Log) multiple causation
Multikollinearität f (Stat) multi-collinearity
multilateraler Handel m (AuW) multilateral trade
multilateraler Saldenausgleich m (AuW) multilateral settlement
multilateraler Zahlungsverkehr m (AuW) multilateral settlements
multilaterales Clearing n (AuW) multilateral clearing
multilaterales Länderkontingent n (AuW) negotiated multilateral quota
multilaterales Wechselkurs-Modell n (AuW) multilateral exchange-rate model
multilaterale Überwachung f (AuW) multilateral surveillance (ie, by the BIS in financing balance-of-payments deficits)
multilaterale Verrechnung f (Fin) multilateral compensation (or settlement)
Multilateralisierung f **des innergemeinschaftlichen Saldenausgleichs** (EG) multilateralization of intra-Community settlements
Multilateralismus m (AuW) multilateralism
Multimikroprozessorsystem n (EDV) multi microprocessor system
Multimomentaufnahme f **mit Leistungsgradschätzen** (IndE) rated-activity sampling

Multimomentverfahren *n*
(IndE) observation ratio method
– ratio delay method
multinationales Unternehmen *n*
(Bw) multinational corporation (*or* company)
– transnational company
multinormale Verteilung *f* (Stat) multi-normal distribution
multiple Erweiterung *f* (Bw) multiple plant expansion
multiple Giralgeldschöpfung *f*
(Vw) multiple bank deposit creation
– multiple expansion of commercial bank money (*or* credit *or* deposits)
multiple Korrelation *f* (Stat) multiple correlation
multiple nichtlineare Korrelation *f* (Stat) multiple curvilinear correlation
multiple Regression *f* (Stat) multiple regression
multipler Korrelationskoeffizient *m* (Stat) coefficient of multiple correlation
multipler Wechselkurs *m* (AuW) multiple (*or* split) exchange rate *(syn, gespaltener od differenzierter Wechselkurs)*
multiples Gleichgewicht *n* (Vw) nonunique equilibrium
Multiplexbetrieb *m*
(EDV) multiplex mode (*or* operation)
– multiplexing
Multiplexer *m* (EDV) multiplexer
Multiplexkanal *m* (EDV) multiplexer channel
Multiplikationsanweisung *f* (EDV) multiply statement
Multiplikationsbefehl *m* (EDV) multiply instruction
Multiplikationseinrichtung *f* (EDV) multiplier
Multiplikationssatz *m* (Stat) multiplication rule *(of probability)*
Multiplikation *f* **von Matrizen** (Math) matrix multiplication
Multiplikator *m* (Math, Vw) multiplier
Multiplikator-Akzelerator-Modell *n* (Vw) multiplier-accelerator model
Multiplikator *m* **für die Ausgaben der öffentlichen Hand** (FiW) government expenditure multiplier
Multiplikatorregister *n* (EDV) multiplier register
Multiplikatorwirkung *f* **e-s ausgeglichenen öffentlichen Haushalts** (Vw) balanced-budget multiplier
Multiplizierwerk *n* (EDV) digital multiplier *(syn, Multiplizierglied)*
Multiplizitätseigenschaft *f* **der Prozesse** (OR) infinite divisibility of activities
Multipointverbindung *f* (EDV) multipoint line *(syn, Netzkonfiguration)*
Multiprogrammverarbeitung *f* (EDV) multiprogramming
Multiprozessorbetrieb *m* (EDV) multiprocessing
Multis *pl* (Bw) multinational corporations
Multisektoren-Multiplikator *m* (Vw) multi-sector multiplier
Multitasking *n* (EDV) multitasking
Multivariaten-Analyse *f* (Stat) multi-variate analysis
Multiwährungsintervention *f* (AuW) multiple currency intervention

Münchener Patentübereinkommen *n* (Pat) Munich Patent Convention
mündelsicher (Fin) eligible for trusts
mündelsichere Kapitalanlage *f* (Fin) eligible investment
mündelsichere Papiere *npl* (Fin) trustee securities, § 1807 I BGB
mündliche Abmachung *f* (Re) = *mündliche Vereinbarung*
mündliche Bestellung *f* (com) oral purchase order
mündliche Kommunikation *f* (Bw) oral (*or* verbal) communication
mündliche Prüfung *f*
(Pw) oral examination
– (GB *also*) viva voce
mündliche Vereinbarung *f*
(Re) verbal agreement (*or* arrangement)
– oral agreement
Mündlichkeitsprinzip *n* (Re) principle of oral presentation
Mundwerbung *f* (Mk) word-of-mouth advertising
Münzeinnahmen *fpl* (FiW) seigniorage
Münzen *fpl* (Vw) coin(s)
Münzfernsprecher *m*
(com) pay station
– (GB) pay telephone
Münzgeld *n* (Vw) specie
Münzgewinn *m* (Vw) profit from coinage
Münzgutschrift *f* (FiW) credit to government on account of coinage
Münzhoheit *f* (FiW) right of coinage
Münzparität *f*
(FiW) mint parity
– mint par of exchange
– mint rate
Münzregal *n* (FiW) right of coinage
Münzumlauf *m* (Vw) coin circulation
Münz- und Barrengold *n* (Vw) gold coin and bullion
Münzverschlechterung *f* (FiW) debasement
Münzverschleiß *m* (FiW) abrasion
Mußbestimmung *f* (Re) mandatory provision
Mußkaufmann *m*
(Re) enterprise commercial by its nature, § 1 II HGB
– merchant by nature of type of business
Muß-Knoten *m* (OR) must-follow node
Mußvorschrift *f* (Re) obligatory disposition
Muster *n* (com) sample
(ie, physical specimen)
Musterarbeitsvertrag *m* (Pw) model employment contract
Mustererkennung *f* (EDV) pattern recognition
Musterkollektion *f*
(com) sample collection
– stock of samples
Musterlager *n* (com) display of samples
Musterlos *n* (Stat) pilot lot
Mustermesse *f* (com) samples fair
Muster *n* **ohne Wert** (com) sample without value
Musterprozeß *m*
(Re) model suit
.– test case litigation
(ie, the nearest American equivalent would be 'class action' or ‚representative action' = one or

more of a large group of persons may sue or be sued as representatives of the class)
Musterrabatt *m* (AuW) sample rebate *(ie, granted to import firm abroad for small quantities of merchandise which were to be used as sales samples)*
Mustersatzung *f* (Re) model articles of association
Musterschutz *m* (Pat) protection of registered design
Mustersendung *f* (com) sample consignment
Mustervertrag *m* (Re) specimen contract *(or* agreement*)*
Muster *npl* **ziehen** (com) to take samples

mutmaßlicher Parteiwille *m* (Re) implied terms
Muttergesellschaft *f* (Bw) parent company
Mutterpause *f* (com) reproducible copy
Mutterschaftsgeld *n* (SozV) maternity allowance
Mutterschaftshilfe *f* (SozV) maternity aid
Mutterschaftsurlaub *m* (SozV) maternity leave
Mutterschutz *m* (Pw) maternity protection
Mutterschutzgesetz *n* (SozV) Maternity Protection Law, of 18 Apr 1968
Mutter *f* **und Tochter** *f* (Re) parent and offspring *(or* subsidiary*)*
Mutungsintervall *n* (Stat) confidence belt *(or* interval *or* range *or* region)

N

nachaddieren (com) to refoot
Nachahmereffekt *m* (Vw) bandwagon effect *(syn, Mitläufereffekt)*
nachaktivieren (ReW) to post-capitalize
Nachaktivierung *f* (ReW) post-capitalization
Nachanmelder *m* (Pat) subsequent applicant
Nachanmeldung *f* (Pat) supplementary application
Nacharbeit *f*
 (com) rework
 (Pw) hours worked to make up for ...
nacharbeiten
 (com) to rework
 (Pw) to make up for ...
Nacharbeitskosten *pl*
 (com, KoR) cost of rework
 (KoR, *sometimes*) cost beyond normal
Nachbardisziplin *f* (Log) neighboring discipline
Nachbarkanten *fpl* (OR) neighboring arcs *(or* cuts*)*
Nachbarschaftseffekt *m* (FiW) neighborhood effect *(ie, all positive and negative effects of an action upon third parties; in a more restricted sense: regional cost-benefit overlapping)*
Nachbarschaftsladen *m* (com) neighborhood shop
Nachbau *m* (Pat) construction under license
nachbearbeiten (com) to rework
Nachbearbeitung *f* (com) reworking
Nachbearbeitungs-Auftrag *m* (IndE) rework order
nach Bedarf (com) call off as required
nachbelasten (ReW) to charge subsequently
Nachbelastung *f*
 (ReW) additional charge
 – subsequent debit
nachbessern
 (com) to rework
 – to rectify faults *(or* defects*)*
Nachbesserung *f*
 (Re) rework
 – rectification of defects *(or* faults*)*
Nachbesserungskosten *pl* (KoR) cost of rework
Nachbesserungspflicht *f* (Re) obligation to remedy defects, §§ 633, 634 BGB
nachbestellen
 (com) to reorder
 – to place a repeat order (for)
Nachbestellung *f*

 (com) reorder
 – repeat order
 (MaW) replenishment order
nach Bestellung angefertigt
 (com) custom-made
 – customized
 – made to order
Nachbesteuerung *f* (StR) supplementary taxation
Nachbewilligung *f* (FiW) supplementary grant
Nachbezugsrecht *n* (Fin) right to prior-year dividends *(ie, on preferred stock, §§ 139ff AktG)*
nach billigem Ermessen (Re) at reasonable discretion
Nachbörse *f* (Bö) after-hours dealing *(or* trading *or* market*)*
nachbörsliche Kurse *mpl* (Bö) after-hours prices
nachbörslich fest (Bö) strong in after-hours trading
Nachbuchung *f* (ReW) completing entry
Nachbürge *m* (Re) collateral *(or* secondary*)* guarantor
Nachbürgschaft *f* (Re) collateral *(or* secondary*)* guaranty
nachdatieren (com) to antedate *(ie, to write a date preceding today's date; opp, vordatieren = to postdate)*
nach Diktat verreist (com) dictated by ... signed in his absence
Nachdruck *m* (com) reprint
Nachemission *f* (Bö) follow-up issue
nachentrichten (SozV) to pay retrospective social insurance contributions
Nachentrichtung *f* (SozV) retrospective payment of contributions
Nacherbe *m* (StR) second heir, § 6 ErbStG
Nacherhebung *f* (Zo) post clearance
Nachfaßaktion *f* (Mk) follow-up procedure
Nachfaßbesuch *m* (Mk) follow-up call
Nachfaßbrief *m* (com) follow-up letter
nachfassen (Mk) to follow up
nachfassende Untersuchung *f* (Stat) follow-up
Nachfaßinterview *n*
 (Mk) callback
 – follow-up interview
Nachfaßwerbung *f* (Mk) follow-up advertising
Nachfeststellung *f*

(StR) subsequent assessment
- subsequent determination of assessed value, § 23 BewG
Nachfeststellungszeitpunkt *m* (StR) time of subsequent assessment
Nachfinanzierung *f* (Fin) supplementary financing
Nachfolgebank *f* (Fin) successor bank
Nachfolgegesellschaft *f* (Bw) successor company
Nachfolgekonferenz *f*
(com) follow-up conference (*or* meeting)
nachfolgendes Ereignis *n* (OR) successor event
nachfolgende Unmöglichkeit *f* (Re) subsequent (*or* supervening) impossibility *(ie, impossibility after a contract is made)*
Nachfolgeorganisation *f* (com) successor organization
Nachfolgeprogramm *n* (EDV) successor program
Nachfolgerin *f* (Bw) = *Nachfolgegesellschaft*
nachfordern (com) to make a further claim
Nachforderung *f*
(com) subsequent (*or* supplementary) claim
(Bö) margin call
Nachfrage *f* (Vw) demand
Nachfrageanalyse *f* (Vw) demand analysis
Nachfrageänderung *f*
(com) change in demand
(Vw) shift in demand
Nachfrageausfall *m* (Vw) demand shortfall
Nachfrage *f* **beleben** (com) to revive (*or* revitalize) demand
Nachfragebelebung *f*
(com) revival of demand
- revitalization of demand
- upswing (*or* upturn) in demand
Nachfragebeweglichkeit *f* (Vw) flexibility of demand
Nachfrageboom *m* (com) boom in (*or* surge of) demand
Nachfrage *f* **decken** (com) to meet (*or* supply) a demand
Nachfrageelastizität *f*
(Vw) demand elasticity
- elasticity of demand
Nachfrageentwicklung *f* (Vw) demand trend
nachfrageerhöhende Maßnahme *f* (Vw) demand-boosting measure
Nachfragefunktion *f*
(Vw) demand function
Nachfragegesetz *n* (Vw) law of demand
Nachfragegleichung *f* (Vw) demand equation
Nachfrageinflation *f*
(Vw) demand inflation
- demand-pull inflation
- demand-shift inflation
- buyers' inflation
Nachfrageinflationsmodell *n* (Vw) demand-inflation model
Nachfrageintensität *f* (com) strength of demand
Nachfragekomponente *f* (Vw) demand component *(eg, des realen BSP = of real gnp)*
Nachfragekurve *f* (Vw) demand curve
Nachfragekurve *f* **des Haushalts** (Vw) individual demand curve
Nachfragekurve *f* **mit konstanter Elastizität** (Vw) isoelastic demand curve

Nachfragekurve *f* **ohne Alternative** (Vw) all-or-nothing demand curve
Nachfragelücke *f* (Vw) deflationary gap
Nachfragemacht *f* (Vw) buyer concentration of power
Nachfragemenge *f* (Vw) quantity demanded
Nachfragemonopol *n* (Vw) monopsony
Nachfragemonopolist *m* (Vw) monopsonist
Nachfrage *f* **nach Arbeitskräften** (Vw) demand for labor
Nachfrage *f* **nach Liquidität** (Vw) demand for cash balances
Nachfrage *f* **nach Produktionsfaktoren** (Vw) factor demand
Nachfrageoligopol *n* (Vw) demand oligopoly
nachfrageorientiert (Vw) demand-oriented *(eg, economic policy)*
Nachfrager *m* (Vw) demander
Nachfragerate *f* (OR) demand rate
Nachfragerückgang *m* (com) drop (*or* fall) in demand
Nachfrage *f* **schaffen** (com) to create demand (for)
Nachfrageschwäche *f* (com) weak demand
Nachfragesog-Inflation *f* (Vw) demand-pull inflation
Nachfragesog-Inflationsmodell *n* (Vw) demand-pull model of inflation
Nachfragesteuerung *f* (Vw) aggregative demand management
Nachfragestruktur *f* (Vw) demand structure
Nachfragetabelle *f* (Vw) demand schedule
Nachfrageüberhang *m* (Vw, Bö) = *Nachfrageüberschuß*
Nachfrageüberschuß *m*
(Vw) excess (in) demand
- excess of demand over supply
- surplus demand
Nachfrageverfall *m* (com) substantial drop in demand
Nachfrageverschiebung *f*
(Vw) shift in demand
- demand shift
Nachfrageverschiebungs-Inflation *m* (Vw) demand shift inflation
Nachfrageverteilung *f* (Vw) demand distribution
Nachfragewandel *m* (Mk) change in demand
Nachfrist *f*
(Re) period of grace
- grace period
- extension of time
- days of grace
- term of grace
- additional period of time
Nachfrist *f* **gewähren** (Re) to extend the original term
Nachfrist *f* **setzen** (Re) to allot a reasonable period within which to make performance *(ie, stating that it would not be accepted after the expiration of this period)*
nachgeben
(com) to dip *(ie, prices, market)*
- to flag
- to sag
- to slip
- to soften

- to weaken
  (Bö) to ease *(ie, securities prices)*
  - to shade
  - to slip back
nachgebend
  (com) dipping *(ie, prices, market)*
  - flagging
  - sagging
  - slipping
  - softening
  - weakening
nachgebende Kurse *mpl* (Bö) easing (*or* shading) prices
Nachgeben *n* **der Zinsen** (Fin) easing of rates
Nachgebühr *f* (com) additional charge *(ie, postage or insufficient postage payable by addressee)*
nachgeholte Abschreibung *f* (ReW) backlog depreciation
nachgelagerte Absatzstufe *f* (Mk) downstream stage of distribution
nachgelagerte Industriezweige *mpl* (Bw) downstream industries
nach geltendem Recht
  (Re) as the law stands
  - under existing law
  - under the law as it now exists
nachgeordnet (Bw) down the line
nachgeordnete Ebenen *fpl* (Bw) lower levels of organization
nachgeordnete Gebietskörperschaften *fpl* (FiW) subordinate units of government
  - state and local units
nachgeordnete Management-Ebene *f* (Bw) subordinate management level
nachgeordneter Linien-Manager *m* (Bw) subordinate line manager
nachgeordnetes Darlehen *n* (Fin) subordinated loan
nachgeschaltete Gesellschaft *f* (StR) second-tier company
nachgiebiges Recht *n*
  (Re) flexible law
  - *(civil law)* jus dispositivum
  (ie, legal obligations which can be excluded by agreement; opp, zwingendes Recht)
nachgiebige Vorschriften *fpl* (re) non-compulsory provisions
Nachgirant *m* (WeR) post-maturity indorser
Nachgründung *f* (Re) post-formation acquisition, § 52 AktG
Nachgründungsbericht *m* (Re) post-formation report, § 52 III AktG
Nachhaftung *f* (Re) secondary liability
nachhaltige Erholung *f* (Vw) sustained pickup *(ie, in economic activity)*
nachhaltige Tätigkeit *f* (StR) sustained (*or* continuous) activity for the purpose of realizing receipts, § 2 UStG
nachhaltige Wiederbelebung *f* (Vw) steady recovery
Nachhaltigkeit *f* (StR) = *nachhaltige Tätigkeit*
Nachholbedarf *m*
  (com) catch-up
  - backlog
  - pent-up ... demand

Nachholwirkung *f* (StR) recapture effect of VAT *(ie, the entrepreneur who buys exempt goods would pay a higher tax because the amount of prior turnover tax he can deduct is reduced by the tax not paid at the preceding stage)*
Nachindossament *n* (WeR) post-maturity indorsement
Nachindossant *m* (WeR) post-maturity indorser
Nachkalkulation *f* (KoR) statistical cost accounting
Nachkosten *pl* (com, KoR) = *Nacharbeitskosten*
Nachkur *f* (SozV) post-cure rest period
Nachlaß *m*
  (com) discount
  - allowance
  - deduction
  - reduction
  (Re) decedent's estate
  (StR) abatement *(eg, of assessed taxes)*
Nachlaß *m* **bei Barzahlung** (com) cash discount
Nachlässe *mpl* (ReW) discounts and price reductions
nachlassen (com, infml) to knock off *(eg, I'll knock $10 off the retail price)*
nachlassende Konjunktur *f*
  (Vw) economy stops expanding
  - economy slipping into recessionary waters
nachlassender Auftragseingang *m*
  (com) flagging (*or* slackening) orders
  - fewer new orders
Nachlassen *n* **der Hochkonjunktur** (Vw) unwinding of boom
Nachlassen *n* **des Inflationsdrucks** (Vw) slackening of inflationary pressures
nachlassende Wirtschaftstätigkeit *f* (Vw) slackening economic activity
Nachlaßgegenstand *m* (Re) asset
Nachlaßkonkurs *m* (Re) bankruptcy of a decedent's estate, §§ 214 ff KO
Nachlaßpfleger *m* (Re) curator of the estate *(ie, appointment is intended to bridge over the period during which it is not yet known who is going to be the heir, §§ 1960 ff BGB)*
Nachlaßsteuer *f* (FiW) estate tax *(ie, tax levied on the decedent's estate and not on the heir receiving the property; the German ErbSt is an ‚Erbanfallsteuer' = inheritance tax)*
Nachlaßverbindlichkeiten *fpl* (Re) debt of decedent's estate
Nachlaß *m* **verwalten** (Re) to administrate a decedent's estate
Nachlaßverwalter *m* (Re) administrator of a decedent's estate
Nachlaßverwaltung *f* (Re) administration of a decedent's estate, §§ 1975 ff BGB
Nachlaß *m* **vom Listenpreis** (com) off list
Nachlauf *m*
  (com) post-carriage
  - off-carriage
  (ie, in container traffic: to final place of arrival)
nachlaufende Reihe *f* (Vw) lagging series
Nachlaufkosten *pl* (com) follow-up costs
Nachlieferung *f*
  (com) additional supply
  - subsequent delivery
nachmachen

(com) to counterfeit
- to fake *(eg, documents, bank notes, products)*
Nachmann *m* (WeR) subsquent indorser *(or holder)*
Nachmärkte *mpl* (Mk) downstream markets
Nachmittagsbörse *f* (Bö) = *Abendbörse*
Nachnahme *f*
(com) cash on delivery, c. o. d., cod
- (US) collect on delivery
Nachnahmebrief *m* (com) c. o. d. letter
Nachnahmekosten *pl* (ReW) c. o. d. expenses
Nachnahmesendung *f* (com) registered c. o. d. consignment
Nachorder *f*
(com) repeat order
- reorder
(MaW) replenishment order
Nachpatent *n* (Pat) subsequent patent
Nachporto *n* (com) additional postage
nachrangige Anleihe *f* (Fin) secondary loan
nachrangige Hypothek *f*
(Re) subordinated
- subsequent
- junior ... mortgage
nachrangiger Gläubiger *m* (Re) secondary *(or* deferred*)* creditor
nachrangiges Pfandrecht *n* (Re) junior lien
nachrechnen
(com) to check a calculation
- to recalculate
Nachrechnung *f* (com) recalculation
Nachrechner *m* (EDV) backend computer
Nachricht *f* (EDV) message
Nachrichten-Speichervermittlung *f* (EDV) message switching
Nachrichtenverarbeitung *f* (EDV) message processing
Nachrichtenvorsatz *m* (EDV) message header
nachrichtlich (com) memorandum item
Nachsaison *f* (com) post-season
Nachsatz *m*
(EDV) end-of-file label
(EDV) trailer record
nachschießen
(Fin) to make a further contribution
(Bö) to remargin
Nachschlageinformationen *fpl* (com) reference information
Nachschlagewerk *n* (com) reference work
Nachschleppwirkung *f* (FiW) fiscal drag
Nachschuß *m* (Fin) supplementary contribution, § 26 I GmbHG
(Fin) additional payment
(Bö) further margin
nachschußfreie Aktien *fpl* (Fin) non-assessable corporate shares
nachschüssige Rente *f*
(Fin) ordinary annuity
- annuity immediate
Nachschußpflicht *f*
(Fin) obligation to make further contributions *(eg, § 26 GmbHG)*
(Vers) assessment to cover unexpected losses
nachschußpflichtig (Fin) liable to make further contributions

nachschußpflichtige Aktien *fpl* (Fin) assessable corporate shares
nachschußpflichtiger Gesellschafter *m* (Fin) contributory partner
Nachschußzahlung *f*
(Fin) additional cover *(or* payment*)*
(Bö) further margin
Nachsendeadresse *f* (com) forwarding address
Nachsendeanschrift *f*
(com) temporary mailing address
- (GB) accommodation address
Nachsendeantrag *m* (com) re-routing request *(ie, made to Post Office)*
nachsenden
(com) to send on
- to forward mail *(ie, to changed address)*
Nachsendung *f* (com) forwarding of mail
Nachsicht-Akkreditiv *n*
(Fin) documentary acceptance credit
- term credit
Nachsichttratte *f* (WeR) usance draft
Nachsichtwechsel *m* (WeR) after-sight bill *(ie, payable at fixed period after sight; syn, Zeitsichtwechsel)*
nachstellige Hypothek *f* (Re) = *nachrangige Hypothek*
nachstelliges Grundpfandrecht *n* (Re) junior mortgage
Nachsteuer *f* (StR) supplementary tax
nächsthöherer Vorgesetzter *m* (Pw) supervisor's supervisor
Nachtarbeit *f* (Pw) night work
Nachtarbeitsverbot *n* (Pw) prohibition of night-work
Nachtbörse *f* (Bö) evening trade
Nachteil *m* (Re) injury
nachteiliger Vertrag *m* (Re) deleterious contract
nachteilige Wirkung *f* (StR) baneful effect *(eg, of regressive tax)*
Nachtrag *m*
(com) postscript *(ie, to letter, report, etc.)*
(com) addendum
nachträgliche Buchung *f*
(ReW) subsequent posting
(ReW) subsequent entry
nachträgliche Genehmigung *f* (Re) subsequent approval
nachträglicher Einbau *m* (IndE) retrofit
nachträglicher Einspruch *m* (Pat) belated opposition
nachträgliche Schichtung *f* (Stat) stratification after sampling
nachträgliche Unmöglichkeit *f*
(Re) subsequent *(or* supervening*)* impossibility of performance
- subsequent frustration
Nachtragsbewilligung *f* (FiW) supplementary appropriation
Nachtragsbuchung *f* (ReW) subsequent entry
Nachtragshaushalt *m*
(FiW) additional *(or* supplementary*)* budget
- (US) deficiency bill
- (GB) deficiency supply bill
Nachtragskredit *m* (FiW) supplementary credit
Nachtragspolice *f* (Vers) additional policy

Nachtrag m zur Police (Vers) indorsement *(ie, provision added to a policy, usu. by being written on the printed page, but also in the form of a rider)*
Nachtschicht *f* (Pw) night shift
Nachttresor *m* (Fin) bank's night safe-deposit box
„Nachtwächterstaat" *m* (Vw) nightwatchman state
– minimal state
Nachunternehmer *m* (com) subordinate contractor *(ie, employed by general contractor)*
Nachvaluten *pl* (Fin) back values
Nachveranlagung *f* (StR) supplementary assessment, § 17 VStG, §§ 18, 21 GrStG
Nachversicherung *f* (SozV) payment of retrospective contributions
(Vers) supplementary insurance
Nachversicherungszeiten *fpl* (SozV) periods for which retrospective contributions are made
Nachversteuerung *f* (StR) supplementary taxation, § 10 VI EStG
nachverzollen (Zo) to pay subsequent duty
Nachverzollung *f*
(Zo) post entry
– subsequent payment of customs duties
nach Wahl des Käufers (com) at buyer's option
nach Wahl des Verkäufers (com) at seller's option
Nachweis *m* **behaupteter Eigenschaften** (Mk) advertising substantiation
Nachweis *m* **der Nettobohrkosten** (ReW) statement of exploration results
nachweisen
(StR) to make a showing
(Re) to prove
– to produce evidence
– to show by submitting suitable documents
Nachweis *m* **von Vorsatz od grober Fahrlässigkeit** (Re) proof of intent or gross negligence
Nachwuchs *m* (Pw, infml) young blood
Nachwuchskräfte *fpl* (Pw) junior staff in training
Nachwuchsmanager *m* (Pw) junior manager
Nachwuchsmann *m* (Pw) junior manager
nachzahlen (com) to pay retrospectively
Nachzahlung *f*
(Fin) back payment
(StR) deficiency in current tax payments
Nachzahlungsaufforderung *f* (Fin) call *(ie, to shareholders for further contributions)*
Nachzahlung *f* **von Steuern aus Vorjahren** (ReW) payment of taxes for prior years
nachziehen
(com, infml) to follow suit
– to play catch-up
nachziehende Lohnerhöhung *f*
(Pw) catch-up increase of wages
– equalizing pay increase
Nachzugsaktien *fpl* (Fin) deferred shares *(or stock)*
nachzuversteuernder Betrag *m* (StR) taxable amount from previous years, § 10a EStG
Nadeldrucker *m* (EDV) wire *(or stylus)* printer
Nadellochkarte *f* (EDV) hand-operated punched card *(syn, Handlochkarte)*
Näherungsfehler *m* (Math) approximation error
Näherungsrechnung *f* (Math) approximate computation
Näherungsvariable *f* (Vw) proxy variable

Näherungswert *m* (Math) approximate(d) value
nahestehende Gesellschaft *f*
(Re) affiliated company
– affiliate
Nahfischerei *f* (com) local fishing
Nahrungsmittelindustrie *f* (com) food (processing) industry
Nahrungsmittelkette *f* (com) food chain
Nahrungs- und Genußmittel *npl* (com) food and kindred products
Nahrungs- und Genußmittelgewerbe *n* (com) food, beverages, and tobacco industry
Nahtstelle *f* (Bw) linkage point
– interface
(EDV) interface *(syn, Schnittstelle)*
Nahverkehr *m*
(com) short-distance traffic
(com) short haulage
naive Mengenlehre *f* (Math) intuitive set theory
naive Quantitätstheorie *f* (Vw) crude quantity theory
Namenliste *f* (EDV) identifier list
namenlose Artikel *mpl* (Mk) no-names
namenlose Handelsmarke *f* (Mk) no-name brand
Namensaktie *f* (WeR) registered share *(or stock)*
Namenskonnossement *n*
(WeR) straight bill of lading *(or B/L)*
– nonnegotiable B/L
Namenslagerschein *m* (WeR) registered warehouse receipt
Namenspapier *n* (WeR) registered security
Namenspfandbrief *m* (WeR) registered mortgage bond
Namensrecht *n* (Re) right to a name, § 12 BGB
Namensscheck *m* (WeR) registered check
Namensschuldverschreibung *f* (WeR) registered bond
namhafter Betrag *m* (com) substantial amount
Nämlichkeit *f* (Zo) identity of goods
Nämlichkeitsbescheinigung *f* (Zo) certificate of identity
Nämlichkeitsnachweis *m* (Zo) proof of unaltered character of temporarily imported goods
Nämlichkeitsschein *m* (Zo) = *Nämlichkeitsbescheinigung*
Nämlichkeitssicherung *f* (Zo) arrangements to prove identity of temporarily imported goods
Nämlichkeitszeichen *n* (Zo) identification mark
Nämlichkeitszeugnis *n* (Zo) = *Nämlichkeitsbescheinigung*
NAND-Schaltung *f* (EDV) NAND circuit *(or element or gate)*
NAND-Verknüpfung *f* (EDV) = *NAND-Funktion*
NAND-Funktion *f*
(EDV) NAND operation
– non-conjunction
– alternative denial
– dispersion
NAND-Glied *n* (EDV) = *NAND-Schaltung*
nasse Stücke *npl* (Fin) mortgage bonds issued but not yet outstanding
Naßgewicht *n* (com) weight in wet condition *(ie, standard allowance 2 percent)*
Nationalbudget *n*

(FiW) national budget
- national income estimate
nationale Buchführung f (VGR) national accounting
nationale Handelsbräuche mpl (com) national trade usages
Nationaleinkommen n (VGR) national income (syn, Volkseinkommen)
nationaler Markt m (Vw) national market
nationales Patent n (Pat) national patent
Nationalökonomie f (Vw) economics (ie, obsolescent term, being superseded by ‚Volkswirtschaftslehre')
Nationalprodukt n (VGR) national product
Naturalerfüllung f (Re) performance in kind
Naturalherstellung f
 (Re) restitution in kind, § 249 BGB
- restoration to the previous condition
- (civil law) restitutio in integrum
Naturalleistungen fpl (Pw) payment in kind
Naturallohn m (Pw) wages (or compensation) in kind (syn, Sachlohn)
Naturalobligation f
 (Re) imperfect obligation
- „natural claim"
 (ie, not enforceable in courts of law; eg, gambling debts, § 762 BGB)
Naturalrabatt m (com) rebate in kind
Naturalrestitution f (Re) = Naturalherstellung
Naturaltausch m (Vw) barter
 (ie, exchance of goods and services without the use of money)
Naturaltilgung f (Fin) repayment of mortgage loan to real-property bank by means of mortgage bonds (if below par) instead of cash
Naturalwirtschaft f
 (Vw) barter
- moneyless
- nonmonetary ... economy
Naturalzins m (Vw) interest in kind (opp, Geldzins = money interest)
natürliche Arbeitslosigkeit f (Vw) natural rate of unemployment
natürliche Kostenarten fpl (KoR) primary cost types (syn, ursprüngliche od reine Kostenarten; opp, zusammengesetzte sekundäre Kostenarten)
natürliche Person f (Re) natural person
natürlicher Abgang m
 (Pw) natural wastage
- attrition
 (Vers) natural wastage
natürliche Rate f **der Arbeitslosigkeit** (Vw) natural unemployment rate
natürliche Ressourcen pl (Vw) natural resources
natürlicher Fehler m (Re) inherent defect (or vice)
natürlicher Griffbereich m (IndE) normal working area
natürlicher Logarithmus m
 (Math) natural logarithm
- Napierian logarithm
- hyperbolic logarithm
natürlicher Lohn m (Vw) natural wage
natürlicher Preis m (Vw) natural price (opp, Marktpreis)
natürlicher Verschleiß m

(Bw) disuse
- natural wear and tear
 (ie, as a factor of depreciation = Abschreibungsursache)
natürlicher Zins m (Vw) natural interest rate (Wicksell)
natürliches Monopol n (Vw) natural monopoly
natürliches Recht n (Re) natural (or inherent) right
natürliche Wachstumsrate f (Vw) natural rate of growth
natürliche Zahl f (Math) natural number
Naturrecht n (Re) natural law
Nebenabrede f
 (Re) ancillary
- collateral
- side
- subsidiary ... agreement
Nebenanspruch m
 (Re) accessory
- additional
- secondary
- subsidiary ... claim
Nebenanschluß m (com) (telephone) extension
Nebenapparat m (com) = Nebenanschluß
Nebenartikel m (com) side-line article
Nebenausfall m (Stat) minor failure
Nebenausgaben fpl (com) incidental expenses
Nebenbedienungsplatz m (EDV) subconsole
Nebenbedingung f
 (Math) constraint
- restriction
- auxiliary considon
- side condition
Nebenberuf m (Pw) secondary (or side-line) occupation
nebenberuflicher Vertreter m (Vers) part-time agent
Nebenbeschäftigung f (SozV) low-paid or side-line employment (eg, 15 hours per week, DM390 per month, or one sixth of total income)
Nebenbetrieb m
 (IndE) auxiliary plant
 (StR) auxiliary enterprise, §§ 34, 42 BewG
Nebenbezüge pl
 (Pw) fringe benefits
- perquisites
- perks
Nebenbörse f (Bö) side-line (or secondary) market
Nebenbücher npl (ReW) subsidiary books of account
Nebenbuchhaltung f (ReW) contributory accounting unit (eg, fixed asset, inventory, and payroll accounting)
Nebenbuchung f (ReW) entry into subsidiary books of account
Nebenbürge m (Re) collateral guarantor
Nebenbürgschaft f (Re) collateral (or secondary) guaranty
Nebendiagonale f (Math) conjugate diagonal
Nebendiagonale f **e-r Matrix** (Math) secondary diagonal
Nebeneinkünfte pl
 (Pw) additional (or extra) income
 (StR) nonemployment income
- income from sources other than employment

(ie, disregarded in computing assessed tax if gross amount does not exceed DM800 in the taxable year, § 46 III EStG)
Nebeneinnahmen *fpl* (Pw) extra income
Nebenertrag *m* (ReW) revenue from disposal of waste, spoilage, and scrap
Nebenerwerbslandwirt *m* (com) part-time farmer
Nebenerwerbsstelle *f* (com) part-time farm *(opp, Haupterwerbsstelle = full-time farm)*
Nebenerwerbstätigkeit *f* (StR) subsidiary gainful activity
Nebenerzeugnis *n*
(IndE) byproduct
– co-product
– residual product
– subsidiary product
– spinoff
(ie, in joint production; syn, Nebenprodukt; opp, Haupterzeugnis)
Nebenfach *n*
(Pw) minor
– (GB) secondary subject
(ie, complementary to a major field of attention; in Britain a student reads his main subject, and elects a secondary subject; opp, Hauptfach)
Nebenfehler *m* (Stat) minor defect
Nebenfiskus *m* (FiW) auxiliary fiscal agent
Nebenforderung *f* (Re) subsidiary claim
Nebengebühren *fpl* (com) extra charges
Nebengewerbe *n* (com) ancillary part of a business
Nebengleis *n*
(IndE) siding
– sidetrack
(ie, opening onto the main track at both ends)
Nebenkapazität *f* (IndE) side-product capacity *(eg, gas output in a steel plant)*
Nebenkasse *f*
(Fin) petty cash fund
(Fin) secondary cash office
Nebenklage *f* (Re) incidental action
Nebenkläger *m*
(Re) co-plaintiff
– intervening party
Nebenklausel *f* (Fin) negative pledge clause
Nebenkosten *pl*
(KoR) incidental expenses *(or* charges)
– incidentals
– attendant expenses
(ie, minor items that are not particularized)
(MaW) expenses incidental to acquisition
(Fin) incidental bank charges
Nebenkostenstelle *f* (KoR) indirect *(or* nonproductive) center
Nebenleistungen *fpl*
(Re) collateral *(or* ancillary) performances
(Pw) additional compensation
– fringe benefits
(StR) auxiliary *(or* ancillary) services, § 8 I No. 8 UStG
Nebenleistungen *fpl* **in Sachform** (Pw) allowance in kind
Nebenleistungspflichten *fpl* (Re) subsidiary obligationen
Nebenmarkt *m* (Bö) secondary market
Nebenpapier *n* (Fin) coupon sheet

Nebenparameter *m* (Stat) incidental parameter
Nebenpatent *n* (Pat) collateral *(or* subordinated) patent
Nebenpflichten *fpl*
(Re) accessory
– secondary
– subsidiary ... duties *(or* obligations)
Nebenplan *m* (Bw) alternative plan
Nebenplatz *m* (Fin) out-of-town place
Nebenprodukt *n* (IndE) = *Nebenerzeugnis*
Nebenprogramm *n*
(EDV) secondary
– side
– subordinate ... program
Nebenrechnung *f* (Math) auxiliary calculation
nebensächlicher Fehler *m* (Stat) incidental defect
Nebenstelle *f* (com) (telephone) extension
Nebenstellenanlage *f* (EDV) private branch exchange, PBX
Nebentätigkeit *f* (Pw) = *Nebenberuf*
Nebenunternehmer *m* (com) = *Nachunternehmer*
Nebenverdienst *m* (Pw) = *Nebeneinkünfte*
Nebenvereinbarungen *fpl* (Re) supplementary stipulations
Nebenverpflichtungen *fpl* (Re) subsidiary duties *(ie, of stockholders)*, §§ 55, 180 AktG
Nebenversicherung *f* (Vers) additional insurance
Nebenvertrag *m* (Re) accessory *(or* secondary) contract
Nebenwerte *mpl* (Bö) second-line stocks
Nebenwirkungen *fpl* (Vw, Bw) side effects
Nebenzeit *f*
(IndE) auxiliary process time
– machine ancillary time
Nebenzweigstelle *f* (Fin) subsidiary branch office *(ie, of savings banks, handling inpayments and outpayments, but no customers' accounts)*
Negation *f*
(Log) negation
(EDV) negation
– NOT operation
– Boolean complementation
(syn, boolesche Komplementierung)
Negationsschaltung *f* (EDV) NOT circuit *(or* element)
Negationsverknüpfung *f* (EDV) NOT operation
Negativattest *n* (Kart) negative clearance
negative Einkommensteuer *f* (FiW) negative income tax
negative Ersparnisse *fpl* (Vw) dissaving
negative Externalitäten *fpl*
(Vw) external diseconomies
– negative externalities
negative externe Effekte *mpl* (Vw) = *negative Externalitäten*
negative externe Ersparnisse *fpl* (Vw) external diseconomies
negative ganze Zahl *f* (Math) negative integer
negative interne Ersparnisse *fpl* (Vw) internal diseconomies
negative Intervention *f* (AuW) negative intervention
(ie, in foreign exchange markets)
negative Korrelation *f* (Stat) negative correlation
negative Leistungsbilanz *f*

(VGR) negative balance on services
- service deficit
negative Orderklausel *f*
(WeR) negative order clause
- „not to order" clause
negative Publizität *f* (Re) notice as against third parties, § 68 BGB
negative Quittung *f* (EDV) negative acknowledge, NAK
negativer Bestätigungsvermerk *m* (ReW) adverse audit opinion
negativer Betrag *m* (ReW) negative amount
negativer Firmenwert *m* (ReW) bad will
negativer Koeffizient *m* (Math) minus coefficient
negativer Mehrwert *m* (Vw) negative valued added
negativer Nutzen *m* (Vw) negative utility
negativer Personal-Nettobedarf *m* (Pw) number of layoffs
negativer Preis *m* (Vw) negative price
negativer Prüfungsvermerk *m* (ReW) negative audit report (*or* certificate)
(*ie, „nothing came to our attention which would indicate that these statements are not fairly presented"*)
negativer Realzins *m* (Vw) negative real interest rate (*ie, less than rate of inflation*)
negatives Dumping *n* (AuW) reverse dumping
negatives Gut *n*
(Vw) discommodity
- disgood
negatives Interesse *n* (Re) negative interest, § 122 BGB (*ie, damage resulting from bona fide reliance on validity of contract; syn, Vertrauensinteresse; opp, Erfüllungsinteresse, positives Interesse*)
negatives Kapital *n* (ReW) negative capital (*ie, excess of liabilities over assets*)
negatives Kapitalkonto *n* (ReW) negative capital account (*ie, recorded on the assets side of a balance sheet*)
negatives Schuldanerkenntnis *n* (Re) agreement by which creditor acknowledges that there is no obligatory relation between him and his debtor, § 397 II BGB
negative Steuern *fpl* (FiW) negative taxes (*ie, publicly financed transfer payments*)
negatives Wachstum *n* (Vw) minus (*or* negative) growth
negative Vorratsinvestitionen *f* (Vw) inventory disinvestment
negative Währungsausgleichsbeträge *mpl* (EG) negative monetary compensatory amounts
negative Wirtschaftsgüter *npl* (ReW) negative assets
negative Zahl *f* (Math) negative number
Negativklausel *f* (Fin) negative pledge clause (*ie, in bond issue business*)
Negativliste *f* (AuW) list of nonliberalized goods
Negativzins *m* (Fin) negative (*or* penal) interest
Negator *m* (EDV) = *NICHT-Glied*
Negotiation *f*
(AuW) discounting of documentary draft
(Fin) issue of public loan (*ie, esp. by selling to bank or banking syndicate*)
Negotiationskredit *m* (Fin) = *Negoziierungskredit*

negotiierbares Akkreditiv *n* (Fin) negotiable credit
Negotiierbarkeit *f* (WeR) negotiability
negotiierende Bank *f* (Fin) negotiating bank
Negotiierungsanzeige *f* (Fin) advice of negotiation
Negotiierungsauftrag *m* (Fin) order to negotiate
negoziierbar (WeR) negotiable (*ie, legally capable of being transferred by indorsement and delivery = übertragbar durch Indossament und Übergabe*)
Negoziierungskredit *m*
(Fin) drawing authorization
- authority to negotiate
(*ie, based on letter of credit and shipping documents*)
nehmen, was der Markt hergibt (com) to charge ‚what the traffic will bear'
Neigung *f* **zur Monopolbildung** (Vw) propensity to monopolize (*ie, ratio of supply elasticity to demand elasticity*)
Nennbetrag *m* (Fin) = *Nennwert*
Nennbetrag *m* **je Aktie** (Fin) par value per share
nennenswerter Wettbewerb *m* (Kart) reasonable degree of competition
Nennkapital *n* (Fin) = *Nominalkapital*
Nennmaß *n* (Stat) basic size (*ie, in quality control*)
Nennwert *m*
(Fin) face value (*or* amount)
- nominal value (*or* amount)
- par value (*syn, Nennbetrag, Nominalwert*)
Nennwertaktie *f*
(Fin) par-value share
- face value share
- nominal value share
nennwertlose Aktie *f*
(Fin) no-par stock
- (GB) nonpar shares
Nennwert *m* **von Münzen** (Fin) denominational value of coins
Neoliberalismus *m*
(Vw) principle of maintaining both ‚order'
(*by necessary and sufficient government intervention*) *and ‚competition' in a social free market economy*
(*ie, the term defies precise translation; it is a tag for West Germany's peculiar post-war brand of neoliberalism, developed by the Freiburg school of economists; syn, Ordoliberalismus*)
Neomerkantilismus *m* (Vw) neomercantilism
Neoquantitätstheorie *f* (Vw) neo-quantity theory of money
Neoricardianische Theorie *f* (Vw) neo-Ricardian theory (*ie, seeks to determine product prices in a multi-sectoral system with highest production coefficients by means of linear equations*)
netto (com) net(t)
Nettoabsatz *m* (Fin) net security sales
Nettoabsatzwert *m* (ReW) sales value (*ie, in inventory valuation*)
Netto-Anlageinvestitionen *fpl*
(VGR) net investment in fixed assets
- net fixed capital formation
Nettoanlagevermögen *n* (Bw) net fixed assets
Netto-Auftragseingang *m* (com) net sales
Nettoauslandsforderungen *fpl*
(Auw) net external assets

Nettoauslandsinvestitionen *fpl* (AuW) net foreign investment
Netto-Auslandsposition *f* (AuW) net external position
Nettoauslandsverschuldung *f* (AuW) net external indebtedness
Nettoausschüttung *f* (Fin) net payment (*or* payout)
Nettoaustauschverhältnis *n* (AuW) net barter terms of trade
Nettoausweis *m*
 (ReW) net statement *(ie, of fixed assets after deducting accumulated depreciation)*
 (ReW) net presentation
Netto-Auszahlung *f* (Fin) net cash investment *(ie, in investment analysis)*
Nettobedarfsermittlung *f* (MaW) assessment of net material requirements
Nettobestand *m* (Bö) net position (*or* holdings)
Nettobetrag *m* (com) net amount
Nettobetriebsgewinn *m*
 (ReW) net operating profit
 – (GB) net trading profit
Nettobetriebsverlust *m*
 (ReW) net operating loss
 – (GB) net trading loss
Nettobilanz *f* **der unsichtbaren Leistungen** (VGR) invisible net balance
Nettobuchwert *m* (ReW) net book value
Netto-Cashflow *m* (Fin) net cash flow *(ie, aftertax profits + dividends + depreciation)*
Netto-Devisenabfluß *m* (AuW) net currency outflow
Nettodevisenposition *f* (AuW) net reserve position
Netto-Devisenzufluß *m* (AuW) net currency inflow
Nettoeinkaufspreis *m* (ReW) net purchase price *(ie, invoice price + cost of acquisition – deductions)*
Nettoeinkaufswert *m* (ReW) net purchases *(ie, cost + freight inward – returns, allowances and discounts)*
Nettoeinkommen *n*
 (Pw) net income (*or* earnings)
 – earnings net of tax *(syn, Reineinkommen)*
Nettoeinkünfte *pl* (Pw) net earnings
Nettoeinnahmen *fpl* (com) net receipts
Nettoerfolgsrechnung *f* (ReW) netted income statement *(opp, Bruttoerfolgsrechnung = grossed income statement)*
Nettoergebnis *n* (ReW) net earnings (*or* result)
Nettoerlös *m* (ReW) net revenue (*or* proceeds)
Nettoerlös *m* **e–s diskontierten Wechsels** (Fin) net avails
Nettoersparnis *f* **der privaten Haushalte** (VGR) net personal savings
Nettoertrag *m* (Fin) net earnings (*or* return)
Nettoertrag *m* **aus Wertpapieren** (Fin) net security gain
Nettoetat *m* (FiW) net budget *(ie, showing only receipt or expenditure surplus; opp, Bruttoetat)*
Nettoforderungen *fpl* **der Kreditinstitute** (Vw) net external assets of banks
Nettoforderungsausfall *m* (Fin) net loan charge-offs
Netto-Fremdmittelbedarf *m* (FiW) net funding needs

Nettogehalt *n*
 (Pw) net salary
Nettogesamtvermögen *n* (Fin) capital employed (*or* invested) *(ie, fixed assets + current assets – current liabilities)*
Nettogeschäfte *npl* (Bö) net price transactions *(ie, commission, handling charges etc. are included in the security price)*
Nettogewicht *n* (com) net(t) weight
Nettogewinn *m*
 (Fin) net earnings
 (KoR) net profit (*or* income) *(ie, revenue minus total cost [= fixed + variable cost])*
Nettogewinne *mpl* **aus Devisentermingeschäften** (Fin) net gains on forward exchange transactions
Nettogewinn *m* **nach Steuern** (ReW) net profit after taxes
Nettogewinn *m* **vor Steuern** (ReW) net profit before taxes
Nettogewinnzuschlag *m* (com) net profit markup
Nettogläubigerposition *f* (AuW) net creditor position
Nettoguthaben *n* **bei der Zentralbank** (Fin) net balance with the central bank
Nettoinlandsinvestitionen *fpl* **ohne Staat** (VGR) net private domestic investment
Nettoinlandsprodukt *n* (VGR) net domestic product
Nettoinventarwert *m* (Fin) net asset value
Nettoinvestition *f* (Fin) net investment *(ie, Bruttoinvestition – Ersatzinvestition = gross investment minus replacement investment)*
Nettoinvestitionen *fpl* (VGR) net private domestic investment
Nettoinvestitionsquote *f* (VGR) net investment ratio
Nettokapitalabfluß *m* (AuW) net outflow of capital
Nettokapitalbildung *f* (Vw) net capital formation
Nettokapitalimporte *mpl* (AuW) net capital imports
Nettokapitalproduktivität *f* (Vw) net capital productivity
Nettokapitalzustrom *m* (AuW) net inflow of capital
netto Kasse ohne Abzug (com) net cash
Nettokreditaufnahme *f*
 (FiW) net borrowing
 – net credit intake
Nettokreditgewährungen *fpl* (Fin) net lendings
Nettokurs *m* (Bö) net price
Nettoliquidität *f* (Fin) net liquid assets *(ie, total of liquid assets – total of current liabilities)*
Nettoliquiditätszufluß *m* (Fin) net liquidity inflow
Nettolohn *m*
 (Pw) net wages
 – disposable earnings
 – take-home pay
Nettoposition *f* (AuW) net position
Nettoprämie *f* (Vers) net premium (*or* rate)
Nettopreis *m* (com) net price
Nettoproduktion *f* (VGR) net output *(ie, gross output minus purchased materials and services)*
Nettoproduktionsindex *m* (Stat) net production index
Nettoproduktionswert *m* (VGR) net output *(ie,*

value added + capital consumption; opp, Bruttoproduktionswert = gross output)
Nettoquote *f* (VGR) net-output/gross-output ratio
Netto-Realisationswert *m* (ReW) net realizable value *(ie, of inventory)*
Nettorechnung *f* (ReW) = *Nettoerfolgsrechnung*
Nettorendite *f* (Fin) net yield
Nettorentenniveau *n* (SozV) level of net pensions
Nettoproduktionsziffer *f* (Stat) net reproduction rate, NNR
Nettoschuldnerposition *f* (AuW) net debtor position
Nettosozialprodukt *n* (VGR) net national product, NNP, nnp
Nettosozialprodukt *n* **zu Faktorkosten** (VGR) net national product (NNP) at factor cost
Nettosozialprodukt *n* **zu Marktpreisen** (VGR) net national product (NNP) at market prices
Nettosteuerbetrag *m* (com) net tax amount
Nettotara *f* (com) net tare
Nettoumlaufvermögen *n* (ReW) (net) working capital *(ie, excess of current assets over current liabilities)*
Nettoumsatz *m*
 (ReW) net sales
 – (GB) net turnover
 (ie, gross sales less deductions = Erlösschmälerungen; syn, Reinumsatz)
Nettoumsatzerlöse *mpl*
 (ReW) net sales (revenues)
 (ReW, EG) net turnover
Nettoumsatzrendite *f* (Fin) net earnings as percentage of sales
netto verdienen (Pw) to net
Nettoverdienst *m*
 (Pw) net income (*or* earnings)
 – take-home pay
Nettoverkaufserlöse *mpl* (ReW) = *Nettoumsatzerlöse*
Nettoverkaufspreis *m* (com) net sales price *(ie, cash price ex stock, not including seller's transport charges and taxes)*
Nettovermögen *n* (Fin) net assets (*or* worth)
Nettoverschuldung *f*
 (FiW) net national debt
 – net indebtedness
Nettoverzinsung *f* (Fin) net return
Nettovolkseinkommen *n* (VGR) net national income, NNI
Nettowährungsreserven *fpl* (AuW) net official monetary assets
Nettowarenwert *m* (com) net value of merchandise
Nettowertschöpfung *f* (VGR) net value added *(ie, net production less depreciation = Nettoproduktionswert abz Abschreibungen –; or: sum of wages, salaries, interest, distributed and undistributed profit)*
Nettowertzuwachs *m* (Fin) net appreciation
Netto-Wohlfahrtsverluste *mpl*
 (Vw) deadweight losses
 – factor excess burden
 – excess burden
Nettozins *m* (Fin) pure interest
Nettozinsaufwand *m* (ReW) interest paid – net
Nettozinsbelastung *f* (Fin) net interest burden

Nettozinsdifferenz *f* (Bö) covered interest-rate differential
Nettozinsklausel *f* (Fin) net interest clause
Nettozinsspanne *f* (Fin) net interest margin
Netzbetriebssystem *n* (EDV) network operating system
Netze *npl* **kürzester Ketten** (OR) multi-terminal shortest chains
Netze *npl* **von Flüssen** (OR) multi-terminal flows
Netz *n* **gegenseitiger Kreditlinien** (AuW) swap network
Netzkonfiguration *f* (EDV) multipoint line *(syn, Multipointverbindung)*
Netz *n* **mit Kapazitätsangaben** (OR) capacitated network
Netzmodell *n* (EDV) network analog
Netzplan *m* (OR) network
Netzplan *m* **mit Entscheidungsereignissen** (OR) generalized network
 – db network
Netzplan *m* **mit Entscheidungsknoten** (OR) decision box network
Netzplantechnik *f* (OR) network planning technique
 (ie, emphasizes scheduled completion time and resource allocation)
Netzwerkanalysator *m* (EDV) network analyzer
Netzwerk *n* **mit Entscheidungsereignissen** (OR) activity network
Netzwerktheorie *f* (OR) network flow theory
neu (Pat) novel
Neuabschlüsse *mpl*
 (com) fresh business
 – new orders booked
 – new order bookings
Neuakquisition *f* (Mk) canvassing of new orders and customers
Neuanschaffung *f* (ReW) new acquisition
Neubautätigkeit *f* (com) new-construction activity
Neubauten *mpl* (StR) new buildings, § 31 GrStDV *(ie, those ready for moving in after 31 Mar 1924)*
Neubegebung *f* (Fin) new issue
Neuberechnung *f*
 (com) recalculation
 – updating
Neubewertung *f*
 (ReW) revaluation
 (com) reappraisal
 – reassessment
 – re-rating
Neubewertung *f* **des Vorratsvermögens** (ReW) inventory revaluation
Neubewertungsrücklage *f* (ReW, EG) revaluation reserve *(ie, set up to earmark the difference between original cost and replacement cost)*
neue Abschlüsse *mpl* (com) = *Neuabschlüsse*
neue Aktie *f* (Fin) new share *(syn, junge Aktie)*
Neueinstellungen *fpl*
 (Pw) new hirings
 – taking on new labor
 – accession (*or* hiring) rate
neu einstufen (com) to reclassify
neue Märkte *mpl* **erschließen** (Mk) to open up (*or* develop) new markets
Neuemission *f*

(Bö) new (*or* fresh) issue
(Bö) primary distribution (*or* offering)
Neuemissionsmarkt *m* (Bö) new issue market
Neuengagements *npl*
(Fin) new loan commitments
(Bö) new buying
Neue Politische Ökonomie *f* (Vw) New Political Economy *(syn, Ökonomische Theorie der Politik, Nichtmarktliche Entscheidungstheorie)*
Neue Weltwirtschaftsordnung *f* (Vw) New World Economic Order
Neufestsetzung *f* **der Leitkurse** (AuW) realignment of central exchange rates
Neufestsetzung *f* **der Steuer** (StR) reassessment of a tax
Neufestsetzung *f* **der Währungsparitäten** (AuW) parity realignment
− realignment of parities
Neufestsetzung *f* **der Wechselkurse** (AuW) currency realignment
Neufinanzierung *f* (Fin) original financing *(ie, provision of fresh funds for capital spending; opp, Umfinanzierung)*
Neugeschäft *n* (com) new business
Neugläubiger *m* (Re) assignee *(syn, Abtretungsempfänger, Zessionar)*
Neugründungen *fpl* (Bw) new businesses
Neuheit *f* (Pat) novelty
Neuheit *f* **der Erfindung** (Pat) novelty of an invention
Neuheitsmangel *m* (Pat) lack (*or* want) of novelty
Neuheitsprüfung *f* (Pat) search for novelty
Neuheitsrest *m* (Pat) inventive difference
neuheitsschädlich
(Pat) detrimental (*or* prejudicial) to novelty
neuheitsschädliche Vorwegnahme *f* **e−r Erfindung** (Pat) anticipation of an invention
Neuheitsschädlichkeit *f* (Pat) bar to novelty
Neuinvestitionen *fpl*
(Bw) investment in new plant and equipment
− new plant and equipment expenditure
(VGR) business outlay for new plant and equipment
Neukredite *mpl* (Fin) new credits
Neukreditgeschäft *n* (Fin) new lendings
Neulieferung *f* (com) replacement
Neunerkomplement *n* (EDV) nine's complement
Neunersprung *m*
(EDV) standing-on-nines carry
− high speed carry
Neunkanten-Zuführung *f* (EDV) nine edge leading *(syn, Zuführung mit Unterkante vorn)*
neunzigspaltige Lochkarte *f* (EDV) ninety column card
Neuordnung *f* (Bw) reorganization and restructuring measures
Neuordnung *f* **der Währungsparitäten** (AuW) currency realignment
Neuordnung *f* **der Wechselkurse** (AuW) currency realignment
Neuordnungsplan *m* (Bw) rationalization program
Neuorganisation *f*
(Bw) fundamental reorganization *(eg, of a plant division)*
− streamlining operations

Neuorientierung *f*
(com) reorientation
− new departure
Neuorientierung *f* **der Wechselkurse** (AuW) currency realignment
Neuregelung *f* (com) new arrangements
neu schreiben (EDV) to rewrite
neutrale Aufwendungen *mpl* (ReW) = *neutraler Aufwand*
neutrale Erträge *mpl* (ReW) nonoperating revenue
neutrale Güter *npl* (AuW) neutral goods *(ie, not subject to international commodity exchange)*
neutraler Aufwand *m* (ReW) nonoperating expense
neutraler Erfolg *m* (ReW) nonoperating income *(ie, nonoperating revenue − nonoperating expense)*
neutraler Gewinn *m* (ReW) nonoperating profit (*or* income) *(ie, total profit − operating profit)*
neutraler technischer Fortschritt *m* (Vw) neutral technical progress
neutraler Zins *m* (Vw) neutral rate of interest *(ie, during full employment)*
neutrales Ergebnis *n* (ReW) nonoperating result
neutrales Geld *n* (Vw) neutral money
neutrales Gleichgewicht *n* (Vw) neutral (*or* metastable) equilibrium
neutrale Steuer *f* (FiW) neutral tax
neutrale Transaktionen *fpl* (EG) blank tranactions
neutralisieren (Fin) to neutralize *(eg, money)*
Neutralität *f* **der Besteuerung** (FiW) neutrality of taxation
(ie, refers to feature of certain taxes not to trigger off unintended substitution effects)
Neutralität *f* **des Geldes** (Vw) neutrality of money *(ie, the assumption that money, serving only as a medium of exchange, is indifferent to real quantities, such as real national income, production, level of employment, relative prices)*
Neuveranlagung *f* (StR) new assessment *(ie, made if material changes occur in taxpayer's conditions, § 16 VStG, §§ 17, 21 GrStG)*
neu verschulden, sich (FiW) to take on new debt
Neuverschuldung *f*
(Fin, FiW) new borrowings
− new indebtedness
− taking on new debt
Neuverteilung *f* **des Steueraufkommens** (FiW) restructuring of the income from the two major sources − income tax and value-added tax
Neuwert *m* (Vers) reinstatement value
Neuwertversicherung *f* (Vers) insurance reinstatement policy
Neuzugangsziffer *f* (Stat) attack rate
Neuzulassungen *fpl* (com) new car registrations
Neuzusage *f* (Fin) new credit commitment
NE-Werte *mpl* (Bö) nonferrous metals stock
nicht abgehobene Dividende *f* (Fin) unclaimed dividends
nicht abgerechnete Leistungen *fpl* (com) uninvoiced sales
nicht abgeschriebene Agiobeträge *mpl* (Fin) unamortized premiums
nicht abgeschriebener Rest *m* (ReW) unamortized balance

nicht abgeschriebenes Damnum *n* (ReW) unamortized debt (*or* bond) discount
nicht abgeschriebenes Disagio *n* (ReW) = *nicht abgeschriebenes Damnum*
Nichtabnahme *f*
(com) nonacceptance
(Re) failure (of buyer) to take delivery of goods
– failure to take up the goods
Nichtabrechnungsteilnehmer *m* (Fin) institutions not participating in the clearing procedure
nicht abzählbar (Math) nondenumerable
nicht abzugsfähige Ausgaben *fpl* (StR) nondeductible expenses, § 12 EStG
Nichtabzugsfähigkeit *f* **langfristiger Verbindlichkeiten** (StR) nondeductibility of long-term debt *(ie, for purposes of the trade tax)*
nicht-additive Schockvariable *f* (Stat) nonadditive disturbance
nicht aktivierungspflichtige Gemeinkosten *pl* (ReW) noncapitalized overhead
nicht-akzeptable Tratte *f* (WeR) nonacceptable draft
nicht akzeptierter Wechsel *m* (WeR) unaccepted bill
nicht am Lager (com) out of stock
nichtamtlicher Handel *m* (Bö) unofficial trading
nichtamtlicher Markt *m* (Bö) unofficial market
Nichtannahme *f* (Re) nonacceptance
nicht an Order (WeR) not to order
nichtanrechenbare ausländische Einkommensteuer *f* (StR) noncreditable foreign income tax
nicht anrechnungsberechtigter Anteilseigner *m* (StR) shareholder not entitled to an imputation credit
Nichtanzeige *f*
(Re) non-disclosure
– non-notification
Nichtarbeitnehmer *m* (SozV) non-employee
nicht aufgabenorientierte Variable *f* (Mk) nontask variable
nicht teilbare Fixkosten *pl* (KoR) joint fixed cost
nicht ausgeglichener Haushalt *m* (FiW) unbalanced budget
nicht ausgeschüttete Gewinne *mpl*
(Fin) earnings (*or* net income *or* profits)
– profit retentions
– reinvested earnings
– retained earnings (*or* income *or* profit)
– undistributed profits
– (GB) ploughed-back profits
(syn, einbehaltene od thesaurierte Gewinne)
nicht ausgetaktetes Montageband *n* (IndE) unbalanced line
Nichtausnutzung *f* **der Kapazität** (IndE) underutilization of capacity
nicht ausschüttungsfähiger Gewinnvortrag *m* (ReW) restricted retained earnings
nicht ausüben (Bö) to abandon *(eg, an option)*
Nichtausübung *f* **e–r Tätigkeit** (StR) nonexercise of a taxable activity, § 24 I b EStG
Nichtausübung *f* **e–s Patents** (Pat) non-working of a patent
Nichtausübung *f* **e–s Rechts** (Re) nonexercise of a right
Nichtausübungsklausel *f* (Fin) no-action clause

nichtautomatische Rallonge *f* (AuW) non-automatic rallonge
nicht-autonome Nachfrage *f* (Vw) derived demand
Nichtbank *f* (Fin) non-bank
Nichtbankengeldmarkt *m* (Fin) intercompany money market
Nichtbankenkundschaft *f* (Fin) nonbank customers
Nichtbankensektor *m* (Vw) nonbanking sector *(ie, private and government sectors)*
nicht bankfähig (Fin) unbankable
Nichtbankplatz *m* (Fin) nonbank place
Nichtbasisvariable *f* (OR) nonbasic variable
Nichtbeachtung *f* (Re) noncompliance (with)
Nichtbeantwortung *f* (Stat) non-response
nicht beeinflußbare Kosten *pl* (KoR) uncontrollable cost
nicht befriedigter Gläubiger *m* (Re) unsatisfied creditor
nichtbeherrschte Fertigung *f* (Stat) process out of control
nicht beobachtbare Grundvariable *f* (Stat) latent variable
nicht berichtigtes Moment *n* (Stat) crude moment
nicht bestreikt
(Pw) not strike-bound
– nonstruck *(eg, steel mills)*
nicht bevorrechtigte Forderung *f* (Re) ordinary debt
nicht bevorrechtigte Konkursforderungen *fpl* (Re) unsecured debt
nicht bevorrechtigter Gläubiger *m*
(Re) ordinary
– general
– nonpreferred
– unsecured ... creditor
nichtbörsenfähig (Fin) nonmarketable *(eg, capital market paper)*
nicht börsenfähige Werte *mpl* (Bö) nonmarketable securities
nicht börsengängige Wertpapiere *n* (Bö) nonmarketable securities
nichtbuchführungspflichtige Landwirte *mpl* (StR) nonbookkeeping farmers, § 13a EStG
nichtdauerhafte Güter *npl* (Vw) nondurable goods
nichtdauerhafte Produktionsmittel *npl* (Vw) nondurable means of production
nichtdeutsche Arbeitnehmer *mpl* (Pw) foreign employees
nichtdichte Menge *f* (Math) nondense set
nicht diskontfähiger Wechsel *m* (Fin) unbankable paper
nicht diskriminierender Zoll *m* (Zo) nondiscriminatory tariff
Nichtdiskriminierung *f* (AuW) nondiscrimination
nichtdokumentäres Akkreditiv *n* (Fin) clean (*or* open) credit
nichtdruckende Funktion *f* (EDV) non-print function
nichteheliche Kinder *npl* (StR) illegitimate children
nicht eingefordertes Kapital *n* (Fin) uncalled capital
nicht eingelöste Police *f* (Vers) policy not taken up
nicht eingelöster Scheck *m* (Fin) unpaid check
nicht eingelöster Wechsel *m* (WeR) dishonored bill

nicht eingetragener Verein *m* (Re) unincorporated association
nicht eingezahlte Einnahmen *fpl* (Fin) undeposited receipts
Nichteinhaltung *f* (Re) noncompliance
Nichteinhaltung *f* **vertraglicher Vereinbarungen** (Re) nonfulfillment of contract stipulations
Nichteinlösung *f* (WeR) nonpayment
Nichteinlösung *f* **e–s Schecks** (Fin) dishonor of a check
Nichteintritt *m* **e–r Bedingung** (Re) failure of a condition *(eg, precedent or subsequent = aufschiebend od auflösend)*
Nichteisenmetalle *npl* (com) nonferrous metals
nicht empfangsbedürftig (Re) effective without communication
nichtendliche Menge *f* (Math) nonfinite set
nichtentartete Basislösung *f* (OR) nondegenerate basic solution
nichtentartete Lösung *f* (OR) nondegenerate solution
nicht entlasteter Gemeinschuldner *m* (Re) undischarged debtor *(or bankrupt)*
nicht entnommene Gewinne *mpl* (ReW) = *nicht ausgeschüttete Gewinne*
nicht entziehbare Betriebsmittel *pl* (EDV) nonpreemptive resources
nicht erfaßte Kosten *pl* (KoR) imputed cost *(syn, unterstellte Kosten, kalkulatorische Kosten)*
nicht erfolgwirksame Kosten *pl* (KoR) unexpired cost
nicht erfüllender Verkäufer *m* (Re) nonperforming seller
Nichterfüllung *f*
(Re) failure of performance *(or to perform)*
– nonfulfillment
– nonperformance
Nichterfüllung *f* **e–s Kaufvertrages** (Re) nonperformance of a sales contract
Nichterwartungstreue *f* (Stat) bias
nicht erwartungstreue Schätzfunktion *f* (Stat) biased estimator
Nicht-Erwerbspersonen *fpl*
(Vw) persons outside the labor force
– non-active population
nichtfiskalische Abgaben *fpl* (FiW) non-revenue regulatory taxes
nichtfiskalische Besteuerung *f* (FiW) nonrevenue regulatory taxation *(ie, employed as an instrument of implementing economic policies)*
nichtflüchtiger Speicher *m* (EDV) non-volatile *(or permanent)* memory
nichtformales Modell *n* (Vw) naive *(or nonformal)* model
Nichtgemeinschaftsländer *npl* (EG) non-Community countries
nicht genehmigter Streik *m* (Pw) unofficial strike
nichtgewerbliche Einfuhr *f* (AuW) non-commercial imports
nichtgewerbliche Investitionen *fpl* (VGR) capital expenditure outside the enterprise sector *(ie, primarily public building and private housing)*
nicht gewinnberechtigte Police *f* (Vers) non-participating policy
NICHT-Glied *n* (EDV) NOT circuit *(or element)*

nichthomogene Flüsse *mpl* (OR) multi-commodity flows
Nichtidentifizierbarkeit *f* (Stat) incomplete identification
nichtig
(Re) void
– null and void
– ineffectual
– having no legal force *(or binding effect)*
– nugatory
– without legal efficacy
Nichtigkeit *f* (Re) nullity *(eg, of legal transaction)*
Nichtigkeitseinrede *f* (Re) defense of nullity
Nichtigkeitserklärung *f* (Re) declaration of nullity
Nichtigkeitsgrund *m* (Re) ground of nullity
Nichtigkeitsgründe *mpl* (Pat) grants for revocation
Nichtigkeitsklage *f* (Re) nullity suit
Nichtigkeitsverfahren *n* (Pat) revocation of patent by court
nicht in Anspruch genommene Nachlässe *mpl* (com) discounts lost
nicht in Anspruch genommener Kredit *m* (Fin) undrawn loan facilities
nichtinflationäres Wachstum *n* (Vw) noninflationary *(or inflation-free)* growth
nichtkommerzielle Einfuhren *fpl* (AuW) non-commercial importations
nichtkommutativer Körper *m* (Math) noncommutative field
nicht konkurrierende Gruppen *fpl* (Vw) noncompeting groups *(Cairnes)*
nichtkonsistente Schätzfunktion *f* (Stat) inconsistent estimator
nicht konsolidierter Abschluß *m* (ReW) deconsolidated statement
nicht konsolidierte Schuld *f* (FiW) floating *(or unconsolidated)* debt
nichtkonvertible Währung *f* (AuW) nonconvertible currency
nichtkooperatives Spiel *n* (OR) noncooperative game
nicht laufend veranlagte Steuern *fpl* (StR) non-recurring taxes *(eg, capital transfer tax, inheritance tax)*
nichtleere Menge *f* (Math) nonnull set
nichtleere Teilmenge *f* (Math) nonnull subset
Nichtlieferung *f* (com) nondelivery
nichtlineare Beschränkung *f* (Math) nonlinear constraint *(or restriction)*
nichtlineare Beziehung *f* (Math) curvilinear relationship
nichtlineare Korrelation *f* (Stat) curvilinear correlation
nichtlineare Programmierung *f* (OR) nonlinear programming
nichtlineare Regression *f* (Stat) curvilinear *(or nonlinear)* regression
nichtlinearer Trend *m* (Stat) curvilinear trend
nicht lösbare Gleichung *f* (Math) inconsistent equation
nichtmarktliche Entscheidungstheorie *f*
(Vw) nonmarket decision theory
– New Political Economy
(syn, Ökonomische Theorie der Politik, Neue Politische Ökonomie)

441

nichtmarktwirtschaftliche Aktivität f (Vw) non-market-directed activity *(eg, output of numerous farm products which is determined by government-decreed price supports)*
nichtmaterielle Investition f (Bw) intangible investment
nichtmechanischer Drucker m (EDV) non-impact printer *(syn, anschlagloser Drucker)*
nichtmonetäre Transaktion f (AuW) non-monetary transaction
nichtmonetäre Überinvestitionstheorie f (Vw) nonmonetary overinvestment theory
Nichtnegativitäts-Bedingung f (OR) nonnegativity condition *(or requirement or restriction)*
nicht normal verteilte Grundgesamtheit f (Stat) nonnormal population
nicht normal verteilte Stichprobe f (Stat) nonnormal sample
nichtnotierte Aktien fpl **und Anteile** mpl (Bö) unlisted shares
nichtnotierte Anteile mpl **an Kapitalgesellschaften** (StR) unlisted investments *(eg, in limited liability companies and in closely held corporations)*
nichtnotiertes Unternehmen n (Bö) unquoted company
nichtnotiertes Wertpapier n
(Bö) unlisted
– unquoted
– off-board ... security
nicht notifiziertes Factoring n (Fin) nonnotification factoring
Nicht-Notwendigkeitsgüter npl
(Vw) nonessential goods
– luxuries
(ie, income elasticity less than unity)
Nichtnullsummenspiel n (OR) nonzero sum game
nichtöffentliche Stiftung f (Re) private endowment
nicht ordnungsgemäße Erfüllung f (Re) incomplete performance
nicht organisiert (Pw) non-unionized
nichtorganisierte Arbeitnehmer mpl
(Pw) unorganized
– non-union
– non-unionized ... employees
nichtperiodischer Dezimalbruch m (Math) nonperiodic *(or nonrepeating)* decimal
nichtplanarer Graph m (OR) nonplanar graph
nichtprogrammierte Entscheidungen fpl (Bw) non-programmed decisions *(ie, novel, singular, ill-structured political decisions that can be addressed only by general problem-solving approaches)*
nicht programmierter Sprung m (EDV) trap
nicht programmierter Stopp m
(EDV) hangup
– unexpected halt
Nichtraucher-Bereich m (Pw) tobacco-free work area
nicht realisierte Gewinne mpl (ReW) unrealized profits *(or* gains)
nicht realisierte Kursverluste mpl (Bö) paper losses
nicht realisierter Kursgewinn m (Bö) paper profit
nicht realisierter Wertverlust m (ReW) unrealized depreciation
nicht realisierter Wertzuwachs m (ReW) unrealized appreciation

nicht realisierte Verluste mpl (ReW) unrealized losses
nicht realisierte Wertsteigerung f (ReW) valuation excess
nichtrechtsfähige Personenvereinigung f (Re) unincorporated association
nichtrechtsfähiger Verein m (Re) unincorporated society
(ie, association without independent legal existence, § 54 BGB)
nicht relevante Kosten pl (KoR) nonrelevant costs
NICHT-Schaltung f
(EDV) NOT circuit *(or* element)
– inverter
nichtselbständige Arbeit f (StR) dependent employment
nichtsinguläre Matrix f (Math) nonsingular matrix
nichtsinguläre Verteilung f (Stat) nonsingular distribution
Nichtstandardkennsatz m (EDV) non-standard labels
nichtstationäre Wirtschaft f (Vw) nonstationary economy
nichtsteuerbare Umsätze mpl (StR, VAT) nontaxable *(or* non-qualifying) turnovers, § 1 Nos. 1 and 2 UStG
nichtsteuerliche Einnahmen fpl (FiW) non-tax receipts
nicht stimmberechtigte Aktie f (Fin) non-voting share
nichtbestimmberechtigte Vorzugsaktie f (Fin) non-voting preferred stock
nicht streuungsfähiges Risiko n (Fin) nondiversifiable risk *(ie, in portfolio analysis)*
nicht strukturierte Aufgabe f (Pw) nonstructured task
nichttarifäre Handelshemmnisse npl (AuW) non-tariff barriers to trade
nicht testierter Abschluß m (ReW) unaudited financial statement
nicht übereinstimmen
(com) to disagree
– not to be in conformity with
nicht übertragbar
(Re) nontransferable
– unassignable
nicht übertragbares Recht n (Re) unalienable right
nicht unmittelbar zurechenbare Schadensregulierungskosten pl (Vers) unallocated loss adjustment expenses
Nichtunternehmer m (Vw) nonfirm
nicht unterscheidungsfähige Warenzeichen npl (Pat) nondistinctive marks
nicht veranlagte Steuern fpl **vom Ertrag** (StR) non-assessed taxes on earnings
nicht verdiente Prämie f (Vers) unearned premium
Nichtverfügbarkeiten fpl (AuW) nonavailabilities
(ie, lack of supply opportunities in importing countries)
NICHT-Verknüpfung f
(EDV) NOT operation
– negation
– inversion
Nichtvermögensschaden m (Re) damage not resulting in pecuniary loss

nicht vermögenswirksame Subvention f (FiW) non-asset-creating subsidy
nicht verrechnete Gemeinkosten pl (KoR) unabsorbed overhead
nicht verschwindender Wert m (Math) nonzero value
nicht versicherbares Risiko n (Vers) noninsurable risk
nicht versicherter Schaden m (Vers) uninsured loss
nicht versicherungspflichtige Beschäftigung f (SozV) noninsurable occupation
nicht vertragsgemäße Waren fpl (Re) nonconforming goods
nichtverzerrende Schätzgleichung f (Stat) unbiased estimating equation
nicht verzögerte Investitionsfunktion f (Vw) unlegged investment function
nicht voll eingezahlte Aktie f (Fin) partly paid share
nicht vorhersehbarer Schaden m (com) unforeseeable damage
Nichtwohngebäude npl (com) non-residential buildings
nichtwirtschaftliche Güter npl (Vw) noneconomic goods
nichtwirtschaftlicher Verein m (Re) association not for profit, §§ 21, 55 BGB
Nichtzahlung f
(Fin) nonpayment
– failure to pay
nicht zerlegbar (Math) non factorable
nichtzinstragende Kassenbestände mpl (Fin) non-interest-bearing cash balances *(ie, currency and sight deposits)*
nicht zolltarifliche Handelshemmnisse npl (AuW) nontariff barriers
nichtzufällige Stichprobe f (Stat) non-random sample
nicht zugegangene Willenserklärung f (Re) uncommunicated intent
nicht zugelassene Wertpapiere npl (Bö) unlisted securities
nicht zugeschriebene Disagiobeträge mpl (ReW) unamortized discounts
nichtzusammenhängende Mengen fpl (Math) disconnecting sets
nichtzusammenhängender Graph m (Math) disconnected graph
nicht zu vertreten haben
(Re) beyond one's control *(eg, for reasons beyond our control)*
– not to be responsible for
nicht zweckgebundene Ausleihungen fpl (Fin) uncommitted lendings
nicht zweckgebundenes Kapital n (Fin) nonspecific capital
nicht zweckgebundene Zuweisung f (FiW) non-specific contribution *(ie, to subordinate government units = nachgeordnete Gebietskörperschaften)*
Niedergangsphase f (Mk) abandonment stage *(ie, in product life cycle)*
niederlassen, sich
(com) to establish *(or* set up) business
(SozV) to settle

– to locate *(eg, physicians or specialists, in big cities or unserved areas)*
Niederlassung f
(com) branch
– branch operation *(or* establishment)
– branch office
– field organization
Niederlassung f **im Ausland** (com) foreign branch
Niederlassungsfreiheit f (EG) freedom of establishment
Niederlassungsrecht n
(Re) law of establishment
(Re) right of establishment
Niedersächsische Börse f (Bö) Hanover Stock Exchange
– Lower Saxony Exchange
Niederschlagung f (StR) temporary tax waiver *(ie, issued if cost of assessing and collecting a tax would be out of proportion to amount that could be assessed, §§ 156 II, 261 AO)*
Niederschrift f **in der Hauptversammlung** (Re) minutes of the shareholders' meeting, § 130 AktG
Niederstwert m
(ReW) lower of cost or market
– cost or market whichever is lower
Niederstwertkurs m (AuW) lower value rate
Niederstwertprinzip n
(ReW) principle *(or* rule) of the lower of cost or market, § 155 AktG
niedrigbesteuernde Gebiete npl (StR) low-tax territories
niedrig besteuernde Länder npl (StR) low-tax countries
niedrig bewertete Aktien fpl (Fin) low-priced shares *(or* stocks)
niedrig bezahlte Arbeitsplätze mpl (Pw) low-paying jobs
niedrige Anfangsbelastung f (Fin) low initial debt service
niedrige Qualität f (com) low quality
niedriger Abschluß m (Pw) low (pay) settlement
niedriger einstufen
(com) to downgrade
– to put into lower group
niedriger notieren (Bö) to trade lower
niedriger Preis m (com) low *(or* soft) price
niedriges Angebot n (com) low bid *(or* price) offer
Niedriglohnland n (AuW) low-wage country
Niedrigpreis m
(com) cut price
– thrift price
Niedrigpreisgeschäft n (com) cut-price store
Niedrigpreis-Waren fpl (Mk) bargain goods
niedrigster Kurs m (Bö) bottom price
niedrigster Preis m
(com) lowest
– bottom
– rockbottom . . . price
Niedrigsteuerland n (StR) low-tax country
Niedrigstkurs m (Bö) bottom price
Niedrigstkurs m **im EWS** (AuW) lower exchange limit in the EMS
niedrigstwertiges Zeichen n (EDV) least significant character

443

niedrigverzinslich
(Fin) carrying a low interest rate
– low-interest yielding
niedrigverzinslicher Kredit m (Fin) low-interest loan
Niedrigverzinsliche pl (Fin) = niedrigverzinsliche Wertpapiere
niedrigverzinsliche Kurzläufer mpl (Fin) low-coupon shorts
niedrigverzinsliche Wertpapiere npl
(Fin) low-yield securities
– low-coupon securities
– low yielders
Niedrigzinspolitik f
(Vw) policy of low interest rates
– easy money policy
Nießbrauch m
(Re) lifelong right of use
– usufruct
– usufructuary right
(ie, right to use another's property and to appropriate the proceeds thereof, §§ 1030–1089 BGB)
Nießbraucher m
(Re) lifelong user of property
– usufructuary
Niveauänderung f **des Produktionsprozesses** (Vw) change in the level of activity
Niveau n **des Produktionsniveaus** (Vw) level of activity
Niveau n **des Tests** (Stat) level of significance
Niveauelastizität f (Vw) scale elasticity (ie, of a process)
Niveaugrenzerträge mpl (Vw) returns to scale
Niveaugrenzprodukt n (Vw) returns to scale (syn, Skalenertrag)
Niveauverschiebungseffekt m (FiW) displacement effect
(A. T. Peacock/J. Wiseman, 1967)
Nivellierungsmethode f (IndE) leveling system (ie, of performance rating = Leistungsgradschätzen; syn, LMS-Verfahren, Westinghouse-System)
n-Nachwirkungsfreiheit f (Stat) n-freedom
Nochgeschäft n
(Bö) call of more
– put of more
– option to double
noch nicht verjährter Anspruch m (Re) claim not yet barred (ie, by the Statute of Limitations)
noch nicht verrechnete Schecks mpl (Fin) uncleared items
Nochstücke npl (Bö) securities requested under a 'call of more'
Nomenklatur f (Zo) customs nomenclature (syn, Zolltarifschema)
Nomenklaturausschuß m (EG) Nomenclature Committee
Nomenklatur f **für den Kapitalverkehr** (Fin) nomenclature of capital movements
Nominaldefinition f (Log) nominal (or syntactical) definition
(ie, a convention providing that a certain symbol or expression shall stand as substitutes for a particular formula of a system; opp, Realdefinition)
Nominaleinkommen n (Vw) nominal income (opp, real income)

Nominaleinkommen n **des Haushalts** (Vw) consumer's money income
nominale Löhne mpl (Vw) money wages
nominale Parität f (AuW) nominal parity
Nominalertrag m (Fin) = Nominalverzinsung
nominales BIP n (VGR) GDP (gross domestic product) in money terms
nominales Einkommen n (Vw) nominal (or money) income
nominales Sozialprodukt n
(VGR) nominal social product
– national product in money terms
Nominalismus m (Vw) nominalism (opp, metallism)
Nominalkapital n (Fin) nominal capital (ie, capital stock of AG and share capital of GmbH as shown in the balance sheets)
Nominallohn m (Vw) nominal (or money) wage (opp, Reallohn)
Nominallohnsatz m (Vw) nominal wage rate
Nominalverzinsung f
(Fin) nominal interest rate
– cash rate
– coupon rate
– yield (ie, of bonds)
Nominalwert m
(Fin) face value (or amount)
– nominal value (or amount)
– par value (syn, Nennbetrag, Nennwert)
Nominalwertprinzip n (Vw, Bw) nominal-value principle
(ie, DM = DM: the value of money is regarded as independent of its real purchasing power; in business accounting, the difference between historical and current costs results in paper profits and thus – via inflation and taxation – in asset erosion = Substanzverlust)
Nominalwertrechnung f (Fin) par value accounting
Nominalzins m (Fin) = Nominalverzinsung
Nominalzoll m (Zo) nominal tariff
nominell (Vw) in money terms (opp, real = in real terms)
nominelle Entschädigung f (Fin) token amount of indemnity
nominelle Kapitalerhaltung f
(Fin) nominal maintenance of capital
– preservation of corporate assets in money terms
– recovery of original cost
(ie, during operating or service life; opp, substantielle Kapitalerhaltung = in real terms)
nomineller Lohnsatz m (Vw) money wage rate
nominelles BSP n
(VGR) nominal gnp
– gnp in money terms (ie, not at constant prices)
Nomogramm n
(Math) alignment chart
– nomogram
Nonaffektationsprinzip n (FiW) principle of non-appropriation of public funds to specific purposes, § 8 BHO
Non-Karbon-Papier n (EDV) noncarbon paper
Nonsense-Korrelation f (Stat) nonsense correlation
Nonvaleurs mpl (Bö) securities of little or no value

NOP-Befehl *m* (EDV) no-operation (*or* no-op)
- blank
- dummy
- skip ... instruction
(*syn, Nulloperationsbefehl, Übersprungbefehl*)
Nord-Süd-Dialog *m* (Vw) North-South dialog
Nordwesteckenregel *f* (OR) northwest corner rule
NOR-Funktion *f* (EDV) = *NOR-Verknüpfung*
NOR-Glied *n* (EDV) NOR circuit (*or* element)
Norm *f* (IndE) standard specification
Normalablage *f* (EDV) = *Normalfach*
Normalableitung *f* (Math) normal derivative
Normalabschreibung *f* (ReW) ordinary (*or* standard) depreciation *(ie, as shown in financial statement)*
Normalarbeitstag *m* (Pw) standard work day
Normalarbeitsvertrag *m* (Pw) standard contract of employment
Normalarbeitszeit *f* (Pw) standard time
Normalauslastung *f* (Bw) standard utilization
Normalbeschäftigung *f*
(Bw) normal level of capacity utilization
(KoR) normal activity (*or* volume)
- standard activity (*or* capacity)
Normalbrief *m* (com) standard letter
Normaldauer *f* (OR) most probable duration
normale Abweichungsstreuung *f* (Stat) normal error dispersion
normale Arbeitszeit *f* (Pw) standard time
normale Fahrlässigkeit *f*
(Re) ordinary negligence, § 276 BGB
- (*civil law*) culpa levis
normale Fehlerkurve *f* (Stat) normal curve of error
normale Geschäftstätigkeit *f* (ReW, EG) ordinary activities
normale Kapazität *f* (Bw) normal sustainable capacity
normale Offenmarktgeschäfte *npl* (Vw) outright transactions
normale Prüfung *f* (Stat) normal inspection
normaler Handelsverkehr *m* (AuW) ordinary course of trade
normaler Weg *m* (EDV) primary route *(syn, Direktweg; opp, Alternativweg)*
normales Akkreditiv *n* (Fin) straight credit
normales Gut *n* (Vw) normal good
Normalfach *n* (EDV) normal stacker
Normalform *f* (Log) normal (*or* standard) form *(ie, of propositional logic = Aussagenlogik)*
Normalfracht *f* (com) ordinary cargo
Normalgewinn *m* (Vw) normal profit
Normalkapazität *f* (KoR) normal (*or* standard plant) capacity
Normalkonditionen *fpl* (com) standard terms and conditions
Normalkosten *pl* (KoR) normal cost *(ie, including an average or normalized chunk of overhead)*
Normalkostenrechnung *f*
(KoR) normal costing
- normal cost system
Normalkostensatz *m* (KoR) normal cost rate
Normallaufzeit *f* (com) original term
Normalleistung *f*
(IndE) normal output
- target performance

Normallochung *f* (EDV) digit punching
Normallohn *m* (Pw) standard wage
Normalpolice *f* (Vers) standard policy
Normalpreis *m* (KoR) normal (*or* standard) price
Normalrendite *f* (Fin) normal return
Normalsteuersatz *m* (StR) regular rate^t, § 12 UStG
Normalstreuung *f* (Stat) normal dispersion
Normaltarif *m* (com) standard rates *(ie, in rail transportation)*
Normalverbraucher *m* (com) average consumer
Normalverdienst *m* (Pw) straight-time earnings
Normalverteilung *f* (Stat) normal (Gaussian) distribution
Normalverzinsung *f* (Fin) nominal yield
Normalwerte *mpl* (KoR) normal quantities *(ie, costed at fixed prices)*
Normalzeit *f*
(IndE) basic
- base
- standard ... time
Normalzoll *m* (Zo) general tariff
Normalzuschlag *m* (KoR) normal percentage rate *(ie, applied to direct cost as derived from past periods)*
normativer Satz *m* (Log) normative statement
normative Wirtschaftswissenschaft *f* (Vw) normative economics *(opp, positive W. = positive economics)*
normen (IndE) to standardize
Normen- und Typenkartell *n* (Kart) standardization cartel *(ie, relating to uniform methods for the specification of goods and services)*
normieren (Math) to normalize *(eg, vector)*
normierte Programmierung *f* (EDV) standardized programming
normierte Zufallsabweichung *f* (Stat) deviate
Normierungsfaktor *m* (EDV) scale (*or* scaling) factor
Normkosten *pl* (KoR) ideal standard cost
Norm-Rediskont-Kontingent *n* (Vw) · standard rediscount quota
Normung *f* (IndE) standardization
Normungsvorhaben *n* (Kart) standardization project, § 5 I GWB
normunterschreitende Qualität *f* (Stat) substandard quality
Normwerte *mpl* (Bw) standards *(ie, mostly longstanding average values, suited to the special conditions of a plant)*
NOR-Schaltung *f* (EDV) NOR circuit (*or* element *or* gate)
NOR-Verknüpfung *f*
(EDV) NOR operation
- nondisjunction
- joint denial
- Peirce function
- rejection
Nostroeffekten *pl*
(Fin) nostro securities
- securities owned by a bank
Nostrogeschäft *n* (Fin) business for own account
Nostroguthaben *n* (Fin) credit balance on nostro account
- nostro balance (*or* account)

(ie, account kept by one commercial bank with another)
Nostrokonten *npl* (Fin) nostro accounts *(ie, liquid balances on deposit with other credit institutions)*
Nostroverbindlichkeit *f*
(Fin) nostro liability
– due to banks
Nostroverpflichtungen *fpl* (Fin) nostro commitments
Notadresse *f* (WeR) referee in case of need
Notakzept *n* (WeR) acceptance in case of need
Notanzeige *f* (WeR) notice of dishonor
Notar *m*
(Re) notary public
– (GB) Commissioner for Oaths
(ie, lawyer, free professional, qualified as a judge, officially appointed; no equivalent in British and American law)
Notar-Anderkonto *n* (Fin) banking account kept by a notary public in his own name for a third party on a trust basis
Notariatsgebühr *f* (Re) notarial fee
Notariatskosten *pl* (Re) notarial charges
notariell beglaubigen
(Re) to notarize
– to record in notarial form
notariell beglaubigt (Re) notarially authenticated
notariell beurkundetes Rechtsgeschäft *n* (Re) notarized legal transaction
notarielle Beglaubigung *f* (Re) notarial authentication
notarielle Bescheinigung *f* (Re) notarial certificate *(or attestation)*
notarielle Beurkundung *f*
(Re) notarial record
– recording by a notary
– authentication by public act
notarieller Vertrag *m* (Re) notarized agreement *(or contract)*
notarielle Urkunde *f* (Re) notarial act *(or instrument)*
Notbestellung *f* (Re) emergency appointment, § 29 BGB
Notbetrieb *m*
(IndE) emergency operation
– plant operation on a care and maintenance basis
Notenausgabe *f* (Vw) issue of bank notes
Notenausgaberecht *n*
(Vw) authority to issue notes
– note-issuing privilege
Notenbank *f* (Vw) central bank
Notenbankausweis *m* (Fin) central bank return
notenbankfähig (Vw) eligible for rediscount with the central bank
Notenbank-Diskont *m* (Vw) discount rate
Notenbankguthaben *npl* (Fin) central bank balances
Notenbank-Intervention *f* **beim Blockfloaten** (AuW) multiple currency intervention
Notenbankkredit *m* (Fin) central bank loan
Notenbankpolitik *f* (Vw) central bank policy
Notenbankpräsident *m* (Vw) central bank governor
Notenbankprivileg *n* (Vw) note-issuing privilege

Notenbankzinssätze *mpl* (Fin) official interest rates
Notendeckung *f* (Vw) cover of notes in circulation
Notenemission *f* (Vw) issue of bank notes
Notenrückfluß *m* (Vw) reflux of bank notes
Notenstückelung *f* (Vw) denomination of notes
Notenumlauf *m* (Vw) notes in circulation
Nothafen *m*
(com) port of distress
– port of necessity
– port of refuge
notieren
(Bö) to list *(ie, on the stock exchange)*
– to quote
notiert
(Bö) listed
– quoted
notierte Aktien *fpl* (Bö) quoted equities
notierter Kurs *m* (Bö) quoted price
notierte Währung *f* (AuW) currency quoted *(ie, on the official foreign exchange markets)*
notierte Wertpapiere *npl* (Bö) listed *(or quoted)* securities
Notierungen *fpl* **an der Börse** (Bö) official prices *(or quotations)*
Notierung *f* **im Freiverkehr** (Bö) over-the-counter *(or unofficial)* quotation
Notierung *f* **im Telefonverkehr** *m* (Bö) off-board quotation
Notierungsmethode *f* (Bö) quotation technique
Notifikation *f* (Fin) notification
notifizieren (com) to notify
notifiziertes Factoring *n* (Fin) notification factoring
Notifizierung *f* (com) notification
Nötigung *f* (Re) duress, § 240 StGB
Notiz *f* (Bö) quotation
Notizblock *m*
(com) scratch pad
– (GB) scribbling block *(or pad)*
Notizblockspeicher *m* (EDV) scratch-pad memory *(syn, Schnellspeicher)*
Notizen *fpl* **machen** (com) to take notes
Notiz *f* **ohne Umsätze** (Bö) nominal quotation
notleidend
(Fin) defaulting
– in default
notleidende Aktiva *npl* (Fin) nonperforming assets
notleidende Branche *f* (com) ailing industry
notleidender Wechsel *m*
(Fin) bill overdue
– dishonored bill
notleidendes Engagement *n* (Fin) default on a loan
notleidende Wirtschaftszweige *mpl* (com) ailing industries
notleidend werden (Fin) to go into default *(eg, loans)*
Notstand *m* (Re) self-defense *(or self-help)* against things, § 228 BGB
Notstandsarbeiten *fpl* (Vw) public relief work *(ie, not ,public work' which is = öffentliche Arbeiten)*
Notstandskartell *n* (Kart) emergency cartel
Notstandspaket *n* (Vw) emergency package
Notstandsplan *m* (Vw) emergency plan
Notverkauf *m*
(com) distress sale

446

- emergency sale
- panic sale
- bail out

notwendige Bedingung *f* (Log) necessary condition

notwendiges Betriebsvermögen *n* (StR) necessary business property *(ie, assets whose use is necessarily limited to business purposes)*

notwendiges Privatvermögen *n* (StR) necessary private property *(ie, assets usually not appropriated to business purposes)*

Notwendigkeitsgüter *npl* (Vw) essential goods
- essentials
- necessities *(ie, income elasticity less than unity)*

Novation *f* (Re) novation, § 364 II BGB *(ie, substitution of a new contract or obligation for an existing one: originally a term of the civil law, but now also in general use in US and GB; syn, Schuldumwandlung)*

Novationsvertrag *m* (Re) substituted contract

Novelle *f* (Re) amending statute

Novelle *f* **einbringen** (Re) to introduce an amendment

Novelle *f* **verabschieden** (Re) to pass an amendment

novellieren (Re) to amend

Novellierung *f* (Re) amendment

NRZ-Schreibverfahren *n* (EDV) non-return-to-zero recording

NRZ/C-Schreibverfahren *n* (EDV) non-return-to-zero change recording

NRZ/M-Schreibverfahren *n* (EDV) non-return-to-zero mark recording

n-stellig
(Log, Math) n-place
- polyadic

n-stelliger Junktor *m* (Log) n-ary connective

n-tes Glied *n* (Math) last term *(ie, of a sequence or series)*

Nullachse *f* (Math) polar axis

Null-Basis-Budgetierung *f* (FiW) zero-base budgeting

Nullelemente *npl* (Math) zeros

Nullfehlerprogramm *n* (Stat) zero defects program *(ie, in quality control)*

Nullhypothese *f* (Stat) null *(or* zero) hypothesis

Nullklasse *f* (Log) null class *(ie, extension of empty concepts)*

Nullkorrelation *f* (Stat) zero order correlation

Nullmatrix *f* (Math) null matrix

Nullmenge *f*
(Math) empty
- null
- void ... set

Nulloperation *f* (EDV) no operation, NOP, no-op

Nulloperationsbefehl *m* (EDV) no-operation
- no-op
- blank
- dummy
- skip ... instruction
(syn, NOP-Befehl, Übersprungbefehl)

Nullpunkt *m* (Math) pole *(ie, in the polar coordinate system)*

Nullpunkt *m* **des Kartesischen Koordinatensystems** (Math) origin of Cartesian coordinates

Nullsaldo *m* (ReW) zero balance

Nullserie *f* (Stat) pilot lot

Nullstellen *fpl* (Math) zeros

Nullsummen-Gesellschaft *f* (Vw) zero-sum society *(ie, phrase coined by L. Thurow)*

Null-Summen-Spiel *n* (OR) zero sum game

Nulltarif *m*
(com) fare-free transport
(Zo) nil tariff

null und nichtig (Re) null and void

Nullunterdrückung *f* (EDV, Cobol) zero suppression

Nullwachstum *n* (Vw) zero growth

Nullzone *f* (FiW) zero bracket amount

Nullzustand *m* (EDV) zero condition *(or* state)

nume§raire (AuW) nume§raire *(ie, denominator for the exchange rate mechanism)*

numerische Analyse *f* (EDV) numerical analysis

numerische Daten *pl* (EDV) numeric data

numerische Direktsteuerung *f* (EDV) direct numerical control, DNC

numerische Größe *f* (Math) numerical quantity

numerische Lochung *f* (EDV) numeric punching

numerischer Code *m* (EDV) numeric (data) code

numerisches Literal *n* (EDV, Cobol) numerical literal

numerische Steuerung *f* (IndE) numerical control, NC

numerisches Wort *n* (EDV) numeric word

numerisches Zeichen *n* (EDV) numeric character
- digit

numerische Ziele *npl* (Bw) numberized *(or* targeted) goals

numerisch gesteuerte Fertigung *f* (IndE) numerically controlled manufacturing

numerisch gesteuerte Maschinen *fpl* (IndE) numerically controlled (NC) machines

Numerus *m*
(Math) antilogarithm
- inverse logarithm

Numerus clausus *m* (Pw) restricted entry *(ie, to university for overcrowded subjects)*

Nummernkonto *n* (Fin) number *(or* numbered) account *(ie, account to be kept secret from tax and currency control authorities)*

Nummernschild *n*
(com) license plate
- (GB) number plate

Nummernschlüssel *m* (EDV) numeric(al) code

Nummernverzeichnis *n* (Fin) list of securities deposited

nutzbare Maschinenzeit *f* (EDV) available (machine) time *(syn, verfügbare Benutzerzeit)*

Nutzbarkeit *f* (EDV) serviceability

Nutzeffekt *m* (com) efficacy

nutzen (com, fml) to avail oneself of *(eg, offer, proposal, opportunity)*
- to make use of

Nutzen *m*
(Vw) utility
- satisfaction

Nutzen *m* **aus der Formveränderung e–s Gutes** (Vw) form utility

Nutzenaustauschverhältnis *n* (AuW) utility terms of trade
Nutzen *m* **e–r Erfindung** (Pat) utility of an invention
Nutzeneinheit *f* (Vw) util
Nutzenentgang *m* (Vw) negative utility
Nutzenfunktion *f* (Vw) utility function
Nutzengebirge *n* (Vw) utility surface
Nutzen-Kosten-Analyse *f* (com) cost-benefit analysis
Nutzen-Kosten-Kennziffer *f* (FiW) cost-benefit ratio
Nutzenmatrix *f* (Bw) payoff matrix
Nutzenmaximierung *f* (Vw) utility maximization
Nutzenmaximierungsannahme *f* (Vw) utility maximizing rule
Nutzenmaximum *n* (Vw) maximum utility
Nutzenmöglichkeitskurve *f* (Vw) utility frontier
– utility possibility curve in the point sense
Nutzenniveau *n* (Vw) level of satisfaction (*or* utility)
Nutzenprinzip *n*
(FiW) benefit principle
– benefits received principle
Nutzentheorie *f* (Vw) utility theory
Nutzenzweigfunktion *f* (Vw) branch utility function
Nutzfahrzeuge *npl* (com) commercial vehicles
Nutzfahrzeugmarkt *m* (com) commercial vehicles market
Nutzlast *f* (com) pay load
Nutzlastexperte *m* (com) payload expert
Nützlichkeit *f* (Pat) usefulness
– utility
Nutznießer *m* (Re) usufructuary
(Re) beneficiary
Nutzschwelle *f* (KoR) breakeven point *(syn, Gewinnschwelle, Kostendeckungspunkt, toter Punkt)*
Nutzung *f*
(Re) use
– enjoyment

Nutzung *f* **der Meere** (Re) use of the seas
Nutzungsausfall *m* (Vers) loss of use
Nutzungsausfall-Versicherung *f* (Vers) use and occupancy insurance
nutzungsbedingte Abschreibung *f* (ReW) depreciation through use
Nutzungsdauer *f*
(Bw) effective life
– operating life
– service (*or* serviceable) life
– useful economic life
– working life
Nutzungsentgang *m* (Bw) loss of use
Nutzungsentschädigung *f* (Vers) compensation for loss of use
Nutzungsgebühr *f* (com) royalty *(ie, compensation for the use of property)*
(FiW) user fee
Nutzungsgüter *npl* (ReW) assets subject to depreciation
Nutzungshauptzeit *f* (IndE) controlled machine time
Nutzungspotential *n*
(Bw) service capacity
– bundle of potential services
Nutzungsrecht *n* (Re) right of use
Nutzungsvergütungen *fpl* **für die Inspruchnahme von Grundstücken für öffentliche Zwecke** (StR) indemnities paid for the requisitioning of real property under the right of eminent domain, § 24 No. 3 EStG
Nutzungsvertrag *m* (Re) contract for the transfer of use and enjoyment
Nutzungsvorrat *m* (Bw) bundle of services
Nutzungswert *m* **e–r Wohnung** (StR) rental value of appartment
Nutzungswert *m* **von Wohnungen im eigenen Haus** (StR) rental value of taxpayer's own home, § 21a EStG
Nutzwert *m* (Vw) utility value
Nutzwertanalyse *f* (Vw, Bw) benefit analysis *(ie, analysis of a set of complex action alternatives)*

O

Oasenländer *npl* (StR) tax havens *(ie, tiny low-tax countries refusing to conclude double taxation treaties; syn, Steueroasen)*
Oberbegriff *m*
(Log) general
– generic
– comprehensive
– overall
– umbrella ... term
(Log) major term *(ie, the predicate of the conclusion in a categorical syllogism)*
obere Entscheidungsgrenze *f* (Stat) upper control limit
obere Grenze *f*
(Math) least upper bound
– limit superior
obere Kontrollgrenze *f* (Stat) upper control limit

obere Leitungsebene *f* (Bw) upper echelon of management
obere Lochungszone *f* (EDV) upper curtate
obere Prüfgrenze *f* (Stat) = *obere Kontrollgrenze*
oberer Goldpunkt *m* (AuW) gold export point
oberer Grenzwert *m* (Math) upper limit
oberer Interventionspunkt *m*
(AuW) upper support point
– upper intervention rate
– buying point
oberer Rand *m* **der Schlange** (AuW) the snake's upper limit
oberer Rand *m* **des Zielkorridors** (Vw) top (*or* upper end) of target range
obere Schranke *f* **e–r Punktmenge** (Math) majorant
obere Zinsgrenze *f* (Fin) interest rate ceiling

Oberfinanzbezirk m (StR) regional revenue district
Oberfinanzdirektion f (StR) Regional Finance Office *(ie, tax administration on the intermediate level, being both federal and state authority, § 8 I FVG)*
Oberfinanzpräsident m (StR) head of a Regional Finance Office, § 9 I FVG
Oberflächenintegral n (Math) surface integral
Obergesellschaft f
(Re) common parent company, § 329 AktG
– controlling company
– umbrella company
Obergraph m (OR) supergraph
Obergutachten n (com) decisive expert opinion
Oberkörper m (Math) extension of a field *(syn, Erweiterungskörper, Körpererweiterung)*
Oberlandesgericht n (Re) Intermediate Court of Appeals *(ie, deciding on questions of fact and of law, §§ 115–122 GVG)*
Obermeister m (Pw) general *(or* senior) foreman
Obermenge f (Math) set including subsets
Oberprüfer m (Pat) chief examiner
Obersatz m (Log) major premise *(or* premiss) *(ie, containing the major term in a categorical syllogism)*
Oberschiedsrichter m (Re) umpire *(ie, third party selected to arbitrate)*
oberste Führungskraft f (Bw) top executive
oberste Geschäftsleitung f (Bw) top management
oberste Leitungsinstanz f (Bw) top management
oberster Koordinator m (Bw) peak coordinator
oberste Unternehmensleitung f (Bw) top management
oberste Unternehmensziele npl (Bw) top corporate goals *(or* objectives)
Oberverwaltungsgericht n (Re) appellate administrative court *(ie, sometimes called ‚Verwaltungsgerichtshof')*
Oberziel n (Bw) top objective
Objekt n (com) item of property
Objektanalyse f (Bw) task-oriented analysis
Objektbesteuerung f (FiW) taxation of specific property *(syn, Real- od Sachbesteuerung)*
objektbezogene Steuern fpl (FiW) in rem taxes
objektgebundene Kreditgewährung f (Fin) earmarked lending
Objektgliederung f (Bw) task structuring *(syn, Aufgabengliederung)*
objektive Entscheidung f (Re) disinterested *(or* objective) decision
objektive Kosten pl (Bw) objective costs *(ie, all relevant costs when factors of production are freely available = all non-opportunity-costs)*
objektiver Wert m (Bw) objective value
objektives Urteil n (com) unbiased judgment
objektive Unmöglichkeit f (Re) impossibility of performance, *(ie, total inability of party to perform for objective reasons, § 306 BGB)*
Objektkredit m (Fin) loan tied to specific property
Objektmodul m (EDV) object module
Objektprogrammkartensatz m (EDV) object deck
Objektsprache f (Log) object language
Objektsteuer f (FiW) impersonal tax
– tax levied on specific property *(syn, Realsteuer)*

Obligation f (Re) obligation *(ie, an undertaking to perform)*
(Fin) bond
– (GB) debenture
Obligationär m
(Fin) bondholder
– (GB) debenture holder
Obligation f **einlösen** (Fin) to redeem a bond
Obligationenagio n (Fin) bond premium
Obligationen fpl **der öffentlichen Hand** (FiW) public bonds
Obligationendisagio n (Fin) bond discount
Obligation f **mit Tilgungsplan** (Fin) sinking fund bond
Obligationsanleihe f
(Fin) bond loan
– (GB) debenture loan
Obligationsausgabe f (Fin) bond issue
Obligationsgläubiger m (Fin) bondholder
Obligationsinhaber m (Fin) bondholder
Obligationsschuldner m
(Fin) obligor
– bond issuer
Obligationstilgungsfonds m (Fin) bond sinking *(or* redemption) fund
obligatorisch
(Re) mandatory
– obligatory
– binding
obligatorische Rückversicherung f (Vers) automatic *(or* obligatory) treaty
obligatorischer Vertrag m
(Re) contract
– obligatory agreement
(ie, creating an obligation at least on one side)
obligatorisches Recht n (Re) obligatory right *(ie, right to have claims satisfied; opp, absolutes Recht = absolute right)*
obligatorisches Streitschlichtungsverfahren m (Re) compulsory settlement of disputes
obligatorische Versicherung f (Vers, SozV) compulsory insurance
Obligo n
(Fin) commitment
– guaranty
– liability
Obligobuch n (Fin) commitment ledger *(ie, kept by bills department of a bank)*
Obligomeldung f (Fin) notification of liablility
Obligoübernahme f (Fin) assumption of commitment *(or* liability)
Obmann m (Re) = *Oberschiedsrichter*
OC-Funktion f **des Prüfplans** (Stat) operating characteristic
OC-Kurve f (Stat) operating characteristic curve
ODER-Funktion f
(EDV) inclusive-OR operation
– disjunction
– logical add
Odergatter n (EDV) inclusive-OR element *(or* circuit) *(syn, Disjunktionsglied, Mischgatter, Oderglied)*
ODER-Glied n
(EDV) exclusive-OR element
– except gate

- non-equivalence element
  (syn, Antivalenzglied)
Oder-Konto *n* (Fin) joint account
(ie, with the instruction ,,either to sign"; opp, Und-Konto)
ODER-Schaltung *f*
  (EDV) OR circuit *(or* element)
  - inclusive-OR circuit
ODER-Verknüpfung *f*
  (EDV) inclusive-OR operation
  - disjunction
  - logical add
ODER-Zeichen *n* (EDV) OR operator
offenbare Mängel *mpl* (Re) patent defects
offenbarte Präferenzen *fpl* (Vw) revealed preferences *(syn, bekundete Präferenzen)*
Offenbarung *f* **e-r Erfindung** (Pat) disclosure of an invention
Offenbarungseid *m* (Re) oath of disclosure *(or* manifestation)
offene Ausfuhrprämie *f* (AuW) open export bounty
offene Bestellungen *fpl* (MaW) outstanding purchasing orders
offene Darlehenszusagen *fpl* (Fin) outstanding loan commitments
offene Deflation *f* (Vw) undisguised *(or* open) deflation
offene Frage *f* (Stat) open-ended question
offene Gruppe *f* (Stat) open-ended class
offene Handelsgesellschaft *f* (Re) general commercial partnership, §§ 105ff HGB *(ie, leading feature is the unrestricted liability of its partners for debt)*
offene Inflation *f* (Vw) undisguised *(or* open) inflation
offene Linie *f* (Fin) unutilized credit line
offene Personalanzeige *f* (Pw) open *(or* signed) ad
(see: Personalanzeige)
offene Police *f*
  (Vers) floating policy
  - floater
  - declaration policy
  - general policy
  - unvalued policy
  (SeeV) open cover
offene Positionen *fpl* (Bö) open commitments *(or* contracts)
Offene-Posten-Buchführung *f*
  (ReW) open item system
  - ledgerless accounting
  (syn, kontenlose od kontoblattlose Buchführung)
offene Punktmenge *f* (Math) open set of points
offener Auftragsbestand *m* (com) open orders
offener Befehl *m* (EDV) open-ended command
offener Betrag *m* (ReW) amount outstanding
offener Buchkredit *m*
  (Fin) open book account
  - charge account
  - open-account financing
  - sales on open-account basis
  - advance account
offener Dissens *m*
  (Re) patent ambiguity
  - open lack of agreement

offene Rechnung *f* (ReW) open *(or* outstanding) account
offener Fonds *m* (Fin) open-ended fund
offener Halbraum *m* (Math) open halfspace
offener Immobilienfonds *m* (Fin) open-ended real estate fund
offener Investmentfonds *m* (Fin) mutual *(or* open-ended) fund *(ie, no fixed capital)*
offener Kredit *m* (Fin) unsecured *(or* open) credit
offener Mangel *m* (Re) patent defect
offener Markt *m* (com) open market
offener Posten *m* (ReW) open item
offener Regelkreis *m* (EDV) open loop
offener Saldo *m* (ReW) balance due
offene Rücklage *f*
  (ReW) open
  - disclosed
  - general . . . reserve
offener Wagen *m*
  (com) open goods waggon
  - (GB) gondola car
  - (GB, infml) truck *(syn, O-Wagen)*
offenes Angebot *n* (com) open bid *(ie, one allowing price reductions)*
offenes Depot *n* (Fin) open deposit
offenes Entscheidungsmodell *n* (Bw) open decision model
offenes Factoring *n* (Fin) notification factoring
offenes Interview *n* (Mk) depth *(or* qualitative) interview
offenes Konto *n* (Fin) open *(or* current) account
offenes System *n*
  (EDV) open-loop system
  (EDV) open-ended system
offene Stelle *f*
  (Pw) job opening *(or* vacancy)
  - opening
  - unfilled job *(or* vacancy)
  - vacant job
  - vacancy
offene Steuerung *f* (EDV) feedforward
offene Subvention *f* (Vw) overt subsidy
offenes Unterprogramm *n* (EDV) open subroutine
offenes Warenlager *n* (com) public warehouse, § 56 HGB
offenes Welthandelssystem *n* (AuW) open world trading system
offenes Wertpapierdepot *n* (Fin) ordinary deposit of securities
offenes Zahlungsziel *n* (Fin) open terms of payment
offenes Ziel *n* (Fin) open account
offene Terminposition *f* (AuW) open forward position
offene Volkswirtschaft *f* (Vw) open economy
offenlegen
  (com) to disclose
  - to reveal
Offenlegung *f* (ReW) disclosure
Offenlegung *f* **e-r Erfindung** (Pat) disclosure of an invention
Offenlegungspflicht *f* (ReW) duty of disclosure, § 18 KWG
Offenlegungsvorschriften *fpl* (ReW) disclosure requirements *(or* rules)

Offenmarktgeschäfte *npl* (Vw) open market operations
Offenmarktkäufe *mpl* (Fin) purchases in the open market
Offenmarktoperationen *fpl* (Vw) = *Offenmarktgeschäfte*
Offenmarktpapiere *npl* (Fin) open market paper (*or* securities)
Offenmarktpolitik *f* (Vw) open market policy
Offenmarkttitel *mpl* (Fin) = *Offenmarktpapiere*
offen od stillschweigend (Re) overtly or tacitly
offen prozeßgekoppelter Betrieb *m* (EDV) open-loop operation
offensichtlicher Mangel *m* (Re) apparent defect
offenstehende Beträge *mpl* (com) open items
öffentlich anbieten (Bö) to offer for public subscription
öffentlich beglaubigen
 (Re) to authenticate officially (*or* by notarial act)
öffentlich beglaubigt
 (Re) publicly attested
 – officially authenticated
öffentlich beglaubigte Abschrift *f* (Re) notarized copy
öffentlich beglaubigte Urkunde *f* (Re) officially authenticated document
öffentlich bestellter Sachverständiger *m* (com) publicly appointed expert
öffentliche Abgaben *fpl*
 (StR) fiscal charges
 – public charges
 – public contributions
öffentliche Abgaben *fpl* **entrichten** (StR) to pay taxes and other public charges
öffentliche Ankündigung *f* **von Preiswirkungen** (Kart) price signaling
öffentliche Anleihen *fpl*
 (FiW) public authority bonds
 – public sector bonds
öffentliche Arbeiten *fpl* (Vw) public works (*ie, not ‚public relief work‘ which is = Notstandsarbeiten*)
öffentliche Auflegung *f*
 (Bö) public offering
 – invitation for general subscription
öffentliche Aufträge *mpl* (FiW) government contracts
öffentliche Auftragsvergabe *f*
 (FiW) public purchasing
 – purchasing by governmental agencies
 (*syn, Staats- od Behördeneinkauf*)
öffentliche Ausgaben *fpl*
 (FiW) government expenditure
 – governmental spending
 – public sector spending
 – public spending
öffentliche Auschreibung *f*
 (com) public invitation to tender
 – advertised bidding
öffentliche Bausparkasse *f* (com) public building society
öffentliche Bautätigkeit *f* (com) public construction activity
öffentliche Bedienstete *mpl*

 (Pw) public-sector employees
 – (US) government employees
 – (GB) civil servants
öffentliche Bedürfnisse *npl* (Vw) public wants
öffentliche Beglaubigung *f*
 (Re) public certification of signature, § 129 BGB
 – official authentication
öffentliche Bekanntmachung *f* (Re) public disclosure
öffentliche Benutzung *f* (Re) public use
öffentliche Beschaffung *f*
 (FiW) public purchasing
 – purchasing by governmental agencies
 (*syn, öffentliche Auftragsvergabe, Staats- od Behördeneinkauf*)
öffentliche Beschaffungsstelle *f* (FiW) public purchasing agency
öffentliche Betriebe *mpl* (FiW) public enterprises
öffentliche Beurkundung *f* (Re) public authentication
öffentliche Druckschrift *f*
 (Pat) printed patent specification
 – printed publication
öffentliche Eingriffe *mpl* (Vw) government interference (*or* intervention)
öffentliche Einnahmen *fpl* (FiW) public revenue
öffentliche Emission *f* (Fin) public issue (offer) by prospectus
öffentliche Finanzen *pl* (FiW) public finances
öffentliche Finanzwirtschaft *f* (FiW) public finance
öffentliche Güter *npl*
 (Vw) collective
 – public
 – social ... goods
 (*ie, goods which the market provides inadequately or not at all*)
öffentliche Hand *f*
 (FiW) public authorities
 – (US) public fisc
öffentliche Haushalte *mpl* (FiW) public authorities
öffentliche Investitionen *fpl*
 (VGR) public (sector) investment
 – government capital expenditure
öffentliche Körperschaft *f* (Re) public-law corporation
öffentliche Kreditaufnahme *f* (FiW) government (*or* public) borrowing
öffentliche Kredite *mpl*
 (FiW) loans extended by public-law corporations
 (FiW) public-sector borrowing
öffentliche Kreditnachfrage *f* (FiW) public borrowing demand
öffentliche Lasten *fpl* (FiW) public charges
öffentliche Meinungsumfrage *f* (Mk) public opinion poll
öffentliche Mittel *pl* (FiW) public funds
öffentliche Nachfrage *f* (Vw) public demand
öffentliche Plazierung *f*
 (Fin) public placement (*or* placing)
 – market flotation
öffentlicher Auftrag *m* (com) government contract
öffentlicher Bereich *m* (Re) public sector
öffentlicher Betrieb *m* (Bw) public enterprise

öffentlicher Dienst *m*
(Re) public service
- (GB) civil service
- (Pw) public-sector labor force *(ie, comprising all public employees)*

öffentlicher Emittent *m* (FiW) public issuer

öffentlicher Fernsprecher *m* (com) public telephone booth

öffentlicher Haushalt *m* (FiW) government budget

öffentlicher Hochbau *m* (com) public construction

öffentlicher Markt *m* (Bö) official market *(syn, amtlicher Markt)*

öffentlicher Schlachthof *m* (FiW) publicly-owned abattoir

öffentlicher Sektor *m* (FiW) public *(or* government) sector

öffentlicher Verbrauch *m* (VGR) public expenditure on goods and services *(syn, Staatsverbrauch)*

öffentlicher Wohnungsbau *m* (com) public *(or* government) housing

öffentliches Beschaffungswesen *n*
(Vw) public procurement
- state purchasing

öffentliche Schulden *fpl* (FiW) public *(or* national) debt

öffentliche Schuldverschreibungen *fpl* (FiW) public bonds

öffentliches Fernsprechnetz *n* (EDV) public telephone network

öffentliches Finanzwesen *n* (FiW) public finance

öffentliches Interesse *n* (Re) public interest

öffentliches Lagerhaus *n* (com) public warehouse

öffentliche Sparkasse *f* (Fin) public savings bank

öffentliches Recht *n* (Re) public law

öffentliche Stellen *fpl* (Re) public bodies

öffentliche Stromversorgung *f* (com) public power supply

öffentliches Unternehmen *n*
(Bw) public enterprise
- public sector company
- public corporation

öffentliches Vermögen *n* (FiW) public wealth *(or* assets)

öffentliches Versorgungsunternehmen *n*
(Bw) public utility company
- public service company
- public utility

öffentliches Zeichnungsangebot *n*
(Fin) public offering
- public issue by prospectus

öffentliches Zollager *n* (Zo) public warehouse

öffentliche Übertragungen *fpl* (VGR) official transfers

öffentliche Urkunde *f* (Re) public document, § 415 ZPO

öffentliche Verkehrsmittel *npl* (com) public transportation

öffentliche Verschuldung *f*
(FiW) public debt
- public sector indebtedness

öffentliche Verschuldung *f* **ohne Auslandsverbindlichkeiten** (FiW) internal public debt

öffentliche Verschwendung *f* (FiW) waste of public funds

öffentliche Versteigerung *f* (com) sale by public auction

öffentliche Verwaltung *f*
(Re) public administration
- (GB) civil service

öffentliche Wirtschaftsbetriebe *mpl* (Bw) public enterprises

öffentliche Zeichnung *f* (Fin) general subscription

öffentliche Zusatzversorgungseinrichtungen *fpl* (SozV) supplementary pension funds for public employees

öffentliche Zustellung *f* (Re) public notice of service, §§ 203 ff ZPO

öffentlich gebundene Unternehmen *npl* (Vw) regulated industries

Öffentlichkeit *f*
(com) public
- general public
- public at large

Öffentlichkeitsarbeit *f* (Mk) public relations work

öffentlich-rechtlich (Re) public-law ...

öffentlich-rechtliche Forderung *f* (FiW) debt due to a federal, state, or communal authority

öffentlich-rechtliche Grundkreditanstalt *f* (Fin) public mortgage bank

öffentlich-rechtliche Körperschaft *f* (Re) public body *(or* corporation)

öffentlich-rechtliche Kreditanstalt *f* (Fin) public credit institution

öffentlich-rechtliches Unternehmen *n* (Bw) public enterprise

öffentlich versteigern
(com) to auction
- to sell by public auction

Offenwerbung *f* (Mk) open advertising *(opp, Schleichwerbung, Tarnwerbung, Schmuggelwerbung)*

Offerent *m* (com) offeror

offerieren
(com) to offer
- to tender

Offerte *f*
(com) offer
- bid
- quotation
- tender

Offerte *f* **machen** (com) to make an offer

Offerte *f* **widerrufen** (Re) to revoke an offer

offizieller Devisenmarkt *m* (Fin) official *(or* regulated) market

offizielle Reservemittel *npl* (AuW) official reserve assets

offizielle Stellungnahme *f* (com) formal statement *(eg, by a company spokesman)*

Offline-Verarbeitung *f*
(EDV) off-line processing *(or* working)
- offlining
- (ICL) spooling *(syn, indirekte Verarbeitung)*

Offshore-Auftrag *m* (com, US) offshore purchase order

Öffnungszeit *f* (com) opening time

Offshore-Bankplatz *m* (Fin) offshore center *(ie, place with a lot of foreign banks – and a beach)*

Offshore-Steuerabkommen *n* (StR) Offshore Tax Agreement

Offshore-Steuergesetz *n* (StR) Offshore Tax Law
Ogive *f* (Stat) ogive
ohne Berechnung
　(com) free of charge
　– at no charge
ohne Berührung des Zollgebiets (Zo) without crossing the customs territory
ohne Bezugsrecht (Fin) ex rights
ohne Dividende
　(Fin) ex dividend
　– dividend off
ohne eigenes Verschulden (Re) through no fault of one's own
ohne Einwendungsausschluß (Re) subject to any defenses connected with the origin of a contract
ohne Gewähr
　(com) without engagement
　(WeR) without recourse *(ie, if prior indorser signs ..., he exempts himself from liability for payment)*
ohne Gratisaktien (Bö) ex bonus
ohne Kosten (WeR) no protest, Art. 46, 25 II WG
ohne Kupon (Fin) ex coupon
ohne Mängelgewähr (Re) with all faults
ohne Notiz (Bö) no quotation
ohne Obligo (com) without engagement
ohne Prämie (Bö) ex bonus
ohne Protest (WeR) = *ohne Kosten*
ohne Rabatt
　(com) without discount
　– straight
Ohne-Rechnung-Geschäft *n* (com, StR) no-invoice deal *(or* transaction)
ohne rechtlichen Grund (Re) without legal justification, § 812 BGB
ohne Regreß (WeR) = *ohne Rückgriff*
ohne Rückgriff (WeR) without recourse, Art. 9 II WG
ohne Stückzinsen (Bö) ex interest
ohne Umsatz (Bö) no sales
ohne Verschulden (Re) through no fault of one's own
ohne Ziehung (Bö) ex drawing
ohne Zinsen notiert (Bö) quoted flat
ohne zureichenden Grund (Re) without cause
Ökologie *f* (Vw) ecology
ökologisch (Vw) ecological
Ökonometrie *f* (Vw) econometrics
Ökonometriker *m* (Vw) econometrician
ökonometrische Methodenlehre *f* (Vw) econometrics
ökonometrisches Modell *n* (Vw) econometric model
ökonomische Aktivität *f* (Vw) economic activity *(ie, production and distribution of goods and services)*
ökonomische Analyse *f* (Vw) economic analysis
ökonomische Aspekte *mpl*
　(Vw) economic factors *(or* aspects)
　– economics (!)
ökonomische Effizienz *f* (Vw) economic efficiency
ökonomische Güter *npl* (Vw) economic goods
ökonomische Interdependenz *f* (Vw) economic interdependenz
ökonomische Rente *f* (Vw) rent

ökonomischer Erfolg *m* (Vw) economic performance
ökonomische Ressourcen *pl* (Vw) economic resources
ökonomischer Horizont *m* (Bw) economic horizon *(J. Tinbergen)*
ökonomischer Sachverstand *m* (Vw) economic expertise
ökonomischer Wert *m* (ReW) economic value
ökonomisches Gesetz *n* (Vw) economic law
ökonomisches Modell *n* (Vw) economic model
ökonomisches Prinzip *n* (Vw, Bw) efficiency rule *(ie, to produce at a given rate with lowest cost; or to produce at the highest rate with the same cost; syn, Wirtschaftlichkeitsprinzip, Rationalprinzip)*
ökonomisches Verhalten *n* (Vw) economic behavior
Ökonomische Theorie *f* **der Politik** (Vw) New Political Economy *(syn, Neue Politische Ökonomie, Nichtmarktliche Entscheidungstheorie)*
ökonomische Transaktion *f* (Vw) economic transaction
ökonomische Variable *f* (Vw) economic variable
Ökonomisierung *f* **der Kassenhaltung** (Fin) efficient employment of money holdings
Ökosystem *n* (Vw) ecosystem
Öleinfuhren *fpl* (AuW) imports of crude oil
Ölfazilität *f* (IWF) oil facility
Ölförderland *n* (com) oil producing country
Oligopol *n* (Vw) oligopoly
Oligopolist *m* (Vw) oligopolist
oligopolistische Interdependenz *f* (Vw) oligopolistic interdependence
oligopolistischer Markt *m* (Vw) oligopolistic market
Oligopoltheorie *f* (Vw) theory of oligopoly
Oligopson *n* (Vw) oligopsony
Ölpreisexplosion *f* (Vw) oil price explosion
Ölpreisschock *m* (Vw) oil price shock
Ölpreisschub *m*
　(Vw) oil shock
　– surge in oil prices
Ölschwemme *f*
　(Vw) glut of oil *(eg, worldwide)*
　– oil glut
Ölunfall *m* (com) accidental oil spill
Omnibusbefragung *f* (Mk) omnibus survey
Online-Verarbeitung *f* (EDV) on-line processing *(or* working) *(syn, direkte Verarbeitung)*
Operand *m* (EDV, Cobol) operand
Operandenadresse *f* (EDV) operand address
Operandenregister *n* (EDV) arithmetic register *(syn, arithmetisches Register, Rechenregister)*
Operandenteil *m* (EDV) operand part
Operandenübertragung *f* (EDV) operand fetch *(ie, in pipelining)*
Operateur *m* (EDV) operator
Operation *f* (Bw) job
operationale Definition *f* (Log) operational definition
operationales Ziel *n* (Bw) operational goal *(ie, one stated in measurable, verifiable, specific terms of quantity, quality, time, and cost)*
operationalisieren (Log) to operationalize

Operationalismus *m* (Log) operationalism
Operationalität *f*
 (Log) operationality
 − degree of specificity
Operationscharakteristik *f* (Stat) operating (*or* performance) characteristic
Operationscode *m* (EDV) operation (*or* instruction) code
Operationsfeld *n* (Bw) business area
Operationsgeschwindigkeit *f* (EDV) computing speed
Operationsplanung *f* (Bw) operations planning
Operations Research *n*
 (OR) operations research
 − (GB) operational research
 (ie, a frequent US substitute is ‚management science')
Operationsschlüssel *m* (EDV) operation (*or* OP) code
Operationsteil *m* (EDV) operation (*or* operator) part
Operationsumwandler *m* (EDV) operation decoder
Operationszeit *f*
 (EDV) operation time
 (EDV) execution time
operative Planung *f* (Bw) operational (*or* operative) planning
operativer Kern *m* (Bw) operational heart
operativer Plan *m* (Bw) operational plan
operativer Rahmenplan *m* (Bw) operating budget *(opp, capital budget)*
operatives Management *n* (Bw) competitive management
operative Ziele *npl* (Bw) operative goals
Operator *m* (Log) operator *(ie, universal and existential quantifiers − Allquantor und Existenzquantor − are the most common examples)*
 − (EDV) operator
Operatorbefehl *m* (EDV) operator command
Operatormeldung *f* (EDV) operator message
Ophelimität *f* (Vw) ophelimity *(ie, introduced by V. Pareto; the term roughly equivalent is ‚utility')*
Ophelimitätsindex *m* (Vw) index of ophelimity
Opportunitätskosten *pl* (Vw, Bw) opportunity (*or* alternative) cost *(syn, Alternativkosten)*
Opportunitätskostenmatrix *f* (Bw) matrix of opportunity costs *(ie, derived from a decision matrix)*
Opportunitätskosten *pl* **pro Einheit der Engpaßbelastung** (KoR) marginal profit opportunity by machine-hour
optieren (Bö) to make use of an option
Optimalbeschäftigung *f* (KoR) optimum level of activity *(syn, Bestbeschäftigung)*
optimale Auflegungszahl *f* (Bw) optimum lot number
optimale Auftragsgröße *f* (Bw) optimum order size
optimale Bedingungen *fpl* (Bw) optimum conditions
optimale Beschäftigung *f*
 (Bw) optimum output
 (KoR) optimum level of activity
optimale Bestellmenge *f*
 (MaW) economic order(ing) quantity, EOQ

 − optimum lot quantity
 − optimum order quantity
optimale Besteuerung *f* (FiW) optimal taxation
optimale Betriebsgröße *f* (Bw) optimum size (*or* scale) of a plant
optimale Codierung *f* (EDV) optimum coding
optimale Depotzusammensetzung *f* (Fin) portfolio selection
optimale Einkommensverteilung *f* (Vw) optimum income distribution
optimale Faktorkombination *f* (Vw) optimum input combination
optimale Fertigungsmenge *f* (IndE) economic manufacturing quantity
optimale Fließbandbelegung *f* (IndE) assembly line balancing
optimale Geltungszahl *f* (Bw) optimum internal price *(ie, used by E. Schmalenbach to arrive at most efficient uses of plant resources)*
optimale Kapazität *f* (Bw) practical plant capacity
optimale Kapazitätsauslastung *f* (Bw) preferred operating rate
optimale Kapitalstruktur *f* (Fin) optimum capital structure (*or* financing mix)
optimale Lebensdauer *f* (Bw) optimum life
optimale Leistung *f* (Bw) optimum performance
optimale Losgröße *f*
 (Bw) economic lot (*or* batch) size
 − optimum lot size
 − standard run quantity
optimale Losgrößenformel *f* (Bw) EOQ formula
optimale Lösung *f* (Bw) optimal (*or* best) solution
optimale Maschinengröße *f* (IndE) optimum size of major plant
 (eg, which for modern blast furnaces is abt 1,200 tons of pig iron per day)
optimale Nutzung *f* **der Produktionsfaktoren** (Vw) optimum allocation of resources
optimale Nutzung *f* **der verfügbaren Zeit** (OR) most profitable loading of available time
optimale Nutzungsdauer *f* (Bw) optimum economic life
optimale Produktionsmenge *f* (Vw) profit maximization output
optimaler Bestand *m* (MaW) optimum size of inventory *(ie, leading to minimum relevant total costs: inventory carrying cost + cost of acquisition)*
optimaler Datendurchsatz *m* (EDV) optimum throughput
optimaler Entscheidungszeitpunkt *m* (Bw) optimum time of decision making
optimaler Griffbereich *m* (IndE) normal working area
optimaler Kostenpunkt *m* (Bw) locus of minimum cost per unit *(ie, intersection of marginal and average cost curves)*
optimaler Lagerbestand *m* (MaW) = *optimaler Bestand*
optimaler Lieferbereitschaftsgrad *m* (MaW) optimum service degree *(ie, of a stock of inventory; depends on optimum mix of holding cost and stockout cost)*
optimaler Preis *m* (com) optimum (*or* highest possible) price

optimaler Verbrauchsplan *m* (Vw) optimum consumption plan
optimaler Währungsraum *m* (AuW) optimum currency area
optimales Angebot *n* (com) optimum offer
optimales Budget *n* (FiW) optimum budget *(ie, seeking to determine optimum resource allocation between private and public sectors and within the public sector itself)*
optimales Programmieren *n* (EDV) optimum programming
optimales Wachstum *n* (Vw) optimum growth *(ie, is achieved if utility of present and future consumption is at a maximum)*
Optimalitätskriterium *n* (OR) criterion of optimality
Optimalitätsprinzip *n* (OR) optimality principle
Optimalitätstest *m* (OR) optimality test
Optimalstandardkosten *pl* (KoR) ideal (*or* perfection) standard cost
Optimalzoll *m* (Zo) optimum tariff
optimieren (Bw) to optimize
Optimierung *f* (Bw) optimization
optimistische Dauer *f* (OR) optimistic time
optimistische Zeit *f* (OR) optimistic time estimate
Option *f*
 (com) right of first refusal
 – right of choice
 (Bö) option
 (StR, VAT) right of entrepreneur to opt for regular turnover taxation
Option *f* **einräumen** (Bö) to grant an option
Optionsanleihe *f*
 (Fin) optional bond
 – option warrant
 – (GB) convertible debenture stock
Optionsaufgabe *f* (Bö) abandonment of option
Option *f* **ausüben** (Bö) to exercise an option
Optionsberechtigter *m* (Bö) option holder
Optionsbörse *f* (Bö) options exchange
Optionsdarlehen *n* (Fin) optional loan
Optionsdauer *f* (Bö) option period
Optionsempfänger *m* (Bö) grantee of an option
Optionsfrist *f* (Bö) = *Optionsdauer*
Optionsgeber *m* (Bö) giver of an option
Optionsgeschäft *n*
 (Bö) option dealing
 (Bö) option bargain
Optionsgeschäft *n* **mit Termindevisen** (Bö) option forward
Optionshandel *m*
 (Bö) trading in options
 – options business (*or* trading)
Optionsklausel *f*
 (com) option clause
 – first refusal clause
Optionskontrakt *m* (Bö) option deal
Optionsnehmer *m* (Bö) taker of an option
Optionspreis *m* (Bö) option price
Optionsrecht *n* (Bö) option right
 (Bö) stock purchase warrant *(ie, when traded on the stock exchange)*
Optionsschein *m* (Bö) stock purchase warrant
Optionsverkäufer *m* (Bö) writer
optische Abtastung *f* (EDV) optical scanning *(opp,*

elektrische und magnetische Abtastung)
optische Datenverarbeitung *f* (EDV) optical data processing
optischer Abtaster *m* (EDV) optical scanner *(syn, optischer Leser)*
optischer Belegleser *m* (EDV) optical character reader
 (syn, Klarschriftleser)
optischer Leser *m* (EDV) optical (character) reader *(syn, optischer Abtaster)*
optischer Markierungsleser *m* (EDV) optical mark reader
optisches Anzeigegerät *n* (EDV) visual display unit (*or* device)
optische Zeichenerkennung *f* (EDV) optical character recognition, OCR
ordentliche Abschreibung *f* (ReW) ordinary depreciation
 (ie, traced into cost accounting; opp, außerordentliche (Sonder-)Abschreibung)
ordentliche Ausgaben *fpl* (FiW) ordinary expenditure
ordentliche Deckungsmittel *pl* (FiW) ordinary budget receipts
ordentliche Einnahmen *fpl* (FiW) ordinary receipts (*or* revenue)
ordentliche Hauptversammlung *f* (Re) ordinary shareholders' meeting, § 175 AktG
ordentliche Kapitalherabsetzung *f* (Fin) ordinary capital reduction *(ie, reduction of nominal value of shares and repayment to shareholders, § 66 III AktG)*
ordentliche Kündigung *f* (Pw) statutory or contractual notice of termination *(opp, außerordentliche, meist fristlose Kündigung aus wichtigem Grund)*
ordentlicher Haushalt *m* (FiW) ordinary budget
ordentlicher Kaufmann *m* (Re) prudent business man, § 347 HGB
ordentliches Betriebsergebnis *n*
 (ReW) operating result
 – (GB) ordinary trading profit
Orderklausel *f* (WeR) pay-to-order clause
Orderkonnossement *n*
 (com) order bill of lading
 – bill of lading (made out) to order
Orderladeschein *m* (WeR) shipping note made out to order, § 363 II HGB
Orderlagerschein *m*
 (WeR) negotiable warehouse receipt
 – warehouse receipt made out to order
Ordermangel *m* (Bö) shortage of buying orders
Orderpapier *n*
 (WeR) order paper
 – instrument to order
 – instrument made out to order *(ie, transferable by indorsement and delivery)*
Orderpolice *f* (Vers) policy made out to order
Orderscheck *m*
 (WeR) check to order
 – order check
Orderschuldverschreibung *f*
 (WeR) order bond
 – registered bond made out to order
Order- und Inhaberpapiere *npl* (WeR) negotiable

instruments
(ie, payable to order or bearer; syn, Wertpapiere i. e. S.)
Ordervermerk *m* (WeR) order clause
Ordervolumen *n* (Bö) total (*or* volume of) buying orders
ordinale Größe *f* (Math) magnitude
ordinale Nutzenfunktion *f* (Vw) ordinal utility function
ordinaler Nutzen *m* (Vw) ordinal utility
ordinales Meßkonzept *n* (Vw) ordinal utility approach
ordinales Nutzenmaß *n* (Vw) ordinal utility measure
ordinale Nutzenmessung *f* (Vw) measurement of ordinal utility
Ordinalzahl *f* (Math) ordinal number
Ordinate *f* (Math) ordinate
Ordinatendifferenz *f* **zweier Punkte** (Math) rise
Ordner *m* (com) standing file
Ordnung *f* **e-r Matrix** (Math) dimension (*or* order) of a matrix
Ordnungsbegriff *m* (EDV) defining argument
Ordnungsgeld *n* (Re) fine
ordnungsgemäß bevollmächtigt (Re) duly authorized
ordnungsgemäß einberufene Versammlung *f* (Re) duly convened meeting
ordnungsgemäße Zahlung *f* (Fin) payment in due course
ordnungsgemäß zugestellt (com) duly served
Ordnungsgütemaß *n* (EDV) ordering bias
ordnungsmäßige Buchführung *f* (ReW) adequate and orderly accounting *(ie, this basic tenet of German accounting practice is untranslatable; it has statutory and commercial sources)*
Ordnungsmäßigkeit *f* **der Buchführung** (ReW) adequacy of accounting *(ie, see §§ 38–47b HGB, § 149 AktG, §§ 140–148 AO, etc.)*
Ordnungsmuster *n* (Vw) general pattern
Ordnungspolitik *f* (Vw) *(no conceptual equivalent outside West Germany:)* Economic policy proceeding from, and taking as its yardstick of performance, an ideal-type free market system; it is subordinated to the requirements, as the case may be, of the economic framework or ‚Ordnung'; concept goes back to W. Eucken; opp, Prozeßpolitik
Ordnungsrelation *f* (Math) ordering relation
Ordnungssteuer *f* (FiW) nonrevenue regulatory tax *(ie, as an instrument of policy; syn, Zwecksteuer)*
Ordnungswidrigkeit *f*
(Re) non-criminal offense
(Kart) administrative offense
Ordoliberalismus *m* (Vw) *(no conceptual equivalent outside West Germany:)* Neoliberal economic order as conceived by the Freiburg school of economists (Eucken, Böhm). Seeks to uphold individual freedom, protect private ownership of productive capital and reasonably free competition in all markets, and provide a basic ‚order' in the country's economic affairs. A middle position between collectivism and unbridled liberalism. Practical result is a ,,socially tempered market economy". Syn, Neoliberalismus.

Organ *n* (Bw) executive body (*or* organ)
Organe *npl* **e-r Gesellschaft**
(Bw) organs of a company
– corporate agents
– agents of a corporation
– properly constituted agents
– high managerial agents *(ie, phrase coined by the American Law Institute)*
Organertrag *m* (ReW) income from subsidiaries
Organgemeinschaft *f* (StR) group of integrated companies
Organgesellschaft *f*
(StR) dependent enterprise
– integrated enterprise (*or* subsidiary)
(ie, financial, economic, and organizational dependency on another enterprise; may have the form of AG, GmbH, KGaA)
Organhaftung *f* (Re) liability of a legal person for its executive organs, §§ 31, 89 BGB
Organisation *f*
(Bw) *(Führungsfunktion:)* organizing
– *(Gebilde:)* organization
(Vers) field organization
– agency plant
(ie, total force of agents representing an insurer)
Organisation *f* **der erdölexportierenden Länder** (AuW) *(Vienna-based)* Organization of the Petroleum Exporting Countries, OPEC
Organisation *f* **der Vereinten Nationen für industrielle Entwicklung** (AuW) *(Vienna-based)* United Nationals Industrial Development Organization, UNIDO
Organisation *f* **für wirtschaftliche Zusammenarbeit und Entwicklung** (AuW) *(Paris-based)* Organization for Economic Cooperation and Development, OECD
Organisation *f* **mit großer Leitungsspanne** (Bw) shallow (*or* flat) organization
Organisation *f* **mit kleiner Leitungsspanne** (Bw) narrow (*or* deep) organization
Organisation *f* **ohne Erwerbscharakter** (Re) non-profit organization
Organisationsabteilung *f* (Bw) organization department
Organisationsanalyse *f* (Bw) organizational analysis
Organisationsebene *f* (Bw) organization level
Organisationseinheit *f* (Bw) unit of organization *(syn, Instanz, Stelle)*
Organisationsentwicklung *f* (Bw) organization development
Organisationsgrad *m*
(Vw, Bw) level of organization
(Pw) degree of unionization
Organisationsformen *fpl* (Bw) forms of organization
Organisationshandbuch *n* (Bw) organization manual
Organisationsinvestition *f* (Bw) capital spending on setting up or improving the organization structure
Organisationsklausel *f* (Pw) clause concerning union membership
Organisationskosten *pl*
(ReW) organization expense

– startup expense
– (GB) preliminary expense
organisationsmäßig (Bw) in matters of organization
Organisationsmitglieder *npl* (Bw) members of an organization
Organisationsmodell *n* (Bw) organization model *(eg, functional, divisionalized, matrix)*
Organisationsplan *m* (Bw) organization(al) chart *(or* tree)
Organisationsprogramm *n*
(EDV) master program
– supervisory program
– supervisor
Organisationsprogrammierer *m* (EDV) application programmer
Organisationsregeln *fpl* (Bw) rules of organization
Organisationsschaubild *n* (Bw) organization chart *(or* tree)
Organisationssoziologie *f* (Bw) sociology of organization
Organisationsstelle *f* (Bw) ultimate unit of responsibility
Organisationsstruktur *f* (Bw) organization(al) structure
Organisationstalent *n* (Pw) organizational ability *(or* skills)
Organisationstheorie *f* (Bw) theory of organization
Organisations- und Geschäftsführungsprüfung *f* (ReW) management audit
Organisationsziele *npl* (Bw) organizational *(or* system-wide) goals
organisatorisch (Bw) organizational
organisatorische Eingliederung *f* (StR) organizational integration
organisatorische Operation *f* (EDV) bookkeeping *(or* red-tape) operation
organisatorischer Befehl *m* (EDV) bookkeeping *(or* red-tape) instruction
organisatorisches Dilemma *n* (Bw) organizational dilemma *(H. Steinmann) (ie, the amount of failure, conflict, and frustration increases from top to bottom, and is larger in a tall than in a flat organizational structure)*
organisatorisches Umfeld *n* (Bw) organizational environment
organisatorische Umstellung *f* (Bw) organizational shakeup
organischer Bestandteil *m* (com) integral part
organische Rohstoffe *mpl* (com) organic raw materials
organisiert (Pw) unionized
organisierte Arbeitnehmer *mpl* (Pw) unionized employees
organisierter Markt *m*
(Vw) market overt
(Bw) regular market
organisierter Streik *m* (Pw) official strike
Organkredit *m* (Fin) credit to related persons and entities, § 15 KWG
Organmitglied *n* (Re) officer
Organogramm *n (pl. Organigramme)*
(Bw) organization(al) chart
– organization tree
Organschaft *f* (StR) (tax device of) ,,integration"
– integrated inter-company relation *(ie, developed by Federal Fiscal Court for purposes of both income tax and turnover tax: exempts intercompany sales and services within a controlled group of enterprises = Konzern)*
(StR) integrated companies
Organschaftsabrechnung *f* (ReW) accounting settlement between integrated companies
organschaftsähnliches Verhältnis *n* (StR) quasi-integration relationship *(ie, combinations of enterprises that do not fully meet the conditions for recognition as an ,,integration")*
Organschaftsverhältnis *n*
(StR) integrated inter-company relationship
– single-entity relationship
Organschaftsverrechnung *f*
(ReW) settlement between integrated companies
Organschaftsvertrag *m* (Re) contract relating to the integration of a subsidiary
Organträger *m* (StR) dominant enterprise *(ie, any enterprise within the meaning of § 2 I UStG: natural and legal persons, unincorporated partnerships and associations)*
Organverhältnis *n* (StR) integrated relationship with a subsidiary
Organverlust *m* (ReW) loss posted by a subsidiary
OR-Geschäft *m* (com, StR) = *Ohne-Rechnung-Geschäft*
Orientierungsdaten *pl* (Vw) guideline data, § 3 StabG
Orientierungspreis *m* (com) introductory *(or* informative) price (EG) guide *(or* target) price
Orientierungsrahmen *m*
(com) guide lines
– long-term program
Original *n* (com) original *(ie, of any document, letter, etc.)*
Originalausfertigung *f* (com) original document
Originalbeleg *m* (EDV) original *(or* source) document *(syn, Urbeleg)*
Originaldaten *pl* (EDV) raw data
Originaldokument *n* (com) source document
Originalfaktura *f* (com) original invoice
Originalfracht *f* (com) original freight
Originalpolice *f* (Vers) original policy
Originalrechnung *f* (com) original invoice
Originaltara *f* (com) original tare
Originalverpackung *f* (com) original package *(or* wrapping)
Originalwechsel *m* (WeR) original bill of exchange
originäre Produktionsfaktoren *mpl* (Vw) natural resources
originäre Kostenarten *fpl* (KoR) primary cost categories
originärer Firmenwert *m*
(ReW) self-generated goodwill, § 153 V AktG
– unpurchased goodwill
– company-developed goodwill
– goodwill developed by the business
(ie, not considered for balance sheet and tax purposes)
originelle Werbung *f* (Mk) original way of advertising
Ort *m* **der Geschäftsleitung** (Bw) place of management

Ort *m* der Leistung (Re) place of performance
Ort *m* der Niederlassung (Bw) place of establishment
Ort *m* der tatsächlichen Geschäftsleitung (Bw) place of actual management
Ort *m* des steuerbaren Umsatzes (StR) place of taxable transaction
Ort *m* des Verbringens (AuW) place (*or* point) of introduction
Ort *m* des Vertragsabschlusses (Re) place of contract
orthogonale Funktion *f* (Math) orthogonal function
orthogonale Koordinaten *fpl* (Math) orthogonal coordinates
orthogonale Matrix *f* (Math) orthogonal matrix
orthogonale Transformation *f* (Math) orthogonal transformation
Orthogonalitätsbedingung *f* (Math) orthogonality restriction
örtlich begrenzter Streik *m* (Pw) localized strike
örtliche Behörde *f* (Re) local authority
örtliche Gebietskörperschaft *f*
  (FiW) municipal government
  – municipality
  – local government (unit)
  – locality
  – unit of local government
  – general-purpose local government
örtliche Gewohnheit *f* (StR) local practices, § 2 BewG
örtliche Zuständigkeit *f* (StR) place for filing returns, § 17 AO
Ortsbrief *m* (com) local letter
Ortsgespräch *n* (com) local call
Ortskraft *f* (Pw) local employee
Ortskrankenkasse *f* (SozV) local health insurance office

ortskundig (com) having local knowledge
Ortsstapelverarbeitung *f* (EDV) local batch processing
ortsübliche Miete *f* (com) local rent
Ortszulage *f*
  (Pw) local bonus
  – residential allowance
  – local cost of living allowance
Ort *m* und Tag *m* der Ausstellung (com) place and date of issuance (*or* issue)
Österreichische Schule *f* (Vw) Austrian school of economists *(ie, led by K. Menger, F. v. Wieser, and E. v. Böhm-Bawerk)*
oszillierende Reihe *f* (Math) oscillating series
„Otto Normalsteuerzahler" *m* (com, infml) John Citizen, the taxpayer *(ie, the average taxpayer left without the benefit of tax loopholes)*
Otto Normalverbraucher *m*
  (com, infml) John Doe
  – John Citizen
  – (GB) Mr. A. N. Onymous
  (ie, the average, anonymous man)
O-Urteil *n*
  (Log) O-proposition
  – particular negative
Output *m* je Arbeitsstunde
  (Vw) man-hour output
  – output per man-hour
output-orientiertes Budget *n*
  (FiW) planning, programming, budgeting system
  – PPBS system
  – output-oriented budget
Outright-Termingeschäfte *npl* (Bö) outright forward transactions
Outright-Terminkurs *m* (Bö) outright price
O-Wagen *m* (com) = *offener Wagen*

P

Paarkorrelation *f* (Stat) intra-class correlation
Paarmenge *f* (Math) pair set
Paarvergleich *m* (Mk) paired comparison
paarweise disjunkt (Math) pairwise disjoint
paarweise Zuordnung *f* **von Elementen** (Math) pairing of elements
Paasche-Preisindex *m* (Stat) Paasche price index-number *(ie, prices being weighted by the quantities of the given period)*
Pacht *f* (Re) lease *(ie, contract by which the right to possess, use and enjoy a thing, as defined in § 90 BGB, and of its fruit, as defined in § 99 BGB, is granted in exchange for payment of a stipulated price, called ‚rent‘, §§ 581–597 BGB. Note that ‚Miete‘ is identical except that the enjoyment of fruit is excluded.)*
Pachtbedingungen *fpl* (Re) terms of a lease
Pachtbesitz *m* (Re) leasehold property
Pachtdauer *f* (Re) term (*or* life) of a lease
pachten
  (Re) to lease *(ie, land or building)*
  – to take on lease
  (Note that ‚to lease‘ also means ‚verpachten‘ in the sense of ‚to let on lease‘)
Pächterpfandrecht *n* (Re) statutory lien of lessee, § 590 BGB
Pachtertrag *m* (Re) rentals
Pächter *m* und Verpächter *m* (Re) lessee *(ie, person to whom conveyed)* and lessor *(ie, person who conveys)*
Pachtgrundstück *n* (Re) leased property
Pachtkosten *pl* (KoR) rentals paid
Pachtvertrag *m*
  (Re) lease
  – lease agreement
Pachtwert *m* (com) rental value
Pachtzins *m*
  (Re) rent
  – rental
  (ie, paid for use of property)
Päckchen *n* (com) small parcel – petit paquet *(ie, up to 2 kg, but 1 kg if sent abroad)*

packen
(com) to pack *(eg, into boxes, cases)*
(EDV) to pack
Packerei *f* (com) packing department
Packkiste *f* (com) packing box
Packliste *f* (com) packing list
Packmaterial *n*
(com) packing
– packing material
(com) dunnage *(ie, other than packaging)*
Packpapier *n* (com) wrapping paper
Packstück *n*
(com) package
– parcel
Packung *f*
(com) pack *(ie, any size)*
– (GB) packet
(Mk) package
Packungsbeilage *f* (Mk) package insert *(eg, small advertising folder, sample, etc.)*
Packungsgestaltung *f* (com) packaging
Packzettel *m* (com) packing *(or* shipping) slip
pagatorische Buchhaltung *f* (ReW) financial *(or* general) accounting
pagatorische Kosten *pl* (Bw) cash-outlay cost
pagatorische Rechnung *f* (ReW) cash basis of accounting
paginieren (com) to number pages
Paginiermaschine *f* (com) (page) numbering machine
Paket *n*
(com) parcel
– (US, *also*) package
(com) package deal *(or* offer)
(Fin) block *(or* parcel) of shares
Paket-Abholstelle *f* (com) parcel pickup station
Paketabschlag *m* (Fin) share block discount
Paketangebot *n* (Bw) bundle bidding *(ie, R & D + production)*
Paketbesitz *m* (Fin) 25-percent block of shares
Paketempfangsschein *m* (com) parcel receipt *(ie, made out by a shipping company)*
Pakethandel *m*
(Bö) block trading
– large-lot dealing
(Pat) package licensing
Paketkarte *f*
(com) parcel dispatch slip
– parcel mailing form
Paketlösung *f* (com) package solution *(ie, detailed treatment of problems)*
Paketpolice *f* (Vers) package policy
Paketpost *f* (com) parcel post
Paketsendung *f*
(com) parcel
– (US) package
Paketumschlagstelle *f* (com) parcel rerouting center
Paketvermittlung *f* (EDV) packet switching
Paketverkaufsgewinn *m* (Fin) gain on disposal of block of shares
Paketzuschlag *m*
(Bö) share block premium
– extra price on block of shares *(ie, percentage × share price)*

(StR) addition to the combined list price or fair market value of shares or membership rights, § 11 BewG
Paketzustellung *f* (com) parcel delivery
Palettenladung *f* (com) palette load
palettieren (com) to palletize
palettierte Güter *npl* (com) palletized goods
Paneleffekt *m* (Mk) panel effect
Panelerhebung *f* (Mk) panel interview
Panelsterblichkeit *f* (Mk) panel mortality
Panikkäufe *mpl* (com) panic *(or* scare) buying
Panikverkäufe *mpl* (Bö) panic selling
Papiere *npl*
(Fin) securities
(Pw, infml) walking papers
– (GB) marching papers *(or* orders)
Papierfabrik *f* (IndE) paper mill
Papiergeld *n* (Vw) paper currency *(or* money)
Papiergeld *n* **mit Edelmetalldeckung** (Vw) representative money
Papiergold *n* (AuW) „paper gold" *(ie, special drawing rights, SDRs)*
Papierhersteller *m* (com) paper maker
Papierindustrie *f* (com) paper industry
Papierkorb *m*
(com) waste basket
– (GB) waste paper basket
papierlose Ablage *f* (EDV) paperless filing
Papier *n* **mit Maßeinteilung** (com) scale paper
Papier *n* **ohne Maßeinteilung** (com) non-scale paper
Papiersack *m* (com) paper bag
Papiertransport *m* (EDV) paper transport
papierverarbeitende Industrie *f* (com) paper converting industry
Papierverarbeiter *m* (com) paper converter
Papiervorschub *m* (EDV) paper feed
Papierwährung *f* (Vw) paper currency
Pappe *f*
(com) paperboard
– cardboard *(ie, nontechnical term)*
Parabel *f* (Math) parabola
Parabelmultiplizierer *m* (EDV) quarter squares multiplier
parabolische Beschränkungen *fpl* (OR) parabolic constraints
parabolische Funktion *f* (Math) parabolic function
Parafiskus *m*
(FiW) intermediate fiscal power
– auxiliary fiscal agent
(eg, churches, social insurance carriers, EC, World Bank; syn, Hilfsfiskus, Nebenfiskus)
Parallelabfragespeicher *m* (EDV) parallel search memory
Parallelanleihen *fpl* (Fin) parallel loans
Parallelbetrieb *m* (EDV) parallel operation
Parallel-Devisenmarkt *m* (AuW) parallel market
Paralleldrucker *m*
(EDV) line printer
– line at a time printer *(syn, Zeilendrucker)*
parallele Abarbeitung *f* (EDV) pipelining
parallele Kanten *fpl* (OR) parallel edges
parallele Massenfertigung *f* (IndE) parallel mass production
(opp, wechselnde Massenfertigung)

Parallelenschar f (Math) family of parallel lines
paralleler Ablauf m (OR) parallel mode of operation
parallel geschaltete Kanäle mpl (OR) servers arranged in parallel
parallel geschaltete Kanten fpl (OR) branches in parallel
Parallellauf m (EDV) parallel operation
parallel laufendes Patent n (Pat) collateral patent
Parallelmarkt m (Bö) parallel (foreign exchange) market
Parallelmodem n (EDV) parallel modem
Parallelpolitik f (FiW) procyclical fiscal policy
Parallel-Seriendarstellung f (EDV) parallel-serial notation
Parallel-Serien-Umsetzer m (EDV) parallel-serial converter
Parallelspeicher m (EDV) parallel memory (or storage)
Parallelstichprobe f (Stat) duplicate sample
Parallelübertragung f (EDV) parallel transfer
Parallelverarbeitung f (EDV) parallel processing
Parallelverschiebung f (Math) parallel shift (or displacement)
Parallelversuch m (Stat) replication
Parallelwährung f (Vw) parallel currency
Parallelzugriff m (EDV) parallel (or simultaneous) access
Paralogismus m (Log) paralogism (ie, any fallacious reasoning)
Parameter m
  (Math) parameter (ie, an arbitrary constant or variable)
  (Stat) parameter (ie, a constant which most usually occurs in expressions defining frequency distributions, such as population parameters, or in models describing a stochastic situation, such as regression parameters)
Parameter m **der Grundgesamtheit** (Stat) population parameter
parameterfreie Statistik f (Stat) nonparametric statistics
parametergesteuert (EDV) parameter-controlled
Parametergleichung f (Math) parametric equation
Parameterkarte f (EDV) parameter (or control) card
Parameter-Matrix f (Math) parameter matrix
Parameterraum m (Stat) parameter space
Parameterschätzung f (Stat) estimation of parameters
parametrieren (EDV) to parameterize
parametrische Programmierung f (OR) parametric programming
parametrischer Test m (Stat) parametric test
parametrische Statistik f (Stat) parametric statistics
paramonetäre Finanzierungsinstitute npl (Fin) nonfinancial (or nonmonetary) intermediaries (syn, sekundäre F.)
Paraphe f (com) initials
paraphieren (com) to initial (eg, a contract)
paratarifäre Handelshemmnisse npl (Auw) non-tariff barriers
pareto-optimal (Vw) Pareto optimal
Pareto-Optimalität f (Vw) Pareto optimality condition

Pari-Bezugsrecht n (Bö) par rights issue
Pari-Emission f
  (Bö) issue at par
  – par issue
Parikurs m
  (AuW) par of exchange
  – par rate
  (Bö) par price
pari notieren (Bö) to quote at par
Parirückzahlung f (Fin) redemption at par
Pariser Club m
  (Vw) Paris Club
  – Group of Ten
Pariser Verband m (Pat) Paris Union
Pariser Verbandsübereinkunft f **(zum Schutz des gewerblichen Eigentums)** (Pat) Union (or Paris) Convention
  (ie, full title: International Convention for the Protection of Industrial Property; concluded in 1883 and frequently revised, most recently at Stockholm in 1967)
Parität f (AuW) parity
Paritätengitter n (AuW) parity grid (of EMS)
Paritätenraster m (AuW) grid parities
paritätische Mitbestimmung f
  (Pw) parity
  – equal
  – 50:50... codetermination
paritätische Vertretung f (Re) parity representation
Paritätsänderung f (AuW) parity change
Paritätsbit n (EDV) parity (or check) bit
Paritätsfehler m (EDV) parity error
Paritätsklausel f (AuW) parity clause
Paritätskurs m (AuW) parity price
Paritätspreis m (EG) parity price (ie, in farming)
Paritätsprüfung f (EDV) parity (or odd-even) check
Paritätssystem n (IWF) par value system
Paritätstabellen fpl (Bö) parity tables
Paritätsziffer f (EDV) parity digit
parken (Fin) to invest temporarily
Parkett n
  (Bö) floor
  – official market (opp, Kulisse)
Parkhochhaus n (com) multi-story car park
Parkplatz m
  (com) car park
  – (GB) parking lot
  (com) parking space
  – (GB) parking bay
  (Fin) temporary investment
Parteien fpl **e-s Rechtsstreits** (Re) parties to a dispute (syn, streitende Parteien)
Parteienvereinbarung f
  (Re) contractual stipulation
  – agreement by the parties
Partei f **ergreifen** (com) to side (with/against)
Parteifähigkeit f (Re) capacity to sue and be sued, § 50 ZPO
Parteispenden fpl (StR) donation to political parties
Parteiwille m (Re) intention of the parties to a contract
Parteninhaber m (com) part owner of a ship

460

Partenreederei *f* (com) shipowning partnership, § 489 HGB
Partialanalyse *f* (Vw) partial analysis
Partialbruch *m* (Math) partial fraction
partiarischer Darlehensgeber *m* (Fin) lender with participation in debtor's profits
partiarisches Darlehen *n* (Fin) loan which entitles the creditor to a profit participation
– loan with profit participation
Partie *f*
(com) consignment
(Bö) parcel
– lot
(IndE) lot
– batch *(syn, Auflage, Los, Serie)*
(Pw) gang of workers
Partiehandel *m* (Bö) spot business
Partiekauf *m* (com) sale by lot
partielle Ableitung *f* (Math) partial derivative
partielle Aussagenlogik *f* (Log) partial propositional calculus
partielle Differentialgleichung *f* (Math) partial differential equation
partielle Faktorproduktivität *f* (Vw) partial factor productivity
(ie, reciprocal of input/output ratio = Produktionskoeffizient)
partielle Gleichgewichtsanalyse *f* (Vw) partial equilibrium analysis
partielle Integration *f* (Math) integration by parts
partielle Korrelation *f* (Stat) partial correlation
partielle Produktionselastizität *f* (Bw) partial elasticity of production
partielle Rangkorrelation *f* (Stat) partial rank correlation
partielle Regression *f* (Stat) partial regression
partieller Grenzertrag *m* (Vw) partial marginal return
partielles Gleichgewicht *n* (Vw) partial equilibrium
partiell geordnete Menge *f* (Math) partially ordered set
Partienstreuung *f* (IndE) batch variation
Partieware *f*
(com) job *(or* substandard*)* goods
– job lot
partikulär-bejahendes Urteil *n*
(Log) particular affirmative
– I-proposition
partikuläres Urteil *n*
(Log) particular proposition
– particular
Partikularisator *m* (Log) particular *(or* existential*)* quantifier
partikulär-verneinendes Urteil *n*
(Log) particular negative
– O-proposition
Partikulier *m* (com) independent barge-owner
Partikulierschiffahrt *f* (com) private inland waterway shipping
Partizipationsgeschäft *n* (com, Fin) joint transaction
Partizipationsgrad *m* (Bw) degree of employee *(or* subordinate*)* participation
Partizipationskonto *n* (Fin) joint account

Partizipationsplanung *f* (Vw) participatory planning *(ie, in regional economics)*
Partizipationsschein *m* (Fin) participating receipt
Partner *m*
(Re) partner
– co-partner
Partnerwährung *f* (AuW) partner currency
Pascal-Verteilung *f* (Stat) Pascal distribution
Passiva *npl* (ReW) total equity and liabilities
passive Abschreibung *f* (ReW) indirect method of depreciation
(ie, debited through separate valuation account; syn, indirekte Abschreibung)
passive Bestechung *f* (com) taking bribes
passive Handelsbilanz *f* (VGR) unfavorable *(or* adverse*)* balance of trade
passive Kreditbereitschaft *f* (Fin) readiness to borrow
passive Kreditgeschäfte *npl* (Fin) = *Passivgeschäfte*
passive Lohnveredelung *f* (AuW) processing of goods abroad for domestic account
passive Rechnungsabgrenzung *f*
(ReW) accrued expense
– deferred income
passiver Transithandel *m* (AuW) passive transit trade
passiver Veredelungsverkehr *m* (Zo) outward processing
passiver Verrechnungssaldo *m* (Fin) debit balance on inter-branch account, § 53 KWG
passives Bauelement *n* (EDV) passive element
passive Vertretung *f* (Re) passive agency *(ie, agent receives a declaration of intent addressed to the principal through his agency)*
passive Zahlungsbilanz *f* (VGR) unfavorable *(or* adverse*)* balance of payments
Passivfinanzierung *f* (Fin) liabilities-side financing
(ie, financing transaction expanding the volume of equity and outside capital; opp, Aktivfinanzierung)
Passivgelder *npl* (Fin) borrowings
Passivgeschäft *n* (Fin) deposit business
(ReW) transaction creating a liability
(Fin) borrowing transaction *(ie, of banks)*
Passivhandel *m*
(AuW) external trade handled by nonresidents
(AuW) passive trade *(ie, imports exceeding exports)*
passivieren (ReW) to carry as liability
Passivierung *f*
(AuW) pushing into definit
– moving *(or* heading*)* into deficit
(ie, said of balanc of payments; opp. Aktivierung)
Passivierungspflicht *f* (ReW) obligation to carry as liability on the balance sheet, § 40 HGB
Passivierungsrecht *n* (ReW) right to carry as liability on the balance sheet
Passivierungsverbot *n* (ReW) prohibition to carry as liability on the balance sheet
Passivierungswahlrecht *n* (ReW) option to show or not to show items on the liabilities side
passiv Innovierender *m* (Bw) client
Passivkonto *n* (ReW) liability account
Passivkredit *m* (Fin) borrowing *(ie, by a bank)*

Passivlegitimation *f* (Re) capacity to be sued, § 50 ZPO
passiv legitimiert
  (Re) capable of being sued
  – having capacity to be sued
Passivposten *m*
  (ReW) liability (*or* debit) item
  (AuW) debit item
Passivsaldo *m*
  (ReW) debit (*or* adverse) balance
  – deficit
Passivsaldo *m* **der Zahlungsbilanz** (AuW) balance of payments deficit
Passivseite *f* (ReW) liabilities side *(ie, of a balance sheet)*
Passivstruktur *f* (Fin) structure of liabilities
Passivtausch *m* (ReW) accounting exchange on the liabilities side *(ie, of financial statements)*
Passivwechsel *m* (Fin) bill payable
Passivzinsen *mpl*
  (Fin) deposit interest rates
  – interest on deposits
Patent *n*
  (Pat) patent
  – letters patent
Patentabteilung *f* (Pat) patent division
Patent *n* **abtreten** (Pat) to assign a patent
Patentabtretung *f* (Pat) patent assignment
Patentamt *n* (Pat) *(Munich-based)* German Patent Office
Patentamtsentscheidung *f* (Pat) ruling of the Patent Office
Patent *n* **anfechten** (Pat) to challenge a patent
Patentanfechter *m* (Pat) patent challenger
Patent *n* **angemeldet** (Pat) patent applied for
Patent *n* **anmelden**
  (Pat) to apply for a patent
  – to file an application for a patent
Patentanmelder *m* (Pat) patent applicant
Patentanmeldung *f*
  (Pat) patent application
  (Pat) filing of a patent application
Patentanmeldung *f* **bearbeiten** (Pat) to process a patent application
Patentanmeldung *f* **einreichen** (Pat) to file a patent application
Patentanmeldung *f* **im Ausland einreichen** (Pat) to file a patent application abroad
Patentanmeldung *f* **zurücknehmen** (Pat) to withdraw a patent application
Patentanmeldung *f* **zurückweisen** (Pat) to refuse a patent application
Patentanspruch *m* (Pat) patent claim *(ie, defines an invention succintly and serves to delimit the scope of the rights requested)*
Patentanwalt *m*
  (Pat) patent lawyer
  – (US) patent attorney
  – (GB) patent agent
Patent *n* **aufrechterhalten** (Pat) to maintain a patent
Patentaustausch *m*
  (Pat) cross-licensing of patents
  – exchange of patents
Patentaustauschvertrag *m*

  (Pat) cross-license agreement
  – patent exchange agreement
Patentausübung *f*
  (Pat) patent exploitation
  – use (*or* working) of a patent
Patent *n* **auswerten** (Pat) to exploit (*or* work) a patent
Patentauswertung *f* (Pat) exploitation (*or* working) of a patent
patentbegründend (Pat) substantiating a patent claim
Patentberichterstatter *m* (Pat) patent investigator
Patentberichtigung *f* (Pat) patent amendment
Patentberühmung *f* (Pat) patent advertising (*or* marking), § 55 PatG
Patentbeschreibung *f* (Pat) patent specification
Patentbüro *n* (Pat) patent law firm
Patentdauer *f* (Pat) term of a patent
Patenteinspruch *m* (Pat) opposition to a patent
Patenteinspruchsverfahren *n* (Pat) opposition proceeding
Patententziehung *f* (Pat) revocation of a patent
Patent *n* **erlischt** (Pat) patent expires (*or* lapses)
Patent *n* **erteilen** (Pat) to grant (*or* issue) a patent
Patenterteilung *f* (Pat) issue (*or* grant) of a patent
patentfähig (Pat) patentable
patentfähige Erfindung *f* (Pat) patentable invention
patentfähiger Teil *m* (Pat) patentable part
patentfähiges Verfahren *n* (Pat) patentable process
patentfähige Verbesserung *f* (Pat) patentable improvement
Patentfähigkeit *f* (Pat) patentability
Patentfähigkeitserfordernis *n* (Pat) patentability requirement
Patentgebühr *f*
  (Pat) patent fee
  – royalty charge
Patentgemeinschaft *f* (Pat) patent pool
Patentgericht *n* (Pat) patent court
Patentgerichtsverfahren *n* (Pat) patent court proceeding
Patentgesetz *n* (Pat) patent law
Patentgesetzgebung *f* (Pat) patent legislation
Patenthindernis *n* (Pat) bar to patentability
Patent-Holdingsgesellschaft *f* (Pat) patent pool
patentierbar (Pat) patentable
Patentierbarkeit *f* (Pat) patentability
patentieren (Pat) to grant a patent
patentieren lassen
  (Pat) to take out a patent (for)
  – to obtain a patent
  – to patent
patentierte Erfindung *f* (Pat) patented invention
patentiertes Verfahren *n* (Pat) patented process
Patentierung *f* (Pat) issue of a patent
Patentinhaber *m*
  (Pat) holder of a patent
  – owner (*or* proprietor) of a patent
  – patentee
Patentkartell *n* (Pat) patent cartel
Patentklage *f* (Pat) patent proceedings
Patentklasse *f* (Pat) patent class (*or* category)
Patentklassifikation *f* (Pat) patent classification
Patentkosten *pl*

(ReW) cost of acquiring a patent *(ie, price to be capitalized and written off)*
(ReW) research expenditure on patents
(ReW) royalties
- patent charges
Patentlaufzeit *f* (Pat) term of patent
Patentlizenz *f* (Pat) patent license
Patentlizenzabgabe *f* (Pat) royalty
Patentlizenzvertrag *m* (Pat) patent license agreement
Patent *n* **löschen** (Pat) to cancel a patent
Patentlöschung *f* (Pat) cancellation of a patent
Patentlösung *f*
(com) patent answer (*or* solution) *(ie, to a problem)*
- ready-made solution
- magic solution
- (infml) quick fix
Patentmonopol *n* (Pat) patent monopoly
Patentnichtigkeitsverfahren *n* (Pat) proceedings for nullification of a patent
Patent *n* **nutzen**
(Pat) to exploit
- to utilize
- to work ... a patent
Patentpool *m* (Pat) patent holding (*or* pool)
Patentprozeß *m* (Pat) patent litigation
Patentprüfer *m* (Pat) patent examiner
Patentrecht *n* (Pat) patent law
patentrechtlich geschützt (Pat) protected by patent
patentrechtlich geschützter Gegenstand *m* (Pat) patented article
patentrechtlich schützen (Pat) to patent
Patentrolle *f*
(Pat) patent register
- (GB) patent rolls
Patentsachen *fpl* (Pat) patent cases
Patentschrift *f* (Pat) printed patent specification
Patentschutz *m* (Pat) patent protection
Patent *n* **übertragen** (Pat) to assign a patent
Patentübertragung *f* (Pat) assignment of patent
Patent- und Lizenzbilanz *f* (VGR) patent and licenses account
(ie, of a balance of payments)
Patent- und Lizenzverkehr *m* (AuW) patent and license trade
Patentunteranspruch *m* (Pat) sub-claim of a patent
Patenturkunde *f*
(Pat) letters patent
- patent document
Patentverbesserung *f* (Pat) improvement of a patent
Patentverfahren *n* (Pat) patent procedure
Patent *n* **verfallen lassen** (Pat) to abandon a patent
Patent *n* **verlängern** (Pat) to extend the term of a patent
Patentverlängerung *f* (Pat) extension of a patent
Patent *n* **verletzen** (Pat) to infringe a patent
Patentverletzer *m* (Pat) infringer of a patent
Patentverletzung *f*
(Pat) patent infringement
- third-party infringement
Patentverletzungsklage *f*
(Pat) suit for infringement
- infringement suit

Patentverletzungsverfahren *n* (Pat) patent infringement proceedings
Patent *n* **versagen** (Pat) to refuse a patent
Patentversagung *f* (Pat) refusal of a patent
Patentvertrag *m* (Pat) patent agreement
Patentverweigerung *f* (Pat) refusal to issue a patent
Patent *n* **verwerten**
(Pat) to exploit
- to utilize
- to work ... a patent
Patentverwertung *f* (Pat) patent exploitation
Patentverwertungsgesellschaft *f* (Pat) patent utilization company or partnership
Patentverwertungsvertrag *m* (Pat) patent exploitation agreement
Patentverzicht *m* (Pat) abandonment of patent
Patentvorwegnahme *f* (Pat) anticipatory reference
Patentwesen *n* (Pat) patent system
Patent *n* **wird versagt** (Pat) patent is denied
Patentzeichnung *f* (Pat) patent drawing
Patentzusammenfassung *f* (Pat) patent consolidation
Pattsituation *f*
(Pw) deadlock *(eg, in trying to reach a decision under the terms of the codetermination law)*
- stalemate situation
pauschal
(com) flat *(eg, amount, rate)*
- across-the-board *(eg, pay rise)*
- lump-sum
Pauschalabfindung *f* (com) lump-sum settlement (*or* compensation)
Pauschalabschreibung *f* (ReW) group depreciation
- composite-life method of depreciation
(ie, applying a single rate to a group of assets of the same general class = Gruppe gleichartiger Wirtschaftsgüter; syn, Sammelabschreibung)
Pauschalabzug *m* (StR) fixed-amount (*or* flat-rate) tax deduction
Pauschalangebot *n* (com) package offer (*or* deal)
Pauschalbeitrag *m* (com) lump-sum contribution
Pauschalbesteuerung *f* (StR) = *Pauschbesteuerung*
Pauschalbetrag *m* (com) lump sum
Pauschalbewertung *f* (ReW) group valuation *(ie, of items similar in kind and price; syn, Sammelbewertung)*
Pauschaldeckung *f* (Vers) blanket coverage
Pauschaldelkredere *n* (ReW) receivables contingency reserve
(ie, set up to provide against contingent receivables losses; syn, Sammelwertberichtigung; opp, Einzelwertberichtigung)
Pauschale *f*
(com) lump sum
- standard allowance
- flat charge
pauschale Absatzprovision *f*
(Mk) flat-rate sales commission
- (US) override
pauschale Kürzung *f* (FiW) overall (*or* across-the-board) cut
pauschale Lohnerhöhung *f* (Pw) package (*or* across-the-board) wage increase
Pauschalentschädigung *f* (com) lump-sum compensation

463

pauschaler Ausbeutesatz *m* (Bw) standard rate of yield
pauschaler Beitrag *m* (com) flat-rate contribution
pauschale Regulierung *f* (Vers) lump-sum settlement
pauschales Delkredere *n* (ReW) = *Pauschaldelkredere*
Pauschalfracht *f* (com) flat-rate freight
Pauschalfreibetrag *m*
  (StR) standard tax deduction
  – flat-rate exemption
Pauschalgebühr *f* (com) flat charge (*or* fee)
Pauschalhonorar *n*
  (com) flat (rate) fee
  – lump-sum payment for professional services
pauschalieren (com) to set down as a lump-sum
pauschalierte Kosten *pl* (KoR) bunched cost
pauschalierte Sonderausgabe *f* (StR) lump-sum allowance for special expenditure
Pauschalierung *f*
  (com) consolidation into a lump sum
  (StR) taxation at a flat rate
  (StR) assessment of a tax in a blanket amount
  (*eg, § 87 GewStR*)
Pauschalkauf *m* (com) basket purchase *(ie, mostly ‚Investitionsgüter' = capital goods)*
Pauschallizenz *f* (Pat) block license
Pauschalpolice *f*
  (Vers) blank (*or* blanket) policy
  – declaration policy
  – floater policy
Pauschalprämie *f*
  (Vers) all-inclusive premium
  – flat-rate premium
Pauschalpreis *m*
  (com) all-inclusive
  – flat-rate
  – lump-sum ... price
Pauschalregulierung *f* (Vers) lump-sum settlement
Pauschalreise *f* (com) package tour *(ie, all-expense tour)*
Pauschalreisender *m* (com) package tourist
Pauschalrückstellung *f* (ReW) = *Pauschalwertberichtigung*
Pauschal-Sachversicherung *f* (Vers) block policy
Pauschalsatz *m* (com) all-in rate
Pauschalsteuer *f* (StR) lump-sum tax
Pauschalvergütung *f* (com) fixed allowance
Pauschalversicherung *f* (Vers) blanket (*or* package) insurance *(ie, covering several risks)*
Pauschalversicherungspolice *f* (Vers) blanket cover insurance
Pauschalvertrag *m* (Re) blanket agreement
Pauschalwert *m* (com) global (*or* overall) value
Pauschalwertberichtigung *f* (ReW) general bad-debt provision *(opp, Einzelabschreibung, Delkredere-Rückstellung für e–e Einzelforderung)*
Pauschalwertberichtigung *f* **zu Forderungen** (ReW) lump-sum valuation adjustment (*or* reserve) on receivables
Pauschalzuweisung *f* (FiW) lump-sum appropriation
Pauschbesteuerung *f*
  (StR) blanket

  – flat-rate
  – lump-sum ... taxation
  – taxation at a special flat rate
  – blanket assessment
  (eg, covering taxpayers who establish residence in Germany, § 31 EStG; see also: § 34c EStG, § 26 KStG, § 13 VStG)
Pauschbetrag *m* (StR) blanket allowance (*or* deduction)
Pauschbeträge *mpl* **für Werbungskosten** (StR) blanket deductions for income-related expenses, § 9a EStG
Pauschbetrag *m* **für Sonderausgaben** (StR) blanket deduction for special expenditures
Pauschfestsetzung *f* (StR) blanket assessment, § 15 GewStG
Pauschgebühren *fpl* (com) lump-sum fees
Pauschsatz *m* (com) lump-sum charge
Pauschsätze *mpl* **für Berufsgruppen** (StR) flat rates for professional groups
Pauschsteuer *f* (StR) special tax on distributions
Pauschvergütung *f* (com) flat-rate compensation
Pause *f* (Pw) break *(eg, coffee/tea break)*
pausfähige Zeichnung *f* (com) reproducible copy
pendeln (com) to commute *(ie, between home and work)*
Pendelverkehr *m* (com) local commuter travel *(eg, as a major source of Bundesbahn losses)*
Pendler *m* (com) commuter
Penetrationspreispolitik *f* (Mk) penetration pricing *(ie, esp. suited to tap a new mass market for consumer goods)*
Pension *f*
  (SozV) retirement pension (*or* benefit)
  – retired pay *(ie, paid to ‚Beamte')*
  (Pw) retirement pay
  – employee pension *(ie, paid to employees)*
Pensionär *m*
  (Pw) retired employee
  – retiree
pensionieren
  (SozV) to pension off
  – to retire
pensionieren lassen, sich (SozV) to retire *(on a pension) (eg, at the age of 65)*
pensioniert
  (Pw) pensioned off
  – retired
pensioniert werden (SozV) to be retired
Pensionierung *f* (Pw) retirement
Pensionsalter *n* (Pw) pensionable (*or* retirement) age
Pensionsanspruch *m* (SozV) entitlement to a pension
Pensionsanwartschaft *f*
  (SozV) pension expectancy
  – expectancy of future pension benefits
  – vested right to future pension payments
pensionsberechtigt
  (SozV) eligible for a pension
  – entitled to a pension
  – pensionable
Pensionsberechtigung *f* (SozV) entitlement to a pension
Pensionsdienstalter *n* (SozV) pensionable age

Pensionsfonds *m*
(Fin) retirement fund
(Pw) pension fund
Pensionsgeschäft *n*
(Fin) security pension transaction
- repurchase operation
- repos
(ie, sale and repurchase scheme by which banks sell securities to the central bank for a limited period)
Pensionskasse *f* (Pw) pension fund *(ie, gives beneficiaries a legal right to future benefits; eg, § 4c EStG)*
Pensionsnehmer *m* (Fin) lender
Pensionsofferte *f* (Fin) tender from banks for a credit against securities
Pensionsplan *m*
(Pw) pension plan (*or* scheme)
- retirement plan
Pensionsrückstellungen *fpl* (ReW) company pension reserves, § 6a EStG
Pensionsverpflichtung *f* (Pw) pension obligation, § 6a I EStG
Pensionsversicherungsverein *m* (Bw) Pension Guaranty Association
Pensionswechsel *m* (Fin) bill pledged *(ie, bill of exchange deposited with a bank as security for a loan)*
Pensionszusage *f* (Pw) employer's pension commitment
per Aval (Fin) ‚as guarantor' *(ie, of bill of exchange)*
peremptorische Einrede *f* (Re) peremptory defense (*or* exception) *(syn, ausschließende od dauernde od zerstörliche Einrede)*
Periode *f* **erhöhter Gefahr** (Vers) apprehensive period
Periodenabgrenzung *f* (ReW) tracing revenue and expense to applicable accounting period
Periodenabgrenzung *f* **vornehmen** (ReW, infml) to pinpoint expenses accurately for a period
Periodenanalyse *f* (Vw) period analysis
periodenbezogene Kosten *pl*
(KoR) expense
- expired cost
Periodenbruchteil *m* (Math) fractional part of a period
Periodenerfolg *m* (ReW) net income of a given period
Periodenertrag *m* (ReW) current income
periodenfremd (ReW) unrelated to accounting period
periodenfremde Aufwendungen *mpl* **und Erträge** *mpl* (ReW) below-the-line items
periodenfremder Gewinn *m* **und Verlust** *m* (ReW) profit and loss unrelated to accounting period
periodengerechte Rechnungslegung *f* (ReW) accounting on an accrual basis
periodengerechter Jahreserfolg *m* (ReW) annual profit on accrual basis
Periodeninventur *f* (ReW) cyclical inventory count
Periodenkosten *pl* (KoR) period cost (*or* expense *or* charge)
- time cost *(ie, proportional to calendar time)*
Periodenleistung *f* (Bw) period output

Periodenvergleich *m* (com) period-to-period comparison
periodische Abschreibungen *fpl* (ReW) periodic depreciation charges
periodische Bestandsaufnahme *f* (ReW) cycle count
periodisch entnommene Stichprobe *f* (Stat) periodic sample
periodische Prüfung *f* (ReW) repeating audit
periodischer Dezimalbruch *m* (Math) repeating (*or* periodic) decimal
periodische Rückzahlung *f* **von Schulden**
(Fin) periodic repayment of debt
- amortization of debt
periodisiertes Modell *n* (Vw) period model
periphere Einheit *f*
(EDV) peripheral unit *(syn, Anschlußgerät)*
peripheres Gerät *n* (EDV) peripheral equipment (*or* unit)
peripherer Speicher *m* (EDV) peripheral storage
peripheres Steuerwerk *n*
(EDV) peripherical control unit
- control unit
periphere Substitution *f* (Vw) peripheral substitution
periphere Übertragung *f* (EDV) peripheral transfer
Peripheriegerät *n* (EDV) peripheral (unit)
Peripheriewinkel *m* (Math) circumferential angle
per Kasse (Bö) cash
per Kasse kaufen (Bö) to buy spot
per Kasse verkaufen (Bö) to sell spot
permanente Einkommens-Hypothese *f* (Vw) permanent-income hypothesis
permanente Inventur *f*
(MaW) continuous
- perpetual
- running ... inventory
(ie, kept in continuous agreement with stock in hand)
permanente Prüfung *f* (ReW) continuous audit
permanenter Gerätefehler *m* (EDV) permanent (device) error
permanente Stichprobe *f* (Mk) panel
Permanentspeicher *m* (EDV) permanent (*or* fixed) storage *(syn, Festwertspeicher, Dauerspeicher)*
permissive Gesellschaft *f* (Vw) permissive society
Permutation *f* (Math) permutation
Permutationsgruppe *f* (Math) permutation group
Permutationsmatrix *f* (Math) permutation matrix
per Nachnahme (com) charges collect (*or* forward)
per Saldo (ReW) on balance
Personal *n*
(Pw) personnel
- employees
- staff
Personalabbau *m*
(Pw) cut (*or* cutback) in employment (*or* staff)
- manpower reduction
- paring workforce
- reduction of personnal (*or* in workforce)
- slimming of workforce (*or* manning levels)
- staff reduction
Personalabbau *m* **durch natürlichen Abgang** (Pw) reduction of workforce through natural wastage

Personal n abbauen
(Pw) to slim
- to pare
- to trim ... workforce
- to reduce personnel
- to cut staff

Personalabgang m (Pw) attrition of workforce *(ie, number of employees dismissed or retired)*

Personalabteilung f
(Pw) personnel
- employee relation
- staff
- human resources ... department
- (US *also*) industrial relations department

Personalakte f
(Pw) personnel file
- personnel folder
- personnel records
- personnel dossier
- employee records

Personalanweisungsproblem n (IndE) manpower assignment problem

Personalanzeige f (Pw) employment ad *(ie, advertising a job opening in a newspaper or trade journal; ads may be open or blind = offene P. or Kennzifferanzeige; syn, Stellenanzeige)*

Personalaufwand m
(ReW, EG) staff costs
(KoR) employment costs
- personnel costs
- payroll costs
- staff costs

Personalauswahl f (Pw) employee selection

Personalbedarf m (Pw) personnel (*or* manpower) requirements

Personalbedarfsdeckung f (Pw) meeting of manpower requirements

Personalbedarfsplanung f (Pw) manpower planing

Personalberater m (Pw) personnel consultant

Personalbereich m
(Pw) „personnel"
- personnel administration
- personnel function
- human resources function

Personalberichtswesen n (Pw) personnel reporting

Personalbeschaffung f
(Pw) recruiting
- recruitment
- personnel recruiting (*or* recruitment)
- personnel procurement

Personalbeschaffungspolitik f (Pw) recruiting policy

Personalbestand m
(Pw) number of persons employed
- manning
- labor force
- workforce
- staff
- staff size

Personalbestand m **verringern** (Pw) = *Personal abbauen*

Personalbeurteilung f (Pw) performance appraisal

Personalbogen m (Pw) personnel record sheet

Personalbuchhaltung f (Pw) personnel accounting

Personalbudget n (Pw) personnel budget

Personalbüro n (Pw) personnel office

Personalchef m (Pw) personnel manager

Personaleinsatz m (Pw) personnel placement

Personal-Einstellungs-Maßnahmen fpl (Pw) hiring procedures

Personalentwicklung f
(Pw) personnel development
- human resources development

Personalentwicklungssystem n (Pw) system of management development

personaler Entscheidungsträger m (Bw) decision maker

Personaletat m (Pw) manpower budget

Personalförderungspolitik f (Pw) staff promotion policy

Personalfortbildung f
(Pw) personnel training
- *(longer-term)* personnel development

Personalfragebogen m (Pw) personal history form

Personalfreisetzung f
(Pw) personnel layoff
- reduction-in-force

Personalfreisetzungs-Volumen n (Pw) number of layoffs

Personalführung f
(Pw) personnel management
- staffing

Personalgemeinkosten pl (KoR) employment overhead

Personalgesellschaft f (Re) = *Personengesellschaft*

Personal n **im Außendienst** (com) field staff

personalintensiv (Pw) requiring large numbers of staff

Personal-Istbestand m (Pw) actual number of personnel

Personalkartei f (Pw) personnel card file

Personalknappheit f
(Pw) shortage of manpower
- personnel shortage

Personalkosten pl
(KoR) employment (*or* labor) cost
- personnel expenses (*or* cost)
- payroll costs

Personalkosten pl **der Lagerverwaltung** (MaW) cost of storekeeping personnel

Personalkostensteigerung f (Pw) increase in employment (*or* labor) costs

Personalkredit m (Fin) personal loan (*or* credit) *(ie, extended by bank on personal security only)*

Personal-Leasing n (Pw) personnel leasing

Personalleiter m
(Pw) personnel manager
- employment manager
- head of personnel department

Personallücke f (Pw) manpower deficit

Personal-Management n
(Pw) personnel management
- human resources management

Personalmangel m (Pw) manpower shortage

Personalnebenkosten pl
(KoR) incidental (*or* supplementary) personnel cost
- fringe benefits

Personalorganisation f
(Pw) task allocation

- task assignment
- work organization

Personalplanung *f* (Pw) personnel planning
- manpower planning
- human resources planning
- forecasting of manpower requirements

Personalpolitik *f* (Pw) personnel management (*or* policy)
- employment policy
- human resources policy

Personalqualität *f* (Pw) quality of personnel

Personalrat *m* (Pw) personnel committee

Personalreduzierung *f* (Pw) personnel reduction
- reduction-in-force

Personalressourcen *pl* (Pw) human resources

Personalsektor *m* (Pw) personnel function
- personnel administration
- human resources function

Personal-Sollbestand *m* (Pw) budgeted manpower

Personalsteuern *fpl* (FiW) personal taxes *(ie, income + wages tax, net wealth tax, inheritance tax, gift tax)*

Personal- und Sachausgaben *fpl* **des Staates** (FiW) nontransfer expenditures

Personalvermögensrechnung *f* (Pw) human resource accounting, HRA

Personalversammlung *f* (Pw) staff meeting

Personalvertretung *f* (Pw) staff representation

Personalvertretungsgesetz *n* (Pw) Personnel Representation Law, 1955 *(ie, established a quasi-shop steward system for public service employees)*

Personalverwaltung *f* (Pw) personnel (*or* manpower) management

Personalvorschüsse *mpl* (ReW) advances to personnel

Personalwerbung *f* (Pw) recruitment

Personalwesen *n* (Pw) = *Personalwirtschaft*

Personalwirtschaft *f* (Pw) personnel management (*or* administration)
- (infml) man management
- *(chiefly US)* human resources management

Personalzugang *m* (Pw) additions to workforce

Person *f* **des öffentlichen Rechts** (Re) legal entity under public law

personell differenzierte Exportförderung *f* (AuW) export promotion restricted to a specified number of exporters

personelle Betriebsorganisation *f* (Bw) person-centered organization *(ie, dominated by a strong personality cutting across functional lines of authority)*

personelle Einkommensverteilung *f* (Vw) personal income distribution *(ie, benefiting individual income recipients)*

personelle Terminplanung *f* (OR) manpower scheduling

Personenbeförderung *f* (com) passenger transport(ation)

personenbezogene Daten *pl* (EDV) personal data

Personendepot *n* (Fin) register of security deposit holders *(syn, persönliches Depotbuch, Ver-*

wahrungsbuch, [obsolete:] lebendes Depot; opp, Sachdepot)

Personen-Fernverkehr *m* (com) long-distance passenger traffic

Personenfirma *f* (Re) family-name firm *(ie, firm name of sole proprietorship, general commercial or limited partnership, §§ 18ff HGB; opp, Sachfirma)*

Personengarantie-Versicherung *f* (Vers) suretyship insurance

Personengesamtheit *f*
(Re) aggregate
- collection
- combination . . . of persons

Personengesellschaft *f*
(Re) association without independent legal existence
- unincorporated firm
- *(roughly)* partnership
(ie, general category comprising OHG, KG, stille Gesellschaft, and BGB-Gesellschaft; opp, Kapitalgesellschaft)

Personenhandelsgesellschaft *f* (Re) commercial partnership *(ie, term covering both OHG and KG)*

Personen-Kautionsversicherung *f* (Vers) fidelity bond insurance *(ie, taken out by the employee who deposits the insurance policy with his employer)*

Personenkonto *n* (ReW) personal account *(opp, Sachkonto = non-personal account)*

Personennahverkehr *m* (com) short-distance passenger traffic

Personenrecht *n* (Re) law of persons, §§ 1–89 BGB

Personenrechte *npl* (Re) personal rights *(opp, Vermögensrechte)*

Personenschaden *m*
(Re) personal (*or* physical) injury
- injury to person
- personal damage

Personensteuern *fpl*
(FiW) taxes deemed to be imposed on a person
- taxes imposed on the person of the taxpayer
(eg, income tax, net wealth tax, corporate income tax, church tax)

Personentarif *m*
(com) passenger tariff
- rate scale for rail passengers

Personenvereinigung *f* (Re) association (of persons)

Personenverkehr *m*
(com) passenger traffic
- transportation of passengers

Personenversicherung *f* (Vers) personal insurance

persönlich
(com) personal
- (GB) private
(ie, on envelopes: nobody but the addressee is to open)

persönliche Befreiung *f* (StR) personal exemption

persönliche Bemessungsgrundlage *f* (SozV) insured person's basis of assessment

persönliche Beteiligung *f* (Fin) personal investment (*or* participation)

persönliche Dienstbarkeit f (Re) personal servitude
persönliche Einrede f (WeR) personal defense *(ie, not good against a holder in due course, but against certain parties: all defenses not real or absolute)*
persönliche Haftung f (Re) personal (*or* individual) liability *(ie, exposing the personal assets of the responsible person to payment)*
persönlicher Arrest m (Re) arrest of debtor, §§ 918, 933 ZPO
persönlicher Barkredit m (Fin) personal loan
persönlicher Dispositionskredit m (Fin) personal drawing credit
persönlicher Freibetrag m (StR) personal tax exemption
persönlicher Gebrauch m (com, Pat) personal use
persönlicher Kleinkredit m (Fin) loan for personal (non-business) use
persönliches Anschaffungsdarlehen n (Fin) personal loan *(ie, medium-term installment credit of DM2,000–25,000, extended to individuals and small businesses)*
persönliches Depotbuch n (Fin) = Personendepot
persönliches Einkommen n (VGR) personal income
persönliches Engagement n (Pw) ego involvement
persönliches Kontrollbuch n (com) truck driver's logger
persönliche Supposition f (Log) personal supposition
persönliche Verteilzeit f (IndE) personal (need) allowance
persönliche Werbung f (Mk) canvassing *(ie, generally regarded as an act of unfair competition)*
persönlich haftender Gesellschafter m
(Re) full
– general
– unlimited ... partner
– personally liable partner
(ie, fully participating in the profits, losses and management of the partnership and fully liable for its debts)
Persönlichkeitsrechte npl (Re) rights of personality
persönlich verfügbares Einkommen n (VGR) personal disposable income *(ie, net national product at factor cost + transfer payments – direct cost and undistributed profits)*
Person f mit Doppelmitgliedschaft (Bw) linking pin *(ie, formal element in business organizations)*
Person f mit Informationsfiltereigenschaft (Bw) gatekeeper
persuasiver Direktverkauf m (Mk) forced selling
per Termin handeln (Bö) to trade for future delivery
per Termin kaufen (Bö) to buy forward
Perzentil n (Stat) percentile
pessimistische Dauer f (OR) pessimistic time
pessimistische Zeit f (OR) pessimistic time estimate
Petition f (Re) written request or complaint *(ie, addressed to competent authorities or to popular representative bodies)*
Petroleum n
(com) kerosene
– (GB) paraffin (oil)
Petrowährung f (Vw) petrocurrency
Pfad m
(EDV) bus
– highway
– trunk *(syn, Bus, Sammelweg)*
Pfand n
(Re) collateral
– pledge
pfändbar (Re) attachable
pfändbare Bezüge pl (Pw) attachable earnings
Pfändbarkeit f (Re) attachability
Pfandbesitzer m (Re) holder of a pledge
Pfandbesteller m
(Re) pledgor
– pawnor
– pledging party
Pfandbestellung f
(Re) pledging
– pawning
Pfandbrief m (Fin) mortgage bond *(ie, serial obligation issued by German mortgage bank, carries a specified maturity and interest rate)*
Pfandbriefabsatz m (Fin) sale of mortgage bonds
Pfandbriefanleihe f (Fin) mortgage-bond issue
Pfandbriefanstalt f (Fin) special mortgage bank (*or* institution) *(ie, arranges the issue of mortgage bonds and lends the money raised to house buyers, mostly organized under public law)*
Pfandbriefausstattung f (Fin) terms of mortgage bonds
Pfandbriefdisagio n (Fin) mortgage bond discount
Pfandbriefemission f (Fin) mortgage bond issue
Pfandbriefgläubiger m (Re) mortgage bondholder
Pfandbriefhypothek f (Re) mortgage serving as collateral for mortgage bonds
Pfandbriefmarkt m (Bö) mortgage bond market *(ie, part of fixed-interest securities market: key indicator of capital market situation)*
Pfandbriefumlauf m (Fin) mortgage bonds outstanding
Pfanddepot n (Fin) pledged-securities depot *(syn, Depot C)*
Pfandeffekten pl (Fin) pledged securities *(syn, Lombardeffekten)*
pfänden (Re) to attach
Pfandgeber m (Re) = Pfandbesteller
Pfandgegenstand m (Re) pledged (*or* pawned) item
Pfandgläubiger m (Re) lien creditor
– pledgee
(ie, whose claim is secured by a lien on particular property)
Pfandindossament n (WeR) pledging indorsement *(ie, made to deliver securities in pledge, esp. instruments made out to order, Art. 19 WG)*
Pfandinhaber m
(Re) holder of a pledge
– pledgee
– pawnee
Pfandkehr f (Re) disregard of security arrangements, § 289 StGB
Pfandleihe f (com) pawn broking, § 34 GewO *(syn, Versatzgeschäft)*

Pfandleiher *m* (Re) pawnbroker *(ie, lending money, usu. in small sums, on security of personal property left in pawn)*
Pfand *n* **nehmen** (Re) to take in pledge
Pfandnehmer *m* (Re) = *Pfandinhaber*
Pfandrecht *n* (Re) right of lien *(ie, right in rem to movable property providing security for the payment of debt, §§§204ff BGB)*
Pfändung *f*
 (Re) attachment
 – levy of execution
Pfändungsanordnung *f* (Re) order of attachment
Pfändungsbeschluß *m*
 (Re) order of attachment
 – distraint order
Pfändungspfandrecht *n* (Re) execution lien
Pfändungsschuldner *m* (Re) debtor under a levy of execution
Pfändungsschutz *m* (Re) exemption from attachment
Pfändungs- und Überweisungsbeschluß *m* (Re) garnishment order
Pfändungsverfügung *f* (StR) garnishment order *(ie, issued by the local tax office, §§ 309ff AO)*
Pfändung *f* **von Forderungen** (Re) attachment of claims, §§ 828ff ZPO
Pfändung *f* **von Sachen** (Re) attachment of (debtor's) property, §§ 808ff ZPO
Pfandverkauf *m* (Re) sale of pledge *(or* pledged article*)*
Pfandvertrag *m* (Re) contract of lien *(or* pledge*) (ie, to secure satisfaction of debt)*
Pfandverwahrung *f*
 (Re) custody of pledged goods, § 1215 BGB
 (Fin) pledging of securities to a ‚merchant' *(ie, who, upon becoming the lien creditor, has the rights and duties of a depositary, § 17 DepG)*
Pfandverwertung *f* (Re) sale or other disposition of pledge *(eg, § 1234 I BGB)*
Pfeil *m* außerhalb von Rückkopplungskreisen (OR) nonfeed branch
Pfeil *m* **e–s Graphen**
 (OR) branch
 – edge
Pfeil *m* **im Rückkopplungskreis** (OR) feedback branch
Pfeilschema *n* (Math) arrow diagram
Pflegeeltern *pl* (Re) foster parents
Pflegegeld *n* (SozV) nursing allowance
Pflegeheim *n* (SozV) foster home
Pflegekinder *npl* (StR) foster children, § 32 EStG
Pflegekosten *pl* (SozV) nursing expenses
Pfleger *m* (Re) curator, §§ 1909ff BGB *(ie, appointed by the court to care for the person or property of a minor, incompetent, etc.)*
Pflegesatz *m* (SozV) operating cost rate *(ie, in hospital)*
Pflegschaft *f* (Re) curatorship
Pflichtaktie *f* (Fin) qualifying share
Pflichtbeitrag *m* (SozV) compulsory contribution
Pflichtbekanntmachung *f* (Bö) obligatory stock exchange notice
Pflichtblatt *n* (Re) official journal for company announcement
Pflichteifer *m* (Pw) devotion to duty

Pflichteinlage *f* (Fin) compulsory contribution to capital *(ie, payable by limited partner of KG)*
Pflichten *fpl* **des Käufers** (Re) obligations *(or* duties*)* of buyer
Pflichten *fpl* **des Treuhänders** (Re) fiduciary duties
Pflichtenheft *n* (EDV) program specification
Pflichtenkollision *f* (Re) conflicting duties
Pflichterfüllung *f* (Pw) discharge of duties
Pflichtfach *n* (Pw) compulsory subject
pflichtgemäß entscheiden (Re) to consider and decide as in duty bound
Pflichthaftpflichtversicherung *f* (Vers) compulsory third-party liability insurance
Pflichtleistungen *fpl* (SozV) standard insurance benefits
Pflichtmitgliedschaft *f* (com) compulsory membership
Pflichtprüfung *f*
 (ReW) statutory audit
 (Vers) compulsory audit *(ie, of insurance companies)*
Pflichtreserven *fpl* (ReW) legal *(or* statutory*)* reserves *(syn, gesetzliche Rücklagen)*
Pflichtreservesatz *m* (Fin) statutory reserve ratio
Pflichtteil *m*
 (Re) legal *(or* statutory*)* portion of an inheritance
 – compulsory portion
 – *(civil law)* portio legitima
Pflichtteilsanspruch *m* (Re) claim of disinherited heir to his legal portion of the inheritance, §§ 2303 ff. BGB, § 3 ErbStG
Pflichtverletzung *f* (ReW) violation of professional ethics, § 67 WPO
Pflichtversicherter *m*
 (SozV) compulsorily insured
 – employed contributor
Pflichtversicherung *f* (SozV) compulsory insurance *(syn, Zwangsversicherung)*
Pflichtwahlfach *n* (Pw) compulsory elective
Pflicht *f* **zur schadenverhütenden Konstruktion** (Re) duty to design
Phantasiepreis *m* (com) fancy price
Phantasiepreise *mpl* **verlangen** (com) to charge fancy prices
Phantasiewerte *mpl*
 (Bö) bazaar securities
 – cats and dogs *(ie, highly speculative stocks)*
Phantasiewort *n* (Pat) fancy word *(ie, in connection with trademarks)*
Phantomfracht *f* (com) phantom freight
Pharmaindustrie *f* (com) pharmaceuticals industry
Pharmaunternehmen *n* (com) drug company
Phasenbibliothek *f* (EDV) phase library
Phasenfunktion *f* (Math) angle function
Phillipskurve *f* (Vw) Phillips curve *(ie, defines the relationship between jobless rate and percentage changes of nominal wages)*
Phonotypistin *f* (com) audio-typist
photographischer Speicher *m* (EDV) photographic storage
physikalische Adresse *f* (EDV) physical address
physische Distribution *f* (Mk) physical distribution
physische Grenzproduktivität *f* (Vw) marginal physical productivity

physischer Aufbau *m* (EDV, Cobol) physical structure
physischer Satz *m* (EDV, Cobol) physical record
physischer Wirkungsgrad *m* (IndE) technical efficiency
physisches Datenendgerät *n* (EDV) data terminal
physisches Grenzprodukt *n* (Vw) marginal physical product
Pigou-Effekt *m*
  (Vw) Pigou(vian) effect
  – real balance effect
  – wealth effect
Pilotanlage *f* (IndE) pilot (*or* demonstration) processing plant
Pilotbefragung *f* (Mk) pilot (*or* throw-away) interview
Pilotfertigung *f*
  (IndE) pilot plant scale production
  – bench scale production
  (*opp, großtechnische Fertigung = commercial production*)
Pilotinterview *n* (Mk) = *Pilotbefragung*
Pilotprojekt *n* (com) pilot project
Pioniergewinn *m* (Vw) innovational profit
Pionierprodukt *n* (Mk) pioneer product
Pionierunternehmer *m* (Vw) innovating entrepreneur *(A. Schumpeter)*
Pipeline-Rechner *m* (EDV) pipeline computer
Pipeline-Verarbeitung *f* (EDV) pipelining
Pivot-Operation *f* (Math) pivot operation *(ie, in matrix calculus = Matrizenrechnung)*
Pivotzeile *f* (Math) pivot row
Placierung *f* (Fin) = *Plazierung*
Plafond *m*
  (com) ceiling
  – limit
plafondieren (Fin) to set a limit
Plafondierung *f*
  (Fin) setting a limit
  – ceiling control
Plakat *n*
  (Mk) bill
  – poster
Plakatwerbung *f* (Mk) poster advertising
Plan *m*
  (com) plan
  – program
  – budget
  – scheme
Planabschnitt *m* (Fin) budget period
Planabweichung *f* (Bw) budget variance
Planansatz *m*
  (FiW) budget estimate
  (Bw) target
planarer Graph *m* (OR) planar graph
Plan *m* **aufschieben** (com) to suspend (*or* shelve) a plan
Plan *m* **bekanntgeben** (com, infml) to unveil a blueprint (for)
Planbeschäftigung *f* (KoR) activity base
Planbilanz *f* (Fin) budgeted balance sheet
Planbudget *n* (Bw) forecast budget
Plandurchführung *f* (Bw) implementation of plan (*or* budget)
planen

  (com) to plan
  – (infml) to figure ahead
Plangröße *f* (Vw, Bw) planned magnitude
Plan-Istabweichung *f* (Bw) out-of-line situation
Plankontrolle *f* (Bw) budget control
Plankosten *pl*
  (KoR) predicted (*or* forecasted) cost *(ie, term used as an umbrella)*
  – standard
  – current standard
  – budget
  – scheduled
  – target ... cost
Plankostenrechnung *f* (KoR) standard costing *(syn, Sollkostenrechnung)*
Plankostenrechnungsbogen *m* (KoR) budget cost estimate sheet
planlose Stichprobenentnahme *f* (Stat) chunk sampling
planmäßig
  (com) on schedule *(eg, project goes ahead on schedule)*
  – according to plan
planmäßige Abschreibung *f* (ReW) regular (*or* scheduled) depreciation, § 154 AktG *(ie, used to allocate cost of fixed assets over estimated useful life; opp, außerplanmäßige Abschreibung)*
planmäßiges Handeln *n* (Bw) planned action
planmäßige Tilgungen *fpl* (Fin) scheduled repayments
planmäßige Wartung *f* (EDV) scheduled (*or* routine) maintenance
Plannutzenkennziffer *f* (KoR) marginal income per scarce factor
Plannutzenziffer *f* (KoR) speed factor *(ie, speed factor × contribution margin = gross income per unit of scarce factor)*
Planperiode *f*
  (Bw) planning period
  – budgeted period
Planrevision *f*
  (Bw) revision of plan
  – replanning
  – budget adjustment
Planspiel *n*
  (Bw) management business game
  – experimental gaming
Planspiel *n* **über alle Unternehmensbereiche** (Bw) general management game
Plantiefe *f* (Bw) level of detail *(ie, overall/detail)*
Planüberholung *f* (Bw) budget review (*or* revision)
Planüberwachung *f* (Bw) budget control
Planumsatz *m* (Bw) sales projections
Planung *f*
  (Bw) planning
  – budgeting *(ie, preparing statements of plans and expected results in numerical terms)*
  – (US, *also*) master minding *(eg, company policy, in detail and cleverly)*
Planung *f* **des Werbebudgets** (Mk) advertising budgeting
Planung *f* **im Gegenstromverfahren** (Bw) mixed top-down/bottom-up planning
Planung *f* **optimaler Kassenhaltung** (Fin) cash projection

Planungsabteilung f (Bw) planning department
Planungsabweichung f (Bw) planning variance *(eg, between ‚Planzustand' and ‚Istzustand' = Ist – Sollvorgabe)*
Planungsansatz m (Bw) planning approach
Planungsausschuß m (Bw) planning committee
Planungsdaten pl (Bw, Mk) anticipations data
Planungsdeterminanten fpl (Bw) planning determinants *(or* factors)
Planungsforschung f (OR) = *Operations Research*
Planungshorizont m (Bw) planning horizon
– time level of planning
(ie, length of time covered in a plan)
Planungskontrolle f (Bw) planning control
Planungskonzept n (Bw) planning concept
Planungsperiode f (Bw) planning period *(syn, Planungszeitraum)*
Planungsphase f
(Bw) planning stage
(OR) precontractual phase
Planungsprozeß m (Bw) planning process
Planungsrechnung f
(Bw) performance measurement and matching subplans in specified planning periods
(Bw) finding optimum solution from among a set of alternative actions
(OR) = *programming*
(OR) decision models
Planungsrisiko n (Bw) planning risk
Planungssystem n (Bw) planning system
Planungstechnologie f (Bw) planning technology
Planungswiderstand m
(Bw) resistance to planning
– antiplanning biases
Planungszeitraum m
(Bw) planning period *(or* horizon)
(KoR) budget span
Planung f **von oben nach unten** (Bw) top-down planning
Planung f **vorbeugender Wartung** (IndE) evaluated maintenance programming
Planwirtschaft f (Vw) planned *(or* controlled) economy
(syn, Befehlswirtschaft, zentralgeleitete Wirtschaft, Einplanwirtschaft)
Planwirtschaftlichkeitsgrad m (KoR) tightness
Planzahl f (Bw) targeted goal *(ie, mandated for a specified planning period)*
Planziel n
(Bw) planned *(or* operational) target
– targeted objective *(or* goal)
Platte f (EDV) (magnetic) disk
Platte-Betriebssystem n (EDV) Disk Operating System, DOS
Plattenabzug m (EDV) magnetic disk dump
Plattenkassette f
(EDV) magnetic disk cartridge *(or* pack)
– disk cartridge
Plattenlaufwerk n (EDV) (magnetic) disk drive
Plattensektor m (EDV) sector *(ie, part of a track on a direct access storage device)*
Plattenspeicher m (EDV) disk storage
Plattenspeicherabzug m (EDV) disk dump
Plattenspur f (EDV) disk track
Plattenstapel m (EDV) disk pack

Platzagent m (com) = *Platzvertreter*
Platzakzept n (Fin) local acceptance
Platzarbeiter m (Pw) yardman
Platzbedingungen fpl (com) berth terms
platzen (Fin, sl) to bounce *(ie, check)*
platzen lassen (WeR) to dishonor *(ie, bill or check)*
Platzgeschäft n
(com) local transaction
– spot contract
Platzhandel m
(com) local trade
– spot business
Platzkarte f (com) seat reservation ticket
Platzkosten pl (KoR) workcenter cost
Platzkostenrechnung f (KoR) workcenter costing
Platzkostensatz m (KoR) workcenter rate
Platzkurs m
(com) spot rate
– spot market price
Platzmakler m (com) spot broker
Platzmeister m (Pw) yard boss
Platzprotest m (WeR) protest for absence (of drawer) *(syn, Abwesenheitsprotest)*
Platzscheck m (Fin) local check
Platzüberweisung f (Fin) local credit transfer
Platzüberweisungsverfahren n (Fin) local transfer procedure
Platzusancen pl (Fin) local practice
Platzverkauf m (com) sale on the spot
Platzvertreter m
(com) local agent
– town traveller
Platzwechsel m (Fin) local bill *(opp, Distanzwechsel)*
Platzzahlungsverkehr m (Fin) local payments *(ie, between banks in towns with a Federal Bank office)*
Plausibilitätsprüfung f (EDV) plausibility check
plazieren
(com) to place *(ie, a product on the market)*
(Fin) to place *(ie, new securities: selling them to the public at large)*
Plazierung f
(com) placing *(ie, a product on the market)*
(Fin) placement *(ie, of securities in the market)*
Plazierung f **durch Konsortium** (Fin) syndication
Plazierung f **e-r Anleihe** (Fin) placement *(or* issue) of a loan
Plazierung f **e-r Emission** (Fin) placement of an issue
Plazierungsgeschäft n (Fin) security placing business
Plazierungskonsortium n (Fin) selling group *(or* syndicate)
Plazierungskurs m (Fin) placing price
Plazierungsprovision f (Fin) selling commission
Plazierungsvertrag m (Fin) placing agreement
Pleite f
(com) bankruptcy
– business failure
(com, infml) flop
– falling by the wayside
– going to the wall
Pleite f **machen**
(com, infml) to go bust

- to fall by the wayside
- to go to the wall

Plenumsdiskussion *f* (com) floor discussion
Plusankündigung *f* (Bö) share price markup
Pluskorrektur *f* (Bö) upward adjustment
Pluskorrekturen *fpl* **überwogen** (Bö) markups dominated
„plus Stückzinsen" (Fin) and interest
Pluswert *m* **der Schiefe** (Stat) positive skewness
Podiumsdiskussion *f* (com) panel discussion
Poisson-Streuung *f* (Stat) Poisson variation
Poisson-verteilte Ankünfte *fpl* (OR) Poisson arrivals
Poisson-Verteilung *f* (Stat) Poisson (probability) distribution
Pol *m* (Math) pole *(ie, in the polar coordinate system)*
Polarachse *f* (Math) polar axis
Polaritätsprofil *n* (Mk) semantic differential
Polarkoordinatenpapier *n* (Math) polar coordinate paper
Polarwinkel *m*
(Math) polar angle
- amplitude
- anomaly
- azimuth
Police *f* (Vers) insurance policy *(syn, Versicherungsschein)*
Police *f* **ausstellen** (Vers) to issue a police
Policedarlehen *n* (Vers) policy loan *(ie, prepayment of sum insured up to the amount of cash surrender value*
Police *f* **mit versicherbarem Interesse** (SeeV) interest policy
Police *f* **mit Wertangabe** (Vers) valued policy
Policenformular *n* (Vers) blank policy
Policeninhaber *m* (Vers) policy holder
Police *f* **ohne versicherbares Interesse**
(Vers) PPI policy
- wager policy
Police *f* **ohne Wertangabe** (Vers) unvalued policy
Politik *f* **der Nachfragebelebung** (Vw) policies of spurring demand
Politik *f* **des billigen Geldes**
(Vw) easy
- cheap
- loose ... money policy
Politik *f* **des teuren Geldes** (Vw) dear *(or* tight) money policy
politische Ökonomie *f* (Vw) political economy
politischer Streik *m* (Pw) political strike
politisches Risiko *n* (Fin, Vers) political risk
polnische Schreibweise *f*
(EDV) Polish
- parenthesis-free
- prefix ... notation
(syn, klammerfreie od Präfixschreibweise)
Polygon *n* (Math) polygon *(ie, figure consisting of n points and of the line segments $p_n p_1$)*
Polynom *n* (Math) polynomial
Polynomial-Verteilung *f* (Stat) multinomial distribution
Polynom *n* **1. Art** (Math) separable polynomial
Polynom *n* **2. Art** (Math) inseparable polynomial
Polyphasensortierung *f* (EDV) polyphase sorting

Polypol *n* (Vw) polypoly *(ie, competition in a market of very many sellers)*
Polypolist *m* (Vw) polypolist
polypolistische Konkurrenz *f* (Vw) atomistic competition *(ie, in an imperfect market; syn, monopolistische Konkurrenz)*
polypolistischer Markt *m* (Vw) polypolistic market
polypolistisch-heterogene Konkurrenz *f* (Vw) imperfect *(or* monopolistic) competition
polypolistisch-homogene Konkurrenz *f* (Vw) perfect *(or* pure) competition *(syn, vollständige Konkurrenz)*
Polyprozessor-System *n* (EDV) polyprocessor system *(eg, consisting of up to several hundred of 16/32-bit microprocessors)*
Pool *m*
(Kart) pool *(ie, higher-order cartel, with pro-rata distribution of centrally reported profits)*
(Fin) pooling of security-holdings
(Vers) insurers' pool *(ie, organized to spread heavy risks)*
Poolkonsortium *n*
(Fin) pool syndicate
- pool management group
Popper-Kriterium *n* (Log) Popper's criterion *(ie, of falsifiable hypotheses in empirical sciences)*
Population *f*
(Stat) population
- universe
POP-Werbung *f* (Mk) point-of-purchase advertising
Portefeuille *n*
(Fin) portfolio
- holdings
Portefeuille-Bewertung *f* (Fin) portfolio valuation
Portefeuille-Effekten *pl* (Fin) portfolio securities
Portefeuille-Prämienreserve *f* (Vers) portfolio premium reserve
Portefeuille-Umschichtung *f* (Fin) portfolio switching
Portefeuille-Umschichtung *f* **auf höherverzinsliche Anleihen** (Fin) coupon switching
Portefeuille-Wechsel *m* (Fin) portfolio bill
Portfolioanalyse *f* (Bw) portfolio analysis
Portfolioinvestitionen *fpl* (Vw) portfolio investments *(syn, indirekte Investitionen; opp, Direktinvestitionen)*
Portfolio-Management *n* (Bw) portfolio management
Portfolio-Matrix *f* (Bw) portfolio matrix
Portfoliotheorie *f* (Vw) theory of portfolio selection
Porto *n* (com) postage
portofrei
(com) postpaid
- (GB) post-free
Portogebühren *fpl* (com) postage charges *(or* fees)
Portokasse *f*
(com) imprest fund
- petty cash
Porto *n* **und Verpackung** *f* (com) postage and packing
Portozuschlag *m* (com) extra postage
Position *f*
(Pw) position

- post
- job *(eg, er hat eine gute P. = he's got a plum job)*
Positionen *fpl* **des Zolltarifs** (Zo) headings in the customs tariff
Positionieren *n* (EDV) positioning
Positionierer *m*
  (EDV) locator
  (EDV) cursor
Positionierungszeit *f* (EDV) seek time
Positionsanforderungen *fpl* (Pw) job requirements
Positionsauflösung *f* (Fin) liquidation of commitments
Positionsbereinigung *f* (Bö) position squaring
Positionspapier *n* (com) position paper
positive Aussagenlogik *f* (Log) positive propositional calculus *(D. Hilbert)*
positive Externalitäten *fpl*
  (Vw) positive externalities
  - external benefits *(or economies)*
positive externe Effekte *mpl* (Vw) = *positive Externalitäten*
positive externe Ersparnisse *fpl* (Vw) = *positive Externalitäten*
positive Forderungsverletzung *f* (Re) = *positive Vertragsverletzung*
positive ganze Zahl *f*
  (Math) positive integer
  - nonnegative integer
positive interne Ersparnisse *fpl* (Vw) internal economies
positive Korrelation *f* (Stat) direct correlation
positive Ökonomie *f* (Vw) positive economics *(opp, normative Ökonomik)*
positive Risikoauslese *f* (Vers) market creaming *(ie, employing methods of unfair competition)*
positives Interesse *n* (Re) positive interest *(ie, claim to indemnity for breach at an amount equal to the full performance of the contract; syn, Erfüllungsinteresse; opp, negatives Interesse, Vertrauensinteresse)*
positive Vertragsverletzung *f*
  (Re) positive violation of contractual duties
  - positive breach of contract
  - defective performance
  (ie, breach of contract other than delay or impossibility = Verzug od Unmöglichkeit)
positive Wirtschaftswissenschaft *f* (Vw) positive economics *(opp, normative Wirtschaftswissenschaft)*
POS-System *n* (Mk) point-of-sales system
Post *f*
  (com) postal service
  - (GB) Post Office
  (com) mail
  - (GB) post
Postabholer *m* (com) caller for mail
Postabholung *f* (com) collection of mail
postalisch (com) postal
Postanschrift *f*
  (com) mailing address
  - (GB) postal address
Postantwortschein *m* (com) international reply coupon
Postanweisung *f* (Fin) postal remittance

Postausgang *m* (com) outgoing mail
Postbarscheck *m* (Fin) postal check
Postbote *m*
  (com) mailman
  - (GB) postman
Posteingang *m* (com) incoming mail
Posteinlieferungsschein *m* (com) post-office receipt
Posten *m*
  (com) item
  - entry
  - lot
  (Pw) post
  - position
  - job
Posten *m* **aktivieren** (ReW) to charge an account (with an item)
Posten *mpl* **der Rechnungsabgrenzung** (ReW) accruals and deferrals
Posten *mpl* **des ordentlichen Haushalts** (FiW) above-the-line items
Postengebühr *f* (Fin) item-per-item charge
Posten *m* **gutschreiben** (ReW) to credit an item
Posten *m* **passivieren** (ReW) to credit an account (with an item)
Posten *m* **verbuchen** (ReW) to pass an entry to an account
Postfach *n*
  (com) post office box,
  - P. O. Box
Postfreistempler *m* (com) franking machine
Postgebühren *fpl*
  (com) mailing charges
  - (GB) postal charges
Postgeheimnis *n* (com) postal secrecy
Postgewerkschaft *f* (Pw) postal workers' union
Post-Giro *n* (com) postal giro transfer *(ie, new term for ‚Postscheckverkehr')*
Postkarte *f* (com) postal card *(ie, sold by post office with a printed stamp on it)*
Postkosten *pl* (KoR) postal expense
postlagernd
  (com) general delivery
  - (GB) poste restante
postlagernder Brief *m* (com) letter to be called for
postlagernde Sendung *f* (com) poste restante mail
Postlaufkredit *m*
  (Fin) mail credit
  - mailing time credit
Postleitzahl *f*
  (com) postal district code number
  - (US) zip code
  - (GB) post-code
Postleitzahlverzeichnis *n* (com) zip code *(or post-code)* register
Post-Mortem-Programm *n* (EDV) postmortem program
Post-Nachsendung *f* (com) mail rerouting *(ie, to temporary address or to changed domicile)*
postnumerando-Rente *f* (Fin) ordinary annuity
Postpaket *n*
  (com) package
  - (GB) packet
Postprozessor *m* (EDV) postprocessor
Postscheck *m*

(Fin) postal transfer check
- (GB) National Giro Transfer Form
Postscheckamt *n*
(Fin) Postal Giro and Savings Office
- (GB) National Giro Centre
Postscheckdienst *m* (Fin) = *Postscheckverkehr*
Postscheckguthaben *n*
(Fin) postal giro account balance
- deposit in postal checking account
Postscheckkonto *n*
(Fin) postal check account
- (GB) national giro account
Postscheckteilnehmer *m* (Fin) postal check account holder
Postscheckverkehr *m* (Fin) postal giro transfer system *(syn, Postscheckdienst; new term: Post-Giro)*
Postsendungen *fpl* (com) postal consignments
Postspardienst *m* (Fin) postal savings scheme
Postsparkasse *f* (Fin) postal savings bank
Postsparkassendienst *m* (Fin) postal savings bank service
Poststempel *m*
(com) date stamp
- postmark
Postübersendung *f* (com) transmission by mail *(or* post), § 375 BGB
Postüberweisung *f* (Fin) postal remittance *(or* giro transfer)
Postversand *m* (com) postal dispatch
Postversandauftrag *m* (com) mail order
Postversandkatalog *m* (com) mail order catalog
Postverteilung *f* (com) routing of incoming mail
Postwagen *m*
(com) mail car
- (GB) postal van
postwendend
(com) by return mail
- (GB) by return post
Postwerbung *f* (Mk) postal advertising
Postwertzeichen *n* (com) postage stamp
Postwurfsendung *f*
(com) direct mail advertising
- unaddressed mailing
- bulk mail
Postzahlungsverkehr *m* (Fin) postal money transfer system
Postzustellbezirk *m* (com) postal delivery zone
Postzustellung *f* (com) postal delivery
Potentialfaktoren *mpl* (Bw) potential factors of production *(ie, providing a steady, unalterable stream of services, such as plant and machinery; opp, Repetierfaktoren)*
Potentialfunktion *f* (Math) potential *(or* harmonic) function
potentialorientierte Geldpolitik *f* (Vw) potential-oriented monetary policy *(ie, based on the production potential)*
potentialorientierte Richtgröße *f* (Vw) potential-oriented target
potentialorientiertes Geldmengenwachstum *n* (Vw) potential-GNP-oriented monetary growth
potentielle Nachfrage *f* (Vw) potential demand
potentieller Geldgeber *m* (com) prospective lender
potentieller Käufer *m*

(com) prospective buyer
- prospect
potentieller Kreditgeber *m* (Fin) potential lender
potentieller Markt *m* (Mk) potential market
potentieller Marktteilnehmer *m* (Vw) potential marketer
potentielles gesamtwirtschaftliches Angebot *n* (Vw) potential aggregate supply *(ie, equal to the overall production potential)*
Potenz *f* (Math) power
Potenzfunktion *f* (Math) potential function
Potenzieren *n* (Math) raising a number *(or* quantity) to a power *(eg, $a^n = a$ to the power of n)*
Potenzmenge *f* (Math) set of all subsets
Potestativbedingung *f* (Re) potestative condition *(ie, one which makes the execution of a contract dependent on an event which it is in the power of the contracting party to bring about)*
Powerfunktion *f* (Stat) power function *(ie, of a test)*
prädeterminierte Variable *f* (Stat) predetermined variable
Prädikat *n* (Log) predicate *(ie, in categorical propositions)*
Prädikatenkalkül *n* (Log) predicate *(or* functional) calculus
Prädikatenkalkül *n* **erster Stufe** (Log) first-order predicate calculus
Prädikatenlogik *f*
(Log) predicate logic
- logic of functional calculus
- logic of quantification
Prädikatenlogik *f* **zweiter Stufe**
(Log) second-order predicate logic
- second-order logic
praenumerando (Fin) in advance
praenumerando-Rente *f* (Fin) annuity due
praenumerando-Zahlung *f* (Fin) payment beforehand
praesumptio iuris et de iure (Re) irrebuttable presumption
präferentieller Handelsvertrag *m* (AuW) preferential trade agreement
Präferenz *f* (Vw, AuW) preference
präferenzbegünstigte Einfuhren *fpl* (AuW) imports eligible for preferential treatment
präferenzbegünstigtes Land *n* (AuW) country enjoying tariff preferences
präferenzberechtigter Ursprung *m* (Zo) preferential origin
Präferenzbereich *m* (Vw) zone of preference
Präferenzordnung *f*
(Vw, Bw) order
- scale
- set ... of preferences
- hierarchy of needs
Präferenzraum *m* (AuW) preference area
Präferenzregelung *f* (AuW) preferential arrangement
Präferenzsatz *m* (Zo) preferential rate
Präferenz-Seefrachtraten *fpl* (com) preferential rates
Präferenzskala *f* (Vw) preference scale
Präferenzspanne *f* (Zo) margin of preference *(ie, difference between preferential tariff and higher general tariff)*

Präferenzsystem *n* (AuW) preferential system
Präferenzzoll *m* (Zo) preferential duty (*or* tariff) *(syn, Vorzugszoll)*
Präferenzzollsatz *m*
(Zo) preferential rate of duty
– preferential tariff rate
Präfixschreibweise *f*
(EDV) prefix
– Polish
– parenthesis-free ... notation *(syn, polnische od klammerfreie Schreibweise)*
Prägegebühr *f* (FiW) brassage
Prägegewinn *m* (FiW) seigniorage
präjudizieren (Re) to set a precedent (for)
Praktiker *m* (com) practical man
Praktikum *n* (Pw) practical *(ie, 6-month period in industry as part of an undergraduate course)*
praktisch anwendbare Ergebnisse *npl* (Log) implementable results
praktische Bedürfnisse *npl* **des Steuerrechts** (StR) practical exigencies of taxation
praktische Erfahrung *f* (Pw) practical experience *(eg, candidate must have had at least 5 years of...)*
praktische Zweckmäßigkeit *f* (com) practical expediency
praktisch-normative Entscheidungstheorie *f* (Bw) normative decision theory
praktisch realisierbare Kapazität *f*
(Bw) practical capacity
– practical attainable capacity
(ie, the maximum level at which a plant can operate efficiently)
praktizieren (com) to practice *(ie, a profession: doctors and lawyers)*
praktizierender Anwalt *m* (Re) practicing lawyer
Prämie *f*
(AuW) bounty
(Pw) bonus
(Vers) premium
(Bö) option money
(EG) bonus
Prämie *f* **für Pauschalpolice** (Vers) blanket rate
Prämienanleihe *f* (Fin) premium (*or* lottery) bond *(syn, Losanleihe)*
Prämienaufgabe *f* (Bö) abandonment
Prämienaufkommen *n*
(Vers) premium income
– premiums received
Prämienaußenstände *pl* (Vers) outstanding premiums
Prämienbefreiung *f* (Vers) waiver of premium
prämienbegünstigter Sparvertrag *m* (StR) premium-aided savings agreement
prämienbegünstigtes Sparen *n* (StR) premium-aided saving
Prämienbrief *m* (Bö) option contract
Prämien-Diskriminierung *f* (Vers) rate discrimination *(ie, different rates for insureds or risks of small class)*
Prämieneinziehung *f* (Vers) collection of premiums
Prämien *fpl* **erhöhen**
(Vers) to increase
– to raise
– to up ... rates (*or* premiums)

Prämienerklärung *f* (Bö) declaration of options
Prämienerklärungstag *m* (Bö) option day
Prämienfestsetzung *f*
(Vers) rate making
– rate setting
– rating
Prämienfestsetzung *f* **nach individuellem Schadensverlauf**
(Vers) experience rating
– manual rating
– merit rating
prämienfreie Police *f* (Vers) free (*or* paid-up) policy
prämienfreie Versicherung *f*
(Vers) fully paid-up policy
– paid-for insurance
Prämie *f* **für Verbesserungsvorschlag** (Pw) suggestion bonus *(ie, usu. a cash bonus for suggestions considered meritorious; tax-free up to DM 200)*
Prämiengeschäft *n*
(Bö) dealing in options
– option dealing
– stock exchange options
(Bö) option bargain
Prämienhändler *m* (Bö) option dealer
Prämienkäufer *m* (Bö) option buyer
Prämienkrieg *m* (Vers) premium rate war
Prämienkurs *m* (Bö) option price (*or* rate)
Prämienlohn *m* (Pw) time rate plus premium wage
Prämienlohnsystem *n*
(Pw) premium bonus wage system
– premium system
– bonus scheme
Prämiennehmer *m* (Bö) taker of option money
Prämienrechnung *f*
(Vers) premium note
– renewal notice
Prämienregelung *f* (EG) bonus scheme
Prämienreserve *f*
(Vers) premium reserve
– unearned premium reserve
– mathematical reserve
(syn, Deckungsrücklage)
Prämienreservefonds *m* (Vers) premium reserve fund
Prämienrückvergütung *f* (Vers) return of premium
Prämienrückvergütung *f* **bei schadenfreiem Verlauf** (Vers) ,,no claim" bonus
Prämiensatz *m*
(Bö) option rate (*or* price)
(Vers) rate of premium
Prämienschuldverschreibung *f* (Fin) premium bond
Prämiensparen *n* (StR) premium-aided saving
Prämienspareinlagen *fpl* (StR) premium-aided savings deposits
Prämienstorno *m* (Vers) cancellation of premium
Prämienstücklohn *m* (Pw) piece incentive rate
Prämienstundung *f* (Vers) deferment of premium payment
Prämientarif *m* (Vers) premium scale
Prämienüberschuß *m* (Vers) net premium income
Prämienüberträge *mpl* (Vers) premiums unearned on balance sheet date, § 14 VAG

475

Prämienverkäufer *m* (Bö) taker of an option
Prämienversicherung *f* (Vers) proprietary insurance
Prämienvolumen *n* (Vers) total of premiums collected
Prämienvorauszahlung *f* (Vers) advance premium
Prämienwerte *mpl* (Bö) option stock
Prämienzahler *m* (Bö) giver of the rate
Prämienzahlung *f* (Vers) payment of premium
Prämienzuschlag *m* (Vers) additional premium
Prämisse *f* (Log) premise (*or* premiss)
pränumerando (Fin) in advance
Pränumerandorente *f* (Math) annuity date
Präsens-Indikator *m*
  (Vw) coincident indicator
  – coincident
Präsentation *f* (Mk) presentation
Präsentationsfrist *f* (WeR) time for (*or* of) presentment (*syn, Vorlegungsfrist*)
Präsentieren *n* (WeR) presentment of bill of exchange *(ie, for acceptance or payment)*
praxisbezogen (com) practical
praxisfremd
  (Pw) academic
  – not belonging to a ‚practical man'
Praxisschock *m* (Pw) reality shock
Praxiswert *m* (ReW) goodwill of free professional *(ie, acquired goodwill depreciable)*
Präzedenzfall *m*
  (Re) precedent
  – leading case
Präzisionsmaß *n* (Stat) modulus of precision
Preis *m*
  (com) price
  – charge
  – rate
  – (infml) tab
Preis *m* **ab Erzeuger** (com) factory price
Preisabrede *f* (Kart) price agreement, § 5 III GWB
Preisabrufverfahren *n* (Mk) price look-up procedure
Preisabsatzfunktion *f* (Vw) price-demand function
Preisabsatzkurve *f* (Vw) price-demand curve
Preisabschöpfung *f* (EG) price adjustment levy
Preisabsprache *f*
  (Kart) price fixing (*or* rigging)
  – common pricing
Preisabweichung *f* (KoR) price (*or* value) variance
Preis *m* **ab Werk**
  (com) factory price
  – ex factory price
  – price ex works
preisaggressives Vorgehen *n* (Mk) aggressive pricing policy
Preisänderungen *fpl* **vorbehalten** (com) prices subject to change without notice
Preisänderungsrücklage *f* (ReW) = *Preissteigerungsrücklage*
Preisanfrage *f* (com) price inquiry
Preisangabe *f*
  (com) price
  (com) quotation
Preis *m* **angeben** (com) to quote a price
Preisangebot *n*
  (com) price quotation

– quotation
– quoted price
– quote
Preisanhebung *f* (com) price rise (*or* increase)
Preisanstieg *m* (com) price increase
Preisaufschlag *m*
  (com) extra price
  (Mk) markup
Preisauftrieb *m*
  (com) upward trend of prices
  – upsurge of prices
Preisausgleichsprinzip *n* (Bw) principle of price equalization
  (ie, between domestic and export prices, between various plant divisions, etc.)
Preis *m* **aushandeln** (com) to negotiate a price
Preisausschläge *mpl* (com) price fluctuations
Preisausschreiben *n* (Mk) sales promotion competition *(ie, correct solutions fetch a prize)*
Preisauszeichnung *f*
  (com) price marking
  – labeling
Preisauszeichnungspflicht *f* (Re) obligation to mark goods with prices
Preisband *n* (MK) spread of competitive prices
Preisbasis *f* (com) basis of quotation
Preis *m* **beeinflussen** (com) to affect a price
Preis *m* **bei Anlieferung** (com) landed price
Preis *m* **bei Ratenzahlung**
  (com) deferred payment price
  – (GB) hire purchase price
Preis *m* **bei sofortiger Lieferung** (com) spot price
Preis *m* **bei Barzahlung** (com) cash price
Preis *m* **berechnen** (com) to charge a price
preisbereinigt
  (Stat) after adjustment for price rises
  – corrected to eliminate the effects of price inflation
  – in real terms
preisbereinigter Umsatz *m* **je geleistete Arbeitsstunde** (Bw) price-adjusted sales per man-hour
Preis *m* **berichtigen** (com) to adjust a price
Preisberuhigung *f* (com) steadying of prices
Preisbeschluß *m* **fassen**
  (com) to take a decision *(eg, to raise or lower prices)*
Preisbestandteil *m* (Kart) price component
Preisbewegung *f* (com) price tendency
Preisbildung *f*
  (com) pricing
  – setting of prices
  (Vw) price formation
Preisbildung *f* **auf Durchschnittskostenbasis** (Bw) average cost pricing
Preisbildung *f* **aufgrund der Nettoprämie** (Vers) pure premium method *(ie, leaving out of account the cost and expense of the insurer's operation)*
Preisbildungsfaktoren *mpl* (com) price determinants
Preisbindung *f* **zweiter Hand** (Kart) resale price maintenance *(syn, vertikale Preisbindung)*
Preisbrecher *m*
  (com) price cutter
  (com) price cutting article
Preisdeflator *m* (Vw) price deflator

Preisdifferenz *f* (com) price difference (*or* differential)
Preisdifferenzierung *f* (Vw) price differentiation *(ie, sale of identical goods at different prices to different buyers)*
Preisdifferenzierung *f* **transnationaler Unternehmen zwischen nationalen Märkten** (AuW) compensatory dumping
Preisdifferenzkonto *n* (ReW) price variance account *(ie, at year end traced to income statement)*
Preisdifferenzrücklage *f* (ReW) = *(obsolete form of:)* Preissteigerungsrücklage
Preisdiskriminierung *f*
  (Kart) price (*or* rate) discrimination
  – discriminatory pricing
Preis-Dividenden-Rate *f* (Fin) price-dividend ratio
Preisdruck *m* (com) pricing pressure *(eg, imposed by exporters)*
Preisdumping *n* (AuW) price dumping *(ie, prices are cut below marginal cost through government export schemes)*
Preise *mpl* **anheben**
  (com) to increase
  – to raise
  – to lift ... prices
Preise *mpl* **auszeichnen** (com) to mark articles with prices
Preise *mpl* **der Basisperiode** (Vw) base-period prices
Preise *mpl* **diktieren** (Kart) to dictate prices
Preise *mpl* **drücken**
  (com) to run down prices
  – (infml) to shave prices
Preise *mpl* **erhöhen**
  (com) to increase
  – to raise
  – to lift
  – to up
  – to send up ... prices
Preise *mpl* **explodieren**
  (com) prices hit the roof
  – prices go through the ceiling
Preise *mpl* **geben nach** (com) prices ease (*or* soften)
Preise *mpl* **gelten für** (com) prices are for ...
Preise *mpl* **hochschleusen** (EG) to push up prices
Preise *mpl* **hochtreiben** (com) to bid up prices
Preiseinbruch *m*
  (com) sharp dip in prices
  – steep fall in prices
  – steep slide of prices *(ie, prices take a tumble)*
preiselastisch (Vw) price sensitive
Preiselastizität *f* **der Nachfrage** (Vw) price elasticity of demand
Preiselastizität *f* **des Angebots** (Vw) price elasticity of supply
Preisempfehlung *f* (com) price recommendation
preisempfindlicher Markt *m* (com) price-sensitive market
Preise *mpl* **niedrig halten** (com) to keep down prices
Preisentwicklung *f* (com) movement (*or* trend) in prices
Preiserhöhung *f*
  (com) price increase
  – price rise
  – price advance
  – (infml) price hike
Preiserhöhung *f* **durchsetzen** (com) to force through a price rise
Preiserhöhungsrücklage *f* (ReW) reserve for price rises on raw materials
Preiserhöhungsspielraum *m*
  (com) scope for raising prices
  (Vw) money-goods gap
Preiserholung *f* (com) price recovery
Preisermittlung *f* (com) pricing
Preisermittlung *f* **auf der Grundlage der angestrebten Kapitalverzinsung** (Vw) target pricing
Preiserwartungen *fpl* (Vw) price anticipations
Preise *mpl* **senken**
  (com) to decrease
  – to cut
  – to cut down
  – to trim
  – to pare down
  – to reduce
  – to slash ... prices
Preise *mpl* **überwälzen** (com) to pass prices on to customers
Preise *mpl* **verfallen** (com) prices tumble precipitously
Preisexplosion *f*
  (com) price explosion
  – price jump
  – (infml) fly-up of prices *(eg, to meet the much higher market clearance level)*
Preise *mpl* **ziehen an**
  (com) prices rise
  ... improve
  ... look up
Preise *mpl* **zurücknehmen** (com) to roll back prices *(ie, in order to cancel an earlier price hike)*
Preis-Faktor-Kurve *f* (Bw) price-factor curve *(ie, shows factor demand in relation to its price)*
Preis *m* **festsetzen**
  (com) to fix
  – to determine
  – to set ... a price
Preisfestsetzung *f*
  (com) price setting
  – pricing
Preisfestsetzung *f* **unter Berücksichtigung e–r angemessenen Rendite** (Bw) rate-of-return pricing
Preisfixierer *m* (Vw) price maker
Preisfixierung *f* (Vw) price setting
Preisflexibilität *f* (Vw) price flexibility *(ie, reciprocal of price elasticity)*
Preis *m* **frei Bestimmungshafen** (com) landed price
Preis *m* **freibleibend**
  (com) price subject to change without notice
  – price without engagement
Preis *m* **frei Haus**
  (com) door-to-door price
  – delivered price
Preisführer *m* (Vw) price leader
Preisführerschaft *f* (Vw) price leadership
Preisfunktionen *fpl* (Vw) functions of price *(ie,*

477

matching, distribution, allocation, announcement, etc.)
Preisgaberecht *n* (SeeV) right to abandon
Preisgarantie *f* (EG) price guarantee
Preisgebot *n* (com) bidding
preisgebundene Waren *fpl* (Kart) price-maintained goods
Preisgefälle *n* (com) price differential
Preisgefüge *n* (Mk) price structure
Preisgestaltung *f* (com) pricing
Preis-Gewinn-Rate *f* (Fin) price-earnings ratio
Preisgleitklausel *f*
   (com) price escalator (*or* escalation) clause
   – escalator clause
   – price redetermination clause
   – rise-and-fall clause
Preisgrenze *f* (com) price limit (*or* barrier)
preisgünstig (com) reasonably priced
preisgünstigster Anbieter *m* (com) lowest bidder
preisgünstigstes Angebot *n* (com) lowest bid
Preisindex *m* (Stat) price index
Preisindex *m* **für die Lebenshaltung** (Stat) cost-of-living index
Preisinflation *f* (Vw) price inflation
Preisinformationsabsprache *f*
   (Kart) information
   – open price
   – price reporting . . . agreement
Preisinformationssystem *n* (Kart) open price system
Preis *m* **je Einheit**
   (com) unit price
   – price per unit
Preiskalkulation *f* (Bw) cost-based pricing *(ie, seeking to cover all fixed and proportional costs + a reasonable profit in the long run)*
Preiskampf *m* (com) price war
Preiskartell *n*
   (Kart) prices cartel
   – price fixing cartel
Preisklausel *f* (com) price clause
Preisklima *n* (com) price climate
Preiskonjunktur *f* (Vw) price-led boom *(ie, situation of soaring prices and quickly rising profits)*
Preis-Konsum-Funktion *f* (Vw) price-consumption function *(syn, Nachfragefunktion = demand function)*
Preis-Konsumkurve *f* (Vw) price consumption curve
Preiskontrolle *f* (Vw) price control *(ie, government regulation of prices of goods and services designed to reduce increases in the cost of living)*
Preis-Kosten-Erwartungen *fpl* (Vw) price-cost expectations
Preis-Kosten-Schere *f* (com) price-cost gap
Preiskreuzelastizität *f* (Vw) cross-price elasticity
Preiskrieg *m*
   (com) price cutting war
   – prices war
   – (US, infml) no-holds-barred price cutting
Preislage *f*
   (com) price range
   (com, infml) (something) at about the same price
Preislenkung *f* (Vw) regulation of prices
Preisliste *f*

(com) price list
– scale of charges
Preismaßstäbe *mpl* (Mk) price-performance standards
Preismechanismus *m* (Vw) pricing mechanism
Preismeldestelle *f*
   (Bw) open price association
   – central agency
   (ie, collating and distributing price information)
Preismeldeverband *m* (Bw) open price system
Preismeßziffer *f* (Stat) price relative
Preis *m* **mit Gleitklausel** (com) escalation price
Preis-Nachfrage-Funktion *f* (Vw) price demand function
Preisnachlaß *m*
   (com) price reduction
   – discount
   – allowance
   – (infml) rake-off
Preisnachlaß *m* **gewähren**
   (com) to grant a price reduction
   – (infml) to knock off *(eg, from total invoice amount)*
Preisniveau *n* (Vw) price level
Preisniveaustabilität *f* (Vw) stability of the overall price level
Preisnotierung *f* (com) quotation of price
   (AuW) direct quotation *(ie, direct method of quoting foreign exchange: amount of domestic currency payable for 100 units of foreign currency; opp, Mengennotierung)*
Preisobergrenze *f*
   (com) highest price
   – ceiling price
   – price ceiling
Preispolitik *f*
   (Vw) price policy
   (Bw) pricing policy
Preisproblem *n* (com) price issue
Preisprüfung *f* (com) price auditing
Preisrisiko *n* (com) price risk
Preisrückgang *m*
   (com) decline
   – drop
   – fall . . . in prices
Preisrückvergütung *f* (com) refunding of price
Preisschere *f* (com) price gap
Preisschild *n* (com) price label (*or* tag *or* ticket)
Preisschleuderei *f*
   (Kart) reckless price cutting *(ie, without any regard to costs)*
   – price slashing
Preisschub *m*
   (com) jump in prices
   – very sharp price rise
   – price surge
   – surge in prices
   – price boost
Preisschwäche *f* (com) weak prices
Preisschwankungen *fpl*
   (com) fluctuation in prices
   – price fluctuations
Preissenkung *f*
   (com) price cut
   – price reduction

- reduction in price
- markdown

Preisspanne f (com) price margin
Preisspannenverordnung f (Bw) price margin ordinance
Preisspirale f
(Vw) spiral of rising prices
- upward spiral of prices

Preisstabilisierung f (Vw) price stabilization *(ie, keeping prices at a stated level)*
Preisstabilität f
(Vw) stable prices
- price stability

Preisstaffel f (com) graduated price range
Preisstarrheit f (Bw) price rigidity
Preisstarrheit f **nach unten** (Vw) downward inflexibility of prices
Preisstatistik f (Stat) price statistics
Preissteigerung f (com) price increase
Preissteigerungsrate f (Vw) rate of price increases
Preissteigerungsrücklage f (ReW) reserve for price increases *(ie, of inventory items whose replacement cost has become substantially greater in the course of the taxable year, § 51 I EStG, § 74 EStDV)*
Preisstellung f
(com) pricing
- quotation

Preisstellung f **frei Haus** (com) delivered pricing
Preisstopp m (Vw) price freeze *(or stop)*
Preisstrategie f **mit vorweggenommener Inflationskomponente** (Bw) anticipatory *(or hedge)* pricing
Preisstruktur f (Bw) price structure
Preissturz m
(com) sharp drop-off *(or tumble)* in prices
- slump in prices

Preisstützung f
(com) pegging of prices
- price maintenance
- price support

Preistaxen fpl (Vw) = *administrierte Preise*
Preistendenz f
(Bö) market trend
- trend in prices

Preistheorie f
(Vw) price theory
- theory of prices

Preistreiber m (com) price booster
Preistreiberei f (com) profiteering *(ie, deliberate overcharging)*
Preisüberwachung f (Vw) price surveillance *(ie, form of government price control)*
Preisunterbieter m (Kart) price cutter
Preisunterbietung f
(Kart) undercutting
- underselling

Preisuntergrenze f
(Bw) lowest-price limit
- bottom price

Preisvektor m (OR) price vector
Preisvereinbarung f (Kart) price fixing agreement
Preisverfall m
(com) collapse of prices
- deep plunge of prices

- dramatic drop in prices
- large-scale *(or* steep) slide of prices
- shakedown in prices
- tumbling down of prices
- crumbling of prices

Preisvergleichskarte f (ReW) comparative price card
Preisvergleichsmethode f (StR) comparable uncontrolled price method *(see: Fremdvergleich)*
Preisverzeichnis n
(com) schedule of prices
- scale of charges

Preisverzerrung f (com) price distortion
Preiswelle f (com) wave of price increases
Preiswettbewerb m (Vw) price competition
Preiszugeständnis n (com) price concession
Preis m **zurücknehmen**
(com) to mark down
- to pull back ... a price

Pressemappe f (com) press kit
Pressemitteilung f (com) press release
Pressestelle f (Bw) public information office
Prestigeartikel m (Mk) prestige item
Prestige-Gut n (Vw) prestige good *(or* merchandise)
Prestigewerbung f (Mk) prestige advertising
Prestigewert m (Mk) prestige value
Prestige-Wirtschaft f (Vw) prestige economy
prima Bankakzept n (Fin) prime bankers' acceptance
Primadiskonten pl (Fin) = *Privatdiskonten*
Prima-facie-Beweis m (Re) prima facie evidence *(syn, Beweis des ersten Anscheins)*
primaler Pivotschritt m (OR) primal pivot step
primaler zulässiger Vektor m (OR) primal feasible vector
primale Variable f (OR) primal variable
primale Zielfunktion f (OR) primal objective function
primal-ganzzahlige Programmierung f (OR) primal integer programming
Primalproblem n (OR) primal problem
Primanota f
(ReW) journal
- daybook

(syn, Grundbuch, Journal, Memorial, Tagebuch)
Primapapiere npl (Fin) first-class money market paper *(esp. Privatdiskonten = prime acceptances)*
Primäranweisung f (EDV) source statement
Primäraufwand m (Vw) primary input *(ie, in input-output analysis)*
Primärbasis f (OR) primal basis
Primärbibliothek f (EDV) source program library
Primärdaten pl (Stat) primary data
Primärdatenerfassung f (EDV) source data acquisition
primäre Aktiva pl (Vw) primary assets *(ie, gold, foreign exchange and fixed-interest securities sold by the central bank under its open market policy)*
primäre Einkommensverteilung f (Vw) primary income distribution *(ie, resulting from market processes)*
primäre Gemeinkosten pl (KoR) primary overhead
primäre Indikatoren mpl (Stat) key indicators

Primäreinkommen *n* (Vw) primary income
primäre internationale Liquidität *f* (Vw) currency reserves held by central banks
primäre Kennziffern *fpl* (Bw) elementary ratios
primäre Kostenarten *fpl* (KoR) primary cost types *(ie, relating to costs which are based on market prices, such as material cost, personnel cost; syn, originäre Kostenarten; opp, zusammengesetzte sekundäre Kostenarten)*
primäre Marktforschung *f* (Mk) field research
Primärenergie *f* (com) primary energy
primärer Sektor *m* (Vw) primary sector of the economy
Primärforschung *f* (Log) first-hand *(or* field) research
Primärgeld *n* (Vw) primary money
– monetary base
(ie, central bank money + demand deposits with central bank; syn, Geldbasis, monetäre Basis, exogenes Geld)
Primärgeschäft *n* (Bö) new issue business
Primärliquidität *f* (Vw) primary liquidity *(ie, equal to central bank money)*
Primärmarkt *m*
(Bö) primary market
– new issue market
(ie, subsequent trading in the security takes place in the secondary market; opp, Sekundärmarkt, dritter Markt)
Primärmaterial *n* (Stat) raw *(or* source) data
Primärmetalle *npl* (com) primary *(or* virgin) metals *(ie, metals obtained directly from the ore, and not previously used; opp, Sekundärmetalle)*
Primärprogramm *n* (EDV) source program
Primärspeicher *m* (EDV) primary *(or* main) storage
Primärsprache *f* (EDV) source language
Primärstatistik *f* (Stat) primary statistics
Primärverteilung *f* (Vw) = *primäre Einkommensverteilung*
Primärziel *n* (Bw) primary objective
Primawechsel *m* (WeR) first of exchange
Primfaktor *m* (Math) prime factor
primitive Einheitswurzel *f* (Math) primitive nth root of unity
primitives Polynom *n* (Math) primitive polynomial *(syn, Einheitsform)*
Primpolynom *n* (Math) prime *(or* irreducible) polynomial
Primzahl *f*
(Math) prime
– prime number
Primzahlsatz *m* (Math) prime number theorem
Primzahlzwillinge *pl* (Math) twin primes
Prinzip *n* **der Bilanzkontinuität** (ReW) principle of the continuity of balance sheets
– (US) consistency concept
(ie, year-to-year effects of different procedures are minimized by requiring that the same alternative be selected each period)
Prinzip *n* **der Denkökonomie**
(Log) principle of parsimony
– Occam's razor
Prinzip *n* **der Fertigung durch autonome Arbeitsgruppen** (IndE) group technology

Prinzip *n* **der Preisunterschiedslosigkeit** (Vw) law of indifference *(W. St. Jevons)*
Prinzip *n* **der Rechtsstaatlichkeit**
(Re) principle of the rule of law
– rule-of-law principle
Prinzip *n* **der reduzierten Durchschnittskosten** (ReW) cost averaging effect
Prinzip *n* **des kürzesten Weges** (Bw) principle of shortest channel
Prinzip *n* **des minimalen Streuungsverhältnisses** (Stat) least variance ratio
Prinzip *n* **vom Maximum des Betrages** (Math) principle of maximum modulus
Priorität *f* (com) priority
Priorität *f* **beanspruchen** (Pat) to claim priority for an application
Prioritäten *fpl* (Fin) = *Prioritätsobligationen*
Prioritäten *fpl* **ändern** (Bw) to reorder priorities
Prioritäten *fpl* **festlegen** (Bw) to assign priorities (to)
Prioritätsaktien *fpl*
(Fin) preferred stock
– (GB) preference shares *(syn, Vorzugsaktien)*
Prioritätsanspruch *m* (Pat) prior *(or* priority) claim
Prioritätsanzeiger *m* (EDV) priority indicator
Prioritätsdatum *n* (Pat) priority date
Prioritätsjobdisponent *m* (EDV) priority scheduler
Prioritätsobligationen *fpl*
(Fin) preferred bonds
– (GB) preference bonds
Prioritätsverarbeitung *f* (EDV) priority processing
Prioritätsstreitverfahren *n* (Pat) interference proceedings
Privatangelegenheiten *fpl* (Re) private *(or* personal) affairs
Privatanleger *m* (Fin) private investor
Privatanschluß *m*
(com) private (telephone) extension
– (infml) home phone
(com) private railroad siding
Privatbahn *f* (com) private railroad
Privatbank *f* (Fin) private bank *(ie, organized under commercial law, as single proprietor, OHG, KG, GmbH, AG, etc.; opp, öffentliche Bank)*
Privatbankier *m* (Fin) private banker *(ie, mostly run as single proprietor, OHG, KG)*
Privatbilanz *f* (ReW) nonstatutory balance sheet
Privatbörse *f* (com) private exchange *(ie, an exchange-like gathering of private individuals)*
Privatdarlehen *n* (Fin) personal loan
Privatdetektiv *m*
(com) private detective *(or* investigator)
– (infml) private eye
Privatdiskont *m* (Fin) = *Privatdiskontsatz*
Privatdiskonten *pl* (Fin) prime (bankers') acceptances
privatdiskontfähig (Fin) qualifying as prime acceptance
privatdiskontfähige Bankakzepte *npl* (Fin) acceptances qualifying as prime paper
Privatdiskontmarkt *m* (Fin) prime acceptances market
Privatdiskontsatz *m* (Fin) prime acceptance rate
private Bautätigkeit *f* (com) private construction

private Bruttoinlandsinvestitionen *fpl* (VGR) gross private domestic investment
private Einkommensübertragungen *fpl* (VGR) personal transfer payments
private Ersparnisbildung *f* (VGR) private savings
private Geschäftsbanken *fpl* (Fin) private commercial banks
private Güter *npl* (Vw) private goods
private Hypothekenbank *f* (Fin) private mortgage bank
Privateinlagen *fpl* (ReW) private-asset contributions
private Investitionen *fpl* (VGR) private investment
private Kosten *pl* (Vw) private costs *(opp, volkswirtschaftliche Kosten = social costs)*
private Kreditnachfrage *f*
 (Fin) private credit demand
 (Vw) private-sector loan demand
private Nachfrage *f* (Vw) private demand
Privatentnahmen *fpl*
 (ReW) (private) withdrawals
 – (private) drawings *(eg, to take ...)*
private Plazierung *f* (Fin) private placement
privater Frachtführer *m* (com) private carrier
privater Haushalt *m* (VGR) = *Privathaushalt*
privater Kapitalverkehr *m* (VGR) private capital flows
privater Sektor *m* (Vw) private sector of the economy
privater Verbrauch *m*
 (Vw) private consumption
 (VGR) personal consumption expenditure
privates Bankgewerbe *n* (Fin) private banking industry
private Schuldübernahme *f* (Re) assumption of debt *(or* liability) in discharge of old debtor *(syn, befreiende Schuldübernahme)*
private Sparquote *f* (Vw) personal savings ratio
privates Wirtschaftssubjekt *n* (Vw) private economic unit *(or* subject)
privates Zollager *n* (Zo) private customs warehouse
private Titel *mpl* (Fin) private paper
private Verbrauchsnachfrage *f* (Vw) private consumer demand
private Wettbewerbsbeschränkungen *fpl* (Kart) private restraints of trade
private Wirtschaft *f* (Vw) private sector of the economy
Privatfirma *f* (com) private firm
privat gebuchter Kostenanteil *m* (StR) private portion of costs recorded
Privatgeschäfte *npl* (StR) transactions in which neither party is a dealer or trader in securities, § 20 III KVStG
Privatgläubiger *m* (Re) private creditor *(ie, of a partner, § 135 HGB)*
Privatgleisanschluß *m* (com) private (railway) siding
Privatgrundstück *n* (com) private property
Privatgüterwagen *m*
 (com) private freight car
 – (GB) private goods waggon
Privathaftpflichtversicherung *f* (Vers) personal liability insurance

Privathaushalt *m* (VGR) private household
Privatindustrie *f* (com) private industry
Privatinteresse *n* (Re) private interest
Privatinvestitionen *fpl* (VGR) private sector investment
privatisieren
 (Vw) to privatize
 – (GB) to denationalize
 – to return to private ownership
Privatisierung *f*
 (Vw) privatization of public enterprises
 – (GB) denationalization
 – return to private ownership
Privatisierung *f* **der Staatsschuld**
 (FiW) privatization of public debt
Privatkapital *n* (Fin) private (equity) capital
Privatklage *f* (Re) private prosecution, §§ 374–394 StPO
Privatkläger *m* (Re) private prosecutor
Privatkonto *n* (ReW) private account *(ie, subaccount of capital account)*
 (Fin) personal account
Privatkunde *m* (com) private customer
Privatkundenbetreuung *f* (Fin) servicing of private customers
Privatkundengeschäft *n* (Fin) retail banking
Privatkundschaft *f* (com) private customers
Privatmakler *m* (Bö) unofficial *(or* private) broker
Privatperson *f* (Re) private individual
Privatpfändung *f* (Re) levy of execution by private creditor
Privatplacements *npl* (Fin) notes *(ie, issued by public-law institutions or industrial undertakings; minimum amount DM50,000)*
Privatplazierung *f* (Fin) = *private Plazierung*
Privatpublikum *n* (Fin) private investors
Privatrecht *n* (Re) private law *(opp, public law)*
privatrechtlich
 (Re) private-law
 – under private law
privatrechtliche Körperschaft *f* (Re) private law corporation
privatrechtlicher Vertreter *m* (Re) attorney-in-fact, § 164 BGB
Privatsatz *m* (Fin) = *Privatdiskontsatz*
Privatschulden *fpl* (Fin) personal debts *(ie, of a partner)*
Privatsekretärin *f* (com) private secretary
Privatsphäre *f* **des Einzelnen** (Re) privacy of an individual person
privat unterbringen (Fin) to place privately
Privatunternehmen *n* (com) private firm *(or* undertaking)
Privaturkunde *f* (Re) private instrument *(opp, öffentliche Urkunde, § 416 ZPO)*
Privatverbrauch *m* (Vw) private consumption
Privatvermögen *n* (Bw) personal *(or* private) assets
Privatversicherer *m* (Vers) private insurer
Privatversicherung *f* (Vers) private *(or* commercial) insurance
Privatwirtschaft *f*
 (VGR) private sector of the economy
 (Vw) private enterprise
privatwirtschaftliche Lösung *f* (Bw) private-enterprise solution *(eg, of keeping a company alive)*

privatwirtschaftliches Dumping *n* (AuW) privately motivated dumping
privilegierter Befehl *m* (EDV) privileged instruction
Proband *m*
(Pw, Mk) interviewee
– participant
– respondent
Probe *f*
(com) sample
– specimen
(IndE) test piece *(ie, to be prepared for testing)*
– test specimen *(ie, as finally prepared for testing)*
Probeabschluß *m* (ReW) trial balance sheet *(ie, statement of credit and debit sums of all accounts; syn, Summenbilanz, Umsatzbilanz)*
Probeabstimmung *f* (Pw) test ballot
Probeanstellung *f* (Pw) probationary employment
Probearbeitsverhältnis *n* (Pw) = *Probeanstellung*
Probeauftrag *m* (com) trial order
Probebefragung *f* (Mk) pilot survey
Probebetrieb *m*
(IndE) pilot plant scale production
– trial operation *(syn, Versuchsbetrieb)*
Probebilanz *f*
(ReW) proforma
– preliminary
– tentative... balance sheet
– trial balance
Probeerhebung *f* (Stat) exploratory *(or* pilot) survey
Probefahrt *f* (com) trial drive, § 28 StVZO
Probeinterview *n* (Mk) pretest interview
Probekauf *m*
(com) sale on approval
– sale by sample
Probekäufer *m* (com) trial buyer
Probelauf *m*
(IndE) trial
– dry
– pilot... run
(EDV) test run
Probelieferung *f* (com) trial shipment
Probenahme *f*
(com) sampling
– taking of samples
Probenahme *f* **mit Rückstellung** (Stat) sampling with replacement
Proben *fpl* **nehmen** (com) to take samples
Probenteilung *f* (Stat) sample division
Probenummer *f* (com) specimen copy
Probenverkleinerung *f* (Stat) sample reduction
Probepackung *f* (Mk) test package
Probepartie *f* (Stat) pilot lot
Probesaldenbilanz *f* (ReW) closing trial balance
Probeverkauf *m* (Mk) store test
probeweise Beschäftigung *f* (Pw) probationary employment
Probezeit *f*
(Pw) probation(ary) period
– trial period
problematische Aussage *f* (Log) problematic statement *(ie, asserting that something may be the case; opp, assertorische* und *apodiktische Aussage)*
problematisches Urteil *n* (Log) problematic proposition
Problembereich *m* (Log) problem *(or* issue) area
Problembeschreibung *f* (EDV) problem description *(or* definition)
Problemdarstellung *f* (EDV) problem definition *(or* description)
Problem *n* **der optimalen Sortenschaltung** (IndE) batch sequencing problem *(syn, Seriensequenzproblem)*
Problem *n* **des Handlungsreisenden**
(OR) traveling salesman problem
– shortest route problem
Problem *n* **des Schwarzfahrers** (Vw) free rider problem
Problemkreis *m*
(Log) problem system *(or* cluster)
– family of problems
– set of problems
Problemlösungspotential *n* (Bw) problem-solving potential
Problem *n* **mehrfacher Entscheidung** (Stat) multi-decision problem
Problem *n* **ohne Nebenbedingungen** (OR) unconstrained problem
problemorientierte Programmiersprache *f* (EDV) problem oriented language
Problemprogramm *n* (EDV) problem program
Problemstatus (Log) status quaestionis (EDV) problem state
Produkt *n* (com) product *(syn, Erzeugnis)*
Produktanalyse *f* (Mk) product analysis
Produktangebot *n*
(Mk) range of products
– product assortment
Produktarten *fpl* (Bw) types of products
Produktauswahl *f* (Mk) product selection
Produktbeschreibung *f* (Mk) product specification
produktbezogene Deckungsbeitragsrechnung *f* (KoR) product-based contribution margin method
Produktbündelrechnung *f* (KoR) batch costing *(ie, in joint production = Kuppelproduktion)*
Produktdifferenzierung *f* (Mk) product differentiation *(ie, horizontal, vertical, over time)*
Produkt-Diversifikation *f* **(od** -diversifizierung *f)* (Mk) product diversification
Produkte *npl* (com) produce *(ie, agricultural products collectively)*
Produktelimination *f* (Mk) product elimination
Produkte *npl* **eliminieren** (Mk) to abandon products
Produkte *npl* **mit hohem Absatz** (Mk) high volume items
Produktenbörse *f* (Bö) produce exchange *(ie, a market in which future agricultural contracts are bought and sold)*
Produktenhandel *m* (com) produce trade
Produktenmarkt *m* (com) produce market
Produktentwicklung *f* (Bw) product development
Produktfeld *n* (Mk) product field
Produktfeldplanung *f* (Mk) product field planning
Produktfluß *m* (IndE) product flow

Produktführer *m* (Mk) product leader
Produktführung *f* (Mk) product leadership
Produktfunktion *f* (Bw) output function
Produktgestalter *m* (Mk) product designer
Produktgestaltung *f* (Mk) product design (*or* layout)
Produktgruppe *f*
(Mk) product line
- product group (*or* grouping)
- product category
Produktgruppen-Manager *m* (Mk) product-line manager
Produktgruppen-Werbung *f* (Mk) institutional advertising
Produkthaftpflichtversicherung *f* (Vers) product liability insurance
Produkthaftung *f* (Re) product(s) liability *(ie, strict liability in tort = verschuldensunabhängige Haftung)*
Produktinformation *f* (Mk) product information
Produktinnovation *f* (IndE) product innovation
Produktion *f*
(Bw) production *(ie, creation of goods and services)*
(Bw) output
- production
(ie, total number or quantity turned out)
Produktion *f* **aufnehmen** (IndE) to start production
Produktion *f* **auf vorliegende Bestellungen** (IndE) make-to-order production
Produktion-Einkommen-Lag *m* (Vw) output-income lag
Produktion *f* **einstellen** (IndE) to close down production
Produktions... (IndE) = (*also*) **Fertigungs...**
Produktionsabgabe *f* (EG) levy on production
Produktionsablauf *m* (Bw) production sequence
Produktionsablaufplanung *f* (IndE) production sequencing
Produktionsabteilung *f*
(IndE) production department
- product (*or* production) division
Produktionsänderungskosten *pl* (IndE) = *Produktionswechselkosten*
Produktionsanlagen *fpl*
(IndE) production equipment
- production facilities
- production plant
- production unit
Produktionsapparat *m* (IndE) = *Produktionsanlagen*
Produktionsaufgabe *f* (IndE) production task
Produktionsauftrag *m* (IndE) production order (*or* release)
Produktionsauftragsplanung *f* (IndE) overall production planning
Produktionsausdehnung *f* (Bw) increased output (*or* production)
Produktionsausfall *m* (IndE) loss of output (*or* production)
Produktionsausweitung *f* (IndE) expansion of production
Produktionsbereich *m* (IndE) branch of production
Produktionsbericht *m* (Bw) production statement

Produktionsbeschränkung *f*
(Vw) output constraint
(Kart) output limitation *(ie, in quota cartels = Quotenkartelle)*
produktionsbezogener Führungsstil *m* (Bw) production-oriented style of leadership *(R. Likert)*
Produktionsbreite *f* (Bw) product diversification
Produktionsbudget *n* (Bw) operational budget
Produktionsdatenverarbeitung *f* (EDV) production data processing
Produktionsdrosselung *f* (Bw) production cutback
Produktionseinheit *f*
(IndE) unit of output
- unit of production
- work unit
Produktionseinrichtung *f* (IndE) production (or manufacturing) facility
Produktionseinschränkung *f*
(IndE) cutback in production
- cut in production
- production cutback
- reduction in output
Produktionseinstellung *f* (IndE) production stop
Produktions-Einzelplanung *f* (IndE) production scheduling
Produktionselastizität *f* (Vw) output elasticity
Produktionsengpaß *m* (IndE) production bottleneck
Produktionserfahrung *f* (IndE) manufacturing know-how
Produktionsergebnis *n* (IndE) output
Produktionserhebung *f* (Stat) quarterly production survey
Produktionsertrag *m* (Bw) production by value *(ie, sales revenue + additions to inventory)*
Produktions-Expansionspfad *m* (Vw) output expansion path
Produktionsfaktoren *mpl*
(Vw, Bw) factors of production
- productive factors
- productive resources
- inputs
Produktionsfaktoren *mpl* **mit konstantem Einsatzverhältnis** (Vw) fixed inputs
Produktionsfaktoren *mpl* **mit variablem Einsatzverhältnis** (Vw) variable inputs
Produktionsfaktorqualität *f* (Bw) input quality
Produktionsfaktorsystem *n* (Bw) input system
Produktionsfaktor-Wanderungen *fpl* (Vw) factor movements
Produktionsfortschrittskontrolle *f* (IndE) production progress control
Produktionsfunktion *f* (Vw, Bw) production function
Produktionsgebirge *n* (Vw) (physical) production surface *(syn, Ertragsgebirge)*
Produktionsgenossenschaft *f* (Vw) producer cooperative
Produktionsglättung *f* (OR) production smoothing
Produktionsglättungs-Modell *n* (OR) production smoothing model
Produktionsgleichung *f* (Bw) production equation *(syn, implizite Produktionsfunktion, Transformationsfunktion)*
Produktionsgruppe *f* (IndE) production group

Produktionsgüter *npl* (Bw) (intermediate) producer goods *(ie, raw materials and semi-finished goods used in the production of capital and consumer goods; classification in business statistics: primary and general producer goods, capital goods, consumer goods)*
Produktionsgüterindustrie *f* (com) producer goods industry
Produktionshilfssystem *n* (IndE) production support system
Produktionsindex *m* (Stat) production index
Produktionskapazität *f*
 (Vw) production (*or* productive) capacity
 – output capacity
Produktionskartell *n* (Kart) production cartel *(ie, under output restriction agreement or quota agreement)*
Produktionskennziffer *f* (Bw) production index
Produktionskoeffizient *m* (Vw) production (*or* technical) coefficient *(ie, ratio of factor input to volume of output; syn, Inputkoeffizient, Faktorkoeffizient)*
Produktionskonferenz *f* (IndE) production planning conference
Produktionskonto *n* (VGR) product account
Produktionskontrolle *f* (Stat) production control *(syn, Fertigungsüberwachung)*
Produktionskosten *pl*
 (KoR) cost of production
 – production cost
 – process cost
 – output cost
Produktionskostentheorie *f* (Vw) theory of production cost
Produktionskürzung *f* (IndE) production cutback
Produktionsleistung *f* (Bw) output
Produktionsleistung *f* **je Arbeitsstunde**
 (Vw) man-hour output
 – output per man-hour
Produktionsleitung *f* (IndE) manufacturing management
Produktionslenkung *f* (Bw) production control
Produktionsmenge *f* (Bw) output *(syn, Ausbringung, Ausstoß)*
Produktionsmengeneinheit *f* (Bw) physical unit of output
Produktionsmittel *npl* (Vw) means of production
Produktionsmittelabweichung *f* (Bw) plant mix variance
Produktionsmittel-Kombination *f* (IndE) production setup
Produktionsmodell *n* (Bw) production model
Produktionsmöglichkeiten *fpl*
 (Vw) production possibilities
 – potential production
Produktionsmöglichkeitskurve *f*
 (Vw) production frontier
 – production possibility boundary (*or* curve *or* frontier)
 – product transformation curve
 – transformation curve
Produktionsniveau *n*
 (Vw) level of production
 – scale of operations
 – scale of productive process

Produktionsphase *f* (IndE) stage of production
Produktionsplan *m* (IndE) production plan (*or* budget)
Produktionsplanung *f*
 (IndE) production planning and scheduling
 – production planning
 – output budgeting
 (Unterbegriffe: Fertigungsprogrammplanung und Fertigungsvollzugsplanung)
Produktionspolitik *f* (Bw) production policy
Produktionspotential *n*
 (Vw) production potential
 – productive capacity
 (ie, attainable net output – Nettoproduktionswert – at constant prices)
Produktionsprogramm *n* (Bw) production program *(syn, Fertigungsprogramm)*
Produktionsprogramm *n* **bereinigen** (Mk) to streamline a production program
Produktionsprozeß *m* (IndE) production process *(ie, turnout of goods and services through operations which may be mechanical, chemical, assembly, movement, treatment)*
Produktionspyramide *f* (IndE) production pyramid (*or* tree)
Produktionsquote *f* (Bw) output quota
produktionsreif
 (Mk) ready to go into production
 – ready for production
Produktionsreserven *fpl* (IndE) capacity reserves
Produktionsrisiken *npl* (IndE) production risks
Produktionsrückgang *m* (Bw) drop in output
Produktionssparte *f* (IndE) area of production
Produktionsstatistik *f* (Stat) census of production
Produktionsstätte *f*
 (Bw) establishment
 – plant
 (ie, place where goods and services are produced)
Produktionssteuer *f* (FiW) production tax *(syn, Fabrikationssteuer)*
Produktionssteuerung *f* (IndE) production/operations management, POM *(ie, applicable to any type of productive system)*
Produktionsstruktur *f* (IndE) pattern of production
Produktionsstufen *fpl* (IndE) stages of production
Produktionssysteme *npl* (IndE) systems of production
Produktionstechnik *f* (IndE) production engineering (*or* techniques)
Produktionstheorie *f*
 (Vw) production theory
 – theory of production
Produktionsumstellung *f* (IndE) production change-over
Produktionsumweg *m* (Vw) circuitous route of production *(ie, term to describe a concept of the Austrian school of marginalists)*
Produktionsunterbrechung *f* (IndE) disruption of production
Produktionsunternehmen *n* (Vw) business undertaking engaged in the production of goods and services
Produktionsverbund *m* (IndE) interrelated production *(syn, Verbundproduktion, Produktionsverbundenheit, verbundene Produktion)*

Produktionsverfahren n (IndE) production process
Produktionsverlagerung f (Bw) relocation of production facilities
Produktionsvollzugsplanung f (IndE) = *Ablaufplanung*
Produktionsvolumen n (Bw) volume of output
Produktionsvorplanung f
 (IndE) pre-planning of production
 – advance production planning
Produktionswechselkosten pl (IndE) production change-over cost *(also: Produktionsänderungskosten)*
Produktionswert m
 (VGR) gross output *(syn, Bruttoproduktionswert)*
 (KoR) value of production *(ie, sum total of production cost accrued during a specified accounting period)*
Produktionswirtschaft f
 (Bw) production
 (Bw) production economics *(syn, Produktionswirtschaftslehre)*
produktionswirtschaftliche Forschung f (Bw) research in production economics
Produktionswirtschaftslehre f (Bw) production economics
Produktionszahlen fpl (Bw) output figures
Produktionszensus m (Stat) census of production *(ie, taken at intervals of several years)*
Produktionsziel n (Bw) production target
Produktionszweig m
 (Bw) industry
 (IndE) line of production
Produktion f **von Gütern** (Vw) production of goods
Produktivbetriebe mpl (Bw) productive establishments *(ie, Sachleistungsbetriebe + Dienstleistungsbetriebe; opp, Haushaltungen)*
produktive Arbeit f (IndE) direct work
produktive Faktoren mpl
 (Bw) factors of production
 – productive factors
Produktivgenossenschaft f (com) producer co-operative
Produktivität f
 (Bw) productivity
 – physical efficiency
 – production efficiency
 – technological efficiency
 – efficiency
 (ie, ratio of output to input)
Produktivität f **der Investition** (Vw) productivity of capital stock *(ie, output per unit of capital stock)*
Produktivität f **der Maschinenarbeit** (IndE) machine efficiency
Produktivitäts-Anreiz-System n (Pw) productivity incentive system
Produktivitätsengpaß m (IndE) productivity constraint
Produktivitätsfortschritt m
 (Vw) productivity gain
 – growth of productivity
 – improvement in productivity
Produktivitätsgefälle n (Vw) productivity gap
Produktivitäts-Kennzahl f (Bw) productivity ratio *(ie, volume output to volume input)*

Produktivitätsklausel f (Pw) productivity clause *(ie, tying wage rises to long-term productivity gains)*
produktivitätsorientierte Lohnpolitik f (Vw) output-related wages policy
Produktivitätsrente f (SozV) retirement pension tied to productivity gains
Produktivitätsreserve f (IndE) productivity reserve
Produktivitätsrückgang m (Vw) productivity slowdown
Produktivitätssteigerung f (Bw) gain in productivity
Produktivitätstheorie f (Vw) productivity theory of income distribution
Produktivitätstrend m (Vw) trend in productivity
Produktivitätsvorsprung m (Bw) edge in productivity
Produktivitätsziel n (Bw) productivity goal *(or* target)
Produktivitätszuwachsrate f (Vw) rate of gain in productivity
Produktivvermögen n (VGR) productive wealth
Produktkonzeption f (Mk) product conception
Produktkopplung f (IndE) product link *(ie, in joint production = Kuppelproduktion)*
Produktlebensdauer f (Mk) product life
Produktlebenszyklus m (Mk) product life cycle *(ie, comprises five market acceptance stages:*
 1. *Einführungsphase* = pioneering stage;
 2. *Wachstumsphase* = growth stage;
 3. *Reifephase* = maturity stage;
 4. *Sättigungsphase* = saturation stage;
 5. *Degenerationsphase* = decline stage)
Produktlinie f (Mk) product line
Produktlinienplanung f (Bw) product line planning
Produktlinien fpl **zusammenlegen** (Bw) to trim back product lines
Produkt-Management n (Bw) product management
Produktmanager m (Mk) product *(or* brand) manager
Produktmärkte mpl (Mk) product markets
Produkt/Markt-Mix m (Mk) product/market mix
Produktmenge f (Vw, Bw) output
Produktmix m (Mk) product mix *(ie, composite of products offered for sale)*
Produkt-Modell n (IndE) preproduction model
Produktmodifikation f (Mk) product modification
Produktmoment n
 (Stat) multi-variate moment
 – product moment
Produktmuster n (IndE) product sample
Produktor m
 (Bw) input
 – factor of production
Produktorfunktion f (Bw) input function *(syn, Faktorfunktion)*
Produktorganisation f (Bw) product-oriented organizational structure
produktorientierte Struktur f (Bw) product-oriented structure
Produktpalette f
 (Mk) range of products
 – product range
 – product spectrum

Produktpalette f verkleinern (Mk) to trim back a range of products
Produktplanung f (Bw) product planning *(syn, Erzeugnisplanung)*
Produktpolitik f (Mk) product policy
Produktprofil n (Mk) product personality
Produktprogramm n (Bw) = *Produktionsprogramm*
Produktqualität f (Bw) product quality
Produktsparte f (Bw) product division
Produktspezialisierung f (Bw) product specialization
Produkt-Stammbaum m (IndE) product tree
Produktstruktur f (Bw) product structure
Produktsystem n (Bw) product system
Produkttest m (Mk) product test
Produkttyp m (Bw) product type
Produktverbesserung f (Bw) product improvement
Produktvereinfachung f (Bw) product simplification
Produkt n **vorstellen** (Mk, infml) to unleash a product *(eg, at an office automation show)*
Produktwechsel m (Bw) product change
Produktwerbung f (Mk) product (*or* competitive) advertising
Produktziel n (Bw) product goal *(ie, output of specified products in specified volume and quality at predetermined times)*
Produkt-Zuverlässigkeit f (Mk) product reliability
Produzent m (com) producer
Produzentenhaftung f (Re) = *Produkthaftung*
Produzentenpreis m (com) producer-fixed price *(eg, set by a price leader)*
Produzentenrente f (Vw) producer's surplus *(Marshall)*
Produzentenrisiko n (Stat) producer's risk
produzierendes Gewerbe n (com) producing sector *(ie, core of the nonfarming sector of the economy)*
Profit m **i. e. S.** (Vw) pure profit
Profitrate f (Vw) rate of profit
Proformarechnung f (com) pro forma invoice
Prognose f (Bw) forecast
Prognose f **erster Ordnung** (Bw) first-order forecast
Prognosefähigkeit f (Stat) predictive power
Prognosefehler m (Stat) forecast error
Prognosegleichung f (Stat) forecast equation
Prognosegültigkeit f (Vw, Bw) predictive validity
Prognoseinstitut n (Vw) forecasting body (*or* institute)
Prognosekorridor m (Bw) prediction interval
Prognosequalität f (Stat) predictive power
Prognostiker m
 (Bw) forecaster
 – prognosticator
prognostische Effizienz f (Stat) predictive record *(eg, of an econometric model)*
Prognostizierbarkeit f (Bw) predictability
Programm n (EDV) computer program
programmabhängiger Fehler m (EDV) program sensitive fault
Programmablauf m (EDV) program run (*or* execution *or* flow)
Programmablaufplan m (EDV) program flowchart

Programmablaufrechner m (EDV) target (*or* object) computer
Programmabschnitt m (EDV) control section
Programmänderung f (EDV) program modification
Programmausführungsanlage f (EDV, Cobol) object computer
Programmausrüstung f (EDV) software
Programmband n (EDV) program tape
Programmbaustein m (EDV) program module
Programmbefehl m (EDV) program instruction
Programmbereich m
 (EDV) program area
 (EDV) partition *(ie, subdivision of storage area)*
Programmbeschreibung f (EDV) program description
Programmbibliothek f (EDV) program library
Programmbudget n
 (FiW) program budget
 – PPB (planning, programming, budgeting) system
 (ie, projection for the budget period; syn, performance budget)
Programmdokumentation f (EDV) program documentation
Programmdurchlauf m (EDV) program run
Programm n **einlesen** (EDV) to load a program
Programm n **erstellen** (EDV) to generate a program
Programmfehler m (EDV) program error
Programmformular n (EDV) coding sheet
Programmgang m (EDV) program cycle
programmgebundene Bedarfsmengenplanung f (MaW) program-based materials budgeting
Programmgenerator m (EDV) program generator
programmgesteuerte Rechenanlage f (EDV) program-controlled computer
Programmidentifikation f (EDV) program identification
programmierbare Datenstation f (EDV) programmable terminal
programmierbarer Festspeicher m (EDV) programmable read only memory, PROM
programmieren (EDV) to program
Programmierer m (EDV) programmer
Programmierfehler m
 (EDV) bug
 – programming error
Programmierhilfen fpl (EDV) programming aids
Programmiersprache f (EDV) program (*or* programming) language
Programmiersystem n (EDV) programming system
programmierte Unterweisung f (Pw) programmed instruction
Programmierung f (OR) programming
Programmierwort n (EDV, Cobol) user defined word
Programmkarte f (EDV) source program card
Programm-Kompatibilität f (EDV) program compatibility
Programmlader m (EDV) = *Lader*
Programmlauf m (EDV) program run
Programmliste f (EDV) program list
Programmlochkarte f (EDV) source program card
Programmlochstreifen m (EDV) program tape

Programm n **mit Minimaldauer** (OR) crashed program
Programmodul m (EDV) program module
Programmname m (EDV, Cobol) program name
Programmpaket n (EDV) program package
Programmparameter m (EDV) program parameter
Programmprotokoll n (EDV) program listing (or record)
Programmprüfung f (EDV) program testing
Programmprüfzeit f (EDV) program development time
Programmschalter m (EDV) program switch
Programmschemata npl (EDV) generic program units
Programmschleife f (EDV) program loop
Programmschritt m (EDV) program step
Programmsegment n (EDV) program segment
Programmspeicher m (EDV) program memory
Programmsprung m (EDV) program branch
Programmstatuswort n (EDV) program status word, PSW
Programmsteuerung f (EDV) sequential control (syn, Ablaufsteuerung, Taktsteuerung)
Programmstop m **durch Dauerschleife** (EDV) loop stop (ie, loop used to stall execution of program)
Programmstreifen m (EDV) program tape
Programmtesten n (EDV) program checkout
Programmtrommel f (EDV) program drum
Programmübersetzung f (EDV) program translation (EDV) compilation
Programmumwandlung f (EDV) program conversion
Programmunterbrechung f (EDV) program interrupt
Programmverknüpfung f (EDV) program linkage
Programmverwaltung f (EDV) program management
Programmvordruck m (EDV) coding sheet
Programmwartung f (EDV) program maintenance
Programmweiche f (EDV) program switch
Progression f
(StR) progression
– progressive scale
Progressionssatz m (StR) rate of progression
Progressionsvorbehalt m (StR) „exemption with progression" rule (ie, incorporated in all German income tax conventions: each country reserves the right to compute its tax on the portion of the decedent's property over which it has jurisdiction at the rate which would apply to the entire transfer)
progressive Abschreibung f (ReW) increasing balance (method of depreciation)
progressive Einkommensteuer f (StR) progressive income tax
progressive Kalkulation f (KoR) progressive cost estimate (ie, cost-based method of determining product prices; opp, retrograde Kalkulation)
progressive Kosten pl (Bw) progressive costs (ie, rising average, unit or total cost for a given level of activity)
progressive Leistungsprämie f (Pw) accelerated premium

progressive Planung f (Bw) bottom-up planning
progressiver Leistungslohn m (Pw) accelerated incentive
progressives Planungsverfahren n (Bw) bottom-up planning
progressive Steuer f (StR) progressive tax
progressive Steuer f **mit Stufentarif** (StR) graduated tax
progressive Verkaufskalkulation f (com) progressive method of determining sales price (ie, standard method in retailing: cost price + selling and administrative expenses + profit markup = sales price; opp, retrograde Verkaufskalkulation)
Progressivität f **der Einkommensteuer** (StR) progressive rate structure of the income tax
Progressivlohn m (Pw) progressive wage rate
prohibitive Steuer f (FiW) penalty tax
prohibitive Zinsen mpl (Fin) inhibitory interest rates
Prohibitivpreis m (Vw, Mk) prohibitive price
Prohibitivzoll m (Zo) prohibitive duty (or tariff)
Projekt n
(com) project
– scheme
Projekt n **ablehnen** (com) to turn down a project
Projektbindung f (AuW) project tying (ie, in granting economic aid)
Projekt n **durchführen** (com) to implement a project
Projekt n **entwickeln** (com) to develop a project
Projekt n **erweitern** (com) to expand a project
Projekt n **fallen lassen** (com) to abandon (or discard) a project
Projekt n **finanzieren**
(Fin) to fund a project
– to arrange funding for a project
Projektfinanzierung f (Fin) project financing (or funding) (opp, general-purpose loans)
projektgebundene Ausleihungen fpl (Fin) project-linked (or project-tied) lendings
projektgebundene Investitionsfinanzierung f (Fin) project-tied investment funding
projektgebundenes Darlehen n (Fin) nonrecourse loan (ie, tying repayment strictly to the revenues of a particular project)
Projekt n **geht schief** (com) project goes awry
Projektgruppe f (com) project team
Projektierungskosten pl (KoR) planning cost
Projekt n **in Gang setzen** (com) to launch a project
Projektion f (Vw) projection (ie, working out estimates based on a specified set of hypotheses)
projektive Eigenschaft f (Math) projective property
Projekt n **konzipieren** (com) to formulate a project
Projektkosten pl (Bw) project cost
Projektlagebericht m (com) project status report
Projektleiter m (Bw) project manager
Projektleitung f (Bw) project (or operative) management
Projekt n **macht Fortschritte** (com) project is taking shape
Projekt-Management n (Bw) = Projektleitung
Projektmanagement-System n (Bw) project management system

Projektmanager *m* (Bw) = *Projektleiter*
Projektorganisation *f* (Bw) project-type organization *(ie, of a company)*
projektorientiert (Bw) project *(or* job) oriented
Projektplanung *f* (Bw) project scheduling
Projektreife *f* (com) preimplementation stage of a project
Projektstudie *f* (com) feasibility study
Projektträger *m* (Fin) project sponsor
Projektüberwachungssystem *n* (Bw) project control system
Projektvorschlag *m* **vorlegen** (com) to submit a project proposal
Projekt *n* **zurückstellen** (com) to shelve a project
pro-Kopf-Bedarf *m* (Vw) per-capita demand
Pro-Kopf-Einkommen *n* (Stat) per capita income
pro-Kopf-Leistung *f* (Bw) per capita output
pro-Kopf-Verbrauch *m* (Stat) per capita consumption
Prokura *f*
  (Re, *no equivalent*) ‚Prokura', §§ 48 ff HGB
  – power of procuration *(abbreviation ‚p.p.' preceding signature of holder)*
  – general commercial power of attorney *(or* representation)
  (ie, under commercial law, it is a far-reaching, almost unrestricted authority defined by law and entered in the Commercial Register)
Prokura *f* **entziehen** (Re) to withdraw power of procuration
Prokura *f* **erteilen** (Re) to grant power of procuration
Prokura-Indossament *n* (WeR) collection indorsement
Prokurist *m*
  (Re, *no equivalent*) ‚Prokurist', § 51 HGB
  – holder of a general commercial power of attorney
Prolongation *f*
  (com) extension
  (WeR) renewal
  (Bö) carryover *(ie, in forward deals)*
Prolongation *f* **e–s Wechsels** (WeR) renewal of a bill
Prolongationsfaktor *m* (Math) accumulation factor, $(1 + i)^n$
Prolongationsgebühr *f* (WeR) renewal charge
Prolongationssatz *m* (Bö) carryover rate
Prolongationswechsel *m* (WeR) renewal bill *(or* note)
prolongieren
  (com) to extend
  (WeR) to renew a bill
  (Bö) to carry over
prolongierte Police *f* (Vers) extended policy
pro Mengeneinheit (com) per volume unit
promoviert werden (Pw) to be awarded a doctor's degree
prompte Zahlung *f* (com) prompt payment *(ie, without delay; in US within 10 working days)*
Promptgeschäft *n* (Bö) sale for quick delivery *(opp, Lieferungsgeschäft)*
Propergeschäft *n* (Fin) trade for one's own account
proportionale Kosten *pl* (KoR) proportional cost *(ie, part of variable total cost changing in step with volume of output)*
proportionale Stichprobennahme *f* (Stat) proportional sampling
Proportionalitätsfaktor *m* (Math) constant *(or* factor) of proportionality
  – slope
Proportionalitätsmethode *f* (KoR) method of allocating joint-product cost *(ie, spreading costs in proportion to specified bases: physical units produced, revenue-generating power of products, etc.; syn, Verteilungsmethode)*
Proportionalregel *f* (Vers) condition of average clause
Proportionalsatz *m* (StR) flat rate
Proportionalsteuer *f* (StR) proportional tax
Prorata-Klausel *f* (Vers) average clause
Prospekt *m*
  (com) prospectus
  – leaflet
  – folder
Prospekthaftung *f* (Fin) liability extending to statements made in issuing prospectus
prospektiver Kunde *m* (com) potential customer
Prospektmaterial *n* (com) descriptive material
Prospektzwang *m* (Fin) duty to publish an issuing prospectus
Prosperität *f* (Vw) prosperity
Protektionismus *m* (Vw) protectionism
protektionistische Maßnahmen *fpl* (AuW) protectionist measures
protektionistisches Instrumentarium *n* (Vw) protectionist tool kit
Protest *m* (WeR) act of protest, Art. 44, 79 WG
Protestanzeige *f* (WeR) notice of dishonor
Protestfrist *f* (WeR) statutory period for noting and protesting a bill
Protestgebühr *f* (WeR) protest fee
Protestkosten *pl* (WeR) protest charges
Protest *m* **mangels Annahme** (WeR) protest for non-acceptance
Protest *m* **mangels Zahlung** (WeR) protest for refusal of payment
Proteststreik *m* (Pw) protest strike
Protesturkunde *f* (WeR) certificate of dishonor
Protestverzicht *m* (WeR) waiver of protest
Protestwechsel *m* (WeR) protested bill
Protokoll *n*
  (com) minutes *(eg, of a meeting)*
  (EDV) log
  – listing
Protokoll *n* **e–r mündlichen Verhandlung** (Re) transcript of proceedings
Protokollführer *m* (com) person taking minutes
protokollieren
  (com) to take minutes *(eg, of a meeting)*
  – to keep the minutes
  (EDV) to log
Protokollprogramm *n* (EDV) trace program
Protokoll *n* **verlesen** (com) to read out the minutes *(eg, of the last meeting)*
Provenienz-Zertifikat *n* (com) certificate of origin *(ie, evidencing origin or quality, esp. of bulk commodities in world trade)*
Provinzbörse *f* (Bö) regional exchange

Provision *f*
 (com) commission
 – brokerage
 – fee
Provisionsagent *m* (com) = *Provisionsvertreter*
Provisionsaufwendungen *mpl* (Fin) commissions paid
Provisionseinnahmen *fpl* (Fin) commissions received
Provisionserträge *mpl* (Fin) commission earnings (*or* earned)
Provisionsforderungen *fpl* (Fin) commissions receivable
provisionsfrei (com) free of commission
Provisionsgeschäft *n* (com) business on a commission basis
provisionspflichtig (Fin) liable to pay commission
Provisionsüberschuß *m* (Fin) net commissions received
Provisionsversicherung *f* (SeeV) commission insurance
Provisionsvertreter *m* (com) commission agent
provisorische Regierung *f* (com) caretaker government
provisorischer Mittelwert *m* (Stat) assumed (*or* working) mean
Prozedur *f* (EDV) procedure
Prozeduranweisung *f* (EDV) procedure statement
Prozedurteil *m* (EDV, Cobol) procedure division
Prozedurvereinbarung *f* (EDV) procedure declaration
Prozent *n*
 (Math) percent
 – (GB) per cent
Prozentkurs *m* (Bö) percentage quotation (*syn, Stückkurs*)
Prozentnotierung *f* (Bö) percentage quotation
Prozentrechnung *f* (com) percentage arithmetic (*ie, problem of finding: Prozent vom Hundert, auf Hundert, im Hundert*)
Prozentsatz *m* (Math) percentage
Prozentsatz *m* **berechnen** (Math) to get the percentage
Prozentsatz *m* **fehlerhafter Stücke** (Stat) percentage defective
Prozentspanne *f* (com) percentage margin
prozentuale Mengenänderung *f* (Vw) percentage change in quantity
prozentuale mittlere Abweichung *f* (Stat) percentage standard deviation
prozentuale Preisänderung *f* (com) percentage change in price
prozentuelle Zunahme *f* **od Abnahme** *f* (Math) percent increase or decrease
Prozentzeichen *n* (com) percent sign
Prozeß *m*
 (Bw) production process implying constant technical coefficients
 (Re) lawsuit
 – legal proceedings
 – action
Prozeßanalyse *f* (OR) activity analysis
Prozeßautomatisierung *f* (EDV) industrial (*or* process) automation (*syn, Prozeßdatenverarbeitung*)

Prozeß *m* **beenden** (Re) to terminate a suit
Prozeßbeender *m* (EDV) terminator
Prozeßdaten *pl* (EDV) process variables (*syn, Prozeßvariable*)
Prozeß *m* **der Zielbildung** (Bw) goal (*or* objective) setting process
prozeß-determinierter Wirtschaftszweig *m* (Vw) process-determined industry (*eg, coal, steel*)
Prozeßfähigkeit *f* (Re) capacity to sue and be sued, § 51 ZPO
Prozeß *m* **führen** (Re) to conduct litigation
Prozeßgerade *f* (OR) = *Prozeßstrahl*
Prozeßkosten *pl*
 (Re) cost of litigation
 – litigation expenses
 – expense of a lawsuit
Prozeßkostenversicherung *f* (Vers) policy covering cost of litigation
Prozeßlawine *f* (Re) spate of lawsuits
Prozeßlawine *f* **auslösen** (Re) to touch off a tangle of lawsuits
Prozeßleitung *f* (EDV) process control (*opp, numerical control*)
Prozeßmaximen *fpl* (Re) procedural principles
Prozeßniveau *n*
 (OR) activity level
 – level of activity (*or* process)
Prozessor *m* (EDV) data processor
Prozeßparteien *fpl*
 (Re) contending
 – contesting
 – litigant
 – opposing ... parties
 – parties to a lawsuit
 – litigants
Prozeßpolitik *f* (Vw) technical policy issues (*W. Eucken*) (*eg, relating to questions of monetary versus fiscal policy, or employment policy; opp, Ordnungspolitik*)
Prozeßrechner *m* (EDV) process control computer
Prozeßstarter *m* (EDV) initiator
Prozeßsteuerung *f*
 (IndE) process control
 (EDV) task management
 – process managment
 – dispatcher
prozessuale Einrede *f* (Re) defense to an action
prozessuales Problem *n* (Bw) functional issue
Prozeßunfähigkeit *f* (Re) disability to sue and be sued
Prozeßvariable *fpl* (EDV) process variables (*syn, Prozeßdaten*)
Prozeßverwaltung *f* (EDV) task management
prozyklische Wirtschaftspolitik *f* (Vw) pro-cyclical economic policy
Prüfanweisung *f* (Stat) inspection order
Prüfanzeiger *m* (EDV) check indicator
Prüfassistent *m* (ReW) assistant auditor
Prüfattest *n* (com) certificate of inspection
Prüfausgabe *f* (EDV) check problem
prüfbare Theorie *f* (Log) testable theory
Prüfbericht *m* (Stat) test report
Prüfbit *n* (EDV) check bit
Prüfdaten *pl* (Stat) test data
Prüfdiagramm *n* (Stat) inspection diagram

prüfen
(com) to examine
- to check
- to inspect
(ReW) to audit
Prüfer *m*
(ReW) auditor
(EDV) verifier
(Pat) official examiner
Prüferbilanz *f* (StR) tax auditors' balance sheet *(ie, part of tax auditors' report; syn, Prüfungsbilanz, Betriebsprüferbilanz)*
Prüfexemplar *n* (com) checking copy
Prüffunktion *f* (Stat) test function
Prüfgebühr *f* (Pat) examination fee
Prüfgegenstand *m* (Stat) test item (*or* unit)
Prüfgröße *f* (Stat) test statistic
Prüfkanal *m* (EDV) test channel
Prüfkopie *f* (EDV) audit copy
Prüfkosten *pl* (MaW) cost of inspecting incoming materials
(IndE) cost of inspecting work-in-process
Prüfling *m* (Stat) test piece
Prüfliste *f* (ReW) audit trail
(EDV) check list
Prüflocher *m* (EDV) card verifier
Prüflos *n* (Stat) inspection lot
Prüfmaß *n* (Stat) test statistic
Prüfnormen *fpl* (Stat) inspection standards
Prüfpanel *n* (Mk) control panel
Prüfplan *m* (Stat) sampling plan
Prüfplan *m* **für kontinuierliche Stichproben** (Stat) continuous sampling plan
Prüfposten *m* (Stat) inspection lot
Prüfprogramm *n*
(ReW) audit program
(EDV) test program
Prüfpunkt *m*
(EDV) checkpoint
Prüfpunktwiederanlauf *m* (EDV) checkpoint restart
Prüfregister *n* (EDV) check register
Prüfschaltung *f* (EDV) test circuit
Prüfspezifikation *f* (Stat) inspection specification
Prüfspur *f* (EDV) parity test track
Prüfstück *n* (Stat) test piece
Prüfstufe *f* (Stat) inspection level
Prüfsystem *n* (Pat) pre-examination system *(ie, this is opposed to the German ‚Anmeldeprinzip‘ = ‚registration system‘)*
Prüfumfang *m* (Stat) amount of inspection
Prüfung *f* (com) inspection
Prüfung *f* **ablegen**
(Pw) to take an examination
- (GB) to sit (for) an examination
Prüfung *f* **der Beschaffenheit** (Kart) qualitative examination, § 5 IV GWB
Prüfung *f* **der Bücher** (ReW) audit of financial records
Prüfung *f* **der Neuheit** (Pat) novelty search
Prüfung *f* **des Erfindungsanspruchs** (Pat) examination of invention
Prüfung *f* **des Jahresabschlusses** (ReW) annual audit
Prüfung *f* **des Rechnungswesens** (ReW) financial audit

Prüfungsaufsicht *f*
(Pw) proctor at school examinations
- (GB) invigilator
Prüfungsauftrag *m* (ReW) audit assignment
Prüfungsbericht *m*
(ReW) audit report, § 166 AktG
- auditors' (examination) report
- accountant's report
- (US) long-form auditors' report
Prüfungsbescheinigung *f* (com) test certificate
Prüfungsbeurteilung *f* (ReW) post-audit review
Prüfungsbilanz *f* (StR) = *Prüferbilanz*
Prüfungsgesellschaft *f*
(ReW) firm of auditors
- auditing company (*or* firm)
Prüfungsgrundsätze *mpl* (ReW) audit(ing) standards
Prüfungshonorar *n* (ReW) audit fee
Prüfungskosten *pl*
(ReW) audit fees
- auditing costs
Prüfungsprogramm *n* (ReW) audit program
Prüfungspunkt *m*
(Stat) point of control
- indifference quality
Prüfungsrichtlinien *fpl* (ReW) auditing standards
Prüfungsstelle *f* (ReW) auditing agency
Prüfungsumfang *m* (ReW) scope of audit
Prüfungsverband *m* (ReW) auditing association
Prüfungsverfahren *n* (Pat) examination procedure
Prüfungsvermerk *m* (ReW) = *Bestätigungsvermerk*
Prüfungswesen *n* (ReW) auditing
Prüfungszeitraum *m* (ReW) period under review
Prüfung *f* **von Angeboten** (com) analysis of bids
Prüfung *f* **vor Inbetriebnahme** (IndE) pre-operation inspection
Prüfverfahren *n*
(Bw) screening process
(Stat) testing procedure
Prüfvorschriften *fpl* (Stat) test requirements
Prüfzahl *f* (ReW) check figure
Prüfzeichen *n* (EDV) check character
Prüfzettel *m* (Stat) inspection ticket
Prüfziffer *f* (EDV) check digit (*or* number)
Prüfzyklus *m* (IndE) cycle test
Pseudo-Abschnitt *m* (EDV) dummy section
Pseudoadresse *f* (EDV) pseudo address
Pseudobefehl *m* (EDV) pseudo (*or* quasi) instruction
Pseudocode *m* (EDV) pseudo code
Pseudodezimale *f* (EDV) pseudo-decimal
Pseudosatz *m* (EDV) dummy record
Pseudozufallsfolge *f* (EDV) pseudo random number sequence
psychologische Konjunkturtheorie *f* (Vw) psychological business-cycle theory
Public Relations-Mann *m*
(Mk) PR man
- (GB) P.R.O. (= *public relations officer*)
Publikationspflicht *f* (ReW) duty to publish the audited year-end financial statements
Publikum *n* (Vw) private sector *(ie, consisting of households and firms)*

Publikumsfonds *m* (Fin) investment fund open to the general public
Publikumsgeschäft *n* (Fin) retail banking
Publikumsgesellschaft *f*
(Re) public corporation
– publicly held corporation
– (GB) public company
Publikumskäufe *mpl* (Bö) public buying
Publikumspapier *n* (Fin) bond offered for general subscription
Publikumsverkehr *m* (com) personal callers *(ie, contacting administrative offices)*
Publikumswerbung *f* (Mk) advertisement to the public
Publikumswerte *mpl* (Bö) leading shares
Publizitätserfordernisse *npl* (Re) disclosure requirements
Publizitätsgesetz *n* (Re) Disclosure Law, 15 Aug 1969
Publizitätspflicht *f* (ReW) compulsory disclosure
Publizitätsprinzip *n* (ReW) principle of public disclosure
Publizitätsvorschriften *fpl* (ReW) statutory disclosure requirements
Puffer *m* (EDV) buffer *(ie, intermediate storage location)*
Pufferspeicher *m* (EDV) buffer store
– cache (memory)
Pufferbestände *mpl* (AuW) buffer stock
Pufferrolle *f* (com) buffering role *(ie, played by international oil companies)*
Pufferspeicher *m* (EDV) buffer storage
Pufferzeit *f* (OR) float time
Punkt *m* **der Minimaldauer** (OR) crash point
Punktdipol *n* (Math) doublet
Punktelastizität *f* (Vw) point elasticity
Punktesystem *n* (com) point system
– (GB) totting-up procedure *(ie, total driving demerits may result in temporary suspension of driving license)*
punktfremde Mengen *fpl* (Math) disjoint sets
Punktgebilde *n* (Math) configuration of points
pünktliche Lieferung *f* (com) on-time delivery
pünktliche Zahlung *f* (Fin) prompt payment
pünktlich zahlen (Fin) to pay promptly
Punktmatrix *f* (EDV) dot matrix
Punktmenge *f* (Math) point set
Punktprodukt *n*
(Math) dot
– inner . . .
– scalar product
Punktprognose *f* (Stat) point forecast
Punktschätzung *f* (Stat) point estimate
Punkt-Stichprobenverfahren *n* (Stat) point sampling
Punkt-zu-Punkt-Verbindung *f* (EDV) point-to-point circuit
Pupillentechnik *f* (Mk) pupil technique
Pupillometrie *f* (Mk) pupillometrics
pyramidenförmiges Kennzahlensystem *n* (Bw) pyramid structure of ratios *(ie, developed by British Institute of Management, 1956)*

Q

Q-Gewinn *m* (Vw) windfall profit *(syn, dynamischer Marktlagengewinn)*
quadratische Ergänzung *f* (Math) completing the square
quadratische Fläche *f* (Math) quadratic surface
quadratische Gleichung *f* (Math) quadratic equation
quadratische Matrix *f* (Math) square matrix
quadratische mittlere Abweichung *f* (Stat) standard deviation
quadratische Programmierung *f* (OR) quadratic programming
quadratische Schätzfunktion *f* (Stat) quadratic estimator
quadratisches Schema *n* (Math) square array
Quadratwurzel *f* (Math) square root
Quadratzahl *f* (Math) square number
Qualifikation *f*
(Pw) qualification
– level of ability
Qualifikationsmerkmal *n* (Pw) performance ability
Qualifikationsprofil *n* (Pw) qualification profile
Qualifikationsstruktur *f* (Pw) qualification pattern
qualifizieren, sich (Pw) to qualify (for)
qualifiziert
(Pw) qualified
– skilled
qualifizierte Arbeitskraft *f* (Pw) qualified employee
qualifizierte Mehrheit *f* (Bw) qualified majority *(ie, more than three quarters of all votes cast)*
qualifizierte Minderheit *f* (Bw) qualified minority *(ie, representing at least 25% of the equity capital)*
qualifiziertes Inhaberpapier *n* (WeR) restricted bearer instrument
Qualität *f* (com) quality
qualitative Arbeitsplatzbewertung *f* (Pw) qualitative job evaluation
qualitativer Personalbedarf *m* (Pw) qualitative personnel requirements
qualitatives Merkmal *n*
(Stat) attribute
– qualitative characteristic
qualitative Untersuchung *f* (com) qualitative analysis
Qualitätsabweichung *f*
(com) off standard
– variation in quality
Qualitätsarbeit *f* (IndE) quality work
Qualitätserzeugnis *n* (com) high-quality product
Qualitätskonkurrenz *f* (com) = *Qualitätswettbewerb*
Qualitätskontrollbeobachtung *f*

(Stat) quality control surveillance
- quality assurance surveillance
Qualitätskontrolle f (Stat) statistical quality control
Qualitätskontrolle f **mehrerer Merkmale** (Stat) multi-variate quality control
Qualitätskontrollkarte f (Stat) quality control chart
Qualitätskosten pl (Stat) quality costs
Qualitätsmangel m (com) quality failure
Qualitätsmarkt m (Mk) quality market *(ie, where quality matters most)*
Qualitätsmerkmal n (Stat) quality characteristic
Qualitätsnorm f (com) quality standard
Qualitätsprämie f (IndE) quality bonus *(syn, Güteprämie)*
Qualitätsprüfung f (Stat) quality test
Qualitätsrisiko n (com) quality risk
Qualitätssicherung f
(Stat) quality management *(ie, covers quality control and quality assurance)*
(Mk) quality protection *(ie, of merchandise)*
Qualitätssteuerung f (Stat) quality assurance and control
Qualitätsstrategie f (Mk) quality-based strategy
Qualitätstypen mpl (com) commodity grades *(eg, middling fair, good middling, etc.)*
Qualitätsvorschrift f (com) quality specification
Qualitätsvorsprung m (vor) (Mk) qualitative edge (over) *(ie, one's competitors or rivals)*
Qualitätsware f (Mk) choice articles
Qualitätswettbewerb m
(com) competition on quality
- quality competition
- competition in terms of quality
Qualitätszeugnis n (com) certificate of quality
Quantifikator m (Log) quantifier
Quantifizierung f (Log) quantification
Quantil n (Stat) quantile
quantisieren (EDV) to quantize
quantitative Daten pl (Stat) quantitative data
quantitative Kreditkontrolle f (Vw) quantitative credit control
quantitativer Faktor m (Stat) quantitative factor
quantitatives geldpolitisches Ziel n (Vw) monetary growth target
quantitatives Merkmal n (Stat) quantitative characteristic
quantitatives Verfahren n (Bw) quantitative technique
quantitative Zielvorgabe f (Vw) quantitative target
Quantitätsgleichung f
(Vw) quantity equation (of exchange)
- equation of exchange
- monetary equation
- transactions equation *(syn, Verkehrsgleichung)*
Quantitätsnotierung f (Bö) = Mengennotierung
Quantitätsprämie f (IndE) quantity bonus *(ie, mixed system of time and piece-rate wages)*
Quantitätstheorie f (Vw) quantity theory of money
Quantitätszusatzprämie f (IndE) production bonus
Quantor m (Log) quantifier
Quantorenlogik f (Log) logic of quantification
Quartalsabschluß m (ReW) quarterly balance sheet
Quartalsdividende f (Fin) quarterly dividend

Quartil n (Stat) quartile
Quartilsabstand m (Stat) interquartile range *(syn, Quartildispersions-Koeffizient)*
Quasi-Aufwertung f (Vw) backdoor revaluation
Quasi-Geld n
(Vw) near money
- quasi money
Quasi-Größte-Dichte-Schätzung f (Stat) quasi-maximum-likehood estimate
Quasi-Monopol n (Vw) quasi monopoly
Quasimonopolgewinne mpl (Vw) windfall gains *(syn, Marktlagengewinne, Q-Gewinne)*
quasi-öffentliche Güter npl (Vw) quasi-collective goods
Quasirente f (Vw) quasi rent
Quecksilberspeicher m (EDV) mercury storage
Quellcode m (EDV) source code (*or* language)
Quellenabzug m
(StR) pay-as-you-go system
- (GB) P.A.Y.E. (pay as you earn) system *(ie, providing for the withholding of income tax by employers)*
(FiW) deduction
- stoppage
- withholding ... at source
Quellenangabe f (com) reference
quellenbesteuertes Einkommen n (StR) income taxed by withholding at the source
Quellenbesteuerung f
(FiW) taxation
- deduction
- stoppage
- withholding ... at source
(StR) source taxation *(opp, Wohnsitzbesteuerung)*
Quellenforschung f (Log) study of source material
Quellenprinzip n (FiW) source principle
Quell(en)sprache f (EDV) source language
Quellenstaat m
(StR) source state
- country of (income) source
Quellensteuer f
(StR) withholding tax
- tax collected at the source
quellensteuerfreie Rendite f (Fin) no-withholding-tax yield
Quellprogramm n (EDV) source program
Queraddition f
(Math) cross adding
- cross casting
Querklassifikation f (Stat) cross classification
Querparität f (EDV) character (or vertical) parity (syn, Zeichenparität)
Querparitätsprüfung f (EDV) vertical redundancy check
Querprüfbit n (EDV) odd parity bit
querrechnen (EDV) to crossfoot
Querrechnen n (EDV) crossfooting
Querschnittsanalyse f (Vw) cross-section analysis
Querschnittsuntersuchung f (Stat) cross-section study
querschreiben (WeR) to accept a bill of exchange
Quersumme f (EDV) horizontal checksum
Querverweis m (com) cross-reference
Quibinärcode m (EDV) quibinary code

Quick-Pick *m* (com) quick service buffet car
quittieren (com) to receipt
quittiert (com) receipted
quittierte Rechnung *f* (com) receipted invoice
Quittung *f*
  (com) receipt
  – (Re) written acknowledgment of performance, § 368 BGB
Quittung *f* **ausstellen** (com) to write out a receipt
Quittungsbetrieb *m* (EDV) handshaking
Quorum *n* (com) quorum *(syn, beschlußfähige Anzahl, qv)*
Quotation *f* (Bö) = *Notierung*
Quote *f*
  (IWF) quota
  (com, AuW) quota
  (Fin) underwriting share
Quote *f* **der Innenfinanzierung** (Fin) internal financing ratio
Quote *f* **einhalten** (Bw) to keep within a fixed quota
Quotenaktie *f* (Fin) no-par-value stock *(opp, Summenaktie)*
Quotenauswahl *f* (Stat) quota sampling
Quoten *fpl* **e–s Kontingents ausschöpfen** (AuW) to exhaust the shares of a quota

Quoten-Exzedentenvertrag *m* (Vers) quota surplus reinsurance agreement
Quotenkartell *n*
  (Kart) quota cartel
  – (US) commodity restriction scheme
Quotenkonsolidierung *f* (Re) proportional consolidation
Quotenkonsolidierungsverfahren *n* (Fin) pro rata consolidation procedure
quotenmäßige Befriedigung *f* (Re) pro rata payment
quotenmäßiges Miteigentum *n* (Re) proportionate share in ownership
Quotenregelung *f* (EG) quota regime *(eg, of steel output)*
Quotenrückversicherung *f* (Vers) quota share reinsurance
Quotenstichprobe *f* (Stat) quota sample
Quotenvertrag *m* (Vers) quota share insurance
Quotient *m* (Math) quotient
Quotientenprogrammierung *f* (OR) fractional programming
Quotientenregister *n* (EDV) quotient register
Quotient *m* **e–r Reihe** (Math) common ratio
quotieren (Bö) to be listed *(or* quoted)
Quotierung *f* (Bö) = *Notierung*

R

Rabatt *m*
  (com) rebate
  – discount
  – allowance
  – deduction
  – reduction
  (Unterbegriffe:
  1. Barzahlungsnachlaß bis zu 3% [Diskont] = cash discount;
  2. (handelsüblicher) Mengenrabatt (als Waren- od Preisrabatt) = bulk or quantity or volume discount;
  3. Sondernachlaß = special rebate or discount;
  4. Treuerabatt (Treuevergütung) = loyalty rebate, esp. for branded goods)
Rabattabweichung *f* (KoR) quantity rebate variance
Rabatt *m* **bei Mengenabnahme** (com) quantity *(or* volume) discount
Rabatt *m* **für Barzahlung** (com) cash discount
Rabattgesetz *n* (Re) Rebates Law, of 25 Nov 1933 and amendments
Rabatt *m* **gewähren** (com) to grant a rebate *(or* discount)
Rabattgewährung *f* (com) granting of rebate
Rabattkartell *n* (Kart) rebate cartel *(ie, on rebates which represent genuine competition for goods delivered)*
Rabattmarke *f* (com) trading stamp
Rabattregelung *f* (Kart) rebate regulation, § 3 II GWB
Rabattsparmarke *f* (com) = *Rabattmarke*

Rabattsparverein *m* (com) retailers' association pursuing a common discount policy *(ie, subject to independent annual audit, § 4 II RabattG)*
Rabattstaffel *f*
  (com) graduated discount scale
  – discount schedule
Rabattvereinbarung *f* (com) rebate agreement
radialer Transfer *m* (EDV) radial transfer *(ie, an input or output process)*
Radiergummi *m*
  (com) eraser
  – (GB) rubber
Radikal *n* (Math) radical
radikale Buchwertabschreibung *f* (ReW) = *geometrisch-degressive Abschreibung*
Radikand *m* (Math) radicand *(ie, quantity under a radical sign; eg,* $\sqrt{2}$*)*
Radiusvektor *m* (Math) radius vector *(ie, in the polar coordinate system)*
Radixpunkt *m* (EDV) radix point
Radixschreibweise *f* (EDV) radix *(or* base) notation
Radixschreibweise *f* **mit fester Basis** (EDV) fixed radix notation
Radizieren *n*
  (Math) extracting
  – finding
  – computing ... a root of a number *(syn, Wurzelziehen)*
Rahmen *m* (EDV) page
Rahmenabkommen *n*
  (Re) framework

- skeleton
- umbrella ... agreement *(see: ,Abkommen')*
Rahmenadresse *f* (EDV) frame address
Rahmenbedingungen *fpl* (Vw, Bw) general setting
Rahmen *m* **e–s Vertrages** (Re) scope of a contract
Rahmengesetz *n* (Re) framework law
Rahmengesetzgebung *f* (Re) framework legislation
Rahmenkredit *m* (Fin) framework (*or* global) credit
Rahmenplan *m* (Vw) overall economic plan
Rahmenplanung *f* (Bw) overall planning
Rahmenpolice *f* (Vers) master policy
Rahmentarifvertrag *m* (Pw) overall wage agreement
Rahmenversicherungsvertrag *m* (Vers) general insurance contract
Rahmenvertrag *m*
   (Re) basic agreement (*or* contract)
   - framework
   - overall
   - outline
   - skeleton ... agreement
Rahmenvorschriften *fpl* (Re) general regulations
Raiffeisenbanken *fpl* (Fin) rural credit cooperatives
Rallonge *f* **im EWS** (AuW) rallonge
Ramschverkauf *m*
   (com) rummage sale
   - (GB) jumble sale
Ramschware *f*
   (com) job goods
   - odds and ends
   - (GB, sl) odds and sods
Randbedingungen *fpl*
   (Log) initial conditions
   (Math) boundary conditions
Rand *m* **e–r Menge** (Math) boundary (*or* frontier) of a set
Randeinteilung *f* (Stat) marginal classification
Ränder *mpl* **des Bereichs** (Math) barriers of the region
Randklasse *f* (Stat) marginal category
Randkurve *f* (Math) contour
Randlochkarte *f*
   (EDV) edge-notched
   - margin-notched
   - margin punched ... card *(syn, Kerblochkarte)*
Random-Buchführung *f* (ReW) random accounting
Randomisierung *f* (Stat) randomization
Randomspeicher *m* (EDV) random (*or* direct) access storage *(syn, Direktzugriffsspeicher)*
Randomtafel *f* (Stat) random table
Random-Walk-Hypothese *f* (Fin) random walk hypothesis
Randpunkt *m* (Math) boundary point *(eg, of a set)*
Randquadrat *n* (Math) boundary square
Randsegment *n* (Mk) marginal segment
Randverteilung *f*
   (Math) boundary
   - initial
   - marginal ... distribution
Randwerbung *f* (Mk) accessory advertising *(syn, flankierende od unterstützende Werbung)*

Randwertproblem *n* (Math) boundary value problem
Rang *m*
   (Re) rank
   - preference
   - priority
Rangänderung *f* (Re) change of priority, § 880 BGB
Rang *m* **e–r Matrix** (Math) rank of a matrix
Rang *m* **e–s Vektorraumes** (Math) rank of a vector space *(syn, Dimension e–s Vektorraumes)*
Rangfolge *f* **der Gläubiger** (Re) ranking of creditors, § 879 BGB
Rangfolgekriterium *n* (Bw) rank criterion
Rangfolgeverfahren *n* (IndE) job ranking method
Ranggröße *f* (Stat) order statistic
Rangierbahnhof *m*
   (com) switchyard
   - (GB) shunting yard
Rangkorrelation *f* (Stat) rank correlation
Rangkorrelationskoeffizient *m* (Stat) coefficient of rank correlation
Rangkriterium *n* (Stat) rank criterion
rangmäßige Bewertung *f* **von Gütern** (Vw) ranking of commodities
Rangordnung *f*
   (Stat) grade
   (Vw) preference scale *(ie, of alternative choices)*
   (Re) order of priorities
   - ranking order
Rangordnung *f* **von Pfandrechten** (Re) ranking of liens
Rangordnung *f* **von Zielen**
   (Bw) hierarchy of goals
   - goal ranking
Rangreduktion *f* (Stat) reduction in rank
Rangreihenverfahren *n* (IndE) ranking method
Rangstelle *f* (Re) rank
Rangstufenprinzip *n* (Log) ranking method
Rangtest *m* (Stat) ranking test
Rangverhältnis *n* (Re) order of preference, § 879 BGB
Rangvermerk *m* (Re) priority entry *(ie, in land register, § 879 III BGB)*
Rangvorbehalt *m* (Re) reservation of priority, § 881 BGB
rasante Talfahrt *f* (Vw) rapid downslide
rasche Lösung *f* (com) quick fix *(eg, is impossible)*
rascher Kursanstieg *m* (Bö) bulge
rasches Wachstum *n* (com) rapid (*or* accelerated) growth
Raster *m*
   (com) grid
   (Math) filter *(ie, family of nonempty subsets of a set; syn, Filterbasis)*
Rasterdrucker *m* (EDV) dot-matrix printer
Rasterfehler *m* (EDV) timing error
Ratchet-Effekt *m*
   (Vw) bottom stop
   - ratchet effect
Rate *f*
   (com) rate *(ie, in inland waterway shipping)*
   (Fin) installment
   - (GB) instalment
   - part payment

(ie, part of payment spread over a period of time)
Rate *f* **der Produkttransformation** (Vw) rate of product transformation
Ratenanleihe *f* (Fin) installment loan
Ratenhypothek *f* (Fin) installment mortgage *(ie, equal annual redemptions and falling interest payments)*
Ratenkauf *m* (com) installment sale *(syn, Abzahlungskauf, Teilzahlungskauf; see: Abzahlungsgeschäft)*
Ratenkredit *m* (Fin) installment credit *(ie, Teilzahlungskredit im weiteren Sinne: extended to consumers and small businesses, repaid in fixed installments)*
Ratenwechsel *m* (WeR) multi-maturity bill of exchange *(ie, one traveling with a sequence of maturity dates; not allowed under German law, Art. 33 II WG; German term sometimes used to describe „Abzahlungswechsel")*
Ratenzahlung *f*
(Fin) payment by installments
(Fin) time payment
Ratenzahlungskredit *m* (Fin) = *Teilzahlungskredit*
rationaler Bruch *m* (Math) rational fraction
rationaler Lag *m* (Vw) rational lag
rationale Zahl *f* (Math) rational number
rationalisieren
(Bw) to rationalize
– to modernize
– to streamline
Rationalisierung *f* (Bw) rationalization measures *(ie, productivity improvements through replacing manpower by machinery)*
Rationalisierungserfolg *m* (Kart) rationalization effect, § 5 II GWB
Rationalisierungsfachmann *m* (IndE) efficiency engineer *(or* expert)
Rationalisierungsinvestition *f*
(Bw) rationalization investment
– investment for plant modernization
– modernization investment
Rationalisierungskartell *n* (Kart) rationalization cartel *(ie, relating to rationalization of economic processes through specialization)*
Rationalisierungsreserven *fpl* (Bw) potential for rationalization
Rationalisierungsverband *m* (Kart) rationalization association, § 5 GWB
Rationalitätsbereich *m*
(Math) domain of rationality
– number field *(or* domain)
– commutative field *(syn, Körper)*
Rationalprinzip *n*
(Vw, Bw) efficiency rule
– universal rule of efficiency
(ie, prescribes to produce at a given rate with lowest cost; or to produce at the highest rate with the same cost; syn, ökonomisches Prinzip, Wirtschaftlichkeitsprinzip)
Rationalverhalten *n* (Vw, Bw) rational behavior
rationell (IndE) efficient
rationieren (Vw) to ration
Rationierung *f* (Vw) rationing
Raub *m* (Re) robbery, § 249 StGB

Raubbau *m* (Vw) destructive exploitation of resources
räuberische Erpressung *f* (Re) extortionary robbery, § 255 StGB
räuberische Preisunterbietung *f* (Vw) predatory price cutting
räuberischer Diebstahl *m* (Re) theft in the nature of robbery, § 252 StGB
räuberisches Dumping *n* (AuW) predatory dumping
Rauchen *n* **aufgeben**
(com) to give up smoking
– (infml) to kick the smoking habit
Rauchwaren-Einheitsversicherung *f* (Vers) all-inclusive fur policy
Raumarbitrage *f* (AuW) arbitrage in space
Raumbedarf *m* (com) space requirements
Raumcharter *f* (com) tonnage affreightment
Raumeinheiten *fpl* (Vw) spatial units
räumen
(Re) to vacate rented property
– to cease occupancy
Raumfahrtindustrie *f* (com) aerospace industry
Raumfracht *f* (com) freight on measurement basis
Raumkoordinaten *fpl* (Math) space coordinates
Raumkosten *pl* (KoR) cost of office and workshop space
räumlich abgegrenzter Teil *m* (StR) physically separated part *(ie, of a property, § 8 GrStG)*
räumliche Konsumentenanalyse *f* (Mk) spatial consumer analysis
räumliche Mobilität *f* (Vw) geographic *(or* spatial) mobility
räumlicher Vektor *m* (Math) space vector
räumliche Strukturierung *f* (Vw) spatial patterning
Raummiete *f* (KoR) rental
Raumordnungspolitik *f* (Vw) urban and regional policy
Raumplanung *f*
(Vw) regional planning
(com) space planning
(IndE) intra-plant layout
Raumpunkt *m* (Math) point in space
Raumtarif *m* (com) bulk freight tariff *(opp, Stück- und Gewichtstarif)*
Raumtransport *m* (com) orbital freight hauling *(ie, by space shuttles)*
Räumung *f* **des Lagers** (Bw) inventory clearance
Räumungsfrist *f*
(Re) time set for vacating rented property, §§ 721, 794a ZPO
– time for moving out
Räumungsverkauf *m*
(com) liquidation sale
– (GB) closing-down sale
Raumwinkel *m* (Math) solid angle
Raum-Zeit-Koordinaten *fpl* (Log) spatio-temporal coordinates
Rayonchef *m* (com, *rare*) head of department
Reaktionsbereich *m* (Bw) domain of response
Reaktionsbereitschaft *f* (Bw) responsiveness
Reaktionsfunktion *f* (Vw) response function
Reaktionsgeschwindigkeit *f* (Vw) speed of response
Reaktionsgleichung *f* (Vw) behavioral equation

Reaktionskoeffizient m (Vw) coefficient of reaction
Reaktionszeit f (Vw) period of adjustment
real
(Vw, Bw) real
– in real terms
– in terms of real value *(opp, nominell = in money terms)*
Realbesteuerung f (FiW) taxation of specific property *(syn, Objekt- od Sachbesteuerung)*
Realdefinition f (Log) real definition
(ie, not a mere convention for introducing new symbols or notations, but a proposition of equivalence between ‚definiendum' and ‚definiens' where the latter embodies the „essential nature" of the definiendum; opp, Nominaldefinition)
reale Adresse f (EDV) real address *(opp, virtual address)*
reale Einkommenseinbußen fpl (Vw) real income losses
reale Güter npl (Vw) = *Realwerte*
Realeinkommen n (Vw) real income *(or* earnings)
Realeinkommenslücke f (Vw) real income gap
Realeinkommensvergleich m (Vw) real income comparison
reale Kapitalerhaltung f
(Fin) preservation of corporate assets in real terms
– maintenance of equity
reale Kassenhaltung f (Vw) real cash balance
reale Löhne mpl (Pw) = *Reallohn*
reale Produktivkräfte fpl (Vw) real resources
realer Außenhandelsüberschuß m (AuW) real trade surplus
realer Einkommensverlust m (Pw) real wage cut
realer Kasseneffekt m (Vw) real balance effect
realer Außenhandelsüberschuß m (AuW) real trade surplus
Realertrag m (Fin) = *Realverzinsung*
realer Zinsfuß m (Vw) real rate of interest
reales Austauschverhältnis n (AuW) terms of trade
reales BIP n (VGR) real gdp *(or* gross domestic product)
reales Bruttosozialprodukt n
(VGR) real gross national product
– real GNP *(or* gnp)
reales Nettosozialprodukt n (VGR) real net national product *(or* NNP)
reales Sozialprodukt n
(VGR) real national product
– national product in real terms
reale Supposition f (Log) real supposition
reales Volkseinkommen n (VGR) real national income
reales Wachstum n
(Vw) real growth
– growth in unit volume
reale Überinvestitionstheorie f (Vw) nonmonetary overinvestment theory
reale Verbrauchsausgaben fpl (Vw) real consumer spending
Realgemeinde f (StR) real property organization *(see: § 3 II KStG)*
Realgüterprozeß m (Bw) logistic process

Realignment n
(AuW) realignment of parities
– parity realignment
– exchange rate adjustment
Realinvestition f (Bw) fixed *(or* real) investment
Realisationsgewinn m (ReW) gain realized by a sale
Realisationsprinzip n (ReW) realization rule *(or* principle) *(ie, valuation rule: prospective future gains and losses remain unrecorded in the accounts)*
Realisationsverkauf m (com) liquidating sale
Realisationswert m (ReW) value on realization *(ie, used in ‚Liquidationsbilanz'; syn, Veräußerungswert)*
realisierbare Aktiva npl (Fin) realizable assets
Realisierbarkeit f (com) feasibility
realisieren
(com) to implement *(eg, plan, project)*
– to carry out
(Fin) to realize
– to liquidate
– to sell
– to convert into money
(Bö) to take profits
realisierte Gewinne mpl
(ReW) realized profits *(or* gains)
– earned income
(Bö) realized price gains
realisierter Arbeitsplatzwechsel m
(Vw) fluctuation
– labor turnover
realisierter Ertrag m (ReW) realized earnings
realisierter Gewinn m (ReW) realized profit
realisierte Wertsteigerung f (ReW) realized appreciation
Realisierung f
(com) implementation
– carrying out *(eg, of a project)*
(Fin) realization
– liquidation
– sale
(Bö) profit taking
(EDV) implementation
Realisierungszeit f (OR) time of realization
Realisierung f **wirtschaftspolitischer Ziele**
(Vw) economic performance
– implementation of economic targets
Realkapital n
(Vw) real *(or* nonmonetary) capital *(syn, Sachkapital)*
(Bw) tangible fixed assets
Realkapitalbildung f (Vw) productive investment *(ie, investment in fixed assets and inventories; opp, financial investment)*
Realkasseneffekt m (Vw) wealth effect
Realkassenhaltungseffekt m (Vw) real balance effect
Realkauf m (com) cash sale
– *(ie, payment being made in full on receipt of goods; syn, Handkauf)*
Realkonsum m (Vw) real consumption
Realkosten pl
(Vw) real cost
– cost in real terms

Realkostenaustauschverhältnis *n* (AuW) real cost terms of trade
Realkredit *m*
  (Fin) collateral loan *(syn, Sachkredit)*
  (Fin) real estate loan
Realkreditgeschäft *n* (Fin) real estate loan business
Realkreditinstitut *n* (Fin) mortgage bank
Reallohn *m* (Pw) real wage *(ie, nominal wage divided by a price index)*
Reallohnsumme *f* (Vw) aggregate real wage
Realprodukt *n* (VGR) real product *(opp, national product at current prices)*
Realsteuer *f*
  (FiW) impersonal (*or* nonpersonal) tax
  – tax levied on specific property *(syn, Objektsteuer)*
Realsteuerbescheid *m* (StR) municipal assessment notice
Realtausch *m* (Vw) barter
  (ie, exchange of goods and services withouth the use of money)
Realteil *m* (Math) real part of a complex number
Realtransfer *m* (VGR) real transfer
Realvermögen *n* (Vw) real wealth *(eg, of a household)*
Realverzinsung *f* (Fin) real yield
Realwerte *mpl*
  (Vw) real assets
  – *(assets)* in real terms
  – in terms of real value
  – in terms of money at constant prices
Realwissenschaft *f* (Log) factual science
Realzeitausgabe *f* (EDV) real time output
Realzeitbetrieb *m* (EDV) real time operation
Realzeiteingabe *f* (EDV) real time input
Realzeitprogrammiersprache *f* (EDV) real time language
Realzeituhr *f* (EDV) real time clock
Realzeitverfahren *n* (EDV) real time processing
Realzins *m*
  (Fin) real rate of interest
  – interest rate in real terms
  (eg, derived from Umlaufrendite für Festverzinsliche + Veränderung des Preisindex für den privaten Verbrauch)
Reassekuranz *f* (Vers) reinsurance
Rechenanlage *f* (EDV) data processing (*or* dp) equipment
Rechenautomat *m* (EDV) = *Rechner*
Rechenbedarf *m* (EDV) computational requirements
Rechenbefehl *m* (EDV) arithmetic instruction
Rechendezimalpunkt *m* (EDV, Cobol) assumed decimal point
Recheneinheit *f*
  (Vw) unit of account
  (EDV) = *Rechenwerk*
Rechenelement *n* (EDV) = *Rechenwerk*
Rechengeschwindigkeit *f* (EDV) calculating speed
Rechenhaftigkeit *f* (Vw) norms of calculability
Rechenkapazität *f* (EDV) computing capacity
Rechenlocher *m* (EDV) calculating punch
Rechenmaschine *f* (EDV) calculating machine
Rechenoperation *f* (EDV) arithmetic operation
Rechenprüfung *f* (EDV) arithmetic check

Rechenregister *n* (EDV) arithmetic register *(syn, arithmetisches Register, Operandenregister)*
Rechenschaftsbericht *m*
  (com) report
  – accounting *(eg, to give an ...)*
  (ReW) statement of account
Rechenstanzer *m* (EDV) calculating punch
Rechensystem *n* (EDV) data processing system
Rechenverstärker *m* (EDV) computing amplifier
Rechenwerk *n*
  (com) set of figures
  (ReW) set of accounting figures *(eg, financial statement, marginal costing, etc)*
  (EDV) arithmetic unit (*or* element *or* section)
Rechenzeit *f* (EDV) computer (*or* machine) time
Rechenzentrum *n* (EDV) computing (*or* DP) center
Recherche *f* (Pat) official search *(ie, for prior patent specifications, § 28a PatG)*
Rechnen *n* **mit doppelter Stellenzahl** (EDV) double-length (*or* double-precision) arithmetic
Rechnen *n* **mit mehrfacher Wortlänge** (EDV) multiple-length (*or* multi-precision) arithmetic
Rechner *m* (EDV) computer
rechnerabhängiger Speicher *m* (EDV) on-line storage
Rechner-Architektur *f* (EDV) computer architecture
Rechnercode *m*
  (EDV) absolute
  – actual
  – specific ... code *(syn, Maschinencode)*
Rechner *m* **der dritten Generation** (EDV) third-generation computer
Rechner *m* **der zweiten Generation** (EDV) second-generation computer *(ie, utilizing solid state components)*
Rechnerfamilie *f* (EDV) computer family
rechnergesteuert (EDV) computer controlled
rechnergestützt
  (EDV) computer-aided (*or* -based)
  – computerized
rechnergestützte Fertigung *f* (IndE) computer-aided manufacturing, CAM
rechnergestützte Simulation *f* (IndE) computer-based simulation
rechnerische Parität *f* (AuW) calculated parity
rechnerische Rendite *f*
  (Fin) accountant's returns
  – book rate of return
rechnerische Restlaufzeit *f* (Fin) computed remaining maturity
rechnerischer Gewinn *m*
  (ReW) accounting
  – book
  – paper ... profit
rechnerischer Wert *m* **von Aktien** (ReW, EG) accounting par value of shares
rechnerische Vereinfachung *f* (Math) computational simplification
Rechnerkapazität *f* (EDV) computer power
Rechneroperation *f* (EDV) computer (*or* machine) operation
Rechnerprogramm *n* (EDV) computer program
Rechnerschaltplan *n* (EDV) set-up diagram

Rechnersprache *f* (EDV) computer language
Rechnersteuerung *f* (EDV) computer forward control
Rechnersystem *n* (EDV) computer system
rechnerunabhängiger Speicher *m* (EDV) off-line storage
Rechnerverbund *m* (EDV) computer network
Rechnerverbundbetrieb *m* (EDV) multiprocessing
Rechnerverbundnetz *n* (EDV) distributed processing system
Rechnerverbundsystem *n* (EDV) multiprocessing system
Rechnung *f*
 (ReW) invoice
 – bill
 – sales bill
 (com) check *(ie, in a restaurant)*
 – (GB) bill
Rechnung *f* **ausstellen**
 (com) to make out an invoice
 – to invoice
 – to bill *(eg, send now and bill me later)*
Rechnung *f* **bearbeiten** (com) to process an invoice
Rechnung *f* **begleichen**
 (com) to pay
 – to settle
 – (infml) to foot ... a bill
Rechnung *f* **prüfen** (com) to check an invoice
Rechnung *f* **quittieren** (com) to receipt a bill
Rechnungsabgrenzung *f* (ReW) accrual and deferral *(ie, year-end adjustment to allocate revenue and expenditure items to proper accounting periods)*
Rechnungsabgrenzungsposten *mpl*
 (ReW) accruals and deferrals
 – prepaid and deferred items
 (ReW, EG) *(Aktivseite)* prepayments and accrued income
 (ReW, EG) *(Passivseite)* accruals and deferred income
Rechnungsabschrift *f* (com) copy of an invoice
Rechnungsausstellung *f*
 (com) invoicing
 – billing
Rechnungsauszug *m* (Fin) statement of account *(syn, Kontoauszug)*
Rechnungsbelege *mpl*
 (ReW) vouchers
 – documentary evidence *(or* support)
 – accounting records
Rechnungsbetrag *m*
 (com) invoice amount
 – amount appearing on an invoice
Rechnungsdatei *f* (com) billing file
Rechnungsdatum *n*
 (com) date of invoice
 – billing date
Rechnungsdoppel *n* (com) duplicate invoice
Rechnungseinheit *f*
 (Fin) accounting unit
 – unit of account, UA
Rechnungseinzugsverfahren *n*
 (Fin) direct debiting *(ie, by banks for trade accounts receivable)*
Rechnungserteilung *f* (com) invoicing

Rechnungsformular *n* (com) billhead
Rechnungsjahr *n*
 (ReW) accounting *(or* fiscal) year
 (FiW) financial year
 – fiscal year
 – fiscal
 – tax year
Rechnungskopie *f* (com) copy of an invoice
Rechnungslegung *f*
 (Re) rendering of accounts *(ie, preparing statement of receipts and expenditures, § 259 BGB)*
 (ReW) preparing and publishing year-end statements, §§ 148 ff AktG
Rechnungslegungsgrundsätze *mpl* (ReW) accounting rules
Rechnungslegungsvorschriften *fpl* (ReW) statutory accounting requirements
Rechnungslegung *f* **zu Wiederbeschaffungskosten** (ReW) replacement cost accounting
Rechnungsnummer *f* (com) invoice number
Rechnungsperiode *f* (ReW) accounting *(or* fiscal) period
Rechnungspreis *m* (com) invoice price
Rechnungspreis *m* **des Lieferanten** (com) vendor's invoice price
Rechnungsprüfer *m* (ReW) auditor
Rechnungsprüfung *f*
 (com) checking and audit of invoices
 (ReW) auditing of accounts
Rechnungssaldo *m* (com) balance of invoice
Rechnungsvordruck *m* (com) billhead
Rechnungsvorlage *f* (com) presentation of an invoice
Rechnungswert *m* (com) invoice value
Rechnungswesen *n*
 (VGR) national accounting
 (ReW) accounting
 – accountancy
Rechnungszinsfuß *m*
 (ReW) interest rate for accounting purposes
 (Vers) assumed rate of interest
Rechnung *f* **über e–e Sendung** (com) invoice on a shipment
Rechnung *f* **vereinfachen** (com) to simplify computation
Recht *n*
 (Re) law *(ie, objektives Recht)*
 (Re) right *(ie, subjektives Recht)*
Recht *n* **abtreten** (Re) to assign a right
Recht *n* **anerkennen** (Re) to acknowledge a right
Recht *n* **auf Forderungsübertragung** (Re) right of subrogation
Recht *n* **aufgeben**
 (Re) to abandon
 – to disclaim
 – to relinquish
 – to waive ... a right
Recht *n* **auf Gewinnbeteiligung** (Fin) right to participation in profits
Recht *n* **auf Leistung** (Re) right to demand contractual performance
Recht *n* **auf Leistungsverweigerung** (Re) right of refusal to perform, § 320 BGB
Recht *n* **auf Prüfung der Bücher** (ReW) right to inspect books and records

Recht n auf Schadenersatz (Re) right to recover damages
Recht n ausüben (Re) to exercise a right
Rechte npl aus unerlaubter Handlung od Vertrag (Re) rights arising from tort or contract
Recht n beeinträchtigen
(Re) to encroach upon a right
– to infringe a right
– to infringe upon (or on) a right
– to interfere with a right
Recht n beschneiden (Re) to curtail (or impair) a right
Recht n bestreiten
(Re) to challenge
– to dispute
– to protest ... a right
Recht n der Erfindereigenschaft (Pat) right of inventorship
Recht n der Schuldverhältnisse (Re) law of obligations
(ie, as laid down in the second book of the German Civil Code = BGB)
Recht n der Wettbewerbsbeschränkungen (Kart) law against restraints of competition
Recht n des Erfüllungsortes (Re) law of the place of performance
Recht n des unlauteren Wettbewerbs (Kart) law on unfair competition
rechteckiges Koordinatensystem n (Math) rectangular coordinate system
rechteckige Verteilung f (Stat) rectangular distribution
Rechte npl Dritter (Re) third-party rights
rechter Winkel m (Math) right angle
Rechtfertigungsgründe mpl
(Re) legal justification
– grounds of justification
(Kart) gateways
Recht n geht über auf (Re) a right passes to
Recht n geltend machen (Re) to assert a right
Recht n gewähren (Re) to grant a right
rechtlich
(Re) legal
– in law
– in contemplation of law
– de iure
(ie, the German term implies the substance of law; it denotes compliance with technical or formal rules; see: ,rechtmäßig')
rechtlich begründet (Re) legally justified
rechtlich bindende Verpflichtung f (Re) legal obligation (ie, one created between the parties)
rechtliche Bedingung f (Re) legal condition
rechtliche Bindung f (Re) legal obligation
rechtliche Einheit f (Re) separate legal unit
rechtliche Fiktion f
(Re) legal fiction
– (GB also) legal figment
rechtliche Folgerungen fpl (Re) conclusions of law
rechtliche Regelung f (Re) legal arrangements
rechtlicher Irrtum m (Re) mistake in law
rechtliches Gehör n (Re) fair hearing
rechtliche Unmöglichkeit f
(Re) legal (or juridical) impossibility
– impossibility of law

rechtlich selbständiges Unternehmen n (Re) legally independent enterprise
rechtlich unzulässige Bedingung f (Re) illegal condition
rechtlich vertretbar (Re) legally justifiable
rechtmäßig (Re) lawful (ie, implies that an act is authorized or not forbidden by law, and it usually imports a moral substance or ethical permissibility; opp, rechtlich)
rechtmäßiger Besitz m (Re) lawful possession
rechtmäßiger Besitzer m
(com) lawful owner
(Re) lawful possessor (or holder)
rechtmäßiger Eigentümer m
(Re) rightful owner
– sole and unconditional owner
(ie, not contingent or conditional)
rechtmäßiger Inhaber m (WeR) holder in due course, Art. 16 WG
rechtmäßiger Vertreter m (Re) lawful representative
Rechtsabteilung f (Re) legal department
Rechtsanspruch m (Re) legal claim
Rechtsanwalt m
(Re) practicing lawyer
– legal counsel
– (US) attorney-at-law
– (US) counselor-at-law
– (GB) barrister (ie, admitted to plead at the bar)
– (GB) solicitor (ie, allowed to practice in most minor courts)
Rechtsanwendung f
(Re) administration of law
(Re) (phrase in contracts:) ,,applicable law"
– ,,law to apply"
Rechtsausübung f (Re) exercise of a right
Rechtsausweis m (Re) proof of ownership
Rechtsbedingung f (Re) condicio iuris
Rechtsbegriff m
(Re) legal concept
– (loosely also) legal term
Rechtsbehelf m (Re) legal remedy
– remedy in law
– legal relief
(ie, Berufung, Revision, sofortige Beschwerde)
Rechtsbehelfbelehrung f (StR) advising taxpayer of applicable remedies
Rechtsberater m (Re) legal counsel
Rechtsberatung f
(Re) legal counseling
(Re) legal consulting service
Rechtsbeschwerde f (Re) appeal on points of law
Rechtsbestand m e–r Forderung (Re) legal existence of a claim
Rechtsbeugung f (Re) intentional misconstruction of the law (ie, to the benefit or detriment of a party, § 336 StGB)
rechtsbündig (EDV) right justified
rechtsbündig machen (EDV) to right-justify
rechtserheblich (Re) material (eg, facts, evidence)
rechtsfähige Gesellschaft (Re) incorporated company
rechtsfähiger Verein m (Re) incorporated society (ie, association with independent legal existence, §§ 21, 22 BGB)

rechtsfähige Stiftung *f* (Re) foundation with independent legal existence, §§ 80 ff BGB
Rechtsfähigkeit *f* (Re) capacity to acquire and hold rights and duties, § 1 BGB
(Note: ‚legal capacity' in English law covers the ability to acquire rights + to transact legal business = Rechtsfähigkeit + Geschäftsfähigkeit)
rechtsfähig werden (Re) become capable of rights and duties
Rechtsfolgen *fpl* (Re) legal consequences
Rechtsform *f* (Re) legal form (*or* structure)
Rechtsformen der Unternehmung (Re) legal forms of business organization
Rechtsformwechsel *m* (Re) change of legal form
Rechtsfrage *f*
  (Re) question of law
  – *(civile law)* quaestio iuris
Rechtsgebiet *n*
  (Re) branch
  – department
  – division
  – field ... of law
Rechtsgelehrter *m*
  (Re) jurist
  – legal scholar
Rechtsgesamtheit *f* (Re) aggregate of rights
Rechtsgeschäft *n*
  (Re) legal transaction
  – legal business
  – legal act
  – (GB) act of the party
  – (GB) act in the law
  (ie, act having legal consequences in the intention of the parties, §§ 104–185 BGB)
rechtsgeschäftliche Abtretung *f* (Re) assignment by act of the parties
rechtsgeschäftliches Schuldverhältnis *n*
  (Re) contractual obligation
  – obligation under a contract
  – *(civil law)* obligatio ex contractu
rechtsgeschäftliches Veräußerungsverbot *n* (Re) prohibition of alienation by legal transaction, § 137 BGB
rechtsgeschäftliche Übertragung *f* (Re) transfer by act of the party
rechtsgeschäftliche Willenserklärung *f* (Re) legal act of the party
rechtsgeschäftlich handeln (Re) to transact legal business
rechtsgeschäftlich übertragen (Re) to transfer title to property
rechtsgeschäftlich vertreten
  (Re) to act for
  – to contract on behalf of
  – to act in the capacity of an agent
Rechtsgeschäft *n* **unter Lebenden** (Re) transaction inter vivos
Rechtsgeschäft *n* **von Todes wegen** (Re) transaction mortis causa
rechtsgestaltender Gesetzesakt *m* (Re) act of law
Rechtsgrundlage *f*
  (Re) legal foundation
  – statutory source (*or* basis)
  (Re) title of a right *(ie, facts or events by reason of which the right has become vested in its owner)*

Rechtsgrundsatz *m* (Re) principle (*or* rule) of law
rechtsgültig
  (Re) legally effective *(eg, contract)*
  – valid
  – having legal force
rechtsgültiges Patent *n* (Pat) valid patent
Rechtsgültigkeit *f* (Re) legal validity
Rechtsgutachten *n* (Re) legal opinion
Rechtshandlung *f*
  (Re) legal act (*or* transaction)
  – juristic act
  (ie, designed to have a legal effect, directed to the origin, termination, or alteration of a right)
rechtshängig
  (Re) pending *(eg, pending suit)* under judicial determination
  – undetermined
  – before a court
  – sub judice
Rechtshängigkeit *f*
  (Re) pendency of a suit
  – pendent suit
  – lis pendens
rechtshemmende Einrede *f* (Re) dilatory defense (*or* exception) *(syn, dilatorische od aufschiebende Einrede)*
Rechtsirrtum *m* (Re) error in law
Rechtskosten *pl*
  (ReW) cost of litigation
  – legal fees and charges *(ie, including attorney fees)*
Rechtskraft *f*
  (Re) legal efficacy
  – validity
rechtskräftig
  (Re) legally effective
  – valid
  (Re) final
rechtskräftige Entscheidung *f* (Re) final decision
rechtskräftiger Anspruch *m* (Re) legally enforceable claim
rechtskräftiges Urteil *m* (Re) final judgment
Rechtskreis *m* (Re) legal system (*or* orbit)
Rechtsmacht *f* (Re) legal power
Rechtsmangel *m*
  (Re) legal infirmity *(eg, of a negotiable instrument)*
  (Re) deficiency in title
  – defect of/in title
Rechtsmangel *m* **beseitigen** (Re) to remove a deficiency in title (*or* defect of title)
Rechtsmängelhaftung *f* (Re) warranty of title
Rechtsmißbrauch *m*
  (Re) abuse of right
  – abusive exercise of a legal right
Rechtsmittel *n* (Re) legal remedy
Rechtsmittel *n* **einlegen**
  (Re) to lodge an appeal
  – to appeal a decision to a higher court
  – to take an appeal from a decision to a higher court
  – to bring an appeal in court from a decision
Rechtsmittel *npl* **finden nicht statt** (Re) decision is not subject to further review
Rechtsmittelverfahren *n* (Re) appeal procedure

Rechtsmittelverzicht m (Re) waiver of legal remedy
Rechtsmultiplikation f (Math) postmultiplication
Rechtsnachfolge f
(Re) legal succession
- succession in title
(ie, act of the parties, or of the law, by which title to property = Vermögensrecht is conveyed from one person to another)
Rechtsnachfolger m
(Re) legal successor
- successor in title
- succeeding party
- transferee
Rechtsordnung f **für den Tiefseebergbau** (Re) deep sea-bed mining regime
Rechtspersönlichkeit f
(Re) legal person (or personality)
- legal entity
- juridic(al) personality
Rechtspflege f (Re) administration of justice
Rechtspfleger m (Re) judical officer outside the regular judiciary
Rechtssprache f (Re) legal parlance
Rechtsprechung f (Re) court decisions
Rechtsprechung f **der Finanzgerichte** (StR) jurisdiction of the fiscal courts
Rechtsquellen fpl **des Steuerrechts** (StR) statutory sources of German tax law
Rechtssatz m (Re) rule of law
Rechtsschraubenregel f (Math) right-hand screw rule
Rechtsschutz m (Re) legal protection
Rechtsschutzversicherung f
(Vers) legal expense insurance
- (GB) legal protection insurance
Rechtssicherheit f (Re) predictability of legal decisions
Rechtsstaatsprinzip n (Re) principle of the ‚rule of law'
Rechtsstellung f (Re) legal position (or status)
Rechtsstreit m
(Re) lawsuit
- legal action (or proceedings)
- litigation
- suit
Rechtssystem n (Re) legal system
Rechtsübertragung f (Re) transfer of a right
Rechtsübertragung f **kraft Gesetzes** (Re) assignment by operation of law
Rechtssubjekt n
(Re) person in law
- legal entity *(ie, capable of rights and duties)*
Rechts- und Beratungskosten pl (ReW) legal and consultants' fees
Rechts- und Sachmängelgewähr f (Re) warranty of title and quality
rechtsunfähig (Re) legally unable to hold rights
Rechtsunfähigkeit f (Re) legal incapacity (or disability) *(ie, the English term includes ‚Geschäftsunfähigkeit')*
rechtsunwirksam
(Re) legally inoperative
- null and void
- invalid

rechtsverbindlich
(Re) legally binding
- binding in law
rechtsverbindliche Fassung f (Re) legally binding formula
Rechtsverbindlichkeit f
(Re) binding effect
- legal force
Rechtsverhältnis n (Re) legal relation(ship)
Rechtsverletzung f
(Re) infringement of a right
(Re) violation of law
Rechtsverlust m (Re) loss (or forfeiture) of right
Rechtsvermutung f (Re) presumption of law *(opp, Tatsachenvermutung)*
Rechtsverweigerung f
(Re) outright abdication (by a court)
- denial (or refusal) of justice
Rechtsverwirkung f (Re) forfeiture *(ie, loss of right by way of penalty)*
Rechtsverzicht m
(Re) disclaimer of right
- waiver of title
Rechtsvorgänger m
(Re) legal predecessor
- predecessor in title
- preceding party
- transferor
Rechtsvorschrift f (Re) legal provision
Rechtsvorschriften fpl (Re) legal requirements
Rechtsweg m **beschreiten** (Re) to have recourse to law
rechtswidrige Bedingung f (Re) illegal condition
rechtswidrige Handlung f
(Re) wrong
- wrongful act
rechtswidriger Besitz m (Re) unlawful possession
rechtswidriger Vertrag m (Re) illegal contract
rechtswirksamer Vertrag m (Re) valid contract
Rechtswirksamkeit f
(Re) legal validity (or efficacy)
- operativeness
Rechtswissenschaft f
(Re) jurisprudence *(ie, not equal to the German concept ‚Rechtsphilosophie' which has no counterpart in English law)*
- general theory of law
- science of law
- juristic theory
- philosophy of law *(ie, philosophy in its extended meaning of ‚branch of knowledge')*
recht und billig
(Re) fair
- fair and proper
- fair and reasonable
- in justice and fairness
- *(civil law)* ex aequo et bono
Recht n **verletzen** (Re) to infringe upon (or violate) a right
Recht n **verkürzen** (Re) to curtail (or impair) a right
Recht n **verlieren** (Re) to lose a right
Recht n **verteidigen** (Re) to defend a right
Recht n **verwirken** (Re) to forfeit a right
Recht n **übertragen** (Re) to confer a right

Recht n vorbehalten (Re) to reserve a right
Recht n wiederherstellen (Re) to restore a right
rechtwinkeliges ebenes Koordinatensystem n (Math) plane rectangular coordinates
Recht n wird erworben
 (Re) a right is acquired
 – a right accrues to
rechtzeitige Leistung f (Re) punctual performance of an obligation, § 287 BGB
rechtzeitige Lieferung f (com) on-time delivery of an order
rechtzeitiger Einspruch m
 (Re) opposition filed in due time
 – opposition entered in time
Recht n zur Beschau der angemeldeten Waren (Zo) right to examine the goods declared
Redakteur m **im Studio**
 (com) presenter
 – commentator
redaktionelle Vorbearbeitung f (EDV) pre-edit
Rediskont m (Fin) rediscount
rediskontfähig
 (Fin) rediscountable
 – eligible for rediscount
Rediskontfazilität f **e–r Zentralbank** (Fin) discount window
rediskontierbar (Fin) = *rediskontfähig*
rediskontieren (Fin) to rediscount
Rediskontierung f (Fin) rediscounting
Rediskontkontingent n (Fin) rediscount quota *(ie, maximum level of trade bills which commercial banks can rediscount at the central bank)*
Rediskontkontingente npl **festsetzen** (Fin) to set rediscount ceilings
Rediskontkredit m (Fin) rediscount credit
Rediskontlinie f (Fin) rediscount line
Rediskontobligo n (Fin) liability on rediscounts
Rediskontplafond m (Fin) rediscount ceiling
Rediskontrahmen m (Fin) rediscount line
Rediskontsatz m (Fin) rediscount rate
Rediskontstelle f (Fin) rediscount agency
Rediskontzusage f (Fin) rediscounting promise
redistributive Steuer f (FiW) redistributive tax
redlicher Erwerber m
 (Re) innocent party
 – transferee in good faith
Reduktion f **von Netzplänen** (OR) reduction
redundanter Code m (EDV) redundant code *(syn, Sicherheitscode)*
redundantes Zeichen n (EDV) redundant character *(syn, selbstprüfendes Zeichen)*
Redundanzprüfung f (EDV) redundancy check
reduzibles Polynom n (Math) reducible polynomial
reduzierte Gleichung f (Math) depressed equation
reduzierte kubische Gleichung f (Math) reduced cubic equation
reduzierte Prüfung f (Stat) reduced inspection
reduzierter Gradient m (OR) reduced gradient
reduzierte Tara f (com) reduced tare
reduzierte Ware f
 (com) goods offered at reduced prices
 – cut-price goods
Reeder m (com) shipowner, § 484 HGB
Reederei f (com) shipping company, § 489 HGB
Reedereibetrieb m (com) shipping business

Reedereivertreter m (com) shipping agent
reelle Achse f (Math) real number axis
reeller Koeffizient m (Math) real coefficient
reelle Zahl f (Math) real number
Re-Export m (AuW) reexport
REFA (IndE) Work Study Association
REFA-Qualifikation f (Pw) certificate in work study
Referentenentwurf m (Re) draft statute
Referenz f (Pw) reference *(ie, may be either written statement or person supplying it)*
Referenzen fpl (com) trade references
Referenzen fpl **angeben** (Pw) to furnish (*or* supply) references
Referenzen fpl **einholen** (Pw) to take up references
Referenzperiode f (Stat) reference period
Referenzpreis m (EG) reference price
Referenzschreiben n (Pw) letter of appraisal
Referenzzoll m (EG) reference tariff
refinanzieren
 (Fin) to refinance
 – to finance loans
Refinanzierung f
 (Fin) refinancing *(ie, paying off existing debt with funds secured from new debt)*
 (Fin) refunding *(ie, replacing outstanding bonds with new issue)*
Refinanzierung f **des Aktivgeschäfts** (Fin) refinancing of lendings *(ie, by banks)*
Refinanzierungsbasis f (Fin) refinancing potential
Refinanzierungsbedarf m (Fin) refinancing requirements
Refinanzierungsinstitut n **der letzten Instanz** (Fin) lender of last resort
 (ie, the central bank)
Refinanzierungskosten pl
 (Fin) cost of refinancing
 – cost of funding
 (Fin) cost of funds *(ie, to banks)*
Refinanzierungskredit m (Fin) refinancing (*or* rediscount) loan
Refinanzierungslinie f (Fin) rediscount line
Refinanzierungsmittel pl (Fin) refinancing funds
Refinanzierungsplafond m (Fin) refinancing line
Refinanzierungspolitik f (Vw) refinancing policy
Refinanzierungssystem n (EG) refinancing arrangements
Refinanzierungszusage f (Fin) promise to provide refinancing
Reflation f (Vw) reflation *(syn, Redeflation)*
Reflektant m (com) prospective buyer
reflektierter Binärcode m
 (EDV) reflected binary code
 – cyclic code
Reflektormarke f (EDV) reflective spot
Reform f „**an Haupt und Gliedern**" (com) root-and-branch reform
Reformhaus n (com) health food store
Reformvorschlag m (EG) reform proposal
Refundierungsanleihe f (Fin) refunding loan
refüsieren (com) to refuse acceptance
Regal n
 (com) shelf
 – rack
Regalfläche f (com) shelf space

Regal-Großhändler *m*
(Mk) rack jobber
– service merchandiser
rege Investitionstätigkeit *f* (com) high capital spending
Regelabweichung *f* (EDV) deviation
Regelanfrage *f* (Pw) automatic vetting *(ie, of applicants for government jobs)*
Regel *f* **der Exportation** (Log) law of exportation *(ie, in propositional logic)*
Regelgerät *n* (EDV) automatic controller
Regelgröße *f* (EDV) controlled (*or* measured) variable
Regelkreis *m*
(EDV) control (*or* feedback) loop
– feedback control system (*or* circuit)
– loop
(syn, Rückkoppelungsschleife)
Regelleistung *f* (SozV) normal benefit
Regellohn *m* (SozV) regular gross earnings
Regellosigkeitsaxiom *n* (Stat) axiom of randomness
regelmäßig wiederkehrende Lasten *fpl* (Re) periodical outgoings, § 103 BGB
regelmäßig wiederkehrende Zahlungen *fpl* (Fin) periodically recurring payments
Regelmechanismus *m* (Vw) built-in flexibility (*or* stabilizer)
Regelsätze *mpl* (Fin) regular rates *(ie, in standard volume banking)*
Regelstrecke *f*
(EDV) controlled system
– process under control
Regel- und Steuerungstechnik *f* (EDV) control system engineering
Regelung *f*
(EDV) automatic (*or* feedback) control
– cycle regulation
Regelung *f* **aushandeln** (com) to negotiate a settlement
Regelungstechnik *f* (EDV) control engineering
Regelung *f* **von Rechtsstreitigkeiten** (Re) settlement of disputes
Regenversicherung *f* (Vers) rain insurance
Regiearbeit *f* (com) scheduled work *(ie, work for which time and materials are charged)*
Regiebetrieb *m*
(FiW) ancillary municipal enterprise
– municipal enterprise operated by an administrative agency
(eg, public slaughterhouses, forestry, farming)
Regiekosten *pl* (KoR) administrative cost
Regierungsauftrag *m* (FiW) government contract
Regiestufe *f* (Bw) level of management
Regionalanalyse *f* (Vw) regional economics
Regionalbank *f* (Fin) regional bank *(opp, Großbanken)*
regional differenzierte Exportförderung *f* (AuW) export promotion restricted to specified importing countries
regionale Börse *f* (Bö) regional stock exchange
regionale Mobilität *f* (Vw) regional (*or* geographical) mobility
regionaler Exportbasiskoeffizient *m* (AuW) economic base ratio

Regionalökonomie *f* (Vw) regional economics
Regionalplanung *f* (Vw) regional economic planning
Regionalpolitik *f* (Vw) regional development policy
Regionaltheorie *f* (Vw) regional economics
Regionalverband *m* (Re) regional association
Regionalwissenschaft *f* (Vw) regional economics
Registerauszug *m* (Re) extract from register
Registerbefehl *m* (EDV) register instruction
Registergericht *n* (Re) registration court
Registerlänge *f* (EDV) register length
Registeroperand *m* (EDV) register operand
Registerrichter *m* (Re) judge in charge of the Commercial Register
Registrator *m* (com) filing clerk
Registratur *f* (com) filing department
Registrierbuchungsautomat *m* (ReW) automatic listing and bookkeeping machine
registrieren (EDV) to record
Registriergerät *n* (EDV) logger
Registrierkasse *f* (com) cash register
registrierte Arbeitsuchende *mpl* (Vw) applicants registered for work
registriertes Gebrauchsmustermodell *n* (Pat) registered model under a utility patent
Regler *m*
(EDV) controller
– automatic controller
– regulator
Regreß *m* (Re) recourse
(Re) *(often used to denote)* claim to damages
Regreßanspruch *m* (Re) right of recourse
Regreßforderung *f* (Re) recourse claim
Regreß *m* **mangels Annahme** (Re) recourse for nonacceptance
Regreß *m* **mangels Zahlung** (Re) recourse in default of payment
Regreßpflicht *f* (Re) liability to recourse
regreßpflichtig (Re) liable to recourse
Regreßschuldner *m* (Re) person liable to recourse
Regressionsanalyse *f* (Stat) regression analysis
Regressionsfläche *f* (Stat) regression surface
Regressionsgerade *f*
(Stat) line of regression
– regression line
Regressionsgleichung *f*
(Stat) equation of regression
– regression equation
Regressionskoeffizient *m*
(Stat) coefficient of regression
– regression coefficient
Regressionskurve *f* (Stat) regression curve
Regressionsparameter *m* (Stat) regression parameter
regressive Kosten *pl* (KoR) regressive cost (*or* expense) *(ie, falling in absolute terms when level of activity goes up, and vice versa)*
regressive Steuer *f* (FiW) regressive tax
Regressivität *f* (FiW) regressivity
regreßlose Exportfinanzierung *f* (Fin) nonrecourse export financing
Regreß *m* **nehmen** (WeR) to take recourse (against)
Regressor *m*

(Math) determining variable
(Stat) predicted variable
– predictor
– regressor
Regreßpflicht f (Re) liability to recourse
Regreßpflichtiger m (Re) party liable to recourse
Regreßrecht n (Re) right to recourse
reguläre Bankgeschäfte npl (Fin) standard banking operations *(ie, lending and deposit business; opp, Finanzierungs- und Gründungstätigkeit, Effekten- und Depotgeschäft, Zahlungsverkehr, Inkassogeschäft)*
reguläre Funktion f (Math) analytic (*or* regular) function
Regularitätsgebiet n (Math) region of analyticity
regulieren
(com) to settle
– to pay
Regulierung f
(com) settlement
– payment
Regulierung f **e–s Schadens**
(Vers) settlement of a claim
– claim settlement
Regulierungsabkommen n (AuW) settlement agreement
Regulierungsbeamter m (Vers) claim adjuster
Regulierungsbeauftragter m
(Vers) adjuster
– claims representative
Regulierungskosten pl
(Vers) claim expense
– cost of claim settlement
Regulierungskurs m (Bö) settlement price
Rehabilitation f (SozV) rehabilitation
Rehabilitationsstätte f (SozV) rehabilitation center
reibungslose Koordination f (Bw) smooth coordination
Reichsversicherungsordnung f (SozV) West German Social Insurance Code, as of 1 Jan 1912, variously amended
Reichweite f
(Re) scope
– comprehensiveness
(ie, of statutory and administrative rules)
Reifephase f (Mk) maturity stage *(ie, of product life cycle)*
reife Volkswirtschaft f (Vw) mature economy
Reihenabschluß m (Bö) chain transaction *(ie, in forward commodity trading)*
Reihenfertigung f (IndE) flow shop production
Reihenfolgemodell n (OR) sequencing model
Reihenfolgeplanung f
(IndE) job shop scheduling (*or* sequencing)
– priority dispatching
– priority routing and scheduling
Reihenfolgeproblem n (OR) sequencing problem
Reihengeschäft n (StR) chain transaction *(ie, series of deliveries each of which constitutes a taxable turnover)*
Reihenkorrelation f (Stat) serial correlation
Reihenregreß m (WeR) = *Reihenrückgriff*
Reihenrückgriff m (WeR) recourse sequence following chain of indorsers
(opp, Sprungrückgriff)

Reihenstichprobenprüfplan m (Stat) sequential sampling plan
Reihenstichprobenprüfung f (Stat) sequential sampling inspection
Reihe f **von Maßnahmen ankündigen** (com) to announce a package of measures
Reindividende f (Fin) net dividend
reine Akkordarbeit f (Pw) straight piecework
reine Algebra f (Math) abstract (*or* pure) algebra
reine Arbitrage f (AuW) pure arbitrage
reine Außenwirtschaftstheorie f (AuW) pure theory of international trade
reine Forschung f (Bw) pure research *(syn, basic research)*
reine Goldumlaufwährung f (Vw) gold specie standard
reine imaginäre Zahl f (Math) pure imaginary number
Reineinkommen n (Pw) net income (*or* earnings) *(syn, Nettoeinkommen)*
Reineinkommen n **nach Steuern** (Pw) net income after taxes
reine Mathematik f (Math) pure (*or* abstract) mathematics
reiner Gedächtnistest m (Mk) unaided (*or* pure) recall test
Reinerlös m (Fin) net proceeds
reiner Stücklohn m (Pw) straight piece rate
Reinertrag m (ReW) = *Reingewinn*
reiner Verrechnungsdollar m (Fin) offset dollar
reiner Zahlungsverkehr m (AuW) clean payment *(ie, ohne zusätzliche sichernde Dienstleistungen der Zahlungsverkehrsmittler)*
reiner Zins m (Fin) pure interest
reiner Zufallsfehler m (Stat) unbiased error
reines Akkreditiv n (Fin) clean credit *(ie, based on the terms ,,documents against payment")*
reines Bordkonnossement n (com) clean shipped on board bill
reines Konnossement n (com) clean bill of lading (*or* B/L)
(ie, containing no notation that goods received by carrier were defective)
reines Monopol n (Vw) pure monopoly
reine Sterbeziffer f (Stat) refined death rate
reine Stücke npl (Bö) good delivery securities *(ie, conforming to stock exchange usages)*
reine Termingeschäfte npl (Bö) outright transactions
reine Theorie f **des internationalen Handels** (AuW) pure theory of international trade
reine Tratte f (com) clean draft
reine Verladedokumente npl (com) clean documents
Reinfall m
(Bö) plunge
reinganzzahlige Programmierung f (OR) pure integer programming
Reingewicht n (com) net weight *(ie, gross weight minus tare which is weight of wrapping, etc.)*
Reingewinn m
(ReW) net profit
– net earnings
– net income
(ie, sum of revenues minus sum of

expenditures; opp, Reinverlust)
(com) net margin
Reingewinnermittlung *f* (ReW) net income calculation
Reingewinn *m* **je Aktie** (Fin) net per share
Reingewinn *m* **vor Fusion** (ReW) profit prior to merger
Reingewinnzuschlag *m* (com) net profit markup
Reinschrift *f* (com) fair copy
Reinüberschuß *m* (Fin) net surplus
Reinumsatz *m*
(ReW) net sales
– (GB) net turnover *(syn, Nettoumsatz)*
Reinverdienst *m* (Pw) net earnings
Reinverlust *m* (ReW) net loss *(ie, sum of expenditures minus sum of revenues; opp, Reingewinn)*
Reinvermögen *n*
(ReW) net assets
– net worth
reinvestieren
(Fin) to reinvest
– to plow back (GB: plough back) profits into the business
Reinvestition *f*
(Bw) replacement investment
(Fin) reinvestment
– plow back (GB: plough back)
Reinvestitionsrücklage *f* (StR) reserve for reinvestment *(ie, gain on disposal of a certain class of fixed assets)*
Reinvestitionszeitpunkt *m* (Bw) reasonable time for replacing plant and equipment
reinzeichnen (com) to sign a clear bill of lading
Reiseakkreditiv *n* (com) = *Reisekreditbrief*
Reisebeschränkungen *fpl* (AuW) traveling restrictions
Reisebilanz *f* (VGR) balance on travel
Reisebuchhandel *m* (com) itinerant book trade
Reisebüro *n* (com) travel agency *(or* bureau)
Reisecharter *f* (com) voyage charter
Reiseentschädigung *f* (Pw) travel allowance
Reisefracht *f* (com) voyage freight
Reisegepäck *n*
(com) luggage
– (GB) baggage
Reisegepäckversicherung *f*
(Vers) baggage *(or* luggage) insurance
– (US *also*) personal effects floater
Reisegewerbe *n* (com) itinerant trade *(previous term: Wandergewerbe)*
Reisegewerbekarte *f* (com) itinerant trade license *(ie, valid for domestic trade; see: Gewerbelegitimationskarte)*
Reisegewerbesteuer *f* (StR) itinerant-trade tax, § 35a GewStG *(previous term: Wandergewerbesteuer)*
Reisehandel *m* (com) traveling salesman's trade *(ie, door-to-door canvassing of mail orders; syn, Vertreterversandhandel, Detailreisehandel)*
Reisekosten *pl*
(com) travel allowance
(StR) traveling expenses
– travel expenses
Reisekostenerstattung *f* (com) refunding of travel expenses

Reisekostenpauschale *f* (com) travel allowance
Reisekosten-Pauschbeträge *mpl* (StR) blanket amounts of traveling expenses, Abschn. 119 EStR
Reisekostenvergütung *f* (com) reimbursement of travel expenses
Reisekostenzuschuß *m* (com) traveling allowance
Reisekreditbrief *m* (com) traveler's letter of credit
Reiselagerversicherung *f* (Vers) insurance of traveling salesman's merchandise collection
Reisender *m*
(com) traveling salesman
– commercial traveler
(Zo) any traveler
Reisepolice *f* (Vers) voyage policy
Reiseprospekt *m* (com) travel brochure (*or* leaflet)
Reisescheck *m* (com) traveler's (*or* circular) check *(syn, Travellerscheck)*
Reisespesen *pl* (com) travel expenses
Reisespesenabrechnung *f* (com) travel expense statement
Reisespesensatz *m* (com) per diem travel allowance
Reiseunfallversicherung *f* (Vers) traveler's accident insurance
Reiseveranstalter *m* (com) tour operator
Reiseverkehr *m* (com) tourist travel *(syn, Fremdenverkehr, Tourismus)*
Reiseverkehrsbilanz *f* (VGR) balance of tourist travel
Reiseverkehrsstatistik *f* (Stat) tourist travel statistics
Reiseversicherung *f*
(Vers) travel insurance
– tourist policy
– voyage insurance
Reiseversicherungspolice *f* (Vers) tourist policy
Reisevertrag *m* (com) tourist travel agreement *(ie, between travel agency or tour operator and traveler)*
Reisevertreter *m* (com) = *Reisender*
Reisewetterversicherung *f* (Vers) tourist weather insurance *(ie, special line of rain insurance)*
Reisezahlungsmittel *npl* (com) tourist's payment media
reißenden Absatz *m* **finden**
(com) to sell briskly
– (infml) to sell like hot cakes
Reißer *m* (EDV) burster *(ie, used to separate individual forms in a set of continuous stationery output)*
Reiter *m* (com) tab *(ie, used as an aid in filing)*
Reitwechsel *m*
(Fin) kite
– windmill
Reklamation *f* (com) complaint
Reklamations-Abteilung *f* (com, US) query department
Reklame *f* (Mk) advertising *(Note that the German term has a slight tinge of ballyhoo)*
Reklamefeldzug *m* (Mk) advertising campaign
Reklameflächen *fpl*
(Mk) billboards
– (GB) hoardings *(syn, Anschlagflächen)*
Rekonzentration *f* (Vw) reconcentration

Rekordergebnisse *npl* (com) bumper performance (*or* results)
Rekordhöhe *f*
(com) record level *(eg, unemployment and lay-offs are at ...)*
(com) all-time high *(ie, prices reached an ...)*
Rekordzinsen *mpl* (Fin) record high interest rates
Rekrutierungspraxis *f* (Pw) recruitment methods
Rektaindossament *n* (WeR) „not to order" indorsement
Rektaklausel *f* (WeR) nonnegotiable clause
Rektakonnossement *n* (com) straight bill of lading (*or* B/L) *(ie, made out to the name of carrier or captain, § 647 HGB)*
Rektalagerschein *m* (WeR) warehouse receipt made out to a specified person
Rektapapier *n* (WeR) nonnegotiable (*or* registered) instrument *(ie, made to a named person)*
Rektascheck *m* (WeR) check payable to named payee, Art. 5 I ScheckG
Rektawechsel *m*
(WeR) nonnegotiable bill of exchange, Art. 11 WG
– „not to order" bill
Rektifikationsposten *m* (ReW, rare) = *Posten der Wertberichtigung*
rektifizieren (com) to rectify
Rekursionsformel *f* (Math) recursion (*or* recursive) formula
Rekursionsverfahren *n* (Bw) roll-back method
rekursive Definition *f* (Log) recursive definition
rekursive Funktion *f* (Math, Log) recursive function
rekursive Programmierung *f* (OR) recursive programming
relative Abweichung *f* (Stat) relative deviate
relative Adresse *f* (EDV) relative address
relative Adressierung *f* (EDV) relative addressing *(ie, 1. operand address + reference address = absolute address; 2. displacement + base address = absolute address)*
relative Ausschußtoleranz *f*
(Stat) lot tolerance per cent defective
– lot tolerance limit
relative Codierung *f* (EDV) relative coding
relative Einkommenshypothese *f* (Vw) relative income hypothesis
relative Einzelkostenrechnung *f* (KoR) relative direct costing
relative Gemeinkosten *pl* (KoR) relative overhead *(ie, used in marginal costing by Riebel)*
relative Häufigkeit *f* (Stat) relative (*or* proportional) frequency
relative Inflation *f* (Vw) relative inflation
relative Konstanz *f* **der Lohnquoten** (Vw) constancy of relative shares
relative Mehrheit *f*
(Re) relative majority
– (US) plurality
relative Meistbegünstigung *f* (AuW) conditional most-favored-nation treatment
relative Preisunterschiede *mpl* (AuW) relative price differences *(ie, equal to 'comparative advantage')*
relative Priorität *f* (OR) nonpreemptive priority *(ie, in waiting-line theory; opp, absolute Priorität)*
relative Prioritäten *fpl* (OR) head-of-the-line priorities
relative Programmierung *f* (EDV) relative programming
relativer Ausdruck *m* (EDV) relocatable expression
relativer Fehler *m* (EDV) relative error *(opp, absolute error)*
relativer Preis *m* (Vw) relative price
relativer Vorrang *m* (OR) nonpreemptive priority
relatives Recht *n*
(Re) personal right
– right in personam
(ie, imposing obligation on a definite person)
relativierbar (EDV) relocatable
Relativierungstabelle *f* (EDV) relocation dictionary
Relativlader *m* (EDV) relocatable program loader
relevante Daten *pl* (Bw) relevant data
relevante Kosten *pl*
(KoR) relevant
– alternative
– current-outlay
– incremental
– marginal ... cost
relevanter Bereich *m* (KoR) relevant range
relevanter Markt *m* (Vw) relevant market *(ie, concept used by J. Robinson and H. v. Stackelberg)*
relevanter Zinsfuß *m* (Fin) relevant rate
Rembours *m* (Fin) payments by mean of documentary acceptance credit
Remboursauftrag *m* (Fin) order to open a documentary acceptance credit
Remboursbank *f* (Fin) accepting bank
Remboursermächtigung *f* (Fin) reimbursement authorization *(ie, authority to open a documentary acceptance credit)*
Remboursgeschäft *n* (Fin) financing by documentary acceptance credit
Rembourskredit *m* (Fin) documentary acceptance credit
Rembourslinie *f* (Fin) acceptance credit line
Remboursregreß *m* (WeR) reimbursement recourse
Remboursschuldner *m* (Fin) documentary credit debtor
Remboursstratte *f* (Fin) documentary acceptance (*or* bill)
Remboursverbindlichkeit *f* (Fin) indebtedness on documentary acceptance credit
Rembourswechsel *m* (Fin) documentary draft
Rembourszusage *f* (Fin) agreement to reimburse
Remittent *m* (WeR) payee, Art. 1, 75 WG *(syn, Wechselnehmer)*
Remonetisierung *f* (Vw) remonetization
Rendement *n* (com) yield
Rendite *f*
(Fin) yield
(Fin) effective yield (*or* rate) *(ie, on bonds)*
(Fin) annual rate of return
(ie, on capital employed, mostly expressed in percentage terms)
Renditeangleichung *f* (Fin) yield adjustment

Rendite *f* auf die Investition (Fin) return on investment
Rendite *f* bei Langläufern
(Fin) yield on long-dated bonds
– yield on longs
Rendite *f* der Gewinnvergleichsrechnung (Fin) accounting rate of return *(ie, average net income/ average net book value over project life)*
Rendite *f* e-r langfristigen Anlage (Fin) maturity yield
Rendite *f* nach Steuern (Fin) after-tax yield
Renditegefälle *n* (Fin) yield differential *(or* gap)
Renditegefüge *n* (Fin) yield structure
Renditenstatistik *f* (Fin) statistics on yields
Renditenstruktur *f* (Fin) yield structure
Renditeobjekt *n* (Fin) income *(or* investment) property *(ie, type of property the primary purpose of which is to produce monetary income)*
Renditespanne *f* (Fin) yield spread
Renditevorsprung *m* (Fin) yield advantage (over)
Rendite *f* vor Steuern
(Fin) yield before taxes
– pretax yield
Renegotiationsklausel *f* (com) renegotiation clause *(ie, in offshore transactions: permits buyer to review prices within 3 years)*
,,Renner" *m*
(Mk) top-selling item *(or* product)
– runner
Rennwett- und Lotteriegesetz *n* (StR) Law Regulating the Tax on Bettings and Lotteries, of 8 Apr 1922, as amended
Rennwett- und Lotteriesteuer *f* (StR) tax on bettings and lotteries
Renommee *n* (com) reputation or goodwill *(ie, of a person or company)*
Rentabilität *f*
(Bw) profitability
– rate of return on capital employed
– rate of profit *(or* profitability)
– return on investment
– RoI *(ie, capital turnover × net income percentage of sales = Kapitalumsatz × Umsatzerfolg)*
– *(in business parlance)* profitable efficiency
Rentabilität *f* des Betriebes (Fin) operating return *(ie, ratio of operating profit to necessary operating capital = betriebsnotwendiges Kapital)*
Rentabilität *f* des Eigenkapitals (Fin) equity return *(ie, ratio of net profit to equity capital)*
Rentabilitätsanalyse *f*
(Fin) return on investment analysis
– RoI analysis
– profitability analysis
Rentabilitätsberechnung *f* (com) profitability calculation *(or* estimate)
Rentabilitätsfaktor *m* (com, *in retailing)* profitability factor *(ie, percentage gross proceeds minus inventory turnover/100)*
Rentabilitätsgesichtspunkte *mpl* (com) profitability aspects *(or* considerations)
Rentabilitätsindex *m* (Fin) index of profitability
Rentabilitätslücke *f* (Fin) profitability gap
Rentabilitätsprüfung *f* (ReW) profitability audit
Rentabilitätsrechnung *f*

(Fin) evaluation of investment alternatives
– investment appraisal
– preinvestment analysis
(syn, Wirtschaftlichkeitsrechnung)
(Fin) average rate of return (RoI) method
(Fin) mathematics of finance *(ie, dealing with corporation stocks, bonds and other investment)*
Rentabilitätsschwelle *f* (Fin) breakeven point
Rentabilitätsverhältnisse *npl* (Fin) profitability
Rentabilitätsziel *n* (Fin) target rate-of-return goal
Rentabilität *f* von Investitionen (Fin) return on investments *(ie, over total life of project)*
Rente *f*
(Vw) economic rent
(StR) annuity *(ie, both civil law and tax law leave the term undefined)*
(SozV) old-age pension
– retirement pension
(Vers) annuity
Rente *f* ablösen (Fin) to redeem an annuity
Rente *f* kapitalisieren (Fin) to capitalize an annuity
Rente *f* mit unbestimmter Laufzeit (Fin) contingent annuity
Renten *pl* (Bö) = *Rentenwerte*
Rentenablösung *f* (Fin) redemption of an annuity
Rentenalter *n* (Pw) pensionable age
Rentenanleihe *f* (Fin) annuity bond
Rentenanpassung *f* (SozV) pension adjustment
Rentenanpassungsgesetz *n* (SozV) Pension Adjustment Law
Rentenanpassungstermin *m* (SozV) pension adjustment date
Rentenanspruch *m* (SozV, Pw) pension claim
Rentenanwartschaft *f* (SozV) expectancy of pension
Rentenaufwand *m* (Pw) annuity cost
Rentenbaisse *f* (Bö) slump in bond prices
Rentenbarwert *m* (Fin) present value of annuity
Rentenbescheid *m* (SozV) pension notice
Rentenbestand *m* (Fin) bond holdings
Rentendauer *f* (Fin) term of annuity
Renteneinkommen *n*
(Vw) unearned income
(SozV) retirement pensions and other social security pensions
Rentenempfänger *m*
(Fin) annuitant
– (SozV) pensioner
Rentenendwert *m*
(Math) amount of annuity
– accumulation of annuity
– accumulated amount of annuity
– final value of annuity
rentenfähig (SozV) eligible for retirement
Rentenfinanzen *pl* (SozV) pension funds' finances
Rentenflaute *f* (Bö) sluggish bond merket
Rentenfolge *f* (Fin) annuity series
Rentenfonds *m*
(Fin) annuity fund
(Fin) bond-based fund
Rentengeschäft *n* (Vers) annuity business
Rentenhandel *m* (Bö) bond trading
Rentenhausse *f* (Bö) upsurge in bond prices
Rentenkurs *m* (Fin) bond price
Rentenleistungen *fpl*

507

(Fin) annuity payments
(SozV) pension benefits
Rentenmarkt *m*
  (Fin) bond market
  – fixed-interest market
  – fixed-income market
Rentenmarkt *m* **in Anspruch nehmen** (Bö) to tap the bond market
Rentenmarkt *m* **versperren** (Bö) to close off the bond market *(eg, to most companies, due to high interest)*
Renten *fpl* **nach Mindesteinkommen** (SozV) pensions based on minimum incomes
Rentennotierungen *fpl* (Bö) bond prices
Rentenpapiere *npl* (Bö) = *Rentenwerte*
Rentenportefeuille *n* (Fin) bond holdings
Rentenrate *f* (Fin) annuity payment
Rentenrechnung *f* (Math) mathematics of annuities
Rentenrecht *n* (SozV) pension law
Rentenreihe *f* (Fin) annuity series
Rentenschein *m* (Fin) interest coupon *(syn, Zinsschein)*
Rentenschuld *f* (Re) annuity land charge, §§ 1199 ff BGB
Rentenschwäche *f* (Bö) weakness in bond prices
Rentenumlauf *m* (Fin) total bonds outstanding
Rentenumsätze *mpl* (Bö) bond turnover
Renten- und Aktienrendite *f* (Bö) stock market yield
Renten *fpl* **und dauernde Lasten** *fpl* (StR) annuities and permanent burdens *(ie, incurred in connection with the organization or acquisition of a business, § 8 Nr. 2 GewStG, § 52 GewStR)*
Rentenverpflichtungen *fpl* (Fin) liabilities for annuity payments
Rentenversicherung *f*
  (SozV) pension insurance fund
  (Vers) annuity insurance
Rentenversicherung *f* **der Arbeiter und Angestellten** (SozV) wage and salary earners' pension insurance funds
Rentenversicherungsträger *m* (SozV) pension insurance institution (*or* carrier)
Rentenvertrag *m* (Fin) annuity agreement (*or* contract)
Rentenwerte *mpl*
  (Bö) bonds
  – fixed-interest securities
Rentenzahlung *f*
  (SozV) pension payment
  (Vers) annuity payment
rentierend (Fin) profitable
rentieren, sich (Fin) to be profitable
Rentner *m* (SozV) pensioner
Rentnerhaushalt *m* (Stat) household of a retired couple
Rentnerkrankenversicherung *f* (SozV) pensioners' health insurance
Reorganisation *f*
  (Bw) reorganization
  – organizational reshuffle
  – restructuring of activities
Reorganisationsprogramm *n* (Bw) restructuring plan (*or* program)
reorganisieren
  (Bw) to reorganize
  – to reconstruct
  – to regroup
  – to reshape
  – to revamp *(eg, manufacturing operations)*
Reparatur *f*
  (com) repair
  – repair work
Reparaturauftrag *m* (com) repair order
Reparaturkosten *pl* (KoR) cost of repair and maintenance
Reparaturschicht *f* (IndE) maintenance (*or* repair) shift
repartieren
  (Fin) to apportion
  – to allot
  – to scale down an allotment
Repartierung *f*
  (Fin) allotment
  – scaling down *(syn, Zuteilung)*
Repatriierung *f* (AuW) repatriation
Repetierfaktoren *mpl* (Bw) consumable factors of production *(ie, raw materials, auxiliary materials, supplies; opp, Potentialfaktoren)*
repetitive Arbeit *f* (Pw) repetitive work
Report *m*
  (Bö) delayed acceptance penalty
  – (GB) contango
  (ie, London Stock Exchange term: percentage of the selling price payable by the purchaser of shares for the privilege of postponing acceptance of their delivery; opp, Deport)
Reportgenerator *m* (EDV) report generator
Reportarbitrage *f* (Bö) commodity arbitrage
Reportgeschäft *n*
  (Bö) carryover business *(ie, continuation of forward transaction: sale and purchase of securities against payment of carryover price; opp, Deportgeschäft)*
  – contango
  – continuation
Reportsatz *m*
  (Bö) carryover rate
  – contango rate
Reporttag *m* (Bö) contango (*or* continuation) day
Repräsentant *m* (com) representative
Repräsentanz *f* (com) representative office
Repräsentationsaufwendungen *mpl* (StR) duty entertainment expense
Repräsentationszulage *f* (StR) duty entertainment allowance
repräsentativer Durchschnitt *m* (com) representative cross-section
Repräsentativerhebung *f*
  (Stat) representative sampling (*or* survey)
  – sample survey
repräsentativer Kurs *m* (EG) representative conversion rate *(syn, grüner Kurs)*
repräsentative Stichprobe *f* (Stat) average (*or* representative sample
reprivatisieren (Vw) to denationalize
Reprivatisierung *f*
  (Vw) retransfer to private ownership
  – (GB) denationalisation
Reproduktions-Index *m* (Stat) reproduction rate

Reproduktionskosten *pl* (ReW) reproduction cost
Reproduktionskostenwert *m* (Bw) reproduction cost value *(ie, sum of current market values of all assets of a business minus liabilities; used in valuation of enterprises as a whole = Unternehmensbewertung)*
Reproduktionsrate *f* (Stat) = Reproduktions-Index
Reproduktionswert *m* (Bw) reproduction value *(ie, value of an enterprise as a whole: sum of all assets minus all liabilities, but excluding goodwill; syn, Teilreproduktionswert [preferable term], Sachwert, Substanzwert)*
Reproduktionsziffer *f* (Stat) = Reproduktions-Index
reproduzierbare Sachanlagen *fpl* (Bw) reproducible fixed capital
reproduzierbares Realvermögen *n* (Vw) reproducible assets
Reproduzierbarkeit *f* (Stat) reproducibility *(ie, of test results)*
Reptilienfonds *m* (FiW) slush fund *(ie, kept by West German Federal Chancellor as ‚Titel 300' for undisclosed public relations work)*
Repudiation *f* (Vw) repudiation *(ie, of money, due to its low purchasing power as a result of inflation, which makes it unsuitable as a medium of exchange)*
Reserveabgänge *mpl* (Vw) outflow of reserves
Reserveaktivum *n* (AuW) reserve asset *(or* instrument*)*
Reservebanken *fpl* (Vw) reserve banks *(ie, where commercial banks are obligated to keep minimum reserve accounts; eg, Deutsche Bundesbank, US Federal Reserve System)*
Reservebetrieb *m* (EDV) backup operation
Reservebildung *f*
 (ReW) amounts set aside for reserves
Reserveeinheit *f* (IWF) reserve unit
Reservefonds *m*
 (Fin) reserve fund *(ie, of a cooperative)*
 (ReW, *obsolete term)* surplus reserve *(syn, Rücklage)*
Reservehaltung *f* (Fin) reserve management
Reservehaltung *f* **in Form von Guthaben** (Vw) compulsory reserve deposits
Reservehaltung *f* **in Form von Wertpapieren** (Vw) compulsory reserves in securities
Reserveinstrument *n* (AuW) reserve instrument
Reservekapazität *f* (IndE) reserve *(or* standby*)* capacity
Reservemedium *n* (IWF) reserve facility
Reservemeldung *f*
 (Fin) reserve statement
 – reserve status report
Reservemittel *pl* (IWF) reserve facility
Reserven *fpl* (ReW, Fin) reserves *(ie, nondescriptive general term covering ‚Rücklagen', ‚Rückstellungen', ‚Mindestreserven', qv.)*
reservepflichtige Verbindlichkeiten *fpl*
 (Fin) liabilites subject to reserve requirements
 – reserve-carrying liabilities
Reserveposition *f*
 (IWF) Net Fund Position
 – reserve position
 (ie, difference between subscription or quota and IMF holdings of domestic currency)
Reservesatz *m* (Vw) minimum reserve ratio
Reserve-Soll *n* (Fin) required reserve *(ie, monthly average of a bank's domestic liabilities subject to reserve requirements)*
Reservespeicher *m*
 (EDV) spare memory
 – backup store
Reservesystem *n* (EDV) standby *(or* fall back*)* system
reservieren
 (com) to reserve
 – (GB) to book
 – (GB, *also)* to reserve
Reservierung *f*
 (com) reservation
 – (GB) booking
Reservetransaktion *f* (Vw) reserve transaction
Reserveverluste *mpl* (Vw) reserve losses
Reservewährung *f* (AuW) (international) reserve currency
Reservewährungsguthaben *npl* (AuW) reserve currency balances
Reservewährungsländer *npl* (AuW) reserve currency countries
residualbestimmtes Einkommen *n*
 (Vw) residual income
 – income determined residually
Residualfaktor *m* (Vw) residual factor
Residualterm *m* (Stat) residual term
Residualtheorie *f* (Vw) residual theory of profit
Residuen *npl* (Stat) residual variables
Respekttage *mpl* (WeR) days of grace *(ie, not recognized under West German law, Art. 74 WG)*
Ressort *n* (Bw) organizational unit
ressortieren (com) to be handled by *(eg, coal liquefaction is ... by the Federal Research Ministry)*
Ressourcen *pl*
 (Vw) resources
 (Bw) resources
 – capabilities
Ressourcen-Allokation *f*
 (Vw) allocation of resources
 – resource allocation
Ressourcen-Bereitstellung *f* (Bw) resourcing
Ressourcen-Inanspruchnahme *f* **durch den Staat** (FiW) resource absorption by government
Ressourcen-Planung *f* (Bw) capability planning
Ressourcen-Transfer *m* (AuW) transfer of resources
Ressourcen *fpl* **verschwenden** (Bw) to waste *(or* dissipate*)* resources
Rest *m* (com) balance *(eg, of contract price)*
Restanlagenwert *m* (ReW) residual cost *(or* value*)*
Restanten *mpl*
 (com) debtor in default *(or* arrears*)*
 – defaulter
 – delinquent debtor
 (Fin) securities called back for redemption but not yet presented
Restarbeitslosigkeit *f* (Vw) = Bodensatzarbeitslosigkeit

Restaurant-Kette *f*
  (com) restaurant chain
  (GB) catering group
Restbetrag *m*
  (com) balance
  – remaining balance
  – residual amount
Restbruch *m* (Math) fractional part
Restbuchwert *m*
  (ReW) net book value *(ie, after deducting previous depreciation provisions)*
  – remaining book value
  – depreciated book value (*or* cost)
  – amortized cost
  – residual value (*or* cost)
  – unrecovered cost
  – balance of asset cost
Restdeckungsbeitrag *m* (KoR) residual contribution margin *(ie, differences between contribution margins and a number of special fixed costs)*
Restfehler *m* (EDV) residual error
Restglied *n* (Math) remainder after n terms
Restgröße *f* (Stat) residual term
Restguthaben *n* (ReW) remaining credit balance
Restitutio *f* **in integrum** (Re) restoration (*or* restitution) to the previous condition
Restkapital *n*
  (Fin) principal outstanding
  – remaining investment
Restkaufgeld *n* (com) balance of purchase price
Restklasse *f* (Log) difference class
Restkosten *pl* (Bw) cost to complete *(ie, in project management)*
Restkostenrechnung *f* (KoR) = *Restwertrechnung*
Restkostenwert *m* (KoR) cost value of major or chief product in joint production *(ie, coke as against gas)*
Restlaufzeit *f*
  (com) remaining life (*or* term)
  – maturing within ...
  – remainder of the term
  – unexpired term
  – residual time to maturity
Restlebensdauer *f*
  (ReW) remaining life expectancy *(ie, of fixed asset)*
  – remaining useful life
  – unexpired life
restliche Sendung *f* (com) remainder of a consignment
restliche Tilgungsschuld *f* (Fin) remaining investment
Restnutzungsdauer *f* (ReW) = *Restlebensdauer*
Restposten *mpl* **der Zahlungsbilanz**
  (AuW) balance of unclassifiable transactions
  – accommodating (*or* balancing) items
  – errors and omissions
  (syn, Saldo der statistisch nicht aufgliederbaren Transaktionen)
Restprüfung *f*
  (EDV) residue check
  – modulo n check
Restriktion *f*
  (Math) constraint
  – restriction

  – side condition
  (Fin) = *Kreditrestriktion*
Restriktionen *fpl* **im Wertpapierverkehr** (Fin) restrictions (*or* constraints) on security transactions
Restriktionsgrad *m* (Vw) restrictiveness *(eg, in quantitative monetary policy)*
Restriktionskurs *m* (Vw) restrictive course
Restriktionsmaßnahmen *fpl* (Vw) restrictive measures
restriktive Eingriffe *mpl*
  (Vw) controls
  – government interference
restriktive Geldpolitik *f*
  (Vw) restrictive monetary policy
  – tight money policy
  – monetary restraint
restriktive Geldpolitik *f* **fortführen** (Vw) to adhere to a tight monetary policy
restriktive Geld- und Kreditpolitik *f* (Vw) restrictive monetary policy
restriktive Kreditpolitik *f*
  (Vw) restrictive credit policy
  – tight credit policy
  – credit control
restriktive Maßnahmen *fpl* (Vw) restraint measures
restriktive Politik *f*
  (Vw) restrictive economic policy
  – restraint
  – tight policy
Restrisiko *n* (Pw) acceptable risk *(ie, in accident prevention)*
Restschlange *f* (AuW) truncated Snake
Restschuld *f*
  (Fin) residual debt
  – unpaid balance in account
Restsumme *f* **der Abweichungsquadrate** (Stat) error sum of squares
Restwert *m*
  (ReW) declining balance of the asset account *(ie, balance after deducting preceding depreciation provisions)*
  (ReW) residual
  – recovery
  – salvage
  – scrap
  – terminal ... value
Restwertabschreibung *f*
  (ReW) declining-balance method (of depreciation)
  – diminishing-provision method
  (syn, Buchwertabschreibung, geometrisch-degressive Abschreibung)
Restwertrechnung *f* (KoR) residual value costing *(ie, method of costing joint products = Kalkulation von Kuppelprodukten; syn, Restkostenrechnung, Subtraktionsmethode)*
Retentionsrecht *n* (Re) right of retention *(ie, right to retain possession until claim is satisfied, § 369 HGB; syn, Zurückbehaltungsrecht)*
Retorsionsmaßnahme *f* (AuW) retaliatory action (*or* measure)
Retorsionszoll *m* (AuW) retaliatory duty (*or* tariff)
Retouren *fpl*

(com) (sales) returns
- returned sales (*or* purchases)
- goods returned
- (AuW) returned merchandise *(ie, to exporter as setoff against exported goods)*
- (Fin) bills and checks returned unpaid

retrograde Planung *f* (Bw) top-down planning

retrograde Rechenmethode *f* (KoR) inverse method of determining joint-product cost *(ie, sales price of final byproduct less separable cost incurred less profit markup = cost of previous product and so on; end result is the main-product cost)*

retrograde Verkaufskalkulation *f* (com) inverse method of determining purchase price *(ie, sales price less profit markup, selling and administrative expenses, and cost of acquisition; opp, progressive Verkaufskalkulation)*

retrozedieren (Vers) to retrocede

Retrozedent *m* (Vers) retrocedent *(ie, reinsurer placing a retrocession; syn, Weiterrückversicherungsnehmer)*

Retrozession *f* (Vers) retrocession *(ie, cession of reinsurance by one reinsurer to another reinsurer; syn, Folgerückversicherung)*

Retrozessionar *m* (Vers) retrocessionaire *(ie, the reinsurer of a reinsurer; syn, Weiterrückversicherer)*

Reugeld *n* (Re) forfeit money, § 359 BGB

Revalvation *f*
- (Vw) revaluation
- upvaluation

revidiertes Simplexverfahren *n* (OR) revised simplex method

Revision *f*
- (ReW) accounting control
- (ReW) audit(ing)
- (StR) appeal
  (ie, carried to the Federal Fiscal Court, § 115 FGO)
- (Re) appeal on law *(opp, Berufung = appeal on facts and law)*

Revisionsantrag *m* (Re) appeal to a court of superior jurisdiction

Revisionsattest *n* (com) certificate of classification *(ie, issued by a classification society, such as Germanischer Lloyd; Klassifikationsattest)*

Revisionsbeklagter *m* (Re) appellee

Revisionsbericht *m* (ReW) = *Prüfungsbericht*

Revisionskläger *m* (Re) appellant

Revisionsklausel *f* (Re) re-opener clause *(ie, in contracts)*

Revisionslehre *f* (ReW) auditing

Revisionsschrift *f* (StR) appeal brief *(eg, submitted to the Federal Fiscal Court)*

Revisionsverband *m* (ReW) auditing association *(ie, of cooperatives)*

Revision *f* **verwerfen** (StR) to dismiss an appeal, § 126 I FGO

Revisor *m*
- (ReW) auditor
- (IndE) inspector

revolvierende Planung *f* (Bw) revolving planning

revolvierender Kredit *m* (Fin) revolving (*or* continuous) credit

revolvierendes Akkreditiv *n* (Fin) revolving letter of credit

revolvierende Swaps *mpl* (Vw) revolving swaps

Revolving-Akkreditiv *n* (Fin) revolving letter of credit

Rezept *n* (SozV) prescription

Rezensent *m* (com) (book) reviewer

rezensieren
- (com) to review *(eg, a book)*
- (GB *also*) to notice *(ie, which implies that the review is brief)*

Rezension *f* (com) book review

rezeptfreie Medikamente *npl* (SozV) nonprescription drugs

Rezeptgebühr *f* (SozV) prescription charge

Rezeption *f*
- (com) reception desk
- front desk *(ie, at a hotel)*
- (GB) reception

rezeptpflichtige Medikamente *npl* (SozV) prescription drugs

Rezession *f*
- (Vw) recession
- slump

Rezession *f* **bekämpfen** (Vw) to combat (*or* fight) a recession

rezessionsbedingter Nachfragerückgang *m* (Vw) recession-led slump in demand

rezessionsbedingtes Defizit *n* (FiW) recession-swollen budget deficit

rezessionsgeschädigter Wirtschaftszweig *m* (Vw) recession-plagued industry

rezessionssicher (com) recession-resistant *(eg, service business)*

Rezession *f* **überstehen** (Bw) to weather a recession

rezessive Tendenzen *fpl* (Vw) recessionary trends

reziproke Gleichung *f* (Math) reciprocal equation

reziproke Konten *npl* (ReW) suspense accounts *(syn, Spiegelbildkonten, Übergangskonten)*

reziproke Matrix *f* (Math) reciprocal (*or* inverse) matrix

reziprokes Gleichungssystem *n* (Math) inverse system of equations

Reziprozitäts-Prinzip *n* (AuW) reciprocity principle

R-Gespräch *n*
- (com) collect call
- (GB) transferred charge call
- (GB, coll) reverse-charge call

Rheinisch-Westfälisches Institut *n* **für Wirtschaftsforschung** (Vw) *(Essen-based)* Rhenish-Westphalian Institute for Economic Research

Ricambio *m*
- (Fin) redrafted bill
- redraft
- re-exchange
(syn, Ricambiowechsel, Rückwechsel)

Richtbestand *m* (MaW) target inventory level

richterliche Auslegung *f* (Re) judicial construction (*or* interpretation)

richterliche Gewalt *f* (Re) judicial authority

richterlich entscheiden (Re) to hear and determine (a case)

richterliches Ermessen *n* (Re) judicial discretion

511

richtigstellen
(com) to rectify
– to straighten out
Richtigstellung f (com) rectification
Richtigkeit f **der Abschrift wird beglaubigt** (com) certified to be a true and correct copy of the original
Richtkosten pl (KoR, *obsolete*) = *Plankosten*
Richtlinien fpl (StR) administrative regulations
Richtlinien fpl **der Programmverknüpfung** (EDV) linkage conventions
Richtlinien fpl **für die Bewertung des Grundvermögens** (StR) Regulations for the Valuation of Real Property, of 19 Sept 1966
Richtlinienkompetenz f (Bw) right to set the broad rules of company policy
Richtpreis m
(com) recommended (*or* suggested) price
(EG) target price
Richtsätze mpl
(Vw) guiding ratios
(eg, ratio of lending to capital reserves, as fixed by central bank)
(StR) comparative data
(ie, experience figures the government collects in tax examinations and from other sources; applied to small businesses not required to keep books and to enterprises whose reported profits are out of line with those of comparable businesses for unexplained reasons)
Richtungsableitung f (Math) directional derivative
Richtungskämpfe mpl
(com) factional disputes
– factions feud
Richtungskoeffizient m (Math) slope
Richtungskosinus m (Math) direction cosine
Richtungsparameter m (Math) direction parameter
Richtungstaktschrift f (EDV) phase encoding
Riesenprojekt n (com) mega-project *(eg, worth $300bn)*
riesige Haushaltsdefizite npl (FiW) gargantuan budget deficits
Rigorosum n (Pw) final oral examination for a doctorate
Rimesse f (Fin) remittance
Rimessenbuch n
(Fin) book of remittance
– bill book
Ringbuch n
(com) loose-leaf notebook
– (GB) ring book
Ringgeschäft n (com) circular forward transaction
Ringschieben n
(EDV) circular
– logical
– non-arithmetic ... shift
Ringschieberegister n (EDV) circulating register
Ringtausch m **der Arbeitsplätze** (Pw) job rotation
Ringübertragung m
(EDV) cyclic
– ring
– circuit
– circular
– end-around
– nonarithmetic ... shift

Rinnverlust m (com) leakage
Risiken npl **streuen** (Bw) to spread (*or* diversify) risks
Risiko n
(com) risk
– hazard
Risiko n **abdecken** (Vers) to cover a risk
Risiko n **ablehnen** (Vers) to reject a risk
Risikoanalyse f (OR) risk analysis
Risikoausgleich m (Vers) balancing of portfolio
Risikoauslese f (Vers) selection of risks
Risikoausschluß m
(Vers) exclusion of risks
– elimination of risks
– policy exclusion (*or* exeption)
– exception
Risikoausschlußklausel f (Vers) excepted risks clause
risikobereites Eigenkapital n (Fin) risk (*or* venture) capital
Risikobewertung f
(Fin) risk assessment (*or* appraisal)
(Vers) risk rating
Risikodeckung f (Fin) risk cover
Risiko n **des Investors** (Fin) exposure
Risiko n **eingehen** (com) to run (*or* incur) a risk
Risiko n **geht über** (Re) risk passes
Risikohäufung f (Vers) cumulation of risk
Risikokapital n (Fin) risk (*or* venture) capital
Risikokapital-Finanzierung f (Fin) risk (*or* venture) capital financing
Risikoklausel f (SeeV) peril clause
Risikolebensversicherung f
(Vers) specific rest-life insurance policy
– renewable term
– term insurance *(see Risikoversicherung)*
Risikomischung f
(Fin) risk spreading
(IndE) risk spreading *(ie, over a number of different products)*
(Vers) diversification of risks
Risikopapier n (Bö) risk paper *(ie, shares and stocks)*
Risikopolitik f (Vers) risk management
Risikoprämie f
(ReW) risk premium *(ie, component of company profit)*
(Vers) net premium (*or* rate)
– expected loss ratio
– risk-absorbed premium
– risk premium
risikoreiche Adresse f (Fin) high-risk borrower
Risikorückstellungen fpl (Vers) contingency reserves
Risikoselektion f (Vers) risk selection
Risikostreuung f
(Bw) diversification of risk
– risk spreading
– spreading of risks
Risikosumme f (Vers) amount at risk
Risiko n **tragen** (com) to carry a risk
Risikotransformation f (Fin) shift in risk spreading
Risikoübergang m (Re) passage of risk *(syn, Gefahrenübergang)*
Risikoübernahme f (Re) assumption of risk

Risiko *n* **übernehmen** (Re) to assume a risk
Risikoversicherung *f* (Vers) term insurance *(ie, life insurance for a stipulated time only, beneficiary receiving the face value of the policy upon death, but nothing upon survival at completion of term; syn, abgekürzte Todesfallversicherung)*
Risikovertrag *m* (Re) hazardous contract
Risikovorsorge *f*
  (com) provision for risks
  (Fin) provision for contingent loan losses
Risikozuschlag *m*
  Fin) risk premium
  (Vers) risk markup
riskieren
  (com) to risk
  – to run a risk
  – to take a chance on *(eg, funds running out)*
Ristornogebühr *f* (Vers) cancellation fee
Ristornoversicherung *f* (Vers) return of premium insurance, § 894 HGB
Roboter *m* (IndE) robot *(ie, reprogrammable, multi-functional manipulator; wider definitions include fixed sequence)*
Roboter-Einsatz *m* (IndE) robot *(or* robotic) applications
Robotersteuerung *f*
  (IndE) robot control
  – robotization *(eg, of machine tools, plants)*
Roboter-Technologie *f*
  (IndE) robot technology
  – robotics
Rohbetriebsvermögen *n* (StR) total gross value (of business property), § 98a BewG
Rohbilanz *f* (ReW) preliminary balance sheet *(syn, Verkehrsbilanz)*
Rohergebnis *n* (ReW) gross profit or loss
Rohertrag *m* (ReW) gross yield *(ie, sales revenue + inventory changes before deductions and total expenditure)*
Rohertragswert *m* (StR) gross rental value, § 79 BewG *(ie, standard of value applied to improved properties listed in § 75 I 1–5 BewG)*
roher Reproduktionsindex *m* (Stat) gross reproduction rate
rohes Moment *n* (Stat) raw moment
Rohgewinn *m*
  (com) gross profit on sales
  – gross margin
  (ie, in trading: net sales less merchandise costs; syn, Warenrohgewinn, Warenbruttogewinn)
Rohgewinnanalyse *f* (ReW) gross profit analysis
Roh-, Hilfs- und Betriebsstoffe *pl* (ReW) raw materials and supplies
Rohmaterial-Anforderung *f* (MaW) raw materials requisition
Rohmateriallager *n* (MaW) raw materials stores
Rohöl *n* (com) crude oil
Rohprobe *f* (Stat) gross sample
Rohrzucker-Einfuhren *fpl* (AuW) cane sugar imports
Rohstahl *m* (com) crude *(or* raw) steel
Rohstahlproduktion *f* (Stat) crude *(or* raw) steel output
Rohstoffabkommen *n* (AuW) commodity agreement *(or* pact)

Rohstoffe *mpl*
  (Vw) raw materials
  – primary products
  – basic commodities
  (IndE) input *(or* charge) materials
Rohstoffhändler *m* (com) commodity trader
rohstoffintensiv (Bw) raw materials intensive
Rohstoffgewinnungsbetrieb *m* (com) extractive enterprise
Rohstoffindustrie *f* (com) natural resources industry
Rohstoffkartell *n* (AuW) commodities cartel
Rohstoffknappheit *f* (Vw) raw materials scarcity
Rohstoffland *n* (Vw) primary-producing country
Rohstoffmarkt *m* (com) raw commodity market
Rohstoffmarktforschung *f* (Mk) commodity marketing research
Rohstoffmonopolist *m* (Vw) raw materials monopolist
Rohstoffpreisindex *m* (com) commodity price index
Rohstoffversorgung *f* **sichern** (Vw) to safeguard supplies of raw materials
Rohüberschuß *m* (com) = *Rohgewinn*
Rohumsatz *m* (ReW) gross sales *(ie, sales before deductions, returns, allowances due to complaints, etc.)*
Rohverlust *m* (ReW) gross loss
Rohvermögen *n* (VGR) gross wealth *(or* assets)
Rohzins *m* (Fin) pure interest
rollende Planung *f*
  (Bw) continuous
  – perpetual
  – rolling ... planning
rollende Prognose *f* (Bw) rolling forecast
rollender Finanzplan *m* (Fin) moving budget
rollendes Budget *n*
  (Bw) continuous
  – perpetual
  – rolling ... budget
rollende Ware *f* (com) goods in rail or road transit *(opp, schwimmende und fliegende Ware)*
Rollenstruktur *f* (Bw) structure of roles
Rollentausch *m* (com) role reversal
Rollfuhrdienst *m* (com) cartage *(or* haulage) service
Rollfuhrunternehmer *m* (com) cartage *(or* haulage) contractor
Rollgeld *n*
  (com) cartage
  – (US) drayage
  – (GB) carriage
rollierendes Budget *n* (Bw) = *rollendes Budget*
Rolltreppe *f* (com) escalator
  – (GB) moving stairway *(or* staircase)
Römische Verträge *mpl* (EG) Treaty of Rome
römische Zahlen *fpl* (Math) Roman numerals
Roosa-Effekt *m* (Vw) locking-in effect
RoRo-Schiff *n* (com) roll-on-roll-off ship *(or* vessel)
roter Ausgang *m* (Zo) red exit
roter Durchgang *m* (Zo) red channel
rote Zahlen *fpl* **schreiben**
  (com) to operate in the red
  – to write red figures

routinemäßige Fertigungsplanung *f*
(IndE) routine production planning
- shop planning
Ruchti-Effekt *m* (Fin) = *Lohmann-Ruchti-Effekt*
Rückantwortschein *m* (com) reply coupon
Rückbehaltungsrecht *n* (Re) = *Zurückbehaltungsrecht*
Rückbelastung *f*
(ReW) billback
- reversal
Rückbuchung *f* (ReW) reverse entry *(syn, Stornobuchung)*
Rückbürge *m* (Re) counter surety
Rückbürgschaft *f*
(Re) back-to-back guaranty
- counter guaranty
rückdatieren
(com) to backdate
- to antedate
rückdatierte Police *f* (Vers) antedated policy
rückdatierter Scheck *m* (Fin) antedated scheck
Rückdatierung *f* (com) backdating
rückdiskontieren (Fin) to rediscount
Rückdiskontierung *f* (Fin) rediscounting
rückerstatten
(Fin) to refund
- to reimburse
Rückerstattung *f*
(Fin) refund
- reimbursement
Rückerstattungsanspruch *m*
(com) claim for reimbursement
- right to refund
Rückerstattungsgarantie *f* (com) money back guarantee
Rückerstattung *f* **von Steuern auf ausländische Erträge** (StR) overspill relief
Rückfahrkarte *f*
(com) round trip ticket
- (GB) return ticket
Rückfall *m* (Re) relapse, § 48 StGB
Rückfluß *m* **auf das investierte Kapital** (Fin) return on capital employed (*or* on investment)
Rückfracht *f*
(com) back freight
- freight home (*or* homeward)
- homeward freight
- return cargo (*or* freight)
Rückführung *f* (Pw) repatriation *(ie, of guest workers)*
Rückführung *f* **e-s Kredits** (Fin) repayment of a loan
Rückführung *f* **von Kapital** (AuW) repatriation of capital
Rückgaberecht *n* (com) return privilege
Rückgang *m*
(com) decline
- decrease
- drop
- fall
- falling off
- lowering
- setback *(eg, in prices)*
Rückgang *m* **auf breiter Front** (Bö) widespread decline in prices

Rückgang *m* **der Steuereinnahmen** (FiW) drop-off in tax revenues
Rückgang *m* **des BSP** (Vw) drop in gnp
Rückgang *m* **des Krankenstandes** (Pw) cut in sick leave
Rückgarantie *f* (Re) back-to-back guaranty
rückgekoppeltes Schieberegister *n* (EDV) feedback shift register
Rückgewährung *f*
(com) repayment
- return
- refunding
- reimbursement
Rückgewinnung *f* **des investierten Kapitals** (Fin) cost (*or* investment) recovery
Rückgewinnung *f* **von Rohstoffen** (Vw) recycling
Rückgriff *m* (com, Re, WeR) recourse (to, against) *(syn, Regreß)*
Rückgriff *m* **gegen Dritte** (Re) recourse to/against third parties
Rückgriff *m* **mangels Annahme** (WeR) recourse for nonacceptance
Rückgriff *m* **mangels Zahlung** (Re) recourse in default of payment
Rückgriff *m* **nehmen** (Re) to have recourse (to/against)
Rückgriffsforderung *f*
(Re) claim for indemnification
- right of recourse
Rückgriffshaftung *f* (Re) liability upon recourse
Rückgriffsrecht *n* (Re) right of recourse
Rückgriffsschuldner *m* (Re) recourse debtor
Rückindossament *n* (WeR) indorsement to prior indorser
Rückkauf *m*
(com) buying back
- repurchase
(Fin) redemption *(ie, of bonds)*
- amortization
- retirement
- callback
(Fin) repurchase *(ie, of stocks)*
(Vers) redemption surrender *(ie, of insurance policy)*
Rückkaufangebot *n* (Fin) repurchase (*or* redemption) offer
Rückkaufdisagio *n* (Fin) redemption (*or* repurchase) discount
Rückkauf *m* **eigener Aktien** (Fin) repurchase of own shares
Rückkauffrist *f* (com) period for repurchase
Rückkaufgesellschaft *f* (com) repurchase company
Rückkaufgewinn *m* (Vers) surrender profit
Rückkaufklausel *f* (Fin) call provision *(ie, referring to bonds)*
Rückkaufkurs *m*
(Fin) redemption
- retirement
- call ... price *(ie, of a bond)*
(Vers) bid price *(ie, fondsgebundene Versicherung)*
Rückkaufsdisagio *n* (Fin) repurchase discount *(ie, accruing when redeemable bonds must be repurchased below par, § 157 AktG)*
Rückkaufsrecht *n* (com) right to repurchase

Rückkaufsvereinbarung *f* (Fin) repurchase agreement
Rückkaufsvertrag *m* (Re) repurchase agreement
Rückkaufswert *m*
(Fin) redemption value *(ie, of securities)*
(Vers) cash surrender value *(ie, amount the insurer is obliged to pay to the insured upon premature termination of the insurance contract)*
Rückkauf *m* **von Schuldverschreibungen** (Fin) bond redemption (*or* call-back)
Rückkaufzeitpunkt *m* (Fin) date at which bonds are callable
Rückkehradresse *f* (EDV) return address
Rückkehrbefehl *m* (EDV) return instruction
Rückkehr *f* **zu festen Wechselkursen** (AuW) return to fixed parities
Rückkopplung *f* (EDV) feedback
Rückkopplungsschleife *f* (EDV) control (*or* feedback) loop *(syn, Regelkreis)*
Rücklage *f*
(ReW) surplus reserve
– reserve
– appropriated retained earnings
(ie, legal reserve: appropriation of surplus for use in future years; part of equity capital!)
Rücklage *f* **auflösen**
(ReW) to dissolve
– to liquidate
– to retransfer ... a reserve
– to return a reserve to source
Rücklage *f* **bilden**
(ReW) to establish
– to form
– to build up
– to set up ... a reserve, § 150 AktG
Rücklage *f* **e-r Bank** (Fin) bank reserve
Rücklage *f* **erfolgswirksam auflösen** (StR) to retransfer a reserve to taxable income
Rücklage *f* **für aufgeschobene Instandhaltung** (ReW) reserve for repairs
Rücklage *f* **für Erneuerung des Anlagevermögens** (ReW) reserve for renewals and replacements
– reserve for plant extensions
Rücklage *f* **für Ersatzbeschaffung** (ReW) replacement reserve (*or* allowance)
Rücklage *f* **für Preissteigerung** (ReW) reserve for price increases
(ie, of inventory items whose replacement cost has become substantially greater in the course of the taxable year, § 51 I EStG, § 74 EStDV)
Rücklage *f* **für Reinvestitionen** (StR) reserve for reinvestments
(ie, gains on disposal of fixed assets may be transferred to the costs of other assets, thereby reducing taxable profit)
Rücklagen *fpl*
(ReW, EG) reserves
(com, infml) nest egg
– rainy-day reserves
Rücklagenauflösung *f*
(ReW) dissolution
– liquidation
– retransfer ... of a reserve
Rücklagenbildung *f* (ReW) forming (*or* setting up) a reserve (for)

Rücklagen *fpl* **dotieren** (ReW) to add to (*or* transfer to) reserves
Rücklagendotierung *f* (ReW) = Rücklagenzuweisung
Rücklagen *fpl* **stärken** (ReW) to beef up reserves
Rücklagenzuweisung *f* (ReW) allocation (*or* transfer) to reserves
Rücklage *f* **speisen** (ReW) to fund a reserve
Rücklage *f* **umwandeln** (ReW) to retransfer a reserve
rückläufig
(com) declining
– decreasing
– dropping
– falling
– going down
– lowering *(ie, all general terms)*
– flagging *(ie, less stiff)*
– sagging
– softening
– weakening
– dipping *(ie, slightly)*
– slipping *(ie, smoothly)*
– plunging *(ie, suddenly)*
– plummeting *(ie, steeply and suddenly)*
– tumbling *(ie, rapidly)*
rückläufige Konjunktur *f* (Vw) declining economic activity
rückläufiger Aktienmarkt *m*
(Bö) shrinking
– receding
– soft ... market
rückläufiger Preis *m* (com) falling price
rückläufige Tendenz *f* (com) declining trend
rückläufige Überweisung *f* (Fin) automatic debit transfer
rückläufige Umsatzentwicklung *f* (com) falling sales
Rücklaufquote *f*
– response rate
(Stat) number of responses
Rücklaufschrott *m* (IndE) return (*or* home) scrap
Rücklauf *m* **wegen unzureichender Lösungen** (Bw) failure cycles
Rücklieferung *f* (com) return delivery (*or* shipment)
Rückmeldung *f* (EDV) acknowledgment, *(ie, confirming receipt of a message; syn, Bestätigungsmeldung)*
Rücknahme *f*
(Fin) redemption
– repurchase
Rücknahme *f* **der Zulassung** (ReW) revocation of license to practice, § 11 WPO
Rücknahmegarantie *f* (Fin) repurchase guaranty
Rücknahmekurs *m*
(Fin) redemption price
(Fin) cash-in (*or* call) price
(Fin) net asset value *(ie, in investmend funds)*
Rücknahmen *fpl* (Fin) repurchases
Rücknahmesätze *mpl* (Fin) buying rates *(ie, paid by the Bundesbank for money market paper; opp, Abgabesätze)*
Rücknahmewert *m* (Bö) bid value
Rückporto *n* (com) return postage

Rückprämie f
 (Bö) put
 − put option
 − premium for the put
 − put premium
Rückprämie f **mit Nachliefern** (Bö) put of more
Rückprämiengeschäft n
 (Bö) put
 (Bö) trading in puts
Rückprämienkurs m (Bö) put price
Rückprämie f **verkaufen** (Bö) to give for the put
Rückrechnungsverfahren n (ReW) application of grossing-up procedure
Rückrechnung f **von brutto auf netto** (com) netback
Rückreise f **e-s Schiffes** (com) return voyage
Rückrufaktion f (com) recall action (eg, automobiles)
Rucksackproblem n (OR) Knapsack problem
Rückschaltzeichen n (EDV) shift-in character, SI
Rückscheck m (Fin) returned check (syn, Retourscheck)
Rückscheckkonto n (Fin) returned checks account
Rückschein m
 (com) return receipt
 − (GB) advice of receipt, A.R.
 − advice of delivery
Rückschlag m (com) setback
Rückschlag m **erleiden** (com) to suffer a setback
Rückschleusung f **von Geldern** (Fin) recycling of funds
Rückschlußwahrscheinlichkeit f (Stat) inverse probability
Rückseite f
 (com) „on the reverse side"
 − (GB) „overleaf"
Rücksendung f (com) return cargo (or shipment)
Rücksendungen fpl
 (com) returns
 − sales returns
 − returned sales (or purchases)
 − goods returned
rücksetzen
 (EDV) to reset
 (EDV) to backspace
Rücksetzen n
 (EDV) reset
 (EDV) backspace
Rücksetzen n **um e-n Abschnitt** (EDV) rewind tape mark
Rückspesen pl (com) back charges
Rücksprung m (EDV) return
Rücksprungadresse f (EDV) = Rückkehradresse
Rücksprungstelle f (EDV) reentry point
rückspulen (EDV) to rewind
Rückstände mpl (Fin) arrears
rückständige Dividende f (Fin) dividend in arrears
rückständige Lieferung f (com) overdue delivery
rückständige Miete f (com) back rent
rückständige Prämie f (Vers) overdue premium
rückständige Rate f (Fin) back installment
rückständige Steuern fpl (StR) delinquent (or unpaid) taxes
rückständige Tilgungszahlungen fpl (Fin) redemption arrears

rückständige Zinsen mpl (Fin) back interest
Rückstellung f
 (ReW) liability reserve
 − provision
 − operating reserve
 − withheld accounts
 − reserve for uncertain liabilities and anticipated losses
 (ie, reasonably foreseeable, but uncertain in amount; eg, litigation, warranties, deductible taxes, etc.)
 (Stat) replacement (ie, in sampling)
Rückstellung f **auflösen**
 (ReW) to dissolve
 − to liquidate
 − to retransfer ... a liability reserve
Rückstellung f **bilden**
 (ReW) to establish
 − to form
 − to set up ... a liability reserve
Rückstellungen fpl (ReW, EG) provision for liabilities and charges
Rückstellungen fpl **für Wechselhaftung** (ReW) reserves for liabilities under drafts or bills of exchange, § 103a BewG
Rückstellung f **für Bürgschaftsverpflichtungen** (StR) reserve for guaranties
Rückstellung f **für drohende Verluste aus schwebenden Geschäften** (ReW) special provision for risks (ie, arising in ventures or in trade abroad, § 152 VII AktG)
Rückstellung f **für Eventualverbindlichkeiten** (ReW) = Rückstellung für ungewisse Verbindlichkeiten
Rückstellung f **für Gewährleistungen** (ReW) reserve for warranties, § 152 VII AktG
Rückstellung f **für Haftungsverpflichtungen** (StR) reserve for third-party liability commitments
Rückstellung f **für künftig fällige Provisionen** (StR) reserve for accrued commissions
Rückstellung f **für mögliche Verluste am Vorratsvermögen** (ReW) reserve for possible future losses on inventories
Rückstellung f **für Patentverletzungen** (StR) reserve for patent infringements
Rückstellung f **für Preisnachlässe** (StR) reserve for price reductions, § 103a BewG
Rückstellung f **für Steuerzahlungen** (StR) reserve for accrued taxes (ie, determined during a future tax audit)
Rückstellung f **für uneinbringliche Forderungen** (ReW) reserve (or allowance) for bad debts
Rückstellung f **für ungewisse Verbindlichkeiten** (ReW) reserve for contingencies, § 152 VII AktG
Rückstellung f **für unterlassene Aufwendungen für Instandhaltung** (ReW) reserve for deferred repairs and maintenance, § 152 VII AktG
Rückstellung f **für verjährte Verbindlichkeiten** (ReW) provision for statute-barred liabilities
Rückstellung f **im Kreditgeschäft** (Fin) provision for possible loan losses
Rückstellung f **wegen Bergschäden** (StR) reserve for mining damage
Rückstufung f **von Arbeitsplätzen**

(Pw) downgrading of jobs
- dilution of labor
Rücktritt *m*
(Re) repudiation (of)
- rescission (of)
- withdrawal (from) ... contract
(Pw) retirement from office
Rücktrittsberechtigter *m* (Re) rescinding party, § 350 BGB
Rücktrittserklärung *f* (Re) notice of rescission (*or* withdrawal), § 349 BGB
Rücktrittsklausel *f* (Fin) market-out clause *(ie, permitting withdrawal from a management group)*
Rücktrittsrecht *n*
(Re) right to claim rescission of contract
- right to rescind a contract, §§ 346 ff BGB
(ie, English law does not provide any close parallel)
Rücktritt *m* **vom Vertrage** (Re) rescission of contract, § 346 BGB
rückübertragen (ReW) to retransfer
Rückübertragung *f* (ReW) retransfer
Rückumschlag *m* (com) business reply envelope
rückvergüten
(com) to refund
- to reimburse
Rückvergütung *f* (com) refund
- reimbursement
(Zo) customs drawback
rückversetzen (Pw) to transfer back
Rückversicherer *m*
(Vers) reinsurer
- reinsurance company
- accepting company
- (GB) reassurance company
(syn, Zessionar; opp, Erstversicherer, Zedent)
Rückversicherer-Kette *f* (Vers) string of reinsurers
rückversichern
(Vers) to reinsure
- to buy (*or* effect) reinsurance
- to cede
Rückversicherung *f*
(Vers) reinsurance
- (GB) reassurance
(Vers) reinsurance company
- reinsurer
Rückversicherung *f* **mit Selbstbehalt des Erstversicherers**
(Vers) participating
- pro rata
- share ... reinsurance
Rückversicherungskonsortium *n* (Vers) reinsurance syndicate
Rückversicherungsmakler *m* (Vers) reinsurance broker
Rückversicherungs-Nachweis *m* (Vers) certificate of reinsurance
Rückversicherungsoption *f* (Vers) facultative reinsurance
Rückversicherungspolice *f* (Vers) reinsurance policy
Rückversicherungsprämie *f* (Vers) reinsurance premium
Rückversicherungsquote *f* (Vers) reinsurance quota share

Rückversicherungsvertrag *m* (Vers) reinsurance contract
Rückwälzung *f* **von Steuern** (FiW) backshifting of taxes
Rückwaren *fpl* (com) goods (*or* merchandise) returned
Rückwärtsintegration *f* (Bw) backward integration *(opp, Vorwärtsintegration)*
Rückwärtsrichtung *f* (EDV) reverse direction flow *(ie, in flowcharting)*
Rückwärtsschrittzeichen *n*
(EDV) backspace character, BS
- back-arrow
Rückwärtssteuerung *f* (EDV) backward supervision *(ie, control signals sent from slave to master station)*
Rückwechsel *m*
(Fin) redrafted bill
- redraft
- re-exchange
(syn, Ricambio, Ricambiowechsel)
Rückweisewahrscheinlichkeit *f* (Stat) probability of rejection
rückwirkend bewilligen (StR) to grant with retroactive effect
rückwirkende Lohnerhöhung *f*
(Pw) retroactive pay rise
- (GB) back-dated pay rise
rückwirkendes Gesetz *n*
(Re) retrospective
- retroactive
- ex post facto ... law
rückwirkend vom ... (Re) retroactively as of ...
Rückwirkung *f* (Re, StR) retroactive (*or* retrospective) effect *(ie, of legal provisions)*
Rückwirkungsfreiheit *f* (EDV) absence of reaction
rückzahlbar
(Fin) refundable
- repayable
- redeemable
rückzahlen (com) to pay back
Rückzahlung *f*
(com) refund
- repayment
(Fin) redemption
- payoff
- sinking
- amortization
Rückzahlung *f* **aufschieben** (Fin) to defer repayment
Rückzahlung *f* **bei Endfälligkeit**
(Fin) final redemption
- redemption at term
Rückzahlung *f* **des Kapitals** (Fin) repayment of principal
Rückzahlung *f* **durch Auslosung** (Fin) drawing
Rückzahlung *f* **e-r Anleihe** (Fin) repayment (*or* retirement) of a loan
Rückzahlung *f* **e-r Schuld** (Fin) extinction (*or* repayment) of debt
Rückzahlung *f* **in gleichen Tilgungsraten** (Fin) straight-line redemption
Rückzahlungsagio *n* (Fin) redemption premium
Rückzahlungsbetrag *m* (Fin) amount repayable
Rückzahlungsdisagio *n* (Fin) redemption discount

Rückzahlungsfrist f (Fin) deadline (or time) for repayment
Rückzahlungskurs m (Fin) = *Rückkaufkurs*
Rückzahlungsoption f (Fin) option of repayment
Rückzahlungsprämie f (Fin) redemption premium
Rückzahlungsprovision f (Fin) redemption commission
Rückzahlungsrendite f (Fin) yield to maturity
Rückzahlungstermin m
(Fin) date of repayment
– date of redemption
– deadline for repaying
– maturity date
Rückzahlungswert m (Fin) redemption value
Rückzahlung f **zum Nennwert** (Fin) redemption at par
Rückzoll m (Zo) customs drawback *(ie, on the duties upon re-exporting)*
Rückzollschein m (Zo) customs debenture
Rufanlage f (com) paging system
Rügefrist f (Re) time limit for lodging a complaint
Ruhegehalt n
(SozV) public-service pension
– retirement pension (or pay)
– retired pay
ruhegehaltsfähige Dienstbezüge pl (SozV) pensionable pay
ruhegehaltsfähige Dienstzeit f (SozV) length of pensionable public employment (or service)
ruhegehaltsfähige Einkünfte pl (SozV) pensionable earnings
Ruhegeld n
(SozV) = *Altersruhegeld*
(Pw) supplementary retirement pay
ruhende Konten npl (ReW) inactive accounts
ruhender Verschleiß m
(ReW) disuse
– loss of utility through action of the elements *(ie, as factor of depreciation = Abschreibungsursache)*
Ruheständler m (Pw) retired person
Ruhestandsalter n (Pw) retirement (or retiring) age
Ruhezeit f (EDV) unused time
ruhiger Verlauf m (Bö) calm (or quiet) trading
ruinöse Konkurrenz f (Vw) cut-throat (or destructive) competition
ruinöse Preise mpl (com) ruinously low prices
Rumpfbelegschaft f (Pw) skeleton staff *(eg, during the vacation down-close of businesses)*
Rumpfgeschäftsjahr n (ReW) short fiscal (or business) year
Rumpfwirtschaftsjahr n (StR) short taxable year
runde Klammern fpl (Math) parentheses (sg, -sis)
Rundfahrtproblem n (OR) traveling salesman problem
Rundruf m (EDV) broadcast (syn, Rundspruch)
Rundschreiben n
(com) circular
– circular letter
– (infml) mail shot
Rundungsfehler m (Math) rounding error
Rundverfügung f (StR) circular issued by federal and state ministers of finance, and other high administrative agencies
Rüstkosten pl
(KoR) preproduction cost
– cost of change-over
Rüstprozesse mpl (IndE) preproduction measures *(ie, to prepare tools and machines)*
Rüstzeit f
(IndE) change-over time
– make-ready time
– setup time
– tear-down time
Rüstzeit f **nach Arbeitsschluß** (IndE) shut-down time

S

Saatgut n (com) seeds
Sabotage f (Bw) sabotage *(ie, underhand interference with work)*
Sachanlagebuch n (ReW) plant (or property) ledger
Sachanlagekonto n (ReW) fixed asset account
Sachanlagen fpl
(ReW) tangible fixed assets
(ReW) property, plant, and equipment
Sachanlagenintensität f (Bw) ratio of tangible fixed assets to total assets
Sachanlageninvestition f (Fin) capital expenditure
Sachanlagen fpl **und immaterielle Anlagewerte** mpl (ReW) property, plant, equipment and intangible assets
Sachanlagenzugänge mpl (ReW) fixed asset additions
Sachanlagevermögen n (ReW) tangible fixed assets *(ie, all movable and immovable physical assets; opp, immaterielle Güter des Anlagevermögens, Beteiligungen, Finanzanlagen = intangible fixed assets, trade and financial investments)*
Sachaufwand m
(Fin) operating expenses
(FiW) operating expenditure
Sachaufwendungen mpl (StR) tangible benefits *(ie, granted to employees)*
Sachausschüttung f (Fin) distribution in kind
Sach-Bargründung f (Re) formation of a company on a combined basis of cash and noncash contributions
Sachbearbeiter m
(com) person in charge (of)
– person handling ...
(Re) official in charge (of)
(ie, this German catch-all term requires a context-linked translation; he or she is found in private businesses no less than in administrative agencies)
Sachbefugnis f (Re) accrual of substantive claim to

plaintiff *(ie, term is an extension of ‚Aktivlegitimation' = capacity to sue, § 50 ZPO; syn, Sachlegitimation)*
Sachbeschädigung *f* (Re) damage (*or* injury) to property, § 303 StGB
Sachbesteuerung *f* (FiW) taxation of specific property *(syn, Objekt- od Realbesteuerung)*
sachbezogen (Bw) task oriented
Sachbezüge *pl*
(Pw) remuneration in kind
– nonmonetary compensation
Sachbezugsverordnung *f* (SozV) Ordinance Regulating the Value of Tangible Benefits for the Purposes of Social Security, as of 1978
Sachdepot *n* (Fin) security deposit
Sachdepotbuch *n* (Fin) register of security deposits *(opp, Personendepot)*
Sachdividende *f*
(Fin) dividend in kind
– commodity (*or* property) dividend
Sache *f* (Re) corporeal thing, § 90 BGB *(ie, includes liquids and gases)*
Sacheinlage *f*
(Bw) contribution in kind
– non-cash contribution
– contribution other than cash
(syn, Apport, Illation; opp, Geldeinlage = cash contribution)
Sacheinlageaktie *f* (Fin) non-cash share
Sachenmehrheit *f* (Re) plurality of things
Sachenrecht *n* (Re) law of (real and personal) property *(ie, third book of German Civil Code, §§ 854–1296 BGB; must be read in conjunction with the first book of the Code dealing with things, §§ 90ff BGB)*
Sachenrechte *npl* (Re) rights in respect of corporeal things *(eg, property, usufruct, servitudes, etc.; syn, dingliche Rechte)*
sachenrechtliche Übertragung *f* (WeR) transfer by agreement and delivery
sachenrechtliche Wertpapiere *npl* (WeR) securities evidencing property rights *(eg, mortgage deed, land charge deed)*
Sache *f* **zurückverweisen** (StR) to remand a case, § 126 III FGO
Sachfirma *f* (Re) firm name derived from the object of the enterprise
Sachgebiet *n*
(com) functional area
– (special) field
(Log) subject area
sachgemäßer Gebrauch *m* (Re) proper use
sachgerechte Bewertung *f* (ReW) proper evaluation
Sachgesamtheit *f*
(Re) conglomeration of property
– aggregate of things
(ReW) group of assets
Sachgesellschaft *f* (Vers) property insurance company *(opp, Lebensversicherer = life insurer)*
Sachgründung *f* (Re) formation of a company on the basis of non-cash contributions
Sachgründungsbericht *m* (Re) non-cash contribution report
Sachgüter *npl*

(Bw) nonmonetary assets
– physical assets
– tangible assets
Sachgüterproduktion *f* (Bw) production of physical goods *(ie, Produktion i.e.S.)*
Sachinbegriff *m* (Re) conglomeration of property
Sachinvestition *f*
(Fin) real investment
(FiW) spending (*or* expenditure) on fixed assets
Sachkapital *n* (Vw) real (*or* nonmonetary) capital *(syn, Realkapital)*
Sachkapitalerhöhung *f* (Fin) increase of noncash capital, §§ 183, 194, 205 ff AktG
Sachkonto *n*
(ReW) impersonal
– nonpersonal
– general ledger ... account
(syn, Hauptbuchkonto; opp, Personenkonto = personal account)
Sachkontonummer *f* (ReW) general ledger account number
Sachkosten *pl* (ReW) cost of materials
Sachkredit *m* (Fin) collateral loan *(opp, Personalkredit)*
Sachlegitimation *f* (Re) = *Sachbefugnis*
Sachleistungen *fpl*
(com) payment in kind
(Re) contribution in kind
– non-cash capital contributions
(SozV) benefits in kind
– benefits other than money
– non-cash benefits
– in-kind benefits
Sachleistungsvertrag *m* (Re) contract for the supply of goods and services
sachlich differenzierte Exportförderung *f* (AuW) export promotion restricted to specified range of commodities
sachliche Abgrenzung *f* (ReW) allocation of expense unrelated to the operational purpose
sachliche Befreiung *f* (Re) exemption in relation to a subject matter
sachliche Entscheidung *f* (com) objective decision
sachliche Richtigkeit *f* (com) substantive accuracy (*or* correctness)
sachlicher Irrtum *m* (Re) mistake of fact
sachlicher Verteilzeitzuschlag *m* (IndE) contingency allowance
sachliche Zuständigkeit *f* (Re) jurisdiction over subject-matter
sachlich gerechtfertigter Grund *m* (Re) justifiable cause
sachlich zuständig (com) functionally competent
Sachlohn *m* (Pw) wages (*or* compensation) in kind *(syn, Naturallohn)*
Sachmangel *m* (Re) redhibitory defect (*or* vice) *(ie, defect in an article against which the seller is contractually bound to warrant)*
Sachmängelhaftung *f*
(Re) liability for defects, §§ 459ff BGB
– warranty of quality
Sachmittel *pl* (Bw) physical resources
Sachmittelanalyse *f* (Bw) analysis of physical resources
Sachpatent *n* (Pat) product patent

519

Sachrückversicherung f (Vers) property reinsurance
Sachschaden m
   (Re) damage to property
   – injury to property
   – physical damage
   (Vers) loss of property
Sachschäden-Haftpflichtversicherung f (Vers) property-damage liability insurance
Sachschadenrisiko n (Vers) property risk
Sachschadenversicherung f (Vers) property damage insurance
Sachsteuern fpl
   (StR) taxes imposed on an object *(ie, a specific object, such as a parcel of real property, or a conglomeration of property, such as a business)*
   – impersonal taxes
Sachübernahme f (Re) aquisition of assets upon formation, § 27 AktG
Sach- und Dienstleistungskosten pl (ReW) cost of materials and services
Sachvergütung f (Pw) payment in kind
Sachverhalt m
   (Re) facts
   (Re) factual frame
Sachvermögen n
   (Vw) fixed capital *(syn, Realvermögen)*
   (ReW) non-financial assets
Sachvermögensbildung f
   (Vw) productive investment
   – investment in fixed assets and inventories
   – formation of material wealth
   (opp, financial investment)
Sachversicherer m (Vers) property insurance company
Sachversicherung f
   (Vers) business
   – commercial
   – non-life
   – property ... insurance
Sachverständigenausschuß m (com) expert committee
Sachverständigenbeirat m (Vw) advisory council of experts
Sachverständigen m **bestellen** (com) to appoint an expert
Sachverständigengutachten n (com) expert opinion
Sachverständigen m **hinzuziehen**
   (com) to call in *(or* consult) an expert
   – to employ the services of an expert
Sachverständigenrat m (Vw) German Council of Economic Experts
Sachverständiger m
   (com) expert
   – outside expert
   – special expert
   (Vers) appraiser
   – valuer
   (Pat) person skilled in the art
Sachwalter m (Re) trustee of creditors, § 91 VerglO
Sachwert m
   (com) physical *(or* tangible) asset
   (StR) asset value *(ie, standard of value applied to ‚sonstige bebaute Grundstücke'* = *other improved properties,* §§ 83 ff BewG)
   (Fin) intrinsic value
Sachwertanleihe f (Fin) commodity-based loan *(ie, secured by staples like potash, coal, timber, sugar; in Germany between 1922 and 1924)*
Sachwertdividende f (Fin) = Sachdividende
Sachwerte mpl
   (Vw) real assets
   (Fin) resource-based assets *(eg, investors sought ...)*
Sachwertklausel f (com) = Warenpreisklausel
Sachwertschwankungen fpl (ReW) fluctuations in real value
Sachwertverfahren n (StR) asset value method *(ie, aggregate tentative values for land, buildings, and other improvements are corrected to arrive at the fair market value of the entire property,* §§ 83 ff BewG)
Sachwucher m (Re) = Leistungswucher
Sachziel n (Bw) substantive goal *(opp, Formalziel = formal objective)*
sachzielorientiertes Verhalten n (Bw) task-oriented behavior
Sack m (com) bag
Safe m od n **mieten** (Fin) to rent a safe deposit box
Safevertrag m (Fin) safe deposit box agreement
saftige Preise mpl (com, sl) fishy prices
Saftladen m (com, sl) inefficiently run establishment
Saisonabweichung f (Stat) = Saisonschwankung
saisonal bereinigen
   (Stat) to adjust seasonally
saisonale Arbeitslosigkeit f (Vw) seasonal unemployment
saisonale Schwankung f (Stat) = Saisonschwankung
Saisonarbeit f (Pw) seasonal work
Saisonarbeiter m (Pw) seasonal worker
Saisonartikel mpl (com) seasonal goods *(or* articles)
Saisonausverkauf m (com) = Saisonschlußverkauf
Saison-Band n (Stat) = Saison-Index
saisonbedingter Aufschwung m (Vw) seasonal recovery
saisonbereinigt (Stat) seasonally adjusted
Saisonbereinigung f (Stat) seasonal adjustment
Saisonbetrieb m (com) seasonal enterprise
Saisonbewegung f (Stat) = Saisonschwankung
Saisonindex m (Stat) seasonal index
   (ie, Unterbegriffe: Monatsdurchschnittsverfahren, Gliedziffernverfahren, Verfahren der Saisonnormalen)
Saisonkoeffizient m (Stat) seasonal coefficient
Saisonkorridor m (Stat) high-low graph
Saisonkredit m (Fin) seasonal credit *(ie, granted to farming and fishery establishments, etc.)*
Saisonschlußverkauf m (com) end-of season clearance sale *(ie, at reduced prices)*
Saisonschwankung f (Stat) seasonal variation
Saisonwanderung f (Stat) seasonal migration
Saisonwaren fpl (com) seasonal products
Saison-Zahl f (Stat) seasonal average
säkulare Inflation f (Vw) secular inflation
säkularer Trend m (Stat) secular trend
säkulare Stagnation f (Vw) secular stagnation

säkulare Stagnationstheorie *f* (Vw) theory of secular stagnation *(J. M. Keynes and A. Hansen)*
Säkulargleichung *f* (Math) secular equation
Saldenabstimmung *f* (ReW) balance reconciliation
Saldenaufstellung *f* (ReW) balance-of account statement
Saldenausgleich *m* (AuW) settlement of balance
Saldenbestätigung *f* (ReW) statement of balance
Saldenbilanz *f* (ReW) list of balances
Saldendatei *f*
  (ReW) open item balance
  – balance file
Saldenkarte *f* (ReW) balance card
Saldenliste *f* (ReW) list of current account balances
Saldenprüfung *f* (ReW) balance control
Saldenumbuchung *f* (ReW) carry forward
saldieren
  (ReW) to balance (out)
  – to net out *(eg, accounts, debits and credits)*
Saldieren *n*
  (ReW) balancing out
  – netting out
Saldierungsverbot *n* (ReW) prohibition to offset accounts payable against accounts receivable
Saldierwerk *n* (EDV) accumulator *(ie, electronic unit for performing arithmetic)*
Saldo *m*
  (ReW) balance
  – account balance
  – balance of account
Saldoanerkenntnis *f* (Re) confirmation of balance
Saldo *m* **der amtlichen Verrechnungen** (AuW) official settlements balance
Saldo *m* **der Erwerbs- und Vermögenseinkommen zwischen Inländern und der übrigen Welt** (VGR) net factor income payments from the rest of the world
Saldo *m* **der Kapitalbilanzen** (VGR) balance of capital transactions
Saldo *m* **der laufenden Übertragungen** (VGR) net current transfers
Saldo *m* **der laufenden Übertragungen zwischen inländischen Wirtschaftseinheiten und der übrigen Welt** (VGR) net current transfer from the rest of the world
Saldo *m* **der laufenden Posten** (AuW) balance of current transactions
Saldo *m* **der Leistungsbilanz** (VGR) balance on current account
Saldo *m* **der nicht erfaßten Posten und statistischen Ermittlungsfehler** (VGR) net errors and omissions *(ie, on current and capital accounts)*
Saldo *m* **der statistisch erfaßten Transaktionen** (VGR) balance of recorded transactions
Saldo *m* **der statistisch nicht aufgliederbaren Transaktionen**
  (VGR) balance of unclassifiable transactions
  – accommodating *(or* balancing) items
  – errors and omissions
  (syn, Restposten der Zahlungsbilanz)
Saldo *m* **der Zahlungsbilanz** (AuW) balance of payments surplus *(or* deficit, *as the case may be)*
Saldovortrag *m*
  (ReW) balance carried forward
  (ReW) balance brought forward

SAL-Pakete *npl* (com) SAL *(surface air lifted)* parcels
salvatorische Klausel *f* (Re) escape clause
Salzsteuer *f* (StR) excise tax on salt
Sammelabschreibung *f*
  (ReW) group depreciation
  – composite-life method of depreciation
  (ie, applying a single rate to a group of assets of the same general class = Gruppe gleichartiger Wirtschaftsgüter; syn, Pauschalabschreibung)
Sammelaktie *f* (Fin) multiple share certificate *(ie, evidencing large share holding, not widely used in Germany; syn, Globalaktie)*
Sammelanleihe *f* (Fin) joint loan issue *(ie, floated by a number of municipalities)*
Sammelanschluß *m* (com) private branch exchange
Sammelaufstellung *f* (com) collective list
Sammelauftrag *m* (Fin) bulk order
Sammelbehälter *m* (MaW) accumulation *(or* assembly) bin *(ie, for allocated materials = für auftragsbezogene Teile)*
Sammelbeleg *m* (ReW) collective-entry voucher
Sammelbestand *m* (Fin) collective security holding
Sammelbestellung *f*
  (com) collective order
  (com) multi-copy order *(ie, of books)*
Sammelbewertung *f* (ReW) group valuation *(ie, of items similar in kind and price; syn, Pauschalbewertung)*
Sammelblatt *n* (ReW) grouping sheet
Sammelbogen *m* (ReW) recapitulation sheet
Sammelbuch *n*
  (ReW) general journal *(syn, Sammeljournal)*
Sammelbuchung *f* (ReW) compound entry
Sammeldepot *n*
  (Fin) collective securities deposit
  (Fin) collective safe deposit
Sammeldepotkonto *n* (Fin) collective deposit account
Sammeleinkauf *m* (com) group buying
Sammelfaktura *f* (com) monthly billing
Sammelgang *m* (EDV) group printing *(opp, Einzelgang)*
Sammelgenehmigung *f* (com) collective authorization
Sammelinkasso *n* (Fin) centralized collection
Sammeljournal *n* (ReW) = *Sammelbuch*
Sammelkonnossement *n*
  (com) grouped
  – omnibus
  – collective ... bill of lading
Sammelkonto *n*
  (ReW) assembly
  – absorption
  – collective
  – control(ling)
  – summary
  – intermediate clearing ... account
Sammelladung *f*
  (com) consolidated shipment
  – consolidation
  – (GB) grouped *(or* collective) consignment
  – (GB) grouped shipment
  – mixed *(or* pooled) consignment
  – joint cargo

Sammelladungs-Konnossement n (com) combined (or groupage) bill of lading
Sammelladungsspediteur m (com) grouped consignment forwarder, § 413 HGB
Sammelladungsspedition f (com) grouped consignment forwarding
Sammelladungsverkehr m (com) groupage traffic
Sammelmappe f (com) loose-leaf binder
Sammelpolice f
  (Vers) general
  – group
  – package ... policy
Sammelposten m (ReW) collective item
Sammelrechnung f (com) unit billing
Sammelschiene f (IndE) bus bar
Sammelsendung f (com) combined shipment
Sammeltarif m (com) group rate
Sammeltransport m (com) collective transport
Sammelüberweisung f (Fin) combined bank transfer
Sammelurkunde f (Fin) global certificate
Sammelversicherung f (Vers) group (or collective) insurance
Sammelversicherungsvertrag m (Vers) general (or group) policy
Sammelverwahrung f
  (Fin) collective safekeeping of securities
  – (US) bulk segregation
Sammelweg m
  (EDV) bus
  – highway
  – trunk (syn, Bus, Pfad)
Sammelwertberichtigung f (ReW) global value adjustment
  – overall contingency reserve
  (ie, set up to provide against contingent receivables losses; syn, Pauschaldelkredere; opp, Einzelwertberichtigung)
Sammelwertberichtigung f **auf Kredite** (ReW) global loan writeoff provision
Sandkastenmodell n (IndE) lilliputian model
sanieren
  (Fin) to reorganize
  – (GB) to reconstruct
  (com, infml) to refloat
  – to reforge
  – to reshape
  – to revamp
  – to revitalize
  – to put new life into
saniertes Baugebiet n (com) rehabilitated (or upgraded) area
Sanierung f
  (com) rescue operation (or package)
  (Fin) recapitalization
  – capital reconstruction
  – capital reorganization (ie, capital writedown + restocking with fresh capital)
Sanierung f **der Rentenfinanzen** (SozV) consolidation of pension funds' finances
Sanierungsbilanz f
  (ReW) recapitalization balance sheet
  – capital reconstruction statement
  – (GB) reconstruction accounts
Sanierungsbündel n (Fin) rescue package

Sanierungsdarlehen n (Fin) reorganization loan
Sanierungsgewinn m
  (ReW) recapitalization gains
  – reorganization surplus
  (ie, from wiping out company debts)
Sanierungs-Konsortium n (Fin) backing (or reconstruction) syndicate
Sanierungskonzept n
  (Bw) recovery strategy
  – rescue package
Sanierungskredit m
  (Fin) reorganization loan
  – (GB) reconstruction loan
Sanierungsplan m (Fin) financial rescue plan
Sanierungsprogramm n
  (Fin) rescue package (or scheme)
  – reorganization scheme
Sanierungsübersicht f (ReW) reorganization statement (ie, listing assets and liabilities valued on three different bases: (1) as shown in the accounts; (2) continued operation; (3) discontinuance and disposal)
Sanierungsumgründung f (Re) reconstruction and reorganization of a company
Sanierungsvergleich m (Re) composition agreement with creditors
Satellitenrechner m (EDV) satellite computer (syn, Vorrechner)
Satellitensteuer f (StR) satellite tax (ie, levied in connection with another tax; eg, church tax based on income tax)
Satellitensystem n (EDV) remote computing processor
  – satellite system
Sattelpunkt m
  (Math) saddle point
  – point of stagnation
Sattelpunktsatz m (OR) minimax theorem
Sattelzug m
  (com) trailer truck
  – (GB) articulated lorry (short: artic)
  – (GB, infml) bender
Sättigung f
  (Mk) saturation of a market
  (Mk) rate of public acceptance
Sättigungsgesetz n (Vw) law of satiety
Sättigungsgrenze f (Mk) absorption point
Sättigungsmenge f (Vw) volume of saturation (ie, at which zero price obtains)
Sättigungsnachfrage f (Vw) saturation demand
Sättigungsphase f (Mk) saturation stage (ie, of product life cycle)
Sättigungspunkt m (Vw) saturation point (ie, where demand function intersects abscissa)
Sättigungswerbung f (Mk) saturation advertising
Satz m
  (com) rate
  (Log) statement
  (EDV) data (or logical) record
Satzadresse f (EDV) record address
Satzadressendatei f (EDV) record address file
Satzanzahl f (EDV) record count
Satzende n (EDV) end of record
Satzendekennzeichen n (EDV) end-of-record label
Satzendewort n (EDV) end of record word

Sätze *mpl* **unter Banken** (Fin) interbank money market rates
Satz *m* **fester Länge** (EDV) fixed length record
Satzfolge *f* (EDV) record sequence
Satzformat *n* (EDV) record format
Satz *m* **für Tagesgeld** (Fin) call (*or* overnight) rate
Satzgruppe *f* (EDV) grouped records
Satzlänge *f* (EDV) record length
Satzlücke *f* (EDV) interrecord gap
Satzmarke *f* (EDV) record marker
Satzname *m* (EDV, Cobol) data record name
Satzprüfung *f* (EDV) record checking
Satzstruktur *f* (EDV) record layout
Satzung *f*
 (Re) charter
 (Re) articles of incorporation, § 2 AktG
 – corporate articles
 – (US) charter and bylaws
 – (GB) memorandum and articles of association
Satzungsänderung *f*
 (Re) alteration of charter
 (Re) amendment to the articles of incorporation, § 119 AktG
satzungsgemäß (Re) in conformity with (*or* conformably to) the charter
satzungsmäßige Befugnisse *fpl* (Re) statutory corporate powers (*ie, transferred by the articles of incorporation*)
satzungsmäßige Benachrichtigung *f* (Re) due notice
satzungsmäßige Einberufung *f* (Re) = *satzungsmäßige Benachrichtigung*
satzungsmäßige Ladung *f* (Re) = *satzungsmäßige Benachrichtigung*
satzungsmäßige Mindesteinlage *f* (Re) statutory minimum contribution
satzungsmäßige Rücklagen *fpl* (ReW, EG) reserves provided for by the articles of association
Satz *m* **variabler Länge** (EDV) variable length record
Satz *m* **Verschiffungspapiere** (com) commercial set (*ie, invoice, draft, bill of lading, insurance policy*)
Satz *m* **vom zureichenden Grunde** (Log) principle of sufficient reason
Satzzählung *f* (EDV) record count
Satzzeichen *n* (EDV) punctuation mark
Satzzwischenraum *m* (EDV) interrecord (*or* record) gap
Säulendarstellung *f* (Stat) = *Säulendiagramm*
Säulendiagramm *n*
 (Stat) bar chart (*or* graph)
 – column diagram
 – histogram
säumig (com) defaulting
säumiger Gesellschafter *m* (Re) defaulting shareholder
säumiger Schuldner *m*
 (com) debtor in arrears (*or* in default)
 – defaulting debtor
 – delinquent debtor
säumiger Zahler *m* (com, infml) tardy payer
säumig sein (com) to default
säumig werden
 (com) to fall (*or* get) behind (*eg, in mortgage payments on a house*)
 (Fin) to default
Säumnisurteil *n* (Re) default judgment
Säumniszuschlag *m*
 (StR) delay penalty (*ie, 1 percent of the delinquent tax, § 240 AO*)
 (Vers) delay penalty
 – delinquency charge
Sauregurkenzeit *f* (com, sl) unhealthy slack period in business
„Saustallquote" *f* (com) rate of inefficiency (*or* muddling through*)
Savage-Axiom *n* (Vw) sure-thing principle (*ie, of decision theory*)
Saysches Theorem *n* (Vw) Say's law
Scanlon-Plan *m* (Pw) Scanlon plan (*ie, incentive plan designed to increase efficiency with opportunity for the accrued savings achieved to be distributed among the workers*)
Scanner-Kassensystem *n* (Mk) checkout scanner
Schachbrettregel *f* (Math) checkerboard rule
Schachtelbeteiligung *f*
 (Fin) equity stake in an affiliated company (*ie, at least 25%*)
 – qualified minority holding
Schachteldividende *f* (Fin) dividend from an interrelated company
Schachtelgesellschaft *f*
 (Re) interrelated company
 (StR) entity claiming the affiliation privilege, § 102 BewG
schachteln (EDV) to nest
Schachtelprivileg *n*
 (StR) „affiliation privilege", § 26 KStG
 – intercompany (*or* intercorporate) privilege (*ie, conditional tax exemption for intercompany dividends, the term applying to income, property, net worth, and trade taxation*)
Schachtelung *f* (EDV) nesting
Schaden *m*
 (Re) damage
 – injury
 – loss
 (*ie, Einbuße an Rechtsgütern = loss or diminution of what is a man's own, occasioned by the fault of another; difference in asset value before and after the event*)
 (Vers) loss (*ie, basis for a claim for indemnity or damages under the terms of an insurance policy*)
Schadenabfindung *f*
 (Re) indemnification
 – claim adjustment
Schadenabteilung *f* (Vers) claims (*or* loss) department
Schadenabwicklung *f*
 (Vers) claims adjustment
 – loss adjustment
 – settlement of claims
Schadenandienung *f* (Vers) = *Schadenanzeige*
Schadenanfall *m* (Vers) incidence of loss
Schaden *m* **anmelden** (Vers) to give notice of claim
Schadenanspruch *m* (Vers) insurance claim
Schadenanzeige *f* (Vers) notification of damage (*or* loss)
Schadenattest *n*

523

(SeeV) certificate of damage
– survey report
Schadenaufmachung *f* (SeeV) average adjustment (*or* statement)
Schadenaufstellung *f* (Re) statement of damage
Schadenausgleich *m*
(Vers) compensation for damage
(SeeV) contributions
Schaden *m* **bearbeiten** (Vers) to handle (*or* process) a claim
Schadenbearbeitung *f*
(Vers) claims handling (*or* processing)
(Vers) claims handling department
schadenbegründende Ursache *f* (Vers) proximate cause
Schaden *m* **beheben**
(com) to repair a damage
– to rectify (*or* remedy) a defect
Schadenbetrag *m* (Vers) amount of loss
Schaden *m* **durch inneren Verderb** (com) damage by intrinsic defects
Schadeneintritt *m* (Vers) occurrence of a loss
Schadeneintrittswahrscheinlichkeit *f* (Vers) probability of loss
Schadenereignis *n* (Vers) damaging event
Schadenermittlung *f* (Re) ascertainment of damage
Schadenersatz *m*
(Re) damages
– compensation in damages
(*ie, the basic rule of ‚Naturalherstellung' is that the person who has suffered loss or injury cannot claim pecuniary compensation, §§ 249–255 BGB*)
Schadenersatzanspruch *m* (Re) claim for damages
Schadenersatzansprüche *mpl* **geltend machen** (Re) to claim damages
Schadenersatz *m* **beantragen** (Re) to advance (*or* put in) a claim for damages
Schadenersatz *m* **erwirken** (Re) to collect (*or* recover) damages
Schadenersatz *m* **für Folgeschaden** (Re) consequential damages
Schadenersatz *m* **in Geld**
(Re) compensation in money
– pecuniary damages
Schadenersatzklage *f* (Re) action to recover damages
Schadenersatz *m* **leisten** (Re) to pay damages
Schadenersatzleistung *f* (Re) payment of damages
Schadenersatzlimit *n* (Vers) aggregate limit
Schadenersatzpflicht *f*
(Re) liability for damages
– obligation to compensate (*or* pay damages)
schadenersatzpflichtig (Re) liable in damages (*or* to pay damages)
Schadenersatz *m* **wegen Nichterfüllung** (Re) (pecuniary) damages for nonperformance
Schadenersatz *m* **wegen unerlaubter Handlung** (Re) damages in tort
Schadenersatz *m* **zuerkennen** (Re) to award damages
Schadenerwartung *f* (Vers) expectation of loss
Schadenexzedent *m* (Vers) excess of loss
Schadenexzedentdeckung *f* (Vers) loss excess cover

Schadenexzedenten-Rückversicherung *f* (Vers) excess of loss reinsurance
Schaden *m* **festsetzen** (com) to assess a damage
Schaden *m* **feststellen** (SeeV) to calculate the individual contributions
Schadenfeststellung *f* (Vers) ascertainment of damage (*or* loss)
Schadenfreiheitsrabatt *m* (Vers) no-claim bonus
Schadenfrequenz *f* (Vers) = *Schadenhäufigkeit*
Schadenhaftung *f* (Re) liability for damages
Schadenhäufigkeit *f* (Vers) incidence of loss
Schadenhöhe *f*
(com) amount of loss
– extent of damage
Schadenmaximum *n* (com) loss limit
Schadenmeldung *f*
(Vers) damage report
– notice of damage
Schadenminderungspflicht *f* (Re) doctrine of avoidable consequences
Schadennachweis *m* (Re) proof of loss
Schadenprüfung *f* (Vers) damage survey
Schadenquote *f*
(Vers) claims percentage
– loss ratio
Schaden *m* **regulieren** (Vers) to adjust a damage
Schadenregulierer *m*
(Vers) claim adjuster
– claims assessor
– claim inspector
– claim representative
– settling agent
– (GB) assessor
(SeeV) average adjuster
Schadenregulierung *f*
(Vers) claim (*or* loss) adjustment
– claim (*or* loss) settlement
– settlement of claims
(SeeV) average adjustment
Schadenregulierungskosten *pl* (Vers) loss adjustment expenses
Schadenreserve *f* (Vers) = *Schadenrückstellung*
Schadenrückstellung *f* (Vers) loss reserve (*ie, set up for losses reported but not yet paid*)
Schadensachbearbeiter *m* (Vers) claim adjuster
Schadensachverständiger *m* (Vers) insurance adjuster
Schadensersatz *m* (Re) = *Schadenersatz*
Schadensfall *m*
(Vers) claim
– damaging event
Schadensfall *m* **tritt ein** (Vers) insured loss (*or* risk) occurs
Schaden *m* **tragen** (com) to bear a loss
Schadenüberschuß *m* (Vers) excess of loss
Schadenumschichtung *f* (Vers) redistribution of loss
schadenunerhebliche Ursache *f* (Re) remote cause
Schadenursache *f* (Vers) cause of loss
Schadenverhütung *f* (Vers) loss prevention
Schadenverlauf *m* (Vers) loss experience
Schadenverlauf *m* **des einzelnen Versicherers** (Vers) individual experience
Schadenversicherung *f* (Vers) casualty insurance (*opp, Summenversicherung*)

Schaden m verursachen (com) to cause loss (or damage)
Schadenwahrscheinlichkeit f (Vers) probability of future losses
Schaden m zufügen (Re) to inflict injury (on)
schädigende Handlung f (Re) harmful (or injurious) act
Schadlosbürge m (Re) collection guarantor
Schadlosbürgschaft f
(Re) guaranty of collection
– (GB) deficiency (or deficit) guarantee
– indemnity bond
schadlos halten
(Re) to indemnify
– to save harmless
Schadloshaltung f
(Re) indemnification
– indemnity
Schadloshaltungsklausel f (Re) hold-harmless clause
Schaffung f **neuer Arbeitsplätze** (Vw) creation of new employment
Schaffung f **von Arbeitsplätzen** (Pw) creation of jobs
Schaffung f **von Ausbildungsplätzen** (Pw) creation of training openings
Schaffung f **von zusätzlichem Geld** (Vw) creation of additional money
Schaltalgebra f (EDV) logic (or switching) algebra
Schaltanweisung f (EDV, Cobol) alter statement
Schaltbrett n
(EDV) plugboard
– patchboard (syn, Steckbrett)
Schaltelement n
(EDV) logic element
– gate
Schalter m
(com) counter
(OR) channel
– server
– service facility
(syn, Bedienungsstation, Abfertigung, Kanal)
Schalterbeamter m (com) cashier
Schaltergeschäft n (Fin) counter transactions (eg, simultaneous purchase and cash payment „at the counter"; syn, Tafelgeschäft)
Schaltermaschine f (EDV) teller terminal
Schalterprovision f (Fin) selling commission (ie, paid by a member of an underwriting syndicate to another for selling part of their securities quota to the public)
Schaltersteuerung f (EDV) switch controller
Schalterterminal n (EDV) counter terminal
Schaltfeld n (EDV) control panel
Schaltglied n
(EDV) logical element
– gate
Schaltplan m (EDV) switching diagram
Schaltplatte f (EDV) plugboard
Schaltschema n (EDV) circuit diagram
Schalttafel f
(EDV) control (or patch) panel
– jackfield
(syn, Stecktafel)
Schalttafelsteuerung f (EDV) panel control

Schaltungstechnologie f (EDV) circuit technology
Schaltvariable f (EDV) switching variable
Schaltwerk n (EDV) sequential logic system
Schaltzeichen n (EDV) gate symbol (eg, UND, ODER, NAND, NOR)
Schaltzeit f (EDV) switching time
scharf ansteigen
(com) to soar
– to leap
– to shoot up
– to bounce up
– to increase sharply
Schärfe f **e-s Tests** (Stat) power of a test
scharfe Konkurrenz f (com) = scharfer Wettbewerb
scharfe Rezession f (Vw) severe recession
scharfer Wettbewerb m
(com) bitter
– fierce
– intense
– keen
– severe
– stiff ... competition
scharf kalkuliert (com) with a low margin
scharf kalkulierter Preis m (com) close price
Scharparameter m (Math) family of straight lines
Schattenpreise mpl (Vw, OR) shadow (or accounting) prices
Schattenspeicher m (EDV) nonaddressable (or shaded) memory
Schattenwirtschaft f
(Vw) underground
– subterranean
– shadow
– dual (or parallel)
– informal (or irregular)
– cash
– moonlight
– (GB) black
– (sl) „Black & Decker" ... economy
(ie, this portion of gnp, being nonreported or under-reported, is not measured by official statistics)
Schatzanweisung f (FiW) treasury note
Schätze mpl (FiW) = Schatzanweisungen
schätzen
(com) to estimate (at)
– to appraise
– to assess (at)
– to put (at) (eg, putting the rise at 4%)
– (infml) to guesstimate
(ReW) to tax
Schätzer m
(com) appraiser
– valuer
– evaluator
– assessor
(Zo) appraising officer
Schätzfehler m (Stat) error of estimation
Schätzfunktion f (Stat) estimate
Schätzgleichung f (Stat) estimating equation
Schätzklausel f (Vers) appraisal clause
Schätzkosten pl (com) estimated cost
Schätzmethode f (Stat) method of estimation
Schatzpapiere npl (Fin) treasury certificates

Schätzung *f*
(com) estimate
– appraisal
(com) estimation
– appraisement
– valuation
(StR) determination of taxable income by estimate, § 162 I AO
Schätzung *f* **bei beschränkter Information** (Stat) limited information estimate
Schätzung *f* **mit kleinstmöglicher Varianz** (Stat) minimum variance estimate
Schätzung *f* **von Besteuerungsgrundlagen** (StR) estimate of tax bases, § 162 AO
– estimated assessment
Schatzwechsel *m* (FiW) Treasury bill *(ie, placed by the Bundesbank with the banks on a tap basis; normally held to maturity – 90 days –, but resold to the Bundesbank if liquidity is short)*
Schatzwechselkredit *m* (FiW) credit based on the purchase of Treasury bills
Schätzwert *m*
(com) estimated value
– estimate
(Stat) estimator
Schaubild *n* (Stat) graph
Schaufenster *n*
(Mk) shop window
– (US) store window
Schaufensterauslage *f* (Mk) window display
Schaufensterwerbung *f* (Mk) shop window advertising
Schaukasten *m* (Mk) display case
Schaumweinsteuer *f*
(StR) champagne tax
– excise tax on champagne
Schaupackung *f* (Mk) display package
Schauwerbegestalter *m* (Mk) display designer
Scheck *m*
(Fin) check
– (GB) cheque
Scheckabrechnungsmaschine *f* (Fin) check processor
Scheckabrechnungsverkehr *m* (Fin) clearance of checks
Scheckabteilung *f* (Fin) check processing and collecting department
Scheck *m* **ausschreiben** (Fin) to write out a check
Scheck *m* **ausstellen** (Fin) to write out a check
Scheck *m* **ausstellen auf** (com) to make check payable to
Scheckaussteller *m* (Fin) maker *(or* drawer*)* of a check
Scheckbetrug *m*
(Fin) check fraud
– (infml) paperhanging
Scheckbuch *n* (Fin) check register
Scheckbürgschaft *f* (Fin) guaranty for checks, Art. 25–27 ScheckG
Scheckdeckungsanfrage *f* (Fin) check authorization *(or* verification*)*
Scheckdiskontierung *f* (Fin) discounting of checks
Scheckeinlösegebühr *f* (Fin) check encashment charge
Scheck *m* **einlösen**

(Fin) to cash a check
(Fin) to pay a check
Scheckeinlösung *f*
(Fin) encashment of a check
(Fin) payment of a check
Scheck *m* **einreichen** (Fin) to present a check
Scheckeinreichung *f* (Fin) presentation of a check
Scheckeinreichungsformular *n* (Fin) check paying-in slip
Scheckeinreichungsfrist *f* (Fin) time limit for presentation of a check
Scheck *m* **einziehen** (Fin) to collect a check
Scheckeinzug *m* (Fin) check collection *(syn, Scheckinkasso)*
Scheckfähigkeit *f* (WeR) capacity to draw or indorse checks, Art. 3, 60ff ScheckG
Scheck *m* **fälschen** (Fin) to counterfeit a check
Scheckformular *n* (Fin) check form
Scheckheft *n* (Fin) check book
Scheckinhaber *m* (WeR) bearer of a check
Scheckinkasso *n* (Fin) check collection *(syn, Scheckeinzug)*
Scheckkarte *f* (Fin) check identification card
Scheckklausel *f* (Fin) check clause *(ie, statutory wording: ,,Zahlen Sie gegen diesen Scheck")*
Scheckleiste *f*
(Fin) counterfoil
– stub
Scheckmißbrauch *m* (Fin) = *Scheckbetrug*
Schecknehmer *m* (Fin) payee of a check
Scheck *m* **nicht einlösen** (Fin) to dishonor a check
Scheckprozeß *m* (Re) check proceedings, § 605a ZPO
Scheckrecht *n* (Re) law relating to checks
Scheckreiterei *f* (Fin) check kiting
Scheckrückgabe *f* (Fin) return of an unpaid check
Scheckrückrechnung *f* (Fin) check return bill
Schecksicherung *f* (EDV, Cobol) check protest
Schecksortiermaschine *f* (Fin) check sorter
Schecksperre *f*
(Fin) stop payment order
– cancellation *(or* countermand*)* of a check
Scheck *m* **sperren** (Fin) to stop a check
Scheckumlauf *m* (Fin) checks in circulation
Scheck-Unterschriftenmaschine *f* (Fin) = *Scheckzeichnungsmaschine*
Scheckverkehr *m* (Fin) check transactions
Scheckverrechnung *f* (Fin) check clearing
Scheck *m* **zum Inkasso** (Fin) check for collection
Scheckzahlung *f* (Fin) payment by check
Scheckzeichnungsmaschine *f* (Fin) check signer *(syn, Scheck-Unterschriftenmaschine)*
Schedulensteuer *f* (FiW, GB) schedular taxes
Scheibenspeicher *m* (EDV) magnetic disk storage
Scheidemünzen *fpl* (Vw) low-value coin *(opp, Kurantgeld = current money)*
Schein-Aktiva *npl* (ReW) fictitious assets
Scheinanbieter *m* (com) by-bidder *(ie, employed to bid at an auction in order to raise the prices for the auctioneer or seller)*
Scheinangebot *n* (com) by-bid *(ie, in order to boost a price)*
Scheinargument *n* (Log) dummy argument
scheinbare Variable *f* (Log) bound variable *(syn, gebundene Variable)*

Scheinereignis *n* (OR) dummy event
Scheinfirma *f* (com) ,,paper" company *(ie, used as a training ground for apprentices and junior clerks)*
Scheingebot *n* (com) sham *(or* straw) bid
Scheingeschäft *n*
  (Re) fictitious
  – dummy
  – ostensible
  – sham ... transaction, § 117 BGB
Scheingesellschaft *f* (Re) ostensible company *(ie, operating under its name, but without charter and bylaws)*
Scheingesellschafter *m*
  (Re) nominal
  – ostensible
  – quasi ... partner
  – (GB) holding-out partner
Scheingewinn *m*
  (ReW) paper
  – phantom
  – fictitious ... profit
  – inventory profit *(= aus Vorratshaltung)*
  – (infml) fool's profit
Scheingewinne *mpl* **aus Lagerhaltung**
  (ReW) phantom inventory gains
  – inventory profits
Scheingründung *f* (Re) fictitious formation of a corporation *(ie, without business purpose or actual operations; set up to create a corporate shell; syn, Mantelgründung)*
Scheinhandelsgesellschaft *f* (Re) = *Scheingesellschaft*
Scheinkaufmann *m* (Re) ostensible merchant *(ie, no statutory term: developed in and out of court, see § 5 HGB)*
Scheinkonflikt *m* (Bw) spurious conflict
Scheinkorrelation *f* (Stat) illusory *(or* spurious) correlation
Scheinkurs *m* (Bö) fictitious security price *(syn, Ausweichkurs)*
Scheinproblem *n* (Log) pseudo problem
Scheinvariable *f* (OR) dummy variable
Scheinverlust *m* (ReW) fictitious loss *(opp, Scheingewinn, qv)*
Scheinvertrag *m* (Re) fictitious contract
Scheinvorgang *m* (OR) dummy activity (or job)
Scheitelwert *m* (Math) vertex
Schema *n*
  (Stat) diagram
  – array
Schemabrief *m* (com) standard letter *(ie, identical wording, but addressed to individual persons or firms)*
Schema *n* **der Elemente** (Math) array of elements
schematisiert (Math, Stat) idealized
Schenker *m* (Re) donor
Schenkung *f*
  (Re) gift
  (Re) donation *(ie, disposition by which one person from his property enriches another person, provided both parties agree that there should be no compensation, §§ 516–534 BGB)*
Schenkungsbilanz *f*
  (VGR) balance on transfer account
  – (US) unilateral payments
  (syn, Transferbilanz, Übertragungsbilanz)
Schenkungsteuer *f* (StR) gift tax *(ie, companion tax to ‚Erbschaftsteuer' = inheritance tax)*
Schenkung *f* **unter Auflage** (Re) gift subject to burdens, § 525 BGB
Schenkung *f* **unter Lebenden**
  (Re) gift inter vivos
  (StR) transfer of property inter vivos, § 1 I ErbStG
Schenkung *f* **von Todes wegen**
  (Re) gift *(or* donation) mortis causa, § 2301 BGB
  (StR) gift in contemplation of death, § 3 I ErbStG
Schere *f* (com) gap *(eg, between receipts and expenditures)*
Scherenbewegung *f* (Stat) scissor movement *(eg, of time series in a business cycle diagram)*
scherzhafte Reklame *f* (Mk) facetious advertising
Schicht *f* (Stat) stratum *(pl* strata)
Schichtarbeit *f* (Pw) shift work
Schichtarbeiter *m* (Pw) shift worker
Schichtband *n* (EDV) ferrous coated tape
Schichtbetrieb *m* (IndE) shift operation
Schichtenbildung *f* (Stat) stratification
Schichtführer *m* (Pw) shift manager *(or* foreman)
Schichtkosten *pl* (KoR) cost of extra shift
Schichtleistung *f* (IndE) output per shift
Schichtplan *m* (IndE) shift schedule
Schichtung *f* (Stat) stratification
Schichtwechsel *m* (IndE) turning of shifts *(eg, in a 7-day backward cycle: night – late – early)*
Schichtzulage *f* (Pw) shift premium
Schicksalsgemeinschaft *f* (SeeV) common adventure
Schickschuld *f* (Re) obligation where debtor must send goods or money to creditor
Schiebebefehl *m* (EDV) shift instruction
Schieberegister *n* (EDV) shift register
Schiebetakt *m* (EDV) shift register clock pulse
Schiedsabkommen *n* (Re) arbitration agreement
Schiedsantrag *m* (Re) request for arbitration
Schiedsausschuß *m* (Re) arbitration committee
Schiedsgericht *n*
  (Re) arbitration tribunal
  – court of arbitration
Schiedsgericht *n* **anrufen** (Re) to refer to arbitration
schiedsgerichtliche Beilegung *f* (Re) settlement by way of arbitration
Schiedsgerichtsbarkeit *f*
  (Re) arbitration
  (Re) arbitral jurisdiction
Schiedsgerichtshof *m* (Re) arbitral court
Schiedsgerichtskosten *pl* (Re) cost of arbitration
Schiedsgerichtsordnung *f* (Re) arbitration code
Schiedsgerichtstermin *m* (Re) time appointed for an arbitration hearing
Schiedsgerichtsvereinbarung *f* (Re) agreement to arbitrate
Schiedsgerichtsverfahren *n* (Re) arbitration proceedings
Schiedshof *m* (Re) court of arbitration
Schiedsinstanz *f* (Re) arbitral authority *(or* body)

Schiedsklausel *f*
(Re) clause of arbitration
(Pw) mediation clause
Schiedskommission *f* (Re) arbitration committee
Schiedsobmann *m* (Re) umpire
Schiedsordnung *f* (Re) rules of arbitration *(ie, ‚Vergleichs- und Schiedsordnung der Internationalen Handelskammer', ‚Rules of American Arbitration', etc.)*
Schiedsort *m* (Re) place of arbitration
Schiedsparteien *fpl* (Re) parties to arbitration
Schiedsrichter *m* (Re) arbitrator
schiedsrichterliche Beilegung *f* (Re) arbitrational settlement
schiedsrichterlich entscheiden (Re) to arbitrate
Schiedsspruch *m*
(Re) arbitration award
– arbitral award
– arbitrator's award
Schiedsspruch *m* **fällen** (Re) to render an award
Schiedsspruchwert *m* (Bw) value of an enterprise as a whole *(ie, as determined by an arbitrating expert; syn, Arbitriumwert)*
Schiedsverfahren *n* (Re) arbitration proceedings
Schiedsvergleich *m* (Re) settlement in arbitration proceedings
Schiedsvertrag *m* (Re) arbitration agreement
Schiefe *f* **e–r Verteilung**
(Stat) asymmetry
– skewness
schiefe Verteilung *f* (Stat) asymmetric *(or* skew) distribution
schiefsymmetrisch (Math) skew symmetrical
schiefwinkeliges Koordinatensystem *n* (Math) oblique reference system
Schienenverkehr *m* (com) rail traffic
Schiene/Straße-Güterverkehr *m* (com) ,,combined transport" freight traffic *(ie, going partly by rail and partly by road)*
Schiffahrt *f* (com) shipping
Schiffahrtsabgaben *fpl* (com) navigation charges, § 754 HGB
Schiffahrtsabkommen *n* (Re) shipping *(or* navigation) agreement
Schiffahrtsagent *m* (com) shipping agent
Schiffahrtsgesellschaft *f* (com) shipping company
Schiffahrtskonferenz *f*
(com) freight conference
(com) shipping conference
Schiffahrtskonferenz *f* **der Trampschiffahrt** (com) Baltic and International Maritime Conference
Schiffahrtslinie *f* (com) shipping line
Schiffahrtsrecht *n* (Re) shipping law
Schiffahrtswege *mpl* (com) ocean routes
schiffbare Gewässer *npl* (com) navigable waters
Schiffbauindustrie *f* (com) shipbuilding industry
Schiffbruch *m* (SeeV) shipwreck
Schiff *n* **chartern** (com) to charter *(or* freight) a ship
Schiffer *m*
(com) master, §§ 511–555 HGB
– carrier *(syn, Kapitän)*
Schifferbörse *f* (com) shipping exchange
Schiffsabfahrtsliste *f* (com) sailing list
Schiffsabgaben *fpl* (com) ship's charges

Schiffsagent *m* (com) shipping agent
Schiffsankunftsavis *n* (com) arrival note
Schiffsanteil *m* (com) share in a ship, § 491 HGB
Schiffsbank *f* (Fin) ship mortgage bank
Schiffsdisponent *m* (com) shipping manager, § 492 HGB
Schiffseigentümer *m* (com) shipowner *(ie, in ocean shipping)*
Schiffseigner *m* (com) shipowner *(ie, in inland waterway shipping)*
Schiffsfracht *f*
(com) freight
– cargo
Schiffsfrachten *fpl* (VGR) shipping services
Schiffsgläubiger *m* (Re) maritime lien holder, §§ 754 ff HGB
Schiffshypothek *f* (Re) ship mortgage
Schiffshypothekenbank *f* (Fin) = *Schiffspfandbriefbank*
Schiffskaskoversicherer *m* (Vers) hull underwriter
Schiffskaskoversicherung *f* (Vers) hull coverage – marine insurance policy *(ie, coverage against loss to a vessel or its machinery or equipment)*
Schiffsklasseattest *n* (Re) classification certificate
Schiffsladung *f* (com) shipment
Schiffsliegeplatz *m* (com) loading berth
Schiffsliste *f* (com) sailing list
Schiffsmakler *m*
(com) shipping agent
– ship broker
Schiffsmanifest *n* (com) ship's manifest
Schiffsmeßbrief *m* (com) tonnage certificate
Schiffspart *m* (com) share in a ship *(ie, one of the shares of joint shipowners = Mitreeder)*
Schiffspfandbriefbank *f* (Fin) ship mortgage bank
Schiffspfandrecht *n* (Re) ship's mortgage
Schiffsraum *m* (com) hold
Schiffsunfälle *mpl* (SeeV) marine casualties
Schiffsverladekosten *pl* (com) lading charges
Schiffszettel *m* (com) shipping note
Schikaneverbot *n* (Re) prohibition of chicanery *(ie, exercise of a right which can have no purpose except the infliction of injury on another is unlawful, § 226 BGB)*
Schlafstadt *f*
(com) commuting town
– bedroom community
– (GB) dormitory town
Schlagseite *f* (SeeV) list of a ship
Schlagwort *n* (Log) keyword
– subject heading
Schlagzeilen *fpl* **machen** (com) to hit the headlines
schlampig arbeiten
(Pw) to do sliphod *(or* shoddy *or* sloppy) work
– (infml) to quit on the job
Schlange *f* **im Tunnel** (AuW) snake in the tunnel
Schlangenwährungen *fpl* (AuW) snake currencies
Schlange *f* **ohne Tunnel** (AuW) blockfloating
schlecht bezahlt (Pw) underpaid
schlechte Adressen *fpl* (Fin) marginal accounts
Schlechterfüllung *f* (Re) defective *(or* faulty) performance
schlechter Kauf *m* (com) bad buy
schlechtes Risiko *n* (Vers) substandard risk

schlechte Stücke *npl* (Stat) spotty quality
schlecht strukturiertes Problem *n* (Log) ill-structured problem
Schlechtstücke *npl*
(Stat) defective items *(or* units)
– rejects
Schlechtwettergeld *n* (Pw) bad-weather compensation
(ie, paid to reduce recorded seasonal unemployment in the German construction industry)
Schlechtwetterzulage *f* (Pw) hard-weather allowance
Schlechtzahl *f* (Stat) rejection number
Schleichhandel *m* (com) black trading *(syn, Schwarzhandel)*
schleichende Inflation *f* (Vw) creeping inflation
Schleichwerbung *f* (Mk) camouflaged advertising *(syn, Schmuggelwerbung)*
Schleife *f* (OR) loop
schleifenloses Netzwerk *n* (OR) loopless network
Schleife *f* **erster Ordnung** (OR) first order loop
Schleife *f* **n–ter Ordnung** (OR) loop of order n
Schleife *f* **ohne gemeinsame Knoten** (OR) disjoint loop
schleppende Nachfrage *f* (com) sagging demand
schleppender Absatz *m* (com) poor market
schleppender Zahlungseingang *m* (Fin) stretching out of accounts receivable *(ie, customers pay more slowly)*
Schlepper *m*
(com) tugboat
– (also) tug
Schleppkahn *m* (com) barge
Schlepplohn *m*
(com) towage
– tug charge
Schleppschiffahrt *f*
(com) tugging
– towage
Schleppschiffahrtsunternehmer *m* (com) towing barges contractor, § 742 HGB
Schleppzug *m* (com) barge train
Schleuderpreis *m*
(com) give-away
– knock-out
– slaughtered ... price
Schleuderverkauf *m* (com) selling at knock-out prices
schlichte Ebene *f* (Math) simple complex plane
schlichten
(Re) to mediate *(ie, general term)*
– to conciliate *(ie, in court and in labor disputes)*
– to settle amicably *(ie, out of court)*
Schlichter *m*
(Re) mediator
– conciliator
Schlichtung *f*
(Re) arbitration
– conciliation
– mediation
– settlement
Schlichtung *f* **in Arbeitskämpfen** (Pw) labor arbitration
Schlichtungsabkommen *n* (Re) conciliation agreement

Schlichtungsausschuß *m* (Re) conciliation committee
Schlichtungsbestimmungen *fpl* (Pw) mediation provisions
Schlichtungskommission *f* (Pw) mediation commission *(or* committee)
Schlichtungsstelle *f* (Re) conciliation board
Schlichtungsverfahren *n* (Pw) conciliation procedure *(ie, in collective bargaining)*
Schlichtungsvorschlag *m*
(Pw) mediation proposal
– offer of conciliation
Schlichtungswesen *n* (Pw) industrial conciliation
schließen
(com) to close down
– to shut down
– to discontinue
(Log) to infer *(ie, deductively or inductively)*
– to conclude
schließende Statistik *f* (Stat) inferential statistics *(syn, Inferenz-Statistik, analytische Statistik)*
Schließfach *n*
(com) P.O. box
– post office box
(Fin) safe deposit box
– (also) safety deposit box
Schließfachmiete *f* (com) safe deposit box rental
Schließfachversicherung *f* (Vers) safe deposit box insurance
Schlitzlochkarte *f* (EDV) slotted card
Schlupf *m* (OR) slack *(syn, Pufferzeit)*
Schlupfvariable *f* (OR) slack variable
Schlupfzeit *f* (OR) slack time
Schluß *m*
(Log) inference *(ie, deductive or inductive)*
– conclusion
(Bö) contract note
(Bö) unit of trading
Schlußabnahme *f* (com) final acceptance
Schlußabrechnung *f*
(com) final account
– final billing
Schlußabstimmung *f* (com) final vote
Schlußbericht *m*
(com) final report
(com) exit presentation *(eg, submitted by outside expert)*
Schlußbesprechung *f* (StR) final conference *(eg, terminates a tax examination, § 201 AO)*
Schlußbestand *m*
(ReW) ending inventory
– end-of-period inventory
– closing stock
Schlußbestimmung *f* (Re) final provision
Schlußbilanz *f*
(ReW) end-of-period
– final
– closing ... balance sheet
Schlußbilanzkonto *n* (ReW) closing-balance account
Schlußbrief *m*
(com) commodity contract
(Bö, *commodity trading*, US) purchase and sale memorandum
(com) fixing letter *(ie, in chartering)*

Schlußbuchung *f* (ReW) closing entry
Schlußdividende *f*
 (Fin) final dividend
 (Vers) terminal bonus
Schlüssel *m*
 (KoR) = *Schlüsselgrößen*
 (EDV) code
Schlüsselarbeiten *fpl* (IndE) reference operations
Schlüsselbegriff *m* (Log) key concept
Schlüsselbranche *f* (com) = *Schlüsselindustrie*
schlüsselfertige Anlage *f* (IndE) turn-key plant
Schlüsselfrage *f* (com) key question
Schlüsselgrößen *fpl*
 (KoR) bases of distribution
 – allocation bases (*or* keys)
Schlüsselindustrie *f*
 (com) key industry
 – (infml, US) bellwether industry
 (eg, autos, chemicals, steel, food, information processing, machinery, oil, paper)
Schlüsselkosten *pl* (KoR) spread-type cost *(ie, traceable to cost centers by applying allocation bases)*
Schlüssellohnsatz *m* (Pw) key job rate
Schlüsselpositionen *fpl*
 (Pw) key positions
 – (infml) key slots *(eg, to bring fresh faces into key slots)*
Schlüsselrohstoffe *mpl* (AuW) core commodities *(ie, UNCTAD term)*
Schlüsseltätigkeit *f* (Pw) key job
Schlüsseltechnologie *f* (IndE) key technology *(eg, based on ICs and microprocessors)*
Schlüsselvariable *f* (Vw) key variable
Schlüsselverzeichnis *n* (Log) scoring manual
Schlüsselwährung *f* (AuW) key currency
Schlüsselwährungsland *n* (AuW) reserve center
Schlüsselwort *n* (EDV, Cobol) keyword
Schlüssel *m* **zur Arbeitsplatzbewertung** (Pw) job evaluation scale
Schlüsselzuweisungen *fpl* (FiW) quota allocations of funds *(ie, based on Ausgangsmeßzahl and Steuerkraftmeßzahl)*
schlußfolgerndes Denken *n* (Log) deductive reasoning
Schlußformel *f* (com) complimentary close *(ie, in business letters)*
schlüssige Begründung *f* (Log) cogent argument
schlüssiges Verhalten *n* (Re) passive manifestation of will
Schlußinventar *n* (ReW) closing inventory
Schlußkurs *m*
 (Bö) closing price
 – closing quotation
 – final quotation
 – close
Schlußkurs *m* **des Vortrages**
 (Bö) previous-day closing price
 – previous quotation
Schlußnote *f*
 (Bö) (broker's) contract note, §§ 94, 102 HGB
 – *(security trading, US)* confirmation slip
 – *(commodity trading, US)* purchase and sale memorandum
 (syn, Schlußschein)

Schlußnotierung *f*
 (com) closing price (*or* quotation)
 (Bö) = *Schlußkurs*
Schlußprüfung *f* (Stat) final inspection
Schlußquote *f* (Re) liquidation dividend
Schlußquote *f* **im Konkurs** (Re) final dividend
Schlußrechnung *f* (Re) final account *(ie, submitted to creditors' meeting, § 86 KO)*
Schlußregel *f* (Log) rule of inference
Schlußschein *m* (Bö) = *Schlußnote*
Schlußtendenz *f* (Bö) final tone
Schlußtermin *m*
 (com) final date
 – time limit
Schlußverkauf *m* (com) end-of-season sale
Schlußverteilung *f* (Re) final distribution, § 161 KO
Schlußvorschriften *fpl* (Re) final provisions
Schlußzahlung *f* (Fin) final payment
Schmiergelder *npl*
 (com) bribe money
 – graft
 – (corporate) payoff
 – (infml) kickback
 – (infml) slush money
 – (sl) boodle
Schmierpapier *n* (com, infml) scratch paper
Schmuggel *m* (StR) smuggling, § 373 AO
Schmuggelwerbung *f* (Mk) camouflaged advertising *(syn, Schleichwerbung)*
schmutziges Floaten *n*
 (AuW) dirty float
 – filthy float
 – controlled (*or* managed) floating
Schmutzzulage *f* (Pw) dirty work bonus (*or* pay)
Schneeballsystem *n* (Mk) snowball sales system *(ie, against bonos mores)*
Schnellbahn *f* (com) fast-rail system (*or* service)
Schnelldrucker *m* (EDV) high-speed printer
schnelle Abfertigung *f* (com) prompt (*or* speedy) dispatch
schneller Papiervorschub *m* (EDV) paper throw
schneller Zugriff *m* (EDV) fast (*or* immediate) access
Schnellfraß *m* (Mk, sl) fast food
Schnellhefter *m*
 (com) folder
 – letter file
Schnellspeicher *m*
 (EDV) high speed memory
 – fast (*or* rapid) access storage
 – zero access storage *(ie, inaccurate term)*
 (EDV) scratch-pad memory *(syn, Notizblockspeicher)*
Schnellstanzen *n* (EDV) gang punching
Schnellstanzer *m* (EDV) gang punch
Schnellübertrag *m*
 (EDV) high-speed carry
 – ripple-through carry
Schnellzugriffsspeicher *m* (EDV) = *Schnellspeicher*
Schnellzugriffsspur *f* (EDV) rapid access loop
Schnitt *m*
 (IndE) section
 – sectional drawing

Schnittebene *f* (Math) cutting plane
Schnittebenen-Algorithmus *m* (OR) cutting-plane algorithm
Schnittkurve *f* (Math) intersecting curve
Schnittmenge *f* (Math) intersection (*or* meet) of sets
Schnittpunkt *m*
  (Math) intersection
  – point of intersection
Schnittstelle *f* (EDV) interface *(syn, Nahtstelle, Anschlußstelle, Verbindungsstelle)*
Schnittstellenleitung *f* (EDV) interface circuit
Schnittstellenvervielfacher *m* (EDV) interface expander
Schnittware *f* (com) yard goods
Schnittzeichnung *f* (com) sectional drawing
Schnittzeile *f* (OR) cut row
Schockvariable *f*
  (Stat) disturbance
  – random disturbance (*or* perturbation)
  – shock
schöpferische Tätigkeit *f* (StR) creative activity, § 96 BewG
Schonfrist *f* (Pat) period of grace *(ie, extended to applicants)*
schraffieren
  (Math) to shade
  – to hatch
schraffierte Fläche *f* (Math) shaded area
schraffierte Graphik *f* (Math) hatched graph
Schräglauf *m* (EDV) tape skew
Schranken *fpl* **für den Marktzutritt** (Vw) barriers to entry into the market
Schreibanweisung *f* (EDV, Cobol) write statement
Schreibautomat *m* (EDV) automatic typewriter
Schreibbefehl *m* (EDV) write instruction
Schreibblock *m* (com) writing pad
Schreibdichte *f* (EDV) record density
Schreiben *n* **e–r Bandmarke** (EDV) write tape mark
Schreibfehler *m*
  (com) clerical error
  (com) typing mistake
Schreibkopf *m* (EDV) write (*or* record) head *(syn, Kugelkopf, Typenkopf)*
Schreib-Lese-Einrichtung *f* (EDV) write-read unit
Schreib-Lesekopf *m*
  (EDV) read-write head
  – head combined
Schreiblocher *m* (EDV) printing card punch
Schreibmarke *f* (EDV) cursor *(ie, movable spot of light on the cathode ray tube of a visual display unit)*
Schreibmarkensteuerung *f* (EDV) cursor control
Schreibmaschine *f* (com) typewriter
Schreibrad *n* (EDV) print wheel
Schreibring *m* (EDV) file protection ring
Schreibsicherungsring *m* (EDV) = *Schreibring*
Schreibstation *f* (EDV) printer terminal
Schreibstelle *f* (EDV) print position
Schreibtischforschung *f* (Mk) desk research
Schreibtischtest *m*
  (EDV) desk (*or* dry) check
  – dry run
Schreibverfahren *n* (EDV) recording mode

Schreibverfahren *n* **ohne Rückkehr zum Bezugspunkt** (EDV) non-return-to-reference (*or* zero) recording
Schreibweise *f* (Log, Math) system of notation
Schrift *f* (com) publication
Schriftart *f*
  (EDV) font
  – (GB) fount
Schriftenreihe *f* (com) publication series
Schriftform *f*
  (com) in writing
  – reduced to a writing
  (Re) in writing
  – written form
  (eg, agreement must be in writing; no writing is required)
Schriftführer *m* (com) keeper of the minutes
Schriftgut *n* (com) documents and records
schriftlich (com) in writing
schriftlich einreichen (com) to submit in writing
schriftlicher Vertrag *m*
  (Re) written agreement (*or* contract)
  – agreement in writing
schriftliches Einverständnis *n* (Re) written consent
schriftliche Stellungnahme *f* (com) comments in writing
schriftliche Vollmacht *f* (Re) written power of attorney
schriftliche Zollanmeldung *f* (Zo) entry in writing
schriftlich fixieren
  (com) to put in writing
  – (fml) to reduce to writing
Schriftlichkeitsprinzip *n* (Re) principle of documentation *(ie, wer schreibt, der bleibt = quod non in actis, non est in mundo)*
Schriftsatz *m* (Re) brief
Schriftstück *n*
  (com) document
  – paper
Schriftträger *mpl* (com) written records
Schriftverkehr *m* (com) correspondence
Schriftwechsel *m*
  (com) correspondence
  – exchange of letters
Schriftzeichenfolge *f* (EDV) character string
Schritt *m* (EDV) signal element
Schrittakt *m* (EDV) signal element timing
schritthaltende Datenverarbeitung *f* (EDV) real time processing
Schrittpuls *m* (EDV) clock pulse (*or* signal)
schrittweise Beseitigung *f* **der Zölle** (Zo) progressive abolition (*or* elimination) of customs duties
schrittweise Einführung *f* **des Gemeinsamen Zolltarifs** (Zo) progressive introduction of the Common Customs Tariff
schrittweise Wechselkursänderung *f*
  (AuW) sliding peg
  – gliding parity
Schrittzähler *m* (EDV) step counter
Schrott *m* (com) scrap
Schrotterlös *m* (KoR) proceeds from sale of scrap
Schrotthandel *m* (com) scrap trade (*or* business)
Schrotthändler *m* (com) scrap merchant
Schrottrücklauf *m* (IndE) return of scrap
Schrottverarbeiter *m* (IndE) scrap metal processor

Schrottverkauf m (KoR) sale of scrap
Schrottwert m
  (ReW) scrap
  – salvage
  – recovery
  – residual
  – disposal
  – junk ... value
Schrottzettel m (IndE) scrap ticket
schrumpfende Gewinne mpl (com) shrinking profits
Schrumpfung f **der Auftragsbestände**
  (com) reduction of orders on hand
  – falling orders
Schub m
  (com) jump
  – wave (eg, of prices, interest rates)
Schubladenpatent n (Pat) blocking patent
Schubladenplan m (Bw, FiW) contingency plan
Schubladenplanung f
  (FiW) contingency planning
  (Bw) contingency (or alternative) planning (syn, Alternativplanung)
Schubverarbeitung f (EDV) batch processing (syn, Stapelverarbeitung)
schubweise Ankunft f (OR) bulk arrival
Schuhindustrie f (com) footwear industry
Schulabgangsalter n (Pw) school leaving age
Schulabgangszeugnis n (Pw) school leaving certificate
Schulausbildung f (Pw) school education
Schulbesuch m (Pw) school attendance
Schulbildung f (Pw) school education
Schuld f
  (Re) obligation
  (Re) debt
  – indebtedness
Schuldabänderung f (Re) change of obligation, § 305 BGB
Schuldanerkenntnis n (Re) acknowledgment of debt (ie, takes debtor's case outside the Statute of Limitations = unterbricht die Verjährung, § 208 BGB)
schuldbefreiende Wirkung f
  (Re) effect of discharging the contract
  – in full satisfaction of debt
  – with full discharge of debtor
Schuldbefreiung f (Fin) discharge of debt
Schuld f **begleichen**
  (Fin) to pay
  – to discharge
  – to settle ... a debt
Schuldbuch n (FiW) Debt Register
Schuldbuchforderungen fpl (FiW) Debt Register claims (ie, Federal Government loans are listed on the stock exchange)
Schuldbuchgiroverkehr m (FiW) transfers of the Federal Debt Register
Schuld f **eingehen**
  (Fin) to contract a debt
  – to incur a liability
Schulden fpl
  (com) debts
  – indebtedness
  (ReW) liabilities

Schulden fpl **abtragen** (com) to pay off debts
Schulden fpl **abzahlen** (com) to pay off debts
Schuldenaufnahme f (FiW, Fin) borrowing
Schuldenberg m (Fin) mountain of debt
Schuldendeckel m (FiW) debt limitation (ie, ceiling placed on amount of borrowings by governments)
Schuldendienst m
  (Fin) debt service (or servicing)
  – debt service bill
  – debt servicing charges
  – repayment and service of existing debt (ie, interest and principal repayments)
Schuldendienstquote f (FiW) debt-service ratio (ie, interest outlay to sum total of public spending)
Schuldenerlaß m
  (Re) release (or remission) of debt
  (AuW) debt relief (ie, release of obligation of LDCs to replay loans)
schuldenfrei
  (com) free from debt (or obligation)
  (com) clear
  – free and clear (eg, house is clear of mortgages)
Schulden fpl **konsolidieren** (Fin) to consolidate debt
Schuldenkonsolidierung f
  (ReW) offsetting of receivables and payables in the consolidated financial statements
  (Fin) consolidation of debt
Schulden fpl **machen** (com, infml) to load up with debt
Schuldenmoratorium n (Fin) deferral of debt repayment
Schuldenpolitik f (FiW) debt management
Schuldenquotient m (Fin) debt-gross assets ratio
Schuldenrückzahlung f
  (Fin) debt repayment
  – debt redemption
  – debt retirement
Schuldenstrukturpolitik f (FiW) debt management
Schulden fpl **tilgen** (Fin) to repay debt
Schuldentilgung f (Fin) repayment of debt
Schuldentilgungs-Fähigkeit f (Fin) debt repaying capability
Schuldentilgungsfonds m (Fin) sinking fund
Schuldenüberhang m (Fin) excess of debt over assets
Schulden fpl **übernehmen** (Fin) to assume debt
Schulden fpl **zurückzahlen** (Fin) to pay off debt
Schuld f **erfüllen**
  (Re) to perform an obligation
  – to satisfy a debt
Schulderlaß m
  (Re) remission of debt
  – waiver by creditor of his right to the performance of a contract, § 397 BGB
Schuld f **erlassen** (Re) to remit a debt
schuldhaft (Re) culpably (eg, to cause damage to third party ...)
schuldhaftes Zögern n (Re) culpable delay, § 121 BGB
Schuldmitübernahme f (Re) = kumulative Schuldübernahme
Schuldner m
  (Re) debtor

- obligor
- *(bei Abtretung auch)* debitor cessus
  (ie, anyone liable on a claim, whether due or to become due)

Schuldnerarbitrage *f* (AuW) debtor arbitrage

Schuldnerbegünstigung *f* (Re) preference of debtors

Schuldnerland *n* (AuW) debtor country (*or* nation)

Schuldnermehrheit *f* (Re) plurality of debtors, §§ 420, 427, 840 BGB

Schuldnerposition *f* (AuW) debtor position

Schuldnerquote *f* **im EWS** (AuW) debtor quota

Schuldnerrallonge *f* (EG) debtor rallonge

Schuldnerverzug *m*
  (Re) debtor's delay, § 284 BGB
- *(civil law)* mora solvendi

Schuldnerzentralbank *f* (AuW) debtor central bank

Schuldrecht *n* (Re) law of obligations
  (ie, second book of the German Civil Code, §§ 241–853 BGB; contains most of the material which an English lawyer is accustomed to find in books on the law of contracts, the law of torts, and in books on special types of legal relations, such as sale of goods, landlord and tenant, etc.)

schuldrechtliche Beziehungen *fpl* (Re) contractual relations

schuldrechtlicher Anspruch *m* (Re) claim under contract

schuldrechtlicher Vertrag *m* (Re) contract

schuldrechtliches Wertpapier *n* (WeR) debt instrument

schuldrechtliche Übertragung *f* (WeR) transfer by assignment and delivery

Schuldsalden *mpl* **im EWS** (AuW) debtor balances

Schuldschein *m*
  (Re) certificate of indebtedness, §§ 371, 952 BGB
- memorandum of debt
- I.O.U.
  (Fin) SD certificate
- DM-denominated promissory note
- note payable (*or simply:* note)
  (ie, qualifies as security but not as evidence of claim; issued in large denominations of not less than DM500,000; issued by public or private borrowers of top-rate standing; purchase or sale by assignment)

Schuldscheindarlehen *n*
  (Fin) loan against borrowers' notes
- loan against SD certificates
  (ie, long-term direct credit where lender is entitled to fixed interest till maturity and to repayment. Transfer of title by written assignment. Notes not being deemed securities, interest is paid without deduction of 25 percent withholding tax.)

Schuldtitel *m* (Re) enforceable legal document *(ie, judgment, attachment order, arbitration award, temporary injunction, etc.; syn, Vollstreckungstitel)*

Schuldübernahme *f*
  (Re) assumption of debt (*or* indebtedness), §§ 414–419 BGB
- transfer of liability

Schuldumwandlung *f*

  (Re) novation *(ie, substitution of a new debt or obligation for an existing one, § 305 BGB; syn, Novation)*
  (Fin) conversion of debt

Schuldurkunde *f*
  (Re) debt instrument
- instrument (*or* certificate) of indebtedness

Schuldverhältnis *n*
  (Re) obligation
- obligatory relation
  (ie, relation between two persons which entitles one of them to claim from the other some act or omission recognized as capable of producing a legal effect)

Schuldverhältnis *n* **aus unterlaubter Handlung**
  (Re) delictual obligation, §§ 823ff BGB
- *(civil law)* obligatio ex delictu

Schuldverhältnis *n* **aus ungerechtfertigter Bereicherung**
  (Re) obligation created by the receipt of unjustified benefits, §§ 812ff BGB
- *(civil law)* condictio sine justa causa

Schuldverschreibung *f* (WeR) bond
  (ie, security evidencing an interest-bearing debt, if the instrument is (1) made out to bearer, (2) transferable by indorsement, (3) made out in serial form, or (4) equipped with interest coupons, § 12 KVStG)

Schuldverschreibung *f* **auf den Inhaber** (WeR) bearer bond

Schuldverschreibung *f* **mit variabler Rendite** (Fin) variable yield bond

Schuldversprechen *n*
  (Re) (abstract) promise to perform an agreement
- promise to pay a debt

Schuldvertrag *m* (Re) contract *(ie, only one type of the wider species of agreements)*

Schuldwechsel *mpl* (ReW) notes payable

Schuldwechsel *m* **gegenüber Fremden** (ReW) notes payable to third parties

Schuldzinsen *mpl*
  (Fin) debt interest
- interest on debt (*or* indebtedness)
- interest on borrowing
  (Vers) fixed charges

schulische Ausbildung *f* (Pw) schooling

schulpflichtiges Alter *n* (Pw) compulsory school age

Schund *m* (com, infml) inferior merchandise

Schürfrechte *npl* (Re) mining rights

Schütt-aus-Hol-zurück-Politik *f* (Fin) pay out/take back policy

Schüttgüter *npl*
  (com) bulk material
- material in bulk
- loose material

Schutzdauer *f* (Pat) time of protection, § 9 WZG

schutzfähig (Pat) patentable

Schutzfähigkeit *f*
  (Pat) eligibility for protection
- patentability

Schutzfrist *f*
  (Pat) period of protection
  (Pat) life (*or* term) of a patent, § 10 PatG

533

Schutzgebühr f (com) nominal charge (or fee)
Schutzklausel f (AuW, GATT) safeguard clause
Schutzmarke f (Pat) trademark
Schutzrecht n **angreifen** (Pat) to contest the validity of a protected right
Schutzrechte npl (Pat, comprehensive term) industrial property rights
Schutzrechtkosten pl (KoR) royalties
Schutzrechtsinhaber m (Pat) holder of an industrial property right
Schutzrechtsverletzung f (Pat) infringement of an industrial property right
Schutzrechtsverwertungsgesellschaft f (Pat) company or partnership commercially utilizing property rights
Schutzumfang m (Pat) scope of protection
schutzwürdige Eigentumsrechte npl (Re) protectable types of ownership rights
Schutzzoll m (AuW) protective duty (or tariff)
Schutzzollpolitik f (AuW) protectionism
Schwäche f **der Binnenwirtschaft** (Vw) weakness of the domestic economy
schwache Konjunktur f (Vw) weakness of economic activity
schwache Konvergenz f (Math) weak convergence
schwache Nachfrage f
 (Vw) weak
 – lagging
 – sluggish ... demand
schwächer bewertete Währung f (AuW) depreciated currency
schwächerer Auftragseingang m (com) thinner order books
schwache Umsätze mpl
 (Bö) low level of trading activity
 – light trading
schwache Währung f (AuW) weak currency
Schwachstelle f
 (com) potential trouble spot
 – weak point
 – danger point (or spot)
Schwangerschaft f (Pw) pregnancy
Schwangerschaftsurlaub m (Pw) prenatal leave
schwankender Zins m (Fin) floating interest rate
schwankende Wechselkurse mpl (AuW) fluctuating exchange rates
Schwankung f **der Chargen** (IndE) batch variation
Schwankung f **e-r Funktion** (Math) oscillation of a function
Schwankungsbreite f
 (Stat) range (syn, Spannweite, Variationsbreite)
 (AuW) fluctuation margin (ie, of foreign exchange rates)
Schwankungsgrenze f (AuW) limit of fluctuations
Schwankungsmarkt m (Bö) variable-price market (syn, variabler Markt; opp, Einheitsmarkt)
Schwankungsreserven fpl (Vers) = Schwankungsrückstellungen
Schwankungsrückstellungen fpl
 (ReW) provision for exchange rate fluctuations
 (Vers) claims equalization reserve
Schwankungswerte mpl (Bö) variable-price securities
Schwänze f (Bö) corner (ie, in forward transactions; möglichst restloser Aufkauf e-r bestimmten Warengattung; eg, make a fortune from a corner in wheat)
schwänzen (Bö) to corner
Schwanzfläche f (Stat) tail area (ie, of a distribution)
Schwarzarbeit f (Pw) moonlighting
 (ie, performed illegally and going undeclared)
schwarzarbeiten
 (com) to moonlight
 – to work ,,off the books"
 – (GB) to go black
Schwarzarbeiter m
 (Pw) moonlighter
 – (infml) fly-by-night worker
schwarze Liste f
 – black list
 (com) denied list (eg, companies are put on the ...)
schwarzes Brett n (Pw) notice board (eg, to put sth up on the ...)
schwarze Zahlen fpl **schreiben** (Fin) to write black figures
Schwarzfahrer m
 (com) free rider (ie, person dodging fares in public transport)
 (Re) unauthorized user of vehicles, § 248b StGB
Schwarzfahrt f (Re) unauthorized use of motor vehicles
Schwarzhandel m (com) black trading (syn, Schleichhandel)
Schwarzmarkt m (com) black market
schwebende Belastung f (Re) floating charge
schwebende Geschäfte npl
 (ReW) pending transactions (or business)
 (ReW) pending projects
schwebende Patentanmeldung f (Pat) patent pending
schwebende Schulden fpl
 (FiW) floating
 – unfunded
 – short-term ... public debt (syn, unfundierte Schulden)
schwebende Verrechnungen fpl (Fin) items in course of settlement
schwebend unwirksam (Re) provisionally ineffective (or invalid)
Schwebezeit f (Re) period of suspense (ie, used to indicate the period of time during which it is uncertain whether a condition will be fulfilled or not)
Schweigepflicht f
 (Re) duty of discretion
 (Pw) duty of secrecy
Schweinezyklus m (Vw) hog (or pig) cycle (ie, illustrating the cobweb theorem)
Schwellenglied n (EDV) threshold element
Schwellenland n (Vw) threshold country (ie, one still below the development level of highly industrialized countries, such as Brazil, Spain, Mexico, Argentina)
Schwellenpreis m (EG) threshold price (ie, fixed for imported grain, rice, sugar, milk, dairy products, and fats)
Schwellenwert m (Stat) cutoff

Schwemme f (com) glut in supplies
schwer absetzbare Ware f (com) slow moving merchandise
schwer absetzbare Wertpapiere npl (Fin) deadweights
Schwerbehindertenausweis m (SozV) severely handicapped person's identity card
Schwerbehindertengesetz n (SozV) Law Relating to the Severely Handicapped, of 29 Apr 1974, as amended
Schwerbehinderter m (SozV) severely handicapped person
Schwerbeschädigte mpl (SozV) = (now) *Schwerbehinderte*
schwere Papiere npl (Bö) heavy-priced shares
schwerer Kursverlust m (Bö, infml) falling out of bed *(ie, refers to a stock that suffers sudden and serious decline)*
Schwergut n (com) heavy cargo
Schwergutladefähigkeit f (com) deadweight cargo capacity
Schwergutschiff n (com) heavy-lift ship
Schwerindustrie f
(com) heavy industry
(com) heavy capital goods industry
Schwerkriegsbeschädigte mpl (SozV) severely handicapped veterans
Schwermetalle npl (com) heavy metals
Schwerpunktstreik m (Pw) selective (*or* key) strike
Schwerpunkt m **verlagern** (com) to shift the focus of activities towards
schwer verkaufen, sich (com) to sell hard
schwer verkäufliche Ware f (com) slow selling merchandise
schwer vermittelbar (Pw) difficult to place
schwer versicherbares Großrisiko n (Vers) target risk
schwerwiegender Fehler m (EDV) unrecoverable error
Schwesterbank f (Fin) sister institution
Schwestergesellschaft f
(Bw) fellow subsidiary
– sister company
Schwesterinstitut n (com) affiliated organization
schwierige Geschäftslage f (Fin) difficult banking conditions
schwimmende Ware f
(com) goods afloat
– afloats
Schwindelfirma f (com) bogus company (*or* firm)
Schwindelgeschäft n (com) fraudulent transaction
Schwund m
(com) shrinkage
– leakage
– ullage
(MaW) inventory shrinkage
Schwundsatz m (com) rate of shrinkage (*or* waste)
Sechseck n
(Math) hexagon
– polygon of six sides
Sechsmonatsgeld n (Fin) six-month money
Sechsspaltenausweis m
(ReW) six-column statement
– fixed-asset transaction statement *(see: Anlagespiegel)*

Sedes materiae f
(Re) source of law
– source of legal provision
seefahrende Nationen fpl (AuW) maritime nations
Seefracht f (com) ocean freight
Seefrachtbrief m (com) ocean bill of lading
Seefrachtgeschäft n
(com) ocean shipping trade, §§ 556–663 HGB
– affreightment
– carriage of goods by sea
Seefrachtrate f (com) shipping rate
Seefrachtvertrag m (com) contract of affreightment
Seefunkverkehr m (com) marine radio service
Seegebiet n (com) waters
Seegefahr f
(com) marine risk
– maritime peril
Seegüterversicherung f (SeeV) marine cargo insurance
Seehafen m (com) maritime (*or* sea) port *(ie, there are 14 of them in West Germany)*
Seehafenplatz m (com) seaport town
Seehafenspediteur m
(com) shipping agent
– (GB) land agent
Seehaftpflichtversicherung f (SeeV) marine liability insurance
Seehandel m
(com) maritime (*or* sea) trade
– ocean commerce
Seehandelskredit m (Fin) maritime commerce credit
Seehandelsrecht n (Re) maritime law *(ie, laid down in the 4th book of the German Commercial Code, HGB)*
Seekargoversicherung f (Vers) marine cargo insurance
Seekaskoversicherung f (Vers) maritime hull insurance
Seekasse f (SozV) sailors' compulsory health insurance scheme *(syn, Seekrankenkasse)*
Seekrankenkasse f (SozV) = *Seekasse*
Seeladeschein m (com) ocean bill of lading *(syn, Konnossement)*
Seelenmassage f (Vw) moral suasion
seemäßige Verpackung f
(com) seaworthy packing
– cargopack
seemäßig verpackt (com) packed for ocean shipment
Seemeile f (com) nautical mile *(ie, 1,853 km)*
Seeprotest m (com) captain's protest, §§ 522 ff HGB *(syn, Verklarung)*
Seerechtsabkommen n (Re) Law of the Sea Convention
Seerechtsgericht n (Re) Law of the Sea Tribunal
Seerechtskonferenz f (Re) Conference on the Law of the Sea
Seerechtsvertrag m (Re) treaty on the law of the sea
Seeschaden m (SeeV) average *(ie, partial loss or damage to ship or cargo)*
Seeschadenberechnung f (SeeV) adjustment of average
Seeschiedsgericht n (Re) marine arbitral tribunal

Seeschiff *n* (com) ocean going vessel
Seeschiffahrt *f* (com) ocean shipping industry
Seeschiffsverkehr *m* (com) ocean going traffic
Seetransport *m* (com) ocean (*or* marine) transport
Seetransportgeschäft *n*
 (com) shipping trade
 – marine transport
Seetransportversicherer *m* (Vers) marine underwriter
seetüchtiges Schiff *n* (com) seaworthy vessel
Seeverpackung *f* (com) seaworthy packing
Seeversicherer *m* (SeeV) marine insurer (*or* underwriter)
Seeversicherung *f* (Vers) ocean marine insurance
Seeversicherungsmakler *m* (Vers) marine insurance broker
Seeversicherungsmarkt *m* (Vers) marine insurance market
Seeversicherungspolice *f* (Vers) marine insurance policy, M.I.P.
Seeversicherungsrecht *n* (Re) marine insurance law
Seeversicherungsvertrag *m* (Vers) marine insurance contract
Seevölkerrechtsabkommen *n* (Re) treaty on the law of the sea
Seewarentransport *m* (com) carriage of goods by sea
Seewurf *m* (SeeV) jettison
Segmentationstheorie *f* (Fin) segmentation theory *(ie, tries to explain the interest rate structure)*
Segmentierung *f* (EDV, Cobol) segmentation
Segmentierung *f* **des Marktes** (Mk) market segmentation *(syn, Marktsegmentierung)*
Segmentmarke *f* (EDV) segment (*or* tape) mark
Sehne *f* (Math) chord
sehr kurzfristige Fazilität *f* (EG) Very Short Term Facility
Seite *f* (EDV) page *(syn, Rahmen, Kachel)*
Seitenansicht *f* (com) end (*or* side) view
Seitenaufriß *m* (com) end elevation
Seitenaustauschverfahren *n* (EDV) demand paging
 – paging algorithm
Seitenwechselspeicher *m* (EDV) paging device
Seitenzuführung *f* (EDV) sideways (*or* parallel) feed
Sekretärin *f* (Pw) secretary
Sektor *m* (EDV) sector of disk track
Sektoradresse *f* (EDV) sector address
sektorale Arbeitslosigkeit *f* (Vw) sectoral unemployment
sektorale (Engpaß-)Inflation *f* (Vw) sectoral inflation
sektorale Verschiebungen *fpl* (Vw) sectoral shifts *(ie, from agriculture to manufacturing to services)*
Sektor *m* **Ausland** (VGR) sector rest-of-the world
Sektor *m* **öffentliche Haushalte** (VGR) government sector
Sektor *m* **private Haushalte** (VGR) consumer (*or* household) sector
Sektor *m* **Staat** (VGR) public sector
Sektor *m* **Unternehmen** (VGR) business sector
Sektsteuer *f* (StR) tax on sparkling wine
Sekundärbedarf *m* (Bw) secondary requirements *(ie, of raw materials and work-in-process)*
Sekundärdaten *pl* (Stat) secondary data

sekundäre Aktiva *npl* (Vw) secondary assets
sekundäre Einkommensverteilung *f* (Vw) secondary income distribution *(ie, government redistribution)*
sekundäre Fixkostenumlage *f* (KoR) secondary fixed-cost allocation
sekundäre Gemeinkosten *pl* (KoR) secondary overhead (expenses)
sekundäre Kennziffer *f*
 (Bw) advanced ratio
 – (GB) supporting ratio
sekundäre Kosten *pl*
 (KoR) secondary
 – composite
 – mixed ... costs
sekundäre Kostenstelle *f* (KoR) indirect (*or* service) cost center *(syn, Hilfskostenstelle)*
sekundärer Sektor *m* **der Volkswirtschaft** (Vw) secondary sector
sekundäres Giralgeld *n* (Vw) derived demand deposit
sekundäre Wirtschaftseinheit *f* (Vw) secondary economic unit
Sekundärforschung *f* (Log) desk research
Sekundärgeschäft *n* (Bö) trading in existing (*or* secondary market) securities
Sekundärliquidität *f* (Vw) secondary liquidity
Sekundärmarkt *m* (Bö) secondary (*or* after) market *(ie, market for transactions in existing securities; opp, Primärmarkt, dritter Markt)*
Sekundärmetalle *npl* (com) secondary metals *(ie, metals recovered from scrap, as distinguished from primary metals, which are obtained direct from the ore)*
Sekundärreserven *fpl* (Vw) secondary reserves
Sekundärspeicher *m* (EDV) secondary storage
Sekundärstatistik *f* (Stat) derived statistics
Sekundärverteilung *f* (Vw) secondary distribution
Sekundawechsel *m* (Fin) second of exchange
selbstadjungierte Transformation *f* (Math) self-adjoint transformation
selbständig bewertungsfähige Güter *npl* (ReW) assets that can be valued separately
selbständige Arbeit *f* (StR) self-employment, § 18 EStG
selbständige Einrede *f* (Re) independent defense
Selbständiger *m*
 (com) self-employed
 – independent
selbständiger Unternehmer *m* (Re) legally independent contractor *(eg, agents, auditors, lottery collectors)*
selbständig Erwerbstätige *pl* (com) self-employed persons
selbständiges Patent *n* (Pat) independent patent
selbständige Sprache *f* (EDV) self-contained language
selbständiges Unternehmen *n* (Bw) independent enterprise
selbständige Tätigkeit *f* (com) self-employment
selbständige Verpflichtung *f* (Re) independent undertaking
Selbstanfertigung *f* (IndE) self-manufacture
Selbstanzeige *f* (StR) self-accusation of tax evasion reported to the local tax office, § 371 AO

Selbstbedienung *f*
(Mk) self-service *(ie, in retail stores)*
– (GB) self-selection
Selbstbedienungsladen *m* (com) self-service store *(or* establishment*)*
Selbstbedienungsstation *f* (com) self-service station *(eg, gas, petrol)*
Selbstbehalt *m*
(Vers) deductible *(ie, portion of insured loss to be borne by the insured)*
(Vers) rentention *(ie, amount of liability assumed by the writing company and not reinsured)*
selbstbehaltene Risiken *npl* (Vers) retained risks
Selbstbehaltquote *f* (Vers) quota share
Selbstbehaltsklausel *f*
(Vers) own-risk clause
– franchise clause
Selbstbeschränkung *f* (AuW) voluntary restraint
Selbstbeschränkungsabkommen *n*
(AuW) orderly market agreement
– voluntary restraint agreement
Selbstbeschuldigung *f* (Re) self-incrimination
Selbstbeteiligung *f* (Vers) = *Selbstbehalt*
Selbstbeteiligungsklausel *f* (Vers) excess coverage
Selbstbeteiligungstarif *m* (Vers) percentage excess policy
Selbsteintritt *m* (Re) self-dealing *(ie, of a commission agent, § 400 I HGB)*
selbsterstellte Anlagen *fpl*
(ReW) self-constructed assets
– assets constructed by a company for its own use
selbsterzeugendes Modell *n* (Vw) self-generating model
Selbstfinanzierung *f*
(Fin) self-financing
– auto financing
– internal generation of funds
(ie, retention of earnings for use in the business)
Selbstfinanzierungsmittel *pl*
(Fin) internally generated funds
– internal equity
– finance provided out of company's own resources
Selbstfinanzierungsquote *f*
(Fin) self-financing ratio
– retention rate
(ie, retained earnings to profits after taxes)
Selbstheilungskräfte *fpl* **des Marktes** (Vw) self-regulating forces of the market
Selbsthilfeverkauf *m* (Re) self-help sale, § 373 HGB
Selbstkontrahent *m* (Re) self-contracting party
selbstkontrahieren (Re) to act as principal and agent
Selbstkontrahieren *n*
(Re) self-contracting
– self-dealing
(ie, an agent cannot as such conclude a transaction between the principal and himself or another party represented by himself, except if he has been granted express authority to do so, § 181 BGB)
selbstkorrigierender Code *m* (EDV) self-correcting code *(syn, Fehlerkorrekturcode)*

Selbstkosten *pl*
(KoR, *in manufacturing*) total production cost *(ie, direct materials, direct labor, direct overhead + selling and administrative overhead)*
(KoR, *in trading*) cost of sales *(ie, cost of goods purchased + storage + selling and administrative expenses)*
Selbstkosten *pl* **des Umsatzes** (ReW) total cost of sales
Selbstkostenpreis *m* (Bw) cost price *(ie, total production cost or cost of sales + profit markup)*
Selbstkostenpreismethode *f* (StR) cost-plus method *(see: Fremdvergleich)*
selbstladendes Programm *n* (EDV) self-loading program
selbstorganisierender Rechner *m* (EDV) self-organizing computer *(ie, able to arrange its internal structure)*
selbstprüfender Code *m*
(EDV) self-checking code
– error detecting code
selbstprüfendes Zeichen *n* (EDV) redundant *(or* check*)* character
selbstprüfende Zahl *f* (EDV) self-checking number
Selbstprüfung *f* (EDV) built-in *(or* hardware*)* check *(syn, automatische Geräteprüfung)*
selbstschuldnerisch (Re) creating a primary liability
selbstschuldnerisch bürgen (Re) to give a guaranty of payment as coprincipal debtor
selbstschuldnerische Bürgschaft *f*
(Re) absolute guaranty
– guaranty of payment
(ie, guarantor = Bürge has primary liability: no defense of ‚beneficium discussionis' = Einrede der Vorausklage, that is, his liability is fixed when debt is due and principal does not pay)
selbstschuldnerischer Bürge *m* (Re) guarantor primarily liable
selbsttätige Regelung *f* (EDV) automatic control
selbsttragender Aufschwung *m* (Vw) self-feeding *(or* self-sustaining*)* recovery
Selbstveranlagung *f* (StR) self-assessment *(ie, taxpayer is allowed to decide whether or not he is liable for tax and for which amount income tax liability exists; this practice is excluded in German tax law by § 150 AO)*
Selbstverbrauch *m* (StR) appropriation of business property for nonbusiness purposes of the owner, § 30 UStG
Selbstversicherer *m*
(Vers) self-insurer
– co-insurer
Selbstversicherung *f*
(Vers) self-insurance
– co-insurance
Selbstversicherungs-Fonds *m* (Vers) self-insurance fund
Selbstversorgung *f* (Vw) self-sufficiency *(eg, of oil)*
Selbstverstümmelung *f* (Vers) self-inflicted injury
Selbstverwirklichung *f* (Pw) self-fulfillment *(eg, at the expense of salary, position, or status)*
Selbstvollzug *m* (Pw) self-constitution
Selbstwählferndienst *m*
(com) direct distance dialing, DDD
– (GB) subscriber trunk dialling

537

Selbstwählvermittlungsstelle *f* (EDV) automatic exchange
Selbstzahler *m* (Vers) self-pay patient
Selektion *f* (EDV) outsorting of cards
selektive Kreditpolitik *f* (Vw) selective credit policy
selektive Kreditkontrolle *f* (Vw) selective credit control
selektive Verzerrung *f* (Stat) selective bias
Selektorkanal *m* (EDV) selector channel
seltene Erden *pl* (com) rare earths
seltene Metalle *npl* (com) rare metals
Semantik *f* (Log) semantics *(ie, extensionale Semantik = theory of reference; intensionale Semantik: theory of meaning)*
semantische Geschlossenheit *f* (Log) semantical closure
semantische Homogenität *f* (Log) semantical consistency
Semiotik *f* (Log) semiotics *(ie, comprises syntax, semantics, pragmatics)*
Semipermanentspeicher *m* (EDV) semi-permanent storage
Sendeabrufzeichen *n*
(EDV) invitation to send, ITS
– polling character
Sendeknoten *m* (OR) emitter *(or* source) node
senden
(com) to send (off)
– to ship
– to forward
– to address
Sendeteil *m* **e–s Knotens** (OR) emitter
Sendung *f*
(com) consignment
– shipment
Seniorität *f* (Pw) seniority
Senke *f*
(Math) sink
(EDV) well
senken
(com) to decrease
– to reduce
– to level down *(eg, prices)*
– to shave *(eg, costs)*
– to cut out *(eg, the use of copper by 75%)*
Senkrechte *f*
(Math) vertical line
– perpendicular
„Senkrechtstarter" *m* (Pw, infml) vertical takeoff tycoon
sensible Güter *npl* (AuW) sensitive commodities *(or* goods)
sensible Rohstoffe *mpl* (AuW) sensitive raw materials *(or* commodities) *(eg, manganese, vanadium, cobolt, chromium)*
Sensitivitätsanalyse *f* (Bw) sensitivity analysis
separable Körpererweiterung *f* (Math) separable *(or* algebraic) extension of a field *(syn, algebraische Körpererweiterung, Körpererweiterung 1. Art)*
separabler Raum *m* (Math) separable (topological) space
separables Polynom *n* (Math) separable polynomial *(syn, Polynom 1. Art)*

Separationstheorem *n* (Vw) separation theorem *(I. Fischer) (syn, Dezentralisationstheorem, Trennungstheorem)*
Sequentialtest *m* (Stat) sequential test
sequentielle Arbeitsweise *f* (EDV) sequential operation
sequentielle Bearbeitung *f* (EDV) stacked job processing
sequentielle Entscheidung *f* **bei Unsicherheit** (OR) sequential ordering decision
sequentieller Ablauf *m* (OR) sequential mode of operation
sequentieller Fortschritt *m* (OR) sequential progress
sequentieller Prüfplan *m* (Stat) sequential sampling plan
sequentieller Rechner *m* (EDV) sequential computer
sequentieller Stichprobenplan *m* (Stat) sequential sampling plan
sequentieller Versuchsplan *m* (Stat) sequential test plan
sequentieller Zugriff *m* (EDV) sequential *(or* serial) access
sequentielle Schätzung *f* (Stat) sequential estimation
sequentielles Stichprobenverfahren *n* (Stat) sequential sampling
sequentielle Steuerung *f* (EDV) sequential control
sequentielle Stichprobe *f* (Stat) item-by-item *(or* sequential) sample
sequentielle Verarbeitung *f* (EDV) sequential processing
Sequentiellrechner *m* (EDV) sequential computer
Sequenzanalyse *f* (Stat) sequential analysis *(or* sampling)
Sequenzprüfung *f* (Stat) = *Sequenzanalyse*
Serie *f*
(IndE) lot
– batch *(syn, Auflage, Los, Partie)*
Serie *f* **auflegen** (IndE) to run a production series
serieller Betrieb *m* (EDV) serial operation
serieller Datentransfer *m* (EDV) serial transfer
serieller Rechner *m* (EDV) serial computer *(ie, having a single arithmetic and logic unit)*
serieller Zugriff *m* (EDV) sequential *(or* serial) access
serielles Addierwerk *n* **für Dualzahlen**
(EDV) addition unit für binary numbers
– serial addition für binary numbers
(syn, serielle Addition von Dualzahlen)
serielle Verarbeitung *f* (EDV) serial processing
seriell wiederverwendbar (EDV) serially reusable
Serienaddierwerk *n* (EDV) serial adder
Serienanleihe *f* (Fin) serial bonds issue
Serienbetrieb *m* (EDV) serial operation *(opp, parallel operation)*
Seriendrucker *m* (EDV) serial printer
Serienfälligkeit *f* (Fin) serial maturity
Serienfertigung *f* (IndE) continuous series-type production
(ie, products differ in combination of parts; opp, Sortenfertigung, Einzelfertigung)
Seriengröße *f* (IndE) batch size *(syn, Losgröße)*
Serienherstellung *f* (IndE) = *Serienfertigung*

Serien-Parallel-Betrieb *m* (EDV) serial parallel operation
Serien-Parallel-Umsetzer *m* (EDV) serial-parallel converter
Seriensequenzproblem *n* (IndE) batch sequencing problem *(syn, Problem der optimalen Sortenschaltung)*
Serienübertragung *f* (EDV) serial transmission
Servicegrad *m* (MaW) service level *(or* degree) *(syn, Lieferbereitschaftsgrad)*
Servituten *pl* (Re) = *Dienstbarkeiten*
Sheffer-Funktion *f* (EDV) NAND operation
– non-conjunction *(syn, NAND-Funktion, NAND-Verknüpfung)*
Shefferstrich *m* (Log) Sheffer stroke
– non-conjunction
sichere Anlage *f* (Fin) sound investment
sichere Mehrheit *f* (com) comfortable majority
sichere Vorräte *mpl* (Vw) proven reserves *(ie, of natural resources; eg, ore, crude oil)*
Sicherheit *f* (Fin) security
(Re) collateral
– collateral security
(Stat) confidence level
Sicherheit *f* **am Arbeitsplatz** (Pw) job safety
– on-the-job security
– workplace safety *(ie, low accident rate)*
Sicherheit *f* **bieten** (Fin) to offer security *(or* collateral)
Sicherheit *f* **des Arbeitsplatzes** (Pw) job security
– security of employment
Sicherheiten *fpl* **bestellen** (Re) to furnish collateral
Sicherheit *f* **leisten** (Fin) to furnish security
Sicherheitsarrest *m* (Re) arrest of debtor, §§ 918, 933 ZPO *(syn, persönlicher Arrest)*
Sicherheitsbedürfnis *n* (Pw) safety need
Sicherheitsbestand *m* (MaW) minimum inventory level
– safety level *(or* stock)
– reserve stock
– inventory buffer
– inventory cushion
– inventory reserve
– inventory reserve stock
– protective inventory
Sicherheitscode *m* (EDV) redundant code
Sicherheitskapital *n* (Vers) surplus to policyholders
Sicherheitskoeffizient *m* (KoR) margin of safety
Sicherheitslager *n* (Bw) buffer stock
Sicherheitsspanne *f* (Bw) margin of error
Sicherheitswechsel *m* (Fin) collateral bill
Sicherheitszuschlag *m* (com) margin of safety
(MaW) safety factor *(ie, in inventory management)*
(Vers) safety loading
– loading for contingencies
sichern (com) to hedge *(eg, against rising costs)*
(com) to provide security

Sicherung *f* (com) protection
– safeguarding
(com) hedging
Sicherung *f* **der Geldwertstabilität** (Vw) safeguarding monetary stability
– stabilization policy
Sicherung *f* **der Realeinkommen** (Pw) safeguarding real incomes
Sicherung *f* **des Arbeitsplatzes** (Pw) job protection
– safeguarding of jobs
Sicherung *f* **gegen Geldwertschwund** (Vw) inflation proofing
Sicherung *f* **gegen Verlust** (com) cover against loss
Sicherungsabtretung *f* (Re) assignment (of a claim) for security *(ie, a type of trustee relationship)*
Sicherungseigentum *n* (Re) ownership by way of security
Sicherungseigentümer *m* (Re) owner of collateral security
Sicherungsformen *fpl* (Fin) security arrangements
Sicherungsgeber *m* (StR) transferor of title to property for purposes of security, § 39 II 1 AO
Sicherungsgegenstand *m* (Re) collateral
Sicherungsgeld *n* (StR) penalty
Sicherungsgelder *npl* (Fin) funds pledged as security
Sicherungsgeschäft *n*
(AuW) covering transaction
(Bö) hedge
Sicherungsgrenze *f* (Fin) protection ceiling
Sicherungsgrundschuld *f* (Re) real estate charge securing a loan
Sicherungshypothek *f* (Re) debt-securing mortgage, § 1184 BGB
Sicherungskäufe *mpl* (Bö) hedge buying
Sicherungsklausel *f* (Fin) safeguarding clause
Sicherungsnehmer *m* (Re) secured party
Sicherungspatent *n* (Pat) confirmation patent
Sicherungsreserve *f* (Fin) deposit security reserve *(ie, set up by the Landesbanken and the Central Giro Institutions)*
Sicherungsübereignung *f* (Re) transfer of ownership by way of security *(ie, used instead of a pledge; permits debtor to remain in possession of the property)*
Sicherungsverfahren *n* (Re) attachment procedure, § 916 ZPO *(syn, Arrestverfahren)*
Sicherungsverkauf *m* (Re) hedge selling
Sicherungsvorkehrungen *fpl* (com) protective measures
Sicherungszession *f* (Re) = *Sicherungsabtretung*
Sichtakkreditiv *n* (Fin) clean credit *(ie, based on the terms 'documents against payment')*
Sichtanzeige *f* (EDV) visual display
sichtbare Ausfuhr *f* (VGR) visible exports
sichtbare Einfuhr *f* (VGR) visible imports
sichtbare Ein- und Ausfuhren *fpl* (VGR) visible items *(ie, of international trade)*
– visibles
Sichtdepositen *pl* (Fin) = *Sichteinlagen*
Sichteinlagen *fpl* (Fin) sight *(or* demand) deposits *(syn, Sichtdepositen; opp, Termineinlagen: Kündigungsgelder und feste Gelder)*

Sichteinlagenkonto n (Fin) sight deposit account
Sichtgerät n (EDV) visual display unit *(syn, Bildschirmgerät)*
Sichtguthaben n (Fin) credit balance payable at call
Sichtkartei f (EDV) visual file
Sichtkontrolle f (EDV) sight check *(ie, of punch pattern)*
Sichtkurs m (Fin) sight *(or* demand) rate *(ie, currency rate for short-term means of payments, esp. checks, telegraphic transfers, sight bills)*
Sichtpackung f (Mk) blister packaging
Sichttratte f (WeR) sight draft, Art. 2 WG
Sichtverbindlichkeiten fpl (Fin) demand liabilities
Sichtverkauf m (com) display selling
Sichtwechsel m
  (WeR) bill on demand, Art. 2 WG
  – bill payable at sight
  – bill payable on demand
Sickerquote f (Vw) leakage
Sickerverluste mpl (Vw) = *Sickerquote*
Siedewasserreaktor m (IndE) boiling water nuclear reactor, BWR
Siegelbruch m (Re) breaking official seals, § 136 StGB
Sigma-Verfahren n (Stat) sigma scoring
signal-adaptive Regelung f (EDV) closed loop adaptation *(opp, adaptive Regelung mit Rückführung)*
Signalausfall m (EDV) drop out *(ie, on magnetic tapes)*
Signalgeber m (EDV) annunciator *(ie, warning device to indicate the status of systems or circuits)*
Signalspeicher m (EDV) latch *(ie, condition indicating that current input value is to be stored)*
Signalwirkung f (Vw, FiW) announcement effect
signieren (com) to autograph *(eg, a book)*
signifikante Ziffer f (Math) significant digit
Signifikanz f (Stat) significance
Signifikanzniveau n (Stat) level of significance
Signifikanzprüfung f (Stat) test of significance
Signifikanzstufe f (Stat) size of the test
Signum n (com) logo
Silberwährung f (Vw) silver standard
Silvesterputz m (Fin) year-end window dressing
Simplexalgorithmus m (OR) simplex algorithm
Simplexbetrieb m (EDV) simplex operation
Simplexkanal m (EDV) simplex channel
Simplex-Verfahren n (OR) simplex method
Simulation f (OR) simulation
simultane Gleichung f (Math) simultaneous equation
simultane lineare Gleichung f (Math) simultaneous linear equation
Simultangründung f (Re) single-step formation (of a stock corporation = AG) *(ie, incorporation and capital issue at the same time; syn, Einheitsgründung; opp, Stufengründung)*
Simultanhaftung f
  (Re) simultaneous liability
  – direct and primary liability
Simultanplanung f (Bw) simultaneous planning
Simultanrechner m (EDV) simultaneous *(or* parallel) computer
Simultanschätzung f (OR) simultaneous estimate
Simultanverarbeitung f

(EDV) multiprocessing
  – parallel processing
  – simultaneous processing
  (syn, Mehrrechnersystem, Mehrprozessor- od Multiprozessorsystem)
Singer-Prebisch-These f (Vw) Singer-Prebisch theorem *(ie, positing that the terms of trade of the developing countries are on an irreversible downslide)*
singuläre Matrix f (OR) singular matrix
singuläres Urteil n (Log) singular proposition
singuläre Verteilung f (Stat) singular distribution
sinken
  (com) to decline
  – to decrease
  – to dip
  – to drop
  – to fall
  – to sag *(eg, prices)*
sinkende Gewinne mpl (Fin) falling profits *(or* profitability!)
sinkende Industrieproduktion f (Vw) falling industrial output
sinkende Rentabilität f (Fin) sagging profitability
sinkender Skalenertrag m (Vw) decreasing returns to scale
sinusförmiger Input-Verlauf m (Vw) sinusoidal input
Sinuskurve f
  (Math) sine curve
  – sinusoid
sittenwidrige Bedingung f (Re) condition contra bonos mores
sittenwidrige Bereicherung f (Re) immoral enrichment
sittenwidriger Vertrag m (Re) agreement contrary to public policy
sittenwidriges Geschäft n (Re) transaction contra bonos mores
sittenwidriges Rechtsgeschäft n (Re) legal transaction violating public policy, § 138 BGB
sittenwidrige Werbung f (Mk) unfair advertising *(ie, against good morals)*
Sittenwidrigkeit f (Re) violation of accepted moral standards, § 138 BGB
Situationsanalyse f (Vw) situational analysis *(ie, in economic policy)*
Situation ungleichgewichtigen Wachstums f (Vw) unsteady-growth situation
situative Entscheidung f (Bw) ad-hoc decision
Sitz m
  (com) headquarters *(eg, headquartered or based at ...)*
  – main office
  (Re) seat
  – statutory *(or* registered) office
  – legal domicile
  – principal place of business
Sitz m **des Käufers** (Re) buyer's place of business
Sitz m **e–r Gesellschaft** (Re) corporate seat *(or* domicile), § 5 AktG
Sitzgemeinde f (StR) community in which the most valuable part of a property is located, § 24 GrStG
Sitzland n (Re) country of incorporation

Sitzstreik *m* (Pw) sitdown (*or* sit-in) strike
Sitzung *f* (com) meeting
Sitzung *f* **abbrechen** (com) to break off a meeting
Sitzung *f* **anberaumen** (com) to fix (*or* schedule) a meeting
Sitzung *f* **aufheben**
(com) to close
– to end
– to terminate ... a meeting
Sitzung *f* **einberufen**
(com) to call a meeting
– (fml) to convene a meeting
Sitzung *f* **leiten** (com) to chair (*or* preside over) a meeting
Sitzungsgeld *n* (com) meeting attendance fee
Sitzungsperiode *f* (com) negotiating session
Sitzungsprotokoll *n* (com) minutes of a meeting
Sitzung *f* **vertagen** (com) to adjourn a meeting (*for, till, until*)
Sitzverlegung *f* (Re) transfer of place of business (*or* seat)
skalare Matrix *f* (Math) scalar matrix
skalares Produkt *n* (Math) scalar (*or* dot) product
skalare Variable *f* (Math) scalar variable
Skalarmultiplikation *f* (Math) scalar multiplication
Skalenelastizität *f* (Vw) scale elasticity *(ie, relative change of output to proportional relative change of all inputs)*
Skalenertrag *m* (Vw) returns to scale *(syn, Niveaugrenzprodukt)*
Skalenfaktor *m* (Vw) catch-all variable *(ie, in the Cobb-Douglas production function)*
Skalentechnik *f* (Log) scale analysis
Skalenvorteile *mpl* (Vw) economies of scale *(syn, Größenvorteile, Degressionsgewinne)*
skalieren (com) to scale
Skalierungsverfahren *n* (Log) scale analysis
Skonto *m* od *n* (*pl* Skonti) (Fin) cash discount
Skonto-Aufwendungen *mpl* (ReW) cash discount paid
Skonto-Erträge *mpl* (ReW) cash discount received
Skontofrist *f* (com) discount period
Skonto *m* **in Anspruch nehmen** (Fin) to take a cash discount
Skontoprozentsatz *m* (Fin) cash discount percentage
Skontration *f*
(MaW) perpetual inventory *(syn, Fortschreibung: updating procedure)*
(Fin) clearing
Skontro *n* (ReW, MaW) auxiliary ledger *(ie, to record daily changes of incoming and outgoing items)*
Skriptum *n* (Pw) course-supporting material
Sockelbetrag *m* (Pw) extra award to the lowest paid
sofern nichts anderes festgelegt (Re) unless otherwise stated
Sofortabschreibung *f*
(StR) writeoff in full (*or* as incurred)
– immediate writeoff
– immediate chargeoff
(ie, to current operations: of an expenditure whose beneficial effects are not exhausted in the current year)

sofort fällige Rente *f* (Fin) immediate annuity
sofortige Beschwerde *f* (Re) immediate complaint, § 793 ZPO
sofortige Lieferung *f*
(com) prompt delivery
(Bö) spot delivery
sofortiger Versicherungsschutz *m* (Vers) immediate cover
sofortige Versicherungsleistung *f* (Vers) immediate benefit
sofortige Zahlung *f* (com) immediate payment
sofort lieferbare Ware *f* (Bö) prompts
Sofort-Liquidität *f* (Fin) spot cash
sofort nach Eröffnung (Bö) within moments of opening
Sofortprogramm *n* (com) crash program
Sofortreaktion *f* (Bw) crash reaction
sofort verfügbare Ware *f* (Mk) actuals
Sofortzugriff *m* (EDV) immediate (*or* fast) access
Solawechsel *m* (WeR) promissory note *(syn, Eigenwechsel)*
Solidarbeitrag *m*
(SozV) social-insurance contribution based on the idea of solidarity among all employees
Solidarbürgschaft *f* (Re) joint and several guaranty
Solidarhaftung *f* (Re) joint und several liability
Solidaritätsbeitrag *m* (Pw) free-rider contribution *(ie, payable by non-unionized employees into an equalization fund; demanded by unions, but disputed by employers)*
Solidaritätsfonds *m* (AuW) solidarity fund *(ie, set up by the Group of Ten with a capital of 20bn SDRs)*
Solidarschuldner *m*
(Re) co-principle debtor
– joint and several debtor
Soll *n* (ReW) debit (side) *(ie, of an account)*
Soll-Ausbringung *f*
(Bw) planned
– predicted
– budgeted ... output
Sollbestand *m* (MaW) target inventory
Solleindeckungszeit *f* (MaW) sum of acquisition lead time + safety margin *(opp, Isteindeckungszeit)*
Soll-Fertigungszeit *f* (IndE) planned direct labor hours
Soll-Ist-Vergleich *m*
(Bw) target-performance comparison
(Bw) performance report
Sollkaufmann *m* (Re) merchant by virtue of registration, § 2 HGB
Sollkosten *pl*
(KoR) budgeted
– target
– attainable standard
– current standard
– ideal standard ... cost
(syn, Vorgabe- od Budgetkosten)
Sollkostenrechnung *f* (KoR) standard costing *(syn, Plankostenrechnung)*
Sollqualität *f* (Stat) program quality
Sollsaldo *m* (ReW) debit balance *(ie, excess of debit over credit entries)*
Sollsatz *m* (Log) ought statement

Sollseite *f*
(ReW) debit side *(ie, of an account)*
– debtor
Sollwert *m* (EDV) set point
Sollzahlen *fpl* (com) target figures
Sollzeit *f* (KoR, IndE) standard time
Sollzinsen *mpl*
(Fin) debtor interest
– debit rate
– interest charges *(or* expenses)
– interest rate charged
Sollzinsen *mpl* **der Banken** (Fin) bank lending rates
Sollzinssatz *m* (Fin) borrowing rate
Solo-Terminkurs *m* (Bö) outright price
solvent
(Fin) solvent
– liquid
Solvenz *f*
(Fin) ability *(or* capacity) to pay
– debt paying ability
– solvency
(syn, Zahlungsfähigkeit; opp, Zahlungsunfähigkeit, Insolvenz)
Solvenzvorschriften *fpl* (Vers) statutory solvency regulations
Sommerloch *n* (Mk, infml) summertime blues
Sommerpreise *mpl* (com) graduated summer prices
Sommerschlußverkauf *m* (com) summer sales *(ie, at knockdown prices)*
Sonderabgabe *f* (StR) special levy *(or* impost)
Sonderabschreibungen *fpl* (ReW, StR) special depreciation allowances
Sonderanfertigung *f* (IndE) item made to order
Sonderangebot *n*
(com) bargain sale
– premium offer
– special bargain
(Mk) flash item
Sonderaufgaben *fpl* (Pw) extra-duty assignments
Sonderauftrag *m* (com) special order
Sonderausgaben *fpl* (StR) special expenses, §§ 10, 10a, 10b EStG
Sonderausgaben-Pauschbetrag *m* (StR) blanket allowance for special expenses, § 10c I EStG
Sonderausschüttung *f* (Fin) extra distribution
Sonderbelastungen *fpl* (FiW) special burden
Sonderbericht *m* (Bw) special-purpose report
Sonderbestellung *f* (com) special order
Sonderbestimmung *f* (Re) special provision
Sonderbetriebsmittel *npl* (ReW) beneficially owned third-party assets
Sonderbetriebsvermögen *n* (Bw) special property *(ie, assets appropriated to the use of a partnership without becoming partnership property)*
Sonderbilanz *f* (ReW) special-purpose balance sheet *(ie, occasions: Gründung, Verschuldung, Sanierung, Fusion, Konkurs, Auseinandersetzung, etc.)*
Sonderdarlehen *n* (Fin) special-term loan
Sonderdepot *n* (Fin) special securities deposit
Sonderdividende *f*
(Fin) extra *(or* special) dividend
– bonus
Sondereigentum *n* (Re) individual ownership *(ie, in a condominium building)*

Sondereinzelkosten *pl* (KoR) special direct cost
Sondereinzelkosten *pl* **der Fertigung** (KoR) special production costs
Sondereinzelkosten *pl* **des Vertriebs** (KoR) special direct sales cost
Sonderermäßigung *f* (com) special price reduction
Sonderfazilitäten *fpl* (IWF) special facilities
Sonderfreibetrag *m* (StR) special tax-free amount
Sondergebühr *f* (com) extra fee
Sondergefahren *fpl* (Vers) extraneous perils
Sondergemeinkosten *pl* (KoR) special overhead expenses
Sondergerichtsbarkeit *f* (Re) limited jurisdiction, Art. 101 II GG
Sondergewinn *m* (Fin) extra profit
Sondergutachten *n* (com) special expert opinion
Sonderhaushalt *m* (FiW) special budget
Sonderkalkulation *f* (KoR) special-purpose cost estimate
Sonderkonjunktur *f* (Vw) special trend of economic activity
Sonderkonkurs *m* (Re) special bankruptcy proceedings, §§ 214ff, 236ff, 238 KO
Sonderkontingent *n* (AuW) special quota
Sonderkonto *n* (Fin) special account
Sonderkonto *n* **gutschreiben** (ReW) to credit to a separate account
Sonderkosten *pl* (KoR) special expenses
Sonderkosten *pl* **der Fertigung** (KoR) special production costs
Sonderkredit *m* (Fin) special credit
Sonderkurs *m* (Bö) put-through price
Sonderlombard *m* (Vw) special Lombard facility *(ie, managed on a day-to-day basis)*
Sonderlombardfenster *n* (Vw) special Lombard window
Sonderlombardkredit *m* (Fin) special Lombard loan
Sonderlombardsystem *n* (Vw) special Lombard system
Sondermetalle *npl* (com) special metals *(ie, rare metals such as titanium, chromium, tungsten, molybdenum, etc.)*
Sondernachfolge *f* (Re) individual succession *(opp, Gesamtrechtsnachfolge = universal succession)*
Sondernachlaß *m* (com) special discount *(or* rebate) *(ie, granted to special groups of final consumers)*
Sonderorganisationen *fpl* (AuW) specialized agencies
Sonderpfanddepot *n* (Fin) special pledged-securities deposit *(syn, Depot D)*
Sonderposten *m* (com) off-the-line item
Sonderposten *mpl* **mit Rücklagenanteil** (ReW) special accounts which in part constitute reserves
– reserves for special purposes
– items with accrual character
Sonderpreis *m*
(com) special
– exceptional
– preferential ... price *(ie, granted to special groups of final consumers)*
Sonderprüfer *m* (ReW) special auditor

Sonderprüfung *f* (ReW) special audit, §§ 142–146, 258–261 AktG
Sonderrabatt *m* (com) special rebate *(eg, Personalrabatt, Vereinsrabatt)*
Sonderrechte *npl* (Re) special membership rights *(ie, granted to stockholders or groups of stockholders)*
Sonderrücklage *f*
(ReW) special-purpose reserve
– surplus reserve
(Vers) special contingency reserve
Sonderrückstellungen *fpl* (ReW) special provisions
Sonderschicht *f* (Pw) extra shift
Sondersitzung *f* (com) special meeting
Sondersparte *f* (Vers) special line (of business) *(eg, medical malpractice, professional indemnity)*
Sonderstatistiken *fpl* (Stat) special-purpose statistics
Sondertarif *m*
(Zo) preferential rate
– special tariff
Sonderumlage *f* (FiW) special assessment
Sonderumsatzsteuer *f* (StR) export levy *(ie, on products destined for export, 4%; syn, Exportsteuer, inapplicable as of 11 Oct 1969)*
Sonderurlaub *m* (Pw) special leave
Sondervergütung *f* (Pw) extra (*or* premium) pay
Sonderverkauf *m* (Mk) special sales at knockdown prices *(eg, Sonderveranstaltungen, Saisonschlußverkauf)*
Sondervermögen *n* **des Bundes** (FiW) special assets of the Federal Government *(ie, Deutsche Bundespost, Deutsche Bundesbahn, ERP-Sondervermögen, Ausgleichsfonds)*
Sonderverwahrung *f* (Fin) individual safe custody of securities, § 2 DepG
(syn, Streifbanddepot)
Sondervollmacht *f* (Re) special authority *(ie, to undertake certain transactions or certain kinds of transactions within the scope of joint representation for an OHG, § 125 II 2 HGB)*
Sondervorteile *mpl* (Re) special advantages, § 26 AktG
Sondervotum *n* (Re) dissenting opinion
Sonderwertberichtigung *f*
(ReW) special valuation account
– special value adjustment
Sonderzeichen *n* (EDV) special character
Sonderziehungsrechte *npl*
(IWF) special drawing rights, SDRs
– (infml) paper gold
Sonderzins *m* (Fin) special interest
Sonderzulage *f* (Pw) special bonus
Sondierungsgespräche *npl* (com) exploratory talks
Sonntagsarbeit *f* (Pw) sunday work
sonstige Aufwendungen *mpl*
(ReW) miscellaneous
– other
– sundry . . . expense
sonstige Aufwendungen *mpl* **und Erträge** *m* (ReW) other revenue and expense
sonstige Aufzeichnungen *fpl*
(ReW) supporting records
– documentation supporting books of accounts
sonstige Ausleihungen *fpl* (ReW, EG) other loans

sonstige bebaute Grundstücke *npl* (StR) other improved properties, § 75 I BewG
sonstige Bezüge *pl* (StR) other earnings, § 7 LStDV
sonstige Einkünfte *pl* (StR) other income *(ie, speculative gains, income of a recurrent nature, miscellaneous income, § 2 I No. 7 and § 22 EStG)*
sonstige Erträge *mpl*
(ReW) miscellaneous
– other
– sundry . . . revenue
sonstige Finanzanlagen *fpl* (ReW) other investments
sonstige Forderungen *fpl*
(ReW) other accounts receivable
– accounts receivable – other
sonstige immaterielle Werte *mpl* (ReW) other intangibles
sonstige kurzfristige Verbindlichkeiten *fpl* (ReW) other current liabilities
sonstige Leistungen *fpl* (StR, VAT) other performances *(ie, mostly services)*
sonstige Nutzzeit *f* (EDV) incidental time
sonstige Posten *mpl* **des Umlaufvermögens** (ReW) other current assets
sonstige Rechtseinheiten *fpl* (Re) other legal entities
sonstige Rückstellungen *fpl* (ReW) sundry accruals
sonstiges Recht *n* (Re) right similar to the right of ownership, § 823 BGB
sonstiges Vermögen *n*
(ReW) other assets
(StR) other property, §§ 110–113a BewG
sonstige Verbindlichkeiten *fpl*
(ReW) other accounts payable, § 151 AktG
– accounts payable – other
– other liabilities
– sundry creditors
sonstige Vermögensgegenstände *mpl* (ReW) miscellaneous other current assets
sonstige Wagnisse *npl* (ReW) miscellaneous risks
Sonst-Regel *f* (EDV) else rule
Sorgerecht *n* (Re) right of custody
Sorgfalt *f* **e–s ordentliches Kaufmanns** (Re) due care and diligence of a prudent businessman, § 347 HGB
– diligence of a careful mercantile trader
Sorgfalt *f* **in eigenen Angelegenheiten** (Re) diligentia quam in suis *(ie, the same degree of care and prudence that men prompted by self-interest generally exercise in their own affairs, § 277 BGB)*
Sorgfaltspflicht *f*
(Re) duty of care
– duty to take care
Sorte *f*
(com) grade
– quality
– variety
(com) brand
– make
Sorten *fpl* (Fin) foreign notes and coin
Sortenabteilung *f* (Fin) foreign currency department

Sortenfertigung *f* (IndE) continuous batch production
(ie, related products differing in single features only; eg, dimensions, special additions, etc.; special type of ‚Serienfertigung')
Sortengeschäft *n* (Fin) = *Sortenhandel*
Sortenhandel *m* (Fin) dealings in foreign notes and coin
Sortenkalkulation *f* (KoR) batch-type costing
Sortenkurs *m* (Bö) exchange rate for foreign notes and coin
Sortenliste *f* (Kart) seed variety catalog
Sortenprogramm *n* (IndE) batch sequencing
Sortenrechnung *f* (KoR) = *Sortenkalkulation*
Sortenschutz *m* (Pat) plant varieties protection
Sortenschutzrechte *npl* (Pat) industrial property rights in seed varieties
Sortensequenzproblem *n* (IndE) batch sequencing problem *(syn, Seriensequenzproblem)*
Sortenwechselkosten *pl* (KoR) batch changeover cost
Sortierargument *n* (EDV) sort key
sortieren (EDV) sort
Sortierfach *n*
 (com) pigeonhole
 (EDV) sorter pocket
Sortierfolge *f* (EDV) collating (*or* collation) sequence
Sortiergenerator *m* (EDV) sort generator
Sortiergerät *n* (EDV) sorter
Sortierkriterium *n* (EDV) sort key
Sortiermaschine *f* (EDV) (card) sorter
Sortiermerkmal *n* (EDV) sort key
Sortier-Misch-Generator *m* (EDV) sort-merge generator
Sortier-Mischprogramm *n* (EDV) sort-merge program
Sortiernadel *f* (EDV) sorting needle
Sortierprüfung *f* (Stat) screening (inspection)
Sortierverfahren *n* (EDV) sorting method
Sortiment *n*
 (Mk) product range (*or* assortment)
 – assortment of goods
 – range of godds
 – line of merchandise
 – business mix
Sortiment *n* **bereinigen** (Mk) to streamline a product range
Sortimenter *m* (com) retail bookseller
Sortimentsabteilung *f* (com) new book department
Sortimentsbuchhandel *m* (com) retail bookselling
Sortimentsbuchhändler *m* (com) retail bookseller
Sortimentshandel *m*
 (com) single-line trade
 – wholesale trade
Sortiment *n* **umstellen** (Mk) to change one's business mix
Souvenirladen *m* (com) gift shop
soweit nicht anders vereinbart (Re) = *mangels . . .*
Sozialabgaben *fpl*
 (SozV) social insurance contributions
 – (US) social security tax
Sozialaufwand *m* (Pw) social welfare expenditure
sozial bedingte Präferenzen *fpl* (Vw) social preferences

Sozialbeirat *m* (SozV) Social Security Advisory Council
Sozialbeiträge *mpl* (SozV) social insurance contributions
Sozialbeiträge *mpl* **der Arbeitgeber** (VGR) employers' contributions to social security
Sozialbeiträge *mpl* **der Arbeitnehmer** (VGR) employees' contributions to social security
Sozialbericht *m*
 (ReW) socio-economic report *(ie, voluntary or statutory; part of annual report)*
 (FiW) social policy report *(ie, prepared by Federal Government)*
Sozialbilanz *f* (ReW) corporate socio-economic accounting *(syn, gesellschaftsbezogene Rechnungslegung)*
Sozialbindung *f* (Re) societal restrictions on individual property rights, Art. 14 GG
Sozialbudget *n* (FiW) social welfare budget
Sozialdumping *n* (AuW) = *soziales Dumping*
soziale Aufwendungen *mpl* (ReW) social welfare expenditure (*or* charges) *(not: soziale Kosten)*
 (ReW, EG) social security costs
soziale Einrichtungen *fpl* (Pw) welfare facilities
soziale Erträge *mpl* (Vw) social benefits *(syn, volkswirtschaftliche Erträge)*
soziale Ertragsrate *f* (Vw) social rate of return
soziale Grundrisiken *npl* (Vw) basic social risks
soziale Indikatoren *mpl* (Vw) social indicators *(ie, quantitative indexes to measure the quality of life of individuals and groups)*
Sozialeinkommen *n* (SozV) income from public sources
soziale Kassen *fpl* (StR) social welfare funds, § 5 I No. 3 KStG 1977
soziale Kosten *pl*
 (Vw) social costs
 – discommodities
 (ie, preferred term in German is ‚externe Kosten')
soziale Krankenversicherung *f* (SozV) social health insurance
soziale Lasten *fpl* (Pw) social charges
soziale Leistungen *fpl* (SozV) = *Sozialleistungen*
soziale Marktwirtschaft *f*
 (Vw) social market economy
 – social free market economy
 – socially tempered (*or* responsible) market economy
 (ie, concept applied in West Germany by K. Adenauer and L. Erhard who tried to steer a middle course between a guided or planned economy and an unfettered free enterprise economy)
sozialer Wohnungsbau *m* (Vw) social welfare housing
 (ie, construction of low-rent apartment houses for the benefit of socially disadvantaged families)
soziales Dumping *n* (AuW) social dumping *(syn, Sozial-Dumping)*
soziale Sicherheit *f* (Vw) = *soziale Sicherung*
soziale Sicherung *f* (Vw) social security
soziale Wahrnehmungsfähigkeit *f* (Bw) social sensitivity
soziale Wohlfahrtsfunktion *f* (Vw) social welfare function

soziale Zeitpräferenzrate f (Vw) social time preference rate
soziale Zusatzkosten pl
(Vw) uncompensated (or unpaid) costs
- uncharged disservices
Sozialfonds m (ReW) = Sozialkapital
Sozialgericht n (Re) first-instance administrative court for social security and related matters
Sozialhilfe f
(SozV) public assistance
- supplementary welfare benefits
(obsolete synonyms: Wohlfahrt, Fürsorge)
Sozialinvestitionen fpl
(Vw) social capital investments
- socially useful investments
Sozialkapital n (ReW) social capital (ie, Sozialrücklagen und Sozialrückstellungen; between 10 and 15% of total capital)
Sozialkosten pl (ReW) social welfare expenditure (ie, part of total labor cost)
Sozialkunde f (Pw, appr) social studies (ie, not ‚social science')
Soziallasten fpl (ReW) = Sozialkosten
Sozialleistungen fpl (SozV) social security benefits
Sozialleistungen fpl **der Arbeitgeber** (SozV) employers' social security contributions
Sozialleistungsquote f (SozV) social expenditure ratio
Sozialleistungsrecht n (SozV) law governing social security benefits
Soziallohn m (Pw) socially subsidized wage (syn, Familienlohn)
Sozialökonomik f (Vw) economics
Sozialpartner mpl
(Bw) corporate economic partners
- mangement and labor
(ie, labor and capital, represented by their umbrella organizations; German term in some quarters treated as an impermissible euphemism that would paper over the ‚logically inherent conflict' between management and labor; nothing short of all-pervasive plant democracy will satisfy such opponents)
Sozialplan m (Pw) social plan
(ie, worked out to mitigate undue hardship resulting from partial or complete plant closure)
Sozialpolitik f (Vw) social policy
Sozialprodukt n
(VGR) national product
- (infml) economic pie
Sozialprodukt n **ohne Budgeteinfluß** (FiW) pure-cycle income
Sozialquote f (SozV) = Sozialleistungsquote
Sozialrente f (SozV) social insurance pension
Sozialrentner m (SozV) social insurance pensioner
Sozialrücklagen fpl (ReW) social reserves (ie, part of Sozialkapital)
Sozialrückstellungen fpl (ReW) provisions for welfare expenditure (eg, pension funds; part of Sozialkapital)
sozial ungerechtfertigte Kündigung f (Pw) socially unjustified dismissal
Sozialversicherung f (SozV) social insurance
Sozialversicherungsbeitrag m
(SozV) social security contribution
- (US) federal social security tax
- (GB) national insurance contribution
Sozialversicherungsgrenze f (SozV) income limit for social insurance
Sozialversicherungshaushalt m (VGR) social insurance sector
Sozialversicherungsleistungen fpl (SozV) social insurance benefits
sozialversicherungspflichtig (SozV) subject to social insurance contributions
Sozialversicherungsträger m (SozV) social insurance carrier
Sozialversicherungszweig m (SozV) sector of social security
Sozialvertrag m (Vw) social compact (ie, between government and autonomous societal groups)
Sozialwissenschaften fpl (Vw) social sciences
Sozialwissenschaftler m (Vw) social scientist
sozialwissenschaftliche Entscheidungstheorie f (Bw) behavioral decision-making theory
Sozialzulage f (Pw) social welfare bonus (eg, Kinderzulage, Alterszulage, Wohnungsgeld)
Sozietät f (Re) professional firm (ie, lawyers, accountants, physicians)
Sozius m (Re) partner
Spalte f (EDV) card column
Spalte f **e–r Matrix** (Math) column of a matrix
Spaltenaufteiler m (EDV) column split (ie, to encode two separate digits in the column of a card)
spaltenbinär (EDV) chinese (or column) binary
Spaltenbitkarte f (EDV) column binary card (syn, Dualkarte)
Spaltenvektor m (Math) column vector
Spaltlagenstreuung f (EDV) gap scatter
spanabhebende Fertigung f (IndE) machining operations (eg, turning, drilling, milling, planing, sawing, filing)
spanlose Fertigung f (IndE) forming operations
Spanne f
(Mk) markup
(Fin) margin
(Bö) spread
Spanne f **zwischen Ausgabe- und Rücknahmekurs** (Bö) bid-offer spread
Spanne f **zwischen Geld und Brief** (Bö) price (or bid-ask) spread
spannungsfreies Wachstum n (Vw) tension-free growth
Spannungsklausel f (Pw) proration clause (ie, pension benefits are to be prorated in relation to an agreed formula; eg, x % of public sector pay)
Spannungspreis m (Bö) spread price
Spannweite f (Stat) range (syn, Schwankungsbreite, Variationsbreite)
Spannweitendarstellung f (Stat) high-low points method
Spannweiten-Kontrollkarte f (Stat) range chart
Spannweitenmitte f
(Stat) center of range
- mid range
Sparanreiz m (Fin) incentive to save
Sparaufkommen n
(Fin) total savings
- volume of savings

Sparbildung *f* (Fin) formation of savings
Sparbrief *m*
 (Fin) bank savings bond
 – savings certificate
Sparbuch *n* (Fin) passbook
Spareckzins *m* (Fin) basic savings rate *(ie, fixed for savings deposits at statutory notice = mit gesetzlicher Kündigungsfrist)*
Spareinlagen *fpl* (Fin) savings deposits
Spareinlagen *fpl* **mit gesetzlicher Kündigungsfrist** (Fin) savings deposits at statutory notice
Spareinlagenzuwachs *m* (Fin) growth in savings deposits
sparen
 (com) to economize
 – to save
 (com, infml) to put aside/by
 – to put away in savings
 – to squirrel away *(eg, for retirement)*
Sparen *n* **der privaten Haushalte** (Vw) consumer savings
Sparer *m* (com) saver
Sparer-Freibetrag *m* (StR) savers' tax-free amount, § 20 IV EStG
Sparförderung *f* (Vw) measures designed to promote savings
Sparfunktion *f* (Vw) savings function
Spargelder *npl* (Fin) total volume of savings *(opp, Geldmarktgelder, Kontokorrenteinlagen)*
Spargeschäft *n* (Fin) savings business
Spargiroverkehr *m*
 (Fin) transfer of funds via the savings banks
 – savings banks' giro system
Sparguthaben *npl* (Fin) savings deposits
Sparinstitut *n* (Fin) savings institution
Sparkassen *fpl*
 (Fin) savings banks *(ie, owned and run by local authorities; huge network of abt. 16,000 branches countrywide, and 12 Girozentralen = central giro institutions)*
 – (US) thrift institutions
 – (GB) Trustee Savings Banks
Sparkassenbrief *m* (Fin) savings bank certificate *(ie, in denominations of DM1,000, 5,000 and 10,000)*
Sparkassenbuch *n* (Fin) = *Sparbuch*
Sparkassenprüfung *f* (Fin) statutory audit of savings banks
Sparkassenrevision *f* (Fin) = *Sparkassenprüfung*
Sparkassenstatistik *f* (Fin) savings bank statistics
Sparkassen- und Giroverband *m* (Fin) savings banks and their clearing association
Sparkonto *n* (Fin) savings account
Sparleistung *f* (Fin) net savings *(ie, new savings deposits less withdrawals)*
Sparmaßnahme *f*
 (com) savings measure
 (Fin, infml) belt-tigthening measure
Sparneigung *f* (Vw) propensity to save
Sparparadoxon *n* (Vw) paradox of thrift
Sparprämie *f*
 (StR) savings premium
 – tax premium for savings
 (ie, premium for savings deposits, contributions to building and loan associations, investment in shares of investment companies, and purchases of the first issue of securities
 (Vers) premium not absorbed by risk
Sparprämiengesetz *n* (Fin) Savings Premium Law *(ie, law on premiums paid by the government on certain savings and investments of resident individuals)*
Sparprodukt *n* (Math) scalar triple product
Sparprogramm *n* (Bw) cost-cutting program
Sparprogramm *n* **der öffentlichen Hand** (FiW) fiscal restraint program
Sparquote *f*
 (Vw, *macroeconomics*) propensity to save *(subterms: durchschnittliche und marginale Sp.)*
 (VGR) savings-income ratio *(ie, ratio of savings to disposable income)*
Sparquote *f* **der privaten Haushalte** (Vw) personal-savings ratio
Sparquote *f* **steigt** (Vw) savings rate picks up
sparsam
 (com) economical
 – economizing
 – saving
 – thrifty
Sparsamkeit *f*
 (com) economy
 – economizing
 – thrift(iness)
 – thrifty management
sparsam wirtschaften (com) to economize
Sparschuldverschreibung *f* (Fin) savings bond
Spartätigkeit *f* (Vw) savings activity
Spartätigkeit *f* **anregen** (Vw) to spur savings
Sparte *f*
 (com) line of business
 (Bw) division
 (Vers) line *(ie, general classification of business; eg, life, fire, health, transport)*
Sparte *f* **Fertigung** (IndE) manufacturing division
Spartenleiter *m* (Bw) divisional manager
Spartenorganisation *f* (Bw) divisional organization
Spartenstruktur *f* (Bw) divisional structure *(syn, divisionale Struktur)*
Spar- und Darlehnsbanken *fpl* (Fin) savings and loan banks *(ie, rural credit cooperatives)*
Sparvertrag *m* (Fin) savings agreement
Sparvolumen *n* (Fin) total volume of savings
Sparzinsen *mpl* (Fin) interest on savings deposits
Sparzulage *f* (Pw) savings bonus
spätere Anmeldung *f* (Pat) subsequent application
späterer Erwerber *m* (Re) subsequent transferee
spätestens bis (com) on or before *(ie, a specified date)*
Spätestens-Klausel *f* (com) „not-later-than" clause *(ie, amount payable upon signing the contract or not exceeding a certain date after shipment)*
spätester Endzeitpunkt *m* (OR) latest completion time
Spätindikator *m*
 (Vw) lagging indicator
 – lagger
 – laggard *(eg, unit labor costs, inventories)*
Spätkapitalismus *m*
 (Vw) late capitalism
 – late capitalist regime

Spätschaden *m* (Vers) belated claim
Spätschadenreserve *f* (Vers) reserve (set up) for belated claims
Spätschicht *f* (Pw) late shift
spätzyklische Reihe *f* (Vw) lagging series
Spediteur *m*
(com) forwarding agent
– forwarder
– freight forwarder
(ie, acting on instructions of a shipper or consignee, § 407 HGB)
– transport company
Spediteurbedingungen *fpl* (com) = *Allgemeine Deutsche Spediteurbedingungen, ADSp*
Spediteurbescheinigung *f* (com) carrier's receipt
Spediteurdokumente *npl* (com) forwarder's documents
Spediteurdurchkonnossement *n* (com) forwarder's through bill of lading (*or* B/L)
Spediteurgeschäft *n*
(com) forwarding business
(com) conclusion of a forwarding contract
Spediteurkonnossement *n* (com) house bill *(ie, made out by forwarder: neither document of title [= Traditionspapier] nor a genuine bill of lading)*
Spediteurofferte *f* (com) forwarder's offer
Spediteur-Pfandrecht *n* (Re) forwarder's lien, § 50 ADSp
Spediteurrechnung *f* (com) forwarder's note of charges
Spediteursammelgutverkehr *m* (com) forwarding agents' collective shipment
Spediteur-Übernahmebescheinigung *f*
(com) forwarder's receipt
– *(international:)* Forwarding Certificate of Receipt, FCR
Spedition *f*
(com) forwarding trade
– freight forwarding
(com) = *Spediteur*
Speditionsagent *m* (com) forwarder's agent
Speditionsauftrag *m* (com) forwarding order *(syn, Speditionsvertrag, Verkehrsauftrag)*
Speditionsbogen *m* (com) forwarding sheet
Speditionsbüro *n*
(com) forwarding office
– shipping agency
Speditionsgeschäft *n* (com) forwarding business (*or* trade)
Speditionsgesellschaft *f* (com) forwarding company
Speditionsgewerbe *n* (com) forwarding industry
Speditionskonto *n* (ReW) carrying account *(ie, balance equal to gross forwarding profit = Brutto-Speditionsgewinn)*
Speditionskosten *pl* (ReW) forwarding expenses (*or* charges)
Speditionsprovision *f* (com) forwarding commission
Speditionsunternehmen *n* (com) freight forwarder
Speditionsversicherungsschein *m* (Vers) forwarder's risk insurance policy
Speditionsvertrag *m* (com) forwarding contract *(syn, Speditionsauftrag, Verkehrsauftrag)*
Speicher *m*

(EDV) memory
– storage
Speicherabzug *m*
(EDV) dump
– memory (*or* storage) dump
(ie, transfer of contents of a memory to a peripheral unit; see: Speicherauszug)
Speicherabzugroutine *f* (EDV) dump routine
Speicheradresse *f* (EDV) memory address
Speicheradreßregister *n* (EDV) memory address register
Speicherausdruck *m* (EDV) = *Speicherabzug*
Speicherauszug *m*
(EDV) selective memory (*or* storage) dump
– snapshot dump
Speicherauszug *m* **der Änderungen** (EDV) change dump
Speicherbank *f* (EDV) memory bank
Speicherbefehle *mpl* (EDV) storage instructions
Speicherbelegung *f* (EDV) memory occupancy
Speicherbereich *m* (EDV) memory area
Speicherbereichsschutz *m* (EDV) memory protect *(syn, geschützter Speicher, Speicherschreibsperre)*
Speicherblock *m* (EDV) storage block
Speicherdichte *f* (EDV) packing density
Speicherdruckroutine *f* (EDV) memory print routine
Speicherebene *f* (EDV) digit plane
Speichereinheit *f* (EDV) memory unit
Speicherelement *n* (EDV) memory (*or* storage) cell
Speichergerät *n* (EDV) storage device
Speichergröße *f* (EDV) memory size
Speicherhierarchie *f* (EDV) storage hierarchy
Speicherinhalt *m* (EDV) memory contents
Speicherkapazität *f*
(EDV) storage (*or* memory) capacity
– capacity
Speicherkern *m* (EDV) memory (*or* magnetic) core
Speicherkosten *pl* (EDV) storage cost
Speichermatrix *f* (EDV) matrix store
Speicher *m* **mit wahlfreiem Zugriff** (EDV) random access memory, RAM
speichern (EDV) to store
Speicherplatz *m*
(EDV) memory (*or* storage) location
– memory space
Speicherplatzbedarf *m*
(EDV) memory requirements
– required storage locations
Speicherplatzzuweisung *f* (EDV) storage allocation
speicherprogrammierter Rechner *m* (EDV) stored program computer
speicherprogrammiertes Rechensystem *n* (EDV) stored program dp system
speicherprogrammierte Steuerung *f* (EDV) stored program control, SPC
Speicherpuffer *m* (EDV) memory buffer *(ie, placed between memory and peripheral units)*
Speicherpufferregister *n* (EDV) memory buffer register
Speicherregister *n* (EDV) storage register
Speicherschlüssel *m* (EDV) storage protection key

Speicherschreibmaschine *f* (com) electronic typewriter
Speicherschreibsperre *f* (EDV) memory protect feature
Speicherschutzschlüssel *m* (EDV) protection key
Speicherseite *f* (EDV) page
Speicherstelle *f* (EDV) storage position
Speichervermittlung *f* (EDV) store and forward switching
(syn, Teilstreckenvermittlung)
Speicherverteilung *f* (EDV) storage allocation
Speicherwerk *n* (EDV) main memory system
Speicherwort *n* (EDV) memory word
Speicherzelle *f* (EDV) storage cell
Speicherzuordnung *f* (EDV) memory (*or* storage) allocation
Speicherzyklus *m* (EDV) memory cycle
Speisekartenfrage *f*
  (Stat) multiple-choice question
  (Mk) precoded question
Speisewagen *m*
  (com) dining car
  – (GB) restaurant car
Spekulant *m*
  (Fin) speculator
  (Bö) operator
  – stock exchange gambler
Spekulation *f*
  (Bö) speculation
  – stock exchange gambling
Spekulationsaktien *fpl* (Fin) speculative shares
spekulationsbedinge Kursschwankungen *fpl* (Bö) speculative price swings
spekulationsbedingte Pluskorrekturen *fpl* (Bö) speculative markups
Spekulationsbewegung *f* (Bö) speculative movement
Spekulationsdruck *m* (Bö) speculative pressure
Spekulationsfieber *n* (Bö) speculative frenzy
Spekulationsgelder *npl* (Bö) speculative funds
Spekulationsgeschäft *n*
  (com) speculative transaction
  (Bö) speculative bargain
Spekulationsgewinne *mpl* (Fin) speculative gains
Spekulationshandel *m* (Bö) speculative trading
(opp, Effektivhandel)
Spekulationskapital *n* (Fin) venture capital
Spekulationsklasse *f*
  (Vw) idle balances (*or* money)
  – speculative balances (*or* holdings)
Spekulationskäufe *mpl* (Bö) speculative buying
Spekulationsmotiv *n* (Vw) speculative motive
Spekulationspapiere *npl* (Bö) speculative securities
Spekulationssteuer *f* (StR) tax on speculative profits, §§ 22, 23 EStG
Spekulationswelle *f* (Bö) speculative surge
Spekulationswert *m* (Fin) = *Spekulationsgewinn*
Spekulationswerte *mpl* (Bö) hot issues
spekulative Anlage *f* (Fin) speculative investment
spekulative Gewinne *mpl* (Fin) paper profits
spekulative Kapitalbewegungen *fpl* (Fin) speculative capital flows (*or* movements)
spekulative Käufe *mpl* (Bö) speculative buying
spekulative Nachfrage *f* (Bö) speculative demand
spekulativer Bestand *m* (MaW) speculative stock of inventory *(ie, for which price rises are anticipated)*
spekulative Zinsarbitrage *f* (AuW) uncovered arbitrage
spekulieren
  (Fin) to speculate
  – to gamble
  – to play the market
spenden
  (com) to make a donation
  – to contribute
Spenden *fpl*
  (StR) donations
  – voluntary contributions *(eg, to charitable institutions, political parties, § 10 b II EStG)*
Spendenabzug *m* (StR) deduction from taxable income of donations for charity or public benefits
Spenden *fpl* **an politische Parteien** (StR) contributions to political parties
Spenden *fpl* **für mildtätige Zwecke** (StR) charitable contributions
Spendenquittung *f* (StR) receipt for donation
Spenden *fpl* **und Schenkungen** *fpl* (ReW) contributions and donations
Sperrauftrag *m* (Fin) stop order
Sperrdepot *n* (Fin) blocked security deposit
Sperre *f* (EDV) lockout
sperren
  (Fin) to block
  – to countermand
  – to freeze
  – to stop
Sperrfrist *f*
  (Re) blocking period, § 28 VerglO
  (Fin) qualifying period
Sperrguthaben *n* (Fin) blocked account (*or* deposit)
sperrige Güter *npl* (com) bulk (*or* bulky) goods
sperrige Ladung *f* (com) bulky cargo
Sperrjahr *n*
  (Re) one-year waiting period
  (ie, assets of a company in liquidation must not be distributed until one year has elapsed from the date of the last of three successive newspaper notices summoning creditors to register their claims with the liquidators of the company, §§ 267, 272 AktG; §§ 65, 73 GmbHG)
  (Kart) one-year waiting period, § 7 UWG
Sperrklinkeneffekt *m*
  (Vw) ratchet effect
  – downward rigidity
  – bottom stop
Sperrkonto *n* (Fin) blocked account
Sperrliste *f* (Fin) black list
Sperrminorität *f* (Bw) blocking minority (stake) *(ie, 25% + 1 share: legal minimum required to block a change in the statutes of a German company)*
Sperrpatent *n* (Pat) blocking (*or* defensive) patent
Sperrstücke *npl* (Fin) blocked securities *(ie, not freely disposable)*
Sperrung *f*
  (Fin) blockage
  – countermand

– stoppage
– freeze
Sperrvermerk *m*
(com) blocking note
(Fin) nonnegotiability clause
(Pw) request to management consultant not to pass job application to a company or to companies named by applicant *(eg, ,,List any company to whom your applications should not be sent")*
Sperrzeiten *fpl* (SozV) periods of ineligibility for benefits
Spesen *pl*
(com) expenses
– out-of-pocket expenses
(Fin) bank charges
Spesenabrechnung *f* (com) expense report
spesenfrei (com) free of expense
Spesenkonto *n* (com) expense account
Spesenpauschale *f* (com) expense allowance
Spesenrechnung *f* (Fin) note of expenses *(ie, sent out by bank buying and selling securities for account of customer; eg, broker's fee, capital transfer tax, commission)*
Spesensatz *m* (com) daily expense allowance
Spezialanfertigung *f* (IndE) special manufacture
Spezialbanken *fpl* (Fin) special-purpose banks
Spezialbilanz *f* (ReW) = *Sonderbilanz*
Spezialbörse *f* (Bö) special exchange
Spezialerzeugnis *n* (com) specialty product
Spezialfonds *m* (Fin) specialized fund
Spezialgebiet *n*
(com) special field *(or* line)
– speciality
Spezialgeschäft *n*
(Mk) specialty store
– single-line store
– one-line business
Spezialgroßhandlung *f* (com) specialized wholesaler
Spezialhandel *m* (AuW) special trade
Spezialindex *m* (EDV, Cobol) index
Spezialindizierung *f* (EDV, Cobol) indexing
Spezialisierung *f* (Vw) specialization
Spezialisierungsgrad *m* (Bw) degree of specialization
Spezialisierungskartell *n* (Kart) specialization cartel
Spezialist *m*
(com) specialist
– expert
Spezial-Kohlepapier *n* (com) special carbon paper
Spezialkreditinstitut *n* (com) specialized bank
Spezial-Lombard *m* (Vw) special (variable) Lombard rate
Spezialmärkte *mpl* (com) specialized markets
Spezialrechner *m* (EDV) special-purpose computer
Spezialrückversicherung *f*
(Vers) special risk reinsurance
– facultative reinsurance
Spezialvollmacht *f* (Re) special agency *(ie, authorizing to conduct a single transaction or a series of transactions, but not continuous service; opp, Generalvollmacht)*

Spezialwert *m*
(Bö) special stock
– specialty
spezielle Abgaben *fpl* (FiW) special fiscal charges *(ie, Gebühren und Beiträge)*
spezielle Nachfragefunktion *f* (Vw) special demand function
spezielle Steuern *fpl* (FiW) narrow-based taxes
Spezieskauf *m* (Re) sale of ascertained *(or* specific) goods *(syn, Stückkauf; opp, Gattungskauf)*
Speziesschuld *f* (Re) specific *(or* specifically defined) obligation
(syn, Stückschuld; opp, Gattungsschuld)
Spezifikation *f* (com) specification
Spezifikationskauf *m* (Re) sale by description
– sale subject to buyer's specifications
(ie, may be both ,Gattungskauf' or ,Stückkauf'; widespread in the iron and steel, yarn, wood, and paper industries; § 375 I HGB)
Spezifikationspaket *n* (com) specification package
spezifisch-allgemeiner Satz *m* (Log) strictly universal statement
spezifischer Deckungsbeitrag *m* (KoR) marginal income per scarce factor
spezifischer Zoll *m* (Zo) specific duty *(or* tariff)
spezifisch öffentliche Güter *npl* (FiW) nonrival goods
spezifizieren
(com) to give full particulars
– to itemize
– to particularize
– to specify
Spezifizierung *f*
(com) specification
– itemization
– detailed statement
Spezifizierung *f* **von Patenteinsprüchen** (Pat) notice of objections
sphärische Konkurrenz *f* (Mk) vertical competition
Spiegelbildkonten *npl* (ReW) suspence accounts *(ie, linking cost and financial accounting systems; syn, Übergangskonten)*
Spiegelpunkt *m* **e-s Punktes** (Math) image of a point
Spiegelung *f* **an der Achse** (Math) reflexion in an axis
Spiel *n* (Stat) clearance
Spielbankabgabe *f* (StR) special tax on gambling casinos
(ie, 80% collected from gross gambling proceeds in lieu of all taxes otherwise payable, such as those on income, turnover, net worth)
Spieler-Indifferenz-Feld *n* (OR) gambler's indifference field
Spielgeschäft *n* (Bö) gambling in futures *(syn, Differenzgeschäft)*
Spielkartensteuer *f* (StR) excise tax on playing cards
Spiel *n* **mit Sattelpunkt** (OR) saddle-point game
Spielraum *m*
(com) freedom
– leeway *(eg, each dealer has a few days' . . .)*
– maneuvering (GB: manoeuvring) room
Spielraum *m* **der Geldpolitik** (Vw) room for manoeuver with monetary policy

549

Spielraumschaltung f (EDV) gating circuit
Spielraumtheorie f (Stat) theory of range
Spielraum m **verlieren** (com) to run out of scope *(eg, for productivity gains)*
spieltheoretisch (OR) game theoretic
Spieltheorie f
  (OR) game theory
  – theory of games
Spiel n **und Wette** f (Re) gaming and betting, § 762 BGB
Spielwarengeschäft n (com) toy store
Spielwarenindustrie f (com) toy industry
Spielwarenmesse f (com) toy fair
Spinngewebe-Theorem n (Vw) cobweb theorem
Spinnwebmodell n (Vw) cobweb model
Spitzen fpl
  (Fin) net claims *(eg, are settled by transfers of central bank money)*
  (Bö) fractional shares
  – fractions
Spitzenanlage f (Fin) first-class investment
Spitzenausgleich m
  (Fin) settlement of balance
  – evening-out of the peaks
  (FinW) compensatory transfer
Spitzenbedarf m
  (com) peak demand *(eg, of coal)*
  (com) peak requirements
  – marginal requirements
Spitzenbelastung f (IndE) peak load
Spitzenbeträge mpl (Fin) residual amounts
Spitzeneinkommen n (Pw) top (or peak) income
Spitzenfinanzierung f (Fin) provision of residual finance
Spitzenführungskraft f (Pw) top executive
Spitzengespräch n
  (com) high-level consultations
  – top-level discussions (or talks)
Spitzengremium n (Bw) top management team
Spitzengruppe f (com) top bracket
Spitzeninstitution f (com) = *Spitzenorganisation*
Spitzenkennzahl f (Bw) key ratio *(eg, RoI)*
Spitzenkräfte fpl
  (Pw) top people
  – top-level personnel
  – high achievers
Spitzenlohn m (Pw) top wage (rate)
Spitzenmarke f (Mk) brand leader
Spitzenmodell n
  (MK) top-of-the line model
  – top model
Spitzennachfrage f
  (Mk) peak demand
  – residual demand
  – topout *(ie, reach a peak and retreat from it)*
Spitzenorganisation f
  (com) umbrella (or central) organization
  – federation
Spitzenorganisationen fpl **der Gewerkschaften** (Pw) central union organizations
Spitzenpapier n (Bö) leading stock
Spitzenposition f (Pw) top-level position
Spitzenqualität f
  (com) best
  – prime
  – top ... quality
  (Mk) top-quality merchandise
Spitzenregulierung f (Bö) settlement of fractions
Spitzenreiter m (com, Bö) market leader
Spitzenrendite f (Fin) top yield
Spitzenstellung f (Pw) top post
Spitzensteuersatz m (StR) top rate
Spitzentechnologie f
  (IndE) high
  – advanced
  – top-flight
  – state-of-the-art ... technology *(syn, Hochtechnologie)*
Spitzenverband m
  (com) central association
  – umbrella organization
Spitzenverkauf m (com) peak sales
Spitzenvertreter m (com) top-level representative
Spitzenwerte mpl
  (Bö) leaders
  – leading equities (or shares)
  – high fliers
Spitzenziel n (Bw) top management objective
spitzer Winkel m (Math) acute angle
Splitting n (StR) splitting
spontane Arbeitsniederlegung f (Pw) spontaneous strike
Spontankauf m (Mk) impulse buying
sporadisches Dumping n (AuW) intermittent dumping
Spotgeschäft n (Bö) spot transaction *(opp, Termingeschäft)*
Spottpreis m
  (com) very small price
  – (infml) song *(eg, ... bought the ailing company for a song)*
Sprachanweisung f (EDV) language statement *(ie, coded by a computer user)*
Sprachausgabeeinheit f (EDV) audio response unit, ARU
Sprache f **der Wirtschaft**
  (com) business (or industry) parlance
  – business jargon
springen
  (EDV) to branch
  – to jump
Springer m (IndE) standby man
Sprosse f (EDV) row
Sprossenteilung f (EDV) row pitch
Sprungadresse f (EDV) branch address
Sprungbedingung f (EDV) branch condition
Sprungbefehl m
  (EDV) branch
  – jump
  – skip
  – transfer
  – conditional transfer ... instruction
  – unconditional branch
Sprung m **e-r Funktion** (Math) saltus of a function
sprungfixe Kosten pl (KoR) = *Sprungkosten*
Sprungfunktion f (Math) jump (or step) function
sprunghaft ansteigen
  (com) to rocket *(eg, prices)*
  – to soar
  – to shoot up

sprunghafter Preisanstieg | **Staatsbetrieb**

- to skyrocket
- to zoom

sprunghafter Preisanstieg *m* (com) steep increase in prices

Sprungklage *f* (StR) immediate litigation brought to reverse an administrative action *(ie, requires the consent of the agency which rendered the contested decision, § 45 I FGO)*

Sprungkosten *pl* (KoR) step *(or* step-variable) cost
- fixed cost rising in steps *(syn, intervallfixe Kosten)*

Sprungregreß *m* (WeR) = *Sprungrückgriff*

Sprungrevision *f* (StR) leap-frog appeal, § 45 FGO

Sprungrückgriff *m* (WeR) recourse against one of the previous indorsers *(ie, other than the last-preceding one, Art. 47 II WG, Art. 44 II ScheckG; syn, Sprungregreß)*

Spur *f* (EDV) track

Spuradresse *f* (EDV) track *(or* home) address

Spur *f* **der Matrix** (Math) trace of matrix

Spurelement *n* (EVD) track element

Spurgruppe *f* (EDV) band

Spurteilung *f* (EDV) track pitch

Spurwechseleinrichtung *f* (EDV) track overflow feature

Staat *m* (VGR) government sector

Staat *m* **der Belegenheit** (StR) state of situs

staatliche Anreize *mpl* (FiW) government incentives

staatliche Beteiligung *f* (Bw) state shareholding

staatliche Bewirtschaftung *f* (Vw) government control

staatliche Einkommensübertragungen *fpl* (VGR) government transfer payments
- government transfers

staatliche Enteignung *f* (AuW) government expropriation

staatliche Exportförderung *f* (AuW) state aid to exports

staatliche Exportgarantie *f* (AuW) government export guaranty

staatliche Förderung *f* (FiW) government aid

staatliche Garantie *f* (FiW) government guaranty

staatliche Genehmigung *f* (Re) governmental authorization *(eg, to carry on business)*

staatliche Handelsförderung *f* (Vw) government-supported trade promotion

staatliche Hilfen *fpl* (FiW) state assistance

staatliche Intervention *f* (Vw) government intervention

staatliche Kapitalmarktpolitik *f* (Vw) government capital market policy

staatliche Kreditbürgschaft *f* (Fin) state loan guaranty

staatliche Kreditgarantie *f* (Fin) state *(or* government) loan guaranty

staatliche Maßnahmen *pfl* (Vw) government action *(or* measures)

staatliche Mittel *pl* (FiW) government funds

staatliche Nachfrage *f* (VGR) government demand

staatliche Nettokreditaufnahme *f* (FiW) government net borrowing

staatliche Organisationen *fpl* (FiW) government organizations *(or* agencies)

staatliche Prüfung *f* (Pw) state examination

staatlicher Eingriff *m* (Vw) government intervention

staatlicher Kreditbedarf *m* (FiW) government borrowing requirements

staatliche Rohstoffbevorratung *f* (Vw) government stockpiling *(ie, of sensitive raw materials: chromium, manganese, cobalt, certain types of asbestos)*

staatlicher Stahlkonzern *m* (Vw) state-owned steel group

staatliches Außenhandelsmonopol *n* (AuW) state-controlled trading monopoly

staatliche Schuldenaufnahme *f* (FiW) government borrowing

staatliches Dumping *n* (AuW) government-supported dumping

staatliches Handeln *n* (Re) government *(or* public) activity

staatliches Konjunkturprogramm *n* (Vw) government scheme set up to stimulate economic activity

staatliches Monopol *n* (Vw) government monopoly

staatliche Subventionen *fpl* (FiW) government subsidies

staatliches Unternehmen *n* (FiW) public enterprise

staatliche Unterstützung *f* (FiW) government *(or* state) aid

staatliche Vorratsstelle *f* (Vw) government storage agency

staatliche Vorschriften *fpl* (Re) government regulations

staatliche Vorschriften *fpl* **einhalten** (Re) to comply with government regulations

staatlich gefördert (FiW) government sponsored

Staatsanleihe *f* (FiW) government bond issue *(ie, sold by Bund, Länder or foreign governments)*

Staatsanwalt *m* (Re) district attorney
- (GB) public prosecutor
(ie, prosecuting officer of the government)

Staatsaufsicht *f* (Re) state supervision

Staatsausgaben *fpl* (VGR) government spending *(or* expenditure)
- public spending

Staatsausgaben-Gleichung *f* (Vw) government spending equation

Staatsausgaben-Multiplikator *m* (FiW) government expenditure multiplier *(ie, in relation to national income)*

Staatsausgabenquote *f* (FiW) public sector share in gnp
- government activity rate
(ie, Verhältnis von Eigenausgaben von Bund, Ländern und Gemeinden zu Volkseinkommen = ratio of expenditures of all government units to national income; in US and GB this ratio is defined as: government expenditures to gnp; syn, Staatsquote)

Staatsbankrott *m* (Vw) national bankruptcy *(Unterbegriffe: (1) offener St. = repudiation of government indebtedness; (2) verschleierter St. = forced conversion or arbitrary inflation)*

Staatsbetrieb *m* (FiW) government-owned enterprise

551

Staatseinkauf m (FiW) public purchasing *(syn, Behördeneinkauf, öffentliche Auftragsvergabe)*
Staatseinnahmen *fpl*
(FiW) public revenue
- government receipts *(syn, öffentliche Einnahmen)*
Staatsfinanzen *pl* (FiW) public finances
Staatshaftung *f* (Re) government liability
Staatshandel m (Vw) state trading
Staatshandelsland *n* (AuW) state-trading country
Staatshaushalt m (FiW) government budget *(syn, öffentlicher Haushalt)*
staatsinterne Effizienz *f* (FiW) intra-government efficiency
Staatskapitalismus m
(Vw) state capitalism
- state capitalist regime
staatskapitalistisch (Vw) state capitalist
Staatskasse *f* (FiW) treasury
Staatspapiere *npl* (FiW) government securities
Staatsquote *f* (FiW) = *Staatsausgabenquote*
Staatsschulden *fpl*
(FiW) government (*or* public) debt
- (GB) national debt
(syn, öffentliche Schulden)
Staatsschuldendienst m (FiW) servicing of public debts
Staatsschuld *f* **nicht anerkennen** (Re) to repudiate a public debt
Staatsschuldverschreibung *f* (Fin) government bond
Staatsverbrauch m
(VGR) public
- government
- collective
- state ... consumption
- government expenditure on goods and services
Staatsverschuldung *f* (FiW) = *Staatsschulden*
Staatswirtschaft *f* (FiW) public sector of the economy
staatswirtschaftliche Einnahmen *fpl* (FiW) public revenues
Stab m (Bw) staff
Stabdiagramm *n*
(Stat) bar graph
- bar chart
- column diagram
Stabdrucker m (EDV) bar printer
stabiles Gleichgewicht *n* (Vw) stable equilibrium
stabiles Preisniveau *n* (Vw) stable price level
stabile Währung *f* (Vw) stable currency
stabile Währungszone *f* (EG) zone of monetary stability
stabile Wechselkursrelationen *fpl* (AuW) stable exchange rate relations
stabile Wirtschaftsbeziehungen *fpl* (AuW) stable economic relations
stabilisiertes Handlungssystem *n* (Bw) boundary-maintaining action system
Stabilisierung *f* **der Märkte** (com) stabilization of markets
Stabilisierung *f* **des Preisniveaus** (Vw) stabilization of the overall price level
Stabilisierungsfonds m (Fin) stabilization fund

Stabilisierungskrise *f* (Vw) stabilization crisis
Stabilisierungspolitik *f* (Vw) = *Stabilitätspolitik*
Stabilität *f* (Vw) economic stability
(ie, high level of employment, stable prices, and external balance)
Stabilitätsanleihe *f* (FiW) stabilization loan
Stabilitätsbedingungen *fpl* (Vw) convergence conditions
Stabilitätsbonus m (AuW) „stability bonus"
Stabilitätsfortschritt m (Vw) progress toward stability
Stabilitätsgesetz *n* (Vw) Stabilization Law
(ie, short for: Gesetz zur Förderung der Stabilität des Wachstums der Wirtschaft = Law Promoting Stability and Growth of the Economy, of 8 June 1967)
Stabilitätskrise *f* (Vw) stabilization crisis
Stabilitätskurs m (Vw) policy of stabilization
Stabilitätspolitik *f* (Vw) stabilization policy *(syn, Stabilisierungspolitik)*
Stabilitätsprogramm *n*
(Vw) stabilization program
- deflationary program
Stabilitätsvorsprung m (Vw) better stability record
Stabilitätszuschlag m (StR) temporary stabilization levy *(ie, expired on 31 Dec 1974)*
Stablinienorganisation *f*
(Bw) line and staff authority relationships
- line-staff organization structure
Stabsabteilung *f*
(Bw) staff unit
- staff and service department
- service department
- (infml) palace guard
Stabsassistent m (Pw) staff assistant
Stabskräfte *fpl* (Bw) staff
Stabspapier *n* (Bw) staff paper
Stabstelle *f* (Bw) staff unit (*or* position)
Stabstätigkeit *f* (Bw) staff activities
Stachelrad *n* (EDV) pin feed platen
Stachelradvorschub m (EDV) pinfeed
Stadtökonomik *f* (Vw) urban economics
Stadtsparkasse *f* (Fin) savings bank run by a municipality
Stadtstaaten *mpl* (FiW) city state Länder *(eg, Hamburg, Bremen)*
Staffelanleihe *f* (Fin) graduated-interest loan
Staffelform *f* **der Gewinn- und Verlustrechnung** (ReW) report
- running
- columnar
- narrative ... form of income statement
Staffelgebühren *fpl* (com) differential rates
Staffelmiete *f* (com) graduated rent
staffeln
(com) to graduate
- to scale
Staffelpreise *mpl* (com) graduated (*or* staggered) prices
Staffelskonto m od *n* (com) progressive discount rate
Staffelspannen *fpl* (Mk) graduated markup scheme
(ie, based on quality, sizes, buyer groups, etc.)
Staffelsumme *f* (Math) progressive total
Staffeltarif m (com) graduated tariff

Staffelung *f*
 (com) differentiation
 – graduation
 – scaling
Staffelung *f* **der Laufzeiten** (Fin) spacing out terms to maturity
Staffelzinsen *mpl* (Fin) graduated interest
Staffelzinsrechnung *f* (Fin) calculation of interest on a day-today basis
Stagflation *f*
 (Vw) stagflation
 – stagnation + inflation
Stagnationsthese *f*
 (Vw) mature economy thesis
 – secular stagnation thesis
 – stagnation theory
Stahlaktien *fpl*
 (Bö) steel shares
 – steels
Stahlgroßhändler *m* (com) steel wholesaler
Stahlhandel *m* (com) steel trading
Stahlindustrie *f* (com) steel industry
Stahlkammer *f* (Fin) safe deposit vault *(syn, Tresor, Panzergewölbe)*
Stahlkartell *n* (Kart) steel cartel
Stahlkonzern *m* (com) steel group
Stahlmoderatoren *mpl*
 (com) moderators
 – (infml) wise men
 (ie, three businessmen devising a plan for the shakeup of the ailing West German steel industry)
Stahl- und Leichtmetallbau *m* (IndE) steel and light metal construction
Stammabschnitt *m* (Zo) counterfoil *(see: Anweisungsblatt)*
Stammaktien *fpl*
 (Fin) common shares
 – common stock
 – common equity
 – (GB) ordinary shares
Stammaktionär *m*
 (Fin) common stockholder
 – (GB) ordinary shareholder
Stammanmeldung *f* (Pat) parent *(or* basic*)* application
Stammband *n* (EDV) master tape
Stammbelegschaft *f* (Pw) = *Stammpersonal*
Stammdatei *f* (EDV) master file
Stammdaten *pl* (Pw) key data
 (EDV) master data
Stammdividende *f* ordinary dividend
Stämme *mpl*
 (Bö) shares of common stock
 – (GB) ordinary shares
Stammeinlage *f*
 (Fin) original capital contribution *(ie, paid to a GmbH)*
 – participating share
 – participation
 – part
 (Fin) original investment
Stammeintrag *m* (EDV) master record
Stammfirma *f* (Bw) parent firm
Stammfunktion *f* (Math) primary *(or* primitive*)* function

Stammgesellschaft *f* (Re) parent company
Stammhaus *n*
 (Bw) parent company
 – company headquarters
Stammkapital *n* **der GmbH** (Fin) share *(or* nominal*)* capital of a GmbH *(ie, total par value of all ‚Stammeinlagen': minimum DM20,000; § 5 GmbHG; do not confuse with ‚Grundkapital' of AG)*
Stammkarte *f* (EDV) master card *(syn, Mutterkarte, Matrizenkarte)*
Stammkunde *m*
 (com) regular customer
 – regular patron
 – (infml) regular
Stammkunde *m* **sein** (com) to patronize
Stammkundschaft *f*
 (com) regular customers
 – established clientele
Stammnummer *f* (Pw) employee pay number
Stammpatent *n* (Pat) original *(or* parent*)* patent
Stammpersonal *n* (Pw) skeleton staff
Stammprioritäten *fpl* (Fin) = *Vorzugsaktien*
Stammsitz *m* (com) group headquarters
Stammtisch-Politiker *m*
 (com) cracker barrel politician
 – (GB) ale-house politician
Stamm *m* **von Facharbeitern** (Pw) permanent staff of skilled workers
Stand *m*
 (ReW) balance *(ie, of an account)*
 (Bö) price (of securities)
Standardabweichung *f* (Stat) standard deviation *(ie, positive square root of the variance σ^2 = positive Wurzel aus der mittleren quadratischen Abweichung)*
Standardabweichung *f* **der Stichprobe** (Stat) standard deviation of the sample
Standardanschluß *m* (EDV) standard interface
Standardbauteile *npl* (EDV) standard components
Standardbrief *m* (com) standard letter
Standardfehler *m* (Stat) standard error
Standard-Finanzierung *f* (Fin, infml) ready-to-wear financial pattern
Standardformular *n* (com) standard form
Standardgemeinkosten *pl* (KoR) standard overhead
Standardgesamtheit *f* (Stat) standard population
Standardgut *n* (Vw) numéraire
standardisieren (Bw) to standardize
standardisierte Zufallsvariable *f* (Stat) normal *(or* standardized*)* variate
Standardisierung *f* (Bw) standardization
Standardkalkulation *f* (KoR) standard costing
Standardkennsatz *m* (EDV) standard label
Standardklausel *f* (Re) standard clause
Standardkorb-Technik *f* (IWF) basket technique *(ie, of daily SDR valuation)*
Standardkosten *pl*
 (KoR) standard cost
 – cost standard
Standardkostenkarte *f* (KoR) product cost card
Standardkostenrechnung *f*
 (KoR) standard cost accounting
 – standard costing
Standardkostensatz *m* (KoR) standard costing rate

Standardleistungsgrad *m* (IndE) standard rating
Standard-Maschinenstunden *fpl* (KoR) standard machine hours
Standardmuster *n* (com) basis grade
Standardnormalverteilung *f* (Stat) standard normal distribution
Standardpreis *m* (KoR) standard price *(syn, fester Verrechnungspreis)*
Standardprogramm *n* (EDV) standard program
Standardqualität *f* (com) standard quality
Standardselbstkosten *pl* (KoR) standard mill cost
Standardsorte *f* (com) basic (*or* standard) grade
Standard-Steuersatz *m* (StR) basic tax rate
Standardtransformation *f* (Stat) standard transformation *(ie, of normal Gaussian distribution)*
Standard-Umsetzprogramm *n* (EDV) standard convension program
Standardunterprogramm *n* (EDV) standard subroutine
Standardverfahren *n* (Bw) standard operating procedure
Standardvertrag *m* (Re) standard-form contract
Standardwerte *mpl* (Bö) leaders
Standardzeit *f* (IndE) standard time
Standby-Abkommen *n* (IWF) standby arrangement
Standby-Kredit *m* (IWF) standby credit (*or* facility)
Stand *m* **der Technik**
(Pat) prior art
– state of the art
– progress of the arts
Standesamt *n*
(Re) marriage clerk's office
– (GB) Register Office
Standespflichten *fpl* (com) professional duties
Standesvertretung *f* (com) professional representation
ständige Arbeitskräfte *fpl* (Pw) permanent workers (*or* labor)
ständige Bevölkerungsstichprobe *f* (Stat) current population survey
ständige Einrichtung *f* (com) permanent institution
ständiger Beirat *m* (Vw) permanent advisory council
ständige Rechtsprechung *f* (Re) long-standing decisions *(eg, of a superior court)*
ständiger Vertreter *m* (StR) permanent representative, § 13 AO
ständiger Wohnsitz *m* (Re) permanent residence
ständig wechselnde Einsatzstelle *f* (StR) regularly changing place of employment
ständische Gesellschaft *f* (Vw) corporatist (*or* corporatively structured) society
Standleitung *f* (EDV) leased line *(opp, Wählleitung)*
Standort *m* (Bw) location
Standortänderung *f* (Bw) relocation
Standortbedingungen *fpl* (Bw) local conditions
Standortbindung *f* (Bw) locational pull (toward)
Standortfaktoren *mpl* (Bw) location factors
standortgebundene Subvention *f* (Vw) location specific subsidy
Standortkonzeption *f* (Bw) locational concept
Standortlehre *f* (Vw) economics of location

Standortplanung *f* (Bw) locational planning
Standortpräferenz *f* (Bw) locational preference
Standorttheorie *f* (Bw) location theory
Standortverlegung *f* (Bw) change of location
Standortvorteil *m* (Bw) locational advantage
Standortwahl *f* (Bw) locational choice
Standverbindung *f* (EDV) point-to-point circuit
stanzen
(EDV) to punch
– to perforate
Stanzgeschwindigkeit *f*
(EDV) card punching rate
– perforation rate
Stanzer *m* (EDV) punch
Stanzmesser *n* (EDV) punch knife
Stanzstation *f* (EDV) punching station
Stapel *m*
(EDV) pack
(EDV) batch
Stapelarbeit *f* (EDV) = *Stapelverarbeitung*
Stapelbetrieb *m* (EDV) = *Stapelverarbeitung*
Stapelfernverarbeitung *f* (EDV) remote batch processing *(or* working)
Stapelgüter *npl* (com) = *Stapelwaren*
Stapelspeicher *m* (EDV) cellar
– push-down store *(syn, Kellerspeicher)*
Stapelverarbeitung *f* (EDV) batch processing *(syn, Batch-Verarbeitung, schubweise Verarbeitung)*
Stapelverkehr *m* (EDV) batch traffic
Stapelwaren *fpl* (com) staple commodities
stapelweise verarbeiten (EDV) to batch
starke Auslandsnachfrage *f* (AuW) strong demand from foreign markets
starke Führung *f* (Bw) strong (*or* stand-up) leadership
starke Kursausschläge *mpl*
(Bö) wild fluctions of prices (*or* rates)
– gyrations
starke Schwankungen *fpl* (com, infml) big swings *(eg, in traditional manufacturing business)*
starke Währung *f* (AuW) strong currency
stark überbewertet (Bö) strongly overvalued
stark unterbewertet (Bö) strongly undervalued
starre Arbeitszeit *f* (Pw) fixed schedule *(opp, flextime)*
starre Budgetierung *f* (Bw) fixed budgeting
starre Kostenvorgaben *fpl* (KoR) basic cost standards
starre Plankostenrechnung *f* (KoR) fixed budget cost accounting
starrer Wechselkurs *m* (AuW) fixed (*or* pegged) exchange rate
starres Budget *n* (KoR) fixed budget *(ie, allowing no contingency items)*
starre Vollkostenrechnung *f* (KoR) absorption costing
Starrheit *f* **der Reallöhne nach unten** (Vw) downward rigidity of real wages *(ie, due to the ratchet principle = Sperrklinkeneffekt)*
Startadresse *f* (EDV) start address
Startbefehl *m* (EDV) initial instruction (*or* order)
Startbit *n* (EDV) start bit
Startereignis *n* (OR) start event
Starthilfe *f* (com) launching aid
Startkarte *f* (EDV) transfer card

Startknoten *m* (OR) starting node
Startroutinespeicher *m* (EDV) bootstrap memory
Startschritt *m* (EDV) start element
Start-Stop-Betrieb *m* (EDV) start-stop operation
Start-Stop-Lücke *f* (EDV) interrecord gap
Start-Stop-Verfahren *n* (EDV) start-stop system
Startzeit *f* (EDV) start (*or* acceleration) time
Statik *f*
 (Vw) statics
 – static analysis
stationäre Behandlung *f* (SozV) in-patient treatment
stationärer Iterationszyklus *m* (OR) stationary cycle
stationärer Kreislauf *m* (Vw) stationary circular flow
stationärer Punkt *m*
 (Math) point of stagnation
 – saddle point
stationärer Zustand *m* (Vw) stationary state
stationäre Verteilung *f* (Vw) stationary distribution
stationäre Wirtschaft *f* (Vw) stationary economy
stationäre Zeitreihe *f* (Stat) stationary time series
Stationskennung *f*
 (EDV) station identification
 – answerback code *(syn, Kennung)*
Stationsschwester *f*
 (Pw) head nurse
 – (GB) charge-nurse
statische Analyse *f*
 (Vw) static analysis
 – statics
statische Außenhandelsgewinne *mpl* (AuW) allocative (*or* static) gains from trade
statische Bedarfselastizität *f* (Mk) static demand elasticity
statische Bilanz *f* (ReW) point-in-time balance sheet
 (see § 39 HGB; theory developed by Schär, Nicklisch, le Coutre)
statische Methoden *fpl* (Fin) static techniques *(ie, of investment evaluation: Kostenvergleich, Gewinnvergleich, Rentabilitätsrechnung, Amortisationsrechnung)*
statischer Schräglauf *m* (EDV) static skew
statischer Speicher *m* (EDV) static storage
statisches Modell *n* (Bw) static model
statische Wirtschaft *f* (Vw) static economy
Statistik *f* (Stat) statistics
Statistiken *fpl* (Stat) statistics
statistische Berechnung *f* (Stat) statistical computation
statistische Daten *pl*
 (Stat) statistical data
 – statistics
statistische Einheit *f* (Stat) statistical (*or* survey) unit *(syn, Merkmalsträger)*
statistische Entscheidungsfunktion *f* (Stat) statistical decision function
statistische Entscheidungstheorie *f* (Stat) statistical decision theory
statistische Erhebung *f* (Stat) statistical recording (*or* survey)
statistische Erklärung *f* (Stat) statistical explanation

statistische Fehlschlüsse *mpl* (Stat) statistical fallacies
statistische Hypothese *f* (Stat) statistical hypothesis
statistische Kausalforschung *f* (Stat) statistical inference
statistische Masse *f* (Stat) population *(Unterbegriffe: Grundgesamtheit = parent population; Teilgesamtheit = population sample)*
statistische Maßzahl *f* (Stat) statistic
statistische Methodenlehre *f* (Stat) theory of statistics
statistische Qualitätskontrolle *f* (Stat) statistical quality control
statistischer Anmeldeschein *m* (Zo) declaration for statistics
statistische Reihe *f* (Stat) statistical series
statistischer Nachweis *m* (ReW) statistical evidence
statistischer Parameter *m* (Stat) statistical parameter
statistischer Wert *m* **der Waren** (Zo) statistical value of goods
Statistisches Bundesamt *n* (Stat) *(Wiesbaden-based)* Federal Statistical Office
statistische Sicherheit *f* (Stat) confidence factor
statistische Strategie *f* (Stat) statistical strategy
statistische Variable *f* (Stat) statistical variable
statistische Veränderliche *f* (Stat) = *statistische Variable*
statistische Verteilung *f* (Stat) statistical distribution
statistische Zahlungsbilanz *f* (AuW) account balance of payments
Stätte *f* **der Geschäftsleitung** (StR) place of management, § 16 II StAnpG *(ie, not equal to ‚Sitz e-s Unternehmens')*
Status *m* (pl. **Staten** *pl*) (ReW) statement of assets and liabilities *(ie, prepared for various purposes, such as reorganization, bankruptcy, liquidation, etc.)*
Status-Güter *npl* (Vw) positional goods
Statuswort *n* (EDV) status word
Statut *n*
 (Re) charter
 (Re) articles of incorporation
Stauguterkontrolleur *m* (com) tallyman
Stauung *f*
 (OR) bunching up
 – congestion
 (SeeV) actual stowage
Stechkarte *f*
 (Pw) time
 – clock
 – time clock ... card
Stechuhr *f*
 (Pw) time
 – punching
 – time stamping ... clock
 – attendance recorder
Steckbaugruppe *f* (EDV) plug-in unit
steckerkompatibel (EDV) plug compatible
steckerkompatible Einrichtungen *fpl*
 (EDV) PCM equipment
 – PCMs
steckerkompatibler Baustein *m* (EDV) plug compatible module, PCM

Stecktafel f (EDV) control panel
Steckverbindung f (EDV) plug connection
stehende Betriebsmittel npl (StR) operating assets, § 33 II BewG
steigende Abschreibung f (ReW) increasing-balance method of depreciation *(opp, degressive Abschreibung)*
steigende Annuität f (Fin) rising annuity
steigende Funktion f (Math) increasing function
steigende Kosten pl (com) rising costs
steigende Lagerbestände mpl (MaW) rising inventories
steigende Nachfrage f (com) rising demand
Steigen n **der Aktienkurse auf breiter Front** (Bö) broad equity advance
steigende Reihe f (Math) ascending series
steigender Lohnsatz m (Pw) ascending wage rate
steigende Rohstoffkosten pl (com) rising raw materials costs
steigender Skalenertrag m (Vw) increasing returns to scale
steigende Tendenz f (com) upward tendency
steigende Verteidigungsausgaben fpl (FiW) rising defence outlays
steigern
 (com) to increase *(eg, prices, wages)*
 – to raise
 – to advance
 – to lift
 (com, infml) to boost
 – to bump up
 – to hike up
 – to step up
Steigerungsbetrag m (com) increment
Steigerungskorridor m (Vw) growth bracket *(ie, fixed for money supply growth)*
Steigerungsrate f (com) rate of escalation *(eg, in material prices)*
Steigung f (Math) slope
Steigungsmaß n
 (Math) slope
 – rate of change
Steilablage f (com) vertical filing *(syn, Vertikalregistratur)*
steil endende Verteilung f (Stat) abrupt distribution
Steine und Erden pl (com) rock, stone, and related mineral products
Steinkohleeinheit f (IndE) coal equivalent *(eg, primary energy input was 300m tonnes of coal equivalent = mtce)*
Steinkohleförderung f (com) hard coal output
Steinkohle-Kraftwerk n (IndE) hard-coal-based power station
Stellage f
 (Bö) put and call
 – straddle
Stellagegeber m (Bö) seller of a spread
Stellage-Geschäft n (Bö) put and call option
Stellagekurs m (Bö) put and call price
Stellagenehmer m (Bö) buyer of a spread
Stelle f
 (Bw) organizational *(or* administrative*)* unit
 – unit of responsibility
 (Pw) job
 – post
 – position
 (EDV) digit position
 (EDV) place
Stelle f **ausschreiben** (Pw) to advertise a job opening *(or* vacancy*)*
Stelle f **besetzen** (Pw) to fill a job *(or* vacancy*)*
Stelle f **des Fertigungsbereichs** (IndE) production department *(or* division*)*
Stellenabbau m (Pw) reduction of staff
Stellenanforderungen fpl (Pw) job requirements
Stellenangebot n
 (Pw) job offer
 – offer of employment
Stellenangebote npl (Pw) vacancies
Stellenanzeige f
 (Pw) job advertisement
 – employment ad
 (ie, advertising a job opening in a newspaper or trade journal; ads may be open or blind = offene Personalanzeige od Kennziffer-Anzeige; syn, Personalanzeige)
Stellenausschreibung f (Pw) job advertisement
Stellenausschreibungspflicht f (Pw) obligation to advertise vacancies
Stellenaussonderung f (Stat) ordinal selection
Stellenbeschreibung f (Pw) job description *(or* specification*)*
Stellenbesetzungsplan m (Pw) job cover plan
Stellenbewerber m (Pw) job applicant
Stelleneinzelkosten pl (KoR) direct cost center costs
Stellengemeinkosten pl
 (KoR) cost center overhead
 – departmental overhead
 – departmental burden
Stellengesuch n (Pw) job application *(syn, Bewerbung)*
Stellengliederung f (KoR) cost center classification *(or* break-down*)*
Stellenimpuls m
 (EDV) commutator pulse
 – position pulse
 – P-pulse
 – digit pulse *(syn, Zyklusimpuls)*
Stelleninhaber m
 (Pw) jobholder
 – incumbent of a job
Stellenkosten pl
 (KoR) cost center cost
 – departmental cost
Stellenleiter m (Pw) activity head
Stellenmarkt m (Pw) employment market
Stellenmaschine f (EDV) character-oriented computer *(or* machine*)*
Stellenplan m
 (Pw) position chart
 – staffing schedule
Stellenschreibweise f (EDV) positional notation *(or* representation*)*
Stellensuche f
 (Pw) job search *(or* seeking*)*
 – (infml) job hunt
Stellensuchende mpl (Pw) job seekers
Stellentaktzeit f (EDV) digit period *(or* time*)*

Stellentausch *m* (Pw) job rotation
Stellenumlage *f* (KoR) departmental charge
Stellenvermittlung *f* (Pw) job placement
Stellenvermittlungsmonopol *n*
  (Pw) monopoly of job placement
  (ie, held by the Nürnberg-based Federal Labor Office and its subordinate agencies)
Stellenwechsel *m* (Pw) job switch
Stellenwertebene *f* (EDV) digit plane
Stellenwertverschiebung *f* (EDV) relocation *(ie, modification of base addresses to compensate for a change in origin of a set of code)*
Stellenzahl *f* (Math) number of terms *(ie, in a progression)*
Stellfläche *f* (com) shelve space
Stellgeschäft *n* (Bö) = *Stellagegeschäft*
Stellglied *n* (EDV) final control element
Stellgröße *f* (EDV) manipulated variable
  – regulation variable
  – set point
Stellkurs *m* (Bö) put and call price
Stellungnahme *f* **abgeben**
  (com) to make
  – to issue
  – to submit ... comments
Stellung *f* **ohne Aufstiegsmöglichkeiten** (Pw) terminal job *(or position)*
stellvertretend
  (com) acting (for)
  – deputizing
stellvertretender Direktor *m* (com) deputy manager
stellvertretender Vorsitzender *m* (com) deputy chairman
stellvertretender Vorstandsvorsitzender *m* (Bw) deputy chairman of the board
stellvertretende Zielvariable *f* (Vw) target variable
Stellvertreter *m*
  (com) deputy
  – substitute
  – standby person
  (Re) attorney-in-fact
  – private attorney
  – agent *(Note that in English law ‚agent' has a much wider meaning: any person acting for another, directly or indirectly)*
  (Fin) proxy
Stellvertretung *f*
  (com) representation
  – agency
  (Fin) proxy
Stempelkarte *f* (Pw) clock card
Stempelkissen *n*
  (com) inkpad
  – inking pad
Stempelmarke *f* (StR) fee stamp
Stempelsteuer *f* (StR) stamp tax
Stempeluhr *f* (Pw) attendance recorder
Stempelvorrichtung *f* **für Gütestempel** (Stat) certificate stamping unit
Stenoblock *m*
  (com) steno pad
  – (GB) jotter
Stenografie *f* (com) shorthand
Sterbefallversicherung *f*
  (Vers) life insurance
  – (GB) life assurance
Sterbegeld *n* (SozV) death benefit
  (ie, payment made to beneficiary of deceased person)
Sterbegeldversicherung *f* (Vers) death benefit insurance
Sterbekasse *f* (SozV) fund distributing death benefits
Sterbetafel *f*
  (Vers) graduated life table
  – mortality chart *(or* table)
Sterbewahrscheinlichkeit *f* (Vers) expected mortality
Sterbeziffer *f* (Stat) death rate
Sterblichkeit *f* (Vers) mortality rate
Sterblichkeitsgewinn *m* (Vers) mortality profit
Sterblichkeitstabelle *f* (Vers) life *(or* mortality) table
Sterblichkeitsverlauf *m* (Stat) mortality experience
Sterblichkeitsziffer *f* (Stat) = *Sterbeziffer*
stetig (Math) continuous
stetige Analyse *f* (Math) continuous analysis
stetige Funktion *f* (Math) continuous function
stetiger Warenfluß *m*
  (com) steady
  – continuous
  – uninterrupted ... flow of goods
stetiges Einkommen *n* (Pw) steady income stream
stetiges Modell *n* (Vw) continuous model
stetiges Wachstum *n*
  (Vw) steady
  – sustained
  – sustainable ... growth
stetige Verteilung *f* (Stat) continuous distribution
stetige Verzinsung *f* (Math) continous conversion of compound interest
stetige Zufallsvariable *f* (Stat) continuous variable *(or* variate)
Stetigkeit *f* **e–r Funktion** (Math) continuity of a function
Stetigkeitsaxiom *n* (Math) axiom of continuity
stets erwartungstreue Schätzfunktion *f* (Stat) absolutely unbiassed estimator
Steuer *f* (StR) = *Steuern*
Steuerabkommen *n* (Re) tax agreement *(or* treaty)
Steuerabwälzung *f* (Fin) tax burden transfer clause
  (ie, in loan agreements)
  (FiW) = *Steuerüberwälzung*
Steuerabwehr *f* (StR) *(comprehensive term to describe:)* all action and attempts to escape or reduce one's tax liability
  (Unterbegriffe: Steuerhinterziehung, Steuerausweichung, Steuereinholung, Steuerüberwälzung)
Steuerabzug *m* (StR) tax deduction
Steuerabzugsbetrag *m* (StR) amount of withholding tax
Steuerabzugsverfahren *n* (StR) tax deduction at source
Steuerabzug *m* **vom Kapitalertrag** (StR) withholding tax on capital revenues
Steueramortisation *f* (FiW) tax capitalization *(syn, Steuertilgung)*
Steueränderungsgesetz *n* (StR) Tax Amendment Law

Steueranpassungsgesetz n (StR) Law for the Adaptation of Taxes, of 16 Oct 1934, as amended
Steueranrechnung f (StR) tax credit *(esp. foreign taxes)*
Steueranrechnungsverfahren n (StR) tax credit procedure
Steueranspruch m (StR) claim under the tax relationship, § 37 I AO
Steueranstoß m (FiW) tax impact (point)
Steueranweisung f (EDV) control statement
Steuerarrest m (StR) attachment for tax debts
Steuer f **auf das Gewerbekapital** (StR) trading capital tax
  (ie, levied on capital employed)
Steuer f **aufheben**
  (StR) to abandon a tax
  – (infml) to scrap a tax
Steueraufkommen n
  (FiW) tax receipts
  – tax revenue
  – tax yield
  – tax collections
  – (infml) tax take
Steueraufschub m (StR) deferral of tax payment date
Steuer f **auf Selbstverbrauch** (StR) temporary investment tax, § 9b III EStG
Steueraufsicht f (StR) general supervision of tax offices
  – general supervisory function of the local tax office
Steueraufwand m (ReW) tax expenditure
Steuerausfall m (FiW) shortfall of tax revenue
  – tax loss
Steuerausländer m (StR) nonresident *(ie, person subject to limited tax liability)*
Steuerausschuß m (FiW) tax committee
Steuerausweichung f (StR) tax avoidance *(ie, taking advantage of tax loopholes, which is legal, up to a point; syn, Steuervermeidung; opp, Steuerhinterziehung = tax evasion)*
Steuerbanderole f (StR) revenue stamp
steuerbare Leistung f (StR) taxable performance, § 3 UStG
steuerbares Einkommen n
  (StR) taxable (*or* chargeable) income
  – income liable in taxes
steuerbare Umsätze mpl
  (StR) qualifying turnovers
  – qualifying transactions
  – taxable activities, § 1 UStG
Steuerbefehl m (EDV) control command
steuerbefreite Kasse f (SozV) exempt (*or* qualified) fund, Abschn. 6, 2 KStR
steuerbefreiter Betrieb m (StR) tax-exempt enterprise
steuerbefreiter Grundbesitz m (StR) exempt real property, § 3 GrStG
steuerbefreite Übernehmerin f (StR) tax-exempt transferee
steuerbefreite Wirtschaftsgüter npl (StR) tax-exempt assets, §§ 101, 114 BewG
Steuerbefreiung f
  (StR) exemption from tax liability
  – tax exemption

Steuerbefreiung f **bei der Ausfuhr** (StR) exemption of export deliveries
Steuerbefreiung f **bei der Einfuhr** (StR) exemption from import tax
Steuerbefreiungen fpl (StR) tax concessions and allowances
steuerbegünstigt
  (StR) tax favored
  – tax privileged
  – tax qualified
  – tax sheltered
steuerbegünstigter nicht entnommener Gewinn m (StR) portion of profit not withdrawn and qualifying for tax benefit
steuerbegünstigter Zweck m (StR) recognized purpose
steuerbegünstigtes Sparen n (StR) tax-favored saving
steuerbegünstigte Umwandlung f (StR) tax-privileged reorganization
steuerbegünstigte Wertpapiere npl (StR) securities with tax benefits attached to them *(opp, tarifbesteuerte Wertpapiere)*
steuerbegünstigte Zwecke mpl (StR) tax-favored purposes, §§ 51–54 AO
Steuerbegünstigung f
  (StR) tax benefit
  – tax concession
  – tax privilege
  – favorable tax treatment
Steuerbehörde f (StR) revenue (*or* tax) authority
Steuerbelastung f (StR) tax burden
Steuerbemessungsgrundlage f
  (StR) tax base *(ie, object to be taxed)*
  (StR, VAT) taxable amount
steuerberatende Berufe mpl (StR) tax advising (*or* consulting *or* counseling) professions•
Steuerberater m
  (StR) tax consultant
  – tax adviser
  – tax counselor
Steuerberatung f
  (StR) tax consultation
  – tax advice
  – tax counseling
Steuerberatungsgesellschaft f (StR) tax consulting company *(ie, organized as AG, GmbH, KG)*
Steuerberatungsgesetz n (StR) Law on Tax Advisers, of 16 Aug 1961, as amended
Steuerberatungskosten pl (StR) fees for tax consulting services
Steuerberechnung f
  (StR) computation of a tax
  – tax accounting
Steuerbescheid m (StR) formal assessment note, §§ 155, 218 AO
Steuerbescheid m **erlassen** (StR) to make (*or* issue) a tax assessment notice
Steuerbetrug m (StR) tax fraud
Steuerbevollmächtigter m
  (StR) agent in tax matters
  (ie, admission closed after 12 Aug 1980)
Steuerbilanz f (StR) tax balance sheet
Steuerblock m (EDV) control block *(syn, Kennblock)*

Steuerdaten *pl* (EDV) control data
Steuerdelikt *n* (StR) tax offense
Steuerdestinatar *m* (StR) intended taxpayer *(ie, need not be identical with the ‚Steuerträger')*
Steuerdiffusion *f* (FiW) tax diffusion *(ie, distribution of a tax burden throughout the economy as a whole)*
Steuerdruck *m* (StR) tax burden
Steuereinheit *f*
(StR) taxable object
(EDV) control unit
Steuereinholung *f* (StR) making up for increased taxes by working even harder
Steuereinkünfte *pl* (FiW) fiscal revenues
Steuereinnahmen *fpl* (StR) = *Steueraufkommen*
Steuereinziehung *f* (StR) collection of taxes
Steuerentlastung *f*
(StR) tax benefit (*or* break)
– (GB) tax relief
Steuerentlastungsgesetz *n*
(StR) Tax Relief Law
– Law on Tax Relief and Support of Families
Steuerentrichtung *f* (StR) payment of taxes
Steuer *f* **erheben** (StR) to levy a tax
Steuererhebung *f* (StR) tax collection
Steuerhebung *f* **nach dem Quellenprinzip** (StR) collection (*or* stoppage) at source
Steuererhöhung *f*
(StR) tax increase
– rise in taxes
Steuererklärung *f* (StR) tax return, § 149 AO
Steuerklärung *f* **abgeben** (StR) to file a tax return, § 149 AO
Steuererklärung *f* **ausfüllen**
(StR) to fill in one's tax return
– (infml) to do one's taxes
Steuererklärungsfrist *f*
(StR) due date for annual income tax return, § 56 EStDV
– filing period for taxpayers
Steuererlaß *m* (StR) forgiveness of a tax *(ie, which may be complete or partial, § 227 AO)*
– mitigation of tax liability
– equitable relief related to the collection of a tax
Steuererleichterung *f*
(StR) tax benefit
– (GB) tax relief
Steuerermäßigung *f* (StR) tax reduction
Steuerermäßigung *f* **bei Auslandsvermögen** (StR) reduction of net worth for foreign business property, § 12 VStG
Steuerermittlungsverfahren *n* (StR) procedure applying to the examination of a taxpayer with respect to a specific taxable year or number of years, §§ 88, 200 AO
Steuerersparnis *f* (StR) tax saving
Steuererstattung *f* (StR) tax refund
Steuerertrag *m*
(FiW) proceeds (*or* yield) of a tax
Steuerfahndung *f* (StR) tax search, § 208 I AO
Steuerfeld *n* (EDV) panel control field
Steuerfestsetzung *f* **unter Vorbehalt der Nachprüfung** (StR) preliminary assessment of taxpayers subject to tax examination, § 164 AO

Steuerfiskus *m* (StR) tax authorities
Steuerflexibilität *f* (FiW) elasticity of tax revenue *(syn, Aufkommenselastizität)*
Steuerflucht *f* (StR) tax evasion by absconding *(ie, a special case of ‚Steuerausweichung')*
Steuerfolge *f* (EDV) control sequence
Steuerfortwälzung *f* (FiW) passing forward of taxes
steuerfrei
(StR) tax free
– tax exempt
– not subject to taxation
– (infml) clear of taxes *(eg, bonds return 5%, ...)*
Steuerfreibetrag *m*
(StR) statutory tax exemption
– tax-free amount (*or* allowance)
steuerfreie Anleihe *f* (Fin) tax-exempt loan issue
steuerfreie Bezüge *pl* (StR) tax-free earnings
steuerfreie Einnahmen *fpl* (StR) non-taxable income, § 3c EStG
steuerfreie Gewinnausschüttung *f* (StR) tax-free distribution of profits
steuerfreie Lieferungen *fpl* (StR) nontaxable turnovers
steuerfreie Obligationen *fpl* (Fin) tax-exempt bonds
steuerfreies Einkommen *n* (StR) tax-free (*or* nontaxable) income
steuerfreie Wertpapiere *npl* (Fin) tax-exempt securities, § 3 Ziff 45, 53, 54 and § 3a EStG
Steuerfreiheit *f*
(StR) tax exemption
– immunity from taxation
Steuerfreijahre *npl* (StR) tax holiday
Steuergefälle *n* (StR) tax differential
Steuergegenstand *m*
(StR) object of a tax
– taxable event (*or* object *or* unit) *(eg, income, property)*
Steuergeheimnis *n* (StR) tax secrecy *(ie, of tax returns and all other data relevant to the determination of tax liability, § 30 AO)*
Steuergelder *npl* (FiW, infml) tax money
Steuergerät *n* (EDV) controller *(syn, Steuerteil)*
Steuergerechtigkeit *f* (FiW) tax equity
Steuergerichte *npl* (FiW) fiscal courts
Steuergesetz *n* (StR) tax law (*or* statute)
Steuergesetzgebung *f* (StR) fiscal (*or* tax) legislation
Steuergläubiger *m* (FiW) tax creditor *(ie, all governmental units)*
Steuergröße *f* (EDV) set point
Steuergrundgesetz *n* (StR) fundamental law of West German taxation *(ie, Abgabenordnung: Fiscal Code)*
Steuergrundsätze *mpl* (FiW) canons of taxation
Steuergutschein *m*
(StR) tax-reserve certificate
– tax anticipation warrant (*or* note)
Steuergutschrift *f* (StR) tax credit
Steuerhaftung *f* (StR) tax liability *(eg, attaching to employer for employee wage taxes)*
Steuerharmonisierung *f*
(EG) harmonization of taxes
– tax harmonization

Steuerhäufung *f* (FiW) tax accumulation *(ie, may happen to an individual taxpayer through tax shifting)*
Steuerhehler *m* (StR) tax receiver
Steuerhehlerei *f* (StR) tax receiving *(ie, dealing in tax-evaded property, § 374 AO)*
Steuerhinterzieher *m*
 (StR) tax evader
 − (infml) tax dodger
Steuerhinterziehung *f*
 (StR) (illegal) tax evasion, § 370 AO
 − tax fraud
 − (infml) tax dodging
 (opp, Steuerausweichung od -vermeidung = tax avoidance)
Steuerhoheit *f*
 (FiW) jurisdiction to tax
 − power to tax
 − power to levy taxes
 − taxing power
 (ie, comprises Gesetzgebungshoheit, Ertragshoheit, Verwaltungshoheit; divided among the various governmental units)
Steuerillusion *f* (FiW) tax illusion
Steuerinflation *f* (Vw) tax inflation
Steuerinformation *f* (EDV) control information
Steuerinländer *m* (StR) resident taxpayer *(ie, person subject to unlimited tax liability)*
Steuerinzidenz *f*
 (FiW) incidence of taxation
 − tax incidence
Steuerjahr *n* (StR) tax (*or* taxable) year
Steuerjurist *m* (StR) tax lawyer
Steuerkarte *f*
 (StR) wage tax card
 (EDV) control
 − parameter
 − job control ... card
Steuerklasse *f* (StR) tax class
Steuerklassifikation *f* (StR) classification (*or* grouping) of taxes
Steuerkraft *f* (StR) taxable capacity
Steuerkraftmeßzahl *f*
 (StR) rate of taxable capacity
 − adjusted collection figure of a state
 (ie, total tax collections of the state for the fiscal year + collections from real property tax and trade tax made by the municipalities located in the state − extraordinary expenditures incurred by the state during the fiscal year)
Steuerkreis *m* (EDV) control circuit *(syn, Steuerschaltung)*
Steuerkurswerte *mpl* (StR) special tax values *(ie, prescribed to determine the assessed value of securities that are business assets, § 113 BewG)*
Steuerkürzung *f* (com) tax cut
Steuerlast *f* (StR) tax burden
Steuerlastquote *f* (FiW) = *Steuerquote*
Steuerlastverteilung *f* (FiW) distribution of tax burden
Steuerlehre *f* (StR) theory of taxation
steuerlich abzugsfähig
 (StR) tax deductible
 − allowable for tax purposes
steuerlich belasten

 (FiW) to tax
 − to subject to taxation
steuerlich befreien (StR) to exempt from taxation *(eg, DM800 of interest on private savings accounts)*
steuerlich beraten (StR) to render tax advice
steuerliche Abschreibung *f*
 (StR) tax depreciation
 − tax write-off
 (ie, depreciation for income-tax purposes, § 7 EStG, § 9 EStDV; syn, Absetzung für Abnutzung, AfA)
steuerliche Abschreibungsmöglichkeiten *fpl* (StR) tax write-off facilities
steuerliche Absetzung *f* (StR) tax deduction
steuerliche Abzugsmöglichkeiten *fpl* (StR) scope for deducting items from tax liability
steuerliche Anreize *mpl* (StR) beneficial tax incentives
steuerliche Aspekte *mpl* (StR) taxation aspects
steuerliche Begriffsbestimmungen *fpl* (StR) definitions for tax purposes, §§ 3ff AO
steuerliche Behandlung *f*
 (StR) treatment for tax purposes
 − tax treatment
steuerliche Belastung *f*
 (StR) tax burden (*or* load)
 − taxation *(eg, of profits or earnings)*
steuerliche Belastungsgrenze *f* (FiW) taxable capacity
steuerliche Benachteiligung *f* (StR) tax discrimination
steuerliche Bewertungsvorschriften *fpl* (StR) tax valuation rules
steuerliche Bilanzierungsgrundsätze *mpl* (ReW) tax-based accounting principles
steuerliche Diskriminierung *f* (StR) fiscal (*or* tax) discrimination
steuerliche Gesamtbelastung *f* (FiW) total tax burden
steuerliche Gestaltungsfreiheit *f* (StR) freedom (of taxpayers) to shape transactions so as to accomplish the most favorable tax result
steuerliche Gewinnermittlung *f* (StR) determination of taxable income
steuerliche Gleichbehandlung *f* (StR) equal tax treatment
steuerliche Höchstbeträge *mpl* (StR) maximum amounts deductible from tax liability
steuerliche Investitionsanreize *mpl* (StR) tax concessions (to business) to spur new investment
steuerliche Konsequenzen *fpl* (StR) tax consequences
steuerliche Nebenleistungen *fpl* (StR) incidental tax payments
 (ie, charges for delayed payment, interest, etc., § 3 AO)
steuerlichen Wohnsitz *m* **begründen** (StR) to establish a tax residence
steuerlicher Anreiz *m* (StR) tax incentive
steuerlicher Grenzausgleich *m* (EG) border adjustment for internal taxes
steuerlicher Grundstückswert *m* (StR) assessable site value
steuerlicher Nachteil *m* (StR) fiscal disadvantage

steuerlicher Verlustrücktrag m (StR) tax loss carryback
steuerlicher Verlustvortrag m (StR) tax loss carryforward
– tax loss credit
steuerlicher Wertansatz m (StR) tax valuation
steuerlicher Wohnsitz m (StR) fiscal (or tax) domicile
– tax residence
steuerliche Sonderabschreibung f (StR) special depreciation allowance for tax purposes
– fast tax write-off
steuerliches Rechtsinstitut n (StR) tax-modifying device (or vehicle) (eg, Organschaft, Schachtelprivileg)
steuerliche Vergünstigung f (StR) tax concession
steuerliche Verrechnungspreise mpl in internationalen Konzernen (StR) international intercompany pricing for tax purposes
steuerliche Vorteile mpl (StR) tax benefits
steuerlich manipulieren (StR) to shift income from a high bracket into a lower one
steuerlich motivierte Umschichtung f e–s Portefeuilles (Fin) tax switching
steuerlich nicht abzugsfähig (StR) disallowable against tax
steuerlich voll abzugsfähig (StR) fully tax deductible
Steuerliste f (FiW) list of tax assessments (ie, open for public inspection)
Steuerlochkarte f (EDV) pilot card
Steuerlochstreifen m (EDV) control paper tape
Steuerlochungen fpl (EDV) control (or function) holes
– control punchings (syn, Leitlochungen)
Steuermannsquittung f (com) mate's receipt
Steuermarke f (StR) tax stamp
Steuermaßstab m (StR) tax base
Steuermaximen fpl (FiW) tax canons
Steuermeßbetrag m (StR) tentative tax (ie, product of applicable tax rate and taxable business profits) (StR) product of assessed value – Einheitswert – and basic rate – Steuermeßzahl – (ie, to which the municipal percentage = Hebesatz is applied, § 13 GrStG)
Steuermeßzahl f (StR) basic federal rate (ie, applying to property and business profits)
Steuermindereinnahmen fpl (FiW) revenue shortfall
– shortfall of tax revenues
Steuer f **mit negativen Leistungsanreizen** (FiW) repressive tax
Steuermittel pl (FiW) funds raised by taxation
– tax revenues
Steuermonopol n (FiW) fiscal monopoly
Steuermoral f (StR) tax morale
Steuermultiplikator m (FiW) tax multiplier
Steuern fpl (StR) taxes (ie, current or nonrecurring payments of money collected by a public authority for revenue purposes and imposed by that authority on all those who fulfill the conditions establishing liability for payment, § 3 AO)
Steuernachlaß m (StR) tax rebate (or abatement)
Steuern n **des Entscheidungsprozesses** (Bw) decision control
Steuern fpl **entrichten** (StR) to pay taxes
Steuern erheben (FiW) to levy taxes
Steuern fpl **erhöhen** (StR) to raise
– to put up ... tax rates (or rates of taxation)
– to increase taxation
Steuern fpl **hinterziehen** (StR) to evade taxes
Steuern fpl **mit örtlichem Geltungsbereich** (FiW) taxes applied locally
– taxes of local application
Steuern fpl **senken** (FiW) to cut taxes
Steuern fpl **umgehen** (StR) to avoid (or to dodge) taxes
Steuernummer f (StR) tax payer's account number
Steuern fpl **und Abgaben** fpl (ReW) taxes and other fiscal charges
Steuern fpl **vom Einkommen, Ertrag und Vermögen** (StR) taxes on corporate income, business profits, and net worth
Steuern fpl **vom Grundbesitz** (StR) real property taxes, § 9 I No. 2 EStG
Steueroase f (FiW) tax haven
Steuerobjekt n (FiW) taxable object
Steuerordnungswidrigkeit f (StR) fiscal (or tax) violation, § 377 AO
Steuerpaket n (FiW) tax package
Steuerpauschalierung f (StR) lump-sum taxation
Steuerpfändung f (StR) tax foreclosure
Steuerpflicht f (StR) liability to pay taxes
steuerpflichtig (StR) taxable
– subject to tax
– liable in taxes
steuerpflichtige inländische Körperschaft f (StR) domestic corporate tax payer
steuerpflichtige Kapitalerträge mpl (StR) taxable investment income
steuerpflichtige Leistung f (StR, VAT) taxable transaction
Steuerpflichtiger m (StR) legal taxpayer, § 33 I AO
steuerpflichtiger Gegenstand m (StR) taxable object
steuerpflichtiger Gewinn m (StR) taxable gain (or profit)
steuerpflichtiger Nachlaß m (StR) taxable estate
steuerpflichtiger Umsatz m (StR) taxable turnover
steuerpflichtiges Einkommen n (StR) taxable (or chargeable) income
– income liable in taxes
steuerpflichtiges Vermögen n (StR) taxable net worth
Steuerpolitik f (StR) tax (or taxation) policy
Steuerpostulate npl (FiW) tax canons
Steuerpräferenzen fpl (StR) tax preferences (ie, part of the promotion of the West Berlin economy: income taxes are lower by 30% and 20%, respectively)
Steuerprogramm n (EDV) control program (syn, Systemsteuerprogramm)
Steuerprogression f (StR) tax progression

Steuerprüfung *f* (StR) tax examination (*or* audit)
Steuerpult *n* (EDV) control console
Steuerquelle *f*
(StR) tax base *(eg, property values are the major ... of local governments)*
(FiW) source of revenue
Steuerquote *f*
(FiW) tax load ratio
– overall tax ratio
(ie, total tax collections to gnp at market prices = Steuern/BSP zu Marktpreisen; opp, individuelle Steuerquote, qv)
Steuerrecht *n*
(StR) law of taxation
– fiscal law
Steuerrecht *n* **der Unternehmen** (StR) company tax law
steuerrechtliche Behandlung *f* (StR) tax treatment *(eg, of inventories)*
steuerrechtliche Bewertung *f* (StR) tax-based valuation *(opp, handelsrechtliche Bewertung = commercial valuation)*
steuerrechtliche Vorschriften *fpl* (StR) tax law provisions (*or* rules *or* regulations)
Steuerreform *f* (StR) tax reform
Steuerregister *n* (EDV) control register (*or* counter)
Steuerregression *f* (StR) tax regression
Steuerrichtlinien *fpl* (StR) administrative tax regulations *(ie, accompanying federal tax statutes and issued by the Federal Ministry of Finance)*
Steuerrückerstattung *f* (StR) refund of overpaid tax, § 36 IV EStG
Steuerrückstände *mpl*
(ReW) tax arrears
Steuerrückstellungen *fpl* (ReW, EG) provisions for taxation
Steuerrückvergütung *f*
(StR) refund of taxes
– tax refund
Steuerrückwälzung *f* (FiW) passing backward of taxes
Steuerrückzahlung *f* (StR) tax refund
Steuersatz *m* (StR) tax rate
Steuersäumnisgesetz *n* (StR) Law on Tax Arrears, of 13 July 1961
Steuerschaltung *f* (EDV) control circuit *(syn, Steuerkreis)*
Steuerschätzung *f* (StR) determination of taxable income by estimate, § 162 I AO
Steuerschlupfloch *n* (FiW) tax loophole
Steuerschraube *f* (FiW) tax load
Steuerschraube *f* **anziehen** (FiW) to turn the tax screw
Steuerschuld *f*
(StR) liability to tax
– tax liability
(StR) tax payable (*or* due)
(StR, VAT) total amount of tax charged on the invoices rendered by the entrepreneur
Steuerschuld *f* **des Rechtsnachfolgers** (StR) transferee liability, § 45 AO
Steuerschuldner *m*
(StR) person subject to a tax
– taxpayer

Steuerschuldverhältnis *n* (StR) government-taxpayer relationship, § 38 AO
Steuersenkung *f* (StR) tax cut (*or* reduction)
Steuerstatistik *f* (StR) tax statistics
Steuerstempel *m* (StR) revenue stamp
Steuersteppen *fpl* (FiW) high-tax countries
Steuerstraftat *f*
(StR) criminal tax violation
– tax offense
Steuerstrafverfahren *n* (StR) criminal tax proceedings, §§ 385–408 AO
steuerstarkes Land *n* (FiW) country with large tax revenues
Steuerstufe *f* (StR) tax bracket
Steuerstundung *f* (StR) tax deferral, § 222 AO
Steuersubjekt *n* (StR) taxable entity
Steuersystem *n*
(FiW) revenue raising system
– tax structure
(StR) system of taxation
(EDV) control system
steuersystematisch (StR) as defined within the German tax system
Steuersystem *n* **mit Rückkopplung** (EDV) closed-loop control system
Steuertabelle *f* (StR) tax-rate table
Steuertarif *m* (StR) tax-rate table
Steuertatbestand *m* (StR) taxable event
Steuerteil *n* (EDV) controller *(syn, Steuergerät)*
Steuertermin *m* (StR) tax payment date
Steuertheorie *f* (StR) theory of taxation
Steuertilgung *f* (FiW) tax capitalization *(syn, Steueramortisation)*
Steuerträger *m* (FiW) actual taxpayer *(ie, the final resting place of the tax)*
Steuer *f* **überwälzen** (FiW) to pass on (*or* to shift) a tax
Steuerüberwälzung *f* (FiW) shifting of taxes
– tax shifting
(Unterbegriffe: Vor-, Rück- und Schrägüberwälzung)
Steuerumgehung *f* (StR) tax avoidance, § 42 AO
Steuerung *f*
(EDV) control
– feed forward control
– open loop control
Steuerung *f* **des Materialdurchlaufs** (MaW) materials management *(ie, procurement, stockkeeping, production, shipping)*
Steuerungsablauf *m* (EDV) control sequence
Steuerungseinrichtungen *fpl* (EDV) selectors
Steuerungsfunktion *f*
(Vw) allocative function
(EDV) control function
Steuerungstechnik *f* (EDV) control engineering
Steuerungsübergabe *f* (EDV) control transfer
Steuerung *f* **von Produktionsprozessen** (IndE) process control
steuerunschädlich (StR) tax neutral
Steuerunschädlichkeit *f* (StR) tax neutrality
Steuerveranlagung *f* (StR) tax assessment
Steuerverbindlichkeiten *fpl*
(StR) tax liabilities
– tax payable
Steuervergehen *n* (StR) = *Steuerstraftat*

Steuervergünstigung *f*
(StR) favorable tax treatment
– tax break (*or* credit *or* relief)
– tax concession
– taxation privilege
Steuervergütung *f* (StR) tax refund, § 4a UStG
Steuervergütungsbescheid *m* (StR) notice of a decision on a refund claim, § 348 AO
Steuerverkürzung *f* (StR) tax deficiency, § 378 AO
Steuervermeidung *f* (FiW) = *Steuerausweichung*
Steuerverpflichtungsgrund *m* (StR) taxable event
Steuerversicherung *f* (Vers) tax insurance
Steuerverwaltung *f* (StR) tax administration
Steuer *f* **von der Steuer** (StR, VAT) tax on tax *(ie, on each subsequent sale)*
Steuervorausschätzung *f* (FiW) tax estimate
Steuervorauszahlung *f* (StR) prepayment of taxes *(ie, estimated tax payment made in advance)*
Steuervordruck *m* (StR) tax form
Steuervorteil *m*
(StR) tax advantage
– tax break
– tax preference
Steuerwerk *n* (EDV) control unit *(syn, Leitwerk, Kommandowerk)*
Steuerwicklung *f* (EDV) drive winding
Steuerwiderstand *m* (StR) resistance to taxation
steuerwirksam
(StR) tax effective *(eg, agreement)*
– affecting tax liability
Steuerwirkungen *fpl* (FiW) effects of taxation
Steuerwohnsitz *m* (StR) = *steuerlicher Wohnsitz*
Steuerwort *n* (EDV) control word
Steuerzahler *m* (StR) taxpayer
Steuerzahllast *f* (StR, VAT) amount of tax payable by the entrepreneur *(ie, Steuerschuld abzüglich Vorsteuer)*
Steuerzahlung *f* (StR) payment of taxes
Steuerzeichen *n*
(StR) revenue stamp
(EDV) control character
Steuerzeitschrift *f* (StR) tax journal
Stibitz-Code *m* (EDV) excess-three code
Stichgleis *n* (com) spur (*or* stub) track *(ie, connected to main track at one end only; opp, totes Gleis)*
Stichkupon *m* (Fin) renewal coupon
Stichprobe *f*
(com) spot check
(Stat) sample
Stichprobe *f* **entnehmen** (Stat) to take a sample
Stichprobe *f* **hochrechnen**
(Stat) to extrapolate
– to blow up
– to raise ... a sample
Stichprobe *f* **mit Selbstgewichtung** (Stat) self-weighting sample
Stichprobeneinheit *f* (Stat) sample unit
Stichprobenentnahme *f* **aus der Masse** (Stat) bulk sampling
Stichprobenerhebung *f* (Stat) sample survey *(ie, relates to only a specified part of the population; ‚sample census', sometimes used, is a misnomer)*
Stichprobenerhebungsgrundlage *f* (Stat) frame
Stichprobenfehler *m* (Stat) sampling error

stichprobenfremder Fehler *m* (Stat) nonsampling error
Stichprobenfunktion *f* (Stat) sample function *(eg, Gauß-Statistik, Stichprobenvarianz, t-Statistik)*
Stichprobenkenngröße *f* (Stat) sample statistic
Stichprobenkorrelogramm *n* (Stat) sample correlogram
Stichprobenkosten *pl* (Stat) cost of sample
Stichprobenkostenfunktion *f* (Stat) sample cost function
Stichprobenmaßzahl *f* (Stat) = *Stichprobenkenngröße*
Stichprobenmethode *f* (Stat) sampling method
Stichprobenmittelwert *m* (Stat) mean of the sample
Stichprobenmoment *n* (Stat) sample moment
Stichprobennahme *f* **aus der Masse** (Stat) bulk sampling
Stichprobennetz *n* (Stat) network of samples
Stichprobenplan *m* (Stat) sampling plan
Stichprobenpopulation *f* (Stat) sample population
Stichprobenprüfplan *m* (Stat) sampling inspection plan
Stichprobenprüfung *f* (Stat) sampling inspection
Stichprobenpunkt *m* (Stat) sample point
Stichprobenraum *m* (Stat) sample space *(syn, Ereignisraum)*
Stichproben-Standardabweichung *f* (Stat) standard deviation of the sample
Stichprobenstruktur *f* (Stat) sampling structure
Stichprobensystem *n* (Stat) sampling system
Stichprobentechnik *f* (Stat) sampling technique
Stichprobentheorie *f* (Stat) theory of sampling
Stichprobenumfang *m*
(Stat) sample size
– range of sample
Stichprobenvariable *f* (Stat) sample value
Stichprobenvarianz *f* (Stat) variance of the sample
Stichprobenverfahren *n*
(Stat) sampling
– sampling procedure
Stichprobenverfahren *n* **mit Klumpenauswahl** (Stat) cluster (*or* nested) sampling
Stichprobenverfahren *n* **mit Unterauswahl** (Stat) subsampling
Stichprobenverteilung *f* (Stat) sampling distribution
stichprobenweise prüfen (ReW) to testcheck
Stichtag *m*
(com) key
– target
– effective
– relevant ... date
(ReW) reporting (*or* cutoff) date
(Fin) call date
Stichtaginventur *f*
(ReW) periodical inventory (*or* stocktaking)
– end-of-period inventory
Stichtagskurs *m*
(Bö) current price
– market price on reporting date
Stichwahl *f*
(Pw) decisive
– final
– second ... ballot
– runoff vote

stiften
(com) to make a contribution
(Re) to donate
– to endow
Stifter *m* (Re) donor
Stiftung *f*
(Re) foundation
– endowment
(ie, foundation is a general term, including endowment which means the particular fund of the institution bestowed for the purpose intended)
Stiftung des öffentlichen Rechts *f* (Re) foundation under public law
Stiftung *f* **des Privatrechts** (Re) private foundation, §§ 80 ff BGB
Stiftung *f* **errichten** (Re) to organize (*or* set up) a foundation
Stiftungsvermögen *n*
(Re) endowment fund (*or* property)
– property of foundation
stille Beteiligung *f* (Fin) dormant equity holding
stille Forderungsabtretung *f* (Re) = *stille Zession*
stillegen (Bw) to shut down (*or* close down) a plant
Stillegen *n* **von Goldbeständen** (AuW) gold sterilization
stille Gesellschaft *f* (Re) dormant partnership, §§ 335 ff HGB
(U.S. law, for instance, differentiates as follows: (1) silent: no voice in the affairs of the business; (2) secret: undisclosed; (3) dormant: both silent and secret. In German law, the partnership is nothing more than an ‚undisclosed participation'. The distinguishing feature is that the German ‚dormant partner' is in no way liable for the debts of the business)
Stillegung *f* (Bw) plant shutdown (*or* close-down)
Stillegung *f* **e–s Anlagegutes** (ReW) retirement of a fixed asset
Stillegung *f* **von Steuereinnahmen** (FiW) immobilization of tax receipts (or revenues)
stille Reserven *fpl*
(ReW) secret
– hidden
– undisclosed ... reserves
(ie, book value is less than the actual realizable value; syn, stille Rücklagen)
stiller Gesellschafter *m* (Re) dormant partner *(see: ‚stille Gesellschaft')*
stiller Teilhaber *m* (Re) = *stiller Gesellschafter*
stille Rücklagen *fpl* (ReW) = *stille Reserven*
stilles Factoring *n* (Fin) non-notification factoring
stille Zession *f* (Re) undisclosed assignment
Stillhalteabkommen *n*
(Re) standstill agreement
(Fin) standby agreement
(AuW, OECD) trade pledge
(AuW) Basle Agreement
– Reciprocal Currency Agreement
(syn, Basler Abkommen; between 1931 and 1962)
stillhalten
(Fin) to grant a moratorium
– to postpone enforcement of claims
Stillhalter *m* (Bö) taker of an option
Stillhaltung *f* (Fin) prolongation of credits

Stillschweigen *n* (Re) silence
(ie, the silence of a party generally implies his refusal)
stillschweigende Bedingung *f* (Re) implied condition
stillschweigende Einwilligung *f* (Re) acquiescence
stillschweigende Gewährleistung *f* (Re) implied (*or* tacit) warranty
stillschweigende Mängelhaftung *f* (Re) = *stillschweigende Gewährleistung*
stillschweigende Mietverlängerung *f* (Re) tacit extension of tenancy
stillschweigendes Einverständnis *n* (Re) connivance
stillschweigende Vereinbarung *f* (Re) tacit agreement (*or* understanding)
stillschweigende Verlängerung *f* (Re) tacit renewal
stillschweigende Voraussetzung *f* (Log) implicit understanding
stillschweigende Willenserklärung *f* (Re) implied manifestation of intent
stillschweigende Zustimmung *f* (Re) implied (*or* tacit) consent
stillschweigend vereinbaren (Re) to stipulate tacitly (*or* by implication)
stillschweigend vereinbarte Leistungspflichten *fpl* (Re) implied obligations
stillschweigend verlängern (com) to extend automatically (*or* by implication)
Stillstandskosten *pl* (KoR) downtime cost
Stillstandszeit *f*
(IndE) downtime
– idle time
– dead time
– lost time
– downperiod
– stoppage
stimmberechtigte Aktie *f* (Fin) voting share (*or* stock)
stimmberechtigter Aktionär *m* (Fin) voting shareholder
stimmberechtigtes Kapital *n* (Fin) voting capital
stimmberechtigte Stammaktien *fpl* (Fin) ordinary voting shares
Stimme *f* **abgeben** (Pw) to cast one's vote
stimmen für (Pw) to vote for
Stimmengleichheit *f* (Pw) equality (*or* parity) of votes
Stimmenkauf *m* (Bw) vote buying, § 405 III AktG
Stimmenmehrheit *f*
(Pw) majority of votes
– majority vote
Stimmenthaltungen *fpl* (Pw) abstentions
Stimmrecht *n* (Bw) voting right, § 12 AktG
Stimmrechtsaktie *f* (Fin) voting stock (*or* share)
Stimmrechtsausübung *f* **durch Vertreter** (com) voting by proxy
Stimmrechtsbevollmächtigter *m* (Re) proxy
Stimmrechtsbindung *f* (Re) voting commitment
stimmrechtslose Aktie *f* (Fin) nonvoting share
stimmrechtslose Vorzugsaktie *f* (Fin) nonvoting preferred stock (*or* GB: preference share)
Stimmrechtsmißbrauch *m* (Re) abuse of voting rights, § 405 III AktG
Stimmrechtstreuhänder *m* (Re) voting trustee

Stimmrechtsübertragung f (Re) transfer of voting rights
Stimmrechtsvertreter m (Re) proxy
Stimmrechtsvollmacht f (Re) voting proxy *(ie, written power of attorney to act for another in a stockholder meeting)*
Stimmschein m (Fin) certificate of proxy *(ie, made out by depositary bank or notary public)*
Stimmung f (Bö) tone of the market
Stimmvieh n (Pw, sl) stupid electorate
stochastische Komponente f (Stat) random component
stochastische Konvergenz f (Stat) convergence in probability
stochastische Programmierung f (OR) stochastic programming
stochastischer Prozeß m (Stat) random process
stochastische Variable f (Stat) chance (*or* random) variable
Stockdividende f
– (Fin) stock dividend
– (GB) free issue of new shares
Stoffeinsatz m (ReW) expenditure on materials
Stoffkosten pl (KoR) cost of materials *(syn, Materialkosten, qv)*
Stoffumwandlung f
(IndE) conversion *(ie, general and chemical)*
(Bw) conversion of resources
Stoffwert m **des Geldes** (Vw) intrinsic value of money
Stoffwirtschaft f (MaW) materials management
Stoffwirtschafts-Ingenieur m (MaW) materials management engineer
Stop-loss-Order f
(Bö) stop loss order
– cutting limit order
Stoppbefehl m (EDV) halt (*or* checkpoint) instruction *(syn, Haltbefehl)*
Stoppbit n (EDV) stop bit (*or* element)
Stoppcode m
(EDV) stop code
– halt instruction
Stopp m **der Reallöhne** (Vw) real wage freeze
Stoppkurs m (Bö) stop price *(ie, applied between 1942 and 1948)*
Stopppreis m (Vw) stop price *(ie, fixed by administrative agencies or cartels)*
Stoppschrittprüfung f (EDV) stop element check
Stopptag m (Fin) record date *(ie, set for transfer of registered securities)*
Stoppzeit f (EDV) stop (*or* declaration) time
Störanfall-Ablauf-Analyse f (Bw) failure mode and effect analysis, DIN 25 419
störanfällig
(com) susceptible to breakdown
– breaking down easily
Störanfälligkeit f
(com) susceptability to breakdown
(OR) probability of failure
(EDV) error liability
störende Kapitalbewegungen fpl (AuW) disruptive capital movements
Störgröße f
(Stat) random disturbance (*or* perturbation)
(EDV) perturbation variable

stornieren
(com) to cancel *(eg, an order)*
(ReW) to reverse an entry
Stornierung f **e–s Auftrages** (com) cancellation of an order
Stornobuchung f (ReW) reversing entry *(syn, Rückbuchung)*
Stornogewinn m (Vers) lapse (*or* withdrawal) profit
Stornoklausel f (Vers) lapse provision
Storno m **mit höherer als der zeitanteiligen Prämie** (Vers) short-rate cancellation
Storno m **mit zeitanteiliger Prämie** (Vers) prorata cancellation
Stornorecht n (Fin) right *(of bank)* to cancel credit entry
Storno m **vor Ablauf** (Vers) flat cancellation
Störsignal n (EDV) drop in *(ie, on magnetic tapes)*
Störungsaufzeichnung f (EDV) failure logging
Störterm m (Stat) = *Störvariable*
störungsbedingte Brachzeit f (IndE) machine downtime
Störungsbericht m (IndE) failure report
störungsfreies Wachstum n
(Vw) undisturbed growth
– disturbance-free growth
Störungsrate f (OR) rate of failure
Stürungsstelle f
(com) telephone repair department
– (GB) faults and service difficulties
Störungssuche f
(IndE) trouble-shooting
– troubleshoot
Störungszeit f (EDV) downtime
Störvariable f
(Stat) random disturbance (*or* perturbation)
– disturbance
– disturbance variable
– shock
strafbarer Eigennutz m (Re) punishable self-interest, §§ 284 ff StGB
straffe Geldpolitik f (Vw) tight monetary policy
straffen
(Bw) to streamline *(eg, an organization)*
– (infml) to take up the slack
straffe Unternehmensleitung f (Bw, infml) hands-on management
straff führen (Bw, infml) to run a „tight ship"
Strafgesetzbuch n (Re) German Penal Code
Strafrecht n (Re) criminal law
strafrechtliche Handlung f (Re) criminal offense
Strafrichter m
(Re) criminal court judge
– (GB) recorder
Strafsteuer f
(StR) penalty tax
– tax penalty
Strafzinsen mpl
(Fin) penalty interest
– penalty rate
(ie, due to early withdrawal of deposits)
Strafzins m **für Rückzahlung vor Fälligkeit** (Fin) repayment with penalty
Strahl m (Math) ray
Strahlspeicher m (EDV) beam store

Strammheit *f* **der Korrelation** (Stat) closeness of correlation
Strandung *f* **mit Bergung** (SeeV) stranding and salvage
Straßburger Patentübereinkommen *n* (Pat) Convention on the Unification of Certain Points of Substantive Law on Patent for Invention
Straßenanliegerbeitrag *m* (FiW) frontage assessment
Straßenbenutzungsgebühr *f* (FiW) road-use tax
Straßenfahrzeug *n* (com) road motor vehicle
Straßenfahrzeugbau *m* (com) road vehicle construction
Straßenfertigung *f* (IndE) line production
Straßengüterverkehr *m* (com) road haulage
Straßengüterverkehrsteuer *f* (StR) road haulage tax *(ie, levied in Germany between 1968 and 1972)*
Straßenhandel *m* (com) street marketing
Straßenverkehrsgesetz *n* (Re) Road Traffic Law
Straße-Schiene-Verbund *m* (com) road-rail link
Strategie *f* (Bw) (corporate) strategy
Strategie *f* **ändern** (Bw) to change *(or* rejig) corporate strategy
Strategie *f* **der externen Flexibilität** (Bw) external flexibility strategy
Strategie *f* **der niedrigen Preise** (Mk) low-price strategy
Strategie *f* **einschlagen** (Bw) to embark on a strategy
strategische Anfälligkeit *f* (Bw) strategic vulnerability
strategische Planung *f* (Bw) strategic planning
strategischer Geschäftsbereich *m* (Bw) strategic business area
strategisches Management *n* (Bw) strategic management
strategisches Modell *n* (Bw) strategic model
strategische Unternehmensplanung *f* (Bw) strategic managerial planning
strategische Ziele *npl* (Bw) strategic *(or* long-run) goals
Strazze *f*
 (ReW) daybook
 – (GB) waste book
 (ie, in which the transactions of the day are entered in the order of their occurrence; syn, Kladde, Vorbuch)
strecken (Fin) to extend maturity date
Streckenfracht *f* (com) freightage charged for transportation between two railroad stations
Streckengeschäft *n*
 (com) transfer orders
 (ie, sale where seller agrees to ship the goods to buyer's destination at the latter's risk, § 447 BGB; basis of transaction may be sample, catalog, or indication of standard quality)
 (com) drop shipment business
Streckenhandel *m* (com) = *Streckengeschäft*
Streckung *f* (com) stretch-out
 (eg, in the buildup of expenditures)
Streckungsdarlehen *n* (Fin) credit granted to cover the discount deducted from a mortgage loan *(ie, which is paid out 100 percent; redemption of loan does not start until discount has been repaid)*

Streifband *n* (com) postal wrapper
Streifbanddepot *n*
 (Fin) individual safe custody of securities, § 2 DepG *(syn, Sonderverwahrung)*
 – (US) segregation
Streifbandgebühr *f* (Fin) individual deposit fee
Streifendiagramm *n* (Stat) band diagram
Streifendoppler *m* (EDV) paper tape reproducer
Streifenende *n* (EDV) trailing end
Streifenleser *m* (EDV) paper tape reader
Streifenlocher *m* (EDV) paper tape punch
Streifenstanzer *m* (EDV) paper tape punch
Streifensteuer *f* (StR) revenue strip tax
Streifen-Stichprobenverfahren *n* (Stat) zonal sampling
Streik *m* (Pw) strike
Streik abbrechen (Pw) to call off a strike
Streikabstimmung *f* (Pw) strike ballot
Streik *m* **abwenden** (Pw) to stave off *(or* avert) a strike
Streik *m* **aufheben** (Pw) to call off a strike
Streikaufruf *m* (Pw) union strike call
Streik *m* **aushalten** (Bw) to ride a strike *(eg, newspaper publishers, Post Office)*
Streik *m* **ausrufen** (Pw) to call a strike
Streikausschuß *m* (Pw) strike committee
Streikbeteiligung *f* (Pw) strike turnout
Streikbrecher *m*
 (Pw) strikebreaker
 – (sl) scab
 – (GB, sl) blackleg
 – (GB, sl) knob
streiken
 (Pw) to strike
 – to go on strike
Streikgeld *n* (Pw) strike pay
Streikkasse *f* (Pw) strike fund
Streikleitung *f* (Pw) strike leadership
streiklustig (Pw) strike prone
Streikposten *m* (Pw) picket
Streiktage *mpl*
 (Stat) man-days of strike idleness
 – lost workdays
Streikverbotsklausel *f* (Pw) no-strike clause
Streikwaffe *f* (Pw) strike weapon
Streikwelle *f* (Pw) wave of strikes
streitende Parteien *fpl*
 (Re) contending
 – contesting
 – litigant
 – opposing ... parties
 – parties to a lawsuit
 – litigants
Streitfrage *f* (com) contentious issue
Streitgegenstand *m* (Re) matter in controversy
Streitigkeiten *fpl*
 (Re) disputes
 (Re) contested matters
 – disputed questions
Streitigkeiten *fpl* **austragen** (Re) to settle disputes
Streitigkeiten *fpl* **beilegen** (Re) to dissolve disputes
Streitigkeiten *fpl* **schüren** (Re) to stoke up a controversy
Streitigkeiten *fpl* **vortragen** (Re) to refer disputes to

Streitpatent *n* (Pat) litigious patent
Streitsache *f*
 (Re) matter in controversy
 – matter in dispute
 – matter in issue
 – subject-matter
Streitwert *m*
 (Re) amount in controversy *(or* dispute *or* litigation)
 – amount involved
 – jurisdictional amount
 – value of property in litigation
strenge Bestimmungen *fpl* (Re) stringent provisions
strenge Devisenbestimmungen *fpl* (AuW) stiff exchange regulations
strenge Disjunktion *f*
 (Log) exclusive disjunction
 – alternation
Strenge *f* **e–s Tests** (Stat) strength of a test
strenge Implikation *f* (Log) strict implication *(ie, in modal logic)*
strenge Objektivität *f* (Log) rigorous objectivity
strengster Test *m* (Stat) most stringent test
streng vertraulich (com) strictly confidential
Streubreite *f*
 (Fin) spread *(eg, of interest rates)*
 (Mk) coverage
Streudiagramm *n* (Stat) = *Streuungsdiagramm*
streuen
 (Stat) to scatter
 (Fin) to spread
 – to diversify
Streugrenzen *fpl* (Stat) limits of variation
Streuung *f*
 (Stat) dispersion
 – scatter
Streuung *f* **der Aktien** (Fin) distribution of shares
Streuung *f* **der Anlagepalette** (Fin) diversification of investments
Streuungsdiagramm *n* (Stat) scatter diagram *(or* chart)
Streuungskoeffizient *m* (Stat) coefficient of variation *(syn, Variationskoeffizient)*
Streuungs-Kovarianz-Matrix *f* (Stat) matrix of variances and covariances
Streuungsmaß *n* (Stat) measure of dispersion
Streuungsmatrix *f* (Stat) dispersion matrix
Streuungsparameter *m* (Stat) parameter of dispersion
Streuungsverhältnis *n* (Stat) variance ratio
Streuung *f* **von Anlagen** (Fin) spreading of investments
Streuwerbung *f* (Mk) nonselective advertising
Strichcode *m* (EDV) bar code *(syn, Balkencode)*
Strichcode-Kennzeichnung *f* (EDV) bar code marking
Strichcodeleser *m* (EDV) bar code scanner *(syn, Balkencodeleser)*
strichcodierte Artikelnummer *f* (Mk) bar coded identification number
strichcodierter Artikel *m* (Mk) bar-marked *(or* bar-coded) product item
Strichcodierung *f*
 (EDV) bar coding
 – bar code marking *(ie, system of product identification)*
Strichelverfahren *n* (Stat) tally-sheet method
Strichkante *f* (EDV) stroke edge
Strichkarte *f* (EDV) mark sense card
Strichliste *f* (Stat) tally sheet
Strichmarkierung *f* (EDV) bar mark
Strichmarkierungsfeld *n* (EDV) mark field
Strichstärke *f* (EDV) stroke width
strikte Implikation *f* (Log) strict implication *(ie, ,,If A then B" is true only when B is deducible from A; syn, strenge Implikation; opp, material implication)*
strittige Angelegenheit *f* (Re) subject in dispute
strittiger Fall *m* (Re) case *(or* matter) in dispute
strittige Verlustzeit *f* (EDV) debatable time
Strohmann *m*
 (Re) dummy
 – straw man
 – man of straw
Strohmann-Aktienbeteiligung *f* (Fin) nominee shareholding
Stromabschaltung *f* (IndE) power cut
Stromausfall *m* (IndE) power failure
Strombedingungen *fpl* (Vw) flow conditions
Stromgröße *f*
 (Vw) flow
 – flow variable
 – rate of flow
Strompreis *m* (com) power rate
Stromrechnung *f*
 (com) electricity bill
 (VGR) statement of flows *(or* flow variables)
Stromtarif *m* (com) = *Strompreis*
Strömungsgleichgewicht *n* (Vw) shifting equilibrium
Strömungsgröße *f* (Vw) = *Stromgröße*
Strömungslinien *fpl* (Math) flow lines
Strom *m* **von Nutzungen** (Vw) flow of services
Strukturanalyse *f* (Vw) structural analysis
Strukturanpassung *f*
 (com) structual adjustment
 – adjustment to meet fundamental changes
Strukturbereinigung *f* (Bw) restructuring *(eg, of an enterprise)*
Struktur *f* **der Weisungsbeziehungen** (Bw) lines of authority
Strukturdimension *f* (Bw) structural aspect *(or* dimension)
strukturelle Anpassung *f* (Vw) structural adaptation
strukturelle Arbeitslosigkeit *f* (Vw) structural unemployment
strukturelle Budgetgrenze *f* (FiW) structural budget margin
strukturelle Fehlanpassung *f* (Vw) structural maladjustment
strukturelle Indikatoren *mpl* (Vw) structural indicators
strukturelle Inflation *f* (Vw) structural inflation
strukturelle Investitionen *fpl* (Vw) structural investment
strukturelle Konstante *f* (Math) structural constant
struktureller Freiheitsgrad *m* (Bw) structural degree of freedom

strukturelles Defizit *n* (FiW) structural (*or* built-in) deficit
strukturelles finanzielles Gleichgewicht *n* (Fin) structural financial equilibrium
strukturelles Problem *n* (Bw) structural issue (*or* problem)
strukturelles Ungleichgewicht *n* (Vw) structural imbalance
strukturelle Überschüsse *mpl* (EG) structural surpluses *(eg, in farming)*
Strukturerkennung *f* (EDV) pattern recognition
Strukturgleichung *f* (Math) structural equation
Strukturhilfe *f* (FiW) state restructuring aid
Strukturhilfegesetz *n* (Re) Law Ruling on the Improvement of Regional Economic Structure (passed in 1969)
strukturierte Adresse *f* (EDV) compound address *(syn, zusammengesetzte Adresse)*
strukturierte Aufgabe *f* (Pw) structured task
strukturierte Programmierung *f* (EDV) structured programming
Strukturierung *f* **von Arbeitsaufgaben** (Pw) job design
Strukturkoeffizient *m* (Stat) structural coefficient
Strukturkonzept *n* (Bw) structual plan (*or* scheme)
Strukturkrisenkartell *n* (Kart) structural-crisis cartel
Strukturparameter *m* (Stat) structural parameter
Strukturpolitik *f*
(Vw) structural policy
– adjustment policy
– (GB) development area policy
Strukturspeicher *m* (EDV) non-erasable storage *(syn, Dauerspeicher)*
Strukturvariable *f* (Stat) structural variable
Strukturverbesserung *f* (Vw) structural improvement
Strukturvorteil *m* (Bw) structural advantage
Strukturwandel *m* (Vw) structural change
Strukturzuschüsse *mpl* (EG) structural grants
Stückaktie *f* (Fin) individual share certificate
Stückdividende *f* (Fin) dividend per share
Stücke *npl*
(Fin) securities
– denominations
Stückdepot *n* (Fin) deposit of fungible securities *(ie, German term replaced by ‚Aberdepot')*
Stückekonto *n* (Fin) = *Stückedepot*
stückeln (Fin) to denominate
stückelose Anleihe *f* (Fin) no-certificate loan
stückelose Lieferung *f* (Fin) delivery of securities with no transfer of certificates
stückeloser Verkehr *m* (Bö) trading in securities with no transfer of certificates
Stückelung *f* (Fin) denomination *(ie, standard of value, esp. of banknotes, stocks, and bonds)*
Stückemangel *m* (Fin) shortage of offerings
Stückerfolg *m* (ReW) unit profit (*or* loss)
Stückeverzeichnis *n* (Fin) schedule of deposited securities
Stückezuteilung *f* (Fin) allotment of securities
Stückgebühr *f* (Fin) charge per item
Stückgeld *n* (Vw) notes and coin *(ie, term now obsolete)*

Stückgeldakkord *n* (Pw) money piece rate *(opp, Stückzeitakkord)*
Stückgewinn *m* (KoR) profit per unit
Stückgut *n*
(com) general (*or* mixed) cargo
– less-than-cargo lot, l. c. l. *(opp, Waggonladung)*
Stückgutfracht *f*
(com) general cargo
– package freight
– freighting by the case
– LCL *(less than carlaod)* freight
Stückguttarif *m* (com) LCL rates
Stückgutversand *m* (com) shipment as LCL lot
Stückkalkulation *f* (KoR) product costing
Stückkauf *m* (Re) sale of ascertained (*or* specific) goods *(syn, Spezieskauf; opp, Gattungskauf)*
Stückkosten *pl*
(KoR) unit cost
– per unit cost
– cost per unit of output (*or* volume)
Stückkostenkalkulation *f* (KoR) product costing
Stückkosten *pl* **kalkulieren** (KoR) to build up product cost
Stückkostennachteile *mpl* (Bw) disadvantages of higher cost units
Stückkostenrechnung *f* (KoR) unit costing
Stückkurs *m*
(Bö) unit quotation
– quotation per share
(syn, Stücknotierung; opp, Prozentkurs)
Stückliste *f*
(MaW) bill of materials
(IndE) master bill of materials
– parts list *(syn, Teileliste)*
Stücklistenauflösung *f* (IndE) bill explosion
Stücklistenprozessor *m* (IndE) bill of material processor
Stücklistenspeicher *m* (EDV) parts list storage
Stücklizenz *f* (Pat) per unit royalty
Stücklohn *m*
(IndE) payment by piece rates
– wage on piecework basis
Stücklohnfaktor *m* (IndE) basic piece rate
Stücklohnsatz *m* (IndE) piece rate
Stücklohnverfahren *n* (IndE) differential piece rate system
Stück *n* **mit kritischem Fehler** (Stat) critical defective
Stücknotierung *f* (Bö) unit quotation *(syn, Stückkurs)*
Stücknummer *f*
(Fin) share certificate number
(Fin) bond certificate number
Stückpreis *m* (com) unit price
Stückrechnung *f* (KoR) product costing
Stückschuld *f* (Re) specific (*or* specifically defined) obligation *(syn, Speziesschuld; opp, Gattungsschuld)*
Stückspanne *f* (Mk) item-related profit margin *(ie, difference between purchase and sales prices of a single article)*
Stückwertaktie *f* (Bö) share quoted per unit
Stückzeit *f*
(IndE) job time
– time required per unit of output

Stückzeitakkord *m* (Pw) time-based piece rate *(opp, Stückgeldakkord)*
Stückzinsen *mpl* (Fin) accrued interest
Stückzoll *m* (Zo) duty per article
Studentisation *f* (Stat) studentization
Student-Verteilung *f* (Stat) Student distribution
studieren
 (com) to study
 – to examine carefully
 (Pw) to study for
 – (GB) to read for a university degree
Stufe *f* (EDV, Cobol) level
Stufen *fpl* **der Unternehmensführung** (Bw) levels of management *(ie, top, middle, lower)*
Stufendurchschnittssatztarif *m* (FiW) = *Stufentarif*
Stufenflexibilität *f*
 (AuW) managed flexibility *(ie, of foreign exchange rates)*
 – moving parity
 – moving peg
Stufenform-Plotter *m* (EDV) incremental plotter
Stufengründung *f* (Re) formation of an AG by incorporators and subscribers *(ie, not permissible under West German Stock Corporation law; syn, Sukzessivgründung, Zeichnungsgründung)*
Stufenleiterverfahren *n* (KoR) step ladder method
Stufenplan *m* (EG) plan by stages
Stufenpreise *mpl* (com) staggered prices
Stufenproduktion *f* (IndE) stepwise adjustment of volume output to seasonal sales variations
Stufenrabatt *m* (com) chain discount
Stufentarif *m* (FiW) graduated scale of taxes *(syn, Stufendurchschnittssatztarif)*
Stufenverfahren *n* (IndE) = *Stufenwertzahlverfahren*
stufenweise Fixkostendeckungsrechnung *f* (KoR) multi-stage fixed-cost accounting
stufenweise Planung *f* (Bw) level-by-level planning
stufenweise Verwirklichung *f*
 (Bw) attainment
 – achievement
 – implementation
 – realization ... by stages
Stufenwertzahlverfahren *n* (IndE) points rating method *(or evaluation)*
stümperhafte Arbeit *f* (Pw, GB) prentice piece of work
stumpfer Winkel *m* (Math) obtuse angle
stunden
 (Fin) to allow delayed debt repayment
 – to defer
 – to grant a respite
Stundenlohn *m*
 (Pw) hourly rate of pay
 – compensation per hour worked
Stundenverdienst *m* (Pw) = *Stundenlohn*
Stundung *f*
 (Re) respite *(ie, agreement between debtor and creditor fixing time or delay for payment, § 509 BGB)*
 (Fin) deferral *(or prolongation)* of debt repayment
 (StR) extension of time for payment, § 222 AO
Stundung *f* **des Kaufpreises** (com) respite *(ie, delay in the payment of purchase price)*

Stundung *f* **gewähren**
 (com) to grant delay in payment
 – to grant a respite
Stundungsantrag *m* (Fin) request for deferring debt repayment
Stundungsfrist *f* (com) period of deferral *(or prolongation)*
Stundungsgesuch *n*
 (Fin) application for a respite
 – request for an extension of time
Stundungszinsen *mpl* (StR) interest on delinquent taxes, § 234 AO
Stundung *f* **von Forderungen** (Fin) prolongation of debts
stürmisches Wachstum *n* (Bw) expansion head-on
Sturmschädenversicherung *f* (Vers) storm and tempest insurance
Stuttgarter Verfahren *n* (StR) Stuttgart method *(ie, of computing the fair value of unlisted securities and membership rights, based on net worth and earning capacity; Abschn. 76ff VStR 1977)*
Stützkurs *m* (Bö) supported price
Stützpreis *m* (com) supported price
Stützpunkt *m*
 (Math) extreme point
 (EDV) restart point
Stützung *f* (Stat) truncation
Stützung *f* **des Wechselkurses** (AuW) pegging of exchange rate
Stützungsaktionen *fpl* (Vw) support action *(or measures)*
Stützungsfonds *m* (Fin) deposit guaranty fund *(ie, set up by the German Giro associations)*
Stützungskäufe *mpl*
 (Fin) support buying *(or operations)*
 (Bö) backing
Stützungskonsortium *n* (Fin) backing syndicate
Stützungskredit *m*
 (Fin) emergency credit
 – stand-by credit
Stützungspreis *m* (Vw) support price *(ie, a government administered price)*
Stützungssystem *n* (EG) Community support system
Stützungsverpflichtungen *fpl* (Fin) support commitments
Stützung *f* **von Währungen** (AuW) monetary support
subjektiv ausgewählte Stichprobe *f* (Stat) judgment sample
subjektive Bedürfnisbefriedigung *f* (Vw) subjective satisfaction
subjektiver Wert *m* (ReW) subjective value
subjektives Recht *n* (Re) legal right
subjektives Risiko *n* (Vers) subjective risk
subjektive Unmöglichkeit *f* (Re) inability to perform *(syn, Unvermögen)*
subjektive Wahrscheinlichkeit *f* (Stat) expectancy
subjektive Werttheorie *f* (Vw) subjective theory of value
Subjektsteuern *fpl* (FiW) = *Personensteuern*
Subjunktion *f*
 (Log) material implication
 – logical conditional
subjunktiver Konditionalsatz *m*

(Log) contrary-to-fact conditional
- counterfactual
- counterfactual conditional
- subjunctive proposition
subkonträre Aussage f (Log) subcontrary proposition
subkonträrer Gegensatz m (Log) inclusive disjunction *(ie, in traditional logic)*
subkritischer Weg m (OR) subcritical path
Submission f
(com) invitation to bid (*or* tender)
- requests for bids
(ie, published notice that competitive bids are requested; syn, Ausschreibung)
Submissionsangebot n
(com) bid
- tender
Submissionsbedingungen fpl (com) tender terms
Submissionsbewerber m
(com) bidder
- tenderer
Submissionsgarantie f
(com) tender guaranty
- bid bond
Submissionskartell n (Kart) bidding cartel
Submissionspreis m (com) contract price
Submissionsschluß m (com) bid closing date
Submissionstermin m (com) opening date
Submissionsverfahren n
(com) tender procedure
- competitive bidding procedure
(Fin) public tender
Submissionsvergabe f (com) award of contract
Submissionsvertrag m (com) tender agreement
Submittent m
(com) bidder
- tenderer
suboptimieren (OR) to suboptimize
Subordinationskonzern m (Bw) group of subordinated affiliates
Subordinationsquote f
(Bw) span of control
- span of command
- span of management
- span of supervision
- span of responsibility
- chain of command
Subrogation f (Re) subrogation
subsidiäre Haftung f (Re) secondary liability
subsidiär haften (Re) secondarily liable
Subsistenzminimum n (Vw) subsistence level
Subskript n (Math) subscript
Subskription f
(Fin) subscription to new securities issue
(IWF) subscriptions *(ie, capital contributions)*
Subskriptionspreis m (com) prepublication price *(ie, of books)*
substantielle Abnutzung f (ReW) physical wear and tear *(ie, of fixed assets)*
substantielle Kapitalerhaltung f
(Bw) maintenance (*or* preservation) of real-asset values *(ie, paper profits and losses being eliminated from results accounting; syn, Substanzerhaltung)*
(Fin) maintenance of equity

(ReW) recovery of replacement cost *(ie, during service life)*
Substanzaushöhlung f (Bw) erosion of assets in real terms
(ie, through inflation)
Substanzbesteuerung f (StR) taxation of property
Substanzbewertung f (StR) net assets valuation *(eg, Einheitswert, Ertragswert, gemeiner Wert, Teilwert)*
Substanzerhaltung f (Bw, Fin) = substantielle Kapitalerhaltung
Substanzerhaltungsrechnung f (ReW) inflation accounting
Substanzerhaltungsrücklage f (ReW) inflation reserve
Substanzsteuern fpl (FiW) taxes on non-income values
Substanzverlust m (Bw) asset erosion
Substanzverringerung f (ReW) depletion
Substanzwert m (Bw) net asset value *(ie, value of an enterprise as a whole: sum of all assets – all liabilities at current market values, but excluding goodwill; syn, Teilreproduktionswert)*
(Fin) intrinsic value
Substanzzuwachs m (Bw) growth in asset volume
substituierbare Güter npl (Vw) substitutable goods
Substitut m od n
(com, *rare term for*) sub-representative
- sub-agent
(Vw) substitute good (*or* product)
substitutionale Produktionsfaktoren mpl (Vw) substitutional factors of production
substitutionale Produktionsfunktion f (Vw) substitutional production function
Substitutionseffekt m (Vw) substitution effect *(ie, subcase of what is known as the Ricardo effect)*
Substitutionselastizität f (Vw) elasticity of (technical) substitution
Substitutionsgrad m (Fin) degree of substitution
Substitutionsgut n (Vw) substitute good (*or* product)
Substitutionskoeffizient m (Vw) substitution coefficient
Substitutionskonkurrenz f (Vw) competition of substitute goods
Substitutionskonto n (IWF) substitution account *(ie, member countries may swap excess dollars for an IMF composite credit)*
Substitutionskosten pl (Vw) opportunity cost
Substitutionskostentheorie f (AuW) theory of substitution cost
Substitutionskredit m (Fin) substitution credit *(ie, any form of credit which a bank grants on its own standing; eg, Avalkredit, Akzeptkredit)*
Substitutionskurve f (Vw) tradeoff curve
Substitutionslücke f (Vw) gap in the chain of substitution
Substitutionsrate f (Vw) rate of commodity substitution
Substitutionsstelle f (EDV) substitution bit
substitutives Gut n (Vw) substitute good (*or* product)
Subtraktionsmenge f (Math) difference set
Subtraktionsmethode f (KoR) residual value costing *(ie, method of costing joint products = Kal-*

kulation von Kuppelprodukten; syn, Restwert- od Restkostenrechnung)
Subtraktion *f* **von Matrizen** (Math) matrix subtraction
Subunternehmer *m* (com) subcontractor
Subunternehmervertrag *m* (com) subcontract
Subvention *f* (Vw) subsidy
Subventionen *fpl* **streichen** (Vw) to quash subsidies
subventionieren (Vw) to subsidize
subventionierte Kreditfinanzierung *f* (Fin) subsidized credit financing
subventionierter Preis *m* (Vw) subsidized (*or* pegged) price
Subventionsbetrug *m* (Re) subsidy fraud, § 264 StGB
Subventionskonto *n* (IWF) Subsidy Account
Suchargument *n* (EDV) search argument
Suche *f* **nach Alternativen** (Vw, Bw) search for alternatives (*or* alternative policies)
Suchkriterium *n* (EDV) = *Suchargument*
Suchphase *f* (Bw) phase of finding alternative solutions *(ie, in decision theory)*
Suchschleife *f* (EDV) search cycle
Suchschlüssel *m* (EDV) search key
Suchverfahren *n* (EDV) search method
Suchzeit *f* (EDV) search (*or* seek) time
Suchzyklus *m* (EDV) search cycle *(syn, Suchschleife)*
Suffix *m* (Math) lower index
Suggestivfrage *f* (Mk) loaded question
Suggestivwerbung *f* (Mk) suggestive advertising *(opp, informative Werbung)*
suggestiv wirkende Voraussage *f* (Log) self-fulfilling prophesy
Sukzession *f* (Re) legal succession
sukzessiver Lagerzugang *m* (MaW) non-instantaneous receipt
Sukzessivgründung *f* (Re) = *Stufengründung*
Sukzessivlieferungsvertrag *m* (Re) multiple delivery contract
– continuing sales contract
– open-end contract
– apportioned contract
Sukzessivplanung *f* (Bw) multi-stage planning
Summandenregister *n* (EDV) addend register *(syn, Addenregister)*
summarische Arbeitsbewertung *f* (IndE) nonanalytic job evaluation
summarische Beschau *f* (Zo) summary examination
summarisches Arbeitsbewertungsverfahren *n* (IndE) factor comparison method
summarisches Verfahren *n* (Re) summary proceedings *(eg, Wechsel- und Urkundenprozesse)*
summarische Zollanmeldung *f* (Zo) summary customs declaration
Summation *f* (Math) summation
Summationsindex *m* (Math) summation index
Summationszeichen *n* (Math) summation sign
Summe *f* **aller Teilmengen** (Math) space of the investigation
Summe *f* **der Abweichungsquadrate** (Stat) deviance
– squariance
– sum of squares

Summe *f* **der Einkünfte beider Ehegatten** (StR) combined net income of the spouses, § 56 I 1 b EStDV
Summe *f* **der gesamten Umsätze** (StR) total turnover, Abschn. 113 EStR *(ie, taxable and nontaxable income)*
Summe *f* **der unendlichen Reihe** (Math) sum to infinity
Summe *f* **Eigen- und langfristiges Kapital** (Vers) total investable funds
Summe *f* **Einzelkosten** (KoR) product cost *(opp, period cost)*
Summenaktie *f* (Re) share certificate issued for a fixed amount, § 6 AktG *(opp, Quotenaktie, which is not permissible in West Germany)*
Summenbilanz *f* (ReW) statement of account transactions *(ie, listing of credit and debit sums of all accounts; syn, Umsatzbilanz, Probeabschluß)*
Summenexzedenten-Rückversicherung *f* (Vers) excess of line reinsurance
Summenhäufigkeit *f* (Stat) cumulative frequency
Summenhäufigkeitspolygon *n* (Stat) cumulative polygon
Summenhäufigkeitsverteilung *f* (Stat) cumulative frequency distribution
Summenkarte *f* (ReW) asset control account (EDV) summary card
Summenkontrolle *f* (EDV) summation check
Summenkurve *f* (Stat) cumulative curve
– ogive
Summenlinie *f* (Stat) cumulative frequency polygon
Summenlochen *n* (EDV) summary punching
Summenlocher *m* (EDV) summary punch
Summenstanzer *m* (EDV) summary punch
Summentabelle *f* (com) cumulative table
Summenversicherung *f* (Vers) fixed sum insurance *(opp, Schadenversicherung)*
Summenverteilung *f* (Stat) cumulative distribution
Summenverwahrung *f* (Fin) deposit of fungible securities *(ie, bank need only return paper of same description and quantity)*
Summenwahrscheinlichkeit *f* (Stat) cumulative probability
Summenzuwachs *m* (Vers) reversionary bonus
summierbar (Math) summable
Summierung *f* (Math) summation
Superdividende *f* (Fin) superdividend
(Fin) surplus dividend *(syn, Überdividende)*
Supergoldtranche *f* (IWF) super gold tranche
superiore Güter *npl* (Vw) superior goods
Superlativ-Werbung *f* (Mk) puff advertising *(syn, übertreibende Werbung)*
Supermarkt *m* (Mk) supermarket
Supermultiplikator *m* (Vw) supermultiplier
Superprovision *f* (com) overriding commission *(ie, paid to a general agent for the benefit of his sub-agents)*
Superspiel *n* (Vw) supergame *(Luca and Raiffa)*
Supplementinvestition *f* (Fin) = *Differenzinvestition*
Supplementwinkel *m* (Math) supplementary angle

Supposition *f* (Log) supposition
supranationale Anleihe *f* (Fin) supranational bond *(eg, World Bank, ECSC, etc.)*
Supremum *n* (Math) supremum
surrogate Produktionsfunktion *f* (Vw) as-if production function
Surrogatsteuer *f* (FiW) tax on a substitute product
sustentative Ausgaben *fpl* (Fiw) stabilizing public expenditure
Süßwarenindustrie *f* (com) sugar confectionery industry
Swap-Abkommen *n* (AuW) swap arrangement
Swap-Abschluß *m* (AuW) swap transaction
Swap-Fazilitäten *fpl* (IWF) swap facilities
Swapgeschäft *n* (AuW) swap transaction (*or* operation)
Swapkarussell *n* (AuW) merry-go-round in central-bank-covered foreign exchange
Swapkonditionen *fpl* (AuW) swap terms
Swapsatz *m*
   (AuW) swap rate
   – forward margin
   (ie, difference between forward and spot price)
Swap-Vereinbarung *f* (AuW) swap agreement between central banks
Swing *m* (AuW) swing *(ie, reciprocal credit lines)*
Switch-Geschäft *n* (AuW) switch
Switch-Prämie *f* (AuW) switch premium
Syllogismus *m* (Log) syllogism *(ie, deductive argument having two premises and a conclusion)*
Sylvesterputz *m* (ReW) window dressing
symbolische Adresse *f* (EDV) symbolic (*or* floating) address *(syn, Distanzadresse; opp, absolute Adresse)*
symbolische Codierung *f* (EDV) symbolic coding
symbolische Instruktion *f* (EDV) symbolic instruction
symbolische Programmiersprache *f* (EDV) symbolic language
symbolische Programmierung *f* (EDV) symbolic programming *(opp, absolute programming)*
symbolischer Befehl *m* (EDV) symbolic instruction
symbolischer Code *m* (EDV) symbolic code
symbolisches Programm *n* (EDV) symbolic program *(opp, absolute program)*
Symbolsprache *f* (EDV) symbolic programming language
Symmetrieachse *f* (Math) axis of symmetry
Symmetriebedingung *f* (Math) symmetry requirement
Symmetrie-Test *m* (Stat) symmetry test *(ie, special type of nonparametric testing)*
symmetrische Determinante *f* (Math) symmetrical determinant
symmetrische Differenz *f* (Math) symmetric difference
symmetrische Matrix *f* (Math) symmetrical matrix
symmetrischer Fehler *m* (EDV) balanced error
symmetrische Verteilung *f* (Stat) symmetric distribution
symmetrisch-zweiseitiger Test *m* (Stat) equal-tails test
Sympathiestreik *m* (Pw) sympathetic (*or* sympathy) strike
synallagmatischer Schuldvertrag *m* (Re) reciprocal (*or* synallagmatic) contract *(ie, bilateral agreement intending to create obligations on both sides)*
synchrone Arbeitsweise *f* (EDV) synchronous operation
synchrone Lochstreifengewinnung *f* (EDV) synchronous punching
synchroner Konjunkturindikator *m* (Vw) coincident indicator
Synchronisierzeichen *n* (EDV) idle character
Synchronlocher *m* (EDV) synchronous punch
Synchronrechner *m* (EDV) synchronous computer
Synchronübertragung *f* (EDV) synchronous transmission
Synchronverfahren *n* (EDV) synchronous mode
Syndikat *n*
   (Kart) centrally managed market sharing cartel, § 5 III GWB *(ie, independent legal existence, and joint purchasing or selling units)*
   (Fin) syndicate
   – consortium
Syndikatsvertrag *m* (Fin) consortium (*or* underwriting) agreement
Syndikus *m*
   (Re) legal officer of a company
   – staff lawyer
syndizierte Anleihe *f* (Fin) syndicated loan
syndizierte Bankfinanzierung *f* (Fin) syndicated bank financing
syndizierter Eurowährungskredit *m* (Fin) syndicated Eurocurrency loan
Syndizierung *f* (Fin) syndication
synkategorematisches Zeichen *n* (Log) syncategorematic sign *(ie, any symbol that has no independent meaning and acquires its meaning only when joined to other symbols)*
Syntaxprüfung *f* (EDV) syntax checking
synthetische Adresse *f* (EDV) synthetic (*or* generated) address
synthetischer Satz *m* (Log) synthetic statement *(ie relating a subject concept with a predicate concept not included within the subject proper; opp, analytischer Satz)*
SYN-Zeichen *n* (EDV) synchronous idle character, SYN
Systemabgang *m* (OR) system output
Systemanalyse *f*
   (Bw) system analysis
   – feasibility study
Systemanalytiker *m* (Bw) systems analyst
Systemanbieter *m* (com) systems seller
Systemansatz *m* (Bw) systems approach
systematische Auswahl *f* (Stat) systematic sampling
systematische Komponente *f* (Stat) systematic component *(ie, in time series)*
systematischer Arbeitsplatzwechsel *m* (Pw) job rotation
systematischer Erhebungsfehler *m* (Stat) procedural bias
systematischer Fehler *m*
   (Stat) systematic error
   – cumulative error
   – inherent bias
systematischer Fehler *m* **im Ansatz** (Stat) specification bias

systematisches Probieren *n* (Log) trial and error
systematische Stichprobe *f* (Stat) systematic sample
Systemaufruf *m* (EDV) supervisor call
Systemausgabeeinheit *f* (EDV) system output device (*or* unit)
Systemband *n* (EDV) system tape
Systembeschreibung *f* (EDV) systems definition (*or* specification)
Systembibliothek *f* (EDV) system library
System *n* **der Ausgleichsfinanzierung** (IWF) facility on compensatory financing
System *n* **der erweiterten reellen Zahlen** (Math) extended real number system
System *n* **der Frachtparitäten** (com) basing-point system
System *n* **der freien Marktwirtschaft** (Vw) free enterprise system
System *n* **der obligatorischen bilateralen Konversion** (AuW) system of obligatory bilateral conversion
System *n* **der Zielzonen** (Vw) target zone system
System *n* **des gespaltenen Steuersatzes** (StR) double rate system
System *n* **des multilateralen Saldenausgleichs durch Reserveaktiva** (AuW) system of multilateral asset settlement
Systemeingabeeinheit *f* (EDV) system input device (*or* unit)
Systemeingabeprogramm *n* (EDV) reader/interpreter
Systementwicklung *f* (EDV) systems design
Systeme *npl* **vorbestimmter Zeiten** (IndE) systems of predetermined times (*eg, MTA, MTM, BMT*)
System *n* **fester Wechselkurse** (AuW) system of fixed exchange rates
Systemforschung *f* (Bw) systems research
Systemgenerierung *f*
 (EDV) system generation
 – sysgen
System *n* **gespaltener Wechselkurse** (AuW) split currency system *(ie, separate rates of exchange for commercial and official transactions)*
System *n* **gleitender Bandbreiten** (AuW) system of crawling (*or* sliding) pegs
System *n* **gleitender Wechselkurse** (AuW) system of floating exchange rates
Systemkern *m*
 (EDV) resident monitor
 – supervisor
System *n* **linearer Ungleichungen** (Math) system of linear inequalities
System *n* **multipler Wechselkurse** (AuW) multiple currency system
 – multiple-rate system
System *n* **niederer Ordnung** (IndE) operating unit
System-Organisation *f* (Bw) system-oriented structure
Systemplanung *f* (EDV) system engineering
Systemplatte *f* (EDV) system (residence) disk
Systemprogramm *n*
 (EDV) system program
 – operating system routine
Systemprüfung *f* (EDV) system check
systemresident (EDV) system resident
Systemresidenz *f* (EDV) system residence
Systemsteuerprogramm *n* (EDV) control program
Systemtest *m* (EDV) system check
Systemtheorie *f*
 (Bw) systems research
 – system engineering
System *n* **überlappender Gruppen** (Bw) overlapping group form of structure
System-Urband *n* (EDV) master tape
Systemverklemmung *f* (EDV) deadlock
Systemzugang *m* (OR) system input
Systemzusammenbruch *m*
 (EDV) abnormal system end
 – system crash
Systemzwänge *mpl* (Vw, Bw) structural constraints
SZR-Korb *m* (IWF) SDR basket

T

Tabakbörse *f* (Bö) tobacco exchange
Tabakernte *f* (com) tobacco crop
Tabakerzeugnisse *npl* (com) tobacco products
Tabakgeschäft *n*
 (com) tobacco store
 – (GB) tobacconist
Tabakmonopol *n* (FiW) tobacco monopoly
Tabaksteuer *f* (StR) tobacco tax
tabakverarbeitende Industrie *f* (com) tobacco processing industry
Tabakwaren *fpl* (com) = *Tabakerzeugnisse*
tabellarisch
 (Stat) tabular
 – in tabular form
tabellarisch darstellen (Stat) to tabulate
tabellarische Darstellung *f*
 (Stat) graph
 – chart
 (Stat) tabulation

tabellarischer Lebenslauf *m*
 (Pw) personal data (*or* record sheet)
 – resume
 (ie, in place of a written-out curriculum vitae)
Tabelle *f*
 (Stat) table
 (Re) schedule of debts, § 164 KO
 (EDV) table
Tabelle *f* **aufstellen** (Stat) to compile a table
Tabellenauszug *m* (Re) extract from schedule of debts, § 164 KO
Tabellenbuchführung *f* (ReW) columnar form of accounting
Tabelleneintragung *f* (Stat) table entry
tabellengesteuert (EDV) table-controlled
Tabellenlesen *n* (EDV) table look-up
Tabellensuchprogramm *n* (EDV) table lookup program
Tabellenwerk *n* (Math) mathematical tables

573

Tabellenzeitwert *m* (IndE) synthetic time standard
Tabelliermaschine *f* (EDV) tabulator
tabellieren
 (com) to tabulate
 – to table
 – to arrange data into a table
Tabulator *m* (EDV) tabulator
Tabulatorzeichen *n* (EDV) tabulation character, TAB
Tachograph *m*
 (com) tachograph
 – vehicle performance recorder *(syn, Fahrtschreiber)*
Tafeldifferenz *f* (Math) proportional part, p. p.
Tafelgeschäft *n* (Fin) counter transactions *(eg, simultaneous purchase and cash payment ,,at the counter"; syn, Schaltergeschäft)*
Tafelmethode *f* (Stat) table method
Tag *m* **der Lieferung** (com) date of delivery
Tag *m* **des Geschäftsabschlusses** (com) contract date
Tag *m* **des Inkrafttretens** (Re) operative date
Tagebau *m*
 (IndE) strip mining *(ie, of coal and ore)*
 – (GB) open-cast mining
Tagebuch *n*
 (ReW) daybook
 – journal
 – blotter
 – business diary
 (syn, Grundbuch, Memorial, Journal, Primanota)
 (com) daily journal *(ie, kept by a commercial broker, § 101 HGB)*
Tagebucheintragung *f* (ReW) journal entry
Tagegeld *n*
 (com) daily allowance
 – per diem allowance
 – per diem
Tagegeldversicherung *f* (Vers) daily benefits insurance
Tagelöhner *m* (Pw) daily paid worker
Tagelohnsatz *m* (Pw) daywork rate
tagen (com) to hold a meeting
tagesaktuelles Geschäft *n*
 (Bw) day-to-day business
 – (infml) nuts and bolts operations
Tagesauftrag *m* (Bö) order valid today
Tagesauszug *m* (Fin) daily statement
Tagesbelastung *f* (IndE) day load
Tagesbericht *m* (com) daily report
Tagesdurchsatz *m* (IndE) daily throughput
Tageseinnahme *f* (com) = *Tageskasse*
Tagesförderung *f* (IndE) daily output
Tagesgeld *n* (Fin) overnight money *(ie, repayable within 24 hours)*
Tagesgeldmarkt *m* (Fin) overnight money market
Tagesgeldsatz *m* (Fin) overnight rate
Tagesgeld *n* **unter Banken** (Fin) interbank call money
Tagesgeschäft *n*
 (Bö) day order
 – today only order *(syn, Tageskauf)*
Tagesgeschäfte *npl* **führen**
 (Bw) to handle the day-to-day operations

 – (infml) to run the show day by day *(eg, said of a managing director)*
Tageskalkulation *f* (KoR) current cost calculation
Tageskasse *f*
 (com) daily cash receipts
 – daily takings
Tageskauf *m* (Bö) = *Tagesgeschäft*
Tageskurs *m*
 (AuW) current rate of exchange
 (Bö) daily quotation
 – current *(or* going) price
Tageskurs *m* **im EWS** (AuW) daily rate
Tagesleistung *f* (IndE) daily output
Tageslosung *f* (com) daily takings
Tagesnotierung *f* (Bö) daily quotation
Tagesordnung *f*
 (com) agenda
 – order of the day
 – business to be transacted
Tagesordnungspunkt *m* (com) item on the agenda
Tagesordnung *f* **vorbereiten** (com) to prepare the agenda
Tagespreis *m* (com) current *(or* ruling) price
Tagespreisprinzip *n* (com) current-price principle *(ie, of cooperatives)*
Tagesproduktion *f* (IndE) daily output
Tagessatz *m* (com) per diem rate
Tagesschwankungen *fpl* (com, Bö) intraday fluctuations
Tagesspesen *pl* (com) per-diem charges
Tagesumsatz *m*
 (com) daily sales
 – (GB) daily turnover
Tageswechsel *m* (Fin) = *Tagwechsel*
Tageswert *m* (ReW) current *(or* market) value *(ie, identical with ‚gemeiner Wert' in tax law, § 9 BewG, and with ‚Zeitwert' in commercial law, § 40 HGB; syn, Marktwert)*
tageweise Verzinsung *f* (Fin) continuous compounding *(ie, on a daily basis)*
tagfertig (ReW) updated *(eg, bookkeeping records)*
täglicher Kassenbericht *m* (ReW) daily cash report
tägliches Geld *n*
 (Fin) call money
 – day-to-day money
 – daily money
 (ie, automatically rolled over to the next day until repayment is demanded)
täglich fällig (Fin) due at call *(or* on demand)
täglich fällige Einlagen *fpl*
 (Fin) deposits payable on demand
 – demand deposits
täglich fällige Forderungen *fpl* (Fin) immediately realizable claims *(eg, against the central bank)*
täglich fällige Gelder *npl* (Fin) deposits at call
täglich fällige Guthaben *npl*
 (Fin) current accounts
 – demand deposits
 (ie, kept with commercial banks)
täglich fällige Verbindlichkeiten *fpl* (Fin) liabilities payable on demand
täglich kündbar (Fin) subject to call
täglich kündbare Kredite *mpl* **aufnehmen** (Fin) to borrow at call
Tagung *f*

(com) meeting
- conference
- (infml) get-together
Tagung *f* **abhalten** (com) to hold a meeting
Tagung *f* **einberufen** (com) to call a meeting
Tagungsbericht *m* (com) proceedings
Tagungsort *m* (com) meeting place
Tagungsteilnehmer *m* (com) participant in a meeting
Tagwechsel *m* (Fin) bill payable at a specified date *(syn, Datumswechsel, Tageswechsel; opp, Datowechsel)*
Takt *m*
(IndE) cycle
- timed sequence
(EDV) clock pulse
Taktabstand *m* (EDV) clock period
Taktfertigung *f* (IndE) cycle operations
Taktfolge *f* (EDV) clock rate
Taktfrequenz *f* (EDV) clock frequency
Taktgeber *m*
(EDV) clock
- clock generator
- internal clock
Taktgeberspur *f* (EDV) clock track
taktisch-dispositive Ziele *npl* (Bw) tactical *(or* short-run) goals
taktische Führung *f* (Bw) tactical execution
taktische Planung *f* (Bw) tactical planning
Taktleitung *f* (EDV) timing line
Taktoperation *f* (EDV) clock operation
Taktspur *f* (EDV) clock track
Taktsteuerung *f* (EDV) sequential control *(syn, Ablaufsteuerung, Programmsteuerung)*
Taktstraße *f* (IndE) transfer *(or* assembly) line
Taktzeit *f* (IndE) cycle time
Tallymann *m* (com) tally clerk
Talon *m*
(Fin) renewal coupon
- coupon sheet
(syn, Erneuerungsschein, Leiste, Leistenschein)
Talsohle *f*
(Vw) bottom *(ie, of recession)*
- trough
- economic tailspin
- pit of slump
Talsohle *f* **verlassen** (Vw) to bottom out
Tandembetrieb *m* (IndE) tandem operation
Tangente *f* (Math) tangent
Tangentenfläche *f* (Math) tangent surface of a space curve
Tangentenkurve *f* (Math) tangent curve
Tangentenlösung *f* (Vw) tangency solution
Tangentensatz *m*
(Math) tangent law
- law of tangents
Tangentialebene *f* (Math) tangent plane
Tangentialpunkt *m* (Math) point of tangency
Tanklager *n* (IndE) fuel depot *(or* store)
Tankstelle *f*
(com) filling station
- (infml) gas station
- (GB) petrol station
(Mk) gasoline retailer
- (GB) petrol retailer

Tante-Emma-Laden *m*
(Mk) mom-and-pop store
- ,,ma and pa" corner store
Tantieme *f*
(Pw) management bonus *(ie, type of profit participation)*
(Pat) author's fee
- royalty
Tantiemesteuer *f* (StR) = *Aufsichtsratsteuer*
Tapetenindustrie *f* (com) wallpaper industry
Tara *f* (com) tare *(ie, (weight of container or packaging material)*
Tarif *m*
(com) scale of charges
(com) freight tariff *(or* rates) *(ie, in railroad and air traffic)*
(Pw) pay scale
(StR) tax scale
(Zo) customs tariff
(Vers) rate *(ie, cost of a given unit of insurance: premium is the rate* × *number of units purchased)*
Tarifabschluß *m*
(Pw) conclusion of a pay agreement
(Pw) wage *(or* labor) settlement
- pay *(or* wage) deal
- wage agreement
Tarifabschluß *m* **im öffentlichen Dienst** (Pw) pay settlement in the public service
Tarifabschluß *m* **in Höhe des Produktivitätszuwachses** (Pw) productivity deal
Tarifangestellter *m* (Pw) salaried employee covered by collective agreement system
tarifäre Handelshemmnisse *npl* (AuW) tariff barriers
Tarifaufsicht *f* (Vers) insurance rate regulation
Tarifausschuß *m* (Pw) collective settlement committee *(ie, appointed by the Federal Minister of Labor; comprised of three members each of employee and employer umbrella organizations, § 5 Tarifvertragsgesetz)*
Tarifautonomie *f*
(Pw, *roughly*) autonomous wage bargaining
- free collective bargaining
- mutual independence of employers and employees
(ie, ,,a sacred cow in West Germany": German labor law recognizes and protects the adversary role of management and unions, forbidding all interference with the bargaining process)
Tarifbelastung *f*
(StR) tariff rate load
- tax rate burden
(ie, corporate tax rate that applies to undistributed profits of a certain type; ranging from zero to 56%)
tarifbesteuerte Wertpapiere *npl* (Fin) fully-taxed securities *(opp, steuerfreie od steuerbegünstigte Wertpapiere)*
Tarifbezirk *m* (Pw) tariff area *(ie, wage negotiation occurs at Länder level)*
Tariferhöhung *f* (Pw) increase of standard wage
Tariffähigkeit *f* (Pw) capacity to negotiate pay deals, § 2 Tarifvertragsgesetz
Tariffrachten *fpl* (com) tariff rates

575

Tariffreibetrag *m* (StR) general allowance, § 32 EStG
Tariffreiheit *f* (Pw) freedom of collective bargaining
Tarif *m* **für Verträge mit kurzer Laufzeit** (Vers) short rate
Tarifgebundenheit *f* (Pw) commitment to the rules of a collective agreement, § 3 Tarifvertragsgesetz
Tarifgestaltung *f* (StR) rate making (*or* setting)
Tarifgrundlohn *m* (Pw) total job rate
Tarifgruppe *f*
  (StR) tax bracket
  (Pw) wage group
Tarifhoheit *f* (com) right to authorized railroad rates
  (Pw) constitutional right to bargain collectively
  – principle of autonomy in collective bargaining
  – principle of independent wage bargaining
  (ie, between management and labor, with no outside interference)
Tarifierung *f*
  (Zo) tariff classification of goods
  (Vers) setting of insurance rates
Tarifierungsgrundlage *f* (com) rate base
Tarifkommission *f* (Pw) union bargaining committee
Tarifkontrollgesetz *n* (Vers) rate regulatory law
Tarifkreis *m* (Pw) employees covered by a collective bargaining contract
Tarifkrieg *m* (com) fares war *(eg, in aviation)*
tarifliche Arbeitszeit *f* (Pw) hours by collective agreement
tarifliche Beschaffenheit *f* (Zo) tariff description
tariflicher Urlaub *m* (Pw) standard holiday with pay
tarifliche Warenbezeichnung *f* (Zo) tariff description
Tariflohn *m*
  (Pw) negotiated standard wage rate
  – agreed (*or* union) wage rate
Tariflohnerhöhung *f* (Pw) increase of union wage rate
Tarifnummer *f* (Zo) tariff heading
Tarifpaket *n* (Pw) pay package deal
Tarifpartner *mpl*
  (Pw) labor and management
  – unions and management
  – parties to a pay deal
Tarifpolitik *f* (Pw) pay rate policy
Tarifpositionen *fpl* (Zo) tariff headings (*or* items)
Tarifprogression *f* (StR) progressive increase in tax scales
Tarifrecht *n* (Re) collective bargaining law
Tarifrunde *f*
  (Pw) round of wage negotiations
  – wage bargaining round
  – negotiating round
  – pay round
  – round of wage claims
Tarifsatz *m* (com) tariff rate *(ie, called ‚Frachtsatz' in railroad traffic)*
Tarifsprung *m*
  (StR) jump in the tax scale
  (Zo) change of tariff heading

Tarifstaffelung *f* (com) rate scale
Tarifstatistik *f* (Zo) tariff statistics
Tarifstelle *f* (Zo) tariff subheading
Tarifstreit *m* (Pw) wage dispute
Tarifstufen *fpl* (StR) tax scale increments
Tarifstundenlohn *m* (Pw) standard hourly rate
Tarifsystem *n* (com) tariff rate system *(ie, in railroad freight business)*
Tariftonnenkilometer *m* (com) ton-kilometer charged
Tarifverband *m* (Vers) rate making association
Tariverdienst *m* (Pw) pay rates
Tarifverhandlungen *fpl*
  (Pw) pay
  – wage
  – contract
  – wage contract ... negotiations
  (ie, carried on between trade unions and employers' associations)
Tarifverhandlungen *fpl* **für gescheitert erklären** (Pw) to break off wage negotiations
Tarifvertrag *m* (Pw) collective agreement
Tarifvertragsgesetz *n* (Pw) Collective Agreements Law, of 25 Aug 1969, as amended
Tarifvertrag *m* **aushandeln** (Pw) to bargain collectively
Tarifwerte *mpl* (Bö) utilities
Tarifzwang *m* (Pw) compulsory collective bargaining
Tarnwerbung *f* (Mk) camouflaged (*or* masked) advertising
Taschengeldparagraph *m* (Re) provision governing ,,pocket money contracts", § 110 BGB
Taschenpfändung *f* (Re) attachment of debtor's purse
  (ie, including all things movable which debtor has about him, § 808 ZPO)
Taschenrechner *m* (EDV) pocket calculator
Tastatur *f* (EDV) keyboard
Tastatureingabe *f* (EDV) keyboard entry
Tastatursperre *f* (EDV) keyboard lockout
tastengesteuert (EDV) key driven
Tastentelefon *n* (EDV) pushbutton telephone
Tastfehler *m* (EDV) keying entry
Tat *f*
  (Re) act
  – offense
Tatbestand *m*
  (com) fact of the matter
  (Re) facts
  – state (*or* set) of facts
  (Re) facts of the case
  (Re) statutory definition of an offense
Tatbestand *m* **feststellen** (Re) to take down the facts of a case
Tatbestandsfeststellungen *fpl* (Re) findings of fact
Täter *m*
  (Re) offender
  – perpetrator
Tatfrage *f*
  (Re) question of fact
  – quaestio facti
tätig
  (com) active
  – acting

tätige Reue f (StR) active regret *(see ‚Selbstanzeige', § 371 AO)*
tätiger Inhaber m (Bw) active proprietor
tätiger Teilhaber m (Re) acting partner
Tätigkeit f
 (IndE) activity
 (Bw) operations
Tätigkeit f **des Exportbasissektors** (Vw) base activity
Tätigkeitsanalyse f (Pw) task analysis
Tätigkeitsbereich m (com) area (*or* field) of operation
Tätigkeitsbericht m (com) activity (*or* progress) report
Tätigkeitsgruppe f (Pw) job cluster
Tätigkeitsknoten m (OR) activity point
Tätigkeitsmerkmale *npl* (Pw) job characteristics
Tätigkeitsnachweis m (Pw) performance record
Tätigkeitsprofil n (Pw) job profile
Tätigkeitszeit f (IndE) total activity time
Tatsachenbehauptung f
 (Re) factual statement
 – statement of fact
Tatsachenfeststellung f (Re) conclusion of fact
Tatsachenfrage f (Log) question of fact
Tatsachenirrtum m (Re) error in fact
Tatsachenvermutung f (Re) presumption of fact *(opp, Rechtsvermutung)*
tatsachenwidrige Annahme f (Log) counterfactual assumption
tatsächliche Adresse f (EDV) actual address *(syn, absolute address)*
tatsächliche Arbeitszeit f (Pw) actual hours worked
tatsächliche Ausfuhr f (Zo) actual exportation
tatsächliche Herrschaft f
 (StR) economic property, § 39 II AO *(opp, legal title)*
 (Re) physical control
tatsächliche Nutzungsdauer f (Bw) actual service life of assets
tatsächlicher Ursprung m **von Waren** (Zo) true origin of goods
tatsächliche Unmöglichkeit f
 (Re) absolute impossibility
 – impossibility of fact
Tausch m
 (com) exchange
 – barter
 – swap
tauschen
 (com) to exchange
 – to barter
 – to swap
Tauschdepot n (Fin) exchangeable securities deposit, §§ 10ff DepG *(syn, Tauschverwahrung)*
Tauschgeschäft n (com) barter transaction
Tauschgewinne *mpl* (AuW) gains from exchange (*or* trade)
Tauschgleichgewicht n (Vw) equilibrium of exchange
Tauschhandel m (Vw) barter trading *(opp, Kaufhandel)*
Tauschkurve f (AuW) offer curve
Tauschmittel n

(Vw) medium of exchange
– circulating medium
Tauschmittelfunktion f **des Geldes**
 (Vw) money as a medium of exchange
 – exchange function of money
Tauschmöglichkeitskurve f (Vw) exchange possibility line
Tauschoptimum n (Vw) exchange optimum *(syn, Handelsoptimum)*
Tauschtransaktion f (Bö) equity switching
Täuschung f (Re) = arglistige Täuschung
Tauschverkehr m (Vw) bartering
Tauschverwahrung f (Fin) = Tauschdepot
Tausch m **von Wirtschaftsgütern** (Bw) exchange of assets
Tauschwert m
 (Vw) value in exchange *(opp, Gebrauchswert = value in use)*
 (Bw) exchange value
Tauschwirtschaft f
 (Vw) barter economy
 (AuW) exchange (*or* nonmonetary) economy
Taxator m
 (com) appraiser
 – valuer
Taxe f
 (Vw) government-fixed price
 (com) appraisal fee
 (Vers) agreement on insured value
 (Vers) amount of loss to be paid *(ie, as determined by insurance valuer)*
Taxgewicht n (com) chargeable weight
Taxi n
 (com) cab
 – (GB) taxi
 – (fml) taxicab
Taxi n **bestellen** (com) to call a cab
taxieren
 (com) to appraise
 – to value
taxierte Police f (Vers) valued policy
Taxierung f
 (com) appraisal
 – evaluation
 – valuation
Taxi n **nehmen** (com) to take a cab
Taxistand m
 (com) taxi stand
 – cab stand
 – (GB) taxi rank
Taxkurs m (Bö) estimated price (*or* quotation)
taxonomische Methode f (Bw) taxonomic method
Taxwert m
 (com) appraised value *(ie, generally equal to ‚Verkehrswert')*
 (SeeV) valuation
Taylorsche Entwicklung f (Math) Taylor expansion
Taylorsche Reihe f (Math) Taylor series
Tayloscher Satz m (Math) Taylor's theorem
Teamarbeit f (com) team work
Teamtheorie f (Bw) theory of teams
Technik f
 (IndE) technology *(ie, branch of science)*
 – engineering *(ie, practical application)*
 – technique *(ie, method)*

Technik *f* wissenschaftlichen Arbeitens (Log) methods of scientific investigation
Techniker *m*
(com) technical man
(IndE) engineer
– technician *(ie, highly skilled worker in industry and science)*
– operator
technisch
(IndE) technological
– technical
– engineering
– industrial
technisch ausgereift (com) sophisticated
technisch bedingte Wertminderung *f* (Bw) wear and tear
technische Abschreibung *f* (ReW) = *Mengenabschreibung*
technische Aktienanalyse *f* (Bö) technical analysis
technische Aktientrendanalyse *f* (Bö) technical analysis of stock trends
technische Anlagen *fpl* **und Maschinen** *fpl* (ReW, EG) plant and machinery
technische Bedarfsprämie *f*
(Vers) burning cost
– pure burning cost
– pure loss cost
(ie, ratio of reinsurance losses to ceding company's subject premiums)
technische Beratung *f*
(com) technical consulting
– advisory services of a technical nature
technische Beratungsfirma *f* (com) consulting engineers
technische Daten *pl* (IndE) engineering data
technische Einzelheiten *fpl*
(com) technical details
– technicalities
technische Entwertung *f* (ReW) physical depreciation of assets
technische Grenzen *fpl* (IndE) engineering constraints
technische Güter *npl* (com) technical goods
technische Handelshemmnisse *npl* (AuW) technical barriers to trade
technisch einwandfrei (com) conforming to specification
technische Kapazität *f* (Bw) technical capacity *(ie, irrespective of cost level at different degrees of utilization)*
technische Kundendienstleistungen *fpl* (com) after-installation service
technische Kurserholung *f* (Bö) technical rally *(ie, turnaround in a generally declining market)*
technische Lieferbedingungen *fpl* (com) engineering specifications
technische Nutzungsdauer *f* (Bw) physical life
technische Produktionsplanung *f* **und -steuerung** *f* (IndE) production engineering
technischer Außendienst *m* (com) customer engineering
technischer Berater *m* (Bw) consulting engineer
technischer Direktor *m*
(com) technical manager
– (US) vicepresident engineering

technische Relation *f* (Vw) engineering relationship
technische Reserven *fpl* (Vers) technical reserves *(ie, incorrect term covering ‚Prämienüberträge' and ‚Schadenreserven')*
technischer Fortschritt *m*
(com) technical progress
– technological progress *(or advance or improvement)*
– engineering progress
(Pat) progress of the arts
– improvement in *(or upon)* the arts
technischer Gewinn *m* (Vers) underwriting profit
technischer Kundendienst *m* (com) customer engineering
technischer Sachverständiger *m* (Vers) surveyor
Technischer Überwachungsverein *m* (com) Engineering Control Association
technischer Verschleiß *m* (Bw) ordinary wear and tear
technischer Wandel *m* (com) technological changes
technischer Wirkungsgrad *m* (IndE) physical *(or engineering)* efficiency
technisches Angebot *n* (com) engineering proposal *(ie, price usually excluded)*
technisches Datenblatt *n* (IndE) specification *(or spec)* sheet
technisches Risiko *n* (Bw) technical risk
technische Substitutionsrate *f* (Vw) rate of technical substitution
technische Überholung *f* (Bw) physical obsolescence *(opp, wirtschaftliche Überholung)*
technische Veralterung *f* (Bw) obsolescence
technische Verbrauchsgüter *npl* (Mk) durable consumer goods
technische Versicherungszweige *mpl* (Vers) technical lines of insurance business *(ie, umbrella term covering engineering risks)*
technische Zeichnung *f* (com) engineering drawing
technische Zusammenarbeit *f* (com) technical cooperation
technisch-pragmatische Lösungen *fpl* technological fixes
technisch-wirtschaftliches Vorstadium *n* e–s Projektes (com) definition phase
technisch-wirtschaftliche Überholung *f* (Bw) obsolescence
Technologie *f* (IndE) technology
Technologiebewertung *f* (IndE) technology assessment
Technologiemenge *f* (IndE) set of production outputs
Technologiepolitik *f* (IndE) technology policies
Technologie-Transfer *m* (Vw) transfer of technology
Technologie-Vertrag *m* (Bw) agreement for general technical exchange
Technologie-Werte *mpl* (Bö) technology equities
Technologiewirkungsanalyse *f* (IndE) technology assessment
technologische Arbeitslosigkeit *f* (Vw) technological unemployment *(ie, not to be equated with ‚structural unemployment')*
technologische Gleichung *f* (Vw) technological equation

technologische Grenzen *fpl* (Vw) technology constraints (*or* limitations)
technologische Kapazität *f* (IndE) technological capability
technologische Lücke *f* (IndE) technological gap
technologischer Berater *m* (Bw) technology consultant
technologische Relation *f* (Vw) = *technische Relation*
technologischer externer Effekt *m* (Vw) technical externality
technologische Vorhersagen *fpl* (Bw) technological forecasting
technologische Zwänge *mpl* (Bw) technological compulsions (*or* constraints)
Teesteuer *f* (StR) excise tax on tea
Teil *n*
  (IndE) part
  – component
Teilabnahme *f* (com) acceptance of part or parts *(eg, of a major project)*
Teilabrechnung *f* (com) partial billing
Teilabschreibung *f* (ReW) writedown *(ie, transfer of portion of asset account balance to profit and loss or to expense account)*
Teilabtretung *f* (Re) partial assignment
Teilakzept *n* (WeR) partial acceptance, Art. 26 I WG
Teilamortisationsvertrag *m* (Mk) non full payout leasing contract
Teilanlage *f* (IndE) operating unit
Teilanlieferung *f* (com) part shipment
Teilanmeldung *f* (Pat) divisional application
Teilannahme *f* (WeR) = *Teilakzept*
Teilarbeitsvorgang *m* (IndE) element *(ie, small logically sequenced subtask for which time is recorded)*
Teilaufgabe *f* (Pw) subtask
Teilausschreibung *f* (com) partial invitation to tender (*or* to bid)
teilautonome Gruppe *f* (Pw) self-managing team
teilbar (Math) divisible
teilbare Leistung *f* (Re) divisible performance, § 427 BGB
teilbarer Vertrag *m* (Re) divisible contract
teilbares Akkreditiv *n* (Fin) divisible credit
Teilbereich *m* (Math) subdomain
Teilbeschäftigte *pl* (SozV) persons holding several qualifying jobs *(syn, Mehrfachbeschäftigte)*
Teilbetrag *m* (com) partial amount
Teilbetrag *m* **des Eigenkapitals** (Fin) portion of equity
Teilbetrieb *m* (StR) independent division of a business
Teilbetriebsergebnis *n*
  (ReW) partial operating result
  (Fin) surplus on interest earnings and on commission business *(of a bank)* less administrative expense
teilbewegliche Kosten *pl* (KoR) semi-variable cost
Teilbudget *n*
  (Bw) sectional budget
  – functional subplan
Teilbudget *n* **des Absatzbereiches** (Bw) sales and marketing budget

Teilbudget *n* **des Fertigungsbereichs** (Bw) manufacturing budget
Teilbudget *n* **des Verwaltungsbereichs** (Bw) office and administration budget
Teilcharter *f* (com) partial charter
Teilebedarfsrechnung *f* (IndE) parts requirements planning *(ie, of parts and assemblies [Baugruppen] required for a planning period)*
Teilefamilie *f* (IndE) family of parts
Teilefertigung *f*
  (IndE) component manufacture
  – production of parts and subassemblies *(ie, Teile und U-Gruppen)*
Teilegruppe *f* (IndE) subassembly
Teileigentum *n* (Re) part ownership
teileingezahlte Aktien *fpl* (Fin) partly paid shares (*or* stock)
Teilelager *n* (MaW) parts inventory (*or* stock)
Teileliste *f* (IndE) parts list *(ie, in production planning)*
Teilemission *f* (Fin) partial issue
Teilemontage *f* (IndE) mechanical components assembly
Teilenummer *f* (IndE) part number
Teileprogrammierung *f* (EDV) parts programming
teilerfremd
  (Math) prime
  – aliquant
Teilerfüllung *f* (Re) part performance
Teilerhebung *f*
  (Stat) sample survey *(syn, Stichprobenerhebung)*
  (Stat) incomplete census
Teilestammdatei *f* (IndE) component master file
Teilestammsatz *m*
  (IndE) basic set of components
  (EDV) component master set
Teilgesamtheit *f*
  (Stat) subpopulation
  – stratum *(pl. strata)*
Teilgewinnabführungsvertrag *m* (Re) agreement to transfer part of profits, § 292 I No. 2 AktG
Teilgruppentrennzeichen *n* (EDV) unit separator character
Teilhaber *m*
  (Re) partner
  – co-partner
Teilhaberbetrieb *m* (EDV) online system
Teilhaberpapiere *npl* (Fin) variable-income securities *(ie, evidencing membership rights)*
Teilhaberschaft *f* (Re) partnership
Teilhafter *m* (Re) limited partner *(syn, Kommanditist; opp, Vollhafter, Komplementär)*
Teilindikator *m* (Vw) partial indicator
Teilindossament *n* (WeR) partial indorsement *(ie, legally ineffective, Art. 12 WG)*
Teilintervall *n* (Math) subinterval
Teilkapitel *n* (Zo) subchapter
Teilkaskoversicherung *f* (Vers) part comprehensive cover *(opp, Vollkaskoversicherung)*
Teilklasse *f* (Log, Math) subclass
Teilkonnossement *n* (com) partial bill of lading (*or* B/L)
Teilkonsolidierung *f* (ReW) partial consolidation, § 330 AktG
Teilkonzern *m* (Bw) subgroup

Teilkonzernabschluß *m*
(ReW) partially consolidated financial statement, § 330 AktG
– (GB) subgroup accounts
Teilkonzernlagebericht *m* (ReW) subgroup annual report
Teilkorrelationskoeffizient *m* (Stat) coefficient of partial correlation
Teilkosten *pl* (KoR) portion of overall costs *(opp, Vollkosten)*
Teilkostenrechnung *f*
(KoR) direct
– marginal
– variable ... costing
Teilladung *f* (com) part shipment
Teilleistungen *fpl* (Re) performance by successive installments, § 266 BGB
Teillieferung *f* (com) part delivery
Teillieferungen *fpl*
(com) part shipments
(Re) delivery by installments
Teillieferungsvertrag *m* (Re) installment contract
Teilliquidation *f* (Bö) partial settlement
Teillosgröße *f* (Bw) split lot
Teilmarkt *m* (Vw) submarket
Teilmasse *f* (Stat) subpopulation
Teilmatrize *f* (Math) component matrix
Teilmenge *f* (Math) subset
Teilmengen-Symbol *n* (Math) set inclusion symbol
Teilmonopol *n* (Vw) partial monopoly
Teilmontage *f*
(IndE) subassembly *(ie, Unterbaugruppe)*
(IndE) assembly of subassemblies
Teilnehmer *m* **am Abrechnungsverkehr** (Fin) participating bank
Teilnehmerbetrieb *m* (EDV) remote computing and time-sharing
Teilnehmersystem *n*
(EDV) time sharing system
– time slicing
Teilnichtigkeit *f*
(Re) partial nullity *(or* invalidity*)*
– severability
– separability *(ie, referring to contracts)*
Teilpaket *n* **von Werbeleistungen** (Mk) service module
Teilplan *m*
(Bw) subplan
– subbudget
Teilplanung *f* (Bw) functional planning
Teilprogramm *n* (EDV) subroutine
Teilprovision *f* (com) partial commission *(ie, for a partly performed transaction)*
Teilreproduktionswert *m*
(Bw) net asset value
– reproduction value
(ie, value of an enterprise as a whole: sum of all assets minus all liabilities at current market values, but excluding goodwill; syn, Substanzwert)
Teilrücktritt *m* (Re) partial cancellation *(or* rescission*)*
Teilschaden *m* (Vers) partial damage *(or* loss*)*
Teilschäden *mpl* **eingeschlossen** (SeeV) with particular average

Teilschnitt *m* (com) part sectional elevation
Teilschuldverhältnis *n* (Re) fraction of an obligatory debt
Teilschuldverschreibung *f*
(Fin) bond
– (GB) debenture
Teilselbstbedienung *f* (Mk) partial self-service
Teilsendung *f* (com) part shipment
Teilstrecken-Vermittlung *f* (EDV) store and forward switching *(syn, Speichervermittlung)*
Teilstreik *m* (Pw) partial strike
Teilsumme *f* (Math) partial sum
Teilübertragung *f* (EDV) partial carry
Teilung *f* **der Patentanmeldung** (Pat) division of a patent
Teilungsmasse *f* (Re) estate to be apportioned, § 107 ZVG
Teilungsplan *m* (Re) scheme of apportionment, §§ 106ff ZVG
Teilungsversteigerung *f* (Re) compulsory partition by public auction
teilvariable Kosten *pl*
(KoR) semi-variable
– semi-fixed
– mixed
– borderline ... costs
Teilvektor *m* (Math) component vector
Teilverlust *m* (SeeV) partial loss
Teilversand *m* (com) part shipment
Teilverschiffung *f* (com) = *Teilversand*
Teilvorgang *m* (IndE) job element
Teilwarteschlange *f* (OR) subqueue
teilweise Abgabenbefreiung *f* (Zo) partial exemption
teilweise Aussetzung *f* **der Zollsätze** (Zo) partial suspension of customs duties
teilweise Befriedigung *f*
(Re) partial payment
– satisfaction in part
– discharge in part
teilweise eingeschränkter Bestätigungsvermerk *m* (ReW) piecemeal audit opinion
teilweise eingezahlte Aktie *f* (Fin) partly paid-up share
teilweise Erfüllung *f* (Re) part performance
teilweise Nichterfüllung *f* (Re) incomplete performance
teilweise Nichtigkeit *f* (Re) partial nullity
teilweise Unmöglichkeit *f* (Re) partial impossibility of performance, § 280 BGB
teilweise zerlegt (IndE) semi-knocked down, SKD
Teilwert *m* (StR) going-concern value
(ie, based on the assumption of the continuation of the business as a whole, not on the existence of a separate and isolated item of property; § 10 BewG, § 6 I 1 EStG)
Teilwertabschreibung *f* (ReW) write-off to the lower going-concern value *(ie, equal to the difference between book value and the going-concern value of the asset)*
Teilwertberichtigung *f* **von Anlagegegenständen** (ReW) = *Teilabschreibung*
Teil-Wiederausfuhr *f* (Zo) split reexportation
Teil-Wiedereinfuhr *f* (Zo) split reimportation
Teilzahlung *f*

Teilzahlungsbank
(com) part (or partial) payment
(Fin) installment
(IndE) progress payment *(ie, in plant engineering and construction)*
Teilzahlungsbank *f* (Fin) installment sales financing institution
Teilzahlungsfinanzierung *f* (Fin) installment financing
Teilzahlungsforderungen *fpl* (Fin) installment debtors
Teilzahlungsgeschäft *n* (Re) installment contract *(ie, seller agrees to deliver goods, while buyer agrees to make initial down payment and to pay balance in installments; type of customer financing; the strictly legal term is ‚Abzahlungsgeschäft')*
Teilzahlungskauf *m* (com) installment sale *(syn, Ratenkauf, Abzahlungskauf; see: Abzahlungsgeschäft)*
Teilzahlungskredit *m* (Fin) = *Ratenkredit (ie, extended by Teilzahlungsbanken, Kreditbanken and Sparkassen)*
(Fin) installment loan *(ie, available as A-Geschäft, B-Geschäft, and C-Geschäft)*
Teilzahlungskreditgeschäft *n* (Fin) installment lending
Teilzahlungskreditinstitut *n* (Fin) installment credit institution *(or organization)*
Teilzahlungskreditversicherung *f* (Vers) installment credit insurance
Teilzahlungspreis *m* (com) total installment contract price
Teilzahlungsverkauf *m* (com) installment sale
Teilzahlungsvertrag *m* (com) credit sale agreement
Teilzeitarbeit *f* (Pw) part-time job *(or work or employment)*
Teilzeitbeschäftigung *f* (StR) short-time work(ing)
Teilzeitkräfte *fpl*
(Pw) part-time employees
– part timers
Teilziel *n*
(Bw) subgoal
– subobjective
Teilzusammenstellung *f* (IndE) subassembly *(ie, in bills of material)*
Tele-Einkauf *m* (Mk) teleshopping
Telefonbuch *n*
(com) telephone directory *(or* book)
– (infml) phone book
Telefondienst *m* (com) telephone service
Telefongebühren *fpl* (com) telephone charges
Telefongespräch *n* **aufnehmen** (com) to tape a telephone conversation
Telefonhandel *m* (Bö) inter-office trading
telefonisch (com) by telephone
telefonische Anweisungen *fpl* (com) directives over the telephone
Telefonist *m* (od –in *f*)
(com) telephone operator
– operator
Telefonnummer *f* (com) telephone (*or* phone) number
Telefonrechnung *f* (com) telephone bill
Telefonverkehr *m*
(com) telephone traffic

(Bö) interoffice trading (or dealings) *(ie, unregulated and unofficial market)*
Telefonvermittlung *f* (com) telephone exchange
Telefonzelle *f*
(com) telephone (*or* phone) booth
– call box
– (GB *also*) telephone kiosk
– phone box
– telephone box
Telefonzentrale *f* (com) telephone exchange
telegrafieren
(com) to telegraph
– to wire
telegrafisch
(com) by telegram
– by wire
telegrafische Auszahlung *f* (Fin) telegraphic transfer, T.T. *(ie, of money amounts)*
telegrafische Mitteilung *f* (com) telegraphic message
Telegramm *n* (com) telegram
Telegrammadresse *f* (com) telegraphic address
Telegrammannahme *f* (com) telegram reception
Telegramm *n* **aufgeben**
(com) to send off a telegram
– to dispatch a cable
Telegrammformular *n* (com) telegram form
Telegrammschalter *m* (com) telegram counter
Telegramm *n* **zustellen** (com) to deliver a telegram
Telekommunikation *f* (Bw) telecommunications
Telekopierer *m*
(EDV) telecopier
– facsimile terminal
Teleoperator *m* (IndE) teleoperator *(ie, remote-controlled manipulator without program control)*
Telex *n* (com) telex
Telexvermittlung *f*
(com) telex exchange
– teleprinter exchange service
tel quel
(com) sale as is
– sale with all faults
– run-of-mine
(ie, purchaser must take article for better or worse, unless seller contrives to conceal any fault)
Telquel-Kurs *m* (Bö) tel quel rate *(ie, in foreign exchange trading)*
temporäre Datei *f* (EDV) temporary data set
Tendenz *f*
(com) tendency
– trend
– general thrust of developments
Tendenzbetrieb *m* (Bw) organization concerned with propagating attitudes *(ie, press, politics, churches)*
Tendenz *f* **überzeichnen** (Vw) to overstate a trend
Tendenzwende *f*
(Vw) trend reversal
– drastic reversal
– turnaround
Tendertechnik *f* (Fin) offer for sale by tender
Tensor *m* (Math) tensor
Tensoralgebra *f* (Math) tensor algebra
Tensoranalyse *f* (Math) tensor analysis

581

Tensorgleichung f (Math) tensor equation
Tensorrechnung f (Math) tensor algebra
Tensor m **zweiter Stufe** (Math) tensor of valence two
Teppichboden m
 (com) wall-to-wall carpeting
 – (GB) fitted carpet
Term m (Math) term
Terme mpl **gruppieren** (Math) to group terms
Term m **e-s kategorischen Urteils** (Log) categorematic word
Termin m
 (com) appointment
 – (infml) time *(eg, let she give you a time to see me)*
 (com) deadline
 – time limit
 – appointed day *(or* time*)*
 – target date
Terminablage f (com) tickler file
Termin m **absagen** (com) to cancel an appointment
Terminabschlag m (Bö) forward discount
Terminabschluß m (Bö) forward contract
Termin m **anberaumen** (Re) to fix a hearing
Termin m **ansetzen** (Re) to set a case down for hearing
Terminauftrag m (Bö) forward order
Termin m **ausmachen** (com) to arrange an appointment
 (eg, for me with the sales manager)
Terminbörse f (Bö) forward exchange *(or* market*)*
Terminbüro n (IndE) progress control department *(or* office*)*
Termindevisen pl (Bö) forward exchange
Termindollars mpl (AuW) forward dollars
Termin m **einhalten**
 (com) to meet a time target *(or* deadline*)*
 – to meet a schedule
Termineinlagen fpl (Fin) time deposits *(ie, feste Gelder od Festgelder + Kündigungsgelder, ohne Spareinlagen; opp, Sichteinlagen)*
Terminengagements npl (Bö) commitments for future delivery
Termin m **festlegen** (com) to fix a deadline
termingebundene Bankguthaben npl (Fin) time balances at banks
Termingeldanlagen fpl (Fin) time deposit investments
Termingelder npl **unter 4 Jahren** (Fin) time deposits and funds borrowed for less than four years
Termingeldkonto n
 (Fin) time deposit account
 – term account
Termingeldsatz m (Fin) time deposit rate
Termingeldzinsen mpl (Fin) interest rates on time deposits
termingemäß (com) on schedule *(eg, plans are going ahead ...)*
Termingeschäft n
 (Bö) dealing in futures
 – (GB) dealings for the account
 (Bö) forward exchange transaction
 (Bö) financial futures
 (Bö) commodity futures

Termingespräch n
 (com) production scheduling meeting
 – delivery dates discussion
Terminhandel m
 (Bö) futures trading
 – trading in futures
 (ie, mostly in commodities)
terminieren (com) to fix a date
Terminierung f (com) setting a deadline *(or* time limit*)*
Terminjäger m
 (com) expediter
 – (infml) progress chaser
Terminkalender m (com) appointments diary
Terminkarte f (IndE) progress card
Terminkauf m
 (Bö) forward buying
 – purchase for forward delivery
Terminkäufer m (Bö) forward buyer
Terminkaufs-Deckungsgeschäft n (Bö) long hedge
Terminkauf m **tätigen** (Bö) to buy forward
Terminkommissionär m (Bö) futures commission broker
Terminkonten npl (Fin) time accounts
Terminkontrakt m
 (Bö) futures contract
 – contract for future delivery
 – (pl) futures
Terminkurs m (Bö) futures price *(or* rate*)*
terminlich festlegen (com) to schedule
Terminlieferung f (Bö) future delivery
Terminmarkt m (Bö) forward *(or* futures*)* market
Terminnotierung f
 (Bö) forward *(or* futures*)* quotation
 – quotation for forward delivery
Terminologie f (Log) terminology
terminologisch (Log) terminological
Terminpapiere npl (Bö) forward securities
Termin-Pfund n (Bö) future sterling
Terminplan m
 (com) time *(or* due date*)* schedule
 (IndE) schedule
Terminplanung f (com) time scheduling
Terminposition f (Fin) official commitment *(ie, of monetary authorities from intervention in the futures market)*
Terminpositionen fpl (Bö) forward commitments
Terminsicherung f
 (Bö) futures hedging
 – forward cover
 – hedging in the forward market
Terminspekulation f
 (Bö) forward speculation
 – speculation in futures
Termintreue f
 (com) faithfulness to deadlines
 – schedule effectiveness
Termin m **überschreiten** (com) to miss a deadline
Terminüberwacher m (IndE) traffic manager
Terminüberwachung f
 (com) progress control
 (MaW) monitoring of inventory levels
 – stockchasing
 (IndE) expediting
 (Fin) tracing of maturities

Terminüberwachungsliste *f*
 (com) deadline control list
 (Fin) maturities control list
Terminverbindlichkeiten *fpl* (Fin) time liabilities
Terminverkauf *m*
 (Bö) forward sale
 – (GB) sale for the account
Terminverkäufer *m* (Bö) forward seller
Terminverkaufs-Deckungsgeschäft *n* (Bö) short hedge
Terminverlagerung *f* (IndE) shifting of target dates
Termin *m* **versäumen** (com) to miss a cut-off date
Terminvorgabe *f* (com) scheduled date
Terminvorschau *f* (com) schedule outlook report
Terminware *f* (Bö) forward (*or* future) commodity
Terminzahl *f* (Math) number of terms *(syn, Zinsdauer, Laufzeit der Verzinsung)*
Termlogik *f* (Log) logic of terms
tertiäre Kennziffern *fpl*
 (Bw) tertiary ratios
 – (GB) explanatory ratios
 (ie, combination of several elementary or advanced ratios used to promote corporate decision making)
tertiärer Sektor *m* (Vw) tertiary (*or* service) sector of the economy
Test *m* (EDV) test
Testament *n* (Re) last will and testament, §§ 1937ff BGB
testamentarischer Erbe *m* (Re) testamentary heir
Testamentsvollstrecker *m* (Re) executor *(ie, his authority rests upon the will of the testator)*
Testat *n* (ReW) = *Bestätigungsvermerk*
Testbefragung *f* (Mk) opinion survey
Testdaten *pl* (EDV) test data
Testdatengenerator *m* (EDV) test data generator
Testfrage *f* (Stat) probe question
Testgebiet *n* (Mk) test area
Testhilfen *fpl* (EDV) program diagnostic routines
Testhypothese *f* (Stat) alternate hypothesis
Testieren *n* (ReW) attestation
testierter Abschluß *m*
 (ReW) certified financial statement
 – audited accounts
Testinterview *n* (Mk) pre-test interview
Testladen *m* (Mk) audit store
Testlauf *m* (EDV) debugging run
Testmarke *f* (Mk) test brand
Testmarkt *m* (Mk) test market
Testmarktaktion *f* (Mk) sales test
Test *m* **mit minimaximalem Schärfeverlust** (Stat) most stringent test
Testmuster *n* (Mk) test specimen
Testprobe *f* (Stat) test sample
Testprogramm *n*
 (EDV) check (*or* test) program
 (EDV) program test routine
Teststärke *f* (Stat) strength of a test
Testsystem *n* (EDV) debugging system
Testwerbung *f* (Mk) pilot (*or* test) advertising
teuer
 (com) expensive
 – (US) high-priced
 – (GB) dear
 – (GB, infml) pricy/pricey

teure Konsumgüter *npl* (Mk) big-ticket items (*or* goods)
teures Geld *n* (Vw) dear money
Teuerungsrate *f* (Vw) rate of inflation
Teuerungszulage *f* (Pw) cost-of-living allowance (*or* bonus)
Teufelskreis *m* **der Unterentwicklung** (Vw) vicious circle of underdevelopment *(ie, due to low rates of capital formation)*
Teufelskreis-Theorem *n* (Vw) vicious-circle theorem
Text *m* (Mk) copy
textabhängig (EDV) contextual
Textabteilung *f* (Mk) copy department
Textanalyse *f* (Mk) content analysis
Texter *m* (Mk) copy writer
Textilindustrie *f* (com) textile industry
Textilmesse *f* (com) textile goods fair
Textilwerte *mpl* (Bö) textiles
Textilwirtschaft *f* (com) textile industry
Textverarbeitung *f* (EDV) word processing
Textverarbeitungsgerät *n* (EDV) word processor
T-Gruppentraining *n* (Pw) sensitivity training
Thekenaufsteller *m* (Mk) counter display
Thekenverkauf *m* (Mk) over-the-counter selling
Theorem *n* (Math, Log) theorem
Theorem *n* **der komparativen Kostenvorteile** (AuW) theorem of comparative cost advantages
theoretische Maximalkapazität *f* (Bw) theoretical maximum plant capacity
theoretische Optimalkapazität *f* (Bw) theoretical optimum plant capacity
theoretisches Konstrukt *n* (Log) theoretical construct
theoretische Statistik *f* (Stat) theory of statistics
Theorie *f* **der absoluten Kostenvorteile** (AuW) theory of absolute cost advantages
Theorie *f* **der administrierten Preise** (Vw) administered price theory
Theorie *f* **der ausleihbaren Fonds** (Fin) theory of loanable funds
Theorie *f* **der Bestimmung von Ersatzinvestitionen** (Bw) replacement (*or* renewal) theory
Theorie *f* **der Eigentumsrechte** (Vw) theory of property rights
Theorie *f* **der Einkommensverteilung** (Vw) theory of income distribution
Theorie *f* **der fallenden Profitrate** (Vw) falling-rate-of-profit theory
Theorie *f* **der Grenzproduktivität** (Vw) marginal theory of distribution
Theorie *f* **der großen Stichproben** (Stat) theory of large samples
Theorie *f* **der kleinen Stichproben** (Stat) theory of small samples
Theorie *f* **der Lagerhaltung** (OR) stockkeeping theory
Theorie *f* **der linearen Filter** (Stat) theory of linear filtering
Theorie *f* **der öffentlichen Entscheidung** (Vw) theory of public choice
Theorie *f* **der öffentlichen Regulierung** (Vw) theory of government regulation of business
Theorie *f* **der öffentlichen Verschwendung** (FiW) theory of public-sector inefficiency

Theory f der quantitativen Wirtschaftspolitik (Vw) theory of quantitative economic policy *(ie, developed by J. Tinberg en and R. Frisch)*
Theorie f der rekursiven Funktionen (Math) recursive function theory
Theorie f der relativen Preise (Vw) theory of relative prices
Theorie f der Schätzung (Stat) theory of estimation
Theorie f der Spiele (Math) theory of games
Theorie f der statistischen Inferenz (Stat) theory of inference
Theorie f der strategischen Spiele (Math) theory of strategic games
Theorie f der Verbraucher-Präferenzen (Vw) theory of consumer preference
Theorie f der vollständigen materiellen Inzidenz (FiW) diffusion theory of taxation
Theorie f der vollständigen Steuerüberwälzung (FiW) diffusion theory of taxation
Theorie f der Wahlakte (Vw) theory (*or* analysis) of choice
Theorie f der Wahrheitsfunktionen (Log) theory of truth-functions
Theorie f der zeitlichen Zinsstruktur (Fin) term structure theory of interest rates
Theorie f des allgemeinen Gleichgewichts (Vw) general equilibrium theory
Theorie f des Haushalts (Vw) consumer theory
Theorie f des partiellen Gleichgewichts (Vw) partial equilibrium theory
Theorie f des Rationalverhaltens (Vw, Bw) theory of rational behavior
Theorie f des Sachbezugs (Log) theory of reference
Theorie f des Stichprobenverfahrens (Stat) theory of sampling
Theorie f öffentlicher Güter (FiW) theory of public goods
Theorie f zentraler Ordnung (Vw) central place theory
thesaurieren
  (ReW) to retain profits (*or* earnings *or* income)
  – to reinvest profits
  – to plow back profits into the business
  – (GB) to plough back profits
thesaurierte Gewinne *mpl*
  (Fin) earnings (*or* net income *or* profits) retained for use in the business
  – retained earnings
  – profit retentions
  – reinvested earnings
  – undistributed profits
  – (GB) ploughed-back profits
Thesaurierung f
  (ReW) earnings (*or* income *or* profit) retention
  – (GB) ploughing back of profits
Thesaurierungsfonds *m*
  (Fin) cumulative
  – growth
  – non-dividend . . . fund *(syn, Wachstumsfonds; opp, Einkommensfonds)*
Ticker-Notierung f (Bö) tape quotation
Tiefbau *m* (com) civil engineering
Tiefbauprojekte *npl* (com) civil engineering projects
Tiefeninterview *n* (Stat) depth interview

Tiefgang *m*
  (com) draft *(of a ship)*
  – (GB) draught
Tiefgarage f (com) underground car park
tiefgegliederte Schichtung f (Stat) deep stratification
tiefgestaffelte Gehaltsstruktur f (Pw) multi-grade salary structure
tiefgestellter Index *m*
  (Math) lower index
  – subscript
tiefgreifende Änderungen *fpl* (com) deep-seated changes
Tiefkühlanlage f (com) freezer center
tiefkühlen (com) to deep freeze
Tiefkühlkost f (com) frozen food
Tiefkühltruhe f (com) deep freezer
Tieflader *m* (com) flat-bed trailer
Tiefpunkt *m* **der Rezession f** (Vw) bottom of the trough
Tiefseebergbau *m* (com) deep sea (*or* seabed) mining
Tiefseeboden *m* (com) deep ocean floor
Tiefseefischerei f (com) deep sea fishery
Tiefstand *m*
  (com) bottom
  – low
Tiefstand *m* **erreichen** (com) to hit a low
Tiefstkurs *m*
  (Bö) lowest price
  – all-time low
Tiefstpreise *mpl*
  (com) bottom
  – lowest
  – rock-bottom . . . prices
tilgbar
  (Fin) amortizable
  – redeemable
  – repayable
tilgen
  (Fin) to amortize
  – to pay back
  – to pay off
  – to redeem
  – to repay
  – (infml) to wipe off a debt
Tilgung f
  (Fin) amortization
  – paying back/off
  – redemption
  – repayment
  – sinking
Tilgung f durch jährliche Auslosungen (Fin) redemption by annual drawings
Tilgung f e-r Anleihe (Fin) redemption of a loan
Tilgung f e-r Hypothek (Fin) repayment of a mortgage
Tilgung f in gleichen Raten (Fin) straight-line redemption
Tilgungsabkommen *n* (Fin) redemption agreement
Tilgungsanleihe f
  (Fin) amortization
  – redemption
  – sinking-fund . . . loan
  – redeemable bond issue *(syn, Zinsanleihe)*

Tilgungsaufforderung *f* (Fin) call for redemption
Tilgungsaufgeld *n* (Fin) redemption premium
Tilgungsaufschub *m* (Fin) deferral of redemption payments
Tilgungsaussetzung *f* (Fin) suspension of redemption payments
Tilgungsbedingungen *fpl* (Fin) terms of amortization
Tilgungsdarlehen *n* (Fin) redeemable loan
Tilgungsdauer *f* (Fin) payback period
Tilgungsdienst *m* (Fin) redemption service
Tilgungserlös *m* (Fin) redemption yield
Tilgungsfälligkeit *f* (Fin) date of redemption
Tilgungsfonds *m*
 (Fin) redemption
 - sinking
 - amortization ... fund *(ie, set aside at regular intervals; syn, Amortisationsfonds)*
Tilgungsfondskredit *m* (Fin) sinking fund loan
tilgungsfreie Jahre *npl* (Fin) redemption-free period
tilgungsfreie Zeit *f* (Fin) grace period for repayment of principal
Tilgungsgewinn *m* (Fin) gain on redemption
Tilgungsgrundschuld *f* (Re) real estate charge to secure a redemption loan
Tilgungshypothek *f* (Fin) redemption mortgage *(ie, debtor repays in equal annual installments; syn, Annuitätenhypothek, Amortisationshypothek)*
Tilgungskapital *n* (Fin) sinking-fund capital *(ie, long-term borrowed capital repayable through depreciation or self-financing facilities)*
Tilgungskredit *m* (Fin) amortizable loan
Tilgungskurs *m* (Fin) redemption price (*or* rate)
Tilgungslebensversicherung *f* (Vers) mortgage redemption life insurance
Tilgungsleistung *f* (Fin) redemption payment
Tilgungsmittel *pl* (Fin) redemption funds
Tilgungsmodalitäten *fpl*
 (Fin) terms of redemption
 - repayment terms
Tilgungsplan *m*
 (Fin) redemption (*or* amortization) schedule
 - redemption table
 - sinking fund table
Tilgungsrate *f*
 (Fin) redemption
 - amortization
 - sinking fund ... installment
Tilgungsrechnung *f* (Math) sinking-fund calculations
Tilgungsrecht *n*
 (Fin) call right
 - right of redemption
Tilgungsrücklage *f*
 (Fin) sinking fund reserve
 - redemption reserve
Tilgungsstreckung *f* (Fin) repayment deferral
Tilgungsstreckungsantrag *m* (Fin) request for repayment deferral
Tilgungstermin *m* (Fin) repayment date
Tilgungs- und Zinslast *f*
 (Fin) debt-servicing burden
 - repayment and service of existing debt

Tilgungsvereinbarung *f* (Fin) redemption agreement
Tilgungsverpflichtungen *fpl* (Fin) redemption commitments
Tilgungsvolumen *n* (Fin) total redemptions
Tilgungszahlung *f* (Fin) redemption payment
Tilgungszeit *f* (Fin) payback period
Tilgung von Verbindlichkeiten *f* (Fin) payment of debts
Tintenstrahldrucker *m* (EDV) ink jet printer
Tippfehler *m* (com) typing mistake
Tischcomputer *m* (EDV) desk-top computer
Tischkopierer *m* (com) desk-top copier
Tischrechner *m* (EDV) desk calculator
Tochtergesellschaft *f*
 (Bw) (majority-owned) subsidiary
 - (infml) offshoot of a company
 (StR) (first-tier) subsidiary, § 102 II BewG *(ie, at present the simple ownership of 50% or more of a company is not enough to require it to be treated as a subsidiary. There is also a requirement that the company should come unter the unified financial management of the parent. Under the EEC's 7th Directive the Germans are more likely to be required to comply with a more rigid ownership criterion.)*
Tochtergesellschaft *f* **im Mehrheitsbesitz** (Bw) majority-owned subsidiary
Tochtergesellschaft *f* **100%** (Bw) wholly-owned subsidiary
Tochtergesellschaft *f* **unter 50%**
 (Bw) affiliate
 - affiliated company
Tochterinstitut *n* (Fin) banking subsidiary
Todesfallrisiko *n* (Vers) death risk
Todesfallversicherung *f*
 (Vers) straight-life (*or* whole-life) insurance
 - (GB) assurance payable at death
Toleranzgrenze *f* (Stat) tolerance limit
Toleranzintervall *n* (Stat) tolerance interval
Toleranzklausel *f* (Kart) minor-merger clause, § 24 VIII GWB
Tonnenfracht *f*
 (com) ton freight
 - freight charged by the ton
Tonnenkilometer *m* (com) ton kilometer
Topologie *f*
 (Math) analysis situs
 - topology
topologische Eigenschaft *f* (Log) contextual property
topologische Gleichung *f* (Math) topological equation
topologische Gruppe *f* (Math) topological group
topologischer Raum *m* (Math) topological space
topologische Skala *f* (Stat) topological scale
torsionsfreie Gruppe *f* (Math) torsion-free group
Torsionskurve *f* (Math) twisted curve
Totalanalyse *f* (Vw) general (*or* total) analysis
Totalausverkauf *m* (com) going-out-of-business sale
totale Ableitung *f* (Math) total derivative
totale Faktorvariation *f* (Vw) total factor variation
totale Partnerschafts-Ideologie *f* (Pw) full partnership ideology

totaler Grenzertrag *m* (Vw) total marginal return
Totalerhebung *f* (Stat) complete-population survey *(syn, Vollerhebung)*
totales Differential *n* (Math) total differential
totale Simultanplanung *f* (Bw) comprehensive simultaneous planning
total geordnet (Math) nested
Totalgewinn *m* (Bw) total profit *(ie, sum total of profits taken over the entire life of a business)*
Totalgleichgewicht *n*
  (Vw) complete
  – total
  – unique steady-state ... equilibrium
Totalrechnung *f* (ReW) total-life accounting *(ie, seeking to determinc results of a business enterprise for its whole life from startup to discontinuance; opp, Periodenrechnung)*
Totalschaden *m* (Vers) actual total loss
Totalverlust *m* (SeeV) total loss
toter Punkt *m* (KoR) breakeven point *(syn, Gewinnschwelle, Nutzschwelle, Kostendeckungspunkt)*
tote Saison *f* (Mk) dead *(or* off) season
totes Gleis *n*
  (com) siding
  – sidetrack
  (ie, opening onto main track at both ends; opp, Stichgleis)
totes Inventar *n*
  (Bw) farm equipment and machinery
  – (GB) dead stock
totes Kapital *n* (Fin) idle funds
totes Konto *n* (ReW) inactive *(or* dormant) account
totes Papier *n* (Bö) inactive security
Totgangfunktionsgeber *m* (EDV) dead zone unit
Totspeicher *m* (EDV) read only memory, ROM *(syn, Festspeicher)*
Totzeit *f* (EDV) dead time
Tourismus *m* (com) tourist travel
Tourismusgewerbe *n* (com) tourist industry
Touristengepäckversicherung *f* (Vers) tourist baggage *(or* luggage) insurance
Touristik *f* (com) tourist industry
Trabantenstation *f* (EDV) tributary station *(syn, Unterstation)*
trabende Inflation *f* (Vw) trotting inflation
traditionelles Verfahren *n* **der Budgetaufstellung** (FiW) traditional budgeting
Traditionspapiere *npl* (WeR) documents of title *(syn, Dispositionspapiere)*
träge Organisation *f* (Bw) sluggish organization
Tragepackung *f* (com) carry-home container
Träger *m*
  (Re) supporting organization
  (Re) supporting public authority
  (com) sponsoring agency
  (Vers) fund, § 4 d EStG
  – insurance carrier
Trägerkosten *pl* (KoR) cost of product, product group, etc.
Trägersprache *f* (EDV) host language
Träger *m* **von Rechten und Pflichten** (Re) subject of rights and duties
Tragetasche *f*
  (com) shopping bag
  – (GB) carrier bag
Tragfähigkeit *f* (com) carrying *(or* cargo) capacity
Trägheitsmoment *n* (Stat) moment of inertia
Trampgeschäft *n*
  (com) tramping
  – tramp shipping
Trampreeder *m* (com) tramp owner
Trampschiff *n* (com) tramp (steamer)
Trampschiffahrt *f* (com) tramp navigation *(syn, Charterschiffahrt)*
Trampverkehr *m* (com) tramping trade
Tranche e–r Anleihe *f* (Fin) tranche of a bond issue
Tranche *f* **e–s Kontingents** (AuW) quota share
Transaktion *f*
  (com) transaction
  – operation
  – deal
Transaktionskasse *f* (Vw) transactions balance *(or* holdings)
  (ie, amount of money an economic unit requires to settle its current transactions)
Transaktionskonto *n* (VGR) transactions account
Transaktionsmotiv *n* (Vw) transactions motive
Transaktionsnachfragefunktion *f* (Vw) transactions demand function
Transaktionsvolumen *n* (Vw) volume of economic transactions
Transaktionswährung *f* (AuW) transactions *(or* trading) currency
Transaktionswerte *mpl* (VGR) transaction values
Transfer *m* (Vw) transfer
Transferabkommen *n* (AuW) transfer agreement
Transferausgaben *fpl* (FiW) transfer payments *(or* expenditure)
Transferbefehl *m* (EDV) transfer *(or* branch) instruction
Transferbeschränkungen *fpl*
  (AuW) transfer restrictions
  – restrictions on transfers
Transferbilanz *f*
  (VGR) balance on transfer account
  – (US) unilateral payments
  (syn, Schenkungsbilanz, Übertragungsbilanz)
Transfereinkommen *n* (Vw) transfer *(or* nonfactor) income
Transfergarantie *f* (AuW) transfer guaranty
Transfergeschwindigkeit *f* (EDV) data transfer rate
transferieren (Fin) to transfer
Transferklausel *f* (AuW) transfer clause
Transferleistungen *fpl* **der Privatwirtschaft** (VGR) private transfers
Transferlockerung *f* (Fin) relaxation of transfer restrictions
Transfermechanismus *m* (AuW) transfer mechanism *(ie, explains the aggregate effects of autonomous capital exports)*
Transfermoratorium *n* (AuW) suspension of transfers
Transfermultiplikator *m* (FiW) transfer multiplier
Transferrisiko *n* (AuW) transfer risk *(syn, Konvertierungs- und Transferrisiko)*
Transferstraße *f* (IndE) transfer line *(or* system)
Transfertheorie *f* (AuW) theory of transfers

Transferwirtschaft f (FiW) transfer economy
Transferzahlungen fpl (Vw) transfer payments
Transferzahlungen fpl **der Unternehmen** (VGR) business transfer payments
Transferzahlungen fpl **des Staates** (VGR) government transfer payments
transfinite Kardinalzahl f (Math) transfinite cardinal number
transfinite Menge f (Math) infinite set
Transformation f (Math) transformation
Transformationsdeterminante f (Math) determinant of transformation
Transformationsgleichung f (Math) equation of transformation
Transformationskurve f
 (Vw) product frontier
 – product transformation curve
 – production-possibility boundary (or curve or frontier)
 – tradeoff curve
Transformationsmatrix f (Math) matrix of transformation
Transformierte f (Math) transform
transformierte Matrix f (Math) transform of a matrix
Transitabfertigung f (Zo) transit clearance
Transitabgaben fpl (Zo) transit charges
Transitabkommen n (AuW) transit convention
Transitausfuhr f (Zo) transit (or third-country) export (ie, channeled through third countries)
Transitbescheinigung f (com) transit bond
Transiteinfuhr f (AuW) transit (or third-country) imports (ie, channeled through third countries)
Transiterklärung f (Zo) transit declaration
Transitfracht f (com) through freight
Transitgüter npl
 (com) goods in transit
 – afloats
Transithafen m
 (com) port of transit
 – intermediate port
Transithandel m
 (AuW) transit
 – merchanting
 – third-country ... trade
Transithandelsgeschäfte npl (AuW) merchanting transactions
Transithandelsgüter npl
 (AuW) transit goods
 – goods in transit
Transithandelsland n (AuW) merchanting country
Transithändler m (AuW) transit (or merchanting) trader
Transitivitätsbedingung f (Math) transitivity requirement
Transitivitätsgebiet n **e–r Matrix** (Math) transitivity set
Transitkonnossement n (com) transit bill of lading
Transitladung f (com) transit cargo
Transitlager n (com) transit store
transitorische Aktiva npl
 (ReW) prepaid expense (or cost)
 – deferred charges (or cost or expense or debit)
 – unexpired expense
 – accounts paid in advance

transitorische Passiva npl
 (ReW) prepaid income
 – deferred income (or credit or revenue or liability or assets)
 – unearned income (or revenue)
 – accounts received in advance
transitorische Rechnungsabgrenzung f
 (ReW) deferral
 – deferment
transitorischer Posten m (ReW) deferred item
Transit-Spediteur m (com) transit agent
Transitverkehr m
 (AuW) transit trade (or traffic)
 – international transit
Transitversand m (AuW) transit dispatch
Transitwaren fpl (AuW) transit goods
Transitweg m (AuW) transit route
Transitzoll m (Zo) duty on goods in transit
transnationale Unternehmungen fpl (AuW) transnational corporation (ie, preferred UN usage)
transparenter Modus m (EDV) transparent mode
Transponierte f **e–r Matrix** (Math) transpose of a matrix
transponierte Matrix f (Math) transposed matrix
transponiertes Gleichungssystem n (Math) transposed set of equations
transponiertes Vektorsystem n (Math) transposed vector set
Transport m
 (com) transport(ation)
 – carriage
 – conveyance
 – haulage
 – shipping
Transportabteilung f (Bw) materials handling department
Transportalgorithmus m (OR) transport algorithm
Transportanweisung f (Bw) transport instruction
Transportarbeit f (Bw) transport operations
Transportart f (com) means of transport (ation)
Transportaufgabe f (Bw) transport assignment
Transportbedingungen fpl
 (com) terms of transportation
 – freight terms
Transportbehälter m (com) container
Transportbeschränkung f (Bw) transport constraint
Transportbilanz f (VGR) net position on transport
Transporteinheit f (Bw) unit of transport
Transportfunktion f
 (Bw) transport function
 – materials handling function
Transportgefährdung f (Re) intentional endangering of public transportation, § 315 StGB
Transportgeschäft n
 (com) transport business
 – shipping trade
Transportgewerbe n
 (com) carrying
 – haulage
 – transport (ation) ... industry (or trade)
Transportgut n (com) cargo
Transportgüter npl (com) goods in transit
Transporthaftung f (Re) carrier's liability
transportintensive Güter npl (com) transport-intensive goods

587

Transportkapazität f (com) transport capacity
Transportkosten pl
  (com) cost of transport
  – carrying charges
Transportleistungen fpl (Vw) transport services
Transportlochung f (EDV) sprocket holes
Transportmakler m (com) freight broker
Transportmittel n (com) means of transportation (or conveyance)
Transportpapiere npl (com) shipping papers (eg, Konnossement, Frachtbrief, Ladeschein)
Transportplanung f (Bw) transport planning
Transportproblem n (OR) transport problem (syn, Verteilungs- od Distributionsproblem)
Transportraum m (com) cargo space
Transportrisiko n (com) transport risk
Transportsachverständiger m (com) transportation expert
Transportschaden m
  (com) transport damage (or loss)
  – damage in transit
Transportunternehmer m
  (com) carrier
  – transport contractor
  – haulier
Transportversicherung f (Vers) transport(ation) insurance
Transportversicherungspolice f **auf den Inhaber** (Vers) transport insurance policy made out to bearer
Transportvertrag m (com) contract of carriage
Transportvolumen n
  (com) total transports
  – freight volume
Transportvorschriften fpl (com) forwarding (or shipping) instructions
Transportweg m (com) transport route
Transportwesen n (com) transportation
Transversalitätsbedingung f (Math) transversality condition (ie, in calculus of variation)
transzendente Funktion f (Math) transcendental function
transzendente Zahl f (Math) transcendent number
Trassant m (WeR) drawer
Trassat m (WeR) drawee
trassiert-eigener Scheck m (WeR) check where the drawer names himself as the drawee, Art. 6 III ScheckG)
trassiert-eigener Wechsel m (WeR) bill of exchange where the drawer is identical with the drawee, Art, 3 II WG
Trassierungskredit m
  (Fin) documentary acceptance credit
  – draft credit
  – drawing credit
  – reimbursement credit
Tratte f (WeR) draft
Trattenbuch n (Fin) draft register
Tratte f **ohne Dokumente** (Fin) clean draft
Travellerscheck m (com) traveler's (or circular) check (syn, Reisescheck)
Treffgenauigkeit f (Stat) accuracy
Treibstoffsteuer f (StR) fuel tax (ie, a special form of the ‚Mineralölsteuer')
Trendanalyse f (Stat) trend analysis

Trendausschaltung f (Stat) trend elimination
Trendbereinigung f (Stat) trend adjustment
Trendextrapolation f (Stat) extrapolating the trend line
Trendverlauf m (Vw) trend path
Trendwende f (Vw) trend reversal
Trennabschnitt m (Zo) voucher (see: Anweisungsblatt)
Trennanalyse f (Stat) discriminatory analysis
trennbare Präferenzen fpl (Vw) separable preferences
Trennbit n (EDV) framing bit
trennen
  (EDV) to decollate
  – to deleave
trennende Supposition f (Log) discrete supposition
trennen von, sich (Pw) to part company with (eg, a chief executive)
Trennfunktion f
  (Math) discriminant function
  – discriminator
Trennmaschine f (EDV) decollator
trennscharf (Stat) powerful
Trennschärfe f (Stat) power
Trennschärfefunktion f (Stat) power function
trennscharfer Konfidenzbereich m (Stat) shortest confidence region
trennscharfes Konfidenz-Verfahren n (Stat) most accurate (or shortest) confidence process
trennschärfster Konfidenzbereich m (Stat) most selective confidence interval (or region)
trennschärfster kritischer Bereich m (Stat) most powerful critical region
trennschärfster Test m (Stat) most powerful test
Trennsymbol n
  (EDV) separator
  – delimiter
Trennung f **nach Funktionsmerkmalen** (Bw) functional grouping
Trennungsentschädigung f
  (Pw) severance pay
  – separation (or isolation) allowance
Trennzeichen n (EDV) data delimiter
Treppendiagramm n (Stat) histogram
treppenförmig ansteigen (Math) to grow in stairlike progression
Treppenfunktion f (Math) step function
Treppenkredit m (Fin) graduated-interest loan
Treppenkurve f (Math) step curve
Treppen-Polygon n (Stat) frequency polygon
Treppenverfahren n (KoR) step ladder method
Tresor m (Fin) safe deposit vault (syn, Stahlkammer)
Treuevergütung f (com) = Treurabatt
Treugeber m
  (Re) trustor
  – transferor (ie, in a ‚Treuhand' relationship)
Treugiroverkehr m (Fin) = Treuhandgiroverkehr
Treuhand f (Re) trust
Treuhandeigenschaft f (Re) fiduciary capacity
Treuhandeigentum n (Re) trust property
Treuhänder m
  (Re) fiduciary
  – trustee
Treuhänderausschuß m (Re) committee of trustees

Treuhänder *m* **bestellen** (Re) to appoint a trustee
Treuhänderdepot *n* (Fin) third-party security deposit
Treuhändereigenschaft *f* (Re) fiduciary capacity
treuhänderisch
(Re) fiduciary
- in trust
treuhänderisch besitzen (Re) to hold as a trustee
treuhänderischer Besitz *m* (Re) fiduciary possession
treuhänderischer Besitzer *m* (Re) holder in trust
treuhänderisches Eigentum *n* (Re) trust property
treuhänderische Verwaltung *f* (Re) trust administration
treuhänderisch verwalten (Re) to administer in a fiduciary capacity
Treuhänderschaft *f* (Re) trusteeship
Treuhandgelder *npl* (Fin) trust fund (*or* monies)
Treuhandgeschäft *n* (Re) trust transaction
Treuhandgesellschaft *f* (Re) trust company *(ie, today mostly auditing and tax consulting firms)*
Treuhandgiroverkehr *m* (Fin) accounts receivable clearing transactions *(syn, Treugiroverkehr)*
Treuhandkonto *n* (Fin) trust (*or* third-party) account *(ie, held in a bank by trustees on behalf of third-party assets; syn, Anderkonto)*
Treuhandkredite *mpl*
(Fin) loans in transit
- loans for third-party account
- conduit credits *(syn, durchlaufende Kredite)*
Treuhandsonderkonto *n* (Fin) special trust account
Treuhandstelle *f* (Re) trust agency
Treuhandverhältnis *n* (Re) trust relationship
Treuhandvermögen *n*
(Re) trust property
(Fin) trust fund
Treuhandvertrag *m* (Re) trust agreement
Treuhandverwaltung *f* (Re) fiduciary management
Treunehmer *m* (Re) trustee
Treurabatt *m* (com) loyalty discount (*or* rebate)
- fidelity rebate
(ie, designed to discourage customers from seeking alternative sources of supply)
Treu und Glauben
(Re) good faith
- bona fide
Trichterinterview *n* (Log) funnel-type interview
Trigonometrie *f* (Math) trigonometry
trigonometrische Funktion *f* (Math) trigonometric function
trigonometrische Reihe *f* (Math) trigonometric (*or* Fourier) series
Trinkgelder *npl* (StR) tips and gratuities, § 3 No. 51 EStG

trockener Wechsel *m* (WeR) promissory note *(syn, eigener Wechsel, Solawechsel)*
trockene Stücke *npl* (Fin) mortgage bonds in circulation
Trockenfracht-Markt *m* (com) dry cargo market *(eg, coal or iron ore trade)*
Trockenschiff *n* (com) dry cargo ship
Trommeldrucker *m* (EDV) barrel printer *(syn, Typenwalzendrucker)*
Trommelmarke *f*
(EDV) drum mark
- home address marker
Trommelspeicher *m* (EDV) magnetic drum storage
Trugschluß *m* (Log) fallacy *(ie, any unsound step or process of reasoning: mistake of formal logic, suppression of an unacceptable premise, lack of adaptation of reasoning to its alleged purpose)*
Trunkenheit *f* **am Steuer**
(Vers) drunken driving
- (GB) drunk in charge
Trustfonds *m* (IWF) Trust Fund
Tschebyscheffsche Ungleichung *f* (Stat) Tschebycheff inequality
Tunnelboden *m* (AuW) floor
Tunneldecke *f* (AuW) ceiling
turbulentes Vektorfeld *n* (Math) solenoidal vector field
Twen-Markt *m* (Mk) youth market
Typenhammer *m* (EDV) print hammer
Typenmuster *n* (com) representative sample
Typenrad *n* (EDV) print (*or* type) wheel
Typenscheibe *f* (EDV) daisy wheel
Typenscheibendrucker *m*
(EDV) daisy wheel printer
- petal printer
Typenschild *n* (IndE) identification plate
Typenstab *m* (EDV) = *Typenstange*
Typenstange *f* (EDV) type bar *(syn, Typenstab, Druckstange, Druckstab)*
Typentheorie *f* (Math, Log) theory of types
Typenträger *m* (EDV) print member
Typentrommel *f* (EDV) type drum
Typenverminderung *f* (IndE) variety reduction
Typenwalzendrucker *m* (EDV) barrel printer *(syn, Trommeldrucker)*
typischer stiller Gesellschafter *m* (Re) typical dormant partner
Typung *f* (IndE) standardization
Typungskartell *n* (Kart) standardization cartel
Typungsvorhaben *n* (Kart) standardization project, § 5 I GWB
TZ-Buchkredit *m* (Fin) installment book credit
TZ-Wechselkredit *m* (Fin) installment credit backed by promissory notes

U

U-Bahn *f*
(com) subway
- (GB) underground
- (GB, infml) tube
Überabschreibung *f*

(ReW) overprovision of depreciation, § 256 V AktG
(ReW) overdepreciation *(ie, writedown beyond the estimated zero value)*
überabzählbar (Math) nondenumerable

über alle Schranken *fpl* **zunehmen**
(Math to grow large (*or* to increase) without bound
− to increase beyond bound (*or* all bounds)
überalterte Bevölkerung *f* (Stat) overaged population
Überalterung *f* (Bw) = *Überholung*
Überangebot *n*
(Vw) excess supply
− oversupply
überarbeiten (com) to rework
Überbau *m* (Re) structure extending over a boundary, § 912 BGB
Überbeschäftigung *f*
(Vw) overemployment
− over-full employment *(opp, Unterbeschäftigung)*
überbesetzt
(Pw) overstaffed
− overmanned
Überbesetzung *f*
(Pw) overmanning
− overstaffing *(ie, emphasis on white-collar workers)*
− excess staff
Überbestand *m*
(MaW) excessive stock (*or* inventory)
− oversupply
− long position
(StR) excess inventory of current assets, § 33 III BewG
Überbesteuerung *f* (FiW) excessive taxation
überbestimmt
(Math) overidentified
− overspecified
überbetrieblich (com) intercompany
überbetriebliche Ausbildung *f* (Pw) extra-plant training
überbetriebliche Mitbestimmung *f*
(Pw) supra-plant codetermination
− codetermination beyond the enterprise
überbetrieblicher Streikausschuß *m* (Pw) umbrella strike committee
überbewerten
(ReW) to overvalue
− to overstate
überbewertete Aktien *fpl* (Bö) overpriced (*or* top-heavy) shares
überbewertete Währung *f* (Vw) overvalued currency
Überbewertung *f*
(ReW) overstating *(ie, balance sheet items)*
(Bw) overvaluation *(ie, of assets)*
(Bö) overpricing *(ie, of securities)*
(Fin) overvaluation *(ie, of a currency)*
überbieten
(com) to outbid
− to overbid
Überbietung *f*
(com) outbidding
− overbidding
Überbord-Auslieferungsklausel *f* (com) overside-delivery clause
überbringen (com) to deliver acceptance to
Überbringer *m* (WeR) bearer

Überbringerklausel *f* (WeR) bearer clause
Überbringerscheck *m* (WeR) bearer check
überbrücken
(com) to bridge
− to tide over
Überbrückungshilfe *f* (Pw) temporary assistance
Überbrückungsfinanzierung *f* (Fin) bridging (*or* interim) financing
Überbrückungskredit *m*
(Fin) bridging loan
− (infml) bridge over
Überdeckung *f*
(Fin) excess (*or* surplus) cover
(KoR) overabsorption
Überdividende *f*
(Fin) superdividend
(Fin) surplus dividend *(syn, Superdividende)*
überdurchschnittlich
(com) above average
− higher than average
(Pw) better than average
überdurchschnittliche Abgaben *fpl* (Bö) oversold positions
überdurchschnittliches Wachstum *n* (Vw) above-average growth
übereignen
(Re) to transfer ownership
− to pass title to
Übereignung *f*
(Re) transfer of ownership, § 929 BGB
(Re) conveyance, § 873 BGB *(ie, transfer of title to land)*
übereinkommen (Re) to agree
Übereinkommen *n*
(Re) convention
− agreement
(ie, mehrseitig = between more than two parties)
Übereinkunft *f* (Re) agreement *(ie, zweiseitig = between two parties)*
Übereinkunft *f* **mit Gläubigern** (Re) arrangement with creditors
übereinstimmen (mit)
(com) to be in agreement with
− to conform to
− to be conformable to
− to answer to
Übereinstimmung *f*
(com) agreement
− conformity
Übereinstimmungskoeffizient *m* (Stat) coefficient of agreement (*or* concordance)
Überemission *f*
(Bö) overissue of securities
− undigested securities
überfällig
(com) oderdue
− past due
überfällige Aufträge *mpl* (IndE) jobs past due
überfällige Ausfuhrforderung *f* (AuW) export claim overdue (*or* past due)
überfällige Forderungen *fpl*
(Fin) claims past due
− delinquent accounts receivables
(Fin) stretched-out receivables *(ie, customers paying more slowly)*

überfälliger Betrag *m* (com) amount overdue
Überfischen *n*
  (com) overfishing
  – over-exploitation of fish
Überfließlager *n* (MaW) flow-over inventory
Überfracht *f* (com) extra freight
Überfremdung *f* (Bw) excessive foreign control
Übergabe *f* (Re) delivery, § 929 BGB
Übergabebescheinigung *f* (com) receipt of delivery
Übergabebilanz *f* (ReW) premerger balance sheet
Übergang *m*
  (Re) transition
  – transmission
Übergang *m* **der Ersatzansprüche** (Vers) subrogation of claims *(ie, right of insurer to step into the shoes of the party whom it compensates)*
Übergang *f* **der Gefahr** *m* (Re) passage of a risk
Übergang *m* **des Eigentums** (Re) passage of ownership
Übergang *m* **kraft Gesetzes** (Re) assignment *(or transfer) by operation of law*
Übergangsbestimmungen *fpl* (Re) transitional provisions
Übergangsbudget *n* (FiW) transitional budget
Übergangskonten *npl* (ReW) suspense accounts *(ie, linking cost and financial accounting systems; syn, Spiegelbildkonten, reziproke Konten)*
Übergangslösung *f*
  (com) provisional solution
  – temporary arrangement
Übergangsposten *m* (ReW) suspense *(or transitory)* item
Übergangsregelung *f* (Re) transitional arrangements
Übergangsstelle *f* (EDV) connector *(ie, in flowcharting)*
Übergangsstellung *f* (Pw) staging post *(ie, phase in career development)*
Übergangsvorschriften *fpl* (Re) transitional provisions
Übergangswahrscheinlichkeit *f* (Stat) transition probability
Übergangswahrscheinlichkeits-Matrix *f* (Stat) transition probability matrix
Übergangszeit *f* (com) transitional period
übergeben
  (com) to deliver
  – to turn over
  – to hand over
  – to transfer
Übergebot *n* (Re) higher bid, § 72 ZVG
übergehen
  (Pw) to pass over *(ie, sb in making appointments)*
  (EDV) to skip *(ie, to ignore instructions in a sequence)*
übergeordnete Instanz *f*
  (Re) court above
  – next higher court
übergeordnete Stelle *f* (Bw) superior unit *(or department)*
Übergepäck *n* (com) excess baggage
Übergewicht *n* (com) overweight *(eg, parcel is 10kg overweight)*
Übergewinnsteuer *f* (FiW, US, GB) excess profits tax

Übergruppe *f* (EDV) supergroup
Übergruppenwechsel *m* (EDV) major control change
Überhitzung *f*
  (Vw) overheating *(ie, of the economy)*
  (Bö) wave of heavy selling
überhöhte Bestände *mpl* (MaW) inflated inventory
überhöhter Preis *m*
  (com) excessive
  – heavy
  – stiff . . . price
Überholung *f*
  (ReW) obsolescence *(ie, of fixed assets; subterms: wirtschaftliche/technische Überholung)*
  (com) overhaul *(ie, through inspection and repair)*
Überholverbot *n*
  (com) No Passing
  – (GB) Do not overtake
überidentifiziert
  (Math) overidentified
  – multiply identified
Überinvestition *f* (Bw) overinvestment
Überinvestitionstheorie *f* (Vw) overinvestment theory
Überkapazität *f*
  (Bw) excess
  – surplus
  – redundant . . . capacity
  – overcapacity
  – capacity overshoot
überkapitalisieren (Fin) to overcapitalize
überkapitalisiert
  (Fin) overcapitalized
  – (infml) top heavy
Überkapitalisierung *f* (Fin) overcapitalization *(opp, Unterkapitalisierung)*
über Kassakurs (Bö) over spot
Überkreuzverflechtung *f*
  (Re) interlocking, § 100 AktG
  – corporate interlock
Überkreuz-Wiederholungsplan *m* (Stat) cross-over *(or switch-back)* design
überladen (com) to overload
Überladung *f* (com) overloading
überlagern
  (com) to fog over
  – to conceal
überlagerte Häufigkeitsverteilung *f* (Stat) compound frequency distribution
überlagerte Poisson-Verteilung *f* (Stat) compound Poisson distribution
überlagerte Stichprobe *f* (Stat) interpenetrating sample
Überlagerung *f*
  (Math) superposition
  (EDV) overlay
Überlagerungsbaum *m* (EDV) overlay tree
Überlagerungseffekt *m* (Mk) carry-over effect
überlappende Brachzeit *f* (IndE) machine interference time
überlappende Planung *f* (Bw) rolling budget
überlappende Schichtarbeit *f* (IndE) coupling-up
überlappte Auswahleinheiten *fpl* (Stat) overlapping sampling units

591

Überlappung f (EDV) overlap
Überlappungsmaß n (Stat) intensity of transvariation
Überlappungssegment n (EDV) overlay segment
Überlassung f **von Wirtschaftsgütern** (StR) transfer of assets or the use thereof, § 15 I No. 3 EStG *(eg, to a partnership)*
Überlauf m (EDV) overflow
Überlaufregister n (EDV) overflow register
Überlaufsatz m (EDV) overflow record
Überlaufstelle f (EDV) overflow position
überlebender Ehegatte m (StR) surviving spouse
Überlebensrente f (Fin) joint and survivor annuity
Überlebensversicherung f (Vers) survivorship insurance
Überlebenswahrscheinlichkeit f (Vers) survivorship probability
Überleitungsbestimmungen fpl (Re) transitional provisions
überlesen (EDV) to skip *(ie, to ignore instructions in a sequence)*
Überliegegeld n (com) demurrage (charges)
Überliegezeit f (com) extra lay days *(ie, allowed for loading and unloading)*
Überliquidität f (Fin) excess liquidity
Überlochung f (EDV) overpunch
Übermittlungsabschnitt m (EDV) communications link
Übermittlungsfehler m (Re) error in communicating a declaration, § 120 BGB
(EDV) error in transmission
Übernachfrage f (Vw) excess *(or* surplus) demand
Übernachtungsgeld n (Pw) overnight accommodation allowance
Übernachtungskosten pl (StR) hotel expense
Übernahme f
 (Bw) takeover
 – acquisition
 – purchase
 – *(also)* merger
 – (infml) corporate marriage
 – (infml) tie-up
 (Fin) underwriting *(ie, of a loan)*
Übernahmeangebot n
 (Bw) takeover bid
 – corporate takeover proposal
 – tender offer
Übernahme f **des Ausfallrisikos** (Fin) assumption of credit risk
Übernahmegarantie f (Fin) underwriting guaranty
Übernahmegerüchte npl (Fin) takeover rumors
Übernahmegewinn m (Fin) gain on takeover
Übernahmegründung f (Re) formation of a company where all shares are subscribed by the incorporators
Übernahmeklage f (Re) action brought to take over the business of a partnership, § 142 I HGB
Übernahmekonnossement n (com) received (for shipment) bill of lading
Übernahmekonsortium n
 (Fin) underwriting group *(or* syndicate)
 – purchase group
 – purchasing syndicate
Übernahmekriterien npl (Fin) acquisition criteria
Übernahmekurs m

(Fin) takeover price
(Fin) underwriting price
Übernahmeofferte f (Fin) = *Übernahmeangebot*
Übernahmepreis m (Fin) = *Übernahmekurs*
Übernahmeprovision f (Fin) underwriting commission
Übernahmeschein m (com) dock receipt
Übernahmeschlacht f
 (Fin) take-over battle *(or* struggle)
 – bidding war
 – bid battle
 – merger contest
Übernahme-Spezialist m (Bw) buy-out specialist
Übernahmestrategie f (Bw) acquisition strategy
Übernahmeverhandlungen fpl (Bw) takeover negotiations
Übernahmeverlust m (Fin) loss on takeover
Übernahmeverpflichtungen fpl
 (Fin) underwriting commitment
 (Fin) firm takeover bid
Übernahmevertrag m
 (Fin) acquisition *(or* takeover) agreement
 (Fin) underwriting *(or* subscription) agreement
 – purchase contract *(ie, relating to securities issue)*
Übernahme f **von Verbindlichkeiten**
 (Re) assumption of debt
 – assumption of liabilities as debtor
übernehmen
 (com) to take over
 (Fin) to take up *(ie, an issue)*
 (Bw) to take over *(ie, a company by acquisition)*
 (KoR) to absorb *(ie, costs)*
übernehmende Gesellschaft f
 (Bw) acquiring
 – purchasing
 – absorbing
 – transferee ... company *(ie, in a merger operation)*
über Nennwert (Fin) above par
übernommene Gesellschaft f
 (Bw) acquired
 – purchased
 – transferor ... company
Überorganisation f (Bw) overorganization
überorganisiert (Bw) overorganized
über pari
 (Fin) above par
 – at a premium
Überparie-Emission f (Fin) issue above par *(or* at a premium)
Überparität f
 (Pw) supra parity
 – union dominance
überparitätische Mitbestimmung f (Pw) overparity in representation
Überproduktion f (Bw) overproduction
überproportionale Kosten pl (KoR) progressively rising variable cost
überproportionale Produktionskosten pl (Bw) convex production cost *(syn, progressive Kosten)*
Überprovision f (Vers) overriding commission *(ie, in reinsurance)*
Überprüfung f
 (com) audit

- check
- review

überragende Marktstellung f (Kart) superior market position
- commanding position over competitors

überragendes Interesse n **der Allgemeinheit** (Re) overriding public interest

Überraschungsbesuch m (Mk) cold call

Überraschungsgewinne mpl (Vw) windfall profits

Überraschungsverluste mpl (Vw) windfall losses

Überredungskunst f (Mk) salesmanship *(ie, skill in persuading)*

überregionale Werbung f (Mk) national advertising

Überrollungsbudget n (FiW) rollover budget

überschäumende Konjunktur f (Vw) runaway boom

Überschlagsrechnung f (com) rough estimate

überschreiben (EDV) to overwrite

Überschreiten n **der Binnengrenzen** (EG) crossing of internal frontiers

Überschuldung f
(Fin) debt overload
- overindebtedness
- liabilities in excess of assets
- financial position where liabilities exceed assets

Überschuldungsbilanz f (ReW) statement of overindebtedness *(ie, for corporate persons equal to Konkurs- od Vergleichsstatus)*

Überschuß m (FiW) surplus

Überschuß m **aus Zinsen und Provisionen** (Fin) net income from interest and commissions

Überschußbeteiligung f (Vers) surplus sharing

Überschuß m **der Dienstleistungsbilanz** (AuW) surplus on invisibles

Überschuß m **des Kaufpreises e-s Unternehmens über seinen Buchwert** (Fin) acquisition excess

Überschußdividende f (Fin) surplus dividend

Überschuß-Dumping n (AuW) surplus dumping

Überschußfinanzierung f (Fin) cash flow financing *(ie, German term introduced by Hasenack)*

Überschußgelder npl (Fin) surplus funds

Überschußguthaben n (AuW) net accumulation of ECUs

überschüssige Arbeitskräfte fpl (Pw) slack labor

überschüssige Kasse f (Vw) excessive cash holdings

überschüssige Prämieneinnahmen fpl (Vers) surplus premiums

Überschußkasse f (Vw) liquidity of a bank

Überschußland n (AuW) surplus country

Überschußnachfrage f (Vw) excess demand

Überschußnachfrage-Inflation f (Vw) excess demand inflation

Überschußproduktion f (EG) surplus production

Überschußrechnung f
(StR) cash receipts and disbursement method, § 4 III EStG
- net income method

Überschußreserve f (Vw) excess reserve *(or* cash) *(ie, cash in excess of the minimum reserve)*

Überschuß-Risiko-Kriterium n (Fin) excess return risk criterion

Überschußrückstellung f (Vers) bonus reserve

Überschwemmungsversicherung f (Vers) flood insurance

Überseeverpackung f
(com) seaworthy packing
- packing for ocean shipment

Überseehandel m (AuW) overseas trade

Überseemärkte mpl (AuW) overseas markets

übersenden
(com) to send
- to transmit

übersendende Bank f (Fin) remitting bank

Übersender m
(com) sender
- consignor

übersetzen
(com) to translate *(ie, texts from a source language into a target language)*
(EDV) to assemble
- to compile
- to translate

Übersetzen n
(com) translating
(EDV) compilation

Übersetzer m
(com) translator
(EDV) translating program
(EDV) compiler
- compiling program *(or* routine) *(ie, for problem-oriented languages)*
(EDV) assembler
- assembly program *(ie, for symbolic languages)*
(EDV) processor *(ie, in numerical control)*

Übersetzungsanweisung f (EDV) directive

Übersetzungslauf m
(EDV) compiler run
(EDV) assembler run

Übersetzungsprogramm n
(EDV) translating program
- translator

Übersichtszeichnung f
(com) general arrangement drawing
- layout plan
- outline drawing

Überspekulation f (Bö) overtrading

Übersprungbefehl m
(EDV) no-operation *(or* no-op)
- blank
- do-nothing
- dummy
- skip ... instruction *(syn, Nulloperationsbefehl, NOP-Befehl)*

überstehen (com, infml) sail through *(eg, the current recession unscathed)*

übersteigen
(com) to exceed
- to top *(eg, sales will ... $2bn)*

Überstunden fpl (Pw) overtime

Überstunden fpl **kürzen** (Pw) to cut overtime

Überstunden fpl **machen** (Pw) to work overtime

Überstundenvergütung f (Pw) overtime pay

Überstundenzuschlag m (Pw) overtime premium

übertarifliche Bezahlung f (Pw) pay *(or* compensation) outside collective bargaining agreement

übertarifliche Leistungszulage f (Pw) excess merit bonus

Übertrag m
(ReW) carry forward

Übertrag auf neue Rechnung
(ReW) brought forward
(EDV) add carry
Übertrag *m* **auf neue Rechnung** *f* (ReW) brought forward to new account
übertragbar
(Re) assignable
(WeR) transferable
(WeR) negotiable
übertragbares Akkreditiv *n* (Fin) transferable letter of credit
Übertragbarkeit *f*
(Re) assignability
(WeR) transferability
(WeR) negotiability *(ie, of order and bearer instruments only)*
übertragen
(Re) to assign
(Re) to convey *(ie, title in real estate)*
(WeR) to transfer *(ie, by assignment)*
(WeR) to negotiate *(ie, by consent and delivery)*
Übertragen *n* (EDV) move mode *(ie, movement of data without delimiters; opp, load mode)*
übertragende Gesellschaft *f* (Re) predecessor *(or transferor)* company *(ie, in takeover or merger)*
Übertragender *m* (Re) transferor
Übertragung *f*
(VGR) transfer *(ie, without specific consideration = Gegenleistung)*
(Re) transfer
(ie, in BGB terminology every transfer of a right arising from an obligation to another creditor, no matter whether the transfer is effected by agreement between the parties or takes place automatically by operation of law)
(Re) conveyance *(ie, of title in land)*
(WeR) transfer *(ie, by assignment)*
(WeR) negotiation *(ie, by consent and delivery)*
(OR) transmittance
Übertragung *f* **durch Abtretung** (Re) transfer by assignment
Übertragung *f* **durch Begebung** (WeR) transfer by negotiation
Übertragungen *fpl* (VGR) transfer payments
– (US) unilateral transfers
Übertragungen *fpl* **zwischen Haushalten** (VGR) interpersonal transfers
Übertragung *f* **e-r Forderung** (Re) assignment of a claim
Übertragung *f* **e-r Sachgesamtheit** (Re) bulk transfer
Übertragung *f* **kraft Gesetzes** (Re) assignment by operation of law
Übertragungsanspruch *m* (Re) claim to transfer of property, § 985 BGB
(syn, Herausgabeanspruch)
Übertragungsbilanz *f*
(VGR) balance on transfer account
– (US) unilateral payments
(syn, Transferbilanz, Schenkungsbilanz)
Übertragungscode *f* (EDV) transmission code
Übertragungsempfänger *m* (Re) transferee
Übertragungsfunktion *f* (Math) transfer *(or* admittance*)* function
Übertragungsgeschwindigkeit *f*
(EDV) transmission speed

Überwachungsrecht
(EDV) bit *(or* data*)* rate *(syn, Bitgeschwindigkeit)*
Übertragungsgewinn *m* (StR) transfer gain *(ie, difference between book value and fair market value – gemeiner Wert – of the assets of a transformed ‚Kapitalgesellschaft'; eg, AG, GmbH)*
Übertragungskanal *m* (EDV) communications channel
Übertragungsmodus *m* (EDV) move mode *(opp, Lademodus)*
Übertragungsprozedur *f* (EDV) transmission line procedure
Übertragungssicherheit *f* (EDV) transmission reliability
Übertragungsstelle *f* (Fin) transfer agent
Übertragungssteuerzeichen *n* (EDV) transmission control character
Übertragungsurkunde *f* (Re) instrument of transfer
Übertragungsverfahren *n* (EDV) transmission method
Übertragungsvermerk *m* (WeR) indorsement
Übertragungswirtschaft *f* (Vw) grants economy *(ie, field of study in welfare economics, developed by K. Boulding)*
Übertragung *f* **von Gütern** (Re) transfer of goods
Übertragung *f* **von Haushaltsmitteln** *pl* (FiW) transfer of budget funds
Übertragung *f* **von Vermögen** (Re) transfer of assets
Übertragung *f* **zu Lebzeiten** (Re) transfer inter vivos
übertreffen
(com) to beat
– to get ahead of
– to leave behind
– to outdistance
– to outperform
– to outstrip
übertreibende Werbung *f*
(Mk) puff advertising
– puffery *(syn, Superlativ-Werbung)*
überversichert (Vers) overinsured
Überversicherung *f* (Vers) overinsurance
– (infml) insurance poor *(ie, carrying more insurance than is really needed)*
Überversorgung *f* (AuW) superabundance *(eg, of international liquidity)*
Übervölkerung *f* (Stat) overpopulation
überwachen
(Bw) to control
– to monitor
– to supervise
Überwacher *m* (EDV) checking program *(or* routine*)*
Überwachung *f*
(Bw) control
– follow-up
– monitoring
– supervision
Überwachung *f* **des Wareneingangs** (MaW) inspection of incoming merchandise
Überwachungsprogramm *n* (EDV) = *Überwacher*
Überwachungsrecht *n* (Re) right of inspection *(ie, of limited partner, § 166 HGB; syn, Kontrollrecht)*

Überwachungszeit f (IndE) machine attention time
Überwachungszollstelle f (Zo) customs office of surveillance
überwälzen (auf)
(com, StR) to pass on to
– to pass along to *(ie, prices, taxes)*
(FiW) to shift *(ie, taxes to . . .)*
Überwälzung f (FiW) shifting of taxes *(subterms: Vorwälzung, Rückwälzung)*
Überwälzungsspielraum m (Vw) shifting potential *(ie, opportunities to pass price and wage increases on to the ultimate consumer)*
überweisen
(Fin) to remit
– to transfer
(Re) to refer *(eg, a dispute to arbitrators)*
Überweisung f
(Fin) remittance
– transfer
(Re) referral
Überweisung f **durch Sammelverkehr** (Fin) bank giro
Überweisungen fpl **ausländischer Arbeitskräfte** (VGR) foreign worker remittances
Überweisungsabteilung f (Fin) giro department
Überweisungsauftrag m (Fin) transfer instruction
Überweisungsbeschluß m (Re) transfer order, § 835 ZPO
Überweisungsempfänger m (Fin) credit transfer remittee
Überweisungsformular n (Fin) credit transfer form
Überweisungsgebühr f (Fin) remittance (*or* transfer) charge
Überweisungsscheck m (Fin) transfer check *(ie, transfer instruction in Bundesbank transactions; no check in its legal sense)*
Überweisungsträger m (Fin) transfer slip
Überweisungsverkehr m
(Fin) bank transfer payments
– giro credit transfers
– cashless transfer payments
(syn, Giroverkehr)
überwiegend schwächer (Bö) predominantly lower
überzahlen (com) to overpay *(eg, taxes)*
überzähliges Material n (MaW) surplus material
überzahlter Betrag m (StR) balance of tax overpayment, § 36 IV EStG
Überzahlung f (StR) overpayment of taxes
überzeichnen (Bö) to oversubscribe *(ie, an issue)*
überzeichnete Emission f (Bö) oversubscribed issue
Überzeichnung f (Bö) oversubscription *(eg, of the second tranche of Carter Notes)*
überziehen (Fin) to overdraw an account
Überziehung f (Fin) overdraft
Überziehungskredit m (Fin) overdraft facility (*or* loan)
Überziehungsprovision f (Fin) overdraft commission (*or* fee)
überzogene Einkommensansprüche mpl (Pw) excessive (*or* unjustified) claims to income rises
üble Nachrede f (Re) damaging a person's reputation, § 186 StGB
üblicher Handelswert m (com) common market value

üblicher Wettbewerbspreis m (com) ordinary competitive price
übrige Gegenstände mpl (ReW) other items
Übungsfirma f (Pw) simulated business enterprise
Ubiquitäten fpl (Vw, Bw) ubiquities *(ie, natural resources everywhere available, such as – previously – air and water)*
Uferstaat m (Re) littoral state *(ie, in Sea Law)*
U-Gruppe f (IndE) subassembly
Ultimo m (Bö) last trading day of a month
Ultimoabrechnung f (ReW) end-of-month settlement
Ultimoausschläge mpl (Bö) end-of-month fluctuations
Ultimobedarf m (com) end-of-month requirements
Ultimodifferenz f (Bö) difference between forward and settlement rate
Ultimogeld n (Bö) end-of-month settlement loan
Ultimogeschäft n (Bö) transaction for end-of-month settlement
Ultimoglattstellung f (Bö) squaring of end-of-month position
Ultimohandel m (Bö) = *Ultimogeschäft*
Ultimokurs m (Bö) end-of-month quotation
Ultimoregulierung f (Bö) end-of-month settlement
umadressieren (com) to redirect
Umadressierung f (com) redirection
umarbeiten (com) to rework
Umbasierung f (Stat) rebasing of index numbers
Umbaufinanzierung f (Fin) financing the re-modelling of a property
umbilden
(Bw) to reorganize
– to reshuffle
Umbildung f
(Bw) reorganisation
– reshuffle
Umbruch m (EDV) make-up *(ie, in text processing)*
umbuchen
(ReW) to transfer to another account
– to reclassify
– to repost
Umbuchung f
(ReW) book transfer
– reclassification
– reposting
umcodieren (EDV) to translate
Umcodierung f (EDV) code translation
umdefinieren (Log) to redefine
Umdeutung f (Re) conversion of a legal transaction *(ie, if transaction is void but requirements for the validity of another transaction of the same effect are complied with, such other transaction will be allowed to take the place of the intended transaction, § 140 BGB)*
umdisponieren
(com) to modify arrangements
– to rearrange
Umdisposition f (com) rearrangement
Umdruckbogen m (IndE) production order master form
Umfang m **der Charge** (IndE) batch size
Umfang m **der Haftung** (Re) scope of liability
Umfang m **der Vertretungsmacht** (Re) scope of power of representation

Umfang m der Vollmacht (Bw) scope of power of attorney
Umfang m e-r Versicherung (Vers) coverage of an insurance policy
Umfang m e-s Patents (Pat) scope of a patent
umfangreiche Abgaben *fpl* (Bö) spate of selling
Umfangsvorteile *mpl* (Vw) economies of scope *(ie, may imply span of production program and depth of production pattern)*
Umfangswinkel *m* (Math) circumferential angle
umfassende Menge *f* (Math) inclusive set
umfassende Reform *f* (com) top-to-bottom reform
umfassendes Patent *n* (Pat) broad patent
Umfeldverschmutzung *f* (Bw) pollution of environment
umfinanzieren
　(Fin) to refinance
　– to refund
　– to switch funds
Umfinanzierung *f*
　(Fin) switch-type financing *(ie, extension, substitution, and transformation of funds; opp, Neufinanzierung)*
　– refunding
　– refinancing
　(Fin) = *Umschuldung*
umformen (Fin) to transform into
umformulieren
　(com) to rephrase
　– to redraft
Umformulierung *f*
　(com) rephrasing
　– redrafting
Umformungsregel *f* (Log) transformation rule
Umfrage *f*
　(Mk) opinion survey
　– public opinion poll
Umfrageergebnisse *npl* (Mk) results of a survey
Umgebungsbasis *f* (Math) base consisting of neighborhoods
Umgebungsremission *f* (EDV) background reflection
　(ie, in optical character recognition)
Umgehungsgeschäft *n* (Re) transaction for the purpose of evading a law
umgekehrte Designierung *f* (AuW) reverse designation
umgekehrtes Dumping *n* (AuW) reverse dumping
umgesetzte Leistungen *fpl* (StR) goods and services sold
umgliedern
　(ReW) to transfer
　– to reclassify
　(ie, to another account; syn, umbuchen)
umgründen (Re) to convert to another legal form
　(ie, of business organization)
Umgründung *f* (Re) change of legal form *(ie, mostly sole proprietorship and general commercial partnership into an AG, or vice versa)*
umgruppieren (Log) to reclassify
Umhüllende *f* (Math) envelope
umkehrbare eindeutige Abbildung *f*
　(Math) one-to-one mapping *(or* function *or* transformation*)*
　– bijection

umkehrbar eindeutige Relation *f* (Log, Math) one-to-one correspondence
umkehrbarer Akzelerator *m* (Vw) reversible accelerator
Umkehrfunktion *f* (Math) inverse function
Umkehrkoeffizient *m* (Stat) tilling coefficient
Umkehrmatrix *f* (Math) inverse matrix
Umladegebühren *fpl* (com) reloading charges
Umladehafen *m* (com) port of tran(s)shipment
Umladekonnossement *n* (com) trans(s)hipment bill of lading *(or* B/L*)*
umladen
　(com) to reload
　– to tran(s)ship
Umladeplatz *m* (com) reloading *(or* transfer*)* station
Umladestelle *f* (com) trans(s)hipment point
Umladung *f*
　(com) reloading
　– tran(s)shipment
Umlage *f*
　(StR) levy
　– contribution
　(KoR) allocation
　– charge
Umlageprinzip *n* (SozV) principle of adjustable contributions
Umlagesatz *m* (FiW) rate of contribution
Umlageschlüssel *m* (KoR) allocation formula
Umlageverfahren *n*
　(SozV) social insurance on a pay-as-you-go basis *(opp, fully-funded basis = Kapitaldeckungsverfahren)*
　(Vers) current disbursement
　(SeeV) proportionate contribution system
　(KoR) method of cost allocation
„Umlauf" (com) please circulate
Umlauf m an Anleihen (Fin) bonds outstanding
umlaufende Betriebsmittel *npl* (StR) (normal inventory of) current assets
　(ie, required for an orderly conduct of farming, § 33 II BewG)
umlaufende festverzinsliche Wertpapiere *npl* (Fin) bonds outstanding
umlaufende Lager *npl* (MaW) transportation inventories
umlauffähig
　(Fin) negotiable
　– marketable
umlauffähiges Wertpapier *n* (WeR) negotiable instrument
Umlauffähigkeit *f*
　(Fin) marketability
　– negotiability
Umlaufgeschwindigkeit *f* (Vw) cash transactions velocity
Umlaufgeschwindigkeit *f* **des Geldes**
　(Vw) velocity of circulation
　– transactions velocity
Umlaufgrenze *f* (Fin) issuing limit
Umlaufmarkt *m*
　(Bö) market for securities outstanding
　– secondary market
Umlaufrendite *f* (Fin) yield on bonds outstanding
Umlaufrichtung *f* (Math) direction of traversal

Umlaufspeicher *m* (EDV) cyclic store *(ie, access available only at fixed points in a basic cycle)*
Umlaufvermögen *n*
 (ReW) current assets
 – (GB) floating assets
umlegen
 (ReW) to allocate
 – to distribute
 – to apportion
Umlegung *f*
 (ReW) allocation
 – distribution
 – apportionment
Umleitung *f* **e-r Sendung** (com) reconsignment
Umlenkung *f* **der Handelsströme** (AuW) deflection of trade
Umorganisation *f* (Re) reorganization
umrechnen
 (ReW) to translate *(ie, currencies; not: to convert!)*
 (Fin) to convert
Umrechnungsfaktor *m* (ReW) translation ratio
Umrechnungsgewinne *mpl* (ReW) translation gains
Umrechnungskurs *m* (Fin) rate of exchange
Umrechnungssätze *mpl* (Bö) conversion rates
Umrechnungstabelle *f* (Fin) table of exchange rates
Umrechnungsverhältnis *n*
 (AuW) ratio of conversion
 – exchange ratio
Umrißplanung *f* (Bw) provisional overall planning
umrüsten (IndE) to refit
Umrüsten *n* (IndE) retrofit
Umsatz *m*
 (com) business
 – sales volume
 – volume of trade
 – (GB) turnover
 (ReW) sales revenue
 – sales
 – revenues
 – (GB) turnover
 (Bö) activity
 – dealings
 – turnover
 (Bö) trading volume
 – volume of trade
 (Mk) billings *(ie, of an advertising agency; eg, annual billings in excess of $2m)*
Umsatzanalyse *f* (Bw) sales analysis
Umsatzaufwendungen *fpl* (ReW) cost of goods sold
Umsatzausgleichsteuer *f* (StR) turnover equalization tax on imported goods *(ie, superseded by VAT = value added tax)*
Umsatzbelebung *f* (com) increase in turnover
Umsatzbesteuerung *f* (StR) taxation of turnover
umsatzbezogene Kapitalrentabilität *f* (Fin) sales-related return on investment *(ie, pretax operating income to sales)*
Umsatzbilanz *f* (ReW) statement of account transactions *(ie, listing of credit and debit sums of all accounts; syn, Summenbilanz)*
Umsatzbonus *m* (com) annual quantity discount *(ie, based on sales volume)*

Umsatzbonussystem *n* (Mk) sales-based bonus system
Umsatz *m* **bringen** (com) to pull in sales *(eg, product pulls in over DM500 m worth of sales this year)*
Umsätze *mpl*
 (com) sales
 – (GB) turnover
 (Fin) movements
 (Bö) trading
Umsatzeinbuße *f* (com) drop in sales
Umsätze *mpl* **in Kurzläufern** (Bö) dealings in shorts
Umsatzergiebigkeit *f* (Fin) = *Umsatzrentabilität*
Umsatzerlöse *mpl*
 (ReW) sales
 – sales revenues
 – revenues
 – (GB) turnover
 – gross annual receipts
 – gross income from sales and services, § 157 AktG
Umsatzertrag *m* (ReW) sales revenue *(opp, unrealized revenue from inventory additions)*
Umsatz *m* **e-r Werbeagentur** (Mk) billings
Umsatz *mpl* **steigen** (com) sales are perking up
Umsatzgeschäfte *npl* (Re) commercial transactions
Umsatzgeschwindigkeit *f* (Bw) = *Umschlagshäufigkeit*
Umsatz-Gewinn-Diagramm *n* (KoR) profit-volume chart
Umsatzgewinnrate *f* (Fin) = *Umsatzrentabilität*
Umsatzgigant *m* (com) sales giant
Umsatzgrößen-Klasse *f* (Bw) turnover-size category
Umsatzhäufigkeit *f* (Bw) = *Umschlagshäufigkeit*
Umsatzkarte *f* (EDV) accounting detail card
Umsatzkasse *f* (Vw) transactions balances *(or cash or holdings)*
Umsatzkostenverfahren *n* (KoR) „cost of sales"-type short-term results accounting *(ie, gross sales revenue – sales deductions = net sales revenue – cost of sales = operating result = Betriebsergebnis; based on either full cost or marginal cost; opp, Gesamtkostenverfahren)*
Umsatz-Leverage *n* (Fin) operating leverage
umsatzloser Markt *m* (Bö) flat *(or* inactive) market
umsatzloses Konto *n*
 (ReW) dead
 – dormant
 – inactive . . . account
Umsatzprovision *f*
 (com) sales commission
 (Fin) account turnover fee
Umsatzrechnung *f* (ReW) = *Gewinn- und Verlustrechnung*
Umsatzrendite *f* (Fin) = *Umsatzrentabilität*
Umsatzrentabilität *f*
 (Fin) percentage return on sales *(ie, component of RoI ratio system)*
 (Also:)
 – net income percentage of sales
 – net operating margin
 – profit on sales
 – profit percentage

597

- profit margin
- (GB) profit-turnover ratio
(syn, Umsatzrendite, Umsatzgewinnrate, Gewinn in % des Umsatzes)
Umsatzrückgang m
(com) decline
- drop
- slump ... in sales
- faltering sales
umsatzschwacher Markt m (com) inactive market
Umsatzspitzenreiter m (Bö) volume leader
Umsatzstatistik f (Mk) sales statistics
Umsatz m **steigern**
(com) to increase
- to boost
- to lift
- (infml) to beef up ... sales (GB: turnover)
Umsatzsteigerung f
(com) increase
- advance
- upswing ... in volume sales
- (GB) turnover growth
Umsatzsteigerung f **durch Ein- und Verkauf billiger Waren** (Mk) trading down
Umsatzsteuer f (StR) turnover tax
Umsatzsteueranteil m (StR) turnover tax component (*or* element) *(ie, of a sales price)*
Umsatzsteuer f **auf den Eigenverbrauch** (StR) turnover tax on appropriation of business property for nonbusiness purposes
Umsatzsteuerbefreiung f (StR) exemption from turnover tax
Umsatzsteuerbelastung f (StR) turnover tax burden
Umsatzsteuer-Durchführungsverordnung f (StR) Ordinance Regulating the Turnover (Value-Added) Tax, of 21 Dec 1979
Umsatzsteuererstattung f (StR) rebate of turnover tax
umsatzsteuerfrei
(StR) zero-rated
- nonchargeable
Umsatzsteuerfreiheit f (StR) exemption from turnover tax
Umsatzsteuer f **für den Eigenverbrauch** (StR) turnover tax on personal use by taxpayer
Umsatzsteuergesetz n (StR) Turnover (Value-Added) Tax Law, of 26 Nov 1979, as amended
Umsatzsteuerharmonisierung f (EG) harmonization of turnover tax
Umsatzsteuerpflicht f (StR) turnover tax liability
umsatzsteuerpflichtig (StR) subject to turnover tax
Umsatzsteuerprüfung f (StR) turnover tax audit
Umsatzsteuerrecht n (StR) law of the turnover tax
Umsatzsteuerreform f (StR) turnover tax reform (1968) *(ie, introducing the value-added tax)*
Umsatzsteuerrückvergütung f (StR) turnover tax refund
Umsatzsteuerschuld f (StR) turnover tax liability
Umsatzsteuerstatistik f (FiW) turnover tax statistics
Umsatzsteuervoranmeldung f (StR) turnover tax advance return
Umsatzsteuer-Zahllast f (StR) amount of turnover tax payable *(ie, to the tax office)*

Umsatz m **stieg** (com) sales posted again
Umsatzstufe f (StR) turnover stage
Umsatzüberschuß m (Fin) funds from operations *(ie, item in funds statement = Kapitalflußrechnung)*
(Fin) cash flow *(ie, Geldzufluß aus Umsatz, if liquid funds are subtracted)*
Umsatzüberschußrechnung f (Fin) cash flow statement
Umsatzverhältnis n (ReW) turnover ratio
Umsatzvolumen n
(com) sales volume
- volume of trade
- (GB) turnover
Umsatzzahlen fpl (Bw) turnover ratios
Umschaltzeichen n
(EDV) escape character, ESC
- shift-out character, SO
umschichten
(Fin) to shift
- to switch
Umschichtung f
(Fin) shifting
- switching
Umschichtung f **des Sozialprodukts** (Vw) shifting of national product *(eg, to job-creating investments)*
Umschichtungsfinanzierung f (Fin) debt restructuring (*or* rescheduling) *(ie, converting short-term into long-term debt)*
Umschichtungstransaktion f (AuW) switching transaction *(eg, from $ in DM)*
Umschichtung f **von Ressourcen** (Vw) reallocation of resources
Umschlag m (com) trans(s)hipment
Umschlagdauer f **von Forderungen** (Fin) days of receivables
Umschlagdauer f **von Verbindlichkeiten** (Fin) days of payables
umschlagen (com) to trans(s)hip *(ie, from one conveyance to another)*
Umschlaghafen m (com) port of trans(s)hipment
Umschlagkennziffer f (Bw) = *Umschlagshäufigkeit*
Umschlagkennziffer f **der Debitoren** (Fin) accounts receivable turnover ratio *(ie, average receivables outstanding to average daily net sales)*
Umschlagplatz m (com) place of trans(s)hipment
Umschlagsgeschwindigkeit f (Bw) = *Umschlagshäufigkeit*
Umschlagshäufigkeit f
(Bw) rate of turnover
- turnover rate
(ie, ratio of annual sales to 1. total capital; 2. equity capital; 3. average inventory; syn, Umsatzhäufigkeit)
Umschlagshäufigkeit f **des Eigenkapitals**
(Bw) rate of equity turnover
- equity-sales ratio
Umschlagshäufigkeit f **des Gesamtkapitals**
(Bw) rate of total capital turnover
- total capital-sales ratio
Umschlagshäufigkeit f **des Warenbestandes**
(Bw) rate of merchandise (*or* inventory) turnover
- inventory-sales ratio

Umschlagskennzahlen *fpl* (Bw) turnover ratios
Umschlagspesen *pl* (com) handling charges
Umschlagszeit *f*
  (Bw) replacement period
  (EDV) turn-around time
umschreiben
  (ReW) to transfer *(ie, to another account)*
  (Fin) to transfer *(ie, securities)*
  (Re) to convey *(ie, property)*
Umschreibung *f*
  (ReW) book transfer *(ie, from one account to another)*
  (Fin) transfer *(ie, of securities)*
  (Re) conveyance *(ie, of property)*
umschulden
  (Fin) to reschedule
  – to restructure
  – to roll over ... debt
  (Fin) to fund
  – to refinance
Umschuldung *f*
  (Fin) debt rescheduling *(ie, postponing payments of future debts)*
  (Fin) debt refunding *(or* conversion*)*
Umschuldungsaktion *f*
  (Fin) rescheduling operation
  (Fin) funding operation
Umschuldungsanleihe *f* (Fin) refunding bond issue
Umschuldungskredit *m* (Fin) refunding credit
Umschulung *f*
  (Pw) job
  – occupational
  – vocational ... retraining
Umschulungsbeihilfe *f* (Pw) retraining allowance
Umschulungsmaßnahmen *fpl* (Pw) retraining measures
Umschwung *m* (Vw) turnaround *(ie, in the business cycle)*
umsetzen (EDV) to convert
Umsetzer *m*
  (EDV) converter
  – conversion equipment *(or* unit*)*
Umsetzprogramm *n* (EDV) conversion program
Umsetzung *f*
  (Pw) transfer
  – transferral
  (EDV) conversion
umsonst
  (com) gratuitous
  – at no charge
  – (infml) for nothing
umspeichern (EDV) to restore
Umstände *mpl* **des Einzelfalles** (Re) circumstances of the case
Umstände *mpl* **liegen vor** (com) circumstances are present
Umstand *m* **tritt ein** (Re) contingency comes to pass
umsteigen (Fin, infml) to shift *(eg, funds into long-term bonds, or deposits into other currencies)*
Umsteigeverbindung *f* (com) transfer connection
Umstellkosten *pl* (KoR) change-over costs
Umstellungsprozeß *m* (Vw) process of readjustment
Umstellungsverluste *mpl* (Bw) readjustment losses

Umstellungszuschlag *m* (IndE) change-over allowance
Umstellzeit *f* (IndE) changeover time
umstempeln (Fin) to restamp *(ie, share certificates; eg, as worth only DM50)*
Umstempelung *f* (Fin) restamping of share certificates
umstrittene Frage *f* (com) contentious issue
umstrukturieren
  (Bw) to restructure
  – to reorganize
  – to reshuffle *(eg, business organization)*
Umstrukturierung *f*
  (Bw) restructuring of operations
  – restructuring and adjustment
  – structural transformation
  – shake-up in the structure *(eg, of the electricity supply industry)*
  – „corporate surgery" *(ie, to eliminate loss-making operations)*
Umstrukturierung *f* **der Staatsausgaben** (FiW) restructuring of government expenditures
Umstrukturierung *f* **des Gebührensystems** (Fin) restructuring of service charge pattern
umstufen (com) to reclassify
Umstufung *f*
  (com) reclassification
  – regrading
Umtausch *m* (Fin) exchange *(ie, of shares)*
Umtauschaktionen *fpl* (Fin) swap transactions
Umtauschangebot *n*
  (Fin) exchange
  – conversion
  – tender ... offer
umtauschen
  (Fin) to change *(eg, money)*
  – (more fml) to exchange *(eg, DM for $)*
  – (fml) to convert *(ie, foreign currency)*
Umtauschobligationen *fpl* (Fin) refunding bonds
Umtauschoperation *f* (Fin) repurchase operation
Umtauschquittung *f* (com) refund check
Umtauschrecht *n*
  (Fin) conversion right *(or* privilege*)*
  – option to convert
  – right of exchange
Umtauschverhältnis *n*
  (Fin) exchange ratio
  (Fin) conversion ratio
Umtauschversicherung *f*
  (Vers) versatile policy
  – (GB) convertible assurance
umverteilen (Vw) to redistribute
Umverteilung *f* (Vw) redistribution
Umverteilungshaushalt *m* (Vw, EG) redistribution mechanism
Umverteilungs-Multiplikator *m* (Vw) redistribution multiplier
Umwandlung *f*
  (Re) transformation
  – reorganization
  (ie, change in legal form without change in identity; eg, from corporation to limited liability company)
Umwandlung *f* **in e-e andere Vermögensform** (Vw) asset transformation

599

Umwandlungsbilanz *f* (ReW) reorganization balance sheet
Umwandlungsgebühr *f* (Pat) conversion fee
Umwandlungsgeschäft *n* (Fin) reorganization business *(ie, of banks cooperating in changes of corporate legal forms)*
Umwandlungsgesetz *n* (Re) Reorganization Law, as amended on 15 Aug 1969
Umwandlungsgewinn *m* (StR) reorganization gain *(eg, accruing to a dependent entity which is merged into the dominant enterprise)*
Umwandlungsrecht *n* (Fin) commutation right
Umwandlungssteuergesetz *n* (StR) Tax Reorganization Law
Umwandlungsverkehr *m* (EG) processing under customs control
Umwandlung *f* **von Rücklagen** (StR) transfer of reserves
Umweglenkung *f* (EDV) alternative routing *(ie, alternative communication path)*
Umwegproduktion *f* (Vw) indirect (*or* roundabout) production
Umwelt *f*
(Vw, Bw) environment
– (infml) outside world
Umweltbedingungen *fpl* (Bw) environmental forces
Umweltbeobachtung *f*
(Bw) monitoring (*or* surveillance) of environment
– external surveillance
umweltbezogene Flexibilität *f* (Bw) external flexibility
Umweltkonstellation *f* (Bw) combination of environmental forces
Umweltökonomie *f* (Vw) environmental economics
Umweltrestriktionen *fpl* (Vw, Bw) environmental restrictions
Umweltpolitik *f* (Vw) environmental policy
Umweltschutz *m*
(Vw) environmental protection (*or* conservation)
Umweltschützer *mpl*
(Vw) environmentalists
– defenders of the environment
Umwelt-Überwachungssystem *n* (Bw) environment surveillance system
Umweltverschmutzung *f* (Vw) environmental pollution
Umweltzustand *m* (Vw) environmental constellation
Umworbene *pl*
(Mk) media public
– (GB) ádmass *(ie, especially the TV proletariat, as it were)*
Umzäunungspatent *n* (Pat) fencing-off patent
Umzugsbeihilfe *f*
(Pw) assistance with removal expenses
– relocation assistance (*or* allowance)
Umzugskosten *pl*
(StR) moving
– removal
– relocation ... expenses
Umzugskostenbeihilfe *f* (Pw) = *Umzugsbeihilfe*

Umzugskosten-Entschädigung *f* (StR) relocation allowance, § 3 No. 16 EStG
Unabdingbarkeit *f* (Re) prohibition to change legal provisions by agreement
unabhängige Banken *fpl* (Fin) independent operators
unabhängige Bedürfnisse *npl* (Vw) independent needs
unabhängige Einrede *f* (Re) independent defense
unabhängige Pufferzeit *f* (OR) independent float
unabhängiger Berater *m* (com) outside consultant
unabhängiger Händler *m* (com) independent trader
unabhängiger Prüfer *m* (ReW) external auditor
unabhängiger Vorgangspuffer *m* (OR) independent float
unabhängiger Wartezustand *m* (EDV) asynchronous disconnected mode, ADM
unabhängiges Ereignis *n* (OR) independent event
unabhängige Variable *f* (Math) independent variable
unabhängige Wirtschaftsprüfungsgesellschaft *f* (ReW) independent accounting firm
Unabhängigkeit *f* **der Bundesbank** (Vw) autonomy of the Deutsche Bundesbank *(ie, its formal independent status)*
unabwendbares Ereignis *n* (Re) inevitable incident (*or* accident)
unanfechtbarer Steuerbescheid *m* (StR) uncontestable tax assessment
unanfechtbare Verfügung *f* (Re) unappealable order
(eg, of the Federal Cartel Office)
unangemeldeter Besuch *m* **e-s Verkaufsvertreters** (Mk) cold call
unangreifbares Patent *n* (Pat) incontestable patent
unärer Operator *m* (EDV) unary (*or* monadic) operator
unaufgebbare Forderung *f* (com) nonnegotiable demand
unausgeglichener Haushalt *m* (FiW) unbalanced budget
unausgeglichene Zahlungsbilanz *f* (AuW) balance of payments in disequilibrium
unausgenutzte Arbeitskräfte *fpl* (Vw) slack labor
unausgenutzte Kapazität *f* (Bw) capacity reserve
unbare Geschäftsvorfälle *mpl* (ReW) noncash transactions
unbarer Zahlungsverkehr *m* (Fin) cashless money transfers (*or* payments)
unbeabsichtigte negative Handlung *f* (Re) omission
unbearbeiteter Markt *m* (Mk) virgin market
unbebaute Grundstücke *npl*
(ReW) land
– land not built-on
– undeveloped real estate
– vacant land
(StR) unimproved real property *(ie, carrying no building, or any building erected thereon is not ready for use, §§ 72, 73 BewG)*
Unbedenklichkeitsbescheinigung *f* (AuW) certificate of nonobjection
unbedingte Annahme *f* (WeR) absolute acceptance
unbedingte Anweisung *f* (EDV, Cobol) imperative statement

unbedingte Meistbegünstigungsklausel *f* (AuW) unconditioned most-favored-nation clause
unbedingter Programmsatz *m* (EDV, Cobol) imperative sentence
unbedingter Sprung *m* (EDV) unconditional jump
unbedingter Sprungbefehl *m* (EDV) unconditional branch (*or* jump) instruction
unbedingtes Urteil *n* (Log) categorical proposition
unbefristete Exportförderung *f* (AuW) export promotion unlimited in time
unbefugter Besitz *m* (Re) unauthorized possession
unbefugter Firmengebrauch *m* (Re) unauthorized use of firm name, §§ 18–24, 30 HGB
unbegründet (Re) without just (*or* sufficient) cause
unbekannter Faktor *m* (Log) factor of disturbance
unbelastetes Grundstück *n* (Re) unencumbered real estate
unbenannte Zahl *f* (Math) absolute (*or* abstract) number
unbequeme Zinsfüße *mpl* (Math) odd interest rates
unbereinigt (Stat) unadjusted
unbeschädigt (com) undamaged
unbeschädigte Ladung *f* (com) sound cargo
unbeschäftigt
(Pw) unemployed
– out of work
unbeschränkte Einkommensteuerpflicht *f* (StR) residents' income tax liability
unbeschränkte Geschäftsfähigkeit *f* (Re) full capacity to contract
– full contractual capacity
(*opp, beschränkte Geschäftsfähigkeit*)
unbeschränkte Haftung *f*
(Re) full
– personal
– unlimited . . . liability
– unlimited exposure to liability
unbeschränkte Lizenz *f* (Pat) non-restricted license
unbeschränkte Meistbegünstigung *f* (AuW) unconditional most-favored-nation clause
unbeschränkte Nachschußpflicht *f* (Re) unlimited liability of members to make additional contributions
unbeschränkter Zugang *m* (Vw) unrestricted entry
unbeschränkte Steuerpflicht *f* (StR) unlimited tax liability
unbeschränkte Zuständigkeit *f* (Re) general (*or* full) juristiction
(*ie, complete jurisdiction over a given subject-matter or class of actions*)
unbeschränkt haftbar (Re) absolutely liable
unbeschränkt konvertierbare Währung *f* (Vw) free currency
unbeschränkt steuerpflichtig (StR) subject to unlimited tax liability (*ie, Steuerinländer = resident individual*)
unbeschränkt steuerpflichtige Kapitalgesellschaft *f* (StR) resident corporation
unbeschränkt steuerpflichtige Körperschaft *f* (StR) resident corporate body
unbesetzt (Pw) vacant
unbesetzter Arbeitsplatz *m*
(Pw) vacant job
– vacancy
– job opening

unbestätigtes Akkreditiv *n* (Fin) unconfirmed letter of credit
unbestätigtes unwiderrufliches Akkreditiv *n* (Fin) unconfirmed irrevocable letter of credit
unbestellte Waren *fpl* (com) unordered merchandise
unbestimmte Gleichung *f* (Math) indeterminate equation
unbestimmte Lösung *f* (Math) indeterminate solution
unbestimmter Rechtsbegriff *m* (Re) gray legal concept
unbestimmtes Gleichgewicht *n* (Vw) indeterminate equilibrium
unbestimmtes Integral *n*
(Math) antiderivative
– improper (*or* indefinite) integral
Unbestimmtheitsmaß *n* (Stat) coefficient of non-determination
unbewegliche Güter *npl* (Re) immovable goods
unbewegliche Sache *f* (Re) immovable thing
unbewegliches Vermögen *n* (Re) real property
unbewegtes Konto *n*
(ReW) dead
– dormant
– inactive . . . account
unbeweisbarer Ausgangssatz *m* (Log) primitive proposition
unbewiesene Behauptung *f* (Re) unproved assertion
unbezahlte Freizeit *f* (Pw) time off without pay
unbezahlte Rechnungen *fpl* (Fin) unpaid bills
unbezahlter Urlaub *m* (Pw) leave without pay
unbillige Härte *f* (Re) undue hardship
unbillig eingeschränkt (Kart) inequitably restrained
Unbilligkeit *f* (StR) inequity (*eg, in assessing a tax, §§ 163, 227 AO*)
undefinierter Grundbegriff *m* (Log) primitive concept (*or* notion *or* term)
UND-Funktion *f*
(EDV) AND operation
– logical conjunction
– logical multiply
– logicial product
– meet (*syn, Konjunktion*)
UND-Gatter *n* (EDV) = *UND-Schaltung*
UND-Glied *n* (EDV) = *UND-Schaltung*
UND-Knoten *m* (EDV) AND node
UND-Konto *n* (Fin) joint account (*ie, with the instruction ,,both or all to sign"*)
UND-Schaltung *f*
(EDV) AND circuit (*or* element *or* gate)
– logical AND circuit
– coincidence gate
undurchsichtige Organisationsstruktur *f*
(Bw) muddled structure
– (infml) higgledy-piggledy organization structure
Undurchsichtigkeit *f* der Bezeichnungsrelation (Log) referential opacity
UND-Verbindung *f* (Log) conjunction
UND-Verknüpfung *f* (EDV) = *UND-Funktion*
unechte Arbeitslosigkeit *f* (Vw) fictitious rate of unemployment (*ie, due to illness, injury, strike*)

unechter Bruch *m* (Math) improper fraction
unechter Durchschnitt *m* (Stat) untrue average
unechtes Abladegeschäft *n* (com) import transaction where port of destination is deemed to be the place of performance
uneigentliche Bedingung *f* (Re) unreal condition *(ie, condition in appearance only: whenever it is absolutely certain that the specified event must happen or absolutely certain that it cannot happen)*
uneigentliches Integral *n* (Math) improper integral
uneinbringliche Forderungen *fpl*
 (ReW) bad debts, § 40 III HGB
 – uncollectibles
 – uncollectible accounts (*or* receivables)
 – unrecoverable accounts
 – irrecoverable debts
uneingeschränkt
 (Re) unrestricted
 – unqualified
uneingeschränkter Bestätigungsvermerk *m* (ReW) unqualified audit certificate (*or* report)
uneingeschränkter Handel *m* (AuW) unhampered trade
uneingeschränkter Wettbewerb *m*
 (Vw) unbridled
 – unfettered
 – unlimited
 – unrestrained
 – unrestricted ... competition
uneingeschränktes Akzept *n*
 (WeR) general
 – unconditional
 – unqualified ... acceptance
uneingeschränktes Recht *n*
 (Re) absolute right
 – full legal right
uneingeschränkte Zufallsstichprobe *f* (Stat) unrestricted random sample
uneinheitliche Leistungsgrade *mpl* (IndE) inconsistent ratings
uneinheitlich tendieren (Bö) to tend mixed
uneinklagbarer Anspruch *m* (Re) unenforceable claim
unelastische Nachfrage *f* (Vw) inelastic demand
unelastischer Bereich *m* **der Nachfragekurve** (Vw) inelastic range of demand
unelastisches Angebot *n* (Vw) inelastic supply
unendliche Abschreibung *f* (ReW) = *Restwertabschreibung*
unendliche Elastizität *f* (Vw) perfect elasticity
unendliche Folge *f* (Math) infinite sequence
unendliche Folge *f* **von Gliedern** (Math) infinite set of terms
unendliche Grundgesamtheit *f* (Stat) infinite population
unendliche Menge *f* (Math) infinite set
unendlicher Dezimalbruch *m* (Math) infinite (*or* nonterminating) decimal
unendlicher Reihe *f* (Math) infinite series
unendlicher Graph *m* (OR) infinite graph
unendlicher periodischer Dezimalbruch *m* (Math) repeating decimal
 – recurring decimal fraction
unendliches Produkt *n* (Math) infinite product

unendliches Spiel *n* (OR) infinite game
unendliche Stichprobe *f* (Stat) infinite sample
unendliche Unstetigkeitsstelle *f* (Math) infinite discontinuity
Unendlichkeit *f* (Math) infinity
unentdeckte Rohstoffreserven *fpl* (com) undiscovered (*or* untapped) raw materials reserves
unentgeltlich
 (com) free
 – free of charge
 – at no charge
 – without payment
 (Re) without legal consideration
 – gratuitous
unentgeltliche Einfuhren *fpl* (AuW) imports free of payment
unentgeltliche Leistungen *fpl*
 (VGR) transfer payments
 – unilateral transfers
 (StR) gratuitous performances, § 1 UStG
unentgeltliche Lizenz *f* (Pat) royalty-free license
unentgeltlicher Erwerb *m* (Re) gratuitous acquisition
unentgeltlich erwerben (Re) to acquire gratuitously
unentgeltliches Rechtsgeschäft *n* (Re) legal transaction unsupported by quid pro quo
unentgeltliche Übertragung *f* (Re) gratuitous transfer
unentschuldigtes Fehlen *n* (Pw) unauthorized absence
unerlaubte Handlung *f*
 (Re) unlawful act
 – tort
 – tortious act
 (ie, the civil-law term 'delict', either intentional or negligent, as used in § 823 BGB, has a more restricted meaning)
unerlaubter Nachbau *m*
 (Pat) unlicensed reproduction
 – unlawful imitation
unerlaubter Wettbewerb *m* (Kart) illegal competition
unerlaubte Werbung *f* (Mk) illicit advertising
unerledigter Auftrag *m*
 (com) back
 – open
 – outstanding
 – unfilled ... order
unerledigter Fall *m* (Re) unsettled case
unerledigte Tagesordnungspunkte *mpl* (com) unfinished business
unerschlossene Grundstücke *npl* (com) raw (*or* undeveloped) land
unerwarteter Gewinn *m* (com) unexpected (*or* windfall) profit
unerwartetes Ereignis *n*
 (Bw) unexpected event
 – fallout
unerwünschter Parameter *m* (Stat) nuisance parameter
Unfähigkeit *f* (Bw) incapacity to manage a business in an orderly manner, § 117 HGB
Unfall außerhalb der Arbeitszeit *m* (Pw) off-the-job accident
Unfallentschädigung *f*

(SozV) compensation for accidents
- accident benefit (*or* indemnity)
unfallgeneigt (Pw) accident prone
Unfallhaftpflicht *f* (Re) accident liability
Unfallhäufigkeitsziffer *f*
(Pw) industrial
- injury
- work ... accident rate
Unfallmeldung *f* (Pw) work accident notification
Unfallneigung *f* (Pw) accident proneness
Unfallrente *f*
(SozV) = *Verletztenrente*
(Vers) accident benefits
Unfallrisiko *n* (Pw) accident hazard (*or* risk)
Unfallursachenforschung *f* (Pw) accident analysis
Unfallverhütung *f* (Pw) industrial accident prevention
Unfallversicherung *f*
(Vers) accident insurance
(SozV) employment injury insurance
- work-related injury insurance
- (US) workmen's compensation
unfertige Erzeugnisse *npl*
(ReW) work in process (*or* progress)
(IndE) in-process items
- partly finished products
- semi-finished products
- unfinished products
unformatierte Daten *pl* (EDV) unformatted data
unfrankiert (com) postage unpaid
unfrankierter Brief *m* (com) unpaid letter
unfrei
(com) freight collect (*or* forward)
- (GB) carriage forward, C/F
(com) postage not prepaid
unfreiwillige Arbeitslosigkeit *f* (Vw) involuntary unemployment
unfundierte Schulden *fpl* (Fin, FiW) unconsolidated (*or* floating) debt
unfundiertes Einkommen *n* (Vw) earned income (*opp, fundiertes Einkommen, Renteneinkommen*)
ungarisches Lösungsverfahren *n* (OR) Hungarian method
ungebundener technischer Fortschritt *m* (Vw) disembodied technical progress
ungebundener Wechselkurs *m* (AuW) freely fluctuating (*or* flexible) exchange rate
ungedämpfte Cobweb-Oszillation *f* (Vw) undamped cobweb oscillation
ungedeckter Blankovorschuß *m* (Fin) uncovered advance
ungedeckter Kredit *m* (Fin) open (*or* unsecured) credit
ungedeckter Scheck *m*
(Fin) bad
- uncovered
- (infml) bum
- (infml) rubber ... check
- (GB, infml) dud cheque
ungedeckter Wechsel *m* (Fin) uncovered bill of exchange
ungedeckte Zinsarbitrage *f* (AuW) uncovered interest arbitrage
ungeeignet

(com) unfit
- unsuitable
- unsuited
- unworkable (*eg, proposal*)
ungehinderter Wettbewerb *m* (Kart) free and unfettered competition
ungeklärte Beträge *mpl* (AuW) accommodating (*or* balancing) items (*ie, in balance of payments*)
ungelernter Arbeiter *m* (Pw) unskilled worker
ungelochte Karte *f* (EDV) blank (*or* dummy) card
ungemilderte Steuerpflicht *f* (StR) unreduced tax liability
ungenutzte Kapazität *f*
(Bw) idle
- unused
- unutilized ... capacity
- margin of spare capacity
ungenutzter Produktionsspielraum *m* (Vw) margin of underutilized capital
ungenutztes Kapital *n* (Fin) dead capital
ungenutzte Taktzeit *f* (IndE) balance time
ungeplante Desinvestition *f* (Vw) unintended disinvestment
ungeplantes Entsparen *n* (Vw) unintended dissaving
ungeplantes Sparen *n* (Vw) unintended saving
ungeprüftes Patent *n* (Pat) patent without examination
ungerade Funktion *f* (Math) odd function
ungerade Parität *f* (EDV) odd parity
ungerade Zahl *f* (Math) odd number
ungerechtfertigte Bereicherung *f*
(Re) unjust (*or* undue) enrichment
- injustified benefit
(*ie, the import of this concept of German law, §§ 812ff BGB, is vastly greater than it is in English law*)
ungerechtfertigte Steuervorteile *mpl* (StR) unjustified tax advantages
ungeregelter Freiverkehr *m* (Bö) offboard trading
ungerichtete Kante *f* (OR) undirected arc
ungerichteter Graph *m* (OR) undirected graph
ungeschichtete Zufallsstichprobe *f* (Stat) simple random sample
Ungesetzlichkeit *f* **des Vertragszwecks** (Re) illegality of purpose
ungesicherte Anleihe *f* (Fin) plain (*or* unsecured) bond issue
ungesicherter Kredit *m* (Fin) unsecured credit
ungesicherter Schuldschein *m* (Fin) straight note
ungesicherte Schuldverschreibung *f*
(Fin) unsecured bond
- (GB) unsecured (*or* naked) debenture
ungesichertes Darlehen *n* (Fin) unsecured loan
ungesicherte Tratte *f* (Fin) unsecured (*or* clean) draft
ungesicherte Verbindlichkeit *f* (Fin) unsecured liability
ungestörter Besitz *m* (Re) quiet possession
ungetilgte Obligationen *fpl* (Fin) outstanding bonds
ungewisse Schulden *fpl* (ReW) contingent debt
ungewisse Verbindlichkeiten *fpl* (ReW) contingent liabilities
Ungewißheitsgrad *m* (Vw, Bw) state of ignorance

ungewogener geometrischer Mittelwertindex *m* (Stat) simple geometric mean of relatives
ungewogener Index *m* (Stat) unweighted index
ungewogener Mittelwert *m* (Stat) simple average
ungewogener Summenindex *m* (Stat) aggregative relative
ungewollte Lagerbildung *f* (Vw) involuntary inventory buildup
ungezielte Kundenwerbung *f* (Mk) cold canvassing
ungezügelte Inflation *f* (Vw) wild inflation
ungleichartige Stichprobennahme *f* (Stat) mixed sampling
ungleiche Verhandlungsmacht *f* (Re) inequality of bargaining power
Ungleichgewicht *n* (Vw) disequilibrium
Ungleichgewicht *n* **der Leistungsbilanz** (AuW) external imbalance on current account
ungleichgewichtiges Wachstum *n* (Vw) unbalanced growth
Ungleichgewichtsmodell *n* (Vw) disequilibrium model
Ungleichheit *f* **von Matrizen** (Math) inequality of matrices
ungleichmäßige Konvergenz *f* (Math) nonuniform convergence
Ungleichung *f* (Math) inequality
Ungleichung *f* **von Fréchet** (Stat) information (*or* Cramèr-Rao) inequality
ungünstige Bedingungen *fpl* (com) unfavorable (*or* disadvantageous) terms
ungünstige Wirtschaftsentwicklung *f* (Vw) weak performance of the economy
– sluggish economy
Unikat *n* (com) unique copy
unimodulare Matrix *f* (Math) unimodular matrix
Unimodularität *f* (Math) unimodular property
Unionspriorität *f* (Pat) Convention priority
unitäre Matrix *f* (Math) unitary matrix
Universalbank *f* (Fin) universal (*or* all-purpose) bank
Universalbank-System *n* (Fin) universal banking system (*ie, offering deposit and investment banking functions under one roof*)
– unibanking
Universalbegriff *m* (Log) universal concept
Universalerbe *m* (Re) sole legatee (*ie, named as such in a last will and testament*)
universales Urteil *n* (Log) universal propositon
– (*short*) universal
Universalien *pl* (Log) universals
Universalmenge *f* (Log, Math) universal set (of reference)
– universe
Universalrechner *m* (EDV) all-purpose (*or* general-purpose) computer
Universalsukzession *f* (Re) universal (*or* general) succession, § 1922 BGB
unklare Verantwortlichkeitsbeziehungen *fpl* (Bw) blurred lines of responsibility
unkontrolliertes Stichprobenverfahren *n* (Stat) accidental (*or* haphazard) sampling
unkörperliche Gegenstände *mpl* (Re) intangibles
– incorporeal objects

Unkosten *pl* (com) charges
– expenses
(KoR) (*outdated term*) = Gemeinkosten
Unkostenzuschlag *m* (Vers) loading (*ie, amount added to the pure insurance cost to cover the cost of operation of the insurer*)
unkündbar (Fin) non-redeemable
– irredeemable
(Pw) not subject to termination
– tenured
unkündbare Rente *f* (Fin) non-terminable (*or* irredeemable) annuity
unkündbares Darlehen *n* (Fin) uncallable loan
unkündbare Wertpapiere *npl* (Fin) noncallable (*or* uncallable) securities
unlautere Mittel *npl* (Re) improper means
unlauterer Wettbewerb *m* (Kart) unfair competition
– dishonest trading
unlauteres Geschäftsgebaren *n* (com) dishonest (*or* dubious) business practices
unlautere Wettbewerbshandlungen *fpl* (Kart) unfair trade practices
– fraudulent trading
unlimitierter Auftrag *m* (Bö) market order (*ie, executed at the best price available*)
– order at best
unmittelbare Adresse *f* (EDV) immediate (*or* zero-level) address
unmittelbare Ausfuhr *f* (com) direct export
unmittelbare Beteiligung *f* (Fin) direct participation
unmittelbare Direktinvestition *f* (VGR) primary direct investment
unmittelbare Durchfuhr *f* (Zo) through transit
unmittelbare Folge *f* (Re) proximate consequence
unmittelbare Interessen *npl* (Log) ultimate (*or* direct) interests
unmittelbare Kreditvergabe *f* **an den Kunden** (Fin) straight lending
unmittelbarer Besitz *m* (Re) actual (*or* physical) possession
unmittelbarer Besitzer *m* (Re) actual (*or* direct) holder (*or* possessor)
(*opp, mittelbarer Besitzer*)
unmittelbarer Bestimmungsgrund *m* (Vw) proximate determinant
unmittelbare Rechtsbeziehung *f* (Re) privity of contract
unmittelbarer Schaden *m* (Re) direct damage (*or* loss)
unmittelbarer Vorgesetzter *m* (Pw) first-line (*or* immediate) supervisor
unmittelbarer Zwang *m* (StR) direct enforcement, § 331 AO
unmittelbare Stichprobennahme *f* (Stat) unitary sampling
unmittelbares Verhalten *n* (Re) outward act
unmittelbare Ursache *f* (Re) proximate cause (*eg, of an injury*)
unmittelbare Verarbeitung *f* (EDV) demand processing

unmittelbare Ziele

- *(sometimes)* in-line processing *(syn, mitlaufende Verarbeitung)*
unmittelbare Ziele *npl* (Log) ultimate goals
Unmittelbarkeitsprinzip *n* (Re) principle of immediate recognition
unmittelbar konkurrierende Waren *fpl* (AuW) directly competitive products
unmodifizierte Wiederkauf-Situationen *fpl* (Mk) straight rebuys *(opp, modifizierte W. = modified buys)*
unmögliche Bedingung *f* (Re) impossible condition
Unmöglichkeit *f* (Re) subsequent impossibility of performance *(ie, for which neither party is responsible; §§ 275 ff, 306 ff, 323 ff BGB)*
Unmöglichkeit *f* **der Leistung** (Re) impossibility of performance
unnotierte Werte *mpl* (Bö) unlisted (*or* unquoted) securities
unparteiischer Gutachter *m* (com) nonpartisan expert
unpfändbar
(Re) exempt from execution
– non-leviable
unpfändbare Bezüge *pl* (Pw) earnings exempt from garnishment
unpfändbare Forderung *f* (Re) claim exempt from judicial attachment, § 394 BGB
unpfändbare Sachen *fpl* (Re) non-attachable items
Unpfändbarkeit *f* (Re) exemption from execution
unplanmäßige Tilgung *f* (Fin) unscheduled redemption
unproduktiv
(com) unproductive
– idle
unproduktive Arbeit *f* (Bw) dead work
unqualifizierte Tätigkeit *f* (Pw) unskilled work
unquittierte Rechnung *f* (com) unreceipted bill (*or* invoice)
unrealisierter Ertrag *m* (ReW) unrealized revenue (from inventory additions) *(opp, Absatzertrag)*
unregelmäßiger Verwahrungsvertrag *m*
(Re) bailment in the nature of a loan, § 700 BGB
– *(civil law)* depositum irregulare
unreines Konnossement *n*
(com) foul
– dirty
– claused ... bill of lading (*or* B/L)
(ie, containing notation that goods received by carrier were defective)
unrentabel (com) unprofitable
unrentables Unternehmen *n* (Bw) marginal enterprise
unrentable Tochtergesellschaft *f* (Bw) marginal subsidiary
unrichtige Angaben *fpl*
(com) incorrect statements
(Re) misrepresentation
Unruhe *f* **auf den Geldmärkten** (Fin) volatility in the money markets
unsachgemäße Verwendung *f* (com) misuse
unschädlich (Re) having no detrimental effect
unschuldiger Dritter *m* (Re) innocent bystander *(ie, in cases of products liability)*
unselbständige Stiftung *f* (Re) endowment fund

Unterbegriff

unselbständiges Zeichen *n* (Log) syncategorematic sign
(ie, having no meaning in isolation)
unselbständige Tätigkeit *f* (Pw) dependent employment
Unsicherheitsmarge *f* (com) margin of uncertainty
unsichtbare Ausfuhr *f* (VGR) invisible exports
unsichtbare Einfuhr *f* (VGR) invisible imports
unsichtbare Ein- und Ausfuhren *fpl* (VGR) invisibles
unsichtbare Exporte *mpl* (VGR) invisible exports
unsichtbare Hand *f* (Vw) invisible hand *(ie, phrase coined by Adam Smith, basic tenet upheld by all economic liberals)*
unsichtbare Importe *mpl* (VGR) invisible imports
unsichtbarer Handel *m* (VGR) invisible trade
unsichtbarer Zoll *m* (AuW) invisible tariff
unsichtbare Transaktionen *fpl* (VGR) invisible transactions
unstabiles Cobweb *n* (Vw) explosive cobweb
unstabiles Gleichgewicht *n* (Vw) unstable equilibrium
unständig Beschäftigte *mpl* (Stat) temporarily employed persons
unständige Beschäftigung *f* (Pw) temporary employment
unstetige Funktion *f* (Math) discontinuous function
Unstetigkeit *f* (Math) discontinuity
Unstetigkeitsstelle *f*
(Math) (point of) discontinuity
– jump
– point break
Untätigkeitsklage *f* (StR) complaint on the ground of excessive delay by the agency concerned *(ie, requires the lapse of six months from the time the administrative procedures were initiated, § 46 FGO)*
untaxierte Police *f* (Vers) open (*or* untaxed) policy
unteilbare Leistung *f* (Re) indivisible performance, § 431 BGB
Unteilbarkeit *f* **der Produktionsfaktoren** (Vw) indivisibility of input factors
Unteilbarkeit *f* **von Gütern**
(Vw) indivisibility
– jointness
– nonappropriability ... of goods
Unterabschreibung *f*
(ReW) underdepreciation
– underprovision of depreciation
Unterabteilung *f* (Bw) subdivision
Unterakkreditiv *n* (Fin) back-to-back credit
Unteranspruch *m*
(Re) subclaim
– subordinate claim
Unterauftrag *m* (com) subcontract
Unteraufträge *mpl* **vergeben**
(com) to subcontract
– to farm out work
Unterauslastung *f*
(IndE) underutilization of capacity
idle capacity
Unterauswahl *f* (Stat) subsample
Unterbaugruppe *f* (IndE) subassembly
Unterbegriff *m*
(Log) subterm

605

Unterbeschäftigung
(Log) minor term *(ie, the term that is the subject of the conclusion in a categorical syllogism)*
Unterbeschäftigung *f*
(Vw) underemployment
– less-than-full employment *(opp, Überbeschäftigung)*
(Bw) underutilization
– operating *(or* working) below capacity
Unterbeschäftigungseinkommen *n* (Vw) underemployment income
Unterbesetzung *f*
(Pw) undermanning
– understaffing *(ie, emphasis on white-collar workers)*
Unterbestellung *f* (com) suborder
Unterbeteiligung *f*
(Fin) subparticipation
– accessory participation
– participation in another's partnership
Unterbeteiligungsvertrag *m* (Fin) subunderwriting agreement *(ie, in a syndicate group)*
Unterbevollmächtigter *m* (com) sub-agent
unterbewerten
(ReW) to undervalue
– to understate
unterbewertet (ReW) undervalued
Unterbewertung *f*
(ReW) understating *(ie, balance sheet items)*
(Bw) undervaluation *(ie, of assets)*
(Bö) underpricing *(ie, of securities)*
(Fin) undervaluation *(ie, of a currency)*
Unterbezahlung *f* (Pw) underpayment
unterbieten
(com) to undercut
– to undersell *(eg, a producer by unfairly low-priced imports)*
(com) to underbid
Unterbietung *f*
(com) undercutting
– underselling
– underbidding
Unterbilanz *f* (ReW) adverse *(or* deficit) balance
unterbrechbar (EDV) interruptable
unterbrechen (EDV) to interrupt
Unterbrechung *f* (EDV) interrupt
Unterbrechung *f* **der Verjährung**
(Re) interruption of the Statute of Limitations
– *(civil law)* interruption of prescription *(ie, a new period of limitations begins to run at the end of the interrupting event; § 217 BGB)*
Unterbrechungsanforderung *f* (EDV) interrupt request
Unterbrechungsmaske *f* (EDV) interrupt mask *(or* trap)
Unterbrechungsmaskenregister *n* (EDV) interrupt mask register, IMR
Unterbrechungsregister *n* (EDV) interrupt register
Unterbrechungssteuerung *f* (EDV) interrupt control
Unterbrechungstaste *f* (EDV) attention key *(syn, Abruftaste)*
Unterbrechungssystem *n* (EDV) interrupt system
Unterbrechungszustand *m* (EDV) interrupt state
unterbringen (com, Fin) to place *(eg, purchase order, securities issue)*

Unterbringung *f* **beim Publikum** (Fin) public placement *(or* placing)
Unterbringung *f* **von Aufträgen** (com) placing orders
unterbrochene Rente *f* (Fin) noncontinuous annuity
Unterdeklarierung *f* (com) short entry
unter dem Strich (ReW) below the line
Unterdeterminante *f*
(Math) minor
– subdeterminant
Unterdrückung *f* **führender Nullen** (EDV) suppression of leading zeros
untere Einkommensgruppen *fpl* (StR) lower income brackets *(or* ranges *or* groups)
untere Entscheidungsgrenze *f* (Stat) lower control limit
untere Gerichte *npl* (Re) inferior *(or* minor) courts
untere Grenze *f*
(Math) greatest lower bound
– limit inferior
Untereinkaufspreisverkäufe *mpl* (Mk) below-cost sales
untere Kontrollgrenze *f* (Stat) lower control limit
untere Leitungsebene *f* (Bw) lower management
untere Lochungszone *f* (EDV) lower curtate
unterer Goldpunkt *m* (AuW) gold import point
unterer Grenzwert *m* (Math) lower limit
unterer Interventionspunkt *m*
(AuW) bottom
– floor
– lower . . . support point
– floor
unterer Rand *m* **der Schlange** (AuW) the snake's lower limit
unterer Rand *m* **des Zielkorridors** (AuW) bottom *(or* lower) end of target range
unterer Wendepunkt *m* (Vw) lower turning point *(ie, in the business cycle)*
untere Schranke *f*
(Math) lower bound
– minorant *(ie, of a point set)*
unteres Preissegment *n* (Mk) lower price segment
untere Zone *f* (EDV) = *untere Lochungszone*
Unterfinanzierung *f* (Fin) *(wrongly used instead of = Illiquidität)*
Unterfischen *n*
(com) underfishing
– under-exploitation of fish
Unterfrachtvertrag *m*
(com) subcontract of affreightment
– subcharter
– subchartering contract
Untergebene *mpl*
(Pw) subordinates
– (infml) (people) down the line
untergebenenbezogener Führungsstil *m* (Bw) employee-oriented style of leadership *(R. Likert)*
untergeordnete Instanz *f*
(Re) court below
– minor court
– lower-instance court
untergeordnete Stelle *f* (Bw) subordinate unit *(or* department)
Untergesellschaft *f*

(Bw) sub-partnership
(Bw) subsidiary (company)
(Bw) controlled company
untergliederte Datei *f* (EDV) partitioned date file
Untergraph *m* (OR) subgraph
Untergraph *m* **mit beschränktem Grad** (Math) degree-constrained graph
Untergruppensumme *f* (Math) minor total
Untergruppentrennung *f* (EDV) minor control change
Untergruppen-Trennzeichen *n* (EDV) record separator
Untergruppenwechsel *m* (EDV) minor control change
Unterhalt *m* **leisten** (Re) to pay support
unterhaltsberechtigte Person *f* (StR) dependent *(ie, person entitled to support by others)*
Unterhaltsbezüge *mpl* **und Renten** *fpl* (StR) annuities
Unterhaltsgeld *n* (SozV) maintenance allowance
Unterhaltsleistungen *fpl* (StR) alimony payments *(ie, between spouses, § 10 I No. 1 EStG)*
Unterhaltspflicht *f* (StR) statutory support obligation
Unterhaltssicherungsgesetz *n* (Re) Law Guaranteeing and Securing Support
Unterhaltszahlungen *fpl* (Re) maintenance payments
Unterhaltung *f*
(com) maintenance
– upkeep
Unterhaltungsselektronik *f* (com) consumer electronics
Unterhaltungsindustrie *f* (com) entertainment industry
Unterhaltungskosten *pl* (com) maintenance expenses
Unterholding *f* (Bw) subholding
Unterkanal *m* (EDV) subchannel
Unterkapazität *f* (Bw) capacity shortage
unterkapitalisiert (Fin) undercapitalized
Unterkapitalisierung *f* (Fin) undercapitalization
unter Kassakurs (Bö) under spot
Unterkonsorte *m* (Fin) sub-underwriter
Unterkonsortium *n* (Fin) sub-syndicate
Unterkonsumtionstheorie *f* (Vw) underconsumption theory
Unterkonto *n*
(ReW) adjunct
– auxiliary
– companion
– detail
– subsidiary ... account
– subaccount
Unterlagen *fpl*
(com) documents
– data and information
– papers
– material
Unterlagenmaterial *n* (OR) book-up material
unterlassen
(Re) to fail to do
– to refrain from doing
– to forbear from doing
– to omit to do/doing

unterlassene Abschreibungen *fpl* (ReW) depreciation shortfall
unterlassene Instandhaltung *f* (ReW) deferred maintenance
unterlassene Patentausübung *f* (Pat) non-use of a patent
unterlassene Wartung *f* **und Instandhaltung** (Bw) deferred repairs and maintenance
Unterlassung *f*
(Re) forbearance, § 241 BGB *(ie, an intentional negative act)*
– omission *(ie, an unintentional negative act)*
– nonperformance of an activity
– failure to do sth
Unterlassungsklage *f*
(Re) action for restraint
– action for restraining the defendant from committing a ‚delict'
Unterlauf *m* (EDV) (arithmetic) underflow
unter Lebenden (Re) inter vivos *(ie, between living persons; eg, gift inter vivos; opp, mortis causa: von Todes wegen)*
Unterlieferant *m* (com) subcontractor
unterliegen (Re) to be subject to
Unterlizenz *f* (Pat) sublicense
Unterlizenzgeber *m* (Pat) sublicensor
Unterlizenznehmer *m* (Pat) sublicensee
Unterlochung *f* (EDV) underpunch
Untermatrize *f* (Math) submatrix
Untermenge *f* (Math) subset
Unternachfrage *f*
(Vw) underdemand
(com) shortfall in demand
Unternehmen *n*
(Bw) business enterprise
– business firm
– business undertaking
– firm
– undertaking
– concern *(ie, any economic unit!)*
– (infml) company *(ie, this informal term does not necessarily connote incorporation in AmE or BrE; it often stands for a partnership or even a sole proprietorship)*
Unternehmen *n* **der gewerblichen Wirtschaft** (com) commercial enterprise
Unternehmen *n* **gründen**
(Re) to form
– to organize
– to create
– to set up
– to establish ... a business
Unternehmen *n* **mit hohem Fremdkapitalanteil**
(Fin) highly levered company
– (GB) highly geared company
Unternehmen *n* **mit hoher Dividendenausschüttung** (Fin) high payout firm
Unternehmen *n* **mit niedriger Gewinnausschüttung** (Fin) low payout firm
Unternehmensberater *m* (Bw) management (*or* business) consultant
– consultant to management
– management (*or* business) counselor
Unternehmensberatung *f* (Bw) mangement consulting (*or* consultancy)

Unternehmensbereich *m*
(Bw) functional area
– operation
– division
– group *(eg, inventory control, finance, sales)*
Unternehmensbewertung *f* (Fin) valuation of an enterprise as a whole
Unternehmensbilanz *f* (ReW) corporate balance sheet
unternehmenseigene Gesellschaft *f* **im Ausland** (Vers) offshore captive
Unternehmensergebnis *n* (ReW) overall company result *(ie, operating result + nonoperating result)*
Unternehmenserträge *mpl* (ReW) company earnings
Unternehmensfinanzierung *f*
– company
– corporate
– enterprise
– managerial ... finance
– business enterprise finance
Unternehmensformen *fpl* (Bw) forms of business organization
Unternehmensforschung *f*
(OR) operations research
– (GB) operational research
(ie, German operations researchers have meanwhile given up this misleading translation and returned to the original American or British term)
Unternehmensführung *f* (Bw) management
Unternehmensgewinn *m* (Fin) business *(or* corporate*)* profit
Unternehmensgliederung *f* (Bw) departmental structure
Unternehmensgründung *f* (Bw) business formation
Unternehmensgruppe *f* (Bw) group (of companies)
Unternehmenshaftung *f* (Re) enterprise liability
Unternehmens-Image *n* (Bw) corporate image
unternehmensinterne Berichterstattung *f* (Bw) internal reporting
unternehmensinterne Flexibilität *f* (Bw) internal flexibility
unternehmensinterne Konstellation *f* (Bw) internal configuration
Unternehmensinvestitionen *fpl* (Vw) industrial *(or* corporate*)* investments
Unternehmenskapital *n* (Fin) total capital *(ie, equity capital + outside capital)*
Unternehmenskonzentration *f* (Kart) corporate concentration
Unternehmensleiter *m*
(Bw) business executive
– top manager
– top executive
– leader
(eg, of a large corporation)
Unternehmensliquidität *f* (Fin) corporate liquidity
Unternehmensmitbestimmung *f* (Pw) codetermination at business enterprise level
Unternehmensmodell *n* (Bw) company model
Unternehmensorganisation *f* (Bw) company organization
Unternehmensplanspiel *n*
(Bw) business
– management decision

– operational
– executive ... game
Unternehmensplanung *f*
(Bw) business
– corporate
– company
– managerial ... planning
Unternehmenspolitik *f*
(Bw) business
– company
– corporate ... policy
Unternehmenssektor *m* (VGR) corporate sector
Unternehmensspitze *f*
(Bw) top management
– (infml) corporate summit *(eg, executives below the ...)*
Unternehmensstrategie *f*
(Bw) business
– corporate
– master ... strategy *(ie, including purposes, objectives, policies)*
Unternehmensteile *mpl* **abstoßen** (Bw) to spin off *(or* hive off*)* operations
unternehmenstypischer Wert *m* (ReW) value to the business
Unternehmensübernahme *f*
(Fin) acquisition
– takeover
– merger *(ie, also as a general term)*
– tie-up
Unternehmensumwelt *f* (Bw) business environment
Unternehmensverband *m* (Bw) federation of commercial or industrial enterprises
Unternehmensverfassung *f* (Bw) corporate legal structure *(ie, term used in discussions of developments marked by ‚Betriebsverfassungsgesetz', ‚Mitbestimmungsgesetz' etc.)*
Unternehmensverluste *mpl* (Fin) company losses
Unternehmensverschuldung *f* (Fin) corporate indebtedness
Unternehmensvertrag *m*
(Re) affiliation agreement, §§ 291–307 AktG
(Re) agreement between enterprises
– inter-company agreement
Unternehmensziele *npl*
(Bw) business
– corporate
– enterprise ... goals *(or* objectives*)*
– goals of the organization
Unternehmenszusammenschluß *m*
(Bw) business combination
– *(as a general term also)* merger
– tie-up
Unternehmenszweck *m* (Bw) nature *(or* purpose*)* of a business
Unternehmen *n* **voll ausbauen** (com, infml) to fully-fledge a company *(eg, it took 18 months to raise the capital needed ...)*
Unternehmer *m*
(Vw) entrepreneur
(Bw) businessman
– contractor
(StR) entrepreneur *(ie, not identical with the general understanding of the term: one who exer-*

cises a business, professional, or other continuing activity, independently and with the intent to realize receipts; § 2 I UStG)
Unternehmer *pl* (Bw) business community *(ie, businessmen collectively: ‚die Wirtschaft')*
Unternehmereinheit *f* (StR) legally independent enterprises owned or controlled by the same interests are treated as an economic unit for turnover tax purposes *(ie, term no longer used in turnover tax law)*
Unternehmereinkommen *n* (VGR) entrepreneurial income
– income of entrepreneuers
– busines income
– earnings from the ownership of the enterprise
Unternehmergeist *m* (Bw) entrepreneurial spirit
Unternehmergewinn *m* (Bw) (corporate) profit
Unternehmerhaftpflicht *f* (Re) employer's liability
Unternehmerin *f* (com) businesswoman
unternehmerische Entscheidungen *fpl* **unter Risiko** (Bw) entrepreneurial risk-taking decisions
unternehmerische Entscheidungsgrundsätze *mpl* (Bw) business (or management) policies
unternehmerische Gesamtplanung *f* (Bw) corporate planning
unternehmerische Investitionsnachfrage *f* (Vw) investment demand of enterprises
unternehmerisches Potential *n* (Bw) operational capabilities
unternehmerisches Risiko *n* (Bw) business risk
unternehmerisches Wagnis *n* (Bw) business risk
unternehmerische Willensbildung *f* (Bw) managerial decision-making
Unternehmerlohn *m*
(Vw) proprietors' income
– wages of entrepreneurship
(ReW) entrepreneurial
– managerial
– management ... wages (or income)
(ie, hypothetical compensation for the services of the owner or owners)
Unternehmertätigkeit *f* (VGR) entrepreneurial activity
Unternehmerverband *m* (Vw) trade association
Unternehmerwagnis *n* (Bw) entrepreneurial risk
Unternehmerwechsel *m* (StR) business changing hands *(ie, deemed to have been discontinued by the transferor and newly commenced by the transferee, § 5 II GewStG)*
Unternehmung *f* (Bw) = *Unternehmen*
Unternehmungsaufspaltung *f* (Bw) split of a (unitary) business *(ie, into a property-holding entity and an operating company; see: Betriebsaufspaltung)*
Unternehmungsberater *m* (Bw) = *Unternehmensberater*
Unternehmungsbewertung *f* (Bw) valuation of an enterprise as a whole
Unternehmungsergebnis *n* (ReW) overall business result *(ie, difference between revenue and expenditure: Betriebserfolg + neutraler Erfolg)*
Unternehmungsformen *fpl* (Bw) forms of business organization
Unternehmungsgewinn *m* (ReW) annual profit *(or* income) *(ie, annual revenues – expenditure)*

Unternehmungsleiter *m* (Bw) enterprise manager *(syn, Unternehmensleiter)*
Unternehmungsmehrwert *m* (Bw) *(rare expression for)* = *Firmenwert*
Unternehmungspolitik *f* (Bw) business policy
Unternehmungsrentabilität *f* (Fin) overall return *(ie, ratio of net profit + interest on borrowed capital to total capital employed)*
Unternehmungswert *m* (Bw) value of an enterprise as a whole
Unternehmungsziele *npl* (Bw) = *Unternehmensziele*
Unternehmungszusammenschluß *m* (Bw) = *Unternehmenszusammenschluß*
unter Nennwert
(Fin) below par
– at a discount
Unternetzplan *m* (OR) subnetwork
Unterordnungskonzern *m*
(Bw) group of subordinated affiliates
– vertical group
(ie, with a unified management at headquarters)
Unterorganisation *f* (Bw) underorganization
unter pari
(Fin) below par
– at a discount
Unterpari-Emission *f* (Fin) issue below par *(or* at a discount)
Unterprogramm *n*
(EDV) subprogramm
– subroutine
Unterprogrammaufruf *m* (EDV) subroutine call
Unterprogrammbibliothek *f* (EDV) subroutine library
Unterprogramm *n* **zweiter Stufe** (EDV) second remove subroutine
unterproportionale Kosten *pl* (KoR) degressively rising variable cost
unterproportionale Produktionskosten *pl* (Bw) concave production cost *(syn, degressive Kosten)*
unterqualifiziertes Personal *n* (Pw) underqualified personnel
Unterraum *m* (Math) subspace
Unterrichtsmaterial *n* (Pw) teaching materials
Untersagungsverfahren *n* (Kart) prohibition proceedings, § 37a GWB
Untersagungsvoraussetzungen *fpl* (Kart) prohibition requirements
Untersatz *m* (Log) minor premise *(ie, containing the minor term in a categorical syllogism)*
Unterscheidungsmerkmal *n* (Log) destinctive feature
Unterschiede *mpl* **in den Zollsätzen** (AuW) tariff differential
unterschiedliche Preisnachlässe *mpl* (Mk) differential discounts
Unterschlagung *f* (Re) embezzlement, § 246 StGB
unterschreiben
(com) to sign
– to undersign
– to subscribe
Unterschriftsberechtigter *m* (com) person lawfully authorized to sign
Unterschriftsberechtigung *f* (com) authority to sign
Unterschriftsprobe *f* (com) specimen signature

Unterschriftsstempel *m* (com) signature stamp
Unterschriftsverzeichnis *n* (com) list of authorized signatures
Unterschriftsvollmacht *f* (com) authority to sign documents
unterschwellige Werbung *f* (Mk) subliminal advertising
Unterstation *f* (EDV) tributary station *(syn, Trabantenstation)*
unterste Leitungsebene *f* (Bw) first-line management
unterstellter Mitarbeiter *m* (Pw) subordinate
unterstellte Transaktion *f* (VGR) imputation
unterstellt sein (Pw) to report to
unterstützende Werbung *f* (Mk) accessory advertising *(syn, flankierende od Randwerbung)*
Unterstützungskasse *f* (Pw) relief fund *(ie, does not give the potential beneficiaries a legal right to the benefits distributed by it, § 4d EStG)*
Unterstützungslinie *f* (Bö) support line *(ie, in chart analysis)*
Unterstützungszahlung *f* (com) maintenance payment
untersuchen
 (com) to examine
 – to analyze
 – to study
 – to investigate
 – to scrutinize *(ie, examine in detail)*
 – to inquire (into)
 – to probe (into)
 – to search (into)
 – (infml) to take a look (at) *(adj: careful, close, good, hard, long)*
Untersuchung *f*
 (com) axamination
 – analysis
 – study
 – investigation
 – scruting
 – inquiry
 – search
Untersuchung der Werbewirksamkeit *f* (Mk) impact study
Untersuchungsgegenstand *m*
 (Log) area under investigation
 – study topic
Untersuchungsgeheimnisse *npl* (Re) investigatory secrets
Untersuchungshaft *f* (Re) pre-trial detention
Untersuchungspopulation *f* (Stat) survey population
Untersuchungsziel *n* (Log) study objective
Untertasse *f* (Bö) saucer *(ie, in chart analysis)*
Unterteilung *f* **des Wertebereiches** (Stat) quantization of a variable
unter üblichem Vorbehalt (Re) with the usual proviso *(or reservation)*
Unterunternehmer *m* (com) subcontractor *(syn, Subunternehmer)*
Untervergabe *f*
 (com) subcontracting
 – farming out
Untervermietung *f* (Re) subletting
Unterversicherer *m* (Vers) subunderwriter

unterversichern (Vers) to underinsure
Unterversicherung *f* (Vers) underinsurance
Untervertreter *m* (com) subagent
Untervertretung *f* (com) subagency
Untervollmacht *f* (Re) substitute power of attorney
unterwegs befindliche Güter *npl* (com) goods in transit
Unterwerfungsverfahren *n* (StR) voluntary submission to tax penalty proceedings
unterwertige Münze *f* (Fin) minor coin
unter Wert verkaufen (com) to sell below value
unterzeichnen
 (com) to sign
 – to subscribe *(ie, one's name to)*
 – (infml) to write one's name on the dotted line
Unterzeichner *m* (com) signer
Unterzeichnerstaat *m* (EG) signatory state
Unterzeichneter *m* (Re) undersigned
Unterziel *n*
 (Bw) subgoal
 – subobjective
unter zollamtlicher Überwachung befördern (Zo) to transport under customs control
unter Zollaufsicht (Zo) under customs supervision
unter Zollbegleitung befördern (Zo) to transport under customs escort
unter Zollverschluß *m* (Zo) in bond *(opp, duty paid)*
unter Zollverschluß *m* **einlagern** (Zo) to store in bonds
untilgbar (Fin) irredeemable
Untilgbarkeit *f* (Fin) irredeemability
Untreue *f* (Re) breach of public trust, § 266 StGB
unübertragbar (Re) nontransferable
unübertragbarer Rentenanspruch *m* (SozV, Pw) unassignable pension right
Unübertragbarkeit *f* (Re) nontransferability
unverändert fest (Bö) continued firm
unverarbeitete Rohstoffe *mpl* (Vw) primary commodities
unverbindlich
 (com) not binding
 – non-committal
 – without engagement
unverbindliche Antwort *f* (com) non-committal answer *(or reply)*
unverbindlich empfohlener Preis *m* (Kart) nonbinding recommended price
unverbindliche Preisempfehlung *f* (Kart) nonbinding price recommendation
unveredelte Ware *f* (Zo) goods in the unaltered state
unverfallbar
 (Vers) non-forfeitable
 – unforfeitable
 (eg, pension rights)
unverfallbare Rentenanwartschaft *f* (Vers) nonforfeitable *(or* unforfeitable) expectancy of a pension
Unverfallbarkeit *f* (Vers) non-forfeitability
 – unforfeitability
unverhältnismäßige Kosten *pl* (com) unreasonable expense
unverjährbar (Re) not subject to the Statute of Limitations

unverjährbarer Anspruch m (Re) unbarrable claim
unverkäuflich
(com) unsalable
– not for sale
unverkäufliche Aktien fpl (Fin) sour stock
unverkäufliche Bestände mpl (com) dead stock
unverkäuflicher Artikel m (com) unsalable article (or item)
Unverkäuflichkeit f (com) unsalability
unverkettbar (Math) nonconformable
unverkürzte Bilanz f (StR) unabbreviated commercial balance sheet
unverkürzte Gewinn- und Verlustrechnung f (StR) unabbreviated profit and loss statement
unverlangtes Angebot n (com) unsolicited offer
unverlangte Sendung f (com) unsolicited consignment
unverlangtes Manuskript n (com) unsolicited manuscript
unvermeidbares Risiko n (Fin) systematic risk
Unvermögen n
(Re) inability to perform
– subjective impossibility
(ie, performance impossible for debtor only; syn, subjektive Unmöglichkeit)
unverrechnete Beistellung f (KoR) uncharged provision of materials
unverriegelbar (EDV) non-locking
unverschuldete Verzögerung f (Re) excusable delay
unversicherbares Risiko n (Vers) prohibited risk
unversicherte Risiken npl (Vers) excepted risks
unversteuert (StR) untaxed
unverteilte Gewinne mpl
(Fin) retained earnings (or income or profits)
– retentions
– undistributed profits
unverteilter Reingewinn m (ReW) undistributed net income
Unverträglichkeit f (Log) alternative denial
unverzerrte Beratung f (Bw) unbiased counseling (activity) (H. Steinmann)
unverzerrte Stichprobe f (Stat) unbiased sample
unverzinslich
(Fin) bearing (or earning) no interest
– non-interest-bearing
unverzinsliche Einlagen fpl (Fin) non-interest-bearing deposits
unverzinsliche Forderungen fpl (StR) non-interest-bearing debts § 12 III BewG
unverzinslicher Kredit m (Fin) interest-free credit
unverzinsliche Schatzanweisungen fpl (Fin) discountable treasury bonds
(ie, issued by the German government, usu. for 6–24 months' maturities; yielding interest by virtue of being issued at a discount on their face value; syn, U-Schätze)
unverzinsliche Schuldverschreibungen fpl (Fin) interest-free bonds
unverzinsliches Darlehen n
(Fin) interest-free loan
– non-interest bearing loan
unverzögerte endogene Variable f (Stat) nonlagged endogenous variable
unverzögerte Funktion f (Math) unlagged function

unverzollt (com) duty unpaid
unverzollte Waren fpl (com) uncleared goods
unverzüglich (Re) in due course, § 121 BGB (ie, term only excludes culpable delay = schuldhaftes Verzögern)
unvollkommene Information f (Vw) incomplete information
unvollkommener Markt m (Vw) imperfect market (syn, unvollkommene Konkurrenz)
unvollkommenes Recht n (Re) imperfect right
unvollkommene Verbindlichkeit f (Re) imperfect obligation
unvollkommen zweiseitiger Schuldvertrag m (Re) imperfectly reciprocal contract
(ie, primarily intended to create an obligation on one side only, but incidentally resulting in the creation of an obligation on the other side)
unvollständige Angaben fpl (com) incomplete statements
unvollständige Disjunktion f (Log) inclusive disjunction
unvollständige Gamma-Funktion f (Math) incomplete gamma function
unvollständige Konkurrenz f (Vw) imperfect competition
unvollständige Lieferung f (com) short delivery
unvollständige Stichprobe f (Stat) defective sample
unwesentliche Beteiligung f (ReW) immaterial holding
unwesentlicher Bestandteil m (Re) non-essential component part
unwesentlicher Wettbewerb m (Kart) insignificant competition, § 7 I GWB
unwesentliches Spiel n (OR) inessential game
unwiderlegliche Vermutung f
(Re) irrebuttable
– conclusive
– absolute ... presumption
– praesumptio juris et de jure
– presumption of law and of right
(ie, no counter-evidence permitted: keine Widerlegungsmöglichkeit zugelassen)
unwiderruflich (com) irrevocable
unwiderrufliche Bezugsberechtigung f (Vers) irrevocable appointment of beneficiary
unwiderrufliche Refinanzierungszusage f (AuW) unqualified agreement to reimburse (ie, by World Bank)
unwiderrufliches Akkreditiv n (com) irrevocable letter of credit
unwiderrufliche Wechselkurse mpl (EG) irrevocable parities
unwirksam
(Re) null
– null and void
– invalid
– legally ineffective
– inoperative
– ineffectual
– not binding in law
– having no legal force
– having no binding effect
– nugatory (eg, legislative act)
unwirksame Rechtsgeschäfte npl (Re) void and voidable transactions, § 41 AO

Unwirksamkeit *f*
(Re) nullity
– invalidity
– inefficacy
– voidness
– inoperativeness
– nugacity
Unwirksamkeitserklärung *f* (Re) declaration of ineffectiveness
unwirtschaftlich
(com) uneconomical
– inefficient
unwirtschaftliche Frachtraten *fpl* (com) uncommercial rates
Unwirtschaftlichkeit *f* (com) inefficiency *(ie, implies wasting scarce resources in all areas of economic activity; syn, Ineffizienz)*
unzerlegbares Polynom *n* (Math) irreducible polynomial
unzulässige Operation *f* (EDV) illegal operation
unzulässiger Befehl *m* (EDV) illegal instruction
unzulässige Rechtsausübung *f* (Re) inadmissible exercise of a right
(ie, violating the principle of equity and fair dealing; special cases: Verwirkung and Wegfall der Geschäftsgrundlage)
unzulässiges Zeichen *n* (EDV) illegal character
unzumutbare Beschäftigung *f* (Pw) unacceptable employment
unzumutbare Härte *f* (Re) undue hardship
unzureichende Auslastung *f* (Bw) (plants) working at unsatisfactory levels
unzustellbar
(com) undeliverable
– undelivered *(eg, if... return to)*
unzustellbarer Brief *m* (com) dead letter
unzuverlässiger Test *m* (Stat) biased test
unzweideutige Aufforderung *f* **zur Leistung** (Re) unconditional request for performance
Urabstimmung *f* (Pw) strike vote *(or* ballot) *(ie, reguires a three quarter majority of all union members of a single company or district)*
Uraufzeichnungen *fpl* (ReW) records of original entry
Urbanistik *f* (Vw) urban economics *(syn, Stadtökonomie)*
Urbeleg *m* (EDV) original *(or* source) document *(syn, Originalbeleg)*
Ureingabe *f*
(EDV) bootstrap
(EDV) bootstrapping
Ureingabeprogramm *n* (EDV) bootstrap loader
Urerzeuger *m* (Bw) primary producer
Urerzeugung *f* (Bw) primary production
Urheberrecht *n* (Pat) copyright
urheberrechtlich geschütztes Werk *n* (Pat) copyrighted publication
urheberrechtlich schützen (Pat) to copyright
Urheberrechtsschutzgesetz *n* (Pat) copyright law
Urheberrechtslizenzgebühren *fpl* (Pat) copyright royalties
Urheberrechtsschutz *m* (Pat) protection by copyright
Urheberrechtsverletzung *f* (Pat) infringement of copyright

Urheberrechtsverwertungsgesellschaft *f* (Pat) copyright association
Urkunde *f*
(Re) instrument
– document
Urkunde *f* **des Handelsverkehrs** (Re) commercial instrument
Urkundenbeweis *m* (Re) proof by documentary evidence
Urkundenfälschung *f* (Re) forgery of documents, § 267 StGB
urkundlicher Beweis *m* (Re) proof by documentary evidence
Urkundsbeamter *m* **der Geschäftsstelle** (Re, appr) clerk of court
Urlader *m* (EDV) initial program loader
Urlaub *m*
(Pw) vacation
– (GB) holiday *(ie, students in GB speak of ‚vacations'; Sommerferien: long vac, or long)*
Urlaubsanspruch *m* (Pw) vacation entitlement
Urlaubsentgelt *n* (ReW) vacation pay – salaries and wages
Urlaubsgeld *n*
(ReW) = *Urlaubsentgelt*
(Pw) vacation bonus
– (GB) holiday (cash) bonus
Urlaubsplan *m* (Pw) vacation schedule, § 87 I 5 BetrVerfG
Urlaubsplanung *f* (Pw) scheduling vacations
Urlaubsvertretung *f* (Pw) vacation replacement
Urmaterial *n* (Stat) primary data
Urnenauswahl *f* (Stat) lottery sampling
Urproduktion *f* (Bw) primary production
Urproduktionsbetriebe *mpl* (Bw) extractive industries *(ie, may include water, gas, and power supply)*
Ursache *f* **e-s Maschinenausfalls** (IndE) force of mortality
ursächliche Variable *f* (Stat) cause variable
Ursprung *m* **des kartesischen Koordinatensystems** (Math) origin of Cartesian coordinates
ursprüngliche Akkumulation *f* (Vw) primary accumulation
ursprüngliche Gemeinschaft *f* (EG) original Community
ursprüngliche Informationsquelle *f* (Bw) original source of information
ursprüngliche Kostenarten *fpl* (KoR) primary cost types *(syn, einfache od primäre Kostenarten)*
ursprünglicher Kapitalbetrag *m* (Math) original principal
ursprünglicher Kapitaleinsatz *m* (Fin) initial investment *(ie, in preinvestment analysis)*
ursprüngliche Unmöglichkeit *f*
(Re) initial *(or* original) impossibility
– impossibility at the time of making
– impossibility ab initio
(Note that the term ‚Unmöglichkeit' in German law is reserved for cases where performance is impossible for everybody, not for debtor only)
Ursprungsangabe *f* (com) statement of origin
Ursprungsbescheinigung *f* (com) = *Ursprungsangabe*
Ursprungsbezeichnung *f*

(com) mark of origin
(Zo) designation (*or* identification) of origin
Ursprungsdaten *pl* (EDV, Stat) raw data
Ursprungsdrittland *n* (Zo) non-member country of origin
Ursprungserklärung *f* (Zo) declaration of origin *(eg, submitted by exporter)*
Ursprungserzeugnisse *npl* (Zo) originating products
Ursprungsfinanzierung *f* (Fin) initial finance
Ursprungskapital *n* (Fin) initial capital
Ursprungsland *n* (com) country of origin
Ursprungsnachweis *m* (com) documentary evidence of origin
Ursprungsnachweise *mpl* **anerkennen** (Zo) to accept the documentary evidence of origin
Ursprungspatent *n* (Pat) original patent
Ursprungsprogramm *n* (EDV) source program
Ursprungsprogrammkartensatz *m* (EDV) source deck
Ursprungssprache *f* (EDV) source language *(syn, Quellsprache)*
Ursprungswert *m* (com) original value
Ursprungswerte *mpl* (Stat) unadjusted figures
Ursprungszeugnis *n* (com) certificate of origin
Urstart *m*
 (EDV) cold start
 – initial program loading

Urteil *n* **aufheben**
 (Re) to set aside
 – to rescind
 – to quash
 – (US) to vacate ... a judgment
 – to reverse a court ruling
Urteiler *m* (Pw) rater *(ie, in performance appraisal)*
Urteilsfindung *f* (StR) deliberations leading to a court decision, § 16 FGO
Urteilslogik *f* (Log) logic of propositions (*or* judgments)
Urwahl *f* (Pw) direct election *(ie, of the works council)*
Usance *f*
 (com) trade
 – business
 – commercial
 – mercantile ... usage
 – custom of the trade
 – mercantile custom
 – usage of the market (*or* trade)
 (Bö) rules and regulations
Usancenhandel *m* (Bö) cross dealing
Usancenkredit *m* (Fin) usage credit
Usancenkurs *m* (Fin) cross rate
U-Schätze *mpl* (Fin) = *unverzinsliche Schatzanweisungen*
utopisch-holistische Sozialplanung *f* (Vw) holistic social engineering

V

vagabundierende Gelder *npl*
 (Fin) hot money
 – footlose funds *(eg, marshaled by the oil-exporting countries)*
vakant (Pw) vacant
Valenz *f* (Log) biconditional
Validierung *f* (Log) validation
Valoren *pl* (Fin) securities *(ie, including bank notes)*
Valorisation *f* (Vw) valorization
Valuta *f*
 (Fin) currency
 (Fin) loan proceeds
 (Fin) value date
Valutaakzept *n* (Fin) foreign currency acceptance
Valutaanleihe *f* (Fin) foreign currency loan *(ie, floated by German issuer; syn, Valutabond, Auslandsbond)*
Valutadumping *n* (AuW) exchange dumping
Valuta-Exporttratte *f* (Fin) export draft in foreign currency
Valutageschäft *n* (Fin) foreign currency (*or* exchange) transaction
Valutagewinn *m* (Fin) gains on foreign exchange
Valutaguthaben *n* (Fin) foreign currency holding
Valutaklausel *f* (Fin) foreign currency clause *(syn, Währungsklausel)*
Valutakonto *n* (Fin) foreign currency account *(syn, Währungskonto)*
Valutakupon *m* (Fin) foreign currency coupon

Valutanotierung *f* (Fin) quotation of exchange
Valutapapiere *npl* (Fin) foreign currency securities
Valutarisiko *n* (Fin) exchange risk
Valutaschuld *f* (Fin) foreign currency debt, § 244 BGB
Valutatag *m* (Fin) value date *(ie, on which bank account entry becomes effective)*
Valutatrassierungskredit *m* (Fin) foreign currency acceptance credit
Valutaversicherung *f* (Vers) foreign currency insurance
Valutawechsel *m* (Fin) foreign exchange bill
Valuten *pl* (Fin) foreign currencies
Valutenarbitrage *f* (Fin) currency arbitrage
Valutengeschäft *n* (Fin) dealing in foreign notes and coin
Valutenkonto *n* (Fin) currency account
valutieren
 (Fin) to fix (*or* state) the value date
 (Fin) to extend a loan
Valutierung *f*
 (Fin) fixing (*or* stating) the value date
 (Fin) extension of a loan
Valutierungstermin *m*
 (Fin) value date
 (Fin) date of loan extension
variabel verzinslich (Fin) on a floating rate basis
Variabilität *f* (Stat) variability
Variabilitätskoeffizient *m* (Stat) = *Variationskoeffizient*

Variable f (Math) variable
variable Absatzgeschwindigkeit f (Mk) variable rate of selling
variable Arbeitszeit f (Pw) = *gleitende Arbeitszeit*
variable Bestellmenge f (MaW) variable-order quantity
variable Durchschnittskosten pl (Vw) average variable cost
variable Fertigungsgemeinkosten pl (KoR) variable factory overhead
variable Kosten pl (KoR) variable cost (*or* expenses *or* charges) *(syn, veränderliche Kosten, beschäftigungsabhängige Kosten; opp, fixe Kosten)*
Variable f mit konstantem Zeitverlauf (Math) continuous time variable
Variablenkontrolle f (Stat) sampling by variables
variable Notierung f (Bö) floating quotation
Variablenprüfung f
(Stat) inspection by variable
– variable gauge
variabler Beschaffungsrhythmus m (MaW) variable cycle
variabler Handel m (Bö) variable-price trading
variabler Markt m (Bö) variable-price market *(syn, Schwankungsmarkt; opp, Einheitsmarkt)*
variables Feld n (EDV) variable (length) field
variable Stückkosten pl (KoR) variable unit costs
variable Substitutionselastizität f (Vw) variable elasticity of substitution
variable Werte mpl (Bö) variable-price securities
variable Wortlänge f (EDV) variable word length
variable Zinsen mpl (Fin) variable (*or* floating) rate
Varianz f (Stat) variance σ^2
Varianzanalyse f (Stat) variance analysis
Varianz f der Grundgesamtheit (Stat) parent variance
Varianz f der Stichprobe (Stat) sampling variance
Varianz f innerhalb der Gruppen (Stat) within-group variance
Varianz f innerhalb der Klassen (Stat) intra-class variance
Varianzkomponente f (Stat) component of variance
Varianz-Quotiententest m (Stat) variance-ratio test
Variationsbreite f (Stat) range *(syn, Spannweite, Schwankungsbreite)*
Variationskoeffizient m (Stat) coefficient of variation
Variationsrechnung f (Math) calculus of variation
Variator m (KoR) factor of expense variability *(ie, in one-stage overhead planning)*
Veblen-Effekt m (Vw) conspicuous-consumption effect *(syn, externer Konsumeffekt)*
Veblen-Gut n (Vw) prestige good (*or* merchandise)
Vektor m (Math) vector
Vektoranalyse f (Math) vector analysis
Vektorbüschel n (Math) cluster of vectors
Vektoren mpl mit gleichem Anfangspunkt (Math) coterminous vectors
Vektorenrechner m (EDV) vector processor
Vektorfeld n (Math) vector field

vektorielle Schreibweise f (Math) vectorial notation
vektorielles Feld n (Math) vector field
vektorielles Produkt n (Math) vector (*or* cross) product
Vektorkomponente f (Math) vector component
Vektoroptimierung f (OR) vector optimization
Vektorraum m (Math) vector space
Vektorrechnung f (Math) vector calculus
Vektorschar f (Math) cluster of vectors
Vektorsystem n (Math) vector set
verabreden (com) to make an appointment
Verabredung f (com) appointment *(eg, I have an appointment to see Mr X)*
verallgemeinerter Mittelwertsatz m (Math) extended mean value theorem
Veränderliche f (Math) variable
veränderliche Kosten pl (KoR) = *variable Kosten*
veränderlicher Auswahlsatz m (Stat) variable sampling fraction
Veränderung f der Konzernrücklagen (ReW) change in consolidated reserves
Veränderung f der Rücklagen (ReW) reserve transfers
Veränderungsrate f (com) rate of change
veranlagende Behörde f (StR) tax assessing authority
veranlagte Steuern fpl (StR) assessed taxes
Veranlagung f (StR) tax assessment *(ie, formal procedure by which the tax office determines the amount of income tax or corporate income tax for a particular taxable year, § 25 I EStG, § 49 I KStG)*
Veranlagungsbescheid m (StR) tax assessment notice
Veranlagungsgrundlage f (StR) basis of assessment
Veranlagungsjahr n (StR) year of assessment
Veranlagungssteuern fpl (StR) = *veranlagte Steuern*
Veranlagungsverfahren n (StR) assessment procedure
Veranlagungszeitpunkt m (StR) effective assessment date
Veranlagungszeitraum m (StR) tax assessment period
veranlassen (com) to prompt *(eg, management to shut down a subsidiary)*
veranschlagen (com) to estimate
Verantwortlichkeit f (Bw) responsibility
Verantwortungsbereich m (Pw) area of responsibility (*or* accountability)
Verantwortungsbewußtsein n (Pw) acceptance of responsibility
verantwortungsvolle Aufgabe f (Pw) position of broad responsibility
verarbeiten (IndE) to process
verarbeitende Industrie f (com) manufacturing (*or* processing) industry
verarbeitendes Gewerbe n (com) manufacturing sector
Verarbeiter m (IndE) processor
Verarbeitung f
(IndE) processing
– conversion *(ie, general and chemical)*
Verarbeitungsart f (EDV, Cobol) processing mode

Verarbeitungsbereich m (EDV) processing area
Verarbeitungsbetrieb m (IndE) processing plant *(opp, Substanzbetrieb)*
Verarbeitungserzeugnisse npl (EG) processed (farm) products
Verarbeitungsgeschwindigkeit f (EDV) processing speed
Verarbeitungskosten pl (KoR) processing cost
Verarbeitungsprogramm n (EDV) processing program
Verarbeitungsrechner m (EDV) host computer
Verarbeitungsschritt m (EDV) processing step
Verarbeitungsstufe f (Bw) production *(or* processing*)* stage
Verarbeitungszustand m (EDV) processing state
Verarmungswachstum n (Vw) immiserizing growth
Verausgabung f **von Mitteln** (Fin) disbursement of funds
Veräußerer m
  (com) seller
  – vendor
  (Re) transferor *(ie, for a consideration)*
  (Re) alienor *(ie, in real property law)*
veräußern
  (com) to sell
  – to dispose of
  (Re) to transfer *(ie, for a consideration)*
  (Re) to alienate *(ie, in real property law)*
Veräußerung f
  (com) sale
  – realization
  – disposal *(or* disposition*) (ie, for a consideration)*
  (Re) transfer *(ie, for a consideration)*
  (Re) alienation *(ie, in real property law)*
Veräußerung f **e-s Betriebes** (Bw) sale of an entire business
Veräußerungsgewinn m (ReW) gain on disposal *(or* sale*)* or other transfer, § 17 EStG
Veräußerungskette f (Re) sales chain
Veräußerungspreis m (StR) disposition *(or* transfer*)* price
Veräußerungs- und Zahlungsverbot n (Fin) order prohibiting disposals and payments, § 46a KWG
Veräußerungsverlust m (ReW) loss on disposal
Veräußerungswert m
  (com) recovery
  – residual
  – scrap ... value
  (ReW) value on realization
  – proceeds on disposal
  (ie, used in ‚Liquidationsbilanzen'; syn, Realisationswert)
Veräußerung f **von Anlagen** (ReW) asset disposal
Veräußerung f **von Beteiligungen**
  (Fin) sale of share holdings
  – (GB) sale of trade investments
Verband m
  (com) trade *(or* professional*)* association
  (com) federation
Verband m **der Automobilindustrie e.V.** (com) *(Frankfurt-based)* German Motor Industry Federation
Verband m **der Chemischen Industrie** (com) Chemical Industry Federation

Verbandsanmeldung f (Pat) Convention application
Verbandsland n
  (Pat) Convention country
  – member country of the Paris Convention
Verbandsmarke f (Pat) collective *(or* certification*)* mark
Verbandspreis m (Kart) price fixed by a cartel or syndicate
Verbandspriorität f (Pat) Convention priority
Verbandstheorie f (Math) lattice theory
Verbandsübereinkunft f **zum Schutz des Gewerblichen Eigentums** (Pat) Convention for the Protection of Industrial Property
Verbandszeichen n
  (Pat) collective mark
  – certification trademark
  (ie, trademark for use by members of a trade association)
Verbandszeitschrift f (com) trade journal
Verband m **zum Schutz des Gewerblichen Eigentums** (Pat) Union for the Protection of Industrial Property
verbegrifflichen (Log) to conceptualize
Verbegrifflichung f (Log) conceptualization
Verbesserung f **des Ausbildungsstandes** (Pw) educational upgrading
Verbesserungserfindung f (Pat) improvement invention
Verbesserungsinvestitionen fpl (Vw) capital deepening *(ie, to increase capital intensity)*
Verbesserungspatent n (Pat) improvement patent
Verbesserungsvorschläge mpl (Bw) suggestions for improvement
verbilligter Kredit m (Fin) subsidized credit
verbinden
  (EDV) to link(age) edit
  – to compose
  – to consolidate
  (ie, to combine separately produced load or object modules into an executable phase)
verbindende Supposition f (Log) common supposition
verbindliche Entscheidung f (Re) binding decision
verbindliches Angebot n (com) firm *(or* binding*)* offer
verbindliche Sprachregelung f
  (Re) language of contract
  (Re) authentic language
Verbindlichkeit f
  (Re) obligation
  (Re) binding force
  – legal validity
Verbindlichkeiten fpl
  (ReW) liabilities
  – indebtedness
  – debts
  – due to
  – accounts payable
  – payables
  (ReW, EG) creditors
Verbindlichkeiten fpl **aus Bürgschaften** (ReW) liabilities on guaranties
Verbindlichkeiten fpl **aus diskontierten Wechseln** (ReW) liabilities on bills discounted

Verbindlichkeiten *fpl* **aus Gewährleistungsverträgen** (ReW) liabilities under warranties
Verbindlichkeiten *fpl* **aus Lieferungen und Leistungen** (ReW, EG) trade creditors
  (ReW) trade accounts payable
  – accounts payable – trade
  – accounts payable for goods and services
Verbindlichkeiten *fpl* **aus Pensionsansprüchen** (ReW) liabilities for pension rights
Verbindlichkeiten *fpl* **aus Währungstermingeschäften** (ReW) liabilities on forward exchange contracts
Verbindlichkeiten *fpl* **aus Wechseln** (ReW, EG) bills of exchange payable
Verbindlichkeiten *fpl* **e-r Gesellschaft**
  (ReW) partnership debts
  (ReW) company debts
Verbindlichkeiten *fpl* **eingehen**
  (Re) to assume obligations
  (Fin) to incur (*or* contract) debts
Verbindlichkeiten *fpl* **erfüllen**
  (Re) to discharge obligations
  (Fin) to repay debt
Verbindlichkeiten *fpl* **gegenüber Banken** (ReW) due to banks
Verbindlichkeiten *fpl* **gegenüber Beteiligungsgesellschaften** (ReW) due to associated companies
Verbindlichkeiten *fpl* **gegenüber Konzernunternehmen** (ReW) due to affiliated companies
Verbindlichkeiten *fpl* **gegenüber Kreditinstituten** (ReW, EG) amounts owed to credit institutions
Verbindlichkeiten *fpl* **gegenüber verbundenen Unternehmen** (ReW, EG) amounts owed to affiliated undertakings
Verbindlichkeiten *fpl* **mit unbestimmter Fälligkeit** (Fin) indeterminate-term liabilities
Verbindlichkeit *f* **mit kurzer Restlaufzeit** (Fin) maturing liability
Verbindlichkeitserklärung *f* (Re) declaration of commitment
Verbindung *f*
  (EDV) link
  – linkage
Verbindungsabbau *m* (EDV) connection cleardown
Verbindungsaufbau *m* (EDV) connection setup (*or* buildup)
Verbindungskapazitätsmatrix *f* (OR) branchcapacity matrix
Verbindungsprogramm *n* (EDV) subscriber connection program
Verbindungsstecker *m* (EDV) connector *(ie, mechanical means of connecting one or more electrical circuits)*
verborgener Mangel *m*
  (Re) hidden defect
  – inherent vice
Verbot *n* **der Werbung** (com) prohibition to advertise
verbotene Eigenmacht *f* (Re) unlawful interference with possession, § 858 BGB
verbotene Kombination *f* (EDV) forbidden combination
Verbotsprinzip *n*

  (Kart) rule of per se illegality
  – per se approach
Verbrauch *m* (Vw, Bw) consumption
verbrauchen
  (com) to consume
  – to use up
Verbraucher *m*
  (Vw, Bw) consumer
  – final consumer
  – ultimate consumer
Verbraucherausgaben *fpl* (Vw) consumer spending (*or* expenditure)
Verbraucherbedürfnisse *npl* (Vw) consumer wants
Verbraucherberatung *f*
  (Vw) consumer counseling
  – consumer advisory service
Verbraucherbewegung *f*
  (Vw) consumer movement
  – consumerism
Verbraucher-Erwartungen *fpl* (Vw) consumer sentiment *(eg, is steadily deteriorating)*
Verbrauchergenossenschaft *f* (Bw) consumer cooperative
Verbrauchergewohnheiten *fpl* (Vw) consumer habits
Verbraucherinformation *f* (Mk) consumer information
Verbraucherkredit *m* (Fin) consumer credit
Verbrauchermarkt *m* (Mk) shopping center
Verbrauchernachfrage *f* (Vw) consumer demand
Verbraucherpolitik *f* (Vw) consumer policy
Verbraucherschutz *m* (Vw) consumer protection
Verbraucherverbände *mpl* (Vw) consumer organizations
Verbraucherverhalten *n* (Mk) consumer behavior
Verbraucherwerbung *f* (Mk) consumer advertising
Verbrauch *m* **für zivile Zwecke** (VGR) public consumption for civil purposes
Verbrauchsabweichung *f*
  (KoR) budget
  – expense
  – spending
  – usage ... variance
verbrauchsbedingte Abschreibung *f* (ReW) = *Mengenabschreibung*
verbrauchsbedingte Wertminderung *f* (ReW) physical depreciation
Verbrauchsfaktor *m* (KoR) power factor
Verbrauchsfläche *f* (Vw) commodity space
Verbrauchsforschung *f* (Vw) consumer research
verbrauchsgebundene Bedarfsmengenplanung *f* (MaW) usage-based materials budgeting
Verbrauchsgerade *f* (Vw) consumption line
Verbrauchsgewohnheiten *fpl*
  (Mk) consumer habits
  – consumption patterns
Verbrauchsgüter *npl* (Mk) consumer (*or* consumption) goods *(ie, either durables or nondurables)*
Verbrauchsgütergewerbe *n* (com) consumer goods sector
Verbrauchsgüterindustrie *f* (com) consumer goods industry
Verbrauchsgütermarkt *m* (Mk) consumer market
Verbrauchsgüterpanel *n* (Mk) consumer goods panel

Verbrauchsland *n* (AuW) country of consumption
Verbrauchsort *m* (AuW) place of final use
– place of consumption
Verbrauchsrate *f* (Bw) rate of usage
Verbrauchsstruktur *f* (Vw) pattern of consumption
Verbrauchsteuer *f* (StR) general tax on consumption
Verbrauchsteueraufkommen *n* (FiW) consumer tax revenue
– revenue from excise duties
verbrauchsteuerpflichtig (StR) liable in consumer taxes
Verbrauchswirtschaftsplan *m* (Vw) purchase plan
verbrauchte Prämie *f* (Vers) earned premium
verbriefen (WeR) to embody
– to evidence ownership
verbrieftes Recht *n* (Re) vested title
verbuchen (ReW) to enter in/on
– to carry on
– to post to
– to recognize on *(ie, books of account)*
(Bö) to register *(eg, price gains)*
Verbuchung *f* (ReW) entry
– posting
Verbund *m* (Bw) association
– combination
Verbunddarlehen *n* (Fin) joint loan extension
Verbunddirektorium *n* (Bw) interlocking directorate *(syn, Überkreuzverflechtung)*
verbundene Kosten *pl* (KoR) related cost
verbundene Lebensversicherung *f* (Vers) joint life policy
verbundene Leistungen *fpl* (KoR) joint products *(syn, Kuppelprodukte)*
verbundene Nachfrage *f* (Vw) joint demand
verbundene Produktion *f* (IndE) joint production
verbundene Rechtsgeschäfte *npl* (Re) linked legal transactions
verbundenes Angebot *n* (Vw) joint supply
verbundene Stichproben *fpl* (Stat) matched samples
verbundene Unternehmen *npl* (Bw) related undertakings *(or* enterprises), § 15 AktG
– allied *(or* associated) companies
verbundene Verteilung *f* (Stat) joint distribution
verbundene Warenzeichen *npl* (Pat) associated trademarks
Verbundenheitsmatrix *f* (OR) connectedness matrix
Verbundkontenkonsolidierung *f* (ReW) consolidation of group accounts
Verbundlieferung *f* (com) intercompany shipment
Verbundlochkarte *f* (EDV) dual card
Verbundnetz *n* (EDV) mixed network
Verbundschulden *fpl* (ReW) group liabilities
Verbundunternehmen *n* (Bw) affiliate
– affiliated company
Verbundverkehr *m* (IndE) intercompany traffic

Verbundwerbung *f* (Mk) association *(or* combined) advertising
Verbundwirtschaft *f* (Bw) vertical integration
Verdacht *m* **des abgestimmten Verhaltens** (Kart) charge of collusion
verdeckte Arbeitslosigkeit *f* (Vw) concealed unemployment
verdeckte Gewinnausschüttung *f* (StR) constructive dividend, § 8 III 2 KStG, Abschn. 31 KStR
– disguised profit distribution
verdeckte Inflation *f* (Vw) camouflaged inflation
verdecktes Factoring *n* (Fin) nonnotification factoring
verdecktes Rechtsgeschäft *n* (Re) concealed transaction, § 117 BGB
verdeckte Steuer *f* (FiW) hidden tax
verdichten (EDV) to collate
– to merge
Verdichten *n* **von Netzplänen** (OR) reduction
Verdichtung *f* (EDV) collation
– merger
Verdichtungsebene *f* (ReW) level of consolidation
Verdichtungsprogramm *n* (EDV) condensing routine
Verdienst *m* (Pw) earnings
Verdienstausfall *m* (Pw) loss of earnings
Verdichtungskurve *f* (Vw) wage curve
Verdienstmöglichkeit *f* (Pw) potential earnings
Verdienstspanne *f* (com) (profit) margin
verdiente Prämie *f* (Vers) earned premium
verdingen, sich (com) to hire out one's services (to)
Verdinglichung *f* **e-s Begriffs** (Log) reification
Verdingung *f* (com) invitation to bid *(or* tender)
– request for bids
(ie, published notice that competitive bids are requested)
Verdoppelung *f* **der Lebensversicherungssumme bei Unfalltod** (Vers) double indemnity
verdrängen (com) to drive
– to eliminate
– to squeeze
– (infml) to freeze *(ie, rivals or competitors out of the market)*
(Fin) to crowd out
(Pw) to turn out of office
Verdrängung *f* (FiW) crowding-out *(ie, of private borrowers from the credit markets)*
Verdrängungswettbewerb *m* (Kart) destructive *(or* predatory) competition
– predatory price cutting
– predatory pricing policy
(ie, elimination of direct competitors in a market)
(Fin) crowding-out competition *(ie, on the capital market: between government and private business)*
veredeln (IndE) to process
veredelte Umsatzsteuer *f* (FiW) refined turnover tax *(ie, phrase coined by W. v. Siemens)*
veredelte Ware *f* (Zo) processed goods
Veredelung *f*

Veredelungsbetrieb
(IndE) materials improvement
- processing
Veredelungsbetrieb m (IndE) processing plant
Veredelungsindustrie f (Vw) processing industry
Veredelungskosten pl (KoR) cost of materials improvement
Veredelungstechnologie f
(IndE) processing
- refining
- transformation ... technology
Veredelungsverkehr m (AuW) across the border processing
Veredelungsvorschriften fpl (AuW) processing regulations
Veredelungswirtschaft f (com) processing industry
vereidigter Buchprüfer m (StR) licensed public accountant
vereidigter Buchsachverständiger m (ReW) sworn accounting expert
verteidiger Dolmetscher m (com) sworn interpreter
vereidigter Makler m (com) sworn broker
Verein m (Re) association *(ie, as a legal person of private law, §§ 21ff BGB)*
vereinbaren
(Re) to agree upon
- to stipulate
vereinbart (Re) mutually agreed upon
vereinbarte Entgelte npl (StR) consideration agreed upon *(ie, taxable turnovers reported on the accrual basis: Solleinnahmen; § 20 I UStG; opp, vereinnahmte Entgelte)*
vereinbarte Frist f
(com) stipulated term (*or* time)
- time agreed upon
vereinbarte Kündigungsfrist f (Re) agreed notice
vereinbarte Qualität f (com) agreed quality
vereinbarter Güterstand m (Re) contractual property system
vereinbarter Preis m (com) price agreed upon
vereinbarter Zinssatz m (Fin) contract rate of interest
vereinbarte Summe f (com) stipulated sum
Vereinbarung f
(Re) agreement
- stipulation
- undertaking
Vereinbarungsdarlehen n (Fin) contractual loan
Vereinbarung f **treffen** (com) to reach (*or* to conclude) an agreement
Vereinbarung f **zur Vermeidung der Doppelbesteuerung** (StR) double taxation agreement
Verein m **Deutscher Maschinenbau-Anstalten** (com) *(Frankfurt-based)* Association of German Machinery Manufacturers, VDMA
Verein m **Deutscher Werkzeugmaschinenfabriken** (com) Association of German Machine Tool Makers
vereinfachte Kapitalherabsetzung f (Fin) simplified capital reduction *(ie, no repayment to shareholders)*
vereinfachter Scheck- und Lastschrifteinzug m (Fin) simplified check and direct debit collection procedure

Verfahrenstechnik
vereinfachte Übertragung f (Re) simplified transfer of ownership
vereinheitlichter EGKS-Tarif m (Zo) unified ECSC-tariff
Vereinigungsmenge f
(Math) union
- sum
- join ... of sets
Vereinigung f **von Unternehmen** (Kart) association of enterprises
vereinnahmte Entgelte npl (StR) consideration collected *(ie, taxable turnovers reported on the cash basis: Isteinnahmen; § 20 I UStG; opp, vereinbarte Entgelte)*
vereinnahmte Mieten fpl (StR) rental income
Vereinsbörsen fpl (Bö) securities exchanges *set up and maintained by private-law associations which act as institutional carriers: Bremen, Düsseldorf, Hannover, München, Stuttgart; opp, Kammerbörsen*
Vereinsregister n (Re) Register of Associations
vereinzelte Kursgewinne mpl (Bö) scattered gains
Vereinzelung f (EDV) single feed
vereiteln (Re) to frustrate
Verengung f **des Geldmarktes** (Fin) tight money market
Verfahren n
(Re) procedure
(Re) = *Klage*
(com) method
- technique
- operation
- process
Verfahren n **aussetzen** (Re) to stay legal proceedings
Verfahren n **der gleichen Abstände** (Stat) method of equal appearing intervals
Verfahren n **der kritischen Methode** (Stat) critical incident technique
Verfahren n **der transferierten Rahmenordnungen** (Stat) ordered metric scales
Verfahren n **der Vorratsbewertung** (KoR) costing method of inventories
Verfahren n **der zeitlichen Abgrenzung** (Bw) cutoff method
Verfahren n **durchführen** (Re) to conduct proceedings
Verfahren n **einleiten** (Re) to open legal proceedings (against)
Verfahren n **einstellen**
(Re) to discontinue proceedings
- to drop a case
Verfahrensabweichung f (KoR) nonstandard operation variance
Verfahrenskosten pl (Re) cost of proceedings
Verfahrensmangel m (Re) material defect of legal proceedings
verfahrensorientierte Programmiersprache f (EDV) procedure oriented language
Verfahrenspatent n (Pat) process patent
Verfahrensrecht n
(Re) procedural
- adjective
- remedial ... law
Verfahrenstechnik f (IndE) process engineering

verfahrenstechnische Auslegung f von Anlagen (IndE) process design
Verfahrenszuschlag m
(IndE) process
− controlled cycle
− excess work ... allowance
Verfahren n **zur Ergänzung fehlender Werte** (Stat) missing plot technique
Verfahren n **zur Feststellung des Prioritätsrechts** (Pat) interference proceedings
Verfall m
(Re) forfeiture *(ie, loss of some right)*
(Fin) maturity
(Vers) lapse
(ie, termination of policy because of failure to pay premium)
verfallbar (Vers) forfeitable *(eg, pension right)*
Verfallbarkeit f (Vers) forfeitability
verfallen
(Re) to forfeit
(Re) to expire
(Fin) to mature
− to fall (*or* become) due
(Bö) to collapse
(Vers) to lapse
verfallener Scheck m (Fin) stale check
verfallenes Patent n (Pat) lapsed patent
Verfall m **e-s Patents** (Pat) forfeiture of a patent
verfallene Versicherungspolice f (Vers) lapsed policy
Verfallklausel f
(Re) forfeiture clause
(Fin) expiration clause
Verfallmitteilung f (Vers) lapse notice
Verfalltag m
(com) date of expiration (*or* expiry)
− cut-off date
− due date
− expiring date
− date of maturity
Verfassung f
(Re) constituent document *(eg, charter, certificate of incorporation)*
(Bö) tone of the market
Verfassungsbeschwerde f (Re) constitutional complaint *(ie, extraordinary legal remedy)*
verfassungsmäßig berufene Vertreter mpl
(Re) properly constituted agents, § 31 BGB
− primary agents
verfassungswidrig (Re) violating basic constitutional principles
verflachen
(Bö) to level off
− to slacken
Verflechtung f
(com) interdependence
− interlacing
− interlinking
− interpenetration
− linkage
− mutual dependence
Verflechtung f **der Volkswirtschaften** (AuW) interpenetration of national economies
Verflechtung f **mit nachgelagerten Sektoren** (Vw) forward linkage

Verflechtung f **mit vorgelagerten Sektoren** (Vw) backward linkage
Verflechtungsbilanz f (Vw) interlacing balance
Verflechtungskoeffizient m (Vw) input-output coefficient
verflüssigen
(Fin) to sell
− to liquidate
− to realize
Verflüssigung f (Fin) liquidation of assets
Verfolgungsrecht n (Re) right of stoppage in transit *(ie, right of seller or buying agent to resume possession of goods as long as they are in course of transit, § 44 KO)*
verfrachten
(com) to freight (goods)
− to send as freight
Verfrachter m (com) ocean carrier *(ie, called 'Frachtführer' in river and land transport)*
Verfrachtung f
(com) ocean transport
− (GB) carriage of goods by sea
Verfrachtungsvertrag m (com) contract of affreightment
verfügbare Arbeitskräfte fpl
(Vw) manpower resources
− labor resources
verfügbare Benutzerzeit f (EDV) available (machine) time *(syn, nutzbare Maschinenzeit)*
verfügbare Betriebszeit f (EDV) serviceable time
verfügbare Mittel pl
(Fin) available cash
− liquid funds
verfügbare Mittel pl **ausgeben** (Fin) to disburse available cash
verfügbares Einkommen n (VGR) disposable income
verfügbares Einkommen n **der privaten Haushalte** (VGR) personal disposable income
verfügbares Realeinkommen n (VGR) real disposable income
Verfügung f (Re) disposition *(ie, transaction by which rights are transferred, altered, encumbered, or terminated)*
verfügungsberechtigt (Re) free to dispose
Verfügungsberechtigung f (Fin) authorization to draw
Verfügungsbeschränkung f (Re) restraint on disposal
Verfügungsbetrag m (Fin) payout amount *(ie, of a loan: nominal amount less loan discount)*
Verfügungsfähigkeit f (Re) disposing capacity (*or* power)
Verfügungsmacht f (Re) power of control
Verfügungsrecht n
(Re) right of diposition
− right of free disposal
− *(civil law)* jus disponendi
Verfügungsverbot n (Re) restraint on disposition
Verfügungsvorbehalt m (Re) reservation of right of disposal
Verfügung f **unter Lebenden** (Re) disposition inter vivos
Verfügung f **von Todes wegen** (Re) disposition mortis causa

Vergabe *f*
(com) award of contract
(com) placing an order
(Fin) extension of a credit
(FiW) allocation of funds
Vergabe im Submissionsweg *f* (com) allocation by tender
Vergeltungsmaßnahmen *fpl*
(AuW) reprisals
- retaliation
- retaliatory measures (*or* action) (*eg, potential threat of ... against*)
Vergeltungsmaßnahmen *fpl* **ergreifen**
(AuW) to retaliate (against)
- to take retaliatory action
Vergeltungszoll *m* (AuW) retaliatory duty (*or* tariff)
Vergleich *m*
(Re) debt composition proceedings
- preventive composition
(*ie, procedure aimed at rehabilitation of an insolvent business by scaling down the indebtedness; a company must get agreement from a qualified majority of the creditors to a new plan of the company and pay back 35% of what it owes within 18 months; if creditors cannot agree terms with the company, it then goes bankrupt; affects only the rights of unsecured creditors*)
- (US) corporate reorganization
(*ie, requires that the whole debt structure be reconstituted; affects also secured creditors*)
(Re) compromise
- settlement
(*ie, mutual waiver made to put an end to a dispute, § 779 BGB; may be achieved in and out of court*)
Vergleich *m* **anmelden**
(Re) to file a voluntary petition in bankruptcy
- (US) to file in court the German equivalent of Chapter 11
(*ie, of the U.S. Federal Bankruptcy Law, for the reorganization of a company*)
vergleichbare Waren *fpl* (com) comparable products
Vergleich *m* **beantragen**
(Re) to apply for court protection from creditors
- to go to the courts for „composition" of debts
- to seek court protection from creditors
vergleichende Rechtswissenschaft *f* (Re) comparative jurisprudence
vergleichender Warentest *m* (Mk) comparative product test
vergleichende Steuerlehre *f* (StR) comparative tax law
vergleichende Warenprüfung *f* (Mk) comparative shopping
vergleichende Werbung *f* (Mk) comparative advertising (*ie, competitive claims inviting comparison with a group of products or other products in the same field*)
Vergleichsabschlüsse *mpl* (ReW) comparative statements
Vergleichsantrag *m* (Re) petition for the initiation of composition proceedings
- application for court protection from creditors

Vergleichsausschuß *m* (Re) board of conciliation
Vergleichsbasis *f*
(com) basis of comparison
- base-line comparison
Vergleichsbefehl *m* (EDV) compare verb
Vergleichsbestätigung *f* (Re) court (*or* official) recognition of composition preceedings
Vergleichsbilanz *f* (Re) = *Vergleichsstatus*
Vergleich *m* **schließen**
(Re) to compromise
- to reach a settlement
Vergleichseröffnung *f* (Re) opening of composition proceedings
Vergleichsgericht *n* (Re) court in charge of composition proceedings
Vergleichsgewinn *m* (ReW) composition gains (*ie, resulting from creditors' waiver of outstanding claims*)
Vergleichsgläubiger *m* (Re) creditor in composition proceedings
Vergleichsgruppenwechsel *m*
(EDV) comparing control change
- control change
Vergleichskalkulation *f* (KoR) comparative costing
Vergleichsmuster *n* (com) reference sample
Vergleichsordnung *f* (Re) Court Composition Law, of 26 Feb 1935, as amended
Vergleichsquote *f*
(Re) dividend in composition
- settlement quota
Vergleichsrechnung *f* (KoR) comparative cost accounting
Vergleichsschuldner *m* (Re) debtor in composition proceedings
Vergleichsstatus *m* (Re) statement of affairs (*ie, submitted in court composition proceedings*)
Vergleichstest *m* (Math) comparison test
Vergleichs- und Schiedsordnung *f* (com) Rules of Conciliation and Arbitration (*ie, laid down by the Paris-based International Chamber of Commerce, ICC*)
Vergleichsverfahren *n*
(Bw) method of comparison
(Re) court composition proceedings
(Re) conciliation procedure
Vergleichsverwalter *m* (Re) trustee in composition proceedings, §§ 38–43 VerglO
Vergleichsvorschlag *m*
(Re) offer for a settlement
- (GB) scheme of arrangement
Vergleichszahlen *fpl* (Stat) benchmark figures
Vergleichszeitraum *m* (com) given period
Vergnügungssteuer *f* (StR) amusements tax
vergriffen
(com) out of stock
- sold out
(com) out of print (*ie, said of books*)
vergüten
(com) to compensate
- to remunerate
(com) to reimburse
- to refund
(com) to indemnify
Vergütung *f*
(com) pay

– fee
– compensation
– remuneration
(com) reimbursement
– refunding
(com) indemnity
Vergütung *f* **für Ausfallzeiten** (Pw) delay compensation
Vergütungsanspruch *m* (Re) right to compensation
Verhaltensflexibilität *f* (Bw) action flexibility
Verhaltensgitter *n* (Bw) managerial grid *(Blake/Mouton)*
Verhaltensgleichung *f* (Vw) behavioral equation
Verhaltenshypothese *f* (Bw) behavioral assumption
Verhaltenskodex *m* (Re) code of conduct
Verhaltensmodell *n* (Bw) behavioral model
Verhaltensweise *f* (Bw) behavior pattern *(eg, of firms)*
Verhältnis *n* **Geldmenge zu Geldbasis** (Vw) money multiplier
Verhältnis *n* **Gewinn zu Dividende** (Fin) earnings-dividend ratio
– dividend cover
– times covered
Verhältnisgröße *f* (Vw) ratio variable
verhältnismäßiger Teil *m* (Re) proportionate part
Verhältnis *n* **Nettoumsatz zu Anlagevermögen ohne Abschreibung** (ReW) fixed-assets turnover
Verhältnis *n* **Reingewinn zu Festzinsen und Dividenden** (Fin) fixed interest cover
Verhältnis *n* **Reingewinn zu Nettoerlös** (ReW) net profit ratio
Verhältnisschätzfunktion *f* (Stat) ratio estimator
Verhältnisschätzung *f* (Stat) ratio estimate
Verhältnis *n* **Standard–Lohneinzelkosten zu Istkosten** (KoR) labor-cost ratio
Verhältnis *n* **von Anlagevermögen zu langfristigen Verbindlichkeiten** (Bw) ratio of fixed assets to fixed liabilities
Verhältnis *n* **von Bestands- zu Stromgrößen** (Vw) stock-flow ratio
Verhältnis *n* **von Forderungen zu Einkäufen** (Bw) ratio of accounts payable to purchases
Verhältnis *n* **von Kapital zu Anlagevermögen** (Bw) ratio of capital to fixed assets
Verhältnis *n* **von Schuldwechsel zu Forderungen a. W. u. L.** (Bw) ratio of notes payable to accounts payable
Verhältnis *n* **Vorräte zur Gesamtproduktion** (Bw) stock-output ratio
Verhältniszahl *f*
(Math) ratio
(Stat) relative
Verhältnis *n* **zwischen Umsatzerlösen und variablen Kosten** (Bw) variable cost ratio
verhandeln
(com) to discuss
– to debate
(com) to negotiate (about/on)
– to bargain (for/about)
(Re) to negotiate
(Re) to hear *(ie, a case)*
Verhandlung *f* (Re) hearing
Verhandlung *f* **aussetzen** (Re) to suspend a hearing

Verhandlungen *fpl*
(com) discussions
– talks
– bargaining
– negotiations
Verhandlungen *fpl* **abbrechen**
(com) to break off negotiations
Verhandlungen *fpl* **beenden** (com) to terminate negotiations
Verhandlungen *fpl* **beginnen**
(com) to start
– to commence
– to open ... negotiations (*or* talks)
Verhandlungen *fpl* **finden statt** (com) negotiations are under way
Verhandlungsangebot *n* (com) offer to negotiate
Verhandlungsauftrag *m* (com) negotiating mandate
Verhandlungsbereich *m* (Bw) bargaining set *(ie, term used in decision theory)*
Verhandlungsführer *m* (com) negotiator
Verhandlungsgrundlage *f* (com) negotiating basis (*or* platform)
Verhandlungsmacht *f* (com) bargaining power
Verhandlungsmandat *n* (com) authority to negotiate
Verhandlungsniederschrift *f* (com) minutes of meeting
Verhandlungspaket *n* (com) package deal
Verhandlungspartner *m* (com) negotiating party
Verhandlungsposition *f* (com) negotiating position
Verhandlungsposition *f* **schwächen** (com) to weaken someone's bargaining hand
Verhandlungsprotokoll *n* (Pw) bargaining records
Verhandlungsrunde *f* (com) round of negotiations
Verhandlungsspielraum *m*
(com) negotiating range
– room to negotiate
(Pw) bargaining room (*or* range)
Verhandlungsstärke *f*
(com) negotiating strength
(Pw) bargaining power
Verhandlungsstruktur *f* (Pw) bargaining structure
Verhandlungsteam *n* (com) negotiating team
Verhandlungstisch *m* (Pw) bargaining table
Verhandlungsvollmacht *f* (com) authority to negotiate
verifizierte Tara *f* (com) verified tare
verjähren
(Re) to act as a bar
– to be struck by the statute of limitations
verjährt
(Re) time-barred
– statute-barred *(eg, claim, action)*
verjährte Forderung *f* (Re) statute-barred debt
verjährter Anspruch *m*
(Re) statute-barred debt
– stale claim
verjährte Verbindlichkeiten *fpl* (Re) statute-barred debt
Verjährung *f*
(Re) statutory limitation
– limitation of liability in time
– limitation on time of bringing suit
– prescription

(opp, Ersitzung) (ie, a claim left dormant for a certain time ceases to be enforceable, §§ 194ff BGB)
Verjährung *f* **hemmen** (Re) to suspend the limitation period
Verjährungsfrist *f*
(Re) period of limitation
– limitation period
– *(civil law)* period of prescription
(ie, the period of time the lapse of which acts as a bar to an action, §§ 194–197 BGB)
Verjährung *f* **unterbrechen** (Re) to interrupt the limitation period
verkalkulieren (com) to miscalculate
Verkauf *m* (com) sale
Verkauf *m* **auf Abruf** (Bö) buyer's call
Verkauf *m* **aufgrund e-r Ausschreibung** (com) sale by tender
Verkauf *m* **auf Kreditbasis** (com) credit sale
Verkauf *m* **auf Ziel**
(com) credit sale
– sale for the account
– (US) charge sale
Verkauf *m* **durch Submission** (Fin) sale by tender
verkaufen
(com) to sell
– to vend
Verkäufe *mpl* **an andere Wirtschaftssubjekte** (VGR) sales to other economic units
Verkäufer *m* (od -in *f*)
(com) salesclerk
– salesman
– saleslady *(or* woman *or* girl) *(ie, to give equal weight to either sex the term ‚salesperson' is nowadays heard more often than not)*
– (GB) (shop) assistent
– (GB, sl) counter jumper
Verkäufermarkt *m* (Vw) seller's market *(opp, Käufermarkt = buyer's market)*
Verkäuferoption *f* (Bö) sellers' option
Verkauf *m* **gegen bar** (com) cash sale
Verkauf *m* **in Bausch und Bogen** (com) outright sale
Verkauf *m* **mit Rückkaufsrecht** (com) sale with option to repurchase
Verkaufsabrechnung *f*
(com) sales accounting
(Bö) contract *(or* sold) note
Verkaufsabschluß *m* (com) conclusion of a sale
Verkaufsagentur *f* (com) sales agency
Verkaufsangebot *n*
(com) offer to sell
(Bö) offer for sale *(ie, of new securities)*
Verkaufsauftrag *m* (Bö) order to sell
Verkaufsauftrag *m* **bestens** (Bö) sell order at market
Verkaufsaußendienst *m* (Mk) sales force
Verkaufsautomat *m*
(com) dispensing machine
– vending machine
– (automatic) vendor
– (infml) slot machine
Verkaufsbedingungen *fpl*
(com) terms and conditions
– conditions of sale and delivery

Verkaufsbezirk *m* (Mk) sales district
Verkaufsbüro *n*
(com) sales office
– selling agency
Verkaufsdatenerfassung *f* (Mk) sales data acquisition *(eg, through POS terminals)*
Verkaufserlös *m* (Bö) sales proceeds
Verkaufserlöse *mpl* (ReW) sales revenue
verkaufsfähige Erzeugnisse *npl* (Mk) salable products
Verkaufsfiliale *f* (Mk) branch store
Verkaufsfläche *f* (Mk) selling space
Verkaufsförderung *f* (Mk) sales promotion
Verkaufsförderungs-Abteilung *f* (Mk) promotion services department
Verkaufsfrist *f* (Fin) subscription period
Verkaufsgebiet *n* (com) sales territory
Verkaufsgemeinschaft *f* (com) selling association
Verkaufsgenossenschaft *f* (Bw) cooperative selling association
Verkaufsgespräch *n* (com) sales talk
Verkaufsgruppe *f* (Fin) selling group *(or* syndicate)
Verkaufsgruppenvertrag *m* (Fin) selling group agreement
Verkaufsjournal *n* (com) sales register
Verkaufskommissionär *m*
(com) factor
– commission agent *(or* merchant)
Verkaufskontor *n* (Bw) independent selling subsidiary *(syn, Werkhandelsgesellschaft)*
Verkaufskurs *m*
(Bö) check rate
(Bö) offering price *(ie, of loan)*
Verkaufsleiter *m* (Mk) sales manager
Verkaufsmethode *f* (Mk) selling technique
Verkaufsmuster *n* (Mk) pattern sample
Verkaufsniederlassung *f* (Mk) sales branch
Verkaufsnote *f* (com) sold note
Verkaufsoption *f*
(com) selling option
(Bö) put option
Verkaufsorder *f* (Bö) order to sell
Verkaufsorganisation *f* (com) sales organization
Verkaufspersonal *n* (com) sales personnel *(or* staff)
Verkaufsprämie *f*
(com) sales premium
– (infml) push money *(ie, in retail trading)*
Verkaufspreis *m* (com) selling price
Verkaufsprospekt *m* (Bö) offering prospectus
Verkaufsprovision *f* (com) sales *(or* selling) commission
Verkaufspunkt *m* (Mk) point of sale, POS
Verkaufsquote *f* (Mk) sales quota
Verkaufsrechnung *f* (com) sales invoice
Verkaufsschlager *m*
(com) hot selling line
– top selling article
– (infml) runner
– (infml) hot number
– (sl) smash hit *(eg, the professional copycat's latest fake is an uncontestable . . .)*
Verkaufsstelle *f*
(Mk) marketing outlet
(Fin) subscription agent
Verkaufssyndikat *n* (Bw) selling syndicate

Verkaufs- und Lieferbedingungen *fpl* (com) conditions of sale and delivery
Verkaufsvergütung *f* (Fin) selling commission
Verkaufsvertrag *m* (Fin) selling agreement
Verkaufsvertreter *m*
(com) salesman
– saleswoman
– (esp. US) salesperson
– (fml) sales representative
Verkaufswert *m* (com) selling (*or* marketable) value
Verkaufswiderstand *m* (Mk) buying resistance
Verkaufsziffern *fpl* (Bw) sales figures
Verkauf *m* **unter Eigentumsvorbehalt** (Re) conditional sale, § 455 BGB
Verkauf *m* **unter Selbstkosten** (com) sale below cost price
Verkauf *m* **wegen Geschäftsaufgabe** (com) closing-down sale
– winding-up sale
Verkauf *m* **zur sofortigen Lieferung** (com) sale for immediate delivery
Verkehr *m*
(com) commercial transactions
(com) traffic
Verkehr *m* **mit ungebrochener Fracht** (Zo) through traffic
Verkehrsampel *f*
(com) street crossing light
– (GB) Belisha beacon
Verkehrsanalyse *f*
(EDV) analysis of traffic
– performance analysis
Verkehrsaufkommen *n* (com) volume of traffic
Verkehrsauftrag *m* (com) forwarding order *(syn, Speditionsauftrag, Speditionsvertrag)*
Verkehrsbedürfnisse *npl* (Re) requirements of ordinary intercourse
Verkehrsbilanz *f* (ReW) preliminary balance sheet *(syn, Rohbilanz)*
Verkehrsdichte *f* (OR) traffic intensity
verkehrsfähig
(com) marketable
(WeR) negotiable
Verkehrsfähigkeit *f*
(com) marketability
(WeR) negotiability
Verkehrsgewerbe *n* (com) transport(ation) industry
Verkehrsgleichung *f*
(Vw) quantity equation of exchange
– transaction equation
(syn, Quantitätsgleichung)
Verkehrshypothek *f* (Re) ordinary mortgage
Verkehrslage *f* (Bw) location in respect of transport facilities
Verkehrsleistungen *fpl* (com) transportation services
Verkehrspapier *n* (WeR) negotiable paper
Verkehrspolitik *f* (Vw) transport(ation) policy
Verkehrssitte *f*
(Re) common
– general
– ordinary ... usage
– local conventions

Verkehrssitten *fpl* **im Handelsverkehr** (Re) customary business practices
Verkehrsstau *m*
(com) traffic jam
– (GB) hold-up
Verkehrsströme *mpl* (com) patterns of traffic movement
Verkehrsteuern *fpl*
(StR) taxes on transactions
– transactions taxes
(eg, turnover tax, inheritance tax, federal excise taxes)
Verkehrstechnik *f* (com) transport(ation) engineering
Verkehrsträger *m* (Vw) traffic carrier *(ie, rail, road, air)*
verkehrsübliche Sorgfalt *f*
(Re) ordinary care
– ordinary diligence
– due diligence
(ie, diligence and care required in ordinary dealings: diligentia quam in suis, § 276 BGB)
Verkehrsverlagerung *f* (Zo) deflection of trade
Verkehrswert *m*
(com) current market value
– salable value
Verkehrswertschätzung *f* (com) estimate of current market value
Verkehrswirtschaft *f*
(Vw) exchange economy
(Vw) transportation sector
Verkettbarkeit *f* (Math) conformability
verketten
(EDV) to chain
– to concatenate
verkettete Datei *f* (EDV) concatenated data file
verkettete Fertigungslinien *fpl* (IndE) interlinked production lines
verketteter Index *m* (Stat) chain index
Verkettung *f* (EDV) chaining
verklagen
(Re) to take (a person) to court
– to proceed against a person
– (infml) to bring charges against
– (GB, infml) to have someone up
Verklarung *f* (com) captain's protest, §§ 522ff HGB
(syn, Seeprotest)
verknüpfte Liste *f* (EDV) chained list
Verknüpfung *f* (EDV) logical operation
Verknüpfungsbefehl *m* (EDV) logical instruction
Verknüpfungsgleichung *f* (Math) coupling equation
Verknüpfungsglied *n* (EDV) logical element
Verknüpfungszeichen *n* (Log) logical connective
verkörpern (WeR) to embody
verkraften (com) to switch traffic from rail to road
verkrustete Organisationsstruktur *f* (Bw) red-tape ridden bureaucracy
verkürzte Arbeitszeit *f* (Pw) reduced hours
verkürzte quadratische Form *f* (Math) abridged quadratic form
verkürzter Block *m* (EDV) short block
Verkürzung *f* **der Arbeitszeit** (Pw) shortening of working hours

Verkürzung f von Lieferfristen (Vw) shortening of delivery periods
Verladeflughafen m (com) airport of dispatch
Verladehafen m (com) port of loading
Verladekosten pl (com) loading expenses
verladen
  (com) to load
  – to ship
Verladeort m (com) place of loading
Verladepapiere npl (com) shipping documents
Verlader m
  (com) shipper
  – forwarder *(ie, neither exporter nor carrier; syn, Ablader)*
  (com, *occasionally*) freighter *(syn, Befrachter)*
Verladeschein m (com) shipping note
Verladung f (com) loading
Verladungskosten pl (com) loading charges
Verlag m
  (com) publishers
  – publishing firm (*or* house)
verlagern (com, EDV) to relocate
verlagerte Investitionen fpl (Vw) humped investment
Verlagerung f des Wohnortes (Pw) change of residence
Verlagerung f von Arbeitsplätzen (Bw) job relocation
Verlagssystem n (Vw) domestic (*or* putting-out) system
Verlagswesen n
  (com) publishing trade
  – book industry
verlängern
  (com) to extend
  – to renew
verlängerte Einfuhr f (StR) extended imports *(ie, under the former Turnover Tax Law)*
verlängerter Eigentumsvorbehalt m (Re) extended reservation of ownership
Verlängerung f
  (com) extension
  – renewal
  – prolongation
Verlängerung f der Abgabefrist (com) filing extension
Verlängerung f der Gültigkeitsdauer (Re) extension of validity
Verlängerung f der Laufzeit (Re) stretchout of term
Verlängerung f der Lieferfrist (com) extension of delivery period
Verlängerung f e-s Patents (Pat) renewal of a patent
Verlängerung f e-s Wechsels (WeR) prolongation of a bill of exchange
Verlängerungsanmeldung f (Kart) notification of extension, § 103 GWB
Verlängerungsgebühr f (Pat) renewal fee
Verlängerungsklausel f (SeeV) continuation clause
Verlängerungspolice f (Vers) extension policy
Verlängerungsrecht n (Re) right to renew
Verlängerung f von Fristen (StR) extensions of time for the filing of returns, § 109 AO

verlangsamen (Vw) to decelerate *(eg, food and housing costs)*
verlangsamtes Wachstum n (Vw) slower economic (*or* industrial) growth
Verlangsamung f (Vw) slowdown *(eg, in the rate of savings)*
Verlauf m (Math) slope
Verlaufsziel n (Vw) year-on-year target
Verlautbarung f (com) pronouncement *(eg, of accounting associations)*
Verlegung f der Geschäftsleitung (Bw) transfer of place of management
Verlegung f des Sitzes (Bw) relocation of a registered office (*or* business premises)
Verlegung f des Wohnsitzes (StR) transfer of residence
Verlegung f lohnintensiver Fertigungen in Niedriglohnländer (AuW) offshore sourcing
verleihen
  (Re) to lend
  – to hire out
Verleiher m (Re) lender
verletzen
  (Re) to violate
  – to be violative of
Verletzung f der Formvorschriften (Re) non-compliance with formal requirements
Verletzung f der Sorgfaltspflicht (Re) violation of the duty of care *(ie, neglect of supervisory duties or obligations, § 276 BGB)*
Verletzung f des Berufsgeheimnisses (Re) violation of professional secrecy
Verletzung f e-s gewerblichen Schutzrechts (Pat) infringement of an industrial property right
Verletzung f e-s Patents (Pat) patent infringement
Verletzung f wesentlicher Formvorschriften (Re) non-observance of essential formalities
verlockende Anlage f (Fin) alluring investment
verlorener Baukostenzuschuß m (Re) non-repayable contribution to building costs (by tenant)
verlorene Streiktage mpl (Vw) total of working days lost through industrial disputes
Verlust m (ReW) loss
Verlust m **abdecken** (com) to cover (*or* to make good) a loss
Verlustabzug m (StR) net operating loss carryoyer and carryback, § 10d EStG
Verlustattest n (SeeV) certificate of loss
Verlustausgleich m (StR) loss compensation, § 2 III EStG
Verlustausweis m (ReW) reporting a loss
Verlust m **ausweisen** (ReW) to report a loss
Verlust m **des Arbeitsplatzes** (Pw) loss of job (*or* employment)
Verlust m **des Geschäftsjahres** (ReW, EG) loss for the financial year
Verluste mpl **abziehen** (StR) to offset losses
Verluste mpl **aus Anlageabgängen** (ReW) losses from fixed-asset disposals
Verluste mpl **ausgleichen** (ReW) to balance out losses *(eg, with earnings from other divisions)*
Verlust m **e-s Rechts** (Re) loss of a right
Verlustfunktion f (Stat) loss function
Verlustgeschäft n

Verlustkonto

(com) money-losing deal
- losing bargain

Verlustkonto n (ReW) deficit account

Verlustrückstellung f (ReW) contingency reserve

Verlustrücktrag m (StR) loss carryback, § 10 d EStG

Verlustübernahme f (StR) transfer of losses

Verlustvortrag m
(ReW) accumulated loss
(ReW) loss brought forward
(StR) loss carryover (or carryforward), § 10 d EStG

Verlustvortrag m **aus dem Vorjahr** (ReW) loss carried forward from previous fiscal year

Verlustzeit f **durch Fehlbedienung** (EDV) operating delays (ie, time lost due to mistakes in operating)

Verlustzone f (KoR) loss wedge (ie, in a breakeven chart)

Verlustzuweisung f (StR) allocation of losses

Vermächtnisnehmer m (Re) specific legatee

vermarkten
(Mk) to market
- to put on the market

Vermarktungsbestimmungen fpl (AuW) marketing provisions

Vermehrungsstufe f (Kart) seed multiplication level

vermeidbares Risiko n (Fin) diversifiable (or systematic) risk

vermeidbare Verzögerung f (IndE) avoidable delay

Vermeidung f **der Doppelbesteuerung** (StR) prevention or mitigation of double taxation

Vermessungsamt n (Re) land surveying office

vermieten
(Re) to let (eg, a house for payment of regular rent)
- to let out (eg, room or part of building)
- (US) to rent out

Vermieter m (Re) lessor

vermietete Erzeugnisse npl (com) equipment leased to customers

Vermietung f (Re) lease

Vermietung f **und Verpachtung** f (StR) rentals or royalties, § 2 I 6 EStG

Vermietung f **vollständiger Betriebsanlagen** (Fin) plant leasing

Vermietung f **von Grundstücken** (Re) rental of real property

Vermietung f **von Investitionsgütern** (com) leasing of capital assets

verminderte Erwerbsfähigkeit f (Pw) partial disability

Vermischung f **vertretbarer Sachen** (Re) confusion (or commingling) of fungible goods, § 948 BGB

vermitteln
(com) to go between
- to act as intermediary
- to bring together
- to bring to an understanding
- to use one's good offices
(Re) to mediate (eg, in a wages conflict)
- to arbitrate (eg, between contending parties, workers and employers)
- to intervene

Vermögensarten

Vermittler m
(com) go between
- intermediary
- middleman
(Re) conciliator
- mediator

Vermittlerprovision f (Vers) production cost

Vermittlung f
(Re) arbitration
- conciliation
- mediation
- good offices

Vermittlung f **der Befrachtung** (com) freight brokerage

Vermittlungsagent m
(Vers) application
- survey
- surveying ... agent (opp, Abschlußagent)

Vermittlungsangebot n (Pw) offer of mediation

Vermittlungsausschuß m (com) mediating committee

Vermittlungsgebühr f (com) introduction charges

Vermittlungsgehilfe m (Re) negotiator of deals, § 75 g HGB

Vermittlungsmakler m **im Edelmetallhandel** (Fin) bullion broker

Vermittlungsperson f (com) middleman

Vermittlungsprovision f
(com) commission for business negotiated by commercial agent, § 87 HGB
(Fin) finder's fee

Vermittlungsverfahren n (Re) joint committee procedure (ie, for further discussion of proposed legislation)

Vermittlungsvertreter m (com) agent appointed to negotiate business transactions (opp, Abschlußvertreter)

Vermittlungsvorschlag m (com) compromise proposal

vermittlungswillige Arbeitslose mpl (Pw) available workers

Vermittlung f **von Geschäften** (com) negotiation of business transactions
- business negotiation

Vermögen n
(com) assets
- wealth
(ReW) net worth (or assets)

Vermögen n **der Gesellschaft**
(Fin) partnership assets
(Fin) corporate assets

Vermögen n **des Haushalts** (Vw) household's stock of wealth

Vermögen n **e-r Unternehmung** (Fin) assets of a business (or enterprise)

Vermögen n **e-r Unterstützungskasse** (Pw) actual endowment of a relief fund, § 5 I No. 3 e KStG

Vermögen n **juristischer Personen** (Fin) corporate assets

Vermögen n **natürlicher Personen** (Fin) assets of natural persons

Vermögensabgabe f (StR) capital levy (ie, imposed under the Equalization of Burdens Law)

Vermögensarten fpl (StR) categories of assets, §§ 17 ff BewG (ie, 1. land- und forstwirtschaft-

liches Vermögen; 2. *Grundvermögen;* 3. *Betriebsvermögen;* 4. *sonstiges Vermögen)*
Vermögensaufstellung *f* (StR) statement of net assets, Abschn. 4 VStR
Vermögensaufstellung *f* e-s **Konkursschuldners** (Re) statement of affairs
Vermögensauseinandersetzung *f* (Re) division of net assets
Vermögensauskehrungen *fpl* **bei Kapitalherabsetzung od Liquidation** (StR) assets paid out in connection with capital reduction or liquidation
Vermögensausweis *m* (ReW) financial statement
Vermögensbewertung *f* (StR) valuation of net assets
Vermögensbilanz *f* (ReW) asset and liability statement
Vermögensbildung *f* (Vw) capital (*or* wealth) formation
Vermögensbildungsgesetz *n* (Pw) Law Promoting Capital Formation by Employees
Vermögensbildungspläne *mpl* (Pw) plans for the redistribution of wealth
Vermögenseinbuße *f* (Re) actual loss or damage *(opp, future loss or expectancy)*
 – *(civil law)* damnum emergens
 – *(Scotch law)* damnum datum
Vermögenseinkommen *n* (Vw) unearned income
Vermögenseinlage *f*
 (Fin) investment
 (Fin) capital contribution
Vermögenserträge *mpl* (Fin) investment income
Vermögensgegenstand *m*
 (Re) item of property
 (Bw) asset
Vermögensinteresse *n* (Re) pecuniary interest
Vermögenslage *f*
 (com) financial situation (*or* position)
 (ReW) net worth position, § 329 II AktG
Vermögensmasse *f* (StR) conglomeration of property, § 138 II AO
Vermögensmehrung *f* (StR) increase in net worth
Vermögensneuanlagen *fpl* (Fin) new investment of funds
Vermögensobjekt *n* (com) asset
Vermögensposition *f* (AuW) external assets
Vermögensrechnung *f*
 (VGR) gross saving and investment account
 – wealth statement
 (ReW) internal balance sheet
Vermögensrecht *n*
 (Re) property
 – proprietary
 – economic ... right
Vermögensschaden *m* (Vers) economic loss *(ie, including, but not limited to, ‚Personenschaden' = injury to persons and ‚Sachschaden' = property damage or loss in property)*
Vermögensschadenversicherung *f* (Vers) consequential loss insurance
Vermögensstatus *m* (ReW) statement of assets and liabilities as of a specified date
Vermögensstruktur *f* (Fin) assets and liabilities structure
Vermögensteuer *f* (StR) net worth tax *(ie, individuals, partnerships, and companies are charge-*

able on their total movable and immovable capital situated inside and outside West Germany)
Vermögensteuer-Durchführungsverordnung *f* (StR) Ordinance Regulating the Net Worth Tax Law
Vermögensteuererklärung *f* (StR) net worth tax return, § 19 VStG
Vermögensteuergesetz *n* (StR) Net Worth Tax Law, as amended 27 July 1978
Vermögensteuerpflicht *f* (StR) liability to pay net worth tax
Vermögensteuer-Richtlinien *fpl* (StR) Net Worth Tax Regulations, as of 31 Mar 1977
Vermögensübersicht *f* (ReW) statement of assets and liabilities
Vermögensübertragung *f*
 (Re) asset transfer
 – assignment of property *(eg, to creditors)*
 – transfer of net worth
Vermögensumschichtung *f* (Fin) restructuring of assets
Vermögensumverteilung *f* (Vw) redistribution of wealth
Vermögens- und Ertragslage *f* (ReW) financial and earnings position
Vermögensveränderungskonto *n* (VGR) investment account
Vermögensvergleich *m*
 (StR) regular method of net worth comparison, § 5 EStG
 (StR) simplified method of net worth comparison, § 4 I EStG *(ie, also called ‚Bestandsvergleich')*
Vermögensverhältnisse *npl* (Fin) financial circumstances
Vermögensverteilung *f*
 (Vw) distribution of wealth
 (Re) division of assets
Vermögensverwalter *m*
 (Re) manager (*or* administrator *or* custodian) of an estate
 (Re) committee of the estate *(ie, of persons non compos mentis)*
 (Fin) investment manager
 (Fin) portfolio manager
Vermögensverwaltung *f*
 (Re) property administration
 – asset management
 (Fin) investment management
 – portfolio management
Vermögensverwaltungsgesellschaft *f* (Fin) property-management company
Vermögensvorteil *m* (Re) financial (*or* pecuniary) benefit
Vermögenswerte *mpl*
 (com) assets
 (Bw) resources
 (Re) property holdings
Vermögenswerte *mpl* **einbringen** (Bw) to bring assets (to)
vermögenswirksame Ausgaben *fpl* (FiW) asset-creating expenditure
vermögenswirksame Leistungen *fpl* (StR) employment benefits to encourage capital formation
Vermögenszensus *m* (VGR) wealth census

Vermögenszuwachs *m* (Bw) capital appreciation
Vermögen *n* **übertragen** (Re) to transfer assets
vermuteter Ausfall *m* (ReW) estimated loss of receivables
Vermutung *f* (Re) presumption
(subterms: einfache, widerlegliche, unwiderlegliche Vermutung)
Vermutung *f* **begründen** (Re) to establish a presumption
verneinendes Urteil *n*
(Log) negative proposition
– negative
veröffentlichter Abschluß *m* (ReW) published (*or* disclosed) accounts
Veröffentlichung *f*
(com) publication
(ReW) disclosure
Veröffentlichungsrechte *npl* (Re) publishing rights
Verordnung *f* **über den Lohnsteuer-Jahresausgleich** (StR) Ordinance Regulating the Annual Recomputation of the Wage Tax of Employees and Workers
Verordnung *f* **über die einkommensteuerliche Behandlung der freien Berufe** (StR) Ordinance Regulating the Income Tax Treatment of Free Professionals
Verordnung *f* **über die Führung e-s Wareneingangsbuches** (StR) Ordinance Regulating the Maintenance of a Merchandise Receiving Book
Verordnung *f* **zum Steuersäumnisgesetz** (StR) Ordinance Implementing the Law on Tax Arrears
verpachten (Re) to lease *(ie, land or building)*
– to let on lease
(Note that ‚to lease' also means ‚pachten' in the sense of ‚to take on lease')
Verpächter *m* (Re) lessor
Verpachtung *f*
(Re) lease
– leasing
Verpachtung *f* **e-s Patents** (Pat) lease of a patent
Verpachtung *f* **von Grundstücken** (Re) rental of real property
verpacken (com) to pack
Verpacken *n* (com) packing
Verpacker *m*
(com) packer
(com) packing agent
Verpackung *f* (com) packing and packaging *(ie, generic term)*
Verpackungsanweisung *f* (com) packing instructions
Verpackungsindustrie *f* (com) packaging industry
Verpackungskiste *f* (com) packing case
Verpackungskosten *pl* (com) packing charges (*or* expenses)
Verpackungsliste *f* (com) packing list
Verpackungstest *m* (Mk) pack test
Verpackungs- und Auszeichnungsbestimmungen *fpl* (AuW) packaging and labeling regulations
verpfänden
(Re) to pledge
– to pawn
(ie, real or personal property as security on a debt)

Verpfändung *f*
(Re) pledge *(eg, of marketable assets)*
– pledging
verpflichten
(Re) to obligate
– to put under an obligation
– to commit
– to bind
verpflichten, sich
(Re) to undertake
– to engage
– to promise *(eg, to be answerable for debt)*
Verpflichteter *m* (Re) obligor *(eg, person bound under a contract)*
Verpflichtung *f*
(Re) commitment
– engagement
– obligation
– promise
– undertaking
Verpflichtung *f* **anfechten** (Re) to dispute an obligation *(eg, to meet a claim in full)*
Verpflichtung *f* **eingehen**
(Re) to assume (*or* enter into) an obligation
(com, Fin) to take on (new) commitments
Verpflichtung *f* **erfüllen**
(Re) to answer
– to discharge
– to fulfill
– to perform
– to meet
– to satisfy ... an obligation
Verpflichtungserklärung *f*
(Re) formal obligation *(eg, to sign a ...)*
(Zo) bond
Verpflichtungsermächtigung *f* (Fin) commitment authorization
Verpflichtungsgeschäft *n* (Re) obligatory contract *(eg, tax is imposed on the ... rather than on the transfer itself)*
Verpflichtungsklage *f* (StR) action to enforce the issuance of an administrative decision, § 40 I FGO
Verpflichtungsschein *m* (WeR) certificate of obligation *(ie, drawn up by a merchant in respect of money, securities or other fungible things, § 363 HGB)*
Verpflichtung *f* **übernehmen** (Re) to assume an obligation
verrechnen
(com) to net (with)
– to set off (against)
– to offset (against)
(ReW) to absorb *(ie, spread through allocation)*
(ReW) to charge *(eg, as an expense)*
(KoR) to allocate
– to apportion
– to spread
– to trace (to)
(Fin) to clear
– to settle
verrechnete Abweichungen *fpl* (KoR) allocated variances
verrechnete Gemeinkosten *pl* (KoR) absorbed overhead

verrechnete Kosten pl (KoR) allocated cost (or expense)
Verrechnung f
(com) netting (with)
– setting off (against)
(ReW) absorption
(ReW) charging
(KoR) allocation
– apportionment
– distribution
(Fin) clearing
– settlement
Verrechnung f **betrieblicher Leistungen** (KoR) distribution of internal services
Verrechnungsabkommen n
(AuW) payments agreement
(Fin) clearing (or settlement) agreement
Verrechnungsabweichungen fpl (KoR) revisions variance
Verrechnungsdollar m (AuW) clearing dollar
Verrechnungseinheit f (Fin) unit of account
Verrechnungsgeschäft n (com) offsetting transaction
Verrechnungsgrundlage f (KoR) allocation base
Verrechnungsguthaben n (Fin) clearing balance
Verrechnungsklausel f (AuW) offset clause
Verrechnungskonto n
(ReW) clearing (or offset) account
(ReW) intercompany clearing account
(KoR) allocation account
Verrechnungskurs m (Fin) settlement price
Verrechnungsposten m (ReW) offsetting item
Verrechnungspreis m (ReW) transfer price
Verrechnungssaldo m (Fin) clearing balance
Verrechnungssatz m (KoR) cost rate
Verrechnungsscheck m (Fin) collection-only check
Verrechnungsspitze f (Fin) clearing fraction
Verrechnungsstelle f (Fin) clearing office
Verrechnungstage mpl (Fin) clearing days
Verrechnungsverkehr m (Fin) clearing transactions
Verrechnungswährung f (Fin) clearing currency
Verrentung f **der Steuerschuld** (StR) payment of tax in annual installments
(ie, comprising amortization installments and interest, § 24 ErbStG)
Verrichtungsgehilfe m (Re) vicarious agent (ie, with respect to tort liability, § 831 BGB)
verringerter Investitionskoeffizient m (Vw) reduced investment coefficient
Verringerung f **des Bestandes** (ReW, EG) reduction in stocks
Verringerung f **des Spezialisierungsgrades** (IndE) despecialization
versagen
(Pw) to fail
– (infml) to fall down on a job
Versager m
(Pw, sl) total loss
– (GB) poor tool (ie, at an activity)
Versagung f **e-s Patents** (Pat) withholding of a patent
Versand m
(com) dispatch
– shipment
– shipping

– forwarding
– sending off
Versandabteilung f (com) shipping (or forwarding) department
Versandanmeldung f (Zo) transit declaration
Versandanschrift f (com) address for shipments
Versandanweisungen fpl (com) forwarding (or shipping) instructions
Versandanzeige f
(com) advice
– delivery
– dispatch
– shipping ... note
– forwarding advice
– letter of advice
Versandauftrag m (com) dispatch (or shipping) order
Versandausschuß m (EG, Zo) Committee on Community Transit
Versandbedingungen fpl (com) shipping terms
versandbereit (com) ready for shipment
Versandbereitstellungskredit m (com) packing credit
Versandbescheinigung f (com) shipping certificate
Versandbestellung f
(com) mail order buying
– (GB) postal shopping
Versand m **durchführen** (com) to effect shipment
Versandgebühr f (com) forwarding charge
Versandhafen m
(com) port of loading
– shipping port
Versandhaus n
(com) mail order house
– (GB) catalogue company
Versandhausgruppe f (com) mail order group
Versandhaushandel m (com) mail order selling
Versandhauswerbung f (Mk) mail order advertising
Versandhauswerte mpl (Bö) mail orders
Versandkosten pl (KoR) delivery (or shipping) cost (ie, cost of sending goods by mail, truck, rail or plane; an element of selling expense in cost accounting)
Versandleiter m (com) shipping supervisor
Versandliste f (com) packing list
Versandmeister m (com) shipping foreman
Versandmeldung f (com) ready-for-shipment note
Versandpapier n (Zo) movement document
Versandpapiere npl (com) shipping documents
Versandprobe f (Stat) shipping sample
Versandschachtel f (com, GB) shipping case
Versandscheck m (Fin) out-of-town check
Versandschein m (Zo) transit bond note
Versandspesen pl (com) forwarding (or shipping) expense
Versandtag m (com) date of dispatch
Versandtermin m (com) date of shipment
Versandverfahren n (Zo) transit procedure
Versandvorschriften fpl (com) forwarding (or shipping) instructions
Versandwechsel m (Fin) out-of-town bill
Versandweg m (com) shipping route
Versandwert m (VGR) value of shipments (ie, value of all products and services sold)

Versandzeichen *n* (com) shipping mark
Versatzgeschäft *n* (com) pawn broking, § 34 GewO *(syn, Pfandleihe)*
Versäumnisurteil *n* (Re) judgment by default, §§ 330–347 ZPO
Verschaffung *f* **der Verfügungsmacht** (Re) transfer of power to dispose of an asset *(ie, putting the recipient in a position to deal with a property in the manner of an owner)*
verschärfen
  (com) to aggravate
  – to exacerbate
  – (infml) to hot up *(eg, air fare war)*
  (com) to sharpen
  – to intensify *(eg, competition)*
  (Fin) to tighten up *(eg, credit policy)*
verschärfte Prüfung *f* (Stat) tightened inspection
verschicken (com) to send out *(eg, offers, advertising materials)*
verschiebbar (EDV) relocatable
Verschiebbarkeit *f* **von Programmen** (EDV) program relocatability
Verschiebebefehl *m* (EDV) shift instruction
Verschiebung *f* (EDV) relocation
Verschiebung *f* **der Angebotskurve**
  (Vw) shift in supply
  – shifting of supply curve
Verschiebung *f* **der Einkommensverteilung** (Vw) distributional shift
Verschiebung *f* **der Nachfragekurve**
  (Vw) shift in demand
  – shifting of demand curve
Verschiebungsoperator *m* (Vw) shift operator
Verschiebungsparameter *m* (Stat) translation parameter
Verschiffung *f* (com) shipment
Verschiffungsauftrag *m* (com) shipping order
Verschiffungs-Bescheinigung *f* (com) certificate of shipment *(ie, substituting a bill of lading)*
Verschiffungsdokumente *npl* (com) shipping documents
Verschiffungsgewicht *n* (com) shipping weight
Verschiffungshafen *m* (com) port of dispatch *(or shipment)*
Verschiffungskonnossement *n* (com) shipped *(or ocean)* bill of lading
Verschlechterung *f* **der Gewinnsituation** (com) weakening of earnings *(or profits)*
Verschlechterung *f* **der Zahlungsbilanz**
  (AuW) deterioration of the balance of payments
  – increase in the deficit of the balance of payments
  – putting the balance of payments in a deficit position
verschleiertes Dumping *n* (AuW) hidden dumping
Verschleißanlagen *fpl* (Bw) depreciable assets *(or property)*
Verschleiß *m* **des Produktionsapparates** (VGR) capital consumption
Verschleißfreiheit *f* (IndE) durability
verschleudern (com) to sell at ruinous prices
Verschleuderung *f* (com) selling at dumping *(or ruinous) prices*
Verschlüsselung *f* (EDV) code

Verschlüsselungsmatrix *f* (EDV) coding matrix
Verschmelzung *f* **durch Aufnahme** (Bw) merger
Verschmelzung *f* **durch Neubildung** (Bw) consolidation
verschmutztes politisches Umfeld *n* (Bw) polluted political environment
verschreibungspflichtige Medikamente *npl* (SozV) prescription drugs
Verschulden *n* (Re) fault
  (ie, general term covering ‚Vorsatz und Fahrlässigkeit' = intention and negligence; in English law the word fault is equivalent with negligence)
Verschulden *n* **bei Vertragsschluß** (Re) culpa in contrahendo *(ie, violation of mutual confidence in the preparation of a contract)*
Verschuldenshaftung *f*
  (Re) liability based on (proof of) fault
  – liability for default
verschulden, sich (Fin) to incur debts
Verschuldensneigung *f* (Fin) propensity to incur debts *(or* liabilities)
verschuldensunabhängige Haftung *f*
  (Re) strict liability in tort
  – liability without fault
verschuldet
  (Fin) indebted
  – (infml) saddled by debt
  – (infml) stuffed with debt
  – (infml) running in the red
Verschuldung *f* (Fin) indebtedness
  – level of debt
  (Fin) contraction of debt
Verschuldung *f* **der öffentlichen Hand** (FiW) public debt
Verschuldungsbereitschaft *f* (Fin) propensity to take up credits
Verschuldungsgrad *m* (Fin) debt-equity ratio *(ie, total liabilities to total equity)*
Verschuldungsgrenze *f* (Fin, FiW) debt limitations *(or* limit) *(ie, ceiling placed on the amount of borrowings by individuals, corporations, or public authorities)*
Verschuldungskoeffizient *m* (Fin) = *Verschuldungsgrad*
Verschuldungspolitik *f* **der öffentlichen Hand** (FiW) debt management
Verschuldungspotential *n* (Fin) borrowing potential
Verschuldungsspielraum *m* (Fin) debt margin
Verschweigen *n* **rechtserheblicher Umstände** (Vers) material concealment
Verschwendung *f* **von Ressourcen** (Bw) dissipation *(or* wasting) of resources
versenden
  (com) to mail
  – (GB) to post
  (com) to dispatch
  – to forward
  – to send off
  – to ship
  – to effect shipment
Versender *m*
  (com) sender
  – consignor
Versendung *f*

(com) dispatch
- shipment
Versendungskauf m (com) sale to destination according to buyer's instructions, § 447 BGB
Versendungskosten pl (com) cost of transportation (or carriage)
Versendungsort m
(com) place of consignment
- shipping point
versetzte Ablage f (EDV) offset stacker
Versetzung f
(Pw) transfer
- transferral
- relocation
Versetzung f ablehnen (Pw) to turn down a transfer
versicherbar (Vers) insurable
versicherbarer Wert m (Vers) insurable value
versicherbares Interesse n
(Vers) insurable interest
- (GB) assurable interest
versicherbares Risiko n (Vers) insurable risk
Versicherer m
(Vers) insurance company
- insurer
- (GB) assurer
- underwriter
Versicherer-Gruppe f (Vers) fleet of companies (ie, common ownership and management)
versichern
(Vers) to insure
- (GB also) to assure
- to write insurance
versicherte Gefahren fpl (Vers) risks covered
Versichertendividende f (Vers) bonus
Versicherter m
(Vers) insured (pl. insureds)
- (GB) assured (pl. assureds)
- insured party
- policyholder
versicherter Gegenstand m (Vers) subject matter insured
versicherter Wert m (Vers) insured value
versichertes Interesse n (Vers) interest insured
Versicherung f
(Vers) insurance
- (GB) assurance
- underwriting
Versicherung f abschließen (Vers) to take out (or effect) insurance
Versicherung f als Vielschutzpaket (Vers) all-in (or all-risk) insurance
Versicherung f an Eides statt
(Re) affidavit
- (GB) statutory declaration
(ie, statement in lieu of an oath, signed and affirmed)
Versicherung f auf den Todesfall (Vers) whole life insurance (ie, either straight/ordinary, or single-premium, or limited-payment; opp, term insurance)
Versicherung f auf den Todes- und Erlebensfall (Vers) endowment life insurance
(ie, payable to the insured at the end of the contract or covered period or to beneficiary if insured dies prior to maturity date)

Versicherung f auf Zeit (Vers) time insurance
Versicherung f für eigene Rechnung (Vers) insurance for own account
Versicherung f für fremde Rechnung (Vers) insurance for third party account
Versicherung f für Rechnung, für wen es angeht (Vers) insurance for account of whom it may concern
Versicherung f gegen außergewöhnliche Risiken (Vers) contingency risk insurance
Versicherung f läuft ab (Vers) policy expires (or matures)
Versicherung f mit Barausschüttung der Dividende (Vers) participating insurance
Versicherung f mit Gewinnbeteiligungsgarantie (Vers) guaranteed dividend policy
Versicherung f mit Selbstbehalt (Vers) participating insurance
Versicherung f ohne Gewinnbeteiligung (Vers) insurance without profit
Versicherungsabschluß m
(Vers) taking out insurance
(Vers) contract of insurance
Versicherungsagent m (Vers) insurance agent
Versicherungsakquisiteur m (Vers) insurance canvasser
Versicherungsaktien fpl (Bö) insurance stocks
Versicherungsanspruch m (Vers) insurance claim
Versicherungsantrag m (Vers) application
Versicherungsaufsichtsamt n (Vers) Insurance Supervisory Office
Versicherungsaufsichtsbehörde f (Vers) Insurance Supervisory Authority
Versicherungsaufsichtsbehörden fpl **der Länder** (Vers) State Insurance Supervisory Agencies
Versicherungsaufsichtsgesetz n (Vers) Law on the Supervision of Insurance Companies
Versicherungsbedingungen fpl
(Vers) insurance conditions
- terms of a policy
Versicherungsbeginn m (Vers) commencement of insurance cover
Versicherungsbeitrag m (Vers) insurance premium
Versicherungsbestand m
(Vers) number of insured persons
- business in force
- insurance portfolio
Versicherungsbetrug m (Re) insurance fraud, § 265 StGB
Versicherungsdarlehen n (Fin) actuarial loan
Versicherungsdauer f (Vers) period insured
- period of coverage
- term of insurance
Versicherungsdeckung f (Vers) insurance cover
versicherungsfähig (Vers) insurable
versicherungsfähige Gefahren fpl (Vers) insurable risks
Versicherungsfähigkeit f (Vers) insurability
Versicherungsfall m (Vers) insured event (eg, disability, age limit)
versicherungsfreie Beschäftigung f (SozV) insurance-exempt employment
Versicherungsgegenstand m (Vers) subject matter of insurance
Versicherungsgeschäft n

(Vers) insurance business
- underwriting
Versicherungsgesellschaft *f* (Vers) insurance company
Versicherungsgesellschaft *f* **auf Gegenseitigkeit** (Vers) mutual insurance company
Versicherungsjahre *npl* (SozV) years of coverage (*or* insurance)
Versicherungskonsortium *n* (Vers) insurers' syndicate
Versicherungskosten *pl*
(ReW) cost of insurance
- insurance charges (*or* expenses)
Versicherungsleistungen *fpl* (Vers) insurance benefits
Versicherungsmakler *m* (Vers) insurance broker
Versicherungsmathematik *f* (Vers) actuarial theory
Versicherungsmathematiker *m* (Vers) actuary
versicherungsmathematisch (Vers) actuarial
versicherungsmathematische Grundlage *f* (Vers) actuarial basis
versicherungsmathematische Kostenermittlung *f* (Vers) actuarial valuation
versicherungsmathematischer Gegenwartswert *mpl* (Vers) present actuarial value
Versicherungsnehmer *m*
(Vers) person taking out insurance
- party contracting insurance
- insured
- policyholder
Versicherungsneugeschäft *n* (Vers) new insurance business
versicherungspflichtige Beschäftigung *f* (SozV) covered (*or* contributory) employment
Versicherungspflichtgrenze *f* (SozV) taxable wage base
(*ie, monthly earnings ceiling for the assessment of social insurance contributions; syn, Jahresarbeitsverdienstgrenze*)
versicherungspflichtiges Entgelt *n* (SozV) eligible income (*or* earnings)
Versicherungspolice *f* (Vers) insurance policy
Versicherungspraktiker *m* (Vers) insurance practitioner
Versicherungsprämie *f* (Vers) insurance premium
Versicherungsrisiko *n* (Vers) insured risk
Versicherungsrückkauf *m* (Vers) redemption of policy
Versicherungsrückkaufwert *m* (Vers) surrender value
Versicherungsschein *m* (Vers) insurance policy
Versicherungsschutz *m*
(Vers) insurance cover (*or* protection)
- coverage
Versicherungssparen *n* (Vers) saving through insurance companies
Versicherungssparte *f*
(Vers) line of insurance business
- insurance class
versicherungsstatistische Tabelle *f* (Vers) actuarial table
Versicherungssumme *f* (Vers) amount (*or* sum) insured
Versicherungstarif *m* (Vers) tariff
versicherungstechnisch (Vers) actuarial

versicherungstechnische Bilanz *f* (Vers) actuarial statement
versicherungstechnische Gewinn- und Verlustrechnung *f* (Vers) revenue account
versicherungstechnische Rücklagen *fpl* (Vers) technical reserves
versicherungstechnisches Ergebnis *n* (Vers) underwriting result
Versicherungsteuer *f* (StR) insurance tax
Versicherungsteuer-Durchführungsverordnung *f* (Re) Ordinance Regulating the Insurance Tax Law, of 20 Apr 1960
Versicherungsteuergesetz *n* (StR) Insurance Tax Law, as republished on 24 July 1959
Versicherungsträger *m*
(Vers) insurer
- insurance carrier
Versicherungsunterlagen *fpl* (Vers) insurance papers (*or* records)
Versicherungsunternehmen *n* (Vers) insurance company
Versicherungsurkunde *f* (Vers) insurance policy
Versicherungsverein *m* **auf Gegenseitigkeit** (Vers) mutual insurance society
Versicherungsverhältnis *n* (Vers) insurance relationship
Versicherungsverlängerung *f* (Vers) extension of policy
Versicherungsvertrag *m* (Vers) contract of insurance
Versicherungsvertrag *m* **schließen** (Vers) to take out an insurance policy
Versicherungsvertrag *m* **über Einmalbetrag** (Vers) single-premium insurance policy, § 30 EStDV
Versicherungsvertreter *m* (Vers) insurance agent (*ie, employee of the insurance company*)
Versicherungswert *m* (Vers) insurable value
Versicherungswert *m* **der Fracht** (Vers) freight insurance value
Versicherungswerte *mpl*
(Bö) insurance stocks
- insurances
Versicherungswirtschaft *f* (Vers) insurance industry
Versicherungszeit *f* (Vers) term of insurance
Versicherungszertifikat *n* (Vers) insurance certificate
Versicherungszweig *m* (Vers) insurance line
versilbern (Fin, infml) to convert into money
Versorgungseinrichtung *f* (Pw) pension organization
Versorgungsengpaß *m* (Vw, Bw) supply bottleneck
Versorgungsfall *m* (SozV, Vers) insured event (*ie, in the case of social insurance or pension fund*)
Versorgungsfreibetrag *m* (StR) personal exemption by way of statutory pensions or social security benefits, § 17 I ErbStG
Versorgungsgrad *m* (Vw) level of satisfaction (*or* utility)
Versorgungslage *f* (com) supply situation
Versorgungsunternehmen *n*
(Bw) utility
- (US) public service corporation
Versorgungswerk *n* (Pw) company pension system
Versorgungswerte *mpl* (Bö) utilities

Versorgungszusage f (Pw) employer's pension commitment
verspätet
 (com) late
 – behind schedule
verspätete Lieferung f (com) delayed (or late) delivery
verspäteter Einspruch m (Pat) late opposition
Verspätungsschaden m (Re) damage due to delayed performance
Verspätungszuschlag m (StR) delay penalty *(ie, up to 10% of the tax as finally determined or DM10,000 if return is not filed within the prescribed period)*
Versprechen n
 (Re) promise
 – engagement
 – undertaking
Versprechensempfänger m (Re) promisee
Versprechensgeber m (Re) promisor
verstaatlichen
 (Re) to nationalize
 – to take into public ownership *(eg, the banking or steel industry)*
verstaatliche Wirtschaftszweige mpl (Re) nationalized industries
Verstaatlichung f (Re) nationalization
verstärkte Absatzbemühungen fpl (Mk) intensified marketing efforts
Verstärkung f **der eigenen Mittel** (Fin) strenghtening of capital resources
verstauen (com) to stow (away)
versteckte Abwertung f (AuW) hidden devaluation
versteckte Arbeitslosigkeit f
 (Vw) disguised
 – hidden
 – camouflaged
 – fictitious ... unemployment
versteckte Aufwertung f (Vw) shadow revaluation
versteckte Ausfuhrprämie f (AuW) hidden (or undisclosed) export bounty *(eg, duty drawback, tax cuts)*
versteckte Besteuerung f (FiW) hidden taxation
versteckte Inflation f (Vw) hidden inflation
versteckte Preissenkung f (com) covered price cut
versteckter Arbeitskräfteüberschuß m (Pw) concealed surplus of labor
versteckter Dissens m
 (Re) latent ambiguity
 – hidden disagreement
versteckter Mangel m (Re) hidden (or latent) defect
versteckter Streik m (Pw) hidden (or camouflaged) strike
versteckte Subvention f (Vw) hidden subsidy
versteckte Überwälzung f (StR) hidden shifting of a tax
Versteifung f **des Geldmarktes** (Fin) tightening of the money market
Versteigerer m (com) auctioneer *(ie, at public sales by auction)*
versteigern
 (com) to auction (off) *(ie, at public sales by auction; eg, materials, stocks, surplus)*
 – to sell by public auction

 – to put up at auction
versteigert (com) sold by public auction
Versteigerung f
 (com) auction
 – sale by public auction *(syn, Auktion, Gant, Vergantung)*
Versteigerungsbedingungen fpl (Re) terms governing forced sale of real property, § 66 ZVG
Versteigerungserlös m (com) proceeds of an auction
Versteigerungsgericht n (Re) court in charge of judicial sale
Versteigerungslimit n (com) limit for bidding
Versteigerungsort m (com) place of auction
Versteigerungstermin m (Re) date of judicial sale, § 36 ZVG
Versteigerungsvermerk m (Re) entry of judicical sale in real estate register
verstetigen (com) to smooth out *(eg, cash flow, order intake)*
Verstetigung f (Vw) increasing steadiness
versteuerbar (StR) taxable
versteuern (StR) to pay tax (on)
versteuert
 (StR) net of tax
 – tax paid
Versteuerung f (StR) payment of tax (on)
verstimmen (Bö) to unsettle *(ie, the market)*
verstoßen gegen
 (Re) to violate
 – to infringe (on/upon)
 – to contravene
 – to disregard
 – to run afoul (of) *(eg, of competition law)*
Verstoß m
 (Re) violation
 – infringement
 – contravention
 – disregard
Verstoß m **gegen die guten Sitten** (Re) violation contra bonos mores
Verstrickung f (Re) attachment by execution *(see: Pfandentstrickung)*
Versuch m
 (Re) attempt *(eg, to commit an offense)*
 (IndE) trial
 – test
 – experiment
Versuch m **der Steuerhinterziehung** (StR) attempt at tax evasion, § 370 II AO
Versuchsabteilung f (Bw) experimental station
Versuchsanlage f (IndE) pilot plant
Versuchsanordnung f (Stat) experimental layout
Versuchsanstalt f (IndE) research department (or center)
Versuchsaufbau m (EDV) breadboard *(ie, experimental or mock-up model of any device)*
Versuchsauftrag m (IndE) experimental order
Versuchsballon m
 (Mk) try-on
 – trial baloon
Versuchsbetrieb m
 (IndE) trial operation
 – pilot plant scale production *(syn, Probebetrieb)*

Versuchsergebnisse *npl* (IndE) test results
Versuchsperson *f* (Mk) respondent
Versuchsplan *m* (Stat) experimental design
Versuchsplan *m* **mit Gittern** (Stat) lattice design
Versuchsstadium *n* (com) experimental stage
Versuchs- und Entwicklungskosten *pl* (ReW) cost of development and experiments
Versuchswerbung *f* (Mk) test marketing
Versuch *m* **und Irrtum** *m* (Log) trial and error
vertagen (com) to adjourn (for/till/until) *(eg, meeting, conference, trial)*
Vertagung *f* (Re) adjournment, § 227 ZPO
Vertagung *f* **auf unbestimmte Zeit** (Re) adjournment sine die
Vertauschung *f* (Math) interchange
Verteidiger *m* (Re) defense counsel
Verteidigungsausgaben *fpl*
 (VGR) public consumption – defense
 (FiW) defense expenditure *(or* outlays *or* spending)
Verteidigungsbeitrag *m* (FiW) defense contribution
Verteidigungsetat *m*
 (FiW) defense budget
 (FiW) defense appropriations
Verteidigungsinvestitionen *fpl* (FiW) capital outlays for defense purposes
verteilbarer Aufwand *m* **für Anlagegüter** (ReW) depreciable *(or* service) cost
verteilen
 (com) to distribute
 – to dole out *(eg, money for export financing)*
 (infml) to pass out *(eg, free samples of merchandise)*
 (KoR) to allocate
 – to assign
 – to distribute
 – to apportion
 – to trace (to)
Verteiler *m*
 (com) mailing *(or* distribution) list
 (com) share-out key
Verteilerkette *f* (Mk) distribution chain
Verteilerliste *f* (com) = **Verteiler**
Verteilernetz *n* (Mk) distribution network
Verteilerschlüssel *m* (com) share-out key
Verteilerzuschlag *m* (Vw) distribution markup
verteilte Kostenabweichungen *fpl* (KoR) redistributed cost
verteilte zeitliche Verzögerung *f* (Vw) distributed lag
Verteilung *f*
 (Vw, FiW) distribution
 (EG) share-out *(eg, of the EEC's limited fish stocks to member states)*
 (Mk) distribution
 (KoR) allocation
 – assignment
 – distribution
 – apportionment
Verteilung *f* **der Anschaffungs- und Herstellungskosten** (ReW) systematic, periodic allocation of cost *(ie, of limited-life assets)*
Verteilung *f* **des Nachlasses** (Re) distribution of the estate

Verteilung *f* **des Restvermögens** (Bw) distribution of remaining assets *(ie, on liquidating a partnership,* § 155 HGB)
Verteilung *f* **des Volkseinkommens** (VGR) distribution of national income
Verteilungsdichte *f* (Stat) frequency of distribution
verteilungsfrei (Stat) distribution free
verteilungsfreier Test *m* (Stat) distribution-free method
verteilungsfreie Statistik *f* (Stat) nonparametric statistics
Verteilungsfunktion *f* (Stat) distribution function
Verteilungsfunktion *f* **des Preises** (Vw) distribution function of prices
Verteilungsmaße *npl* (Stat) measures of distribution
Verteilungsmethode *f* (KoR) method of allocating joint product costs *(syn, Proportionalitätsmethode)*
Verteilungsmodus *m* (com) distribution formula
Verteilungspolitik *f* (Vw) distributional policy
Verteilungsproblem *n* (OR) transport problem
Verteilungsquote *f* (Vw) distributive share
Verteilungsrechnung *f* (VGR) incomes received method *(opp, Entstehungsrechnung, Verwendungsrechnung)*
Verteilungsschlüssel *m* (KoR) allocation base *(or* formula)
Verteilungsseite *f* (VGR) earnings side
Verteilungsspielraum *m*
 (Vw) distributive margin
 – room for distributive policy moves
 – scope for income redistribution
Verteilungstheorie *f* (Vw) theory of distribution
verteilungsunabhängiges Verfahren *n* (Stat) distribution-free method
Verteilungsverfahren *n* (Re) distribution proceedings, §§ 105 ff ZVG
Verteilung *f* **von Kostenabweichungen** (KoR) circulation of costs
Verteilzeitzuschlag *m* (IndE) delay allowance
verteuern (com) to raise prices
Verteuerung *f* (com) price increase
Vertikale *f* (Math) vertical line
vertikale Arbeitsmobilität *f* (Pw) vertical labor mobility
vertikale Diversifikation *f* (Bw) vertical diversification
vertikale Funktionssäule *f* (Bw) vertical functions
vertikale Gleichheit *f* (FiW) vertical equity *(syn, vertikale Gerechtigkeit)*
vertikale Integration *f* (Bw) vertical *(or* upward) integration
vertikale Konkurrenz *f* (Mk) vertical competition *(syn, sphärische Konkurrenz)*
vertikale Konzentration *f* (Bw) = *vertikale Integration*
vertikale Mobilität *f* (Vw) vertical *(or* upward) mobility
vertikale Preisbindung *f*
 (Kart) resale price maintenance
 – vertical price fixing
vertikale Prüfung *f* (EDV) vertical redundancy check, VRC
vertikaler Finanzausgleich *m* (FiW) vertical dis-

tribution of tax revenue *(ie, operating on the principle of general and special fiscal grants)*
vertikaler Kommunikationsweg *m* (Bw) vertical communication channel
vertikaler Zusammenschluß *m* (Re) vertical combination
vertikale Steuergerechtigkeit *f* (FiW) vertical equity
vertikales Wachstum *n* (Bw) vertical growth *(eg, forward or backward integration)*
vertikale Verflechtung *f* (Bw) vertical integration
vertikale Vorwärtsintegration *f* (Bw) forward vertical integration
vertikale Wettbewerbsbeschränkungen *fpl* (Kart) vertical restraints of competition
vertikale Zeichenachse *f* (EDV) stroke centerline
Vertikalkonzern *m* (Bw) vertical group (of affiliated companies)
Vertikalregistratur *f* (com) vertical filing *(syn, Steilablage)*
Vertikaltabulator *m* (EDV) vertical tabulation character, VT
Vertikalverbund *m* (Bw) vertical link *(ie, comprising all stages of production up to the final consumer)*
Vertrag *m*
(Re) agreement *(ie, general term)*
(Re) contract *(ie, schuldrechtlicher Vertrag)*
(Re) treaty *(ie, made between countries)*
Vertrag *m* **abschließen** (Re) = *Vertrag schließen*
Vertrag *m* **ändern** (Re) to reform a contract
Vertrag *m* **anfechten** (Re) to avoid a contract
Vertrag *m* **annehmen** (Re) to accept a contract
Vertrag *m* **aufheben**
(Re) to cancel
– to annul
– to nullify ... a contract
Vertrag *m* **aufkündigen** (Re, infml) to pull out of an agreement
Vertrag *m* **aufsetzen** (Re) to draft *(or* draw up) a contract
Vertrag *m* **aushandeln** (Re) to negotiate an agreement *(or* contract)
Vertrag *m* **auslegen** (Re) to construe *(or* interpret) the terms of a contract *(ie, to analyze it into its essential features)*
Vertrag *m* **brechen** (Re) to break *(or* violate) a contract
Vertrag *m* **einhalten**
(Re) to honor an agreement
– to meet the conditions of a contract
– to stand by a contract
– comply with the terms of a contract
Verträge *mpl* **mit Preisfestsetzung nach Kosten + Verrechnung fester Zuschläge** (com, US) cost-plus-a-fixed-fee contracts
Vertrag *m* **erfüllen**
(Re) to perform
– to fulfill
– to discharge ... a contract
– to perform one's duties under a contract
Vertrag *m* **kündigen** (Re) to terminate a contract
Vertrag *m* **läuft ab** (Re) contract expires
vertraglich
(Re) contractual

– by contract
– by agreement
vertraglich binden (Re) to bind by contract
vertragliche Anreize *mpl* (Bw) contractual incentives
vertragliche Beziehungen *fpl* (Re) contractual relations
vertragliche Bindung *f* (Re) contractual commitment *(or* engagement)
vertragliche Einigung *f* (Re) contractual agreement
vertragliche Frist *f* (Re) time specified by a contract
vertragliche Garantie *f* (Re) contractual guaranty
vertragliche Haftung *f* (Re) contractual liability
vertragliche Indexklausel *f* (Re) contractual indexing clause
vertragliche Laufzeit *f* (Re) contract period
vertragliche Lizenz *f* (Pat) contractual license
vertraglicher Anspruch *m*
(Re) claim under a contract
– contract claim
– contractual claim
vertragliche Rechte *npl* **und Pflichten** *fpl* (Re) contractual rights and duties
vertragliche Regelung *f* (Re) contractual arrangement
vertraglicher Güterstand *m* (Re) matrimonial regime elected by agreement
vertraglicher Haftungsausschluß *m* (Re) contractual exclusion of liability
vertraglicher Unternehmenszusammenschluß *m* (Kart) contract combination
vertraglicher Zinssatz *m* (Fin) contract rate of interest
vertraglicher Zusammenschluß *m* (Re) contractual association
vertragliches Nutzungsrecht *n* (Re) contractual right to use property
vertragliche Vereinbarung *f* (Re) contractual arrangement
vertragliche Verpflichtungen *fpl* **eingehen** (Re) to contract liabilities
vertraglich festgelegt
(Re) contract...
– contracted
– stipulated by contract
vertraglich festgelegter Zinssatz *m* (Fin) contract rate of interest
vertraglich festlegen (Re) = *vertraglich vereinbaren*
vertraglich geschuldete Leistung *f*
(Re) contractual obligation
– contract debt
Verträglichkeit *f* (EDV) compatibility
vertraglich vereinbaren
(Re) to agree
– to agree *(or* stipulate) by contract
– to agree contractually
vertraglich verpflichten, sich (Re) to bind oneself by contract
vertraglich verpflichtet (Re) bound by contract
Vertrag *m* **mit Preisgleitklausel** (Mk) fluctuation price contract
Vertrag *m* **paraphieren** (Re) to initial an agreement
Vertragsablauf *m* (Re) expiration of a contract

Vertragsabrede *f* (Re) contractual stipulation
Vertragsabschluß *m* (Re) conclusion of a contract
Vertragsänderung *f* (Re) alteration of a contract
Vertragsangebot *n* (Re) offer of a contract *(syn, Offerte)*
Vertragsannahme *f* (Re) acceptance of a contractual offer
Vertragsanspruch *m* (Re) contractual claim
Vertragsaufhebung *f* (Re) rescission of a contract
Vertragsauflösung *f*
 (Re) cancellation
 – discharge
 – termination ... of a contract
Vertragsaufsage *f* (Re) anticipatory breach of contract *(ie, serious and final refusal to perform in the future; special case of ‚positive Vertragsverletzung')*
Vertragsauslegung *f* (Re) interpretation (*or* construction) of (the terms of) a contract
Vertragsbedingungen *fpl*
 (Re) terms
 – conditions
 – provisions
 – stipulations ... of a contract
Vertragsbeendigung *f* (Re) termination of a contract
Vertragsbeginn *m* (Re) commencement of a contract
Vertragsbeitritt *m* (Re) accession to a treaty
Vertragsbestand *m* (Vers) total policies outstanding
Vertragsbestandteil *m* (Re) element of a contract
Vertragsbestimmung *f* (Re) contractual provision (*or* stipulation)
Vertragsbeteiligter *m* (Re) party to an agreement (*or* contract)
Vertragsbeziehungen *fpl* (Re) contractual relations
Vertragsbruch *m* (Re) breach of a contract
Vertrag *m* **schließen**
 (Re) to conclude
 – to contract
 – to enter into
 – to make
 – to sign ... an agreement
Vertragsdauer *f* (Re) contractual period *(ie, period for which the contract is to run)*
Vertragsentwurf *m* (Re) draft contract (*or* agreement)
Vertragserfüllung *f*
 (Re) completion
 – discharge
 – fulfillment
 – performance ... of a contract
Vertragserfüllung *f* **ablehnen** (Re) to repudiate a contract
Vertragsformeln *fpl* (com) trade terms *(see: Incoterms)*
Vertragsformen *fpl* (Vers) types of cover
Vertragsforschung *f* (Bw) contract research *(ie, awarded to research institutes, universities, or other firms)*
Vertragsfreiheit *f* (Re) freedom of contract
Vertragsgebiet *n* (com) contractual territory
Vertragsgegenstand *m* (Re) subject matter of a contract

Vertragsgegner *m*
 (Re) contracting party
 – party to an agreement (*or* contract)
vertragsgemäß
 (Re) as per agreement
 – conformable to the contract
 – contractual
vertragsgemäße Erzeugnisse *npl* (Re) contract products
vertragsgemäße Güter *npl* (Re) conforming goods
vertragsgerechte Funktionstüchtigkeit *f* (Re) performance as stipulated
vertragsgerechte Ware *f* (Re) = *vertragsgerechte Güter*
Vertragsgrundlage *f* (Re) basis of agreement (*or* contract)
Vertragshaftung *f* (Re) contract(ual) liability *(ie, liability founded upon the express or implied terms of a contract)*
Vertragshändler *m* (Mk) authorized (*or* franchised) dealer
Vertragshändlervertrag *m* (Re) dealer's contract
Vertragskonzern *m* (Bw) contract-based group of affiliated companies *(opp, Beteiligungskonzern)*
vertragsmäßiges Rücktrittsrecht *n* (Re) right of rescission under a contract, § 327 BGB
Vertragsparteien *fpl*
 (Re) contracting parties
 – parties to an agreement (*or* contract)
 – the parties hereto *(ie, in contract wording)*
Vertragspartner *m* (Re) = *Vertragsparteien*
Vertragspfandrecht *n* (Re) contractual lien *(ie, arising by stipulation of the parties; opp, gesetzliches Pfandrecht)*
Vertragspflichten *fpl*
 (Re) contractual duties (*or* obligations)
 – duties under a contract
Vertragspreis *m* (com) contract price
Vertragsrecht *n* (Re) law of contracts
Vertragsrechte *npl*
 (Re) contractual rights
 – rights under a contract
Vertrags-Rückversicherung *f* (Vers) treaty reinsurance
Vertragsschluß *m*
 (Re) conclusion
 – formation
 – making ... of a contract
Vertragssparen *n* (Fin) scheme-linked saving
Vertragsstrafe *f*
 (Re) contract penalty
 – penalty for nonperformance of contract
 – time penalty under a contract
 – (GB) liquidated damages
 (ie, promise to pay a stipulated sum of money if work is not completed on schedule, §§ 339ff BGB, § 348 HGB; syn, Konventionalstrafe. Note that ‚liquidated damages' is a sum fixed as an estimate of the extent of the injury which a breach of contract will cause.)
Vertragstarif *m* (Zo) conventional tariff
Vertragsteil *m* (Re) = *Vertragspartner*
Vertragstermin *m*
 (com) contract deadline
 – deadline for performance of contract

635

vertragstreue Partei f (Re) nondefaulting (or nonbreaching) party
Vertragstyp m (Re) type of contract
Vertrag m **sui generis** (Re) contract sui generis
Vertragsurkunde f (Re) contractual document
Vertragsverhältnis n
  (Re) contractual relationship
  – relation ex contractu
Vertragsverlängerung f (Re) extension (or renewal) of a contract
Vertragsverletzung f
  (Re) breach (or violation) of contract
  – breach of duty to perform
Vertragsverpflichtung f (Re) contractual obligation
Vertragswerk n (Re) set of agreements
vertragswidrig
  (Re) contrary to
  – not conforming to
  – not conformable to
  – not in keeping with
  – in violation of ... a contract
Vertragswidrigkeit f
  (Re) contractual defect
  – lack of conformity with the contract
Vertragswille m
  (Re) meeting (or union) of minds of the contracting parties
  – intention of the parties to a contract
Vertragszollsatz m (Zo) contractual (or conventional) rate of customs duty
Vertrag m **über den Zuschlag** (com) purchase award contract
Vertrag m **unterzeichnen** (Re) to sign a contract
Vertrag m **verlängern** (Re) to renew a contract
Vertrag m **verletzen** (Re) to violate a contract
Vertrag m **widerrufen** (Re) to repudiate a contract
Vertrag m **zugunsten Dritter** (Re) third-party beneficiary contract
Vertrag n **zur Gründung der Europäischen Gemeinschaft** (EG) Treaty establishing the European Economic Community
Vertrag m **zur Gründung der Europäischen Gemeinschaft für Kohle und Stahl** (EG) Treaty establishing the European Coal and Steel Community
Vertrag m **zur Gründung der Europäischen Wirtschaftsgemeinschaft** (EG) Treaty establishing the European Economic Community
Vertrauensarzt m (SozV) physician acting as medical referee under social insurance legislation, § 369b RVO
Vertrauensbereich m (Stat) confidence belt (or interval or range or region) (syn, Konfidenzbereich)
Vertrauensbruch m (Re) breach of faith
Vertrauensentzug m **durch die Hauptversammlung** (Re) vote of no-confidence of a shareholders' meeting
Vertrauensgrenze f (Stat) confidence limit
Vertrauensinteresse n (Re) negative interest, § 122 BGB (ie, damage resulting from bona fide reliance on validity of contract; syn, negatives Interesse; opp, Erfüllungsinteresse, positives Interesse)
Vertrauensintervall n (Stat) = Vertrauensbereich

Vertrauenskoeffizient m (Stat) confidence coefficient
Vertrauensmänner mpl (Pw) union shop stewards
Vertrauensniveau n (Stat) confidence level (syn, Konfidenzniveau)
Vertrauensschaden m (Re) = Vertrauensinteresse
Vertrauensschaden-Versicherung f (Vers) commercial fidelity insurance
Vertrauensstellung f (Pw) confidential (or fiduciary) position
Vertrauensverhältnis n (Re) confidential (or fiduciary) relation
Vertrauenswerbung f (Mk) institutional advertising
vertraulicher Bericht m (com) confidential report
vertrauliches Schriftstück n (com) confidential document
vertretbar
  (Re) justifiable
  – defensible
  – reasonable
  (com) fungible
vertretbare Sachen fpl (Re) fungible goods, § 91 BGB
vertretbare Waren fpl (Re) fungible (or merchantable) goods
vertretbare Wertpapiere npl (Fin) fungible securities
Vertretbarkeit f
  (Re) justifiability
  (com) fungibility
vertreten
  (com) to act for (or in place of)
  – to deputize for
  – to substitute for
  (Re) to represent (ie, said of lawyers)
  – (GB) to act for
  (Re) to answer for
  – to be responsible for
Vertretener m (Re) principal
  (ie, person for whom someone else acts as a representative, § 70 AO)
Vertreter m
  (Re) attorney-in-fact, § 164 BGB
  – agent
  (com) deputy
  – substitute
  – proxy
  (Mk) salesman (saleswoman)
  – sales representative
  (Mk) traveling salesman
  – (GB) commercial traveller
  (Vers) insurance agent
Vertreterbericht m
  (com) agent's report
  – call slip
Vertreterbesuch m (com) sales call
Vertreterbezirk m (com) agent's territory
Vertreterkosten pl (KoR) agency expenses
Vertreter m **ohne Vertretungsmacht** f
  (Re) unauthorized agent
  – (civil law) falsus procurator
  (ie, attorney-in-fact without proper authority, § 179 BGB)
Vertreterorganisation f (Mk) sales force
Vertreterprovision f

(com) agency fee
- agent's commission
Vertreterstab *m* (com) staff of representatives
Vertreterversandhandel *m* (com) traveling salesman's trade *(ie, door-to-door canvassing of mail orders)*
Vertretervertrag *m* (Re) agency agreement
Vertretervollmacht *f* (Vers) commission of authority
Vertretung *f*
(com) substitution
- deputizing
- proxy
(Re) agency, § 164 BGB *(ie, used for cases in which agent is acting openly in the name of principal)*
(com) representation
Vertretung *f* **gemeinsamer Interessen** (Bw) promotion *(or* furtherance) of common interests
Vertretungsberechtigter *m*
(Re) person acting for and on/in behalf of
- authorized representative
Vertretungsgrundsatz *m* (Re) principle of representation
Vertretungsmacht *f* (Re) power of representation *(or* to represent) *(opp, Geschäftsführungsbefugnis)*
Vertretungsmacht *f* **überschreiten**
(Re) to act in excess of authority
- to exceed one's instructions as an agent
(ie, to do an act outside the scope of the purpose for which agent has been appointed)
Vertretungsverhältnis *n* (Re) agency
Vertretungsvertrag *m* (Re) contract of agency
Vertretungszwang *m* (Re) mandatory representation *(ie, by lawyer in court)*
Vertrieb *m*
(Mk) distribution
- selling
- marketing
(Mk) marketing department
Vertrieb *m* **nach dem Schneeballprinzip**
(Mk) multi-level distributorship
- pyramid selling
Vertriebsabteilung *f* (Mk) marketing department
Vertriebsaufwendungen *fpl* (ReW) selling expenses
Vertriebsberater *m* (Mk) marketing consultant
Vertriebsbereich *m* (Bw) sales function *(or* sector)
Vertriebsbindung *f* (Kart) distributional restraint
Vertriebsbüro *n* (com) selling agency
Vertriebseinrichtung *f* (Kart) selling organization, § 5 III GWB
Vertriebseinrichtungen *fpl* (Kart) distribution facilities
Vertriebsergebnis *n* (Bw) sales results
Vertriebsfunktion *f* (Mk) marketing function
Vertriebsgebiet *n* (Mk) sales territory
Vertriebsgemeinkosten *pl* (KoR) selling overhead *(or* expense)
Vertriebsgesellschaft *f* (Bw) selling *(or* marketing) company *(ie, preferred form: Vertriebskapitalgesellschaft, either AG or GmbH)*
Vertriebskartell *n* (Kart) sales cartel
Vertriebskonsortium *n*

(Fin) selling group
- selling *(or* trading) syndicate
Vertriebskosten *pl*
(KoR) distribution *(or* selling) expense
- sales cost
Vertriebskostenanalyse *f* (Mk) distribution cost analysis
Vertriebskostenrechnung *f* (Mk) distributive costing
Vertriebskostenstelle *f* (KoR) sales department cost center
(syn, Vertriebsstelle)
Vertriebslager *n* (Mk) sales depot
Vertriebsleiter *m* (Mk) sales *(or* marketing) manager
Vertriebsleitung *f* (Mk) sales *(or* marketing) management
Vertriebsmittel *npl* (Mk) marketing tools
Vertriebsnetz *n* (Mk) marketing network
Vertriebsorganisation *f* (Mk) marketing organization
Vertriebsplan *m*
(Mk) marketing plan
- sales budget
Vertriebspolitik *f* (Mk) distribution *(or* marketing) policy
Vertriebsrecht *n* (Re) right of sale
Vertriebsrisiken *npl* (Mk) general marketing risks
Vertriebsschulung *f* (Mk) marketing training
Vertriebsspanne *f* (Mk) sales margin
Vertriebsstelle *f* (Mk) sales outlet
Vertriebsstrategie *f* (Mk) marketing strategy
Vertriebstochter *m* (Mk) marketing subsidiary
Vertriebs- und Verwaltungsgemeinkosten *pl*
(KoR) selling and administrative expense
- general operating expense
Vertriebswagnis *n* (ReW) accounts receivable risk
(syn, Debitorenwagnis)
Vertriebsweg *m*
(com) distributive channel
- channel of distribution
Verursachungsprinzip *n* (Vw) principle of causation
vervielfältigen (com) to duplicate
Vervielfältiger *m*
(Math) multiplier
(com) duplicator
vervielfältigte Unterschrift *f* (com) facsimile signature
verwahren (com) to hold in safe custody
verwahrende Bank *f* (Fin) custodian bank
Verwahrer *m* (Re) depositary
Verwahrung *f*
(Re) custody
(Fin) safekeeping *(eg, of securities)*
- (GB) safe custody *(or* storage)
Verwahrungsbuch *n* (Fin) custody ledger
Verwahrungsgebühr *f* (Fin) custody fee
Verwahrungsgeschäft *n* (Fin) custody transactions
Verwahrungslager *n* (Zo) temporary store
Verwahrungsstücke *npl* (Fin) custody items
Verwahrungsvertrag *m* (Re) custody agreement
(ie, for the safekeeping of movables, whether for reward or otherwise, § 688 BGB)
verwalten

(Bw) to administer
– to manage
verwaltende Funktionen *fpl* (Bw) administrative (*or* custodial) functions
verwaltetes Vermögen *n* (Fin) agency fund
Verwaltung *f* (Bw) administration
– management
(Bw) administrative department
Verwaltungsakt *m* (StR) administrative act (*or* decision)
Verwaltungsakt *m* **aufheben** (StR) to vacate an administrative decision
Verwaltungsaktien *fpl* (Fin) management shares *(ie, held in treasury, usu. by an underwriting group on behalf of company's management)*
Verwaltungsapparat *m* (Bw) administrative machinery
Verwaltungsarbeiten *fpl* (com) administrative work
Verwaltungsaufwand *m* (ReW) administrative expense
Verwaltungsausschuß *m* (EG) management committee
Verwaltungsbehörde *f* (Re) administrative agency
Verwaltungsbeirat *m* (Re) advisory council
Verwaltungsbeschwerde *f* (Re) appeal taken against an administrative decision
Verwaltungsentscheidung *f* (Re) administrative decision
Verwaltungsermessen *n* (Re) administrative discretion
Verwaltungsfachmann *m* (Bw) administrator
Verwaltungsgebäude *n* (Bw) administrative (*or* commercial) building
Verwaltungsgebühr *f*
(Re) administrative fee (*or* charge)
(Fin) management fee
Verwaltungsgemeinkosten *pl* (KoR) general and administrative overhead (*or* expense)
Verwaltungsgericht *n*
(Re) first-instance administrative court
– administrative court of original jurisdiction
Verwaltungsgerichtsbarkeit *f* (Re) system of administrative jurisdiction
Verwaltungsgerichtshof *m* (Re) appellate administrative court *(ie, term allowed under provincial law for ‚Oberverwaltungsgericht')*
Verwaltungsgerichtsordnung *f* (Re) Code of Administrative Procedure, of 21 Jan 1960
Verwaltungsgesellschaft *f* (Fin) management company
Verwaltungsinvestitionen *fpl* (FiW) government capital expenditure
Verwaltungskosten *pl* (KoR) administrative expense
Verwaltungskostenanteil *m* (Vers) portion of administrative expense included in premium income
Verwaltungskostenstelle *f* (KoR) administration cost center *(syn, Verwaltungsstelle)*
Verwaltungskostenzuschlag *m* (Vers) (margin of) loading
Verwaltungskredit *m* (Fin) transmitted loan
Verwaltungskredite *mpl* (FiW) borrowing to smooth out budgetary irregularities

Verwaltungsorgan *n* (Re) administrative body
Verwaltungsrat *m*
(Re) administrative board
– board of administration
(ie, of public bodies; opp, supervisory board of stock corporations)
(Bw) board of directors *(ie, of companies outside Germany)*
Verwaltungsrecht *n* (Re) administrative law
Verwaltungsrechtsweg *m* (Re) recourse to administrative tribunals *(opp, recourse to ordinary courts)*
– administrative remedies
Verwaltungsstelle *f* (KoR) = Verwaltungskostenstelle
Verwaltungtreuhand *f* (Re) administrative trust
Verwaltungsverfahren *n* (Re) administrative procedural practise
Verwaltungsverfahrensgesetz *n* (Re) Law on Administrative Procedure, of 25 May 1976
Verwaltungsvermögen *n* (Re) assets serving administrative purposes *(ie, schools, hospitals, barracks, etc.)*
Verwaltungsverordnung *f* (Re) administrative decree
Verwaltungsverfahrensgesetz *n* (Re) Law on Administrative Procedures, of 25 May 1976
Verwaltungsvertrag *m*
(Bw) business management agreement *(syn, Betriebsführungsvertrag)*
(Fin) investment contract
Verwaltungsvorschriften *fpl* (Re) administrative regulations
Verwaltungszwangsverfahren *n* (Re) administrative execution procedure
verwandte Erfindung *f* (Pat) cognate invention
verwässertes Grundkapital *n* (Fin) diluted (*or* watered) capital
Verwässerung *f* **des Aktienkapitals**
(Fin) dilution of equity
– stock watering
Verwechslungsgefahr *f* (Re) risk of confusion *(ie, of firm names)*
Verwechslung *f* **von Warenzeichen** (Pat) confusion of trade mark
Verweigerung *f* **des Bestätigungsvermerks** (ReW) disclaimer of audit opinion
Verweigerungsliste *f* (AuW, US) denial list
Verweildauer *f* (SozV) length of stay *(ie, in hospital)*
Verweilzeit *f*
(OR) expected waiting + service time
(EDV) elapsed (*or* job around) time *(syn, Auftragsumlaufzeit)*
Verweis *m* (ReW) censure, § 68 WPO
Verweisadresse *f* (EDV) chaining address
verweisen an (Re) to refer to
Verweisung *f* **an ein Schiedsgericht** (Re) reference to arbitration
verwendbares Eigenkapital *n* (StR) distributable equity capital
– available net equity
(ie, generic term for all balance-sheet items that can be the object of a corporate distribution, § 27 KStG 1977)

Verwender *m* (com) user
Verwendung *f* **des BIP** (VGR) use of GDP (*or* gross domestic product)
Verwendung *f* **des Bruttosozialprodukts** (VGR) expenditure on gross national product
Verwendung *f* **des Reingewinns** (ReW) appropriation of net income
Verwendungen *fpl* (Re) outlays for the maintenance or improvement of property
Verwendungsdauer *f* (Bw) service life
Verwendungsrechnung *f*
  (VGR) consumption-plus-investment method
  – (GB) consumption-savings method
Verwendungsschein *m* (EG) document for temporary importation
Verwendungsseite *f* (VGR) expenditure side
Verwendungszwang *m* (AuW) mixing and tying requirements
Verwerfen *n*
  (Stat) refusal
  – final rejection
Verwerfung *f* **der Buchführung** (StR) rejection of the accounting system *(ie, by tax authorities, Abschn. 29 II No. 6 EStR)*
verwerten
  (com) to utilize
  (Re) to realize
Verwertung *f*
  (com) utilization
  (Re) realization *(ie, by judicial sale or otherwise)*
Verwertung *f* **e-s Patents**
  (Pat) exploitation
  – use
  – working ... of a patent
Verwertungsaktien *fpl* (Fin) = *Vorratsaktien*
Verwertungsgesellschaft *f* (Bw) company or partnership exploiting third-party rights
Verwertungskonsortium *n* (Fin) selling syndicate
Verwertungsrechte *npl* (Pat) rights of exploitation, §§ 15 ff UrhG
verwirken
  (Re) to forfeit
  (Re) to incur *(eg, a penalty)*
verwirkte Strafe *f* (Re) forfeited penalty, § 343 BGB
Verwirkung *f* (Re) forfeiture *(eg, of contractual rights, § 360 BGB)*
Verwirkung *f* **des Rücktrittsrechts** (Re) forfeiture of right of rescission
Verwirkungsklausel *f* (Re) forfeiture clause
Verwürfler *m* (EDV) scrambler
verzahnen
  (EDV) to interlace
  – to interleave
verzahnt ablaufende Verarbeitung *f*
  (EDV) concurrent processing
  – multi-processing
Verzahnung *f*
  (EDV) interlacing
  – interleaving
Verzahnung *f* **zwischen System und Struktur** (Bw) crosswalk
verzeichnen
  (com) to record

(com) to post *(eg, large increases in orders received)*
Verzeichnis *n* **der Patentklassen** (Pat) class index of patents
verzerrende Schätzfunktion *f* (Stat) biased estimator
verzerrte Auswahl *f* (Stat) selective bias
verzerrte Prüfung *f* (Stat) biased test
verzerrte Stichprobe *f* (Stat) biased sample
Verzerrungen *fpl* **des internationalen Handels** (AuW) nontariff distortions of international trade *(ie, wider than ‚nontariff barriers')*
Verzerrung *f* **nach oben** (Stat) upward bias
Verzerrung *f* **nach unten** (Stat) downward bias
Verzicht *m*
  (Re) disclaimer
  – waiver
  (Re) release agreement, § 397 I BGB *(syn, Erlaßvertrag, qv)*
Verzicht *m* **auf die gesetzmäßigen und satzungsmäßigen Formalitäten und Fristen für die Einberufung der Hauptversammlung** (Re) waiver of notice
Verzicht *m* **auf Ersatzansprüche** (Re) waiver of claims for damages
Verzicht *m* **auf Steuerbefreiungen** (StR) waiver of exemption, § 4 No. 6 ff UStG
Verzicht *m* **auf Stundungszinsen** (StR) waiver of interest on delinquent taxes, § 234 II AO
verzichten auf
  (com) to pass up *(eg, cheap prices offered by subcontractors)*
  (Re) to disclaim
  – to waive
Verzichterklärung *f*
  (Re) (notice of) disclaimer
  – waiver
verzinsen
  (Fin) to pay interest (on)
  (Fin) to bear (*or* yield) interest
verzinslich (Fin) bearing interest
verzinsliche Forderung *f* (Fin) interest-bearing debt
verzinsliches Darlehen *n* (Fin) interest-bearing loan
verzinsliches Guthaben *n* (Fin) money drawing interest *(ie, in a bank account)*
verzinsliches Sonderdarlehen *n* (Fin) special interest-bearing loan
verzinslich mit (Fin) bearing interest at the rate of
Verzinsung *f*
  (Fin) rate of interest
  (Fin) return
  (Fin) interest payment
Verzinsung *f* **des eingesetzten Kapitals** (Fin) return on capital employed
Verzinsungsverbot *n* (Vw) ban on interest payments *(ie, in deposits of nonresidents)*
verzögern
  (com) to delay
  – to retard
  – to slow
  – (infml) to hold up
  – to put back *(eg, decision, production, delivery)*
verzögernde Einrede *f* (Re) dilatory defense (*or*

639

exception) *(ie, not tending to defeat an action, but only to retard its progress; syn, dilatorische Einrede)*
verzögerte Anpassung *f* (Vw) lagged adjustment
verzögerte Ausstoßvariable *f* (Vw) lagged output term
verzögerte Auszahlung *f* **des Akkreditivbetrages** (Fin) deferred payment
verzögerte endogene Variable *f* (Stat) lagged endogenous variable
verzögerte Funktion *f* (Vw) lagged function
verzögerte Investitionsfunktion *f* (Vw) lagged investment function
verzögerte Konsumfunktion *f* (Vw) lagged consumption function
verzögerte Variable *f* (Vw) lagged variable
Verzögerung *f*
  (com) delay
  – retardation
  (OR) slip
  – slippage
Verzögerungsleitung *f* (EDV) delay line
Verzögerungstaktik *f* (com) delaying *(or* postponement) tactics
Verzögerungszeit *f* (EDV) deceleration time
verzollen (Zo) to clear through the customs
verzollt
  (Zo) customs cleared
  – duty paid
verzollte Ware *f* (com) goods out of bond
Verzollung *f* (Zo) customs clearance
Verzollung *f* **bei Auslagerung** (Zo) clearance from bonded warehouse
Verzollungsförmlichkeiten *fpl* (Zo) customs clearance formalities
Verzollungsgebühren *fpl* (Zo) customs clearance charges
Verzollungskosten *pl* (Zo) clearance charges
Verzollungsmaßstäbe *mpl* (Zo) bases of customs duties *(ie, percentages, quantities)*
Verzollungspapiere *npl* (Zo) clearance papers
Verzollungswert *m*
  (Zo) customs *(or* declared) value
  – current domestic value
Verzug *m*
  (Re) delayed performance
  – delay in performance
  (ie, term unknown in English law; the legal consequences of delayed performance depend on ,whether time is of the essense of the contract or not')
  (Fin) default *(eg, on loan agreement)*
Verzugsschaden *m* (Re) damage caused by delayed performance, § 286 BGB
Verzugsstrafe *f* (Re) penalty for delayed delivery
Verzugszinsen *mpl*
  (Fin) (penalty) interest on arrears, § 288 BGB
  – interest on defaulted payment
verzweigen (EDV) to branch
verzweigte Phasenfolge *f* (OR) branched-phase sequence
Verzweigung *f* (EDV) branch *(syn, jump)*
Verzweigungsadresse *f* (EDV) branch address
Verzweigungsbefehl *m* (EDV) branch instruction
Verzweigungspunkt *m*

(Math) branch *(or* winding) point *(ie, of Rieman surface)*
(EDV) branch(ing) point
Verzweigungsschnitt *m* (Math) branch cut
Video-Recorder *m* (com) video tape recorder, VTR
vieldeutige Abbildung *f* (Math) relation
vieldeutige Funktion *f* (Math) many-valued function
Vieleck *n* (Math) polygon
Vielfachleitung *f*
  (EDV) highway
  – bus
Vielfachzugriffssystem *n* (EDV) multi-user system
vielflächiger Graph *m* (Math) polyhedral graph
Vielkanten-Netzplan *m* (OR) multi-branch network
Vielschutzdeckung *f* (Vers) multiple-protection insurance
vielseitig (com) versatile
Vielseitigkeit *f* (com) versatility
Vieradreßbefehl *m* (EDV) three-plus-one address instruction
Vieradreßcode *m* (EDV) four address code
Vierfeldertafel *f* (Stat) two-by-two table
Vierschaltungseinheit *f* (EDV) quad *(ie, four separately insulated conductors twisted together)*
Vier-Sektoren-Wirtschaft *f* (VGR) four-sector economy
vierstelliger Junktor *m* (Log) quaternary connective
Vierteljahresbericht *m* (ReW) quarterly statement
Vierteljahresbeträge *mpl* (com) quarterly contributions
Vierteljahresdividende *f* (Fin) quarterly dividend
Vierteljahresgeld *n* (Fin) three-month (money)
Vierteljahresprämie *f* (Vers) quarterly premium
vierteljährliche Kreditnehmer-Statisitk *f* (Fin) quarterly summary reports on credits extended to resident borrowers as per the end of each calendar quarter
Vierzig-Stunden-Woche *f* (Pw) forty-hour week
Vinkulationsgeschäft *n* (com) lending on goods in rail transit
vinkulieren (Fin) to restrict transferability
vinkulierte Namensaktie *f* (Fin) registered share not freely transferable *(ie, transfer inter vivos contingent upon the consent of the corporation, § 68 AktG)*
Vinkulierung *f* (Fin) restriction of transferability
Virement *n* (FiW) virement
virtuelle Adresse *f* (EDV) virtual address *(syn, real address)*
virtueller Speicher *m* (EDV) virtual memory
virtuelle Verbindung *f* (EDV) virtual circuit
Visitenkarte *f* (com) calling *(or* visiting) card
visueller Trend *m* (Stat) visual trend
Vitationskonflikt *m* (Bw) minus-minus conflict
Vogel-Strauß-Politik *f* (com) ostrich approach
Volksbank *f* (Fin) people's bank
Volkseinkommen *n* (VGR) national income *(eg, net national product at factor cost)*
Volkseinkommensgleichung *f* (Vw) income and expenditure equation
Volkshochschule *f* (Pw, appr) adult evening classes
Volksvermögen *n* (VGR) national wealth

Volksvermögensrechnung *f* (VGR) national balance sheet
Volkswirtschaft *f*
(Vw) economy
– economy as a whole
(Vw) = *Volkswirtschaftslehre*
Volkswirtschaft *f* **im Gleichgewicht** (Vw) balanced economy
volkswirtschaftlich (Vw) economic
volkswirtschaftliche Erträge *mpl* (Vw) social returns
volkswirtschaftliche Gesamtanalyse *f* (VGR) macroeconomic analsysis
volkswirtschaftliche Gesamtausgaben *fpl* (VGR) national expenditure
volkswirtschaftliche Gesamtgrößen *fpl* (Vw) aggregates *(ie, of economic activity)*
– broad totals
– economy-wide totals
volkswirtschaftliche Gesamtnachfrage *f* (Vw) aggregate demand
volkswirtschaftliche Gesamtplanung *f* (Vw) overall economic planning
– ‚planification'
volkswirtschaftliche Gesamtrechnung *f* (VGR) national accounting (system)
– national accounts
– macroeconomic accounting
volkswirtschaftliche Indifferenzkurve *f* (Vw) community indifference curve
volkswirtschaftliche Indikatoren *mpl* (Vw) social indicators
volkswirtschaftliche Kosten *pl* (Vw) social (*or* external) costs
volkswirtschaftliche Liquiditätsquote *f* (Vw) liquidity ratio of the economy
volkswirtschaftliche Nutzen *mpl* (Vw) social benefits
volkswirtschaftliche Planung *f* (Vw) economic planning
volkswirtschaftlicher Produktionsprozeß *m* (Vw) aggregate production process
volkswirtschaftliche Sparquote *f* (VGR) aggregate savings ratio
volkswirtschaftliches Rechnungswesen *n* (VGR) aggregate economic accounting
volkswirtschaftliche Theorie *f* (Vw) economic theory (*or* analysis)
volkswirtschaftliche Theorie *f* **der Firma** (Vw) theory of the firm
volkswirtschaftliche Verflechtungsmatrix *f* (Vw) input-output table
volkswirtschaftliche Vermögensbildung *f* (Vw) aggregate wealth formation
volkswirtschaftliche Wertschöpfung *f* (VGR) aggregate value added
Volkswirtschaftslehre *f* (Vw) economics *(syn, Wirtschaftswissenschaft, Nationalökonomie, Sozialökonomie, Politische Ökonomie)*
Volkswirtschaftspolitik *f* (Vw) = *Wirtschaftspolitik*
Volkszählung *f* (Stat) population census
Vollabschreibung *f* (ReW) immediate writeoff
voll abzugsfähig (FiW) fully tax deductible
voll abzugsfähige Sonderausgaben *fpl* (StR) fully deductible special expenses

Volladdierer *m* (EDV) full (*or* digital) adder *(syn, Addierglied, Addierwerk, Volladdierglied)*
Volladdierglied *n* (EDV) digital adder
Vollamortisationsvertrag *m* (Mk) full payout leasing contract
Vollanrechnungssystem *n* (StR) full credit system
Vollarbeitskräfte *fpl* (Fw) full-time employees
voll ausgebildet (Pw) fully trained
Vollauslastung *f* (Bw) full capacity operation (*or* use)
Vollauslastung *f* **des Produktionspotentials** (Bw) full capacity use of capital stock
vollautomatisch (IndE) fully automatic
vollautomatische Fabrik *f* (IndE) fully automatic plant
vollautomatische Fertigung *f* (IndE) fully automatic assembly
vollautomatischer Betrieb *m* (IndE) fully automatic operation
Vollautomatisierung *f* (IndE) full automation
Vollbeendigung *f* **e-r Gesellschaft** (Re) final acts of liquidation, § 157 I HGB
Vollbeschäftigung *f*
(Vw) full employment *(ie, full utilization of resources; usu. limited to labor)*
(KoR) full capacity utilization (*or* use *or* operation)
– capacity working (*or* output *or* production)
Vollbeschäftigungsbudget *n* (FiW) full employment budget
Vollbeschäftigungsdefizit *n* (Vw) full employment deficit
Vollbeschäftigungsgrad *m* (Vw) full employment ratio
(ie, effective use of labor force to 100% full employment)
Vollbeschäftigungslücke *f* (Vw) gross national product gap
Vollbeschäftigungs-Output *m* (Vw) potential gross national product
Vollbeschäftigungspolitik *f* (Vw) full employment policy
Vollbeschäftigungsüberschuß *m* (FiW) full employment budget surplus
Vollbeschäftigungsüberschußbudget *n* (FiW) full employment surplus budget
Vollbeschäftigungswirtschaft *f* (Vw) full employment economy
Vollbeschäftigungsziel *n* (Vw) full employment goal
Vollcharter *f* (com) complete charter
volle Deliktsfähigkeit *f* (Re) unlimited capacity to commit unlawful acts
volle Haftung *f*
(Bw) unlimited
– full
– personal . . . liability *(syn, unbeschränkte Haftung)*
Volleindeckung *f* (Fin) unqualified cover
voll eingezahlte Aktien *fpl* (Fin) fully paid-up shares
voll eingezahltes Kapital *n* (ReW) fully paid-up capital
voll eingezahlte Versicherung *f* (Vers) paid-up insurance (*or* policy)

volle Konvertierbarkeit f (AuW) full (*or* unrestricted) convertibility
Vollerhebung f (Stat) full census *(ie, complete-population survey; opp, Teilerhebung)*
voller Lohnausgleich m (Pw) no loss of pay *(eg, when working time is cut)*
voller Satz m (com) full set *(eg, of bills of lading)*
voller Schluß m (Bö) full (*or* even) lot
volles Eigentum n (Re) unrestricted ownership
Vollfamilie f (Stat) full family *(opp, Kernfamilie)*
Vollfinanzierung f (Fin) 100% outside financing
voll gezeichnete Anleihe f (Fin) fully subscribed loan
Vollhafter m (Re) general partner *(syn, Komplementär; opp, Teilhafter, Kommanditist)*
Vollindossament n
(WeR) full indorsement
– indorsement in full *(opp, Blankoindossament)*
Volljährigkeit f
(Re) full
– legal
– legal . . . age
– majority *(ie, generally 18 years of age)*
Volljährigkeitserklärung f (Re, US) decree of full emancipation
volljährig werden
(Re) to come of age
– to attain majority (*or* full age)
Volljurist m (Re) fully trained lawyer *(opp, German facetious term: Schmalspurjurist)*
Vollkaskoversicherung f
(Vers) fully comprehensive cover *(opp, Teilkaskoversicherung)*
– full coverage insurance
– deductible clause collision insurance
Vollkaufmann m (Re) full (*or* fully qualified) merchant *(ie, registered in the Commercial Register and subject to all provisions of the HGB)*
volkommene Elastizität f (Vw) perfect elasticity
vollkommene homogene Konkurrenz f (Vw) pure competition
vollkommene Information f (Vw) complete information *(ie, of relevant events in past, present and future; opp, unvollkommene Information)*
vollkommene Konkurrenz f (Vw) = *vollständige Konkurrenz*
vollkommen elastisch (Vw) perfectly elastic
vollkommener Markt m (Vw) perfect market
vollkommen unelastisch (Vw) perfectly inelastic
Vollkonsolidierung f (ReW) full consolidation, § 329 AktG
Voll-Konvertibilität f (AuW) unrestricted convertibility
Vollkonzession f (Fin) unlimited banking license *(ie, issued by the banking supervisory authority)*
Vollkosten pl (KoR) full cost *(opp, Teilkosten)*
Vollkostenbasis f (KoR) absorbed (*or* full cost) basis
Vollkostenkalkulation f
(KoR) full cost pricing
– markup pricing *(ie, average variable cost + markup)*
Vollkostenprinzip n
(KoR) full cost principle
– markup principle

Vollkostenrechnung f (KoR) absorption (*or* full) costing
Vollkostenübernahme f
(Vers) comprehensive coverage
– (infml) „first-dollar" coverage
– provision of comprehensive benefits
Vollmacht f (Re) power of attorney *(ie, authority to act for and on/in behalf of)*
Vollmacht f **ausstellen** (Re) to execute a power of attorney (to)
Vollmachtsaktionär m (Fin) proxy shareholder, § 129 AktG
Vollmachtsformular n (Fin) form of proxy
Vollmachtsindossament n (WeR) collection indorsement
Vollmachtsinhaber m (Re) holder of a power of attorney
Vollmachtsstimmrecht n (Fin) proxy voting right
Vollmacht f **überschreiten** (Re) to exceed (*or* overstep) one's authority
Vollmachtsurkunde f
(Re) power of attorney
– letter of attorney (*or* authorization)
Vollmachtswiderruf m
(Re) rescission
– revocation
– withdrawal . . . of a power of attorney
Vollmitglied n (Re) full member
voll nutzen (com) to exploit to the fullest practicable extent
Volloperation f (EDV) complete operation
Vollprüfung f
(Stat) 100% (*or* screening) inspection
(ReW) detail audit
Vollsortiment n (Mk) full range of products
vollständig ausgezahlter Kredit m (Fin) fully paid-out loan
vollständig austauschen
(com) to replace completely
– (infml) to replace lock, stock and barrel
vollständige Abgabenbefreiung f (Zo) total exemption
vollständige Aussetzung f **der Zollsätze** (Zo) total suspension of customs duties
vollständige Disjunktion f
(Log) exclusive disjunction
– alternation
vollständige ganzzahlige Matrix f (OR) all-integer matrix
vollständige Induktion f (Log, Math) weak induction
vollständige Invalidität f (SozV) complete disablement
vollständige Konkurrenz f (Vw) perfect (*or* pure) competition
(syn, vollkommene Konkurrenz)
vollständige Operation f (EDV) complete operation
vollständiger Satz m (com) = *voller Satz*
vollständiger Übertrag m (EDV) complete carry
vollständiger Wettbewerb m (Vw) = *vollständige Konkurrenz*
vollständiges Monopol n (Vw) absolute monopoly
vollständiges Programm n (EDV) complete routine

vollständige Unelastizität f (Vw) complete (or perfect) inelasticity (ie, of supply and demand)
vollständig ganzzahliger Algorithmus m (OR) all-integer algorithm
vollständig gezeichnete Anleihe f (Fin) fully subscribed loan
vollständig zerlegt (IndE) completely knocked down, CKD
vollstreckbar (Re) enforceable by execution
vollstreckbare Ausfertigung f (Re) enforceable proof of indebtedness, § 724 ZPO
vollstreckbare Entscheidung f
  (Re) decision capable of execution
  – enforceable decision
vollstreckbare Forderung f (Re) enforceable claim
vollstreckbarer Titel m (Re) = *Vollstreckungstitel*
vollstreckbare Urkunde f (Re) enforceable instrument (ie, allowing creditor to have execution levied upon debtor, § 794 I 5 ZPO)
Vollstreckbarkeit f (Re) enforceability by execution
Vollstreckung f
  (Re) judicial enforcement
  – execution
Vollstreckung f **aussetzen** (Re) to stay execution of decision
Vollstreckungsabwehrklage f (Re) = *Vollstreckungsgegenklage*
Vollstreckungsbefehl m (Re) (obsolete) = *Vollstreckungsbescheid*
Vollstreckungsbehörde f (Re) law enforcement authority
Vollstreckungsbescheid m (Re) judicial order for execution (ie, für vollstreckbar erklärter Mahnbescheid)
Vollstreckungsgegenklage f (Re) action opposing judicial enforcement, § 767 ZPO (syn, *Vollstreckungsabwehrklage*)
Vollstreckungsgericht n (Re) court in charge of enforcement procedures, § 764 ZPO
Vollstreckungsgläubiger m (Re) execution creditor
Vollstreckungsmaßnahme f (StR) forcible tax collection
Vollstreckungsschuldner m (StR) execution debtor, § 253 AO
Vollstreckungsschutz m (Re) protection against unfair judicial execution, § 765a ZPO
Vollstreckungstitel m (Re) enforceable legal document (ie, judgement, attachment order, arbitration award, temporary injunction, etc.; syn, *Schuldtitel*)
Vollstreckungsvereitelung f (Re) frustration of a writ of execution, § 288 StGB
Vollstreckungsverfahren n (Re) execution proceedings
voll überwälzen (com) to pass (ie, rising costs) on fully (eg, in higher product prices)
Vollversicherung f (Vers) = *Vollwertversicherung*
voll verwässerter Gewinn m **je Aktie** (Fin) fully diluted earnings per share
vollwertige Münze f (Vw) full-bodied coin
Vollwertversicherung f (Vers) insurance at full value (ie, insured value = insured sum)
Vollzeitbeschäftigung f (Pw) full-time employment (or job)

vollziehen
  (Re) to enforce
  – to execute
vollziehende Behörde f (Re) executive public agency
vollziehende Funktion f (Bw) operating function
Vollziehung f **aussetzen** (Re) to suspend enforcement
Vollzugsbudget n (Bw) operative budget
Volumen n
  (Bw) volume
  (Fin) total lendings
  (Bö) turnover
  – volume
Volumenbudget n (Mk) volume budget (syn, *Absatzbudget*)
Volumenverluste mpl (com) losses in business volume
Vomhundertsatz m (com) percentage rate
vom Parteiwillen unabhängige Umstände mpl (Re) events beyond the reasonable control of the parties
von Amts wegen
  (Re) ex officio
von Anfang an nichtig (Re) void from the beginning (or ab initio)
von der Tagesordnung absetzen (com) to remove from the agenda
von Fall zu Fall (com) on a case-by-case basis
von Haus zu Haus (com) from warehouse to warehouse
von Lehre und Rechtsprechung entwickelt (Re) developed in and out of court
von links multiplizieren (Math) to premultiply
von Null verschiedener Wert m (Math) nonzero value
von rechts multiplizieren (Math) to postmultiply
von Rechts wegen (Re) as of right
von Todes wegen (Re) mortis causa (ie, by reason of death; eg, donation mortis causa: a gift under apprehension of death; opp, inter vivos: unter Lebenden)
Vorausabtretung f (Re) assignment in advance
Vorabausschüttung f (StR) advanced distribution (of profit)
Vorabbericht m (ReW) flash report
Vorakten fpl (Re) previous files
Voranmelder m (Pat) prior applicant
Voranmeldung f
  (com) advance notice
  (StR) monthly prepayment notice (or report), § 18 I UStG
  (Pat) previous application
Voranmeldungszeitraum m (StR) current prepayment period, § 13 UStG
Voranschlag m
  (com) cost estimate (syn, *Kostenvoranschlag*)
  (Fin) preliminary budget (ie, part of financial planning)
Voranzeige f (com) advance notice
Vorarbeiter m
  (Pw) assistant (or petty) foreman
  – subforeman
  – (infml) gang (or straw) boss
  (ie, does not hold any formal qualification)

Vorausabtretung *f*
  (Re) assignment in advance
  – blanket assignment
Vorausbestellung *f* (com) advance order
vorausbezahlen (com) to pay in advance
vorausbezahlt (com) prepaid
vorausdisponieren
  (com) to make arrangements in advance
  (com) to buy ahead
Vorausdispositionen *fpl* (com) advance arrangements
vorauseilender Indiaktor *m*
  (Vw) leader
  – leading indicator *(syn, vorlaufender Konjunkturindikator)*
Vorausfestsetzung *f* (Zo) advance fixing
Vorausfestsetzungsbescheinigung *f* (Zo) advance fixing certificate
vorausgehende Anmeldung *f* (Pat) prior application
vorausgeschätzte Gesamtprojektkosten *pl* (OR) projection of costs to product completion
vorausgeschätzte Kosten *pl* (KoR) formula cost
Vorausinformation *f* (Bw) upstream information
Vorausleistung *f* (com) advance performance
Vorausplazierung *f* (Fin) advance selling *(ie, of a securities issue)*
Vorausprämie *f* (Vers) premium paid in advance
Vorausrechnung *f* (com) advance invoice *(or* bill)
Voraussagespanne *f* (Stat) prediction interval
voraussetzungslos (Log) free of preconceptions
voraussichtliche Ausfälle *mpl* (ReW) contingent losses *(eg, on receivables)*
voraussichtlicher Bedarf *m* (com) anticipated requirements
Vorausveranlagung *f* (StR) advance assessment
Vorauswahl *f* (Pw) preliminary screening *(ie, of job applicants)*
Vorauswertung *f* (com) initial evaluation
Vorauszahlung *f*
  (com) advance payment
  – payment in advance
  – prepayment
Vorauszahlungen *fpl* (StR) tax prepayments
Vorauszahlungsbescheid *m*
  (StR) notice of current prepayment of tax
  – notice of tax prepayment *(ie, issued by local finance office, § 37 III EStG)*
Vorauszahlungsfinanzierung *f* (Fin) financing by customer advances
Vorauszahlungs-Geschäft *n* (com) sale against cash in advance
Vorbehalt *m*
  (Re) limiting condition
  – reservation
  – proviso *(ie, with the proviso that . . .)*
vorbehaltlich
  (com) subject to
  – with the provisio that . . .
  – provided that
vorbehaltlose Abtretung *f* (Vers) absolute assignment
Vorbehaltskauf *m* (com) conditional sale
Vorbehaltskäufer *m* (com) conditional purchaser
Vorbehaltsurteil *n* (Re) final judgment issued subject to a proviso, § 219 BGB

Vorbemerkungen *fpl* (Log) preliminary notes
Vorbenutzungsrecht *n* (Pat) right of prior use, § 7 PatG
vorbereitende Arbeiten *fpl* (IndE) make-ready work *(ie, prior to start of production)*
Vorbereitungshandlung *f* (StR) preparatory action
Vorbereitungsphase *f* (com) lead-up
Vorbereitungs- und Prüfzeit *f* (IndE) check time
Vorbescheid *m*
  (StR) preliminary decree, § 90 III FGO
  (Pat) preliminary ruling
Vorbesitzer *m* (Re) prior holder
Vorbesprechung *f*
  (com) preliminary discussion
  – preparatory conference
Vorbestellung *f* (com) advance order
vorbestimmte Zeiten *fpl* (IndE) predetermined times *(ie, in MTA, MTM, BMT)*
vorbeugende Instandhaltung *f* (IndE) preventive maintenance
vorbeugende Prüfung *f* (Stat) preventive inspection
vorbeugende Unterlassungsklage *f* (Pat) prohibitory suit, § 47 I PatG
Vorbörse *f*
  (Bö) before-hour dealings
  – market before official hours
vorbörslicher Kurs *m* (Bö) pre-market price
Vorbuch *n*
  (ReW) daybook
  – (GB) waste book *(ie, in which the transactions of the day are entered in the order of their occurrence; syn, Kladde, Strazze)*
vordatieren (com) to postdate *(ie, to write a date following today's date; opp, nachdatieren = to antedate)*
vordatierter Scheck *m* (Fin) postdated *(or* forward-dated) check *(ie, cannot be cashed before the date appearing on its face)*
Vordergrundprogramm *n* (EDV) foreground program
Vordersatz *m* (Log) premise
  – premiss
  (Log) antecedent
  – condition
vorderste Front *f* (com, infml) leading edge *(eg, of technological development)*
Vordividende *f* (Fin) interim *(or* initial) dividend
Vordruck *m* (com) form
Vordrucksatz *m* (com) multipart form
Vorentwicklung *f* (Bw) advance development
Vorentwurf *m* (com) preliminary draft
Vorerbe *m* (Re) first heir, §§ 2105 ff BGB
Vorerfinder *m* (Pat) prior inventor
Vorerhebung *f* (Stat) exploratory survey
vor Fälligkeit
  (Fin) ahead of schedule *(eg, repayment of loan)*
  – prior to maturity *(or* due date)
Vorfakturierung *f* (com) prebilling
vorfinanzieren (Fin) to provide advance *(or* preliminary) financing
Vorfinanzierung *f* (Fin) advance financing *(ie, by short-term funds; esp, in the construction industry)*

Vorfinanzierungskredit *m* (Fin) preliminary loan
Vorfinanzierungszusage *f* (Fin) promise to grant preliminary credit
Vorfracht *f* (com) original freight *(ie, up to a point of trans(s)hipment)*
vorführen (Zo) to produce *(ie, goods to the customs: bei der Zollstelle)*
Vorgabe *f*
 (Bw) performance target
 – standard
 (Mk) checklist *(syn, Standardvorgabe)*
Vorgabeermittlung *f* (KoR) determination of standards
Vorgabekalkulation *f* (IndE) determination of standard time
Vorgabekosten *pl*
 (KoR) budgeted
 – target
 – attainable standard
 – current standard
 – ideal standard ... cost *(syn, Soll- od Budgetkosten)*
Vorgabestunde *f* (IndE) standard hour
Vorgabezeit *f*
 (IndE) standard
 – standard operation
 – all-in
 – allowed
 – incentive ... time
Vorgabezeitkalkulation *f* (IndE) = *Vorgabekalkulation*
Vorgang *m*
 (Bw) operation
 (com) job file *(ie, in office organization)*
 – job
 (OR) activity *(DIN 69 900)*
Vorgänger *m*
 (Re) predecessor
 (Re) predecessor company
Vorgang *m* **mit Puffer** (OR) floater
Vorgangselement *n* (IndE) job element
Vorgangspuffer *m* (OR) float
vorgegebene Hauptzeit *f* (IndE) standard running time
vorgegebene Variable *f*
 (Stat) predictive
 – predicated
 – determining ... variable
 – predictor
 – regressor
vorgehen (Re) to rank prior to
vorgelagerte Absatzstufe *f* (Mk) upstream stage of distribution
vorgelagerte Industriezweige *mpl* (Bw) upstream industries
vorgelagerte Preise *mpl* (com) prices charged at earlier stages
vorgeordnet (Bw) up the line
 – upstream
vorgeordnete Buchhaltung *f* (ReW) central accounting unit
vorgesehener Beförderungsweg *m* (Zo) intended route
Vorgesellschaft *f* (Bw) stock corporation existing prior to registration, § 41 AktG

Vorgesetztenbeurteilung *f* (Pw) appraisal by subordinates
Vorgesetztenschulung *f* (Pw) supervisory training
Vorgesetzter *m* (Pw) superior
Vorgespräche *npl* **führen** (com) to hold preliminary *(or* exploratory) talks (with)
Vorgründungsgesellschaft *f* (Bw) = *Vorgesellschaft*
Vorgründungsgewinn *m* (Fin) profit prior to company formation
Vorgründungsvertrag *m* (Re) pre-formation agreement
vorherbestimmte Variable *f* (Stat) predetermined variable
vorhergehendes Glied *n* (Math) next preceding term *(eg, of a progression)*
vorherige Mitteilung *f* (com) advance notification
vorherige schriftliche Zustimmung *f* (Re) prior written approval
vorherige Zustimmung *f* (Re) previous consent
Vorhersage *f*
 (Vw, Bw) forecast
 – prediction
Vorhersagefehler *m* (Stat) forecast error
Vorindossant *m* (WeR) previous indorser
Vorinstanz *f* (Re) lower court
Vorjahr *n* (com) previous year
Vorjahresergebnis *n* (ReW) prior year results
Vorjahresgewinn *m* (ReW) prior year earnings *(or* income)
Vorkalkulation *f*
 (KoR) preliminary costing
 (KoR) cost estimating department
Vorkalkulationskarten *fpl* (KoR) estimated cost cards
Vorkalkulator *m* (KoR) cost estimator
vorkalkulierte Kosten *pl* (KoR) estimated cost
Vorkasse *f* (com) cash in advance
Vorkaufsrecht *n*
 (Re) right of preemption
 – preemptive right
 – right of first refusal *(ie, see §§ 504ff and §§ 1094ff BGB)*
Vorkommenswahrscheinlichkeit *f* (OR) probability of occurrence
Vorkompilierer *m* (EDV) preprocessor
Vorkonto *n* (ReW) preliminary account
Vorkosten *pl* (com) preliminary expense
Vorkostenstelle *f* (KoR) indirect *(or* service) cost center *(syn, Hilfskostenstelle)*
Vorlage *f*
 (com) submission
 – presentation
 (WeR) presentation
 – production
 (Fin) advance
Vorlage *f* **des Jahresabschlusses** (ReW) presentation of year-end financial statement
Vorlagefrist *f* (com) time limit for submission *(or* presentation)
Vorlagen *fpl* (Zo) manufacturing documents *(ie, plans, drawings, designs, patterns, manuscripts, etc.)*
Vorlage *f* **von Dokumenten** (com) tender of documents

Vorlagezinsen *mpl* (Fin) interest on outpayment of unmatured savings account *(syn, Vorschußzinsen, Zwischenzinsen)*
Vorlage *f* **zum Inkasso** (Fin) presentation for collection
Vorlasten *fpl* (Re) prior charges
Vorlauf *m*
(com) pre-carriage
– on-carriage
(ie, in container traffic: to port of dispatch)
(EDV) leader
vorlaufender Konjunkturindikator *m*
(Vw) leader
– leading indicator *(eg, new orders, money supply, stock prices; syn, vorauseilender Indikator)*
vorläufige Berechnung *f* (com) provisional estimate
vorläufige Bescheinigung *f* (com) interim (*or* provisional) certificate
vorläufige Beschreibung *f* (Pat) provisional specification
vorläufige Bilanz *f* (ReW) trial balance sheet
vorläufige Deckungszusage *f*
(Vers) provisional cover
– cover note
– binder
– slip
vorläufige Ergebnisse *npl* (com) provisional figures
vorläufige Patentschrift *f* (Pat) provisional patent specification
vorläufige Prämie *f* (Vers) provisional rate (*or* premium)
vorläufiger Abschluß *m* (ReW) preliminary financial statement
vorläufiger Bescheid *m* (Re) provisional ruling
vorläufiger Versicherungsschein *m* (Vers) insurance note
vorläufiges Aktienzertifikat *n* (Fin) temporary stock certificate
– (GB) scrip *(ie, a scrip in US usage is a formal certificate representing a fraction of a share)*
vorläufiges Budget *n* (Bw) tentative (*or* trial) budget
vorläufige Schätzung *f* (com) provisional estimate
vorläufiges Schutzrecht *n* (Pat) right of provisional protection
vorläufige Steuerfestsetzung *f* (StR) preliminary tax assessment, § 165 AO
vorläufige Vereinbarung *f* (Re) interim (*or* provisional) agreement
vorläufige Versicherungspolice *f*
(Vers) binding receipt
– slip
– binder
vorläufige Vorgabezeit *f* (IndE) temporary standard
vorläufige Zielfestsetzung *f* (Bw) preliminary setting of objectives
Vorlaufinformation *f* (com) header information
Vorlaufkarte *f* (EDV) header card
Vorlaufkosten *pl* (KoR) preproduction cost *(ie, related to individual orders)*
Vorlaufprogramm *n* (EDV) preparatory program
Vorlaufzeit *f*

(Bw) lead time
(Mk) gap between product conception and introduction
Vorlaufzeit *f* **der Fertigung** (IndE) manufacturing lead time
vorlegen
(com) to submit *(eg, application, plan)*
(Re) to produce *(eg, written power of attorney)*
(WeR) to present *(ie, for acceptance or payment)*
(Fin) to advance *(eg, a certain amount of money)*
Vorlegung *f* **e-s Schecks** (WeR) presentation of a check
Vorlegung *f* **e-s Wechsels** (WeR) presentation of a bill
Vorlegungsfrist *f* (WeR) time for (*or* of) presentment
Vorlegungsort *m* (Fin) place of presentation
Vorlegungsverbot *n* (Fin) instruction not to present
Vorlegungsvermerk *m* (WeR) notice of dishonor
Vorlegung *f* **zum Akzept** (WeR) presentation for acceptance
Vorlegung *f* **zur Zahlung** (Fin) presentation for payment
Vorleistungen *fpl* (VGR) purchased materials and services *(ie, current purchases of materials and services from other enterprises)*
Vorleistungen *fpl* **erbringen** (com) to make advance deliveries or payments
Vorleistungskoeffizient *m* (Vw) input coefficient
Vorlieferant *m* (com) supplier
vorliegender Fall *m* (Re) case at issue (*or* under consideration)
Vorlizenz *f* (Pat) preliminary license
Vormann *m*
(Re) predecessor in interest, § 65 AktG
(WeR) prior indorser
Vormaterial *n*
(IndE) feedstock
– start material
vormerken
(com) to note
– to put down
– to put somebody's name down
(Pw, infml) to pencil in *(eg, for a job, task, advancement)*
Vormerkung *f* (Re) provisional entry in the real estate register, §§ 883–888 BGB
Vormund *m*
(Re) guardian
– (US) committee of the person
Vormundschaft *f* (Re) guardianship, §§ 1773 ff BGB
Vormundschaftsgericht *n* (Re) guardianship court
vornumeriert (com) prenumbered
Vorpatent *n* (Pat) prior patent
Vorperiode *f* (ReW) previous period
Vorprämie *f*
(Bö) call
– call option
– premium for the call
Vorprämie *f* **kaufen** (Bö) to give for the call
Vorprämiengeschäft *n* (Bö) trading in calls
Vorprämienkäufer *m* (Bö) giver for the call
Vorprämienkurs *m* (Bö) call price
Vorprämien *f* **verkaufen** (Bö) to take for the call

Vorprodukte *npl*
(com) primary products
(IndE) feedstock
− intermediate products *(ie, used for further processing)*
Vorprojektierung *f* (com) preliminary study
Vorprüfer *m* (Pat) primary examiner
Vorprüfung *f*
(com) feasibility study
(ReW) preaudit
(StR) preliminary tax audit
Vorrangebene *f* (Bw) priority level
vorrangige Belastung *f* (Re) prior charge
vorrangige Hypothek *f* (Re) prior (*or* senior) mortgage
vorrangiges Pfandrecht *n* (Re) prior lien
vorrangiges Ziel *n* (Bw) prime (*or* priority) goal
Vorrangmatrix *f* (OR) precedence matrix
Vorrangregel *f* (OR) preference rule
Vorrangsteuerung *f* (EDV) priority control
Vorrangverarbeitung *f* (EDV) priority processing
Vorräte *mpl*
(MaW) inventory
− stock of inventory
− inventory stocks
− goods on hand
− (GB) stock-in-trade
(ReW, EG) stocks
Vorräte *mpl* **abbauen**
(MaW) to cut inventories
− to destock
Vorräte *mpl* **aufstocken** (MaW) to build up inventory
Vorrätekonto *n* (ReW) inventory account
Vorräte-Versicherung *f* (Vers) inventory insurance
vorrätig (com) in stock
Vorratsabbau *m*
(Vw, MaW) destocking
− inventory reduction
− reduction in stocks
Vorratsaktien *fpl* (Fin) company's own shares *(ie, held in treasury, § 71 AktG; syn, Verwertungsaktien)*
Vorratsaufstockung *f* (MaW) inventory buildup
Vorratsbewertung *f* (ReW) inventory valuation
Vorratsbewertungs-Rückstellung *f* (ReW) stock adjustment reserve
Vorratsgrundstücke *npl* (Bw) nonplant land *(ie, held for speculative purposes or for future plant extensions)*
vorratsintensiv (Bw) inventory-intensive
Vorratsinvestition *f* (VGR) inventory investment
Vorratskäufe *mpl* **auf lange Sicht** (com) long-term stocking up
Vorratskredit *m* (Fin) inventory financing loan
Vorratsplan *m* (MaW) inventory budget
Vorratsproduktion *f*
(IndE) make-to-stock production
− production for inventory
Vorratsstelle *f* (Vw) storage agency
Vorratsstellenwechsel *m* (Fin) storage agency bill
Vorratsveränderung *f* (MaW) change in inventories (*or* stocks)
Vorratsvermögen *npl*
(ReW) inventories

− stock on hand
− (GB) stock-in-trade
Vorratswirtschaft *f* (MaW) inventory management
Vorrechner *m*
(EDV) front-end processor
− host computer
(EDV) satellite computer
Vorrechtsaktien *fpl* (Fin) = *Vorzugsaktien*
Vorrechtsgläubiger *m* (Re) preferred creditor
Vorrichtungspatent *n* (Pat) device patent
Vorsaison *f* (com) early season
Vorsatz *m*
(Re) intent
− intention
(ie, willful or intentional default made by the debtor with the consciousness of the consequences of his conduct)
(EDV) header record
− *(sometimes)* leader
vorsätzliche Steuerumgehung *f* (StR) deliberate tax avoidance
vorsätzliche unerlaubte Handlung *f* (Re) intentional tort
Vorschaltdarlehen *n* (Fin) preliminary loan *(eg, in financing the construction of commercial buildings)*
Vorschaltgesellschaft *f* (Bw) holding company
Vorschaubilanz *f* (ReW) projected balance sheet
Vorschauergebnisrechnung *f* (ReW) projected earnings statement
Vorschaurechnung *f*
(Bw) forecasting
(ReW) budgetary accounting
vorschießen (com) to advance *(eg, money)*
Vorschlag *m*
(com) proposal
− suggestion
Vorschlag *m* **annehmen** (com) to accept a proposal
Vorschlag *m* **ausarbeiten**
(com) to draft
− to prepare
− to work out ... a proposal
vorschlagen
(com) to propose
− to suggest
Vorschlag *m* **machen**
(com) to bring forward
− to put forward
− to put up ... a proposal (*or* suggestion)
Vorschlagsentwurf *m* (com) draft proposal
Vorschlagswesen *n* (Pw) suggestion system *(ie, company program providing employees the chance to present ideas, methods, or plans for the improvement of the company's products or services)*
Vorschlag *m* **unterbreiten** (com) to submit (*or* put) a proposal (to)
Vorschlag *m* **verwerfen** (com) to reject a proposal
Vorschrift *f*
(Re) provision
− regulation
− rule
Vorschriften *fpl* **des Einkommensteuerrechts** (StR) rules of income-tax law
Vorschrift *f* **e-s Vertrages**

647

(Re) provision of a contract
- contractual provision
Vorschriften *fpl* **entsprechen** (Re) to conform to (statutory) regulations
Vorschriften *fpl* **über die Bildung von Rücklagen** (ReW) reserve requirements
Vorschriften *fpl* **über die Kennzeichnung des Ursprungslandes** (Zo) marks of origin prescriptions
Vorschrift *f* **verletzen** (Re) to disobey a rule
Vorschub *m* (EDV) feed
Vorschubband *n* (EDV) = *Lochbandschleife*
Vorschubbefehl *m* (EDV) feed instruction
Vorschubloch *n* (EDV) feed (*or* sprocket) hole (*syn, Führungsloch*)
Vorschublochband *n* (EDV) printer carriage tape
Vorschubraupe *f* (EDV) paper tractor
Vorschuß *m*
(Fin) advance disbursement
(Pw) wage advance
vorschüssige Rente *f* (Fin) annuity due
Vorschuß *m* **leisten** (com) to make advance payment
Vorschußwechsel *m* (Fin) collateral bill (*syn, Depotwechsel*)
Vorschußzinsen *mpl* (Fin) = *Vorlagezinsen*
Vorsetzen *n* **um e-n Abschnitt** (EDV) unwind tape mark
vorsichtige Dispositionen *fpl* (com) guarded market activities
vorsichtiger Kostenansatz *m* (ReW) conservative cost estimate
vorsichtig eröffnen (Bö) to open cautiously
vorsichtiger Optimismus *m* (Bö) guarded optimism
vorsichtige Schätzung *f* (com) conservative estimate
Vorsichtskasse *f* (Vw) precautionary balances (*or* holdings)
Vorsichtsprinzip *n* (ReW) principle of caution (*or* conservatism)
Vorsitz *m*
(com) chair
- chairmanship
- presidency
Vorsitzender *m* (com) chairman (*ie, Americans now generally prefer 'chairperson' if the term is understood to include both male and female*)
Vorsitzender *m* **des Aufsichtsrats** (Bw) chairman (*or* head) of supervisory board
vorsitzender Richter *m* (StR) presiding judge, § 10 I FGO
Vorsitzer *m* (Bw) chief executive
Vorsitz *m* **führen**
(com) to chair (*eg, a meeting*)
- to be in the chair
- to act as chairman
- to preside over (*eg, a meeting*)
Vorsitz *m* **übernehmen** (com) to take the chair
Vorsorgeaufwendungen *fpl* (StR) expenses of a provident nature (*ie, insurance premiums and payments to business and loan associations, § 10 I Nos. 2, 3 EStG; deductible as blanket allowances*)
Vorsorgepauschale *f*
(com) provisional lump sum (*ie, in construction contracts*)

(StR) blanket allowance for expenses incurred to safeguard the future of employee taxpayers, § 10c III EStG
Vorsorgepauschbetrag *m* (StR) blanket allowance for expenses incurred to safeguard the future of taxpayers other than employees, § 10c II EStG
Vorsorgeuntersuchung *f* (SozV) precautionary checkup
Vorsorgeversicherung *f* (Vers) insurance including future risks
vorsortieren (EDV) to presort
Vorspannband *n* (EDV) tape leader
Vorspiegelung *f* **falscher Tatsachen** (Re) false pretenses (*eg, to obtain goods by . . .*)
Vorstand *m* (Bw) managing board, §§ 76–94 AktG
- board of management
(*ie, in charge of day-to-day operations of a company; US equivalent: top management executive committee*)
Vorstand *m* **Produktion**
(Bw) production director
- (US) vice president production
Vorstandsaktien *fpl* (Fin) management shares
Vorstandsbericht *m* (Bw) management report
Vorstandsbeschluß *m* (Bw) resolution of managing board
Vorstandsbezüge *pl* (Pw) managing board members' remuneration
Vorstandsfunktion *f* (Bw) top-executive function
Vorstandsmitglied *n* (Bw) member of managing board
Vorstandssprecher *m*
(Bw) spokesman of managing board
- management board spokesman
- company spokesman
Vorstandsvorsitzender *m*
(Bw) chairman of managing board (*ie, chief operating officer*)
- (US) chief executive officer, ceo, CEO
- (US) company president
- (GB) managing director
Vorstand *m* **Technik**
(Bw) technical director
- (US) vice president engineering
Vorstellungsgespräch *n* (Pw) selection interview
Vorstellungskosten *pl* (Pw) applicant's interview expenses
Vorsteuer *f*
(StR, VAT) prior (turnover) tax, § 15 I UStG
- input tax
Vorsteuerabzug *m*
(StR, VAT) prior-tax deduction
- deduction of prior turnover tax
Vorsteuerverfahren *n* (StR) prior-turnover-tax method
(*ie, used in determining the actual amount of VAT to be paid*)
Vorstrafe *f* (Re) previous conviction
Vorstudie *f*
(com) pilot
- preliminary
- feasibility . . . study
Vortagesnotierung *f* (Bö) previous quotation
Vorteile *mpl* **der Massenfertigung** (Vw) economies of mass production

vorteilhafte Investition f (Fin) profitable investment
Vorteilhaftigkeit f (Fin) profitability *(ie, of investment projects)*
Vorteilsausgleichung f (Re) adjustment of profit *(ie, compensatio lucri cum damno)*
Vorteilskriterium n (Fin) yardstick of profitability *(ie, used in preinvestment analysis)*
Vorteilsprinzip n (FiW) benefit *(or* benefits-received*)* principle
Vorteilsvergleich m (Fin) comparison of profitabilities *(ie, made in preinvestment analysis)*
Vortest m (Mk) pretest
Vortrag m
(com) paper *(ie, read a paper)*
– talk *(ie, give a talk)*
(ReW) (amount) carried forward
(ReW) (amount) brought forward
Vortrag m **auf neue Rechnung** (ReW) balance carried forward (to new account)
Vortrag m **aus letzter Rechnung** (ReW) balance brought forward
vortragen
(ReW) to carry forward
– to carry over
– to bring forward
Vortragsreise f
(com) lecture tour
– tour to carry out speaking engagements *(eg, he is off on a ...)*
vorübergehende Ausfuhr f (Zo) temporary exportation
vorübergehende Ausfuhr f **zur passiven Veredelung** (Zo) temporary exportation for outward processing
vorübergehende Einfuhr f
(AuW) temporary importation
(Zo) temporary admission
vorübergehende Einfuhr f **zur aktiven Veredelung** (Zo) temporary admission for inward processing
vorübergehende Einlagerung f (Zo) temporary warehousing
vorübergehende Erweiterung f **der Bandbreiten** (AuW) temporary widening of the margins of fluctuation
vorübergehende Kapitalanlage f (Fin) temporary investment
vorübergehender Fehler m (EDV) transient error
vorübergehende Verwahrung f (Zo) temporary storage
vorübergehende Verwendung f (com) temporary use
vorübergehende Verwendung f **bei teilweiser Abgabenerhebung** (EG) temporary importation with partial payment of duty
Vorumsätze mpl (StR) prior turnovers (including imports)
Vorumsatzverfahren n (StR) prior-turnover method *(ie, gross turnovers less prior turnovers = net turnovers on which applicable VAT rate is payable)*
Vor-und Nachsaison f (com) off-season
Vor- und Nachteile mpl (com) assets and drawbacks *(eg, of a market-oriented economy)*
Vor- und Nachteile mpl **abwägen** (com) to add up the benefits and disadvantages *(eg, of a contemplated merger)*
Vorvaluten pl (Fin) forward values
Vorverfahren n (Re) preliminary proceedings
Vorverhandlungen fpl (com) preliminary negotiations
Vorverkauf m (Mk) advance sale
vorverkaufte Schuldverschreibungen fpl (Fin) bonds sold prior to issue
Vorveröffentlichung f
(Pat) prior publication
– prior public printed description
vorverrechnete Auftragskosten pl (KoR) job order costs billed in advance
Vorversicherung f (Vers) previous insurance
Vorvertrag m
(com) letter of understanding
(Re) preliminary *(or* tentative*)* agreement
vorvertragliche Rücklagen fpl (StR) reserves set up prior to effective date of agreement
vor Vertragsablauf (Re) prior to the time the contract is due to expire
Vorwahl f (com) dialing code
Vorwälzung f (FiW) forward shifting
vorwärtsdatieren (Math) to compound
Vorwärtsintegration f (Bw) forward integration *(opp, Rückwärtsintegration)*
vorwärtskommen (Pw) to get ahead *(eg, on the corporate ladder)*
Vorwärtsstrategie f (Mk) forward strategy
vorweggenommene Erfindung f (Pat) anticipated invention
vorweggenommener Gewinnanteil m (Vers) anticipated bonus
Vorwegnahme f (Pat) anticipation
vorwiegende Schadensursache f
(Re) proximate
– decisive
– preponderant ... cause of injury
Vorzeichen n
(Math) algebraic sign
(EDV, Cobol) operational sign
Vorzeichenbit n (EDV) sign bit
Vorzeichenstelle f (EDV) sign position
Vorzeichenziffer f (EDV) sign digit
vorzeitige Abwicklung f (com) advance termination
vorzeitige Arbeitsunfähigkeit f (Pw) premature disablement *(or* incapacity*)*
vorzeitige Ausfuhr f (Zo) prior exportation
vorzeitige Beendigung f (com) premature termination *(eg, of contract or agreement)*
vorzeitige Fälligkeit f (Fin) accelerated maturity
vorzeitige Kündigung f (Re) premature termination
vorzeitige Pensionierung f (Pw) early retirement
vorzeitige Rückzahlung f (Fin) advance redemption *(or* repayment*)*
vorzeitiger Rückkauf m (Fin) repurchase prior to maturity
vorzeitiges Kündigungsrecht n (Fin) right to call a loan prior to maturity
vorzeitiges Veralten n (Bw) obsolescence
vorzeitige Tilgung f (Fin) = *vorzeitige Rückzahlung*

vorzeitige Zahlung f (Fin) payment before due date
vorzeitig tilgbar (Fin) repayable in advance
vorzeitig zurückzahlen (Fin) to repay ahead of schedule
Vorzimmer n
(com) anteroom
– antechamber
Vorzüge pl (Fin) = *Vorzugsaktien*
Vorzugsaktien fpl
(Fin) preferred stock
– (GB) preference shares
(syn, Stammprioritäten, Vorrechtsaktien, Prioritätsaktien)
Vorzugsaktionär m
(Fin) preferred stockholder
– (GB) preference shareholder
Vorzugsangebot n (com) preference offer
Vorzugsbedingungen fpl (com) preferential conditions
Vorzugsbehandlung f (com) preferential arrangements
Vorzugsdividende f
(Fin) dividend on preferred stock
– preferred dividend

Vorzugsdividendendeckung f (Fin) times preferred dividend earned
Vorzugsgläubiger m (Re) preferred creditor
Vorzugskauf m (Mk) accommodation purchase
Vorzugskonditionen fpl (com) preferential terms
Vorzugskurs m (Bö) preferential price *(ie, below market quotation)*
Vorzugsobligationen fpl (Fin) priority bonds
Vorzugspreis m (com) special price
Vorzugsrabatt m (com) preferential discount
Vorzugsrechte npl (Re) rights of priority
Vorzugssätze mpl (Fin) preferential rates
Vorzugsstammaktien fpl (Fin) preferred ordinary shares
Vorzugszeichnungsrecht n (Fin) preferential right of subscription
Vorzugszins m (Fin) preferential interest rate
Vorzugszoll m (Zo) preferential duty *(or* tariff) *(syn, Präferenzzoll)*
Vostrokonto n (Fin) vostro account *(opp, Nostrokonto)*
V-Steuern fpl (StR) assessed taxes

W

wachsende Wirtschaft f (Vw) growing economy
Wachstum n (Vw, Bw) growth
Wachstumsaktien fpl (Fin) growth stocks
Wachstumsanleihe f (Fin) premium-carrying loan
Wachstumsbranche f (com) growth industry
Wachstumsfonds m
(Fin) growth
– cumulative
– no-dividend ... fund
(syn, Thesaurierungsfonds; opp, Einkommensfonds)
Wachstumsgleichgewicht n (Vw) steady-state growth
Wachstumsindustrie f (Vw) growth industry
Wachstumskurve f (Stat) growth curve
Wachstumsmarkt m (Mk) growth market
Wachstumsmodell n (Vw) growth model
Wachstumsmotor m (Vw) engine of economic growth
Wachstumspfad m (Vw) growth path
– pathway growth
Wachstumsphase f (Mk) growth stage *(ie, of product life cycle)*
Wachstumspolitik f (Vw) growth policy
Wachstumsprojektion f (Vw) growth projection
Wachstumsprozeß m (Vw) growth process
Wachstumsrate f (Vw) rate of growth *(or* expansion)
Wachstumsschranken fpl (Vw) barriers to economic growth
wachstumsschwacher Wirtschaftszweig m (Vw) flat-growth industry
Wachstumsspielraum m (Vw) growth potential
Wachstumsstufen fpl (Bw) stages of expansion *(ie, refers to growth rate of business correspondence)*

Wachstumstheorie f (Vw) theory of economic growth
Wachstumstrend m (Vw) trend rate of growth
Wachstumswerte mpl (Fin) growth stocks
Wachstumsziel n (Vw) *(numberized)* growth target
Wafer m (EDV) wafer *(syn, Halbleiterscheibe)*
Waffenexporte mpl (AuW) arms exports
Waffengleichheit f **der Tarifpartner** (Pw) balance of firepower of the bargaining partners
Wagedrift f (Vw) earnings drift
Wagenachskilometer mpl (com) car axle kilometers *(ie, product of freight train axles and kilometers covered)*
Wagenladung f
(com) carload
– (GB) waggon-load
(ie, minimum weight, 5,000kgs; opp, Stückgut)
Wagenteilladung f (com) less-than-car-load, LCL
Wagenpark m
(com) car pool
– automobile fleet
– vehicles park
Wagenrücklauf m (EDV) carriage return, CR
Wagenstandgeld n (com) track storage charge
Waggon m
(com) freight car
– (GB) waggon *(US spelling: wagon)*
Waggonladung f (com) carload lot *(opp, Stückgut)*
Wagnis n
(Bw) risk
– hazard
Wagnisse npl **wegen Schwankungen der Fremdwährungskurse** (Fin) risks due to fluctuation in currency exchange rates
Wagnisverluste mpl (ReW) encountered risks

Wagnisverzehr *m* (Bw) catastrophic losses of plant and inventory
Wagniszuschlag *m* (Vers) risk premium
Wahl *f* **des Arbeitsplatzes** (Vw) job choice
Wahlfach *n*
– (Pw) elective
– (GB) optional subject
wahlfreier Zugriff *m* (EDV) random (*or* direct) access
wahlfreie Verarbeitung *f* (EDV) random processing
Wahlhandlung *f* (Vw) choice
Wahlhandlungstheorie *f* (Vw) theory of choice
Wählleitung *f* (EDV) dial (*or* switched) line
Wahlmann *m* (Pw) elector
Wahlparadoxon *n* (Vw) paradox of choice
Wahlrecht *n* (Re) right of election *(ie, right to choose one of several promised acts, §§ 262, 263 BGB)*
Wahlschuld *f* (Re) alternative obligation *(ie, an obligation that allows obligor to choose which of two or more things he will do; § 262 BGB)*
wahre mittlere Qualitätslage der Fertigung (Stat) true process average
während der Gültigkeit des Angebots (com) during the continuance of the offer
während der Laufzeit (Re) during the term (*or* continuance *or* currency) *(eg, of contract or agreement)*
während der Vertragsdauer (Re) at all times during the term of this contract
wahrgenommenes Risiko *n* (Vw) perceived risk
Wahrheit *f* **in der Werbung** *f* (Mk) truth in advertising
Wahrheitsfunktion *f* (Log) truth function
Wahrheitsmatrix *f* (Log) truth table
Wahrheitsmenge *f* (Log) truth set
Wahrheitswert *m* (Log) truth value
Wahrheitswertetafel *f*
(Log) truth table
(EDV) Boolean operation table
Wahrheitswertfunktor *m* (Log) truth-functional connective (*or* operator)
Wahrnehmung *f* **von Aufgaben** (com) discharge of duties (*or* responsibilities)
Wahrnehmung *f* **von Interessen** (Re) safeguarding of interests
Wahrnehmung *f* **von Rechten** (Re) protection of rights
wahrscheinliche Abweichung *f* (Stat) = *wahrscheinlicher Fehler*
wahrscheinliche Lebensdauer *f* (Vers) life expectancy
wahrscheinliche Restnutzungsdauer *f* (ReW) probable life
wahrscheinlicher Fehler *m* (Stat) probable error *(ie, 0.67449 σ)*
wahrscheinlicher Höchstschaden *m* (Vers) probable maximum loss *(ie, under normal conditions)*
wahrscheinlicher Nutzungsgrad *m* (OR) interval availability (of machines)
wahrscheinliche Vorräte *mpl* (Vw) potential reserves *(eg, of mineral resources)*
Wahrscheinlichkeit *f* **des Rückgangs der Aktienkurse** (Bö) downside risk

Wahrscheinlichkeit *f* **e-s Ereignisses** (Stat) probability of an event
Wahrscheinlichkeitsaussage *f* (Stat) probability statement
Wahrscheinlichkeitsdichte *f* (Stat) probability density
Wahrscheinlichkeitsdichte *f* **der Ausfallzeit** (OR) rate of failure
Wahrscheinlichkeitsdichtefunktion *f* (Stat) probability density function
Wahrscheinlichkeitsdichte *f* **in e-m Punkt** (Stat) point density
Wahrscheinlichkeitsfunktion *f* (Stat) probability function
Wahrscheinlichkeitsgrad *m* (Stat) degree of probability
Wahrscheinlichkeitsgrenze *f* (Stat) probability limit
Wahrscheinlichkeitsintegral *n* (Math) probability integral
Wahrscheinlichkeitslimes *m* (Stat) probability limit
Wahrscheinlichkeitslogik *f* (Log) probability logic
Wahrscheinlichkeitsnetz *n* (Stat) probability grid
Wahrscheinlichkeitspapier *n* (Math) probability paper
Wahrscheinlichkeitsrechnung *f* (Stat) calculus of probability
Wahrscheinlichkeitssätze *mpl* (Stat) probability theorems *(ie, some of them being axioms and definitions of modern probability theory)*
Wahrscheinlichkeitsschluß *m* (Stat) probable inference
Wahrscheinlichkeits-Stichprobe *f* (Stat) probability sample
Wahrscheinlichkeitstheorie *f* (Stat) theory of probability
Wahrscheinlichkeitsverteilung *f* (Stat) probability distribution
wahrscheinlichste Dauer *f*
(OR) most likely time
– most probable duration
Währung *f* (Vw) currency
Wahrung *f* **gesamtwirtschaftlicher Belange** (Vw) safeguarding interests of the national economy
Währungsabkommen *n* (AuW) currency (*or* monetary) agreement
Währungsabwertung *f*
(AuW) currency depreciation
– currency devaluation
– exchange depreciation
Währungsakzept *n* (Fin) foreign currency acceptance
Währungsanleihe *f* (Fin) foreign currency (*or* external) loan
Währungsaufwertung *f* (AuW) currency (*or* revaluation *or* upvaluation)
Währungsausgleich *m* (EG) Monetary Compensatory Amounts *(ie, in farm trade; syn, Grenzausgleich, qv)*
Währungsgleichsfonds *m*
(AuW) equalization fund
– (GB) Exchange Equalization Account
Währungsausschuß *m* (EG) Monetary Committee
Währungsbandbreiten *fpl* (AuW) currency bands
Währungsbehörden *fpl* (Vw) monetary authorities
Währungsbeistand *m* (AuW) monetary support

651

Währungsbestände *mpl*
(AuW) currency (*or* monetary) reserves
– holdings of currency
Währungsblock *m* (AuW) currency (*or* monetary) bloc
Währungsdeckung *f* (AuW) currency cover
Währungsdumping *n* (AuW) exchange-rate dumping *(ie, through lower rate of foreign currency)*
Währungseinheit *f* (Vw) unit of currency
Währungseinlagen *fpl* (Fin) foreign currency deposits
Währungsexperte *m* (Vw) expert on foreign exchange markets
Währungsfonds *m* (IWF) = *International Monetary Fund*
Währungsgebiet *n* (AuW) currency area
Währungsgewinn *m*
(Fin) foreign exchange earnings
– exchange gain
Währungsgold *n* (AuW) monetary gold
Währungsguthaben *npl* (Fin) foreign exchange balances *(syn, Fremdwährungsguthaben)*
Währungshüter *m* (Vw, infml) guardian of the currency *(ie, the central bank)*
Währungsklauseln *fpl* (Fin) currency clauses *(syn, Valutaklauseln)*
Währungskonto *n* (Fin) foreign exchange account *(syn, Fremdwährungskonto, Devisenkonto)*
Währungskonvertibilität *f* (Vw) currency convertibility
Währungskorb *m*
(AuW) currency basket
– (infml) currency cocktail
Währungskorb *m* **des EWS** (AuW) ECU basket
Währungskredit *m* (Fin) foreign currency loan
Währungskrise *f* (AuW) monetary (*or* currency) crisis
Währungskurs *m* (Fin) exchange rate
Währungskursstabilität *f* (Vw) exchange stability
Währungsmechanismus *m* (Vw) monetary mechanism
Währungsoption *f* (Fin) currency option
Währungsordnung *f* (Vw) = *Währungssystem*
Währungsparität *f* (AuW) monetary (*or* currency) parity
Währungspolitik *f* (Vw, AuW) monetary policy
währungspolitisch (Vw) in terms of monetary policy
währungspolitisches Instrumentarium *n* (Vw) instruments of monetary policy
währungspolitische Zusammenarbeit *f* (AuW) monetary cooperation
Währungsreform *f* (Vw) currency reform
Währungsrelationen *fpl* (AuW) currency relations
Währungsreserven *fpl*
(AuW) currency (*or* monetary) reserves
– foreign exchange reserves (*or* holdings)
– reserve balances
– reserve (asset) holdings
Währungsrisiko *n*
(AuW) foreign exchange risk
– currency risk
Währungsscheck *m* (Fin) foreign currency check
Währungsschlange *f* (AuW) currency snake
Währungsspekulant *m* (Fin) currency speculator

Währungsstabilität *f* (Vw) monetary stability
Währungsstabilitätszone *f* (EG) zone of monetary stability
Währung *f* **stützen**
(AuW) to support
– to prop up
– to underpin ... a currency
Währungssystem *n*
(Vw) monetary system
– currency regime
Währungsumrechnung *f*
(ReW) currency translation
– translating foreign currency accounts
Währungsumstellung *f* (Vw) = *Währungsreform*
Währungsunion *f* (AuW) monetary (*or* currency) union
Währungsverbund *m* (AuW) currency bloc
Währungsverfall *m* (Vw) currency erosion (*or* decline)
Währungsverlust *m* (AuW) loss on exchange
Währungszuschlag *m* (com) exchange markup *(ie, added to base rates in ocean shipping)*
Wahrung *f* **von Gläubigerinteressen** (ReW) protection of creditors' claims
Waisenbeihilfe *f* (SozV) orphan's one-off allowance *(ie, in statutory accident insurance)*
Waisengeld *n* (SozV) orphan's pension *(ie, paid under pension schemes for public employees and for farmers)*
Waisenrente *f* (SozV) orphan's pension *(ie, paid under statutory pension and accident insurance schemes)*
Wandelanleihen *fpl* (Fin) = *Wandelschuldverschreibungen*
Wandelgeschäft *n* (Bö) callable forward transaction *(ie, formulas: ,,per ultimo täglich'' or ,,per ultimo auf Kündigung'')*
Wandelprämie *f* (Fin) conversion premium
Wandelrecht *n*
(Fin) conversion privilege
– right of conversion
Wandelschuldverschreibungen *fpl*
(Fin) convertible bonds
– convertibles
– (GB) convertible loan stock
(syn, Wandelobligationen, Wandelanleihe)
Wandelschuldverschreibung *f* **mit Aktienbezugsrecht** (Fin) detachable stock warrant
Wandelvorzugsaktien *fpl* (Fin) convertible preferred stock
Wanderarbeitnehmer *m* (Pw) migrant worker
Wandergewerbe *n* (com) ambulatory (*or* itinerant) trade
Wandergewerbeschein *m* (com) *now* = *Reisegewerbekarte*
Wandergewerbesteuer *f* (StR) = *Reisegewerbesteuer*
Wanderung *f* (Stat) migration
Wandlung *f*
(Re) cancellation of sale *(ie, right to rescind contract of sale, § 462 BGB)*
(Re) cancellation of contract for work, § 634 BGB
Wandlungsaufgeld *n* (Fin) conversion premium
Wandlungsbedingungen *fpl* (Fin) conversion terms

Wandlungspreis *m* (Fin) conversion price
Wandlungsrecht *n*
  (Fin) conversion privilege
  – right of conversion
Wandlungsverhältnis *n* (Fin) conversion ratio
Ware *f* **abnehmen** (com) to take delivery of goods
Ware *f* **absenden**
  (com) to send off
  – to dispatch
  – to ship ... goods
  – to dispatch an order
Ware *f* **liefern** (com) to deliver goods
Waren *fpl*
  (com) goods
  – commodities
  – merchandise
  (Mk) articles
  – products
  (ReW, EG) goods for resale
Warenakkreditiv *n* (Fin) documentary letter of credit
warenanalytischer Ansatz *m* (Mk) commodity approach of distribution
Warenanmeldung *f* (Zo) declaration of goods
Warenannahme *f*
  (MaW) receipt of goods
  (MaW) goods receiving department
Warenarbitrage *f* (Bö) commodity arbitrage
Warenart *f* (Zo) class of goods
Warenausfuhr *f* (AuW) exportation of goods
Warenausfuhren *fpl* (AuW) merchandise exports
Warenausgang *m* (ReW) sale of withdrawal of goods
Warenausgangsbuch *n* (StR) merchandise sales book, § 144 AO
Warenausgangskontrolle *f* (Stat) outgoing-lot control
Warenausgangslager *n*
  (MaW) outgoing merchandise inventory
  – finished goods warehouse
Warenausstattung *f* (Mk) presentation of goods
Warenaustauschverhältnis *n* (Vw) commodity terms of trade
Warenautomat *m*
  (com) vending machine
  – (GB) slot machine
Warenbeförderung *f* **durch Rohrleitungen** (com) carriage of goods by pipeline
Warenbeförderung *f* **im Luftverkehr** (com) carriage of goods by air
Warenbeförderung *f* **unter Zollverschluß** (Zo) carriage of goods under customs seal
Warenbegleitschein *m* (com) document accompanying goods
  (AuW) accompanying document *(ie, may be used instead of ‚Ausfuhrgenehmigung', § 21 AWV)*
  (Zo) bond note
Warenbeleihung *f* (Fin) lending on goods *(syn, Warenlombard)*
Warenbeschaffungskosten *pl* (ReW) merchandise procurement cost
Waren *fpl* **beschauen** (Zo) to examine (*or* inspect) the goods
Warenbescheinigung *f* (EG) movement certificate

Warenbeschreibung *f* (com) description (*or* identification) of goods
Warenbestand *m*
  (MaW) stock on hand
  – stock in trade
Warenbestandskonto *n* (ReW) = *Wareneinkaufskonto*
Warenbevorschussung *f* (Fin) advance on commodities
Warenbewegungen *fpl* (Zo) movement of goods
Warenbezeichnung *f*
  (com) description (*or* identification) of goods
  (Mk) trade name
Warenbezugskosten *pl* (ReW) cost pertaining to the acquisition and receipt of goods
Warenbilanz *f* (AuW) trade balance *(syn, Handelsbilanz)*
Warenbilanzdefizit *n* (AuW) visible trade deficit
Warenbilanzüberschuß *m* (AuW) visible trade surplus
Warenbörse *f* (Bö) commodity exchange *(ie, the vast majority are markets in which a single item is traded, such as sugar, coffee, grain, cotton, jute, copper, tin, etc.)*
Warenbruttogewinn *m* (com) = *Warenrohgewinn*
Warendelkredere-Versicherung *f* (Vers) accounts receivable insurance
Warendividende *f* (com) = *Warenrückvergütung*
Warendurchfuhr *f* (AuW) transit of goods
Wareneinfuhr *f* (AuW) importation of goods
Wareneinfuhren *fpl* (AuW) merchandise imports
Wareneingang *m*
  (MaW) receiving
  – receipt of goods
  (MaW) incoming merchandise
Wareneingangsbescheinigung *f*
  (AuW) delivery verification
  (MaW) delivery receipt
Wareneingangsbuch *n* (StR) merchandise purchase book, § 143 AO
Wareneingangskontrolle *f*
  (MaW) inspection of incoming shipments
  – incoming-lot control
Wareneingangsschein *m* (MaW) receiving slip (*or* ticket)
Wareneinheitsversicherung *f* (Vers) combined-risk insurance *(Einheitsversicherung)*
Wareneinkaufskonto *n* (ReW) merchandise purchase account
Wareneinsatz *m* (com) sales input *(ie, volume of goods required to achieve a given turnover, valued at cost price)*
Wareneinstandswert *m* (com) cost of merchandise sold
Wareneinzelspanne *f* (Mk) item-related margin *(ie, difference between purchase and sales prices of a single article)*
Warenexporte *mpl* (AuW) merchandise exports
Waren *fpl* **freigeben** (com) to release goods *(eg, to the importer on a trust receipt)*
Warenführer *m* (Zo) carrier
Warengeld *n* (Vw) commodity money
Warengeschäfte *npl* (com) commodity trade *(ie, wholesale and retail, including external trade)*
Warengruppe *f*

(Stat) class of products
- products category

Warengruppenspanne f (Mk) profit margin of commodity group

Warengruppenverzeichnis n (AuW) schedule of 99 product groups

Warenhandel m
(AuW) commodity (*or* merchandise) trade
(Bö) commodities trading

Warenhandelsbetrieb m (com) trading establishment

Warenhändler m (com) trader

Warenhaus n
(com) department store
- (GB) departmental store

Warenhauskonzern m (com) department store chain (*or* group)

Waren fpl **im freien Verkehr**
(Zo) goods in free circulation
- goods cleared for home use

Warenimporte mpl (AuW) merchandise imports

Waren fpl **in Kommission verkaufen** (com) to sell goods on a consignment basis

Warenkalkulation f (KoR) costing of merchandise sold

Warenkonto n (ReW) merchandise account

Warenkorb m (Stat) basket (*or* set) of commodities

Warenkredit m
(Fin) commodity (*or* trade) credit
(Fin) lending on goods (*syn*, Warenlombard)

Warenkreditversicherung f (Vers) credit sale insurance

Warenkunde f (Mk) merchandise technology

Warenlager n (MaW) merchandise inventory

Warenlombard m (Fin) advance (*or* lending) on goods (*ie, loan collateralized by commodities*)

Warenmuster n (com) commercial sample

Warenmuster n **von geringem Wert** (com) sample of small value

Warennebenkosten pl (MaW) incidental procurement costs

Waren fpl **ohne Ursprungseigenschaft** (Zo) non-originating products

Warenpapiere npl
(com) shipping documents
- documents of title

Warenpartie f
(com) parcel of goods
- lot

Warenpreisindex m (Stat) commodity price index

Warenpreisklausel f
(com) stable-value clause based on commodity price (*syn*, Sachwertklausel)

Warenproben fpl (com) merchandise samples

Warenrechnung f (Zo) commercial invoice

Warenreingewinn m (ReW) net profit on sales

Warenrembourskredit m (Fin) commercial acceptance credit

Warenreservewährung f (Vw) commodity reserve currency

Warenrohgewinn m
(com) gross profit on sales
- gross margin
(*ie in trading: net sales less merchandise costs; syn, Rohgewinn, Warenbruttogewinn*)

Warenrücksendungen fpl (com) return of goods

Warenrückvergütung f (com) rebate on purchased goods

Warensendung f (com) consignment of goods

Warensortiment n (com) assortment (*or* line) of goods

Warensteuer f (FiW) commodity tax

Warenterminbörse f (Bö) commodity futures exchange

Warentermingeschäft n (Bö) commodity futures transaction

Warenterminhandel m
(Bö) commodity forward dealings (*or* trading)

Warentest m (com) comparative products test

Warenumsatz m (com) merchandise turnover

Warenumschließung f
(StR) packing
- packaging (*ie, term used in turnover tax law*)

Waren fpl **unbestimmbaren Ursprungs** (Zo) products of undetermined origin

Waren- und Dienstleistungsverkehr m (AuW) movement of goods and services

Warenuntergruppe f (com) products subcategory

Waren fpl **unter Zollverschluß**
(Zo) bonded goods
- goods in bond

Warenursprung m (com) origin of goods

Warenverkaufskonto n (ReW) merchandise sales account

Warenverkehr m
(AuW) merchandise movements
(Zo) trade

Warenverkehrsbescheinigung f (EG) movement certificate

Warenverpfändung f (Re) pledge of goods

Warenversand m
(com) shipping of goods
(Zo) transit operation

Warenvertreter m (com) agent dealing in commodities (*opp, Vertreter für Hilfsgeschäfte des Handels: Bankvertreter, Versicherungsvertreter*)

Warenverzeichnis n (Stat) product classification

Warenvorräte mpl
(MaW) inventories
- goods (carried) in stock
- merchandise on hand

Warenvorschüsse mpl (Fin) advances on goods

Warenwährung f (Vw) commodity currency (*or* standard)

Warenwechsel m
(Fin) commercial
- commodity ... bill (*syn*, Handelswechsel)

Warenwerbung f (Mk) product advertising

Warenwert m (com) invoiced value of goods

Warenzeichen n (Pat) trademark, § 1 WZG

Warenzeichen n **anmelden** (Pat) to apply for registration of a trademark, § 2 WZG

Warenzeichenfälschung f (Pat) commercial counterfeiting, §§ 24, 26 WZG

Warenzeichenlizenz f (Pat) trademark license

Warenzeichenmißbrauch m (Pat) trademark infringement, § 24 WZG

Warenzeichenrecht n (Pat) law of trademarks, §§ 1–36 WZG

Warenzeichenrolle f (Pat) trademark register, § 3 WZG
Warenzeichenschutz m (Pat) trademark protection
Warenzeichenverletzung f (Pat) infringement of a trademark, § 24 WZG
Warenzeichenvorschriften fpl (Pat, US) Trademark Rules of Practice
Waren fpl **zollamtlich behandeln** (Zo) to clear goods through the customs
Waren fpl **zur Vermietung** (Zo) goods imported on hire terms
Ware f **verbringen** (com) to introduce products *(eg, into a market)*
Wärmestelle f (IndE) fuel control department
Warmstart m
  (EDV) warm start
  – system restart
Warngrenze f
  (Stat) warning limit
  – peril points *(ie, on control charts)*
Warnstreik m
  (Pw) demonstration
  – protest
  – spontaneous
  – token ... strike *(eg, workers staged a ...)*
Warrantdiskont m (com) = *Warrantlombard*
Warrantlombard m (Fin) lending on goods *(ie, against delivery of warrant; rarely used in Germany)*
Warteaufruf m (EDV) wait call
Wartebelastung f (EDV) mean queue size
Wartekosten pl (OR) cost of waiting time *(ie, often equal to opportunity costs)*
Warteliste f
  (com) waiting list
  – rooster
Warteraum m (OR) waiting space *(ie, in waiting-line models)*
Warteschlange f
  (OR) waiting line
  – queue
  – line-up
Warteschlangendisziplin f (OR) queue discipline
Warteschlangenmodell n (OR) waiting-line *(or* queuing) model
Warteschlangentheorie f (OR) waiting-line *(or* queuing) theory *(syn, Bedienungstheorie)*
Warteschlangenverlustfaktor m (OR) queuing loss factor
Wartesystem n
  (OR) waiting-line system
  – queuing system
Wartetheorie f (Vw) waiting theory of interest *(G. Cassel)*
Wartezeit f
  (com) waiting period
  (SozV) qualifying period *(ie, minimum period of credit for contributions needed to qualify for benefits, 180 calendar months)*
  (Pw, Vers) qualifying *(or* waiting) period
  (Or) waiting time
  (Mk) latency period
Wartezeitminimierung f (IndE) minimization of waiting time
Wartezeitproblem n (OR) congestion problem

Wartezimmerverfahren n (AuW) „waiting room" method *(ie, temporary suspense of transfer of fund to a given country)*
Wartezustand m
  (EDV) wait state
  – disconnected mode, DM
Wartung f
  (IndE) maintenance
  – servicing
  – upkeep
Wartung f **durch Fremdfirmen** (com) third-party maintenance *(or* service)
Wartungsdienst m (com) maintenance service
Wartungsfeld n (EDV) maintenance control panel
Wartungskosten pl
  (KoR) maintenance cost *(or* charges)
  – cost of upkeep
Wartungsprogramm n (EDV) maintenance program
Wartungsprozessor m (EDV) service processor
Wartungsrückstellung f (ReW) maintenance reserve
Wartungsunternehmen n (com) service contractor
Wartungsvertrag m (com) service *(or* maintenance) agreement
Wartungszeit f (EDV) maintenance time
Waschzettel m (Mk) blurb *(ie, relating to books)*
Wasseraktien fpl (Bö) heavily diluted stocks
Wasserkosten pl (KoR) cost of water consumption
Wasserschadenversicherung f (Vers) water damage insurance
Wasserstraßen fpl (com) waterways
Wechsel m (WeR) bill of exchange
Wechselabrechnung f (Fin) bill discount note
Wechselabschrift f (WeR) copy of a bill *(syn, Wechselkopie)*
Wechselabteilung f (Fin) bill discount and collection department
Wechselagent m (Fin) = *Wechselmakler*
Wechselakzept n (WeR) acceptance of a bill
Wechsel m **akzeptieren** (WeR) to accept a bill
Wechselannahme f (WeR) acceptance of a bill
Wechselarbitrage f
  (AuW) arbitration of exchange
  – cross exchange
Wechsel m **auf kurze Sicht** (Fin) short (dated) bill
Wechselausfertigung f (WeR) duplicate of a bill *(eg, first, second, third of exchange)*
Wechsel m **ausstellen** (WeR) to make out *(or* draw) a bill
Wechselaussteller m (WeR) drawer of a bill
Wechselbad n (com) continual alternations between good and bad years
wechselbarer Speicher m (EDV) interchangeable memory
Wechsel m **begeben** (WeR) to negotiate a bill
Wechselbestand m (Fin) bill holdings
Wechselbetrieb m (EDV) half duplex operation *(syn, Halbduplexbetrieb)*
Wechselbezogener m (WeR) drawee of a bill
Wechselblankett n (WeR) blank bill
Wechselbuch n (ReW) = *Wechselkopierbuch*
Wechselbürge m
  (WeR) guarantor of a bill
  – collateral acceptor

655

Wechselbürgschaft f (WeR) bill guaranty
Wechseldebitoren pl (ReW) bills receivable
Wechseldiskont m (Fin) bank discount
Wechsel m **diskontieren lassen** (Fin) to get a bill discounted
Wechseldiskontierung f
  (Fin) discounting of a bill
  – bill discounting
Wechseldiskontkredit m (Fin) discount credit
Wechseldiskontlinie f (Fin) discount line
Wechseldiskontsatz m (Fin) bill discount rate
Wechseldomizil n (WeR) domicile of a bill *(ie, place where a bill is made payable)*
Wechsel m **domizilieren** (WeR) to domicile a bill
Wechseldrittausfertigung f (WeR) third of exchange
Wechselduplikat n (WeR) duplicate of a bill *(eg, first, second, third of exchange)*
Wechsel m **einlösen**
  (Fin) to discharge
  – to honor
  – to meet
  – to pay
  – to take up ... a bill
Wechseleinlösung f (Fin) payment of a bill
Wechseleinreicher m (WeR) party presenting a bill
Wechseleinzug m (Fin) collection of bill *(syn, Wechselinkasso)*
Wechseleinzugsspesen pl (Fin) bill collection charges
Wechselfähigkeit f (WeR) capacity to draw bills
Wechselfälligkeit f (WeR) maturity of a bill
Wechselfälschung f (WeR) counterfeit of a bill
Wechselforderungen fpl (ReW) bills (or notes) receivable
Wechselfrist f (WeR) time limit for payment of a bill
Wechselgeld n
  (com) change
  – small change
  (Fin) change fund *(ie, at disposal of cashier)*
Wechselgeschäft n (Fin) bill business
wechselgeschäftsfähig (WeR) capable of drawing bills
Wechselgesetz n (WeR) Law on Bills of Exchange, of 1 Apr 1934
Wechselgirant m (WeR) indorser of a bill
Wechselgiro n (WeR) indorsement of a bill
Wechselgläubiger m (Fin) bill creditor
Wechselhaftung f (WeR) liability under a bill of exchange
Wechselhandel m (Fin) bill brokerage
Wechselhereinnahme f (Fin) acceptance of a bill
Wechsel m **hereinnehmen** (Fin) to accept a bill
Wechsel m **honorieren** (WeR) = *Wechsel einlösen*
Wechsel mpl **im Bestand** (ReW) bills of exchange on hand
Wechsel mpl **im Umlauf** (Fin) bills in circulation
Wechselinhaber m (WeR) holder of a bill
Wechselinkasso n (Fin) collection of a bill *(syn, Wechseleinzug)*
Wechselklage f
  (WeR) action on a dishonored bill
  – suit upon a bill
  – (GB) action under the Bills of Exchange Act

Wechselkommission f (Fin) bill broking
Wechselkopie f (WeR) = *Wechselabschrift*
Wechselkopierbuch n (ReW) discount ledger
Wechselkredit m (Fin) acceptance *(or* discount) credit
Wechselkreditvolumen n (Fin) total discounts
Wechselkurs m
  (AuW) exchange rate
  – rate of exchange
Wechselkursabwertung f (AuW) exchange rate depreciation *(or* devaluation)
Wechselkurs-Adjustierung f (AuW) exchange rate realignment
Wechselkursänderung f (AuW) parity change
Wechselkursanpassung f (Vw) exchange rate adjustment *(or* rearrangement)
Wechselkursarbitrage f (AuW) = *Wechselarbitrage*
Wechselkursberichtigung f (AuW) = *Wechselkursanpassung*
Wechselkursbewegungen fpl (AuW) currency movements
Wechselkurse mpl (Fin) currency rates *(ie, quoted as interbank exchange rates, excluding bank service charges)*
Wechselkursfreigabe f (AuW) floating of the exchange rate
Wechselkursgarantie f (AuW) exchange rate guaranty
Wechselkursgefüge n (AuW) pattern of exchange rates
Wechselkursgewinne mpl (ReW) gains on currency translations
Wechselkurskorrektur f (AuW) = *Wechselkursanpassung*
Wechselkursmechanismus m (AuW) exchange rate mechanism
Wechselkursnotierung f (AUW) exchange rate quotation
Wechselkursparität f (AuW) exchange rate parity
Wechselkurspolitik f (AuW) exchange rate policy
Wechselkursregime n (IWF) exchange regime
Wechselkursrelationen fpl
  (AuW) exchange rate relations
  – currency parities
Wechselkursrisiko n (Fin) exchange risk
Wechselkursschwankungen fpl
  (AuW) exchange rate *(or* currency) fluctuations
  – currency movements
Wechselkursstabilisierung f (AuW) stabilizing the exchange rate
Wechselkursstabilität f (AuW) exchange rate stability
Wechselkurssystem n (AuW) exchange rate system
Wechselkursumrechnung f
  (AuW) conversion of exchange rates
  (ReW) currency translation
Wechselkursumrechnungsgewinne mpl (ReW) translation gains
Wechselkursverlust m (ReW) loss on exchange
Wechselkurtage f (Fin) bill brokerage
Wechsellagen fpl **der Konjunktur** (Vw) ups and downs of economic activity
Wechsellombard m (Fin) lending on bills *(ie, loans collateralized by notes outstanding)*

Wechselmakler m
(Fin) discounter
- factor
- (GB) bill broker
Wechselmaterial n (Fin) bills (of exchange)
wechselnde Massenfertigung f (IndE) alternative mass production *(opp, parallele Massenfertigung)*
Wechselnehmer m (WeR) payee of a bill *(syn, Remittent)*
Wechsel m **nicht einlösen** (WeR) to dishonor a bill
Wechselobligo n
(ReW) notes payable
(Fin) bill commitments
- (liability on) bills discounted
Wechselparität f (Vw) parity of exchange
Wechselpensionsgeschäft n (Fin) presentment of bills at Bundesbank under prepurchase agreements
Wechselportefeuille n (Fin) bill holdings (*or* portfolio)
Wechselprolongation f (WeR) renewal of a bill
Wechsel m **prolongieren** (WeR) to renew a bill
Wechselprotest m (WeR) bill protest
Wechselprotestanzeige f
(WeR) mandate of protest
- notice of protest
- protest jacket
Wechselprotestkosten pl (WeR) protest fees
Wechselprovision f (Fin) bill brokerage
Wechselprozeß m (Re) legal proceedings related to a bill of exchange, § 602 ZPO
Wechselrechnung f (Math) computation of simple discount *(syn, Diskontrechnung)*
Wechselrecht n (WeR) legal provisions on bills of exchange and promissory notes
Wechselrediskont m (Fin) redisounting of bills
Wechsel m **rediskontieren** (Fin) to rediscount a bill
Wechselregreß m (WeR) recourse to a party liable on a bill
Wechselreiterei f
(WeR) bill jobbing
- kite flying
- kiting
Wechselrembours m (Fin) documentary acceptance credit
Wechselrückgriff m (WeR) = *Wechselregreß*
Wechselschicht f
(Pw) swing
- rotating
- alternate ... shift
Wechselschicht-Arbeiter m (Pw) swing-shift worker
Wechselschicht-Gruppe f (Pw) alternating shift
Wechselschriftverfahren n (EDV) non-return-to-zero (*or* NRZ) recording
Wechselschuldner m (WeR) debtor on a bill
wechselseitig beteiligte Unternehmen npl (Re) interlocking enterprises, § 19 AktG
wechselseitige Beteiligung f (Fin) mutual participation
wechselseitige Haftung f (Re) cross liability
wechselseitige Überlebensversicherung f (Vers) joint insurance
Wechselsekunda f (WeR) second of exchange

Wechselskontro n (Fin) bill ledger
Wechselspesen pl (Fin) bill charges
Wechselsteuer f (StR) tax on drafts and bills of exchange
Wechselsteuergesetz n (Re) Law regulating the Tax on Drafts, Bills of Exchange, and Acceptances, as republished on 24 Juli 1959
Wechselstube f (Fin) exchange office *(ie, of a bank)*
Wechseltaktschrift f (EDV) two-frequency recording mode
Wechselumlauf m (Fin) bills in circulation
Wechselverbindlichkeiten fpl (ReW) bills payable
Wechselverbindlichkeiten fpl **eingehen** (Fin) to enter obligations on a bill of exchange
Wechselverbindlichkeiten fpl **gegenüber Banken** (ReW) notes payable to banks
Wechselverpflichteter m (WeR) party liable on a bill of exchange
Wechselvorlage f (WeR) presentment of a bill
Wechsel m **vorlegen** (WeR) to present a bill
Wechsel mpl **weitergeben** (Fin) to rediscount bills of exchange
Wechselwinkel m (Math) alternate angle
Wechsel m **ziehen (auf)** (WeR) to draw a bill of exchange (on)
Wechselziehung f (WeR) drawing of a bill
Wechselzinsen mpl (Fin) interest paid on a bill
Wechsel m **zum Diskont einreichen** (Fin) to discount a bill with a bank
Wechsel m **zu Protest gehen lassen** (WeR) to have a bill protested
Wechsel m **zur Annahme vorlegen** (WeR) to present a bill for acceptance
Wechselzweitschrift f (WeR) second of exchange
Weg m (OR) path
Weg m **beschreiten** (com) to start down a path
Wegegeld n (com) traveling expenses
Wegelagererpatent n (Pat) free-lance (*or* shortgun) patent
Wegerecht n (Re) right-of-way
Wegeunfall m (Pw) travel accident
Wegezeit f
(Pw) home-to-office time
(IndE) site-to-quarters time
Wegfall m **der Geschäftsgrundlage**
(Re) frustration of contract
- lapse of purpose
(ie, a vital change in circumstances assumed by the parties at the time the contract was concluded)
Wegfall m **von Anteilen** (Fin) retirement of shares
Wegintegral n (Math) contour integral
wegloben (Pw, infml) to kick sb up the stairs
Wegmatrix f (Math) path matrix
Wegnahmerecht n (Re) jus tollendi *(ie, right to remove an article affixed to a thing, § 258 BGB)*
Wegproblem n (OR) routing problem
wegrationalisieren (Pw) to abolish jobs by technological advance
wegsteuern (FiW) to skim off by taxation
Wegwerfbecher m (com) disposable cup
Wegwerfgesellschaft f (Vw, infml) throw-away society
Wegwerfgüter npl
(Mk) disposable products
- disposables

wegziehen
(com, infml) to move away
– to pull up one's roots
weibliche Führungskräfte *fpl* (Pw) women executives
weiches Interview *n* (Stat) permissive interview
weiche Technologien *fpl* (Vw) small-scale (*or* ,,soft") technologies (*usu. implying a sort of updated arts-and-crafts vision*)
weiche Währung *f* (AuW) soft currency (*ie, not freely convertible or fluctuating in the exchange markets*)
Weichwährungsland *n* (AuW) soft-currency country
Weihnachtsfreibetrag *m* (StR) tax-free Christmas allowance (*ie, DM400, § 19 III EStG*)
Weihnachtsgratifikation *f* (Pw) = *Weihnachtszuwendung*
Weihnachtszuwendung *f*
(Pw) Christmas bonus
– cash bonus at Christmas
weiße Ware *f* (com) white goods (*ie, washing machines, freezers, cookers, dishwashers; opp, braune Ware*)
Weisungen *fpl*
(Pw) instructions
– orders
weisungsgebunden
(Pw) bound by directives
– reporting to
Weisungsgewalt *f* (Bw) authority
Weisungskompetenz *f* (Bw) managerial authority
Weisungsrecht *n* (Pw) right to issue instructions to employees
weit auslegen (Re) to put a broad (*or* liberal) construction upon
weite Auslegung *f*
(Re) broad construction
– liberal interpretation
Weiterbegebung *f* (WeR) renegotiation
Weiterbehandlungsgebühr *f* (Pat) fee for further processing
Weiterbenutzung *f* (Pat) continued use
weiterbeschäftigen
(Pw) to continue to employ
– to keep on
Weiterbildung *f* **in e-m nicht ausgeübten Beruf** (StR) reacquiring or updating skills used in a former profession, vocation, or business activity, § 10 I No. 7 EStG
Weiterbildungskosten *pl* (StR) retraining expenses
Weiterbildung *f* **von Führungskräften**
(Pw) executive development (*or* training)
– management development
weiterführender Zyklus *m* (OR) transition cycle
Weitergabe *f* **von Handelswechseln** (Fin) rediscounting of commercial bills
Weitergabe *f* **von Kompetenzen von oben nach unten** (Bw) top-down delegation of authority
weitergeleiteter Eigentumsvorbehalt *m* (Re) transferred reservation of ownership
weiterleihen
(Fin) to gon on lending
(Fin) to on-lend money (*eg, deposited with banks*)

weiterleiten an
(com) to pass on
– to transmit
(com) forward to
– (GB) redirect to (*ie, instructions to post office on envelope*)
Weiterleitungskredit *m* (Fin) flow-through credit
Weiterlieferung *f* (com) delivery (*or* supply) to third party
Weiterrückversicherer *m* (Vers) retrocessionaire (*ie, the reinsurer of a reinsurer; syn; Retrozessionar*)
Weiterrückversicherungsnehmer *m* (Vers) retrocedent (*ie, reinsurer placing a retrocession; syn, Retrozedent*)
weiterverarbeiten (com) to reprocess
Weiterverarbeiter *m*
(com) processing firm
– processor
Weiterverarbeitung *f*
(com) processing
(IndE) downstream operations (*eg, refining and petrochemical plants*)
weiterveräußern (com) to resell
Weiterveräußerung *f* (com) resale
Weiterveräußerung *f* **an Dritte** (com) resale to third parties
Weiterveredelung *f* (com) supplementary processing
Weiterverkauf *m* (com) resale
weiterverkaufen (com) to resell
weitervermieten (Re) to re-let
Weitervermietung *f* (Re) re-letting
Weiterversendung *f* (com) redispatch
Weiterversicherung *f* (Vers) continued insurance
weitreichende Marktdurchdringung *f* (Mk) blanket market penetration
Weittechnik *f* (IndE) telecommunications
Weitverkehr *m* (IndE) = *Weittechnik*
,,Wellblech-Konjunktur" *f* (Vw) saw-tooth pattern of economic activity
Wellpappe *f*
(com) corrugated fiberboard
– (*short form*) corrugated
Wellpappenfabrikant *m* (com) boxmaker
Weltabschluß *m*
(ReW) worldwide financial statements
– (GB) worldwide annual accounts
Weltbank *f* (AuW) World Bank (*short for: International Bank for Reconstruction and Development*)
Weltbilanz *f*
(ReW) worldwide balance sheet
– global financial statement
Weltbruttosozialprodukt *n* (VGR) gross world product
Welteinkommensprinzip *n* (FiW) principle of income-source neutrality
Weltfangertrag *m* (com) world fish catch
Weltfischereiertrag *m* (com) world harvest of fish (*ie, comprising demersal fish = Bodenfisch, caught near the ocean floor, and pelagic fish = pelagische Fische, caught near the surface*)
Weltgetreidehandel *m* (AuW) world grain trade
Welthandel *m*

(AuW) world
- international
- global ... trade
Welthandelskonferenz f (AuW) UNCTAD: United Nations Conference on Trade and Development
Welthandels-Konjunktur f (AuW) cyclical movements in world trade
Welthandelssystem n (AuW) world trading system
Weltindustriezensus m (Stat) worldwide industrial census
Weltkonjunktur f (Vw) worldwide economic activity *(eg, in the absence of a revival of ...)*
Welt-Konzernbilanz f
(ReW) consoldated world accounts
- worldwide consolidated financial statement
- global annual accounts
Weltmarkt m
(AuW) global
- international
- world ... market
Weltmarktbedingungen fpl (AuW) conditions of world markets
Weltmarktpreis m (AuW) world market price
Weltmarktstrategie f (Bw) world-wide market strategy
Weltpatent n (Pat) universal patent
Weltumsatz m
(com) worldwide sales
- sales worldwide
- world group sales
Weltunternehmen n
(Bw) international company *(or* corporation)
- globe-spanning business enterprise
Welt-Urheberrechts-Konvention f (Pat) Universal Copyright Convention, of 6 Sept 1952
Weltvorräte mpl (Vw) global reserves *(eg, minerals, petroleum)*
Weltwährungsfonds m (IWF) International Monetary Fund, IMF
Weltwährungssystem n (AuW) international monetary system
Weltwarenmärkte mpl (com) world commodity markets
weltweite Handelsbeziehungen fpl (Bw) far-flung trade connections *(ie, covering the whole world)*
weltweite Inflation f (Vw) worldwide inflation
weltweite Knappheit f (AuW) worldwide shortage (of)
weltweite Liquiditätsschwierigkeiten fpl (Fin) worldwide financial crunch
weltweite Rezession f
(AuW) global downturn
- world recession
Weltwirtschaft f
(AuW) global
- international
- world ... economy
weltwirtschaftliche Lage f (AuW) international economic condition
Weltwirtschaftsgipfel m (Vw) world economic summit
Weltwirtschaftsinstitut n (Vw) *(Kiel-based)* Institute for World Economics
Weltwirtschaftskrise f

(Vw) world-wide economic crisis
(Vw) the Great Depression
- the Depression years *(ie, limited to the crisis of the 1930s)*
Weltwirtschaftsordnung f (AuW) international economic order *(or* system)
Wendepunkt m
(Math) turning point
- point of inflection
weniger gute Adresse f
(Fin) borrower of lesser standing
- lesser-rated borrower
Wenn-dann-Beziehung f (Log) action-consequence relation
Wenn-Satz m (Log) if statement
Werbeabteilung f (Mk) advertising department
Werbeagent m
(Mk) advertising man
- adman
Werbeagentur f (Mk) advertising agency
Werbeaktionen fpl (Mk) advertising measures
Werbeanalyse f (Mk) advertising analysis
Werbeantwort f (Mk) business reply
Werbeaquisiteur m (Mk) advertising canvasser
Werbeaufwand m (Mk) advertising expense *(syn, Werbeaufwendungen)*
Werbebeilage f
(Mk) advertising supplement
- (infml) stuffer
Werbeberater m (Mk) advertising consultant
Werbeberatung f (Mk) advertising agency
Werbebranche f (Mk) advertising industry
Werbebrief m (Mk) advertising letter
Werbebroschüre f (Mk) brochure
Werbebudget n (Mk) advertising budget *(syn, Werbeetat)*
Werbedrucke mpl (Mk) printed advertising material
(syn, Werbedrucksachen)
Werbeerfolg m (Mk) advertising effectiveness
Werbeerfolgskontrolle f (Mk) control of advertising effectiveness
Werbeerfolgsprognose f (Mk) forecast of advertising effectiveness
Werbeerfüller m (Mk) adopter
Werbeetat m (Mk) advertising budget *(syn, Werbebudget)*
Werbefachmann m (Mk) advertising specialist *(or* expert)
Werbefeldzug m (Mk) advertising campaign
Werbefernsehen n (Mk) advertising TV
Werbefläche f
(Mk) hoarding
- (GB) billboard
Werbeforschung f (Mk) advertising research
Werbegag m (Mk) advertising *(or* publicity) stunt
Werbegeschenke npl (Mk) give-away articles
Werbegrundsätze mpl (Mk) standards of advertising practice
werbeintensive Produkte npl (Mk) highly advertised products
Werbekampagne f (Mk) advertising campaign
Werbekonkurrenz f (Mk) competition through advertising
Werbekontrolle f (Mk) = *Werbeerfolgskontrolle*

Werbekosten *pl* (Mk) advertising expense *(syn, Werbeaufwand)*
Werbeleiter *m* (Mk) advertising manager
Werbemaßnahmen *fpl* (Mk) advertising efforts
Werbematerial *n* (Mk) advertising material
Werbemittel *n* (Mk) advertising medium
Werbemittelanalyse *f* (Mk) analysis of advertising media
Werbemuster *n* (Mk) advertising sample
werben
 (Mk) to advertise
 – to promote
werbende Aktiva *npl*
 (Bw) earning assets
 (Fin) interest-bearing assets
werbende Ausgaben *fpl* (FiW) productive expenditure *(opp, transfer expenditure)*
werbendes Kapital *n* (Vw) reproductive capital
werbendes Vermögen *n* (Fin) earning assets
Werbeplakat *n* (com) show bill
Werbeplanung *f* (Mk) planning of advertising
Werbepreis *m* (Mk) advertising price
Werbepsychologie *f* (Mk) advertising psychology
Werber *m* (Mk) solicitor
Werberabatt *m* (Mk) advertising rebate
Werberendite *f* (Mk) advertising return
Werberevision *f* (Mk) review of promotional activities
Werberiese *m* (Mk) media tycoon *(eg, Kenneth Thompson)*
Werbesendungen *fpl*
 (com) advertising mail
 (Mk) broadcast of commercials
Werbeslang *m* (Mk) advertising slang
Werbeslogan *m* (Mk) advertising slogan
Werbespot *m* (Mk) advertising spot
Werbe-Stückkosten *pl* (Mk) unit advertising cost
Werbeträger *mpl* (Mk) advertising media *(syn, Werbemedia, Media)*
Werbeträgeranalyse *f* (Mk) media analysis
Werbevertreter *m* (Mk) advertising salesman
Werbewirkung *f* (Mk) impact of advertising
Werbewirtschaft *f* (Mk) advertising industry
Werbung *f* (Mk) advertising
Werbung *f* **durch Postwurfsendungen** (Mk) direct mail advertising
Werbung *f* **ohne postalischen Werbemittelversand** (Mk) unmailed direct advertising
Werbungskosten *pl* (StR) income-related expenses, § 9 EStG
Werbungskosten-Pauschbetrag *m* (StR) blanket deduction for income-related expenses, § 9a EStG
Werbungsmittler *m* (Mk) advertising agency *(or office)*
Werbungstreibender *m* (Mk) advertiser
Werdegang *m*
 (Pw) personal background
 – career
Werk *n*
 (IndE) production facility
 – plant
 – factory
Werkbahn *f* (Bw) plant-owned railroad feeder system

Werkfernverkehr *m* (com) plant-operated long-distance traffic *(opp, Werkverkehr, Werknahverkehr)*
Werkhandelsgesellschaft *f* (Bw) independent selling subsidiary *(syn, Verkaufskontor)*
Werkleistungsvertrag *m* (Re) contract under which goods are improved, processed or converted
Werklieferung *f*
 (Re) sale under a contract for goods and services
 (StR) sale for turnover tax purposes, § 3 IV UStG
Werklieferungsvertrag *m* (Re) work performance contract *(ie, contract constituting mixture of sale and contract of work, § 651 BGB)*
Werklohn *m* (Re) compensation for work, § 651 BGB
Werknahverkehr *m* (com) plant-operated short-haul traffic *(opp, Werkverkehr, Werkfernverkehr)*
Werknormen *fpl* (IndE) plant-developed standards
Werksabholung *f* (com) factory pickup
Werksanlagen *fpl* (IndE) plant facilities
Werksarzt *m* (Pw) plant physician
Werksbescheinigung *f* (com) works (*or* mill) certificate
Werksbuchhaltung *f* (ReW) plant accounting department
Werkschutz *m* (Bw) plant security guard
werkseigener Güterverkehr *m* (com) private freight traffic
Werksferien *pl* (Bw) vacation close-down *(ie, complete stopping of work during the holiday period; syn, Betriebsferien)*
Werksgebäude *n* (com) factory building
Werksgrundstück *n*
 (com) plant site
 – factory-site land
werksintern (com) intra-plant
Werkskantine *f* (Pw) works canteen
Werkskontrolle *f* (Stat) manufacturer's quality control
Werkskosten *pl* (KoR) manufacturing cost *(ie, fixed cost + variable cost related to manufacturing)*
Werksleiter *m* (IndE) plant manager
Werksleitung *f* (IndE) plant management
Werksparkassen *fpl* (Bw) company savings banks
Werkspionage *f* (Bw) industrial espionage
Werksprüfung *f* (Stat) manufacturer's inspection
Werksrabatt *m* (com) factory rebate
Werksselbstkosten *pl* (KoR) factory cost price
Werkstatt *f* (IndE) shop
Werkstattauftrag *m* (IndE) job shop order
Werkstattfertigung *f*
 (IndE) job shop production *(ie, custom manufacturing operation; eg, tool and die making)*
 – cellular organization of production
 – intermittent production
Werkstattleistungen *fpl* (IndE) production shop services
Werkstattzeichnung *f* (com) workshop drawing
Werkstoffe *mpl* (Bw) materials
Werkstoffgemeinkosten *pl* (KoR) indirect material costs
Werkstoffplanung *f* (Bw) materials planning

Werkstoffverlust *m* (IndE) loss of feedstock *(ie, difference between startup volume and finished weight)*
Werkstoffzeit *f* (IndE) door-to-door time
Werkstor *n* (com) plant gate
Werksvertreter *m* (com) manufacturer's agent *(ie, not independent)*
Werkswohnung *f*
  (Pw) factory-owned apartment
  – (GB) factory-owned flat
Werkszeitung *f*
  (Bw) in-house
  – company
  – employee ... magazine
  – house organ
Werkszeugnis *n* (com) mill certificate
Werkverkehr *m*
  (com) plant-operated traffic *(ie, companies carrying their own goods)*
  – (US) private carriage
  (subterms: Werknahverkehr, Werkfernverkehr)
Werkverkehrsversicherung *f* (Vers) private carriage insurance
Werk *n* **verlegen** (Bw) to relocate a plant
Werkvertrag *m* (Re) contract for work *(ie, one by which one party, the contractor, promises to produce a work and the other party, the customer, promises to pay for it, §§ 631ff BGB; the chief criterion being that the contractor is not subject to any control by the customer)*
Werkverwaltungsgemeinkosten *pl* (KoR) plant management overhead
Werkzeichnung *f* (com) workshop drawing
Werkzeuganforderung *f* (IndE) tool (issue) order
Werkzeugentnahmeschein *m* (MaW) tools requisition slip
Werkzeugkosten *pl* (ReW) cost of tools
Werkzeuglager *n* (MaW) tools stores
Werkzeugmacher *m* (Pw) toolmaker
Werkzeugmaschine *f* (IndE) machine tool
Werkzeugmaschinen-Hersteller *m* (com) machine tool maker
Werkzeugwechselzeit *f* (IndE) tool allowance
Wert *m* (Vw, Bw) value
Wertanalyse *f* (Bw) value analysis *(or* engineering*)*
Wertansatz *m* (ReW) valuation *(eg, of fixed assets; § 40 HGB)*
Wertaufbewahrungsmittel *n* (Vw) store of value *(or* purchasing power*)*
Wertaufholung *f* (StR) increased valuation on previous balance-sheet figures
Wert *m* **beilegen** (ReW) to attribute value to
Wertberichtigung *f* (ReW) valuation adjustment *(ie, entry on the liabilities side of a balance sheet, made to offset overvaluation of assets)*
Wertberichtigung *f* **auf Anlagevermögen** (ReW) value adjustment of fixed assets
Wertberichtigung *f* **auf Beteiligungen** (ReW) allowance for loss on investments
Wertberichtigung *f* **auf Finanzanlagevermögen** (ReW) (indirect) writedown of permanent investment
Werberichtigung *f* **auf Forderungen** (ReW) discount on accounts receivable
Wertberichtigung *f* **auf Sachanlagevermögen** (ReW) (indirect) provision for depreciation, depletion, and amortization of plant, property and equipment
Wertberichtigung *f* **auf Substanzverringerung** (ReW) allowance for depletion
Wertberichtigung *f* **auf Umlaufvermögen** (ReW) current-asset valuation adjustment
Wertberichtigung *f* **auf uneinbringliche Forderungen** (ReW) provision for bad debts
Wertberichtigung *f* **auf Vorratsvermögen** (ReW) inventory valuation adjustment
Wertberichtigung *f* **auf zweifelhafte Forderungen** (ReW) allowance for doubtful accounts
Wertberichtigungen *fpl* (ReW, EG) value adjustments
Wertberichtigungen *fpl* **auf Forderungen und Wertpapiere** (Fin) losses incurred or provided for on loans and securities
Wertberichtigungen *fpl* **im Kreditgeschäft** (Fin) losses on loans
Wertberichtigungskonto *n* (ReW) value adjustment account
Wert *m* **der Grundgesamtheit** (Stat) parental value
Wert *m* **der Zentraltendenz** (Stat) central value
Wertebereich *m* (Math) range
Wert erhalten (WeR) value received *(syn,* Wert in Rechnung; *obsolete phrase)*
Wert *m* **e–s Anlagegegenstandes bei Außerbetriebnahme** (ReW) exit price
Wert *m* **e–s Schnittes** (Math) capacity of a cut
Wertermittlung *f* **bei mehreren Beteiligten** (StR) valuation of an asset owned by more than one person, § 3 BewG
Werterneuerungsfonds *m* (ReW) earmarked taxable reserve for future price increases of plant and machinery *(syn,* Maschinenerneuerungskonto, Werterneuerungskonto*)*
Wertetafel *f* (Math) value matrix
Wertetupel *n* (Math) set of variables
Wertfortschreibung *f* (StR) adjustment of assessed value, § 22 BewG
Wertgrenze *f* (Zo) value limit
Wertgrenzprodukt *n* (Vw) marginal product in terms of value
Wertkontingent *n* (Zo) quota by value
Wertkorrektur *m* (ReW) value adjustment
Wertlehre *f* (Re, VW) axiology
wertlose Informationen *fpl* (EDV, infml) garbage
wertmäßig
  (com) in terms of value
  – in value *(eg, exports rose 16% in value)*
  – by value *(eg, 30% of the market by value)*
wertmäßige Konsolidierung *f* (ReW) consolidation in terms of value
Wertmaßstab *m* (Vw) *(money as)* measure of value
Wertminderung *f*
  (Bw) lost usefulness
  – loss of serviceability
  – decline in economic usefulness *(ie, of fixed-asset items)*
Wertminderung *f* **durch Schwund** (com) shrinkage loss
Wertnachnahme *f* (com) delivery by forwarder against payment
Wertnachweis *m* (com) evidence of value

Wertpapier n
(WeR) security
– (US + GB) negotiable instrument *(ie, the English concept is more restricted: English law speaks of it only if holder in due course is prejudiced neither by defects in title of previous holder nor by defenses which might be available against previous holders = Wertpapier i. e. S. = Order- und Inhaberpapier)*
Wertpapierabsatz m (Fin) sale of securities
Wertpapierabschreibung f (ReW) securities write-off
Wertpapierabteilung f (Fin) securities department *(syn, Effektenabteilung)*
Wertpapieranalyse f (Fin) security analysis
Wertpapieranalytiker m (Fin) security analyst
Wertpapieranlage f (Fin) investment in securities
Wertpapierarbitrage f (Fin) arbitrage in securities
Wertpapieraufstellung f (Fin) statement of securities
Wertpapierauftrag m **ohne Limit** (Bö) unlimited order
Wertpapierauslieferung f (Fin) delivery of securities
Wertpapierberatung f (Fin) investment counseling
Wertpapierbesitz m (Fin) security holdings
Wertpapierbesitzer m (Fin) security holder
Wertpapierbestand m (Fin) security holdings *(or* portfolio*)*
Wertpapierbewertung f (Fin) valuation of securities
Wertpapierbörse f
(Bö) stock exchange
– stock market
– securities exchange
– market
(ie, exchanges on the European Continent are often called Bourses)
Wertpapierdarlehen n (Fin) loan on collateral securities
Wertpapierdepot n
(Fin) securities portfolio
(Fin) security deposit account
Wertpapiere npl (ReW, EG) investments
Wertpapiere npl **beleihen** (Fin) to advance money on securities
Wertpapiere npl **der öffentlichen Hand** (Fin) public sector paper
Wertpapiere npl **des Anlagevermögens**
(ReW) permanent *(or* long-term*)* investments
(ReW, EG) investments held as fixed assets
Wertpapiere npl **des Umlaufvermögens**
(ReW) marketable securities
– temporary investments
– investments held as current assets
Wertpapiere npl **i. e. S.** (WeR) negotiable instruments *(ie, payable to order or bearer; syn, Order- und Inhaberpapiere)*
Wertpapiereigengeschäfte npl (Fin) securities transactions for own account
Wertpapiere npl **lombardieren** (Fin) to advance money on securities
Wertpapieremission f (Fin) security issue
Wertpapiere npl **mit kurzer Laufzeit** (Fin) short-dated securities *(syn, Kurzläufer)*

Wertpapierengagement n (Fin) security portfolio
Wertpapiererträge mpl (ReW) income from securities
Wertpapiere npl **und Anteile** mpl (StR) securities and membership rights, § 11 BewG
Wertpapierfernscheck m (Fin) securities transfer order
Wertpapierfinanzierung f (Fin) financing through securities
Wertpapierfonds m (Fin) security-based investment fund
Wertpapiergeschäft n
(Fin) security transaction
(Fin) dealing *(or* trading*)* in securities
– securities business
Wertpapiergiroverkehr m (Fin) securities clearing transactions
Wertpapierhandel m (Bö) securities trading
Wertpapierhändler m **im Freiverkehr** (Bö) securities dealer
Wertpapierinhaber m (Fin) holder of securities
Wertpapierkaufabrechnung f (Fin) bought note
Wertpapierkennummer f (Fin) securities code number
Wertpapier-Kommissionsgeschäft n (Fin) stock broking business
Wertpapierkonto n (Fin) securities account
Wertpapierkredit m (Fin) credit based on purchase of securities
Wertpapierkurs m (Bö) security price *(or* quotation*)*
Wertpapierlombard m (Fin) loan on securities
Wertpapiermakler m (Fin) stock broker
Wertpapiermarkt m (Fin) securities market
Wertpapier n **mit geringen Umsätzen** (Bö) low-volume security
Wertpapiernotierung f (Bö) quotation
Wertpapier n **öffentlichen Glaubens** (WeR) negotiable instrument
Wertpapierpaket m (Bö) block of shares
Wertpapierpensionsgeschäft n (Fin) sale and repurchase scheme *(ie, borrowing short-term against securities under a ,,pension" agreement by which banks sell securities to the central bank for a limited period: pledging/purchase today, repurchase/reselling later)*
Wertpapierplazierung f (Fin) placing of securities
Wertpapierportefeuille n
(Fin) security holdings
– securities portfolio
Wertpapierrechnung f (Fin) computation of effective interest rate *(syn, Effektenrechnung)*
Wertpapierrecht n (WeR) law of negotiable instruments
Wertpapierrendite f (Fin) yield *(ie, on stocks or bonds)*
Wertpapierrückkauf m (Fin) repurchase of securities
Wertpapiersammelbank f (Fin) financial institution operating collective security deposits and giro transfer systems *(syn, Kassenverein, Effektengirobank)*
Wertpapierscheck m (Fin) securities transfer order
Wertpapiersparen n (Fin) investment saving
Wertpapierstatistik f (Bö) securities statistics

Wertpapierstückelung *f* (Fin) denomination of securities
Wertpapiertausch *m* (Fin) exchange of securities
Wertpapiertermingeschäft *n* (Bö) forward deal in securities
Wertpapiertransaktion *f* (Fin) securities transaction
Wertpapierübertragung *f* (Fin) transfer of securities
Wertpapierumsatz *m* (Bö) volume of trading
Wertpapierverkäufe *mpl* **des Berufshandels** (Bö) shop selling
Wertpapierverkaufsabrechnung *f* (Fin) sold note
Wertpapierverrechnungskonto *n* (Fin) securities clearing account
Wertpapierverwaltung *f* (Fin) portfolio management
Wertpapierzuteilung *f*
 (Fin) allotment of securities
 (Fin) scaling down
Wertparadoxon *n* (Vw) paradox of value
Wertrechtanleihe *f* (FiW) government-inscribed debt *(syn, Wertschriftanleihe)*
Wertrechte *npl* (Fin) loan stock rights *(ie, not evidenced by certificates; used, for instance, in ‚Treuhandgiroverkehr')*
Wertschöpfung *f*
 (Bw) value added
 – real net output
 (ie, output minus input, calculated as a firm's total sales less expenditure on goods and services purchased from other firms = Verkaufserlöse – Vorleistungen)
 (VGR) value added *(ie, net value added + nonfactor charges; Unterbegriffe: Bruttowertschöpfung und Nettowertschöpfung, qv)*
Wertschöpfungsstruktur *f* (Vw) value added pattern *(eg, of the total private sector of the economy)*
Wertschriftanleihe *f* (FiW) = *Wertrechtanleihe*
Wertschriftenclearing *n* (Fin) securities clearing
Wertschwankungen *fpl* (ReW) fluctuations in value
Wertsicherungsklausel *f*
 (Fin) escalation
 – index
 – stable-value ... clause
Wertsteigerung *f*
 (com) appreciation
 – increase *(or* rise) in value
 – gain *(or* rise) *(eg, in the value of the DM against the $)*
Wertsteigerung *f* **durch Neubewertung** (Bw) revaluation surplus
Wertsteigerungsklausel *f* (com) escalation clause
Wertstellung *f* (Fin) value (date) *(syn, Valutierung: ,,Val. per ..." or ,,Wert per ...")*
Werttheorie *f* (Vw) theory of value
Wertumsatz *m* (ReW) sales in terms of value
Wert- und Ursprungszertifikat *n* (com) certificate of value and origin
Werturteil *n* (Log) value judgement
Wertverlust *m*
 (com) depreciation
 – decrease in value
 – loss *(or* fall) *(eg, in the value of the DM against the $)*
Wertzahlen *fpl* (StR) special factors applied to arrive at the fair market value of real property, § 90 BewG
Wertzeichen *n* (com) postage stamp
Wertzoll *m*
 (Zo) customs duty ad valorem
 – ad valorem duty
wertzollbare Waren *fpl*
 (Zo) goods subject to ad valorem duty
 – ad valorem goods
Wertzollrecht *n* (Re) valuation legislation
Wertzolltarif *m* (Zo) ad valorem tariff
Wertzuschlagklausel *f* (Vers) premium escalator clause *(ie, to take account of later appreciations)*
Wertzuwachs *m*
 (com) appreciation
 – increase in value
 – increment
Wertzuwachssteuer *f* (FiW) property increment tax
Wesensgleichheit *f* (Pat) identity
wesentlich (Re) material
wesentlich Beteiligte *mpl* (StR) substantial investors, § 17 EStG
wesentliche Bedingung *f* (Re) essential condition
wesentliche Bestandteile *mpl*
 (com) essential features *(or* traits)
 (Re) integral parts *(eg, of a contract)*
 (Re) essential component parts, § 93 BGB
 – immovable fixtures
wesentliche Beteiligung *f* (StR) substantial investment *(or* equity holding), § 17 EStG
wesentliche Formvorschriften *fpl* (Re) essential requirements of form
wesentlicher Inhalt *m* (Re) main provisions *(eg, of a contract)*
wesentlicher Wettbewerb *m* (Kart) substantial competition, § 5a I GWB
wesentliches Beschaffenheitsmerkmal *n* **e–r Ware** (Zo) essential character of an article
wesentliches Spiel *n* (OR) essential game
wesentliche Vereinbarungen *fpl* (Re) essential contract arrangements
wesentliche Vertragsverletzung *f* (Re) fundamental breach of contract
Wesentlichkeit *f* (ReW) materiality
Westeuropäische Union *f* (EG) Western European Union, WEU
Westinghouse-System *n* (IndE) leveling system
Wettbewerb *m* (Vw) competition *(syn, Konkurrenz; may be: tough, intense, powerful, stiff, fierce)*
Wettbewerb *m* **ausschalten** (Bw) to eliminate competition
Wettbewerb *m* **beschränken** (Kart) to impair competition
Wettbewerb *m* **erhalten** (Kart) to preserve competition
Wettbewerb *m* **fördern** (Bw) to promote competition
Wettbewerb *m* **lähmen** (Kart) to render competition inoperative
wettbewerbliche Anreize *mpl* (Bw) competitive incentives

wettbewerbliche Verhaltensmotivation f (Vw) spirit of competition
Wettbewerb m **regeln** (Kart) to regulate competition
wettbewerbsbeschränkende Abrede f (Kart) conspiracy in restraint of competition
wettbewerbsbeschränkender Vertrag m (Kart) agreement in restraint of competition
wettbewerbsbeschränkender Zusammenschluß m (Kart) combination in restraint of competition
wettbewerbsbeschränkendes Verhalten n (Kart) competition restraining activities
- (US) restraint of trade
- (GB) restrictive trade practices
wettbewerbsbeschränkende Vereinbarung f (Kart) agreement in restraint of competition
wettbewerbsbeschränkender Vertrag m (Kart) contract in restraint of competition
Wettbewerbsbeschränkung f
(Kart) restraint of competition
- (US) restraint of trade
- (GB) restrictive practices
wettbewerbsdämpfend (Kart) tending to restrain competition
Wettbewerbsdruck m (com) competitive pressures *(eg, to be immune to ...)*
wettbewerbsfähig (com) competitive
wettbewerbsfähig bleiben (com) to stay competitive
wettbewerbsfähiger Preis m (Mk) competitive price
Wettbewerbsfähigkeit f (com) competitiveness
- competitive strength
- competitive edge
- ability to compete (*or* to meet competition) effectively
Wettbewerbsfähigkeit f **erhalten**
(com) to keep one's competitive edge
- to retain competitiveness
Wettbewerbsfähigkeit f **stärken** (com) to reinforce one's competitive position *(eg, domestically and internationally)*
Wettbewerbsfähigkeit f **wiederherstellen** (Bw) to restore competitiveness
wettbewerbsfeindlich (KartR) detrimental to effective competition
wettbewerbsfeindliches Verhalten n (Kart) anti-competitive behavior (*or* practices) *(ie, practices calculated to prevent or distort competition)*
Wettbewerbsförderung f (Vw) promotion of competition
Wettbewerbsfreiheit f (Vw) freedom of competition (*or* to compete)
Wettbewerbsfunktionen fpl (Vw) functions of competition
Wettbewerbsgesetz n (Kart) Law Against Restraints of Competition, 1957
Wettbewerbsgesetze npl (Kart) competition laws
Wettbewerbsgrad m (Vw) level of competition
Wettbewerbshüter mpl (Kart) competition watchdogs *(ie, Berlin-based Federal Cartel Office; Antitrust Division and Federal Trade Commission in U.S.A., Monopolies and Mergers Commission in Great Britain)*
wettbewerbsintensiv (com) intensely competitive

Wettbewerbsklausel f
(Kart) restraint of competition clause
- non-competition clause
- exclusive service clause
- ancillary covenant against competition
(ie, in employment contracts; syn, Konkurrenzklausel)
Wettbewerbsklima n (Bw) competition (*or* competitive) climate
Wettbewerbslage f (Bw) competitive position
Wettbewerbsmarkt m (Vw) competitive market
Wettbewerbsnachteil m (Kart) competitive disadvantage (against)
wettbewerbsneutral (Bw) not affecting competition
Wettbewerbsneutralität f **herstellen** (StR) to eliminate competitive distortion
Wettbewerbsneutralität f **verletzen** (StR) to distort competition
Wettbewerbsnorm f (Kart) norm for competition
Wettbewerbspolitik f (Vw) competition (*or* competitive) policy
wettbewerbspolitische Gesichtspunkte mpl (Vw) aspects of market competition policy
Wettbewerbsposition f (Bw) competitive position
Wettbewerbspreis m (Mk) competitive price
Wettbewerbspreisbildung f (Mk) competitive pricing
Wettbewerbsrecht n
(Kart) law on competition
- (US) antitrust law
- (GB) restrictive trade practices law
wettbewerbsrechtliche Konsequenzen fpl (Kart) competitive consequences *(eg, of corporate conduct)*
Wettbewerbsregeln fpl (Kart) rules of competition
wettbewerbsschädlicher Zusammenschluß m (Kart) combination restraining competition
Wettbewerbsschutz m (Kart) protection of fair competition
wettbewerbsschwache Branchen fpl (Vw) industries ill-equipped to meet competition
Wettbewerbsschwächung f (Vw) decline of competitiveness
Wettbewerbsstrategie f (Mk) competitive strategy
Wettbewerbsstruktur f (Vw) pattern of competition
Wettbewerb m **stärken** (Kart) to reinforce competition
Wettbewerbstheorie f (Vw) theory of competition
Wettbewerbsverbot n (Re) prohibition to compete *(ie, applies to commercial clerks, voluntary apprentices, personally liable partners of OHG and KG, and managing board members, §§ 60, 82a, 112 HGB, § 88 AktG)*
Wettbewerbsvereinbarungen fpl (Bw) agreements to limit competition
Wettbewerbsverfälschung f (Kart) distortion of competition
Wettbewerbsverhalten n (com) competitive behavior
Wettbewerbsverschiebung f (com) shift in competitive strength
Wettbewerbsverzerrung f
(Vw) distortion of competitive positions *(eg, among the main industrial countries)*

(Kart) distortion of competition
- distorted competition
- competitive distortion
Wettbewerbsvorschriften *fpl* **verletzen** (Kart) to violate (*or* fall foul of) competition rules
Wettbewerbsvorteil *m* (com) competitive advantage (*or* edge) (over)
wettbewerbswidrig (Kart) anticompetitive
wettbewerbswidriges Verhalten *n* (Re) anticompetitive practice
Wettbewerbswirtschaft *f* (Vw) competitive economy
Wettbewerb *m* **verdrängen** (com) to cut out (all) competition
Wettbewerb *m* **verzerren** (Kart) to distort competition
Wettbewerb *m* **zwischen verschiedenen hierarchischen Ebenen** (Bw) vertical strain
wichtiger Grund *m*
(Re) compelling (*or* substantial) reason
(Pw) cause (*eg, dismissed for cause*)
wichtiger Kunde *m* (com) key customer
Wicksellscher Prozeß *m* (Vw) Wicksellian cumulative process
Wicksells Idealbank *f* (Vw) Wicksell's ideal bank
Widerklage *f* **erheben** (Re) to advance a counterclaim in legal proceedings, § 33 ZPO
widerlegliche Vermutung *f*
(Re) rebuttable
- inconclusive
- disputable ... presumption
(*ie, may be invalidated by proof or stronger presumption; opp, unwiderlegliche Vermutung*)
Widerlegung *f* (Log) refutation
widerrechtliche Aneignung *f* (Re) misappropriation
widerrechtliche Drohung *f* (Re) unlawful threat, § 123 BGB
widerrechtlicher Besitz *m* (Re) unlawful possession
Widerruf *m*
(Re) cancellation
- rescission
- revocation
Widerruf *m* **der Zulassung** (ReW) revocation of license to practise, § 11 WPO
widerrufen
(Re) to revoke
- to rescind
- to annul
- to nullify
- to void
widerrufliche Bezugsberechtigung *f* (Vers) revocable appointment of beneficiary
widerrufliches Akkreditiv *n* (Fin) revocable letter of credit
Widerspruch *m* **einlegen** (Re) to file an objection
widersprüchliche Aussage *f* (Log) inconsistent statement
widersprüchliche Gleichung *f* (Math) inconsistent equation
widerspruchsfreie Gleichungen *fpl* (Math) consistent equations
Widerspruchsfreiheit *f* (Log) consistency
Widerspruchsklage *f* (StR) third-party action against execution, § 262 AO

Widmungsexemplar *n*
(com) complementary
- courtesy
- author's ... copy
(*syn, Autorenexemplar, Dedikationsexemplar*)
Wiederanlage *f* (Fin) reinvestment
Wiederanlagerabatt *m* (Fin) reinvestment discount
Wiederanlagerecht *n* (Fin) reinvestment privilege
Wiederanlage *f* **von Ertragsausschüttungen** (Fin) reinvestment of distributed earnings
Wiederanlauf *m*
(EDV) rerun
- restart
wieder anlaufen lassen (EDV) to restart
Wiederanlaufkosten *pl* (Bw) restarting costs
Wiederanlaufpunkt *m* (EDV) restart point
Wiederanlaufroutine *f* (EDV) restart routine
wiederanlegen (Fin) to reinvest
wieder ansteigen (com) to rebound (*eg, index, sales*)
Wiederaufbaubank *f* (Fin) = Kreditanstalt für Wiederaufbau
Wiederauffinden *n* **von Informationen** (EDV) information retrieval (*ie, esp. through the use of a computerized system*)
wiederaufgenommene Anmeldung *f* (Pat) renewal application
Wiederaufleben *n* **e-r Versicherung** (Vers) reinstatement of a policy
Wiederaufschwung *m* (Vw) economic recovery
Wiederaufstockung *f* **des Kapitals** (Fin) issue of additional stock
Wiederausfuhr *f* (Zo) re-exportation (*syn, Re-Export*)
Wiederausfuhranmeldung *f* (Zo) re-export document
Wiederausfuhrbehandlung *f* (Zo) clearance on re-exportation
Wiederausfuhrbescheinigung *f* (Zo) re-exportation certificate
wiederausführen (Zo) to re-export
Wiederausführer *m* (Zo) re-exporter
Wiederausfuhrhandel *m* (AuW) re-export trade
Wiederberufung *f* (Re) reappointment
Wiederbeschaffung *f* (Bw) replacement
Wiederbeschaffungskosten *pl* (ReW) replacement cost (*syn, Wiederbeschaffungswert*)
Wiederbeschaffungsmodell *n* (OR) replacement model
Wiederbeschaffungspreis *m* (ReW) replacement price (*syn, Wiederbeschaffungskosten*)
Wiederbeschaffungsrestwert *m* (ReW) written-down current replacement cost
Wiederbeschaffungsrücklage *f* (ReW) replacement reserve
- amount set aside for replacement
Wiederbeschaffungsversicherung *f* (Vers) replacement insurance
Wiederbeschaffungswert *m* (ReW) replacement value
Wiederbeschaffungszeit *f* (Bw) reorder cycle
Wiedereinfuhr *f* (Zo) re-importation
wieder einführen
(Vw) to reimpose (*eg, exchange controls*)
(Zo) to re-import

Wiedereinführer *m* (Zo) re-importer
Wiedereingliederung *f* **in das Erwerbsleben** (Pw) vocational reintegration
Wiedereinsetzung *f* **in den vorigen Stand** (Re) restoration (*or* restitution) to the previous condition
— (*civil law*) restitutio in integrum
wiedereinstellen
  (Pw) to rehire
  — to reinstate
  — to reemploy
Wiedereinstellung *f*
  (Pw) rehiring
  — re-engagement
  — re-employment
Wiedererkennungsverfahren *n* (Mk) recognition test (*syn*, Wiedererkennungsprüfung)
wiedereröffnen (com) to reopen
Wiedereröffnung *f* (com) reopening
wiedererstatten
  (com) to pay back
  — to refund
  — to reimburse
  — to repay
  — to return
Wiedererstattung *f*
  (com) refund
  — reimbursement
  — repayment
  — return
Wiederfangstichprobe *f* (Stat) capture-release sample
Wiedergewinnung *f*
  (Fin) recovery
  — payoff
Wiedergewinnungsfaktor *m* (Fin) capital recovery factor (*ie, applied in preinvestment analysis* = *Investitionsrechnung*)
Wiedergewinnungszeit *f*
  (Fin) recovery time
  — payback time (*or* period)
  — payout time
Wiederherstellungsklausel *f* (Vers) replacement clause
Wiederherstellungswert *m* (ReW) = *Reproduktionswert*
Wiederholbarkeitsvarianz *f* (Stat) repeatability variance
wiederholen (EDV) to rerun
wiederholte Folgeausbildung *f* (Pw) recurrent education
Wiederholungsadressierung *f* (EDV) repetitive addressing
Wiederholungsanforderung *f* (EDV) automatic request for repetition
Wiederholungsbefehl *m* (EDV) repetition instruction
Wiederholungsbudget *n* (FiW) rollover budget
Wiederholungsgenauigkeit *f* (Stat) precision
Wiederholungskäufe *mpl* (com) repeat buying
Wiederholungslauf *m* (EDV) rerun
Wiederholungslesungen *fpl* (EDV) re-read cycles
Wiederholungsnachfrage *f* (Mk) repeat demand
Wiederholungsrabatt *m* (Mk) rebate granted for repeat advertising (*syn, Malrabatt*)

Wiederholungsstichprobe *f* (Mk) replication
Wiederholungsverfahren *n* (Stat) test-retest technique
Wiederinkraftsetzung *f*
  (Vers) reinstatement
  — renewal
wiederkaufen (com) to repurchase
Wiederkäufer *m* (com) repurchaser
Wiederkaufsrecht *n* (Re) right of repurchase, §§ 497ff BGB
wiederkehrende Bezüge *pl* (StR) = *wiederkehrende Leistungen*
wiederkehrende Leistungen *fpl* (StR) recurrent benefits (*or* payments)
wiederkehrende Nutzungen *fpl* **und Leistungen** *fpl* (StR) recurrent payments and other benefits, §§ 13–16 BewG
wiederkehrende Zahlungen *fpl* (Fin) periodical payments
Wiederverheiratung *f* (StR) remarriage
Wiederverkauf *m* (com) resale
wiederverkaufen (com) to resell
Wiederverkäufer *m* (com) reseller
Wiederverkäuferrabatt *m*
  (com) trade discount
  (Fin) re-allowance
Wiederverkaufspreis *m* (com) resale price
Wiederverkaufspreismethode *f* (StR) resale price method (*see Fremdvergleich*)
Wiederverkaufsrecht *n* (com) right of resale
Wiederverkaufswert *m* (com) resale value
Wiederverwertung *f*
  (com) recycling
  — salvage
Wiedervorlage *f* (com) re-submission
Wiedervorstellung *f* (Stat) re-submission (*ie, of an inspection lot*)
Wiederwahl *f*
  (Pw) re-election
  — recall
  (*eg, of an elected board member*)
wie die Ware liegt und steht (com) as is
Wiegegeld *n* (com) weighting charge
Wiegezertifikat *n* (com) weight certificate
Wiener Schule *f* (Vw) Austrian School of Economic Thought
wilder Eigenkapitalmarkt *m* (Fin) unorganized equity market
wilder Streik *m*
  (Pw) illegal
  — wildcat
  — unauthorized ... strike
Wille *m* **der Parteien** (Re) intention of the parties
Willensbildung *f* (Bw) decision making
Willensbildungszentrum *n* (Bw) decision-making center
Willenseinigung *f*
  (Re) agreement
  — mutual assent
  — meeting (*or* union) of minds
  — (*civil law*) assensio mentium
  (*ie, necessary for the creation of a valid contract*)
Willenserklärung *f*
  (Re) declaration of intention
  — manifestation of intent

Willensmängel *mpl* (Re) defects of legal intent *(eg, Irrtum, Täuschung, Drohung)*
Willenstheorie *f* (Re) doctrine of real intention *(ie, invoked in formation of contract)*
Willensübereinstimmung *f* (Re) = *Willenseinigung*
Wille *m* **zum Wettbewerb** (Kart) spirit of competition
willkürliche Annahme *f* (Log) arbitrary assumption
willkürliche Funktion *f* (Math) arbitrary function
willkürliche Konstante *f* (Math) arbitrary constant
willkürlicher Parameter *m* (Math) arbitrary parameter
Windhandel *m* (Bö) = *Leerverkauf*
Windhundverfahren *n* (FiW) allocation of funds on a first come-first served basis
Windprotest *m* (WeR) protest for absence (of drawer) *(syn, Abwesenheitsprotest)*
Windungspunkt *m* (Math) branch point *(ie, of Rieman surface)*
Winkeltransformation *f* (Math) angular transformation
Winkelverwandtschaft *f* (Math) angular relationship
Winterbauförderung *f* (Vw) promotion of winter construction
Wintergeld *n* (Pw) winter bonus
Winterschlußverkauf *m* (com) winter sales
wir behalten uns vor ... (Re) we reserve the right to ...
wirkliche Adresse *f* (EDV) real address *(opp, virtual address)*
wirklicher Totalverlust *m* (SeeV) actual total loss
wirkliche Tara *f* (com) real tare *(syn, reelle Tara)*
wirksam
  (Re) effective
  – operative
wirksame Nachfrage *f* (Vw) effective demand
Wirksamkeit *f*
  (Stat) effectiveness
  (Bw) efficiency
  – effectiveness
  – efficacy
wirksam werden
  (Re) to become effective (*or* operative)
  – to take effect
  – to come (*or* enter) into force
wirkt für und gegen (Re) is operative for and against
Wirkung *f* **e-s Vertrages** (Re) effect (*or* operation) of a contract
Wirkung *f* **gegenüber Dritten** (Re) effect (*or* operation) as against third parties
Wirkung *f* **kraft Gesetzes** (Re) operation by law
Wirkungsanalyse *f* (Bw) impact (*or* consequences) analysis *(eg, in project evaluation)*
Wirkungsvariable *f* (Stat) effect variable
Wirkungsverzögerung *f*
  (Vw) operational
  – policy-effect
  – time ... lag
Wirtschaft *f*
  (Vw) economy (as a whole)
  – trade and industry
  – business sector
  (Bw) business community (*or* world)

Wirtschaft *f* **ankurbeln** (Vw) to give a boost to the economy *(eg, by fiscal action)*
Wirtschaft *f* **in Ordnung bringen** (Vw, infml) to put the economy to rights
wirtschaftlich
  (Vw) economic *(ie, related to trade and industry and to economics)*
  (Bw) economical
  – economy ...
  – cost-effective
  – low-cost
  – money-saving
wirtschaftlich (com, adv) economically (speaking)
wirtschaftlich abhängig (com) economically dependent
wirtschaftlich angemessene Darstellung *f* (ReW) fair representation
wirtschaftliche Abschreibung *f* (Bw) functional depreciation
wirtschaftliche Beratung *f*
  (com) commercial consulting
  – advisory services of a commercial nature
wirtschaftliche Betrachtungsweise *f* (StR) economic approach
  (ie, fundamental rule controlling the application and interpretation of all West German tax laws, § 1 I StAnpG)
wirtschaftliche Bewegungsfreiheit *f*
  (Kart) scope of economic activity, § 13 I GWB
  – freedom of economic action
wirtschaftliche Druckmittel *npl* (Kart) economic pressure
wirtschaftliche Eingliederung *f* (Vw) economic integration
wirtschaftliche Einheit *f* (StR) economic unity *(ie, the object of valuation, consisting of one or several assets belonging to the same owner, § 2 BewG)*
wirtschaftliche Entwertung *f* (ReW) non-physical depreciation (of assets)
wirtschaftliche Entwicklung *f*
  (Vw) economic development
  (Vw) course of the economy
  – general thrust of the economy
wirtschaftliche Erholung *f*
  (Vw) economic recovery
  – pickup in economic activity
  – rebound in the economy
  – upswing in the economy
wirtschaftliche Hauptsektoren *mpl* (Vw) main economic sectors *(ie, primary, secondary, and tertiary sectors)*
wirtschaftliche Kapazität *f* (Bw) economic capacity *(ie, output potential at the cost optimum, mostly 85% of maximum capacity)*
wirtschaftliche Konzentration *f* (Vw) economic (*or* industrial) concentration
wirtschaftliche Leistung *f* (Vw) economic performance
wirtschaftliche Nutzungsdauer *f* (Bw) economic life
wirtschaftlicher Aufstieg *m* (Vw) takeoff *(ie, of a developing economy, W. Rostow)*
wirtschaftlicher Dualismus *m* (Vw) dual economy
wirtschaftliche Rechtsstreitigkeiten *fpl* (Re) business disputes

wirtschaftlicher Eigentümer *m* (Re) beneficial (*or* equitable) owner *(opp, legal or nominal owner)*
wirtschaftliche Restriktionen *fpl* (Bw) economic constraints
wirtschaftlicher Geschäftsbetrieb *m* (StR) planned economic activities, § 2 III GewStG *(ie, wider in scope than the term ‚business'; it may include hospitals, homes for the aged or sick, and recreation centers operated by organizations)*
wirtschaftlicher Sektor *m*
(Vw) branch of economic activity
– economic sector
wirtschaftlicher Umsatz *m* (VGR) sales on an accrual basis
wirtschaftlicher Verein *m* (Re) incorporated society established for economic purposes *(ie, this need not include the acquisition of profits, § 22 BGB)*
wirtschaftlicher Wert *m* (Vw) want-satisfying ability *(ie, of goods)*
wirtschaftlicher Zusammenbruch *m* (Vw) complete economic breakdown
wirtschaftlicher Zusammenhang *m* (StR) economic connection (*or* relationship), § 9 I No. 1 EStG
wirtschaftliche Sanktionen *fpl* (Vw) = *Wirtschaftssanktionen*
wirtschaftliches Eigentum *n* (StR) beneficial ownership
wirtschaftliches Ergebnis *n* (Vw) economic performance
wirtschaftliches Gut *n*
(Vw) economic good
– commodity
wirtschaftliches Klima *n* (Bw) economic climate
wirtschaftliches Risiko *n* (Bw) commercial risk
wirtschaftliche Streitigkeiten *fpl* (Re) commercial disputes
wirtschaftliche Struktur *f* (Vw) economic structure
wirtschaftliches Ungleichgewicht *n* (Vw) economic disequilibrium
wirtschaftliches Verhalten *n* (Vw) economic behavior
wirtschaftliche Tätigkeit *f* (com) economic activity *(ie, of any person or entity)*
wirtschaftliche Tätigkeit *f* **des Staates** (FiW) public-sector economic activity
wirtschaftliche Überholung *f* (Bw) economic obsolescence *(ie, due to causes other than wear and tear)*
wirtschaftliche und monetäre Integration *f* (EG) economic and monetary integration
wirtschaftliche Untereinheit *f* (StR) economic subunit, § 19 BewG
wirtschaftliche Vergeltungsmaßnahmen *fpl* (Vw) economic reprisals
wirtschaftliche Vorgänge *mpl* (Vw) economic processes
wirtschaftliche Ziele *npl* (Vw) economic goals (*or* objectives *or* ends)
wirtschaftliche Zusammengehörigkeit *f* (StR) appropriation of several individual assets to a common economic purpose, § 2 BewG
Wirtschaftlichkeit *f* (Bw) economic (*or* operational) efficiency
Wirtschaftlichkeitsanalyse *f*
(Bw) economic feasibility study
(Bw) economic analysis
Wirtschaftlichkeitsberechnung *f* (Bw) = *Wirtschaftlichkeitsrechnung*
Wirtschaftlichkeitsprinzip *n* (Vw, Bw) efficiency rule
(ie, to produce at a given rate with lowest cost; or to produce at the highest rate with the same cost; syn, ökonomisches Prinzip, Rationalprinzip)
Wirtschaftlichkeitsrechnung *f*
(Bw) economy (*or* efficiency) calculation
– evaluation (*or* assessment) of economic efficiency
– estimate of operating economy
– feasibility study
(Fin) capital budgeting
– capital expenditure evaluation
– evaluation of investment alternatives
– investment appraisal
– preinvestment analysis
(ie, method of comparing the profitability = Vorteilhaftigkeit of alternative investment projects; syn, Rentabilitätsrechnung)
Wirtschaftlichkeitsstudie *f* (Bw) economic analysis
wirtschaftlich selbständig (Bw) economically independent
Wirtschaftsabkommen *n* (Re) economic accord *(eg, on cooperation in trade and science)*
Wirtschaftsablauf *m* (Vw) workings of the economy
Wirtschaftsausschuß *m* (Pw) joint management-employee economic committee
Wirtschaftsbarometer *n* (Vw) business barometer
Wirtschaftsbau *m* (com) commercial-construction sector
Wirtschaftsbelebung *f* (Vw) economic recovery
Wirtschaftsberater *m* (com) economic adviser
Wirtschaftsbereich *m*
(Vw) sector of the economy
– economic sector
– branch of the economy
– industry
(Vw) branch of economic activity
Wirtschaftsbereichspolitik *f* (Vw) sectoral economic policy
Wirtschaftsbetriebe *mpl* **der öffentlichen Hand** (FiW) = *öffentliche Wirtschaftsbetriebe*
Wirtschaftsbeziehungen *fpl* (Vw) economic (*or* trade) relations
Wirtschaftsblockade *f* (AuW) economic blockade
Wirtschaftsdemokratie *f* (Vw) economic democracy
Wirtschaftseinheit *f*
(Vw) economic unit (*or* entity)
– business entity
(opp, legal entity)
Wirtschaftsentwicklung *f* (Vw) economic development
Wirtschaftsergebnis *n* (ReW) operating result
wirtschaftliche Mobilität *f* (Vw) industrial mobility
Wirtschaftsfachverband *m* (com) trade association
Wirtschaftsförderungsmaßnahmen *fpl* (Vw) measures to spur the economy
Wirtschaftsform *f* (Vw) economic system
Wirtschaftsforschung *f* (Vw) economic research

Wirtschaftsforschungsinstitut *n* (Vw) economic research institute
Wirtschaftsgebiet *n* (AuW) economic area
Wirtschaftsgenossenschaft *f* (Re) commercial cooperative
Wirtschaftsgeographie *f* (com) commercial (*or* economic) geography
Wirtschaftsgeschehen *n* (Vw) economic affairs (*or* matters)
Wirtschaftsgeschichte *f* (Vw) economic history
Wirtschaftsgesellschaft *f* (Vw) economic society
Wirtschaftsgesetz *n* (Re) law affecting the economy as a whole *(opp, law regulating restricted areas, such as a tax law)*
Wirtschaftsgipfel *m* (Vw) economic summit (conference)
Wirtschaftsgut *n*
(Vw) commodity
– *(sometimes also)* a good
(StR) (income-producing) asset
(ie, all items of economic value that are appropriated to the use of a business and can be capitalized, including privileges, rights, concessions, § 2 BewG)
Wirtschaftsgüter *npl*
(ReW) assets and liabilities
(Mk) merchandise *(syn, Handelsgüter)*
Wirtschaftsgüter *npl* **zur Erzielung von Einkünften**
(StR) income-producing assets
Wirtschaftsgut *n* **mit begrenzter Nutzungsdauer**
(Bw) limited-life asset
– wasting asset
Wirtschaftshilfe *f* (AuW) economic aid
Wirtschaftsjahr *n*
(com) business
– financial
– fiscal ... year
(StR) taxable year
Wirtschaftsjournalist *m* (com) business journalist
Wirtschaftsjurist *m* (Re) industrial lawyer
Wirtschaftskreise *mpl* (Bw) business community
Wirtschaftskreislauf *m* (Vw) circular flow
Wirtschaftskrieg *m* (Vw) economic warfare
Wirtschaftskriminalität *f* (Re) white-collar crimes
Wirtschaftskrise *f* (Vw) economic crisis
Wirtschaftskurs *m* (Vw) general thrust of economic policy
Wirtschaftsleistung *f* (Vw) economic performance
Wirtschaftsmagazin *n* (com) business magazine
Wirtschaftsministerium *n* (com) Economics Ministry
Wirtschaftsordnung *f* (Vw) economic order *(ie, no conceptual equivalent in English; near-synonyms: Wirtschaftssystem, Wirtschaftsverfassung)*
Wirtschaftspädagogik *f*
(Pw, *roughly*) economic and business pedagogics
(ie, deals with principles and practice of training teachers for technical and vocational schools)
Wirtschaftsplanung *f* (Vw) economic planning
Wirtschaftspolitik *f* (Vw) economic policy
Wirtschaftspolitiker *m* (Vw) economic policy-maker
wirtschaftspolitische Bedingungen *fpl* (Vw) economic policy conditions

wirtschaftspolitische Beratung *f* (Vw) economic counseling
wirtschaftspolitische Grundprobleme *npl* (Vw) fundamental issues concerning the management of the national economy
wirtschaftspolitisches Instrumentarium *n* (Vw) instruments of economic policy
– economic policy mix
wirtschaftspolitisches Rezept *n* (Vw) economic policy solution
wirtschaftspolitische Ziele *npl*
(Vw) economic goals
(Vw) economic targets *(ie, usu. numberized)*
wirtschaftspolitische Zusammenarbeit *f*
– economic cooperation
(Vw) policy collaboration
Wirtschaftspotential *n* (Vw) economic strength
Wirtschaftspraxis *f*
(com) business *(eg, in actual business)*
(Bw) business practices
(Re) mercantile custom
Wirtschaftspresse *f* (com) business press
Wirtschaftsprozeß *m* (Vw) economic process
Wirtschaftsprüfer *m*
(ReW, US) certified public accountant *(ie, almost always referred to as CPA)*
– (GB) chartered accountant, CA
Wirtschaftsprüferverordnung *f* (Re) Law Regulating the Profession of. Certified Public Accountants, of 24 July 1961
Wirtschaftsprüfung *f*
(ReW) auditing
(ReW) audit
Wirtschaftsprüfungsgesellschaft *f*
(ReW) audit company (*or* firm)
– CPA partnership (*or* company)
(ie, either incorporated or unincorporated)
Wirtschaftsprüfungsstelle *f* (ReW) auditing agency
Wirtschaftsrechnen *n* (com) business arithmetic
Wirtschaftsrechnung *f* (Stat) sample survey *(ie, made by the Federal Statistical Office)*
Wirtschaftsrecht *n*
(Re) Law of the Economy
– Economic Law
(ie, the majority view in Germany is that ‚Wirtschaftsrecht' is to be a subdivision of Administrative Law)
Wirtschaftsredakteur *m*
(com) financial editor
– (GB) City editor
Wirtschaftssanktionen *fpl*
(Vw) economic (*or* trade) sanctions
– economic reprisals
Wirtschaftssektor *m* (VGR) sector of economic activity
Wirtschaftsspionage *f* (Bw) economic espionage
– industrial spying
Wirtschaftsstabilität *f* (Vw) economic stability
Wirtschaftsstatistik *f* (Stat) business (*or* economic) statistics
Wirtschaftsstrafrecht *n* (Re) company criminal law
Wirtschaftsstruktur *f* (Vw) economic structure
Wirtschaftsstufe *f* (Vw) stage in the economic process
Wirtschaftssubjekt *n*

(Vw) economic unit
- transactor
Wirtschaftssystem n (Vw) economic system *(ie, Wirtschaftssystem and Wirtschaftsordnung are often used side by side; generally the term is variously defined, depending upon the school of economic thought)*
Wirtschaftsteil m (StR) operating properties *(ie, of an agricultural establishment, § 34 I BewG)*
Wirtschaftstheoretiker m (Vw) economic theorist
Wirtschaftstheorie f (Vw) economic theory
Wirtschaftstypen mpl (Bw) types of economic units
Wirtschafts- und Sozialausschuß m (EG) Economic and Social Committee
Wirtschafts- und Währungsintegration f (EG) economic and monetary integration
Wirtschafts- und Währungsunion f (EG) economic and monetary union
Wirtschaftsunion f (Vw) economic union
Wirtschaftsunternehmen n (Bw) business enterprise
Wirtschaftsverband m
(com) industrial (or trade association
- federation of . . .
Wirtschaftsverbrechen n (Re) white-collar crime
Wirtschaftsverfassung f (Re) constitution of the economy
(ie, covering relations between government and private enterprise, fundamental rights such as freedom of contract and of industrial/commercial activity, and the definition of public power)
Wirtschaftsverwaltung f (Re) administration of the economy *(ie, concerned with the machinery and the procedures necessary for the exercise of public powers)*
Wirtschaftswachstum n
(Vw) economic growth
- expansion of business activity
Wirtschaftswert m (StR) economic value *(ie, of an agricultural establishment: assessed value reduced by the rental value of the residential buildings that belong to it)*
Wirtschaftswissenschaft f (Vw) economics *(syn, Volkswirtschaftslehre, Nationalökonomie, Sozialökonomie)*
wirtschaftswissenschaftliche Fachsprache f (Vw) economic jargon
wissenschaftliche Unternehmensführung f (Bw) scientific management
Wirtschaftszeitreihe f (Stat) economic time series
Wirtschaftszeitung f (com) business paper
Wirtschaftszweig m
(Vw) branch of economic activity
(Bw) industry
- branch of industry
- trade
Wirtschaft f **unterbeschäftigen** (Vw) to operate the economy below its supply capabilities
Wirtschaft f **wächst** (Vw) economy expands *(eg, at a 1.7% rate)*
Wissenschaftlicher Beirat m (Vw) Scientific Advisory Council *(eg, attached to the Ministry of Economics)*
wissenschaftlicher Rechner m (EDV) scientific computer

wissenschaftlicher Zoll m (Zo) scientific tariff
Wissenschaftstheorie f (Log) general philosophy of science
Wissensstand m (Log) present body of knowledge
Witteveen-Fazilität f (IWF) Witteveen facility *(ie, official term ,,zusätzliche Finanzierungsvorkehrung")*
Witwenabfindung f (SozV) lump-sum settlement paid to widows on remarriage
Witwengeld n (SozV) widow's pension *(ie, paid to widows of public employees)*
Witwenrente f (SozV) widow's pension *(ie, paid under statutory social insurance and accident insurance schemes)*
Wochenausweis m (Fin) weekly return
Wochengeld n (SozV) = *(now) Mutterschaftsgeld*
Wochenhilfe f (SozV) = *(now) Mutterschaftshilfe*
Wochenmarkt m
(com) weekly market
- (GB) market
wöchentliche EG-Ausschreibung f (EG) weekly EEC tender
wohlerworbener Besitz m (Re) vested possession
wohlerworbene Rechte npl (Re) vested interests (or rights)
Wohlfahrtseinrichtungen fpl (Pw) welfare facilities
Wohlfahrtserträge mpl (Vw) welfare returns
Wohlfahrtsimplikationen fpl (Vw) welfare implications
Wohlfahrtsökonomik f (Vw) welfare economics
Wohlfahrtsstaat m (Vw) welfare state
Wohlfahrtstheorie f (Vw) welfare economics *(syn, Wohlfahrtsökonomik, Allokationstheorie)*
wohlgeordnete Menge f (Math) well-ordered set
Wohlordnungssatz m (Math) well-ordering theorem
Wohlstandsgesellschaft f (Vw) affluent society
Wohlstandsgrenze f (Vw) utility possibility curve in the situation sense
wohlstandsnegative Abschließungseffekte mpl (AuW) trade diversion
wohlstandspositive Aufschließungseffekte mpl (AuW) trade creation
Wohltätigkeitsorganisation f
(com) charitable organization
- (US, infml) do-good organization
Wohngebäude npl (com) residential buildings
Wohnheim n
(Pw) dormitory
- (GB) hall of residence
Wohnort m (Re) place of residence
Wohnsitz m (StR) habitual residence *(ie, place where an individual occupies a residence under circumstances which indicate that he will retain and use it not merely temporarily, § 8 AO)*
Wohnsitz m **aufheben** (Re) to discontinue a residence
Wohnsitz m **begründen** (Re) to establish a residence
Wohnsitzbesteuerung f (StR) residence taxation
Wohnsitzfinanzamt n (StR) local tax office for the taxpayer's residence or customary place of abode, § 19 AO
Wohnsitzprinzip n (FiW) principle of income-source neutrality *(ie, applied in double taxation)*

Wohnsitzstaat *m* (StR) country of ordinary residence *(opp, Quellenstaat)*
Wohnsitzvoraussetzung *f* (StR) residence requirement
Wohnteil *m* (StR) residential properties *(of an agricultural establishment)*, § 34 I BewG
Wohn- und Wirtschaftsgebäude *npl* (StR) residential and farm buildings, § 33 II BewG
Wohnungsbau *m* (com) residential *(or* housing) construction
– construction of residential property
(com) residential construction industry
Wohnungsbaudarlehen *n*
(Fin) house-building loan
– housing loan
Wohnungsbaufinanzierung *f* (Fin) housing finance
Wohnungsbaugenossenschaft *f* (com) residential building cooperative
Wohnungsbaugesetz *n* (Re) Law on Public Subsidies for the Construction of Low-Rental Apartments
Wohnungsbaukredit *m* (Fin) housing loan
Wohnungsbau-Prämiengesetz *n* (Re) Law on the Payment of Premiums for Financing the Construction of Residential Properties
Wohnungseigentum *n*
(StR) home ownership
(StR) condominium property
– ownership right in a condominium, § 68 BewG
Wohnungseigentümergemeinschaft *f* (Re) condominium owners' association
Wohnungseigentumsgesetz *n* (Re) Law on Cooperative Apartments and Proprietary Leases, of 15 March 1951, as amended
Wohnungsgrundstück *n* (com) residential real estate
Wohnungsknappheit *f* (Vw) housing shortage
Wohnungsmarkt *m* (Vw) housing market
Wohnungsneubauten *mpl*

(com) newly constructed housing
– new construction
Wohnungsprämiengesetz *n* (Re) Law on the Payment of Premiums for Financing the Construction of Residential Properties, as republished on 22 June 1979
Wohnungsunternehmen *n* (com) housing company
Wohnungswert *m* (StR) assessed value of residential properties, § 47 BewG
Wölbung *f* (Stat) kurtosis *(syn, Exzeß)*
wortadressierter Speicher *m* (EDV) word addressed storage
Wortadressierung *f* (EDV) word addressing
Wörterbucheintrag *m* (EDV) dictionary entry
Wort *n* **erteilen** (com) to give the floor (to)
Wortlänge *f* (EDV) word length
Wortmarke *f* (EDV) word mark
Wortmaschine *f* (EDV) word-oriented computer
wortorganisierter Speicher *m* (EDV) word-organized storage
Wortprozessor *m* (EDV) word processor
Wortzeit *f* (EDV) word time
Wucher *m* (Re) usury, § 138 II BGB
Wuchermiete *f*
(Re) extortinate rent
– (GB) rackrent *(see: Mietwucher)*
Wucherzinsen *mpl*
(Fin) usurious interest
– loan shark rates
Wuchsaktie *f* (Fin) growth stock
Wuchswerte *mpl* (Fin) = *Wuchsaktien*
Wurschtelquote *f* (com, sl) rate of muddling through
Wurzelgleichung *f* (Math) radical equation
Wurzelsegment *n* (EDV) root segment
Wurzelzeichen *n* (Math) radical sign
Wurzelziehen *n*
(Math) extracting
– finding
– computing ... a root of a number *(syn, Radizieren)*

X

xerografischer Drucker *m* (EDV) xerographic printer
X-Lochung *f*
(EDV) X punch
– eleven punch *(syn, Elfer-Lochung)*

Y

Y-Lochung *f*
(EDV) Y-punch
– twelve punch

Z

Zahl f (Math) number
zahlbar (com) payable
zahlbar an Inhaber (WeR) payable to bearer
zahlbar an Order (WeR) payable to order
zahlbar bei Aufforderung (Fin) payable on demand
zahlbar bei Fälligkeit
 (Fin) payable at maturity
 – payable when due
zahlbar bei Lieferung (Fin) payable on delivery
zahlbar bei Sicht (WeR) payable on demand *(ie, at sight or on presentation)*
zahlbar bei Vorlage (Fin) payable on presentation
zahlbar nach einem Jahr (ReW, EG) becoming due and payble after more than one year
zahlbar nach Sicht (WeR) payable after sight
zahlbar stellen (Fin) to domiciliate
Zahlbarstellung f (Fin) domiciliation
Zählbogen m (Stat) census paper
Zahl f **der Beschäftigten**
 (Pw) number of employees *(or* of people employed)
 – number of people on payroll
 – labor force
Zahl f **der geschätzten Nutzungsjahre** (ReW) number of years of expected life *(ie, in depreciation accounting)*
Zahl f **der leerverkauften Aktien** (Bö) short interest *(or* position)
Zahl f **der Neuabschlüsse** (com) number of new contracts
zahlen
 (com) to pay
 (Fin) to effect
 – to make
 – to meet ... payment
Zahlencode m (EDV) numeric (data) code
Zahlendarstellung f (Math) number notation *(or* representation)
Zahlendarstellung f **mit fester Basis** (EDV) fixed base notation
zahlende Mitglieder npl (com) paid-in membership
Zahlengerade f (Math) real number axis
Zahlenlochung f (EDV) numeric punching
Zahlensystem n (Math) number system
Zahlenwerk n (com) set *(or* system) of figures
Zahler m (Fin) payer, *(also)* payor
Zähler m
 (Math) numerator
 (EDV) counter
 (EDV, Cobol) tally
Zahlgrenze f
 (com) bus fare zone limit
 – (GB) fare stage
Zahlkarte f (Fin) postal money order
Zahllast f (FiW) regular tax burden
Zählregister n (EDV) counter register
Zahlstelle f
 (WeR) domicile
 (Fin) appointed paying agent *(or* payment office) *(ie, for dividend payout)*
 (Fin) branch office
Zahlstellenabkommen n (Fin) paying agency agreement *(ie, between bond issuer and bank)*
Zahlstellengeschäft n (Fin) interest and dividend payout business
Zahlstellenprovision f (Fin) paying agency commission
Zahlstellenvereinbarung f (Fin) paying agency agreement
Zahlstellenverzeichnis n (Fin) list of paying agencies
Zahltag m
 (Pw) payday
 (WeR) date of payment, Art. 38 WG *(syn, Zahlungstag)*
Zahlung f (Fin) payment
Zahlung f **ablehnen** (Fin) to refuse payment
Zahlung f **auf erstes Anfordern** (Fin) payment upon first demand
Zahlung f **aufschieben** (Fin) to defer payment
Zahlung f **bei Auftragserteilung** (Fin) cash with order, c.w.o.
Zahlung f **bei Bestellung** (Fin) = *Zahlung bei Auftragserteilung*
Zahlung f **bei Erhalt der Ware** (Fin) payment on receipt of goods
Zahlung f **bei Fälligkeit** (Fin) payment when due
Zahlung f **bei Lieferung** (Fin) payment on delivery
Zahlung f **bei Vorlage** (Fin) payment on presentation
Zahlung f **durch Akzept** (Fin) payment by acceptance
Zahlung f **durch Dauerüberweisung** (Fin) automatic bill paying
Zahlung f **durch Scheck** (Fin) payment by check
Zahlungen fpl **einstellen** (Fin) to stop *(or* suspend) payments
Zahlungen fpl **wieder aufnehmen** (Fin) to resume payments
Zahlung f **gegen Dokumente** (Fin) payment against documents
Zahlung f **gegen Nachnahme** (Fin) cash on delivery, COD
Zahlung f **gegen offene Rechnung** (Fin) clean payment
Zahlung f **im voraus** (Fin) payment in advance
Zahlung f **in offener Rechnung** (Fin) payment on open account
Zahlung f **in Raten** (Fin) payment by installments
Zahlung f **leisten**
 (Fin) to pay
 (Fin) to effect
 – to make
 – to meet ... payment
Zahlungsabkommen n (AuW) payments agreement
Zahlungsanweisung f (Fin) instruction *(or* order) to pay

Zahlungsaufforderung f
(Fin) demand for payment
– request to pay

Zahlungsaufschub m
(Fin) extension of time for payment
– respite *(ie, delay obtained for payment of sums owed)*

Zahlungsaufschub m **bewilligen** (Fin) to grant deferred payment

Zahlungsauftrag m (Fin) payment order

Zahlungsbedingungen fpl (com) terms of payment
– terms *(eg, to sell at reasonable terms)*

Zahlungsbefehl m (Re) *(replaced by „Mahnbescheid')*

Zahlungsberechtigter m (Fin) party entitled to payment

Zahlungsbereitschaft f (Fin) ability to pay

Zahlungsbeschränkungen fpl (AuW) exchange restrictions on payments

Zahlungsbevollmächtigter m (Fin) principal responsible for...

Zahlungsbilanz f
(AuW) balance of payments
– international balance of payments
– external accounts

Zahlungsbilanzausgleich m
(AuW) balance of payments adjustment
– adjusting the balance of payments

Zahlungsbilanz f **ausgleichen** (AuW) to adjust *(or square)* the balance of payments

Zahlungsbilanzdefizit n
(AuW) balance of payments deficit
– payments deficit
– external deficit

Zahlungsbilanz f **ex post** (AuW) accounting balance of payments

Zahlungsbilanzgleichgewicht n (AuW) balance of payments equilibrium

Zahlungsbilanzlücke f (AuW) gap in the balance of payments
– payments gap *(eg, between the U.S. and its trading partners)*

Zahlungsbilanzmechanismus m (AuW) external payments mechanism

Zahlungsbilanzmultiplikator m (AuW) balance of payments multiplier *(syn, Leistungsbilanzmultiplikator)*

Zahlungsbilanzpolitik f (AuW) balance of payments policy

Zahlungsbilanzsaldo m (AuW) balance of payments outcome *(ie, surplus or deficit)*

Zahlungsfähiger m (Fin) person able to pay

zahlungsfähig
(Fin) able to pay
– solvent

Zahlungsfähigkeit f
(Fin) ability *(or* capacity) to pay
– debt paying ability
– solvency
(syn, Solvenz; opp, Zahlungsunfähigkeit)

Zahlungsfrist f
(com) period of payment
– time limit for payment

Zahlungsgarantie f (Re) payment bond *(or* guaranty)

Zahlungsgewohnheiten fpl
(Fin) payment behavior *(or* habits)
– prior payment pattern

zahlungshalber
(Re) on account of payment
– *(civil law)* datio solutionis causa

Zahlungsintervalleffekt m (Vw) payment interval effect *(ie, in liquidity theory)*

Zahlungsklausel f (Fin) payment clause

Zahlungsmittel n
(Vw) means of payment
(ReW) cash

Zahlungsmittelmenge f (Vw) quantity of money in the economy

Zahlungsmittel-Surrogat n (Vw) substitute for cash

Zahlungsmittelumlauf m (Vw) money supply *(syn, Geldvolumen)*

Zahlungsmodalitäten fpl (Fin) payment policies *(or* terms) *(eg, due within 30 days and 2% discount allowed if paid in less than 10 days)*

Zahlungsmodus m (Fin) method of payment

Zahlungsmoral f (Fin) payment behavior

Zahlungsmoratorium n (Fin) standstill agreement

Zahlungsobergrenze f (Fin) maximum limit for payment

Zahlungsort m (Re) place of payment, § 270 BGB

Zahlungspapiere npl (Fin) financial documents

Zahlungspflicht f (Fin) obligation to pay

Zahlungspflichtiger m (Fin) party liable to pay

Zahlungsplan m (Fin) cash income and outgo plan

Zahlungsplanung f (Fin) cash planning

Zahlungsreihe f
(ReW) expenditure-receipts columns *(or* accounts)
(Fin) series of payments

Zahlungsrhythmuseffekt m (Vw) payment pattern effect

Zahlungsrückstände mpl
(Fin) backlog of payments
– payments in arrears

Zahlungsschwierigkeit f (Fin) temporary shortage of liquid funds

Zahlungssitten fpl (Fin) payment habits

Zahlungsstockung f (Fin) liquidity crunch

Zahlungssystem n (Fin) payments system

Zahlungstag m (WeR) day of payment, Art. 38 WG

Zahlungstermin m (Fin) payment date

Zahlung f **stunden** (Fin) to grant a respite for payment of debt

Zahlungsüberweisung f (Fin) payments transfer

zahlungsunfähig
(Fin) insolvent
– unable to meet one's obligations
– (GB) unable to comply with one's bargains *(esp. in the matter of stock exchange firms)*

zahlungsunfähiger Schuldner m (Fin) defaulting *(or* bad) debtor

Zahlungsunfähigkeit f
(Fin) inability to pay
– insolvency
(syn, Insolvenz; opp, Zahlungsfähigkeit, Solvenz)

Zahlungsunion f (AuW) payments union

Zahlungsverjährung f (StR) prescription of tax

payments, § 228 AO *(opp, Festsetzungsverjährung)*
Zahlungsverkehr *m*
  (Fin) money
  – monetary
  – payment ... transactions
  – payments
Zahlungsverkehr *m* **mit dem Ausland** (AuW) external payments
Zahlungsverkehrabwicklung *f* (Fin) handling of payments
Zahlungsverkehr *m* **zwischen Banken** (Fin) interbank payment transactions
Zahlungsverpflichtung *f*
  (Fin) obligation *(or* duty) to pay
  – payment commitment
  – financial obligation
Zahlungsverpflichtung *f* **eingehen**
  (com) to undertake a financial commitment
  – to promise to pay
Zahlungsverpflichtungen *fpl* **nachkommen** (Fin) to meet one's payments
Zahlungsverschiebungen *fpl* (Fin) shift in the pattern of payments
Zahlungsversprechen *n* (WeR) promise to pay
Zahlungsverweigerung *f* (WeR) dishonor by non-payment
Zahlungsverzug *m* (Fin) default *(or* delay) in payment
Zahlungswährung *f* (Vw) money of payment
Zahlungsweise *f* (Fin) method *(or* mode) of payment
Zahlungsziel *n*
  (com) date of required payment
  – period of payment
  – time allowed for payment
Zahlungsziel *n* **einräumen**
  (com) to allow time for payment
  – to allow a time of credit for settlement
  – to grant credit
Zahlung *f* **verweigern** (Fin) to refuse payment
Zahlung *f* **vor Fälligkeit** (Fin) payment before maturity
Zählwerk *n* (EDV) counter
Zangenpolitik *f* (Vw) pincer-like policy *(ie, of central bank)*
Zebrastreifen *m*
  (com) crosswalk
  – pedestrian crossing
  (GB) Zebra (crossing)
Zedent *m*
  (Re) assignor
  (Vers) ceding company
  – original insurer
  – reinsured *(or* reassured)
  (ie, in reinsurance; syn, Erstversicherer, Direktversicherer)
zedieren
  (Re) to assign
  – to make an assignment
  (syn, abtreten)
  (Vers) to cede *(ie, to reinsurer)*
zedierende Gesellschaft *f* (Vers) ceding company *(ie, in reinsurance)*
Zehnergruppe *f*

  (IWF) Group of Ten
  – Paris Club
Zehnerkomplement *n* (EDV) ten's complement
Zehner-Logarithmus-Funktion *f* (EDV) log 10 function
Zehnertastatur *f* (EDV) numeric keyboard
Zeichen *n* (EDV) character
Zeichenabfühlung *f* (EDV) mark sensing
Zeichenbegrenzung *f* (EDV) character boundary
Zeichencode *m* (EDV) character code
Zahlendarstellung *f* (EDV) number notation
Zeichendichte *f* (EDV) character density
Zeichendrucker *m*
  (EDV) character printer
  – character-at-a-time printer *(syn, Buchstabendrucker)*
Zeichenerkennung *f* (EDV) character recognition
Zeichenfehlerwahrscheinlichkeit *f* (EDV) character error probability
Zeichenfolge *f*
  (EDV, Cobol) string
  (EDV) bit *(or* character) string
zeichengebunden (EDV) character oriented
Zeichengerät *n* (EDV) data plotter *(opp, video terminal)*
Zeichenkontur *f* (EDV) character outline
Zeichenkonzentrator *m* (EDV) pack/unpack facility
Zeichenleser *m*
  (EDV) character reader
  (EDV) mark sensing device
Zeichenlocher *m* (EDV) mark sensing reproducer
Zeichenlochkarte *f* (EDV) mark sense card
Zeichenmaschine *f* (EDV) character-oriented computer
Zeichenpapier *n* **mit Maßeinteilung** (com) chart paper
Zeichenreihe *f* (Log) string of symbols
Zeichenschablone *f* (EDV) flowcharting template
Zeichenschutz *m* (Pat) protection of brand names
Zeichensteuer *f*
  (StR) revenue strip tax
  – revenue stamp tax
Zeichenteilmenge *f* (EDV) character subset
Zeichenverdichtung *f*
  (EDV) character crowding
  – digit compression
Zeichenvorrat *m* (EDV) character repertoire *(or* set)
zeichnen (Fin) to subscribe (for)
Zeichnerbank *f* (Fin) subscribing bank
Zeichner *m* **von Aktien** (Fin) subscriber to shares
Zeichnung *f*
  (com) signature
  (Fin) subscription *(ie, written obligation to buy a certain amount of newly issued bonds or shares)*
  (IndE) engineering drawing *(ie, from which bill of materials is prepared)*
Zeichnungsagio *n* (Fin) subscription premium
Zeichnungsangebot *n* (Fin) subscription offer
Zeichnungsantrag *m* (Fin) subscription application
Zeichnungsbedingungen *fpl* (Fin) terms of subscription *(eg, stating nominal rate, subscription rate, redemption, repayment, relating to newly issued shares)*

zeichnungsberechtigt (com) authorized to sign
Zeichnungsberechtigung f (com) signature power
Zeichnungsbevollmächtigter m (com) duly authorized signatory
Zeichnungseinladung f
 (Fin) invitation to prospective subscribers
 – invitation to subscribe
Zeichnungsformular n (Fin) subscription blank
Zeichnungsfrist f (Fin) subscription period
Zeichnungsgebühr f (Fin) subscription charges
Zeichnungsgründung f (Re) formation of an AG by incorporators *and* subscribers
 (syn, Stufengründung)
Zeichnungskartei f (com) file of engineering drawings
Zeichnungskurs m
 (Fin) offering price
 – subscription rate
Zeichnungsprospekt m (Fin) issue prospectus
Zeichnungsrecht n (Fin) subscription right
Zeichnungsregistratur f (com) filing system for engineering drawings
Zeichnungsrendite f (Fin) yield on subscription
Zeichnungsschein m (Fin) subscription slip *(ie, through which purchaser of new securities agrees to payment on stipulated conditions, to issue price, etc., § 185 AktG)*
Zeichnungsschluß m (Fin) closing of subscription
Zeichnungsstelle f (Fin) subscription agent *(ie, bank accepting subscriptions for newly issued securities)*
Zeichnungsurkunde f (Fin) letter of subscription
Zeichnungsvollmacht f (com) authority to sign *(eg, company documents with legally binding effect)*
Zeile f **e–r Matrix** (Math) row of a matrix
Zeilendifferenz f (Math) row difference
Zeilendruck m (EDV) line printing
Zeilendrucker m (EDV) line printer
Zeilennummer f (EDV) line number
Zeilenstandsanzeige f (EDV) line count
Zeilentransportunterdrückung f (EDV) space suppression
Zeilenvektor m (Math) row vector
Zeilenvorschub m (EDV) line feed
Zeilenvorschubzeichen n
 (EDV) new line character
 – NL character
zeitabhängige Kosten pl (KoR) time costs
Zeitablauf m (Bw) lapse *(or* passage*)* of time
Zeitabschnitt m (Math) payment interval *(ie, in computation of annuities)*
Zeitabschnittsbetrieb m (EDV) time slicing mode
Zeitabweichung f (KoR) time variance
Zeitallokation f (Vw) allocation of time
zeitanteilig (KoR) pro rata temporis
Zeitarbeit f (Pw) temporary work *(or* employment*)*
Zeitarbitrage f (AuW) time arbitrage
Zeitaufnahmebogen m (IndE) time observation *(or* study*)* sheet
Zeitbestimmung f (Re) stipulation as to time, § 163 BGB
Zeitcharter f (com) period time charter *(eg, two-year commitments)*
Zeit f **der Aussetzung** (EG) suspension period *(ie, relating to the value of the unit of account*

Zeitermittlung f (IndE) time measurement
Zeitfracht f (com) time freight
Zeitfrachtvertrag m (com) time charter
Zeit f **für auftragsfremde Tätigkeit** (IndE) diverted time
Zeitgeber m (EDV) timer
Zeitgeberregister n (EDV) timer register
Zeitgeschäfte npl
 (Bö) dealings in futures *(or* for the account*)*
 – forward dealings *(or* transactions*)*
Zeithorizont m
 (Vw, Bw) level of time
 – time horizon *(or* shape*)*
Zeitkarte f (com) season ticket
Zeitkauf m (com) sale on credit terms
Zeitkomponenten fpl (Vw) temporal constructs
Zeitkosten pl (KoR) period cost *(ie, independent of level of activity)*
zeitlich begrenzter Streik m (Pw) limited duration strike
zeitliche Abgrenzung f (ReW) allocation of expense unrelated to accounting period
zeitliche Beschränkung f (com) limitation in time
zeitlicher Ablauf m (Bw) time sequence
zeitlicher Bezug m (Bw) goal period
zeitlicher Korrekturfaktor m (Stat) time comparability factor
zeitlicher Verlauf m (Fin) time shape *(eg, of cash flows)*
zeitliche Umschichtung f **von Ausgaben** (Fin) rephasing of expenditures
zeitliche Unterschiede mpl (Fin) different time horizons
zeitliche Veränderung f **von Variablen** (Vw) time path of variables
zeitliche Verteilung f (Vw) time distribution *(eg, of receipts and expenditures)*
zeitliche Verteilung f **von Arbeitsgängen** (IndE) balancing of works
Zeitlohn m
 (Pw) time (wage) rate
 – time-related payment
Zeitlohnarbeit f (Pw) time work
Zeitlohnsatz m (Pw) time work rate
Zeitlohnstundenanteil m (IndE) time on daywork
Zeitmengenbestand m (MaW) inventory level as function of time
Zeitmengendefizit n (MaW) inventory stockout as function of time
Zeitmessung f
 (IndE) time measurement
 (EDV) timing
Zeitmultiplexverfahren n (EDV) time-division multiplex method
Zeitnehmer m (IndE) time study man
Zeitnorm f (IndE) standard time
zeitoptimales Programmieren n
 (EDV) minimum access
 – minimum delay
 – minimum latency ... coding
Zeitparameter m (OR) time parameter
Zeitplanung f (Bw) (time) scheduling
Zeitpräferenz f (Vw) time preference
Zeitpräferenzrate f (Vw) rate of time preference
Zeitprämie f (Vers) time premium

Zeitpunkt m der Anleihebegebung (Fin) = *Zeitpunkt der Emission*
Zeitpunkt m der Anmeldung (Pat) filing date
Zeitpunkt m der Besteuerung
(StR) effective date
– (GB) tax point *(eg, tax point is the delivery date, not the date of the order)*
Zeitpunkt m der Emission (Fin) date *(or* time) of issue
Zeitpunkt m der Fälligkeit (Fin) date of maturity
Zeitpunkt m der Lieferung (com) time of delivery
Zeitpunkt m der Versandbereitschaft (com) ready date
Zeitraffungsfaktor m (Stat) acceleration factor
Zeitreihe f (Stat) time series
Zeitreihenanalyse f (Stat) time series analysis
Zeitrente f
(Fin) annuity certain
– temporary annuity *(opp, ewige Rente)*
Zeitscheibe f (EDV) time slice
Zeitscheibenverfahren n (EDV) time slicing
Zeitschriftenraum m
(com) periodical room
– (GB) news-room
Zeitsichtwechsel m (WeR) bill payable at fixed period after sight *(syn, Nachsichtwechsel)*
Zeitspanne f für die Verdrängung e–s älteren Produktes (Mk) takeover time
Zeitstudie f (IndE) time study
Zeitumkehrprobe f (Stat) time reversal test
Zeit- und Bewegungsstudien fpl (IndE) time and motion study
Zeitungsanzeige f
(Mk) newspaper advertisement *(or* ad)
– (GB) advert *(ie, stress on first syllable!)*
Zeitungsausschnittbüro n
(com) clipping bureau
– (GB) press cutting agency
– cutting service
Zeitungswerbung f (Mk) newspaper advertising
Zeitverhalten n (EDV) time behavior
Zeitverschleiß m (ReW) depreciation based on time *(ie, if time value of money is recognized, which typically it is not, one of the compound interest methods is appropriate; opp, Gebrauchsverschleiß)*
Zeitvorgabe f (IndE) time standard
Zeitwechsel m (WeR) time draft
zeitweilige Aussetzung f der Zollsätze (Zo) temporary suspension of customs duties
zeitweiliges Floaten n (AuW) temporary floating
zeitweiser Arbeitsplatzwechsel m (Pw) job rotation
Zeitwert m
(Math) end value
(ReW) current market value *(syn, Tageswert, qv)*
Zeit-Wirkungs-Verteilung f (Stat) response time distribution
Zeitzähler m (EDV) time counter
Zeitzuschlagfaktor m (IndE) allowances factor
Zeitzuschlag m für Ausschuß (IndE) reject allowance
Zelle f (EDV) cell *(ie, smallest unit of a store)*
Zensus m (Stat) census
Zensusjahr n (Stat) census year

Zentralabteilung f
(Bw) central department
– staff department *(or* division *or* unit)
Zentralausschuß m der Deutschen Werbewirtschaft (Mk) *(Bonn-based)* Central Committee of the German Advertising Industry
Zentralbank f (Vw) central bank
zentralbankfähig (Vw) eligible for rediscount with the central bank
zentralbankfähige Aktiva npl (Fin) eligible assets *(ie, assets which the central bank is willing to monetize)*
zentralbankfähiger Wechsel m
(Fin) eligible bill
– bill eligible for rediscount
zentralbankfähige Wertpapiere npl (Fin) eligible paper
Zentralbankgeld n (Vw) central bank money *(ie, central bank notes + current accounts with the central bank)*
Zentralbankgeldmenge f (Vw) central bank money supply *(or* stock)
Zentralbankgeldsteuerung f (Vw) central bank money control
Zentralbankguthaben n (Vw) uncommitted reserves
Zentralbank f in Anspruch nehmen (Fin) to have recourse to the central bank
Zentralbankrat m (Vw) Central Bank Council
Zentralbankrat m der Deutschen Bundesbank (Vw) Central Bank Council of the Bundesbank
Zentralbankreserven fpl (Vw) central bank reserves *(ie, gold + own reserves)*
Zentralbearbeitung f (Bw) centralized processing *(eg, of transferred funds)*
Zentralbegriff m (Log) key concept
Zentralbereich m (Bw) central division
Zentralbüro n (Bw) executive office
Zentrale f (Bw) headquarters
zentrale Abrechnungsstelle f
(ReW) accounting center
– central accounting unit
zentrale Arbeitszuweisung f (IndE) centralized dispatching
zentrale Auftragsbearbeitung f (Bw) central order processing system, COP
zentrale Datenbank f (EDV) data center
zentrale Haushalte mpl (FiW) central and regional authorities
Zentraleinheit f
(EDV) central processing unit, CPU
– frame
– main frame
Zentraleinkauf m
(Bw) central buying
– centralized purchasing
zentrale Investitionsplanung f (Vw) central investment planning
zentrale öffentliche Stellen fpl (FiW) central and regional authorities
zentraler Einkauf m (Bw) = *Zentraleinkauf*
zentrale Reserven fpl (AuW) official reserves
zentraler Grenzwertsatz m (Math) central limit law *(or* theorem)
Zentraler Kapitalmarktausschuß m (Fin) Central

Zentraler Kreditausschuß

Capital Market Committee *(ie, presently 11 members representing the largest West German issue banks: advises one-time issuers on time, volume and terms of a loan issue; syn, Kapitalmarktkommission, Kleine Kapitalmarktkommission)*
Zentraler Kreditausschuß *m* (Fin) Central Loans Committee
zentrales Lager *n* (MaW) central stores
zentrales Leitwerk *n* (EDV) central control unit
zentrale Steuereinheit *f* (EDV) central control unit *(syn, Hauptleitwerk)*
zentrale Wartung *f* (IndE) centralized maintenance
zentralgeleitete Wirtschaft *f* (Vw) centrally administered economy *(W. Eucken)*
Zentralgenossenschaft *f* (com) central cooperative
Zentralisierungsgrad *m* (Bw) degree of centralization
Zentralismus *m* (Bw) centralization
Zentralkartei *f* (com) central card index
Zentralkasse *f* (Fin) central organization of credit cooperatives
Zentralmarktausschuß *m* (Fin) Central Market Committee *(ie, voluntary agency comprising representatives from commercial, savings, and mortgage banks + one observer from Deutsche Bundesbank)*
Zentralmärkte *mpl* (com) central markets
Zentralnotenbank *f* (Vw) = Zentralbank
Zentralordinate *f* (Stat) pivot *(ie, of a linear trend)*
Zentralplanwirtschaft *f* (Vw) centrally planned economy
Zentralprozessor *m* (EDV) central processor, CP
Zentralrat *m* **der Bundesbank** (Vw) Bundesbank Central Council
Zentralregistratur *f* (com) central filing department *(syn, Hauptablage)*
Zentralspeicher *m* (EDV) main memory
Zentralstelle *f* **für die Vergabe von Studienplätzen** (Pw) *(Dortmund-based)* Central Clearing-House for University Applicants
Zentralverband *m* **der Elektrotechnischen Industrie** (com) Central Association of the Electrical Industry
Zentralverband *m* **des Deutschen Handwerks** (com) Central Association of German Handicrafts
Zentralverwaltungswirtschaft *f* (Vw) centrally planned economy
Zentralwert *m* (Stat) median
zentriertes Interview *n* (Mk) focussed interview
zentriertes Moment *n* (Math) central moment
Zentriwinkel *m* (Math) central angle
zerbrechlich, mit äußerster Sorgfalt behandeln (com) fragile, handle with extreme care
Zerfällen *n* **der Tage** (Math) breaking up the time element *(ie, in interest rate computation)*
zerlegen
 (IndE) to disassemble
 – to break down into
zerlegte Vektoren *mpl* (Math) partitioned vectors
Zerlegung *f* (IndE) disassembly
Zerlegung *f* **des Steuermeßbetrages** (StR) allocation of the tax base *(ie, among various municipalities, §§ 28ff GewStG, § 22 GrStG)*

Ziel

Zerlegung *f* **e–r Kantenmenge** (Math) edge partition
Zerlegung *f* **e–r Menge** (Math) partition of a set
Zerlegung *f* **e–r Menge gerichteter Kanten** (OR) arc partition
Zerlegungsalgorithmus *m* (OR) partitioning algorithm
Zerlegungsbescheid *m* (StR) formal notice of apportionment *(ie, served by the tax office on the taxpayer, § 188 AO)*
Zerlegung *f* **von Zeitreihen** (Stat) time series decomposition
zerrüttete Finanzen *pl* (Fin) shattered finances
Zerschlagungswert *m* (ReW) breakup value *(ie, term turning up in ‚Liquidationsbilanzen')*
zerstörende Einrede *f* (Re) peremptory defense *(or exemption)*
 (ie, insisting that plaintiff never had the right to institute the suit or that the original right is extinguished or determined)
zerstörendes Lesen *n* (EDV) destructive read(ing)
zerstörende Werkstoffprüfung *f* (Stat) destructive materials testing
zerstörungsfreies Lesen *n* (EDV) non-destructive read, NDR
zerstörungsfreie Werkstoffprüfung *f* (Stat) non-destructive testing
Zession *f*
 (Re) assignment of claim *(or* debt*)*, §§ 398ff BGB *(syn, Abtretung)*
 (Vers) cession *(ie, in reinsurance)*
Zessionar *m*
 (Re) assignee
 – assign
 – *(Scot)* cessionary
 (syn, Abtretungsempfänger)
Zessionskredit *m* (Fin) advance on receivables
Zessionsurkunde *f* (Re) instrument of assignment
Zeta-Transformation *f* (Math) zeta transform
Zettelbuchhaltung *f* (ReW) slip system of accounting *(syn, Belegbuchhaltung, qv)*
Zeugnis *n*
 (Pw) testimonial
 – letter of reference
Zickzackpapier *n* (EDV) fanfold stationery
ziehen (com) to sample
Ziehen *n* **mit Zurücklegen** (Stat) sampling with replacements
Ziehen *n* **ohne Zurücklegen** (Stat) sampling without replacements
Ziehkartei *f* (EDV) tub file
Ziehung *f* (Fin) drawing
Ziehung *f* **auf das Generalkonto** (IWF) drawing on the General Account
Ziehungsavis *n* (Fin) draft advice
Ziehungsermächtigung *f*
 (Fin) authority to draw
 – drawing authorization
Ziehungsliste *f* (Fin) list of drawings
Ziehungsrechte *npl* (IWF) drawing rights
Ziel *n*
 (Bw) goal
 – objective
 – target
 (ie, the basic idea of each term is the same; target

often means ‚numerisches Ziel')
(Fin) time for payment
Zieladresse *f* (EDV) destination address
Zielanalyse *f* (Bw) goal analysis
Zielantinomie *f* (Vw) conflicting goals
Zielausmaß *n*
(Bw) targeted goal
– target range
Zielband *n* (Vw) target range *(ie, of money supply growth)*
Zielbestand *m* (MaW) target inventory
Zielbeziehungen *fpl* (Vw) relations between economic policy goals *(ie, identity, neutrality, compatibility, inconsistency, conflict)*
Zielbildung *f* (Bw) goal *(or* objective) setting process
Zieldifferenz *f* (Vw) indifference *(or* neutrality) of goals *(syn, Zielneutralität)*
Zielentscheidungsprozeß *m* (Bw) goal formation process
Zielereignis *n* (OR) target event
Zielerfüllungsgrad *m* (Bw) degree of goal performance
Zielerreichung *f* (Bw) achievement of objectives
Zielerreichungsgrad *m* (Bw) degree of goal accomplishment
Zielerreichungs-Restriktion *f* (Bw) goal constraint *(or* restriction)
Ziele *npl* **überschreiten** (Vw) to overshoot targets *(eg, of monetary growth)*
Zielfestsetzung *f* (Bw) establishment *(or* setting) of company objectives
Zielformulierung *f*
(Bw) policy formulation
– statement of objectives
Zielfunktion *f* (Math) objective function
zielgerichtet (Bw) goal-directed
Zielgesamtheit *f* (Mk) target population
zielgesteuerte Unternehmensführung *f* (Bw) management by objectives
Zielgrößen *fpl* (com) target figures
Zielgruppe *f* (Mk) target group
Zielharmonie *f* (Vw) compatible *(or* complementary) goals *(syn, Zielkomplementarität od -kompatibilität)*
Zielhierarchie *f* (Bw) hierarchy of goals
Zielidentität *f* (Vw) identity of goals
Zielinhalt *f* (Bw) goal content
Zielinkompatibilität *f* (Vw) = *Zielkonflikt*
Zielkatalog *m* (Vw) goal system *(syn, Zielsystem)*
Zielknoten *m* (OR) terminal node
Zielkompatibilität *f* (Vw) = *Zielkomplementarität*
Zielkomplementarität *f* (Vw) complementary *(or* compatible) goals *(syn, Zielharmonie, Zielkompatibilität)*
Zielkonflikt *m*
(Bw) goal conflict
– conflicting *(or* competing) goals
– inconsistency of goals
Zielkonkurrenz *f* (Vw) = *Zielkonflikt*
Zielkorridor *m* (Vw) target range *(eg, of monetary growth)*
Ziel-Kurs-Zonen *fpl* (IWF) target zones
Zielmarkt *m* (Mk) target market

Ziel-Mittel-Dichotomie *f* (Vw) means-ends dichotomy
Zielnachfolge *f* (Bw) goal succession
Zielneutralität *f* (Vw) neutrality *(or* indifference) of goals *(syn, Zielindifferenz)*
zielorientiertes Budget *n* (FiW) performance budget
Zielplanung *f*
(Bw) goal formation process
(Bw) target planning
Zielpreis *m*
(EG) target price
(Zo) norm price
Zielprogramm *n* (EDV, Cobol) target *(or* object) program
Zielprogrammierung *f* (OR) goal programming
Zielpunkt *m* (OR) arrival point
Ziel *n* **realisieren**
(Bw) to accomplish
– to achieve
– to attain ... a goal
Zielrealisierung *f*
(Bw) accomplishment of goals
– achievement of objectives
Zielrevision *f* (Bw) goal analysis and review
Zielrichtung *f* (Bw) goal direction
Zielsetzung *f* (Bw) = *Ziel*
Zielspanne *f* (com) target range
Zielsprache *f* (EDV) target language
Zielsuche *f* (Bw) goal search
Zielsystem *n*
(Bw) system of objectives
– goal system
Zielüberprüfung *f* (Bw) = *Zielrevision*
Zielunabhängigkeit *f* (Vw) independence of goals
Zielvariable *f*
(Bw) goal variable
(OR) target variable
(Stat) explained variable
Zielvereinbarung *f* (Bw) agreement on (operational) targets
Zielverschiebung *f* (Bw) goal displacement
Zielvorgaben *fpl*
(Bw) defined goals and objectives
(FiW) public-sector goals and objectives
Zielwechsel *m* (Fin) time bill
Zielwidersprüchlichkeit *f*
(Vw) inconsistency of goals
– inconsistent goals
Zielzonen *fpl* (Vw) target zones
Ziffer *f* (EDV) digit
Ziffernanzeige *f* (EDV) digital display
Zifferncode *m* (EDV) numerical code
Zifferndarstellung *f* (EDV) digital notation
Ziffernrechner *m* (EDV) digital computer *(opp, Analogrechner)*
Ziffernsicherungscode *m* (EDV) number protection code
Ziffernstelle *f* (EDV) digit place *(or* position)
Ziffernumschaltung *f* (EDV) figures shift
Zigarettensteuer *f* (StR) excise tax on cigarettes
Zimmermiete *f* **am Arbeitsort** (StR) room rent at place of work
Zinnabkommen *n* (Vw) tin agreement *(or* accord)
Zins *m* (Fin) interest

Zinsabbau *m* (Fin) lowering rates
zinsabhängiges Geschäft *n* (Fin) interest-based business *(ie, of banks; opp, service-based business)*
Zinsabstimmung *f* (Fin) collusion (among banks) in changing their interest rates *(eg, delay in raising rates paid on savings deposits)*
zinsähnliche Aufwendungen *mpl* (ReW) interest-related expense
zinsähnliche Erträge *mpl* (ReW) interest-related income
Zinsanleihe *f* (Fin) loan repayable on a fixed date *(ie, with or without premium; opp, Tilgungsanleihe)*
Zinsanpassung *f* (Fin) interest rate adjustment
Zinsanstieg *m* (Fin) upstick in interest rates
Zinsarbitrage *f* (Bö) interest-rate arbitrage
Zinsarbitrage-Geschäfte *npl* (Bö) interest-rate arbitrage dealings
Zinsauftrieb *m*
 (Fin) improvement
 – upsurge
 – upswing
 – upturn ... in interest rates
Zinsaufwendungen *fpl* (ReW) interest paid *(or* expense*)*
Zinsausfall *m* (Fin) loss of interest
Zinsausfallrisiko *n* (Fin) interest loss risk
Zinsausgleichsteuer *f* (Fin) interest equalization tax *(US 1964)*
Zinsausschläge *mpl* (Fin) erratic rate movements
Zinsausstattung *f*
 (Fin) rate of interest
 (Fin) coupon rate
Zinsbeihilfen *fpl* (Fin) interest subsidies
Zinsbelastung *f* (Fin) interest load
Zinsberechnung *f* (Fin) calculation of interest
Zinsbewußtsein *n* (Fin) interest-mindedness *(eg, of investors)*
Zinsbogen *m* (Fin) coupon sheet
Zinsbonifikation *f* (Fin) additional interest
zinsbringend (Fin) interest bearing
Zinsdauer *f* (Math) number of terms
Zinsdruck *m* (Fin) interest rate pressure
Zinseffekt *m* (Vw) rate of interest effect *(ie, of open market operations)*
Zinselastizität *f* (Vw) interest-rate elasticity *(ie, of money demand)*
zinsempfindlich (Fin) interest sensitive
Zinsen *mpl* **aus Bauspartguthaben** (StR) interests from savings accounts with building associations
Zinsen *mpl* **aus Hypotheken und Grundschulden** (StR) interests from mortgages and other encumbrances of real property
Zinsen *mpl* **aus Sparanteilen bestimmter Versicherungsbeiträge** (StR) interest on savings portion of certain insurance premiums
Zinsen *mpl* **aus Teilschuldverschreibungen** (Fin) interest on bonds
Zinsen *mpl* **bei Aussetzung der Vollziehung** (StR) interest due while forcible collection of a tax is suspended, § 237 AO
Zinsen *mpl* **berechnen**
 (Fin) to calculate interest
 (Fin) to charge interest

Zinsen *mpl* **bezogen auf 365 Tage** (Math) exact interest *(ie, used in Great Britain and in German Civil Code)*
Zinsen *mpl* **bezogen auf 360 Tage** (Math) ordinary interest *(ie, applied in German and French)*
Zinsen *mpl* **bringen** (Fin) = *Zinsen tragen*
Zinsendienst *m* (Fin) interest service
Zinsen *mpl* **für Festgeldanlagen** (Fin) time deposit rates
Zinsen *mpl* **senken**
 (Fin) to ease back
 – to bring down
 – to relax ... interest rates
Zinsen *mpl* **sinken** (Vw) interest rates decline *(or* fall*)*
Zinsenstamm *m* (Fin) renewal coupon *(syn, Talon, Erneuerungsschein)*
Zinsen *mpl* **tragen**
 (Fin) to bear
 – to yield
 – to generate
 – to produce ... interest *(ie, on the principal = Kapital)*
Zinsentspannung *f* (Fin) easing of interest rates
Zinsen *mpl* **und Tilgung** *f* (Fin) interest and repayment (of principal)
Zinsen *mpl* **und zinsähnliche Aufwendungen** *mpl* (Fin) interest and related expenses
Zinsergebnis *n* (ReW) net interest income
Zinserhöhung *f* (Vw) increase in interest rates
Zinserneuerungsschein *m* (Fin) renewal coupon
Zinserträge *mpl*
 (Fin) interest income *(or* earnings*)*
 – interest earned *(or* received*)*
 (Vers) investment income *(ie, earned in short-term money markets)*
Zinserträge *mpl* **aus Darlehen** (Fin) interest yield on loans
Zinserträge *mpl* **aus Wertpapieren** (Fin) interest on securities
Zinsertragsbilanz *f* (Fin) interest income statement
Zinsertragskurve *f* (Fin) yield curve
Zinserwartungen *fpl* (Fin) interest-rate expectations
Zinseszins *m* (Fin) compound interest
Zinseszinsperiode *f* (Fin) accumulation *(or* conversion*)* period
Zinseszinsrechnung *f* (Fin) compound interest calculation
Zinseszinstabelle *f* (Fin) compound interest table
Zinsfälligkeitstermin *m* (Fin) interest due date
Zinsflexibilität *f* (Fin) interest rate flexibility
Zinsforderungen *fpl* (ReW) interest receivable
zinsfrei
 (Fin) free of interest
 – paying no interest (on)
zinsfreies Darlehen *n*
 (Fin) interest-free loan
 – non-interest-bearing loan
zinsfreies Darlehen *n* **aufnehmen** (Fin) to borrow interest-free (from)
zinsfreies Darlehen *n* **gewähren** (Fin) to lend money interest-free (to)
Zins *m* **für Ausleihungen** (Fin) lending rate
Zins *m* **für Festgeld** (Fin) fixed period interest rate

679

Zinsfuß *m*
 (Fin) interest rate
 – rate of interest
Zinsgarantie *f* (Fin) interest payment guaranty
zinsgebundener Kredit *m* (Fin) fixed rate loan
Zinsgefälle *n* (Fin) interest-rate differential (*or* gap *or* spread)
Zinsgefüge *n* (Fin) structure (*or* pattern) of interest rates
Zinsgipfel *m* (Fin) interest peak
Zinsgleitklausel *f* (Fin) interest escalation clause
zinsgünstige Finanzierung *f* (Fin) reduced-interest financing
zinsgünstiger Festkredit *m* (Fin) low-fixed-rate loan
zinsgünstiges Darlehen *n* (Fin) low-interest (*or* reduced-interest) loan
Zinsgutschrift *f* (Fin) credit for accrued interest
Zinshöhe *f* (Fin) level of interest rates
Zinshypothek *f* (Fin) redemption mortgage *(ie, debtor repays in equal annual installments; syn, Annuitätenhypothek, Tilgungshypothek, Amortisationshypothek)*
zinsinduzierte Kapitalzuflüsse *mpl* (AuW) capital inflows triggered by interest rate differentials
Zinsinflation *f* (Vw) interest inflation
Zinskonditionen *fpl* (Fin) lending (*or* interest) terms
Zinskontrakte *mpl*
 (Fin) futures contracts in interest rates
 – interest rates futures
 – financial futures contracts
 (ie, evidencing purchase or sale of a fixed amount of a financial commodity, at a price agreed at the present, on a specified future date; it facilitates the transfer of risks from parties that do not wish to bear it (hedgers) to those who are prepared to bear it (speculators); risk of loss – or possibility of gains – arises from movement in prices, interest rates, or exchange rates)
zinskongruent (Fin) at identical rates
Zinskonversion *f* (Fin) interest-rate reduction through conversion *(ie, not to be confounded with ‚Zinsreduktion' and ‚Zinssenkung')*
Zinskosten *pl* (Fin) interest cost
Zins-Kredit-Mechanismus *m* (AuW) interest-credit mechanism
Zinskupon *m* (Fin) interest coupon
Zinslast *f* (Fin) interest burden (*or* load)
Zinsleiste *f* (Fin) renewal coupon
Zinsleistungen *fpl* (Fin) interest payments
zinslos (Fin) interest-free
zinsloses Darlehen *n*
 (Fin) interest-free loan
 – (infml) flat (*or* gift) credit
zinsloses Guthaben *n* (Fin) free balance
Zinsmarge *f* (Fin) interest margin
Zinsniveau *n* (Vw) level of interest rates
Zinsniveau *n* **senken**
 (Vw) to lower the interest rate level
 – to peg interest rates at a lower level
Zinsnote *f* (Fin) interest statement *(syn, Zinsrechnung)*
Zinsobergrenze *f* (Fin) interest ceiling
Zinsparität *f* (Vw) interest parity

Zinsperiode *f* (Fin) interest (*or* conversion) period
Zinspolitik *f* (Vw) interest rate policy
zinspolitische Abstimmung *f* (Fin) = *Zinsabstimmung*
zinsreagibel (Fin) interest sensitive
Zinsrechnung *f* (Fin) computation of interest
Zinsreduktion *f* (Fin) reduction of nominal interest rate
Zinsregulierungsklausel *f* (Fin) interest adjustment clause
zinsrobust (Fin) insensitive to interest rate fluctuations
Zinssatz *m*
 (Fin) interest rate
 – rate of interest
Zinssätze *mpl* **bleiben hoch** (Fin) interest rates stay at present high levels
Zinssätze *mpl* **für Ausleihungen** (Fin) lending rates
Zinssätze *mpl* **für Bankkredite** (Fin) bank loan rates
Zinssätze *mpl* **für Eurodollareinlagen** (Fin) Eurodollar deposit rates
Zinssatz *m* **für Festverzinsliche** (Fin) coupon rate
Zinssätze *mpl* **für Kurzläufer** (Fin) short rates
Zinssätze *mpl* **für Langläufer** (Fin) long rates
Zinssätze *mpl* **für Spareinlagen** (Fin) savings deposit rates
Zinssätze *mpl* **geben nach** (Fin) interest rates start moving down
Zinssatz *m* **steigt**
 (Fin) interest rate ...
 – moves up
 – rises
 – goes up
 – increases
Zinsschein *m*
 (Fin) interest coupon (*or* warrant)
 – coupon
Zinsscheine *mpl* **einlösen** (Fin) to collect coupons
Zinsscheineinlösungsdienst *m* (Fin) coupon service
Zinssenkung *f* (Vw) interest rate cut
Zinsspanne *f*
 (Fin) interest spread (*or* margin)
 – rate spread
 (ie, difference between interest paid by banks on deposits and received for credits)
Zinsspannenrechnung *f* (Fin) margin costing
Zinsspirale *f* (Vw) spiral of rising interest rates
Zinssteigerung *f*
 (Fin) increase in interest rates
 – (infml) run-up in interest rates
Zinsstopp *m* (Fin) interest freeze
Zinsströme *mpl* (ReW) interest flows
Zinsstruktur *f*
 (Vw) interest rate regime
 – structure of interest rates
Zinsstrukturkurve *f* (Fin) yield curve
Zinssturz *m* (Fin) nosedive of interest rates *(ie, sudden large drop)*
Zinssubvention *f* (Fin) interest subsidy
Zinssubventionierung *f* (Fin) subsidizing interest rates
 (eg, for loans in foreign trade)
Zinstermin *m*
 (Fin) due date for interest payment

- interest (due) date
- coupon date

Zins-Terminkontrakt m (Fin) interest rate futures contract

Zinsterminmarkt m (Fin) interest rate futures market

Zinstheorie f (Vw) theory of interest

zinstragend
(Fin) interest earning (or yielding)
- bearing interest

zinstragendes Aktivum n (Fin) interest earning asset

zinstragendes Wertpapier n (Fin) active paper

zinstreibend (Fin) driving up interest rates

Zinsüberschuß m
(Fin) net interest received
- net interest revenue
- surplus on interest earnings

Zinsübertragungsmechanismus m (Vw) cost-of-capital channel

Zinsumschwung m (Fin) interest rebound

zinsunabhängige Geschäfte npl (Fin) non-interest business

zinsunelastisch (Fin) interest inelastic

Zinsuntergrenze f (Fin) interest floor

zinsverbilligter Kredit m (Fin) interest-subsidized loan

Zinsverbilligung f (Fin) subsidizing interest rates

Zinsverbindlichkeiten fpl (Fin) interest payable

Zinsverzicht m (Fin) waiver of interest

Zinswende f (Fin) turnaround in interest rate movements

Zinswettbewerb m (Fin) interest rate competition

Zinswettlauf m (Vw) interest rate war

Zinswucher m (Re) usurious interest

Zinszahlung f (Fin) interest payment

Zinszuschuß m (Fin) interest rate subsidy

Zinszyklus m (Vw) interest rate cycle

Zirkakurs m (Bö) approximate price

Zirkular n (com) circular letter

zirkulare Konkurrenz f (Vw) circular competition

Zirkularkreditbrief m (Fin) circular letter of credit

zivile Luftfahrt f (com) civil aviation

Zivilkammer f (Re) Chamber for Civil Matters

Zivilprozeß m (Re) civil action (or litigation)

Zivilprozeßordnung f (Re) Code of Civil Procedure, of 12 Sept 1950

zögerliche Aufwärtsentwicklung f (com) sluggish rise (ie, in interest rates)

zögernde Erholung f (Vw) fledgling recovery

zögernde Wiederbelebung f (Vw) hesitant economic revival

Zoll m
(Zo) customs duty
- (US, also) custom duty
- duty
- tariff
(Zo) customs (ie, in the sense of Zollverwaltung)

Zollabbau m
(Zo) duty (or tariff) reduction
- tariff dismantling
- reduction in tariff rates

Zollabfertigung f (Zo) customs clearance

Zollabfertigungsgebühren fpl (Zo) customs clearance charges

Zollabfertigungshafen m (Zo) port of clearance (or entry)

Zollabfertigungsförmlichkeiten fpl (Zo) customs clearance procedures

Zollabfertigungsschein m
(Zo) customs declaration
- clearance certificate

Zollabkommen n
(Zo) tariff agreement
- customs convention

Zolladungsverzeichnis n (Zo) customs manifest

Zollagent m (Zo) customs agent

Zollager n (Zo) bonded (or customs) warehouse

Zollagergut n (Zo) bonded goods

Zollagerung f (Zo) customs warehouse procedure

zollähnliche Hemmnisse npl (AuW) quasi-tariff barriers

Zollamt n (Zo) customs office

zollamtlich abfertigen (Zo) to clear through the customs

zollamtlich deklarieren (Zo) to declare officially

zollamtliche Abfertigung f (Zo) customs clearance

zollamtliche Bearbeitung f (Zo) customs treatment

zollamtliche Bescheinigung f (Zo) customs certificate

zollamtliche Bewertung f (Zo) customs valuation

zollamtliche Erfassung f **der Waren** (Zo) customs treatment of goods

zollamtliche Überwachung f (Zo) customs control (or supervision)

Zollamtsvorsteher m (Zo) head of customs office

Zollandungsplatz m (Zo) customs wharf

Zollanmelder m (Zo) declarant

Zollanmeldung f (Zo) customs declaration (or entry)

Zollanmeldung f **berichtigen** (Zo) to amend the goods declaration

Zollanmeldung f **für die Abfertigung zum freien Verkehr** (Zo) entry for release for free circulation

Zollanpassung f (Zo) tariff adjustment

Zollanschlüsse mpl (Zo) customs enclaves, § 2 II ZG

Zollantrag m (Zo) customs application

Zollantrag m **für Inlandsverbrauch** (Zo) entry for home use

Zollantrag m **stellen** (Zo) to file an entry

Zollaufkommen n (Zo) customs revenue

Zollaufschlag m (Zo) customs surcharge

Zollaufsicht f (Zo) customs supervision

Zollausfuhrerklärung f (Zo) declaration outwards

Zollauskunft f (Zo) = Zolltarifauskunft

Zollausland n (Zo) foreign customs territories, § 2 ZG

Zollauslieferungsschein m (Zo) customs warrant

Zollausschluß m (Zo) part of the customs area of an adjacent country, § 2 ZG

Zollaussetzung f (Zo) suspension of customs duties

Zollbeamter m (Zo) customs officer

Zollbefreiung f (Zo) customs duty-free admission

Zollbefund m (Zo) official certification of customs treatment, § 19 ZG

Zollbegleitpapiere npl (Zo) customs documents accompanying a consignment

Zollbegleitschein m (Zo) bond note

Zollbegünstigungsliste f (Zo) preferential tariff list
Zollbehandlung f
 (Zo) customs treatment
 – clearance of goods by customs
Zollbehörden fpl (Zo) customs authorities
Zollbelastung f (Zo) incidence of customs duties
Zollbeleg-Nummer f (Zo) import entry registration number
Zollbeschau f (Zo) customs examination, §§ 16, 17 ZG
Zollbescheid m (Zo) notice of assessment, § 36 III ZG, § 155 I AO
Zollbeschränkung f (Zo) customs restriction
Zollbestimmungen fpl (Zo) customs provisions (or regulations)
Zollbewertung f (Zo) valuation for customs purposes
Zollbezirk m (Zo) customs district
Zollbinnenland n (Zo) inland customs territory, § 68 ZG
Zollbinnenlinie f (Zo) borderline between customs district and inland customs territory
Zollbürge m (Zo) customs guarantor
Zollbürgschaft f (Zo) customs guaranty
Zollboot n (Zo) revenue cutter
Zolldeklaration f
 (Zo) customs declaration
 – declaration
 – bill of entry
Zolldisparitäten fpl (Zo) disparities of tariff structures
Zolldokument n (Zo) customs document
Zolldoppeltarif m (Zo) two-column tariff
Zölle mpl
 (Zo) customs duties
 – duties
 – tariff
Zolleinfuhrdeklaration f
 (Zo) declaration inwards
 – inward manifest
Zolleinnahmen fpl (FiW) customs collections (or receipts or revenues)
Zolleinnahmeverlagerung f (Zo) deflection of customs receipts
Zollerhebung f (Zo) collection of customs duties
Zollerklärung f (Zo) customs declaration
Zollerlaß m (Zo) remission of duty, §§ 38 II, 40 ZG
Zollerleichterungen fpl (Zo) customs facilities
Zollermäßigung f
 (Zo) abatement of customs duty
 – tariff reduction
Zollermittlung f (Zo) duty assessment
Zölle mpl **und Abgaben** fpl **gleicher Wirkung** (Zo) customs duties and charges having equivalent effect
Zollfahndung f (Zo) customs investigation
Zollfahndungsdienst m (Zo) customs investigation service, § 152 GVG
Zollfahndungsstelle f (StR) Customs Investigation Division
Zollfaktura f (Zo) customs invoice
Zollfestsetzung f (Zo) assessment of duty
Zollflughafen m (Zo) airport of entry
Zollformalitäten fpl (Zo) = Zollförmlichkeiten

Zollförmlichkeiten fpl (Zo) customs formalities
Zollformular n (Zo) customs form
zollfrei
 (Zo) duty free
 – free of duty
zollfreie Einfuhr f
 (Zo) duty-free importation (or entry)
 – free entry
zollfreies Jahreskontingent n (Zo) annual tariff quota free of customs duties
zollfreie Ware f (Zo) duty-free goods
zollfreie Wiedereinfuhr f (Zo) duty return
Zollfreigebiet n (Zo) free zone, § 2 III ZG
Zollfreiheit f
 (Zo) customs exemption
 – exemption from customs duties
zollfremde Hemmnisse npl (AuW) non-tariff barriers to trade
Zollgebiet n (Zo) customs territory
Zollgebühren fpl (Zo) clearance charges
Zollgesetz n (Zo) Customs Law, of 14 June 1961, as amended
Zollgesetzgebung f (Zo) tariff legislation
Zollgewahrsam m (Zo) customs custody
Zollgewicht n (Zo) dutiable weight, § 34 ZG
Zollgrenzbezirk m
 (Zo) customs district, §§ 68–72 ZG
 – customs surveillance zone
Zollgrenze f (Zo) customs frontier
Zollgut n (Zo) dutiable goods, § 6 AZO
Zollgutlager n (Zo) customs warehouse
Zollgutlagerung f (Zo) customs warehousing
Zollgutumwandlung f (Zo) conversion of dutiable goods, § 54 ZG
Zollgutversand m (Zo) customs transit
Zollgutversandanmeldung f (Zo) customs transit declaration
Zollhafen m
 (Zo) point of entry
 – (US) port of entry
zollhängige Waren fpl (Zo) goods in process of clearing
Zollharmonisierung f (EG) tariff harmonization
Zollherabsetzung f (Zo) reduction of customs duties
Zollhinterlegung f (Zo) customs deposit
Zollhinterziehung f
 (Zo) customs fraud
 – evasion of customs duties
Zollhoheit f (Zo) customs (or tariff) jurisdiction
Zollinformation f (Zo) tariff information
Zollinhaltserklärung f (Zo) customs declaration
Zollinland n (Zo) domestic customs territory
Zollinspektion f (Zo) customs inspection
Zollkartell n (Kart) customs cartel
Zollkennzeichnungs-Vorschriften fpl (Zo) marking (or marks-of-origin) requirements
Zollkontingent n (Zo) tariff (rate) quota
Zollkontingent n **ausschöpfen** (Zo) to exhaust a tariff quota
Zollkontingent n **eröffnen** (Zo) to grant a tariff quota
Zollkontrolle f (Zo) customs control (or inspection)
Zollkontrollzone f (com) customs supervision zone

Zollkonzession f (Zo) tarif concession
Zollkrieg m (Zo) tariff war
Zollmakler m (Zo) customs-house broker
Zollmaßnahme f
 (Zo) tariff measure
 – customs action
Zollmauer f (Zo) tariff wall
Zollnämlichkeitsbescheinigung f (Zo) certificate for entry of returned products
Zollniederlage f (Zo) public customs warehouse
Zollniederlassung f (Zo) customs (or bonded) warehouse
Zollpapier n **bereinigen** (Zo) to regularize (eg, a temporary importation paper)
Zollpapiere npl (Zo) customs (or clearing) documents
Zollpapiere npl **für die vorübergehende Einfuhr** (Zo) temporary importation paper
zollpflichtig
 (Zo) dutiable
 (Zo) liable to duty
zollpflichtiges Gewicht n (Zo) dutiable weight
zollpflichtige Waren fpl
 (Zo) dutiable (or duty-bearing) goods
 – bonded goods
Zollplafond m (Zo) tariff ceiling
Zollplombe f (Zo) customs seal
Zollpolitik f (AuW) tariff policy
zollpolitisches Gleichgewicht n (AuW) tariff equilibrium
Zollpräferenzen fpl (Zo) tariff preferences
Zollpräferenzregelung f (Zo) preferential tariff arrangement
Zollpräferenzspanne f (Zo) preference margin
Zollquittung f
 (Zo) customs receipt (or voucher)
 – (GB) customs-house docket
Zollrechnung f (Zo) customs' invoice
Zollrecht n (Zo) customs legislation
zollrechtliche Behandlung f (Zo) customs treatment
zollrechtliche Behandlung f **der Waren** (Zo) customs treatment applicable to goods
zollrechtliche Freigabe f **der Waren** (Zo) release of goods for free circulation
Zollrückerstattung f (Zo) refund of customs duties
Zollrückschein m (Zo) customs debenture
Zollrückvergütung f (Zo) customs drawback
Zollrunde f (AuW) round of tariff reductions
Zollsatz m
 (Zo) rate of customs duty
 – tariff rate
Zollsätze mpl **angleichen** (Zo) to adjust (or align) tariff rates
Zollsatz m **Null anwenden** (Zo) to apply a zero rate
Zollsatz m **wiederanwenden** (Zo) to reimpose customs duties
Zollschloß n (Zo) customs lock
Zollschnur f (Zo) customs seal string
Zollschranke f (Zo) customs (or duty) barrier
Zollschuld f
 (Zo) customs debt
 – due to customs
Zollschuppen m (Zo) customs shed
Zollschutz m (AuW) tariff protection

Zollsenkung f
 (AuW) tariff cut (or reduction)
 – duty reduction
Zollsicherheit f (Zo) customs security
Zollstatus m (Zo) customs status
Zollstelle f **an der Grenze** (Zo) customs office at the frontier
Zollstelle f **der Bürgschaftsleistung** (EG) office of guaranty
Zollstelle im Landesinneren (Zo) inland customs office
Zollstellen fpl
 (Zo) customs authorities (or offices)
 – (GB) customs station (ie, Hauptzollämter und Zollämter)
Zollstrafe f (Zo) customs penalty
Zollstraße f (Zo) customs route, § 3 II ZG
Zollsystem n (Zo) tariff structure
Zolltara f (Zo) customs tare
Zolltarif m
 (Zo) customs tariff
 – tariff schedule
 – tariff
 – tariff number
Zolltarifangleichungen fpl (Zo) tariff adjustments
Zolltarifauskunft f (StR) ruling in a customs tariff classification matter § 348 AO
Zolltarifbestimmungen fpl (Zo) tariff provisions
Zolltarife mpl **ausgleichen** (AuW) to harmonize tariffs
Zolltarifgesetz n (Zo) tariff law
Zolltarifierung f (Zo) customs classification
Zolltarifkennziffer f (Zo) tariff code
zolltarifliche Behandlung f **der Waren** (Zo) tariff treatment of goods
zolltarifliche Benennung f (Zo) tariff description
zolltarifliche Einstufung f (Zo) tariff classification
Zolltarifrecht n (Zo) tariff laws
Zolltarifschema n (Zo) tariff nomenclature
Zolltheorie f (AuW) customs tariff theory
Zoll m **umgehen** (Zo) to avoid customs duty
Zoll- und Verbrauchsteueraufsicht f (StR) duty and consumption tax control
Zollunion f (Zo) customs union
Zollveredelung f (Zo) processing in bond
Zollverfahren n (Zo) customs procedure
Zollverfahrensvorschriften fpl (Zo) customs procedural requirements
Zollverfahren n **zuführen** (Zo) to place under a customs procedure
Zollvergehen n (Zo) infringement of customs regulations
Zollvergünstigung f (Zo) tariff advantage
Zollverhandlungen fpl (AuW) tariff negotiations
Zollverkehr m (Zo) customs procedure (or system)
Zollversandgut n (Zo) goods in customs transit
Zollverschluß m (Zo) customs seal
Zollverschlüsse mpl **anlegen** (Zo) to affix customs seals
Zollverschlüsse mpl **beschädigen** (Zo) to damage the customs seals
Zollverschlußsystem n (Zo) customs sealing device
Zollvertrag m (Zo) tariff agreement
Zollverwaltung f (Zo) customs administration
Zollvollmacht f (Zo) customs power of attorney

Zollvorschriften fpl (Zo) customs regulations (*or* requirements)
Zollwarenverzeichnis *n* (Zo) tariff nomenclature
Zollwert *m*
  (Zo) customs (*or* dutiable) value
  – valuation for customs purposes
Zollwertabkommen *n* (AuW) Convention on the Customs Valuation of Goods
Zollwertanmelder *m* (Zo) declarant
Zollwertausschuß *m* (EG) Valuation Committee
Zollwertbemessung *f* (Zo) customs valuation
Zollwertbestimmung *f* (Zo) = *Zollwertbemessung*
Zollwertermittlung *f* (Zo) method of valuation for duty purposes
Zollwertkompendium *n* (Zo) Valuation Compendium
Zollwertnachprüfung *f* (Zo) verification of dutiable value
Zollzugeständnisliste *f* (AuW) schedule of concessions *(ie, within GATT)*
Zollzugeständnisse *npl* (AuW) tariff concessions
Zölle *mpl* **und Verbrauchsteuern** *fpl* (FiW) customs duties and excise taxes
Zollzuschlag *m* (Zo) additional duty
Zollzuwiderhandlung *f* (Zo) offense against customs legislation
Zollzwecke *mpl* (Zo) duty payment purposes
Zollzweigstelle *f* (Zo) customs suboffice
Zone *f* (EDV) curtate
Zonenbit *n* (EDV) zone bit
Zonenlochung *f* (EDV) zone punch
Zonenrandförderungsgesetz *n* (Re) Law for the Promotion of the Economy of the Border Regions, of 5 Aug 1971, as amended
Zonenrandgebiet *n* (FiW) border area *(ie, between the Federal Republic of Germany and the German Democratic Republic)*
Zonentarif *m* (com) zone rates
Zubehör *n*
  (com) accessories
  (Re) removable fixtures
  – accessory property
  (ie, not firmly attached to the realty, but serving the purpose of the latter, § 97 BGB, § 68 I BewG)
zubilligen (com) to allow *(eg, reasonable time)*
Zubringeranlage *f* (EDV) feeder equipment
Zubringerspeicher *m* (EDV) auxiliary (*or* backing) store *(syn, Ergänzungsspeicher, Hilfsspeicher)*
Zubringerverkehr *m* (com) feeder traffic
Zubuße *f* (StR) contribution to a mining company
Zuckerabschöpfung *f* (Zo) levy on sugar
Zuckerbörse *f* (Bö) sugar exchange
Zuckerhersteller *m* (com) sugar producer
Zuckerindustrie *f* (com) sugar industry
Zuckerrübenernte *f* (com) sugar beet production
Zuckersteuer *f*
  (StR) sugar tax
  – excise duty on sugar
Zufall *m*
  (Stat) random event
  (com) chance
  – coincidence
  – accident
zufällige Ordnung *f* (Stat) randomization

zufälliges Unmöglichwerden *n* **der Leistung** (Re) accidental impossibility of performance
Zufälligkeitsgrad *m* (Stat) degree of randomness
Zufallsabweichung *f* (Stat) random variation
zufallsähnliches Stichprobenverfahren *n* (Stat) quasi-random sampling
Zufallsanordnung *f* (Stat) random order
Zufallsauswahl *f* (Stat) random sampling (*or* selection)
Zufallsbeschränkungen *fpl* (Stat) chance constraints
Zufallseinflüsse *mpl* (Stat) random factors
Zufallsereignis *n* (Stat) random event
Zufallsexperiment *n* (Stat) random experiment
Zufallsfehler *m* (Stat) random error
Zufallsfolge *f* (Math) random sequence
Zufallsgewinn *m* (com) windfall profit
Zufallsgrenze *f* (Stat) critical ratio
Zufallskomponente *f* (Stat) random component
Zufallsparameter *m* (Stat) incidental parameter
Zufallsprozeß *m* (Stat) random process
Zufallsreihe *f* (Stat) random series
Zufallsstichprobe *f* (Stat) random sample
Zufallsstichprobenfehler *m* (Stat) random sampling error
Zufallsstreuung *f* (Stat) chance variation
Zufallstheorie *f* (Stat) chance theory
Zufallsvariable *f*
  (Stat) stochastic
  – random
  – chance
  – aleatory ... variable
  – variate
Zufallsverteilung *f* (Stat) random distribution
Zufallszahl *f* (EDV) random number
Zufallszahlen *fpl*
  (Stat) random numbers (*or* digits)
  – random sampling numbers
Zufallszahlengenerator *m* (EDV) random number generator
Zufallszahlentafel *f* (Stat) random number table
zufließen (Re) to accrue
Zufluß *m* **von Kapital** (AuW) inflow (*or* influx) of capital
Zuführeffekte *mpl* (Vw) injections
zuführen
  (ReW) to carry
  – to allocate
  – to transfer
  – to make appropriation *(ie, to reserves)*
  (EDV) to gate (to)
Zuführung *f*
  (ReW) allocation
  – appropriation
  – carrying
  – transfer *(ie, to reserves)*
  (EDV) feed
Zuführungen *fpl* **zu Rückstellungen im Kreditgeschäft** (Fin) provision for possible loan losses
Zuführung *f* **mit mehrfachem Lesen** (EDV) multi-read (*or* multi-cycle) feeding
Zuführung *f* **mit Oberkante vorn** (EDV) Y-leading edge
Zuführung *f* **mit Unterkante vorn** (EDV) nine edge leading *(syn, 9-Kanten-Zuführung)*

Zuführung *f* **mit Vorderseite oben** (EDV) face up feed
Zuführung *f* **mit Vorderseite unten** (EDV) face down feed
Zuführung *f* **neuen Eigenkapitals** (Fin) injection of new equity capital
Zuführungsfehler *m* (EDV) misfeed
Zuführung *f* **von Finanzmitteln** (Fin) provision of finance
Zuführung *f* **zu Rückstellungen für Gewährleistungs- und Schadenersatzansprüche** (ReW) provision for warranty and liability claims
Zuführung *f* **zu Rückstellungen für Wechselobligo** (ReW) provision for accrued notes payable
Zugabe *f*
  (com) bonus *(ie, sth in addition to what is usual or expected)*
  (Mk) free gift
Zugänge *mpl* (ReW) additions *(eg, of fixed assets)*
Zugänge *mpl* **bei den Beteiligungen** (Fin) additional investment in subsidiaries and associated companies
Zugänge *mpl* **im Sachanlagevermögen** (ReW) additions to property, plant, and equipment
Zugänger *m* (OR) branch leading into node
zugangsbedürftig (Re) requiring communication
Zugangsbeschränkungen *fpl*
  (Vw) barriers to entry
  – restrictions of entry
Zugangseinheiten *fpl* (OR) input
Zugangserleichterungen *fpl* (Mk) greater ease of entry into a market
Zugangsjahr *n* (ReW) year of acquisition
Zugangsrate *f* (OR) arrival rate
Zugangsprozeß *m* (OR) arrival process
Zugangswert *m* (ReW) value of additions
Zugang *m* **zu Finanzmärkten** (Fin) access to the financial markets
Zugang *m* **zur Beschäftigung** (Pw) access to employment
Zugartikel *m* (Mk) = *Lockartikel*
zugelassener Empfänger *m* (EG) authorized consignee
zugelassener Satz *m* **der Ausfuhrabschöpfung** (EG) tendered rate of export levy
zugelassener Versender *m* (EG) authorized consignor
zugelassenes Wertpapier *n* (Bö) registered security
zugeordneter ungerichteter Graph *m* (Math) associated undirected graph
zugesagte Mittel *pl* (Fin) promised funds
zugesicherte Eigenschaft *f* (com) warranted quality
zugesicherte Qualität *f* (com) promised quality
Zugeständnis *n*
  (com) concession
  (com) shading *(ie, pricing and other conditions)*
Zugewinn *m* (StR) increase in the combined net worth of spouses during marriage, § 5 I ErbStG
Zugewinngemeinschaft *f*
  (StR) statutory property regime between married individuals
  – equalization of combined net worth
  (ie, property regime = Güterstand by which each spouse retains ownership and management of his or her property during marriage, but the increase in the combined net worth of the spouses during marriage is distributed equally, § 1363 BGB, § 5 I ErbStG)
Zugriff *m* (EDV) access
Zugriffsarm *m* (EDV) access arm
Zugriffsart *f* (EDV, Cobol) access mode
zugriffsfreie Speicherung *f* (EDV) zero access storage
Zugriffsgeschwindigkeit *f* (EDV) = *Zugriffszeit*
Zugriffsmethode *f* (EDV) access method
Zugriffszeit *f* (EDV) access time
zugrundeliegendes Geschäft *n* (Re) underlying transaction
Zug-um-Zug-Bedingung *f* (Re) concurrent condition
Zug-um-Zug-Geschäft *n* (Re) transaction requiring simultaneous performance
Zug um Zug leisten (Re) to perform contemporaneously (with) *(eg, delivery is to be concurrent with payment)*
Zug-um-Zug-Leistung *f* (Re) contemporaneous performance
Zug-um-Zug-Order *f* (Bö) alternative order
zugunsten von
  (ReW) to the credit of
  – credited to
zu hoch ausweisen (ReW) to overstate
zu jeweiligen Preisen (VGR) at current (*or* ruling) prices
Zukauf *m*
  (com) complementary purchase
  (Bö) fresh buying
zu konstanten Preisen
  (VGR) at constant prices
  – in real terms
  – in volume terms
zukünftiger Schaden *m* (Re) future damage (*or* injury)
Zukunftserfolgswert *m* (ReW) present value of future profits
  (ie, used in valuation of enterprises as a whole; syn, Zukunftsertragwert)
Zukunftsforschung *f* (Vw) futurology
Zulage *f*
  (Pw) bonus
  – premium
  – extra pay
zulässige Abweichung *f* (com) allowance
zulässige Ausschußzahl *f* (Stat) allowable defects
zulässige Bandbreite *f* (Fin) admissible range of fluctuations
zulässige Basis *f* (OR) admissible (*or* feasable) basis
zulässige Fangquote *f* (com) allowable catch
zulässige Gesamtfangquote *f* (com) total allowable catch
zulässige Hypothese *f* (Stat) admissible hypothesis
zulässige Lösung *f* (OR) feasible solution
zulässiger Vektor *m* (OR) feasible vector
zulässiges Beweismaterial *n* (Re) competent evidence
zulässiges Kassenvermögen *n* (Pw) permissible endowment of a fund, § 4d No. 2 EStG
zulässige Untergruppe *f* (Math) admissible subgroup

zulässige Werte *mpl* **e–r Variablen** (Math) permissible values of a variable
zulässige Zahl *f* (Math) admissible number
Zulassung *f* (ReW) admission to practice *(ie, as Wirtschaftsprüfer)*
Zulassungsantrag *m* (Bö) request for listing on a stock exchange
Zulassungsausschuß *m* (Bö) Listing Committee
Zulassungsbedingungen *fpl* (Bö) requirements for having a security traded on a stock exchange
Zulassungsbedingungen *fpl* **für die Einfuhr** (Zo) eligibility of goods for entry
Zulassungsbescheid *m* (Bö) listing notice
Zulassungsbescheinigung *f* (Zo) certificate of approval
Zulassungsbestimmungen *fpl* (Re) licensing requirements *(eg, for the establishment of new businesses)*
Zulassungsprüfung *f* (Pw) entrance examination
Zulassungsstelle *f* (Bö) Listing Board, § 36 BörsG
Zulassungsverfahren *n*
  (Bö) listing procedure
  (Zo) approval procedure
Zulassungsvorschriften *fpl* (Bö) listing requirements
Zulassung *f* **von Kraftfahrzeugen** (com) car registration
Zulassung *f* **von Wertpapieren zum Börsenhandel** (Bö) admission to listing, §§ 36–49 BörsG
Zulassung *f* **zum Geschäftsbetrieb** (Re) license to conduct business
Zulassung *f* **zum Handel** (Bö) acceptance for trading on a stock exchange
zu Lasten
  (ReW) to the debit of
  – charged to
zulegen (Bö) to move ahead *(eg, security prices)*
Zuleitungsauftrag *m* (IndE) subsidiary order
Zulieferbetrieb *m* (com) = *Zulieferer*
Zulieferer *m*
  (com) supplier
  – component supplier
  – outside supplier
  – subcontractor
Zulieferindustrie *f* (com) components supplying industry
Zulieferteile *npl* (com) supplied parts
Zulieferungen *fpl* (com) supplies
Zuliefervertrag *m* (com) subcontract
zum Akzept vorlegen (WeR) to present for acceptance
zum Anschaffungs- od Herstellungswert *m* (ReW) at cost
zum Diskont einreichen (Fin) to present for discount
zum Diskont gegebene Wechsel *mpl* (ReW) notes receivable discounted
zum Einzug (Fin) for collection *(ie, form of indorsement on a note or check)*
zum freien Verkehr abfertigen
  (Zo) to clear for homse use
zum freien Verkehr freigeben
  (Zo) to release for *(or* put into) free circulation
  – to put on the market
zum gemeinschaftlichen Versandverfahren abfertigen (Zo) to place under a Community transit procedure
zum Inkasso (Fin) for collection
zum Inkasso vorlegen (Fin) to present for payment in cash
zum Nennwert (Fin) at par
zumutbare Belastung *f* (StR) amount of extraordinary expenditure (= *außergewöhnliche Belastungen*) which the taxpayer can reasonably be expected to bear himself, § 33 EStG
zumutbare Eigenbelastung *f* (StR) = *zumutbare Belastung*
Zumutbarkeit *f* (Re) equitableness
zum Verkauf anbieten (com) to offer for sale
zum zollrechtlich freien Verkehr anmelden (Zo) to enter for free circulation
Zunahme *f* **der Lagerbestände** (MaW) inventory buildup *(or* pile-up)
Zündwarenmonopol *n* (FiW) matches monopoly
Zündwarensteuer *f* (StR) excise tax on matches and tapers
zunehmende Niveaugrenzerträge *mpl* (Vw) = *zunehmende Skalenerträge*
zunehmender Grenznutzen *m* (Vw) increasing marginal utility
zunehmender Wettbewerb *m* (com) mounting competition
zunehmende Skalenerträge *mpl* (Vw) increasing returns to scale
zu niedrig ausweisen
  (ReW) to understate
  – to underreport
zu niedrig bewertete Aktie *f* (Bö) underpriced share
zuordnen
  (com) to allocate
  – to assign
  – to attribute
Zuordnung *f*
  (com) allocation
  – assignment
  – attribution
  (Math) matching *(eg, of elements)*
Zuordnungsdefinition *f* (Log) ostensive *(or* applicative) definition
Zuordnungsfehler *m* (Stat) error of reference
Zuordnungsmeßzahl *f* (Stat) classification statistic
Zuordnungsproblem *n* (OR) allocation *(or* assignment) problem *(syn, Zuweisungsproblem)*
Zuordnungstabelle *f* (EDV) symbol table
zu pari (Fin) at par
zu Protest gehen lassen (WeR) to dishonor a bill
zur Ansicht
  (com) on approal
  – (GB, infml) on áppro *(ie, accented on first syllable)*
zurechenbar
  (KoR) allocable to
  – chargeable to
  – identifiable with
  – traceable to
zurechenbare Fahrlässigkeit *f* (Re) imputed negligence
zurechenbare Kenntnis *f* (Re) constructive notice
zurechenbare Kosten *pl* (KoR) separable cost

zurechenbare Ursache f (Stat) assignable cause
zurechnen
 (KoR) to allocate to
 – to apportion to
 – to assign to
 – to charge to
 – to identify with
 – to trace to
Zurechnung f
 (Vw) allocation
 (KoR) allocation
 – apportionment
 – assignment
 (StR) attribution *(ie, property is attributed to its owner for tax purposes, § 39 AO, §§ 108, 120 BewG)*
Zurechnungsfähigkeit f (Re) capacity to be responsible for civil delicts
Zurechnungsfortschreibung f (StR) adjustment of assessed values on account of changed conditions, § 22 BewG
Zurechnungsproblem n (Log) classification problem
Zurechnungsregeln fpl (StR) attribution rules *(ie, applying to family foundations)*
zur Konkurrenz abwandern
 (com) to switch to a rival
 – to take one's custom elsewhere
zur Sache kommen
 (com, sl) to get down to brass tacks
 – (GB) to get down to the put-to *(ie, taking action after all)*
zur Tagesordnung übergehen (com) to pass to the order of the day
Zurückbehalt m (Re) withholding delivery *(ie, of goods)*
Zurückbehaltungsrecht n
 (Re) right of retention (*or* lien)
 – retaining lien
 (ie, right to retain possession of property until claim is satisfied, § 273 BGB, § 369 HGB)
Zurückbehaltungsrecht n **beim gegenseitigen Vertrag**
 (Re) right to refuse performance
 – right of refusal to perform
 (ie, unless the other party is willing to perform the whole of his promise at the same time, § 320 I BGB)
zurückerstatten
 (com) to pay back
 – to refund
 – to reimburse
 – to repay
 – to return
Zurückerstattung f
 (com) refund *(eg, on defective goods)*
 – repayment
 – reimbursement
zurückfordern
 (com) to claim back
 – to reclaim
zurückgehen
 (com) to decline
 – to decrease
 – to fall (off)

 – to come down
 – to drop (off) *(eg, prices, demand)*
zurückgelegte Beitragszeiten fpl (SozV) periods of coverage completed
zurückgesandte Waren fpl (com) goods returned
zurückgestaute Inflation f (Vw) repressed (*or* suppressed) inflation
zurückgestaute Preiserhöhungen fpl (Vw) bottled-up price increases *(ie, due to price controls)*
zurückgewiesene Lieferung f (Stat) rejected lot
zurückgewinnen
 (com) to get back
 – to regain
 – to recover
 – to recapture
 – to recoup
zurückhalten, sich (Bö) to move to (*or* stay on) the sidelines
Zurückhaltung f **der Anleger**
 (Bö) buyers' resistance
 – investor restraint
zurückkaufen
 (com) to buy back
 – to repurchase
 – to purchase back
zurücklegen
 (com) to put aside
 – to put on one side *(ie, article for customer)*
Zurücknahme f **e–s Angebots** (Re) revocation of offer
Zurücknahme f **e–s Patents** (Pat) withdrawal of a patent
zurücknehmen
 (Re) to revoke *(eg, an offer)*
 (Bö) to mark down *(ie, a stock)*
zurückrufen
 (Fin) to recall
 – to withdraw
zurücksenden
 (com) to send back
 – to return
zurückspulen (EDV) to rewind
zurückstellen
 (com) to put off
 – to put aside (for the time being)
 – to put on the shelf
 – to shelve
 – to pigeonhole
 – to lay aside
zurückstufen (Pw) to downgrade
Zurückstufung f
 (Pw) downgrading
 – (fml) demotion
zurücktreten
 (Re) to cancel
 – to repudiate
 – to rescind
 – to withdraw (from)
 – (infml) to pull out of
 – (infml) to back out of ... a contract
 (Pw) to retire
 – to resign
 – to withdraw
 – (infml) to step down (as/from)
zurückverweisen (Re) to remand a case

Zurückverweisung *f* **e–er Sache** (StR) remand of a case, § 126 III FGO
Zurückweisung *f* (Stat) rejection
Zurückweisung *f* **e–r Anmeldung** (Pat) refusal of a patent application
Zurückweisungswahrscheinlichkeit *f* (Stat) probability of rejection
Zurückweisungszahl *f* (Stat) rejection number
zurückzahlen
  (com) to pay back
  – (infml) to pay off *(= pay back)*
  – to refund
  – to reimburse
  – to repay
  – to return
  – (GB) to pay off *(ie, the whole of a debt)*
Zurückzahlung *f*
  (Fin) reimbursement
  – refund
  – repayment
  – return
zur Unterschrift vorlegen (com) to present for signature
zur Vertretung berufen (Re) appointed to act for
zur Vorlage (com) ,,please re-present"
zur weiteren Veranlassung (com) for further action
zur Zeichnung auflegen (Fin) to invite subscriptions
Zusage *f*
  (com) promise
  – commitment
  – engagement
  – undertaking
zusagen
  (com) to promise *(to do/that)*
  – to undertake *(to do)*
  – to engage *(oneself, to do)*
  – to commit *(to/to doing)*
Zusagen *fpl* **aus Eigenmitteln** (Fin) lendings from own resources
Zusageprovision *f* (Fin) commitment commission *(or fee)*
Zusammenarbeit *f* (com) cooperation
zusammenarbeiten
  (com) to cooperate *(eg, to counter competition from abroad)*
  – to work together
  – to act jointly *(or in concert)*
  – to join forces
  – to band together
  – to team up
  – to pull together
zusammenbrechen
  (com) to collapse
  – to breakdown
  – to fail completely
Zusammenbruch *m*
  (com) collapse
  – complete failure
  – breakdown
Zusammenbruch *m* **e–s Marktes** (com) collapse of a market
zusammenfassen
  (com) to sum up
  – to summarize
  – to outline
  – to cut down
  – to boil down
  (com) to condense
  – to combine
  – to mold into *(eg, departmental budgets into a preliminary budget)*
zusammenfassender Bericht *m*
  (com) summary report *(or statement)*
  – condensed report
Zusammenfassung *f*
  (com) summary
  – brief outline
  – précis
  – résumé
Zusammenfassung *f* **der Fehlerquadrate** (Stat) pooling of error
Zusammenfassung *f* **von Klassen** (Stat) pooling of classes
zusammengefaßte Buchung *f* (ReW) compound bookkeeping entry
zusammengefaßte Europäische Einheit *f* (EG) European Composite Unit
zusammengefaßte Sektorenkonten *npl* (VGR) consolidated sector accounts
zusammengeschlossene Unternehmen *npl* (Bw) consolidated companies
zusammengesetzte Arbitrage *f* (AuW) compound arbitration
zusammengesetzte Ausdrücke *mpl* (Math) combination of terms
zusammengesetzte Buchung *f* (ReW) compound entry
zusammengesetzte Dividende *f* (Fin) compound dividend
zusammengesetzte Größe *f* (Math) complex quantity
zusammengesetzte Häufigkeitsverteilung *f* (Stat) compound frequency distribution
zusammengesetzte Hypothese *f* (Stat) composite *(or* nonsimple) hypothesis
zusammengesetzte Kostenarten *fpl* (KoR) composite cost types
zusammengesetzte Nachfrage *f* (Vw) composite demand
zusammengesetzter Buchungssatz *m* (ReW) compound entry formula *(ie, in double-entry bookkeeping)*
zusammengesetzte Reise *f* (com) combined voyage
zusammengesetzter Index *m* (Stat) composite index number
zusammengesetzter Multiplikator *m* (Vw) compound multiplier
zusammengesetzter Satz *m* (Log) compound proposition *(or* sentence)
zusammengesetztes Angebot *n* (Vw) composite supply
zusammengesetzte sekundäre Kostenarten *fpl* (KoR) composite secondary cost types
zusammengesetzes Ereignis *n* (OR) composite event
zusammengesetztes Stabdiagramm *n* (Stat) component bar chart
zusammengesetzte Zahl *f* (Math) composite number

zusammenhängender Graph *m* (Math) connected graph
Zusammenlegung *f* **von Aktien** (Fin) grouping of shares, § 222 AktG
Zusammenlegung *f* **von Kapazitäten** (IndE) reduction and relocation of production capacities
zusammenreißen, sich
(com, infml) to pull oneself together
– to start moving
– to show more stuff
– (GB) to pull one's socks up
zusammenschließen, sich (com) = *zusammenarbeiten*
Zusammenschluß *m*
(Bw) combination
– joining of two companies
(Kart) merger *(ie, comprises mergers, acquisitions of assets or participations, as well as other forms of affiliations between enterprises, § 23 II GWB)*
Zusammenschlußkontrolle *f* (Kart) merger control
Zusammenschlußvorhaben *n* (Kart) merger plan
Zusammenstoß *m* (EDV) contention *(ie, when more than one device wishes to use another device at the same time)*
zusammenstreichen
(com) to reduce steeply
– to slash
– to pare down *(eg, budgets)*
Zusammenveranlagung *f* (StR) filing joint returns
Zusatz *m* (Re) addendum
Zusatzabschöpfung *f* (EG) variable additional farm levy *(ie, collected for various farm products imported from nonmember countries)*
Zusatzaktie *f* (Fin) bonus share *(syn, Gratisaktie)*
Zusatzanmeldung *f* (Pat) additional application
Zusatzauswertung *f* (com) additional evaluation
Zusatzbefehl *m* (EDV) additional instruction
Zusatzdatensatz *m* (EDV) addition record *(ie, resulting from the creation of a new record during file processing)*
Zusatzdividende *f* (Fin) additional dividend
Zusatzeinrichtungen *fpl* (IndE) auxiliary equipment
Zusatzerfindung *f* (Pat) additional invention
Zusatzgeräte *npl* (EDV) auxiliary equipment *(ie, operated off-line)*
Zusatzinformation *f* (com) ancillary information
Zusatzkante *f* (OR) additional branch
Zusatzkapazität *f* (Bw) excess productive capability *(eg, for manufacturing on a real-time demand basis)*
Zusatzkapital *n* (Fin) additional capital *(ie, generated by self-financing; shown on the books as open reserves)*
Zusatzklausel *f* (Re) additional clause
Zusatzkontingent *n* (Zo) additional quota
Zusatzkosten *pl* (KoR) additional cost
Zusatzlast *f* (FiW) excess burden *(eg, imposed by a special consumption tax)*
zusätzliche Finanzierungsvorkehrung *f* (IWF) additional financing facility *(syn, Witteveen facility)*
zusätzliche Informationsschritte *mpl* (EDV) overhead bits
zusätzliche Mittel *pl* (Fin) fresh finance

zusätzlicher Aufschlag *m* (Mk) additional markon *(ie, in retailing)*
zusätzlicher Urlaub *m* (Pw) extra leave
Zusatzlieferanten *mpl* (AuW) marginal contributors
Zusatzpatent *n*
(Pat) additional (*or* supplementary) patent
– patent of addition
(ie, improvement of a patented invention)
Zusatzpfad *m* (OR) flow augmenting path
Zusatzpfeil *m* (OR) additional branch
Zusatzprämie *f* (Vers) extra premium
Zusatzprogramm *n* (EDV) add-on program
Zusatzprovision *f* (com) extra commission
Zusatzprüfung *f* (Stat) penalty test *(ie, in quality control)*
Zusatzrente *f* (SozV) supplementary pension
Zusatzspeicher *m* (EDV) auxiliary storage
Zusatzsteuer *f*
(FiW) additional tax
– surcharge
– surtax
Zusatzvergütung *f* (Pw) extra pay
Zusatzversicherung *f*
(Vers) additional
– collateral
– supplementary ... insurance
– (infml) ,,gap filler'' insurance
Zusatzversorgung *f* (SozV) supplementary benefits
Zusatzversorgungseinrichtungen *fpl* **im öffentlichen Dienst** (SozV) supplementary pension funds for public employees
Zusatzvertrag *m* (Re) collateral (*or* accessory) contract
Zusatzzoll *m* (Zo) additional duty
Zuschätzung *f* (StR) supplementary estimate *(ie, of missing or incorrect information in a taxpayer's accounting system, Abschn. 29 II No. 6 EStR)*
Zuschlag *m*
(com) award of contract (*or* purchase order)
– bid award
– acceptance of bid (*or* tender)
(Pw) bonus
– premium
(StR) addition
(StR) surcharge
Zuschlag *m* **an den Meistbietenden** (com) knockdown to the highest bidder
Zuschlag *m* **bei Auftragswechsel** (IndE) job changeover allowance
Zuschlag *m* **bei Serienwechsel** (IndE) batch changeover allowance
zuschlagen
(com) to award a contract
(com) to knock down *(ie, to the highest bidder)*
Zuschlag *m* **erhalten**
(com) to win (*or* obtain) a contract
– be awarded a contract *(eg, for supplying a petrochemical plant)*
Zuschlag *m* **erteilen**
(com) to award a contract
– to let contract *(eg, to lowest bidder)*
Zuschlag *m* **für ablaufbedingte Wartezeit** (IndE) unoccupied-time allowance

Zuschlag *m* **für fixe und variable Gemeinkosten** (KoR) combined overhead rate
Zuschlag *m* **für zusätzliche Arbeiten** (IndE) extra work allowance
Zuschlagsatz *m* (KoR) costing rate
Zuschlagsempfänger *m* (EG) successful tenderer
Zuschlagsgrundlage *f* (KoR) allocation base
Zuschlagskalkulation *f*
  (KoR) job (order) costing
  – job cost system
  – order cost system
  – specific-order cost system
  – job lot system
  – production-order accounting
Zuschlagsprozentsatz *m* (KoR) percentage overhead rate
Zuschlagskosten *pl* (KoR) = *Gemeinkosten*
Zuschlagsprämie *f* (Vers) additional premium
Zuschlagssatz *m* (KoR) indirect manufacturing rate
zuschneiden auf (com) to tailor to *(eg, individual requirements)*
Zuschnittproblem *n* (OR) trim problem
Zuschreibung *f*
  (ReW) appreciation in value
  – write-up
  – revaluation
Zuschreibung *f* **aus Höherbewertung** (ReW) write-up due to appreciation of assets
Zuschreibung *f* **von Gegenständen des Anlagevermögens** (ReW) write-up of fixed assets
Zuschuß *m*
  (FiW) grant
  – subsidy
  (com) contribution
  – premium
  – allowance
Zuschuß *m* **an Entwicklungsländer** (Vw) grant-in-aid to LDCs
Zuschußbetrieb *m*
  (Bw) deficient operation
  (Bw) subsidized enterprise
Zuschüsse *mpl* **aus öffentlichen Mitteln** (StR) subsidies from public funds
zusichern (com) to warrant
Zusicherung *f* (Re) undertaking
Zusicherung *f* **e–r Eigenschaft** (Re) warranty of a quality
Zustandekommen *n* **e–s Vertrages** (Re) formation of contract
zuständig (Re) competent
zuständige Behörde *f* (Re) appropriate (*or* competent) authority
zuständige Organe *npl* (Re) appropriate organs
zuständiges Gericht *n*
  (Re) court in charge
  – court of competent jurisdiction
  – appropriate court
zuständige Zollstelle *f* (Zo) competent customs office
Zuständigkeit *f*
  (Re) jurisdiction
  – jurisdictional reach *(eg, of laws)*
  (Bw) responsibility
  – scope of authority

Zuständigkeit *f* **des Finanzamts** (StR) jurisdiction of tax office, § 20 AO
Zustandsaufzeichnung *f* (EDV) environment record
Zustandsbaum *m* (Bw) stochastic tree
Zustandsparameter *m* (Bw) state parameter
Zustandsraum *m* (Bw) stochastic decision space
Zustandsregister *n* (EDV) status register
Zustandsvariable *f* (Stat) state variable
Zustandswahrscheinlichkeit *f* (OR) state probability
Zustellbezirk *m* (com) postal delivery zone
zustellen
  (com) to deliver
  (Re) to serve upon
  – to notify by service
Zustellgebühr *f*
  (com) delivery fee
  – postage
  (com) carriage
  – cartage
  (Re) fee for service
Zustellpostamt *n* (com) delivery post office
Zustellung *f*
  (com) delivery
  (Re) service (upon)
  – serving
  – notice of service
Zustellung *f* **e–r Ladung** (Re) service of a summons
Zustellungsadresse *f* (Re) address for service
Zustellungsbevollmächtigter *m*
  (Re) person authorized to accept service
  (StR) resident party to whom communications can be directed
Zustellungsurkunde *f* (Re) affidavit of service
zustimmen
  (Re) to agree
  – to consent
  – to assent
Zustimmung *f* (Re) (affirmative) consent *(ie, general term covering both ‚Einwilligung' and ‚Genehmigung', § 182 BGB)*
Zustimmungsfrist *f* (Re) time allowed for final consent (*or* agreement)
zuteilen
  (Fin) to allot
  – to scale down *(syn, repartieren)*
Zuteilung *f*
  (Fin) allotment
  – scaling down *(syn, Repartierung)*
Zuteilung *f* **knapper Mittel über den Preismechanismus** (Vw) rationing by the purse
Zuteilungsanzeige *f* (Fin) allotment letter
Zuteilungsbetrag *m* (Fin) allotment money
Zuteilungsempfänger *m* (Fin) allottee
Zuteilungskurs *m* (Fin) allotment price
zuteilungsreif (Fin) available for draw-downs *(ie, on building society deposits)*
Zuteilungsschein *m* (Fin) certificate of allotment
Zuteilungsstrategie *f* (EDV) scheduling discipline
Zuteilungssystem *n* (com) allocation system
Zuteilung *f* **von Fangquoten** (com) allocation of fishing
Zuteilung *f* **von Wertpapieren** (Fin) issuance of securities *(eg, to the first purchaser thereof)*

Zuverlässigkeit f (EDV) reliability
  (OR) reliability *(ie, mathematical probability that a product will function for a stipulated time)*
Zuverlässigkeitsangaben fpl (Stat) reliability data
Zuverlässigkeitsgrad m (IndE) dependability *(ie, of machines)*
Zuverlässigkeitsrechnung f (Stat) calculus of reliability
Zuverlässigkeitstheorie f (OR) reliability theory
zu versteuerndes Einkommen n (StR) taxable income, §§ 2 and 32 EStG
zu viel berechnen (com) to overcharge
zuvorkommen
  (com) to win against *(ie, competitors)*
  – (infml) to scoop *(eg, a trade and technology agreement with Russia, esp. by being faster than competitors)*
Zuwachs m
  (com) growth
  – addition
  (Fin) appreciation
  – gain
  – increment
Zuwachsmindestreservesatz m (Vw) marginal reserve requirements
Zuwachsrate f
  (com) growth rate
  – rate of growth
  – rate of increase
zuweisen
  (ReW) to allocate *(eg, to reserves)*
  (EDV) to allocate
  – to assign
Zuweisung f
  (ReW) allocation
  – transfer
  (eg, allocations from profit to reserves; provision for cost of replacing assets out of current revenues)
Zuweisungsformel f (FiW) basic allocation formula *(ie, determining amounts distributed to other governmental entities)*
Zuweisungsproblem n (OR) = *Zuordnungsproblem*
Zuweisung f von Mitteln (Fin) allocation *(or* appropriation*)* of funds
Zuweisung f zu Rücklagen
  (ReW) allocation to reserves
  – transfer to accruals
Zuwendungsempfänger m (Re) donee beneficiary
Zuwendungsgesetz n (Re) Pension Contributions Law, 26 March 1952
Zuwiderhandlung f (Re) contravention
Zuzahlungen fpl der Aktionäre (Fin) additional contributions of shareholders
zuzurechnendes Einkommen n (StR) attributable income
zuzurechnendes Einkommen n der Organgesellschaft (StR) amount of income transferred by integrated company
zwangloses Treffen n (com) informal get-together
Zwangsanleihe f
  (FiW) forced loan
  (FiW) mandatory loan
  – investment aid deduction
(ie, interest-free loan by high-income earners to the government, equal to 5% of income tax burden, to help encourage a general economic upswing; syn, Investitionshilfeabgabe)
Zwangsebene f (Math) constraint plant
Zwangseinziehung f (Fin) forced retirement of shares
Zwangsgeld n
  (StR) coercive fine *(or* penalty*) (ie, imposed by the local tax office, §§ 328, 329 AO)*
  (Kart) enforcement fine
Zwangshypothek f (Re) forced registration of a mortgage, § 867 ZPO)
Zwangskartell n (Kart) compulsory cartel
Zwangskonversion f (Fin) forced conversion
zwangsläufige Bedienungsfolge f (EDV) enforced transaction sequence
Zwangsliquidation f
  (Re) involuntary liquidation
  – compulsory winding-up
Zwangslizenz f (Pat) compulsory license, § 15 I PatG
Zwangsmitgliedschaft f (com) compulsory membership *(eg, in chambers of industry and commerce)*
Zwangsmittel npl (StR) enforcement measures, § 328 AO
Zwangspensionierung f (Pw) compulsory *(or* mandatory*)* retirement
Zwangsregulierung f (Bö) forced settlement *(syn, Exekution)*
Zwangsrücklauf m (Fin) compulsory redemption of bonds
Zwangsschlichtung f
  (Re) compulsory arbitration
  (Pw) compulsory settlement of disputes
Zwangssparen n (Vw) forced saving
Zwangssyndikat n (Kart) government-enforced syndicate *(ie, prohibited after 1945)*
Zwangsverfahren n (StR) enforcement procedure, §§ 328 ff AO
Zwangsvergleich m (Re) legal settlement in bankruptcy, §§ 173–201 KO
Zwangsverkauf m (Re) judicial sale
Zwangsversicherung f (SozV) compulsory insurance
(syn, Pflichtversicherung, obligatorische Versicherung)
zwangsversteigern (Re) to sell by public auction
Zwangsversteigerung f
  (Re) forced
  – foreclosure
  – execution ... sale *(ie, by way of public auction, §§ 814–824 ZPO)*
Zwangsverwaltung f (Re) forced administration of property, §§ 146ff ZVG
Zwangsverwertung f (Pat) compulsory working
Zwangsvollstreckung f (Re) compulsory execution
  – levy upon property
  (ie, against/into property, §§ 704–945 ZPO)
Zwangsvollstreckung f durchführen (Re) to execute against *(or* levy upon*)* the judgment debtor's property
Zwangsvollstreckung f in das bewegliche Vermögen (Re) levy of execution on movable property

Zwangsvorsorge *f* (SozV) coercive system of social security
Zwangswahlverfahren *n* (Stat) forced choice method
Zwangswirtschaft *f* (Vw) command economy
Zwanziger-Ausschuß *m* (IWF) Committee of Twenty *(ie, set up to reform the International Monetary System; disbanded in 1974)*
Zwanziger-Klub *m* (IWF) Group of Twenty *(ie, constituting the Interim Committee of the IMF)*
Zweckbestimmung *f* (com) purpose which sth is appointed to serve
Zweckbindung *f*
 (AuW) project tying *(ie, in granting economic aid to developing countries)*
 (Fin, FiW) earmarking
 – appropriation
zweckentfremdete Mittel *pl* (Fin) diverted *(or misused)* funds
Zweckforschung *f* (Bw) applied research
zweckgebundene Einnahmen *fpl* (Fin) earmarked *(or restricted)* receipts
zweckgebundene Mittel *pl* (Fin, FiW) earmarked funds
zweckgebundener Liquiditätsüberschuß *m* (Fin) reserve fund
zweckgebundene Rücklagen *fpl* (ReW) appropriated reserves
zweckgebundenes Kapital *n* (Fin) specific capital
zweckgebundenes Material *n* (MaW) earmarked material
Zweckgliederung *f* (Bw) task structuring *(syn, Aufgaben- od Objektgliederung)*
Zweck-Mittel-Beziehung *f* (Log) means-end relation
Zweck-Mittel-Hierarchie *f* (Bw) means-end hierarchy *(or chain)*
Zweckrationalität *f* (Log) instrumental rationality
Zwecksparen *n* (Fin) special-purpose saving
Zwcksparunternehmen *n* (Fin) special-purpose savings bank
Zwecksteuer *f* (FiW) nonrevenue regulatory tax *(ie, as an instrument of policy; syn, Ordnungssteuer)*
Zweckverband *m* (Re) special-purpose association
Zweckvermögen *n*
 (Fin) special-purpose fund
 – assets earmarked for a special purpose
 – conglomeration of property for a specific purpose
Zweckzuwendung *f* (StR) transfer of property for a particular purpose, § 1 I 3 ErbStG
Zwei-Abweichungs-Methode *f*
 (KoR) two-way overhead analysis
 – two-variance method
Zweiadreßbefehl *m*
 (EDV) two-address instruction
 – one-plus-one (address) instruction
Zweiadreßcode *m* (EDV) two-address code
Zweiadreßmaschine *f* (EDV) two-address machine
Zweiadreßsystem *n* (EDV) two-address system
Zwei-aus-fünf-Code *m* (EDV) two-out-of-five code
Zwei-Behälter-System *n* (MaW) two-bin system
Zweideutigkeit *f* (Log) equivocation

zweidimensionale Verteilung *f* (Stat) bivariate distribution
Zweidrittelwert *m* (StR) two-thirds appraisal of unmatured insurance claims *(ie, based on total premiums paid, § 12 IV BewG)*
Zweierkomplement *n* (EDV) two's complement
Zweier-Logarithmus *m* (Math) binary logarithm
Zweiersystem *n* (EDV) binary system
zweifache Einteilung *f* (Stat) two-way classification
zweifach teilbarer Graph *m* (Math) bipartite graph
Zweifamilienhaus *n* (StR) two-family home *(ie, residential property with two apartments, § 75 VI BewG)*
zweifelhafte Forderungen *fpl* (ReW) doubtful accounts receivable
Zweiganstalt *f* (Fin) branch
 (eg, Landeszentralbanken as branches of Deutsche Bundesbank)
Zweigbetrieb *m* (Bw) branch operation
Zweiggeschäft *n* (Mk) branch store
zweigipfelige Verteilung *f* (Stat) bimodal distribution
zweigleisiger Vertrieb *m* (Mk) marketing at two different price levels
zweigliedrige Gesellschaft *f* (Bw) = *Zweimanngesellschaft*
Zweigniederlassung *f* (Bw) branch establishment
Zweigstelle *f* **im Kreditwesen** (Fin) branch *(ie, replacing the older term ‚Depositenkasse')*
Zweigstellenleiter *m* (com) branch manager
Zweigstellennetz *n* (Fin) network of branch offices *(eg, widespread . . .)*
Zweigstellensteuer *f* (StR) branch tax *(ie, declared unconstitutional in 1967)*
Zwei-Güter-Fall *m* (Vw) two-commodity case
Zweigwerk *n* (IndE) branch plant
Zweikanalschalter *m* (EDV) two-channel switch
Zweikreissystem *n* (ReW) dual accounting system *(ie, financial accounting and cost accounting as two separate systems, connected by an offsetting account; syn, dualistisches System)*
Zwei-Länder-Fall *m* (Vw) two-country case *(or model)*
Zwei-Länder-Zwei-Güter-Zwei-Faktoren-Modell *n* (AuW) two-by-two-by-two model
Zwei-mal-Zwei-Einteilung *f* (Stat) double dichotomy
Zweimanngesellschaft *f* (Bw) two-man company, § 142 HGB
 (syn, zweigliedrige Gesellschaft)
Zweipersonen-Nullsummenspiel *n* (OR) two-person zero-sum game
Zweipersonenspiel *n* (OR) two-person game
Zwei-Phasen-Methode *f* (OR) two-phase method *(of linear programming)*
zweiphasiges Stichprobenverfahren *n* (Stat) double *(or* two-phase*)* sampling
Zweiprodukttest *m* (Mk) diadic product test
Zweireihenkorrelation *f* (Stat) biserial correlation
Zweischichtler *m* (IndE) two-shift worker *(ie, working early and late shifts; opp, Einschichtler, Dreischichtler, Kontiarbeiter)*
zweiseitige exponentielle Verteilung *f* (Stat) double exponential distribution
zweiseitige Handelsgeschäfte *npl* (com) bilateral *(or* two-sided*)* commercial transactions

zweiseitiger Prüfplan *m* (Stat) bilateral sampling
zweiseitiger Schuldvertrag *m* (Re) bilateral contract
zweiseitiger Test *m* (Stat) two-way test
zweiseitige Willenserklärung *f* (Re) bilateral act of the party
Zwei-Sektoren-Wirtschaft *f* (VGR) two-sector economy
Zweispaltenjournal *n* (ReW) two-column journal
Zweispaltentarif *m* (AuW) double-column tariff
zweistellig (Log) two-place
zweistellige Hypothek *f* (Re) second mortgage
zweistellige Inflation *f* (Vw) two-digit (*or* double-digit) inflation
zweistellige Inflationsrate *f* (Vw) double-digit inflation rate
zweistellige Relation *f* (Log) dyadic relation
zweistelliger Funktor *m* (Log) binary connective
zweistelliges Prädikat *n* (Log) binary predicate
Zweistufen-Markt *m* (AuW) two-tier exchange market
zweistufiger Stichprobenplan *m* (Stat) double-phase sampling plan
zweistufiges Leitungssystem *n* (Bw) two-tier board structure (*or* system) *(ie, separates supervisory from executive functions)*
zweistufiges Stichprobenverfahren *n* (Stat) = zweiphasiges Stichprobenverfahren
zweistufige Stichprobe *f* (Stat) two-stage (*or* double) sample
zweistufiges Unterprogramm *n* (EDV) two-level subroutine
zweistufiges Wechselkurssystem *n* (AuW) dual exchange rate system
Zweitakkreditiv *n* (com) back-to-back credit
Zweitausfertigung *f* (com) duplicate
zweitbeauftragte Bank *f* (Fin) intermediate (*or* paying) bank *(ie, in handling letters of credit)*
Zweitbegünstigter *m*
 (Re) contingent beneficiary
 (Vers) secondary beneficiary
Zweitbeschäftigung *f*
 (Pw) double
 – secondary
 – subsidiary . . . employment
Zweitbest-Theorie *f* (Vw) second-best theory
zweite Ableitung *f* (Math) second-order derivative
zweite Alternative *f* (Bw) challenger *(ie, in evaluating replacement investment alternatives)*
zweite Hypothek *f*
 (Re) junior
 – second
 – secondary . . . mortgage
Zweitemission *f* (Fin) secondary offering
zweite Originalausfertigung *f* (com) duplicate original
zweite partielle Ableitung *f* (Math) second-order partial derivative
zweiter Grenzwertsatz *m* (Stat) second limit theorem
Zweites Deutsches Fernsehen *n* (Mk) Second German Television Network
zweite Wahl *f*
 (com) second-class quality
 – (infml) seconds

Zweithand-Leasing *n* (Fin) second hand leasing
zweitklassig
 (com) second rate
 – second string
 (eg, business school)
Zweitmarke *f* (Mk) secondary brand name
Zweitproduzent *m* (Bw) second source
Zweitschrift *f*
 (com) duplicate
 – second copy
Zweitschuldner *m* (Re) secondary debtor
2-Tupel *n* (Log, Math) ordered pair
Zwei-Weg-Kommunikation *f* (EDV) two-way communication
zweiwertige Logik *f* (Log) two-valued logic
Zweiwertigkeit *f*
 (Log) two-valuedness
 – divalence
Zwillingsprüfung *f* (EDV) duplication check *(syn, Doppelprüfung)*
zwingende Bestimmung *f* (Re) mandatory provision
zwingender Beweis *m* (Log) conclusive proof
zwingend erfüllte Bedingung *f* (Log) a fortiori satisfied condition
zwingende Schlußfolgerung *f*
 (Log) inescapable (*or* compelling) conclusion
zwingendes Interesse *n* (Re) compelling interest
zwingendes Recht *n* (Re) binding law
 (ie, legal obligations which cannot be excluded by agreement; opp, nachgiebiges Recht)
Zwischenabnahme *f* (IndE) in-process inspection
Zwischenabrechnung *f* (ReW) intermediate account
Zwischenabschluß *m*
 (ReW) interim closing
 (ReW) interim financial statement
 – (GB) interim accounts
Zwischenankunftszeit *f* (OR) interarrival time
Zwischenausweis *m* (Fin) interim return
Zwischenbericht *m*
 (com) intermediate (*or* interim) report
 (ReW) half-yearly report
Zwischenberichterstattung *f* (ReW) interim financial reporting
Zwischenbescheid *m* (com) interim comments, reply, statement, etc.
zwischenbetriebliche Kooperation *f* (Bw) interplant cooperation
zwischenbetriebliche Mobilität *f* (Pw) interplant mobility
zwischenbetrieblicher Gewinn *m* (Fin) intercompany profit
zwischenbetrieblicher Vergleich *m*
 (Bw) comparative external analysis
 – interfirm comparison
Zwischenbilanz *f* (ReW) interim balance sheet
Zwischendividende *f*
 (Fin) interim dividend
 (Vers) interim bonus (*or* dividend)
Zwischenergebnis *n* (ReW) intermediate result
Zwischenerzeugnisse *npl* (IndE) intermediate products
Zwischenfinanzierung *f*
 (Fin) bridging

- interim
- intermediate ... financing (*or* finance)

Zwischenfinanzierungskredit *m* (Fin) bridging loan

zwischengeschaltete Gesellschaften *fpl* (StR) interposed companies

zwischengeschaltetes Kreditinstitut *n* (Fin) intermediary banking institution

Zwischengesellschaft *f* (StR) intermediate company

Zwischenglieder *npl* **e-r Folge od Reihe** (Math) intermediate terms

Zwischengruppenvarianz *f* (Stat) between-group variance

Zwischenhafen *m* (com) intermediate port

Zwischenhandel *m*
(AuW) transit trade
(com) intermediate (wholesale) trade

Zwischenhändler *m*
(com) intermediary
- intermediate dealer
- middleman

Zwischenholding *f* (Re) intermediate holding company

Zwischenkalulation *f* (KoR) intermediate costing

Zwischenkonsolidierung *f* (ReW) intercompany consolidation

Zwischenkonto *n* (ReW) intermediate (*or* suspense) account

Zwischenkredit *m*
(Fin) bridging
- bridge-over
- interim
- intermediate ... loan

Zwischenlager *n*
(MaW) intermediate inventory (*or* store)
- in-process material stores
- operational stock
- bumper store
- entrepot facilities

Zwischenlagerung *f* (MaW) intermediate (*or* in-process) storage

Zwischenlochung *f* (EDV) interstage punching

Zwischenlösung *f* (com) interim arrangement

Zwischenmaterial *n* (com) intermediate materials

zwischenmenschliche Beziehungen *fpl* (Pw) human relations

Zwischenprodukt *n* (Bw) intermediate product

Zwischenprüfung *f* (MaW) interim check

Zwischenraum *m*
(EDV) space character, SP
- space
- blank

zwischenschalten (com) to interpose

Zwischenschein *m*
(Fin) temporary stock certificate, § 10 AktG
- (GB) scrip

Zwischenspediteur *m* (com) intermediate forwarder

Zwischenspeicher *m* (EDV) intermediate (*or* temporary) storage

zwischenstaatliche Einrichtung *f* (AuW) inter-governmental agency

zwischenstaatliches Abkommen *n* (Re) inter-governmental agreement

zwischenstädtischer Güterverkehr *m* (com) domestic intercity freight traffic

Zwischenstufe *f* (Bw) intermediate level

Zwischensumme *f*
(com) subtotal
(EDV) batch total

Zwischentermin *m*
(com) provisional deadline
(Fin) intermediate maturity

Zwischenurteil *n* (Re) interlocutory judgment, § 304 ZPO

Zwischenverkäufer *m* (com) intermediate seller

Zwischenverkauf vorbehalten (com) subject to sale

Zwischenvertrag *m* (Re) provisional agreement

Zwischenwert *m* (ReW) intermediate value

Zwischenzeugnis *n* (Pw) provisional testimonial

Zwischenziel *n* (Vw) intermediate target

Zwischenzielvariable *f* (Vw) target variable

Zwischenzinsen *mpl* (Fin) = *Vorlagezinsen*

Zwischenzollstelle *f* (Zo) intermediate office

Zwischenzyklus *m* (EDV) intercycle

Zwölferlochung *f*
(EDV) twelve punch
- Y-punch

Zyklenzählerrückstellung *f* (EDV) cycle reset

zyklisch abfragen (EDV) to poll (*ie, to interrogate a remote terminal*)

zyklische Arbeitslosigkeit *f* (Vw) = *konjunkturelle Arbeitslosigkeit*

zyklische Entwicklung *f* (Vw) cyclical movements

zyklische Konkurrenz *f* (Vw) cyclical competition (*R. Triffin*)

zyklische Permutation *f*
(Math) cyclic (*or* circular) permutation
- (*or simply*) a cycle

zyklische Permutation *f* **vom Grade 2** (Math) transposition

zyklische Programmierung *f* (EDV) loop coding

zyklischer Budgetausgleich *m* (FiW) cyclical budgeting

zyklischer Code *m* (EDV) cyclic code

zyklisches Abfragen *n* (EDV) polling

zyklisches Verhalten *n* (Vw) cyclicality

zyklisches Wachstum *n* (Vw) cyclical growth

zyklische Verlaufsstruktur *f* (Vw) cyclical pattern

zyklische Verschiebung *f* (EDV) cycle (*or* cyclic) shift

zyklische Verteilung *f* (Stat) circular distribution

Zyklus *m*
(OR) cycle
- closed chain
- loop
(IndE) cycle

Zyklusimpuls *m*
(EDV) commutator pulse
- position pulse
- P-pulse
- digit pulse *(syn, Stellenimpuls)*

Zykluszähler *m* (EDV) cycle index counter

Zykluszählung *f* (EDV) cycle count

Zykluszeit *f*
(EDV) cycle time

Zylinderadresse *f* (EDV) cylinder address

Zylinderindex *m* (EDV) cylinder index

Anhang

Anhang

9.1 Rentabilitätsbegriffe

1.0 Kapitalrentabilität

    1.1 Gesamtkapitalrentabilität (GKR) $= \dfrac{\text{Kapitalgewinn}}{\text{Gesamtkapital}}$

    1.2 Eigenkapitalrentabilität (EKR) $= \dfrac{\text{Jahresüberschuß vor Steuern}}{\text{Eigenkapital}}$

    1.3 Umsatzbezogene Kapital- $= \dfrac{\text{Betriebsergebnis vor Steuern}}{\text{Umsatzbezogener Kapitaleinsatz}}$
        rentabilität

2.0 Umsatzrentabilität (UR) $= \dfrac{\text{Betriebsergebnis vor Steuern}}{\text{Umsatz}}$

3.0 Betriebsrentabilität (BR) $= \dfrac{\text{kalkulatorisches Betriebsergebnis vor Steuern}}{\text{betriebsnotwendiges Kapital}}$

*

9.2 Du Pont-(RoI)-Kennzahlensystem

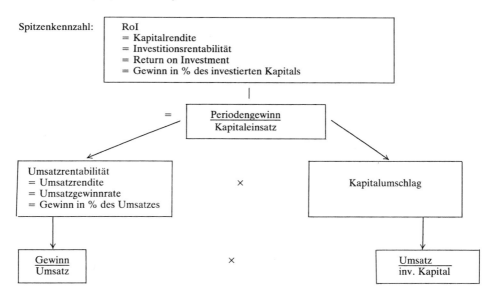

Erläuterungen:

1. Gewinn: Deckungsbeitrag − fixe Kosten
2. investiertes Kapital: Umlaufvermögen + Anlagevermögen
3. Umlaufvermögen: Zahlungsmittel + Forderungen + Bestände
4. Deckungsbeitrag: Nettoumsatz − variable Kosten
5. Nettoumsatz: Bruttoumsatz − Erlösschmälerungen

9.1 Profitability Concepts

1.0 Return on investment

    1.1 Total return on investment   = $\dfrac{\text{net income}}{\text{total capital}}$

    1.2 Equity return   = $\dfrac{\text{pretax annual net income}}{\text{equity capital}}$
        (= rate of return on stockholders' equity)

    1.3 Sales-related return on investment   = $\dfrac{\text{pretax operating income}}{\text{sales-related capital}}$

2.0 Percentage return on sales   = $\dfrac{\text{pretax operating income}}{\text{sales}}$

3.0 Operating return   = $\dfrac{\text{pretax ,,as if'' operating income}}{\text{necessary operating capital}}$

*

9.2 Du Pont Ratio System of Financial Control

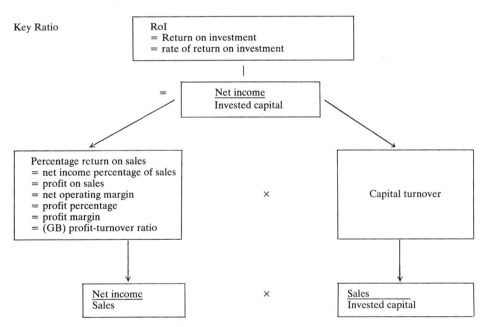

Definitions:

1. Net income: Contribution margin – fixed expenses
2. Invested capital: Current assets + fixed assets
3. Current assets: Cash + receivables + inventories
4. Contribution margin: Net sales – all variable expenses
5. Net sales: Gross sales – deductions

9.3 Kapitalflußrechnung

Mittelverwendung	Mittelherkunft
I. <u>Eigenkapitalminderung</u> 　1. Gewinnausschüttung 　2. Kapitalentnahmen 　3. Bilanzverlust	I. <u>Kapitaleinlagen</u> 　Außenfinanzierung 　– Innenfinanzierung
II. <u>Investitionen</u> 　1. Anlagevermögen 　　netto 　　+ <u>Abschreibungen</u> 　　brutto 　2. Finanzinvestition 　　netto 　　+ <u>Abschreibungen</u> 　　brutto	II. <u>Cash Flow</u> (Umsatzüberschuß) 　1. Gewinn 　2. Rücklagen 　3. Abschreibungen 　4. Rückstellungen
III. <u>Betriebsmittelzunahme</u> 　1. Vorrätemehrungen 　2. Krediteinräumungen	III. <u>Betriebsmittelabnahme</u> 　Finanzierung durch Kapitalfreisetzung 　1. Vorrätebau 　2. Kreditabbau 　3. Sonstiges Umlaufvermögen
IV. <u>Schuldentilgung</u>	IV. <u>Schuldenaufnahme</u> 　Außenfinanzierung 　– Fremdfinanzierung
V. <u>Erhöhung liquider Mittel</u>	V. <u>Minderung liquider Mittel</u>

9.3 Funds Statement

Uses of funds
  I. <u>Decrease in equity</u>
    1. profit distribution
    2. withdrawals
    3. loss for the year

  II. <u>Capital spending</u>
    1. purchase of plant assets
       net
      + <u>depreciation</u>
       gross
    2. financial investments
       net
      + <u>writeoff</u>
       gross

  III. <u>Current operations</u>
    1. increase in inventory
    2. lendings

  IV. <u>Repayment of debt</u>

  V. <u>Increase in net funds</u>

Sources of funds
  I. <u>Increase in equity</u>
    external finance
    – internal finance

  II. <u>Cash flow</u>
    1. net income
    2. change in reserves
    3. depreciation, depletion and amortization
    4. change in provisions

  III. <u>Current operations</u>
    capital set free by
      1. inventory destocking
      2. loan repayment
      3. other current assets

  IV. <u>New long-term debt</u>
    external finance
    – borrowed capital

  V. <u>Decrease in net funds</u>

9.4 Gliederung der Bilanz nach § 151 AktG

AKTIVSEITE
I. Ausstehende Einlagen auf das Grundkapital, davon eingefordert:
II. Anlagevermögen:
   A. Sachanlagen und immaterielle Anlagewerte
      1. Grundstücke und grundstücksgleiche Rechte mit Geschäfts-, Fabrik- und anderen Bauten;
      2. Grundstücke und grundstücksgleiche Rechte mit Wohnbauten;
      3. Grundstücke und grundstücksgleiche Rechte ohne Bauten;
      4. Bauten auf fremden Grundstücken;
      5. Maschinen und maschinelle Anlagen;
      6. Betriebs- und Geschäftsausstattung;
      7. Anlagen im Bau und Anzahlungen auf Anlagen;
      8. Konzessionen, gewerbliche Schutzrechte und ähnliche Rechte sowie Lizenzen an solchen Rechten.
   B. Finanzanlagen:
      1. Beteiligungen;
      2. Wertpapiere des Anlagevermögens;
      3. Ausleihungen mit einer Laufzeit von mindestens vier Jahren; davon durch Grundpfandrechte gesichert:
III. Umlaufvermögen:
   A. Vorräte:
      1. Roh-, Hilfs- und Betriebsstoffe;
      2. unfertige Erzeugnisse;
      3. fertige Erzeugnisse, Waren.
   B. Andere Gegenstände des Umlaufvermögens:
      1. geleistete Anzahlungen;
      2. Forderungen aus Lieferungen und Leistungen; davon mit einer Restlaufzeit von mehr als einem Jahr;
      3. Wechsel;
         davon bundesbankfähig;
      4. Schecks;
      5. Kassenbestand, Bundesbank- und Postscheckguthaben;
      6. Guthaben bei Kreditinstituten;
      7. eigene Aktien unter Angabe ihres Nennbetrages;
      8. Anteile an einer herrschenden oder an der Gesellschaft mit Mehrheit beteiligten Kapitalgesellschaft oder bergrechtlichen Gewerkschaft unter Angabe ihres Nennbetrages, bei Kuxen ihrer Zahl;
      9. Forderungen an verbundene Unternehmen;
    10. Forderungen aus Krediten;
    11. sonstige Vermögensgegenstände.
IV. Rechnungsabgrenzungsposten

V. Bilanzverlust

PASSIVSEITE
I. Grundkapital

II. Offene Rücklagen
   1. gesetzliche Rücklagen;
   2. andere Rücklagen (freie Rücklagen).

III. Wertberichtigungen

IV. Rückstellungen
   1. Pensionsrückstellungen;
   2. andere Rückstellungen.
V. Verbindlichkeiten mit einer Laufzeit von mindestens vier Jahren:
   1. Anleihen;
      davon durch Grundpfandrechte gesichert;

9.4 Layout of Balance Sheet, as per § 151 AktG

ASSETS
- I. Subscriptions to capital stock, called DM ...
- II. Fixed and Financial Assets:
  - A. Tangible and intangible assets
    1. Land and leasehold rights together with office, factory, and other buildings thereon;
    2. Land and leasehold rights together with dwellings thereon;
    3. Land and leasehold rights without buildings;
    4. Buildings on land owned by others;
    5. Machinery and equipment;
    6. Fixtures, furniture, and office equipment;
    7. Construction in progress and advances on fixed assets;
    8. Franchises, patents, trademarks, and similar rights, as well as licenses thereto.
  - B. Financial Assets
    1. Investments;
    2. Securities evidencing long-term investments;
    3. Loans receivable not due within four years; DM ... secured by mortgages.
- III. Current Assets:
  - A. Inventories:
    1. Raw materials and supplies;
    2. Work in process;
    3. Finished goods, merchandise.
  - B. Other current assets:
    1. Advances to suppliers;
    2. Accounts receivable; DM ... not due within one year;
    3. Notes receivables; DM ... discountable with Deutsche Bundesbank;
    4. Checks;
    5. Cash on hand and on deposit with Deutsche Bundesbank and in postal checking accounts;
    6. Cash in other bank accounts;
    7. Treasury stock, par value DM ...
    8. Shares in a controlling company (including mining enterprises) or in one holding the majority interest, par value DM ..., or, in the case of mining shares, number of shares;
    9. Due from affiliated companies;
    10. Loans and advances;
    11. Other assets.
- IV. Prepaid Expenses and Deferred Charges

- V. Balance-sheet Loss

LIABILITIES
- I. Capital Stock
- II. Open Reserves (= appropriated surplus)
  1. Legal reserves
  2. Other reserves (free reserves)

- III. Valuation Reserves

- IV. Accrued Liabilities
  1. Provision for pensions
  2. Other provisions (= for estimated liabilities and other accrued expenditure)
- V. Liabilities Maturing Within Four Years:
  1. Loans; DM ... secured by mortgages;

2. Verbindlichkeiten gegenüber Kreditinstituten;
   davon durch Grundpfandrechte gesichert:
3. sonstige Verbindlichkeiten.

VI. <u>Andere Verbindlichkeiten</u>
1. Verbindlichkeiten aus Lieferungen und Leistungen;
2. Verbindlichkeiten aus der Annahme gezogener Wechsel und der Ausstellung eigener Wechsel;
3. Verbindlichkeiten gegenüber Kreditinstituten;
4. erhaltene Anzahlungen;
5. Verbindlichkeiten gegenüber verbundenen Unternehmen;
6. sonstige Verbindlichkeiten.

VII. <u>Rechnungsabgrenzungsposten</u>
VIII. <u>Bilanzgewinn</u>

2. Due to banks;
    DM ... secured by mortgages;
3. Other liabilities.
VI. Other Liabilities
   1. Accounts payable;
   2. Notes payable;
   3. Due to banks;
   4. Advances from customers;
   5. Due to affiliated companies;
   6. Other liabilities.
VII. Deferred Income
VIII. Balance Sheet Profit (= unappropriated retained earnings)

Anhang

9.4 Gliederung der Gewinn- und Verlustrechnung nach § 157 AktG

1. Umsatzerlöse
2. Erhöhung oder Verminderung des Bestands an fertigen und unfertigen Erzeugnissen
3. andere aktivierte Eigenleistungen
4. Gesamtleistung
5. Aufwendungen für Roh-, Hilfs- und Betriebsstoffe sowie für bezogene Waren
6. Rohertrag/Rohaufwand
7. Erträge aus Gewinngemeinschaften, Gewinnabführungs- und Teilgewinnabführungs-Verträgen
8. Erträge aus Beteiligungen
9. Erträge aus anderen Finanzanlagen
10. sonstige Zinsen und ähnliche Erträge
11. Erträge aus dem Abgang von Gegenständen des Anlagevermögens und aus Zuschreibungen zu Gegenständen des Anlagevermögens
12. Erträge aus der Herabsetzung der Pauschalwertberichtigung zu Forderungen
13. Erträge aus der Auflösung von Rückstellungen
14. sonstige Erträge, davon außerordentliche
15. Erträge aus Verlustübernahme

16. Löhne und Gehälter
17. soziale Abgaben
18. Aufwendungen für Altersversorgung und Unterstützung
19. Abschreibungen und Wertberichtigungen auf Sachanlagen und immaterielle Anlagewerte
20. Abschreibungen und Wertberichtigungen auf Finanzanlagen
21. Verluste aus Wertminderungen oder dem Abgang von Gegenständen des Umlaufvermögens außer Vorräten und Einstellung in die Pauschalwertberichtigung zu Forderungen
22. Verluste aus dem Abgang von Gegenständen des Anlagevermögens
23. Zinsen und ähnliche Aufwendungen
24. Steuern
    a) vom Einkommen, vom Ertrag und vom Vermögen
    b) sonstige
25. Aufwendungen aus Verlustübernahme
26. sonstige Aufwendungen
27. auf Grund einer Gewinngemeinschaft, eines Gewinnabführungs- und eines Teilgewinnabführungsvertrages abgeführte Gewinne
28. Jahresüberschuß/Jahresfehlbetrag
29. Gewinnvortrag/Verlustvortrag aus dem Vorjahr
30. Entnahmen aus offenen Rücklagen
    a) aus der gesetzlichen Rücklage
    b) aus freien Rücklagen
31. Einstellungen aus dem Jahresüberschuß in offene Rücklagen
    a) in die gesetzliche Rücklage
    b) in freie Rücklagen

32. Bilanzgewinn/Bilanzverlust

Anhang

9.4 Layout of Balance Sheet, as per § 151 AktG

1. Sales revenues (net of sales returns and allowances)
2. Inventory changes in finished goods and work in process
3. Capitalized cost of self-constructed assets
4. Total output
5. Expired cost of raw materials, supplies, and acquired merchandise
6. Net amount
7. Income from profit-pooling agreements, profit-transfer contracts, and partial-profit-transfer contracts
8. Income from investments
9. Income from other long-term investments
10. Other interest and similar income
11. Gains on disposal and appreciation writeup of fixed and financial assets
12. Gains from reduction of lump-sum valuation adjustments on receivables
13. Gains from retransfer of accrued liabilities
14. Other income, including extraordinary income
15. Compensation in connection with loss-absorption agreements

16. Wages and salaries
17. Social security levies
18. Cost of retirement plans and related benefits
19. Depreciation and writedowns on property, plant, and equipment as well as intangible assets
20. Writedown on investments
21. Losses from decline in value or retirement of current assets except inventories and additions to lump-sum valuation adjustments on receivables
22. Losses on disposal of fixed assets
23. Interest and similar expenses
24. Taxes
    a) on income and net worth
    b) other
25. Losses under loss-absorption agreements
26. Other expenses
27. Income transferred under profit-pooling agreements, profit-transfer contracts, and partial-profit-transfer contracts
28. Net income/net loss for the year
29. Balance-sheet profit/loss carried forward from the previous year
30. Withdrawals from open reserves
    a) from legal reserves
    b) from free reserves
31. Transfer to open reserves out of net income
    a) to legal reserves
    b) to free reserves

32. Balance-sheet profit/loss

9.5 Gliederung der Bilanz nach Art. 9 der 4. EG-Richtlinie

AKTIVA

A. Ausstehende Einlagen auf das gezeichnete Kapital

B. Aufwendungen für die Errichtung und Erweiterung des Unternehmens

C. Anlagevermögen
  I. Immaterielle Anlagewerte
    1. Forschungs- und Entwicklungskosten.
    2. Konzessionen, Patente, Lizenzen, Warenzeichen und ähnliche Rechte und Werte.
    3. Geschäfts- oder Firmenwert, sofern er entgeltlich erworben wurde.
    4. Geleistete Anzahlungen.
  II. Sachanlagen
    1. Grundstücke und Bauten.
    2. Technische Anlagen und Maschinen.
    3. Andere Anlagen, Betriebs- und Geschäftsausstattung.
    4. Geleistete Anzahlungen und Anlagen im Bau.
  III. Finanzanlagen
    1. Anteile an verbundenen Unternehmen.
    2. Forderungen gegen verbundene Unternehmen.
    3. Beteiligungen.
    4. Forderungen gegen Unternehmen, mit denen ein Beteiligungsverhältnis besteht.
    5. Wertpapiere des Anlagevermögens.
    6. Sonstige Ausleihungen.
    7. Eigene Aktien oder Anteile (unter Angabe ihres Nennbetrages oder, wenn ein Nennbetrag nicht vorhanden ist, ihres rechnerischen Wertes).

D. Umlaufvermögen
  I. Vorräte
    1. Roh-, Hilfs- und Betriebsstoffe.
    2. Unfertige Erzeugnisse.
    3. Fertige Erzeugnisse und Waren.
    4. Geleistete Anzahlungen.
  II. Forderungen
    1. Forderungen aus Lieferungen und Leistungen.
    2. Forderungen gegen verbundene Unternehmen.

PASSIVA

A. Eigenkapital
  I. Gezeichnetes Kapital
  II. Agio
  III. Neubewertungsrücklage
  IV. Rücklagen
    1. Gesetzliche Rücklage.
    2. Rücklagen für eigene Aktien oder Anteile.
    3. Satzungsmäßige Rücklagen.
    4. Sonstige Rücklagen.
  V. Ergebnisvortrag
  VI. Ergebnis des Geschäftsjahres

B. Rückstellungen
  1. Rückstellungen für Pensionen und ähnliche Verpflichtungen.
  2. Steuerrückstellungen.
  3. Sonstige Rückstellungen.

C. Verbindlichkeiten
  1. Anleihen, davon konvertibel.
  2. Verbindlichkeiten gegenüber Kreditinstituten.
  3. Erhaltene Anzahlungen auf Bestellungen.
  4. Verbindlichkeiten aus Lieferungen und Leistungen.
  5. Verbindlichkeiten aus Wechseln.
  6. Verbindlichkeiten gegenüber verbundenen Unternehmen.
  7. Verbindlichkeiten gegenüber Unternehmen, mit denen ein Beteiligungsverhältnis besteht.
  8. Sonstige Verbindlichkeiten, davon Verbindlichkeiten aus Steuern und Verbindlichkeiten im Rahmen der sozialen Sicherheit.
  9. Rechnungsabgrenzungsposten.

D. Rechnungsabgrenzungsposten

9.5 Layout of Balance Sheet as itemized in Art. 9, 4th EEC Council Directive

ASSETS
A. Subscribed capital unpaid

B. Formation expenses

C. Fixed assets
  I. Intangible assets
    1. Cost of research and development.
    2. Concessions, patents, licences, trade marks and similar rights and assets.
    3. Goodwill, to the extent that it was acquired for valuable consideration.
    4. Payments on account.
  II. Tangible assets
    1. Land and buildings.
    2. Plant and machinery.
    3. Other fixtures and fittings, tools and equipment.
    4. Payments on account and tangible assets in course of construction.
  III. Financial assets
    1. Shares in affiliated undertakings.
    2. Loans to affiliated undertakings.
    3. Participating interests.
    4. Loans to undertakings with which the company is linked by virtue of participating interests.
    5. Investments held as fixed assets.
    6. Other loans.
    7. Own shares (with an indication of their nominal value or, in the absence of a nominal value, their accounting par value).

D. Current assets
  I. Stocks
    1. Raw materials and consumables.
    2. Work in progress.
    3. Finished goods and goods for resale.
    4. Payments on account.
  II. Debtors
    1. Trade debtors.
    2. Amounts owed by affiliated undertakings.

LIABILITIES
A. Capital and reserves
  I. Subscribed capital
  II. Share premium account
  III. Revaluation reserve
  IV. Reserves
    1. Legal reserve.
    2. Reserve for own shares.
    3. Reserves provided for by the articles of association.
    4. Other reserves.
  V. Profit or loss brought forward
  VI. Profit or loss for the financial year

B. Provisions for liabilities and charges
  1. Provisions for pensions and similar obligations.
  2. Provisions for taxation.
  3. Other provisions.

C. Creditors
  1. Debenture loans, showing convertible loans separately.
  2. Amounts owed to credit institutions.
  3. Payments received on account of orders.
  4. Trade creditors.
  5. Bills of exchange payable.
  6. Amounts owed to affiliated undertakings.
  7. Amounts owed to undertakings with which the company is linked by virtue of participating interests.
  8. Other creditors including tax and social security.
  9. Accruals and deferred income.

D. Accruals and deferred income

Anhang

      3. Forderungen gegen Unternehmen, mit denen ein Beteiligungsverhältnis besteht.
      4. Sonstige Forderungen.
      5. Gezeichnetes Kapital, das eingefordert, aber noch nicht eingezahlt ist.
      6. Rechnungsabgrenzungsposten.
  III. <u>Wertpapiere</u>
      1. Anteile an verbundenen Unternehmen.
      2. Eigene Aktien oder Anteile (unter Angabe ihres Nennbetrages oder, wenn ein Nennbetrag nicht vorhanden ist, ihres rechnerischen Wertes).
      3. Sonstige Wertpapiere.
  IV. <u>Guthaben bei Kreditinstituten, Postscheckguthaben, Schecks und Kassenbestand</u>

E. <u>Rechnungsabgrenzungsposten</u>   E. <u>Gewinn des Geschäftsjahres</u>

F. <u>Verlust des Geschäftsjahres</u>

9.5 Gliederung der Gewinn- und Verlustrechnung nach Art. 24 der 4. EG-Richtlinie

A. <u>AUFWENDUNGEN</u>
   1. Verringerung des Bestandes an fertigen und unfertigen Erzeugnissen.
   2. a) Materialaufwand.
      b) Sonstige externe Aufwendungen.
   3. Personalaufwand:
      a) Löhne und Gehälter.
      b) Soziale Aufwendungen, davon für Altersversorgung.
   4. a) Wertberichtigungen zu Aufwendungen für die Errichtung und Erweiterung des Unternehmens und zu Sachanlagen und immateriellen Anlagewerten.
      b) Wertberichtigungen zu Gegenständen des Umlaufvermögens, soweit diese die in den Unternehmen üblichen Wertberichtigungen überschreiten.
   5. Sonstige betriebliche Aufwendungen.
   6. Wertberichtigungen zu Finanzanlagen und zu Wertpapieren des Umlaufvermögens.
   7. Zinsen und ähnliche Aufwendungen, davon an verbundene Unternehmen.
   8. Steuern auf das Ergebnis der normalen Geschäftstätigkeit.
   9. Ergebnis der normalen Geschäftstätigkeit nach Abzug der Steuern.
  10. Außerordentliche Aufwendungen.
  11. Steuern auf das außerordentliche Ergebnis.
  12. Sonstige Steuern, soweit nicht unter obigen Posten enthalten.
  13. Ergebnis des Geschäftsjahres.

B. <u>ERTRÄGE</u>
   1. Nettoumsatzerlöse.
   2. Erhöhung des Bestandes an fertigen und unfertigen Erzeugnissen.
   3. Andere aktivierte Eigenleistungen.
   4. Sonstige betriebliche Erträge.
   5. Erträge aus Beteiligungen, davon aus verbundenen Unternehmen.
   6. Erträge aus sonstigen Wertpapieren und Forderungen des Anlagevermögens, davon aus verbundenen Unternehmen.
   7. Sonstige Zinsen und ähnliche Erträge, davon aus verbundenen Unternehmen.
   8. Ergebnis der normalen Geschäftstätigkeit nach Abzug der Steuern.
   9. Außerordentliche Erträge.
  10. Ergebnis des Geschäftsjahres.

3. Amounts owed by undertakings with which the company is linked by virtue of participating interests.
4. Other debtors.
5. Subscribed capital called but not paid.
6. Prepayments and accrued income.

III. Investments
1. Shares in affiliated undertakings.
2. Own shares (with an indication of their nominal value or, in the absence of a nominal value, their accounting par value).
3. Other investments.

IV. Cash at bank and in hand

E. Prepayments and accrued income

F. Loss for the financial year

E. Profit for the financial year

9.5 Layout of Profit and Loss Account as itemized in Art. 24, 4th EEC Council Directive

A. CHARGES
1. Reduction in stocks of finished goods and in work in progress.
2. a) raw materials and consumables;
   b) other external charges.
3. Staff costs:
   a) wages and salaries;
   b) social security costs, with a separate indication of thoss relating to pensions.
4. a) Value adjustments in respect of formation expenses and of tangible and intangible fixed assets.
   b) Value adjustments in respect of current assets, to the extent that they exceed the amount of value adjustments which are normal in the undertaking concerned.
5. Other operating charges.
6. Value adjustments in respect of financial assets and of investments held as current assets.
7. Interest payable and similar charges, with a separate indication of those concerning affiliated undertakings.
8. Tax on profit or loss on ordinary activities.
9. Profit or loss on ordinary activities after taxation.
10. Extraordinary charges.
11. Tax on extraordinary profit or loss.
12. Other taxes not shown under the above items.
13. Profit or loss for the financial year.

B. INCOME
1. Net turnover.
2. Increase in stocks of finished goods and in work in progress.
3. Work performed by the undertaking for its own purposes and capitalized.
4. Other operating income.
5. Income from participating interests, with a separate indication of that derived from affiliated undertakings.
6. Income from other investments and loans forming part of the fixed assets, with a separate indication of that derived from affiliated undertakings.
7. Other interest receivable and similar income, with a separate indication of that derived from affiliated undertakings.
8. Profit or loss on ordinary activities after taxation.
9. Extraordinary income.
10. Profit or loss for the financial year.

9.6 VGR: Produktionskonto eines Unternehmens

↑
 	
Brutto-
wert-
schöpfung
 	
=
 	
Nettoproduk-
tionswert
↓
	1. Käufe von Vorleistungen
	   1.1 aus dem Ausland
	   1.2 im Inland
	
	2. Abschreibungen
	
	3. Indirekte Steuern
	   – Subventionen
	
	4. Nettowert-
	   schöpfung: 4.1 Löhne, Gehälter / 4.2 Zinsen / 4.3 verteilter Gewinn / 4.4 unverteilter Gewinn
		1. Verkäufe
		   1.1 an Unternehmen
		   1.2 an Staat
		
		2. Verkäufe von
		   Konsumgütern
		
		3. Verkäufe von Investitions-
		   gütern
		
		4. Bestandsänderungen an eigenen Erzeugnissen
		
		5. Selbsterstellte Anlagen
			↑
			
			Brutto-
			produktions-
			wert
			↓

9.6 National Accounting:
Product Account of a Business Enterprise

↑
Gross
value
added
=
Net
output
↓
	1. Purchased materials and services
	  1.1 from abroad
	  1.2 domestic
			1. Sales
			  1.1 to enterprises
			  1.2 to government
				↑
				Business
				gross
				output
				↓

	2. Depreciation		2. Sales of consumer goods	
	3. Indirect taxes less subsidies		3. Sales of capital goods	
	4. Net value added	4.1 Wages, salaries	4. Increase in inventories	
		4.2 Interest	5. Self-constructed assets (for own use of the enterprise)	
		4.3 Distributed profit		
		4.4 Undistributed profit		

Anhang

9.7 VGR: Sozialprodukt und Volkseinkommen (1)

1 Einkommen aus unselbständiger Arbeit
2 Einkommen aus Unternehmertätigkeit und Vermögen
3 Abschreibungen
4 Indirekte Steuern
5 abzüglich: Subventionen

6 **Bruttoinlandsprodukt zu Marktpreisen**
7 + Saldo der Erwerbs- und Vermögenseinkommen zwischen Inländern und der übrigen Welt

8 **Bruttosozialprodukt zu Marktpreisen**
9 − Abschreibungen

10 **Nettosozialprodukt zu Marktpreisen**
11 − indirekte Steuern (abzüglich: Subventionen)

12 **Nettosozialprodukt zu Faktorkosten**
= **Volkseinkommen**

*

Sozialprodukt und Volkseinkommen (2)

I. Entstehung
   1 Land- und Forstwirtschaft
   2 Bergbau, Gewinnung von Steinen und Erden
   3 Energieversorgung und Wasserversorgung
   4 Verarbeitendes Gewerbe
   5 Baugewerbe
   6 Handel, Gaststätten- und Beherbergungsgewerbe
   7 Verkehr und Nachrichtenübermittlung
   8 Übrige Bereiche
   9 Einfuhrabgaben

  10 **Bruttoinlandsprodukt zu Marktpreisen**

II. Verteilung
   1 Einkommen aus unselbständiger Arbeit
   2 Betriebsüberschuß (Einkommen aus Unternehmertätigkeit und Vermögen)
   3 Saldo der Erwerbs- und Vermögenseinkommen zwischen Inländern und der übrigen Welt
   4 **Nettosozialprodukt zu Faktorkosten (= Volkseinkommen)**
   5 Indirekte Steuern (abzüglich: Subventionen)
   6 **Nettosozialprodukt zu Marktpreisen**
   7 Saldo der laufenden Übertragungen zwischen inländischen Wirtschaftseinheiten und der übrigen Welt

   8 **Verfügbares Einkommen**

III. Verwendung
   1 Privater Verbrauch
   2 Staatsverbrauch
   3 Anlageinvestitionen
   4 Vorratsveränderung
   5 Außenbeitrag

   6 **Bruttoinlandsprodukt zu Marktpreisen**

Anhang

9.7 National Product and National Income (1)

1 Compensation of employees
2 Income from property and entrepreneurship
3 Capital asset consumption
4 Indirect taxes
5 less: subsidies

6 **Gross domestic product at market prices**
7 + Net factor income payments from the rest of the world

8 **Gross national product at market prices**
9 − Capital asset consumption

10 **Net national product at market prices**
11 − Indirect taxes (less: subsidies)

12 **Net national product at factor cost
= National income**

*

National Product and National Income (2)

I. Industrial origin of gross domestic product
   1 Agriculture and forestry
   2 Mining and quarrying
   3 Electricitiy, gas, and water
   4 Manufacturing
   5 Construction
   6 Wholesale and retail trade, hotels and restaurants
   7 Transportation and communication
   8 Others
   9 Levies on imports

  10 **Gross domestic product at market prices**

II. Distribution of national income
   1 Compensation of employees
   2 Operating surplus (income from property and entrepreneurship)
   3 Net factor income from the rest of the world
   4 **Net national income at factor cost (= national income)**
   5 Indirect taxes (less: subsidies)
   6 **Net national product at market prices**
   7 Net current transfers from the rest of the world

   8 **Disposable income**

III. Expenditure on gross national product
   1 Private consumption expenditure
   2 Government consumption expenditure
   3 Gross fixed capital formation
   4 Increase in stocks
   5 Net export of goods and services

   6 **Gross domestic product at market prices**

Anhang

9.8 Schema der Zahlungsbilanz der Bundesrepublik Deutschland

A. Leistungsbilanz
  1.0 **Handelsbilanz**
    1.1 Ausfuhr (fob)
    1.2 Einfuhr (cif)
    Saldo
  2.0 **Dienstleistungsbilanz**
    2.1 Einnahmen
    2.2 Ausgaben
    Saldo
  3.0 **Übertragungsbilanz** (= Schenkungsbilanz, Bilanz der unentgeltlichen Leistungen)
    3.1 Privat
    3.2 Öffentlich
    Saldo
  Saldo der Leistungsbilanz

B. Langfristiger Kapitalverkehr
  1.0 Privat
    1.1 Direktinvestitionen
    1.2 Portfolioinvestitionen
    1.3 Kredite und Darlehen
  2.0 Öffentlich
  Saldo

C. Grundbilanz (A + B)

D. Kurzfristiger Kapitalverkehr
  1.0 Kreditinstitute
  2.0 Wirtschaftsunternehmen
  3.0 Öffentliche Hand
  Saldo

E. Saldo der statistisch nicht aufgegliederten Transaktionen (Restposten)

F. Ausgleichsposten zur Auslandsposition der Bundesbank
  1.0 Ausgleichsposten für zugeteilte Sonderziehungsrechte
  2.0 Bewertungsänderungen der Auslandspositionen
  Saldo

G. Auslandsposition der Bundesbank = Devisenbilanz
  1.0 Währungsreserven
    1.1 Gold
    1.2 Reserveposition im IWF und Sonderziehungsrechte
    1.3 Devisen und Sorten
    1.4 Verbindlichkeiten
    Änderung der Währungsreserven
  2.0 Kredite und sonstige Forderungen an das Ausland
  Änderung der Auslandsposition nach Bewertungsänderungen

9.8 System of Balance of Payments Accounts

A. **Current Account**
　1.0 **Trade Balance**
　　1.1 Merchandise exports
　　1.2 Merchandise imports
　　　Balance
　2.0 **Services**
　　2.1 Receipts
　　2.2 Expenditures
　　　Balance
　3.0 **Transfer** (or **Unilateral**) **Payments**
　　3.1 Private
　　3.2 Government
　　　Balance
　Balance on Current Account

B. **Long-term Capital**
　1.0 Private
　　1.1 Direct investment
　　1.2 Portfolio investment
　　1.3 Advances and loans
　2.0 Government
　Balance

C. **Basic Balance** (A + B)

D. **Short-term Capital**
　1.0 Banks
　2.0 Business enterprises
　3.0 Government
　Balance

E. Statistical Discrepancies (Balancing Item)

F. Balancing Item to External Position of Bundesbank
　1.0 Balancing item to allocations of IMF special drawing rights
　2.0 Changes in valuation of external position
　Balance

G. External Position of Bundesbank
　1.0 Reserve assets
　　1.1 Gold stock
　　1.2 Reserve position in IMF and special drawing rights (SDRs)
　　1.3 Foreign currency holdings
　　1.4 Liabilities to foreigners
　　Change in reserve assets
　2.0 Credits and other claims on foreigners
　Change in external position after valuation changes

Währungsbezeichnungen/List of Local Currencies

Land	Währungseinheit	Place	Local Unit
Afghanistan	Afghani = 100 Puls	Afghanistan	Afghani (Af) = 100 puls (Pl)
Ägypten	Ägyptisches Pfund (ägypt.£) = 100 Piaster = 1000 Milliemes	Egypt	Egyptian Pound (£E) = 100 piasters (Pt) = 1000 milliemes
Albanien	Lek = 100 Qindarka	Albania	Lek = 100 quintar
Algerien	Algerischer Dinar = 100 Centimes	Algeria	Dinar (DA) = 100 centimes
Angola	Kwanza = 100 Lwei	Angola	Kwanza (Kz) = 100 lwei (lw)
Argentinien	Argentinischer Peso (argent$) = 100 Centavos	Argentina	Ar.Peso ($) = 100 Centavos (c)
Äquatorial-Guinea	Ekuele = 100 Centimos	Equatorial Guinea	Ekuele (Ek) = 100 centimos
Äthiopien	Birr = 100 cents	Ethiopia	Birr (Br) = 100 cents (ct)
Australien	Australischer Dollar = 100 Cents	Australia	Australian dollar ($, $A) = 100 cents (c)
Bahama-Inseln	Bahama-Dollar = 100 Cents	Bahamas	Ba.dollar (B$) = 100 cents (c)
Bahrain	Bahrain-Dinar = 1000 Fils	Bahrain	Bahrain dinar (BD) = 1000 fils
Bangladesch	Taka = 100 Paisha	Bangladesh	Taka (Tk) = 100 paise (ps)
Barbados	Barbados-Dollar = 100 Cents	Barbados	Barbados $ (BD$) = 100 cents (c)
Belgien	Belgischer Franc = 100 Centimes	Belgium	B. Franc (fr, F, FB) = 100 centimes (c)
Belize	Belize-Dollar = 100 Cents	Belize	Belize $ (Bz$) = 100 cents (c)
Benin	CFA-Franc = 100 Centimes	Benin	C.F.A. Franc (FF.C.A.) = 100 centimes (c)
Bermuda-Inseln	Bermuda-Dollar = 100 Cents	Bermuda	Bermudian dollar (Bda$, BD$) = 100 cents
Bhutan	Ngultrum (NU, nu) = 100 Chetrum (Ch, ch)	Bhutan	Indian Rupee
Birma	Kyat = 100 Pyas	Burma	Kyat (K) = 100 pyas (p)
Bolivien	Peso Boliviano = 100 Centavos	Bolivia	Bolivian Peso ($b) = 100 centavos (cts)
Botsuana (Betschuanaland)	Pula = 100 Thebe	Botswana (= Bechuanaland)	Pula (P) = 100 thebe (t)
Brasilien	Cruzeiro = 100 Centavos	Brazil	Cruzeiro (Cr$) = 100 centavos (cts)
Brunei	Brunei-Dollar = 100 Cents	Brunei	Brunei $ (BR$) = 100 cents (c)
Bulgarien	Lew = 100 Stótinki	Bulgaria	Lev (Lv) = 100 stotinki (st)
Burundi	Burundi-Franc = 100 Centimes	Burundi	Burundi Franc (F.Bu.) = 100 Centimes (c)
Cayman-Inseln	Kaimann-Dollar = 100 Cents	Cayman-Islands	Cayman $ (CI$) = 100 cents (c)
Chile	Chilenischer Peso = 100 Centavos	Chile	C. Peso ($) = 100 centisimos
China (Volksrepublik)	Renminbi ¥uan (RMB.¥) = 10 Jiao	China, Peoples Republic of	Renminbi Yuan = 100 fen

Anhang

Land	Währungseinheit	Place	Local Unit
Costa Rica	Costa Rica-Colón = 100 Céntimos	Costa Rica	Colon (C) = 100 centimes (c)
Curaçao	Niederl. Antillen-Gulden (NAf) = 100 Cents	Curacao	Dutch Antilles Guilder (DAf) = 100 cents (c)
Dänemark	Dänische Krone = 100 Öre	Denmark	Danish Krone (dkr) = 100 ore
Deutschland (West)	Deutsche Mark (DM) = 100 Deutsche Pfennig (Pf)	Germany (West)	Deutsch Mark = 100 pfennig
Deutschland (Ost)	Ostmark (M) = 100 Pfennig (Pf)	Germany (East)	Ostmark = 100 pfennig
Dominica	Ostkaribischer Dollar = 100 Cents	Dominica	East Caribbean $ (EC$) = 100 cents (c)
Dominikanische Republik	Dominikanischer Peso = 100 Centavos	Dominican Republic	Dominican Peso (dom$) = 100 centavos (cts)
Dschibuti	Dschibuti-Franc = 100 Centimes	Djibuti	Djibouti Franc (FDjib) = 100 centimes (c)
Ecuador	Sucre = 100 Centavos	Ecuador	Sucre = 100 centavos (ctvs)
Elfenbeinküste	CFA-Franc = 100 Centimes = 100 centimes (c)	Ivory Coast,	C. F. A. Franc
Republic of El Salvador	El Salvador-Colón = 100 Centavos	El Salvador	Colon ($\mathcal{C}$) = 100 centavos
Falkland-Inseln	Falkland-Pfund = 100 New Pence	Falkland Islands	Falkland Is £ (FI£) = 100 new pence
Fidschi-Inseln	Fidschi-Dollar = 100 New Pence	Fiji Islands	Fij Is $ ($F) = 100 cents
Finnland	Finnmark = 100 Penni	Finland	Markka = 100 penis (p)
Frankreich	Französischer Franc = 100 Centimes	France	French Franc (FF) = 100 centimes (c)
Französisch-Guyana	Franc = 100 Centimes	French Guiana	Local Franc (F)= 100 centimes (c)
Französisch-Ozeanien	CFP-Franc = 100 Centimes	French Pacific	C. F. P. Franc = 100 centimes (c)
Gabun	CFA-Franc = 100 Centimes	Gabon Republic	C. f. A. Franc = 100 centimes (c)
Gambia	Dalasi = 100 Bututs	Gambia	Dalasa, Dalasis (D) = 100 bututs (b)
Ghana	Cedi = 100 Pesewas	Ghana	New Cedi ($\mathcal{C}$) = 100 pesewa (p)
Gibraltar	Gibraltar-Pfund = 100 New Pence	Gibraltar	Gibraltar £ (Gib£) = 100 new pence
Grenada	Ostkaribischer Dollar = 100 Cents	Granada	East Caribbean $ (EC$) = 100 cents (c)
Griechenland	Drachme = 100 Lepta	Greece	Drachma (Dr., dr.) = 100 lepta
Großbritannien und Nordirland	Pfund Sterling = 100 New Pence	Great Britain and Northern Ireland	Pound Sterling (£) = 100 new pence
Guadeloupe	Franc = 100 Centimes	Guadeloupe	Local Franc = 100 centimes (c)
Guatemala	Quetzal = 100 Centavos	Guatemala	Quetzal (Q, $\mathcal{Q}$) = 100 centavos (cts)
Guinea	Syli = 100 Cauris	Guinea, Republic of	Syli (SY) = 100 kori
Guinea-Bissau	Guinea-Peso = 100 Centavos	Guinea-Bissau	Guinea Peso (PG) = 100 centavos (cts)
Guyana	Guyana-Dollar = 100 Cents	Guyana	Guyanese $ (G$) = 100 cents

Anhang

Land	Währungseinheit	Place	Local Unit
Haiti	Gourde = 100 Centimes	Haiti	Gourde (Gde, G) = 100 centimes (c)
Honduras	Lempira = 100 Centavos	Honduras Republic	Lempira (L) = 100 centavos (cts)
Hongkong	Hongkong-Dollar = 100 Cents	Hong Kong	Hong Kong $ (HK$) = 100 Cents
Indien	Indische Rupie = 100 Paise	India	Indian Rupee (IR) = 100 paise (p)
Indonesien	Rupiah = 100 Sen	Indonesia	Rupiah (Rp) = 100 sen (s)
Irak	Irak-Dinar = 1000 Fils	Iraq	Iraq Dinar (ID) = 1000 fils
Iran	Rial = 100 Dinars	Iran	Rial (RI) = 100 dinars (d)
Irland	Irisches Pfund = 100 New Pence	Irish Republic	Irish Pound (Ir£) = 100 new pence
Island	Isländische Krone = 100 Aurar	Iceland	New Krona (IKr, Kr) = 100 aurar (aur)
Israel	Schekel = 100 New Agorot	Israel	shekel (IS) = 100 agorot
Italien	Italienische Lira = 100 Centesimi	Italy	Lira (Lit, L) = 100 centesimi (cent)
Jamaika	Jamaika-Dollar = 100 Cents	Jamaica	Jamaican Dollar (J$) = 100 cents (c)
Japan	Yen = 100 Sen	Japan	Yen (¥) = 100 sen
Jemen (Arabische Republik)	Jemen-Rial = 100 Fils	Yemen Arab Republic	Yemini Ryal (Y. Rl) = 100 fils
Jemen (Demokratischer)	Jemen-Dinar = 1000 fils	Yemen (South)	S. Yemen Dinar (YD, Y£) = 1000 fils
Jordanien	Jordan-Dinar = 1000 Fils	Jordan	Jordan Dinar (JD) = 1000 fils (FLS)
Jugoslawien	Jugoslawischer Dinar = 100 Para	Yugoslawia	New Y Dinar (Din) = 100 paras (p)
Kaimanninseln	Kaimann-Dollar = 100 Cents	Cayman Islands	Cayman Dollar (CI$) = 100 cents (c)
Kamerun	CFA-Franc = 100 Centimes	Cameroon, Republic of	C. F. A. Franc (F C. F. A.) = 100 centimes (c)
Kanada	Kanadischer Dollar = 100 Cents	Canada	Candian Dollar (Can$) = 100 cents (c)
Kap Verde	Kap-Verde-Escudo = 100 Centavos	Cape Verde Isle	Cape V. Escudo (Esc) = 100 centavos (cts)
Katar	Katar-Riyal = 100 Dirhams	Qatar	Qatar Riyal (QR) = 100 dirhams
Kenia	Kenia-Schilling = 100 Cents	Kenya	Kenya shilling (K. Sh.) = 100 cents (cts)
Kolumbien	Kolumbischer Peso = 100 Centavos	Colombia	Peso ($) = 100 centavos (cvs)
Kongo	CFA-Franc = 100 Centimes	Congo	C. F. A. Franc (F C. F. A.) = 100 centimes (c)
Korea (Süd)	Won = 100 Chon	Korea (South)	Won (W) = 100 jeon
Kuba	Kubanischer Peso = 100 Centavos	Cuba	Cuban Peso (Cuban $) = 100 Centavos (¢)
Kuwait	Kuwait-Dinar = 100 Dirhams	Kuwait	Kuwait dinar (KD) = 1000 fils = 100 dirhams
Laotische Demokratische Volksdemokratie	Kip de libération = 100 At	Laos	New Kip = 100 At

Anhang

Land	Währungseinheit	Place	Local Unit
Lesotho (= Basutoland)	(Südafrikanischer) Rand od Loti = 100 Cents	Lesotho	Loti = 100 cents (c) od lisente (s)
Libanon	Libanesisches Pfund = 100 Piastres	Lebanon	Lebanese £ (L£) Livre libanaise (L.L.) = 100 piastres (P.L.)
Liberia	Liberianischer Dollar = 100 Cents	Liberia	Liberian $ (Lib$) = 100 cents (c)
Libyen	Libyscher Dinar = 1000 Dirhams	Libya	Dinar (LD., DL) = 1000 milliemes
Liechtenstein	Schweizer Franken = 100 Rappen	Liechtenstein	Swiss Franc = 100 centimes
Luxemburg	Luxemburgischer Franc = 100 Centimes	Luxembourg	Lux Franc (lfr) = 100 centimes (c)
Macau	Pataca = 100 Avos	Macao	Pataca (M$, Pat) = 100 avos
Madagaskar	Madagaskar-Franc = 100 Centimes	Malagasy Republic	Franc Malgache (FMG) = 100 centimes (c)
Malawi	Malawi-Kwacha = 100 Tambala	Malawi	Kwacha (MK) = 100 tambala (t)
Malaysia	Malaysischer Ringgit = 100 Sen	Malaysia	Malaysian Ringgit (M$) = 100 cents (c)
Malediven	Malediven-Rupie = 100 Laris	Maldive Island	Rufiyaa Maldivian Rupee (Re) = 100 laris
Mali	Mali-France = 100 Centimes	Mali, Republic	Mali Franc (FM) = 100 centimes (c)
Malta	Malta-Pfund = 100 Cents = 1000 Mils	Malta	Maltese Pound (£M) = 20 shillings = 240 pence
Marokko	Dirham = 100 Centimes	Marocco	Dirham (DH) = 100 francs
Mauretanien	Ouguiya = 5 Khoums	Mauritanian Islamic Republic	Ougiya (UM) = 100 centimes
Mauritius	Mauritius-Rupie = 100 Cents	Mauritius	M. Rupee (MR) = 100 cents (c)
Mexiko	Mexikanischer Peso = 100 Centavos	Mexico	Mexican peso (mex$) = 100 centavos (cts)
Mongolische Volksrepublik	Tugrug = 100 Mongo	Mongolia	Tugrik, Tughrik = 100 mongo
Mosambique	Metical, Escudo = 100 Centavos	Mozambique	Metical, Escudo = 100 centavos
Nepal	Nepalesische Rupie = 100 Paisa	Nepal	Nepalese Rupee (N.Re.) = 100 pice
Neuseeland	Neuseeland-Dollar = 100 Cents	New Zealand	N.Z. Dollar (NZ$) = 100 cents (c)
Nicaragua	Córdoba = 100 Centavos	Nicaragua	Cordoba = 100 cents (c)
Niederlande	Holländischer Gulden (hfl) = 100 Cents	Netherlands, the	Guilder (Gld) = 100 cents (c)
Niederländische Antillen	Niederl. Antillen-Gulden = 100 Cents	Netherlands Antilles (Aruba-Curaçao)	Antillian Guilder, N.A. florin = 100 cents (c)
Niger	CFA-Franc = 100 Centimes	Niger, Republic of the	C.F.A. France (F C.F.A.) = 100 centimes (c)
Nigeria	Naira = 100 Kobo	Nigeria, Federation of	Naira (N) = 100 kobo (k)
Norwegen	Norwegische Krone = 100 Øre	Norway	Norway Krone (nkr) = 100 ore (Ø)
Obervolta	CFA-Franc = 100 Centimes	Upper Volta (Republic)	C.F.A. Franc (F C.F.A.) = 100 centesimos

Anhang

Land	Währungseinheit	Place	Local Unit
Österreich	Schilling = 100 Groschen	Austria	Schilling (S) = 100 groschen (Gr)
Oman	Rial Omani = 1000 Baizas	Oman	Rial Omani (R. O.) = 1000 baizas (bz)
Pakistan	Pakistanische Rupie = 100 Paisa	Pakistan	Pakistan Rupee (Pak. Re.) = 100 paisa (ps)
Panama	Balboa = 100 Centesimos	Panama	Balboa (B/.) = 100 cents (c)
Paraguay	Guarani = 100 Céntimos	Paraguay	Guaraní (G̶, G) = 100 centimos (cts)
Peru	Sol = 100 Centavos	Peru	Sol (de oro) (S/.) = 100 centavos (cts)
Philippinen	Philippinischer Peso = 100 Centavos	Philippine Islands (Philippines)	Philippine Peso (P) = 100 centavos (c)
Polen	Zloty = 100 Groszy	Poland	Zloty (Zl) = 100 groszy (gr)
Portugal	Escudo = 100 Centavos	Portugal	Portuguese Escudo (Esc, $) = 100 centavos (ctvs)
Ruanda	Ruanda-Franc = 100 Centimes	Rwanda	Rwanda Franc (F. Rw.) = 100 centimes
Rumänien	Leu = 100 Bani	Roumania	Leu (I) = 100 bani
Sambia	Kwacha = 100 Ngwee	Zambia	Kwacha (K) = 100 ngwee (n)
San Marino	San Marino-Lira = 100 Centesimi	San Marino	Italian Lira = 100 centesimi
Saudi-Arabien	Saudi Riyal = 20 Quirshes = 100 Hallalas	Saudi Arabia	Riyal (Rl) = 20 qursh = 100 halalas
Schweden	Schwedische Krone (skr) = 100 Öre	Sweden	Krona (Kr, kr) = 100 ore
Schweiz	Schweizer Franken (sfr) = 100 Rappen = 100 Centimes	Switzerland	Swiss Franc = 100 centimes
Senegal	CFA-Franc = 100 Centimes	Senegal, Republic of	C. F. A. Franc = 100 centimes (c)
Seychellen	Seychellen-Rupie = 100 Cents	Seychelles	S. Rupee (SR) = 100 cents (c)
Sierra Leone	Leone = 100 Cents	Sierra Leone	leone (Le) = 100 cents (c)
Simbabwe (Rhodesien)	Simbabwe-Dollar = 100 Cents	Zimbabwe (Rhodesia)	Zimbabwe Dollar (Z$) = 100 cents (c)
Singapur	Singapur-Dollar = 100 Cents	Singapore	Singapore Dollar (S$) = 100 cents (c)
Somalia	Somalischer Schilling = 100 Centesimi	Somalia	Somali Shilling (So. Sh.) = 100 cents (c)
Sowjetunion	Rubel = 100 Kopeken	U.S.S.R.	Ruble (Rbl) = 100 kopecks
Spanien	Peseta = 100 Céntimos	Spain	Peseta (Pta) = 100 centimos (cts)
Sri Lanka (Ceylon)	Sri-Lanka-Rupie = 100 Sri Lanka Cents	Sri Lanka	S. L. Rupee (S. L. Re.) = 100 cents (S. L. Cts.)
Sudan	Sudanesisches Pfund = 100 Piastres = 1000 Milliemes	Sudan, Republic of the	Sudanese Pound = 100 piastres (PT) = 1000 milliemes (mms)
Südafrika	Rand = 100 Cents	South Africa (Republic)	Rand (R) = 100 cents (c)
Südwestafrika	Rand = 100 Cents	South West African Territories	Rand (R) = 100 cents (c)
Surinam (Niederländisch-Guyana)	Surinam-Gulden = 100 Cents	Surinam (Neth. Guiana)	Surinam Guilder (Sf) = 100 cents

Land	Währungseinheit	Place	Local Unit
Swasiland	Lilangeni = 100 Cents	Swaziland	Lilangeni, (Plural:) Emalangeni = 100 cents (c)
Syrien	Syrisches Pfund = 100 Piastres	Syria	Syria Pound (syr$) = 100 piastres (PS)
Taiwan	Neuer Taiwan-Dollar = 100 Cents	Taiwan	New Taiwan Dollar (NT$) = 100 cents (¢)
Tansania	Tansania-Schilling = 100 Cents	Tanzania	Tanzania Shilling (T. Sh.) = 100 cents (Ct)
Thailand	Baht = 100 Stangs	Thailand	baht (B) = 100 stangs (St)
Togo	CFA-Franc = 100 Centimes	Togo Republic	C. F. A. Franc = 100 centimes (c)
Tonga	Pa'anga = 100 Seniti	Tonga Islands	Ha'anga (T$) = 100 seniti (s)
Trinidad und Tobago	Trinidad-und-Tobago-Dollar = 100 Cents	Trinida & Tobago	Trinidad & Tob. Dollar (TT$) = 100 cents (cts)
Tschad	CFA-Franc = 100 Centimes	Chad, Republic of	C. F. A. Franc = 100 centimes (c)
Tschechoslowakei	Tschechoslowakische Krone = 100 Haleru	Czechoslovakia	Koruna (Kčs) = 100 heller (h)
Tunesien	Tunesischer Dinar = 1000 Milliemes	Tunesia	Tunisian Dinar (tD) = 1000 milliemes (M)
Türkei	Türkisches Pfund = 100 Kurus	Turkey	Lira (TL) = 100 kurush (krs)
Uganda	Uganda-Schilling = 100 Cents	Uganda	Shilling (Sh) = 100 Cents (Ct)
Ungarn	Forint = 100 Filler	Hungary	Forint (Ft) = 100 filler (f)
Uruguay	Uruguayischer Neuer Peso = 100 Céntesimos	Uruguay	New Peso (N$) = 100 centimes
Venezuela	Bolivar = 100 Céntimos	Venezuela	Bolivar (B) = 100 centimos (cts)
Vereinigte Arabische Emirate	Dirham = 100 Fils	United Arab Emirates	Dirham (DH) = 100 fils
Vereinigte Staaten	US-Dollar = 100 Cents	United States	U. S. Dollar (US-$) = 100 cents (c)
Zaire	Zaire = 100 Makuta, (Singular:) Likuta = 10000 Sengi	Zaire Republic	Zaire = 100 makuta (K)
Zypern	Zypern-Pfund = 1000 Mils	Cyprus	Cyprus Pound (C£) = 1000 mils (m)